Waterfowl Ecology and Management: Selected Readings

Waterfowl Ecology and Management: Selected Readings

Compiled by:
John T. Ratti
Washington State University
Lester D. Flake
South Dakota State University
W. Alan Wentz
National Wildlife Federation

Illustrated by Dean Rocky Barrick

A Publication of The Wildlife Society

Library of Congress Catalog Card Number: 82-70782
ISBN: 0-933564-09-0
Printed in the United States of America by Allen Press, Inc.,
Lawrence, Kansas

For information, or to order, write to: The Wildlife Society, Inc.,
5410 Grosvenor Lane, Bethesda, Maryland 20814.

DEDICATION

This book of readings was prepared for use by students and wildlife managers who have an interest in North American waterfowl. No single individual has contributed more to the subject of waterfowl management and ecology over the last 40 years than Frank C. Bellrose.

Frank Bellrose has devoted his life to the study of waterfowl and he has influenced many biologists through his work and publications. It is difficult to single out any one area to identify as Frank's most prominent contribution because his work has touched nearly every area of waterfowl biology. Through the years he has received many awards for his writings and his professional efforts to understand and increase waterfowl populations. Frank's contributions are recognized both nationally and internationally, and we are pleased to dedicate this book to him.

FOREWORD

A major objective of The Wildlife Society is to disseminate biological information useful to the understanding and management of wildlife and their environments. For nearly 45 years this effort has been accomplished in large part by *The Journal of Wildlife Management*, supplemented more recently by *Wildlife Monographs* and the *Wildlife Society Bulletin*.

In addition to its serial publications, The Wildlife Society has published several books aimed at readers ranging from the professional wildlife biologist to the elementary grade school student. The objective here has been to provide in comprehensive form information not readily retrievable by those persons requiring it.

Probably no more extensive a body of literature exists for a discrete group of wildlife species than for waterfowl. The difficulty of identifying and locating pertinent, important waterfowl literature is a problem for the practicing biologist and student alike. John Ratti, Les Flake, and Al Wentz faced a formidable task in establishing guidelines for content, examining the literature, and making the final selection of papers to be included in this book.

If six other groups of three compilers drew up their lists of what ought to be included in a book of this type, one could predict six different lists of papers. Nevertheless, this book serves a genuine need of the waterfowl biologist and enthusiast by providing many of the significant waterfowl papers in one volume. I predict *Waterfowl Ecology and Management: Selected Readings* will receive its deserved welcome and will be widely used.

THEODORE A. BOOKHOUT
President
The Wildlife Society

PREFACE AND ACKNOWLEDGMENTS

Waterfowl are one of the most cherished groups of wildlife species in North America and are enthusiastically sought by hunters, scientists, photographers, and bird watchers. In 1979, waterfowl hunters paid over $15,000,000 for U.S. Migratory Bird Conservation and Hunting Stamps—clear testimony to the recreational and economic importance of these species. Consumptive and non-consumptive demand for the waterfowl resource continues to increase as does habitat destruction, primarily due to agricultural and industrial activities; under these circumstances, waterfowl represent an especially important challenge to wildlife scientists and managers.

A vast body of literature exists on the history, biology, and management of waterfowl. Our primary objective was to compile a comprehensive group of readings suitable as an academic textbook and as a professional reference book. This book is not intended for the highly trained waterfowl specialist, although many may find it useful. Due to space limitations, we attempted to select shorter, concise, and "readable" papers with an obvious message.

Each section and subsection of the book contains a selected bibliography that is intended to direct the reader to additional papers on specific subjects. Many monographs and other publications of excessive length are included in these selected bibliographies. As an additional aid to restrict the overall length of the book, we have limited our selection of papers primarily to those on North American populations of ducks, geese, and swans.

We began our project by developing an extensive waterfowl bibliography, which was slowly and systematically reduced to a workable first draft. Many waterfowl specialists commented on various drafts of the book. We would like to thank the following individuals for the valuable criticisms they provided:

DAVID R. ANDERSON, Leader, Utah Cooperative Wildlife Research Unit, Utah State University, Logan

FRANK C. BELLROSE, Wildlife Specialist, Illinois Natural History Survey, Havana

LEIGH H. FREDRICKSON and PATRICK W. BROWN, Gaylord Memorial Laboratory and the University of Missouri, Puxico

LAURENCE R. JAHN, Vice President, Wildlife Management Institute, Washington, D.C.

JOHN A. KADLEC, Department of Wildlife Science, Utah State University, Logan

HARVEY W. MILLER, Central Flyway Representative, U.S. Fish and Wildlife Service, Denver, Colorado

DENNIS G. RAVELING, Chairman, Department of Wildlife and Fisheries Biology, University of California, Davis

DAVID L. TRAUGER, Chief, Division of Wildlife Ecology Research, U.S. Fish and Wildlife Service, Washington, D.C.

We also received many helpful suggestions from The Wildlife Society Council members serving during 1977–80, TWS Publications Committee, and graduate students of waterfowl ecology and management at South Dakota State University. We also acknowledge William Clark, Tim Fendley, Thomas McCabe, Al Sargeant, and Gary White for comments on several papers that were difficult for us to assess. This project was initiated while all 3 compilers were employed at South Dakota State University and we were blessed with the dedicated, expert, and cheerful secretarial help of Alice Molengraaf and Kathy Lytle.

We extend sincere thanks to Dean Rocky Barrick for the excellent art work that illustrates our book. And last, but most importantly, we thank all of the authors whose dedicated research in waterfowl ecology and management has provided the nucleus of this book.

JOHN T. RATTI
LESTER D. FLAKE
W. ALAN WENTZ

CONTENTS

Land Use and Habitat

Broods

Behavior

Population Ecology

Sex Ratios

Disease and Environmental Contaminants

Physiology and Energetics

IV. FOOD HABITS AND FEEDING ECOLOGY

Artificial Structures

Economic Impacts

VI. MOVEMENT AND MIGRATION

VII. WINTERING WATERFOWL

VIII. EVOLUTION, HYBRIDIZATION, AND SPECIATION

HISTORICAL

A DISCUSSION FOR MANAGEMENT[1]

H. A. HOCHBAUM[2]

A few years ago there was clamor for a set of rules by which we could manipulate the land for the benefit of waterfowl. Fortunately, although much we needed to know of habits and life histories was lacking, and still is for that matter, it was clear that three steps had to be taken to build up the dwindling populations of these birds, viz., restoration of lost breeding marshes, improvement of wintering waters, and less gunfire. It was by these means, plus the grace of Providence, that ducks pulled out of their deep depression.

More water and less gunfire have done the job; but this is not management. These first steps only set the stage. There may come a time when ducks will have adequate water, north and south and along their flyways. But the time will never arrive when management of waterfowl resources is out of date.

I speak of management in the broad sense. Between the Lake of the Woods, and the Rocky Mountains there are, perhaps, a million duck marshes, large and small. These will never be counted, much less individually controlled. Management of waterfowl must develop as a part of the master plan of land use for this prairie country. Everywhere the breeding marshes border or overlap the realm of man's activities; and man is one of the most important factors limiting waterfowl success. His marsh fires when ducks are nesting, the grazing of his cattle, the early mowing of hay lands, and many other activities destroy thousands of duck nests, or render marshes second-rate or worthless.

The most important tool of management today is education to show the landowner—whether municipality, county, state, province or farmer—how to use the land without destroying its resources. Such instruction is now being undertaken, and I count the educational program of Ducks Unlimited, which is making the people of the prairies conscious of their wealth in marshland, their greatest achievement.

But educators must be educated, or must teach themselves. At present we do not have many of the essential facts upon which management is to be based. I can show you (Fig. 1) when the first ducks start nesting in the Delta region, and thus obtain a reasonable date for the close of spring burning. But the same date may not apply to a region 300 or 400 miles to the northwest. A schedule of waterfowl activities, as these dovetail with land use throughout the prairies, is but one small step towards an over-all plan for management.

There are many questions, all vitally important, still unanswered. And in the present scheme of operations they will not be answered for many years to come. On my bookshelf, which is essentially a waterfowl library, I have ten pounds of literature on farm game management for every ounce on ducks. And I can find more of the life history facts on the Song Sparrow than on the Redhead or Ruddy Duck, neither of which has yet fully recovered from their dangerous position of the last decade.

---

[1] Originally published in The canvasback on a prairie marsh, pages 148–169. The Stackpole Co., Harrisburg, Pennsylvania and The Wildlife Management Institute, Washington, D.C., 1944.

[2] Present address: Delta, Manitoba R1N 3A1, Canada.

This book is but a small step towards the attainment of facts necessary for management. In carrying the discussion by seasons, I have unavoidably spread some important topics, such as sex ratio and courtship behavior, through several chapters. At the expense of some repetition, these are here drawn together and discussed briefly from the aspect of management. For each topic, however, one will find more hints for research than tools for management.

Sex Ratio.—The existence of an excess of males in the populations of North American waterfowl has been established beyond doubt.[3] This preponderance of drakes apparently is greatest in the diving ducks, where a sex ratio of 60:40 or more seems to prevail in most species. There is less disparity between the sexes in some of the river ducks, notably the Mallard, but in some the situation appears to be much the same as in the deep-water species.

What are the reasons for this preponderance of males? The studies of secondary sex ratios in the Canvasback, Redhead, Mallard and Pintail at Delta (Table 1) suggest that the unbalance is not primarily due to any large difference in the numbers of each sex at hatching. The Delta records show a slight preponderance of males at birth, such as exists also in man, and in some domestic animals. But this difference is not great enough to account for the severe distortion in adults.

The Delta bag tally (Table 2) shows that the kill of juveniles for all species was 1,502 males and 1,522 females, almost a perfect 50:50 sex ratio. This even

[3] For evidence of unbalanced ratios and discussions of sex ratios in waterfowl refer to: Lincoln (1932:3–4, 16–17, 1933:335–337), Leopold (1933:110–111, 339), Mayr (1939:156–179), McIlhenny (1940:87–93), Erickson (1943:20–34).

Table 1. Secondary sex ratio of wild ducks hatched in the Delta incubator.

Species	Number hatched		Percentage ratio
	Male	Female	
Canvasback	266	258	51:49
Redhead	219	193	53:47
Mallard	332	298	53:47
Pintail	276	243	53:47
Total	1,093	992	52:48

kill in the total bag of young birds is a balance between a slight excess of males in some species and of females in others. Such disparities suggest that, while hunting pressure in juveniles may contribute to an unbalanced ratio, severe disproportions cannot be attributed to such mortality. We are led to the conclusion that the heavy loss in females takes place sometime after young birds have made their first southward departure from the breeding grounds.

McIlhenny (1940:93) traced the sex of Pintails, Lesser Scaups and Ring-necked Ducks which had lived four years after banding. In each species his evidence shows "that a considerable percentage of males live longer than females, indicating that the females have more hazards to overcome than the males."

Mayr (1939:175) suggests that the lack of females may be due to deaths during incubation. In 512 duck nests studied in Alberta and Saskatchewan, Kalmbach (1937:16) found 9 females killed at the nest. In 209 duck nests studied at Delta, Sowls (unpublished manuscript) found 2 dead females. While we know almost nothing of losses in territorial drakes, it seems logical to conclude that a ground-nesting female, bearing the full burden of incubation, would be more vulnerable to predators than the male during the nesting period. I suspect such losses in hens sometimes are high when fire, mov-

Table 2. Sex ratio of the Delta shooting bag, 1938 to 1941.[1]

Species	Year	Male	Female	Ratio	Adult male	Adult female	Ratio	Juvenile male	Juvenile female	Ratio
Mallard	1938	167	225	43:57[2]						
	1939	347	309	53:47	106	98	52:48	241	211	53:47
	1940	89	118	43:57	14	45	[3]	75	73	50:50
	1941	233	174	57:43	96	32	75:25	137	142	49:51
Total		836	826	50:50	216	175	55:45	453	426	51:49
Gadwall	1938	32	42							
	1939	31	37		8	13		23	24	
	1940	19	26		2	6		17	20	
	1941	20	35		5	13		15	22	
Total		102	140	42:58	15	32		55	66	45:55
Baldpate	1938	9	9							
	1939	13	22		1	8		12	14	
	1940	5	8		0	3		5	5	
	1941	8	4		1	2		7	2	
Total		35	43	45:55	2	13		24	21	
Pintail	1938	21	52							
	1939	29	41		6	20		23	21	
	1940	11	29		2	12		9	17	
	1941	23	32		12	21		11	11	
Total		84	154	35:65	20	53		43	49	47:53
Green-winged Teal	1938	20	23							
	1939	14	16		1	2		13	14	
	1940	15	19		3	10		12	9	
	1941	15	11		6	6		9	5	
Total		64	69	48:52	10	18		34	28	
Blue-winged Teal	1938	32	49		6	16		25	30	
	1939	33	32		1	14		32	18	
	1940	18	25		3	7		15	18	
	1941	39	44		7	17		32	27	
Total		122	150	45:55	17	54		104	93	53:47
Shoveler	1938	11	18							
	1939	26	28		6	10		20	18	
	1940	10	13		4	7		6	6	
	1941	34	34		3	10		31	24	
Total		81	93	47:53	13	27		57	48	54:46
Redhead	1938	23	11							
	1939	46	47		7	8		39	39	
	1940	14	13		1	1		13	12	
	1941	94	63	60:40	3	2		91	61	60:40
Total		177	134	57:43	11	11		143	112	56:44
Canvasback	1938	111	100	53:47						
	1939	204	263	44:56	27	57		177	206	46:54
	1940	19	33		1	3		18	30	
	1941	135	157	46:54	9	24		126	133	49:51
Total		469	553	46:54	37	84	31:69	321	369	47:53
Lesser Scaup	1938	171	166	51:49	36	52		135	114	54:46
	1939	64	84	43:57	14	15		50	69	42:58
	1940	13	19		1	4		12	15	
	1941	90	127	41:59	19	15		71	112	39:61
Total		338	396	46:54	70	86	45:55	268	310	46:54

[1] Age identified only in Blue-winged Teal and Lesser Scaup in 1938; age identified in all species 1939 to 1941.

[2] Figures have been carried to the second decimal in computing percentage ratios. In this table the remaining fraction has been dropped when less than 0.05, and the higher unit adopted when more than 0.05. Thus the 43:57 ratio given for the Mallard is 42.60:57.39.

[3] Percentage ratios not given for yearly totals of less than 100 birds.

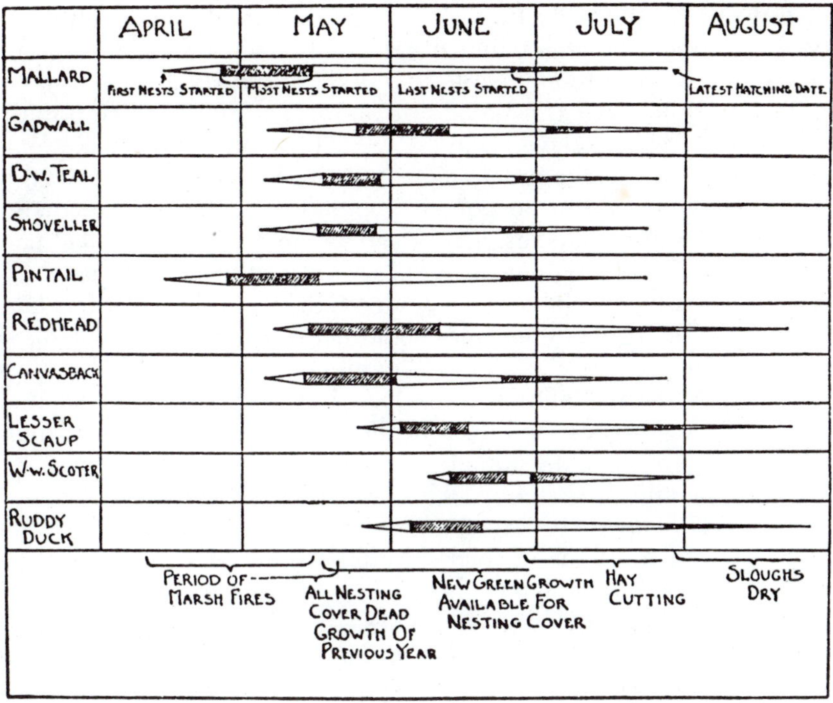

Fig. 1. Total span of the nesting period. Earliest nesting dates were based upon nest observations in all species except the White-winged Scoter. The periods during which most nests were started were determined by a study of nests, by observations of territorial pairs, and by deductions based upon the appearance of newly-hatched broods. The periods when the last nests were started were determined by observations of nests and territorial pairs as well as by deductions from brood observations. The latest hatching dates were based on nest or brood observations. In most instances where the date was based on brood observations I was able to determine the presence of the egg-tooth in young of the latest broods.

ing before a stiff wind, sweeps over the marsh edge. The relatively small number of deaths observed by Kalmbach and Sowls indicates, however, that nesting deaths, although a contributing factor, probably are not the sole cause of unequal ratios.

A heavy hunting-season loss of adult females is clearly indicated in Table 2. Until it has been disproved by studies elsewhere, we must assume that wherever ducks are shot on northern breeding grounds, a larger kill of adult females will prevail. This is due to the greater abundance of hens after the midsummer departure of the drakes, and to their delayed wing molt which, under some conditions, makes the hen more vulnerable to gun pressure. It is true, on the other hand, that the midsummer movements of the males from the breeding marshes in the North, may cause a balancing kill of drakes farther south. Whether such a balanced kill exists can be determined only by examining sex and age ratios in bags in many parts of the land.

Leopold (1933:339) says: "It is possible that the heavy preponderance of drakes found by Lincoln to obtain in wild ducks all over the continent will be traced in part to differential sex mortality from duck disease and lead poisoning." Furthermore, he points out that "any marked disturbance of the sex ratio may be considered as circumstantial evidence of disease, unless some other 'visible' form of differential mortality can be adduced to explain it." The delayed wing molt of the female suggests the probability of her greater vulnerability to botulism in northern breeding marshes. This remains in the realm of theory, however, until someone actually checks sex and age of botulism losses in many marshes throughout a season.

Drought may take a heavy toll of brood females and of those that are flightless. Speaking of drought losses in the pothole country of Alberta and Saskatchewan, Cartwright (1941:379) says: "It is no exaggeration to say that millions of ducklings died in this type of country in the last ten years." The loss in ducklings, and probably in their mothers, is reported to have run into thousands at Many Island Lake, Alberta, before that famous breeding area was restored by Ducks Unlimited. Lincoln (1937:174) speaks of heavy drought losses of ducks in Alberta during the summer of 1936. The loss of ducklings is emphasized in most reports, but I suspect that the mortality in adult hens is considerable. The fact that many brood hens are saved with their offspring in rescue operations, suggests that many probably remain to die with their charges when rescue is not forthcoming. Certainly we may assume that whatever losses occur in adults during late-summer drought, they are heaviest in the female.

There may be other lethal factors operating against the female. No single cause of mortality is responsible for the lack of hens, but many contribute to a differential death rate resulting in the existing ratios.

The significance of an unequal sex ratio is apparent to anyone who can handle round numbers in his head. It means, for one thing, that the potential breeding population of a species is considerably less than indicated by census. Take, for example, a theoretical population of 100,000 ducks, with a male-female ratio of 65:35. Instead of a potential breeding population of 50,000 pairs, there actually can be no more than 35,000 pairs at the very most. With some females not breeding their first year and others harassed by the heavy excess of unmated males, the number probably would be considerably less. In such populations a species might not be able to reproduce its numbers in a season, much less increase.

In some birds a heavy preponderance of males is associated with a reduction in numbers and reduced productivity. Thus Leopold (1933:111) writes: "A heavy excess of males is definitely known to have been associated with the decline of the Heath Hen and possibly represents the final cause of the decline." An excess of males has been observed to accompany a down-trend in numbers in the Bobwhite and Pinnated Grouse as well as in other birds. I am astounded annually at the excess of males in the Ruddy Duck at Delta. Sex ratios are difficult to obtain in this species, since the birds arrive after the ice has left the bays, and the transient flocks far from shore are not easily tallied. In careful counts made at the height of the 1941 and 1942 migrations, I saw 329 male Ruddy Ducks and 35 females, 9 drakes for every hen. This greater number of males undoubtedly was influenced to a certain extent by the earlier arrival of drakes in this species. Nevertheless, the excess is very noticeable throughout the breeding season. In mid-June, when most Ruddy hens are nesting and still are attended by their mates, I have seen hundreds of loose, unattached males in an afternoon paddle through the marsh. Often, in June, I have watched a band of more than 100 drakes emerge from a tule island as my canoe approached. Unmated drakes are more numerous than pairs in Delta Ruddy Ducks.

In his discussion of animal numbers, Elton (1927:113) wrote: "As Hewitt (1921) has pointed out, . . . great abundance is no criterion that a species is in no danger of extinction. Just as an animal can increase very quickly in a few years under good conditions, so on the other hand it may be entirely wiped out in a few years, even though it is enormously abundant. The argument that a species is in no danger because it is very common, is a complete fallacy." The demonstrated failure of abundance to save a species, and the evidence pointing to an excess of males as a symptom of population decline, should lead us still to view the status of some of our ducks solemnly. The Redhead, Canvasback and Ruddy Duck, despite large wintering concentration in some regions, show numbers considerably less than "great abundance," and all are top-heavy with drakes.

What can we do about these unbalanced ratios? The answer is "not much" until we determine the causes of the distortion. Here lies one of the most important and still largely unexplored fields of waterfowl biology.

Courtship.—The courtship behavior of ducks is the "pulse" of the marsh by which one can detect the throb of the season in any given area, North or South, East or West. A task for the waterfowl biologist, be he confined to a single marsh, or assigned to study breeding conditions in a vast region, is to understand the rhythm of habit and movement, species by species, during the critical spring period. It is only through an understanding of courtship and breeding behavior that he can appraise spring populations.

Between early April and early July on any breeding marsh one finds ducks in seven distinct categories: (1) Unmated birds not yet courting; (2) unmated birds in prenuptial courtship; (3) mated pairs: (4) unmated sexually active drakes; (5) novice drakes; (6) summering males; (7) unsuccessful or nonbreeding females. The following is a resumé of the behavior characteristics that distinguishes each group.

1. Unmated ducks not yet courting.—Seen most frequently in early spring in mixed companies of drakes and hens, neither sex offering courtship display. There is no evidence of sexual awareness among these birds; drakes pay no attention to the females, and drakes and hens do not associate together as pairs.

2. Unmated ducks in prenuptial courtship.—The drakes display in company before the hen, the most common situation being a party of two to eight males courting a single female. The hen shows no attachment to any male, except in the final stages. She repels the advances of her suitors with a thrust, or evades them by diving or by taking flight.

The courtship pursuit-flight is the most conspicuous phase of prenuptial courtship, except in the Ruddy Duck. Two other types of pursuit-flights, however, bear a superficial resemblance to the true prenuptial actions. Sometimes, for instance, when a pair moves in nuptial flight, unmated or territorial drakes lift from the marsh to follow, thus giving rise to a situation similar to prenuptial behavior. The nuptial flight begins with the pair, the extra males not joining until after drake and hen are in the air. The males usually lag behind the pair, only the mated drake being able to maneuver close to the hen. Eventually the other males, one by one, return to the marsh, finally leaving the pair alone. In prenuptial flights on the other hand, the party of drakes always leaves the water together. No one male, except in the final stages, outmaneuvers the others; and the group remains intact until its return to water at the conclusion of the chase.

It sometimes happens that only two males court a single female. Prenuptial flights of such trios may be mistaken for the actions of a territorial drake driving off an intruding pair. As pointed out earlier, such flights may be considered truly prenuptial when the three birds remain together. If one male breaks away, returning to the marsh, he is probably a territorial drake, and the others a mated pair.

3. Mated pairs.—The drake and hen, when paired, always remain together when loafing, feeding, or when in flight. On the wing the female usually leads her mate. Two distinct periods in the life of a pair may be recognized by behavior characteristics; the period of non-display in transients and the period of nuptial courtship in the territorial pairs.

Transient pairs are gregarious, frequently traveling, feeding or loafing in bands. Display is infrequent or lacking entirely, and the male is not hostile towards others of his kind. Individual pairs do not become attached to one small portion of the marsh for an extended period.

Territorial pairs isolate themselves from others of their kind, and the drake is hostile towards the intrusion of pairs or sexually active unmated birds of his own species. The pair displays mutually, and the drake challenges intruders with display actions. Drake and hen are found daily on their territory, which they are reluctant to leave in the face of human intrusion.

The behavior of the territorial pair betrays the position of the two in the nesting cycle. When seen together in nesting cover, the hen is searching for a nest site. When the male is seen alone on his territory, or on an out-of-territory waiting site in the morning, but when the pair rests on the territory later in the day, the hen is laying. After incubation has started the drake is found alone throughout the day, being visited only at intervals by the hen. Some drakes abandon the territory soon after the beginning of incubation, others may remain a week or ten days, while occasionally one may linger throughout the period of incubation. The latter behavior is regular, however, only in the Ruddy Duck.

4. Novice drakes.—These are sexually inactive birds tolerated on the territory. They do not regularly display, nor do they attempt possession of the territorial female. Usually they feed or loaf at a slight distance from the pair, and are the first to depart in the presence of a human intruder.

5. Sexually active unmated males.—Such drakes intrude upon the territory, from which they invariably are evicted by the resident male. They display intensely in the presence of a female. These loose birds may be seen alone or in small, roving bands which show no attachment to any given portion of the marsh.

6. Summering drakes.—Postbreeding males gather in small bands in May, increasing to large flocks in June. These are sexually inactive birds that do not display regularly and exhibit no sexual awareness of females. They are molting, and, as the season progresses, may be distinguished easily by their "ragged" plumage as the eclipse replaces the nuptial garb.

7. Unsuccessful or nonbreeding females.—With the exception of the hens seen in groups of noncourting, unmated birds in early spring, I have never en-

countered unattached females of any species during late April and early May. At this time all hens are being courted, are paired, or are incubating. As the numbers of postbreeding males increase, however, one sees with them an occasional female, such hens always being greatly outnumbered by drakes. These, like the males, are sexually inactive, showing no sexual awareness of their associates. Some undoubtedly have been unsuccessful in their first or second nesting attempts, and have reached the end of the reproductive chain. Others, possibly yearlings, may be individuals which never mated. In no Delta species have I seen unattached females in sufficient numbers to suggest the nonbreeding of yearling hens as a group. In the White-winged Scoter, however, companies of birds far out on the lake in June may include nonbreeding yearlings of both sexes.

In his study of the Lesser Scaup in British Columbia, Munro (1941:132) distinguished yearling hens among July and August gatherings of molting drakes. In the Barrow's Golden-eye, which Munro concludes does not nest its first year, he found some evidence of sexual activity in yearling females; one became attached to a territorial pair, while another attempted to usurp the brood of an older hen (Munro 1939:272). In the Buffle-head, Munro (1942:140) says "Large numbers of second year females associate in flocks on the breeding grounds at the time when breeding females are incubating or caring for young."

Territory.—In the earlier literature one finds scattered references which clearly indicate the territorial behavior of ducks. Thus in 1909 Stansell (quoted by Bent 1925:26) says of the Buffle-head: "When two or more pairs occupy a single pond, the males are usually very pugnacious, often quarreling and trying to drive each other off the pond for hours at a time." Munro (quoted by Bent 1925:15) writes that the drakes of two mated pairs of Barrow's Golden-eyes in a small lake "acted as if extremely jealous of each other and on several occasions left their mates and engaged in spirited encounters." Wetmore (1920:228), comparing the behavior of summering drakes with that of mated males, said: "The mated birds when found alone are not far from the site of the nest, are more alert and watchful at the approach of an intruder, and often call a warning to the female. When flushed they may fly only a short distance and then drop into the water again, and in any case usually circle around and seem loath to leave the neighborhood."

Despite the fact that Eliot Howard's classic work *Territory in Bird Life,* published in 1920, revolutionized the life history study of birds in general, it had little impact in America in the field of waterfowl biology. In the many duck-nesting studies undertaken during the last 20 years, there is, with the following exceptions, little mention of territory. Bennett (1936:495), in discussing the relation between shore line and nesting populations, writes: "Territories and territorial difficulties in relation to the shore line and water are or may be the controlling factors in duck-nesting concentrations." Later he speaks briefly of the "home base" of a nesting pair, the "nesting territory" and the "waiting territory," and he shows that counts of waiting drakes give a reliable index to the nesting population (Bennett 1938:43, 51, 123, 130). Bennett's definitions and descriptions of territory in ducks, however, are not clear-cut. Munro (1939:265, 270, 273, 279, 281) speaks more precisely of territory in the Barrow's Golden-eye. And of the Buffle-head he writes: "A breeding pair establishes a definite territory which the male vigorously defends from encroachment by other males. The territory may be an entire pond or, on larger waters, an area along several hundred yards of shore line" (Munro 1942:142).

The concept of territory in ducks eventually will effect changes in waterfowl research and management techniques. In the past, as evidenced by the reports of many duck-nesting studies, we have thought and worked largely in terms of the nest and nesting cover. The productive capacity of an area frequently has been measured in terms of nesting densities. I do not wish to undervalue the importance of the nest and its site, but it is clear that the first requirement of a pair is the territory, of which nesting cover is but one component. Management of cover is but one phase of the more important manipulation of territorial terrain. In some areas, plowed or heavily grazed, the absence of shore-line vegetation may limit the distribution of pairs, and populations may be increased by improvement of cover. In others, however, nesting facilities are adequate, with deficiencies in food, water or loafing spots limiting the number of pairs. In such a situation, further improvement of cover will not increase the number of breeding pairs.

It is clear that, despite friction over territorial sites, there is little or no competition in placing nests. High nesting densities reveal specific preferences for certain plant associations, but cannot be used as an index to the breeding capacity of a marsh; low nesting densities do not necessarily indicate low breeding numbers. At Delta, for instance, in meadowland broken by islands of Phragmites, hens converge from many widely separated territories to nest in a small area. In another portion of the marsh, where Phragmites prevails, the nests of the same number of hens are widely distributed. Only the territorial population is constant.

This, of course, is a great advantage to the marsh manager who is studying waterfowl on a small area, or over a wide region. Determination of nesting populations by a count of nests is tedious, slow and never complete. Measurement by a study of territorial pairs gives a much broader picture within a shorter period and, for one who studies behavior characters carefully, is considerably more accurate than a nest count.

Let me cite an example of the importance of territory over nests as an index to population. In 1942, as already mentioned, there were 37 territorial pairs of ducks per mile of shore line on Cadham Bay. On the lake shore, 400 yards away, there were but 9 pairs per mile. The vegetation available for the nesting of bay and lakeshore birds was exactly the same; both nested in the same meadows. But the other components were inferior on the lake shore. There, because of wave action, food plants were scarce near the shore, and, due to the wind tides, neither the water nor the loafing spots were stable. On the bay, food was plentiful, while loafing spots and water were stable.

Territorial occupation might tell us much we wish to know regarding the breeding status of a species. Thus, in 1943, on a square mile of Delta marsh there were 4 territorial pairs of Canvasbacks as compared with 41 territorial pairs of Mallards. The fact that the Mallards appeared to completely fill their available territorial sites, while the Canvasbacks did not occupy much first-rate territorial water suggests that breeding numbers of the latter species are still low and the marsh underpopulated. The wide

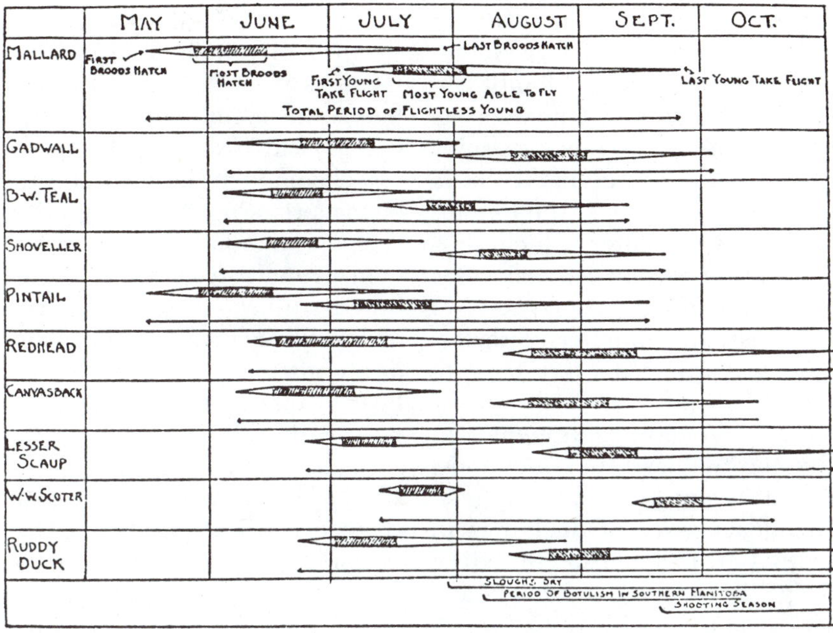

Fig. 2. Total span of the brood period. Earliest hatching dates were based on nest observations in all species except the White-winged Scoter. Periods when most young hatch, and date of latest hatchings were based largely on brood observations. Periods when first young and most young take wing were based on field observations, which checked closely with observations of captive-reared young. Dates when last young take wing were deduced from the wing development of ducklings collected during the shooting season.

dispersal of Canvasback pairs throughout the marsh, together with the accounts of much larger breeding concentrations in the past given by older residents, strengthen this conclusion. In some species the problem of the moment is to build up populations to the point where they may use the breeding facilities already available.

Territory offers unlimited possibilities for research in almost totally unexplored fields of waterfowl biology. What follows when the territorial drake is killed before the nest is started, or during the egg-laying period? What is the "turnover" in territorial males? R. D. Harris (unpublished notes), of Ducks Unlimited, has developed a simple technique for trapping females at the nest so that they may be marked for identification. With such marked females we can learn what follows when the nest is destroyed (or removed by the investigator) during various stages of the egg-laying and incubation periods. Does the hen obtain a new mate and nest again when the clutch is destroyed after the departure of her drake?

Broods.—Figure 2 deserves more than a passing glance. It shows, among other things, that the great bulk of young ducks of the two most successful species, the Mallard and Pintail, are on the wing by the end of July. They have the remainder of the summer and the early autumn in which to condition themselves for the southward migration. Most of the young Blue-winged Teal and Shovellers are flying by the middle of August. Among the river ducks, only the Gadwall is delayed.

But look at the diving ducks. Only a

few of the early-hatched broods are flying by the middle of August, and most youngsters do not take their first flight until late August or early September. This suggests that the difference in flying schedules between river ducks and diving ducks is one reason for the success of the former, and the failure of the latter, which, during the "duck depression" of ten years ago, brought some deep-water species to such dangerously low numbers. Species, such as the Mallard, that bring most of their young to wing before midsummer, are much less vulnerable to drought than others, like the Redhead, in which most young do not fly until after mid-August. The tremendous losses of ducklings in the western portions of the breeding range during dry years probably have been heaviest in the diving ducks.

Furthermore, because of their longer flightless period, the diving ducks are vulnerable to predators and other hazards for a longer period than most of the river ducks. A Canvasback stands less chance of reaching the flying stage in nine weeks than a Blue-winged Teal in six weeks.

This situation at Delta is most serious in the Redhead which, year after year, shows the largest percentage of flightless ducklings after the end of August. Many local residents refer to these late broods as "second or third hatchings." Undoubtedly some are products of late nests which followed first unsuccessful attempts. The fact remains, however, that some Delta Redheads do not start nesting until late June or early July, hence some late broods are the products of first nests.

This delayed development is by no means confined to the latitude of Delta, but apparently prevails throughout the land. Thus Wetmore (1921:4) says that on the Bear River Marshes, Utah: "Redheads less than a third grown were common as late as September 7; a large number of young Redheads were unable to fly until after September 25." Rowan (letter) tells me of a brood of Lesser Scaups he saw near Edmonton, Alberta, September 14, which were "still in the down."

Delayed flight in the diving ducks is as characteristic of the group as their big feet, and this fact must be recognized in management. It modifies the analysis of brood studies, it demands maintenance of water on breeding marshes through September, and it should have some bearing on shooting policy when drought prevails in the prairies.

A phase of management which has received much attention in recent years is the censusing of waterfowl. The problem is complex and the techniques, on the breeding grounds at least, poorly developed. At the North American Wildlife Conference in 1936 it was suggested that the census of the breeding grounds should take place "when the old ducks are with the young." A glance at Fig. 2 shows that this period extends from mid-May, when the first Mallards and Pintails hatch, until mid-August, when most of the young diving ducks have been abandoned by their parents. There is no confined period during the spring or summer when all broods of all species may be seen. As already pointed out, the first young Pintails are awing at the same time the first Lesser Scaups and Ruddy Ducks are hatching, while the earliest-hatched Pintails are in flight before the last Pintail nests have hatched. A reliable study of summer populations can be made only when the same area is covered at frequent intervals throughout the course of a season.

Maill (quoted by Elton 1927:2) writes: "Natural history . . . is encumbered by multitudes of facts which are recorded only because they are easy to record." I would qualify this statement by adding that the encumbrance frequently is not so much in the nature of the material but in the manner in which the record is made and analyzed. Counting broods is one of the easiest and most pleasant tasks of the summer, but the figures obtained often are quite meaningless. It is common practice, for instance, to count the number of young per brood, add, then divide to obtain an average. Such averages have been interpreted as significant evidence of the degree of brood success. On almost any summer day, broods encountered will range from newly-hatched, to those almost ready to fly. Since brood mortality is progressive, averages drawn from all age classes give a figure having little importance.

Bennett (1938:73–74) gave meaning to his brood records by analyzing them by weekly averages through the season, and his figures clearly show the progressive decline in brood size. When possible, an estimate of age should be made for each brood, thus further qualifying the time element. Age determination is difficult, even in hatchery-reared ducklings at one's feet. Besides, possible variations in growth rate in different latitudes means that age criteria may not be everywhere the same. In all ducklings, however, there are two "constants": newly-hatched young, and young almost ready to fly. Most field workers, with some practice, can learn to identify these two classes with a small margin of error. Hence brood counts may be made and analyzed in three distinct groups, newly-hatched young, intermediate young, and young almost ready to fly. The average of the youngest class will give a fair picture of brood size at hatching; the average of the oldest young gives a more accurate figure for the number reaching the flying stage than an average of all groups.

Conclusions regarding the number of young per brood attaining flight may be drawn most accurately in the river ducks, where the hen usually remains with her charges until they are ready to fly. In the diving ducks, where the hen frequently abandons her young before flying age, the parentless brood may split up or join with other stray ducklings. Such bands cannot be considered as units. This early abandonment of ducklings in the diving ducks probably is a universal trait in Delta species. I have seen parentless bands of Canvasbacks, Lesser Scaups and Ruddy Ducks in the marshlands near The Pas, in northern Manitoba. On the Bear River Marshes of Utah, Wetmore (1923:11) says of the Redhead: "The parent may forsake her charges when they are less than half grown, and it is the rule for them to be left to their own devices at an early age."

Brood counts do not always give a fair appraisal of brood populations. Thus at Delta the river ducks, which outnumber the diving ducks, are seen with less frequency because the young are reared to a greater extent in edge cover. Nor are brood counts an indication of the productivity of any given portion of an area such as Delta, where there is a movement of broods from the sloughs to the larger bays.

The Postbreeding Season.—The postbreeding habits and movements of ducks present the waterfowl biologist with the following facts which must be recognized in any management plan, whether it is local, regional or continental in scope.

1. After they have completed their marital duties, drake river ducks foregather on marshes where loafing spots are found adjacent to feeding areas. These bands eventually concentrate in large marshes to pass the flightless period in waters abundant in food and supplied with protective cover growths along the shore

line. Drake diving ducks likewise assemble in marshes, but move to certain lakes to molt the wing feathers.

2. This movement of males to their gathering and molting waters constitutes the largest population shift between the spring and fall migrations. Censuses made without recognition of this change do not give a valid picture of breeding numbers in any given region. In some marshes, numbers are greatly increased by an influx of males, and a species uncommon or absent as a breeder, may become abundant. Other areas, adequate as breeding marshes, may appear underpopulated as drakes move elsewhere. Late spring and summer appraisals may be severely misleading unless due attention is given to this early-summer "shuffle."

3. Although the flightless period of the individual is relatively short, seldom lasting more than a month, the molt for ducks as a group is extended throughout much of the summer and early autumn. At Delta it extends from the second week in June, when the first Mallard and Pintail drakes lose their wing feathers, until the second week in October when the last Redhead and Canvasback females have gained the use of their new wings. Drakes molt earlier than the females, hence may be less vulnerable to drought and botulism.

4. Many adult females have not completed the change when the shooting season opens. This is true not only of southern Canada, but also of marshes to the south. In Utah, Wetmore (1921:7) found flightless females after the hunting season opened on October 1.

5. The postbreeding separation of the sexes influences the make-up of late summer and early autumn populations. In all Delta river ducks except the Mallard, most adult males depart for points unknown shortly after the flightless period and do not again return in large numbers. This leaves an autumn preponderance of females. Likewise drake diving ducks do not return to the breeding marsh in large numbers after leaving the molting lakes.

A number of important questions concerning the postbreeding period await study. What is the pattern of molting marshes on the breeding grounds? In Manitoba I know of but two marshes to which large numbers of drake river ducks regularly come to pass the flightless period: the Netley Marsh, at the south end of Lake Winnipeg, and the Delta Marsh. Probably other large marshes in the province serve the same function, e.g., the marshes of Lake Winnipegosis, those of the Saskatchewan River Delta, and the vast breeding areas in the region of The Pas.

What lakes, among the countless thousands of the prairie provinces, are molting waters for the diving ducks? In summer surveys, an appraisal of molting populations of drake diving ducks should be made.

What are the movements of the drakes after they depart from the molting waters? Of ducks at Avery Island, Louisiana, McIlhenny (1940:91) says: "A study of the birds as trapped points to the conclusion that the females and young come south in advance of the adult males." Since the old males molt earlier, and depart from their breeding marshes earlier, we might wonder where they "hang out" while the females overtake them in the journey to the wintering grounds. Dawson (1923:1796) speaks of an "early and abundant autumnal return of the male Pintails while still in the eclipse plumage" in California. He says: "Probably the Santa Barbara coast is unusually favored in this respect, because annually, in the month of August, before other reported localities are talking, or even thinking of ducks, we are visited by hundreds, sometimes thousands, of returning migrants, invariably males. Gadwalls are among them, and on the 25th of August, 1915, I encountered upon the Estero ponds, within the city limits, a close-set flock of twenty-five Blue-winged Teal. But Pintails outnumbered all other ducks (save resident Ruddies) a hundred to one at this season."

How long do these males remain together? In Texas, Arthur Hawkins (unpublished manuscript) saw a flock of 500 Pintails on November 9 composed almost entirely of drakes. Robert H. Smith (letter) says that in the first northward flights of Pintails reaching the rice section of Arkansas, he has seen flocks showing almost 100 per cent males, and in the first spring flights reaching northern Iowa he has seen flocks of males. B. W. Cartwright tells me he has seen transient flocks of Pintail drakes in early May in southern Manitoba. Do some bands retain their identity throughout the winter, or are such spring aggregations made up of yearling males?

What is the schedule of the wing molt among birds which breed within the Arctic Circle, as do many Mallards and Pintails? There spring comes late and the freeze-up early, and the entire routine of breeding and molting must fall within a considerably shorter span than that which prevails on the prairies to the south. Is the flightless period shortened for the species as a whole, or for the individual? The former would be true if the span of the nesting season is compressed, as it must be in the Arctic. If all Arctic-breeding females nest at about the same time, there would not be as much individual variation in the time of the wing molt. This fact is suggested by the observations of Angus Gavin (unpublished manuscript) who says that drake Pintails in the region of the Perry River complete the wing molt by the middle of July. This is three weeks before the last Pintail drake has regained his new flight feathers at Delta.

For the individual bird a shorter period required for the development of new flight feathers may be influenced by the greater amount of daylight prevailing in the Arctic.

Autumn and the Shooting Season.—In 33 states and Provinces where the Ring-necked Pheasant is legal game, the average length of the shooting season in 1942 was less than four weeks, the average daily bag was three birds, and in most regions the female was protected. Furthermore, because this bird is not migratory, shooting pressure ended for any given group of birds when the state or provincial season closed. In ducks the open season for the same year averaged more than two months throughout the land. The daily bag was 10 birds in the United States and 12 in Canada (where, in many provinces, there is no Sunday shooting and ice closes the season long before the legal deadline). Females were not protected. Hunting began September 1 in Alaska and closed January 10 in Delaware, Maryland, Texas and the 12 other states of the "southern zone." Some ducks, therefore, were under fire for considerably longer than two months in passage from their breeding marshes to their wintering waters.

I have no object in comparing the more stringent policy that governs the shooting of a successful exotic with the far less restrictive regulations for our native waterfowl, except to emphasize two points: (1) The sportsman can thank ducks, not pheasants, for the fact that his hunting coat on the back of the kitchen door is ready for use during a good part of the autumn. Regulations governing the take of waterfowl allow the hunter "more for his money" than do the laws controlling the harvest of any other game bird. (2) The administrator of waterfowl policy should view his laws with deep respect. It is possible, on the basis of statistics, for the people of North America to wipe out the waterfowl population in the course of one autumn under existing seasons and bag limits. The fact that this seems improbable on the basis of observed practice does not remove the burden of responsibility.

Probably no phase of game policy is more encumbered with conflicting opinion than that which governs the harvest of waterfowl. Besides the mass of hunters who accept existing laws as just, there are two large opposing groups, one of which will forever believe that shooting regulations are too tight, and the other which will never be satisified that they are restrictive enough. Shooting laws, the sportsman should understand, are not drawn to balance between the pressures of the two extremist groups. The harvest of North American waterfowl is governed, first, by treaties between the citizens and governments of the three interdependent North American countries, Canada, the United States and Mexico. These delegate the broad responsibilities of each country, giving each, within treaty limits, the freedom to regulate its waterfowl shooting laws according to the status of the species involved. To this end, each country cooperates with the others in a year-around survey of waterfowl resources—on the breeding grounds, along the flyways, and on the wintering waters—bringing together facts and evidence for the purpose of determining a safe and just harvest.

While much is thus accomplished in appraising the year's production from which the harvest is to be taken, we know very little regarding the nature of the harvest itself. For instance: We know almost nothing of the sex and age make-up of autumn populations, nor how the movements of the different groups fit in with the pattern of zoned open seasons. It is agreed that if we are to have duck hunting we cannot, as in pheasants, protect the hen by selective shooting laws. But in a group of birds in which the males so greatly outnumber the females, it is important that we know something of the impact our present system has upon the sex balance of living populations.

Nor do we know very much regarding the harvest by species. Are all species shot in proportion to their existing numbers? Probably not. Witness the heavy kill of Canvasbacks at Delta as compared with that of the Mallard, a species which, locally and continentally, far outnumbers the Canvasback. I suspect that the diving ducks, measured in relative numbers, receive heavier shooting pressure than the river ducks. Hawkins and Bellrose (1939:181–182) estimated that, although Lesser Scaups were far less numerous than Mallards in the Illinois Valley during the autumn of 1938, the kill of Lesser Scaups ranked second or third to that of Mallards. More information regarding the harvest might tell us how opening or closing dates might be manipulated to favor some species. Thus Hawkins and Bellrose (1939:180, 186) have shown that in Illinois the illegal kill of Wood Ducks, which was greater in 1938 than the legal kill of Blue-winged Teal, might have been greatly reduced if the opening date for shooting had been delayed one week. And merely shortening the season does not always mean that the kill will be lighter. Wilson (1938:638) shows that the kill of Canvasbacks on the Bear River Marshes, although relatively small, was greater in 1934, under a 30-day season, than it was the previous year during a shooting period of 60 days.

Years ago, Cook (1906:12) said: "An important question in connection with the protection of ducks is the time when they pair for the breeding season, since it is evident that if shooting is continued after the birds are paired a decided decrease in the number of broods will result." It is clear that in the "southern zone" of the United States, where duck hunting continues until January 10, pairing takes place in the Mallard, and possibly in other species, while these birds are under pressure of gunfire. Are pairs more, or less, vulnerable than unmated birds; and if one mate is killed, does the survivor obtain a new partner?

One of the most perplexing problems concerning autumn populations is that of damage by ducks to certain domestic crops. Now, in period of war, with the shortage of manpower and the need for all foods, this problem has received wide publicity; and some sporting groups echo the complaints of farmers with suggestions that shooting regulations be relaxed so that "overpopulations," supposedly responsible for the damage, may be reduced. The problem is difficult to appraise from all its viewpoints—that of the farmer, who stands a heavy loss, that of the sportsman, who would like to help the farmer and at the same time improve his own shooting, that of the biologist, who sees the overlap between the realm of ducks and man as an unavoidable conflict if we are to have ducks and rice or barley fields along the same flyways, or that of the administrator, who must be fair in his dealings with ducks and men alike. All interested in this subject must accept the following facts: (1) "Locally or periodically wild fowl have caused losses to grain and certain truck crops ever since agriculture became established in their migration flyways" (Kalmbach 1935:1). (2) Farm damage by ducks is not necessarily evidence that waterfowl have reached a point of "overabundance." Kalmbach (1935:1) pointed out that "duck damage (sometimes of serious proportions to the individual farmer) [has occurred] during a period when the national supply of waterfowl [was] becoming precariously low." (3) While such destruction of crops is generally referred to as "duck damage," many species are quite innocent. The country over, Mallards and Pintails are the chief offenders, with the Black Duck and Baldpate and some of the other river ducks causing severe damage in some localities. (4) Measures directed at all ducks throughout the country will not solve the problem. (5) Damage to domestic crops is not always an indication of a failure of the natural food supply. At Delta, for instance, despite the presence of one of the finest stands of natural foods in the land, the thousands of Mallards that crowd the lake shore each autumn ignore this wild supply to feed on domestic fields by preference. Many cultivated grains are preferred foods for some species, and, as Kalmbach points out (1935:5): "One cannot set out a banquet table for the birds and then expect them not to use it."

Of the many fields for study of our ducks in autumn not all are for the state, federal or university agencies alone. Each duck hunter has a research problem of his own—that of determining how he may reduce his crippling loss. Even the most skillful hunters lose some birds by crippling; and the losses by the great mass of gunners attain staggering proportions. Sportsmen often speak vehemently against the crow, the skunk and other predators. Yet with crippling losses sometimes reaching the tremendous figure of one bird lost for every one bagged, it is clear that the hunter may at times fall below the plane of the natural predator which, to say the least, usually kills cleanly without waste. The law allows each hunter a certain number of birds and never asks him how many he crippled to attain the legal limit. Hunting skill is not to be measured in the size of the bag, but in the manner in which the kill was made. Many cripples are the result of poor, slovenly shooting by inexperienced hunters; but many more are lost through plain carelessness—shooting at birds beyond killing range, firing into flocks, or failure to leave the hide to retrieve a cripple that has dropped beyond shot range. Crows, skunks and other predators can be, and are, controlled where their numbers cause severe damage to waterfowl. But there is no simple method to control the crippling loss. It will always remain a personal issue with the individual hunter.

EPILOGUE

The bays are closed with ice; the ducks are gone. Where bluebills rode a week ago, a Snowy Owl now sits in the middle of an ice field. The ducks are gone; for five months to come there will be only the music of the north wind in the maples. It is winter and rough winter every day, until sometime in late March when Georgie Storey will strain with hand in air from the last seat in the last row of the little building housing the marsh-side school.

"Yes, George?"

"I seen four Mallards this morning."

"*Saw*, George. I *saw* four Mallards. The past participle is —."

The lesson is never finished. From far away comes the bark of geese. The children run for the schoolyard, the teacher for the stoop.

"There they are! There they are! Canada Grays over Slacks' bluff!"

Over by the shed the men stop their work and step into the sun to watch the birds in silence. They see them swing over the bay, flare above the schoolyard, then head north across the frozen lake. Old Ernie Cook, gravely taking pipe from mouth, says "A week early."

There is no sound except of geese and the south wind in the maples, the coming of another spring.

LITERATURE CITED

BENNETT, LOGAN J. 1936. Duck nesting carrying capacities in Iowa. Trans. First N. Am. Wildlife Conf.: 494–498.

———. 1938. The Blue-winged Teal, its ecology and management. 144pp. Collegiate Press, Ames, Iowa.

BENT, ARTHUR CLEVELAND. 1925. Life histories of North American wild fowl, order Anseres (Part II). U.S. Nat. Mus. Bull. 130, 376pp.

CARTWRIGHT, B. W. 1941. Restoration of waterfowl habitat in western Canada. Trans. Fifth N. Am. Wildlife Conf.: 377–382.

COOKE, WELLS W. 1906. Distribution and migration of North American ducks, geese, and swans. U.S. Dept. Agr. Biol. Survey Bull. 26, 90pp.

CRAIG, W. 1908. The voices of pigeons regarded as a means of social control. Am. Jour. Sociol. 14:86–100.

DAWSON, WILLIAM LEON. 1923. The birds of California. Booklovers' Ed. Vol. 4. South Moulton Co., San Diego.

ELTON, CHARLES. 1927. Animal ecology. 209pp. Macmillan, New York.

ERICKSON, ARNOLD B. 1943. Sex ratios of ducks in Minnesota. Auk 60:20–34.

HAWKINS, ARTHUR S., AND FRANK C. BELLROSE. 1939. The duck flight and kill along the Illinois River during the fall of 1938. American Wildlife 28:178–186.

HEWITT, C. GORDON. 1921. The conservation of wildlife in Canada. 344pp. Scribner's, New York.

HOWARD, H. ELIOT. 1920. Territory in bird life. 308pp. Murray, London.

KALMBACH, E. R. 1935. Protecting grain crops from damage by wild fowl. U.S. Dept. Agr. Wildlife Research Leaflet. BS-13, 7pp. (Mimeographed.)

———. 1937. Crow-waterfowl relationships based

on preliminary studies on Canadian breeding grounds. U.S. Dept. Agr. Circ. 433, 36pp.

LEOPOLD, ALDO. 1933. Game management. 481pp. Scribner's, New York.

LINCOLN, FREDERICK C. 1932. Do drakes outnumber Susies? American Game 21:3–4, 16–17.

———. 1933. A decade of bird banding in America: a review. Smithsonian Report (1932):327–351.

———. 1937. The waterfowl situation. Trans. Second N. Am. Wildlife Conf.: 168–179.

MAYR, ERNST. 1939. The sex ratio in wild birds. The American Naturalist 73:156–179.

MCILHENNY, E. A. 1940. Sex ratio in wild birds. Auk 57:85–93.

MUNRO, J. A. 1939. Studies of waterfowl in British Columbia; Barrow's Golden-eye and American Golden-eye. Trans. Royal Can. Institute 22: 259–318.

———. 1941. Studies of waterfowl in British Columbia; Greater Scaup Duck and Lesser Scaup Duck. Can. Jour. of Research 19:113–138.

———. 1942. Studies of waterfowl in British Columbia; Buffle-head. Can. Jour. of Research 20:133–160.

WETMORE, ALEXANDER. 1920. Observations on the habits of birds at Lake Burford, New Mexico. Auk 37:221–247, 293–412.

———. 1921. Wild ducks and duck foods of the Bear River Marshes, Utah. U.S. Dept. Agr. Bull. 936, 20pp.

———. 1923. Migration records from wild ducks and other birds banded in the Salt Lake Valley, Utah. U.S. Dept. Agr. Bull. 1145, 14pp.

WILSON, VANEZ T. 1938. Management of waterfowl public shooting grounds. Trans. Third N. Am. Wildlife Conf.: 633–639.

THE PERMANENT VALUE OF REFUGES IN WATERFOWL MANAGEMENT[1]

J. CLARK SALYER II, Fish and Wildlife Service, Chicago, IL

Since the dark days of the early 30's when the continental waterfowl population, through a combination of adverse factors, was so seriously threatened that duck hunting appeared to be relegated to the "now I can remember when" status, conditions have so improved that some raise the question: "Are waterfowl refuges necessary?" The answer is not hard to find. Waterfowl refuges, and for that matter refuges for other forms of wildlife, are a necessity. The continued expansion of intensive land utilization in the United States forces maintenance of the wildlife refuge program as a sort of life insurance policy for the nation's wildlife resources. The national wildlife refuge program provides the most concrete and lasting safeguard against possible depletion of the waterfowl population. Without the refuges, and with less successful management, it is certain that the present liberal hunting regulations would not have been possible.

The most outstandingly successful programs for wildlife conservation have been based in part upon refuges. The original purpose of the national waterfowl refuge program was sound, namely to restore as much breeding ground as was possible under existing land and land-use conditions. Those conditions vary, hence some of the lands that are necessary from a long-time conservation viewpoint are not restorable now but may be in the future.

The second purpose of the program was to provide suitable areas at intervals along the four great flyways where the birds could find rest and food, and the third was to preserve or restore as much of the wintering ground as possible. The birds can be substantially benefited only when provisions are made for their welfare at all seasons.

An important form of insurance provided by the refuge program is the preservation of habitat against the deterioration or complete destruction that so often follows intensive land-use development. Individually such developments may not affect large acreages of waterfowl habitat but collectively they have a far-reaching effect by decreasing below the essential minimum the area necessary to furnish adequate nesting, feeding, and resting habitat for these birds—an important national resource. Industrialization along the Atlantic seaboard during the past few decades, together with the drainage of marshes for resort development and mosquito control have eliminated more than 7 million acres of wintering grounds formerly available to the waterfowl of the Atlantic Flyway. Forty years ago the public would have scoffed at the idea that the drainage of coastal marsh lands could have such a far-reaching effect on the waterfowl population. We have profited, in a measure, from the mistakes of past exploitation but nonetheless, continued vigilance is necessary to protect the remaining waterfowl habitat. Flood control, irrigation and power projects, and ill-advised drainage projects now directly menace vast acreages of the remaining waterfowl territory in the United States.

[1] Originally published in Trans. North Am. Wildl. Conf. 10:43–47, 1945.

These continued threats emphasize the necessity of permanent wildlife refuges.

Providing refuges for wildlife is not a new activity. That the principle is sound is demonstrated by the general practice by gunning clubs for many years of alternating shooting periods with intervals during which there is no gunning on actual hunting lands, and of protecting a reasonable proportion of the total acreage controlled by the club against all shooting. The logic behind the refuge program is not that of locking up wildlife and attempting to protect it absolutely and forever; rather, refuges should be considered as reservoirs that assure a sustained annual yield from a renewable resource. Many sportsmen, one time generally opposed to the waterfowl refuge idea, have learned by experience that these closed areas have permanent value in creating better shooting locally. Thus, instead of the birds being "burned out" of a district during the early part of the hunting season, their movements along the migration route are more leisurely because of the presence of resting areas protected from shooting. They filter out gradually from such rest areas and feeding grounds and provide a more uniform and longer shooting season than would prevail if the refuges were not available.

The preservation of the residual brood stock necessary to populate the nesting grounds is far more important than is generally recognized by gunners who have an opportunity to make observations on only isolated sections of the waterfowl habitat. Destruction of waterfowl resorts through industrial and other land-use developments results in the concentration of waterfowl on remaining areas, these giving to the local observers an impression of plenty. Right now we are faced with a real possibility of having too few feeding grounds to accommodate the waterfowl raised in Canada and Alaska, but which must depend to a large extent on the United States as a winter resort. Waterfowl must eat 12 months out of the year and unless they are properly cared for and well fed during the winter months they cannot fully populate the breeding grounds the succeeding season. Controlled water levels, management practices which have been developed and put into effect on the refuges, permit the production of more waterfowl food per acre than is possible on lands not so intensively managed. While a good job is being done with what we have, the refuges cannot provide all the feed necessary for the continental population of waterfowl; they do, however, feed a sufficient number to guarantee a reasonable annual crop of young birds. In districts where vast acreages of waterfowl habitat have been converted to agricultural use, restriction of natural feeding grounds has led to destruction of crops. Concentrated production of food on refuge lands has acted as a buffer, however, has minimized depredations, and helped to prevent the serious losses of grain and other crops that would have resulted in the absence of such a program.

The principle of multiple use applies fully to the Service's national wildlife refuges. While the majority of the refuge areas were acquired and developed primarily for waterfowl, their contribution to the protection and increase of other wildlife is sometimes equally important and in many instances of greater importance locally. The lakes and marshes developed for waterfowl are highly productive of fish and fur animals. The annual yield of muskrats from some of our refuges constitutes an important economic contribution to the community. Sport and commercial fishing has developed locally on a large scale where nonexistent before. To date more than 40,000 pheasants have been made available from waterfowl refuges for restocking under the direction of state conservation departments. More than 5,000 deer have been supplied from refuge properties for stocking by state conservation officers.

From the beginning of the national emergency the federal refuge properties have contributed substantially to the growing of war food crops and the grazing of livestock. Economic use of refuge lands is a part of our basic management program. The regulated grazing of pasture lands contained within refuges promoted recovery of forage to the extent that the additional grazing required for expansion of beef production was available locally. It is significant that even though many of our national waterfowl refuges were restoration projects in the fullest sense of the word, many having been developed on land once classed as submarginal, the yields from cropland upon them which has been devoted to food production compare favorably with those of the best land in the vicinity. The same is true of the range land. Thus, the refuge acreages are not closed to economic or recreational use, but are utilized to the extent consistent with primary management of the properties for waterfowl and other wildlife. The harvesting of timber from refuges has yielded a large volume of high grade lumber now urgently needed by war industries. Thus, the national wildlife refuges not only have a permanent value to local economy but in an hour of need have provided resources of vital national importance.

A permanent value of refuge properties that is frequently overlooked is their function as field laboratories wherein experimentation is constantly carried on to determine the most efficient and most practical means of managing wildlife populations and wildlife habitat.

Their most fundamental value, of course, is that they provide homes for the birds. We have a considerable part of the breeding population of some of the most important waterfowl species in the United States and for at least half of each year we must feed an overwhelming percentage of the waterfowl of North America, not only those which breed in the United States, but also in Canada, Alaska, and Greenland. Practically all of the geese winter in the United States and their fate depends upon our treatment of them.

The waterfowl refuges always give us a necessary margin of safety in continental conservation, hence it's just as good business to keep them as it is to keep life insurance. They supply the margin of safety which makes possible sound management of a commodity so unpredictable as a wildlife population. So far as I can see we are always going to need the national refuge program.

To summarize:

1. The national waterfowl refuge system preserves waterfowl habitat, thus providing a place for the birds over large areas where suitable habitat has practically disappeared.

2. The waterfowl refuges are necessary to save the breeding stock essential for repopulating the nesting grounds each year.

3. The waterfowl refuges have proved themselves to be one of the important tools of waterfowl management, spreading the birds with fair uniformity over the entire country, extending the length of the shooting period locally, and making shooting opportunities more democratic.

4. The waterfowl refuges provide a habitat for many interesting and impor-

tant nongame species of wildlife, some of which, as the fur bearers, are of great economic importance.

5. The refuges have become very important to the economic life and success of surrounding communities and are making a very appreciable contribution to the war effort in foodstuffs, furs, lumber, and fibers.

RECOVERY POTENTIALS IN NORTH AMERICAN WATERFOWL

H. ALBERT HOCHBAUM, Delta Waterfowl Research Station, Delta, Manitoba, Canada

The great wildlife tragedy of the past decade is the false optimism that has attended the rise in waterfowl populations. On every hand we are offered superlatives describing the situation: *"the miracle of conservation," "production boosted 500 per cent," "overpopulations,"* increases reaching *"almost to the full carrying capacity of the environment."* If any disturbing news attended the flights of recent years it was blamed on the weather: *"record crop heads southward"* but *"haywire weather produces freaky duck season."* And then comes the "grand slam." In a recent press release (Gabrielson 1946) we are told by the Fish and Wildlife Service that it sees "in the situation a threat to the future of migratory waterfowl hunting." One bad season and "pop" goes the waterfowl balloon.

How could this happen? Management has taken much credit for the rise in waterfowl populations. But management has failed. We have gone from reported overpopulations to poor flights in 2 years. Even before the shotgun shells are off the ration lists, even before all the hunters in the armed services have returned to the marshes, the situation marks the future of waterfowl hunting as jeopardized. This is not management! The "miracle" is not the restoration of waterfowl; the miracle is that in 10 years we did not have the "know-how" to avoid the present situation which could have been avoided had management functioned. The miracle is that we could so steep ourselves in manufactured optimism that the current situation (which management should have foreseen) comes as a deep shock and surprise to most of us.

Management has failed in one of its most important functions. It has failed to foresee the current plight of waterfowl; it has failed to predict (as successful management of any domestic crop must predict), to manage and regulate the harvest in accordance with prevailing conditions that were measurable and predictable. Let us hope that we may learn. The future of waterfowl as game birds still depends upon management.

Waterfowl management admittedly is far more complex than in other game birds. The vast, mobile population is spread over our entire continent, the joint property of three nations. When we manage waterfowl we do not work with one species in one environment, as in quail or pheasants, managing and hunting one kind. Ducks in their many species are not alike. Each is unlike the others in behavior, in physical makeup and in its relationship to man, the hunter and would-be manager. As one small step, then, in setting the stage for future management, let us study some of the factors governing the potential recovery rates in the several species of American ducks. "Recovery," incidentally, is the proper word. Ducks are still in the recovery stage in their climb from the deep low of 10 years ago. Now and for some time to come management must concern itself with recovering lost populations rather than maintaining stable numbers.

When we manage the environment for "waterfowl" we must know that each

---

[1] Originally published in Trans. North Am. Wildl. Conf. 11:403–416, 1946.

species or group of species reacts differently according to its innate makeup. We must know that waterfowl management is not necessarily redhead management. We must know that factors responsible for an increase in mallards may not induce similar gains in canvasbacks. If we are to manage the harvest we must learn to predict why and when some species have produced substantial gains while others have not.

The following discussion attempts to describe some of the reasons for the differential recovery rate in our important game ducks. An understanding of the variation in productivity is essential, not only in the management of the environment, but in the establishment of sound waterfowl policy governing the harvest.

NUMBERS

Great numbers by no means insure large populations. Indeed, in cyclic species, such as grouse and rabbits, population peaks are followed by drastic "crash" declines. In our migratory waterfowl, however, we know of no such spectacular drops in population. The recent deep low developed over a long period of years and its cause, in contrast to other game cycles, was known. In waterfowl we see security rather than disaster in numbers.

Numbers in waterfowl probably have an important bearing on recovery rates. The larger the population, the better its chance to increase its numbers. This is due to the nature of the breeding environment. At no time are breeding conditions favorable throughout the range, as we know all too well from our studies in recent years. When abundant water renders marshes in dry regions safe, floods are apt to strike elsewhere in the range. At no time is the entire breeding area safe from drought and flood, fire and agriculture.

When numbers are large, the spread of the breeding population is such that it can absorb local adversities. It can suffer regional setbacks and still show an overall gain. When numbers are low, local adversities may seriously impair the entire population, as in 1945 when the redhead breeding grounds in Canada suffered drought and flood during the same season. We can draw a comparison with the rich and the poor investor. The rich man may scatter his investments widely, never chancing to lose all and always building his total securities. The poor man with his few investments chances meager gains and heavy loss.

While we cannot quote figures of relative waterfowl abundance, it is clear that those species which had the largest populations 10 years ago, the mallard and pintail, have shown the greatest recovery. This undoubtedly is due in part to their original advantage of greater numbers.

Management must direct its efforts towards improvement of conditions for small populations with their limited breeding area and their hazardous "investments." If management favors the small investor, so to speak, the species rich in numbers will take care of themselves.

BREEDING RANGE

Breeding range varies widely according to species. There is a vast center of waterfowl breeding activity in the northern tier of the United States and in the prairie provinces of Canada where there is great specific overlap and where most of the important game species (with the exception of the black duck and wood duck) nest. Some, but not all species, have ranges extending far beyond this central region. Clearly the most successful species, such as the mallard and pintail, have the widest ranges. The much less successful ducks, as the redhead and canvasback which suffered so severely during the "duck depression," are much more restricted in range (Gabrielson and Lincoln 1941). The present breeding concentrations of these two diving ducks is at the northern edge of the original pattern of their continental breeding range.

One of the most serious pressures of this northern region is clear when we examine growth rates. Young canvasbacks and redheads require several more weeks to reach the flying stage than young mallards and pintails. They are favored by the longer spring and summer of the lower latitudes where, however, their breeding habitat is now greatly reduced through conflict with agriculture. Even in the latitude of northern Utah the main hatch of redheads is not awing until mid-September (Williams 1944:254). In the northern tier of states and in southern Canada many young redheads are not awing until October while some do not fly until ice comes (Hochbaum 1944:109). It is possible that there is some compensation in the longer days of northern regions, but evidence now at hand suggests that the northern portion of the breeding range cannot produce optimum crops in these species. Management must be directed towards the improvement of southern ranges for species with long growth periods.

A glance at any range map (Kalmbach 1937, Kortright 1942) shows the main breeding area of redheads and canvasbacks overlapping the agricultural regions and hazardous drought areas. Management has attempted to create drought-proof waters within this region; but the 1945 drought struck with such force in Saskatchewan and Alberta that even some of the newly-created areas were left dry or nearly so. The much-publicized Many Island Lake in southern Alberta is but one example of the failure of management to conquer drought. As yet we have been unable to provide drought-proof areas on more than a fraction of the dry regions. We are unable to control drought much beyond the established irrigation districts. But with the knowledge of the breeding ranges and with current information on water conditions we can predict seasonal production according to variations in water. This is an important function of management. Yet this year, despite drought in the west, and floods in important areas on the eastern prairies, and despite reports of poor production in the redhead, there were no steps to make compensating regulations. This is not management.

To one who knows the prairies of the northwest, it is clear that the cross-hatched range maps are most deceiving. Vast regions within these designated areas are untenable. The area acceptable to breeding ducks is but a fraction of the area indicated on the maps. This is particularly true in the diving ducks, notably the redhead, canvasback, and ruddy duck. These are primarily water-nesters; they nest over water in emergent vegetation. Their range in large measure is restricted to areas where there are acceptable stands of emergent growths. Hence their range is greatly restricted within its over-all pattern; their numbers are concentrated. And because of their intolerance they do not respond rapidly to changing conditions. Emergent growths require a year or more to produce their stands. When management or natural forces increase the water supply, there is a lag between the appearance of water and response by breeding birds of these species.

River ducks, on the other hand, being primarily land-nesters, do not demand the close relationship between the aquatic territorial site and the nest; they are much more tolerant in their choice of breeding situations. Thus their breeding range is much less restricted within the over-all pattern; their numbers are seldom as concentrated as in the diving ducks. When new water is available their reaction is immediate. An outstanding example of this great difference between river ducks and diving ducks was seen on the agricultural prairie of southern Manitoba in 1945. There was the most bountiful runoff in at least 8 years. Throughout the southern portion of the province were scattered thousands of small waters, many of them persisting through the season. To all of these areas came river ducks (mostly mallards and pintails but all the prairie species in this group were present), and there was the heaviest farmland nesting population in a decade. Territorial pairs were numerous where they had not been seen for years. But the new breeding population consisted only of river ducks. An extensive survey of this region revealed but one pair of diving ducks (lesser scaup) breeding on new water.

Thus we see that river ducks are spread, diving ducks concentrated. Concentrations are dangerous. When disaster strikes it may impair production in a considerable portion of a population. We must look with grave concern at the recent floods on the great Netley Marsh in Manitoba where breeds one of the largest redhead concentrations in the land.

PIONEERING

We know very little about the role of tradition in waterfowl behavior. We do not accept the stand that the breeding ground of a given species is an inherent range; yet we do not have full understanding of the land use shown by the different ducks.

We do know this, when new water areas are created there is a response on the part of certain ducks which come to nest at these new places. We see this in the new refuge marshes. It was shown by the 1945 behavior of river ducks on Manitoba farmland. These birds, in their many thousands, bred on new waters which had not existed within their individual life spans. In other words, these ducks moved to areas with which they could have had no previous experience and which had not been used by ducks for at least one waterfowl generation. This is pioneering. Through its ability to pioneer a species responds rapidly to management. If it pioneers slowly, it responds slowly to management.

Clearly the most successful river ducks are the most rapid pioneers. The diving ducks pioneer slowly. River ducks being more tolerant in their choice of breeding environment than diving ducks find a wider variety of ecological patterns acceptable. Hence new waters, as we have seen, are accepted more rapidly by river ducks.

I suspect, however, that variation in the pioneering trait reflects more than variations in breeding tolerances. The ability to pioneer is a part of the specific makeup and there is much variation species by species. The ability to pioneer is highly developed in the mallard and pintail, poorly developed in the redhead and canvasback.

To place the matter in different light, some species probably are more closely bound to traditions than others. Tradition-bound species pioneer slowly. We know, for instance, that the Canada goose is tradition-bound. When, as we know to have occurred, an entire local population is killed, the breeding traditions are killed with the birds and the area is barren of breeders no matter how attractive it may be. There are hundreds of "burned-out" marshes which are ecologically suitable for nesting geese, but which do not hold breeding populations because of broken traditions. When new traditions are established, as Pirnie (1938) has established goose traditions at the Kellogg Bird Sanctuary, in Michigan, a new local breeding population is created.

I suspect that similar traditions obtain in ducks and that river ducks are less tightly bound to them than diving ducks.

The importance of traditional behavior to management is great. It means that in species with strong traditional ties, we must build up "seed" populations on new or uninhabited areas, thus establishing new local breeding populations through the creation (or reestablishment) of traditions. We refer to burned-out marshes. Here traditions have been burned-out with the vanished birds. While we may not overrate the importance of the great Canadian breeding grounds, certainly we underrate the importance of breeding areas within the United States. The rebuilding of traditions here, I believe, is just as important as the rebuilding of marshes.

SEX PROPERTIES

In examining sex properties, as outlined by Leopold (1933:95), we find the ledger partly balanced.

All American game ducks are monogamous in the wild.

Except for the long period in the wood duck (30 days), incubation requires between 3 and 4 weeks, with most species bringing off their young in 21 to 25 days.

All species produce but one brood a year.

The meager information at hand suggests only a slight unbalance of the sex ratio at hatching (Hochbaum 1944:51).

In adult populations we know that an unbalanced ratio obtains in many species of ducks. Here the ledger favors the river ducks, where the preponderance of drakes is not so great as in the diving ducks (Lincoln 1932, 1933; Leopold 1933; Mayr 1939; MaIlhenny 1940; Erickson 1943; Hochbaum 1944; Petrides 1944; Smith 1946). This difference between the two groups becomes all the more apparent when we examine sex ratios of birds arriving on the breeding grounds (Table 1).

We know very little about sex ratios beyond the fact that they exist. From studies in other game birds (Leopold 1933:110, 339) and in ducks we infer that an unbalanced ratio is a symptom of a low population. Logically, this same unbalance is an important factor in keeping population levels low.

We cannot manage sex ratios since we do not know what distorts them. But where there is serious unbalance, this knowledge should have an important bearing on regulations when populations are low and the reproductive season poor. Sex ratio is one of the fundamentals governing management policy for all domestic stock. It must be a fundamental in regulating the management of wild populations.

In the age of maturity we again find the ledger slightly unbalanced in favor of the river ducks. All river ducks breed their first year. Redheads, canvasbacks, and lesser scaups likewise breed their first year; but studies of the lesser scaup by Munro (1941) indicate that some individuals do not attain breeding maturity their first spring.

The American golden-eye, Barrow's golden-eye and the buffle-head all re-

Table 1. Sex ratios of river ducks and diving ducks, Delta, Manitoba.[1]

Species	Male	Female	Percentage		Ratio		
			Male	Female	Male		Female
Mallard	1,226	1,197	50.6	49.4	1.02	to	1
Pintail	1,687	1,563	51.9	48.1	1.09	to	1
Redhead	538	388	58.2	42.8	1.38	to	1
Canvasback	1,908	1,008	65.4	34.6	1.89	to	1
Lesser scaup	6,940	3,447	66.8	33.2	2.01	to	1

[1] Sample counts of migrant flocks during the last 2 weeks of April and the first week of May, 1939 to 1945, inclusive.

quire more than one year to attain sexual maturity (Munro 1939, 1942). This, of course, greatly reduces the breeding potential in these species which, however, do not hold first rank as game ducks.

NESTING

A. Time

The time of nesting has an important bearing on productivity. In southern Manitoba the mallards and the pintails are the earliest nesters; the lesser scaup, the ruddy duck and the white-winged scoter are the latest nesters, while the remainder of the species are the "middle" nesters (Hochbaum 1944:94).

The late nesters suffer a severe disadvantage in the tardy appearance of offspring; young lesser scaups are just hatching when early-hatched pintails are taking their first flights. The redhead, too suffers the disadvantage of late nestings for, while its season begins with the canvasback, the span of nesting is spread over a much longer period.

The products of late nestings suffer the hazards of late summer, as we shall discuss more thoroughly in our consideration of broods.

In general we might say that early nesting is the most hazardous; and it is in the time of nesting that the mallard and pintail suffer their greatest disadvantage over other species. Clutches during the early egg-laying stage are subject to frost damage. All nesting cover during the early season is dead growth of the previous year, hence more hazardous; it is more vulnerable to fire and to predator. During periods of heavy runoff, early nests are subject to disastrous flooding. Early nests are more vulnerable to agricultural hazards (with the exception of mowing) than late nests; through much of the range the period of early nesting coincides with the beginning of farm work.

Nests of the middle period are the safest. New growth makes better nesting cover. Farm work is already established. Fire is less ravaging in green growth. Predators find more buffer prey available.

Late season nests suffer from mowing and, in important parts of the range, from floods. The breeding waters of the lower Saskatchewan River and the Winnipeg River, for instance, reach their peak levels during summer rather than in spring.

The early-season disadvantage of mallards and pintails does not hold in the reign of management. These species receive the greatest benefits from nesting-ground management and the recovery rate under management is greater, because of this, than in middle- and late-season nesters. Fire can be and is widely controlled through education. The same applies to a lesser degree in agricultural offenses and predator control favors the early nesters.

B. Place

The important game species nest either on dry land or over water in emergent vegetation. The wood duck, the buffle-head and the two golden-eyes nest in tree cavities.

All of the river ducks are land-nesters; the redhead, canvasback and ruddy duck nest predominantly in emergent vegetation. The lesser scaup regularly nests on land or over water.

The land-nesters apparently are vulnerable to the most severe hazards. Fire is more destructive; the pressure of agriculture more severe. The threat of predators is greater in land-nesters. Of the important nest predators, the ground squirrel, skunk, fox, coyote, and snake prey more heavily on land nests than on the insular nests in emergent vegetation. Water-nesters suffer the consequences of their concentrations, and are more seriously affected by fluctuations in water level.

The disadvantages of the land-nesters, however, are reversed under management. Management of fire and of farming improves conditions for river ducks tremendously. Control of predators, restriction of grazing and mowing and most other management practices favor river ducks. Thus the land-nesters may respond rapidly to management while the situation for the water-nesters remains fundamentally unchanged. Under management, the productivity rate of the river ducks is increased while there is little change in the diving ducks.

C. Waste

Nature "anticipates" some waste in reproduction. The potential wild duck crop is not 100 per cent of the eggs, as some highly popularized "duck mathematics" would have us believe. But in a few species there is added wastage over and above all other accountable losses. Two or more females deposit eggs in the same nest; when a number of 20 or more eggs is reached, the nest generally is abandoned and the potential output of two or more hens wasted.

This behavior, which we are unable to explain, is particularly frequent in the redhead and ruddy duck; wasted "dump" nests in these two species are found wherever they breed. Such behavior no doubt limits productivity considerably. It cannot be controlled, but it has a bearing on policy.

REARING

The age and date of the first flights of young ducks is an important factor in the productivity rate. Birds with short growth periods and early hatching dates obviously have greater chances for success than those with long growth periods and late hatching dates. The successful mallards and pintails have early hatching dates and short growth periods; the less successful diving ducks have late hatching dates and long growth periods (Hochbaum 1944:109).

Young which reach the flying stage by midsummer have almost 2 months in which to condition themselves for the autumn migration. The basic pattern of a duck's behavior is inborn, but it learns to direct its innate behavior to objects and places in its environment through experience. Thus young ducks flying by midsummer have much more time to condition themselves to their environment than those species which do not take flight until they are on the threshold of the autumn movements and the shooting season.

It may be that the early flying date in the mallard and the pintail is related to tradition. These young birds, we know, make extensive movements during late summer prior to their southward journey. They are familiar through experience with a much larger portion of the breeding range than the diving ducks which have much less time for "exploratory" movements.

Late flying dates overlap with the periods of severe late-summer drought and its attendant hazards. Diving ducks are far more vulnerable to drought than river ducklings.

The longer growing period and later hatching date in diving ducks apparently conflicts with the moulting period of the mother. In river ducks most hens remain with the brood until the youngsters are awing. There is still sufficient time to molt the wing feathers before the autumn flights. In diving ducks, however, the hen usually abandons her children before they take flight, this being necessary that she may molt her flight feathers in time for the fall passage. Young attended by the mother are much more wary in the presence of enemies than unattended young. A heavier brood mortality in diving ducks may result because they become orphans before they can fly.

Flight is an efficient means of escape from many enemies. River ducks being able to escape in flight at an earlier age than diving ducks probably suffer to a lesser degree from predator losses during the preflight period.

Clearly the river ducklings are favored during the growth period; undoubtedly the slower recovery in the diving ducks is due in large measure to their disadvantages as ducklings. Management cannot control growth rates, but it must recognize the importance of providing stable water levels for diving ducks through the critical period of late summer.

HUNTING

The pressure of hunting is not the same on all species. Even under similar conditions at the same time on the same marsh, the kill in one species may be much greater than the kill in another; a species with a low population may suffer heavier losses in proportion to its continental numbers than an abundant species (Hawkins and Bellrose 1939). There is strong evidence, for instance, that the redhead, newly replaced in the full bag, is being shot in greater proportion than some of the more common species. The Fish and Wildlife Service reports rather casually (1945) that "more returns were received for the redhead than for the lesser scaup although a smaller number of redheads had been banded." Hunting, then contributes heavily to the differentials in recovery rates.

Current regulations do little to favor species by the manipulation of time and place. Game laws have not kept pace with other advances in conservation; there is much to be done, much to be learned, and waterfowl policy must undergo some serious and drastic changes. The ultimate regulations will aim at controlling the *time* and the *place* of the kill *in favor of certain ducks* without placing a heavier weight on hunter and warden. For instance, in the important breeding regions of the West the duck season opens the last day of summer, September 20, in the northern tier of states. Opening day finds established aggregations of adults and well-matured juvenile mallards and pintails feeding on the upland fields. But in the breeding marshes, now shooting grounds, the young of many species of diving ducks are just taking their first flights, while many adult females are just recovering from the wing-molt. To hunt on these marshes in late September places this important seed stock in jeopardy. Wetmore, who made an exhaustive survey of western waterfowl marshes, said (1921:10): "To make the opening date earlier than October 1 would be a great mistake, as it would inevitably lead to killing a large number of young ducks before they are in condition, while at the same time many of the adult birds would be molting." Dr. Wetmore was speaking of the Utah region; but his statement applies to the entire northern tier of states. If the officials who open the season on breeding marshes the 20th of September cannot follow the advice of their own technical reports, I implore them to spend a hot September afternoon examining marshland duck bags. They will find many young of redheads and of other species, birds in such poor condition that some are hardly worth plucking. How can Wisconsin and Minnesota ever hope to rebuild the breeding stock and the breeding traditions on their marshlands if they begin their shooting before the young and the molting adults are conditioned? Officials complain that they are slaves of public opinion. But if it is imperative to open the shooting September 20, the marsh species could be saved and the hunters given well-conditioned game by limiting early-season shooting to the uplands where mallards and pintails feed on agricultural land. Stubble shooting is to be had in most of the states now hunting ducks before the end of September. I am not trying to suggest this example as a regulation. I am merely trying to show how pressure on a species or group can be reduced by manipulating time and place in favor of ducks. This also gives hunting without undue complications in regulations. Indeed, it is much easier to protect a species such as the redhead by regulating place than regulating number. If there is no marsh shooting until October 1, a substantial redhead population has been spared. Limiting the bag on redheads but permitting marsh shooting, places the species under much greater hazard. This is the type of regulation we must adopt ultimately if we are going to enjoy duck shooting in the future.

Besides our failure to heed such warnings as given by Dr. Wetmore, the lack of information is a great handicap to advances in waterfowl policy. We don't have the information we need. There must be larger staffs of trained men to study waterfowl on the breeding grounds so that information is available *before* the annual regulations are made. The present waterfowl situation, which is in large measure a direct result of hand-made overoptimism, could have been avoided had we been able to obtain annual reports from the vast breeding grounds that gave a true picture of existing conditions and numbers. *We have not even developed the techniques for appraising waterfowl populations on the breeding grounds.* Many states have more manpower and far better techniques for the preseason appraisal of the pheasant populations than the United States government has for the appraisal of breeding waterfowl populations.

Waterfowl policy is further complicated by the frequent over-optimistic and often unsubstantiated reports on waterfowl conditions in Canada issued by Ducks Unlimited. The good which has been done (which is considerable) is overweighed by a propaganda policy which rocks the very foundations of game management. Fake duckling rescues for publicity, thousands of acres credited to management where little or no improvement has been enforced—these do not contribute to sound waterfowl policy.

Table 2. Conditions influencing recovery rates in mallard and redhead.

Condition	Mallard	Advances recovery	Retards recovery	Redhead	Advances recovery	Retards recovery
Numbers	Relatively high	x		Relatively low		x
Breeding range						
A. Regional	Extensive	x		Limited		x
B. Local	Spread	x		Concentrated		x
Pioneering	Rapid	x		Slow		x
Sex properties	More evenly balanced sex ratio gives mallard advantage	x				x
Nesting						
A. Time	Early nesting hazardous		x	Middle nesting less hazardous	x	
B. Place	Land nests vulnerable to more hazards		x	Water nests vulnerable to fewer hazards	x	
C. Waste	Little	x		Great		x
D. Response to management	Rapid	x		Slow		x
Rearing						
A. Hatching date	Early	x		Late		x
B. Growth rate	Rapid	x		Slow		x
C. Period with hen	Full brood period	x		Abandoned before full grown		x
Hunting						
A. Condition	Young in good condition when season opens	x		Young poorly conditioned when season opens		x
B. Hunting pressure	Relatively light in proportion to numbers	x		Relatively heavy in proportion to numbers		x
C. Wariness	One of the most wary game birds	x		One of the least wary game birds		x

We have got to pull in our belts, forget about miracles, stop taking credit for the good of weather and blaming bad weather for poor flights. We must put an end to the stream of unsubstantial optimism that floods the land and build a program that operates on science and speaks with plain common sense. After 10 years we still are at the threshold of management.

DISCUSSION

I have attempted to show how different species react differently to the same situations. Waterfowl management must recognize and study these differences more carefully so that policy serves special species as well as "waterfowl" generally.

The discussion is general, the species many, so that we cannot draw up a precise table here showing the differences in potential recovery rates species by species. But let us apply the various conditions in two species to point up our discussion. We will compare the successful mallard with the unsuccessful redhead (Table 2).

We see in Table 2 the overwhelming

advantages enjoyed by the mallard—advantages that are further enhanced by management to a far greater degree than in the redhead. We see why the mallard is the more abundant species. The reasons for its more rapid recovery from the last depression are obvious. We know why future management must be directed towards the redhead and other species with low productivity rates. We see why merely placing the redhead on a protected list, as it was until a short time ago, is not enough to speed recovery. Waterfowl management must learn to measure productivity rates species by species, and it must know enough about habits to adjust policy according to these.

After 10 years we cannot blame the current plight of ducks on predators or on weather or on water conditions or on the combination of natural forces we know to be working. Certainly we cannot blame sportsmen to whom we have given ever-optimistic reports and whose hunting we regulate. Management is at fault. Never has management been permitted to do so much; never has it failed so completely. If we are going to have ducks in sufficient numbers to hunt we must find out what is wrong with our management plan—right now! We must make the necessary changes as soon as possible. There is much to learn. There is much to do. Let us forget miracles and seek facts.

LITERATURE CITED

ERICKSON, ARNOLD B. 1943. Sex ratios in ducks in Minnesota. Auk 60:20–34.

GABRIELSON, IRA N. 1946. Press notice 124100, Dept. of the Int. Information Service.

———, AND FREDERICK C. LINCOLN. 1941. What is behind the waterfowl regulations? Committee Print No. 1, Senate, 77th Congress, 1st Session. 34pp.

HAWKINS, ARTHUR S., AND FRANK C. BELLROSE. 1939. The duck flight and kill along the Illinois River during the fall of 1938. Am. Wildlife 28(4):178–186.

HOCHBAUM, H. ALBERT. 1944. The canvasback on a prairie marsh. American Wildlife Institute.

KORTRIGHT, FRANCIS H. 1942. The ducks, geese and swans of North America. American Wildlife Institute.

LEOPOLD, ALDO. 1933. Game management. Scribner's, N.Y.

LINCOLN, FREDERICK C. 1932. Do drakes outnumber Susies? Am. Game 21:3–4, 16–17.

———. 1933. A decade of bird banding in America: a review. Smithsonian Report (1932):327–351.

MCILHENNY, E. A. 1940. Sex ratio in wild birds. Auk 57:85–93.

MAYR, ERNST 1939. The sex ratio in wild birds. The Am. Naturalist 73:156–179.

MUNRO, J. A. 1939. Studies of waterfowl in British Columbia; Barrow's golden-eye and American golden-eye. Trans. Royal Can. Institute 22:259–318.

———. 1941. Studies of waterfowl in British Columbia; greater scaup duck and lesser scaup duck. Can. Jour. of Research 19:113–138.

———. 1942. Studies of waterfowl in British Columbia; buffle-head. Can. Jour. of Research 20:133–160.

PIRNIE, MILES D. 1938. Restocking of the Canada goose successful in southern Michigan. Trans. 3rd N. Am. Wildlife Conf. 624–627.

PETRIDES, GEORGE A. 1944. Sex ratios in ducks. Auk 61:564–571.

SMITH, J. DONALD 1946. The canvasback in Minnesota. Auk 63:73–81.

U.S. FISH AND WILDLIFE SERVICE 1945. Status of migratory birds: 1944–1945. Wildlife Leaflet 274. U.S. Dept. of the Int.

WETMORE, ALEXANDER 1921. Wild ducks and duck foods of the Bear River Marshes, Utah. U.S. Dept. Agri. Bull. 936. 20pp.

WILLIAMS, CECIL S. 1944. Migration of redheads from the Utah breeding grounds. Auk 61:252–259.

THE COMEBACK OF THE WOOD DUCK

FRANK C. BELLROSE, Illinois Natural History Survey, Havana 62644

Abstract: The wood duck (*Aix sponsa*) has shown a remarkable recovery in abundance from the low population level of the early 1900's. It is alternately either the second or third most important duck in hunters' bag east of the Great Plains, aggregating almost 750,000 of the current kill. A closed season, 1916–40, followed by limited hunting regulations since then is apparently responsible for the comeback of this species. Because of the extensive drainage of timbered bottomlands and swamps, the wood duck will never be as abundant as it was prior to 1900.

Most wildlife managers do not realize that the comeback of the wood duck rivals that of the white-tailed deer (*Odocoileus virginianus*). Conservationists point with pride to the return in abundance of the whitetails and the wild turkey (*Meleagris gallopavo*); they herald the tremendous increase in the numbers of Canada geese (*Branta canadensis*) in recent years. But amid all the self-congratulation on the role that wildlife management has exercised in the current abundance of these species, the past status of the wood duck is all too often overlooked.

HISTORICAL ASPECTS

Forgotten is the fact that in the first decades of the 20th century, it was feared that the wood duck would follow the Labrador duck (*Camptorhynchus labradorius*) into extinction. As witness comments by naturalists of that period: Cooke (1906:8) noted, "So persistently has this duck (wood duck) been pursued that in some sections it has been practically exterminated. . . . As a result the wood duck is constantly diminishing in numbers, and soon is likely to be known only from books or by tradition." The famous hunter and naturalist George Bird Grinnell (1901:142) remarked, "Being shot at all seasons of the year they are becoming very scarce and are likely to be exterminated before long." Forbush (1913), an eminent Massachusetts ornithologist, wrote (p. 353) that "the Wood Duck . . . is now rapidly growing rare in most of the State," adding that "only the most rigid enforcement of the law can save this, the most beautiful of American wild ducks, from extermination."

These and many more remarks written in the same vein by naturalists in the early 1900's attest to the dangerously low level reached by wood duck populations during that period. So alarmed were conservationists by this decline that they insisted wood ducks be given complete protection under the Federal Migratory Bird Act of 1916, and subsequently, the broader Migratory Bird Treaty Act of 1918 with Canada. Under these legislative provisions the wood duck enjoyed complete legal protection until 1941, when one wood duck was permitted in the daily bag and possession limits of hunters in 15 states. Hunters in all states were given the privilege of taking one in 1942.

RECOVERY IN ABUNDANCE

Wood ducks were permitted in the bag in 1941 because they had dramatically increased in abundance during the years they were legally protected. This increase was evident to us in our early years (1938–41) of waterfowl investigation in Illinois. Wood ducks breeding in the area of our observations appeared to be approaching a saturation point in utilization of their nesting

Originally published in Wildl. Soc. Bull. 4(3):107–110, 1976.

habitat: nests were found in cottage chimneys and in poorly situated natural cavities; one was found on an open-stick hawk nest. It was apparent that suitable nest sites were in short supply.

Consequently, in 1939 we erected several hundred nest houses for wood ducks. Indicative of the high wood duck population was the occupancy rate of almost 52 percent the first season. Probably because nest success in houses was higher than in natural cavities, the use of nest houses increased each year up to 1942, when an occupancy rate of 65 percent was recorded (Bellrose 1955:46).

Moreover, in late summer thousands of wood ducks were observed in bottomland lakes of the Illinois Valley. During September 1938, we saw over 10,000 feeding in wheat stubble fields near Havana, Illinois.

In the East, also, their numbers had rebounded. For example, in the Concord area of Massachusetts, Griscom (1949:188) reported that by 1938 the wood duck had made a recovery from the verge of extinction and fully occupied all nesting habitats.

In 1942 we circulated a questionnaire concerning the status of the wood ducks to several hundred wildlife biologists and ornithologists. There were 220 replies; the respondents reported that their observations during the previous 10 years indicated the following trends in wood duck populations: In states of the Atlantic Flyway, 64 percent reported an increase, 27 percent no apparent change, and 9 percent a decrease. In the Mississippi Flyway, 62 percent of the observers reported an increase, 31 percent little or no change, and 7 percent a decrease.

TEMPORARY SETBACK IN RECOVERY

Although all indications pointed to a remarkable recovery in wood duck populations by the early 1940's, the comeback of the wood duck suffered a reverse in the Midwest in the early 1950's. In spite of the fairly high nest success in 1947 and 1948, the use of houses by wood ducks decreased markedly in central Illinois in 1949 and remained low through 1955.

A measure of the decline was in the bag checks made throughout the Mississippi Flyway in 1953, which showed that wood ducks composed only 3.9 percent of the bag. To appreciate the depressed state of wood duck populations at that time it is only necessary to compare their part in the bag in 1953 with the 11 percent for 1963–74.

The decline in wood duck abundance in the Mississippi Flyway was so apparent by 1954 that the season on wood ducks was closed in this flyway. One wood duck was again permitted in the bag in 1955, when 167,000 were killed in the Mississippi Flyway. The season on wood ducks was again closed in 1956 and remained closed in certain states of this flyway in 1957 and 1958. When one wood duck was permitted in the bag of all hunters in the Mississippi Flyway in 1959, the kill amounted to 141,000. It remained below 165,000 until 1963; that season the kill of wood ducks in the flyway zoomed to 371,000. From 1964 through 1974, the kill in the Mississippi Flyway averaged an astounding 505,000 birds.

RECENT STATUS

Partly responsible for the high kill of wood ducks in 1963 and subsequent years (1964–74) was an increase in the daily bag limit from one to two. The mere fact that two wood ducks were permitted in the bag in 1963 is indicative of the rapid population recovery that occurred since the season was last closed throughout the flyway in 1956. Moreover, wood duck populations since 1963 have sustained an average annual kill of 500,000 in the Mississippi Flyway without an obvious depletion in abundance.

Linear regression analysis indicates that there has been no significant trend in the wood duck kill in either the Mississippi or the Atlantic flyways during 1963–74. A similar analysis of the calculated preseason population of wood ducks (Martinson and Henny 1966, Kimball 1972) also indicates that in these two flyways there has been no significant trend in population abundance during 1960–71.

Available evidence suggests that over the last decade the wood duck has been able to sustain a kill of about 500,000 in the Mississippi Flyway and 225,000 in the Atlantic Flyway without jeopardizing its contemporary status. It has composed 11 percent of the duck hunters' bags in the Mississippi Flyway, 1963–74, ranking as the second most important duck in 9 years and third most important in 3 years. In the Atlantic Flyway, the wood duck has made up 15 percent of the duck bag, 1963–74, ranking second in 4 years and third in 8 years. Wood ducks are clearly one of the most important species to duck hunters east of the Great Plains.

EFFECT OF HABITAT DESTRUCTION

Adequate protection from excessively high kills must surely be the most important reason for the recovery of the wood duck from the dangerously low levels it reached during the first quarter of the 20th century. Because of the drainage of swamps and the clearing of bottomland timber, however, the wood duck will never return to its pre-1900 abundance; breeding habitat destruction has been too enormous.

Although there are no figures on the numbers of wood ducks during the late 1800's, early naturalists were rapt in describing their tremendous abundance in many areas. Here are some of their comments:

In a book on Michigan bird life, Barrows (1912:88) stated that in the 1890's, the wood duck was one of the most abundant ducks in the state. At Buckeye Lake, Ohio, Trautman (1940:189) quoted former market hunters to the effect that it was such an abundant duck during the summer between 1850 and 1890 that a "profitable business was made of hunting fledglings and flightless adults in the flapper stage."

According to John McGovern, an early market hunter in south-central Wisconsin, wood ducks were the most abundant duck, with the mallard (*Anas platyrhynchos*) a close second (Hawkins 1940:50). About 1883, he killed over 1,000 ducks, up to 77 in 1 day. Askins (1931) described a spring trip through the lowlands of Arkansas in the 1890's. On a 20-mile horseback ride he observed that wood ducks were never out of sight and commented that thousands of them were nesting in the trees of the swampland, and that no one envisaged a time when this could not be true.

Sufficient time has not elapsed to measure the effects of the slow but steady destruction of habitat upon wood duck populations from 1960 through 1971. Population data—calculated from a combination of kill data, age ratios, and band-recovery rates—are too imprecise to permit adequate short-term evaluation. The effect of habitat destruction on waterfowl populations can be likened to the drip of a leaky faucet, whereas the effect of an excessive kill upon the subsequent breeding population could be compared to turning on the faucet for a second or two.

Increased production of young wood ducks has resulted from the erection of nest houses that reduce nest losses. To what extent there has been a "trade off" between an increase in production as a result of management (e.g., nest houses) and a decrease in production from the loss of nesting habitat is beyond the scope of this paper. Moreover, habitat destruction exerts its depressing force on wood duck populations beyond the nesting season.

POPULATION RESILIENCE

But with all the hunting pressure and habitat destruction the wood duck has experienced in this century, it has shown a remarkable resilience to the adversities that beset it. The resilience of wood duck populations stems from an astounding ability to produce large clutches, and, when the occasion demands, frequently to renest. It is the only species of waterfowl in North America known to sometimes raise two broods to flight stage during the same season (Hester 1965, Hansen 1971:108).

The comeback of the wood duck from near extinction provides another example of the importance to posterity of preventing this fate from befalling other species. If the wood duck had become extinct in the early 1900's, the loss of a species that has become alternately the second or third most important game duck to hunters east of the Great Plains would detract considerably from the present level of hunting. No other species of waterfowl has the capability to expand into the range and habitats occupied by the wood duck.

LITERATURE CITED

ASKINS, CAPT. C. 1931. Game bird shooting. The MacMillan Co., New York. 321pp.

BARROWS, W. B. 1912. Michigan bird life. Michigan Agric. Coll. Spec. Bull., Lansing. 822pp.

BELLROSE, F. C. 1955. Housing for wood ducks. Illinois Nat. Hist. Surv. Circ. 45. Second printing, rev. 48pp.

COOKE, W. W. 1906. Distribution and migration of North American ducks, geese, and swans. U.S. Bur. Biol. Surv. Bull. 26. 90pp.

FORBUSH, E. H. 1913. Useful birds and their protection. 4th ed. Massachusetts State Board of Agriculture. 451pp.

GRINNELL, G. B. 1901. American duck shooting. Forest and Stream Publishing Co., New York. 627pp.

GRISCOM, L. 1949. The birds of Concord. Harvard University Press, Cambridge. 340pp.

HANSEN, J. L. 1971. The role of nest boxes in management of the wood duck on Mingo National Wildlife Refuge. M.A. Thesis. Univ. of Missouri, Columbia. 159pp.

HAWKINS, A. S. 1940. A wildlife history of Faville Grove, Wisconsin. Trans. Wisconsin Acad. Sci., Arts, and Letters 32:29–65.

HESTER, F. E. 1965 (1962). Survival, renesting, and return of adult wood ducks to previously used nest boxes. Proc. Annu. Conf. Southeastern Assoc. Game and Fish Commissioners 16: 67–70.

KIMBALL, C. F. 1972. Wood ducks band recovery data for 1971 and population trend in the eastern United States and Ontario, 1966–1971. U.S. Bur. Sport Fish. Wildl. Adm. Rep. 219. 7pp.

MARTINSON, R. K., AND C. J. HENNY. 1966. Band recovery data (1965) and pre-season population estimates for wood ducks (1960–65). U.S. Bur. Sport Fish. Wildl. Adm. Rep. 114. 16pp.

TRAUTMAN, M. B. 1940. The birds of Buckeye Lake, Ohio. Univ. Michigan Mus. Zool. Misc. Publ. 44. 466pp.

SELECTED BIBLIOGRAPHY

Historical

ALISON, R. M. 1978. The earliest records of waterfowl hunting. Wildl. Soc. Bull. 6(4):196–199.

BELLROSE, F. C., AND T. G. SCOTT. 1955. Waterfowl conservation in the decade following World War II. Wilson Bull. 67(4):310–312.

COLLS, D. G. 1951. The conflict between waterfowl and agriculture. Trans. North Am. Wildl. Conf. 16:89–93.

COTTAM, C. 1944. The role of impoundments in postwar planning for waterfowl. Trans. North Am. Wildl. Conf. 9:288–295.

———. 1947. Waterfowl at the crossroads. Trans. North Am. Wildl. Conf. 12:67–82.

———. 1949. Limiting factors of present waterfowl knowledge. Trans. North Am. Wildl. Conf. 14:42–57.

———. 1951. Waterfowl's future depends upon management. Trans. North Am. Wildl. Conf. 16:109–117.

DAY, A. M. 1946. The problem of increased hunting pressure on waterfowl. Trans. North Am. Wildl. Conf. 11:55–61.

ERICKSON, R. C. 1959. Diving ducks—Their past and future. Proc. 13th Annu. Conf. S.E. Assoc. Game Fish Comm. 13:277–282.

HICKEY, J. J. 1955. Is there scientific basis for flyway management? Trans. North Am. Wildl. Conf. 20:126–150.

JAHN, L. R. 1961. The status of waterfowl conservation. Wilson Bull. 73(1): 96–106.

———. 1961. The future of waterfowl. Proc. 15th Annu. Conf. S.E. Assoc. Game Fish Comm. 15:68–70.

LINCOLN, F. C. 1937. The waterfowl situation. Trans. North Am. Wildl. Conf. 2:168–179.

RYSGAARD, G. N. 1941. A short history of waterfowl. Conserv. Volunteer 2(9): 75–79.

SHERWOOD, G. A. 1960. The whistling swan in the West with particular reference to Great Salt Lake Valley, Utah. Condor 62(5):370–377.

TIMM, D. E., R. G. BROMLEY, D. MCKNIGHT, AND R. S. RODGERS. 1979. Management evolution of dusky Canada geese. Pages 322–330 *in* R. L. Jarvis and J. C. Bartonek, eds. Management and biology of Pacific flyway geese. A symposium. Northwest Section of The Wildlife Society. Oregon State Univ. Book Stores, Inc., Corvallis.

REPRODUCTIVE ECOLOGY
General Biology

REPRODUCTIVE OUTPUT OF BLACK DUCKS IN THE ST. LAWRENCE ESTUARY

AUSTIN REED, Canadian Wildlife Service, 1141 route de l'Eglise, Quebec, Canada G1V 3W5

Abstract: The breeding biology of black ducks (*Anas rubripes*) was studied in an estuarine habitat over the period 1963–73. Nests were located on islands and on the mainland in the vicinity of tidal marshes. Of 590 nests, 248 (42 percent) reached the hatching stage; the mainland-nesting portion of the population showed a nest success of 28 percent ($N = 83$ nests), those using the main nesting island, Ile-aux-Pommes, 44 percent ($N = 478$ nests), and those using other islands 52 percent ($N = 29$ nests). On Ile-aux-Pommes annual nest success varied between 30 and 71 percent. Unsuccessful clutches were lost to predation (mainly gull [*Larus* sp.] and crow [*Corvus brachyrhynchos*] on islands, red fox [*Vulpes fulva*] and crow on mainland) or desertion. Fifty-two nests (9 percent of total) were judged to have been abandoned as a direct result of disturbance by the investigator. Annual fluctuations in nesting success could not be clearly attributed to weather factors, the quantity or quality of concealing cover, or to predator or competitor density. Nesting success did not vary according to laying date, but did vary in relation to the stage of nesting; the probability of loss was much greater during egg-laying than during incubation. Through renesting, nest losses were compensated for in some years but not in others. On the average, 65 percent of island nesting pairs brought off broods. Using capture-recapture techniques and visual observation, I estimated that 55 percent of all broods produced flying young, and 34 percent of ducklings that hatched reached flight age. On the basis of these estimates, 100 breeding pairs would produce 183 fledged young, a rate much lower than reported for this species in other studies; the discrepancy of results is attributed mainly to losses of entire broods which were unaccounted for in other studies.

J. WILDL. MANAGE. 39(2):243–255

To manage animal populations with the aim of assuring a harvestable surplus, knowledge of the species' reproductive output (rate of production of fledged young) is essential. Attempts to modify waterfowl habitat to favor increased production of young should be aimed at minimizing the effects of those factors which cause most prefledge losses. Detailed knowledge of the stages at which losses occur and the circumstances in which they occur should form the basis for attempts to preserve or modify habitat and to manipulate predator or competitor populations. Both nesting and brood-rearing phases of the breeding cycle must be considered. This paper, based on the results of 11 years' study of the black duck in the St. Lawrence estuary, Quebec, attempts to evaluate the rate of production of fledged young per nesting female.

Intensive hunting of the relatively small population of black ducks in eastern North America (the fall flights in recent years being about 1 to 1.5 million birds) necessitates careful management based on close surveillance. Information on the rate of breeding success and its range of annual variation should be taken into account in formulating regulations designed to control the harvest.

Many studies of the nesting of various species of dabbling ducks have provided information on the proportion of nests or eggs which produce young, but, because most species are able to renest following the loss of an initial nest (Sowls 1955), the rate of egg or nesting success does not necessarily reflect the rate of production of young per breeding female, which is the parameter of greater importance. An island-nesting segment of the study population was studied in particular detail over a full decade; the resulting data permitted estimation of production of newly-hatched young per nesting female.

Originally published in J. Wildl. Manage. 39(2):243–255, 1975.

Detailed estimates of brood and duckling survival were carried out by intensive visual observation and by capture-recapture techniques over four years (1968 to 1971), and the results were compared with those obtained by direct observation of color-marked hens with broods and other data gathered over the full course of the study (1963–73). Many researchers have produced estimates of survival based on the difference between the average number of ducklings per brood at nest exodus and the average number per class III brood, without providing evidence that no entire broods were destroyed. Such an approach is likely to result in serious over-estimation of the number of young reared to the fledging stage. I placed special emphasis on estimating the proportion of broods which produced no fledged young in order to arrive at a more realistic evaluation of productivity.

G. Moisan, Université Laval (presently Quebec Dept. Tourism Fish and Game), suggested the project and provided direction during the early stages. H. Boyd, Canadian Wildlife Service, offered useful suggestions and encouragement during later stages. M. Lepage conducted graduate studies on brood survival in 1970 and 1971 under the joint supervision of J. Bédard (Université Laval) and myself; I am grateful to him for having made his data available. Field assistance was provided by R. Ouellet, Quebec Wildlife Service, and several undergraduate and graduate students from l'Université Laval. The study was supported by l'Université Laval (1963), the Quebec Wildlife Service (1964–69), and the Canadian Wildlife Service (1969–72), and by grants from Canadian Industries Limited, the Quebec Wildlife Federation, the National Research Council of Canada (grant to J. Bédard), and the Frank M. Chapman Fund of the American Museum of Natural History. Mrs. B. Déry and her sons kindly granted permission to carry out studies on Ile-aux-Pommes. C. D. MacInnes, I. Newton, H. Boyd, and J. Bédard provided helpful comments on the manuscript.

THE STUDY AREA AND POPULATION

The population which I studied inhabited the tidal marshes of the south shore of the St. Lawrence estuary, 120–240 km downstream from Quebec City. Their nests were located on adjacent dry mainland and on islands, but brood rearing took place in tidal marshes on the mainland shore. The breeding population of that area was evaluated at approximately 1,500–2,000 pairs (Reed 1973). Detailed nesting studies were carried out on Ile-aux-Pommes, a 9-ha grassy island 5.6 km off shore (48°N, 69°10′W), and on a nearby mainland plot (3,150 ha) containing farmland, forest, and peat bog, extending inland from a 16-km stretch of tidal marsh shoreline (Fig. 1). Ile-aux-Pommes is the site of a large breeding colony of herring gulls (*Larus argentatus*), great black-backed gulls (*L. marinus*), and common eiders (*Somateria mollissima*). Intensive investigations on brood rearing were undertaken along an 8-km stretch of *Spartina* marsh shoreline near Isle Verte (48°N, 69°W). Detailed descriptions of the area and the breeding population can be found in Reed (1970, 1973), Reed and Moisan (1971), and Lepage (1973).

METHODS

Nests were located by systematic searching through potential cover, thrashing the vegetation with bamboo poles to flush nesting ducks. The location of nests was carefully recorded in relation to recognizable landmarks; occasionally small unobtrusive markers were placed in the field to aid in

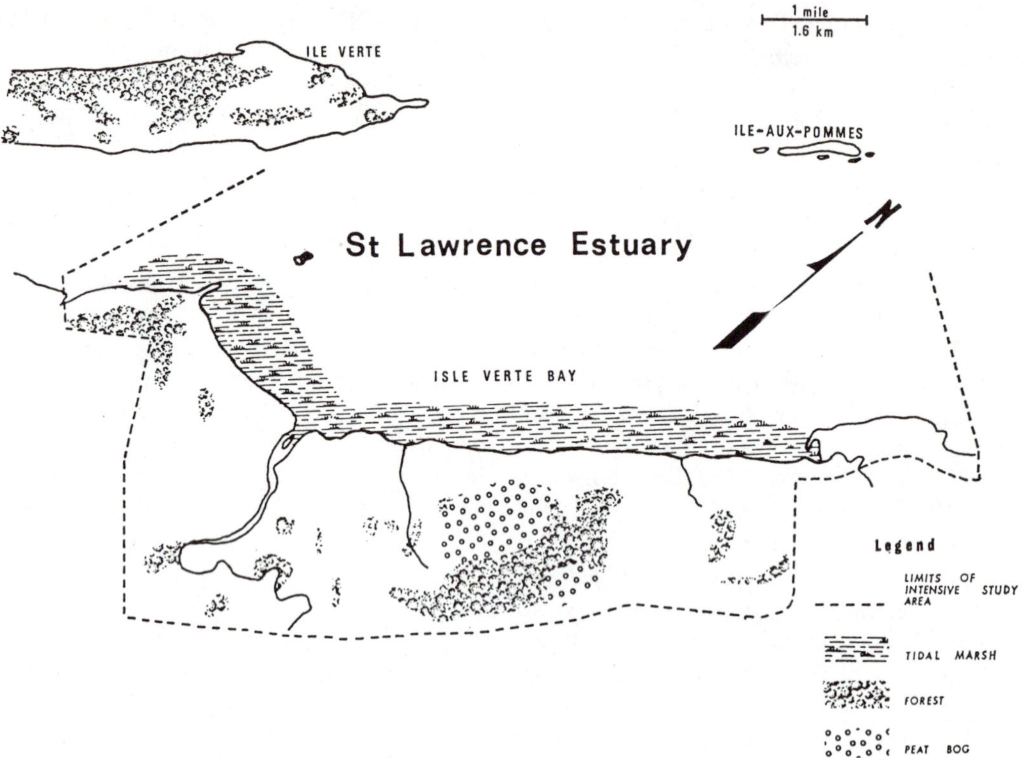

Fig. 1. The intensive study area.

relocating nests. The stage of incubation of eggs was determined with a field candler and criteria described by Weller (1956). Extreme care was taken to disturb concealing vegetation as little as possible and to cover eggs with down or nest material before leaving the site.

The fates of nests were determined by revisiting them according to the following schedule: Ile-aux-Pommes, once a week (6–9 days), except in 1963 when nests were checked every 2–3 days; mainland and other islands, once (if found during incubation) or twice (if found during laying) prior to the expected date of hatching, and once thereafter.

Adult females were caught on the nest during late incubation with long-handled dip nets and various types of nest traps, and color marked for individual recognition with neck bands (1964–65), spray paint on primaries (1966–71), nasal saddles (1972–73), and plastic leg bands (1966–71). Twelve nesting females were fitted with transmitters in 1972 to permit their radio location through the brood rearing period.

Ducklings were captured by hand by a small crew walking through the tidal marsh (1964–69); this technique was rendered more efficient by using a pointing dog (German shorthair) to aid in locating ducklings (1970–73). The sex of ducklings was determined by cloacal examination. Early in the study (1964–68) age of ducklings was determined by plumage characteristics following the criteria proposed by Gollop and Marshall (1954, unpublished report to Mississippi Flyway Council Technical Sec-

Table 1 Fate of black duck nests by nesting location, St. Lawrence estuary, 1963–72.

Fate of nest	% nests[a]			
	Ile-aux-Pommes	Other islands	Main-land	Total
Hatched	43.9	51.7	27.7	42.0 (248)[b]
Destroyed	38.7	44.8	55.4	41.4 (244)
Abandoned	17.4	3.4	16.9	16.6 (98)

[a] Based on 590 nests of known fate; an additional 23 nests were found for which the fate could not be determined.
[b] The number of nests is indicated in parentheses.

tion); more precise aging was possible thereafter by measuring right tarsus and bill length (culmen) of all ducklings and comparing them to growth curves established from wild ducklings of known age (Reed 1970, Lepage 1973). Ducklings less than three weeks old were marked with numbered fingerling fish tags placed in the web of the foot, and older ones were fitted with conventional aluminum leg bands.

Many hours of observation of nesting and brood-rearing black ducks were made from natural elevations and towers close to the marsh and from blinds on the island. From 1966 to 1970 brood counts were conducted from a low flying helicopter. Ducklings observed on these occasions were aged by Gollop and Marshall's (1954, unpublished report to Mississippi Flyway Council Technical Section) technique.

Analytical techniques will be discussed in the appropriate sections of the paper.

RESULTS

Nesting

From 1963 to 1972, inclusive, 613 black duck nests were found on the island and along the south shore of the estuary. The fates of 590 were determined (Table 1). The data from Ile-aux-Pommes were of greatest volume and consistency (478 nests) and permitted detailed year-to-year comparisons (Table 2).

Table 2. Black duck nesting success by year, Ile-aux-Pommes, 1963–72.

Year	% nests			Total no. of nests[a]
	Hatched	Destroyed	Abandoned	
1963	30.2	44.3	25.5	106
1964	52.8	30.6	16.7	72
1965	36.0	40.0	24.0	50
1966	52.2	39.1	8.7	46
1967	50.0	42.5	7.5	40
1968	39.4	45.5	15.2	33
1969	53.3	37.8	8.9	45
1970	71.4	9.5	19.0	21
1971	38.2	50.0	11.8	34
1972	41.9	32.3	25.8	31
Total	43.9	38.7	17.4	478

[a] Excluding 7 nests for which the fate could not be determined.

Of the 98 nests which were abandoned, 52 were judged to have been abandoned as a direct result of my interference (Table 1), although capturing and marking of nesting females, performed only during late incubation, did not contribute appreciably to nest losses.

On Ile-aux-Pommes, the losses were largely attributed to egg predators (gulls and occasionally common crows) or to nest-site competitors (eiders, which occasionally take over black duck nests). On the mainland, where the red fox and the common crow are the chief predators, human scent and disturbed vegetation may have resulted in a greater degree of observer-induced losses than on the island. Several instances of predation were believed to have been caused by an opportunistic fox that followed my tracks from nest to nest. The data did not permit assessment of success rates in undisturbed conditions, but they suggested that the recorded values must be considered as minimum estimates of that rate

Nesting success fluctuated considerably from year to year (Table 2: χ^2, 9 df =

23.17, $P < 0.01$). Since similar rates of observer interference prevailed through the period 1964–72, and marked annual differences occurred in the proportion of nests reaching hatching, most of the variation must have been natural.

Although nesting cover was distinctly reduced in 1963 (due to a grass fire which swept the island in the fall of 1962), no annual changes in the quantity and quality of cover were noted over the rest of the study period. The density of resident predators (roughly 4,500 pairs of breeding gulls) was relatively stable over the study period, and the number of nesting eiders, which compete with black ducks for nesting sites, fluctuated from year to year within the range 1,700–3,000 pairs (Reed 1973); neither gull nor eider numbers were correlated with annual nesting success rates of black ducks. In 1970 a fox was present on the island for the early part of the nesting season, but, although it killed many gulls and eiders and ate many of their eggs, it apparently took only one black duck female and no black duck eggs. A substantially higher proportion of nests hatched that year. Thus, annual fluctuations in success could not be explained clearly by changes in the availability of concealing cover or by changes in predator and competitor density. Further, no relationship was found between weather (average temperature and total rainfall—recorded at the Trois-Pistoles weather station 9.6 km away) and rates of nest loss on either a bimonthly or total season basis.

Nesting success rates did not vary in relation to laying dates; the 10-year averages for nests initiated early- (prior to 2 May), mid- (3–13 May) and late-season (after 24 May) were 46.6 percent, 49.2 percent, and 40.7 percent, respectively (χ^2, 2 df = 1.67, $P > 0.25$: numbers of nests 174, 197, and 81—Ile-aux-Pommes data only).

Nest losses did not occur at a constant rate throughout the nesting cycle. Of 240 nests (Ile-aux-Pommes data) lost through predation and abandonment and for which the records were complete, 22.1 percent (53 nests) were lost during egg laying, 52.9 percent (127 nests) during the first half of the incubation period, and 25.0 percent (60 nests) during the second half of incubation. These data were examined in more detail to provide a measure of nest losses per unit time of exposure. The estimated total number of "nest-days" (see Mayfield 1961) to which nests in the laying stage were exposed to the risk of loss was approximately 754, giving a daily rate of nest loss of 53/754 = 0.070; values for nests in the first and second halves of the incubation stage were 0.030 and 0.018, respectively. Clearly the probability of loss decreases with advancing stages of the cycle.

In terms of documenting reproductive output in a species such as the black duck, which is capable of compensating for nest losses by renesting (Stotts and Davis 1960, Coulter and Miller 1968), it is more useful to express output in terms of the number of eggs hatched (or broods produced) per breeding female than to use the nest as the basic unit. The nest records of females nesting on Ile-aux-Pommes were examined to provide for each year (1) daily tallies of active nests, (2) corresponding daily numbers of females judged to be in the renesting interval (the period between the loss of a nest and the initiation of a replacement clutch [Sowls 1955:132]), and (3) daily cumulative totals of nests already hatched. The maximum daily sum of these three figures provided the estimate of that year's breeding population (number of nesting females). In an earlier study (Reed 1970), where the technique was described in detail, it was shown that consistently accurate estimates were obtained.

Table 3. Black duck breeding success and production of newly hatched ducklings, Ile-aux-Pommes, 1963–72.

Year	Est. breeding pop. (no. ♀♀) (A)	Total clutches hatched (B)	Renesting effort[a] (no. nests/♀)	% ♀♀ producing broods (B/A × 100)	Total ducklings produced (at nest exodus) (C)	Duckling production rate (no. ducklings/♀) (C/A)	Brood size at nest exodus (C/B)
1963	53	32	2.0	60.4	277	5.23	8.66
1964	62	38	1.2	61.3	348	5.61	9.16
1965	35	18	1.5	51.4	130	3.71	7.22
1966	33	24	1.4	72.7	198	6.00	8.25
1967	24	20	1.7	83.3	152	6.33	7.60
1968	19	13	1.7	68.4	105	5.53	8.08
1969	32	24	1.4	75.0	182	5.69	7.58
1970	19	15	1.2	78.9	128	6.74	8.53
1971	24	13	1.5	54.2	112	4.87	8.62
1972	24	13	1.3	54.2	119	4.96	9.15
Mean	32.5	21	1.5	64.6	175.1	5.39	8.33

[a] Renesting effort: total number of nests found/estimated breeding population (no. ♀♀).

The estimates are reproduced in Table 3 along with other pertinent parameters of reproductive output also established from the detailed nest records from Ile-aux-Pommes. A comparison of the estimated proportions of nesting females producing broods (column 5, Table 3) with the nesting success rates (column 2, Table 2) showed that they were correlated (linear regression equation $\hat{Y} = 35.45 + 0.656\ X$; $t = 2.70$, 9 df, $P < 0.05$ where $\hat{Y}$ is the proportion of females producing broods and X is the nesting success rate), but in some years important variations occurred. The proportion of females producing broods was much higher in 1967 than would have been predicted by the regression equation (83.3 percent compared to an expected value of 68.3 percent), and somewhat higher than expected in 1968 (68.4 percent compared to 61.3 percent); values lower than expected on the basis of nest success rates were recorded in 1964 (61.3 percent vs. 70.1 percent). These differences from expected rates of brood production were caused by varying rates of renesting persistency (column 4, Table 3). In 1967 a high rate of renesting accompanied high nesting success to allow an exceptionally large proportion of the females to bring off broods, whereas in 1968 persistent renesting partially compensated for heavy nest losses. In 1964 excellent nesting success was attained, but those females that lost their nests did not renest with great frequency.

Renesting rates were negatively correlated with nesting success rates ($r_s = -0.75$, $N = 10$, $P < 0.01$), suggesting that high renesting rates could be explained by a greater availability of renesters because of heavy nest losses.

Strong correlations occurred between population size and both the number of nests hatched and the number of ducklings produced (r_s = +0.87 and +0.84, respectively, $N = 10$, $P < 0.01$). A very strong correlation was noted between the rate of brood production (percentage of females hatching out nests) and the rate of duckling production ($r_s = +0.96$, $N = 10$, $P <$ 0.01), as was the case for the number of nests hatched vs. the number of ducklings produced ($r_s = +0.98$, $N = 10$, $P < 0.01$). The influence of annual variations in clutch size, partial predation, embryonic mortality, and egg infertility was relatively unimportant in modifying the rate of duckling production and initial brood size.

Brood Rearing

The study area and the behavior of the population offered exceptional possibilities for the study of survival. An 8-km stretch of tidal marsh shoreline was conveniently closed off to the east by 3.2 km of shoreline that was unsuitable for brood rearing and to the west by a wharf and river; visual observation and capture adjacent to the study area confirmed that little, if any, emigration of broods occurred. Furthermore, capture-recapture indicated that broods usually spent the entire rearing period along short stretches of shoreline; few broods were known to have undertaken movements exceeding 1.6 km, excluding initial movements from nest to rearing marsh. Visual observations and capture-recapture of ducklings indicated strong ties within broods; interchange of ducklings or uniting of broods was recorded or suspected in less than one percent of several hundred broods handled.

From 1968 to 1971 a comparison was made of expected numbers of broods and observed numbers at two-week intervals through the brood rearing season. Expected numbers were determined mainly by capture-recapture analyses of data obtained by banding ducklings. Usually, we were able to locate, capture, and release ducklings as discrete family units. In this way each marked duckling could be assigned to a specific brood; the recapture of one or more ducklings of a given brood constituted a recapture of that brood. To determine "observed" numbers we carried out intensive observation at strategically located sites to record all broods present. These visual searches were conducted at 2-week intervals, based on a natural schedule of high tide coinciding with dawn; under these conditions (which occurred for only a few hours every two weeks) most concealing vegetation was submerged and broods were most active, maximizing the possibility of seeing all broods. These data were expanded to cover the whole area on the basis of extensive (but less intensive) observations covering the entire marsh. Alternatively, and as a check, "observed" numbers were calculated by capture-recapture analysis. The sources of the data are further explained in Reed (1970) and Lepage (1973).

The results of brood capture and recapture were analyzed by Schaefer's method (Schaefer 1951) and stratified by age, which yielded total estimated brood numbers of 98, 69, 95, and 111 for the years 1968 to 1971, respectively. These values were our estimates of the number of broods entering the population (i.e., that reached the rearing marsh) each year. Nest records were used to establish the proportions of these totals which entered the population at given time periods each year. Thus, for any specific date, we could estimate the number of broods that would have been present if no broods had been entirely destroyed ("expected" number of broods).

Brood surveys, adjusted for unobserved broods, provided estimates of the number of broods present at two-week intervals throughout the season in all four years ("observed" number of broods). As an example, the 1970 data are presented in Table 4 along with that year's estimates of the expected numbers of broods on the corresponding dates. Comparison of these figures indicated mean survival rates of 48 percent (1968), 50 percent (1969), 60 percent (1970), and 67 percent (1971), and an overall mean of 56 percent. The high value estimated for 1971 was caused by an exceptionally high and apparently

Table 4. Survival of black duck broods in 1970 as estimated by comparing numbers of broods "present" with expected numbers, where "present" numbers were determined by field observation.

Date	Class I (1–18 days)			Class II (19–43 days)			Class III (44–60 days)			Total		
	No. broods present	Expected no. broods	Survival (%)	No. broods present	Expected no. broods	Survival (%)	No. broods present	Expected no. broods	Survival (%)	No. broods present	Expected no. broods	Survival (%)
5–9 June	8	20	40	0	0		0	0		8	20	40
21–22 June	17	34	50	6	14	43	0	0		23	48	48
7–9 July	22	34	65	27	46	59	0	1	0	49	81	60
20–24 July	14	17	82	30	51	59	30	26	115	74	94	79
3–4 Aug.	9	5	180	22	43	51	19	33	58	50	81	62
18–19 Aug.	0	0		16	16	100	3	34	9	19	50	38
Mean survival (%)			64			59			55			60

erroneous number of "observed" class III broods during late-season surveys (poor visibility likely caused us to tally some groups of fledged young and adults as class III broods).

The increased efficiency of the dog-assisted crew, directed by M. Lepage in 1970 and 1971, yielded capture-recapture data of sufficient volume for analysis by Jolly's stochastic method (Jolly 1965). This provided alternative estimates of numbers of broods present ("observed" numbers) at different time periods (see example in Table 5). When these values were compared to expected numbers, mean survival rates of 61 percent (1970) and 48 percent (1971) were obtained.

From 1968 to 1973, 47 color-marked nesting females were known to have hatched clutches and to have led their broods away from the nest. At least 34 percent were known to have produced fledged young and 26 percent were known to have lost all ducklings before attaining age class II; the fate of 40 percent could not be determined.

These analyses indicated that about 55 percent of broods that reached the rearing marsh produced one or more fledged young. The evidence also indicated that most losses occurred at an early age (see Table 4); on average roughly 80 percent of all brood losses occurred in age class I, 20 percent in age class II, and negligible losses in class III.

Since brood size was recorded for all visual and capture-recapture observations, it was possible to analyze survival of ducklings by the same techniques. Thus, in 1968 and 1969 we estimated that 34 percent and 38 percent of all ducklings that reached the rearing marsh survived to fledge. The corresponding rates for 1970 and 1971 were 32 percent and 34 percent, respectively. Using "observed numbers" calculated by Jolly's stochastic method (Jolly 1965), we estimated the duckling survival rates in 1970 and 1971 to be 40 percent and 25 percent, respectively. The mean of these 6 values was 34 percent. The basic data and details of analyses can be found in Reed (1970) and Lepage (1973).

I concluded that approximately one-third of the ducklings that reached the rearing marsh survived to fledge.

DISCUSSION

Several workers have reported rates of nesting success for black ducks in other areas. Stotts and Davis (1960:148) reported 38 percent success for a sample of 574 nests on mainland and islands in Chesapeake Bay, Maryland; if nest lossess attributed to the observer are included in the calculations, as they have been in this study, the rate drops to 30 percent. Coulter and Mendall (1968:95) recorded a success rate of 55 percent for 340 nests, prinicipally in marshes in Maine, and on islands in Lake Champlain, Vermont, they found 67 percent to 84 percent success for 231 nests. Laperle (1974:26) found black duck nesting success on islands in the St. Lawrence near Montreal, Quebec (Iles-de-la-Paix National Wildlife Area), to be 54 percent (*N* = 112, 1968–70). Young's (1968:211) records indicated 57 percent success (*N* = 28 nests) for black ducks near Sudbury, Ontario; the island nesting component of the population achieved 72 percent success.

Those results, recorded in different areas throughout the southern half of the range, showed widely varying values of nesting success. Although different study techniques may have been a contributing factor, this variation must reflect natural phenomena, perhaps most likely the types and abundance of local predators and the accessibility of nesting sites. This and other studies indicate that heavy nest losses often occur; most recorded instances of high success rates relate to birds nesting on islands or in flooded forests that usually are devoid of ground predators. Undoubtedly most black ducks nest in sites which can be reached by ground predators (in my study area more than 75 percent nested on the mainland).

The data from Ile-aux-Pommes indicated that in some years renesting largely may compensate for nest losses but in others it does not. Thus the annual rate of nest survival does not necessarily foreshadow that year's level of duckling production. The rate of duckling production (number of newly hatched ducklings produced per breeding female) is regulated mainly by the combined effect of nesting success and renesting persistency. None of the parameters assessed locally (weather, density of predators, density of competitors, and quality and quantity of nesting cover) could be clearly shown to affect this rate. Recent studies on nesting geese in northern areas (Ryder 1970, Harvey 1971, MacInnes et al. 1974, Newton personal communication) and common eiders (Milne 1974) have suggested that breeding output may be influenced by conditions at earlier dates (on the wintering grounds or along migration routes) which influence the physical condition of the breeding female. Ryder (1970) and MacInnes et al. (1974) each postulated that both nesting success and clutch size might be affected similarly, suggesting that the fitness of the female at the start of the nesting period would be reflected in several parameters of her performance. In this study, however, neither annual clutch size nor rates of renesting persistency were positively correlated with nesting success.

The most important conclusions to be drawn from this analysis of the nesting cycle are that some breeding females do not bring off broods and that the proportion of females which are unsuccessful varies from year to year. Annual variations in the rate of production of newly hatched young are governed largely by nesting success rates and renesting persistency; annual variations in clutch size, embryonic mortality, and egg infertility are unimportant in this respect.

Waterfowl managers may wish to evaluate or predict production of newly hatched ducklings either on the basis of production per breeding female or total production for a given geographic area. The results of this study show that the parameter providing the best estimation of the production rate per female is the female success rate (percentage of females hatching out broods) ($r_s = +0.96$) which is a difficult and time-consuming parameter to measure (both the number of breeders and the number of hatches must be determined); a simpler index could be obtained from the nesting success rates ($r_s = +0.79$). The parameter best reflecting total production of newly hatched young is the number of nests hatched ($r_s = +0.98$); a simpler but less precise index could be provided by the number of breeding females ($r_s = +0.84$). This last correlation suggests that an accurate census of breeding pairs could provide a reasonably reliable index of the expected crop of newly hatched ducklings. However, the lack of marked sexual dimorphism, a wide spacing of nesting pairs, and the frequent use of forested habitat render large scale census difficult and subject to large errors. On small areas such as wildlife refuges and managed marshes, a careful and detailed census of breeding pairs should provide an efficient and reliable predictive index to the number of broods produced.

The study of survival from hatching to fledging involved several indirect measurements (e.g., capture-recapture estimates) which can be considered valid only if certain requirements regarding marking and sampling are met (Southwood 1966:75). In an earlier report Lepage (1973) showed that the underlying assumptions and requirements had been sufficiently fulfilled. All evidence indicated that brood losses recorded in this study were almost entirely due to death and not to emigration.

It is remarkable that my intensive investigations failed to reveal adequately the causes of duckling mortality. On several occasions great black-backed gulls were observed attempting, unsuccessfully, to catch ducklings; the remains of two banded ducklings were found at gull nests on a nearby island. Common crows were also seen attempting unsuccessfully to capture young ducklings. One duckling found in the marsh was believed to have been killed by a marsh hawk (*Circus cyaneus*). Red fox and raccoon (*Procyon lotor*) were fairly numerous in the area and were known to visit the marsh. Other potential mammalian predators observed in the area were mink (*Mustela vison*), weasel (*M. frenata, M. erminea*), and striped skunk (*Mephitis mephitis*).

There is evidence to suggest that chilling and/or exhaustion of young ducklings is an important cause of death. Early-hatched broods are often subjected to cold weather; in addition many must travel 3 to 6 km from the nest site to the rearing marsh (Reed 1970). In good weather these movements presumably do not deplete the energy reserves of the ducklings, for I have numerous records of fledged young which were known to have been hatched in nests on Ile-aux-Pommes, 5.6 km from the marsh. However, in bad weather chilling and exhaustion may have eliminated some broods before they reached the marsh and may have left others badly weakened. The case of a radio-marked hen which nested on Ile-aux-Pommes is particularly revealing in this respect: her nest was the earliest hatch recorded in 1972 and exceptionally cold, rainy, and windy weather prevailed at hatching and at the time the brood made the crossing from the island. The initial brood of 12 ducklings had been reduced to 8 when first located in the rearing marsh 3 days later; the following day only 6 remained, and they did not display the vigor typical of ducklings of that age when feeding and following the hen. By the following afternoon all ducklings had disappeared, presumably dead from the effects of chilling and exhaustion.

Combining the results of the nesting and brood rearing studies permits an appraisal

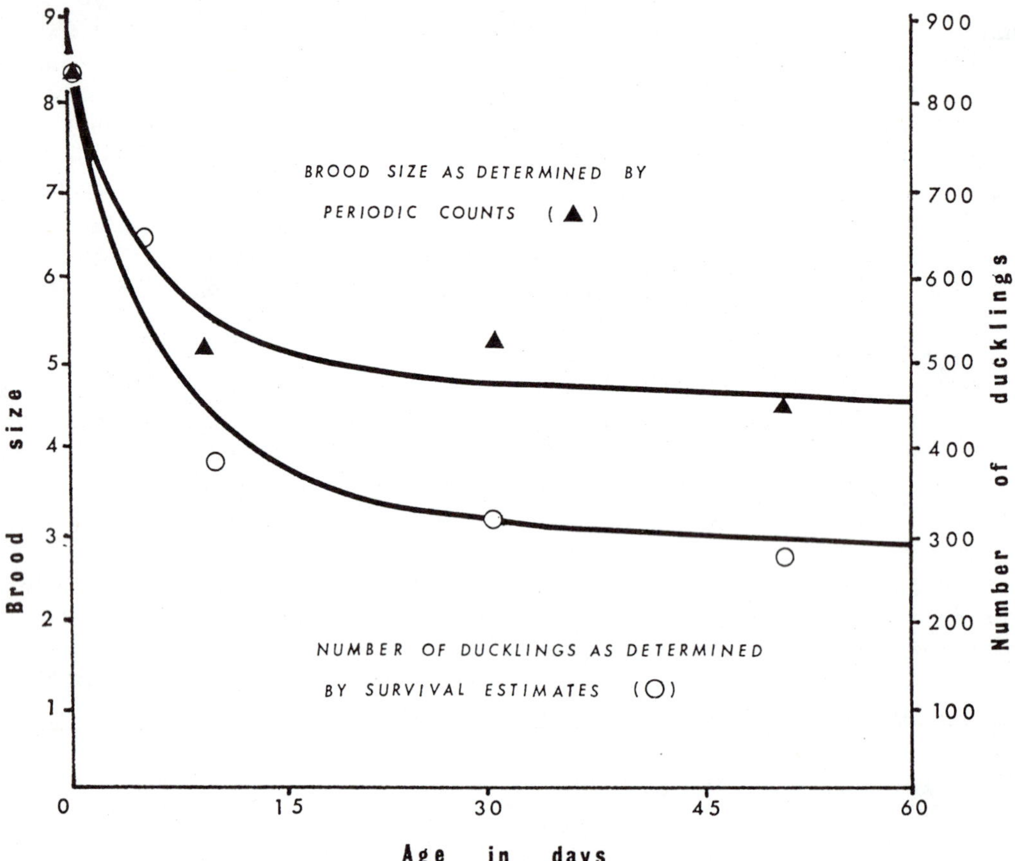

Fig. 2. Black duck brood size and survival of a hypothetical population of 100 broods with 8.3 ducklings each at nest exodus, Isle Verte Bay.

of production of fledged young. An hypothetical population of 100 nesting pairs would have produced on average about 65 broods of which 36 (55 percent) would have reached flight age, a total of 183 ducklings (34 percent survival of 65 broods with 8.3 ducklings). If no adult mortality occurred during the breeding season the fall age ratio would be 200 adults:183 juveniles (1:0.92).

My study indicated a much lower rate of survival than has generally been attributed to the species. Valid comparisons with studies in other regions are not possible, however, since other workers have failed to take losses of entire broods into account (Stotts 1968, Stotts and Davis 1960, Wright 1954). Annual appraisals of production of young dabbling ducks in the prairies and parklands of western North America (Cooch 1969, Crissey 1969) did not account for losses of entire broods; if the proportion of brood losses varies annually in that area, the production index could be erroneous in some years. Two studies on the mallard (*Anas platyrhynchos*) have indicated the importance of loss of entire broods, those of Eygenraam (1957) in the Netherlands and Dzubin and Gollop (1972) in western Canada. The latter authors presented data

Table 5. Survival of black ducks broods in 1970 as estimated by comparing numbers of broods "present" with expected numbers, where "present" numbers were determined by capture–recapture analyses using Jolly's (1965) method.

Capture–recapture period	No. broods present	Expected no. broods[a]	Survival (%)
11 June–16 June	13	32	41
17 June–25 June	26	47	55
26 June–2 July	44	57	77
3 July–10 July	68	78	87
14 July–24 July	53	92	58
25 July–30 July	48	93	52
31 July–10 Aug.	48	79	61
11 Aug.–20 Aug.	25	56	45
Mean survival (%)			61

[a] Estimated as in Table 4.

that clearly illustrated the degree of error which can occur by estimating survival by changes in brood size (Dzubin and Gollop 1972:131). I have illustrated this type of error by applying my data to a hypothetical population of 100 broods (Fig. 2). Estimated production (hatching to fledging), by the techniques described in this paper, of 100 broods with 8.3 ducklings per brood at nest exodus would yield 282 fledged young (34 percent survival of young). Using only changes in brood size would have yielded 450 ducklings (100 broods × 4.5 ducklings, class III [Reed 1970]), a much greater estimated production.

The results of this study and that of Dzubin and Gollop (1972) indicate the importance of losses caused by unproductive nesting and of losses of entire broods in waterfowl. The significance of these findings is far reaching. Most previous studies, which have not accounted for those factors, undoubtedly have furnished greatly exaggerated estimates of production rates. The ability of some waterfowl populations to replace postfledge losses through reproduction requires serious re-analysis. Commonly used criteria of production such as clutch size, nesting success rates, and class III brood size no longer can be accepted unless they can be related to the number of breeding birds in a manner permitting estimation of the unproductive segment of that population.

LITERATURE CITED

COOCH, F. G. 1969. Waterfowl-production habitat requirements. Pages 5–10 *in* Saskatoon wetlands seminar. Can. Wildl. Serv. Rep. Ser. 6.

COULTER, M. W., AND H. L. MENDALL. 1968. Habitat and breeding ecology: Northeastern States. Pages 90–101 *in* P. Barske, ed. The black duck; evaluation, management and research: a symposium. Atlantic Waterfowl Council and Wildlife Management Institute, Washington, D.C.

———, AND W. R. MILLER. 1968. Nesting biology of black ducks and mallards in northern New England. Vermont Fish Game Dept. Bull. 68-2. 74pp.

CRISSEY, W. F. 1969. Prairie potholes from a continental viewpoint. Pages 161–171 *in* Saskatoon wetlands seminar. Can. Wildl. Serv. Rep. Ser. 6.

DZUBIN, A., AND J. B. GOLLOP. 1972. Aspects of mallard breeding ecology in Canadian parkland and grassland. Pages 113–152 *in* Population ecology of migratory birds. U.S. Fish Wildl. Serv. Res. Rep. 2.

EYGENRAAM, J. A. 1957. The sex-ratio and the production of the mallard (*Anas platyrhynchos* L.). Ardea 45(3–4):117–143.

HARVEY, J. M. 1971. Factors affecting blue goose nesting success. Can. J. Zool. 49(2): 223–234.

JOLLY, G. M. 1965. Explicit estimates from capture-recapture data with both death and immigration-stochastic model. Biometrika 52(1–2):225–247.

LAPERLE, M. 1974. Effects of water level fluctuations on duck breeding success. Pages 18–30 *in* H. Boyd, ed. Waterfowl studies. Can. Wildl. Serv. Rep. Ser. 29.

LEPAGE, M. 1973. Survie et croissance du Canard noir (*Anas rubripes*) durant la période d'élevage. M.S. Thesis. L'Université Laval, Québec. 128pp.

MACINNES, C. D., R. A. DAVIS, R. N. JONES, B. C. LIEFF, AND A. J. PAKULAK. 1974. Reproductive efficiency of McConnell River small Canada geese. J. Wildl. Manage. 38(4): 686–707.

MAYFIELD, H. 1961. Nesting success calculated from exposure. Wilson Bull. 73(3):255–261.

MILNE, H. 1974. Breeding numbers and reproductive rate of eiders at the Sands of Forvie National Nature Reserve, Scotland. Ibis 116 (2):135–154.

REED, A. 1970. The breeding ecology of the black duck in the St. Lawrence estuary. D.S. Thesis. L'Université Laval, Québec. 175pp.

———. 1973. Aquatic bird colonies in the St. Lawrence estuary. Quebec Wildl. Serv. Bull. 18. 54pp.

———, AND G. MOISAN. 1971. The *Spartina* tidal marshes of the St. Lawrence estuary and their importance to aquatic birds. Naturaliste Can. 98(5):905–922.

RYDER, J. P. 1970. A possible factor in the evolution of clutch size in Ross' goose. Wilson Bull. 82(1):5–13.

SCHAEFER, M. B. 1951. Estimation of size of animal populations by marking experiments. U.S. Fish Wildl. Serv. Fish. Bull. 69. 52:191–203.

SOUTHWOOD, T. R. E. 1966. Ecological methods. Chapman and Hall, London. 391pp.

SOWLS, L. K. 1955. Prairie ducks. The Stackpole Co., Harrisburg, Pa. 193pp.

STOTTS, V. D. 1968. Habitat and breeding ecology: east central United States. Pages 102–112 *in* P. Barske, ed. The black duck; evaluation, management and research: a symposium. Atlantic Waterfowl Council and Wildlife Management Institute, Washington, D.C.

———, AND D. E. DAVIS. 1960. The black duck in the Chesapeake Bay of Maryland: breeding behavior and biology. Chesapeake Sci. 1(3–4):127–154.

WELLER, M. W. 1956. A simple field candler for waterfowl eggs. J. Wildl. Manage. 20(2): 111–113.

WRIGHT, B. S. 1954. High tide and an east wind. The Stackpole Co., Harrisburg, Pa. 162pp.

YOUNG, C. M. 1968. Island nesting of ducks in northern Ontario. Can. Field-Nat. 82(3): 209–212.

Accepted 19 November 1974.

FACTORS INFLUENCING NESTING SUCCESS OF EIDERS IN PENOBSCOT BAY, MAINE[1]

JERRY S. CHOATE, Maine Cooperative Wildlife Research Unit, Orono[2]

Abstract: Histories were recorded for 1,030 American eider (*Somateria mollissima dresseri*) nests on five islands during two breeding seasons in Penobscot Bay, Maine. Nesting success was 39 percent in 1964 and 36 percent in 1965. Predation by gulls was responsible for most nest losses. Five factors were found to be related to nesting success: nesting cover, clutch size, partial predation, gull populations, and human disturbance. Nests in hardwood shrubs and cow parsnip (*Heracleum maximum*) had relatively high success while those in grasses and nightshade (*Solanum dulcamara*) were much less successful. Nests with a complete clutch of fewer than four eggs were less successful than those with four or more eggs. When part of a clutch was lost to predators the chance of ultimate success of the remaining eggs was reduced. The number of nesting gulls per nesting eider on a given island was inversely related to the nesting success of the eiders on that island. Human disturbance was indirectly responsible for lowered nesting success.

During a study of the breeding biology of the American eider in Penobscot Bay, Maine, in the spring and summer of 1964 and 1965 (Choate 1966), data were collected on several factors believed to influence nesting success of the species. The objective of this paper is to point out these factors and the extent of their influence.

The author is grateful to Howard L. Mendall and Malcolm W. Coulter, Professors of Game Management, University of Maine, who assisted with field work and reviewed the manuscript. Professor Mendall also served as project supervisor. Credit is likewise due to many University students and staff members, and residents of the island of Islesboro, without whose aid in the field this project would have been impossible.

THE STUDY AREA

Penobscot Bay is approximately 30 miles long, and, at its mouth, 28 miles wide. It primarily drains the Penobscot River and is located about midway between the easternmost and westernmost points on the Maine coast. Mean high tide is around 10 ft.

Eider nests were studied on five islands which range from approximately 0.25 to 4 acres in area. The islands are named Flat Island, Mouse Island, Goose Island, East Goose Rock, and Robinson Rock. All are rather long and narrow. Flat Island is low lying and very level. The others, especially Robinson Rock, are steep sided and rise abruptly out of the water. However, the central portions are more level and slope gently toward the steep edges.

Each island is composed of bed rock covered with a thin layer of soil. The rock is exposed at the edges and sometimes near the center of the islands. Wherever the soil has accumulated sufficiently it supports dense growths of vegetation.

Excluding Flat Island, the soils are mainly humus. Flat Island apparently has a layer of more sterile mineral soil as evidenced by its vegetation. Bayberry (*Myrica pensylvanica*), a shrub which grows on sterile soil (Fernald 1950), is abundant.

The major plant species present on the study islands are: cow parsnip (*Hera-*

[1] Contribution from the Maine Cooperative Wildlife Research Unit, Orono, Maine: Maine Department of Inland Fisheries and Game, University of Maine, Wildlife Management Institute, and the U. S. Bureau of Sport Fisheries and Wildlife, cooperating.

[2] Present address: 1553 Crittenden Street, Alden, New York.

Originally published in J. Wildl. Manage. 31(4):769–777, 1967.

cleum maximum); several grasses—timothy (*Phleum pratense*), witch-grass (*Agropyron repens*), redtop (*Agrostis alba*), Kentucky bluegrass (*Poa pratensis*), and wild rye (*Elymus virginicus*); miscellaneous small herbs, primarily common ragweed (*Ambrosia artemisiifolia*) and pineapple weed (*Matricaria matricarioides*); nettle (*Urtica viridis*); nightshade (*Solanum dulcamara*); goldenrod (*Solidago rugosa*); and shrubs composed of rose (*Rosa* sp.), bayberry, and raspberry (*Rubus* sp.).

Nesting on the study islands are several other species of birds: black duck (*Anas rubripes*), great black-backed gull (*Larus marinus*), herring gull (*L. argentatus*), double-crested cormorant (*Phalacrocorax auritus*), black guillemot (*Cepphus grylle*), and song sparrow (*Melospiza melodia*). Meadow voles (*Microtus pennsylvanicus*), found in abundance on Flat Island, are the only small mammals known to inhabit the study area.

METHODS

During the 1964 season eider nests were studied on Mouse Island, Goose Island, East Goose Rock, and Robinson Rock. In 1965, Flat Island was substituted for Robinson Rock in order to determine differences in nesting success in shrubby vegetation on Flat Island as contrasted to success in herbaceous vegetation on the other islands.

Commencing in the early spring of both seasons, visits were made at least once a week to each island to search for eider nests, except when adverse weather prevented. Searches were limited to a maximum of 3 hours in an attempt to prevent overexposure of eggs to adverse temperatures when unattended by females.

This procedure was altered somewhat in 1965 to test the effect of human disturbance on nesting success. Goose Island and East Goose Rock, which had about the same success and same number of visits in 1964, were checked an unequal number of times in 1965. Goose Island was visited 27 times spaced throughout the season and East Goose Rock 12 times. On the basis of 1964 data, I assume that if there had been no human disturbance in 1965 nesting success would have been about equal on the two islands.

Eider nests were marked with numbered wooden stakes, and pertinent data were recorded for each nest on every visit, including: date, island, number of eggs, nesting cover, and concealment. Nesting cover was recorded as the type of vegetation immediately surrounding the nest and included the following: cow parsnip, grass, nettle, miscellaneous herbs, nightshade, barren rock,[3] goldenrod, nettle–grass, and shrubs. If two or more plant species surrounded a nest, the one that provided the most cover was recorded. In the case of the nettle–grass type there were enough nests where neither grass nor nettle predominated to justify the use of this mixed-cover type.

Concealment was evaluated by looking directly down on the nest from a standing position and estimating what percent of the nest area was blocked from view by the vegetation. The four concealment classes used were poor, fair, good, and excellent, representing respectively 0–25, 26–50, 51–75, and 76–100 percent of the nest hidden.

Fecal matter was wiped off the eggs if the female had defecated on them when she flushed. The clutch was then covered with down to insulate the eggs and to help camouflage them from predators.

Nests were periodically rechecked until the eggs hatched, were destroyed, or were

[3] Arbitrarily included as a cover type.

deserted. Nest fate was ascertained by Girard's (1939) method of looking for shell membranes in recently abandoned sites. A nest was considered successful when one or more membranes could be found in or near it. If there were no signs of success or there was evidence of disturbance, the nest fate was recorded as destroyed. If there was no indication of recent activity at a nest containing eggs, it was considered deserted. Eggs were recorded as infertile when the female incubated them much beyond 4 weeks and, when the eggs were subsequently opened, there was no apparent embryo development. A partially developed embryo was interpreted as having died from overexposure to adverse weather or some other factor which was not determined.

Eider and gull populations were estimated from nest counts made throughout the study except at Flat Island. Since the extent of renesting was unknown, only approximations of the breeding populations could be made. Since both sexes of gulls incubate the eggs it was assumed that two gulls occupied a nest. Male eiders left the islands when nesting began and only one eider was considered to occupy a nest.

When feasible, birds were observed from a blind, so that predatory activities of gulls on eider nests could be viewed.

In order to determine nesting densities, each island except Flat Island was mapped, using a plane table and alidade.

RESULTS

Histories were recorded for 1,030 eider nests (569 in 1964 and 461 in 1965). Of this total the fate was determined in 963 cases. Overall success was quite similar in the two years. In 1964, 39 percent of the nests produced one or more young and 39 percent of the eggs hatched. The corresponding figures for 1965 were 36 percent nest success and 39 percent hatching success.

Table 1. Fate of 963 eider nests in the Penobscot Bay study area, 1964 and 1965, expressed in percentages.

	Percent of Nests				
Year	Hatched	Destroyed	Deserted	Infertile or Exposed to Heat	Total
1964 (515 nests)	39	52	8	1	100
1965 (448 nests)	36	58	3	3	100

Predation caused the greatest proportion of nest losses (Table 1). Crows (*Corvus brachyrhynchos*) often visited the study islands, but it is believed that gulls were the chief predators. Whenever crows were observed on an island they were feeding along the shoreline and were not near active eider nests. On the other hand, personnel who aided in field work observed gulls preying upon eider nests. As shown in Table 1, some clutches did not hatch because they were infertile, deserted by the female, or possibly were overheated (see Rolnik 1943:157) by exposure to direct sunlight.

There is disagreement as to the effect of avian predators on eider production. According to Cooch (1966) such effect is negligible when an eider population is maintaining itself at carrying capacity. If the population is depressed, however, predation may be important in maintaining low numbers. In the Grand Manan Archipelago, New Brunswick, Pimlott (1952) found little evidence that gulls preyed on eider eggs. On the other hand, Belopol'skii (1957:269) analyzed 25 stomachs of the glaucous gull (*Larus hyperboreus*) and found that eider ducklings and eggs made up 12 percent of

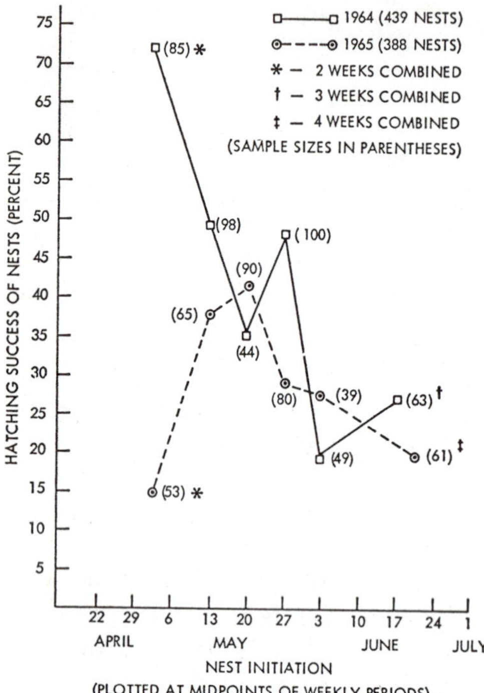

Fig. 1. Hatching success of eider nests in relation to date of nest initiation, Penobscot Bay, Maine.

Table 2. Hatching success of 946* eider nests, by cover types.

Cover Type	1964		1965	
	No. of Nests	Percent Hatched	No. of Nests	Percent Hatched
Cow parsnip	222	48	204	39
Grass	133	33	88	19
Nettle	32	41	—	—
Miscellaneous herbs	25	32	12	17
Nightshade	23	26	22	14
Rock	24	25	35	26
Goldenrod	15	40	21	33
Nettle–Grass	32	31	—	—
Shrubs	—	—	58	74
Total	506	39	440	36

* This number differs by 17 from the number of nests included in Table 1 because 17 nests did not fit any of the cover categories, being in driftwood, seaweed, etc.

the contents. On many occasions Reed (1964) observed herring and black-backed gulls preying on eider nests.

Since production was limited primarily by nest predation, several factors were examined which might have a bearing on predation.

Nesting Cover

Percent success in the various cover types was considered (Table 2). Success for nests in a given type was compared to success in all other types combined. Chi-square values showed that in 1964 nesting success was significantly higher for nests in cow parsnip than for those in the other types ($P < 0.005$) while nests in grass had lower success ($P < 0.10$). The 1965 data showed nests in grass and nightshade to have significantly lower nesting success ($P < 0.005$ for grass and 0.025 for nightshade) than nests in the other types. Success of nests in shrubs was much higher ($P < 0.005$) than in the other types.

Apparently these differences in predation were directly related to the physical characteristics of the plant species. The broad leaves of cow parsnip provided more concealment than any other cover plant. Although the relationship was not precise, data collected on concealment of nests in the herbaceous cover types indicated greater success for those better concealed. Shrubs provided little concealment until nesting was near completion. However, the thick barrier produced by the stems and branches of the shrubs apparently discouraged gulls from preying upon eider nests by hindering their movement through the vegetation.

Other studies have shown cover type and degree of concealment to be related to nesting success. Lewis (1959) observed sheltered and concealed eider nests on wooded islands, and there was practically no predation, but on treeless islands about 20 percent of the nests were destroyed. Belopol'skii (1957:272) and Grenquist (1959) also

Table 3. Success of eider nests by clutch size* (complete clutches only).

YEAR	LESS THAN FOUR EGGS		FOUR OR MORE EGGS		ALL COMPLETE CLUTCHES	
	No. of Nests	Percent Success	No. of Nests	Percent Success	No. of Nests	Percent Success
1964	129	53	190	67	319	62
1965	107	50	159	66	266	60

* See text explanation for apparent discrepancy with Tables 1 and 2.

found higher success in sheltered as opposed to open sites.

The effect of dense cover (such as the shrub type of the present study) in reducing predation is also pointed out by Reed (1964) in a study of black ducks; nests in dense cover were protected from gulls because the gulls' long wings appeared to hinder their movement in such cover.

Nesting success might be expected to increase as the season progressed and vegetation developed. However, this held true only for the early part of the 1965 season (Fig. 1). Success increased in nests initiated up to the last part of May, after which it declined. In 1964, nesting success was at its height early in the season and dropped as the season progressed. There is no satisfactory explanation for this decrease later in the season.

Greater nest loss late in the season indicated a lack of success in renests (nests with little down and small clutches in the last part of the season indicated that renesting occurred). Thus, renesting may not have made up to any great extent for nests lost earlier in the season.

In contrast to the present study, Lewis (1939:73) found that egg destruction decreased to almost none about the middle of June. He attributed the decline to two factors: (1) vegetation development provided more shelter and (2) large schools of small fish arrived, supplying readily available food to nest predators. Paynter (1951:505), on the other hand, concluded that early and late nests were equally successful in producing young.

Nest Densities

Considering entire islands, nest densities ranged from 3.8 per 1,000 square ft (166 nests/acre)[4] on Mouse Island in 1965 to 8.9 per 1,000 square ft (389 nests/acre) on East Goose Rock in 1964. No relationship was found between nest density on an island and success of the nests on that island. Nest densities on small, arbitrarily chosen areas of each island ranged from 4.3 to 136.4 per 1,000 square ft (187 to 5,940 nests/acre). In these areas also, no relation could be found between nest density and nest success.

In contrast to the present study, Belopol'skii (1957:272, 294) found higher nesting success in a large, densely populated eider colony than on islands where eider nests were sparse. A larger sample of islands with like vegetation and a greater range of nest densities might have shown a similar relationship in the present study.

Clutch Size

In both years, those nests with an above-average clutch size (four or more eggs)

[4] Most of the nest densities expressed in nests per acre are based on an area of less than 1 acre and are therefore unreal figures. They are presented merely to provide comparison with other waterfowl species where densities are usually measured in nests per acre.

were more successful than those with below-average clutch size (Table 3). A Chi-square test showed the differences in success to be significant ($P < 0.025$). Possible reasons for these differences are: (1) the larger clutches were laid by older birds which had more capability and/or desire to bring off a brood successfully; (2) eiders, regardless of age, were more strongly attached to nests with larger clutches.

At Kent Island, New Brunswick, Paynter (1951:504) showed that the size of complete clutches of eider eggs was not related to the survival rate. Paynter (1949:152) found a contrasting situation, however, for herring gulls where success was higher in three-egg clutches than in two-egg clutches. He believed that in two-egg nests the female lacked the full measure of stimulation provided by a full clutch which causes broodiness and parental care, so that the nests were poorly guarded and more susceptible to predation.

The figures for nesting success in Table 3 are considerably higher than overall nesting success. This difference results because Table 3 includes only complete clutches, and rate of success in nests where clutches were completed was greater than for all nests. Of those nests destroyed in 1965, 66 percent were lost before the clutch was complete. (The nature of the data tabulation prevented calculation of the corresponding figure for 1964.) Thus, once a full clutch of eggs was laid there was less chance the nest would be destroyed. A lower rate of destruction after completion is to be expected since the female is more attentive to the nest when incubation begins.

Partial Predation

In some nests only part of the clutch was lost to predators. In 1964, partial predation was recorded in 13 percent of the nests; in 1965 it was noted in 9 percent. Once a gull located a nest and took part of the eggs, it might be expected that the nest would more likely be lost on subsequent visits by the same gull. Partial predation was recorded for nests only after incubation started. Thus, success for partially destroyed clutches was compared to success among incubated clutches where either no eggs or all eggs were destroyed (Table 4). In 1964, success was significantly lower ($P < 0.01$) in the partially destroyed clutches. Although success was also lower in 1965, the difference was not significant ($P > 0.01$).

Milne (1963) found in Scotland that some partial predation occurred without nest desertion but the subsequent success of these nests is not known. No other studies are known of eider nesting where partial predation has been considered in relation to nesting success.

Gull Populations

It was suspected that the numerical ratio of gulls to eiders might influence nesting success. It appears that this was the case in 1964 (Table 5) when success decreased as the gull : eider ratio increased. Although this did not hold true in 1965, the differential effects that year of human disturbance (discussed in next section) probably overshadowed any effects of the gull : eider ratios.

Based on a small number of observations, it is believed that black-backed gulls preyed more heavily than herring gulls on eider nests. There was an apparent relation between all gull : eider ratios and nesting success, but it may well be that most nest destruction was by black-backed gulls even though, based on rough estimates, they

Table 4. Eider nest success in relation to loss of part of the clutch during incubation (complete clutches only).

	CLUTCHES WITH PARTIAL PREDATION		CLUTCHES WITHOUT PARTIAL PREDATION	
YEAR	No. of Records	Percent Success	No. of Records	Percent Success
1964	52	44	260	65
1965	40	50	224	61

made up only about a fourth of the total gull population.

Human Disturbance

In many waterfowl production studies human influence is a factor, although its importance is often hard to measure. In the present study, human disturbance appeared to influence nesting success to a great extent. Observations from a blind showed that after an investigator left an island, the gulls returned much sooner than the eiders. Of course, before the eiders returned, the nests were highly vulnerable to predation by the gulls.

Observations during a nest-trapping and banding operation on Robinson Rock in 1965 also indicated the effect of human disturbance. When the island was revisited one or more times on the same day, after setting nets or banding eiders, many newly destroyed nests were evident. Gulls were seen flying back to the island as soon as the workers left, and they no doubt destroyed many nests before the eiders returned. Grenquist (1959) also believed that flushing a female eider from her nest gave crows a chance to destroy the nest. Black-backed gulls were observed by Todd (1963) to break up an eider nest after a man flushed the female.

Human disturbance did not appear to cause much nest desertion. Only a small percentage of nests was considered deserted (Table 1) and it is not known how many of these were actually the result of human disturbance. It should be pointed out that nests could have been abandoned and subsequently destroyed before they were labeled deserted. Thus, the actual percentage of abandoned nests could have been somewhat higher than shown in Table 1.

There is disagreement as to the effect of human disturbance on nest desertion. Paludan (1962), who captured breeding female eiders on the nest and banded them, noted that few abandoned. Usually the females returned to the nests in a short time. However, Hildén (1964) studied several species of ducks and observed that the eider was the species most apt to desert its nest. In a number of cases the nest was abandoned after the female was flushed only once.

A few clutches apparently were lost because of overexposure to heat when nests were checked on hot, sunny days. Several cases of partially developed embryos were

Table 5. Eider nest success related to the ratio of gulls (including both herring and black-backed) to eiders.

	1964			1965		
		EIDER NESTS			EIDER NESTS	
ISLAND	Gull : Eider	No.	% success	Gull : Eider	No.	% success
Mouse Island	1.3 : 1	247	47	1.5 : 1	223	29
Goose Island	1.9 : 1	86	36	2.0 : 1	113	27
East Goose Rock	2.0 : 1	64	34	3.5 : 1	52	40
Robinson Rock	2.2 : 1	118	28	—	—	—

suspected to be the result of this exposure. Overheating occurred when many eiders were flushed from their nests and it was 2 hours or more before the observer could cover all the eggs.

During artificial incubation of eider eggs, a temperature of 42 C or higher may kill all the embryos (Rolnik 1943:157). This temperature was occasionally exceeded in the present study. Overheating occurred primarily in sparse cover where the eggs were not sufficiently shaded from the direct sunlight. There was no evidence that any losses were caused by excessive cooling of the eggs.

As with desertion, losses to overexposure may have been greater than indicated in Table 1. Embryos could have died and the eggs been eaten by predators before it was known that the embryos had perished. In such cases the nests would have been included in the predation category.

As mentioned in Methods, there was differential human disturbance on two islands in 1965. Goose Island, with more than twice as many visits, had 27 percent nest success—about two-thirds that for East Goose Rock (40 percent). Chi-square showed the difference to be significant ($P < 0.10$). Thus, with greater human disturbance on Goose Island, nesting success was significantly lower.

In the Cape Dorset Area, Northwest Territories, egg loss was heavier than normal when the eiders were frequently disturbed (Cooch 1966). Paynter (1951) believed that an observer's presence contributed to decreased eider nesting success.

Milne (1963) attempted to measure the effect of disturbance on success in a manner similar to that of the present study. A study area that was visited daily was compared with a relatively undisturbed control area. Although success was somewhat lower (3 percent) in the disturbed area, the difference was not significant.

LITERATURE CITED

BELOPOL'SKII, L. O. 1957. Ecology of sea colony birds of the Barents Sea. Acad. Sci., U.S.S.R. English trans. (1961) by Israel Prog. Sci. Transl. Office Tech. Serv., U. S. Dept. Commerce, Washington, D. C. 346pp.

CHOATE, J. S. 1966. Breeding biology of the American eider in Penobscot Bay, Maine. M.S. Thesis. Univ. Maine, Orono. 173pp.

COOCH, F. G. 1965. The breeding biology and management of the northern eider (*Somateria mollissima borealis*) in the Cape Dorset area, Northwest Territories. Canadian Wildl. Service, Wildl. Mgmt. Bull. Ser. 2, No. 10. Ottawa. 68pp.

FERNALD, M. L. 1950. Gray's manual of botany. 8th ed. Am. Book Co., New York. 1,632pp.

*GIRARD, G. L. 1939. Notes on life history of the shoveler. Trans. N. Am. Wildl. Conf. 4:364–371.

GRENQUIST, P. 1959. On the damage done by crow to the eider population in the bird sanctuary of Soderskar 1953–1959. Abstract of articles published in Suomen Riista 13:9–10.

HILDÉN, O. 1964. Ecology of duck populations in the island group of Valassaaret, Gulf of Bothnia. Annales Zoologici 1:153–279.

LEWIS, H. F. 1939. Size of sets of eggs of the American eider. J. Wildl. Mgmt. 3(1):70–73.

———. 1959. Predation on eider ducks by great black-backed gulls in Nova Scotia. Nova Scotia Dept. Lands and Forests. 16pp. Typewritten.

MILNE, H. 1963. Seasonal distribution and breeding biology of the eider, *Somateria mollissima mollissima* L., in the northeast of Scotland. Ph.D. Thesis. Aberdeen Univ., Aberdeenshire, Scotland. 235pp.

PALUDAN, K. 1962. [Eider-ducks (*Somateria mollissima*) in Danish waters.] (In Danish; English summary.) Danske Vildtundersøgelser Hefte 10. 87pp.

PAYNTER, R. A., JR. 1949. Clutch-size and the egg and chick mortality of Kent Island herring gulls. Ecology 30(2):146–166.

———. 1951. Clutch-size and egg mortality of Kent Island eiders. Ecology 32(3):497–507.

PIMLOTT, D. H. 1952. The economic status of the herring gulls of the Grand Manan Archipelago, New Brunswick, 1949. Canada Dept. Resources and Dev., Natl. Parks Branch, Wildl. Mgmt. Bull. Ser. 2, No. 5. 76pp.

REED, A. 1964. A nesting study of the black duck (*Anas rubripes*) at Ile aux Pommes, Quebec. M.S. Thesis. Laval Univ., Quebec City. 160pp.

ROLNIK, VERA. 1943. Instructions for the incubation of eider duck eggs. J. Wildl. Mgmt. 7(2):155–162.

TODD, W. E. C. 1963. Birds of the Labrador Peninsula. Univ. Toronto Press. 819pp.

Received for publication October 17, 1966.

SURVIVAL OF WOOD DUCK BROODS FROM DUMP NESTS[1]

H. W. HEUSMANN, Massachusetts Division of Fisheries and Game, Westboro

Abstract: Recapture rates of web-tagged wood ducks (*Aix sponsa*) hatched on the Great Meadows National Wildlife Refuge in Concord, Massachusetts, were 26.3 and 26.5 percent for ducklings hatched in dump nests during the periods 1952–54 and 1964–66. During these same periods, recapture rates of ducklings hatched in normal nests were 27.7 and 24.3 percent.

The purpose of this paper is to report on survival of wood duck broods hatched in dump nests and in normal nests during two 3-year periods at the Great Meadows National Wildlife Refuge in Concord, Massachusetts. The role of dump (compound or community) nesting in wood duck production has not been definitely established. Grice and Rogers (1965:41) and Morse and Wight (1969) indicated that dump nesting contributed to the population, whereas Jones and Leopold (1967) concluded that it was detrimental. However, all these observations were based on rates of hatch and not on survival of broods to the flight stage.

I acknowledge the activities of D. Grice who conducted the fieldwork during the periods covered and thank him for his review of this manuscript. I also thank W. W. Blandin and C. H. Bridges of the Massachusetts Division of Fisheries and Game for their many comments and suggestions and extend my appreciation to R. Bellville, P. Pekkala, and W. MacCallum for their involvement in the project. I especially acknowledge J. Pottie for his work in compiling the statistical data involved in this report.

HISTORY

The Great Meadows refuge was a former hay and cranberry meadow of about 150 acres that was diked and flooded in the early 1930's. The extensive stands of aquatic vegetation present during the early 1950's are described by Grice and Rogers (1965). A vegetational die-off started in the 1960's, and wood duck brood cover decreased by 1964.

Two periods were selected for this study. The first, 1952 through 1954, represented a rapidly expanding wood duck population. The number of ducklings produced on the Great Meadows refuge increased from less than 300 in 1951 to more than 750 in 1956. During the period from 1952 through 1954, the number of nest attempts increased from 44 to 95, with 72, 72, and 71, respectively, nest boxes available each of the 3 years. A dramatic decrease in the population occurred in 1959.

The second period, from 1964 through 1966, was selected as representative of a stable population, although evidence based on recruitment of web-tagged hens indicated that the population actually may have been declining (Grice 1966). During this period, the number of nest attempts fluctuated from 38 in 1964, to 35 in 1965, to 45 in 1966, and then declined to 6 by 1970.

---

[1] A contribution of Massachusetts Federal Aid in Wildlife Restoration Projects W–19–R, W–35–R, and W–42–R.

Originally published in J. Wildl. Manage. 36(2):620–624, 1972.

Table 1. Abandonment rates of wood duck nests on the Great Meadows National Wildlife Refuge.

	1952	1953	1954	TOTAL	1964	1965	1966	TOTAL
NORMAL NEST								
Number of nests	27	30	35	92	31	21	34	86
Number abandoned	1	14	18	33	4	1	4	9
Percentage abandoned	3.7	46.7	51.4	35.7	12.9	4.8	11.8	10.6
DUMP NEST								
Number of nests	18	44	55	117	6	10	6	22
Number abandoned	4	10	24	38	1	0	1	2
Percentage abandoned	22.2	22.7	43.6	32.5	16.7	0.0	16.7	7.7

There were 99, 99, and 96 nest boxes available in 1964, 1965, and 1966, respectively.

METHODS

Data for this paper were collected from 237 wood duck nests during the six breeding seasons of 1952 through 1954 and 1964 through 1966. Wooden nest boxes with tunnel predator guards, as described by McLaughlin and Grice (1952:248), were used during all breeding seasons. Web-tagging of ducklings for future identification was carried out according to the methods described by Grice and Rogers (1965). Ducklings were recaptured during the summer and fall by the use of several small traps with funnel entrances. The traps were baited with whole kernel corn. Both stationary and floating traps were used.

A dump nest was arbitrarily defined by Grice and Rogers (1965:39) as any nest with 16 or more eggs. Morse and Wight (1969:286) checked wood duck nests to determine rates of egg deposition and found "no nest with 16 or more eggs to have a normal rate of egg deposition . . . ." They also found many nests with fewer than 16 eggs to be dump nests, based on rates of egg deposition and other criteria. For the present paper, the data on numbers of dump nests represent minimal figures and the use of the term dump nest refers only to nests of 16 or more eggs.

RESULTS

Jones and Leopold (1967), dealing with a rapidly expanding wood duck population and a scarcity of nest sites, found that less than half of the dump nests checked produced ducklings, whereas approximately two-thirds of the normal nests resulted in duckling production. Data on abandonment rates for Great Meadows are presented in Table 1. The rates varied greatly from year to year and were much higher during the first 3-year period, when the population was expanding. When totals for the two periods were considered, abandonment rates for dump nests were lower than for normal nests. When a normal nest hen abandoned a nest, the clutch was lost, but when a dump nest hen abandoned a nest, there was a possibility that a second hen might incubate the clutch. Since abandonment of dump nests was not a critical factor during this study, it was excluded from further consideration.

A second area considered when comparing production of dump nests and normal nests was hatchability. If no more ducklings hatched from each of the larger nests than from each of the normal nests, the importance of survival of broods from dump nests would be minimal. Table 2 presents data on the rates of hatch of normal and dump nests for the two periods involved in this study. During both periods, the average hatch success for dump nests was

Table 2. Wood duck nest data for Great Meadows National Wildlife Refuge, 1952–54 and 1964–66.

	1952–54		1964–66	
	Dump Nest	Normal Nest	Dump Nest	Normal Nest
Number of nests	79	57	20	89
Number of eggs	1,652	610	382	918
Number hatched	1,232	501	330	840
Average clutch	20.9	10.7	19.1	11.8
Average number hatched	15.6	8.8	16.5	10.7
Percentage hatched	74.6	82.1	86.4	91.5

lower than for normal nests. There was a correlation between the size of clutch and the size of hatch in both normal and dump nests (Figs. 1 and 2). This agrees with the findings of Morse and Wight (1969).

McGilvrey (1969) observed wood duck broods and found that over 90 percent of the preflight mortalities occurred during the first 2 weeks after hatching. He felt that Class II ducklings provided a reliable estimate of production to flight stage. Therefore, in considering trapped ducklings, only birds of this development or higher were included in the data.

The results of the two trapping periods are presented in Table 3. There were more normal nests than dump nests with no recaptures (21 versus 14 for 1952–54 and 25 versus 2 for 1964–66). This resulted in similar recapture rates for both types of nests during the two study periods. During the 1950's, 26.3 percent of all web-tagged ducklings from dump nests were recaptured compared with 27.7 percent of ducklings from normal nests. During the mid-1960's, these percentages from dump and normal nests were 26.5 and 24.3, respectively.

DISCUSSION

There is no evidence to indicate that smaller wood duck broods are more prone to leave an area than larger broods. If the assumption is made that ducklings from both dump nests and normal nests are equally available for trapping, then survival rates of wood ducks to flight stage were similar for both types of nests. Therefore, dump nests produced more flying birds per nest than normal nests.

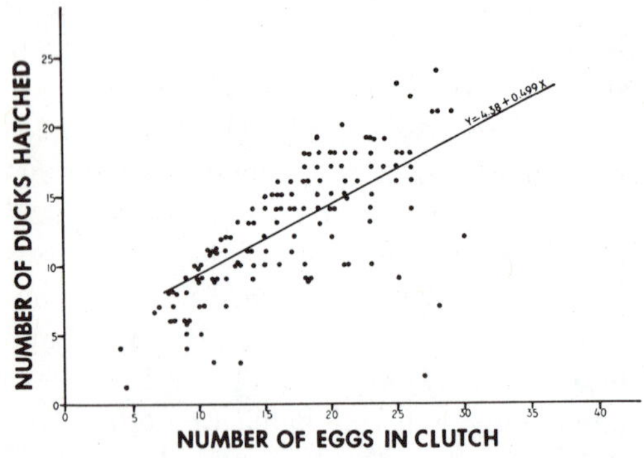

Fig. 1. Linear regression analysis of 1952–54 hatching rates of wood duck nests on the Great Meadows National Wildlife Refuge.

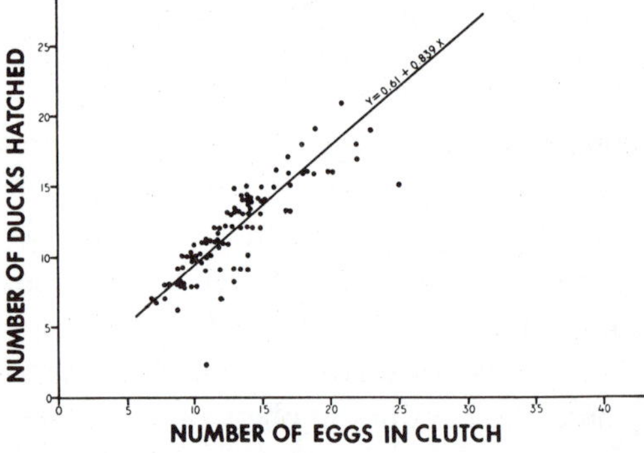

Fig. 2. Linear regression analysis of 1964–66 hatching rates of wood duck nests on the Great Meadows National Wildlife Refuge.

Table 3. Recapture rates for all successful dump and normal wood duck nests on the Great Meadows National Wildlife Refuge, 1952–54 and 1964–66.

	DUMP	NORMAL	DUMP	NORMAL	DUMP	NORMAL	DUMP	NORMAL
	1952		1953		1954		Total	
Number of nests	14	24	34	16	31	17	79	57
Number of ducks tagged	190	200	514	100	417	137	1,121	437
Number of ducks recaptured	41	83	167	23	87	15	295	121
Percentage recaptured	21.5	41.5	32.5	23.0	20.9	10.9	26.3	27.7
Number of recaptured ducklings per nest	3.4	3.8	5.2	2.0	3.1	0.9	4.1	2.4
	1964		1965		1966		Total	
Number of nests	5	27	10	21	5	30	20	73
Number of ducks tagged	81	236	140	175	84	315	305	726
Number of ducks recaptured	25	56	44	40	12	80	81	176
Percentage recaptured	30.8	23.7	31.4	22.9	14.3	25.4	26.5	24.3
Number of recaptured ducklings per nest	5.0	2.1	4.4	2.4	2.4	2.8	4.4	2.6

The role that dump nesting plays in total production varies. During the years of rapid population growth from 1952 through 1954, dump nests made up 58.1 percent of the successful nests and produced 70.9 percent of the ducklings recaptured. During the mid-1960's, when the population was much lower and more nest boxes were available, dump nests comprised only 20.4 percent of the total nests and produced 31.5 percent of the recaptures.

No observations were made to determine if a single female raised her brood by herself or if there was a tendency for ducklings from large broods to join small broods.

Before any definite conclusions can be reached concerning the role of dump nesting in wood duck production, further research needs to be carried out concerning the status of the egg-dumping female. Consider a case where a hen begins laying in a nest already containing 6 eggs. If the original hen lays a clutch of 12 eggs, the dumping hen will have a chance to lay 6 eggs before the original nester begins incubation. Grice and Rogers (1965:40–41) suggested that the incubating hen is in the dominant position and will force the other bird out. The ousted hen may then scatter the rest of her clutch, make no attempt to incubate, and begin to molt. A second possibility is that she may dump her remaining eggs in a second occupied nest and succeed in ousting the other hen, or she may again be ousted and go into molt. A third possibility is that she may also establish her own nest and successfully incubate her remaining clutch, perhaps producing additional eggs.

If the dumping hen renests, she will make an extra contribution to the population by dump nesting. However, if the dumping hen does not renest, then dump nesting is beneficial only to the extent that it results in a contribution from hens that would otherwise make no contribution to production. Even if the hen renests, Grice and Rogers (1965:66) found that the later in the season a nest hatches, the greater the mortality suffered by broods.

Investigations should be made to determine if it is feasible to create artificial dump nests by adding eggs from game-farm wood ducks to clutches in the wild, prior to incubation. It is possible that such a technique would increase the production of wood ducks in a natural environment.

LITERATURE CITED

GRICE, D. 1966. Wood duck nesting success and brood survival. Massachusetts Div. Fisheries and Game P–R Rept., Project W–35–R–9. 7pp. Mimeo.

———, AND J. P. ROGERS. 1965. The wood duck in Massachusetts. Massachusetts Div. Fisheries and Game P–R Rept., Project W–19–R. 96pp.

JONES, R. E., AND A. S. LEOPOLD. 1967. Nesting interference in a dense population of wood ducks. J. Wildl. Mgmt. 31(2):221–228.

MCGILVREY, F. B. 1969. Survival in wood duck broods. J. Wildl. Mgmt. 33(1):73–76.

MCLAUGHLIN, C. L., AND D. GRICE. 1952. The effectiveness of large-scale erection of wood duck boxes as a management procedure. Trans. N. Am. Wildl. Conf. 17:242–259.

MORSE, T. E., AND H. M. WIGHT. 1969. Dump nesting and its effect on production in wood ducks. J. Wildl. Mgmt. 33(2):284–293.

Received for publication June 3, 1971.

POST-BREEDING ACTIVITIES OF MALLARDS AND WOOD DUCKS IN NORTH-CENTRAL MINNESOTA[1]

DAVID S. GILMER, Department of Ecology and Behavioral Biology, University of Minnesota, St. Paul 55108[2]
RONALD E. KIRBY, Department of Ecology and Behavioral Biology, University of Minnesota, St. Paul 55108[3]
I. J. BALL, Department of Entomology, Fisheries and Wildlife, University of Minnesota, St. Paul 55108[4]
JOHN H. RIECHMANN, Department of Ecology and Behavioral Biology, University of Minnesota, St. Paul 55108[5]

Abstract: We used radio telemetry to monitor the post-breeding activities of 129 mallards (*Anas platyrhynchos*) and 118 wood ducks (*Aix sponsa*) on a 932-km² area in north-central Minnesota from 1968 to 1974. Upon completion of breeding activities and before the flightless period, all mallard drakes departed the area; this exodus peaked during early June. Of the non-brood hens 8 of 23 remained on the area, whereas 26 of 51 of the hens raising broods spent the flightless period on their breeding areas. Thirty-nine percent of the mallard hens on the area in the spring were present at the beginning of their flightless period. Fifty percent of the drake wood ducks and 41 percent of the hens left the breeding area before flightlessness. Their timing was similar to that of mallards. The flightless period began in mid-June for wood duck drakes and lasted into early October for some mallard hens. All late molting mallard and wood duck hens reared broods that same year. A minimum of 35 percent of the spring mallard hens remained on the area at the beginning of hunting season (early October). About 17 percent of the wood duck males and 42 percent of the females breeding locally remained on the area until hunting began. Eleven of 51 mallards and 4 of 25 wood ducks that reared broods were killed on the study area compared with 2 of 23 for non-brood mallards and 1 of 20 for non-brood wood duck hens. Principal habitats used by post-breeding mallards were bays of large lakes and river marshes. Wood ducks tended to use similar habitat but also frequented small woodland ponds. During the flightless period both species remained mostly in areas with abundant emergent cover.

J. WILDL. MANAGE. 41(3):345–359

Activities of ducks are generally less well understood during the post-breeding period than during the breeding season. Mobility following the termination of breeding and secretive behavior during the flightless period have discouraged intensive studies. In spite of these difficulties, biologists have described some aspects of post-breeding ecology in waterfowl. Hochbaum (1944: 111, 1955:139) and Sowls (1955:151) discussed the post-breeding activities of North American prairie ducks. Oring (1964) studied the post-breeding behavior of several species in Idaho. An extensive review of the movements to molting areas in waterfowl was produced by Salomonsen (1968). Munro (1943), Boyd (1960), Raitasuo (1964), and Coulter and Miller (1968) discussed some aspects of the post-breeding ecology of mallards. Grice and Rogers (1965) described molting and late summer activities of wood ducks in Massachusetts.

The primary objectives of this paper are to describe the movements and behavior of a population of mallards and wood ducks from the termination of breeding or brood-rearing to the onset of the fall migration. The study was conducted as a part of an investigation of the ecology of ducks breeding in the forested habitat of north-central Minnesota (Ball et al. 1975, Gilmer et al. 1975, Kirby et al. 1976).

[1] This research was supported by the U.S. Fish and Wildlife Service, University of Minnesota, National Institute of Health Training Grant 5 T01 GM01779, and the U.S. Atomic Energy Commission (C00-1332-117).

[2] Present address: Northern Prairie Wildlife Research Center, U.S. Fish and Wildlife Service, Jamestown, North Dakota 58401.

[3] Present address: Migratory Bird and Habitat Research Laboratory, U.S. Fish and Wildlife Service, Laurel, Maryland 20811.

[4] Present address: Department of Zoology, Washington State University, Pullman 99163.

[5] Present address: R.R. #1, Valmeyer, Illinois 62295.

Originally published in J. Wildl. Manage. 41(3):345–359, 1977.

We thank G. L. Krapu for critically reviewing the manuscript and J. B. Gollop and R. L. Jessen for providing suggestions in manuscript preparation. L. M. Cowardin provided assistance and guidance in all phases of the field work. We were assisted in statistical analyses by D. H. Johnson and in computer processing by D. A. Davenport. C. W. Shaiffer prepared the figures. Telemetry equipment was constructed and maintained by the engineering staff, Cedar Creek Bioelectronics Laboratory, University of Minnesota. Banding data examined in this paper were collected by the Minnesota Department of Natural Resources and the U.S. Fish and Wildlife Service. Extensive use was made of aircraft operated by pilots of the U.S. Fish and Wildlife Service and Bemidji Aviation Inc., T. S. Klodfelter, R. S. Stott, T. W. Schoenfelder, and C. A. Punke assisted with data collection.

STUDY AREA

The center of the study area was in the northwest portion of the Chippewa National Forest, Beltrami County, about 25 km east of Bemidji, Minnesota. Ducks were trapped and intensively studied on a 106-km² area between 1968 and 1971 and on a 236-km² area during 1972–74. These were included within a 932-km² area in which regular aerial searches for radio-equipped ducks were conducted from 1969 to 1974. Aerial searches also were conducted in several counties in northwestern Minnesota in August and September during 5 field seasons. To obtain a better sample of banding data, we examined all bandings and recoveries in an area (15,000 km²) enclosing the Chippewa National Forest. Lakes (>4 ha) and wetlands (excluding wooded swamps) 0.8 ha and larger made up approximately 25 and 13 percent of the area respectively. The remaining surface area (62%) consisted mostly of forest cover with scattered upland clearings. Wetland densities were approximately 2.1 wetlands/km². About 950 km of stream and river habitat was present on the area (unpubl. U.S. Forest Service records, Cass Lake, Minnesota). Cowardin and Johnson (1973) developed a preliminary classification of the wetland plant communities common to the area.

METHODS

Adult ducks were captured during the nesting, brood rearing, flightless, and post-flightless periods (April–September). A variety of methods was used to trap birds during the nesting season (Gilmer 1971); however, the nightlighting technique (Cummings and Hewitt 1964) proved most effective for capturing hens with broods and flightless birds. A breast-mounted radio package (Gilmer et al. 1974) with a circuitry similar to that described by Cochran and Lord (1963) was attached to each bird. All ducks were fitted with leg bands.

Birds were tracked with fixed antennas as well as with motor vehicles, boats, and aircraft equipped with receiving antennas. Conventional methods were used to determine the location of birds from surface receiving stations (Ball 1971, Gilmer 1971). During 1969–71 aerial searches were conducted an average of once per week from July through mid-September in a 518-km² area surrounding the trapping sites. In 1972–74, aircraft searches were increased to an average of 5 per week and the area expanded to include 932-km².

Birds we could not locate easily with surface receivers were located with aircraft by first searching the area of the bird's most recently known location. If this attempt was unsuccessful the search was expanded to cover all areas the bird had used previously. Finally, adjacent drainages, large lakes, and other known preferred areas for the species were searched. Absence of the duck was confirmed by a search of all water areas within the study area boundary. When a bird was located, its position was determined by techniques similar to those described by Seidensticker et al. (1970). Several times during August and September in most years, aerial surveys were made of selected waterfowl habitat within a radius of approximately 160 km from the center of the study area.

We divided the post-breeding portion of the annual cycle into 3 periods for analysis; (1) the pre-flightless period, which began when all reproductive related activities terminated (i.e., nesting ceased, the brood was abandoned, or the pair bond terminated) and ended when the bird became flightless during wing molt; (2) the flightless period; and (3) the post-flightless period from completion of wing molt to beginning of fall migration.

Hens unsuccessful in their nesting efforts began the pre-flightless period when their last nest was destroyed or 1 July was arbitrarily used when no nest could be found. Successful hens began this period upon leaving their broods; however, occasionally a pre-flightless period did not occur when a hen's flight feathers were shed before she left the brood. Dates that drakes abandoned nesting hens usually were determined by tracking pairs in which both the hen and drake were instrumented. In a few other situations we were able to determine abandonment dates when only the hen was instrumented by visually confirming the absence of the drake. Drakes began the pre-flightless period when they abandoned their hen; otherwise we arbitrarily used 1 July. All birds monitored during the pre-flightless period were local breeders. Breeding status for drakes and for some hens was ascertained by observing the birds for a minimum of 10 days during the breeding season. An observed nest or brood confirmed local status for most hens. About 60 percent of the birds studied during the flightless period were confirmed local breeders. Our post-flightless observations included some birds that may have entered the study area from elsewhere. We treated these birds separately if their activities were different from those of local birds.

Most transmitters were operational for 75 days; many units operated up to 90 days. This meant that birds marked early in the season could be tracked until mid-July. If we were unable to locate a duck carrying a transmitter that had operated less than 75 days, we assumed that the bird had left the study area. The probability of a transmitter failing prematurely or being rendered inoperative by a predator during the 75-day period was considered slight. When transmitters ceased operating the status of these birds during the pre-flightless period became "unknown" unless they were by then known to be flightless.

For band recovery analysis we examined all normal and experimental (birds also fitted with transmitters, nasal saddles, or patagial tags) bandings from 1954 to 1974 recorded in the geographic area approximately bounded by the Chippewa National Forest. Direct recoveries considered in the analysis consisted of banded birds killed or found dead during the migratory movement following banding. Also included with direct recoveries for this analysis were birds recaptured the following spring and reported killed later that fall.

For purposes of backdating to estimate the date of loss of flight feathers or to estimate the date a bird was capable of flight we considered the flightless period in both mallards and wood ducks to be 26 days (Boyd 1960:140, Palmer 1972:94).

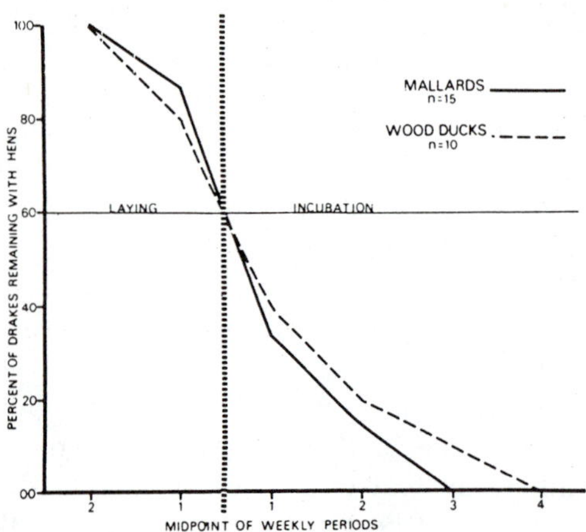

Fig. 1. Stage at which drake mallards and wood ducks deserted nesting hens on the study area 1968–72. Incubation periods for mallards and wood ducks were 26 and 30 days, respectively.

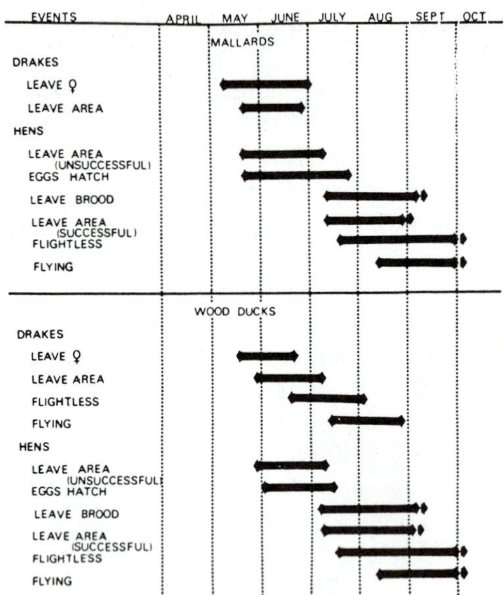

Fig. 2. Sequence of post-breeding events based on data collected on radio equipped mallards and wood ducks on the study area 1968–74. Double arrows designate events where termination dates were not determined. No radio equipped mallard drakes molted on the area.

RESULTS AND DISCUSSION

During the pre-flightless period we monitored 101 mallards consisting of 27 drakes, 51 brood hens, and 23 non-brood hens; and 66 wood ducks consisting of 21 drakes, 25 brood hens, and 20 non-brood hens. In addition we obtained movement and behavior data on 28 mallard hens and 53 wood ducks (30 hens and 23 drakes) during their flightless and/or post-flightless periods. This latter group of birds included ducks whose breeding histories that season were known plus others of unknown breeding histories captured on the study area.

Termination of the Pair and Hen-Brood Bonds

We monitored 15 mallard pairs and found that drakes remained with their hens an average of 4.1 days into incubation, ranging from 5 days before the clutch was completed to 17 days after the start of incubation (Fig. 1). Hen abandonment occurred from 5 May to 1 July with a mean of 6 June (Fig. 2). Most investigators have indicated that mallard pair bonds usually last until the onset of incubation (Munro 1943, Hochbaum 1955:140, Sowls 1955:96, Evans and Black 1956:21, Oring 1964, Salomonsen 1968), but Hochbaum (1944:83) suspected that some mallard drakes leave their hens several days before clutches are completed. Dzubin (1955) reported that the pair bond may be maintained into the second week of incubation. Oring (1964) observed 13 mallard pairs and noted that only 1 pair remained together beyond the second week.

The drakes of 10 wood duck pairs remained with their hens an average of 6.5 days into incubation; the time ranged from 4 days before the clutch was completed to 25 days after the start of incubation (Fig. 1). Date of hen abandonment occurred from 14 May to 23 June with a mean of 27 May (Fig. 2). Drakes observed in Missouri abandoned their hens by the fourth week (Clawson 1975:108).

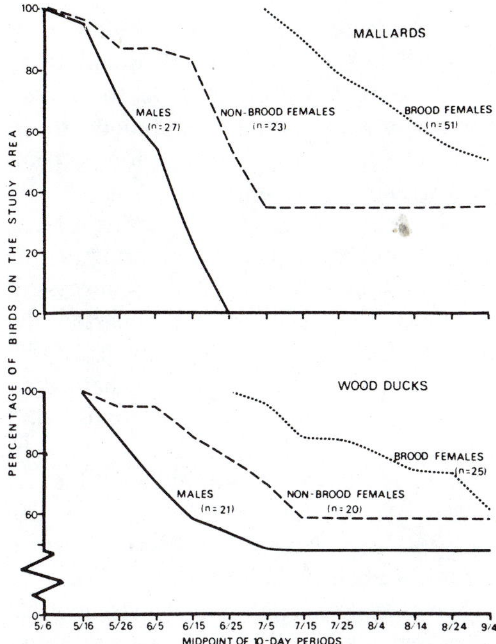

Fig. 3. Percentages of paired drakes, brood hens, and non-brood hens remaining on the study area during the period 21 April through 9 September 1968–72.

We were unable to detect a relationship between the number of days a drake mallard or wood duck remained with an incubating hen and the timing of laying. Our small sample sizes affected this analysis. Departure of the drake may depend on several factors in addition to the sexual activity of the pair (Raitasuo 1964), or the onset of molt (Bezzel 1959). Stimulus provided by other pairs, the influence of nearby flocked males, or changes in habitat conditions as well as the effect of the radio package may influence pair bond duration and departure by the male.

We observed a wood duck pair in 1969 and 1970 that remained together after an unsuccessful season (no nest was found but we suspected a nesting attempt was made). Mallard pairs, after loss of a nest, occasionally behaved as though they had ceased nesting efforts (i.e., loafing, little feeding activity, few movements), but subsequent nest attempts might have been made without our knowledge. Maintenance of the pair bond after an unsuccessful breeding season may explain how migrational homing of pairs could occur (Dwyer et al. 1973).

Radio tracking indicated that a hen mallard abandoned her brood as early as 7 July. One mallard hen still accompanied her brood at the time we discontinued field work on 10 September in 1 year. The earliest known brood abandonment by a wood duck occurred on 3 July. The latest a wood duck hen attended a brood was 7 September (Fig. 2). On the average, mallard hens remained with their broods significantly longer (50.7 days) than wood duck hens (30.8 days) (Ball et al. 1975: 778).

Pre-flightless Period

Mallards.—The number of adult mallards on the study area declined markedly as the breeding season progressed (Fig. 3). Males departed as early as 17 May, but some marked drakes remained as late as 28 June and a few unmarked pairs and lone males were observed through the first week in July. The appearance of the first broods corresponded approximately with the departure of the first drakes. Wright (1954: 58) reported that concentrations of drake black ducks (*Anas rubripes*) in New Brunswick usually appeared about the date the first broods were seen. Other evidence indicated that drakes were scarce on our area during summer. Of 406 adult mallards banded on the Chippewa National Forest during July and August 1954 to 1974 only 20 were drakes.

Movements of post-breeding ducks away from the breeding grounds have been reported for several dabbler species in North America (Hochbaum 1944:122, Wright 1954:58, Evans and Black 1956). Movements to molting areas may consist of a northward shift of up to hundreds of kilometers from the breeding grounds. Furthermore, among dabbling ducks only the males and a few non-breeding females participate (Salomonsen 1968).

The destination of post-breeding mallard drakes leaving their breeding ranges on the study area is unknown. Of 11 direct recoveries from 71 males banded in spring and early summer one was from Roseau, Minnesota, about 190 km north of the banding site, and one return was reported from Bonneyville, Alberta, 1,800 km northwest of the study area. The other nine recoveries were from states south or west of Minnesota. Gollop (1965:40) stated that 16 of 88 direct recoveries of drake mallards banded as adults near Kindersley, Saskatchewan, were reported from north of the banding site. Movements of birds out of our study area may contribute to the large numbers of molting mallard drakes reported each summer in southern Manitoba at Delta Marsh (Hochbaum 1944:122, Sowls 1955:154) and Whitewater Lake (Bossenmaier and Marshall 1958), and J. Clark Salyer National Wildlife Refuge (NWR) in north-central North Dakota (J. Malcolm, personal communication).

The majority of hens that were unsuccessful in their nesting efforts or that lost their broods within a few days of hatching eventually left the study area prior to the flightless period (Fig. 3). Few hens joined departing drakes; rather, most gathered into small flocks that traveled independently of the drakes. In 2 instances in May hens that associated with small groups of drakes were seen paired later. Therefore, at least some hens in mixed flocks in May were not post-breeding birds but were actively seeking to establish a pair bond with a male.

The number of brood hens on the study area gradually declined from mid-July until early September (Fig. 3). Initially, hens departed the study area individually or in small flocks; however, later in the season some hens terminating their brood attachment may have left the study area in company with immature birds.

We monitored hens over 5 nesting seasons to determine their success in rearing broods (Fig. 4). Using the proportion of successful and unsuccessful hens that departed the area we estimated that 39 percent of the mallard hens present in spring remained on the study area at the end of August and molted locally. This figure did not consider hens that left the study area but returned later in the summer or for the few hens that may have left the study area in September before they became flightless.

Tracking data suggest that most mallard hens remained within northwestern Minnesota during the post-breeding period. Supporting this hypothesis is the fact that of 71 direct recoveries of adult hens banded on the Chippewa National Forest between 1954 and 1974, 41 were reported shot on the area in October and November. The high proportion of recoveries near the banding site is indicative of heavy hunting pressure (Jessen 1970) as well as vulnerability of these hens on their breeding marshes. Direct recoveries also suggest that some hens move out of the area before the southward migration. Six of the hens were shot at points 50 to 320 km north of the study area. The farthest bird was an unsuccessful nester that departed the area in mid-June and was recovered in southern Manitoba.

Using aircraft we found 2 hens after they had left the study area. One was at Agassiz NWR, 140 km northwest of the study area, 8 days after departing and 27 days after abandoning her brood. This hen was shot near that refuge later the same fall. A second hen was 60 km west, at Lower Rice Lake on 11 September having left a brood

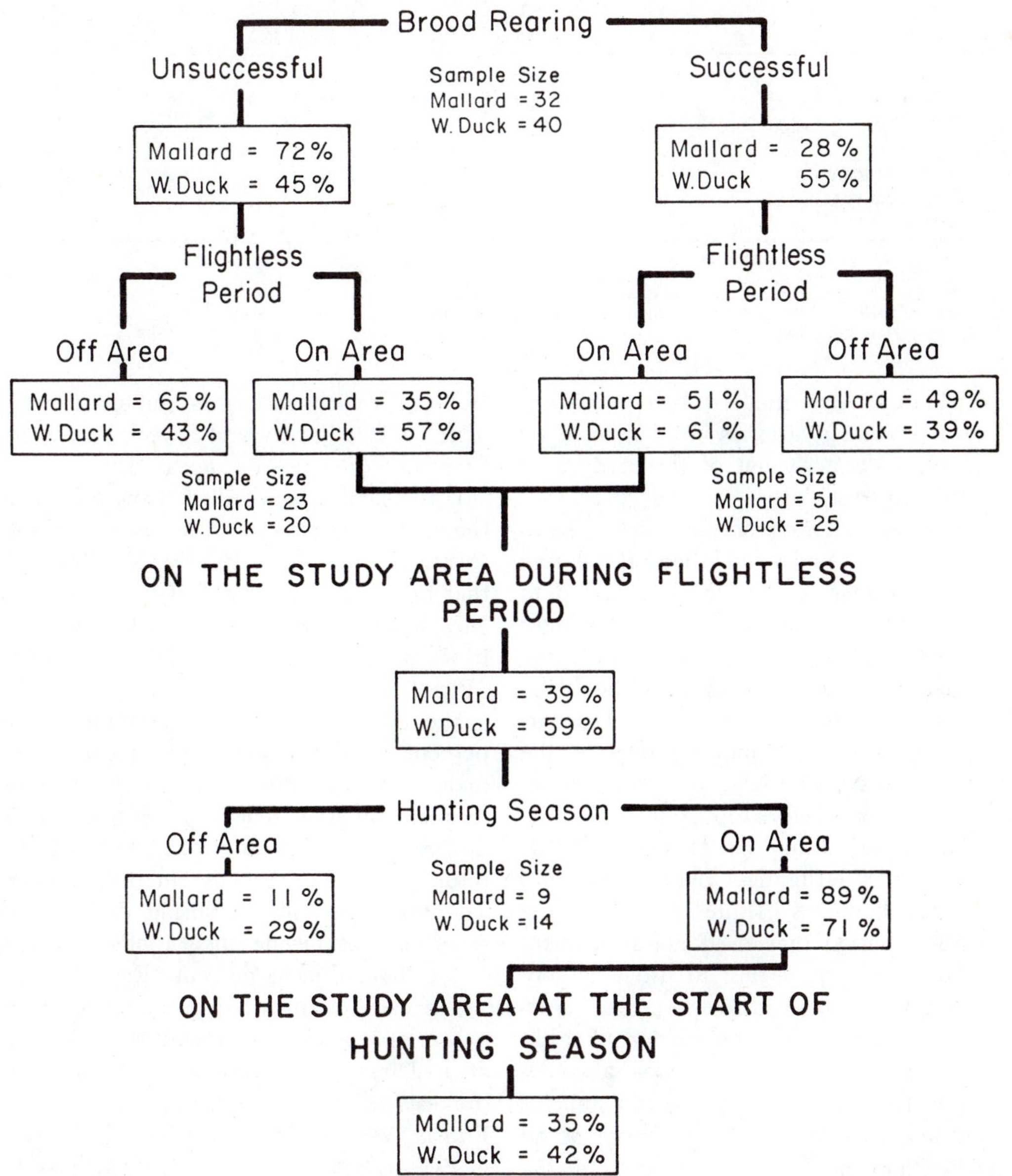

Fig. 4. Flow diagram based on radio tracking data showing the percentages of mallard and wood duck hens breeding on the study area that were successful rearing broods, present on the area during the flightless period and at the start of hunting season in early October.

Table 1. Habitats used by radio equipped and unmarked mallards and wood ducks during post-breeding.

Habitat	Post-breeding periods					
	Pre-flightless		Flightless		Post-flightless	
	Mallard	Wood duck	Mallard	Wood duck	Mallard	Wood duck
Lakes:						
Shorelines/mud bars	**[1,2]				**	**
Emergent vegetation[3]		**	**	**[4]	**	**
River-stream:						
Shorelines/mud bars	**				**	
Emergent vegetation[3]		**	**	**	**	
Non-permanent wetlands	*	*		**[5]		**

[1] **—frequent use, *—occasional use.
[2] Lakes >100 hectares.
[3] Wild rice (*Zizania aquatica*) preferred cover when available after July.
[4] Lakes as small as 40 ha. were used by individuals and small groups.
[5] Shrub swamps bordering lakes.

on 21 July. Two mallard hens with unknown breeding histories were tracked 20 and 41 km easterly out of the study area but subsequently lost.

Four hen mallards left the study area in July or August and were killed on the area in the fall. One of these birds returned to molt on the study area, because the flight feathers were reported to be partially developed when the bird was shot. The others might have done likewise or returned during migration after molting outside the study area. No drakes were known to return to the area before or during hunting.

The principal habitat of hen mallards during the pre-flightless period was mud bars and shorelines (Table 1). Nearing the flightless period they used non-permanent wetlands less, preferring to use emergent vegetation on lakes and rivers.

Wood Ducks.—The population of adult wood ducks on the study area also decreased throughout the spring and summer (Fig. 3); however, relatively more wood ducks than mallards remained into the flightless period. Wood duck males began leaving as early as 25 May, about 1 week after mallard drakes, and 1 week before the first wood duck broods appeared.

Unsuccessful wood duck hens left with the first drakes on 26 May and continued to depart until about 10 July. The first hen that had raised a brood left the area on 3 July. Brood hens departed at a low rate until numbers stabilized in early September (Fig. 3).

We determined that a minimum of 59 percent of all hens present in spring remained on the study area at the end of August and molted locally (Fig. 4). This did not account for any hens that left but returned to the area later in the summer. The proportion of the spring drakes that were present during the flightless period was estimated at 48 percent (Fig. 5).

We were unable to determine the destination of wood ducks leaving the breeding area. Direct recoveries of 7 of 19 adult drakes banded on the Chippewa National Forest were reported locally; the others were recovered farther south in Minnesota and other states in the Mississippi (10) and

→

Fig. 5. Flow diagram based on radio tracking data showing the percentages of mallard and wood duck drakes breeding on the study area that were present on the area during the flightless period and at the start of hunting season.

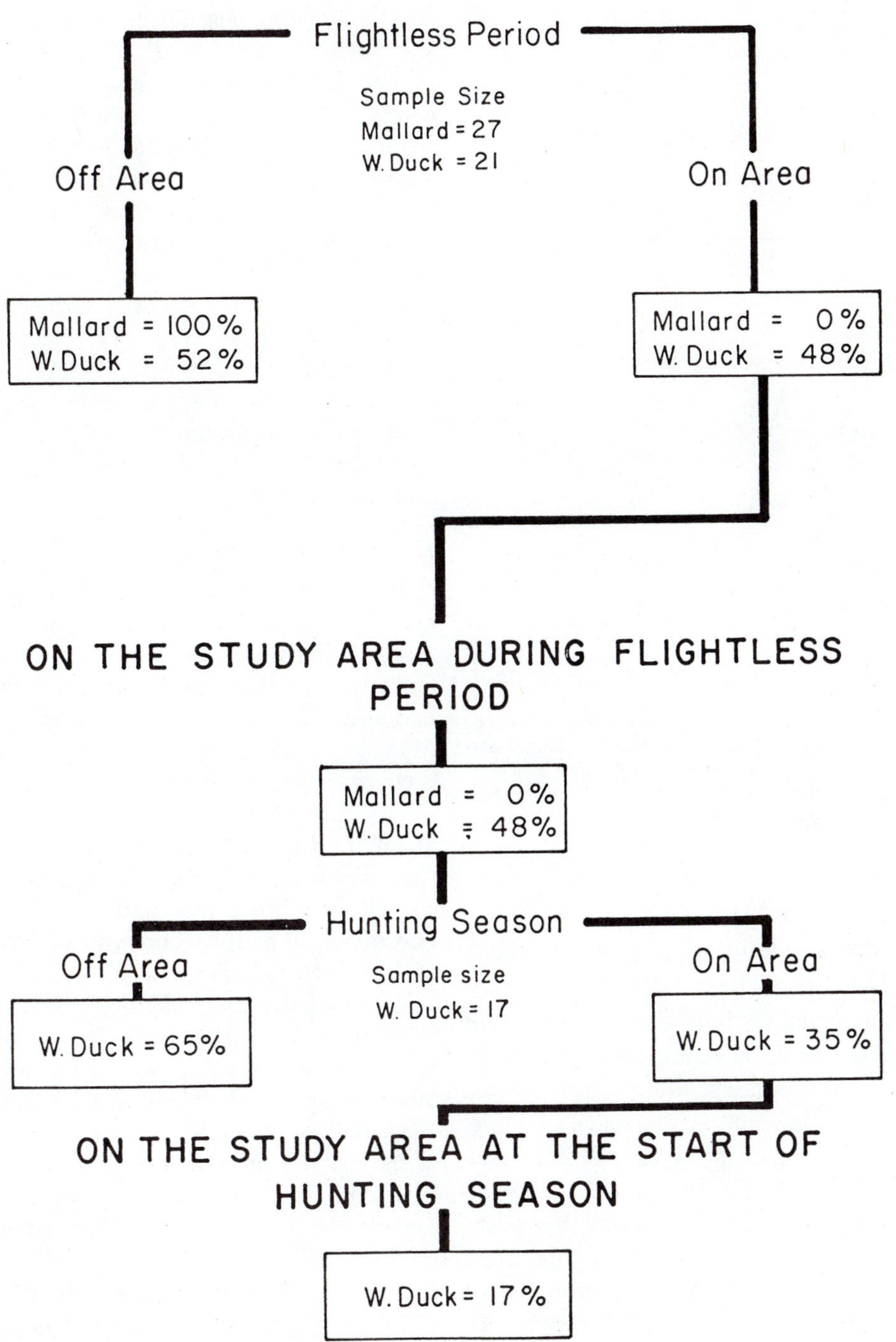
DRAKES BREEDING ON THE STUDY AREA
Flightless Period
Sample Size
Mallard = 27
W. Duck = 21
Off Area
On Area
Mallard = 100%
W. Duck = 52%
Mallard = 0%
W. Duck = 48%
ON THE STUDY AREA DURING FLIGHTLESS PERIOD
Mallard = 0%
W. Duck = 48%
Hunting Season
Sample size
W. Duck = 17
Off Area
On Area
W. Duck = 65%
W. Duck = 35%
ON THE STUDY AREA AT THE START OF HUNTING SEASON
W. Duck = 17%

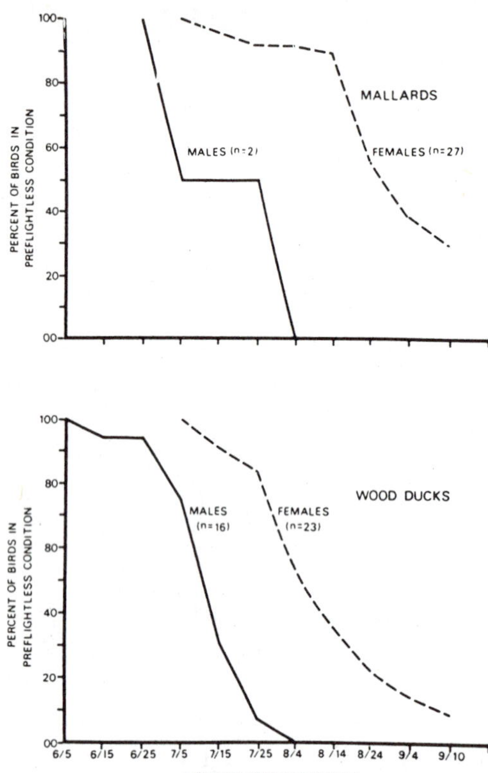

Fig. 6. Percentage of mallards and wood ducks in the preflightless condition on the study area 1968–74. About 30 percent of the mallard hens and 9 percent of the wood duck hens were still in the pre-flightless condition when last observed on 10 September. All birds were radio equipped except for mallard males.

Central (2) Flyways. Marshes at the Agassiz NWR, which have no breeding wood ducks, experience large influxes of molting wood ducks during June and July each year (T. Atkins, personal communication). Postbreeding and molting adult males are reported to congregate in the Lac Qui Parle Wildlife Management Area (WMA) 260 km southwest of the study area. Lac Qui Parle banding data also indicate that postbreeding birds move into Minnesota from as far away as Missouri (R. Benson, personal communication). Drakes which left our study area may contribute to wood duck concentrations in those areas.

Banding recoveries indicated that many locally breeding hens are on the area during the hunting season. Of 21 direct recoveries of hens banded on the Chippewa National Forest, 14 were shot on the study area, most being birds that had molted locally and remained there until the hunting season; however, some hens that left before molt may have returned to the area and subsequently were shot in the fall. The other recoveries were reported from locations farther south in the Mississippi Flyway.

Pre-flightless wood ducks were most commonly found in emergent cover associated with shallow bays of lakes and river and stream marshes as well as small (<40 ha) wetlands (Table 1).

Flightless Period

Mallards.—Few drakes were known to molt locally. Only 2 of 71 adult males captured on the study area were flightless. Examination of these birds indicated that 1 had shed flight feathers as early as 10 July (Fig. 6). Neither bird carried a radio and their breeding histories were unknown.

The first mallard hen became flightless about 15 July. Of 27 monitored hens 15 shed flight feathers after 1 September (Fig. 6). All were brood hens and 5 had not begun the wing molt by our last observations on 10 September (Fig. 2).

The tendency for drake mallards to molt flight feathers earlier and more simultaneously than hens has been described by other biologists (Hochbaum 1944:118, Balat 1970, Bellrose 1976:242). About 50 percent of the mallard hens on a study area in Finland were still flightless by 20 August (Raitasuo 1964). A number of authors noted, as we did, that hen mallards are occasionally flightless as late as October (Boyd 1960, Balat 1970, Eygenraam 1957). This situation was common on our study area and gives rise to speculation that some hens may delay the wing molt until during migration or until they arrive on the wintering grounds as occasionally observed in gadwall (*Anas strepera*) (Lebret 1952, Chabreck 1966), European wigeon (*A. penelope*) (Lebret 1952), and green-winged teal (*A. crecca*) (Rogers 1967).

Most broods were abandoned before the hen commenced wing molt; 2 hen mallards remained with their young into the flightless period. Elsewhere this was rare but has been observed occasionally (Salomonsen 1968, Raitasuo 1964).

Flightless mallard hens were extremely wary and sought seclusion in emergent cover. They were usually solitary; only a few small groups were noted. One exceptional hen remained with her brood when flightless and was frequently observed using open areas.

Mallard hens passed their flightless period in large lakes and river marshes. Extensive emergent vegetation, particularly wild rice, was used by most birds (Table 1).

Large, permanent shallow waters with dense cover, food, and seclusion are important habitat needs for dabbling ducks during the flightless period (Salomonsen 1968, Hochbaum 1944:122, Lebret 1971). The best wetlands in our study area did not meet all of these requirements. Wild rice beds were not available until August, long after mallard drakes departed.

Home ranges of flightless mallard hens varied considerably as during the breeding season (Gilmer et al. 1975). Some flightless birds were quite sedentary, whereas others used sites on large lakes that required overwater travel distances exceeding 3 km. Of 13 mallard hens that remained on the study area to molt, the movement between the brood rearing and molting areas ranged from 0 to 4 km ($\bar{X} = 1.6$ km).

Wood Ducks.—Drake wood ducks began the flightless period in mid-June (Fig. 6). Sixty days was the span of the flightless period for all drakes we monitored; this was at least 10 days shorter than noted for either hen mallards or wood ducks (Fig. 2).

The first wood duck hen became flightless in mid-July. Of 23 hens, 5 (all brood hens) did not begin wing molt until after 1 September, and 2 of these had not shed their old feathers when last observed on 10 September (Fig. 6).

Some adult wood duck drakes trapped in central Illinois were in breeding plumage in early August, but others were still flightless as late as 29 September (Bellrose 1976:194). In Massachusetts, most drakes regained flight in August and a few were flightless as late as mid-September; hens showed greater variation—some were flightless by mid-July and others wore old plumage in September (Grice and Rogers 1965:75).

Habitat used by flightless wood ducks was similar to that used by mallards; however, wood ducks also were found commonly on small lakes as well as shrub swamps (Table 1). Flightless birds were very secretive and many used inaccessible habitat which effectively isolated them from disturbance.

Tracking data on 26 molting wood ducks suggested that they were usually sedentary; however, during the course of the entire flightless period, shorelines of up to 2 km in length were used by some birds.

Post-flightless Period

Mallards.—About 10 days before the opening of hunting season the first fall influx of mallards appeared on the study area each year. Presence of these birds on the area may have been influenced by the discontinuation of feeding programs established each year on refuges in northwestern Minnesota in order to reduce grain depredation by field feeding ducks. It was in these flocks that we again observed adult drake mallards; a group which had been absent since their departure as post-breeding birds in May and June.

After completing wing molt, most hen mallards joined flocks of adult hens and immatures that made daily flights of up to 13 km between several areas used for resting and feeding (Kirby et al. 1976). Many hens used their old molting sites as night roosts but spent days in other isolated areas.

During the 1972–74 field seasons we monitored 9 resident mallard hens that had molted locally (at least 5 reared broods that same year). Eight of 9 remained on the area until the hunting season began in early October, after which none could be found. Most mallards left when disturbed by hunters (Kirby et al. 1976); the post-flightless hens still present during the hunting season shifted to smaller isolated areas during daytime but continued to use their original night roosting sites (Table 1).

Six of 11 adult hen mallards with unknown breeding and molting histories remained on the study area at least until hunting began; the others left up to 60 days before that. Hens that left early in the season probably had not yet molted. Three departing hens were eventually relocated; two had joined large flocks using extensive wild rice areas, 43 km east of the study area. The other had moved north and was shot at Agassiz NWR. The extent of travel by flocks during premigration movements in late summer and early fall is suggested by direct recoveries in Manitoba of 16 of 46 immatures banded in 1968 in northwestern Minnesota (Jessen 1969). Of 465 mallards banded as locals in Minnesota by Lensink (1964:41), 10 were reported as direct recoveries in Canada. The possibility of late summer movements to the north by mallards was also indicated by Sugden et al. (1974) in Alberta, Gollop (1960) in Saskatchewan, and in the prairie provinces in general by Cartwright and Law (1952). In the fall of 1948 Mann (1950) reported a reverse migration of ducks from North Dakota into Manitoba.

Hen mallards on the study area during September included flightless and post-flightless birds originating there and elsewhere. The proportion of hens present in the spring that remained until hunting season was estimated at 35 percent (Fig. 4). Data collected from 3 samples of hens monitored during all portions of the post-breeding period were used to determine this percentage. This estimate is conservative because some birds left the breeding area but returned later in the season.

Band recoveries from mallards monitored on the study area suggest that brood-rearing hens experienced higher hunting mortality rates near the breeding site than did non-brood hens. Of 51 mallard hens that were monitored during the brood rearing period on the study area, 11 were later shot on the area. Only 2 of 23 hens known to be unsuccessful breeders were recovered locally. Recovery rates off-area were similar at 8 (16%) and 7 (17%) for the brood and non-brood hens, respectively.

Wood Ducks.—Of 17 drake wood ducks carrying transmitters during the post-flightless period, 11 left the study area before the hunting season opened. Nine of these left the area during apparent migratory movements during the last week of September (the timing of these migratory movements occurred within 5 days of 24 September each year during 1972–74). Our last wood duck drake disappeared on 11 October.

We monitored 14 wood duck hens during their post-flightless period. Four hens left before October. Three of these birds departed during apparent migratory movements in the last week of September. Ten of the marked birds remained into October, with the last departing on 22 October. Our data suggested that most hens initiated migratory movements after the drakes. Recoveries of birds banded at Lac Qui Parle WMA indicate that adult hens and immature wood ducks migrated out of Minnesota later than do adult males (R. Benson, personal communication).

The proportion of wood ducks present in the spring that remained until the hunting season was estimated at 42 percent for hens (Fig. 4) and 17 percent for drakes (Fig. 5). We did not consider birds that left but may have returned later in the summer.

We were unable to determine the destination or dispersal patterns of any birds leaving the study area during the post-flightless period. Direct band recoveries indicated only that birds were killed on the study area or to the south; no evidence indicated that post-flightless wood ducks moved north. Because wood ducks began migration before the hunting season, analysis of direct recoveries was of limited value in determining their late summer activities. Grice and Rogers (1965:77–78) noted that wood ducks were difficult to locate in late summer and fall in Massachusetts except in the evening because these birds dispersed to secluded streams, ponds and small marshes during the day.

After maturation of flight feathers, wood ducks developed daily movement patterns similar to those we observed in mallards. Wood duck groups seldom exceeded 12 birds, whereas mallards frequently were observed in flocks of several hundred. Isolated small wetlands and beaver impoundments were used frequently by wood ducks but not by mallards (Table 1). Wood ducks and mallards made roosting flights similar to those documented by Hein and Haugen (1966). Movement patterns indicated infrequent changes in roosting sites but use of daytime areas shifted throughout the season. The small flock size, use of isolated areas, and overall sedentary nature of wood ducks during mid-day resulted in this species being much less disturbed by hunters than mallards.

As with mallards, brood rearing wood ducks suffered higher hunting mortality near the breeding sites than did non-brood hens. Of 25 wood duck brood hens monitored on the study area, 4 were shot locally, but only 1 of 20 non-brood hens was recovered on the area. We did not have sufficient data to compare wood duck recovery rates off the study area.

CONCLUSIONS

By early summer, major groups of ducks (i.e., drakes, unsuccessful hens) may leave the breeding grounds and travel considerable distances to molting areas. Biologists have argued about the function of the separation of non-breeding birds from the young. Salomonsen (1968) suggested that the departure of adults will increase the food sources available to the young. Another possibility is that post-breeding ducks may seek areas for molting that are more suitable than the breeding marshes. Areas selected for molting may be unsuitable for brood rearing. Exodus of post-breeding mallards out of our areas was a more distinct behavior than what we observed in wood ducks. The purpose of the movements may be quite different in the 2 species. The ultimate explanation for this kind of behavior may consist of a complex of factors including the above, and perhaps others unknown at this time.

Hochbaum (1944:138), Cartwright and Law (1952:22), and Anderson and Henny (1972:81) reported that adult females are vulnerable to shooting mortality on breeding marshes. Our investigation confirmed that many females present in the spring were still present in the fall and harvested in larger proportion on the breeding grounds compared to birds that had left before hunting season. In late summer most of the birds remaining from the spring were hens that had successfully reared broods. Overharvest of these experienced breeders may seriously impair attempts to sustain satisfactory production on a marsh (Hochbaum 1947). In this situation maintenance of production may depend heavily on the pioneering of the species into the area. One underlying cause of the vulnerability of brood hens in our area is that nest predation often results in repeated renesting; consequently the hen's brood rearing and molting chronology may be retarded into the early fall. A delay in the opening date of the hunting season, particularly in years of late nesting, may provide for a longer time span between completion of the hen's molt and hunting. This respite may permit adult females to regain flight strength and join flocks that may be less vulnerable than the solitary hen.

Investigations of what happens to ducks between the breeding season and fall migration may be difficult and at best provide fragmentary information. In spite of this, such information will provide an appreciation for the dynamic nature of the postbreeding period, aid in an understanding of the basic biology of waterfowl, and improve our ability to more effectively manage locally breeding ducks.

LITERATURE CITED

ANDERSON, D. R., AND C. J. HENNY. 1972. Population ecology of the mallard. I. A review of previous studies and the distribution and migration from breeding areas. U.S. Fish Wildl. Serv. Resour. Publ. 105. 166pp.

BALAT, F. 1970. On the wing-molt in the mallard, (*Anas platyrhynchos*), in Czechoslovakia. Zoologicke Listy 19(2):135–144.

BALL, I. J., JR. 1971. Movements, habitat use and behavior of wood duck (*Aix sponsa*) broods in north-central Minnesota as determined by radio tracking. M.S. Thesis. Univ. of Minnesota, St. Paul. 56pp.

———, D. S. GILMER, L. M. COWARDIN, AND J. H. RIECHMANN. 1975. Survival of wood duck and mallard broods in north-central Minnesota. J. Wildl. Manage. 39(4):776–780.

BELLROSE, F. C. 1976. Ducks, geese and swans of North America. The Stackpole Co., Harrisburg, Pa. 543pp.

BEZZEL, E. 1959. Beitrage zur biologie der Geschlechter bei entenvogeln. Anz. Orn. Ges. Bayern. 5:269–355.

BOSSENMAIER, E. F., AND W. H. MARSHALL. 1958. Field-feeding by water fowl in southeastern Manitoba. Wildl. Monogr. 1. 32pp.

BOYD, H. 1960. The flightless period of the mallard in England. Wildfowl Trust Annu. Rep. 12:140–143.

CARTWRIGHT, B. W., AND J. T. LAW. 1952. Waterfowl banding 1939–1950 by Ducks Unlimited. Ducks Unlimited, Winnipeg. 53pp.

CHABRECK, R. H. 1966. Molting gadwall (*Anas strepera*) in Louisiana. Auk 83(4):664.

CLAWSON, R. L. 1975. The ecology of dump nesting in wood ducks. M.S. Thesis. Univ. of Missouri, Columbia. 122pp.

COCHRAN, W. W., AND R. D. LORD, JR. 1963. A radio-tracking system for wild animals. J. Wildl. Manage. 27(1):9–24.

COULTER, M. W., AND W. R. MILLER. 1968. Nesting biology of black ducks and mallards in northern New England. Vermont Fish Game Dept. Bull. 68-2. 74pp.

COWARDIN, L. M., AND D. H. JOHNSON. 1973. Preliminary classification of wetland plant communities in north-central Minnesota. U.S. Fish Wildl. Serv. Spec. Sci. Rep. Wildl. 168. 33pp.

CUMMINGS, G. E., AND O. H. HEWITT. 1964. Capturing waterfowl and marsh birds at night with light and sound. J. Wildl. Manage. 28(1):120–126.

DWYER, T. J., S. R. DERRICKSON, AND D. S. GILMER. 1973. Migrational homing by a pair of mallards. Auk 90(3):687.

DZUBIN, A. 1955. Some evidences of home range in waterfowl. Trans. N. Am. Wildl. Conf. 20:278–298.

EVANS, C. D., AND K. E. BLACK. 1956. Duck production studies on the prairie potholes of South Dakota. U.S. Fish Wildl. Serv. Spec. Sci. Rep. Wildl. 32. 59pp.

EYGENRAAM, J. A. 1957. The sex-ratio and the production of the mallard (*Anas platyrhynchos*) L. Ardea 45(3–4):117–143.

GILMER, D. S. 1971. Home range and habitat use of breeding mallards (*Anas platyrhyn-*

chos) and wood ducks (*Aix sponsa*) in north-central Minnesota as determined by radio tracking. Ph.D. Thesis. Univ. Minnesota, St. Paul. 142pp.

———, I. J. BALL, L. M. COWARDIN, AND J. H. RIECHMANN. 1974. Effects of radio packages on wild ducks. J. Wildl. Manage. 38(2): 243–252.

———, ———, ———, ———, AND J. R. TESTER. 1975. Habitat use and home range of mallards breeding in Minnesota. J. Wildl. Manage. 39(4):781–789.

GOLLOP, J. B. 1960. Mallard goes north after nesting. Blue Jay 18(2):77.

———. 1965. Dispersal and annual survival of the mallard (*Anas platyrhynchos*). Ph.D. Thesis. Univ. of Saskatchewan, Saskatoon. 174pp.

GRICE, D., AND J. P. ROGERS. 1965. The wood duck in Massachusetts. Massachusetts Div. Fish Game P-R Rep., Proj. W-19-R. 96pp.

HEIN, D., AND A. O. HAUGEN. 1966. Autumn roosting flight counts as an index to wood duck abundance. J. Wildl. Manage. 30(4):657–668.

HOCHBAUM, H. A. 1944. The canvasback on a prairie marsh. The American Wildlife Institute, Washington, D.C. 201pp.

———. 1947. The effect of concentrated hunting pressure on waterfowl breeding stock. Trans. N. Am. Wildl. Conf. 12:53–64.

———. 1955. Travels and traditions of waterfowl. University of Minnesota Press, Minneapolis. 301pp.

JESSEN, R. L. 1969. Wrong way mallards. Minnesota Div. Game and Fish. News and Notes 71. 14pp.

———. 1970. Mallard population trends and hunting losses in Minnesota. J. Wildl. Manage. 34(1):93–105.

KIRBY, R. E., J. H. RIECHMANN, AND M. E. SHOUGH. 1976. A preliminary report on Minnesota's innovative 1973 waterfowl season. Wildl. Soc. Bull. 4(2):55–63.

LEBRET, T. 1952. Pre-moult migration of a female Gadwall (*Anas strepera* L.) and two female wigeon (*A. penelope* L.). Ardea 40 (1–2):75–76.

———. 1971. Observations of surface feeding ducks (Anatinae) in wing molt in tidal habitat in the Biesbosch Hollands Diep Haringbliet area. Limosa 44(1–2):29–44.

LENSINK, C. J. 1964. Distribution of recoveries from bandings of ducklings. U.S. Fish Wildl. Serv. Spec. Sci. Rep. Wildl. 89. 146pp.

MANN, G. E. 1950. Reverse fall migration. J. Wildl. Manage. 14(3):360–362.

MUNRO, J. A. 1943. Studies of waterfowl in British Columbia, Mallard. Can. J. Res. 21(8): 223–260.

ORING, L. W. 1964. Behavior and ecology of certain ducks during the postbreeding period. J. Wildl. Manage. 28(2):223–233.

PALMER, R. S. 1972. Patterns of molting. Pages 65–102 *in* D. S. Farner and J. R. King, eds. Avian biology. Vol. II. Academic Press, New York.

RAITASUO, K. 1964. Social behavior of the mallard (*Anas platyrhynchos*) in the course of the annual cycle. Pap. Game Res. 24. 72pp.

ROGERS, J. P. 1967. Flightless green-winged teal in southeast Missouri. Wilson Bull. 79(3):339.

SALOMONSEN, F. 1968. The moult migration. Wildfowl Trust Annu. Rep. 19:5–24.

SEIDENSTICKER, J. C., M. G. HORNOCKER, R. R. KNIGHT, AND S. L. JUDD. 1970. Equipment and techniques for radio tracking mountain lions and elk. Idaho For. Wildl. Range Exp. Stn. Bull. 6. 20pp.

SOWLS, L. K. 1955. Prairie ducks. The Stackpole Co., Harrisburg, Pa. 193pp.

SUGDEN, L. G., W. L. THURLOW, R. D. HARRIS, AND K. VERMEER. 1974. Investigations of mallards overwintering at Calgary, Alberta. Can. Field-Nat. 88(3):303–311.

WRIGHT, B. S. 1954. High tide and an east wind. The Stackpole Co., Harrisburg, Pa., and The Wildlife Management Institute, Washington, D.C. 162pp.

Received 5 April 1976.
Accepted 7 April 1977.

EFFECT OF PREDATOR REDUCTION ON WATERFOWL NESTING SUCCESS[1]

DONALD S. BALSER, U. S. Bureau of Sport Fisheries and Wildlife, Wildlife Research Center, Denver, Colorado
HERBERT H. DILL, U. S. Bureau of Sport Fisheries and Wildlife, Division of Wildlife Refuges, Minneapolis, Minnesota
HARVEY K. NELSON, U. S. Bureau of Sport Fisheries and Wildlife, Wildlife Research Center, Jamestown, North Dakota

Abstract: A 6-year study to determine the effect of nest-predator removal on waterfowl nesting success was conducted at the Agassiz National Wildlife Refuge in northwestern Minnesota from 1959 through 1964. Predators were removed from the west side of the Refuge while the east side served as a control area. At the end of 3 years, these areas were reversed to reduce the effects of environmental influences. The effect of predator removal was measured by a simulated nest study to determine predation pressure, a check of natural nest success, and weekly breeding pair and brood counts. Results indicated that 60 percent more Class I ducklings were produced on the units where predator control was conducted. Until more is known, reduction of predators to increase waterfowl nesting success should be limited to intensively managed production areas where substantial nest losses are demonstrated.

Earlier in the century, Kalmbach (1939: 601) reported an average waterfowl nesting success of 60 percent in 22 studies across the North American continent. However, in recent years a number of investigators have indicated an apparent low rate of nesting success among waterfowl. Anderson (1957:88), for example, gave a figure of 38.4 percent, and Keith (1961:82), summarizing work by several authors, reported that nest success for dabbling ducks averaged 39 percent. A nesting study conducted by J. C. Carlsen in 1956 at Agassiz National Wildlife Refuge in northwestern Minnesota (personal communication) showed that only 33 percent of 30 duck nests located in a 68-acre study area were successful. According to Agassiz Refuge reports for 1958 and 1959 (the first year of this study at Agassiz), the nesting success rate ranged from 30 to 40 percent, with primary losses due to predation.

With predation apparently increasing, and with waterfowl so much in demand for sport hunting at the same time their habitat and breeding populations are decreasing, a point may have been reached where it is economically feasible to improve nesting success by reducing nest-predator populations, provided (1) that the area is under intensive management and the major management objective is to obtain maximum waterfowl production, and (2) that demonstrated nest losses are serious enough to allow a worthwhile increase in productivity when predator control is applied.

A number of studies with other types of birds have indicated that predator control under such circumstances may increase productivity. For example, Darrow (1947:349) indicated that predator control experiments have been effective in reducing nest losses among grouse. Hickey (1955) summarized much of the work on other predator control experiments with gallinaceous birds. A study similar to the one reported here to determine the effects of predator control on pheasant nest success in Minnesota is reported by Chesness et al. (1968).

In 1959, this study was initiated at Agassiz to determine the effects of predator con-

[1] This study was conducted by the U. S. Bureau of Sport Fisheries and Wildlife in cooperation with the Minnesota Division of Game and Fish and was partly financed under Pittman–Robertson Projects W11-R-19 through 23.

Originally published in J. Wildl. Manage. 32(4):669–682, 1968.

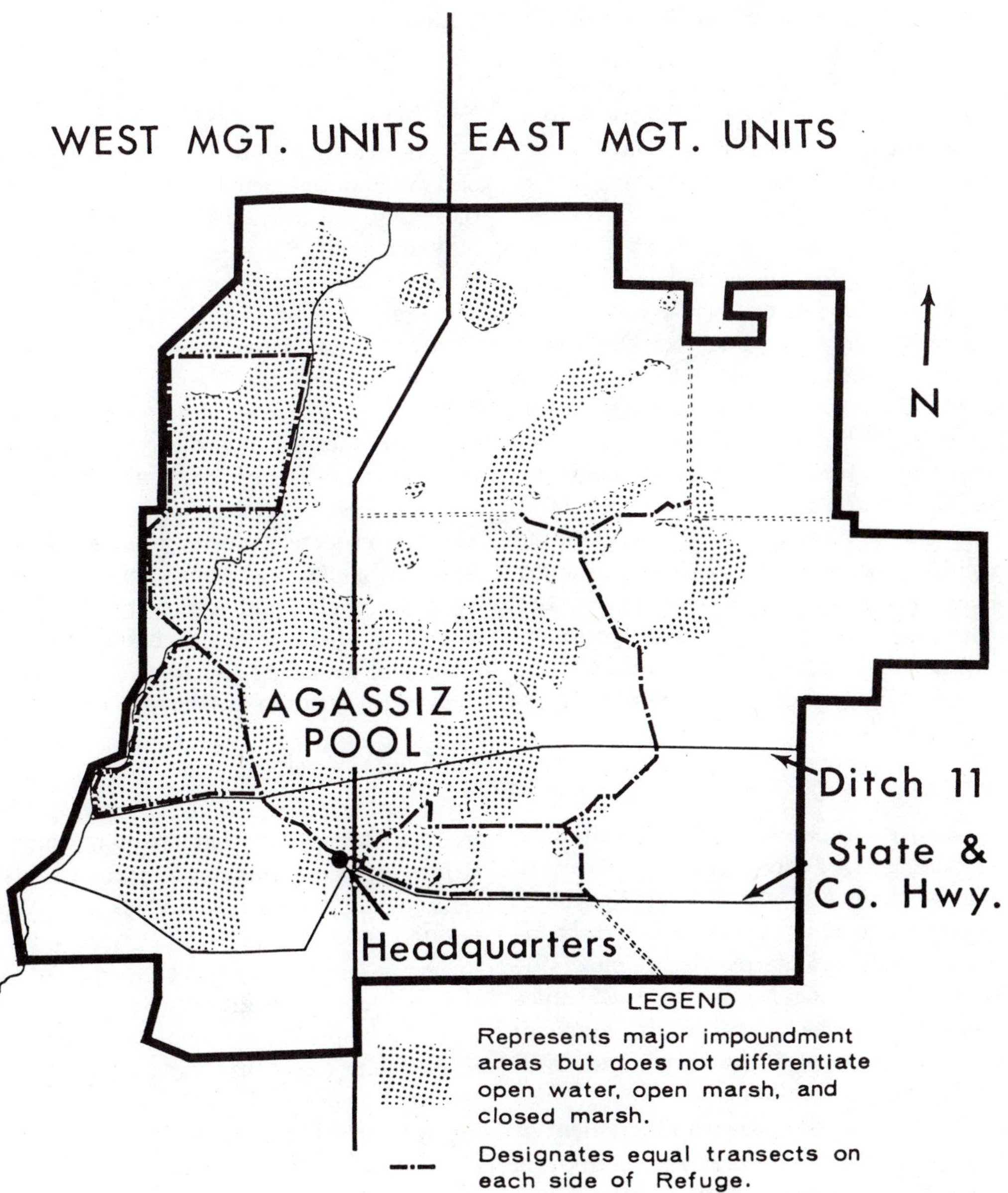

Fig. 1. Schematic map of Agassiz National Wildlife Refuge. (Scale approximately 3/8 inch per mile.)

trol on waterfowl nesting success. Among the major questions we sought to answer were: How great were nest losses when predation was and was not controlled? Does the presence of high predator densities prevent the successful use of otherwise suitable nesting cover? Does renesting compensate for the bulk of nest predation?

And finally, is it economically feasible to increase waterfowl production on a limited area by the removal of nest predators?

We sincerely thank Ralph Town, Marvin Mansfield, Don Perkuchin, and David Olsen of the Division of Wildlife Refuges; Berkeley Peterson of the Division of Wildlife Services, U. S. Bureau of Sport Fisheries and Wildlife; Biologists William H. Longley, John P. Lindmeier, Charles Kinsey, and Marius Morse of the Minnesota Division of Game and Fish, who carried out the bulk of the field work during portions of this study; and trappers Carl Burrell and Glen Bernstein, whose diligent efforts contributed to the success of the control program.

Special thanks are due the cooperating agencies for their patience and encouragement, which allowed completion of this work in spite of numerous personnel changes, and to Charles M. Loveless of the Denver Wildlife Research Center for statistical analysis.

DESCRIPTION OF AREA

The Agassiz National Wildlife Refuge, containing 61,009 acres, lies at the eastern edge of the bed of glacial Lake Agassiz in the transition zone between northern coniferous forests and the prairie region of the Red River of the North. It is 25 miles northeast of Thief River Falls, Marshall County, Minnesota. The Thief and Mud rivers traverse the Refuge.

The topography is flat with a gradient of 1 to 2 ft/mile. The drainage pattern is toward the southwest, with Judicial Ditch No. 11 and the Thief River the primary drains.

The vegetation and other features are described in the work of Harris and Marshall (1963) and Perkuchin (1964). Marginal farms and an abundance of hay, rock, stump piles, and ditch spoil banks surrounding the Refuge create excellent habitat for small carnivores.

METHODS

This investigation was begun in the spring of 1959 and conducted through 1964. For the study, we divided the Agassiz Refuge into two areas, the west and east management units consisting of 19,129 and 19,155 acres respectively (Fig. 1). The basic study plan consisted of removing nest predators on the west half for 3 years with the east half serving as a control area. At the end of 3 years the plan was reversed and predator control was applied to the east half with the west half serving as a control area. This reversal was expected to offset differences in habitat and waterfowl population dynamics that might affect study results. The area where predator control was applied will be called the *treated area,* and the control area the *untreated area.*

Predator Control

Control was directed at the entire predator complex except that snapping turtles (*Chelydra serpentina*) and northern pike (*Esox lucius*), which prey on ducklings, were omitted because their densities were judged to be too low to have much effect. We attempted to remove all other actual and potential nest predators completely, not only to eliminate the actual losses they caused, but to prevent their disturbing nests. Baiting with strychnine-poisoned eggs was initiated soon after spring breakup each year to effect a reduction before nesting began, and was continued throughout the season (Table 1).

The formula and procedure for preparing the poisoned eggs were modified from unpublished techniques used by the Division of Wildlife Services, U. S. Bureau of Sport Fisheries and Wildlife. One-half ounce

Table. 1. Predator control methods used, Agassiz National Wildlife Refuge, Minnesota, 1959–64.

Year	Control Period	Strychnine Eggs		Live Traps	Steel Traps
		No. of Stations	Total* Eggs		
1959	April 29–June 17	241	1,538	—	—
1960	May 3–June 10	258	2,409	—	—
1961	March 27–June 27	—	—	92	27
	April 15–June 27	134	477	—	—
1962	April 2–August 7	—	—	152	44
	April 25–August 6	123	1,124	—	—
1963	April 2—July 31	—	—	154	19
	April 8–July 31	148	672	—	—
1964	April 3–July 31	—	—	148	11
	April 20–July 31	141	774	—	—

* Destroyed eggs were regularly replaced; hence total number of eggs used does not agree with number of stations times eggs set per station.

strychnine sulfate, 9 ounces honey, and ½ ounce water were thoroughly mixed and heated in a saucepan. A purple dye was added to the mixture and 1½ cc was injected with a syringe into the large end of a chicken egg that had been perforated with two holes to allow the extrusion of surplus albumen. The strychnine was dispersed through the egg by running the needle to the small end of the egg and injecting the solution as it was withdrawn. The holes were then sealed by drying the albumen in the sun, and the shell of each egg was rubber-stamped with the word "poison."

A strychnine egg station consisted of two or three treated eggs placed in an artificial nest site along major predator travel lanes. In the last 3 years of the study the strychnine egg stations were grouped at major dike intersections and predator access points to save on labor. The number of strychnine egg stations varied between 123 and 258 during the study years. At the termination of each station, any eggs remaining were picked up and buried.

After control efforts were completed in 1959 and 1960, it was apparent that strychnine eggs alone would not provide the desired degree of control. Steel traps to take red foxes and live traps to take raccoons were added during succeeding years (Table 1). Records were maintained on methods and number of predators taken for all these control operations. In addition, two trappers were hired each year of the study to conduct predator control during the entire nesting season, April through July, at an average cost of $3,000 per year for salaries and expenses. Additional control in the fall was carried out in 1960 and 1961.

Since public relations are a vital part of any control program, adjacent landowners were contacted in person and by letter to acquaint them with the program, and the reasons and methods of the study were carefully explained in order to minimize misunderstandings.

Waterfowl Surveys

Surveys were conducted to determine the effects of predator control on waterfowl production. Before the study was begun, trial aerial surveys were conducted to determine the best method for censusing breeding pairs on the Refuge and to develop correction factors for the differences in distribution and species composition in aerial and ground counts. Procedures used in the cooperative waterfowl breeding ground survey in the northern states and Canada were adopted with slight modifications to meet the needs of this study. Initially, an aerial survey of breeding populations was conducted for the entire Refuge by flying transects along every quarter-section line across the Refuge and recording all ducks observed within ⅛ mile on each side of the flight line. This could be done quite accurately on the Refuge because of existing roads, ditches, and fence lines. Ducks were recorded by location along flight lines or within designated units, and these data were used to indicate the size of transects needed to meet statistical requirements. It was determined that a one-third random sample of quarter-section lines (transects) was adequate for aerial censusing of the annual breeding population. A separate flight was made to determine the species composition on the Refuge as seen from the air. This was followed by simultaneous runs of the ground transects both on the ground and from the air to develop an annual "air–ground" ratio, which was also corrected for differences in species observability.

For the ground surveys, a 19-mile-long ground transect, stratified by habitat types, was established on each half of the Refuge. The transects were selected on the basis of available access roads, maximum possible length, and equal proportions of four waterfowl habitat types: (1) open water, (2) open ditch, (3) open marsh, and (4) closed marsh. Observations along the ground transects were made from a raised platform mounted on a pickup truck driven at a slow speed along the dike roads. This permitted the observers to cover a ⅛-mile strip on each side of the road. The ground transects were not beat out, so the breeding population recorded from the ground represented a minimum, and projections made from it tended to underestimate the total breeding population on the Refuge.

Blue-winged teal (*Anas discors*), mallard (*A. platyrhynchos*), and gadwall (*A. strepera*) made up 69 percent of the breeding population on the Refuge. Of this percentage, 55 percent were blue-winged teal, 27 percent mallards, and 18 percent gadwalls. The remaining 31 percent were primarily divers and less abundant species of puddle ducks. The three principal species served as the basis for all waterfowl surveys in this study.

Differences in waterfowl production and predation pressure were evaluated by treatment, area, and year from (1) breeding pair counts, (2) brood counts, (3) fate of natural nests, and (4) fate of simulated nests.

Breeding pair counts were made weekly during May on both ground transects (Dill et al. 1957:11–17), and the count for the date when most migrants had left the Refuge and before nesting began in earnest was selected as best representing the number of breeding pairs. This date was between May 25 and June 1 in all years for both aerial and ground transects.

Weekly brood counts were made from the time the first brood appeared until the last brood was observed late in August (Dill et al. 1960:4–8, 17–22). Broods were recorded by species, number of ducklings, and age-classes (Gollop and Marshall 1954). To reduce the influence of brood movement, Class I broods (ducklings under 19 days old, except blue-winged teal under 14 days) or Class IA broods (ducklings under 7 days old) were used as a measure of total ducklings produced on each transect. Since the total number of ducklings observed throughout the entire nesting season included those produced by renesting, use of this figure automatically corrected for any changes in brood sizes resulting from renesting.

A search for duck nests was made each year on the transects by ground crews and a tractor-mounted flush bar, but accidental observations made both on the transects and elsewhere during the course of other work were also recorded. A data sheet was kept for each nest. Weller's (1956) technique was used for candling eggs to determine the stage of incubation.

Simulated nests were used on each ground transect to determine differences in predation pressure. This technique was similar to that described by Rearden (1951) and gave us control over the number of nests studied and their location.

At least 100 simulated nests containing three chicken eggs each were placed on each transect every year. Each nest was placed in a cleared, slight depression under a small clump of dead grass, thistle, or sedge, so as to appear as natural as possible. Each nest was marked with a numbered tag attached to a stake. The minimum distance between nests on a transect was approximately 75 ft; the average was 150 ft. Nests placed along dikes were as close as 3 ft and as far as 30 ft from the water's edge or the edge of the road; the usual distance was between 5 and 15 ft. Nests in "upland cover" habitat were placed at a minimum of 30 ft from the maintained edge of roads or from shorelines, but usually at least 150 ft.

To avoid leaving trails that predators could follow, we approached each nest site individually from the bare dike road, took large steps not in line, avoided crushing vegetation, spaced visits at least 8 days apart, and passed by the nest at a distance of 3–4 ft. The activity of the trappers, placing of poison egg stations, and general activity of the biologists was believed to further confound any tendency to follow human trails.

A simulated nest was recorded as destroyed when any egg was missing or damaged by a predator. Nests lost or flooded were not counted in the sample.

RESULTS AND DISCUSSION

Predator Control

The type and extent of control methods necessarily varied, and thus the results attributed to each method are not comparable. The main objective was to attain as complete control as possible so that potential differences in nesting success could be determined. No single method alone was sufficiently effective to achieve the desired control, and strychnine eggs, live traps, steel traps, and Conibear traps all played a part. Strychnine eggs appeared the most effective for reducing avian predation and removing skunks, but were not as effective in removing raccoons or foxes. A specially constructed live trap, 11 × 12 × 42 inches, proved effective for raccoons and skunks. No. 2 steel traps were the most reliable for foxes.

The total number of animals taken increased during the first 3 years as control was intensified (Table 2). The strychnine

Table 2. Number of principal mammalian nest predators taken during each nesting season by all methods at Agassiz National Wildlife Refuge, Minnesota, 1959–64.

YEAR	RACCOON	SKUNK	FOX	TOTAL
1959	28	46	5	79
1960	61	96	39	196
1961	95	155	21	271
1962	100	205	58	363
1963	94	162	8	264
1964	66	97	6	169
Totals	444	761	137	1,342

egg stations were consolidated and reduced in number, and in the third year live traps were added.

The total number of raccoons, skunks, and foxes known to have been removed by all methods is shown by species and year in Table 2; so few predators of other species were taken that they were not included. In addition, 277 raccoons, skunks, and foxes were taken during the fall of 1960 and 1961 to aid the spring control effort, but immigration by the next spring made this effort appear impractical, so no further attempts at fall control were made.

Potential nest predators, obtained from the records of animals killed by strychnine eggs, were: striped skunk (*Mephitis mephitis*), raccoon (*Procyon lotor*), red fox (*Vulpes fulva*), dog, badger (*Taxidea taxus*), mink (*Mustela vison*), short-tailed weasel (*Mustela erminea*), woodchuck (*Marmota monax*), Franklin's ground squirrel (*Citellus franklinii*), thirteen-lined ground squirrel (*Citellus tridecemlineatus*), crow (*Corvus brachyrhynchos*), magpie (*Pica pica*), marsh hawk (*Circus cyaneus*).

All of these species except the marsh hawk have been previously reported as nest predators. Normally, only a few marsh hawks were taken, but 19 were recovered at strychnine egg stations in 1963.

The resident breeding population of these hawks appeared to be quickly eliminated after the poisoned eggs were set out. Dead marsh hawks were observed at egg stations with egg shells and purple dye in their throats. Although crows were observed on the untreated areas during the control program, relatively few were seen or recovered in the treated areas; we believe that most of them were repelled by the crows that weie poisoned. Egg punctures by other small avian species were noted, but the species were not identified.

In 1959 and 1960, predators were recovered at only 16 and 20 percent of the destroyed strychnine egg stations. Although some nest predators were probably killed by strychnine eggs and not found, every destroyed egg station did not necessarily represent a predator kill. Tests on live-trapped raccoons indicated that they would salivate and spit out the strychnine from treated eggs, thus receiving a sublethal dose from which they recovered in a day or two. This, coupled with the numerous broken eggs whose contents were not ingested, suggests that many eggs were destroyed for every predator killed.

Each year the catch of predatory animals dropped after the first few weeks. We felt that essentially the entire resident population was controlled by our methods the last 4 years, and that continued catches (one or two animals per day per 150 traps) represented immigration. Most of these were caught on the perimeter while the interior

Table 3. "Success" (freedom from predation) of simulated duck nests on areas with predator control (treated) and without control (untreated) on Agassiz National Wildlife Refuge, Minnesota, 1959–64.

YEAR	TREATED		UNTREATED		COMPUTED χ^2
	No. Nests Successful	Total Nests	No. Nests Successful	Total Nests	
	West		*East*		
1959	82	100	23	125	87.64
1960	122	171	48	192	76.44
1961	92	100	36	91	56.9
	East		*West*		
1962	79	112	37	107	36.97
1963	93	100	45	100	51.6
1964	63	71	50	84	15.2
All years	531	654	239	699	

Total $\chi^2 = 30.3$, $P < 0.99$, 1 df

Ratio treated to untreated = (531/654)/(239/699) = 2.38:1

Mean nest success rate:

Treated	Untreated
81%	34%

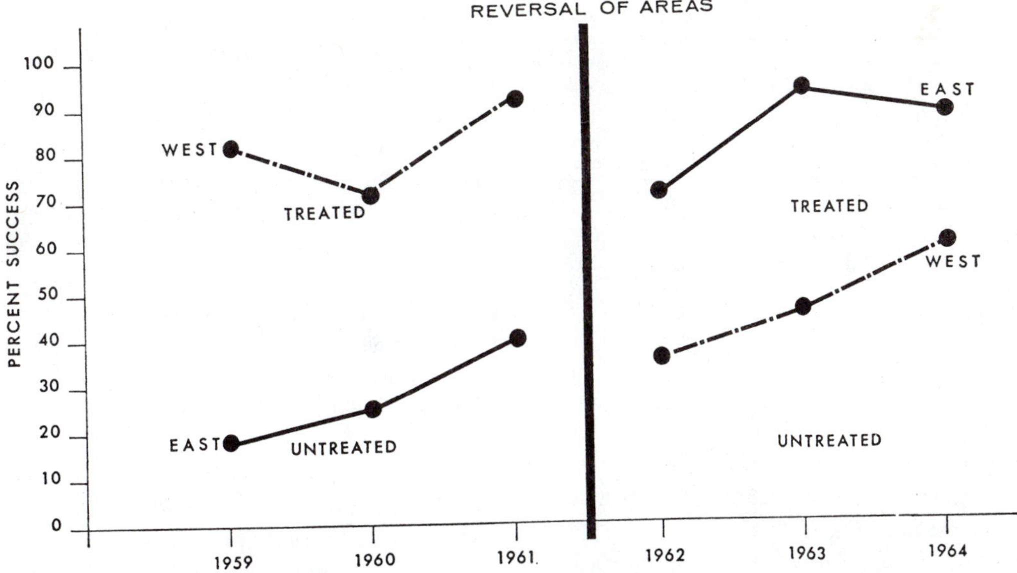

Fig. 2. Percent "success" of simulated duck nests on treated and untreated areas (with and without predator control).

traps went untouched and the area was devoid of animal sign.

Most control efforts are usually terminated when the catch drops and trappers become discouraged; this is suggested as a reason why many control attempts have failed to produce results when predation was a principal cause of nest losses. We believe continuous control is required throughout the nesting season to maintain reduced predation pressure. It appears probable that intensive control may have played a part in inducing this ingress.

Although predation was reduced, no noticeable increase in meadow voles (*Microtus pennsylvanicus*), Franklin's ground squirrels, or woodchucks was detected during this study. Woodchucks, in fact, appeared to decrease, presumably because of limited control efforts along dikes. A special study conducted in 1964 with snap traps to sample small-rodent populations on the treated and untreated areas was inconclusive. It is possible that periodic spring floods in the waterfowl units limit terrestrial rodent numbers more than predators do. During such critical periods, their habitat is restricted to dikes, with little freeboard.

Simulated Nest Studies

Simulated nests were used to indicate predation pressure and to determine the degree of nest protection afforded by predator removal. The rate of predation on simulated nests is not necessarily proportional to the number of predators, but may relate to their level of skill and egg-eating proclivities.

Results of the 6 years of simulated nest studies on treated and untreated areas are shown in Table 3. Freedom from predation for these nests, or their "success," was 2.38 times greater on the treated area than on the untreated area, and the mean rate of "success" increased from 34 to 81 percent.

Fig. 2 represents the assumed "success" of simulated nests during the two alternate

Table 4. Hatching success of natural duck nests of three principal species—blue-winged teal, mallard, and gadwall—on areas with predator control (treated) and without control (untreated) on Agassiz National Wildlife Refuge, Minnesota, 1959–64.

YEAR	TREATED		UNTREATED	
	% Success	No. Nests	% Success	No. Nests
	West		*East*	
1959	57.3	68	80.0	15
1960	35.0	31	56.0	16
1961	75.7	33	16.6	6
	East		*West*	
1962*	48.2	29	2.2	45
1963	65.3	52	16.6	18
1964*	70.5	34	0.0	12

1959–60 computed $\chi^2 = 0.126$, $P \leqq 0.25$, 1 df

1961–64 computed $\chi^2 = 20.842$, $P \leqq 0.99$, 3 df

Mean nest success rate:

	Treated	Untreated
1959–64	352/6 = 58.7	171.4/6 = 28.6
1961–64	259.7/4 = 64.9	35.4/4 = 8.8

Ratio of treated to untreated (6 years): 58.7/28.6 = 2.05:1

* Years of severe flooding.

3-year periods of the study. An upward trend can be noted in the untreated area for each period, and an unprecedented high of 60-percent "success" occurred the last year. It appears that predator control on the treated area affected results on the untreated area because of an inadequate buffer zone between them. This buffer zone was the Mud Lake Unit, a 10,000-acre marsh of predominantly open water, 2¾ miles at the widest point and narrowing on the north to a 3,000-acre tamarack spruce swamp. If it was inadequate, the difference indicated in the "success" of simulated nests between treated and untreated areas is conservative.

Natural Nest Success

The hatching success of natural duck nests during the 6 years is presented in Table 4. Control efforts the first 2 years (strychnine eggs only, for a 6-week period) did not achieve the intensity or duration of control desired. In addition, high success occurred on the untreated area in these years, presumably because of an unusually high land–water ratio, resulting in greater dispersion of nests and predators. A chi-square test indicated that the difference in success of natural nests between the treated and untreated areas was not significant the first 2 years, but was significant the last 4 years. For these reasons, the last 4 years of nesting data are treated separately in Table 4.

Although the sample size of natural nests in some years on the untreated area was small, when totaled for 6 years it allows comparison of natural and simulated nests, and so is included. More nests were recorded on the treated area because of accidental findings during control operations and because ducks nested in more obvious and open locations, when predators were removed. For example, four incubated nests were found in a 15-ft circle, and many nests were found along the wheel tracks and along predator travel lanes on dike edges in previously untenable sites.

In spite of a higher success rate for natural nests on the untreated area (east) during the first 2 years, the success rate for the 6 years was 2.05 times greater on the treated than on the untreated area. Since this figure does not consider the effect of renesting (which should be higher on the untreated area), it is believed to overestimate the success due to treatment.

Breeding Pair Counts

Total breeding pair counts of the three principal species from complete aerial surveys for the Refuge are shown in Table 5. Counts varied from approximately 9,000 to 14,000 pairs the first 5 years of the study

Table 5. Total aerial counts of breeding pairs of the three principal species of ducks on Agassiz National Wildlife Refuge, Minnesota, 1959–64.

SPECIES	1959	1960	1961	1962*	1963	1964*
Blue-winged teal	6,041	5,584	7,684	7,346	5,614	1,673
Mallard	2,504	4,450	4,228	918	1,748	1,195
Gadwall	1,179	2,217	2,858	1,974	2,488	1,110
Totals	9,724	12,251	14,770	10,238	9,850	3,978

* Severe floods occurred in 1962 and 1964.

down to about 4,000 pairs in 1964. The average number was 10,133.

Breeding pair counts of the three principal species on ground transects are shown in Table 6. The west half of the Refuge showed consistently higher counts, thereby indicating a more attractive habitat. However, an analysis of variance for breeding pairs per mile indicated no significant difference ($P > 0.05$) between treated and untreated areas (Table 7). This fortunately allowed comparison of total numbers of ducklings produced on each transect for the 6 years without weighting the data for breeding pairs. The analysis of variance on this and succeeding tests was a mixed model, with species and treatments considered as fixed effects and the years as random effects.

Table 6. Ground transect counts of breeding pairs of the three principal species of ducks—blue-winged teal, mallard, and gadwall—on areas with predator control (treated) and without control (untreated) on Agassiz National Wildlife Refuge, Minnesota, 1959–64.

YEAR	TREATED AREA	UNTREATED AREA
	West	*East*
1959	809	507
1960	606	351
1961	786	505
	East	*West*
1962	274	449
1963	330	551
1964	371	777
Total	3,176	3,140
Total for West:	3,978	
Total for East:	2,338	

Brood Counts

An analysis of variance for Class IA broods counted per mile is given in Table 8. The number of ducklings recorded was significantly higher ($P < 0.05$) on the treated area than on the untreated area. The total count of all Class I broods is shown in Table 9 (expressed as total ducklings to allow for any differences in brood sizes). Possible changes in brood sizes due to renesting were considered, but a *t* test indicated no significant differences ($P > 0.05$) in brood sizes between treated and untreated areas for any of the three principal species.

Floods in 1962 and 1964 severely curtailed production in comparison with other years (see natural nest success, Table 4, and total duckling counts, Table 9). How-

Table 7. Analysis of variance for breeding pairs/mile of the three principal species of ducks—blue-winged teal, mallard, and gadwall—Agassiz National Wildlife Refuge, Minnesota, 1959–64.

SOURCE	DF	MS	COMPUTED F VALUES
Species (S)	2	448.8284	24.79*
Treatments (T)	1	0.0241	< 1
Years (Y)	5	33.2609	6.39*
S × T	2	1.6307	< 1
S × Y	10	18.1040	3.48*
T × Y	5	34.0765	6.55*

* Difference significant ($P < 0.05$).

Table 8. Analysis of variance for counts of Class IA broods of ducklings of the three principal species—blue-winged teal, mallard, and gadwall—per mile, Agassiz National Wildlife Refuge, Minnesota, 1959–64.

SOURCE	DF	MS	COMPUTED F VALUES
Species (S)	2	8.91	3.59†
Treatments (T)	1	1.78	9.88*
Years (Y)	5	3.78	4.26*
S × T	2	1.07	1.21
S × Y	10	2.48	2.79†
T × Y	5	0.18	< 1.0

* Significantly different ($P < 0.05$).
† Significantly different ($P < 0.10$).

Table 10. Analysis of variance for total number of ducklings in Class I broods of the three principal species—blue-winged teal, mallard, and gadwall—on Agassiz National Wildlife Refuge, Minnesota, 1959–64.

SOURCE	DF	MS	COMPUTED F VALUES
Species (S)	2	962930.59	4.31*
Treatment (T)	1	204454.69	4.77†
Years (Y)	5	468442.58	12.03*
S × T	2	158182.19	5.06†
S × Y	10	223439.22	5.74*
T × Y	5	42837.30	1.10

* Significantly different ($P < 0.05$).
† Significantly different ($P < 0.10$).

ever, production on the treated area almost equaled that on the untreated area in spite of much lower breeding pair counts. The flooding in both years was protracted, lasting through the peak of the nesting season and well into July. It greatly reduced freeboard on the dikes and concentrated both predators and waterfowl nests on restricted land areas, thereby increasing nest losses. This suggests that predation can be additive to losses from flooding, particularly when the high water is of long duration, and is an exception to the theory that predation is of benefit in distributing the hatch over a period of time to avoid catastrophes (Cartwright 1952:133).

Table 9. Number of ducklings counted on transects as Class I broods of the three principal species—blue-winged teal, mallard, and gadwall—on areas with predator control (treated) and without control (untreated) on Agassiz National Wildlife Refuge, Minnesota, 1959–64.

YEAR	TREATED	UNTREATED
	West	*East*
1959	865	524
1960	1,427	1,276
1961	3,057	1,975
	East	*West*
1962*	297	307
1963	1,615	520
1964*	310	256
Totals	7,571	4,858
Ratio—Treated:Untreated = 1.56:1		

* Severe floods occurred in 1962 and 1964.

The treated areas produced 1.56 times as many Class I ducklings and 1.65 times as many Class IA ducklings as the untreated area (Table 9). The average increase of both classes in actual productivity due to treatment was 60 percent.

The total production of Class I ducklings on the treated and untreated areas was significantly different ($P < 0.01$) (Table 10). Since no significant difference was demonstrated in the number of breeding pairs between the areas, it seems reasonable to conclude that the increase in duckling production occurred as a result of control of nest predators.

General Discussion

Comparing nest success as determined by the three methods used shows that simulated nests were 2.38 times more "successful," natural nests 2.05 times more successful, and duckling counts 1.56 and 1.65 times higher on treated than on untreated areas. The average increase shown by nesting studies was slightly over twice that of total duckling counts (2.2:1 as compared with 1.6:1). This indicates that renesting compensated for approximately half the nest losses in this study. We believe

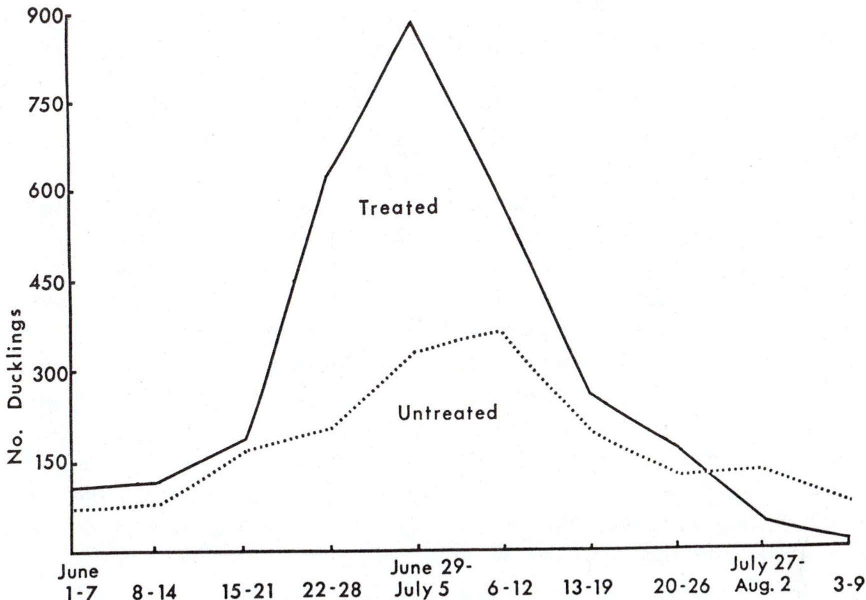

Fig. 3. Hatching curve for 1959–64 based on number of Class IA ducklings of the three principal species—blue-winged teal, mallard, and gadwall.

that total duckling counts are a more accurate assessment of the effects of predator control on nesting success than nest studies.

Errington (1942) indicated that renesting may largely compensate for earlier severe losses from predation and other causes. Cartwright (1952) referred to this premise when establishing models to compare potential with actual waterfowl production. The premise is true if it is assumed that most pairs attempt to renest and low rates of predation are involved. However, where predation continues, or the latitude does not allow time for successful renesting when nests are lost during incubation, successful renesting may be a negligible factor. However, duckling production resulting from nests destroyed and reestablished before incubation started may be important.

Sowls (1949:271) reported a minimum of 13 renests from 66 nests terminated during incubation. In contrast, the combined peak of hatching for the Class IA broods of the three principal species in this study on the treated and untreated areas (Fig. 3) shows little evidence of late renesting. The peak of hatching of the three principal species varies by only one week at this latitude, so the curves were consolidated to show on one graph the periods when control is most applicable and to compare the effect of treatment and nontreatment on the total hatching pattern. Note that the portion on the graph representing the untreated area is slightly skewed to the right, presumably due to renesting. The major effects of treatment appear to occur 2 weeks on either side of the peak of hatch, with little effect on early and late broods. From this, we judge predator control should be conducted for at least the 3 months of May, June, and July. April was also included to prevent predators from disturbing incoming pairs. The curve indicates that the control periods were terminated too early in 1959, 1960, and 1961 (Table 1) to provide the most benefit to nesting success.

Ideally, the effects of treatment in a study of this kind should be expressed in terms of increased production of ducklings per breeding pair, but it is difficult to equate total ducklings produced on ground transects with breeding pair counts on ground transects. While the breeding pair counts are believed quite accurate, we are not sure how many of the breeding pairs counted along the ground transects actually nested within range of the dikes and produced broods for later counts; some pairs may even have migrated. For these reasons, breeding pair counts along the ground transects appear to be too high and brood counts too low to adequately express productivity in ducklings per pair. Of the estimates used in this study, total duckling counts appear to be the most reliable indicator of treatment effect. If further research of this type is undertaken, it should be limited to areas where an accurate ratio of breeding pairs to broods can be determined.

The cost of control in terms of additional ducklings produced can be fairly well approximated by this model:

1. Average number of pairs of three principal species per year from complete aerial counts (Table 5) .... 10,000+ pairs
2. Original success rate (40%) .. 4,000 pairs
3. Indicated increase in breeding pairs producing broods (60% of item 2) .... 2,400 additional pairs
4. 2,400 additional pairs producing an average of 6 ducklings per brood .... 14,400 additional ducklings
5. At a cost of $3,000 per year for control (including trappers' salary and expenses) each additional duckling produced costs approximately 21 cents.

Expressed another way, a 60-percent increase in ducklings produced without predator control would require acquisition, development, and maintenance of 36,000 additional acres of similar habitat.

CONCLUDING REMARKS

Where predator control is to be considered as a management technique to increase nesting success on intensively managed waterfowl production areas, the following recommendations are offered:

1. Measurements of predation pressure or nest destruction should be made before initiating control and again during control to insure (a) that nest destruction rates are severe enough to allow a significant increase in nesting success, including the effect of renesting; (b) that the control program is effective in reducing predation; and (c) that the cost and effort of predator control are economically justified.

2. The entire predator complex should be controlled or compensatory predation may occur by a species not under control.

3. No one method of control will give adequate reduction over long periods, or be efficient under all conditions. Raccoons became shy of strychnine-treated eggs after the first season; steel traps were difficult to keep functioning during the early nesting period because of freezing and thawing. For such reasons, it is advisable to use a combination of the most effective control methods.

4. Strychnine-treated eggs should be carefully placed, under responsible supervision and within the legal limits of the state and local community.

5. Other means of alleviating predator losses should be investigated such as predator-proof, over-water nest structures and manipulation of habitat to favor waterfowl nesting while discouraging predators.

6. Careful attention should be given to public relations to prevent misunderstanding, accidents, or over-optimism.

7. Results of this study should not be

arbitrarily applied to other locations or predator–prey situations. The situation under which this study was conducted at Agassiz National Wildlife Refuge may be unique. However, it is hoped that this work will stimulate investigation of predator–prey relationships before control programs are initiated or condemned.

LITERATURE CITED

ANDERSON, W. 1957. A waterfowl nesting study in the Sacramento Valley, California, 1955. California Fish and Game 43(1):71–90.

CARTWRIGHT, B. W. 1952. A comparison of potential with actual waterfowl production. Trans. N. Am. Wildl. Conf. 17:131–137.

CHESNESS, R. A., M. M. NELSON, AND W. H. LONGLEY. 1968. The effect of predator removal on pheasant reproductive success. J. Wildl. Mgmt. 32(4):683–697.

DARROW, R. W. 1947. Predation. Pp. 307–350. *In* G. Bump, R. W. Darrow, F. C. Edminster, and W. F. Crissey, The ruffed grouse: life history, propagation, management. New York State Conserv. Dept. 915pp.

DILL, H. H., R. M. ABNEY, H. K. NELSON, AND A. D. GEIS. 1957. Narrative Report, Agassiz National Wildlife Refuge May–Aug. 35pp. Typewritten.

———, H. K. NELSON, AND A. D. GEIS. 1960. Narrative Report, Agassiz National Wildlife Refuge May–Aug. 30pp. Typewritten.

ERRINGTON, P. L. 1942. On the analysis of productivity in populations of higher vertebrates. J. Wildl. Mgmt. 6(2):165–181.

GOLLOP, J. B., AND W. H. MARSHALL. 1954. A guide for aging duck broods in the field. Mississippi Flyway Council Tech. Sec. 14pp. Mimeo.

HARRIS, S. W., AND W. H. MARSHALL. 1963. Ecology of water-level manipulations on a northern marsh. Ecology 44(2):331–343.

HICKEY, J. J. 1955. Some American population research on gallinaceous birds. Pp. 326–396. *In* A. Wolfson (Editor), Recent studies in avian biology. Univ. Illinois Press, Urbana. 479pp.

KALMBACH, E. R. 1939. Nesting success: its significance in waterfowl reproduction. Trans. N. Am. Wildl. Conf. 4:591–604.

KEITH, L. B. 1961. A study of waterfowl ecology on small impoundments in southeastern Alberta. Wildl. Monogr. 6. 88pp.

PERKUCHIN, D. R. 1964. The dummy waterfowl nest as an index to predation. M.S. Thesis. Michigan State Univ., East Lansing. 23pp.

REARDEN, J. D. 1951. Identification of waterfowl nest predators. J. Wildl. Mgmt. 15(4):386–395.

SOWLS, L. K. 1949. A preliminary report on renesting in waterfowl. Trans. N. Am. Wildl. Conf. 14:260–273.

WELLER, M. W. 1956. A simple field candler for waterfowl eggs. J. Wildl. Mgmt. 20(2):111–113.

Received for publication August 25, 1966.

RED FOX SPATIAL CHARACTERISTICS IN RELATION TO WATERFOWL PREDATION

ALAN B. SARGEANT, Northern Prairie Wildlife Research Center, Jamestown, North Dakota

Abstract: Radio-equipped red foxes (*Vulpes vulpes*) on the Cedar Creek area in Minnesota were spatially distributed, with individual families occupying well defined, nonoverlapping, contiguous territories. Territory boundaries often conformed to natural physical boundaries and appeared to be maintained through some nonaggressive behavior mechanism. Individual foxes traveled extensively throughout the family territory each night. Fox territories appeared to range from approximately 1 to 3 square miles in size, dependent largely on population density. Red foxes used a sequence of dens to rear their pups, and the amount and location of food remains at individual dens changed as the pups matured. The denning season was divided into pre-emergence, confined-use, and dispersed-use periods of 4 to 5 weeks each. Remains of adult waterfowl were collected at rearing dens on six townships in three ecologically different regions of eastern North Dakota. Remains of 172 adult dabbling ducks and 16 adult American coots (*Fulica americana*) were found at 35 dens. No remains from diving ducks were found. The number of adult ducks per den averaged 1.6, 5.9, and 10.2 for paired townships in regions with relatively low, moderate, and high duck populations, respectively. Eighty-four percent of the ducks were females. The species and sex composition of ducks found at dens during early and late sampling periods reflected the nesting chronology of prairie dabbling ducks. Occupied rearing dens were focal points of red fox travel, and the locations of dens may have had considerable influence on predation. Thirty-five of 38 dens found on the six township study areas were on pastured or idle lands. The distribution of rearing dens on the Sand Lake and Arrowwood national wildlife refuges suggested that, on these areas, fox dens were concentrated because of the topography and land-use practices.

Red foxes are abundant throughout much of the prairie waterfowl production areas in the United States and Canada. They prey on waterfowl and their eggs, but few data are available that document the use of these food sources by red foxes.

The purposes of this paper are to discuss certain spatial characteristics of red foxes that relate to their population densities and predator–prey interactions, and to portray and discuss red fox utilization of adult waterfowl during the nesting season. Data included in this paper came primarily from (1) literature on the subject, (2) a study on the ecology and behavior of radio-equipped red foxes on the Cedar Creek Natural History Area in east-central Minnesota, (3) a study of red fox utilization of adult waterfowl on six townships in eastern North Dakota, and (4) observations on locations of red fox dens on Sand Lake National Wildlife Refuge, South Dakota, and Arrowwood National Wildlife Refuge, North Dakota. Only certain aspects of these studies that demonstrate specific characteristics of red foxes in relation to their interactions with waterfowl populations are presented. A more detailed and comprehensive report on the Cedar Creek study is being prepared for publication.

STUDY AREAS

The Cedar Creek study area consisted of 16 square miles centering on the Cedar Creek Natural History Area in Anoka and Isanti counties, Minnesota. This area contains a mixture of deciduous woodlots, cultivated and idle fields, and open and wooded swamps. Several lakes and marshes, a permanent stream, and numerous small farms and well-traveled roads are scattered throughout the area. The heterogeneous makeup of this study area provided a varied environment for the resident fox population.

Six township study areas were selected in three ecologically different prairie regions of eastern North Dakota (Fig. 1). These sites were not intended to represent broad

Originally published in J. Wildl. Manage. 36(2):225–236, 1972.

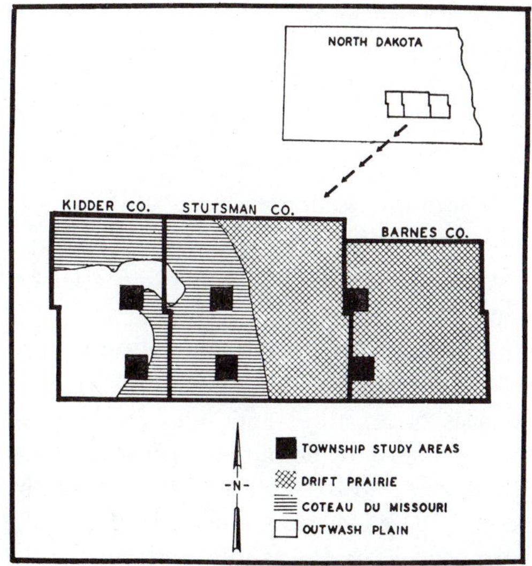

Fig. 1. Location of six township study areas in North Dakota.

geographic areas. Two of the townships were in Barnes County on the Drift Prairie, two in Stutsman County on the Coteau du Missouri, and two in Kidder County, predominately an Outwash Plain area of the Coteau du Missouri (Bradley et al. 1963, Huxel and Petri 1965, Kelly 1966).

The Barnes County townships were intensively farmed for small grain production and had relatively little pasture or idle lands. Agriculture on the Stutsman and Kidder county townships was an interspersion of small grain farming and livestock grazing. Because of heavy snowfall during the winter of 1968–69 and rapid spring runoff, both the Barnes and Stutsman county townships had an abundance of water areas and supported high populations of nesting waterfowl during the spring of 1969. The Kidder County townships each contained a large alkaline lake but relatively few freshwater areas, and waterfowl population densities were relatively low.

Arrowwood National Wildlife Refuge is located in Stutsman and Foster counties in eastern North Dakota. Sand Lake National Wildlife Refuge is in Brown County in northeastern South Dakota. Both refuges, comprised of narrow zones of land bordering impounded lakes and marshes along the James River, are surrounded by cultivated lands.

For the Cedar Creek study I am indebted to D. W. Warner and B. R. Peterson, who were primarily responsible for the author's participation and provided guidance and support throughout the study; W. W. Cochran and V. B. Kuechle provided the necessary electronics assistance; D. B. Siniff contributed much help in the development of computerized data-processing methods; J. E. Forbes was the principal field assistant; and R. L. Himes captured the necessary study animals. This study was generously supported by the Louis W. and Maud Hill Family Foundation of St. Paul, Minnesota; the National Institutes of Health, U. S. Public Health Service Training Grant 5T1 AI 188; and the Bureau of Sport Fisheries and Wildlife, Division of Wildlife Services.

I appreciate the help of Refuge Manager L. J. Schoonover for assistance in locating red fox rearing dens on the Sand Lake National Wildlife Refuge, and the help of Refuge Manager A. D. Kruse and graduate student G. L. Rohde for assistance on the Arrowwood Refuge.

For help in documenting red fox population densities and their utilization of waterfowl on the six townships in North Dakota, I am grateful to C. M. Pfeifer, who served as both pilot and observer, and to W. K. Pfeifer, who served as an experienced observer on all aerial flights. R. T. Eberhardt and S. H. Allen assisted in collecting and examining food remains found at red fox dens, and R. E. Stewart and H. A. Kantrud provided information on waterfowl composition and population densities in eastern North Dakota.

For editorial assistance in preparing this

paper I am particularly grateful to P. F. Springer and F. B. Lee.

METHODS

The movements of 32 radio-equipped red foxes were followed on the Cedar Creek study area from 1963 through 1965 with the use of portable radio-tracking equipment and the Cedar Creek automatic radio-tracking system (Cochran et al. 1965). Most of these foxes were captured in steel traps with attached tranquilizer tabs (Balser 1965). The automatic tracking equipment enabled simultaneous, semicontinuous recording of the location of most study animals. Data recorded on photographic film by the tracking system were extracted manually and placed on punch cards for computer processing. Because of the large amount of data, analysis was based on a sampling of fox movements at 10-minute intervals, whenever possible. Signal losses due to equipment limitations occurred periodically, with resultant minor gaps in the data, but these losses did not prevent me from obtaining an accurate record of fox movements.

Systematic aerial searches to locate red foxes and active rearing dens were conducted over each of the six township study areas during April 10–12, May 20–24, and June 16–18, 1969. Individual townships were flown at elevations of approximately 150 to 250 feet during periods of favorable light and weather conditions on transects spaced 0.25 mile apart. Dense habitats were circled for more complete checks. The same pilot and two observers participated in all flights. After each flight, landowners were contacted, and rearing dens were visited and partially or completely excavated. All food remains were collected for future identification. When pups were captured they were ear-tagged and released back into the dens.

Red fox dens were located by ground observations on Sand Lake Refuge during May 1968 and on Arrowwood Refuge during May and June 1969.

RESULTS

Fox Spatial Occupancy and the Social Group

An understanding of red fox spatial occupancy requires consideration of the social structure of the species. The red fox family, which forms the basic social group, typically consists of an adult male and female, and their pups from whelping to dispersal. Seton (1929) referred frequently to the fox family. Scott (1943:444–446) emphasized the importance of the fox family unit and recognized the tendency of individual families to occupy relatively exclusive ranges on the Moingona area in Iowa. Ables (1969) used radiotelemetry and documented the movements of two spatially separated but adjacent groups of red foxes on the 1,200-acre University of Wisconsin Arboretum, an area of mixed prairie, forest, and marshes, surrounded in part by a residential area.

Scott (1943:441) suggested that if "positive reaction to a particular place and familiarity with the environment are manifestations of territory then territorialism is characteristic of the red fox." Territorialism as used in this paper incorporates Scott's definition but also denotes exclusive occupation of specific areas by discrete families.

Unpublished results from the Cedar Creek study established that individual red fox social groups (families) mutually occupied well-defined, nonoverlapping, contiguous territories. Territorial integrity appeared to be maintained through some nonaggressive behavior mechanism. Boundaries of territories were not patrolled, yet there appeared to be an acute awareness of the presence and a mutual avoidance between family members holding adjacent territories.

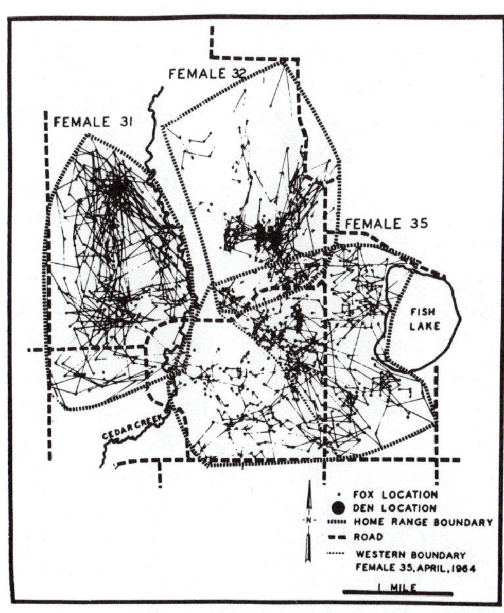

Fig. 2. Home ranges of three red foxes in east-central Minnesota during May 6–June 3, 1964. The lines between fox locations connect consecutive points in travel separated by no more than a 1-hour difference in time.

Territorial boundaries were well established and often conformed to natural physical boundaries such as roads, streams, and lake shores. Wet habitats such as marshes and swamps were avoided to varying degrees during the ice-free seasons but were used during the winter. All other habitats were occupied by foxes during all seasons. Except for the seasonal avoidance of wet habitats near territory boundaries, contiguous red fox territories encompassed nearly all land area.

Individual foxes generally traveled throughout much of the family territory each night. The home range of any adult family member during a 2-week period portrayed the entire family territory. Thus, individual home ranges and family territories were similar in their spatial attributes.

The territories of three fox families on the Cedar Creek area are shown in Fig. 2 by the home ranges of three adult females during May 6–June 3, 1964. The indicated areas of overlap between females 32 and 35 and females 31 and 35 were caused by minor changes in boundaries of home ranges during the study period, errors in locations of foxes due to limitations of the telemetry system and inaccuracies in recording data (Heezen and Tester 1967), and the method used to delineate the boundaries of the home range. At any specific time there was little overlap of the home ranges of these three females. The unoccupied area between females 31 and 32 was the result of a seasonal avoidance of swampy areas along Cedar Creek by female 32.

Females 31 and 32 whelped and were caring for pups, whereas female 35 was without pups. An adult male resided in each territory. An additional adult female (without pups) lived in the territory with female 32. Thus, three different types of social groups are represented in these data.

The inclusion of at least two adult females in a social group was also observed by Ables (1969), who documented the attachment of two female littermates to the natal area for over a year. Sheldon (1950) suggested the possibility of polygamy in red foxes and presented several instances of communal denning by two litters and one instance where a *barren* female was caught at an active rearing den. Murie (1961:152–154) reported observing one or more *supplemental* adults at three dens in Alaska. Three supplemental adult females were seen at one of Murie's dens, and the supplemental adult at another was a male.

Certain red fox spatial characteristics of relevance to this paper were evident from the findings at Cedar Creek and in the literature. Red foxes were highly territorial, and their territories were occupied by all members of the family. Territorial boundaries often conformed to natural physical boundaries, territories often encompassed areas avoided by foxes in their daily movements, and contiguous red fox territories sometimes occupied nearly all land area.

Territory Size and Population Densities

Few detailed descriptions of the size of red fox home ranges are found in the literature. Seton (1929:475) suggested that individual red foxes occupied areas not more than 5 miles in diameter but did not ordinarily range that far. Murie (1936:43) found a pair of red foxes occupying 1,200 acres of the George Reserve in Michigan, plus an undetermined area outside the Reserve. Scott (1943:441) concluded that on the Moingona area in Iowa, "an arc drawn on a one-mile radius would ordinarily circumscribe the movements of the resident individual, pair or family" of red foxes. The *daily range* of Michigan red foxes, determined by following their trails in the snow, was calculated as 1.4 square miles in southern Michigan (Arnold and Schofield 1956) and 2.8 square miles in northern Michigan (Schofield 1960). Storm (1965) found home ranges of 910 and 1,040 acres for two adult male red foxes in northern Illinois. Ables (1969) found the range of an adult male living in a *typical* Wisconsin farming area to be 1,460 acres, but the largest *range* of seven red foxes residing on the confined Wisconsin Arboretum was 400 acres. He suggested that the *richness* of the habitat, in terms of food abundance and availability, was a possible explanation for the small ranges. The Arboretum, however, may have represented an *island* of habitat in a suburban environment that confined the movements of the resident foxes.

The home range sizes for the Cedar Creek foxes shown in Fig. 2 were 2.5, 2.3, and 3.3 square miles for foxes 31, 32, and 35, respectively. The home range of female 35, however, nearly doubled in size between mid-April and mid-May 1964. The area to the west of the western boundary of female 35 was part of the territory of an adjacent family prior to late April 1964. On April 28 a radio-equipped adult male and six pups from this adjacent family were killed. After these deaths, female 35 and her mate rapidly expanded their territory to include part of the area previously occupied by this family. This major adjustment in the territory boundaries suggested that the mother of the six pups had either left the area or was dead.

As previously discussed, the size of the home range of individual red foxes was similar to the size of the territory of the family. Thus, these findings and the home range data previously cited suggested that red fox families tended to occupy territories approximately 1 to 3 square miles in size.

Low red fox population densities with numerous uninhabited areas developed in eastern North Dakota during the winter of 1968–69. Spring population densities on the six township study areas ranged from approximately two to seven families on each township. However, these families appeared to occupy distinct areas despite the low population densities. Red foxes have been abundant in these counties since the early 1940's and were estimated at 0.8 to 1.4 adult foxes per square mile during the spring of 1944 (North Dakota Game and Fish Dept. 1949). Their decline in 1968–69 occured during a severe winter when snow cover was optimum for ground and aerial hunting and red fox fur prices were high, ranging up to $13.50 each for unskinned foxes (S. H. Allen, personal communication).

The findings of this and other studies suggested that red foxes have an innate minimum and maximum spatial requirement that was manifested in their territoriality. Within these limits, territory size was a reflection of population density, which in turn was dependent on overall environmental conditions. As densities of red fox populations diminished, the size of territory of the remaining animals increased. Only when population densities fell below the level at which maximum territory size occurred did uninhabited areas appear in suitable habitat.

Den Ecology

Food remains that accumulated at red fox rearing dens have been used to determine the minimal numbers and the species and sex composition of certain prey used by adult foxes in feeding their pups. Several authors have shown that food remains at dens do not accurately represent the diet of pup foxes, because desirable small items may be totally consumed (Errington 1937, Scott 1947, North Dakota Game and Fish Dept. 1949, Drieslien 1967). The observed incidence of downy ducklings at dens has little meaning, because ducklings are easily consumed. Generally, however, pup foxes leave at least some feathers of adult waterfowl brought to the dens.

Whelping usually occurs during late March or April in eastern North Dakota (North Dakota Game and Fish Dept. 1949), and for 10–15 weeks the pups are confined in or near a sequence of several rearing dens. Scott (1943:444–446, 1947:438) and Scott and Klimstra (1955:13–15) found that individual litters used from three to seven different rearing dens.

Physical and behavioral characteristics of fox pups changed rapidly during the denning season. The denning season was divided into three periods: (1) from whelping to emergence of the pups from the underground burrows (pre-emergence), (2) when all pup activity was confined to the immediate den vicinity (confined-use), and (3) when pup activity was more widely dispersed in the den area and several dens were often used simultaneously (dispersed use). During each of these periods, one or more dens might be used by individual litters.

The three periods of den use lasted approximately 4 to 5 weeks each and were characterized by differences in pup feeding behavior. Pups were nursed during much of the pre-emergence period, and few food remains were present at dens. During the confined-use period, pups consumed whole food items, but the remains were often located underground, and complete excavation of the den was necessary for their retrieval. Most food remains occurred on the surface during the dispersed-use period, but the remains of many waterfowl brought to these dens may have been missed, because they were often almost totally consumed by the pups and the remains scattered over large areas.

Incidence and Abundance of Waterfowl at Rearing Dens

Aerial and ground observations showed that a minimum of 25 red fox families inhabited the six township study areas. The total number of dens noted during each of the three aerial survey periods, and afterwards confirmed as being active or used by the foxes earlier in the season, were 3, 12, and 21, respectively. Two additional dens were located by ground observers. Other studies previously cited showed that red foxes used from three to seven different rearing dens. The township families appeared to follow this same pattern of multiple den use. Thus, the 38 dens visited on the townships were only part of the total number of dens used by the 25 families known to occupy these areas. The total number of adult waterfowl found at the township dens is presented in Table 1. The three dens located during the first aerial survey period were not included since they

Table 1. Numbers of adult waterfowl as determined from remains at red fox rearing dens in eastern North Dakota.

Den Site	Number of Active Dens	Number of Families	Total Coots	Coots per Den	Total Ducks	Ducks per Den
Barnes County						
Township 1	7	3	7	1.0	51	7.3
Township 2	4	3	2	0.5	14	3.5
Subtotal	11	6	9	0.8	65	5.9
Stutsman County						
Township 3	6	4	3	0.5	75	12.5
Township 4	2	2	1	0.5	7	3.5
Subtotal	8	6	4	0.5	82	10.2
Kidder County						
Township 5	9	6	2	0.2	13	1.4
Township 6	7	6	1	0.1	12	1.7
Subtotal	16	12	3	0.2	25	1.6
Total or average	35	24	16	0.5	172	4.9

were visited during the period of pre-emergence, when few or no food remains were found at dens.

The total number of adult waterfowl utilized by all the families under study on the six townships was unknown. These data represented only a partial count because (1) the identification methods provided minimal counts on the number of waterfowl represented in retrieved remains, (2) many rearing dens used by the families were doubtless not found or were not completely excavated, (3) food remains at the dens represented only food items brought to the dens and did not include food that was consumed or cached elsewhere by the adults, and (4) the denning season terminated prior to the end of the waterfowl nesting season.

Data gathered between May 20 and June 17, 1969, in a study by R. E. Stewart and H. A. Kantrud (personal communication), indicated dabbling duck densities of approximately 32 and 69 pairs per square mile for larger areas of the Drift Prairie and Coteau du Missouri, which included the Barnes County and Stutsman County townships, respectively. Applicable density data for waterfowl were not available for the Kidder County townships on the Outwash Plain. Stewart and Kantrud also found that dabbling ducks represented 95, 83, and 91 percent of the total duck population in the three regions encompassing the Barnes, Stutsman, and Kidder county townships, respectively.

The average number of ducks per den for the Barnes and Stutsman county townships (Table 1) was approximately proportionate to the corresponding duck population densities. The average number of ducks per den (4.9) for the combined data from all six townships was similar to previous findings in 1943–47, when 5.0 ducks per den were identified at 62 dens in eastern North Dakota (North Dakota Game and Fish Dept. 1949).

Differences in red fox utilization of waterfowl between the Barnes and Stutsman county townships with high waterfowl densities and the Kidder County townships with relatively low waterfowl densities were also reflected in the total number of dens with duck remains and the maximum number of ducks at individual dens. Duck remains were found at 18 of 19 dens on the four high-density townships during the confined-use and dispersed-use denning periods and at only 9 of 16 dens on the two low-density townships. The maximum number of ducks found at a single den on the low-density townships was six. Eight dens on the high-density areas contained remains of 8 to 33 ducks.

Successive dens used by six litters on the high-waterfowl-density townships showed accumulated totals of 1, 12, 18, 19, 24, and 27 ducks for each litter. In no instance, however, were visits made to all of the dens used by a litter. Strangely enough, the family for which only one duck was found lived adjacent to a large marsh with an abundance of waterfowl. Although the foxes appeared to use ducks in proportion to their abundance, no diving ducks were found in the food remains at dens. Diving ducks occurred in all areas, and their nonuse by foxes is ascribed to their almost totally aquatic nesting and feeding habits, which made them unavailable to foxes. The relatively high vulnerability of dabbling ducks is discussed in the following section.

American coots represented 12, 5, and 11 percent of the total waterfowl remains at dens in the Barnes, Stutsman, and Kidder county townships, respectively (Table 1). Stewart and Kantrud (personal communication) found that coots represented 6, 27, and 4 percent of the total waterfowl in the regions encompassing these same townships, respectively. The abundance of coots at dens was lowest in the Stutsman County townships, where their actual number and their population composition were apparently highest (Table 1). These results appear inconsistent with the nonuse of diving ducks by foxes, since coots also were almost totally aquatic. Coots, however, unlike diving ducks, were frequently observed walking on the shores of many marshes, where they may have been vulnerable to predation by foxes.

Red foxes utilized a variety of prey species (Errington 1937, Scott 1943, 1947, Scott and Klimstra 1955) and thus were not dependent on waterfowl for their survival. Their utilization of waterfowl was dependent not only on the abundance of vulnerable waterfowl but on the abundance of other vulnerable prey and the predatory behavior of individual foxes. In Barnes and Stutsman counties, waterfowl were undoubtedly the most abundant, large, wild prey species. Meadow mouse (*Microtus pennsylvanicus*) populations were abnormally high in the spring of 1969, and they were heavily used by the foxes in all six townships. They may have buffered red fox utilization of waterfowl.

Species and Sex Composition of Dabbling Ducks at Rearing Dens

The species and sex composition of adult ducks found at the township dens are given in Table 2. The sex ratios of ducks on the townships were unknown, but Bellrose et al. (1961:405–408) determined that males usually predominated among adults in most duck species. It was evident from these data that red fox utilization of adult waterfowl during the nesting season was directed toward female dabbling ducks. The fact that females made up 84 percent of all ducks that were identified as to sex, and that females never comprised less than 75 percent of any single species, clearly indicated selective predation on females.

The physical condition and cause of death of the waterfowl utilized by the township foxes could not be determined. No nonpredator mortality, however, such as *roadkills* was known to occur in sufficient magnitude to account for the number of ducks found at the rearing dens. Agricultural practices, particularly haying, were known to inflict losses on nesting hens, but haying was just beginning in mid-June when the last den surveys were being made. There

Table 2. Species and sex composition of adult ducks at red fox rearing dens in six townships in eastern North Dakota.

	Number of Ducks (May 26–June 4)	Species Composition (percent)	Number of Ducks (June 16–July 9)	Species Composition (percent)	Number of Sex-determined Ducks	Female Ducks (percent)
Blue-winged teal	19	26	27	32	39	85
Pintail	28	38	18	21	43	79
Shoveler	10	13	13	15	11	100
Mallard	9	12	9	11	16	87
Gadwall	3	4	12	14	13	78
Green-winged teal (*Anas carolinensis*)	2	3	5	6	4	75
American widgeon (*Mareca americana*)	3	4	1	1	3	100
Total or average	74	100	85	100	129	84

was also little evidence of remains from waterfowl utilized by other animals.

Sowls (1955:83, 86–87), comparing the nesting chronology of prairie dabbling ducks, showed that mallards (*Anas platyrhynchos*) and pintails (*Anas acuta*) were early nesters, blue-winged teal (*Anas discors*) and shovelers (*Spatula clypeata*) were mid- to late-season nesters, and gadwalls (*Anas strepera*) were late-season nesters. This trend in nest chronology was reflected in the relative species composition of ducks found at the township dens during the sampling periods of May 26–June 4 and June 16–July 9 (Table 2). These differences in species composition were minimized, since many of the dens visited during the late sampling period undoubtedly contained remains from earlier periods.

The high incidence of female dabbling ducks and their change in species composition in accordance with their nesting chronology suggested that most of the waterfowl found at the rearing dens represented selective predation by red foxes on nesting hens.

Den Location in Relation to Waterfowl Predation

Individual red fox movement was distributed throughout the family territory, but certain behavioral and life history events resulted in specific areas becoming focal points of activity. Foremost among these areas were the active rearing dens. The concentration of movement around rearing dens is illustrated in Fig. 2 by the movement patterns of foxes 31 and 32 on the Cedar Creek area.

Since occupied rearing dens were focal points of red fox travel, the probability of foxes encountering nesting waterfowl near the dens would seem greater than in most areas within the territory. Thus, two areas of similar habitat and similar waterfowl densities in the same fox territory might experience different predation rates, depending on their proximity to the rearing den. This factor became increasingly important during the late stages of the denning season when pup movement was distributed throughout the den area.

Natal den sites may be located anywhere within the red fox territory, but successively used dens were often in the natal area. Red fox dens frequently had a history of previous use, and the site selection appeared unrelated to prey abundance. The locations of the 38 active rearing dens on the six townships were 35 on pasture and idle lands and 3 on cropland. The high use of pastured and idle lands for denning occurred even on the Barnes County townships that were almost completely cultivated.

The distribution of occupied rearing dens

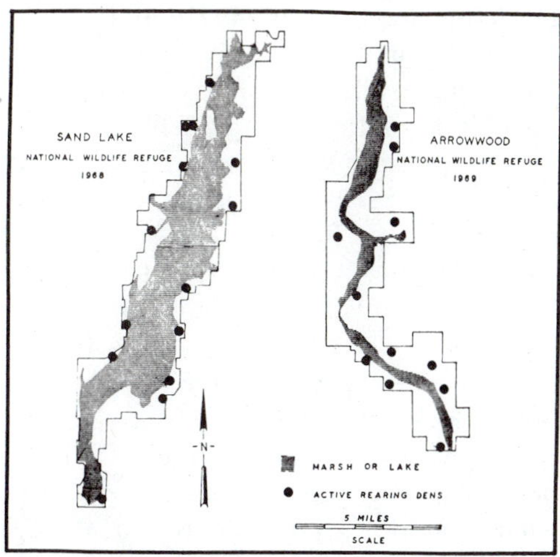

Fig. 3. Location of active red fox rearing dens on Sand Lake National Wildlife Refuge, South Dakota; and Arrowwood National Wildlife Refuge, North Dakota.

on the Sand Lake and Arrowwood national wildlife refuges is shown in Fig. 3. These data showed a concentration of red fox dens in good waterfowl nesting habitat as a result of certain land features and land-use practices. The refuge lands were managed as wildlife habitat and were subject to relatively little human disturbance, whereas the surrounding lands were intensively cultivated and subjected to greater disturbance. The James River flowing through both refuges formed a natural boundary separating the foxes into subpopulations on each side of the river. The refuge lands also had an abundance of well-drained slopes that provided good denning sites. These topographical features and land-use practices resulted in an apparent selection of the refuge lands as denning areas and a spacing of occupied dens within the refuge boundaries. No systematic searches were made to locate all dens on either refuge, and it is assumed that some were missed. The location of these dens concentrated fox movement on the refuge lands and may have resulted in considerably more predation on nesting waterfowl than would have occurred if the dens had been located outside the refuge boundaries.

DISCUSSION

Red fox–waterfowl interactions in the prairie wetland region result from the annual influx of migratory waterfowl into areas already occupied by spatially distributed red fox family groups. Thus, unlike many predator–prey relationships, an annual cycle of renewed encounters occurs between foxes and waterfowl. Although red foxes (a terrestrial species) and waterfowl (an aquatic group) occupy different environmental niches during much of the nesting season, dabbling ducks utilize terrestrial habitat for egg-laying and incubation. During this period, nesting hens appear quite vulnerable to predation by foxes and, as shown in Table 1, are used for food.

Red fox predation on waterfowl is related in part to fox population densities. The territorial characteristics of the red fox family group result in complete occupancy of nearly all land areas in the prairie wetland region during periods of moderate to high population densities and the occurrence of uninhabited areas during periods of low densities. However, even during periods of high fox population densities, individual waterfowl engaged in egg-laying and incubation may be exposed to predation by only a single family of foxes. Areas of good habitat that concentrate nesting waterfowl may also be utilized by only the red fox family occupying that area as part of its territory.

During periods of low red fox population densities, predation on individual sites is highly variable, depending upon whether the sites are located inside or outside of territories occupied by foxes. Within territories occupied by foxes, predation may be of similar intensity to that occurring during periods of moderate fox population densities, whereas outside the territory, no predation from foxes ordinarily occurs unless it is from transient or displaced individuals. Thus, as was observed on the township study areas, although predation by individual red fox families appears substantial, the impact on the total township waterfowl populations was relatively minor because much of the area was unoccupied by foxes.

Red fox predation on waterfowl occurs as the result of encounters between family members and vulnerable waterfowl. Red fox movement within the territory serves two fundamental needs: to maintain the territory and to simultaneously fulfill the necessities of life. Thus, all movement by foxes must not be interpreted as representing or being motivated by hunting behavior. Red foxes travel in and occupy areas not normally used for hunting, and predation may occur in these areas as a result of a circumstantial encounter with vulnerable prey.

CONCLUSIONS

In considering the impact of red foxes on nesting waterfowl, a careful distinction must be made between waterfowl survival and waterfowl abundance. Waterfowl have built-in mechanisms that favor survival in areas of suitable habitat. Thus, renesting by waterfowl compensates in part for egg losses; homing and pioneering are factors in repopulation of depleted areas; and large clutch sizes provide an annual population increment to compensate for various mortality factors.

Red fox population densities appear regulated by inherent species characteristics and overall environmental conditions. Areas with little or no use are often included in fox territories, and uninhabited areas develop between territories during periods of low population densities. Hunting characteristics of individual foxes and the abundance and availability of other prey species possibly are reflected in variable predation rates on nesting waterfowl. These characteristics favor survival of waterfowl in areas occupied by red foxes.

A high priority objective of most waterfowl management programs is to maintain or increase waterfowl populations for recreational use. The loss of adult hen dabbling ducks to foxes affects the annual waterfowl production potential of an area because it occurs at that time of the year when waterfowl populations are at their lowest levels and losses are largely noncompensatory. Furthermore, red fox predation is not restricted to adult waterfowl but also occurs on waterfowl eggs and ducklings. The significance of these losses in terms of waterfowl abundance and the harvestable surplus is unknown but may prove to be substantial in some areas.

Red foxes have considerable economic values and sporting qualities that rank them high as fur and game species. Reduction in fox population densities as a means to alleviate predation has biological, economic, and moral implications. In any attempts to reduce population densities, consideration must be given to the social and spatial characteristics of the species that under *normal* fox population densities result in the rapid inclusion of uninhabited areas into existing territories. Certainly much more information is needed to understand fox–waterfowl relationships before any measures are employed to prevent red fox predation on waterfowl.

LITERATURE CITED

ABLES, E. D. 1969. Home-range studies of red foxes (*Vulpes vulpes*). J. Mammal. 50(1): 108–120.

ARNOLD, D. A., AND R. D. SCHOFIELD. 1956 (1955). Home range and dispersal of Michigan red foxes. Michigan Acad. Sci., Arts, and Letters Papers 41(pt. 2):91–97.

BALSER, D. S. 1965. Tranquilizer tabs for capturing wild carnivores. J. Wildl. Mgmt. 29 (3):438–442.

BELLROSE, F. C., T. G. SCOTT, A. S. HAWKINS, AND J. B. LOW. 1961. Sex ratios and age ratios in North American ducks. Illinois Nat. Hist. Survey Bull. 27(art. 6):391–474.

BRADLEY, E., L. R. PETRI, AND D. G. ADOLPHSON. 1963. Geology and ground water resources of Kidder County, North Dakota. Part III. Ground water and chemical quality of water. North Dakota Geol. Survey Bull. 36. 38pp.

COCHRAN, W. W., D. W. WARNER, J. R. TESTER, AND V. B. KUECHLE. 1965. Automatic radiotracking system for monitoring animal movements. BioScience 15(2):98–100.

DRIESLIEN, R. L. 1967. Fox-prey relationships in eastern South Dakota. M.S. Thesis. South Dakota State Univ. 89pp.

ERRINGTON, P. L. 1937. Food habits of Iowa red foxes during a drought summer. Ecology 18 (1):53–61.

HEEZEN, K. L., AND J. R. TESTER. 1967. Evaluation of radio-tracking by triangulation with special reference to deer movements. J. Wildl. Mgmt. 31(1):124–141.

HUXEL, C. J., JR., AND L. R. PETRI. 1965. Geology and ground water resources of Stutsman County, North Dakota. Part III. Ground water and its chemical quality. North Dakota Geol. Survey Bull. 41. 58pp.

KELLY, T. E. 1966. Geology and ground water resources Barnes County, North Dakota. Part III. Ground water resources. North Dakota Geol. Survey Bull. 43. 67pp.

MURIE, A. 1936. Following fox trails. Univ. of Michigan Museum of Zool. Misc. Publ. 32. 45pp.

———. 1961. A naturalist in Alaska. The Devin–Adair Company, New York. 302pp.

NORTH DAKOTA GAME AND FISH DEPARTMENT. 1949. The red fox in North Dakota. North Dakota Game and Fish Dept. P–R Rept., Project 7–R. 31pp.

SCHOFIELD, R. D. 1960. A thousand miles of fox trails in Michigan's ruffed grouse range. J. Wildl. Mgmt. 24(4):432–434.

SCOTT, T. G. 1943. Some food coactions of the northern plains red fox. Ecol. Monographs 13(4):427–479.

———. 1947. Comparative analysis of red fox feeding trends on two central Iowa areas. Iowa State Coll. Agr. Expt. Sta. Research Bull. 353:427–487.

———, AND W. D. KLIMSTRA. 1955. Red foxes and a declining prey population. Southern Illinois Univ. Monograph Ser. 1. 123pp.

SETON, E. T. 1929. Lives of game animals. Vol. 1. Doubleday Company, Garden City, New York. 640pp.

SHELDON, W. G. 1950. Denning habits and home range of red foxes in New York State. J. Wildl. Mgmt. 14(1):33–42.

SOWLS, L. K. 1955. Prairie ducks: a study of their behavior, ecology and management. The Stackpole Company, Harrisburg, Pennsylvania. 193pp.

STORM, G. L. 1965. Movements and activities of foxes as determined by radio-tracking. J. Wildl. Mgmt. 29(1):1–13.

Received for publication April 30, 1971.

THE ECOLOGICAL RELATIONS OF PIKE, *ESOX LUCIUS* L., AND WATERFOWL[1]

VICTOR E. F. SOLMAN,[2] Department of Zoology, University of Toronto

The interrelations of waterfowl and fish have been discussed in the literature for many years. The present study deals with the relation only from the standpoint of pike predation on young waterfowl. In this connection observations were made on certain aspects of the life histories of both pike and waterfowl, as well as a more detailed study of the food habits of the pike.

METHOD

During the summers of 1940 and 1941, four months were spent by the author in studying the relations of pike and waterfowl on the water areas of the Saskatchewan River delta. During this period over 3,000 pike were caught and determinations of age, sex, length, weight and stomach contents were made.

Pike held in confinement were fed specimens of ducklings, chicks, young grebes, young terns, shrews, mice, pieces of muskrat flesh, goldeyes and perch. The pike were examined at intervals after feeding in order to determine the rate of digestion of different types of food.

By intensive fishing in one body of water data concerning the total pike population were obtained. Observations on the feeding habits of the pike were made by using wooden and metal lures armed with multiple hooks.

A study was made of waterfowl brood sizes, nesting habits, time of broods reaching the water and susceptibility to destruction by pike.

Information regarding the distribution of pike and of pike predation on young waterfowl was received from 207 observers at selected points in the Prairie Provinces in answer to questionnaires.

PHYSIOGRAPHY OF THE AREA STUDIED

The field investigation was carried out on six water areas on the lower Saskatchewan River delta, southeast of The Pas, Man. This delta (Fig. 1) comprises an area about 90 miles long from northwest to southeast and with an average width of 35 miles. A large part of this area is flooded by water from the Saskatchewan River during periods of high water, which may occur in spring, midsummer or at both times.

The average altitude of the area is about 835 feet above sea level, with a gradual slope downward from northwest to southeast. The forest cover is limited to the higher regions and is not subject to flooding except on rare occasions (Fig. 2).

The depth of water in the channels and lakes of the area varies with the season by as much as 10 feet, according to the level of the Saskatchewan River, and local precipitation and evaporation. The average annual precipitation for the area, as recorded by the meteorological station at The Pas, Man., amounts to 15.44 inches, of which 4.49 inches occur during the winter as snow. The temperature varies between −54.0°F and 100.6°F with an annual average of 30°F.

The water supply of the area is provid-

---

[1] Originally published in Ecology 26(2):157–170, 1945.

[2] Present address: Migratory Birds Branch, Canadian Wildlife Service, Place Vincent Massey, Hull, Quebec K1A 0E7.

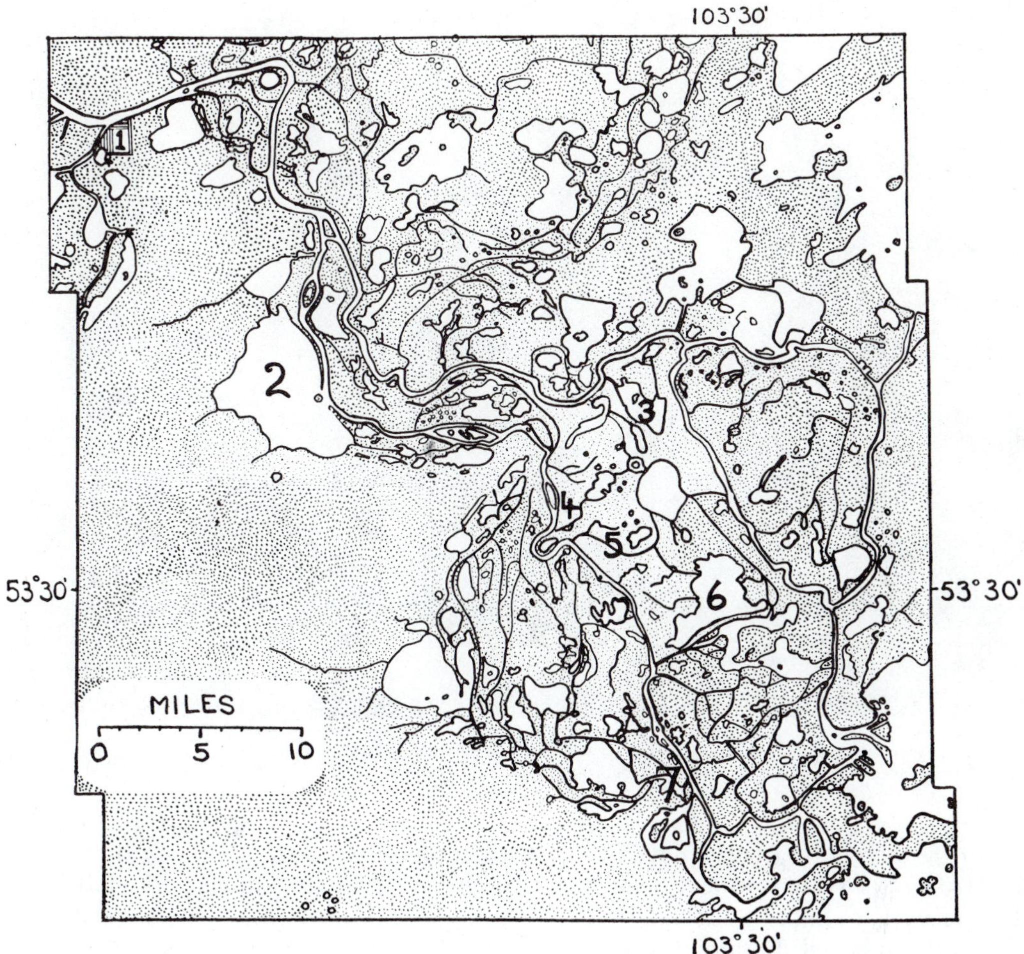

Fig. 1. Map of the Lower Saskatchewan River Delta. Clear areas—water; stippled areas—woods and marsh. 1. The Pas, Manitoba; 2. Kelsey Lake; 3. Red Rock Lake; 4. Saskatchewan River; 5. Baptizing Creek; 6. Littlefish Lake; 7. Willow Creek.

ed by the Saskatchewan River in addition to local precipitation. The volume of water passing down the river is in the order of 60,000 cu. ft. per sec. during the spring period of high water and falls to less than 50 per cent of this amount during the low water periods of late summer and early autumn. The water is turbid at all times, the turbidity increasing at times of increased volume of flow.

Water levels are controlled in many of the lakes of the area to create conditions more favourable for the production of muskrats, *Ondatra zibethica* L., and in these the water becomes clear owing to the settling of the suspended silt. The temperature of the water varies from a winter minimum of the order of 32 to 39°F under the ice to a summer maximum of about 75°F for the Saskatchewan River and a higher maximum (about 84°F) in the shallower lakes.

Fig. 2. Aerial view of a small portion of Saskatchewan River delta showing Saskatchewan River in the foreground and several small lakes and dry lake beds in the background.

During the course of the investigation in 1940 and 1941 six water areas were studied with respect to the relations of pike and waterfowl. Data on these water areas are given in Table 1 and the location of the areas is shown in Fig. 1.

As seen from Fig. 2 the banks of the river channels in the delta are lined to a large extent by deciduous and evergreen trees while the lakes are usually surrounded by small deciduous trees and shrubs and several species of emergent aquatic plants. Since these water areas are all in connection with the Saskatchewan River their flora and fauna are almost identical.

Table 1. Size and depth of six water areas studied on the lower Saskatchewan River delta, Manitoba.

Name of area	Approximate area (acres)	Width (feet)	Depth (feet)
Littlefish Lake	6,600		4
Kelsey Lake	17,700		2
Red Rock Lake	2,300		6
Baptizing Creek	18	30	3
Willow Creek		200	5
Saskatchewan River		800	15

DISTRIBUTION OF BREEDING DUCKS IN THE PRAIRIE PROVINCES

Ducks have been observed to nest at almost all water areas in the Prairie Provinces that are present at the time of the spring influx of ducks from the southern wintering grounds. The deep lakes of the

Precambrian regions of southern Manitoba and of northern Manitoba, Saskatchewan and Alberta attract relatively few waterfowl on account of their comparative lack of waterfowl food and nesting cover, but with these few exceptions, any water area, permanent or temporary, which provides food and nesting cover, is occupied by ducks during the breeding season. This applies to small temporary ponds and water-filled ditches and sloughs as well as to large lakes and river systems. Variations in temperature, salinity and pH of the water seem to have no effect on the nesting of waterfowl except as such factors may influence food and nesting cover.

This almost ubiquitous nesting of waterfowl throughout the Prairie Provinces is one factor assuring their survival, since no one environmental factor except absence of water is capable of causing an extensive reduction of the population. Although large areas have suffered from drought in the past, only a portion of the duck breeding range has been rendered untenable at any one time.

Owing to their more or less uniform water supply, the great river deltas of the Prairie Provinces and the Northwest Territories are now very important duck breeding areas since much of what was formerly breeding area has become useless through lack of water. The combined annual average duck population (all ages) of the Saskatchewan and Athabaska deltas has amounted to about 14,500,000 for each of six years (1936–41 inclusive) according to Ducks Unlimited (Canada).

A great deal of the decrease in water areas during the past forty years can be attributed to the tremendous increase in the acreage of land devoted to the production of cereal crops during that time. The total acreage has increased from approximately 3,500,000 acres in 1900 to over 40,000,000 acres in 1940; an elevenfold increase. In addition to destroying waterfowl breeding grounds directly, the cereal crops, by removing more water from the soil than the prairie grasses they replaced (Briggs and Shantz 1913, Bailey 1940), have contributed to a lowering of the water table. The continued growth of cereal grains has depleted the supply of humus in the soil (Shutt 1925) and this has also caused a lowering of the water table by allowing a more rapid run-off of the surface water through the decreased water-holding capacity of the soil. A lowered water table causes surface water areas to dry up or what is even worse, in terms of waterfowl losses, to become temporary in nature.

In addition to the large amount of water utilized in agricultural production, there has been a decrease in the annual amount of precipitation on the prairie areas where the great increase in agriculture took place, as shown by the precipitation records of the Meteorological Service of Canada.

The reduction in available nesting area on the prairies thus brought about is probably the greatest factor enhancing the importance of the northern areas as duck breeding areas.

Since the large deltas of the Athabaska River (Alberta), the Saskatchewan River (Manitoba) and the Slave River (North West Territories) and to a lesser extent of the Red River (Manitoba) are beyond the agricultural areas, crows, magpies and other waterfowl predators characteristic of the prairie agricultural areas are almost absent. These delta areas, however, with their shallow lakes and channels, and abundant plant and animal food are the home of large numbers of pike. Since these delta areas have become more important as waterfowl producers on account of the reduction of the prairie breeding areas, the predation of pike on young waterfowl has increased in importance.

DISTRIBUTION OF PIKE IN THE PRAIRIE PROVINCES

The pike has a very wide distribution. Weed (1927) reports the distribution being circumpolar north of 40° N. latitude. Williams (1922) and Preble (1908) report the pike as occurring in the Mackenzie River north to the Arctic Ocean. It occurs throughout the three Prairie Provinces from the Northwest Territories to the United States, being more widely distributed in the east than in the west, and probably reaches its greatest abundance in terms of numbers per unit water area on the great deltas of the Athabaska and Saskatchewan Rivers in Alberta and Manitoba respectively.

Pike frequent shallow weedy waters and are considered by some authors as being typical of this type of habitat (Dymond 1926), often being found to be the most abundant fish in areas where they occur. Pike are not found in the saline lakes of the Prairie Provinces according to Moore (unpublished). Pike weighing as much as 49 pounds have been reported by Chambers (1896) but the largest taken on the delta of the Saskatchewan River by the author weighed 14¾ pounds. Ross (1940) reports a pike weighing 20½ pounds from the delta of the Athabaska River.

LIFE HISTORY OF THE PIKE

The spawning of the pike is well described in the literature by Kendall (1917), Embody (unpublished), Rawson (1932) and McNamara (1937). Bajkov and Shortt (1939) stress the fact that on the Saskatchewan River delta at least, the pike spawn in very shallow water, the depth often being only a few inches. Rawson reported spawning in Lake Waskesiu, Saskatchewan as occuring between May 1 and 15. Spawning was not observed by the author but it is probable that it occurred during the first weeks of May since the latitude and other conditions of the area are almost identical with the location in which Rawson observed spawning.

Rate of Growth.—The young pike hatch about May 25 (Rawson 1932) and grow rapidly. Several young pike were captured during the investigation and the remains of others were recovered from the stomachs of larger pike. The lengths and approximate ages of these small pike are recorded in Table 2.

Of the 3,001 pike examined during the investigation scales were removed from 1,702 and these were used to determine the ages of the pike. The results of these age determinations are summarized in Table 3.

It will be noted that female fish were longer than male fish in the age groups from 3 to 8 years inclusive. The difference is significant as shown by the "*t*" test of Fisher (1936).

Food Habits.—The food of the pike in the early stages of its development has been well described by Embody (unpublished) and Rawson (1932). The food of the adult pike has been studied by many authors including Day (1880–84), Robertson (1886–88), Marshall and Gilbert (1904), Forbes and Richardson (1908), Clemens, Dymond and Bigelow (1924), McNamara (1937) and Allen (1939).

In connection with the special food habits referred to in this paper some previous work has been done. Bajkov and Shortt (1939) report that two percent of the pike they examined contained young ducks while 0.6 per cent contained young

Table 2. Date of capture, approximate age and length of pike fry from water areas on the Saskatchewan River delta, 1940 and 1941.

Date	Year	Location	Approximate age (days)	Number	Average length (inches)
21 to 25 June	1940	Littlefish Lake	30	2	2.50
4 to 5 July	1940	Littlefish Lake	45	6	2.84
6 July	1941	Baptizing Creek	47	1	3.75
7 to 14 July	1940	Littlefish Lake	50	8	3.82
11 to 23 July	1941	Willow Creek	57	6	4.04
25 to 29 July	1940	Red Rock Lake	65	3	6.08
5 to 8 Aug	1940	Red Rock Lake	75	3	6.75

muskrats. They stressed the fact that pike between two and four pounds in weight were responsible for most of this predation. About 500 pike were examined in this study.

Ross (1940) reported that of 1,758 pike he examined 13 or 0.74 per cent contained young ducks, 9 or 0.51 per cent contained young coots and 2 or 0.16 per cent contained young muskrats. He also pointed out that pike 22 to 27 inches long and weighing from 2½ to 4 pounds were responsible for the greater part of the predation (77 per cent) that he observed. Both Ross and Bajkov and Shortt noted that young diving ducks were found more often in pike stomachs than young surface feeding ducks. Predation on young waterfowl was reported from 44 per cent of the areas in which pike were reported by a series of 207 observers scattered over the Prairie Provinces.

In working on the food habits of the pike on the delta of the Saskatchewan River during the summers of 1940 and 1941 a few observations were made by the author on the methods of feeding of the pike. The feeding appeared to be based to a large extent on visual stimuli as suggested by Embody, though the range of vision of the pike appeared to be limited to about 10 to 15 feet, judging by observations made in the clear water of one area studied during the summer of 1941. Here a pike ignored a brightly painted wooden lure if it passed at a distance greater than 10 to 15 feet in front of the fish, even though this operation was repeated several times in rapid succession. The same fish would almost invariably seize the lure if it passed within 2 to 8 feet of it. This observation was repeated at least 30 times during the course of the summer. Smitt (1892) reports that the prey is seized crosswise, held until dead and then swallowed head first. This seizing of the prey crosswise was noted in the use of the lure as all 54

Table 3. Age, sex and length relation of pike from the Saskatchewan River delta (1940 and 1941).

Age (years)	No.	Male average length (inches)	No.	Female average length (inches)
1	3	4.00		
2			1	8.25
3	541	14.79	516	14.92
4	142	19.21	106	20.04
5	135	21.36	41	22.35
6	84	22.54	29	23.69
7	33	22.97	25	26.24
8	14	25.36	15	28.82
9	1	33.00	6	29.54
10			4	31.44
11			2	36.37
12			2	35.50
13			1	39.00
14			1	37.00
Total	953		749	
Grand total	1,702			

Table 4. Sex ratios, food habits and parasites of the pike from six water areas (1940 and 1941).

	Littlefish Lake	Kelsey Lake	Red Rock Lake	Baptizing Creek	Willow Creek	Sask. River	Total
Sex of pike							
Male	1,048	40	185	292	36	15	1,616
Female	1,072	32	99	141	25	13	1,382
Number of pike with empty stomachs							
Male	762	29	74	191	38	12	1,006
Female	748	24	40	83	25	7	927
Number of pike containing:							
Waterfowl	9		12	13			34
Mammals				6			6
Amphipods	399		81	1			481
Crayfish		12	1		5		18
Insect remains	173		27	9			204
Fish remains	32	7	54	31	34	6	164
Leeches	54		40	12			106
Digested material				97	8		105
Misc. items	30						30
Cestode worms	2		22	31		2	57
Nematode worms			38	17		1	56

of the fish taken on the wooden lure became impaled on the central hooks of the lure rather than on the tail hooks. The idea of visual stimuli for feeding was supported further by the fact that a brightly painted wooden lure attracted pike at a greater distance than a dark coloured one, other conditions being similar, and a chromium plated metal lure was more effective than a brightly painted one. In almost all cases that were observed, the pike swam from a position behind the lure to one beside it immediately before seizing it; and then turning sharply toward it, seized the lure at about the middle of its length.

During the 1940 study, 2,353 pike were taken in gill nets of 2½, 4 and 4½ inch mesh. During the 1941 study 546 pike were taken in gill nets of 2½, 3 and 3½ inch mesh and 102 were taken by angling. The pike were opened immediately following capture and an examination made of stomach contents.

Qualitative data on stomach contents were recorded during the 1940 study while during 1941 quantitative data were recorded in addition. A summary of the food items found in the pike is given in Table 4.

The weight of individual stomach contents varied from 0.1 to 368 g, the heaviest single items being fish. Of the 648 stomachs examined in 1941, 265 contained food material. Of the number containing food 182 stomachs contained food that could be classified and weighed accurately. A summary of the contents of the 182 stomachs is given in Table 5.

The average weight of food per stomach was nearly three times as great in female as in male pike (Table 5). This difference in amount of food per stomach may explain the observed difference in rate of growth of male and female pike as shown in Table 3 since pike with larger quantities of food in their stomachs would have more available for assimilation. The average lengths of the pike of which the stomach contents are summa-

Table 5. Average weight of food per stomach which contained food in different areas on the Saskatchewan River delta, 1941.

Location	Average weight of food per stomach (g)			Number of stomachs in which food was found		
	Male	Female	Total	Male	Female	Total
Red Rock Lake	9.0	8.6	8.9	59	26	85
Baptizing Creek	8.9	18.5	13.0	38	28	66
Saskatchewan River	6.2	148.9	91.3	4	6	10
Willow Creek	5.8	5.5	5.7	10	11	21
Average	8.6	23.8	13.9	111	71	182

rized in Table 5 were 19.58 inches for the male pike and 20.72 inches for the female pike. The small difference in average size of the male and female pike is in marked contrast to the 1:3 difference in average quantity of food per stomach.

The details of the young waterfowl found in pike stomachs during the investigation are summarized in Table 6.

As seen from Table 6 pike between 19 and 30 inches (inclusive) in length comprised 71.5 per cent (25 out of 35) of the fish which had eaten young waterfowl (32 out of 42 young waterfowl eaten or 76.2 per cent of the total) while representing only 23.3 per cent (620 out of 2,658) of the total number of pike examined that were large enough to be capable of eating young waterfowl. No young waterfowl were eaten by pike less than 14 inches in length (Table 6) and this excludes from the above total 343 pike that were examined but were less than 14 inches long.

Of the 34 pike which were found to contain young waterfowl 19 were females. Female pike were responsible for 56 per cent of the predation on young waterfowl while comprising only 47.8 per cent of the total number of pike that were large enough (over 14 inches in length) to prey on young waterfowl.

The availability of young waterfowl was different on the different areas studied and Table 7 summarizes these differences on the three areas on which large numbers of pike were examined.

Of the 2,658 pike taken during the study that were large enough to prey on young waterfowl 29 or 1.08 per cent had eaten young ducklings and 5 or 0.20 per cent had eaten young coots and grebes. In a number of cases pike were found which contained more than one young waterfowl at one time as shown in the following list:

29 pike (85 per cent) each contained 1 young waterfowl.
3 pike (9 per cent) each contained 2 young waterfowl.
1 pike (3 per cent) contained 3 young waterfowl.
1 pike (3 per cent) contained 4 young waterfowl.

From the above list it is seen that 15 per cent of the pike that contained young waterfowl contained more than one, or an average of 2.6 young waterfowl per pike.

The age and species of young waterfowl found in pike stomachs during the investigation are summarized in Tables 8 and 9.

From Table 8 it is seen that 45 per cent (19 out of 42) of the young waterfowl found in pike stomachs were less than one week old. This is probably because the small waterfowl tend to spend most

Table 6. Length, weight, sex and age of pike caught during 1940 and 1941 that contained young waterfowl.

		(Pike)						
			Weight					
Pike no.	No., age and kind of waterfowl	Length in.	Lb.	Oz.	Sex	Age years	Date	Location
94	1 Canvasback (under 1 wk.) 2 Redheads (under 1 wk.)	19½	2	4	M	5	18/6/40	Littlefish Lake
143	1 Canvasback (under 1 wk.)	22½	3	7	F	4	20/6/40	Littlefish Lake
237	1 Unidentifiable (age unknown)	14¾	0	14	M	3	21/6/40	Littlefish Lake
314	1 Canvasback (under 1 wk.)	21	2	12	F	4	22/6/40	Littlefish Lake
344	1 Teal (2–3 wk.)	22¾	2	14	M	4	25/6/40	Littlefish Lake
345	1 Redhead (under 1 wk.)	15¾	1	3	M	3	25/6/40	Littlefish Lake
1444	1 Canvasback (age unknown)	15¼	1	1	M		10/7/40	Littlefish Lake
1528	1 Lesser Scaup (age unknown)	16½	1	3	M		11/7/40	Littlefish Lake
1722	1 Lesser Scaup (about 2 wk.)	16¼	1	3	F		12/7/40	Littlefish Lake
2212	1 Diver (about 2 wk.)	24½	3	13	F	5	28/7/40	Red Rock Lake
2213	1 Ruddy (under 1 wk.)	21¾	2	11	M	5	29/7/40	Red Rock Lake
2220	1 Baldpate (age unknown)	31½	8	2	F	8	29/7/40	Red Rock Lake
2243	1 Unidentifiable (age unknown)	24	3	1	F	4	29/7/40	Red Rock Lake
2244	1 Lesser Scaup (age unknown)	23¼	3	8	F	5	29/7/40	Red Rock Lake
2253	1 Diver (3–4 wk.)	24¾	3	12	M	4	30/7/40	Red Rock Lake
2279	1 Unidentifiable (age unknown)	23	4	0	F	7	5/8/40	Red Rock Lake
2301	1 Ruddy (2–3 wk.)	22	3	3	M	6	6/8/40	Red Rock Lake
2325	1 Unidentifiable (age unknown)	29½	6	0	F	7	8/8/40	Red Rock Lake
2327	1 Unidentifiable (age unknown)	22½	2	14	M	4	8/8/40	Red Rock Lake
2328	1 Ruddy (3 wk.)	24	3	14	M	5	8/8/40	Red Rock Lake
2345	1 Lesser Scaup (3 wk.)	25	3	14	M	4	18/8/40	Red Rock Lake
A165	1 Mallard (1–2 wk.)	30	5	15	F	10	13/6/41	Baptizing Creek
A183	1 Redhead (1 wk.) 1 Baldpate (2 wk.) 1 Redhead (1 wk.) 1 Unidentified (3 wk.)	27½	5	14	F	9	15/6/41	Baptizing Creek
A196	1 Coot (1 wk.) 1 Canvasback (1 wk.)	25½	4	12	M	8	15/6/41	Baptizing Creek
A208	1 Canvasback (3 days)	32½	7	10	F	8	15/6/41	Baptizing Creek
A282	1 Gadwall (1 wk.) 1 Mallard (5 wk.)	29½	7	3	F	7	17/6/41	Baptizing Creek
A290	1 Coot (1 wk.) 1 Coot (3 days)	22¼	3	0	F	5	17/6/41	Baptizing Creek
A311	1 Redhead (1 wk.)	22¾	3	4	M	7	18/6/41	Baptizing Creek
A366	1 Ruddy (adult)	34½	9	13	F	12	20/6/41	Baptizing Creek
A383	1 Canvasback (1 wk.)	23¾	3	8	F	6	21/6/41	Baptizing Creek
A480	1 Coot (3 wk.)	29½	7	3	F	6	1/7/41	Baptizing Creek
A497	1 Grebe (3 days)	19½	2	0	F		3/7/41	Baptizing Creek
A498	1 Coot (age unknown)	18¾	1	11	F	3	4/7/41	Baptizing Creek
A602	1 Baldpate (1 wk.)	17¾	1	9	M	4	16/7/41	Baptizing Creek

Table 7. Availability of young waterfowl, number of pike examined and degree of predation on young waterfowl on three water areas of the Saskatchewan River delta.

	Baptizing Creek 1941	Littlefish Lake 1940	Red Rock Lake 1940
Number of brood observed	9	80	68
Number of duckings	73	447	457
Area in acres	18	6,600	2,300
Acres per duckling	0.25	14.7	5.1
Number of pike examined	433	2,120	161
Percentage of pike which had eaten ducklings	2.1	0.42	7.5
Number of acres per pike	0.04*	0.25?	?

* See Population Densities, page 122.

of their time in the shallow water areas where the pike are more abundant and also because the small waterfowl cannot move as rapidly nor for as great a distance when pursued. The very young waterfowl of all species tend to dive when pursued while the older waterfowl tend to travel away from the pursuer over the surface of the water.

The diving ducks, canvasback, redhead, lesser scaup and ruddy are preyed upon by the pike three times as heavily as are the surface feeding ducks, baldpate, mallard, teal and gadwall (Table 9). This marked difference in predation on diving and surface feeding ducks is probably due to the greater proportion of time spent under water by the divers and their consequent greater accessibility to the pike. This greater predation on diving than on surface feeding ducks has also been observed by Ross (1940) and Bajkov and Shortt (1939). Redhead ducklings were not abundant on the areas studied so the fact that 6 were found in pike stomachs (Tables 6, 9) indicates that they are particularly susceptible to predation by pike.

In addition to the young waterfowl listed in Table 6, 2 mice and 4 shrews were found in pike stomachs during the investigation, indicating that even animals that spend only a part of their time in the water are not safe from predation by the pike. A young yellow-headed blackbird, *Xanthocephalus xanthocephalus* Bonaparte was found in the stomach of pike no. 369 taken from Littlefish Lake during the 1940 investigation, while the duckling found in pike no. 237 had not yet

Table 8. Number and age of young waterfowl found in pike stomachs during 1940 and 1941.

Age (wk.)	Number in pike stomachs
0–1	19
1–2	4
2–3	6
3–4	1
4–5	1
Over 5	1
Undetermined	10
Total	42

Table 9. Number and species of young waterfowl found in pike stomachs during 1940 and 1941.

Number	Species		
7	Canvasback	Total divers	21
6	Red Head		
4	Lesser Scaup		
4	Ruddy		
3	Baldpate	Total surface ducks	7
2	Mallard		
1	Teal		
1	Gadwall		
5	Coot		
1	Grebe		
8	Unidentified		
42	Total		

hatched and still had a yolk sac attached. How these two items became available to the pike is not known.

Muskrats were abundant on the area, 190,000 having been trapped from the area during the spring of 1941 but none were found in pike stomachs. Bajkov and Shortt (1939) and Ross (1940) reported finding muskrat in pike stomachs.

Young waterfowl are available to pike in this area for a period of 60 to 80 days during an average summer. The numbers of ducklings eaten by pike are related to the speed of digestion of ducklings by pike, and to the abundance of pike in the area.

Rates of Digestion.—Some observations made in the field indicated that digestion of ducklings by pike might be a slow process.

Feeding experiments were carried on in the field and in the laboratory in an attempt to obtain more accurate information on this question. In the field pike were confined in cages 4 feet square made of 1 inch mesh poultry wire supported by a frame of 2 inch square lumber. These cages were suspended in water, some in the Saskatchewan River where the flow of water through the cage maintained an almost constant temperature and some in Baptizing Creek where shade was provided to prevent undue heating of the water by the sun.

In the laboratory metal tanks 4 feet long, 1 foot wide and 1 foot deep were used through which water flowed at a rate of 1 to 4 cu. feet per hour. Temperature was maintained uniform by means of electric heaters.

Since the fish refused to feed normally in captivity, food items were forced down the oesophagus with a blunt instrument. Care was taken to avoid injury to the fish and also to avoid keeping the fish out of water longer than necessary. None of the fish showed any marked loss of vigour on being returned to the water after feeding.

After feeding, the fish were left undisturbed for a variable interval of time and then dissected to observe the degree of digestion that had taken place. In a few of the field experiments the fish died before it was intended to terminate the experiment. While the cause of death could not be determined from an intensive examination of the fish immediately after death, it is thought that the experiences of the fish prior to being placed in the feeding cages were responsible for death because several fish that were intended for experimental use died before being fed. It is possible that struggling to escape, before removal from the gill net might have produced a state of exhaustion from which complete recovery was impossible even though death did not follow immediately.

The foods used were allowed to remain in the pike stomachs for intervals ranging from 8 to 236 hours. The weight of the partly digested food item remaining in the stomach at the end of the experiment was deducted from its initial weight. The loss of weight expressed as a percentage of the initial weight was used as an index of the degree of digestion that had taken place.

In all 67 experiments were carried out of which 54 were performed in the field and 13 in the laboratory. Positive results were obtained in 40 of the experiments while the remaining 27 failed to show any measurable digestion though the material remained in the stomachs for periods of 8 to 71 hours. The lack of digestion in these 27 experiments was probably due to a disturbance of the normal metabolism of the fish through confinement, handling and a history previous to capture.

Some idea of the speed of digestion of

Table 10. Average per cent digestion for specified time intervals.

Time of digestion (hours)	Average amount digested (per cent)
0–20	5.1
20–40	11.3
40–60	19.9
100–130	55.2

waterfowl by pike can be gained from the data presented in Table 10.

In Table 11 the rates of digestion of four different types of animal material are shown in terms of average per cent digestion per hour. This was calculated in each case by dividing the loss in weight expressed as a percentage of the initial weight, by the number of hours during which digestion had been taking place.

The rate of digestion of fish is about 68 per cent greater than that of ducklings. Other birds and mammals are also digested more rapidly than ducklings. This may be due to the water-resistant nature of the down covering the body of the ducklings which probably slows the digestive process by preventing the digestive juices from coming into contact with the body tissues of the ducklings until some time after they reach the pike stomach. This protection by a water-resistant covering of feathers or fur is shown to a lesser extent by the other birds used and to a still lesser extent by the mammals. In the fish this type of protection is absent and digestion is more rapid.

The digestion is carried on at the posterior end of the stomach as pointed out by Jung (1899) and only the part of the food adjacent to this area is in process of being digested at any time. The food is passed backward to this "digestive region" as fast as the material already digested passes through the pyloric valve. Once digestion has begun and the flesh of the animal is exposed at the digested surface, the rate of digestion of birds and mammals may be similar to that of fish.

Table 11. Average rates of digestion, temperature and number of experiments performed using four types of food material.

Material fed	Number of experiments	Per cent digestion per hour (average)	Temperature °F (average)
Ducklings	17	0.44	72.8
Birds other than ducklings	6	0.51	69.8
Mammals	10	0.66	63.9
Fish	7	0.74	68.0

Waterfowl showed an average rate of digestion amounting to 0.44 per cent of the weight per hour at 72°F which would indicate a time of about 230 hours or almost 10 days for complete digestion.

The temperature range included in the experiments was too narrow to permit any generalizations on the effect of temperature on the rate of digestion except in the experiments in which mammals were fed. Of the 10 experiments in this group 5 were performed at an average temperature of 53°F and had an average percentage digestion per hour of 0.61, while the other 5 were performed at an average temperature of 74°F and had an average percentage digestion per hour of 0.70. This increase of 15 per cent in the rate of digestion for a 21°F increase in temperature is considerably less than would be expected in view of Vant Hoff's law.

Clausen (1936) has shown that the body temperatures of 10 species of fish with which he worked tended to assume the temperature of the surrounding water. All previous references to temperatures of digestion have assumed that a similar relation holds in the case of the pike with respect to the temperature of the surrounding water.

As shown by Mellanby (1940) the rate of a vital process depends to a large extent on the temperature to which the animal was subjected previous to the beginning of the measurements. This effect of acclimatization probably also applies to rates of digestion and may explain the small difference between the rates of digestion at the two temperatures used.

Population Densities.—During the 1941 investigation an effort was made to determine the density of population of pike in one of the water areas studied. A section of Baptizing Creek was investigated which had a surface area of approximately 18 acres. From this section of creek 485 pike were taken during a 39 day period. The number of pike caught per unit of fishing effort decreased from 10 fish per hour on June 13 to 1 fish per 24 hours on July 21, using the same net under similar conditions. This decrease indicated that the pike population had been almost completely removed from the section of creek investigated. Assuming a uniform population, at least 27 pike must have been present per acre of creek surface at the beginning of the investigation.

WATERFOWL PIKE RELATIONS

During the course of the study carried out at Baptizing Creek 13 pike were taken which contained 19 young waterfowl. The removal of young waterfowl by pike amounted to 1 waterfowl per 0.95 acres of water area of this type during a 39 day period. As the total water area of the Saskatchewan River delta is at least 600,000 acres, the loss of young waterfowl through pike predation becomes an important factor in the economy of the waterfowl population of this delta.

Since young waterfowl small enough to be eaten by pike are present on the water for a period of 60 to 80 days during the average season (May 23 to Sept. 8, 1941) the number eaten by pike in a given area would be greater than was found during the course of the 39 day investigation.

By "fishing out" an 18 acre section of Baptizing Creek during the 1941 investigation it was found that the initial pike population must have contained at least 27 fish, large enough to eat ducklings, per acre. On the basis of such a population and the fact that slightly over 1 per cent of the total number of pike taken during the investigation contained young waterfowl, and assuming (as indicated by experiments on the rate of digestion) that a pike might eat waterfowl as often as 8 times during one season, the loss amounts to about 1 waterfowl per 0.5 acres of water per season. This is of the same order of magnitude as that of the observed loss at Baptizing Creek, so probably something between the observed and calculated losses represents the true state of affairs, since it is unlikely that the observed loss represented the complete picture of the predation on waterfowl by pike.

Assuming a similar pike and waterfowl population throughout the water areas of the Athabaska and Saskatchewan River deltas, which together contain about 900,000 acres of water at normal summer water levels, and assuming a loss of one water fowl per 0.6 acres of water per season, then the total number of waterfowl destroyed yearly on these areas amounts to 1,500,000. The yearly average production of waterfowl on these delta areas is about 14,500,000 (data from Ducks Unlimited Canada). Pike predation may account for the destruction of 9.7 per cent of the waterfowl produced on these deltas or about 3.2 per cent of the total number produced in the Prairie Provinces.

CONTROL OF THE PIKE

Several methods have been suggested by means of which it was hoped pike populations could be reduced in numbers or eliminated from areas in which they are particularly destructive to waterfowl.

Fishing, electrical methods of destruction, poisoning, screening and biological control were all considered as methods of reducing the pike population in certain areas. Most of these methods have been used successfully in the control of fish populations but in view of the large areas of shallow water and the dense populations of pike involved it was thought that expense would be prohibitive to the use of any of these methods for control of the numbers of pike on the Saskatchewan River delta.

SUMMARY

The increase of agriculture on the Prairies during the last few decades, together with a decrease of precipitation, has reduced the availability of the Prairies as a breeding ground for waterfowl. The northern breeding areas have therefore become more important in maintaining the waterfowl population of North America.

Predation on young waterfowl by pike was reported from 44 per cent of areas under observation by 207 observers. Its intensity varied, for instance at Littlefish Lake 0.42 per cent of pike taken contained waterfowl, at Redrock Lake 7.5 per cent, and at Baptizing Creek 3.0 per cent. Forty-five per cent of the waterfowl eaten were less than one week old, and diving ducklings were taken three times as often as surface species.

Pike between 19 and 30 inches long were responsible for 71.5 per cent of all predation on waterfowl, although this size range was only 23.3 per cent of all pike taken which were large enough to prey on waterfowl.

Female pike contained on the average three times the weight of food found in males, although they were on the average but 1.14 inches longer; females comprised 47.8 per cent of the population, but were responsible for 56 per cent of the predation. This greater predation and greater food content are probably related to their greater observed growth rate.

Predation by pike may destroy one young waterfowl per 0.6 acre (1.7 per acre) of water per season in areas like the Saskatchewan River delta. Since the combined areas of this and the Athabaska River delta comprise over 900,000 acres at normal summer levels, the destruction of young waterfowl by pike may amount to 1,500,000 per year, or 9.7 percent of the average annual production of these areas.

ACKNOWLEDGMENTS

The author is deeply indebted to the staffs of Ducks Unlimited (Canada), Winnipeg, Man., the Department of Zoology, University of Toronto, Toronto, Ont., the Royal Ontario Museum of Zoology, Toronto, Ont. and the Department of Mines and Natural Resources of Manitoba at The Pas, Manitoba for the cooperation in time, personnel and funds provided by them. Particular thanks are due Professor A. F. Coventry of the Department of Zoology, University of Toronto, Toronto, Ont. who directed the research and provided guidance throughout the course of the study.

LITERATURE CITED

ALLEN, K. R. 1939. A note on the food of the pike (*Esox lucius*) in Windermere. Journ. Anim. Ecol. 8:72–75.

BAILEY, L. F. 1940. Some water relations of three western grasses. 1. The transpiration ratio. Am. Journ. Bot. 27:122–128.

BAJKOV, A. D., AND A. H. SHORTT. 1939. Northern pike (jackfish) as predator on waterfowl and muskrats. Pub. of Ducks Unlimited (Canada), Winnipeg, Man.

BRIGGS, L. J., AND H. L. SHANTZ. 1913. The water

requirement of plants. U.S. Dept. of Agr., Bureau of Plant Industry, Bull. 284.

CHAMBERS, E. D. T. 1896. The ouananiche and its Canadian environment. The pike: 283–288.

CLAUSEN, R. G. 1934. Body temperature of fresh water fishes. Ecology 15:139–144.

CLEMENS, W. A., J. R. DYMOND, AND N. K. BIGELOW. 1924. Food studies of Lake Nipigon fishes. Pub. Ont. Fish. Res. Lab. 25:103–165.

DAY, F. 1880–84. The fishes of Great Britain and Ireland. Vol. 2.

DYMOND, J. R. 1926. The fishes of Lake Nipigon. Pub. Ont. Fish. Res. Lab. 27:3–108.

EMBODY, G. C. Unpublished data on the "Ecology, Habits and Growth of the pike, *Esox lucius.*" Cornell University, Ithaca, N.Y. 1910.

FISHER, R. A. 1936. Statistical methods for research workers. Oliver and Boyd, London and Edinburgh.

FORBES, S. A., AND R. E. RICHARDSON. 1908. The fishes of Illinois. Nat. Hist. Surv. of Illinois, 3.

KENDALL, W. C. 1917. The pikes—Their geographical distribution, habits and commercial importance. U.S. Bureau of Fisheries Report, 1–45.

MARSHALL, W. S., AND N. C. GILBERT. 1904. Notes on the food and parasites of some fresh water fishes from the lakes at Madison, Wisconsin. Rept. U.S. Fish Comm. 513–522.

MCNAMARA, F. 1937. Breeding and food habits of the pikes, *Esox lucius* and *Esox vermiculatus.* Trans. Am. Fish. Soc. 66:372–373.

MELLANBY, K. 1940. Temperature coefficients and acclimatization. Nature 146:165–166.

MOORE, J. E. Unpublished data on 60 saline lakes of Saskatchewan. University of Saskatchewan, Saskatoon, Saskatchewan, 1941.

PREBLE, E. A. 1908. A biological investigation of the Athabaska-MacKenzie region. U.S. Dept. of Agr., North American Fauna 27:1–574.

RAWSON, D. S. 1932. The pike of Waskesiu Lake, Saskatchewan. Trans. Am. Fish. Soc. 62: 323–330.

ROBERTSON, D. 1886–88. The pike *Esox lucius* L. Proc. and Trans. Nat. Hist. Soc. Glasgow, N.S. 2:212–214.

ROSS, D. A. 1940. Jackfish investigation, 1940, Athabaska Delta, Alberta. Pub. of Ducks Unlimited (Canada), Winnipeg, Man.

SHUTT, F. T. 1925. Influence of grain growing on the nitrogen and organic matter content of the western prairie soils of Canada. Dom. of Can., Dept. of Agr., Bull. 44, new series.

SMITT, F. A. 1892. A history of Scandinavian fishes. The pike 2:997–1010. Stockholm.

WEED, A. C. 1927. Pike, pickerel and muskellunge. Field Museum of Nat. Hist., Zool. Leaflet 9.

WILLIAMS, M. Y. 1922. Biological notes along 1400 miles of the Mackenzie River System. Canad. Field Nat. 36:61.

YUNG, E. 1899. Recherches sur la digestion des poissons. Archiv. de Zool. Exp. et Generale, 3e Ser. 7:121–201.

PREDATION BY SNAPPING TURTLES UPON AQUATIC BIRDS IN MAINE MARSHES[1]

MALCOLM W. COULTER, Maine Cooperative Wildlife Research Unit, ORONO 04469

The purpose of this report is to present the findings of a study of predation by the common snapping turtle (*Chelydra serpentina* Linnaeus) upon aquatic birds. Persons interested in the welfare of ducks and other aquatic birds have often referred to this reptile as a predator, although there is little specific information to indicate to what extent losses are incurred. The overall food habits of the snapping turtle have been discussed in detail by Alexander (1943) and Lagler (1943). These and other studies indicate that the usual diet consists largely of vegetation, several kinds of invertebrates, and nongame fishes. Birds or mammals are, as a rule, incidental foods taken infrequently. Alexander (*op.cit.*) seems to have aptly summarized the status of the snapping turtle by stating: "The economic importance of this turtle depends largely upon the habitat in which it lives, because there is a high correlation between the availability of various food items taken and the amounts of each taken . . . "

It appears that there has been little opportunity to study the turtle under conditions where large numbers of birds might be readily available. Lagler (1943) trapped 21 snapping turtles from a pond in Michigan that contained about 20 acres of surface water, with a nesting waterfowl population in excess of one pair per acre. Four young mallards (*Anas platyrhynchos*) were present in three turtles. It was concluded that despite the high concentration of avian prey, the reptiles turned to more available aquatic vegetation for food. Miller (1952) found ducklings in four of 10 snapping turtles collected from the Sandbar Waterfowl Refuge in Vermont in 1950, but birds occurred in only 2 of 23 turtles taken during 1951.

The present investigation was designed to study habitats where birds, especially waterfowl, were known to be abundant in Maine and where high snapping turtle populations were believed to exist. In addition, collection of specimens was limited to the peak of the brood season for ducks.

METHODS

Turtles were captured with Smith Standard Turtle Traps (manufactured by Robert G. Smith, East Killingly, Connecticut). These traps are about the size and shape of a 50-gallon steel drum and consist of a frame of three metal hoops over which cord netting is stretched. A funnel at one end permits access by turtles attempting to reach the bait. The bait is enclosed in a perforated tin can suspended about two-thirds of the distance from the funnel to the back of the trap. These traps are staked in 1½ to 4 feet of water with the funnel facing downstream or offshore. Scraps of marine fish, canned sardines, and locally caught fish and frogs were used as bait. In general, canned sardines and scraps from marine fish were slightly more effective than were frogs or locally caught coarse fish. Canned sardines were used much of the time because they resulted in good catches and were convenient to use in the field. However, regardless of the kind of bait, it was attractive to the turtles only when fresh. Tainted bait greatly reduced the catch, or often resulted in no catch. For this reason the bait was generally replaced at least every other day.

Traps were tended at least once each day. Captured turtles were shot before removal

[1]The writer expresses his appreciation to Howard L. Mendall, leader, Maine Cooperative Wildlife Research Unit, for identification of bird remains, suggestions during the study, and in preparation of the manuscript. Several persons assisted with the field or laboratory work, especially former graduate assistants Fred Dean, Frank Haseltine, Robert Hyers, and J. William Peppard; graduate students William Nicholson and David O'Meara; and State Game Biologist Richard Parks. Contribution from the Maine Cooperative Wildlife Research Unit, Orono, Maine; Maine Department of Inland Fisheries and Game, University of Maine, Wildlife Management Institute, and the U.S. Fish and Wildlife Service cooperating.

Originally published in J. Wildl. Manage. 21(1):17–21, 1957.

from the traps. The entire gastrointestinal tract was preserved for detailed study.

Laboratory study of the digestive tracts involved repeated washing, screening, and flotation of food materials to separate the various components and to permit thorough search for evidence of birds. Identification of bird remains was pursued as far as accurately possible. For some specimens the species and approximate age could be determined; in others only the general group to which it belonged could be stated and, in several cases, the remains did not permit any classification other than unidentified bird.

Information concerning the abundance of birds, especially ducks, was recorded from the areas where turtles were collected. At Corinna Stream, one of the major sample areas, studies of breeding pairs of ducks, nesting success, and rearing were made by observers who were on the area daily during the summer months.

All habitats studied were acid-water marshes located in central and eastern Maine. These marshes consisted of shallow expanses of warm water with abundant stands of emergent and floating vegetation. Relatively small proportions of open water, sluggish currents, and soft bottoms were typical.

RESULTS

A total of 171 turtles was collected from eight areas. Food was present in 157 specimens used for this discussion. The colon was the most valuable portion of the gastrointestinal tract for studying foods eaten. Almost all of the colons contained food, whereas many of the stomachs were empty. Food items in the colon included entire leaves and shoots of plants, fish bones and scales, whole insects, mollusks, and bones and feathers from birds. Generally much of the material in the upper portion of the colon was not as finely broken as that in the lower portion. The latter frequently consisted of vegetation reduced to a mucky mass, but containing fish scales, bones, feathers, parts of insects, and other hard material. A summary of the frequency of occurrence of the major groups of foods is presented in Table 1.

Plants were found most frequently and also made up a high percentage of the volume. Some individuals contained over 700 c.c. of vegetation. Fish, insects, mollusks, and amphibians varied in frequency of occurrence much more than did vegetation. Abundant plant life was characteristic of all areas from which turtles were taken. However, the abundance of other foods varied considerably, not only by areas, but in the same area under different water levels.

Bird remains were found in about one of every four turtles. Forty-two specimens contained evidence of a minimum of 52 birds including 25 ducks, 11 grebes, 3 rails, and 13 unidentified birds. The ducks were represented by 7 black ducks (*Anas rubripes*), 5 ring-necked ducks (*Aythya collaris*), 3 golden-eyes (*Bucephala clangula*), 2 wood ducks (*Aix sponsa*), 2 blue-winged teals (*Anas discors*), 2 surface-feeding ducks of unknown species, and 4 unidentified ducks. While most of the duck remains were from young birds up to six weeks of age, at least three adults were positively identified.

In most instances evidence of only a single bird was found. However, one 31-pound turtle had consumed five birds including one ring-necked duck, one golden-eye, and three pied-billed grebes (*Podilymbus podiceps*). A 24-pound specimen contained two black ducks, one unidentified surface-feeding duck, and one grebe. Four additional turtles, ranging in size from 11 to 41 pounds, had each eaten two birds.

Thirty-seven of the birds taken could be classified as either those that habitually feed on the surface or in the shallows, or birds that usually dive to feed in deeper water. The two groups are about equally represented. However, among the ducks, surface-feeding species were taken almost twice as often as divers, although both groups were well represented on the areas studied.

DISCUSSION

In examining gastrointestinal tracts, there is always the question as to how much of the material represents carrion. There was no way to determine this from the evidence at hand. However, field observations of turtles actually catching birds, together with this reptile's preference for fresh food, constitute strong circumstantial evidence that a noteworthy proportion of this material very likely resulted from direct predation. Experiments reported by Lagler (1943) and

TABLE 1. — SUMMARY OF SNAPPING TURTLE FOOD HABITS BY AREAS

	Frequency of Occurrence; Per Cent Occurrence in Brackets						
	1949	Corinna 1950	1951-53	Pocamoonshine 1950	Scammon 1953	Misc. Areas	Totals
No. Specimens	31	59	17	14	25	11	157
Vegetation	26	51	12	13	18	6	126
	(84)	(86)	(71)	(93)	(72)	(55)	(80)
Insects	25	48	3	7	5	5	93
	(81)	(81)	(18)	(50)	(20)	(46)	(59)
Mollusks	26	23	5	2	2	1	59
	(84)	(39)	(29)	(14)	(8)	(9)	(38)
Fish	18	35	8	12	22	8	103
	(58)	(59)	(47)	(86)	(88)	(73)	(66)
Amphibians	1	23	0	0	0	1	25
	(3)	(39)	(0)	(0)	(0)	(9)	(16)
Birds	13	10	5	4	8	2	42
	(42)	(17)	(29)	(29)	(32)	(18)	(27)
Misc. vert.	4[1]	2[1]	2[1]	0	2[2]	2[2]	12
	(13)	(3)	(12)	(0)	(8)	(18)	(8)

[1] Unidentified
[2] Muskrat

Alexander (1943), as well as the experiences of those who trapped turtles during the present study, have demonstrated a preference by this reptile for fresh food when available. While it is felt that much of the material represents kills by the reptiles, it should be borne in mind that undoubtedly a few of the birds died from other causes.

The highest incidence of birds in turtles occurred at Corinna Stream in 1949 when the water was very low. The density of birds and of turtles, when expressed in terms of number per acre of surface water, was high (Table 2). Thirty-one usable turtle specimens were taken during a 9-day period representing 54 trap nights. Thirteen, or 42 per cent, of these contained a total of 18 birds.

During the following season, water levels were higher at Corinna Stream, although still below normal. The density of birds and of turtles was slightly less. The incidence of birds in turtles dropped sharply. The results suggested that predation might be correlated with habitat conditions and that the incidence of predation decreases during high water levels when, as a rule, more favorable rearing habitat is provided for aquatic birds. However, further data from Corinna Stream in years when high water increased the surface acreage to three times that of 1949 and 1950 indicate that predation was still common. Only a small sample of turtles was taken during seasons of high water, yet about one in every three had eaten birds. The turtle population no doubt was much less than during previous years, since 106 specimens totaling 2,103 pounds had been removed in 1949 and 1950.

Similar results were obtained from Scammon Pond. This marsh is a State Game Management Area, and the water level was carefully regulated to maintain conditions considered optimum for duck broods. Of 25 turtles taken in 13 days, 8 (32 per cent) contained evidence of 10 ducks and 2 grebes. There are no data to compare this to the incidence of birds in turtles in the same area under conditions of low water levels.

An attempt was made to study a third area that was much larger than Corinna Stream or Scammon Pond. This marsh, known as the Pocamoonshine–Crawford Lake Thoroughfare contains close to 2,000 acres and is a productive waterfowl-breeding marsh. The 1950 population of breeding ducks was about one pair per 30 acres. Only 14 turtles could be collected, despite intensive trapping efforts. No ducks were found in the digestive tracts, but 4 grebes were present in 4 of the 14 specimens. Despite the fact that snapping turtles are frequently seen on this marsh, in contrast to a paucity of sight records in the other areas, the turtle population is believed to be relatively low

TABLE 2. — A COMPARISON OF FREQUENCY OF OCCURRENCE OF BIRDS IN TURTLE DIGESTIVE TRACTS BY AREAS

Study Area / Habitat	Turtle Density	Density[1] Ducks	Density[1] Grebes	No. Turtles[2]	Per Cent Occur. of Birds	Breakdown of Birds Found
Corinna 1949 Plants—abundant Fish—abundant locally Water—very low Other birds[3]—very common	Catch = 1:8.0 A. Trap success 1 turtle / 1.6 trap nights for 9 days	1:6.5 acres	1:25 acres	31	42	9 ducks 5 grebes 1 rail 3 unident.
Corinna 1950 Plants—abundant Fish—abundant locally Water—low, but higher than 1949 Other birds[3]—very common	Catch = 1:4.0 A. Trap success 1 turtle / 4 trap nights for 30 days	1:8.0 acres	1:35 acres	59	17	4 ducks 7 unident.
Corinna 1951-53 Plants—abundant Fish—abundant Water,very high, surface acreage increased 3 times Other birds[3]—very common	Catch = 1:100 A. Trap success 1 turtle / 40 trap nights for 55-60 days	1:30 acres	Prob. close to 1:100 acres	17	29	2 ducks 3 unident.
		Total Corinna		107	29	15 ducks 5 grebes 1 rail 13 unident.
Pocamoonshine 1950 Plants—very abundant Fish—very abundant Water—high Other birds[3]—common	Catch = 1:130 A. Trap success 1 1 turtle / 4 trap nights for 8 days	1:30 acres	Believed fairly low	14	29	4 grebes
Scammon Pond Game Mgmt. Area 1953 Plants—very abundant Fish—very abundant Water—moderately high Other birds[3]—common	Catch = 1:12 A. Trap success 1 turtle / 7 trap nights for 13 days	1:20 acres	Believed low	25	32	10 ducks 2 grebes
		Grand Total		146	25	25 ducks 11 grebes 1 rail 13 unident.

[1] Number breeding pairs
[2] Only those with food used
[3] Rails, herons, bitterns

in comparison to the other marshes studied.

It is difficult to determine the magnitude of such predation upon the duck population of a given marsh. Little is known of the size of turtle populations. Also, there are no data to indicate the total period during which predation may occur. With the data at hand some minimum estimates can be made.

Based upon detailed productivity studies at Corinna Stream, an estimated 192 ducklings were produced on the area during 1949. Eight ducklings, or about four per cent of the estimated population of ducklings, plus one adult duck, were taken by turtles during a 9-day period. However, experiments with captive turtles that were fed ducks and killed at intervals after feeding, indicate that evidence of ducks may remain in the digestive tracts as long as 12 days. Thus, the period sampled by the specimens examined includes at least 21 days. The 31 specimens, representing a 21-day feeding period, yielded four per cent of the estimated total duckling population. But, if we assume that the residual turtle population was also taking ducks at the same rate during the sample period, the probable mortality among ducklings is much greater.

For the Corinna Stream study area a conservative estimate of the remaining turtle population can be made. Despite the fact that during 1949, one turtle was taken for every eight acres of surface water, 73 additional specimens were taken in 1950. Trapping was discontinued in 1950 only because of a lack of time and the fact that some broods were awing. Trapping success was still high when collection ceased. These data would indicate that at least 100 turtles were present during 1949, and probably very many more. If we assume, for purposes of this discussion, that the residual turtle population after collections in 1949 was 70 individuals and that they preyed upon ducklings at the same rate of those captured, mortality of ducklings during the 21-day sample period is calculated at about 13 per cent of the estimated duckling population.

At Scammon Pond 10 ducks were taken by turtles during a 25-day sample period. The estimated duckling population was 100, thus indicating known mortality of 10 per cent. Considering that a sizeable residual turtle population was also present at this area, the actual loss was probably much higher during that period.

During the present investigation it was possible to study only a few areas where turtles and ducks were abundant. There is need for further investigation in regions where a greater variety of habitats can be studied with varying densities of ducks and turtles. There is also need for more details concerning the density of these reptiles and simple methods for appraising their abundance. It became apparent during the present investigation that observation of snapping turtles was not a clue to their abundance under the conditions studied. At Corinna Stream less than two dozen sight records of turtles were accumulated by observers who were on the area daily during two summers, yet during that period over a ton of snapping turtles (106 individuals) was removed during 39 days of trapping. The degree of utilization of gravel and sand banks for nesting grounds adjacent to the marsh seemed to offer a better indication of the local abundance of these reptiles.

The results from the areas studied suggest that sizeable losses to waterfowl and other birds may be expected in some habitats. But it should be emphasized that this study was designed to investigate environments where predation would be expected to be highest if it occurred at all. In Maine there appear to be few areas where both ducks and snapping turtles are actually abundant. Widespread control of snapping turtles would be both impractical and undesirable. Control on a local basis or in marshes under intensive management for waterfowl production may be worthwhile, especially if other predators are also controlled.

SUMMARY

The gastrointestinal tracts of 157 snapping turtles taken in central and eastern Maine during the waterfowl brood season were examined. About one in every four turtles (27 per cent) contained evidence of birds. Up to 13 per cent of the estimated duckling population was taken by turtles during sample periods of 25 days or less. Significant mortality of ducklings is believed to be limited to local areas where both turtles and ducklings are abundant. Widespread control of snapping turtles is not recommended. Control on areas managed intensively for waterfowl production appears desirable if other predators are also controlled.

LITERATURE CITED

ALEXANDER, MAURICE M. 1943. Food habits of the snapping turtle in Connecticut. J. Wildl. Mgmt., 7(3):278-282.

LAGLER, KARL F. 1943. Food habits and economic relations of the turtles of Michigan with special reference to fish management. Amer. Mid. Nat., 29(2):257-312.

MILLER, WILLIAM R. 1952. Aspects of wood duck nesting box management. Proc. Northeastern Fish and Game Conf., Jackson's Mill, W.Va., 6 pp. (mimeo.).

Received for publication January 5, 1956

INTERPRETING THE RESULTS OF NESTING STUDIES

HARVEY W. MILLER, Northern Prairie Wildlife Research Center, U.S. Fish and Wildlife Service, Jamestown, North Dakota 58401[1]
DOUGLAS H. JOHNSON, Northern Prairie Wildlife Research Center, U.S. Fish and Wildlife Service, Jamestown, North Dakota 58401

Abstract: Nesting studies are used to assess the production of birds and to evaluate nesting habitats. Most such studies involve finding nests in a given area and subsequently determining the proportion that hatched. Unfortunately, the results are often biased by unrecognized differences in the probabilities of finding successful and unsuccessful nests. The observed hatch rates of 1,900 nests of blue-winged teal (*Anas discors*) are presented to illustrate the relationship of hatch rates to time remaining until the nests should hatch. The Mayfield method of correcting for these biases is illustrated. Other examples demonstrate the possible effects of sampling procedures on observed hatch rates and nest density.

J. WILDL. MANAGE. 42(3):471–476

Nesting studies are common in investigations of waterfowl and other birds. Most are undertaken to assess the production of breeding birds and to evaluate nesting habitats and the techniques of managing such habitats. The objectives are to determine hatch rates and density of nests in selected habitats. The procedures commonly used are searching selected areas to find nests and subsequently checking those nests to ascertain whether or not the eggs were hatched.

Unfortunately, the nests of most species are initiated over periods of at least several days during which some of the nests may be destroyed. If nests are destroyed, many females will renest 1 or more times; consequently, it is common to find newly initiated nests after others of the same species have hatched. Continuous searches over such prolonged periods generally are impractical; hence, most studies involve periodic searches. If some nests were missed because they were initiated and destroyed between searches, the observed nest density clearly would be biased downward. Less obviously, but more importantly, the observed nesting success would be biased upward. We have restricted our discussion to these biases.

These potential biases, among several commonly occurring in nesting studies, were recognized previously by Hammond and Forward (1956) and Mayfield (1960, 1961). Mayfield (1961) elaborated the method of estimating nesting success from nests observed during all or any portion of the period between initiation and hatch. The method has not been widely adopted. Mayfield therefore published the method again 14 yr later and noted correctly (Mayfield 1975:456) that "not every published report shows awareness of the problem." At least 2 other investigators (Townsend 1966, Reed 1975) acknowledged the problem in waterfowl studies; Townsend used Mayfield's method in his analysis.

Our purpose is to bring the potential biases associated with periodic searching to the attention of investigators who may consider undertaking nesting studies. Our studies will exemplify the magnitude of these biases. We will also illustrate how the inconsistency of the biases invalidates many comparisons commonly made within and among nesting studies. We will demonstrate Mayfield's method for obtaining better estimates of the success and density of nests.

[1] Present address: U.S. Fish and Wildlife Service, 1978 South Garrison Street, Denver, Colorado 80227.

Originally published in J. Wildl. Manage. 42(3):471–476, 1978.

We hereby acknowledge the support and guidance of H. K. Nelson, former Director, and W. R. Goforth, Director of the Northern Prairie Wildlife Research Center, in the studies which led to this paper. We are especially grateful for the use of the nest records provided by, and for the constructive comments of, H. F. Duebbert, K. F. Higgins, L. M. Kirsch, A. T. Klett, and J. T. Lokemoen. Our thanks to D. A. Davenport for assistance with computer programing, to C. W. Shaiffer for drafting the figures, and to H. F. Mayfield for reviewing an earlier draft of this report. Our special thanks to L. M. Cowardin for perceptive technical and editorial comments on the manuscript.

METHODS

The records we present were obtained from studies of duck nesting conducted in North and South Dakota during 1967–72. The study areas included upland habitats on public and private lands selected to provide a broad range of the habitat types and land uses available to nesting ducks.

Searches to locate nests were conducted 15 May–15 July and generally between 0700 and 1400 h when ducks, laying as well as incubating, were most likely to be at the nest. Most areas were searched from 2 to as many as 4 times at intervals of approximately 3 weeks. Most searches were made with cable-chain flushing devices as described by Higgins et al. (1969), although a "Varty Drag" (Martz 1967:240) was used on some roadsides and a rope drag (Earl 1950:336) was used in some croplands. These methods of finding nests depended upon flushing the ducks; therefore, nests were not detected if they were not attended at the time of the search or if the duck did not flush (Higgins et al. 1969).

The site from which a duck flushed was examined, and if at least 1 egg was present, it was considered a nest. The number of eggs and stage of development (Weller 1956) were recorded along with details of the nest site. A marker was placed near each nest and the nest was reexamined on or soon after the anticipated hatching date. Nests in which at least 1 egg hatched were classified as successful. A few nests in which development ceased after they were found were classified as abandoned. All other nests were destroyed, usually by predators.

We emphasize that these methods were designed solely to measure the proportion of successful nests among all nests in an area, including those from renesting efforts. The methods are not in themselves adequate to determine the proportion of successful females (productivity) if renesting occurs.

RESULTS AND DISCUSSION

We limit our discussion to 1,900 nests of blue-winged teal found during the studies and classified both by stage of development when found and by fate as either hatched or destroyed (Table 1). Abandoned nests were excluded from analysis. Thirteen nests had hatched (ducklings were in the nest) when found, and the remainder were almost equally divided between the laying (934) and incubation (953) stages. The observed hatch rate of all nests (a common product of nesting studies) was 0.441.

In studies reported here, the nests were examined on or soon after the anticipated hatching date; thus, the maximum possible exposure was the number of days between finding and hatching. We observed that blue-winged teal generally laid an egg each day, that there was an average of 10.2 eggs in the nests being incubated when found, and that the eggs were hatched typically on the 24th or 25th day of incubation. Therefore, we used an average of 35 days from initiation of the nest to hatching and calculated that, for example, a nest found with 4 unincubated eggs would hatch 31 days hence. When observed, the actual hatching dates corresponded closely with those calculated in this manner.

The data in Table 1 display a strong inverse relationship between observed hatch rates and the period remaining until the nests are due to hatch. The hatch rate, for example, of nests for which the period till hatch was 8 days (0.795) was nearly double that of nests for which the period till hatch was 16 days (0.471). To be successful, nests must survive the combined laying and incubation periods. The hatch rate (0.237) of 1-egg nests, which had 34 days to go before hatching, would suggest that if all nests had been found when they were initiated (35 days to go), somewhat less than 24 percent of them would have hatched.

The data in Table 1 also demonstrate that the greater the proportion of nests found in the later stages of development, the more the composite hatch rate will be biased upwards. Conversely, nesting density will be biased further downward as the proportion of unsuccessful nests not found increases.

Mayfield (1961) recognized the improbability of finding a reasonably large sample of nests at the time they were initiated. Therefore, instead of lifetime survival rates, he measured daily survival rates during the periods he was able to observe the nests. For this, he considered each day that a nest existed to be 1 nest-day of exposure. For example, a nest found on 10 May and still existing on 18 May would have survived 8 nest-days. If the nest had been destroyed, he assumed

Table 1. Observed hatch rates of blue-winged teal nests found in North and South Dakota, 1967–1972.

Stage when found	Days until hatch	Number of nests		Hatch rate
		Hatched	Destroyed	
Laying				
1 egg	34	9	29	0.237
2 eggs	33	9	23	0.281
3 eggs	32	9	29	0.237
4 eggs	31	9	37	0.196
5 eggs	30	27	57	0.321
6 eggs	29	23	75	0.235
7 eggs	28	29	79	0.269
8 eggs	27	26	93	0.218
9 eggs	26	34	76	0.309
10 eggs	25	40	87	0.315
10+ eggs	24	53	81	0.396
Incubating				
4 days	20	120	166	0.420
8 days	16	128	144	0.471
12 days	12	57	33	0.633
16 days	8	93	24	0.795
20 days	4	111	27	0.804
22 days	2	28	2	0.933
Pipped	1	19	1	0.950
Hatched	0	13	0	1.000
Total		837	1,063	0.441

it had survived until midway through the period, an exposure of 4 nest-days. The number of nests destroyed divided by the total exposure of both surviving and destroyed nests would be the estimated daily mortality rate. That rate subtracted from 1.0 (which represents perfect survival) would be the daily survival rate which could then be projected to the lifetime of the nests studied as the expected nest hatch rate.

We calculated the expected hatch rate for 1-egg nests (Table 1) by Mayfield's method as he described. The resulting rate, 0.277, appeared somewhat inconsistent with the observed rate of 0.237 (for a 34-day period). This inconsistency and other evidence suggested that the assumption that destroyed nests had survived until midway through the exposure period was incorrect, a possibility that Mayfield recognized but did not believe

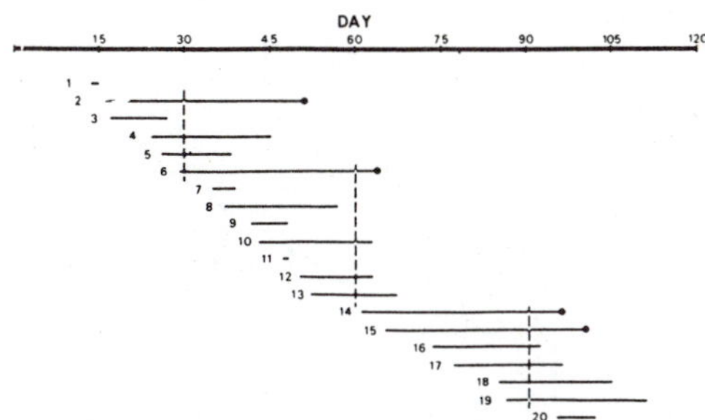

Fig. 1. Hypothetical survival times of a population of 20 nests initiated during a 120-day breeding season. Nests that hatch (survive 35 days) are indicated by a survival line ending with a dot (•). The results of searches for nests on days 30, 60, and 90 are also shown.

significant in the relatively short exposure periods of his studies. We calculated the expected survival of a nest that did not ultimately hatch, and found it to be much closer to 40 percent of the exposure period, rather than to 50 percent of the period.

The calculation of the hatch rate represented by the data in Table 1 will illustrate Mayfield's method. The exposure of nests that hatched is determined: 9 × 34 + 9 × 33 + 9 × 32 + . . . + 19 × 1 = 13,712 nest-days. Likewise, the exposure of nests that were destroyed is determined: (29 × 34 + 23 × 33 + 29 × 32 . . . + 1 × 1 = 24,848) × 0.40 (to account for the portion of the possible exposure period the nests had survived) = 9,939 nest-days. The number of destroyed nests (1,063) divided by the total exposure (23,651 nest-days) equals the daily mortality rate (0.045) which, when subtracted from 1.0, yields a daily survival rate of 0.955. The probability that a nest would survive from initiation to hatching is the daily survival rate over the 35-day lifetime or $0.955^{35} = 0.200$.

A 20 percent expected hatch rate is consistent with that suggested by the 1-egg nests. We emphasize the great difference between this rate and the composite hatch rate (0.441) which is ordinarily reported; the observed rate is 220 percent of the value estimated by the Mayfield method.

An improved estimate of nest density is also possible. The number of successful nests (837) was, according to the Mayfield method, about 20 percent of those initiated. Therefore, the number found represented 4,185 (837 ÷ 0.20) nests actually initiated.

The difference between the observed and true hatch rates reflects more or less the sampling procedures used to find the nests. This relationship is illustrated by the hypothetical but not unlikely histories of 20 nests (Fig. 1). Nest 1 was initiated on day 14 and was destroyed 1 day later, Nest 2 started on day 16 and hatched, etc. We assumed for the sake of the example that all nests active on the search date were discovered. Our first hypothetical search was on day 30 when 4 nests were found; 2 hatched resulting in an observed hatch rate of 50 percent. On day 60, again 4 nests were found; 1 hatched resulting in an observed hatch rate of 25 percent. On day 90, 6 nests were found; 2 hatched and the observed hatch rate would be 33 percent. Had we conducted all 3 searches, we would have found only 13 of the 20 nests (Nest 6 would have been found on both day 30 and day 60) and observed a hatch rate of 31 percent. Actually, 4 of our 20 hypothetical nests hatched and the true hatch rate was only 20 percent. Obviously neither a single search nor 3 searches were adequate in this example. Even if searching had been at weekly intervals, some short-lived nests would have been missed. Because unsuccessful nests were less likely to be found, the observed hatch rate was consistently too high and the density too low.

Furthermore, differences in sampling

Table 2. Hypothetical hatch rates of nests in 2 fields subjected to different treatments.

Fate	Stage of development						Total
	Laying	Incubation (days)					
		4	8	12	16	20	
Treatment A							
Hatch	16	20	24	7	8	9	84
Fail	24	20	16	3	2	1	66
Hatch rate (%)	40	50	60	70	80	90	56
Treatment B							
Hatch	3	4	5	24	28	32	96
Fail	7	6	5	16	12	8	54
Hatch rate (%)	30	40	50	60	70	80	64

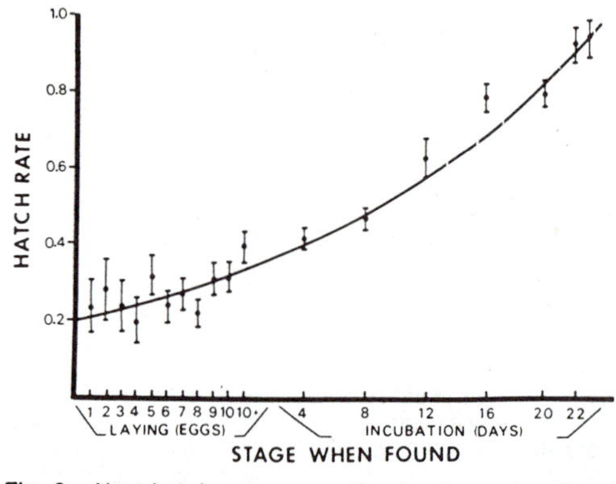

Fig. 2. Nest hatch rates according to stage when found (±1 SE) and estimated hatch rates determined from Mayfield method as described in text.

procedures also could preclude valid comparisons of hatch rates and nest densities between areas. This can best be illustrated by hypothetical data (Table 2) representing the success of nests found in 2 fields subjected to Treatments A and B. Although all nests regardless of age are grouped in most studies, we have grouped these by stages of development to illustrate better the problems. Under Treatment A, arbitrarily assigned hatch rates were 40 percent for nests found in the laying stage, 50 percent for nests found 4 days along, etc., up to 90 percent for nests 20 days into incubation. The composite rate for all nests found was 56 percent. Under Treatment B, hatch rates were a uniform 10 percent lower at each stage. Despite this difference, the composite rate was 64 percent, *higher* than Treatment A. These strange results simply reflect the majority of nests having been found in early stages of development in Treatment A and in later stages in Treatment B. This could be caused by more frequent searches in A with the result that most nests were found before they reached later stages of development.

The hypothetical data in Table 2 illustrate that the observed composite hatch rates may be misleading. Under Treatment B, for example, the hatch rate of "laying" nests, observed through most of their life span, is 30 percent, which suggests that the true hatch rate is not anywhere near 64 percent. Furthermore, comparison of the 2 treatments on the basis of the composite hatch rates would imply that Treatment B is better than Treatment A, a clearly erroneous conclusion. A misleading conclusion can be avoided if the hatch rates in each treatment are compared only within stage of development categories (laying, 4 days incubation, etc.), as displayed in Table 2. However, the Mayfield method enables all observations to be used in a simple comparison of the effects of the 2 treatments. If we assume that the total exposure period was 35 days and that all "laying" nests were found 30 days prior to hatching, we find the estimated hatch rates show Treatment A (34%) to be clearly better than Treatment B (21%).

An assumption in using Mayfield's method is that the daily survival rate of nests is constant among nests (Green 1977) and throughout the laying and incubation periods. We suspected some variation in the daily survival rates when, for example, the female started incubation and first occupied the nest overnight. There was, however, no important difference between the estimated survival rates of nests (Table 1) found during laying (daily survival rate = 0.9548) and those found during incubation (daily survival rate = 0.9555). Additionally, no consistent deviation was noted between expected and observed hatch rates (Fig. 2).

We have demonstrated the probable biases intermittent searches cause in the results of a nesting study. Pooling nests found at different stages of development resulted in an observed hatch rate biased upward and an observed density biased downward. These biases varied according to the procedures used to obtain the sample of nests and the results from pooled data could lead to erroneous conclusions. We have illustrated a simple procedure, the Mayfield method, of correcting for such biases and avoiding possibly erroneous conclusions. The corrected results obtained in our examples appeared to be consistent with our observations of blue-winged teal nests throughout the laying and incubation period. We therefore recommend the use of Mayfield's or similar methods of correcting the observed nesting success and density in future analyses.

LITERATURE CITED

EARL, J. P. 1950. Production of mallards on irrigated land in the Sacramento Valley, California. J. Wildl. Manage. 14(3):332–342.

GREEN, R. F. 1977. Do more birds produce fewer young? A comment on Mayfield's measure of nest success. Wilson Bull. 89(1):173–175.

HAMMOND, M. C., AND W. R. FORWARD. 1956. Experiments on causes of duck nest predation. J. Wildl. Manage. 20(3):243–247.

HIGGINS, K. F., L. M. KIRSCH, AND I. J. BALL, JR. 1969. A cable-chain device for locating duck nests. J. Wildl. Manage. 33(4):1009–1011.

MARTZ, G. F. 1967. Effects of nesting cover removal on breeding puddle ducks. J. Wildl. Manage. 31(2):236–247.

MAYFIELD, H. 1960. The Kirtland's Warbler. Cranbrook Institute of Science, Bloomfield Hills, Michigan. 242pp.

———. 1961. Nesting success calculated from exposure. Wilson Bull. 73(3):255–261.

———. 1975. Suggestions for calculating nest success. Wilson Bull. 87(4):456–466.

REED, A. 1975. Reproductive output of black ducks in the St. Lawrence Estuary. J. Wildl. Manage. 39(2):243–255.

TOWNSEND, G. H. 1966. A study of waterfowl nesting on the Saskatchewan River Delta. Can. Field Nat. 80(2):74–88.

WELLER, M. W. 1956. A simple field candler for waterfowl eggs. J. Wildl. Manage. 20(2):111–113.

Received 1 September 1977.
Accepted 20 February 1978.

RENESTING[1]

L. K. SOWLS[2]

Ducks are "indeterminate" layers, capable of producing large clutches of eggs, as contrasted with the "determinate" layers such as doves, pigeons, and plovers where clutch size is a nearly predictable number. While those birds usually have more than one brood per year, ducks have but one. However, ducks are persistent renesters and will try again if their first nest is destroyed.

While the extent of nest losses among ducks has been studied thoroughly, the details of the renesting phenomenon in waterfowl have received little attention. Studies of renesting in waterfowl were started at Delta in 1946 and continued through 1950. The preliminary findings of this study have been published (Sowls 1949). This chapter is a continuation of the earlier paper with the same procedures extended to a larger sample size. Work since 1949 also was directed toward the problem of renesting following the loss of downy young.

Previous Work.—Bennett (1938:57–58) and Low (1945:50) have distinguished renesting attempts from first nests by smaller clutch size, less down and the general appearance of the nest, and the lateness of the season. In predation studies, Kalmbach (1937:21) classified the nests into "early" and "late season" nests, the latter group apparently representing renests. Cartwright (1944:327) and Errington (1942:170–171) discussed some of the theoretical aspects of the importance of renesting in game birds, including waterfowl. Hochbaum (1944:158) pointed out the need for renesting information about ducks and suggested nest-trapping and marking of hens as a means of study.

Barnes (1948:449) described the occurrence of a banded wood duck nesting twice in one season. Engeling (1949:6) said of a mottled duck in Texas, "I observed a pair build five nests in succession and lay a total of 34 eggs before finally hatching a brood of nine."

During the year 1950, I concentrated on the behavior of hens after nests were destroyed during the *later stages* of incubation in order that this aspect of the problem could be treated more thoroughly.

Clutch Size, First Nests Versus Renests.—Lack (1947) pointed out that the tendency for clutches of renests to be smaller than clutches of first nests among ducks has been known for many years in Europe. I already have mentioned Bennett's and Low's work on clutch size.

My data on clutch size of both first nests and renests for 21 individual hens are given in Table 1. On analysis, the apparent drop in clutch size was found to be statistically significant.

Although the average number of eggs in first clutches is greater statistically than the average number of eggs in renests, the difference is not great enough to distinguish first clutches from renests.

Some known renests of gadwalls, blue-winged teal and pintails had more eggs than the first clutch of another individual of the same species. One pintail had the same size clutch in her first nest and her renest.

---

[1] Originally published in Prairie ducks, pages 129–142. The Wildlife Management Institute, Washington, D.C., 1955.

[2] Present address: Arizona Cooperative Wildlife Research Unit, U.S.D.I., 214 Biological Sciences East, University of Arizona, Tucson, AZ 85721.

Table 1. Clutch size of first nests and renests of individual hens.

Species	Number eggs first nest	Number eggs second nest	Number eggs third nest
Mallard	10	9	
Pintail	10	9	
	10	8	8
	10	7	
	9	8	7
	9	7	
	9	6	
	9	4	
	8	8	
	8	7	
	8	7	
	8	6	
	7	6	
	7	3	
Gadwall	11	9	
	10	9	
	8	5	
Shoveller	12	9	
	12	8	8
B-w Teal	12	10	
	10	9	

In Table 2, I have divided the nesting season into three arbitrary parts and have included under each part of the nesting season, all clutches known to be full sets of eggs. It is apparent that a decrease in size occurs in all species as the season advances.

Bennett's "normal" nests of the blue-winged teal averaged only 9.3 eggs. One blue-winged teal at Delta in 1948 had more eggs (10) in her second nest than Bennett's average for all first nests. The other teal in this study had about the same number of eggs (9) in her second nest as Bennett's average first clutch in a species where clutches of 12 or more are common. The above instances may indicate that many of what Bennett called "normal" nests actually were renests.

The accumulated evidence appears to show that clutch size is not a valid criterion for distinguishing first nests from re-

Table 2. Differences in clutch size in the early, middle and late periods of the nesting season.

Species	Completed by May 15		Completed May 15–June 15		Completed after June 15	
	No.	Ave.	No.	Ave.	No.	Ave.
Mallard	23	10.0	25	8.3	3	9.1
Pintail	45	9.0	46	7.1	14	7.0
Gadwall	—	—	17	10.5	10	9.5
Shoveller	—	—	15	10.8	14	8.5
B-w Teal	—	—	54	10.6	42	8.8

nests. Many renests would fall into the category of first nests if judged on the basis of clutch size alone. Low (1945:50) recognized this in his study of the redhead and suggests that his classification of renests does not include all of the renests but only those of which he was certain.

There are other complicating factors which may be inherent in all duck-nesting studies. For example, the number of eggs in a nest may not represent the actual number laid by the hen. A reduction of the clutch occurs when (1) a predator removes an egg, (2) the hen removes an egg broken by a predator, and (3) the hen is disturbed at laying time and drops an egg away from the nest.

Appearance, First Nests Versus Renests.—Some renests were as well constructed and as well concealed as first nests. In some cases there was no noticeable change in appearance between first nests and renests. In two or three gadwall nests there was as much down in the second nest as in the first. In the case of both blue-winged teal nests and mallard nests I could distinguish some reduction of down, but it was not great. In the case of pintails, the species for which I have the most data, there was a noticeable decrease in the amount of down in some renests when compared with the first nests of the same individuals. However,

Figs. 1, 2. First and second nests of pintail hen No. 47-604106 for 1948.

Fig. 3. Third nest of pintail hen No. 47-604106 for 1948.

without having seen and recorded the first nest, it would have been impossible to say whether or not the nests were first attempts or renests (Figs. 1–3).

One of the difficulties in distinguishing renests by appearance is that in order to do so one would have to compare all nests at the same stage of incubation, because down and other materials accumulate gradually.

Renesting Interval.—The time between the destruction of the first nest and the laying of the first egg in the second nest might well be called the *renesting interval.* That this time varies with the stage of incubation has been described for other groups of birds than waterfowl. Stieve (1918) studied the anatomical basis of the re-laying capacity of the jackdaw in Poland. Laven (1940:131) discussed Stieve's findings in relation to renesting. Laven says that when the first clutch is destroyed shortly after the first laying period, re-laying occurs more promptly than when the first clutch is well advanced in incubation. The remaining follicles after cessation of laying soon are resorbed. For a time, however, the larger follicles are capable of being rebuilt. Later in incubation, they are so regressed that they can no longer be used for replacement purposes, and thereafter the smaller follicles must go through a construction process. Accordingly, re-laying takes longer.

For the ringed plover, a two-brooded species, Laven (1940:132) in Germany found an increase in the length of this period which I have called the renesting interval after nests were destroyed, but also found a shortening of the interval again in the very late stages of incubation. When the stage of incubation of the first clutch was 6–12 days, the renesting

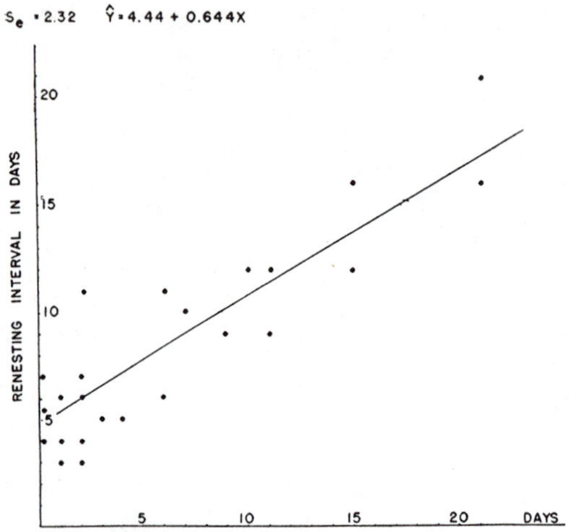

Fig. 4. Regression of length of renesting interval on stage of incubation at destruction of first nest.

interval was 5–6 days. When incubation was advanced to 14–21 days, the interval was 11–20 days. When a clutch was 26 days incubated, however, the interval was only 6–7 days. Laven points out that this indicates a renewed regular growth of the follicles toward the end of the incubation period in this species, which normally raises two broods a year.

Not all groups of birds show a lengthening of the renesting interval as the incubation-stage-at-destruction advances. Nice (1937:111) found that the renesting interval in song sparrows usually is five days. The incubation period of this species is 11 to 12 days, and it normally lays three or more clutches a year.

Data gathered at Delta on the renesting interval between 24 first and second duck nests are plotted graphically in Fig. 4.

All hens waited at least three days before renesting. For each additional day of incubation at the time of destruction of first nest, these hens waited an average of 0.62 days before beginning to lay their second clutches.

Continuous Laying.—All data so far presented have dealt with the renesting which follows the destruction of a complete clutch after incubation has begun. When nests are destroyed during the laying period, another situation exists.

Information on this phase of renesting behavior has been more difficult to obtain because hens are hard to capture and mark during the laying time. When laying, a hen's attachment to her nest is weaker than it is during incubation, and disturbance often causes desertion. The robbing of a nest each day to determine how many eggs a hen will lay continuously has not been successful in the field because of heavy predation which terminated experiments in all cases.

In 1949, three records were obtained of continuous laying in the wild. A blue-winged teal hen was captured and marked on May 24 after she had laid five eggs. One egg was warm when I found the nest. The eggs were taken from her at the time. On June 2, the same hen was found on a new nest 50 yards from the first nest site. At that time she had nine eggs, but continued laying until she had a clutch of 13. The number of eggs found on June 2 indicated that the hen had continued laying in her new nest the day following the destruction of her first nest. Thus, a total of 18 eggs was laid continuously.

In 1949 also, continuous laying by shovellers was noted twice. On May 20, a banded hen was flushed from her nest where she had laid one egg. She abandoned her nest, moved 80 yards, and began a new nest, this time laying 12 eggs. The first egg in this latter nest was laid the day following abandonment of the first nest.

Incidentally, this individual hen, which was well known to me, nested for four consecutive years on the study area. All four of her first nests, each of which had a complete clutch, held 12 eggs.

The other record of a shoveller laying continuously in 1949 was of a banded hen found on June 27 with four fresh eggs. She abandoned her nest then and continued to lay in another nest 150 yards away on June 28. This time she produced a clutch of six eggs. This late-season nest probably was a second renest, since the clutch was small.

It seems likely from these observations that continuous laying usually occurs when nests are broken up during the laying period, and that there is no renesting interval then.

Further observations concerning continuous laying were made by autopsy. The reproductive system of a laying hen is shown in Fig. 5. A shell was about to be deposited on an egg in the oviduct. Other eggs in various stages were in the process of development. Several ovulated follicles were visible, and the largest one (indicated by an arrow), probably was the source of the egg about to be laid. This mallard hen had laid four eggs when she was killed. Since I wished to compare the condition found in this laying mallard hen with a hen that I believed to be nearly through laying her clutch of eggs, I collected a gadwall hen on June 19, 1950, as she settled down on a nest at 7:00 a.m. The nest held 10 cold eggs when she arrived. Since the clutch size for Delta gadwalls did not exceed 11 eggs, I believed that the hen was ready to lay her last egg. When I autopsied this hen, I found a completely developed egg ready to be laid but found no follicles over 5 millimeters in diameter. Incubating hens were collected also. It was found that a rapid regression in the size of follicles occurred when incubation began.

From this anatomical evidence it seems likely that continuous laying cannot occur when the nest is destroyed at the time that the last egg is about to be laid, and definite that it cannot occur when the nest is destroyed during the incubation period. Just when, in the laying period, clutch size is determined is unknown. But it is evident, that regression of follicles and their increase again to egg-laying size happen rapidly.

The lengthening period of the renesting interval as the ovaries regress during the incubation period is consistent with anatomical data existing on domestic fowl. Aside from the fact that the smaller ova have more growing to do than the larger ones, the rate of growth of the larger ova has been found to be faster. Of this, Riddle (1916:388) says, "... the rate of growth is not uniform, or continuous, and may be divided into a number of periods. In a previous study, I found some evidence that the growth period in the fowl is not a steady, unbroken one—not even among the larger continuously growing ova of a functioning ovary; but at a certain point, the rate changes quite suddenly to a rate apparently eight to 20 times faster than before; and further, that the change in rate normally occurs five to

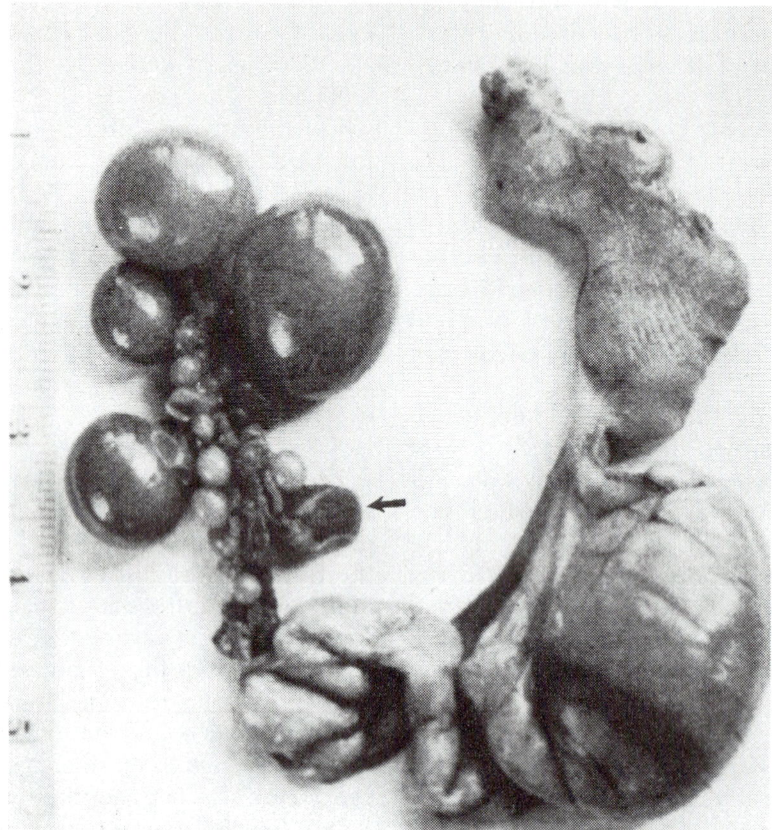

Fig. 5. Reproductive tract of a laying mallard hen. The arrow indicates an ovulated follicle from which the large egg in the oviduct probably came.

eight days before ovulation, and when the ova have reached a diameter of about 6mm."

Renesting After Loss of Brood.—In 1949 and in 1950, I made an effort to determine what happened to a hen after her brood was taken from her.

In order to answer this question, I nest-trapped and marked 10 hens and left them to incubate their eggs. Then, just as the young had hatched and were dry enough to leave the nest, they were taken from the hen. The procedure was carried out with six pintails, three blue-winged teal and one mallard. Of this group, two of the pintail hens were known to renest following loss of brood. One waited for a period of 18 days and then laid a clutch of three. Her first clutch had been seven. The second waited for 16 days and produced a clutch of eight. Her first clutch had been 10.

From these observations we see that some hens will renest even after their eggs have hatched and the brood is destroyed. How long after hatching a hen will do so is unknown. Variation in the reaction of the hen to early-season brood-loss and late-season brood-loss may be considerable. This likewise is unknown.

Location of Renests.—The locations of first nests and renests of 31 hens are plot-

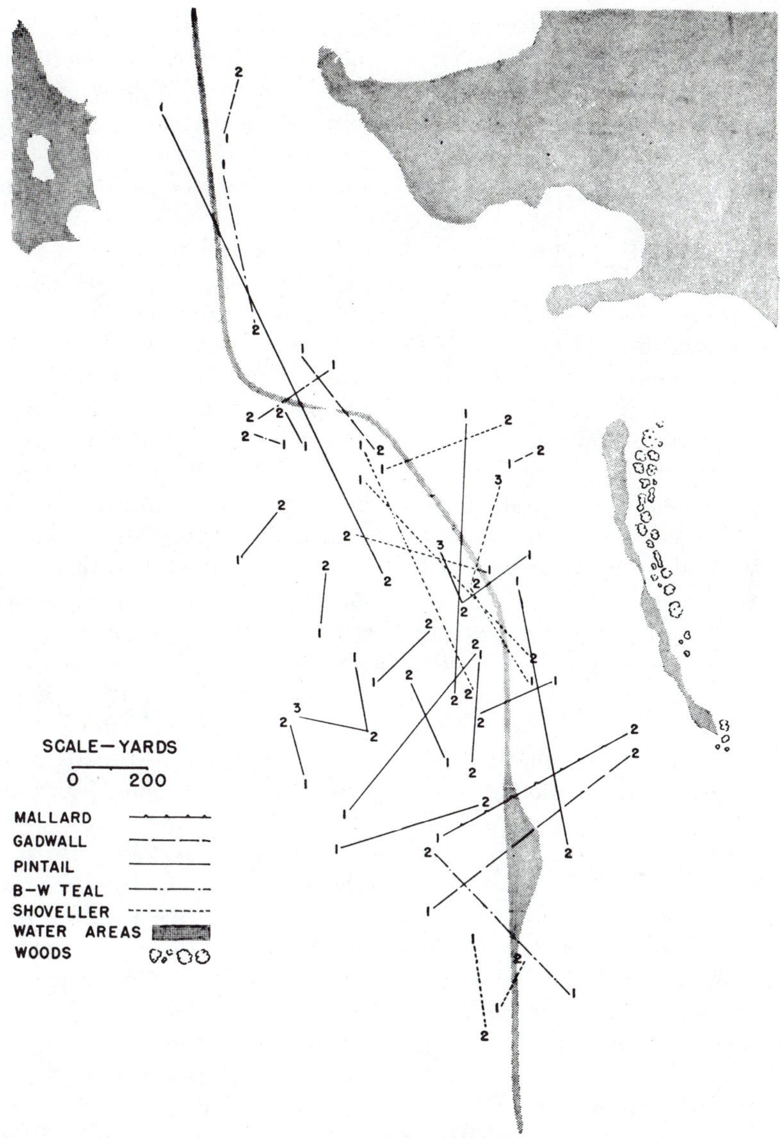

Fig. 6. Locations of first nests and renests of 31 hens of 5 species, 1947–50.

ted in Fig. 6. Of these hens, all but one had located their second nests within a relatively short distance from their first nests. The maximum, minimum, and average distances between first nests and renests of 31 hens of five species are given in Table 3. Only one hen moved over 700 yards. This bird was a pintail which located her second nest 1,500 yards from her first nest. In this case, rising marsh waters flooded the area around the site of the first nest so that the hen was forced to move.

It is of interest to note that the pattern

Table 3. Distances in yards between different nests of the same hen during the same year.

Species	Number of hens	Maximum distance	Minimum distance	Average distance
Mallard	1	700	700	700
Gadwall	3	600	45	320
Pintail	15	1,500	85	282
Shoveller	7	765	135	355
B-w Teal	5	405	135	270

of nest sites in Fig. 6 (first nests and renests in a single year) is similar to the pattern of nest sites in Fig. 7 (nests of returning hens, two or more years).

Number of Unsuccessful Hens Which Renest.—How many unsuccessful hens renest is unknown. The fact that only 42 of our 220 marked hens were known to do so does not mean that the others did not. I have no doubt that there were renests on the study area that I did not discover. This is indicated clearly by the fact that six of my 42 renest records resulted from seeing a brood with a marked hen rather than by finding the second nests. Other hens may have nested outside the study area; still others may not have renested at all.

Low (1945:48) in his study of the redhead divided the nesting season into 10-day periods and showed the number of hens in each period which terminated their breeding efforts because of nest failures.

Laven (1940:131) in his study of the ringed plover in Germany says that one pair produced four additional layings after the loss of its first clutch, while other pairs in the area produced one clutch and departed when that was lost. He also points out that great variation between individuals and birds of different ages must be expected.

That some pairs of ducks wander following nest destruction may account for the large gatherings of pairs which one often sees on the breeding grounds late in the nesting period. As has been mentioned, this may follow changes in environment of first nesting. Arthur S. Hawkins and I saw such a gathering of pairs and lone hens of gadwalls, pintails, mallards and blue-winged teal at Whitewater Lake, Manitoba, on June 26, 1946. For three springs, I saw such gatherings of pintails south of the study area at Delta. Similar flocks have been observed by Stoudt and Davis (1948:134) who say, "Apparently the South Dakota area had a large number of either transient or non-breeding birds on the transects during the first week in June and these consisted mainly of pintails, mallards and shovellers . . . . It may be that this state has more than her share of non-breeding birds which may consist of either infertile or sexually immature ducks or bachelor drakes. . . . The fact that 135 pairs of pintails were seen on Transects F and B in June and only four broods were found in July illustrates the need for future studies along these lines."

Renesting and Inventory Counts.—The presence of birds of undetermined status as described above may confuse the counting of breeding pairs for inventory purposes. Smith and Hawkins (1948:62) ask the question, "How many times during the season does the population of an area renew itself; i.e., what is its turnover rate? If a given drake defends his territory against all other drakes of his kind for only two weeks and the nesting period for the species spans six weeks, there is the theoretical possibility that the area appraised at ten pairs per section had a total season's population of thirty pairs (three turnovers)."

To what extent this wide span of nesting is accounted for by late first nesters, and to what extent by renesters who failed earlier, is not known. If one con-

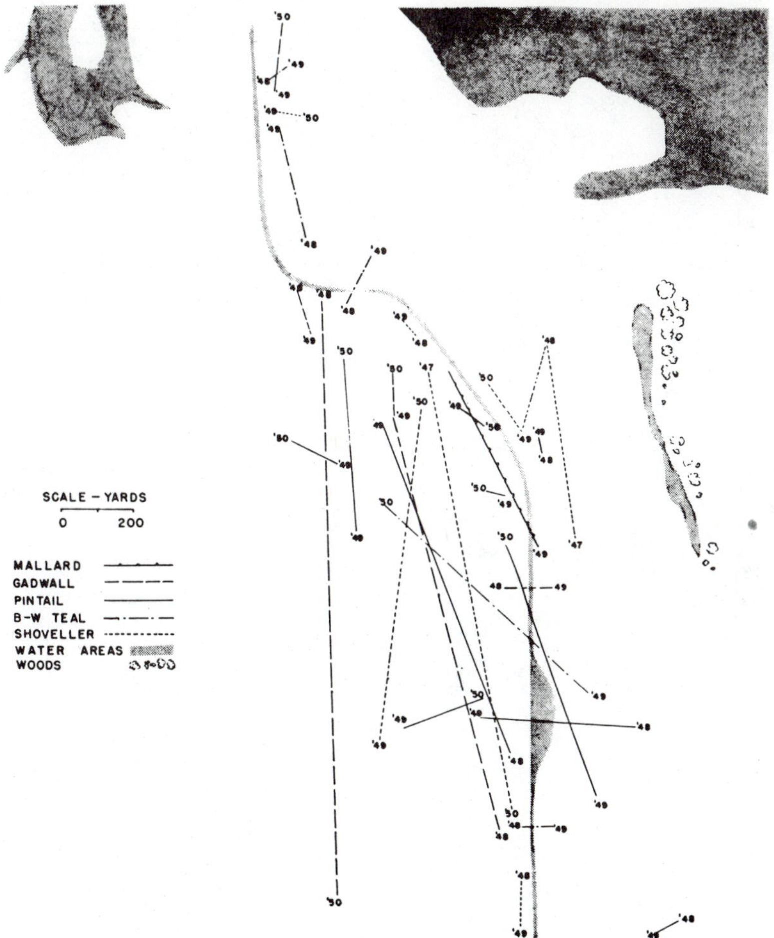

Fig. 7. Nest locations of returning individual hens of five species during different years.

siders the ducks' persistence to renest, however, it seems likely that a large number of the late nesters are merely the same birds which failed earlier. Hence, rather than having a "turnover" of hens, we have an extension of the nesting season brought about through renesting.

Persistence in Renesting.—Not all species exhibit the same persistency to renest following the destruction of their first nests. The measurement of this comparative persistency is not made easily, however, because of several factors. The number of hens marked in the renesting study was not the same for all species. The time of season in which they were marked was not always the same. Many hens probably were marked for the first time when they already were on their second nests. Mallards were difficult to handle, deserted readily, and did not offer good opportunity for comparison.

In my studies, I repeatedly found that of all species, the pintail was the most persistent renester, and the blue-winged teal the least persistent renester. Of 62

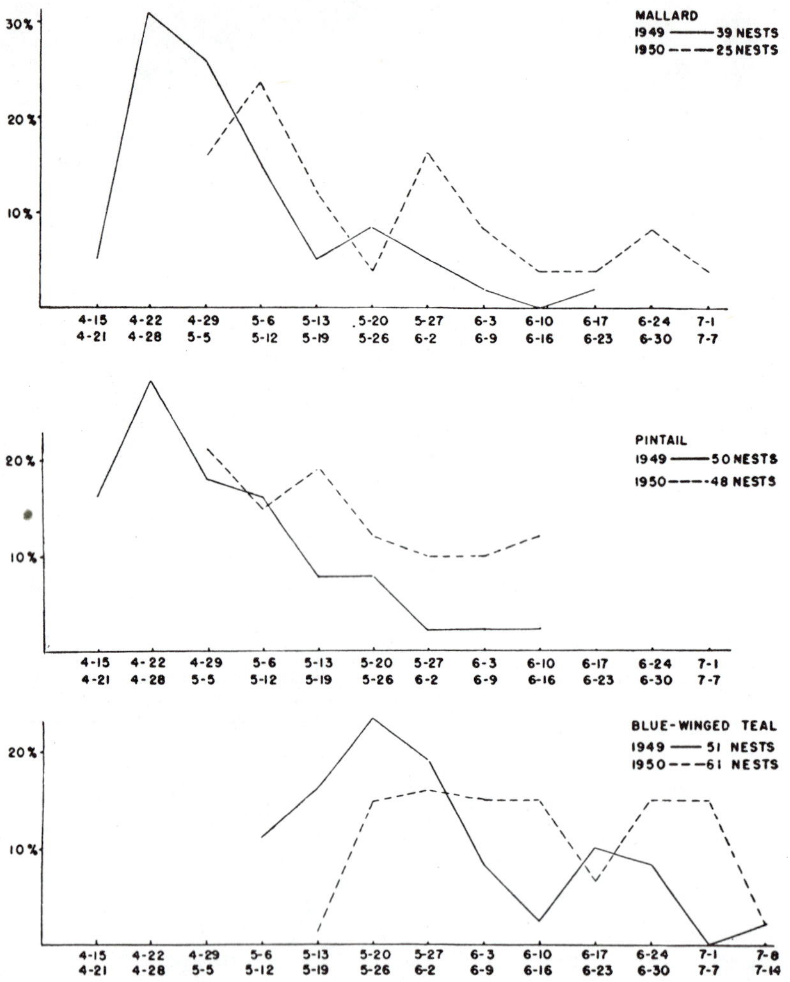

Fig. 8. Nesting chronology of mallard, pintail, and blue-winged teal for the years 1949 and 1950 determined by the percentage of nests started by weeks of the season.

pintail hens marked, I obtained definite renesting records on 19, or 30 per cent. Two of these were known to renest a second time following destruction of their second nest. It was the pintail which gave me positive information that renesting not only follows nest destruction but sometimes also follows destruction of a hatched brood.

In the five years of my study, I nest-trapped and marked 88 blue-winged teal hens. Of this number, only five, or about 6 per cent, were known to renest. This sample of marked hens was larger than the number of marked hen pintails, but the renesting number was only about one-sixth as great.

Only one renesting mallard was recorded of 20 hens marked. Of 33 shovellers marked, only seven were known to

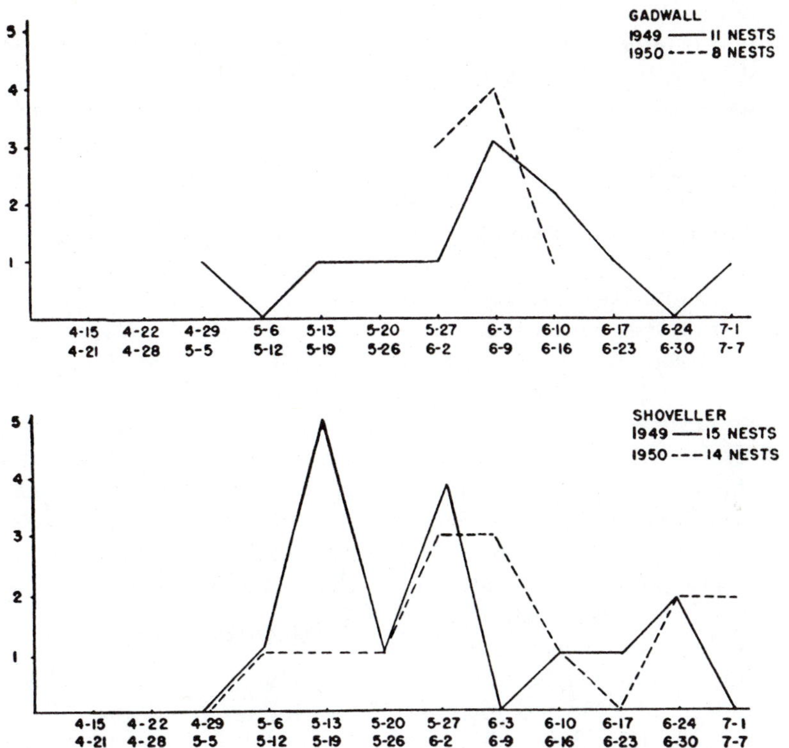

Fig. 9. Nesting chronology of gadwall and shoveller for the years 1949 and 1950 determined by number of nests started by weeks of the season.

renest. One of these, however, was persistent enough to renest twice in one year. This shoveller, and two pintail hens, were the only three individuals in my study known to do this. The gadwall was a persistent renester; 23 per cent of 16 gadwalls marked were known to renest. For these three species just mentioned, a relatively small amount of data was obtained. Although only one mallard was known to renest, I am certain, from dates of nesting, that they readily do so. Williams and Marshall (1938:41) working at Bear River, Utah, found that 70 per cent of the duck eggs found hatched successfully. Sowls (1948:130), however, working at Delta, found that only 35 per cent of nests found hatched successfully. Thus we see that there is a variation in early-season nest losses between regions and between years.

In 1940, heavy early-season nest losses at Delta resulted from spring floods. In 1946, spring fires wiped out all early nests over large parts of the Delta marsh, and only renesting could have maintained population numbers that year. In 1950, spring plowing on the Portage plains took an abnormally heavy toll of pintail nests during the peak of the nesting season.

Evidence that early losses are compensated for by renesting is obtained from an analysis of nesting data. To interpret such data we might set an arbitrary date after which all nests started would be considered renests. For the Delta marsh area, I would set this date for mallards and pintails at May 20. (This date would vary with early and late years but would be correct for the latest season I have seen at Delta.) From Fig. 8, it is evident that 17 per cent of all mallard nests, and 25 per cent of all pintail nests in 1949, were started after this date and would therefore be considered renests. In 1950, 48 per cent of the mallard and 44 per cent of the pintail nests were begun after May 20 and would be, therefore, renests. I believe that this is a conservative interpretation. As has been pointed out earlier, these figures do not include renests of marked hens which renested after my disturbance of the first nest. Furthermore, nests destroyed very early in incubation and nests destroyed during the laying period could have led to renestings which would have been begun before this date.

For the later-nesting blue-winged teal, I would set June 24 as the arbitrary date after which all nests begun could be considered renests. Figure 8 then shows us that 9 per cent of the blue-winged teal nests found in 1949 were renests, and in 1950, more than 30 per cent were renests.

I believe that the data on the gadwall and shoveller given in Fig. 9 are insufficient for such an analysis.

During the spring of 1950, I determined from embryo dating of eggs found in early-season nests that a large hatch of mallards and pintails would occur during the period between June 6 and June 12. This prediction was fulfilled when the majority of early-collected eggs hatched in the Delta incubator during this period. Contrary to the prediction that large numbers of pintail and mallard broods would appear in the wild, no broods were seen until July 8. At least a half-dozen observers had been in the field during this time. I believe that only on the basis of early and heavy nest loss can this lack of early broods be explained.

Analysis of brood data on the dates of hatching within arbitrarily set periods would give an estimate of the percentage of young which resulted from renesting. In my study, I was unable to gather enough brood data to do this.

Although we cannot determine from the data now available the percentage of thwarted hens which renest, and the percentage of production which results from renesting, it is clear that renesting at Delta is of major importance in maintaining the waterfowl population there.

SUMMARY

1. Ducks have but one brood a year but readily renest if their first nest is destroyed. While the extent of nest destruction has been studied thoroughly in the United States and Canada, the details of the renesting phenomenon have received slight attention.

2. In 1946, a study to answer basic questions in regard to renesting in ducks was started at Delta, Manitoba. Hens were captured on their nests, banded, feather-marked, their nests robbed, and hens released. After this operation, the area was watched for renesting birds.

3. Of 220 birds so trapped, 42 were known to nest again. Of the 42 renesters, three hens were known to have three nests during one season. Two of these were pintails and one was a shoveller.

4. Although the average number of eggs in first clutches is greater statistically than the number of eggs in renests, the difference is not great enough to distinguish first clutches from renests. Some

renests have as many or more eggs than other first nests.

5. Renests cannot be distinguished safely from first nests by their appearance. Many renests look like first nests.

6. The time between the destruction of the first nest and the laying of the first egg in the second nest (*the renesting interval*) varies with the stage of incubation at which the nest is destroyed. The farther advanced incubation is, the longer the hen waits before renesting. All hens whose nests had been destroyed after incubation had begun, waited at least three days before laying again. For each additional day of incubation hens waited an average 0.62 days before renesting.

7. Continuous laying without a renesting interval occurs when the first nest is destroyed during the early part of the laying period. A renesting interval probably is required before laying again if nest destruction occurs on the day the last egg of the first clutch is due to be laid.

8. Two pintails, whose young were taken from them after hatching, renested following the robbing of their young. Thus, renesting may follow the destruction of a hatched brood.

9. The percentage of unsuccessful hens which renest has not been determined. In this study some may have renested outside the study area and some may not have renested at all.

10. Hens located their renests in the vicinity of their first nests. All hens located their renests within 700 yards of their first nests except one pintail which moved 1,500 yards to renest.

11. Of the five species studied, the pintail was the most persistent renester, and the blue-winged teal the least persistent.

12. Inventory counts made by the transect method are complicated by the renesting phenomenon in that birds counted as breeders at one time may be counted as breeders again at a later time when they are in reality renesters that failed earlier.

13. Renesting varies in its importance to production with locality and year depending upon the extent of nest loss. In some areas during some years it may account for nearly the entire production.

14. The number of nests found which were renests was estimated by regarding all nests begun after an arbitrarily set date as renests. The arbitrary date for mallards and pintails at Delta is May 20; for blue-winged teal, June 24. Thus, in 1949, it was estimated that at least 17 per cent of all mallard nests, 14 per cent of all pintail nests, and 9 per cent of all blue-winged teal nests were renests. In 1950, at least 48 per cent of the mallard nests, 44 per cent of the pintail nests, and 30 per cent of the blue-winged teal nests were estimated to be renests.

LITERATURE CITED

BARNES, WILLIAM B. 1948. Unusual nesting behavior of a wood duck. Auk 65:449.

BENNETT, LOGAN J. 1938. The blue-winged teal, its ecology and management. Collegiate Press, Inc., Ames, Iowa. 144pp.

CARTWRIGHT, B. W. 1944. The "crash" decline in sharp-tailed grouse and Hungarian partridge in western Canada and the role of the predator. Trans. 9th N. Amer. Wildl. Conf.:324–330.

ENGELING, GUS A. 1949. The mottled duck—A determined nester. Texas Game and Fish 7(8):6–7.

ERRINGTON, PAUL L. 1942. On the analysis of productivity in populations of higher vertebrates. Jour. Wildl. Mgt. 6:165–181.

HOCHBAUM, H. ALBERT. 1944. The canvasback on a prairie marsh. Amer. Wildlife Inst., Washington, D.C. 201pp.

KALMBACH, E. R. 1937. Crow-waterfowl relations. U.S. Dept. Agr. Circular 443.

LACK, DAVID. 1947. The significance of clutch-size. Ibis Apr. 1947:302–353.

LAVEN, H. 1940. Ueber Nachlegen und Weiterlegen. Ornith. Monatsber. 48:131–136.

LOW, JESSOP B. 1945. Ecology and management of the redhead (*Nyroca americana*) in Iowa. Ecol. Monog. 15(1):35–69.

NICE, MARGARET MORSE. 1937. Studies in the life history of the song sparrow. I. Trans. Linnaean Soc. N.Y. 4. 247pp.

RIDDLE, OSCAR. 1916. Studies on the physiology of reproduction in birds. I. The occurrence and measurement of a sudden change in the rate of growth of avian ova. Amer. Jour. Physiology 41(3):337–396.

SMITH, ROBERT H., AND ARTHUR S. HAWKINS. 1948. Appraising waterfowl breeding populations. Trans. 13th N. Amer. Wildl. Conf.:57–62.

SOWLS, LYLE K. 1948. The Franklin ground squirrel (*Citellus franklinii*) and its relationship to nesting ducks. Jour. Mamm. 29:113–137.

———. 1949. A preliminary report on renesting in waterfowl. Trans. 14th N. Amer. Conf.:260–275.

STIEVE, H. 1918. Die Entwicklung des Eierstockeies der Dohle (Coloeus mondedula). Arch. Mikr. Anat. 92. Ab. II:137–288.

STOUDT, JEROME H., AND FLOYD H. DAVIS. 1948. 1948 Waterfowl breeding ground survey north central region. *In* Waterfowl populations and breeding conditions, summer 1948. Spec. Scient. Rep. No. 60, U.S. Dept. Int., Fish & Wildlife Service, Washington, D.C.:123–148.

WILLIAMS, CECIL S., AND WILLIAM H. MARSHALL. 1938. Duck nesting studies, Bear River migratory bird refuge, Utah, 1937. Jour. Wildl. Mgt. 2:29–48.

BREEDING AGE OF CANADA GEESE[1]

JOHN J. CRAIGHEAD, U. S. Fish and Wildlife Service, Missoula, Montana
DWIGHT S. STOCKSTAD, Montana State Fish and Game Department, Kalispell

Abstract: This study was designed to determine what percent of 1-, 2-, and 3-year-old wild geese (*Branta canadensis moffitti*) nest in a population of limited size; to compare results with similar information from captive flocks; and, by applying the breeding-age data obtained, to determine the percent of breeding geese in the Flathead Valley population. Five hundred forty-eight known-age Canada geese in the Flathead Valley population were color-marked during four breeding seasons, and the survivors were observed for breeding activity over a 5-year period. Most of the marked known-age geese were located prior to nesting; then the number of nesting birds in each age group was determined by censuses throughout the breeding seasons. A similar experiment was conducted on two captive flocks. No 1-year-old birds nested in either the wild or the captive populations. Between 27 and 36 percent of the 2-year-old wild geese nested, but only 17 percent of the captive 2-year-olds did so. All of the 3-year-old wild birds nested, but only 64 percent of the captives nested. Since the proportion of birds breeding in captive and in wild flocks appears to be markedly different, the breeding data from captive flocks cannot be used to determine the breeding age or the percent of breeding birds in a wild population. The breeding-age statistics obtained from the wild population, when applied to life-table data, showed that during a population-turnover period of 5 years only 10.2 percent of a generation of geese in the Flathead Valley, Montana, attained breeding age and survived to nest. This calculation was made on the assumption that one-third of all 2-year-old geese nest.

In order to understand the population dynamics of Canada geese and to interpret more accurately life equations and life tables constructed for the species, it is essential to evaluate breeding-age data on captive flocks and to obtain more precise information on the breeding age of wild birds. Various authors have studied the breeding age of Canada geese in captive and semicaptive flocks. Elder (1946:105) stated that none of the pinioned geese in the flock at Bright Land Farm, Illinois, nested in their first or second years and only 25 percent nested in their third year. Kossack (1950:628), studying the same flock, found that none nested as 1-year-olds, 7.8 percent nested as 2-year-olds, and 20 percent nested as 3-year-olds. Kossack apparently included in his findings both wing-clipped and full-winged birds. Balham (1954), working with a flock in Manitoba, stated that only a small percentage of geese nested as 2-year-olds.

Hanson (1949:181–182), working with captured wild geese (*Branta canadensis interior*) on the Horseshoe Lake Game Refuge in Illinois, separated 1-year-old females from older females by determining the presence or absence of an occluding membrane over the opening of the oviduct. All but one of 2½-year-old females had open oviducts. If this was an accurate way of judging whether these females had nested, then about 94 percent had nested at 2 years. In his most recent publication, Hanson (1962:15) indicates uncertainty as to breeding among 2-year-olds and points out the need to determine more precisely what percent of the 2-year-old females nest in their third spring. He says, however, "At the present stage of our knowledge, predictions of populations must be based on the assumption that all females attempt to nest

[1] Contribution from the Montana Cooperative Wildlife Research Unit, U. S. Fish and Wildlife Service, Montana State Fish and Game Department, Montana State University, and Wildlife Management Institute cooperating. The study was partially supported with Federal Aid in Wildlife Restoration funds under Pittman–Robertson Project W-71-R, Montana State Fish and Game Department.

Originally published in J. Wildl. Manage. 28(1):57–64, 1964.

Fig. 1. Color-marked goose at nest.

at approximately 2 years of age in their third spring of life." If this assumption is incorrect, or cannot be applied to other populations, it may, of course, introduce error into estimates of productivity based on breeding age and into calculations of number and percent of breeding birds.

The purpose of the present study was threefold: (1) to determine from marked known-age birds what percent of 1-, 2-, and 3-year-old wild geese nest in a population of limited size, (2) to compare the results with similar information from captive flocks in the area, and (3) by applying breeding-age data to a life table, to determine the percent of a generation of wild birds surviving to breed.

We were working with the population of wild geese in the Flathead Valley in Montana (Geis 1956, Craighead and Stockstad 1961) and with two captive flocks, one on the National Bison Range at Moiese, Montana, and the other at Warm Springs, Montana.

The Flathead Valley wild goose population is sufficiently small and well defined to lend itself to population analysis. Its average size in the spring was approximately 800 birds from 1953 through 1960. During this 8-year period, 1,609 nests were located. These represent a near-total count and an average of 201 nests per year.

The captive flocks varied in size from year to year but seldom exceeded 60 birds. Only a small proportion of the data was obtained from the Warm Springs flock, thus we have combined data from the two flocks.

We are grateful to Bob Brown, Bob Gustafson, Ralph Stockstad, John Morrison, Glen Beckman, and Maurice Hornocker for their help in capturing and color-marking goslings and for their assistance in locating nests of marked geese. Thanks are due John Schwartz and Victor B. May of the National Bison Range for helping us to mark and observe captive geese. Robert Green and Hank Engbrecht helped in a

Table 1. Size of wild gosling population and marked sample.

YEAR	SIZE OF GOSLING POPULATIONS*	NUMBER OF COLOR-MARKED GOSLINGS	PERCENT COLOR-MARKED
1955	755	245	32.5
1956	517	99	19.1
1957	462	112	24.2
1958	464	92	19.9
Total	2,198	548	

* The size of the gosling populations was determined by numerous counts on the brood areas.

similar manner at the Warm Springs Game Farm.

METHODS

Each year, goslings from both the wild and the captive flocks were sexed by use of the technique described by Elder (1946: 102–105) and marked with neck bands as described by Craighead and Stockstad (1956*b*). Table 1 shows the number of wild goslings captured and color-marked each year from 1955 through 1958. With the exception of the 1958 cohort, males and females of each generation were marked with different-colored, highly visible neck markers (Fig. 1). The sample consisted of 249 males, 207 females, and 92 of undetermined sex. We color-marked and leg-banded 24.9 percent of all goslings produced by the wild population over a 4-year period. The percentages marked and banded each year appear in Table 1.

Most of the marked known-age geese were located prior to nesting; then the number of nesting birds in each age group was determined by censuses throughout the breeding seasons. From 1956 through 1959, 662 nests of wild geese were located; 23 of these were nests of marked known-age birds.

A bird was considered as nesting and its breeding age recorded only if a nest with eggs or goslings was found and a marked bird of known age definitely associated with it. The status of marked females flushed from nests was easily determined, but the status of males was harder to discover. When females were flushed from nests, the males generally joined them. A marked male's joining an unmarked nesting female showed the probable nesting status of the male. Close observation of pairs in this category, over a period of time, yielded precise evidence. The nesting status of three marked males and two marked females, however, remained undetermined (Table 2). The breeding condition of these birds could have been discovered by collecting or trapping them for examination of oviducal openings (Elder 1946:105–108; Hanson 1949:179–180, 181–182), but sacrificing known-age birds or disturbing them by trapping had obvious disadvantages.

Nearly all the goslings produced by the captive flocks were color-marked and leg-banded each season. Fourteen nests of known-age birds were located, and the breeding age of these geese determined.

RESULTS

Wild Population

In designing the study, we recognized that heavy hunting would reduce the sample of color-marked birds over the years, but we had no way of estimating in advance what the magnitude of the kill or the mortality rate for each age would be. Table 2 shows that only 83 of the 548 geese originally captured and marked returned as yearlings. This fact indicates that mortality in the first year of life averaged 85 percent among the marked birds. This figure is probably somewhat too high, however, since we know that a small percentage of 1-year-old geese lost neck markers, and we recognize that some may not have returned to the Flathead Valley. Our band-return data (unpublished) indicate a first-year mortality rate of 60–70 percent in

Table 2. Breeding age of marked known-age geese in a wild population in Flathead Valley, Montana.

	Number in Population				Nesting Status				
Age	Year	Male	Female	Total	Males Nesting	Females Nesting	Undetermined Status	Total Nests	Percent Nesting
1 year	1956	5	6	11	0	0	0	0	
	1957	4	6	10	0	0	0	0	
	1958	17	13	30	0	0	0	0	
	1959	–	–	32	0	0	0	0	
	Total	26	25	83	0	0	0	0	0
2 years	1957	2	4	6	1	2	0	3	
	1958	5	4	9	0	1	1-M	1	
	1959	9	4	13	2	0	3-2M, 1F	2	
	1960	1	4	5	1	2	1-F	3	
	Total	17	16	33	4	5	5	9	27
3 years	1958	2	6	8	2	6	0	8	
	1959	0	0	0	0	0	0	0	
	1960	3	1	4	2	2	0	4	
	Total	5	7	12	4	8	0	12	100
4 years	1959	1	2	3	0	2	1-M	2	
	1960	0	0	0	0	0	0	0	
	Total	1	2	3	0	2	1	0	67
5 years	1960	0	1	1	0	0	1	0	
	Total	0	1	1	0	0	1	0	0

some cohorts. At Horseshoe Lake, Hanson and Smith (1950:177) computed a first-year mortality rate of 74 percent after fall banding.

Among our birds there was no important difference between the number of males and the number of females either at 1 year of age or among the birds of breeding age (Table 2). Hanson and Smith (1950:170–171) found an excess of males 2 years or older in the Horseshoe Lake flock; however, we found no concentration of nonnesting birds composed largely of males. We believe that a favorable sex ratio existed among both the marked and the unmarked birds in the Flathead Lake population. Unpublished band-recovery data further support this belief.

The heavy, first-year mortality left us with a relatively small sample of known-age geese that we could observe during their first spring Consequently, our sample of known-age birds with known breeding history proved to be too small for statistical treatment. Nevertheless, much valuable information concerning the breeding age of geese in a wild-population unit is recorded in Table 2.

Among 83 1-year-old marked geese of both sexes, none nested; most were paired, however, some to marked geese of the same age, and others to unmarked geese of unknown age. Some, though not all, of the 1-year birds selected territories, made scrapes, and defended these weakly. Only 40 percent of these 1-year-old marked birds survived to the age of 2 years.

Of the 33 2-year-old marked geese, 9 (5 females and 4 males) nested. In addition, five marked 2-year-olds defended territories, but their nesting status could not be precisely determined. Evidence indicates that at least two of these and possibly three may have nested and then had their nests destroyed before we located them, but, because other geese were nesting close by, we

Table 3. Breeding age of marked known-age geese in a captive flock at Moiese, Montana.

	Number in Population				Nesting Status				
Age	Year	Male	Female	Total	Males Nesting	Females Nesting	Undetermined Status	Total Nests	Percent Nesting
1 year	1957	4	3	7	0	0	0	0	
	1958	9	2	11	0	0	0	0	
	1959	1	4	5	0	0	0	0	
	1960	6	6	12	0	0	0	0	
	1961	17	8	25	0	0	0	0	
	Total	37	23	60	0	0	0	0	0
2 years	1958	1	2	3	0	0	0	0	
	1959	7	5	12	1	2	0	3	
	1960	0	2	2	0	0	0	0	
	1961	8	5	13	2	0	0	2	
	Total	16	14	30	3	2	0	5	17
3 years	1959	1	2	3	0	0	0	0	
	1960	0	2	2	1	1	0	2	
	1961	5	4	9	4	3	0	7	
	Total	6	8	14	5	4	0	9	64
4 years	1960	1	2	3	0	0	0	0	
	1961	0	1	1	0	0	0	0	
	Total	1	3	4	0	0	0	0	0
5 years	1961	1	1	2	0	0	0	0	
	Total	1	1	2	0	0	0	0	0

could not be certain. We are reasonably sure that they did not attempt to renest. If, as we believe, these three birds actually nested, then 36 percent or roughly one-third of all the 2-year-old birds nested. All marked 2-year-old birds had unmarked mates of unknown age.

All 12 of the 3-year-olds (8 females and 4 males) nested. All marked birds had unmarked mates of unknown age.

The sample size of the 4- and 5-year-old geese (Table 2) is too small for use in population analysis. There seems little doubt, however, that all the 4- and 5-year-old wild geese were sexually mature. These normally nest, unless prevented from doing so by lack of suitable nesting conditions or by failure to pair effectively.

Captive Flocks

Five years' data from the Moiese flock and 1 year's data from the Warm Springs flock are combined in Table 3. There appeared to be no basic differences in the flocks, although the Moiese birds had a larger nesting area and a wider selection of nest sites. The conditions are thought to be reasonably comparable to those described by Kossack (1950) for Bright Land Farm, Illinois, where he determined breeding age and described behavior of captive Canada geese. The Moiese flock contained both pinioned and full-winged birds. It was situated in the Flathead Valley; hence weather and habitat conditions closely paralleled those prevailing for the wild population already discussed.

Among 60 1-year-old geese of both sexes, none nested the first year; their behavior was similar to that of the same age-class in the wild. One first-year bird paired with a 3-year-old but nesting did not occur. Most 1-year-olds selected mates of the same age, but others paired with older birds, as found by Kossack (1950:628).

Five of 29 2-year-olds and 8 of 14 3-year-olds nested. None in the 4- and 5-year age-classes nested. We did not make sufficiently detailed observations of these older birds to discover precisely why they failed to nest, but we suspect that they failed to pair successfully. At least one was paired with a 2-year-old, and the others were paired with birds of unknown age.

DISCUSSION

Breeding Ages in Wild and Captive Flocks

Comparing the breeding ages of wild geese, as established in this study, with the findings of Kossack (1950:628) and our own data on captive birds (Table 3), we conclude that a much higher percentage of wild birds than of captive birds breed at 2 and 3 years of age. Between 27 and 36 percent of the wild 2-year-olds nested, while only 17 percent of the captives of that age did so. All of the wild 3-year-olds but only 64 percent of the captives in that age group nested. Kossack (1950:628) found only 8 and 20 percent nesting at 2 and 3 years of age respectively. Captive birds apparently do not breed in the same proportion as wild birds; hence, data from such flocks cannot be used to calculate the percent of breeding birds in a wild population.

Percent of Breeding Birds

To analyze productivity, we must know as accurately as possible the percentage of breeding geese in a population. This can be determined by direct census during the breeding season, by recapture of banded birds (Hanson and Smith 1950:163–172), or by applying breeding-age statistics to life-table data. The latter method has been hampered by lack of precise data on the breeding of 2-year-olds. If we apply breeding-age statistics to a dynamic life table, then we obtain the percentage of one cohort or generation that survives to breed during the life of the cohort.

When the same method is applied to a composite life table, we can calculate the percent of breeding birds more accurately since the data represent a number of cohorts. Such a calculation will show whether enough geese are surviving to maintain the population level. Unfortunately, we cannot construct a composite life table at this time; we can, however, apply our breeding data to a single generation of geese in the Flathead Valley and calculate the percent of this generation that survived to breed. We have selected the 1953 cohort because it illustrates the fate of a generation of geese experiencing high first- and second-year mortality and a rapid population turnover (Table 4). The data we have presented on breeding age within the population are not conclusive, but we believe them to be sufficiently accurate to be used in calculating the percent of breeding birds.

We propose to apply the following generalizations: (1) no geese breed as yearlings; (2) one-third of the 2-year-olds breed; (3) all of the 3-, 4-, and 5-year-olds breed.

The 1953 cohort consisted of 116 banded goslings from a population of 634. None of these was color-marked. Hunting pressure from 1953 through 1955 was excessive (Craighead and Stockstad 1956*a*). In 1953, resident birds comprised 80 percent of the total known kill for the hunting season, with a disproportionate kill of goslings. If we apply the proposed breeding-age statistics to the life-table data constructed for the 1953 generation of geese (Table 4), we can compute that:

(1) Six hundred sixty-one goslings or 66.1 percent of the cohort did not survive a year.

(2) None of the 339 geese surviving to the age of 1 year nested as yearlings ... 0

Table 4. Abbreviated dynamic life table constructed from band recoveries of 1953 cohort.

Age Inter-val (x)	Number of 1,000 Born Dying in Age Inter-val (d_x)	Number of 1,000 Born Surviving at Start of Age Inter-val (l_x)	d_x as a Percentage of $l_x(100q_x)$
0–1	661	1,000	66.1
1–2	196	339	57.8
2–3	107	143	74.8
3–4	18	36	50.0
4–5	18	18	100.0
5–6	0	0	

(3) One-third of 143 geese surviving to the age of 2 years nested as 2-year-olds 48

(4) All of the 36 geese surviving to the age of 3 years nested as 3-year-olds 36

(5) All of the 18 geese surviving to the age of 4 years nested as 4-year-olds 18

(6) None survived to 5 years 0

Total 102

Thus, only 102 geese or 10.2 percent from a theoretical population of 1,000 birds attained breeding age and survived to nest during a population-turnover period of 5 years. If we had assumed that *all* 2-year-olds nested (Hanson 1962:15), then the figure would have been 19.7 percent or nearly twice as many. But both percentages lie far below the proportion necessary to maintain the population level.

To show more exactly what happened to the 1953 cohort, we can apply the mortality rates from Table 4 and the breeding-age data presented earlier in the text to the actual number of goslings counted on the brood areas in mid-July. In 1953, 634 goslings reached the flying stage. Survival rates were roughly 34 percent the first year, and 42, 25, 50, and 0 percent for the second, third, fourth, and fifth years respectively. Thus, 216 of the 634 goslings survived 1 year; 91 survived 2 years; 23, 3 years; 12, 4 years; and none survived 5 years. Then assuming that only one-third of the 2-year-olds bred, we can compute that only 65 of the original 634 goslings survived to breed. Other generations in the Flathead population may have fared better, but the fate of this cohort well illustrates the effect of heavy hunting pressure on a species that does not attain full breeding potential until 3 years of age. Furthermore, the fate of the 1953 generation shows that if conditions are right, a single generation can be so heavily harvested that it can contribute little to the productive effort of the population. For the population to maintain itself, succeeding generations must have much higher survival rates; otherwise the population must be supplemented by birds of breeding age immigrating from other areas. From 1953 through 1960, the Flathead Valley goose population actually maintained an average level of 800 birds in the spring of the year, fluctuating from a high of 1,077 to a low of 490. The answer to the question of whether the breeding-season level of 800 birds was maintained principally by members of the population unit, or by a combination of these and immigrant geese from other areas, must await recoveries of six generations of banded geese and the construction of a composite life table.

LITERATURE CITED

BALHAM, R. W. 1954. The behavior of the Canada goose (*Branta canadensis*) in Manitoba. Ph.D. Thesis. Univ. of Missouri, Columbia.

CRAIGHEAD, J. J., AND D. S. STOCKSTAD. 1956*a*. Measuring hunting pressure on Canada geese in the Flathead Valley. Trans. N. Am. Wildl. Conf. 21:210–238.

———, AND ———. 1956*b*. A colored neck-band for marking birds. J. Wildl. Mgmt. 20(3):331–332.

———, AND ———. 1961. Evaluating the use of aerial nesting platforms by Canada geese. J. Wildl. Mgmt. 25(4):363–372.

ELDER, W. H. 1946. Age and sex criteria and weights of Canada geese. J. Wildl. Mgmt. 10(2):93–111.

GEIS, MARY BARRACLOUGH. 1956. Productivity of Canada geese in the Flathead Valley, Montana. J. Wildl. Mgmt. 20(4):409–419.

HANSON, H. C. 1949. Methods of determining age in Canada geese and other waterfowl. J. Wildl. Mgmt. 13(2):177–183.

———. 1962. Characters of age, sex, and sexual maturity in Canada geese. Illinois Nat. Hist. Surv. Biol. Notes 49. 15pp.

———, AND R. H. SMITH. 1950. Canada geese of the Mississippi Flyway with special reference to an Illinois flock. Illinois Nat. Hist. Surv. Bull. 25(3):67–210.

KOSSACK, C. W. 1950. Breeding habits of Canada geese under refuge conditions. Am. Midland Naturalist 43:627–649.

Received for publication November 11, 1962.

PREDATION ON CANADA GOOSE NESTS AT McCONNELL RIVER, NORTHWEST TERRITORIES[1]

CHARLES D. MacINNES, Department of Zoology, University of Western Ontario, London
RAJ K. MISRA, Department of Zoology, University of Western Ontario, London

Abstract: Predation losses from nests of small Canada geese (*Branta canadensis*) were observed from 1965 to 1969, on a 62-square-km study area at the mouth of the McConnell River, Northwest Territories. The lack of significant regression of logarithm of clutch size at first observation on date indicated that partial loss of a clutch did not occur in the absence of disturbance by humans. Partial clutch losses comprised 55 percent of all eggs observed lost after repeated visits to individual nests. The proportion of nests completely destroyed did not vary among years, but the proportion losing some eggs did change significantly. The latter difference was due to changes in the activity of predators, or of their interaction with humans, and not due simply to changes in human activity. The number of eggs lost per visit was the same (0.65 egg per visit) for all clutch sizes except six, which lost 0.26 egg per visit. This resulted in greater total destruction of small clutches, because the eggs lost represented a higher proportion of the initial clutch. It was concluded that in the absence of human disturbance, predation losses of eggs would have been small (approximately 10 percent) and would have varied little from year to year despite demonstrated changes in predator activity. A major exception to this might occur because of a high arctic fox (*Alopex lagopus*) population, which was not observed in the course of this study.

An important facet in the study of the reproductive output of a wildlife population is the estimation of the proportions of all life-cycle stages that are taken by predators. In 1964, we began a study designed to measure factors that cause annual variations in the reproductive output of a population of small Canada geese nesting near the mouth of the McConnell River (60° 50′ N, 94° 25′ W) near Eskimo Point, Northwest Territories. This paper deals with the biological properties of predation on nests and with the operational and statistical problems encountered during the analysis of predation.

A major difficulty in the estimation of natural egg loss arises when predators are accidently assisted in finding study nests by actions of human observers (Hammond and Forward 1956). This problem is acute in arctic studies, where the low and sparse vegetative cover enables the common predators to detect disturbances at great distances. Jaegers (*Stercorarius* spp., chiefly *S. parasiticus*), gulls (*Larus argentatus* and *L. thayeri*), and arctic foxes are particularly attracted by human activity and learn to follow biologists in the field.

Field observations were contributed by several graduate and undergraduate students. The assistance and support of all persons and agencies are acknowledged. Special thanks are due Dr. H. W. Norton, University of Illinois, whose critical reading of the manuscript helped to clarify several parts of the statistical analysis.

Classification of Thayer's gull (*L. thayeri*) follows Smith (1966).

THE STUDY AREA

In 1964 and 1965, a study area was chosen to encompass most of the Canada goose habitat within 1 day's walk of a base camp located on the south branch of the McConnell River approximately 4 km from the shore of Hudson Bay. No attempt was made to select an area to be statistically repre-

[1] The studies from which this paper is derived were supported by contracts from the Canadian Wildlife Service and grants from the National Research Council of Canada (A–1980 and A–3912), the Arctic Institute of North America, the Canadian National Sportsmen's Show, and the Wildlife Management Institute.

Originally published in J. Wildl. Manage. 36(2):414–422, 1972.

sentative of the Canada goose habitat of the whole costal plain of western Hudson Bay.

The area is marked with aluminum poles placed at 1-km intervals. It now comprises 62 square kilometers. Although some of the peripheral markers were placed in 1968 and 1969, the area searched for Canada goose nests since 1965 has been consistent.

SURVEY METHODS

Attempts were made (on foot) to find every nest within the marked study area during the incubation period of each season and to visit each nest at least twice. Because nests were widely dispersed, we concentrated on finding incubating females. There were far too many potential nest sites to allow systematic checking of all places where nests might be located. The number of personnel and their experience varied from one season to the next. For several reasons, we could not allocate the searching time and effort equally to all parts of the study area. Two large sections were virtually devoid of landmarks so that it was extremely difficult even to relocate a nest found earlier. In other places, nests located on prominent islands with low vegetation were easily seen from more than 500 m. The delta of the McConnell River was dangerous to traverse at times of high water, and searching effort there was minimal. We are confident that no more than five percent of active nests on the study area escaped detection in the years 1965–69. This confidence stems from the small number of new nests found at hatch, when the adult pairs stayed close to the nests and were most conspicuous.

Any nest from which the female was seen to flush was visited. Nests close to common travel routes were therefore visited many times. Some females sneaked away from their nests while the observer was a long way off. Such nests required long searching efforts, and they may have been exposed to predators several times before they were found.

It became evident early in the study that parasitic jaegers were actively exploiting the opportunities provided when an observer drove the adult geese away from a nest (MacInnes 1962). We took no direct action to prevent predation but made our visits as quickly as possible to reduce the length of disturbance. Damaged eggs were recorded as destroyed, but we did not remove partially eaten eggs from the nest. Eggs were numbered with a felt pen. Each nest site was marked permanently with a small wooden stake placed inconspicuously to avoid attracting predators.

To avoid mathematical difficulties due to the laying of additional eggs after the first visit, all observations were adjusted to contain the maximum number of eggs known to have been laid, less the known losses. This adjustment may have introduced bias due to the addition of eggs laid to replace losses that occurred before completion of the clutch, but our observations indicated that replacement was rare or absent. Cooch (1958:79) observed little replacement laying among blue geese (*Chen caerulescens*) nesting under similar conditions on Southhampton Island, Northwest Territories.

To provide estimates of clutch size, which would be free of bias caused by human activity, several searches were made in regions outside the marked study area. Each search encompassed at least 5 square km, and an effort was made to include at least 20 nests. With limited time, we may not have found all active nests in the regions examined.

METHOD OF ANALYSIS

We considered two hypotheses as to the way in which predators would remove eggs:

1. The number of eggs lost to predators might be proportional to the initial number of eggs present. This hypothesis would obviously be correct if every predator attack resulted in loss of all the eggs in the nest.

2. The number of eggs lost to a single predator attack might be independent of clutch size. In cases where jaegers or gulls followed a human in the field, loss of eggs occurred during the time between the departure of the adult geese at the observer's approach, and the return of the geese after the disturbance. It is possible that this time interval would allow destruction of only a few eggs. The number of eggs destroyed would then depend on the time they were exposed and should be independent of clutch size, unless geese with larger clutches, in contrast to geese with smaller clutches, behaved differently towards human intrusion.

To examine the first hypothesis, a rate of predation independent of initial clutch size must be calculated. The method of Ricker (1958:24–25) is appropriate:

$$N_t = N_o e^{\beta t}. \qquad (1)$$

N_o is the initial number of eggs, N_t the number of eggs remaining at time t, and β is the coefficient of predation. By logarithmic transformation this equation becomes

$$\ln N_t = \ln N_o + \beta t, \qquad (2)$$

and the analysis is accomplished using linear regression.

Two kinds of data were subjected to this analysis:

1. We examined the regression of the logarithm of clutch size at our first visit on time to provide an estimate of predation unbiased by the effect of human visits. For convenience, time was measured in days after June 1.

2. Potentially, more exact information was available in the form of repeated visits to individual nests, allowing the calculation of a predation coefficient for each nest. However, since the results of analysis 1 indicated that the predation observed was due to human visits to the nests, we tested the regression of logarithm of clutch size on visits rather than on time. Because the effect of a visit could be observed only at the subsequent visit, the first visit was scored as 0 (no previous visit), the second as 1, and so on. Due to the difficulty in using the value $-\infty$ of ln 0 in statistical analysis, a nest that was completely destroyed was assigned a clutch size of 0.49. This number has the smallest absolute value of its natural logarithm of any two-place decimal number that rounds to 0.

The second hypothesis was also examined by two methods:

1. The homogeneity of the ratio eggs hatched:eggs lost before hatching was tested for the different clutch sizes. This analysis was applied only to eggs lost between the first and second visit.

2. Egg losses due to the first visit were estimated from the predation rate of equation (1) as follows:

$$L = N_o (1 - e^{\beta}), \qquad (3)$$

where L is the number of eggs lost.
The standard error of L is

$$\text{SE}(L) = (N_o e^{\beta}) (\text{SE of } \beta). \qquad (4)$$

RESULTS

The ultimate objective in this analysis was to estimate the predation losses that would have occurred naturally in the absence of human disturbance. Because a majority of nests were not found during laying, we examined loss of eggs before the nests were visited, by method 1. This analysis included all nests seen, whether in or outside the marked study area. The results are presented in Table 1.

Table 1. Estimates of the regression of the logarithm of clutch size upon the date on which the nest was first visited. This table includes nests outside the main study area.

YEAR	NUMBER OF NESTS	MEAN CLUTCH ± SE	PREDATION COEFFICIENT ± SE[a]
1965	88	4.1 ± 0.16	–0.0040 ± 0.0054
1966	144	4.0 ± 0.11	–0.0017 ± 0.0033
1967	136	4.0 ± 0.10	–0.0018 ± 0.0042
1968	125	3.7 ± 0.12	–0.0077 ± 0.0050
1969	419	3.7 ± 0.06	–0.0025 ± 0.0031

[a] Regression equation $\ln(\text{eggs}) = a + b\,(\text{date})$.

Table 2. Numbers of Canada goose nests observed within the marked study area at McConnell River.

YEAR	NESTS VISITED ONCE	Nests Visited Two or More Times: No Egg Lost	Some Eggs Lost	All Eggs Lost	Mean Visits per Nest	OTHER NEST ATTEMPTS	TOTAL NEST ATTEMPTS
1965	24	26	24	14	3.5	7	95
1966	27	52	26	8	3.9	13	126
1967	15	41	11	10	3.4	18	95
1968	10	20	18	7	4.1	10	65
1969	9	39	8	8	3.6	7	71

For two reasons, such an analysis could produce only an approximate result:

1. For most nests, the starting dates were unknown, and no useful estimate of the time a nest was exposed to predation before the first visit was available. The regression analysis can be applied only because Canada goose nesting at the McConnell River was highly synchronous. In eight seasons (1959–60, 1964–69) the egg-laying period averaged 12.8 days (range, 10 to 15 days), hatching averaged 7.8 days (range, 5 to 12 days), and there was a mean period of 18.4 days (range, 15 to 20 days) between laying of the last egg on the study area and the first hatch. Surveys used for the present analysis were well spaced from the period of late laying until the beginning of the hatch.

2. Nests that were completely destroyed before they were found could not be included in the analysis. Such nests were sometimes easily found because of the fresh down, visible at some distance. However, more frequently the down blew away, or was matted by rain, rendering a recently destroyed nest indistinguishable from one that hatched successfully the previous season. We observed that marked nests reach that condition within 1 day after destruction. For this reason, we had no confidence in our ability to estimate consistently the total number of destroyed nests in a previously unvisited area.

In no year did the predation coefficient differ from zero (Table 1). Since the estimates for individual years proved homogeneous ($F = 2.05$ with 4, 26 df, $P > 0.1$), a pooled estimate for all years was calculated. This value, –0.0020 ± 0.0026, did not differ from zero. Because the analysis did not include completely destroyed nests, lack of regression cannot be interpreted as a total lack of predation. (In one survey outside the marked study area, on June 21, 1968, 17 active and 5 recently destroyed nests were found.) However, the lack of regression showed that nests undisturbed by human activities did not lose only parts of their clutches. *Thus, we concluded that partial loss of the clutch was entirely attributable to human-assisted predation*, and in subsequent analyses we considered partial loss to be artificial. Because Canada geese sometimes desert their nests after disturbance by humans (Brakhage 1965:764), we could not assume that completely destroyed nests would all have been lost in the absence of humans, because eggs left exposed would be destroyed by avian predators within hours of desertion.

On the marked study area, we divided the nests into several classes (Table 2). Two types provided no further information on predation but must be discussed because of difficulties they raise with respect to estimation of predation rates. The category *other nest attempts* contained all nests with

Table 3. The numbers of Canada goose nests found destroyed in relation to the number of times each nest was visited. Data for 1965–69, from the McConnell River study area, are pooled in this table.

VISIT	NEST INTACT[a]	NEST DESTROYED Number	NEST DESTROYED Percent
2	290	22	7.1
3	200	12	5.7
4	139	9	6.1
5	76	3	3.8
6	34	1	2.9
7	13	0	0
8	5	0	0
9	3	0	0

[a] A nest was considered intact if it retained at least one undamaged egg.

Table 4. Summary of Canada goose eggs lost to predators on the McConnell River study area.

YEAR	HATCHED Number	HATCHED Percent	EGGS LOST AS PART OF CLUTCH Number	EGGS LOST AS PART OF CLUTCH Percent	EGGS LOST AS WHOLE CLUTCH Number	EGGS LOST AS WHOLE CLUTCH Percent
1965	262	74	48	14	42	12
1966	289	81	41	11	27	8
1967	191	80	17	7	31	13
1968	129	74	22	13	22	13
1969	177	82	29	14	9	4

anomalous histories. Two-thirds of these were nests in which one egg was laid and then was lost soon after. We believe that most of these were *dump* eggs, an hypothesis supported by three cases that involved neckbanded geese. Although the eggs were taken by predators, it is probable that they had been abandoned before predation. The remaining nests in this category included nests on inaccessible sites and nests known to be active but that were destroyed by floods or unknown causes before they could be visited. The latter were observed during behavior studies from elevated observation towers. These nests would probably not be detected during normal search procedures. Since the observation towers provided only limited coverage and changed from year to year as additional towers were built, we do not have consistent estimates of the frequency of such nests.

Nests visited once could cause serious bias to predation estimates if the reason they were not examined again was that they were destroyed after the first visit and could not subsequently be found, because the adult geese abandoned the sites. Examination of field notes revealed that this was rarely the case. In most instances, nests visited once were in groups on parts of the study area apparently examined only once. We know that some one-visit nests hatched, because the neckbanded adults were seen with broods.

The relative proportions of nests visited once and more than once did not change significantly (χ^2, 4 df = 4.78, $P > 0.3$).

For nests visited twice or more, the proportion that were completely destroyed did not vary from one year to the next (χ^2, 4 df = 4.62, $P > 0.3$). The proportion that lost part of the clutch did vary between years (χ^2, 4 df = 14.50, $P < 0.01$), showing that egg loss due to human-assisted predation changed substantially. However, the mean number of visits per nest (excluding nests visited once) did not vary (χ^2, 4 df = 1.98, $P > 0.50$), and we could find no significant relation between visit number and nest destruction (χ^2, 4 df = 3.17, $P > 0.50$). This test was performed on the data of Table 3, with observations for six or more visits pooled. Therefore we concluded that the variation in partial clutch loss was due to changes in the activity of predators, or their interaction with humans, and not due to changes in human activity. Further information on abundance and activity of jaegers may be found in Angstadt (1961) and J. M. Harvey (unpublished data).

Over the years 1965–69, 1,048 (78 percent) Canada goose eggs hatched on the marked study area; 288 (22 percent) were lost. Of the latter group, 131 (45 percent of losses) were in nests that were com-

Table 5. Unweighted mean predation rates (±SE) of Canada goose nests on the marked study area at McConnell River. The numbers in parentheses are sample sizes.

	Clutch Size					
	2	3	4	5	6	Mean ± SE
1965	−0.447 ± 0.139 (11)	−0.325 ± 0.089 (9)	−0.236 ± 0.132 (12)	−0.172 ± 0.069 (17)	−0.073 ± 0.021 (12)	−0.251 ± 0.045 (61)
1966	−0.549 ± 0.317 (3)	−0.154 ± 0.107 (13)	−0.152 ± 0.057 (20)	−0.093 ± 0.032 (27)	−0.024 ± 0.014 (20)	−0.194 ± 0.068 (83)
1967	−0.350 ± 0.157 (9)	−0.220 ± 0.108 (18)	−0.265 ± 0.153 (11)	−0.113 ± 0.105 (17)	−0.084 ± 0.057 (6)	−0.206 ± 0.054 (61)
1968	−0.041 ± 0.041 (5)	−0.343 ± 0.167 (11)	−0.212 ± 0.108 (15)	−0.077 ± 0.023 (10)	−0.023 ± 0.023 (2)	−0.139 ± 0.041 (43)
1969	−0.366 ± 0.366 (3)	−0.255 ± 0.109 (21)	−0.129 ± 0.123 (13)	−0.199 ± 0.129 (15)	−0.019 ± 0.019 (4)	−0.193 ± 0.084 (56)
Mean ± SE *n*	−0.351 ± 0.106 (31)	−0.260 ± 0.053 (72)	−0.199 ± 0.053 (71)	−0.131 ± 0.037 (86)	−0.045 ± 0.014 (44)	

pletely destroyed, whereas the remainder (55 percent of losses) could be directly attributed to human-assisted predation. Annual variations are shown in Table 4. Although these variations indicated that much of the predation may have been artificial, we proceeded to examine predation coefficients for individual nests (by analysis method 1) in order to discover whether predation was related to clutch size. Only clutch sizes of two to six were considered, due to inadequate observations outside this range.

The predation coefficients (β) were arranged in 25 groups (5 years with five clutch sizes each), as shown in Table 5. These estimates had heterogeneous variances. For further analyses, the group means were weighted inversely as to their variances and compared by analysis of variance. There were significant differences between mean predation coefficients among both years and clutch sizes (Table 6). The differences among years confirmed the earlier result that the proportion of nests losing part of the clutch varied significantly. The differences among clutch sizes showed that the rate at which eggs were lost was not proportional to the initial clutch.

Therefore, we proceeded to test the second hypothesis: that the predation rate was independent of clutch size. The number of eggs lost as a result of the first visit (Table 7) was homogeneous for all clutch sizes (χ^2, 4 df = 4.59, $P > 0.3$). A more correct approach was to estimate egg loss from the

Table 6. Weighted analyses of variance for rates of predation due to visits to nests.

Source	DF	MS	F	P
Among years	4	0.866	6.23	<0.001
Among clutch sizes	20	2.398	17.25	<0.001
Within clutch sizes and years (error)	279	0.139		
Among clutch sizes				
1965	4	4.096	29.46	<0.001
1966	4	2.926	21.05	<0.001
1967	4	1.001	7.20	<0.001
1968	4	2.018	14.52	<0.001
1969	4	1.949	14.02	<0.001

Table 7. Observed and estimated loss of Canada goose eggs due to the first visit to a nest. The estimated values are calculated from the weighted mean predation coefficients from Table 5.

	Observed Loss			Estimated Loss
Clutch	Eggs Lost	Nests	Eggs Lost per Nest	Eggs Lost per Nest ± SE
2	18	31	0.58	0.59 ± 0.15
3	33	72	0.46	0.69 ± 0.12
4	31	71	0.44	0.72 ± 0.17
5	36	86	0.42	0.61 ± 0.16
6	10	44	0.23	0.26 ± 0.08

Table 8. The fate of Canada goose nests of different clutch sizes within the McConnell River study area.

Clutch	Number of Nests		
	Some Eggs Hatched	No Egg Hatched	Percent Destroyed
2	19	12	41
3	56	16	22
4	60	11	15
5	80	6	7
6	44	0	0

mean predation coefficients (β) from Table 5. This procedure was necessary because the year differences (Table 6) biased the tests of pooled data. Egg loss estimates (Table 7) from clutches of two and five were obviously homogeneous, so we pooled them and tested the mean loss against loss from clutches of six eggs. The test ($t = 3.56$, ∞ df) showed that six-egg clutches lost fewer eggs per visit than any other size of clutch. The difference was difficult to assess in this context, because of the obvious changes in frequency of six-egg clutches from year to year. We suspect that a partial explanation may be found in the hypothesis proposed by Ryder (1970) that geese in the best condition in spring will lay large clutches and be more attentive.

A consequence of egg loss per visit being largely independent of clutch size was that smaller clutches were more likely to be destroyed than larger ones. An average two-egg clutch will be gone after 4 visits, but at the same rate of loss, five eggs will disappear only after 10 visits. As is shown in Table 8, small clutches were destroyed more frequently (χ^2, 4 df $= 62.4$, $P < 0.001$) than large clutches. Failure to recognize the cause of this relationship would lead to an erroneous conclusion if, for example, it were shown that younger geese laid smaller clutches and that the greater loss of these was interpreted as showing dependence of nest loss on age of the geese.

DISCUSSION

The major conclusion of this study is that predation losses would contribute little (about 10 to 12 percent) to the loss of productivity of Canada geese on the McConnell River study area if human disturbance was absent. In addition, the rate of loss would vary little from year to year, despite changes in predator abundance or activity.

Possibly even this small loss is not correctly termed predation, since it may have resulted from nest desertion, with the avian *predators* acting only as scavengers. Jaegers and gulls rarely harassed incubating geese and were never observed to succeed in driving a Canada goose from her nest during this study. Thus, the only opportunity for egg-eating would arise when both geese left the nest area simultaneously to feed. During the egg-laying period, the adult geese were frequently absent from the nest for periods of several hours, and during this period blue geese lost many eggs (Cooch 1958:89). However, Canada geese covered their nests with extreme care before leaving, often taking an hour or more to arrange dead vegetation over the eggs. This rendered the nest difficult to detect even from a distance of 2 or 3 feet and presumably served to minimize the loss of eggs to predators. We were unable to detect whether losses during the laying period were heavier than during the incubation period, but observations were few because of the difficulty of finding unattended nests. Nests were conspicuous, covered or not, once incubation began and the female had deposited down in the nest lining.

Arctic foxes might provide an important exception to the conclusion that predation would not be an important source of nest loss at McConnell River in the absence of human disturbance. However, the fact that heavy fox damage to Canada goose nests did not occur during nine (1959–61, 1964–69) seasons that biologists were at the McConnell River nest area indicated that serious predation by foxes would occur infrequently.

In 1961, on a 20-square-kilometer study area west of the Boas River on Southampton Island, Northwest Territories (63° 45′ N, 86° 0.5′ W), foxes removed more than 95 percent of Canada goose eggs found (MacInnes, unpublished data). It was impossible to determine how many eggs were taken, because in several cases eggs were removed one at a time, on the day they were laid. Only 11 nests were located on the study area, although it was evident that there were far more nesting pairs active in the area. Three of the 11 nests were located because the females were sitting on empty nests that contained fresh down. Down is normally deposited only after the clutch is complete or nearly so. At McConnell River, we infrequently observed females sitting on the nest for a day or more after a clutch was destroyed. The last survey of the area on Southampton Island occurred on June 26, about 10 days before hatching was predicted. Of the 11 original nests, only 2 remained containing a total of four eggs.

In 1967, a single arctic fox destroyed, within 5 days, over 200 blue goose nests in 3 square km of the McConnell River study area. Students watched the fox systematically remove and bury eggs from one goose nest after another, until no active nest remained. Three of 30 Canada goose nests in adjacent areas disappeared during this period, but the fox was not observed near them.

Although an individual fox may obviously cause serious destruction among goose nests in a local area, widespread damage rarely occurred because foxes were scarce in nesting areas of Canada geese. Only four den sites of foxes were known on or within 5 km of the McConnell River study area. We never confirmed more than one to be occupied in any season, and all dens were empty in at least two seasons between 1965 and 1969. However, arctic fox populations are known to undergo large fluctuations and occasionally to reach high levels (Macpherson 1969:36–44). The fox catch on Southampton Island in the winter of 1960–61 was the highest for over 30 years. In addition, although lemmings (*Lemmus trimucronatus*) were abundant in late May, a die-off was observed during the thaw, and numbers appeared much reduced when the Canada geese began to lay on June 11. Similar observations on fox populations were made by Macpherson (1969:38) in 1961 near Baker Lake, Northwest Territories. Barry (1967:154–156) observed heavy destruction of blue goose and brant (*Branta bernicla*) nests on a colony in the delta of the Anderson River, Northwest Territories (69° 40′ N, 128° 00′ W). This destruction coincided with occupancy of a den site within the colony. Since Canada goose nests at McConnell River are more widely dispersed than those of blue geese, widespread destruction will occur only when foxes are numerous.

LITERATURE CITED

ANGSTADT, R. B. 1961. Predation by jaegers in a blue goose colony. M.S. Thesis. Cornell Univ. 49pp.

BARRY, T. W. 1967. Geese of the Anderson River Delta, Northwest Territories. Ph.D. Thesis. Univ. of Alberta. 212pp.

BRAKHAGE, G. K. 1965. Biology and behavior of tub-nesting Canada geese. J. Wildl. Mgmt. 29(4):751–771.

COOCH, F. G. 1958. The breeding biology and management of the blue goose *Chen caerulescens*. Ph.D. Thesis. Cornell Univ. 246pp.

HAMMOND, M. C., AND W. R. FORWARD. 1956. Experiments on causes of duck nest predation. J. Wildl. Mgmt. 20(3):243–247.

MACINNES, C. D. 1962. Nesting of small Canada geese near Eskimo Point, Northwest Territories. J. Wildl. Mgmt. 26(3):247–256.

MACPHERSON, A. H. 1969. The dynamics of Canadian arctic fox populations. Canadian Wildl. Serv. Rept. Ser. 8. 52pp. (French and Russian summaries.)

RICKER, W. E. 1958. Handbook of computations for biological statistics of fish populations. Fisheries Research Board Canada Bull. 119. 300pp.

RYDER, J. P. 1970. A possible factor in the evolution of clutch size in Ross' goose. Wilson Bull. 82(1):5–13.

SMITH, N. G. 1966. Evolution of some arctic gulls (*Larus*): an experimental study of isolating mechanisms. Ornithol. Monographs 4. 99pp.

Received for publication May 25, 1970

POPULATION STRUCTURE AND PRODUCTIVITY OF WHISTLING SWANS ON THE YUKON DELTA, ALASKA[1]

CALVIN J. LENSINK,[2] Bureau of Sport Fisheries and Wildlife, Box 346, Bethel, AK 99559

Whistling Swans *Cygnus c. columbianus* are the most conspicuous of wildfowl of the Yukon-Kuskokwim Delta, the principal nesting grounds for swans wintering in western states. They are readily visible from low flying aircraft, and local pilots or their passengers frequently remark on their abundance, the occurrence of large flocks, or even of numbers of young in broods, or of eggs in nests.

The occurrence of a large population, and the ease with which swans are viewed from the air, permits detailed observations of many individuals with relatively small effort or cost. Because the various factors which may affect the welfare of Whistling Swans may affect other species similarly, much information on swans should be of significant value in understanding the ecology of species that are more difficult to study.

METHODS

Most observations were obtained during routine flights over the Delta for several purposes, including hauling of freight and passengers from point to point, as well as systematic aerial census of wildfowl populations. Flights intended primarily for observing swans include only those conducted for censusing random plots in 1968 and 1971, and occasional flights in late fall to ensure adequate sampling of broods just prior to their migration. The observation and recording techniques used are described by King (1973).

Results are summarized for intervals of 10 days to provide reasonable sample sizes and still permit detection of changes in the structure of population units that may occur over the summer. The basic data are deposited in tabular form at the Wildfowl Trust, Slimbridge, being too extensive to publish with the present paper. The consistency of recording observations and the proportion of swans tallied in the flight path varied with the purpose and altitude of the flight, weather conditions, motivation and ability of observers and many other factors. Consistency has much improved in recent years of the study, as compared to years prior to 1967.

RESULTS

Distribution and Behaviour

First swans appear on the Yukon Delta in late April and most have arrived by mid-May. Pairs are soon dispersed widely across the tundra in all suitable habitats, with densities higher in areas near the coast between Nelson Island and Cape Romanzof, an area which, incidentally, is the most productive for several species of geese and ducks as well as swans. Nonterritorial swans, presumably mostly subadults, gather in large flocks along coastal estuaries or occasionally on large inland lakes.

Nesting begins almost immediately in normal years, although late springs may delay nesting by 10 days or more. Hatching has begun as early as 20 June, or as late as 6 July—but, in either event, co-

[1] Originally published in Wildfowl 24:21–25, 1973.

[2] Present address: SRA, Box 921, Anchorage, AK 99502.

Table 1. Survival of cygnets as indicated by changes in size of broods expressed as percentage of the average clutch size for year.

	Clutches		Survival (%)					
Year	No.	Average	June	July	Aug.	Sept.	Oct.	Winter
1963	47	4.32	—	(78.6)	(66.1)	66.4	59.1	—
1964	52	3.30	—	(78.5)	(72.1)	—	—	57.0
1965	44	4.34	—	(44.7)	(75.3)	61.5*	—	50.2
1966	21	4.14	—	(73.2)	(57.2)	60.6*	58.9	50.5
1967	42	4.95	(73.3)	(83.2)	60.2	61.4*	58.8	50.5
1968	59	4.80	(85.0)	77.3	75.8*	75.6*	—	53.5
1969	33	4.67	—	75.4	75.8*	75.1*	—	58.0
1970	20	4.45	—	(77.1)	77.5	75.0*	—	53.0
1971	36	3.34	—	(79.6)	78.1*	75.4*	86.5	—

Samples of less than fifty broods are in parentheses, * those with more than 200. The winter observations, in California and Utah during December or January, are summarized in various reports by J. J. Lynch.

incides with early growth of green vegetation and maximum activity of insects and other invertebrates.

During nesting incubation, paired swans are frequently separated from their mates and many enter our tally as singles. At hatching, the population structure changes abruptly—members of pairs are less commonly separated and the large nonbreeding flocks break up into smaller flocks that begin dispersing over the Delta as they enter the moult.

Although we have not studied individual broods throughout the season, numerous observations suggest that many may remain with their parents near the nesting site (100–400 m) until fledging.

Nonbreeders remain in small flocks of three to fifteen individuals, but as flight is regained in late August they begin congregating in larger premigrant flocks along the coasts or in favourable foraging areas on large inland lakes. Pairs remain scattered until early September when those without broods join the larger flocks, causing a distortion in the apparent proportion of pairs with broods. By late September most swans have left the Delta but some, particularly those with late broods, may remain until freeze-up in October. The number which linger is clearly the direct result of spring conditions—a late spring retarding all events throughout the summer.

Size of Clutches and Broods

Sizes of clutches have varied from an average of 3.30 in 1964 to 4.95 in 1967 (Table 1). Modal size of clutches has varied from three to five. Average size of broods varies directly with size of clutches. Broods observed in the month following the hatch average only 75% of average clutch size. During the remainder of the summer, attrition to broods is relatively small, and at migration, broods still average between 60 and 75% of clutch size. Both the initial loss of cygnets and attrition to broods during the summer appear to be independent of clutch size.

A second sharp reduction in brood size is indicated by censuses of family groups in California and Utah, where broods observed in December average only a little more than 50% of clutch size (Lynch 1972). Again, losses appear to be independent of original clutch or brood size.

Number of Productive Swans

When nesting is completed in late May or early June, the percentage of pairs observed with nests or broods becomes sta-

Table 2. Percent of pairs with nest or brood.

Year	May	June	July	Aug.	Sept.	Oct.
1963	—	—	35.4	(16.1)	52.1	(64.5)
1964	—	29.4	—	15.1	—	—
1965	—	(53.3)	(34.0)	36.6	(62.0)	—
1966	—	(25.4)	(39.5)	34.1	44.7	(60.0)
1967	16.8	47.0	(48.1)	30.1	46.3	(18.3)
1968	(19.5)	50.7	55.9	47.8	61.1	—
1969	(39.2)	48.3	51.6	45.4	71.7	—
1970	(25.4)	36.1	36.2	38.6	65.2	—
1971	—	27.9	24.3	19.2	23.5	(38.4)

Samples of less than 100 pairs are in parentheses.

ble and remains relatively constant through August, suggesting that few pairs lose entire clutches or broods (Table 2). An apparent increase in the percentage of pairs with broods in September results from desertion of territories by idle pairs. The numbers of pairs with nests may vary considerably from year to year, and in the 9 years of our study, swans with broods in August ranged from 15.1 to 47.8% and averaged 31.4% of estimated total pairs.

Estimates of the proportion of productive swans in the population are somewhat more tenuous than our analysis of productive pairs, because of the difficulty in sampling the nonbreeding flocks which are not randomly distributed. During July and August, however, when flocks are smaller and more dispersed than in other months, our samples seem adequately large, and between 40 and 60% of swans appear to be paired and on territories (Table 3). Occasional pairs are observed in nonbreeding flocks, but these are not considered as potential breeders. Although they may be adult swans, the companion birds may be together by chance, or they may be siblings, as most nonbreeders must be of yearling or other subadult age classes.

The proportion of swans occurring in flocks appears relatively stable and does not seem much affected by changes in the number of nesting pairs. We suspect that variation in productivity during preceding years changes the relative sizes of subadult age classes.

If we assume that approximately 50% of swans are paired and on territories, estimates of the proportion of productive adults range from about 9% of the total population in 1964 to 25% in 1968. This

Table 3. Percent of adult or subadult swans identified as singles or pairs.

Year	May	June	July	Aug.	Sept.	Oct.
1963	—	—	(57.2)	(22.1)	13.7*	(24.2)
1964	—	(85.6)	—	64.7	—	—
1965	—	(29.8)	(94.0)	(61.6)	(41.0)	—
1966	—	(59.5)	—	(25.8)	44.7	—
1967	(24.2)	56.3	—	(94.6)	49.4	—
1968	(23.9)	61.1	47.1	43.8*	39.2**	—
1969	(25.5)	50.8*	41.7*	52.6*	8.9**	—
1970	12.1	37.4**	62.6	(39.5)	16.2**	—
1971	—	39.1**	44.0	55.2*	44.4*	(13.2)

Samples of less than 1,000 swans are in parentheses; * those larger than 2,000; ** larger than 3,000.

Table 4. Comparison of climatic factors and productivity.

Year	Ice breakup		Mean temp. (°F at Bethel)				Average clutch	Pairs with broods (%)	Survival	
	Bethel	Chevak	April	May	June	July			Sept.	Winter
1963	5/19	—	19.4	40.6	47.1	54.2	4.32	33.7	66.4	—
1964	6/3	6/16	19.5	31.0	52.5	56.6	3.30	18.3*	72.1	5.0
1965	5/19	6/15	26.5	32.6	48.6	51.6	4.34	39.5	61.5	50.2
1966	5/23	6/15	23.0	33.2	51.8	53.2	4.14	31.5	60.6	50.5
1967	5/11	6/2	30.9	42.5	54.0	53.6	4.95	42.4*	61.4	50.5
1968	5/14	6/5	23.1	41.6	52.3	57.9	4.80	50.9**	75.6	53.5
1969	5/11	5/30	27.1	45.5	52.4	53.7	4.67	48.2**	75.1	58.0
1970	5/14	6/3	22.3	43.3	51.9	51.6	4.45	36.5**	75.0	53.0
1971	5/27	6/15	17.0	35.2	50.0	52.8	3.34	23.4**	75.4	—
Norm.	5/14	?	25.5	40.3	52.1	54.6				

The percentage of pairs with broods is derived from all observations June through August. * Sample exceeding 500 pairs; ** exceeding 1,000. Survival is calculated as percentage of average clutch size for year.

difference is proportionately much larger than differences in clutch size, hence it is a primary factor in determining annual productivity. As both clutch size and number of productive swans normally vary in the same direction, changes in productivity are larger than either. Thus, estimated production in 1964 was only 0.15 eggs per adult, but in 1968 was 0.62 eggs per adult.

DISCUSSION

Climatic conditions in spring are invariably the most important of factors which affect the productivity of swans. Predators, disease, hunting, or other obvious factors do not cause significant annual variation in production. Hunting may have a controlling influence on the population if Klein's (1966) estimate of an illegal harvest of 5,000 swans on the Delta is correct. A late breakup of ice on rivers and ponds or lakes, caused by low temperatures in April or May, results in a reduction in both the size of clutches and the proportion of swans that nest (Table 4). Differences in survival of cygnets during the summer are comparatively small and seem also to be affected partly by spring conditions, as well as weather during summer months. However, our data are confusing and at present no conclusion can be drawn. With the exception of 1964, a year when the reliability of our data is doubtful, survival of cygnets during migration was highest in years with early springs. Examination of many cygnets indicates that a few may not be fledged and others are only just fledging at the normal time for migration to begin. At this point in the cygnets' growth they are without fat reserves and muscle development is poor, and it is apparent that many cygnets are unable to survive the excessive demands of long, migration flights. It seems surprising that so many can.

The low productivity and the hazards to survival of cygnets on the Yukon Delta in years with late springs suggest that swans nesting in more northern areas of Alaska, where shorter seasons are characteristic, are occupying habitat that is marginal for their survival. The relatively large population of swans on the Yukon Delta as compared to these areas (King 1970), may be due entirely to the difference in length of the summer season.

Comparative data are limited to observations by Sladen (personal communication) in Bristol Bay in August 1969 and on the Arctic Slope in 1971. Swans from

Bristol Bay are part of the western population while those from the Arctic Slope migrate to the Atlantic coast (Sladen 1973). In these years spring conditions in Bristol Bay were about normal and comparable to the Yukon Delta, but on the Arctic Slope they were unusually mild, although later than would be normal for the Yukon Delta. In Bristol Bay 31.4% of 156 pairs had broods averaging 3.57 cygnets. On the Arctic Slope 34.5% of 101.5 pairs had broods averaging 2.51 cygnets. Bristol Bay data were well within the normal range for that from the Yukon Delta. Although the season on the Arctic Slope was mild, the percentage of productive pairs was about normal for the Yukon Delta, and average brood size was similar to that observed there in late years.

Productivity appraisals reported by Lynch (1972) for the swans wintering on the Atlantic coast indicate consistently poorer nesting success than western swans, averaging only 11.8% cygnets in wintering populations as compared to 20.6% cygnets for western swans. The number of cygnets in family groups also differs, averaging 2.02 for the Atlantic population and 2.33 for the western. These data confirm our observation on the Delta that the length of the summer season is critical to production among Whistling Swans.

Weather conditions of early spring affect productivity of other wildfowl in Alaska as well as that of Whistling Swans. The deleterious effect of late springs was conclusively demonstrated for ducks of several species during my studies on the Yukon Flats between 1961 and 1964, but on the Yukon Delta our data for most species are too meagre to permit adequate comparison with that of swans. Studies now in progress should meet the necessary data requirements if continued for a sufficient period.

Because of the dominating effect of spring conditions, we can predict production by swans with reasonable accuracy before the first egg is laid. Subsequent observations during the summer essentially confirm and increase the accuracy of earlier predictions. We are satisfied that we can also predict trends in productivity for other species, but cannot at present estimate accurately the magnitude of change that may occur—even after the fact.

Productivity of geese on the Yukon Delta (Black Brant *Branta bernicla orientalis*, Cackling Geese *Branta canadensis minima*, Emperor Geese *Anser canagicus* and White-fronted Geese *Anser albifrons frontalis*) appears generally to be much more stable than that of swans. Perhaps adaptation of these species to changing conditions may not have to be nearly as great as for swans which require a significantly longer period of time between nesting and fledging of young. Among ducks, productivity of late nesting species such as Scaup *Aythya marila* and *A. affinis* seem less affected by late springs than that of earlier nesting dabbling ducks, particularly Mallard *Anas platyrhynchos* and Pintail *Anas acuta,* our earliest migrants and nesters.

Maximum changes in productivity that we have noted for any species occurs among Snow Geese *Anser caerulescens,* which we can observe only during their migration. Bands that we have recovered indicate that the population passing through the Delta nests primarily on Wrangel Island in the Soviet Arctic, and its productivity as indicated by percentage of immatures in the population has ranged from near 0 to 54%. As Wrangel Island has a much shorter season than the

Yukon Delta, productivity of Snow Geese there may be analogous to that of swans in northern Alaska.

SUMMARY

Observations of Whistling Swans from low flying aircraft on the Yukon Delta, Alaska, provide records which permit analysis of annual variations in productivity. Climatic conditions of early spring are the most important factor affecting production, a late spring resulting in a reduced number of nests and reduced clutch size. The percentage of territorial pairs with broods has varied from about 15 to 50%. The average number of cygnets in broods at time of fledging has varied from 2.52 to 3.63.

ACKNOWLEDGMENTS

Many persons have contributed observations summarized in this report. James King, former Refuge Manager, initiated the study in 1962 and 1963. In addition, King (1973) has contributed observations made during annual surveys of breeding populations on the Delta and elsewhere in Alaska. All members of the refuge staff, particularly Jerry Hout, and several visitors to the Wildlife Range have participated as observers.

LITERATURE CITED

KING, J. G. 1960. The swans and geese of Alaska's Arctic Slope. Wildfowl 21:11–17.

———. 1973. The use of small airplanes to gather swan data in Alaska. Wildfowl 24:15–20.

KLEIN, D. R. 1966. Waterfowl in the economy of the Eskimos on the Yukon-Kuskokwim Delta, Alaska. Arctic 19:319–336.

LYNCH, J. J. 1972. Productivity and mortality among geese, swans and brant: Part II. Historical records from productivity appraisals, 1950–1971. Unpublished report. Bureau of Sport Fisheries and Wildlife, Patuxent Wildlife Research Center, Laurel, Md.

SLADEN, W. J. L. 1973. A continental study of Whistling Swans using neck collars. Wildfowl 24:8–14.

SELECTED BIBLIOGRAPHY

Reproductive Ecology: General Biology

ALLISON, R. M. 1975. Breeding biology and behavior of the oldsquaw (*Clangula hyemalis* L.). Ornithol. Monogr. 18. 52pp.

BANKO, W. F. 1960. The trumpeter swan: its history, habits and population in the United States. Bur. Sport Fish. and Wildl. North Am. Fauna 63. 214pp.

BARRY, T. W. 1962. Effect of late seasons on Atlantic brant reproduction. J. Wildl. Manage. 26(1):19–26.

BARSKE, P., editor. 1969. Black duck/ evaluation, management and research: a symposium. Atlantic Waterfowl Council and The Wildl. Manage. Inst., Washington, D.C. 193pp.

BOLEN, E. G., B. MCDANIEL, AND C. COTTAM. 1964. Natural history of the black-bellied tree duck (*Dendrocygna autumnalis*) in southern Texas. Southwest. Nat. 9(2):78–88.

BOURGET, A. A. 1973. Relation of eiders and gulls nesting in mixed colonies in Penobscot Bay, Maine. Auk 90:809–820.

BOUVIER, J. M. 1974. Breeding biology of the hooded merganser in southwestern Quebec, including interactions with common goldeneyes and wood ducks. Can. Field-Nat. 88:323–330.

BROWN, P. W., AND M. A. BROWN. 1981. Nesting biology of the white-winged scoter. J. Wildl. Manage. 45:38–45.

CALVERLEY, B. K., AND D. A. BOAG. 1977. Reproductive potential in parkland- and arctic-nesting populations of mallards and pintails (Anatidae). Can. J. Zool. 55(8):1242–1251.

CLAWSON, R. L., G. W. HARTMAN, AND L. H. FREDRICKSON. 1979. Dump nesting in a Missouri wood duck population. J. Wildl. Manage. 43:347–355.

COOCH, F. G. 1965. The breeding biology and management of the northern eider (*Somateria mollissima borealis*) in the Cape Dorset Area, Northwest Territories. Can. Wildl. Serv. Wildl. Manage. Bull. Ser. 2, No. 10. 68pp.

COOPER, J. A. 1978. The history and breeding biology of the Canada geese of Marshy Point, Manitoba. Wildl. Monogr. 61. 87pp.

———, AND J. R. HICKIN. 1972. Chronology of hatching by laying sequence in Canada geese. Wilson Bull. 84(1):90–92.

CRAIGHEAD, F., AND J. CRAIGHEAD. 1949. Nesting Canada geese on the Upper Snake River. J. Wildl. Manage. 13(1):51–64.

CULBERTSON, J. L., L. L. CADWELL, AND I. O. BUSS. 1971. Nesting and movements of Canada geese on the Snake River in Washington. Condor 73: 230–236.

DANE, C. W. 1966. Some aspects of breeding biology of the blue-winged teal. Auk 83(3):389–402.

DIMMICK, R. W. 1968. Canada geese of Jackson Hole, their ecology and management. Wyoming Game and Fish Comm. Bull. 11. 86pp.

DZUBIN, A., AND J. B. GOLLOP. 1972. Aspects of mallard breeding ecology in Canadian parkland and grassland. Pages 113–151 *in* Population ecology of migratory birds: a symposium. U.S. Dep. Inter. Bur. Sport Fish and Wildl., Wildl. Res. Rep. 2.

EISENHAUER, D. I., AND C. M. KIRKPAT-

RICK. 1977. Ecology of the emperor goose in Alaska. Wildl. Monogr. 57. 62pp.

EWASCHUK, E., AND D. A. BOAG. 1972. Factors affecting hatching success of densely nesting Canada geese. J. Wildl. Manage. 36:1097–1106.

FJETLAND, C. A. 1974. Trumpeter swan management in the national wildlife refuge system. Trans. North Am. Wildl. Resour. Conf. 39:136–141.

FLAKE, L. D. 1978. Wetland diversity and waterfowl. Pages 312–319 *in* P. E. Greeson, J. R. Clark, and J. E. Clark, eds. Wetland functions and values: the state of our understanding. Proc. National Symposium on Wetlands. Am. Water Resour. Assoc., Minneapolis, MN.

GATES, J. M. 1962. Breeding biology of the gadwall in northern Utah. Wilson Bull. 74(1):43–67.

GLOVER, F. A. 1956. Nesting and production of the blue-winged teal (*Anas discors* Linnaeus) in Northwest Iowa. J. Wildl. Manage. 20(1):28–46.

GRIEB, J. R. 1970. The shortgrass prairie Canada goose population. Wildl. Monogr. 22. 49pp.

HANSEN, H. A. 1962. Canada geese of coastal Alaska. Trans. North Am. Wildl. Conf. 27:301–320.

———, P. K. E. SHEPHERD, J. G. KING, AND W. A. TROYER. 1971. The trumpeter swan in Alaska. Wildl. Monogr. 26. 83pp.

HANSON, H. C., AND R. H. SMITH. 1950. Canada geese of the Mississippi flyway, with special reference to an Illinois flock. Ill. Nat. Hist. Survey Bull. 25:59–210.

HANSON, W. C., AND L. L. EBERHARDT. 1971. A Columbia River Canada goose population. Wildl. Monogr. 28. 61pp.

HARVEY, J. M. 1971. Factors affecting blue goose nesting success. Can. J. Zool. 49(2):223–234.

HEUSMANN, H. W. 1975. Several aspects of the nesting biology of yearling wood ducks. J. Wildl. Manage. 39(3):503–507.

HINES, J. E. 1977. Nesting and brood ecology of lesser scaup at Waterhen Marsh, Saskatchewan. Can. Field-Nat. 91(3):248–255.

JONES, R. D., JR. 1970. Reproductive success and age distribution of black brant. J. Wildl. Manage. 34(2):328–333.

KEITH, L. B. 1961. A study of waterfowl ecology on small impoundments on southeastern Alberta. Wildl. Monogr. 6. 88pp.

LAGLER, K. F. 1956. The pike, *Esox lucius* Linnaeus, in relation to waterfowl on the Seney National Wildlife Refuge, Michigan. J. Wildl. Manage. 20(2):114–124.

LEMIEUX, L. 1959. The breeding biology of the greater snow goose on Bylot Island, Northwest Territories. Can. Field-Nat. 73(2):117–128.

LIVEZEY, B. C. 1980. Effects of selected observer-related factors on fates of duck nests. Wildl. Soc. Bull. 8:123–128.

LOKEMOEN, J. T. 1966. Breeding ecology of the redhead duck in western Montana. J. Wildl. Manage. 30(4):668–681.

LOW, J. B. 1940. Production of the redhead (*Nyroca americana*) in Iowa. Wilson Bull. 52(3):153–164.

———. 1941. Nesting of the ruddy duck in Iowa. Auk 58(4):506–517.

———. 1945. Ecology and management of the redhead *Nyroca americana,* in Iowa. Ecol. Monogr. 15:35–69.

MACINNES, C. D. 1962. Nesting of small Canada geese near Eskimo Point,

Northwest Territories. J. Wildl. Manage. 26(3):247–256.

———, R. A. DAVIS, R. N. JONES, B. C. LIEFF, AND A. J. PAKULAK. 1974. Reproductive efficiency of McConnell River small Canada geese. J. Wildl. Manage. 38(4):686–707.

MCCAMANT, R. E., AND E. G. BOLEN. 1979. A 12-year study of nest box utilization by black-bellied whistling ducks. J. Wildl. Manage. 43:936–943.

MCGILVREY, F. B., compiler. 1968. A guide to wood duck production habitat requirements. U.S. Bur. Sport Fish and Wildl. Res. Publ. 60. 32pp.

MCKNIGHT, D. E., AND J. B. LOW. 1969. Factors affecting waterfowl production on a spring-fed salt marsh in Utah. Trans. North Am. Wildl. Nat. Resour. Conf. 34:307–314.

MICKELSON, P. G. 1975. Breeding biology of cackling geese and associated species on the Yukon-Kuskokwim Delta, Alaska. Wildl. Monogr. 45. 35pp.

MORSE, T. E., J. L. JAKABOSKY, AND V. P. MCCROW. 1969. Some aspects of the breeding biology of the hooded merganser. J. Wildl. Manage. 33(3):596–604.

———, AND H. M. WIGHT. 1969. Dump nesting and its effect on production in wood ducks. J. Wildl. Manage. 33(2):284–293.

MUNRO, J. A. 1939. Studies of waterfowl in British Columbia. Barrow's golden-eye, American golden-eye. Trans. Royal Can. Inst. 22(2):259–318.

———. 1941. Studies of waterfowl in British Columbia. Greater scaup duck, lesser scaup duck. Can. J. Res. Sec. D 19(2):113–138.

———. 1942. Studies of waterfowl in British Columbia. Buffle-head. Can. J. Res. Sec. D 20(3):133–160.

———. 1943. Studies of waterfowl in British Columbia. Mallard. Can. J. Res. Sec. D 21(4):223–260.

———. 1944. Studies of waterfowl in British Columbia. Pintail. Can. J. Res. Sec. D 22(3):60–86.

———. 1949. Studies of waterfowl in British Columbia. Green-winged teal. Can. J. Res. Sec. D 27(3):149–178.

———. 1949. Studies of waterfowl in British Columbia. Baldpate. Can. J. Res. Sec. D 27(5):289–307.

———, AND W. A. CLEMENS. 1939. The food and feeding habits of the red-breasted merganser in British Columbia. J. Wildl. Manage. 3(1):46–53.

NUDDS, T. 1978. Comments on Calverley and Boag's (1977) hypothesis on displaced ducks and an evolutionary alternative. Can. J. Zool. 56:2239–2241.

O'BRIEN, G. P. 1975. A study of the Mexican duck (*Anas diazi*) in southeastern Arizona. Ariz. Game Fish Dep. Spec. Rep. 5. 50pp.

ORING, L. W. 1969. Summer biology of the gadwall at Delta, Manitoba. Wilson Bull. 81:44–54.

POSTON, H. J. 1974. Home range and breeding biology of the shoveler. Can. Wildl. Serv. Rep. Ser. 25. 49pp.

RAVELING, D. G. 1976. Status of giant Canada geese nesting in southeast Manitoba. J. Wildl. Manage. 40(2): 214–226.

———. 1977. Canada geese of the Churchhill River basin in north-central Manitoba. J. Wildl. Manage. 41(1): 35–47.

REESE, J. G. 1980. Demography of European Mute Swans in Chesapeake Bay. Auk 97:449–464.

RIENECKER, W. C., AND W. ANDERSON. 1960. A waterfowl nesting study on

Tule Lake and Lower Klamath National Wildlife Refuges, 1957. Calif. Fish and Game 46(4):481–506.

ROLLO, J. D., AND E. G. BOLEN. 1969. Ecological relationships of blue and green-winged teal on the high plains of Texas in early fall. Southwest. Nat. 14(2):171–188.

RYDER, J. P. 1969. Nesting colonies of Ross' goose. Auk 86(2):282–292.

———. 1971. Distribution and breeding biology of the lesser snow goose in central Arctic Canada. Wildfowl 22:18–28.

———. 1972. Biology of nesting Ross' geese. Ardea 60(3/4):185–215.

———, AND F. COOKE. 1973. Ross' geese nesting in Manitoba. Auk 90(3):691–692.

SARGEANT, A. B. 1978. Red fox prey demands and implications to prairie duck production. J. Wildl. Manage. 42(3):520–527.

SCHRANCK, B. W. 1972. Waterfowl nest cover and some predation relationships. J. Wildl. Manage. 36(1):182–186.

SHERWOOD, G. A. 1968. Factors limiting production and expansion of local populations of Canada geese. Pages 73–85 *in* R. L. Hine and C. Schoenfeld, eds. Canada goose management. Dembar Educational Research Service, Inc. Madison, WI.

SIEGFRIED, W. R. 1976. Breeding biology and parasitism in the ruddy duck. Wilson Bull. 88(4):566–574.

SOWLS, L. K. 1949. A preliminary report on renesting in waterfowl. Trans. North Am. Wildl. Conf. 14:260–275.

STEEL, P. E., P. D. DALKE, AND E. G. BIZEAU. 1957. Canada goose production at Gray's Lake, Idaho, 1949–1951. J. Wildl. Manage. 21(1):38–41.

STEWART, P. A. 1967. Wood duck ducklings captured by bullfrogs. Wilson Bull. 79(2):237–238.

STEWART, R. E., AND H. A. KANTRUD. 1973. Ecological distribution of breeding waterfowl populations in North Dakota. J. Wildl. Manage. 37:39–50.

———, AND ———. 1974. Breeding waterfowl populations in the prairie pothole regions of North Dakota. Condor 76(1):70–79.

STRANGE, C. A. 1980. Incidence of avian predators near people searching for waterfowl nests. J. Wildl. Manage. 44:220–222.

VERMEER, K. 1968. Ecological aspects of ducks nesting in high densities among larids. Wilson Bull. 80(1): 78–83.

YOCOM, C. F., AND H. A. HANSEN. 1960. Population studies of waterfowl in eastern Washington. J. Wildl. Manage. 24(3):237–250.

Land Use and Habitat

DUCK NESTING IN INTENSIVELY FARMED AREAS OF NORTH DAKOTA

KENNETH F. HIGGINS, U.S. Fish and Wildlife Service, Northern Prairie Wildlife Research Center, Jamestown, North Dakota 58401

Abstract: A study to determine the major factors limiting duck nesting and production on intensively farmed areas in eastern North Dakota was conducted from 1969 through 1974. A total of 186 duck nests was found during searches on 6,018 ha of upland. Nest density per km² for 5 major habitat types was 20.2 in untilled upland, 3.7 in standing grain stubble, 1.6 in mulched grain stubble, 1.2 in summer fallow, and 1.1 in growing grain. Pintails (*Anas acuta*) nested in cultivated cropland types in greater prevalence than other duck species. Nest densities were 12 times greater on untilled upland (20.2/km²) than on annually tilled cropland (1.7/km²), and hatched-clutch densities were 16 times greater on untilled upland (4.8/km²) than on annually tilled cropland (0.3/km²). Hatching success was greater on untilled upland (25%) than on tilled cropland (17%). Of 186 nests found, 77 percent did not hatch; 76 percent of the failures were attributed to predators and 19 percent to farming operations. Poor quality nesting cover, the result of intensive land use practices, and nesting failures caused by machinery and predators, mainly mammals, were the principal factors limiting duck nesting and production on intensively farmed areas.

J. WILDL. MANAGE. 41(2):232–242

The glaciated prairie pothole region encompasses about 207,200 km² of the north-central United States and about 569,800 km² in south-central Canada. The conversion to monotype small grain farming in this region has been stimulated by demands for more small grains from rising human populations and by greater farm economic pressures. Lodge (1969) pointed out that economic pressures, including the rising costs of production inputs, such as land, fertilizer, machinery, and fuel, and increasing farm income expectations, resulted in a greater farm efficiency requirement. This increased efficiency is being achieved by greater grain production on each unit of cropland, and by the conversion of formerly uncultivated natural wetlands, grasslands, haylands, and parklands into cropland. As a result of efforts to produce more grain, at least 50 percent or 388,500 km² of the formerly uncultivated habitats in the glaciated prairie pothole region have been converted to cropland; this is an area nearly twice in size of all the glaciated prairie pothole region in the U.S. As another result of the efforts to produce more grain in this region, probably between 20 and 40 percent of the natural wetlands have been wholly or partly drained and many of these have been converted into cropland.

High duck production from annually tilled cropland occurred very infrequently in the prairie pothole region of North America, only about once every 10 to 20 years. Hochbaum (1955:229) reported that in 1945 the surface water remained on the farmland of the Portage Plains and Red River Valley through the spring and summer for the first time in at least a decade and nesting ducks settled down on these areas where none had been seen for several waterfowl generations. Gollop et al. (1952) reported that a phenomenal duck hatch in Saskatchewan was the result of abundant surface water and the largest over-wintering grain crop in history.

In contrast to annually tilled cropland, high nest densities and good duck production occurred frequently on untilled upland habitats in the prairie pothole region of North America. Summaries of several studies that found good duck production on untilled upland were presented by Kalmbach

Originally published in J. Wildl. Manage. 41(2):232–242, 1977.

(1939), Keith (1961), Moyle (1964), and Oetting and Cassel (1971). Two long-term duck production studies in Canada by Stoudt (1971) and Smith (1971) showed that good nesting success occurred on untilled upland habitats during most years, the highest in wet years and lowest in drought years. Higgins (1975) also found greater nest and successful-nest densities and nesting success of shorebirds and game birds on untilled upland than on annually cultivated land.

Successful duck production from cropland has been reported to be very dependent on either of two conditions: enough moisture to supply wetlands and delay of field tillage operations on cropland during fall and spring so that water and stubble remain throughout the nesting season (Hammond unpublished data, Colls and Lynch 1951, Hawkins 1954, Smith and Jensen 1956, Lynch 1956) or good wetland conditions and early establishment of grain crops that provide early cover for late nesting and renesting ducks.

High duck production from untilled habitats is dependent on the upland vegetative conditions, which in turn influence predator activity. Habitat conditions can range from excellent to poor depending on spring-summer moisture, vegetative cover form, and intensity of land use. High duck nesting densities and hatching success have been reported on undisturbed grass-legume cover with a tall, dense form by Duebbert (1969), Duebbert and Kantrud (1974), and Duebbert and Lokemoen (1976). The condition of most upland habitats is controlled by the intensity of land use, including idling, grazing, mowing, haying, burning, and tilling. Miller (1971) compared hatching success on idled, grazed, mowed, and cultivated land and found that significantly higher hatching success was achieved on idled land than on land subject to other uses.

Although annual cultivation is the major land use in this region where an average of 63 percent of the North American breeding duck population occurred from 1955 through 1964 (Crissey 1969:161), few studies assessed duck nesting on intensively farmed land. Most of the early surveys on cultivated land provided basic information about duck population trends and land use changes. Before 1960 a few nesting studies (Hammond unpublished data, Milonski 1958) provided quantitative data on ducks nesting on cultivated lands. Since 1960 no such major studies have been published. Additional basic information has been reported occasionally in conjunction with other duck nesting studies. Evans and Wolfe (1967), Smith (1971), Stoudt (1971), and Duebbert and Kantrud (1974). Recently, Higgins and Kantrud (1973) reported quantitative data relating to duck nesting on intensively cultivated land in the Dakotas and, like Milonski (1958), they suggested means by which land operators could help increase the chances of nesting success.

The objectives of this study were to assess the principal factors limiting duck production on intensively cultivated land. This was part of a waterfowl-land use study project of the Northern Prairie Wildlife Research Center. Permission to conduct field investigations on privately owned land was provided by the following farmers: L. Anderson, R. Anderson, V. Anderson, G. Bohl, J. Bohl, Jr., A. Brunsch, P. Bryn, R. Cook, A. Goter, E. Goter, R. Goter, S. Goter, J. Harrington, J. Hoggarth, L. Hoggarth, O. Hoggarth, R. Hoggarth, S. Johnson, G. Norden, R. Unruh, M. Walen, and A. Young.

My thanks go to H. W. Miller for guidance and supervision; to L. M. Kirsch,

H. F. Duebbert, A. T. Klett, and 18 student employees, especially to L. Strecker, for assisting with data collection; to H. Clark for equipment maintenance; to the following federal wetland managers for their assistance in the cooperative farming agreements: T. Atkins, R. Fries, V. Hall, J. Heinecke, M. Mansfield, G. Patton, and H. Troester; to D. H. Johnson for statistical assistance; and to J. C. Bartonek, J. B. Gollop, P. F. Springer, G. L. Krapu, and W. N. Ladd, Jr. for reviewing the manuscript.

STUDY AREAS

Duck nesting data were gathered on four different study areas in the prairie pothole region (Stewart and Kantrud 1973) of North Dakota. Data were collected on the Glenfield Study Area (GSA) during 1971–72, on the Woodworth Study Area (WSA) during 1969–74, on Waterfowl Production Areas (WPA) during 1969–70 and 1973–74 and on the New Home Study Area (NHSA) during 1970–73.

The New Home Study Area was in northwestern Stutsman County on the Missouri Coteau and included 12.95 km^2 of privately owned land. Township or county roads bordered each section. The terrain was gently rolling and interspersed with 322 natural wetland basins. Basin size ranged from 0.004 to 10.125 ha and averaged 0.38 ha. Mean basin density was 24.7 per km^2. There were 2 stock dams and many drainage ditches. Two natural drainages crossed the area.

Land use was 84 percent annually tilled cropland, 4 percent untilled upland, and 12 percent wetlands. Principal crops were durum and hard red spring wheat, barley, oats, rye, flax, and sunflower. Cattle ranching was the secondary land use. Native and tame grasslands were pastured during spring, summer, and fall. Road rights-of-way, dry wetland basins, and abandoned farmyards were hayed during late summer and fall. Rights-of-way that were not hayed were either mowed or burned annually to reduce snow accumulation.

The Glenfield Study Area was in southwestern Foster County on the Drift Plain and included 10.36 km^2 of privately owned land. Land use was 89 percent cultivated cropland, 8 percent nontilled upland, and 3 percent wetlands. The proposed 4-year study on the Glenfield Study Area was terminated prematurely in 1973 because of drought.

The Woodworth Study Area was in northwestern Stutsman County on the Missouri Coteau and included 12.30 km^2 of which 86 percent was federally owned and 14 percent privately owned. Land use was 12 percent annually tilled cropland, 71 percent nontilled upland, and 17 percent wetlands. The terrain is slightly rolling and contains 548 wetland basins. Previous descriptions of the wetlands, upland, and land-use practices were reported by Kirsch (1969). Data from WSA pertain only to the annually tilled cropland, wetlands, and untilled upland located within the cropland field borders.

Federally owned Waterfowl Production Areas were in Dickey, Eddy, Grand Forks, Logan, McIntosh, Ramsey, Steele, Stutsman, and Traill counties. Because private land operators would not permit nest searching in their seeded grain fields, data on duck nesting in growing grain were gathered on federally owned land. These grain fields were sharecropped by private land operators, and the nesting data obtained were believed to be representative of those from privately owned fields.

METHODS

Hectarages of fields, wetland basins, and natural drainages were determined from aerial photographs. Current and past land

Table 1. Hectares of habitats searched on each study area in eastern North Dakota, 1969–1974.

Habitat type	No. hectares searched				Total	%
	NHSA	WSA	GSA	WPA's		
Summer fallow	758	93	132	20	1,003	17
Mulched stubble	1,287	75	319	383	2,064	34
Standing stubble	314	285	131	6	736	12
Growing grain	0	376	0	1,378	1,754	29
Untilled upland	176	67	92	126	461	8
Total	2,535	896	674	1,913	6,018	100

uses were determined from aerial photographs, land operators, and the County Agricultural Stabilization and Conservation Service records in Jamestown, Cooperstown, Valley City, and Fessenden.

Nest searches were made between 15 April and 15 July to comply with farming operations. Except for shelterbelts and rock piles which were examined on foot, all fields were searched with a 53-m cable-chain device similar to that described by Higgins et al. (1969). Areas of the major habitat types that were searched on each study area are presented in Table 1. A nest was defined as a hollowed scrape containing one or more eggs, and a successful clutch was a nest in which at least one egg hatched. Nests were marked with a small red flag, usually 6 steps north. Ecological data were recorded on needle-sort punch cards. The incubation stage of each clutch was aged by field candling with a piece of radiator hose (Weller 1956). Fate of nests was determined on a subsequent visit, and identification of nest fate employed techniques described by Rearden (1951) and Einarsen (1956). The comparisons of nest densities, densities of hatched nests, and hatching success among and within land uses were tested for significant differences with the Kruskal-Wallis one-way analysis of variance test on ranks (Hollander and Wolfe 1973:115).

In this paper, the terms "cultivated" or "tilled" refer to croplands that undergo *annual* tillage or cultivation, e.g., summer fallowing or small grain cropping or row cropping, and "uncultivated" or "untilled" refer to all other types of upland.

RESULTS

Nesting Species

The estimated average density of nesting pairs were: New Home Study Area, 7/km^2; Woodworth Study Area, 36; Glenfield Study Area, 4; and Waterfowl Production Areas, 14. Ninety-three percent were upland nesting species and 7 percent were over-water nesting species. The following data pertain only to upland nesting duck species including mallard (*Anas platyrhynchos*), gadwall (*A. strepera*), American wigeon (*A. americana*), green-winged teal (*A. crecca*), blue-winged teal (*A. discors*), shoveler (*A. clypeata*), pintail, and lesser scaup (*Aythya affinis*).

Habitat Attractiveness

Major indicators of habitat attractiveness for nesting ducks are species composition of nests and nest density when all habitat units in an area have equal chance of being selected. Because of their mobility and the proximity of wetlands to fields, all ducks on the areas had equal chance to nest in any of the habitat units.

Species Composition.—Species composition of 186 duck nests is in Table 2. No American wigeon nests were found during

Table 2. Percentage composition by species of 186 duck nests found in 5 major habitats in an agricultural region of North Dakota during 1969–1974.

Species	Summer fallow (11)[a]	Mulched stubble (34)	Standing stubble (27)	Growing grain (21)	Untilled uplands (93)	Total (186)
Mallard		3	11	10	25	16
Gadwall				19	22	13
Green-winged teal					3	2
Blue-winged teal	9	9	37	48	37	31
Shoveler			4	10	3	3
Pintail	91	88	48	10	8	33
Lesser scaup				5	3	2
Total	100	100	100	102	101	100

[a] Sample size.

searches, but the occasional presence of a brood indicated that they did nest in or near the study areas. Pintails were the prevalent nesting species in fields of summer fallow, mulched stubble, and standing stubble. Blue-winged teal were most prevalent in growing grain, and untilled uplands. The greatest diversity of nesting species occurred in untilled uplands (Table 2) followed by growing grain, standing stubble, mulched stubble, and summer fallow. These findings corroborate the results obtained by Milonski (1958) in Manitoba.

Species Preference.—Seventy-two percent or more of all nests except pintail were in untilled upland (Table 3). Pintails nested in almost equal density in all habitats except growing grain. Only 15 percent or less of the mallards, gadwalls, green-winged teal, blue-winged teal, shoveler, and lesser scaup nested in tilled habitat types.

Nest Densities.—Densities of nests of 7 species of ducks in the upland habitat types are shown in Table 4. Nest density in summer fallow was 1.2/km^2, one of the lowest among the 5 major habitat types. Milonski (1958:222) reported a nest density of 2.5/km^2 on summer fallow fields in Manitoba. Eighteen percent of the nests were in mulched stubble that made up 34 percent of the acreage searched. These were fields of grain stubble that had been either disced or chisel-plowed the previous fall. Density was 1.6 nests/km^2. Because farmers now can harvest grain crops in less time and till more stubble before freeze-up, there is much less stubble left standing than a decade or more ago, yet standing stubble still constitutes a major habitat type. Standing stubble fields comprised 12 percent of the searched area and contained 15 percent of the 186 duck nests, a density of 3.7 nests/km^2.

In several early studies on intensively farmed lands no distinction was made between mulched and standing stubble. As a

Table 3. Habitat preference by species in five major habitats in an agricultural region of North Dakota during 1969–1974.

		Nests per km^2											
		Summer fallow		Mulched stubble		Standing stubble		Growing grain		Untilled uplands		Total	
Species	No. nests	No.	%	No.	%	No.	%	No.	%	No.	%	No.	%
Mallard	29			0.05	1	0.41	7	0.11	2	4.98	90	0.48	100
Gadwall	24							0.23	5	4.33	95	0.40	100
Green-winged teal	3									0.65	100	0.05	100
Blue-winged teal	58	0.10	1	0.15	2	1.36	14	0.57	6	7.37	78	0.97	101
Shoveler	6					0.14	15	0.11	13	0.65	72	0.10	100
Pintail	62	1.00	17	1.45	25	1.77	30	0.11	2	1.52	26	1.03	100
Lesser scaup	4							0.06	8	0.65	92	0.07	100
Total	186	1.10	4	1.65	6	3.67	13	1.20	4	20.15	73	3.10	

Table 4. Duck nest densities and hatching success in various habitat types in an intensively farmed agricultural region in eastern North Dakota during 1969–1974.

Habitat type	No. hectares searched	No. nests found	No. nests/km²	No. nests hatched	No. hatched nests/km²	% success
Annually tilled cropland						
Summer fallow	1,003	12	1.2	1	0.1	8
Mulched stubble	2,064	34	1.6	3	0.1	9
Standing stubble	736	27	3.7	4	0.5	15
Growing grain	1,754	20	1.1	8	0.5	40
Untilled upland						
Idled grassland	57	9(1)[a]	15.8	2	3.5	25
Heavily grazed pasture	66	3	4.5	0	0.0	0
1st year idled pasture	17	3	17.6	2	11.8	67
2nd year idled pasture	9	1	11.1	0	0.0	0
Road rights-of-way	118	43(1)[a]	36.4	8	6.8	19
Abandoned wooded farmsteads	9	4	44.4	1	11.1	25
Dry wetland basins and borders	127	18(2)[a]	14.2	7	5.5	44
Fence rows, rock piles, waterways	1	3	300.0[b]	0	0.0	0
Idled alfalfa	53	9	17.0	2	3.8	22
Subtotal						
Annually tilled cropland	5,557	93	1.7	16	0.3	17
Untilled upland	461	93(4)[a]	20.2	22	4.8	25
Grand total	6,018	186(4)[a]	3.1	38	0.6	21

[a] These 4 nests are included in nest density figures but excluded from the percent success figures since they were destroyed during search operations.
[b] There are insignificant acreages of these habitat types available to nesting ducks.

result, early records on ducks nesting in stubble fields are not directly comparable to these results. Lynch (1947), however, reported that stubble fields, especially fields with combine (standing) stubble, were very attractive to early nesting pintails and mallards. Gollop (1952) reported that pintails and mallards apparently used swaths and (standing) stubble the most; however, gadwalls, green-winged teal, blue-winged teal, and shovelers also were found nesting there.

Spring-planted fields of grain first became available to nesting ducks in late May and early June in most years. By 15 June, grain fields usually made up the major habitat type. Because of its late development as nesting cover, grain was more important to late nesting and renesting ducks than to early nesters. Of the 186 nests, 11 percent were in grain fields that made up 29 percent of the area searched, at a density of 1.1/km². Based on percent composition (Table 2) and nest density (Table 4) growing grain appeared to be an acceptable nesting habitat for gadwalls, blue-winged teal, shovelers, and lesser scaup, all of which are later nesting species.

Earl (1950) reported that winter wheat and barley were important nesting covers for mallards in the Sacramento Valley of California and in the same area Anderson (1957:78) found 19 percent of 333 duck nests in barley fields. Hunt and Naylor (1955:303) reported 4 percent of nests at Honey Lake Valley, California were in cereal crops. Milonski (1958:223) found 2 percent (11 pintail and 1 shoveler) of 608 nests in Manitoba in growing grain fields. During a 5-year nesting study in Nebraska,

Evans and Wolfe (1967:790) found an average of 6 percent of the duck nests in grain, with a maximum of 28 percent in 1960.

Untilled upland was the smallest habitat category on my study areas (8%) of the hectarage searched, but it attracted proportionately more nesting ducks than did annually tilled cropland. The nest density on untilled upland was 20.2/km². Heavily grazed pasture, road rights-of-way, and dry wetland basins and borders were the major components of the untilled uplands. Although the highest nest densities were found in fence rows, rock piles, grassy waterways, and abandoned farmsteads with treegroves, these habitats represented a tiny proportion of the total nesting area and are becoming scarcer with increases in monotype and clean farming practices. Of the various untilled upland habitats remaining on these intensively farmed study areas (Table 4), road rights-of-way that were 3 m wide or wider were most important. Evans and Wolfe (1967:792) reported that during 5 years, 28 percent of the duck nests were found in roadside cover that constituted only 1.2 percent of the study area. Borders of wetland basins accounted for 2.7 percent of their study area and 5.3 percent of the nests were found in this cover type. In Wisconsin, Gates (1965:518) found 95 percent of 139 upland duck nests in wetland basins or hayfields on an area that was 71 percent cultivated.

Duck nest densities on my areas were 12 times greater ($P < 0.01$) on untilled uplands than on cultivated croplands (Table 4). However, duck nest densities did not vary significantly among habitats within either ($P > 0.10$). Milonski (1958) also found highest nest densities on the untilled portion of his intensively farmed study area.

Table 5. Cause of duck nest failures on different habitat types in an intensively farmed agricultural region in eastern North Dakota during 1969–1974.

Habitat type	No. nest failures	Cause of failure: Machinery N	Machinery %	Predators N	Predators %	Unknown N	Unknown %
Annually tilled cropland	77	26	34	45	58	6	8
Untilled upland	67	1	2	65	97	1	2
Total	144	27	19	110	76	7	5

Habitat Productiveness

Densities of Hatched Clutches.—Hatched-clutch densities were 16 times greater ($P < 0.01$) on untilled upland (4.8) than on cropland (0.3) (Table 4) showing that untilled upland produced, per unit of area, significantly more ducklings than cropland. Apparently the intensity of land use affected hatched-clutch densities on both habitats. On cropland, the lowest densities (Table 4) were in summer fallow and mulched stubble fields and the highest densities were in standing stubble and growing grain. On untilled upland the lowest density was in heavily grazed pastures and highest densities were in first-year idled pasture, abandoned wooded farmsteads, road rights-of-way, and dry wetland basins and borders.

Hatching Success.—Hatching success on untilled upland (25%) was greater than on tilled cropland (17%), but the difference was not statistically significant ($P > 0.10$) among or within the habitat types (Table 4). Overall hatching success (21%) was low in comparison with an average of several other studies (Keith 1961:69) (39%) and Moyle (1964:15) (33%).

Cause of Nest Failures

Of the 186 nests found, 144 (77%) did not hatch (Table 5). Predators, principally red foxes (*Vulpes vulpes*), were the major cause of nest failure on tilled and untilled upland. Tillage destroyed 34 percent of all nests and 93 percent of the active nests on cropland. In one instance, a nest was successful because of its location next to a piece of wood which the farmer by-passed with his machinery and, in another situation, a pintail salvaged 5 of 7 eggs that were tilled under by machinery and subsequently hatched 4 of them.

Milonski (1958:220) reported that farming operations destroyed 57 percent (1956) and 41 percent (1957) of the pintail nests on his intensively farmed study area in Manitoba. Crows (*Corvus brachyrhynchos*) and foxes were the principal predators in Manitoba stubble fields, whereas skunks (*Mephitis mephitis*) worked mainly roadsides and field edges.

DISCUSSION

All my areas contained or were adjacent to complexes of natural wetlands. Many intensively farmed areas in the prairie pothole region are devoid of wetlands, because of glacial phenomena or drainage. Such areas do not attract or produce ducks; therefore, projection of duck production for the entire region based on these results would be misleading until the proportion of the area which is productive is evaluated. Further projection to a species level would be even more complex. Apparently, some duck species do not produce in certain nesting habitats even though wetlands are present within an intensively farmed area. For example, Milonski (1958) and I found that 5 of 7 upland nesting species of ducks avoided nesting in summer fallow fields.

Keith (1961:69) stated that an average hatching success of 39 percent would, with renesting, be "more than adequate" to maintain population levels of ducks. According to his criteria the overall 21 percent hatching success on the areas I studied was not sufficient; in fact, the mean productivity rate was 46 percent less than his proposed maintenance threshold. In my opinion, upland nesting duck populations are not capable of maintaining themselves by reproduction during most years on areas that are 85 percent or more annually tilled; more probably their numbers are an annual result of the longevity of homing hens plus recruitment of pioneering ducks from other, more productive, habitats.

Predation, both avian and mammalian, was the greatest cause of egg losses in this study and in most reported studies of duck production. In one study, bullsnakes (*Pituophis sayi*) were the principal cause of egg loss (Imler 1945). Few studies evaluated the effects of predator control (Kalmbach 1939, Imler 1945, Balser et al. 1968, Duebbert and Kantrud 1974), but in every case, duck production was enhanced after predator reduction.

Good duck production from untilled, good quality, upland habitats occurs frequently and consistently with good water conditions. Poor production is most often associated with drought or poor upland vegetative conditions. Intensity of land use (heavy grazing) and predation can also suppress production in these habitats. When the nest densities and success on annually tilled cropland are compared with those on untilled upland, it is apparent that, during most years, the maintenance of duck populations in the prairie pothole region is largely dependent on water conditions and production on untilled upland habitats.

Several years ago Hammond (1964) pointed out that the future of waterfowl was principally in the hands of the small grain farmers. The trend then and now is toward fewer but larger farms with more area under intensive tillage, including wetlands as well as upland. This study, projected with this land use trend, predicts a dismal future for the prairie waterfowl resource.

CONCLUSIONS AND RECOMMENDATIONS

In the prairie pothole region of the United States and Canada, where an estimated 63 percent of the North American duck population nests, 50 percent or more of the land is annually tilled. All relevant studies have shown that duck production is less on annually tilled cropland than on other upland. Poor nesting cover resulting from intensive land use practices, and nesting failures caused by farm machinery and predators, are the principal factors limiting nesting and production on these areas. To help correct the situation, I submit the following recommendations for consideration:

(1) Wetland preservation programs should be expanded to assure an adequate base for future waterfowl. Wetlands are still the primary factor in waterfowl management because land with no water in proximity yields no duck production but land with wetlands interspersed will yield production during some years.

(2) Efforts should be made to increase the amount of stubble residue on annually tilled land. Tilled land makes up about one-half of the glaciated prairie pothole region nesting habitat and usually about 20 percent of this is summer fallow (mostly bare-soil). There is little doubt that large areas of cultivated land will continue to be needed to sustain the burgeoning human population. The amount of stubble remaining over-winter and through the nesting season could be increased by leaving stubble standing over-winter, by limiting fall stubble mulching to one operation, and by delaying any mulch operation of fields programmed for summer fallowing until about 1 June. Agricultural scientists in the Northern Great Plains have indicated that summer fallow operations can be delayed until about 1 June without any significant loss of soil water or increase in normal weed problems (Hass et al. 1974).

(3) Efforts should be continued to preserve and restore, in part, the untilled cover base. The annual loss of untilled upland nesting cover is a major factor that suppresses duck production regardless of existing water conditions. Unlike water, this has not been a fluctuating factor among the waterfowl production requirements but has declined continuously. In addition, sizeable units (32 ha or larger) of untilled habitats could be established and maintained in farmed areas where an adequate wetland base is already protected but where less than 10 percent of the land is untilled. Unnecessary cultivation of public lands, including road rights-of-way, should be discontinued where possible.

(4) The intensity of land use practices on untilled habitats should be planned to provide good quality vegetation for nesting. Waterfowl production on some public lands, including road rights-of-way, is being suppressed due to the intensity of haying, mowing, and grazing, which usually occur annually.

(5) An inventory of land use trends, including intensity of use and size and quality of uplands suitable for nesting ducks should be an integral part of continental waterfowl management plans.

LITERATURE CITED

ANDERSON, W. 1957. A waterfowl nesting study in the Sacramento Valley, California, 1955. California Fish Game 43(1):71–90.

BALSER, D. S., H. H. DILL, AND H. K. NELSON. 1968. Effect of predator reduction on waterfowl nesting success. J. Wildl. Manage. 32(4): 669–682.

COLLS, D. G., AND J. J. LYNCH. 1951. Waterfowl breeding ground survey in Saskatchewan, 1951. Pages 35–40 *in* Waterfowl populations and breeding conditions—summer 1951. U.S. Fish Wildl. Serv. Spec. Sci. Rep. Wildl. 13.

CRISSEY, W. F. 1969. Prairie potholes from a continental viewpoint. Pages 161–171 *in* Saskatoon wetlands seminar. Canadian Wildl. Serv. Rep. Ser. 6.

DUEBBERT, H. F. 1969. High nest density and hatching success of ducks on South Dakota CAP land. Trans. N. Am. Wildl. Nat. Resour. Conf. 34:218–229.

———, AND H. A. KANTRUD. 1974. Upland duck nesting related to land use and predator reduction. J. Wildl. Manage. 38(2):257–265.

———, AND J. T. LOKEMOEN. 1976. Duck nesting in fields of undisturbed grass-legume cover. J. Wildl. Manage. 40(1):39–49.

EARL, J. P. 1950. Production of mallards on irrigated land in the Sacramento Valley, California. J. Wildl. Manage. 14(3):332–342.

EINARSEN, A. S. 1956. Determination of some predator species by field signs. Oregon State Monogr. Stud. Zool. 10. 34pp.

EVANS, R. D., AND C. W. WOLFE, JR. 1967. Waterfowl production in the rainwater basin area of Nebraska. J. Wildl. Manage. 31(4): 788–794.

GATES, J. M. 1965. Duck nesting and production on Wisconsin farmlands. J. Wildl. Manage. 29(3):515–523.

GOLLOP, J. B. 1952. Waterfowl breeding ground survey in Saskatchewan Kindersley-Eston Study Area. Pages 41–51 *in* Waterfowl populations and breeding conditions—summer 1952. U.S. Fish Wildl. Serv. Spec. Sci. Rep. Wildl. 21.

———, J. J. LYNCH, AND W. HYSKA. 1952. Waterfowl breeding ground survey in Saskatchewan. Pages 33–40 *in* Waterfowl populations and breeding conditions—summer 1952. U.S. Fish Wildl. Serv. Spec. Sci. Rep. Wildl. 21.

HAAS, H. J., W. O. WILLIS, AND J. J. BOND. 1974. Summer fallow in the northern great plains (spring wheat). Pages 12–35 *in* Summer fallow in the western United States. U.S. Dept. Agr. Conserv. Res. Rep. 17.

HAMMOND, M. C. 1964. Ducks, grain, and American farmers. Pages 417–424 *in* J. P. Linduska, ed. Waterfowl tomorrow. U.S. Government Printing Office, Washington, D.C.

HAWKINS, A. S. 1954. Waterfowl breeding ground survey in Manitoba. Pages 74–80 *in* Waterfowl populations and breeding conditions—summer 1953. U.S. Fish Wildl. Serv. Spec. Sci. Rep. Wildl. 25.

HIGGINS, K. F. 1975. Shorebird and game bird nests in North Dakota croplands. Wildl. Soc. Bull. 3(4):176–179.

———, AND H. A. KANTRUD. 1973. Increasing bird nesting success on cultivated lands. North Dakota Outdoors 35(9):18–21.

———, L. M. KIRSCH, AND I. J. BALL, JR. 1969. A cable-chain device for locating duck nests. J. Wildl. Manage. 33(4):1009–1011.

HOCHBAUM, H. A. 1955. Travels and traditions of waterfowl. University of Minnesota Press, Minneapolis. 301pp.

HOLLANDER, M., AND D. A. WOLFE. 1973. Nonparametric statistical methods. John Wiley and Sons, Inc., New York. 503pp.

HUNT, E. G., AND A. E. NAYLOR. 1955. Nesting studies of ducks and coots in Honey Lake Valley. California Fish Game 41(4):295–314.

IMLER, R. H. 1945. Bullsnakes and their control on a Nebraska wildlife refuge. J. Wildl. Manage. 9(4):265–273.

KALMBACH, E. R. 1939. Nesting success: its significance in waterfowl reproduction. Trans. N. Am. Wildl. Conf. 4:591–604.

KEITH, L. B. 1961. A study of waterfowl ecology on small impoundments in southeastern Alberta. Wildl. Monogr. 6. 88pp.

KIRSCH, L. M. 1969. Waterfowl production in relation to grazing. J. Wildl. Manage. 33(4): 821–828.

LODGE, R. W. 1969. Agricultural use of wetlands. Pages 11–15 *in* Saskatoon wetlands seminar. Canadian Wildl. Serv. Rep. Ser. 6.

LYNCH, J. J. 1947. Waterfowl breeding conditions in Saskatchewan, 1947. Pages 21–38 *in* Waterfowl breeding conditions—summer 1947. U.S. Fish Wildl. Serv. Spec. Sci. Rep. 45.

———. 1956. Waterfowl breeding ground survey—southern Saskatchewan, 1955. Pages 45–53 *in* Waterfowl populations and breeding conditions—summer 1955. U.S. Fish Wildl. Serv. Spec. Sci. Rep. Wildl. 30.

MILLER, H. W. 1971. Relationships of duck nesting success to land use in North and South Dakota. Trans. Int. Congr. Game Biol. 10: 133–141.

MILONSKI, M. 1958. The significance of farmland for waterfowl nesting and techniques for reducing losses due to agricultural practices. Trans. N. Am. Wildl. Conf. 23:215–228.

MOYLE, J. B., ed. 1964. Ducks and land use in Minnesota. Minnesota Dept. Conser. Tech. Bull. 8. 140pp.

OETTING, R. B., AND J. F. CASSEL. 1971. Waterfowl nesting on interstate highway right-of-way in North Dakota. J. Wildl. Manage. 35 (4):774–781.

REARDEN, J. D. 1951. Identification of waterfowl nest predators. J. Wildl. Manage. 15(4):386–395.

SMITH, A. G. 1971. Ecological factors affecting waterfowl production in the Alberta parklands. U.S. Fish Wildl. Serv. Resour. Publ. 98. 49pp.

———, AND G. H. JENSEN. 1956. Aerial waterfowl breeding ground survey—Alberta, 1955. Pages 26–32 *in* Waterfowl populations and breeding conditions—summer 1955. U.S. Fish Wildl. Serv. Spec. Sci. Rep. 30.

STEWART, R. E., AND H. A. KANTRUD. 1973. Ecological distribution of breeding waterfowl populations in North Dakota. J. Wildl. Manage. 37(1):39–50.

STOUDT, J. H. 1971. Ecological factors affecting waterfowl production in the Saskatchewan parklands. U.S. Fish Wildl. Serv. Resour. Publ. 99. 58pp.

WELLER, M. W. 1956. A simple field candler for waterfowl eggs. J. Wildl. Manage. 20(2):111–113.

Received 12 February 1976.
Accepted 19 January 1977.

HIGH DUCK NESTING SUCCESS IN A PREDATOR-REDUCED ENVIRONMENT

HAROLD F. DUEBBERT, Northern Prairie Wildlife Research Center, U.S. Fish and Wildlife Service, Jamestown, ND 58401
JOHN T. LOKEMOEN, Northern Prairie Wildlife Research Center, U.S. Fish and Wildlife Service, Jamestown, ND 58401

Abstract: Duck nesting and production were studied during 1969–74 on a 51-ha field of undisturbed grass-legume cover and a surrounding 8.13-km² area in north-central South Dakota. The principal mammalian predators of ducks were reduced within a 259-km² zone from May 1969 through August 1971. Dabbling duck nest densities, hatching success, and breeding populations attained high levels. Seven duck species produced 1,062 nests on the 51-ha field during 6 years; 864 (81%) hatched, 146 (14%) were destroyed, and 52 (5%) had other fates. During 1970–72, when predator reduction was most effective, the hatching success for 756 nests was 94%. The number of mallard (*Anas platyrhynchos*) nests increased from 37 (0.7/ha) in 1969 to 181 (3.5/ha) in 1972. Mallard pairs increased from 2.8/km² to 16.8/km² on the 8.13-km² area during the same period. A minimum of 7,250 ducklings hatched on the 51-ha field during the 6 years, including 2,342 ducklings in 1972. Exceptionally high duck nesting densities and hatching rates occurred when predators were controlled.

J. WILDL. MANAGE. 44(2):428–437

Studies in the prairie pothole region of North America have shown that predation is often a primary cause of reduced nesting success of dabbling ducks (Keith 1961, Smith 1971, Stoudt 1971, Higgins 1977). Conversely, other studies have shown that duck nesting success or production increased when predation was temporarily reduced (Kalmbach 1939, Ellig 1955, Balser et al. 1968, Lynch 1972, Schranck 1972, Duebbert and Kantrud 1974). Waterfowl biologists, managers, and administrators have often speculated about the effects of organized predator control on duck production.

During 1969–74 we studied a population of breeding dabbling ducks that included mallards, gadwalls (*Anas strepera*), pintails (*A. acuta*), green-winged teal (*A. crecca*), blue-winged teal (*A. discors*), northern shovelers (*A. clypeata*), and American wigeon (*A. americana*) on an 8.13-km² study area near Hosmer, South Dakota, here termed the Hosmer Study Area (HSA). Primary emphasis was placed on nesting studies in a 51-ha field of undisturbed grass-legume cover. The objective of this study was to investigate the nesting ecology and population responses of dabbling ducks in a glaciated prairie wetland region where the principal predators were rigidly controlled.

We express our appreciation for assistance during the study to our supervisor, H. W. Miller; to F. Ulmer for allowing access to the study area; to P. Dosch who conducted the predator control for the South Dakota Department of Game, Fish, and Parks; to K. F. Higgins, L. M. Kirsch, and A. T. Klett and several other biologists for assistance with field work; to D. A. Davenport and D. H. Johnson for help with data analysis; and to G. A. Swanson and L. M. Kirsch, who reviewed our manuscript and gave editorial assistance.

STUDY AREA

The nesting study was conducted on a 51-ha field (here termed nesting field, NF) of tall, dense cover composed primarily of intermediate wheatgrass and alfalfa. This cover was established on a cropland field in 1965 under the U.S. Department of Agriculture's Cropland Adjustment Program, and remained undisturbed for the duration of our study.

The study area was within a 259-km² (16 × 16-km) area (here termed predator

---

Originally published in J. Wildl. Manage. 44(2):428–437, 1980.

Fig. 1. The 51-ha nesting field and the 8.13-km² Hosmer Study Area, 16 May 1972.

control area, PCA), where red foxes (*Vulpes vulpes*), striped skunks (*Mephitis mephitis*), raccoons (*Procyon lotor*), and badgers (*Taxidea taxus*) were intensively controlled from May 1969 to August 1971. These mammals were the major predators of duck nests, hens, and ducklings in the area (Duebbert and Lokemoen 1976). Data on dabbling duck breeding populations and broods, wetland conditions, and land use were recorded on the 8.13-km² circular HSA, with a radius of 1.6 km, centered on the NF (Fig. 1).

The HSA contained a complex of 74 wetland basins, of which 14 were Class I (ephemeral), 21 were Class II (temporary), and 39 were Class III (seasonal) according to Stewart and Kantrud (1971). Wetlands ranged in size from 0.04 ha to 4.05 ha ($\bar{x}$ = 0.92 ha). Total area of the wetland basins was 67.9 ha, of which 0.9 ha was Class I, 6.5 ha were Class II, and 60.5 ha were Class III. Water conditions during mid-May and mid-July varied widely among years (Table 1). Wetland habitats were excellent for duck production in 1969 and 1970, good in 1971, excellent in 1972, and poor in 1973 and 1974. Agricultural drainage had not affected the area, and original wetland complexes remained intact. Aquatic vegetation in the wetlands was mostly undisturbed, grazed, or hayed. Only a few ephemeral or temporary wetlands were tilled. Giant burreed (*Sparganium eurycarpum*), slough sedge (*Carex atherodes*), and marsh smartweed (*Polygonum coccineum*) dominated the vegetation of undisturbed seasonal wetlands. Invertebrate populations were not quantified, but our observations indicated abundant snails (Lymnaeidae), midges (Chironomidae), and other food organisms used by breeding hens and ducklings associated with seasonal wetlands (Swanson et al. 1974).

Land use on the HSA was typical of the diversified grain-livestock farms in the region. Percentages of the total area in various land uses were: grazed mixed-grass prairie, 28; cropland, 24; domestic

Table 1. Number and area of wetlands on the 8.13-km² Hosmer Study Area in May and July 1969–74.[a]

Year	Mid-May		Mid-July	
	N	Area (ha)	*N*	Area (ha)
1969	40	53.4	66	60.9
1970	36	42.3	15	15.4
1971	19	19.5	15	12.2
1972	53	55.6	16	18.2
1973	11	7.0	3	0.2
1974	16	3.7	5	0.4

[a] Based on 74 wetland basins with a total area of 67.9 ha.

pasture, 9; wetlands, 8; domestic hay, 8; townsite, 7; undisturbed grass-legume cover (NF), 6; and miscellaneous, 9. The land use pattern and farming practices were consistent throughout the study.

METHODS

Intensive predator control was conducted continuously from May 1969 through August 1971 on the PCA. The HSA was situated within the PCA, which was part of a study of relationships between predation and ring-necked pheasants (*Phasianus colchicus*) conducted by the South Dakota Department of Game, Fish, and Parks (Trautman et al. 1974). Predator control methods included strychnine-treated baits, trapping, and shooting. Ducks breeding on our study area were in an essentially predator-free environment during 4 nesting seasons, as indicated by few observations of predators, tracks, scats, active dens, or road-killed animals. There were few avian predators on the area; and small mammals, other than those controlled, were of minor importance as nest or duck predators.

Nests were found by flushing hens with a 53-m cable-chain device towed between 2 vehicles (Higgins et al. 1969). Two complete searches were made of the NF each year at about 30-day intervals. Dates ranged from 25 May to 3 June for the 1st search and 25 June to 8 July for the 2nd. Eggs were candled to determine their stage of development (Weller 1956). The duck population was counted in mid-May and in early June according to techniques outlined by Hammond (1969). Wetland and land use conditions were recorded during the mid-May and mid-July surveys.

Nest densities were totaled from all nests of each species that were found. We calculated hatching rates for each species by the conventional method of dividing the number of hatched nests by the sum of hatched plus destroyed nests. Nests that were deserted or destroyed because of our disturbance, or whose markers were lost, were omitted in calculations of nest success.

Mayfield (1961, 1975) pointed out that conventional methods of analyzing nesting data tend to overestimate success and underestimate density because all nests were not found. Recently, Miller and Johnson (1978) discussed problems inherent in interpreting the results of nesting studies, and recommended use of the Mayfield method. In addition to the conventional method, our data were analyzed by the Mayfield method with a computer program developed by D. A. Davenport at the Northern Prairie Wildlife Research Center to determine the probability of a nest hatching.

Tests were performed to determine the spatial relationships of mallard nests that were simultaneously active about 1 June each year. The principal method was the nearest-neighbor test, which compared the average distance between nearest nests to the value expected if nests were located randomly (Clark and Evans 1954).

Nest searches were timed so that each hen would be flushed only once or twice, and nest fates were not checked until af-

Table 2. Numbers and percentages of nests hatching for duck nests on 51-ha field on the Hosmer Study Area, 1969–74.[a]

	1969		1970		1971		1972		1973		1974		Total/Average	
Species	*N*	%	*N*	%	*N*	%	*N*	%	*N*	%	*N*	%	*N*	%
Mallard	37	79	93	99	79	95	181	90	96	56	13	69	499	84
Gadwall	47	71	50	90	60	100	82	90	24	59	23	86	286	86
Pintail	14	43	25	91	14	100	23	91	11	89	2	100	89	84
Green-winged teal	3	100	3	100	2	100	2	100	2	100	0		12	100
Blue-winged teal	17	59	61	98	14	91	19	84	3	33	0		114	87
Northern shoveler	7	71	18	100	5	100	10	90	3	67	0		43	90
American wigeon	1	0	4	75	6	83	5	100	2	50	1	0	19	78
Total/average	126	69	254	96	180	96	322	90	141	59	39	78	1,062	85
Nests/100 ha	247		498		353		631		276		76		347	

[a] Percentages of hatching success may be based on slightly fewer nests because some were lost, deserted, or destroyed by searchers.

ter calculated hatch dates. Fates of nests were determined by methods outlined by Rearden (1951) and Einarsen (1956) and our own extensive field experience.

Ducks were observed from a blind located in the NF during 2 hours after sunrise on 4 and 14 May 1971 to obtain information on pursuit flights, aerial displays, and other behavior. Vegetation in the NF was analyzed by a series of 1-m^2 quadrats and cover board readings along line transects as described by Duebbert and Lokemoen (1976).

RESULTS AND DISCUSSION

Hatching Success and Other Nesting Factors

High success of dabbling duck nests occurred on the Hosmer Study Area (HSA) during 4 nesting seasons in the near-absence of mammalian predation (Table 2). Eggs hatched in 758 of 842 nests (90%) during 1969–72 when predator control was in effect. Predator reduction was most nearly complete during the 1970 and 1971 nesting seasons, and in those years, 395 of 411 nests (96%) hatched successfully. In 1969, a few predators were present because control had just been initiated. In 1972, predators began to reinvade the area, but populations remained low from residual effects of control activities during the previous 3 years.

Comparative data on duck nesting success in similar habitats not subject to predator control are available from a concurrent study in 9 fields of undisturbed grass-legume cover with a total area of 271 ha outside of the predator control area (PCA) (Duebbert and Lokemoen 1976). The vegetation on these fields was much like that on the HSA, and the nesting plots were surrounded by similar land-use patterns and wetland complexes. Fields were situated an average of 20 km from the HSA and from 3 to 10 km from the boundary of the PCA. In 1971, 1972, and 1973, eggs in 320 of 570 nests hatched, for an average success rate of 56% in the 9 fields without predator control (Duebbert and Lokemoen 1976). During 1971–72, nesting success on the HSA averaged 93%; on the 9 fields outside of the PCA, it averaged 63%.

In 1971, average duck nesting success was 51% in a variety of habitats on agricultural land outside the PCA about 10 km from the nesting field (NF) (Duebbert and Kantrud 1974). Nest densities were low on the agricultural lands, averaging

Table 3. Hatching success (%) of nests as calculated by conventional (C) and Mayfield (M) methods, 1969–72.

Year		Mallard	Gadwall	Blue-winged teal
1969	C	79	71	59
	M	46	53	35
1970	C	99	90	98
	M	96	81	100
1971	C	95	100	91
	M	84	100	76
1972	C	90	90	84
	M	78	74	77

14/km^2. Higgins (1977) reported hatching success of 25% on untilled habitats and 17% on tilled habitats for duck nests in intensively farmed areas of North Dakota.

Nest destruction rates were relatively low during most years of our study. Thus, there was less difference between nesting success as calculated by the conventional or the Mayfield method on the HSA, than in areas with higher nest losses (Table 3). For example, in 1971, mallard nesting success for 79 nests was 95% by the conventional method and 84% by the Mayfield method. In 1971, gadwall nesting success for 60 nests was 100% by both methods. In 1969, when nest destruction rates were higher, there was a greater difference between nest successes determined by the 2 methods.

Abandonment rates were low: 21 of 1,062 nests (2%) were abandoned during all years, indicating that nest-site fidelity was not adversely affected by the high nest density. Nearly all abandonments were a result of our interference when nests contained 1–5 eggs. Another 31 nests had other fates: 6 had complete clutches of infertile eggs, 4 were destroyed by search vehicles, and 21 had unknown fates because markers were lost.

Clutch sizes were normal for the species of ducks that nested on the HSA, indicating that egg laying was not influenced by high-density nesting, concentration of pairs, or long-distance flights. Average clutch size in 1971 for mallards was 8.1 in the NF and 8.2 in fields of similar cover outside of the PCA (Duebbert and Lokemoen 1976), and gadwall mean clutch size was 10.7 on both areas. In 1972, clutch sizes for mallards and gadwalls were slightly lower in the NF than in the other fields (8.1 vs. 8.6 and 10.1 vs. 10.8, respectively). Mallard clutch size during the study averaged 8.4 (338 nests), which is the same average reported for long-term studies in Saskatchewan by Stoudt (1971).

Hatchability rates of eggs were high in successful nests on the HSA. During all years, 7,250 of 7,594 eggs (95%) hatched in successful nests. The 7,250 figure represents the minimum number of ducklings hatched on the field. Only 5 of 1,062 nests contained an abnormally large number of eggs or eggs of different species, and that indicated a low incidence of intraspecific or interspecific egg laying.

For mallard hens in the predator-reduced environment on the HSA, the nesting chronology was relatively early. In 1970 and 1971, 89% and 84% of the mallard nests were started before 1 June. In 1972, when predator populations remained low, 97% of the mallard nests were started before 1 June and 42% before 1 May. About ½ of the young mallards would be fledged by 1 August under this early nesting schedule.

Nest Densities and Spacing

Dabbling ducks normally nest solitarily, but aggregations of some species may be formed where the nesting environment is safe (Lack 1968:118). The nesting field on the HSA contained unusually

Table 4. Indicated dabbling duck pairs on the 8.13-km² Hosmer Study Area, 1969–74.

Species	1969		1970		1971		1972		1973		1974		Total	
	N	%	*N*	%	*N*	%	*N*	%	*N*	%	*N*	%	*N*	%
Mallard	23	12	90	23	59	30	137	27	67	32	18	50	394	26
Gadwall	39	20	61	16	28	14	54	11	48	23	6	17	236	15
Pintail	35	18	80	21	39	20	107	21	54	25	7	19	322	21
Green-winged teal	6	3	6	2	3	2	8	2	2	1	0	0	25	2
Blue-winged teal	63	33	109	28	40	20	130	26	13	6	4	11	359	23
Northern shoveler	25	13	41	11	24	12	60	12	24	11	1	3	175	11
American wigeon	1	tr[a]	3	tr	4	2	6	1	4	2	0	0	18	1
Total	192	99	390	101	197	100	502	100	212	100	36	100	1,529	99
Pairs/km²	24		48		24		62		26		4		31	

[a] Less than 1%.

dense aggregations of nests during 1969–72, when the ducks were in a predator-reduced environment (Table 2). Nests of all species of resident dabbling ducks were found, but mallard nests made up 47% (499 nests) and gadwalls 27% (286 nests) of the total of 1,062 nests. In 1968, the year before intensive predator reduction began, 61 nests (120/100 ha) were found on the NF (Duebbert 1969). In 1969, 126 nests (247/100 ha) were found, and the density increased to 322 nests (631/100 ha) in 1972. The number of mallard nests increased from 37 in 1969 to 181 in 1972. Gadwall nests increased from 47 to 82 during the same period.

Comparison between density of mallard nests on the NF and pairs counted in the surrounding HSA indicated that nests were aggregated in the NF. During all years, the number of mallard nests on the 51-ha NF closely approximated the pair population in the 8.13-km² HSA. Mallard pairs were observed flying to the NF from wetlands up to 3.2 km away. When hens were flushed from nests, they did not always go to the nearest wetland, but often flew 1.6 km or more.

Mallard nests were spaced in various patterns throughout the NF in different years. Results of the nearest-neighbor tests showed the following nest distribution patterns for the respective years: 1969, random; 1970, aggregated (P = 0.14); 1971, random; 1972, aggregated (P = 0.013); 1973, aggregated ($P < 0.001$); 1974, spaced ($P < 0.01$).

On the basis of 6-year averages, there was a general tendency toward higher nest densities (2.29/ha) on the soil zones with higher capability ratings (according to the U.S. Soil Conservation Service classification) and lower (0.65/ha) on those with lower capability ratings. Soils with higher capability ratings supported taller, more dense cover, and slopes ranged 0–6%. Soils with lower capability ratings supported shorter, less dense cover, and slopes ranged 6–12%. This indicated a tendency for nesting hens to select nest sites in zones of taller, more dense cover within the NF.

The highest known density of active mallard nests in the NF at 1 time was 154 (3.0/ha) on 24 May 1972. Then, the average distance between nests was 27 m, and 119 (78%) of the nests were less than 30 m apart. We found 3 mallard nests that were closer to other nests than 6 m; the intervals were 2.1 m, 3.0 m, and 4.6 m. Newton and Campbell (1975) found that 2 m was about the closest nest spacing mallard hens would tolerate without strife. We concluded there was unoccu-

Table 5. Densities of dabbling duck pairs in relation to surface water in mid-May on the 8.13-km² Hosmer Study Area, 1969–74.

Species	Pairs per ha of surface water					
	1969	1970	1971	1972	1973	1974
Mallard	0.43	2.12	3.03	2.46	9.57	4.86
Gadwall	0.73	1.44	1.44	0.97	6.86	1.62
Pintail	0.66	1.89	2.00	1.92	7.71	1.89
Green-winged teal	0.11	0.14	0.15	0.14	0.29	
Blue-winged teal	1.18	2.58	2.05	2.34	1.86	1.08
Northern shoveler	0.47	0.97	1.23	1.08	3.43	0.27
American wigeon	0.02	0.07	0.21	0.11	0.57	
Total	3.60	9.22	10.10	9.03	30.29	9.73

pied nesting cover for mallards on the NF even with the high densities we recorded.

Breeding Populations

Breeding populations of dabbling ducks, especially mallards, increased to high densities on the HSA (Table 4). In 1969, populations of all dabblers were similar to those generally found in the northern Coteau du Missouri in South Dakota (Brewster et al. 1976, Duebbert and Lokemoen 1976). Blue-winged teal were the most numerous, followed by gadwalls, pintails, mallards, and northern shovelers.

Between May 1969 and May 1970, we recorded a 103% increase in dabbling duck pairs and a 291% increase in mallard pairs, but a 10% decrease in HSA wetlands with water. Mallards changed from 12% to 23% of the breeding population and from 5th to 2nd in abundance. During the same period, in eastern South Dakota, Pospahala et al. (1974:67), reported a 32% decrease in wetlands with water, a 5% increase in total ducks, and an 8% increase in breeding mallards.

Mallards became the most abundant breeding species in 1971, and maintained that position until the end of the study. Gadwalls and other dabblers also increased, but less markedly than mallards. Numbers of ponds in May 1971 decreased 12% in eastern South Dakota (Pospahala et al. 1974:67) and 48% on the HSA (Table 1).

In 1972, the dabbling duck breeding population increased to 502 pairs, or 62 pairs/km², which was the highest density recorded on our area. Mallard pairs increased to 137, for a density of 16.8 pairs/km² (Table 4). In 1972, use of available water by breeding pairs of all species averaged 9.0/ha; mallard pairs averaged 2.5/ha (Table 5). Wetlands with water and total breeding pairs also increased on nearby study areas (Duebbert and Lokemoen 1976) and in eastern South Dakota (Pospahala et al. 1974). The large increases in breeding populations, especially mallards, occurred only on the HSA.

Some wetlands on the HSA contained extremely high densities of breeding ducks. For example, on 17 May 1972 we counted 40 indicated pairs of ducks on a 1.4-ha seasonal wetland. Other high populations on seasonal wetlands were 47 pairs on 3.2 ha, 45 pairs on 2.4 ha, and 65 pairs on 4.0 ha.

In 1973 there was a large reduction in water area (Table 1), and effects of predation increased after control ceased in August 1971. The area of surface water decreased 88%, and only 11 of 76 wetlands contained water in mid-May. Numbers of breeding ducks declined, but crowded on the remaining water in dense aggregations. In 1973, total duck pairs averaged 30.3/ha of water and mallard pairs averaged 9.6/ha of water (Table 5). Water conditions deteriorated further in 1974, and in mid-May there was only 3.7 ha of water.

The highest mallard pair density on the HSA was 16.8/km² in 1972. The highest recorded mallard pair density we found in our literature search was 36.2/km² at Lousana, Alberta, in 1958 (Smith 1971). The pair density of all dabbling duck species was 84.5/km² at Lousana in 1958, compared with the 1972 density of 61.8/km² on the HSA. On the basis of density per area of water, the 1973 HSA mallard pair population of 9.6/ha and dabbler pair population of 30.3/ha were higher than any we found in the literature. When Smith (1971) recorded the high populations in 1958, the mallard pair density per area of water was 5.4/ha, and the dabbler pair density was 12.8/ha.

During the May 1971 observations, we obtained information on behavioral interactions of ducks that were nesting in high densities. Of 63 mallard hens that arrived at the field as members of a pair or a group, 46 (73%) were not accompanied or chased by male mallards. The entire sequence of 5 pursuit flights was observed, and hens eventually landed in the cover, suggesting that behavioral interactions did not prevent those hens from nesting in the field. Of 53 gadwall hens that arrived at the field as members of a pair or group, 38 (72%) were not accompanied or chased by male gadwalls. The great amount of duck activity that accompanied the high concentration of nests is emphasized by the fact that a dabbling duck pair, lone drake, or group flight arrived at the field on the average of 1 each 0.7 minute. A mallard pair, lone drake, or group flight was seen each 1.4 minutes.

Mallards and gadwalls in the breeding population apparently adapted in 2 ways to the high nesting densities: sizes of defended areas were reduced so that more pairs were accommodated on the available wetlands near the NF, and some birds used wetlands located more than 1.6 km from the NF. Many birds flew to the NF from several wetlands about 2.4 km away. On the HSA, pairs were spaced throughout the available wetland habitat, but at higher than normal densities. Hens selected nest sites in the most attractive and secure nesting cover, and that contributed to aggregations of nests. After hatching of nests, the hens and broods dispersed into the complex of wetlands within 1.6–3.2 km of the nesting field.

Nesting Cover

Vegetation in the NF was composed of about 90% intermediate wheatgrass, 8% alfalfa, and 2% other plants. Loosely arranged litter composed of residual vegetation from previous growing seasons covered 100% of the ground and averaged 13 cm (range 6–52) in depth. The number of dead plant stems averaged 104/m² (range 12–254), with an average height of 80 cm (range 50–133). The average height of dead leaves on plants that remained standing from the previous year was 60 cm (range 31–79), and that of green leaves 30 cm (range 28–37).

Mallard nests were in tall cover. Of 499 nests, 490 (98%) were in cover that exceeded 30 cm in height. Four hundred four (81%) were in 30- to 60-cm cover, 86 (17%) were in cover taller than 60 cm, and 9 (2%) were in 15- to 30-cm cover. No mallard nests were in cover shorter than 15 cm, but such cover was available in the field.

Gadwall nests were in tall cover similar to that used by mallards. Of 286 nests, 147 (51%) were in 30- to 60-cm cover, 135 (47%) were in cover taller than 60 cm, 4 (1%) were in 15- to 30-cm cover, and none was in cover shorter than 15 cm.

MANAGEMENT IMPLICATIONS

For many years, managers of waterfowl production areas have sought management practices to increase duck production on small units of habitat. In the future, maintenance of desirable duck populations may require greater emphasis on intensive management of lands dedicated to waterfowl production. As Bellrose and Low (1978:64) stated: "If waterfowl are to be maintained at anywhere near existing levels, it is absolutely imperative to increase the waterfowl yield per unit of habitat." Cooch (1969:6) suggested additional study of the degree to which breeding ducks can be crowded on available habitat.

Our study showed that a dabbling duck nest density of 631/100 ha (1972) and hatching success of 96% (1971) occurred on a 51-ha field of undisturbed grass-legume cover. The major environmental factors that contributed to the high nest density and hatching success included a complex of high quality natural wetlands; a field of undisturbed tall, dense vegetation for nesting; and rigid control of predators. Habitats available for ducks in the production of 7,250 hatched ducklings in 6 years included 51 ha of nesting cover and 74 wetlands totaling 68 ha.

High nest densities and hatching success of dabbling ducks on islands are well documented (Hammond and Mann 1956, Duebbert 1966, Vermeer 1968). This study indicated that by the judicious use of habitat management and predator management, it is possible to create highly productive islands of habitat for duck nesting on the mainland. We documented 2 facts relevant to the management of habitats to increase duck production above that which occurs normally. First, mammalian predator populations were effectively reduced and maintained at low levels on a 259-km^2 area including the HSA by 1 man for 3 years. However, regulations are now in effect that restrict the use of strychnine on federal lands, and strychnine was the most effective control method. Second, dabbling ducks, especially mallards, responded to the reduced predation with increased nest densities, hatching success, and breeding populations.

The manipulation of factors that influence the inherent rate of increase of game populations is a basic concept of wildlife management. During the past 20 years, there has been a steady decline in the quantity and quality of waterfowl production habitat on private lands in the prairie pothole region of the United States. Therefore, we suggest that maintenance of high-quality nesting cover, protection and management of wetlands, and predator management should be emphasized on areas intensively managed for waterfowl production. In our opinion, predator management should not be limited to direct control of animals, but could include the use of mechanical and natural barriers to protect nesting habitats and other management techniques to reduce predation.

LITERATURE CITED

BALSER, D. S., H. H. DILL, AND H. K. NELSON. 1968. Effect of predator reduction on waterfowl nesting success. J. Wildl. Manage. 32:669–682.

BELLROSE, F. C., AND J. B. LOW. 1978. Advances in waterfowl management research. Wildl. Soc. Bull. 6:63–72.

BREWSTER, W. G., J. M. GATES, AND L. D. FLAKE. 1976. Breeding waterfowl populations and their distribution in South Dakota. J. Wildl. Manage. 40:50–59.

CLARK, P. J., AND F. C. EVANS. 1954. Distance to

nearest neighbor as a measure of spatial relationships in populations. Ecology 35:445–453.

COOCH, F. G. 1969. Waterfowl production habitat requirements. Pages 5–10 *in* Saskatoon wetlands seminar. Can. Wildl. Serv. Rep. Ser. 6. Ottawa.

DUEBBERT, H. F. 1966. Island nesting of the gadwall in North Dakota. Wilson Bull. 78:12–25.

———. 1969. High nest density and hatching success of ducks on South Dakota CAP land. Trans. North Am. Wildl. Nat. Resour. Conf. 34:218–229.

———, AND H. A. KANTRUD. 1974. Upland duck nesting related to land use and predator reduction. J. Wildl. Manage. 38:257–265.

———, AND J. T. LOKEMOEN. 1976. Duck nesting in fields of undisturbed grass-legume cover. J. Wildl. Manage. 40:39–49.

EINARSEN, A. S. 1956. Determination of some predator species by field signs. Oreg. State Monogr. Stud. Zool. 10. 34pp.

ELLIG, L. J. 1955. Waterfowl relationships to Greenfields Lake, Teton County, Montana. Mont. Fish Game Comm. Bull. 1. 35pp.

HAMMOND, M. C. 1969. Notes on conducting waterfowl breeding population surveys in the north central states. Pages 238–254 *in* Saskatoon wetlands seminar. Can. Wildl. Serv. Rep. Ser. 6. Ottawa.

———, AND G. E. MANN. 1956. Waterfowl nesting islands. J. Wildl. Manage. 20:345–352.

HIGGINS, K. F. 1977. Duck nesting in intensively farmed areas of North Dakota. J. Wildl. Manage. 41:232–242.

———, L. M. KIRSCH, AND I. J. BALL, JR. 1969. A cable-chain device for locating duck nests. J. Wildl. Manage. 33:1009–1011.

KALMBACH, E. R. 1939. Nesting success: its significance in waterfowl production. Trans. North Am. Wildl. Conf. 4:591–604.

KEITH, L. B. 1961. A study of waterfowl ecology on small impoundments in southeastern Alberta. Wildl. Monogr. 6. 88pp.

LACK, D. 1968. Ecological adaptations for breeding in birds. Methuen and Co., Ltd., London. 409pp.

LYNCH, G. M. 1972. Effect of strychnine control on nest predators of dabbling ducks. J. Wildl. Manage. 36:436–440.

MAYFIELD, H. 1961. Nesting success calculated from exposure. Wilson Bull. 73:255–261.

———. 1975. Suggestions for calculating nest success. Wilson Bull. 87:456–466.

MILLER, H. W., AND D. H. JOHNSON. 1978. Interpreting the results of nesting studies. J. Wildl. Manage. 42:471–476.

NEWTON, I., AND C. R. G. CAMPBELL. 1975. Breeding of ducks at Loch Leven, Kinross. Wildfowl 26:83–102.

POSPAHALA, R. S., D. R. ANDERSON, AND C. J. HENNY. 1974. Population ecology of the mallard: II. Breeding habitat conditions, size of the breeding populations, and production indices. U.S. Fish Wildl. Serv. Resour. Publ. 115. 73pp.

REARDEN, J. D. 1951. Identification of waterfowl nest predators. J. Wildl. Manage. 15:386–395.

SCHRANCK, B. W. 1972. Waterfowl nest cover and some predation relationships. J. Wildl. Manage. 36:182–186.

SMITH, A. G. 1971. Ecological factors affecting waterfowl production in the Alberta parklands. U.S. Fish Wildl. Serv. Resour. Publ. 98. 49pp.

STEWART, R. E., AND H. A. KANTRUD. 1971. Classification of natural ponds and lakes in the glaciated prairie region. U.S. Fish Wildl. Serv. Resour. Publ. 92. 57pp.

STOUDT, J. H. 1971. Ecological factors affecting waterfowl production in the Saskatchewan parklands. U.S. Fish Wildl. Serv. Resour. Publ. 99. 58pp.

SWANSON, G. A., M. I. MEYER, AND J. R. SERIE. 1974. Feeding ecology of breeding blue-winged teals. J. Wildl. Manage. 38:396–407.

TRAUTMAN, C. G., L. F. FREDRICKSON, AND A. V. CARTER. 1974. Relationship of red foxes and other predators to populations of ring-necked pheasants and other prey, South Dakota. Trans. North Am. Wildl. Nat. Resour. Conf. 39:241–255.

VERMEER, K. 1968. Ecological aspects of ducks nesting in high densities among larids. Wilson Bull. 80:78–83.

WELLER, M. W. 1956. A simple field candler for waterfowl eggs. J. Wildl. Manage. 20:111–113.

Received 2 December 1977.
Accepted 11 January 1979.

WATERFOWL PRODUCTION ON STOCK-WATERING PONDS IN THE NORTHERN PLAINS[1]

JOHN T. LOKEMOEN, Northern Prairie Wildlife Research Center, Bureau Sport Fisheries & Wildlife, Jamestown, ND

Abstract: In a 5-year study of stock-watering ponds in western North Dakota, pond size was found to be the major factor influencing duck use. As pond size increased, total pair and brood use per pond increased. Pairs used ponds as small as 0.1 acre in size, but broods were seldom seen on ponds of less than 1.0 surface acre. Dam-type ponds larger than 1.0 surface acre comprised only 29% of all man-made ponds on the study area but received 65% of the pair use and 87% of the brood use. Utilization of fenced ponds by pairs and broods was not significantly different from utilization of unfenced ponds. Grazing rates of 2 to 3 acres per AUM and lower rates permitted the development of grassy shoreline cover preferred by pairs and brushy and emergent shorelines preferred by broods. Duck pairs were significantly more numerous on older ponds and ponds with grassy shorelines but less numerous on ponds that had heavy deposits of sediment or were isolated from other wetlands. Broods were significantly more numerous on ponds with brushy shorelines and emergent vegetation than on those without. Broods were less numerous on turbid and newly constructed ponds. The most suitable stock-watering units for maximum waterfowl production were dam-type ponds of 1.5 surface acres, or larger, built in gentle to rolling terrain away from major sources of siltation.

Land-use agencies involved with building ponds to water livestock are becoming more interested in including features that will enhance the value of these man-made wetlands for wildlife. Planning for these programs has prompted questions including: (1) what design criteria result in the most attractive waterfowl pond, and (2) how should ponds and the adjacent uplands be managed? To answer these questions, a study was initiated in 1966 to ascertain the relationships between breeding waterfowl and the design, location, and management of man-made wetlands.

STUDY AREA

From 1967 through 1970 the study was generally confined to the 9- by 4-mile Tracy Mountain Study Area located in western North Dakota, 9 miles southwest of Belfield. Data gathered in 1966 from other ponds located in the vicinity of Belfield and west of Pierre, S. Dak., were also used.

The Tracy Mountain Study area lies in a region with cold winters and warm summers. The growing season averages 120 days. The average annual temperature at Dickinson, 25 miles northeast of the study area, is 40.7°F, and the average annual precipitation 15.4 inches (U.S. Dep. of Commerce 1970). Approximately 75% of the study area was in the Little Missouri River watershed, made up of Bainville-Morton Association soils on a hilly and extensively eroded badlands topography. The remainder was in the Heart River watershed, consisting of Rhoades-Morton Association soils on a rolling topography,

Eighty-eight percent of the study area was rangeland on which the dominant vegetation was blue grama (*Bouteloua gracilis*), western wheatgrass (*Agropyron smithii*), and threadleaf sedge (*Carex filifolia*). The remainder was cropland planted primarily to feed grains and hay, mainly smooth brome (*Bromus inermis*)

---

[1] Originally published in J. of Range Manage. 26(3):179–184, 1973.

[2] Present address: Box 1747, Jamestown, ND 58401.

Table 1. Duck breeding population and brood production on the Tracy Mountain Study Area, 1967–70.

Species of duck	Breeding pairs		Broods		Productivity rate (%)
	Total	Percent	Total	Percent	
Mallard (*Anas platyrhynchos*)	234	50	94	46	40
Gadwall (*Anas strepera*)	18	4	10	5	56
Pintail (*Anas acuta*)	59	13	13	6	22
Green-winged teal (*Anas carolinensis*)	20	4	11	5	55
Blue-winged teal (*Anas discors*)	55	12	37	18	67
American widgeon (*Mareca americana*)	70	15	34	17	49
Shoveler (*Spatula clypeata*)	15	3	7	3	47
Total or average	471	101	206	100	44

and alfalfa (*Medicago sativa*). About 60% of the land is managed by the U.S. Forest Service as part of the Little Missouri River National Grasslands.

For this report, stock-watering ponds were classified into three types similar to those defined by Bue et al. (1964): Stock ponds, formed by building dams across waterways; dugouts, consisting of steep-sided excavations filled by runoff water or ground water; and diked-dugouts, constructed like dugouts except with the spoil placed in a downstream embankment so that a shallow area around the excavation may be flooded. Natural wetlands were mainly small, temporary creek pools.

METHODS

The pond turbidity rating was the depth at which a submerged white disc 3 inches in diameter disappeared from view. Pond size and distance between water areas were measured from aerial photographs. Ponds were considered silted when clay sediment deposits covered the majority of the impoundment bottom. At each pond the percent of surface water with emergent vegetation was estimated visually; and the amount of shoreline that was bare, grassy (grasses and sedges 1 to 24 inches in height), or brushy was measured. Changes in water levels in relation to the spillway elevation were measured during each pond visit. The amount of pond area that was 0.0–1.0, 1.1–2.0, and 2.1–3.0 ft deep was determined by computing the average width of the contour and multiplying by the length. The height and density of shoreline vegetation 6 ft from the water was measured with a cover board similar to that used by Jones (1968).

Each year between late April and early June, two to four counts of breeding pairs of waterfowl were made on all ponds on the study area, including creek pools. The highest pair count for each species for the entire study area was chosen to represent the breeding population. Mallard and pintail breeding pairs were chosen from the April and early May counts, and the breeding pairs of the later nesting species were taken from the mid and late May counts.

Two complete brood counts were made each year, one in mid-July and one in early August. Production was the total number of broods observed on the two counts less possible duplicate broods on the second count. The productivity rate was obtained by dividing the number of broods by the number of breeding pairs.

For analyzing duck-habitat relationships, "pair use" of a pond was the average of two pair counts; mallards and

Fig. 1. Pintail brood of nine on a western North Dakota stock pond.

pintails were totaled from the first two counts and the other species from two of the later counts. The average number of broods seen on the pond during the two brood counts was considered "brood use."

Analyses of duck use by species with pond habitat measurements were made on an IBM System 360/50 using a correlation and multiple linear regression program.

RESULTS AND DISCUSSION

Of the 68 man-made ponds on Tracy Mountain Study Area, 50 were stock ponds, 6 were dugouts, and 12 were diked-dugouts. The ponds ranged in size from 0.04 to 5.9 surface acres and averaged 1.0 acre. Stock ponds averaged 1.4 surface acres, dugouts 0.2 acre, and diked-dugouts 0.3 acre. Creek pools comprised an average of 6% of the water acreage on the study area during the 4 years.

Duck Breeding Population and Production

The duck breeding population on the study area averaged 3.3 pairs per square mile, 1.8 pairs per acre of stock-watering ponds, and 1.9 pairs per acre of all water. This compares with 7.0 pairs per square mile and 2.3 pairs per acre of stock-watering pond in western South Dakota (Bue et al. 1952). The mallard was the most numerous of the seven species of breeding ducks, comprising 50% of the population (Table 1). Other important species included the American widgeon, pintail, and blue-winged teal. Twelve percent of the breeding pairs were found on natural wetlands; the rest were on man-made ponds.

Broods averaged 1.4 per square mile,

Table 2. Breeding pair use* related to pond size (acres) and type.

	Stock pond			Diked-dugout			Dugout		
Pond size	Total no. pond counts	Pair use per acre	Pair use per pond	Total no. pond counts	Pair use per acre	Pair use per pond	Total no. pond counts	Pair use per acre	Pair use per pond
0.04–0.24	20	4.1	0.6	17	2.5	0.5	47	2.3	0.4
0.25–0.54	52	2.4	1.0	31	2.9	1.1	10	1.5	0.5
0.55–1.0	53	1.4	1.0	5	**	**	0	—	—
1.1 –2.0	60	1.8	2.9	0	—	—	0	—	—
2.1 –5.0	48	1.4	4.3	0	—	—	0	—	—
5.1+	15	0.9	7.1	0	—	—	0	—	—
Total	248			53			57		
Average		1.9	2.4		2.5	0.8		2.2	0.4

* Pair use of a pond was the average of two pair counts for each year.
** Too few pond counts to calculate use.

0.79 per acre of stock-watering pond and 0.83 per acre of all water (Fig. 1). In comparison, Bue et al. (1952) found 4.5 broods per square mile and 1.5 broods per acre of man-made pond on their study area. Productivity on the Tracy Mountain Study Area averaged 44% during the 4 years. This is in the higher range of productivity reported in recent prairie studies (Keith 1961) but below the 65% productivity found by Bue et al. (1952). Ten percent of the broods were observed on creek pools and 90% on man-made ponds.

Duck Use by Pond Size and Type

Of the habitat features considered, pond size was most highly correlated ($r = 0.71$) with duck use. Pairs used ponds as small as 0.1 acre; however, the average number of pairs was higher on the larger ponds (Table 2). Sixty-five percent of the pair use was on 29% of the ponds that were larger than one surface acre. Smith (1953) and Berg (1956) reported similar findings in Montana. The increase in duck use was less than proportional to the increase in pond size; the smaller ponds had the lightest average number of pairs per surface acre. Evans and Black (1956) reported that duck use per acre of natural wetlands varied inversely with size and that, although most of the pairs were on larger ponds, the smallest areas received the heaviest use per acre.

On a surface-acre basis, pair use did not differ significantly ($P = 0.05$) among the three pond types. On a unit-pond basis, stock ponds, being larger, were by far the most important to breeding pairs. The excavated ponds were small, and the average pair use per dugout was only one-sixth that per stock pond. The average pair use per diked-dugout was one-third that per stock pond.

Brood use was also related strongly to pond area but somewhat differently from pair use (Table 3). As pond area increased, the number of broods per pond increased; but the highest number of broods per acre was found on intermediate-sized ponds 1.1–2.0 acres in size not on the smallest ponds, as was the case with pairs. Ponds under 0.25 acre received virtually no use by broods and those under 1 acre little use. Two other studies, one of man-made ponds (Berg 1956), and one on natural wetlands (Evans and Black 1956), also recorded few broods on ponds less than 0.5 acre. Only 29% of the man-made ponds on the study

Table 3. Brood use* related to pond size (acres) and type.

	Stock pond			Diked-dugout			Dugout		
Pond size	Total no. pond counts	Brood use per acre	Brood use per pond	Total no. pond counts	Brood use per acre	Brood use per pond	Total no. pond counts	Brood use per acre	Brood use per pond
0.01–0.24	26	0.00	0.00	20	0.00	0.00	53	0.09	0.02
0.25–0.54	44	0.13	0.06	25	0.12	0.04	7	0.00	0.00
0.55–1.0	56	0.37	0.27	5	**	**	0	—	—
1.1 –2.0	54	0.68	1.02	0	—	—	0	—	—
2.1 –5.0	46	0.56	1.78	0	—	—	0	—	—
5.1+	14	0.27	2.11	0	—	—	0	—	—
Total	240			50			60		
Average		0.38	0.77		0.06	0.02		0.08	0.02

* Brood use of a pond was the average of two brood counts for each year.
** Too few pond counts to calculate use.

area were over 1.0 acre in size, yet they contained 87 percent of the brood use. Average brood use per dugout and diked-dugout was 2 to 3% of that per stock pond.

The average brood size for four pond size classes was calculated from observations in which the entire brood was sighted (Table 4). When Sheffe's multiple comparison test was applied, average brood size was significantly smaller on the 0.0- to 1.0-acre class ($P < 0.05$) and the 5.1-acre and larger class ($P < 0.10$) than on the 2.1- to 5.0-acre class. Average brood size on ponds 2.1–5.0 acres in size was greater than on ponds 1.1–2.0 acres, but the difference is not significant ($P = 0.05$). Thus, brood sizes and apparent survival of young were higher on the intermediate-size ponds, which also received the highest brood use per acre. Small ponds may contain insufficient surface area for brood security. In Canada, Stoudt (1971) found that broods forced to use dugouts about 0.1 acre in size survived less than 1 week. On the Tracy Mountain Area, ponds over 5.0 acres may contain smaller broods than intermediate-size ponds because they generally form a harsher environment for broods by often being deep, open, and windswept.

Duck Use of Fenced and Unfenced Shorelines

Because of compacting by winter snows, the height and density of standing shoreline vegetation in spring along fenced ponds was not significantly greater ($P = 0.05$) than that along unfenced ponds (Table 5). Pair use per wetland acre did not differ significantly ($P = 0.05$) between the two shoreline types. However, by summer, the plants were higher on fenced ponds, and the plant density was apparently greater (Fig. 2). Brood use per wetland acre, however, was the same on both fenced ponds and unfenced ponds.

The shoreline comparisons were made on grasslands utilized by cattle from May 1 to November 30 at a moderate rate of about 1.5 to 3.0 acres per AUM. Water-

Table 4. Average brood size for four sizes (acres) of ponds.

Pond aize	Number broods	Average size
0.0–1.0	22	4.7
1.1–2.0	35	5.9
2.1–5.0	47	7.0
5.1+	15	5.1
Total or average	119	6.0

Fig. 2. Fenced stock pond showing the type of fence erected and the response of vegetation inside the exclosure.

fowl might respond positively to vegetation protected from livestock on ranges with heavier grazing pressure. However, the increase in waterfowl use would have to be considerable to justify the expense, because the average cost to fence each pond on the study area was estimated at $500.

Duck Use of Watersheds

Pair use in the rugged Little Missouri River watershed was compared to that in the rolling Heart River watershed. The average pond size was the same in each of the two watersheds; however, the Heart River watershed had 3.1 ponds per square mile, while the Little Missouri had only 1.5. Ponds in the Heart River watershed had significantly ($P < 0.05$) more stable water levels, less bare shore, more emergent vegetation, and more grassy shoreline than those in the Little Missouri River watershed.

Mallards were equally distributed on the two watersheds and were apparently little affected by habitat differences (Table 6). According to a contingency table analysis, pintails, blue-winged teal, American widgeon, and shovelers were significantly ($P < 0.05$) more common per wetland in the Heart River drainage. Gadwall were more numerous in the rolling terrain but not significantly so, while green-winged teal were more common in

Table 5. Comparison of vegetation measurements and waterfowl use on fenced and unfenced ponds, 1967–70.

Season	Pond treatment	Number of ponds surveyed	Average plant height (inches)	Average plant density (%)	Average waterfowl use
Spring	Fenced	21	3	11	3.0 pairs/acre
	Unfenced	27	3	8	3.6 pairs/acre
Summer	Fenced	30	12**	48	1.4 broods/acre
	Unfenced	35	7**	28	1.4 broods/acre

** Significant difference at the 0.05 probability level.

Table 6. Comparison of pair populations on stock-watering ponds in the Little Missouri and Heart River watersheds.

Species of duck	Little Missouri River			Heart River			Ratio of pairs/acre between watersheds
	Number pairs	Pairs/ acre	Percent pairs	Number pairs	Pairs/ acre	Percent pairs	
Mallard	123	.88	68	85	.89	36	1.0:1
Gadwall	7	.05	04	11	.12	05	0.4:1
Pintail	8	.06	04	41	.43	18	0.1:1
Green-winged teal	13	.09	07	6	.06	03	1.5:1
Blue-winged teal	9	.06	05	38	.40	16	0.2:1
American widgeon	20	.14	11	40	.42	17	0.3:1
Shoveler	2	.01	01	12	.13	05	0.1:1
Total or average	182	1.29	100	233	2.45	100	0.5:1

badland ponds. In all, pairs occupied Heart River ponds at twice the density of Little Missouri River ponds.

Although breeding pairs preferred the more marsh-like Heart River ponds, no direct correlation between the amount of pond shoal area and pair use was evident. In Montana, Gjersing (1971) found that brood numbers per pond increased as the amount of pond area 2 ft deep and less increased.

Duck-use and Pond Feature Relationships

The *t* values of the more important relationships between pair use and pond habitat factors are shown in Table 7. Pairs of mallards and of all species combined were positively related to pond age. The removal of topsoil and plants during construction possibly resulted in lower use of ponds less than 5 years old. As plants and nutrients gradually increased in the pond, use by pairs increased. In the eastern United States the reverse usually occurs, duck numbers decreasing as ponds increase in age (Benson and Foley 1956, Kadlec 1962). This results from a combination of factors, including less fertile water and soil, less seasonal drying, increased humic staining, and higher soluble iron concentrations (Cook 1964).

As the distance from a pond to other water increased, use of the pond by pairs generally decreased. Mallards, which have large breeding territories (Dzubin 1955), were an exception and used even the most isolated ponds in the study area. Most species, however, apparently were unable to utilize a pond providing mainly

Table 7. Computed *t* values of multiple regression coefficients between pair use and certain pond characteristics.[1]

Pond characteristics	Species of duck				
	Mallard	American widgeon	Blue-winged teal	Pintail	All species
Age	2.59**	0.86	1.34	0.18	2.51**
Distance to other water	0.58	−1.47	−1.70*	−2.70**	−1.80**
Bare shore	0.87	1.84*	−1.40	0.97	1.31
Grassy shore	1.48	2.19**	−1.23	1.21	1.75*
Silted bottom	−1.81*	−2.32**	1.83*	−1.15	−1.66*

[1] The size of the *t* value indicates the significance of the association, and the minus sign indicates an inverse relationship; * and ** indicate probabilities at the 0.10 and 0.05 levels, respectively.

Table 8. Computed *t* values of multiple regression coefficients between brood use and certain pond characteristics.[1]

Pond characteristics	Species of duck				
	Mallard	American widgeon	Blue-winged teal	Pintail	All species
Age	4.40**	2.14**	0.77	1.69*	4.73**
Distance to other water	−1.35	−2.60**	−1.84*	−1.81*	−3.18**
Turbidity	−2.43**	−0.60	1.14	0.05	−1.53
Emergent vegetation	0.85	−3.55**	0.69	2.89**	0.29
Brushy shore	2.45**	2.21**	0.12	1.18	3.02**

[1] The size of the *t* value indicates the significance of the association, and the minus sign indicates an inverse relationship; * and ** indicate probabilities at the 0.10 and 0,05 levels, respectively.

territorial space which was separated from water providing the other needs for pair support. In studies of small excavated ponds, Cooch (1950) and Hammond and Lacy (1960) found more pairs on those near marshes. Cooch concluded that pair use of dugouts was related to the density of natural wetlands in the vicinity.

It was difficult to determine the shoreline preferences of breeding pairs because of the combination of cover types encircling each pond. However, pairs seemed to prefer open shorelines, with American widgeon positively related to bare and grassy shorelines and all species combined significantly associated with grassy shorelines. Bue et al. (1952) noted that grassy shorelines had more mallard, pintail, and blue-winged teal pairs than did bare shores. On his study area, shorelines that were partly grass and partly bare had intermediate use by pairs.

Pair use by mallards, American widgeon, and all species combined was significantly less in silted ponds. A significant positive correlation between blue-winged teal and siltation resulted because one silted pond developed a new fertile substrata and received heavy use by blue-wings. Heavy siltation covers vegetation, increases turbidity, and shortens the pond life.

The more important relationships between brood use and pond habitat features are shown in Table 8. As with pairs, brood use increased as pond age increased, but decreased notably as the distance between ponds increased. Newly built ponds in Montana also had less use by broods (Gjersing 1971). Broods, unlike pairs, were not significantly influenced by siltation, but mallard broods were significantly less numerous on turbid ponds.

Pintail broods generally use vegetation for escape cover. They were positively related to ponds with emergent vegetation. Blue-winged teal and American widgeon broods usually move to open water for safety. Blue-winged teal were not significantly associated with ponds containing emergent vegetation, and American widgeon were negatively related to this feature.

Broods of most species were positively correlated with brushy shorelines. The optimum in brood cover for most species appeared to be flooded brush or emergent vegetation which allows a brood to remain on the water but with overhead protection. Berg (1956) found that while pond size was more important to broods than plant cover, broods preferred ponds with emergent vegetation. Bue et al. (1952) noted that broods, as did pairs, preferred grassy shorelines rather than

Fig. 3. This stock pond is attractive to waterfowl because it is situated on a moderately rolling site near other water, has a grassy shoreline, emergent vegetation, no sediment problem, and is an excellent size for this area of 4 surface acres.

bare shorelines. In central Montana, Gjersing (1971) concluded that "brood numbers seemed to respond in a positive manner to increases in residual vegetation" on the shoreline.

MANAGEMENT SUGGESTIONS

On the basis of the findings of this and other studies, small reservoirs constructed for watering livestock can be made more beneficial to waterfowl (Fig. 3) if the following points are kept in mind:

1) Pond size is the most important feature affecting waterfowl use. In any given unit of rangeland, only a set number of ponds are constructed, so to be of the greatest value to waterfowl each pond should be designed to obtain maximum use by duck pairs and broods.

   The smallest pond size recommended is 1.5 acres because it usually would not be reduced to less than 1.0 acre in summer, the minimum size suggested for brood support. The maximum pond size need be restricted only by the site available and economics; however, large ponds have fewer ducks per unit area, and more pair and brood use will occur on two ponds with the same total surface area as one large pond.

2) Of the three pond types examined, stock ponds are most important to breeding waterfowl because of their larger average size. Dugouts and diked-dugouts are of little use to broods and have low unit-pond use by breeding pairs. If an excavated pond is the only alternative, diked-dugouts are more valuable to ducks than are dugouts.

3) Ponds should not be built on sites where large volumes of sediment from eroding clay buttes or coulees will wash into the impoundment. Thick deposits of sediment reduce food and cover plants, shorten the pond life, and reduce duck use.

4) Breeding pairs of most species prefer grassy rather than bare shorelines, and broods generally seek shorelines with clumps of brush or emergent vegetation. An important part of any plan to increase waterfowl productivity is the management of upland cover for nesting. Although nest-vegetation

relationships were not a part of this study, other authors have noted that lightly used or unused upland vegetation containing dead litter from the previous year forms the best nesting cover for ducks (Moyle 1964, Kirsch 1969, Gjersing 1971).

5) As much topsoil as possible should be allowed to remain in the impoundment site. Topsoil removed during construction should be replaced on the fill and emergency spillway and seeded to reduce erosion and dam loss.
6) Ponds, particularly smaller ones, should be constructed near other ponds or wetlands. The needs of breeding waterfowl are often obtained from several closely associated ponds. Isolated ponds lacking one important requirement may be unused.
7) Impoundments should be built in rolling terrain rather than rugged terrain or badlands.

Many of the new ponds being built in western North Dakota are dugouts or diked-dugouts of little value to waterfowl. If ponds are built on federal lands or with federal assistance, wildlife production can be benefited by constructing stock ponds that are 1.5 acres or larger. On private land the current federal cost-sharing rate for construction of stock-watering ponds is 60 to 70%. To encourage the construction of ponds that have the greatest value to breeding waterfowl, the rate should be increased to 90% for dam-type ponds and 70% for diked-dugouts. For federal lands, guidelines should be changed to encourage construction of types and sizes in the above management suggestions.

ACKNOWLEDGMENTS

The author would like to thank Harvey Miller and Paul Springer for their suggestions during the study and their constructive reviews of the manuscript, Douglas Johnson for statistical treatment of the data, and personnel of the U.S. Forest Service for assistance in various aspects of the study.

LITERATURE CITED

BENSON, D., AND D. FOLEY. 1956. Waterfowl use of small, man-made wildlife marshes in New York State. New York Fish and Game J. 3:217–224.

BERG, P. F. 1956. A study of waterfowl broods in eastern Montana with special reference to movements and the relationship of reservoir fencing to production. J. Wildl. Manage. 20:253–262.

BUE, I. G., L. BLANKENSHIP, AND W. H. MARSHALL. 1952. The relationship of grazing practices to waterfowl breeding populations and production on stock ponds in western South Dakota. Trans. N. Amer. Wildl. Conf. 17:396–414.

———, H. G. UHLIG, AND J. D. SMITH. 1964. Stock ponds and dugouts. Pp. 391–398. *In* Waterfowl tomorrow. U.S. Dep. of the Interior, Bur. Sport Fish. and Wildl., J. P. Linduska, editor. 770pp.

COOCH, G. 1950. The Prairie Farm Rehabilitation Act dugouts of Manitoba and their role in waterfowl production. Thesis submitted to Queen's Univ., Kingston, Ont., Canada. 140pp.

COOK, A. H. 1964. Better living for ducks—Through chemistry. Pp. 569–578. *In* Waterfowl tomorrow. U.S. Dep. of the Interior, Bur. Sport Fish. and Wildl., J. P. Linduska, editor. 770pp.

DZUBIN, A. 1955. Some evidences of home range in waterfowl. Trans. N. Amer. Wildl. Conf. 20:278–298.

EVANS, C. D., AND K. E. BLACK. 1956. Duck production studies on the prairie potholes of South Dakota. U.S. Fish and Wildl. Serv. Spec. Sci. Rep. Wildl. No. 32. 59pp.

GJERSING, F. M. 1971. A study of waterfowl production on two rest rotation grazing units in northcentral Montana. M.S. Thesis. Montana State Univ. Bozeman. 42pp.

HAMMOND, M. C., AND C. H. LACY. 1960. Ducks from artificial water areas. Conservation Volunteer 23(135):21–26.

JONES, R. E. 1968. A board to measure cover used by prairie grouse. J. Wildl. Manage. 32:28–31.

KADLEC, J. A. 1962. Effects of a drawdown on a waterfowl impoundment. Ecology 43:267–281.

KEITH, L. B. 1961. A study of waterfowl ecology on small impoundments in southeastern Alberta. Wildl. Monogr. 6. 88pp.

KIRSCH, L. M. 1969. Waterfowl production in relation to grazing. J. Wildl. Manage. 33:821–828.

MOYLE, J. B. 1964. Ducks and land use in Minnesota. Minnesota Dept. Conserv. Tech. Bull. 8. 140pp.

SMITH, R. H. 1953. A study of waterfowl production on artificial reservoirs in eastern Montana. J. Wildl. Manage. 17:276–291.

STOUDT, J. H. 1971. Ecological factors affecting waterfowl production in the Saskatchewan parklands. U.S. Dep. of the Interior, Bur. Sport Fish. and Wildl., Res. Pub. No. 99. 58pp.

U.S. DEP. OF COMMERCE, WEATHER BUREAU. 1970. Climatological data—North Dakota. Annu. Summary, Vol. 75. Asheville, N.C.

WATERFOWL NESTING ON INTERSTATE HIGHWAY RIGHT-OF-WAY IN NORTH DAKOTA[1]

ROBERT B. OETTING, Zoology Department, North Dakota State University, Fargo, and Northern Prairie Wildlife Research Center, Jamestown, North Dakota[2]

J. FRANK CASSEL, Zoology Department, North Dakota State University, Fargo

Abstract: We studied 630 acres of roadside along 23 miles of Interstate 94 in Stutsman County, North Dakota, to assess wildlife values of highway rights-of-way. We found 422 duck nests that had an overall success of 57 percent in 1968, 1969, and 1970. Mammalian predators were responsible for 85 percent of the destroyed nests. To test the effect of mowing on duck nest initiation and success, alternate 1-mile blocks of the study area were not mowed in the fall of 1968. In 1969 and 1970, significantly more ducks chose unmowed vegetation in preference to mowed vegetation for nest sites. Mallards (*Anas platyrhynchos*), pintails (*A. acuta*), and gadwalls (*A. strepera*) were especially responsive to unmowed vegetation. Success of duck nests in unmowed vegetation was 62 percent compared with 51 percent in mowed vegetation. Sixteen percent of the nests were unhatched by July 5, the beginning mowing date previously recommended by the North Dakota Highway Department. Wildlife killed by traffic did not increase when half the mile blocks were unmowed, and no significant difference was observed in buildup of snow between mowed and unmowed blocks in the winter of 1968–69. Of 182 motorists interviewed in the study area, 82 percent had not noticed the unmowed rights-of-way. We strongly recommend no mowing of ditch bottoms or back slopes, minimal mowing of inslopes, and no mowing before July 20 to enhance waterfowl nesting and to reduce maintenance costs of highway rights-of-way in duck-producing regions.

Whereas wildlife agencies buy, lease, mitigate the loss of, and beg for wildlife habitat, other lands of promise await development. These lands are on the rights-of-way of the nation's roads, highways, railroads, pipelines, utility transmission lines, strip mines, gravel pits, and irrigation and flood control projects. Some are publicly owned and some are potential wildlife habitat that has been largely ignored.

Egler (1957) estimated the area of the nation's rights-of-way at 50 million acres. The increase in rights-of-way since Egler's estimate has been swift and diverse.

Walterson (1966) estimated primary and secondary highway right-of-way in North Dakota at 789,000 acres and railroad right-of-way at 70,600 acres. These two areas are double the combined acreage (425,000 acres) of state game management areas and federally owned waterfowl production areas and wildlife refuges in North Dakota.

National interstate highway right-of-way is estimated at one million acres, and the figure is still growing. It embraces 23,000 acres in Minnesota, 18,000 acres in Iowa, 18,000 acres in North Dakota, 15,000 acres in Kansas, 12,000 acres in Nebraska, and 10,000 acres in South Dakota.

The cost of right-of-way maintenance has increased in recent years, and today it is a large budgetary item for maintaining agencies. Costs for mowing interstate highways were reported as $15 million annually by Butler and Yoerger (1962). In 1964, Illinois spent an average of $1,026 per mile to maintain vegetation on interstate highways (Joselyn 1969).

Data are available on the use of rights-of-way by wildlife, but comparative studies are rare. Joselyn et al. (1968) compared mowed and unmowed rights-of-way on

[1] Major financial support for this doctoral study program came from funds from the National Defense Education Act Title IV and from scholarships of the National Wildlife Federation.

[2] Present address: Department of Mines, Resources and Environmental Management, Norquay Building, Winnipeg, Manitoba.

Originally published in J. Wildl. Manage. 35(4):774–781, 1971.

secondary gravel, blacktop, and dirt roads in Illinois and found higher densities of pheasant nests and higher nest success in the unmowed portions. Many other investigators, in general nest studies, have included observations of game birds along rights-of-way. In nearly every case, a high proportion of the nesting population was found along rights-of-way that constituted a small portion of the area searched (Table 1).

We initiated a study in Stutsman County, North Dakota, to (1) inventory ground-nesting game birds, (2) test the effect of normal maintenance procedures on nest density and success, (3) measure the response of nesting by game birds to altered maintenance patterns, (4) document wildlife killed by traffic and compare snow buildup in mowed and unmowed portions of the right-of-way, (5) determine opinions of motorists concerning the appearance of unmowed vegetation on rights-of-way, and (6) recommend maintenance procedures for optimum game bird production and minimum maintenance expense.

We appreciate the efforts of J. O. Kyser, Maintenance Engineer, North Dakota Highway Department, whose interest in right-of-way ecology nurtured this project. The study was encouraged by the North Dakota Chapter of The Wildlife Society, North Dakota Game and Fish Department, North Dakota State University, National Wildlife Federation, and the Northern Prairie Wildlife Research Center, Bureau of Sport Fisheries and Wildlife. The Center assisted with project design, technical assistance, equipment, and partial funding for 1970. Special thanks are extended to L. Kirsch, H. Miller, H. Duebbert, and other personnel of the Center and to E. DeGroot, K. Olson, R. Page, and L. Voorhees of NDSU for advice and assistance in the field work.

Table 1. Game bird nests found on rights-of-way compared with other areas searched.

STATE	PERCENT OF STUDY AREA AS ROADSIDE	PERCENT OF NESTS FOUND IN ROADSIDE	SOURCE
Nebraska	1.2	28	Evans and Wolfe (1967)
Nebraska	<1.0	25.1	Wolfe and Evans (1967)
Minnesota	2.0	25	Chesness (1965)
Nebraska	<2.0	24	Linder et al. (1960)
North Dakota	1.4	57	Fisher (1955)
North Dakota	2.0	43	Fisher (1954)
North Dakota	2.6	27	Bach and Stuart (1942)
North Dakota	Shorelines and roadside had highest nest densities.[a]		Martz (1967)
South Dakota	Pheasant nest densities were highest on roadsides and fencerows.[a]		Trautman (1960)
Manitoba	Duck nest densities were highest on roadsides and hayfields.[a]		Milonski (1958)
Iowa	Roadsides were best for production of pheasants.[a]		Klo[n]glan (1955)
Michigan	Majority of pheasants produced in roadsides and ditch banks.[a]		Shick (1952)
Wisconsin	Roadsides were preferred by nesting gray partridge.[a]		Hawkins (1937)

[a] Quantitative data could not be compared in the manner shown above.

THE STUDY AREA

The study area consisted of 630 acres of roadsides along I-94 from the Oswego interchange to the Northern Pacific Railroad overpass east of Crystal Springs. It also included 24, 0.6-acre triangles at 6 interchanges.

Vegetation of the study area formed a rather uniform community of smooth bromegrass (*Bromus inermis*) with an understory of Kentucky bluegrass (*Poa pratensis*). Scattered stands of crested wheatgrass

(*Agropyron cristatum*), slender wheatgrass (*A. trachycaulum*), volunteer yellow sweet clover (*Melilotus officinalis*), and alfalfa (*Medicago sativa*) were also present. Shrubs and other woody vegetation were absent.

Birds nesting in this cover included mallards, blue-winged teal (*Anas discors*), gadwalls, pintails, shovelers (*Spatula clypeata*), lesser scaup (*Aythya affinis*), mourning doves (*Zenaidura macroura*), killdeer (*Charadrius vociferus*), American bitterns (*Botaurus lentiginosus*), gray partridge (*Perdix perdix*), and upland plovers (*Bartramia longicauda*). Also seen were broods of sharp-tailed grouse (*Pedioecetes phasianellis*) and ring-necked pheasants (*Phasianus colchicus*). Other animals observed in the study area were white-tailed jack rabbits (*Lepus townsendii*), striped skunks (*Mephitis mephitis*), Richardson's ground squirrels (*Citellus richardsonii*), white-tailed deer (*Odocoileus virginianus*), long-tailed weasels (*Mustela frenata*), and a variety of gulls, hawks, shorebirds, mice, voles, and songbirds.

MATERIALS AND METHODS

The study area was searched for nests of game birds three times each year with a cable-chain drag (Higgins et al. 1969). Locations of nests were marked by painting numbers on fence posts. The stage of incubation was determined by the flotation method (Westerskov 1950). Data were recorded on Burrough's 91-hole Unisort punch cards to facilitate retrieval and analysis.

The study area was completely mowed in 1967. In September 1968, through an agreement with the North Dakota Highway Department, alternate 1-mile blocks and half the triangles at interchanges were left unmowed to test the effect of this reduced maintenance on initiation and success of game bird nests in 1969 and 1970. This pattern of maintenance resulted in 312 mowed and 318 unmowed acres. Twenty feet of all in slopes were mowed to retard buildup of snow. Our criterion for a nest was one with at least one egg. Our criterion for a successful nest was one in which at least one egg hatched.

Data on wildlife killed by traffic were recorded for May, June, and July of 1968 and 1969. Snow measurements were taken at the edge of the driving surface, ditch bottom, and fence at 48 stations four times in the winter of 1968–69. Interviews with motorists were conducted at a rest area near the west end of the study area in May and June 1969, when differences in the appearance of the mowed and unmowed blocks could be appreciated. Motorists were asked four questions: Have you noticed the mowed and unmowed right-of-way condition? Which do you prefer? Why? Do you prefer the mowed treatment in the face of high mowing costs?

RESULTS

Nesting Activity

During the 3 years, 447 nests were found for a mean annual nest density of 23 nests per 100 acres or 7 nests per mile of highway. Included were 422 duck nests (22 nests per 100 acres or 6 nests per mile). Nests of blue-winged teal were the most abundant (173), followed by nests of mallards (95), gadwalls (83), and pintails (35).

Waterfowl exhibited peak nest initiation during the fourth week of May and peak hatching the fourth week of June. The first duck nests were initiated the second week of April and only five were started after the first week of July. The first clutch hatched the third week of May, and by the second week of August only three nests

Table 2. Selection of nest sites in 1968 compared with 1969 and 1970.

	1968				1969 and 1970			
	Nests in Blocks to be Mowed		Nests in Blocks to be Unmowed		Nests in Mowed Blocks		Nests in Unmowed Blocks	
Species	N	Percent	N	Percent	N	Percent	N	Percent
Mallard	13	54	11	46	13	18	58	82
Pintail	1	13	7	87	5	19	22	81
Gadwall	7	29	17	71	20	34	39	66
Scaup	–	–	–	–	–	–	2	–
Blue-winged teal	32	63	19	37	56	46	66	54
Shoveler	6	46	7	54	11	52	10	48
Total	59[a]	49	61[a]	51	105[b]	35	197[b]	65

[a] Not significantly different.
[b] Significantly more ducks chose unmowed blocks ($P < 0.001$).

were still being incubated. The chronology of initiation and hatching showed the typical pattern of mallards and pintails first, shovelers next, and blue-winged teal and gadwalls last.

Nest Location

The distribution of 120 waterfowl nests in the spring of 1968 was nearly equal between 1-mile control blocks designated to be mowed (59 nests) and experimental blocks designated to be unmowed (61 nests). Significantly more nests (197) were found in unmowed blocks than in mowed blocks (105) in 1969 and 1970, after the 1968 mowing versus nonmowing treatment. Mallards, pintails, and gadwalls were especially responsive to unmowed vegetation, but the response was less definite for blue-winged teal and shovelers (Table 2).

Nest Success

Nest success was 59 percent for all nests and 57 percent for duck nests. Pintails had the highest success (65 percent) and mallards had the lowest (47 percent). Success for 13 upland plover nests was 100 percent. Mammalian predators destroyed 145 nests (35 percent of all active nests), mowing destroyed 10, desertion terminated 10, and avian predators destroyed 6 (Table 3).

The success of waterfowl nests was

Table 3. Species composition and success of nests along I-94, 1968–70.

Species	Number of Nests	Crushed or Deserted[a]	Success		Cause of Nest Failure			
			N	Percent	Mammal	Bird	Mower	Desertion[b]
Mallard	95	5	42	47	43	1	2	2
Pintail	35	1	22	65	12	–	–	–
Gadwall	83	8	41	55	27	1	4	2
Lesser scaup	2	1	1	100	–	–	–	–
Blue-winged teal	173	12	98	61	49	4	4	6
Shoveler	34	4	17	57	13	–	–	–
Total ducks	422	31	221	57	144	6	10	10
Mourning dove	8	2	5	83	1	–	–	–
Killdeer	2	0	2	100	–	–	–	–
Upland plover	13	0	13	100	–	–	–	–
American bittern	1	0	1	100	–	–	–	–
Gray partridge	1	1	0	–	–	–	–	–
Total	447	34	242	59	145	6	10	10

[a] Nests crushed or deserted due to search and nests of unknown fate. These nests are not included in success ratios.
[b] Normal nest desertions. These nests are included in success ratios.

Table 4. Comparative hatching success of active nests between mowed and unmowed blocks, 1969–70.

Species	Nests in Mowed Blocks	Success N	Success Percent	Nests in Unmowed Blocks	Success N	Success Percent
Mallard	13	7	54	54	30	56
Pintail	5	3	60	21	16	76
Gadwall	16	4	25	37	24	65
Lesser scaup	0	–	–	1	1	–
Blue-winged teal	53	31	58	62	37	60
Shoveler	11	5	45	9	6	67
Total	98	50[a]	51	184	114[a]	62

[a] Significantly more nests hatched in unmowed vegetation ($P < 0.10$).

higher in unmowed blocks than in mowed blocks. Nest success was 51 percent for all ducks in mowed areas compared with 62 percent in unmowed areas for 1969 and 1970 combined. Gadwalls showed the largest difference in nest success between unmowed blocks (65 percent) and mowed blocks (25 percent). Success of mallard and blue-winged teal nests was nearly equal in the two types of vegetation (Table 4).

Wildlife Killed by Traffic

The entire highway in the study area was searched daily for road-kills during May, June, and July. Traffic killed 42 animals in the study area in 1968, when all vegetation on the right-of-way was in the mowed condition. The list included 23 striped skunks, 5 white-tailed deer, 4 raccoons, and 4 ducks. During the same period in 1969, when half the right-of-way was unmowed, 37 dead animals were recorded, including 16 ducks, 12 jack rabbits, and 3 white-tailed deer.

Snow Measurements

Snow depth on the mowed miles averaged 3.8 inches on the top of the in slope, 11.6 inches on the in slope, and 13.1 inches at the outer boundary of the right-of-way. Depths on the unmowed miles averaged 4.2 inches, 14.5 inches, and 15.2 inches at these positions. Prompt and continuous blading kept driving surfaces equally free of snow on both areas.

Opinions of Motorists

Eighty-two percent of the motorists interviewed had not detected a difference between mowed and unmowed portions of the right-of-way. When the two conditions were pointed out, 72 percent preferred the mowed strips because they were neater. Many respondents wanted to change their answers after the interview, when the study was explained, to a preference for unmowed vegetation, because they feared their first answers might jeopardize wildlife using the right-of-way.

DISCUSSION

We found higher densities of duck nests and higher nest success in unmowed right-of-way areas than in mowed areas. The importance of unmowed, ungrazed, upland nest cover for waterfowl has been shown by other investigators. Kirsch (1969) and Page (1971) reported lower densities of duck nests in hayed or grazed areas than in standing vegetation in Stutsman County. Duebbert (1969) found 61 nests in a 125-acre retired cropland field in South Dakota during a study in 1968. Many other studies have shown conclusively that nesting puddle ducks prefer, and are more successful in, ungrazed and unmowed vegetation than in grazed and mowed vegetation.

Nest success achieved by ducks during our study is relatively high in comparison with other recent studies in the prairie region (Table 5). We believe that high-speed traffic and other barriers associated with the highway corridor probably acted as a deterrent to the activity of red foxes and thus reduced the predation influence of this species on the right-of-way. The absence of red foxes (*Vulpes fulva*) among the animals killed by traffic also suggests reduced travel by this animal across the highway.

Previous to this study, the North Dakota Highway Department recommended July 5 as a beginning date for mowing on all primary and secondary roads. The chronology of waterfowl nest initiation and hatching shows that this date conflicts with the peak hatching period for ducks in North Dakota.

Problems anticipated by the Highway Department from the cessation of mowing of rights-of-way, such as increased wildlife-vehicle collisions and snow buildup, did not materialize during this study. The unmowed blocks, with only 20 feet of the inslopes mowed, caused no snow problems for the Highway Department.

Changes in the species composition of wildlife killed by traffic, especially the absence of jack rabbits in 1968 and striped skunks in 1969, suggest that these kills were more a function of movement or population fluctuations than of unmowed vegetation on the right-of-way.

Most motorists were unaware of the condition of the right-of-way. Their expressed interest in wildlife suggested that they would accept the appearance of an unmowed right-of-way for the benefit of ducks and other wildlife. Publicity programs, highway signs, and displays on bulletin boards at rest areas could help educate the motoring public as to the values of vegetation on unmowed rights-of-way, especially if the costs of mowing were portrayed. Statewide cessation of mowing on primary and secondary highway rights-of-way has saved the North Dakota Highway Department over $300,000 since 1968 (J. O. Kyser, personal communication, 1970).

Table 5. Reported success of duck nests in North America.

Location	Percent Nest Success	Source
North Dakota	57	Present study
North Dakota (railroad right-of-way)	83	Page (1971)
North Dakota	22	Kirsch (1969)
North Dakota	25	Martz (1967)
South Dakota	79	Duebbert (1969)
Central Minnesota	34	Moyle (1964:14)
North-central Iowa	35	Burgess et al. (1965)
Northwest Iowa	21	Glover (1956:38)
Wisconsin	27	Labisky (1957)
Southeast Alberta	35	Keith (1961)
Southern Manitoba	35	Sowls (1955:114)

We offered the following management recommendations to the North Dakota Highway Department for enhancing waterfowl nesting and minimizing maintenance costs on rights-of-way along I-94 in duck-producing regions: (1) ditch bottoms, secondary slopes, and back slopes should remain unmowed and inslope mowing for reduced snow hazard should be minimal, (2) interchange triangles should remain unmowed except to the toe of the inslope or less, and (3) mowing of inslopes should be delayed until well after the peak of waterfowl nesting—at least until July 20.

It is gratifying to report that the Highway Department responded to these recommendations and altered maintenance methods on the right-of-way of I-94 from Tower City to Tappen, a distance of 78 miles and an area of about 2,000 acres. Habitat in this area supports moderate to high duck production. The Department also delayed the start of mowing on primary and secondary roads from July 5 to July 15, to allow more duck nests to hatch.

We found officials of the Highway Department interested in ecological roadside management, and, for intensified efforts to manage other rights-of-way for wildlife, we urge wildlife biologists to seek the cooperation of personnel responsible for maintenance of highways and railroads.

How much and what kind of wildlife can be managed on the diverse network of rights-of-way remains to be seen. In many areas, land use is so intense that rights-of-way offer virtually the only habitat for wildlife. Some rights-of-way, especially those maintained with herbicides, or narrow types where predators are highly effective, may be less desirable for wildlife.

The possibility of planting interstate rights-of-way to native flora should also be explored. Several thousand acres of memorial native grassland, readily accessible to the public, could be the result of such work.

As America's environmental awareness sharpens, the citizenry, who own most of the right-of-way resource, will demand an audit of the management record. So far, in many states, this record is dismally lacking in ecological discipline. We commend the state of North Dakota and other states that have taken steps to enhance use of highway rights-of-way by wildlife. A unique opportunity exists for highway officials to provide millions of acres of native biota to the public in the form of better managed rights-of-way. A similar opportunity exists for wildlife biologists and administrators to encourage management of America's right-of-way resource for optimum production of wildlife and native flora.

LITERATURE CITED

BACH, R. N., AND R. W. STUART. 1942. North Dakota upland game nesting studies, 1941. North Dakota Game and Fish Dept. P–R Rept., Project 7R. 41pp.

BURGESS, H. H., H. H. PRINCE, AND D. L. TRAUGER. 1965. Blue-winged teal nesting success as related to land use. J. Wildl. Mgmt. 29(1): 89–95.

BUTLER, J. B., AND R. R. YOERGER. 1962. Current trends in equipment for roadside cover establishment and maintenance. Roadside Development Com. Rept. 41:59–91.

CHESNESS, R. A. 1965. Ringneck nesting . . . *southern* Minnesota style. Conserv. Volunteer 28(162):48–51.

DUEBBERT, H. F. 1969. High nest density and hatching success of ducks on South Dakota CAP land. Trans. N. Am. Wildl. and Nat. Resources Conf. 34:218–228.

EGLER, F. E. 1957. Rightofways and wildlife habitat: a progress report. Trans. N. Am. Wildl. Conf. 22:133–142.

EVANS, R. D., AND C. W. WOLFE, JR. 1967. Waterfowl production in the Rainwater Basin area of Nebraska. J. Wildl. Mgmt. 31(4): 788–794.

FISHER, R. J. 1954. Pheasant nesting, production and movement studies in southwestern North Dakota, 1953. North Dakota Game and Fish Dept. P–R Rept., Project W–35–R–1. 17pp.

———. 1955. Pheasant nesting studies in southwestern North Dakota, May–October, 1954. North Dakota Game and Fish Dept. P–R Rept., Project W–35–R–2. 27pp.

GLOVER, F. A. 1956. Nesting and production of the blue-winged teal (*Anas discors* Linnaeus) in northwest Iowa. J. Wildl. Mgmt. 20(1): 28–46.

HAWKINS, A. S. 1937. Hungarian partridge nesting studies at Faville Grove. Trans. N. Am. Wildl. Conf. 2:481–484.

HIGGINS, K. F., L. M. KIRSCH, AND I. J. BALL, JR. 1969. A cable–chain device for locating duck nests. J. Wildl. Mgmt. 33(4):1009–1011.

JOSELYN, G. B. 1969. Wildlife—an essential consideration determining future highway roadside maintenance policy. Highway Research Record 280:1–14.

———, J. E. WARNOCK, AND S. L. ETTER. 1968. Manipulation of roadside cover for nesting pheasants—a preliminary report. J. Wildl. Mgmt. 32(2):217–233.

KEITH, L. B. 1961. A study of waterfowl ecology on small impoundments in southeastern Alberta. Wildl. Monographs 6. 88pp.

KIRSCH, L. M. 1969. Waterfowl production in relation to grazing. J. Wildl. Mgmt. 33(4): 821–828.

KLO[N]GLAN, E. D. 1955. Pheasant nesting and production in Winnebago County, Iowa, 1954. Proc. Iowa Acad. Sci. 62:626–637.

LABISKY, R. F. 1957. Relation of hay harvesting to duck nesting under a refuge-permittee system. J. Wildl. Mgmt. 21(2):194–200.

LINDER, R. L., D. L. LYON, AND C. P. AGEE. 1960. An analysis of pheasant nesting in south-central Nebraska. Trans. N. Am. Wildl. and Nat. Resources Conf. 25:214–229.

MARTZ, G. F. 1967. Effects of nesting cover removal on breeding puddle ducks. J. Wildl. Mgmt. 31(2):236–247.

MILONSKI, M. 1958. The significance of farmland for waterfowl nesting and techniques for reducing losses due to agricultural practices. Trans. N. Am. Wildl. Conf. 23:215–227.

MOYLE, J. B. (ed.) 1964. Ducks and land use in Minnesota. Minnesota Dept. Conserv., Div. Game and Fish Tech. Bull. 8. 140pp.

PAGE, R. D. 1971. Waterfowl nesting on a railroad right-of-way in North Dakota. J. Wildl. Mgmt. 35(3):544–550.

SHICK, C. 1952. A study of pheasants on the 9,000-acre prairie farm Saginaw County, Michigan. Michigan Dept. Conserv., Game Div. 134pp.

SOWLS, L. K. 1955. Prairie ducks: a study of their behavior, ecology and management. 1st ed. The Stackpole Company, Harrisburg, Pennsylvania, and the Wildlife Management Institute, Washington, D. C. 193pp.

TRAUTMAN, C. G. 1960. Evaluation of pheasant nesting habitat in eastern South Dakota. Trans. N. Am. Wildl. and Nat. Resources Conf. 25:202–213.

WALTERSON, J. E. 1966. Land use study. North Dakota Outdoor Recreation Agency. 115pp.

WESTERSKOV, K. 1950. Methods for determining the age of game bird eggs. J. Wildl. Mgmt. 14(1):56–67.

WOLFE, C. W., JR., AND R. D. EVANS. 1967. Characteristics of roadside pheasant nests. Nebraska Game and Fish Dept. P–R Rept., Project W–28–R. 14pp.

Received for publication February 8, 1971.

WATERFOWL PRODUCTION IN RELATION TO GRAZING

LEO M. KIRSCH, Northern Prairie Wildlife Research Center, Jamestown, North Dakota

Abstract: A 4-year production study of upland nesting waterfowl on the Missouri Coteau area of North Dakota showed that pair numbers, nesting densities and nest success were generally reduced by grazing. It is suggested that cover removal such as regular grazing and mowing be discontinued on areas managed primarily for waterfowl production and that management practices which create dense rank cover be substituted.

Wetland drainage is rapidly reducing waterfowl production in the prairie pothole region of North America where Smith et al. (1964) estimated that half of the continental duck population is produced in an average year. Efforts to preserve prairie wetlands include programs of Federal, state, and provincial governments and private conservation organizations in the United States and Canada. Despite these efforts, an average of 138,000 acres are drained each year in the Dakotas and Minnesota (Morgan 1969).

A less obvious but no less harmful loss of waterfowl production in prairie areas results from changes in agricultural land use. This is especially true on private lands where potholes remain but lack of nesting cover may be seriously inhibiting production (Dwyer 1969).

This paper presents the results of a 4-year study from 1965 through 1968 on the relationship of waterfowl production to land use, with emphasis on grazing. Its purpose is to provide habitat management guidelines for increasing waterfowl production.

I would like to acknowledge the following persons for their help on field work: K. D. Bayha, K. F. Higgins, A. T. Klett, and H. W. Miller of the Northern Prairie Wildlife Research Center, and I. J. Ball, S. A. Mickley, M. E. Westfahl, R. J. King, and S. D. Wilds, summer employees. Appreciation is extended to H. L. Clark, of the Northern Prairie Wildlife Research Center, for building and maintaining equipment used in this work, and special thanks to C. W. Dane, H. F. Duebbert, H. K. Nelson, A. T. Klett, H. W. Miller, and P. F. Springer for editorial assistance.

STUDY AREA

The Woodworth Study Area is situated in northwestern Stutsman County, North Dakota, in the Missouri Coteau physiographic area. Land use on the 3,840-acre study area is primarily diversified farming. The approximate acreages in each land-use category during the study were: pasture—1,360; cropland—770; "idle land"—740 (not grazed or mowed); and hayland—240. Wetlands covered from 250–570 acres. Building sites, roads, railroad rights-of-way, and shelterbelts totaled about 160 acres.

The 640 wetland basins on the study area covered about 592 acres and had widely varied characteristics. Their size ranged from a fraction of an acre to slightly more than 53 acres and averaged 0.92 acre. The depth of some is regulated by natural spillways while others seldom, if ever, overflowed. Maximum water depths ranged from a few inches to over 10 ft. A few contained fresh water but the majority were slightly to moderately brackish.

Pasture and idle lands were either native grassland containing exotic grasses and forbs, or tame mixtures of bromegrass (*Bromus inermis*), quackgrass (*Agropyron*

Originally published in J. Wildl. Manage. 33(4):821–828, 1969.

Table 1. Characteristics of sample plots for waterfowl nest study, Woodworth Study Area, 1967–68.

Plot No.	Upland Vegetation	Land Use	Upland Acres	Wetland Acres	No. of Wetland Basins	Feet of Shoreline
Grazed						
8	Native grassland and alfalfa-grass	Lightly grazed	60.5	30.9	22	13,185
7	Native grassland	Moderately to heavily grazed	35.0	6.7	19	5,260
11	Native grassland	Heavily grazed	68.0	11.3	33	11,930
		Total	163.5	48.9	74	30,345
Ungrazed						
5	Native grassland and alfalfa-grass	Idle	57.0	8.8	18	7,890
6	Native grassland	Idle	36.0	4.5	22	6,390
10	Native grassland	Idle	64.0	20.2	26	12,575
		Total	157.0	33.5	66	26,765

repens), and alfalfa (*Medicago sativa*). Hayland was either native grassland or alfalfa mixed with tame grasses. Scattered clumps of brush of the following genera are found on both idle and grazed native grasslands: *Symphoricarpus*, *Elaeagnus*, *Crataegus*, *Prunus*, and *Rosa*. Croplands were used for producing small grains. About one-quarter of the cropland was summer fallowed each year.

METHODS

Six plots ranging in size from 41 to 91 acres were selected for intensive nesting studies in 1967 and 1968. An attempt was made to minimize variables other than land-use by selecting plots having similar terrain, wetland distribution and classification, and upland vegetation. Characteristics of the plots are presented in Table 1.

Grazing intensity was judged by visual inspection of residual vegetation in the spring before the current year's growth began. Pastures with ⅔ or more of the previous year's growth remaining were classified as lightly grazed, those with ⅓ to ⅔ as moderately grazed, and those with less than ⅓ as heavily grazed. In terms of livestock use, lightly grazed plots were stocked at a rate of one cow per 9 to 15 acres or one animal unit month (A.U.M.) per 6 acres, moderately grazed plots at one cow per 5 to 8 acres (one A.U.M. per 1.35 acres), and heavily grazed plots at one cow per 2 to 4 acres (one A.U.M. per fraction of an acre).

Surveys of water areas and counts of waterfowl pairs were made at 10-day intervals between late April and late June. These were conducted by walking or driving to each wetland basin and recording pairs, lone males, lone females, and groups of each species. Duplication in counting was avoided by not flushing ducks or by watching them until they landed if they were flushed. Observation of pairs, lone drakes, or combinations indicative of pairs were used to estimate the breeding population (Hammond, unpublished instruction manual on file at the Northern Prairie Wildlife Research Center).

Table 2. Numbers of pairs of dabbling ducks on sample plots during mid-May, Woodworth Study Area, 1967–68.

Plot No.	Number of Dabbler Pairs			Dabbler Pairs per 10,000 Feet of Shoreline		
	1967	1968		1967	1968	Average
Grazed						
8	18	12		13	11	12
7	11	8		22	18	20
11	15	9		15	9	12
Total	44	29	Avg.	17	13	15
Ungrazed						
5	18	15		28	23	26
6	12	5		19	8	14
10	25	30		20	25	23
Total	55	50	Avg.	22	19	21

Four nest searches were made each year at approximately 2-week intervals from late May through July. Searching was done between 7:00 AM and 1:00 PM with the use of a cable-chain drag described by Higgins et al. (1969). Paired plots in ungrazed and grazed vegetation were searched either on the same or subsequent days.

All nests located were examined to determine species, stage of incubation, number of eggs, cover type, cover condition, and location with respect to water. Each nest was marked by a strip of colored tape or a surveyor's flag attached to vegetation or a stake 10 to 20 ft from the site. Nests were visited after calculated hatching dates to determine their fates.

Brood production was estimated on the basis of surveys of all water areas during mid-July and mid-August and augmented by incidental observations. The minimum number of broods was estimated by eliminating from the records all duplicate observations as indicated by species, date, location, age-class, and number of young.

Predator activity in and near drag tracks was monitored by clearing all vegetation from 3- × 3-ft plots and covering the exposed areas with about 3 inches of dirt sieved through ¼-inch hardware cloth. The plots were then smoothed and dusted with fine dirt sieved through window screen. Plots prepared in this manner were examined after 24 hours for evidence of predator activity.

RESULTS

Pair Populations

Pair populations of dabbling ducks, principally blue-winged teal (*Anas discors*), gadwall (*A. strepera*), mallard (*A. platyrhynchos*), shoveler (*Spatula clypeata*), and pintail (*A. acuta*) on grazed and ungrazed plots are compared in Table 2. An average of 21 pairs per 10,000 ft of shoreline was found on ungrazed plots and 15 pairs on grazed plots. The observed differences would have been greater if the population on plot 6 had not been especially low in 1968. This low population may have been caused by the presence of red foxes (*Vulpes fulva*) which had a den on this 36-acre plot. Fox dens were not observed on or near other plots. No apparent relationships existed between grazing intensity and pair densities on the grazed plots.

Further evidence of the difference in pair populations on idle and grazed areas was obtained by comparing pair data for 100 additional Woodworth Study Area ponds from each of these land-use categories during 1967 and 1968. Ponds on grazed areas averaged 17 pairs compared to 21 pairs per 10,000 ft of shoreline on ponds in idle areas.

Similar observations have been made by other workers. Salyer (1962:40) studied pair use on 6 sections of land on or near the Lostwood National Wildlife Refuge in North Dakota. He observed approximately twice as many pairs on idle land as he did on similar units of moderately grazed or lightly

Table 3. Effect of cattle on numbers of pairs and nests of ducks, Woodworth Study Area, 1967.

	PLOT 8—CATTLE[a]		PLOT 5—NO CATTLE	
DATE	Pairs	Nests	Pairs	Nests
June 1–3	20	14	21	10
June 26–28	9	6	20	9
Percent change	–55	–57	–5	–10

[a] Twenty-one yearling cattle entered on June 9.

Table 4. Densities of duck nests on sample plots, Woodworth Study Area, 1967 and 1968.

PLOT NO.	NO. ACTIVE NESTS FOUND	NESTS/ACRE
Grazed		
8	30	0.23
7	8	0.09
11	22	0.16
Total	60	Average 0.17
Ungrazed		
5	34	0.26
6	25	0.34
10	30	0.23
Total	89	Average 0.28

grazed lands. Martz (1967:242) noted that activity of prenesting pairs was greater on unmowed than on mowed units in his North Dakota study area. Drewien (1968:39) found more pairs per pond in Soil Bank and other idle land in South Dakota than on hayed, cultivated, or grazed lands.

In addition to this effect of cover removal on breeding populations, pairs are apparently also disturbed by cattle and tend to move from areas where cattle graze or concentrate. In 1967, the pair population counted on plot 8 was 20 during the June 1–3 pair survey (Table 3). Cattle were placed in this plot on June 9, and only 9 pairs were found during the June 26–28 survey. Conversely, the pair population on plot 5, where cattle were excluded, was 21 during the first survey and 20 during the latter.

The effects of disturbance by cattle were also reflected in nest densities on the above plots. There were 14 active nests on plot 8 during the first survey and 6 during the latter while on plot 5 nest densities were 10 and 9 during the first and latter survey, respectively. The change in nest density on plot 8 was not a result of nests hatching. Hammond (Personal communication) observed a similar reaction of breeding ducks to cattle on Lostwood and LaCreek National Wildlife refuges. He reported that female ducks tended to avoid sites where cattle were present during the prenesting period and when selecting nest sites. He noted a movement of females from potholes in pastures to those in surrounding ungrazed areas on Lostwood National Wildlife Refuge.

Nest Densities

Average nest densities on sample plots during 1967 and 1968 were 0.17 nest per acre on grazed plots and 0.28 nest per acre on ungrazed plots (Table 4). The lightly grazed plot had a higher nest density than the heavily or moderately grazed plots. The lowest nest density on idle plots was equal to the highest on grazed plots.

When comparing nest densities one should consider that the cable-chain drag was more efficient in grazed than in idle cover. Ninety percent of 10 previously located hens on nests were flushed when dragged over in grazed cover, while 67 percent of 15 hens were flushed by the drag in idle cover.

Other observers have reported high nest densities in idle cover. R. I. Benson in Moyle (1964:117) found undisturbed upland grassy areas and Soil Bank fields to be

Table 5. Duck-nesting success by land use, Woodworth Study Area, 1965–1968 (all nests located on upland sites).

			Land Use			
	Ungrazed	Grazed	Odd Areas[a]	Hayland	Cropland	Totals
Nests hatched	61	17	4	1	1	84
Nests destroyed or deserted	160	105	24	4	5	298
Total nests	221	122	28	5	6	382
Percent hatched	28	14	14	20	17	22

[a] Includes isolated clumps of vegetation containing less than 5 acres and strips of cover 200 ft or less in width such as slough margins, fencerows, roadsides, and railroad right-of-ways. Most such areas were in an idle condition.

the most favored nesting sites for dabbling ducks in Minnesota. A density of 0.7 acre per nest was found by Keith (1961:65) on an ungrazed area in Alberta. Nest densities found on Valentine National Wildlife Refuge, Nebraska, by Campbell (Unpublished report on file at the Refuge) were from three to five times greater on idle than on grazed and mowed areas. Martz (1967: 244) found consistently higher nest densities on unmowed than on mowed areas at Lower Souris National Wildlife Refuge in North Dakota. In Iowa, "the heaviest concentration of [blue-winged] teal nests, one per 1.3 acres, was found on the 30-acre ungrazed island . . ." (Glover 1956:34). Ungrazed meadows, which made up 14 percent of the study area, accommodated 87 percent of the 593 nests found by Sowls (1955:67) during studies in Manitoba, Canada. Ungrazed meadows studied by Sowls included mowed and unmowed vegetation.

Nest Success

Nest success was calculated from 382 duck nests located on upland areas in all land-use categories of the study area during 1965–68 (Table 5). Nest success on ungrazed areas was twice as high as on grazed areas. Samples for hayland, cropland, and odd areas were too small for comparison, but the relatively poor success when compared to the larger areas of undisturbed cover is probably indicative of a true difference.

I believe that actual nest success in ungrazed cover was even greater than the 100-percent difference the data show. Repeated nest searches with the cable-chain drag during 1967 made vehicle trails through the dense ungrazed cover. These trails remained throughout the winter of 1967–68 and nest searching activities during 1968 kept them open, increasing the extent of predation.

Evidence that red foxes used the vehicle trails as access routes into idle cover was obtained by placing 19 dust plots in the vehicle trails during 1968. Fox tracks were found during 43 percent of 56 exposures. Twenty plots were placed out of the vehicle trails in ungrazed areas for comparison, and fox tracks were found on only 8 percent of 60 exposures. Capel (1965:64) found that dummy nests located close to cattle trails suffered higher losses from predators than those located some distance away.

The adverse effect of vehicle trails in ungrazed cover was suggested by other information. In 1965 and 1966 prior to use of the drag, observed nesting success for 25 nests located in grazed areas was 20 percent compared to 46 percent for 46 nests found on idle lands. In 1967, the year the cable-chain drag was first used, observed success for 51 nests in grazed areas was 10 percent and nest success for 81 nests in ungrazed areas was 28 percent. In 1968, when cleared trails were present during the entire nesting season, 15 percent of 46 nests found in grazed areas hatched compared to 17 percent of 93 nests in ungrazed areas.

Another factor which may increase nest losses in ungrazed cover was reported by Hammond (Personal communication). He found that walking to nests in grazed areas did not increase predation rates as much as walking to nests in ungrazed cover.

Other workers have found higher nesting success in ungrazed than on grazed areas. Imler (Unpublished report on file at the Refuge) studied 377 duck nests on Crescent Lake National Wildlife Refuge, Nebraska. He found nesting success ranging from a low of 2 percent on summer grazed areas to a high of 21 percent in idle areas. The second highest success observed by Imler was on hayed and lightly grazed areas where 14 percent of the nests hatched. Anderson (1957:78) reported that 42.2 percent of 116 nests on idle land in California hatched while none of 7 nests on grazed land hatched. Glover (1956:41) found 24.4 percent nesting success on idle and lightly grazed areas in Iowa compared to only 10.5 percent success on heavily and moderately grazed areas.

Burgess et al. (1965) reported higher success on moderately grazed areas on Union Slough National Wildlife Refuge, Iowa, than on idle areas. Most of the idle cover studied, however, consisted of narrow strips or small clumps which this study (Table 5), as well as that of Moyle (1964), found to be especially vulnerable to predation. A more recent study in Iowa compared nest survival for 60 simulated nests in each of 3 land use categories (Weller, personal communication). On grazed lands survival was 10 percent, on lands grazed the previous year 17 percent, and on idle lands 30 percent.

Relatively low nest success (22 percent) was reported by Keith (1961:78) in 90 acres of ungrazed cover. This area contained about 54 water areas which occupied about a third of the land and resulted in a pattern of narrow bands of upland cover between water areas or between water areas and the perimeter fence. He also noted that nests 25 ft or less from water were subject to higher predation than elsewhere on the study area. This, coupled with the pattern of upland cover, apparently made nests on this area especially vulnerable to predation. He observed comparatively high nesting success (38 percent) on another ungrazed area of 43 acres.

Errington (1963:187) pointed out that half to three-quarters of the nests of some birds may fail and still allow the breeding female to raise a brood, and Stoddard (1932:225) found that when observed nesting success was between 20 and 40 percent nearly all female bobwhite (*Colinus virginianus*) produced young because of renesting. On the Woodworth Study Area in 1966, when at least 50 percent of an estimated population of 633 pairs of ducks produced broods, the observed nesting success for 63 nests was 33 percent. In 1967, when at least 31 percent of an estimated population of 664 pairs of ducks produced broods, the observed nesting success for 152 nests was 20 percent. I suspect that the actual production during 1966 and 1967 was higher than the data indicate because all broods were not seen, but even so, the 14 percent observed nesting success on grazed areas found during this study would not maintain the duck population. The 28 percent success observed on idle areas would maintain and perhaps increase the population.

CONCLUSIONS AND RECOMMENDATIONS

In reviewing literature I was unable to find a single example where grazing or other cover removal activities increased waterfowl production. An outstanding example of the importance of undisturbed cover was reported by Mihelsons (1968:45) on three islands in a Latvian Lake where duck nesting increased from 6 to 9 times when mowing and grazing were discontinued. He found 5 to 7 mallard, shoveler, and pintail nests per year before grazing and mowing were stopped. This average increased to 40 nests after cessation of these activities. In his concluding remarks Mihelsons (1968:46) stated: "The above examples show that in places where breeding of ducks is desirable, economic activity is not permissible."

In our North Dakota study, higher pair populations, higher nest densities, and higher nesting success were found in ungrazed cover than in any other land-use type studied. Another important advantage of ungrazed cover was suggested by Leopold (1933). He noted that since most waterfowl begin to nest before new growth is suitable for nesting, the presence of residual cover from the previous year permits birds to begin nesting earlier and allows a longer time for renesting. Any activity which reduces residual cover from the previous year may adversely affect waterfowl production. Elimination of grazing and mowing activities will result in increased waterfowl production.

Other types of manipulations may result in further increases in waterfowl production. Rank cover, such as provided by the Soil Bank Program, appears to be an ideal objective. In Minnesota, Moyle (1964) demonstrated the value of Soil Bank cover to nesting ducks. Similarly, Duebbert (1969) found higher duck nest densities and success in rank, dense cover created under the Cropland Adjustment Program in South Dakota than on any other cover studied. Other wildlife species benefit from rank cover. Dahlgren (1967) reported that Soil Bank land was highly beneficial to ring-necked pheasants (*Phasianus colchicus*) in South Dakota. I found high populations of sharp-tailed grouse (*Pedioecetes phasianellus*) on North Dakota Soil Bank and Cropland Adjustment fields, and the highest greater prairie chicken (*Tympanuchus cupido*) populations I have observed in North Dakota were on Soil Bank lands.

Based on the above findings I recommend:

1. That grazing and haying be discontinued as regular land-use practices on areas managed primarily for upland nesting ducks and upland game birds.
2. That dense, rank cover similar to Cropland Adjustment Program cover described by Duebbert (1969) be established on reverted cropland areas managed for duck production.
3. That periodic burning or soil disturbance to alter plant succession, fertilization, or combinations of these be tested as means of creating dense, rank cover.
4. That studies be continued to refine methods for creating and maintaining the most productive nesting cover for upland nesting ducks.

LITERATURE CITED

ANDERSON, W. 1957. A waterfowl nesting study in the Sacramento Valley, California, 1955. California Fish and Game 43(1):71–90.

BURGESS, H. H., H. H. PRINCE, AND D. L. TRAUGER.

1965. Blue-winged teal nesting success as related to land use. J. Wildl. Mgmt. 29(1): 89–95.

CAPEL, S. W. 1965. The relationship between grazing and predator activity in four types of waterfowl nesting cover. M.A. Thesis. Univ. Missouri, Columbia. 78pp.

DAHLGREN, R. 1967. The pheasant decline. South Dakota Dept. Game, Fish and Parks. 44pp.

DREWIEN, R. C. 1968. Ecological relationships of breeding blue-winged teal to prairie potholes. M.S. Thesis. South Dakota State Univ., Brookings. 98pp.

DUEBBERT, H. F. 1969. High nest density and hatching success of ducks on South Dakota CAP land. Trans. N. Am. Wildl. and Nat. Resources Conf. 34:(In press).

DWYER, T. J. 1969. Waterfowl breeding habitat in agricultural and non-agricultural land in Manitoba. M.S. Thesis. Univ. Wisconsin, Madison. 23pp.

ERRINGTON, P. L. 1963. The phenomenon of predation. Am. Scientist 51:180–192.

GLOVER, F. A. 1956. Nesting and production of the blue-winged teal (*Anas discors* Linnaeus) in northeast Iowa. J. Wildl. Mgmt. 20(1): 28–46.

HIGGINS, K. F., L. M. KIRSCH, AND I. J. BALL. 1969. A cable-chain device for locating duck nests. J. Wildl. Mgmt. 33(4):1009–1011.

KEITH, L. B. 1961. A study of waterfowl ecology on small impoundments in southeastern Alberta. Wildl. Monograph 6. 88pp.

LEOPOLD, A. L. 1933. Game management. Charles Scribner's Sons, New York and London. 481pp.

MARTZ, G. F. 1967. Effects of nesting cover emoval on breeding puddle ducks. J. Wildl. Mgmt. 31(2):236–247.

MIHELSONS, H. A. 1968. Methods of increasing the duck populations on lakes in Latvia. Pp. 41–55. *In* Birds of the Baltic region: ecology and migrations. Proc. Baltic Ornithol. Conf., 1960. 4. Riga, U.S.S.R. (Transl. from Russian by Israel Program for Scientific Transl.). 336pp.

MORGAN, R. 1969. Habitat development project. North Dakota Outdoors 31(7):22–23.

MOYLE, J. B. 1964. Ducks and land use in Minnesota. Minnesota Dept. Conserv. Tech. Bull. 8. 140pp.

SALYER, J. W. 1962. The ecological effects of drought and grazing on prairie nesting ducks. M.S. Thesis. Univ. Missouri, Columbia. 70pp.

SMITH, A. G., J. H. STOUDT, AND J. B. GOLLOP. 1964. Prairie potholes and marshes. Pp. 39–50. *In* J. P. Linduska (Editor), Waterfowl tomorrow. U. S. Government Printing Office, Washington, D. C. 770pp.

SOWLS, L. K. 1955. Prairie ducks, a study of their behavior, ecology and management. The Stackpole Company, Harrisburg, Pennsylvania. 193pp.

STODDARD, H. L. 1932. The bobwhite quail, its habits, preservation and increase. Charles Scribner's Sons, New York. 559pp.

Received for publication May 5, 1969.

USE OF NATURAL BASIN WETLANDS BY BREEDING WATERFOWL IN NORTH DAKOTA

HAROLD A. KANTRUD, U.S. Fish and Wildlife Service, Northern Prairie Wildlife Research Center, Jamestown, North Dakota 58401

ROBERT E. STEWART, U.S. Fish and Wildlife Service, Northern Prairie Wildlife Research Center, Jamestown, North Dakota 58401

Abstract: Use of basin wetlands by breeding populations of 12 species of waterfowl was investigated in 1965 and during 1967–69 throughout the prairie pothole region of North Dakota. Data were obtained primarily by random sampling techniques. Of the total population occupying natural basin wetlands 55 percent occupied seasonal and 36 percent occupied semipermanent wetlands. Seasonal wetlands contained 60 percent of the population of dabbling ducks, while semipermanent wetlands supported 75 percent of the population of diving ducks. On basins with ponded water, highest concentrations of breeding pairs occurred on temporary, seasonal, and semipermanent wetlands; moderate concentrations were recorded on ephemeral, fen, and undifferentiated tillage wetlands; and low concentrations occurred on permanent and alkali wetlands. The proportion of basins that retained ponded water had a direct bearing on the value of each type of wetland to breeding waterfowl. Relative values of the more intermittent types of wetlands are greatly increased during years of ample precipitation.

J. WILDL. MANAGE. 41(2):243–253

Shallow basin wetlands in the prairie pothole region of south-central Canada and north-central United States represent the principal breeding habitats of many waterfowl species in North America. Climatic instability and natural differences in the capacity to retain ponded water cause drastic annual and seasonal variations in the distribution and number of ponds, and in the area of ponded water among various types of basins.

Densities of breeding waterfowl as related to wetland habitat were investigated in the prairie pothole region by a number of biologists, including Evans and Black (1956), Jenni (1956), Benson (1964), Jessen et al. (1964), Drewien and Springer (1969), Sauder (1969), Smith (1971), and Stoudt (1971). The results of these studies are not comparable because each investigator used his own wetland classification system or a modified version of the systems of Bach (Bach, R. N. 1950. Some general aspects of North Dakota water areas and their study. North Dakota Game and Fish Dept. 13pp. Mimeo.) or Martin et al. (1953). Moreover, most of these studies were restricted to short transects or small blocks of land. Regardless of length, roadside transects may not provide a representative sample of wetlands because of changes in wetland characteristics and densities caused by road construction. Small blocks of land usually contain too few wetlands to make meaningful comparisons of waterfowl use among wetland types.

In this paper, we report the use by breeding waterfowl of wetlands classified according to a system designed specifically for the prairie pothole region (Stewart and Kantrud 1971). About 14 percent of the glaciated prairie pothole region of central North America (Fig. 1) occurs in North Dakota. This particular area contained a yearly average of 1,619,000 pairs of breeding ducks (27.6 pairs/km^2) during 1967–69 (Stewart and Kantrud 1974).

Two earlier reports (Stewart and Kantrud 1973, 1974) utilized nearly the same data in documenting population estimates of breeding waterfowl and their proportional distribution among various wetland types and biotic sections within the prairie pothole region. We hope the information on

Originally published in J. Wildl. Manage. 41(2):243–253, 1977.

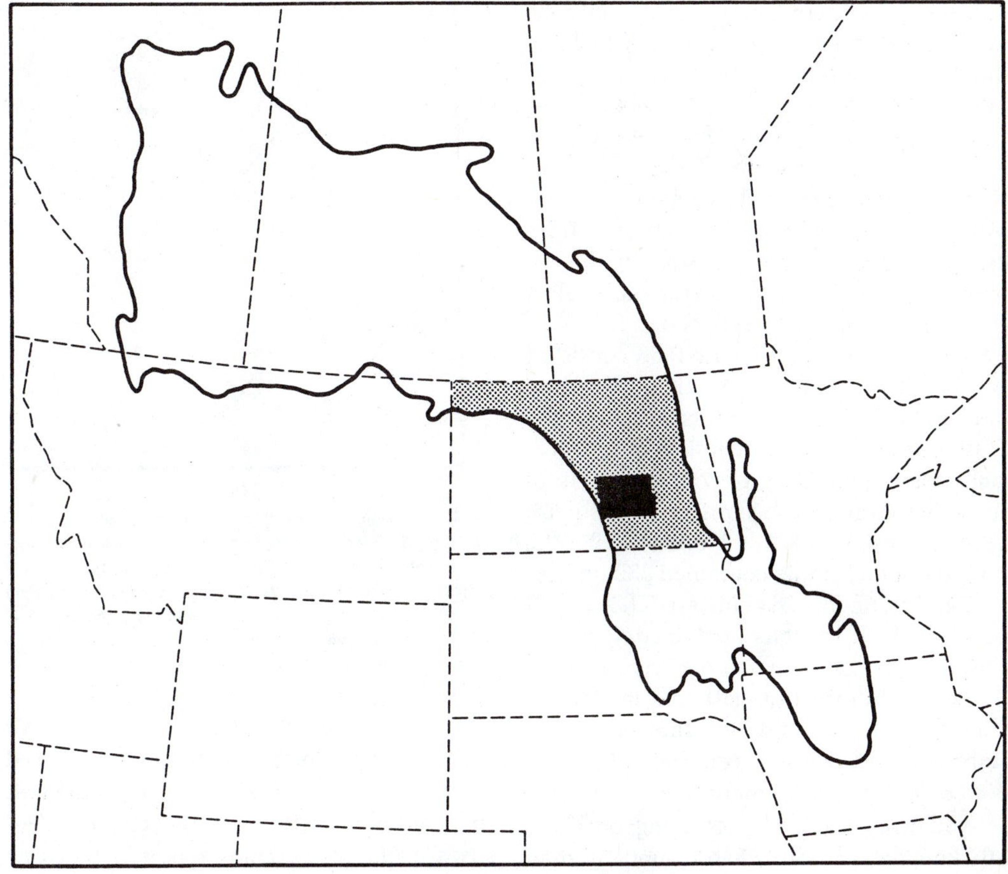

Fig. 1. Prairie pothole region of central North America, showing portion lying within North Dakota. Location of Stutsman and Kidder counties, where supplementary information was gathered, is shown in black.

pair densities contained in this paper will aid biologists to determine the effectiveness of habitat acquisition or manipulation programs and to quantify impacts to populations of breeding waterfowl caused by various private or public works projects.

We thank D. A. Davenport for the development and use of computer programs to process the data collected during 1967–69. D. W. Larson and C. R. Madsen assisted with the general field work in 1965, and personnel (34 in number) from the U.S. Fish and Wildlife Service, U.S. Soil Conservation Service, and North Dakota Game and Fish Department aided in the waterfowl censuses and habitat surveys in 1969. We acknowledge editorial assistance by D. H. Johnson.

METHODS

Census

Censuses were conducted during 1965 and 1967–69. In general, the proportion of wetland basins containing ponded water was about average in 1965, above average in 1967 and 1969, and below average in 1968. The investigation did not cover wetland basins without ponded water in 1968 nor those on a portion of the area in 1969. During the 1967–69 period, data were obtained from wetlands lying within sample plots selected at random from the prairie pothole region of North Dakota. This region was described and mapped in detail previously (Stewart and Kantrud 1972*b*, 1973). Procedures used to stratify the region, determine sample sizes, and select the sample units were described.

Sample units in 1967 and 1968 consisted of legal, 160 acre quarter sections (64.7 ha) and totaled 68 and 194 units, respectively. Cluster sampling was employed in 1969, each cluster consisting of four quarter sections that formed the corners of a square with dimensions of 2 × 2 miles (3.2 × 3.2 km); the total sample contained 332 quarter sections, grouped as 83 clusters. The several minor wetland habitats inadequately represented in the random sample were supplemented by information gathered in 1965 on discrete wetlands selected subjectively in Stutsman and Kidder counties (Fig. 1). Water depth measurements (Fig. 2) were derived from wetlands occurring on three 1.61 km^2 areas in Stutsman County studied during 1961–66.

The stratified random sample surveys provided estimates of breeding duck populations and the total amount of wetland habitat. However, when data for specific wetland habitats were analyzed, the unequal representation of some habitats among the strata caused large variances. For some uncommon wetland habitats, data from both random and nonrandom studies were combined. These two conditions precluded calculation of precision estimates.

Waterfowl censuses were conducted by two observers between half hour after sunrise and half hour before sunset when sustained wind velocities did not exceed 25 km/hr. Each observer was responsible for the census of ducks on a rectangular half

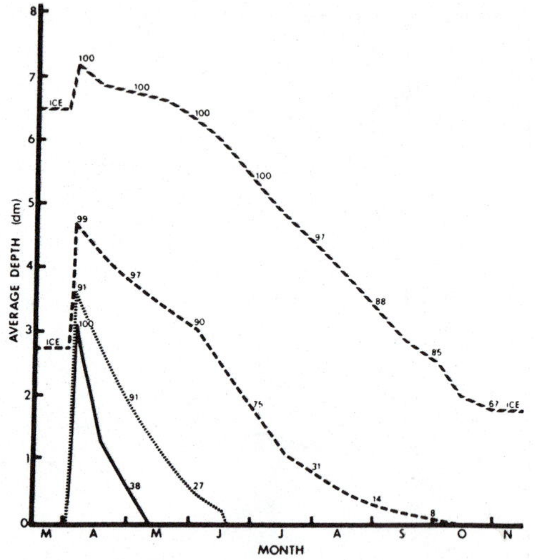

Fig. 2. Average water depth of 4 classes of basin wetlands during 1963. During a 6-year period (1961–66) average mid-spring water levels were higher in 2 years and lower in 3 years. Proportion of wetlands containing ponded water during the ice-free season is shown above the lines. The lines are, from top to bottom, semi permanent (N = 33), temporary (N = 22), seasonal (N = 72) and ephemeral (N = 8).

(32.4 ha) of the quarter section. Notes were kept of ducks flushed and were compared at the end of each coverage of a sample unit to avoid duplications in the counts. Censuses on large wetlands required that one observer record flushed ducks from a high vantage point while the other observer waded in a zigzag course through the wetland. During the censuses, our interpretation of segregated pairs, lone males, and mixed flocks of both sexes was in general agreement with the guidelines established by Hammond (1969). Flocks of male mallards (*Anas platyrhynchos*) or pintails (*A. acuta*) containing as many as 10 individuals were occasionally observed on large wetlands during principal breeding periods. In these cases we considered each male to indicate a pair, as recommended by Dzubin (1969*b*).

We varied the chronology of the censuses slightly each year to compensate for variable phenological conditions. In 1965, two censuses were conducted. The mallard, pintail, green-winged teal (*Anas crecca*), shoveler (*A. clypeata*), American wigeon (*A. americana*), ring-necked duck (*Aythya collaris*), and canvasback (*A. valisineria*) were counted from 5 May to 16 May, and the gadwall (*Anas strepera*), blue-winged teal (*A. discors*), redhead (*Aythya americana*), lesser scaup (*A. affinis*), and ruddy duck (*Oxyura jamaicensis*) were counted from 7 June to 24 June. During 1967–68, sample units were covered once or twice during the breeding season. Single coverage was restricted to those sample units covered during the overlapping period of early-, mid-, and late-nesting species. The mallard and pintail, both early-nesting species, were censused from 24 April to 7 June 1967 and from 23 April to 7 June 1968; mid-nesting species, including the gadwall, green-winged teal, blue-winged teal, shoveler, American wigeon, ring-necked duck, and canvasback were censused from 14 May to 10 July 1967 and from 15 May to 15 July 1968; and late-nesting species, including the redhead, lesser scaup, and ruddy duck were censused from 22 May to 19 July 1967 and from 20 May to 23 July 1968. In 1969, because of the limited time available for cooperation by other investigators, a single census was conducted during the overlapping portion of the principal breeding periods for groups of early-, mid-, and late-nesting species; this composite period extended from 20 May to 10 June.

Data are not included for the cinnamon teal (*Anas cyanoptera*) and wood duck (*Aix sponsa*), since these species were represented in the count totals by fewer than 10 pairs. Other relatively rare breeding waterfowl including the Canada goose (*Branta canadensis*), common goldeneye (*Bucephala clangula*), bufflehead (*B. albeola*), and hooded merganser (*Lophodytes cucullatus*) were not recorded on the study areas.

Wetland Classes

The seven classes of natural-basin wetlands referred to in this report were previously described in detail (Stewart and Kantrud 1971). In this classification, five classes were distinguished on the basis of water permanence (degree of retention of ponded water) as indicated by the vegetative zone occupying the central or deepest part of the wetland basin. These classes are ephemeral, temporary, seasonal, semipermanent, and permanent. Other classes included alkali, characterized by the intermittent occurrence of shallow, highly saline surface water, and fen, recognized by a characteristic zone of vegetation that developed on areas containing surficial exposures of alkaline groundwater.

In North Dakota, many ephemeral, temporary, and seasonal wetlands were tilled for agricultural purposes. Cultivation of bottom soils of ephemeral wetlands during dry periods frequently resulted in soil movement and siltation that virtually eliminated these wetlands. We often could not assign tilled wetlands to a particular class because indicator plant species were not present. Such wetlands were called undifferentiated tillage ponds.

The density of wetlands per square kilometer was highest for undifferentiated tillage ponds (12.7). Average densities for the prevalent differentiated classes of wetlands were: ephemeral—2.5, temporary—2.9, seasonal—5.6, and semipermanent—0.8. Densities were also determined, with less accuracy, for those classes that are comparatively uncommon: permanent—0.023, alkali—0.023, and fen—0.015.

Average size (in ha) of basin wetlands varied as follows (figures in parentheses indicate number of wetlands in sample): ephemeral—0.04 (272), temporary—0.25 (356), seasonal—1.15 (782), semipermanent—9.34 (151), undifferentiated tillage

Table 1. Proportional distribution (%) of breeding duck pairs on basin wetlands, derived from wetlands occurring on sample plots censused during 1967–69.

	Wetland type							
Species[a]	Ephemeral	Temporary	Seasonal	Semi-permanent	Permanent	Alkali	Fen	Undifferentiated tillage
Dabbling ducks								
Mallard (811)		4.2	59.1	29.5	0.6	0.6		6.0
Gadwall (746)		3.6	54.6	35.4	2.0	0.4		4.0
Pintail (1013)	0.1	4.1	61.7	22.4	0.9	0.3	0.1	10.4
Green-winged teal (214)		1.4	64.0	22.0	5.6			7.0
Blue-winged teal (2089)	T[b]	2.7	61.2	31.2	2.5	0.3		2.0
Shoveler (608)		3.0	59.2	33.1	0.3			4.4
American wigeon (86)		3.5	61.6	25.6		1.2		8.1
Diving ducks								
Redhead (326)			22.1	76.4	0.6			0.9
Ring-necked duck (33)			21.2	69.7	6.1			3.0
Canvasback (92)			18.5	78.3	3.3			
Lesser scaup (74)			37.8	52.7	5.4		2.7	1.4
Ruddy duck (297)			13.1	78.5	8.1			0.3
Total dabbling ducks (5567)	T	3.3	60.0	29.7	1.7	0.3	T	4.9
Total diving ducks (822)			19.8	74.9	4.3		0.2	0.7
Total ducks (6389)	T	2.9	54.8	35.5	2.0	0.3	T	4.4

[a] Numbers in parentheses indicate total number of pairs in sample.
[b] Indicates <0.05%.

wetlands—0.21 (598), permanent—32.92 (21), alkali—48.04 (11), and fen—3.63 (11).

Out of the total area of ponded water during the peak breeding period for early-nesting ducks in 1967–69, 44 percent was in seasonal wetlands, 36 percent was in semipermanent wetlands, and 0.1 percent in ephemeral, 2 percent in temporary, 5 percent in permanent, 7 percent in alkali, 0.2 percent in fen, and 6 percent in undifferentiated tillage wetlands.

RESULTS

Distribution of Breeding Ducks

A previous report (Stewart and Kantrud 1973) indicated that, in the prairie pothole region of North Dakota, during 1967–69, about 84 percent of the pairs of breeding ducks occurred on natural-basin wetlands, 6 percent were on streams and oxbows, and 10 percent occupied various manmade wetlands.

Out of the total breeding population occurring on natural-basin wetlands 55 percent was on seasonal, 36 percent on semipermanent, 2.9 percent on temporary, 2 percent on permanent, 0.3 percent on alkali, and 4.4 percent on undifferentiated tillage wetlands (Table 1). Noticeable differences in the use of basin wetlands by the two ecological groups of species—dabblers and divers—were apparent: while a majority (60%) of the dabbling duck population occupied seasonal wetlands, a vast majority (75%) of the diving duck population occupied semipermanent wetlands.

Table 2. Density (pairs/km^2 of wetland) of breeding ducks on wetlands containing ponded water.

Species	Wetland type							
	Ephemeral[a]	Temporary[a]	Seasonal[a]	Semi-permanent[a]	Permanent[b]	Alkali[b]	Fen[b]	Undifferentiated tillage[a]
Dabbling ducks								
Mallard		66.7	44.9	28.6	4.3	1.5	27.3	29.5
Gadwall		54.3	38.8	29.5	7.9	13.4	17.6	21.1
Pintail	49.2	82.4	58.6	27.0	3.6	6.8	24.8	63.3
Green-winged teal		6.0	13.1	5.2	1.7	0.6		10.5
Blue-winged teal	137.7	112.6	122.4	73.7	14.5	5.1	42.7	29.5
Shoveler		36.2	34.4	22.7	1.7	7.8	12.6	34.4
American wigeon		6.0	5.0	2.4	2.0	3.2		4.9
Diving ducks								
Redhead			7.4	29.6	3.3	0.4	4.9	3.7
Ring-necked duck			0.7	2.6	0.9	0.2		0.7
Canvasback			1.6	8.1	2.2	0.2		
Lesser scaup			2.9	4.7	6.1	1.3	4.9	1.2
Ruddy duck			4.0	28.2	4.8		17.2	1.2
Total dabbling ducks	186.9	364.2	317.2	189.1	35.7	38.4	125.0	193.2
Total diving ducks			16.6	73.2	17.2	2.1	27.0	6.8
Area (km^2) of habitat during breeding								
Min.	0.0007	0.449	9.66	7.70	6.91	5.28	0.398	0.82
Max.	0.0203	0.509	10.65	9.03	6.99	5.28	0.409	1.66

[a] Data from random plots studied 1967–69.
[b] Data from 1965 on subjectively selected wetlands added to 1967–69 results.

Densities of Breeding Pairs

Waterfowl use of wetlands was restricted almost entirely to those basins that contained ponded water. Annual variations in the number of basins with ponded water was positively correlated with changes in breeding waterfowl populations in many areas of the prairie pothole region (Evans and Black 1956; Jenni 1956; Salyer 1962; Rogers 1964; Drewien and Springer 1969; Stoudt 1969, 1971; Schroeder 1971; Smith 1971; Stewart and Kantrud 1974).

The value of each wetland type as related to habitat preferences is expressed as pairs per square kilometer of basins with ponded water (Table 2). High densities were found to be characteristic of both major classes of basin wetlands. For total ducks, the density was 27 percent higher on seasonal than on semipermanent wetlands. The composition of duck species also differed markedly. The prevalent species with respect to density in decreasing order were the blue-winged teal, pintail, mallard, gadwall, and shoveler on seasonal wetlands; and the blue-winged teal, redhead, gadwall, mallard, ruddy duck, pintail, and shoveler on semipermanent wetlands. The habitat affinities of dabbling ducks and diving ducks were in sharp contrast. Comparative data for seasonal and semipermanent wetlands showed that the density of dabbling ducks was about 68 percent higher on seasonal wetlands, whereas the density of diving ducks was 341 percent higher on semipermanent wetlands.

Several other wetland types were of considerable importance, particularly for dabbling ducks. Temporary wetlands supported highest densities of dabbling ducks; principal species in decreasing order of density, included the blue-winged teal, pintail, mallard, gadwall, and shoveler—a composition the same as that of seasonal wetlands. Rather high densities also were recorded for ephemeral, fen, and undifferentiated tillage wetlands. Predominant species on these wetlands, listed in decreasing order of density, were the blue-winged teal and pintail on ephemeral wetlands; the blue-winged teal, mallard, and pintail on fens; and the pintail, shoveler, mallard, blue-winged teal, and gadwall on undifferentiated tillage wetlands. Comparatively low densities of breeding waterfowl were recorded for permanent and alkali wetlands.

The more favorable habitats for each species are also shown in Table 2. Densities of the ubiquitous blue-winged teal were especially high on ephemeral, temporary, and seasonal wetlands. Mallards and gadwalls were in highest densities on temporary and seasonal wetlands. The higher concentrations of the pintail, green-winged teal, shoveler, and American wigeon occurred on temporary, seasonal, and undifferentiated tillage wetlands. Most of the diving duck species, including the redhead, ring-necked duck, canvasback, and ruddy duck were well represented only on semipermanent wetlands. The greater densities of the lesser scaup, however, were found on permanent and fen wetlands as well as on semipermanent wetlands.

Relationship of Water Retention to Pair Densities

Since waterfowl were attracted only to those basins with ponded water, it follows that the proportion of basins with ponded water had a direct bearing on the value or usefulness of each type of basin wetland to waterfowl. This was not taken into account in previous evaluations (Table 2), because they were based entirely on average densities of breeding waterfowl on basins with ponded water. A more realistic approach in appraising the value of each wetland type was to calculate the average density of breeding waterfowl occurring on all basins of each type without regard to the presence or absence of ponded water. For most wetland types, densities calculated in this manner differed greatly from one year to the next because the proportions of basins with ponded water are so changeable.

In general, the value of the more intermittent types of basin wetlands to breeding waterfowl greatly increased during years with ample precipitation and decreased during drought years. These intermittent types include ephemeral, temporary, seasonal, alkali, and undifferentiated tillage wetlands. To a much lesser degree, these trends were also apparent for semipermanent and fen wetlands. Permanent wetlands differed from other types in that densities of breeding pairs normally remained fairly constant every year, regardless of changing climatic conditions.

Information concerning the use of the more common types of basin wetlands during years with ample (above average) precipitation is included in Table 3. These densities (pairs/km^2) of breeding waterfowl were calculated from combined population data obtained in 1967 and 1969 on basins with or without ponded water. The data clearly show that densities of total ducks were highest on seasonal wetlands and fairly high on semipermanent wetlands, only moderate on temporary wetlands, rather low on undifferentiated tillage wetlands, and very low on ephemeral wetlands. Though seasonal wetlands were the principal habitat utilized by all species of dabbling ducks, semipermanent wetlands also supported moderate numbers, particularly of mallard, gadwall, pintail, blue-winged teal, and shoveler. Appreciable use of undifferentiated tillage wetlands by pintails and mallards also was recorded. Semipermanent wetlands were of paramount importance for all species of diving ducks. Rather limited use by redheads and ruddy ducks occurred on seasonal wetlands.

DISCUSSION

The combined effects of many variable ecological factors were reflected by differences in the distribution and density of breeding waterfowl among the types of basin wetlands. Perhaps the most important of these factors was water permanence, the length of time that ponded water was maintained in wetland basins. Water permanence had a direct bearing on the species composition and prevalence of wetland plant communities so important to waterfowl habitat (Stewart and Kantrud 1971). The fertility of ponded water in several types of basin wetlands was also determined in part by water permanence, because nutrients bound in organic matter were released through oxidation of bottom soils when wetlands went dry. In response to increased water fertility, greater populations of invertebrate food organisms appeared, making the ponds more attractive to breeding waterfowl (Moyle 1961). Salinity was important in some types of wetlands, sometimes closely correlated with differences in vegetation (Stewart and Kantrud 1972*a*). It may influence the occurrence and abundance of invertebrates (Serie and Swanson 1976, Swanson et al. 1974). The attractiveness of some wetlands to waterfowl may be related to annual changes in the ratio of emergent vegetation to open water, which have been attributed to fluctuations in water depth (Stewart and Kantrud 1971).

Table 3. Density (pairs/km² of wetland) of breeding ducks on wetlands without regard to presence or absence of ponded water. Data from sample plots studied in 1967 and 1969.

	Wetland type				
Species	Ephemeral	Temporary	Seasonal	Semipermanent	Undifferentiated tillage
Dabbling ducks					
Mallard		29.7	37.7	23.5	16.4
Gadwall		20.3	34.5	24.5	2.5
Pintail	10.0	29.7	46.6	23.1	29.5
Green-winged teal		1.6	10.9	5.0	0.8
Blue-winged teal	10.0	31.2	109.4	67.2	4.1
Shoveler		14.1	28.0	15.2	2.5
American wigeon			3.9	1.9	0.8
Diving ducks					
Redhead			6.0	31.0	
Ring-necked duck			0.3	1.9	
Canvasback			1.7	11.2	
Lesser scaup			3.0	6.9	
Ruddy duck			5.2	29.9	
Total dabbling ducks	20.0	126.6	271.0	160.4	56.6
Total diving ducks			16.2	80.9	

Water depth and temperature affected the abundance and availability of waterfowl foods (Krapu 1974, Swanson et al. 1974). Other environmental variables that undoubtedly influenced breeding waterfowl included wetland size, land use, and the composition of local wetland complexes, particularly in regard to the number, size and types of basin wetlands. In addition, observed differences in utilization of wetlands by breeding ducks may be partly related to extrinsic factors such as population size, mortality, and homing rates (Dzubin 1969*a*, Dzubin and Gollop 1972).

Seasonal wetlands undoubtedly provided the greatest abundance of high-quality wetland habitat for breeding ducks during years of average or above-average water. In such years nearly all seasonal wetlands retained ponded water throughout the spring and early summer and their value to breeding waterfowl was maximized. During years of below-average water conditions the value of seasonal wetlands may be reduced greatly. The moderately shallow central and peripheral vegetative zones of seasonal wetlands probably were the main feeding areas for breeding dabbling ducks during most years. The nutrient availability remained high because seasonal wetlands were usually dry by late summer, resulting in the annual oxidation of organic matter which would otherwise remain stable (Swanson et al. 1974). Seasonal wetlands were very numerous and widely distributed and thus provided isolation for pairs during courtship as well as waiting sites for males near their nesting hens. The dense stands of shallow-marsh emergents including burreed (*Sparganium eurycarpum*), slough sedge (*Carex atherodes*), and whitetop (*Scolochloa festucacea*) were also utilized as nesting sites by some diving ducks, especially during wet years (Stewart 1975, Stoudt in prep.).

Semipermanent wetlands comprised the principal breeding habitat for diving ducks throughout the North Dakota portion of the prairie pothole region. During years with below-average water, they often served as the principal breeding habitat for dabbling ducks as well (Stewart and Kantrud 1973). They normally retained ponded water throughout the breeding season. For this reason, their value for breeding waterfowl remained relatively stable except during very dry years. Diving ducks normally spent the greater part of their time on the relatively deep open-water areas where luxuriant beds of submerged aquatic plants occurred (Bartonek and Hickey 1969, Rogers and Korschgen 1966). Stands of tall, coarse emergent plants such as common cattail (*Typha latifolia*) and hardstem bulrush (*Scirpus acutus*), furnished the over-water nesting cover that was required by diving ducks. Shallow, peripheral areas were used as feeding and resting sites by dabbling ducks. Although semipermanent wetlands were not as abundant as seasonal wetlands, they were relatively large; as a consequence, their long shorelines might be occupied simultaneously by numerous breeding pairs.

Temporary wetlands containing ponded water were unique in that they supported greater densities of breeding dabbling ducks than any other wetland type. This was indicative of their fertility as reflected by the abundance and availability of invertebrate food organisms. Temporary ponds were usually the first to develop an invertebrate population each spring due to the rapid warming of the shallow water which is characteristic (Swanson et al. 1974). Following this initial spring period, the use by waterfowl of temporary wetlands was generally quite low because ponded water was not maintained for more than 2 or 3 weeks. Although temporary ponds were numerous, the proportion of the total basin wetland area they contributed was low because of their small average size.

Undifferentiated tillage wetlands are cultivated because of a low degree of water permanence, and, like temporary wetlands, their use by breeding ducks was low. They comprised about one-fourth of the total area of basin wetlands (Stewart and Kantrud 1973). However, the amount of suitable waterfowl habitat provided was small because of the rapid loss of ponded water. Water volume in ponds located in crop fields was often reduced by heavy siltation from adjacent uplands. In spring, the value of tillage wetlands to breeding waterfowl was dependent in part on the presence of stubble, dead weeds, and crop residue. Waterfowl use of tilled wetlands devoid of old growth was much reduced because these ponds lacked the organic substrate that is vital for production of an abundant invertebrate fauna. Krapu (1974) showed that frequently tilled wetlands did not produce sufficient invertebrate proteins to supply the needs of pintail hens during egg-laying. Tillage wetlands containing stubble or other dead vegetative debris were capable of producing large populations of invertebrates and thus attracted breeding dabbling ducks, at least temporarily.

Ephemeral, permanent, alkali, and fen wetlands were of minor importance. Their combined basins were occupied by only 2.3 percent of the total population of breeding waterfowl. Ephemeral wetlands usually held ponded water for only a few days following snow-melt or for a few hours following heavy summer rainstorms. At the opposite extreme, permanent wetlands provided a constant source of water with stable levels, but their value to breeding waterfowl was low. This poor utilization probably resulted from a combination of factors including excessive water depth, low rates of nutrient recycling, competition for invertebrates by minnows (Swanson and Nelson 1970), and the scarcity of vegetated, shallow-water feeding areas because of steep, rocky shorelines or severe wave action. Alkali wetlands often contained shallow, highly fertile expanses of surface water that supported abundant, easily accessible invertebrates for food. However, because their shorelines were largely devoid of emergent vegetation significant use by breeding pairs was probably limited by lack of protective cover. Fens supported moderate densities of breeding ducks, but their overall value was insignificant owing to their scarcity.

The relative values of various types of basin wetlands, as specified in this report, apply only to breeding pairs of ducks. Evaluations based on use by duck broods and migrant waterfowl, and on use by breeding and migrating populations of other marsh or aquatic birds may differ greatly.

LITERATURE CITED

BARTONEK, J. C., AND J. J. HICKEY. 1969. Food habits of canvasbacks, redheads, and lesser scaup in Manitoba. Condor 71(3):280–290.

BENSON, R. I. 1964. A study of duck nesting and production as related to land use in Pope County, Minnesota. Minnesota Dept. Conserv. Div. Game and Fish Tech. Bull. 8(Sect. IV): 107–126.

DREWIEN, R. C., AND P. F. SPRINGER. 1969. Ecological relationships of breeding blue-winged teal to prairie potholes. Pages 102–115 *in* Saskatoon wetlands seminar. Can. Wildl. Serv. Rep. Ser. 6.

DZUBIN, A. 1969*a*. Comments on carrying capacity of small ponds for ducks and possible effects of density on mallard production. Pages 138–160 *in* Saskatoon wetlands seminar. Can. Wildl. Serv. Rep. Ser. 6.

———. 1969*b*. Assessing breeding populations of ducks by ground counts. Pages 178–230 *in* Saskatoon wetlands seminar. Can. Wildl. Serv. Rep. Ser. 6.

———, AND J. B. GOLLOP. 1972. Aspects of mallard breeding ecology in Canadian parkland and grassland. Pages 113–152 *in* Population ecology of migratory birds. U.S. Bur. Sport Fish. Wildl. Wildl. Res. Rep. 2.

EVANS, C. D., AND K. E. BLACK. 1956. Duck production studies on the prairie potholes of South Dakota. U.S. Fish Wildl. Serv. Spec. Sci. Rep. Wildl. 32. 59pp.

HAMMOND, M. C. 1969. Notes on conducting waterfowl breeding population surveys in the north central states. Pages 238–254 *in* Saskatoon wetlands seminar. Can. Wildl. Serv. Rep. Ser. 6.

JENNI, D. A. 1956. Pothole water levels in relation to waterfowl breeding populations and production. M.S. Thesis. Utah State Univ., Logan. 55pp.

JESSEN, R. L., J. P. LINDMEIER, AND R. E. FARMES. 1964. A study of duck nesting and production as related to land use in Mahnomen County, Minnesota. Minnesota Dept. Conserv. Div. Game and Fish Tech. Bull. 8(Sect. II): 26–85.

KRAPU, G. L. 1974. Feeding ecology of Pintail hens during reproduction. Auk 91(2):278–290.

MARTIN, A. C., N. HOTCHKISS, F. M. UHLER, AND W. S. BOURN. 1953. Classification of wetlands of the United States. U.S. Fish Wildl. Serv. Spec. Sci. Rep. Wildl. 20. 14pp.

MOYLE, J. B. 1961. Aquatic invertebrates as related to larger water plants and waterfowl. Minnesota Conserv. Dept. Invest. Rep. 233. 24pp.

ROGERS, J. P., AND L. J. KORSCHGEN. 1966. Foods of lesser scaups on breeding, migration, and wintering areas. J. Wildl. Manage. 30(2):258–264.

SAUDER, D. W. 1969. An evaluation of the roadside technique for censusing breeding waterfowl. M.S. Thesis. South Dakota State Univ., Brookings. 60pp.

SERIE, J. R., AND G. A. SWANSON. 1976. Feeding ecology of breeding gadwalls on saline wetlands. J. Wildl. Manage. 40(1):69–81.

SMITH, A. G. 1971. Ecological factors affecting waterfowl production in the Alberta parklands. U.S. Bur. Sport Fish. Wildl. Resour. Publ. 98. 49pp.

STEWART, R. E. 1975. Breeding birds of North Dakota. Tri-college Center for Environmental Studies, North Dakota State Univ., Fargo, North Dakota. 295pp.

———, AND H. A. KANTRUD. 1971. Classification of natural ponds and lakes in the glaciated prairie region. U.S. Bur. Sport Fish. Wildl. Resour. Publ. 92. 57pp.

———, AND ———. 1972*a*. Vegetation of prairie potholes, North Dakota, in relation to quality of water and other environmental factors. U.S. Geol. Surv. Prof. Pap. 585-D. 36pp.

———, AND ———. 1972*b*. Population estimates of breeding birds in North Dakota. Auk 89 (4):766–788.

———, AND ———. 1973. Ecological distribution of breeding waterfowl populations in North Dakota. J. Wildl. Manage. 37(1):39–50.

———, AND ———. 1974. Breeding waterfowl populations in the prairie pothole region of North Dakota. Condor 76(1):70–79.

STOUDT, J. H. 1971. Ecological factors affecting waterfowl production in the Saskatchewan parklands. U.S. Bur. Sport Fish. Wildl. Resour. Publ. 99. 58pp.

———. (in prep.). Habitat relationships of breeding canvasbacks on a Manitoba study area. U.S. Fish Wildl. Serv. Resour. Publ.

SWANSON, G. A., AND H. K. NELSON. 1970. Potential influence of fish rearing programs on waterfowl breeding habitat. Pages 65–71 *in* Edw. Schneberger, ed. A symposium on the management of midwestern winterkill lakes. Am. Fish. Soc. N. Central Div.

———, M. I. MEYER, AND J. R. SERIE. 1974. Feeding ecology of breeding blue-winged teals. J. Wildl. Manage. 38(3):396–407.

Received 19 April 1976.
Accepted 27 January 1977.

COMMENTS ON CARRYING CAPACITY OF SMALL PONDS FOR DUCKS AND POSSIBLE EFFECTS OF DENSITY ON MALLARD PRODUCTION[1,2]

ALEX DZUBIN[3]

The purposes of this presentation are (1) to examine the concept of carrying capacity as it pertains to small ponds habitat; (2) to summarize some of the available literature from ground study areas on pond occupancy by mallards; (3) to suggest possible effects of increasing pair density on production of mallard young. I have attempted to give my documented results and undocumented theories on two of the multitide of questions asked by the convener of this seminar, Dr. J. B. Gollop.

My comments are based on a literature review of published and unpublished ground study reports and 4 years of field work on each of two study areas, one in the parkland of Manitoba, 9 miles south of Minnedosa, Manitoba, and the other in the grassland, 12 miles southwest of Kindersley, Saskatchewan. Descriptions of both study blocks are found in Dzubin (1969). From 1952 to 1959 observations on marked and unmarked breeding waterfowl pairs have been made from their first arrival in spring to their departure to moulting areas in July and August. My review of the population dynamics literature is not exhaustive but readers are referred to recent major reviews by Wynne-Edwards (1962) and Lack (1966). For descriptions of mallard behaviour see Weidmann (1956), Lebret (1961), and Raitasuo (1964).

The concept that animal populations themselves control their densities is not new. The works of Nicholson, Solomon, Elton, Lack, Kluijver, and others clearly show that abundance of birds and animals in communities is self-limiting (for other views see Andrewartha and Birch 1954, Wynne-Edwards 1962). Associated with the concept of density-dependent population growth are Errington's (1951) views on inversity, i.e., production of young per animal is higher when populations per unit area are lower and decreases as population density increases.

The concepts of carrying capacity and critical limiting factors, after Liebig's "Law of the minimum," were presented by Leopold (1933). Carrying capacity was utilized by Errington (1934) in reference to bobwhite quail and was defined as "the heaviest population that a specific environment could be expected to winter." Later Errington and Hamerstrom (1936) elaborated the concept and defined it as the "upper limit of survival possible in a given covert territory under the most favorable conditions." The upper limit was mainly determined by predation upon adult, vigorous birds. In the same paper (p. 309), weighing the effects of social interactions, they re-define carrying capacity "as the level beyond which simple predation upon adult birds, their own territorial intolerances and their tendencies to depart from coverts overcrowded with their own or some oth-

[1] Originally published in Saskatoon Wetlands Seminar, pages 138–160. Can. Wildl. Serv. Rep. 6, 1969.

[2] Reproduced by permission of the Minister of Supply and Services Canada.

[3] Present address: Canadian Wildlife Service, Migratory Bird Research Center, University of Saskatchewan Campus, Saskatoon, Saskatchewan S7N 0X4, Canada.

er species do not permit continued maintenance of population." The *Wildlife Investigational Techniques Manual* defines carrying capacity twice: (1) "the maximum number of animals a given area can support during a given period of the year" and (2) "the maximum number of animals which can be maintained indefinitely on a given area." Edwards and Fowle (1955) discussed at some length the various definitions found in the literature and concluded that most were vague and meaningless. Furthermore, since more than one limiting factor is involved in placing an upper limit on population potential and since those limiting factors vary constantly, carrying capacity is not a stable attribute of the environment. From census data it is obvious that yearly mallard populations vary between some low and high figure. Mallards are not found on small pond habitats above a certain number of pairs per square mile. The maximum pair population in any spring may be determined by the limited capacity of the habitat to support pairs, whether the limit is imposed by food, predators, land use, juxtaposition of ponds and nest cover, climate and pond numbers, or social interactions. Also, although habitat can often support maximum numbers of adult birds, the true measure of carrying capacity in the spring is the proportion of adults that raise young to flying or breeding age without irreparable damage to the environment, i.e., habitats can support adults but not necessarily yearly maintain a viable breeding population. If carrying capacity of habitat is surpassed, then the habitat deteriorates because of the presence of a superabundance of animals, or the animals themselves suffer some increased mortality to balance the inability of the environment to support them, or their reproductive capacity is lowered.

POND HABITAT CARRYING CAPACITY

The apparent relationship of pond numbers to breeding pair populations has been widely studied. That a general relationship exists on the Canadian prairies between high May and July pond numbers with high breeding populations, and good production is apparent from examination of pond and population figures published by the U.S. Bureau of Sport Fisheries and Wildlife from 1953 through 1963 (Bellrose et al. 1961; Lynch et al. 1963; Gollop 1963; Crissey 1963*a,b*, 1969). However, critical examination of pond figures and breeding population numbers for individual study blocks and transects shows wide variations in ponds available per species and pairs censused per pond. Valid comparisons of breeding pair and pond aerial survey data from different areas are nearly impossible to make in that ponds varying in size from 0.1 to over 10 acres are each classified as one pothole and no quantitative record is kept of water or habitat quality on each transect. Similarly, the percentage of each breeding species seen by aerial crews varies yearly with stage of development of vegetation and other factors (Stewart et al. 1958, Diem and Lu 1960, Crissey 1963*a*). Because of the inherent biases in pond–pair data gathered by aerial surveys and lack of supplementary data on yearly pond and habitat quality, I examined published and unpublished data from a number of ground studies to determine: (1) if any constant or maximum relationship exists on any one area between spring pond numbers and mallard breeding pairs utilizing these ponds; (2) if space in the form of pond numbers available is limiting populations.

Sowls (1947) believed that the number of breeding pairs per unit of marsh is a precise biological figure for "when a pothole, slough, or bay holds its limit of breeding pairs it has reached its full carrying capacity." He also noted that tolerance between species varies, and concluded

> A pothole large enough for one pair of Mallards and one pair of Pintails might have room enough for two pairs of Shovelers and four pairs of Blue-winged Teal. Mallards and Pintails require more space, they are quicker to defend. Blue-wings are the most tolerant of all.

Stoudt (1952*a*) was the first to propose that there are density-dependent factors affecting duck breeding numbers in pothole habitat. Stoudt, after studying waterfowl populations for a number of years in the Dakotas and then initiating a study at Redvers, Saskatchewan, in the southern parklands, noted that

> there is increasing evidence each year to the effect that breeding pairs on the prairie breeding grounds tend to make maximum use of the available small water areas and spill over into less favorable or submarginal habitat when maximum capacity has been reached. The data suggest that these small (one acre or less) water areas were populated about to the saturation point or to carrying capacity and possibly the utilization of them may provide an index to the status of the population.

The terms "submarginal," "saturation point," "carrying capacity" were not defined.

Stoudt (1954) reported a drop of water areas from 306 in 1953 to 232 in 1954 and a parallel 18 per cent drop in breeding mallards from 258 to 215 on five square miles. He concluded that "apparently the water areas on Redvers area had reached maximum carrying capacity in 1952 and the reduction in numbers of areas in 1954 forced some breeders to move elsewhere." Stoudt (1952*b*) noted that "in general it can be stated that the breeding pair population of waterfowl in the Dakotas has varied directly with the number of water areas per square mile during the past five years," i.e., 1948 to 1952 inclusive. He noted further that "the number of water areas per square mile is more important than the total acreage per square mile."

Later, Stoudt (1964) noted that in 1955, 1960, and 1964 there were more ponds than ducks available to use them, also that low water levels in ponds are a deterrent to waterfowl use. He concludes (p. 15) that duck populations on the Redvers area "did not decrease seriously until the number of Type 3 (i.e., permanent) ponds began to disappear in 1959." A close relationship existed between all pair populations and the number of Type 3 ponds.

Bellrose et al. (1961) discussed the relationship between ponds and productivity of breeding pairs and speculated that an inverse relationship exists between population density and production of young ducks (i.e., Errington's inversity principle). They concluded that

> when the grassland and aspen parklands have reached the limit of their carrying capacity as a result of population increase and/or habitat deterioration, the production of juveniles per adult Mallard declines for two to four years until the breeding population has declined to a point where population density is no longer a limiting factor. Then, when a decrease in population or an increase in water areas result in some increased space per breeding pair, the production of young per breeder increases for one to three years, until population density again becomes a limiting factor.

Changes in density of mallard breeding pairs on the breeding grounds were thought to affect production by altering (1) the rate of nest destruction and desertion, and (2) the relative number of ducks that can be accomodated by prime breeding habitats.

Evans and Black (1956) consider that breeding pairs show little preference for potholes especially attractive from the standpoint of food, cover, or any other measurable factor. The major reason behind pond use was that pairs "sought space and freedom from interference and that the ability to find such isolation had an effect on the productivity of the birds as individuals, as well as on the carrying capacity of a given area." They also state (p. 45) that "the conflict between pairs when they come into proximity leads them to space themselves out and is very probably the factor which determines the carrying capacity of the habitat." No data are presented to show how lack of isolation or constant contacts between the same species on the same pothole directly or indirectly affected production.

The need for "space" in spring was considered to be paramount in pothole habitats of Minnesota and the Dakotas (Ducks and drainage in the prairie pothole region, 1953). Small temporary potholes allowed the breeding population to disperse. Space requirements of ducks were considered to be a limiting factor. Nesting was considered a function of the hen alone, and her choice of nest location appeared to be influenced by a desire for isolation. Land nests did not appear to bear any particular relation to any pothole type. Pairs were highly mobile and utilized any suitable sites within or near their breeding territory. The author(s) concluded that:

1. Maximum waterfowl production in the pothole country results from the inter-relation of a number of different pothole types, each fulfilling certain needs of the population.

2. The waterfowl habitat of the pothole region, therefore, can be evaluated only on the basis of the entire community of potholes and surrounding lands, rather than by individual water units.

The apparent effects of spring breeding-pair density on nesting and production of young are described by Smith (1961) for the Lousana Study Area, although both crowding and drought conditions occurred simultaneously. Smith felt that there was a "psychological and possibly a physiological shock" which takes place when mallards return to dried breeding grounds. In May of 1959 and 1961 he observed mallard pairs flocking on the little available water, making no apparent attempt to breed. He notes that "densities [of pairs] on these ponds increased tremendously over and above customary populations found on those ponds and continued to remain high until late May . . . ." "One pond that held one or two Mallard pairs in wet years held 15 pairs in 1961" (p. 5). Ducks in drought-stricken parkland were unable to adjust to local disasters. Flocks of pairs remained on the area until mid-June when there was a general exodus of mallards (Smith, 1961). Either density of pairs affected nesting or drought affected habitat, which in turn indirectly influenced the internal physiological state of hens. Phillips and Van Tienhoven (1960, 1962) have discussed the physiological mechanisms involved in gonad inactivity in wild pintails. Rogers (1964) showed that lesser scaup hens failed to nest when suitable nesting substrate was unavailable because of drought. The latter study parallels the work of Hinde (1966) on various environmental stimuli affecting gonad growth in canaries (*Serinus canarius*).

Crissey (1965) has suggested that the growth of mallard populations in North America is density dependent. He felt that if hunting were to cease for several years, at first production would exceed mortality and the population would increase rapidly. As population increased more crowded conditions would exist in the migration and wintering areas. Mallard populations would expand to the extent of their breeding habitat, as populations would be unable to find suitable breeding areas. He predicted that the North American mallard population might rise from two to four times its present size. At this level it would exceed the "capacity" of its breeding range, so that production ratios would be about 0.25 young per adult. This level of production would balance natural mortality and population would become stable. With blue-winged teal, Crissey also suggested that during the recent drought period there have been more blue-winged teal breeders than could find suitable places to nest. With scaup he proposed that northern habitats may be overstocked as low adult : immature ratios indicate poor productivity.

Mendall (1958:65) suggested that territorialism was limiting pair populations of ring-necked ducks on certain streams in Maine, in spite of the low evident overt conflict between pairs. Stoudt (1965), in a study of small pond habitats at Minnedosa, Manitoba, postulated that canvasback pairs may have reached their "maximum carrying capacity" at about 10 pairs per square mile in 1963 through 1965.

All authors suggest that various pond habitat units do indeed have a carrying capacity for each species. Although predators, nesting cover, brood ponds, spring weather, pond numbers, and man's activities are key factors operating to prevent duck species from realizing their biotic potential, these authors suggest that space and spacing mechanisms affect breeding pair densities and resultant production of young. However, few waterfowl biologists have clearly defined carrying capacity or experimentally shown how density of pairs and spacing mechanisms affect pair abundance and production.

SPECIES POPULATIONS AND POND NUMBERS

On any unit of small pond habitat the number of observed mallard pairs fluctuates yearly between certain limits. Rarely, except in grasslands, do they become extinct, and then only because of a lack of spring or brood ponds. The fluctuations may reflect the ability of the habitat to support only a certain pair density, hunting mortality with resultant poor homing, excellent production with high homing rates, population shifts, or pioneering by yearlings.

Average pair per pond figures based on total pair populations from a study area tend to mask any variations in tolerance between various species. Little pair intolerance has been noted between diver pairs (Hochbaum 1944; Sowls 1955; Mendall 1961; McKinney 1965; Dzubin, pers. obs.); therefore divers can well crowd on available deep-water ponds. Pintail pairs can and do successfully crowd into preferred ponds as there is little overt aggression between pairs (Smith 1963). Shovelers and blue-winged teal show much aerial and overt aggression (McKinney 1965) and partially isolate themselves on pothole habitat, but a number of pairs (e.g., five pairs on a 3.6-acre pond) tend to utilize one pothole and not utilize apparently similar ponds nearby. There is in effect a natural clumping of pairs of blue-winged teal in small pond habitat (Dzubin 1955). Pairs of mallards, baldpate, and gadwall show by far the greatest intolerance of other pairs of their own species. Density effects should be determined on the basis of these three species as the other dabbler and diver species show a far greater predisposition to tolerate the presence of pairs of their own species in the same pond. In effect, a 100 per cent increase in blue-winged teal numbers might lead to little or no increase in the amount of pair interaction, whereas a 50 per cent increase in baldpate pairs might increase pair interactions (i.e., flights, fights, fleeing) many-fold. If need for space and pair intolerance affect both size of breeding population utilizing a definite number of ponds and subsequent production of young, the pair per pond figure should be calculated for each species and associated production figures should be utilized. It is apparent that high pair per pond figures need not have any meaning if production from these pairs is affected by the crowding. The mere presence of pairs does not immediately reflect a high production rate of young.

Crissey (1963), in an unpublished report (An Evaluation of Type One Water Areas), questions the usefulness of Type 1 transient ponds in the spring as "necessary parts of waterfowl breeding habitat." He plotted relationships of water areas per square mile and ducks per square mile from a number of prairie aerial strata from 1951 to 1963. His graphs show little or no positive relationship between numbers of spring water areas and associated breeding populations. This was especially evident in Saskatchewan parkland strata in those years in which water densities were in excess of 10 areas per square mile. Other conclusions were:

1. The ratio between temporary and permanent types of ponds should be examined in the light of spring breeding populations, especially production of young.

2. Size of breeding population utilizing the pothole breeding areas may depend on quality of breeding habitat, strength of homing tendencies of a species, and postbreeding season mortality.

Although a comparison of spring breeding-pair densities and water area numbers can be made from available aerial or ground data, I question the validity of such comparisons as a measure of optimum use or carrying capacity because:

1. Populations are unable to take immediate advantage of available ponds. Hunting mortality may decimate a population homing to a particular strata, leading to an underpopulation even though habitat is optimum. Also, there may be a lag of 1 to 2 years in high production after high pair populations home to a wet region.

2. Quality and size of ponds on an acreage basis are not weighted in the comparison, nor is the upland nesting cover or food resources of areas considered.

3. Shifts of populations do occur from "dry" strata to strata containing more favourable water supplies and in no way reflect the "attractiveness" of the ponds.

4. All species are lumped even though some show a greater predisposition and "need" for isolation than others. If isolation on small temporary ponds is a necessary prerequisite for mallards, gadwall, and baldpate (the three most aggressive species with most pair contacts) even for a short, 20-day period, and if the lack of it precludes successful breeding, then the value of such ponds in creating nothing more than "space" should be recognized. One of the main criteria of use should be, what space does a particular species require (i.e., pond numbers and types) to successfully and consistently produce maximum number of young?

5. Pond × breeding pair correlations and relationships should be made on an individual species and data not lumped (e.g., not ducks per pond but mallards per pond). Also, quality of ponds, size, distribution, frequency and degree of pond ag-

gregations, plus availability of nesting cover should all be considered. Indicated pairs enumerated should be known to be breeding and not migrating or summering in a unit of habitat.

POND OCCUPANCY

I have assumed that during the breeding season a mallard pair occupies a pond because of some requisite available there, i.e., resting and loafing, feeding, waiting, or because of its close proximity to nesting cover or nesting site (cf. Evans and Black 1956). Also, choice may be influenced by some species-specific "habitat releasing mechanism" (Svardson 1949). The single pond may be one of six to ten utilized on the home range, and the percentage of time spent on any one pond varies daily and seasonally. For example, once the feeding requisite is met the pair moves elsewhere or after the hen has flown into nesting cover the drake may move to the primary waiting area. Ponds are also utilized because of spatial requirements especially as "escape areas" where pairs are able to land and not be pursued by other drakes. Pairs therefore occupy some ponds in order to isolate themselves from other pairs of the same species. Such occupied ponds may not be the primary choice of the pair but may be the only available pond from which they are not pursued, i.e., on which there is no interference with their utilization of the breeding requisite. Evans and Black (1956) have concluded that the desire for isolation by breeding pairs on their Waubay Study Area, South Dakota, led to a dispersal of the population and to an intensive use of parts of the habitat which would not otherwise have been used.

For South Dakota, Murdy and Anderson (1951) showed that in 1950 and 1951 an average of 78 per cent and 74 per cent, respectively, of the potholes in various counties was occupied by breeding pairs of ducks. Since mallards made up only 17 to 18 per cent of the total number of pairs censused the percentage occupancy of mallards must have been low indeed—probably less than 15 per cent of the ponds available. In Wisconsin, Jahn and Hunt (1964) show only 12 to 18 per cent of water areas occupied in cross-country road transects for 1948 to 1950, while from 63 to 79 per cent of water areas are shown occupied in North and South Dakota. Smith (1956) indicated a percentage occupancy in May ponds of 51, 55, and 54 per cent for all types of some 200 water areas on the Lousana Study Area for 1953, 1954, and 1955. He also noted (p. 48) that "certain physical characteristics of potholes attract or repel waterfowl. Regardless of water levels some ponds are not of value to ducks. No matter how prevalent the ponds nor how great the population of ducks, crowding seems to occur on certain areas rather than pioneering into hitherto unused ponds."

Gollop (1954) noted a cluster problem in census of pairs at Kindersley, Saskatchewan: "88 per cent of the 474 indicated pairs (including some 197± Mallard pairs) were located on 10 per cent of the 195 water areas" and "75 per cent of the 474 pairs were recorded on seven large sloughs . . . ." Between May 11 and June 10, on 43 Saskatchewan ground transects containing 12,465 ponds, Soper (1948) found the percentage occupancy of ponds per transect to vary between 2.6 and 89.3 per cent and to average 30.9 per cent. He tallied 13,408 ducks in this time, of which about 15 per cent were mallards. On the Kindersley Study Area, from 1956 to 1959, when number of late April ponds varied from 102 to 35 and mallard populations from 418 to 176 per square mile (Table 1), pond occupancy by one or more mallards was always

Table 1. Comparison of pothole numbers, water acreage per mallard pair, and shore line available per pair on two study areas during laying and early incubation periods.

	Roseneath, Manitoba (895 acres)					Kindersley, Saskatchewan (6,720 acres)				
Year	1952	1953	1954	1955	Average	1956	1957	1958	1959	Average
Census date	5/9 to 5/15	4/25 to 5/10	4/25 to 5/10	4/25 to 5/10	1952 to 1955	5/14 to 5/15	5/12	5/10	5/11	1956 to 1959
Number of indicated mallard pairs	54	49	41	33	44	290	418	191	176	269*
Total number of potholes with water on April 25 to 30	101	149	150	162	140.5	102	63	43	35	60.8
Pairs per pond	0.53	0.33	0.27	0.20	0.33	2.84	6.63	4.44	5.03	4.74
Total pothole acreage	116.4	124.2	123.6	125.8	122.5	642.2	573.5	377.7	207.8	450.3
Water acreage per pair	2.16	2.53	3.02	3.81	2.88	2.21	1.37	1.98	1.18	1.69
Pairs per acre	0.46	0.39	0.33	0.26	0.36	0.45	0.73	0.51	0.85	0.64
Total shore-line distance of ponds (feet)	82,327	97,804	98,422	101,064	94,904	131,090	106,807	85,464	54,665	94,507
Shore lines per pair (feet)	1,525	1,996	2,400	3,063	2,246	452	256	478	311	374
Total pothole basins	181					114				
Average basin size (acres)	0.7					5.7				

* Kindersley data include unmated drakes, not sex-ratio corrected (see Dzubin 1969).

greater than 85 per cent. It tended to vary with time of day and nesting phenology. During mid-morning counts, when many hens were laying and pairs were spaced from other pairs, from 92 to 98 per cent of all ponds would be occupied by mallards, although it should be noted that pond sizes varied from 0.1 to 226 acres.

It is difficult to weigh the accuracy of pond-occupancy data. Most censuses are carried out but once through the breeding season during varying periods of the day. Therefore, any consistent pattern of pond use seasonally or daily is not adequately measured by one instantaneous count. A pair may utilize a small pond for a loafing or feeding area for 1 hour a day, immediately after sunrise. The presence of the pond may be a prime reason for the hen remaining to breed in an area. Yet its over-all value to the pair is not weighed by the sampling procedures now utilized. More intensive daily and seasonal evaluation of pond use by pairs of different species must be made, especially during periods of maximum pair and drake intolerance. The present widely divergent views on pond use and pond occupancy are probably the result of varying sampling methods utilized by workers. In all, what most ground studies of ponds available and pair utilization show is that:

1. Not all ponds are occupied 100 per cent of the time. Pairs or drakes may utilize one or two ponds exclusively for a short time during the laying period. Before or after this period six to ten other ponds are occupied for requisites during any one time interval of any day.

2. Some are occupied more than others and for longer periods of the day. There are seasonal differences in use associated with breeding phenology. Larger ponds (i.e., 5+acres) are nearly always occupied after they are ice free. Smaller ponds are used heavily in April when pairs are dispersed or nesting. Small ponds are also used in early spring as they are first to become ice free.

3. There is some species difference in occupancy; dabblers choose smaller, shallower areas whereas divers are found in larger, deeper ponds. Density of pairs may affect pothole use. Poorer quality ponds may be heavily utilized under dense populations because of spacing effects.

4. One pond does not generally contain all the breeding requisites for a pair (unless it is over 3.0 acres in size). Even if it apparently does, pairs will travel elsewhere and utilize other ponds, i.e., they have some inherent tendency to move. A "community of potholes" relationship exists, each pothole having one or more requisites and each contributing to the successful breeding of the pair. In some instances a superabundance of requisites exists; in fact pairs can successfully nest and produce young with less water than they utilize in high water years.

5. The correlation of pond numbers with numbers of mallard breeding pairs from one sample may be meaningless in that no objective measure of pond size or water quality is considered. Ponds per square mile figures are relatively meaningless for yearly comparative purposes unless acreage of water is given or pond sizes remain the same. However, this statistic can be used in a general way for long-term comparisons on the same transects or blocks and within the same area.

6. In nearly all ground studies there were usually more ponds available than mallard pairs occupying them. Where data are presented to show that more than one pair of mallards per pond was censused in early May (e.g., Kindersley), pond size influenced these figures. A small number of ponds over 3.5 acres in size can distort average pair per pond fig-

ures. No measure is made of large ponds immediately off a one-eighth- or one-quarter-mile transect and well within the home range of most species pairs. The need for consideration of pond size when discussing average pair use is obvious.

7. The yearly fluctuations in pond numbers primarily reflect the drying and refilling of the temporary transient waters with most permanent ponds remaining relatively available for pairs until major droughts.

8. After a year of drought and poor production and then a return to higher pond numbers the low pair population does not make immediate use of the additional water, i.e., there is a lower pair per pond ratio. There may be a lag of 1 to 2 years while production increases and pairs homing to an area reoccupy all potholes to "carrying capacity" (Bellrose et al. 1961).

9. Mallard and other pairs may be forced to crowd into available waters and be unable to isolate themselves at times of (a) local droughts which force homing pairs to use available water, (b) droughts elsewhere which shift a segment of the population into a new breeding area and result in crowding, or (c) heavy local production and low mortality leading to a high homing rate to a particular breeding area in the following year.

10. Intolerance and hostile behaviour between pairs, as a possible population-density control has largely been speculative with no concrete evidence yet presented to show that pair interactions consistently interfere with pair settling, thus forcing some pairs to move elsewhere, perhaps into suboptimal habitat with a corresponding reduction in productivity. Kluijver and Tinbergen (1953) and Lack (1966) have discussed territorial effects in adjusting density of pairs of great tits (*Parus major*). Pairs preferred broad-leafed areas but occupied conifer plantations as territories filled. Jenkins, Watson, and Miller (1963) record red grouse (*Lagopus l. scoticus*) being forced out of prime breeding habitat by territorial behaviour into submarginal habitat where they died.

That pairs of mallards, baldpate, and gadwall interfere with the successful utilization of breeding requisites by other pairs of the same species is regularly apparent. The total effects of such interference on production have not yet been shown under the population densities studied in parkland areas. Also, because of yearly mortality due to hunting the number of pairs returning to the breeding area may be appreciably lower than could potentially breed in any locality (Moyle 1964). Therefore parkland ponds might be considered "underpopulated" with few apparent density effects on production. However, there is a suggestion that subtle density effects are operating even under intermediate population levels.

11. Any pond–pair density relationship must be determined at peak of intolerance period of drakes, i.e., prenesting, laying, and early incubation periods. For early breeding mallards these periods vary but should run April 15 to May 10. Spacing mechanisms come into play most intensely then, and more ponds may be required or used by a pair or drake during this interval. For baldpate the most intolerant period of drakes would be May 10 to 30, and for gadwall May 15 to June 5. After peak periods of intolerance drakes become social and more drakes will utilize a smaller number of ponds. Periods of pair intolerance may extend over 20 to 30 days but because all of a mallard population does not nest synchronously nesting may extend over a 2-month period. Pond numbers decrease

through April and May as ephemeral potholes dry. The attempted correlation of a decreasing number of ponds with a dynamic population of different spatual requirements leads to many incongruities.

12. In one spring the actual capacity of the habitat to maintain a breeding population can be exceeded. Number of breeding pairs on ponds without supplementary data on productivity of pairs and numbers of young which reach fledging age gives an erroneous measure of the carrying capacity. In grassland habitat pairs crowd beyond the limit at which they can produce optimum number of young. Any self-regulatory mechanism is imperfect, or there is a time lag before its effects are visible. Before numbers of water areas and breeding pairs are related, yearly comparisons of average production of breeding pairs under various levels of density per unit area should be made. Although pairs per unit area can be used as a general index to carrying capacity for a specific time period, we might consider less superficial measures such as clutch or brood size and percentage of hens fledging broods.

MALLARD PAIRS PER POND

I examined a number of data from waterfowl ground study areas with the object of determining the number of mallard pairs per spring pond observed by the census takers. I had hoped to determine if on the average more than one mallard pair was found per pond. The examination was hampered by a lack of published supplementary data on pond size, pond configuration, and percentage of pond covered with vegetation. Also, both pairs and lone drakes are censused as "indicated pairs." These criteria are warranted but the relationship between two pairs and between two drakes whose hens are away laying are not the same, i.e., drakes with incubating hens are "social" while those with laying hens are not. Although there is an apparent general relationship between high pond numbers with high pair populations, and excellent production of young (Bellrose et al. 1963), I tried to determine if the relationship between high pond numbers and high mallard populations was consistent.

Hochbaum (1944), Stoudt (1949), Smith (1956), and Evans et al. (1952) have shown that there was a decrease in intensity of use by breeding river ducks with increase in pothole size. On the Roseneath Study Area, Evans et al. (1952) noted wide variations in occupancy of certain pothole types and sizes by breeding pairs. Certain small ephemeral "D" areas were occupied 100 per cent of the time. The highest pair per acre figure, 2.9, was for ponds less than 0.5 acres in size. Ponds between 1 and 4 acres contained from 0.3 to 1.5 breeding pairs per acre of water. Since mallards made up about one-third of the breeding population, mallard pairs per acre probably varied between 0.1 and 0.5 for all pond sizes and types.

Leitch (1954) reported on pair counts made by Ducks Unlimited staff in Alberta from 1951 to 1954. His data show that of 275 square miles of habitat sampled an average of 11 potholes per square mile was found in May 1953, and 10 in May 1954. On the same transects an average of 25 breeding pairs per square mile was recorded of which nearly 25 per cent were mallards. There were, therefore, some 1.6 to 1.8 ponds per mallard pair (i.e., 11/6 and 10/6) in the sampled areas in Alberta. In the grassland sections an average of 1.2 ponds per mallard pair was recorded while in the parkland 2.5 ponds per pair were noted in May. Number of ponds per mallard pair in grassland ranged from 0.6 to 2.2 while in the parkland it varied from 1.0 to 5.5. No indication is given of type, quality, or size of potholes.

Similar transect data collected by Ducks Unlimited in Saskatchewan showed that of 161 square miles sampled in 1952 and 177 square miles sampled in 1953 and 1954, there were on the average 21, 13, and 8 potholes, respectively, per square mile in May (Leitch 1954). These ponds contained some 22, 37, and 30, respectively, breeding pairs of which mallard again made up about 25 per cent. In 1952 there were approximately four ponds per mallard pair, 1.4 in 1953 and 1.0 in 1954. In the grassland section number of ponds per pair averaged 1.4 and ranged from 0.4 to 5.5 while in the parkland it averaged 2.0 ponds per pair and ranged from 0.6 to 7.0. His data clearly show a wide variation in number of ponds per mallard pair in both grassland and parkland habitats, with invariably more ponds available than indicated mallard pairs on them.

For some of the most intensively studied transect and block study areas reported on by waterfowl biologists during the "wet" years, 1949 to 1954, it is apparent that the number of indicated mallard pairs per pond varies markedly between areas in the grassland and parkland (Table 2). Valid comparisons between areas are difficult to make because yearly pond size or quality of ponds is not described. On a parkland study area of Manitoba, Pospichal et al. (1954) reported a relatively stable figure of 0.6 to 1.0 mallards per pond from 1949 to 1954. However, for a Saskatchewan grassland block, Leitch (1951 to 1954) recorded an ever increasing number of mallard pairs per pond, 0.12 to 1.39, in spite of yearly decreases in production. Occupancy may therefore reflect not only water conditions on the study area but also water conditions in the immediate environs of the area and elsewhere on the breeding grounds (Lynch 1948, Stoudt 1958). Local and long-distance shifts of breeding populations into well-watered areas may occur with some frequency on the Canadian prairies and locally distort "average" pair per pond figures (Crissey 1963*a*, Hansen 1960, Hansen and McKnight 1964).

On two parkland study areas followed for over 10 years, Smith (1964) and Stoudt (1964, pers. comm.) report very wide variations in numbers of mallard pairs per pond. Stoudt showed that the number of mallard pairs per early May pond ranged from .09 to .93, while Smith showed from .20 to 1.84 (Table 3). The number of ponds per pair varied from 1.15 to 10.91 and averaged 2.31 for Stoudt's area, while it varied from .54 to 4.92 and averaged 1.22 on Smith's area.

Data from Roseneath and Kindersley (Table 1) also show a wide yearly variation in mallard pairs per pond and water acreage per mallard pair. On the parkland study area, Roseneath, the number of mallard pairs per pond varied from 0.20 to 0.53 and averaged 0.33, whereas on the grassland area it varied from 2.84 to a maximum of 6.63 and averaged 4.7. The data merely reflect the differences in average pond size for the two blocks, 0.70 acres for parkland and 5.65 acres for grassland, and do not necessarily confirm wide apparent variations in number of mallard pairs per pond.

The shore line available per pair on the parkland area varied from 1,525 feet to 3,063 and averaged 2,246. On the grassland block shore line available per pair varied from 256 to 478 feet and averaged 374 (Table 1). The average shore line per

Table 2. Comparison of pothole numbers and breeding mallard pairs for pothole regions of Canada and United States.

Area	Year	Area square miles	Number early May ponds	Number indicated mallard pairs	Average mallard pairs per pond	Type of area	Grass-land or park-land	Author
Newdale–Erickson, Man.	1954	50.4	1,100*	734	0.7	Transect	P	Pospichal *et al.* 1954
	1953	50.4	1,200+	798	0.7	Transect	P	Pospichal *et al.* 1954
	1952	50.4	800*	807	1.0	Transect	P	Pospichal *et al.* 1954
	1951	50.4	1,000*	594	0.6	Transect	P	Pospichal *et al.* 1954
	1950	50.4	1,200+	712	0.6	Transect	P	Pospichal *et al.* 1954
	1949	50.4	1,200	718	0.6	Transect	P	Pospichal *et al.* 1954
Southey, Sask.	1952	2.0	84	13	0.15	Block	P	Leitch 1952
	1953	2.0	120*	19	0.16	Block	P	Sterling 1953
	1954	2.0	124*	27	0.22	Block	P	Sterling 1954
South Dakota	1951	88.0	739	292	0.40	Transect	G	Stoudt 1953
	1952	88.0	1,091	335	0.31	Transect	G	Stoudt 1953
	1953	88.0	1,154	329	0.29	Transect	G	Stoudt 1953
North Dakota	1951	146	1,800	586	0.33	Transect	G	Stoudt 1953
	1952	146	1,732	682	0.39	Transect	G	Stoudt 1953
	1953	146	1,809	599	0.33	Transect	G	Stoudt 1953
Success, Sask.	1955	11.2	340	234	0.69	Transect	G	Reeves *et al.* 1955
Kindersley, Eston, Sask.	1952	20.5	219	241	1.1	Transect	G	Gollop 1952
	1953	20.5	250	293	1.2	Transect	G	Gollop 1953
	1954	20.5 (20 used)	195	197	9.9	Transect	G	Gollop 1954
Caron, Sask.	1950	4.25	261	31	0.12	Block	G	Leitch 1951
	1951	4.25	261	34	0.13	Block	G	Leitch 1951
	1952	4.25	261	111	0.43	Block	G	Leitch 1952
	1953	4.25	261	154	0.59	Block	G	Leitch 1953
	1954	4.25	139	193	1.39	Block	G	Leitch 1954
	1955	4.25	261+	106	0.41	Block	G	Leitch 1955

* Estimated from area descriptions. Data from yearly *Waterfowl Populations and Breeding Conditions*, U.S. Department of the Interior, Washington.

pair is not a particularly good statistic in that the centre of ponds which are over 50 yards wide can also be used by pairs for escape.

The data from all ground study areas showed:

1. There were generally more ponds than indicated mallard pairs to utilize them (although it is recognized that one instantaneous count does not measure the daily and seasonal use of a single pond by a species).

2. On any area there was a wide yearly variation in number of ponds available per pair.

3. There were wide variations in average water acreage available per mallard pair—0.89 acres per pair for the Lousana area, 1.45 acres per pair for the Redvers area, 2.88 acres per pair for the Roseneath block, and 1.69 acres for the Kindersley area.

4. There is no apparent consistent relationship on the Redvers, Lousana, or Roseneath study areas between high mallard pair populations and productivity as measured by percentage of successful hens. Either pair densities had not reached "critical" levels at which production is affected by pair interactions, or other limiting factors are more severe. In 1958, at Lousana, 338 mallard pairs (i.e.,

Table 3. Yearly variations in mallard pairs per pond on two parkland study areas. (After Stoudt 1964, Tables 4 and 7, pers. comm.; Smith 1964, Tables 2 and 3, pers. comm.)

	Redvers, Saskatchewan					Lousana, Alberta				
Year	May mallard breeding pair population	Early May ponds	Mallard pairs per pond	Ponds per pair	% successful females	May mallard breeding pair population	Early May ponds	Mallard pairs per pond	Ponds per pair	% successful females
1952	265	306	0.87	1.15	46					
1953	258	306	0.84	1.18	39	103	196	0.53	1.90	61
1954	215	232	0.93	1.08	21	151	191	0.79	1.26	45
1955	174	445	0.39	2.56	42	152	204	0.75	1.34	92
1956	218	443	0.49	2.03	34	155	201	0.77	1.30	77
1957	208	327	0.64	1.57	31	153	189	0.81	1.24	68
1958	205	314	0.65	1.53	22	338	198	1.71	0.59	46
1959	95	172	0.55	1.81	22	241	131	1.84	0.54	15
1960	125	369	0.34	2.95	32	228	168	1.36	0.74	21
1961	39	73	0.53	1.87	31	112	78	1.44	0.70	19
1962	30	122	0.25	4.07	70	66	50	1.32	0.76	24
1963	56	236	0.24	4.21	41	55	174	0.32	3.16	44
1964	78	574	0.14	7.36	21	75	114	0.66	1.52	47
1965	58	375	0.15	6.47		60	295	0.20	4.92	
1966	45	491	0.09	10.91		84	217	0.39	2.58	
Total	2,069	4,785				1,973	2,406			
Average	138	319	0.43	2.31	34.8	141	172	0.82	1.22	46.6
Range	30–265	73–574	0.09–0.93	1.15–10.91	21–70	55–338	50–204	0.20–1.84	0.54–4.92	15–92

Stoudt (1952) shows 306 ponds containing 202 acres of water and 1.31 mallard pairs per acre of water. If an average of 138 pairs is found on the 200 acres of water there was an average of 1.45 acres of water per pair.

One hundred and seventy-two May ponds probably contained some 121 acres. On these 141 mallard pairs were found for an average of 0.89 acres of water per mallard pair.

93 pairs per square mile or .61 pairs per acre) were noted on 152 acres of water (Table 3). This was the highest pair population ever recorded, i.e., the upper "limit," but still the number of successful hens producing broods approached 50 per cent. Because of droughts and poor water conditions, in 1959 densities were higher (i.e., 2.6 pairs per acre on 82 acres of water) but the number of successful hens dropped to 15 per cent. Habitat conditions, due in great part to density-independent climatic factors, probably played a major indirect role in limiting production, although the effect of high densities per acre cannot be discounted. At Kindersley, there is evidence from 1956 through 1958 that pair interactions themselves had an indirect effect on productivity.

5. Pair per pond data need not reflect optimum or maximum pair populations. They may be distorted by population shifts, i.e., immigration, due to droughts elsewhere on the breeding grounds. Production per pair under different densities per pond should be used as criteria for carrying capacity.

6. Other factors besides pond availability, e.g., excessive hunting and natural mortality of pairs during the previous year may result in fewer pairs homing to an area. (See Moyle [1964] for discussion of hunting mortality effects on spring breeding populations.) Mallards are unable to make immediate use of all available ponds. In wet years following droughts and low population levels, there were usually more than two ponds available per pair. There may be a lag of

several years before continuing high production of young and homing of these young can take advantage of available water. The pair population response to high pond numbers is not instantaneous.

7. Data on mallard pairs per pond (Tables 1, 2, and 3) indicate that generally in the parkland habitat less than one mallard pair per pond has been enumerated (i.e., except for a 5-year period at Lousana when more than one but less than two pairs per pond was counted). In grasslands of North and South Dakota less than one-half pair per pond was seen, while in Canada usually over one pair per pond and as many as 6.6 were counted at Kindersley. This may merely reflect a greater average pond size in grassland with more crowding of pairs per pond. It is imperative that pond size and quality be considered in any such comparisons between habitats.

8. At Roseneath, rarely were there more than two mallard pairs on open ponds less than 1.5 acres in size during the maximum pair dispersal interval, April 20 to May 15. More than two mallard pairs could utilize ponds larger than 1.5 acres and covered with emergents. At Kindersley aggregations of pairs usually occurred on all ponds over 3.5 acres in size, but rarely did two pairs successfully utilize ponds less than 1.5 acres.

PAIR SPACING IN GRASSLAND AND PARKLAND HABITAT

Under low or intermediate population levels of 22 to 36 pairs per square mile of parkland pond habitat (i.e., on 66 to 112 ponds per square mile), mallard pairs space themselves through hostile and sexual chases and avoidance of occupied ponds. Drakes are eminently successful in keeping from one to three ponds clear of other pairs as the number of other pairs attempting to use or flying over an occupied pond is small (e.g., two to ten pairs per day resulting in a maximum of 10 to 20 drake–pair contacts per day). Drakes are able to pursue all hens of pairs. Open ponds 1.5 acres or less generally have only one mallard pair using them as waiting areas. Ponds larger than 2 acres, containing vegetation clumps, may occasionally be utilized by two pairs (but two to ten drakes whose hens were incubating could utilize them). For 20 to 30 days drakes might be considered dominant over all other drakes on their own activity centres even though they may be displaced occasionally by more aggressive ones. Spacing (1) lessens competition for breeding requisites and interference with resource use, (2) distributes pairs into both favourable and unfavourable portions of the habitat, and (3) aids in dispersing nests which may serve an antipredator function (McKinney, 1965).

Under slightly higher population levels of 17 to 40 pairs per square mile of grassland pond habitat but containing only three to ten large ponds per square mile, homing mallard pairs aggregate on available water. Pairs are spaced from other pairs but at closer distances than those in parkland. Populations of pairs may approach one pair per acre on ponds over 3.5 acres in size. One studied 5.3-acre pond contained a maximum of five mallard pairs per acre. In these dense pair situations, drakes are incompletely dominant, as the number of pairs attempting to utilize or move through an activity centre may rise to 20 to 30 per day. The drake is unable to chase all pairs and still retain the close pair-bond relationship with his hen or his own hen is consistently chased by other drakes. Here threshold distance for attacked hens is much reduced. Pairs adapt to more crowded conditions by reducing tolerance distances. Weeden (1965) noted that willow ptarmigan (*Lagopus lagopus*) also respond less to territorial transgressions of other pairs when densities are high.

Although mallard drakes may keep a bay or point clear of other pairs for hours or even days they are invariably displaced by other more aggressive drakes (who may also be displaced). There is then a constant seasonal shifting of activity centres of pairs or drakes with first one and then another aggressive drake usurping a favoured waiting site. The social structure of dense pair populations of mallards on a single pond is extremely complex, while the social hierarchy of aggregated pairs is not constant. Age of drake, i.e., adult or yearling, may be a factor. The dominant position of drakes is allied to the breeding condition of hen and some periodic "bursts" in hostility which peak and wane daily and seasonally. However, a few marked drakes were noted to be dominant over all other drakes for 2- to 5-day periods.

Spacing mechanisms other than the ordinary mated-female or individual distance (Conder 1949) are attributes of most dabbler species. In spring mallard pairs are attracted to shallow ice-free ponds with clumps of grass and shrub nesting cover around them. Many pairs attempt to utilize such localities, and hens attempt to settle in nesting cover. Through a series of pursuits and avoidance of occupied areas by newly arrived pairs, only one pair is able to utilize the most attractive site. Others disperse themselves into other nearby ponds. Since not all pond aggregations in a square-mile block appear to contain optimum habitat, i.e., dense nesting cover and brood ponds to assure maximum survival of clutch or brood to fledging, some localities are considered less suitable or suboptimal. Climatic factors and availability of water make certain aggregations of ponds more optimum in one year than another. A number of mallard pairs may not compete for space or requisites one year but do so the next because of much reduced pond numbers forcing pairs to use available potholes. As pair densities increase or if habitat deteriorates because of droughts more pairs may be forced by the spacing mechanisms into suboptimal localities or forced to emigrate to new habitat elsewhere. Because of instability of water, runoff ponds may be optimum one year and suboptimum the next. Both density-dependent regulators, in the form of increased pair interaction, and density-independent regulators, i.e., climate affecting pond numbers and quality, limit pair densities on parkland and grassland ponds. Density effects do not become evident until certain critical levels are exceeded.

LETHAL BROOD AREAS

Over the Canadian prairies mallard and pintail pairs are yearly observed to nest in the vicinity of ephemeral sheet waters and shallow ditches. High temperatures, winds, and evaporation rates dry these waters and leave no brood areas for the hatched young. Flat, glacial lake bottoms with poor drainage are periodically flooded with snowmelt water, e.g., Red River plains of Manitoba and Regina plains of Saskatchewan. Such areas attract breeding waterfowl but rarely provide sufficient permanent brood ponds to fledge ducklings. I have termed these areas "lethal brood areas." These lethal areas may also be tracts of habitat which were previously capable of sustaining breeding pairs and broods but which, because of droughts, no longer provide the necessary brood requisites. For example, a mallard hen may continue to home to a lone grassland pond area which previously could sustain her brood to fledging but because of drought the pond and all nearby ones dry before the brood hatches. In such circumstances, the hen loses her brood but may continue to home to the area in subsequent years. Yearling hens nesting for the first time may also pioneer to such transient pond habitat. Nearby high pair densities might also force hens into using this suboptimal habitat. Similar lethal territory has been described by Nice (in Errington and Hamerstrom 1936), who recorded that "apparently the birds [i.e., song sparrows] will take up these territories that prove lethal to them—partly through attachment to a former territory, even when considerably changed, partly because there is so little really good Song Sparrow territory in the vicinity." However, with song sparrows, the adults themselves succumbed. Jahn and Hunt (1964) note that duck pairs "on poorer quality habitat or on good quality wetlands attractive to pairs but lacking water to ensure brood survival may be less efficient in producing ducklings." Gates (1965) has also concluded that some farmland in central Wisconsin constituted a "trap" for nesting ducks as temporary waters attract pairs in spring but insufficient brood waters do not ensure adequate brood survival in most years. Thus breeding home ranges, with ephemeral waters, are lethal for broods but not necessarily for the adults which are more mobile.

MALLARD PAIR DENSITY AND PRODUCTION OF YOUNG

Does density of pairs have an effect on final production of young from a locality? Does pair density directly affect the habitat occupied by all pairs?

It is obvious from observational evidence that mallard pairs tend to space themselves in any habitat they utilize. The spacing is a result of attack, escape, and sexual tendencies, and the distribution of land nesting cover and water components of the habitat. The degree of spacing (i.e., distance between pairs) varies with population densities, but mallards have a wide range of adaptability to density pressures. Spacing promotes the utilization of all portions of a habitat, although some portions may be more optimum for population survival than others (optimum here meaning the animal, land, water, and vegetational make-up of the habitat which leads to a maximum sustained utilization by breeding birds, i.e., the sum total of all environmental factors in the habitat that affect a maximum survival of young to fledging). As such, localities need not be optimum every year but vary yearly in their ability to sustain maximum numbers of breeders and produce maximum numbers of young which survive to breeding age. The yearly changes in the capacity of the habitat to hold pairs and produce young vary markedly depending on water conditions, predator populations, the activities of man, and the interactions of pairs themselves.

Mallard pairs restrict their breeding activities to a locality and utilize various portions of the water and upland contained in their breeding home range. Drakes show general hostility from a number of different points on the home range which may be used by the drake or pair for feeding, loafing, nesting, or gravelling. However, most hostility is shown from a specific waiting area whose main function, I submit, revolves about the reestablishment of the pair bond whenever the hen is away from the nest. Hens which are pursued by drakes showing either hostile or sexual tendencies flee the area and retire elsewhere. Any discussion of the cause–effect relationship of density on reproduction revolves about the effect of hostility and sexual tendencies of drakes on the successful settling and nesting of a hen or the fleeing of a hen away from the pond, locality, or region. Two conflicting tendencies need to be considered. One is the hen's "urge" to settle in the natal area (i.e., homing) or choice of species-specific habitat, and the other is her tendency to flee from the area because of the hostile sexual attacks of drakes.

In parkland habitat where ponds and nesting cover are found in superabundance, hens are observed to flee from ponds after being pursued by drakes but are apparently not deterred from settling on some other unoccupied nearby pond. Hens of pairs are also observed to avoid ponds already occupied by other mallard pairs. The pursuits of drakes are mainly directed toward the hen. Drakes therefore interfere with the exploitation of the breeding requisites of other nearby pairs. Hostile and sexual chases lead to some lessening of competition for resources and breeding space by pairs; the severity of the competition increases as population density increases. Because pairs are mobile they may utilize for requisites any pond within a mile or two of the pond from which they were chased. There must be a point at which continued interference with settling and exploitation of the resources results in excess energy expenditures for fleeing and less for breeding activities. Yet under the population levels studied in parkland, 22 to 36 pairs per square mile on 66 to 112 ponds, I gathered little evidence to suggest that continued harassment led to a home range abandonment and to lack of breeding. Shifting of the waiting area sites does occur occasionally due to pair interactions of dominant and less dominant drakes, but conclusive evidence that such shifting negatively affected the pair which moved is lacking. There is some observational evidence to suggest that some pairs locate themselves on more "optimal" home ranges than others, i.e., those which contain much nesting cover, have many deep ponds for broods, and contain two or three excellent feeding areas. (This is especially true of adult (2+ years) mallards which come into breeding condition earlier than yearlings.) Conclusive data are unavailable to indicate that fertility (i.e., viability of clutches), or fecundity (i.e., clutch size or brood survival to fledging) are reduced as a direct result of continued interference by drakes in resource use by hens. The data from the Roseneath Study Area suggest that mallard pair populations have not yet reached a critical density at which social interactions have a marked effect on fertility or fecundity. Other density-independent limiting factors are more evidently depressing summer increase, while fall hunting mortality itself serves as a major control of spring pair abundance (Moyle 1964).

The question of the effects of social interactions on reproduction resolves itself to how frequently is a hen or drake pursued before the time and energy regularly channelled to reproductive purposes are negatively interfered with. One might expect the critical point at which a hen or drake spends most of her or his time fleeing or pursuing other mallards to the detriment of the normal sequence of events leading to nesting and hatching to vary between each bird because of its physiological condition and also because of varying availability of requisites in each breeding home range.

The experimental evidence to show

the critical point at which rechannelling of energy and time expenditures worked to the detriment of reproduction is singularly lacking. Little is understood of the physiological condition of each pair on its arrival from the south and, further, we have no measure of the need for, and relative availability of, the various resources within the home range to which the pair confines its activities. The evidence weighed in the present study concerned itself with a comparison of mallard breeding behaviour and efficiency of reproduction in two areas. One was a parkland habitat where pairs are spaced and which is well endowed with water and nesting cover. Here, production of young was nearly sufficient to keep the population in balance. The second was a grassland area in which pairs are forced to aggregate and nesting cover is not dispersed but is confined to small areas both near to and at some distance from water. Here, production was never sufficient to keep population in balance, with immigration of pioneers and drought-displaced birds keeping spring populations high. At best, the evidence for a measurable relationship between high pair populations with a high number of social interactions, and a decrease in number of fledged young is indefinite. That the two are somehow correlated is now obvious but the correlation itself is nearly impossible to weigh because of the many interrelated facets and subtleties of pair coactions.

In certain grassland localities breeding drakes do interfere with the continued exploitation of water, food, and nesting cover by both resident hens and hens attempting to settle for the first time. The degree of interference in resource use, through hostile and sexual pursuits, is governed largely by the density of the local breeding population. It follows that when populations are dense and where hens in the same breeding condition are attempting to exploit various requisites of the environment, more interference will result. We do not know at what point or how often a hen must be pursued and forced to vacate a resource before she fails to breed, moves elsewhere or disperses her nest at some distance from the source of interference. Nor do we know at what densities she and her brood are affected physiologically and psychologically. Any anti-predator function of spacing nests which the three bird flight and attempted rape flight may have (McKinney 1965) would work under high population densities to the ultimate regulation of density, through over-dispersal of nests and increased brood losses on the journey to the water.

Some Negative Effects of Increased Pair Densities

From 1956 to 1959, I observed possible density effects on reproductive behaviour and production rates of immature mallards in grassland habitat (Dzubin, ms.). I have utilized the following observational data in support of my proposal:

1. "Three bird flights" (McKinney 1965) are the main mechanisms of mallard pair spacing. Avoidance of occupied areas, "attempted rape flights," and dispersion of suitable habitat also tend to space pairs. Spacing activity of mallards is most evident during the prenesting and laying periods.

2. As pair populations increase on a pond the number of pair contacts increases and hens are chased more often by drakes.

3. Many hens in laying condition (but certainly not all) are not permitted by frequent drake activity to nest in cover close to ponds utilized by groups of drakes. Hens must therefore withdraw some dis-

tance from ponds in order to find nesting cover in which they are unmolested.

4. Mallard nests are found farther from ponds in grassland under dense population numbers than mallard nests reported in studies where breeding populations were much lower (Girard 1941, Hochbaum 1944, Sowls 1955, Keith 1961).

5. Any increase in the distance hens nest away from water works to the detriment of brood survival. That is, the probability of a brood successfully moving to water from a nest 1,000 yards from a pond is lower than that of one moving 200 yards or less to a pond. In North Dakota, Salyer (1962) reported increased brood mortality resulting from longer distances from nest to water in drought years. Mortality of broods on the Kindersley Study Area from nest to water has approached 50 per cent.

I therefore propose the following hypothesis:

Although mallard breeding pairs can and do adapt to increasing pair numbers by decreasing the hostile-tolerance distances around them, the increasing pair density on ponds leads to what may be called an over-dispersion of nests away from water. The over-dispersion of nests at great distances from water leads to lower brood survival which in effect decreases reproductive rates of dense populations. I propose, therefore, that higher brood mortality, indirectly due to pair interactions on water, is one of the proximate population regulatory mechanisms for mallards breeding under exceedingly dense pair numbers.

In parkland habitat spacing mechanisms may force some hens and pairs into less optimum localities, i.e., the chances of a hen nesting in poorer cover adjacent to poorer brood ponds to produce flying young are proportionally reduced. Preliminary evidence from early spring collections suggest that adult hens come into breeding condition first and such hens and their drakes may usurp the optimum habitat. Later nesting yearling hens may therefore be forced to utilize the remaining suboptimum habitat with a concomitant reduction in proportion of successful yearling hens producing broods. This postulate needs further corroboration. Grice and Rogers (1965) have established that yearling wood ducks (*Aix sponsa*) nested later than adults but some even failed to establish nests when population densities were high. Yearling wood duck hens were unable to compete successfully with older females for a restricted number of nest sites. Later nesting in yearlings may have some adaptive significance in that habitat used first by breeding adults may then become available for the yearling segment when the aggressive responses of adult drakes wane. In mallards, selection of spring breeding habitat and the accurate measure of optimum and suboptimum tracts require more study.

Management Implications

If nesting sites close to water are critical for brood survival and if hostile and sexual pursuits of drakes force females away from water during the nest-searching interval, an obvious solution would be to present nest sites on ponds. This might ensure that females would not have to rise into the air, leave the activity centre, and be visible to drakes. Spaced nesting structures in ponds should be tested to determine if hens will utilize them and if brood survival is materially increased. Stoudt (in litt.) has recorded five mallard nests in cattail cover in one end of a 2.2-acre pond, and I have observed three mallard hens nesting in a

400-foot strip of cattail on a 10-acre pond. If wild mallard hens can nest together in ponds this might be an obvious solution to raising "two ducks where we raised one before." The anti-predator function of nest spacing might, however, be thwarted, and predator control would be necessary in intensively managed pond units. Various types of nests have been successfully used by semi-tame mallard hens (Burger and Webster 1964), but need testing on wild populations.

Possible Density Regulators

With increasing density of mallard breeding pairs brought on by high survival of young homing to natal areas, or shifts of breeding populations from drought-stricken areas, or reduction of number of pond water areas by drought, a number of regulators could affect the immediate and subsequent population density in an area. These are as follows:

1. Some pairs make long-distance emigrations to new habitats and successfully breed and produce young in these newly colonized areas. Emigration may be selectively advantageous if the move from dense to less dense populated areas confers some added chance of survival on the parents or their young (Lidiker 1962). Emigration may not only be triggered by density effects but by density-independent factors, e.g., climate and its effect on pond availability and pond quality. (Density control through emigration.) (Crissey 1957, 1969).

2. Some pairs remain in the densely populated locality and do not attempt to breed or nest only once, and are not predisposed to renest. (Density control through nonbreeding or low renesting rates.) (Smith 1959).

3. Some pairs are forced into or choose to use suboptimal portions of the habitat and fail to produce any young. Grassland and parkland pairs may be forced into the forested areas where production in these displaced pairs is much reduced (Hansen and McKnight 1964). (Density control through emigration and no recruitment of young.)

4. Some pairs adapt to increasing density by reducing tolerance distance and are able to nest successfully. Yet with increasing densities birth rates are reduced indirectly through self-regulatory mechanisms associated with long distance, over-dispersion of nests from water, and high loss of young. (Density control through low recruitment of young.) (Kindersley area, 1957).

5. Parental stress may increase and affect later survival of young, i.e., survival of broods is predetermined by the physiological and psychological condition of the parents. Direct contact between pairs is not necessary as even visual stimuli may somehow affect parent birds. (Jenkins 1961, 1963, on gray partridge.) (Density control through increased brood mortality.)

6. Mortality of broods reared in overcrowded ponds increases and reduces over-all recruitment rate. Constant brood mixing leads to more orphaned young. (Density control through lower recruitment of young.) (Kindersley area; see also Beard 1964.)

7. Mortality of adults may increase associated with density-dependent effects on physiology of birds and with continued interference of birds attempting to utilize food, loafing spots, or nesting cover resources which are in short supply. Pairs may channel more time and energy toward pair encounters or fleeing than to breeding purposes. Also, in dense wild populations, rape of incubating and brood hens by gangs of drakes leads to

added hen mortality, especially in pintails, more rarely in mallards. Broods may be dispersed by frequent molestation of hens. (Density control through increased mortality of adults.)

8. Some pairs may be able to adapt to dense population levels through asynchronous breeding periods staggered through the season so that the habitat is being utilized to its fullest potential. Dense pair populations and associated aggressive coactions may in some way affect ovulation in hens and prevent laying. As the breeding season progresses pair densities and chasing decrease, and ovulation may again occur. (Density control through staggered or protracted breeding seasons.) (McKinney, in litt.—shovelers).

9. On dense nesting islands gadwall ducks may show increased desertion rates of clutches or increased incidence of dropped eggs (Hammond and Mann 1956). The number of infertile eggs and a tendency toward nest parasitism may also increase. However, vastly increased hatching success on islands outweighs any density effects on egg production or number of eggs hatched. Deubbert (1966) suggests an increase in embryonic mortality associated with increased harassment of hens by males. Similar studies on Canada geese are summarized by Munro (1960) and Collias and Jahn (1959). (Minor density control through increased effects on fertility.)

Density-independent Regulators

Although self-regulatory mechanisms could become important after pair densities reach "critical" levels (i.e., where competitive exploitation of resources in short supply, whether food, space, nest cover, etc., leads to summer population decrease), climate acting as a density-independent factor is paramount in supplying the water base of the pond habitat. Without it pairs would not be attracted to nest and broods would succumb quickly, leading to extirpation of local populations. Spring weather also influences timing and success of breeding season and, indirectly, availability of aquatic foods, although waste grain foods appear superabundant in both grassland and parkland habitats. Food on wintering grounds may be more critical. Since much of prairie Canada, especially the grasslands, lies in a rainfall-deficient area where summer precipitation does not balance the loss through evaporation, snow and rain exert the major controlling effect on pond habitat availability and quality and therefore on any waterfowl population increase. Since May and July pond numbers increase and decrease in relation to periodic runoff and evaporation rates, the effects of climatic factors vary seasonally and yearly. Other density-independent factors, e.g., activities of man and predation (although only the doomed surplus may be taken) also greatly control local population levels. Fall hunting mortality appears to be a major population decrease factor with 65 to 70 per cent of the immature mallards and 35 to 40 per cent of the adults succumbing from one year to the next (Keith 1961). In Minnesota, Moyle (1964) has documented a study block on which hunting mortality exceeded production rates of young; this worked to markedly reduce spring pair numbers. Hunting mortality may thus keep parkland populations well below the critical density level although circumstantial evidence suggests that density factors operate even under intermediate population levels leading to some dominant pairs being more successful producers of young than others which are less dominant.

SPACING MECHANISMS LIMITING PAIR DENSITY

Do spacing mechanisms and "territorial" behaviour place an upper limit on the mallard pair density in small water habitat?

Students of ornithology have for decades discussed the phenomena of incompressibility of territory sizes. Howard (1920) suggested that territoriality regulated density of breeding birds, while Nicholson (1933) concluded that "in any given area there is room for only a limited number of territories. Consequently, the surplus individuals are continually harried by their more fortunate brethren or are forced into unsuitable environments and so their chance of survival and of producing offspring is greatly reduced." Territories were likened to rubber discs by Huxley (1934), who suggested that the more these defended areas were compressed by the activity of other pairs the stronger becomes the resistance against further compression. It was postulated that the holding of territories by birds, especially passerines, defined some upper limit to the number of successful breeding pairs any block of habitat could sustain. Later Svardson (1949) discussed how individual pairs of the same species competing for breeding requisites encouraged the spread of the population from optimum to marginal habitats. Errington (1956) also noted that because of intraspecific competition, species may be forced into a greater variety of habitats, some of which may be "scarcely defined as habitable for the species trying to live in them." Kluijver and Tinbergen (1953) concluded that territorial behaviour in the great tit (*Parus major*) forced some pairs from a more "favorable" broadleafed habitat to a suboptimal pine plantation, with resultant lower clutch sizes and renesting rates, although Lack (1966:77) has questioned this view of population regulation. In British Columbia, Tompa (1962) has also concluded that song sparrow densities were limited by territorialism on an island breeding habitat where immigrant pairs were forced elsewhere. Beer et al. (1956) determined that some island-nesting passerines successfully fledged young on territories well below the minimum size found in mainland habitats. There is still much controversy as to the function of territorialism as it pertains to reserving an adequate food supply for parents and young and how food resources may ultimately regulate density (Klopfer 1964, Wynne-Edwards 1962, Lack 1966).

Mallard pairs themselves have an incomplete dominance relationship in that a drake may or may not be dominant through the breeding season on his activity centre. Some drakes are, however, dominant and others subdominant for periods of days. Mallard activity centres are not analogous to passerine territories with some irreducible size limit (Kluijver and Tinbergen 1953; Hinde 1956; Tinbergen 1957; Tompa 1962, 1963; Lack 1966) and are not completely mutually exclusive areas. Therefore, crowding of mallard pairs can occur on ponds, especially as aftermaths of good previous production and high homing rates, shifts of population from drought-stricken areas to better watered ones, and spring droughts which force pairs to use available ponds more intensely. Can this crowding occur indefinitely? I have observed pairs successfully nesting which were crowded up to five pairs per acre of water under severe drought conditions, but crowding may also lead to nonbreeding, emigration, lower reproductive succession of adults, increased mortality of adults, and generally lower survival of resultant broods. For each habitat unit some operational or critical level of density must occur before pair interactions themselves depress population growth. Density effects are only minor or nonexistent before this operational level is reached.

Crowding under favourable and dispersed water conditions as found in parkland is prevented by spacing mechanisms (i.e., TBF, ARF, and avoidance) so that all pairs are not found in the most attractive ponds but are spaced over the countryside. There are two conflicting tendencies noted with mallard hens or pairs during the breeding season: (1) hens of pairs attempt to utilize all favourable and attractive ponds, nesting cover, and feeding areas; (2) drakes of resident pairs interfere in the exploitation of these resources by hens and pairs. The interference by drakes and avoidance of hens leads to spacing. Since not all localities are endowed with suitable tracts of nesting cover or deep brood ponds, I suggest some hens are forced into utilizing the poorer tracts for breeding, i.e., spacing mechanisms lead to maximum use of all possible localities of the breeding habitat by forcing some pairs into suboptimum portions.

In short, spacing mechanisms do not lead directly to immediate limitation of mallard pair densities as various degrees of crowding can occur. As Solomon (1949) has pointed out, there may be a lag between the time a population reaches critical or operational levels and the resultant observable density effects. The most obvious lag is the interval between high density of breeders in one spring leading to low recruitment of young and a lower returning number of breeders the following year, because of post-breeding season mortality on the adults. However, spacing mechanisms must control upper densities, as rarely is there a complete breakdown of the mated-female distance leading to flocked aggregations of pairs. Short-range dispersal or long-range emigration are the possible alternatives.

Observations indicate that mallards will successfully nest under dense pair levels with little apparent effect on fertility but an increasing effect on fecundity, i.e., brood survival. There must, however, be some "optimum" density of pairs per unit of each pond habitat throughout the prairies. Assuming that all environmental factors are yearly constant (which they are not) this would be at some pair level which would result in the maximum number of eggs hatched and young fledged. Because most environmental factors are inter-related the critical or operational level of density cannot be accurately ascertained. There appears to be an increasing scale of negative effects on population growth paralleling density increases.

Optimum pair levels per square mile of habitat would vary yearly and prairie-wide depending on pothole numbers, their sizes, shapes, and vegetational component, predator populations, spring weather, land use, nesting cover, etc. Spacing effects on reproductive efficiency would occur even under "intermediate" population levels and become more severe as pair density increases. Therefore, there is probably some upper limit of pair density beyond which the reproductive efficiency of mallard pairs drops to a level where birth rate does not balance death rate.

Mallards may not be capable of regulating their immediate population density under severe environmental conditions (i.e., droughts). Although emigration to new habitat and use of suboptimum or even lethal brood areas does occur, some mallards can adapt to more dense levels and attempt breeding. The efficiency of production is, however, much reduced indirectly through the effects of spacing and increased pair interactions. On the parkland and grassland study areas it appeared that a varying percentage of spring mallard pairs contribute fewer or no young to the fall population simply because they utilized or were forced into poorer quality habitat.

Drake intolerance, three bird flights (territoriality), and sexual chases (attempted rape flights) are seasonal and usually restricted to short 30-day periods of the 3-month breeding season. Any adaptation that mallards have toward delay of breeding under dense pair levels or toward asynchrony of breeding season, i.e., early, intermediate, or late breeders, would work to the ultimate survival of the species in an area. Smith and Hawkins (1948) had earlier discussed the possibilities of three turn-overs of pairs during a 6-week breeding season. A unit of small pond habitat could theoretically serve an early breeding pair from April 15 to May 15, an intermediate breeder from May 15 to June 15, and a late breeder, perhaps a yearling, from June 15 to July 15 with little or no pair interaction, even though three different pairs utilized the resources of one home range.

SUMMARY

1. The concept of "carrying capacity" has been utilized in the waterfowl literature for years. Although a number of environmental and density-independent limiting factors are recognized, workers have continually suggested that "space" limits pair densities and places an upper limit on numbers of pairs utilizing a unit of pond-type habitat. Carrying capacity has been based on maximum spring pair counts, whereas percentage of hens successful in producing fledged young should, in fact, be the criteria.

Long-term ground studies by J. Stoudt, A. Smith, and others indicate that mallard pair populations fluctuate yearly between some high and low values. The fluctuations may or may not reflect the ability of the habitat to sustain pairs while upper pair limits may be set by a number of factors. Hunting mortality, low homing rates, population shifts, and poor production of young the previous year, all affect spring breeding pair abundance. I suggest a better measure of carrying capacity be clutch sizes and viability of eggs plus the number of fledged young produced or number of hens successful in producing broods to flying stage by a known spring breeding population. Although possessing various spacing mechanisms, mallard pairs will crowd beyond the density which produces maximum numbers of young, especially where habitats deteriorate because of droughts. Spacing mechanisms help place an upper limit on pair densities although upper densities themselves would vary with habitat units. The visible results of high density are not instantaneous but there could be immediate emigration of "surplus" pairs which are unable to compete successfully for breeding space. There may be a lag of a year between attainment of densities beyond the "optimum" and the resultant negative effects on reproduction and general population. The summer decrease, especially on young produced, is theoretically reflected in a decreased density of pairs the following spring. Therefore, enumeration of breeding pairs only may lead to erroneous conclusions about the ability of the habitat to sustain a pair population or its resultant young. Mallard habitat, itself, is relatively unstable and this instability makes accurate measures of carrying capacity difficult.

2. Any correlations between pond numbers and breeding pairs should be tempered with data on pond size, quality, and density. Individual species and not ducks as a whole should be compared. Spacing mechanisms and space requirements are most evident during the prenesting, nesting, and early incubation periods of the mallard, i.e., the period of strongest site attachment. Comparisons of pond numbers and pair populations should be made at a time when the greatest proportion of the population is in these three breeding phases. All species are variable in their time of initiation of nesting and therefore periods of maximum intolerance vary.

3. Pond occupancy or importance values of pond types to a species cannot be measured by one count. Pairs and drakes localize their activity to six to ten ponds during the prenesting through early incubation period but restrict over three-quarters of their movements to one or two ponds (i.e., waiting areas) plus a feeding area and nesting site. Studies in a number of grassland and parkland areas indicate that from one to ten ponds per mallard pair have been available during the period 1950 to 1960. Mallard populations have fluctuated yearly about some mean value in parkland study areas but have become nonexistent in grassland blocks which are completely devoid of spring ponds. The wide yearly population fluctuations in grassland habitats reflect the relative instability of numbers and quality of May and July ponds. Studies of waterfowl habitat selection and species preferences for certain upland cover and pond types, similar to those of Beecher (1942), Svardson (1949), Weller and Spatcher (1965), and Hilden (1965) should be undertaken. We must obtain some accurate measures of mallard environment. What do mallard pairs require to successfully produce optimum numbers of young in parkland, grassland, forest, marsh, lake, or pond habitats, in terms of water acreage, food, nesting cover, dispersion of water and land, etc.

4. Two related systems of density control are postulated, both based on spring spacing mechanisms of mallards. One, in parkland, under intermediate pair levels, operates when increasing pair density leads to more pair interactions forcing a proportion of pairs into suboptimal pond areas where production of young is reduced. The second, in grassland habitat, where high pair aggregations on restricted numbers of ponds lead to high pair coactions around these ponds, forces some hens to nest at great distances (500+ yards) from water to escape hostile and sexual pursuits by drakes (i.e., suboptimal nest sites). Any increased distance hens nest from water leads to lower survival of newly hatched broods to water. Under low and intermediate pair densities, spacing mechanisms function to disperse pairs and nests and this in itself may serve as an anti-predator device. With high pair densities there is in effect an "over-dispersion" of nests with subsequent negative effects on brood survival. In both pond habitats, parkland or grassland, high pair densities associated with poor habitat quality or droughts may lead to emigration of pairs to the forested habitat of the north where again production is reduced or pairs fail to breed (Lidiker 1962, Hansen and McKnight 1964). However, density-independent factors, such as weather and its effect on pond numbers and quality, must also play a major role in control of spring density and emigration to new habitat.

Densities of breeding pairs are controlled in part by the interactions of the pairs themselves, especially where optimum habitat is limited. The critical point at which continuous hostility of pairs leads to competition for limited resources or space, contributing to the lowering of birth rates, varies between habitat types and pond blocks. Other limiting factors besides density and spacing effects tend to control pair levels and brood production in parkland habitat.

ACKNOWLEDGMENTS

I have benefited from discussions of density effects on mallard production with a number of federal, state, and provincial waterfowl biologists. Frank McKinney of the University of Minnesota has been especially helpful. Jerry Stoudt and Allen Smith, U.S. Bureau of Sport Fisheries and Wildlife biologists, have allowed me to quote extensively from unpublished material. Financial support for the 1952 to 1955 parkland study was received from the Delta Waterfowl Research Station, National Research Council of Canada, and University of Wisconsin. The 1956 to 1959 grassland study was conducted under auspices of the Canadian Wildlife Service. Dr. R. A. McCabe of the Department of Wildlife Management, University of Wisconsin, supervised the study. Dr. J. B. Gollop of the Canadian Wildlife Service helped with all phases of the work.

LITERATURE CITED

ANDREWARTHA, H. G., AND L. C. BIRCH. 1954. The distribution and abundance of animals. Univ. Chicago Press, Chicago. 782pp.

BEARD, E. H. 1964. Duck brood behaviour at the Seney National Wildlife Refuge. J. Wildl. Mgmt. 28(3):492–521.

BEECHER, W. J. 1942. Nesting birds and the vegetative substrate. Chicago Ornith. Soc. 69pp.

BEER, J., L. FRENGEL, AND N. HANSEN. 1956. Minimum space requirements of some nesting passerines. Wilson Bull. 68:200–209.

BELLROSE, F. C., JR., T. G. SCOTT, A. S. HAWKINS, AND J. B. LOW. 1961. Sex ratios and age ratios in North American ducks. Illinois Nat. Hist. Surv. Bull. 27(6):391–474.

BURGER, G. V., AND C. G. WEBSTER. 1964. Instant nesting habitat. *In* Waterfowl tomorrow. Ed. J. J. Linduska. U.S. Dep. Int., Washington. Pp. 655–666.

COLLIAS, N. E., AND L. R. JAHN. 1959. Social behavior and breeding success in Canada Geese (*Branta canadensis*) confined under seminatural conditions. Auk 76:478–509.

CONDER, P. J. 1949. Individual distance. Ibis 91:649–655.

CRISSEY, W. F. 1963*a*. Wildlife population management. *In* Hearings before Subcommittee on Fisheries and Wildlife Conservation. 88 Congress, First Session. July 18, 19, August 5, 1963. Serial 88-9. U.S. Govt. Print. Office, Washington, D.C. Pp. 136–166.

———. 1963*b*. Exploitation of migratory waterfowl populations in North America. Proc. First European Meeting on Wildlife Conserv. Pp. 105–120. St. Andrews, The Nature Conservancy, London.

———. 1965. Waterfowl species management: problems and progress. Trans N. Amer. Wildl. and Nat. Res. Conf. 30:229–246.

———. 1969. Prairie potholes from a continental viewpoint. Saskatoon Wetlands Seminar, Can. Wildl. Serv. Rep. 6.

DEUBBERT, H. F. 1966. Island nesting of gadwall in North Dakota. Wilson Bull. 78:12–25.

DIEM, K. L., AND K. H. LU. 1960. Factors influencing waterfowl censuses in the parklands, Alberta, Canada. J. Wildl. Mgmt. 24(2):113–133.

DUCKS AND DRAINAGE IN THE PRAIRIE POTHOLE REGION. 1953. U.S. Fish and Wildlife Service.

DZUBIN, A. 1955. Some evidence of home range in waterfowl. Trans. N. Amer. Wildl. Conf. 20:278–298.

———. 1969. Assessing breeding populations of ducks by ground counts. Saskatoon Wetlands Seminar, Can. Wildl. Serv. Rep. 6.

EDWARDS, R. Y., AND C. D. FOWLE. 1955. The concept of carrying capacity. Trans. N. Amer. Wildl. Conf. 20:589–602.

ERRINGTON, P. L. 1934. Vulnerability of bobwhite populations to predation. Ecology 15:110–127.

———. 1951. Concerning fluctuations in populations of the prolific and widely distributed muskrat. Amer. Nat. 85:273–292.

———. 1956. Factors limiting higher vertebrate populations. Science 124(3216):304–307.

———, AND F. N. HAMERSTROM, JR. 1936. The northern bobwhites winter territory. Iowa Agr. Exp. Sta. Res. Bull. 201:301–443.

EVANS, C. D., AND K. E. BLACK. 1956. Duck production studies on the prairie potholes of South Dakota. U.S. Fish and Wildl. Serv. Spec. Sci. Rep. Wildl. No. 32. 59pp.

———, A. S. HAWKINS, AND W. H. MARSHALL.

1952. Movements of waterfowl broods in Manitoba, U.S. Fish and Wildl. Serv. Spec. Sci. Rep. Wildl. No. 16. 63pp.

GATES, J. M. 1965. Duck nesting and production on farmlands. J. Wildl. Mgmt. 29:515–523.

GIRARD, G. L., 1941. The mallard: its management in western Montana. J. Wildl. Mgmt. 5(3): 233–259.

GOLLOP, J. B. 1954. Waterfowl breeding ground survey—Saskatchewan, 1954. Special Study Area—Kindersley-Eston. *In* Waterfowl populations and breeding conditions, summer 1954. U.S. Fish and Wildl. Serv. Spec. Sci. Rep. Wildl. No. 27, Washington, D.C. Pp. 66–70.

———. 1963. Wetland inventories in western Canada. Int. Union Game Biol. Trans. Congr. VI: 249–264.

GRICE, D., AND J. P. ROGERS. 1965. The wood duck in Massachusetts. Mass. Div. Fisheries and Game. Final Rep. Proj. W-19-R. 96pp.

HAMMOND, M. C., AND G. E. MANN. 1956. Waterfowl nesting islands. J. Wildl. Mgmt. 20: 345–352.

HANSEN, H. A. 1960. Changed status of several species of waterfowl in Alaska. Condor 62(2):136–137.

———, AND D. E. MCKNIGHT. 1964. Emigration of drought displaced ducks to the Arctic. Trans. N. Amer. Wildl. and Nat. Res. Conf. 29:119–127.

HILDEN, O. 1965. Habitat selection in birds. A review. Ann. Zool. Fennici 2(1):53–75.

HINDE, R. A. 1956. The biological significance of territories in birds. Ibis 98:340–369.

———. 1966. Animal behaviour. McGraw-Hill Book Co., London. 534pp.

HOCHBAUM, H. A. 1944. The canvasback on a prairie marsh. Amer. Wildl. Inst., Washington, D.C. 201pp.

HUXLEY, J.S. 1934. A natural experiment on the territorial instinct. British Birds 27:270–277.

JAHN, L. R., AND R. A. HUNT. 1964. Duck and coot ecology and management in Wisconsin. Wisconsin Dep. Conserv. Tech. Bull. No. 33, 212pp.

JENKINS, D. 1961. Social behaviour in the partridge, *Perdix perdix*. Ibis 103a:155–188.

———. 1963. Chick survival in a partridge population. Animal Health 7:6–10.

———, A. WATSON, AND G. R. MILLER. 1963. Population studies on Red Grouse, *Lagopus lagopus scoticus* (Lath.) in northeast Scotland. J. Anim. Ecol. 32:317–376.

KEITH, L. B. 1961. A study of waterfowl ecology on small impoundments in southeastern Alberta. Wildl. Monogr. No. 6. 88pp.

KLOPFER, P. H. 1964. Behavioral aspects of ecology. Prentice-Hall, Englewood Cliffs, N.J. 166pp.

KLUIJVER, H. N., AND L. TINBERGEN. 1953. Territory and the regulation of density in titmice. Arch. Neerl. Zool. 10:265–289.

LACK, D. 1966. Population studies of birds. Clarendon Press, Oxford. 341pp.

LEBRET, T. 1961. The pair formation in the annual cycle of the Mallard, *Anas platyrhynchos* L. Ardea 49:97–158.

LEITCH, W. G. 1954. Waterfowl breeding ground survey of Ducks Unlimited (Canada) in Alberta, Saskatchewan and Manitoba. *In* Waterfowl populations and breeding conditions, summer 1954. U.S. Fish and Wildl. Serv. Spec. Sci. Rep. Wildl. No. 27. Washington, D.C. Pp. 99–105.

LEOPOLD, A. 1933. Game management. Charles Scribner's Sons, New York. 481pp.

LIDIKER, W. J. 1962. Emigration as a possible mechanism permitting the regulation of population below carrying capacity. Amer. Nat. 96:29–33.

LYNCH, J. 1949. Waterfowl breeding ground survey in Saskatchewan, 1949. *In* Waterfowl populations and breeding conditions, summer 1949. U.S. Fish and Wildl. Serv. Spec. Sci. Rep. Wildl. No. 2. Washington, D.C. Pp. 48–82.

LYNCH, J. J., C. D. EVANS, AND V. C. CONOVER. 1963. Inventory of waterfowl environments of prairie Canada. Trans. N. Amer. Wildl. and Nat. Res. Conf. 28:93–109.

MCKINNEY, F. 1965. Spacing and chasing in breeding ducks. Wildfowl Trust Ann. Rep. 16:92–106.

MENDALL, H. L. 1958. The ring-necked duck in the northeast. Univ. of Maine Studies, Sec. Series No. 73. 317pp.

MOYLE, J. B., editor. 1964. Ducks and land use in Minnesota. Minnesota Dep. Conserv. Tech. Bull. No. 8. 140pp.

MUNRO, D. A. 1960. Factors affecting reproduction of the Canada Goose. Proc. Int. Ornith. Cong. 12:542–556.

MURDY, R., AND M. ANDERSON. 1951. Waterfowl breeding ground survey in South Dakota. *In* Waterfowl populations and breeding conditions, summer 1951. U.S. Fish and Wildl. Serv. Spec. Sci. Rep. Wildl. No. 13. Washington, D.C. Pp. 151–158.

NICHOLSON, A. J. 1933. The balance of animal populations. J. Anim. Ecol. 2:132–178.

PHILLIPS, R. E., AND A. VAN TIENHOVEN. 1960. Endocrine factors involved in the failure of Pintail ducks *Anas acuta* to reproduce in captivity. J. Endocrinol. 21:253–261.

———, AND ———. 1962. Some physiological correlates of Pintail reproductive behavior. Condor 64:291–299.

POSPICHAL, G., B. M. CRAM, AND G. PARSONS. 1954. Waterfowl breeding population and production studies. Newdale-Erickson Study Area, Manitoba, 1954. *In* Waterfowl populations and breeding conditions, summer 1954. U.S. Fish and Wildl. Serv. Spec. Sci. Rep. Wildl. No. 27. Pp. 82–91.

RAITASUO, K. 1964. Social behaviour of the mallard

Anas platyrhynchos, in the course of the annual cycle. Papers on Game Res. 24. 72pp.

ROGERS, J. P. 1964. Effect of drought on reproduction of the Lesser Scaup. J. Wildl. Mgmt. 28(2):213–220.

SALYER, J. W. 1962. Effects of drought and land use on prairie nesting ducks. Trans. N. Amer. Wildl. and Nat. Res. Conf. 27:69–79.

SMITH, A. G. 1956. A progress report on the Lousana Waterfowl Study Area, 1953–1955. Lousana, Alberta, Canada. Unpublished report. U.S. Fish and Wildl. Serv., Brigham City, Utah. 89pp.

———. 1959. Progress report. The 1959 waterfowl surveys on the Lousana Study Area, Lousana, Alberta, Canada. U.S. Fish and Wildl. Serv., Wildl. Res. Lab., Denver, Colo. Unpublished mimeo rep. 15pp.

———. 1961. Waterfowl survey of the Lousana Study Area, Alberta, Canada. U.S. Fish and Wildl. Serv., Wildl. Res. Lab., Denver, Colo. Unpublished rep. 33 pp. mimeo.

———. 1964. Progress report. The 1964 waterfowl survey on the Lousana Study Area, Alberta, Canada. U.S. Fish and Wildl. Serv., Wild. Res. Lab., Denver, Colo. Unpublished mimeo rep. 25pp.

SMITH, R. H., AND A. S. HAWKINS. 1948. Appraising waterfowl breeding populations. Trans. N. Amer. Wildl. Conf. 13:57–69.

SMITH, R. I. 1963. The social aspects of reproductive behavior in the Pintail (*Anas acuta acuta*, L.). Ph.D. thesis. Utah State Univ., Logan. 72pp.

SOLOMON, M. E. 1949. The natural control of animal populations. J. Anim. Ecol. 18:1–35.

SOPER, J. D. 1948. Waterfowl breeding conditions in Saskatchewan, 1948. *In* Waterfowl populations and breeding conditions, summer 1948. U.S. Fish and Wildl. Serv. Spec. Sci. Rep. No. 60. Washington, D.C. Pp. 56–75.

SOWLS, L. K. 1955. Prairie ducks. The Stackpole Co., Harrisburg, Pa. 193pp.

STEWART, R. E., A. D. GEIS, AND C. D. EVANS. 1958. Distribution of populations and hunting kill of the canvasback. J. Wildl. Mgmt. 22(4):333–370.

STOUDT, J. H. 1949. Waterfowl breeding ground survey in the Dakotas—1949. *In* Waterfowl populations and breeding conditions, summer 1949. U.S. Fish and Wildl. Serv. Spec. Sci. Rep. Wildl. No. 2. Washington, D.C. Pp. 143–153.

———. 1952*a*. Waterfowl breeding ground survey of Redvers Area, Saskatchewan. *In* Waterfowl populations and breeding conditions, summer 1952. U.S. Fish and Wildl. Serv. Spec. Sci. Rep. No. 21. Washington, D.C. Pp. 52–60.

———. 1952*b*. Waterfowl breeding ground survey in the Dakotas. *In* Waterfowl populations and breeding conditions, summer 1952. U.S. Fish and Wildl. Serv. Spec. Sci. Rep. Wildl. No. 21. Pp. 203–211.

———. 1964. Factors affecting waterfowl breeding populations and the production of young in the parklands of Canada. Ann. Progress Rep. Wildl. Res. Work Unit A-8.2. U.S. Fish and Wildl. Serv., Jamestown, N.D. Unpublished mimeo rep. 55pp.

———. 1965. Habitat requirements of the canvasback during the breeding season. U.S. Fish and Wildl. Serv., Jamestown, N.D. Unpublished mimeo rep. 6pp.

SVARDSON, G. 1949. Competition and habitat selection in birds. Oikos 1:157–174.

TINBERGEN, N. 1957. The functions of territory. Bird Study 4:14–27.

TOMPA, F. S. 1962. Territorial behavior: the main controlling factor of a local Song Sparrow population. Auk 79:687–697.

———. 1963. Behavioral responses of Song Sparrows to different environmental conditions. Proc. Int. Ornith. Cong. 13:729–739.

WEEDEN, J. S. 1965. Territorial behaviour of the Tree Sparrow. Condor 67(3):193–209.

WEIDMANN, U. 1956. Verhaltens studien an der Stockente (*Anas platyrhynchos* L.). I. Das Aktionsystem. Zschr. Tierpsychol. 13:208–271. (English translation, Dep. of State, Ottawa).

WELLER, M. W., AND C. S. SPATCHER. 1965. Role of habitat in the distribution and abundance of marsh birds. Iowa State Univ., Dep of Zool. and Entom. Spec. Rep. No. 43. 31pp.

WYNNE-EDWARDS, V. C. 1962. Animal dispersion in relation to social behaviour. Oliver and Boyd, London. 653pp.

THE ROLE OF ENVIRONMENTAL HETEROGENEITY IN THE REGULATION OF DUCK POPULATIONS

J. H. PATTERSON, Canadian Wildlife Service, Edmonton, Alberta T5J 1S6

Abstract: Behavioral spacing of breeding pairs and the availability of energy resources have been proposed as major factors that regulate duck populations. To compare the relative importance and interaction of the two mechanisms, the seasonal distribution of duck populations was determined in an edaphically heterogeneous system of beaver (*Castor canadensis*) ponds west of Ottawa, Ontario, near a boundary of the Ottawa-St. Lawrence Lowland and the Precambrian Shield. Ponds were selected in a number of geological substrates, so that within a relatively small geographical area a variety of water chemical conditions was represented. The seasonal production of submerged vegetation was a function of water hardness and formed the basis of the assumption that water chemistry could be employed quantitatively as a measure of pond fertility. Numbers of breeding pairs of ducks were dependent only on the amount of surface water available, indicating that the major population regulatory mechanism was behavioral spacing. Fledged ducks, on the other hand, selected fertile wetlands regardless of pond size, indicating that populations were regulated by the availability of energy resources. Habitat requirements of broods were intermediate, because both behavioral escape cover and food availability were important. It is postulated that the different environmental requirements of the three life history stages are an evolutionary adaptation to a temporarily unpredictable environment. The adaptations allow duck populations to maintain equilibrium in a temporarily unpredictable environment, and to attain high population size in a spatially heterogeneous environment.

J. WILDL. MANAGE. 40(1):22–32

Behavioral spacing mechanisms and the availability of food resources are two factors considered to be of major significance in the regulation of duck populations (Evans and Black 1956, Moyle 1956, Hawkins 1964, Jahn and Hunt 1964:16, Dzubin 1969, Dzubin and Gollop 1972). Although there is a considerable body of knowledge concerning duck population dynamics and the regulatory effects of specific environmental factors, there is a lack of consensus on the relative importance, or relationships, of the various factors known to regulate population size. The question of what overall environmental factors regulate duck populations was asked repeatedly by contributors to the Saskatoon Wetlands Seminar published in 1969. In summarizing the seminar, Jahn (1969:177) stated that for progress to be made in waterfowl research "Seasonal needs of the birds must be related to the physical, chemical and biotic features of the ecosystem."

Recent developments in theoretical ecology have stressed the importance of the abiotic environment in determining many basic biotic properties (Loucks 1970, Sanders 1969, Slobodkin and Sanders 1969, Smith 1970, Wiegert and Owen 1971). Such fundamental biological phenomena as niche differentiation and mechanisms of population regulation may evolve in response to environmental characteristics.

The theoretical evidence that mechanisms of ecosystem organization and population regulation can respond to environmental characteristics provided the conceptual basis for this study. Research emphasis was placed on determining environmental parameters that would quantitatively indicate the seasonal requirements of breeding ducks. To this end, a study area was selected that provided a continuum of wetlands ranging from biologically productive hardwater ponds to less productive soft water ponds, yet was small enough to avoid geographical influences on populations. The presence of numerous beaver ponds

Originally published in J. Wildl. Manage. 40(1):22–32, 1976.

overlying a variety of geological substrates provided a natural outdoor laboratory. Ponds of specific chemical regimes and sizes could be selected to provide the treatments necessary for field experiments to determine the environmental requirements of ducks.

This work is from a Ph.D. thesis submitted to Carleton University. Financial support was provided by research contracts and graduate scholarships from the Canadian Wildlife Service and Ontario Graduate Fellowships. I thank L. P. Lefkovitch, Director, Statistical Research Service, Agriculture Canada, for performing the statistical analyses and A. T. Prince, Director, Inland Waters Branch, Environment Canada, whose laboratory conducted the water chemical analyses. E. Grinnell's hard work and enthusiasm as my field assistant are greatly appreciated. I also thank H. G. Merriam and J. D. H. Lambert, Department of Biology, Carleton University, and N. G. Perrett and H. Boyd, Canadian Wildlife Service, for advice during the study. H. G. Merriam, H. Boyd, L. P. Lefkovitch, and W. J. D. Stephen critically reviewed the paper.

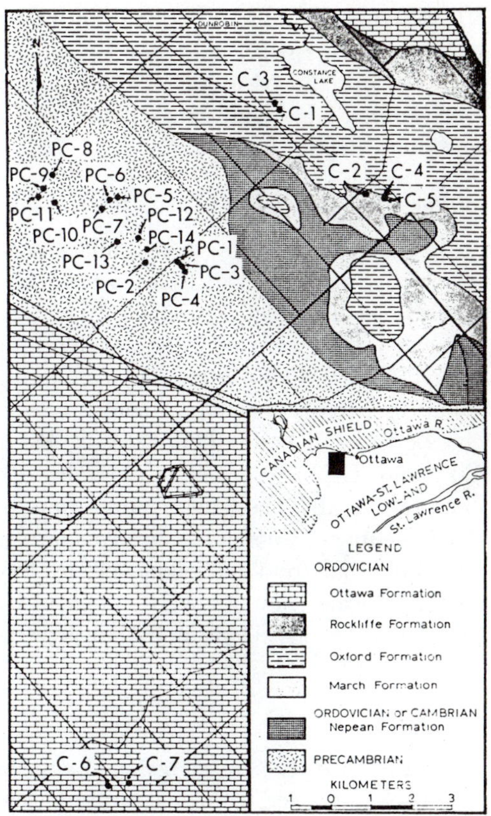

Fig. 1. Bedrock geology of the study area and the location of the 7 carbonate (C) ponds and 14 Precambrian (PC) ponds. After Wilson (1946:map 588A) and Livingstone et al. (1969:map 69-1).

METHODS

The Study Area

Field investigations were conducted during the summers of 1966, 1967, 1969, and 1970 in March and Huntley Townships, Carleton County, Ontario, approximately 32 km west of Ottawa, in an area bounded by 75°55′ to 76°05′W and 45°15′ to 45°25′N. The study area was located in the western portion of the Ottawa-St. Lawrence Lowland close to its contact with the Canadian Shield (Fig. 1). The sedimentary and Precambrian geology were described by Wilson (1946) and Livingstone et al. (1969), respectively.

Study Ponds

Field studies were conducted on 21 beaver ponds selected from the numerous ponds present in the area. Seven carbonate ponds were located in the sedimentary lowland and 14 in the Precambrian Shield (Fig. 1). Five ponds (PC-1, PC-2, PC-3, C-1, and C-3), studied in 1966 and 1967, were selected from either Precambrian or sedimentary areas. As the study progressed, however, it became possible to choose ponds of specific water chemical regimes on the basis of more detailed geological information. More ponds (12 in 1969 and 21 in

1970) were selected to provide a continuum of both water quality and pond size. All ponds were required to have open water, a well defined edge with gentle slope, and a maximum depth of 1.5 m.

Water Chemistry

Water chemical data were collected to provide a quantitative index of habitat fertility. In 1966, 1967, and 1969, 10 surface water samples were collected at monthly intervals from May to August in each pond. In 1970, detailed chemical analyses were conducted on 5 ponds (PC-1, PC-2, PC-3, C-2, and C-3) at 2-week intervals. To characterize the chemical composition of the remaining 16 ponds, 2 surface samples were collected from each pond on 10 July 1970. All water samples were analyzed by the Water Quality Division Laboratory in Ottawa.

Vegetation

To establish the relationship between water chemistry and biological productivity, I estimated the 1970 production of submerged macrophytes in four ponds chosen to represent the range of water chemical conditions in the study area.

Macrophyte production estimates were made from seasonal changes in plant biomass, essentially following the procedures of Westlake (1969). Random numbers were used to select 15 sampling stations in C-3, PC-1, and PC-3, and 20 in PC-2. Collections were made six times between mid-May and mid-August. Macrophyte samples were taken by pushing a 20.3-cm-diameter cylinder into the substrate and removing all the enclosed plant material. In the laboratory, samples were separated into species, encrusted carbonates were removed with 0.02 N HCl, and dry weights were taken. Results were expressed as grams of dry plant material per square meter.

Duck Populations

Ducks were censused weekly from early May through early September each year. Counts usually were made in early morning and were supplemented with observations made during other work. The methods of counting ducks depended on the season and the nature of the pond. The usual technique was to travel around the pond periphery in a canoe with two retrievers working the edge. In counting broods, one man walking on the shoreline with the dogs between him and another man in a canoe proved most efficient. The locations of all duck sightings were recorded on copies of base maps of the ponds. From these data, estimates were made of the total populations of breeding pairs, broods, and late summer fledged and adult ducks. Duck species observed in the study were mallards (*Anas platyrhynchos*), black ducks (*A. rubripes*), blue-winged teals (*A. discors*), green-winged teals (*A. crecca*), wood ducks (*Aix sponsa*), ring-necked ducks (*Aythya collaris*), and hooded mergansers (*Lophodytes cucullatus*).

RESULTS

Water Chemistry

All study ponds contained water of the bicarbonate type but showed considerable pond-to-pond variability in ionic concentrations (Table 1). Cation composition was generally in the order Ca > Mg > Na > K with the exception of ponds C-4, PC-8, and PC-14 where Na > Mg. In relation to the modified standard Wisconsin categories of Brooks and Deevey (1963:134) (HCO_3 < 10 mg/liter, extremely soft; 10–27, soft; 28–84, medium hard; > 84, hard) all carbonate ponds contained hard water. Of the Precambrian ponds, PC-2, PC-8, and PC-14 were near the division of hard and medium hard, PC-1, PC-3, PC-4, PC-9, and

Table 1. Summary of spring 1970 morphometry and mean 1970 surface water chemistry. Chemical values are expressed as mg/liter with the exception of pH.

Pond	Size (ha)	Shore length (m)	pH	Ca	Mg	HCO_3
C-1	1.9	1,250	7.25	40.8	14.0	189.7
C-2	2.6	1,050	7.26	32.9	6.2	101.8
C-3	1.3	1,090	7.39	47.7	14.9	187.2
C-4	3.0	1,378	7.30	33.2	6.3	104.5
C-5	1.9	1,165	7.95	27.4	6.0	84.4
C-6	4.5	1,558	7.30	43.1	8.8	145.3
C-7	6.6	1,493	7.25	43.1	8.9	145.5
PC-1	2.5	2,212	6.67	15.9	1.9	39.3
PC-2	6.2	4,399	6.99	28.2	2.7	80.7
PC-3	1.3	1,296	6.58	12.7	0.8	32.0
PC-4	1.7	1,418	6.60	14.1	1.5	41.8
PC-5	1.0	1,286	6.45	10.7	1.2	26.5
PC-6	0.7	526	6.40	9.3	1.1	22.3
PC-7	2.2	3,019	6.30	7.6	0.7	18.2
PC-8	1.4	920	7.20	24.7	3.2	90.8
PC-9	2.8	1,452	6.60	10.3	2.3	33.9
PC-10	2.2	1,604	6.60	8.4	0.8	25.7
PC-11	1.9	1,557	6.45	8.6	0.8	23.6
PC-12	2.9	1,467	6.55	11.0	1.3	32.0
PC-13	3.9	2,633	6.35	8.6	0.8	22.0
PC-14	5.6	4,101	7.25	27.1	2.7	83.7

PC-12 were medium hard, and the remaining ponds were of the soft water type.

Vegetation

Maximum seasonal standing crops of submerged macrophytes ranged from 44 g/m^2 in PC-1 to 61 g/m^2 in PC-2 (Fig. 2). These data alone would suggest that macrophyte production was similar under all water chemical regimes. However, when growth rates were considered, seasonal production showed a marked response to water chemistry. In hard water C-3, rapid spring growth produced maximum biomass levels in May that persisted for much of the growing season. Growth rates in the other three ponds decreased in proportion to decreasing water hardness. In the most dilute pond, PC-3, maximum production was not reached until July, and there was no biomass plateau (Fig. 2).

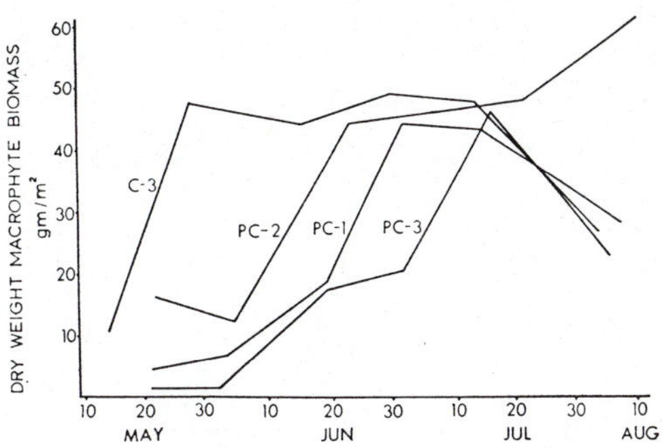

Fig. 2. Seasonal production of total submerged macrophyte biomass (g dry weight/m^2) in the four core ponds, May–August 1970.

When macrophyte production is considered as an energy resource base for consumer organisms, the temporal dimension of biomass provides a more valid expression of productivity than maximum seasonal biomass. In this respect macrophyte productivity is clearly a function of water quality. These data formed the basis of the assumption that, within the study area, water chemistry could be employed quantitatively as a measure of pond fertility.

Duck Populations

Results of the 1966, 1967, and 1969 duck censuses indicated that the patterns of pond utilization varied from pond to pond and were not constant throughout the breeding season (Tables 2, 3). The data suggested that densities of breeding pairs were dispersed evenly on all ponds, whereas broods and fledged ducks were aggregated on the more biologically productive ponds. To further define the apparent spatial and temporal changes in habitat utilization, I designed a field experiment for the 1970 field season. With existing geological and water chemical information it was possible to select a continuum of 21 ponds that varied in both biological production and surface water area where the seasonal pat-

Table 2. Numbers and densities of breeding pairs (BP), broods (BR), and fledged ducks (FL) observed on study ponds in 1966 and 1967. BP census not made on ponds C-1 and C-3 in 1966.

	1966						1967					
	Total			Density/ha			Total			Density/ha		
Pond	BP	BR	FL	BP	BR	FL	BP	BR	FL	BP	BR	FL
C-1		7	95		3.68	73.4	3		40	0.94		16.8
C-3		5	7		5.36	11.6	3	3	38	2.40	2.40	40.8
PC-1	9	4	35	3.58	2.05	26.9	4	3	20	1.61	1.19	10.4
PC-2	8	3	210	1.28	0.62	57.6	6	4	336	0.96	0.64	68.0
PC-3	2	2	13	1.51	2.15	1.7	3		2	2.25		2.2

terns of pond utilization could be monitored (Table 3).

Changes in the environmental requirements of duck populations in the study area were quantified by analyses of variance, i.e., by the method of fitting constants placed in a multiple regression context to relate duck numbers, x (transformed by $\log [x + 1]$), to physical and chemical pond characteristics. To determine whether there was a temporal shift in environmental requirements, I analyzed the three life history stages of the breeding cycle separately. In each of the 3 analyses, data from all 4 years were included, so that a pond that was studied for more than 1 year was treated as a separate pond for each year.

Pond areas and shoreline lengths were calculated for each pond in all years during early May, mid-June, and mid-August to

Table 3. Numbers and densities of breeding pairs (BP), broods (BR), and fledged ducks (FL) observed on study ponds in 1969 and 1970.[a]

	1969						1970					
	Total			Density/ha			Total			Density/ha		
Pond	BP	BR	FL	BP	BR	FL	BP	BR	FL	BP	BR	FL
C-1	4	5	67	1.26	2.10	28.2	2	1	44	1.06	1.75	217.5
C-2		4	101		1.56	64.0	4	4	121	1.56	2.55	124.5
C-3	4	4	18	3.19	3.19	19.3	1	5	51	0.79	5.36	84.0
C-4							4	3	99	1.36	1.48	68.0
C-5							3			1.56		
C-6							6	6	204	1.33	1.33	68.9
C-7							10	10	210	1.53	2.45	78.6
PC-1	5	1	31	2.00	0.40	16.1	8		20	3.19		15.6
PC-2	9	5	316	1.43	0.79	64.0	10	1	349	1.61	0.20	95.9
PC-3	3		2	2.25		2.2	4	1	2	2.92	1.09	2.7
PC-4	2	1	16	1.19	0.59	17.3	1			0.59		
PC-5	5	2	13	4.94	1.98	16.8	2		3	1.98		7.4
PC-6	1		1	1.38		5.9	1			1.38		
PC-7	9	2	16	4.05	0.89	8.9	5	1	19	2.25	0.54	12.1
PC-8	4	4	29	2.92	3.66	44.7	3	2	25	2.17	1.83	38.5
PC-9							6	5	38	2.13	1.75	13.8
PC-10							4		16	0.35		8.2
PC-11							5	2	16	2.62	1.06	9.4
PC-12							4	2	26	1.38	1.06	12.6
PC-13							2	2	20	0.52	0.54	5.9
PC-14							10	5	47	1.78	1.36	17.1

[a] In 1969 ponds C-4, 5, 6, 7 and PC-9, 10, 11, 12, 13, 14 not examined; BP census not made on pond C-2. In 1970 BP and FL censuses not made on pond C-5.

Table 4. Summary of analyses of variance for the three life history stages of ducks on the study area.[a]

Source of variation	Variance ratio		
	Breeding pairs	Broods	Fledged ducks
Area	+117.16***	-2.62	-0.35
Shore length	-0.96	+4.11*	+1.06
Calcium	-8.082**	+16.75***	+21.14***
Magnesium	+2.65	+0.72	-10.41**
Iron	-3.11	-2.67	-7.49**
Manganese	+0.16	-6.96*	-0.68
Chloride	-8.93**	-7.74**	-9.83**
Silica	+2.59	+6.92*	+6.74*
Year	3.09	1.18	6.23*
Season	154.97***	61.24**	99.40***
Reduction in sum of squares (%)	86.4	73.5	80.2

[a] Variance ratios are presented for sources of variation which were significant in one or more of the analyses. Signs are those of the associated partial regression coefficients.
* $P < 0.05$.
** $P < 0.01$.
*** $P < 0.001$.

represent conditions during the peak periods of habitat selection by breeding pairs, broods, and fledged ducks, respectively.

Conversely, it did not appear necessary to establish water chemical concentrations separately for the three periods. It was assumed that the biological characteristics of the ponds that would be important to ducks would integrate the water chemical conditions over the season. Thus, in the 1966, 1967, and 1969 ponds, and the five 1970 core ponds, the water chemical concentrations used in the analyses were the seasonal means of surface samples. The values for the remaining 1970 ponds were the means of two surface samples from each pond, collected on 10 July 1970. The chemical variables employed in the analyses were calcium, magnesium, sodium, potassium, total iron, total manganese, chloride, nitrate, and silica, all expressed as mg/liter.

A summary of the three analyses is given in Table 4. The high positive *F* value for pond area in the breeding pair analysis indicated the strong relationship between pair numbers and pond size. Associated with this response, however, were significant negative relationships with calcium and chloride. Since concentrations of both of these ions were lower in the soft water ponds, the negative relationships indicated a trend towards selection of more sterile waters by breeding pairs.

Significant factors in the analysis for broods were distinct from those for pairs (Table 4). Brood numbers were positively related to concentrations of calcium and silica, and negatively related to total manganese, indicating selection of harder water ponds. Since brood numbers were high in some of the non-dolomitic ponds that have low chloride concentrations, there was a negative relationship between brood numbers and chloride. Although broods did select more fertile ponds, the positive relationship with shoreline length indicated that they still were associated with pond morphometry.

The distribution of fledged ducks was independent of the morphometric characteristics of the ponds (Table 4). The positive associations with calcium and silica and the negative relationship with iron reflected the selection of harder water ponds. There were also negative relationships with magnesium and chloride, both of which had low concentrations in the non-dolomitic hard water ponds, C-6 and C-7. The significant year effect in this analysis indicated that there was some annual variation in the fledged duck populations. However, the relatively high total reduction in sums of squares for the three analyses indicated that the selected environmental characteristics accounted for a large proportion of the variability in the distribution of duck populations within the study area.

DISCUSSION

The results showed a definite seasonal shift in the environmental requirements of duck populations. The number of breeding pairs that a given pond can accommodate is primarily a function of pond surface area. There was no evidence of selection of edaphically rich wetlands. The fact that pair densities were relatively constant in a spatially heterogeneous environment indicated dispersion of the population by behavioral spacing. Although territoriality and the resulting spacing of breeding ducks generally are acknowledged, there are various interpretations of the effects on populations. A common conclusion is that ducks prefer fertile wetlands and inhabit less fertile areas only when they are forced into them by overcrowding. In Wisconsin, where breeding populations were low as a result of heavy hunting pressure, Jessen et al. (1964) concluded that breeding pairs selected more fertile habitats. However, in the Waubay region of South Dakota, Evans and Black (1956) found that breeding ducks were evenly dispersed over all available habitat. Dzubin (1969) concluded that spacing mechanisms function to disperse pairs and nests, but usually result in the utilization of less stable habitat with resulting decreased production. According to Dzubin and Gollop (1972), spacing behavior dispersed mallard breeding pairs in the numerous small ponds of the prairie parkland and may have played an important role in determining breeding densities. However, they suggested that spacing mechanisms played a minor role in influencing continental reproductive output.

In this study, it can be concluded that spacing mechanisms dispersed the breeding pair population in relation to the availability of water, and that habitat fertility was not a factor in pond selection by pairs.

In contrast with the evenly dispersed breeding pairs, brood densities were highest on the harder water ponds. The positive relationship established between submerged macrophyte productivity and water hardness reflects brood selection of the more biologically productive wetlands in response to greater availability of food.

Although the distribution of broods showed a movement to more fertile ponds, the selection was not complete. There was an associated relationship with shoreline length, which indicated the behavioral requirement of broods for escape cover. Most brood sightings were near the shoreline, in or close to cover of some sort. Evans and Black (1956) concluded that the selection of brood rearing habitat depended on the availability of a means of escape from predators. In the case of dabbling ducks, this was furnished primarily by emergent vegetation.

By late summer, fledged and adult ducks showed an even stronger selection of fertile ponds than did broods. Highest densities consistently were found on the hard and medium-hard water ponds, regardless of pond size or configuration. The conclusion from these data is that wetland fertility is

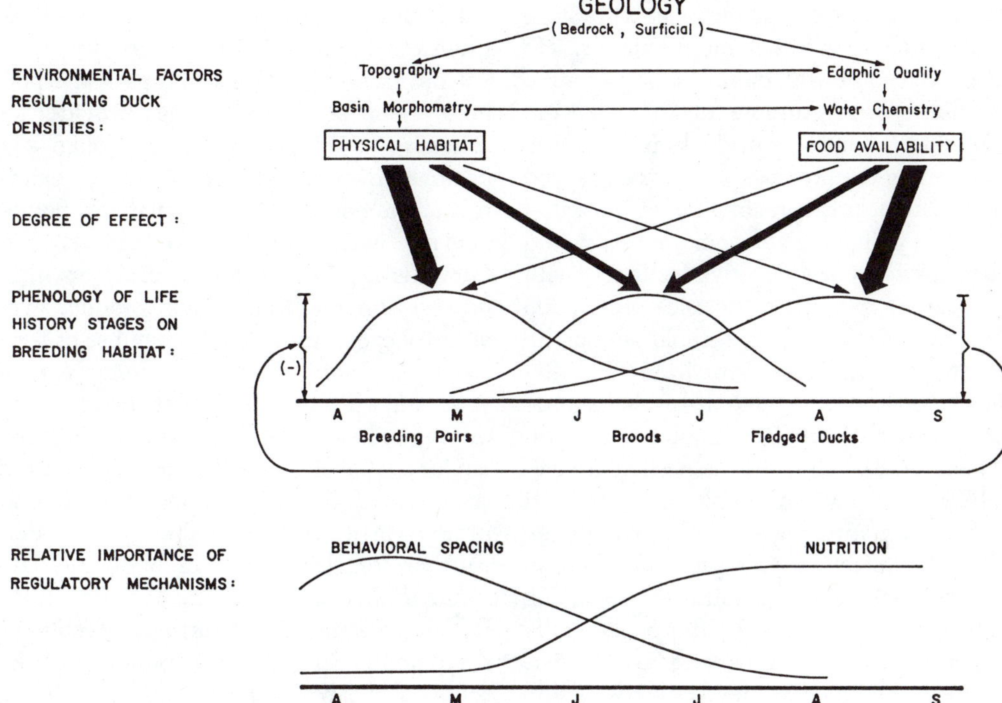

Fig. 3. A conceptual model describing the environmental regulation of duck populations in the study area.

the most important environmental factor in habitat selection by fledged ducks.

A MODEL OF DUCK POPULATION REGULATION

The quantification of seasonal changes in the environmental requirements of breeding ducks was facilitated by the unique nature of the study area. The close juxtaposition of ponds of different water chemical conditions provided an array of habitat types in which seasonal patterns of habitat selection could be documented. However, the agreement of the results with concepts in the waterfowl literature suggests that these patterns are not unique to the study area, but, in general terms, reflect an overall strategy of population regulation evolved by dabbling ducks.

An interpretation of such a strategy, and a seasonal differentiation of component factors in the environmental regulation of dabbling duck populations, is shown in the conceptual model in Fig. 3. The purpose of the model is to illustrate, in the most general of terms, that the environmental requirements of each stage of the reproductive cycle are distinct, yet they interact to influence overall population regulation. Although the components of the model are derived from the results of this study, the phenomenon of homing provides the key mechanism which links together the temporally changing regulatory factors. Homing of breeding female ducks to the area in which they were fledged frequently has been documented with banded birds (Hochbaum 1944:62, Sowls 1955:25, Dzubin and Gollop 1972). In a regional population context Smith (1969) considered homing to be an important factor equilibrating local populations to habitat conditions. He concluded that the numbers of potential breeding pairs returning to an area were related to the number of ducks produced in that area in the previous year. As expressed in the model, the regulation of potential breeding pair populations in an area would be in the form of a negative feedback, with a 1-year lag, relative to the duck production that the habitat resources could support in the intervening year. Actual pair densities then would be regulated by behavioral spacing mechanisms in relation to the available breeding habitat of the particular year.

In this study area, the seasonal shift in habitat requirements allows a high degree of utilization of a spatially heterogeneous system of wetlands. By not being confined to fertile ponds, the behaviorally dispersed breeding pairs can make full use of even the most sterile wetlands where they can have isolation from other pairs. The broods and fledged ducks, which require more abundant food resources, then can be accommodated on the more fertile waters in the area. The occupancy of all study ponds by breeding pairs (mean of 1.71/ha water in 1970) indicates the high degree of utilization of the area as a whole.

In the vast igneous areas of the Precambrian Shield, water bodies are characterized by relatively stable water levels, low biological productivity, and low densities of breeding ducks (Wellein and Lumsden 1964). The concepts developed in this study suggest that the major factor regulating populations in the Shield would be the lack of energy resources for broods and fledged ducks. Food regulation of duck production would result in relatively low numbers of birds returning in the spring to breed. Thus, breeding pair densities likely would be below levels where behavioral spacing mechanisms would influence population size significantly.

Conversely, the prairie and parkland pothole region of North America provides an extensive regional system of biologically productive wetlands for breeding waterfowl. The pothole region is relatively homogeneous with respect to wetland fertility, but it is far from being a stable environment. Climatic fluctuations produce wet and dry cycles in which the number of wetlands can vary drastically from year to year and within years. Under drought conditions, when water becomes limiting, behavioral spacing would function to keep the successful breeding population low, in proportion to the availability of water. Further loss of habitat in mid- and late summer would affect brood survival to fledging and result in a further reduction of the potential breeding pair populations the following year. Thus, regulation at all life history stages could function to rapidly equilibrate the population with declining habitat resources. Conversely, in a period of increasing water availability, high rates of production and homing would cause the population to expand rapidly to fill the available habitat.

The validity of this type of relationship is illustrated by the high annual correlation between available water in the pothole region and the size of the breeding population (Crissey 1969). If the population were not regulated behaviorally, then in dry years, when there are fewer wetlands, large breeding populations would be crowded into the remaining habitat with resultant heavy mortality rates of young ducks and possible damage to the environment.

Recent developments in theoretical ecology have stressed the importance of the nature of the abiotic environment in determining many basic ecological functions

(Loucks 1970, Sanders 1969, Slobodkin and Sanders 1969, Smith 1970, Wiegert and Owen 1971). Such fundamental biological phenomena as niche differentiation and mechanisms of population regulation may evolve in response to environmental characteristics. I suggest that the strategy of population regulation of dabbling ducks evolved as an interrelated set of mechanisms which, in combination, serve to maintain duck populations in equilibrium with an unpredictable environment.

The evolutionary importance of temporal environmental variability to ecosystems has been stressed by Odum (1969) and Loucks (1970). Loucks advanced the hypothesis that evolution in ecosystems has brought about an adaptation to both heterogeneous environments and to a repeating pattern of changing environments. He suggested that high levels of ecosystem diversity and productivity can be due to temporal environmental heterogeneity which triggers the recycling and rejuvenation of the biotic systems. Loucks concluded that the periodicity of such environmental changes can range from several centuries in the northern lake forest to a few decades or even annually in the grasslands.

Wetland ecosystems in the pothole region, where the majority of North American ducks are produced, illustrate Loucks' hypothesis. Wetlands in this fertile area are highly productive. Succession here should be short-lived. However, environmental change in the form of drought cycles results in the drying out of many of the basins, and the ecosystems are periodically rejuvenated. Thus, the wetlands are maintained at early successional stages and provide productive breeding habitat for ducks.

Sanders (1969) and Slobodkin and Sanders (1969) characterized such physically controlled and unpredictable ecosystems as being low in species diversity and unstable. Because of the changing environment, component species have broad, flexible niches. Slobodkin and Sanders (1969: 88) stated that "for species in 'unpredictable' environments it is generally the case that different life history stages show different sensitivity to environmental changes."

The long term persistence and high productivity of prairie wetland ecosystems, which provide most of the breeding habitat for dabbling ducks, is due in great part to temporal environmental heterogeneity. Such wetlands are dependent on periodic climatic changes, and, as such, they are unpredictable ecosystems. I consider the seasonal variations in the environmental requirements of the different life history stages of dabbling ducks to be an evolutionary adaptation to temporal environmental heterogeneity that allows rapid equilibration of populations with habitat availability. While such a strategy of population regulation may have evolved in a temporally heterogeneous environment, it allows populations to exist at relatively high densities in a spatially heterogeneous environment, fully utilizing both the available water area and food resources.

LITERATURE CITED

BROOKS, J. L., AND E. S. DEEVEY, JR. 1963. New England. Pages 117–162 *in* D. G. Frey, ed. Limnology of North America. University of Wisconsin Press, Madison.

CRISSEY, W. F. 1969. Prairie potholes from a continental viewpoint. Pages 161–171 *in* Saskatoon wetlands seminar. Can. Wildl. Serv. Rep. Ser. 6.

DZUBIN, A. 1969. Comments on carrying capacity of small ponds for ducks and possible effects of density on mallard production. Pages 138–171 *in* Saskatoon wetlands seminar. Can. Wildl. Serv. Rep. Ser. 6.

———, AND J. B. GOLLOP. 1972. Aspects of mallard breeding ecology in Canadian parkland and grassland. Pages 113–151 *in* Population ecology of migratory birds: a symposium. U.S. Fish Wildl. Serv. Wildl. Res. Rep. 2.

EVANS, C. D., AND K. E. BLACK. 1956. Duck production studies on the prairie potholes of South Dakota. U.S. Fish Wildl. Serv. Spec. Sci. Rep. Wildl. 32. 59pp.

HAWKINS, A. S. 1964. Mississippi flyway. Pages 185–207 *in* J. P. Linduska, ed. Waterfowl tomorrow. U.S. Government Printing Office, Washington, D.C.

HOCHBAUM, H. A. 1944. The canvasback on a prairie marsh. The American Wildlife Institute, Washington, D.C. 201pp.

JAHN, L. R. 1969. Summary: Part III. Pages 172–177 *in* Saskatoon wetlands seminar. Can. Wildl. Serv. Rep. Ser. 6.

———, AND R. A. HUNT. 1964. Duck and coot ecology and management in Wisconsin. Wisconsin Dept. Conserv. Tech. Bull. 33. 212pp.

JESSEN, R. L., J. P. LINDMEIER, AND R. E. FARMES. 1964. A study of duck nesting and production as related to land use in Mahnomen County, Minnesota. Pages 26–85 *in* J. B. Moyle, ed. Ducks and land use in Minnesota. Minnesota Dept. Conserv. Tech. Bull. 8.

LIVINGSTONE, K. W., P. A. HILL, AND J. I. KIRWAN. 1969. Preliminary map and notes Arnprior, Ontario, Canada. Carleton Univ. Geological Paper 69-1. 13pp.

LOUCKS, O. L. 1970. Evolution of diversity, efficiency, and community stability. Am. Zool. 10(1):17–25.

MOYLE, J. B. 1956. Relationships between the chemistry of Minnesota surface waters and wildlife management. J. Wildl. Manage. 20(3):303–320.

ODUM, E. P. 1969. The strategy of ecosystem development. Science 164(3877):262–270.

SANDERS, H. L. 1969. Benthic marine diversity and the stability-time hypothesis. Pages 71–81 *in* Diversity and stability in ecological systems. Brookhaven Symp. Biol. 22.

SLOBODKIN, L. B., AND H. L. SANDERS. 1969. On the contribution of environmental predictability to species diversity. Pages 82–95 *in* Diversity and stability in ecological systems. Brookhaven Symp. Biol. 22.

SMITH, A. G. 1969. Waterfowl-habitat relationships on the Lousana, Alberta, waterfowl study area. Pages 116–122 *in* Saskatoon wetlands seminar. Can. Wildl. Serv. Rep. Ser. 6.

SMITH, F. E. 1970. Analysis of ecosystems. Pages 7–18 *in* D. E. Reichle, ed. Analysis of temperate forest ecosystems. Springer-Verlag, New York.

SOWLS, L. K. 1955. Prairie ducks. The Stackpole Co., Harrisburg, Pa., and The Wildlife Management Institute, Washington, D.C. 193pp.

WELLEIN, E. G., AND H. G. LUMSDEN. 1964. Northern forests and tundra. Pages 67–76 *in* J. P. Linduska, ed. Waterfowl tomorrow. U.S. Government Printing Office, Washington, D.C.

WESTLAKE, D. F. 1969. Primary production rates from changes in biomass. Macrophytes. Pages 103–107 *in* R. A. Vollenweider, ed. A manual on methods for measuring primary production in aquatic environments. I.B.P. Handb. 12. Blackwell Scientific Publications, Oxford.

WIEGERT, R. G., AND D. F. OWEN. 1971. Trophic structure, available resources and population density in terrestrial vs. aquatic ecosystems. J. Theor. Biol. 30(1):69–81.

WILSON, A. E. 1946. Geology of the Ottawa-St. Lawrence Lowland, Ontario and Quebec. Geol. Surv. Canada Mem. 241. 66pp.

Accepted 16 September 1975.

WATERFOWL NESTING ISLANDS[1]

M. C. HAMMOND AND G. E. MANN, U.S. Fish and Wildlife Service, Upham, North Dakota, and Fergus Falls, Minnesota

There has recently been an increasing amount of interest in the development of islands for nesting waterfowl, as evidenced by inquiries received by the Fish and Wildlife Service.

Questions have primarily involved the following: (1) island construction—size, shape, location, and cost; (2) the use that might be expected; (3) values of points or other land masses surrounded by a channel or moat; (4) territorial characteristics of nesting concentrations; and (5) the relationships between island waterfowl nesting concentrations and reduction of habitat, as through drainage.

These notes have assembled the data available on some 70 Lower Souris National Wildlife Refuge (North Dakota) islands constructed in 1935 and general observations made by the senior author in North Dakota, South Dakota, Nebraska, and the Prairie Provinces.

It is well established that nesting waterfowl are frequently attracted to islands in numbers seldom found on the mainlands. Bent (1923, 1925) describes this habit for many wildfowl species; Gross (1945) reported concentrations of nesting black ducks (*Anas rubripes*) on the outer coastal islands of Maine; Miller and Collins (1954) recorded heavy use of islands by ducks on the Tule Lake and Lower Klamath National Wildlife refuges. There are many examples for the Canada Goose (*Branta canadensis*) (Jensen and Nelson *in* Williams, *et al.*, 1948; Craighead and Craighead, 1949; Kossack, 1950; Miller and Collins, 1953; and Naylor, 1953). Nevertheless, the simple fact that a land mass is surrounded by water does not guarantee its acceptance by ducks and geese or the success of nesting upon it.

Factors Responsible for Island-nesting Concentrations

There is some question as to whether or not islands hold any basic attractiveness as a habitat type and if they are instinctively selected as optimum nesting sites. F. C. R. Jourdain (in notes supplied Bent, 1925:201) suggests that certain geese have acquired the habit of nesting in inaccessible places to avoid molestation by foxes in the Arctic. We may say, at least, that geese and many ducks quickly learn to take advantage of the sites where predation is avoided.

Certain characteristics of many true islands have obvious values. Among them are: (1) relative freedom from disturbances by mammals or birds; (2) a greater capacity for territorial occupancy because of the high ratio of water-land edge to land mass; and (3) close proximity of water, food, loafing (or lookout) sites, and nesting cover.

When nest losses are low for a period of several years, high production may lead to good annual survival and, through "homing" (Sowls, 1949), increase the number of potential nesting birds.

The gradual build-up of populations may reach a point where a scarcity of good nest sites occurs, and heavy use is made of those available. This sequence was observed with the Lower Souris Canada goose flock which originated from 11 hand-raised, pinioned pairs acquired in 1937 and 28 full-winged, wild-captured birds released in 1939 (Hammond, 1950).

[1] Some of the field data were recorded by C. J. Henry and Donald V. Gray, Fish and Wildlife Service. We also wish to acknowledge suggestions and editorial advice by H. A. Hochbaum and Frank McKinney, Delta Waterfowl Research Station; Lyle K. Sowls, Arizona Coop. Wildl. Res. Unit, Univ. of Arizona; Mrs. Margaret M. Nice, Chicago, Ill.; Laurence R. Jahn, Wisconsin Conservation Dept.; C. T. Rollings, J. D. Smith and J. J. Wilson of the Fish and Wildlife Service; and J. W. Kimball, Minnesota Department of Conservation.

Originally published in J. Wildl. Manage. 20(4):345–352, 1956.

Goose nesting in early years was dispersed to one, or occasionally two, nests per island. If two per area, they occurred 200 to 300 feet or more apart. By 1953, with a breeding population of about 65 pairs, the birds had adjusted to relatively close nesting, in a few instances 50 to 60 feet apart (7 to 12 nests per island, about 16 per acre). The increasing tolerance extended through 8 years, the recent period of rapid population increase.

There has been a decided tendency for ducks to concentrate on only a few of the open-water islands. While most may have 10 to 30 nests, only two are known to have had a hundred or more. We suspect that social attractions play an important part in this and that the territorial and breeding displays may tend to draw pairs from surrounding areas, once the aggregations reach a certain level (Armstrong, 1947:175-182, 344-347).

Gadwalls (*Anas strepera*) seem particularly responsive to this phenomenon (Bent, 1923:77-79; Miller and Collins, 1954:31; and, we suspect, the Bear River Refuge concentrations described by Williams and Marshall, 1938).

As the population builds up, there is constriction of (1) territorial activity by birds occupying the island margin and (2) use of other areas during the brief period required for coition. The eventual limits are reached through (1) increasing social conflicts and attending egg loss; (2) exodus of pairs to other islands or mainland areas for nesting purposes; (3) gradually increasing losses to minor predators; and (4) periodic catastrophic loss, e.g., predation, flooding, and weather.

Our information about the various aspects of gadwall territoriality was rather sketchy. It did appear that birds from the margins of the impoundment flew to the islands to nest. The frequent pursuits by "resident" drakes failed to prevent the new-coming hens from nesting.

TABLE 1. — SPECIES COMPOSITION OF DUCK NESTS FOUND ON ISLANDS OF LOWER SOURIS NATIONAL WILDLIFE REFUGE (1935-1953)[1]

Species	Number of nests	Per cent
Gadwall (*Anas strepera*)	356	61
Mallard (*Anas platyrhynchos*)	135	23
Pintail (*Anas acuta*)	45	8
Scaup (*Aythya affinis*)	13	2
Redhead (*Aythya americana*)	12	2
Blue-winged teal (*Anas discors*)	9	
American widgeon (*Mareca americana*)	3	
Shoveller (*Spatula clypeata*)	3	3
Canvas-back (*Aythya valisineria*)	2	
Ruddy duck (*Oxyura jamaicensis*)	2	
Totals	580	99

[1] In the North Dakota duck-breeding population blue-wings and pintails are about equal in abundance, followed by mallards, shovellers, and gadwalls (Hjelle, *in* Crissey, 1951:149).

SPECIES COMPOSITION

While all resident waterfowl species commonly nest on islands, it appears that geese and gadwalls have the greatest inclination to attain unusual densities. Mallards (*Anas platyrhynchos*), and sometimes pintails (*A. acuta*), reach greater proportions than would be expected from their normal behavior in other environments (Table 1). Bent (1923: 90) describes a small concentration of baldpates (*Mareca americana*). The numbers of blue-wings (*Anas discors*) and shovellers (*Spatula clypeata*) he found on the Crane Lake island (p. 113) are about what might be expected on the basis of the length of shoreline involved.

Redheads (*Aythya americana*) and lesser scaup ducks (*A. affinis*) are attracted to the smaller islands. The few redhead dry-land nesting sites we have observed were only a foot or so from the water's edge on mainland areas. Island nests are frequently found 15 to 20 feet from water and on Lacreek Refuge (South Dakota) an extreme distance of 50 feet was noted by Hammond. A series of small mounds thrown up in the early drainage of the Souris marshes provides secure sites a foot or so above the water line for many nesting redheads. In Bent (*loc. cit.*, 208, 218) are further descriptions of island-nesting scaup.

Greater scaups (*Aythya marila*) and oldsquaws (*Clangula hyemalis*) were apparently the commonest island nesters on Mývatn, a lake in northeastern Iceland (Scott, 1952: 125-132).

These notes would indicate that only moderate use of islands would normally be expected for most ducks. But where gadwalls were common, there would be a good possibility of finding the spectacular concentrations. Considering their frequent use by this species, the Canada goose, mallards, scaups, and redheads, it would seem that island construction would often be an important management practice.

VEGETATION

Preferred goose-nesting sites are usually so located that vegetative cover seems of minor importance. At times the cover may be too dense and tall; however, it may be used as a base upon which the nest is constructed. Nests are often built upon bare ground (Miller and Collins, 1953:391; Naylor, 1953; Kossack, 1950; Yocom, 1952; Craighead and Craighead, 1949).

The last-mentioned writers found some nests that were well concealed (p. 54). The only well-concealed nests found on Lower Souris were two known renestings in 1954. The original nests were on the island crest in low, dead weeds and grass. Following their destruction, the new nestings were located 5 feet and about 100 feet away in depressions, in one case just inside the edge of a moderately dense *Phragmites* patch. Laying was still in progress when the nests were found, and the eggs were completely covered with about two inches of dead leaves and stems.

Yocom (1952) noted that Canadas on the Snake River (Washington) "... show a preference for nest sites near logs or driftwood." In 1956 a few Lower Souris geese built their nests on small hay piles placed on several bare, newly constructed islands.

In general, cover also seemed of secondary importance to the common island-nesting ducks. Where there was a choice between dense weeds (Canada thistle, *Cirsium arvense,* and nettle, *Urtica procera*) and grass, the weeds were clearly preferred by both gadwalls and mallards. With a choice between these weeds and open, thinly vegetated sites, the dense cover was also preferred. On all islands many nests were started when cover was insufficient to provide much screening for them. Miller and Collins (1954:34-35) also recorded a preference for cover sites, such as nettle, offering good concealment for gadwalls and mallards.

Management of the Lower Souris islands has principally involved the removal of willow (*Salix* spp.) growth by cutting and spraying with weed killers. Natural revegetation by weeds and grasses has been adequate to prevent serious top erosion from rains.

Extensive beds of pondweed (*Potamogeton* spp.) in the shallow waters surrounding the islands may have been important in their concentrated use. An abundance of food has been available during the gadwall nesting season.

NESTING LOSSES

Island nesters are subject to the same vagaries of the weather as those birds nesting on the mainland. In addition there is sometimes a greater danger from flooding. Errington (1946: 175-177) discusses the hazards to which island- and colonial-nesting birds may be subjected. Predation remains the primary mortality factor, whether it occurs periodically through accidental stranding or invasion of the island by a mammal, or through chronic susceptibility to egg-eating birds.

Bent (1923:78-79) describes an island (approximately 9 acres in size) in Crane Lake, Saskatchewan, visited with H. K. Job in June 1905. This supported an estimated 150 pairs of nesting ducks. In 1906 he found the site practically deserted and evidence that a coyote (*Canis latrans*) living there had ". . . cleaned out all of the nests, and driven the ducks away."

Salter (*in* Williams, *et al.*, 1950: 126-127) found high mammalian nest predation on islands in the Glenns Ferry area of the Snake River, Idaho, in 1950.

Kalmbach (1937:4, 26) found crows (*Corvus brachyrhynchos*) to be the principal hazard to island-nesting ducks in the Cooking Lake District of Alberta. These islands either furnished crow-nesting sites or were regularly visited by crows from the mainland one-half or one mile away.

On June 30, 1936, C. J. Henry, E. R. Kalmbach, W. F. Kubichek, and Neil Hotchkiss found 63 birds [including 59 ducks and coots (*Fulica americana*)] and 4 mammals killed by one or more weasels (*Mustela frenata*) stranded on a small Lower Souris island. In later years, mink (*Mustela vison*), when present, usually preyed heavily upon nesting ducks and ducklings. Skunks (*Mephitis mephitis*), badgers (*Taxidea taxus*), raccoons (*Procyon lotor*), foxes (*Vulpes fulva*), and crows were relatively efficient in excluding nesting from islands accessible to them.

During a late freeze on April 16, 17, and 18, 1953, a fox (or foxes) crossed about one-fourth mile of new thin ice to reach Ding Island where they destroyed 11 of 12 active goose nests. In that year low water levels in Unit 326 permitted access to several islands. On these, all observed goose nests were destroyed.

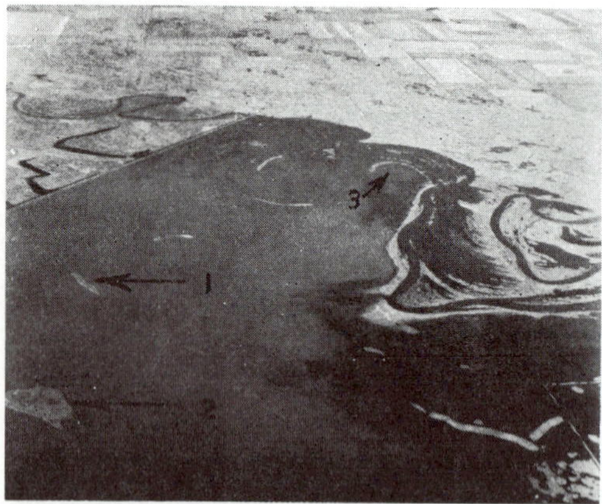

FIG. 1. Aerial view of Gadwall (1) and Ding (2) islands, Lower Souris Refuge. Islands close to bars or marsh (3) are accessible to predators and seldom have successful nesting.

While the nests of many colonial species are relatively secure as long as they are attended by the adults, when the latter are forced to leave their nests, the exposed eggs are subject to increased losses from gulls (*Larus* spp.) and crows. Under normal circumstances a pair of geese can successfully defend their nest against crows and the smaller mammals. We have had reported instances of geese driving crows away from the nest site and of a mallard hen defending its nest against an attack by crows.

Most large marshes in the Prairie States and Provinces probably support a wider variety and greater number of egg-eating mammals and birds than is found in many other agricultural districts of the continent. Since the recent drought (1930's), raccoons and foxes have increased and extended their ranges into all suitable habitat.

When nest predators are naturally in low numbers, or where intensive predator control is carried on, islands may not be of great importance. It appears, however, that the low rate of reproduction and heavy hunting pressure operating with geese require high nesting success if populations are to attain satisfactory levels in settled areas.

Colonial island-nesting birds, such as gulls, pelicans (*Pelecanus erythrorhynchos*), and cormorants (*Phalacrocorax auritus*) frequently prevent waterfowl from nesting. Leon Snyder (interview) described the regular desertion of nests by geese as soon as pelicans began nesting in numbers (Bowdoin National Wildlife Refuge, Malta, Montana). Goose nests at Lower Souris were usually near hatching by the time cormorants and great blue herons (*Ardea herodias*) began nesting, however. Duck nests are usually not found on the island used by nesting pelicans on Lacreek Refuge.

The losses that arise from increasing social tension as a nesting population builds up are often severe. Naylor (1953:90-91) describes an island 30 by 75 yards in dimensions, upon which 16 of 31 goose nests were deserted, mostly due to the overcrowded condition. Successful pairs often left the nest with two or three young and deserted the remaining eggs. Some of the nests were as close as 6 feet. Miller and Collins (1953:392) reported: "Desertion, the greatest factor causing nest failure in this study, was attributed mainly to intraspecific strife on heavily populated islands where competition for nest sites was acute. The desertion of nests on crowded islands amounted to 13 nests or 56.6 per cent of the total nests deserted."

Kossack (1950:638) observed 10 and 12 goose nests per acre on a 2.3-acre island in 1945 and 1946. "The shortest distance between nests was 40 feet and the longest 90 feet." Desertions accounted for 5 of 24 nests in 1945, ". . . because of floods, crows, or unknown reasons." In 1946, with 28 pairs ". . . one nest was broken up by a pair trying to reclaim their nest site of 1945, and one nest was deserted." He concluded that, except for these instances, the birds nested in harmony.

On mainland areas Johnson (1947:24) found that Canada geese should not be crowded beyond one-half or one acre per pair.

Only 4 of 94 Lower Souris goose nestings were deserted in 1951 and 1952 (some were 50 to 60 feet apart).

Over a period of time, geese will adjust to very close quarters, apparently depending upon the satisfactory establishment of the flock social order. Leading to this point, nestings separated by only short distances seem to result in appreciable amounts of desertion.

With Lower Souris island duck-nesting concentrations, desertions amounted to 8 per cent (29 of 370 nests) during 1947 and 1953. Mainland rates for dabblers have regularly been 3 to 4 per cent or less. Accompanying the increased losses to this factor are layings by more than one hen in a single nest, successful incubation of only part of the multiple clutches, irregularities in incubation by some hens, and an increased incidence of dropped eggs.

Infertile eggs and dead embryos comprised 16 per cent of the total eggs in a sample of 90 terminated island gadwall nests examined by Hammond and L. J. Harrison, August 1, 1947. A three-year average (1938 to 1940) for 934 eggs was only 4.8 per cent for unhatched eggs in successful mainland nests.

The absence of predation on Lower Souris islands isolated by open water has led to some exceptional duck-nest densities. On islands averaging 0.3 to 1.0 acre in size, there have regularly been 20 to 80 nests per acre.

Gadwall Island (0.8 acre), with at least 160 nesting pairs in 1947, exceeded a rate of 200 nests per acre (Henry, 1948). About 90 per cent of the nests hatched, and 1,350 young were produced. This rate of hatching success has usually been equaled by both ducks and geese on all of the open-water islands. Averages for mainland nest samples have rarely exceeded 50 per cent in recent years.

Flooding and erosion in 1949 caused many ducks to move from Gadwall to Ding Island, 500 yards south. Since that time the nesting population has been reduced to about 40 to 60 pairs.

Ding Island, a 7.0-acre natural area, maintained a population of about 100 nesting pairs or more through 1949 to 1955. Many pintails and mallards, as well as gadwalls, have nested upon it.

Gadwall clutch sizes were higher for island than for mainland nests (10.5 as compared with 9.2 for a six-year average, 1935-1940, for 200 nests). This may arise from either (1) the absence of loss of partial clutches to predators, (2) the addition of eggs by hens other than the rightful owner, (3) fewer renestings because of the higher nesting success on islands (Sowls, 1949: 263, shows that first clutches contain more eggs, on the average, than renestings), or (4) a true increase in clutch size. We tried to exclude from the tabulation all clutches known to have been laid by two or more hens in a single nest.

ISLAND NESTING AND DRAINAGE

The question has been raised: "Do not the island-nesting concentrations observed in certain large marshes indicate that the number of small water areas might be greatly reduced by widespread agricultural drainage, yet by crowding provide an equal waterfowl population?"

While this may seem, at first glance, to be an absurd question, it is true that we do not know the limits to crowding in waterfowl populations. The breeding concentration at Mývatn (Scott, 1952:129) is of interest: ". . . The farmers of the nineteen farms round the lake . . . take all eggs in excess of four from each nest. They have been doing this for about 700 years and figures for the egg-crop over the last fifty years show no overall decline. . ." It would appear that predation must be of very minor importance there. Considering waterfowl behavior alone, it is likely that breeding densities could be increased somewhat above present and recent population levels.

The territorial and nesting aspects of islands are not comparable to those of pothole and slough environment, however. Concentrations on land masses are extremely vulnerable to predation and to the various types of land use employed by our farmers and ranchers. Normally, we may expect that the greatest dispersal of nests into the widest variety of nesting habitat will insure the best survival.

Even the island concentrations are subject to catastrophic losses. Except under management or natural conditions, which exclude predation, flooding and other major decimating factors, they are not apt to continue uninterrupted over a long period of years.

In the light of our present knowledge we must conclude that reduction in habitat will result in proportionate declines in the waterfowl population.

ISLAND CONSTRUCTION

The initial island construction on Lower Souris was completed prior to first flooding of the marshes. Widths varied from 20 to 100 feet and lengths from 20 feet to nearly a mile. Earth was moved from each side to the center making a borrow pit or ditch that served to hold water for nesting ducks during years when impoundments were partly dry. The height above the surrounding bottom flats averaged four to six feet, but this was reduced in some cases by later settling and erosion.

In October 1955, a private contractor furnished D-7 bulldozer and operator for $10.00 an hour. In 48 working hours an island was constructed having a top surface 27 ft. by 264 ft. in dimensions, 6 ft. high with a slope of 1:7. Cost per cubic yard was about $0.12 (a total of 4,020 cu. yds.), and per running foot, $1.82. Costs for dragline construction would be somewhat higher, depending upon size of equipment and operating conditions.

FIG. 2. Some "push-ups" built with bulldozer in 1953. These small islands in emergent vegetation can be built for $10.00 to $30.00, depending upon size.

We believe that this island could easily last 100 years and could average five goose nests each year. This figures out at about $0.20 for each goose produced. If nesting ducks are considered, the cost of $5.00 a year should produce about 100 ducks in addition to 20 geese.

After 14 years of flooding, the more exposed "dragline" islands have had an estimated surface loss of about 65 to 75 per cent due to waves and ice movement. To reduce future erosion, projects in 1953 and 1955 were planned so that each island would be protected from waves by other islands, dikes, or natural windbreaks. We believe that close spacing will prolong the life of the development, hold down construction costs, and provide for greatest waterfowl use per acre of impounded area. There are further economies in use of bulldozers to push up small islands suitable for a single goose pair in such protected areas. Ray Erickson (interview) reported immediate acceptance of them as goose nesting sites on Malheur Refuge, Oregon. He found that they should be higher than the surrounding marsh cover and should be constructed in pairs a few hundred feet apart to provide for both nest and a lookout stand for the male. About 18 inches of water was believed desirable to reduce access by predatory animals.

We have also built a few of these "push-ups" in isolated patches of emergent vegetation. One of the more attractive of them was used in 1956.

On some projects log booms or stone riprap may be needed to hold light soils in place. Scattered stands of emergents probably do not detract and would be of value as wave barriers.

It is usually important that islands be separated from the mainland by at least several hundred feet of open water if they are to remain predator free. Even then they should be inspected each spring to remove animals that may have moved onto them during the winter. We have not seen any tendency for concentrated island duck nesting on any marginal or shallow marshy locations. Raccoons and coyotes were observed to cross channels of 100 feet and less. Skunks and foxes are not barred by deep channels 20 feet in width.

In shallow marshes sufficient isolation through the goose nesting season may be obtained if a belt of vegetation 200 to 300 feet wide can be removed from around the island. This may be done through burning or mechanical means when water levels permit.

Water depth is undoubtedly of considerable importance; raccoons and most animals will probably wade greater distances than they will swim. Twelve to 18 inches of water seems to be a desired range, considering both isolation and damage from waves. In deeper waters the island height must be increased to compensate for increased erosion and to provide freeboard. Pondweeds provide effective protection during several months of each year; they are usually in better stands in the shallower waters.

Size and shape are of importance chiefly

with regard to diminishing returns as certain limits are exceeded. Islands with surfaces 15 to 30 feet wide will usually have more use, per acre, than those much larger.

The proximity of food may be of greater importance to ducks than to geese. All of the favored Lower Souris gadwall island concentrations were in sites having an abundance of pondweeds. Geese nest prior to pondweed development and sometimes fly a mile to feeding sites in grain fields or flooded meadows.

While we have several graveled islands under observation, we cannot see that they have been disproportionately selected. In marshes lacking grit they would serve as a good source of supply, and this may favor heavier nesting use. Gravel will also aid in stabilizing the slopes and binding silt and muck materials thrown up in island construction.

FIG. 3. A close view of Gadwall Island in 1947. At this time there were at least 160 ducks and a colony of common terns (*Sterna hirundo*) nesting upon it. (Photo by C. J. Henry)

In the past, small brush-hay mounds and elevated tubs (Yocom, 1952) have been placed in the marsh. Up to the present time they have not been used, but we feel that further trials of nesting devices of this type should be made because of their low cost.

We did not observe any use of muskrat houses for nesting until 1956. The two nests found that spring suggest that the importance of these sites may increase in future years.

There are decided advantages in planning for and completing island construction during the early development of any impoundment. Equipment would be on the spot and dry working conditions would favor relatively low costs. Many water areas, unproductive because of their shoreline type, could support important breeding goose populations if islands could be provided.

SUMMARY

Nesting islands play an important role in the production rates of certain populations of Canada geese, and locally of some ducks.

Waterfowl quickly learn to take advantage of predator-free nesting sites such as islands. Other factors favoring heavy island use are the high ratio of water-land edge to land mass and the close proximity of water, food, loafing sites, and nesting cover. Concentrations arise through good annual survival and probably the social attractions of breeding displays. Vegetation is of minor importance as a nesting factor, unless it becomes too tall and rank. Gadwalls and mallards do choose the denser growth of weeds if they are available. The principal island-nesting losses are due to predation, competition of other birds, and intraspecific strife. Lesser losses arise through irregularities in laying and incubation by some hens under crowded conditions.

On the Lower Souris refuge only the islands well surrounded by open water have been particularly attractive and have had high nesting success. They are believed to be primarily responsible for the build-up of a resident Canada goose flock from 22 to about 370 birds between 1937 and 1954, despite a severe set-back in 1945. In 1954 only about 50 to 60 feet separated nesting pairs on some islands, and closer crowding will probably result in increased friction and nest loss. In the gadwall-nesting concentrations (which reached a rate of 200 nests per acre on one favored island), there are some pairs using the islands through the day. Other pairs, having part of their home ranges elsewhere, fly to the islands to nest, resulting in a great deal of aerial pursuit and other breeding displays. The "resident" drakes are not able to prevent the intruders from nesting.

We do not feel that the occurrence of island concentrations justifies the belief that waterfowl on mainland areas can make a similar adjustment if habitat is decreased through drainage. More likely, reduction in water areas will cause a proportionate decline in waterfowl populations. In new island construction the important considerations are: (1) isolation from mainland areas by several hundred feet of open water at least 12 inches in depth; (2) control of erosion through close spacing, proximity to protective structures, treatment of margins with resistant materials, or use of natural vegetative wave breaks; and (3) a size apt to furnish the greatest waterfowl use for the money expended. Costs in 1955 were $1.82 a running foot for a large island constructed by bulldozer. With a life expectancy of 100 years this comes to about $0.20 for each goose and $0.05 for each duck we would expect to be produced.

LITERATURE CITED

ARMSTRONG, E. A. 1947. Bird display and behaviour. Oxford Univ. Press. N. Y.

BENT, A. C. 1923. Life histories of North American wild fowl. U.S. Natl. Mus., Bull. 126.

———. 1925. Life histories of North American wild fowl. U.S. Natl. Mus., Bull. 130.

CRAIGHEAD, F. C., JR. AND J. J. CRAIGHEAD. 1949. Nesting Canada geese on the upper Snake River. J. Wildl. Mgmt., 13:51-64.

CRISSEY, W. F. AND OTHERS. 1951. Waterfowl populations and breeding conditions – summer 1951. U.S. Fish and Wildl. Service; Canadian Wildl. Service; Spec. Sci. Rept. Wildlife No. 13.

ERRINGTON, P. L. 1946. Predation and vertebrate populations. Quart. Rev. Biol., 21:144-177.

GROSS, A. O. 1945. The black duck nesting on the outer coastal islands of Maine. Auk, 62:620-622.

[HAMMOND, M. C.] 1950. Canadas in N. D. N. Dak. Outdoors, 12(11):6-7.

HENRY, C. J. 1948. Summer on the Souris marsh. Audubon Mag., 50:242-249.

JOHNSON, C. S. 1947. Canada goose management, Seney National Wildlife Refuge. J. Wildl. Mgmt., 11:21-24.

KALMBACH, E. R. 1937. Crow-waterfowl relationships. Circ. U.S. Dept. Agric., No. 433. 36 pp.

KOSSACK, C. W. 1950. Breeding habits of Canada geese under refuge conditions. Amer. Midl. Nat., 43:627-649.

MILLER, A. W. AND B. D. COLLINS. 1953. A nesting study of Canada geese on Tule Lake and Lower Klamath National Wildlife refuges, Siskiyou County, California. Calif. Fish and Game, 39:385-396.

———. 1954. A nesting study of ducks and coots on Tule Lake and Lower Klamath National Wildlife refuges. Calif. Fish and Game, 40:17-37.

NAYLOR, A. E. 1953. Production of the Canada goose on Honey Lake Refuge, Lassen County, California. Calif. Fish and Game, 39:83-94.

SCOTT, P. 1952. Mývatn 1951. Fifth Annual Report of the Severn Wildlife Trust, 1951-1952, pp. 125-132. Country Life Ltd., London.

SOWLS, L. K. 1949. A preliminary report on renesting in waterfowl. Trans. N. Amer. Wildl. Conf., 14:260-273.

WILLIAMS, C. S. AND WM. H. MARSHALL. 1938. Duck nesting studies, Bear River Migratory Bird Refuge, Utah, 1937. J. Wildl. Mgmt., 2:29-48.

——— AND OTHERS. 1948. Waterfowl populations and breeding conditions–summer 1948. U.S. Fish and Wildl. Service; Canadian Wildl. Service; Spec. Sci. Rept. No. 60.

——— AND ———. 1950. Waterfowl populations and breeding conditions–summer 1950. U.S. Fish and Wildl. Service; Dominion Wildl. Service; Spec Sci. Rept.: Wildlife No. 8.

YOCOM, C. F. 1952. Techniques used to increase nesting of Canada geese. J. Wildl. Mgmt., 16: 425-428.

Received for publication February 11, 1956.

SELECTED BIBLIOGRAPHY

Reproductive Ecology: Land Use and Habitat

BEARD, E. B. 1953. The importance of beaver in waterfowl management at the Seney National Wildlife Refuge. J. Wild. Manage. 17:398–436.

BELLROSE, F. C. 1977. Species distribution, habitats, and characteristics of breeding dabbling ducks in North America. Pages 1–15 *in* T. A. Bookhout, ed. Waterfowl and wetlands—An integrated review. Proc. of a Symp. at the 39th Midwest Fish and Wildl. Conf., Madison, WI. LaCrosse Printing Co., Inc., LaCrosse.

BENSON, R. I. 1964. A study of duck nesting and production as related to land use in Pope County, Minnesota. Pages 107–126 *in* Symposium on ducks and land use in Minnesota. Minnesota Dep. Conserv. Tech. Bull. 8.

BREWSTER, W. G., J. M. GATES, AND L. D. FLAKE. 1976. Breeding waterfowl populations and their distribution in South Dakota. J. Wildl. Manage. 40(1):50–59.

BURGESS, H. H., H. H. PRINCE, AND D. L. TRAUGER. 1965. Blue-winged teal nesting success as related to land use. J. Wildl. Manage. 29(1):89–95.

COULTER, M. W., AND H. L. MENDALL. 1968. Black duck habitat and breeding ecology—Northeastern states. Pages 90–101 *in* The black duck; a symposium. The Wildl. Manage. Inst., Washington, D.C.

CRISSEY, W. F. 1969. Prairie potholes from a continental viewpoint. Pages 161–171 *in* Saskatoon Wetlands Seminar. Can. Wildl. Serv. Rep. 6.

DREWIEN, R. C., AND P. F. SPRINGER. 1969. Ecological relationships of breeding blue-winged teal to prairie potholes. Pages 102–105 *in* Saskatoon Wetlands Seminar. Can. Wildl. Serv. Rep. Ser. 6.

DUEBBERT, H. F. 1966. Island nesting of the gadwall in North Dakota. Wilson Bull. 78(1):12–25.

———, AND H. A. KANTRUD. 1974. Upland duck nesting related to land use and predator reduction. J. Wildl. Manage. 38(2):257–265.

———, AND J. T. LOKEMOEN. 1976. Duck nesting in fields of undisturbed grass-legume cover. J. Wildl. Manage. 40(1):39–49.

DWYER, T. J. 1970. Waterfowl breeding habitat in agricultural and nonagricultural land in Manitoba. J. Wildl. Manage. 34(1):130–136.

———, G. L. KRAPU, AND D. M. JANKE. 1979. Use of prairie pothole habitat by breeding mallards. J. Wildl. Manage. 43(2):526–531.

DZUBIN, A. 1969. Comments on carrying capacity of small ponds for ducks and possible effects of density on mallard production. Pages 138–160 *in* Saskatoon Wetlands Seminar. Can. Wildl. Serv. Rep. 6.

EVARD, J. O. 1975. Waterfowl use of dug ponds in northwestern Wisconsin. Wildl. Soc. Bull. 3(1):13–18.

FLAKE, L. D. 1979. Perspectives on man-made ponds and waterfowl in the Northern Prairies. 31st Annu. Meet. For. Comm., Great Plains Agric. Counc., Colorado State Univ., Fort Collins. Pp. 33–36.

FREDRICKSON, L. H., AND R. D. DROBNEY. 1977. Habitat utilization by postbreeding waterfowl. Pages

119–131 *in* T. A. Bookhout, ed. Waterfowl and wetlands—An integrated review. Proc. Symp. at 39th Midwest Fish and Wildl. Conf., Madison, WI. LaCrosse Printing Co., Inc., LaCrosse.

FRITZELL, E. K. 1975. Effects of agricultural burning on nesting waterfowl. Can. Field-Nat. 89(1):21–27.

GILMER, D. S., I. J. BALL, L. M. COWARDIN, J. H. RIECHMANN, AND J. R. TESTER. 1975. Habitat use and home range of mallards breeding in Minnesota. J. Wildl. Manage. 39(4):781–789.

———, R. E. KIRBY, I. J. BALL, AND J. H. RIECHMANN. 1977. Post-breeding activities of mallards and wood ducks in north-central Minnesota. J. Wildl. Manage. 41(3):345–359.

HAMMOND, M. C., AND G. E. MANN. 1956. Waterfowl nesting islands. J. Wildl. Manage. 20(4):345–352.

HAWKINS, A. S., AND W. E. GREEN. 1966. Waterfowl management opportunities in forested areas of the Lakes States. Proc. Soc. Am. For. Meet. Pp. 54–58.

HEITMEYER, M. E., AND L. H. FREDRICKSON. 1981. Do wetland conditions in Mississippi Delta hardwoods influence mallard recruitment? Trans. N. Am. Wildl. Nat. Resour. Conf. 46:(In Press).

HIRST, S. M., AND C. A. EASTHOPE. 1981. Use of agricultural lands by waterfowl in southwestern British Columbia. J. Wildl. Manage. 45:454–462.

JARVIS, R. L., AND S. W. HARRIS. 1971. Land-use patterns and duck production at Malheur National Wildlife Refuge. J. Wildl. Manage. 35(4):767–773.

KAISER, P. H., S. S. BERLINGER, AND L. H. FREDRICKSON. 1979. Response of blue-winged teal to range management on waterfowl production areas in southeastern South Dakota. J. Range Manage. 32(4):295–298.

KAMINSKI, R. M., AND H. H. PRINCE. 1981. Dabbling duck and aquatic macroinvertebrate responses to manipulated wetland habitat. J. Wildl. Manage. 45:1–15.

KIEL, W. H., Jr., A. S. HAWKINS, AND N. G. PERRET. 1972. Waterfowl habitat trends in the aspen parkland of Manitoba. Can. Wildl. Serv. Rep. Ser. 18. 63 pp.

KIRSCH, L. M., AND A. D. KRUSE. 1973. Prairie fires and wildlife. Pages 289–303 *in* Tall timbers fire ecology conference. Tall Timbers Res. Station, Tallahassee, FL.

KRAPU, G. L. 1977. Pintail reproduction hampered by snowfall and agriculture. Wilson Bull. 89(1):154–157.

———, L. G. TALENT, AND T. J. DWYER. 1979. Marsh nesting by mallards. Wildl. Soc. Bull. 7(2):104–110.

MCCABE, T. R. 1979. Productivity and nesting habitat of Great Basin Canada geese, Umatilla, Washington. Pages 117–129 *in* R. L. Jarvis and J. C. Bartonek, eds. Management and biology of Pacific flyway geese. A symposium. Northwest Sec. of The Wildl. Soc. Oregon State Univ. Book Stores, Inc., Corvallis.

MCKNIGHT, D. E. 1974. Dry-land nesting by redheads and ruddy ducks. J. Wildl. Manage. 38(1):112–119.

MUNDINGER, J. G. 1976. Waterfowl response to rest-rotation grazing. J. Wildl. Manage. 40(1):60–68.

POSTON, H. J. 1969. Relationship between the shoveler and its breeding habitat at Strathmore, Alberta. Pages 132–137 *in* Saskatoon Wetlands Seminar. Can. Wildl. Serv. Rep. Ser. 6.

RENOUF, R. N. 1972. Waterfowl utilization of beaver ponds in New Brunswick. J. Wildl. Manage. 36(3):740–744.

RUWALDT, J. J., L. D. FLAKE, AND J. M. GATES. 1979. Waterfowl pair use of natural and man-made wetlands in South Dakota. J. Wildl. Manage. 43(2):375–383.

SMITH, A. G. 1971. Ecological factors affecting waterfowl production in the Alberta Parklands. Bur. Sport Fish. and Wildl. Res. Publ. 98, Washington, D.C.

STEWART, R. E., AND H. A. Kantrud. 1973. Ecological distributions of breeding waterfowl populations in North Dakota. J. Wildl. Manage. 37(1):39–50.

STOUDT, J. H. 1969. Relationships between waterfowl and water areas in the Redvers Waterfowl Study Area. Pages 123–131 *in* Saskatoon Wetlands Seminar, Can. Wildl. Rep. Ser. 6.

———. 1971. Ecological factors affecting waterfowl production in the Saskatchewan Parklands. U.S. Bur. Sport Fish. Wildl. Res. Publ. 99. 58pp.

TRAUGER, D. L., AND J. H. STOUDT. 1978. Trends in waterfowl populations and habitats on study areas in Canadian parklands. Trans. N. Am. Wildl. Nat. Resour. Conf. 43:187–205.

VERMEER, K. 1970. A study of Canada geese, *Branta canadensis,* nesting on islands in southeastern Alberta. Can. J. Zoo. 48(2):235–240.

VOORHEES, L. D., AND J. F. CASSEL. 1980. Highway right-of-way: mowing versus succession as related to duck nesting. J. Wildl. Manage. 44:155–163.

WELLER, M. W. 1979. Density and habitat relationships of blue-winged teal nesting in northwestern Iowa. J. Wildl. Manage. 43:367–374.

Broods

HEN AND BROOD BEHAVIOR[1]

L. K. SOWLS[2]

The behavior of the hen and her young during the brood season lacks the aggressive aspects of the hen's and drake's behavior during the territorial period. It lacks the complete solitude of the incubating period but does not approach the gregariousness which is typical of all waterfowl in autumn.

Broods are raised in waters bordering or near to the meadows where they hatched. There they must survive many dangers between hatching and flying. They survive only because of their instinctive and learned behaviors associated with the ability to escape danger, to hide, and to follow the protective calls and signals of their mother. From the simplest instinctive response to the complex learned behaviors which develop slowly with time, all play an important part in survival. The climax of this period comes when the instinct to fly develops by practice into strong, alert and precise flight.

Hatching.—In the incubator at Delta, thousands of clutches of wild duck eggs have been hatched; and it has been easy to watch and record the hatching process. In the wild, however, and under natural conditions, few hatching nests have been observed. In my study at Delta, I watched four pintail nests and two blue-winged teal nests from the time the first egg pipped until the young were ready to leave.

In 1949, I recorded the incubator hatching of 15 clutches. Of this group, seven clutches had a hatching period of less than one day, all eggs of each clutch hatching on the same day. Two clutches required a period of two days and six required a period of three days. Of six clutches hatching in the wild, all eggs of each clutch began pipping at the same time, and all young emerged within an hour of each other. Clutches hatched in the wild and under natural conditions hatched uniformly. Some incubator-hatched clutches required up to three days to complete the process.

Brood Movements.—The intentional robbing of nests in the renesting study at Delta curtailed the collection of mass brood-movement data. On the study area, I saw one pintail hen move her brood 800 yards within the first 24 hours after hatching. Several others moved their broods lesser distances to the nearest slough or ditch. Three pintail broods that were hatched by marked hens on the study area were known to grow to flying age within 500 yards of the nest site.

Important information on brood movements has been given by Evans (1951) who studied the movements of marked ducklings in the glaciated pothole country near Minnedosa, Manitoba. Evans found that movements between potholes occurred in a random direction. Of pintail broods he wrote (1951:47–48): "This brood travelled 0.42 miles from the nest in 16 days. . . . These three broods were observed to travel 0.78 miles in 71 days for an average of 0.011 miles per day. No brood of this species was known to occupy a single pothole for more than 14 days." Of mallard broods, Evans (1951:49) said: "These two broods travelled a total

[1] Originally published in Prairie ducks, pages 143–150. The Wildlife Management Institute, Washington, D.C., 1955.

[2] Present address: Arizona Cooperative Wildlife Research Unit, U.S.D.I., 214 Biological Sciences East, University of Arizona, Tucson, AZ 85721.

of 0.48 miles in 38 days for an average of 0.013 miles per day. . . . No mallard brood was known to occupy a single pothole for more than 20 days." And Evans (1951:49) wrote about the blue-winged teal: "The longest time a brood of this species was known to occupy a single pothole was 28 days." Evans (1951:50–51) also observed a shoveller brood that spent 16 days in one pothole, and a gadwall brood that spent 17 days in one pothole. He was able to determine which species moved their broods most readily. "Pintail broods were the most mobile, followed in order by canvasback, mallard, redhead, blue-winged teal, and baldpate, while ruddy ducks broods were the least mobile," according to Evans (1951:108).

Brood Reactions to Calls of Hen.—The reactions of the young to different calls of the hen were observed in the field. There was the freezing reaction in which the young remained quiet and immobile, and the huddling reaction in which the young moved close to the hen and stayed near her in a solid group.

On July 13, 1950, I attempted to identify a pintail hen which was known to be banded and which had a brood with her. She was known to be somewhere in a small whitetop-edged pothole with nine ducklings about three weeks old. At 6:45 a.m. two other observers and I stationed ourselves at three points around the pothole and slowly drove the hen and brood out into the center where there was open water. The hen and brood had been hidden in heavy flooded whitetop on the south side of the pothole. The hen flushed and issued a long rasping call, which apparently served to alert the young; all of them remained stationary with heads high. They made no effort to join the hen or to escape to cover. After several minutes we withdrew to about 40 yards from the pond and allowed the hen to return. After returning to the pond, the hen continued to emit her loud, rasping call and the young remained immobile and alert. The hen moved slowly to the south side of the pond and changed her loud rasping call to one resembling a low *cheep-cheep*. At that moment, the entire brood dashed toward the flooded whitetop cover.

When working in heavy stands of flooded whitetop on the study area, I often heard the cheeping of ducklings. But as soon as a disturbed mother took to the air and circled the area making loud rasping calls, the young ceased their cheeping and were quiet.

The reactions of the young to the calls of the hen apparently were learned during the first few hours after hatching. This point has been demonstrated adequately by various students of bird behavior. Lorenz (1937:262) believed: ". . . that most birds do not recognize their own species 'instinctively,' but that by far the greater part of their reactions, whose normal object is represented by a fellow-member of the species, must be conditioned to this object during the individual life of the bird." In his experiments with young geese and ducks, Lorenz found that in some cases he was able to induce young birds to take for their parent-companion whatever living thing they were exposed to first. The process whereby this attachment originated, he called "imprinting."

Nice (1953:33) has called the early hours of life a period of rapid learning of the characters of the parent and credits Heinroth as the first to discover that the newly hatched grey goose (*Anser anser*) adopts as its parent the first living being it sets eyes upon. Tinbergen (1951:150) has termed these first few hours of an animal's life a period of critical learning.

Fabricius (1951) was able to imprint

Fig. 1. Brood of blue-winged teal ducklings one hour after hatching.

young ducklings to follow him and come to his calls, and also to get young ducklings of one species to be imprinted to the older ducklings of another species. He found that the period during which young tufted ducks could be imprinted was from birth up to at least 36–38 hours. Both Fabricius and Lorenz focused considerable attention on the releasing mechanisms of the "following" reactions. Nice (1953), using the techniques developed by Fabricius, succeeded in imprinting to human beings 12 ducklings of five different species. These ducklings accepted human beings as parent-companions when subjected to visual signs and acoustic signals during the first few hours of life.

During my studies, most nests were robbed intentionally in order to gather data on renesting. Consequently, few nests were left to be observed as they hatched normally. In wild nests, I found that the young showed no fear reactions immediately upon hatching and while still wet. After the young were dry and presented a downy appearance, they showed an awareness of intrusion and responded by attempting to scurry out of the nest to hide in the grass at the edge of the nest. Figures 1 and 2 show a brood of blue-winged teal young just after hatching, and the same brood eight hours after hatching. Although some variation existed in the time required for drying off and leaving the nest, I suspect that most ducklings left the nest within 12 hours after hatching. The drying-off period normally was spent cuddled under the hen.

Tolling of Intruder by Hen.—A hen is said to toll when she diverts an intruder's attention from her brood by moving de-

Fig. 2. Same brood of blue-winged teal eight hours after hatching.

liberately and conspicuously from it. While working a dog in the nesting meadows at Delta, I saw on many occasions hens try to draw my dog away from a brood that was hidden in the grass. The most spectacular observation of this occurred on July 5, 1948. On that afternoon, I saw a pintail hen circling and quacking loudly over my head as I walked through a flooded whitetop meadow on the study area. I could identify the hen by the colored bands on her legs and was anxious to learn whether she had renested and now had a brood in the heavy grass. When I encouraged my dog to find the young, the hen immediately began luring him away. She accomplished this by swooping low over the dog and flying slowly in front of him in a direction away from where the brood apparently was hidden. By continued search one young pintail was found.

The broods of young ducklings show a remarkable timing or synchronization of activities. In his descriptions of the "imprinting" of young ducklings, Fabricius (1951:165) has made note of this: "All the young birds of one group generally perform the same kind of activity simultaneously, such as preening, eating or sleeping. This synchronization is very important for successful conduction of a brood." Just as it is important to the investigator who has conditioned young birds to follow him, so it is important to the safe conduct of the brood when led by their mother in the wild.

Hiding of Young by Hen.—On a number of occasions it was clear that the mother intentionally hid her young before attempting to toll away an intruder. Sometimes the hen alerted them with a call producing the freezing response. Sometimes the hen actually guided the young into a safe place before attempting to lead the intruder away.

On a July day in 1950, Dr. W. J. Breckenridge, James Houston and I watched a redhead hen and brood of eight 4-day-old ducklings. The hen was swimming down the middle of a ditch with the young close by her. We watched her for a short time until she swam into a small side channel where the ditch had overflowed and flooded phragmites cover was available. Almost immediately the hen swam out alone and continued down the ditch while the young remained hidden in dense reeds.

Hiding of Hen with Brood.—In my observations at Delta, I found that a hen, when disturbed in a flooded area, usually attempted to hide her young and then draw me away from the place where the young were hidden. Sometimes, however, the hen hid herself with her young.

On June 7, 1947, a hen mallard with a brood of 8-week-old ducklings was seen in a part of the Delta ditch where the edges were relatively bare because of grazing. This mallard hen led her brood down the ditch for 20 yards and then attempted to hide them against a tiny clump of wild barley on the bank. In doing so, the hen stretched her neck out over the shore in the shadow of the grass clump and remained quiet. The young huddled close to her.

When puddle ducks with young were disturbed by a canoe, hiding behavior was more common than tolling, or leading away. But when they were disturbed in shallow, flooded meadows, tolling was to be expected. When diving ducks with young are disturbed, they take their young to open water instead of into reeds (Hochbaum 1944:105).

Feigning Behavior of Hen.—A hen is said to feign when she exhibits a spectacular flapping movement across water or land similar to the escape behavior of flightless molting birds. This behavior serves to attract attention away from a hen's brood as in tolling, but the hen uses a flapping movement across land or water, whereas in tolling she swims or flies.

Hochbaum (1944:105) describes the feigning of puddle ducks and says: "Feigning behavior is most intense in pintail and blue-winged teal . . . and is less intense in the gadwall, shoveller and mallard." I have seen feigning behavior in all species at Delta on open water and on dry land but have not witnessed it in flooded meadows where the hen invariably took to the air and attempted to lead me away by flying.

The feigning behavior of a hen with a brood is the same as that which frequently is exhibited by incubating hens during the late stages of incubation.

Defense of Young by Mother.—Hens have been known to defend their young against intruders without making an attempt to draw the intruder away. The best example of this that I know of was an instance in which a mallard hen successfully defended her brood against a mink. The observation was made at Delta and was described to me in a letter dated January 22, 1947, by Arthur S. Hawkins who wrote:

"On June 25, 1946, I saw a mink attack 8 newly hatched ducklings belonging to a mallard. The fight which lasted at least 10 minutes was staged within 50 yards of my observation station and at times it came much closer to me.

"The hen's strategy was to keep her

brood bunched. Each time the mink approached she swam between her brood and the invader. She quacked constantly and flapped her wings repeatedly in his face giving the ducklings a chance for a wild dash across the ditch."

Brood Habitat.—Areas of flooded vegetation formed the most important brood cover at Delta. On the study area, large flooded fields of whitetop were preferred rearing grounds for the surface-feeding species. Open waters were not used extensively by the surface-feeders with broods, but they were used by diving duck broods. In the flooded grassy meadows, small hummocks formed loafing places where the mother and young spent much of their time. These dry loafing places are important to the young ducks and are a necessary part of any rearing ground. In the larger bays, muskrat houses and mud bars served this purpose. On the long narrow ditch which ran through the study area, the loafing logs and platforms put out for breeding-season adults were used extensively by the broods as loafing sites.

In the pothole country of Manitoba, Evans (1951:104) found that the large open potholes with sedge-whitetop margins were favored as brood rearing areas while similar areas with bulrush cover were a close second. He also found that depth was an important factor influencing pothole selection; and that during periods of low water, potholes over two feet deep definitely were preferred to shallower areas.

SUMMARY

1. The hatching of clutches in the wild and hatching in the Delta incubator were compared. Six clutches hatched in the wild and under natural conditions hatched uniformly. Some incubator-hatched clutches required up to three days to complete the process.

2. The first 12 hours of the life of a newly hatched brood was observed in the wild and the behavior noted.

3. The reactions of the young to the calls of the hen apparently were learned during the early hours of life.

4. Brood movements were watched by me at Delta and by Evans at Minnedosa. Broods moved in random directions and varying distances. One pintail hen moved her brood 800 yards within 24 hours of hatching. Three pintail broods grew to flying age within 500 yards of the nest site. Evans found pintail broods to be the most mobile, followed by canvasback, mallard, redhead, blue-winged teal, baldpate, and ruddy duck.

5. Brood reactions to the calls of the hen were watched in the wild. There was a "freezing reaction," "huddling reaction," and a reaction in which the young joined the hen and swam with her. The reactions of the young to the calls of the hen apparently were learned during the first few hours after hatching.

6. Sometimes brood hens "toll" when intruded upon. By moving deliberately and conspicuously from the intruder they attempt to divert attention from their broods.

7. Hens were known to hide their broods before attempting to toll an intruder away. Sometimes they hid themselves with their young.

8. Among the surface-feeders, hiding behavior was to be expected when water was deep; tolling behavior was to be expected when it was shallow.

9. Feigning behavior differs from tolling behavior in that a feigning hen exhibits spectacular flapping movements

across the water or land, whereas a tolling hen swims or flies.

10. Hens sometimes defend their young against intruders.

11. Areas of flooded vegetation, such as whitetop, were preferred rearing grounds for the surface-feeding species at Delta. In the pothole country, large open potholes with sedge-whitetop margins and good depth (over 2 feet) were preferred.

LITERATURE CITED

EVANS, CHARLES D. 1951. A study of the movements of waterfowl broods in Manitoba. Unpub. thesis. University of Minnesota. 134pp.

FABRICIUS, E. 1951. Zur Ethologie junger Anatiden. Acta Zoologica Fennica 68:1–175.

HOCHBAUM, H. ALBERT. 1944. The canvasback on a prairie marsh. Amer. Wildlife Inst., Washington, D.C. 201pp.

LORENZ, KONRAD Z. 1937. The companion in the birds' world. Auk 54:245–273.

NICE, MARGARET MORSE. 1953. Some experiences in imprinting young ducklings. Condor 55:33–37.

TINBERGEN, N. 1951. The study of instinct. Oxford, London. 228pp.

SURVIVAL OF WOOD DUCK AND MALLARD BROODS IN NORTH-CENTRAL MINNESOTA[1]

I. J. BALL, Department of Entomology, Fisheries and Wildlife, University of Minnesota, St. Paul 55108[2]

DAVID S. GILMER, Department of Ecology and Behavioral Biology, University of Minnesota, St. Paul 55108[3]

LEWIS M. COWARDIN, U. S. Fish and Wildlife Service, Northern Prairie Wildlife Research Center, Jamestown, North Dakota 58401

JOHN H. RIECHMANN, Department of Ecology and Behavioral Biology, University of Minnesota, St. Paul 55108[4]

Abstract: Duckling survival in wood duck (*Aix sponsa*) and mallard (*Anas platyrhynchos*) broods was estimated from data obtained from 71 radio-marked brood hens on a study area in north-central Minnesota. Radio-marked hens produced 30 broods during the study, and 41 hens already leading broods were captured and radio-marked. Production estimates based on brood size counts were inflated by about 38 percent for wood ducks and 30 percent for mallards if total-brood losses were not taken into account. Mortality during the first 2 weeks of life was most severe, accounting for 86 percent of total recorded mortality in wood ducks and 70 percent in mallards. Rearing success was about 41 percent for wood ducks and 44 percent for mallards. Duckling survival was negatively correlated with distance of overland travel by young broods. Wood ducks had a shorter hen-brood bond than mallards, and presence of the hen appeared to affect duckling survival less in wood duck broods than in mallards.

J. WILDL. MANAGE. 39(4):776–780

Counting the number of young in duck broods and estimating their age traditionally has been used to calculate survival. As Reed (1970:119) pointed out, however, survival or production estimates based on the average number of ducklings per unmarked brood fail to take into account cases where all ducklings in a brood are lost. This paper reports on survival and related behavioral characteristics of wood duck and mallard ducklings, with special reference to the influence of total-brood loss on production estimates.

J. R. Tester provided support and guidance throughout the study; he, D. H. Johnson, and H. W. Miller critically reviewed the manuscript. R. S. Stott and T. Clodfelter assisted with collection of data. Radiotracking equipment was constructed and maintained by the engineering staff, Cedar Creek Bioelectronics Laboratory, University of Minnesota.

METHODS

During the summers of 1968–72, brood hens were radiotracked and observed on a 98-km² study area in north-central Minnesota (Gilmer et al. 1974, Gilmer 1971, Ball 1971, 1973). We also recorded the number and age of ducklings in all unmarked broods seen (Gollop and Marshall 1954, Dreis 1954, Steffan 1969, unpublished data, Northern Prairie Wildlife Research Center, Jamestown, North Dakota). Because some broods were very difficult to see during daylight hours, we occasionally used a night vision scope (Swanson and Sargeant 1972) or a nightlighting boat to aid in observing and counting ducklings.

In all marked broods and in the unmarked broods which could be tentatively identified by location, size, and number of ducklings, duplicate counts of a brood in

[1] Funded by the U. S. Fish and Wildlife Service, University of Minnesota, National Institutes of Health Training Grant 5T01 GM01779-08, and U. S. Atomic Energy Commission, C00-1332-105.

[2] Present address: Department of Zoology, Washington State University, Pullman 99163.

[3] Present address: U. S. Fish and Wildlife Service, Northern Prairie Wildlife Research Center, Jamestown, North Dakota 58401.

[4] Present address: R. R. 1, Valmeyer, Illinois 62295.

Originally published in J. Wildl. Manage. 39(4):776–780, 1975.

one age-class were eliminated from calculations unless ducklings were lost during the class interval; then the mean of the two extreme counts was used.

Apparent survival to each age-class was calculated by dividing the observed mean brood size for the class by mean initial brood size (from clutch size information). True survival was calculated as apparent survival times the percentage of total broods with at least one duckling surviving. When hens were radio-marked for the first time with ducklings already more than an estimated two days old, the record was not used in calculating total-brood loss rates.

RESULTS

Twenty-one wood duck and nine mallard broods were produced by radio-marked hens during the study. In addition, 5 wood duck and 36 mallard hens were captured and radio-marked while already leading broods. Usable (nonduplicate) duckling counts in unmarked wood duck and mallard broods totaled 45 and 265, respectively.

We were able to determine accurately the number of hatched eggs in only 5 of the 21 successful wood duck nests because all but 1 nest were in natural tree cavities. Many cavities were quite deep, and our attempts to cut examination holes were unsuccessful. Thus our estimate of 10.0 ducklings per successful wood duck nest is open to question because of small sample size and high variability ($n = 5$, SE = 1.67). However, McGilvrey (1969:74) reported an average of 9.8 young per successful wood duck nest and Heusmann (1972:623) found that normal wood duck nests averaged 8.8 and 10.7 young per successful nest during 2 study periods, with an overall average of 9.96. The estimate of 9.4 young per successful mallard nest ($n = 12$, SE = 0.40) is based on the number of hatched eggs in 8 successful nests and on clutch size minus an 8 percent non-hatch expectation (Dzubin and Gollop 1972:150) in 4 nests which were destroyed prior to hatching.

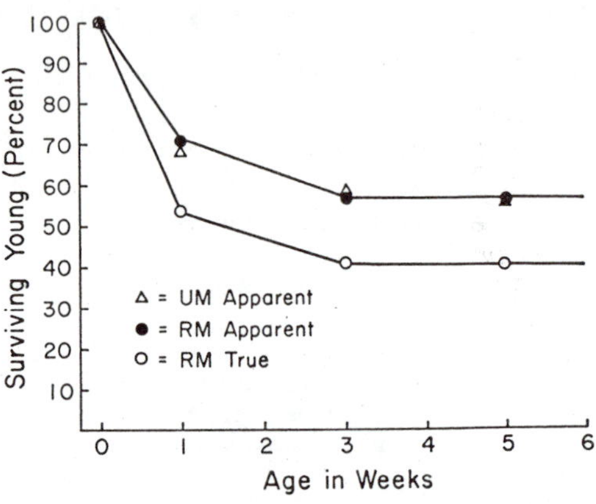

Fig. 1. Survival of wood duck broods in Minnesota based on information from 26 radio-marked (RM) broods and 45 usable sightings of unmarked (UM) broods. Initial mean brood size was assumed to be 10.0. Apparent survival to each age-class equals observed mean brood size for the age-class divided by initial mean brood size. True survival equals apparent survival times the percentage of total broods with at least one duckling surviving.

Survival Estimates

Apparent mean survival was similar between radio-marked and unmarked wood ducks in all age-classes (Fig. 1). These means, however, fail to account for those situations where all ducklings in a brood are lost, because the "zero" size category is obviously not observable and hence is not figured in the average. Production estimates based on our apparent survival data were inflated 38 percent by failure to account for the total loss of 5 of 21 wood duck broods. On average, wood duck hens raised about 41 percent of the ducklings they initially produced. The possibility that being radio-marked lowered rearing efficiency in female ducks must be considered, but this seems unlikely since apparent sizes of marked broods were not significantly different from unmarked broods for either species in any age-class (*t*-tests, $P > 0.05$). Failure to account for total-brood losses in mallards would result in overestimating production by about 30 percent (Fig. 2). Mallard rearing success, including total-brood mortality, averaged about 44 percent.

Mortality during the first 2 weeks after hatching was most severe, accounting for 86 percent of total recorded mortality in wood ducks and 70 percent in mallards. This situation is typical of many areas and duck species (Keith 1961, McGilvrey 1969, Reed 1970), although the causes of these early deaths are poorly understood (see Bengston 1972). We saw only 4 predation attempts (all by mink [*Mustela vison*] and all unsuccessful), and found one 42-day-old mallard incapacitated by a mink.

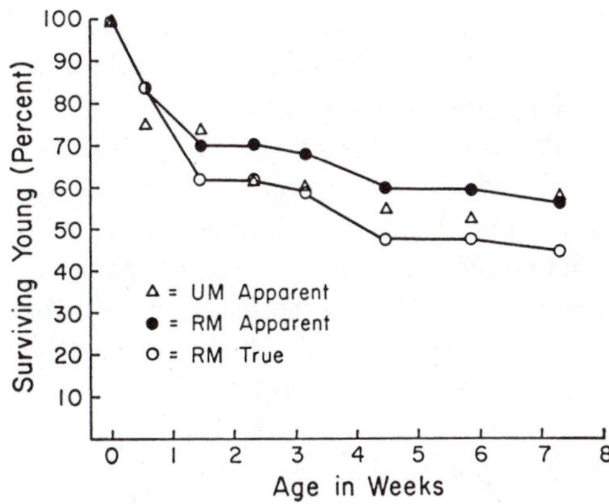

Fig. 2. Survival of mallard broods in Minnesota based on information from 45 radio-marked (RM) broods and 265 usable sightings of unmarked (UM) broods. Initial mean brood size was assumed to be 9.4. Apparent survival to each age-class equals observed mean brood size for the age-class divided by initial mean brood size. True survival equals apparent survival times the percentage of total broods with at least one duckling surviving.

Overland Movements

Young ducklings logically would seem to be most vulnerable to accidents, predation, and losses due to exhaustion or scattering during overland moves (Bellrose 1953, Keith 1961, Odom 1970, Dzubin and Gollop 1972). However, Evans and Black (1956) found no evidence that duck broods moving between prairie wetlands suffered more mortality than did sedentary broods. A significant negative linear correlation existed between distance of overland moves completed prior to 2 weeks of age and number of surviving ducklings in broods of radio-marked hens ($r = -0.39$, 28 df, $P < 0.05$). Broods undertaking overland moves of 0.8 km or less averaged 8.53 young vs. 6.77 in more mobile broods. A measure of variability is inherent in these analyses, because we often did not know how many ducklings left the nest and hence could not make the more precise test of correlation between the number of ducklings lost and overland distance moved. Also, there was often a lag of several days or more after a move was completed before we could obtain a count without disturbing the brood.

Hen-Brood Bonds

Female dabbling ducks usually remain with their ducklings until near fledging (Evans et al. 1952), but wood duck hen-brood bonds usually are terminated at about five weeks or less (McGilvrey 1969: 75, Beard 1964:513). Radio-marked mallard females stayed with their offspring for an average of 50.7 days, significantly longer than the 30.8-day average for wood ducks ($t = 2.95$, 61 df, $P < 0.01$). Because the hens were radio-marked, we were unlikely to interpret temporary absence as permanent abandonment. Several mallard hens left their 5- to 6-week-old ducklings during daylight but returned and escorted them on feeding forays during the night. These broods probably would have been considered abandoned had the hens been unmarked or only color-marked. Numerous radio-marked mallards remained with fledged ducklings for a week or more, and two were known to associate with their offspring after entering molt.

In addition to having relatively short hen-brood bonds, wood ducks seem to have loose bonds in that ducklings behave in an independent fashion very early (McGilvrey 1969, Ball 1973). In contrast, young mallard ducklings tend to stay close to their hen and respond promptly to her attempts to gather or lead them. Stewart (1958, 1974) reported that wood duck hens regularly leave even young ducklings for morning and evening feeding. From these clues, one might expect that absence of a hen would affect duckling survival less in wood ducks than in mallards. Unmarked wood duck broods 2 to 4 weeks old numbered about the same whether led by a female or not ($\bar{x} = 5.70$ vs. 5.57 ducklings per brood, $t = 0.98$, 15 df, $P > 0.30$). On the other hand, 2- to 5-week-old mallard broods led by females tended to average more ducklings than parentless broods of the same age class ($\bar{x} = 5.53$ vs. 3.76, $t = 2.69$, 91 df, $P < 0.10$). Further evidence of this tendency may be found by considering only parentless broods. We used 4 weeks in wood ducks and 5 weeks in mallards as the dividing lines between "young" and "old" parentless broods and found that young wood duck broods averaged about the same size as old broods ($\bar{x} = 5.14$ vs. 5.13, $t = 0.01$, 13 df, $P > 0.40$). Parentless mallards, however, averaged fewer ducklings per young brood than per old brood ($\bar{x} = 4.21$ vs. 5.25, $t = 1.48$, 44 df, $0.10 > P > 0.05$). The level of significance is not particularly high, but it seems meaningful in that the difference between means is in the opposite direction from that expected in broods led by a hen, where brood size tended to decrease with increasing age (Fig. 2). This suggests that mallard broods which were abandoned very early suffered high mortality, whereas those abandoned closer to fledging age were able to survive without a parent. Some total-brood mortality probably occurred in abandoned young broods. Aggregation of older parentless broods is a possible alternative explanation, but this rarely was seen in mallards until after fledging.

DISCUSSION AND MANAGEMENT IMPLICATIONS

Reed (1970:136) estimated that about half the female black ducks (*Anas rubripes*) which produced broods on his study area lost all of their ducklings. He suggested that production estimates based on brood counts be interpreted with caution, pending further information on the extent of total-brood losses in other situations. Dzubin and Gollop (1972:130) estimated that only 48 percent of all mallard broods hatched on 1 of their Canadian study areas survived the initial move from nest site to water, and that only 58 percent of the broods reaching water ultimately survived to fledging. Brood survival thus varies from species to species and area to area, but we agree that total-brood losses make production estimates based solely on brood-size counts decidedly liberal, perhaps about one-third too high for wood ducks and mallards breeding in the lake-forest region of the North Central states. In studies of wood duck survival, average brood sizes as low as 3.1 and 4.3 have been reported (Odom 1970:115, Decker 1959:312). If females vary in their ability to rear their broods successfully, or even if mere chance variations in survival are considered, some total-brood losses logically would be expected.

Timber management to produce wood duck nest trees within 0.8 km of brood water has been recommended (McGilvrey 1968:5, Gilmer 1971:123). In view of the capabilities of wood duck broods for successful overland travel, this seems to be a reasonable management guideline. Any other management procedures to minimize duckling mortality obviously must focus on the first two weeks of life but will be difficult to formulate without further knowledge of the causes of early mortality.

Female mallards usually remain with their ducklings until near fledging; early breaks in the hen-brood bond seem to decrease duckling survival. Relatively short and loose hen-brood bonds are normal in wood ducks, however, and seem to have little or no adverse effect on survival of the young.

LITERATURE CITED

BALL, I. J. 1971. Movements, habitat use and behavior of wood duck (*Aix sponsa*) broods in north-central Minnesota as determined by radio tracking. M.S. Thesis. Univ. of Minnesota, St. Paul. 56pp.

———. 1973. Ecology of duck broods in north-central Minnesota. Ph.D. Thesis. Univ. of Minnesota, St. Paul. 67pp.

BEARD, E. B. 1964. Duck brood behavior at the Seney National Wildlife Refuge. J. Wildl. Manage. 28(3):492–521.

BELLROSE, F. C. 1953. Housing for wood ducks. Illinois Nat. Hist. Surv. Circ. 45. 47pp.

BENGSTON, S. A. 1972. Reproduction and fluctuations in the size of duck populations at Lake Myvatn, Iceland. Oikos 23(1):35–58.

DECKER, E. 1959. A 4-year study of wood ducks on a Pennsylvania marsh. J. Wildl. Manage. 23(3):310–315.

DREIS, R. E. 1954. A field observation method of aging broods of wood ducks. J. Wildl. Manage. 18(2):280–281.

DZUBIN, A., AND J. B. GOLLOP. 1972. Aspects of mallard breeding ecology in Canadian parkland and grassland. Pages 113–152 *in* Population ecology of migratory birds. U.S. Fish Wildl. Serv. Wildl. Res. Rep. 2.

EVANS, C. D., AND K. E. BLACK. 1956. Duck production studies on the prairie potholes of South Dakota. U.S. Fish Wildl. Serv. Spec. Sci. Rep. Wildl. 32. 59pp.

———, A. S. HAWKINS, AND W. H. MARSHALL. 1952. Movements of waterfowl broods in Manitoba. U.S. Fish Wildl. Serv. Spec. Sci. Rep. Wildl. 16. 47pp.

GILMER, D. S. 1971. Home range and habitat use of breeding mallards (*Anas platyrhynchos*) and wood ducks (*Aix sponsa*) in north-central Minnesota as determined by radio tracking. Ph.D. Thesis. Univ. of Minnesota, St. Paul. 142pp.

———, I. J. BALL, L. M. COWARDIN, AND J. H. RIECHMANN. 1974. Effects of radio packages on wild ducks. J. Wildl. Manage. 38(2):243–252.

GOLLOP, J. B., AND W. H. MARSHALL. 1954. A guide for aging duck broods in the field. Mississippi Flyway Tech. Sect. 14pp. (Mimeogr.)

HEUSMANN, H. W. 1972. Survival of wood duck broods from dump nests. J. Wildl. Manage. 36(2):620–624.

KEITH, L. B. 1961. A study of waterfowl ecology on small impoundments in southeastern Alberta. Wildl. Monogr. 6. 88pp.

MCGILVREY, F. B. (compiler). 1968. A guide to wood duck production habitat requirements. U. S. Bur. Sport Fish Wildl. Resour. Publ. 60. 32pp.

———. 1969. Survival in wood duck broods. J. Wildl. Manage. 33(1):73–76.

ODOM, R. R. 1970. Nest box production and brood survival of wood ducks on the Piedmont National Wildlife Refuge 1969. Proc. Southeastern Assoc. Game and Fish Commissioners 24:108–117.

REED, A. 1970. The breeding ecology of the black duck in the St. Lawrence estuary. D. Sc. Thesis. Universite Laval, Quebec. 175pp.

STEWART, P. A. 1958. Local movements of wood ducks (*Aix sponsa*). Auk 75(2):157–168.

———. 1974. Mother wood ducks feeding away from their broods. Bird Banding 45(1):58.

SWANSON, G. A., AND A. B. SARGEANT. 1972. Observation of nighttime feeding behavior of ducks. J. Wildl. Manage. 36(3):959–961.

Accepted 25 June 1975.

OLDSQUAW BROOD BEHAVIOR[1,2]

R. M. ALISON, Wildlife Branch, Ministry of National Resources, Queen's Park, Toronto, Ontario M7A 1W3, Canada

Oldsquaw (*Clangula hyemalis*) brood behavior was investigated in the vicinity of Churchill, Manitoba in 1974 and 1975 by means of a banding-marking program. In May and June of these years, 35 adult females were captured and marked. In addition, in July and August, 128 immatures were caught and banded, 46 of which were also marked with nasal saddles (Alison 1975*a*). Brood behavior was monitored through sightings of marked birds and recaptures of banded, unmarked individuals.

Communal broods of Oldsquaws were commonly observed, especially from mid-July to mid-August. Several instances of brood adoption were also noted. In one of these instances (22 July), a marked female, which successfully hatched a clutch of five eggs on 7 July 1975, adopted four other Oldsquaw ducklings; these about two days younger than her brood. An adult female was not present with the second brood and it is likely that the four adopted ones were from a brood of six which had previously vanished from a nearby pond subsequent to the death of the adult female. Two other instances of brood adoption involving marked adult females and banded broods were noted in 1975. Such behavior is not uncommon among waterfowl (Hochbaum 1944).

Communal broods of Oldsquaws comprising as many as 135 individuals were observed. Frequently, the number of adult females accompanying these broods was insufficient to account for the total number of young assuming only combination of specific broods, each with the appropriate adult. In one communal flock of 56, 93% were immatures whereas another contained 32 immatures and only one adult female. Many of the young birds had evidently been adopted, perhaps through separation from their own parent. The composition of individual communal broods changed often, as individuals and groups of immatures and adults walked about from pond to pond.

BROOD BEHAVIOR

Although anecdotal accounts of the brood behavior of this and other species are recorded (Bent 1923, Phillips 1925), detailed studies of the activities of the young of diving species are available only for Redheads (*Aythya americana*) (Low 1945, Lokemoen 1966) and Canvasbacks (*Aythya valisineria*) (Hochbaum 1944, 1960). In this study, older females marked in previous years tended to be more successful in rearing young than younger females, and the older birds and their broods possibly formed a nucleus for communal broods. Frequently some of the oldest females accompanied communal broods; very old females and their broods were seldom observed alone.

Certain females were exceptionally aggressive towards specific kinds of predators. One female, for example, routinely attacked and chased Herring Gulls (*Larus argentatus*) from the lake in which a large communal brood was present. Such attacks were frequently conducted in the air. When threatened by a winged predator, the entire brood always dove and while submerged, swam towards shore,

---

[1] Originally published in Bird-Banding 47(3): 210–213, 1976.

[2] Reproduced with permission of the Northeastern Bird-Banding Association.

eventually surfacing among dense shoreline vegetation. The birds never left the water to escape such an attack. If the pond was shallow, winged predators were often able to see the submerged ducklings and could dive beneath the surface and capture them. The young always swam very close to the pond bottom during escape attempts, usually causing debris to "boil up" and cloud the water. Ducklings often reversed direction and vanished into the turbid water. Such behavior may be of selective advantage in predator avoidance. Broods tended to occur on ponds with much bottom sediment, which might readily be agitated, rather than in ponds with rocky bottoms. Also, in most instances the adult female attempted to attract the predator away from the escaping ducklings. If the brood was surprised in deep water, far from shore, the female invariably dove, swimming in a zig-zag fashion close to the bottom causing agitation of bottom sediment. The young birds, unable to swim to protective shoreline vegetation, dove continuously into the turbid water, their activities increasing the turbidity. In these circumstances, immatures were very seldom captured by the predator.

When confronted by a human or large carnivore, the female and brood always swam to the center of the pond, remaining above the surface in alert posture. As the threat approached quite near the brood (within 25 m) the female, or in the case of a communal brood, all the adult females, swam toward the threat, frequently diving when within about 10 m and almost invariably surfacing beside the intruder in an apparent attempt to distract attention from the young. Movement by the intruder toward the young caused the female to approach more closely and continue this behavior, frequently calling and splashing violently on the water surface. During these activities, broods usually remained stationary.

When a threat approached to within about 10 m of the young, the brood immediately scattered and dove, behaving in the manner described previously. In these instances, attempts to drive the brood for banding purposes were totally ineffective. Although the birds dove continuously, once submerged, they did not progress in any particular direction nor did they venture beyond the area clouded by their diving and swimming activities. Frequently, the clouded area did not exceed 10 m in diameter and yet, whenever I approached a brood and caused it to scatter and dive in this manner, the birds continued to dive and surface within the turbid area rather than swim away to clear water. This diving behavior always continued until the departure of the threat.

Before each dive and while submerged, the female and young vocalized regularly, uttering the warning call "urk" (Alison 1975*b*). In this manner, the birds communicated under water without visual contact.

BROOD MOVEMENTS

Daily movements of 22 broods (adult female and at least five ducklings marked) were recorded. Typically individual broods remained on relatively small ponds (about 750 m^2) for about 1.5 weeks after hatching. During this interval, few communal broods were seen. However, at an age of about 1.5–2 weeks (and older), broods were frequently led by the adult female to nearby ponds. During the prefledging period (average 35 days) each brood might move to 10–20 different ponds. With increasing age, the broods frequented larger ponds. In some instances, relatively large distances were travelled. One brood walked 2.0 km in one night; another walked 5.2 km through dense cover in three nights, remaining on suitable ponds during the day.

Movement between ponds or lakes always occurred at night (between 2300 and 0600). Prior to movement, the adult females frequently flew about the vicinity apparently searching for another suitable pond or water area. Several such exploratory flights were conducted by individual females in a single afternoon; these were the only occasions when they abandoned the brood before fledging. At dusk, the broods were led overland to the chosen destination (not necessarily the nearest open water). Sometimes, involving communal broods, the entire flock did not follow one female and thus the congregation split. Even after fledging, flocks comprised solely of immatures frequently appeared on the study area, although such visits from Hudson's Bay occurred only between 0900 and 1650.

About mid-July, communal broods began to occur on large lakes, although the number of birds comprising these flocks varied daily as birds arrived and departed. Broods usually remained on individual lakes for only about 8–10 days before departing, sometimes en masse, for nearby lakes. Eventually, the fledged birds flew (or perhaps walked) to Hudson's Bay. Individual females invariably led their broods over the same route year after year. Thus, certain lakes traditionally supported large flocks of immatures whereas others supported none.

DISCUSSION

Although communal broods occur among Oldsquaws, such behavior being presumably of selective advantage, the mechanism enhancing survival of immatures is unknown. The defensive actions of adult female Oldsquaws, although apparently relatively ineffective when performed by one female in the presence of more than one predator (Salomonsen 1950), frequently succeed in protecting the young when performed by several associated females. Similarly, predation upon adult females in such congregations may be reduced as compared to the loss by predation of lone females or females with one brood.

Certain escape behavior performed by immatures involving activities which tend to cause bottom sediment to cloud the water would be of greater escape value when performed by large numbers of individuals (i.e., communal broods). Therefore, despite the possible increased predation of flightless immatures walking in large congregations between ponds, escape behavior performed by the young and defensive behavior of the adult females are more effective when performed in large assemblages and apparently, as a result, such flocking behavior is of selective value. It is possibly disadvantageous, however, in those instances where frequent overland movements between ponds are necessary as food supplies are depleted by large numbers of congregated Oldsquaws. It is unknown whether interpond movements are stimulated by declining food supplies. Furthermore, frequent brood movements between ponds do not apparently occur among other species of diving ducks (Poston 1974), particularly in areas where ponds are more productive nutritionally.

Adult females conduct their broods to the same ponds year after year. Older females probably produce more fledged young than younger females, because the former, in addition to locating their nests so as to minimize predation loss, conduct their broods to ponds or lakes in which the young might escape predation more readily than elsewhere. Thus, the breeding nucleus of an Oldsquaw population may comprise only the oldest, most experienced adult females, possibly not more than 10–20% of the breeding females. One of the most productive females was at least seven years old. Increased breeding success with age has also been reported for Canvasbacks and Lesser Scaup (*Aythya affinis*) (D. Trauger, pers. comm.).

Suitable management of Oldsquaws on the breeding grounds would therefore comprise identification and retention of those lakes traditionally frequented by Oldsquaw broods in those areas in which they might be threatened by development.

LITERATURE CITED

ALISON, R. M. 1975*a*. Capturing and marking Oldsquaw. Bird-Banding 46:248–250.

———. 1975*b*. Breeding biology and behavior of the Oldsquaw (*Clangula hyemalis* L.). Ornithol. Monogr. 18, 52pp.

BENT, A. C. 1925. Life histories of North American wildfowl, order Anseres. U.S. Natl. Mus., Bull. 130:32–50, Vol. 2.

HOCHBAUM, H. A. 1944. The Canvasback on a prairie marsh. Washington, D.C., Wildl. Mgmt. Inst.

———. 1960. The brood season. Nat. Hist. June–July, pp. 54–61.

LOKEMOEN, T. 1966. Breeding ecology of the Redhead duck in western Montana. J. Wildl. Manage. 30:668–681.

LOW, S. B. 1945. Ecology and management of the Redhead, *Nyroca americana,* in Iowa. Ecol. Monogr. 15:35–69.

PHILLIPS, J. C. 1925. The natural history of the ducks, vol. 3. Boston, Houghton Mifflin Co.

POSTON, H. J. 1974. Home range and breeding biology of the shoveler. Canadian Wildl. Serv. Report Series 25. Ottawa, Queens Printer.

SALOMONSEN, F. 1950. The birds of Greenland. Kobenhavn. Ejnar Munksgaard.

LACK OF ASSOCIATION AMONG DUCK BROODMATES DURING MIGRATION AND WINTERING[1]

R. K. MARTINSON,[2] Migratory Bird Populations Station, Laurel, MD 20810
A. S. HAWKINS, U.S. Bureau of Sport Fisheries and Wildlife, Minneapolis, MN 55408

Male (Lensink 1964:19) and female ducks tend to return to the area where they last bred or were raised (Sowls 1955). Band recovery data show a similar tendency for ducks to return to wintering areas (Stewart et al. 1958, Martinson 1966). Wintering British Columbia Mallard (*Anas platyrhynchos*) populations may be definite associations of birds that breed in the same general locality, migrate together, and use the same wintering area (Munro 1943). On the other hand Gollop (1965:36–37) showed that Mallards reared in Saskatchewan or breeding there returned in subsequent years, but "neither migrated nor wintered as definite associations." He based his conclusions on recovery data from groups of Mallards banded on the same slough and from broodmates. His data showed, by date or area of recovery, that the birds migrated independently and sometimes to different wintering localities. This paper presents additional data suggesting that ducks banded as broodmates may migrate independently.

We obtained records from banders and from the banding schedule files at the Bird Banding Laboratory, Laurel, Maryland, for several hundred groups of flightless ducklings that were identified as broodmates when banded. All were released at or near the point of capture but not neccessarily in a group. Of the 31 broods yielding recoveries of two or more broodmates, 21 were recovered at places or dates of no significance to the problem. Table 1 shows the recovery details for the remaining 10 broods, in which the recoveries of broodmates on different migration and wintering areas or in different migration or wintering periods suggest they had not migrated together. The first three broods yielded recoveries in different migration or wintering areas during the same migrational or wintering period: Mallards in Idaho and Arkansas, Gadwalls (*Anas strepera*) in southwestern Illinois and eastern Virginia, and Canvasbacks (*Aythya valisineria*) in southeastern Michigan and California. Recoveries from the other three broods of Canvasbacks also suggest separate migration by both date and location. The recoveries from the last four broods of Mallards in different migrational or wintering areas but in different years are equally suggestive because of the tendency of ducks to return to the same wintering area they first visit.

If, as these data indicate, ducklings do not travel together as a family unit, and therefore not with the parent hen, it can be speculated that homing to the natal area (Sowls 1955, Lensink 1964:19) is not accomplished by the leadership of the parent. It might also be concluded that, although a wintering area tradition is established after the first migration, wintering populations of ducks are interrelated through the mingling of their progeny.

---

[1] Originally published in Auk 85(4):684–686, 1968.

[2] Address correspondence to this author. Present address: 10875 N.W. Rainmont, Portland, OR 97229.

Table 1. Recovery details of ducks believed to be members of the same brood when banded.

Species	Banding location and date	Recovery information: Sex	Location of recovery	Date of recovery
Mallard	Success, Saskatchewan	Male	Southwestern Saskatchewan (Eston)	3 October 1955
	27 July 1955	Male	Southwestern Idaho (Emmett)	20 November 1955
		Male	Northeastern Arkansas (Walnut Ridge)	20 December 1955
Gadwall	Abound, Saskatchewan	Male	Southwestern Illinois (Alton)	15 November 1958
	4 August 1958	Female	Eastern Virginia (Montross)	December 1958
Canvasback	Waldeck, Saskatchewan	Female	Southeastern Michigan (Lake St. Clair)	11 November 1958
	4 July 1958	Male	Central California (San Pablo Bay)	12 December 1958
		Male	Southeastern Michigan (Detroit River)	6 March 1960
Canvasback	Oak River, Manitoba	Female	Southwestern Manitoba (Sandy Lake)	28 September 1953
	14 July 1953	Male	Eastern Michigan (Saginaw Bay)	26 October 1953
		Female	North-central North Dakota (Anamoose)	29 October 1953
Canvasback	Sandy Lake, Manitoba	Male	Southeastern Wisconsin (Fox Lake)	1 November 1953
	16 July 1953	Male	Southwestern Minnesota (Yellow Medicine Co.)	15 November 1953
		Female	Chesapeake Bay, Maryland (St. Marys Co.)	7 January 1954
Canvasback	Minnedosa, Manitoba	Female	Southwestern Manitoba (Amaranth)	21 September 1953
	24 July 1953	Female	Eastern South Dakota (Kingsbury Co.)	4 October 1953
		Female	East-central Wisconsin (Lake Poygan)	8 November 1953
		Male	Southeastern Michigan (Lake St. Clair)	7 November 1953
Mallard	Lucky Lake, Saskatchewan	Male	Northwestern Wyoming (Powell)	11 March 1964
	10 July 1957	Male	Southeastern Nebraska (Beatrice)	23 November 1957
Mallard	Abound, Saskatchewan	Male	Southeastern Arkansas (Stuttgart	31 December 1960
	3 August 1960	Female	North-central Texas (Seymour)	"Hunting season" 1962
Mallard	Bradwell, Saskatchewan	Female	Central Saskatchewan (Bradwell)	6 September 1958
	27 July 1958	Male	Northeastern Nebraska (Verdel)	27 November 1958
		Male	Southwestern British Columbia (Vancouver)	8 December 1962
Mallard	Minnedosa, Manitoba	Female	Southeastern Saskatchewan (Moosomin)	20 October 1952
	9 July 1952	Adult female	Southeastern Arkansas (Stuttgart)	12 December 1952
		Male	Northeastern Texas (Dallas)	23 November 1953

LITERATURE CITED

GOLLOP, J. B. 1965. Dispersal and annual survival of the mallard (*Anas platyrhynchos*). Canadian Wildlife Service (mimeo.).

LENSINK, C. J. 1964. Distribution of recoveries from banding of ducklings. U.S. Fish and Wildlife Service, Special Sci. Rept., Wildlife No. 89.

MARTINSON, R. K. 1966. Some characteristics of wintering mallard populations and their management. Migratory Bird Populations Station, Laurel, Maryland, Administrative Rept. No. 116.

MUNRO, J. A. 1943. Studies of waterfowl in British Columbia mallard. Canadian J. Research D 21:223–260.

SOWLS, L. K. 1955. Prairie ducks. Harrisburg, Pennsylvania, Stackpole.

STEWART, R. E., A. D. GEIS, AND C. D. EVANS. 1958. Distribution of populations and hunting kill of the canvasback. J. Wildl. Mgmt. 22:333–370.

SELECTED BIBLIOGRAPHY

Reproductive Ecology: Broods

BAKER, J. L. 1970. Wood duck brood survival on the Noxubee National Wildlife Refuge. Proc. Annu. Conf. S.E. Assoc. Game Fish Comm. 24:104–108.

BEARD, E. B. 1964. Duck brood behavior at the Seney National Wildlife Refuge. J. Wildl. Manage. 28(3):492–521.

BEDARD, J., AND J. MUNRO. 1977. Brood and creche stability in the common eider of the St. Lawrence Estuary. Behaviour 60(3–4):221–236.

BERG, P. F. 1956. A study of waterfowl broods in eastern Montana with special reference to movements and the relationship of reservoir fencing to production. J. Wildl. Manage. 20:253–262.

COWAN, P. J. 1974. Individual differences in alarm calls of Canada geese leading broods. Auk 91(1):189–191.

HEALEY, R. F., F. COOKE, AND P. W. COLGAN. 1980. Demographic consequences of snow goose brood-rearing traditions. J. Wildl. Manage. 44:900–904.

HEUSMANN, H. W. 1972. Survival of wood duck broods from dump nests. J. Wildl. Manage. 36(2):620–624.

JOYNER, D. E. 1977. Behavior of ruddy duck broods in Utah. Auk 94(2):343–349.

KITCHEN, D. W., AND G. S. HUNT. 1969. Brood habitat of the hooded merganser. J. Wildl. Manage. 33(3):605–609.

LAHART, D. E., AND G. W. CORNWELL. 1970. Habitat preference and survival of Florida duck broods. Proc. Annu. Conf. S.E. Assoc. Game Fish Comm. 24:117–121.

MACK, G. D., AND L. D. FLAKE. 1980. Habitat relationships of waterfowl broods on South Dakota stock ponds. J. Wildl. Manage. 44:695–699.

MCGILVREY, F. B. 1969. Survival in wood duck broods. J. Wildl. Manage. 33(1):73–76.

RINGELMAN, J. K., AND L. D. FLAKE. 1980. Diurnal visibility and activity of blue-winged teal and mallard broods. J. Wildl. Manage. 44:822–830.

SMART, G. 1965. Development and maturation of primary feathers of redhead ducklings. J. Wildl. Manage. 29(3):533–536.

YOUNG, C. M. 1967. Overland migration of duck broods in a drought-free area. Can. J. Zool. 45(3):249–251.

Behavior

ECOETHOLOGICAL ASPECTS OF REPRODUCTION[1]

FRANK MCKINNEY[2]

The past decade saw new and exciting developments in areas of research in which evolution, ecology, and ethology overlap. Studies of avian reproduction played a key role in promoting new ways of thinking (Cullen 1957; von Haartman 1957; Tinbergen 1959; Orians 1961; Immelmann 1961, 1962; Crook 1964). These studies evolved through a blending of interests and ideas derived mainly from the long-term studies of Lack (1954, 1966, 1968, 1971) on avian ecology, especially population regulation, and those of Tinbergen (1953, 1954, 1959, 1963, 1967) on the evolution and adaptive significance of behavior.

Investigators using these new approaches have referred to their field as "ecoethology" or "behavioral ecology." Although there are still somewhat different emphases among investigators, depending on whether their interests are primarily ecological or behavioral, it is obvious that an important field of biology, focusing on the study of adaptations, has developed rapidly.

This new field had its roots in ornithology and already occupies a dominant place in the thinking of avian biologists. There have been parallel developments among field biologists of all types. In particular, it has been stimulated, among mammalogists, by the rapid growth of field studies on primates (e.g., Jay 1968, Altmann 1971, Crook 1970). These developments have had profound influences on the orientation of research programs with ultimate objectives bearing on conservation, control, or management; this is especially apparent in Britain (Murton 1971).

The blend of interests, stemming mainly from the research programs of Lack and Tinbergen, is illustrated by current attention to such topics as feeding ecology and behavior (e.g., Watson 1970), spacing behavior (Watson and Moss 1970, Brown and Orians 1970), social systems (Crook 1965, Orians 1969), flocking behavior (Crook 1961, Moynihan 1962), habitat selection (Hildén 1965), and communication (Crook 1964, Marler 1968). Many of these areas of research have been reviewed recently, primarily from an ecological aspect, by Orians (1971), and since other participants in this symposium will discuss important ecological and physiological aspects of reproduction, I will take an ethological viewpoint. Since my task is neither to present the latest products of research nor to provide a detailed review, I will concentrate on an attempt to illustrate the ecoethological approach.

THE HISTORY OF ECOETHOLOGY

Ethology had its roots in natural history and zoology, stemming from the early work of such biologists as Charles Darwin, C. O. Whitman, Oskar Heinroth, Wallace Craig, and Julian Huxley. It became a recognized branch of biology largely under the influence of Konrad Lorenz and Niko Tinbergen. Since the interests and discoveries of these two zoologists are well known through their many books and papers, I will not attempt to give a résumé of their research.

---

[1] Originally published in D. Farner, ed. Breeding biology of birds, pages 6–21. National Academy of Sciences, Washington, D.C., 1973.

[2] Present address: Bell Museum of Natural History, University of Minnesota, Minneapolis, MN 55455.

It is essential to note, however, that both have applied concepts of organic evolution to the study of animal behavior. A concern with how behavior has evolved and how it is adaptive has been central to their ideas and research. To this end, they applied to behavior the methods of comparative anatomy, especially the concepts of homology, adaptive radiation, and convergent evolution. Both Lorenz and Tinbergen have consistently stressed the need for careful observation and description of natural behavior and, because of their training as systematists, they tend to think of behavior patterns as though they were "organs" possessed by a species.

This zoological approach was, and still very largely is, completely different from the way that most psychologists think about behavior. As many reviewers (e.g., Klopfer and Hailman 1967) have pointed out, there are fundamental differences in interests. In general, for example, psychologists tend to have little interest in the evolution and adaptive significance of behavior.

Lorenz and Tinbergen laid great stress on the desirability of asking all four types of biological questions (causation, development, evolution, and function) about behavior and, for many years, attention was focused on their ideas about causation and development, the very areas where their interests overlapped with those of psychologists and physiologists. This produced endless controversy over such matters as the distinction between instinct and learning and the reality and nature of "drives." From this interaction there emerged a flourishing interdisciplinary field (sometimes called "psychobiology"), centered around such problems as motivation and imprinting, to which both ethologists and psychologists were attracted. These fields are brilliantly reviewed by Hinde (1970), whose research program has had a major catalytic effect in bridging these two disciplines.

Meanwhile, many ethologists slanted their research toward problems of evolution and adaptive significance. They followed the classic ethological orientation toward behavior as an attribute of a species, and it is understandable that they found their closest ties with evolutionists, ornithologists, and ecologists, rather than with neurophysiologists and psychologists. Splitting within the ethological ranks has been resisted vigorously, largely intuitively I think, because of the basic conviction of zoologists that all aspects of biology are interrelated. But specialization has been inevitable, as methods and techniques have become more sophisticated and as the volume of research has increased steeply. The basic ecoethological methods—field observation, description and analysis of natural behavior, field and laboratory experimentation (e.g., with models and playback of tape recordings), and comparisons between species—require prolonged, specialized training and distinctive attitudes. Most researchers in this field cannot handle with equal competence the laboratory techniques used by neurophysiologists, endocrinologists, and learning psychologists. Fortunately, interdisciplinary contact between these fields is possible through symposia such as this, and there are increasing signs of fruitful team approaches being instituted.

In the broadest sense, everyone uses comparative methods, but there have been important differences in the way that these methods have been applied by psychologists and ethologists. Comparative psychologists and physiologists frequently compare representatives from different animal groups, as they do, for example, in studying learning abilities in fish, frogs, chickens, cats, and monkeys. Such studies usually focus on a fundamental process, rather than on the particular species selected as a class representative. Ethologists, in contrast, have come to rely heavily on two specialized ways of comparing different species: They study *adaptive radiation* in a group of closely related species, or they search for *convergence* among distantly related forms living under similar environmental conditions. Both of these methods are basic to all evolutionary studies and are certainly of fundamental importance in ecoethology.

Classic examples of the approach via adaptive radiation are those of Lorenz (1941) on the comparison of duck displays and Tinbergen (1959) on gulls. The use of the convergence approach is well illustrated in von Haartman's (1957) study of hole-nesting adaptations in different groups of birds.

The investigations of Lorenz on ducks showed that courtship displays can be homologized from species to species and that many are useful taxonomic characters. This discovery caused considerable excitement among systematists, and there has been widespread application of the method in other groups of animals. Many of these studies were carried out on captive animals and interesting information was gathered on the distribution of homologous displays, often providing insights as to how these signal movements have evolved from such everyday actions as feeding and preening movements. The view of Lorenz, however, that the signal repertoires are "mere conventions," their characteristics being largely accidental in any one species, was generally accepted. This mode of thinking was reinforced by strong emphasis by evolutionary biologists on the role played by courtship displays in species isolation.

This point of view was changed radically by Cullen (1957) in a study of the Black-legged Kittiwake (*Rissa tridactyla*). Her ideas on the influence of environmental factors, in this case cliff-nesting, on all aspects of social behavior developed for two reasons: (a) the behavior of many gull species had been described and the descriptions were available to provide a contrast with the Kittiwake, and (b) these comparative studies of gulls were carried out in the field, where ideas on the adaptive significance of behavior developed naturally as selective forces were observed in action.

The ideas of Cullen were quickly confirmed and extended by studies on other bird groups, especially by Crook (1964) in extensive comparative investigations on weaver birds (Ploceinae). This has led to broader statements (e.g., Crook 1965, Lack 1968, Orians 1971) of relationships between seasonal and spatial distribution of food, feeding methods, characteristics of the breeding habitat and the nest-site, vulnerability to predators, mating systems, characteristics of the pair-bond, and communication methods. It is now recognized that the behavior of each species has evolved as a compromise between many competing selection pressures and that morphological, physiological, ecological, and behavioral adaptations must be thought of as coadapted systems.

One is tempted to use the term "breakthrough" in considering these advances in thinking about adaptive aspects of avian reproduction; the effects have indeed been far-reaching. The fundamental importance of observation and description of the behavior of each species (the building of "ethograms") is now easy to justify. The need to study birds in the field in their natural habitats can be argued logically. The comparative method

Table 1. Major behavioral differences between Steller's Eider and Common Eider.

Characteristic	Steller's Eider	Common Eider
Body size	Small	Large
Feeding habitat	Shallow water	Deep water
Food	Small invertebrates	Large invertebrates
Diving flocks	Large, densely packed; synchronize dives	Small not densely packed; dives not synchronized
Response to birds of prey	Flocks fly up readily	Fly less readily; may dive to escape
Precopulatory behavior	Brief; single shake; final display invariable	Up to several minutes; conspicuous wing-flap; many shakes; some calls by male; final display variable
Postcopulatory behavior	Pair flies back to flock; male displays silent	Male calls
Courtship behavior	Preflight movements; short flights; aerial pursuits; displays rapid; males silent	Underwater pursuits; displays slower; some compound displays; males give cooing calls

need no longer be used tentatively and intuitively, as it was for many years, but can now be applied deliberately with specific objectives in mind. In short, the study of species-specific behavior, as pioneered by species-oriented ornithologists and ethologists, seems to have finally come of age and has taken a key place in adaptation research.

A COMPARISON OF STELLER'S EIDER AND COMMON EIDER

Studies of the behavior of the Common Eider (*Somateria mollissima*) in England and Alaska (McKinney 1961) and of Steller's Eider (*Polysticta stelleri*) in Alaska (McKinney 1965*b*) disclosed many differences (Table 1). On the Alaska Peninsula in spring, the small Steller's Eider feeds mostly in shallow water, apparently on small molluscs and crustacea. Some feeding is done along shorelines but mostly the birds dive to take food off the bottom. It is an extremely sociable species at this time of year, living in very large, densely packed flocks. When diving for food, there is a marked tendency for birds to dive synchronously, and at times a whole flock, including several thousand birds, will submerge almost simultaneously. The birds are very easily flushed by the appearance of such birds of prey as eagles and gyrfalcons, flocks taking to the air when the predator is still a speck on the horizon. In summary, the Steller's Eider shows strong tendencies to be sociable and to take wing readily, both characteristics probably being primarily antipredator adaptations.

In contrast, the large Common Eider feeds mainly by diving in deep water, often bringing large food items (e.g., crabs, razor-shells) to the surface to swallow. Feeding flocks are usually quite small, less densely-packed, and there is much less pronounced synchronous diving than in Steller's Eider. In general, they seem less likely to fly in response to birds of prey and there are reports that they will dive to escape. Thus, these large birds are less markedly sociable,

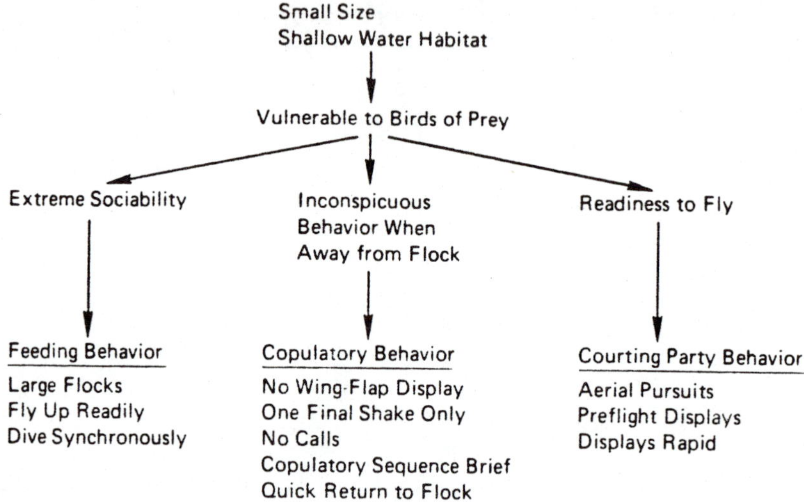

Fig. 1. Suggested relationships between body size, habitat characteristics, vulnerability to predators, and various characteristics of social behavior in Steller's Eider.

less ready to fly, and, in general, their preference for deep-water feeding probably makes them less vulnerable to surprise attacks from predators.

These differences seem to have had repercussions on the characteristics of their social behavior and signaling methods, notably the behavior associated with pair formation and copulation (Fig. 1). In courting groups, Steller's Eider males frequently adopt erect preflight postures, they perform ritualized "short flights," and aerial pursuit flights are common. Furthermore, the courtship displays are rapid and males give no calls. In Common Eider, preflight and aerial components are absent, and courting parties indulge in underwater pursuits instead. The male displays are slower and more elaborate and many are accompanied by cooing calls.

To copulate, a pair of Steller's Eider flies out several hundred meters from the flock, quickly performs precopulatory displays, mounting occurs, and almost immediately they fly back to the flock. Presumably, while away from the flock, the pair is much more vulnerable to attack by birds of prey, and their uneasiness is often apparent. Selection has apparently favored the use of inconspicuous displays in this situation, and the evolutionary changes that have occurred in the precopulatory displays are nicely shown by comparing them to the displays of the Common Eider. In the latter species, Shakes are frequent, and Bathing movements are usually followed by a conspicuous ritualized Wing-flap. In Steller's Eider, only a single Shake occurs, immediately before mounting, and while Bathe is very frequent, a ritualized Wing-flap is absent.

Thus there is good evidence to suggest that the small size and shallow-water feeding habits of Steller's Eider make this species more vulnerable to predators. This has favored extreme sociability and a general readiness to take wing. These tendencies are reflected in the kinds of display used and selection has favored the use of inconspicuous displays

Table 2. Major differences in ecology and breeding behavior between the Shoveler and the Pintail.

Behavior	Shoveler	Pintail
Habitat	Permanent water areas rich in plankton	Temporary pools and widely dispersed permanent water areas
Nest site	Concealed in dense cover near water	In open or sparse cover often far from water
Feeding methods	Mainly strains plankton	Up-ends frequently
Breeding home range	Small discrete territories with little overlap	Large with much overlap
Brood movements	Short distances	Can move long distances
Distant threat signals	Head-pumping and calls; wing noise	—
Hostility between paired males	Highly developed ritualized circular fighting	Rare
Strength of pair-bond	Strong	Weak
Duration of pair-bond	Throughout incubation	Breaks early in incubation
Aerial chases	Brief and short-range; male hostility common	Prolonged and wide-ranging
Rape attempts	Rare	Common
Copulation frequency in pairs	Daily before and during laying	Rarely observed
Courtship displays	Ritualized feeding movements; Jump Flight	Grunt-whistle; Head-up-tail-up

when birds are away from the safety of the flock.

BREEDING BEHAVIOR OF THE SHOVELER AND PINTAIL

Territorial behavior and aerial pursuit activity in dabbling ducks on the breeding grounds have been topics of controversy for many years. There have been strong disagreements on whether ducks do defend territories, whether chasing activity disperses breeding pairs, and whether the motivation of chasing males is primarily aggressive or sexual. Strong observational evidence in favor of territorial behavior was presented by Hochbaum (1944), Sowls (1955), Dzubin (1955), and others, but it is now clear that generalizations about such behavior in ducks, or even in dabblers and divers, are very dangerous. There are important specific differences and, apparently, each species has evolved somewhat different breeding strategies in response to selection pressures of several kinds (McKinney 1965*a*).

It has been recognized for some time, for example, that the average size of the "home range" of a breeding pair varies from species to species (Dzubin 1955), but progress has been very slow in discovering *why* each species behaves differently. It now seems likely that specific differences in such factors as food requirements and feeding methods, seasonal and spatial distribution of food, nesting cover and brood rearing habitat, physical characteristics of the habitat, and vulnerability of nests to predation have placed different demands on each

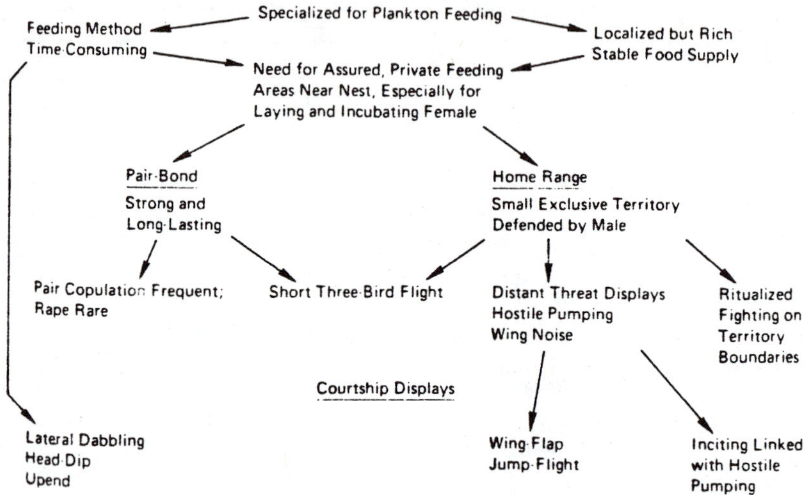

Fig. 2. Suggested relationships between feeding strategy and social behavior in the Shoveler.

species, resulting in a variety of breeding strategies. The complexity and subtlety of the relationships between such factors can be illustrated by comparing two extreme types in the dabbling duck group, the Shoveler (*Anas clypeata*) and the Pintail (*A. acuta*) (Table 2).

The Shoveler, with its large spatulate bill, specializes in feeding by straining plankton at the surface. This appears to be a time-consuming feeding method and breeding pairs prefer prairie habitats, where there is a rich supply of suitable food available within a restricted area throughout the breeding season. Also it must be especially important for females during the prelaying, laying, and incubation periods to have assured feeding areas, close to the nest site, where they are free from harassment by conspecific individuals. Observations on *A. clypeata*, both in the wild (McKinney 1965*a*, Poston 1969) and in captivity (McKinney 1967), and on the closely related Cape Shoveler (*A. smithi*) (McKinney 1970) have shown that these requirements are met by a classical territorial arrangement. Breeding-pair ranges are small, well defended by the male, and there is usually little overlap between neighboring territories. Associated with this system, Shovelers have long-lasting pair-bonds, the male often behaving aggressively on his territory until the time of hatching.

These pair-bond and territorial characteristics have widespread repercussions on all aspects of breeding behavior in Shovelers (McKinney 1970) (Fig. 2). Pair-bond copulations occur daily, promiscuous tendencies of males are weak, and rape of strange females is rare. Aerial chases involving a territorial male pursuing an intruding pair (three-bird flights) are frequent but brief and of short range; the pursuer quickly returns to his territory and mate. Males threaten intruders at a distance with conspicuous Hostile Pumping movements accompanied by calls. Their wings make a characteristic, loud buzzing sound, especially at takeoff; this also appears to have a threat function, discouraging intrusions. At territo-

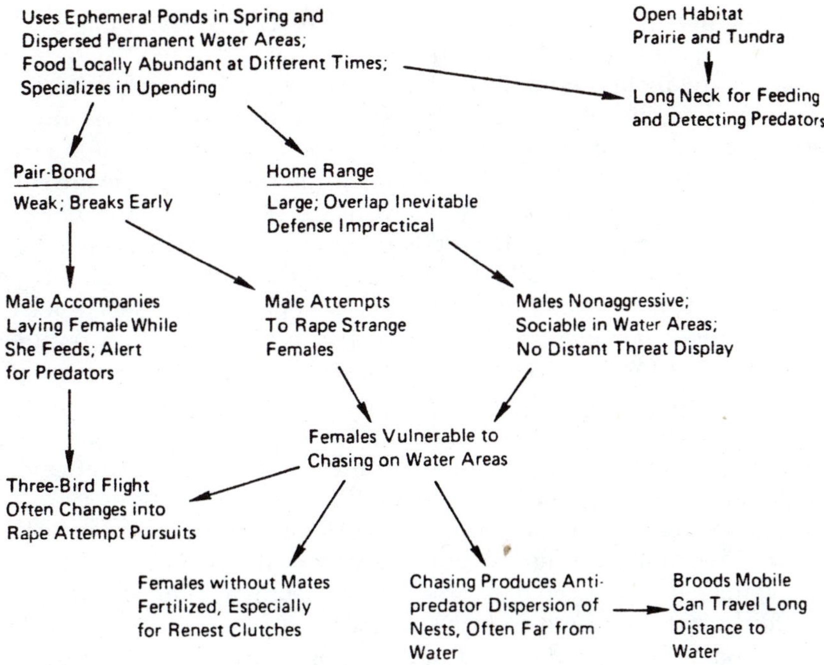

Fig. 3. Suggested relationships between species ecology and breeding strategy in the Pintail.

rial boundaries, disputes between males are resolved through highly ritualized circular fighting.

The evolution of Hostile Pumping, wing noise, and the time-consuming feeding method appear to have influenced the courtship displays. Thus the form of the female's Inciting movement is quite different from that of other *Anas* species, including a mixture of head-pumping and head-low pointing movements, clearly influenced by Hostile Pumping. Males have conspicuous Wing-flap and Jump-flight displays, reinforced by wing noise. The Shoveler, and its relatives in the blue-winged duck group, have used three feeding movements as the basis for the courtship displays: Lateral Dabbling, Head-dip, and Up-end. Presumably, the evolution of these signals was facilitated by the possibility they offered of continuing to feed while signaling, and this may still be the case in Lateral Dabbling.

The Pintail strategy is completely different, though as yet it is not so well understood. The following account is based on Smith's (1968) important study, although Fig. 3 has been worked out in collaboration with Mr. Scott Derrickson who is currently studying this species.

Pintails seem best adapted to open prairie or tundra habitats. Although they are early spring migrants and make use of temporary pools, they are able to breed in areas with sparse, widely scattered permanent water areas. Mobility is their specialty and pairs range widely, using locally abundant food sources as they become available throughout the breeding season. The broods are mobile and the cryptically colored ducklings often make long overland journeys from nest to water. The long neck is probably an adaptation for feeding by up-ending, which they do a great deal, and it may also be an important aid to vision in grassland habitats. The diet is probably more vegetarian than that of the Shoveler.

In contrast to the Shoveler, discrete defended territories are impossible and the home ranges of many pairs overlap. Males are strikingly nonaggressive and are sociable at the water areas. There are no distant threat displays, and fighting between males is rare.

The pair-bond is much "weaker" than in the Shoveler, and it breaks early in incubation. Males do accompany their mates much of the time during the prelaying and laying periods, when they presumably afford protection both from harassing males and from predators. But paired males also spend much time pursuing the females of other pairs. These aerial pursuits may begin as three-bird flights, but they are so prolonged that they often attract other males and change into "rape-attempt flights" that may end, after great distances are covered, in rape of the female by several males when the party lands.

Because of their localized nature, the same water areas are used by many males and females, and the latter are very vulnerable to being chased when they come to feed. Because the vigorous, persistent chasing seems to result in many females moving far from water to lay, nests are dispersed. This must be especially important for the Pintail since the site is often very open (e.g., they will use burns and ploughed fields).

Raping is likely important in fertilizing eggs, especially in the case of females without a mate who are preparing to lay renest clutches.

RESEARCH STRATEGIES

There is evidence from these comparative studies of eiders and dabbling ducks to suggest that differences in feeding ecology, habitat characteristics, and vulnerability to predators have had wide-ranging repercussions on territorial behavior, characteristics of the pair-bond, and other aspects of social behavior. The picture is still only dimly outlined for any species of waterfowl, but the possibility of really "understanding how everything fits" is tantalizing. Progress so far has come mainly from the strategy that I have outlined and has stemmed from an interest in the evolution of displays. Now, however, the need is apparent for much more detailed information on waterfowl foods and feeding methods, on predation, on time and energy budgets, on home ranges and their features, on the physical characteristics of different habitats for communication by various methods, on the process of pair formation and the duration of pair-bonds, on the functions of individual displays, and so on. Any one of these topics, however, could occupy a team of investigators for years, even if they devoted all of their energy to a single species.

The worth of intensive research on single species over many years has been well illustrated by the studies of Watson and Moss (1970), Murton (1965) and Tinbergen (1967) and the need for experimental approaches that involve models, playback of tape-recorded vocalizations, and habitat manipulations is obvious. But insights on adaptation seem to come mainly from comparative study, and there are strong tendencies these days to neglect this approach in favor of detailed analytical and experimental work on single species. Individual choice will no doubt lead different workers in different directions, and some ecoethologists will certainly continue to search for broad correlations through comparative methods. As Scott (1968) has expressed it, "the game of assigning adaptive significance to either structure or behavior is one of the rare areas still open to the free imaginations of scientists" and it is likely that many will continue to be attracted to this pursuit.

There are practical difficulties in deciding which groups should be studied, how much detail is needed in behavioral descriptions for each species, how many species should be examined, and in what sequence. Should ecological information be collected simultaneously and, if so, what parameters must be measured, and how precisely? After preliminary comparative studies of behavior and ecology have been made, should attention then be given to (a) analytical, (b) experimental, or (c) further comparative study? How far do we need to go, for example, with preliminary motivational analyses on the social behavior of each species?

Not the least obligation is that of keeping abreast of the literature. On birds alone, the literature relating to adaptations is widely scattered in a multitude of journals. Comparative, descriptive papers tend to be long and filled with details that are of interest mainly to people working on the same or closely related species.

The answer is obvious, I think, i.e., team approach will be essential. All techniques must be applied in such a way that they are complementary; we can afford to neglect none. Studies of captive birds have an important role in many groups, but field studies of each species must also be made. Long-term intensive investigations, along many analytical and experimental lines, are needed on single species, but comparative studies are essential to provide the ideas. Morphological and physiological studies on each species are necessary, as well as ecological and ethological investigations. None of these studies will ever be truly "complete." The price we pay for being interested in evolutionary problems is that every study we make will be "preliminary." The best we can hope for is to set the stage for deeper understanding.

IMPLICATIONS FOR WILDLIFE MANAGEMENT

For many years, the comparative study of displays seemed far removed from the practical tasks of monitoring population levels; predicting production; controlling depredations; preserving, manipulating, and creating habitat; regulating harvests; and saving species from extinction. This held true as long as ethologists were primarily interested in taxonomic questions. With broadening of interests to include the relationships between signaling methods and adaptive strategies of each species, however, this is no longer the case. Ethologists have had to blend their interests with those of ecologists and, conversely, ecologists have found that many problems lead them to study behavior. It is obvious now that we cannot hope to understand what makes a species "tick" without knowing how its ecology, behavior, morphology, and physiology are interrelated. This is surely the only firm basis for sound conservation, control, and management of its populations.

For example, the problems involved in censusing breeding pairs, interpreting the significance of male aggregations, pursuit flights and raping activity, and home range characteristics must be quite different for the Shoveler and the Pintail.

In spite of much research, we do not yet seem to have a clear understanding of the relationships between breeding behavior and the ecological requirements of such important game species as the Mallard (*Anas platyrhynchos*), Baldpate (*A. americana*), Gadwall (*A. strepera*), Green-winged Teal (*A. crecca*), or Wood Duck (*Aix sponsa*). Perhaps the clues to understanding the breeding strategies of these species will come from comparing and contrasting their behavior with that of the Shoveler and Pintail.

CONCLUSION

By combining intensive studies of ecology and behavior of single species with comparative studies of closely related species, new ideas can emerge on the adaptive radiation of ecoethological strategies in the study group. Long-term field studies on each species are essential, and they should be deliberately directed toward questions of adaptive significance. Beyond the early exploratory stages, the breadth of this approach will usually require team effort, combining the talents of specialists in such fields as feeding ecology, nutrition, and reproductive physiology. Comparative ethologists can play a key role in such teams by revealing specific differences that require explanation. The adaptive characteristics of each species are interrelated in complex and often unexpected ways, and overemphasis on one source of selection, or on one research strategy, is likely to lead to an unbalanced picture. Ecoethological research is time-consuming, and long-term programs are essential; but there seems to be no alternative if we wish to understand why each species behaves as it does.

ACKNOWLEDGMENT

The research reported here was in part supported by the Atomic Energy Commission through Grant COO-1332-77.

LITERATURE CITED

ALTMANN, S. A. 1971. Baboon ecology. University of Chicago Press, Chicago.

BROWN, J. L., AND G. H. ORIANS. 1970. Spacing patterns in mobile animals. Ann. Rev. Ecol. Syst. 1:239–262.

CROOK, J. H. 1961. The basis of flock organization in birds, pp. 125–149. *In* W. H. Thorpe and O. L. Zangwill, eds. Current problems in animal behaviour. Cambridge University Press, London.

———. 1964. The evolution of social organisation and visual communication in the weaver birds (Ploceinae). Behaviour Suppl. 10.

———. 1965. The adaptive significance of avian social organizations. Symp. Zool. Soc. London 14:181–218.

———. 1970. The socio-ecology of primates, pp. 103–166. *In* J. H. Crook, ed. Social behaviour in birds and mammals. Academic Press, New York.

CULLEN, E. 1957. Adaptations in the Kittiwake to cliff-nesting. Ibis 99:275–302.

DZUBIN, A. 1955. Some evidences of home range in waterfowl, pp. 278–298. *In* Transactions of the 20th North American Wildlife Conference. Wildlife Management Institute, Washington, D.C.

HILDÉN, O. 1965. Habitat selection in birds. Ann. Zool. Fenn. 2:53–75.

HINDE, R. A. 1970. Animal behaviour: a synthesis of ethology and comparative psychology. McGraw-Hill, New York. 876pp.

HOCHBAUM, H. A. 1944. The Canvasback on a prairie marsh. American Wildlife Institute, Washington, D.C. 187pp.

IMMELMANN, K. 1961. Beiträge zur Biologie und Ethologie australischer Honigfresser (Meliphagidae). J. Ornithol. 102:164–207.

———. 1962. Beiträge zu einer vergleichenden Biologie australischer Prachtfinken (Spermestidae). Zool. Jahr. Abt. Syst. Oekol. Geogr. Tiere 90:1–96.

JAY, P., editor. 1968. Primates: studies in adaptation and variability. Holt, Rinehart and Winston, New York. 529pp.

KLOPFER, P., AND J. P. HAILMAN. 1965. Habitat selection in birds. Adv. Study Behav. 1:279–303.

———, AND ———. 1967. Ethology's first century. Prentice-Hall, Englewood Cliffs, New Jersey. 297pp.

LACK, D. 1954. The natural regulation of animal numbers. Oxford University Press, London. 343pp.

———. 1966. Population studies in birds. Oxford University Press, London. 341pp.

———. 1968. Ecological adaptations for breeding in birds. Methuen, London. 409pp.

———. 1971. Ecological isolation in birds. Blackwell's, Oxford. 404pp.

LORENZ, K. 1941. Vergleichende Bewegungsstudien an Anatinen. J. Ornithol. Suppl. 89: 194–294.

MARLER, P. 1968. Visual systems, pp. 103–126. *In* T. A. Sebeok, ed. Animal communication. University of Indiana Press, Bloomington.

MCKINNEY, F. 1961. An analysis of the displays of the European Eider *Somateria mollissima mollissima* (Linnaeus) and the Pacific Eider *Somateria mollissima v. nigra* Bonaparte. Behaviour Suppl. 7:1–24.

———. 1965*a*. Spacing and chasing in breeding ducks, pp. 92–106. *In* Wildfowl Trust 16th Annual Report. Country Life Ltd, London.

———. 1965*b*. The spring behavior of wild Steller's Eiders. Condor 67:273–290.

———. 1967. Breeding behaviour of captive Shovelers, pp. 108–121. *In* Wildfowl Trust 18th Annual Report. The Wildfowl Trust, Slimbridge, England.

———. 1970. Displays of four species of blue-winged ducks. Living Bird 9:29–64.

MOYNIHAN, M. 1962. The organization and probable evolution of some mixed species flocks of neotropical birds. Smithsonian Misc. Collect. 143(7):1–140.

MURTON, R. K. 1965. The Wood Pigeon. New Naturalist Monograph. Collins, London. 256pp.

———. 1971. Man and birds. Collins, London. 364pp.

ORIANS, G. H. 1961. The ecology of blackbird (*Agelaius*) social systems. Ecol. Monogr. 31:285–312.

———. 1969. On the evolution of mating systems in birds and mammals. Am. Nat. 103:589–603.

———. 1971. Ecological aspects of behavior, pp. 513–546. *In* D. S. Farner and J. R. King, eds. Avian biology. Vol. 1. Academic Press, New York.

POSTON, H. J. 1969. Relationships between the Shoveler and its breeding habitat at Strathmore, Alberta, pp. 132–137. *In* Saskatoon wetlands seminar. Rep. Ser. No. 6. Canadian Wildlife Service, Ottawa, Canada.

SCOTT, J. P. 1968. Observation, pp. 17–30. *In* T. A. Sebeok, ed. Animal communication. University of Indiana Press, Bloomington.

SMITH, R. I. 1968. The social aspects of reproductive behavior in the Pintail. Auk 85:381–396.

SOWLS, L. K. 1955. Prairie ducks. Stackpole, Harrisburg, Pennsylvania. 193pp.

TINBERGEN, N. 1953. The Herring Gull's world. Collins, London. 255pp.

———. 1954. The origin and evolution of courtship and threat display, pp. 233–250. *In* J. S. Huxley et al., eds. Evolution as a process. Allen & Unwin, London.

———. 1959. Comparative studies of the behaviour of gulls (Laridae): a progress report. Behaviour 15:1–70.

———. 1963. On adaptive radiation in gulls (Tribe Larini). Zool. Mededelingen 39:209–223.

———. 1967. Adaptive features of the Black-headed Gull *Larus ridibundus* L., pp. 43–59. *In* Proceedings of the XIV International Ornithological Congress. Almquist & Wiksells, Uppsala.

VON HAARTMAN, L. 1957. Adaptation in hole-nesting birds. Evolution 11:339–347.

WATSON, A., editor. 1970. Animal populations in relation to their food resources. Blackwell's, Oxford. 477pp.

———, AND R. MOSS. 1970. Dominance, spacing behaviour and aggression in relation to population limitation in vertebrates, pp. 167–220. *In* A. Watson, ed. Animal populations in relation to their food resources. Blackwell's, Oxford.

CHRONOLOGY OF PAIR FORMATION IN SOME NEARCTIC *AYTHYA* (ANATIDAE)[1,2]

MILTON W. WELLER,[3] Department of Zoology and Entomology, Iowa State University, Ames, IA

The chronology of pair formation in ducks has been little studied in spite of sizable concentrations of waterfowl on wintering areas and relative ease of observation. This is, perhaps, a result of the rather deep-seated concept that pairing in birds occurs mainly in spring. It may be true that the intensity of courtship is more conspicuous in spring on migration stops and in breeding areas, because conflict situations are common and conspicuous aerial displays are more prevalent. However, it appears that many species arrive on the breeding areas paired, although the permanence of these pair bonds is unknown. It is well known that ducks in the Northern Hemisphere have a transient "winter" plumage ("basic" plumage of Humphrey and Parkes 1959) which is shifted forward in the sequence to late summer and commonly is called the "eclipse" plumage. The breeding (or alternate) plumage then develops in fall or early winter. Obviously, this sequence must have evolved simultaneously with early pair formation in the Anatinae and in relation to the chronology of winter flocking.

In the North American members of the genus *Aythya* (the "pochards" or "inland divers"), some distinct differences are apparent in the comparative chronology of nesting. The usual sequence in these species appears to be: Canvasback (*A. valisineria*), followed very closely in most areas by the Ring-necked Duck (*A. collaris*), Redhead (*A. americana*), and still later by the Lesser Scaup (*A. affinis*) (Bent 1923, Hochbaum 1944, Mendall 1958). Of special interest is the laying pattern of the Redhead, a semiparasitic bird. Some individuals start nesting as early as do Canvasbacks, but most start parasitic laying when Canvasbacks begin nesting and construct nests later in the season (Weller 1959).

Although less is known of the sequence of plumages than of the sequence of nesting, it appears that there is less difference between species in the attainment of breeding plumages. The Lesser Scaup probably is the last to attain complete breeding plumage (especially in yearlings, which often are recognizable in spring migration and on breeding areas) while no dramatic difference seems to occur in the other three species. Redheads possibly precede Ring-necks and Canvasbacks (October versus November according to Bent 1923, Mendall 1958, and Weller 1957). However, too little detailed information is available for comparable areas.

The purpose of this study was to determine whether differences in biology are reflected in the comparative chronology of pair formation. Preliminary observations of Redheads were made in southern Manitoba during the springs of 1953 and 1954, at Chesapeake Bay and Cayuga Lake during February and March of 1954, and at Spring Lake near Havana, Illinois, in March of 1957. Intensive ob-

---

[1] Originally published in Auk 82(2):227–235, 1965.

[2] Journal Paper No. J-4843 of the Iowa Agricultural and Home Economics Experiment Station, Ames, Iowa. Project No. 1504.

[3] Present address: Department of Entomology, Fisheries, and Wildlife, University of Minnesota, St. Paul, MN 55101.

servations of Redheads and other species on wintering areas were started during the winter of 1960. Southern Texas was selected for the study of wintering birds because of the concentrations of Redheads as well as smaller numbers of the other species of the genus *Aythya*. Brief observations of Ring-necked Ducks were made in southern Louisiana in early January of 1961. Some notes made on three dabbling ducks serve for comparison with the diving ducks: Pintails (*Anas acuta*) and Mottled Ducks (*A. fulvigula*) in Texas and Mallards (*A. platyrhynchos*) in Louisiana. Observations of divers were made in Iowa during the spring migration of 1961 and 1962 and in Michigan in 1963.

This project was financed by the Permanent Science Fund of the American Academy of Arts and Sciences of Boston, Massachusetts, and preliminary observations were supported by the Wildlife Management Institute through the Delta Waterfowl Research Station. The study was assisted greatly by the use of facilities of the Welder Wildlife Foundation of Sinton, Texas. Clarence Cottom and the late Bobby J. Wilks of the latter organization suggested study areas as did T. L. Clark of the Texas Game and Fish Commission and L. E. Beatty and E. B. Chamberlain of the U.S. Bureau of Sports Fisheries and Wildlife. Workers at the Laccasine National Wildlife Refuge in southern Louisiana were helpful in arranging for observation of Ring-necked Ducks and Mallards.

THE PAIRING PROCESS

Acquiring a mate appears to be a gradual process in most ducks and apparently starts in midwinter on the southern wintering areas. Pairing appears to be a result of many temporary associations within a flock of rather consistent members. Individual recognition is assumed. As sexual drives increase, pairs which remain together are "tested" constantly by aggressive unpaired and, possibly, paired males. Changes in mates probably are common early in the pairing periods, as noted in marked Mallards by Weidmann (1956). In species of *Aythya*, as in most ducks, the female plays a major role in the regulation of the pairing process, showing interest or lack of interest by leading, following, attacking, or fleeing. Johnsgard (1960*a*) has described the similarity of this type of behavior in species of *Anas* and *Aythya*.

Pairing displays are common in migration areas in the central United States and continue in the breeding areas. Whether these pairs remain together on the breeding areas and in migration is unknown, but pairs are conspicuous even in large flocks on wintering areas and in early migration. Although many of these pairs may have only a temporary bond, the action clearly indicates the sexual stimulation essential to the permanent pairing process. This behavior differs markedly from that of individuals in flocks of one sex and flocks of both sexes in which no pair association exists.

CHRONOLOGY OF PAIRING

I attempted to measure the chronology of pairing quantitatively by determining the percentage of females which were associated with a male, regardless of the length of time of the association. This seemed to be the only way to record quickly the association of sexes in large flocks, since marking of birds was impractical. Obviously, some errors were due to chance association of males with females, but the obvious tolerance of females for males and the attraction of males to females was conspicuous. The duration of this bond was measured by observing "pairs" through a telescope and timing (by means of a stop-watch) the duration of the pair association. Such pairs were observed until: (1) they were lost from view among other birds, (2) members of the pair separated, or (3) observations were interrupted for some reason. In addition, notes were made on courtship to determine which displays were present in early pairing, whether aggressiveness between males was apparent, and whether copulation occurred.

Midwinter, 1960–61

The first observations were made on Redheads during late December and early January, 1960–61, at the Laguna Atascosa Refuge near San Benito, Texas. Because the time of pairing was unknown, the time to initiate observations was a guess, but I considered it best to precede the display period rather than arrive after it had started. Surprisingly, I found that numerous pairs were already in evidence and that courtship parties were common among Redheads in this period. Most known displays, as described by Hochbaum (1944) for Canvasbacks and Johnsgard (1960*a*, 1961) for the genus *Aythya*, were noted except for aerial displays and copulation.

During the same period, 25 to 30 Canvasbacks were viewed at Sarita, Texas, and were predominantly females. However, males present were not seen to display. Several hundred Lesser Scaup were observed near Corpus Christi, Texas, for considerable periods. Scaup of both sexes were scattered as individuals and in small flocks of up to 30 birds but I observed no sexual activity.

Also, in early January, several refuges in southern Louisiana were visited to observe Ring-necked Ducks. A small number of Ring-necks was observed at Laccasine National Wildlife Refuge. The only display seen was the *head throw* by males. However, this display could not be related clearly to reproductive behavior. Moreover, in this particular situation, females did not seem especially attached to males nor did males spend much time following females.

Late February–Early March, 1961

Because of the status of pairing on the first trip to the wintering areas, I made a second trip during the last two weeks of February in an attempt to measure the rate of pair bond formation. Because of changes in water conditions and a major northward shift in the Redhead population, most observations were made near Corpus Christi, Texas. This may well have been a different flock, but courtship display was more intense and pairs were more in evidence than had been previously noted. However, aerial displays and copulation still were not witnessed.

Observations made on Lesser Scaup in February were more satisfactory than those of early January. Several hundred scaup were observed at close range and no evidence of pairs or displays was seen.

A few Canvasbacks were again observed in southern Texas and more males were in evidence than before. Males clearly showed more interest in females, but no intensive courtship activities were observed.

In the same period, about 40 Ring-necked Ducks were observed at the Welder Wildlife Refuge. During the day, birds were scattered about the lake and small groups of females were conspicuous, while males were in twos or threes. However, after sunset, the entire flock of Ring-necks moved, along with other ducks and coots, into a grove of trees, apparently to roost. In doing so, they all met and, on occasions, *head throws* were seen.

Thus, in late February, Lesser Scaup had not started pairing activities and Canvasbacks and Ring-necks showed only a slight attraction of males to females. Redheads, however, were strongly activated, and pairs made up a large percentage of the premigratory flock. Apparently, Lesser Scaup are still not actively courting in the southern United States even in mid-March. Observations in Louisiana by Frank McKinney (in litt.), of the Minnesota Museum of Natural History, indicated only one possible pair among 66 males and 22 females counted.

Spring, 1961–62

Observations on pairing of Ring-necks, Lesser Scaup, and Redheads were made in central Iowa in late March and early April, 1961 and 1962. At that time, pairs of Redheads were conspicuous and lone hens were rare. Numerous Ring-necks and scaup were in pairs and courtship was seen commonly. Dr. John Rogers (in litt.), of the Gaylord Memorial Laboratory at Puxico, Missouri, made observations on Lesser Scaup in February of 1961 and found no pairing activity. But in Iowa in early April, not only were displays common, but I observed copulation in both Ring-necked Ducks and Lesser Scaup. Thus, courtship activity of Lesser Scaup and Ring-necks seemed to be of the same intensity in Iowa in early April as occurred in Redheads in Texas in early January. It appears that, in Redheads and, probably, Canvasbacks, courtship starts on the wintering areas well ahead of similar activity in Lesser Scaup and possibly Ring-necks, which seem to start courtship in early migration. However, both copulation and aerial chases were common in all species by the time they arrived in central Iowa. It must be recognized, however, that not all flocks or even all birds in flocks are at the same stage in the reproductive cycle and that the origin of these flocks as well as their destinations were unknown. Moreover, Hochbaum (1944) has pointed out that early migrants often are paired birds.

Efforts to show "pairing" quantitatively are summarized in Table 1 and are compared, in Fig. 1, with some data on dabbling ducks collected by other workers. Among Redheads, 35 per cent were "paired" during late December and early January, in comparison with 9 to 13 per cent in other divers and 87–100 per cent in dabbling ducks. By late February, 58 per cent of the Redheads were considered "paired," although little evidence of increased pair tendencies was noted among other divers. In spring migration at the latitude of Iowa and Illinois, 80 to 84 per cent of all female Redheads were "paired," and 41 to 55 per cent of other diving ducks were "paired." Obviously, these figures are only a gross measure of sexual associations, but they demonstrate increased tolerance by females for the attention of males.

Limited observations on dabbling ducks demonstrate the significantly earlier pair formation in this group compared with that of pochards. Data here presented agree more closely with the estimates of Johnsgard (1960*b*) than with those of Stotts (1958). However, Stotts' observations were made in the field upon large flocks, and the lack of clear-cut sexual dimorphism in Black Ducks (*Anas rubripes*) limited observations. The general pattern presented here agrees with that of European species of *Anas* and *Aythya* shown by Bezzel (1959). Pairing of the Mallard occurred mainly from September through November, Tufted Ducks (*Aythya fuligula*) paired mainly in March, and Common Pochards (*Aythya ferina*) did not pair until May.

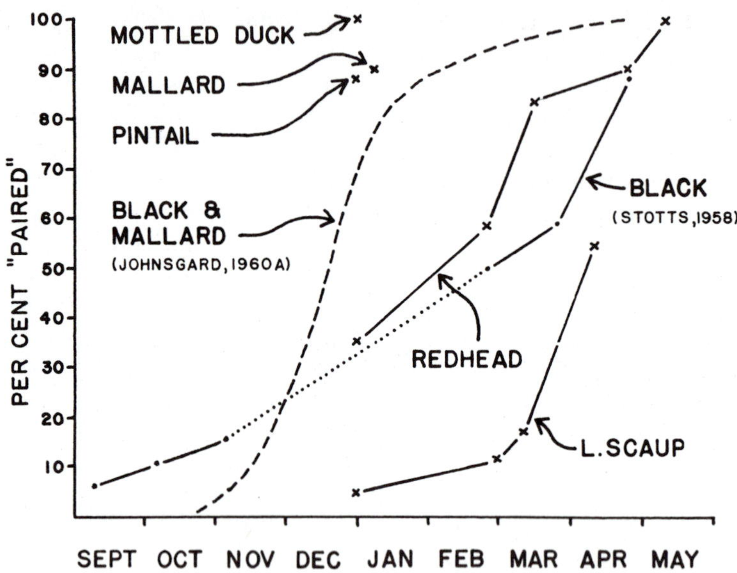

Fig. 1. A comparison of data from this and other studies on the percentages of ducks "paired" at various times of the year.

Another measure of the tendency of members of the pair to remain together is suggested by data on the duration of the pair relationship (Table 2). These data do suggest that the duration of the pair bond is longer for Redheads in March and April than in January and February. Of greater significance is that the duration of this bond in Redheads is more than three times that of the scaup at the same time.

DISCUSSION

The observations on Canvasbacks and Ring-necked Ducks are not considered satisfactory because they involve small and somewhat isolated groups studied under conditions poor for observation. Some general observations in the Chesapeake Bay area in late February of 1954 indicated considerable courtship activity in Canvasbacks whereas relatively little was seen in Texas. However, the observations on Ring-necks agree generally with those of Zirrer (1945) who noted that some Ring-necks arrived in Wisconsin in pairs but that courtship was very intense in mid-April.

Although further observations are needed, the sequence of display and pairing seems generally correlated with the onset of breeding plumage and nesting. There is close agreement in data for Lesser Scaup while those for Canvasback and Ring-necks agree only in a more general way. Better data on chronology of nesting and plumage development of all species in the same area would help materially to clarify conclusions. The major exception is the pairing of the Redhead, which clearly is more nearly correlated with its establishment of home range on the breeding area and parasitic laying than with its major breeding period. Moreover, pairing activities in the Redhead seem to begin well in advance of those species which begin normal nesting at the time the Redhead lays parasit-

Table 1. Observations of the percentage of female ducks paired in winter and spring.

Species	Per cent of females paired	Number of females seen	Number of females paired	Number of females unpaired	Number of males unpaired	Locality	Month
Mottled Duck	100	22	22	0	0	Texas	Dec.–Jan.
Mallard	90	31	28	3	6	Louisiana	January
Pintail	87	216	187	29	393	Texas	Dec.–Jan.
Redhead	35	709	249	460	733	Texas	Dec.–Jan.
	58	408	238	170	533	Texas	February
	84	37	31	6	19	Illinois	March
	89	27	24	3	31	Iowa	March–April
Ring-necked Duck	13	47	6	41	34	Texas–La.	January
	12	49	6	43	34	Texas	February
	55	172	94	78	149	Iowa	March–April
Lesser Scaup	9	35	3	32	119	Ill.–Missouri	December
	4	125	5	120	161	Texas–La.	Dec.–Jan.
	12	462	58	404	487	Texas	February
	17	166	29	137	185	Michigan	March
	56	259	146	113	427	Iowa	March–April
Canvasback	10	10	3	10	66	Ill.–Missouri	December
	0	48	0	48	59	Texas	January
	10	86	9	77	83	Texas	February
	4	27	1	26	61	Michigan	March
	41	19	8	11	41	Iowa	March–April

ically. The relationship of this early courtship period to the parasitic habits of the Redhead is still obscure, but it suggests further abnormality in the reproductive cycle.

It is important to note that relatively little information is available on age of maturity in these species. Not all species acquire full breeding plumage as yearlings prior to the display period. This is especially conspicuous in Lesser Scaup which may be very brown in spring. Munro (1941) questioned whether yearling Lesser Scaup males mated in their first year but suggested that some females did. McKnight and Buss (1962) have presented some better evidence that some females do so. As in many species of animals, it is probable that older and experienced males mate with most females and that yearling males rarely compete successfully. Moreover, the same situation may occur in the other divers, but it is less conspicuous because of less con-

Table 2. Duration of the pair relationship in four species of the genus *Aythya*.

Species	December (Missouri–Illinois)	January–February (Texas–Louisiana)	March–April (Iowa)
Redhead	—	9.9[1] (0.5–84)[2] (33)[3]	13.3 (4.0–22) (8)
Ring-neck	—	7.7 (1.0–22) (5)	12.2 (0.9–44.8) (19)
Canvasback	2.7 (0.4–5.0) (4)	1.9 (0.5–5.0) (16)	3.9 (1.7–5.0) (3)
Scaup	0.5 (0.1–1.2) (6)	3.2 (0.5–15) (16)	8.1 (0.3–44) (16)

[1] Average numbers of minutes.
[2] Range in minutes.
[3] Sample size.

trast between first and later breeding plumages.

Available data on dabbling ducks of the genus *Anas* suggests that pairing precedes that of the divers by several months. Males of Mallards and Pintails often assume their adult plumages in early fall, nearly two months prior to that of the divers, and nesting starts in early April or about one month prior to that of Canvasbacks. Thus, a general correlation exists in acquisition of breeding plumage, chronology of pairing, and initiation of nesting in both Anatini and Aythyini.

SUMMARY

Observations on four species of inland diving ducks (genus *Aythya*) demonstrated considerable difference in chronology of pairing. There was a general correlation between the comparative chronology of pairing, acquisition of breeding plumage, and initiation of nesting among most species but at least one irregularity seems to exist. Redheads, which normally follow Canvasbacks in initiation of nesting, preceded in courtship activities the Canvasbacks observed in this study. Compared with Redheads, Canvasbacks, and Ring-necked Ducks, Lesser Scaup were the last to start pairing activities and the last to nest. Limited observations on Ring-necks suggested that the pairing period was slightly later than that of Canvasbacks, as is their nesting period. Limited observations on three species of dabbling ducks (*Anas*) suggested a considerably earlier period of pairing in comparison with the divers.

LITERATURE CITED

BENT, A. C. 1923. Life histories of North American wild fowl, Vol. 1. U.S. Natl. Mus., Bull. 126. 243pp.

BEZZEL, E. 1959. Beiträge zur Biologie der Geschlechter bei Entenvögeln. Anzeiger der Ornithologischen Gesellschaft im Bayern 5: 269–355.

HOCHBAUM, H. A. 1944. The Canvasback on a prairie marsh. Amer. Wildl. Inst., Washington, D.C.

HUMPHREY, P. S., AND K. C. PARKES. 1959. An approach to the study of molts and plumages. Auk 76:1–31.

JOHNSGARD, P. A. 1960*a*. Pair-formation mechanisms in *Anas* (Anatidae) and related genera. Ibis 102:616–618.

———. 1960*b*. A quantitative study of sexual behavior of Mallards and Black Ducks. Wilson Bull. 72:133–155.

———. 1961. The taxonomy of the Anatidae—A behavioural analysis. Ibis 103:71–85.

MCKNIGHT, D. E., AND I. O. BUSS. 1962. Evidence of breeding in yearling female Lesser Scaup. J. Wildl. Mgmt. 26:328–329.

MENDALL, H. L. 1958. The Ring-necked Duck in the northeast. Univ. of Maine Bull. 60:1–317.

MUNRO, J. A. 1941. Studies of waterfowl in British Columbia: Greater Scaup duck and Lesser Scaup duck. Canadian J. Res. D 19:113–138.

STOTTS, V. 1958. The time of pair formation in Black Ducks. Trans. N. A. Wildl. Conf. 23:192–197.

WEIDMANN, U. 1956. Verhaltensstudien an der Stockente (*Anas platyrhynchos* L.), I. Das Aktionsystem. Zeits. f. Tierpsychol. 13:208–271.

WELLER, M. W. 1957. Growth, weights, and plumages of the Redhead (*Aythya americana*). Wilson Bull. 69:5–38.

———. 1959. Parasitic egg laying in the Redhead (*Aythya americana*) and other North American Anatidae. Ecol. Monogr. 29:333–365.

ZIRRER, F. 1945. The Ring-necked Duck. Passenger Pigeon 7:41–46.

THE EVOLUTION OF DUCK DISPLAYS[1]

F. MCKINNEY[2]

The social signals of waterfowl have been well known to students of behaviour evolution since the pioneer studies of Heinroth (1911) and Lorenz (1941) revealed their spectacular diversity. Most of the special movements, postures, calls, and mechanical noises used by these birds in a variety of social situations are easy to study under captive conditions and these 'displays' have been especially well catalogued for the family Anatidae. The form of many, such as the 'grunt-whistle,' is so distinctive that they can be used with confidence as taxonomic characters, and waterfowl displays provide especially convincing illustrations of the phenomenon of behavioural homology. As a result, the family has become famous as the classic example of the successful use of comparative behaviour studies in systematics (Lorenz 1941, Delacour and Mayr 1945, Johnsgard 1965).

Much less attention has been given to explaining the sources and significance of specific differences in display activities, however, and in many ways the waterfowl are ideally suited for study of the adaptive radiation of signalling methods. As shown by the now famous work along these lines in gulls (Tinbergen 1959, 1963) and weaver-birds (Crook 1964), and similar studies on sulids (Nelson 1970), icterids (Orians and Christman 1968), and tetraonids (Hjorth 1970), a blend of ethological, ecological, and evolutionary approaches is essential. A great deal of ecological information is available on waterfowl, especially on species of economic significance to wildfowlers, and although there have been many behaviour studies, the results have not generally been integrated and interpreted in an evolutionary framework.

Each species has to be examined separately as a product of a unique evolutionary history, its specializations being viewed as repercussions of certain major 'decisions' during its history. As argued by Hinde (1959), these are most likely to have been related to changes in habitat or food, as new 'niches' became available. As these changes were taking place, in many cases selection must have favoured new breeding strategies requiring different social signals. Thus while changes in feeding methods and habitat-preferences may have been of basic significance, the modifications in display repertoires that accompanied them have to be interpreted in the light of variations in mating systems, pair-spacing patterns, parental roles, and related phenomena. This crucial area of 'social systems' has not been given the attention it deserves by students of waterfowl behaviour.

In respect to the dabbling ducks (tribe Anatini, including 36 species of *Anas*), with which I will be primarily concerned here, two facets of the social system have remained enigmas since the beginning of this century. First, the significance of 'social courtship' (Gesellschaftsspiel), in which several males perform displays

---

[1] Originally published in G. Baerends, C. Beer, and A. Manning, eds. Function and evolution in behaviour, pages 331–357. Oxford University Press, London, 1975.

[2] Present address: Bell Museum of Natural History, University of Minnesota, Minneapolis, MN 55455.

around a female, and especially its relationship to pair formation, have been unclear. Secondly, the aerial pursuits of males after females, during the breeding season, have been confusing for the mixture of aggressive and sexual motivation they seem to betray, and their relevance to male promiscuity and to the defence of territories has been much debated. Recent reviews of the controversies are included in McKinney (1969) and Weidmann and Darley (1971*a*). I think that the time is ripe for an attempt to formulate a series of working hypotheses embracing these aspects of duck behaviour and the most promising approach seems to lie in exploring the implications of natural selection at the level of individuals.

Three overlapping questions are discussed here: why do ducks need displays, why do displays have the characteristics they have, and what factors have been most important in producing specific differences in display repertoires? Displays are regarded as 'signalling devices,' the performance of each being advantageous to the performer in dealing with his or her personal social relationships, primarily with conspecifics. Behavioural traits are assumed to be under ultimate genetic control and selection is viewed as operating through differential survival and reproduction of individuals. Not only is there co-operation between the members of a pair for breeding but there is also competition between the interests and investments of males and females, as argued by Trivers (1972).

The point of view presented in this discussion was developed while I studied the breeding behaviour of captive Green-winged Teal, *Anas crecca carolinensis*, in May and June 1973. Preliminary conclusions from this research are summarized here but the detailed results will be published separately.

CONSTRAINTS AND PRE-ADAPTATIONS

The 36 species of *Anas* occupy a variety of aquatic habitats around the world. Their structure and life-styles are basically similar, indicating that the ancestral stock from which they arose must have had pre-adaptive commitments to exploiting ecological niches associated with marshes, ponds, rivers, and lagoons. As adults and as ducklings they are dependent on shallow waters for their main foods, and they need water every day for drinking and bathing. Aquatic plants and invertebrates are taken at or near the water surface and, although a few species gather food on land or by diving, dabbling ducks spend their lives, first and foremost, surface-swimming.

The members of several duck tribes have specialized in diving for food (for example, Aythyini, Mergini, Oxyurini) and to varying degrees have sacrificed efficiency in walking through changes in body proportions and leg position. In contrast, the Anatini have remained adept walkers and associated with this ability is their potential for nesting far from water. Their agility out of water enables them to use a variety of nesting sites, including tree-stumps, and other elevated sites. But most nest on the ground, in vegetation, and this can entail hazardous trips away from the safety of water both for adults, when selecting the nest-site or for females while laying and incubating, and for ducklings, when leaving the nest or crossing between water areas.

Anatidae are built for strong, direct flight. They have high wing-loading and a requirement for steady flapping. This flying method evidently evolved in association with a life-style demanding rapid changes in location, often over long distances. Most living anatids travel extensively, making daily journeys between feeding grounds or between water and nest-site, and seasonal movements between areas used for breeding and moulting and other areas used outside the breeding season. For the dabbling ducks, in particular, the use of shallow fresh water habitats demands adaptability and mobility when conditions change. Feeding areas and brood-rearing habitat can be created or disappear almost overnight when rivers flood or ponds dry up, and these events can seldom be predicted with certainty from week to week or from year to year.

These specializations for feeding from the water surface while swimming and the use of flight primarily for changing location have had many repercussions on the signalling methods of dabbling ducks. Maintenance of feathers for waterproofing and flight are vitally important and these birds spend much time bathing, preening, shaking, and oiling their plumage. These activities often occur in close temporal association with social interactions (pair formation, hostile encounters, copulations) and many comfort movements have been adapted for signalling purposes (reviewed in McKinney 1965*a*). The flying method, involving constant flapping, precludes soaring, and aerial manoeuvre such as hovering or sailing are possible only momentarily. As a result, aerial displays are limited mainly to the giving of vocalizations and to the ritualization of complete short flights performed just above the water surface (Lebret 1958, McKinney 1970). On the other hand, rapid direct flight involves the risk of separation for mates or flock members and alarm calls, pre-flight signals promoting synchronous take-off, and contact calls given when flying, are well developed in waterfowl. In turn, the attention-getting potential of these signals has favoured their further adaptation for use in courtship situations.

Changes in the roles of the sexes in care of the eggs and young have evidently been of fundamental significance in the evolution of waterfowl social systems and signalling methods. The main tasks to be accomplished are incubating the eggs, leading the young, brooding and oiling them in the early days, warning them of danger, and protecting them from predators. The young feed for themselves (for exceptions, see Kear 1970) and they can be cared for either by one or by both parents. Co-operative parental care is highly developed in the swans, geese, and Whistling Ducks (subfamily Anserinae) while in the sheld-ducks, sheld-geese, and all the other duck tribes (subfamily Anatinae) the female plays the major role, males never sharing in incubation.

Johnsgard (1962) and Kear (1970) have discussed evolutionary trends in waterfowl breeding systems, basing their conclusions on a phylogenetic arrangement derived from comparative studies of living forms. While there is still much room for argument about the probable characteristics of the two ancestral stocks, commitment in the Anatinae to incubation by the female only seems to have had especially far-reaching consequences. This system could have been favoured by a need for males to specialize in defence (as Kear suggests) or by a need for females to specialize in incubation. The latter could have been associated with anti-predator nest-concealment where the danger of betrayal of the nest-site was greater if two individuals had to make flights to and from adjacent water areas. In this event, females would have been pre-adapted for the role of incubator through their knowledge of local topography (and perhaps also the local predators) through their experiences during the egg-laying period.

The divergence in the roles of males and females in breeding in Anatinae has evidently involved differences in the vulnerability of the sexes to predation and perhaps to other sources of mortality. Unbalanced adult sex-ratios, with a preponderance of males, are well known in many duck species (for example, Bellrose et al. 1961) and are generally attributed to heavier losses to predators among incubating females, as reflected strikingly in a recent study of fox kills by Sargeant (1972). In species where the male is very aggressive in defense of mate, territory, nest, or young (for example, sheld-ducks and sheld-geese), on the other hand, the risks entailed in advertisement and fighting could be greater than those to which nesting females are exposed. In either case, unbalanced adult sex-ratios may be expected to increase competition for the sex partners in shortest supply. Such competition is likely to have been the main driving force behind the evolution of conspicuous male plumage features, elaborate male courtship displays, and the phenomenon of social courtship itself in those duck species where males predominate. Conversely the type of courtship found in some sheld-duck, where females aggressively compete for mates (Heinroth 1911, Johnsgard 1965) has presumably been favoured by an adult sex-ratio with a preponderance of females.

Among the dabbling ducks, no species is known to be completely promiscuous and, apart from his role in copulation, the male's presence is evidently required by the female for other supporting activities. Most important are probably his roles in protecting the female in which he will invest or has invested his genes (1) from predators, (2) from stolen matings by other males, and (3) by defending a food source for her during the egg-laying and incubation phases. Each of these roles has favoured a pair-bond system and most of the social signals that have evolved in this group appear to be necessary to accomplish pairing, to maintain bonds, to protect females from predators and stolen matings, and to defend areas for the female's use.

However, the demand on a paired male's time required to safeguard his mate's breeding effort must vary between different *Anas* species. In some, the male stays close to his mate throughout incubation, but in others, paired males spend much time and energy exploiting a second method of reproduction—stolen matings. Specific diversity in male social behaviour seems to have many of its roots in the extent to which males have combined these two breeding strategies—pair-bonding and promiscuous rape.

Predation on eggs is heavy in *Anas* species and females regularly lay two, or even three, clutches in a breeding season before succeeding in bringing off a brood. Thus females may require the services of a male for copulation at various, unpredictable times and, in species where the pair bond breaks early, there may be many opportunities for males to inseminate females. Again, competition between males is inevitable.

Males are observed accompanying females with broods in some duck species (Weller 1968, 1972; Kear 1970; Siegfried 1974) but the significance of this behaviour is not yet clear. The male's presence may contribute in some way to survival of the young or the mate, or it may reflect persistence of the pair bond with benefits for the male in future breeding attempts.

LIFE-STYLE AND SOCIAL SYSTEMS

Many of the freshwater habitats used by dabbling ducks around the world have been modified by human activities and it is no longer a simple matter to reconstruct the ecological conditions to which each living species is primarily adapted. In southern Africa, for example, waterfowl now depend heavily on irrigation dams (Siegfried 1970) and artificial water areas are widely used in many countries. In the North American prairies, duck ecology has been influenced greatly both by agricultural practices (for example, pothole drainage, grain farming) and by wildlife management practices (local and seasonal control of hunting, preservation of refuge areas, creation of new breeding habitat). Nevertheless, specific differences in preferences for feeding areas, food, habitats, and nest-sites are well-known to field workers who have studied the ecology of several sympatric species simultaneously (see, for example, Sowls 1955, Keith 1961, Hildén 1964). Although it is often difficult to decide which of these differences reflect ancestral predilections and which are relatively recent adaptations to changing environments, much of the picture may still emerge through comparative eco-ethological work.

Major characteristics of the adaptive radiation of *Anas* are obvious, however, if species or groups of species with very distinctive morphological adaptations or habitat-preferences are considered. Specialization for plankton-straining in Shovelers and for grazing in wigeons are two of the clearest examples. The African Black Duck, *A. sparsa,* uses primarily river habitats. The Pintail *A. acuta,* is an open-country bird often nesting far from water in sparse cover, and ranging widely to use temporary water areas. Mallards (*A. platyrhynchos* and related species) use many different habitats, both wooded and open, but their agility in using wooded ponds, their ability to nest in trees, and their preference for more permanent water areas suggest quite a different historical background from that of the Pintail.

Specific differences in feeding habits and habitat preferences appear to have had basic repercussions on breeding strategies, as illustrated by the contrasting social systems seen in the Shoveler *A. clypeata,* and the Pintail *A. acuta.* Of prime importance here seems to be the concept of 'economic defendability' (Brown 1964, Brown and Orians 1970). Breeding Shoveler pairs have small, discrete territories, defended by the males, the pair bond is strong and long-lasting, and males spend little time attempting promiscuous matings with other females. In the Pintail system, on the other hand, males divide their time between accompanying the mate and trying to rape other females; paired males do not defend areas, and females suffer heavy harassment (R. I. Smith 1968). These differences seem to be related to the use of rich, localized food sources (plankton in relatively permanent ponds) by Shovelers and the exploiting of temporarily available and widely scattered feeding places by Pintails (see McKinney 1973 and subsequent discussion in the same symposium by G. H. Orians). Defence of an area is feasible in the former, and I suspect that it is advantageous in providing an assured, secure feeding site for the female of the pair during the pre-laying,

laying, and incubation phases. Studies of feeding ecology and bioenergetics are needed to test this hypothesis, the suggestion being that plankton-straining is a time-consuming feeding method entailing special problems for breeding females.

My current observations on the breeding behaviour of captive Green-winged Teal have revealed a Pintail-like system involving a similar combination of pair bonding and male promiscuity, but they suggest that characteristics of feeding ecology are unlikely to provide a complete explanation for the evolution of this type of breeding system. Conflicts between the breeding strageties of males and females are evidently involved and the advantages to males of investing their time and energy in the reproductive effort of one female (through a pair bond) and the advantages of trying to inseminate as many females as possible (through raping) seem likely to vary in response to various other factors as well (for example, habitat characteristics, availability of females, vulnerability to predators). The importance of time and energy budgeting in European Teal, *A. crecca crecca*, while they are on their wintering grounds in France is well shown by Tamisier (1972) and his studies strongly reinforce the need to view time spent in courtship as an expense that individuals must balance against the dangers and effort involved.

The behaviour of Shoveler pairs and Green-winged Teal pairs, confined in the same densities under similar conditions in large flight-pens (described in McKinney 1967) is dramatically different. Male Shovelers spend much of their time threatening, chasing, and fighting with neighbouring males, with the result that each pair comes to occupy more or less exclusive areas in the pen. Paired males do not perform courtship displays to other females and they spend little time actively trying to rape them; almost all of their activities centre round the mate and the territory. Male Green-winged Teal, in contrast, maintain similar strong pair bonds, but they spend very little time chasing other males and essentially there is no 'defended area.' From time to time, a male leaves his mate, approaches another female, and performs courtship displays to her; if his mate should approach, however, displays are then directed to her almost exclusively. Males also leave their mates to engage in vigorous pursuits after other females, frequently culminating in attempts to rape. After these pursuits, each male returns to his mate.

These rape attempts were so frequent and persistent in the Green-winged Teal that females deserted their eggs and spent much of their time hiding from males. Unfortunately we underestimated the seriousness of their plight and four of eight females died, from direct or indirect effects of harassment, before they could be removed from the pens.

Intermediate between these two systems is that adopted by the Mallard. Males are very aggressive and attempt to defend exclusive areas, but they do not usually maintain these areas through the incubation period, as Shovelers do. They become involved in rape attempts much more frequently than Shovelers, but their investment in territorial defense probably leads to somewhat less investment in raping activity than is the case in the Pintail or Green-winged Teal.

Raping activity is very widespread, perhaps universal, in the genus *Anas*, and specific variations in its frequency are probably dependent largely on whether paired males can afford to neglect their mates or their territories. This, in turn, must depend on the needs of females, though, in some species, there may be relationships between male behaviour in defence of an area and the subsequent survival of the brood. For most species, such an effect seems unlikely since broods are highly mobile, but defence of a brood-rearing area may prove to be important in species such as the resident, river-dwelling *A. sparsa* (Siegfried 1968).

In addition, many ecological and behavioural factors must influence the risks, rewards, and energy expenditures involved in rape attempts for the males of each species, and variation in male mating systems will not be fully understood until the 'compromises' concerned have been worked out.

SOCIAL SYSTEMS AND SIGNALLING NEEDS

Signals promoting synchronous take-off and the co-ordination of a male and female in copulation are unlikely to be influenced greatly by variations in social systems and the movements serving these functions are essentially uniform throughout the genus. On the other hand, with differences in the character of the pair bond and varying needs for territorial defence, the associated signals might be expected to vary.

In the Blue-winged Ducks (Shovelers and their allies), conspicuous 'hostile pumping' movements are used both as long-range and short-range threat signals, and they appear to have evolved in response to the need of these species to defend territories. Non-territorial species such as the Pintail and Green-winged Teal lack a conspicuous long-range threat signal.

Orientation components have often been noted in the courtship displays of ducks (for example Fig. 1) but little attention has been given to the factors promoting these characteristics from species to species or from one display to another. The care with which males aim their displays at a specific female achieves its ultimate refinement in those species that use the grunt-whistle. At the peak of this movement, the male directs a spray of water droplets, flipped up by the tip of his bill, toward the female. In order to achieve this, the bird must first align his body laterally to the female, and clear signs of the male's preoccupation with 'aiming' can be detected in the ritualized shaking movements that precede the display (Simmons and Weidmann 1973). The importance of this precise orientation of male displays is apparent when the male has 'interests' in more than one female at a time and rapid alternation in the direction of signalling is required. Probably this display (and perhaps other highly directional displays associated with it in species such as the Green-winged Teal and Mallard) evolved in response to situations involving more than one female (see p. 338).

Arguments such as these could be carried further, but they are perhaps premature until more is known about *Anas* social systems. Rather than pursuing them further here, I will stress the different signalling needs of males and females, since these are basic to the interpretation of display repertoires in all duck species.

SIGNALLING NEEDS OF MALES

A great deal can be inferred about the information that is probably being transmitted by displays through observation of the situations in which they are given, their characteristics, and the effects they appear to have on other animals present. These methods have been used by many ethologists and the possibilities of this

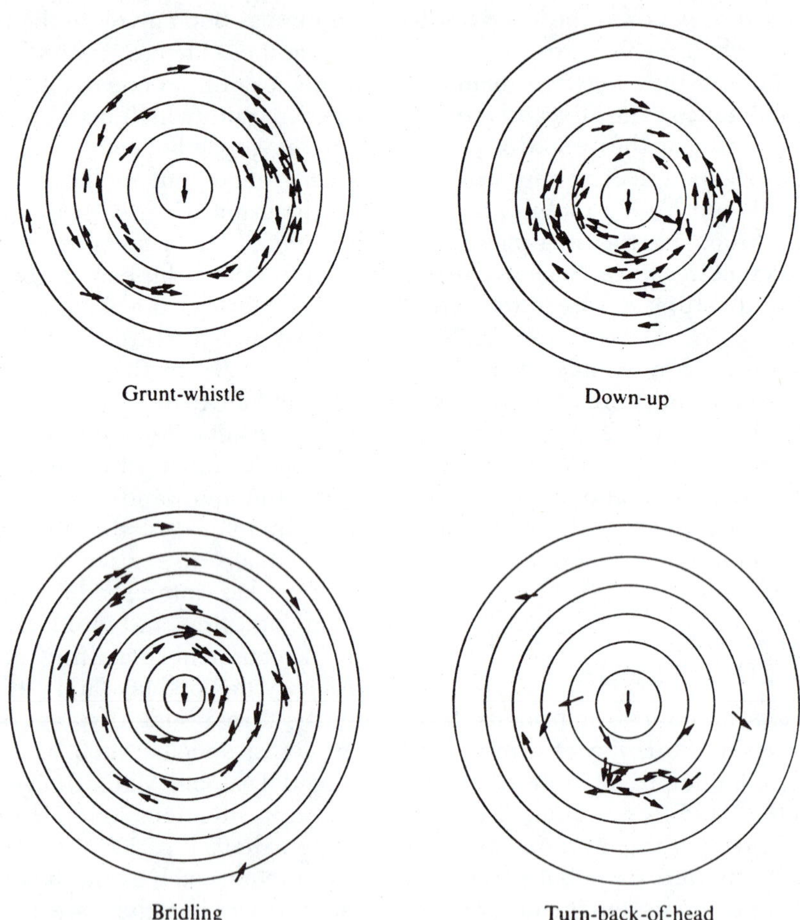

Fig. 1. Positions of male Green-winged Teal in relation to the female (centre arrow) during performances of grunt-whistle, down-up, bridling, and turn-back-of-head displays. Note the precise lateral body orientation of males when performing the grunt-whistle, shorter distance from the female in the case of the down-up, variability in distance for bridling, and positioning in front of the female for turn-back-of-head. Grunt-whistle, bridling, and turn-back-of-head can occur when only one male is present, but down-up is performed only when a second male is present also. The distance between concentric circles is one foot; a swimming teal measures slightly less from bill-tip to tail-tip.

functional approach to signals have become clearer recently (see W. J. Smith 1968). In some cases, experimental testing of hypotheses is possible, as has been done for only one duck display, the Mallard's 'decrescendo call' (Lockner and Phillips 1969, Abraham 1974). For interpreting displays occurring in complex social interactions, however, we must rely on indirect evidence and natural experiments.

Courtship and Establishment of Bonds with Females

In order to maximize their reproductive effort, it must be advantageous for both males and females to choose their sexual partners with care. Except for individuals that were paired in a previous year, females must be using indirect methods of evaluating the potential of males as breeding partners. The most likely criteria would seem to be (1) vigour, skill, and persistence in courtship, (2) healthy physical condition, as reflected in quality of plumage, (3) attentiveness, compatibility, and constancy in reaffirmation of the bond, (4) success in competition with other males, and (5) efficiency in copulation. Female ducks could well make use of all these qualities in choosing among potential mates, and Johnsgard (1960*c*) has given some suggestive evidence in respect to plumage features, but experimental evidence is lacking.

The most likely method of achieving efficient mate-selection would seem to be through a series of trial liaisons, and the earliest bonds among Mallards (Weidmann 1956) and captive Shovelers (pers. observ.) are temporary. In northern-hemisphere *Anas* species, courtship begins several months before the birds move to the breeding area, and individuals that begin testing potential mates early must, on average, be at an advantage. Among the captive Shovelers I observed, adult males came into breeding plumage and began giving displays earlier than yearlings. Adults are heavier and more experienced and on average may be expected to be superior to yearling males in all the qualities used by females for assessment.

To establish a bond with a female, a male (1) must attract her attention to him and let her know that he is interested in her; (2) he must compete successfully with other males in holding her interest until she allies herself with him and follows him; (3) he must discourage rival males by threatening and, if necessary, fighting them; (4) he must overcome the female's aggressive tendencies toward him. To accomplish all of these things, preferably simultaneously, and to be able to maintain them whether the female is swimming, walking or standing on land, or flying, requires a complex series of signals. All four accomplishments are important, each requires different kinds of signals, and none can be over-emphasized at the expense of the others. In general, the male's behaviour relating to the female is incompatible with his hostile behavior toward other males, and the two activities must either alternate rapidly or be combined in behaviour patterns meaning different things to females and males.

It must be to the advantage of unpaired males to explore on-going courtship activities, since these indicate that at least one other male has discovered a female worthy of his attention and the chances are good that, even if she has established a bond already, she has been judged to offer 'possibilities.' Thus courting groups (which are noisy and conspicuous because of the competing males' attention-getting signals) tend to attract other males. But each male must have to make decisions, throughout the pairing season, on which female to devote his attention to. As with males, females must vary in 'quality' and, by judging behaviour and appearance, males may be expected to become expert in reading the signs governing the expenditure of their courting effort.

By studying the situations in which each male courtship display is performed, the effects they appear to have on other birds, and the form of the displays, it is possible to classify them in relation to their probable functions. I have made a preliminary attempts to do this for the Green-winged Teal (Table 1), and the same principles should apply to all ducks although many variants may be expected.

The discussion above obviously concerns the phenomenon known in the lit-

Table 1. A simplified attempt to classify Green-winged Teal displays according to their probable functions; displays of ducklings, juveniles, and females with broods are not included (see McKinney 1965*b* for descriptions and photographs of many of the displays).

	Male	Female
(A) Pre-flight intention	Head-shake Head-thrusting	Head-shake Head-thrusting
(B) Bond establishment		
(1) Pre-display warning	Head-shake Shake	
(2) Attracting attention, specifying interest, holding attention, leading away	Repeated calls Grunt-whistle Head-up-tail-up Turn-toward-female Turn-back-of-head Wing-flap Jump-flight Bridling (on land)	Nod-swim Quacks coinciding with male displays
(3) Interest in female, threat toward rival combined	Down-up	
(4) Threat toward rival	Bill-up	
(5) Indicating preference for one male, threat toward other birds		Inciting
(6) Retreat from rival, jockey for position	Nod-swim	
(7) Appease female's hostility	Bill-down	
(C) Bond maintenance		
(1) Re-affirm bond		
(a) Mates alone	Preen-behind-wing Belly-preen (on land) Bill-dip; drink	Preen-behind-wing
(b) Other birds present	Grunt-whistle, etc. Down-up	Inciting
(2) Warning and contact in flight	Repeated calls	Repeated quacks
(3) Contact when separated	Repeated calls	Descrescendo call
(4) Post-copulation	Bridling	
(D) Intention to copulate	Head-pumping	Head-pumping Prone posture
(E) Combating rape attempts	(Fights would-be rapist)	Inciting Repulsion

erature as 'social courtship,' but I have avoided reifying this concept as has often been done in the literature. It seems better to regard these group activities as the results of simultaneous attempts on the part of individual males to court one female, rather than some sort of organized performance with a raison d'être of its own. The activities of the group are explainable, I believe, on the basis of the individual interests and responses of the birds present.

A major problem in understanding social courtship has arisen with the observation that paired male Mallard will leave their mates to join such a group (Weidmann 1956). This has led to the impression that the activity is 'infectious,' that participation may be important in stimulating 'interest' in pairing, or that there are psychosomatic effects related to gonad maturation and breeding synchronization. Also, since 'pairs' of ducks can be seen in autumn before social courtship has really begun (Lebret 1961) there has been some discussion of whether group activity is 'necessary' for pair formation. It seems more profitable to work from the assumption that a male does not participate in social courtship unless he has an interest in trying to form a bond or a liaison with the female, or that he is exploring these possibilities.[3]

This is supported by my recent observations on captive Green-winged Teal. Throughout May and early June 1973, paired males frequently left their mates to perform displays (grunt-whistle, head-up-tail-up, turn-toward-female, turn-back-of-head, bridling) to other females. Once several females began to show pre-nesting activities, males also began raping assaults, but displays continued to be given to females which had not reached this phase. If a male's mate joined such a group, he switched the orientation of his displays to her; thus, at times, four pairs might be swimming together, each male repeatedly giving displays to his own mate.

I interpret these activities as attempts by paired males to establish personal liaisons with females other than their mates. Such relationships could be of benefit in the event that re-pairing with a new mate becomes desirable or necessary, and perhaps they help to increase a male's chances of success in future raping attempts with these females. Occasionally, a male might have an opportunity to acquire two mates simultaenously, and such trios may prove to be commoner than we now think (see Lebret 1961).

Observations of apparent 'pairs' in Mallards in autumn, before social courtship has really begun (Lebret 1961) might suggest that social courtship is not 'necessary' for pairing to occur. It seems more likely that some bonds remain intact after an unsuccessful breeding attempt and occasionally, even in migratory species, like the Mallard, the same birds breed together in successive years (Lebret 1961, Dwyer et al. 1973). In these instances, strong personal bonds must have existed, but I suspect that they were retested, through competitive courtship, during winter. This phenomenon may well be more common in non-migratory populations and information is badly needed on species reported to have long-lasting bonds.

Bond-maintenance and Defence of the Mate

In the Green-winged Teal, paired males evidently re-affirm their bonds by performing the same kinds of displays to the mate as they use in pair formation. At other times, however, when the members of a pair are alone together, there are special displays apparently serving this function. 'Preen-behind-wing,' 'shake + belly-preen,' 'preen-dorsally,' 'drinking,' and 'bill-dipping' are especially common in *Anas* species. Brief nibbling or touching of the female may also occur ('Tendieren'), as described by von de Wall (1965), as a form of 'directed courtship.'

Males perform bursts of repeated calls when separated from the mate and especially when they are searching for her. This is the response given by a paired male to his mate's decrescendo call, and

[3] Social courtship activity in groups of males only, as reported by Lorenz (1941), Weidmann and Darley (1971*b*), and others, seems to be abnormal, if not pathological. It can be triggered by homosexual, captive-reared males, but I have seen it occasionally also in wild-caught Green-winged Teal deprived of females in captivity.

these calls provide the main mechanism for maintaining contact between mates when they are apart.

Males protect their mates, as best they can, by threatening, chasing, or fighting with males attempting to court or rape the mate. As might be expected, the close-range threat displays used are variable in intensity and duration (for example, bill-up in the Green-winged Teal, rab-rab calling in the Mallard) depending on the situation.

Territorial Defence

Highly territorial species, such as the Shoveler, have conspicuous threat signals and they use ritualized fighting methods in boundary disputes (McKinney 1970).

Pre-copulatory Signals

In most *Anas* species, intention to copulate is signalled by vertical 'head-pumping' movements; in other ducks a variety of ritualized movements are used (see Johnsgard 1965). These displays are usually inconspicuous and rarely are there vocalizations. In general, male ducks perform pre-copulatory displays much more often than their mates and mounting is likely to follow only when the female has taken the initiative, or when she indicates her readiness by responding to the male's displays with similar ones or by assuming the 'prone' posture. Thus the frequency of copulations between the members of a pair appears to be regulated by the female.

In at least some species (for example, Mallard: Raitasuo 1964) copulations occur months before egg-laying begins, and presumably they are part of the pair-bond testing procedure. Just before and during the egg-laying period, well established pairs of captive Shoveler (McKinney 1967) and Mallards (Barrett 1973) copulated only once or a few times each day. Such a rate, governed by the female, is presumably a minimum required to ensure fertilization of the eggs since copulating birds must be especially vulnerable to predators.

After his mate has been assaulted (and perhaps inseminated) by other males, however, it must be to a male's disadvantage to allow her to decide whether or not she will permit him to copulate. In such situations, Barrett (1973) has recorded rape-like, 'forced pair-copulations,' involving mated birds, in captive Mallards. Similar behaviour occurred frequently in captive Green-winged Teal, paired males attempting to rape their own mates a few minutes after the latter had been assaulted by other males. Pre-copulatory 'pumping' is absent in these situations where selection for a prompt response by the mated male must be very strong.

Post-copulatory Signals

Immediately after an apparently successful copulation, male ducks usually perform one or a series of displays with obvious orientation of the male's body in relation to the female. In *Anas* species, the performance can include such displays as bridling, turn-toward-female, nod-swim, turn-back-of-head, and at least one call is given (for example, a loud whistle accompanying bridling). Attempts to explain the occurrence of these displays in terms of motivational conflict theory (McKinney 1961) or isolating mechanism function (Johnsgard 1963) have not been very convincing, and it seems more likely that they are functioning to re-affirm individual identity, thereby helping to maintain the pair-bond.

The characteristics of male post-copulatory displays in ducks suggest that they are designed to draw the female's attention to the performer and they seem to demonstrate structural features and voice characteristics that could be used by females to identify their mates individually. There can be no better time for a male to draw attention to his identity than immediately after he has accomplished a successful copulation if, by so doing, he increases his mate's confidence in his competence as a breeding partner and reduces the risk that she will desert him. If this is the case, post-copulatory displays should be especially well developed in birds which can least afford to lose a mate and in those where the danger of doing so is great.

In general terms, comparative evidence seems to support this argument. In swans, geese, and Whistling Ducks, which have long-term pair-bonds and the investment of individuals in their mates must be great, both male and female usually perform post-copulatory displays in unison. In sheld-ducks, where competition for mates may be severest in females, both sexes also perform, but Johnsgard (1965) reports that the female calls loudly, and in *Tadorna ferruginea* and *T. cana* she starts calling before the male begins his displays. In the remaining duck tribes, where competition for mates appears to be greatest among males, post-copulatory displays are usually given exclusively by males.

SIGNALLING NEEDS OF FEMALES

Pairing

At times during periods of social courtship in Green-winged Teal, females perform nod-swimming (repeated forward and back movements of the head) and they give loud, single quacks almost coinciding with, but clearly in response to, male displays. Johnsgard (1965) has noted similar calls in other *Anas* species, and Weidmann and Darley (1971*a*) have analysed the effects of female nod-swimming in Mallards. These movements and calls appear to stimulate and hold the interest of males in the female, although they are by no means essential triggers for male courtship. Moreover, these attention-getting devices could be important in competition between females during pairing.

Pair formation in ducks is usually regarded as a process in which females make a selection from the males that court them. Certainly this is going on, but males also must be exercising choice in their decisions to court certain females. Although there will usually be an excess of males in the flocks when pairing is taking place, this is not the 'cause' of male competition for females. Rather it must increase the intensity of the competition that is inevitably present when the males and females in a population sort themselves out into pairs. Early in the pairing season especially, we should expect to see females 'making advances' toward particularly desirable males and encouraging them to court. Late in the season, when most females have established bonds and yearling males have become active in courtship, competition between males is certainly the most conspicuous aspect of the phenomenon. Nevertheless, the female must be able to change her mind (for example, if the mate becomes sick or injured), and she will need signals indicating her interest in other males.

Instances of active 'courtship' on the part of females might also be expected in captive flocks where choice of mates is limited. Among Shovelers and Blue-winged Teal, *A. discors,* I have occasionally seen females direct displays typical of the male repertoire (belly-preen, lateral dabbling, turn-back-of-the-head) at males (McKinney 1970).

For pairing to occur, females must have a method of indicating preference for one male over another so that both favoured and rejected males are informed of the female's decision. This is accomplished in most *Anas* species by 'inciting'—sideways movements of the head performed beside the favoured male with the bill directed away from him, often pointing toward the rejected male. In the full performance, rattling calls accompany these movements. Although ritualized to a considerable degree (Lorenz 1958), there is much variability in the intensity of the movements and calls, and at times the performance grades into threat and even short chases.

Bond-maintenance and Contact Between Mates

Once a female has indicated a preference for one male she re-affirms the liaison by repeatedly performing 'inciting' beside him when other males approach. Especially when the bond has recently formed, females may respond to the ritualized 'preen-behind-wing' of the male by giving the same display while the two birds stand close together. If the mates become separated, the female gives decrescendo calls, the male repeated calls, and the two come together again.

When the pair takes wing, especially as a result of a disturbance, the female gives a series of loud, evenly-spaced quacks ('going-away call' of Lorenz 1953) and the male often gives repeated calls. These responses to being flushed occur in pairs before they move to the breeding grounds, and they must be functioning mainly in keeping the birds together.

During the breeding season, however, females give much longer bouts of similar evenly-spaced quacks in two contexts: (1) during flights by the pair over nesting cover (or when swimming before flights) during the days immediately before laying of the first egg, and (2) in late incubation or when females are leading broods, associated with mobbing or distraction displays in the presence of a predator.

While there are striking differences in context between the going-away call, 'persistent quacking' during nest-site selection, and the broody calls of an alarmed, defensive female, I suspect that they have a common motivational basis. Clearly, however, they must be serving different functions. The going-away call apparently functions in maintaining contact with the mate, broody calls presumably warn the brood of danger and distract the predator, and perhaps persistent quacking serves both to ensure attendance by the mate and to lure predators during nest-site selection.

Persistent quacking is a loud, conspicuous signal with characteristics suggesting a 'broadcast' function rather than simply a mate-contact function. Since it occurs in both territorial and non-territorial species (for example, Shoveler and Green-winged Teal) it seems not to be advertisement associated with defence of an area. Its frequent occurrence in twilight and at night suggest that it undoubtedly keeps the mate informed of his female's location and, since decrescendo calls are also given during this phase (in Green-winged Teal) and persistent quacking is given especially in flight, it appears important that the male be informed in this way. Indeed, nesting cover seems always to be inspected by the pair as a unit (for example, in Shoveler, Mallard, and Green-winged Teal), and the male must play an important role at this time in being watchful for predators and warning his mate of danger. Also, since persistent quacking does seem to be stimulated by appearance of a potential predator (though often such a stimulus is certainly not present), I believe that it may have a luring effect on mammals, resulting in betrayal of their presence. The decision on exactly where to locate the first nest of the season must be an extremely important one for females, and it would be surprising to find that the decision was not influenced by her knowledge of the local predators.

The male usually accompanies the female very closely during inspection of cover. In the beginning, they are very alert and they often seem to take turns in moving into patches of grass for brief periods. On subsequent days, more and more time is spent moving around in cover (McKinney 1967). In my captive Green-winged Teal, it was not always the female who made the first move into cover; frequently the male seemed highly motivated to do so and he often preceded the female. Evidently these excursions into unknown terrain, where predators are at home, are dangerous and strong cooperation between the mates is favoured.

Incubation, Rape Assaults, and Re-nesting

Once the clutch has been laid females incubate steadily with one or two brief periods off the nest each day to feed, drink, and bathe. During these periods, so long as a strong bond persists, the male is alert for the arrival of his mate on their favourite feeding waters, and he is active in joining her and accompanying her while she feeds. His presence presumably is important to both members of the pair, in warning the female of predators and in guarding her against rape attempts. In the latter respect, however, females are victims of the social system, and there may be little they can do to prevent harassment by alert males intent on raping.

In species where paired males specialize in promiscuous activities, it is not yet clear whether they discriminate between laying and incubating females although, from the point of view of fathering progeny, the latter are inappropriate targets for assault. On average, however, it may be a good strategy for males to chase all females in view of the high rate of predation on eggs and the steady 'supply' of females in the 're-nest interval' phase throughout the breeding season. From the female's point of view, on the other hand, it would seem to be advantageous to signal her broody condition and this appears to be achieved through 'repulsion behaviour' (Lorenz 1953). This involves characteristic hunched, ruffled postures and distinctive loud 'broody' calls. Females give this response to harassing males once they begin to incubate, and their aggressiveness increases throughout incubation, culminating in vigorous attack on conspecifics in defence of the brood. Presumably some would-be rapists are 'repulsed' by such behaviour and, if a choice is available, they would be expected to direct their chases toward females which are not performing in this way, since these are more likely to be laying birds.

The fertilization of females for re-nest clutches is extremely difficult to study in wild birds, and it is still not clear how this is accomplished. There are surely specific differences, since male Shovelers usually remain faithful to their mates throughout the incubation period, and thus will be available to father the eggs in replacement clutches. In other species, such as the Mallard and Pintail, bonds are thought to break in mid-incubation, and females must either re-pair or be inseminated through raping. Sowls (1955) believed that females 'tease' males during the re-nest interval, encouraging males to pursue them, but behavioural changes in females during this phase need further careful study.

CHARACTERISTICS OF DISPLAYS WITH DIFFERENT FUNCTIONS

If the displays of each species serve different functions, each display must have evolved under a different combination of selective pressures. Thus it is not sufficient to suppose that selection has favoured individuals with efficient sets of 'courtship displays.' Each display must have evolved, to some extent, independently, and the ritualization processes determining its present form should reflect its special functions.

Male Courtship Displays

These displays appear to serve at least five different functions: attracting the female's attention to the performer, specifying which female is being courted, holding the female's attention, leading her away, and helping males to compete with other males.

Attention-getting displays tend to be sudden, startling performances, involving motions that are distinctly different from predictable, everyday activities. Loud, brief calls (for example whistles) usually coincide with movements involving the head, wings, or the whole body. Plumage features often reinforce the optical effect (for example, the Pintail's tail in the head-up-tail-up posture). Many of these displays are derived from, or are related to alert, alarm, or escape behaviour (for example, repeated calls, nod-swimming). These are predictable sources since birds are naturally responsive to signs of alarm in their companions.

Most male courtship displays in *Anas* species are performed with a deliberate orientation component in relation to the female; often the whole body is either broadside or pointing directly at the female, or the head only is turned toward or away from her. This seems to be the main method whereby males specify which female interests them, and water-splashing, as in the grunt-whistle, is the highest development of this phenomenon.

The main technique used in holding the female's attention on the performer seems to be through the use of display-chains. Body-shakes or head-shakes are often used as a 'warning' that a display is likely to be performed. These are often described as being 'introductory to a bout of courtship,' but it seems better to regard them as preliminary moves in the attention-getting strategy of each male. This is well illustrated by the linkages of displays associated with the grunt-whistle in the Green-winged Teal (Fig. 2). Males often give only preliminary head-shakes, as they 'jockey' for position in the group, waiting until the female and the other males are appropriately placed before proceeding with the major movements in the sequence (grunt-whistle + head-up-tail-up + turn-toward-female + turn-back-of-head or nod-swim). The male can break off the sequence at various points, however, depending on the changing positions and activities of the other birds.

As pointed out by Johnsgard (1960*b*), turn-back-of-head is a very widespread display in ducks of many tribes, performed by a male as the female swims toward him and apparently serving to encourage her to follow him. In the grunt-whistle sequences described above, it comes toward the end, culminating in the ideal procedure of catching-attention + holding-attention + leading-away. Other displays may serve similar functions in other ducks, for example, the jump-flights of *Anas* species and the rit-

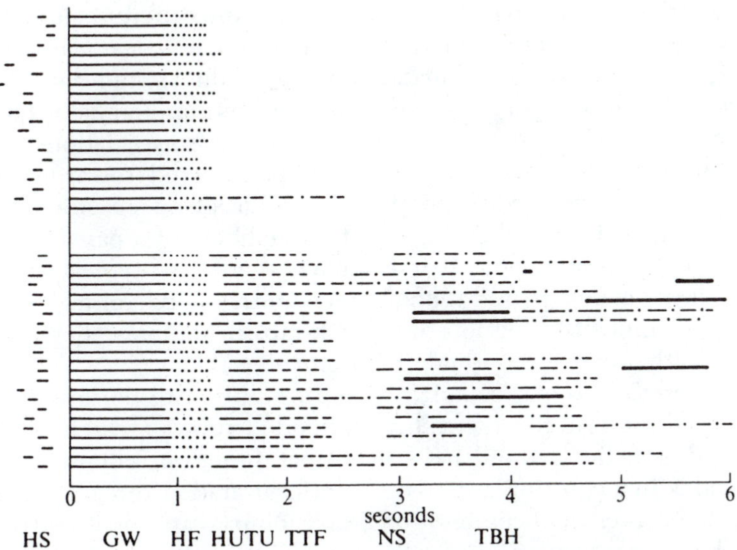

Fig. 2. Forty-four grunt-whistle sequences performed by one male Green-winged Teal during one session of social courtship. A preliminary head-shake (HS) is followed by the grunt-whistle (GW) and a head-flick (HF) in all cases. Head-up-tail-up (HUTU) and turn-toward-female (TTF) may (lower sequences) or may not (upper sequences) follow. Occurrence, order, and duration of nod-swimming (NS) and turn-back-of-head (TBH), shown as a solid line vary greatly depending on the positions and behaviour of the female and other males in the group. (From a 16 mm cine film, exposed at 24 frames per second. See McKinney [1965*b*] for descriptions and photographs of the displays.)

ualized short-flights of the Goldeneye, *Bucephala clangula.* The evolution of such displays entailing moving away in front of the female was presumably facilitated by the basic tendency of these social birds to follow others.

Although the idea of competition between males was inherent in the views of Heinroth (1911) and Lorenz (1941), this aspect of duck social courtship has often been neglected. Clues to the presence of hostility between males are subtle in many species and easily missed when attention is focused on the displays. This is especially well illustrated by three types of study on the displays of Goldeneyes, *Bucephala clangula,* with emphasis on the displays as fixed action patterns (Dane et al. 1959, Dane and van der Kloot 1964), as products of motivational conflict (Lind 1959), and as signals used in pairing (Nilsson 1969). Each approach has its merits, and the results are complementary, but the most recent study by Nilsson is especially valuable in interpreting displays in the light of competition between males. The recent work of Weidmann and his colleagues on the Mallard, and my own studies on Eider Ducks, Blue-winged Ducks, and the Green-winged Teal agree closely on the important role of aggression in duck courtship. In fact, as Heinroth concluded long ago, social courtship in *Anas* makes no sense unless it is viewed as a consequence of competition between males for mates.

Lebret (1961) has argued that social courtship functions not only in pairing but as a method of canalizing aggression during autumn and winter when Mallard Ducks must live in flocks. His careful observations can be interpreted in another way, however, if males are assumed to benefit from extra-pair-bond liaisons. He noted that 'many paired males may take part in social display, while their mates are sleeping on the banks' and 'we may not conclude that a certain drake is unpaired because of the absence of a possible mate.' Such behaviour corresponds to that described earlier for the Green-winged Teal, and is explainable if it is assumed that these males (paired though they may be) are indeed trying to establish liaisons with other individual females. Thus Lebret's idea of a 'canalizing of aggression' function for courtship should be modified: the over-all behaviour of the males in a courting group appears always to be a result of competition between males for the attention of a female but male displays can have different functions. These can be distinguished most easily by comparing the simplest possible situations, namely, when only one male or two males are involved.

Association of the down-up display of the Mallard with hostile situations has been known for a long time (for example, Weidmann 1956), and this is readily confirmed by its linkage with the obviously hostile rab-rab palavers of threatening males. The Green-winged Teal has exact parallels in the bill-up threat display and the down-up display. However, I have never seen these displays performed by a single male to a female; for a male to perform the down-up, he must be close to both a female and another male. In the simplest situations, a male gives this display when his mate is close beside him and another male is nearby, all three birds often having their bodies aligned parallel. I conclude that this display has both threat function in relation to other males, and attention-getting function (including bond-affirmation) for the female.

This phenomenon of a single male display having different signal functions for males and females may well be widespread in ducks, and it may be suspected where there are signs of hostile motivation in close association with a display that is directed toward females. Thus many 'greeting ceremonies' involving the members of a pair include male displays that occur typically during hostile encounters between males (for example, rab-rab in Mallards; hostile pumping in Shovelers).

In addition to performing highly ritualized displays, which appear to have threat function, competing males also perform graded threat signals during social courtship (especially when two males become preoccupied with one another rather than with the female), they swim off or chase one another (especially when provoked by performance of an attention-getting display), and they are constantly jockeying for position, interrupting one another's display-chains, and occasionally fighting vigorously. The tendency to synchronize their displays in 'bursts' is most famous (at least in Mallards and the Green-winged Teal) in the case of the down-up—suggesting again the high level of male–male interaction involved when this display is given. Presumably synchronization is a 'tactic' resulting from the competition between males; a solitary performance of an attention-getting display is likely to be advantageous to a male in capturing the female's undivided attention, a result countered by synchronizing. Repeated calls also tend to occur in bouts during social courtship in these two species—a prime attention-getting display. The grunt-whistle, on the other hand, tends to be solitary performance, each male concentrating on timing and orientating the display precisely in relation to the female, moving further away from her and beginning only when other males seem unlikely to interrupt.

Many of the complexities of social courtship have been omitted here since I have been concerned with arguing a point of view. Each species must be examined carefully to test the validity of the ideas, and many complicating factors will no doubt emerge.

FACTORS RESPONSIBLE FOR SPECIFIC DIFFERENCES

Sibley (1957) and Johnsgard (1960*a*, 1963, 1965) have argued that diversity in the display movements, calls, and male plumage patterns of ducks has evolved in response to selection for specific distinctiveness. They point to the ease with which closely related sympatric species can be hybridized in captivity, reasoning that effective isolating mechanisms must be operating to prevent this in wild birds. The male displays used in courtship vary much more between species than do precopulatory displays and female vocalizations, as it should be if the former are functioning to prevent hybrid matings. The argument is further supported by the frequent occurrence of reduced sexual dimorphism in plumage on islands (where closely related species are absent) and in the southern hemisphere (where pair bonds are thought to be long, pairing seasons may be more distinct, there may be more ecological separation, and in general there seems to be less danger of hybridization).

There are alternatives to this argument, however, and it does not provide a convincing explanation for many kinds of specific differences. I have tried to show that signalling devices have evolved in response to needs of males and females to communicate varied kinds of information of vital importance in resolving their individual relationships. While some (perhaps all) of these signals undoubtedly do give information on the species and sex of the bird performing them, a great deal more is involved. Signalling needs are different in species with different life-styles and social systems, and display repertoires have evidently been moulded by a great variety of selection pressures. Such things as vulnerability to predators (McKinney 1965*c*), degree of territoriality (McKinney 1970), proportion of courtship performed on land (Kaltenhäuser 1971), characteristics of pair bonding and male promiscuity have evidently been involved. For most duck species, we do not have enough information on signalling needs nor on social systems to judge the full extent of their repercussions on display movements, sounds, or morphology.

There is still much to be discovered about species-recognition and factors influencing mate-choice in ducks. The work of Schutz (1965) on sexual imprinting suggests that preferences for a type of mate are heavily influenced by the social environment during the brood phase, and it now seems likely that male courtship displays may have little to do with prevention of hybrid matings.

Many male displays involve a combination of movements, sounds, and an exhibition of plumage features, and there has been a tendency to think of all three as though they have evolved in concert. Linkages there are to be sure, but it seems more important to recognize that changes in each of these categories have surely been influenced by quite different blends of selective forces, and changes in each have proceeded at different rates.

Judging from their occurrence in many living species, most male courtship display movements seem to have been relatively conservative features, although they have been combined in various sequences and some movements have been dropped from adult repertoires. There have probably been constraints on repertoire size, as suggested by Moynihan (1970), but differences of this type are unlikely to be understood until signalling needs, and the functions of each display have been worked out for each species. It seems particulary dangerous to assume that the presence or absence of a grunt-whistle or a down-up in one species has come about as a result of selection for specifically distinct courtship repertoires, as Johnsgard (1965) proposes for the two sympatric South American Pintails, *A. georgica* and *A. bahamensis*.

The sources of selection that have moulded male vocalizations and plumage patterns now seem likely to be much more difficult to investigate than those involved in the evolution of display movements. We know very little about the biological functions of these characteristics and this must be the first step in working out why they have evolved.

CONCLUSIONS

The displays of ducks are viewed as signalling devices evolved through selection of individuals gaining advantages in their personal social relationships from performance of these behaviour patterns. Signalling is needed for many purposes (for example, pairing, territory defence, flight-intention, copulation-intention, pair-bond maintenance). The signal characteristics required vary with the situation. Males and females often have to communicate different kinds of information. Signalling needs vary from species to species in relation to differences in the social system.

The breeding system involving incubation by the female only has apparently had fundamental repercussions on social behaviour in the Anatinae. Breeding entails different risks for males and females; unbalanced adult sex-ratios are common, and competition for mates and copulations is strong. Seasonal pair bonding is apparently usual in *Anas* species but the extent to which males defend territories, engage in promiscuous matings, and attend the female and brood vary from species to species.

Social courtship in *Anas* species is interpreted as a consequence of competition between males for breeding partners. Highly directional displays, such as the grunt-whistle, may have evolved to enable males to specify which female interests them in situations where they are attempting to establish or maintain bonds or liaisons with more than one female. The extent to which males are able to combine promiscuous raping activity with maintenance of a pair bond seems to have been an important factor in the evolution of *Anas* social systems.

In spite of much study, duck displays continue to pose some of the most challenging problems in the fields of animal communication and behaviour evolution. A deeper understanding of the factors that have shaped their evolution may come especially from comparative studies of social systems and investigations of the signalling needs of individuals.

ACKNOWLEDGMENTS

Niko Tinbergen's approach has inevitably influenced the way all ethologists think about behaviour evolution and his comparative programme on gull behaviour has provided the model for these duck studies. I am grateful to him for inspiration and encouragement in the fascinating but frustrating task of trying to figure out why each species behaves differently. Julie Barrett, Scott Derrickson, Walter Graul, Cathy Laurie, Roy Siegfried, and Scott Stalheim gave very helpful, detailed criticisms of the manuscript, and Paul Stolen helped in many ways with the Green-winged Teal study. The research was supported by the Graduate School, University of Minnesota, the National Science Foundation (Grant GB-36651X), and the U.S. Atomic Energy Commission (Contract AT(11-1)-1332; Publication COO-1332-98).

LITERATURE CITED

ABRAHAM, R. L. 1974. Vocalizations of the Mallard (*Anas platyrhynchos*). Condor 76:401–420.

BARRETT, J. 1973. Breeding behavior of captive Mallards. M.S. Thesis, University of Minnesota.

BELLROSE, F. C., T. G. SCOTT, A. S. HAWKINS, AND J. B. LOW. 1961. Sex ratios and age ratios in North American ducks. Bull. Ill. Nat. Hist. Survey 27:385–474.

BROWN, J. L. 1964. The evolution of diversity in avian territorial systems. Wilson Bull. 76: 160–169.

———, AND G. H. ORIANS. 1970. Spacing patterns in mobile animals. A. Rev. Ecol. Syst. 1:239–262.

CROOK, J. H. 1964. The evolution of social organization and visual communication in the weaver birds (Ploceinae). Behaviour Suppl. 10.

DANE, B., AND W. G. VAN DER KLOOT. 1964. An analysis of the display of the Goldeneye duck (*Bucephala clangula* L.). Behaviour 22:282–328.

———, C. WALCOTT, AND W. H. DRURY. 1959. The form and duration of the display actions of the goldeneye (*Bucephala clangula*). Behaviour 14:265–281.

DELACOUR, J., AND E. MAYR. 1945. The family Anatidae. Wilson Bull. 57:3–55.

DWYER, T. J., S. R. DERRICKSON, AND D. S. GILMER. 1973. Migrational homing in a pair of Mallards. Auk 90:687.

HEINROTH, O. 1911. Beitrage zur Biologie, namentlich Ethologie und Psychologie der Anatiden. Proc. Int. Orn. Congr. 5:589–702.

HILDÉN, O. 1964. Ecology of duck populations in the island group of Valassaaret, Gulf of Bothnia. Ann. Zool. Fenn. 1:153–279.

HINDE, R. A. 1959. Behaviour and speciation in birds and lower vertebrates. Biol. Rev. 34: 85–128.

HJORTH, I. 1970. Reproductive behaviour in Tetraonidae with special reference to males. Viltrevy 7:183–596.

JOHNSGARD, P. A. 1960*a*. Hybridization in the Anatidae and its taxonomic implications. Wildfowl Trust 11th Annual Report, pp. 31–45.

———. 1960*b*. Pair-formation mechanisms in Anas (Anatidae) and related genera. Ibis 102:616–618.

———. 1960*c*. A quantitative study of sexual behavior in Mallards and Black Ducks. Wilson Bull. 72:133–145.

———. 1962. Evolutionary trends in the behaviour and morphology of the Anatidae. Wildfowl Trust 13th Annual Report, pp. 130–148.

———. 1963. Behavioral isolating mechanisms in the family Anatidae. Proc. Int. Orn. Congr. 13(1):531–543.

———. 1965. Handbook of waterfowl behavior. Cornell University Press, Ithaca, New York.

KALTENHÄUSER, D. 1971. Über Evolutionsvorgänge in der Schwimmentenbalz. Z. Tierpsychol. 29:481–540.

KEAR, J. 1970. The adaptive radiation of parental care in waterfowl. *In* Social behaviour in birds and mammals (ed., J. H. Crook). Academic Press, New York.

KEITH, L. 1961. A study of waterfowl ecology on small impoundments in south-eastern Alberta. Wildl. Monogr. 6.

LEBRET, T. 1958. The 'Jump-flight' of the Mallard, *Anas platyrhynchos* L., the Teal, *Anas crecca* L. and the Shoveler, *Spatula clypeata* L. Ardea 46:68–72.

———. 1961. The pair formation in the annual cycle of the Mallard, *Anas platyrhynchos* L. Ardea 49:97–158.

LIND, H. 1959. Studies on courtship and copulatory behavior in the goldeneye (*Bucephala clangula* (L.)). Dansk. Orn. Foren. Tidssk. 53:177–219.

LOCKNER, R. F., AND R. E. PHILLIPS. 1969. A preliminary analysis of the decrescendo call in female mallards (*Anas platyrhynchos* L.). Behaviour 35:281–287.

LORENZ, K. 1941. Vergleichende Bewegungsstudien an Anatinen. J. Orn., Lpz. 89:194–294.

———. 1953. Comparative studies on the behaviour of the Anatinae. Reprinted from Avicultural Magazine.

———. 1958. The evolution of behavior. Scient. Am. 199:67–78.

MCKINNEY, F. 1961. An analysis of the displays of the European Eider *Somateria mollissima mollissima* (Linnaeus) and the Pacific Eider *Somateria mollissima v. nigra* Bonaparte. Behaviour, Suppl. 7.

———. 1965*a*. The comfort movements of Anatidae. Behaviour 25:120–220.

———. 1965*b*. The displays of the American Green-winged Teal. Wilson Bull. 77:112–121.

———. 1965*c*. The spring behavior of wild Steller Eiders. Condor 67:273–290.

———. 1967. Breeding behaviour of captive Shovelers. Wildfowl Trust 18th Annual Report, pp. 108–121.

———. 1969. The behaviour of ducks. *In* The behaviour of domestic animals (ed., E. S. E. Hafez) (2nd ed.). Ballière, Tindall, and Cox, London.

———. 1970. Displays of four species of blue-winged ducks. Living Bird 9:29–64.

———. 1973. Ecoethological aspects of reproduction. *In* Breeding biology of birds, pp. 6–21. National Academy of Sciences, Washington, D.C.

MOYNIHAN, M. 1970. Control, suppression, decay, disappearance and replacement of displays. J. Theor. Biol. 29:85–112.

NELSON, J. B. 1970. The relationship between behaviour and ecology in the Sulidae with reference to other sea birds. Oceanogr. Mar. Biol. A. Rev. 8:501–574.

NILSSON, L. 1969. Knipans *Bucephala clangula* beteende under vinterhalvaret. Vår fågelvärld 28:199–210.

ORIANS, G. H., AND G. M. CHRISTMAN. 1968. A comparative study of the behavior of Red-winged, Tricolored, and Yellow-headed Blackbirds. Univ. Calif. Publs. Zool. 84.

RAITASUO, K. 1964. Social behaviour of the mallard, *Anas platyrhynchos*, in the course of the annual cycle. Papers on Game Research, Helsinki, No. 24.

SARGEANT, A. B. 1972. Red fox spatial characteristics in relation to waterfowl predation. J. Wildl. Mgmt. 36:225–236.

SCHUTZ, F. 1965. Sexuelle Prägung bei Anatiden. Z. Tierpsychol. 22:50–103.

SIBLEY, C. G. 1957. The evolutionary and taxonomic significance of sexual dimorphism and hybridization in birds. Condor 59:166–191.

SIEGFRIED, W. R. 1965. The Cape Shoveler *Anas smithii* (Hartert) in southern Africa. Ostrich 36:155–198.

———. 1968. The Black Duck in the south-western Cape. Ostrich 39:61–75.

———. 1970. Wildfowl distribution, conservation and research in southern Africa. Wildfowl 21:89–98.

———. 1974. Brood care, pair bonds and plumage in southern African Anatini. Wildfowl 25:33–40.

SIMMONS, K. E. L., AND U. WEIDMANN. 1973. Directional bias as a component of social behaviour with special reference to the Mallard, *Anas platyrhynchos*. J. Zool. Lond. 170:49–62.

SMITH, R. I. 1968. The social aspects of reproductive behavior in the Pintail. Auk 85:381–396.

SMITH, W. J. 1968. Message-meaning analysis. *In* Animal communication (ed., T. A. Sebeok). Indiana University Press, Bloomington.

SOWLS, L. K. 1955. Prairie ducks. Wildlife Management Institute, Washington, D.C.

TAMISIER, A. 1972. Rythmes nycthemeraux des sarcelles d'hiver pendant leur hivernage en Camargue. Alauda 40:109–159.

TINBERGEN, N. 1959. Comparative studies of the behaviour of gulls (Laridae): a progress report. Behaviour 15:1–70.

———. 1963. On adaptive radiation in Gulls (Tribe Larini). Zool. Med. 39:209–223.

TRIVERS, R. L. 1972. Parental investment and sexual selection. *In* Sexual selection and the descent of man 1871–1971 (ed., B. G. Campbell). Aldine, Chicago.

VON DE WALL, W. 1965. 'Gesellschaftsspiel' und Balz der Anatini. J. Orn. 106:65–80.

WEIDMANN, U. 1956. Verhaltensstudien an der Stockente (*Anas platyrhynchos* L.). I. Das Aktionsystem. Z. Tierpsychol. 13:208–271.

———, AND J. DARLEY. 1971*a*. The role of the female in the social display of mallards. Anim. Behav. 19:287–298.

———, AND ———. 1971*b*. The synchronization of signals in the 'social display' of Mallards. Rev. Comp. Anim. 5:131–135.

WELLER, M. W. 1968. Notes on some Argentine anatids. Wilson Bull. 80:189–212.

———. 1972. Ecological studies of Falkland Islands' waterfowl. Wildfowl 23:25–44.

SITE ATTACHMENT IN THE NORTHERN SHOVELER[1]

NORMAN R. SEYMOUR,[2] Department of Biology, Saint Francis Xavier University, Antigonish, Nova Scotia, Canada

Territory typically refers to "any defended area" (Mayr 1935, Noble 1939, Tinbergen 1939, Nice 1941) that is thought to arise as the outcome of two distinct tendencies, site attachment and hostility (Tinbergen 1957). Although the concept has been considered to be generally valid for ducks (McKinney 1965), controversy exists over the use and validity of the concept in some species (Dzubin 1955, Bezzel 1959, Lebret 1961, Hori 1963). Although hostility of male ducks towards conspecifics has been shown to occur in several species, the question of the male's attachment to a site has remained unresolved and largely uninvestigated. The present study was designed to assess the possibility that such site attachment does occur in a manner consistent with the territory concept.

Demonstration of site attachment in ducks is rendered difficult under natural conditions because, as McKinney (1965) pointed out, the possibility cannot normally be excluded that a male is defending the female rather than a site to which he is attached. To separate these two variables, I tried an experimental approach that involved moving a female away from the defended area. I chose as the study bird the Northern Shoveler (*Anas clypeata*), which appears to be territorial in the classical sense (McKinney 1967, Seymour MS).

The experiment was conducted between 27 May and 10 June 1970 on the Delta Marsh, Manitoba, Canada. The birds under test were watched for a total of 27 hours and, in addition, hourly checks of the study area from 05:00 to 22:00 (darkness prevented earlier and later observation) were made on 10 days. The study area was a flooded grass meadow of approximately 20 ha that never exceeded 0.5 m in depth. Prior to the experiment, I had counted from two to seven unmated male shovelers on the meadow feeding and courting females of transient pairs. Seven males, including those referred to below as males 1 and 2, were caught on the meadow in a clover trap described by Lincoln and Baldwin (1929), marked with nasal markers (Bartonek and Dane 1964), and released where captured.

An unmated female, hatched from a wild-procured egg and held in captivity for a year, was placed in the trap to decoy the unmated males. Three trapping sites referred to as sites A, B and C were chosen. Site B was 65 m from Site A, site C was 150 m from site B and 185 m from site A. Laths located at 5-m intervals from the trap, which I refer to as the trap site, allowed me to determine where interactions occurred relative to the trap site. Specific objectives, details of procedures, and observations are reported below in five parts that correspond to shifts in the location of the decoy female.

(1) The female was placed at site A for 4 days, then removed from the meadow for 2 days, to determine (a) whether unmated males would be attracted to her, (b) whether one male would become dominant over the others and establish a territory, and (c) to assess the behavior of the male(s) after removal of the female.

Within one day of placing the female at site A, a male (male 1) became domi-

[1] Originally published in Auk 91(2):423–427, 1974.

[2] Present address: McGill University, Sainte Anne de Bellevue, Quebec H0A 1C0, Canada.

nant in the area and chased and pecked other males with which he had previously shown no apparent hostility. After the first day, the other males tended to avoid him. By the second day male 1, who had learned how to pass freely into and out of the trap, could approach the female and not be threatened or pecked by her. The female reacted to other males by adopting an inciting posture and by an avoidance response as they approached the trap. Thus, an association suggesting a typical pair bond appeared to have been established between male 1 and the female. Male 1 remained with the female until she was removed from the study area 4 days later.

After the female was removed, male 1 remained at site A. During hourly checks he was typically seen within 5 m of a lath that marked the former location of the female. This male threatened, chased, and made pursuit flights after virtually all shoveler males that flew or swam within approximately 30 m of site A. He invariably returned to site A after each pursuit flight. During this time the unmated males, who formerly had been attracted to site A by the female, fed together elsewhere on the meadow and showed little of the hostility among themselves that they had exhibited previously when in association with the female.

(2) Two days after I had removed the decoy female I returned her to the meadow at site B for 2 days to determine if male 1 would desert site A to follow her to site B. The female in the trap at site B was readily visible from site A where male 1 was located.

Male 1 deserted site A and joined the female within 2 hours after she was placed at site B. On arrival at site B he immediately chased several unmated males, most of which had also been at site A, from near the trap and quickly assumed dominance in the area. I did not see him return to site A while the female was at site B.

(3) Two days after putting the female at site B, I shifted her for 2 days to site C, which was visually isolated from Site B. This made it possible for me to test further whether male 1 would locate and follow the female even though she was not directly visible to him so long as he stayed at site B.

Male 1 remained at site B in the absence of the female and continued to chase conspecifics that flew or swam within approximately 30 m of the site. At site C another male (male 2) became dominant over other males, although the female threatened and avoided him. The female, in apparent agitation, swam almost continuously around the trap at site C.

After 36 hours, male 1 found the female at site C, but was prevented from approaching closer than approximately 15 m of the trap by male 2, who maintained his dominance over all males, including male 1. While the female was at site C male 1 typically remained 5 to 30 minutes at the site and then returned to site B where he remained within 1 or 2 m of the site. Male 1 also chased male shovelers at site C when he was there, but was never seen trying to chase male 2 after what I believe was their initial encounter, in which male 2 forced male 1 to retreat.

(4) After the female had been 2 days at site C, I shifted her back to site B for 3 days to determine whether male 2 would follow the female or remain at site C, and to determine the behavior of males.

Male 1 joined the female within 30 minutes after she was placed back at site B. Male 2 deserted site C the next day and also flew to site B. This time male 2 was prevented from approaching close to the female by male 1, who remained dominant over all males at site B. Male 1 was obviously more aggressive towards other males at site B than he had been at site C. Male 2 showed a corresponding lack of hostility at site B.

(5) I removed the female from the study area to determine how long males 1 and 2 would remain in the area in the absence of the female. Male 1 remained at site B for at least 2 days after removal, but male 2 left the study area on the day of removal. This final move terminated the experiment.

In agreement with the literature, the behavior of males 1 and 2 demonstrated the initial importance of the female in determining where the defensive behavior of the male occurs. Certainly it was the female and not the particular topographic site that attracted the males to the trap site. Additional evidence was provided for this view by the fact that both males deserted their former areas of dominance to follow the translocated female. Attachment of the male to the female prior to the establishment of the territory, which occurs naturally, presumably ensures that the male will follow the female until her activity becomes localized in an area that the male could then begin to defend (see Hochbaum 1944). The behavior of both males 1 and 2 showed that unmated males can undergo a rapid change to courtship and defensive behavior, as required by the above interpretations.

The behavior of males 1 and 2 also demonstrated that once they were established on a physical site, it then held special significance for them in the absence of the female. Both males, but particularly male 1, remained at the trap sites for periods of up to 2 days after the female was removed, and both males exhibited typical territorial defense and dominance at this time. These results therefore provide definite evidence that a site per se, and not just the female, may provide a basis for attachment and apparent defensive behavior in this species. The fact that at site C male 1 could see and presumably hear the female with whom he had formed a definite bond, yet was unable to dominate male 2, suggests further that the mere presence of the mate does not ensure that the male will be dominant at a given site. Unrestrained paired females would be expected to flee with the mate from a site which the mate does not control. At both sites B and C, prior ownership apparently gave one male the advantage over the other, further demonstrating the importance of site attachment.

The survival value of territorial behavior and site attachment has been the subject of controversy (see Hinde 1956, Tinbergen 1957). In the shoveler, localization of the male's activities on the territory presumably enables the female to return there to seek her mate's protection from not infrequent harassment by territorial and unmated male shovelers that she may encounter while off the nest (Seymour MS). Perhaps of equal importance Tinbergen suggested that site attachment allows males to advertise their presence in a territory. Although I have not presented here proof of territorial advertisement in the shoveler, the conspicuous coloration of the male suggests that this occurs. If so, then site attachment that localizes the male on the territory presumably functions to allow conspecifics to identify and associate the territory with the hostile male, thereby reducing encroachment and harassment, and possibly limiting breeding pair density.

This study was supported by the National Research Council of Canada, the Manitoba Department of Mines, Resources and Environmental Management, and the Delta Waterfowl Research Station. Thanks are extended to Roger M. Evans and W. Roy Siegfried for their comments and assistance in writing the manuscript.

LITERATURE CITED

BARTONEK, J. C., AND C. W. DANE. 1964. Numbered nasal discs for waterfowl. J. Wildl. Mgmt. 28:688–692.

BEZZEL, E. 1966. Zur Ermittlung von Gelegerösse und Schlüpferfolg bei Entenvögeln. Volgelwelt 87:97–106.

DZUBIN, A. 1955. Some evidences of home range in waterfowl. Trans. 20th North Amer. Wildl. Conf.:278–298.

HINDE, R. 1956. The biological significance of the territories of birds. Ibis 98:340–369.

HOCHBAUM, H. A. 1944. The Canvasback on a prairie marsh. Washington, D.C., Amer. Wildl. Inst.

HORI, J. 1963. Three-bird flights in the Mallard. Wildfowl Trust Ann. Rept. 14:124–132.

LEBRET, T. 1961. The pair formation in the annual cycle of the Mallard, *Anas platyrhynchos L.* Ardea 49:97–158.

LINCOLN, F. C., AND S. P. BALDWIN. 1929. Manual for bird banders. U.S. Dept. Agr., Misc. Publ. 58.

MAYR, E. 1935. Bernard Altum and the territory theory. Proc. Linnaean Soc. New York. Nos. 45, 46:24–38.

MCKINNEY, F. 1965. Spacing and chasing in breeding ducks. Wildfowl Trust Ann. Rept. 16:92–106.

———. 1967. Breeding behaviour of captive Shovelers. Wildfowl Trust Ann. Rept. 18:108–121.

NICE, M. M. 1941. The role of territory in bird life. Amer. Midl. Naturalist 26:441–487.

NOBLE, G. K. 1939. The role of dominance on the social life of birds. Auk 56:263–273.

TINBERGEN, N. 1939. Field observations of East Greenland Birds. 2. The behaviour of the Snow Bunting (*Plectrophenax nivalis subnivalis* (Brehm)) in spring. Trans. Linnaean Soc. New York 5:1–94.

———. 1957. The function of territory. Bird Study 4:14–27.

SOCIAL BEHAVIOR OF BREEDING GADWALLS IN NORTH DAKOTA[1]

THOMAS J. DWYER,[2] Bureau of Sport Fisheries and Wildlife, Northern Prairie Wildlife Research Center, Jamestown, ND 58401

Responses of duck pairs encountering other ducks were categorized by McKinney (1965*b*) as displays, attack, escape and avoidance, sexual pursuit, and sociability. Gadwalls (*Anas strepera*) show all these responses on the breeding grounds, and characteristic behavior patterns occur depending on the reproductive state of the birds involved. The responses of paired ducks to unpaired males on the breeding grounds have not been described for the Gadwall or any other species. The function of aerial flights (McKinney 1965*b*) is also confused in the literature. The objectives of this paper are to describe the responses of paired breeding Gadwalls to other Gadwall pairs and unmated drakes and to discuss the possible reasons for the type of spacing behavior Gadwall pairs exhibit.

STUDY AREA AND METHODS

The 36-square-mile study area is in south central North Dakota, 6 miles south of Medina. The topography results from extensive stagnation of the last ice sheet and consists mainly of stagnation moraine with smaller patches of perched lacustrine plain and glacial outwash (Winters 1963). The land is characterized by numerous low hills interspersed with small undrained depressions that contain wetlands of various sizes and types. The number of wetland basins per square mile ranges from 5 to 30 with an average size of about 4 acres. According to the classification of Stewart and Kantrud (1971), 10% of the wetlands are ephemeral, 33% temporary, 35% seasonal, and 15% semipermanent. Three permanent lakes over 50 acres in size and several dugouts and fens occur on the area. Approximately 40% of the land is grazed pasture and 60% is farmed for small grains.

Data for this paper were gathered during 1972 and 1973 by visual study of marked and unmarked Gadwall pairs and unmated drakes. Ducks were trapped at baited shoreline sites and marked with back-mounted radio packages (Dwyer 1972) and/or nasal saddles. Transmitter signals were used primarily to locate birds quickly for periods of extended visual observation. Studies on seven pairs and three unmated drake Gadwalls that were marked during the prenesting period showed that members of pairs spend virtually 100% of the time together. Therefore for purposes of this study, I considered a drake unmated if he was absent from a female for 5 min or longer during the prenesting period. Unmated drakes showed no tendency to remain at any specific location and were quite mobile.

Intraspecific social responses of Gadwalls on the breeding grounds are described for the spring arrival, prenesting, and laying to early incubation periods (Table 1). Responses of marked pairs to other pairs and unmated drakes were correlated to the stage of the breeding cycle

[1] Originally published in Auk 91(2):375–386, 1974.

[2] Present address: Migratory Bird and Habitat Research Lab, U.S. Fish and Wildlife Service, Laurel, MD 20811.

Table 1. Summary of responses of Gadwalls to conspecifics during three time periods of the breeding season.[1]

Interaction between	Responses		
	Spring arrival	Prenesting	Laying
Pair-pair	Chin-lift Threat	3-bird flight Chin-lift	3-bird flight Chin-lift
Pair-unmated drake	Chin-lift Threat Inciting Courtship displays Courtship flight Preening-behind-the-wing	Chin-lift Threat Inciting Courtship displays Preening-behind-the-wing	Chin-lift Threat Preening-behind-the-wing
Paired drake[2]-pair	—	—	3-bird flight Chin-lift
Paired drake[2]-lone drake[3]	—	—	Chin-lift Fighting Preening-behind-the-wing

[1] Exact quantitative data on frequencies or sequences of these responses were not gathered in this study.
[2] Hen at nest.
[3] Either paired or unpaired drake.

when nests of the marked females were found and the laying or incubation stage determined. During the breeding season the reproductive states of individual birds overlap in any local population, but Gadwalls seem to be more synchronized in the start of breeding than other duck species (Duebbert 1958, Bezzel 1962, Oring 1969). Thus data from interactions between unmarked pairs were usable because most birds were in the same reproductive state at any particular time. Behavior patterns resulting from interactions were quite consistent during any one time period.

A sex ratio and breeding chronology survey was conducted weekly on a sample group of 24 potholes during April and May of both 1972 and 1973. Observations of flights and behavioral interactions were written directly as notes or dictated to a portable tape recorder. Flights involving both marked and unmarked birds were timed with a stopwatch or the second hand of a wristwatch. Three-bird flights were timed from initiation of the flight to the breakoff point of the pursuing male.

In 1973 a metronome timing device (Wiens et al. 1970) set at a 15-sec interval was used to establish a sampling interval for time budget studies of Gadwall pairs. The activity of both members of a pair was coded directly on a columnar form each time the tone sounded. Two 1-h sampling periods were picked at random for each of three separate time periods of the day, 0600 to 1100, 1100 to 1600 and 1600 to 2100. I tried to watch a pair each day for 1 h in each of the three time periods, but succeeded in only about half of these attempts.

I succeeded in observing unmarked pairs of Gadwalls for purposes of time budget analysis during 34.8 h in the prenesting period. I watched two other pairs for 23.4 additional h during the laying period. Both drakes of these two pairs were identifiable by plumage characters, and I confirmed that the females were nesting by watching them fly to the nest site in the early morning while the drake remained at the activity center alone. I also gathered 6 h of data on the two paired drakes while their females were at the nest.

Three pairs of Gadwalls were introduced into a flight pen similar to that used by McKinney (1967) on 1 May 1973 and watched for 6 to 10 h per week until the hens were incubating. This procedure yielded information on vocalizations and permitted better interpretation of some behavior patterns seen in the wild.

RESULTS AND DISCUSSION

Lorenz (1953) first described the courtship behavior of the Gadwall. Gates (1958) elaborated on Lorenz's descriptions and related some displays to social situations in which they occur. Both Gates (1958) and Johnsgard (1965) illustrated displays. Displays characteristically given by paired Gadwalls to conspecifics on the breeding grounds are: preening-behind-the-wing, chin-lifting, and inciting. Courtship displays most often given by unmated drakes on the breeding grounds include burp, grunt-whistle, head-up-tail-up, down-up, and turn-back-of-head. Displays involved in copulatory behavior are not discussed.

Spring Arrival Period

Small flocks of paired Gadwalls began to arrive at the study area during the first week of April 1972 and the fourth week of March 1973. Among these early arrivals sex ratios were almost equal, and this ratio continued through the peak of migration in April. Numbers declined in early May, and the sex ratio became much more imbalanced in favor of males, primarily because many transient pairs left the area.

Duebbert (1966) working at J. Clark Salyer National Wildlife Refuge in northern North Dakota noted average spring arrival dates of Gadwalls to be about the same as in this study and showing a similar early season sex ratio. Gates (1962) found two major influxes of birds through his study tract in Ogden Bay, Utah. Many of the early arrivals were unpaired, and an unequal sex ratio prevailed among them. The second group of birds to arrive there was composed almost entirely of mated pairs.

Gadwall pairs usually arrive on their breeding grounds as much as a month or more before egg-laying begins (Gates 1962, Duebbert 1966, Oring 1969). A similar interval occurred in this study. This long residency before nesting allows many opportunities for social interactions between pairs. McKinney (1965*b*) pointed out that social responses play an important role in determining patterns of pair spacing.

Pairs of Gadwalls were usually seen in the company of other species including Redheads (*Aythya americana*), Canvasbacks (*A. valisineria*), American Wigeon (*Anas americana*), and American Coots (*Fulica americana*). The spatial pattern of pairs in the flocks appeared to conform to Condor's (1949) concept of "individual distance." During April of both years, when the sex ratio did not exceed 1.2 males per female, hostile interactions between pairs usually consisted of open-bill threat movements by males, mutual chin-lift postures by pairs, and avoidance responses by other birds during feeding activities. Early in May when smaller groups of pairs were present on potholes, very short three-bird chases (female of a pair chased by a paired male and followed by her mate) became common.

In flock situations paired hens are sometimes approached by unpaired males who attempt to court them. The hen incites and alternately chin-lifts in unison with her mate. Pairs seem vulnerable to unmated drakes at this time and are sometimes harassed for long periods as the drakes perform the complete repertoire of the species' courtship displays. Sometimes the drakes press the hen too closely, and she takes flight followed by her mate and the courting drakes. Other drakes in the vicinity that appear to be unmated are immediately attracted by the sight and sounds of the flight and a swift erratic display flight ensues involving a changing number of drakes and lasting several minutes. First one, then another drake maneuvers to catch up with the hen, sets his wings, thrusts his head up and back, and utters the harsh nasal sound characteristic of the burp display. Much fighting between males takes place in the air behind the hen as the paired male tries to drive the other drakes away. The female gives the inciting call (Lebret 1958) during the flight as she tries to elude the pursuing drakes. Upon returning to a pond, the female incites against the remaining drakes, and the pair moves away.

Wüst (1960) and Gates (1958) describe courtship flights that derive from swim courtship during pair formation in the fall and winter. Neither author distinguishes these flights from spring courtship flights involving an already paired hen. Dzubin (1957) describes Mallard (*Anas platyrhynchos*) spring courtship flights that seem essentially the same as in the Gadwall in that they are caused by encounters between loosely paired hens and unmated drakes, but Mallard flights lack the ingredient of male-to-male aggression so characteristic of Gadwall flights. Lebret (1955) describes how intraspecific encounters of unmated drakes and pairs of several species, including Gadwalls, give rise to courting flights in the winter. He also mentions that spring courtship flights are no different than those in the winter except they occur less frequently because most birds are paired.

Prenesting Period

The prenesting period begins when pairs from flocks of Gadwalls have dispersed to smaller wetlands. At this time two categories of pairs are distinguishable. One group has already selected one or more preferred feeding and loafing spots, called activity centers or core areas (Gates 1958), where they spend virtually the entire day. The other group consists of those pairs actively seeking such centers. Mated drakes initiate most three-bird chases, so characteristic of this period, from activity centers.

Responses of Mated Drakes to Pairs.— Throughout the prenesting period the degree of intraspecific tolerance mated drakes exhibit steadily decreases. Early in the prenesting period paired drakes usually tolerate other pairs to within 20 to 30 yards with no aggression. But when a pair approaches closer, the resident drake immediately becomes alert, swims rapidly toward the approaching pair for approximately one-half the distance separating them, and then flies the remaining distance. He lands close to the hen, assumes the chin-lift posture, and gives a rapid burplike call. The hen immediately takes flight chased by the resident drake and followed by her drake. During the chase, the female's mate continually tries to position himself between the attacker and his mate.

Later in the prenesting period, the attacking drake flies at the hen on the water and sometimes lands directly on her. At this time a paired drake's attack threshold

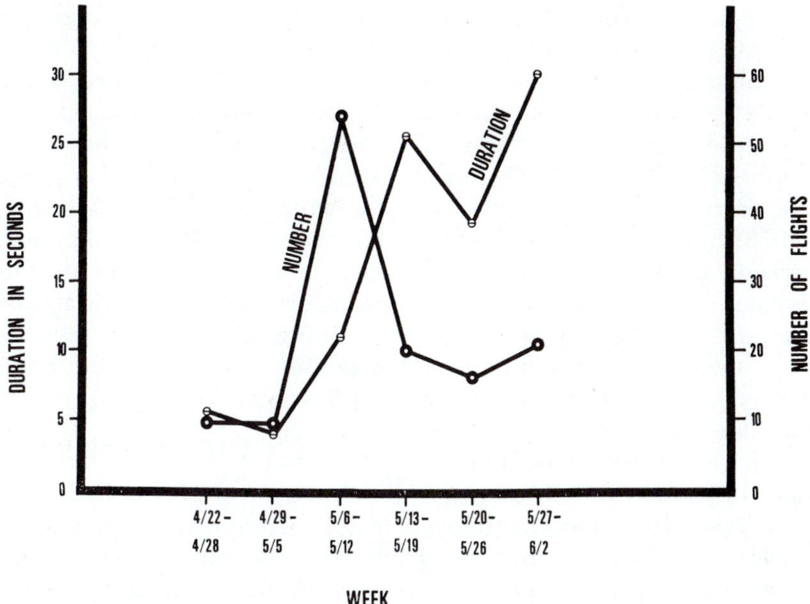

Fig. 1. Number of Gadwall three-bird chases recorded during 12 h of observation per week and average duration of flights in seconds during 1973.

is lower, and he will chase pairs flying overhead or those that approach to within 50 to 60 yards. Also at this time, hens aware of mated drakes flying at them take flight before the drake can approach them too closely.

The frequency, intensity, and length of three-bird chases all increase as nesting approaches. The peak of chasing activity occurs during the second week of May when pairs are establishing themselves at activity centers (Fig. 1). Chases increase in length until about the last week in May and first week of June when most hens are laying (Fig. 1). In 1972 one marked drake's chases lasted from 5 to 20 sec 3 weeks prior to nesting (seven chases), 15 to 30 sec 2 weeks prior to nesting (five chases) and 30 to 50 sec the week before and during early laying (seven chases).

A drake whose hen is being chased readily attacks the pursuing drake in the air as his hen gives the inciting call. During early prenesting this male-to-male aggression is usually enough to deter the pursurer, and he returns to his hen. Later the pursuits are so vigorous that the drake of the pursued hen rarely catches up to the pursuer before the chase ends. The hen gives the inciting call much more rapidly during these high intensity chases as she frantically maneuvers to escape the pursuing drake.

The pursuing drake gives one or more burp calls as he glides back to the site from which he initiated the attack and also burps as he swims back to his hen. The burp may function as a recognition call whereby the hen can recognize her approaching drake. In over 150 three-bird chases, I have never seen a paired drake fail to give the burp display on completion of the flight.

Unpaired males occasionally fly up to follow three-bird chases and may display to the hen in the air. They do not burp when returning to a pond and may break off in midflight to follow other birds.

Responses of Pairs to Unmated Drakes.—The sex ratio of Gadwalls on the study area in 1972 averaged 1.6 males per female during the first 3 weeks of May. In 1973 there were 1.3 males per female present during the same period. These unmated drakes frequently associated in groups of two or three and attempted to associate with mated pairs.

While pairs are selecting an activity center, they are sometimes approached by unmated drakes. Pairs usually tolerate an unmated drake to within a few yards with no aggression, but when the unmated male approaches closer, the mated male swims between his hen and the intruder and chin-lifts. If the intruder persists, the pair chin-lifts in unison, and the hen incites against him. Occasionally two unmated drakes approach and try to court a hen. This situation elicits inciting by the hen coupled with chin-lifting by her mate and alternating with mutual chin-lifting by the pair. The paired drake threatens each approaching drake after the hen incites against him. The hen at times is much more aggressive in these situations than her mate. I have rarely seen these encounters result in a courting flight as occurs regularly during flock situations in the spring arrival period.

After pairs have selected activity centers, they appear more secure from the harassment of unmated males. A chin-lift by the mated male is enough to make unmated males stop their approach. I theorize that unmated males recognize pairs at activity centers as secure.

The actions of unpaired males change quite rapidly. After several minutes of harassing a pair, they may stop and begin to feed and allow the pair to move away. The high frequency of preening-behind-the-wing by unmated males during the harassment of a pair may show conflicting tendencies to associate with the pair and to retreat from the pair's threats. Members of the pair also preen-behind-the-wing at this time. McKinney (1965*a*) has shown that ritualized preening movements occur during and after hostile encounters in the Anatidae. Ritualized preening and drinking movements also occur as displays in courtship (Gates 1958, von de Wall 1965).

Laying to Early Incubation Period

Response of Mated Drakes to Pairs.—Pairs spend virtually all their time at one or two activity centers (Gates 1958; Dwyer, pers. observ.). Mated drakes chase hens of other pairs from the general vicinity of the activity center as described in the section on prenesting. Three-bird flights are lengthy until the midpoint of the laying period, when male aggression seems to taper off and the flights become shorter. During laying of the first half of the clutch, the four paired drakes under observation usually did not leave the activity center while their hens were at the nest. They remained very alert and gave the burp display often. Time budget analysis shows that a mated drake alone on an activity center spends over 5% of the time giving the burp display. He also makes short, low flights over the general vicinity of the nest giving the burp call.

A drake seems preoccupied during his hen's absence and he does not initiate as many pursuits against other pairs as when his hen is present (Gates 1958). The few three-bird flights I have seen initiated by males alone at activity centers lasted approximately half as long as flights when the hen was present. As lay-

Table 2. Social behavior and some characteristics of pursuit flights in the Gadwall.[1]

	Stage of mate's breeding cycle		
	Prenesting	Laying	Early incubation
Amount of time paired male spends			
Alone on waiting area	0	XX	X
Associating with other males	0	X	XX
Attacking other pairs	XXX	XX	0
Attacking other males	X	X	X
Attempting to rape strange females	0	0	X
Characteristics of pursuit flights			
Frequency of 3-bird flights by paired males	XXX	XX	X
Frequency of flights involving many males	X	X	X
Aggression between males in flight	XXX	X	X

[1] Table format adapted from McKinney (1965*b*). The ratings X, XX, XXX (0 = absent), represent low, moderate, and high frequency of occurrence of the behavior pattern or characteristic. These approximate ratings are based on observations of marked birds.

ing progresses, the drake spends more time away from the activity center. He associates peacefully with other males, and pairs treat him as an unmated drake.

Hens in the late laying or incubation stage sometimes become involved in chases that involve more than one pursuing male. These flights usually occur when a female returns to her activity center from the nest and her mate is not there. She is then vulnerable to other paired males who are usually associating in small groups at this time. Gates (1958) called these flights "harrying chases." They are long and may last over 4 min. I have seen only six of these flights, and none resulted in rape of the female as occurs regularly in the Mallard or Pintail (*Anas acuta*). Gates (1958) saw attempted rape in only two out of many Gadwall "harrying chases" he watched. The great amount of male-to-male aggression in the flights or the fact that the extra males drop out of the flight after varying lengths of time may prevent rape from occurring.

Responses of Mated Drakes to Other Drakes.—When pairs are together in activity centers mated drakes tolerate lone drakes to within a short distance. A chin-lift or threat posture by a mated drake is enough to make a lone drake retreat. No harassment of pairs by unmated drakes occurs as in the early prenesting period.

When a drake is alone on his activity center, he is hostile to other lone drakes who approach. Chin-lifting and sometimes bill grabbing and pushing are common for the first few days of laying. In all cases I have seen, the resident drake was the victor in these contests, and the other drake usually left the site. After the midpoint of laying, mated drakes seek out other lone drakes. Groups of several drakes feeding or loafing together are common at this time, but later in the day these same drakes may return to their activity centers and be reunited with their hens.

Spacing Behavior in the Gadwall

Brown (1964) pointed out that competition for some essential ecological requisite is the most important factor in maintaining intraspecific aggression in a population. The type of territoriality or aggressive behavior that a species exhibits is probably the result of the kinds

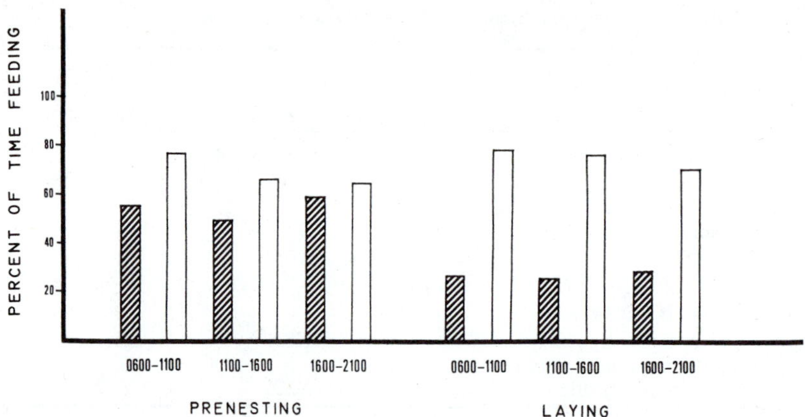

Fig. 2. Percentage of time pairs of Gadwalls spent feeding during the prenesting and laying periods. Males are indicated by crosshatching.

of ecological requisites that are in short supply (Brown 1964).

McKinney (1965*b*) reviewed the theories on the function of chasing in ducks and surmised that pair spacing tended to reduce predation rates because nests would probably be spaced. Siegfried (1968) in his paper on the Black Duck (*Anas sparsa*) of South Africa, speculated that the survival value of spacing in this species was based on a sparse food supply. Spacing, as Brown (1969) has pointed out, must be a secondary consequence of competition for some essential requirements, such as a foraging site. McKinney (1973) in a later paper modified his theory on the function of chasing to include the feeding requirements of female ducks during the breeding season. He concluded, without data on feeding rates, that it would be important for Northern Shoveler (*A. clypeata*) females to have assured feeding grounds during the prenesting, laying, and incubation periods.

Breeding female ducks, including Gadwalls, require a high-protein diet (Holm and Scott 1954) and consume aquatic invertebrates in much greater proportion before and during egg-laying than at other times of the year (Swanson and Nelson 1970, Swanson and Meyer 1974). Breeding hens probably also need an increased amount of feeding time to select this high quality diet. Several characteristics of Gadwall social behavior (Table 2) and general behavior provide evidence that chasing ensures the breeding hen an opportunity to utilize a needed food supply. Gates (1958) first described how a pair of Gadwalls spend the greater part of each day in one particular place. He emphasized that they used this site mainly for loafing or sleeping and occasionally for feeding. In this study I found that the greatest amount of feeding activity also takes place at the activity center. Time budget analyses of pairs during the prenesting and laying periods show significantly greater ($P < 0.05$) feeding rates by the females regardless of the time of day. On the average females spend 17% and 48% more time feeding than males during the prenesting period and laying period, respectively (Fig. 2). Bengtson (1972) showed that female Harlequin Ducks (*Histrionicus histrionicus*) spend 30% more time feeding than their mates prior to nesting.

As shown previously three-bird chases

are most frequent when pairs select activity centers, but a male is aggressive toward other pairs and unmated drakes until his hen is well into laying. Thus a mated drake by protecting his female from unmated drakes intent on courtship may provide more time for her to feed unmolested. By protecting his female from the approach of pairs he eliminates competitors for the food source at the activity center. I theorize that the most important function of chasing is to protect the food supply and secondarily to provide for undisturbed feeding time. Young (1970) showed that Sheld-Ducks (*Tadorna tadorna*) most likely protect an adequate food supply as they do not establish their exclusive feeding areas where the snail density is below 30 snails/m^2.

Orians (1971:534) postulated that for birds living in habitats with a reasonably uniform distribution of food, "foraging time will be minimized" if no other individuals are feeding on the same food in the same area. Natural selection should favor behavior patterns that would eliminate other individuals as long as the energetic costs are not too great (Orians ibid.). Food resources in small wetlands vary in abundance owing to physical and chemical properties of each wetland. Once a paired female selects a spot, it could be advantageous for her mate to expel other Gadwalls from it to assure her food supply. She could then quickly build up her metabolic reserves for nesting with a minimum of disturbance.

SUMMARY

The social behavior of the Gadwall on the breeding grounds in North Dakota is described in terms of the responses of mated drakes to other pairs and unmated drakes. During the spring arrival period, intraspecific aggression is limited to threat postures by paired males and avoidance responses by other birds. Spring courtship flights occur when paired hens are pressed by unpaired males who are displaying to them.

During the prenesting period the degree of intraspecific tolerance mated drakes exhibit steadily decreases. The chin-lift posture is the most important indication of aggressive tendencies in a mated drake. Mated drakes tolerate other pairs to within about 20 to 30 yards in the early prenesting period but chase them when they approach to within 50 to 60 yards or fly overhead as their hens near laying. The frequency, intensity, and length of three-bird chases all increase as the nesting period approaches. Male-to-male aggression is common during three-bird flights. Nesting females are occasionally harassed by paired males, but rape appears to be very rare in contrast to the Mallard and Pintail.

While the hen lays the first half of the clutch, the drake remains at the activity center and is most aggressive toward other pairs while his mate is present. As laying progresses he spends more and more time away from the activity center and associates with other males. Time budget analyses show that paired females spend 17% and 48% more time feeding than their mates during the time they are together in the prenesting and laying periods, respectively. A paired drake provides the seclusion necessary for this increased amount of feeding by chasing other Gadwalls from the vicinity of his female.

ACKNOWLEDGMENTS

Scott Derrickson contributed many ideas during the course of this study and helped edit the manuscript. I especially thank Charles Dane for editorial advice. Harold Duebbert and David Gilmer read the manuscript critically. Douglas Johnson provided statistical advice. The Bioelectronics Lab of the James Ford Bell

Museum, University of Minnesota, provided the telemetry equipment through a cooperative agreement with the Northern Prairie Wildlife Research Center. This paper was subsidized by the Northern Prairie Wildlife Research Center.

LITERATURE CITED

BENGTSON, S. A. 1972. Breeding ecology of the Harlequin Duck *Histrionicus histrionicus* (L.) in Iceland. Ornis Scand. 3:1–19.

BEZZEL, E. 1962. Beobachtungen über Legebeginn und Legezeit bei Entenpopulationen. Anz. Ornithol. Ges. Bayern. 6:218–233.

BROWN, J. L. 1964. The evolution of diversity in avian territorial systems. Wilson Bull. 76: 160–169.

———. 1969. Territorial behavior and population regulation in birds, a review and re-evaluation. Wilson Bull. 81:293–329.

CONDOR, P. J. 1949. Individual distance. Ibis 91:649–655.

DUEBBERT, H. F. 1958. Island nesting of the Gadwall (*Anas strepera*) in North Dakota. Unpublished M.A. thesis, Columbia, Univ. Missouri.

———. 1966. Island nesting of the Gadwall in North Dakota. Wilson Bull. 78:12–25.

DWYER, T. J. 1972. An adjustable radio-package for ducks. Bird-Banding 43:282–284.

DZUBIN, A. 1957. Pairing display and spring and summer flights of the Mallard. Blue Jay 15:10–13.

GATES, J. M. 1958. A study of the breeding behavior of the Gadwall in northern Utah. Unpublished M.S. thesis, Logan, Utah State Univ.

———. 1962. Breeding biology of the Gadwall in northern Utah. Wilson Bull. 74:43–67.

HOLM, E. R., AND M. L. SCOTT. 1954. Studies on the nutrition of wild waterfowl. New York Fish and Game J. 1:171–187.

JOHNSGARD, P. A. 1965. Handbook of waterfowl behavior. Ithaca, Cornell Univ. Press.

LEBRET, T. 1955. Die verfolgungsflüge der Enten. J. Ornithol. 96:43–49.

———. 1958. Inciting ("Hetzen") by flying ducks. Ardea 46:73–75.

LORENZ, K. 1953. Comparative studies on the behavior of the Anatinae. Reprinted from Avicult. Mag. 57:157–182; 58:8–17, 61–72, 86–94, 172–184; 59:24–34, 80–91.

MCKINNEY, F. 1965*a*. The comfort movements of Anatidae. Behaviour 25:120–220.

———. 1965*b*. Spacing and chasing in breeding ducks. Wildfowl 16:92–106.

———. 1967. Breeding behavior of captive Shovelers. Wildfowl 18:108–121.

———. 1973. Ecoethological aspects of reproduction. Pp. 6–21 *in* Breeding biology of birds (D. S. Farner, ed.). Washington, D.C., Natl. Acad. Sci.

ORIANS, G. 1971. Ecological aspects of behavior. Pp. 513–546 *in* Avian biology, vol. 1 (D. S. Farner and J. R. King, eds.). New York, Academic Press.

ORING, L. W. 1969. Summer biology of the Gadwall at Delta, Manitoba. Wilson Bull. 81:44–54.

SIEGFRIED, W. R. 1968. The Black Duck in the South-western Cape. Ostrich 39:61–75.

STEWART, R. E., AND H. A. KANTRUD. 1971. Classification of natural ponds and lakes in the glaciated prairie region. Resource Publ. 92, Bur. Sport Fisheries and Wildl.

SWANSON, G. A., AND M. I. MEYER. 1974. The role of invertebrates in the feeding ecology of Anatinae during the breeding season. Waterfowl Habitat Mgmt. Symp., Spec. Publ. Wildl. Mgmt. Inst.

———, AND H. K. NELSON. 1970. Potential influence of fish rearing programs on waterfowl breeding habitat. Pp. 65–71 *in* A symposium on the management of midwestern winterkill lakes (E. Schneberger, ed.). Madison, Wisconsin, Special Publ., Amer. Fisheries Soc., North Central Div.

VON DE WALL, W. 1965. "Gesellschaftsspiel" und Balz der Anatini. J. Ornithol. 106:65–80.

WIENS, J. A., S. G. MARTIN, W. R. HOLTHAUS, AND F. A. IWEN. 1970. Metronome timing in behavioral ecology studies. Ecology 51:350–352.

WINTERS, H. A. 1963. Geology and ground water resources of Stutsman County, North Dakota, part I: Geology. North Dakota Geol. Survey Bull. No. 41.

WÜST, W. 1960. Das problem des Reihens der Enten besonders von *Anas strepera*. Proc. 12th Intern. Ornithol. Congr. 2:795–800.

YOUNG, C. M. 1970. Territoriality in the Common Shelduck *Tadorna tadorna*. Ibis 112:330–335.

THE SOCIAL ORGANIZATION OF A MALLARD POPULATION IN NORTHERN IOWA[1]

DALE D. HUMBURG, Department of Fisheries and Wildlife, Michigan State University, East Lansing 48824[2]
HAROLD H. PRINCE, Department of Fisheries and Wildlife, Michigan State University, East Lansing 48824
RICHARD A. BISHOP, Iowa Conservation Commission, Clear Lake 50428

Abstract: Twenty-two hen and 134 drake mallards were marked during a 2-year study of mallard (*Anas platyrhynchos*) breeding activity on Ventura Marsh in north-central Iowa. During April, sex ratios of mallards observed on breeding areas (54% drakes) were lower than those observed in fields or on open water areas (58% drakes). Numbers of mallards observed declined after the initial influx, and remained relatively constant throughout the breeding season. The number of breeding mallards appeared to be limited by pursuit flights. Sixty-four marked drakes, observed at least once with a hen spent an average of 17.6 days on the marsh whereas 70 drakes, not seen with hens averaged 1.3 days on the area. There was a continual turnover of lone drakes on the study area throughout the breeding season. The nests of 22 marked hens were destroyed between day 10 and 17 of incubation. Four of the hens left the study area, 3 remained but did not remate, and 15 remated. Of 11 identified rematings, 8 hens (73%) returned to their original drake and 3 (27%) changed drakes after losing their nest.

J. WILDL. MANAGE. 42(1):72–80

The social organization of mallard breeding populations is not clearly understood. Studies concerning courtship behavior, interaction between pairs, and nesting provide a base for understanding mallard mate selection and production.

The pair is fundamental to mallard reproduction. Weidman and Darley (1971) reviewed the range of attitudes among investigators concerning the role of the mallard male and female in display and courtship. They concluded that the female is essential in directing display and that social display promotes pair formation, which occurs for the most part before spring migration (Hawkins *in* Hochbaum 1944:121; Weller 1965:227). Hochbaum (1944:16) and Sowls (1955:21) reflected the general acceptance by biologists that most mallards are paired upon arrival at spring breeding areas. Lebret (1961:105) defined a hen and drake as paired when they maintained close proximity when together and when the drake defended the female from other mallards.

Pair interaction in the form of pursuit flights (3-bird flights) was described by Dzubin (1957), McKinney (1965) and Titman (1973). Pursuit and avoidance were believed responsible for the spacing of breeding pairs (Dzubin 1969*a*). The ultimate consequence of spacing appears to be a lessened competition for breeding requisites and dispersion of nests as an antipredator mechanism. Those pairs unable to enter a breeding system may attempt to nest elsewhere, delay the breeding effort, or molt.

During the reproductive effort, drakes were observed with hens on breeding areas throughout the laying period and for an average of 8 days into incubation (Lebret 1961:127). Dzubin (1955:286) reported drakes present in the vicinity of nests until day 14 of incubation. Unless the nest is destroyed or abandoned, the hen continues incubating until the eggs hatch. Nest destruction, which appears to be a limiting factor in the annual production of mallards, was reported by Dzubin and Gollop (1972) to

[1] Support provided by Iowa Conservation Commission P-R Project W-115-R-2 and the Michigan Agricultural Experiment Station; Journal Article Number 7689.

[2] Present address: Missouri Department of Conservation, Fish and Wildlife Research Center, Columbia 65201.

Originally published in J. Wildl. Manage. 42(1):72–80, 1978.

range from 22 to 73 percent, depending upon the area studied, nesting cover condition, predator density, water level, weather, and human disturbance. Renesting, as high as 77 percent (Keith 1961:67), plays an important role in maintaining annual production in breeding mallard populations.

A pair bond is necessary for successful culmination of egg laying and clutch incubation (Dzubin 1970), so hens losing nests probably will not renest without remating, even though they can lay fertile eggs up to 17 days after insemination (Elder and Weller 1954:501). Renesting hens could select a drake from a variety of sources; the original mate, a drake originally paired with a different female, or a previously unpaired drake. Although few data are available concerning the breeding activity of unpaired drakes, Titman (1973:41) observed marked unpaired males for a short time in localized areas on a breeding marsh. He speculated that there may be a selective advantage for an unpaired drake to be available for breeding with renesting hens. Elder and Weller (1954) suggested that unpaired drakes are essential to high productivity by supplying mates to renesting hens. In studying pintails (*Anas acuta*) Smith (1968) found that pursuit flights may often result in rape of the female, insuring fertilization. However, unpaired drakes could be harmful to production by harrassing nesting hens (Titman and Lowther 1975).

Investigations by Bellrose (1961) revealed mallard sex ratios generally favor drakes and ranged from 68 to 233 drakes: 100 hens, depending upon latitude, season, and data collection method. The percentage of drake mallards appears to have increased since 1970 (Bellrose 1976:230). Some biologists have advocated harvest of the excess drakes. Dzubin (1970) suggested that harvest of surplus drakes may be biologically justified if (1) no difference exists in the time required for sexual maturity in both sexes, (2) surplus drakes have no significance in providing mates for renesting hens, and (3) harvest of hens would not parallel drake harvest. With the advent of the point system in waterfowl hunting regulations, which allows for the harvest of surplus drakes, controversy has arisen concerning the biological implication that increased drake harvest could have on mallard production.

This study was designed to describe the structure and relationships between various components of a mallard breeding population on a breeding area. Specifically, the breeding activity of drake and hen mallards relative to the nesting cycle of unsuccessful nesting hens is described.

We gratefully acknowledge the assistance of V. Wright with the project design, E. Peloquin and B. Batt for assistance with methods and data analysis, and G. Dudderar and D. Beaver for evaluating the final manuscript. Field assistance was provided by T. Willson, A. Woodward, R. Andrews, and J. Cash.

STUDY AREA

Field observations were conducted on Ventura Marsh, a 305 ha state-owned area, and small wetlands (less than 2 ha) within a 2.5 km radius. Although there are many semi-permanent wetlands within 16 km of Ventura Marsh, the 2 nearest wetlands larger than 4 ha in size are 18 and 21 km from the marsh. Aerial telemetry was conducted within a 16 km radius of Ventura Marsh and over waters greater than 4 ha in size located within 48 km.

The marsh is located at the west end of a 1,457 ha glacial lake in Cerro Gordo and Hancock counties in north-central Iowa. Emergent vegetation consisted of sedges (*Carex* spp.), cattail (*Typha* spp.), bullrush (*Scirpus* spp.), and various species of annual plants. Uplands utilized by nesting mallards and blue-winged teal (*Anas discors*) consist of the adjacent 121 ha of bluegrass (*Poa pratensis*) and brome-grass (*Bromus inermis*) in state ownership and alfalfa fields on private land. The majority of private land was planted in row crops.

MATERIALS AND METHODS

Trapping and Marking

All drakes and one-half of the hen mallards marked were captured in clover-leaf traps containing a live mallard hen as a decoy (11 traps in 1974, 13 in 1975). Hens were also captured on nests. Trapping was accomplished in early incubation with a bail trap (Doty and Lee 1974). We removed an egg from each nest and aged the embryo (Prince et al. 1968). We determined nesting chronology by back-dating clutches and class Ia broods (Gollop and Marshall 1954) to date of nest initiation (Sowls 1955:82).

Eight hens and 69 drakes in 1974 and 14 hens and 63 drake mallards in 1975 were banded with U.S. Fish and Wildlife Service bands and tagged with polyvinyl nasal saddles marked for individual identification. We sprayed flourescent paint on the undersides of wings and on the tail, to allow identification in flight. During the 2 years, radio transmitters, similar to those described by Dwyer (1972), were attached to 13 drakes and 21 hens. After the first week of trapping, marked mallards comprised an average of 35 and 40 percent of the total mallards observed.

Observations

We conducted systematic population counts and observed marked and unmarked mallards from first arrival until the end of breeding. In 1975 we determined mallard sex ratios on breeding areas and of individual flocks on fields and open water areas within 24 km of Ventura Marsh. Weekly ground counts (Dzubin 1969*b*) taken from the end of April until July recorded the number of mallard pairs, single drakes and groups of drakes on Ventura Marsh. Mallard activity and numbers on the marsh also were measured during 5-day periods with observations from fixed locations. We attempted to observe activity on Ventura Marsh from 6 different locations during daylight hours each 5 days. We observed marked and unmarked mallards, and avoided recounting the same individual within the hour-long observation period. We categorized activity into locomotion, feeding, social behavior, and comfort movements. When possible, location, duration, and intensity was described. Using these observations we calculated the total number of mallards seen per hour. We also determined the number of days individual mallards spent on the area and the breeding status of each bird. The number of days marked drakes were paired with hens, as defined by Lebret (1961), will be referred to as a pair sequence.

Drakes paired with incubating females were identified by flushing the hen and determining the identity of the male that joined her in flight. We monitored hen remating activity after we destroyed nests around 14 days of incubation. Daily, we located hens that lost nests, recorded association with drakes, and determined renesting activity and subsequent nest success. We made at least 1 flight per week throughout the breeding season in search of birds that were no longer present on the study area.

Statistical Analysis

Standard statistical procedures were according to Snedecor and Cochran (1967). We calculated observation randomness of marked drakes by Chi-square tests comparing actual and expected variance of days individuals were observed during subsequent 5-day periods after capture (Southwood 1966:77).

RESULTS

Population Observations

Each year, the greatest number of birds observed per hour occurred soon after spring arrival (Fig. 1). Eighty-eight percent of these mallards were paired. Sex ratios ranged from 126 to 154 drakes: 100 hens and averaged 138 drakes:100 hens ($N = 5{,}695$). During the same period, mallard sex ratios spaced on breeding areas averaged 115 drakes:100 hens. Mallard numbers declined but remained fairly constant after 20 April both years, averaging 8.7 ± 3.5 per hour in 1974 and 10.6 ± 3.2 per hour in 1975. Totals of 78 (1974) and 84 (1975) mallards were counted during the first ground counts in late April. In contrast to the fixed-point observations, numbers of mallards observed during ground counts continued to decline throughout the season.

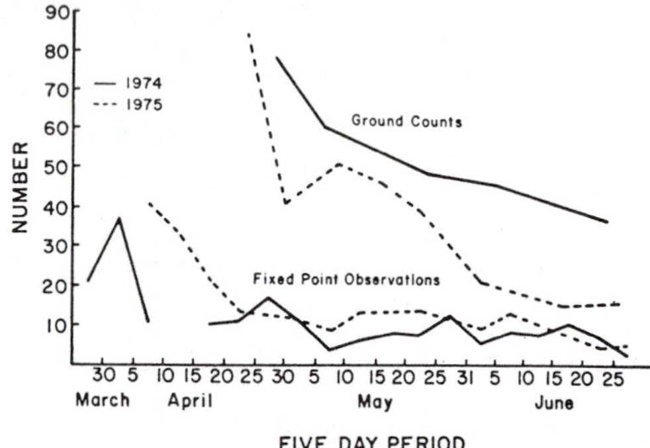

Fig. 1. Total number of mallards seen during ground counts, and number observed per hour per 5-day period during fixed-point observations on Ventura Marsh.

Marked Drake and Pair Observations

We began trapping in early April of each year and marked about 75 percent of the drakes by 1 May. Although we observed 64 marked drakes in pair sequences during the 2 years, less than 14 were observed during any 5-day period. Averages of 10.3 ± 3.4 and 11.0 ± 1.6 marked drakes in 1974 and 1975 were paired during the 8 periods following 20 April. The trends of the number of marked drakes and the total number of mallards observed per hour during fixed-point observations appeared similar. Although the ground counts and cumulative number of drakes marked suggested that the potential number of mallards was high for the area, the actual number of birds present and visible on the marsh remained at a lower and relatively constant level.

From the information collected on marked pairs, we were able to estimate the total number of pairs on the area during a 5-day period with a modified Lincoln Index:

$$\hat{N} = MC/R$$

where $\hat{N}$ = estimated number of pairs present during a 5-day period, M = number of paired marked drakes known present during a 5-day period, C = total number of single drakes plus pairs observed during a 5-day period, and R = number of marked single drakes plus pairs observed during a 5-day period. Utilizing this index, we calculated the number of pairs present on the area after trapping and marking began (Fig. 2). The number of indicated pairs (pairs plus lone drakes) calculated from ground counts were included as an independent check for comparison with estimated pairs. The counts and pair estimates were significantly correlated ($r = 0.67$, 9 df, $P < 0.05$). The number of pairs appeared to decline gradually as the season progressed. The abrupt drop in the number of pairs between 5 and 10 May, 1974 was due

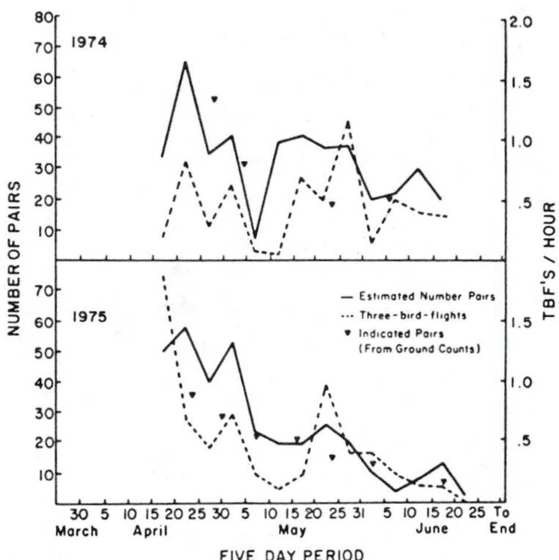

Fig. 2. Total number of mallards estimated present, compared to number of indicated pairs determined from ground counts, and mean number of 3-bird-flights (TBF's) per hour on Ventura Marsh.

to birds dispersing to surface water outside the study area created by a week of heavy rainfall. We expanded the total number of marked pairs and the average proportion of marked to unmarked birds on the area to give an estimate of the total number of pairs on Ventura Marsh for the season. From this calculation, we estimated that at least 70 pairs utilized the system each year.

We observed a range of 0.04 to 1.88 flights per hour over the 2 years (Fig. 2). We calculated the number of 3-bird flights per hour from the fixed-point observations and found the number of estimated pairs and the number of flights to be significantly correlated ($r = 0.61$, 25 df, $P < 0.05$).

Over the 2-year study, we captured and marked 134 drakes. We observed 48 percent (64) in at least 1 pair sequence for an average of 10.4 ± 8.2 days. We observed 11 percent (15) of the males in at least 2 pair sequences and 2 males in 3 pair sequences. The second pair sequences averaged 6.9 ± 6.9 days in length and there was a significant decrease ($P < 0.01$) in the time individual drakes spent in second contrasted with first pair sequences. Over the 2 years, 3 of 8 drakes were known to be paired with 2 different hens during the season. Chronologically, 76 percent of the 64 first pair sequences were initiated before 10 May, whereas 87 percent of the second pair sequences did not occur until after 20 May.

The length of time that paired drakes were observed on the study area proved to be significantly different from what would be expected randomly. Marked drakes, which we observed at least part of the time with hens, spent an average of 17.5 ± 11.8 and 17.8 ± 13.7 total days on the area during the 1974 and 1975 seasons. Of the 64 marked drakes that we observed with a hen, 20 percent (13) were observed as single drakes before they were observed in a pair sequence.

Marked drakes, which were never observed with a hen, were not contacted on the study area for more days than would be expected randomly. Fifty-seven percent of the drakes (39) in 1974 and 52 perecnt (31) in 1975 were not observed with a hen after they were captured and marked. We observed drakes, never seen with hens, for averages of 1.2 ± 2.1 and 1.3 ± 1.2 days during 1974 and 1975. During the 14 5-day periods after 15 April, we observed 6.1-± 4.5 unpaired drakes in 1974 and 6.7 ± 4.8 drakes in 1975 per period.

Nesting and Remating

Nests were initiated between 5 April and 15 June in 1974, and 15 April and 10 June in 1975. Fifty percent of the nests were initiated by 30 April, 1974 and 5 May, 1975 (Fig. 3). According to our design, we destroyed, at mid-incubation, 5 nests in 1974 and 6 in 1975. We also monitored 11 hens losing nests to predation and weather. The large number of nests lost between 5 and 10 May in 1974 were the result of wet and cold

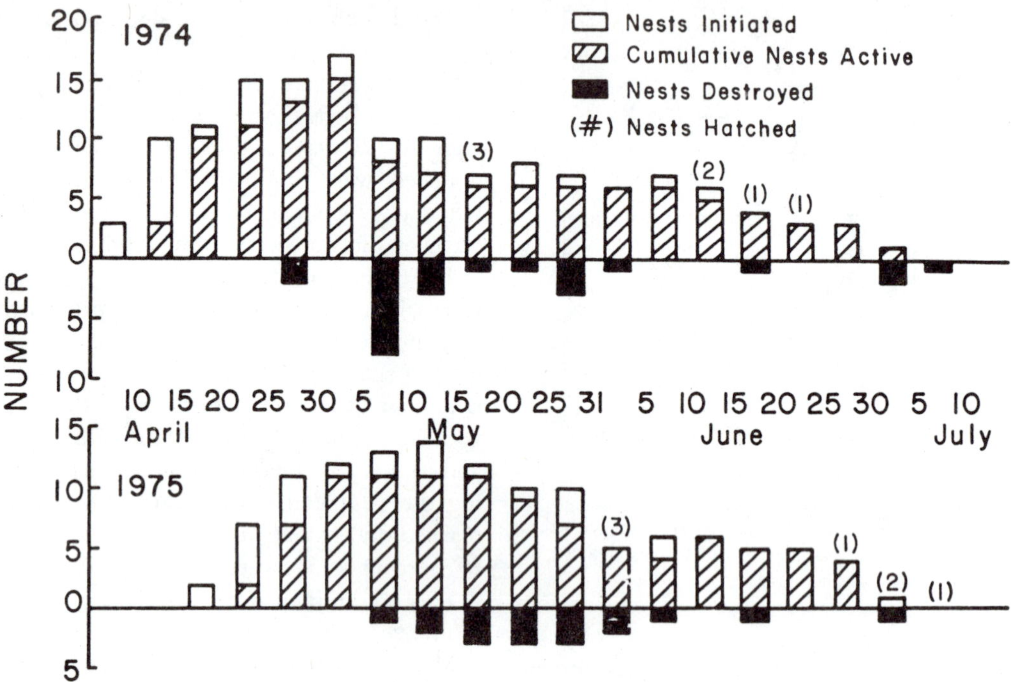

Fig. 3. The chronology and status of nesting attempts observed on Ventura Marsh.

weather during that period. The loss corresponded to the abnormal drop in the number of pairs during the same period.

The nests of 22 marked mallard hens, each equipped with a working transmitter were destroyed both naturally and by design between days 10 and 17 of incubation during 1974 and 1975 (Table 1). Four emigrated from the study area after nest destruction and were not located from the air. Three remained on the study area after nest loss, but were not again observed with a drake. After nest loss, we observed 15 of the hens with a drake. Four hens were with unmarked drakes both before and after nest loss. In 11 identified remating sequences, 8 hens returned to their original drake and 3 remated with different drakes. Two of these 3 drakes were marked; 1 had been previously paired and 1 had not been observed with a hen. The third hen was observed with an unmarked drake in her second pair sequence.

Table 1. Breeding activity of hen mallards after destruction of nest between day 10 and 17 of incubation.

Year	Observed with a drake: Previous mate	Observed with a drake: New mate	Observed with a drake: Unknown	Observed without a drake	Not observed on study area	Total
1974	2[a]	2	1	1	1	7
1975	6	1[a]	3	2	3	15

[a] Data from 2 females with nests destroyed before day 6 of incubation are included.

DISCUSSION

Eighty-eight percent of the mallards arriving in northern Iowa in late March and early April were paired. This is consistent with the 90 percent paired mallards observed by Weller (1965) on wintering areas and agrees with the general concensus among biologists that most mallards arrive paired on breeding areas in the spring.

Sex ratios on (115:100) and off (138:100) Ventura Marsh suggested segregation of paired from unpaired drakes. Dzubin's (1969*a*:188) ratio of 112:100 for spaced mallards on wetlands near Kindersley, Saskatchewan was similar to those we observed on the north Iowa breeding area. It appears that sex ratios of mallards utilizing breeding areas may tend toward 50:50, whereas spring sex ratios of mallards not associated with breeding areas may reflect the extent of sex ratio disparity in North American mallard populations.

After nesting pairs were established on Ventura Marsh, the number of mallards remained relatively constant throughout the breeding season. Dzubin (1969*a*) discussed carrying capacity for pothole habitats and suggested that, for low to intermediate population levels of mallards, chases and avoidance are responsible for limiting pair abundance. In our study, the numbers of pairs and of pursuit flights were positively correlated. Pair interaction increased when a greater number of birds were present, so it appeared that spacing mechanisms, in the form of pursuit flights, were important on Ventura Marsh. Our information appears to be consistent with the idea that an upper limit exists on the density of pairs that can utilize a breeding area (Dzubin 1969*a*:156). Our data also suggest that, depending upon breeding status, the time individual mallards spend on the area is limited. Twice as many paired as unpaired drakes were observed on the marsh throughout the season and paired drakes were observed for an average of 16 days longer than unpaired drakes.

We observed a continuous turnover of lone drakes and pairs on Ventura Marsh throughout the breeding season. The number of pairs that used Ventura Marsh as a breeding area and the turnover of pairs during the season could not be enumerated directly. However, we estimated, with the aid of a modified Lincoln Index, that at least 70 pairs utilized the marsh during each breeding season. The number of pairs using a breeding area over the season appeared to be greater than ground counts conducted after 1 May would indicate.

In addition to population turnover effects, hens that lost nests and renested further confounded the clarity of understanding mallard breeding. Besides new pairs entering a system, renesting pairs probably accounted for a large proportion of the pairs utilizing breeding areas later in the season. The number of hens losing nests and the incidence of renesting were documented by Keith (1961), Coulter and Miller (1968), and Dzubin and Gollop (1972), but few data are available on remating activity of hens thwarted in initial nesting attempts. Our observations of individual hens after nest loss showed hens obtained mates in a variety of ways. A majority (73%) returned to the original drake, suggesting that paired drakes were available for remating at least until mid-incubation.

Observations of marked drakes also suggested flexibility in remating activity; although the majority of drakes were involved in 1 pair sequence, 23 percent were observed in 2 or 3 pair sequences. Three of 8 drakes paired to marked hens were known to have paired with different hens during the same breeding season. Twenty percent of the marked paired drakes were observed for a period of time on the marsh without a hen before they were observed in a pair sequence. None were seen in more than 1 sequence as a paired drake. This suggested that a certain proportion of drakes arrived unpaired in the spring and a limited number were successful in mating with a hen later in the season.

Hen mallards clearly have a flexible reproductive strategy, and exploit a number of alternatives for remating after nest destruction. In this study, renesting hens most commonly remated with their original mate. Less commonly, a hen remated with a drake previously paired to another female, or with an unpaired drake. Other hens which lost nests did not remate or emigrated from the area. There appeared to be an upper limit on the number of pairs utilizing the breeding area at 1 time. Turnover of individuals and pairs, and the resultant temporal spacing, allowed a larger number of pairs to use the marsh over the season. There was always a supply of unpaired drakes present for short periods on Ventura Marsh. The actual number of surplus males was greater than that utilized by renesting hens. Although surplus drakes appeared available for breeding, they did not seem to interfere with breeders in the system. Additional work involving different population densities, changes in sex ratios, different habitats and different locations within the breeding range is needed to determine (1) the effects these factors have on mallard productivity, and (2) the range of associations that exist between breeding mallards.

LITERATURE CITED

BELLROSE, F. C., T. G. SCOTT, A. S. HAWKINS, AND J. B. LOW. 1961. Sex ratios and age ratios in North American ducks. Bull. Illinois Nat. Hist. Surv. 27(6):391–474.

———. 1976. Ducks, geese and swans of North America. Stockpole Books. Harrisburg, Pennsylvania. 544pp.

COULTER, M. W., AND W. R. MILLER. 1968. Nesting biology of black ducks and mallards in northern New England. Vermont Fish and Game Dept. Bull. 63-2. 73pp

DOTY, H. A., AND F. B. LEE. 1974. Homing to nest baskets by wild female mallards. J. Wildl. Manage. 38(4):714–719.

DWYER, T. J. 1972. An adjustable radio-package for ducks. Bird-Banding 43(4):282–284.

DZUBIN, A. 1955. Some evidences of home range in waterfowl. Trans. N. A. Wildl. Conf. 20: 278–298.

———. 1957. Pairing display and spring and summer flights of the mallard. Blue Jay 15(1): 10–13.

———. 1969*a*. Comments on carrying capacity of small ponds for ducks and possible effects of density on mallard production. Pages 138–171 *in* Saskatoon wetlands seminar. Can. Wildl. Serv. Rep. Ser. 6.

———. 1969*b*. Assessing breeding populations of ducks by ground counts. Pages 178–230 *in* Saskatoon wetlands seminar. Can. Wildl. Serv. Rep. Ser. 6.

———, AND J. B. GOLLOP. 1972. Aspects of mallard breeding ecology in Canadian parkland and grassland. Pages 113–151 *in* Population ecology of migratory birds: a symposium. U.S. Fish Wildl. Serv. Wildl. Res. Rep. 2.

ELDER, W. H., AND M. W. WELLER. 1954. Duration of fertility in the domestic mallard hen after isolation from the drake. J. Wildl. Manage. 18(4):495–502.

GOLLOP, J. B., AND W. H. MARSHALL. 1954. A guide to aging duck broods in the field. Miss. Flyway Council Tech. Sect. Rept. (Mimeo). 14pp.

HOCHBAUM, H. A. 1944. The canvasback on a prairie marsh. Amer. Wildl. Inst., Washington, D.C. 201pp.

KEITH, L. B. 1961. A study of waterfowl ecology on small impoundments in south-eastern Alberta. Wildl. Monogr. 6. 88pp.

LEBRET, T. 1961. The pair formation in the annual cycle of the mallard, *Anas platyrhynchos* L. Ardea 49(3–4):97–158.

MCKINNEY, D. R. 1964. Spacing and chasing in breeding ducks. Wildfowl Trust Ann. Rept. 16:92–106.

PRINCE, H. H., P. B. SIEGAL, AND G. W. CORNWELL. 1968. Embryonic growth of mallard and pekin ducks. Growth 32(3):225–233.

SMITH, R. I. 1968. The social aspects of reproductive behavior in the pintail. Auk 85(3): 381–396.

SNEDECOR, G. W., AND W. G. COCHRAN. 1967. Statistical methods. Sixth ed. Iowa State University Press, Ames. 593pp.

SOUTHWOOD, T. R. E. 1971. Ecology methods. Chapman and Hall, London. 391pp.

SOWLS, L. K. 1955. Prairie ducks. Stackpole Co., Harrisburg, Pennsylvania. 193pp.

TITMAN, R. 1973. The role of the pursuit flight in the breeding biology of the mallard. Ph.D. Thesis. Univ. of New Brunswick, Fredericton. 201pp.

———, AND J. K. LOWTHER. 1975. The breeding behavior of a crowded population of mallards. Can. J. Zool. 53(9):1270–1283.

WEIDMANN, U., AND J. DARLEY. 1971. The role of the female in the social display of mallards. Animal Behavior 19(2):287–298.

WELLER, M. W. 1965. Chronology of pair formation in some nearctic *Aythya* (Anatidae). Auk 82(2):227–235.

Received 17 May 1976.
Accepted 10 August 1977.

PAIR-BOND TENURE IN THE BLACK-BELLIED TREE DUCK

ERIC G. BOLEN, Department of Range and Wildlife Management, Texas Tech University, Lubbock

Abstract: Evidence of lifelong pair bonds for black-bellied tree ducks (*Dendrocygna autumnalis*) was determined from instances of year-to-year mate retention and, indirectly, from renesting studies.

Waterfowl (Anatidae) include some species that mate for life as well as those that select new mates prior to each breeding attempt. The tree ducks (Anserinae: Dendrocygnini of Delacour and Mayr 1945:10), like other anserines, maintain a viable pair bond lasting at least through the rearing period of their young. This form of parental behavior has in turn led to the general assumption that tree ducks also mate for life. This relationship, however, has not been more than casually recorded in captive flocks of tree ducks; no supporting data from field studies are available as confirmation for any of the eight species in the tree duck group. This paper accordingly reports observations of pair bond relationships in the black-bellied tree duck, originating from field studies in southern Texas.

I am indebted to Frank C. Bellrose for reviewing this manuscript.

CRITERIA AND METHODS

Direct evidence for examining pair-bond tenure primarily stems from the return of two mates banded on a nest and subsequently found together on a nest the next year. Known pairs can be determined in the black-bellied tree duck, as the males share incubation duties with their hens; both sexes are thus alternately available for capture and banding at the nest site. Mortality between nesting seasons, however, certainly leads to new matings by the survivors, so that the opportunities for recovering an intact pair for a second time are lessened. Hence, recapturing a bird with a new mate does not necessarily mean that an earlier pair bond was voluntarily dissolved.

Supporting data on pair-bond tenure may also be obtained when the same two birds remain as mates between an unsuccessful first nesting attempt and a subsequent renesting effort during the same breeding season. The effects of year-to-year mortality are minimized in renesting data, although conclusions as to pair tenure, based on renesting, are only inferential.

To explore these and other relationships, nesting black-bellied tree ducks were caught and banded with standard aluminum leg bands. Some nesting pairs were additionally marked with plastic neck collars modified from Sherwood (1966). The banding data, as used here, are an adjunct to other studies of this species, and were collected during periodic inspections of nest boxes erected in Cameron, Nueces, San Patricio, and Live Oak counties, Texas.

The nest boxes, described elsewhere (Bolen 1967), were located in groups of six or more per study area so that potential sites for renesting efforts were locally available. Searches for renests were limited to the nest boxes. Renesting was experimentally induced by collecting a partially incubated clutch after previously banding both the male and female.

RESULTS AND DISCUSSION

Seven instances of year-to-year mate retention are now available to establish from field records that black-bellied tree ducks form permanent pair bonds (Table 1). Six of these pairs were recaptured on nests 1 year after they were initially recorded as nesting pairs. These instances thus rep-

Originally published in J. Wildl. Manage. 35(2):385–388, 1971.

Table 1. Banding data for black-bellied tree ducks paired for at least two nesting seasons.

BAND NO.	SEX	INITIAL NEST CAPTURE		NEST RECAPTURE[c]		STUDY AREA[d]
		Date[a]	Box No.[b]	Date	Box No.[b]	
607-07395	M	6-14-65	6	5-28-66	38	MPW-Nueces Co.
607-07398	F	6-19-65	6	5-31-66	38	MPW-Nueces Co.
607-07397	M	6-19-65	52	6-18-66	74	MPW-Nueces Co.
607-47804	F	6-27-65	52	6-27-66	74	MPW-Nueces Co.
607-47819	M	5-19-66	78	6-17-67	80	WST-Cameron Co.
797-70414	F	6-05-66	78	6-08-67	80	WST-Cameron Co.
797-70437	M	7-27-66	73	6-03-69	74	MPW-Nueces Co.
797-70440	F	8-03-66	73	5-31-69	74	MPW-Nueces Co.
747-17817	M	8-02-66	49	8-05-67	88	VHL-San Patricio Co.
797-70443	F	8-11-66	49	8-10-67	88	VHL-San Patricio Co.
847-41025	M	7-17-67	27	7-09-68	28	HLY-Live Oak Co.
847-41020	F	7-12-67	27	7-23-68	28	HLY-Live Oak Co.
897-94234	M	8-10-68	93	6-10-69	93	MGT-Cameron Co.
897-94240	F	8-21-68	93	6-17-69	93	MGT-Cameron Co.

[a] In a few instances, individuals had been caught earlier in spring by cannon net and were already banded when handled on the nest.

[b] The nest boxes are not necessarily consecutively numbered at each study area. Hence the box numbers may not designate any spatial relationships between nest locations for a given pair in subsequent years.

[c] Date and location for last recapture only; intervening recaptures, if any, are not shown here.

[d] The initials preceding the counties (MPW-Nueces Co.) indicate the landowners and the specific study areas. All recaptures in subsequent years were in the same areas as the initial nest captures.

resent at least 2 consecutive years of pair-bond maintenance. As mentioned previously, the chances of finding pairs over longer periods of time are lessened by annual mortality. Nonetheless, the pair designated by band numbers 797-70437 and 797-70440 were nesting together in 1966—and perhaps even earlier—and again in 1968 and 1969; neither bird was located in the nesting season of 1967.

Supplemental information from preliminary renesting data involves three cases where the same mates remained paired for a second nesting attempt after the first nest was artificially destroyed. These records are shown in Table 2.

Pair 607-47819 and 797-70414 were involved in both the year-to-year recovery data and the renesting data (Tables 1 and 2, respectively). The incubating birds were caught on separate occasions in June 1966; the male had been previously banded in 1965 in a nearby nesting box, but the female was not caught. The first clutch in 1966 was a compound or *dump* nest of 41 eggs. Destruction of this nest was simulated by collection of the eggs on June 10 to induce renesting, and the nest box was accordingly abandoned by the pair. In July the same pair was found incubating a clutch of 15 eggs that later successfully hatched.

One year later, in 1967, these birds were again recovered as a nesting pair incubating another compound clutch of 65 eggs.

Two additional lines of information, still of inferential value, further indicate lifetime tenure in pair bonds of black-bellied tree ducks. First, in the years 1962–65, 31 banded black-bellied tree ducks were known to have returned a second year to the place where they were originally banded; these records include birds banded both on nests and after capture with a cannon net. Of these 31 birds, 42 percent were males and 58 percent were females. Thus, the homing tendencies in the black-bellied tree duck

Table 2. Renesting data for black-bellied tree ducks illustrating retention of the pair bond between nesting attempts in the same season.

Initial Nest Attempt				Renest Attempt		
Band No.	Sex	Date[a]	Box No.[b]	Date[c]	Box No.[b]	Study Area[d]
607-47898	M	6-07-66	1	8-05-66	89	MNT-Cameron Co.
797-70401	F		1		89	MNT-Cameron Co.
607-47899	M	6-07-66	27	8-C8-66	33	HLY-Live Oak Co.
797-70412	F		27		33	HLY-Live Oak Co.
607-47819	M	6-10-66	78	7-27-66	2	MNT-Cameron Co.
797-70414	F		78		2	MNT-Cameron Co.

[a] The date when nest destruction was simulated by collection of the eggs for artificial incubation.
[b] See *b*, Table 1.
[c] The date when one of the banded pair was first caught during renesting.
[d] The first two pairs renested in the same specific areas as the initial nest capture; the third pair's initial nest was on WST-Cameron Co.

seem equally strong in both sexes, a condition necessarily expected in a species with year-to-year pair-bond tenure. It appears that species that change mates each year are also those in which only the females exhibit marked homing behavior (Hochbaum 1955: 239, Sowls 1955:40–41) whereas mutual homing tendencies are an a priori expectation for waterfowl taxa with lifetime pair bonds. Hence, the relationship between sex-specific homing behavior and pair-bond tenure emerges for waterfowl with short or permanent tenure in the pair bond.

Secondly, the 50:50 balance found in adult sex ratios (Bolen 1970) is a characteristic one would expect to find each spring if black-bellied tree ducks mate for life. Such a balance can be contrasted with the unbalanced sex ratios found in many populations (Bellrose et al. 1961:427), the latter in turn supporting the idea that an *excess* of drakes may function as a reserve pool of mates for renesting hens (Elder and Weller 1954:500). Renesting data for the black-bellied tree duck (Table 2) thus correlates well with the 50:50 adult sex ratio present in the spring population: an excess of male tree ducks is not required for renesting activities, as the pairs remain intact between nesting attempts.

Thus, the direct and indirect evidence now available from field studies of the black-bellied tree duck indicates that this species maintains a pair-bond tenure of lifelong duration.

LITERATURE CITED

BELLROSE, F. C., T. G. SCOTT, A. S. HAWKINS, AND J. B. LOW. 1961. Sex ratios and age ratios in North American ducks. Illinois Nat. Hist. Survey Bull. 27(art. 6):391–474.

BOLEN, E. G. 1967. Nesting boxes for black-bellied tree ducks. J. Wildl. Mgmt. 31(4): 794–797.

———. 1970. Sex ratios in the black-bellied tree duck. J. Wildl. Mgmt. 34(1):68–73.

DELACOUR, J., AND E. MAYR. 1945. The family Anatidae. Wilson Bull. 57(1):3–55.

ELDER, W. H., AND M. W. WELLER. 1954. Duration of fertility in the domestic mallard hen after isolation from the drake. J. Wildl. Mgmt. 18(4):495–502.

HOCHBAUM, H. A. 1955. Travels and traditions of waterfowl. Charles T. Branford Co., Newton, Massachusetts. 301pp. (Also, The University of Minnesota Press, Minneapolis. 1955. 301 pp.)

SHERWOOD, G. A. 1966. Flexible plastic collars compared to nasal discs for marking geese. J. Wildl. Mgmt. 30(4):853–855.

SOWLS, L. K. 1955. Prairie ducks: a study of their behavior, ecology and management. The Stackpole Company, Harrisburg, Pennsylvania, and the Wildlife Management Institute, Washington, D. C. 193pp.

Received for publication September 21, 1970.

EFFECTS OF INTERSPECIFIC NEST PARASITISM BY REDHEADS AND RUDDY DUCKS[1]

DAVID E. JOYNER, School of Life Sciences, University of Nebraska, Lincoln 68508[2]

Abstract: Of 809 duck nests found at Farmington Bay Waterfowl Management Area, Farmington, Utah, 290 were parasitized interspecifically—264 by redheads (*Aythya americana*) and 62 by ruddy ducks (*Oxyura jamaicensis*). Pintail (*Anas acuta*) and cinnamon teal (*A. cyanoptera*) nests most frequently incurred redhead parasitism, whereas cinnamon teal and redhead nests were most often parasitized by ruddy ducks. Mallard (*A. platyrhynchos*), pintail, and cinnamon teal nests parasitized interspecifically by ruddy ducks and redheads had significantly reduced ($P < 0.05$) egg successes. Egg success of cinnamon teal was significantly reduced ($P < 0.05$) through host egg displacement, primarily as a result of redhead parasitism. Egg displacement resulting from interspecific parasitism had a negligible effect on mallard, pintail, and redhead egg success. Redhead and ruddy duck interspecific parasitism did not decrease significantly ($P > 0.05$) host nesting success by increasing the occurrence of nest abandonment and nest predation.

J. WILDL. MANAGE. 40(1):33–38

Parasitic nesting behavior among Anatidae has generated interest among biologists, especially concerning the effects of facultative parasitism on waterfowl productivity. Obligate parasitic nesting has been reported for five families of birds (Lack 1968: 82). Within the five families, the South American black-headed duck (*Heteronetta atricapilla*) is the only known anatid obligate parasite (Weller 1968). Facultative parasitism has been reported for other genera of Anatidae, most notably in *Oxyura* (Hochbaum 1944:48, Joyner 1973) and *Aythya* (McKinney 1954, Weller 1959), and to a lesser extent in *Anas* (Weller 1959), *Dendrocygna* (Bolen and Cain 1968), and *Branta* (Hanson and Eberhardt 1971, Prevett and MacInnes 1973).

Increased nest abandonment has been regarded as one adverse consequence of interspecific facultative parasitism (Low 1941, Miller and Collins 1954, Ryder 1961). Additional detrimental effects attributed to interspecific parasitism are reduced clutch-size of host species (Weller 1959) and loss of eggs through displacement and breakage (Low 1940, Weller 1959).

The purpose of this study was to ascertain the effects of ruddy duck and redhead interspecific parasitism on waterfowl productivity at Farmington Bay Waterfowl Management Area, Farmington, Utah. I thank A. F. Regenthal, F. C. Jensen, R. Dietz, and T. Provan of the Utah Division of Wildlife Resources for their assistance. I am indebted to P. A. Johnsgard and R. M. Case for critically reviewing the manuscript.

STUDY AREA AND METHODS

Field investigations were conducted at Farmington Bay Waterfowl Management Area from 1972 through 1974. Farmington Bay was selected because of its large nesting populations of ruddy ducks and redheads. The refuge, encompassing 4,310 ha of Great Salt Lake shore area, is located near the delta of the Jordan River. Nesting habitat consisted predominantly of alkali bulrush (*Scirpus paludosus*), cattail (*Typha*

[1] Financial support was provided through research grants from the Frank M. Chapman Memorial Fund of the American Museum of Natural History, the Society of Sigma Xi, and the Josselyn Van Tyne Memorial Fund of the American Ornithologists' Union.

[2] Present address: Department of Zoology, University of Guelph, Guelph, Ontario N1G 2W1.

Originally published in J. Wildl. Manage. 40(1):33–38, 1976.

Table 1. Nesting success for five species of ducks parasitized interspecifically by the redhead, ruddy duck, or both (1972–74).

Host species	Total no. nests found	Parasite species	No. nests parasitized	No. parasitized nests			
				Hatched	Abandoned	Destroyed	Undetermined[a]
Mallard	29	Ruddy duck	2(7)[b]	1(50)	1(50)		
		Redhead	8(28)	5(83)		1(17)	2
		Both	1(3)		1(100)		
		Total	11(38)	6(67)	2(22)	1(11)	2
Pintail	48	Ruddy duck	3(6)	3(100)			
		Redhead	20(42)	10(76)	1(8)	2(16)	7
		Both	1(2)		1(100)		
		Total	24(50)	13(77)	2(12)	2(12)	7
Cinnamon teal	474	Ruddy duck	11(2)	6(55)	3(27)	2(18)	
		Redhead	194(41)	92(57)	46(28)	24(15)	32
		Both	32(7)	9(28)	19(59)	4(13)	
		Total	237(50)	107(52)	68(33)	30(15)	32
Redhead	93	Ruddy duck	10(11)	1(10)	9(90)		
Ruddy duck	158	Redhead	6(4)	2(33)	4(67)		

[a] Redhead nesting success for 1972 was not available and therefore was listed as undetermined.
[b] Percentage of sample is given in parentheses.

latifolia), hardstem bulrush (*S. acutus*), and saltgrass (*Distichlis stricta*).

Duck nests were located by periodically searching all available nesting habitat within the study area. Once located, all parasitized nests were marked with numbered yellow flags (12.5 × 5.0 cm) placed 5 m from the nest site. White flags were used to mark unparasitized nests. Flagging tape was tied to the vegetation near each nest site to facilitate relocation. Nests were revisited once each week until the eggs hatched, or until the nests were abandoned or destroyed. Statistical analyses were according to Steel and Torrie (1960:73) and Sokal and Rohlf (1969:503, 585, 607).

RESULTS

Of 809 nests of mallards, pintails, cinnamon teal, redheads, and ruddy ducks, 290 were parasitized interspecifically by either the redhead or the ruddy duck. Redheads parasitized 264 nests of 4 species, and 812 parasitic redhead eggs were found. This total was 50 percent of the 1,637 redhead eggs found over the 3-year period. The 62 nests of 4 species parasitized by ruddy ducks contained 146 parasitic eggs, or 9 percent of the total 1,618 ruddy duck eggs found. Table 1 lists percentage and success of nests parasitized by ruddy ducks and redheads. Dual parasitism affected only 6 percent of all 809 duck nests, but 55 percent of the 62 nests parasitized by ruddy ducks also were parasitized by redheads. In contrast, only 13 percent of the 264 nests affected by redhead parasitism also were parasitized by ruddy ducks.

The effects of ruddy duck and redhead parasitism on host clutch-size are shown in Table 2. Mallard and pintail clutch-sizes were not significantly reduced ($P > 0.05$) by redhead and ruddy duck parasitism. Clutch-sizes of parasitized cinnamon teal, redhead, and ruddy duck nests were found to be significantly less ($P < 0.05$) than unparasitized nests. Egg success of hosts (Table 3) was affected not only by the number of parasitic eggs deposited within the nest, but also by the parasitic species

Table 2. Mean clutch-size and number of parasitic eggs per nest for five species of ducks parasitized interspecifically by the redhead, ruddy duck, or both (1972–74).

Host species	Parasite species	No. nests	No. host eggs	No. parasite eggs	Mean clutch-size of host	Mean no. of parasite eggs
Mallard	Ruddy duck	2	11	11	5.5	5.5
	Redhead	8	56	41	7.0	5.1
	Both	1	8	11	8.0	11.0
	Total	11	75	63	6.8	5.7
	Unparasitized	18	130		7.2	
Pintail	Ruddy duck	3	14	12	4.7	4.0
	Redhead	20	114	55	5.7	2.8
	Both	1	8	6	8.0	6.0
	Total	24	136	73	5.7	3.0
	Unparasitized	24	156		6.5	
Cinnamon teal	Ruddy duck	11	71	28	6.5	2.5
	Redhead	194	1,386	547	7.1	2.8
	Both	32	188	163	5.9	5.1
	Total	237	1,645	738	6.9*	3.1
	Unparasitized	237	1,830		7.7	
Redhead	Ruddy duck	10	62	17	6.2*	1.7
	Unparasitized	83	825		10.0	
Ruddy duck	Redhead	6	42	10	7.0*	1.7
	Unparasitized	152	1,419		9.3	

* Significantly different ($P < 0.05$) from unparasitized clutch-sizes; *t*-test, $s_1^2 = s_2^2$, $n_1 \neq n_2$ (Steel and Torrie 1960: 73).

Table 3. Egg success of five species of ducks parasitized interspecifically by the redhead, ruddy duck, or both (1972–74).

Host species	Parasite species	Total no. eggs		No. host eggs		No. parasitic eggs	
		host	parasite	hatched	sub-sample[a]	hatched	sub-sample[b]
Mallard	Ruddy duck	11	11	2	11(18.2)[c]	4	11(36.4)
	Redhead	56	41	33	45(73.3)	6	28(21.4)
	Both	8	11		8		11
	Total	75	63	35	64(54.7)*	10	50(20.0)
	Unparasitized	130		43	66(65.2)		
Pintail	Ruddy duck	14	12	4	14(28.6)	11	12(91.7)
	Redhead	114	55	39	78(50.0)	13	40(32.5)
	Both	8	6		8		6
	Total	136	73	43	100(43.0)*	24	58(41.4)
	Unparasitized	156		83	125(66.4)		
Cinnamon teal	Ruddy duck	71	28	44	71(62.0)	3	28(10.7)
	Redhead	1,386	547	561	1,158(48.0)	91	469(19.4)
	Both	188	163	37	188(19.7)	20	163(12.3)
	Total	1,645	738	642	1,417(45.3)*	114	660(17.3)
	Unparasitized	1,830		744	1,271(59.0)		
Redhead	Ruddy duck	62	17	2	62(3.2)*	3	17(17.7)
	Unparasitized	825		187	508(36.8)		
Ruddy duck	Redhead	42	10	14	42(33.3)	1	10(10.0)
	Unparasitized	1,419		443	1,419(31.2)		

[a] Sub-sample pertains to 1973–74 data for nests parasitized by the redhead.
[b] Sub-sample pertains to 1973–74 data for redhead parasitic egg success.
[c] Figures in parentheses are hatching percentages.
* Significantly different ($P < 0.05$) from unparasitized nests.

Table 4. Effects of interspecific parasitism on duck nest abandonment and predation, 1973–74.

Host species	Unparasitized nests: Total no.	Unparasitized nests: No. abandoned or destroyed	Parasitized nests: Total no.	Parasitized nests: No. abandoned or destroyed
Cinnamon teal	166	72	168	73
Mallard	9	3	6	1
Pintail	19	3	13	3

involved. Clutches parasitized by both species exhibited lower host egg success than those affected by either species singly. Host egg success also was dependent on rates of predation, nest abandonment, egg displacement, individual clutch-size, and egg fertility.

Although ruddy ducks and redheads had access to five potential host species, each of the two parasitic species expressed some degree of host preference, whether through actual preference or as a result of similar habitat requirements. Pintail and cinnamon teal nests differed significantly in rates of parasitism by the two parasitic species (pintail, $\chi^2 = 15.63$, 1 df, $P < 0.01$; cinnamon teal, $\chi^2 = 175.46$, 1 df, $P < 0.01$). Twenty-one of 48 pintail nests and 226 of 463 cinnamon teal nests were parasitized by redheads, compared to 4 pintail nests and 43 cinnamon teal nests parasitized by ruddy ducks. Such differences in parasitism rates were not found for mallards ($\chi^2 = 3.78$, 1 df, $P > 0.05$). Ruddy duck and redhead pair counts were approximately equal for the 3-year period, totaling 1,104 and 1,037 pairs, respectively.

Ruddy duck and redhead parasitism had little effect on rates of nest abandonment by host species. A chi-square analysis (Sokal and Rohlf 1969:585) revealed no significant differences ($P > 0.05$) in the extent of nest abandonment and nest predation for parasitized and unparasitized nests regardless of host species involved (Table 4). However, the nests of mallards, pintails, and cinnamon teal parasitized by redheads and ruddy ducks had significantly reduced ($P < 0.05$) egg successes. Mallard and pintail egg losses resulted from increased rates of egg predation which did not result in increased rates of nest abandonment. Unlike mallards and pintails, the decrease in cinnamon teal egg success resulted primarily from increased egg displacement. A significantly ($P < 0.05$) greater number of cinnamon teal eggs was displaced from parasitized nests than from unparasitized nests (Table 5). Eggs were considered displaced if they were pushed out of the nest bowl, buried underneath the clutch with nest material separating the two, or missing from the nest.

Increasing the number of parasitic eggs

Table 5. Effects of parasitism on cinnamon teal egg displacement, 1973–74.

Parasitized nests: Total no. eggs	Parasitized nests: No. displaced eggs	Unparasitized nests: Total no. eggs	Unparasitized nests: No. displaced eggs	t_s[a]
1,147	192(16.7)[b]	1,177	48(4.1)	10.54*

[a] Test of equality of two percentages (Sokal and Rohlf 1969:607).
[b] Values in parentheses are percentages.
* $P < 0.01$.

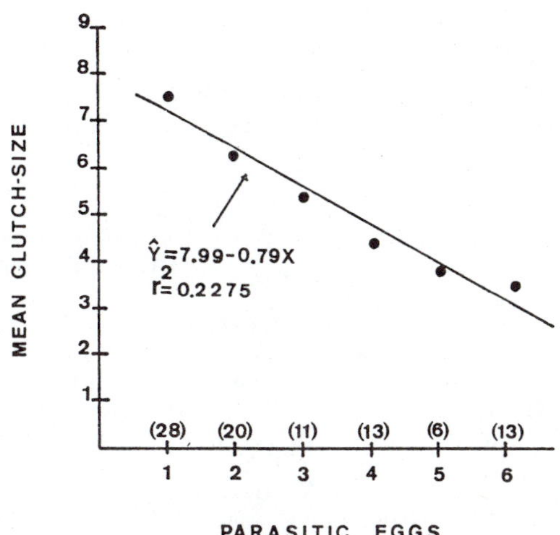

Fig. 1. Effects of ruddy duck and redhead parasitism on mean clutch-size of cinnamon teal at time of hatching. Sample sizes used in calculating mean values are in parentheses.

per nest, regardless of parasitic species, decreased the number of cinnamon teal eggs remaining at the time of hatching. A significant reduction ($P < 0.01$) in mean clutch-size of cinnamon teal at time of hatching occurred (Fig. 1) as the number of parasitic eggs increased from one to six. The addition of each parasitic egg, regardless of species, reduced the mean egg success of cinnamon teal by 0.79 egg per nest. Even though ruddy duck and redhead egg deposition depressed cinnamon teal egg success significantly ($P < 0.01$), the extent of suppression resulting from parasitic egg deposition accounted for less than 23 percent of the variability in cinnamon teal mean clutch-size ($r^2 = 0.2275$, Sokal and Rohlf 1969:503).

DISCUSSION

The impact of parasitism varied with the parasite, host species, and extent of parasitism. Mallard and pintail nests were parasitized readily by redheads and to a lesser extent by ruddy ducks. However, the activity of neither parasite significantly increased mallard and pintail nest loss through abandonment or predation. Although the rates of nest abandonment by cinnamon teal were high, redhead and ruddy duck parasitism was not considered to be a significant cause (see Table 4).

Parasitism at Farmington Bay had an insignificant effect on mallard and pintail total clutch-size, primarily because parasite egg deposition generally followed the initiation of host incubation. Cinnamon teal, redhead, and ruddy duck clutch-sizes were significantly less in parasitized nests than unparasitized nests, although the deposition of parasitic eggs into ruddy duck and redhead nests was not believed to have been the cause of that reduction. Both ruddy ducks and redheads readily abandoned their nests during the egg-laying period, especially as a result of repeated disturbances from nest examination. Cinnamon teal clutch-sizes were reduced through egg displacement. Reduced clutch-sizes and egg successes resulted not entirely from the possible suppression of host ovulation (Weller 1959), but rather from associated egg displacement and increased rates of egg predation and breakage. Weller (1959:355) indicated that excessive parasitism may depress host ovulation rates if 60–70 percent of the available nests are parasitized with an average of 4–6 eggs per nest. In this study, parasitism did not appear to be of sufficient magnitude during host egg-laying to produce a noticeable effect on the average clutch-size of hosts, even though 40–50 percent of the available mallard, pintail, and cinnamon teal nests were parasitized with 3 or more alien eggs. Egg deposition by both parasitic species generally occurred during host incubation rather than during host egg-laying, a circumstance also reported by Weller (1959) and Miller and Collins (1954).

Nest parasitism did have a significant suppressive effect on cinnamon teal hatching success through egg displacement, although the hatching success of mallards and pintails was not significantly affected by this factor. Displacement of eggs from ruddy duck nests was encountered rarely, whereas eggs frequently were pushed out of redhead nests which accounted for much of their egg loss.

It is evident that interspecific nest parasitism by ruddy ducks at Farmington Bay had a negligible effect on the overall hatching success of mallards, pintails, and redheads. The high incidence of naturally occurring redhead nest abandonment (Weller 1959) may have obscured the detrimental effects resulting from ruddy duck parasitism of redhead nests. Cinnamon teal hatching success was influenced less by ruddy duck parasitism than by redhead or dual parasitism, the assumption being that parasitism by the larger redhead resulted in a greater number of cinnamon teal eggs being broken or pushed out of the nest. However, few parasitized nests showed structural damage attributable to parasite-host interaction. Most nests appeared normal and could not be identified as having been parasitized by either redheads or ruddy ducks until the vegetation was moved aside and the eggs revealed.

In contrast, redhead parasitism had a more detrimental effect on host egg success, regardless of the host species involved. The crowding of waterfowl into preferred habitat, whether managed or natural, may enhance the potential for excessive parasitism by redheads. The high rate of redhead parasitism of mallard, pintail, and cinnamon teal nests observed at Farmington Bay probably reflected such crowding. Redhead parasitism of other species, most notably the canvasback (*A. valisineria*), may be unavoidable due to similarities in habitat preferences where the species are sympatric.

LITERATURE CITED

BOLEN, E. G., AND B. W. CAIN. 1968. Mixed wood duck-tree duck clutch in Texas. Condor 70(4):389–390.

HANSON, W. C., AND L. L. EBERHARDT. 1971. A Columbia River Canada goose population, 1950–1970. Wildl. Monogr. 28. 61pp.

HOCHBAUM, H. A. 1944. The canvasback on a prairie marsh. The American Wildlife Institute, Washington, D.C. 201pp.

JOYNER, D. E. 1973. Interspecific nest parasitism by ducks and coots in Utah. Auk 90 (3):692–693.

LACK, D. 1968. Ecological adaptations for breeding in birds. Methuen and Co. Ltd., London. 409pp.

LOW, J. B. 1940. Production of the redhead (*Nyroca americana*) in Iowa. Wilson Bull. 52(3):153–164.

———. 1941. Nesting of the ruddy duck in Iowa. Auk 58(4):506–517.

MCKINNEY, D. F. 1954. An observation on redhead parasitism. Wilson Bull. 66(2):146–148.

MILLER, A. W., AND B. D. COLLINS. 1954. A nesting study of ducks and coots on Tule Lake and Lower Klamath National Wildlife Refuges. California Fish Game 40(1):17–37.

PREVETT, J. P., AND C. D. MACINNES. 1973. Observations of wild hybrids between Canada and blue geese. Condor 75(1):124–125.

RYDER, R. A. 1961. Coot and duck productivity in northern Utah. Trans. N. Am. Wildl. Nat. Resour. Conf. 26:134–146.

SOKAL, R. R., AND F. J. ROHLF. 1969. Biometry. W. H. Freeman and Co., San Francisco. 776pp.

STEEL, R. G. D., AND J. H. TORRIE. 1960. Principles and procedures of statistics. McGraw-Hill Book Co., Inc., New York. 481pp.

WELLER, M. W. 1959. Parasitic egg laying in the redhead (*Aythya americana*) and other North American Anatidae. Ecol. Monogr. 29(4):333–365.

———. 1968. The breeding biology of the parasitic black-headed duck. Living Bird 7: 169–207.

Accepted 29 August 1975.

CRÈCHE FORMATION IN THE COMMON EIDER[1]

J. MUNRO and J. BÉDARD,[2] Département de Biologie, Faculté des Sciences et de Génie, Cité Universitaire, Université Laval, Québec, Québec, Canada G1K 7P4

Abstract: The formation of crèches was studied in the Common Eider (*Somateria mollissima*) nesting at high density on Bicquette Island in the St. Lawrence River estuary. Aspects of social behavior relevant to crèche formation are examined in detail. Data from 293 individually tagged females aided in elucidating the breeding history and in understanding the parental behavior of previously recognized categories of adult females ('B—Brooding,' 'A—Associate,' 'V—Visiting,' and 'N—Neutral'). Crèches resulting from the encounter between two or more broods begin to form immediately after the nest exodus and last well into the rearing period (about 10 weeks). The encounters themselves may be stimulated by alarm or predation or may sometimes result from the mutual attraction of ducklings. Our figures reveal that the rate of fixation of such encounters into permanent crèches decreases from a high of 88% in broods reaching the shore of the nesting island to a low of 0–6% in encounters between groups meeting during the latter half of the rearing period (between the 4th and the 10th weeks). Agonistic interactions among B-status females tending crèches provoke a hitherto unexplained lowering of the ratio of females to ducklings in such groups. Instead of a loose system of cooperation between females rearing crèches as was previously surmised, we found rather that the organization of these groups is based upon a hierarchical ranking of females involved in tending. The crèche is thus seen as an accidentally expanded family.

A number of Anatinae display crèching behavior (see Gorman and Milne 1972 for a recent review). Crèche was defined elsewhere as the grouping of any number of parentally unrelated adult female(s) and young (Munro 1975). In the Common Eider (*Somateria mollissima*) of the St. Lawrence estuary, amalgamation of broods into crèches sometimes resulted from accidental encounters between two or more broods and sometimes represented a spontaneous tendency to regroup in the face of larid predation. In the latter case, the behavior conferred a distinct survival advantage to the young in most cases (Munro 1975). Once formed, a crèche was very stable from the time of settling in the coastal rearing areas at about 1 week of age, to fledging, at about 10 weeks of age (Munro 1975). Even a crèche consisting of up to 35 ducklings and 2 females behaved as a cohesive family unit.

In the present paper, we seek to understand the social and ecological conditions that prevail at and shortly after hatching and lead, within a few days, to the fixation of familial bonds and thus to numerically aberrant family units (crèches). To this end, we describe in fairly minute detail various aspects of the behavior of the various categories of birds involved in crèching. We also discuss the influence of duckling age on crèche formation and the proportion of encounters resulting in permanent amalgamation.

STUDY AREA AND METHODS

About 20,000 pairs of Common Eiders breed in the St. Lawrence estuary, 92% being found on 6 nesting islands (see Reed 1973 and Munro 1975 for details). A discrete peak of hatching occurs between 10 and 20 June and the majority of broods and/or crèches are rapidly led by adult females to mainland littoral areas for the duration of the rearing period. The length of the sea crossings involved varies between 3 and 14 km. Most ducklings are reared along the southern shore of the river between Kamouraska and Matane, with smaller numbers remaining

[1] Originally published in Auk 94(4):759–771, 1977.

[2] Address correspondence to this author.

around the largest islands or moving to the northern shore between the Saguenay River and Forestville.

Over 1,400 breeding females were marked with patagial tags during 1972 and 1973, and a few entire broods and/or crèches were marked as they were leaving nesting islands. The ducklings were marked with colored nape tags, which did not disrupt brood unity but did cause a significant increase in predation. Therefore, the tagging of broods was discontined after marking 140 young in 24 different groups.

Four discrete categories of female behavior were recognized. (1) *Broody* (B). Assumes the leadership of the brood/crèche. She does all or most of the vocalization and surveillance and swims in a central or fore position in the group; does not abandon ducklings except under most extreme disturbance. Two, or rarely three, B-status birds may accompany a crèche on a permanent basis with little or no aggression between them. (2) *Associate* (A). Assumes a subordinate role to the B-female. Swims in a peripheral or rear position in a crèche. Readily leaves the ducklings in the case of moderate disturbance. Generally associates with the same crèche over several consecutive days. (3) *Visiting* (V). Has a very low and transitory broodiness. Such females are temporarily attracted to a nearby brood or crèche. Show ambiguous (care-giving and agonistic) behavior towards ducklings. May swim alongside a crèche for variable lengths of time but leave at the slightest disturbance. May visit a number of different crèches in the same day. (4) *Neutral* (N). Displays no broodiness whatsoever and is not attracted by a nearby crèche or brood. Some of the V-females may probably assume an N-status at certain times and vice versa. Generally 5 min of continuous observation are sufficient to classify a female. Further explanations of these categories are found in Munro (1975).

Most of the observations were obtained during June 1973 on the NE coast of Bicquette Island, a 9.1-ha wooded islet 30 km SW of Rimouski and inhabited by approximately 7,500 pairs of Common Eiders.

RESULTS

Crèche Size.—Crèches encountered during the present study comprised between 1 and 5 females of Broody or Associate status and between 1 and 60 ducklings. The most commonly encountered assemblage contained 2 females and 7–9 ducklings. We divided the period from laying to fledging into time intervals of different lengths that corresponded to discrete stages in the life history of the young ducks. These stages are labeled A–F in Fig. 1 and are discussed further below.

BEHAVIOR OF CRÈCHING BIRDS

On the Nest (Stages A–B).—The incubating female is normally silent. A few hours before the ducklings are either seen or heard, she emits soft low calls at variable intervals. These calls seem to mesmerize V-females. The latter often leave the shore of the inlet in groups of 2–5 individuals, loudly chorusing bisyllabic notes of increasing intensity towards the end of the phrase. These parties roam under the forest canopy or amidst the thick brush and finally converge upon a hatching clutch of eggs to settle down. The V-birds come and go, sometimes as many as 10 of them competing with one another for position, the most aggressive individuals settling as close as possible to the incubating female. The latter will not tolerate such V-birds any closer than about 1 m. Other

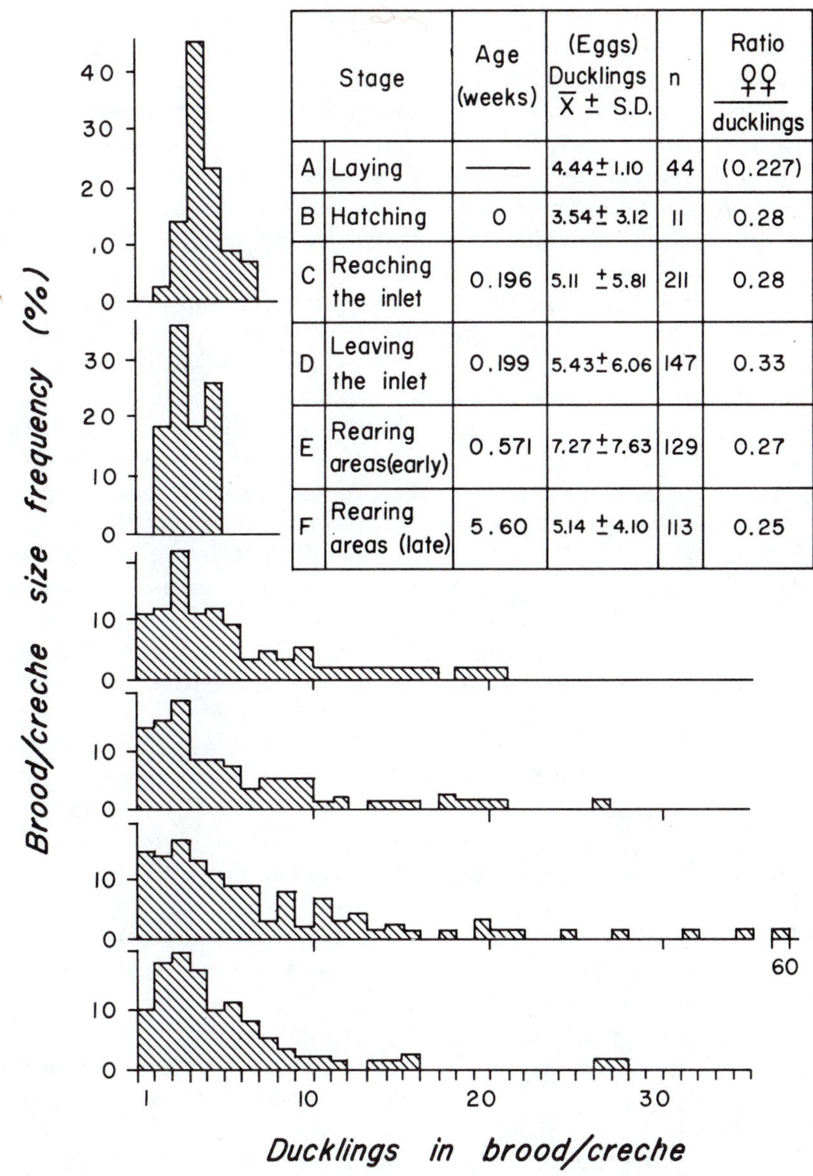

	Stage	Age (weeks)	(Eggs) Ducklings $\overline{X} \pm$ S.D.	n	Ratio ♀♀/ducklings
A	Laying	——	4.44 ± 1.10	44	(0.227)
B	Hatching	0	3.54 ± 3.12	11	0.28
C	Reaching the inlet	0.196	5.11 ± 5.81	211	0.28
D	Leaving the inlet	0.199	5.43 ± 6.06	147	0.33
E	Rearing areas (early)	0.571	7.27 ± 7.63	129	0.27
F	Rearing areas (late)	5.60	5.14 ± 4.10	113	0.25

Fig. 1. Frequency of brood/crèche size, female/ducklings ratio (summing only females with B- or A-status); Bicquette Island, 1973.

incubating females on immediately surrounding nests show no concern whatsoever for such activities. Most of the V-females disappear towards nightfall.

A minimum average of 25 hours (N = 9, range 9–27) elapses between hatching of the first egg and nest exodus; over this period, the ducklings acquire their full mobility and perfect their vocal abilities. The female adopts a brooding posture with partly opened wings and spread tail; in this position the energetic ducklings roaming on her back and around the female must be exposed to the two whitish wingbars. These wingbars are much less evident on neighboring V-females.

From Nest to Shore (Stages B–C).—Over the average 38 m that separate the nest from the shore, the family party will pass by about 100 nests, 10 of which perhaps will be hatching. If hatching occurs towards the peak of the season, the brood will also meet with two or three more broods also on their way to the shore. The mother, or B-status bird leads the brood with the same low-pitched calls that she emitted on the nest. She vocalizes to indicate departure, to maintain vocal contact with dispersed young, and to respond to a distressed duckling. The V-females often join the brood, walking alongside or slightly at the rear of the brood, all the time emitting vocalizations of the type already described. The group makes many stops, some of these lasting 10 or 15 minutes, particularly in the grassy rim that surrounds the forested core of the island. In this sparse cover, Herring Gulls (*Larus argentatus*) make predation attempts. Upon reaching the inlet, the group size has increased from 3.54 ± 3.12 to 5.11 ± 5.81 (Fig. 1). Although these two figures do not differ significantly from each other ($t = -1.64$, $0.2 < P < 0.1$), the histograms in Fig. 1 instantly reveal that important changes in group composition have happened.

In the Inlet (Stage C).—During the next moments—traversing the inlet in its whole length requires an average of 30 min ($N = 211$, extremes 5 and 120)—the brood or crèche will make many costly encounters with gulls. Upon attack, only the B-females accompanying the group emit a loud, rolling alarm call. The ducklings respond by clustering under the opened wings and tail of the B-female(s). Out of the 211 groups observed, 201 had an escort of V-status birds. In most cases, the small number that came with the group from the nest is augmented by another 10–20 upon reaching the inlet. The numbers of this escort will change continuously thereafter by the constant addition and departure of individual birds. Sometimes the entire escort will detach itself and converge towards a neighboring group whose B-female is emitting alarm calls in the face of gull attacks. These V-females strive to contact the ducklings, fight among themselves to get closer, and often manage to dislocate the crèche in the process. In such a case isolated ducklings wander from one V-female to the other, emitting distress calls and eliciting at first great interest among the escort; but this interest dwindles rapidly once a given female has managed to approach the duckling(s) and often after delivering aggressive jabs at the lone young.

Visiting females might by their mere presence act as deterrents to the attacking gull(s), but their actual influence upon protection of the crèche was assessed as "slight" elsewhere (Munro and Bédard 1977).

In only 9 cases out of 211 did we notice that the female(s) leading the group adopted a tolerant attitude towards the escorting V-birds. Normally, these are greeted harshly by the leading B-bird(s), which stive to maintain a free radius around the ducklings (Fig. 2). Even in absence of gull predation and harassment by V-females, the brooding female will emit soft calls to maintain contact with the ducklings. She also maintains a semi-brooding posture, the wingbars clearly displayed.

In the event of a disruption created by the activities of V-females, the leading bird is normally able to regroup her party and to continue towards the mouth of the

Fig. 2. Typical aggressive reaction of a "Broody" (B-status) female towards a "Visiting" (V-status) bird that came too near the ducklings.

inlet of the island. Most of the V-females abandon the brood/crèche as it nears the sea, individual birds joining incoming crèches or simply hauling out for a rest.

Around the Island (Stage D).—A modal brood size of 3.0 among broods leaving the inlet suggests that at this time real broods still make up a substantial proportion of the groups. Although predation pressure has been very strong between stages C and D, the average size of the group has remained unchanged during the interval (Fig. 1).

From now on, predation pressure is reduced considerably (Munro and Bédard 1977), and harassment from V-females is almost over. But over the 2–24 hours that the crèche will spend around the island before launching on the 5-hour journey that will take it to the south shore of the estuary, 13 km away, it will encounter many broods and crèches and may temporarily or permanently amalgamate with some of them. Ducklings first begin feeding along the shoreline of their natal island, even though they may pass only a few hours in this region.

Coastal Rearing Areas (Stages E–F).—Once in the rearing areas, the groups, either brood or crèche, have a remarkable stability as well as, in general, a strict preference for a very specific rearing site. We sighted 47 marked broods or crèches a total of 264 times throughout the summer of 1973: 91% of these successive sightings were obtained from the same sites. This phenomenon is further examined in Munro (1975). This site and social stability lasts until the ducklings are 9–10 weeks old. Towards the middle and the end of the rearing period, feeding ducklings may disperse over an area 25–30 m in diameter; yet, upon alarm and during roosting, the maintenance of family links is obvious. It is only during the 9th or 10th week that these links seem to disintegrate, at which time large groups of molting females and fully grown ducklings begin to move eastward along the south shore of the estuary.

From the above description, it appears that eider groups, broods or crèches, behave as real family units; one category of female, the B-status birds, always accompanies the group and performs protection and attraction displays that exert a strong effect upon the ducklings.

BREEDING HISTORY OF CRÈCHING FEMALES

Origin of Broody and Associate Females.—The appearance of brooding behavior in a female eider coincides with her hatching a clutch of eggs. Three marked females followed for at least 30 days each while tending crèches and broods in the coastal rearing areas displayed broody behavior (in the sense understood for the B-category) characteristic of B-status females. These 3 marked birds were sighted a total of 11 times on and around Bicquette prior to hatching their brood and leaving the island with it. In the 5 cases when they could be assigned to a behavioral category, they fell into the N-category as is proper for incubating females.

Like B-hens, A-females have successfully hatched a clutch of eggs. But abundant circumstantial evidence suggests that the latter are more or less broody hens that have been displaced from leadership by broodier and more aggressive females. As witnessed in the records from 10 marked birds, both B- and A-status are stable at least throughout the entire 30-min interval between the arrival in the inlet and their departure. A total of 304 females of these two categories accompanied the 211 groups reaching the shore of the inlet. Of these, 30 were catalogued as Associates and 274 as Broody. Following instances of predation and particularly during brood mixing, some of the broody females were in turn displaced by broodier birds and adopted in turn the status of Associate bird.

Out of 18 B-status females that suffered total predation on the brood they accompanied, 16 displayed a remarkable parental behavior in vacuo: they kept calling intensely while patrolling the area where the loss occurred. Such birds also adopted a brooding attitude with partly opened wings and lunged towards passing gulls. More interesting still, 7 of these 16 birds joined another crèche within 20 min of the loss of their young and assumed therein the previously held B-status (5 cases) or a newly acquired A-status (2 cases). The remaining 9 birds were not presented such an occasion of a group passing by, and their parental attitude decreased while they were joining V- and N-females at rest, so that they were lost among them. Thus, very clearly, these behavioral attitudes are very discrete and likely correspond to hormonal conditions and the social feedback brought about by the breeding history of the individual. The permanence of the B-status in 40 marked females followed in the rearing areas lasted an average of 36 days (Munro 1975). Thus V-females cannot, under the circumstances prevailing in our study area, become incorporated in a brood or a crèche in the manner that B- or A-birds can.

Origin of Visiting and Neutral Females.—In view of the high density of nesting birds, the contingent of females resting from incubation duties in the inlet at any one time may be quite considerable. Could these simply assume V-status while off duty? Not likely, for we found that marked incubating females, either on or off the nest are oblivious of ducklings. Seven marked females in various stages of incubation were assigned the Neutral status when confronted with incoming broods while resting on the shore of the inlet between incubation bouts. Such indifference towards ducklings will also develop in birds failing to breed early during incubation, as we shall explain below.

Moreover, we found that marked incubating females left the nest for periods lasting less than 10 min at a time. Since V-females harass crèches or surround hatching nests, sometimes for hours at a time, it is unlikely then that V-birds are actively engaged in incubation.

Other workers (Lewis 1959, Robertson 1929) suggested that V-females were subadult birds, but this is untenable as in 4 years of field study, we never collected or observed more than a few dozen subadult (mostly males) Common Eiders in the St. Lawrence estuary.

Visiting females are thought to be failed nesters on the basis of the following evidence. Three marked females accorded this status in the inlet had been trapped with their mates (thus in the very first stages of breeding) on Bicquette Island 20 days earlier. V-females were also frequently seen settling into empty nest bowls for periods of up to 30 min suggesting an attraction to nest sites and perhaps a tendency to renest. Finally, we also analyzed resightings of 16 females marked in our trap that were never seen as Broody or Associate birds but were later found displaying V- or N-status. The average time interval between tagging and first resighting (both events on Bicquette Island) with V-status was 19.8 ± 10.11 days ($N = 10$); the remaining 6 birds when first resighted assumed N-status (7.83 ± 7.24 days). This difference ($P < 0.025$) leads us to think that V-status birds were resighted much later because they were engaged in incubation longer and hence, much less likely to be observed loafing in the inlet.

Admittedly, more evidence is needed to support this interpretation, but the data would be very tedious to gather. As we have established elsewhere (Munro 1975), birds losing nests or young slowly shift over time from one behavioral category to the next, the evidence indicating that the transition is directional from B through A, then V and finally N.

BROOD MIXING

Circumstances in Which Mixing Occurs.—The thickness of the vegetation kept us from witnessing directly the mixing of broods heading toward the inlet shore. We noted above (Fig. 1) that a degree of mixing took place in such circumstances, but nothing suggests that predation could account for such mixing. Departing broods are sometimes temporarily halted by obstacles in the footpath (our trapping device being one of these) and thus have an opportunity to meet another brood. In 9 such cases of two broods coming together along our trap, permanent mixing resulted in 6 and was followed by aggression among B-status birds leading the broods. In one case, a B-status bird completely expelled the other.

Once in the narrow inlet, random movements of broods also lead to contact with one another. These contacts may result in any of the following. The two groups may separate immediately or they may swim or walk alongside each other for some time without ever mixing. The two groups may amalgamate and remain together as a stable crèche. The groups may combine briefly, and then separate, perhaps with an exchange of ducklings between the groups having taken place. The relative frequency of these various instances of encounters between broods are examined in Table 1 and will be further discussed below. Quite often the

Table 1. Outcome of encounters[1] between Common Eider broods and/or crèches.[2]

Location	Age[3] hours (weeks)	Total number of encounters observed	Encounters resulting in amalgamation		Amalgamation transitory[7]		Amalgamation transitory original groups reform	
			N	%	N	%	N	%
I Nesting grounds[5]	26 (0.155)	—	26	—	3	12	—	—
II Inlet, NE Bicquette	27 (0.161)	75	50	67	14	28	13	93
III Around Bicquette Is. and outer reefs	30–40 (0.208)	68	35	51	25	71	16	64
IV Around Bic Is.	41–65 (0.315)	12	4	33	3	75	2	67
V Rearing areas	(1.5)[6]	49	17	35	13	76	13	100
	(6.5)[7]	28	2	7	2	100	2	100
(groups of mixed age)		88	17	19	16[8]	94	16	100

[1] Approaching groups are involved in an "encounter" provided they came within 8 m of each other.
[2] On Bicquette Island and on the neighboring shore of the St. Lawrence estuary. Bic Island (IV) is on the normal route to the rearing areas.
[3] Age 0 is the complete hatching of the first duckling of a brood.
[4] Mixing results in a new group and is considered transitory when the latter separate within 30 min.
[5] These cases are of groups already formed by the time they reached the shore of the inlet. Note that 211 groups reached the inlet of which 26 were mixed, implying an original cohort of about 234 broods. The number of encounters among these cannot be established.
[6] Mixing involves groups of even age in their 1st, 2nd, or 3rd week after hatching.
[7] Mixing involves groups of even age in their 4th–10th week after hatching.
[8] One permanent mixing involved 1 group of 4 ducklings aged 9–10 weeks joining another of one B-female and 5 ducklings aged 7–8 weeks.

mixing seems to be the result of mutual attraction, but most cases of mixing coincide with harassment by larid predators. This matter is discussed, and figures on the subject are presented elsewhere (Munro and Bédard 1977).

Feeding broods or crèches often come into contact after leaving the inlet. Such contacts are enhanced by greater dispersal of the ducklings, probably as a response to reduced predation pressure. During sea crossings, we have also noticed a tendency to regroup: in 3 instances we saw 2 groups leaving the shore of Bicquette Island for the mainland simultaneously but independently, a few hundred meters apart. Upon noticing each other some distance away from the shore, both converged towards each other and swam as a single party for at least 300 m before disappearing out of sight.

Along the coast, in the rearing areas, encounters are frequent but amalgamations resulting from these are rare (Table 1). Only in cases of alarm did we observe large, but short-lived grouping taking place (sometimes as many as 150 ducklings could become involved in such grouping).

Behavior of Females and Ducklings During Mixing.—In the inlet, ducklings mix spontaneously either as they naturally follow their B-female or, else, as they converge towards the most defensive bird and the one adopting the most obvious brooding posture in the case of a gull attack. On the rearing grounds and especially as they reach older age, ducklings may show aggression towards a foreigner attempting to join their brood or crèche, but usually ducklings show no resentment toward the company of other ducklings of similar age. They will, however, soon respond very specifically to the vocalizations of their B-female, which (depending upon whether or not mixing has occurred) may or may not be their

Table 2. Changes in the number of females tending broods and/or creches in groups leaving Bicquette Island in June 1973.[1]

	Behavioral status	
	B— Brooding	A— Associate
A. Changes in crèche structure without changes in (relative) numbers		
I. i. Gains resulting from the amalgamation of two or more broods under continuous observation	58	4
ii. Expected gain following splitting of a crèche under observation (23 cases)	24	3
II. Status change within a group under observation		
i. Brooding female becomes Associate	−7	+7
ii. Associate female becomes Brooding	+3	−3
B. Changes in crèche structure and numbers		
I. Losses		
i. Following disintegration after total predation	45	8
ii. Departure of tending females (A- or B-)		
1. Resulting from aggression by resident or newly arrived B-status female	5	13
2. Does not follow arrival in crèche of a new B-status female	2	7
3. Does not follow arrival of new B-status bird and no aggression noted among females in crèche	0	5
4. Unaccounted for	3	3
II. Gains		
i. Unknown origin but not left over after mixing or splitting	25	33
ii. Shift from neighboring brood	0	1
iii. Female freed after loss of ducklings joining a new group	6	1

[1] A total of 211 groups containing 303 females were followed in detail. The time interval examined cover steps C and D in Fig. 1.

mother. During mixing (or immediately following predation), agonistic relations between B-females in the newly formed crèche are commonplace. These events seem to determine a hierarchy reflected in the position of the birds in the floating group. The result of this aggression may go from one extreme, that is, the expulsion of one of the broody females (Table 2, BIii1) to the mutual tolerance of two birds of nearly equivalent status in the same crèche. The latter will usually be the outcome of a rather major clash between two evenly matched birds. Occasionally, the subordinate B-female will remain as Associate and swim either near the rear of the sides of a crèche containing perhaps some or all of her ducklings. The duration of her status as Associate is not well established.

Relations among several B-females within a crèche are coordinated by a number of minute agonistic attitudes and movements, many of which must have escaped our attention. In Table 2, the statistics on attendance of B- and A-females are pooled for the 211 cases observed in detail. Only two cases (BIii2) are interpreted as representing spontaneous departures for a B-status bird and were quite certainly not the result of agonistic activities of the other B-female. In most cases—and this also perhaps includes poorly documented cases (BIii4) and even some cases when no aggression was detected (BIii3)—the losses of B- and A-females from a crèche must be accounted for by agonistic activities from broodier and more aggressive females.

The 58 cases (AIi) of females of unknown origin joining crèches very likely included both females who had recently lost their brood and thus still retained a strong maternal drive, and B-females expelled from their own group. But most are probably B-females of various tendencies that have lost their entire brood or crèche as a consequence of predation: 58 females thus freed were seen to join loafing birds on the sides of the inlet. We must remark that it is also from these groups of loafing birds that most of these 58 incomers originate. Section A in Table 2 is a straightforward compilation of all gains and losses occurring in groups followed without interruption. For all the groups involved, the result of mixing is nil as the gains of one group are created by the losses of the other. Changes in status among crèche females are thus generally the result of agonistic relations. The rate of departure of B- and A-females can be estimated by comparing the measured B- and A-females/ducklings ratio to the expected one considering duckling mortality rate and forced (by complete mortality of the group) departure rate. Duckling mortality at the end of the 6th week was estimated at 67.7% (Munro 1975). When this percentage is applied to the initial brood size of 3.54 (Fig. 1), one finds a final expected brood size of 1.14. If we ignore crèche formation and the loss of entire broods, we can predict that on the average, by the 6th week after hatching, one female would care for this reduced brood. But we know from Table 2 (BIi) that the loss of entire broods frees 17.5% (53/303) of all the females (B- and A-status) while duckling mortality over the same time interval amounts to 23% (Munro 1975). Assuming that such a rate of entire brood losses is prevalent over the first 6 weeks of brood rearing, we can estimate that 51.5% of all the females would be freed from parental duties while total duckling mortality would amount to 67.7% during the same time. Thus if broods remained broods and if any female that suffered the loss of its whole brood departed, we would expect a females/ducklings ratio of 0.425 or 42.5%. The observed value is a mere 0.25 or 25% (Fig. 1), and this important decline in female involvement cannot be accounted for by our calculations. According to our behavioral observations and our earlier discussion, these departures result almost exclusively from aggressive interactions within the crèche and, secondarily from spontaneous abandonment by weakly motivated females. An examination of mortality data in Munro and Bédard (1977) and the data in Fig. 1 suggest that about two thirds of these departing females leave between reaching the inlet and the 5th day (first age class) of the young.

Brood Mixing Frequency: Changes With Time.—When one considers the already established case for group stability on the coast on the one hand and the familial character of the relations described above on the other, one is led to conclude that crèches are nothing but numerically aberrant family units. Table 1 shows the progression of group stability with time. The decreasing amalgamation rate and the increasing separation rate can be accounted for by invoking age, the only factor that changes uninterruptedly. The correlation coefficient between age on the one hand and the proportion of permanent amalgamation on the other is -0.843 ($P < 0.05$).

The role of predation in the process of crèche stabilization with age can be dismissed. Actually, while no predation was observed on the nesting site, crèche formation still took place there. In the inlet, newly formed crèches and those arriving already formed (on the nesting grounds) suffered the same predation pressure, yet the latter did show a greater stability. Afterwards, predation diminished in parallel with actual mixing but no longer paralleled age. Thus around Bicquette, predation pressure is low, yet encounters are still numerous. But splits leading to the *statu quo ante* are the rule (13 cases out of 14 encounters) at an age of 27 hours. Even at this early age, the ducklings are able to recognize and choose to follow a given B-female leader.

DISCUSSION

Crèching behavior and the environmental conditions leading to it are not found exclusively on Bicquette Island. Though nesting density is higher there than anywhere else, great densities are also encountered on at least five islands or island groups in the St. Lawrence estuary (see Reed 1973 for details). On every one of these islands, conditions of topography, vegetation, and exposure create locally and to a varied extent conditions leading to brood pile-ups or brood convergences. Distinct forest paths used by departing broods are known for every one of the nesting islands. Protected bays or inlets where broods tend to converge for minutes or hours after hatching before undertaking the sea crossing are also known for most islands and in particular Ile aux Pommes, Brandypot, and the Pèlerins.

Stonehouse (1960) established that parental links in the King Penguin (*Aptenodytes patagonica*) develop over the first week while real "crèches" form after about the youngs' 6th week of age. Crèching in that species has evolved apparently as an antipredator device. The same pattern has been found in the White Pelican (*Pelecanus erythrorhynchos*) (Schaller 1964) and the Great White Pelican (*P. onocrotalus*) (Brown and Urban 1969) except that in the latter crèche form at 20–30 days of age. Adult birds recognize their own progeny among the crèche as in the penguins, and the crèche is thought to have evolved to ease thermoregulatory problems of isolated young. In the Gentoo Penguin (*Pygoscelis papua*), Roberts (1940) described crèching behavior and ascribed to it an energy saving value. In these three species at least, crèching behavior is seen as an evolved feature of the rearing period, normal interfamily aggression being reduced so that members of the crèche can secure certain advantages against predation or heat loss.

The crèching in the Common Eider has nothing in common with what has been just described. In our opinion, the only evolved trait of this behavior is the spontaneous tendency for females to regroup their ducklings in the face of predation with concurrent lowering of normal aggressiveness among them (Munro 1975). The contingent stabilization of groups formed following encounters (be these due to predation, chance, or alarm) seems to be a fortuitous consequence of overcrowding at the precise period when family links tend to crystallize. The two factors that correlate best with crèche formation are age and predation rate but, as discussed previously, the latter agent cannot be held responsible for the familial fixation itself. In an Anatidae, the Mallard (*Anas platyrhynchos*), Raitasuo (1964) felt that relations between members of a brood seemed to be based upon imprinting and had stabilized permanently by the 3rd day of age after which foreign ducklings were rejected. In the Anatidae (Cushing and Ramsay 1949, Collias and Collias 1956) and the Coot (*Fulica atra*) (Alley and Boyd 1950), 4–7 days are required for the formation and stabilization of family links. Our estimate of the time required in the Common Eider is nearly equivalent or perhaps slightly shorter, but our views that crèching is nothing but the aberrant hardening of oversize family links are perfectly harmonized with the views expressed by these authors. In *The King Penguin* Stonehouse (1960) also noted that prior to the fixation of family links (1 week) exchange of young and the resulting crèche formation in the sense discussed here also occurs. Koskimies (1957) also believed that the Velvet Scoter (*Melanitta fusca*) the high density prevalent upon or soon after hatching interfered with normal family development and provoked crèche formation. Thus time is a necessary component of crèching: predation alone or alarm or chance encounters while provoking mixing of broods does not necessarily result in the formation of crèches. Birds within these groups must further develop mutual or reciprocal links between adult females and young, and perhaps later between young themselves. Presumably the circumstances in the St. Lawrence estuary, where the ducklings must all undertake lengthy sea crossings lasting several hours under the leadership of B-female(s) before reaching the rearing areas must be greatly conducive to the stabilization of links within such groups.

It is impossible to say without experimentation, whether or not the ducklings can recognize each other at age 27–35 hours. Evidence from captive birds suggests that individual recognition is not possible before several days at least and more likely before several weeks. Thus the leadership of the B-female would be the determinant factor in crèche stability at least in the early stages of crèche life. On the other hand, two femaleless groups of 8- and 9-week-old ducklings were seen repeatedly in the rearing grounds preserving great stability and going through a number of encounters with crèches and broods but always maintaining their original composition. Thus reciprocal links between the ducklings had developed at that age. Besides female leadership, these mutual links must play a role in the cohesion of the group and may account at least partly for the growing avoidance with age or even repulsion of groups in face of other groups. The marked tendency to avoid mixing is reflected in the column "Encounter resulting in amalgamation" in Table 2 where the percentage decreases steadily from 67 to 7 over the first 6 weeks of age. We have circumstantial evidence suggesting that beyond 30 ducklings, a crèche becomes increasingly unstable. Perhaps at this size, the mutual abilities of ducklings and of females to cope with so many social elements are exceeded.

Among factors playing a role in mixing and crèche formation, the polarizing effect of a superbroody female (the "mother-effect" as some workers call it) has been recognized by Bergman (1956) in the Goosander (*Mergus merganser*) and in the Red-breasted Merganser (*Mergus serrator*), by Koskimies (1957) in the Velvet Scoter (*Melanitta fusca*), by Williams (1974) in the Shelduck (*Tadorna tadorna*), and in the Common Eider by Ahlén and Andersson (1970). This effect is also manifested in data provided by Boase (1938) in *Tadorna* as the females/ducklings ratio is much smaller in his data in large crèches than in small ones. This strongly suggests that very maternal and broody females may draw to them many more ducklings than can more modestly aggressive and less broody females. Recent work on *Tadorna* in the Ythan estuary in northeastern Scotland largely confirms these views and further documents the existence of vast differences in the aptitude of individual females to attract ducklings and to establish parental relations with them (I. J. Patterson, pers. commun.).

The latter fact has been noted in *Somateria* by Koskimies (1957) and by Ahlén and Andersson (1970) who report that the ducklings will spontaneously cluster behind the most stimulating female. Our observations lead us to similar conclusions. We further believe that this 'stimulating' character of certain females is primarily mediated through her vocalizations, secondarily through her postures, and thirdly through her vigor in chasing neighboring females.

According to Gorman and Milne (1972) crèches in the Common Eider constitute an example of a genuine cooperative system in which the care of the young is left to newly arrived breeding females thus freeing the early arrivals to move to supposedly better feeding grounds. The behavior is thus characterized by a total and rapid (3.88 days) dissolution of family links. We believe that the departure of some females is caused by the encounter itself resulting in either agonistic expulsion or loss of contact with known ducklings. Thus aggression among successfully breeding females results in a rapid loss of position of the subordinate and less broody/aggressive individuals. The latter may remove themselves entirely from the group and then rapidly lose all attachment to young, or they may attempt to regain a leadership position in another brood or crèche. Thus there appears to be no sign of "cooperation" whatsoever among females. Quite to the contrary, a marked hierarchy exists among them in the case of crèches tended by more than one bird. Over 200 resightings of 45 marked females confirmed the existence and the stability of such a hierarchical organization amongst females sharing the supervision of crèches. Once again, the only cooperation that we have established is in instances of predation when several B-females will spontaneously regroup.

McAloney (1973) felt that in crèches, no one female was totally responsible for the care of the ducklings and conversely, the ducklings did not generally appear to be imprinted on any particular female. Similar views were proposed by Milne (1963) but until experimental evidence becomes available, support for such views as "imprinting on a general female model" are entirely lacking. We have circumstantial evidence suggesting that within a crèche, some of the females may be attached only to some (perhaps in some cases their own) ducklings. Such birds usually leave the crèche if all their ducklings disappear. Similar observations have been made in Scotland by Mendenhall (pers. commun.).

Ahlén and Andersson (1970) claim that females leave the brood or crèche under the combined influences of a decrease in maternal behavior and a simultaneous increase in hunger, but they present no quantitative evidence to support their claim. We may add that the spontaneous loss of broodiness in such circumstances would be a rather stunning event, as the ducklings themselves whose presence must create a powerful stimulus to develop this broodiness are always present. Only in cases when more aggressive females persistently hold or prevent this reciprocal linkage with ducklings to develop will a female be forced to leave.

ACKNOWLEDGMENTS

The study was supported by a grant from the Ministère de l'Education du Québec (Formation des chercheurs et action concertée). Jean Munro received financial support from la Société Zoologique de Québec Inc. and the Ministère de l'Education du Québec for which he is grateful. We also thank a number of persons who have helped with the field work: Gaétan Rochette, Michel Durand, Francine Munro, François Caron, and Jean Gauthier. We also thank Y. Desbiens and M. Thibault for hospitality and unfailing generosity while on Bicquette Island. We thank Mr. M. Boulanger, Superintendent of the Lighthouse Operations with the Ministry of Transport, for authorization to establish caches and to work on Bicquette. We finally thank Jeremy McNeil and Laurence Ellison for suggesting useful improvements on early drafts on this manuscript.

LITERATURE CITED

AHLÉN, I., AND A. ANDERSSON. 1970. Breeding ecology of an eider population on Spitsbergen. Ornis Scandinavica 1:83–106.

ALLEY, R., AND H. BOYD. 1950. Parent-young recognition in the Coot, *Fulica atra*. Ibis 92:46–51.

BERGMAN, G. 1956. Om kullsammanslagning hos skrakar, *Mergus serrator* och *Mergus merganser*. Fauna och Flora (1956):97–110.

BOASE, H. 1938. Further notes on the habits of the shell-duck. Brit. Birds 31:367–371.

BROWN, L. H., AND E. K. URBAN. 1969. The breeding biology of the Great White Pelican *Pelecanus onocrotalus roseus* at Lake Shala, Ethiopia. Ibis 111:199–237.

COLLIAS, N. E., AND E. C. COLLIAS. 1956. Some mechanisms of family integration in ducks. Auk 73:378–400.

CUSHING, J. E., AND A. O. RAMSAY. 1949. The noninheritable aspects of family unity in birds. Condor 51:82–87.

GORMAN, M. L., AND H. MILNE. 1972. Crèche behaviour in the Common Eider, *Somateria m. mollissima* L. Ornis Scandinavica 3:21–26.

KOSKIMIES, J. 1957. Verhalten und Okologie der Jungen und der Jungenführenden Weibchen der Samtente. Ann. Zoologici Fennici 18:1–69.

LEWIS, H. F. 1959. Predation of Eider Ducks by Great Black-backed Gulls in Nova Scota. Unpubl. Rep. for the Nova Scotia Dept. of Lands and Forests, Halifax.

MCALONEY, R. K. 1973. Brood ecology of the Common Eider (*Somateria mollissima dresseri*) in the Liscombe area of Nova Scotia. Unpubl. M.S. Thesis. Wolfville, Nova Scota, Acadia Univ.

MILNE, H. 1963. Seasonal distribution and breeding biology of the Eider *Somateria mollissima mollissima* L., in north-east of Scotland. Unpubl. Ph.D. Thesis. Aberdeen, Univ. Aberdeen.

MUNRO, J. 1975. L'élevage des jeunes chez l'Eider commun (*Somateria mollissima*) dans l'estuaire du Saint-Laurent. Unpubl. M.S. Thesis. Québec, Université Laval.

———, AND J. BÉDARD. 1977. Gull predation and crèching behavior in The Common Eider. J. Anim. Ecol. 46:124–136.

RAITASUO, K. 1964. Social behaviour of the Mallard *Anas platyrhynchos* in the course of the annual cycle. Papers on Game Research No. 24, Helsinki.

REED, A. 1973. Aquatic bird colonies in the Saint Lawrence estuary. Publ. No. 18, Ministère du tourisme, de la chasse et de la pêche, Québec.

ROBERTS, B. B. 1940. The breeding behaviour in penguins with special reference to *Pygoscelis papua* (Forster). Sci. Rept. Brit. Graham Land Exped. 1934–7 3:195–254.

ROBERTSON, D. J. 1929. Notes on the breeding habits of the Eiders in the Orkneys. Brit. Birds 23:26–30.

SCHALLER, G. 1964. Breeding behaviour of the White Pelican at Yellowstone Lake, Wyoming. Condor 66:3–23.

STONEHOUSE, B. 1960. The King Penguin *Aptenodytes patagonica* of South Georgia. Part 1. Breeding behaviour and development. Sci. Rept. Falkland Island Depend. Surv. No. 23.

WILLIAMS, M. J. 1974. Crèche behaviour of Shelduck (*Tadorna tadorna* L.). Paper presented at the 14th Intern. Ornithol. Congr. Canberra.

SELECTED BIBLIOGRAPHY

Reproductive Ecology: Behavior

BAILEY, R. O., N. R. SEYMOUR, AND G. R. STEWART. 1978. Rape behavior in blue-winged teal. Auk 95:188–190.

COLLIAS, N. E., AND E. C. COLLIAS. 1956. Some mechanisms of family integration in ducks. Auk 73(3):378–400.

COOKE, F., AND C. M. MCNALLY. 1975. Mate selection and colour preferences in lesser snow geese. Behaviour 53(1–2):151–170.

———, P. J. MIRSKY, AND M. B. SEIGER. 1972. Color preferences in the lesser snow goose and their possible role in mate selection. Can. J. Zool. 50(5):529–536.

DANE, B., AND W. G. VAN DER KLOOT. 1964. An analysis of the display of the goldeneye duck (*Bucephala clangula* L.). Behaviour 22(3–4): 282–328.

DES LAURIERS, J. R., AND B. H. BRATTSTROM. 1965. Cooperative feeding behavior in red-breasted mergansers. Auk 82(4):639.

DZUBIN, A. 1957. Pairing display and spring and summer flights of the mallard. Blue Jay 15(1):10–13.

HANSON, H. C. 1953. Inter-family dominace in Canada geese. Auk 70(1):11–16.

HESS, E. H. 1959. Imprinting. Science 130(3368):133–141.

HORI, J. 1963. Three-bird flights in the mallard. 14th Annu. Rep. Wildfowl Trust 1961–62. pp. 124–132.

JOHNSGARD, P. A. 1960. Pair formation mechanisms in *Anas* (Anatidae) and related genera. Ibis 102:616–618.

———. 1960. A quantitative study of sexual behavior of mallards and black ducks. Wilson Bull. 72(2):133–155.

———. 1961. The sexual behavior and systematic postion of the hooded merganser. Wilson Bull. 73(3):227–236.

———. 1963. Behavioral isolating mechanisms in the family Anatidae. Proc. XIII Int. Ornithol. Congr. pp. 531–543.

———. 1964. Comparative behavior and relationships of the eiders. Condor 66(2):113–129.

———, AND J. KEAR. 1968. A review of parental carrying of young by waterfowl. Living Bird 7:89–102.

KORSCHGEN, C. E., AND L. H. FREDRICKSON. 1976. Comparative displays of yearling and adult male wood ducks. Auk 93(4):793–807.

LEBRET, T. 1958. The "jump-flight" of the mallard, *Anas platyrhynchos* L., the teal, *Anas crecca* L. and the shoveler, *Spatula clypeata* L. Ardea 46 (1/2):68–72.

———. 1961. The pair formation in the annual cycle of the mallard, *Anas platyrhynchos* L. Ardea 49(3/4):97–158.

MARTIN, E. M., AND A. O. HAUGEN. 1960. Seasonal changes in wood duck roosting flight habits. Wilson Bull. 72(3):238–243.

MATTSON, M. E., AND R. M. EVANS. 1974. Visual imprinting and auditory-discrimination learning in young of the canvasback and semiparasitic redhead (Anatidae). Can. J. Zool. 52(3):421–427.

MCKINNEY, F. 1965. The comfort movements of Anatidae. Behaviour 25(1–2):120–220.

———. 1965. The spring behavior of wild steller eiders. Condor 67(4): 273–290.

———. 1970. Displays of four species of bluewinged ducks. Living Bird 9:29–64.

NICE, M. M. 1953. Some experiments in imprinting ducklings. Condor 55(1):33–37.

ORING, L. W. 1964. Behavior and ecology of certain ducks during the postbreeding period. J. Wildl. Manage. 28(2):223–233.

PREVETT, J. P., AND C. D. MACINNES. 1980. Family and other social groups in snow geese. Wildl. Monogr. 71. 46pp.

RAVELING, D. G. 1969. Preflight and flight behavior of Canada geese. Auk 86(4):671–681.

———. 1969. Social classes of Canada geese in winter. J. Wildl. Manage. 33(2):304–318.

———. 1970. Dominance relationships and agonistic behavior of Canada geese in winter. Behaviour 37:291–319.

RYDER, J. P. 1975. The significance of territory size in colonial nesting geese—An hypothesis. Wildfowl 26:114–116.

SIEGFRIED, W. R. 1974. Time budget of behavior among lesser scaups on Delta Marsh. J. Wildl. Manage. 38(4):708–713.

SMITH, R. I. 1968. The social aspects of reproductive behavior in the pintail. Auk 85(3):381–396.

STEWART, G. R., AND R. D. TITMAN. 1980. Territorial behavior by prairie pothole blue-winged teal. Can. J. Zool. 58(4):639–649.

WELLER, M. W. 1959. Parasitic egg laying in the redhead (*Aythya americana*) and other North American Anatidae. Ecol. Monogr. 29:333–365.

———. 1967. Courtship of the redhead (*Aythya americana*). Auk 84(4):544–559.

Drought

EFFECT OF DROUGHT ON REPRODUCTION OF THE LESSER SCAUP

JOHN P. ROGERS, Gaylord Memorial Laboratory, University of Missouri, Puxico

Abstract: Responses of the lesser scaup (*Aythya affinis*) to severe drought were studied on a 1-square-mile pothole area in southwestern Manitoba from 1957 to 1960. The population decreased 63 percent in 1959 and 29 percent in 1960. The decline resulted from an abrupt decrease in water level. This caused an abnormally early departure of pairs from their nesting potholes, which were either dry or had wide mud flats exposed around the perimeters early in the season. Another important factor in the decline was a failure in production. In 1959, when habitat conditions were poorest, nesting was inhibited in most of the resident pairs. Searching by hens for nest sites decreased in intensity, and only 8 percent of the pairs nested. Groups of pairs loafed on the larger potholes throughout the season. Inhibition was reflected in low ovarian weights and follicular atresia. The presence of mud flats, rather than lack of nesting cover around the pothole perimeters, appeared to be the inhibitory factor. In 1958 and 1960, strong nesting efforts were made but were broken up by excessive predation, mostly by skunks (*Mephitis mephitis*). Scaups appear to be more vulnerable than other ducks to nest predators because they nest late in the season when predators are more abundant, and they nest close to the edge of the water where predators frequently hunt. The effect of nest predation on scaup production is especially severe because few hens renest if the first nest is lost.

Although the lesser scaup is one of the most abundant ducks in North America, information on its ecology is scarce. This is partly because most of its breeding range is in northwestern Canada and Alaska, where it is not easily accessible, and partly because waterfowl biologists have been concerned with other, more important, game ducks.

Most lesser scaups breed in the far north, but many nest in the parklands of southwestern Canada where drought is frequent. This paper reports the effect of drought on a breeding population of lesser scaup on a 1-square-mile study area in southwestern Manitoba, Canada. Observations were made during four breeding seasons, 1957–60, in which extreme differences in water conditions prevailed. Changes in reproductive behavior and success are described, and an attempt is made to relate these to changes in water conditions during the drought. A preliminary report on the first 2 years of this study was given earlier (Rogers 1959), and pertinent data from that paper are included in this report.

This paper presents one aspect of a general study of the lesser scaup. Financial support was provided by the Missouri Cooperative Wildlife Research Unit and the Delta Waterfowl Research Station. Additional support was received in 1958 from the Frank M. Chapman Memorial Fund of the American Museum of Natural History. I am indebted to William H. Elder, University of Missouri, and H. Albert Hochbaum, Delta Waterfowl Research Station, for advice and assistance throughout the study. Thanks are also due Thomas S. Baskett, U. S. Bureau of Sport Fisheries and Wildlife, and D. Frank McKinney and Peter Ward of the Delta Station.

LOCALE

The study was made in the Minnedosa pothole country—site of several previous waterfowl studies (Evans et al. 1952, Kiel 1955). General descriptions of the country have been given by these workers, as well as by Ehrlich et al. (1958), and need not be repeated here.

The most intensive observations were made on a square-mile block of potholes 2

Originally published in J. Wildl. Manage. 28(2):213–222, 1964.

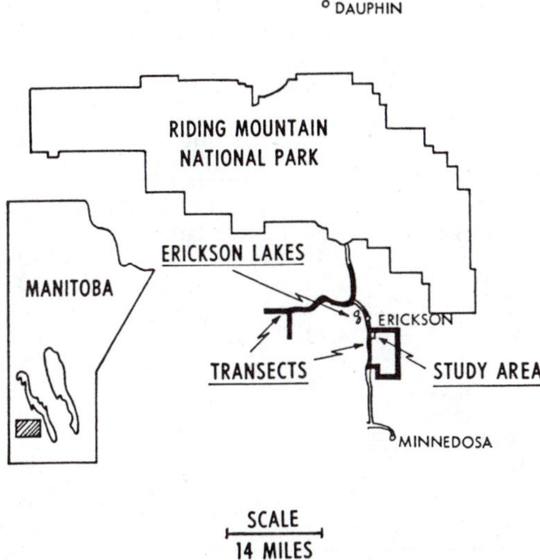

Fig. 1. Location of the Study Area, Erickson Lakes, and Transects, near Erickson, Manitoba.

miles south of the town of Erickson. Supplementary observations were made on two nearby lakes of 150 and 200 acres maximum size, and along two roadside transects running 50 miles through the pothole country. These areas are shown in Fig. 1 and will be referred to as the Study Area, Erickson Lakes, and the Transects.

The lesser scaup is a common nester here, even though the region lies near the southeastern border of this scaup's breeding range. On the Study Area it was the most abundant breeding duck, and, on the other areas, it ranked second or third in abundance. Thirteen other species of breeding ducks were present; most abundant were the mallard (*Anas platyrhynchos*) and the blue-winged teal (*Anas discors*).

The 26 potholes on the Study Area are described and classified in Table 1, and their size and distribution are shown in Fig. 2. They depend on surface runoff for their water supply, and they lose water by evaporation. Water levels are usually highest in spring but fall during the summer, when high temperatures and dry winds prevail. Occasionally, the water level is raised in autumn by heavy rains but otherwise remains relatively stable until the following spring.

METHODS

Population counts were made weekly on the Study Area and the Erickson Lakes. Counts were begun between 8:00 and 9:00 AM and required 2–3½ hours for completion on each area.

Lesser scaups were recorded as pairs, lone males, or lone females. Lone females were assumed to represent pairs. This assumption was not made in the case of males, because they outnumbered females, indicating that many males were not mated.

Pairs present the first week of June were considered resident, because spring migration was over and nesting began about this time in southern Manitoba. However, in 1957, the first census on the Study Area was not made until June 26, when some females were known to be incubating. Since these females represented pairs not seen during the census, the pair count was considered low. Accordingly, the number of resident pairs for 1957 is based on the number of broods produced (27)

Table 1. Classification and description of potholes on the Study Area.

CLASS	NUMBER	FEATURES
Permanent	7	Water 4 feet deep or more; emergent vegetation confined to perimeter; open water persistent after several years of drought.
Semipermanent	6	Water 2–4 feet deep; emergent vegetation not confined to perimeter; dry after 1 or 2 years of drought.
Temporary	13	Water 2 feet deep or less; usually dry each summer.

divided by the known percentage of successful nests (50 percent).

We located nests by observing females in the morning as they left or returned to their nests, and by searching cover with the aid of a Labrador retriever. Because few lesser scaup nested more than 50 feet from water, nest searching was concentrated within this zone of cover around each pothole. It is unlikely that many nests were overlooked.

Production was measured by counting broods. On the Study Area and the Erickson Lakes, they were counted during the weekly census. On the Transects, a single roadside count was made just before the oldest young on the other two areas could fly. This provided a sample of production over an extensive area, for comparison with counts on the two smaller areas.

Hatching dates were calculated by estimating the age of each brood and backdating from the day of observation. Age estimates were based on size and plumage development, criteria similar to those presented by Weller (1957) for the redhead (*Aythya americana*).

Lesser scaups were collected in spring

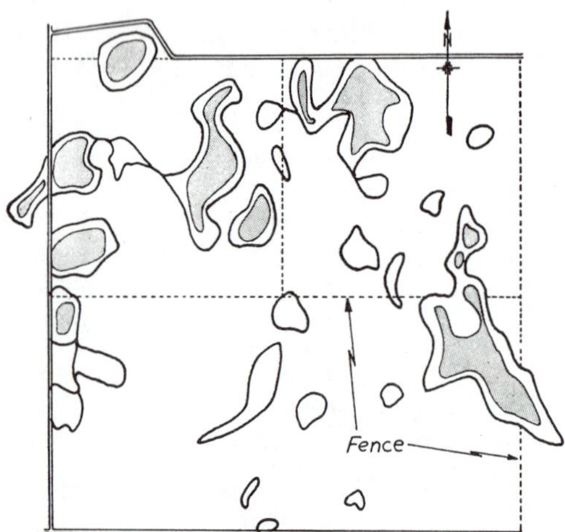

Fig. 2. The size and distribution of Study Area potholes on June 20, 1957 (outline) and June 20, 1959 (shaded).

Table 2. Precipitation at Dauphin, Manitoba, 1951–60, the nearest weather station, 44 miles north of Erickson. (Courtesy of the Canadian Department of Transport, Meteorological Branch, Toronto.)

Month	Ten-year Mean	Mean 1953–56	Mean 1957–60
January	1.21	1.83	0.71
February	0.72	0.98	0.51
March	0.98	1.20	0.76
April	1.12	1.12	1.20
May	1.82	2.39	1.90
June	4.20	6.72	2.63
July	1.77	1.97	1.65
August	2.61	1.93	2.45
September	1.98	2.89	2.45
October	1.24	1.25	1.39
November	1.15	1.47	1.00
December	1.09	1.40	1.00
Totals	19.89	25.14	16.43

and summer, 1959 and 1960, for examination of the gonads. They were collected on potholes near Erickson, where shooting did not interfere with other observations. Gonads were removed in the field, preserved in Bouin's fluid or in 10 percent formalin, and examined later in the laboratory. After blotting excess moisture from the gonads, they were weighed on a torsion balance. Ovarian follicles were measured with a vernier caliper, and ovulated and atretic follicles were counted.

Residence was maintained on the Study Area during each field season except in 1960, when brief but regular visits were made from Delta. Periods of observation were as follows: June 16–September 4, 1957; April 18–September 4, 1958; April 29–August 20, 1959; May 13–August 1, 1960.

OBSERVATIONS AND DISCUSSION

Changes in Water Level and Vegetation

As a result of more than average precipitation from 1953 to 1956 (Table 2), unusually high water levels prevailed in the lakes and potholes of southern Manitoba when this study began. Around Erickson,

Table 3. Annual change in resident pairs of lesser scaup on the Study Area.

YEAR	NUMBER OF PAIRS	PERCENT CHANGE FROM PREVIOUS YEAR
1957	54	—
1958	65	+20
1959	24	-63
1960	17	-29

water overflowed the pothole basins and flooded the surrounding sedge meadows.

During the period of rising water, stands of emergent vegetation were drowned out and new ones were formed near the edges of expanded water areas. Old roots and stubble, exposed when the water receded, showed where vegetation had been. Occasionally, old grain stubble was found where pothole edges had been dry enough to be cultivated. In most cases the area of old roots was continuous with the area of living vegetation, indicating that relocation had kept pace with the edge of advancing water.

In the summer of 1957, the period of abundant precipitation ended. On the Study Area, the water level began falling in July and by mid-August had retreated from the meadows surrounding the potholes.

Water supplies were not replenished during fall and winter, and the spring and summer precipitation was extremely light in 1958. Most potholes were still full, but the surrounding meadows were dry when scaups began nesting in June. From then on the water level in the potholes dropped rapidly. Bulrush and cattail stands were partially dry by mid-June, and, in July, they were isolated by gradually increasing areas of bare mud. Only 9 of 26 potholes on the Study Area still contained water by mid-August.

The same nine potholes, with wide mud flats interposed between the edge of the water and the nearest vegetation, were the only ones available to the ducks in the spring of 1959. Light, but timely, rains during the summer reduced water loss and prevented complete desiccation of more potholes.

Heavy rains in September, 1959, followed by more than 50 inches of snow in October, provided the first significant additions of water to the potholes since 1957. More was added by rainfall in May, 1960. In June, all but two recently ditched potholes were full, the mud flats were submerged, and water extended to, but did not flood, the surrounding meadows. Thus, conditions were quite similar to those at the beginning of the lesser scaup nesting season in 1958.

The great change in water conditions during the study is illustrated by the difference in number and size of potholes on the Study Area between June, 1957, and June, 1959 (Fig. 2). The decrease in water area was approximately 63 percent. An aerial photograph was used to determine pothole sizes in 1957. The change in each subsequent year was measured and mapped in the field against 1957 boundaries. Water area was estimated from the maps with a dot-grid. In mid-June each year, the following acreages of water were present: 1957—135; 1958—85; 1959—50; 1960—95.

With the filling of the potholes again in 1960, emergent vegetation was greatly improved. During the summer, hardstem bulrush (*Scirpus acutus*) extended out into the water in the most flourishing stands since 1957. Nevertheless, many potholes were bare of cover because the edges were cultivated or mowed and grazed during 1958 and 1959. Such practices are common in this region when water is low; it is probable that 2 or more years of high water are necessary before good cover is reestablished.

Decrease in Scaup Population

One of the most obvious changes in the lesser scaup population was an abrupt decrease beginning in 1959. Table 3 shows that the number of resident pairs on the Study Area suddenly declined 63 percent in 1959 and 29 percent in 1960.

A decline in lesser scaup numbers in 1959 is also shown by counts on the Erickson Lakes (Fig. 3), but there was no change in the year preceding or the year following. These lakes were concentration areas for large numbers of transient scaups indistinguishable from residents. Variations in the rate of movement of transients may have obscured all but very large annual differences in population levels.

Early Departure of Pairs from Breeding Areas

An important factor in the sudden population decrease on the Study Area in 1959 was an abnormally early departure of resident pairs from their nesting potholes. Fig. 4 shows that the number of pairs declined rapidly in late May and early June, 1959, in contrast to the relatively stable population during the same period in 1958. Resident pairs apparently arrived on the Study Area in the spring of 1959, but instead of remaining and nesting, as in 1958, they moved on after a brief stay. Furniss

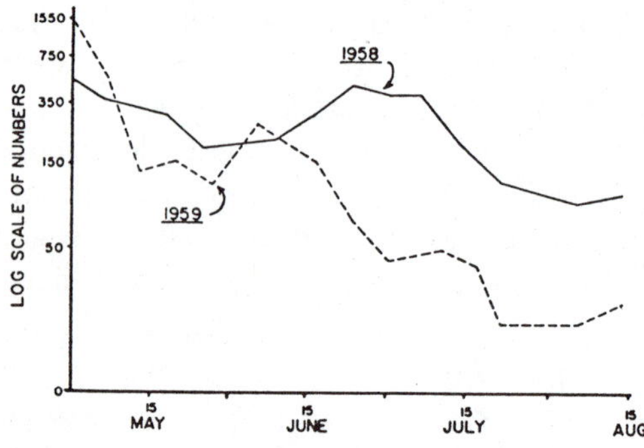

Fig. 3. Counts of lesser scaup on the Erickson Lakes from spring migration to late summer.

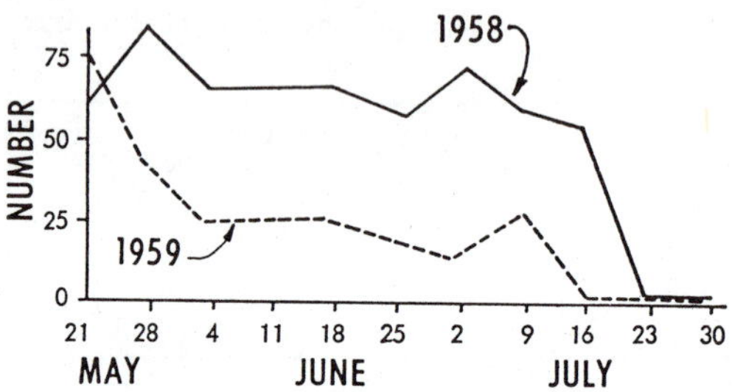

Fig. 4. Seasonal change in number of resident pairs on the Study Area.

(1938:22–23) observed a decrease of 40 percent in adult lesser scaups when the water level declined on his study area, and he conjectured that this "decrease may have been due to a movement farther north than during previous years. . . ."

Extremely low water levels on the Study Area in the period just prior to nesting probably caused the decrease in population. Many potholes were completely dry, and wide mud flats were exposed in the few that contained water. Mendall (1958: 241) found that low breeding populations of ring-necked ducks (*Aythya collaris*) and black ducks (*Anas rubripes*) often resulted if water levels were unfavorable during a brief critical period just before nesting.

A direct relationship between the number of breeding pairs of ducks and the number of water areas has been noted by Evans and Black (1956), Schroeder (1959), and Salyer (1962). Lesser scaups probably were similarly affected. However, the suddenness of the decrease, coupled with the fact that resident pairs increased in 1958 in spite of a decrease in water area, suggests that lesser scaups were responding to the poor quality of the potholes as well as to the decrease in number. Stoudt (1959) apparently reached a similar conclusion for various species of ducks in Saskatchewan.

No direct evidence was obtained to show an early departure of pairs from other pothole areas in 1959, but population counts on the Erickson Lakes suggest that such a movement was widespread. After transients reached a peak of abundance during migration in early May, a second concentration of scaups occurred, usually in late June or early July. In 1959, however, it occurred in the first week of June—3 weeks earlier than in 1958 (Fig. 3).

The June–July concentration of scaups consisted mostly of males that were beginning the postnuptial molt. Presumably, they were en route to traditional molting lakes farther north (Hochbaum 1944), after having completed or given up their reproductive efforts for the year. The proportion of females accompanying them varied annually, apparently depending on the success of the breeding season. In 1957, when many females nested successfully and remained on the breeding areas with broods, the ratio of males to females was 14:1; in 1959, when many pairs abandoned the potholes early without making a nesting attempt, it was 3.2:1.

The counts on the Erickson Lakes thus show an influx of lesser scaup pairs into an area known to be used mainly by transients. The influx occurred in early June when scaups should have been on their breeding areas preparing to nest. It seems likely that the early movement of pairs away from breeding areas was widespread in the region around Erickson in 1959.

Inhibition of Nesting

Of the pairs that remained on the Study Area during the nesting season of 1959, only a few attempted to nest; most appeared to be inhibited by the extremely low water conditions.

Intensive observations on the four best nesting potholes on the Study Area revealed inhibition of nesting. The resident pairs on these potholes were watched closely from late May to late July for signs of nesting activity. In 1958 and 1959, observations were made 3 or 4 mornings per week and, in 1960, 2 or 3 mornings every other week. No comparable observations were made in 1957. Whenever a female was thought to be going to a nest, the location was carefully noted. When the cover around these potholes was searched for nests, particular attention was given to these probable nest locations.

Table 4. Percent of resident pairs that nested on four potholes, 1958–60.

Year	Number of Pairs	Number of Nests Found	Percent of Pairs Nesting
1958	25	16	64
1959	12	1	8
1960	5	3	60

The results of these observations (Table 4) show that only 8 percent of the resident pairs nested in 1959, whereas 60–64 percent nested in the other years. Nests were not found for every pair in 1958 and 1960, which may indicate that some inhibition occurred in these years as well. However, it is probable that some nests were overlooked, especially if the eggs were taken by predators, and that some pairs nested elsewhere. This could not account for the scarcity of nests in 1959, because cover was more thoroughly searched that year and fewer surrounding potholes contained water.

The behavior of pairs observed during the morning watches indicated that the intensity and duration of the search for nest sites was low in 1959. During the nesting season, scaup pairs often walked into the nesting cover or landed in it after flying about in low circles. Presumably they were searching for nest sites. The females could often be seen exploring clumps of vegetation. In 1958, this be-

Table 5. Weights of ovaries of lesser scaup collected near Erickson, Manitoba. Numbers in parentheses represent sample size.

MONTH	AVERAGE WEIGHT (GRAMS)	
	1959	1960
May	0.84 (5)	0.89 (4)
June	6.22 (5)	13.95 (3)
July	0.96 (7)	3.06 (3)
Totals	2.47 (17)	7.46 (10)

havior was seen in 57 percent of 94 observations of pairs from May 14 to July 18. The data for 1960, though less complete, indicated a similar level of activity. In 1959, searching for nest sites was observed in only 40 percent of 73 observations of pairs, and it began 22 days later and ended a week earlier than in 1958 and 1960.

Other changes in behavior reflected poor nesting conditions. In the years of low production, groups of pairs were commonly seen loafing on the larger potholes throughout the nesting season. In contrast, pairs disappeared at a steady rate beginning in late June, 1957, and few remained by mid-July. This was because increasing numbers of females were incubating and were no longer with males. In years when few nests were successful and some females did not nest, many pairs remained intact until the second or third week in July, then suddenly broke up.

Gonadal Inhibition

Inhibition of nesting was associated with incomplete ovarian development. Weights of ovaries collected on breeding areas near Erickson were much lower in 1959 than in 1960 (Table 5). Only one of eight females collected during the nesting period (June 1–July 18, 1959) was laying. Ovarian weights of the other seven females ranged from 0.4 to 4.6 grams, and only three had follicles as large as 10 mm in diameter. In contrast, fully developed ovaries of other lesser scaups examined during this study weighed nearly 30 grams, and mature follicles measured approximately 30 mm in diameter.

In 1959, follicles 10 mm in diameter or more were often atretic and being absorbed. The largest follicles in the three most advanced ovaries of nonlaying hens were atretic, and, even in the laying hen, two large follicles were atretic. Two laying hens collected in 1960 had no atretic follicles, but the largest follicles in the ovaries of two nonlaying hens were atretic.

Gonads were not collected in 1958. However, one marked female that had completed laying on June 26, 1958, was accidentally killed at a power line on June 25, 1959. An examination of her ovary revealed that she had laid no eggs in 1959; the ovary weighed only 3.2 grams and the three largest follicles were atretic.

No difference in average testicular weights in 1959 and 1960 was found. Histological examination of the testes showed that in both years primary spermatocytes in synizesis were present in the earliest May collections, indicating that spermatogenesis had begun. Large clusters of spermatozoa were abundant in testes collected in June.

The data presented above show that the female, but not the male, reproductive cycle was depressed in 1959. There seemed to be no depression of early stages of ovarian development, for weights of ovaries collected in May of 1959 did not differ from those collected in May of 1960.

Role of Environmental Factors in Reproductive Inhibition

Marshall (1959) summarized evidence showing that the presence or absence of critical environmental factors may delay or completely inhibit reproduction in

Table 6. Distance of lesser scaup nests from water.

Year	Number of Nests	Distance from Nearest Water (feet)	
		Average	Range
1957	12	7	1–45
1958	26	109	3–900
1959	16	125	15–600
1960	8	21	3–35

birds. Among ducks and other marsh birds, the most important factors are those associated with changes in water level (Johnsgard 1956, Mendall 1958, Weller et al. 1958).

It is difficult to determine by observation alone which aspect of the change in water level is detrimental. In some Australian ducks, water level apparently directly influences the reproductive cycle. Thus, during periods of drought, the gonads of the grey teal (*Anas gibberifrons*) and the pink-eared duck (*Malacorhynchus membranaceus*) remained small and inactive (Frith 1959). With a rise in water level, the gonads enlarged, sexual display occurred and was followed by breeding, regardless of the season of the year.

Since these Australian ducks nest in tree cavities, the change in water level presumably did not exert its influence by altering the nesting habitat. On the other hand, data presented by Mendall (1949, 1958) indicate that water level indirectly influenced black duck and ring-necked duck nesting by its effect on the quality and quantity of nesting cover. Similar findings were reported by Barry (1962: 23) for the Atlantic brant (*Branta bernicla*). When snow and water covered their nesting habitat, many brant did not breed and the nearly mature ovarian follicles became atretic and were resorbed.

In the lesser scaup, also, water level appears to be important because of its effect on nesting habitat. The wide mud flats present in 1959 were inhibitory because of the unsuitable nesting conditions they created. Lesser scaups usually nest very close to the edge of the water; more than half of the 40 nests observed by Gehrman (1951) in Washington, and of the 98 nests observed by Keith (1961) in Alberta, were within 15 feet of the water's edge. The location of nests in relation to water during the present study is shown in Table 6. Only one nest was found more than 8 feet from water in 1957, but in 1959 no nest was closer than 15 feet, because bare mud flats, rather than nesting cover, occupied a zone 15–75 feet wide around the potholes. Apparently most lesser scaups will not nest under these conditions.

Although nests were located almost as far from water in 1958 as in 1959, no inhibition of nesting was found, apparently because mud flats were not exposed until after nesting began. In 1959, mud flats were present prior to the start of nesting.

Role of Predation

Scaup made strong efforts to nest every year, except at the peak of the drought in 1959. Only in 1957 were their efforts successful. Production of young near Erickson decreased 93 percent from 1957 to 1958 and remained low in the subsequent 2 years (Table 7).

The main reason for this poor production was excessive nest predation. Although predators destroyed 50 percent of observed nests in 1957, they destroyed 74

Table 7. Number of lesser scaup ducklings counted near Erickson.

Year	Location			Total
	Study Area	Erickson Lakes	Transects	
1957	237	551	169	957
1958	20	6	39	65
1959	11	0	9	20
1960	22	6	45	73

percent in the next 3 years (Table 8). In many cases the specific predator was unknown, but the appearance of nest and egg remains (Sowls 1948, Rearden 1951) and the presence of hairs showed that nearly all nests were destroyed by mammals. Skunks were the principal predator with weasels (*Mustela* sp.) and mink (*Mustela vison*) implicated in some cases.

In this study, as in those by Furniss (1938), Ellig (1955), and Stoudt (1959), increased skunk predation was associated with dry nesting cover. However, it is not clear why predation increased. No evidence was obtained to show that it was due to an increase in the skunk population. An unusual number of skunks may have been attracted to the nesting cover by the large number of meadow voles (*Microtus* sp.) present in the dry years. Although no population measurements were made, the number of voles observed in the vegetation around the potholes was much greater from 1958 to 1960 than in 1957. While hunting for voles, skunks could have found and destroyed many duck nests.

Even if more skunks were not attracted to the nesting cover, scaup nests may have been easier to find in the dry years because the female scaups had to walk to their nests instead of swim. Predators may have followed these land trails to the scaup nests.

Scaups are more susceptible to nest predation than are other ducks because of their tendency to nest close to the edge of the water. In Alberta, Keith (1961:61–63) found that, in the nesting cover used by scaups, predation was greater within 25 feet of the water than beyond 25 feet.

The fact that most lesser scaups do not begin nesting until June also exposes them to greater nest predation. Ellig (1955) found that in Montana predation became more severe as the season progressed. He believed that this was due to the appearance of foraging juvenile skunks in late June. Keith (1961:60) observed a similar situation in Alberta.

Table 8. Fate of lesser scaup nests found near Erickson.

YEAR	NUMBER OF NESTS	HATCHED	DESTROYED BY PREDATORS	OTHER LOSSES*	PERCENT SUCCESS
1957	12	6	6	0	50.0
1958	26	1	21	4	3.8
1959	16	1	10	5	6.3
1960	8	1	6	1	12.5

* Grazing, mowing, and four nests collected in 1959.

The effect of nest predation is further exaggerated in the lesser scaup because few hens renest. Keith (1961:67) calculated that 39 percent of unsuccessful lesser scaup hens renested on his study area as compared with 100 percent of unsuccessful mallard hens. In the present study, no evidence of lesser scaup renesting was found. Renesting must not be a very important factor in the productivity of this species. As Kalmbach (1937) pointed out, most scaup renesting would occur too late to enable the young to fly before freeze-up.

LITERATURE CITED

BARRY, T. W. 1962. Effect of late seasons on Atlantic brant reproduction. J. Wildl. Mgmt. 26(1):19–26.

EHRLICH, W. A., L. E. PRATT, E. A. POYSER, AND F. P. LECLAIRE. 1958. Report of reconnaissance soil survey of Westlake map sheet area. Manitoba Soil Survey Soils Rept. 8. 100pp.

ELLIG, L. J. 1955. Waterfowl relationships to Greenfields Lake, Teton County, Montana. Montana Fish and Game Dept. Tech. Bull. 1. 35pp.

EVANS, C. D., AND K. E. BLACK. 1956. Duck production studies on the prairie potholes of South Dakota. U. S. Fish and Wildl. Serv. Spec. Sci. Rept.—Wildl. 32. 59pp.

———, A. S. HAWKINS, AND W. H. MARSHALL. 1952. Movements of waterfowl broods in Manitoba. U. S. Fish and Wildl. Serv. Spec. Sci. Rept.—Wildl. 16. 47pp. + [18].

FRITH, H. J. 1959. The ecology of wild ducks in inland New South Wales. IV. Breeding. C.S.I.R.O. Wildl. Research 4(2):156–181.

FURNISS, O. C. 1938. The 1937 waterfowl season in the Prince Albert district, central Saskatchewan. Wilson Bull. 50(1):17–27.

GEHRMAN, K. H. 1951. An ecological study of the lesser scaup duck (*Aythya affinis*, Eyton) at West Medical Lake, Spokane Co., Washington. M.S. Thesis. State Coll. of Washington, Pullman. 94pp.

HOCHBAUM, H. A. 1944. The canvasback on a prairie marsh. The American Wildlife Institute, Washington, D. C. xii + 201pp.

JOHNSGARD, P. A. 1956. Effects of water fluctuation and vegetation change on bird populations, particularly waterfowl. Ecology 37 (4):689–701.

KALMBACH, E. R. 1937. Crow–waterfowl relationships. U. S. Dept. Agr. Circ. 433. 35pp.

KEITH, L. B. 1961. A study of waterfowl ecology on small impoundments in southeastern Alberta. Wildl. Monographs 6. 88pp.

KIEL, W. H., JR. 1955. Nesting studies of the coot in southwestern Manitoba. J. Wildl. Mgmt. 19(2):189–198.

MARSHALL, A. J. 1959. Internal and environmental control of breeding. Ibis 101(3–4): 456–478.

MENDALL, H. L. 1949. Breeding ground improvements for waterfowl in Maine. Trans. N. Am. Wildl. Conf. 14:58–63.

———. 1958. The ring-necked duck in the northeast. Univ. of Maine Studies, Second Ser. 73. xv + 317pp.

REARDEN, J. D. 1951. Identification of waterfowl nest predators. J. Wildl. Mgmt. 15 (4):386–395.

ROGERS, J. P. 1959. Low water and lesser scaup reproduction near Erickson, Manitoba. Trans. N. Am. Wildl. Conf. 24:216–223.

SALYER, J. W. 1962. Effects of drought and land use on prairie nesting ducks. Trans. N. Am. Wildl. Conf. 27:69–79.

SCHROEDER, C. H. 1959. No water! No ducks! North Dakota Outdoors 22(4):4–5.

SOWLS, L. K. 1948. The Franklin ground squirrel, *Citellus franklinii* (Sabine), and its relationship to nesting ducks. J. Mammal. 29(2):113–137.

STOUDT, J. H. 1959. 1959 progress report: Redvers waterfowl study area with comparative data for seven previous years. U. S. Bur. Sport Fisheries and Wildl. Wildl. Research Lab., Denver, Colorado. 110pp.

WELLER, M. W. 1957. Growth, weights, and plumages of the redhead, *Aythya americana*. Wilson Bull. 69(1):5–38.

———, B. H. WINGFIELD, AND J. B. LOW. 1958. Effects of habitat deterioration on bird populations of a small Utah marsh. Condor 60 (4):220–226.

Received for publication April 27, 1963.

RESPONSE OF PINTAIL BREEDING POPULATIONS TO DROUGHT

ROBERT I. SMITH, Bureau of Sport Fisheries and Wildlife, U.S. Department of the Interior, Washington, D.C.

Abstract: An inverse relationship ($r = -0.91$) between numbers of water areas on the prairies of Alberta and Saskatchewan and the portion of the pintail (*Anas acuta*) population moving north of the prairies and parklands is apparent for the years 1959–68. As the portion of the pintail population moving into northern areas increased, an index of annual production declined ($r = -0.92$).

Northward shifting of duck populations during periods of drought has been discussed by Hansen and McKnight (1964) and Crissey (1969). The pintail is an interesting species in this regard, for it is known to nest north of the Arctic Circle as well as on the prairies. Hansen and McKnight (1964), in a discussion of northward shifts of dabbling ducks, suggested that these species must have responded in this manner to drought over the ages. Waterfowl surveys that recorded shifts of pintails northward first occurred during the drought of 1949. Changes in the distribution of pintails were reported by Smith (1949) and Smith and Lawrence (1949). Similar drought conditions occurred in 1959 and continuously from 1961 through 1964. Water conditions on the prairies were relatively good in 1960 and during the 1965–67 period. The purpose of this paper is to explore the relationships between shifts of pintail populations and the abundance of water on the prairies; and to examine the annual production of pintails, which has varied, apparently as a result of drought and the subsequent population shifts.

PROCEDURES AND RESULTS

The distribution of breeding populations of pintails, 1959–68, was examined using results of waterfowl surveys conducted by the United States Bureau of Sport Fisheries and Wildlife (Martinson et al. 1968). These surveys are made from aircraft flown at speeds of 95–110 miles/hr along standardized transects. The proportion of waterfowl on the ground that are not visible from aircraft is determined by concurrent air and ground counts on selected areas. This results in two estimates of population density, one that is corrected for visibility and one that is not corrected. The indexes of pintail populations used in this study do not include adjustments for visibility bias, because visibility correction factors for areas north of the prairies and parklands are based upon small samples and are of questionable accuracy.

Numbers of ponds are recorded from aircraft during the waterfowl surveys, and pond densities are expanded to the total area within each stratum. This indicator of surface-water abundance was examined for the southern portion of Saskatchewan and Alberta. The areas selected for population indexes and pond densities do not represent all of the breeding range of the pintail; however, they include those portions that were most important in determining the distribution of the species during the 1959–68 period. Survey coverage of northern waterfowl areas has never been complete, but transects in major waterfowl breeding areas north of the parklands provide data that are comparable from year to year over the 1959–68 intervals. These data provide a measure of the relative magnitude of northward shifts when years are compared, but they do not measure the absolute magnitude of such shifts.

Originally published in J. Wildl. Manage. 34(4):943–946, 1970.

Table 1. Pintail breeding population indexes, prairie pond indexes, and age ratios.

Year	Population Indexes in May (Thousands)		Ratio Northern/Southern	Prairie Pond Index in May (Millions)	Im./Ad. in U.S. Harvest
	Northern	Southern			
1959	1402	917	1.52	1.28	—[a]
1960	609	1207	.50	3.09	—[a]
1961	913	510	1.79	1.29	0.76
1962	647	448	1.44	1.87	1.10
1963	532	611	.87	1.81	1.29
1964	561	528	1.06	1.82	0.97
1965	399	640	.62	2.68	1.54
1966	360	968	.37	2.72	1.45
1967	308	1182	.26	2.84	1.50
1968	705	435	1.62	1.30	0.65

[a] Information on age ratios was not available until 1961.

The relationship between numbers of pintails in northern areas and numbers in the prairies and parklands was calculated and expressed as the following ratio:

$$\text{Ratio northern/southern populations} = \frac{\text{Population indexes for northern Alberta, British Columbia, Northwest Territories, and Alaska}}{\text{Population indexes for southern Alberta and southern Saskatchewan}}$$

This ratio was used rather than the indexes, to eliminate yearly variation in the size of the continental population of pintails.

To examine the northward shifts of pintail populations in relation to annual production, the ratio of immatures per adult in the United States harvest of pintails was used as an index of pintail production (Croft and Carney 1969, U.S.D.I. Migratory Bird Pop. Sta.; and Smart, 1965, U.S.D.I. Migratory Bird Pop. Sta.). Since immatures are more vulnerable than adults to shooting pressure, and it was assumed that this relative vulnerability to gunning pressure was constant from year to year, the age ratios used merely reflect production trends. Information on age ratios prior to 1961 was not available.

A summary of pintail population indexes in May, prairie ponds in May, and age ratios from the fall harvest, is presented in Table 1. A regression analysis (Fig. 1) using data from Table 1 indicates that the proportion of the pintail population moving to northern areas varied inversely with the number of ponds on the prairie ($r = -0.91$, $P \leqslant 0.01$). A regression of age ratios on ratios of northern to southern populations (Fig. 2) shows an inverse relationship ($r = -0.92$, $P \leqslant 0.01$). When prairie ponds are scarce, pintails tend to move northward; and in northern areas pintail production is low.

DISCUSSION

Two noticeable characteristics of pintail habitat are shallow water (Smith 1968) and the absence of tall emergent aquatic plants (Sowls 1955). On the prairie, pintail habitat recurs at intervals as the distribution of surface water changes during periods of water abundance and scarcity. Pintails seem to prefer types of wetland that are subject to seasonal and annual instability. One might expect that animals adapted to such conditions would be quick to respond to change. Also, it seems appropriate for such animals to avoid strong attachments to specific locations.

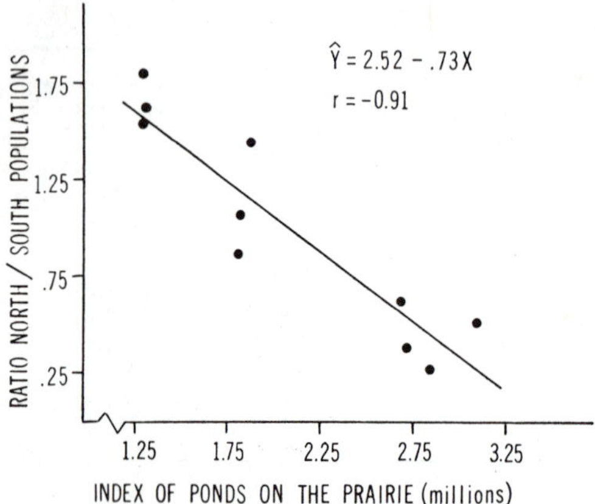

Fig. 1. Shifts in the distribution of pintails in relation to numbers of ponds on the prairies of Alberta and Saskatchewan in May.

Each spring a large segment of the North American pintail population arrives in flocks on the prairies of Alberta and Saskatchewan. These flocks are composed of pairs, and it would appear that they are confronted with several alternatives. All pairs could disperse over the available habitat and begin nesting, or some pairs could occupy the available water areas while social pressures force others to disperse widely and perhaps randomly. The data presented indicate that varying proportions of the pintail population continue to move northward, depending upon the abundance of prairie ponds. Since pintail production in northern areas appears to be low, it can be surmised that survival of adult pintails must become paramount during droughts. Stating the point another way, northern areas contain a reservoir of pintails which supplies the prairies with breeding populations when conditions there are favorable. Lynch et al. (1963) drew a somewhat similar conclusion regarding the role of northern areas in prairie waterfowl production.

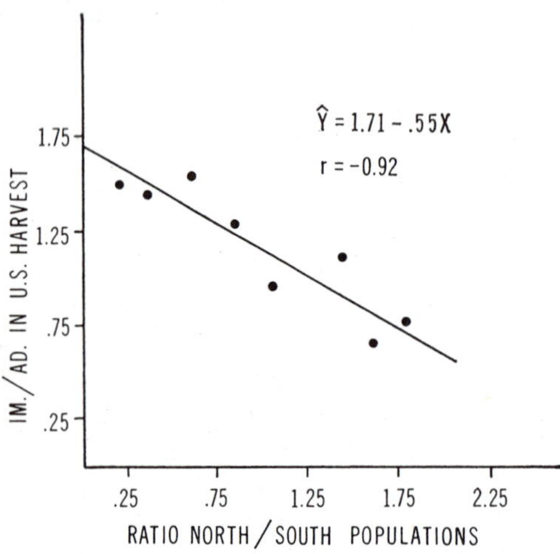

Fig. 2. Changes in an index of pintail production in relation to changes in the distribution of the population.

LITERATURE CITED

CRISSEY, W. F. 1969. Prairie potholes from a continental viewpoint. Canadian Wildl. Serv. Rept. Ser. 6:161–171.

HANSEN, H. A., AND D. E. MCKNIGHT. 1964. Emigration of drought-displaced ducks to the Arctic. Trans. N. Am. Wildl. Conf. 29:119–127.

LYNCH, J. J., C. D. EVANS, AND V. C. CONOVER. 1963. Inventory of waterfowl environments of prairie Canada. Trans. N. Am. Wildl. Conf. 28:93–109.

MARTINSON, R. K., J. F. VOELZER, AND MILDRED R. HUDGINS. 1968. Waterfowl status report 1968. U. S. Fish Wildl. Serv., Spec. Sci. Rept. Wildl. 122. 158pp.

SMITH, A. G. 1949. Waterfowl populations and breeding conditions, summer 1949. U. S. Fish Wildl. Serv., Spec. Sci. Rept. Wildl. 2. Pp.43.

SMITH, R. H., AND C. H. LAWRENCE. 1949. Waterfowl populations and breeding conditions, summer 1949. U. S. Fish Wildl. Serv., Spec. Sci. Rept. Wildl. 2. Pp.5–9.

SMITH, R. I. 1968. The social aspects of reproductive behavior in the pintail. Auk 85 (3):381–396.

SOWLS, L. K. 1955. Prairie ducks. The Wildlife Management Institute, Washington, D. C. 193pp.

Received for publication January 20, 1970.

EMIGRATION OF DROUGHT-DISPLACED DUCKS TO THE ARCTIC[1]

HENRY A. HANSEN[2] and DONALD E. MCKNIGHT, Bureau of Sport Fisheries and Wildlife, Juneau, AK

When the prairie pothole region is periodically seared by drought what happens to the ducks which ordinarily use this area for nesting? How far will they travel to find suitable conditions and what is their reproductive success in the new environment?

These questions are of primary concern both in immediate and in long-range management plans. Current regulations should reflect reproductive success throughout the range of all species, and particularly the most vulnerable. For the future, acquisition and/or safeguarding of habitat should be emphasized on the very important periphery of the breeding range as well as on the prairies.

Progress has been made during the most recent drought in the plains states and Canadian prairie provinces to determine the emigration pattern of drought-displaced ducks. This paper is based upon data from aerial surveys in general and from specific ground studies in east-central Alaska, the terminus for several species of displaced prairie ducks. The evidence from aerial surveys is massive and circumstantial. That from the ground studies is a collection of minutiae corroborating the aerial.

MASSIVE EVIDENCE OF NORTHWARD MOVEMENT

For purposes of illustration, only the dabbling ducks will be considered in this instance. They are conveniently grouped in the summary reports and are more nearly representative of the prairies than the divers. Although canvasback and redhead are largely prairie oriented, to include the entire group of diving ducks would throw the analogy out of perspective. The northern breeding population is weighted heavily with scaup and scoter and to a lesser extent with goldeneye and bufflehead, none of which would be affected greatly by adverse conditions on the prairies.

The cumulative aerial survey data show an inverse relationship between duck populations on the southern prairies and in the northern habitat during periods of duress in the former (Crissey 1961). As prairie potholes disappear and their associated waterfowl population diminishes, the duck population expands in the north. When the prairie becomes re-watered, it absorbs ducks at the expense of the north. These population shifts move rather consistently in the same direction, but not in the same magnitude, and only for a limited number of years (Fig. 1). The prairie pothole dabbling duck breeding population index dropped from a high of 12.6 million birds in 1956 to 6.5 million in 1959, a loss of 6 million. During the same period, the dabbler index in northern Alberta, NWT and Alaska climbed from 1.6 million to 3.9 million, a gain of only 2.3 million.

A temporary respite in the prairie drought reversed the downward trend there slightly in 1960 where a breeding population index of 6.6 million dabbling ducks was calculated, up 0.1 million from the previous year. The northern index in 1960 decreased from 3.8 to 1.9 million dabblers, a loss far greater than the in-

[1] Originally published in Trans. North Am. Wildl. Nat. Resour. Conf. 29:119–126, 1964.

[2] Address correspondence to this author. Present address: 1563 E. Polnell Rd., Oak Harbor, WA 98277.

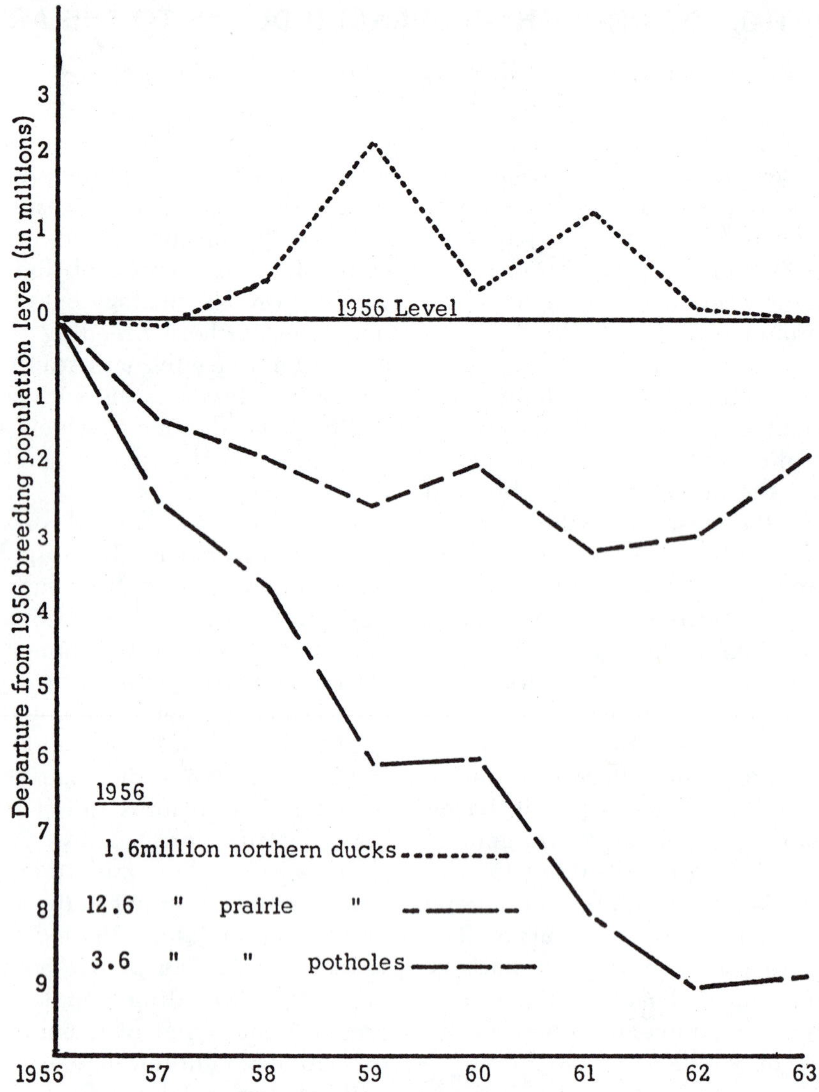

Fig. 1. Inverse relationship of dabbling duck breeding population between prairie and northern habitat.

crease in the south. The drought intensified in 1961 with a further decrease of 2.0 million in the prairie index. There was a concurrent increase in the north but of only 1.1 million. In 1962, the prairie population lost another 1.1 million dabblers. The inversion between north and south had apparently run its course by now, however, because the northern habitat also lost 1.2 million dabblers, returning that population almost to its 1956 level. The northern population remained static in 1963 when the downward trend on the prairies was reversed with an increase in surface water for the second consecutive year. Whether or not the prairie population rebuilds explosively to its 1955–56 peak, there is no reason to

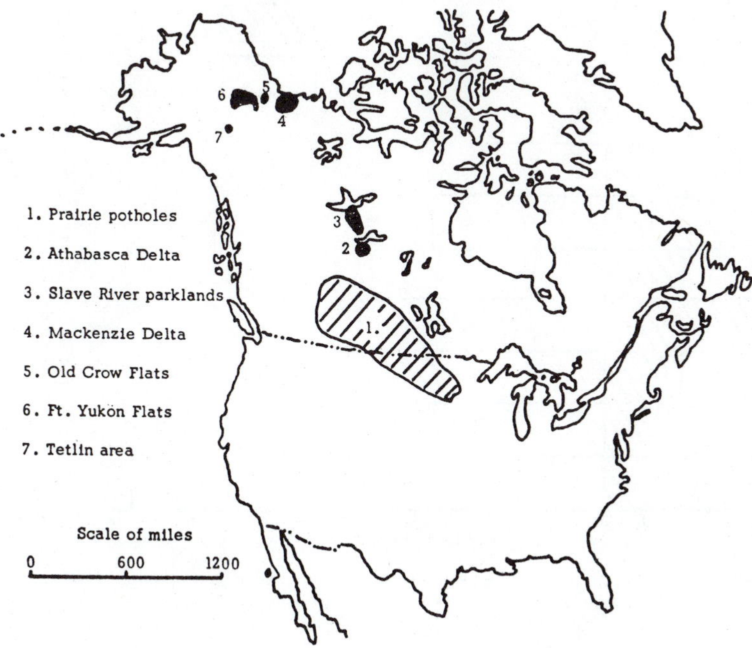

Fig. 2. Area of reference.

believe that it will do so at the further expense of its reservoir area in the north.

When drought forces ducks from the prairies many of them probably go no farther north than necessary to find suitable unoccupied habitat. The late-comers keep pushing north and west and some terminate in east-central Alaska. When the mass movement is viewed through some of its component parts the evidence looks thus. The basic population index on the 1,625 square-mile Athabaska Delta was 84,000 ducks (all species) in 1955, a year of abundant surface water on the prairies. In the drought year of 1961 the population index for the same area peaked at 250,000 ducks.

On the Slave River parklands, 7,500 square miles in extent and some 200 miles farther north, the change between 1955 and 1961 was an increase from 40,000 to 230,000 ducks. Across the Continental Divide lies the Old Crow Flats near the confluence of the Old Crow and Porcupine Rivers. The population index in this mountain-rimmed valley of 2,000 square miles increased from a base of 77,000 ducks to a high of 170,000 in 1961 (Smith et al. 1964). In approximately 11,000 square miles of habitat in eastern Alaska the population index increased from 200,000 to 320,000 during the same period (Fig. 2).

DETAILED EVIDENCE OF PRAIRIE DUCKS IN ALASKA

Production studies and banding have been conducted near Ft. Yukon in eastern Alaska from 1953 through 1956 and from 1960 to date. A similar project has been in progress near Tetlin on the upper Tanana River since 1957. During these studies, blue-winged teal, redhead, ruddy ducks, ring-necked ducks, canvasback and shovelers were recorded either for the first time or in much greater abun-

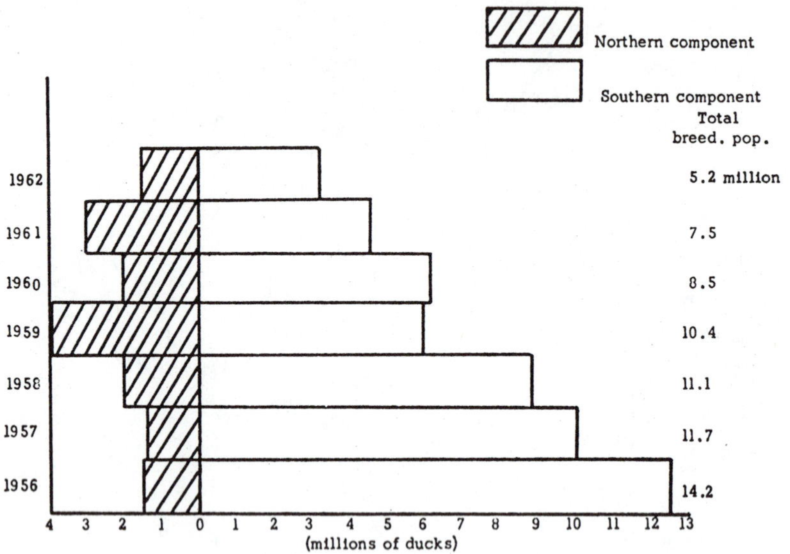

Fig. 3. Dabbling duck breeding population index as derived from aerial surveys on prairies, NWT and Alaska.

dance than formerly (Hansen 1960), but not until after the onset of the current drought in the prairies. The species—new to Alaska—reached their peak abundance in 1959 and 1960. They have decreased steadily in the three subsequent years. Canvasback are common summer residents in eastern Alaska every year, but in 1959 and 1960 they were observed regularly along the Bering Sea coast as well. In addition to the regular breeding population in the upper Yukon and Tanana valleys, large rafts of idle canvasback were observed. The shoveler is also common in the eastern part of the state, but in 1959 they were observed in unprecedented numbers and large rafts were present in an idle status. Shovelers declined in abundance in subsequent years, but not in proportion to the decline in number of broods counted in Tetlin.

During the eastern Alaska banding operations, several species of ducks banded elsewhere were caught. In addition to banded birds recovered in traps, many out-of-state bands have been recovered from hunting activities. From an analysis of all these band recoveries, some appear to be useful in proving the existence in Alaska of drought-displaced ducks and others are of no value whatever. Pintail and widgeon fall into the latter category. Of 33 Alaska recoveries of pintails banded since 1948 in the prairie drought area, 16 were taken through 1957 (years of abundant water) and 17 were taken from 1958–62 (years of drought). Neither sex nor age seems to have any bearing on the pintail's erratic pattern of dispersion. The pattern of widgeon recoveries is somewhat less erratic than pintails, but is not conclusive.

In contrast, five mallards banded as locals on the Canadian prairies have been recovered in Alaska, one in 1957 and the remaining four from 1959–62. In addition, two adult prairie mallards were recovered in the latter period. This is interesting in light of the distribution of mallards banded in Alaska. Of 384 banded from 1948–59, there have been 49 recoveries, all in the Pacific Northwest or enroute down the coast of Alaska. From 1959–62, 100 mallards were banded with 14 recoveries, three from the Central Flyway, one from Utah and 10 from the Pacific Coast. There were four direct recoveries from 64 redheads banded at Tetlin in 1959; one each from Saskatchewan, Wisconsin, Nebraska and Texas. Additionally, there was one second-recovery from southern Alberta and one in 1963 from South Dakota. Green-winged teal and lesser scaup banded on the prairies have also been retrapped in subsequent years in eastern Alaska.

REPRODUCTIVE SUCCESS OF DISPLACED DUCKS

The stable northern habitat not only serves as a reservoir for drought-displaced ducks from the capricious prairies, but some of them will nest successfully after having extended their migration far beyond their home territory. Prior to 1959 there was only one record of blue-winged teal nesting successfully in Alaska (Kessel 1955). Twelve broods were counted in the Tetlin area in 1959, three the following summer, four in 1961, and none since. Three redhead broods were observed in 1959, six in 1960 and none since. These are the only redhead nesting records from Alaska. One ruddy duck brood and one ring-necked duck brood were also recorded in 1959 with none observed since. With the exception of ruddy ducks, all these species have either been observed regularly or trapped in considerable numbers since 1962 when broods were no longer observed or at least in greatly reduced numbers (Table 1).

The relatively low production of these immigrant ducks is not due to small broods, but rather it seems to be a lack of effort from the outset on the part of most individuals. The average size of Class I and II broods at Tetlin from 1958 to 1961 was 7.2 for 19 blue-winged teal, 7.9 for 41 shoveler, 6.8 for 107 canvasback and 4.6 for 7 redhead broods. These compare well with broods in the prairie habitat under optimum conditions. A stronger nesting effort seems to be made in the first year or two these ducks arrive in the north than in subsequent years. This is based on the observation that the number of broods counted among the key species (redhead, blue-winged teal, shoveler) decreases at a faster rate than the total number of adults observed in the same area. Thus, no redhead nor blue-winged teal broods were observed in either 1962 or 1963 although adults of both species were still recorded regularly, though in smaller numbers than in the previous years. During 1962 and 1963, respectively, 24 and 18 flightless adult redheads were banded near Ft. Yukon. Teal were not taken because there was no early season banding when they would have been flightless.

Table 1. Broods of key immigrant species counted at Tetlin.

Species	1958	1959	1960	1961	1962	1963
Shoveler	5	24	7	5	1	0
B. W. Teal	0	12	3	4	0	0
Redhead	0	3	6	0	0	0
Canvasback	22	24	18	18	18	14
Ruddy	0	1	0	0	0	0

Many of these displaced ducks arrive quite late as far north and west as Alaska. In fact, we have observed a "second wave" arrive after many of the early migrants already started to nest. These would have been missed entirely in the northern aerial breeding population surveys and this omission could account, in part at least, for the differential between birds absent from the prairie and not counted elsewhere during the first year or two of the drought. It is possible that the late arrivals wander considerably enroute, dissipate their energies and have passed their physiological primeness before settling down. Whatever process, then, triggers a renesting effort in more southern latitudes has been lost by the time these birds have settled onto Arctic marshes.

Although some individuals can and will nest successfully under displaced circumstances, not enough of them do to maintain an abundance commensurate with that attained in their normal environment. This is apparent when the breeding population index of 14.2 million dabbling ducks in 1956 had dwindled to 5.2 million in 1962 even though the northern component remained at or above the 1956 level throughout the period. As various decimating factors caught up with the displaced prairie ducks, they died out of the population without having contributed sufficiently to maintain their original abundance. By then, however, the stable northern habitat may already have served one of its most important, recurrent functions. As Lynch (1963) pointed out, "What makes the prairies so spectacular is the fact that now and then they explode their production. We can't have an explosion without detonators and I think that these (stable northern areas) . . . are the detonators that kick off these explosions when other conditions decree that it can happen."

Based upon our expanded knowledge of the country and greater field experience of the past few years, we are quite certain that the recent influx of displaced prairie ducks into Alaska is nothing new. A similar movement surely occurred during the drought of the 1930's and others of like magnitude back through history and would already be a matter of written record if a naturalist had been in the field to observe the event.

Studies in the north should be accelerated generally so we may better determine what the basic waterfowl population structure is and how it contributes to the continental supply from year to normal year. Knowledge of weather cycles on the prairies may be progressing to the extent that they can be forecast with reasonable accuracy within the foreseeable future. Toward this end the northern studies should also be oriented to a better understanding of the factors affecting production among drought-displaced ducks when they are super-imposed upon a stable population already in residence.

The future of duck hunting may very well hinge on what is now the peripheral habitat beyond the "heartland" of production. The importance of this vast area should be clearly recognized and fully understood. As civilization and its attendant industrialization move northward at an accelerating pace, the "progress" they engender will pose a threat not only to the pristine condition of many of these areas but to their very existence. The best defense against destructive aspects of these developments should be a well-informed public standing firmly behind dedicated administrators.

LITERATURE CITED

CRISSEY, W. F. 1961. The 1961 status of waterfowl as presented to the waterfowl advisory committee. Mimeographed leaflet, pp. 1–31. U.S. Fish and Wildlife Service, Washington, D.C.

HANSEN, H. A. 1960. Changed status of several species of waterfowl in Alaska. The Condor 62:(2):136–137.

KESSEL, B. 1955. Distributional records of waterfowl from the interior of Alaska. The Condor 57(6):372–373.

LYNCH, J. J. 1963. Waterfowl environments of prairie Canada. 28th North American Wildlife Conference, pp. 93–109.

SMITH, R. H., F. DUFRESNE, AND H. A. HANSEN. 1964. Northern watersheds and deltas *in* Waterfowl tomorrow. U.S. Fish and Wildlife Service, Washington, D.C.

SELECTED BIBLIOGRAPHY

Reproductive Ecology: Drought

DERKSEN, D. V., AND W. D. ELDRIDGE. 1980. Drought displacement of pintails to the Arctic coastal plain, Alaska. J. Wildl. Manage. 44(1):224–229.

HANSEN, H. A. 1960. Changed status of several species of waterfowl in Alaska. Condor 62(2):136–137.

HENNY, C. J. 1973. Drought displaced movement of North American pintails into Siberia. J. Wildl. Manage. 37:23–29.

MURDY, W. H. 1966. When the prairies go dry. Naturalist 17(1):8–13.

SALYER, J. W. 1962. Effects of drought and land use on prairie nesting ducks. Trans. North Am. Wildl. Nat. Res. Conf. 27:69–79.

POPULATION INFLUENCES AND CHARACTERISTICS
Hunting

DIFFERENTIAL VULNERABILITY PATTERNS AMONG THREE SPECIES OF SEA DUCKS[1]

RICHARD S. STOTT, Department of Animal Sciences, University of New Hampshire, Durham
DAVID P. OLSON, Institute of Natural and Environmental Resources, University of New Hampshire, Durham

Abstract: During the 1969 and 1970 hunting seasons, 1,530 white-winged scoters (*Melanitta deglandi*), surf scoters (*M. perspicillata*), and common scoters (*Oidemia nigra*) were observed responding to decoys in typical scoter hunting situations on the New Hampshire coastline. Results indicated that the common scoter was extremely vulnerable to actual hunting, the surf scoter was intermediate, and the white-winged scoter was the least vulnerable. These differences in vulnerability patterns influenced the composition of the scoter harvest as compared with the relative abundance of the three species on the study area. The literature indicates that changes in population levels and winter distribution of scoters have occurred. The described differences in vulnerability, coupled with past hunting pressure, provide a mechanism by which these changes could have happened. To more fully understand the future dynamics of scoter populations in relation to harvest, more accurate population measurements are needed.

The sport of sea duck hunting is old and well established, especially along the New England coast, and many hunters enjoy the challenge of ocean shooting with the long seasons and liberal bag limits. Despite this long history of sport hunting, there is little available information concerning the effect of hunting on sea duck populations because of the presently inadequate sampling of the harvest by such surveys as wing collections, hunter mail questionnaires, and band recovery data.

Differences in vulnerability of waterfowl, based on observations in hunting situations, were first described in 1965 (Olson 1965). From this work, Olson concluded that disproportionate sex ratios in canvasbacks (*Aythya valisineria*) were the result of differences in vulnerability between sex- and age-groups. He further suggested that differences in vulnerability probably affected the population structure of other waterfowl such as lesser scaup (*Aythya affinis*).

The objective of the present study was to measure the differences in vulnerability among three species of sea ducks (white-winged, surf, and common scoters) during actual hunting situations and to discuss the implications of these differences in relation to scoter distribution and population structure. This study was part of a larger investigation concerning the winter ecology of sea ducks on the New Hampshire coastline (Stott and Olson, Unpublished data). In this report, reference to *scoters* will include white-winged, surf, and common scoters.

We are indebted to the numerous hunters who donated their scoters for the harvest study and shared their knowledge of sea duck hunting with us. We also acknowledge the assistance of H. P. Nevers, graduate student, Department of Forest Resources, for conducting scoter population counts in the fall of 1967. The New Hampshire Agricultural Experiment Station provided partial support during the investigation.

METHODS

This investigation was conducted on a study area comprising 22 miles of open coastline from Portsmouth, New Hampshire, to Salisbury, Massachusetts.

During the sea duck hunting seasons

[1] Published with the approval of the Director of the New Hampshire Agricultural Experiment Station as scientific contribution No. 597.

Originally published in J. Wildl. Manage. 36(3):775–783, 1972.

Fig. 1. Typical hunting method for scoters and setup for decoying observations.

Fig. 2. Scoter silhouettes employed in decoy trails; these silhouettes are commonly used by sea duck hunters.

(September 25 to January 10) of 1969 and 1970, observations were made of the behavior of the three scoter species as they encountered hunters with boats and decoys on the open ocean (Figs. 1, 2) in the typical scoter hunting pattern employed all along the study area. Binoculars were used to identify the species, age, and sex of waterfowl. Age and sex categories consisted of two groups: adult males and a combined group of adult females and juvenile males and females. The latter group was used since juveniles and adult females have similar plumages.

Observations included species, flock size, age and sex, and response to decoys. For this report, a flock was considered to be one or more scoters. Response to decoys was characterized in five ways: landing (in or near decoys), low, medium, wide, and no response. Low, medium, and wide are subjective ratings in relation to shotgun range. In general, low corresponded to 40 yards or less; medium, 40 to 60 yards; and wide, beyond 60 yards. No response designation was recorded when it was judged that scoters were close enough to see the decoys but showed no visible sign of decoying or changing flight direction due to the decoys.

During the 1967–69 hunting seasons, coastal waterfowl hunters were interviewed and scoter carcasses or wings were obtained. The interviews and collection of specimens were used to estimate the scoter harvest on the study area.

At the same time, populations of scoters were censused weekly, utilizing ground observation points along the coastline. Thus, populations of the three species of scoters were known during the hunting season, and comparisons between actual populations and composition of the scoters harvested were possible. In a previous study (Stott and Olson 1972), we found that the ground census technique was much more accurate and reliable than aerial censuses. Ninety-eight percent of the sea ducks counted by aerial surveys were within 500 yards of shore, and they were easily identified with field glasses and spotting scope.

RESULTS

Decoy Observations

A total of 1,530 scoters in 571 flocks were observed responding to decoys in typical scoter hunting situations on 36 occasions during October, November, and December 1969 and October and November 1970 (Table 1). Approximately half of the decoy observations were conducted during actual shooting situations and the other half with no shooting. Only 13 flocks (2.3 percent) of mixed species were observed, and these

Table 1. Comparative behavior of 1,530 scoters in hunting encounters during the 1969–70 hunting seasons on the New Hampshire coastline.

	Adult Males					Adult Females and Juveniles				
	Landing and Low	Medium	Wide	No Response	Total	Landing and Low	Medium	Wide	No Response	Total
White-winged Scoter[a, b]										
Number	8	29	53	124	214	166	95	58	53	372
Percent	4	13	25	58		44	26	16	14	
Surf Scoter[b]										
Number	8	16	3	1	28	306	88	42	10	446
Percent	29	57	11	3		69	20	9	2	
Common Scoter[b]										
Number	6	1	0	0	7	335	128	0	0	463
Percent	86	14	0	0		72	28	0	0	

[a] Differences between adult male and adult female and juvenile white-winged scoters were significant at 99 percent level (3 df), using a chi-square test.
[b] Differences among the three species were significant at the 99 percent level (6 df), using a chi-square test.

consisted of two species in all possible combinations among the three scoters.

The common scoter decoyed more readily (100 percent of all common scoters observed decoyed either at the landing or low or medium distances) than the surf scoter (88 percent) and the white-winged scoter (51 percent). There was also a marked contrast between the decoy responses of the adult male white-winged scoter (17 percent) and the adult female and juvenile white-winged scoters (70 percent). These behavioral differences were similar to responses previously observed in canvasbacks (Olson 1965). The decoy responses between age- and sex-groups of surf and common scoters appeared to be similar, although there was a small sample of adult males for both of these species. Using a chi-square test, we found the differences in the decoy responses of the scoter species to be significant at the 99 percent level.

Flock Size in Relation to Vulnerability

From information gathered during the decoy observations that involved actual shooting, an indication of mortality in relation to flock size for the three species of scoters during a shooting opportunity could be made. A shooting opportunity was one in which one or more birds responded in the low or medium range to the decoys. Of a total of 58 white-winged scoters in 27 shooting opportunities, 19 (32.8 percent) were killed; of 74 surf scoters in 40 shooting opportunities, 32 (43.2 percent) were killed; and of 196 common scoters in 33 shooting opportunities, only 23 (11.7 percent) were killed. This marked difference in mortality was related to flock size in that scoters in small flocks had a greater probability of death than those in larger flocks. Seventy-six and 74 percent of white-winged and surf scoters occurred in flocks of singles and doubles (Table 2). In contrast, only 51 percent of common scoters were observed as singles and doubles. The average flock size of the white-winged scoter was 1.9 (range, 1–8); of the surf scoter, 2.7 (range, 1–25); and of the common scoter, 5.2 (range, 1–35). There was no significant difference in flock size between adult female and juvenile white-winged scoters.

Table 2. Percentage of scoters in each size of flock responding to decoys during the 1969–70 hunting seasons on the New Hampshire coastline.

	Number of Birds in Flock																			Total Number of Flocks
	1	2	3	4	5	6	7	8	9	10	11	12	13	14	15	16–20	21–25	26–30	31–35	
WHITE-WINGED SCOTER																				
Adult males	62	21	9	2	4	2	–	–	–	–	–	–	–	–	–	–	–	–	–	53
Adult females and juveniles	51	23	10	8	4	3	–	1	–	–	–	–	–	–	–	–	–	–	–	157
All	54	22	10	6	4	3	–	1	–	–	–	–	–	–	–	–	–	–	–	210
SURF SCOTER	46	28	9	6	3	2	0.5	–	–	0.5	0.5	2	–	–	1	1	0.5	–	–	173
COMMON SCOTER	27	24	8	5	10	1	2	1	3	5	1	2	1	1	5	1	2	–	1	91

Bent (1925:140) stated that the young and adults of the common and surf scoters provided the best shooting since they decoyed well, particularly when in small flocks, and that a pair or a single bird of these two species would often circle about the decoys several times. We found that small flocks of these two species did decoy more readily as compared with the larger flocks and that the repeated decoying behavior of these two species was prominent, especially in the common scoter.

Although the flock sizes of the white-winged scoter and surf scoters were somewhat similar, the difference in mortality of these two species (32.8 percent and 43.2 percent, respectively) may be related to body size. The white-winged scoter is noticeably larger than the surf scoter (3 pounds, 8 ounces, average weight of seven adult male white-winged scoters; 2 pounds, 3 ounces, average weight of 10 adult male surf scoters; Kortright 1953:386), and the mortality difference may be related to the amount of lead shot needed to kill the larger scoter. Elder (1950, 1955) suggested that a small duck may be killed more easily than a large duck—for example, a blue-winged teal (*Anas discors*) versus a mallard (*A. platyrhynchos*).

Composition of Harvest in Relation to Populations

During the 1967–69 hunting seasons, the population of scoters on the study area was compared with the composition of the harvest for typical hunting weekends (Table 3). This comparison revealed that the common scoter was extremely vulnerable to actual hunting, whereas the white-winged scoter was the least vulnerable. The common scoter made up only 6 percent or less of the October, November, and December scoter population. However, the percentage of common scoters killed each month in relation to its population level indicated that this species was likely to be killed at least four times as readily as the white-winged scoter and at least twice as readily as the surf scoter. Chi-square tests performed on the monthly proportions of scoters in the population and kill were all significant at the 99 percent level.

The obvious explanation for the higher proportion of common scoters harvested lies in its extreme vulnerability to decoying; however, there are other possibilities. Since the common scoter was always the least abundant species on the study area, one could hypothesize that it was more vulner-

Table 3. Composition of population and kill of scoters from typical hunting weekends during the 1967–69 hunting seasons on the New Hampshire coastline.

								TOTALS	
								Number[a]	Percent
	1968		1969						
	Oct. 13	Oct. 27	Oct. 10	Oct. 19	Oct. 26	Oct. 31			
White-winged scoter	87/0[b]	87/5	72/39	140/44	317/21	307/4		1,010/113	11.2
Surf scoter	25/5	55/7	308/78	141/31	157/25	353/6		1,039/152	14.6
Common scoter	3/1	3/3	4/3	3/3	12/8	20/2		45/20	44.4
								($X^2 = 37.6, P < 0.01$, 2 df)	
	1967		1968		1969				
	Nov. 9	Nov. 20	Nov. 3	Nov. 23	Nov. 15	Nov. 21	Nov. 26		
White-winged scoter	235/3	136/5	234/14	173/11	295/2	411/4	677/3	2,161/42	1.9
Surf scoter	55/3	29/4	24/16	64/7	256/3	113/4	78/3	619/40	6.5
Common scoter	16/3	63/6	3/5	10/3	7/8	10/2	22/2	131/29	22.1
								($X^2 = 145.4, P < 0.01$, 2 df)	
	1968		1969						
	Dec. 1	Dec. 9	Dec. 17	Dec. 30					
White-winged scoter	411/8	356/9	329/6	910/2				2,006/25	1.2
Surf scoter	137/2	130/7	107/1	64/1				438/11	2.5
Common scoter	8/7	15/0	103/1	41/0				167/8	4.8
								($X^2 = 13.0, P < 0.01$, 2 df)	

[a] Totals are the summation of all recorded observations for each month.
[b] The ground census/kill on or near the census date.

able when alone or in small groups. It is a common observation of waterfowl hunters that singles decoy more readily than larger flocks. The analysis of flock size for the three species of scoters (Table 2) indicated that common scoters approached the decoys in larger flock sizes than the other two species. Furthermore, the behavior of common scoters in these larger flocks was similar to that of singles and doubles.

Another possible explanation for the higher proportion of common scoters harvested is that this species might pass through the study area at a greater rate than surf or white-winged scoters. During the study period, censuses were conducted weekly, and all flying birds and direction of flight were recorded. There were no observations that indicated the migration of common scoters was greater than that of the other species, especially close to shore where hunting took place. The scoter migration commonly occurred during early and mid-October, with birds in large groups (100–300 in number) flying through the study area at an average distance of 2 to 4 miles from shore. Scoter movements near shore, where hunting occurred, appeared to be a trading back and forth of smaller flocks (5–40 in number), with similar proportions passing north and south.

Thus, the differences in vulnerability measured in the decoy study appeared to result in the disproportionate harvest of common and surf scoters; however, these differences are somewhat modified by variations in migration and hunting activity.

Migration Patterns and Harvest

The 1969 sea duck harvest on the study area was 310 scoters consisting of 50 percent surf scoters, 40 percent white-winged scoters, and 10 percent common scoters. These percentages were derived from a representative sample taken from the most consistent sea duck hunters.

From daily observations during the entire 1969 sea duck hunting season, it was ascertained that approximately 83 percent of the hunting pressure occurred from the opening day (September 25) to the second week of November, which corresponded with the opening of the deer season. This same sequence of hunting pressure until mid-November was also noted during the 1968 and 1970 hunting seasons.

The period of October to mid-November was the peak of the surf scoter population on the study area, with adult males, females, and juveniles all being present. It was during this same period that 87 percent of the scoter harvest occurred. The moderate vulnerability and peak population levels of surf scoters during this time accounted for this species making up a majority of the kill. White-winged scoters did not reach their peak population on the study area until the end of November and early December. At this time, the surf scoters had decreased to a low wintering population level. The common scoter's low population level remained stable throughout the hunting season except for a slight increase in late December and January.

Even though the population of scoters in December and January was at its highest of the entire hunting season, scoter hunting was very limited due to adverse seas and cold weather. The scoter population during this period consisted of approximately 84 percent white-winged scoters, which had a substantial proportion of adult males. Decoy trials during this period indicated that although scoters were active, there were few shooting opportunities because of the consistent flaring off of the adult male white-winged scoters that usually took any adult females and juveniles with them. In short, scoter hunting was at its poorest in December and January, even though it was the peak of the wintering scoter population.

DISCUSSION

Hunting Patterns and Past and Present Scoter Populations

Although the literature concerning scoters is scant, there are several references that suggest that the vulnerability patterns described here, together with past hunting pressures, may have produced changes in scoter population levels and shifts in wintering populations among the three species of scoters.

Richards (1952) and Silver (1957) reviewed the literature concerning sea duck populations and stated that the surf scoter was probably more abundant than the other two species during the 1800's, with the common (American) scoter being the least abundant. Mackay (1891) also described the same proportion of abundance in the three scoters.

Mackay (1897), Forbush (1925), Richards (1952), and Silver (1957) all stated that there was an apparent reverse in scoter population levels during the 1890's and early 1900's. They indicated that the white-winged scoter was the most abundant on the New England coast and the common scoter the least abundant. Mackay (1897) further stated that the common scoter was becoming a scarce bird on the Massachusetts and Rhode Island coasts.

Presently, on the New England coast, the white-winged scoter appears to be the most abundant, with much lesser numbers of surfs and even fewer common scoters. On our study area, we found that the scoter population of 600–800 birds during the winters of 1968–70 consisted of 84 percent white-winged scoters, 12 percent surf scoters, and 4 percent common scoters. Similar observations were also made during the winters of 1966–68. R. Billard and E. Moses (personal communication) in their aerial surveys for the Connecticut Fisheries and Game Department and the U. S. Fish and Wildlife Service indicated that the white-winged scoter was the most common scoter species on the Connecticut and Massachusetts coastlines. Aerial surveys of the southern coast of Maine by the authors also indicated that white-winged scoters were more abundant than the other species of scoters.

Thus, the evidence suggests that there has been a change in the species composition of scoters in New England. The changes appear to have been caused by a decrease in surf scoters in relation to white-winged scoters and an even greater decline in the common scoter. These changes in scoter populations occurred during a period when market hunting was common and sea ducks were hunted in the fall, winter, and spring, particularly on the New England coast. Bent (1925:140) stated that at this time 15 or 20 scoters a day was considered a good day's kill, although many more have been killed in a single day by some hunters. On the New Hampshire coast, Great Boar's Head, for many years, has been a traditional spot for hunting scoters, and formerly it was common to observe 30 boats on an average morning hunt (personal communication with coastal residents). At the time of this study, on the best weekends, only five or six boats were set up for sea ducks at Boar's Head. People who hunted years ago state that there are not as many scoters as there used to be. These recollections of the past may be exaggerated, but to keep 30 boats occupied, there must have been more scoters than during our study, when a bag limit of seven sea ducks a day was difficult to obtain.

Winter Distribution of Scoters

Bent (1925) described the past winter ranges of all three species of scoters. The white-winged scoter ranged from the Gulf of St. Lawrence to South Carolina; the surf scoter ranged from the Bay of Fundy southward to Florida, most abundantly from Massachusetts to New Jersey; and the common scoter ranged regularly from Maine south to Long Island Sound and New Jersey, rarely to South Carolina.

Presently, the mid-Atlantic coastal area appears to winter the majority of surf scoters. Stewart (1962) indicated that surf scoters were much more abundant than white-winged and common scoters along the Maryland and southern Delaware coasts. He also mentioned that the common scoter was the least abundant of the three species. Sprunt (1931:258) stated that "For three consecutive winters American [common] Scoters have been noted on the South Carolina coast and are probably to be included in the number of winter residents." He also described huge flocks of common scoters in December and January of 1930–31. O. Dewberry (personal communication), in his winter coastal aerial surveys for the Georgia Fish and Game Department, found that of approximately 10,000–30,000 scoters using the open coast during the winters of 1968–70, common scoters made up the entire number.

Thus, there is some evidence that scoters have changed in numbers and less compelling evidence that changes in winter distribution may also have occurred. The differences in vulnerability described in the present study provide a mechanism by which these changes could have happened. Hockbaum (1955) suggested that broken traditions can account for the disappearance, due to severe overhunting, of waterfowl species from suitable habitat.

Management Implications

It is possible that hunting pressure, migration patterns, and differences in vulnerability to hunting are maintaining scoter populations and winter distributions in a kind of dynamic equilibrium. Surf and common scoters, which are the most vulnerable to hunting along the New Hampshire coastline and hence probably along the entire New England coastline, may survive better if they winter farther south, where they are less affected by hunting. White-winged scoters, which appear to be least affected by hunting, are the most common in winter along the New Hampshire coastline.

Although the hunting pressure on the study area remained somewhat stable over three hunting seasons (1968–70), it is our opinion that scoter hunting will increase in the near future. Sea duck hunting has a long tradition in New England; it is still popular among coastal hunters, and increasing numbers of sportsmen are obtaining boats suitable for ocean use. The present sea duck season is in effect from Maine to Long Island, New York, and recently, also in Maryland, where reports (V. Stotts, personal communication) indicate that the season is becoming popular among some hunters. Such changes in hunting pressure or patterns will probably cause further changes in scoter populations.

Because of the nature of sea duck hunting techniques, we have few suggestions for changes in regulations to decrease the pressure on common and surf scoters. Species identification is difficult even for expert observers; hence it is doubtful if average sportsmen could master it. The problem is compounded by the fact that many juveniles of all three species decoy into sea duck hunting setups and are all quite similar in appearance. Consequently, different bag limits for the three species may not be effective. A later season opening would decrease pressure on surf and common scoters, but to be effective, the season would probably have to open in late October or November. Such a late season would eliminate the bulk of the scoter hunting because by this time of the year, hunting opportunities are becoming limited by weather conditions in New England.

It might be possible to selectively decoy the various species if different kinds of decoys and arrangements of decoys were employed. In this study, we tried to duplicate the hunting method (Fig. 1) used by the majority of sea duck hunters, and no modifications were tried. Olson (1965) found that the less vulnerable adult male canvasbacks could be encouraged to enter shooting setups by using larger numbers of male decoys. Gallon plastic jugs painted black for sea duck decoys are becoming more common along the New Hampshire coastline. There is need for considerably more study of the responses of scoters and other sea ducks to various numbers and kinds of decoys both on the present study area and in other situations.

Perhaps the biggest problem in effective management of scoter populations, or even to the complete understanding of the implications of this study, is that there are no accurate population measurements for sea ducks. Likewise, there are few other measures of population status such as bag checks, band recovery data, or measures of production in breeding areas. In another part of this study (Stott and Olson 1972), we found that aerial surveys of scoters were extremely variable and that, depending on weather conditions, between 6.5 percent and 75.8 percent of the population was counted. Hence, the one *census* of scoter populations conducted each year, the midwinter aerial survey, probably provides little, if any, reliable information concerning population status.

Crissey (1965:231) in his report concerning waterfowl species management stated, "Longer seasons and larger bag limits also have been established for species that either are not particularly vulnerable to shooting or are not highly prized by hunters. Scoters and mergansers are good examples of this." Our study indicated that common scoters are particularly vulnerable to hunting and that changes in scoter populations and distribution may have already occurred. Thus, there is need for better information concerning these species. This information would come with the initiation of banding studies, accurate winter population censuses, and improved harvest analyses.

LITERATURE CITED

BENT, A. C. 1925. Life histories of North American wild fowl: order Anseres (part). U. S. Natl. Museum Bull. 130. 376pp.

CRISSEY, W. F. 1965. Waterfowl species management: problems and progress. Trans. N. Am. Wildl. and Nat. Resources Conf. 30: 229–245.

ELDER, W. H. 1950. (Discussion after presentation of a report.) Trans. N. Am. Wildl. Conf. 15:504.

———. 1955. Fluoroscopic measures of hunting pressure in Europe and North America. Trans. N. Am. Wildl. Conf. 20:298–321.

FORBUSH, E. H. 1925. Birds of Massachusetts and other New England states. Part I. Water birds, marsh birds and shore birds. Massachusetts Department of Agriculture. 481pp.

HOCHBAUM, H. A. 1955. Travels and traditions of waterfowl. The University of Minnesota Press, Minneapolis. 301pp.

KORTRIGHT, F. H. 1953. The ducks, geese and swans of North America. The Stackpole Company, Harrisburg, Pennsylvania, and the Wildlife Management Institute, Washington, D. C. 476pp.

MACKAY, G. H. 1891. The scoters (*Oidemia americana, O. deglandi* and *O. perspicillata*) in New England. Auk 8(3):279–290.

———. 1897. Sundry notes. Auk 14(2):228–229.

OLSON, D. P. 1965. Differential vulnerability of male and female canvasbacks to hunting. Trans. N. Am. Wildl. and Nat. Resources Conf. 30:121–134.

RICHARDS, T. 1952. The waterfowl of New Hampshire, their history and present status. M.S. Thesis. Univ. of Michigan. 194pp.

SILVER, HELENETTE. 1957. A history of New Hampshire game and furbearers. New Hampshire Fish and Game Dept. Survey Rept. 6. 466pp.

SPRUNT, A., JR. 1931. The American scoter (*Oidemia americana*) again in winter on the South Carolina coast. Auk 48(2):258.

STEWART, R. E. 1962. Waterfowl populations in the upper Chesapeake region. U. S. Fish and Wildl. Serv. Spec. Sci. Rept.: Wildl. No. 65. 208pp.

STOTT, R. S., AND D. P. OLSON. 1972. An evaluation of waterfowl surveys on the New Hampshire coastline. J. Wildl. Mgmt. 36(2):468–477.

Received for publication December 13, 1971.

MALLARD POPULATION TRENDS AND HUNTING LOSSES IN MINNESOTA

ROBERT L. JESSEN, Minnesota Department of Conservation, St. Paul

Abstract: The abundance of the mallard (*Anas platyrhynchos*) as a breeding duck in Minnesota is known only from general reports until about 20 years ago when systematic censuses began. Records suggest an early decline in abundance prior to 1900. More recently, there has been a slight increase to a level of approximately one pair per square mile in the ten better duck-breeding counties of the western and northcentral portion of the state. During the 1950s, the first-year total mortality of wild young mallards reared in the state was high (75–85 percent). Most of this mortality was from hunting (55–65 percent) and about 70 percent of this was reported from Minnesota. Mallard reproductive success in the state is considered average, or better than average, compared with other breeding localities, but productivity of young per acre of wetland indicates an under-use of suitable habitat. A review of kill statistics and hunting regulations clearly indicates that in years of highly restrictive regulations, especially those having a daily limit of one mallard, there has been a reduction in the harvest of local mallards and increased survival of local birds. Within large refuge units, survival and subsequent production of mallards has been higher than in non-refuge areas of Minnesota. There is a conflict between maximum sport-hunting use of wetlands and maximum production of mallards. It is suggested that this conflict can be resolved in part by setting aside a portion of the state wetlands in a pattern of small refuges. Additional protection thus gained locally in Minnesota, together with judicious hunting regulations throughout the Flyway, can increase the breeding population and harvestable surplus of mallards.

INTRODUCTION

The mallard has long been highly regarded by hunters and has made up a large proportion of the waterfowl harvest both in North America and in the Mississippi Flyway. In 1967, mallards made up 34 percent of the ducks taken in North America (excluding Mexico) and 38 percent of those in the Mississippi Flyway (Martin and Carney 1968, Benson 1968, Canadian Wildlife Ser. 1968). Management of the mallard in the Mississippi Flyway must include the breeding grounds (largely in northern states and Canada), and waters frequented during migration and wintering (mostly in the central states). It is obviously of prime importance that there be a sizeable population of breeders and suitable habitat for them if the mallard is to remain an important hunting resource in the future.

Minnesota occupies a critical position in the Mississippi Flyway management pattern. It is not only a breeding ground (about a half million ducks are estimated to have bred in Minnesota in 1968, of which about one-fifth were mallards) but is a state in which there is a high mallard harvest (435,000 in 1967, as calculated from Martin and Carney 1968, Croft and Carney 1969). Also, in Minnesota, many refuge areas have been established and many wetlands have been purchased by both state and federal agencies for waterfowl and for public hunting.

Flyway-wide, mallard populations have been in serious trouble in recent years (1962–1968) because of continual loss of breeding areas in the United States and Canada, drought over much of the prairie, and (in the opinion of at least some waterfowl biologists) overshooting. Because Minnesota is both a breeding ground and a heavily hunted area, this summary of the history and status of the mallard in Minnesota has been prepared. The results suggest that current management practices must be changed to insure and enhance the status of this important species.

This paper is based on studies made by

Originally published in J. Wildl. Manage. 34(1):93–105, 1970.

many individuals in Minnesota. Special credit is due to J. D. Smith and F. Lee, who began documenting the status of the mallard in Minnesota, and to L. Johnson, J. Lindmeier, N. Ordal, and R. Benson who gathered much of the data. Appreciation is also extended to J. B. Moyle for aid in preparing the manuscript.

ABUNDANCE, PAST AND PRESENT

Only general statements can be made as to the number of mallards in Minnesota (or elsewhere in North America) before and for some time after settlement of the country. The mallard, or "common duck," as it was called by some early naturalists, was rated as "abundant" in Minnesota by P. L. Hatch (1880:371), State Ornithologist. He assigned a lesser rating to the blue-winged and green-winged teal (*A. discors* and *A. crecca*). A decade later, Hatch (1892:39) described the mallard as easily studied "as they breed extensively in nearly every portion of the state . . . ." T. S. Roberts, long-time student of Minnesota's birds, recalled "back to a time when this duck (the mallard) was so abundant that almost every pothole had its breeding pair and the prairie sloughs were full of them" (Roberts 1936:224). Roberts' first work on Minnesota bird life was published in 1875; his experiences span this early period.

By 1900, and perhaps some time before, the population of breeding mallards and other ducks in Minnesota had declined. Most of the better land on the prairies was in agricultural use, and drainage of wetlands was under way. Prior to 1900, market hunting and spring shooting were still legal. Breckenridge (1949:15) estimated that by 1880 there were perhaps 65,000 duck hunters "ranging Minnesota marshes". Also many pioneers supplemented their food supply with wild ducks. By 1898, T. Miller, a long-time resident of Heron Lake in southwestern Minnesota, commented that there were "sadly diminished numbers" of mallards, pintails (*A. acuta*) and spoonbills (*A. clypeata*) on this famous hunting area (Roberts 1919:62). Later, about 1915, it was noted by C. Avery (1916:26) that there was an increase of breeding teal, mallard, pintail, wood duck (*Aix sponsa*) and other ducks. This was attributed, among other things, to the "prevention of some spring shooting."

In 1919, Minnesota hunters were required to report the number of game animals taken. In that year, the kill was estimated from hunters' report cards at 489,000 mallards taken by 76,355 hunters. Mallards made up about a quarter of the total duck kill—less than for "blue-bill ducks" (primarily lesser scaup *Aythya affinis*) but more than for blue-winged teal (Avery 1920). Annual raw kill figures for mallards, as calculated from hunter report cards, averaged about 400,000 during the 1920s, ranged from 164,000 to 1,118,000 in the 1930s, averaged about 750,000 in the 1940s and were somewhat less than 500,000 in the 1950s. In the 1960s, harvests ranged from 159,000 to 468,000. Data from report cards of Minnesota hunters for recent years, when adjusted for 10 percent non-hunting license holders, closely approximate federal figures having a different sampling base (Benson 1966).

The contribution to the total take of mallards by those reared in Minnesota is not known for earlier years but may well have been at least 10–20 percent of this total. The take of such birds in recent years, as will be shown later, has been about 80,000 or about one-fourth of the total kill. In early years, the waterfowl hunting season opened as early as September 16, which favored the taking of locally reared birds.

Systematic censusing of breeding ducks began in Minnesota in 1948 with 10,400 miles of roadside count (automobile transects). Aerial surveys began in 1951. The roadside census originally included most of the state, excluding only the unglaciated regions in the southeast and southwest, the Precambrian shield of the northeast and parts of the Red River valley in the Northwest. This extensive coverage was later reduced to the 10 more important duck breeding counties in the western and north-central parts of the state. Aerial censuses were made throughout the prairie portions of the state until 1966 (see Lee et al. 1964: 87) when they were revised to include central Minnesota and exclude prairie regions with wetlands. Aerial survey counts have been adjusted for birds not seen by comparing them with ground counts. The average density for pairs of breeding mallards along 550 miles of ground transects in the 10 better waterfowl counties was 0.6 pairs per square mile in the early 1950s. This increased in an irregular fashion to 1.5 pairs in 1966, declined to 0.8 in 1967, and increased again to 1.1 in 1968. The proportion of mallards in the total duck count has increased from about 20 to 25 percent during the past 20 years. Aerial surveys also show a slight upward trend in the counts of breeding mallards during this same period.

It seems likely from the surveys that the mallard breeding populations using the main waterfowl breeding areas of Minnesota have ranged between 40,000 and 80,000 pairs in recent years and that the breeding population was probably around 55,000 pairs in the spring of 1968. These figures are minimal because they do not include birds nesting outside the censused half of the state. They are also subject to a considerable amount of sampling error.

MORTALITY AND MOVEMENT

Mortality of mallards, hunting and total, as here reported is based on the recovery of bands. Calculations follow the dynamic method described by Geis and Taber (1963). The earliest banding of mallards in Minnesota was by State Game Warden, Martin Nelson, at Thief Lake, in northwestern Minnesota. He banded 507 birds during the hunting season in 1933, and 407 before the season in 1935 (Minnesota Department of Conservation records). Nelson did not record the age of the birds. Return of bands (first year direct recovery) was high: 26 percent for those banded in 1933 and 22 percent for those banded in 1935. In these 2 years, the hunting season opened on October 1 and October 21, respectively. The calculated first year total mortality from bands recovered is high, 72 and 70 percent. Most of these birds were not killed locally. In 1933, 77 percent of the bands were returned from out of state (mostly from Illinois), and in 1935, 76 percent.

During this same period, band recoveries from ducks banded elsewhere were generally lower and usually were between 9 and 20 percent (Pirnie 1935, Phillips and Lincoln 1930, Cartwright 1945). This suggests especially high hunting pressure in the 1930s on Minnesota mallards. In 1942, however, when 218 immature mallards were banded at Thief Lake, the direct band-recovery rate was lower, only 11.5 percent (Minnesota Department of Conservation records).

In the 1950s, the direct band-recovery rate from mallards, banded as flightless young in Minnesota, was about 19 percent; that for mallards, banded as flying young in the late 1950s, was somewhat less, about 17 percent; and that for older pre-season banded birds, about 10 percent.

Using these data and correcting for non-

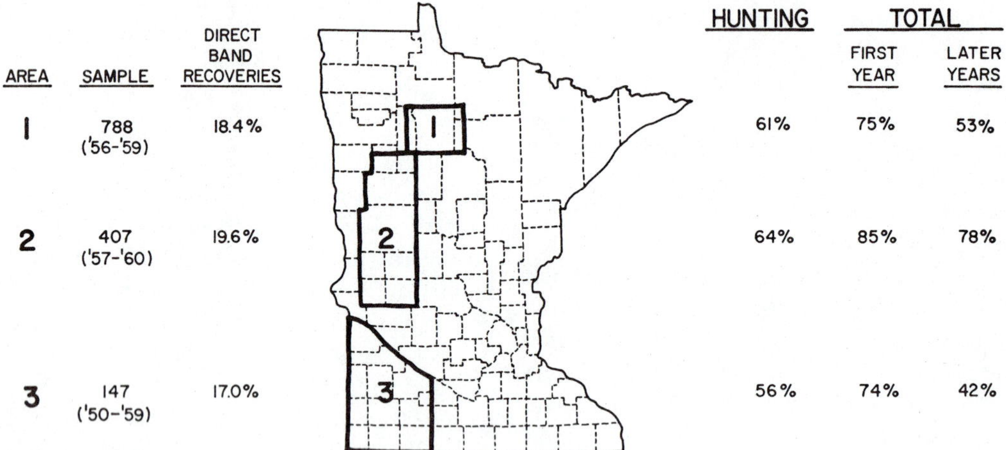

Fig. 1. Estimated hunting and total mortality of flightless young of mallard ducks banded in three areas of Minnesota, as calculated from band recoveries.

reporting by using a factor of 2.5 (Bellrose and Chase 1950, Bellrose 1955, Hunt et al. 1958, Geis and Atwood 1961) and adding one-third for crippling loss (Atwood and Wells 1960, Atwood 1961, Mendall 1958, Bellrose 1953, Low 1945, Sowls 1955), hunting and total mortality have been calculated (Fig. 1). Such calculations indicate that during the 1950s, 56–64 percent of the locally-reared birds were killed by hunting (not counting indirect loss from lead poisoning).

Immature flying mallards banded before the hunting season, especially in northern Minnesota, are of uncertain origin and some may have been reared elsewhere, especially in Canada. It is probable, however, that most birds considered here were reared in Minnesota because Lensink (1964) reported that only 2.5 percent of the direct band recoveries for mallards raised in Manitoba (the nearest out-state source) came from Minnesota. This is in contrast to the 53 percent recovered in Minnesota from our bandings.

Much of the hunting mortality for mallards banded as flightless young in Minnesota is the result of shooting birds within the state—averaging 70 percent for the period 1948–1961 (Lee et al. 1964:84). A considerable portion of the bands were returned from areas close to the banding site. When the banding and recovery data are considered by 10-minute-degree blocks (areas of 7.5 × 11 miles or 82.5 square miles in central Minnesota), 10 percent of the males and 19 percent of the females that were later reported came from within the same block. Band returns for following years (indirect recovery) to the same blocks was less for males (4 percent) but greater for females (28 percent). This indicates considerable return to waters within 5 miles of natal areas (Table 1). Lensink (1964) reports similar recovery of bands near banding sites in Canada.

In Minnesota, a high proportion (61 percent) of mallards banded as flightless young and shot that same fall are taken by October 15. After this date, the proportion of recoveries from all areas progresses at a rate of about 1 percent a day until late in November. Few locally reared mallards are taken in Minnesota after November 1 because by then shallow marshes, even along the Mississippi River in southeastern Minnesota, have usually frozen over at least once.

Immature mallards, banded in extreme northwestern Minnesota in September, usually leave the state first. Some of these birds may have been reared in Canada. Generally, however, mallards reared in Minnesota are among the last to leave the state, staying throughout the fall and often remaining close to their natal marshes. This is especially true for hens that have nested. Such attachment to natal areas makes locally-reared mallards especially vulnerable to local hunters.

BREEDING SUCCESS

Nesting studies in three areas of Minnesota during the period 1957–1960 indicate that half or more of the hens are successful in hatching at least one egg (Lee et al. 1964:13). This is a fairly high success rate (Crissey 1967), but the estimate is strengthened by counts of lone males. Stoudt (1959) found, in a June tally, that the 70 percent lone males in breeding pair counts was related to an active nesting success of 40 percent. Lone males found in breeding pair counts in Minnesota, during the third and fourth week in May in recent years, have averaged 69 percent for ground tallies and 81 percent for those made from the air.

If, on the average, hens in Minnesota rear a brood of six to flying stage (and this seems likely), a fall flight ratio of 1.5 young: 1.0 adult (assuming a 50:50 sex ratio of breeders), or 3.0 young per adult hen would result. This is higher than the average ratio of about 1.0 for North America during the period 1959–1965 (Crissey 1967) and indicates better than average hatching of young on Minnesota breeding areas.

Table 1. The percentage of flightless young mallards banded and subsequently recovered within the same 10-minute block of land.[a]

	Recoveries Same Year Banded		Recoveries in Later Years	
Sex	Total recoveries	Percentage same block	Total recoveries	Percentage same block
Males	243	10	81	4
Females	160	19	58	28
Both	403	13	139	14

[a] A ten-minute block of land approximates an area of 7.5 × 11.0 miles. Included in these recoveries are birds retrapped. Reports are for birds banded 1948–1961.

Average production of mallards on Minnesota wetlands that have been studied has ranged from 0.11 to 0.21 flying young per acre during the period 1957–1960 (Lee et al. 1964:22). The better production on similar prairie waters in Canada (which, however, may possibly have a higher basic fertility) has ranged from 0.7 young mallards per acre, for a large impoundment and associated potholes in Alberta (Keith 1961), to 4.0 per acre in the Redvers area of Saskatchewan (J. H. Stoudt personal communication), and 6.0 per acre from the Lousana area of Alberta (calculated from Smith 1958).

It appears, therefore, that prairie wetlands in Minnesota are often underutilized by mallards, probably because of a shortage of breeding stock.

EFFECTS OF HUNTING REGULATIONS

During the 1950s, the effect of hunting regulations on the mallard in Minnesota were generally similar each year. Variation in both season length and bag limit showed no evident relationship to band recovery or mortality (Lee et al. 1964:86). Judging from band recoveries, a week's delay in the opening of the season in 1955 and 1956, and a fifth duck in the bag in 1956, made

Table 2. Band recovery rates of mallard ducks banded in Minnesota as flightless young.

YEAR	NUMBER BANDED	PERCENTAGE OF BANDS RECOVERED IN YEARS AFTER BANDING									
		0–1	1–2	2–3	3–4	4–5	5–6	6–7	7–8	8–9	9–10
No special mallard regulations:											
1955–1961	1109 males	19.6	4.0	2.0	0.8	0.5	0.3	0.1	0.2	0.3	0.1
1955–1961	696 females	18.5	3.9	1.6	0.6	0.3	0.3	0.1	0.0	0.1	0.1
1955–1961	1805 both sexes[a]	19.2	3.9	1.8	0.7	0.4	0.3	0.1	0.1	0.2	0.1
Special mallard regulations:											
1962	268 both sexes	8.2	2.6	4.1	1.9	1.9	1.2	–	–	–	–
1963	442 both sexes	13.8	4.3	0.9	0.7	0.9	–	–	–	–	–
1964	738 both sexes	14.1	2.6	2.2	0.8	–	–	–	–	–	–
1965	523 both sexes	7.8	4.2	1.7	–	–	–	–	–	–	–
1966	509 both sexes	13.8	2.0	–	–	–	–	–	–	–	–
1967	567 both sexes	12.7	–	–	–	–	–	–	–	–	–
1962–1967	1564 males	11.8	3.0	1.8	1.1	1.4	1.6	–	–	–	–
1962–1967	1447 females	12.4	3.2	2.3	0.8	1.1	0.7	–	–	–	–

[a] The number of local mallards banded in 1960 and 1961 totalled 67. This number has little influence in the overall results.

little difference in mallard hunting mortality. The direct band-recovery rate for both 1955 and 1956 was 19 percent compared to a long-term average of 19.6 percent (Lee et al. 1964:86).

Greater hunting restrictions, modifications of regulations, and resulting variation in number of hunters in the 1960s produced measurable differences in hunting mortality as calculated from band recoveries. During 1962 and 1965 when the daily limit for mallards was one bird, the direct band-recovery rate was only 8 percent. In other years, when two or more mallards were permitted in the daily bag, the direct band-recovery rate was about 14 percent, even though there was considerable difference each year in the number of hunters afield and the total number of ducks harvested (Tables 2 and 3).

In recent years, the band-reporting (response) rate has declined (Martinson 1966, Martinson and McCann 1966, Henny 1967). Correcting the Minnesota returns in the light of these recent findings and adding one third for crippling loss, it appears that hunting mortality for Minnesota mallards was 35 percent in 1962, 61 in 1963, 63 in 1964, 35 in 1965, 61 in 1966, and 56 percent in 1967. Hunting mortality of young mallards was about the same in 1963, 1964, and 1966, as it had been in the 1950s, but in 1962 and 1965, when only one mallard was permitted, hunting mortality was about half as great. In 1967, hunting mortality was intermediate —about 56 percent.

The 1962 season, which was the most restrictive in the history of Minnesota waterfowl hunting, had the lowest hunting mortality ever recorded for mallards—35 percent—and, on the basis of bands now in, probably also the lowest total mortality —about 40 percent. It has not been possible to calculate total mortality for more recent years since all bands have not yet been reported. For 1962, the calculated natural mortality was 5 percent as compared to 14–21 percent in the 1950s. It appears, therefore, that decreased hunting mortality, because of a daily bag limit for mallards of one duck, was not compensated for by an increase in natural mortality as

Table 3. Minnesota waterfowl hunting regulations, hunter participation, and duck harvests during the 1960s.

YEAR	SEASON LENGTH	DAILY DUCK BAG	DAILY MALLARD BAG	NUMBER DUCK STAMPS SOLD	NUMBER DUCKS BAGGED[a]	NUMBER MALLARDS BAGGED
1960	40	4	4	139,000	996,000	468,000
1961	30	2	2	85,000	487,000	253,000
1962	25	2	1	78,000	376,000	159,000
1963	35	3	2	112,000	741,000	286,000
1964	40	4	2	129,000	1,151,000	352,000
1965	40	4	1	126,000	831,000	221,000
1966	45	4	2	150,000	1,244,000	363,000
1967	40	4	2	158,000	1,290,000	435,000

[a] Number of ducks bagged is not adjusted for response bias in hunter reports. Total duck harvests here are taken from federal calculations in Waterfowl Status Reports, U. S. Dept. Interior, Fish and Wildlife Service, Washington, D.C.

might theoretically be expected. This indicates, perhaps, that natural mortality includes delayed losses from shot carried by birds and that such delayed mortality is less when fewer hunters are afield.

If we assume hunting mortality to be about 60 percent in most years, and natural mortality about 20 percent, then total mortality from one year to the next approximates 80 percent. Even with a production of 1.5 young per adult, as has been estimated, it is obvious that the local breeding population cannot perpetuate itself and can be maintained only by augmentation from other sources.

REFUGES

The decline in populations of mallards and other waterfowl, as a result of unrestricted shooting, has long been observed. This led to the establishment of refuges on wintering grounds in the early 1900s and later, on migration routes and breeding areas. In such areas necessary habitat was retained or enhanced and the kill was often limited. In the breeding range, the assumption was made that refuges provided protected areas to which breeding ducks could return and raise broods. Providing support for this assumption, Salyer and Gillett (1964) gave annual production figures totaling over a quarter of a million birds for eight large federal refuges. This figure includes an annual production figure of 30,000 ducks of all kinds for Agassiz National Refuge in Minnesota.

There are few well-documented published studies on production of refuge areas, especially smaller areas, that consider the fate of the birds after they have been reared. This is the case despite the fact that in 1963 there were, in the United States, 220 federal refuges totaling about 2.6 million acres (about half of these in the Mississippi Flyway) and 1,360 state management areas, in 1961, totaling about 4.5 million acres, of which nearly half featured some refuge design (Salyer and Gillet 1964, Jorgensen et al. 1964). By 1969, Minnesota had 757 state-owned wetlands totaling about 220,000 acres (located in 81 of the 87 counties) and 56,000 acres of federally-owned smaller waterfowl production areas located mostly in the western part of the state. In addition, there were 164,000 acres of waterfowl habitat on six federal refuge units and 150,000 acres on larger state units. This provides about 600,000 acres of upland and aquatic habitat managed primarily for waterfowl. About two-thirds of this total area, including most of the state and federally owned small wetlands, was public hunting area. In 1968, there were 95 state statutory game refuges totaling 736,340 acres, many of which contained some waterfowl habitat.

The usual annual hunting kill of ducks in Minnesota is about one million birds. Perhaps one-fourth of these are raised here. There are at present slightly more than 2 acres of managed waterfowl habitat in Minnesota for each locally reared duck taken, about one-tenth of which is closed refuge. This amount of closed refuge area has not prevented an excessive kill of mallards reared in the state.

There has been doubt as to the effectiveness of refuges for protection of locally reared ducks. Jahn and Hunt (1964) concluded that refuges were of little benefit to locally reared ducks in Wisconsin primarily because birds, in their post-breeding wandering, left both refuge and non-refuge areas alike. The 20,000-acre Horicon National Wildlife Refuge failed to provide for the needs of mallards and they continued, during the hunting season, to travel up to 15 miles for preferred agricultural foods. Immature wild mallards, banded at Horicon from 1949 to 1955, had a 75-percent first-year mortality and 49 percent of the bands came from within 20 miles of the banding site (Jahn and Hunt 1964:129). Size of refuge, however, may make a difference. In Illinois, data from the banding of mallards on two widely separated refuges indicated that birds displaced from the smaller refuge (McGinnis Slough) experienced a "slightly higher" mortality than those which remained on the larger refuge (Bellrose and Chase 1950). Mallards leaving the smaller refuge apparently found less secure surroundings elsewhere than those remaining on the larger refuge. Displacement of birds is inferred from bandings made at a later date and recorded by Bellrose (1954).

Pirnie (1935) was of the opinion that refuges served useful functions, both to protect waterfowl from shooting and to increase hunting opportunity. Bellrose (1954) also valued refuges for both the welfare of the birds and enhancement of local hunting. These seemingly incongruous conclusions are taken to mean that hunting quality rather than quantity improved and that the harvest rates on the birds were reduced. The Federal Refuge Program has, as one of its functions, the reduction of hunting take. This role has been questioned by Crissey (1966). Factual information to establish the protective function of refuges under a variety of conditions, especially for breeding birds, seems to be lacking. LaCreek National Wildlife Refuge, South Dakota, and Seney National Wildlife Refuge, Michigan, both were inadequate to assure survival of hand-reared redheads (*Aythya americana*) released on these areas (Weller and Ward 1959). It appears that enhancement of breeding populations by establishing a refuge largely depends upon how well the needs of the birds can be provided for within the refuge during the hunting season.

In Minnesota, the largest contiguous land area closed to waterfowl hunting is the urban and suburban land which surrounds Minneapolis and St. Paul. This refuge has an area of nearly 500 square miles. During 1955 and 1956, censuses of breeding waterfowl populations were made and flightless young ducks were banded in northern Ramsey County (Minnesota Department of Conservation records). The mallard was the most numerous breeding duck, but the blue-winged teal was nearly as abundant. Mallards occupied 25–35 percent of the 140 available ponds checked, and occupancy by teal was somewhat higher. This rate of pond occupancy by mallards may be compared to an average of 7 percent in seven surrounding counties open to hunting

(582 ponds checked), and with 6.5 percent for ponds in six better western counties during these same years (309 ponds checked). It is evident that ponds in the closed area of Ramsey County had a substantially greater use by breeding mallards than ponds in other areas of the state.

For 66 flightless young mallards banded within this refuge, the first-year direct band-recovery rate was 23 percent and calculated first-year mortality 68 percent. Fifty-nine percent of all bands reported were from birds taken within Minnesota compared to 70 percent for the state as a whole. These findings by themselves should only be regarded as suggestive of the refuge effect since so few birds were banded.

The Agassiz National Wildlife Refuge in northwestern Minnesota encompasses 61,000 acres of which 25,000 acres are classified as wetland. In the summer of 1954, under a banding program by state and federal personnel, 241 flightless young mallards were captured within the refuge (Minnesota Department of Conservation records). A comparison of band recoveries from these birds with those of 191 local mallards banded in 1954 elsewhere in Minnesota indicates the following differences:

1. The direct band-recovery rate for mallards banded on the refuge was 16 percent. This is 12 percent less than the 28 percent recorded for birds banded elsewhere in the state.

2. The calculated first-year total mortality rate of young from the refuge was 71 percent as contrasted to 86 percent for those banded elsewhere in the state that same year.

3. The proportion of bands recovered from within Minnesota was 39 percent from the refuge mallards and 75 percent from those banded elsewhere in the state that same year.

These data indicate that large refuges provide some protection to local birds by reducing harvest rates and that there is a tendency to shift harvests of mallards reared on them to areas outside of Minnesota. It seems likely that smaller refuges could have been as effective if they contained within them enough habitat of high quality to satisfy the birds' needs. Additional protection would have been provided to birds reared on the large refuges discussed here had a number of smaller refuges been available in the surrounding countryside.

PRESENT AND POTENTIAL CONTRIBUTION OF LOCALLY-REARED MALLARDS TO FALL HARVEST

The present contribution of Minnesota-reared mallards to the fall harvest, both within and outside the state, can be approximated from statewide breeding-population estimates and application of the nesting-success rate as found on Minnesota study areas. Therefore, for purposes of calculation, about half of the 55,000 breeding pairs are assumed to ultimately rear six young to flying age. This would provide a fall flight of 275,000 local birds consisting of 110,000 adults and 165,000 young. Of these, about one-third of the young and one-fourth of the adults, or about 80,000 mallards, are typically bagged in Minnesota. An additional 30 thousand are taken outside the state. The Minnesota kill so calculated is equivalent to one fourth the average state kill of mallards during the 4 years, 1964–1967. Most of the remaining three-fourths come from Canada.

The Minnesota production estimates may be too high because of the relatively high estimated-reproduction rate, but certainly local mallards are an important part of the fall hunting take in Minnesota, and to a lesser extent, elsewhere in the Mississippi

Flyway. This could be expected to increase if greater occupancy of Minnesota breeding areas could be assured.

Substantial increase in state breeding populations of mallards can be expected with better habitat utilization and management (especially adjustment of harvest rates). It seems likely, considering data cited from other areas, that the more fertile prairie marshes of Minnesota have a potential productivity of 2–3 mallard ducklings a year, several times their present production. On a statewide basis, such increased production would probably require a breeding population of one-half to three-fourths of a million breeding pairs and could supply waterfowl hunters with a harvestable surplus in excess of a half million birds annually. It is unlikely, however, that such maximum utilization of Minnesota areas could be achieved within the limitations of present management capabilities without complete elimination of waterfowl hunting within the state.

Data on breeding mallard populations on the Agassiz National Wildlife Refuge in northwestern Minnesota, near the prairie edge, provide a more realistic and achievable indication of production potentials of Minnesota waters. Here, on 25,000 acres of wetland, the number of mallard breeding pairs has ranged from less than 1,000 to about 4,000, with an average of 2,500 in recent years (Balser et al. 1968). This is about one pair for 10 acres of wetland. The relationship of the size of the breeding population of mallards on the Agassiz Refuge to the statewide inventory of wetlands having high waterfowl value (Mann 1955), suggests that there is sufficient habitat for 200,000 or more breeding pairs of mallards in Minnesota—about four times the present number. This estimate is conservative since it only considers high-value wetlands. It seems reasonable, therefore, that the production of mallards in Minnesota could be doubled or quadrupled if local birds could selectively be protected from overharvesting. That this is possible is also evidenced by the figures cited earlier which show pond occupancy in the Minneapolis-St. Paul refuge area four times that in the adjacent non-refuge areas.

An eventual increase of mallard production in Minnesota that would increase the present harvest two to four times would benefit hunters in Minnesota and to a lesser extent throughout the Flyway, but it could come only with some limitation of hunting opportunities, at least intially, on breeding, migration, and wintering areas used by these ducks.

DISCUSSION FOR MANAGEMENT

The use of Minnesota wetlands by breeding mallards is less than that of some other areas, especially those in Canada. Also, the present breeding population in the state is evidently maintaining itself by augmentation from birds reared elsewhere. To increase the use of wetlands by breeding mallards and to produce more birds for hunting requires use of one or more of the following techniques:

1. Attraction of additional breeding mallards to Minnesota waterfowl habitat during spring migration as suggested by Girard (1941:234).
2. Increasing the reproductive success of mallards in Minnesota, especially the proportion of hens rearing a brood. This approach by itself would provide only a partial solution at the present level of hunting take.
3. Reduction of the harvest rates on Minnesota-reared mallards by regulation. This could be accomplished by reducing the harvest rate within Minnesota to that of other breeding

areas supplying the Mississippi Flyway, and/or by reduction of hunting kill on migration and wintering areas.

Considering these techniques, reduction of harvest by regulation, would probably most successfully increase breeding populations and ultimate production. Regulations are best suited to widespread application at minimal costs.

Regulations to reduce harvest rates must essentially involve: (1) limiting the daily bag; (2) limiting the period of hunting; (3) limiting the available areas to hunt; or (4) directly limiting the number of hunters participating.

Application of regulations which reduce daily bag or season length are non-selective to Minnesota-reared mallards. Reductions in the hunting take by these methods would reduce the take for all mallards frequenting the state each fall. Because of this non-selective effect, it is improbable that reduced seasons, such as those employing a one-mallard daily limit, could be held without strong objections when applied selectively in Minnesota. An objective of maximum recreational use of the total waterfowl resource in the state would have to be considered secondary to that of maximum production if statewide regulations are used to reduce local harvest rates.

Increased survival of mallards reared on large refuges in Minnesota indicate a selective reduction of harvest rates. The establishment of a pattern of small refuge units (limiting of areas to hunt) would likely favor scattered local birds over flocked migrants. Such a pattern would also be most compatible with existing hunter use of marshlands and with an objective of maximum use of the total waterfowl resource. It is uncertain, however, as to the extent to which such a program would have to be employed before accomplishing the needed reduction of harvest rates on local mallards.

This review has shown that mallard harvest rates have been excessive when the major take of birds has occurred on migration and wintering areas (historically); and, also, when the major take of birds has occurred within the state (current situation). It is proposed that a limitation of places to hunt near breeding marshes will more evenly distribute the hunting impact between breeding grounds and wintering areas. The success of such a program in conjunction with judicious hunting regulations throughout the breeding, migration, and wintering areas will enhance mallard survival and future production of these birds in Minnesota. If the goal of increased mallard production in Minnesota and maximum use of the total waterfowl resource is found to be unattainable by these methods, its resolution will then require direct limitation of hunter numbers according to a planned approach of harvest distribution.

LITERATURE CITED

ATWOOD, E. L. 1961. Waterfowl harvests in the Mississippi Flyway States during the 1960–61 hunting season. U. S. Fish and Wildl. Ser., Spec. Sci. Rept. Wildlife No. 56. 49pp.

———, AND C. F. WELLS, JR. 1960. Waterfowl harvests in the United States during the 1959–60 hunting season. U. S. Fish and Wildl. Ser., Spec. Sci. Rept. Wildlife No. 52. 25pp.

AVERY, C. 1916. Biennial report of the State Game and Fish Commission of Minnesota for the biennial period ending July 31, 1916. Syndicate Printing Co., Minneapolis. 83pp.

———. 1920. Biennial report of the State Game and Fish Comm. of Minnesota for the biennial period ending June 30, 1920. Syndicate Printing Co., Minneapolis. 92pp.

BALSER, D. S., H. H. DILL, AND H. K. NELSON. 1968. Effect of predator reduction on waterfowl nesting success. J. Wildl. Mgmt. 32(4): 669–682.

BELLROSE, F. C. 1953. A preliminary evaluation of cripple losses in waterfowl. Trans. N. Am. Wildl. Conf. 18:337–360.

———, AND ELIZABETH B. CHASE. 1950. Population losses in the mallard, black duck, and blue-winged teal. Illinois Nat. Hist. Surv., Biol. Notes 22. 27pp.

———. 1954. The value of waterfowl refuges in Illinois. J. Wildl. Mgmt. 18(2):160–169.

———. 1955. A comparison of recoveries from reward and standard bands. J. Wildl. Mgmt. 19(1):71–75.

BENSON, D. A. 1968. Waterfowl harvest and hunter activity in Canada during the 1967–68 hunting season. Canadian Wildl. Serv., Progr. Notes No. 5. 39pp.

BENSON, R. I. 1966. Waterfowl harvests 1960–63. Minnesota Conserv. Dept. Game Research Quart. Prog. Rept. 25(4):1–13.

BRECKENRIDGE, W. J. 1949. A century of Minnesota wildlife. Reprint—Minnesota Hist. Soc., June–Sept. 24pp.

CANADIAN WILDLIFE SERVICE. 1968. Species of waterfowl killed in Canada during the 1967–68 hunting season. Prog. Notes No. 7. Ottawa. 3pp.

CARTWRIGHT, B. W. 1945. Some results of duck banding in western Canada by Ducks Unlimited. N. Am. Wildl. Conf. 10:332–338.

CRISSEY, W. F. 1966. Present and future role of refuges. U. S. Dept. of Interior, Bur. Sport Fisheries and Wildl., paper presented Region 5 Conf., Boston, Massachusetts. 6pp.

———. 1967. Prairie potholes from a continental viewpoint. Seminar on small water areas in the prairie pothole region. Feb. 20–22, Saskatoon, Saskatchewan, Canada. 21pp.

CROFT, R. L., AND S. M. CARNEY. 1969. Species composition of the duck kill by states for the 1967–68 and 1968–69 hunting season. U. S. Dept. Interior, Bur. Sport Fisheries and Wildl., Migratory Bird Pop. Sta., Admin. Rept. No. 169. 17pp.

GEIS, A. D., AND E. L. ATWOOD. 1961. Proportion of recovered waterfowl bands reported. J. Wildl. Mgmt. 25(2):154–159.

———, AND R. D. TABER. 1963. Measuring hunting and other mortality. Pp. 284–298. *In* Wildlife Investigational Techniques. 2nd ed. The Wildlife Society, Washington, D. C. 419pp.

GIRARD, G. L. 1941. The mallard: its management in western Montana. J. Wildl. Mgmt. 5(3):233–259.

HATCH, P. L. 1880. A list of the birds of Minnesota. A report to N. H. Winchell, State Geologist, included in State Geologists Annual Rept. Pp. 359–383.

———. 1892. Notes on the birds of Minnesota. First report of the state zoologist. Geol. and Nat. Hist. Surv. of Minn. Harrison and Smith, Minneapolis. 487pp.

HENNY, C. J. 1967. Estimating band-reporting rates from banding and crippling loss data. J. Wildl. Mgmt. 31(3):533–538.

HUNT, R. A., L. R. JAHN, R. C. HOPKINS, AND G. H. AMELONG. 1958. An evaluation of artificial mallard propagation in Wisconsin. Wisconsin Conserv. Dept., Game Mgmt. Div., Tech. Wildl. Bull. No. 16. 79pp.

JAHN, L. R., AND R. A. HUNT. 1964. Duck and coot ecology and management in Wisconsin. Wisconsin Conserv. Dept., Tech. Bull. No. 33. 212pp.

JORGENSEN, S. E., F. T. STEINER, AND D. F. LAPOINTE. 1964. Places to hide—and seek: state areas. Pp. 509–518. *In* Waterfowl Tomorrow, U. S. Dept. of Interior, Bur. Sport Fish, and Wildl., J. P. Linduska (Editor). 770pp.

KEITH, L. B. 1961. A study of waterfowl ecology on small impoundments in southeastern Alberta. Wildl. Monograph No. 6. 88pp.

LEE, F. B., R. L. JESSEN, N. J. ORDAL, R. I. BENSON, J. P. LINDMEIER, R. E. FARMES, AND M. M. NELSON. 1964. Ducks and land use in Minnesota. Minnesota Dept. Conserv., Tech. Bull. No. 8. 140pp.

LENSINK, C. J. 1964. Distribution of recoveries from bandings of ducklings. U. S. Fish and Wildl. Ser., Spec. Sci. Rept. Wildl. No. 89. 146pp.

LOW, J. B. 1945. Ecology and management of the redhead, *Nyroca americana*, in Iowa. Ecol. Monographs 15:35–69.

MANN, G. E. 1955. Wetland inventory of Minnestoa. U. S. Dept. of Interior, Fish and Wildl. Serv., Office of River Basin Stud. 43pp.

MARTIN, E. L., AND S. M. CARNEY. 1968. Waterfowl kill survey. *In* Waterfowl Status Report—1968. U. S. Dept. of Interior, Bur. Sport Fisheries and Wildl., Spec. Sci. Rept. Wildl. No. 122. 158pp.

MARTINSON, R. K. 1966. Proportion of recovered duck bands that are reported. J. Wildl. Mgmt. 30(2):264–268.

———, AND J. A. MCCANN. 1966. Proportion of recovered goose and brant bands that are reported. J. Wildl. Mgmt. 30(4):856–858.

MENDALL, H. L. 1958. The ring-necked duck in the Northeast. Univ. of Maine Studies, Orono Second Ser., No. 73. 317pp.

PHILLIPS, J. C., AND F. C. LINCOLN. 1930. American waterfowl; their present situation and the outlook for their future. Houghton Mifflin Co., New York. 312pp.

PIRNIE, M. D. 1935. Michigan waterfowl management. Michigan Dept. of Conserv., Lansing. 328pp.

ROBERTS, T. S. 1919. Waterbirds of Minnesota; past and present. *In* Bien. Rept. of the State Game and Fish Comm. of Minnesota, for the biennial period ending July 31, 1918. Pp. 56–91.

———. 1936. The birds of Minnesota, Vol. I. Univ. of Minnesota Press, Minneapolis. 718pp.

SALYER, J. C., II, AND F. G. GILLETT. 1964. Places to hide—and seek: federal refuges. Pp. 497–508. *In* Waterfowl Tomorrow. U. S.

Dept. of Interior, Bur. Sport Fish. and Wildl., J. P. Linduska (Editor). 770pp.

SMITH, A. G. 1958. A progress report on the 1958 waterfowl surveys on the Lousana study area, Lousana, Alberta, Canada. U. S. Bur. Sport Fisheries and Wildl., Wildl. Research Lab., Denver, Colo. 12pp.

SOWLS, L. K. 1955. Prairie ducks: a study of their behavior, ecology, and management. The Wildlife Management Institute, Washington, D. C. 193pp.

STOUDT, J. H. 1959. Progress report: Redvers waterfowl study area with comparative data for several previous years. U. S. Bur. Sport Fisheries and Wildl., Wildl. Research Lab., Denver, Colo. 110pp.

WELLER, M. W., AND P. WARD. 1959. Migration and mortality of hand-reared redheads (*Aythya americana*). J. Wildl. Mgmt. 23(4): 427–433.

Received for publication July 14, 1969.

FIELD EVALUATION OF THREE TYPES OF WATERFOWL HUNTING REGULATIONS[1]

EDWARD J. MIKULA, Michigan Department of Natural Resources, Lansing
GERALD F. MARTZ, Michigan Department of Natural Resources, Lansing
CARL L. BENNETT, JR., Michigan Department of Natural Resources, Lansing

Abstract: Duck hunting regulations in the 1960's required hunters to identify species in flight. Violation rates were often high, and there was criticism of the federal government's management policies. In 1969, a Michigan experiment on a state game area compared the merits of three regulations: the point system, a simple two-bird limit, and the current species-oriented Mississippi Flyway-wide hunting regulations. Control of hunter activity permitted a complete bag check and an opinion poll. Observations of hunter performance provided estimates of violation rates and hunter selectivity in shooting. Crippling losses were not different between regulations. The highest duck harvest rates occurred under the two-bird limit, the point system had an intermediate harvest rate, and the flyway regulations, the lowest. Proportionately fewer high-point ducks were taken with the point system than with other regulations, but more low-point ducks and scarce black ducks (*Anas rubripes*) were taken under the flyway regulations. Mallards (*Anas platyrhynchos*) made up 73, 74, and 54 percent, respectively, of the harvests under the point system, two-bird limit, and flyway regulations. Mallard sex ratios were 2.53 males per female under the point system, 1.31 under the two-bird limit, and 1.36 under the flyway regulations. Observations of hunter performance confirmed the data for harvest rates among systems from the bag checks, with some exceptions noted under the flyway regulations. More hunter parties violated the flyway regulations (33 percent) than the point system (16 percent) or the two-bird limit (18 percent) regulations. Most violations under all systems were for overbagging or attempted overbagging. Opinions of 2,727 hunters were obtained on 6,778 ballots. Sixty-nine percent preferred the point system; 20 percent, the flyway regulations; and 11 percent, the two-bird limit. Opinions were influenced by experience with the systems and with the harvest rates obtained with each. We concluded that of the three regulations tested, the point system came closest to achieving the optimum utilization and manipulation of the waterfowl resource. It provided reasonable hunting opportunity, maximum hunter satisfaction, and acceptable hunter behavior.

During the 1960's, the demand for ducks outstripped the supply. Severe habitat deterioration—the result of widespread drought in the prairies of Canada and the United States—markedly reduced duck populations, particularly that of the mallard, the preferred target of most duck hunters.

During this period, federal, state, and provincial conservation agencies and the flyway councils employed restrictive regulations that were species-oriented and based on selective shooting. The objectives were to reduce the kill of several important duck species (including the mallard) and maintain adequate breeding stock, and, at the same time, to maintain hunter opportunity by maximum utilization of the available waterfowl resource. Thus, species management was explored extensively by manipulation of annual shooting regulations and through special seasons.

Large-scale data-gathering efforts involving breeding ground surveys, duck banding, duck wing collections, and kill surveys documented the capability of species management regulations to control changes in continental duck populations (Geis et al. 1969*a*, Geis 1963, Martinson et al. 1968, Geis and Crissey 1969). However, the species management concept had some serious shortcomings. Observations of hunter performance demonstrated that many hunters shot at certain ducks in disregard of regulations (Martin and Kaczinski 1968, Kimball 1969). Subsequent studies by Martz et al. (1969), Cooper (1969), and Evrard

[1] A contribution of the Michigan Department of Natural Resources, Wildlife Division, Research and Development Division, and P–R Project W–96–R.

Originally published in J. Wildl. Manage. 36(2):441–459, 1972.

(1970) demonstrated that most waterfowl hunters did a poor job of identifying ducks. These findings prompted many responsible officials to urge a return to simple harvest regulations (a small but set number of ducks of any species per day, with no identifications required) and to urge closing the season when necessary.

Against this background, a new species-oriented approach to duck hunting regulations was tested in 1968, during a special waterfowl season in the San Luis Valley of Colorado. Designated the *point system*, the regulation required only inhand identification of ducks after they were shot, to maintain legal bags. However, hunters capable of making inflight identification could increase the size of their bags by selecting certain ducks. The daily limit of ducks was determined by total points, with birds needing protection assigned high-point values, and those ducks for which increased gunning pressure was possible assigned low-point values. The hunter was required to stop hunting when the point value of the last duck killed, when added to the point values of previously killed ducks, reached or exceeded the daily point limit. This was a modification of the old and well-used fishing rule of "10 pounds plus one fish." To our knowledge, its application to duck hunters was first suggested in 1966 by John Rose of the Minnesota Wildlife Federation.

Analysis of data from the 1968 season in the San Luis Valley under the point system suggested that hunters liked the new system and that it had considerable promise for directing gunning pressure away from or toward specific species and sexes of ducks (Geis et al. 1969*b*). In 1969, the Bureau of Sport Fisheries and Wildlife and the Mississippi Flyway Council agreed to a test of the point system concept under controlled hunting conditions at the Shiawassee River State Game Area in Michigan.

The Shiawassee area offered a unique opportunity not only to test the point system but to test other alternative regulations; namely, a simple two-duck daily bag limit and the species-oriented Mississippi Flyway regulations of 1959. This was a pilot study on a unique area to gain information as to which class of regulation was the best for waterfowl harvest management in Michigan. The three regulations featured inhand identification and species orientation, simple count and no species differentiation, and inflight identification and species orientation. We also wished to determine to what degree data collected in a bag check were mirrored by observations of hunter performance. There are many different specific sets of rules possible within each class of regulation. The rules we used were arrived at in conjunction with the Bureau of Sport Fisheries and Wildlife.

We believe the ideal regulations should provide a maximum harvest of abundant ducks while protecting those in short supply, provide maximum hours of hunter recreation (opportunity), promote minimum illegal behavior, be enforceable, be simple and understandable, be acceptable to hunters, and enhance sport quality.

The authors thank Dr. A. D. Geis, U. S. Bureau of Sport Fisheries and Wildlife, for his numerous ideas and suggestions that were incorporated into the experiment. Many personnel from the Michigan Department of Natural Resources and the U. S. Bureau of Sport Fisheries and Wildlife made major contributions to the data collection phase of the experiment. We particularly thank M. Johnson and H. Dykema, district wildlife biologists associated with the Shiawassee River State Game Area, who facilitated collection of the checking station data. Drs. F. W. Stuewer, R. I.

Blouch, and D. W. Douglass of the Michigan Department of Natural Resources reviewed and edited the final manuscript.

THE STUDY AREA

The 7,635-acre Shiwassee River State Game Area, in east-central Michigan, about 10 miles southwest of the city of Saginaw, was selected for this study because of several unique characteristics. Because of good soils, production of cereal grains and soybeans, and water level control, this area and the adjacent 8,800-acre Shiawassee National Wildlife Refuge combine to attract 80,000–100,000 ducks each fall. A harvest of 2,000–6,000 birds is obtained from this population. One-half to two-thirds are mallards, but black ducks, green-winged teal (*Anas carolinensis*), and pintails (*Anas acuta*) are also important. Dabbling ducks make up about 85–90 percent of the harvest. We expected, therefore, that hunters would have opportunities to be selective and that sample sizes in the kill would be adequate to measure differences among the experimental systems in terms of species composition and harvest rates. Harvest rate, a term used throughout this paper, is defined as the kill of ducks per 1,000 hunter trips.

Water levels on approximately 3,000 acres of the game area can be controlled. Half of this acreage is lowland hardwood timber, another 600 acres is in natural marsh, and the remaining 900 acres is cropland. Much of the hunting is done in the flooded cropland, where strips of corn, left for hunter concealment, are surrounded by open water 1–2 feet deep. Quality hunting is provided by regulating hunter numbers and hunter spacing. The dikes, corn strips, and hunter spacing make the area an ideal place to observe hunter behavior at close range.

The opportunity to hunt on the game area is regulated by a random drawing held twice daily for separate morning and afternoon hunts. Hunters choose their hunting locations according to their order in the drawing. Permittees are required to stay in their assigned corn strips or hunting zones. Hunter spacing is designed to provide a minimum of 10 acres per hunter. At the end of their hunt, all permit holders are required to return their permits and present all game bagged for examination and to supply data on hunting hours and crippling loss. Other special rules also regulated hunter activity and controlled hunter access; for example, there was a limit of 25 shells per man, and shooting from dikes and using outboard motors in the hunting zones were prohibited.

METHODS

The three regulations tested in this experiment were as follows:

1. Point system. The daily limit was 60 points. The limit was reached when the point value of the last bird bagged, when added to point values of previously bagged birds, reached or exceeded 60 points. The 60-point birds were female mallard, black duck, female wood duck (*Aix sponsa*), redhead (*Aythya americana*), canvasback (*A. valisineria*), and hooded merganser (*Lophodytes cucullatus*). The 20-point birds were male mallard, male wood duck, American widgeon (*Mareca americana*), and ring-necked duck (*Aythya collaris*). The 10-point birds were all other ducks (including mergansers) and coots (*Fulica americana*).

2. Two-bird limit. The daily bag limit was two birds: any species or sex of duck (including mergansers) or coots.

3. Flyway regulations. The daily bag limit of ducks (except mergansers) was four, but it could not include more than one mallard, one black duck, two wood

Table 1. Comparisons of checking station statistics and hunter performance data by system of regulations.

	POINT SYSTEM	TWO-BIRD LIMIT	FLYWAY REGULATIONS	TOTAL OR AVERAGE
CHECK STATION DATA				
Number of Hunting Periods	38	20	12	70
October 10–27	17	10	7	34
Oct. 28–Nov. 14	21	10	5	36
Hunter Trips	4,774	1,732	1,189	7,695
Hours Hunted	15,782	5,299	3,733	24,814
Hours per Hunt	3.30	3.06	3.14	3.23
Reported Duck Kill	3,641	1,514	894	6,049
Female mallards	756	483	203	1,442
Black Ducks	221	140	126	487
All 60-point ducks	1,083	664	363	2,110
Male mallards	1,913	633	276	2,822
All 20-point ducks	2,114	705	370	3,189
All 10-point ducks	444	145	161	750
Total mallards	2,672	1,121	480	4,273
Coot Kill	149	23	73	245
Reported Crippling Loss (percent)[a]	18.7	18.5	18.6	18.6
HUNTER PERFORMANCE DATA				
Number of Parties Observed	129	79	46	254
Hunters per Party	2.37	2.20	2.35	2.31
Average Observation (hours)	3.06	2.98	3.12	3.04
Hunter Hours Observed	935	518	337	1,789
Waterfowl Flights Observed	1,206	581	714	2,501
Waterfowl Knocked Down	441	266	215	922

[a] Expressed as the proportion lost of all birds knocked down.

ducks, or one canvasback or redhead. The daily limit of mergansers was five, of which no more than one could be a hooded merganser. The daily limit of coots was 10.

The 1969 duck hunting season at the Shiawassee River State Game Area was designed to provide 70 half-day hunting periods, starting on the afternoon of October 10 and extending through November 14, but excluding the morning of October 20 (opening day of Michigan's pheasant season). Because the point system was such a new concept for Michigan hunters, we decided that 50 percent of the hunting periods should be devoted to the point system and approximately 25 percent each to the two-bird limit and the Mississippi Flyway regulations. On this basis, the three regulations were randomly assigned to the hunting periods, with the actual distribution skewed toward the point system and the two-bird experiment (Table 1). As a result of this distribution, the three regulations were not tested equally between the first and second halves of the season.

The system to be tested during each hunting period was listed, placed in a dated envelope, and sealed. After each morning and afternoon drawing, which determined the order of every party to select hunting locations on the managed area, the appropriate envelope was opened and the hunting system to be used was announced. This procedure was followed to minimize any possibility that hunters would avoid a particular system if the list was published in advance of the season.

To prevent confusion among hunters, because the hunting system could change from one hunting period to the next, a description of the rules being tested and the reasons for the experiment were announced over the public address system after each drawing. Each hunter also received a color-coded card describing the rules of the system being tested. These information cards matched identical cards of a large scale posted in the game area check station. The point system card also contained examples of permissible bags, and under all systems, the cards served as special transport permits for the birds bagged, after validation by check station personnel.

These procedures and the experimental design enabled us to conduct three separate data-collection programs for evaluating regulations—a bag check, observations of hunter performance, and an opinion survey. The hunter bag check was conducted at the check station. For each regulation, it gave us data on the total harvest, composition of the harvest, harvest rates, reported crippling loss, and mallard sex ratios.

A survey of hunter performance supplied data on many of those factors examined by the hunter bag check program and provided a check for comparing field activity with check station statistics. It also provided estimates of hunter compliance with the regulations and their shooting selectivity.

More than 90 percent of the observations were made by wildlife biologists of the Department of Natural Resources and by personnel from the Bureau of Sport Fisheries and Wildlife. A few qualified Michigan State University wildlife students also made observations. Observers used the Standard Hunter Performance Survey Card (USDI Form 3–171, revised August 1968) for recording observations of hunter performance. Observers recorded the time, the number and species of ducks in each flight of birds judged to be in range of the hunters being watched, plus those flights fired at that were out of range. The performance card also provided space for recording the number of shots fired, whether birds fell, and the fate of birds seen to fall (found and kept, found and discarded, not found, not searched for, or status unknown). Other data recorded included results of the post-observation bag check, violation information, and routine items on number of hunters, type and location of hunting, dog use, and time and weather features.

The entire hunt was observed for most parties selected for observation. The majority of observations were conducted in flooded cropland areas because, with the aid of binoculars, it was easy to observe hunters from the dikes or shooting strips at distances of approximately 200 yards. Observations were made only where we expected the greatest bird activity, so as to accumulate maximum data for the manpower expended. We believe the check station drawing sufficiently randomized permit holders and precluded exclusive use of desirable areas by a particular group or type of hunter. About half of the hunter observations were made in the first 2 weeks of the season (October 10 through October 27), because our records showed that waterfowl use and harvest were highest during this period. Through an oversight in planning, observations were distributed evenly throughout all days of the week, even though half of the hunting pressure and kill occurred on weekends.

The species and status of birds seen to fall during observations of hunter performance were corrected according to subsequent bag check information. For example, the fate of birds recorded as *status unknown* was often determined later to be *found and kept*. Similarly, a bird originally recorded only as *unidentified teal* could, for example, be determined later as a green-winged or a blue-winged teal (*Anas discors*). We estimate that about 20 percent of the species identification and status data from observations of hunter performance were corrected by subsequent bag checks. Therefore, conclusions reached in this study about the harvest rate and the species fired at, based on observations of hunter performance, also have a dependent relationship with the bag check.

A hunter-opinion program was conducted at the check station to measure hunter acceptance of each regulation. Upon termination of his hunt, each hunter was asked to complete a simple questionnaire that asked, "Which of the regulations under item 1 do you prefer?" Following this question were check (√) boxes for point system, two-birds daily, and statewide regulation, in that order. This questionnaire was completed after every hunt regardless of the number of times a person hunted. The questionnaires were not signed except for the small game license number by which we determined the number of different individuals registering opinions and related their opinions to their hunting success and experience with each of the systems.

After the season, we transcribed bag check, hunter performance, and opinion data from the field records to keypunch cards for computer tabulation, processing, and printout.

RESULTS

A total of 7,695 hunter trips involving 24,814 hours of hunting were recorded at the Shiawassee River State Game Area check station during the 1969 experimental season (Table 1). A harvest of 6,049 ducks was recorded: 3,641 under the point system regulation, 1,514 under the two-bird limit, and 894 under the Mississippi Flyway regulation. The average hunting trip was slightly longer under the species-oriented point system and the flyway regulations than under the two-bird limit, but crippling losses, averaging 18.6 percent of all birds knocked down, were not significantly different among the three hunting systems.

Personnel made observations on 254 hunting parties during the experiment. They observed 2,501 flights of waterfowl and recorded 922 ducks and coots knocked from the air by hunters, or about 12 percent of the combined check station kill and reported crippling loss.

Bag Check

Calculated harvest rates by hunting system for the entire season and for the first and second halves of the experiment are presented in Table 2. Data for the entire season suggested that the simple two-bird limit yielded higher harvest rates than either of the species-oriented regulations. This occurred for the total number of ducks, mallards, hen mallards, and all 60-point ducks. The flyway regulations produced the highest harvest rates on only black ducks, 10-point ducks, and coots. They also had the lowest harvest rates on the total number of ducks, mallards, male mallards, and all 20-point ducks. It is perhaps significant that, of the three regulations tested, the point system yielded the lowest harvest rates on the 60-point ducks (those assigned a high degree of protection), including both the important female mallard and the black duck. However, the point system yielded the highest harvest rates of any system for the abundant male mallard and all 20-point ducks, and it utilized 10-point ducks and coots at a rate second to the flyway regulations. Mallards comprised 73 and 74 percent, respectively, of the point system and two-bird limit bags, but the one-mallard daily limit of the flyway regulations was instrumental in limiting mallards to only 54 percent of that bag.

Table 2. Harvest of ducks and coots per 1,000 hunter trips and associated species and sex ratios based on birds examined at the Shiawassee River State Game Area checking station in 1969.

SPECIES, POINT CATEGORY, OR SPECIES AND SEX RATIOS	POINT SYSTEM			TWO-BIRD LIMIT			FLYWAY REGULATIONS		
	Oct. 10–27	Oct. 28–Nov. 14	Full Season	Oct. 10–27	Oct. 28–Nov. 14	Full Season	Oct. 10–27	Oct. 28–Nov. 14	Full Season
Female mallard	202	96	158	292	241	279	181	147	171
Black duck	47	45	46	70	111	81	114	88	106
All 60-point ducks	278	153	227	385	378	383	328	252	305
Male mallard	520	230	401	382	320	365	237	221	232
All 20-point ducks	582	243	443	429	346	407	333	261	311
All 10-point ducks	122	52	93	90	65	84	165	65	135
Total mallards	723	326	560	678	561	647	417	371	404
Total ducks	983	448	763	905	789	874	825	578	752
Coots (10-points)	38	21	31	17	4	13	79	20	61
Percent mallards	73	73	73	75	71	74	51	64	54
Mallard sex ratio (males : female)	2.6	2.4	2.5	1.3	1.3	1.3	1.3	1.5	1.4
Mallard : black duck ratio	15.4	7.2	12.1	9.7	4.7	8.0	3.7	4.2	3.8

The first half of the 1969 hunting season was a period of unusually high duck abundance at the Shiawassee area, particularly of mallards and the 10-point species. During this period, calculated harvest rates for the point system actually surpassed those of the two-bird limit and flyway regulations for the total number of ducks, mallards, male mallards, and 20-point ducks. This was different from the data for the entire season. However, the point-system harvest rates for 60-point ducks were still lower than the harvest rates recorded for the flyway regulations (intermediate) and the two-bird limit (highest). The best utilization of 10-point ducks and coots during this early period still occurred with the flyway regulations. Mallards constituted nearly three-fourths of the kill for the point system and the two-bird limit but only half of the harvest under the flyway regulations.

During the latter half of the 1969 season, the availability of mallards and 10-point ducks to Shiawassee hunters was considerably reduced due to departures of birds and changes in feeding patterns. Harvest rates were lower for all hunting systems compared with the first half of the season. Howver, this decline was not as severe for the two-bird limit, resulting in the two-bird system having the highest harvest rates of the three systems tested during the October 28–November 14 period. The flyway regulations had the next highest harvest rates during this late period, for all species and point categories (except male mallards and 10-point ducks). The point system had the lowest harvest rates. This represented a sharp reversal in the harvest rates for the point system for male mallards, total mallards, and total ducks, when compared with the first half of the experiment. Despite these changes, mallards still constituted almost three-fourths of the duck harvest for the point system and the two-bird limit but made up 64 percent of the bag under the flyway regulations.

As mallard sex ratios varied little between the first and second half of the experiment within the hunting systems, they are reported for the entire season. Mallard sex ratios were similar under the two-bird limit and flyway regulations (1.31 and 1.36 drakes per hen, respectively), but they were

Table 3. Numbers of waterfowl bagged, composition of the kill, and calculated harvest rates by hunting system, based on observations of hunter performance at the Shiawassee River State Game Area.

Species, Point Category, or Sex and Species Ratios	Point System			Two-bird Limit			Flyway Regulations		
	Birds Knocked Down		Birds Downed per 1,000 Hunter Trips	Birds Knocked Down		Birds Downed per 1,000 Hunter Trips	Birds Knocked Down		Birds Downed per 1,000 Hunter Trips
	Number	Percent		Number	Percent		Number	Percent	
Female mallard	82	20	268	73	28	420	30	15	278
Black duck	19	5	62	28	11	161	37	18	343
All 60-point ducks	115	27	376	107	41	615	71	35	657
Male mallards	227	54	742	98	37	563	69	34	639
All 20-point ducks	241	58	788	107	41	615	87	43	806
All 10-point ducks	52	12	170	28	11	161	36	18	333
Unknown mallards	4	1	13	17	6	98	10	5	93
Other unknown ducks	7	2	23	4	2	23	0	0	0
Total mallards	313	75	1,023	188	71	1,080	109	53	1,009
Total ducks	419	100	1,369	263	101	1,511	204	101	1,888
Coots	22	—	72	3	—	17	11	—	102
Mallard sex ratio (males : female)	2.8			1.3			2.3		
Mallard : black duck ratio	16.5			6.7			2.9		

highly distorted in favor of drakes under the point system (2.53 males per female). Mallard sex ratios in the two previous years of managed hunting at the Shiawassee River State Game Area had been 1.25 males per female in 1967 and 1.26 males per female in 1968 (Dykema 1968, 1969). In the point system, the sex ratio of 2.53 males per female represented a significant departure from these previous statistics. Colorado also experienced a sex ratio that shifted heavily to drakes (2.85 males per female) in a test of the point system at the San Luis Valley in 1968. During 1963–66, the San Luis Valley special hunts did not yield a sex ratio more distorted than 1.75 males per female, when seasons had no special restrictions on mallard sexes (values calculated from data in BSFW, Admin. Rept. 175, Table 8). During the 1970 waterfowl season at the Shiawassee area, when additional testing of the point system was conducted, the mallard sex ratio was only 1.56 drakes per hen in the harvest (Mikula et al. 1971). The 1970 season had vastly increased hunting pressure compared with 1969 and a reduced availability of male mallards. Under these circumstances, hunters were less selective in shooting than they were in 1969.

The ratio of mallards to black ducks during the experiment was highest under the point system (15.4) and lowest (3.7) with the flyway regulations. These differences suggested a strong interaction between mallard and black duck hunting rules, bird availability, and hunter selection.

Observation of Hunter Performance

Harvest rates for birds knocked down during observations of hunter performance were calculated in the same manner as for the bag check. This was done for comparative purposes. However, as a result of observations being concentrated in areas of maximum bird activity, harvest rates determined from observations of hunter performance were higher than harvest rates determined from checking station data. Hunter performance data also involved some unidentified ducks and some illegal

Table 4. Estimated numbers of waterfowl and associated species and sex ratios that would have occurred in the kill at the Shiawassee River State Game Area in 1969, by hunting system, had the measured kill rates for each system (birds bagged per 1,000 hunter trips) been applied for the whole season.

Species, Point Category, or Species and Sex Ratios	Point System			Two-bird Limit			Flyway Regulations		
	Oct. 10–27	Oct. 28–Nov. 14	Full Season	Oct. 10–27	Oct. 28–Nov. 14	Full Season	Oct. 10–27	Oct. 28–Nov. 14	Full Season
Female mallard	993	267	1,260	1,436	669	2,105	890	408	1,298
Black duck	231	135	366	344	308	652	561	244	805
All 60-point ducks	1,367	425	1,792	1,893	1,050	2,943	1,613	700	2,313
Male mallard	2,557	639	3,196	1,878	889	2,767	1,165	614	1,779
All 20-point ducks	2,862	675	3,537	2,109	961	3,070	1,637	725	2,362
All 10-point ducks	600	144	744	443	181	624	811	181	992
Total mallards	3,555	906	4,461	3,334	1,558	4,892	2,050	1,031	3,081
Total ducks	4,833	1,245	6,078	4,450	2,192	6,642	4,057	1,606	5,663
Coots	187	58	245	84	11	95	388	56	444
Percent mallards	73	73	73	75	71	74	51	64	54
Mallard sex ratio (males: female)	2.6	2.4	2.5	1.3	1.3	1.3	1.3	1.5	1.4
Mallard: black duck	15.4	7.2	12.2	9.7	5.1	7.5	3.7	4.2	3.8

ducks not reported to the check station. The hunter performance data were only sufficient to compare with the bag check for the entire season, without a breakdown for the early (October 10–27) and late (October 28–November 14) periods.

The relative harvest rates of ducks and coots between the point system and the two-bird limit regulations, as determined from observations of hunters, showed remarkable similarities to bag check data, as did the percentages of mallards in the bag, mallard sex ratios, and mallard: black duck ratios (compare Table 3 with Table 2). However, only a portion of the harvest rates, as determined from observations of hunters, for the flyway regulations matched results of the bag check. Similarities included harvest data for the hen mallard and the total number of mallards. When compared with the bag check, the harvest rates for the total number of ducks, black ducks, all 60-point ducks, male mallards, and all 20-point ducks, were proportionally greater than would be expected. We believe the discrepancies between hunter performance observations and bag check data under the flyway regulations were the result of sampling bias related to the small number of observations obtained in the hunter performance program.

We compared both the performance observations and the check station data for 233 parties of hunters. The kill per party reported at the check station was 0.988 bird per hour. In the field, we recorded 0.911 legal duck per hour as found and kept by these same parties. These statistics are so similar that we believe the changes in harvest rates recorded at the check station were fair approximations of changes in hunter behavior in the field as influenced by different regulations.

Projected Harvest Estimates

The ability to predict the total duck harvest with any set of regulations is vital to modern waterfowl management. Having previously determined the validity of harvest rates recorded at the check station, we applied data for each of the three regulations to the total number of hunting trips recorded in 1969, to arrive at a total estimated harvest for each system. These sta-

Table 5. Examination of hunter selectivity in shooting based on single species flights recorded during observations of hunter performance. (Percentage values listed only for sample sizes of 20 or more flights.)

Species or Point Category	Point System		Two-bird Limit		Flyway Regulations	
	Number of Flights	Percent Shot at	Number of Flights	Percent Shot at	Number of Flights	Percent Shot at
Female mallard	174	59	85	82	102	35
Male mallard	312	95	114	94	173	45
Unknown mallard	92	78	125	83	114	48
Subtotal	578	81	324	81	389	43
Black duck	79	61	41	100	53	79
Other puddlers	134	63	43	74	66	83
Subtotal (puddlers)	791	76	408	87	508	52
Subtotal (divers)	48	63	20	90	10	—
Unknown ducks	28	89	27	100	3	—
Total	867	76	455	88	521	53
60-point ducks	272	60	134	89	163	52
20-point ducks	343	92	129	92	194	49
10-point ducks	123	62	39	74	47	83
Coot	115	33	15	—	25	76

tistics were calculated for the first and second halves of the season and added for the final values (Table 4). This was done in recognition of the unequal distribution of hunting periods for each system between the first and second halves of the experimental season.

Instead of the actual harvest of 6,049 ducks recorded at the Shiawassee area in 1969, we estimated that 6,642 ducks would have been taken with a full season of the two-bird limit, 6,078 with the point system, and 5,663 under flyway regulations.

Hunter Selectivity in Shooting

Data in Tables 5–7 suggest a strong difference in hunter behavior among experimental systems involving the ducks shot at. With some exceptions, all types and point categories of ducks in flights containing only one species were shot at most frequently under the two-bird limit experiment (Table 5). The exceptions were 10-point and other dabbling ducks shot at most frequently under the flyway regulations and drake mallards, total mallards, and all 20-point ducks shot at with equal frequency under the two-bird limit and the point system. Sixty- and 20-point ducks were shot at less frequently under the flyway regulations. Data involving most of the ducks recorded during observations of hunter performance, including flights of more than one species, are presented in Table 6. The proportions of 60-, 20-, and 10-point birds observed to be knocked down by hunters during hunter performance checks agreed closely with bag check data for all three regulations. However, examination of the proportions of those birds that observers actually identified in flight suggested that hunters avoided shooting the protected 60-point ducks under the point system and actively sought the male mallard that had a medium point value. Under the point system, 10-point birds appeared to have been harvested in proportion in their availability.

Under the two-bird limit, birds in the various point categories were apparently taken in proportion to their availability. Under the flyway regulations, protected 60-point ducks were taken as they were avail-

Table 6. The influence of hunter selectivity in shooting on species composition of the kill, based on comparisons of observations of hunter performance and checking station records.

		Hunter Performance Observations				Bag Check	
		Flights of Identified Waterfowl		Waterfowl Knocked Down			
Regulations	Point Value	Number of Birds	Percent of Total	Number of Birds	Percent of Total	Waterfowl Reported	Percent of Total
Point system							
	60	1,418	37.3	115	26.7	1,083	28.6
	20	1,762	46.4	241	56.0	2,114	55.8
	10[a]	617	16.2	74	17.2	593	15.6
Total		3,797	99.9	430	100.0	3,790	100.0
Two-bird limit							
	60	596	47.6	107	43.7	664	43.2
	20	558	44.5	107	43.7	705	45.9
	10[a]	99	7.9	31	12.7	168	10.9
Total		1,253	100.0	245	100.1	1,537	100.0
Flyway regulation							
	60	614	35.1	71	34.6	363	37.5
	20	922	52.6	87	42.4	370	38.3
	10[a]	216	12.3	47	22.9	234	24.2
Total		1,752	100.0	205	99.9	967	100.0

[a] Includes coots.

able; however, 20-point ducks (mostly male mallards) were available to hunters at a rate higher than they were harvested. Under the flyway regulations, hunters would have to select some 10-point ducks to legally complete the daily four-bird bag allowed, since there was a limit of only one mallard and one black duck. As a result, 10-point ducks were found to be taken at a rate twice as great under the flyway regulations as their availability suggested.

Shooting selectivity by hunters strongly influenced mallard sex ratios in the kill under the point system experiment (Table 7). The mallard sex ratio for birds observed inflight was 1.61 drakes per hen, significantly less than the 2.77 drakes per hen recorded as shot down ($\chi^2 = 19.73$, 1 df), or the 2.53 drake:hen ratio of mallards recorded at the check station.

These data indicated no significant selection for drake mallards over hens under the

Table 7. The influence of hunter selectivity in shooting on mallard sex ratios, based on observations of hunter performance and checking station data.

	Hunter Performance Observations						Bag Check		
	Number of Mallards Observed in Flights			Number of Mallards Knocked Down			Number of Mallards		
Regulations	Males	Females	Males: Female	Males	Females	Males: Female	Males	Females	Males: Female
Point system	1,700	1,054	1.61	227	82	2.77	1,913	756	2.53
Two-bird limit	515	437	1.18	98	73	1.34	633	483	1.31
Flyway regulations	844	385	2.19	69	30	2.30	276	203	1.36

Table 8. Violation record of hunter parties observed during field performance checks.

Type of Violation	Percentage of Hunter Parties in Violation		
	Point System (129 parties observed)	Two-bird Limit (79 parties observed)	Flyway Regulations (46 parties observed)
Overbagging or attempted overbagging	7.8[a]	10.1	19.6
Discarding birds	7.8	3.8	17.4
Shot outside time limit	2.3	3.8	6.5
Other	1.6	2.5	0.0
Total[b]	15.5	17.7	32.6

[a] Five parties or 3.9 percent of those observed reordered their bags.
[b] The total (party) violation rate is less than the addition of component violations, since some parties violated more than one regulation.

non sex-oriented, two-bird limit or the flyway regulations. In the two-bird limit, 1.18 drake mallards per hen were observed among flying birds, whereas 1.34 drake mallards per hen were shot down ($\chi^2 = 0.72$, 1 df), and 1.31 drakes per hen were recorded at the check station. In the flyway regulations experiment, 2.19 mallard males per female were observed inflight, whereas 2.30 males per female were shot down ($\chi^2 = 0.01$, 1 df). These values were substantially greater than the 1.36 males per female ratio recorded in the bag check but were probably biased as a result of the small number of hunter performance observations.

Illegal Activity

It was impractical in the field to determine, under any of the systems tested, which hunters shot which ducks. Therefore, only the illegal behavior of hunting parties was recorded. Undoubtedly, this minimized the actual rate of technical violations that occurred, but party hunting,

Table 9. Retrieval status of all ducks and coots seen knocked down during the observations of hunter performance, by system and point category, as determined by the field observers.

Regulations and Status	60-point Birds		20-point Birds		10-point Birds		Point Category Unknown	All Birds	
	Number	Percent	Number	Percent	Number	Percent	Number	Number	Percent
Point System									
Found and kept	99	86.1	220	91.3	61	82.4	2	382	86.6
Not Found	11	9.6	15	6.2	6	8.1	3	35	7.9
Discarded[a]	4	3.5	3	1.2	6	8.1	5	18	4.1
Status Unknown	1	0.9	3	1.2	1	1.4	1	6	1.4
Total	115	100.1	241	99.9	74	100.0	11	441	100.0
Two-bird Limit									
Found and kept	93	86.9	92	86.0	27	87.1	6	218	82.0
Not Found	8	7.5	11	10.3	1	3.2	10	30	11.3
Discarded[a]	6	5.6	3	2.8	3	9.7	0	12	4.5
Status Unknown	0	0.0	1	0.9	0	0.0	5	6	2.3
Total	107	100.0	107	100.0	31	100.0	21	266	100.1
Flyway Regulations									
Found and Kept	61	85.9	76	87.4	35	74.5	3	175	81.4
Not Found	8	11.3	7	8.0	4	8.5	1	20	9.3
Discarded[a]	0	0.0	4	4.6	7	14.9	3	14	6.5
Status Unknown	2	2.8	0	0.0	1	2.1	3	6	2.8
Total	71	100.0	87	100.0	47	100.0	10	215	100.0

[a] Includes birds found and discarded and not searched for (when birds fell directly).

Table 10. Legal status of the ducks and coots knocked down during observations of hunter performance.

REGULATION	Number and Category of Birds Shot Down					
	Found and Kept	Not Found	Discarded	Status Unknown	Total	Percent
POINT SYSTEM						
Legal	374	33	—	1	408	92.5
Illegal	8	2	18	1	29	6.6
Other[a]	—	—	—	4	4	0.9
Total	382	35	18	6	441	100.0
TWO-BIRD LIMIT						
Legal	208	29	—	1	238	89.5
Illegal	10	1	12	0	23	8.6
Other[a]	—	—	—	5	5	1.9
Total	218	30	12	6	266	100.0
FLYWAY REGULATIONS						
Legal	165	18	—	1	184	85.6
Illegal	10	1	15	0	26	12.1
Other[a]	—	—	—	5	5	2.3
Total	175	19	15	6	215	100.0

[a] No determination possible as to legality.

although illegal, is traditionally practiced. Hunter performance observations indicated (Table 8) that the violation rates by parties were essentially similar under the point system and the two-bird limit, 15.5 and 17.7 percent, respectively. These values were about half the violation rate of 32.6 percent observed under the flyway regulations. Under the one-mallard daily bag of the flyway regulations, two-thirds of the violations were associated with overbagging. Under the point system, 5 of the 129 parties observed (3.9 percent) were involved in rearranging the order of the birds they shot, so that when they appeared at the check station they reported their bags as legal. The second most important violation of the species-oriented regulations was the discarding of ducks or coots. This violation was least prevalent under the two-bird limit.

We analyzed the fate of all birds shot down during the observations of hunter performance. The data (Table 9) suggested little difference among systems for the proportion of birds found and kept. Under all systems, the incidence of discarding birds (mostly coots) was highest for birds in the 10-point category.

Birds taken under the flyway regulations were more often judged to be illegal, based on their association with overbagging and discarding of birds, than were those taken under the two-bird limit and the point system (Table 10). Illegal birds constituted 12.1 percent of all birds downed under the flyway regulations, compared with 6.6 percent under the point system. The figure for the two-bird limit was intermediate.

Most hunters did not have the opportunity to take their legal limit (Table 11). About two-thirds of the hunters under the point system and the two-bird limit did not achieve a daily limit, and fewer than half the parties under the restrictive one-mallard flyway regulation failed to achieve their daily bag limit. Of those parties that had the opportunity to overbag, most left the field without attempting to take additional birds (62 percent under the flyway regulations and 73 and 78 percent, respectively,

Table 11. Bag limit achievements and bag limit violations by hunter parties observed during performance checks.

ACHIEVEMENT CATEGORY	POINT SYSTEM		TWO-BIRD LIMIT		FLYWAY REGULATIONS	
	Number	Percent	Number	Percent	Number	Percent
Hunter parties observed	129	—	79	—	46	—
Party bag limit not obtained (therefore no opportunity to overbag)	88	68	50	63	20	43
Parties with opportunity to overbag (total limit or minimum mallard limit attained)	41	32	30	37	26[a]	57
Parties with opportunity that did not attempt to overbag (includes parties leaving the field)	32	78	22	73	16	62
Parties with opportunity that attempted to overbag	9	22	8	27	10	38
Parties with opportunity that achieved excess bags	8[b]	20	6	20	9	35

[a] In these cases the four-bird bag, or maximum limit, contained the one-bird mallard limit, but only one party (2.2 percent of the total) achieved the maximum legal bag of four birds per man.
[b] Includes parties that reordered their bags.

under the two-bird limit and point system). Of those parties staying on after achieving a bag limit and attempting to overbag, 35 percent hunting under the flyway regulations actually did so, whereas only 20 percent of the parties under the point system and the two-bird limit exceeded their limits.

Hunter Opinions

We recorded 6,778 opinions of hunter preference regarding the experimental regulations. These opinions, which we viewed as ballots, were cast by 2,727 individual hunters. Hunters favored the species and sex-oriented point system (69.2 percent). In second place, with 20.0 percent of the votes, was the species-oriented flyway regulation. Least preferred, with 10.8 percent of the votes, was the simple, uncomplicated, but seemingly restrictive, two-bird limit. A comparison of data for the first and second halves of the season showed no significant shift in the proportion of opinions favoring the two-bird limit but suggested that the point system gained in popularity during the late part of the experiment at the expense of the flyway regulations.

In an attempt to better understand this voting, we examined the votes registered, the actual experience of hunters with each system (Table 12), and the harvest rates achieved by hunters under each system

Table 12. The relationship between experimental systems hunted under and the preferences expressed toward them by hunters.

SYSTEM(S) OF EXPERIENCE[a]	HUNTER PREFERENCES RECORDED							
	Point System		Two-bird Limit		Flyway Regulations		Total	
	Number	Percent	Number	Percent	Number	Percent	Number	Percent
1	361	73.2	46	9.3	86	17.4	493	99.9
2	41	39.0	32	30.5	32	30.5	105	100.0
3	100	48.5	21	10.2	85	41.3	206	100.0
1, 2	174	59.8	53	18.2	64	22.0	291	100.0
1, 3	1,304	69.2	130	6.9	451	23.9	1,885	100.0
2, 3	177	53.3	74	22.3	81	24.4	332	100.0
1, 2, 3	2,531	73.0	378	10.9	557	16.1	3,466	100.0
Total or average	4,688	69.2	734	10.8	1,356	20.0	6,778	100.0

[a] 1 = point system, 2 = two-bird limit, 3 = flyway regulations.

Table 13. The relationship between kill rates and the preferences expressed by hunters toward the experimental systems.

Greatest Kill per Hour	Hunter Preferences Recorded							
	Point System		Two-bird Limit		Flyway Regulations		Total	
	Number	Percent	Number	Percent	Number	Percent	Number	Percent
Point system	1,705	75.5	200	8.9	353	15.6	2,258	100.0
Two-bird limit	1,368	70.8	252	13.0	312	16.1	1,932	99.9
Flyway regulations	651	67.7	83	8.6	228	23.7	962	100.0
Systems tied or no kill	964	59.3	199	12.2	463	28.5	1,626	100.0
Total or average	4,688	69.2	734	10.8	1,356	20.0	6,778	100.0

(Table 13). Both experience and kill influenced hunter opinions. All but two of the experience categories of hunters (Table 12) cast majority opinions favoring the point system concept, but those people who experienced only the two-bird limit or flyway regulations voted less frequently for the point system. However, 73 percent of those hunters experiencing at least one trip under all three hunting systems chose the point system.

When hunters were placed into categories of harvest rates, and their opinions examined accordingly (Table 13), 59 to 76 percent of all groups (even unsuccessful hunters) preferred the point system. However, these data also suggested that the two-bird limit and the flyway regulations received a larger proportion of favorable opinions when hunters experienced higher harvest rates with those two systems than with the point system.

DISCUSSION AND CONCLUSIONS

Having determined characteristics of the harvest and hunter attitudes and behavior toward the three hunting systems tested, we feel it pertinent to make a determination as to which of the three regulations tested appears best suited to current waterfowl management needs in Michigan, and possibly elsewhere. Thus, our discussion is based on the desired characteristics for what we believe are ideal harvest regulations.

1. The regulations should provide for maximum utilization of abundant ducks while protecting those in scarce supply (selective shooting principle).

The harvest statistics from the test of the point system demonstrated that most hunters were capable of selectively shooting the common drake mallard inflight, while avoiding the female mallard and black duck. Data obtained under the flyway regulations showed that hunters not only recognized and avoided mallards but sought and increased the proportion of nonmallard ducks in their bags. It was possible with a complex regulation, such as the point system or flyway regulations, to successfully direct shooting pressure toward or away from the species or sexes of ducks common to a geographical area and therefore familiar to many of the hunters.

When selective shooting was not required, as with the two-bird limit, hunters did little or no selecting of the birds they shot. Therefore, both the point system and flyway regulations offered greater flexibility in utilizing and manipulating waterfowl populations than the simple two-bird limit.

The point system was designed and tested as a mallard-oriented regulation, both in this Michigan test and in the San Luis Valley test. Substantial increases in gunning pressure were placed upon male mallards with relatively little increase in pressure on other low or medium value species. This resulted from hunter preferences for male mallards but could be altered by different point allocations for species.

Most recent estimates encompassing the 1967–69 period suggest that in the prehunting season, the sex ratio of mallards in the United States has been approximately 1.0 male per female for immatures and 1.5 males per female for adults (Anderson et al. 1970). If one assumes that a reasonable fall flight contains 22 million mallards, with a ratio of 1.10 young per adult, and then applies the 1967–69 sex ratio to these data, one can calculate that somewhat more than 2 million male mallards are in excess of an even sex ratio. This surplus seems large in comparison with the annual harvest of about 4 million mallards in the United States; it is probably the accumulated product of 5–10 years of differential mortality. Should this surplus be dissipated without an increase in hen survival and subsequent total mallard production, then the benefit of selective mallard drake shooting could be short-lived. We are also uncertain of the biological implications of an even sex ratio versus excess males, for maintaining mallard productivity. Additional research is needed to resolve these important questions.

The use of selective shooting regulations does create a problem, in that restrictions or liberalizations of harvest regulations for a target species may have significant and perhaps unwanted effects on the harvest of other species. We found substantial decreases in mallard harvest rates when changing from the point system (1–3 mallards a day) to the flyway regulations (one-a-day mallard limit). However, apparent hunter preference for big ducks or the effect of bag limit differentials caused hunters to substitute a black duck for a second mallard under the flyway regulations, and as a result, the one-a-day black duck provision was ineffective in holding down the black duck harvest. In previous years, mallards acted as a buffer on the black duck kill. This phenomenon has probably been operating in the Mississippi Flyway, where, in 7 of the last 11 years (1960–70), black duck limits have been more liberal than mallard limits. This may be a contributing factor in the reduction of the black duck population (Addy 1968:4), at least in the western portion of its range.

2. The regulations should provide maximum hunter time in the field (opportunity).

Because the two-bird limit yielded a higher duck harvest rate and would have yielded a greater total harvest than either of the species-oriented regulations, any hunting season employing a simple bag limit would need to be short for a given harvest of birds, if other factors such as hunter participation or shooting hours were not drastically altered. In effect, the passing up of some shooting opportunities because of species-identification requirements in either the point system or flyway regulations saves some birds to be harvested at a later time. In this study, the hours per hunt were slightly greater for both the point system and flyway regulations than for the two-bird limit. We feel that the species regulations provided a reasonable trade-off of birds bagged for additional time in the field. If hunter recreation can be equated with maximum time spent afield, then species regulations appear to be most advantageous.

3. The regulations should promote minimum illegal behavior and be enforceable.

Many individuals have been concerned that the incentive of the point system—big bag limits for some species and sexes of ducks—will tempt hunters to discard high-point birds until they achieve a bag of the desired species. The practice of discarding birds was higher under the point system than under the simple two-bird limit, but it was highest of all under the flyway regulations. Managing the harvest by the point system, therefore, reduced the discarding of birds and violations of the bag limit substantially, when compared with the flyway regulations, to a degree almost as low as with the two-bird limit.

Reordering, a form of overbagging unique to the point system, is accomplished by rearranging the order of ducks as they are actually killed from a sequence that is illegal to one that appears legal in a bag check. Reordering will be more difficult and time-consuming for enforcement officers to detect than conventional overbagging and might become a more serious problem in expanded use of the point system. We feel, however, that the low percentage of reordering observed in this experiment does not present a real threat to the orderly management of the resource in view of the gains obtained in selective shooting behavior.

4. The regulations should be simple and understandable.

For the hunter, the two-bird limit was the simplest and most understandable regulation tested, since no qualifications were added to the bag limit, not even the separation of coots from ducks. In our opinion, the point system is more complicated than the current flyway regulations, and the addition of sex features to species requirements is sufficient reason to conclude that this is the most complicated regulation we used.

Nonetheless, we believe that the point system was understood because (1) today's hunter has been associated with complex flyway regulations for at least 10 years; (2) a careful explanation of the point system, including distribution of a regulations card, was provided to hunters; (3) few complaints were voiced that the regulations were complex; and (4) violation rates were about as low with the point system as they were with the easily understood, two-bird limit.

5. The regulations should be acceptable to hunters.

We cannot pretend, especially by use of our simplified questionnaire, to fully understand all factors that contribute to a rewarding hunting experience. However, if taken at face value, the preference poll of the Shiawassee area hunters demonstrated that the point system regulations incorporated features that pleased them. Harvest rates were better for many hunters under the two-bird limit and flyway regulations, yet these hunters still voted overwhelmingly for the point system. We believe that the maximum possible bag (whether attained or not) had a marked influence on hunter decisions. For the point system, the maximum possible bag was six ducks; for the flyway regulations, four ducks; and for the two-bird limit, two ducks.

There are other logical reasons that may explain the acceptability of the point system. Essential duck identifications are changed from inflight to inhand specimens when compared with the flyway regulation. The point system is the first species-oriented hunting regulation that incorporates a provision for a true mistake for the hunter. The last duck shot always becomes the control bird that determines whether hunting can continue or whether a point limit has been reached. Geis et al. (1969:7) have stated that the honest hunter achieves freedom from fear of accidental violation—the killing of a protected duck. Perhaps this is so, and instead of a mistakenly shot duck being discarded or bootlegged, it serves as a lesson in duck identification and can be taken home legally.

6. The regulations should enhance sport quality.

This item was not directly tested in the Shiawassee Game Area experiment, but some relationships can be discussed. Duck hunting can be defined, in part, as those values that provide human satisfaction through opportunities to be afield and to bag ducks. Satisfaction is achieved when the rewards of the sport, the opportunity, and the bag are reasonable. Hunters, being individualistic, have different expectations concerning these values. Some hunters are easily satisfied, but others must attain a high return. Therefore, if wildfowling is to be preserved, it must appeal to a wide range of hunters to obtain the interest and economic support needed to maintain habitat in the face of other human demands.

If we accept this premise as valid, then regulations play an important role in a satisfying experience. In this regard, the simple two-bird limit has serious shortcomings. For reasons stated earlier, the two-bird limit cannot provide as long a season for the supply of ducks available; therefore, it does not provide the opportunity of a species- or sex-oriented regulation, or both. The two-bird limit provided a reasonable minimum daily bag for Shiawassee Game Area duck hunters, as evidenced by the low violation rates. However, the two-bird limit cannot provide the challenge of high bag limits to the more sophisticated and skillful hunters. In fact, skills evidenced in the choice of hunting location, in shooting ability, in artful use of calls, decoys, dogs, and watercraft, in duck identification, and in birds bagged, are downgraded. The quality of wildfowling is undermined through loss of traditional values.

In contrast, the point system appears to offer a unique potential for satisfying expectations of a variety of hunters with regard to the bag limit. A minimum bag limit is provided (in this experiment, one 60-point bird). However, a high limit is possible, if it is made up of low-point, abundant species, and it can be achieved only by increased effort and skill. Most Shiawassee Game Area hunters accepted this latter provision as a greater challenge to the shooting of scarce species. Thus, the point system enhanced quality.

All the regulations we tested had certain deficiencies. However, in this pilot study, the species- and sex-oriented point system regulation most closely fitted the criteria selected as important for modern waterfowl management in our state. It seemed to be a better regulation than the complex system previously used in Michigan and better than the simple regulation tested. On this basis, we recommended the point system for statewide testing. If further experience during statewide testing reveals no more significant shortcomings of the regulation than were witnessed in this study, it appears to be the system best suited to manipulate and to fully utilize waterfowl populations, to provide the hunter ample time in the field (opportunity), to provide the most hunter satisfaction, and to promote acceptable hunter behavior.

LITERATURE CITED

ADDY, C. E. 1968. General review: the black duck, evaluation, management, and research. Symp. Atlantic Waterfowl Council, Chestertown, Maryland. 193pp.

ANDERSON, D. R., R. S. POSPAHALA, H. M. REEVES, J. P. ROGERS, AND W. F. CRISSEY. 1970. Estimates of the sex composition of the 1967–69 mallard population. Migratory Bird Populations Sta. Admin. Rept. 182. 14pp.

COOPER, J. A. 1969. An evaluation of species identification levels for a sample of Massachusetts waterfowl hunters. M. S. Thesis. Univ. of Massachusetts. 140pp.

DYKEMA, H. 1968. 1967 waterfowl season in Shiawassee River State Game Area. Michigan Dept. Nat. Resources Wildl. Div. Rept. 2622. 7pp.

———. 1969. 1968 waterfowl season at Shiawassee River State Game Area, Saginaw County. Michigan Dept. Nat. Resources Wildl. Div. Rept. 2638. 7pp.

EVRARD, J. O. 1970. Assessing and improving the ability of hunters to identify flying waterfowl. J. Wildl. Mgmt. 34(1):114–126.

GEIS, A. D. 1963. Role of hunting regulations in migratory bird management. Trans. N. Am. Wildl. and Nat. Resources Conf. 28:164–171.

———, AND W. F. CRISSEY. 1969. Effect of restrictive hunting regulations on canvasback and redhead harvest rates and survival. J. Wildl. Mgmt. 33(4):860–866.

———, R. K. MARTINSON, AND D. R. ANDERSON. 1969*a*. Establishing hunting regulations and allowable harvest of mallards in the United States. J. Wildl. Mgmt. 33(4):848–859.

———, E. M. MARTIN, R. HOPPER, H. FUNK, AND R. BULLER. 1969*b*. Progress report: 1968 experimental duck hunting season in the San Luis Valley of Colorado—an evaluation of the "Point System" in regulating the harvest. Migratory Bird Populations Sta. Admin. Rept. 175. 18pp.

KIMBALL, C. F. 1969. Mallard bag violation by hunter parties limited to a daily bag of one mallard during the 1965 and 1968 hunting seasons, based on the hunter performance survey. Migratory Bird Populations Sta. Admin. Rept. 180. 3pp.

MARTIN, E. M., AND C. F. KACZINSKI. 1968. Hunting activity and success during the 1967 experimental September teal hunting season. Migratory Bird Populations Sta. Admin. Rept. 155. 15pp.

MARTINSON, R. K., A. D. GEIS, AND R. I. SMITH. 1968. Black duck harvest and population dynamics in eastern Canada and the Atlantic Flyway: the black duck, evaluation, management, and research. Symp. Atlantic Waterfowl Council, Chestertown, Maryland. 193pp.

MARTZ, G., G. L. ZORB, AND M. K. JOHNSON. 1969. Qualifying to hunt waterfowl through testing and training. Michigan Research and Development Div. Rept. 173. 18pp.

MIKULA, E. J., G. MARTZ, C. BENNETT, JR., AND M. K. JOHNSON. 1971. The 1970 point system experiment, Shiawassee River State Game Area, Saginaw County, Michigan. Michigan Dept. Nat. Resources Wildl. Div. Rept. 2680. 21pp.

Received for publication June 28, 1971.

MANAGED GOOSE HUNTING AT HORICON MARSH[1]

RICHARD A. HUNT[2] and J. G. BELL, Wisconsin Conservation Department, Horicon, WI
L. R. JAHN,[3] Wildlife Management Institute, Horicon, WI

In recent years, goose hunting activities on and in the vicinity of the Horicon National Wildlife Refuge, located in southeastern Wisconsin, have attracted the attention of hunters, wildlife managers and conservationists. The principal objective of this paper is to trace developments in goose hunting at Horicon Marsh and review some of the management practices involved. In describing developments, we will concentrate on two aspects, (1) hunting opportunities and (2) goose harvest.

As a state agency, the Wisconsin Conservation Department has the basic obligation of providing an adequate and flexible system for the protection, development and use of the outdoor resources of the state. With respect to the Canada goose (*Branta canadensis interior*) resource, the challenge to meet this obligation has increased in magnitude during the last 10 years. Canada geese have always been a much sought-after species and a highly-prized game bird. The species has always been a common spring and fall migrant. Its relative unimportance, prior to 1950, was due to the limited numbers attracted to refuge areas during hunting seasons. At the time of their publication, "Canada Geese of the Mississippi Flyway," Hanson and Smith (1950) considered only two fall concentration sites of importance in Wisconsin, (1) the Rock Prairie Refuge in the extreme south-central area and (2) the Greenwood Farms Refuge in the central area. While several thousand geese used these state-controlled refuges each fall, hunters harvested only a few hundred birds at each area. The Horicon National Wildlife Refuge, which was established in 1940, was not mentioned. Rapid development of the Horicon Refuge as a fall goose concentration site in 1949 resulted in the Wisconsin Conservation Department taking greater interest in goose management and research.

DESCRIPTION OF AREA

Horicon Marsh lies immediately north of the City of Horicon in Dodge and Fond du Lac counties. The marsh is 14 miles long, averages 3.5 miles in width, and totals 31,653 acres. As the goose flies, it is approximately 800 miles south of the breeding range along the Hudson Bay coast and about 475 miles due north of the principal winter range in the Horseshoe Lake, Illinois area. The southern one-third (10,857 acres) of Horicon Marsh is state-owned and serves primarily as a public hunting and fishing grounds. The northern two-thirds (20,796 acres) is federally owned and is known as the Horicon National Wildlife Refuge. Because of high public use of the state-owned portion and the emphasis on duck management, relatively few geese concentrate there in fall. This paper deals with fall populations of Canada geese on the federally owned portion, unless otherwise specified.

Within the federal refuge, approximately two-thirds of the area is covered by 1–2 feet of water and is highly pro-

[1] Originally published in Trans. North Am. Wildl. Nat. Resour. Conf. 27:91–106, 1962.

[2] Address correspondence to this author. Present address: 309 Birchcrest Rd., Horicon, WI 53032.

[3] Formerly Wisconsin Waterfowl Research Project Leader stationed at Horicon from 1950 through 1959.

ductive aquatic habitat. Emergent aquatic vegetation is dominant, but does not completely cover the flooded area. A variety of management practices are used to maintain or manipulate the aquatic vegetation for duck and coot use, and in some years for muskrat populations. Geese use the aquatic areas for watering, roosting and loafing, and some feeding. Most of the feeding activities are concentrated on the 1,500 acres of agricultural land located along the periphery of the refuge.

Some of Wisconsin's best agricultural lands surround the Marsh. Dairying is the principal form of farming. Hay and corn are the important crops. Canada geese and dairy farming are highly compatible. Geese make feeding flights to farm lands as far as 15 miles from the refuge. Most off-refuge flights are west and north. Contributing importantly to the northern flight pattern is the Thornton Closed Area, a privately developed refuge of about 900 acres located 8 miles northeast of the marsh. In some years, daily feeding flights between the Thornton Area and Horicon Marsh contribute significantly to goose hunting opportunities.

GOOSE POPULATIONS

Basically, the Canada geese using Horicon Marsh are part of the Mississippi Valley population. A major portion of the Canada goose band recoveries occurring at Horicon Marsh are primarily from unpublished Illinois studies conducted on the winter range. A few recoveries also occur from the work at Jack Miner Sanctuary in Kingsville, Ontario, and from the large banding program being carried out at the Swan Lake National Wildlife Refuge in Missouri. Our own banding work in the early 1950's yielded recoveries well within the limits of the Mississippi Valley population (Hanson and Smith 1950:76).

Although part of the Horicon Marsh was established as a federal refuge in 1940, Canada geese did not start concentrating on the area in large numbers until the late 1940's. A peak fall population of over 10,000 Canadas occurred for the first time in 1949. Almost every year since then has seen a continuing increase, with 1961 being the highest when over 100,000 Canadas used the refuge (Table 1). Increased numbers of Canada geese at Horicon Marsh have resulted from a combination of factors. Development of the refuge has created greatly improved food and water conditions, as well as furnishing protection to the birds. Refuge farming operations have stressed increasing acreages of alfalfa and fall-planted greens for browse and increasing corn acreages and yields. Other important factors include: (1) a greater availability of geese due to the increased flyway populations, (2) manipulation of hunting regulations to permit an early build-up of fall goose-use on the refuge and surrounding areas and (3) gradual changes in farming operations on private lands around the refuge aimed at providing feeding areas to attract geese.

DEVELOPMENT OF GOOSE HUNTING

Goose hunting interest began to develop in the years immediately after World War II, when a few thousand geese started using the refuge each fall. Road-side hunter checks were established in 1949 and continued through 1952. During that period, free-lance goose hunting was largely eliminated. Peripheral farms offering good hunting were leased, and daily fee shooting developed on many other farms. Establishing the actual status of hunting privileges (i.e., lease, daily fee,

Table 1. Fall Canada goose population data Horicon National Wildlife Refuge 1949–61.

Year	Date geese arrived	Number geese Oct. 1	Opening of goose hunting		Peak goose pop.		Close of goose hunting		Average fall goose population[1]
			Date	No. geese	Date	Number	Date	No. geese	
1949	Sept. 12	1,600	Oct. 14	3,900	Nov. 1	12,000	Nov. 22	100	5,600
1950	Sept. 22	1,000	Oct. 14	8,000	Nov. 14	20,500	Nov. 16	20,000	12,100
1951	Sept. 18	5,000	Oct. 13	12,500	Oct. 25	24,000	Nov. 25	1,000	12,000
1952	Sept. 18	4,000	Oct. 4	5,000	Oct. 21	17,500	Nov. 27	13,000	14,000
1953	Sept. 16	3,000	Oct. 3	3,000	Nov. 1	30,000	Nov. 26	15,000	21,500
1954	Sept. 16	5,000	Oct. 2	5,000	Nov. 3	47,000	Nov. 25	30,000	37,800
1955	Sept. 15	20,000	Oct. 1	20,000	Nov. 1	31,200	Dec. 9	1,000	23,400
1956	Sept. 16	3,000	Oct. 1	3,000	Oct. 31	67,300	Dec. 9	1,000	40,200
1957	Sept. 20	5,000	Oct. 15	32,000	Oct. 21	37,400	Dec. 9	700	22,900
1958	Sept. 16	4,000	Oct. 15	47,100	Oct. 20	50,300	Nov. 16	28,000	48,200
1959	Sept. 15	14,200	Oct. 15	75,000	Oct. 15	75,000	Dec. 2	6,000	47,500
1960	Sept. 12	12,000	Oct. 7	40,000	Nov. 2	73,300	Oct. 16	70,000	62,300
1961	Sept. 12	41,000	Oct. 7	57,000	Nov. 1	100,200	Oct. 25	92,000	83,500

[1] The average number of Canada geese present between October 10 and November 15.

hunting by permission, etc.) was complicated by lack of any licensing system or special regulation of such hunting areas. By 1952 many hunters had only two places to hunt geese. They either stood on the roads or railroad tracks around the refuge, or they hunted along the south boundary of the refuge on the state-owned portion of the marsh. Under such conditions, poor sportsmanship, wild shooting, high crippling loss, and trespassing on private or refuge lands were common occurrences.

In recognizing the need for improving the goose hunting situation at Horicon Marsh, the Wisconsin Conservation Department considered the purchase of a strip of land completely around the periphery of the federal refuge. Estimated cost of these farm lands in 1952 was about 1½ million dollars. An expenditure of this magnitude for goose hunting was considered impractical. Nor chould such lands be leased at the $0.20 per acre rate the Conservation Department was authorized to pay under its public hunting and fishing grounds program.

Fortunately, federal officials also recognized the need for improving hunting conditions, and in 1953 permitted the state to establish a managed hunting unit along the north and west boundary of the refuge. Since 1953, efforts have been concentrated on developing this unit in the best interest of the hunting public and the geese.

From a physical standpoint, the managed hunting unit in 1953 had 114 blinds in an 8-mile long strip averaging 125 yards in width. Blinds were spaced 125 yards apart. Experience quickly showed that goose hunters need much more space. Hunters in adjoining blinds frequently fired at geese passing between blinds and often claimed any geese knocked down. The 125-yard width for retrieving downed birds also proved inadequate. These conditions led to three changes in 1954: (1) an extension of the managed hunting unit along the entire east boundary, which increased the total length to 17 miles, (2) an increase in maximum width of the hunting unit to 440 yards, and (3) retention of the 114 blinds, with a minimal spacing of 200 yards between blinds. The managed hunting unit

Table 2. Chronology of goose hunting regulations at Horicon Marsh 1949–61.[1]

Year	Regulations
1949–52	Canada goose hunting developed on private lands surrounding the refuge. Only statewide waterfowl hunting regulations in effect. Leasing and daily fee shooting dominated the area by 1952. Shot size limited to BB and smaller in 1952.
1953	Limited public hunting permitted in state managed hunting unit on periphery of federal refuge. First-come, first-serve used for 114 blinds on a 8-mile strip 125 yards wide. Blinds 125 yards apart; limit of 3 hunters per blind; blinds refilled at any time; $1.00 hunter fee. Season limit of two Canada geese per hunter for the managed unit. No dogs allowed; duck hunting permitted.
1954	Managed hunting unit increased to 17 miles in length, 440 yards in width and blinds were spaced 200 yards apart. Guns must be enclosed in case when hunters are not in blind.
1955	Managed hunting unit blinds were closed every Monday of season at request of private-land hunters (only in 1955).
1956	Hunting in managed unit limited to 3 trips per season rather than 2 Canada geese per hunter. Blinds were refilled only during the period from noon to 1:00 p.m. (only in 1956). Duck shooting was prohibited (continuous since 1956).
1957	Opening of waterfowl hunting delayed to October 15 (continuous through 1959). Daily hunting hours curtailed to 2:00 p.m. closing in zone around refuge (continuous, with minor alterations, through 1961). A mail-type blind reservation system was initiated, based on earliest post mark. Fee changed to $3.00 per reservation. Blinds not used by reservations filled from waiting line. Limit of 3 reservations, but no limit on number of trips per hunter if blinds are available.
1958	Reservation system changed to permit random selection of applicants. Limit of one reservation per hunter. Blinds reduced to 110. Goose hunting stopped in 2-county area around Horicon Marsh after 33 days of 70-day season and harvest of 11,500 Canadas.
1959	Daily bag limit reduced in mid-season from 2 Canadas to 1 to reduce goose kill. Goose hunting stopped in 2-county area after 49 days of 70-day season and harvest of 25,000 Canadas.
1960	Kill quota of 7,000 established for Horicon and Necedah refuge areas in Wisconsin. No delayed opening. Blinds reduced to 106. Reservations assigned only through October 31 in anticipation of short season due to quota. Waterfowl hunting eliminated from road and railroad right-of-ways. Daily bag limit set at 1 goose of any species in the managed unit and 2:00 p.m. zone. Daily bag limit set at 1 Canada goose for entire state. Blinds on private lands moved back 75 yards from refuge boundary. Goose hunting stopped in 2-county area after 10 days of 60-day season and harvest of 13,000 Canadas.
1961	Applicants for blind reservation required to possess current hunting license. Kill quota of 10,000 Canada geese set for Horicon marsh area. When total kill reaches 8,500 hunting stops in 2:00 p.m. zone. No delayed opening. Bag limit set at 1 goose of any species in managed hunting unit and 1 Canada goose in the 2-county area surrounding the refuge. Hunting in private lands limited to blinds spaced 200 yards apart, 100 yards from property boundary, and 75 yards from refuge. Hunters limited to three per blind. Hunting stopped in 2:00 p.m. zone after 11 days and a kill of 8,500 Canada geese. Complete closure after 18 days, when total kill reached 11,000

[1] Regulations continue from year to year unless changes are indicated. Statewide waterfowl regulations prevail unless otherwise indicated.

now totals 1,485 upland acres, or 7 per cent of the refuge area. While the managed unit has remained essentially constant since 1954, hunting regulations for the area have varied considerably (Table 2). The effects of these regulations on goose hunting opportunities and harvest are considered in the balance of this paper.

DISTRIBUTION OF HUNTING OPPORTUNITIES

From 1950 through 1952 estimates of goose hunting trips to the immediate

Table 3. Horicon Marsh goose hunting statistics, 1953–61.

Item	Year								
	1953	1954	1955	1956	1957	1958	1959	1960	1961
Statewide season length (days)	55	55	70	70	70	70	70	70	60
Days hunted Horicon marsh area	55	55	70	70	56[1]	33[1]	49[1]	10	18
Hunter trips to area[2]	28,900	26,400	28,100	34,100	23,900	25,100	55,300	16,900	15,100
Total harvest in area[3]	2,000	2,300	6,000	7,400	11,500	16,000	25,000	13,000	13,300
Managed hunting unit									
Hunter trips	16,713	17,685	16,254	11,746	13,318	11,158	15,299	4,921	5,118
Canada geese bagged	655	1,115	2,302	2,159	3,308	5,401	8,664	3,002	2,453
Crippling loss (%)[4]	42	22	23	15	17	18	14	16	14
Geese per trip	0.04	0.06	0.14	0.18	0.25	0.48	0.57	0.48	0.61
Hours per trip	4.5	4.9	5.4	5.1	5.1	5.3	—	—	—
Shots per goose bagged	40	25	22	13	15	—	—	—	—

[1] Federal regulations permitted a 70-day statewide season. The delayed opening in the Horicon Marsh Area—1959, subtracted 14 days. In 1958 and 1959 the goose season was also closed when a large kill occurred.

[2] Based on car counts around the periphery of the refuge. All yearly totals rounded to the nearest 100.

[3] Includes estimated kill and crippling loss.

[4] Calculated by dividing the number of geese reported knocked down and lost by the sum of the geese bagged and lost.

Horicon area increased from 15,900 to 24,300. The estimated Canada goose harvest was 1,800, 2,800 and 2,400 for the respective years in this period. Much of the increase in hunters occurred on roads and railroad track right-of-ways. By 1952, approximately 60 per cent of the hunting trips and 32 per cent of the goose kill occurred in this limited zone, an acreage representing no more than a few per cent of the total hunting territory. Approximately half of the hunting trips were made by hunters living within 10 miles of the marsh. Hunters contacted averaged 0.08 geese per trip, fired 27 shots per goose bagged, averaged 6.5 trips per season, and hunted slightly more than 2 hours per trip.

Canada geese at Horicon are on the wing shortly after daylight and are moving from aquatic roosting sites to feeding areas on and around the refuge. These natural feeding activities, which last for two to three hours in the morning and occur again in the late afternoon, limit the amount of time large numbers of hunters will wait along refuge boundaries for a chance to shoot at geese. When geese establish flight patterns out of the refuge, hunters concentrate along the flight lanes. The harvest is limited by highly competitive shooting and the geese soon learn to confine their movements to the refuge. As a consequence, most goose hunting activities terminate by 9:00 a.m. in the entire area.

With the establishment of the managed hunting unit on federal lands in 1953, a considerable change occurred in the distribution of hunting pressure along the refuge boundary. From 1953 through 1959, when hunting seasons were unaffected by kill quotas, there was an average of 31,700 hunter trips to the immediate refuge area, and a peak of 55,300 in 1959 (Table 3). The managed hunting unit accounted for 46 per cent of the trips during that 7-year period, and hunters averaged about 5 hours per trip. From 1958 through 1961, hunters averaged 0.52 geese per trip.

It is not our intent to imply that the managed hunting unit is providing one-half of the goose hunting opportunities at Horicon Marsh. In the first few years of its operation, most of the goose hunting occurred on the farms on the immediate periphery of the refuge and the managed unit played a very important role. While hunting pressure on private lands was unaffected for some years, there was a visible reduction in hunter use of the roads and railroad tracks. However, with continuing increase in popularity of goose hunting, hunting pressure increased, and subsequently public hunting had to be regulated by other means. In later years, changes in hunting regulations resulted in more hunting occurring in outlying areas and a shift in hunters to these areas. In terms of the total estimated hunting effort in 1961, the managed unit accounted for a little more than 10 per cent of the hunter trips (C. W. Lemke, personal communication, 1962).

For several years, we determined the number of individual hunters using the managed unit. This ranged from a low of 7,019 in 1956 to a high of 10,008 in 1958. When considering that Wisconsin averages approximately 100,000 waterfowl hunters, the 1,485-acre managed hunting unit makes a significant contribution by providing goose hunting opportunities for 7.0 to 10.5 per cent of the hunters. Admittedly, opportunities to hunt are limited to one or two trips per year. But we consider the system good for this very reason. Our regulations have been designed to spread hunting opportunities.

In view of the trend toward controlled goose hunting, a brief review is presented of experiences with various regulations used to spread hunting opportunities in the managed hunting unit.

(1) From 1953 through 1955, a season bag limit of 2 Canada geese was in effect. In that period, only 2 per cent of the hunters bagged the limit. This regulation probably would have had a considerably greater effect with higher goose populations and regulations employed since 1957.

(2) In 1956, a 3-trip limit was established as a more equitable means of distributing hunting opportunities. Only 13 per cent of the hunters actually made three trips that year. The 3-trip limit remained in effect in 1957 but was modified to allow more trips per individual if blinds were available. This procedure has been used through 1961. With other changes in obtaining a chance to hunt, hunters making three or more trips decreased to 2 per cent in 1959.

(3) A mail-type reservation system was established in 1957 to replace the first-come, first-served system of obtaining blinds. In 1957 reservations were selected on the basis of earliest postmark. Unequal chances occurred due to variations in time of stamping mail at different classes of post offices. Beginning in 1958, applications were accepted during a specified period and a random selection of applications was made. Unlimited reservation requests were permitted in 1957. In subsequent years only one request was permitted. Until 1961, a reservation could be obtained without possession of a current hunting license. Requiring a person to possess a license before applying for a reservation probably reduced applications received by 35 per cent, from 25,879 in 1960 to 16,731 in 1961. Use of reservations was lowest in 1957, when only 52 per cent were hon-

ored. A long hunting season and low goose populations were responsible for the limited use of reservations. Blind reservation use increased after 1957 and reached a high of 92.5 per cent in 1961. The reservation system's major effect was to reduce the number of trips made by hunters of the city of Milwaukee from 45 to 30 per cent and to permit a corresponding increase from other sources. Local hunters were unaffected by the reservation system and continued to contribute about 8 to 10 per cent of the hunter trips. Apparently a major portion of the local hunters have access to private lands in the area.

(4) Two restrictions considered desirable, but which have been difficult to evaluate, are (1) a ban on duck shooting since 1956 and (2) a daily bag limit of 1 goose, regardless of species, since 1960. In 1955 over 3,700 ducks were killed in the managed unit. Prohibiting duck hunting reduces the amount of shooting and increases turnover of blinds after hunters have killed their geese. In 1959 over 380 blue and snow geese were killed, with some hunters bagging limits of 5 geese. Establishing a 1 goose limit was aimed at preventing hunters from waiting for blue and snow geese after killing their limits of Canadas, and also at distributing the goose harvest among the greatest number of hunters.

Since 1957 the distribution of hunting opportunities outside the managed hunting unit has improved. In 1957 a delayed opening and a 2:00 p.m. closing zone were established for the first time. The delayed opening zone was an area around the marsh that included most of the daily off-refuge feeding flights of geese. The 2:00 p.m. closing zone was smaller in area and was designed to encourage some geese to leave the refuge in the afternoon feeding periods. Early migrant Canada geese arriving at Horicon Marsh readily adapted to the protected area offered, and established extensive feeding flights to the surrounding countryside. Hunters naturally took advantage of the hunting opportunities created by these feeding activities. Estimates indicate that over 3,000 geese were bagged in the first 3 days of hunting in 1957. About one-third of the kill was made by hunters on outlying farms.

While the above techniques were successful in spreading hunters over a bigger area, the increased kill also attracted more goose hunters. Many of these hunters had only roads and railroad tracks from which to shoot at geese. Increasing hunting pressure resulted in poor quality hunting on easily accessible areas. For example, late in the 1959 season, hunters standing almost shoulder to shoulder on a ¼-mile stretch of road along the west boundary bagged 160 and 136 Canada geese on successive days. In 1960, hunting from roads and railroad track right-of-ways was prohibited. Now goose hunting must occur on private lands or in the managed hunting unit.

Where did the hundreds of goose hunters who used the roads and railroad tracks go to hunt geese in 1960? Many were forced to shift to the more outlying areas. Generally, a hunting fee of some sort was charged, but this imposed no great burden. Geese used these areas and hunters were willing to pay for the hunting opportunities. A majority of landowners on the periphery of the refuge also provided more blinds as a result of the road hunting restriction. With the competition that existed for goose hunting space along the refuge, hunters readily made use of these added blinds. To cite an extreme example, on one farm of 140 acres along the eastern edge of the refuge there were 55 blinds, or 1 blind per 2.5

acres. Most of these blinds were used throughout the 1960 season.

The logical solution to discourage crowded conditions was to encourage adequate spacing of blinds on private land. Regulations for this purpose were established in 1961. These regulations immediately reduced daily hunting pressure. For example, in the same length of refuge boundary behind 106 state-operated blinds, private blinds were reduced from 495 to 194, or 61 per cent.

The question of where the evicted hunters on private land hunted in 1961 is also pertinent. We have no data to answer this question. We know from personal contact that the effect of blind spacing in the immediate refuge area was not as great in reducing the number of individuals who hunted as it was in reducing the number of trips per season per hunter.

As yet, there has been no indication that the regulations employed are actually reducing the opportunity to hunt geese. Increasing goose populations, along with changes in regulations, have spread hunting efforts over a much larger area. This greater space has absorbed many hunters who previously used the peripheral areas, both public and private.

HARVEST ASPECTS

One of the principal objectives at Horicon Marsh has been to increase the harvest of Canada geese within the limits of their annual production. In the early 1950's, heavy hunting pressure in the area appeared to be the most important factor holding down the kill. The early October hunting-season openings, daylight-to-dark shooting hours, and the ring of blinds around the marsh quickly confined geese to the refuge. Perhaps of equal importance was the fact that a great many of the hunters had little or no goose hunting experience. Many hunters simply did not know when a goose was in killing range. As a consequence, shooting "too soon" was as common as shooting at geese which were really out of range.

Several techniques for increasing the goose kill became apparent. While there was no way to control shooting by hunters, regulations could be established to permit more access to the geese. Recommendations following the 1954 season were: (1) to delay opening the hunting season until mid-October in a large area around the marsh and (2) to stop hunting at 2:00 p.m. each day within this zone. While these two regulations were not adopted until 1957, they were the two principal techniques which resulted in a significant increase in the harvest.

The geese themselves aided in increasing the kill in 1955 and 1956. Many Canada geese migrated early in 1955, with the result that a natural delayed opening effect occurred. Approximately 20,000 geese were present and feeding in the general refuge area when the hunting season opened on October 1. A large number of geese were bagged in the early part of the season and the total kill increased to 6,000. In 1956 the migration was more on schedule, but the refuge goose population reached a peak of 67,300. Sheer numbers of geese accounted for a continuing increase in the kill.

In 1957, when the delayed opening and 2:00 p.m. daily closing zone were established, the kill increased to 11,500 despite a drop in peak goose numbers to about half the 1956 level. These regulations were used again in 1958 and 1959, but with considerably more geese present than in 1957. In 1958 the kill rose to 16,000 and goose hunting was closed by the Wisconsin Conservation Department after 33 days of a 70-day season. In 1959, the kill increased to 25,000 and hunting was stopped after 49 days of a 70-day season. The important point to note in the years of rapidly increasing kill was the number of geese in the area when the hunting season opened (Table 1). Without constant harassment, near-peak numbers of geese were present and off-refuge feeding flights were well established when the hunting season opened.

Local hunters were, of course, enthused over the increased goose harvest. They were now getting "their fair share of geese." However, criticism developed from some people because they feared a "slaughter" was occurring. The early closing of the hunting seasons in 1958 and 1959 demonstrated the intent of the Wisconsin Conservation Department to protect the goose resource.

As it turned out, the increased kill near Horicon Marsh in 1959 was important to Illinois as well as Wisconsin hunters. For the first time, the Mississippi Valley goose population was being subjected to heavy harvests in two states. Previously, Illinois had taken the major share of the kill, averaging over 30,000 geese for the 10-year period 1950–59 (Arthur 1960). Horicon's greatly increased kill caused a decline in the Illinois kill, and the combined harvest from all states resulted in a decline in the annual mid-winter goose inventory to its lowest level since 1952. As a result of these developments, a Canada goose harvest-quota system was established in 1960 through joint efforts of the U.S. Bureau of Sports Fisheries and Wildlife and the states in the upper Mississippi Flyway.

HARVEST QUOTA SYSTEM

Nelson (1961) has presented the most recent review of this important management of waterfowl. The immediate objective of the quota system is to hold the kill on the Mississippi Valley population below the annual reproductive gains. Current thinking is that both the wintering and breeding ranges can support many more geese. Harvesting fewer geese than are produced should permit an increase in the population to take advantage of the carrying capacity of the range. In brief, the system involves (1) determining the age structure of the wintering population, (2) estimating the production gains and mortality, (3) calculating the population available for harvest in the next hunting season, and (4) determining how the harvest will be divided between states. Distribution of the available harvest is worked out to the mutual satisfaction of the Bureau of Sport Fisheries and Wildlife and the states in the upper Mississippi Flyway. Specific quotas have been set only in the major harvest areas in the states of Illinois and Wisconsin.

Establishment of the harvest-quota system created a new challenge at Horicon Marsh. The problems were to decrease the total kill and slow down the daily kill. In 1960 a quota of 7,000 Canada geese was set for two areas in Wisconsin: (1) the Horicon National Wildlife Refuge and (2) the Necedah National Wildlife Refuge, located in the central part of the state.

In view of increasing goose use in the Horicon area, some changes were needed in regulations to decrease the daily kill. With the objective of prolonging the 1960 season, goose hunting was permitted as early as possible and a daily bag limit of 1 goose of any species was established. As it developed, an early migration occurred and over 40,000 geese were in the area on opening day October 7, 1960. Hunters killed geese at a rate of about 1,000 per day. Kill surveys (Lemke 1960, Green 1960) revealed the need to stop hunting within a week, but administrative action to close the season required an additional 3 days. Consequently, the season lasted 10 days and the harvest reached 13,000, including crip-

Table 4. Distribution of Canada goose harvest Horicon Marsh Area 1953–61.

Item	Year								
	1953	1954	1955	1956	1957[1]	1958	1959	1960[2]	1961[2]
Number of geese bagged[3]	1,211	1,862	5,072	6,237	9,503	13,746	22,035	10,900	11,141
Percentage distribution of total bag									
Managed hunting unit	50	60	45	33	35	39	33	28	22
Peripheral farms[4]	42	35	53	65	63	59	33	48	24
Outlying areas							33	21	49
State end of Horicon Marsh	8	5	2	2	2	2	1	3	5
Total in 2:00 p.m. zone[5]							66	76	46

[1] Established 2:00 p.m. closing zone around Horicon Marsh and continued it through 1961.
[2] Established harvest quotas of 7,000 Canada geese in 1960 and 10,000 in 1961.
[3] Excludes crippling loss.
[4] Includes percentages in outlying areas for years 1953 through 1958.
[5] Data from unpublished report on "1961 Goose Harvest, Horicon National Wildlife Refuge," by W. F. Green.

pling loss. Controlling the kill in 1960 was further complicated by the rapidly expanding refuge goose population, which increased from 40,000 to 70,000 during the 10-day period of hunting. An unfortunate result of the rapid kill at Horicon Marsh was the early closing at the Necedah area, where only 300 geese were bagged.

A somewhat similar pattern followed in the 1961 hunting season. The quota was somewhat higher, 12,000 for Wisconsin, of which 10,000 were actually assigned to the Horicon area. Horicon's 10,000 quota was further divided to permit closing the 2:00 p.m. zone after the kill had reached 8,500 in the entire area. The remaining 1,500 geese were allotted to an area outside the 2:00 p.m. zone. Regulations were comparable to 1960, except that (1) daily shooting started at sunrise instead of one-half hour before and (2) blind spacing on private lands was established for the first time. When the hunting season opened on October 7, over 57,000 geese were present and many geese had well developed feeding flights outside the refuge. Despite intensive hunting, the refuge goose population increased to 92,000 by October 15. Containing this large population inside the refuge appears to be impossible. Hunting was over in 11 days in the 2:00 p.m. zone. An additional 7 days were required to take 1,500 geese in outlying areas.

One important objective in the short 1961 season was accomplished. A considerably greater portion of the kill was taken in outlying areas than in any previous year (Table 4). Contributing most importantly to the wider distribution of kill, was the sunrise opening of daily shooting hours. A major part of the geese making morning feeding flights out of the refuge were well beyond the immediate periphery of the refuge when shooting started.

Limitations on hunting imposed by the quota have had some important side effects. Goose-use at Horicon Marsh has developed to the point where the refuge in 1961 held approximately one-half of the entire Mississippi Valley Canada goose population, and two-thirds of the population that eventually reached the Illinois winter range. Much of this increased use is due to the effectiveness of the federal refuge management program. Perhaps of equal importance has been the early and rapid kill that has occurred in the area. Some geese arriving at Horicon Marsh in the latter part of the normal migration period never were subjected to hunting. In the absence of continuous shooting and an abundance of food and water, migration from Horicon Marsh was delayed. Consequently, fewer geese were present in Illinois, where hunting pressure declined in both 1960 and 1961. Whether or not additional goose-use should be encouraged at Horicon Marsh is a question needing careful study.

FUTURE MANAGEMENT

In our estimation, Canada goose harvest quotas should be a continuing practice. No better method is known to help maintain both satisfactory goose hunting and an optimum-sized Mississippi Valley Canada goose population. Management and hunting regulations should be aimed not only at spreading the available kill among as many hunters as possible, but also at providing the maximum hunting opportunities. Since the 1962 mid-winter inventory revealed no increase in Canada geese, despite restrictive quotas in Illinois and Wisconsin, another very limited harvest appears necessary. As yet, regulations have not been established for 1962. However, the main concern will be to design regulations to prolong hunting opportunities. Three other regulations should be considered:

1. A compulsory form of goose-hunter and goose-kill registration.
2. A season bag limit of 4 or 5 Canada geese.
3. A shell limit for individual hunters in the managed hunting unit.

To some people, our use of the terms "managed" and "hunting" are probably misnomers. We frankly admit that goose "shooting" is a more descriptive term. We also admit that much of the hunting is not of high quality. However, by standards in other goose hunting areas, management of hunters and control of harvest are considered good. Distribution of hunting effort and harvest are also good. While the quality of goose hunting in the vicinity of Horicon Marsh is not ideal, it is considerably better than it would be if only statewide waterfowl regulations applied.

The unfortunate part of the goose hunting picture in the past few years is that too much emphasis has been placed on the actual killing of geese and not enough on the opportunity to hunt geese. The bird is no longer considered a trophy by many hunters. Possibly too many geese have been attracted to Horicon Marsh, especially during the past few years. Hunting regulations have also made it too easy to bag geese. Changing the major emphasis from killing geese to that of increasing opportunities to hunt geese is now the foremost challenge.

SUMMARY

This paper traces developments in goose hunting opportunities and regulation of goose harvest in the vicinity of the Horicon National Wildlife Refuge from 1949 through 1961. Peak Canada goose populations on the refuge increased in that period from 12,000 in 1949 to 100,000 in 1961. Basically the Canada geese using Horicon Marsh are part of the Mississippi Valley population.

By 1952, 60 per cent of the hunter trips and 32 per cent of the goose kill occurred on the limited space provided by roads and railroad right-of-ways. Hunters averaged 6.5 trips per year, 2 hours per trip, 0.08 geese per trip, and fired 27 shots per goose bagged.

In 1953 a state-operated managed hunting unit was established on the periphery of the federal refuge to improve the distribution of hunting opportunities. From 1953 through 1959 the managed unit accounted for 46 per cent of the hunter trips to the area. From 1958 through 1961 hunters in the managed unit averaged 0.52 geese per trip. Regulations used to increase hunting opportunities in the managed unit included (1) a season bag limit of 2 Canada geese (1953–55), (2) a season limit of 3 trips per hunter, (3) a mail-type reservation system, and (4) restricting the daily bag limit to 1 goose of any species (1960–61).

Regulations to improve hunting conditions on private lands around the refuge included (1) prohibiting hunting on roads and railroad tracks, (2) moving blinds 75 yards back from the refuge boundary, and (3) requiring a 200-yard spacing of blinds on private lands.

Two regulations were very effective in increasing the goose harvest at Horicon Marsh in the years 1957 through 1959: (1) a delayed zone opening to mid-October, and (2) a 2:00 p.m. daily closing in a zone around the refuge.

As a result of the increased harvest at Horicon Marsh and a continuing heavy kill in Illinois, a Canada goose harvest-quota system was developed in 1960. In both 1960 and 1961, the quota was instrumental in preventing excessive harvests of the Mississippi Valley Canada goose population in Wisconsin and Illinois. In the future, regulations in Wisconsin will have to be designed to contain the allowable kill within quota limits and at the same time provide maximum hunting opportunities.

ACKNOWLEDGMENTS

Many individuals of the Wisconsin Conservation Department and the U.S. Bureau of Sport Fisheries and Wildlife contributed to the development and improvement of goose hunting at Horicon Marsh. We are particularly indebted to Lloyd Gunther, Robert F. Russell and Lester H. Dundas, who were refuge managers at the Horicon National Wildlife Refuge from 1950 through 1961.

A note of special appreciation is due Wisconsin sportsmen for their support and cooperation in the goose hunting program. They are to be commended for their acceptance of the restrictions on Canada goose hunting imposed by harvest quotas. They have helped advance an essential part of a basic goose management program.

LITERATURE CITED

ARTHUR, G. C. 1960. Canada goose populations, harvests, regulations and management—Southern Illinois, 1927–1959. Ill. Dept. of Cons. March 28, 1960. 2pp. (Multilith.)

GREEN, W. E. 1960. 1960 goose harvest—Horicon Refuge. U.S. Bur. Sport Fish. & Wildl., Minneapolis. Oct. 31, 1960. 7pp. (Photo copy.)

HANSON, H. C., AND R. H. SMITH. 1950. Canada geese of the Mississippi Flyway. Ill. Nat. Hist. Surv., Bull. 25, Art. 3:67–210.

LEMKE, C. W. 1960. Summary of mailed goose kill questionnaire, 1960. Wis. Cons. Dept., Dec. 19, 1960. 3pp. (Mimeo.)

NELSON, H. K. 1961. New approaches in Canada goose management. Presented at Mid-west Wildl. Conf., Lincoln, Neb., Dec. 4–6, 1961. 24pp. (Multilith.)

LEAD SHOT IN SOME SPRING MIGRANT DUCKS[1]

ROBERT L. JESSEN,[2] Minnesota State Department of Conservation
DWAIN W. WARNER, Museum of Natural History, University of Minnesota
FRANCIS A. SPURRELL, University of Minnesota
JOHN P. LINDMEIER, Minnesota State Department of Conservation
BERTIN W. ANDERSON, University of South Dakota

Abstract: The incidence of lead shot in 1,687 lesser scaup (*Aythya affinis*) and 416 ring-necked ducks (*Aythya collaris*) in spring migration in Minnesota and the implications as related to the bird population and hunting harvest the preceding fall are considered in this study. The ducks, which were examined for shot by photofluorographic radiography had died as a result of oil pollution on the Mississippi River in the vicinity of Red Wing in the spring of 1963. The birds were separated into two age groups and by sex. Yearling lesser scaup had a body shot incidence (proportion of birds containg shot) of 5.5 percent and yearling ring-necked ducks 17.8 percent. For both species, yearling males had a higher incidence of shot than yearling females, and the most common location of shot was just beneath the skin on the back and abdomen. By using shot incidence in conjunction with other data, the harvest rate during the preceding hunting season (1962) was estimated as being 15 to 20 percent of the population for yearling lesser scaup of both sexes; 30 to 35 percent for yearling female ring-necked ducks, 60 to 70 percent for yearling males, and 45 to 55 percent for yearlings of both sexes of ring-necked ducks combined. Incidence of ingested shot in the digestive tracts of the birds (mostly gizzard) was low, being 1.7 percent for lesser scaup and 1.6 percent for ring-necked ducks.

In December 1962 an estimated million gallons of fuel oil were lost from an oil storage facility at Savage, Minnesota. The spilled oil largely remained under the snow until spring melt waters carried the oil into the adjacent Minnesota River. On January 23 the same winter, during a period of extremely cold weather, there also had been an accidental release of 1 to 1.5 million gallons of soybean oil from storage facilities at Mankato on the Blue Earth River, a tributary of the Minnesota River. Subsequently, this oil flowed into the Mississippi River (Moyle et al. 1963).

Following breakup of ice in March and early April 1963, many waterfowl (especially ducks) were killed by coming in contact with these oils on the backwaters of the Mississippi River. Other birds became uncapable of flying as their feathers became coated with oil. Waterfowl losses were estimated at about 10,000 birds and were noted for about 60 miles from the mouth of the Minnesota River downstream to Lake Pepin.

In rescue operations 1,369 live and 1,842 dead birds were recovered. Many of the live birds died later even though they were washed with detergent and housed in warm quarters. As a result, 2,745 dead birds became available for examination for incidence of body shot that they had previously received.

Most of the waterfowl were diving ducks (Tribe Aythyini). Of the 2,388 ducks originally examined, only 49 were dabbling ducks (Tribe Anatini). The few dabbling ducks killed indicate a differential response to oil pollution by the two groups of birds. Of the diving ducks, 76 percent were lesser scaup and 19 percent ring-necked ducks. These two species were the most numerous spring migrants at the time.

METHODS OF INVESTIGATION

In August 1963 all dead birds were taken from cold storage, examined, and in-

[1] Originally published in J. Minn. Acad. Sci. 35(2/3):90–94, 1969.

[2] Address correspondence to this author. Present address: Box 378, Rt. 5, Bemidji, MN 56601.

dividually marked with metal leg bands. The birds were then tallied according to species, sex, relative amount of oil on the feathers, and condition of the carcass. Two examinations were then undertaken: (1) photofluorographic images from two projections to determine the presence and location of lead pellets; and (2) internal examination for identifying the yearling birds.

Photofluorographic images were prepared by use of an automatic sequencing 70 mm Westinghouse photofluorographic unit. The primary beam was provided by a Picker radiograph activated at 66 kilovolts peak and 90 milliampere seconds. Anode focal spot to screen distance was 100 centimeters. These units had been designed to military specifications. Great care in establishment of exposure routine, equipment location, and lead shielding was necessary. This care was needed to reduce the occupational exposure below 6.25 milliroentgens per hour of x-ray production received by any of the technical assistants.

Two photofluorographs were taken of each bird. A lateral (L-R) and a dorsal to ventral view provided for three-dimensional localization of pellets within the birds. This method also provided a check for occasional pellets found within areas of heavy bone density as projected on the photofluorographs.

Sex determination was made on the basis of external plumage characteristics. Age criteria were those established by Anderson (1966) and used by him on these birds. Birds having relative bursa depths of 29 or less were considered to be at least 20 months old, and those having a relative bursa depth of 32 or more, yearling birds. Relative bursa size is the product of greatest width and greatest length as measured in millimeters.

Birds in which body parts were missing or tissue decay prevented age identification are not included in the tabulations. In all, 1,687 lesser scaup and 416 ring-necked ducks were satisfactorily aged and sexed. In the calculations it is assumed that there was no differential response by sex of the birds coming in contact with the oils and that there was no differential survival of rescued birds related to sex, age, or condition.

INCIDENCE AND LOCATION OF SHOT

Of the yearling lesser scaup 5.5 percent were found to have one or more imbedded lead shot pellets per bird (Table 1). Adult scaup that had survived two or more hunting seasons had a 9.1 percent incidence. There was a slightly higher incidence of pellets in adult males (9.6 percent) than in females (7.1 percent). The higher occurrence of shot pellets in males is similar to that reported for this same species by Elder (1955), and this suggests that male lesser scaup are selected as targets by some hunters. A small portion of this difference may be due to the somewhat larger size of the males—30 as compared to 28 ounces average weight.

Ring-necked ducks had a substantially higher shot incidence than did lesser scaup for both age groups. Adults had a 21.6 percent shot incidence (Table 1). Yearling birds had a 17.8 percent shot incidence and showed a significant difference in shot incidence between the sexes, the well-marked males having a 25.4 percent and females 8.6 percent (t value 2.60 at the 1 percent level).

The number of shot pellets per bird varied considerably. The most found in a single bird was eight. Sixty-seven percent of the birds carrying shot had only one pellet; 20 percent, two pellets; and 7 percent, three.

Table 1. Percentage of spring migrant ducks killed by oil pollution in 1963 which had one or more lead shot pellets imbedded in their bodies.

Species and age	Males	Females	Both
Ring-necked ducks			
Adult	20.7 (*N* = 193)	23.4 (*N* = 94)	21.6
Yearling	25.4 (*N* = 71)	8.6 (*N* = 58)	17.8
Lesser scaup			
Adult	9.6 (*N* = 1,087)	7.1 (*N* = 309)	9.1
Yearling	5.8 (*N* = 156)	5.2 (*N* = 135)	5.5

The location of lead pellets in the bodies of birds was generally similar for ring-necked ducks and lesser scaup (Table 2). The most frequent site of lodged shot was the back (23.8 percent) and abdomen (22.5 percent). Other common sites of lodging were breast (14.3 percent), head (11.2 percent), neck (10.6 percent), and wings (10.5 percent). Many pellets were lodged just beneath the skin, where they presumably stopped without having done much physical damage to the birds. The distribution of lodged pellets is remarkably similar to that recorded by Bellrose (1953) in live-trapped mallard ducks. He found 22.2 percent of the body shot lodged in the back and 15.6 percent in the belly and flank area. Most pellets in these mallards were externally lodged—that is, in skin or flesh without having broken bones. Bellrose was handicapped in his classification by use of a fluoroscope which allowed only one view of the birds, so his classifications of the shot locations were somewhat arbitrary.

Scarcity of shot in the massive breast muscles of the oil-sticken birds is strong evidence that birds wounded in this area are unable to complete their migration and are taken by hunters or predators. The high incidence of pellets in the abdomen is indicative of the non-essential functions of this area to flight and a high resistance to peritonitis among these ducks.

INGESTED SHOT

The examination showed ingested lead shot in 1.6 percent of the male lesser scaup and in 1.8 percent of the females

Table 2. Location of shot pellets in birds killed by oil pollution.

	Lesser scaup			Ring-necked ducks				
	Number of birds			Number of birds			All birds	
Location	Male	Female	Percentage[1] both	Male	Female	Percentage[1] both	Number	Percentage
Head	16	4	10.0	16	1	13.3	37	11.2
Neck	16	6	11.0	10	3	10.2	35	10.6
Breast	22	6	14.0	10	9	14.8	47	14.3
Back	37	12	24.5	19	10	22.6	78	23.8
Wings	15	2	8.5	15	3	14.0	35	10.5
Thorax	4	1	2.5	1	0	0.8	6	1.8
Abdomen	40	6	23.0	19	9	21.8	74	22.5
Legs	4	1	2.5	0	0	0.0	5	1.5
Side	7	1	4.0	2	1	2.3	11	3.4

[1] Percentage of birds containing shot that had at least one shot in a particular location.

Table 3. Proportion of ducks containing one or more ingested lead shot.

Species	Number examined	Number with shot	Percentage with shot
Ring-necked duck			
Male	264	2	0.8
Female	152	5	3.3
Lesser scaup			
Male	1,243	20	1.6
Female	444	8	1.8
All kinds	2,103	35	1.7

(Table 3). Similar examination of ring-necked ducks disclosed an average of 0.8 percent for males and 3.3 percent for females. This is a statistically significant higher occurrence in the females (t value 1.85 with a 6 percent level of significance).

The presence of ingested shot pellets in 1.7 percent of the lesser scaup and 1.6 percent of the ring-necked ducks is somewhat similar to that reported for wintering ducks in Michigan, where Whitlock and Miller (1947) reported 1.0 percent for all species. It is considerably less than that reported by Bellrose (1959) for lesser scaup and ring-necked ducks in the fall (usually in excess of 10 percent). Reid (1947) has also reported a high incidence of ingested shot in fall migrant ducks in Minnesota—14 percent for diving ducks and 8 percent for dabbling ducks.

In the sample of birds available for photofluorographic radiography there were two sources of bias. First, birds that have ingested lead shot are less capable of survival because of the stress of lead poisoning. Secondly, some of the birds rescued from the oil pollution, 900 in total, survived for various lengths of time before dying and may have eliminated shot pellets from their digestive tracts (especially the lumen of the gizzard) prior to death. These two biases tend to mitigate each other, but the magnitude of each is unknown.

The significantly higher occurrence of ingested lead shot in female ring-necked ducks (3.3 percent) than in males (0.8 percent) is apparently associated with the females seeking greater amounts of grit prior to laying eggs. Such behavior has been reported for the ring-necked pheasant by Kopischke (1966). The lack of a marked difference between male and female scaup is probably because many yearling scaup do not breed, and the egg laying period of those that do is later than for ring-necked ducks.

In general these spring migrant ducks did not have an unusually high incidence of ingested lead shot even though they had traversed heavily used public hunting grounds. Bellrose (1959) suggests that lethal poisoning does not occur until birds have ingested 4 to 5 pellets of lead shot, varying somewhat with diet. Therefore, it appears few of these ducks would have died of lead poisoning from ingested shot.

BODY SHOT AND HUNTING KILL

The incidence of imbedded shot in game birds that have survived a hunting season has long been recognized as being related to hunting pressure and kill (Whitlock and Miller 1947, Elder 1950). This relationship is most amenable to interpretation for young-of-the-year birds that have gone through only one hunting season. However, the authors know of no attempt to express this relationship quantitatively. Such a relationship cannot be exact, but it can serve as a useful indicator and perhaps as a wildlife management tool. To relate the incidence of body shot to the proportion of the population killed by hunting (total hunting mortality) requires information of several kinds, each of which has associated error.

Table 4. Reference to estimates of game birds harvests and body shot incidence in the surviving population used in Fig. 1.

Code[1] Population	References	Comment
1—Continental mallard population, 1963	Several sources[2]	Immature males only
2—Continental mallard population, 1964	Several sources[2]	Immature males only
3—Continental mallard population, 1965	Several sources[2]	Immature males only
4—Cock pheasants, South Dakota, 1952 and 1959	Chesness and Nelson 1964	Includes adults
5—Cock pheasants, North Dakota, 1957–59	Chesness and Nelson 1964	Includes adults
6—Cock pheasants, Minnesota, 1958–60	Chesness and Nelson 1964	Includes adults
7—Cock pheasants, Wisconsin, 1953–56	Chesness and Nelson 1964	Includes adults
8—Hen pheasants, South Dakota, 1952–59	Chesness and Nelson 1964	Includes adults
9—Hen pheasants, North Dakota, 1957–59	Chesness and Nelson 1964	Includes adults
10—Hen pheasants, Minnesota, 1958–60	Chesness and Nelson 1964	Includes adults
11—Hen pheasants, Wisconsin, 1953–56	Chesness and Nelson 1964	Includes adults
12—Mallards, Illinois, 1949–52	Bellrose 1953	Immature males
13—Mean of six species, early 1950's	Elder 1955	Calculations from table 4

[1] Numerals shown in Fig. 2.
[2] Especially Brakhage (1966), Hansen (1964), Crissey (1967), Hansen and Hudgins (1965), and Grieb (pers. commun.).

In the following calculations, population and kill statistics are used at face value, and crippling loss is assumed to equal 30 percent of the birds bagged. The latter assumption is based on the work of Mendall (1958) on ring-necked ducks as is supported by Minnesota data of Lee et al. (1964).

The basic question to be considered is—"What is the general quantitative relationship between the percentage of living birds containing one or more lead shot in body tissues after a hunting season to the percentage of birds in the hunted population that were killed by hunters?"

In an attempt to interpret shot incidence found in lesser scaup and ring-necked ducks and relate this to hunting kill, similar data were compiled or calculated from other sources (Table 4). These represent situations in which incidence of shot in surviving birds is known and where information on hunting kill (including crippling loss) is available or can be calculated and in which data is also available or can be calculated on the size of the population hunted. Using this information, the percentage of birds (ducks and pheasants) in a population that were killed by hunting has been plotted against the percentage of survivors carrying body shot (Fig. 1). The unmodified circles in this graph represent values for young-of-the-year birds (birds hunted in the same year they were hatched), and circles with arrows pointing to the left are values for populations of birds of mixed ages. The arrows indicate that the values are too high when applied to yearling birds and that the true value lies to the left. It should be pointed out, however, that in all cases a large part of the hunting kill was of yearling birds.

After plotting the data, several curves or mathematical models were calculated to obtain a curve that would best represent the data, and that shown in Fig. 1 was selected. It is based on hunting mortalities (including crippling loss) ranging from 5 to 80 percent of the population hunted and incidence of body shot ranging from 3 to 35 percent of the surviving birds. The curve selected in this model represents a relationship in which the number of birds that survive with embed-

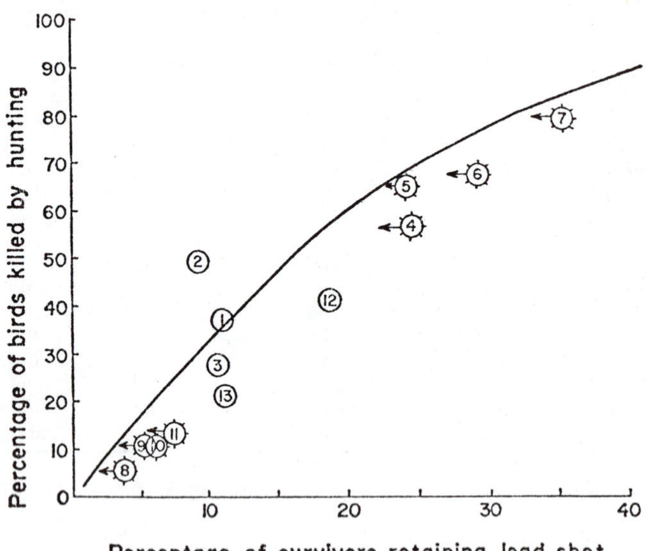

Fig. 1. Percentage of surviving yearling game birds (ducks and pheasants) retaining body shot after the hunting season as related to the percentage of birds killed by hunting (including crippling loss). Circles with rays are based on data for pheasants; those without rays on data for ducks. Arrows signify data for birds of mixed ages and that the true value for yearling birds lies to the left; absence of arrows indicates young-of-the-year birds. Data are from sources cited in Table 4.

ded pellets is equivalent to 25 percent of the hunting kill. That is, for every three birds killed, one bird will be struck, survive its wound, and carry at least one lead pellet in its body. The slope of the curve represents a series of segments each representing 2.5 perccent of the total kill and flattens out as the population is thinned by hunting. It was calculated in this way since such population thinning occurs as ducks migrate down the flyway or, in the case of pheasants, as the hunting season progresses.

From this curve, for example, it can be estimated that if 20 percent of the birds surviving the hunting season carry shot, it is likely that 60 percent of the birds in the population were killed by hunting. Applying it to the incidence of shot already given for yearling lesser scaup and ring-necked ducks, it is estimated that the hunting kill of yearling scaup in the fall of 1962 was about 20 percent of the population and that for ring-necked ducks about 55 percent. The kill figure for ring-necked ducks suggests overshooting of this type.

BODY SHOT AND POPULATION SIZE

Theoretically, the curve in Fig. 1 can also be used to estimate the size of the population from which the hunting kill came providing that the following pieces of information are known: (1) the hunting take of yearling birds; (2) crippling loss as a percentage of the hunting take; (3) the proportion of yearling to adult birds taken by hunters; and (4) the post-season incidence of shot in surviving yearling birds. These relationships will be considered for lesser scaup and ring-necked ducks and compared with estimates obtained in other ways.

Lesser Scaup

It will be recalled that 5.5 percent of the yearling lesser scaup examined carried body shot. Referring to Fig. 1, this indicates a take hunting kill of about 20 percent of the pre-season population. The total U.S. hunting kill of yearling lesser scaup in 1962 was estimated by Glover and Smith (1963) to be 55,000 birds, to which should be added a crippling loss of 30 percent plus an estimated 12,000 kill in Canada. This gives an estimated total kill of 85,000 birds. Since the curve indicates this represents 20 percent of the total pre-season population of yearling birds the total population is estimated at 425,000 (5 × 85,000) birds.

The population of lesser scaup of all ages (other than ducklings) on the breeding grounds the previous summer (1962) as tallied by aerial counts was estimated as 2.7 million birds (Glover and Smith 1963). This is probably too low. Martinson (personal communication) estimated that if it is corrected on the basis of ground counts, the real population size may have been 4.4 million. Lesser scaup populations contain more male than female ducks. The ratio was 3.5 males to 1.0 females for adult oil-killed birds, but was nearly equal for yearling birds. From these data and findings of other workers (Erickson 1943, Bellrose et al. 1961:419, Benson 1963) it appears likely that about 70 percent of the lesser scaup population on the breeding grounds was of male ducks. On this basis the number of paired breeding birds on the breeding grounds would be about 2.6 million (using the corrected aerial count as a base) of which about 0.8 million were yearling birds (based on the age ratio of the oil-killed ducks and further corrected for seasonal changes as reported by Benson 1963). This estimate for yearling birds (750,000) is considerably higher than that already calculated from incidence of shot (425,000) by use of Fig. 1.

If, however, the figures for the original aerial count were used as a base without any corrections, the estimate for yearling birds on the breeding grounds in 1962 becomes 460,000—a figure quite comparable to the 425,000 calculated from shot incidence.

Ring-necked Ducks

The incidence of body shot found in yearling ring-necked ducks killed by the oil spill was 24.5 percent for males, 8.6 percent for females and 17.8 percent for both sexes combined. Again referring to the curve in Fig. 1, a hunting kill of about 55 percent is indicated among yearling ring-necked ducks both sexes combined.

The 1962 hunting kill (including that estimated for Canada and the crippling loss) is estimated at about 230,000 birds, of which about 60 percent (138,000) were young-of-the-year. It is estimated, as was done in the previous section, that the fall population was about 250,000 yearling birds. Judging from the ratio of the yearling to adult birds in the U.S. hunter's bag (1.36:1) and making allowance for immatures being more easily shot (1.7 times as reported by Lee et al. 1964:86), it appears that the adult population was around 275,000 in a total of about 500,000 birds in the fall flight. Probably almost half were killed.

The surviving population as estimated from shot incidence is in fairly close agreement with the uncorrected aerial counts made in 1963, when there were 313,000 ring-necked ducks counted on the wintering grounds and 216,000 on spring breeding grounds (Glover and Smith 1963). It should be emphasized that the uncorrected aerial counts are minimal because of the difficulty of seeing the birds from the air.

LITERATURE CITED

ANDERSON, B. W. 1966. A morphological anaysis of a large sample of lesser scaup (*Aythya affinis*) and ring-necks (*Aythya collaris*). M.A. Thesis, Univ. of Minn. 92pp.

BELLROSE, F. C. 1953. A preliminary evaluation of crippling losses in waterfowl. Trans. N.W. Wildl. Conf. 18:337–359.

———. 1959. Lead poisoning as a mortality factor in waterfowl populations. Ill. Nat. Hist. Surv. Bull. 27(3):235–288.

———, T. G. SCOTT, A. S. HAWKINS, AND J. B. LOW. 1961. Sex and age ratios in North American ducks. Ill. Nat. Hist. Surv. Bull. 27(6):391–474.

BENSON, R. I. 1963. Spring waterfowl sex ratios, 1962. Min. P-R Job Comp. Rpt., Wildl. Surveys. pp. 65–67.

BRAKHAGE, G. K. 1966. An evaluation of the fluoroscopic technique for measuring hunting pressure in Mississippi Flyway mallards. Fluoroscopic Committee Rpt. Miss. Fly. Council, Minutes Miss. Fly. Council, March 13:61–64.

CHESNESS, R. A., AND M. M. NELSON. 1964. Illegal kill of hen pheasants in Minnesota. J. Wildl. Mgmt. 28(2):249–253.

CRISSEY, W. F. 1967. Prairie potholes from a continental viewpoint. Seminar on small water areas in the prairie pothole region. Feb. 20–22, Saskatoon, Saskatchewan, Canada. 21pp.

ELDER, W. H. 1950. Measurement of hunting pressure in waterfowl by means of X-ray. Trans. N. Am. Wildl. Conf. 15:490–504.

———. 1955. Fluoroscopic measures of hunting pressure in Europe and North America. Trans. N. Am. Wildl. Conf. 20:298–321.

ERICKSON, A. B. 1943. Sex ratios of ducks in Minnesota, 1938–40. Auk 60:20–34.

GEIS, A. D., AND E. L. ATWOOD. 1961. Proportion of recovered waterfowl bands reported. J. Wildl. Mgmt. 25(2):154–159.

GLOVER, F. A., AND J. D. SMITH. 1963. Waterfowl status report, 1963. U.S. Fish and Wild. Serv., Spec. Sci. Rpt., Wildlife No. 75. 178pp.

HANSEN, H. A. 1964. Waterfowl status report, 1964. U.S. Fish and Wildl. Serv., Spec. Sci. Rpt., Wildlife No. 86. 142pp.

———, AND MILDRED HUDGINS. 1965. U.S. Fish and Wildl. Serv., Spec. Sci. Rpt., Wildl. No. 90. 110pp.

KOPISCHKE, E. D. 1966. Selection of calcium- and magnesium-bearing grit by pheasants of Minnesota. J. Wildl. Mgmt. 30(2):276–279.

LEE, F. B., R. L. JESSEN, N. J. ORDAL, R. I. BENSON, J. P. LINDMEIER, R. E. FARMES, AND M. M. NELSON. 1964. Ducks and land use in Minnesota. Minn. Dept. Cons., Tech. Bull. No. 8. 140pp. John B. Moyle, editor.

MENDALL, H. L. 1958. The ring-necked duck in the northeast. Univ. of Maine Studies, Second Series, No. 73. 317pp.

MOYLE, J. B., D. B. VESALL, B. R. JONES, R. L. JESSEN, AND M. CASEY. 1963. Waterfowl mortality caused by oil pollution of the Minnesota and Mississippi Rivers in 1963. Minn. Dept. Cons., Spec. Pub. 21. 19pp.

REID, V. H. 1948. Lead shot in Minnesota waterfowl. J. Wildl. Mgmt. 12(2):123–127.

WHITLOCK, S. C., AND H. J. MILLER. 1947. Gunshot wounds in ducks. J. Wildl. Mgmt. 11(3):279–281.

A COMPARISON OF LEAD AND STEEL SHOT FOR WATERFOWL HUNTING

EDWARD J. MIKULA, Michigan Department of Natural Resources, Wildlife Division, Lansing 48926
GERALD F. MARTZ, Michigan Department of Natural Resources, Wildlife Division, Lansing 48926
LAWRENCE A. RYEL, Michigan Department of Natural Resources, Surveys and Statistics, Lansing 48926

Abstract: During the 1973 waterfowl hunting season, a field test of steel and lead shot was conducted at the Shiawassee River State Game Area near Saginaw, Michigan. The experiment was part of a nationwide study to evaluate the relative efficiency of steel as compared with lead. It took more shots with steel to down waterfowl than it did with lead, but both shot materials were nearly identical in efficiency up to 31.5 m (35 yards). Crippling loss for steel was 16.0 percent compared with 13.6 percent for lead. There was no significant differences in the crippling loss between the two shot materials ($0.50 > P > 0.25$).

HISTORY AND INTRODUCTION

The lead poisoning problem in waterfowl and its toxicology has been thoroughly described and discussed by Bellrose (1959), Jordan and Bellrose (1950), the Mississippi Flyway Council (1965), and other authors. Research to find a suitable substitute for lead shot has been reported by Andrews and Longcore (1969), the Mississippi Flyway Council (1965), Kozicky and Madson (1973), Irwin et al. (1973) and Kimball (1974).

The controlled shooting tests of lead and steel shot conducted by Winchester in 1972–73 resulted in an expanded field testing program of lead and steel shot by the U.S. Fish and Wildlife Service during the 1973–74 waterfowl hunting season. These tests were designed to focus on the differences in crippling of waterfowl under actual hunting conditions in various regions of the country. The Shiawassee River State Game Area in Michigan was selected as one of the test sites. A good data base of past hunter use and performance, including crippling loss and harvest, has been accumulated for this area.

The authors thank personnel of the Fish and Wildlife Service for their assistance in planning the study. Special thanks are extended to Department of Natural Resources' personnel who assisted in gathering field data and to F. W. Stuewer and R. I. Blouch for editorial review of the manuscript.

A description of the Shiawassee River State Game Area, as well as specific management and hunting programs has been described elsewhere (Mikula et al. 1972*a*).

METHODS

Between 10 October and 4 November 1973, steel and lead shot field tests were scheduled for 47 half-day hunting periods. A daily bag limit of four ducks (any species or sex) was used for those hunters participating in the tests. This provided maximum data by eliminating the restrictive effects of regulations.

In each of the half-day hunting periods, matched tests were scheduled with one hunting party using lead shot loads and the other steel shot loads. Five shooting posts where hunting harvest opportunities were expected to be the greatest, were selected for each hunting period. Lead or steel shot was randomly assigned to the highest blind numbers prior to the tests. The assignments for each half-day period were sealed in separate dated envelopes. These envelopes were opened only after the test hunting parties were selected.

Originally published in Wildl. Soc. Bull. 5(1):3–8, 1977.

Before each drawing for shooting posts, hunters were briefed about area rules, general waterfowl regulations and the purpose and conditions of the lead vs. steel shot field test. Everyone was told that all members of a party must use a 12-gauge shotgun. Volunteers had to further agree to accompany a biologist who would observe their hunt, to use ammunition furnished by the Department, and to answer a questionnaire. Hunters were advised that steel shot was recommended only for a single barrel shotgun of modern manufacture.

Potential participants did not know which blinds had been chosen for the tests until they picked such a blind as part of the regular blind selection procedure. The hunting parties selecting test blinds were asked if they had the appropriate shotguns and would agree to other experimental conditions. If so, they were issued a hunting permit for that blind and were briefed by the biologist observer. If they could not qualify or did not want to participate, they were required to select another blind. The test blind then remained open for selection by a subsequent party.

Hunters were instructed that they could use only the test ammunition provided and that the observer would bring the test shells with him and would meet them at their blind. Ammunition used was 1⅛ oz. steel and 1¼ oz. lead No. 4 shot shells in standard 2¾ inch 12 gauge, manufactured and furnished by the Federal Cartridge Corporation, Minneapolis, Minnesota. From outward appearances the steel and lead shells looked identical. There were no markings on the shells indicating which type of shot hunters were using; only the boxes were coded to aid in distributing the proper shells to the observer. One box of 25 shells was issued for each person in the party.

Hunting parties were not told which type of shot they were using until the completion of their hunt. In many of the tests, the observer did not know what material was being used.

During the hunt, the observer positioned himself immediately behind the hunters in the blind area and recorded information on the hunt. He was instructed to be passive and not to participate by giving advice, information or any aid to the hunters. Data of the hunt were recorded on U.S. Fish and Wildlife Service standard Hunter Performance Observation Form No. 3-171. In addition, the ranges at which birds were shot at was taken with optical Ranging Rangefinders (Ranging Co., Rochester, New York) whenever possible and estimated in other situations.

At the completion of the hunt each member of the party filled out a short questionnaire. Information asked for included the type of hunting, guns and ammunition, hunting success and satisfaction with loads used.

Table 1. Number of hunts and characteristics of parties participating in the 1973 steel/lead shot experiment.

	Steel shot	Lead shot
No. of morning hunts	22	23
No. of afternoon hunts	24	22
Total no. of hunts	46	45
No. of hunter trips	120	121
Hunters per party	2.6	2.7
Average length of hunt (hours)	3.70	3.62
Parties using a dog (percent)	39	24

RESULTS

Hunter Participation and Weapons

An almost equal number of hunting parties were observed using the two kinds of shot (Table 1). The 241 total hunter trips in the experiment were made by 195 individuals. Only 15 individuals used both types of ammunition during the tests (24 steel-shot trips and 21 lead-shot trips). Eighty-seven hunters participated in the steel test and 93 in the lead test. Just over 86 percent of the hunters participated in the steel test and 93 in the lead test. Eighty-six percent of the hunters participated in the experiment once. The maximum number of hunts by any participant was six.

Nearly all of the 47 hunts programmed for each of the test materials were accomplished. Resulting data are based on 45 paired hunts where steel and lead shot were used under similar weather, habitat, bird behavior and species composition conditions.

Average hunter party size and length of hunt were nearly identical between the steel and lead tests.

A total of 117 parties had the opportunity to participate in the tests. Of that total 26 parties declined the opportunity to participate. Seventeen of the 26 parties could not qualify because one or more of the

Table 2. Flight data, shooting statistics and crippling losses experienced in the 1973 steel/lead shot experiment.

	Steel shot	Lead shot
No. of flights shot at	466	394
Total no. of birds in flights	1,201	1,042
Birds per flight	2.58	2.65
No. of shots fired	1,209	986
No. of birds knocked down	268	273
No. of shots per bird knocked down	4.3	3.6
No. of birds retrieved	225	236
Unretrieved birds[1] (number)	43	37
(percent)	16.0	13.6
Birds lost per 100 birds bagged	19.1	15.7

[1] Includes birds where no range data recorded.

party had a shotgun other than a 12 gauge. Six parties did not want to participate because they did not want to take the chance of using steel shot. Two parties had members who did not wish to use steel shot in their double barrel shotguns, and one party had a magnum shotgun that would not eject standard loads.

Eight percent of the hunters in the steel-shot tests actually used double barrel guns. In both the lead and steel tests auto-loaders and pumps were far the most common weapons. Most hunters used guns with full choke barrels.

Field Data

Hunters using steel fired more shells and shot at more flights of ducks than those using lead (Table 2). It took 4.3 shots to down a bird in the steel tests and 3.6 in the lead tests. Hunters using steel retrieved fewer of the birds brought down than those using lead, 16.0 and 13.6 percent respectively. The difference, however, was not significant ($P > 0.05$). The percentage of unretrieved birds downed with steel and lead shot was well within the range of 14.9 to 19.9 percent for the previous 4 years reported by hunters in similar habitat at this area.

Over 80 percent of the birds fired at in the tests were mallards (*Anas platyrhynchos*). The remaining flights were composed of ring-necked ducks (*Aythya collaris*), green-winged teal (*Anas crecca*), blue-winged teal (*A. discors*), black ducks (*A. rubripes*), pintails (*A. acuta*) and a small number of other species. There were no discernible differences between steel and lead in the proportions of the species observed, the species brought down, and those retrieved. Eight Canada geese (*Branta canadensis*) were retrieved of 8 knocked down with lead and 3 of 4 knocked down with steel.

Shot Shell Efficiency

The number of shooting opportunities taken by hunters and the proportion of all opportunities in which waterfowl were brought down were plotted against shooting ranges (Table 3). Range data were recorded for 98 percent of all shooting opportunities, with slightly more than 60 percent of the measurements made with rangefinders and the balance by ocular estimation. It should be emphasized that range data represents the distances at which shooting began. The second and third shots of repeating weapons were often at birds 9.2 to 18.5 m (10–20 yards) beyond the recorded ranges. However, it was impossible to keep track of which birds were downed or lost with the first or the subsequent shots.

Most "first shots" taken by hunters were at ranges between 19.4 m (21 yards) and 41.5 m (45 yards). On a cumulative basis, the first shots for both steel and lead shot shells were similar (83 percent for steel and 82 percent for lead) at birds within 41.5 m (45 yards) (Table 3).

Table 3. A summary of shooting opportunities taken at various ranges and the proportions in which waterfowl were knocked down in the 1973 steel/lead shot experiment.

	STEEL			LEAD		
Minimum estimate of shooting ranges (m)[1]	No. of shoot. oppor. taken	No. of shoot. oppor. where birds were downed	% of shoot. oppor. where birds were downed	No. of shoot. oppor. taken	No. of shoot. oppor. where birds were downed	% of shoot. oppor. where birds were downed
9.2–27.7 (10–30 yds.)	152	108	71	131	106	81
28.6–41.5 (31–45 yds.)	205	105	51	171	117	68
42.5+ (46 yds.)	73	29	40	66	18	27
Unknown range	36	1	–	26	13	–
All ranges	466	243	52.1	394	254	64.4

[1] Recorded ranges were commonly taken when the first shots were fired and may not have been at the range when the birds were hit. Mean shooting range for steel shot was 32.7 m (35.4 yards) and 34.3 m (37.2 yards) for lead shot.

Beyond 41.5 m (45 yards) steel shot appeared to be more efficient: Steel shot users downed birds on 40 percent of their shooting opportunities compared with 27 percent for lead users. Lead, because of its greater density, retains greater pellet energy at longer ranges resulting in a greater "knock-down" ability beyond 41.5 m. What we observed may be due to experimental chance, differences in hunter shooting skill, shot pattern density or in shot velocity. It could also be a combination of any or all of these factors.

Based on the experiences of biologist observers, it was their consensus that the presence of the observer had only a minimal impact on hunter performance or on the distance at which first shots were taken. In most instances the hunters were so absorbed in their hunt, they were unaware of the observer. We feel hunters performed as might be expected for a cross section of the waterfowl-hunting public.

With both steel and lead the lowest rate of crippling loss occurred when birds were initially shot at from 9.2 to 27.7 m (10–30 yards), and the highest rate of crippling loss occurred when birds were initially shot at beyond 41.5 m (45 yards) (Table 4). Losses, therefore, essentially paralleled the ranges at which shooting opportunities were taken.

Over half of the birds downed as "sailers" were lost by hunters, while 7 to 9 percent of the birds falling directly were lost. Not all "sailers" are pursued by hunters.

When all hunters using steel shot were compared with those using lead there was no significant difference ($P > 0.05$) between the crippling rate.

Hunter Attitudes

Most hunters who participated in the steel/lead experiment answered questionnaires following their hunt. All hunters were asked to answer questions about lead poisoning and the steel-shot hunters were asked to complete the steel-shot questionnaire. Of those replying, 99 percent had heard of the lead poisoning problem in waterfowl. Fourteen percent of the respondents were undecided as to the seriousness of the problem, while 85 percent believed it to be serious. Only 1 percent of the responding hunters did not believe lead poisoning to be a serious problem.

Of those hunters who used steel shot, 64.6 percent expressed satisfaction with its

Table 4. Fate of waterfowl knocked down following shooting opportunities taken at various ranges.

	Distance (m)[1]							
	Steel shot				Lead shot			
Category	9.2–27.7	28.6–41.5	42.5 +	Total	9.2–27.7	28.6–41.5	42.5 +	Total
Direct fall								
No. retrieved	103	87	19	209	106	89	11	206
No. unretrieved	9	8	3	20	7	7	1	15
% unretrieved	8.0	8.4	13.6	8.7	6.2	7.3	8.3	6.8
Sailers								
No. retrieved	4	7	4	15	4	12	2	18
No. unretrieved	9	9	4	22	1	13	5	19
% unretrieved	69	56	50	59	20	52	71	51
Total unretrieved	18	17	7	42	8	20	6	34
% unretrieved	14	15	23	15.8	7.0	17	32	13.2

[1] Equivalent yardage shown in Table 3, column 1.

performance. Twenty-five percent were undecided about the performance of steel shot and 10.3 percent of the hunters said they were dissatisfied with steel. Most of the dissatisfied group had lost cripples or complained of lack of "knock-down" power.

Hunters using steel, as well as those using lead, experienced occasional failure of the shells to eject from the chamber of the shotgun. In such instances, a second or third shot was impossible. As far as we know, this problem occurred only in automatic weapons chambered for 3-inch magnum shells. Since the test shells were standard 3¾ dram loads, it was possible that the ejection mechanism of some autoloaders was not properly adjusted for non-magnum loads. Hunters who complained about this problem usually stated they normally used "magnum" shells, considering them superior to the standard loads used in the tests.

In these tests, no misfired or "blooper" rounds, or burst barrels occurred with either steel or lead shot shells.

DISCUSSION AND CONCLUSIONS

While it took more rounds to bring down waterfowl with steel shot than with lead, both materials showed nearly equal efficiency up to 32.3 m (35 yards). The field test also showed no significant differences ($P > 0.05$) in the crippling rate for either shot material. Most crippling losses occurred at moderate shooting ranges, not at extreme ranges. The results from other areas conducting similar tests in 1973 also showed similar results.

Observations suggest that shooting opportunities for Michigan hunters is limited, and as a result, hunters shoot at most of the birds that pass within shotgun range. Statewide hunter performance observations made during the 1971 and 1972 hunting season showed that only 5.4 and 5.8 percent, respectively, of Michigan waterfowl hunting parties achieved a daily bag limit (Mikula et al. 1972*b*, 1973).

During 1971 and 1972 hunters shot at 84 and 85 percent, respectively, of all ducks flights within range. Under the point system used in those years hunters shot at 74 and 82 percent, respectively, of the high-point birds, 94 and 97 percent, respectively, of the mid-point birds and 88 and 89 percent, respectively, of the low-point birds. If steel shot were used statewide, probably fewer ducks would be downed by

Michigan hunters. Although a greater proportion of the downed birds might be lost as cripples, Michigan hunters using steel shot would subject waterfowl populations to less mortality than is occurring at the present time with lead shot.

If Bellrose (1959) is correct in concluding that a high percentage of deposited lead shot is unavailable to the waterfowl after 1 year, there should be a reduced drain on the resource from lead poisoning if a conversion to steel shot is made. Michigan has experienced significant lead poisoning mortalities, and any shift to a non-toxic shot material for waterfowl hunting should result in some savings of birds that might be reflected in some increase in the population of waterfowl breeding within the state.

Hunter attitudes and ethics about shooting at unreasonable ranges, not using a retriever and the lack of skill in the use of a shotgun are some of the major factors that may influence the success of any program converting to non-toxic shot material. Coupled with these factors is the ability of a state wildlife agency to provide the necessary education and information on the lead poisoning, waterfowl populations and habitat, hunter attitudes and ethical problems and their solutions. We, as an agency, must be capable of monitoring changes, and to properly convey to the hunting public information on what has and is happening to the resource due to the continued use of lead shot and what they can expect in the future. This approach should ensure a smooth transition to a non-toxic shot material.

Poor hunter performance and hunter ethics, the continued use of lead shot coupled with a continued shrinkage of the waterfowl population and its habitat base could lead to more restrictive harvest regulations. We believe the total drain on the waterfowl resource would be less if steel shot for the hunting of waterfowl was mandatory throughout the country.

LITERATURE CITED

ANDREWS, R. AND J. R. LONGCORE. 1969. The killing efficiency of soft iron shot. N. Am. Wildl. Conf. 34:337–345.

BELLROSE, F. C. 1959. Lead poisoning as a mortality factor in waterfowl populations. Illinois Nat. Hist. Sur. 27(3):235–288.

IRWIN, J. C., D. DENNIS, AND N. G. PERRET. 1973. Lead-iron shot a possible solution to the lead poisoning problem in waterfowl. Midwest Wildl. Conf. 13pp.

JORDAN, J. S., AND F. C. BELLROSE. 1950. Shot alloys and lead poisoning in waterfowl. Trans. N. Am. Wildl. Conf. 15:115–168.

KIMBALL, C. F. 1974. Comparisons of steel and lead shot from controlled field tests and from questionnaires 1973–74. U.S. Fish and Wildl. Serv. 19pp.

KOZICKY, E., AND J. MADSON. 1973. Nilo shotshell efficiency test and experimental mallard ducks, 1972–73. Proc. Int. Assoc. Game, Fish and Conserv. Com. 100–116.

MIKULA, E. J., G. MARTZ, AND C. BENNETT, JR. 1972a. Field evaluation of three types of waterfowl hunting regulations. J. Wildl. Manage. 36(2):441–459.

———, ———, AND ———. 1972b. Michigan 1971 point system experiment. Michigan Dept. Nat. Resour. Wildl. Div. Rep. 2686. 18pp.

———, ———, AND ———. 1973. Michigan 1972 point system experiment. Michigan Dept. Nat. Resour. Wildl. Div. Rep. 2697. 18pp.

MISSISSIPPI FLYWAY COUNCIL. 1965. Wasted waterfowl. Mississippi Flyway Council Planning Committee. 87pp.

SELECTED BIBLIOGRAPHY

Population Influences and Characteristics: Hunting

ALLEN, W. R. 1967. Development and management of the Blythe Ferry Goose Management Area, Meigs County, Tennessee. Proc. Annu. Conf. S.E. Assoc. Game Fish Comm. 21:155–160.

BELLROSE, F. C. 1944. Duck populations and kill. Ill. Nat. Hist. Survey Bull. 23:327–372.

———. 1953. A preliminary evaluation of cripple losses in waterfowl. Trans. North Am. Wildl. Conf. 18:337–359.

BRACE, R. K., R. S. POSPAHALA, AND R. J. BLOHM. 1981. Cooperative programs for evaluating stabilized migratory bird hunting regulations in Canada and the United States. Trans. North Am. Wildl. Nat. Resour. Conf. 46 (In Press).

CHAPMAN, J. A., C. J. HENNY, AND H. M. WIGHT. 1969. The status, population dynamics, and harvest of the dusky Canada goose. Wildl. Monogr. 18. 48pp.

CRISSEY, W. F. 1957. Forecasting waterfowl harvest by flyways. Trans. North Am. Wildl. Conf. 22:256–268.

EVRARD, J. O. 1970. Assessing and improving the ability of hunters to identify flying waterfowl. J. Wildl. Manage. 34:114–126.

GEIS, A. D., AND F. G. COOCH. 1972. Distribution of the duck harvest in Canada and the United States. U.S. Fish Wildl. Serv. Spec. Sci. Rep. 151. 11pp.

———, AND W. F. CRISSEY. 1973. 1970 Test of the point system for regulating duck harvests. Wildl. Soc. Bull. 1(1):1–27.

———, R. K. MARTINSON, AND D. R. ANDERSON. 1969. Establishing hunting regulations and allowable harvest of mallards in the United States. J. Wildl. Manage. 33(4):848–859.

GRIEB, J. R. 1964. Effect of season length and bag size on central flyway duck harvest. Proc. 44th Annu. Conf. West. Assoc. State Game Fish Comm. pp. 197–205.

———, H. D. FUNK, R. M. HOPPER, G. F. WRAKESTRAW, AND D. WITT. 1970. Evaluation of the 1968–1969 experimental mallard drake season in Montana, Wyoming and Colorado. Trans. North Am. Wildl. Nat. Resour. Conf. 35:336–348.

HOCHBAUM, H. A. 1947. The effect of concentrated hunting pressure on waterfowl breeding stock. Trans. North Am. Wildl. Conf. 12:53–62.

———. 1948. Harvesting the waterfowl crop. Trans. North Am. Wildl. Conf. 13:481–491.

HOPPER, R. M., A. D. GEIS, J. R. GRIEB, AND L. NELSON, JR. 1975. Experimental duck hunting seasons, San Luis Valley, Colorado, 1963–1970. Wildl. Monogr. 46. 68pp.

MACAULAY, A. J., AND D. A. BOAG. 1974. Waterfowl harvest by slave Indians in northern Alberta. Arctic 27(1):15–26.

NELSON, L., JR., AND J. B. LOW. 1977. Acceptance of the 1970–71 point system season by duck hunters. Wildl. Soc. Bull. 5(2):52–55.

OLSON, D. P. 1965. Differential vulnerability of male and female canvasbacks to hunting. Trans. North Am. Wildl. Conf. 30:121–135.

PETERSON, S. R. AND R. S. ELLARSON.

1975. Incidence of body shot in Lake Michigan oldsquaws. J. Wildl. Manage. 39(1):217–219.

REEVES, H. M., H. H. DILL, AND A. S. HAWKINS. 1969. A case study in Canada goose management: the Mississippi Valley population. Pages 150–165 *in* R. L. Hine and C. Schoenfeld, eds. Canada goose management; current continental programs. Dembar Educational Res. Services, Inc., Madison, WI.

SCHIERBAUM, D. L., AND D. D. FOLEY. 1957. Differential age and sex vulnerability of the black duck to gunning. New York Fish and Game J. 4(1):88–91.

SIMPSON, S. G., AND R. L. JARVIS. 1979. Comparative ecology of several subspecies of Canada geese during winter in western Oregon. Pages 223–241 *in* R. L. Jarvis and J. C. Bartonek, eds. Management and biology of Pacific flyway geese. A symposium. Northwest Sect. of the Wildl. Soc. Oregon State Univ. Book Stores, Inc., Corvallis.

TACHA, T. C., G. F. MARTZ, AND J. PARKER. 1980. Harvest and mortality of giant Canada geese in southeastern Michigan. Wildl. Soc. Bull. 8(1):40–45.

TIMM, D. E., AND C. P. DAU. 1979. Productivity, mortality, distribution and population status of Pacific flyway white-fronted geese. Pages 280–298 *in* R. L. Jarvis and J. C. Bartonek, eds. Management and biology of Pacific flyway geese. A symposium. Northwest Sect. of the Wildl. Soc. Oregon State Univ. Book Stores, Inc., Corvallis.

VAN DYKE, F. 1981. Mortality in crippled mallards. J. Wildl. Manage. 45:444–451.

Population Ecology

POPULATION DYNAMICS AND THE EXPLOITATION OF DUCKS AND GEESE[1]

H. BOYD,[2] Wildfowl Trust, Slimbridge, Gloucestershire

The family Anatidae, comprising about 145 species, is of world-wide distribution, but statistical information is limited almost entirely to species living in the Arctic and temperate regions of Europe and North America. The family is by taxonomic standards a homogeneous one in which current opinion favours the recognition of relatively few genera, and the geographical limits of the sample restrict attention to the occupants of a small range of habitats. Thus a comparative study of present knowledge of the dynamics of different species might be expected to reveal similarities rather than differences. In the first section of this paper I assemble information about the fecundity and survival to maturity of twenty populations of fourteen species. A second section is devoted to estimates of the mean adult survival rate of populations of twenty-three species. The third section discusses specific studies of the relation between the kill by man and losses from other causes against this comparative background.

THE PRODUCTION OF YOUNG BIRDS AND THEIR SURVIVAL TO MATURITY

In comparing specific characteristics of fertility and survival it is desirable to restrict attention to populations which are in a steady state. So few long and intensive studies of wildfowl populations have been made it is impracticable to set up very rigorous criteria for selection. The results used here have been obtained from studies during at least three years of entire specific or subspecific populations or of breeding groups in clearly-defined areas, and are limited to breeding populations which varied very little in size, or if they fluctuated more widely showed no upward or downward trend.

The most economical method I could find of presenting the information is the series of histograms in Fig. 1, which record average annual production by a hypothetical group of 100 mature females from each population. The average number of eggs actually laid is substantially less than the number expected on the hypothesis that the output is equal to (mean clutch × 100) because a proportion of the mature females fail to lay. There are five genera represented in Fig. 1: two 'grey' and two 'snow' geese, all in *Anser*; three 'black' geese, *Branta*; the common shelduck, *Tadorna tadorna*; four 'dabbling ducks,' *Anas*; and four pochards, *Aythya*. The sequence of the species is that in the classification by Scott (1957).

The histograms suggest that the fecundity of very closely related species is similar and that there are much greater differences between genera (and tribes). Geese (*Anser, Branta*) lay few eggs. Not only are their clutches small, but they are usually unable to produce more than one clutch a year and a significant proportion of mature birds fail to lay. In the case of Arctic nesting species (such as *Branta bernicla* and *Anser caerulescens*) years in which very few females breed successfully occur frequently. These non-breeding years seem usually to be due to a de-

---

[1] Originally published in E. LeCren, ed. The exploitation of natural populations, pages 85–94. John Wiley & Sons, New York, 1962.

[2] Present address: 1032 Pinewood Crescent, Ottawa, Ontario K2B 5Y5, Canada.

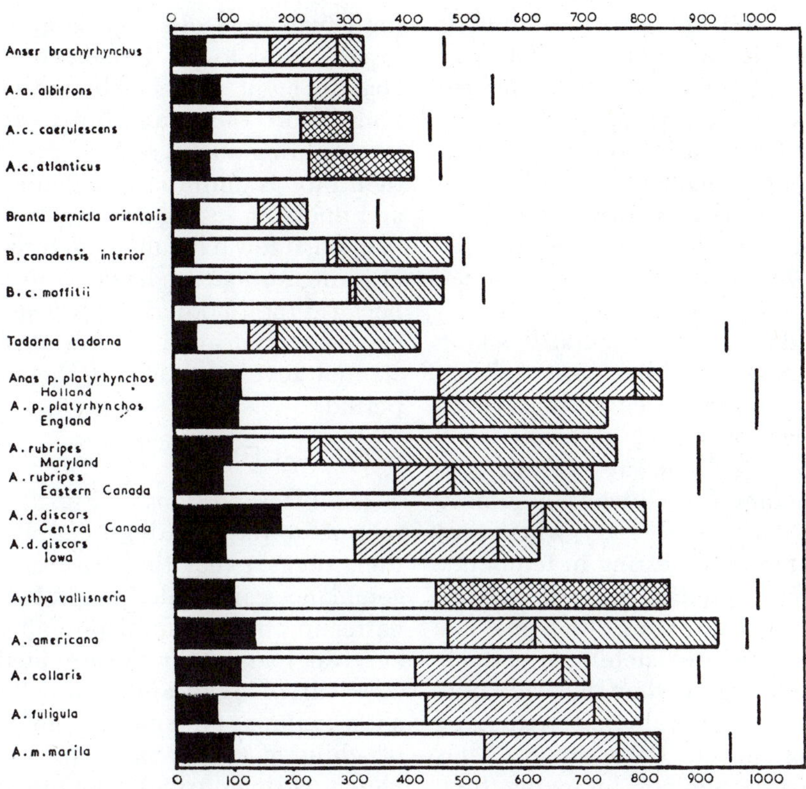

Fig. 1. The average production of eggs by some wildfowl populations and the survival of offspring to breeding age. The theoretical egg production of 100 mature females is shown by the vertical bar. The average actual output is indicated by the total length of each column. Losses between laying and fledging are shown by diagonal shading; losses of eggs to the right, of young before flying to the left. Where there is doubt about the relative size of losses before and after hatching the two patterns of shading are combined to show losses between laying and fledging. The unshaded area shows losses between fledging and maturity and the black area is proportional to the number of young surviving to maturity.

layed thaw in the spring causing nesting sites to be unavailable or to severe weather in the early nesting phase of the breeding cycle inhibiting laying or destroying eggs. In species breeding further south (*B. canadensis*) catastrophes such as losses of nests due to flooding may affect particular colonies, but non-breeding years rarely, if ever, occur and failure to breed is usually a result of unsuccessful competition for nest sites or other limiting social behaviour. So far as is known at present losses of eggs during incubation and of young between hatching and fledging are relatively small in northern-breeding geese. In Canada geese egg losses may be substantial but gosling deaths are few. Geese do not become mature until at least two years old (*A. brachyrhynchus* and *A. albifrons* not until three) so that fullgrown young birds are 'at risk' for at least twenty months before possible entry to the breeding population. Yet in *Anser* pre-breeding losses are relatively few. Though geese in their first winter suffer substantially heavier losses than do older birds, the first year mortality rates of the Arctic breeding species are well below those found in ducks. There is some evidence that in *A. brachyrhynchus* and *A. c. caerulescens* individuals in their second year of life survive better than mature geese. The examples of *B. canadensis* cited here appear to be affected by very heavy juvenile mortality: in the *moffitti* population this 'mortality' may well have included substantial emigration.

The shelduck has a goose-like low mortality-rate after hatching, and delayed sexual maturity (at three or four years) but loses eggs on a duck-like scale.

The dabbling ducks are prolific, supplementing their first clutches by re-nesting attempts when necessary, which they can do by virtue of nesting in temperate regions and beginning nesting activity early in the spring. They suffer massive losses of eggs before hatching or of ducklings before fledging, though steady populations apparently do not withstand large losses in both these stages. They mature in the summer following their birth, so that the pre-breeding period is short, but nevertheless juvenile losses are usually heavier than in geese, as are those of mature birds.

The diving ducks of *Aythya* seem to resemble *Anas*, with the possible distinction that losses before fledging seem to be inflicted more on ducklings than on eggs. The pochards, though not Arctic species, nest late in the summer and do not re-nest so freely as *Anas*, but their output of eggs seems to be as high. This is apparently because, despite the lower frequency of re-nesting, the proportion of complete breeding failures or non-breeding among mature females is low. The situation is rather obscure, because populations of *Aythya* typically show greater fluctuation than those of *Anas*, while in some of them (*A. fuligula*, *A. marila*), and possibly in most, females may not mature until two years old. The large duckling losses seem to be associated with the abandonment of broods by their mothers long before the young birds can fly. In the dabbling ducks, mothers remain with their broods until they are flying strongly and duckling losses are largely confined to the first few days after hatching. Losses of young *Aythya* are less easy to measure, because the (motherless) broods tend to aggregate, but seem to continue at a substantial level throughout the pre-flight period.

ADULT SURVIVAL

The black portions of Fig. 1, showing recruits to the (steady) breeding population, suggest that there are generic resemblances in adult losses. It is rather easier to obtain information about adult survival than about the production and survival of eggs and young. Table 1 shows values of the mean annual survival of adults of twenty-three species in ten genera of seven tribes. The examples are confined to populations not showing marked trends. It has not been possible to use 'adult' here in a wholly consistent way. In most cases the survival rate shown applies to birds at least one year old, rather than to birds known to be sexually mature. Differences in survival between pre-breeders more than a year old and older birds are slight, normally much less than the fluctuations in adult survival between one year and another.

This extended sample strengthens the inference that closely related species have similar adult mortality rates ($d = 1 - s$, where s is survival) and that differences between genera may be substantial. On the view that the death-rate balances the birth-rate, rather than the other way about, this is equivalent to support for the hypothesis that the effective fertility (as defined by Capildeo and Hal-

Table 1. Estimates of the mean annual survival rates of adult wildfowl. Only one estimate is given for each form (species or subspecies): where several independent estimates were available a mean value has been used. Standard deviations are given wherever the method of estimation permits their calculation. All estimates are based on recoveries of marked birds, except those marked *, derived from censuses and age-ratios.

Form	Adult survival-rate	Regional population
Tribe Anserini		
Anser brachyrhynchus	0.74 ± 0.02	Iceland
A. a. albifrons	0.72 ± 0.11	W Siberia
A. a. flavirostris	0.66 ± 0.04	Greenland
A. a. anser	0.77 ± 0.02	Iceland
*A. c. caerulescens**	0.63	Entire
*A. c. atlanticus**	0.67	Entire
Branta c. canadensis	0.78 ± 0.03	England
*B. c. moffitti**	0.82	Washington
*B. b. bernicla**	0.86	British-wintering
B. b. hrota	0.83 ± 0.08	Spitzbergen
B. b. orientalis	0.85 ± 0.05	Alaska
Tribe Tadornini		
Tadorna tadorna	0.80 ± 0.05	German-ringed
Tribe Anatini		
Anas a. acuta	0.52 ± 0.01	Russia
A. crecca crecca	0.49 ± 0.03	British-wintering
A. crecca carolinensis	0.52 ± 0.02	Utah
A. p. platyrhynchos	0.52 ± 0.02	NW Europe
A. rubripes	0.50 ± 0.02	Illinois-marked
A. penelope	0.53 ± 0.04	NW Europe
A. d. discors	0.55 ± 0.04	Manitoba
A. clypeata	0.56 ± 0.06	Britain
Tribe Somateriini		
Somateria m. mollissima	0.61	NW Europe, Greenland
Tribe Aythyini		
Aythya vallisineria	0.59	Central Canada
A. americana	0.51 ± 0.04	Utah
A. fuligula	0.54 ± 0.07	NW Europe
A. m. marila	0.48 ± 0.06	Iceland
Tribe Cairinini		
Aix sponsa	0.64	Ohio
Tribe Mergini		
Melanitta n. nigra	0.77 ± 0.04	Iceland
Clangula hyemalis	0.72 ± 0.04	Iceland
Mergus m. merganser	0.60 ± 0.07	British-wintering

dane 1954) of closely related species is similar.

Another inference from the general observation that geese are bigger than ducks is that large wildfowl survive better, and produce fewer offspring, than small ones. Using average weight as a crude but simple measure of size, the Spearman rank coefficient between body weight and adult survival for the twenty-six species in the sample is +0.579, $P \ll 0.01$.

Males survive appreciably better than females in some species, especially among the diving ducks, in which there seem usually to be an excess of males in the adult population, despite the parity of the sexes at hatching.

EXPLOITATION

The statistics so far presented, though inadequate for constructing a detailed working model of any specific population, provide a 'natural history' background for the study of exploitation, which in Europe and North America consists almost entirely of the shooting of full-grown ducks and geese for sport. (It is of interest to note that public opinion, and legislation, in most countries is hardening against the commercial use of wildfowl, so far as this amounts to offering the killed birds for sale.) The motives of sportsmen are more complex than those of commerical exploiters, but initially it seems best to assume that their principal requirements are to have available the largest possible number of full-grown individuals each season and to be allowed to kill as many of them as they can without detriment to their chances in future years.

Very few wildfowl populations in Arctic and temperate regions of the north are sedentary and many of them perform lengthy annual migrations. Thus sportsmen shooting in the autumn and winter have, in general, no direct means of influencing recruitment to the populations they are pursuing. Moreover, these populations are often heterogeneous assemblies of birds from many different breeding places. For a large safe kill shooting men should favour those species rearing relatively large numbers of young and particularly those in which a high rate of loss in the first year after fledging is still consistent with the maintenance of the breeding population. But this view will only be appropriate if losses from causes other than shooting are small in these species, or if shooting losses can be substituted for natural ones.

The mallard *Anas platyrhynchos* has been marked on a large scale in many countries so that much information on the survival of different sub-populations is available. From a survey (unpublished) of this material I conclude that the species is not capable of sustaining itself when adult losses exceed about 55 per cent, although some authors (e.g., Hickey 1952, Lauckhart 1956) do not concede this. Self-maintaining populations of this species show close similarities in their rates of recruitment and loss, despite great differences in the shooting pressure to which they are subjected.

The relation between the kill by man and other mortality is not easily investigated but in recent years the problems have received much attention in North America and results are beginning to be announced. The most impressive studies so far are those of the U.S. Bureau of Sport Fisheries and Wildlife on the canvasback *Aythya vallisineria* (Stewart et al. 1958, Geis 1959, Atwood 1959). This is a valued game species subjected to heavy shooting pressure, which accounts for more than a half of the deaths of all canvasbacks of flying age. In North America shooting pressure is subject to legislative control through the imposition of bag limits and seasons of varying lengths and the Bureau studies have taken advantage of this situation to demonstrate not only that shooting regulations have been effective in influencing the size of the kill but also that the size of the kill has influenced the size of the breeding population. This work is notable for dealing with the entire wide-ranging specific population of the order of half a million birds.

The canvasback is an example of a species with a high turnover which shows large changes in abundance from year to year, apparently due mainly to variations in breeding success. The mallard and the green-winged teal *Anas crecca* have a similarly large turnover, but show less striking numerical fluctuations because their breeding success is more consistent. (No convenient summary of the varied data on success could be devised for inclusion here.) A study of the survival of marked teal (Boyd 1957*a*) in Europe suggested that about three-fifths of male and one-half of female losses are due to shooting, mostly in winter, and that the kill directly affected annual survival rates. But it also indicated that heavy winter losses due to shooting are offset by reduced losses in subsequent months (including a higher proportion of 'natural deaths' than occur in winter), with the implication that non-shooting mortality should not be regarded as constant and independent of the kill, as some investigators have taken it to be.

No studies of non-shooting mortality among full-grown geese have yet been published but it appears that in several species the kill must constitute a much higher proportion of the total deaths than in these ducks. Some of the geese wintering in Britain which have similar adult mortality rates (see Table 1) show interesting differences in the annual distribution of shooting losses. In the pinkfoot *Anser brachyrhynchus* the kill is largely confined to the period October to February, with peaks in October and January. In the Icelandic greylag *A. anser* losses are spread more nearly uniformly through the period September to April. In the Siberian-breeding whitefront *A. albifrons albifrons* the kill in April to June seems to be as great as that in autumn and winter, while in the Greenland-breeding *A. albifrons flavirostris* most losses occur in May, July, and November to February. Despite these differences in distribution the end results appear to be similar.

Geese, with their low reproductive capacity and delayed maturity, present problems to the prudent exploiter which are particularly acute in cases like that of the brent *Branta bernicla* in which recruitment is highly erratic. In geese, and in other large aquatic birds, as Austin (1957) has pointed out, 'maintenance of the adult population seems of greater importance to the survival of the species than the success of any particular year's crop of young.' If brent are to maintain themselves it would seem to be highly desirable to regulate shooting pressure on a seasonal basis so that in years of poor breeding success the kill is kept small. Greylags or Canada geese on the other hand do not greatly need frequent adjustments of the permissible take.

CONCLUSION

Understanding of the dynamics of wildfowl populations is so imperfect that students can as yet contribute little to population research on a broader scale, but the comparative treatment of closely-related forms which is possible in the Anatidae should prove of value.

ACKNOWLEDGMENTS

Though most of the sums are my own and I have drawn perhaps too heavily on unpublished material in the files of the Wildfowl Trust, a review of this kind is largely dependent on the work of others. The list of references is, I hope, complete enough to record my indebtedness to published work. I am particularly grateful to Dr. Daniel L. Leedy, Chief, Branch of Wildfowl Research and to Dr. John Lynch and Dr. Allen G. Smith, all of the Bureau of Sport Fisheries and Wildlife, U.S. Fish and Wildlife Service, for permission to make use of unpublished information.

LITERATURE CITED

ATWOOD, E. L. 1959. A report on the canvasback and redhead retrieved shooting kill during the 1958–59 season. Section of Wildlife Biometry, Bureau of Sport Fisheries and Wildlife, August 1959.

AUSTIN, O. L. JR. 1957. Review of Boyd (1957*b*). Bird-Banding 28:232.

BELLROSE, F. C., AND E. B. CHASE. 1950. Population losses in the mallard, black duck and blue-winged teal. Biol. Notes Urbana, Illinois. No. 22, 27pp.

BENNETT, L. J. 1938. The blue-winged teal, its ecology and management. Ames, Iowa. 144pp.

BOYD, H. 1956. Statistics of the British population of the pink-footed goose. J. Anim. Ecol. 25:253–273.

———. 1957*a*. Mortality and kill amongst British-ringed teal *Anas crecca*. Ibis 99:157–177.

———. 1957*b*. Mortality and fertility of the white-fronted goose. Bird Study 4:80–93.

———. 1957*c*. Recoveries of British-ringed greylag geese. Rep. Wildf. Tr. 8:51–54.

———. 1958. The survival of white-fronted geese (*Anser albifrons flavirostris* Dalgety & Scott) ringed in Greenland. Dansk. Orn. Foren. Tidsskr. 52:1–8.

———. 1959. The composition of goose populations. Ibis 101:441–445.

———, AND B. KING. 1960. A breeding population of the mallard. Rep. Severn Wildf. Tr. 11:137–143.

CAPILDEO, R., AND J. B. S. HALDANE. 1954. The mathematics of bird population growth and decline. J. Anim. Ecol. 23:215–223.

COOCH, F. G. 1958. The breeding biology and management of the blue goose *Chen caerulescens*. Ph.D. thesis, Cornell U. Abstract in Wildl. Rev. 96:65.

DEMENTIEV, G. P., AND N. A. GLADKOV, editors. 1952. The Birds of the Soviet Union, vol. 4. Moscow. 640pp. (in Russian)

ELDER, W. H. 1955. The relation of age and sex to the weights of pink-footed and grey-lag geese. Rep. Wildf. Tr. 7:127–132.

EYGENRAAM, J. A. 1957. The sex-ratio and the production of the mallard *Anas platyrhynchos* L. Ardea 45:117–143.

GEIS, A. D. 1959. Annual and shooting mortality estimates for the canvasback. J. Wildlife Mgmt. 23:253–261.

GOETHE, F. 1957. Über den Mauzerzug der Brandenten (*Tadorna tadorna* L.) zum Grossen Knechtsand. Funfzig Jahre Seevogelschultz, 96–106. Hamburg.

HALDANE, J. B. S. 1955. The calculation of mortality rates from ringing data. Acta XI Congr. Internat. Orn. 454–458.

HANSEN, H. A., AND U. C. NELSON. 1957. Brant of the Bering Sea—Migration and mortality. Trans. N. Amer. Wildl. Conf. 22:237–256.

HANSON, H. C., AND R. H. SMITH. 1950. Canada geese of the Mississippi flyway. Bull. Ill. Nat. Hist. Surv. 25:63–210.

HANSON, W. C., AND R. L. BROWNING. 1959. Nesting studies of Canada geese on the Hanford Reservation, 1953–56. J. Wildlife Mgmt. 23:129–137.

HICKEY, J. J. 1952. Survival studies of banded birds. U.S. Fish & Wildlife Service Special Scientific Report: Wildlife No. 15. 177pp.

KORTRIGHT, F. H. 1943. The ducks, geese and swans of North America. Washington. 476pp.

LAUCKHART, J. B. 1956. Calculating mortality rates for waterfowl. Murrelet 37:31–34.

LEMIEUX, L. 1959. Histoire naturelle et aménagement de la grande oie blanche *Chen hyperborea atlantica*. Canadian Naturalist 86:133–192.

LOW, J. B. 1945. Ecology and management of the redhead, *Nyroca americana* in Iowa. Ecol. Monogr. 15:35–69.

MEDNALL, H. L. 1958. The ring-necked duck in the northeast. U. Maine Studies, 2nd series, No. 73. 317pp.

SCOTT, P. 1957. A coloured key to the waterfowl of the world. Slimbridge, Glos.

STEWART, P. A. 1957. The wood duck, *Aix sponsa* (Linnaeus), and its management. Ph.D. thesis, Ohio State U. Abstract in Wildl. Rev. 93:72.

STEWART, R. E., A. D. GEIS, AND C. D. EVANS. 1958. Distribution of populations and hunting kill of the canvasback. J. Wildlife Mgmt. 22:333–370.

TAMANTSEVA, L. C., AND T. P. SHEVAREVA. 1957. On the biology of the pintail and the mallard (ringing information). Proc. 3rd Baltic. Orn. Congr. (1954), 27–54. (in Russian)

TAYLOR, S. M. 1959. Shelduck survey, 1958. Bristol Nat. Soc. Orn. Section, Field Work Review, 1958, 8–17.

WRIGHT, B. S. 1954. High tide and an east wind. Harrisburg, Penn. 162pp.

APPENDIX: SOURCES OF DATA AND NOTES ON CALCULATIONS

1. Species included in Fig. 1

Anser brachyrhynchus Baillon. Boyd (1956).

A. a. albifrons (Scopoli). Boyd (1957*b*).

A. c. caerulescens (L.). Data mostly from unpublished material of U.S. Fish and Wildlife Service, supplemented from Cooch (1958), recalculated.

A. c. atlanticus Kennard. Lemieux (1959).

Branta canadensis interior Todd. Hanson and Smith (1950), recalculated.

B. c. moffitti Aldrich. Hanson & Browning (1959), recalculated.

B. bernicla orientalis Tougarinov. Hansen and Nelson (1957), recalculated.

Tadorna tadorna (L.). Taylor (1959), with survival calculations by the author from records by Goethe (1957) and British ringing results.

Anas p. platyrhynchos L. Dutch data calculated from Eygenraam (1957) and published ringing recoveries. British data from Boyd and King (1960) and unpublished material. North American data after Hickey (1952).

A. rubripes Brewster. Wright (1954), Bellrose and Chase (1950).

A. d. discors L. Iowa data from Bennett (1938); Prairie Provinces, recalculated from unpublished material of Allen G. Smith, U.S. Fish and Wildlife Service, with survival calculations from unpublished recoveries collected by Dr. M. Arellano at Delta Waterfowl Research Station, Manitoba.

Aythya vallisineria (Wilson). Geis (1959).

A. americana (Eyton). Low (1945) and Hickey (1952).

A. collaris (Donovan). Mendall (1958), recalculated.

A. fuligula (L.). Unpublished material on British birds.

A. m. marila (L.). Calculated from published recoveries of Iceland-ringed birds and Russian material (Y. A. Isakov *in* Dementiev and Gladkov 1952).

2. Additional species in Table 1

Anser anser. Boyd (1957*c*) and unpublished.

A. albifrons flavirostris Dalgety and Scott. Boyd (1958).

Branta c. canadensis (L.). Unpublished English data.

B. b. bernicla (L.) and *B. b. hrota* (O. F. Müller). Boyd (1959).

Anas a. acuta L. Tamantseva and Shevareva (1957), recalculated.

A. c. crecca L. Boyd (1956).

A. crecca carolinensis Gmelin. From published recoveries.

A. penelope L. From unpublished British and published Icelandic recoveries.

A. clypeata L. From unpublished British data.

Somateria m. mollissima (L.) Published Swedish and Dutch, and unpublished British, recoveries.

Aythya ferina (L.). From unpublished British data.

Aix sponsa (L.) Stewart (1957).

Melanitta n. nigra (L.). From published Icelandic recoveries.

Clangula hyemalis (L.). From published Swedish, Icelandic and Russian recoveries.

Mergus m. merganser (L.). From published Swedish and British recoveries.

Information on adult weights taken from Kortright (1943), Elder (1955) and unpublished material.

Original calculations of survival from recoveries followed the maximum-likelihood method of Haldane (1955).

DISTRIBUTION, HARVEST AND SURVIVAL OF AMERICAN WIGEON BANDED IN CALIFORNIA[1,2]

WARREN C. RIENECKER,[3] Wildlife Management Branch, California Department of Fish and Game

Abstract: Population distribution, sex ratio, kill rate and survival were determined from 32,097 American wigeon banded in California from 1951 to 1969. There are two wigeon populations that winter in California; one is in the Central Valley and the other in the Imperial Valley. The Sacramento Valley is the main wintering area in California. Since 1971 a marked decrease has occurred in wigeon wintering in the Imperial Valley with an increase in Mexico. The true sex ratio of wigeons in the Sacramento Valley is probably close to the 55.0% males found in hunter bag checks and the 56.4% males found in the trapped sample. The male has a higher band recovery rate and survival rate than the female. The mean recovery rate for adult male wigeons banded on the Gray Lodge Wildlife Area is 4.42 ± 0.23% and the mean survival rate is 66.04 ± 1.65% as compared to the Gray Lodge female recovery rate of 3.26 ± 0.28% and the mean survival rate of 58.24 ± 3.63%. The mean life span for adult males is 2.32 years and 1.66 years for adult females.

The American wigeon (*Anas americana*) nests across much of Canada and Alaska and winters in all four North American flyways. This report analyzes wigeon band recoveries from birds banded in California. The objective was to increase our knowledge of migration patterns, survival rates and population turnover, and thus provide a more sound basis for management of this species.

From 1951 through 1971 the California Department of Fish and Game banded, or assisted in banding, 32,097 wigeon during the posthunting season period. Of these, 11,576 were banded on the Gray Lodge Wildlife Area in the Sacramento Valley, 566 on the Grasslands of the San Joaquin Valley and 19,955 on the Wister Wildlife Area and the Salton Sea National Wildlife Refuge in the Imperial Valley. Except for the years 1968, 1969 and 1970 wigeon banding on Gray Lodge has been continuous since 1953. On the Grasslands area wigeon trapping and banding were conducted only during 1955, 1956 and 1958. In the Imperial Valley the banding has been continuous since 1951 except that in 1962 an adequate sample was not obtained. Every year an attempt was made on each area to band at least 1,000 wigeon, but was not always successful. Formerly stationary wire bait traps were utilized to catch the ducks. More recently, cannon nets proved more efficient in trapping wigeon.

METHODS

Seber's (1970) model for band recovery analysis was used to estimate band recovery rate, survival rate and life span of wigeons wintering in California. The method can be used where survival rates, band reporting rates and hunting pressure vary from year to year. All birds alive in a given year, regardless of when they were banded, are assumed to have similar hunting pressure and band reporting rates in that year. Only data from adult birds is used with this method. The method assumes survival and recovery rates are independent of the age of the mature bird. The data were analyzed using a Fortran program (Anderson et al. 1974) on an IBM 360/65 computer. Com-

---

[1] Originally published in Calif. Fish and Game J. 62(2):141–153, 1976.

[2] A contribution of Federal Aid in Wildlife Restoration Project W-30-R, "Waterfowl Studies."

[3] Present address: 1022 Celestial Way, Yuba City, CA 95991.

puter summaries of the recovery data by sex and banding area were supplied by the U.S. Fish and Wildlife Service, Laurel, Maryland.

During the years 1968–70 insufficient samples of wigeon were banded on Gray Lodge and, therefore, the period 1953 through 1967 was used in the analyses. Only a few wigeon were banded during 1962 in Imperial Valley, and therefore the data were divided into the two periods of 1951–61 and 1963–69 and analyzed separately. The San Joaquin Valley data were not used in determining recovery rates and survival rates due to insufficient samples. Only bands recovered from birds shot or found dead during the hunting seasons of September 1 to February 1 were used in determining the kill rate.

RESULTS AND DISCUSSION

Migration

The Pacific Flyway has more wigeon than any other flyway and California winters most of the wigeon in the flyway. Over 50% of the wigeon harvest in the United States is concentrated in the Pacific Flyway and about 25% of this occurs in California (Geis and Cooch 1972). The annual winter waterfowl survey shows that on the average, the California wigeon population is nearly 750,000. Wigeon generally ranks second to the pintail (*Anas acuta*) as the most numerous duck in California. In some years it is replaced by the mallard (*Anas platyrhynchos*) as the second most numerous duck in the population.

There are two wigeon populations wintering in California. The larger of the two occurs in northern California, mostly in the Sacramento and San Joaquin valleys (Central Valley). The smaller population is in the Imperial Valley of southern California.

Those wigeons wintering in northern California nest in Alberta, British Columbia, the western part of the Northwest Territories and central Alaska to the Bering Sea. Few nest in the Pacific Flyway states. Their southern fall migration is mainly through Washington, Idaho, and Oregon to the Central Valley of California. A segment of the population migrates offshore from Alaska to California and winters on the bays of California. However, some wigeon of the Pacific Flyway spend the winter in Washington and Oregon. In fact, the wigeon is second on Washington's winter waterfowl inventory.

California wigeon migrate later than the pintails (*Anas acuta*) but not as late as the canvasback (*Aythya valisineria*). They do not appear in appreciable numbers on the wintering grounds until after the hunting season starts in mid-October.

It was noted that 83.8% of the band recoveries of male wigeon banded in the Sacramento Valley were recovered in California, whereas only 70% of the females were recovered in the same area. The data are consistent in that band recoveries from Washington, Idaho and Oregon revealed a high percentage of females. This could indicate that the females take a more leisurely trip to the wintering grounds than the males and therefore are more vulnerable to hunting en route. Except for a slightly higher harvest of females in October which accounts for the larger number of females in the bag in states north of California, the monthly distribution of harvest for males and females is quite similar (Fig. 1).

Studies have shown that for many species, e.g., mallard, gadwall (*Anas strepera*), pintail, green-winged teal

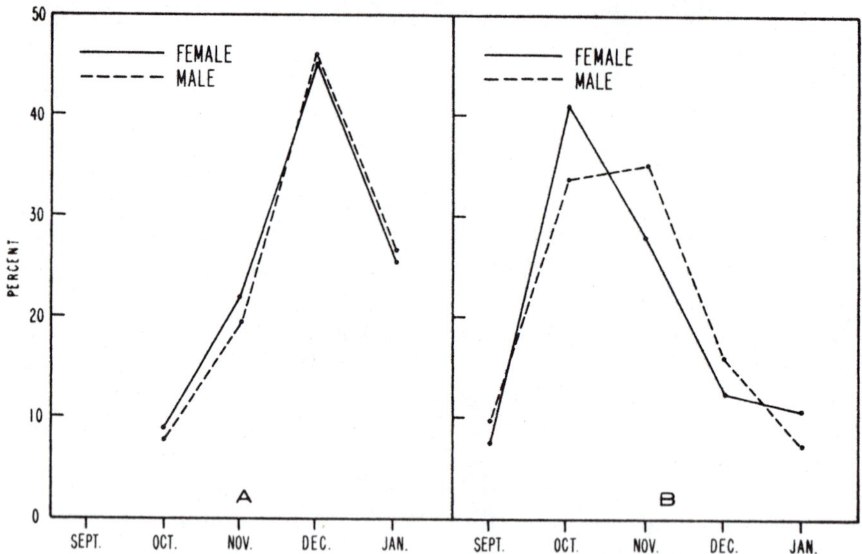

Fig. 1. The chronological harvest of male and female wigeon banded on Gray Lodge Wildlife Area. A = recoveries in California, B = recoveries outside California.

(*Anas crecca*), shoveler (*Anas clypeata*) and canvasback, the hunter bag in Canada contains more females than males. This results from the departure of many adult males prior to the opening of the hunting season (Bellrose et al. 1961). The wigeon follows a similar pattern. Data from California banded wigeon indicate that the females have a significantly higher band recovery rate in Alaska and Canada than the males (7.9% versus 3.0%).

No females were recovered south of the San Joaquin Valley, whereas 2.8% of the males were recovered along the southern California coast and in the Imperial Valley.

The Sacramento Valley is the main wintering ground in California with 54.9% recoveries of wigeons banded on Gray Lodge recovered in the valley in later years. The Sacramento-San Joaquin River Delta with 9.1% and the San Joaquin Valley with 9.6% are also important wigeon wintering areas. Another indication of the value of the Sacramento Valley as a wigeon wintering area is that of those ducks banded in San Joaquin Valley, 32% of the band returns were recovered in the Sacramento Valley in later years. Harold McKinnie concluded in his study on wigeon of California (unpublished report, California Department of Fish and Game) that wigeon wintering in the Sacramento and San Joaquin valleys appear to be the same migratory population with the San Joaquin Valley as the southern boundary of their wintering grounds.

The wigeon population wintering in the Imperial Valley nests in the same general areas, except for a slight shift to the east, compared to those which winter in the Sacramento Valley. There are fewer Imperial Valley birds nesting in British Columbia and more nesting in Saskatchewan than those of the Sacramento Valley populations. Lensink (1964) states that most wigeons from Alaska, British Columbia and Alberta that were shot in the United States were harvested in the

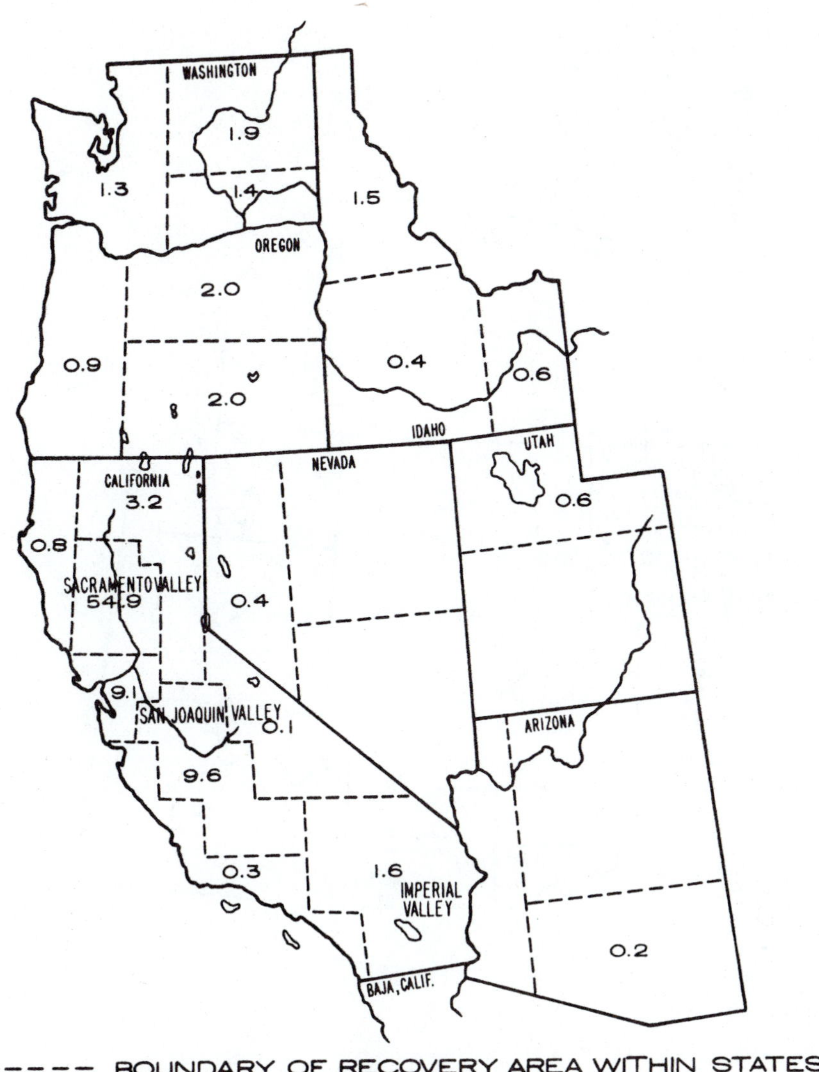

Fig. 2. Band recoveries, by percentage, of 1,183 wigeon banded in the Sacramento Valley 1953–67 and 1971. Additional returns were from Alaska 0.5, Northwest Ter. 0.5, British Columbia 2.2, Alberta 2.5, Saskatchewan 0.5, Montana 0.9 and Tennessee 0.1.

Pacific Flyway, while those from Saskatchewan were recovered nearly equally from hunters in the Mississippi, Central and Pacific flyways. The migration to the Imperial Valley is also slightly more oriented toward the east than that of the Sacramento wigeon populations. There seem to be two main comparisons of the two populations (Figs. 2, 3). First, the Imperial wigeon population is more prone to scatter than the Sacramento wigeon population. Approximately 10% of the band returns from the Imperial Valley population are recovered on the wintering grounds of northern California, whereas less than 2% of the northern Cal-

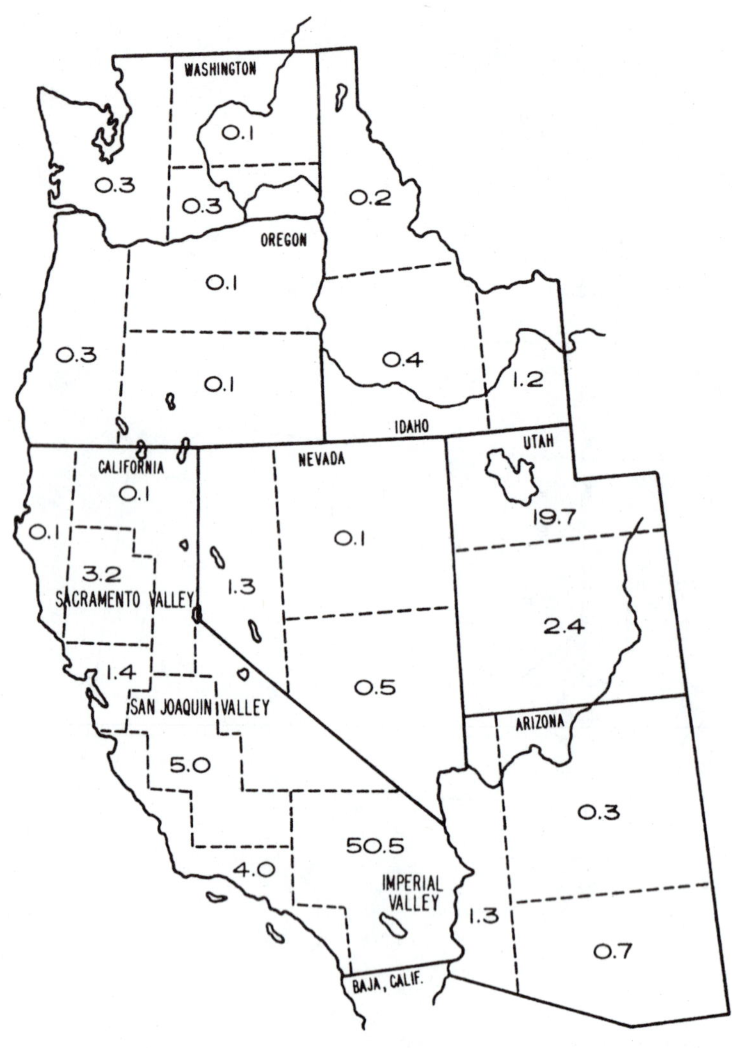

Fig. 3. Band recoveries, by percentage, of 2,208 wigeon banded in Imperial Valley 1951–69. Additional returns were from Alaska 0.4, Northwest Ter. 0.1, British Columbia 0.5, Alberta 1.7, Saskatchewan 0.5, Montana 0.7, Wyoming 0.2, Colorado 0.1, New Mexico 0.1, Texas 0.1, Lousiana 0.1, Iowa 0.1, Kansas 0.1, Baja Calif. 1.2, Sonora 0.5 and Chihuahua 0.2.

ifornia population band returns are recovered in southern California. This trend was also found in the lesser snow goose (*Anser caerulescens hyperborea*) (Rienecker 1965) and is probably typical of all species of waterfowl using these two areas. Secondly, Utah, especially in the vicinity of the Great Salt Lake, is the most important recovery area with 22.1% of the band recoveries from the Imperial Valley wigeon population from outside of the Imperial Valley. Only 0.6% of the band recoveries from wigeon banded in the Sacramento Valley were recovered in this same area. The annual winter waterfowl inventories indicate that Utah winters very few wigeon, usually less than 2,000. Therefore, the assumption might be made that they stay in the area until inclement weather forces them to continue their migration southward to the Imperial Valley or Mexico. Limited recoveries from wigeon banded preseason in Colorado (Ryder 1955) suggest that they migrate southwestward from Colorado into southern California and Mexico. This is also indicated by the Imperial Valley banded wigeons although the returns from Colorado amounted to only two bands or 0.1%.

The annual winter waterfowl inventory has shown that since 1971 a marked decrease has occurred in the number of wigeon wintering in the Imperial Valley and an increase in Mexico. From 1961 through 1970 the wigeon population wintering in the Imperial Valley averaged 21,500 birds. From 1971 through 1973 the average had a drastic drop to 5,200 wigeons; and in 1974, the most recent survey, the population dropped to a low of 1,700 wintering in the Imperial Valley. During this same 10-year period of 1961 through 1970 the wigeon population wintering on the west coast of Mexico averaged 48,200 birds. From 1971 through 1973 the average increased to 54,500. This population shift of wintering grounds has affected all species of ducks wintering on these areas. However, it has become most obvious in the wigeon population.

Much of this population shift probably can be attributed to increased habitat due to development of farm irrigation in Mexico during recent years. Less harassment from hunters in Mexico could be another reason for the shift.

Few band recoveries during the spring migration made it extremely difficult to follow migration patterns to the breeding grounds. However, there is no reason to believe, from the limited data available, that there is any difference between the spring and fall migration routes.

Sex Ratios

The sex ratio of trapped samples of wigeon wintering in the Imperial Valley had more males at 70.0% than samples obtained in the Sacramento Valley at 56.4% or the San Joaquin Valley at 62.0%.

Since the trapping methods were presumably identical on all areas, if there was a bias in trapping with regard to sex, the degree of bias would be similar with all trapping stations. Thus, the sex ratio of the trapped sample would not necessarily be an indication of the true sex ratio of the whole population. A general consensus among waterfowl biologists is that there is a trapping bias towards males, especially with baited wire traps.

By comparing hunter bag check data with trapping data by area and by year (Table 1) it became clear that the sex ratio of 70% males in the trapped sample of wigeons in the Imperial Valley was not indicative of the total population. A theory is that, although the sex ratio of the hunter bag is nearer to that of the population, bag checks can also be biased towards one sex, usually males. The percentage of males in the hunter bag is similar for all areas, i.e., Sacramento Valley 55.0%, San Joaquin Valley 52.9% and Imperial Valley 57.2% (Table 1).

Note also that the percentage of males in the hunter bag and in the trapped sample for the Sacramento Valley are very similar (55.0% and 56.4%). These figures in all probability are close to the true sex ratio of the untrapped population in the Sacramento Valley but not at the Imperial Valley.

The yearly sex ratios for the trapped

Table 1. A summary of sex ratios of wigeons in the hunter bag as compared with sex ratios of wigeons trapped and banded post-season.

	Sacramento Valley						San Joaquin Valley						Imperial Valley					
	Hunter bag			Trapped and banded			Hunter bag			Trapped and banded			Hunter bag			Trapped and banded		
		Percent			Percent			Percent			Percent			Percent			Percent	
Year	Total	Male	Female	Total	Male	Female	Total	Male	Female	Total	Male	Female	Total	Male	Female	Total	Male	Female
1951	—	—	—	—	—	—	—	—	—	—	—	—	749	53.3	46.7	195	63.1	36.9
1952	—	—	—	—	—	—	—	—	—	—	—	—	1,672	51.6	48.4	1,590	63.3	36.7
1953	—	—	—	—	—	—	—	—	—	—	—	—	529	55.2	44.8	3,007	70.4	29.6
1954	2,389	57.0	43.0	1,087	57.3	42.7	—	—	—	—	—	—	700	61.6	38.4	1,195	77.1	22.9
1955	1,852	52.0	48.0	312	61.5	38.5	726	51.2	48.8	271	59.4	40.6	1,983	60.1	39.9	2,017	76.8	23.2
1956	7,592	53.4	46.6	1,059	55.3	44.7	948	56.8	43.2	135	65.2	34.8	1,571	61.1	38.9	939	72.5	27.5
1957	5,057	54.2	45.8	296	46.6	53.4	—	—	—	—	—	—	783	57.5	42.5	1,202	71.8	28.2
1958	8,104	52.9	47.1	616	58.3	41.7	1,114	50.8	49.2	160	63.8	36.2	641	49.6	50.4	1,382	73.8	26.2
1959	4,497	52.3	47.7	600	59.0	41.0	—	—	—	—	—	—	445	60.4	39.6	300	66.7	33.3
1960	4,949	58.0	42.0	1,110	53.1	46.9	—	—	—	—	—	—	835	56.6	43.4	698	66.6	33.4
1961	4,989	60.3	39.7	1,007	53.5	46.5	—	—	—	—	—	—	376	58.5	41.5	1,000	74.6	25.4
1962	1,857	58.6	41.4	1,022	54.4	45.6	—	—	—	—	—	—	—	—	—	—	—	—
1963	3,061	61.6	38.4	1,029	57.8	42.2	—	—	—	—	—	—	344	53.2	46.8	1,000	62.5	37.5
1964	2,154	49.6	50.4	483	63.1	36.9	—	—	—	—	—	—	391	63.9	36.1	1,000	70.0	30.0
1965	2,602	54.8	45.2	232	62.5	37.5	—	—	—	—	—	—	458	55.7	44.3	432	74.1	25.9
1966	2,922	51.9	48.1	1,022	59.7	40.3	—	—	—	—	—	—	479	55.1	44.9	1,000	70.1	29.9
1967	5,122	51.9	48.1	701	59.3	40.7	—	—	—	—	—	—	845	57.8	42.2	999	70.6	29.4
1968	—	—	—	—	—	—	—	—	—	—	—	—	540	56.3	43.7	1,000	60.9	39.1
1969	—	—	—	—	—	—	—	—	—	—	—	—	710	60.1	39.9	999	62.3	37.7
1970	—	—	—	—	—	—	—	—	—	—	—	—	—	—	—	—	—	—
1971	6,164	57.4	42.6	1,000	52.0	48.0	—	—	—	—	—	—	—	—	—	—	—	—
Total	63,311	—	—	11,576	—	—	2,788	—	—	566	—	—	14,051	—	—	19,955	—	—
Mean	—	55.0	45.0	—	56.4	43.6	—	52.9	47.1	—	62.0	38.0	—	57.2	42.8	—	70.0	30.0

Table 2. Summary of band recovery rate and survival for adult male wigeon banded at Gray Lodge Wildlife Area 1953–67.

Year banded	Number banded	Number recovered	Recovery rate: Estimate	Recovery rate: Standard deviation	Survival rate: Estimate	Survival rate: Standard deviation
1953	290	43	5.517	1.341	73.42	15.51
1954	623	79	4.187	0.728	49.42	9.98
1955	192	33	5.454	1.167	80.89	16.10
1956	586	85	4.742	0.723	74.85	18.56
1957	138	18	4.242	1.083	63.20	16.65
1958	359	50	3.875	0.742	93.65	19.56
1959	354	38	4.406	0.815	52.50	10.64
1960	589	71	4.420	0.683	67.46	11.84
1961	539	61	3.410	0.585	70.91	12.61
1962	556	62	4.043	0.634	63.12	11.10
1963	595	67	4.095	0.624	70.50	15.03
1964	305	31	2.843	0.616	55.87	15.55
1965	145	19	5.585	1.331	51.53	12.77
1966	610	89	4.955	0.732	57.26	9.00
1967	416	70	6.731	0.963	—	—
Mean	—	—	4.412	0.236	66.04	1.65

Mean 90% confidence interval for recovery rate: 4.03–4.80.
Mean 90% confidence interval for survival rate: 63.33–68.75.
Goodness of fit test that the data fit Seber's model: $\chi^2 = 73.96$, 75 df.
Mean life span as an adult: 2.32 ± 0.14 years.

samples on all three areas are reasonably close to the average for each area (Table 1) which implies that whatever the cause for this unbalanced sex ratio in trapped birds, it seems to remain constant for each area. This unbalanced sex ratio is also true of green-winged teal wintering in the Imperial Valley. Moisan et al. (1967) pointed out a preponderance of 73% male green-winged teal in the trapped samples from Imperial Valley, whereas those samples trapped in the Central Valley contained 63.8% males.

Harvest and Survival

California hunters rank the wigeon third in popularity, behind the favored mallard and pintail. Size of a bird and its table qualities determine rank. However, availability is probably more important than popularity in determining hunter bag composition. A hunter might prefer a limit of mallards or pintails, but if these are scarce will usually take other species. The annual band recovery and survival rates by sex and banding area are recorded (Tables 2–7). Chi-square tests of the data to Seber's model are also included.

Numerous studies of ducks and geese have shown that female mortality rates tend to be higher than male although their band recovery rates are lower than those of males. The assumption is that the female has a higher nonhunting mortality, particularly during the nesting period than that of the male. The male, in turn, has a higher harvest rate, thus the greater band recovery rate. Differential migration with the male moving into a high harvest area earlier than the female and hunter selectivity on ducks are two possible causes for this greater harvest rate. The data used in this report suggest that the American wigeon follows this pattern.

The mean band recovery rate for adult male wigeons banded at Gray Lodge is 4.42 ± 0.24% and the mean survival rate

Table 3. Summary of band recovery rate and survival for adult female wigeon banded at Gray Lodge Wildlife Area 1953–67.

Year banded	Number banded	Number recovered	Recovery rate Estimate	Recovery rate Standard deviation	Survival rate Estimate	Survival rate Standard deviation
1953	135	17	8.148	2.355	51.56	22.00
1954	464	40	3.373	0.803	104.95	46.36
1955	120	6	2.500	1.083	31.12	14.33
1956	473	38	3.214	0.729	84.62	31.79
1957	158	9	2.306	0.862	79.22	36.13
1958	257	11	1.665	0.602	35.75	14.13
1959	246	18	3.110	0.908	59.24	18.27
1960	521	37	3.669	0.740	53.55	14.58
1961	468	30	2.173	0.551	70.52	19.11
1962	466	28	3.318	0.709	35.38	10.01
1963	434	33	3.138	0.706	72.26	25.49
1964	178	11	2.575	0.871	52.27	26.41
1965	87	6	3.245	1.408	55.71	25.89
1966	412	27	3.204	0.771	34.09	10.12
1967	285	28	4.045	0.993	—	—
Mean	—	—	3.260	0.277	58.24	3.63

Mean 90% confidence interval for recovery rate: 2.81–3.71.
Mean 90% confidence interval for survival rate: 52.29–64.18.
Goodness of fit test that the data fit Seber's model: $\chi^2 = 26.69$, 29 df.
Mean life span as an adult: 1.66 ± 0.28 years.

is 66.04 ± 1.65% (Table 2) as compared to the Gray Lodge female mean recovery rate of 3.26 ± 0.28% and mean survival rate of 58.24 ± 3.63% (Table 3). Average life span for adult males is 2.32 years and 1.66 years for adult females. The wigeon banded in Imperial Valley follow the same general pattern as those of Gray Lodge except for a slight difference in the survival rates of the 1963–69 samples. The male had a mean survival rate of 62.62 ± 2.11% (Table 6) whereas the fe-

Table 4. Summary of band recovery rate and survival for adult male wigeon banded in Imperial Valley 1951–61.

Year banded	Number banded	Number recovered	Recovery rate Estimate	Recovery rate Standard deviation	Survival rate Estimate	Survival rate Standard deviation
1951	123	23	9.756	2.675	58.42	17.36
1952	1,006	154	4.824	0.659	78.15	8.32
1953	2,117	284	4.765	0.416	61.76	6.51
1954	921	129	5.748	0.586	68.45	7.86
1955	1,550	187	5.449	0.476	50.97	0.559
1956	681	89	3.888	0.510	50.62	6.49
1957	863	120	5.001	0.556	66.03	8.93
1958	1,020	114	4.128	0.469	79.67	10.27
1959	200	24	5.538	1.130	58.74	12.63
1960	465	50	4.765	0.753	60.09	14.49
1961	746	93	4.438	0.610	48.03	8.56
Mean	—	—	5.386	0.331	63.00	2.00

Mean 90% confidence interval for recovery rate: 4.84–5.93.
Mean 90% confidence interval for survival rate: 59.71–66.28.
Goodness of fit test that the data fit Seber's model: $\chi^2 = 83.37$, 59 df.
Mean life span as an adult: 2.11 ± 0.25 years.

Table 5. Summary of band recovery rate and survival for adult female wigeon banded in Imperial Valley 1951–61.

			Recovery rate		Survival rate	
Year banded	Number banded	Number recovered	Estimate	Standard deviation	Estimate	Standard deviation
1951	72	8	2.778	1.937	124.79	52.46
1952	584	47	2.968	0.675	47.85	11.23
1953	890	69	3.299	0.549	53.06	13.11
1954	274	23	4.034	0.936	58.18	16.28
1955	467	35	3.697	0.741	65.31	20.88
1956	258	15	2.194	0.672	47.20	15.64
1957	339	26	3.120	0.766	86.69	27.00
1958	362	19	2.624	0.686	65.61	36.43
1959	100	4	2.710	1.369	13.07	7.70
1960	233	23	6.581	1.534	52.24	20.79
1961	254	16	3.033	0.952	—	—
Mean	—	—	3.400	0.342	58.92	6.35

Mean 90% confidence interval for recovery rate: 2.84–3.96.
Mean 90% confidence interval for survival rate: 48.51–69.33.
Goodness of fit test that the data fit Seber's model: $\chi^2 = 26.51$, 20 df.
Mean life span as an adult: 1.58 ± 0.30 years.

Table 6. Summary of band recovery rate and survival for adult male wigeon banded in Imperial Valley 1963–69.

			Recovery rate		Survival rate	
Year banded	Number banded	Number recovered	Estimate	Standard deviation	Estimate	Standard deviation
1963	625	74	4.800	0.855	53.57	9.37
1964	700	92	4.542	0.694	70.57	13.36
1965	320	39	4.570	0.862	73.04	14.51
1966	700	73	2.454	0.449	66.14	10.38
1967	705	85	4.417	0.607	63.74	10.13
1968	609	73	4.711	0.662	48.66	7.60
1969	622	93	5.216	0.696	—	—
Mean	—	—	4.249	0.287	62.62	2.11

Mean 90% confidence interval for recovery rate: 3.78–4.72.
Mean 90% confidence interval for survival rate: 59.15–66.09.
Goodness of fit test that the data fit Seber's model: $\chi^2 = 23.47$, 25 df.
Mean life span as an adult: 2.09 ± 0.31 years.

Table 7. Summary of band recovery rate and survival for adult female wigeon banded in Imperial Valley 1963–69.

			Recovery rate		Survival rate	
Year banded	Number banded	Number recovered	Estimate	Standard deviation	Estimate	Standard deviation
1963	375	34	3.733	0.979	59.26	16.87
1964	300	27	2.872	0.808	98.04	41.32
1965	112	7	3.205	1.275	76.12	37.36
1966	300	12	1.548	0.561	37.94	14.67
1967	294	19	2.721	0.795	48.76	15.35
1968	391	30	4.279	0.918	79.96	27.10
1969	377	16	3.156	0.827	—	—
Mean	—	—	3.060	0.374	66.68	6.01

Mean 90% confidence interval for recovery rate: 2.45–3.67.
Mean 90% confidence interval for survival rate: 56.83–76.53.
Goodness of fit test that the data fit Seber's model: $\chi^2 = 8.99$, 11 df.
Mean life span as an adult: 2.20 ± 0.75 years.

Table 8. Summary of average parameter estimates for adult wigeon banded in California.

		Gray Lodge*	Imperial Valley†
Survival rate	Males	66.04 ± 1.65	63.00 ± 2.00 62.62 ± 2.11
	Females	58.24 ± 3.63	58.92 ± 6.35 66.68 ± 6.01
Recovery rate	Males	4.41 ± .24	5.39 ± .33 4.25 ± .29
	Females	3.26 ± .28	3.40 ± .34 3.06 ± .37
Mean life span	Males	2.32 ± .14	2.11 ± .25 2.09 ± .31
	Females	1.66 ± .28	1.58 ± .30 2.20 ± .75

* 1953–67.
† 1951–61 (top).
1963–69 (bottom).

male had a higher rate of 66.68 ± 6.01% (Table 7); however, the difference is not significant. Note that the standard deviation for the female is much greater than that of the male, because there are fewer females trapped and also fewer females shot than males. In turn, there are fewer female band recoveries, hence less precision, resulting in the greater standard deviation and confidence interval. The wide variation in annual recovery rates and survival rates (Tables 2–7) is mostly due to small sample sizes.

Estimates of parameters on an annual basis are subject to large sampling variances and therefore, average values are summarized (Table 8). Males have a significantly higher survival than females at Gray Lodge; however, no difference was found for wigeon banded in the Imperial Valley. Males banded in the Imperial Valley and at Gray Lodge had significantly higher recovery rates than females. In general, survival of the two banded populations appear to be similar. The effect of varying hunting regulations on survival could not be studied due to the large sampling variances of the annual estimates.

During the period of the study no apparent trend in annual recovery rates was noted other than what might be expected from changes in hunting regulations.

To obtain an estimate of the average kill rate, the band reporting rate and the rate of crippling loss must be known. A band reporting rate of 50% was estimated from the results of the first year band recoveries of the recent reward band study on mallard conducted by Dr. Charles J. Henny, Migratory Bird and Habitat Research Laboratory, Laurel, Maryland. Charles Kimball of the Migratory Bird and Habitat Research Laboratory, Laurel, Maryland (pers. comm.), stated that there are too little hunter performance survey data to estimate crippling loss for wigeon. The overall rate of a 17% loss appears to be the best estimate for dabbling ducks except for the wood duck (*Aix sponsa*).

The average kill rate for adult male wigeons banded on Gray Lodge Wildlife Area is estimated by dividing the band recovery rate of 4.4% by the band reporting rate of 50% which yields the harvest rate at 8.8%, which in turn is adjusted for the 17% crippling loss which results in an average kill rate of 10.3%. This compares to 12.2% for adult males banded in Imperial Valley during the 1951–61 period and 9.9% during the later period of 1963–69. The Gray Lodge female kill rate amounted to 7.6% compared to 8.0% for Imperial Valley female early period and 7.1% for the late period.

A survival rate of 66.04%, e.g., Gray Lodge males, indicates an overall mortality rate of 33.96%. By subtracting the 10.3% hunter kill rate from the 33.96% mortality rate, the data suggest a nonhunting mortality rate of 23.66% for males banded at Gray Lodge. The Gray Lodge females had an expected higher nonhunting mortality of 34.16%. The Imperial Valley wigeon mortality data are comparable to the Gray Lodge data.

Differences in the kill rate and the survival rate between the two wintering populations of wigeon are reasonable. Although their survival is not as high as the 70.77% found for adult male pintail wintering in California (Anderson and Sterling 1974), it is comparable to the continent-wide estimate of 62% suggested for adult male mallards (Anderson, pers. comm.).

SUMMARY

From 1951 through 1971 personnel of the California Department of Fish and Game banded or assisted in banding 32,097 American wigeon during the posthunting season period.

Seber's (1970) method for band recovery analysis was used to determine band recovery rate, survival rate and life span of wigeon populations wintering in California.

Over 50% of the wigeon harvest in the United States is concentrated in the Pacific Flyway and about 25% of the total harvest occurs in California.

There are two wigeon populations in California: those wintering in the Sacramento and San Joaquin valleys and those wintering in the Imperial Valley.

The main fall migration route of wigeon wintering in northern California funnels mainly through Washington, Idaho and Oregon to the Central Valley of California.

The Sacramento Valley is the main wintering area in California.

The wigeon migration to the Imperial Valley is slightly more easterly oriented than that of the northern California wigeon.

Utah, in the vicinity of the Great Salt Lake, is the most important band recovery area for the Imperial Valley wigeon population other than the Imperial Valley.

Since 1971, a marked decrease has occurred in the number of wigeon wintering in the Imperial Valley with a corresponding increase in Mexico.

The sex ratio of trapped samples of wigeon wintering in the Imperial Valley has more males at 70% than samples obtained in the Sacramento and San Joaquin valleys.

The true sex ratio of wigeon in the Sacramento Valley is probably close to the 55.0% males found in hunter bag checks and the 56.4% males found in the trap samples.

The mean recovery rate for adult male wigeons banded at Gray Lodge is 4.42 ± 0.24% and the mean survival rate is 66.04 ± 1.65% as compared to the Gray Lodge female mean recovery rate of 3.26 ± 0.28% and the mean survival rate of 58.24 ± 3.63%. The mean life span for adult males is 2.32 years and 1.66 years for adult females.

Although the Imperial Valley 1963–69 samples show the female to have a slightly higher survival rate of 66.68 ± 6.01% as compared to 62.62 ± 2.11% for the male, it was not significant.

The mean kill rate for adult male wigeon banded at Gray Lodge is 10.3% compared to 12.2% for adult males banded in Imperial Valley 1951–61 and 9.9% during the later period of 1963–69. The Gray Lodge female kill rate amounted to 7.6% compared to 8.0% for Imperial Valley female early period and 7.1% for the late period.

The 10.3% kill rate for Gray Lodge males subtracted from their 33.96% mortality rate suggests a nonhunting mortality of 23.66% compared to the higher 34.16% for females banded at Gray Lodge.

ACKNOWLEDGMENTS

I wish to express my sincere appreciation to David Anderson for his time and patience in assisting me on the statistical phase of the study and for reviewing the manuscript. Thanks are also due to Frank M. Kozlik, John Chattin and Merton N. Rosen for reviewing the manuscript, to personnel of PR Project W30R for assistance in the trapping and banding program and to personnel of the Salton Sea National Wildlife Refuge for cooperating in the program.

LITERATURE CITED

ANDERSON, D. R., C. F. KIMBALL, AND F. R. FIEHRER. 1974. Estimation of population parameters from banding and recovery data. J. Wildl. Manage. 38(2):369–370.

———, AND R. T. STERLING. 1974. Population dynamics of molting pintail drakes banded in south-central Saskatchewan. J. Wildl. Manage. 38(2):266–274.

BELLROSE, F. C., T. G. SCOTT, A. S. HAWKINS, AND J. B. LOW. 1961. Sex ratios and age ratios in North American Ducks. Illinois Natural History Survey Bull. 27(6):391–474.

GEIS, A. D., AND F. G. COOCH. 1972. Distribution of the duck harvest in Canada and the United States. U.S. Fish Wildl. Serv. Spec. Sci. Rep. Wildl. 151. 11pp.

LENSINK, C. J. 1964. Distribution of recoveries from bandings of ducklings. U.S. Fish Wildl. Serv. Spec. Sci. Rep. Wildl. 89. 146pp.

MOISAN, G., R. I. SMITH, AND R. K. MARTINSON. 1967. The green-winged teal: its distribution, migration and population dynamics. U.S. Fish Wildl. Serv. Spec. Sci. Rep. Wildl. 100. 247pp.

RIENECKER, W. C. 1965. A summary of band returns from lesser snow geese (*Chen hyperborea*) of the Pacific Flyway. Calif. Fish Game 51(3):132–146.

RYDER, R. A. 1955. A preliminary analysis of waterfowl recoveries in Colorado with notes on trapping and banding. Completion Report—Federal Aid Project W-37-R Game Bird Survey (Work Plan No. II, Job No. 10).

SEBER, G. A. F. 1970. Estimating time-specific survival and reporting rates for adult birds from band returns. Biometrika 57(2):313–318.

A REWARD BAND STUDY OF MALLARDS TO ESTIMATE BAND REPORTING RATES

CHARLES J. HENNY, Migratory Bird and Habitat Research Laboratory, Laurel, Maryland 20811[1]
KENNETH P. BURNHAM, Migratory Bird and Habitat Research Laboratory, Laurel, Maryland 20811[2]

Abstract: Reward bands ($10) were placed on 2,122 hatching-year mallards (*Anas platyrhynchos*), and an additional 11,490 received conventional bands (controls) to estimate band reporting rates. An analysis of band recoveries indicated that the reporting rate was dependent primarily upon three factors: (1) the distance banded birds were recovered from the banding site, (2) band collecting activities of conservation agencies (usually near banding sites), and(3) the intensity of banding effort in the region (frequency of banded birds in the population of the region). Reporting rates were uniformly depressed near the banding sites, but they showed an east-west cline at distances greater than 80 km from the banding sites. The reporting rate was highest in the west. Limited data on historical band reporting rates were compiled. Recommendations are given for adjusting band recoveries to account for the nonreporting of bands for 1957–73.

J. WILDL. MANAGE. 40(1):1–14

The importance of determining the proportion of waterfowl taken by hunters each year from populations in North America is widely recognized. For more than a decade we have used the first-year recovery rate of banded birds to estimate harvest rates. However, it also has been known for many years that hunters failed to report all the bands from birds they shot (Bellrose 1945, 1955); therefore, an adjustment for the band reporting rate (proportion of bands encountered that were reported to the Bird Banding Laboratory [BBL]) was needed. In more recent years, the band reporting rate was estimated by comparing estimates of banded waterfowl bagged (based on the Mail Questionnaire Survey) with numbers of bands reported to the BBL (Geis and Atwood 1961, Martinson 1966, Martinson and McCann 1966). The first-year recovery rate adjusted for band reporting rate yields the harvest rate, and the harvest rate adjusted for crippling loss yields the kill rate (proportion of population dying as a result of hunting).

The Mail Questionnaire Survey technique may be subject to several biases. Estimates based on the survey suggest that the band reporting rate declined from an estimated 50 percent in the 1950's to approximately 30 percent by 1969 (Anderson and Henny 1972:59), and to 23–25 percent in more recent years. Part of this change may have resulted from modifications in the survey. Two important questions remained unanswered: (1) is the estimate of the present reporting rate accurate, and (2) does the reporting rate vary among locations in North America? This reward band study was begun in 1972 to answer these questions. Band reporting rates that vary from area to area also can bias estimates of survival, distribution of the harvest, and indirect estimates of population size, in addition to nearly all other parameters derived from banding data.

This study was a cooperative effort because waterfowl biologists and administrators in 16 states and 5 provinces assisted.

[1] Present address: Denver Wildlife Research Center, Building 16, Federal Center, Denver, Colorado 80225.

[2] Present address: U.S. Fish and Wildlife Service, Fort Collins, Colorado 80521.

Originally published in J. Wildl. Manage. 40(1):1–14, 1976.

Coordinators for the project included R. Allison, K. Bednarik, S. Browne, J. Chattin, B. Dawson, J. Ellis, H. Funk, C. Gruener, R. Hopper, R. Hunt, R. Jeffrey, R. Jessen, E. Mikula, T. Myers, H. Roberts, D. Sheffer, M. Smith, J. Wilson, and G. Wrakestraw. The efforts of these individuals in coordinating the study at a local or regional level and in making sure that the bands were applied in the proper place, time, and sequence are very much appreciated. Planning sessions with D. Anderson, W. Crissey, G. Cooch, E. Martin, R. Pospahala, H. Reeves, J. Rogers, and R. Smith improved the design of the study and led to better techniques for analyzing the results. B. Gillas and R. Perry also provided considerable assistance by recording all reward band recoveries and processing the letters for payment.

METHODS

Banding Study Design

Hatching-year mallards were banded at 76 sites in 16 states, 4 provinces, and the Northwest Territories during the preseason (July–September) banding periods of 1972 and 1973. The ratio of conventional (control) bands to reward bands applied was approximately 4:1 in Canada and 9:1 in the United States. The reward band (anodized green) was stamped "REWARD $10" and was placed on the leg opposite that carrying the conventional band (i.e., each bird with a reward band was doublebanded). Reward and conventional bands were distributed within each state or province approximately in proportion to the banding effort on hatching-year mallards during the last 3 or 4 years. In general, the banding occurred at sites that had been in operation for many years. Birds marked during the operational banding program were used in the study; therefore, no special banding effort was required. We applied 1,056 reward bands in 1972 and 1,066 in 1973. Conventional bands applied in the 2 years were 5,725 and 5,765, respectively. Basically the ratio of conventional bands to reward bands reported to the BBL was used to estimate the band reporting rate (e.g., 10 percent conventional bands vs. 20 percent reward bands sent to BBL equal a band reporting rate of 50 percent).

Definitions and Assumptions Used in Data Analysis

Generally, bands are reported in two ways: from conservation agencies which solicit bands from hunters (generally at the hunting site), or directly from those hunters who do not surrender their bands through solicitation. For any band recovery the reporting source is known; almost all solicited bands are reported. Consequently, we define band reporting rate as the probability that a hunter voluntarily reports a band, provided he does not turn it over to a conservation agency. For greater clarity this may be called "hunter band reporting rate."

An unadjusted or total band reporting rate is defined as the probability that a band from a bird shot or found dead during the hunting season is reported. Such a rate does not distinguish the source of the reported band. Details of the estimation of these band reporting rates are in the appendix. The following two assumptions were made in the analysis: hunters directly reported all reward bands they obtained, and all solicited bands were reported.

Recoveries (of mallards shot and found dead) used in this analysis included those processed through 20 June 1974. More first-year recoveries probably will be reported from the 1973 bandings, but such late reports would have negligible effects on the band reporting rate estimates.

Table 1. Direct (1st-year) recoveries of immature mallards banded with reward and conventional (control) bands, 1972–73.

Location	Reward bands			Control bands			Total band reporting rate[a]
	1972–73 banded	1st year recovered	Recovery rate	1972–73 banded	1st year recovered	Recovery rate	
Alberta	393	59	0.1501	1,575	136	0.0863	0.575
Saskatchewan	322	50	0.1553	1,269	98	0.0772	0.497
Manitoba	333	69	0.2072	1,386	104	0.0750	0.362
Ontario	387	92	0.2377	1,749	171	0.0978	0.411
NWT	85	13	0.1529	273	24	0.0879	0.575
Canada (total)	1,520	283	0.1862	6,252	533	0.0853	0.458
Washington	60	17	0.2833	540	90	0.1667	0.588
Oregon	43	10	0.2326	388	32	0.0825	0.355
California	52	5	0.0962	478	48	0.1004	1.044
Idaho	22	4	0.1818	192	17	0.0885	0.487
Montana	10			93	5	0.0538	
Wyoming	9	1	0.1111	86	4	0.0465	0.419
Colorado	27	8	0.2963	243	14	0.0576	0.194
North Dakota	54	9	0.1667	280	18	0.0643	0.386
South Dakota	38	3	0.0789	350	20	0.0571	0.724
Western U.S. (total)	315	57	0.1810	2,650	248	0.0936	0.517
Minnesota	60	14	0.2333	540	47	0.0870	0.373
Wisconsin	75	17	0.2267	680	72	0.1059	0.467
Michigan	43	8	0.1860	387	46	0.1189	0.639
Ohio	22	2	0.0909	198	14	0.0707	0.778
Pennsylvania	30	7	0.2333	270	17	0.0630	0.270
New York	44	15	0.3409	396	41	0.1035	0.304
Vermont	13	3	0.2308	117	18	0.1538	0.666
Eastern U.S. (total)	287	66	0.2300	2,588	255	0.0985	0.428
U.S. (total)	602	123	0.2043	5,238	503	0.0960	0.470

[a] Treats all bands reported by conservation agencies the same as those submitted by hunters.

RESULTS

Geographical Variation in Harvest Rates

The first-year recovery rate of reward-banded mallards (submission of all reward bands is assumed) provides an opportunity to evaluate directly hunting pressure on immature mallards banded in certain geographical locations (Table 1). In locations with large numbers of reward-banded birds in both 1972 and 1973, the recovery rates for the 2 years were not significantly different; e.g., in Canada the highest recovery rates were from Ontario and Manitoba bandings each year. Therefore, the data for the 2 years were pooled. The hunting pressure appeared to increase from west to east, and it was significantly different ($P < 0.05$) between Alberta and Ontario (Table 1).

Only small numbers of mallards were reward-banded in each state; threfore, a comparison of reward band recovery rates by states would be meaningless (Table 1). However, the 2-year pooled estimate of the 1st-year recovery rates for reward bands in each flyway did show an interesting pattern. The recovery rate in the Central Flyway was lowest (0.1522 ± 0.0306), with the Mississippi and Pacific Flyways intermediate (0.2050 ± 0.0285 and 0.2034 ± 0.0302, respectively), and the Atlantic Flyway the highest (0.2874 ± 0.0485). With the exception of the Central Flyway, harvest rates of mallards generally increased

Table 2. Indirect recoveries of immature mallards banded with reward and conventional (control) bands, 1972.

Location	Reward bands			Control bands			Total band reporting rate[a]
	1972 banded	2nd year recovered	Recovery rate	1972 banded	2nd year recovered	Recovery rate	
Alberta	231	3	0.0130	1,007	21	0.0209	1.608
Saskatchewan	196	7	0.0357	825	20	0.0242	0.678
Manitoba	160	7	0.0438	772	24	0.0311	0.710
Ontario	200	10	0.0500	997	28	0.0281	0.562
NWT	50	1	0.0200	140	1	0.0071	0.355
Canada (total)	837	28	0.0335	3,741	94	0.0251	0.749
Washington	20			180	5	0.0278	
Oregon	13	2	0.1538	117	5	0.0427	0.278
California	23	1	0.0435	217	8	0.0369	0.848
Idaho	9			81	3	0.0370	
Montana	8			74	3	0.0405	
Colorado	7			63	1	0.0159	
North Dakota	16	1	0.0625	145	5	0.0345	0.552
South Dakota	25	2	0.0800	225	6	0.0267	0.334
Western U.S. (total)	121	6	0.0496	1,102	36	0.0327	0.659
Minnesota	20	1	0.0500	180	4	0.0222	0.444
Wisconsin	25	3	0.1200	225	5	0.0222	0.185
Michigan	13	2	0.1538	117	4	0.0342	0.222
Ohio	7	2	0.2857	63	1	0.0159	0.056
Pennsylvania	15			135	1	0.0074	
New York	15	1	0.0667	135	4	0.0296	0.444
Vermont	3	1	0.3333	27			
Eastern U.S. (total)	98	10	0.1020	882	19	0.0215	0.211
U.S. (total)	219	16	0.0731	1,984	55	0.0277	0.379

[a] Treats all bands reported by conservation agencies the same as those submitted by hunters.

from west to east in both Canada and the United States.

Band Reporting Rates

General.—An evaluation of the first year of data from bandings in 1972 led to a preliminary conclusion that total band recovery rates probably were influenced by at least three factors: (1) band collecting activities of conservation agencies (usually near banding sites), (2) the distance from the banding site at which birds were shot (this affected hunter reporting rate, especially if the site was in operation for a number of years), and (3) the general intensity of banding effort in the region (i.e., the probability that a hunter encounters a banded bird).

The numbers of mallards banded during the 2-year study and the resulting number of recoveries reported to the BBL are shown in Tables 1 and 2. Total band reporting rates were calculated for each political unit. These rates treat all recoveries equally, regardless of who submitted the band, i.e., many areas have large band collecting programs which tend to inflate total band reporting rates locally. For example, only 56 percent of the conventional bands reported from bandings in New York and Vermont were submitted directly by the hunters, as opposed to 86 and 89 percent in Saskatchewan and Manitoba, respectively. This indicated that the data on conventional bands would have to be stratified by "who reported" before

Table 3. Data on recoveries of banded mallards at various distances from banding sites in Canada.

Banding location	No. banded	Numbers and rates of band recoveries by kilometers from banding site								
		0–8	9–31	32–79	80–256	257–803	804–1,609	1,610+	Unknown	Total
					Control					
Ontario	1,749	30(20)[a]	20(13)	29(25)	45(35)	41(31)	30(26)	3(3)	1(0)	199(153)
Manitoba	1,386	4(4)	14(14)	17(14)	22(19)	16(15)	30(23)	22(22)	3(3)	128(114)
Saskatchewan	1,269	5(4)	12(10)	11(10)	21(21)	13(9)	21(18)	29(24)	6(6)	118(102)
Alberta	1,575	5(4)	34(24)	13(11)	12(6)	17(14)	38(26)	36(32)	2(1)	157(118)
NWT	273	3(2)				1(1)	9(9)	12(9)		25(21)
Total	6,252	47(34)	80(61)	70(60)	100(81)	88(70)	128(102)	102(90)	12(10)	627(508)
Recovery rate (total)		0.0075	0.0128	0.0112	0.0160	0.0141	0.0205	0.0163		0.1003
Recovery rate (hunters)		0.0054	0.0098	0.0096	0.0130	0.0112	0.0163	0.0144		0.0813
					Reward					
Ontario	387	15	21	13	16	18	17	2		102
Manitoba	333	4	10	13	13	10	17	9		76
Saskatchewan	322	3	6	4	8	7	10	18	1	57
Alberta	393	12	7	6	5	3	16	12	1	62
NWT	85	1	2				3	8		14
Total	1,520	35	46	36	42	38	63	49	2	311
Recovery rate		0.0230	0.0303	0.0237	0.0276	0.0250	0.0414	0.0322		0.2046
Band reporting rate (total)		0.326	0.422	0.473	0.580	0.564	0.495	0.506		0.490
Band reporting rate (hunters)		0.260	0.358	0.434	0.528	0.506	0.438	0.475		0.438
			0.393			0.481				
% controls reported by conservation agencies		28	24	14	19	20	20	12		19

[a] Numbers reported by hunter's own volition are in parentheses.

Table 4. Data on recoveries of banded mallards at various distances from banding sites in two regions of the United States.

Banding location	No. banded	Numbers and rates of band recoveries by kilometers from banding site: 0–8	9–31	32–79	80–256	257–803	804–1,609	1,610+	Unknown	Total
					Control					
Western U.S.	2,650	24(13)[a]	50(36)	45(28)	56(42)	71(58)	19(17)	11(10)	7(5)	283(209)
Eastern U.S.	2,588	34(13)	47(32)	44(35)	39(34)	59(47)	43(37)	6(4)	2(2)	274(204)
Total	5,238	58(26)	97(68)	89(63)	95(76)	130(105)	62(54)	17(14)	9(7)	557(413)
Recovery rate (total)		0.0111	0.0185	0.0170	0.0181	0.0248	0.0118	0.0032		0.1063
Recovery rate (hunters)		0.0050	0.0130	0.0120	0.0145	0.0200	0.0103	0.0027		0.0788
					Reward					
Western U.S.	315	5	16	10	14	10	4	4		63
Eastern U.S.	287	10	11	15	11	19	10			76
Total	602	15	27	25	25	29	14	4		139
Recovery rate		0.0249	0.0449	0.0415	0.0415	0.0482	0.0233	0.0066		0.2309
Western U.S.										
Band reporting rate (total)		0.572	0.372	0.536	0.475	0.845	0.567	0.331		0.534
Band reporting rate (hunters)		0.418	0.298	0.418	0.405	0.817	0.537	0.306		0.458
			0.342 (9–79)		0.532 (80–1,610+)					
Eastern U.S.										
Band reporting rate (total)		0.376	0.475	0.325	0.394	0.344	0.477			0.400
Band reporting rate (hunters)		0.188	0.380	0.277	0.361	0.295	0.440			0.332
			0.319 (9–79)		0.361 (80–1,610+)					
% Controls reported by conservation agencies										
Western U.S.		46	28	38	25	18	11	9		26
Eastern U.S.		62	32	20	13	20	14	33		26

[a] Numbers reported by hunter's own volition are in parentheses.

meaningful analyses could be made. Such stratification was not necessary for reward band returns, because almost all were submitted directly by the hunters.

The 1972 recovery data indicated that the hunter reporting rate was depressed near banding sites. The potential effects of this phenomenon can be illustrated from bandings in Canada where 41 percent of the 1st-year recoveries of reward bands (assumed to be reported at a 100 percent rate) were reported within 80 km of the banding site, whereas only 8 percent of the 2nd-year recoveries were reported within 80 km. Consequently, the estimated band reporting rate from the second-year recoveries was much higher because of the lower proportion of birds being harvested in the area where the hunter reporting rate was depressed. Apparently immature mallards have a relatively low fidelity to preseason banding sites. We concluded that the nearness of the location of recovery to the banding site was extremely important, so for analysis we stratified recoveries according to the distance from the banding site as well as by reporting category.

Finally, we evaluated geographical variation in the reporting rates at distances greater than 80 km from the banding site (away from the local depressed area) for the 4 flyways by attempting to correlate reporting rates with the probability that a hunter encountered a banded bird (frequency of banded birds in the flyway).

Influence of Conservation Agency Solicitation of Bands.—Band solicitation occurred with the highest frequency near the banding sites in both Canada and the United States, but it was less common in Canada (Tables 3, 4). Band solicitation decreased progressively with distance from the banding site. This pattern of band solicitation tended to minimize somewhat the depressed effects of the hunter reporting rate near the banding sites; however, band solicitation activities varied considerably among political units.

Influence of Distance Recovered from Banding Site.—Band recoveries were recorded for seven distance categories from the banding site, and the control bands were segregated into two additional categories: those submitted directly by a hunter (who reported code "21"), and all other reports (primarily conservation agency reports). Using this breakdown, we computed band reporting rates for the various recovery distances from the banding sites (Tables 3, 4). These reporting rates for hunters showed a marked depression near the banding site in all geographical regions (i.e., Canada, western United States, and eastern United States), with a gradual increase to about 80 km, and then a stabilization at greater distances.

We believe that a loss of hunter curiosity causes the reporting rate to be depressed near banding sites. If a hunter over the years encounters several banded birds and learns that they were banded locally, his curiosity diminishes, resulting in less interest in reporting succeeding bands. Moreover, his loss of curiosity may be compounded by hunters interchanging information. For example, it was common knowledge among hunters in the lower Willamette Valley of Oregon that banded mallards they encountered most likely were marked locally at the Sauvies Island Wildlife Management Area. Although a sportsman hunting 80 km or more from a banding site may encounter several bands over the years, the chances that 2 birds originated at the same site are diminished. Therefore, the hunter at a distance remains more curious about recovered bands and is more likely to report them.

Geographical Estimates of Band Reporting Rates.—Birds banded in western

Table 5. Estimated average hunter band reporting rates for eastern and western continental bandings by distance from the banding site. The standard deviation of estimate is shown in parentheses.

Location	Distance (km)		
	0–8	9–79	80+
Eastern[a]	0.25(0.072)	0.29(0.044)	0.40(0.044)
Western[b]	0.24(0.066)	0.40(0.077)	0.54(0.065)
Average	0.24(0.049)	0.35(0.044)	0.47(0.040)

[a] Bandings in Manitoba, Ontario, Mississippi Flyway, and Atlantic Flyway.
[b] Bandings in Alberta, Saskatchewan, Northwest Territories, Pacific Flyway, and Central Flyway.

Canada and the western United States were reported at consistently higher rates than their eastern counterparts. In Canada, a natural break occurred at the Manitoba-Saskatchewan border (Table 1), and, therefore, the data from east and west of the border were treated separately. The pooled data from bandings in the two eastern flyways and the two western flyways showed a similar pattern, although the differences near the dividing line were not as pronounced. In fact, the reporting rates from several states in the Mississippi and Central Flyways appeared quite similar (Table 1). Therefore, to obtain the best band reporting rate estimate for various regions of North America, we pooled and weighted the data from western Canada and the western United States; the eastern counterparts were treated similarly (Table 5).

Because of the similarity in reporting rates in the Central and Mississippi Flyways, we propose that the North American average apply for recoveries in the two middle flyways (Table 5). The eastern reporting rate would apply to the Atlantic Flyway recoveries as well as Manitoba eastward in Canada. The western reporting rate would be used for the Pacific Flyway recoveries as well as those from Saskatchewan westward in Canada.

Reporting rates near banding sites were depressed similarly throughout North America, with a major east-west trend occurring at distances greater than 80 km from the banding site. The higher reporting rates in the west were readily apparent (Table 5).

Influence of Banding Intensity in Flyways.—In the United States, it was possible with the aid of the Mail Questionnaire Survey, conducted by the U.S. Fish and Wildlife Service, to attempt to relate the hunter band reporting rates to the numbers of hunters, their success, and other related parameters. We believed that the frequency of banded mallards in a population, or the probability of a hunter encountering a band in a given year, may be most important. This probability is related directly to two factors: the percentage of the duck population banded in a region and the number of ducks that a hunter bags (i.e., hunter success in various portions of the country).

Band reporting rates initially were estimated for the eastern and western portions of the United States with the division occurring at the boundary between the Central and Mississippi Flyways. Small sample sizes made further subdivisions meaningless. The data for the two middle flyways were pooled for a third estimate (Table 6). This approach tended to smooth any difference between the east-west relationship. The data revealed an inverse relationship when plotted against the probability of a hunter encountering a band (Fig. 1). It appears that away from the depressed areas near banding sites the probability of encountering a band is important, with a smaller percentage of the bands reported (lower band reporting rate) in areas where bands are more common.

Annual Trend in Band Reporting Rates.—This was not the first reward band study of mallards. Bellrose (1955:72–73) banded mallards at 2 sites in Illinois between 1948

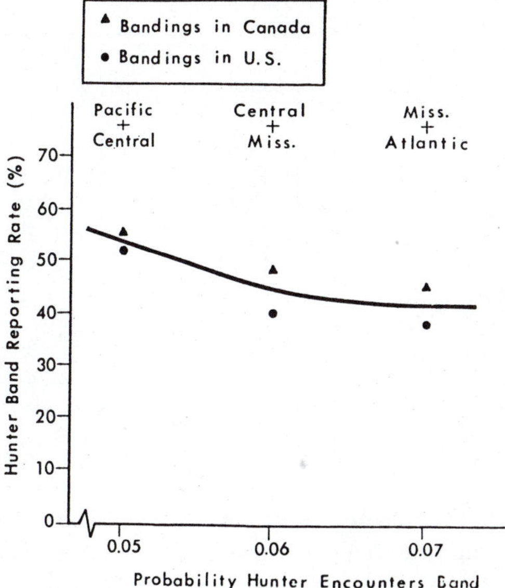

Fig. 1. The inverse relationship between band reporting rate and the probability of a hunter encountering a banded bird.

and 1951 and subsequently estimated total band reporting rates at about 47 to 54 percent from 1st-year recoveries, and approximately 62 or 63 percent from the indirect recoveries (Table 7). "Who reported" codes were not in existence at that time, thus only the total reporting rate could be estimated. A depressed reporting rate near banding sites apparently was prevalent in Illinois by 1948 (i.e., first-year recoveries were closer to the banding site). Bellrose (1955) analyzed in more detail the recoveries from reward bands applied at Chautauqua NWR in 1950 and 1951. He divided the area of the recoveries into 4 subdivisions and estimated the following total band reporting rates (reflecting the early 1950's): Canada 52.1 percent, Northern United States 47.4 percent, Central United States (region of the banding site) 38.4 percent, and Southern United States 47.6 percent. The reporting rate was definitely lower in the region which included the banding site. Bellrose (1955:74) made an additional estimate for the area within 40 km of the banding site and presented data suggesting a total band reporting rate there of 39.4 percent. Illinois was the first state where a large-scale waterfowl banding program was begun (Bellrose and Compton 1970), hence we might expect it to be one of the first states to show a depressed reporting rate bias around banding sites. Thus, the data presented by Bellrose showed that the total band reporting rate in the early 1950's appeared to be depressed near banding sites in Illinois (about 39 percent) but improved at greater distances from the banding sites (range of 47 to 63 percent).

Data from this study would be much more meaningful if they could be compared with the Bellrose (1955) data of 2 decades earlier. Since Bellrose did not differentiate who reported, the total band reporting rate is the only comparable statistic. We believe our data from the eastern United States, excluding New York and

Table 6. East-west trend in hunter band reporting rate estimates for portions of the United States.

Location of recovery	Bandings in Canada (U.S. recoveries)	Bandings in U.S. (≥ 80 km)	Probability hunter-shot banded bird[a]
Pacific & Central flyways	0.547(59)[b]	0.532(32)	0.051
Central & Mississippi flyways	0.476(97)	0.382(42)	0.060
Mississippi & Atlantic flyways	0.426(77)	0.361(40)	0.070

[a] Based on 8-yr average (1964–71) from Mail Questionnaire Survey.
[b] Number of reward bands in estimate is in parentheses.

Table 7. Data from the 1948, 1949, and 1950 reward band study in Illinois by Bellrose (1955).

Location and year banded	Reward	Control	Total band reporting rate
Spring Lake NWR (1948)			
No. banded	200	200	
1st-year recoveries	55(0.2750)[a]	26(0.1300)	0.473
2nd-year and later recoveries	38(0.1900)	24(0.1200)	0.632
Chautauqua NWR (1949)			
No. banded	759	360	
All recoveries[b]	241(0.3175)	71(0.1972)	0.621
Chautauqua NWR (1950)			
No. banded	389	884	
1st-year recoveries	50(0.1285)	61(0.0690)	0.537

[a] Percentage of recoveries is in parentheses.
[b] In-season banding and few recoveries the first year.

Vermont, where band soliciting was exceptionally high, would provide the most meaningful comparisons. Our estimates of the total band reporting rate in 1972–73 were 34.0 percent within 32 km of the banding site and 45.2 percent at distances greater than 32 km.

These estimates compared quite favorably with the earlier Bellrose (1955:74) estimates of 39.4 percent within 40 km of the banding site and 47 to 63 percent at greater distances. This represented a moderate decrease (6 to 10 percentage points) at each distance interval during the last 2 decades. Reliable estimates based on indirect recoveries could not be made for the 1972–73 bandings. Information regarding the average distance a band was reported from the banding site provided further support of the "uniform decrease at all distances hypothesis" during the last 2 decades. If the reporting rate was becoming more depressed each year only near banding sites, the average distance from the banding site for a recovery would be greater. The average distance did not change appreciably during the last 15 years (Table 8). These indices were influenced to some extent by changes in banding sites; however, the consistent values suggested that the decline was uniform at all distances from the banding sites. These data suggested a moderate decline at all distances of 6 to 10 percentage points in the total band reporting rate during the last 2 decades.

In contrast, total band reporting rates, estimated annually in recent years from data in the waterfowl questionnaire survey, suggested a greater decline during the last 2 decades. During the late 1950's, the rate was estimated at approximately 50 percent for mallards, but it decreased to approximately 30 percent by 1969 (Anderson and Henny 1972) and continued to decline more recently (23–25 percent). Questionnaire-based data suggest that the present reporting rate is considerably lower than this reward study indicates.

We feel a change in wording of the questionnaire survey (re banded birds) in 1962 probably was responsible for an abrupt artificial lowering (by approximately 10 percentage points) of the band reporting rate estimates. Answers placed on federal questionnaires are dependent upon many factors, and the wording of the questionnaire may be most important. If the above-mentioned word change caused an artificial drop, then the changes detected by both

Table 8. An index to the distance from the banding site that conventional mallard bands were reported in the United States, 1957–71.

Year	No. recoveries	Distance index[a]
1957	6,502	2.20
1958	6,155	2.22
1959	4,209	2.22
1960	4,608	2.25
1961	3,891	2.30
1962	3,603	2.31
1963	5,519	2.31
1964	8,045	2.24
1965	5,847	2.28
1966	10,989	2.27
1967	10,873	2.25
1968	8,402	2.28
1969	8,760	2.29
1970	10,665	2.26
1971	7,972	2.25
Mean		2.26

[a] Includes "hunter reported" 1st-year and later recoveries. Weights were assigned as follows: 0–8 km, weight 3.89; 9–31 km, weight 2.79; 32–79 km, weight 2.27; and greater than or equal to 80 km, weight 2.01.

approaches during the last 2 decades were quite similar (a change of approximately 10 vs. 15 percentage points). We tend to favor the moderate change obtained from the reward band studies, rather than the severe one suggested by the waterfowl questionnaire survey. The actual estimates of the former may be slightly inflated as a result of the nonreport of reward bands (possibly by 3–5 percentage points).

DISCUSSION AND RECOMMENDATIONS

Now we are left with the following questions. How do we analyze the current mallard band recovery data and the data which have accrued during the last 2 decades? What band reporting rates should be used and how should the adjustment for band reporting rates be made?

The nonrandom solicitation of bands by conservation agencies makes it imperative to adjust for "who reported" the bands. However, the "who reported" codes were begun only in 1957; thus, our band reporting rate recommendation, of necessity, must be restricted to the period 1957–73. We recommend that the hunter band reporting rates (Table 5) be used as a base for all

Table 9. Suggested hunter band reporting rates to use for mallard recoveries during the years 1957–73.[a]

Year of recovery	Distance (km) and location of recoveries: Manitoba eastward in Canada and Atlantic Flyway			Central and Mississippi flyways			Saskatchewan westward in Canada and Pacific Flyway		
	0–8	9–79	80+	0–8	9–79	80+	0–8	9–79	80+
1957	0.3500	0.3900	0.5000	0.3400	0.4500	0.5700	0.3400	0.5000	0.6400
1958	0.3433	0.3833	0.4933	0.3333	0.4433	0.5633	0.3333	0.4933	0.6333
1959	0.3367	0.3767	0.4867	0.3267	0.4367	0.5567	0.3267	0.4867	0.6267
1960	0.3300	0.3700	0.4800	0.3200	0.4300	0.5500	0.3200	0.4800	0.6200
1961	0.3233	0.3633	0.4733	0.3133	0.4233	0.5433	0.3133	0.4733	0.6133
1962	0.3167	0.3567	0.4667	0.3067	0.4167	0.5367	0.3067	0.4667	0.6067
1963	0.3100	0.3500	0.4600	0.3000	0.4100	0.5300	0.3000	0.4600	0.6000
1964	0.3033	0.3433	0.4533	0.2933	0.4033	0.5233	0.2933	0.4533	0.5933
1965	0.2967	0.3367	0.4467	0.2867	0.3967	0.5167	0.2867	0.4467	0.5867
1966	0.2900	0.3300	0.4400	0.2800	0.3900	0.5100	0.2800	0.4400	0.5800
1967	0.2833	0.3233	0.4333	0.2733	0.3833	0.5033	0.2733	0.4333	0.5733
1968	0.2767	0.3167	0.4267	0.2667	0.3767	0.4967	0.2667	0.4267	0.5667
1969	0.2700	0.3100	0.4200	0.2600	0.3700	0.4900	0.2600	0.4200	0.5600
1970	0.2633	0.3033	0.4133	0.2533	0.3633	0.4833	0.2533	0.4133	0.5533
1971	0.2567	0.2967	0.4067	0.2467	0.3567	0.4767	0.2467	0.4067	0.5467
1972–73	0.2500	0.2900	0.4000	0.2400	0.3500	0.4700	0.2400	0.4000	0.5400

[a] These estimates refer to who reported code "21" only. All others are assumed to be reported at a 100% rate. The "who reported" codes were initiated in 1957.

regions and that solicited bands (for practical purposes, all those not reported by who reported code "21") be added at a 100 percent band reporting rate. The suggested hunter band reporting rates for the years 1957–73 are presented in Table 9. Here we assume a gradual decline of 10 percentage points during the time interval in all regions and at all distances. This is an admittedly crude interpolation from the early reward band study of Bellrose (1955); however, the information is reinforced to some degree by the Mail Questionnaire Survey data after 1962, and we have projected the uniform decline back to 1957. To adjust band returns in years after 1973, we recommend using the hunter reporting rates of 1972–73. Because this adjustment may become less satisfactory in future years, another reward band study around 1980 is desirable.

A computer program that will adjust mallard band recoveries according to the above criteria (i.e., region of harvest, year of harvest, distance recovered from banding site, and who reported the band) is available from the Migratory Bird and Habitat Research Laboratory, Laurel, Maryland.

APPENDIX

Estimation of Hunter Band Reporting Rate and Adjustment of Banding Data

In recent years there have been very significant improvements in methods for analyzing band recovery data. These analytic methods are based on a series of new, realistic models describing band recoveries (Seber 1970, Robson and Youngs 1971, Brownie and Robson 1976, Anderson 1975). The analysis of recoveries from this reward band study is based on these new methods; however, mathematical details will be avoided.

First, we give an heuristic explanation of the estimation of hunter band reporting rate. Let NR and NO be the numbers of reward and conventional bands applied in a given year and banding area. With respect to a given recovery area and hunting season after banding, let R and O represent the number of recovered reward and conventional bands, respectively. The relative recovery rate

$$\frac{O}{NO} \Big/ \frac{R}{NR} \qquad (1)$$

estimates *total* band recovery rate. This formula has been used by Bellrose (1955) and Tomlinson (1968), but it does not estimate hunter reporting rate, λ, because band soliciting is not accounted for.

Let h be the harvest rate and S be the survival rate to the start of the given hunting season. Then Sh is the probability that a banded bird is harvested that season. Let H be the total harvest of conventional-banded birds; its expected value is $E(H) = NO(Sh)$. Of these conventional bands recovered, let SO be the number recovered by solicitation and HO be those reported directly by the hunters. Assume that a proportion p of the conventional bands is solicited and that all these bands then are reported by the conservation agencies. Then the conditional expected value of SO is $E(SO|H) = Hp$. Finally, of the remaining $H - SO$ conventional bands, assume that a proportion λ are reported, hence $E(HO|H, SO) = (H - SO)\lambda$.

It is necessary to know the proportion of reward bands reported. We believe that this proportion is very high, hence we assume it is 1. Therefore, $E(R) = NR(Sh)$.

Equating the quantities R, H, SO, and HO to their expectations in the four equations developed above, we can solve for the estimators $\hat{p} = (SO)(NR)/(R)(NO)$ and

$$\hat{\lambda} = \frac{HO}{NO(R/NR) - SO} \qquad (2)$$

Comparison of formulae (1) and (2) (recall that $0 = SO + HO$) shows the nature of the correction for band soliciting. If band soliciting is absent, then $SO = 0$, making formulae (1) and (2) equivalent.

If band recoveries are assumed to have a multinomial distribution (an assumption common to methods of Seber 1970, Robson and Youngs 1971, Brownie and Robson 1976), a variance estimator for $\hat{\lambda}$ is

$$\hat{V}(\hat{\lambda}) = (\hat{\lambda})^2 \cdot$$

$$\left[\frac{1}{HO} + \left(\frac{\hat{\lambda}}{HO}\right)^2 \left\{\left(\frac{NO}{NR}\right)^2 (R) + SO\right\}\right] \qquad (3)$$

If hunter reporting rate is constant over a period of years, then the above results apply to estimation of λ using all recoveries over this period of years from a banded cohort. We merely interpret R, SO, and HO as the total numbers of bands returned over all years and use these new values in formulae (2) and (3). In this use of the formulae, the annual band soliciting rate may vary arbitrarily.

The above results apply only to the recoveries from one cohort, i.e., a given year of banding. Efficient estimates of λ, from all years of banding, do not exist in closed form. Our approach was to estimate λ separately, based on the 1972 and 1973 bandings, and then compute the average weighted inversely to the estimated variances.

Band recovery data are useful for estimating annual survival rates S and annual recovery rates f. Let a banding study be conducted over k years with N_i birds banded in year i and O_{ij} recoveries in year j. The model structure for the expected value of O_{ij}, for birds banded as adults, using Robson and Youngs' (1971) notation is

$$E(O_{ij}) = N_i(S_i S_{i+1} \ldots S_{j-1}) f_j$$

where $O_{ij} = SO_{ij} + HO_{ij}$. The breakdown of returns by who reported affects the model only through the recovery rate parameters f_j. Specifically

$$E(SO_{ij}) = N_i(S_i S_{i+1} \ldots S_{j-1})(h_j p_j)$$

and

$$E(HO_{ij}) = N_i(S_i S_{i+1} \ldots S_{j-1}) h_j (1 - p_j) \lambda_j$$

hence we have

$$f_j = h_j p_j + h_j (1 - p_j) \lambda_j$$

To adjust the recovery rate f to a harvest rate, it is necessary to weight the hunter-reported bands by the reciprocal of the appropriate reporting rate. Solicited bands receive a weight of unity under the assumption they all are reported. Symbolically then, the adjustment we recommend to estimate harvest rates is given by

$$O^*_{ij} = SO_{ij} + HO_{ij}/\lambda_j$$

consequently

$$E(O^*_{ij}) = E(SO_{ij}) + E(HO_{ij})/\lambda_j$$
$$= N_i(S_i S_{i+1} \ldots S_{j-1}) h_j$$

In practice an estimated reporting rate $\hat{\lambda}$ must be used, and each band recovery is individually adjusted (weighted for reporting rate). Solicited bands (any "who reported" code other than 21) get a weight of 1. Hunter-reported bands are weighted by the reciprocal of the appropriate reporting rate from Table 9. For example, from Table 9 a hunter-reported band recovered (shot) in the Central Flyway in 1970 at a distance greater than 80 km from the banding site would get a weight of $1/0.4833) = 2.07$.

Statistical analysis methods for band recovery data (Seber 1970, Brownie and Robson 1976) have been developed for unadjusted data. However, for harvest rate estimates we believe only adjusted data (O^*_{ij}) should be analyzed.

Analysis for survival rates presents additional problems. Most models currently used assume the same band reporting rates for direct and indirect recoveries. We believe this assumption is not met when a high percentage of direct recoveries is taken within 80 km of the banding site and a low percentage of indirect recoveries is taken in this distance region. These circumstances result in a survival rate estimator that is biased high when unadjusted data are analyzed with Seber's (1970) model. We believe this bias can be eliminated by analyzing the adjusted data. Unfortunately, the extensive hypothesis testing and estimation of standard errors of survival rates are valid only for unadjusted data. Thus, we recommend two analyses on data from banding sites with heavy local hunting pressure: one on the unadjusted data and another on the adjusted data. Survival rate estimates should be taken from the analysis of adjusted data. The variance estimates from adjusted data are not valid (they are grossly underestimated), however; thus we recommend taking the sampling variances for the survival rate estimator from the analysis of unadjusted data.

LITERATURE CITED

ANDERSON, D. R. 1975. Population ecology of the mallard V. Temporal and geographic estimates of survival, recovery and harvest rates. U.S. Fish Wildl. Serv. Resour. Publ. 125. (In press)

———, AND C. J. HENNY. 1972. Population ecology of the mallard I. A review of previous studies and the distribution and migration from breeding areas. U.S. Fish Wildl. Serv. Resour. Publ. 105. 166pp.

BELLROSE, F. C., JR. 1945. Ratio of reported to unreported duck bands in Illinois. J. Wildl. Manage. 9(3):254.

———. 1955. A comparison of recoveries from reward and standard bands. J. Wildl. Manage. 19(1):71–75.

———, AND R. D. COMPTON. 1970. Migrational behavior of mallards and black ducks as determined from banding. Illinois Nat. Hist. Surv. Bull. 30(3):167–234.

BROWNIE, C., AND D. S. ROBSON. 1976. Models allowing for age-dependent survival rates for band return data. Biometrics. (In press)

GEIS, A. D., AND E. L. ATWOOD. 1961. Proportion of recovered waterfowl bands reported. J. Wildl. Manage. 25(2):154–159.

MARTINSON, R. K. 1966. Proportion of recovered duck bands that are reported. J. Wildl. Manage. 30(2):264–268.

———, AND J. A. MCCANN. 1966. Proportion of recovered goose and brant bands that are reported. J. Wildl. Manage. 30(4):856–858.

ROBSON, D. S., AND W. D. YOUNGS. 1971. Statistical analysis of reported tag-recaptures in the harvest from an exploited population. Biometrics Unit Publ. BU-369-M, Cornell Univ., Ithaca, N.Y. 15pp.

SEBER, G. A. F. 1970. Estimating time-specific survival and reporting rates for adult birds from band returns. Biometrika 57(2):313–318.

TOMLINSON, R. E. 1968. Reward banding to determine reporting rate of recovered mourning dove bands. J. Wildl. Manage. 32(1):6–11.

Accepted 16 September 1975.

ROLE OF HUNTING REGULATIONS IN MIGRATORY BIRD MANAGEMENT[1]

AELRED D. GEIS, Migratory Bird Populations Station, Bureau of Sport Fisheries and Wildlife, Laurel, MD

The gradual accumulation of evidence that hunting regulations do not have an important effect on fall population levels of most resident small game species is probably the greatest accomplishment thus far in the history of wildlife research. This concept removed the incentive to change hunting regulations annually in response to changes in population levels and simplified the task of game managers. It has also stimulated skepticism concerning the justification for migratory game bird regulations. With migratory game birds, an attempt has been made to control through regulations the size of the kill in relation to the status of populations. When populations were low, regulations were made more restrictive in an attempt to reduce the kill. When populations were high, more liberal regulations were enacted.

Recently the view has been expressed that such changes in regulations are unneccessary. This idea apparently has stemmed from information secured through studies of resident game species. The purpose of this paper is to discuss how well the phenomena that prevent hunting mortality from affecting population levels of resident species apply to migratory game birds.

[1] Originally published in Trans. North Am. Wildl. Conf. 28:164–172, 1963.

[2] Present address: Patuxent Wildlife Research Ctr., Laurel, MD 20811.

HUNTING PRESSURE (AND THEREFORE THE KILL) IS SELF LIMITING REGARDLESS OF SEASON LENGTH

Self regulation of hunting pressure is a phenomenon that prevents hunting pressure from unduly reducing populations levels of resident game. Before population levels have been reduced to the point that inadequate breeding stock is left, hunting is no longer sufficiently productive to stimulate continued hunting pressure. In other words, hunting becomes so poor that hunters stop hunting long before population levels are reduced to a critical point. Many hunters tend to lose their enthusiasm for hunting soon after the season opens and hunting pressure naturally tapers off. This concept is well illustrated by the pheasant hunters who show a tremendous early effort but lose interest long before an excessive kill has occurred. The basic cause for this appears to be a reduction in hunter success as the season progresses. Apparently as populations of resident species are reduced by hunting, the remaining individuals become more widely distributed and are contacted by hunters less frequently. Migratory game birds do not benefit in this manner because they usually are gregarious and utilize a specific, limited type of habitat. Despite relatively low population levels, hunters are able to locate and harvest waterfowl effectively. Information on the hunting kill for the canvasback (Geis 1959) clearly shows that despite a substantial kill in October and November, canvasbacks were still being harvested at a high rate in December. The pattern of hunting activity for waterfowl is not the same as that for resident species.

In the southern states, shooting pressure holds up throughout the entire season. Both the Bureau's Mail Questionnaire Survey of waterfowl hunters and the Duck Wing Collection Survey show that for states such as Florida and California, hunting activity persists throughout the season. Even in northern states, a substantial kill can occur late in the season if conditions are right. For example, the waterfowl kill in Ohio is normally heavily concentrated early in the season, yet in 1960 when a split season was placed in effect, a very substantial kill occurred in late December. Another example occurred in New York in 1958 when a heavy kill of canvasbacks occurred late in the season. Waterfowl hunters are apparently very opportunistic, and when the birds can be taken late in the season, they do not hesitate to do so. Such behavior is contrary to the indifference or lack of effort shown late in the season by hunters of resident species.

Another important difference between resident and migratory game birds is that resident species are subjected to a single hunting season and only one "opening day," while migratory game birds may have a true season length many times longer than that in any single state and which involves several "opening days" with new groups of hunters. For example, normally the shooting pressure on the mallard starts in Canada in September (or earlier in crop depradation areas) and continues in the southern states until mid-January. This is a true season length of at least four months.

The fact that hunting regulations influence the proportion of waterfowl population harvested has been clearly shown by band recovery rates. In studies conducted on the mallard (Hickey 1952), canvasback (Geis 1959), and black duck (Smith and Geis 1962), there has been a strong relationship between regulations and band recovery rates. This leads to the inescapable conclusion that regulations do have an effect on the proportion of the population harvested, which leads logically to the question, "Does increased hunting skill have any effect on overall survival?"

NON-HUNTING MORTALITY FACTORS ARE DENSITY DEPENDENT; THEREFORE THEY DECREASE AS SHOOTING MORTALITY INCREASES

The second consideration that prevents shooting pressure from influencing resident species is that if hunting mortality is increased, non-hunting mortality is reduced. As a result, the annual rate of mortality is unchanged by shooting pressure. In contrast, studies of migratory game birds have indicated that shooting pressure influences annual mortality rates. Hickey (1952) noticed the relationship between band recovery rates and mortality rates in the mallard, based on data going back to the 1920's. Lauckhart (1956) showed that one mallard population in the State of Washington with a 13.1 percent direct recovery rate had an annual mortality rate of 57.0 percent, while another population with a 25.6 percent recovery rate had a 78.1 percent annual rate of mortality. More recently an analysis of black duck banding data, now in progress at the Migratory Bird Populations Station, has shown a strong correlation between shooting pressure and annual mortality rates (Fig. 1). This also

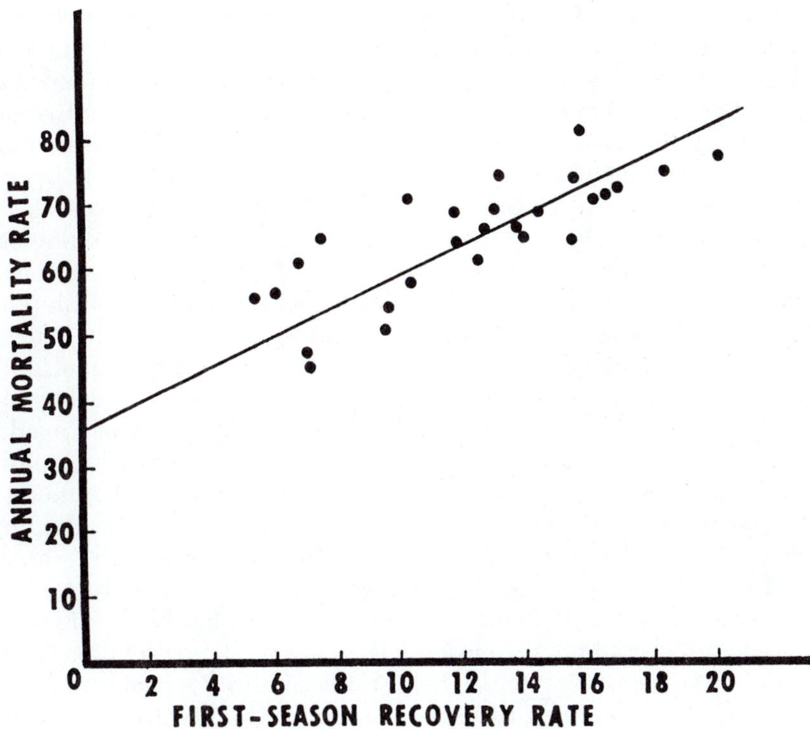

Fig. 1. Relationship between rate of hunting kill and annual mortality rate for black ducks banded as immatures (from Smith and Geis 1962).

illustrates that shooting pressure is not responsible for all mortality and that non-hunting mortality makes up a greater fraction of the total deaths under conditions of low-shooting pressure. Thus, Fig. 1 suggests that non-hunting mortality occurs in addition to and not in place of hunting mortality.

Apparently about the same fraction of the birds going into a year will be killed due to such things as accidents, oil pollution, lead poisoning, and botulism, regardless of shooting pressure. Figure 1 also implies that for black ducks during their first year, this proportion is about 37 percent and that all mortality above that level is due to hunting. Again, the gregarious nature of migratory game birds may be responsible for non-hunting mortality being independent of population size.

Striking evidence that non-hunting mortality does not replace hunting mortality was noted for the white-winged dove. The banding of nestling white-winged doves by the Texas Game and Fish Commission made it possible to determine whether or not the closed seasons from 1954 through 1956 increased the survival rate for this bird. This was done by comparing recovery rates of samples of birds surviving similar periods of time during periods having open and closed seasons. These data are shown in Table 1. For example, the birds banded in 1954 and recovered in 1957, which had lived through three closed seasons before entering an open season, had a recovery rate of 0.9 percent. In contrast, white wings banded in 1957 and 1958, which had lived through three years in which hunting was allowed in Texas, had a less than 0.2 percent fourth-year recovery rate. Similar comparisons were made for birds taken three and two years following banding, and the same relationship was evident. The birds, a portion of whose life included closed seasons, had a higher recovery rate than those subject to annual hunting. Since the recovery rate reflecting the number of birds surviving the period of closed seasons always related to the 1957 hunting season, a different type of comparison was made to examine the possibility that the higher recovery rate following the closed seasons was due to a heavy kill in 1957. This was done by using recovery rates for the 1958 hunting season, since survivors of both the closed seasons and open seasons would be adults at time of recovery during this season and hence comparable. The recovery rates of white-winged doves banded in 1955 and 1956 averaged 1.2 percent, while those banded in 1957 had a 0.7 percent recovery rate. Although the birds banded in 1955 and 1956 were four and three years old, respectively, they had a higher recovery rate than birds banded in 1957. Despite the small sample sizes upon which these comparisons are based, it can be safely concluded that closure of the hunting season increased the survival rate of white-winged doves produced in Texas. Available information indicates that shooting pressure appears to affect mortality rates of migratory game birds, which leads to the next consideration.

INVERSITY

The third phenomenon causing regulations to have little influence on the status of resident species is the discovery that increased mortality is compensated for by increased productivity. As a result, the size of the breeding population does not affect fall population levels due to an inverse relationship between size of breeding population and rate of production. This relationship has been found in resident species by a number of investigators (Errington 1945, Bump et al. 1947, Baskett 1947). In order to consider how well this inverse relationship applies to migratory game birds, it is necessary to consider the factors responsible for production. In regard to ducks produced in the Prairie Provinces of Canada and the North Central States, which provide most of the continent's duck hunting opportunity, it is obvious that the dominant factor affecting production is the status of breeding habitat resulting from climate conditions. It has been evident that there is a strong direct relationship between water conditions, measured by numbers of ponds and waterfowl production. Since climatic conditions can in no way be influenced by the size of the waterfowl population, this phenomenon of an inverse relationship between population levels and production cannot operate for those species nesting primarily in moisture-deficient areas. Bellrose et al. (1961) pointed out that mallard age ratios in the Mississippi Flyway were directly related to the number of ponds per mallard in southern Manitoba and southern Saskatchewan for the period 1955 through 1959. This might be regarded as evidence that population levels influence production. The number of ponds per duck, however, is a measure of the amount of habitat in relationship to the population rather than a measure of population level. It again emphasizes the importance that the amount of suitable habitat has on mallard production. This relationship also implies that under constant habitat conditions, a greater rate of

Table 1. Comparison of recovery rates of Texas white-winged doves following closed versus open hunting seasons in Texas.

Comparison	Status of seasons	Year of banding	Number banded	Number recovered	Recovery rate	Average (unweighted) recovery rate
Fourth hunting season recovery rates	Closed	1954	642	6	0.0093	0.0093
	Open	1957	1,877	3	0.0016	
		1958	3,601	6	0.0017	0.0017
Third hunting season recovery rates	Closed	1955	383	5	0.0130	0.0130
	Open	1957	1,877	10	0.0053	
		1958	3,601	7	0.0019	
		1959	2,809	7	0.0025	0.0032
Second hunting season recovery rates	Closed	1956	180	5	0.0278	0.0278
	Open	1957	1,877	13	0.0069	
		1958	3,601	48	0.0133	
		1959	2,809	18	0.0064	
		1960	3,041	10	0.0033	0.0075
Recovery rates during 1958 season	2 closed, 1 open	1955	383	3	0.0078	
	1 closed, 1 open	1956	180	4	0.0222	0.0124
	1 open	1957	1,877	13	0.0069	0.0069

production will occur with lower population levels. Bellrose et al. concluded, however, that the number of water areas and temperatures and associated weather conditions in April and May were the factors of major importance in production.

Although the dominant factors affecting production of Prairie nesting ducks appear to be clear, much needs to be learned about the factors influencing production of other species of migratory game birds. There is scattered evidence, however, that suggests that there is not an inverse relationship between breeding population densities and production. Mourning doves frequently nest successfully under conditions of high population density. Arctic nesting waterfowl frequently experience almost total failures in production, which is apparently due to adverse weather and flooding during the nesting season. Barry (1962) found that the timing of the spring thaw had a marked influence on brant production. Apparently the major factors influencing production of Arctic nesting waterfowl are not related to the density of the birds.

The black duck, which nests in an environment less subject to severe habitat changes, provides an interesting comparison with prairie nesting ducks in regard to the possibility that production may be influenced by population density. Also, breeding black ducks normally do not occur in high densities. Even for this species, however, available information does not suggest an inverse relationship between population density and production. Mendall and Spencer (1961) found that black duck age ratios in the kill in Maine varied just as widely during the period 1948 through 1957 (from 0.9 to 3.3 immatures per adult) as Bellrose et al. (1961) found that mallard age ratios varied in Illinois during the period 1937 to 1955 (from 0.8 to 3.2 immatures to adult). This suggests that the factors responsible for black duck production are just as variable as those for the mallard which nests in the unstable waterfowl habitat of the

Praire Provinces in Canada and in the North Central States. Furthermore, Stotts and Davis (1960) found that apparently normal production occurred under very high breeding population densities on islands in the Chesapeake Bay. On the other hand, Banko (1960) found a clear inverse relationship between breeding population size and production in Trumpeter swans. This supports the conclusion of Bellrose et al. (1961) that an inverse relationship exists within certain undefined limits. Research is needed for a better understanding of these limits. It is hoped that this information will be obtained by annual determinations of the age composition of the fall waterfowl population through the recently inaugurated Duck Wing and Goose Tail Collection Surveys, combined with an effective pre-season banding program to indicate the extent to which immatures are more vulnerable than adults to shooting.

CONCLUSIONS

Information available thus far suggests that the phenomena that cause hunting regulations to have little effect on the status of resident game species do not apply to migratory game birds. Hunting regulations influence the proportion of migratory game bird populations that are harvested which in turn influences annual mortality rates. Furthermore, there is little evidence to suggest that increased hunting mortality is compensated for by either a reduction in non-hunting mortality or by increased production. This emphasizes the important role of hunting regulations in migratory bird management.

LITERATURE CITED

BANKO, W. E. 1960. The trumpeter swan. U.S. Fish and Wildlife Service, Bureau of Sport Fisheries and Wildlife, North American Fauna, No. 63, Washington, D.C.

BARRY, T. W. 1962. Effect of late seasons on Atlantic brant reproduction. J. Wildl. Mgmt. 26(1):19–26.

BASKETT, T. S. 1947. Nesting and production of the ring-necked pheasant in north-central Iowa. Ecol. Monog. 17(1):1–30.

BELLROSE, F. C., T. G. SCOTT, A. S. HAWKINS, AND J. B. LOW. 1961. Sex ratios and age ratios in North American ducks. Ill. Nat. Hist. Bul. 27(6):391–474.

BUMP, G., R. W. DARROW, F. C. EDMINSTER, AND W. F. CRISSEY. 1947. The ruffed grouse: life history, propagation, management. New York State Cons. Dept. (Albany). 915pp.

ERRINGTON, P. L. 1945. Some contributions of a fifteen-year local study of the northern bobwhite to a knowledge of population phenomena. Ecol. Monog. 15(1):1–34.

GEIS, A. D. 1959. Annual and shooting mortality estimates for the canvasback. J. Wildl. Mgmt. 23(3):253–261.

HICKEY, J. J. 1952. Survival studies of banded birds. U.S. Fish and Wildlife Serv. Spec. Sci. Rep.: Wildlife 15. 177pp.

LAUCKHART, J. B. 1956. Calculating mortality rates for waterfowl. Washington Game Department, The Murrelet, Vol. 37(3):31–34.

MENDALL, H. L., AND H. E. SPENCER, JR. 1961. Waterfowl harvest studies in Maine (1948–1957). Game Div. Bul. No. 7 (Augusta), 60pp.

SMITH, R. I., AND A. D. GEIS. 1962. Comparison of black duck recovery and annual mortality rates. U.S. Fish and Wildlife Serv., Bureau of Sport Fisheries and Wildlife, Administrative Report No. 1.

STOTTS, V. D., AND D. E. DAVIS. 1960. The black duck in the Chesapeake Bay of Maryland: breeding behavior and biology. Chesapeake Science, Vol. 1(3 and 4):127–154.

EFFECT OF RESTRICTIVE AND LIBERAL HUNTING REGULATIONS ON ANNUAL SURVIVAL RATES OF THE MALLARD IN NORTH AMERICA[1]

DAVID R. ANDERSON,[2] Utah Cooperative Wildlife Research Unit,[3] Logan, UT
KENNETH P. BURNHAM, Office of Biological Services, U.S. Fish and Wildiife Service, Fort Collins, CO

This paper presents some research results on the effect of hunting on annual survival rates of the mallard (*Anas platyrhynchos*) in North America. Sport hunting is a very significant mortality factor in mallard populations in North America. Waterfowl hunters have killed about one-quarter of the mallard population in some years. The fraction of total deaths associated with hunting varies from year to year, area to area, and by age and sex of the birds (Anderson 1975). However, as an average in any year, about one-third to one-half of all mallard deaths are due to sport hunting, including unretrieved kill.

It is important to recognize that waterfowl hunting regulations affect the size of the harvest and harvest rate (and kill rate) of mallards in North America. Changes in hunting regulations, numbers of active hunters, and the size of the harvest of mallards have been well documented by Martin and Carney (1977). Band recovery rates reflect both harvest rates (and kill rates) and hunting regulations. Results of the recent reward band study (Henny and Burnham 1976) support the long-held assumption that recovery rates are an index to harvest rates and hence to kill rates. Substantial annual variation has occurred in hunting regulations, harvest rates, and population size. Therefore, we begin with the following basic premises: (1) hunting regulations affect both the size and rate of harvest of mallards; (2) deaths associated with sport hunting represent a very significant fraction of the total deaths in most years.

METHODS

The statistical methodology and underlying theory are detailed in Anderson and Burnham (1976:61–62). Definition of various technical terms are fairly standard and are summarized by Anderson and Burnham (1976:2–3). We will use f, M and S to denote band recovery rates, annual mortality rates and annual survival rates, respectively. We note that the annual survival rate for birds banded during the pre-hunting-season period is approximately September 1 to August 30 the following year.

Two definitions are necessary: *liberal year*, a year when waterfowl hunting regulations were liberal and harvest and harvest rates were high; and *restrictive year*, a year when waterfowl hunting regulations were very restrictive and harvest and harvest rates were low.

The test statistic used to examine differences in average annual survival rates in liberal and restrictive years is fairly simple. If $\hat{\bar{S}}_L$ and $\hat{\bar{S}}_R$ represent estimates of these averages then the test statistic is

$$z = \frac{\hat{\bar{S}}_L - \hat{\bar{S}}_R}{\sqrt{\hat{\text{V}}\text{ar}(\hat{\bar{S}}_L) + \hat{\text{V}}\text{ar}(\hat{\bar{S}}_R) - 2\,\hat{\text{C}}\text{ov}\,\hat{\bar{S}}_L, (\hat{S}_R)}}$$

[1] Originally published in Trans. North Am. Wildl. Nat. Resour. Conf. 43:181–186, 1978.

[2] Address correspondence to this author. Present address: Utah State University, UMC 52, Logan, UT 84322.

[3] U.S. Fish and Wildlife Service, Utah Division of Wildlife Resources, Utah State University, and the Wildlife Management Institute cooperating.

where the sampling variances and covariances in the denominator are those from the Maximum Likelihood methods of Seber (1970, 1973) and Brownie and Robson (1976) (also see Brownie et al. 1977).

Information on the power of these tests can be found in Brownie and Robson (1974). For the one-sided tests used in this report the power is easily approximated. Using $\hat{\delta} = \hat{S}_L - \hat{S}_R$, these test statistics are of the form

$$z = \frac{\hat{\delta}}{\sqrt{\hat{V}\text{ar}(\hat{\delta})}}$$

with the null hypothesis being $H_0{:}E(\hat{\delta}) \geqslant 0$, and the alternative being $H_1{:}E(\delta) < 0$. For a 5 percent level test the rejection criterion is $z < -1.645$. If δ is the true value of $E(\hat{\delta})$ the power of the test is given by

$$P\left[\frac{\hat{\delta} - \delta}{\sqrt{\text{Var}(\hat{\delta})}} \leqslant -1.645 - \frac{\delta}{\sqrt{\text{Var}(\hat{\delta})}}\right]$$

Assuming z is approximately normal $(\delta, \sqrt{\text{Var}(\hat{\delta})})$, then the power is easily computed.

The empirical data analyzed in the present report are banding and recovery data from mallards banded each year before the hunting season in a number of reference areas in North America (see Anderson and Henny 1972:31–32). Analyses were prepared separately for young and adults and for males and females. Parameter estimates of annual survival and recovery rates of young and adults and their sampling variances are from Anderson (1975).

RESULTS

Survival in Years of Liberal and Restrictive Hunting Regulations

Martin and Carney (1977) have presented detailed summaries of waterfowl hunting regulations and mallard harvest statistics. An examination of this information shows that waterfowl hunting regulations were very restrictive in 1962, 1965, and 1968, particularly in the Central and Mississippi Flyways. Hunting seasons in these years opened late, were short in length, and the mallard bag limit was usually restricted within a small total-bag limit. It was estimated that the size of the harvest in these three years was substantially reduced (Martin and Carney 1977). Table 1 presents a summary of hunting regulations and mallard harvest for selected states for 1962 (a restrictive year) and 1970 (a liberal year) as an example of the substantial differences among years. Mallard harvest in the United States was 2.2 million in 1962 and 4.1 million in 1970 (Martin and Carney 1977). Band recovery rates, harvest rates, and kill rates were low in 1962, 1965, and 1968 reflecting the restrictive hunting regulations (Anderson 1975:11)

The opposite extreme is represented by liberal waterfowl hunting regulations in 1964 and 1970 (Martin and Carney 1977). In 1970, hunting seasons opened early, were of longer duration, and permitted a substantially larger daily bag limit. Regulations in 1964 were quite liberal considering that the size of the fall population was not large. The harvest of mallards increased as did recovery rates, harvest rates, and kill rates. It has been known for some time that hunting regulations affect both the harvest and rate of harvest. Here we attempt to determine if harvest and harvest rate affect the annual survival rate of the population.

The restrictive years (1962, 1965 and 1968) and liberal years (1964 and 1970) represent the two extremes in the historical record (Anderson 1975). These years were used to test the null hypothesis that the average annual survival rate in years

Table 1. Summary of waterfowl hunting regulations and mallard harvest estimates for selected states in 1962 and 1970.[a]

Flyway/state	1962 (restrictive) Opening date	Season length	Mallard bag limit	Mallard harvest[b]	1970 (liberal) Opening date	Season length	Mallard bag limit	Mallard harvest[b]
Pacific								
Washington	Oct. 13	75	4	177	Oct. 10	93	6	311
California	Oct. 13	68	5	168	[c]	[c]	7	372
Central								
Colorado	Nov. 9	25	1	12	Oct. 17	90	[d]	115
North Dakota	Oct. 12	25	1	59	Oct. 3	70	5	203
Mississippi								
Minnesota	Oct. 13	25	1	114	Oct. 3	45	4	299
Arkansas	Dec. 6	25	1	41	Nov. 27	45	4	542
Louisiana	Nov. 30	25	1	54	Nov. 7	55	[e]	500
Atlantic								
New York	Oct. 20	45	2	24	Nov. 16	50	4	83
Pennsylvania	Oct. 20	50	2	20	Oct. 10	60	3	66

[a] The estimated size of the continental mallard population was 7.6 million in 1962 and 11.6 million in 1970 (Pospahala et al. 1974:70–71).
[b] In thousands.
[c] Variation by zone within the state.
[d] Point-system season.
[e] Total bag limit was 6 per day.

with restrictive hunting regulations was equal to the average annual survival rate in years with liberal regulations. The test statistic described in the methods section was computed for each age and sex for each geographic area where adequate data were available for analysis. The z test statistics are each distributed normally with a mean of 0 and a variance of 1 under the null hypothesis.

The test statistics were pooled across geographic areas as

$$z = \frac{\sum_{i=1}^{n} z_i}{\sqrt{n}}$$

where n is the number of areas, to form a composite test statistic for each age and sex class. The results of this test are given in Table 2. Also shown in Table 2 is the approximate power (see methods section) of these composite tests based on an assumed 10 percent difference in kill rate between restrictive and liberal years. That is, if H_0 is false, and in fact $\hat{\bar{S}}_L - \hat{\bar{S}}_R = -0.1$, then the power is the probability of rejecting the null hypothesis of no difference in average annual survival rates.

Information presented in Table 2 provides no basis for the rejection of the null hypothesis. The composite z values (an optimal one-tailed test statistic in this case) range from -0.450 to 1.059 and are not significant even at a low significance level. Pooling the final z values for the four age and sex classes yields a test statistic value of 0.258, also not even close to significance. The power of this overall test is approximately 90 percent. We cannot demonstrate that survival was increased in years when very restrictive hunting regulations were enacted. Let it be clear, the harvest and harvest rate decreased as a result of very restrictive hunting regulations. Nevertheless, the effect on annual survival appears negligible. This, of course, implied a compen-

Table 2. Summary of the test results of the null hypothesis that survival rates in years of restrictive hunting regulations (1962, 1965, and 1968) were equal to survival rates in years of liberal hunting regulations (1964 and 1970).

	Test statistic z values			
	Adults		Young	
Reference area	Males	Females	Males	Females
S.W. Alberta (031)	2.283	—	0.409	—
N.E. Southern Alberta–S.W. Saskatchewan (041)	1.662	−0.054	—	—
E. Ontario–W. Quebec (081)	−0.721	−0.605	−0.093	−0.427
E. Washington (092)	—	0.235	—	0.777
E. Oregon (094)	—	−0.300	—	0.086
N. California (101)	0.564	−0.018	−0.243	—
E. Colorado (126)	−1.397	—	—	—
E. North Dakota (131)	−0.854	—	−0.522	—
E. South Dakota (132)	0.611	−0.688	−0.661	0.219
W. Minnesota (133)	−0.372	0.737	1.085	−0.152
Wisconsin–N. Illinois (142)	1.324	−0.561	0.355	−0.477
Michigan–N. Ohio–N. Indiana (143)	−1.085	0.831	−0.643	−0.660
Western Mid-Atlantic (151)	0.625	−0.320	−0.047	0.403
N.E. United States (161)	1.028	0.443	0.669	−1.120
n	12	11	10	9
Mean	0.306	−0.090	0.034	−0.150
$\Sigma\ z_i/\sqrt{n}$ (a composite test statistic)	1.059	−0.027	0.107	−0.450
Approximate power of overall test	0.60	0.41	0.52	0.35

satory mortality process. Such a process might be expected on ecological grounds (see Nicholson 1954, Silliman and Gutsell 1958, Slobodkin and Richman 1956).

Estimates of Average Annual Survival in Years of Liberal and Restrictive Hunting Regulations

Estimates of average annual survival rates in liberal and restrictive years used in the previous section were pooled over geographic areas (Table 3). These overall average survival estimates demonstrate further that extremes in hunting regulations, harvests and harvest rates have not appreciably influenced annual survival rates during the past two decades. The difference between annual survival rates under the two extremes for all age-sex classes combined is estimated to be 0.0004.

DISCUSSION

The primary implication of the concept of compensatory forces of mortality is a further recognition of the importance of environmental variables. Hunters have killed about one-fifth to one-quarter of

Table 3. Estimates of average annual survival rates in years of restrictive and liberal waterfowl hunting regulations.

Age-sex	Number of reference areas	Average survival in restrictive years	Average survival in liberal years	Difference (liberal − restrictive)
Adult males	12	0.6573	0.6366	−0.0207
Adult females	11	0.5500	0.5587	0.0087
Young males	10	0.5175	0.5204	0.0029
Young females	9	0.5263	0.5371	0.0108
All combined	—	0.5628	0.5632	0.0004

the mallard population in an average year. This represents perhaps nearly one-half of the total deaths of mallards. For this substantial mortality to be largely compensatory implies that a set of environmental variables are limiting the population. The identification of these variables and the time of the year when they are critical represent important research needs.

A second implication of these results is that mallards cannot be effectively stockpiled. Very restrictive hunting seasons have not increased annual survival rates nor, therefore, the size of the breeding population the following year.

A third consideration is that of a threshold point. Hunting mortalities can be compensated for by nonhunting mortalities *only to a point.* This crucial concept has been discussed by Anderson and Burnham (1976) at some length. We can barely speculate regarding the threshold point for mallards, much less other waterfowl species.

The analysis of empirical data provides support for the hypothesis that hunting mortality for the mallard has been largely compensated for by variations in natural mortality. The forces of hunting and nonhunting mortality appear to be inversely related below a threshold level. Furthermore, we could not detect increased survival rates during years when hunting regulations were very restrictive and when harvest rates were very low.

Although our results indicate that hunting is a compensatory form of mortality, they do not support the contention that "hunting makes no difference" or that "hunting in year t does not affect the size of the population in year $t + 1$." The concept of a limit or a threshold point is crucial here. Harvest or harvest rates become excessive if they exceed the threshold point. Beyond this point, overharvest can be severe. We know little, at this time, concerning the threshold point for mallards or how this point might vary geographically.

If the evidence for a compensatory mortality process seems convincing, it is not totally conclusive. There are important areas, particularly in northern Canada, that are not represented by banded samples. Band reporting rates, and therefore harvest and kill rates, are not known. These and other problems make analyses and inferences difficult. We freely admit to the limitations of the empirical data available to us, even for mallards. Nevertheless, the analysis of over 683,000 mallards banded before the hunting season provides reasonable evidence that hunting mortality is largely compensated for by nonhunting mortality.

We continue to worry that our results will not be carefully and correctly interpreted. This implication of a compensatory nonhunting mortality process should be carefully and deliberately tested in the field. Furthermore, research must be conducted to identify the environmental factors that limit waterfowl population. Initial attention might focus on the period of the year when limitation takes place. Even this information would have substantial impacts on the waterfowl research and management programs in North America.

LITERATURE CITED

ANDERSON, D. R. 1975. Population ecology of the mallard: V. Temporal and geographic estimates of survival, recovery and harvest rates. U.S. Fish Wildl. Serv., Resour. Publ. 125, Washington, D.C. 110pp.

———, AND K. P. BURNHAM. 1976. Population ecology of the mallard: VI. The effect of exploitation of survival. U.S. Fish and Wildl. Serv., Resour. Publ. 128, Washington, D.C. 66pp.

———, AND C. J. HENNY. 1972. Population ecology of the mallard: I. A review of previous studies and the distribution and migration from breeding areas. U.S. Fish and Wildl. Serv., Resour. Publ. 105, Washington, D.C. 166pp.

BROWNIE, C., D. R. ANDERSON, K. P. BURNHAM, AND D. S. ROBSON. 1978. Statistical inference from band recovery data: A handbook. U.S. Fish and Wildl. Serv., Resour. Publ. 130, Washington, D.C. 212pp.

———, AND D. S. ROBSON. 1974. Testing for the equality of the annual survival rates in the SRY model for band return data. Biometrics Unit, Cornell University, Ithaca, N.Y. BU-521-M. 18pp.

———, AND ———. 1976. Models allowing for age-dependent survival rates for band-return data. Biometrics 32(2):305–323.

HENNY, C. J., AND K. P. BURNHAM. 1976. A mallard reward band study to estimate band reporting rates. J. Wildl. Manage. 40(1):1–14.

MARTIN, E. M., AND S. M. CARNEY. 1977. Population ecology of the mallard: IV. A review of duck hunting regulations, activity and success, with special reference to the mallard. U.S. Fish and Wildl. Serv., Resour. Publ. 131, Washington, D.C. 137pp.

NICHOLSON, A. J. 1954. Compensatory relations of populations to stresses, and their evolutionary significance. Aust. J. Zool. 2:1–8.

POSPAHALA, R. S., D. R. ANDERSON, AND C. J. HENNY. 1974. Population ecology of the mallard: II. Breeding habitat conditions, size of the breeding populations, and production indices. U.S. Fish and Wildl. Serv., Resour. Publ. 115, Washington, D.C. 73pp.

SEBER, G. A. F. 1970. Estimating time-specific survival and reporting rates for adult birds from band returns. Biometrika 57(2):313–318.

———. 1973. The estimation of animal abundance and related parameters. Charles Griffin and Co. Ltd., London. 506pp.

SILLIMAN, R. P., AND J. S. GUTSELL. 1958. Experimental exploitation of fish populations. U.S. Fish. and Wildl. Serv., Fish. Bull. 58(133):214–252.

SLOBODKIN, L. B., AND S. RICHMAN. 1956. The effect of removal of fixed percentages of the newborn on size and variability in populations of *Daphnia pulicaria* (Forbes). Limno. Oceanogr. 1(3):209–237.

THE COMPOSITE DYNAMIC METHOD AS EVIDENCE FOR AGE-SPECIFIC WATERFOWL MORTALITY

KENNETH P. BURNHAM, U.S. Fish and Wildlife Service, Fort Collins, CO 80521
DAVID R. ANDERSON, Utah Cooperative Wildlife Research Unit, Logan, UT 84322

Abstract: For the past 25 years estimation of mortality rates for waterfowl has been based almost entirely on the composite dynamic life table. We examined the specific assumptions for this method and derived a valid goodness of fit test. We performed this test on 45 data sets representing a cross section of banded samples for various waterfowl species, geographic areas, banding periods, and age/sex classes. We found that: (1) the composite dynamic method was rejected ($P < 0.001$) in 37 of the 45 data sets (in fact, 29 were rejected at $P < 0.00001$) and (2) recovery and harvest rates are year-specific (a critical violation of the necessary assumptions). We conclude that the restrictive assumptions required for the composite dynamic method to produce valid estimates of mortality rates are not met in waterfowl data. Also we demonstrate that even when the required assumptions are met, the method produces very biased estimates of age-specific mortality rates. We believe the composite dynamic method should not be used in the analysis of waterfowl banding data. Furthermore, the composite dynamic method does not provide valid evidence for age-specific mortality rates in waterfowl.

J. WILDL. MANAGE. 43(2):356–366

The composite dynamic (CD) life table has been the primary method used to estimate annual mortality rates of waterfowl populations for the past 25 years. Early descriptions and use of the method are found in Bellrose and Chase (1950) and Hickey (1952). The model underlying this estimation method, the properties of the method, and explicit computing formulas are usually not specified clearly (see Geis and Tabor 1963; Geis 1972*a,b*). Nevertheless, use of the method has been widespread (e.g., Moisan et al. 1967; Geis et al. 1971) and not at all restricted to waterfowl. Anderson and Burnham (1976), Eberhardt (1972), and Seber (1972, 1973) present recent material on the validity and usefulness of the method.

Three crucial assumptions are necessary for the composite dynamic method to be valid: (1) annual mortality rate (M_i) varies only by the age (i) of the bird, no time-specific variation of the M_i is allowed; (2) annual recovery rate is a constant fraction of annual mortality rate; and (3) virtually none of the banded birds remains alive when the data are analyzed (Geis 1972*a*:16).

A variety of implications follow from these assumptions, perhaps the most important one is that no year to year (time-specific) variation in either harvest rates, or band reporting rates is allowed. These 2 implicit assumptions are generally recognized as untrue (e.g., Anderson 1975; Henny and Burnham 1976). Assumption (3) means the recovery data from a banding study cannot be validly analyzed with the CD method for many years after banding has stopped. We believe that few biologists recognize the assumptions implicit in the method nor the degree to which the estimators of M_i may be sensitive to departures from these important assumptions.

In addition to these specific assumptions needed for the CD method, a number of general assumptions are necessary for meaningful analysis of banding data under any model (Brownie et al. 1978:6–7). In particular there must be no band loss. Band loss is indistinguishable from age-specific mortality, and is especially serious under the CD method of analysis.

A large scientific literature on various species of birds contains the results from a CD analysis of band recovery data. It

Originally published in J. Wildl. Manage. 43(2):356–366, 1979.

has focused on 3 main areas: (1) the estimation of 1st-year mortality rate (M_1) from birds banded as young and estimation of average annual mortality rate from birds banded as adults (i.e., for adults, M_1 is interpreted as an average); (2) studying age-specificity of the mortality process; i.e., estimating M_1, M_2, M_3, . . . ; and (3) studying the effect of hunting on total annual mortality rates. We wish to address the 1st and 2nd of these as the 3rd has already been discussed by Anderson and Burnham (1976).

It is surprising that no one has reported results of any statistical tests of the assumptions required for the CD method to perform validly. Recently, Hickey (1972:264) believed, ". . . it seems particularly necessary that the basic assumptions underlying these calculations be subjected to an adequate review." That is our purpose here. The 4 objectives of this paper are: (1) to present the specific assumptions and model necessary for the CD method to be valid; (2) to present 2 statistical tests of these assumptions: (a) a goodness of fit test of the CD model to data, and (b) a test that recovery rates are year-independent; (3) to judge the validity of the CD model by analyzing a cross section of waterfowl data; and (4) to reflect on the CD method as evidence for age-specific mortality in waterfowl.

STATISTICAL CONSIDERATIONS

Assumptions and Model

To specify clearly the assumptions and the model underlying the CD method, and the method itself, we must present some mathematical background. First, we introduce our basic notation; for a more detailed discussion of some of these terms and basic background on analysis of recovery data see Anderson (1975), Anderson and Burnham (1976), and Brownie et al. (1978):

k = Number of years of banding,

l = Number of years during which recoveries are recorded, $l \geqslant k$,

$S_i = 1 - M_i$ = Annual survival rate (probability) for birds of age i,

$M_i = 1 - S_i$ = Annual mortality rate (probability) for birds of age i,

f_i = Annual band recovery rate (probability) for birds of age i,

N_i = Number of birds banded in year i, $i = 1, \ldots, k$,

R_{ij} = Number of birds recovered in year j from birds banded in year i, $i = 1, \ldots, k$, $j = 1, \ldots, l$,

$R_{i\cdot}$ = Total number of band recoveries from the ith banded cohort (i.e., birds banded in year i) $= \sum_{j=1}^{l} R_{ij}$,

D'_i = All recoveries of bands exactly i years after banding (corresponds to i years of age for birds banded as young) $i = 1, \ldots, l$, and

TN_i = Total number of banded birds that could have contributed to the recoveries D'_i exactly i years after banding (often called "banded birds available" in year i), $i = 1, \ldots, l$.

The above 2 quantities are computed from the R_{ij} and N_i, respectively. In the case of $k = l$ they are (for $i = 1, \ldots, k$)

$$D'_i = \sum_{j=1}^{k-i+1} R_{j,j+i-1}\,,$$

$$TN_i = \sum_{j=1}^{k-i+1} N_j\,.$$

For example, for $i = 1$, $TN_1 = N_1 + N_2 + \cdots + N_k$ and $D'_1 = R_{11} + R_{22} + \cdots + R_{kk}$, while for $i = k$, $TN_k = N_1$ and $D'_k = R_{1k}$. The mathematical definitions of D'_i and TN_i for $l > k$ are complex and will not be given here. For the general computing formulas of D'_i and TN_i see Anderson and Burnham (1976:55).

Finally we define

$D_i = D'_i/TN_i$ = the proportion of recoveries of all birds aged i, $i = 1, \ldots, l$.

In the wildlife literature, the CD method is often presented only as a sequence of calculations based on the tabulated banding and recovery data. The formula representing these computations for estimating the mortality rate of birds in their ith year of life is:

$$\hat{M}_i = D_i/(D_i + D_{i+1} + \cdots + D_l) \qquad i = 1, \ldots, l - 1. \quad (1)$$

Seber (1972) has given a formalization of this method and some of its properties (also see Seber 1971). Our use of the notation D'_i and D_i is the reverse of Seber's use of this same notation.

Given the estimator of formula (1), we specify the exact model necessary for this to produce valid estimates of age-specific mortality rates. It is beyond the scope of this paper to present all the needed background material on modeling band recovery data (see Brownie et al. 1978). Only key results will be given.

The CD procedure is meant to apply only in cases of age-specific survival and recovery rates. Therefore the general model structure in terms of expected band recoveries is

$$E(R_{ij}) = \begin{cases} N_i f_1 & i = 1 \\ N_i S_1 S_2 \ldots S_{j-i} f_{j-i+1} & i > 1. \end{cases} \quad (2)$$

To complete the statistical model for the recoveries R_{ij}, we note that the recoveries from each banded cohort are multinomial random variables. Thus given N_i birds banded in year i, we have R_{ii}, $R_{i,i+1}, \ldots, R_{il}$, $N_i - R_{i\cdot}$ are multinomial random variables with expectations given by (2). Note that:

$$E(R_{i\cdot}) = E(R_{ii}) + E(R_{i,i+1}) + \cdots + E(R_{i,l}).$$

Recognition of this multinomial model as the correct sampling model for the data allows rigorous consideration of estimation of parameters and tests of the assumptions (see Brownie et al. 1978).

We mention that a special case of the CD model is that of assuming constant recovery and survival rates; that is $f_i \equiv f$ and $S_i \equiv S$ for all i.

From formula (2) we derive:

$$E(D_i) = \begin{cases} f_1 & i = 1 \\ S_1 S_2 \ldots S_{i-1} f_i & i > 1. \end{cases} \quad (3)$$

A fundamental property of estimators is that they should be consistent; that is for large samples their expected value converges to the true parameter value (this is related to unbiasedness). Based on formulas (1) and (3) and the requirement of consistency, Anderson and Burnham (1976:54–55) showed that the CD method is valid only if the ratio f_i/M_i is constant for all i. Thus we must assume that:

$$\frac{f_i}{M_i} \equiv a \qquad i = 1, \ldots, l \quad (4)$$

for some constant a. This is a very restrictive assumption, and unless it is tested there is no reason to believe it is true for waterfowl (Anderson and Burnham 1976:55–56). Finally, the CD estimator of the parameter a is

$$\hat{a} = D_1 + D_2 + \cdots + D_l.$$

Estimation

The CD estimation method was developed long before the complete statistical model given above was formalized. The question of optimal inference under the CD assumptions has never been considered in the literature, nor have sampling variances been developed for $\hat{M}_i$ of formula (1). In fact the estimator of (1) can be improved upon in several ways; e.g., standard maximum likelihood theory.

Identifiability of parameters is an important subject, albeit a quite technical one (cf. Brownie et al. 1978:112). A key result in this regard is Seber's (1971) proof that the parameters $M_1, M_2, \ldots, M_l$ and a of the CD model are not even uniquely identifiable. The basic problem is that given any set of banding data or expected recoveries, numerous different sets of parameters under the CD model could generate exactly these same data. For example, let $k = l = 3$; the following parameters will produce exactly the same expected values, $E(R_{ij})$, for any numbers banded N_i:

$$a = 0.1, \quad S_1 = 0.6, \quad S_2 = 0.5, \quad S_3 = 0.4$$

and

$$a = 0.2, \quad S_1 = 0.8, \quad S_2 = 0.8125, \quad S_3 = \frac{11.2}{13} = 0.86154.$$

In order to estimate the parameters of the CD model at least 1 constraint must be imposed. The types of constraint allowable are to either (1) arbitarily specify 1 (or more) mortality rate(s), or (2) set 2 or more mortality rates equal. Seber (1971) assumed $M_{l-1} = M_l$ and derived estimators which differ from those of the CD method. A thorough statistical treatment of this model will require sequential testing for differences in age-specific mortality rates. Thus one would adopt constraints such as $M_j = M_{j+1} = \cdots = M_l$ and test the adequacy of the model for increasing values of j.

The CD method employs the first approach; arbitrarily specifying that $M_l = 1$. This implicit constraint is unrealistic. It also implies that all products such as $S_iS_{i+1} \ldots S_l$ are are zero, and this implies the usually stated condition required for validity of the CD estimators.

Using formula (3) we can show the estimator $\hat{M}_i$ is consistent for the parameter

$$M_i^* = \frac{M_i}{1 - S_iS_{i+1} \ldots S_l} \qquad i = 1, \ldots, l-1.$$

This means that the expected value of $\hat{M}_i$ is approximately M_i^*, with the approximation getting better for large samples of banded birds. Another way to say this is that $\hat{M}_i$ is a biased estimator (it overestimates M_i) unless the product $S_iS_{i+1} \ldots S_l$ is zero. This will be true only if l is much larger than i, i.e., one does not analyze the data until several years after the last cohort is banded (cf. Seber 1972). Two facts are apparent: (1) the bias in $\hat{M}_i$ is due to the implicit constraint $M_l = 1$, and (2) if a realistic constraint such as $M_{l-1} = M_l$ were used, the statistical bias would vanish as sample size increases.

Goodness of Fit Test

Let $\hat{E}(R_{ij})$ be an (asymptotically efficient) estimator of the expected value of the random variable R_{ij} under the assumptions of the CD method. Then the general goodness of fit test for this model is simply the classical chi-square test based on (observed − expected)²/expected. Symbolically the test statistic is:

$$\chi^2 = \left\{ \sum_{i=1}^{k} \sum_{j=1}^{l} \frac{[R_{ij} - \hat{E}(R_{ij})]^2}{\hat{E}(R_{ij})} \right\} + \left\{ \sum_{i=1}^{k} \frac{[R_{i\cdot} - \hat{E}(R_{i\cdot})]^2}{[N_i - \hat{E}(R_{i\cdot})]} \right\}. \quad (5)$$

The 1st term is based on the recoveries, while the 2nd term accounts for those bands that were never recovered. The quantity $\hat{E}(R_{i\cdot})$ is computed as

$$\hat{E}(R_{i\cdot}) = \sum_{j=i}^{l} \hat{E}(R_{ij}).$$

Under the null hypothesis that the CD model fits the data this test statistic has a chi-square distribution with

$$\frac{k(k+1)}{2} + k(l-k) - l$$

degrees of freedom. Often the expectations for j much greater than i will be very small. If they are less than 2, the chi-square approximation is of doubtful validity. Therefore, it becomes necessary to pool expected values within a row, and corresponding data, if $\hat{E}(R_{ij})$ is less than 2. This results in a valid test, but loses 1 degree of freedom for each pooled R_{ij} value.

Usually the values of $\hat{E}(R_{ij})$ are found by substituting estimated parameter values in the formula for $E(R_{ij})$ (formula 2); in so doing we use $\hat{f}_i = \hat{a}\hat{M}_i$. Using the CD estimators of these parameters (and the constraint $M_l \equiv 1$) leads to the simple formulas:

$$\hat{E}(R_{ij}) = N_i D_{j-i+1} \qquad i = 1, \ldots, k \quad j = i, \ldots, l\,.$$

For example,

$$\hat{E}(R_{ii}) = N_i\hat{f}_1 = N_i\hat{a}\hat{M}_i = N_i D_1.$$

We note that $E(R_{ij})$ is estimable without constraints needed to allow identifiability of the parameters. Therefore, the goodness of fit test (5) is not dependent upon how the parameters are estimated. In fact, this test can be computed without estimating any parameters by computing the conditional expectation of R_{ij} given the statistics $D_1, \ldots, D_l$ (many of the goodness of fit tests in Brownie et al. (1978) were constructed following this procedure). It can be shown that:

$$E(R_{ij} | D_1, \ldots, D_l) = N_i D_{j-i+1}\,,$$

and mathematically a valid goodness of fit test results from using $\hat{E}(R_{ij}) = E(R_{ij} | D_1, \ldots, D_l)$. The validity of this test is unaffected by truncation; i.e., it is valid for all values of k and l.

This goodness of fit test provides a valid test of the 2 assumptions critical to the CD model (the M_i are age-specific only, and $f_i = aM_i$). If the test indicates that the model does not fit we are saying 1 or both of these assumptions is false. Therefore, the method cannot be used in the analysis of data and the estimates of parameters are not useful.

A more specific test can be used to assess the assumption that 1st-year recovery rates are constant, i.e., are age-dependent only, hence not varying with time. Under the assumptions of the CD method we must have $E(R_{ii}) = N_i f_1$ or the ratios R_{ii}/N_i have a constant expectation, independent of the year (i) of banding. A simple k by 2 chi-square contingency table test of this assumption can be written as:

$$\chi^2 = (N.)^2 \sum_{i=1}^{k} \frac{\left[R_{ii} - N_i\left(\frac{R..}{N.}\right)\right]^2}{N_i(R..)(N. - R..)}\,, \qquad (6)$$

where $R..$ = total 1st-year recoveries and $N.$ = total number banded $\equiv TN_1$. This test has $k - 1$ degrees of freedom. If this test rejects the null hypothesis of constant first-year recovery rate then the CD model is invalid. This is because of time variation in the 1st-year recovery rates as would result if harvest rates vary over time.

SELECTION OF WATERFOWL DATA

An objective of this paper is to assess the validity of the CD model for waterfowl banding data in general (excepting geese and swans). Thus we want to test the null hypothesis that the CD model generally fits waterfowl data, versus it does not generally fit such data. This is not the same as testing whether the model fits a given set of data. To meet this more general objective a proper scientific approach is to select a representative sample of all banded waterfowl populations and conduct the tests of assumptions on these data sets. The inference is then not just that the model does or does not fit these given data sets but that it does or does not fit waterfowl banding data in general.

To meet this objective we started with a large tabulation of most of the duck banding data in Canada and the United States from 1955 to 1972. Then we established criteria for selecting data sets. The 2 primary criteria were that the data sets selected be representative of (banded) waterfowl populations and that the banded samples be large enough to yield a reliable test of the assumptions.

To be representative of waterfowl banding we sought to cover a variety of geographic areas, ages, sexes, species, and banding periods (i.e., preseason vs. winter). Before selecting these data sets we established some criterion for a "good" data set; by "good" we mean sufficient numbers of birds banded and of recoveries to yield a meaningful test of the CD method assumptions. Our target goals for each data set were to have at least 5 years of banding ($k \geqslant 5$), an average number banded per year of at least 300, and an average 1st-year recovery rate of at least 3%. In general we met these criteria, however, occasionally we used $k = 4$ and for some data sets average recovery rate was lower than 3% (but in these cases annual numbers banded were in the thousands).

Using these guidelines we selected 45 data sets relating to 9 species from the large tabulation. We emphasize that the tabulation showed only raw data and had never been analyzed by us. Thus we made our selection of data sets before ever knowing the outcome of the tests of assumptions. Once these 45 data sets were selected, we used all of them; there was no subsequent deletion or addition of data sets after the analyses. Thirty-four data sets were from preseason banding (8 adult and 26 young data sets) and 11 sets were from winter banding (all adults). Table 1 provides detailed information on each data set.

RESULTS

Year-specific Recovery Rates

The CD model allows recovery rates to be age-specific only, and these rates must be directly proportional to the age-specific mortality rates. However, waterfowl hunting regulations in North America have fluctuated greatly over the past 25 years (Martin and Carney 1977). It seems logical that recovery rates do vary by year—a violation of a necessary condition of the CD method (Anderson and Burnham 1976:13).

We tested the null hypothesis that 1st-year recovery rates are constant across years using (6); the results appear in Table 1. The test results indicate a sound rejection of the null hypothesis. We conclude that recovery rates in ducks vary significantly by years, a major violation of the CD model assumptions. The idea that year-specific variation is "averaged out" by combining data over a number of years in a "composite" is not correct. For example, this procedure produces severe overestimates of age-specific mortality rates and severe underestimates of their sampling variances. In other words, a highly precise, incorrect estimate is produced.

Goodness of Fit Test of the CD Method

Valid inferences must stem from a model employing valid assumptions. We tested the assumptions necessary for the CD method to be valid using the simple goodness of fit test (formula 5; Table 2). Information in Table 2 provides conclusive evidence that the assumptions of the

Table 1. Results of the test that 1st-year recovery rates are constant across years for 45 sets of waterfowl banding data in North America.

Banding period	Species	State or province	Age and sex	Banding years	k[a]	Total banded	Total recoveries	Significance level
Preseason	Mallard	Montana	Adult ♂	1959–69	11	12,105	1,512	0.00189
		Saskatchewan	Adult ♂	1961–72	12	21,015	2,236	0.00000
		Minnesota	Adult ♀	1959–72	14	10,949	1,077	0.00000
		Wisconsin	Adult ♀	1961–72	12	16,803	1,682	0.00000
		Minnesota	Young ♂	1961–72	12	19,645	3,014	0.00000
		New York	Young ♂	1960–72	13	13,466	2,150	0.00000
		Ontario	Young ♂	1965–72	8	19,792	2,790	0.00140
		Saskatchewan	Young ♂	1955–72	18	30,627	4,263	0.00000
		Minnesota	Young ♀	1961–72	12	16,731	1,993	0.00000
		New York	Young ♀	1960–72	13	13,221	1,837	0.00000
		Ontario	Young ♀	1965–72	8	16,417	2,002	0.00019
		Saskatchewan	Young ♀	1955–72	18	28,198	2,770	0.00000
Preseason	Blue-winged teal	Iowa	Young ♂	1963–72	10	15,510	910	0.00000
		Manitoba	Young ♂	1962–72	11	17,115	691	0.00032
		Minnesota	Young ♂	1963–71	9	10,458	468	0.09759
		Ontario	Young ♂	1963–72	10	11,765	523	0.00108
		Iowa	Young ♀	1963–72	10	13,928	947	0.00000
		Manitoba	Young ♀	1962–72	11	15,723	686	0.00270
		Minnesota	Young ♀	1963–71	9	9,683	520	0.00063
		Ontario	Young ♀	1963–72	10	10,977	583	0.00295
Preseason	Pintail	California	Adult ♂	1955–72	18	34,788	3,356	0.00000
		Saskatchewan	Adult ♂	1955–58	4	22,279	1,403	0.00000
		California	Young ♂	1955–58	4	15,405	1,940	0.07258
		Alberta	Young ♀	1965–71	7	6,386	415	0.41488
		California	Young ♀	1955–58	4	10,216	1,015	0.50003
		Saskatchewan	Young ♀	1964–71	8	9,245	464	0.02668
Preseason	Wood duck	Wisconsin	Adult ♂	1962–72	11	8,126	818	0.00041
		Illinois	Young ♂	1962–72	11	11,690	1,081	0.00375
		Iowa	Young ♂	1962–72	11	9,342	1,026	0.00000
		Wisconsin	Young ♂	1960–70	11	9,197	1,067	0.00000
		Illinois	Young ♀	1962–72	11	10,335	716	0.00410
		Iowa	Young ♀	1962–72	11	8,661	855	0.00000
		Wisconsin	Young ♀	1960–70	11	7,894	816	0.00000
Preseason	Lesser scaup	Alaska	Adult ♂	1960–66	7	26,135	1,012	0.00002
Winter	Mallard	Illinois	Adult ♂	1963–72	10	27,691	2,905	0.00000
		Nebraska	Adult ♂	1965–72	8	15,272	1,562	0.00002
		Illinois	Adult ♀	1963–72	10	12,911	787	0.00723
		Nebraska	Adult ♀	1965–72	8	7,880	322	0.53884
Winter	Green-winged teal	California	Adult ♂	1955–70	16	13,731	919	0.00006
Winter	Pintail	California	Adult ♂	1955–72	18	27,727	2,263	0.00001
		California	Adult ♀	1957–72	16	17,747	764	0.01416
Winter	Redhead	New York	Adult ♂	1955–72	13	20,549	1,776	0.00000
		New York	Adult ♀	1963–72	10	4,629	371	0.00146
Winter	Canvasback	New York	Adult ♂	1955–59	5	6,123	808	0.00000
Winter	Wigeon	California	Adult ♂	1955–68	14	16,992	1,754	0.30970
				TOTALS:		685,079	62,869	

[a] Number of years of banding.

Table 2. Results of goodness of fit test for the composite dynamic model and modern methods applied to 45 sets of waterfowl-banding data in North America.

Banding period	Species	State or province	Age and sex	Banding years	Composite dynamic model: Significance level	Modern methods[a]: Significance level	Modern methods[a]: Model
Preseason	Mallard	Montana	Adult ♂	1959–69	0.00006	0.59843	1
		Saskatchewan	Adult ♂	1961–72	0.00000	0.18843	1
		Minnesota	Adult ♀	1959–72	0.00000	0.00425	1
		Wisconsin	Adult ♀	1961–72	0.00000	0.00834	1
		Minnesota	Young ♂	1961–72	0.00000	0.17011	0[b]
		New York	Young ♂	1960–72	0.00000	0.00836	0
		Ontario	Young ♂	1965–72	0.00027	0.07432	0
		Saskatchewan	Young ♂	1955–72	0.00000	0.00631	0
		Minnesota	Young ♀	1961–72	0.00000	0.13044	0
		New York	Young ♀	1960–72	0.00000	0.28056	0
		Ontario	Young ♀	1965–72	0.00270	0.58030	0
		Sakatchewan	Young ♀	1955–72	0.00000	0.85574	0
Preseason	Blue-winged teal	Iowa	Young ♂	1963–72	0.00000	0.40978	0
		Manitoba	Young ♂	1962–72	0.00015	0.94543	0
		Minnesota	Young ♂	1963–71	0.05430	0.54376	0
		Ontario	Young ♂	1963–71	0.00042	0.01402	0
		Iowa	Young ♀	1963–72	0.00000	0.23395	0
		Manitoba	Young ♀	1962–72	0.00000	0.63155	0
		Minnesota	Young ♀	1963–71	0.00050	0.06369	0
		Ontario	Young ♀	1963–72	0.01422	0.27058	0
Preseason	Pintail	California	Adult ♂	1955–72	0.00000	0.00003	0
		Saskatchewan	Adult ♂	1955–58	0.00000	0.72319	1
		California	Young ♂	1955–58	0.00000	0.00590	0
		Alberta	Young ♀	1965–71	0.00889	0.01171	0
		California	Young ♀	1955–58	0.01128	0.00677	0
		Saskatchewan	Young ♀	1964–71	0.03752	0.30592	0
Preseason	Wood duck	Wisconsin	Adult ♂	1962–72	0.00000	0.96056	0
		Illinois	Young ♂	1962–72	0.00000	0.06970	0
		Iowa	Young ♂	1962–72	0.00001	0.94273	0
		Wisconsin	Young ♂	1960–70	0.00000	0.42157	0
		Illinois	Young ♀	1962–72	0.00014	0.22382	0
		Iowa	Young ♀	1962–72	0.00000	0.35093	0
		Wisconsin	Young ♀	1960–70	0.00000	0.02904	0
Preseason	Lesser scaup	Alaska	Adult ♂	1960–66	0.00000	0.00064	1
Winter	Mallard	Illinois	Adult ♂	1963–72	0.00000	0.42132	1
		Nebraska	Adult ♂	1965–72	0.00001	0.28064	1
		Illinois	Adult ♀	1963–72	0.00023	0.28552	1
		Nebraska	Adult ♀	1965–72	0.68993	0.61217	1
Winter	Green-winged teal	California	Adult ♂	1955–70	0.00000	0.33859	1
Winter	Pintail	California	Adult ♂	1955–72	0.00000	0.04601	1
		California	Adult ♀	1957–72	0.00000	0.02080	1
Winter	Redhead	New York	Adult ♂	1955–72	0.00000	0.01708	1
		New York	Adult ♀	1963–72	0.00489	0.64865	1
Winter	Canvasback	New York	Adult ♂	1955–59	0.00000	0.52254	1
Winter	Wigeon	California	Adult ♂	1955–68	0.00051	0.11472	0

[a] See Brownie et al. (1978).

[b] Tests of assumptions can be made for bandings of only young birds via Model 0; however, estimation is not possible unless a matching sample of adults is also available for analysis (Brownie et al. 1978:33–34).

CD method are not met (e.g., an adequate fit is rejected for 37 of the 45 data sets [82%] at the 0.001 level). This is an overall test of the assumptions necessary for the CD model. Moreover, the test results are not dependent on the particular estimation method used (the same conclusions would be reached if the constraint $M_{l-1} = M_l$ were used, rather than $M_l \equiv 1$). We conclude that the CD method is not appropriate for the analysis of waterfowl-banding data.

Goodness of Fit Tests of Modern Methods

Brownie et al. (1978) present a series of recently developed (i.e., "modern") estimation models and testing procedures to allow selection of the "best" model for a specific data set. It seems appropriate to assess the assumptions made by these modern methods. Relevant information is presented in Table 2 to allow comparisons. Only 8 data sets (18%) are rejected at the 0.01 level and only 2 data sets (4%) are rejected at the 0.001 level. Additional information of this type is given for mallards by Anderson (1975). These results generally indicate that modern methods are adequte for the analysis of waterfowl data—at the very least, they are a considerable improvement over the older methods. In addition, these modern procedures provide statistical tests (i.e., goodness of fit tests, likelihood ratio tests, and contingency-type tests) to assess the assumptions being made for a particular model. If these tests indicate that the assumptions are not met for a particular data set, the model should not be used for the analysis of that data set. Finally, none of the modern methods is affected by truncation of the recovery data and most are not affected by changes or trends in annual band reporting rates.

Bias in Age-specific Mortality Rate Estimates

We pointed out that bias will occur in the mortality rates estimates $\hat{M}_i$ unless $S_i S_{i+1} \ldots S_l$ is essentially zero. This product has not been zero in the vast majority of analyses of banding data. Truncation has occurred almost without exception (e.g., Moisan et al. 1967; Geis et al. 1971). To illustrate the effect of truncation, consider a case where mortality rate for all ages is 0.4 (i.e., $S_i \equiv S$ for all ages). Expected values of the estimator of mortality rate under the CD method can be computed using

$$E(\hat{M}_i) \doteq \frac{M}{1 - S^{k-i+1}} .$$

Although the true $M_i \equiv 0.4$, the CD method would produce the following average estimates for $i = 1, \ldots, 7$: 0.412, 0.420, 0.434, 0.460, 0.510, 0.625, and 1.000. This bias in the CD estimation procedure has frequently been incorrectly interpreted as evidence for age-specific mortality in waterfowl.

We stress that these biases occur even when the assumptions required by the CD model are true; they are an inherent property of the estimation method (primarily because of the implicit constraint $M_l = 1$). One might conclude that mortality rates increase with age when, in fact, only bias increases with age when the CD method is used.

DISCUSSION AND RECOMMENDATIONS

We contend that valid estimates and sound inference must come from a proper model and estimation procedure based on reasonable assumptions. We have found the CD model to be inappropriate as a basis for analysis of waterfowl banding data because: (1) the assumption that recovery rates do not vary by time is unrealistic; there is substantial direct information that hunting regulations influence harvest and harvest rate, and that recovery rate is closely correlated with harvest rate (Henny and Burnham 1976); (2) goodness of fit tests soundly reject the restrictive assumptions required; and (3) logical inconsistencies occur, as for example in applying the method to adults which are a mix of unknown ages when banded (cf. Anderson and Burnham 1976:55–56). Thus, our main point is that the necessary assumptions behind the CD method are logically and demonstratively invalid. Therefore, the CD method should not be used.

A 2nd point, of lesser significance, is that the estimation method itself is poor even if the necessary assumptions are true. It must be recognized that the $l + 1$ parameters $M_1, \ldots, M_l$ and a are not separately estimable unless the mortality rates are subjected to at least 1 appropriate constraint (cf. Seber 1971). The CD method is implicitly based on the constraint $M_l \equiv 1$, which is simply not justified. If there are situations where the CD assumptions are tenable (e.g., recovery data from a few species of nongame birds) improved estimators should be developed for the analyses. We note, however, that the goodness of fit test (5) is valid and independent of the specific estimation method used and is not affected by truncation of the data.

It seems important to recognize that 2 results commonly found in the literature are now suspect. First, the estimates of 1st-year mortality rates of birds banded as young are severely overestimated (e.g., Jessen 1970) because the necessary condition $a = f_i/M_i$ is violated. Second, the notion that mortality increases with age is not validly supported. This notion is an artifact of the CD method due to truncation of data and the implied constraint $M_l = 1$. The concept that mortality in waterfowl is age-specific is not validly supported by analyses using the CD method.

We recommend against the use of the CD method in the analysis of waterfowl banding data. We suggest caution in interpreting published results based on CD method concerning estimate of age-specific mortality rates; differences between mortality rates by sex and geographic areas; and the effect of hunting on total annual mortality rates. We recommend use of the more modern methods. Their advantages are discussed by Anderson and Burnham (1976:18).

LITERATURE CITED

ANDERSON, D. R. 1975. Population ecology of the mallard: V. Temporal and geographic estimates of survival, recovery, and harvest rates. U.S. Fish Wildl. Serv., Resour. Publ. 125. 110pp.

———, AND K. P. BURNHAM. 1976. Population ecology of the mallard: VI. The effect of exploitation on survival. U.S. Fish Wildl. Serv., Resour. Publ. 128. 66pp.

BELLROSE, F. C., AND E. B. CHASE. 1950. Population losses in the mallard, black duck, and blue-winged teal. Ill. Nat. Hist. Surv. Biol. Notes 22. 27pp.

BROWNIE, C., D. R. ANDERSON, K. P. BURNHAM, AND D. S. ROBSON. 1978. Statistical inference from band recovery data: A handbook. U.S. Fish Wildl. Serv., Resour. Publ. 131. 212pp.

EBERHARDT, L. L. 1972. Some problems in estimating survival from banding data. Pages 153–171 *in* Population ecology of migratory birds—A symposium. U.S. Fish Wildl. Serv., Wildl. Res. Rep. 2. 278pp.

GEIS, A. D. 1972*a*. Use of banding data in migratory game bird research and management. U.S. Fish Wildl. Serv., Spec. Sci. Rep. Wildl. 154. 47pp.

———. 1972*b*. Role of banding data in migratory bird population studies. Pages 218–228 *in* Population ecology of migratory birds—A symposium. U.S. Fish Wildl. Serv., Wildl. Res. Rep. 2. 278pp.

———, R. I. SMITH, AND J. P. ROGERS. 1971. Black duck distribution, harvest characteristics, and survival. U.S. Fish Wildl. Serv., Spec. Sci. Rep. Wildl. 139. 241pp.

———, AND R. D. TABOR. 1963. Measuring hunting and other mortality. Pages 284–298 *in* H. S.

Mosby ed. Wildlife investigation techniques. The Wildlife Society, Washington, D.C. 419pp.

HENNY, C. J., AND K. P. BURNHAM. 1976. A mallard reward band study to estimate band reporting rates. J. Wildl. Manage. 40:1–14.

HICKEY, J. J. 1952. Survival studies of banded birds. U.S. Fish Wildl. Serv., Spec. Sci. Rep. Wildl. 15. 177pp.

———. 1972. Population ecology of migratory birds: Symposium summary. Pages 263–271 *in* Population ecology of migratory birds—A symposium. U.S. Fish Wildl. Serv., Wildl. Res. Rep. 2. 278pp.

JESSEN, R. L. 1970. Mallard population trends and hunting losses in Minnesota. J. Wildl. Manage. 34:93–105.

MARTIN, E. M., AND S. M. CARNEY. 1977. Population ecology of the mallard: IV. A review of duck hunting regulations, activity and success, with special reference to the mallard. U.S. Fish Wildl. Serv., Resour. Publ. 130. 137pp.

MOISAN G., R. I. SMITH, AND R. K. MARTINSON. 1967. The green-winged teal: Its distribution, migration, and population dynamics. U.S. Fish Wildl. Serv., Spec. Sci. Rep. Wildl. 100. 248pp.

SEBER, G. A. F. 1971. Estimating age-specific survival rates from bird-band returns when reporting rate is constant. Biometrika 58:491–497.

———. 1972. Estimating survival rates from bird-band returns. J. Wildl. Manage. 34:405–413.

———. 1973. The estimation of animal abundance and related parameters. Charles Griffin and Co. Ltd., London. 506pp.

Received 14 November 1977.
Accepted 27 September 1978.

ASSESSMENT AND POPULATION MANAGEMENT OF NORTH AMERICAN MIGRATORY BIRDS[1]

FANT W. MARTIN,[2] Migratory Bird and Habitat Research Laboratory, U.S. Fish and Wildlife Service, Laurel, MD 20811
RICHARD S. POSPAHALA, Office of Migratory Bird Management, U.S. Fish and Wildlife Service, Laurel, MD 20811
JAMES D. NICHOLS, Migratory Bird and Habitat Research Laboratory, U.S. Fish and Wildlife Service, Laurel, MD 20811

Abstract: Migratory birds are an abundant renewable resource of great economic, recreational, and aesthetic value. They present unique and difficult management problems because of numbers of species and individuals, widespread distribution, seasonal migration, and differences in population characteristics. In this paper we discuss the types of information needed for effective migratory bird management. We describe cooperative surveys in North America used to monitor the status of migratory birds and estimate different population parameters. We then use parameter estimates for the North American mallard to explore functional relationships affecting this population.

More than 700 species of migratory birds occur in North America north of Mexico. Of this number, nearly 100 species are classified as game birds. It is estimated that the fall population of ducks averages 100 million and that of mourning doves (*Zenaida macroura*) may average 500 million birds. When the myriads of individuals in non-hunted species are considered, it is apparent that migratory birds represent an enormously abundant renewable resource.

Hunting of waterfowl in the United States provided more than 17 million days of hunting recreation for some 2.4 million hunters in 1970 (Chamberlain et al. 1972). That same year, hunting of migratory shore and upland game birds (such as doves and woodcock (*Philohela minor*)) supplied more than 17.5 million days of hunting recreation for an estimated 3.3 million American hunters. Although a measurement of the overall harvest (retrieved kill) of all migratory game birds is not available, it has been estimated to exceed 68 million birds in recent years (U.S.D.I. 1975).

Migratory game birds clearly are an important recreational resource of considerable economic value. The value of both game and nongame birds for nonconsumptive use by the hunting and nonhunting public is also an important consideration. Migratory birds are a treasured resource valued for different reasons by many people. They add an important dimension to the human environment and no doubt play an important if imperfectly understood role in the ecosystem.

At one season or another, migratory birds occur in virtually all habitats in North America. Many species breed in Canada, migrate through the United States, and winter in Mexico, Central or South America. Their varied economic and social values, wide-spread distribution, migratory habits, behavior, and population and morphological differences pose unique and complex problems in their conservation.

Within the United States, the U.S. Fish and Wildlife Service has primary national responsibility for preservation and man-

[1] Originally published in J. Cairns, Jr., G. P. Patil, and W. E. Waters, eds. Environmental biomonitoring, assessment, prediction, and management—Certain case studies and related quantitative issues, pages 187–239. Int. Co-op. Publishing House, Fairland, MD, 1978.

[2] Address correspondence to this author. Present address: Patuxent Wildlife Research Ctr., Laurel, MD 20811.

agement of migratory birds. This authority was assigned as the result of a number of legal actions, including international treaties dating from conventions between the United States and Great Britain (for Canada) in 1916, to various national acts passed by the Congress over the years. These different international and national mandates identified the different birds to be protected, all of which are considered for practical purposes to be migratory. The protection and management of migratory birds within the United States has been, through necessity, a partnership between the Federal government and the various States. Similarly, the Fish and Wildlife Service and Canadian Wildlife Service cooperate on many migratory bird problems of mutual concern.

Many different management activities are underway in the United States and Canada which affect migratory birds. Within the Fish and Wildlife Service, for example, there are major programs directed toward evaluating the effects of different environmental pollutants upon migratory birds, restoring species that have become threatened or endangered, and providing habitat and protection for migratory game and nongame species on national wildlife refuges. It is beyond the scope of this paper to discuss these varied and important activities. Instead, we identify the different types of information needed for population management, describe major data-collection activities, and discuss our current state of knowledge concerning the population dynamics of the mallard (*Anas platyrhynchos*), the most abundant species of North American waterfowl.

It will soon become apparent to the reader that management emphasis has been placed on game species, especially heavily-hunted birds such as the mallard. However, activities are being expanded to provide information required to monitor status of nongame populations.

CONCEPTUAL BASIS AND PRESENT MANAGEMENT

Management Goals

The goals of managing a migratory bird species generally can be expressed in terms of a desired numerical abundance, and for game species, a desired level of harvest (exploitation). With respect to abundance, management may be directed at (1) reducing population sizes of species which cause undesirable economic problems such as crop depredations; (2) increasing numbers of desirable species which are declining or persisting at low levels; and (3) maintaining sizes of populations judged to be at desirable levels. Among game species important for hunting, these abundance-oriented goals must also be considered in the context of (4) creating or maintaining a harvest level consistent with recreational interests.

Factors Affecting Population Size

Establishment of management policies requires knowledge of factors that cause increases and decreases in abundance. At the most general level, population size is influenced by four fundamental demographic variables: recruitment (fecundity), mortality, immigration, and emigration. The relationship between these variables and population change can be expressed by the following difference equation:

$$N_{t+\Delta t} = N_t + R_t - M_t + I_t - E_t, \quad (1)$$

where N_t is population size at time t, R_t and I_t are numbers of animals added to the population during the period t to $t + \Delta t$ due to reproduction and immigration, and M_t and E_t represent numbers of animals lost because of mortality and emigration. We usually consider migratory birds on a continent-wide basis and essentially can ignore immigration and emigration. Thus, management goals must be accomplished through manipulation of recruitment and mortality rates.

Many factors affect the abundance of migratory birds. Mortality rates are thought to be affected by such factors as hunting, weather, habitat quality and availability, predation, accidents, disease, and environmental contamination. However, the specific impacts of these different factors and the degree to which they interact are poorly understood. Recruitment is affected by such factors as weather, habitat condition and availability, predation, and environmental contamination. In addition to these extrinsic factors, both recruitment and mortality are possibly affected by population density and by the behavior and physiological condition of individual birds. As noted earlier, one of the principal problems in managing migratory bird populations involves obtaining a detailed understanding of the factors that affect abundance and effecting management policies that bring about desired changes in such factors.

Information Needed for Management

The role of management is to implement practices to bring about desired changes in abundance of migratory birds. An important function of research is to develop requisite methodology which can be used to monitor population status, determine cause and effect relationships, and in particular, produce reliable predictive capability. If the effects of management policies on recruitment and mortality were adequately known, population size alone would constitute sufficient information for management. However, such effects are poorly known and a greater understanding of population dynamics must be achieved in the future. To attain this understanding it is necessary to use more detailed population parameters than overall recruitment, mortality, and abundance. Predictive capability for management purposes also depends to a large extent upon the availability of detailed population parameters. In this paper we refer to 'parameter' as an attribute or value associated with a particular population (or in some cases with a particular model).

Ideally, information on the following parameters would provide the input needed for effective management: (1) Time-, area-, and source-specific mortality for each functionally distinguishable category of individuals in the population. (2) Time- and area-specific recruitment for each distinguishable category. (3) Time- and area-specific frequency distribution of each distinguishable category. (4) Time- and area-specific total population abundance. As used here, 'functionally distinguishable categories' refers to classes of individuals in a population which have similar demographic attributes (i.e., survival and recruitment rates). Age and sex classes represent the most commonly used categories. It should be noted that the dynamics of a population can best be understood if the time intervals to which parameters pertain are short. For example, seasonal measurements of mortality and recruitment would be more instructive than annual estimates. The specificity of the above parameters to geographic areas is only important to the extent that demographic attributes vary geographically. Such parameter specificity is unimportant for geographically isolated populations, but can be quite important for continentally-distributed populations.

Collectively, the information gathered from the set of parameters listed earlier would provide the basis for an effective management program for migratory birds. More specifically, the information gathered would permit us to monitor population status, identify populations experiencing large increases and declines, and evaluate causes of population change.

Current Management Program

Although we can identify specific parameters for which requisite information could lead to ideal management, in actual practice it is difficult to obtain the required data even for key migratory bird species. The widespread distribution, daily mobility, seasonal migration, and the large variety of species involved make it impossible to allocate our efforts evenly on all migratory birds. Consequently, priorities have been set in the past and must continue to be set for use of the limited manpower and funds available for migratory bird research and management.

Historically, management activities in North America have been directed at migratory game birds, especially waterfowl, because of their great importance in hunting recreation and because of interest in maintaining huntable numbers. Population management of waterfowl and other game species has consisted of regulation of harvest through daily limits, season lengths and dates, shooting hours, species quotas and closures, and methods by which the birds legally may be hunted. Over the years, extensive surveys have been initiated to obtain information on such parameters as abundance, recruitment, annual survival, and for waterfowl, size and distribution of harvest. It was recognized that harvest regulations alone were not adequate to maintain waterfowl numbers unless their habitats also were protected. Consequently, funds derived from Migratory Bird Hunting and Conservation Stamps ('Duck Stamps') were earmarked for acquisition of important wetland habitats. Many State conservation agencies also have actively acquired wetland habitats. The limited funds provided for acquisition have not been adequate to offset the loss of wetlands. It has been estimated that a pristine base of 127 million acres of wetlands in the United States had been reduced to fewer than 75 million acres by the late 1960's and the rate of drainage has increased in recent years (Pospahala et al. 1974). Additional habitat preservation programs have been initiated in recent years as a result of Congressional action; however, it is doubtful if these programs will be able to reverse the increasing loss of habitats caused by agricultural, industrial, and other activities. Since a high fraction of North American waterfowl is produced in Canada, there also is a great need to preserve breeding habitat in that country. Canadian agencies and 'Ducks Unlimited,' a private organization, are attempting to preserve wetland habitats; however, in Canada as in the United States, it is unlikely that these efforts will be able to curtail the trend toward conversion of wetlands for agricultural and other purposes. In recent years, management of migratory game birds has been oriented toward species and population units. We believe this approach will become increasingly important in the future, especially for waterfowl, because of a declining habitat base.

Acquisitions of waterfowl habitat and establishment of sanctuaries and national wildlife refuges have benefitted other migratory game and nongame birds. Nonetheless, with the exception of certain threatened or endangered species, there has been no major effort underway to acquire habitats specifically for nongame species. However, programs recently enacted in the United States will make it possible to acquire limited acreages of unusual habitat important to a wide variety of nongame and other wildlife species.

Most remaining management efforts have been directed at certain migratory birds considered as pests, largely because of depredations on cereal crops, and except for major studies of effects of pesticides and other contaminants on migratory birds, limited consideration was given to the many species of migratory nongame birds. Recently, however, these species have begun to receive greater attention, in part because of legal mandates, but also because of increased public interest, and concern within State and Federal agencies over the impacts of pollution, habitat destruction, and other factors upon the well-being of this important resource. Species which are threatened with extinction are of special interest and efforts are underway to restore their numbers. A major new goal in migratory bird management is to identify species which are in a troubled condition so that remedial action can be taken to restore their numbers before they reach a threatened or endangered status. For most other migratory nongame species, management efforts currently are directed at monitoring their numbers, determining their habitat requirements, and identifying habitats that should be protected and enhanced. These efforts are at a modest level now but are likely to expand substantially in the future. Surveys now underway to monitor many nongame species are described in the following section.

ESTIMATING POPULATION AND RELATED PARAMETERS

In this section we describe the major surveys conducted on North American migratory birds and briefly present some representative findings. The attributes which are measured most often are population size, annual recruitment, and annual survival. Inferences and relationships among the various survey results and their value in assessing population dynamics of mallards are discussed in a later section.

Population Inventories

There are three general classes of surveys which are conducted to assess the population size of various migratory bird species. The first consists of situations where a statistically valid attempt is made to count all individuals within a sampling unit. The second class consists of surveys in which counts are made of birds heard calling and/or observed within sample units. Results of such counts, in which the same proportion of individuals is counted in different sampling units each year, are assumed to provide indices rather than absolute measures of abundance. Finally, the third class is represented by total counts made of certain species without a designed sampling scheme, especially in areas where they may concentrate in large numbers. Examples of each class of survey are described below.

Class I.—Waterfowl Breeding Ground Counts: Aerial surveys of waterfowl on breeding areas were initiated in 1947, but it was not until 1955 that these surveys became operational and were expanded to include most of the continent's principal breeding areas. This is probably the most extensive annual wildlife survey in the world. Each year over 3.37 million km^2 (1.3 million $mi.^2$) of breeding habitat in Canada and the United States are systematically sampled to estimate the breeding population of some 20 species of ducks (Fig. 1). The survey is a result of the cooperative efforts of the

Fig. 1. Transects and strata associated with aerial waterfowl breeding population and production surveys.

U.S. Fish and Wildlife Service, the Canadian Wildlife Service, and various State and Provincial wildlife agencies. The data gathered constitute the most important information considered in developing waterfowl hunting regulations each year.

The sampling scheme is a modification of a double sampling plan with stratification. A systematic sample of units was selected with a random location of the first transect in each stratum. These transects are flown in fixed-wing aircraft at a height of 30.5–45.7 m (100–150 ft.) above the ground and all observed, identified waterfowl are counted 201 m (⅛ mi.) on each side of the aircraft. A subsample of the aerial sample then is taken on the ground. The relationship between the air and ground counts is used to adjust the much larger sample of air counts to a ground-count basis, accounting for birds on the ground that are not seen from the air. The efficiency of this design depends on the relative cost of taking the two measurements, the strength of the relationship between the two procedures, and the variability of the estimates from each sample within a stratum. Presently, the ground subsample is often purposively selected and represents varying fractions of the aerial sample (transect). Since the detailed statistical properties of the survey results are quite extensive, only the general applications are presented here.

The actual field procedures employed complicate, to some extent, the development of the parameter estimates and their variances. The 49 strata are surveyed by eight aerial crews and ground subsam-

Table 1. Coefficients of variation of the population estimates of several species of ducks from aerial breeding ground surveys, 1967–77.

Species	1967	1968	1969	1970	1971	1972	1973	1974	1975	1976	1977	1967–77 Avg.
Mallard (*Anas platyrhynchos*)	6.18	7.72	6.35	7.98	6.65	6.04	6.89	7.38	7.08	6.40	9.02	7.06
Gadwall (*Anas strepera*)	13.48	15.19	12.05	11.88	11.35	10.27	15.45	11.34	9.26	10.36	13.15	12.16
Blue-winged teal (*Anas discors*)	11.56	20.23	12.77	11.51	10.79	10.62	12.41	10.95	9.64	9.82	13.74	12.19
Northern shoveler (*Anas clypeata*)	9.58	12.70	9.13	7.59	8.16	11.07	9.81	8.43	7.54	8.91	12.09	9.55
Pintail (*Anas acuta*)	9.70	15.55	7.17	8.36	8.15	8.71	12.40	8.40	7.70	9.22	17.31	10.24
Redhead (*Aythya americana*)	15.44	24.45	17.41	20.02	24.04	16.51	17.39	19.24	18.62	25.17	23.44	20.16
Canvasback (*Aythya valisineria*)	17.78	25.10	24.39	19.80	16.99	15.69	19.74	16.49	14.63	16.97	19.45	18.82
Scaup (*Aythya* sp.)	23.54	23.28	22.01	21.53	23.72	26.75	24.16	21.44	21.90	19.09	20.05	22.50

ples are conducted only in five of these crew areas (strata 26–49). Additionally, since ground access to some transects is not practical, some of the normal assumptions regarding randomness and subsequent independence among the various estimators are not met. Consequently, the variances are biased, but we do not feel that this is a serious drawback. Unfortunately, since an adequate number of ground counts cannot be made in each stratum, the individual visibility ratios pertain to a crew area rather than a stratum.

The estimator of the population size for a particular species in a stratum is:

$$\hat{Y} = A \cdot \hat{B} \cdot \hat{R}, \tag{2}$$

where A = area of the stratum,
$\hat{B}$ = aerial count density of birds per km^2,
$\hat{R}$ = visibility rate for the species in the stratum.

Let x_{i1} be the population size and m_i be the area of the ith aerial transect. Then,

$$\hat{B} = \bar{x}_1/\bar{m}, \tag{3}$$

where on n transects

$$\bar{x}_1 = \left(\sum_{i=1}^{n} x_{i1}\right)/n \tag{4}$$

and

$$\bar{m} = \left(\sum_{i=1}^{n} m_i\right)/n. \tag{5}$$

Similarly, let x_{2j} be the population size from the air count and y_j be the population size from the ground count on the jth transect of the l subsampled transects in crew area j. Then,

$$\hat{R} = \bar{y}/\bar{x}_2, \tag{6}$$

where

$$\bar{y} = \left(\sum_{j=1}^{l} y_j\right)/l, \tag{7}$$

and $$\bar{x}_2 = \left(\sum_{j=1}^{l} x_{2j}\right)/l. \quad (8)$$

The variances of the estimators are calculated using standard methods as follows:

$$\hat{V}(\hat{Y}) = A^2[\hat{R}^2 \cdot \hat{V}(\hat{B}) + \hat{B}^2 \cdot \hat{V}(\hat{R}) - \hat{V}(\hat{B}) \cdot \hat{V}(\hat{R})] \quad (9)$$

and

$$\hat{V}(\hat{B}) = \frac{1}{\bar{m}^2}\left(\sum_{l=1}^{n} x^2_{i1} - 2\hat{B}\sum_{i=1}^{n} x_{i1}m_i + \hat{B}^2 \sum_{i=1}^{n} m_i^2\right)/n(n-1) \quad (10)$$

$$\hat{V}(\hat{R}) = \frac{1}{(\bar{x}_2)^2}\left(\sum_{j=1}^{l} y_j^2 - 2\hat{R}\sum_{j=1}^{l} x_{2j}y_j + \hat{R}^2 \sum_{j=1}^{l} x_{2j}^2\right)/l(l-1). \quad (11)$$

In those strata in crew areas where no ground:air subsamples are available, overall visibility rates for a species are used. In estimating variances for the total population, the variance per sampling unit is used rather than the variance of the overall ratio to ensure a conservative approach. The estimates of the population size of each species in all strata combined are:

$$\hat{Y}_c = \sum_{k=1}^{K}\sum_{j=1}^{J_k} A_{kj}\hat{B}_{kj}\hat{R}_k \quad (12)$$

with an estimated variance of

$$\hat{V}(\hat{Y}_c) = \sum_{k=1}^{K}\left[\hat{Y}_k{}^2 \frac{V(\hat{R}_k)}{\hat{R}_k{}^2} + \sum_{j=1}^{J_k} \hat{Y}^2{}_{jk} \cdot \frac{V(\hat{B}_{kj})}{\hat{B}^2{}_{kj}}\right] \quad (13)$$

where K is the number of strata and J_k denotes the number of strata characterized by a single visibility rate (indexed by k).

We have reviewed the design of the survey, have evaluated the efficiency of the double sampling approach, and have investigated many of the statistical problems encountered (Bowden 1973). However, there are many known improvements which cannot be implemented in such an extensive field program and many biological aspects relating to bird behavior, population characteristics, and distribution that can be resolved only by new research. Observed waterfowl are identified to species and tabulated as singles (mostly lone males), pairs, and grouped birds. Since 20 or more species, which migrate, pair, breed, and nest at different times are counted simultaneously, the quality of the resulting estimates varies among species. For example, we know that many waterfowl populations, particularly diving ducks, contain more males than females. The practice of assuming that lone males represent breeding pairs causes over-estimates of these populations. Corrections are made, however, for those species which nest after the survey, but little can be done about those which initiate nesting early in the season.

Waterfowl populations fluctuate markedly among years, primarily as a result of varying reproduction, and habitat conditions in breeding areas, hence the need for annual censuses. Figures 2 through 5 show the long-term trends in continental populations of total game ducks and several of the most important individual species. The relative precision of breeding population estimates varies considerably depending on abundance, distribution, and visibility of the species involved. Representative examples of the relative precision of population estimates for several species are shown in Table 1.

Class II.—Mourning Dove Call Count Survey: Indices of breeding population size of mourning doves have been estimated annually since 1953 by Federal, State, and independent observers. Orig-

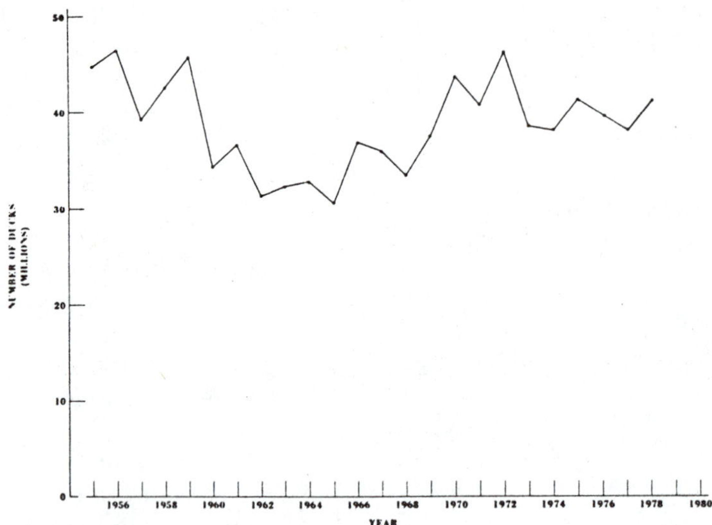

Fig. 2. The trend in principal game duck breeding populations in North America, 1955–78 (adjusted for birds not recorded by aerial crews; includes areas with comparable annual surveys; excludes scoters (*Melanitta* sp.), eiders (*Somateria* sp.), and oldsquaws (*Clangula hyemalia*)).

inal survey routes frequently were selected in areas of high dove density. These were gradually replaced with 'randomly' selected routes and currently there are more than 1,000 routes throughout much of the United States (Dolton 1977). Each call-count route has 20, 3-minute listening stations (stops) spaced at

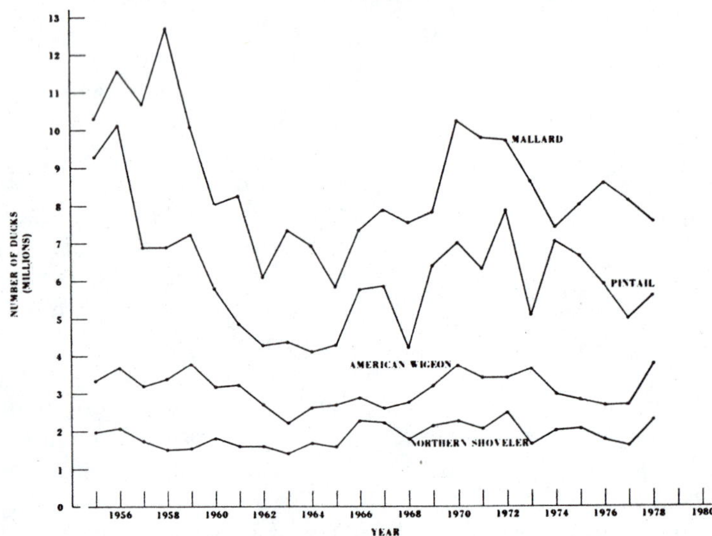

Fig. 3. Mallard (*Anas platyrhynchos*), pintail (*Anas acuta*), American wigeon (*Anas americana*), and northern shoveler (*Anas clypeata*) breeding population estimates, 1955–78.

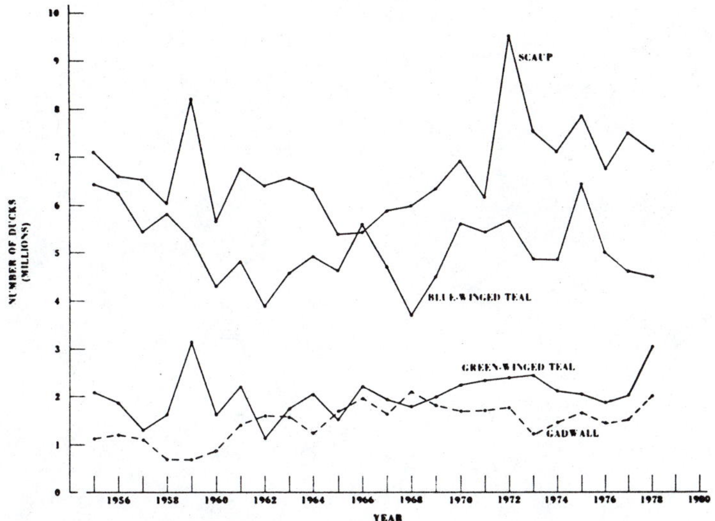

Fig. 4. Scaup (*Aythya* sp.), blue-winged teal (*Anas discors*), American green-winged teal (*Anas crecca carolinensis*), and gadwall (*Anas strepera*) breeding population estimates, 1955–78.

1.6 km (1 mi.) intervals. The routes are located along lightly-traveled roads for purposes of traffic safety and to facilitate hearing calling birds. The birds are censused for approximately 2 hours beginning ½ hour before sunrise. The counts are made one time each June under prescribed conditions.

Call count data are analyzed on the basis of number of birds heard per route

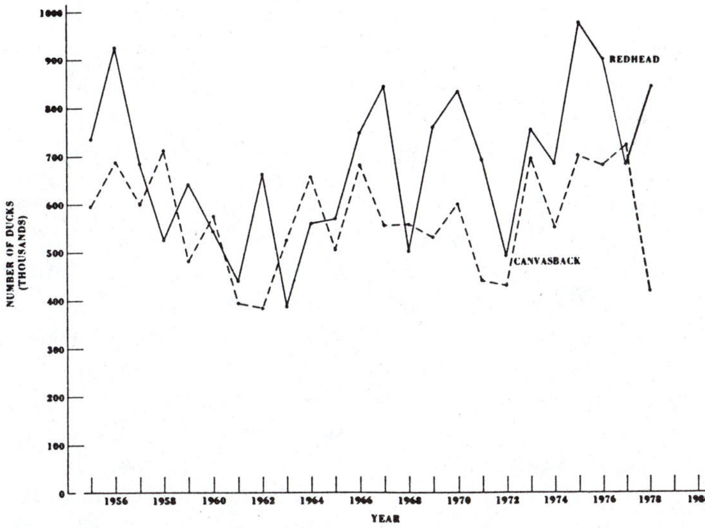

Fig. 5. Redhead (*Aythya americana*) and canvasback (*A. valisineria*) breeding population estimates, 1955–78.

Fig. 6. Administrative management units for the mourning dove (*Zenaida macroura*).

and are weighted by land area within states and regions. Earlier research based upon distribution of band recoveries reported by hunters revealed that doves could be managed as three separate population segments. Consequently, call count results are analyzed and hunting regulations are set within three different management units (Fig. 6). Population indices derived from the Call Count Survey are believed adequate to detect major year-to-year changes in breeding population levels within management units and to monitor long-term trends within states and management units.

A considerable amount of biological research has been made to improve our understanding of the reliability of the survey in relation to mourning dove calling behavior. However, it has been difficult to determine the relationship between calling doves and breeding pairs. For example, research has demonstrated that unmated males call more frequently than do paired males and are more likely to be heard on call count routes (Baskett et al. 1978). Consequently, any major annual changes in the fraction of mated males and females in the breeding population may lead to an erroneous interpretation of survey results. The Call Count Survey is the only method now being used to assess the annual status of mourning doves, and for this reason there is a special need to determine its reliability. In the practical sense, however, there probably is no pressing need for a highly reliable survey to measure annual changes in the breeding population of this species. The mourning dove has a high reproductive rate and young birds typically form some 75% of the fall population when the hunting season begins in September. Conditions during the lengthy nesting season thus may be a major factor affecting population size. We believe that the most important need for improving our understanding of mourning dove population dynamics is a standardized nation-wide mandatory hunting permit which would permit a Federal harvest survey. Among other things, such a survey probably would make it possible to evaluate the important relationship between size of the breeding population and subsequent levels of harvest during the following hunting season, a subject which was explored by Brown and Smith (1976).

Woodcock Singing Ground Survey: Each spring, cooperators conduct counts along approximately 1,400 randomly selected routes to obtain an index to comparative size of the American woodcock breeding population (Artmann 1977). The routes are located along secondary roads throughout the woodcock's major breeding range in eastern Canada and northern states in the Eastern United States. Routes consist of 10 listening points spaced at 0.6 km (0.4 mi.) intervals. Observers count the number of different males heard 'singing' during a 2-minute period at each stop. The number of birds heard calling per route, weighted for land area, is used to obtain an annual index of breeding abundance. The survey is similar in many respects to the Call Count Survey conducted for mourning doves except that counts begin at dusk and continue for only about 30 minutes.

As is true with the Call Count Survey employed to census mourning doves, we have a limited understanding of the reliability of the Singing Ground Survey. It is believed reliable to measure major annual changes and to monitor long-term trends. There are difficult biological and statistical problems associated with evaluating both this survey and the mourning dove survey. Limited research has suggested that some 'sub-dominant' males do not call during the survey period. However, preliminary findings have suggested that the proportion of calling males does not change markedly over time (Whitcomb and Bourgeois 1974). Perhaps the most straightforward approach in evaluation of the survey would be through use of a harvest survey. Such information is needed especially for the woodcock which is rapidly increasing in importance as a game species. Unlike the mourning dove, the recruitment rate in woodcock is comparatively low. Thus the potential ability to recover from large losses in numbers is expected to be less than for doves.

Breeding Bird Survey: The Breeding Bird Survey is a cooperative census designed to monitor changes in distribution and abundance of North American birds during the nesting season. It is the most important means of assessing population trends of migratory nongame birds. The survey is sponsored by both the U.S. Fish and Wildlife Service and the Canadian Wildlife Service and involves the annual censusing of bird populations along some 2,000 routes. The routes are located on secondary roads and were established by a stratified random sampling design. As is the case with other surveys of this type, in the Breeding Bird Survey, roadside habitats and not all habitats in the States and Provinces are sampled. Field procedures have been standardized; most censusing is done in June. Routes are 40.2 km (25 mi.) long with 50 stops at intervals of 0.8 km (0.5 mi.). At each stop, the observer stands near the vehicle and records the total number of birds heard or seen during a 3-minute period. Counts begin ½ hour before sunrise and under normal conditions between 4 and 4.5 hours are required to complete the 50 stops on a route.

The Breeding Bird Survey was initiated in the United Sates on a large scale in 1966, and by 1973 all States except Hawaii and all Provinces except Newfoundland were included (Robbins and Van Velzen 1967, Erskine 1978). The Breeding Bird Survey is unique in that coverage of most of the routes is made by am-

Fig. 7. Southward spread of the breeding range of the barn swallow (*Hirundo rustica*). Southern limit in 1967 is shown by the solid line and in 1977 by the dotted line.

ateur ornithologists. The survey is believed to provide information on population trends of a large number of nongame birds. Only arctic nesters, colonial seabirds, rare species, species with localized distribution, or species found in habitats without adequate roads for coverage are not included in the survey. For example, 499 species were recorded on routes in 1976. Information on population trends measured by the survey is summarized in a number of publications, including Robbins and Erskine (1975), Bystrak and Robbins (1977), and Erskine (1978).

Examples of population trends and distribution measured from the survey are shown in Figs. 7–11. The solid lines in Figs. 8–11 represent least squares fits. Although the survey reliability has not been assessed, results seem quite useful for a number of species and have been supported by supplementary information. For example, Fig. 7 illustrates the dramatic southward range expansion of the barn swallow (*Hirundo rustica*) in the United States during the past decade. Until recently, this species was a very uncommon breeder in the Southeastern United States (Bystrak and Robbins 1977). The Breeding Bird Survey is useful in documenting changes in species considered as pests. For instance, the red-winged blackbird (*Agelaius phoeniceus*) evidently has increased considerably in abundance during the past decade (Fig. 8), probably as a result of changes in agricultural practices throughout North America (Robbins and Erskine 1975, Erskine 1978). However, certain beneficial insectivorous farmland species, such as the eastern kingbird (*Tyrannus tyrannus*) appear to be declining (Fig. 11). Trends in data for interacting species can also be used to suggest hypotheses about the reasons for population changes. The brown-headed cowbird (*Molothrus ater*), for example, parasitizes nests of various North American migratory birds, including the yellow warbler (*Dendroica petechia*). The declining population trend of the yellow warbler (Fig. 10) and the increasing trend in the cowbird (Fig. 9) have led workers to hypothesize that the decline of warblers is a direct result of the cowbird's increase (Robbins and Erskine 1975).

Class III.—Wintering Waterfowl: Extensive surveys of wintering waterfowl have been conducted annually since the mid-1930's. Less frequent surveys have been made in Mexico, Central America, and the West Indies. Until the mid-1950's, winter surveys provided the primary source of information used in development of waterfowl hunting regulations. However, with the development of breeding ground surveys to estimate breeding population sizes of ducks and their expected recruitment, winter survey data have received less emphasis for use in regulatory actions. Canada geese

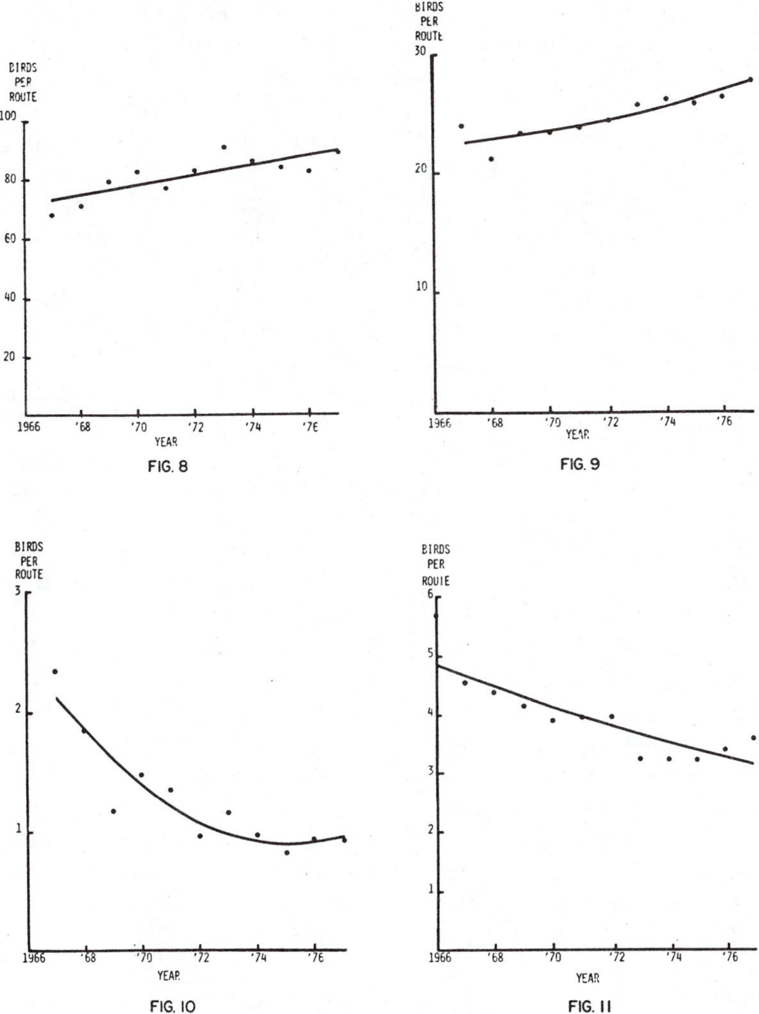

Figs. 8–11. Fig. 8. Population trend for the red-winged blackbird (*Agelaius phoeniceus*) in the Central Region. Fig. 9. Increase in the Central Region of the brown-headed cowbird (*Molothrus ater*), an abundant bird which lays eggs in nests of other species. Fig. 10. Decrease in the Central Region of the yellow warbler (*Dendroica petechia*), a frequent victim of egg-laying parasitism by the brown-headed cowbird (*Molothrus ater*). Fig. 11. Decrease of the insectivorous eastern kingbird (*Tyrannus tyrannus*) in the Eastern Region.

(*Branta canadensis*) are an exception. Since most Canada goose subspecies breed in remote areas throughout much of northern Canada and Alaska, surveys to measure their breeding abundance are not practicable. However, wintering counts of different population segments have proved to be an effective way to measure population trends and to evaluate other management actions. In addition to wintering counts of Canada geese, other special surveys are made to measure abundance of waterfowl species which also breed in inaccessible northern habitats, or which are not sufficiently abundant to be measured with adequate precision during the conventional breeding ground surveys in the spring. Reliability of these special surveys is not known but probably varies among species.

Other Species: In addition to wintering counts of ducks and geese, special surveys now are being conducted at different times, especially at concentration areas, to measure abundance of a variety of species including sandhill cranes (*Grus canadensis*), eagles (*Aquila chrysaetos* and *Haliaeetus leucocephalus*), and white-winged doves (*Zenaida asiatica*). In general, these surveys and the wintering waterfowl surveys are made from aircraft and are supplemented by ground counts.

Measuring Annual Recruitment and Harvest

Since changes over time in migratory bird populations are a function of recruitment and mortality, it is desirable that both of these parameters be estimated. This section describes the various surveys which are conducted each year to estimate recruitment and harvest of migratory game birds. Primary emphasis is given to waterfowl because their reproduction is highly variable and a substantial proportion of the population may be harvested each year.

Aerial Breeding Ground Surveys.—Aerial surveys are conducted each year to provide data on habitat conditions and indices to expected duck production (see Henny et al. 1972 for complete discussion). These surveys are less extensive than those conducted in May but the major and most variable waterfowl production areas are observed each year. Survey techniques are similar to those used in May, but the transect width is reduced to 0.2 km (⅛ mi.) due to the density of vegetation in mid-summer and its effect upon visibility.

During the July Production Survey, estimates are made of the following waterfowl and habitat conditons: (1) the number of broods of different ages (Class I, Class II, and Class III) (Gollop and Marshall 1954); (2) the average number of ducklings in Class II and III broods; (3) the number of paired and lone male ducks by species; and (4) the number of ponds. Information on the numbers of pairs and singles in breeding areas during July that have not moved to molting areas is used as an indicator of the comparative amount of renesting underway. The timing of the July Production Survey is determined by the date on which information must be available for the U.S. regulations meetings, which occur in early August. Therefore, not all young have been hatched at the time field work is terminated about July 25 each year. Consequently, an index to the number of young produced cannot be calculated directly. Rather, the approach taken is to obtain indices relating to factors which either affect or reflect current production success when compared with similar data collected during prior years.

Fall and Winter Surveys.—Annual recruitment of several species of interest cannot be determined on the breeding grounds. Consequently, several surveys are conducted in fall staging areas, during migration and in wintering areas. In many instances the ages of snow and blue geese (*Anser caerulescens*), brant (*Branta* sp.), swans (*Cygnus* sp.) and sandhill cranes may be determined by differences in plumage. Flocks may be sampled in concentration areas and the relative proportion of young in the population determined. In some situations, aerial photographs may be useful, especially for white birds.

Parts Collection Surveys.—Since 1961,

the U.S. Fish and Wildlife Service has conducted a waterfowl Parts Collection Survey in which selected hunters are requested to submit duck wings and goose tails for examination. The Canadian Wildlife Service initiated a similar survey in 1967. The species, age, and in some instances, the sex of birds killed by hunters may be determined from feather characteristics. The age ratios of these samples provide an index to the relative recruitment. Since young birds are more vulnerable to hunting than adults, this survey is not a direct measure of recruitment. If an intensive and representative preseason banding program is conducted in the late summer, the age ratio in the fall population may be estimated by dividing the age ratio in the shot sample by the relative recovery rates of adults and immatures. The relative recovery rates reflect the degree to which the young birds are more vulnerable to hunting than adults. Although this rate varies markedly from year to year depending upon the number of birds, reproduction and hunting conditions, young mallards are normally about 20% more vulnerable than adults. In contrast to waterfowl in which the recruitment varies considerably from year to year, wing collections of woodcock indicate relatively stable recruitment (Martin et al. 1965). These woodcock surveys have been conducted annually since 1959. Similar methods to estimate mourning dove recruitment were employed in the Southeastern United States from 1966 until 1971 (Hayne 1975).

Harvest Surveys.—Surveys to estimate the annual harvest of waterfowl were initiated in the United States in 1952 and in Canada in 1966. In the U.S., hunters buying Duck Stamps at selected post offices are asked to maintain a record of their hunting activity and success (Croft et al. 1971). Canadian waterfowl hunters are required to purchase a Federal migratory bird hunting permit and a sample of these hunters is surveyed each year. The species composition of the harvest is estimated by applying the various proportions of waterfowl from the Parts Collection Surveys to the reported kill. For some species where there is very limited and controlled hunting, such as sandhill cranes and whistling swans (*Cygnus columbianus*), permits are required each year and all hunters are queried as to their hunting activity and success.

Survival, Recovery, and Harvest Rates

Each year in North America large numbers of migratory birds are banded by personnel of the U.S. Fish and Wildlife Service, the Canadian Wildlife Service, and State and Provincial conservation agencies, as well as by other professional and amateur ornithologists. Detailed records of these bandings and of subsequent encounters or recoveries of individual banded birds are processed and maintained by the U.S. Fish and Wildlife Service, Bird Banding Laboratory, Laurel, Maryland, USA. As an example of the magnitude of the data base resulting from these banding efforts, a current study involving mallards banded during winter from 1950 to 1977 will include analysis of nearly 848,000 bandings and 88,000 recoveries. An example of annual banded samples and resulting recoveries for selected species is presented in Table 2. The amount of information resulting from a banding program is generally a function of the proportion and numbers of banded birds that are recovered, and recovery rates are usually higher for game birds. For example, in Table 2, the mallard, canvasback (*Aythya valisineria*), wood-

Table 2. Numbers of birds banded in 1972 and recoveries resulting from 1972 bandings for selected species.

Species	Number banded in 1972	Number of recoveries resulting from 1972 bandings[a]
Herring gull (*Larus argentatus*)	15,807	460
Mallard (*Anas platyrhynchos*)	109,812	14,965
Canvasback (*Aythya valisineria*)	5,068	455
American woodcock (*Philohela minor*)	5,563	345
Mourning dove (*Zenaida macroura*)	123,160	4,163
Red-tailed hawk (*Buteo jamaicensis*)	2,947	135
Red-winged blackbird (*Agelaius phoeniceus*)	27,796	183
Yellow-throated warbler (*Dendroica dominica*)	8,231	6

[a] Recovery totals do not include birds trapped and released during banding operations in the same 10-minute block where originally banded.

cock, and mourning dove are hunted, whereas the other listed species are not.

Source-specific and total (all sources) mortality rates (probabilities) represent important population parameters and can be useful in managing a population. Generally, mortality or survival rates are estimated from banding data in conjunction with either harvest recovery or multiple recapture data (see bibliography of Anderson 1972; reviews of Taylor 1966, Cormack 1968, Seber 1973, Brownie et al. 1978).

Multiple Recapture Models.—Multiple recapture estimation models are based on periodic sampling efforts in which both unmarked and previously banded birds are captured in random samples. Unmarked birds are banded and released and records are kept of recaptures of previously banded birds. All animals captured during each sampling period can then be classified according to when they were last captured. Probability models describing such sequences of sampling efforts and their corresponding maximum likelihood estimators for survival rate and population size were presented by Jolly (1965) and Seber (1965) (also see Darroch 1959, 1961; Seber 1962; Jolly 1963; Robson 1963, 1969; Cormack 1964; Manly and Parr 1968; Arnason 1973; Pollock 1975). The survival rates estimated from multiple recapture data generally represent the probability that an animal alive at the approximate mid-point of one banding period will survive until the mid-point of the next banding period and will be in a geographical location exposed to capture efforts. Mortality rates estimated from multiple recapture data thus represent both mortality and permanent emigration. It should also be noted that currently used multiple recapture models are generally restricted to a single age class of animals (but see Manly and Parr 1968).

The use of multiple recapture data to estimate population parameters of migratory birds has not been nearly as widespread as in sedentary animal populations but includes the efforts of Hammersley (1953), Boyd (1956), Orians (1958), Roberts (1971), and Anderson and Sterling (1974). Multiple recapture methodology may prove valuable for migratory birds that breed or winter in relatively discrete geographic areas. In addition, these methods represent perhaps the best potential means of estimating survival rates of nonhunted species. However, for widespread continental populations of migratory game birds, estimation methods based on harvest recovery data appear to be more generally applicable.

Harvest Recovery Models.—Estimation models using harvest recovery data also are based on periodic banding efforts in which birds are trapped, tagged with individually marked bands, and released. Most banding programs involve annual efforts; most birds are banded during the preseason (July, August, September; before the opening of northern hunting seasons) and winter (January, February) periods. Recovery data are obtained when banded birds are shot by hunters and the bands mailed or otherwise reported to the Bird Banding Laboratory. Recoveries can then be categorized in terms of the year banded and the year recovered, and the number of recoveries in each such category can be modeled as a multinomial random variable. Single age class models and corresponding maximum likelihood estimators were obtained by Haldane (1955), Chapman and Robson (1960), Seber (1970), Robson and Youngs (1971), and Brownie et al. (1978). Models were developed for populations with two and three age classes (i.e., birds during the first and second years or periods of life exhibit different survival or recovery probabilities than older birds) by Brownie and Robson (1974*a*, 1976), Johnson (1974), and Brownie et al. (1978).

These harvest recovery models permit the estimation of two parameters of importance: survival rate and recovery rate. The survival rate (S_i) represents the probability that a bird alive at the time of banding in period i will survive until the time of banding in period i + 1. Specific migratory bird populations or subpopulations are generally banded annually, and the estimated survival rates thus correspond to a one-year time interval. Unlike the survival estimates resulting from the multiple recapture models, those obtained from the harvest recovery models include only losses from mortality, and losses attributable to emigration are not included. Recovery rate (f_i) as estimated in the harvest recovery models, represents the probability that a banded bird alive at the time of banding in year i will be legally shot or found dead during the hunting season of year i and reported. Estimated survival and recovery rates and their standard errors for selected game species are presented in Table 3.

Recovery rate estimates are important because of their relationship to harvest rate, which is essentially a source-specific mortality rate associated with legal hunting. Recovery rate is the product of two separate rates, the reporting rate, λ_i, and the harvest rate H_i (thus $f_i = \lambda_i H_i$). Reporting rate represents the probability that a banded bird which is shot and retrieved by a hunter will be reported to the Bird Banding Laboratory. Harvest rate represents the probability of a banded bird alive at the time of banding in year i being killed and retrieved by a hunter during the hunting season of year i. Harvest rate is thus a relatively important parameter for game birds and generally is calculated from estimates of recovery rate and reporting rate (i.e., $\hat{H}_i = \hat{f}_i/\hat{\lambda}_i$). Recovery rates for such computations are estimated from the harvest recovery models previously cited (see examples in Table 3). Historically two principal methods have been used for estimating band reporting rate (but also see Henny 1967). The first method involves a comparison of estimates of the numbers of birds harvested (based on the Mail Questionnaire Survey) with actual numbers of bands reported to the Bird Banding Laboratory (Geis and Atwood 1961, Martinson 1966, Martinson and McCann 1966). The other method perhaps is more precise. It basically involves a comparison of the proportion of standard bands reported, with the proportion of special 'reward bands' reported from birds banded in the same geographic location (Bell-

Table 3. Mean annual survival and recovery rate estimates for various species of migratory game birds.

Species	Sex[a]	Age class	Banding location and period[b]	Total number banded	Survival rates[c] $\hat{S}$	Survival rates[c] $SE(\hat{S})$	Recovery rates[c] $\hat{f}$	Recovery rates[c] $SE(\hat{f})$
Mallard (*Anas platyrhynchos*)	M	Adult	Southwestern Manitoba, 1967–75	12,266	.680	.016	.062	.002
Mallard	M	Young	Southwestern Manitoba, 1967–75	8,202	.608	.040	.081	.003
Mallard	F	Adult	Southwestern Manitoba, 1958–75	7,099	.504	.033	.054	.004
Mallard	F	Young	Southwestern Manitoba, 1958–75	9,539	.588	.079	.078	.003
Pintail (*Anas acuta*)	M	Adult	Southwestern Alberta, 1955–60	5,426	.693	.026	.030	.002
Pintail	F	Adult	Southeastern Alberta, 1955–61	2,827	.600	.041	.025	.003
Green-winged teal (*Anas crecca*)	M	Adult	Central Saskatchewan, 1955–61	5,402	.495	.041	.023	.003
Canvasback (*Aythya valisineria*)	M	Adult	Delaware-Maryland-Virginia, 1967–75	9,522	.694	.043	.021	.002
Canvasback	F	Adult	Delaware-Maryland-Virginia, 1967–71	2,184	.563	.051	.028	.003
Canada goose[d] (*Branta canadensis*)	M&F	Adult	Swan Lake Refuge, Missouri, 1949–57	4,909	.767	.017	.074	.004
Canada goose[d]	M&F	Young	Swan Lake Refuge, Missouri, 1949–57	6,512	.688	.034	.096	.004
Mourning dove[e] (*Zenaida macroura*)	M&F	Adult	Central North and South Carolina, 1968–74	5,652	.430	.034	.021	.002
Mourning dove[e]	M&F	Young	Central North and South Carolina, 1968–74	20,760	.263	.028	.034	.039
Woodcock[f] (*Philohela minor*)	M	Adult	Maine, 1967–73	1,166	.380	.055	.037	.006
Woodcock[f]	F	Adult	Maine, 1967–73	1,329	.371	.051	.040	.007

[a] M denotes male and F denotes female.

[b] With two exceptions, all banding reported here was conducted during the preseason banding period (i.e., during the summer and early fall). The canvasback banding occurred during the winter (January–February) and the Canada goose banding occurred during the hunting season.

[c] Survival and recovery rates and their standard errors were estimated by the methodology and algorithms summarized in Brownie et al. (1978).

[d] Information source: Brownie et al. (1978:80–85).

[e] Information source: G. Haas (unpublished).

[f] Information source: Krohn et al. (1974).

rose 1955, Tomlinson 1968, Henny and Burnham 1976). 'Reward bands' are bands stamped with a message that any person returning the band will receive a reward. For example, in the 1972–73 mallard reward band study, 'REWARD $10' was stamped on anodized green bands. In estimating the reporting rate of conventional bands, it is assumed that the reporting rate of reward bands is 1.0 (i.e., all retrieved reward bands are assumed to have been reported). A discussion of factors influencing band reporting rate is presented in Henny and Burnham (1976).

APPLICATION OF SURVEY RESULTS IN MALLARD MANAGEMENT

Earlier, we listed the population parameters that would be desirable as an information base for effective management. As pointed out, manpower, funding, and biological constraints have made it difficult to obtain the needed data for key species and have precluded obtaining necessary information for all species of migratory birds.

The mallard has received more attention than all other North American migratory birds, and for many years a major effort has been made to assess its annual status and understand its population dynamics. This species is the most abundant duck in North America and is highly prized by hunters. In this section, we describe the parameter estimates that are available for mallards and discuss our successes and limitations in understanding the population dynamics of this important species.

Population and Related Parameters

The following set of parameters is available for the North American mallard population:

1) year- and area-specific annual survival rates by age (young and adult) and sex as estimated from banding and recovery records (see Anderson 1975*a*, Anderson and Burnham 1976, Hopper et al. 1978);
2) year- and area-specific annual harvest and recovery rates by age and sex, as estimated from banding and recovery data used in conjunction with reward band study information (see Anderson 1975*a*, Hopper et al. 1978);
3) year- and area-specific size and age and sex structure of the harvest, as estimated from the Mail Questionnaire Survey and the Parts Collection Survey (see Martin and Carney 1977);
4) year-specific continental recruitment (expressed as number of young per adult in the September population), as estimated from banding and recovery data, Breeding Ground Survey data, and Parts Collection Survey results (see Pospahala et al. 1974);
5) year- and area-specific breeding population size, as estimated from the Breeding Ground Survey (Pospahala et al. 1974), and January population size, as estimated from the winter survey (e.g., Benning et al. 1978).

In addition to these population parameters, other information relating to mallard population ecology is also collected. For example, habitat data (May and July pond counts) and additional information on production of young ('brood indices') are collected during the Breeding Ground Surveys and the July Production Surveys (Pospahala et al. 1974, Henny et al. 1972).

Some of the mallard population parameters are estimated with greater reliability and precision than others. Some are estimated directly (e.g., May and winter population size), while others (recruitment and harvest rates) are derived from other estimates. With respect to mortality, the population is only subdivided into two age categories, young and adult, reflecting the assumption that mortality is constant for adults and that senescent decline is unimportant (e.g., see Deevey 1947, Ricklefs 1973). Although the generality of this assumption has been challenged (Botkin and Miller 1974) it seems to hold true for mallards (Anderson 1975*a*). Comparison of this set of parameters with the previously described 'highly desirable' set provides some insight to the strengths and shortcomings of the mallard data. Most of the parameter estimates pertain to an annual time interval, and it would be desirable to partition some of the parameters (especially mortality) to correspond to shorter periods. Source-specific mortality is available for only one source—hunting. In addition, recruitment estimates are not available on the basis of specific geographic areas but pertain to the entire continent. Despite these shortcomings, the set of parameter estimates for mallards is better and more complete than that available for any other North American migratory bird and forms a solid base for efforts to understand and manage the population.

Internal Consistency of Parameter Estimates

Time Invariant Matrix Model.—Here, we use two general approaches to determine if our estimates of survival and recruitment rates for North American mallards seem consistent with our estimates of spring population size and rate of increase. The first approach is similar to that of Anderson (1975*a*:27–31) and involves the use of average annual survival and recruitment rates in conjunction with a general population projection matrix (e.g., see Bernardelli 1941; Lewis 1942; Leslie 1945, 1948).

We define the following notation and mean parameter estimates:

S_{AM} = 0.681 = Average annual survival rate for adult males
S_{AF} = 0.555 = Average annual survival rate for adult females
S_{YM} = 0.621 = Average annual survival rate for young males
S_{YF} = 0.563 = Average annual survival rate for young females
P = 1.03 = Average annual recruitment rate or preseason age ratio (young/adult in the fall population)
R = 0.50 = Sex ratio of young birds expressed as proportion male
M_i = Number of adult males in year i
F_i = Number of adult females in year i
Y_i = Number of young in year i

The anniversary date of the projection model is approximately September 1, and the time step is 1 year. All parameter estimates were obtained for the period 1961–74. The survival estimates were computed from a series of annual survival estimates (from banding and recovery data analysis) corresponding to specific breeding reference areas (geographic areas used for mallard data summarization, Anderson and Henny 1972). Annual survival estimates of specified precision (coefficient of variation ≤ 0.30) were weighted by the May population sizes of the corresponding reference areas (as estimated from Breeding Ground Survey data, Pospahala et al. 1974) to produce these average continental estimates. Continental recruitment rates were estimated from banding and recovery data used in conjunction with Parts Collection Survey data. The sex ratio in young of 0.50 is an assumption supported by both empirical data (e.g., Bellrose et al. 1961:403–405, Aldrich 1973:484–485, Anderson et al. 1970) and evolutionary theory (e.g., Fisher 1958, Crow and Kimura 1970, Charnov 1975).

We define the projection matrix as:

$$\underset{\sim}{A} = \begin{bmatrix} S_{AM} & 0 & RS_{YM} \\ 0 & S_{AF} & (1-R)S_{YF} \\ PS_{AM} & PS_{AF} & (RPS_{YM} + (1-R)PS_{YF}) \end{bmatrix}. \quad (14)$$

We define the population vector for year i as:

$$\underline{x}_i = \begin{bmatrix} M_i \\ F_i \\ Y_i \end{bmatrix}. \qquad (15)$$

The equation $x_{i+1} = Ax_i$ constitutes the basic population model and can be used to step the population vector through time. If A has a dominant eigenvalue, λ, which is larger than all other eigenvalues, then the population will ultimately grow at the finite annual rate λ. In addition, the population structure will ultimately be defined by the right eigenvector, v, associated with λ. The application of theory based on the existence of a dominant eigenvalue seems reasonable when projection matrix parameters represent empirically based estimates (see Werner and Caswell 1977:1107), as is true with our matrix.

The dominant eigenvalue and its corresponding right eigenvector for the mallard projection matrix were approximated iteratively (e.g., Searle 1966:182–184). Computed values for the eigenvalue and eigenvector were $\lambda = 1.24$ and $v = (0.558, 0.412, 1.000)$, respectively. The $\lambda = 1.24$ represents the finite annual rate of increase that a population characterized by the constant parameters of the projection matrix would ultimately attain. The long-term average rate of increase for any extant animal population must eventually approach 1.0 (see Reddingius and den Boer 1970:282), and the parameters producing the 1.24 value thus appear to be unreasonable. The parameters were estimated from data covering the period 1961–74, and the geometric mean of the realized annual rates of increase over that period (as computed directly from Breeding Ground Survey population estimates) was 0.998. Thus, the transient behavior of the population over the period of interest was quite similar to that expected over the ecological long run. Of course, the values used in the projection matrix were merely estimates, and sampling error was associated with all of them. In addition, the actual parameters themselves may have varied over the period of estimation. It is important to remember that the projection matrix λ only applies, in the strict sense, to a population exhibiting an asymptotic age-sex structure corresponding to v, and that it is highly unlikely that such a structure existed over the entire period of interest (if at all). Nevertheless, despite these disclaimers and potential sources of error, we were still somewhat disturbed because the projection matrix λ deviated rather considerably from 1.0, and we will return to this point later. Anderson (1975*a*:27–31) employed a similar approach (the structure of his matrix differed slightly from ours), with different parameter estimates obtained from data extending through 1970, and computed $\lambda = 1.06$. The parameter estimates that he used generally were lower than ours, and the resulting λ was thus closer to 1.0.

Another check on the consistency of the parameter estimates used in our matrix can be made by examining the September adult sex ratio which it defines. The asymptotic adult sex ratio is obtained from the first two elements of the eigenvector, v, and is approximately 0.575 (proportion male) or 1.35 adult males per adult female. Modeling efforts by Anderson (1975*a*) have yielded values of 1.21 and 1.27 adult males per adult female, and a modeling effort by Johnson and Sargeant (1977:21) suggested that the fall sex ratio of mallards must be 'more highly distorted' than their spring ratio of 1.26. Anderson et al. (1970) used banding and recovery data as well as Parts Collection Survey data to estimate a preseason sex ratio for North American mallards of 1.52 adult males per adult female. We used the same methodology of Anderson et al. (1970) with more recent data and obtained an estimate of 1.39 adult males per adult female. Thus, our asymptotic sex ratio seems generally consistent with our estimates.

Year-specific Projection Model.—Our second approach to examining the internal consistency of the estimated population parameters was quite similar to the first and again involved the use of a deterministic population projection model. In this case we were interested in using annual survival and recruitment rate estimates to project May population sizes for comparison with Breeding Ground Survey results. Before presenting the model we define model parameters as follows:

$M_{m,i}$ = number of adult males present in the population in May of year i

$M_{s,i}$ = number of adult males present in the population in September of year i

$F_{m,i}$ = number of adult females present in the population in May of year i

$F_{s,i}$ = number of adult females present in the population in September of year i

$N_{s,i}$ = number of young males present in the population in September of year i

$W_{s,i}$ = number of young females present in the population in September of year i

$S_{AM,i}$ = annual survival probability for an adult male in year i

$S_{AF,i}$ = annual survival probability for an adult female in year i

$S_{YM,i}$ = annual survival probability for a young male in year i

$S_{YF,i}$ = annual survival probability for a young female in year i

α_{AM} = exponent specifying the proportion of total annual mortality of adult males occurring during the period May–September

α_{AF} = exponent specifying the proportion of total annual mortality of adult females occurring during the period May–September

P_i = annual recruitment rate of year i, expressed as number of young birds per adult in the population in September

R = sex ratio of young birds in September, expressed as proportion male.

Given these definitions, we can specify a simple population model with the following state equations:

$$M_{s,i} = M_{m,i}(S_{AM,i-1})^{\alpha_{AM}} \quad (16)$$

$$F_{s,i} = F_{m,i}(S_{AF,i-1})^{\alpha_{AF}} \quad (17)$$

$$N_{s,i} = RP_i(M_{s,i} + F_{s,i}) \quad (18)$$

$$W_{s,i} = (1 - R)P_i(M_{s,i} + F_{s,i}) \quad (19)$$

$$M_{m,i+1} = M_{s,i}(S_{AM,i})^{(1-\alpha_{AM})} + (N_{s,i}S_{YM,i})/(S_{AM,i})^{\alpha_{AM}} \quad (20)$$

$$F_{m,i+1} = F_{s,i}(S_{AF,i})^{(1-\alpha_{AF})} + (W_{s,i}S_{YF,i})/(S_{AF,i})^{\alpha_{AF}}. \quad (21)$$

The first two equations simply define the number of adult birds alive in the population in September, as functions of adults alive in May and the survival probabilities of the May–September interval. The third and fourth equations define the number of young birds in the population in September, as functions of annual recruitment rate, sex ratio of young, and number of adults alive in the population in September. The last two equations define the number of adult birds alive in

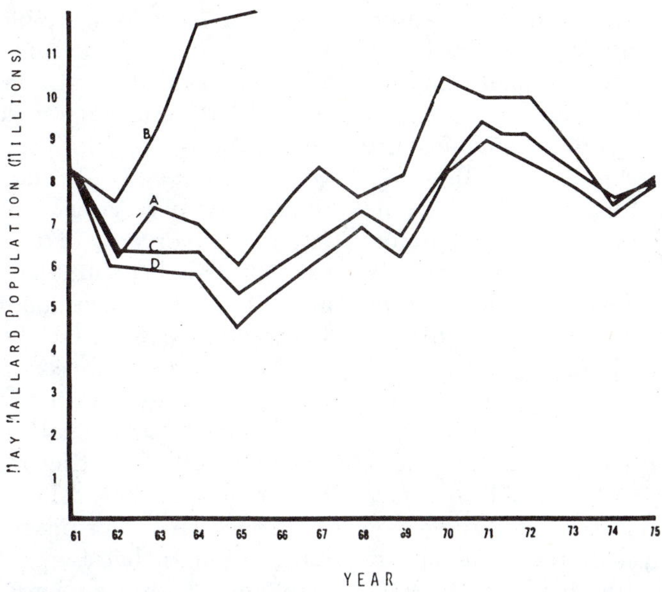

Fig. 12. Comparison of projected May population sizes of mallards (*Anas platyrhynchos*) (see model equations 16–21) with Breeding Ground Survey estimates. Plot A represents Breeding Ground Survey estimates. Plot B represents the projection obtained using annual survival and recruitment estimates. Plot C is the projection obtained using unaltered survival rates and reduced (42%) recruitment rates. Plot D represents the projection obtained using unaltered recruitment rates and reduced (21%) survival rates.

May as functions of September–May survival rates and the number of adults and young present in the population in September of the previous year. Young birds are assumed to achieve adulthood in May of their first year, and the last two equations thus include the assumption that adult survival rates apply to first-year birds during the May–September interval.

Annual continental recruitment and survival rates were estimated as described for the matrix model. However, annual point estimates were used in these projections, rather than the average annual estimates of the matrix model. Information on the seasonal partitioning of mortality in mallards is virtually nonexistent, and appropriate values for α_{AM} and α_{AF} were not known. We chose $\alpha_{AM} = 0.50$ and $\alpha_{AF} = 0.70$. These values correspond approximately to the relative seasonal breakdown of annual mortality hypothesized by Johnson and Sargeant (1977:15). Model projections using various other values of α_{AM} and α_{AF} suggested that the model was fairly robust to biologically reasonable changes in these parameters, with respect to population size.

Initial conditions required by the model included a May population size and sex ratio. All projections covered the period 1961–75 and were thus initiated with the May 1961 breeding population estimate of 8.29 million mallards. A spring sex ratio of 1.28 males per female was assumed for the 1961 population. This value represented somewhat of a compromise between sex ratios presented in Anderson et al. (1970), Anderson (1975*a*), and Johnson and Sargeant (1977), but corresponds closely to the 1.26 value presented in the latter report. Experimental projections with varied initial sex ratios suggested that the model was robust with respect to biologically reasonable changes in this initial condition.

Results of three model projections are presented with a plot of actual Breeding Ground Survey estimates in Fig. 12. The projection employing estimates of annual recruitment and survival rates (plot B) deviated considerably from the population estimates, yielding May population sizes that were too high. Again, it would be naive to expect model projections using parameter estimates to mimic empirical estimates too closely. Nevertheless, results of this simple modeling effort, like those of the matrix model, suggested that either survival or recruitment estimates or both were probably too high. In an effort to investigate the magnitude of the bias that may have existed in the parameter estimates, we determined the amount by which estimates would have to be reduced in order to produce reasonable projections. The appropriateness of the reduction factors was determined simply by examining the product-moment correlation coefficient between projected data and May estimates. The highest correlation coefficients were produced with unaltered recruitment rates by reducing all annual survival rates by approximately 21% (Fig. 12, plot D). When annual survival rates were not altered, a reduction in annual recruitment rates of approximately 42% was required to produce the most reasonable projection (Fig. 12, plot C). It is possible that both survival and recruitment rate estimates are too high and that the appropriate reduction factors are lower than the two extremes presented here.

Continental recruitment rate estimates are generally thought to be fairly good. However, as with all continental estimates derived from banding and recovery data, there is a problem associated with the lack of adequate banding in some areas of the continent. Differences in mallard reproduction apparently do occur among geographic areas (e.g., Calverley and Boag 1977), and such variation in areas with varying banding representation may serve to bias recruitment estimates. The distribution of banded birds also affects the representativeness of the survival rate estimates. In addition, another source of bias in survival estimates has been noted by Anderson (1975*a*:28–31) and involves problems associated with reporting rate differences near banding sites. After correcting for differences in reporting rates, Anderson (1975*a*) found that average survival rate estimates of adult mallards decreased by approximately 1%, while those of young birds decreased about 3%. Of course, this relatively small bias is not equivalent to the 21% required to produce reasonable model projections with unaltered recruitment rates. Currently, we have not resolved the problem associated with high parameter estimates. We intend to examine the effect of reporting rate differences on our survival estimates more closely. In addition, the comparison of these survival estimates with those obtained from winter banded birds should provide a further check on survival rates.

Despite the bias believed to be associated with the recruitment and/or survival rates, it is still of interest to ask if observed annual fluctuations in May population estimates seem to be more closely associated with annual survival or recruitment rates. This question was superficially addressed by using the projection with the reduced (21%) survival rates and unaltered recruitment rates as a basis for comparison with projections using survival and recruitment estimates averaged over all years (the estimates used in the projection matrix). For the original projection with reduced survival estimates (Fig. 12, plot D), the correlation coefficient between projected population sizes and May population estimates was $r \simeq 0.84$. When average survival rates for each age-sex class computed over all years were substituted for the annual survival rates, the resulting projection yielded $r \simeq 0.82$. Thus, the use of average survival rates in the model did not greatly reduce the ability of the projections to mimic May population estimates. However, when the average recruitment rate of 1.03 was used in conjunction with the annual survival estimates, the resulting projection did not mimic May population fluctuations nearly as well ($r \simeq 0.64$). Annual recruitment rates thus seem to be more important than annual survival rates in projecting population patterns that resemble actual May population fluctuations.

Functional Relationships

Once a reasonable set of parameter estimates is obtained, it becomes possible to investigate factors associated with variation in these parameters. Indeed, most of the science involved with managing a natural animal population is associated with investigating the functional relationships that underlie population fluctuations and in developing the ability to predict population changes.

Relationship Between Regulations and Mallard Harvest.—The annual harvest of mallards in the United States has varied from a low of 2.7 million to a high of 5.3 million during the period 1952–77. The mallard harvest in Canada ranged from 1.3 million to slightly over 2 million since 1967. The goal of regulating harvest is to make certain that removal by hunting is not, in itself, the factor limiting the capability of a population to respond to available habitat. To this end, a wide range of regulatory elements has been used to influence harvest. Among these are shooting hours, framework dates, season lengths, split seasons, special seasons, zoning, designation of opening days, bag limits, area and species closures, and harvest quotas. It is of considerable interest and importance to understand the effect of these hunting regulations on harvest rates, survival rates, and size and composition of the mallard harvest.

It is often impossible to isolate the effect of changing one element of regulations, since several are often changed simultaneously. Season length and bag limits are generally considered the most important variables affecting the harvest. In addition to limiting harvest opportunity, short seasons and low bag limits discourage hunters who have only a marginal interest in hunting from participating at all. Simple linear regression analyses with season length as the independent variable account for a large proportion of the variation in annual mallard harvest. For the period 1961–76 these models had correlation coefficients of .77, .91, and .88 for the Pacific, Central, and Mississippi Flyways, respectively. When interpreting these results, however, it must be remembered that season length is determined to some extent by the number of mallards judged to be available for harvest.

Effects of historic regulations on the size and sex composition of the mallard harvest have been investigated in some detail by Martin and Carney (1977). Their analyses suggested that sex composition is affected by sex-specific bag limit regulations and possibly by actual dates of the hunting season. Daily bag limits, season length, season dates, and opening day characteristics (time of day,

day of week) were all believed to affect the size of the annual mallard harvest. Despite these conclusions, however, an attempt to develop a predictive equation describing the relationship between harvest and various aspects of regulations met with little success (Martin and Carney 1977:73).

Relationship Between Hunting Effort, Population Size, and the Mallard Harvest.—Recently, we investigated mallard harvest as a function of hunting effort and population size. The relationship employed was a modification of a production equation described by Beverton and Holt (1957:49). Harvest was hypothesized to be dependent upon hunting effort and the number of adult mallards in the fall, as described in the following relationship:

$$B_t = (1/N_t + c/E_t)^{-1}, \qquad (22)$$

where: B_t = harvest of adult mallards in the United States in year t as estimated using Mail Questionnaire Survey results

N_t = fall population of adult mallards

E_t = hunting effort (thousands of hunter-days afield) as estimated from the Mail Questionnaire Survey.

This model is realistic in that the upper limit of harvest is the number of adults in the population and the simplicity adds to its usefulness. We used data for the years 1961–76 since parts collection information was first available from the 1961 hunting season. The parameter, c, was estimated using a Gauss-Newton nonlinear least squares algorithm. Results are summarized as follows:

$$B_t = (1/N_t + 0.6396/E_t)^{-1}$$
$$r \simeq .98 \qquad (P < .01).$$

The model accounts for a large proportion of the variation in the annual harvest (97%), but as previously mentioned many extrinsic variables such as season length and bag limit, and their effect on hunter participation, are not explicitly included.

Relationship Between Regulations and Recovery Rates.—One simple approach to investigating the effects of regulations on mallard harvest rates and survival rates is to compare parameter estimates obtained during years characterized by dissimilar regulations. This approach alleviates the need to describe regulations in terms of numerous component variables and permits a general characterization of annual regulations as either 'liberal' (conducive to a large harvest) or 'restrictive.' Anderson and Burnham (1976) have used this approach, as well as others, to examine the relationship between regulations and mallard survival rates (see subsequent discussion). Here, we employ this approach to investigate the regulations-harvest rate relationship.

Characterization of annual regulations as being either liberal or restrictive is, to some extent, subjective, so only years representing extremes in regulations were used. For comparative purposes, we chose the same years selected by Anderson and Burnham (1976) for their survival rate tests. The years 1964 and 1970 were categorized as liberal (longer seasons, greater daily bag limits) and 1962, 1965, and 1968 were classified as restrictive. Detailed information on mallard regulations for these years is presented in Martin and Carney (1977), whereas summary data intended to justify the liberal-restrictive classification are provided by Anderson and Burnham (1976:22).

As previously discussed, harvest rates are estimated as the quotient of recovery rates divided by band reporting rates. Because of the well-developed theory as-

Table 4. Results of testing the hypothesis that mallard recovery rates were greater during years of liberal harvest regulations (1964, 1970) than during years of restrictive regulations (1962, 1965, 1968).

Reference area[a]		Test statistic (z value)[b]			
		Adult		Young	
Name	Code	Male	Female	Male	Female
SW Alberta	031	−0.00	—	0.08	—
NE Southern Alberta–SW Saskatchewan	041	−6.16**	−3.44**	−4.00**	−4.70**
SW Manitoba	061	—	−1.11	—	−1.01
E Ontario–W Quebec	081	—	−0.07	—	—
E Washington	092	—	−0.75	—	0.05
E Oregon	094	−2.25*	0.13	−3.24**	−1.79*
N California	101	−0.88	−2.67**	1.84	—
Idaho	111	−3.71**	−0.46	−1.06	0.28
E Colorado	126	−1.07	—	—	—
E North Dakota	131	−5.06**	−3.00**	−2.55**	−1.78*
E South Dakota	132	−5.24**	−3.10**	−0.99	−0.70
W Minnesota	133	−4.53**	−5.05**	−6.25**	−5.34**
Michigan–N Ohio–N Indiana	143	−1.74*	−0.89	−1.95*	−2.70**
Western Mid-Atlantic	151	−1.10	−0.43	−1.57	0.19
NE United States	161	1.94	−0.24	−0.90	−0.67
n (areas tested)		12	13	11	11
$\Sigma z_i/\sqrt{n}$ (composite test statistic)		−8.60**	−5.85**	−6.21**	−5.48**

[a] Reference areas are defined in Anderson and Henny (1972).

[b] The z_i statistics (Brownie *et al.* 1978:180–182) were computed for each reference area i, as

$$z_i = (\hat{f}_R - \hat{f}_L)/\sqrt{[\hat{V}ar(\hat{f}_R) + \hat{V}ar(\hat{f}_L)]},$$

where $\hat{f}_R$ and $\hat{f}_L$ denote the mean annual recovery rate estimates for 1962, 1965, 1968 and 1964, 1970, respectively. $\hat{V}$ar denotes sampling variance. One-tailed tests were used.

* $0.01 < P < 0.05$; ** $P < 0.01$.

sociated with recovery rate estimation, we prefer to use recovery rate estimates rather than harvest rate estimates for hypothesis testing. We thus assumed that harvest rate differences would be reflected by similar differences in recovery rates.

Recovery rate estimates were obtained for mallard breeding reference areas (Anderson and Henny 1972) using banding and recovery data, and methodology summarized in Brownie et al. (1978). We used z statistics (Brownie et al. 1978:180–182) in conjunction with one-tailed tests to test the hypothesis that recovery rates were lower during years of restrictive regulations than during years of liberal regulations. The z statistics were computed for each mallard age-sex category and reference area for which recovery rate estimates for the five selected years could be computed. Results indicated that recovery rates were indeed lower during the restrictive years, as compared with the liberal years, in a number of reference areas for specific age-sex classes (Table 4). Composite test statistics (see Anderson and Burnham, 1976:32) were computed over all areas for each age-sex class, and they suggested that recovery rates were significantly lower during restrictive years in all classes.

Relationship Between Hunting and Survival Rates.—Perhaps the most important question regarding the management of migratory game birds concerns the effect of hunting on survival rates. This subject has been thoroughly addressed by Anderson and Burnham (1976), and here we briefly summarize results of their four types of hypothesis tests. First, they used banding and recovery data to test the null hypothesis that mallard survival rates remained constant from year to year, given that recovery rates varied over time (Anderson and Burnham 1976:20–21). Likelihood ratio tests (Brownie and Robson 1974*b*) of models embodying the null and alternative hypotheses indicated rejection of the null hypothesis for all age-sex classes. Thus, it was concluded that survival rates did vary over time, although hunting was not necessarily a causal factor. Anderson and Burnham (1976:22–25) next selected survival rate estimates for years of restrictive and liberal regulations and computed z statistics to test the null hypothesis that survival rates during years of liberal regulations were not lower than those during restrictive regulations. Composite test statistics indicated that the null hypothesis could not be rejected for any age-sex class. Liberal regulations thus did not appear to result in lower survival rates during the years tested.

Anderson and Burnham (1976:25–31) then used a linear model ($V = V_0 + bK$) to express natural mortality rate (V) as a function of hunting mortality rate (K). The term V_0 denotes natural mortality rate in the absence of hunting, while b represents the slope of the relationship. If hunting mortality is completely compensated for by decreases in natural mortality then $b = -1$. However, if hunting represents a completely additive form of mortality then b should assume a value close to 0. Anderson and Burnham (1976:25–31) estimated b from banding and recovery data and concluded that it was significantly different from the slope expected under the completely additive hypothesis, but not from the -1 expected under the completely compensatory hypothesis. Their final test involved the use of an index of harvest rate derived from estimates of total U.S. harvest (from the Mail Questionnaire Survey and Parts Collection Survey) and total spring population size (from the Breeding Ground Survey). Simple linear correlation analysis was then used to examine the relationship between this harvest rate index and continental survival rate estimates (Anderson and Burnham 1976:31–33). No significant relationship was found. We repeated this analysis using more recent data and similarly found no significant relationship. In summary, results of the analyses of Anderson and Burnham (1976) strongly indicate that hunting does not represent a completely additive form of mortality. Some of their results suggest that hunting may represent a largely compensatory form of mortality.

Predicting Fall Mallard Populations

In August of each year, the U.S. Department of the Interior establishes duck hunting regulations for the subsequent fall and winter. The size of mallard populations expected to exist in the fall (e.g., September) is one of the most important factors considered in the development of mallard regulations. However, the size of the September population is not known in August and must be predicted from data collected during previous months (May–July). For predictive purposes, the September population can be divided into two components, surviving adults and young of the year.

Recruitment Rates.—The number of young in the fall of year t cannot actually be estimated until after the hunting season of year t. Here, we will discuss two models used to predict young of the year present in the fall population from data obtained during May–July. Reproduction in any population can be thought of as a function of factors both intrinsic and extrinsic to the population. For an extensively distributed continental population such as that of the North American mallard, the only intrinsic characteristic of the population that can be reasonably estimated at the time of breeding and nesting is total numbers, and it is certainly reasonable to model reproduction as a function of this parameter. With respect to extrinsic factors, field studies have repeatedly demonstrated the importance of spring and summer water conditions to mallard reproduction (e.g., Mayhew 1955; Stoudt 1969, 1971; Smith 1971; Dzubin and Gollop 1972). On a continental basis, a positive relationship between the number of July ponds in the southern Prairie Provinces of Canada and continental mallard recruitment was demonstrated by Crissey (1969). Thus, both July ponds and spring population size can be used to predict recruitment. One additional parameter that relates directly to recruitment (it is actually an index to recruitment) is the Brood Index for the southern Prairie Provinces from the July Production Survey.

Two basic models are used annually to predict mallard recruitment. The models perform well and generally yield very similar predictions. The first model is linear and is expressed as:

$$\hat{Y}_t = a + bB_t + cP_t + dN_t, \qquad (23)$$

where $\hat{Y}_t$ is the predicted number of fall young (in millions) in year t, B_t represents the July Brood Index (thousands) for the southern Prairie Provinces in year t, P_t denotes the number (in millions) of July ponds in the southern Prairie Provinces in year t, N_t is May population size (millions) in year t, and a, b, c, and d are model constants. Data on $\hat{Y}_t$, B_t, P_t, and N_t are available since 1955. Each July, data from an additional year are added, and the constants a, b, c, and d are estimated using stepwise multiple regression analysis. Using data for the period 1955–77, this basic linear model yielded $r^2 \simeq 0.83$, which was significant ($P < 0.01$). Geis et al. (1969) discussed the use of a similar linear model.

Table 5. Predicted and empirically estimated[a] production rates (fall age ratios expressed as immatures/adult) for mallards, 1967–77.

Year	Recruitment rate		Year	Recruitment rate	
	Prediction	Estimate		Prediction	Estimate
1967	0.8–1.0	1.1	1973	0.8	1.0
1968	0.7	0.8	1974	1.4	1.4
1969	1.2	1.5	1975	1.3	1.1
1970	1.2	0.9	1976	1.1	1.1
1971	0.9–1.0	1.0	1977	0.9–1.0	0.7
1972	0.9	0.9			

[a] The empirical estimate is obtained by adjusting the age ratio of the harvest (obtained from the Parts Collection and Harvest Surveys) for differential age-specific vulnerability (obtained as the ratio of young to adult recovery rates estimated from banding data).

The other predictive model is nonlinear and was adapted for use with mallards by Hammack and Brown (1974) from a general production model suggested by Beverton and Holt (1957:49). The general model is expressed as:

$$\hat{Y}_t = (1/aP_t^{\,b} + c/N_t)^{-1}, \qquad (24)$$

where $\hat{Y}_t$, P_t, and N_t are defined as in the linear model, and a, b, and c are model constants. The ecological implications of this model and its underlying rationale are discussed in Hammack and Brown (1974), Anderson (1975*a,b*), and Brown et al. (1976). Briefly, the model implies that recruitment of mallard young is a function of both important environmental factors ($aP_t^{\,b}$) and the size of the breeding population (c/N_t). For a fixed number of ponds, the number of young increases and approaches an environmentally determined asymptote ($aP_t^{\,b}$) as breeding population size increases. However, the rate of recruitment decreases with increasing breeding population size. The hypotheses about environmental limitation and density dependence implied by the recruitment model thus are quite reasonable from an ecological viewpoint. As with the linear model, data for use in the estimation of model parameters are available since 1955. Similarly, upon inclusion of data from an additional year each July, model parameters are estimated via a Gauss-Newton nonlinear least squares algorithm. Using data for the period 1955–77, the algorithm yielded $r^2 \approx .96$, which was significant ($P < .01$).

We chose not to present parameter estimates for the two general models because of their dynamic nature. Each year, the inclusion of data from an additional year results in new model parameters. In most years, predictions from thse two general models agree reasonably well. In years for which different predictions are obtained, either a range of possible recruitment rates is used or a choice is made based on other relevant biological information. Predicted and empirically estimated recruitment rates for the years 1967–77 are presented for comparison in Table 5.

Total Fall Population.—As mentioned earlier, the total fall mallard population can be subdivided into two components (young and adults) for predictive purposes. The number of adults present in the fall population can be represented as the product of the number of adults present in May, and the summer adult survival rate during the period May–September. The number of adults present in May is estimated annually in the Breeding Ground Survey. However, we currently know of no model which is useful in predicting seasonal or even annual survival as a function of either intrinsic factors such as population size or extrinsic factors such as environmental variables. Thus, our best estimates of annual survival rate are sex-specific, continental averages (i.e., the average survival rates used in the matrix model).

The total fall (September) mallard population in year i ($T_{s,i}$) can be expressed as:

$$T_{s,i} = Y_{s,i} + M_{s,i} + F_{s,i}, \qquad (25)$$

where $Y_{s,i}$, $M_{s,i}$, and $F_{s,i}$ denote the numbers of young, adult males, and adult females, respectively, present during September of year i. We have already outlined two models used to predict $Y_{s,i}$. Retaining the notation of the previously described population projection models, we can write:

$$M_{s,i} = M_{m,i}(S_{AM,i-1})^{\alpha}AM, \qquad (26)$$
$$F_{s,i} = F_{m,i}(S_{AF,i-1})^{\alpha}AF, \qquad (27)$$

where $M_{m,i}$ and $F_{m,i}$ denote May populations of adult males and females, respectively, and $(S_{AM,i-1})^{\alpha}AM$ and $(S_{AF,i-1})^{\alpha}AF$ denote the May–September survival rates of adult males and females, respectively. Thus, equations (23), (24), (26), and (27) are used, in conjunction with equation (25), to predict the fall mallard population. Although there are no empirical estimates of the fall mallard population with which to compare the predictions, there has been a high degree of subjective agreement between forecasted fall populations and harvest during the subsequent hunting seasons.

SUMMARY

More than 700 species of migratory birds occur in North America, constituting a renewable resource of great economic, recreational, and aesthetic value. The harvest of migratory game birds by hunters in the United States is now estimated to exceed 68 million birds annually. The varied economic and social values, widespread distribution, migratory habits, behavior, and population and morphological differences among the many species pose unique and complex problems in their management and conservation. Historically, management efforts have been primarily directed toward migratory game birds.

The goals of managing migratory bird species can be stated rather simply in terms of some desired abundance, which is influenced by four fundamental variables: recruitment, mortality, immigration, and emigration. Since we often focus on continental populations, immigration, and emigration are considered inconsequential and management efforts are directed toward influencing recruitment and mortality. However, the major difficulty is to evaluate the effects of various management policies and programs on the fundamental demographic variables. These variables differ markedly over time, among geographic areas, and among the various age and sex categories in a population. Past and present management activities have emphasized the control of hunting, and habitat protection and enhancement.

Extensive survey programs have been developed to annually estimate population size, recruitment, and survival. In many instances several species are censused simultaneously during one survey, whereas other surveys are oriented toward single species. Some waterfowl surveys are based on well-founded statistical designs involving direct counts of individual birds, while other surveys result in an index to relative abundance. Population estimates of many species are also obtained in concentration areas without the benefit of a designed sampling scheme. Recruitment is estimated each year, either directly or indirectly by various methods. Most efforts to estimate survival involve a series of marking and recapture or recovery experiments. Harvest surveys of some migratory game birds are conducted each year to provide some information regarding the size of harvest of these species. Data from harvest surveys are also used to estimate recruitment and to aid in determining relationships between hunter activity and success and annual game bird abundance.

Since the mallard is abundant and highly sought by hunters, it has received more attention than any other North American migratory bird species. Also, more data have been accumulated for mallards than for any other species. We describe the various parameters that have been estimated for continental mallard populations and our efforts to understand the dynamics of this species. Two population models are described which indicate that estimates of survival and/or recruitment may be too high. Some potential sources of bias have been identified and these will receive greater attention in the future. Since sex ratios derived from the matrix model appear to agree well with other modeling and empirical approaches, the relationship between parameters seems reasonable. Functional relationships between mallard population parameters and various elements of the hunting program are discussed. The size of the mallard harvest can be described very well in terms of regulations, hunter activity, and mallard abundance, but the absolute effect of hunting on mallard survival rates is not explicitly understood. The number of young in the fall mallard population is predicted from estimates of May population size, brood indices, and the number of July ponds in southern Canada. Adults in the fall mallard population are then predicted from estimates of May population size and average adult survival rates.

ACKNOWLEDGMENTS

We gratefully acknowledge assistance from the following people in preparation of this paper: Chandler S. Robbins and Danny R. Bystrak provided material dealing with the Breeding Bird Survey; James E. Hines and Sharon L. Rhoades provided programming and computational assistance; Rebecca C. Perry, Ethel A. Chapman, and Marylu Lammers typed the manuscript.

LITERATURE CITED

ALDRICH, J. W. 1973. Disparate sex ratios in waterfowl. *In* Breeding biology of birds: proceedings of a symposium on breeding behavior and reproductive physiology in birds, D. S. Farner, ed. National Academy of Sciences, Washington, D.C. Pages 482–489.

ANDERSON, D. R. 1972. Bibliography on methods of analyzing bird banding data. U.S. Fish and Wildlife Service, Special Scientific Report, Wildlife No. 156.

———. 1975*a*. Population ecology of the mallard. V. Temporal and geographic estimates of survival, recovery, and harvest rates. U.S. Fish and Wildlife Service, Resource Publication 125.

———. 1975*b*. Optimal exploitation strategies for an animal population in a Markovian environment: a theory and an example. Ecology 56:1281–1297.

———, AND K. P. BURNHAM. 1976. Population ecology of the mallard. VI. The effect of exploitation on survival. U.S. Fish and Wildlife Service, Resource Publication 128.

———, AND C. J. HENNY. 1972. Population ecology of the mallard. I. A review of previous studies and the distribution and migration from breeding areas. U.S. Fish and Wildlife Service, Resource Publication 105.

———, R. S. POSPAHALA, H. M. REEVES, J. P. ROGERS, AND W. F. CRISSEY. 1970. Estimates of the sex composition of the 1967–69 mallard population. U.S. Bureau of Sport Fisheries and Wildlife, Migratory Bird Populations Station Administrative Report 182.

———, AND R. T. STERLING. 1974. Population dynamics of molting pintail drakes banded in south-central Saskatchewan. Journal of Wildlife Management 38:266–274.

ARNASON, A. N. 1973. The estimation of population size, migration rates, and survival in a stratified population. Researches on Population Ecology 15:1–8.

ARTMANN, J. W. 1977. Woodcock status report, 1976. U.S. Fish and Wildlife Service, Special Scientific Report, Wildlife No. 209.

BASKETT, T. S., M. J. ARMBRUSTER, AND M. W. SAYRE. 1978. Biological perspectives for the mourning dove call-count survey. Transactions of the North American Wildlife and Natural Resources Conferences, 43. In Press.

BELLROSE, F. C., JR. 1955. A comparison of recoveries from reward and standard bands. Journal of Wildlife Management 19:71–75.

———, T. G. SCOTT, A. S. HAWKINS, AND J. B. LOW. 1961. Sex ratios and age ratios in North American ducks. Illinois Natural History Survey Bulletin 27:391–474.

BENNING, D. S., S. L. RHOADES, L. D. SCHROEDER, AND M. M. SMITH. 1978. Waterfowl status report, 1974. U.S. Fish and Wildlife Service, Special Scientific Report, Wildlife No. 211.

BERNARDELLI, H. 1941. Population waves. Journal of the Burma Research Society 31:1–18.

BEVERTON, R. J. H., AND S. J. HOLT. 1957. On the dynamics of exploited fish populations. Her Majesty's Stationery Office, London.

BOTKIN, D. B., AND R. S. MILLER. 1974. Mortality rates and survival of birds. American Naturalist 108:181–192.

BOWDEN, D. C. 1973. Review and evaluation of May waterfowl breeding ground survey. Unpublished manuscript. 74pp.

BOYD, H. 1956. Statistics of the British population of the pink-footed goose. Journal of Animal Ecology 25:253–273.

BROWN, D. E., AND R. H. SMITH. 1976. Predicting hunting success from call counts of mourning and white-winged doves. Journal of Wildlife Management 40:743–749.

BROWN, G. M., JR., J. HAMMACK, AND M. F. TILLMAN. 1976. Mallard population dynamics and management models. Journal of Wildlife Management 40:542–555.

BROWNIE, C., D. R. ANDERSON, K. P. BURNHAM, AND D. S. ROBSON. 1978. Statistical inference from band recovery data: A handbook. U.S. Fish and Wildlife Service, Resource Publication 130.

———, AND D. S. ROBSON. 1974*a*. Models allowing for age-dependent survival rates for band-return data. Biometrics Unit, Cornell University, Ithaca, New York. BU-514-M.

———, AND ———. 1974*b*. Testing for equality of the annual survival rates in the SRY model for band return data. Biometrics Unit, Cornell University, Ithaca, New York. BU-515-M.

———, AND ———. 1976. Models allowing for age-dependent survival rates for band return data. Biometrics 32:305–323.

BYSTRAK, D., AND C. S. ROBBINS. 1977. Bird population trends detected by the North American Breeding Bird Survey. Polish Ecological Studies 3:131–143.

CALVERLEY, B. K., AND D. A. BOAG. 1977. Reproductive potential in parkland- and arctic-nesting populations of mallards and pintails (Anatidae). Canadian Journal of Zoology 55:1242–1251.

CHAMBERLAIN, E. B., D. S. BENNING, E. L. FERGUSON, M. M. SMITH, AND J. L. HALL. 1972. Waterfowl status report, 1972. U.S. Fish and Wildlife Service, Special Scientific Report, Wildlife No. 166.

CHAPMAN, D. G., AND D. S. ROBSON. 1960. The analysis of a catch curve. Biometrics 16:354–368.

CHARNOV, E. L. 1975. Sex ratio in an age-structured population. Evolution 29:366–368.

CORMACK, R. M. 1964. Estimates of survival from the sighting of marked animals. Biometrika 51:429–438.

———. 1968. The statistics of capture-recapture methods. Oceanographic Marine Biology Annual Review 6:455–506.

CRISSEY, W. F. 1969. Prairie potholes from a continental viewpoint. Saskatoon Wetlands Seminar, Canadian Wildlife Service Report Series No. 6. Pages 161–171.

CROFT, R. L., S. M. CARNEY, AND E. M. MARTIN. 1971. Waterfowl kill survey. *In* Waterfowl status report, 1970, E. B. Chamberlain, R. K. Martinson, and S. L. Clark, eds. U.S. Fish and Wildlife Service, Special Scientific Report, Wildlife No. 138. Pages 35–41.

CROW, J. F., AND M. KIMURA. 1970. An introduction to population genetics theory. Harper and Row, New York.

DARROCH, J. N. 1959. The multiple recapture census. II. Estimation when there is immigration or death. Biometrika 46:336–351.

———. 1961. The two sample capture-recapture census when tagging and sampling are stratified. Biometrika 48:241–260.

DEEVEY, E. S., JR. 1947. Life tables for natural populations of animals. Quarterly Review of Biology 22:283–314.

DOLTON, D. C. 1977. Mourning dove status report, 1976. U.S. Fish and Wildlife Service, Special Scientific Report, Wildlife No. 208.

DZUBIN, A., AND J. B. GOLLOP. 1972. Aspects of mallard breeding ecology in Canadian parkland and grassland. *In* Population ecology of migratory birds—A symposium. U.S. Fish and Wildlife Service, Wildlife Research Report 2. Pages 113–152.

ERSKINE, A. J. 1978. The first ten years of the cooperative Breeding Birds Survey in Canada. Canadian Wildlife Service Report Series No. 42.

FISHER, R. A. 1958. The genetical theory of natural selection, 2nd ed. Dover, New York.

GEIS, A. D., AND E. L. ATWOOD. 1961. Proportion of recovered waterfowl bands reported. Journal of Wildlife Management 25:154–159.

———, R. K. MARTINSON, AND D. R. ANDERSON. 1969. Establishing hunting regulations and allowable harvest of mallards in the United States. Journal of Wildlife Management 33:848–859.

GOLLOP, J. B., AND W. H. MARSHALL. 1954. A guide for ageing duck broods in the field. Mississippi Flyway Council Technical Section (mimeo).

HALDANE, J. B. S. 1955. The calculation of mortality rates from ringing data. Acta Congress International Ornithologists 11:454–458.

HAMMACK, J., AND G. M. BROWN, JR. 1974. Waterfowl and wetlands: toward bioeconomic analysis. Resources for the Future, Inc. Washington, D.C.

HAMMERSLEY, J. M. 1953. Capture-recapture analysis. Biometrika 40:265–278.

HAYNE, D. W. 1975. Experimental increase of mourning dove bag limit in eastern management unit. Southeastern Association of Game and Fish Commissioners, Technical Bulletin No. 2.

HENNY, C. J. 1967. Estimating band-reporting rates from banding and crippling loss data. Journal of Wildlife Management 31:533–538.

———, D. R. ANDERSON, AND R. S. POSPAHALA. 1972. Aerial surveys of waterfowl production in North America, 1955–71. U.S. Fish and Wildlife Service, Special Scientific Report, Wildlife No. 160.

———, AND K. P. BURNHAM. 1976. A reward band study of mallards to estimate band reporting rates. Journal of Wildlife Management 40:1–14.

HOPPER, R. M., H. D. FUNK, AND D. R. ANDERSON. 1978. Age specificity in mallards banded postseason in eastern Colorado. Journal of Wildlife Management 42:263–270.

JOHNSON, D. H. 1974. Estimating survival rates from banding adult and juvenile birds. Journal of Wildlife Management 38:290–297.

———, AND A. B. SARGEANT. 1977. Impact of red fox predation on the sex ratio of prairie mallards. U.S. Fish and Wildlife Service, Wildlife Research Report 6.

JOLLY, G. M. 1963. Estimates of population parameters from multiple recapture data with both death and dilution—Deterministic model. Biometrika 50:113–128.

———. 1965. Explicit estimates from capture-recapture data with both death and immigration—Stochastic model. Biometrika 52:225–247.

KROHN, W. B., F. W. MARTIN, AND K. P. BURNHAM. 1974. Band-recovery distribution and survival estimates of Maine woodcock. American Woodcock Workshop 5. Georgia Center for Continuing Education. University of Georgia, Athens. (mimeo).

LESLIE, P. H. 1945. On the use of matrices in certain population mathematics. Biometrika 33:183–212.

———. 1948. Some further notes on the use of matrices in population mathematics. Biometrika 35:213–245.

LEWIS, E. G. 1942. On the generation and growth of a population. Sankhyā 6:93–96.

MANLY, B. J. F., AND M. J. PARR. 1968. A new method of estimating population size, survivorship, and birth rate from capture-recapture data. Transactions for the Society for British Entomology 18:81–89.

MARTIN, E. M., AND S. M. CARNEY. 1977. Population ecology of the mallard. IV. A review of duck hunting regulations, activity, and success, with special reference to the mallard. U.S. Fish and Wildlife Service, Resource Publication 130.

MARTIN, F. W., A. D. GEIS, AND W. H. STICKEL. 1965. Results of woodcock wing collections, 1959 to 1962. Journal of Wildlife Management 29:121–131.

MARTINSON, R. K. 1966. Proportion of recovered duck bands that are reported. Journal of Wildlife Management 30:264–268.

———, AND J. A. MCCANN. 1966. Proportion of recovered goose and brant bands that are reported. Journal of Wildlife Management 30:856–858.

MAYHEW, W. W. 1955. Spring rainfall in relation to mallard production in the Sacramento Valley, California. Journal of Wildlife Management 19:36–47.

ORIANS, G. H. 1958. A capture-recapture analysis of a shearwater population. Journal of Animal Ecology 27:71–86.

POLLOCK, K. H. 1975. A K-sample tag-recapture model allowing for unequal survival and catchability. Biometrika 62:577–583.

POSPAHALA, R. S., D. R. ANDERSON, AND C. J. HENNY. 1974. Population ecology of the mallard. II. Breeding habitat conditions, size of the breeding population, and production indices. U.S. Fish and Wildlife Service, Resource Publication 115.

REDDINGIUS, J., AND P. J. DEN BOER. 1970. Simulation experiments illustrating stabilization of animal numbers by spreading of risk. Oecologia 5:240–284.

RICKLEFS, R. E. 1973. Fecundity, mortality, and avian demography. *In* Breeding biology of birds: proceedings of a symposium on breeding behavior and reproductive physiology in birds, D. S. Farner, ed. National Academy of Sciences, Washington, D.C. Pages 366–435.

ROBBINS, C. S., AND A. J. ERSKINE. 1975. Population trends in nongame birds in North America. Transactions of the North American Wildlife and Natural Resources Conference 40:288–293.

———, AND W. T. VAN VELZEN. 1967. The Breeding Bird Survey, 1966. U.S. Fish and Wildlife Service, Special Scientific Report, Wildlife No. 102.

ROBERTS, J. O. L. 1971. Survival among some North American wood warblers. Bird-Banding 42:165–184.

ROBSON, D. S. 1963. Maximum likelihood estimation of a sequence of annual survival rates from a capture-recapture series. *In* North Atlantic Fish Marking Symposium, International Commission of Northwest Atlantic Fisheries, Special Publication 4. Pages 330–335.

———. 1969. Mark-recapture methods of population estimation. *In* New Developments in Survey Sampling, N. L. Johnson and H. Smith, eds. Wiley, New York. Pages 120–140.

———, AND W. D. YOUNGS. 1971. Statistical analysis of reported tag-recaptures in the harvest from an exploited population. Biometrics Unit, Cornell University, Ithaca, New York. BU-369-M.

SEARLE, S. R. 1966. Matrix algebra for the biological sciences. Wiley, New York.

SEBER, G. A. F. 1962. The multi-sample single recapture census. Biometrika 49:339–350.

———. 1965. A note on the multiple recapture census. Biometrika 52:249–259.

———. 1970. Estimating time-specific survival and reporting rates for adult birds from band returns. Biometrika 57:313–318.

———. 1973. The estimation of animal abundance and related parameters. Griffin, London.

SMITH, A. G. 1971. Ecological factors affecting waterfowl production in the Alberta parklands. U.S. Fish and Wildlife Service, Resource Publication 98.

STOUDT, J. H. 1969. Relationships between waterfowl and water areas on the Redvers Waterfowl Study Area. Saskatoon Wetlands Seminar, Canadian Wildlife Service Report Series 6, Pages 123–131.

———. 1971. Ecological factors affecting waterfowl production in the Saskatchewan parklands. U.S. Fish and Wildlife Service, Resource Publication 99.

TAYLOR, S. M. 1966. Recent quantitative work on British bird populations. The Statistician 16:119–170.

TOMLINSON, R. E. 1968. Reward banding to determine reporting rate of recovered mourning dove bands. Journal of Wildlife Management 32:6–11.

U.S.D.I. 1975. Final environmental statement for the issuance of annual regulations permitting the sport hunting of migratory birds. U.S. Fish and Wildlife Serivce, Washington, D.C.

WERNER, P. A., AND H. CASWELL. 1977. Population growth rates and age versus stage-distribution models for teasel (*Dipsacus sylvestris* Huds.). Ecology 58:1103–1111.

WHITCOMB, D. A., AND A. BOURGEOIS. 1974. Studies of singing male surveys on High Island, Michigan. American Woodcock Workshop 5. Georgia Center for Continuing Education. University of Georgia, Athens. (mimeo).

CAN COUNTS OF GROUP SIZES OF CANADA GEESE REVEAL POPULATION STRUCTURE?[1]

DENNIS G. RAVELING[2]

Determination of annual reproductive success of Canada goose populations is one of several phases of data collection necessary for an understanding of population dynamics and for the implementing of effective harvest management. This is especially true when increasing knowledge of the identity of various population units and subspecies (Hanson and Smith 1950, Hanson 1965) has led to the development of differential regulations (quota zones, e.g.) and to recognition of the misleading nature of data representing a composite from two or more divergent populations.

Population structure is used here to indicate proportion of age classes (adults, yearlings, immatures) and proportion of breeding age adults successful in rearing a brood, and average brood size. Collection of data on population structure is a difficult task. Many nesting areas are remote, and it is presently difficult, if not impossible, to gather information on population structure before hunting. Present population statistics are usually based on age ratios of geese killed by hunters or live-trapped, combined with analyses of banding and harvest data. All these methods may introduce large bias to results (Hanson and Smith 1950:168, Nass 1964, Sherwood 1966, Raveling 1966, Martinson and McCann 1966). Furthermore, most data cannot be gathered until after large shooting losses have occurred. This makes extrapolation of results to prehunting estimates difficult.

Another method of gathering population composition data relies on visual identification of the size and number of families in a flock. Until recently, little conclusive evidence existed to prove the continuing unity of goose families (Boyd 1953:88), even though most authors accepted and utilized the concept of family cohesiveness. Recent studies with individually marked Canada geese have amply demonstrated the intact-unit nature of families (Martin 1964:9–10, Sherwood 1966:100–122, Raveling 1967:41–47). Because it had long been thought that geese maintained close family ties for almost a year, interest developed in methods of identifying families in a flock.

Phillips (1916) concluded that groups of flying Canada geese were families or aggregates of family units. Elder and Elder (1949) and Hanson and Smith (1950:152–153, 172) demonstrated that the frequency of different sizes of flying groups changed after hunting. They suggested that group counts might be used to assess production and hunting mortality. Hewit (1950) observed fall migrating blue and snow geese (*Anser caerulescens*) and substantiated the Elders' opinion that many small flocks were made up of families, but pointed out that the presence of nonbreeding adults in these flocks prevented determination of the average numbers of young per brood. Based on similar work with white-fronted geese (*Anser albifrons*), Lebret (1956) concluded that Elder and Elder (1949) had

[1] Originally published in R. Hine and C. Schoenfeld, eds. Canada goose management, pages 87–91. Dembar Educational Research Services, Inc., Madison, WI, 1968.

[2] Present address: Wildlife and Fisheries Biology, Univ. of California–Davis, Davis, CA 95616.

underestimated the abundance of nonbreeding geese and barren pairs and that group counts would not be useful indices to production or shooting losses. Hanson (1965:159) concluded that data from group counts were less reliable than results from trapping.

Lynch and Singleton (1964) formulated an extensive program of investigations on population dynamics based on group counts of blue, snow, and white-fronted geese in which immatures were identifiable in the field because of plumage differences. Unlike previous group counting efforts, Lynch and Singleton's method of identifying families involved the recording of functional groups in the period between breakup of larger flocks and actual landing. While landing groups were considered the first choice for such analyses, these authors also suggested that groups departing from a settled flock would be suitable, as would birds in the air, if they moved only a short distance and did not merge. Lynch and Singleton proposed that average group counts might reveal the percentage of young in a Canada goose flock.

The purpose of this paper is: (1) to report results of observation of Canada geese of known social status (i.e. single, pair, family) in their flight behavior; (2) evaluate techniques of counting groups; and (3) discuss what criteria and further data are necessary for meaningful utilization of group counts as a measure of production.

METHODS

Canada geese (*B. c. interior*) of known social status were regularly observed through the winters of 1963–64 and 1964–65 in their daily activities at Crab Orchard National Wildlife Refuge, Williamson County, Illinois. Individuals and families were color- and radio-marked. Details of these techniques and results relating to unity of families and other behavior may be found elsewhere (Raveling 1967). The marked geese were frequently observed at the moment of taking flight, and their formations during flight to and from feeding areas were observed through a spotting scope. Because Lynch and Singleton (1964) suggested that the group formation at the time of landing was most revealing of family size and relationships, much time was spent in attempting to view marked geese when landing. Most sightings were made at an observation post where some of the radio- and color-marked geese were known to be regularly feeding. The receiver was kept on and the frequency range continually scanned until a signal from a marked goose was heard. I then attempted to observe the goose (or family) descend and land.

RESULTS AND DISCUSSION

During this study it was apparent that counts of groups of geese in the air had little significance in determining average family size, percentage of singles, etc. Frequently, groups of geese in the air changed numbers. Numerous observations of the radio-and color-marked geese demonstrated that sizes of groups taking off or in flight often did not represent true family sizes or ratio of singles and pairs (Tables 1, 2). Even though family members flew next to each other, it was common for other nearby geese to take off at virtually the same time and several groups of singles often coalesced and flew with each other. This behavior causes higher than true average group sizes to be counted. Assuming that one would count only groups of 10 or less as families, the results of this study demonstrate that 75 percent of the time the true size of the group would be identified at take

Table 1. Behavior of radio- and color-marked Canada geese of known social status at the time of flight initiation.

Group	Number of observations	Number observations when individual or group at take-off was: Positively identified[a]	In a group of 10 or less or family was separated[b]	In a group of more than 10
Singles	36	19 (53%)	7 (19%)	10 (28%)
Pairs	8	4 (50%)	—	4 (50%)
Families of 3	21	12 (57%)	5 (24%)	4 (19%)
Families of 4	16	6 (38%)	5 (31%)	5 (31%)
Families of 5	25	20 (80%)	3 (12%)	2 (8%)
Totals	106	61 (58%)	20 (19%)	25 (23%)

[a] E.g., single took off as a single, family of 3 took off as a 3, etc.
[b] Occasionally there was slight delay and separation of family members at take off that might cause an unmarked group to be interpreted as 1 and a 3 instead of a 4, for example.

off and only 45 percent of the time would identification of a group in flight be correct.

Observations of marked geese landing, however, yielded different results. On 10 occasions geese known to be singles were observed landing and on 9 of these the bird landed alone. The other observation was inconclusive in that the goose landed when great numbers of other geese were alighting at the same time and group counts were impossible. On 6 of the 10 observations the marked single was observed while descending, and on 5 of these, it was in close formation with other geese, yet it veered off and landed as a single. Pairs were observed landing on 4 occasions and on 3 of these the individuals landed right next to each other. Once a pair was split about 15–20 feet and they settle on the ground at slightly different times and might have been counted as singles. A family of 3 was twice observed descending in a larger group, but the family separated and landed as a distinct group of 3. On both occasions the adult female made a quick turn and "braked" and the gander and young followed in unison. The other geese in the flock continued gliding and landed elsewhere. A family of 4 was observed landing on one occasion. They broke apart from a flock and landed as a closeknit unit. A family of 5 was twice observed landing as a distinct unit. On one of these occasions the family split from a flock as it glided in to land.

In summary, geese of known social status landed according to their functional group on 17 of 18 different observations.

Table 2. Behavior of radio- and color-marked Canada geese of known social status when in steady flight.

Group	Number of observations	Number observations when individual or group while flying was: Positively identified[a]	In a group of 10 or less	In a group of more than 10
Singles	22	5 (23%)	12 (54%)	5 (23%)
Pairs	5	2 (40%)	2 (40%)	1 (20%)
Families of 3	19	6 (31%)	8 (42%)	5 (27%)
Families of 4	16	4 (25%)	2 (12.5%)	10 (62.5%)
Families of 5	18	7 (39%)	5 (28%)	6 (33%)
Totals	80	24 (30%)	29 (36%)	27 (34%)

[a] E.g., single flying as a single, family of 3 flying as a 3, etc.

Table 3. Counts of landing groups of Canada geese at Crab Orchard National Wildlife Refuge, 1964–65.

Time period	No. of counts	Total no. geese counted (avg. per sample)	Median percent single geese (93% confidence limits)[a]	Median percent pairs (93% confidence limits)[a]	Median group size—groups of 3 or more[b] (93% confidence limits)[a]
Prior to hunting	10	4,195	9.4	17.1	4.12
Oct. 17–23		(420)	(8.6–10.1)	(16.9–19.5)	(4.02–4.13)
Range		244–601			
After hunting	10	5,746	20.1	25.1	3.78
Dec. 19–Jan. 2		(575)	(18.7–21.6)	(24.2–27.4)	(3.68–3.81)
Range		454–683			
Prior to spring migration	10	7,164	22.6	29.9	3.62
Feb. 22–Mar. 5		(716)	(20.8–23.7)	(28.3–30.5)	(3.60–3.64)
Range		499–949			

[a] Walker and Lev (1953:440).
[b] Only groups of 9 birds or less were considered families.

While limited, these results offer confirmation of Lynch and Singleton's (1964) method of analyzing family sizes based on geese at the moment of landing, but not at the time of take off or in steady flight.

Close unity at the moment of landing does not always occur, however. Once an unmarked family landed at the same time a single landed 25 or 30 yards away, and this family and single ran toward each other and met in a Triumph Ceremony, an almost positive indication of familial relationship (Raveling 1967:18–33). Nevertheless it appears that in the great majority of cases families land as close-knit units and split from unrelated geese. It was expected that family members would remain very close to each other, but not that multiples of families and singles flying together would almost always split apart completely enough to be identified. Singles apparently avoided landing right next to other geese with which they were flying. Family members apparently responded only to the final preparatory landing movements and vocalizations within the family. A key observation on the nature of goose behavior was provided by Konrad Lorenz who could not get his imprinted geese to land near him until he wildly spread his arms and fell after running (Tinbergen 1953:111–112). This spreading of the arms more closely resembled movements a goose would make and the geese reacted by landing right beside Lorenz. The almost continual "contact" vocalizations within a family and the "braking" wing movements provide the cues that enable close physical proximity of family members to be maintained while landing.

A further proof that geese regularly land as recognizable groups was provided by a series of counts made within short time intervals at different periods of the winter (Table 3). These counts were made on the same "subflock" of geese which radio-tracking had demonstrated was habitually using the same roost area and flight pattern to feeding areas (Raveling 1967:111–134). These results demonstrated a high degree of regularity in landing associations and the effects of mortality.

Census records in Wisconsin and Illinois showed that the geese observed prior to hunting at Crab Orchard were present before the Wisconsin hunting season. Since fall hunting mortality in Ontario was believed to be very slight relative to the total numbers in this Mississippi Valley population (J. B. Dawson and H. G. Lumsden, pers. comm.), I concluded that the pre-hunt sample was representative of the population prior to hunting, but after migration. Results (Table 3) thus represent the population available for harvest and most meaningful in terms of final reproductive success for the summer of 1964.

Families of geese maintained their unity throughout the winter (Raveling 1967:41–47) and the group counts reflected this behavior in quantitative terms which suggest population structure. Most groups of 3 to 9 represent adult pairs with their offspring. Pairs are mostly adult mated pairs without young; singles mostly represent unmated geese (especially yearlings). Comparison of the number of adult pairs with young to pairs without young thus indicates the proportion of adults successful in bringing a brood, or part of a brood, south and the average family size. However, certain obstacles must be overcome before these data may be utilized as the most accurate measure of production. Most yearling geese are singles (Raveling 1967:47–55) and most singles are yearlings (Raveling, unpubl. data) prior to hunting. However, yearlings may also be in pairs (sibling or mated), in sibling groups, or integral members of families (Raveling 1967:47–55). The prevalence of yearlings in each of these associations affects the ratio of young to old, thus making it difficult to derive age structure. Continued collection of data on group sizes before hunting will allow the computation of mortality and production rates when combined with kill estimates and mid-winter inventory. This, in turn, should enable estimation of presently unknown parameters or ones on which sparse data are available (e.g. percentage of singles which are yearlings). Additional data on the status of yearlings are needed along with information on the percentage of unmated adults (e.g. whether there is a disproportionate sex ratio) and of immatures lacking parents because of "natural" causes.

The technique of counting landing groups has great potential as it may produce precise population information quickly and economically (Lynch and Singleton 1964). For example, harvest quotas for the Mississippi Valley population are presently based on long-term averages of winter population numbers, kill estimates, and apparent average production indices, but not on data for the current year. Group counts before hunting can provide data on the current crop, although after the time regulations are now set. Ultimately, these data may be utilized in determining allowable harvest. Group counts have been conducted every autumn before hunting since 1964 at Horicon National Wildlife Refuge in Wisconsin, in southern Illinois, or both (Raveling, unpubl. data). Results have paralled population trends evident from retrospective analysis of harvest and inventory figures and have borne out prediction of poor reproductive success in 1967, based on observations in the nesting grounds of Ontario (Raveling and Lumsden, unpubl. data). Group counts can lead to the accumulation of data basic to understanding population oscillations and the formulation of life equations. Coupled with information on age ratios of the previous season's kill, magnitude of the kill, and winter population size, pre-hunt population structure appraisals have enabled population size estimates prior to hunting to be made that were in close agreement with a figure obtained by adding the kill to the winter inventory population number (Raveling, unpubl. data). Continued compilation of these data are needed, however, before I can conclude that the prediction procedure is completely satisfactory; this research is continuing.

The Mississippi Valley population of *B. c. interior* is ideal in many ways for the use of group counts in analyzing production and prediction of total population size. Group counts on many other populations of Canada geese, unfortunately, would not be meaningful. Counts must be made prior to the times when significant mortality by hunting has occurred. Once families are disrupted, singles and pairs may represent many different combinations of different age geese.

Another prerequisite for the most meaningful type of group counts is that almost total migration away from nesting areas and concentration in large numbers at another area must occur before hunting. If counts are made on the first migrants, they may be biased to high numbers of yearlings and unsuccessful nesting adults (Vaught and Kirsch 1966:42), especially in years with retarded spring weather and delayed nesting. Flocks nesting in high densities may have large and "unnatural" brood sizes due to "adoption" and thus group counts may be misleading (Williams and Marshall 1938, Brakhage 1965, Sherwood 1966:124–132; and many others). Brood-mixing is not considered prevalent among *B. c. interior* nesting in Ontario (Hanson 1965:152–154, Raveling 1967:45). Counts on nesting areas must be delayed until the young have developed full coordination of their flight abilities. Also, counts on nesting areas may be highly misleading as large numbers of the population representing yearlings and unsuccessful nesting geese may have gone elsewhere to molt (Hanson 1965:78–82, Kuyt 1966). Counts on areas which contain a mixture of subspecies or population units which could not be clearly identified may be highly misleading as these units may have widely differing reproductive success in any one year.

Further factors conducive to reliable results such as counting undisturbed birds landing a few at a time, not counting when strong winds prevail, etc., were discussed by Lynch and Singleton (1964). All these items must be kept in mind when considering undertaking group counts, and care in the selection of time and place of such counts is essential to obtaining meaningful results.

SUMMARY

Counting groups of Canada geese while they are initiating flight, in flight, or landing have all been suggested as means of analyzing population structure based on the number and size of families in a flock. Observations of radio- and color-marked Canada geese during winter proved family unity in daily activities, but revealed that size of functional groups could not be regularly or accurately measured by counts of geese at the moment of take off or in steady flight. However, group size could be identified at the moment of landing. Consecutive counts on the same "subflock" of geese made before and after hunting, and before spring migration, further proved the regularity with which geese land according to a pattern reflecting families, pairs, and singles.

Provided several criteria are met, group counts of landing geese can provide an accurate measure of production prior to hunting, and, coupled with reasonable estimates of the past year's harvest and post-hunting population size, indicate total population size before hunting. Certain prerequisites for use of this technique on other flocks and the need for additional information vital to accurate analysis of population structure are discussed.

LITERATURE CITED

BOYD, H. 1953. On encounters between wild white-fronted geese in winter flocks. Behavior 2:85–129.

BRAKHAGE, GEORGE K. 1965. Biology and behavior of tub-nesting Canada Geese. J. Wildl. Mgmt. 29:751–771.

ELDER, WILLIAM H. AND NINA ELDER. 1949. The role of the family in the formation of goose flocks. Wilson Bull. 61(3):132–140.

HANSON, HAROLD C. 1965. The Giant Canada Goose. So. Ill. Univ. Press, Carbondale. 226 p.

HANSON, HAROLD C. and ROBERT H. SMITH. 1950. Canada geese of the Mississippi Flyway with special reference to an Illinois flock. Bull. Ill. Nat. History Survey 25(3):67–210.

HEWITT, OLIVER H. 1950. Recent studies of blue and lesser snow goose populations in James Bay. Trans. N. Amer. Wildl. Conf. 15:304–309.

KUYT, E. 1966. Further observations on large Canada geese moulting on the Thelon River, Northwest Territories. Can. Field Naturalist 80(2): 63–69.

LEBRET, T. 1956. Are group size counts of wild geese an index of productivity? Ardea 44:284–288.

LYNCH, JOHN J. AND J. R. SINGLETON. 1964. Winter appraisals of annual productivity in geese and other water birds. p. 114–126. *In* The Wildfowl Trust, 15th Ann. Rep.

MARTIN, FANT W. 1964. Behavior and survival of Canada geese in Utah. Utah State Dept. Fish and Game. Pub. No. 64-7 (Fed. Aid Proj. W-29-r). 89 p.

MARTINSON, R. K. AND J. A. MCCANN. 1966. Proportion of recovered goose and brant bands that are reported. J. Wildl. Mgmt. 30:856–858.

NASS, ROGER D. 1964. Sex and age-ratio bias of cannon-netted geese. J. Wildl. Mgmt. 28:522–527.

PHILLIPS, JOHN C. 1916. Two problems in the migration of waterfowl. Auk 33(1):22–27.

RAVELING, DENNIS G. 1966. Factors affecting age ratios of samples of Canada geese caught with cannon-nets. J. Wildl. Mgmt. 30:682–691.

RAVELING, D. G. 1967. Sociobiology and ecology of Canada geese in winter. Ph.D. Dissertation, So. Ill. Univ., Carbondale. 213pp.

SHERWOOD, GLEN A. 1966a. Canada geese on the Seney National Wildlife Refuge. Ph.D. Thesis. Utah State Univ. 300p.

TINBERGEN, N. 1953. Social Behavior in Animals. John Wiley and Sons, Inc., New York. 150p.

VAUGHT, RICHARD W. AND LEO M. KIRSCH. 1966. Canada geese of the eastern prairie population with special reference to the Swan Lake flock. Missouri Dept. Conserv., Tech. Bull. 3. 91p.

WILLIAMS, C. S. AND WILLIAM H. MARSHALL. 1938. Survival of Canada goose goslings, Bear River Refuge, Utah, 1937. J. Wildl. Mgmt. 2:17–19.

NONHUNTING MORTALITY OF FLEDGED NORTH AMERICAN WATERFOWL

I. JACK STOUT, Division of Forestry and Wildlife Resources, Virginia Polytechnic Institute and State University, Blacksburg 24061[1]

GEORGE W. CORNWELL, Division of Forestry and Wildlife Resources, Virginia Polytechnic Institute and State University, Blacksburg 24061[2]

Abstract: A survey of nonhunting mortality of wild waterfowl was conducted by the Delta Waterfowl Research Station, Delta, Manitoba, 1963–65. Records of reported mortality (n = 2,108,880) for the period 1930–64 were assembled from open literature, unpublished federal reports, and a questionnaire. In addition, nonhunting mortality band recoveries (n = 25,817) for the period 1930–63 were analyzed. Data were compiled on mortality from collisions, weather, predation, pollution, diseases and poisons, and miscellaneous factors. Collision mortality (n = 3,015) was 0.1 percent of the total sample and was reported most commonly from the Central Flyway. Collisions with utility wires and automobiles were the most frequent causes of mortality. Weather-related mortality (n = 158,723) was attributed to 7.4 percent of the total sample. Hail was the most important factor during summer. In other seasons various factors operated in concert with cold weather. Predation (n = 2,621) accounted for 0.1 percent of the total mortality reported. Losses appeared to be of similar magnitude in all flyways and peaked during summer. Mortality from pollution (n = 13,944) was 0.6 percent of the total sample. Losses were concentrated on the Atlantic coast and were proportionally heavier among diving ducks (Aythyinae). Mortality from disease (n = 1,873,970) was 87.7 percent of the total mortality studied. Losses were most prevalent in the Central and Pacific flyways during summer and fall. Mortality from miscellaneous causes (n = 82,424) was 3.8 percent of the total sample. Losses were confined largely to the Mississippi Flyway and to the summer–fall period. The seasonal losses peaked during winter and spring.

J. WILDL. MANAGE. 40(4):681–693

This paper summarizes a survey of *reported* nonhunting mortality of wild waterfowl conducted by the Delta Waterfowl Research Station, Delta, Manitoba, 1963–65. A preliminary discussion of waterfowl nonhunting mortality was given by Cornwell and Hochbaum (1962, paper presented at 24th Midwest Fish Wildl. Conf., Des Moines, Iowa), and a detailed study, including an extensive literature review, was completed by Stout (1967). Boyd (1962) provided further impetus for our study.

The objective of the survey was to review and compile qualitative evidence from the available records on nonhunting mortality in waterfowl. Hopefully, this data base will aid in the design of future quantitative studies of nonhunting mortality.

Acknowledgment is made to The Wildlife Management Institute for providing a graduate fellowship and other budgetary support and to the Division of Forestry and Wildlife Resources, Virginia Polytechnic Institute and State University, for funding and use of facilities.

METHODS

Observations of nonhunting mortality were tabulated under these categories: collisions, weather, predation, pollution, disease and poisons, and miscellaneous. Data (sources defined below) were compiled on ducks, geese, and swans native to North America. Deaths not attributed to shooting were regarded as nonhunting mortality; cripple losses and deaths likely to have been confused with hunting losses were excluded

[1] Present address: Department of Biological Sciences, Florida Technological University, P. O. Box 25000, Orlando 32816.

[2] Present address: Ecoimpact, Inc., 6615 S.W. 13th Street, Gainesville, Florida 32608.

Originally published in J. Wildl. Manage. 40(4):681–693, 1976.

from consideration, as were data on unfledged waterfowl.

Questionnaires were directed to approximately 800 waterfowl biologists (state, federal, private, and university) to obtain yearly summaries of observations of nonhunting mortality made during 1963 and 1964. Details on the questionnaire design and cooperators were reported in Stout (1967:61). Three hundred eighty-one questionnaires were returned and 326 contained usable data.

Long-term data for the period from 1954 to 1963 were obtained from the files of the U. S. Fish and Wildlife Service, primarily from refuge narrative and biological reports and necropsy reports.

Waterfowl band-recovery data for the period from 1930 to 1963 were secured on magnetic tape for analysis by IBM 1740 computer through the cooperation of the Migratory Bird Populations Station, Laurel, Maryland. The recovery codes used were reported in Stout (1967:63). Recoveries were tabulated by species, recovery code, year, month, sex, age, and flyway.

Observations of mortality, other than band recoveries, were punched on key-sort cards by species, cause of death, number of deaths, age, sex, year, month, locality, and flyway. Further interpretative information was written on the card.

An observation of nonhunting mortality in this paper refers to an individual anatid that died of nonhunting causes. For example, a single event may have caused the loss of several hundred waterfowl, but each death would be regarded as an observation.

Questionnaire data, unpublished reports, and literature records of nonhunting mortality were combined and subsequently will be referred to as survey data. Every effort was made to avoid duplication of records. Initially band recoveries were analyzed as a separate unit. The survey data and band recovery data sampled different populations and were largely independent measures of nonhunting mortality. The data were pooled when useful for the purpose of analysis.

Accumulated data were tabulated for analysis by mortality factor, species or broader taxonomic grouping, flyway or region, season, and sex. Many observations of mortality were incomplete with regard to one or more variables. Accordingly, totals for the various categories are not consistent among the tables, because the maximum number of complete observations has been used in each.

The two sources of nonhunting mortality data, survey data and band recoveries, have intrinsic biases. These limitations must be recognized and considered in evaluating the data and their meaning. For example, the survey data were more likely to reflect factors spectacular in occurrence, i.e., disease die-offs and kills associated with weather. Conversely, individual cases of predation or collisions were less likely to be reported. Band recoveries were completely dependent upon man for discovery and documentation. Obviously, the probability of a given mortality event being found and reported by man varied markedly among the factors causing mortality. In general, over the years more puddle ducks (Anatinae) have been banded and may have been recovered than diving ducks, geese, and swans. More males than females have been banded over the years (W. Crissey, personal communication).

RESULTS AND DISCUSSION

Collisions

The survey data and band recoveries reported as killed by collision are given in Table 1. Wire strikes and collisions with autos accounted for a majority of the casualities. The Central Flyway reported 55

Table 1. A summary of the nonhunting mortality of waterfowl by category of mortality and source of data.

	Survey data		Band recoveries	
Mortality factor	*n*	%	*n*	%
Collision				
Automobiles	539	23.0	239	33.0
Telephone and power lines	1,487	65.0	20	3.0
Television and radio towers	93	4.0		
Aircraft	40	2.0	10	1.0
Farm machinery	95	4.0	147	21.0
Fences and buildings	20	1.0		
Other objects	25	1.0	300	42.0
Total	2,299		716	
Weather				
Wind	124	0.1		
Hail	148,111	92.9		
Ice	1,016	1.0		
Cold	9,271	6.0		
Heat	7	0.0		
Other			194	100.0
Total	158,529		194	
Predation				
Mammalian	1,012	76.0	898	70.0
Avian	252	19.0	384	30.0
Other vertebrates	74	5.0	1	0.0
Total	1,338		1,283	
Pollution				
Oil	7,911	58.0	251	100.0
Detergents	418	4.0		
Chemicals	2,414	17.0		
Domestic waste	16	0.0		
Other	2,934	21.0		
Total	13,693		251	
Diseases and poisoning				
Botulism	1,679,771	89.7	1,093	63.3
Lead poisoning	69,732	3.8	87	5.0
Fowl cholera	99,066	5.3		
Aspergilliosis	3,860	0.2		
Miscellaneous diseases	12,169	0.6		
Unknown diseases			502	29.1
Parasites	2,516	0.1		
Poisons			45	2.6
Pesticides	5,129	0.3		
Total	1,872,243		1,727	
Miscellaneous factors				
Nets	50,451	83.0	555	2.6
Mammal traps	3,112	5.1	3,131	14.5
Banding mortality	1,994	3.3	794	3.6
Scientific specimens	1,799	3.0	236	1.1
Illegal kills	793	1.3	1,307	6.0
Adverse environmental factors			15,623	72.2
Unknown	1,781	2.9		
Uncommon	848	1.4		
Total	60,778		21,646	
Total mortality	2,108,880		25,817	

percent of the observations, with each of the other strata accounting for 7 to 13 percent (Table 2). Observation of mortality from collision is probably more likely in the Central Flyway owing to the terrain features. Losses from collision may be unrelated to season; however, the data suggest a possible diminution of casualties during spring (Mar–May) (Table 3). Puddle ducks were most evident among the reported mortality (Table 4). There was no evidence that the sexes were differentially vulnerable to fatal collision (Table 5).

Most mortality of waterfowl from collisions is attributable to man, his activities, or his physical additions to the environment. The overall importance is probably minimal. Spectacular losses of migrating passerines (Stoddard and Norris 1967) are in sharp contrast to waterfowl casualties that tend to be isolated events (Tordoff and Mengel 1956). Most of the collisional factors listed in Table 1 do not pose a serious threat to waterfowl.

Collision with utility wires was important. Two factors, migration and inclement weather, probably accentuate wire strikes during the fall–winter period. Others (Quortrup and Shillinger 1941, Harrison 1963) have noted the association between prevalency of wire strikes and inclement weather, particularly fog. In part, learned response to the environment (Hochbaum 1955:14) may prevent many of the potential collisions on familiar areas, viz., nesting grounds and wintering grounds. Cornwell and Hochbaum (1971) suggested removing unnecessary fences and wires from waterfowl production marshes to reduce mortality from collisions.

No quantitative data are available on waterfowl collisions with autos. Data presented elsewhere (Stout 1967:71) suggest that such mortality may be common during the breeding season and periods of disper-

Table 2. Distribution of nonhunting mortality of waterfowl according to flyway or region and source of data.

Mortality factor	Source		%
	Bands	Survey	
Collision (3,140)[a]			
Atlantic	101	132	7.4
Mississippi	159	214	11.9
Central	154	1,565	54.7
Pacific	116	276	12.5
Canada	328	95	13.5
Weather (158,722)			
Atlantic	63	4,863	3.1
Mississippi	47	3,323	2.1
Central	52	150,020	94.6
Pacific	6	322	0.2
Canada	26		0.0
Predation (2,621)			
Atlantic	327	399	27.7
Mississippi	283	291	21.9
Central	113	517	24.0
Pacific	116	132	9.5
Canada	443		16.9
Pollution (14,350)			
Atlantic	48	7,249	50.9
Mississippi	164	3,121	22.9
Central	15	2,933	20.5
Pacific	6	796	5.6
Canada	18		0.1
Disease (1,874,102)			
Atlantic	117	6,115	0.3
Mississippi	115	84,874	4.5
Central	368	902,490	48.2
Pacific	988	878,918	47.0
Canada	117		0.0
Miscellaneous (81,915)			
Atlantic	3,947	2,040	7.3
Mississippi	4,836	54,324	72.2
Central	2,843	3,026	7.2
Pacific	4,344	1,239	6.8
Canada	5,316		6.5

[a] Sample size.

Table 3. Distribution of nonhunting mortality of waterfowl according to season and source of data.

Mortality factor	Source		%
	Bands	Survey	
Collision (3,135)[a]			
Spring	277	225	16.0
Summer	256	594	27.1
Fall	113	797	29.0
Winter	100	773	27.9
Weather (158,693)			
Spring	45	517	0.4
Summer	30	148,000	93.3
Fall	23	350	0.2
Winter	96	9,632	6.1
Predation (2,620)			
Spring	282	177	17.5
Summer	349	730	41.2
Fall	432	90	19.9
Winter	218	342	21.4
Pollution (13,913)			
Spring	172	1,447	11.6
Summer	5	25	0.2
Fall	11	3,676	26.6
Winter	63	8,514	61.6
Disease (1,871,192)			
Spring	162	18,243	1.0
Summer	650	1,252,251	67.0
Fall	681	432,142	23.1
Winter	233	166,830	8.9
Miscellaneous (81,940)			
Spring	7,470	710	10.0
Summer	2,769	2,300	6.0
Fall	4,839	52,371	70.0
Winter	6,437	5,044	14.0

[a] Sample size.

sal. Three hundred band recoveries (Table 1, other objects) were attributed either to wire strikes or auto collision, but a specific cause of death could not be assigned.

Nesting duck mortality from farm machinery does not appear to be serious, although nest loss is of considerable importance. Previous authors (Milonski 1958, Ordal 1964) have reached similar conclusions.

Weather

Waterfowl mortality associated with inclement weather represented 7.4 percent of the total sample, and hail was the most significant individual weather factor (Table 1). Mortality from weather was most represented in the Central Flyway and most was caused by hail (Table 2). These losses, spectacular and readily counted, tended to exaggerate the regional total. Mortality in each of the other geographic strata amounted to 1 to 3 percent. The latter casualties were due largely to cold weather (Tables 1, 2). Ice, cold temperatures, and wind generally acted in concert during the

Table 4. Distribution of nonhunting mortality of waterfowl by species group and source of data.

Mortality factor	Source		%
	Band	Survey	
Collisions (3,016)[a]			
Puddle ducks	1,131	566	56.3
Diving ducks	396	66	15.3
Geese	110	84	6.4
Swans	12		0.4
Unidentified		651	21.6
Weather (158,723)			
Puddle ducks	149	3,013	2.0
Diving ducks	32	1,184	0.8
Geese	13	3,325	2.1
Swans		4	0.0
Unidentified		151,003	95.1
Predation (2,625)			
Puddle ducks	1,109	698	68.8
Diving ducks	81	89	6.5
Geese	94	50	5.5
Swans	2	15	0.6
Unidentified	1	486	18.6
Pollution (3,351)			
Puddle ducks	26	12	1.2
Diving ducks	73	61	4.0
Geese	1	3	0.1
Swans		1	0.0
Unidentified		3,174	94.7
Disease (1,873,970)			
Puddle ducks	1,462	187,929	10.1
Diving ducks	134	5,939	0.3
Geese	128	18,767	1.0
Swans	3	2,097	0.1
Unidentified		1,657,511	88.5
Miscellaneous (82,424)			
Puddle ducks	15,054	2,638	21.5
Diving ducks	3,563	54,357	70.3
Geese	2,968	1,085	4.9
Swans	61	78	0.1
Unidentified		2,620	3.2

[a] Sample size.

winter (Dec–Feb) to cause mortality not readily attributed to any individual factor (Tables 1, 3). The species composition of the casualties ascribed to weather factors was predominantly unidentified (Table 4). Male anatids (288) were more frequent in the reported losses than were females (179) (Table 5).

Factor interactions often complicate the identification of a given weather factor as the ultimate or proximate cause of death.

Table 5. Distribution of nonhunting mortality of waterfowl according to sex.

Mortality factor	Bands		Survey	
	M	F	M	F
Collisions	271	256	219	224
Weather	288	179		
Predation	632	488		
Pollution	149	56	1,837	773
Disease	1,001	413	3,078	2,486
Miscellaneous	10,655	6,002	814	653

When waterfowl habitat is covered with ice, losses result because food, shelter, and escape cover become unavailable. Observations by Trautman et al. (1939) documented ice as the ultimate mortality factor. During freezes of short duration, losses occurred among underweight, diseased, and otherwise injured waterfowl. Healthy birds died only after habitats had frozen over for long periods (Jahn and Hunt 1964:103). High winds have been reported to kill waterfowl in unusual circumstances (Rate 1957, Wooten 1954).

Scattered reports suggested hail as a frequent cause of mortality, principally affecting preflight birds. Smith and Webster (1955:374) in Alberta attributed the loss of up to 148,000 waterfowl to 2 hail storms. Fyfe (1957) presented similar observations from Saskatchewan. Hail losses were shown by Ordal (1964) to have a marked influence on duck production on a Minnesota study area where the number of broods was decreased to one-half of the 4-year average following a severe hail storm. Hochbaum (1955:167) cited an example of migrating waterfowl being killed in flight by hail.

Waterfowl seldom if ever suffer fatal hypothermia unless accompanied by, or as a culmination of, the influence of another stressor. Most observations in the literature cite mortality as having been caused by starvation; in contrast, Roseberry (1962) suggested that predation was the principal source of mortality to upland game. Extensive observations from Great Britain and the United States supported the hypothesis that starvation is the principal cause of hypothermia in waterfowl (Boyd 1964, Harrison and Hudson 1964, Kalmbach and Coburn 1937, Trautman et al. 1939).

Waterfowl species undoubtedly differ in their resistance to cold-weather stress. Boyd (1964) showed that certain waterfowl species in Britain suffered disproportionally heavy losses to cold weather. Evidence presented by Beer (1964) suggested differences at the tribal level in resistance to cold: Dendrocygnini showed the highest mortality, Anserini showed little mortality, and other tribes were intermediate.

Canada geese (*Branta canadensis*) sustained the greatest cold losses reported in the survey. Most observations were from the Atlantic Flyway, specifically the Pea Island area of North Carolina, where studies (Cowan and Herman 1956) revealed that heaviest mortality was associated with cold weather, malnutrition owing to food of low crude protein content, and heavy parasitism by gizzard worms (*Amidostomum anseris*).

Weather factors most often may act to disturb the overall density-regulating process in waterfowl populations. However, with regard to mortality, specific factors may operate under different circumstances as either density-independent or density-proportional effects (Wagner et al. 1965).

Predation

Predation losses represented 0.1 percent of the total nonhunting mortality reported (Table 1). Data suggested that mammals prey on waterfowl three to four times as heavily as do avian predators. Regional variation in predation was small in contrast to other categories of mortality (Table 2). Reported losses were lowest in the Pacific Flyway and highest in the Atlantic Flyway. Survey-reported predation upon waterfowl appeared to peak during summer (Jun–Aug), but band recoveries were more frequent in the fall (Sep–Nov) (Table 3). Losses were represented largely by puddle ducks in the data examined (Table 4). Predation among puddle ducks was probably more likely to be discovered and/or reported than among other anatids. More male (632) than female (488) anatids were observed killed by predators (Table 5).

Errington (1946) reviewed the early literature on vertebrate predation upon waterfowl. He concluded that so-called "surplus" birds comprised most of the mortality. Much of the literature concerned with predation upon waterfowl deals with egg and nesting losses (Bennett 1938, Low 1945, numerous others). Studies providing data on nesting female losses showed that roughly 1 percent of the ground nesters and 5 percent of the cavity nesters may succumb to predation (Keith 1961:44, Milonski 1958:223, Stotts and Davis 1960:149, Glover 1956:41). These losses alone do not appear to have a major influence on waterfowl sex ratios (Bellrose et al. 1961). Post-nesting losses may be frequent among molting birds, for Oring's (1964) observations suggested high vulnerability during flightless periods.

Over 90 percent of the band recoveries attributed to mammalian predation were from puddle ducks. Although more puddle ducks were present in banded populations, the high recovery rate probably reflected the amount of time spent on the ground in nesting and other activities where vulnerability was greater. Twice as many banded geese as diving ducks were recovered.

Previous studies (Hecht 1951, Wright 1953, Bennett 1938:66) suggested low rates of avian predation during the breeding season. Little work has been done on avian predator-waterfowl relationships during winter, but scattered reports document minor losses (Sharp 1951, Imler and Kalmbach 1955).

Recent quantitative studies of red-tailed hawk (*Buteo jamaicensis*) predation in Alberta (Luttich et al. 1970:196) demonstrated that flying-age waterfowl comprised from 3.6 to 16.5 percent of the dietary biomass over the years 1965 through 1968. Predation upon flying-age waterfowl by fish and reptiles does not appear to be of any consequence (Coulter 1958, Lagler 1956, Solman 1945).

Pollution

Data on waterfowl mortality associated with five categories of pollution are presented in Table 1. Oil pollution was a major factor according to the survey data; few band recoveries were reported, but all were attributed to oil pollution. Losses were greatest in the Atlantic Flyway (51 percent), least in the Pacific Flyway (5 percent), and similar in the Mississippi and Central flyways, 23 and 20 percent, respectively (Table 2). Little mortality was reported from Canada. Winter was the season associated with most of the waterfowl losses (Table 3). Reported observations diminished during summer and spring. Waterfowl classed as "unknown species" comprised 95 percent of the combined sample (Table 4). Mortality identified to species, largely from band recoveries, involved principally diving ducks. Mortality from pollution was largely among males (Table 5).

Previous studies of oil pollution (Hawkes 1961, Erickson 1963) reported the greatest regional losses of waterfowl on the coasts of North America, principally the Atlantic coast. Eighty-nine percent of the survey observations were from the Atlantic Flyway. Observations on oil mortality are given by Hadley (1930) and Lincoln (1936). Wilson (1960, unpubl. rep., New York Dept. Environ. Conserv., Albany) showed that significant numbers of waterfowl harvested in the eastern portion of Lake Erie were contaminated by oil, but direct evidence of mortality was not cited.

Band recoveries associated with oil pollution were more than three times more common in the Mississippi Flyway than the Atlantic Flyway. Hunt and Cowan (1963) discussed the hazards of oil pollution to waterfowl wintering on the Detroit River-Lake Erie complex. F. B. Lee (Unpublished data) also observed extensive waterfowl losses to oil in the vicinity of Red Wing, Minnesota. An oil spill on the Mississippi River in 1963 (Jessen 1963, p. 5 *in* Minutes of Technical Section, Mississippi Flyway Council, St. Louis, Mo.) was estimated to have killed 10,000 waterfowl; of 2,000 examined casualties, 85 percent were scaup (*Aythya affinis* and *A. marila*) and 95 percent were males. Hartung and Hunt (1966) suggested that oil losses were still important in the Detroit River area. Pacific Flyway recoveries of oil-contaminated birds were insignificant, although Richardson (1956: 20) reported up to 2,000 white-winged scoters (*Melanitta deglandi*) were killed by a single oil spill.

Occurrence of oil spills on waterways or coasts does not follow any observable seasonal cycle but is random, because most pollution is man-made (Erickson 1963) and in part accidental. Rather, the seasonal movements of waterfowl determine their vulnerability and mortality in the randomly appearing foci of oil pollution. Thus migration may make waterfowl especially vulnerable to oil spills. Hartung (1967) showed that the probability of survival following oil contamination is related directly to the fat reserves of cold-stressed ducks. During the breeding season, only five band recoveries were reported.

Diving ducks sustain most of the casualties attributed to oil pollution. Eiders (*So-*

materia sp.), scoters, and oldsquaws (*Clangula hyemalis*) long have been implicated in these losses (Hadley 1930). Of the total band recoveries, 47 percent were scaup and 20 percent canvasback (*Aythya valisineria*). The black duck (*Anas rubripes*) is probably the most vulnerable of the puddle ducks to oil losses, for it commonly winters on salt water (Wright 1954:109).

Various chemicals and detergents were reported to have killed waterfowl (Table 1, survey data). Major losses (84 percent) were from the Central Flyway where mine pollution was prevalent. Most of the observations were made during the winter season. Mortality appeared to be concentrated on the wintering grounds.

Waterfowl mortality caused by sundry forms of pollution was greatest during the spring (96 percent) (Stout 1967:151). Water pollution by unknown agents also killed mainly diving ducks.

The tendency of pollution to cause mortality during winter and spring (after shooting losses) and prior to the breeding season would be of concern only in those species that otherwise might be reduced to low numbers. Any variation in the number of returning breeding birds then would be of importance.

Diseases and Poisoning

Disease mortality was 87.8 percent of the total nonhunting mortality studied, and band recoveries accounted for less than 1 percent of the diseased sample (Table 1). Botulism was the major pathogen represented in the survey data and band recoveries. Fowl cholera and lead poisoning also were significant factors. Disease and poisoning casualties were greatest in the Central and Pacific flyways, 48.2 and 47 percent, respectively (Table 2); fewest losses were reported from the Atlantic Flyway. Study of the seasonal dynamics of waterfowl losses revealed a unimodal peak in summer and a gradual decline until the following summer (Table 3). Most of the reported mortality (88 percent) was not identified to species (Table 4). Puddle ducks were over 95 percent of the identified sample. Male anatids were reported more frequently than females in the disease sample (Table 5).

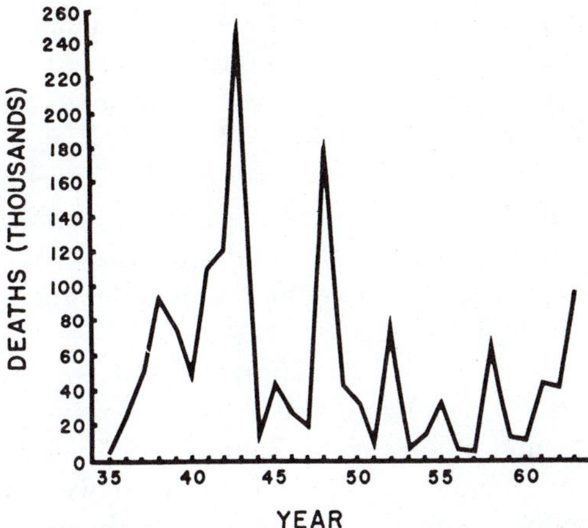

Fig. 1. Trend of waterfowl mortality from botulism principally on federal refuges, 1935–63; survey data and band recoveries combined.

Except for a few local case histories, information on year-to-year variation in mortality caused by botulism is not available. A great quantity of data was abstracted from U. S. Fish and Wildlife Service files, and the long-term trend (29 years) of botulism losses (Fig. 1) showed marked fluctuations every 2 to 5 years. This cycle may be generated by population fluctuations of the invertebrates that harbor the botulism toxin (Jensen and Allen 1960) or by changes in the number of susceptible waterfowl.

The great significance of botulism as a mortality factor in the Pacific and Central flyways was corroborated by the survey; in addition, losses were found to be common in the Mississippi Flyway and limited in the Atlantic Flyway (Reilly and Boroff 1967).

Puddle ducks made up 92 percent of the band recoveries attributed to botulism. The pintail (*Anas acuta*) was the most common species among the band recoveries (44 percent) and in the survey (49 percent). Quortrup and Shillinger (1941) and Hammond (1950) also supported this conclusion. The diving ducks, geese, and swans suffered occasional botulism losses, but nothing comparable to the puddle ducks (Bossenmaier et al. 1954).

The results of the study on lead poisoning (Table 1) supported in several respects the definitive work of Bellrose (1959). The survey indicated the Mississippi Flyway to be the major site of mortality (76 percent); the Central Flyway made up an additional 21 percent. Survey observations were predominantly from winter (79 percent), as also reported by Bellrose (1959:284). The mallard (*A. platyrhynchos*) accounted for 54 percent (47) of the band recoveries and 60 percent (42,135) of the survey observations. Few deaths of banded birds (87) were attributed to lead poisoning. Additional data on the species composition of losses by flyway and season were reported in Stout (1967:168). Overall importance of lead poisoning as a mortality factor affecting waterfowl was estimated by Bellrose (1959:286) as a 2–3 percent annual loss of the total population. This appears to be the best estimate available.

Fowl cholera was generally limited to the Central and Pacific flyways (Quortrup et al. 1946, Rosen and Bischoff 1949). Outbreaks in the Mississippi Flyway were unusual (Vaught et al. 1967), and serologic evidence supports this conclusion (Donahue and Olson 1969). The first published report for the Atlantic Flyway was Gershman et al. (1964); however, Locke et al. (1970) found fowl cholera among waterfowl on the Chesapeake Bay.

Outbreaks of fowl cholera were associated consistently with winter (Quortrup et al. 1946, Rosen and Bischoff 1950, Petrides and Bryant 1951). Gershman et al. (1964) reported the only instance of an outbreak during the breeding season. Survey and band recovery data were inadequate to demonstrate differential losses to fowl cholera by species.

After contamination with the cholera agent, a given area seems to remain a focus in which an outbreak may recur. For example, the Muleshoe area in Texas has had a long history of fowl cholera, and as recently as 1956–57, 60,000 waterfowl were estimated to have died there (Jensen and Williams 1964:339). Data given by Rosen (1969) showed cholera mortality to be density-independent.

An extensive amount of information on waterfowl losses attributed to miscellaneous and unknown diseases and parasites was given by Stout (1967:185, 196). The nature of the data does not lend itself to discussion here.

Pesticide kills of waterfowl were largely seasonal and concentrated during spring migration. Coincidence of mortality, spring migration, and the application of toxic chemicals to agronomic crops also was reported from England (Cramp and Conder 1960, Cramp et al. 1962). The English studies showed the principal losses to be among birds feeding on vegetation. The band recoveries reported here were primarily of vegetation-eating species (94 percent). Geese were especially vulnerable. Direct mortality caused by pesticides appears to be among the breeding stock and superimposed on the losses over winter. More subtle effects may be operating on the breeding biology (Heath et al. 1969), and the impact could be far greater than the direct mortality (Longcore et al. 1971, Friend and Trainer 1972).

Botulism losses are probably the best documented of the nonhunting mortality factors. Areas regularly experiencing waterfowl losses to botulism tend to be watched carefully. Accordingly, the survey data have underestimated the magnitude of other nonhunting mortality compared to botulism losses.

Disease may be an important factor limiting waterfowl numbers. Conclusive evidence to support the presumption of disease acting on waterfowl as a density-dependent factor is not available. Lack (1954:166) speculated that North American waterfowl populations might be controlled in part by disease.

Miscellaneous

Miscellaneous mortality was 3.8 percent of the total nonhunting mortality; however, 83.8 percent of the total band recoveries were included in this category (Table 1). Waterfowl drowned in fish nets represented 83 percent of the survey data sample and 2 percent of the band recoveries (Table 1). Waterfowl losses attributed to mammal traps, banding procedures, scientific collections, and unknown factors were of similar magnitude in the survey sample (Table 1). A major portion of the band recoveries (15,623) was reported as killed by adverse environmental factors (Table 1). Miscellaneous mortality was associated strongly with the Mississippi Flyway (72 percent); the remaining geographic strata reported losses of the same proportion (Table 2). Mortality was associated largely with fall (70 percent) (Table 3), and diving ducks composed 70 percent of the sample (Table 4). Considerable disparity was apparent in the frequency with which the sexes were reported killed by miscellaneous factors (Table 5).

Mortality of waterfowl from commercial fishing nets frequently has been reported (Schorger 1947, Ellarson 1956:105, Jahn and Hunt 1964:102, Bartonek 1965). The survey indicated that the Mississippi Flyway was the principal site of the mortality (99 percent). Losses tended to be most common among wintering populations (McMahan and Fritz 1967), particularly among redheads (*Aythya americana*) and oldsquaws.

Mammal trapping, largely for muskrats (*Ondatra zibethicus*), takes a heavy annual toll of waterfowl. Of the band recoveries, 64 percent were from Canada; 88 percent of the survey reports were from the Mississippi Flyway. Jahn and Hunt (1964:172) reported 1 duck/500 trap-nights in Horicon Marsh, Wisconsin, in 1952. Losses were most common during spring (Mendall 1958: 213, Wright 1954:26).

A major portion of the band recoveries (60.5 percent) was attributed to adverse environmental factors and grouped in this section on miscellaneous mortality (Table 1). If these recoveries could have been ascribed to specific mortality factors the results might have modified some of our conclusions with regard to other mortality factors. Furthermore, the fact that these recoveries (15,623) could not be qualified as to cause of death emphasized the serious limitation imposed on any study of nonhunting mortality, i.e., determination of the cause of death.

Other miscellaneous factors listed in Table 1 were further detailed by Stout (1967) and will not be discussed here. Generally the miscellaneous mortality was associated with man and his activities. The importance of such losses may be expected to grow in the future.

Seasonal Distribution of Band Recoveries

The seasonal trend of nonhunting mortality band recoveries from 1930 to 1963 is shown in Fig. 2. Recoveries of geese and swans peaked in December and January, diving ducks in March, and puddle ducks in

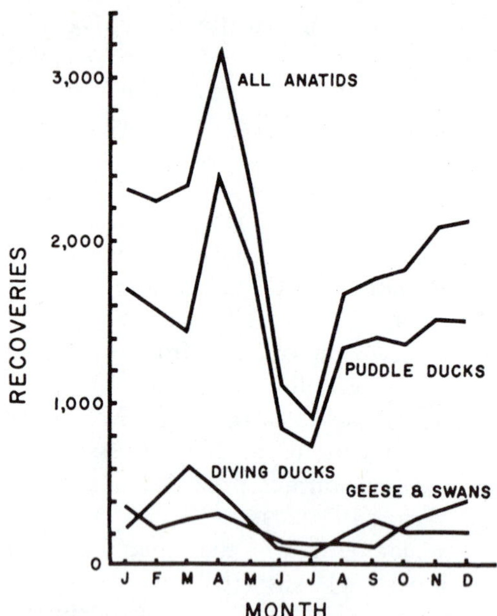

Fig. 2. The seasonal trend of nonhunting mortality of waterfowl according to band recoveries, 1930–63 (n = 25,817).

April. Band recoveries were minimal in July for diving ducks and puddle ducks. Observed mortality of geese and swans was low during the summer months and minimal in September. Recoveries of puddle ducks showed a marked seasonal effect, whereas losses of geese and swans varied slightly by season.

The observed seasonal trend of nonhunting mortality has important implications with regard to annual mortality. Implicit in the harvesting policy for North American waterfowl is the notion that insignificant mortality occurs following the hunting season. That is, nonhunting mortality is assumed to be largely replaced by shooting losses. Some nonhunting mortality is replaced by shooting losses, but we believe the data suggest that important winter and spring losses occur after hunting mortality has reduced the populations.

Buss et al. (1952) discussed spring mortality in ring-necked pheasant (*Phasianus colchicus*) populations and concluded that these losses were the most critical of the year. Similarly, Stewart and Manning (1958) regarded spring and summer mortality as important sources of variation in whistling swan (*Cygnus columbianus*) populations. Conversely, Jahn and Hunt (1964) found winter mortality of waterfowl to be minor in Wisconsin. Mendall's (1958) work on ring-necked ducks (*Aythya collaris*) suggested spring and summer as key periods of mortality. Jennings (1961) plotted the seasonal distribution of death of wild birds ($n = 1{,}000$) examined over a 7-year period. His observations showed a sharp but steady rise in number of deaths from March until a peak was reached in June.

LITERATURE CITED

BARTONEK, J. C. 1965. Mortality of diving ducks on Lake Winnipegosis through commercial fishing. Can. Field-Nat. 79(1):15–20.

BEER, J. 1964. Wildfowl mortality in the Slimbridge collection during the winters of 1961–62 and 1962–63. Wildfowl Trust Annu. Rep. 15:50–56.

BELLROSE, F. C. 1959. Lead poisoning as a mortality factor in waterfowl populations. Illinois Nat. Hist. Surv. Bull. 27(3):235–288.

———, T. G. SCOTT, A. S. HAWKINS, AND J. B. LOW. 1961. Sex ratios and age ratios in North American ducks. Illinois Nat. Hist. Surv. Bull. 27(6):391–474.

BENNETT, L. J. 1938. The blue-winged teal: its ecology and management. Collegiate Press, Ames, Iowa. 144pp.

BOSSENMAIER, E. F., T. A. OLSON, M. E. RUEGER, AND W. H. MARSHALL. 1954. Some field and laboratory aspects of duck sickness at Whitewater Lake, Manitoba. Trans. N. Am. Wildl. Conf. 19:163–175.

BOYD, H. 1962. Population dynamics and the exploitation of ducks and geese. Pages 85–95 *in* E. D. LeCren and M. W. Holdgate, eds. The exploitation of natural animal populations. John Wiley and Sons, Inc., New York.

———. 1964. Wildfowl and other water-birds found dead in England and Wales in January–March 1963. Wildfowl Trust Annu. Rep. 15: 20–22.

BUSS, I. O., C. V. SWANSON, AND D. H. WOODSIDE. 1952. The significance of adult pheasant mortalities in spring to fall populations. Trans. N. Am. Wildl. Conf. 17:269–284.

CORNWELL, G., AND H. A. HOCHBAUM. 1971. Collisions with wires—a source of anatid mortality. Wilson Bull. 83(3):305–306.

COULTER, M. W. 1958. Distribution, food and weight of the snapping turtle in Maine. Maine Field Nat. 14(3):53–62.

COWAN, A. B., AND C. M. HERMAN. 1956 (1955). Winter losses of Canada geese at Pea Island, North Carolina. Proc. Southeastern Assoc. Game and Fish Commissioners 9:172–174.

CRAMP, S., AND P. J. CONDER. 1960. The deaths of birds and mammals connected with toxic chemicals in the first half of 1960. Royal Soc. for Protection of Birds Rep. 1. 20pp.

———, ———, AND J. S. ASH. 1962. Deaths of birds and mammals from toxic chemicals—January–June, 1961. Royal Soc. for Protection of Birds Rep. 2. 24pp.

DONAHUE, J. M., AND L. D. OLSON. 1969. Survey of wild ducks and geese for *Pasteurella* spp. Bull. Wildl. Dis. Assoc. 5(3):201–205.

ELLARSON, R. S. 1956. A study of the old-squaw duck on Lake Michigan. Ph.D. Thesis. Univ. of Wisconsin, Madison. 231pp.

ERICKSON, R. C. 1963. Oil pollution and migratory birds. Atlantic Nat. 18(1):5–14.

ERRINGTON, P. L. 1946. Predation and vertebrate populations. Q. Rev. Biol. 21(2):144–177.

FRIEND, M., AND D. O. TRAINER. 1972. Duck hepatitis virus interactions with DDT and dieldrin in adult mallards. Bull. Environ. Contam. Toxicol. 7(4):202–206.

FYFE, R. W. 1957. Hail damage in the June 17 storm. The Blue Jay 15(4):170–171.

GERSHMAN, M., J. F. WITTER, H. E. SPENCER, JR., AND A. KALVAITIS. 1964. Case Report: epizootic of fowl cholera in the common eider duck. J. Wildl. Manage. 28(3):587–589.

GLOVER, F. A. 1956. Nesting and production of the blue-winged teal (*Anas discors* Linnaeus) in northwest Iowa. J. Wildl. Manage. 20(1): 28–46.

HADLEY, A. H. 1930. Oil pollution and sea-bird fatalities. Birdlore 32(3):241–243.

HAMMOND, M. C. 1950. Some observations on sex ratio of ducks contracting botulism in North Dakota. J. Wildl. Manage. 14(2):209–214.

HARRISON, J. 1963. Heavy mortality of mute swans from electrocution. Wildfowl Trust Annu. Rep. 14:164–165.

———, AND M. HUDSON. 1964. Some effects of severe weather on wildfowl in Kent in 1962–63. Wildfowl Trust Annu. Rep. 15:26–32.

HARTUNG, R. 1967. Energy metabolism in oil-covered ducks. J. Wildl. Manage. 31(4):798–804.

———, AND G. S. HUNT. 1966. Toxicity of some oils to waterfowl. J. Wildl. Manage. 30(3): 564–570.

HAWKES, A. L. 1961. A review of the nature and extent of damage caused by oil pollution at sea. Trans. N. Am. Wildl. Nat. Resour. Conf. 26:343–355.

HEATH, R. G., J. W. SPANN, AND J. F. KREITZER. 1969. Marked DDE impairment of mallard reproduction in controlled studies. Nature 224(5214):47–48.

HECHT, W. R. 1951. Nesting of the marsh hawk at Delta, Manitoba. Wilson Bull. 63(3):167–176.

HOCHBAUM, H. A. 1955. The travels and traditions of waterfowl. University of Minnesota Press, Minneapolis. 300pp.

HUNT, G. S., AND A. B. COWAN. 1963. Causes of deaths of waterfowl on the Lower Detroit River—winter 1960. Trans. N. Am. Wildl. Nat. Resour. Conf. 28:150–163.

IMLER, R. H., AND E. R. KALMBACH. 1955. The bald eagle and its economic status. U.S. Fish Wildl. Serv. Circ. 30. 51pp.

JAHN, L. R., AND R. A. HUNT. 1964. Duck and coot ecology and management in Wisconsin. Wisconsin Dept. Conserv. Tech. Bull. 33. 212pp.

JENNINGS, A. R. 1961. An analysis of 1,000 deaths in wild birds. Bird Study 8(1):25–31.

JENSEN, W. I., AND J. P. ALLEN. 1960. A possible relationship between aquatic invertebrates and avian botulism. Trans. N. Am. Wildl. Nat. Resour. Conf. 25:171–180.

———, AND C. S. WILLIAMS. 1964. Botulism and fowl cholera. Pages 333–341 *in* J. P. Linduska, ed. Waterfowl tomorrow. U.S. Government Printing Office, Washington, D.C.

KALMBACH, E. R., AND D. R. COBURN. 1937. Disease factors in reported cases of starvation in waterfowl. Trans. N. Am. Wildl. Conf. 2: 404–410.

KEITH, L. B. 1961. A study of waterfowl ecology on small impoundments in southeastern Alberta. Wildl. Monogr. 6. 88pp.

LACK, D. 1954. The natural regulation of animal numbers. Oxford University Press, London. 343pp.

LAGLER, K. F. 1956. The pike, *Esox lucius* Linnaeus, in relation to waterfowl on the Seney National Wildlife Refuge, Michigan. J. Wildl. Manage. 20(2):114–124.

LINCOLN, F. C. 1936. The effect of oil pollution on waterfowl. Proc. N. Am. Wildl. Conf. 1: 555–559.

LOCKE, L. N., V. STOTTS, AND G. WOLFHARD. 1970. An outbreak of fowl cholera in waterfowl on the Chesapeake Bay. J. Wildl. Dis. 6(4):404–407.

LONGCORE, J. R., F. B. SAMSON, AND T. W. WHITTENDALE, JR. 1971. DDE thins eggshells and lowers reproductive success of captive black ducks. Bull. Environ. Contam. Toxicol. 6(6):485–490.

LOW, J. B. 1945. Ecology and management of the redhead, *Nyroca americana*, in Iowa. Ecol. Monogr. 15(1):35–69.

LUTTICH, S., D. H. RUSCH, E. C. MESLOW, AND L. B. KEITH. 1970. Ecology of red-tailed hawk predation in Alberta. Ecology 51(2): 190–203.

MCMAHAN, C. A., AND R. L. FRITZ. 1967. Mortality to ducks from trotlines in Lower Laguna Madre, Texas. J. Wildl. Manage. 31(4):783–787.

MENDALL, H. L. 1958. The ring-necked duck in the northeast. Univ. Maine Stud. 2nd. Ser., No. 73. 317pp.

MILONSKI, M. 1958. The significance of farmland for waterfowl nesting and techniques for reducing losses due to agricultural practices. Trans. N. Am. Wildl. Conf. 23:215–228.

ORDAL, N. J. 1964. A study of duck nesting and production as related to land use in Otter Tail County, Minnesota. Pages 82–106 *in* J. B. Moyle, ed. Ducks and land use in Minnesota. Minnesota Dept. Conserv. Tech. Bull. 8.

ORING, L. W. 1964. Predation upon flightless ducks. Wilson Bull. 76(2):190.

PETRIDES, G. A., AND C. R. BRYANT. 1951. An analysis of the 1949–50 fowl cholera epizootic in Texas panhandle waterfowl. Trans. N. Am. Wildl. Conf. 16:193–216.

QUORTRUP, E. R., AND J. E. SHILLINGER. 1941. 3,000 wild bird autopsies on western lake area. J. Am. Vet. Med. Assoc. 99(776):382–387.

———, F. B. QUEEN, AND L. J. MEROVKA. 1946. An outbreak of pasteurellosis in wild ducks. J. Am. Vet. Med. Assoc. 108(827):94–100.

RATE, H. 1957. Redheads killed by a downdraft. Auk 74(3):391.

REILLY, J. R., AND D. A. BOROFF. 1967. Botulism in a tidal estuary in New Jersey. Bull. Wildl. Dis. Assoc. 3(1):26–29.

RICHARDSON, F. 1956. Sea birds affected by oil from the freighter Seagate. The Murrelet 37 (2):20–22.

ROSEBERRY, J. L. 1962. Avian mortality in southern Illinois resulting from severe weather conditions. Ecology 43(4):739–740.

ROSEN, M. N. 1969. Species susceptibility to avian cholera. Bull. Wildl. Dis. Assoc. 5(3): 195–200.

———, AND A. L. BISCHOFF. 1949. The 1948–49 outbreak of fowl cholera in birds in the San Francisco Bay area and surrounding counties. California Fish Game 35(3):185–192.

———, AND ———. 1950. The epidemiology of fowl cholera as it occurs in the wild. Trans. N. Am. Wildl. Conf. 15:147–154.

SCHORGER, A. W. 1947. The deep diving of the loon and old-squaw and its mechanism. Wilson Bull. 59(3):151–159.

SHARP, W. M. 1951. Observations on predator-prey relations between wild ducks, trumpeter swans, and golden eagles. J. Wildl. Manage. 15(2):224–226.

SMITH, A. G., AND H. R. WEBSTER. 1955. Effects of hail storms on waterfowl populations in Alberta, Canada—1953. J. Wildl. Manage. 19(3):368–374.

SOLMAN, V. E. F. 1945. The ecological relations of pike, *Esox lucius* L., and waterfowl. Ecology 26(2):157–170.

STEWART, R. E., AND J. H. MANNING. 1958. Distribution and ecology of whistling swans in the Chesapeake Bay Region. Auk 75(2):203–212.

STODDARD, H. L., SR., AND R. A. NORRIS. 1967. Bird casualties at a Leon County, Florida TV tower: an eleven-year study. Tall Timbers Res. Stn. Bull. 8. 104pp.

STOTTS, V. D., AND D. E. DAVIS. 1960. The black duck in the Chesapeake Bay of Maryland: breeding behavior and biology. Chesapeake Sci. 1(3, 4):127–154.

STOUT, I. J. 1967. The nature and pattern of nonhunting mortality in fledged North American waterfowl. M.S. Thesis. Virginia Polytechnic Inst. and State Univ., Blacksburg. 329pp.

TORDOFF, H. B., AND R. M. MENGEL. 1956. Studies of birds killed in nocturnal migration. Univ. Kansas Mus. Nat. Hist. Publ. 10(1):1–44.

TRAUTMAN, M. B., W. E. BILLS, AND E. L. WICKLIFF. 1939. Winter losses from starvation and exposure of waterfowl and upland game birds in Ohio and other northern states. Wilson Bull. 51(2):86–104.

VAUGHT, R. W., H. C. MCDOUGLE, AND H. H. BURGESS. 1967. Fowl cholera in waterfowl at Squaw Creek National Wildlife Refuge, Missouri. J. Wildl. Manage. 31(2):248–253.

WAGNER, F. H., C. D. BESADNY, AND C. KABAT. 1965. Population ecology and management of Wisconsin pheasants. Wisconsin Conserv. Dept. Tech. Bull. 34. 168pp.

WOOTEN, W. H. 1954. Waterfowl losses in the surf along the northern California coast. J. Wildl. Manage. 18(1):140–141.

WRIGHT, B. S. 1953. The relation of bald eagles to breeding ducks in New Brunswick. J. Wildl. Manage. 17(1):55–62.

———. 1954. High tide and an east wind: the story of the black duck. The Stackpole Co., Harrisburg, Pa., and The Wildlife Management Institute, Washington, D.C. 162pp.

Accepted 12 April 1976.

SELECTED BIBLIOGRAPHY

Population Influences and Characteristics: Population Ecology

ANDERSON, D. R. 1975. Optimal exploitation strategies for an animal population in a Markovian environment: a theory and an example. Ecology 56(6):1281–1297.

———. 1975. Population ecology of the mallard/V. Temporal and geographic estimates of survival, recovery, and harvest rates. U.S. Dep. Inter. Fish and Wildl. Serv. Resour. Publ. 125. 110pp.

———, AND K. P. BURNHAM. 1976. Population ecology of the mallard/VI. The effect of exploitation on survival. U.S. Dep. Inter. Fish and Wildl. Serv. Resour. Publ. 128. 66pp.

———, AND C. J. HENNY. 1972. Population ecology of the mallard/I. A review of previous studies and the distribution and migration from breeding areas. U.S. Bur. Sport Fish Wildl. Resour. Publ. 105. 166pp.

———, P. A. SKAPTASON, K. G. FAHEY, AND C. J. HENNY. 1974. Population ecology of the mallard/III. Bibliography of published research and management findings. U.S. Bur. Sport Fish Wildl. Resour. Publ. 119. 46pp.

———, AND R. T. STERLING. 1974. Population dynamics of molting pintail drakes banded in southcentral Saskatchewan. J. Wildl. Manage. 38(2):266–274.

BAILEY, R. O. 1981. Theoretical approach to problems in waterfowl management. Trans. N. Am. Wildl. Nat. Resour. Conf. 46. In Press.

BARTONEK, J. C. 1965. Mortality of diving ducks on Lake Winnipegosis through commercial fishing. Can. Field-Nat. 79(1):15–20.

BELLROSE, F. C. 1955. A comparison of recoveries from reward and standard bands. J. Wildl. Manage. 19(1):71–75.

BOWERS, E. F., AND F. W. MARTIN. 1975. Managing wood ducks by population units. Trans. North Am. Wildl. Nat. Resour. Conf. 40:300–324.

BOYD, H. 1981. A fair future for prairie ducks; cloudy further north. Trans. N. Am. Wildl. Nat. Resour. Conf. 46. In Press.

BROWN, G. M., JR., J. HAMMACK, AND M. F. TILLMAN. 1976. Mallard population dynamics and management models. J. Wildl. Manage. 40(3):542–555.

COWARDIN, L. M., AND D. H. JOHNSON. 1979. Mathematics and mallard management. J. Wildl. Manage. 43(1):18–35.

DZUBIN, A. 1969. Assessing breeding populations of ducks by ground counts. Pages 178–230 *in* Saskatoon Wetlands Seminar. Can. Wildl. Serv. Rep. Ser. 6.

EBERHARDT, L. L. 1972. Some problems in estimating survival from banding data. Pages 153–171 *in* Population ecology of migratory birds: a symposium. U.S. Dep. Inter. Bur. Sport Fish. and Wildl. Res. Rep. 2.

GEIS, A. D. 1972. Role of banding data in migratory bird population studies. Pages 213–228 *in* Population ecology of migratory birds: a symposium. U.S. Dep. Inter. Bur. Sport Fish. and Wildl. Res. Rep. 2.

———, AND E. L. ATWOOD. 1961. Proportion of recovered waterfowl bands reported. J. Wildl. Manage. 25(2):154–159.

———, AND W. F. CRISSEY. 1969. Effect of restrictive hunting and regulations on canvasback and redhead harvest rates and survival. J. Wildl. Manage. 33(4):860–866.

KROHN, W. B., AND E. G. BIZEAU. 1980. The Rocky Mountain population of the western Canada goose: its distribution, habitats, and management. U.S. Fish and Wildlife Service, Special Scientific Report—Wildlife No. 229, Washington, D.C. 93pp.

MARCH, J. R., AND R. A. HUNT. 1978. Mallard population and harvest dynamics in Wisconsin. Wis. Dep. Nat. Resour. Tech. Bull. 106. 74pp.

MARTIN, E. M., AND S. M. CARNEY. 1977. Population ecology of the mallard/ IV. A review of duck hunting regulations, activity and success, with special reference to the mallard. U.S. Dep. Inter. Fish and Wildl. Serv. Resour. Publ. 130. 137pp.

MARTINSON, R. K. 1966. Proportion of recovered duck bands that are reported. J. Wildl. Manage. 30(2):264–268.

———, AND J. A. MCCANN. 1966. Proportion of recovered goose and brant bands that are reported. J. Wildl. Manage. 30(4):856–858.

MELINCHUK, R., AND J. P. RYDER. The distribution, fall migration routes and survival of Ross' geese. Wildfowl 31:161–171.

MILLER, H. W., A. DZUBIN, AND J. T. SWEET. 1968. Distribution and mortality of Saskatchewan-banded white-fronted geese. Trans. North Am. Wildl. Nat. Resour. Conf. 33:101–119.

MOISAN, G., R. I. SMITH, AND R. K. MARTINSON. 1967. The green-winged teal: its distribution, migration, and population dynamics. U.S. Fish and Wildl. Serv. Spec. Sci. Rep. 100. 248pp.

POSPAHALA, R. S., D. R. ANDERSON, AND C. J. HENNY. 1974. Population ecology of the mallard/II. Breeding habitat conditions, size of the breeding populations, and production indices. U.S. Dep. Inter. Bur. Sport Fish Wildl. Resour. Publ. 115. 73pp.

RATTI, J. T., D. E. TIMM, AND D. R. ANDERSON. 1978. Reevaluation of survival estimates for Vancouver Canada geese: application of modern methods. Wildl. Soc. Bull. 6(3):146–148.

WALTERS, C. J., R. HILBORN, E. OGUSS, R. M. PETERMAN, AND J. M. STANDER. 1974. Development of a simulation model of mallard duck populations. Can. Wildl. Serv. Occas. Pap. 20. 35pp.

Sex Ratios

WATERFOWL SEX RATIOS DURING SPRING IN WASHINGTON STATE AND THEIR INTERPRETATION

PAUL A. JOHNSGARD and IRVEN O. BUSS, Department of Zoology, State College of Washington, Pullman, Washington

Sex-ratio studies have received much attention from research workers in recent years. The contributions of Hochbaum (1944), Petrides (1944) and others have yielded considerable information on sex ratios in waterfowl; Beer (1945) and Yocom (1949) have presented data for the state of Washington. To interpret regional data on waterfowl sex ratios adequately, it is necessary to obtain a series of uninterrupted observations covering the entire migration period of the species concerned. In 1954, an ecologic study was conducted in the Potholes area, Grant County, central Washington (Johnsgard, 1956). During the period February 15 to May 16, sex-ratio data were collected for more than 15,000 ducks, including 17 species to be discussed in this paper. Nearly all these species wintered in the region and were present in small numbers when field work began in February (Johnsgard, 1954).

Sex counts were obtained for several types of habitat during this study. Among these were the potholes which occur between the sand dunes that were deposited in the region during glacial times (Bretz, 1928). Following the recent construction of O'Sullivan Dam and the subsequent filling of Potholes Reservoir, many of these potholes were inundated by the rapid rise of the reservoir. However, seepage below the dam has resulted in the formation of numerous lakes and smaller water areas in the scabland channels previously covered with sagebrush (*Artemisia tridentata*) and associated vegetation. Counts on these new seepage areas, as well as counts obtained on Potholes Reservoir, were recorded separately from those obtained on the sand-dune potholes.

Methods

Sex counts were made directly with the aid of a six-power binocular during daily surveys of the study areas. Only birds definitely identified as to sex were included. There is little likelihood that many birds were overlooked because of the relative scarcity of emergent vegetation in most of the habitats studied. However, it is probable that a certain amount of unavoidable duplication did occur. Ratios have been calculated (males per 100 females, total sample in parenthesis) in all cases where 100 or more individuals were recorded for a given time interval or habitat. In cases where fewer than 100 birds were recorded the total number of males and females is presented, but no ratios were calculated. Choosing 100 individuals as the minimum acceptable sample is wholly arbitrary and is not based on statistical tests.

Observations

As is usual among waterfowl, diving ducks observed in this study tended to exhibit a more disproportionate sex ratio than surface-feeding ducks. Furthermore, ratios of several diving duck species (redhead, common golden-eye, buffle-head, common merganser) tended to become less disproportionate as the migration period progressed. The ruddy duck exhibited a more disproportionate sex ratio near the end of the migration period.

Sex ratios of any single species varied at any given time as a result of at least two influences. First, sex ratios were more unbalanced on areas subject to human disturbance. Paired birds were the first to flush and the last to return to a disturbed area. Birds preoccupied in courtship display were noticeably less wary than paired birds. This same behavior was manifested by field-feeding mallards. Whenever a flock of these birds was flushed, a definite sequence of events could be observed. The first birds to return to the field were invariably a few single males, apparently searching for mates from which they had been separated during flushing. These birds would circle a few times, calling occasionally, but never landing. Later, numerous small flocks of unpaired birds would arrive, typically a single female and two or more males. These birds were the first to land, and were later followed by large groups of mostly paired birds. Thus the

Originally published in J. Wildl. Manage. 20(4):384–388, 1956.

obtaining of sex counts on disturbed areas during the mating period is likely to be markedly influenced as a result of this phenomenon. Yocom (1949) indicated that sex counts of mallards obtained in winter and early spring on the Snake River near Clarkston, Washington, were usually more disproportionate than those obtained along portions of the river which are less frequented by humans.

Second, sex ratios during any single period varied with the characteristics of the habitat. Most mating activities of the surface-feeding ducks occurred on the shallow seepage areas below O'Sullivan Dam; diving ducks courted on the deeper lakes below the dam, along the edge of the reservoir, or on the deeper sand-dune potholes (Johnsgard, 1956). Following mating, many pairs separated from the main flocks and moved to the smaller *Scirpus-* and *Juncus*-lined sand-dune potholes, where food and cover were more available. Perhaps the greater seclusion and freedom from disturbance by bachelor drakes partially accounted for this behavior. Hochbaum (1944) mentioned that paired canvas-backs usually separate from the unpaired birds and frequent the tule edges. In spring observations on the Snake River near Clarkston, Washington, Stout *et al.* (1955) reported: "Early in the study most of the mallards observed in the eddy were unmated. As the study progressed the mated birds tended to move on down the river. The bachelor drakes remained in the eddy."

As a result of the behavior described above, the sex ratios obtained in the more densely vegetated sand-dune potholes were more nearly equal than those counts obtained on the reservoir and seepage areas below O'Sullivan Dam. These differences in sex ratios are presented in Table 1 to illustrate this point. Data for the period February 15-21 are not included in the table, since the sand-dune potholes were still frozen at that time and all waterfowl were congregated in the seepage areas.

A certain degree of habitat preference is demonstrated in this table, the case of the ring-necked duck and canvas-back being most evident. The canvas-back used the seepage lakes almost exclusively during the courting period; since very few birds paired before departure, they were rarely observed in the sand-dune potholes. On the other hand, the ring-necked ducks moved from the seepage areas into the sand-dune potholes as soon as these were free of ice, where the birds continued courtship display. Common mergansers were never recorded in the potholes, but remained on the deeper lakes where they undoubtedly fed on fish and other aquatic animal life. Although the common golden-eye and buffle-head courted in the potholes as well as the seepage lakes, in the former they inhabited only those potholes that were deep and free of most vegetation.

As indicated in Table 2, there were only

TABLE 1. — LOCATIONAL VARIATIONS IN SEX RATIOS

Species	February 22 to May 16			
	Potholes		Reservoir and Seepage Areas	
Mallard (*Anas platyrhynchos*)	118:100	(2,709)	150:100	(1,545)
Gadwall (*A. strepera*)	113:100	(117)	109:100	(367)
Baldpate (*Mareca americana*)	112:100	(138)	139:100	(661)
Pintail (*Anas acuta*)	113:100	(428)	135:100	(564)
Green-winged Teal (*A. carolinensis*)	105:100	(485)	121:100	(287)
Blue-winged Teal (*A. discors*)	(20:20)		(1:1)	
Cinnamon Teal (*A. cyanoptera*)	(48:50)		(8:8)	
Shoveller (*Spatula clypeata*)	113:100	(185)	(64:28)	
Redhead (*Aythya americana*)	128:100	(476)	248:100	(111)
Ring-necked Duck (*A. collaris*)	158:100	(432)	(6:1)	
Canvas-back (*A. valisineria*)	(8:6)		418:100	(294)
Lesser Scaup (*A. affinis*)	177:100	(411)	379:100	(1,423)
Common Golden-eye (*Bucephala clangula*)	97:100	(382)	170:100	(310)
Barrow's Golden-eye (*B. islandica*)	—		(26:14)	
Buffle-head (*B. albeola*)	81:100	(350)	(51:38)	
Ruddy Duck (*Oxyura jamaicensis*)	(30:23)		147:100	(951)
Common Merganser (*Mergus merganser*)	—		161:100	(615)

TABLE 2. — SEASONAL VARIATIONS IN SEX RATIOS

	Feb. 15-March 28		March 29-May 16		Total Feb. 15-May 16	
Mallard	132:100	(3,018)	129:100	(1,996)	131:100	(5,014)
Gadwall	111:100	(175)	108:100	(335)	109:100	(510)
Baldpate	135:100	(443)	147:100	(408)	140:100	(851)
Pintail	122:100	(534)	130:100	(501)	126:100	(1,035)
Green-winged Teal	123:100	(202)	112:100	(667)	114:100	(869)
Blue-winged Teal	–		(21:21)		(21:21)	
Cinnamon Teal	–		97:100	(114)	97:100	(114)
Shoveller	(16:7)		135:100	(254)	141:100	(277)
Redhead	198:100	(175)	140:100	(463)	152:100	(638)
Ring-necked Duck	171:100	(152)	159:100	(329)	163:100	(481)
Canvas-back	416:100	(558)	(15:7)		404:100	(580)
Lesser Scaup	279:100	(528)	317:100	(1,327)	305:100	(1,855)
Common Golden-eye	124:100	(689)	87:100	(170)	116:100	(859)
Barrow's Golden-eye	(8:3)		(18:11)		(26:14)	
Buffle-head	103:100	(189)	81:100	(299)	89:100	(488)
Ruddy Duck	99:100	(173)	153:100	(865)	142:100	(1,038)
Common Merganser	228:100	(479)	51:100	(136)	161:100	(615)

minor variations in the sex ratios of surface-feeding species between the first and second half of the migration period. Although there are several inherent weaknesses in applying statistical tests to determine the significance of such variations, such tests suggest that the seasonal variations of the redhead, common golden-eye, ruddy duck and common merganser sex ratios are of a significant magnitude.

A differential sex migration would explain some of these variations in those species that pair on the breeding grounds (cf. Nice, 1937; and Tinbergen, 1939), but this explanation has limited application to waterfowl, which are usually paired before their arrival on the breeding grounds. Possible exceptions to this are the ruddy duck and the common merganser, both of which apparently exhibit a true differential sex migration.

An early spring preponderance of males followed by approximately equal numbers of males and females has been noticed in blue-winged teal in Minnesota (Erickson, 1943) and in teal (*Anas crecca*), shoveller, and pintail in the Netherlands (Lebret, 1950). This suggests to us that females may winter somewhat farther south than the males. Females are apparently more sensitive to cold than males (Harrison and McLean, 1947), often beginning their fall migration southward before the drakes (Leopold, 1919).

A differential migration between adult and juvenile birds would help account for a late spring equalization in sex ratios for those cases where immature plumages of males closely resemble those of the female. This later migration of juveniles has been noted in redwings (*Agelaius phoeniceus*) (Allen, 1914), buffle-head (Munro, 1942) and other species, and very likely contributed to the apparent sex-ratio variation in the common golden-eye, buffle-head and common merganser in our study. Although juvenile males of these species were separated whenever possible, some were probably confused with females. For this reason the sex ratios presented for these species during the period February 15 to March 28 are considered most accurate.

An alternate explanation for the seasonal variations in sex ratios concerns a differential migratory behavior between paired and unpaired birds. Hochbaum (1944) mentioned that paired canvas-backs arrive at Delta marsh before the unpaired birds; this would tend to result in an increased proportion of males in later sex counts. Beer (1945) noted that paired baldpates were the first to depart from wintering grounds in southwestern Washington, and McIlhenny (1940) observed that female blue-winged teal began migrating north as soon as they were paired. A later preponderance of males was observed in the study area in the case of the ruddy duck. However, observations of the redhead indicated that most wintering birds and early migrants were not paired, and later flocks were composed largely of paired birds. Fuller (1953) noted a similar situation with migrating pintail in Utah.

It is therefore apparent that any general statement to the effect that paired birds migrate earlier or faster than unpaired birds (or vice versa) is subject to considerable debate. However, it is possible that, through the differences in habitat preferences by paired vs. unpaired birds, sufficient cleavage of migratory routes in these two components of the populations occurs to account for paired (or unpaired) birds arriving at a particular location first. If such an influence is actually operative, it would appear logical to suspect that unpaired birds would tend to select habitats suitable for courtship but unsuited for breeding, whereas paired birds would go directly to breeding areas and other habitats that offer most opportunities for food and shelter.

In all likelihood no single explanation will suffice; it is highly probable that all of the above complexities enter into the variations usually encountered in waterfowl sex-ratio counts. As a means of summarizing and comparing some of the available data on sex ratios, ratios observed in this study are compared with samples obtained by direct count in other areas (Table 3). Although ratios based on larger samples obtained from banding and hunter-kill data are available for

TABLE 3. —A COMPARISON OF NORTH AMERICAN WATERFOWL SEX RATIOS

Species	Sex Ratio	Location	Source
Mallard	131:100 (5,014)	Washington	Present Paper
	126:100 (6,810)	Ore., Calif., Nev.	Evenden (1952)
	109:100 (8,805)	Washington	Yocom (1949)
Gadwall	109:100 (510)	Washington	Present Paper
	101:100 (271)	Ore., Nev., Ariz.	Evenden (1952)
Baldpate	140:100 (851)	Washington	Present Paper
	114:100 (4,999)	Washington	Beer (1945)
Pintail	126:100 (1,035)	Washington	Present Paper
	126:100 (12,336)	District of Columbia	Petrides (1944)
	133:100 (11,687)	Utah	Fuller (1953)
Green-winged Teal	114:100 (869)	Washington	Present Paper
	108:100 (4,264)	British Columbia	Munro (1949)
Blue-winged Teal	144:100 (5,090)	Iowa	Bennett (1938)
Cinnamon Teal	97:100 (114)	Washington	Present Paper
	87:100 (2,379)	Utah	Spencer (1953)
Shoveller	141:100 (277)	Washington	Present Paper
	152:100 (3,190)	Ore., Calif., Nev.	Evenden (1952)
Redhead	152:100 (613)	Washington	Present Paper
	142:100 (3,400)	Iowa	Low (1945)
Ring-necked Duck	163:100 (481)	Washington	Present Paper
	193:100 (1,495)	Wisconsin	Buss & Mattison (1955)
Canvas-back	404:100 (580)	Washington	Present Paper
	162:100 (8,936)	Minnesota	Smith (1946)
Lesser Scaup	305:100 (580)	Washington	Present Paper
	201:100 (10,664)	Manitoba	Sowls (1955)
Common Golden-eye	116:100 (859)	Washington	Present Paper
	141:100 (140)	Minnesota	Erickson (1943)
Buffle-head	89:100 (484)	Washington	Present Paper
	142:100 (384)	British Columbia	Munro (1942)
	158:100 (520)	Iowa	Low (1941)
Ruddy Duck	142:100 (1,038)	Washington	Present Paper
	141:100 (850)	Iowa	Low (1941)
Common Merganser	161:100 (615)	Washington	Present Paper
	138:100 (773)	Washington	Beer (1945)

some of these species, such ratios have been shown to produce biased results (Petrides, 1944; Yocom, 1949). Thus, with the exception of Bennett's (1938) data (which are based partially on hunter-kill), the samples included are the largest available based on direct counts.

ACKNOWLEDGMENTS

These data were obtained as part of a research project sponsored by the State College of Washington and the State of Washington Department of Game. The project was financed in part by funds provided for biological and medical research by the State of Washington Initiative Measure No. 171.

SUMMARY

During the spring of 1954, sex-ratio studies were conducted in the Potholes area, Grant County, central Washington. Data were collected on over 15,000 ducks, including 17 species. Sex ratios during any single period were found to vary as a result of different habitat preferences and tolerance of disturbance between paired and unpaired birds. Changes in sex ratios as the migration period progressed were attributed to be the probable result of a differential migratory behavior between ages, sexes, and paired vs. unpaired birds.

LITERATURE CITED

ALLEN, A. A. 1914. The red-winged blackbird: a study in the ecology of a cat-tail marsh. Abst. Proc. Linn. Soc. N. Y., No. 24-25: 43-128.

BEER, J. R. 1945. Sex ratios of ducks in southwestern Washington. Auk, 62:117-124.

BENNETT, L. J. 1938. The blue-winged teal, its ecology and management. Collegiate Press Inc., Ames, Iowa. 144 pp.

BRETZ, J. H. 1928. The channeled scablands of eastern Washington. Geog. Rev., 18:446-477.

BUSS, I. O. AND H. M. MATTISON. 1955. A half century of change in bird populations of the lower Chippewa River, Wisconsin. Milwaukee Public Museum, Milwaukee. 319 pp.

ERICKSON, A. B. 1943. Sex ratios of ducks in Minnesota, 1938-1940. Auk, 60:20-34.

EVENDEN, F. G., JR. 1952. Waterfowl sex ratios observed in the western United States. Jour. Wildl. Mgt., 16:391-393.

FULLER, R. W. 1953. Studies in the life history and ecology of the American pintail (*Anas acuta tzitizhoa* Vieillot) in Utah. M.S. thesis, Utah State Agricultural College, Logan. 181 pp.

HARRISON, J. AND A. MCLEAN. 1947. The effect of severe weather on wigeon. Brit. Birds, 40:218.

HOCHBAUM, H. A. 1944. The canvasback on a prairie marsh. American Wildlife Institute, Washington, D.C. 201 pp.

JOHNSGARD, P. A. 1954. Birds observed in the Potholes region during 1953-54. Murrelet, 35(2): 25-31.

———. 1955. Courtship activities of the Anatidae in eastern Washington. Condor, 57(1):19-27.

———. 1956. The effects of water fluctuation and vegetation change on bird populations, particularly waterfowl. Ecology (in press).

LEBRET, T. 1950. The sex ratios and the proportion of adult drakes of teal, pintail, shoveler and wigeon in the Netherlands, based on field counts made during autumn, winter, and spring. Ardea, 38(1-2):1-18.

LEOPOLD, A. 1919. Differential sex migration of mallards in New Mexico. Condor, 21:182-183.

LOW, J. B. 1941. Spring flight of the diving ducks through northwestern Iowa. Condor, 43(3): 142-151.

———. 1945. Ecology and management of the redhead, *Nyroca americana*, in Iowa. Ecol. Mong., 15(1):35-69.

MCILHENNY, E. A. 1940. Sex ratio in wild birds, Auk, 57(1):85-93.

MUNRO, J. A. 1942. Studies of waterfowl in British Columbia. Bufflehead. Canad. J. Res., 20(D): 133-160.

———. 1949. Studies of waterfowl in British Columbia. Green-winged teal. Canad. J. Res., 27 (D):149-178.

NICE, M. M. 1937. Studies in the life history of the song sparrow (I). Trans. Linn. Soc. N.Y., 4:1-247.

PETRIDES, G. A. 1944. Sex ratios in ducks. Auk, 61:564-571.

SMITH, J. D. 1946. The canvas-back in Minnesota. Auk, 63:73-81.

SOWLS, L. K. 1955. Prairie ducks: a study of their behavior, ecology and management. Wildlife Management Institute, Washington, D. C. 193 pp.

SPENCER, H. F. 1953. The cinnamon teal (*Anas cyanoptera* Vieillot): its life history, ecology, and management. M.S. thesis, Utah State Agric. Coll., Logan. 184 pp.

STOUT, R., A. SOLBERG, K. BRAGET, J. PACE AND R. WALLACE. 1955. Waterfowl study on the Snake River. Unpublished report filed in Dept. Zoology, State Coll. of Wash., Pullman.

TINBERGEN, N. 1939. The behavior of the snow bunting in spring. Trans. Linn. Soc. N. Y., 5:1-94.

YOCOM, C. F. 1949. A study of sex ratios of mallards in the state of Washington. Condor, 51: 222-227.

Received for publication August 2, 1955.

INFLUENCE OF WINTER TEMPERATURES ON PINTAIL SEX RATIOS IN TEXAS[1]

JOHN R. ALFORD III and ERIC G. BOLEN,[2] Department of Range and Wildlife Management, Texas Tech University, Lubbock, TX 79409

Waterfowl sex ratios have been of interest to biologists for several decades. Lincoln (1932) was among the first to note that males outnumbered females in several species of ducks. Sex ratios have since received considerable attention, especially in the extensive review by Bellrose et al. (1961), and in the more recent control of waterfowl harvests (i.e., the point system). However, Bellrose et al. (1961) noted various sampling biases associated with obtaining sex ratios (e.g., trapping vulnerability, hunter selectivity, etc.). Our work reports the apparent effect of a natural phenomenon, the influence of cold, on the sex ratios of pintails wintering on the High Plains of the Texas Panhandle.

SAMPLING METHODS

We sampled pintails wintering on the High Plains Region of the Texas Panhandle. The sites included Muleshoe National Wildlife Refuge, Buffalo Lake National Wildlife Refuge, and playa lakes near the refuges and near Lubbock, Texas (see Rollo and Bolen 1969 and Soutiere et al. 1972 for habitat descriptions). Sampling dates are shown in Table 1.

A variable power spotting scope was used to view the birds at rest on water or on exposed mud flats. The numbers of males and females in the spotting scope's field of vision constituted one sample; 10 initial samples were randomly selected across the breadth of the pintail flocks. We kept a cumulative total of the samples so that the percentage of males could be calculated with a slide rule. The sampling procedure was thus somewhat similar to the concept of species-area curves used by plant ecologists; when additional samples failed to alter the percentage of males (i.e., flattening of the "curve"), the observations were terminated. As the samples did not utilize birds attracted to bait, those already in traps, or those in the hunter's bag, little experimental error was encountered because of social strife, trapping vulnerability, or hunter selectivity. Observations made between late October and February also precluded difficulties associated with the identification of juvenile pintails of each sex or with the eclipse plumage of adult males. Moreover, sex ratios obtained on the wintering ground are presumably free of the local variations occurring in spring on northern breeding marshes (see Hammond *in* Bellrose et al. 1961:402).

Our data were collected under a variety of temperature conditions. The High Plains Region of Texas is subject to temperatures varying each winter from balmy, warm days to cold fronts or blizzards of usually short but extreme proportions. Hence, the sex ratio data we collected enabled us to quantify the influence that minimum daily temperatures might exert on this parameter in pintail populations.

Each of the sex ratio observations was compared with the minimum daily temperature from the Department of Com-

[1] Originally published in Southwest. Nat. 21(4):554–556, 1977.

[2] Address correspondence to this author. Present address: % Dean's Office, The Graduate School, Texas Tech University, Lubbock, TX 79409.

Table 1. Sampling locations, dates, minimum daily temperatures, and sex ratios for wintering pintails, High Plains Region, Texas, 1971–72.

Location	Date	Sample size	Minimum temperature, F	Percent males
Muleshoe playas*	Oct. 23	146	38	47
Muleshoe playas*	Nov. 6	148	34	48
Muleshoe playas*	Nov. 8	99	34	46
Muleshoe playas*	Nov. 11	227	28	55
Buffalo Lake playas*	Dec. 30	358	22	54
Buffalo Lake NWR†	Jan. 10	654	26	53
Buffalo Lake playas*	Jan. 29	538	16	59
Buffalo Lake playas*	Apr. 30	287	14	68
Muleshoe NWR†	Feb. 3	493	5	68
Muleshoe NWR†	Feb. 4	398	4	68
Lubbock playas*	Feb. 5	985	26	70
Muleshoe NWR†	Feb. 10	325	20	69
Lubbock playas*	Feb. 11	499	23	73
Muleshoe playas*	Feb. 18	720	23	66
Muleshoe playas*	Feb. 25	871	33	69

* Playa lakes in vicinity of named locality where pintails congregated.
† NWR = National Wildlife Refuge.

merce records from the nearest weather station for the 24-hour period on the day the sex ratios were obtained.

RESULTS AND DISCUSSION

A correlation test yielded a significant negative relationship ($r = -0.58$, $P < 0.05$); the percentage of males in the winter pintail population on the Texas High Plains increased as temperature decreased (Table 1). The variation in sex ratios attributable directly to minimum daily temperatures is thus 34 percent.

Obviously care must be exercised interpreting these data. For example, each succeeding cold front seemingly pushed female pintails southward (see following references) so that the proportion of males steadily increased throughout the winter months. Accordingly, as the winter progressed there was an ever-larger percentage of males even though the minimum temperatures were by then sometimes higher than in the preceding weeks. The steady increase in the proportion of males would seem most pronounced at locations on the northern edge of the wintering grounds as is the case for our High Plains study areas. The influx of cold-displaced female pintails must also change, a priori, local sex ratios farther south although we have no supporting data on this subject.

The phenomenon that temperature affects the sex ratios of duck populations has been suggested in other studies. Harrison and McLean (1947) suspected that female European wigeon (*Anas penelope*) in Britain suffered more in their physical condition from cold than did males. This suggested to Lebret (1950) that female ducks wintering in the Netherlands are more likely to move southwards under the pressure of severe weather than are males. The effect on regional sex ratio samples is obvious. After examining sex ratios for pintails wintering in Texas, Bellrose et al. (1961:416) concluded that pintail drakes tend to winter farther north, a conclusion we can now more specifically relate with winter temperature regimes. This relationship may exist for species other than puddle ducks as Anderson and Timken (1972) recently found that the proportion of adult males in common merganser (*Mergus merganser*) populations increased as temperatures dropped.

We suggest that any study of winter sex ratios of waterfowl lacking life-long pair bonds (e.g., *Anas* spp. and others) should consider the interaction of ambient temperatures on the proportion of males present in the samples. Our findings suggest a marked influence of cold on this important aspect of waterfowl biology and management.

We appreciate the assistance of B. E. Blair, Manager, Muleshoe National Wildlife Refuge, and P. E. Ferguson, Manager, Buffalo Lake Wildlife Refuge. The manuscript was helpfully reviewed by F. C. Bellrose and the late C. Cottam. This is Technical Note T-9-119 of the College of Agricultural Sciences, Texas Tech University.

LITERATURE CITED

ANDERSON, B. W., AND R. L. TIMKEN. 1972. Sex and age ratios and weights of common mergansers. J. Wildl. Manage. 36:1127–1133.

BELLROSE, F. C., T. G. SCOTT, A. S. HAWKINS, AND J. B. LOW. 1961. Sex ratios and age ratios in North American ducks. Illinois Nat. Hist. Surv. Bull. 27:391–474.

HARRISON, J., AND A. MCLEAN. 1947. The effect of severe weather on wigeon. British Birds 40:218.

LEBRET, T. 1950. The sex-ratios and proportion of adult drakes of teal, pintail, shoveler and wigeon in the Netherlands, based on field counts made during autumn, winter and spring. Ardea 38(1–2):1–18.

LINCOLN, F. C. 1932. Do drakes outnumber susies? Am. Game 21:3–4, 16–17.

ROLLO, J. D., AND E. G. BOLEN. 1969. Ecological relationships of blue and green-winged teal on the High Plains of Texas in early fall. Southwestern Nat. 14:171–188.

SOUTIERE, E. C., H. S. MYRICK, AND E. G. BOLEN. 1972. Chronology and behavior of American widgeon wintering in Texas. J. Wildl. Manage. 36:752–758.

DISPARATE SEX RATIOS IN WATERFOWL[1]

JOHN W. ALDRICH[2]

The issue of disparate sex ratios was singled out for special discussion because of its interest from the standpoint of application to wildlife management, and because it brings to bear a multidisciplinary scrutiny of the reproductive biology of birds. The reason for current interest is the growing sentiment favoring special hunting regulations of wild ducks that encourage the shooting of more males than females. The rationale here is that there is a disproportionately large number of males in wild duck populations and that it would increase hunting opportunities and at the same time tend to reduce the excess males, which are considered either of no value or even detrimental to reproduction. But the assumption that the extra male ducks have no value in reproduction has not been adequately tested and considerable effort will be required to do this. Some hypotheses requiring testing follow:

1. An excess of drakes may be damaging to production because they harass the hens, either causing them to fail to nest or to disperse too far from water to nest during drought periods, with resulting hazard to ducklings.
2. An excess of drakes in group courtship is necessary to stimulate behavior—endrocrine reactions leading to pair formation and synchrony of breeding condition in pairs.
3. An excess of drakes is necessary to ensure a mate for renesting of hens that lose their first clutches of eggs at a time after their first mates have departed.
4. An excess of drakes is necessary to ensure that there will be at least one available male to pair with each female in species the males of which mature at an older age than females.

Harvey K. Nelson commented on the work of a committee of the Central Flyway Technical Section that was formed in 1970 to investigate the function of excess drakes in various waterfowl populations. In particular, he summarized a draft of a paper by Alex Dzubin, titled "Biological Implications of Spring Drake Removal on Productivity of Hen Waterfowl" that was prepared for this committee. Dzubin raised seven questions that are still pertinent to the overall subject as far as ducks are concerned:

1. What is the impact of unnatural sex ratios upon the continued survival and growth of a breeding population?
2. Is a sex ratio distorted above 53:47 (112 ♂♂ : 100 ♀♀) biologically meaningful in terms of providing renesting hens with readily available males after their primary drakes have abandoned the home ranges at midincubation?
3. Does the presence of the male with the hen in a pair-bond confer some positive advantage to successful laying of a fertilized clutch when we consider that, in semitame flocks, one drake can successfully fertilize 6–10 hens?
4. Does a hen with an accompanying male have some advantage in siting her home range, activity center, and waiting area in an optimum location (i.e., for survival of herself and her progeny)?
5. Are unmated drakes in the spring

---

[1] Originally published in D. S. Farner, ed. Breeding biology of birds, pages 482–489. National Academy of Sciences, Washington, D.C., 1973.

[2] Present address: 6324 Lakeview Drive, Falls Church, VA 22041.

mostly yearling or adult birds? Are they capable of fertilizing ova?

6. Most Mallards (*Anas platyrhynchos*) now breed in artificially altered habitats under greatly increased spring grain food resources but under restricted acreages of nesting cover. Mallard populations are now subject to "unnatural" hunting mortality. We must ask the unanswerable questions: What were sex ratios in the pristine breeding habitats before the coming of the white man? Are the present day distorted ratios favoring males an "unnatural" condition due to increased hen mortality from hunting or from higher loss to predators incurred while nesting in suboptimal habitats?

7. Can we, in fact, do as Crissey (1969) proposes; i.e., can we distort the sex ratios to favor hens and thus decrease pair interaction and pair spacing and increase production?

Nelson suggested that the following additional questions need to be answered:

1. When does the greatest female mortality occur and does this vary for different geographic areas and species?

2. What is the difference in waterfowl sex ratios in the northern portions of the breeding range as against the southern portion of the breeding range?

3. Since there is some evidence that drakes, particularly Mallards, winter farther north, is there any indication of a greater excess of hens in the more southern wintering populations?

4. What is the actual potential to harvest excess drakes, in view of some of the experimental seasons that have been tried?

5. Do we really understand the role of male waterfowl as they influence breeding biology and behavior?

In attempting to determine what is really known about waterfowl sex ratios, Dzubin's paper is one of the most useful resources. He presented the following summary information based on his own field experience and an intensive literature review.

Sex ratios can be separated into four categories: primary at fertilization, secondary at hatching, tertiary in immatures, and quaternary in adults. Spring sex ratios of most adult ducks, divers or dabblers, are distorted and favor males (Bellrose et al. 1961, Hochbaum 1944, Sowls 1955). Generally, diver sex ratios are more heavily distorted than dabblers. Secondary sex ratios of incubator-hatched wild Mallard eggs show a 53:47 ratio (N = 630) (Hochbaum 1944:51).

The tertiary sex ratio of the juvenile Mallard component is apparently close to 1:1. Low (1957), summarizing bandings from prairie Canada, showed a sex ratio of 50.9:49.1 (1,138:1,097) for Alberta-banded locals and 51.6:48.4 (4,796:4,505) for Saskatchewan locals. Using only ducklings banded in the years 1950–61, Lensink (1964:93–97) reported a sex ratio of 51.2:48.8 (16,102:15,227) for the western interior of Canada and 50.5:49.5 (12,040:11,721) for the northern plains. In the Kindersley area of Saskatchewan, for the period 1952–59, Gollop (1965) gives a sex ratio of 50.4:49.6 (6,523:6,408) for locally banded young. In all, of some 79,726 Mallard ducklings sexed (an unknown proportion duplicated in above three studies), 50.92 percent were drakes.

The sex ratio in the harvest (1964–67) shows a preponderance of adult drakes per female harvested, i.e., Mississippi Flyway: 2.04, 2.17, 1.74; Central Flyway: 2.02, 2.08, 1.72, 1.85 ♂♂/♀♀ (Croft and Carney 1968). The comparable figures for immatures are Mississippi Flyway—1.20, 1.23, 1.12, 1.22 immature ♂♂/immature

♀♀; Central Flyway—1.46, 1.35, 1.41, 1.46 immature ♂♂/immature ♀♀. Male : female relative recovery rates indicated that in the United States males were more likely to be shot than females (Anderson 1968). Anderson also points out that both the Arkansas and Washington banding data corroborate the general pattern of males being taken in a relatively greater extent in the United States and hens being taken to a greater extent in Canada.

The Canadian species composition survey showed the following sex ratios in the harvest for 1967, 1968, and 1969: Alberta—Ad ♂♂/Ad ♀♀ 1.13, 1.6l, 1.52; Saskatchewan—2.41, 2.44, 1.75 (*N* + 500 + per year) Kaiser et al. (1970). The sex ratio in the harvest need not reflect the true "wild" ratio, as there may be an active choice of drakes by hunters.

As reported by Geis et al. (1969:852), Mallard hens banded in winter through North American generally show a higher first season band recovery rate and show higher average annual mortality rates than do drakes. The processes leading to distorted sex ratios are fairly evident.

Bellrose et al. (1961) concluded that "the effect of hunting on the sex ratios of the entire North American duck population is probably insignificant" while other authors (*in* Olson 1965) have argued that hunting may be a major contributory factor to the disproportionate sex ratios of ducks. Olson (1965) concluded that differences in vulnerability to hunting, especially the high vulnerability of adult hens and juveniles, may be the cause of an unbalanced sex ratio in Canvasbacks (*Aythya valisineria*). The same may be happening with Mallards. Early opening dates for hunting on breeding or molting areas may lead to more of the vulnerable adult female component being killed. To date, we have no extensive evidence to show that natural mortality rates of hens during the breeding season are substantially higher than drakes, except for the preliminary results provided by Keith (1961) and Dzubin and Gollop (in press), who reported approximately 5 percent mortality in drakes and 8–10 percent in hens, May through July. Differential sex mortality on molting lakes is undocumented. Postmolting hens may be more available to Canadian hunters.

There is a differential distribution of sexes and ages on the wintering grounds. Generally, females and juveniles winter further south than do drakes and adults (Bellrose et al. 1961, Gollop 1965). In the Central Flyway states, wintering Mallard flocks at the northern edge of the wintering range are predominantly drakes (60–75 percent). Since most display and pairing activity occurs during December through February and since all hens arriving on the breeding grounds in April are associated with drakes, do these extra drakes join into breeding activities; that is, are they biologically meaningful?

Dzubin's conclusions were that the Mallard pair-bond is a necessary prerequisite for successful breeding in a wild population of Mallards and that there is insufficient behavioral evidence to suggest that a higher proportion of unmated Mallard hens could nest successfully and produce more progeny if the sex ratio were artificially altered to favor hens.

Nelson stressed that it is obvious that the relationship of waterfowl sex ratios to breeding behavior and production rates is not fully understood and that future research on this subject should be directed specifically at determining these relationships for each of the principal species presently involved in sex-oriented regulations. There is ample evidence to indicate the need for caution in encouraging specific sex-oriented waterfowl

Table 1. Summaries of mallard sex ratios.

	1967–68		1968–69		1969–70	
	Adults	Immature	Adults	Immature	Adults	Immature
Prehunting season population	1.60	0.88	1.33	1.13	1.62	0.99
Hunting season harvest	1.87	1.23	1.94	1.27	2.00	1.29
Posthunting season population	1.08	[a]	1.16	[a]	1.12	[a]

[a] Immatures combined with adults in postseason period.

hunting regulations directed at the harvest of excess males and assumed protection of females on a *broad-scale basis,* until there are better answers to the questions raised.

John P. Rogers commented on seasonal change in sex ratios in Mallards. His remarks follow.

For more than three decades ornithologists and wildlife biologists have been puzzling over the significance of uneven sex ratios among ducks. In reviewing this subject today it is apparent that while we now have more data to look at, we have not progressed very far in resolving many of the questions raised years ago. John Aldrich and Harvey Nelson have discussed some of these, and their importance to waterfowl management, especially as they relate to recent interest in increasing the harvest of drake Mallards. My remarks will be concerned with briefly describing a recent evaluation of sex ratios in the North American Mallard population which we believe is pertinent to an understanding of Mallard population dynamics.

The general approach used in this evaluation was described in an unpublished administrative report by Anderson et al. (1970). The figures presented below were developed by W. F. Crissey for a presentation to the Mississippi Flyway Council Technical Committee at Biloxi, Mississippi, in 1972.

In the past, information on sex ratios usually has been obtained by direct field observations. The methods used and the biases caused by the mobility of the birds, as well as differences in seasonal and geographic distribution of sex and age groups have been discussed by Bellrose et al. (1961). These factors make it extremely difficult to obtain a measure of sex ratio representative of the population.

The method used for estimating sex ratios presented here begins with a determination of the size and sex composition of the kill by hunters during the fall and winter hunting season. This is used in conjunction with direct recovery rates from prehunting season banding which, when adjusted to account for unreported bands, yields an estimate of harvest rate by age and sex. With an estimate of harvest and harvest rate it is possible to estimate the size of the population by age and sex from which the kill was taken. Subtraction of the harvest by age and sex from the preseason population yields an estimate of the sex ratio for adults and immatures immediately following the hunting season.

Table 1 summarizes Mallard sex ratios calculated for different times of the year for three years beginning with the hunting season of 1967–68.

These figures show that in early fall, just prior to the hunting season, the sex ratio among adult Mallards is strongly unbalanced in favor of males, while that for immatures is nearly even. It is probable that a sex ratio of 1.6 males per female among adults, and 1.0 males per female among immatures closely approximates the true situation, and that differences between years appearing in the table reflect deficiencies in the data.

Sex ratios in the harvest (second line) show that, for both age groups, hunting takes a higher proportion of the males than of the females present in the population. This is due partly to hunter selectivity but other factors, related to males being more accessible than females to hunters, are believed to play a role, also. Regardless of the reasons, the differential harvest of males and females is sufficiently great that by the end of the hunting season the sex ratio is nearly even, and there is only a relatively slight preponderance of males.

At present, there is no evidence that population losses between the end of the hunting season and the beginning of the breeding season affect one sex more than the other. Thus, it is believed that the sex ratio in the posthunting season population is practically identical to that at the beginning of the breeding season.

The following conclusions are suggested by this analysis: In the annual cycle of the Mallard, large and significant changes in sex ratio occur (1) during the hunting season and (2) during the breeding season. During the hunting season, losses of males (due to hunting) change the sex ratio from a strongly unbalanced to a nearly balanced condition. During the breeding season, losses of females (due to natural mortality) are sufficiently great to cause a return to a strongly unbalanced sex ratio favoring males.

It appears that there is (1) no great excess of males in the continental Mallard population in terms of the population available to begin breeding; and (2) natural mortality of females, associated with breeding, is greater than previously suspected.

Gordon H. Orians of the University of Washington presented a number of points concerning natural selection for sex ratios in birds.

LITERATURE CITED

ANDERSON, D. R. 1968. Summary of first hunting season recovery rates of Mallards banded during winter, summer and early fall of 1967. Administrative Report 165. Bureau of Sport Fisheries and Wildlife, U.S. Department of the Interior. 4pp. (unpublished)

———, R. S. POSPAHALA, H. M. REEVES, J. P. ROGERS, AND W. F. CRISSEY. 1970. Estimates of the sex composition of the 1967–1969 Mallard population. Administrative Report 182. Bureau of Sport Fisheries and Wildlife, U.S. Department of the Interior. 8pp. (unpublished)

BELLROSE, F. C., JR., T. G. SCOTT, A. S. HAWKINS, AND J. B. LOW. 1961. Sex ratios and age ratios in North American ducks. Ill. Nat. Hist. Sur. Bull. 27:391–474.

CRISSEY, W. S. 1969. Prairie potholes from a continental viewpoint. Saskatoon wetlands seminar, pp. 161–177. *In* Canadian Wildlife Service Report Series. No. 6. Canadian Wildlife Service, Ottawa.

CROFT, R. L., AND S. M. CARNEY. 1968. Sex ratios of ducks in the hunting kill, 1966–1967. Administrative Report 153. Bureau of Sport Fisheries and Wildlife, U.S. Department of the Interior. 43pp. (unpublished)

DZUBIN, A., AND J. B. GOLLOP. In Press. Population ecology and spacing of Mallards on a Canadian grassland and parkland area. American Institute of Biological Sciences and Bureau of Sport Fisheries and Wildlife, U.S. Department of the Interior. U.S. Government Printing Office, Washington, D.C.

GEIS, A. D., R. K. MARTINSON, AND D. R. ANDERSON. 1969. Establishing hunting regulations and allowable harvest of Mallards in the United States. J. Wildlife Manage. 38:848–859.

GOLLOP, J. B. 1965. Dispersal and annual survival of the Mallard. Canadian Wildlife Service, Saskatoon, Saskatchewan. 104pp. (unpublished)

HOCHBAUM, H. A. 1944. The Canvasback on a prairie marsh. American Wildlife Institute, Washington, D.C. 201pp.

KAISER, G. W., L. WIGHT, AND F. G. COOCH. 1970. Hand tally—1969 species composition survey. Canadian Wildlife Service, Ottawa, Ontario. (unpublished)

KEITH, L. B. 1961. A study of waterfowl ecology on small impoundments in southeastern Alberta. Wildlife Monogr. 6:1–88.

LENSINK, C. J. 1964. Distribution of recoveries from bandings of ducklings. Special Scientific Report—Wildlife No. 89. Bureau of Sport Fisheries and Wildlife, U.S. Department of the Interior, Washington, D.C. 146pp.

LOW, S. H. 1957. Waterfowl banding in the Canadian prairie provinces. Special Scientific Report—Wildlife No. 36. Bureau of Sport Fisheries and Wildlife, U.S. Department of the Interior, Washington, D.C. 30pp.

OLSON, D. P. 1965. Differential vulnerability of male and female Canvasbacks to hunting. Trans. Thirtieth N. Am. Wildlife Nat. Res. Conf. 30: 121–135.

SOWLS, L. K. 1955. Prairie ducks. Stackpole Co., Harrisburg, Pa. 193pp.

SELECTED BIBLIOGRAPHY

Population Influences and Characteristics: Age and Sex Ratios

ANDERSON, B. W., T. E. KETOLA, AND D. W. WARNER. 1969. Spring sex and age ratios of lesser scaup and ring-necked ducks in Minnesota. J. Wildl. Manage. 33(1):209–212.

BEER, J. 1945. Sex ratios of ducks in southwestern Washington. Auk 62(1):117–124.

BELLROSE, F. C., T. G. SCOTT, A. S. HAWKINS, AND J. B. LOW. 1961. Sex ratios and age ratios in North American ducks. Ill. Nat. Hist. Survey Bull. 27(6):391–474.

BOLEN, E. G. 1970. Sex ratios in the black-bellied tree duck. J. Wildl. Manage. 34(1):68–73.

IMBER, M. J. 1968. Sex ratios in Canada goose populations. J. Wildl. Manage. 32(4):905–920.

JOHNSON, D. H., AND A. B. SARGEANT. 1977. Impact of red fox predation on the sex ratio of prairie mallards . U.S. Fish Wildl. Serv. Wildl. Res. Rep. 6. 56pp.

PETRIDES, G. A. 1944. Sex ratios in ducks. Auk 61(4):564–571.

WELLING, C. H., AND W. J. L. SLADEN. 1979. Canvasback sex ratios on Rhode and West rivers, Chesapeake Bay, 1972–78. J. Wildl. Manage. 43(3):811–812.

Disease and Environmental Contaminants

THE IMPORTANCE OF LEAD POISONING IN WATERFOWL[1]

J. E. SHILLINGER and CLARENCE C. COTTAM, Division of Wildlife Research, Bureau of Biological Survey

Our knowledge of the destructive action of lead when taken into the digestive tracts of waterfowl dates back as far as 1901 when Dr. George B. Grinnell described this condition with its characteristic symptoms in birds on Currituck Sound on the coast of North Carolina. He also reported his observation of similar occurrences on lakes in Texas. Later J. H. Bowles called attention to this condition in the Puget Sound district in Washington. W. L. McAtee likewise noted similar losses in Texas. U.S. Department of Agriculture Bulletin, No. 793, by Wetmore, and miscellaneous reports from various parts of the country 20 years ago showed a general recognition of loss of birds from this cause in various parts of the country.

Lead shot when picked up by birds feeding on marshes over which considerable shooting has been done are rapidly eroded by the grinding action of sharp grit under the powerful action of the gizzard muscles. The finely divided particles of lead cut off by this erosion process become partly absorbable in the presence of the digestive fluids, are absorbed over a long period, and result in plumbism, or lead poisoning. The symptoms as observed in birds, with minor variations, are not unlike those seen in man. General weakness of the voluntary muscles with definite paralysis gradually ensuing. When a sufficient number of these muscles are put out of action in chronic cases, progressive starvation follows. Other than the weakness or paralysis referred to, and a greenish diarrhea, no pronounced symptoms are observable ante-mortem.

On autopsy the gizzard is frequently found to contain shot in various stages of erosion. Often the lead pellets which were originally round are found to be ground flat like a disc, or in a more advanced stage become small shapeless particles not recognizable as shot but having the outward appearance of dark grit. The contents of the gizzard are usually about normal. Due, however, to the apparent paralyzed state of the muscles of the gizzard, and a reverse action of the upper intestinal tract, the gizzard contents are often stained quite green. The appetites of birds suffering from lead poisoning show no apparent decrease, and in some instances an actual stimulation is apparent. This regular intake of food and the paralyzed state of the gizzard muscles results in an over-filling of the upper digestive tract anterior to this organ. This over-filling may be so pronounced as to distend the true stomach, or proventriculus, and the aesophagus to proportions several times their normal size.

Tests have been made by Wetmore, Green, and Shillinger, proving that it is the lead and not impurities contained therein that is responsible for the sickness and losses described. The usual quantity of lead necessary to constitute a fatal dose for an average sized duck has not been definitey determined since it is apparent there are a great many factors which influence this type of poisoning. In some instances it has been observed that a single No. 5 shot was sufficient to kill a mallard drake, while other birds ap-

[1] Originally published in Trans. North Am. Wildl. Conf. 2:398–403, 1937.

pear to withstand the effect of several times this amount for weeks without showing serious injury.

As has been previously mentioned, the destructive action of lead shot upon ingestion is not confined to any restricted locality. Biologists in all sections of the country have reported losses from this cause. It is probable that the greatest losses take place on the feeding and resting grounds where considerable shooting is done. Those areas where the birds nest and raise the young broods are not generally the choice hunting sites and, hence, do not carry the high degree of pollution.

Since, however, the losses are more prominent in the winter months, the affected birds represent the breeding stock from which next year's supply will be produced. While the ducks accustomed to feeding in shallow water are most commonly affected, Canada geese and whistling swans are also frequent victims.

During December 1936, eight ducks from the coast of North Carolina were examined, and all showed on autopsy the effect of lead poisoning. In the same month five mallards from the Pamlico Sound area of Virginia were also examined, and showed the same condition to be the cause of death. During the fall of the same year 14 ducks from the Delaware Bay region in northern Delaware and southern New Jersey were autopsied. Shot were found in all gizzards, the numbers of shot ranging from 3 to 19 per bird.

Earlier in the year 12 ducks which were taken from the area of the Erie Fish and Hunting Club grounds in northern Ohio were examined post-mortem, and all showed unmistakable evidence of lead poisoning. Their organs contained from 2 to 34 shot per bird.

At about the same time at Boyd Lake, Colorado, approximately 100 ducks, mostly mallards, were found sick or dead. Autopsy of 25 birds showed a range of from 1 to 15 shot per bird. Some of these shot were worn down to mere fragments of the original pellets.

From data in the files of the Biological Survey it is apparent the lead poisoning among waterfowl is far more common and more serious than is generally supposed even among most waterfowl conservationists. The lead pellets that have been expelled into the water during the hunting season may have been accidentally sieved out of the mud by the birds or perhaps they may have been taken for gravel or as food, as they are about the size and shape of a number of important duck food seeds. Baiting undoubtedly has had its effect, particularly at important feeding points and near certain blinds where there has been a large yearly accumulation of lead. Where the mud is deep and soft the lead shot gradually sinks out of reach of the birds, but where the bottom is sufficiently hard there is often a marked concentration of the metal.

In such an area in the Chesapeake Bay, Cottam found that 2 birds out of 20 examined contained lead in their stomachs and 2 more showed evidence of lead poisoning. Even though a sub-lethal dose of lead is taken, experimental evidence indicates that the poison so upsets the normal physiological processes that interference with reproduction may result. It is well known that lead acts as an abortifacient in mammalian females and there is evidence that leads us to believe it may induce sterility in birds. Consequently, lead poisoning may be a factor of considerable importance in the decline of our waterfowl.

As would be expected, ingestion of

Table 1.

Species of duck	Total no. of stomachs	No. containing shot	Per cent containing shot	Total no. of shot	Av. of shot in shot containing stomachs
Mallard	2,156	52	2.41	244	4.69
Mottled duck (incl. Florida)	62	3	4.83	6	2.00
Pintail	965	11	1.14	135	12.27
Redhead	414	13	3.14	34	2.61
Ring-necked duck	759	25	3.29	47	1.88
Canvasback	430	42	9.77	525	12.50
Greater scaup duck	808	13	1.61	59	4.54
Lesser scaup duck	1,233	486	39.42	5,720	11.77
Barrow's golden-eye	86	1	1.16	1	1.00
Harlequin duck	72	1	1.39	2	2.00
Pacific eider	72	1	1.39	1	1.00
White-winged scoter	913	23	2.52	30	1.30
Surf scoter	239	4	1.67	4	1.00
American scoter	168	2	1.19	11	5.50

shot is more common late in the winter or early spring after the close of the gunning season than earlier in the fall after a blanket of sediment has covered the shot. The unfortunate part of this trouble lies in the fact that the more attractive the habitat the greater the concentration of birds, with more hunting and consequently a greater deposition of lead.

It seems that it is among the diving species of waterfowl rather than among "tippers" or surface feeders where the greater frequency and more serious effects of lead poisoning are recognized. Of 6,471 diving duck stomachs analyzed in the Food Habits Laboratory of the Biological Survey, 616, or 9.52 per cent showed the presence of lead shot. This figure would appear the more serious if we deleted the more typical sea ducks such as the eiders, harlequins, oldsquaws, and scoters, which, because of their coastal distribution and feeding habits, have little or no opportunity to ingest shot. The more choice inland diving species—the members of the genus *Nyroca*, including the scaups, canvasback, redhead and ringneck—are the birds most seriously affected by lead poisoning. It is indeed surprising that nearly 16 per cent (15.88 per cent) of all of the stomachs of these birds that have yet been analyzed for food habit studies have shown the presence of lead. It is, of course, possible that a large series of birds taken from an area known to be badly polluted with shot may have shown this condition at its worst.

The lesser scaup seems to have been more seriously affected than any other species. In areas of excessive shooting high mortality may result. Perhaps because of the scaup's method of feeding on bottom ooze it often obtains more shot than is ingested by other species of waterfowl inhabiting the same general area. In a series of 477 lesser scaup taken during the gunning season in April 1909 (before the enactment of a Federal law prohibiting spring shooting), on lakes in the vicinity of Marquette, Wis., it was found that 365 of the birds—76.5 per cent—had consumed a total of 4,191 lead pellets or an average of 11½ shot per bird. Varying numbers from 1 to 58 shot pellets were found in individual stomachs. It is not improbable that some of the birds which had no free lead in the gizzard had passed the poison into the intestines and had become affected by it. Of 1,233 stomachs of the lesser scaup examined for food content 486, or 39.42 per cent, contained one or more lead pellets. It is, of course, hoped that the Marquette series of birds has shown the condition at its worst and is really not representative of the general situation.

Canvasbacks seemed to have been next most seriously affected, as 9.77 per cent of all stomachs examined contained lead. This figure should be significant as the birds have been taken at widely different sections of the country and at all seasons of the year. Three and twenty-nine hundredths per cent of the ringnecked duck stomachs contained lead, while 3.14 per cent of the redheads were similarly affected. Because the greater scaup is more commonly a sea bird, it has escaped the ravages of this inland scourge; even so, 1.61 per cent of the stomachs analyzed showed the presence of lead.

While the surface feeders (the Anatinae) are less frequently the victims of lead poisoning, they are by no means immune to its ravages. Fifty-two out of 2,156 mallard stomachs examined, or 2.41 per cent, have been found to contain lead, while 1.14 per cent of the pintails have been similarly affected. Table 1 gives the list of stomachs of all species of ducks examined that have shown as much as 1 per cent containing lead.

Lead poisoning is known to be a serious cause of duck mortality in the north central states. Pirnie (Michigan Waterfowl Management, p. 75, 1935) concludes that it "is the disease which takes the greatest toll of adult ducks in this (Great Lakes) section of the country." "In the spring of 1928," he writes, "hundreds of migrating ducks died soon after their arrival at Houghton Lake, evidently from the effects of lead poisoning." Ten such sick ducks averaged nearly 50 shot in each gizzard. While lead poisoning is widely distributed throughout all sections of this country, evidence seems to indicate that it is more severe in those sections where there is a deficiency of available gravel that may serve as grit in the gizzard of the birds. Under such circumstances the lead seems to be more persistently retained. More than a hundred lead pellets have been found in a single gizzard.

Table 2.

Number of birds showing symptoms and lesions	Number of shot found
12	0
18	1
18	2
16	3
8	4
8	5
2	6
1	7
7	8
2	9
4	12
1	13
2	14
1	15
1	20
1	35
1	38

During November and December 1935, John J. Lynch, working at the Sand Lake Migratory Waterfowl Refuge, at Columbia, S. Dakota, observed about 450 mallard ducks on two air holes after a freeze-up on the first of November. Sick and dead birds were plentiful among them, and green feces indicative of lead poisoning were noted in these locations. One hundred and thirteen dead birds were examined post mortem, and 91 of these contained shot in their digestive organs. Twelve of the others showed definite evidence of lead poisoning even though no shot or fragments could be detected macroscopically in the ingesta with the facilities at hand.

His count of shot in the digestive organs are listed in Table 2.

In addition, 2 canvasbacks held, respectively, 2 and 6 shot; 2 redheads, 5 and 4 shot; 1 pintail, 7 shot, and 1 black duck, 7 shot. Earlier in the season 1 mallard at Mud Lake held 39 shot, and 2 pintails from the same place had, respectively, 179 and 61 shot.

In the disease research laboratories of the Bureau of Biological Survey it is apparent that in the process of diagnosing the causes of deaths among waterfowl in the eastern and central States which are sent to the Department for autopsy, approximately 50 per cent are found to have died from lead poisoning. It is true that most of these come in during the winter months soon after a new supply of shot has been added to the original accumulations on the marshes from previous seasons.

In a memorandum by Mr. J. Clark Salyer, In Charge of the Migratory Waterfowl Refuge Division, Bureau of Biological Survey, dated February 23, 1937, he stated that at the time of his recent visit to the Lake Mattamuskeet area they were picking up on the Refuge an average of eight dead geese and swans per day which were victims of lead poisoning.

It should be pointed out that most of the losses due to lead poisoning are found in the late fall, winter, and early spring, after the hunting season. Since these losses appear to take place after sportsmen have made their kill, taking out the portion of the duck crop estimated by trained conservationists to be the maximum number that may be killed without impairing the necessary supply of breeding stock, the losses occasioned by unusual conditions in the winter must be considered as a loss of valuable breeding stock. In all forms of economic propagation of animal life the breeding stock is regarded as the most valuable. Hence we must look upon the deleterious effect of lead poisoning in waterfowl as of major importance in maintaining an adequate supply of these birds.

IMPACT OF INGESTED LEAD PELLETS ON WATERFOWL[1]

FRANK BELLROSE, Wildlife Specialist, Illinois Natural History Survey, Havana, IL 62644

Lead poisoning results when waterfowl swallow lead shot pellets while feeding upon seeds and animal life on the bottoms of ponds, lakes, and marshes. Laboratory experiments as well as the relationship between food habits and the incidence of ingested shot pellets are mistakenly ingested as food items and not as items of grit.

Once in the gizzard the hydrochloric acid in the digestive juices aided by grit commences to erode the lead. The rate of erosion is governed by the amount and kind of food eaten, and the kind and amount of grit. The erosion rate per day varies from 1 to 5 percent, averages about 3 percent, and remains fairly constant per pellet regardless of the number ingested. Soluble lead salts are formed from the erosive material, and these are absorbed in the blood stream producing an anemic condition: a reduction in the hemoglobin content and in the number of red blood cells. Lesions greatly increase in the liver and kidney. A loss of appetite develops within a day or two after the ingestion of lead, and is followed by a decline in body weight.

The information presented in this paper was obtained as part of a cooperative study between the Illinois Natural History Survey and Olin Industries, 1948–53. Most of the findings of this study have appeared in papers by Jordan and Bellrose (1950, 1951), Bellrose (1959), and Jordan (1968). For the purpose of this paper the data in the files of the INHS were reviewed and are presented in an abstracted form and a more visual format.

MEASURING THE EFFECT OF LEAD

Three levels of lead poisoning are apparent in waterfowl. At the highest level all birds die within 1 to 2 weeks of infection after losing one-sixth of their body weight or less. Usually the ingestion of over six shot pellets is required to produce such a rapid toxic effect. At the medium level of toxicity, the birds gradually waste away losing about one-third of their body weight over a 3-week period. Most die but some recover, and in particular those that have voided shot pellets before becoming moribund. From 1 to 6 ingested lead pellets usually produce this medium level of toxicity. At the low level of toxicity, a slight weight loss occurs and is initially followed by a return to normal weight within 2 or 3 weeks. All of these birds recover. Most of them have ingested but 1 or 2 shot pellets.

There are a number of ways of measuring the effect of lead shot on waterfowl: direct mortality, weight loss, the packed cell volume and hemoglobin content of the blood, the occurrence of lesions in the liver and kidney, and the lead content of the liver, kidney, and leg and wing bones. A comparison of the various indicators of lead poisoning from controlled experiments point to changes in body weight as one of the better and more obvious ways of measuring the level of lead toxicity.

Many factors regulate the effect of ingested lead upon waterfowl survival, making it difficult to assess its importance. Some of the factors that have been found to influence the degree of lead tox-

[1] Originally published in Proc. 1st Int. Waterfowl Symp., pages 163–167. Ducks Unlimited, St. Louis, MO, 1975.

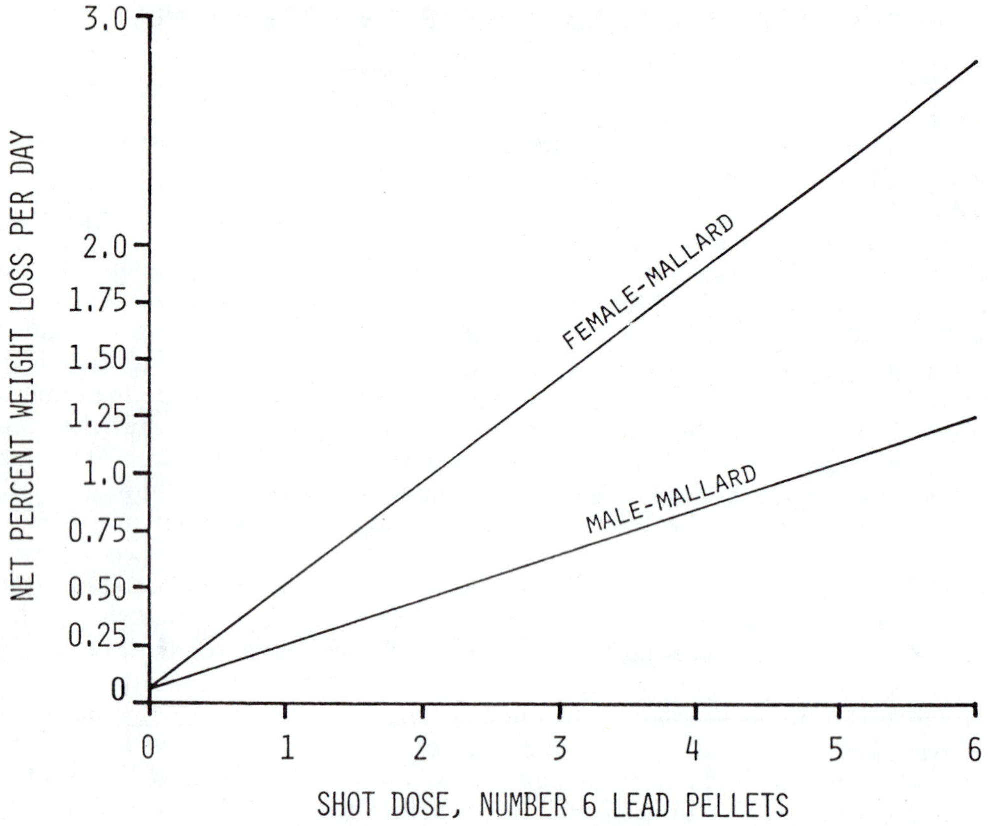

Fig. 1. The net percent of daily body weight loss in game farm mallards with increasing levels of No. 6 lead shot pellets.

icity are: the number and size of ingested shot pellets; the size, age, and sex of the bird; and the composition and volume of the food consumed.

Not only does the size of lead shot determine the surface area exposed to erosion, but the smaller the shot, the greater the possibility that it may be expelled from the gizzard. As shot become smaller from erosion, about 25 percent are passed, but in many instances the bird dies anyway. From 10 to 25 percent of the ducks found in large scale lead poisoning die-offs appear to have passed all shot prior to death.

The effect of from 1 to 6 No. 6 shot pellets on the net daily weight loss of male and female game farm mallards on a corn diet is shown in Fig. 1. As the number of pellets increases, the daily loss of body weight increases at the rate of 0.20 percent per pellet for males and 0.46 percent for females.

The relationship of shot size, diet, age and sex, and size of the duck is shown in Fig. 2. It is apparent that one No. 4 shot induces a larger weight loss than one No. 6 shot. The rate of weight loss in females is almost twice as great as that in males.

INFLUENCE OF FOOD

Early in our experiments it was evident that the composition of food played an important role in survival of waterfowl

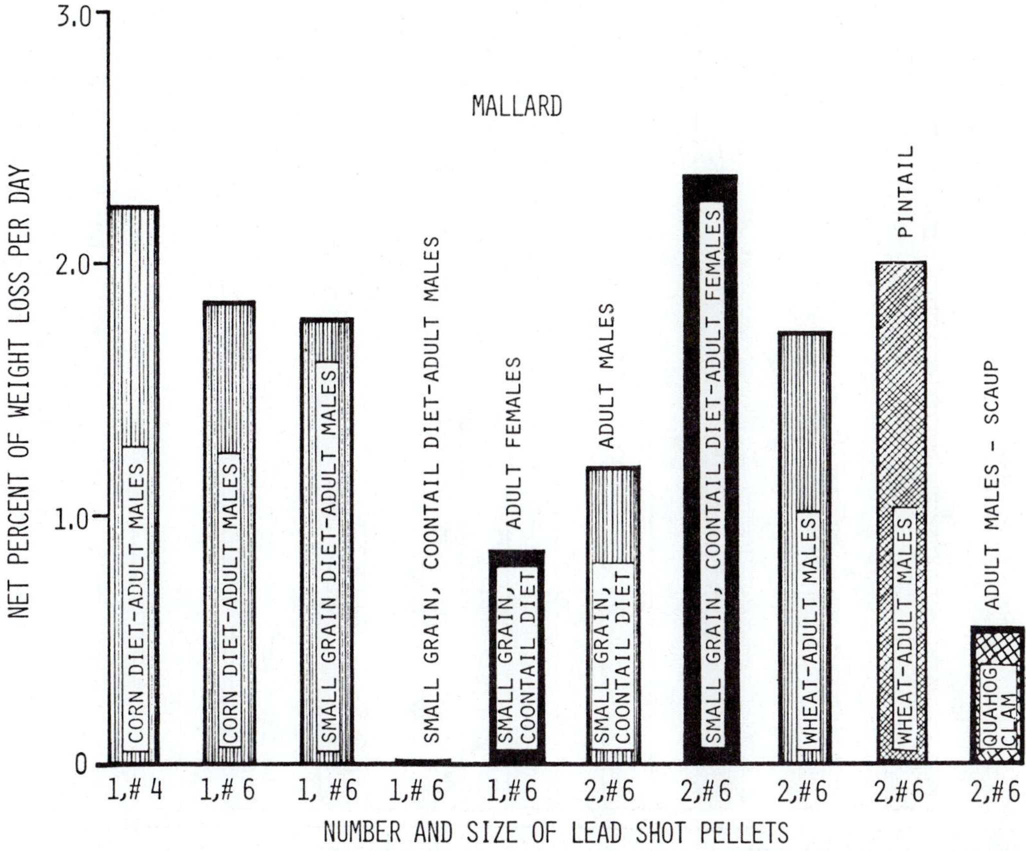

Fig. 2. The average daily net percent body weight loss among ducks dosed with one and two No. 4 and No. 6 lead shot on various diets.

ingesting lead (Jordan and Bellrose 1951, Jordan 1968). We found that commercial duck food pellets suppressed the toxicity of lead the most and corn the least. Between these two extremes ranged other foods. But it is evident from data in Fig. 2 that all diets, except for quahog clam meat fed lesser scaup, result in serious weight losses. Even the best diet that mallards might conceivably find in the wild, small grains and coontail, failed to suppress lead toxicity from two No. 6 lead pellets: net weight loss per day amounted to 1.2 percent in males and 2.3 percent in females. Pintails suffered a greater weight loss from lead toxicity than did mallards while both were on a wheat diet.

Perhaps the dietary makeup of foods results in the combining of certain elements with the lead molecules to reduce their assimilation. But, in addition, the physical properties of the food are known to have an effect. Corn and corn meal were fed two different groups of game farm mallards that were dosed with four No. 6 shot. Those on corn meal showed less effect from lead poisoning than those on whole corn (Jordan 1968).

The quantity of food consumed by an individual bird also has an influence upon the expression of lead toxicity. In-

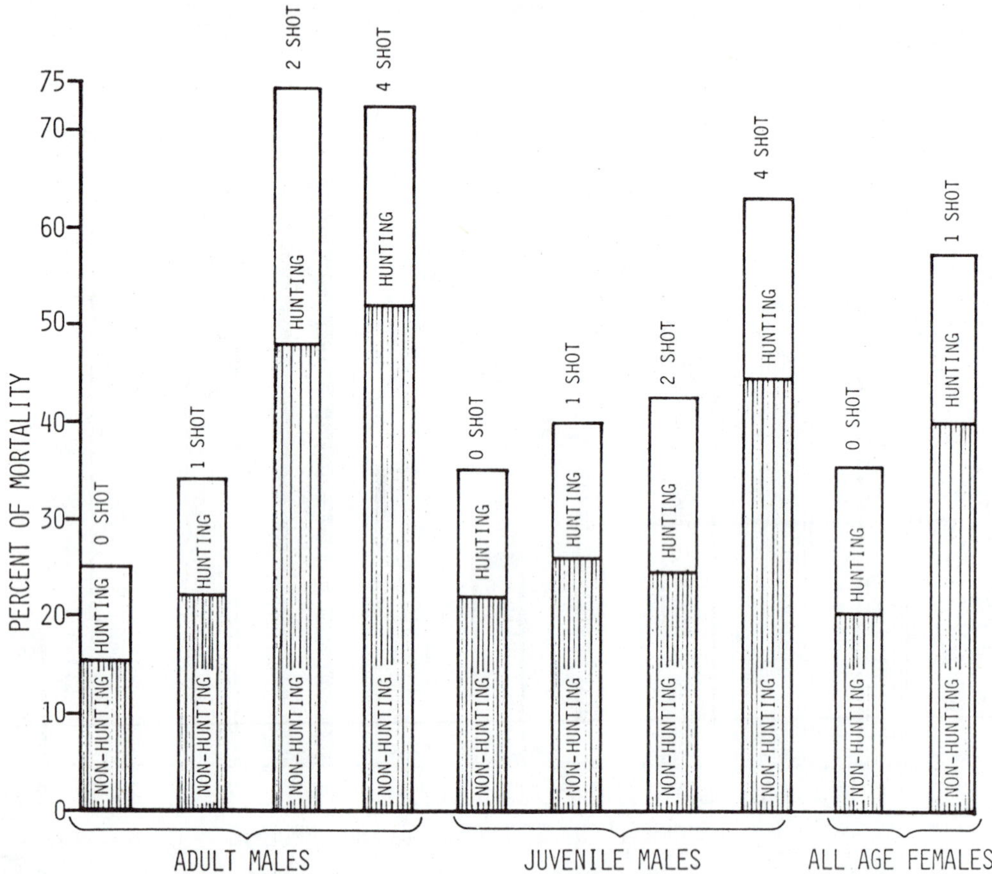

Fig. 3. Mortality in wild mallards during the first 9 months after their release when they were dosed with zero, one, two, or four No. 6 lead shot.

dividuals that habitually eat the most food show the least weight loss when exposed to dietary lead. For a short time in the spring, when female mallard consume more food than males, they are the ones least susceptible to lead poisoning. Likewise, juveniles in the fall eat more food than adults and are less susceptible to lead poisoning at that time, but by midwinter there is little difference between the age groups.

Because of multiplicity of variables encountered in the expression of lead toxicity in laboratory experiments, we decided that it would be tenuous to attempt to determine the importance of lead poisoning in the field on the basis of laboratory findings. Therefore, we undertook experiments under field conditions.

FIELD EXPERIMENTS

Over a period of three autumns we captured more than 6,000 wild mallards which were fluoroscoped for lead shot and weighed for an indication of health. The 4,307 that met the necessary requirements were banded and dosed with one, two, and four No. 6 shot pellets with suitable numbers of lead-free birds used as controls. In a matter of minutes after dosing the ducks were returned to the wild.

Dynamic life tables were prepared from the 558 banded recoveries received over the next 4 years. Reward bands were used to increase the rate of return 2.2 times over the rate of returns for standard bands. To adjust for hunting losses, the band recovery rates were raised to compensate for the nonreporting rate by hunters of 66 percent (Bellrose 1955). This analysis showed that one No. 6 shot resulted in a shrinkage during the first 9 months in mallard hens of mixed ages that was 22 percent greater than the shrinkage in a lead-free control group. The shrinkage at the same shot level averaged 12.3 percent for adult drakes and 4.1 percent for juvenile drakes. At the two No. 6 shot levels of infection, the shrinkage during the first 9 months in the banded sample was 43.6 percent greater in adult drakes and 3.4 percent greater in juvenile drakes than in the lead-free sample. The shrinkage between the adult and juvenile drakes dosed with four No. 6's amounted to 41.3 percent and 31.6 percent respectively above that of the lead-free control groups (Fig. 3).

However, not all of the greater shrinkage in the lead dosed groups represented a waste of the resource. Because of the weakness in flight caused by lead toxicity, hunters killed birds dosed with shot more readily than those ducks that were lead-free. Many of these birds I am sure were emaciated and not as suitable for human food as healthy ducks. Moreover, waterfowl ingesting lead after the hunting season would not have shooting to serve as a source of eliminating weakened birds prior to mortality. Predators would substitute for man in many cases.

Adult males suffered nonhunting mortality that at the one shot level was 3.3 percent higher than the lead-free controls; at the two shot level the nonhunting mortality was 23.5 percent above the control level; and at the four shot level it was 30.0 percent higher (Fig. 3).

Juvenile male mallards experienced little increase in nonhunting mortality with the administration of gizzard lead until the four shot level. At the one shot level, nonhunting losses increased by only 4.7 percent, 0.7 percent at the two shot level, and 37.7 percent at the four shot level.

The controls for mallard hens consisted of recovery rates for bandings made in 1939–43, prior to the dosing of 501 in 1951. A percentage of these control birds had undoubtedly ingested lead shot in nature. Nonetheless, the hens dosed with one No. 6 shot pellet experienced a nonhunting mortality that was 13.9 percent greater than that of the controls.

Recoveries during the hunting season of banding indicate that 26.5 percent of the lead-free controls migrated south while 23.6 percent of those with two, and only 4.1 percent of those with No. 6 lead shot migrated south. It is apparent that one shot did not significantly impair the migration departure of wild mallards. However, as the frequency of ingested lead increases above the one shot level, the ability to migrate is increasingly curtailed. Part of this difference, as shown by laboratory experiments, is a reduction in the time span of toxicity that results as the shot level increases. This is one reason for the development of "hot spots" when larger than usual numbers of shot are ingested.

PROPORTION OF POPULATION INGESTING LEAD

In order to determine the exposure of waterfowl populations to the ingestion of lead shot we solicited the assistance of wildlife biologists across the United

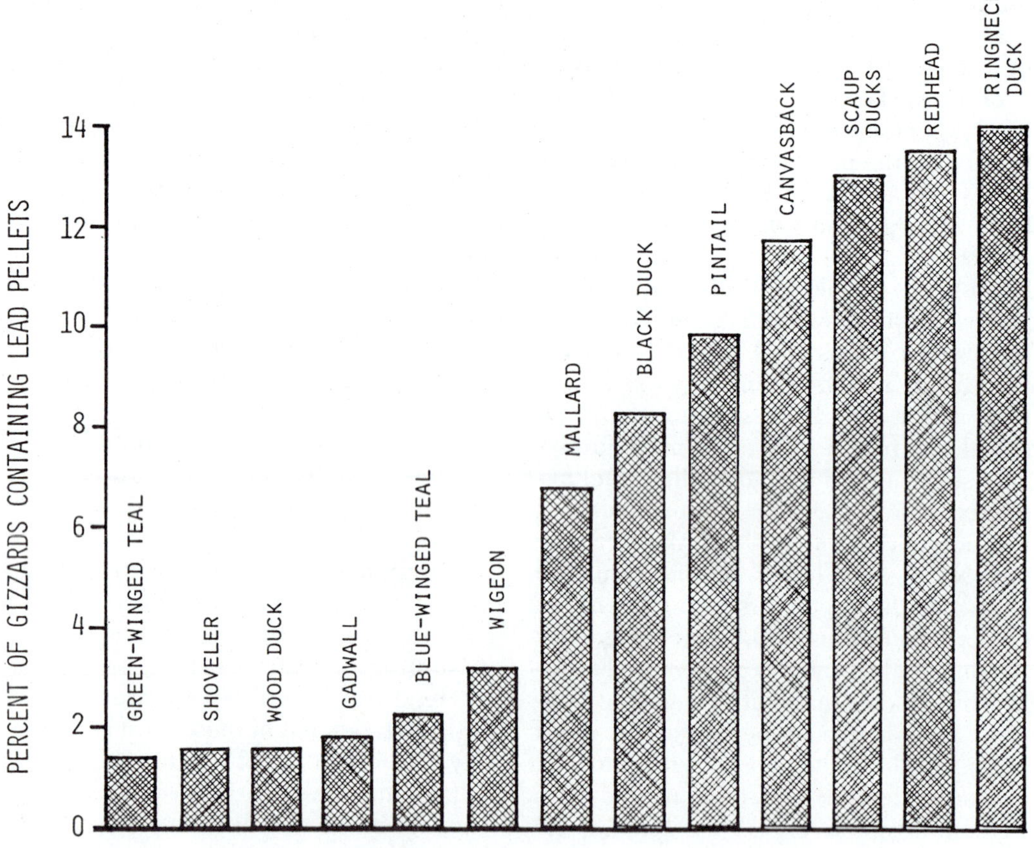

Fig. 4. The incidence of ingested lead shot in 35,000 gizzards of various duck species collected at many locations in North America.

States, 1938–54. As a result of splendid cooperation by many people, 36,145 gizzards were obtained; mallards made up 47 percent of all waterfowl gizzards. Figure 4 shows the indicence of ingested lead shot found in the gizzards of the more abundant game duck species. Among dabbling ducks the incidence of ingested lead was at a high level for mallards, black ducks, and pintails; among diving ducks it was at a high level for canvasbacks, scaups, redheads, and ringnecked ducks. Fortunately two-thirds of the gizzards containing ingested lead shot had but one pellet.

There was a regional variation in the rate of lead occurrence in duck stomachs, Fig. 5. On the Atlantic Flyway 6.1 percent of the mallards and black duck gizzards contained lead, 6.7 percent of all the other ducks. The level of mallard and black duck ingestion in the Mississippi Flyway was 8.6 percent and identical for all other ducks. Mallard gizzards in the Central Flyway contained lead at the rate of 2.7 percent, other ducks 4.1 percent. In the Pacific Flyway, 8.8 percent of the mallard gizzards held ingested lead compared to 6.4 percent of those from all other duck species.

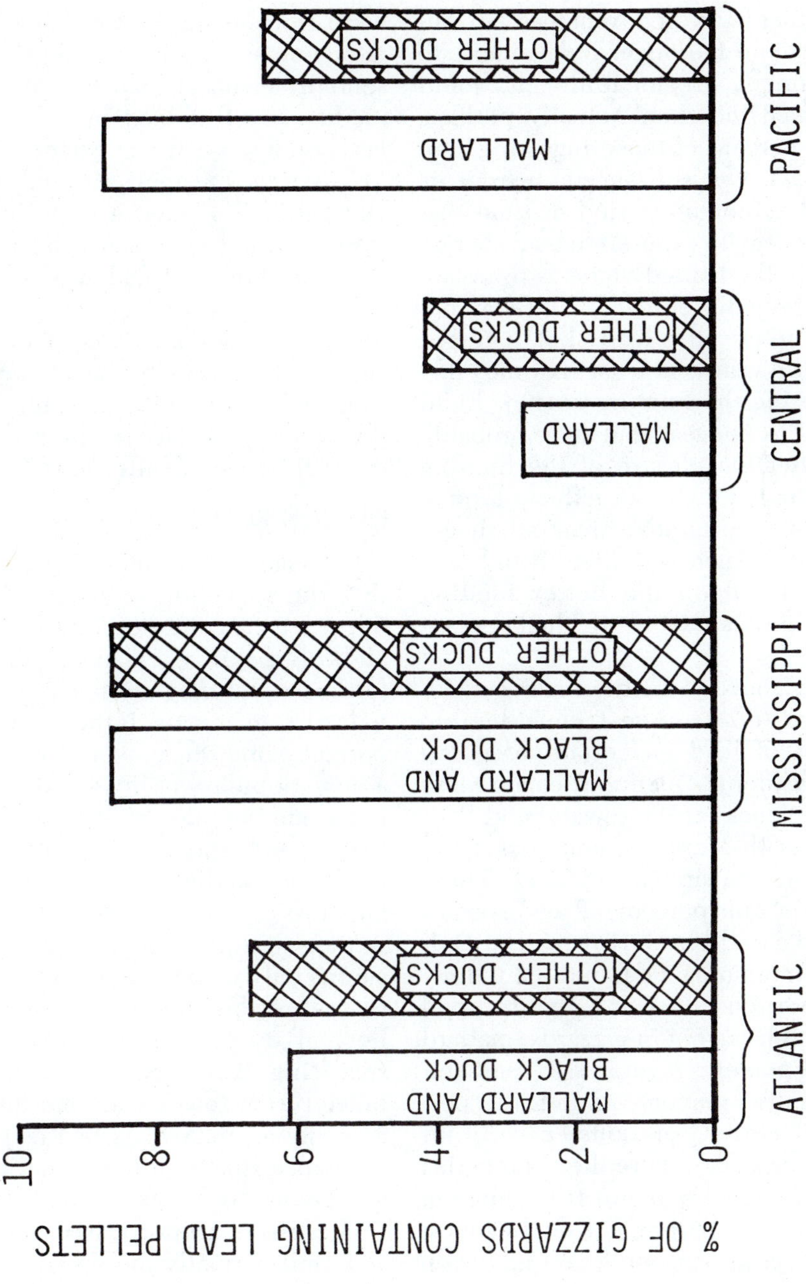

% OF GIZZARDS CONTAINING LEAD PELLETS

0
2
4
6
8
10

ATLANTIC
MALLARD AND BLACK DUCK
OTHER DUCKS

MISSISSIPPI
MALLARD AND BLACK DUCK
OTHER DUCKS

CENTRAL
MALLARD
OTHER DUCKS

PACIFIC
MALLARD
OTHER DUCKS

Fig. 5. A regional comparison of the proportion of lead ingested by mallards and black ducks versus all other ducks.

These levels of shot ingestion represent about a 20-day span during the hunting season. After that time span the bird would either have died from lead poisoning and would no longer be available to hunters or, in all probability, it would have passed the shot. Actually perhaps up to 20 percent of those ingesting shot pass it, and, yet, still succumb from its effects. A minimum period of time that ducks are heavily exposed to lead shot on marshes in the United States is from November through February, a 120-day period. Therefore, the lead shot ingested through the year is at least six times that found during the hunting season. Field observations suggest that it is probably higher after the closure of the hunting season than before because ducks tend to feed in heavily hunted areas when not disturbed by such activities. Blinds are usually placed on the better feeding grounds most attractive to ducks when not in use.

Although outside the time span considered here, ducks ingest considerable quantities of lead on certain breeding grounds. Elder (1950) fluoroscoped more than 3,300 ducks at Whitewater and Eyebrow lakes in Manitoba and Saskatchewan during the summer of 1947. There fewer than one percent of any species contained gizzard lead. However, at Delta Marsh, Manitoba, he found the following proportions of 1,529 live-trapped ducks with lead shot in gizzards: mallard adults 13 percent, juveniles 27 percent; pintail adults 7 percent, juveniles 22 percent; blue-winged teal adults 4 percent, juveniles 5 percent; and redhead juveniles an astounding 49 percent. It is apparent that varying proportions of ducks ingest lead shot on the breeding grounds even during the summer.

The bones from about 41,000 wings provided by hunters during the 1972 and 1973 seasons have been analyzed by the U.S. Fish and Wildlife Service for lead content (Anon. 1974:39–40). Half of these were from mallards. Lead levels in the radius-ulna wing bones ranged from essentially clean of lead to 400 ppm. The median level of lead in immature mallards by flyways were: Atlantic 5.2 ppm., Mississippi 2.2 ppm., Central 0.8 ppm., and Pacific 2.4 ppm. A regional comparison of the occurrence of lead levels in the wing bones of mallards with the incidence of gizzard lead found by us two decades earlier resulted in the conclusion: "There was a statistically significant and positive relationship between the two sets of data in spite of the time interval between collections."

DISCUSSION

Both laboratory and field data indicate that the ingestion of lead pellets produces a toxic condition in waterfowl. Not all birds that ingest lead shot die. We are fortunate that they are not as susceptible to lead as mammals. If they were, our important game ducks would indeed be at a low population level. Nevertheless, large numbers do die directly from lead toxicity and others undoubtedly succumb later when under additional environmental stress.

Many waterfowlers associate lead poisoning only with large die-offs where carcasses are abundantly in evidence. Numbers of ducks found dead in die-offs resulting from lead poisoning have ranged from fewer than one hundred to as many as 16,000. As bad as the documented losses are, they are a fraction of the day-to-day losses that pass unnoticed.

Because of almost instant predation, a sick bird normally disappears quickly in the wild. Almost as many mallards die in the wild each year as are killed by hunters. Yet how often is a dead bird found?

In all the years I have visited marshes populated by hundreds of thousands of ducks, I have seldom seen dead or sick ducks except where die-offs have occurred from lead poisoning.

Not one bird that we dosed with lead shot was ever reported as found dead. Nor did we find any in the area of the experiment. Yet we know that the ducks dosed with lead disappeared from the population at higher rates than those without lead at the time of the experiment. It is reasonable to conclude that the greater disappearance of lead dosed mallards from the wild population than those lead-free occurred because of the ensuing lead toxicity.

When our study was completed in 1959, I made the statement that: "At the present time, lead poisoning losses in waterfowl do not appear to be of sufficient magnitude to warrant such drastic regulations as, for example, prohibiting the use of lead shot in waterfowl hunting" (Bellrose 1959:283). Why has my view on this problem changed? The principal reason is that our waterfowl populations have declined. Like all of our disappearing natural resources they are relatively more valuable today than they were then.

Breeding ground population surveys by the U.S. Fish and Wildlife Service from 1955–74, show that during this 20-year period the ten most abundant species of game ducks have declined 6.2 percent. But mallards have declined 23.3 percent during the same period. Winter inventories indicate a decline of similar magnitude for the black duck. And these two species make up about 35 percent of the ducks killed in the United States.

During this same 20-year period, the number of ponds on the prairies of the United States and Canada have declined 16 percent. The status of the fall prairie duck flight has been inimically related to the abundance of prairie ponds in May. Over 50 percent of the mallards in North America breed there. And yet the decline in mallard breeding numbers during the past 20 years has been greater than the decline in the number of May ponds. Apparently the total mallard mortality from all causes is higher than desirable. If hunting is not to be curtailed further, we need to reduce nonhunting losses. The elimination of lead poisoning as an important mortality factor in waterfowl would greatly assist in improving the status of the mallard, and probably several other species.

LITERATURE CITED

ANON. 1974. Dept. of Interior draft environmental statement DES 74-76. Proposed use of steel shot for hunting waterfowl in the United States. U.S. Fish & Wildl. Serv. 79pp. + 5 appendices.

BELLROSE, F. C. 1955. A comparison of recoveries from reward and standard bands. J. Wildl. Manage. 19:71–75.

———. 1959. Lead poisoning as a mortality factor in waterfowl populations. Ill. Nat. Hist. Surv. Bull. 27(3):235–288.

ELDER, W. H. 1950. Measurements of hunting pressure in waterfowl by means of X-ray. N. Am. Wildl. Conf. Trans. 15:490–503.

JORDAN, J. S. 1968. Influence of diet on lead poisoning in waterfowl. Trans. NE Sec. Wildl. Soc., 25th NE Fish Wildl. Conf.:143–170.

———, AND F. C. BELLROSE. 1950. Shot alloys and lead poisoning in waterfowl. N. Am. Wildl. Conf. Trans. 15:155–168.

———, AND ———. 1951. Lead poisoning in wild waterfowl. Ill. Nat. Hist. Surv. Biol. Notes 26. 27pp.

BOTULISM IN WATERFOWL[1]

G. R. SMITH, Nuffield Institute of Comparative Medicine, The Zoological Society of London, Regent's Park, London NW1 4RY, England

The literature on botulism in wild birds—mainly waterfowl—is extensive, and that related to the disease in man and other species vast. This review will attempt only to indicate and comment upon the more important aspects of the disease in waterfowl and gulls, paying some regard to the general context of botulism in man and other animal species.

NATURE OF BOTULISM

Botulism is almost always a pure intoxication, caused by ingestion of the lethal neurotoxin produced by *Clostridium botulinum,* a bacterium whose natural habitat is soil and mud. If a suitable substance becomes contaminated with the bacterial spores, the organism will, given anaerobic conditions and a favourable temperature, multiply and produce lethal amounts of toxin. This is rapidly destroyed by boiling, but if the contaminated substance should be eaten without adequate heat treatment, some of the toxin may then be absorbed from the small intestine. Depending on the susceptibility of the species, lethal amounts of toxin may pass via the lymph and blood to receptor sites at the ends of the efferent autonomic and somatic nerves that act by the release of acetylcholine. Hence, botulism is a paralytic disease.

There are six types of *C. botulinum,* designated A–F, and a seventh, G, provisionally designated by Giménez and Cicarelli (1970). The toxins of the various types can readily be distinguished by neutralization tests with specific antitoxins. All exert similar pharmacological effects, but their relative toxicities for various animal species often differ widely (Roberts 1959). Those of certain strains, for example types E and F (Duff et al. 1956, Iida 1968), are activated by trypsin. Strains of *C. botulinum* vary in respect of their somatic antigens, the heat resistance of their spores, and their capacity produce proteolytic enzymes.

Types A, B, E and F are mainly, though not exclusively, of importance in relation to human disease; types C and D produce botulism in animals. Type D is an important cause of disease in cattle in South Africa, and type C is responsible for botulism in birds, both wild and domesticated, and in cattle and other animals, especially mink. Type E spores are found particularly in the mud of marine and other aquatic environments and human type E botulism is usually associated with eating fish in which toxin has been produced after death. The feeding of spoiled trash derived from marine fish has resulted in type E botulism in farmed trout (Huss and Eskildsen 1974). Carp, and to a lesser degree eels, were susceptible to type E toxin given by mouth, and carp were also slightly susceptible to type C toxin (Haagsma 1975).

The causal organism of botulism in waterfowl is almost invariably *C. botulinum* type C, though type E is thought to have been implicated on occasion (Fay 1966).

SOME PROPERTIES OF *C. BOTULINUM*

This anaerobic bacterium is a Gram-positive rod, measuring about 4–6

[1] Originally published in Wildfowl 27:129–138, 1976.

μm × 0.9 μm. It forms thick-walled resistant spores that are wider than the bacillus and usually subterminal. Vegetative cells are sluggishly motile and sensitive to oxygen. Colonies on agar plates are glistening and translucent with an indefinite reticular edge. Studies of types A, B (Bonventre and Kempe 1960) and C (Boroff 1955) suggest that break-down of ageing vegetative cells releases the toxin. For the production of large amounts of type C toxin Cardella et al. (1958) incubated cultures at 33°C for 5 days and Boroff and Reilly (1959) at 37°C for 9–10 days. Type C apparently does not grow below 10°C (Segner et al. 1971). Toxin can be converted to a harmless but immunogenic toxoid by formalin.

In the light of recent work, three aspects are worthy of special mention; they are (1) the relationship between the subtypes Cα and Cβ of *C. botulinum,* (2) the slight antigenic overlap between the toxins of types C and D (Dolman and Murakami 1961) and (3) the tendency (Smith 1955, McKee et al. 1958) for cultures of some types, including C, to lose their toxigenicity on repeated subculture. Type C was isolated by Bengston (1922), from the larvae of the blowfly *Lucilia caesar*, in the USA, and by Seddon (1922) in Australia. These isolates were representatives of two subtypes that came to be known as Cα and Cβ respectively (Gunnison and Meyer 1929), the work of Pfenninger (1924) having indicated that Cα antitoxin neutralized the toxin of both subtypes, whereas Cβ antitoxin neutralized Cβ but not Cα toxin. Botulism in waterfowl was usually attributable to the Cα type (Meyer 1956) although Cβ was occasionally thought to be involved (Pullar 1934, Reilly and Boroff 1967).

The composition of the toxins of types Cα, Cβ and D has been the subject of studies by Mason and Robinson (1935), Bulatova et al. (1967), Jansen (1971) and Eklund and Poysky (1972). Schantz and Sugiyama (1974) concluded that Cα toxin consists of a main component C1, together with components C2 and D; Cβ toxin contains the single component C2; D toxin contains a major component D, together with C1 and C2. Jansen (1971) found that the International Standard Type C Antitoxin contained antibodies against C1, C2 and D; D Antitoxin contained C1 and D antibodies. Jansen and Knoetze (1971) and Eklund and Poysky (1972) found that the toxicity of C2 in type Cβ was increased by trypsinization, and the latter authors described type C and D strains of *C. botulinum* that on subculture discontinued the production of C1 and D respectively but continued to produce C2. It is now known that the toxigenicity of types C and D depends upon a continuing association between specific bacteriophages and the clostridia, and that loss of such bacteriophage results in loss of toxin producion (Inoue and Iida 1970, 1971; Eklund et al. 1971, 1972). Eklund and Poysky (1974) demonstrated the interconversion of types C and D by manipulations involving specific bacteriophages, and this work was extended further (Eklund et al. 1974) to include interspecies conversions between *C. botulinum* (types C and D) and *Clostridium novyi* (*oedematiens*) type A.

HISTORICAL AND GEOGRAPHICAL PERSPECTIVE

The disease in man became recognized by medical authorities in Europe, particularly Germany, towards the end of the 18th century. Because of its frequent association with the consumption of sausage, it became known as botulism (from the Latin *botulus*, meaning sausage). The true aetiology was discovered in Belgium in 1896 (van Ermengem 1897). Since that time, numerous outbreaks in humans have been reported in Europe, America, Japan and elsewhere. Although the disease in man is quite rare, it attracts considerable attention because of its dramatic and often fatal nature, and because the widespread distribution of the causal organism necessitates constant care in the food manufacturing industry.

From about 1910, reports appeared in the literature of mortality occurring annually—often on a massive scale—amongst waterfowl on certain lakes and mud flats in the western states of the USA. Kalmbach (1935) wrote 'Although no single outbreak has equaled [sic] in sheer intensity the memorable one that occurred in the marshes about Great Salt Lake in the summer of 1910, there have been years in which the mortality, even in single areas, has exceeded 100,000 birds.' The 'western duck sickness' was at first thought to be some form of chemical poisoning and toxic concentrations of alkaline salts were strongly suspected. It was not until some 20 years after the initial description that intensive and sustained research revealed the disease to be botulism (Giltner and Couch 1930, Hobmaier 1930, Kalmbach 1930, Kalmback and Gunderson 1934) due to the organism now known as *C. botulinum* type Cα. Much of our present knowledge of botulism in waterfowl rests upon the very comprehensive American research (Kalmbach 1968) of the last half century.

Botulism in waterfowl is known also (Meyer 1956) in Canada, Argentina, Mexico, Uruguay, Australia, Germany (Lüthgen 1972), South Africa (Blaker 1967, Hay et al. 1973), Sweden (Niléhn and Johannsen 1965), the Netherlands (Haagsma et al. 1972, Haagsma 1974), Britain (Roberts et al. 1972, G. R. Smith 1975) and Spain (Mountfort 1973, Anon. 1975). Recent serious outbreaks in Western Europe have attracted considerable attention but the disease has probably existed there for many years (G. R. Smith 1975).

DISTRIBUTION OF *C. BOTULINUM* IN NATURE

The pioneer soil surveys of Meyer and Dubovsky (1922*a,b,c*) and Dubovsky and Meyer (1922) have been followed by numerous others. The chemical and biological nature of soil or mud samples is inevitably diverse, and Meyer (1956) stressed that failure to demonstrate *C. botulinum* was no proof of the organism's absence. Nevertheless, surveys have proved of value in indicating the prevalence of various types of the organism and the strikingly regional distribution of some of them (Baird-Parker 1969). Meyer (1956) suggested that the failure to demonstrate types C, D and E in early surveys may have been due to excessive preliminary heating of the samples. He considered that an exceptionally high incidence was exemplified by the figure of 30% obtained from Californian samples by Meyer and Dubovsky (1922*a*).

The geographical range of botulism in waterfowl demonstrates the wide distribution of type C spores in mud. Type C was once thought (Quortrup and Sudheimer 1942, Roberts 1959) to be confined in general to areas where botulism had occurred. It is certainly true that in aquatic areas following an outbreak in waterfowl, type C can readily be demonstrated in the mud for years afterwards. However, the organism has also been identified in lakes or waterways that have no known history of the disease. In such areas Haagsma (1974) found that 30% of mud samples from a number of Dutch inland waters contained *C. botulinum* type B, C or E, but that E prodominated. Smith and Moryson (1975) found that

72.5% of the lakes and waterways of London contained types B, C, D or E, but that B occurred between two and three times more frequently than C or E; D was found on one occasion only. In further unpublished studies, using constant techniques, their results varied from the uniform contamination of a large aquatic area with one or more of types B, C and E to the very low prevalence of type E in another area. In London, soil samples taken 200–300 yards from lakes positive for *C. botulinum* were usually negative (for further information see Smith, G. R., Br. Vet. J. 134:407–411, 1978). It is known (Segner et al. 1971) that type C organisms occur also in marine environments.

The occurrence of *C. botulinum* in soil and mud results in the not infrequent presence of the organism in the guts of birds, mammals and fish. Gunderson (1933) concluded that ducks occasionally carried types A, B and C in their livers; Dolman (1964) mentioned the isolation of types B and C from the livers of lemmings. Müller (1967) reported the presence of type Cβ in the livers of 4% of slaughtered cattle and 3% of pigs. These findings are given perspective by the knowledge that clostridial species other than *C. botulinum* sometimes occur in the internal organs and tissues of normal animals.

EPIDEMIOLOGY

It seems possible that the original contamination of a lake or waterway with any type of *C. botulinum* could occur through the intermediary of waterbirds that fly from one aquatic environment to another. Any bird leaving a lake on which an outbreak of avian botulism is in progress is likely to carry type C spores on its external surfaces and in its alimentary tract (Haagsma 1974). Such a bird may just have ingested a lethal dose of toxin and die after reaching a hitherto uncontaminated lake; if so, type C organisms are likely to invade the putrefying carcase from the gut and multiply profusely, thus seeding the new environment with massive numbers of organisms. Microbiological factors that might militate either for or against the establishment of various types of *C. botulinum* in a new environment have been described by Dack (1926), Quortrup and Sudheimer (1943), Grecz et al. (1959), Crisley and Helz (1961), Kautter et al. (1966), Wentz et al. (1967) and L. DS. Smith (1975). Chemical and other factors may also play a part.

The factors that favour the precipitation of an outbreak of botulism in waterfowl include a prolonged spell of warm weather, enlarged areas of shallow stagnant water, alkalinity, an abundance of aquatic invertebrates, and oxygen depletion associated with large amounts of rotting vegetation or other organic matter (Kalmback and Gunderson 1934, Coburn and Quortrup 1938, Quortrup and Holt 1941, Quortrup and Sudheimer 1942, Bell et al. 1955, McKee et al. 1958, Jensen and Allen 1960, Rosen 1971). Manmade influences such as thermal pollution of water by power stations (Haagsma et al. 1972) or irrigation procedures that involve the creation of shallow areas of stagnant water over stubble or other vegetation (McLean 1946) may also play a part. If type C is already present in the mud, the factors outlined above may stimulate sudden and rapid multiplication of the organism with the consequent production of lethal quantities of toxin. Whilst multiplication may occur in sludge and rotting vegetation, decaying invertebrates or waterfowl are very favourable as growth media and provide a suitable micro-environment in inhospitable surroundings (Bell et al. 1955). Multiplication of the organism in the carcases of birds may result in high concentrations of toxin that are then available to give rise to further deaths. In some instances the toxin may be transferred to other birds by the intermediary of dipterous fly larvae, which are not themselves susceptible but can accumulate considerable amounts by ingesting and crawling through decaying flesh. The eating of such larvae by waterfowl, pheasants and other birds may result in botulism (Lee et al. 1962, Rosen 1971, Smith et al. 1975). Occasional deaths from botulism may continue for many weeks after the peak mortality of an outbreak has subsided. Quortrup and Sudheimer (1942) were convinced that toxin was rapidly destroyed under natural conditions, but Haagsma (1974) found that it was undiminished after nine months. During an outbreak, the contamination of the environment with spores increases greatly, thus enhancing the possibility of a future outbreak.

Gulls are known to suffer from type C botulism and refuse dumps may well be the source of toxin. Evidence regarding the possible occurrence of type E botulism in gulls and other birds on Lake Michigan is discussed by Herman (1964), Kaufmann and Fay (1964), Fay et al. (1965), Fay (1966), Kaufmann and Crecelius (1967) and Monheimer (1968).

Botulism in waterfowl has been described in South Africa, but reports from the tropics are rare. This may be because mortality remains unreported or undiagnosed, but mud and water temperatures in the tropics, unlike those in temperate zones, will remain comparatively high and fluctuate little.

AVIAN SPECIES AFFECTED

The very wide range of species affected is illustrated by numerous reports, including those of Kalmbach and Gunderson (1934), Fay et al. (1965), Blaker (1967) and Keymer et al. (1972). Certain carrion-eating species have been described as resistant to botulism (Kalmbach 1939, Holdeman 1970).

ASPECTS OF PATHOGENESIS

The manner in which the disease usually arises has already been outlined, but a number of points deserve special mention either because of their intrinsic interest or because they require further study.

The likelihood that a fatal dose of toxin will be ingested in any outbreak of botulism in waterfowl may depend upon the feeding habits of particular species, but in addition it is probable that different species vary in their susceptibility to type C toxin (Haagsma et al. 1972, Haagsma 1974).

Although it is generally accepted that botulism is most often a pure intoxication, 'wound botulism' of man (Merson and Dowell 1973) shows that multiplication of *C. botulinum* can occur in the tissues under certain circumstances. Minervin (1967) and others (see Petty 1965) believe that elaboration of toxin in the alimentary tract may play a part in certain cases of human botulism, and Roberts (1959) mentioned ruminants and birds in the same context. This is however a controversial point (Dolman 1964) and one on which direct evidence from animal experimentation is largely lacking. The administration of toxin-free type A and B spores by mouth to guinea-pigs was shown by Coleman and Meyer (1922) and Orr (1922) to produce botulism only when very large doses were used. Sugiyama et al. (1970) obtained no evidence of multiplication of *C. botulinum* type E in the intestinal tract of live fish. However, Bullen et al. (1953) and Bullen and Scarisbrick (1957) found that dietary factors influence profoundly the multiplication of *Clostridium perfringens (welchii)* in the alimentary tract of sheep and that *C. perfringens* is also not infrequently found in tissues remote from the gut. Several workers (Hobmaier 1932, Kalmbach and Gunderson 1934, Bell et al. 1955, Boroff and Reilly 1962, Dolman 1964, Haagsma 1974) have commented that the livers of some birds dying from botulism contain type C organisms. This matter deserves further study paying particular attention to (1) rigid aseptic precautions in technique, (2) the absolute exclusion of any possibility of invasion after death, (3) the purity of isolates, (4) the degree of invasion, and (5) the reports, already mentioned, that the livers of normal birds and animals may contain *C. botulinum* spores.

Cooch (1961, 1964) observed that the functioning of the salt gland possessed by ducks and geese that use the alkaline waters of the prairies is impaired by the action of type C toxin; a sublethal dose of toxin given by mouth to such birds became lethal if sodium chloride solution was administered at the same time.

Although *C. botulinum* types B, C and E are by no means uncommon in inland aquatic environments, the literature indicates that except for the possible occasional involvement of type E all outbreaks of botulism in waterfowl are due to type C. The reasons for this apparent paradox may well be complex, but in studies with gallinaceous birds Gross and Smith (1971) found that type C toxin was more readily absorbed through the gut wall than B or E toxin and that B toxin possessed little toxicity; type A and E toxins possessed the greatest toxicity, and D and F were nontoxic.

Experiments by Jensen and Gritman (1967) demonstrated a reinforcing effect between type C and E toxins when they were administered together to Mallard *Anas platyrhynchos*, and Jensen and Micuda (1970) found that administration of the pesticide malathion to Mallard decreased the effects of type C toxin.

CLINICAL SIGNS

Depending on the amount of toxin ingested, and perhaps also on species susceptibility, the signs of botulism in waterfowl may progress from nothing more than slight difficulty in flying to complete flaccid paralysis of the limbs and neck, followed by acute respiratory distress and death. The clinical features may include eye disturbances such as rapid dilation and contraction of the pupil, paralysis of the iris, immobilization of the nictitating membrane, disappearance of the eye closure reflex, and conjunctivitis. Paralysis of the neck muscles will result in drowning of birds that are on water. Ingestion of small doses of toxin may be followed by recovery after illness lasting up to a week.

DIAGNOSIS

No characteristic lesion is seen at necropsy and diagnosis of botulism in waterfowl depends primarily on the demonstration and identification of type C toxin in the serum or tissues, or in the alimentary tract although this is less conclusive and usually less successful. The possibility of type E botulism should not be overlooked.

It must always be borne in mind that the alimentary tracts of birds dying from other causes may contain *C. botulinum,* especially if the immediate environment is heavily contaminated. If the organism is present in the gut, it may invade the carcase after death and produce toxin in the tissues. Thus, the demonstration of toxin in a carcase in which putrefaction has begun does not constitute a satisfactory diagnosis. Preferably several birds showing advanced symptoms consistent with a diagnosis of botulism should be killed to provide serum samples for examination. Some birds dying from botulism have insufficient toxin in their serum to permit a diagnosis. If the collection of blood presents difficulty, tissues, for example liver, may be homogenized in gelatine-phosphate buffer, though this is less satisfactory because of the dilution involved. After collection, the samples should be refrigerated without delay, or frozen if they cannot be examined within a day or so.

Intraperitoneal inoculation of mice with up to 1.0 ml of serum containing toxin will produce within four days—and usually much sooner—a characteristic 'wasp-waist,' followed by progressive paralysis, respiratory distress and death. Very small amounts of toxin produce nothing more than a slight wasp-waist. If the initial test proves positive, the toxin in the remainder of the sample must be typed by neutralization tests with specific antitoxins in mice. To ensure complete specificity, the antitoxins should be diluted to the levels recommended by the supplier (Baird-Parker 1969). As little as 0.1 unit of type C antitoxin will effectively neutralize any toxin likely to be present in 1.0 ml of avian serum.

Where mortality is suspected retrospectively to have been due to botulism, it may be of interest to examine mud samples by methods such as those described by Smith and Moryson (1975). With experience, such methods may be expected always to give a positive result if several samples are examined from an area where the disease has occurred in recent years. While demonstration of type C in the mud does not confirm the original suspicion of botulism, failure to demonstrate it is good presumptive evidence that the mortality was due to some other cause.

IMMUNITY

After recovery from botulism waterfowl remain susceptible to the disease. Rosen (1971) observed ducks that suffered three attacks within a single season. Haagsma (1974) found that Mallard failed to resist one minimal lethal dose of type C toxin after recovery from botulism, and even after multiple sublethal doses of type C toxin detectable levels of antitoxin were not produced. Shave (1970) reached similar conclusions from studies on pheasants. Lamanna (1970) failed to demonstrate antitoxin in the sera of normal persons and considered that the development of antitoxic immunity as a result of sublethal exposures to toxin was unlikely. Dolman et al. (1949) failed to immunise mice against *C. botulinum* toxin by administering formol-toxoid by mouth.

On the other hand, there is some evidence to suggest that an immune response can occur as a result of the ingestion of antigenic material. Thus, although Jansen et al. (1970) failed to induce a primary immune response in rabbits by giving large quantities of type C toxin by mouth, in animals that were already basically immune a secondary type response resulted. Kaufmann and Crecelius (1967) reported experiments indicating that gulls may acquire immunity to type E toxin as a result of the repeated ingestion of sublethal doses over a period of time. Resistance to the toxins of *C. botulinum* has been observed in carrion-eating birds such as the Turkey Vulture *Cathartes aura* (Kalmbach 1939). Holdeman (1970) cited work by Pates and her colleagues showing that vulture serum contained a substance—probably antibody—that neutralized type C toxin, and that exposure of vultures to sublethal doses of type A toxin resulted in the production of antitoxin.

Vaccines consisting of toxoid with a reinforcer are used to protect laboratory workers against various types of *C. botulinum* toxin, and to protect cattle (Sterne and Wentzel 1950, 1952) and mink (Appleton and White 1959) against naturally occurring botulism. The immunization of pheasants and ducks against type C toxin has also been studied (Boroff and Reilly 1959, 1962; Rosen 1959; Fish et al. 1967) and vaccination is occasionally used to protect valuable collections of waterfowl. In many developed countries, stocks of antitoxin are held at central points for emergency use in the treatment of human botulism, and type C antitoxin is sometimes used in the treatment of naturally affected waterfowl (Kalmbach 1968, Rosen 1971). The international standards for the antitoxins type A–E have been discussed by Bowmer (1963).

TREATMENT

Individual rescue and treatment of birds can be an expensive exercise in terms of manpower. Sick birds that are removed to an uncontaminated environment and given toxin-free water and food will often recover. Treatment with type C antitoxin is often effective and may sometimes be economically feasible (Kalmbach 1968, Haagsma et al. 1972). The artificial administration of water by mouth is useful in diluting the toxin and flushing the intestinal tract (Rosen 1971). Birds in a state of collapse seldom respond to treatment.

CONTROL

Control of botulism in waterfowl is often very difficult. It depends either on eliminating as many as possible of those factors favouring the precipation of an outbreak, or upon keeping birds away from areas in which outbreaks are already in progress. Methods of control have been discussed by Kalmbach and Gunderson (1934), Hobmaier (1932), Quortrup and Holt (1941), Quortrup and Sudheimer (1942), McLean (1946), Sperry (1947), Rosen and Bischoff (1953) and Rosen (1971).

Various forms of water manipulation have been suggested: the permanent drainage of heavily contaminated marshes; the construction of embankments to eliminate shallow marginal water and thus prevent recession of the waterline in hot weather; maintenance of a constant water level by withdrawals from reservoirs; circulation of water by pumping. The early removal and burning of carcases during an outbreak is important and the removal of mats of drifting vegetation has also been considered helpful. It may be feasible to drain and clean small lakes such as those in public parks. Attempts have sometimes been made to keep birds away from dangerous areas by baiting elsewhere, or by putting them up with thunderflashes, flares or power boats and herding them by aircraft.

Surveys of the prevalence of *C. botulinum* in wetlands might with advantage be used in the planning stages of certain projects concerned with waterfowl. Surveys repeated at intervals would be of interest in relation to the management of refuges, as well as providing valuable epidemiological data. Thus, Smith and Moryson (unpublished) were unable to demonstrate type C in any of the eight refuges of the Wildfowl Trust in England and Scotland.

PUBLIC HEALTH AND BOTULISM IN WATERFOWL

Despite the enormous annual mortality from botulism that occurs in waterfowl, the literature contains only three reports of type C botulism in man and none is entirely conclusive (Gilbert 1974). The reasons for this state of affairs are not well understood (Lamanna 1970) and Gunnison and Meyer (1928) found type C toxin to be pathogenic for rhesus monkeys. In our present state of knowledge it would seem wise to regard *C. botulinum* type C as a potential human pathogen. It has been shown that types B and E are sometimes widespread in inland freshwater environments and it seems possible that they might increase under the influence of those factors that cause multiplication of type C. On general grounds, the unbridled proliferation of *C. botulinum* in any aquatic environment must be considered undesirable.

ACKNOWLEDGMENTS

Research at the Nuffield Institute of Comparative Medicine on botulism in waterfowl is supported by the Wellcome Trust and the Natural Environment Research Council.

SUMMARY

A brief review is given of the bacteriology of the disease of botulism, its distribution, epidemiology, diagnosis, treatment and control in waterfowl.

LITERATURE CITED

ANON. 1975. Coto Donana, Spain. Bull. Int. Waterfowl Res. Bur. 39/40:43–44.

APPLETON, G. S., AND P. G. WHITE. 1959. Field evaluation of *Clostridium botulinum* type C toxoids in mink. Am. J. Vet. Res. 20:166–169.

BAIRD-PARKER, A. C. 1969. Medical and veterinary significance of spore-forming bacteria and their spores. *In* The bacterial spore, ed. G. W. Gould and A. Hurst. London and New York: Academic Press, pp. 517–548.

BELL, J. F., G. W. SCIPLE, AND A. A. HUBERT. 1955. A microenvironment concept of the epizoology of avian botulism. J. Wildl. Mgmt. 19:352–357.

BENGSTON, I. A. 1922. Preliminary note on a toxin-producing anaerobe isolated from the larvae of Lucilia caesar. Publ. Hlth. Rep., Wash. 37:164–170.

BLAKER, D. 1967. An outbreak of botulinus poisoning among waterbirds. Ostrich 38:144–147.

BONVENTRE, P. F., AND L. L. KEMPE. 1960. Physiology of toxin production by *Clostridium botulinum* types A and B. I. Growth, autolysis and toxin production. J. Bact. 79:18–23.

BOROFF, D. A. 1955. Study of toxins of *Clostridium botulinum*. III. Relation of autolysis to toxin production. J. Bact. 70:363–367.

———, AND J. R. REILLY. 1959. Studies on the toxin of *Clostridium botulinum*. V. Prophylactic immunization of pheasants and ducks against avian botulism. J. Bact. 77:142–146.

———, AND ———. 1962. Studies on the toxin of *Clostridium botulinum*. VI. Botulism among pheasants and quail, mode of transmission and degree of resistance offered by immunization. Int. Arch. Allergy 20:306–313.

BOWMER, E. J. 1963. Preparation and assay of the international standards for *Clostridium botulinum* types A, B, C, D and E antitoxins. Bull. Wld. Hlth. Org. 29:701–709.

BULATOVA, T. I., K. I. MATVEEV, AND V. S. SAMSONOVA. 1967. Biological characteristics of *Cl. botulinum* type C strains isolated from minks in the USSR. *In* Botulism 1966, Proc. 5th Int. Sympos. Food Microbiol., ed. M. Ingram and T. A. Roberts. London: Chapman and Hall, pp. 391–399.

BULLEN, J. J., AND R. SCARISBRICK. 1957. Enterotoxaemia of sheep: experimental reproduction of the disease. J. Path. Bact. 73:495–509.

———, ———, AND A. MADDOCK. 1953. Enterotoxaemia of sheep: the fate of washed suspensions of *Clostridium welchii* type D introduced into the rumen of normal sheep. J. Path. Bact. 65:209–219.

CARDELLA, M. A., J. T. DUFF, C. GOTTFRIED, AND J. S. BEGEL. 1958. Studies on immunity to toxins of *Clostridium botulinum*. IV. Production and purification of type C toxin for conversion to toxoid. J. Bact. 75:360–365.

COBURN, D. R., AND E. R. QUORTRUP. 1938. The distribution of botulinus toxin in duck sickness areas. Trans. 3rd N. Am. Wildl. Conf., pp. 869–876.

COLEMAN, G. E., AND K. F. MEYER. 1922. Some observations on the pathogenicity of *B. botulinus* X. J. Infect. Dis. 31:622–649.

COOCH, F. G. 1961. Avian salt gland and botulism. Can. Wildl. Serv. Res. Prog. Rep., p. 27.

———. 1964. A preliminary study of the survival value of a functional salt gland in prairie Anatidae. Auk 81:380–393.

CRISLEY, F. D., AND G. E. HELZ. 1961. Some observations of the effect of filtrates of several representative concomitant bacteria on *Clostridium botulinum* type A. Can. J. Microbiol. 7:633–639.

DACK, G. M. 1926. Influence of some anaerobic species on toxin of *Cl. botulinum* with special reference to *Cl. sporogenes*. J. Infect. Dis. 38:165–173.

DOLMAN, C. E. 1964. Botulism as a world health problem. *In* Botulism. Procedings of a symposium, ed. K. H. Lewis and K. Cassel, Jr. Cincinnati, Ohio: U.S. Dept. Hlth. Educ. and Welf., Publ. Hlth. Serv., pp. 5–32.

———, L. C. JENKINS, AND J. E. WOOD. 1949. Observations on the problem of oral immunization against *Clostridium botulinum* toxin. Can. J. Publ. Hlth. 40:37.

———, AND L. MURAKAMI. 1961. *Clostridium botulinum* type F with recent observations on other types. J. Infect. Dis. 109:107–128.

DUBOVSKY, B. J., AND K. F. MEYER. 1922. An experimental study of the methods available for the enrichment, demonstration and isolation of *B. botulinus* in specimens of soil and its products, in suspected food, in clinical and in necropsy material. I. J. Infect. Dis. 31:501–540.

DUFF, J. T., G. G. WRIGHT, AND A. YARINSKY. 1956. Activation of *Clostridium botulinum* type E toxin by trypsin. J. Bact. 72:455–460.

EKLUND, M. W., AND F. T. POYSKY. 1972. Activation of a toxic component of *Clostridium botulinum* types C and D by trypsin. Appl. Microbiol. 24:108–113.

———, AND ———. 1974. Interconversion of type C and D strains of *Clostridium botulinum* by specific bacteriophages. Appl. Microbiol. 27:251- 258.

———, ———, J. A. MEYERS, AND G. A. PELROY. 1974. Interspecies conversion of *Clostridium botulinum* type C to *Clostridium novyi* type A by bacteriophage. Science 186:456–458.

———, ———, AND S. M. REED. 1972. Bacteriophage and the toxigenicity of *Clostridium botulinum* type D. Nature New Biol. 235:16–17.

———, ———, ———, AND C. A. SMITH. 1971. Bacteriophage and the toxigenicity of *Clostridium botulinum* type C. Science 172:480–482.

FAY, L. D. 1966. Type E botulism in Great Lakes waterbirds. Trans. 31st N. Am. Wildl. Conf. pp. 139–149.

———, O. W. KAUFMANN, AND L. A. RYEL. 1965. Mass mortality of water-birds in Lake Michigan 1963–64. Pubn. No. 13, Great Lakes Research Division, University of Michigan, pp. 36–46.

FISH, N. A., W. R. MITCHELL, AND D. A. BARNUM. 1967. A report of a natural outbreak of botulism in pheasants. Can. Vet. J. 8:10–16.

GILBERT, R. J. 1974. Staphylococcal food poisoning and botulism. Postgrad. Med. J. 50:603–611.

GILTNER, L. T., AND J. F. COUCH. 1930. Western duck sickness and botulism. Science 72:660.

GIMÉNEZ, D. F., AND A. S. CICCARELLI. 1970. Another type of *Clostridium botulinum*. Zentbl. Bakt. Parasitkde., I Abt. Orig. 215:221–224.

GRECZ, N., R. O. WAGENAAR, AND G. M. DACK. 1959. Inhibition of *Clostridium botulinum* by culture filtrates of *Brevibacterium linens*. J. Bact. 78:506–510.

GROSS, W. B., AND L. DS. SMITH. 1971. Experimental botulism in gallinaceous birds. Avian Dis. 15:716–722.

GUNDERSON, M. F. 1933. Presence of *Clostridium botulinum* in livers of birds not affected with botulism. Proc. Soc. Exp. Biol. Med. 30:747–750.

GUNNISON, J. B., AND K. F. MEYER. 1928. Susceptibility of *Macacus rhesus* monkeys to botulinum toxin types B, C and D. Proc. Soc. Exp. Biol. Med. 26:89–90.

———, AND ———. 1929. Cultural study of an international collection of *Clostridium botulinum* and *parabotulinum* XXXVIII. J. Infect. Dis. 45:119–134.

HAAGSMA, J. 1974. Etiology and epidemiology of botulism in water-fowl in the Netherlands. Tijdschr. Diergeneesk. 99:434–442.

———. 1975. Sensitivity of eels (*Anguilla anguilla*) and carp (*Cyprinus carpio*) to type C and E botulinum toxin. Zentbl. Bakt. Parasitkde., I Abt. Orig. 230:59–66.

———, H. J. OVER, T. SMIT, AND J. HOEKSTRA. 1972. Botulism in waterfowl in the Netherlands in 1970. Neth. J. Vet. Sci. 5:12–33.

HAY, C. M. E., H. N. VAN DER MADE, AND P. C. KNOETZE. 1973. Isolation of *Clostridium botulinum* type C from an outbreak of botulism in wild geese. J. S. Afr. Vet. Ass. 44:53–56.

HERMAN, C. M. 1964. Significance of bird losses on Lake Michigan during November and December 1963. Pubn. No. 11, Great Lakes Research Division, University of Michigan, pp. 84–87.

HOBMAIER, M. 1930. Duck disease caused by the poison of the *Bacillus botulinus*. Calif. Fish Game 16:285–286.

———. 1932. Conditions and control of botulism (duck disease) in waterfowl. Calif. Fish Game 18:5–21.

HOLDEMAN, L. V. 1970. The ecology and natural history of *Clostridium botulinum*. J. Wildl. Dis. 6:205–210.

HUSS, H. H., AND U. ESKILDSEN. 1974. Botulism in farmed trout caused by *Clostridium botulinum* type E. Nord. Vet.-Med. 26:733–738.

IIDA, H. 1968. Activation of *Clostridium botulinum* toxin by trypsin. *In* Toxic Micro-Organisms, Proc. 1st US–Japan Conf. Toxic Micro-organisms, 7–10 October 1968, ed. M. Herzberg. Washington D.C.: UJNR Joint Panels on Toxic Micro-organisms and the U.S. Department of the Interior, pp. 336–340.

INOUE, K., AND H. IIDA. 1970. Conversion of toxigenicity in *Clostridium botulinum* type C. Jap. J. Microbiol. 14:87–89.

———, AND ———. 1971. Phage conversion of toxigenicity in *Clostridium botulinum* types C and D. Jap. J. Med. Sci. Biol. 24:53–56.

JANSEN, B. C. 1971. The toxic antigenic factors produced by *Clostridium botulinum* types C and D. Onderstepoort J. Vet. Res. 38:93–98.

———, AND P. C. KNOETZE. 1971. Tryptic activation of *Clostridium botulinum* type Cβ toxin. Onderstepoort J. Vet. Res. 38:237–238.

———, ———, AND F. VISSER. 1970. The antigenicity of *Clostridium botulinum* type C toxin administered *per os*. Onderstepoort J. Vet. Res. 37:169–172.

JENSEN, W. I., AND J. P. ALLEN. 1960. A possible relationship between aquatic invertebrates and avian botulism. Trans. 25th N. Am. Wildl. Conf. 171–179.

———, AND R. B. GRITMAN. 1967. An adjuvant effect between *Cl. botulinum* type C and E toxins in the mallard duck (*Anas platyrhynchos*). *In* Botulism 1966, Proc. 5th Int. Sympos. Food Microbiol., ed. M. Ingram and T. A. Roberts. London: Chapman & Hall, pp. 407–413.

———, AND J. M. MICUDA. 1970. The effect of malathion on the susceptibility of the mallard duck (*Anas platyrhynchos*) to *Clostridium botulinum* type C toxin. *In* Toxic Micro-Organisms, Proc. 1st US–Japan Conf. Toxic Micro-organisms, 7–10 October 1968, ed. M. Herzberg. Washington D.C.: UJNR Joint Panels on Toxic Microorganisms and the U.S. Department of the Interior, pp. 372–375.

KALMBACH, E. R. 1930. Western duck sickness produced experimentally. Science 72:658–659.

———. 1935. Will botulism become a world-wide hazard to wild fowl? J. Am. Vet. Med. Ass. 87:183–187.

———. 1939. American vultures and the toxin of *Clostridium botulinum*. J. Am. Vet. Med. Ass. 94:187–191.

———. 1968. Type C botulism among wild birds—A historical sketch. Bur. Sport Fish. Wildl. Rep., Wash., Wildlife No. 110:1–8.

———, AND M. F. GUNDERSON. 1934. Western duck sickness: a form of botulism. USDA Tech. Bull. No. 411:1–81.

KAUFMANN, O. W., AND M. S. CRECELIUS. 1967. Experimentally induced immunity in gulls to type E botulism. Am. J. Vet. Res. 28:1857–1862.

———, AND L. D. FAY. 1964. *Clostridium botulinum* type E toxin in tissues of dead loons and gulls. Mich. State Univ. Agric. Exp. Sta. Quart. Bull. 47:236–242.

KAUTTER, D. A., S. M. HARMON, R. K. LYNT, JR., AND T. LILLY, JR. 1966. Antagonistic effect on *Clostridium botulinum* type E by organisms resembling it. Appl. Microbiol. 14:616–622.

KEYMER, I. F., G. R. SMITH, T. A. ROBERTS, S. I. HEANEY, AND D. J. HIBBERD. 1972. Botulism as a factor in waterfowl mortality at St James's Park, London. Vet. Rec. 90:111–114.

LAMANNA, C. 1970. Critical comment on research needs in botulism: ecology, nature and action of toxin. *In* Toxic Micro-Organisms, Proc. 1st US–Japan Conf. Toxic Micro-organisms, 7–10 October 1968, ed. M. Herzberg. Washington D.C.: UJNR Joint Panel on Toxic Micro-organisms and the U.S. Department of the Interior, pp. 230–235.

LEE, V. H., S. VADLAMUDI, AND R. P. HANSON. 1962. Blow fly larvae as a source of botulinum toxin for game farm pheasants. J. Wildl. Mgmt. 26:411–413.

LÜTHGEN, W. VON. 1972. Verluste von wasservögeln durch botulismus-C-intoxikationen auf geschlossenen gewässern. Proc. 14th Int. Sympos. Dis. Zoo Anim. Berlin: Akademie-Verlag, pp. 89–93.

MASON, J. H., AND E. M. ROBINSON. 1935. The antigenic components of the toxins of *Cl. botulinum* types C and D. Onderstepoort J. Vet. Sci. Anim. Indust. 5:65–75.

MCKEE, M. T., J. F. BELL, AND B. H. HOYER. 1958. Culture of *Clostridium botulinum* type C with controlled pH. J. Bact. 75:135–142.

MCLEAN, D. D. 1946. Duck disease at Tulare lake. Calif. Fish Game 32:71–80.

MERSON, M. H., AND V. R. DOWELL, JR. 1973. Epidemiological, clinical and laboratory aspects of wound botulism. New Engl. J. Med. 289:1005–1010.

MEYER, K. F., AND B. J. DUBOVSKY. 1922*a*. The distribution of the spores of *B. botulinus* in California. II. J. Infect. Dis. 31:541–555.

———, AND ———. 1922*b*. The distribution of the spores of *B. botulinus* in the United States. IV. J. Infect. Dis. 31:559–594.

———, AND ———. 1922*c*. The distribution of the spores of *B. botulinus* in Belgium, Denmark, England and the Netherlands, VI. J. Infect. Dis. 31:600–609.

MINERVIN, S. M. 1967. On the parenteral-enteral method of administering serum in cases of botulism. *In* Botulism 1966, Proc. 5th Int. Sympos. Food Microbiol., ed. M. Ingram and T. A. Roberts. London: Chapman & Hall, pp. 336–345.

MONHEIMER, R. H. 1968. The relationship of Lake Michigan waterbird mortalities to naturally occurring *Clostridium botulinum* type E toxin. Wildlife Dis. 4:81–85.

MOUNTFORT, G. 1973. Wildlife disaster in Spain. The Times, October 9th.

MÜLLER, J. 1967. On the occurrence of *Clostridium botulinum* type C beta in the livers of slaughter animals in Denmark. Bull. Off. Int. Epiz. 67:1473–1478.

NILÉHN, P. O., AND A. JOHANNSEN. 1965. Ett utbrot av aviär botulism. Nord. Vet-Med. 17:685–692.

ORR, P. F. 1922. The pathogenicity of *B. botulinus*. J. Infect. Dis. 30:118–127.

PETTY, C. S. 1965. Botulism: the disease and the toxin. Am. J. Med. Sci. 249:345–359.

PFENNINGER, W. 1924. Toxico-immunologic and serologic relationship of *B. botulinus*, type C, and *B. parabotulinus*, 'Seddon.' XXII. J. Infect. Dis. 35:347–352.

PULLAR, E. M. 1934. Enzootic botulism amongst wild birds. Aust. Vet. J. 10:128–135.

QUORTRUP, AND A. L. HOLT. 1941. Detection of potential botulinus-toxin-producing areas in western duck marshes with suggestions for control. J. Bact. 41:363–372.

———, AND R. L. SUDHEIMER. 1942. Research notes on botulism in western marsh areas with recommendations for control. Trans. 7th N. Am. Wildl. Conf., pp. 284–293.

———, AND ———. 1943. Some ecological relations of *Pseudomonas aeruginosa* to *Clostridium botulinum* type C. J. Bact. 45:551–554.

REILLY, J. R., AND D. A. BOROFF. 1967. Botulism in a tidal estuary in New Jersey. Wildlife Dis. 3:26–29.

ROBERTS, R. S. 1959. Clostridial diseases. *In* Infectious diseases of animals: diseases due to bacteria, ed. A. W. Stableforth and I. A. Galloway. London: Butterworths, pp. 160–228.

ROBERTS, T. A., I. F. KEYMER, E. D. BORLAND, AND G. R. SMITH. 1972. Botulism in birds and mammals in Great Britain. Vet. Rec. 91:11–12.

ROSEN, M. N. 1959. Immunization of pheasants with botulinum toxoid. Calif. Fish Game 45:343–350.

———. 1971. Botulism. *In* Infectious and parasitic deseases of wild birds, ed. J. W. Davis, R. C. Anderson, L. Karstad, and D. O. Trainer. Ames: Iowa State University Press, pp. 100–117.

———, AND A. L. BISCHOFF. 1953. A new approach towards botulism control. Trans. 18th N. Am. Wildl. Conf. pp. 191–199.

SCHANTZ, E. J., AND H. SUGIYAMA. 1974. The toxins of *Clostridium botulinum. In* Essays in toxicology, vol. 5, ed. W. J. Hayes. London and New York: Academic Press, pp. 99–119.

SEDDON, H. R. 1922. Bulbar paralysis in cattle due to the action of a toxicogenic bacillus, with a discussion on the relationship of the condition to forage poisoning (botulism). J. Comp. Path. 35:147–190.

SEGNER, W. P., C. F. SCHMIDT, AND J. K. BOLTZ. 1971. Minimal growth temperature, sodium chloride tolerance, pH sensitivity and toxin production of marine and terrestrial strains of *Clostridium botulinum* type C. Appl. Microbiol. 22:1025–1029.

SHAVE, H. J. 1970. Progressive pathologic signs of botulism in pheasants. J. Wildl. Dis. 6:402–403.

SMITH, G. R. 1975. Recent European outbreaks of botulism in waterfowl. Bull. Int. Waterfowl Res. Bur. No. 39/40:72–74.

———, J. M. HIME, I. F. KEYMER, J. M. GRAHAM, P. J. S. OLNEY, AND M. R. BRAMBELL. 1975. Botulism in captive birds fed commercially-bred maggots. Vet. Rec. 97:204–205.

———, AND C. J. MORYSON. 1975. *Clostridium botulinum* in the lakes and waterways of London. J. Hyg., Camb. 75:371–379.

SMITH, L. DS. 1955. Introduction to the pathogenic anaerobes. University of Chicago Press and Cambridge University Press, p. 115.

———. 1975. Inhibition of *Clostridium botulinum* by strains of *Clostridium perfringens* isolated from soil. Appl. Microbiol. 30:319–323.

SPERRY, C. C. 1947. Botulism control by water manipulation. Trans. 12th N. Am. Wildl. Conf., pp. 228–233.

STERNE, M., AND L. M. WENTZEL. 1950. A new method for the large-scale production of high-titre botulinum formol-toxoid types C and D. J. Immunol. 65:175–183.

———, AND ———. 1952. Botulism in animals in South Africa. Rpt. 14th Int. Vet. Congr., 8–13 August 1949. London: HMSO, pp. 329–331.

SUGIYAMA, H., T. L. BOTT, AND E. M. FOSTER. 1970. *Clostridium botulinum* type E in an inland bay (Green Bay of Lake Michigan). *In* Toxic Micro-Organisms, Proc. 1st US–Japan Conf. Toxic Micro-organisms, ed. M. Herzberg. Washington D.C.: UNJR Joint Panels on Toxic Micro-organisms and the U.S. Department of the Interior, pp. 287–291.

VAN ERMENGEM, E. 1897. Ueber einen neuen anaëroben Bacillus und seine Beziehungen zum Botulismus. Z. Hyg. Infectkrankh. 26:1–56.

WENTZ, M. W., R. A. SCOTT, AND J. W. VENNES. 1967. *Clostridium botulinum* type F: seasonal inhibition by *Bacillus licheniformis.* Science 155:89–90.

DUCK PLAGUE (DUCK VIRUS ENTERITIS) IN WILD WATERFOWL[1]

MILTON FRIEND,[2] Bureau of Sport Fisheries and Wildlife, Denver Wildlife Research Center, Denver, CO
GARY L. PEARSON, Bureau of Sport Fisheries and Wildlife, Northern Prairie Research Center, Jamestown, ND

Duck plague which has come to be known in the United States as duck virus enteritis (DVE), is an acute, contagious, and often fatal, herpesvirus infection of domestic ducks, geese, and swans. DVE has recently been identified in free-flying waterfowl and is now considered to be a serious threat to our North American waterfowl resource. This brief description of DVE is intended as a guide to aid in the prompt recognition and reporting of future outbreaks in wild waterfowl, which must be the first steps in our efforts to control the disease.

BACKGROUND

DVE was first recognized in the Netherlands as a disease of domestic waterfowl in 1942. The virus responsible for this disease was identified in 1949, and the name "duck plague" was proposed that year at the 14th International Veterinary Congress. In retrospect, it now appears that DVE has been present in the Netherlands since at least 1923. It is also known to have been present in Belgium, India, England, and the United States and is suspected to have occurred in France and China. All reports of DVE have been in captive or domestic waterfowl except in the United States, where it has recently occurred in wild waterfowl. Presently, DVE is known to occur only in waterfowl.

HISTORY OF DVE IN THE UNITED STATES

DVE was first diagnosed in the United States in January 1967, when it appeared among commercial flocks of Pekin ducks (*Anas platyrhynchos domesticus*) on Long Island, New York. Nearly 40 percent of Long Island's commercial Pekin flocks were infected that year, and small numbers of wild waterfowl on Long Island died from the disease. DVE also appeared in two widely separated areas in upstate New York; Muscovy ducks (*Cairina moschata*) were involved at one location and mute swans (*Cygnus olor*) at the other.

During 1968 DVE recurred in domestic flocks of ducks on Long Island and appeared in Maryland and Pennsylvania. Widely scattered outbreaks involving small numbers of captive waterfowl have continued on Long Island and in Pennsylvania since that time. In 1972 DVE appeared in a lagoon in front of the Palace of Fine Arts in San Francisco, California, killing about 100 captive waterfowl. The next report came in January 1973, when a severe outbreak occurred among wild waterfowl at the Lake Andes National Wildlife Refuge in South Dakota (Fig. 1). This was the first major outbreak in wild waterfowl. More than 40,000 ducks, primarily mallards (*Anas platyrhynchos*), died at Lake Andes, dramatically illustrating the potential impact of this disease on the North American waterfowl resource.

The eradication of DVE from the United States is a desirable but probably

[1] Originally published by U.S. Dep. Inter. Bur. Sport Fish. and Wildl., 1973. 16 pp.

[2] Address correspondence to this author. Present address: National Wildlife Health Laboratory, 1655 Linden Dr., Madison, WI 53706.

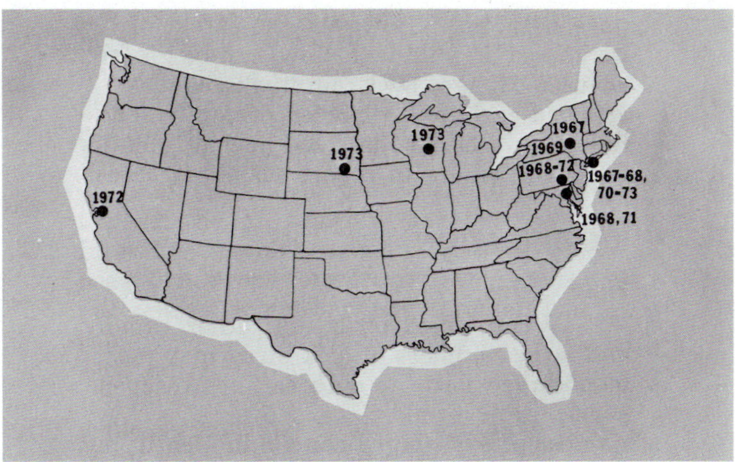

Fig. 1. Distribution of duck virus enteritis in the United States (laboratory-confirmed cases through June 30, 1973).

unrealistic goal. However, the extent of its impact on wild waterfowl can be greatly reduced if new DVE outbreaks can be detected early and reported promptly. The following sections describe how to identify DVE and where to report suspected cases.

IDENTIFICATION

Field Signs

DVE-infected birds die rather rapidly, and large numbers of sick birds may not be observed until an outbreak has reached considerable proportions. However, a number of early signs can aid in identifying possible outbreaks.

Because of the severe enteritis associated with DVE, bloody feces or blotches of blood ranging in size to several inches in diameter may be seen on the ground before any dead birds are observed. Resting areas used by concentrations of waterfowl should be routinely checked for these signs.

The first noticeable signs associated with the birds' behavior are droopy appearance, increased thirst, slow movements, reduced wariness, and reluctance to fly. Often the birds may attempt to hide in sparse cover and will let an observer almost touch them before they fly. Birds lose their ability to stand before they lose the power of flight, so that those that cannot fly may be seen propelling themselves along the ground with their wings.

Death is often immediately preceded by a series of convulsions that might be misinterpreted as chemical (pesticide) poisoning. These convulsions are more easily observed if the bird is on the water. A typical sequence starts with the head being extended over the back and pointed towards the tail, which is elevated and fanned as the bird swims in a circle. The head then drops forward into the water, the tail relaxes somewhat, and the wings flap rapidly as the bird holds its bill upward. This entire sequence may repeat itself several times before the bird dies, either while on the water or after swimming slowly to the shore. Sometimes affected birds hide in dense vegetation, perhaps because they have become hypersensitive to light. When a dead bird is found on land, careful ex-

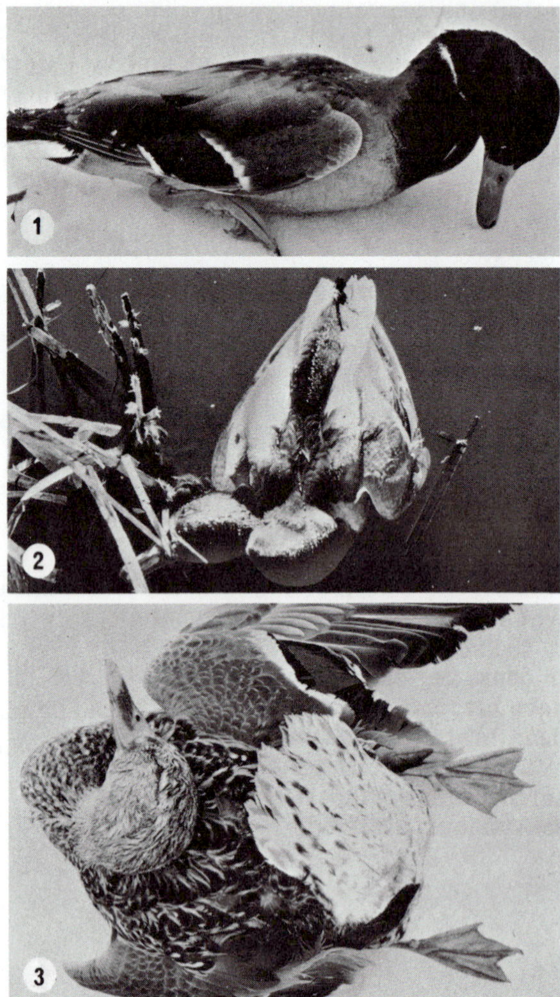

Fig. 2. Typical death positions of ducks infected with duck virus enteritis. Numbers correspond to positions described in the text.

amination of its terminal position and surroundings will often disclose that convulsions occurred just before death.

Affected birds generally die in one of three rather characteristic positions (Figs. 2, 3): (1) With the neck arched and bill perpendicular to the supporting surface, wings slightly drooped, and legs often extended to the rear with the bottom surfaces of the webs up; (2) with the neck twisted and head lying to one side of the midline of the back, upper portions of the wings slightly extended away from the body, and tail closed; and (3) with the head fully extended towards the tail and often lying on the midline of the back, the wings at least partially extended and the primaries fully or partially fanned, and the tail generally elevated and fanned. Birds in this third position have

Fig. 3. Typical death position of a Canada goose infected with duck virus enteritis.

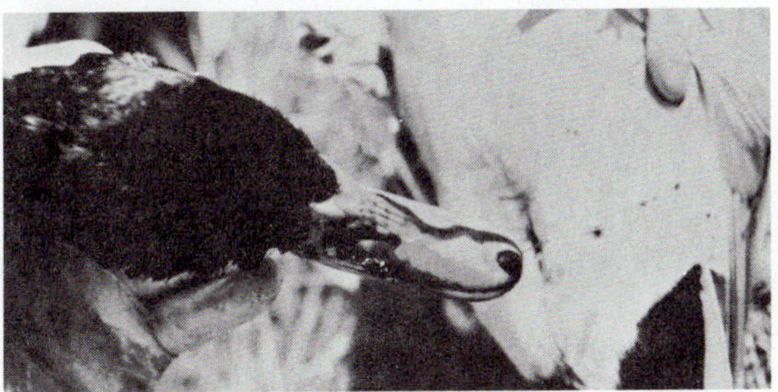

Fig. 4. Blood dripping from the nares of a mallard infected with duck virus enteritis.

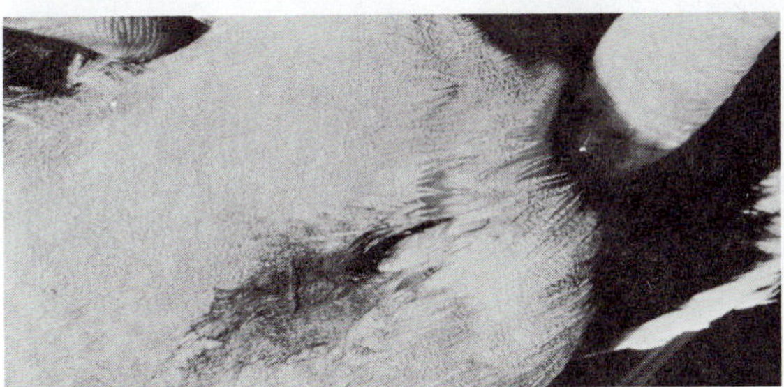

Fig. 5. Blood-stained vent of a mallard infected with duck virus enteritis.

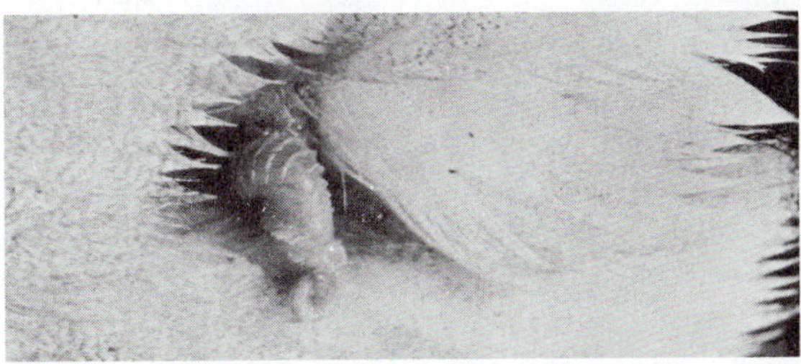

Fig. 6. Prolapsed penis of a duck virus enteritis infected mallard.

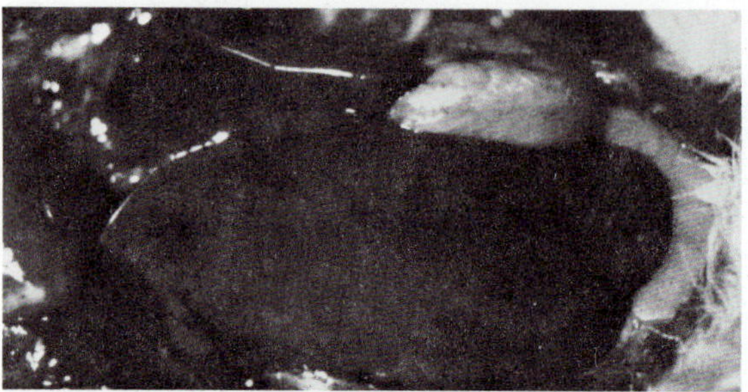

Fig. 7. Focal necrosis (yellow spots) in the liver of a mallard infected with duck virus enteritis.

Fig. 8. Hemorrhages on the liver of a mallard infected with duck virus enteritis.

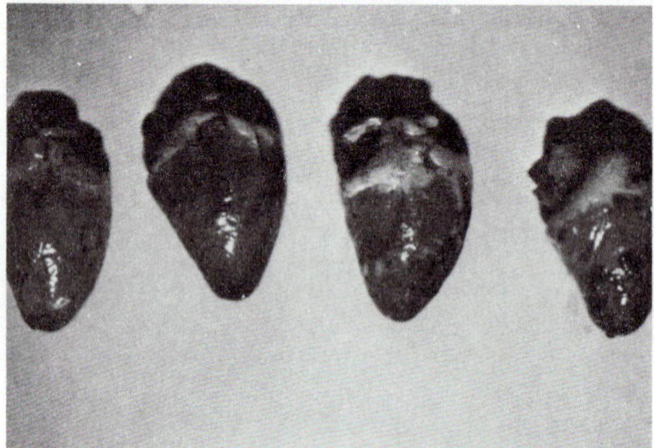

Fig. 9. Degrees of hemorrhaging on the heart ranging from pinpoint (left) to large areas of surface (right) of mallards infected with duck virus enteritis.

all the characteristics of having died in convulsion.

External Lesions

Examination of dead waterfowl often discloses a bloody discharge from the nares and bill, especially when the bird is held by its feet (Fig. 4). In addition, the vent may show evidence of blood staining (Fig. 5) and, in the case of male mallards, the penis may be prolapsed (Fig. 6). None, all, or any combination of these lesions may be present in a particular bird. Canada geese (*Branta canadensis*) that die from DVE usually have blood-stained vents but not bloody discharges from the bill.

Fig. 10. Gross appearance of viscera in a mallard infected with duck virus enteritis. Note hemorrhages on the heart and syrinx, focal necrosis of the liver, and large amount of fat covering the gizzard.

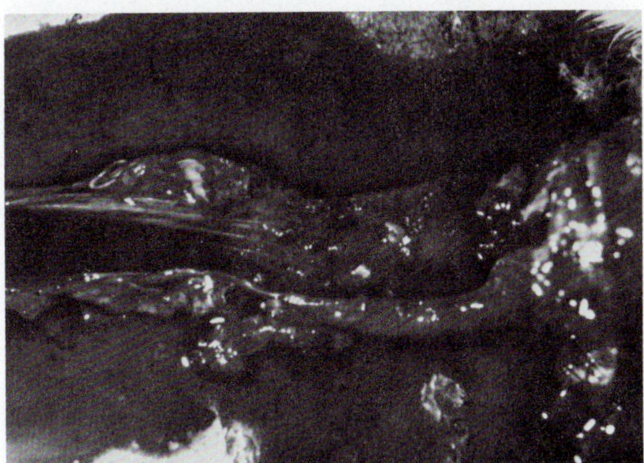

Fig. 11. Blood from the lumen of the esophagus and proventriculus of a mallard infected with duck virus enteritis. This blood is the source of bloody bills and blood-stained vents observed in some duck virus enteritis infected birds.

Internal Lesions

Upon necropsy, gross examination of the viscera often discloses multiple areas of focal necrosis (yellow or whitish spots of pinhead size or larger) on the liver (Fig. 7) or a discolored liver (copper rather than mahogany color) with patches of hemorrhage (Fig. 8). Hemorrhages that vary from pinpoint to pinhead in size may also appear on fatty areas of the heart, and larger hemorrhages may be present on the heart muscle (Fig. 9). Edema may be present around the syrinx, and the surface of the syrinx may also contain numerous pinhead-size or larger hemorrhages (Fig. 10). The spleen is darkened and often reduced in size. All of the preceding lesions are also consistent with a diagnosis of avian cholera (*Pasteurella multocida*) and thus, by themselves, are not diagnostic for either disease.

Additional internal lesions, however, are characteristic of DVE and are not seen in avian cholera.

In cases of DVE the intestines are often hemorrhagic or distended and ap-

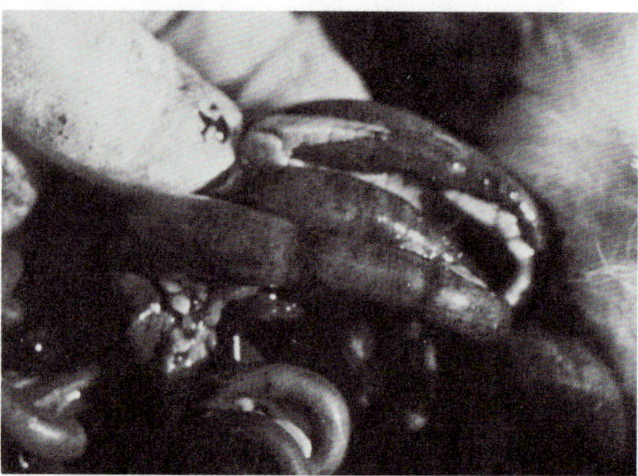

Fig. 12. Hemorrhagic band in the intestine (serosal surface) of a mallard infected with duck virus enteritis.

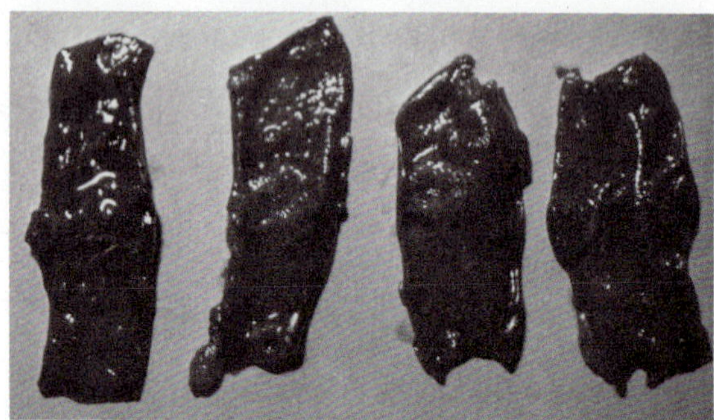

Fig. 13. Lymphoid disks in the intestine (mucosal surface) of a mallard infected with duck virus enteritis.

pear dark blue to purple because of free blood within the lumen. It is this blood that results in the blood-stained vents and bloody bills seen in some birds (Fig. 11). One of the most diagnostic lesions is hemorrhage wherever lymphatic tissue is concentrated in the intestine. In mallards, this process results in the formation of four hemorrhagic bands circumscribing the intestine that are obvious from the serosal (external) surface (Fig. 12). In Canada geese, the lymphatic tissue is concentrated in disks scattered along the intestinal tract; in infected birds, these areas appear as large dark blotches from the serosal surface but as discrete buttons or ulcer-like lesions from the mucosal (inner) surface (Fig. 13). The mucosal surface of the esophageal-proventricular junction is also often hemorrhagic and necrotic in DVE-infected waterfowl.

In addition, the lower regions of the intestinal tract (cloaca, cecum, and rectum) in DVE-afflicted waterfowl often show enanthematous (eruptive or raised) lesions on their mucosal surfaces. These lesions are discrete and scattered and may be scab-like or have a cheesy appearance (Figs. 14–15). This area of the intestine may also contain numerous hemorrhagic and necrotic foci. Similar enanthematous lesions may occur on the surface of the esophagus. These lesions tend to follow the longitudinal folds of

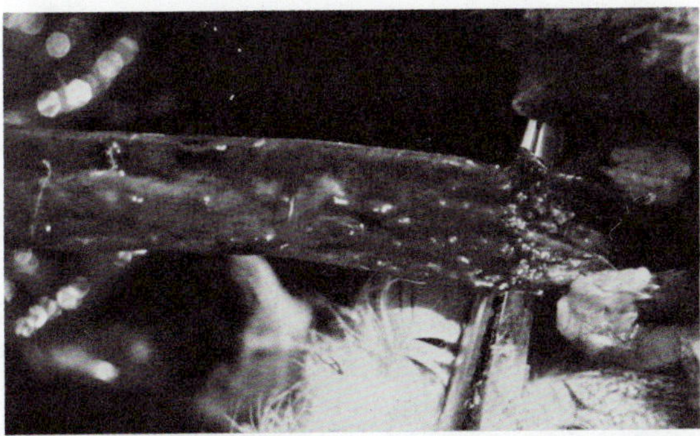

Fig. 14. Eruptive lesions of the lower intestine of a mallard infected with duck virus enteritis.

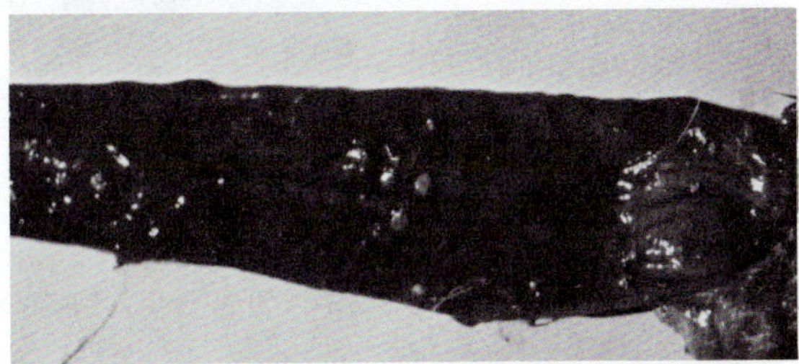

Fig. 15. Raised lesions of the lower intestine of a mallard infected with duck virus enteritis.

Fig. 16. Diphtheritic-like lesions covering the mucosal surface of the esophagus of a mallard infected with duck virus enteritis. This degree of esophageal involvement is limited to chronic cases.

the esophageal tissue and, in more chronic cases of DVE, may eventually coalesce to form a diphtheritic-like membrane over the entire mucosal surface (Fig. 16).

THE DISEASE

The incubation period of DVE in waterfowl appears to be about 6 to 10 days. After affected birds develop clinical signs, they generally die within a week, most probably within 1 to 3 days. Infected birds may feed up to a few hours before death.

Mortality rates in infected flocks will vary. They have ranged from 5 to 10 percent for domestic waterfowl although, in the Netherlands, they have generally exceeded 90 percent. During the original outbreaks on Long Island in 1967, only about 6 percent of the Flanders Bay populations of wild black ducks (*Anas rubripes*) and mallards died, but mortality exceeded 40 percent of the 100,000 mallards present during the 1973 Lake Andes outbreak.

Survivors are thought to be immune, possibly serving as asymptomatic carriers capable of maintaining the disease between outbreaks. DVE is thought to be spread primarily by infected waterfowl that shed the virus in feces or other bodily discharges. Susceptible waterfowl may become exposed either directly through contact with these birds or indirectly through contact with a contaminated environment. Stagnant or slow-moving shallow bodies of water contaminated with the virus are believed to be an important vehicle of transmission in domestic duck outbreaks. Water may also have been an important vehicle in the Lake Andes outbreak since ingestion is probably the most common route of virus exposure.

All species of ducks, geese, and swans are assumed to be susceptible to DVE, and outbreaks may occur at any season of the year. Many of the outbreaks in domestic and captive waterfowl have followed a period of inclement weather; other physical or biological stress factors may also be important in either precipitating or maintaining outbreaks. Little is known about the epizootiology (natural history) of DVE in wild waterfowl. However, the disease is apparently density-dependent; crowding of waterfowl onto limited areas undoubtedly facilitates the transmission of the virus once an outbreak begins.

REPORTING SUSPECTED DVE OUTBREAKS

The photographs provided in this report should allow a tentative field diagnosis of DVE. If, after preliminary investigations, you feel DVE may be involved, notify immediately the nearest Regional Office of the U.S. Bureau of Sport Fisheries and Wildlife. It will provide instructions for obtaining an investigation by a diagnostic laboratory.

The addresses, telephone numbers, and States served by the Bureau Regional Offices are as follows:

PACIFIC REGION

1500 Plaza Building, 500 N.E. Multnomah St., Portland, OR 97232 (503-231-6118).

Washington, Oregon, Idaho, California, Nevada, Hawaii.

SOUTHWEST REGION

Federal Building, U.S. Post Office and Court House, 500 Gold Avenue S.W., Albuquerque, NM 87103 (505-766-2321).

Arizona, New Mexico, Oklahoma, Texas.

NORTH CENTRAL REGION

Federal Building, Fort Snelling, Twin Cities, MN 55111 (612-725-3563).

Minnesota, Wisconsin, Michigan, Illinois, Indiana, Ohio.

SOUTHEAST REGION

75 Spring St., S.W., Atlanta, GA 30303 (404-221-3588).

Arkansas, Louisiana, Kentucky, Tennessee, Mississippi, Alabama, Georgia, North Carolina, South Carolina, Florida.

NORTHEAST REGION

One Gateway Ctr. Suite 700, Newton Corner, MA 02158 (617-965-5100).

Maine, Vermont, New Hampshire,

Massachusetts, Connecticut, Rhode Island, New York, Pennsylvania, New Jersey, Delaware, Maryland, West Virginia, Virginia.

DENVER REGION

134 Union Blvd, Denver, CO 80225 (303-234-2209).

Montana, Wyoming, North Dakota, South Dakota, Nebraska, Iowa, Utah, Colorado, Kansas, Missouri.

ALASKA AREA

1011 E. Tudor Rd., Anchorage, AK 99503 (907-276-3800).

Alaska.

Several fresh specimens should be collected at the time of your preliminary investigation. Place each bird in a separate plastic bag and then place each of these bags in separate bags, taking care not to contaminate the outside of the second bag. Freeze at least 2 or 3 specimens, and hold at least 2 or 3 specimens in refrigeration until the Regional Office is notified. Extreme care must be taken when examining these birds to avoid transporting the virus to other susceptible waterfowl. Disinfect clothing by washing. Disinfect all instruments and all contaminated surfaces, either by liberally applying a strong household bleach or by burning.

ASPERGILLOSIS IN WINTERING MALLARDS[1]

GARY L. PEARSON, Bureau of Sport Fisheries and Wildlife, Northern Prairie Wildlife Research Center, Jamestown, ND 58401

Losses among mallards (*Anas platyrhynchos*) wintering on a seepage ditch below the Garrison Dam on the Missouri River at Riverdale, North Dakota, were reported on February 24, 1968. In early February, while conducting their annual winter banding operation, personnel of the North Dakota Game and Fish Department observed approximately 1,000 mallards on the ditch. Approximately 200 mallards were banded after being captured in a walk-in trap baited with corn and wheat located on the bank of the ditch. Snow covered the area and caused the ducks to concentrate at the bait site from the time of the banding operation until the reporting of the losses.

A total of 135 recently dead mallards (97 males, 38 females) were collected on February 24 and 25. An additional 42 mallard carcasses in various stages of decomposition were also found. There was evidence that predators had fed on some of the carcasses, and this prevented an accurate total count of the mortality. One sick drake mallard was captured on the 24th, but no affected birds were seen among an estimated 500 live ducks flushed from the trap site on the 25th. Subsequent searches failed to reveal further losses; this indicates that the major mortality may have been limited to a period of a few days. However, dispersion of the ducks during the moderate weather of the last few days of February may have been partially responsible for the apparent sudden cessation of losses.

Examination of 23 recently dead mallards revealed a general absence of subcutaneous and visceral fat and slight atrophy of the pectoral muscles. Fifteen males weighed an average of 1,012 g. and 8 females averaged 843 g. Ecchymotic hemorrhages were present in the myocardium of many specimens. The lungs of all ducks examined were severely congested and contained multiple small (1–2 mm), creamy-white, firm nodules. Interclavicular and anterior and posterior thoracic air sacs of most ducks were cloudy and thickened. In several cases the air sacs contained plaques up to 5 mm in diameter, and some exhibited definite mycelia. Occasionally, plaques were present on kidneys and other abdominal organs.

Histologically, sections of lung tissue which were stained with hematoxylin and eosin showed a generalized hemorrhagic pneumonia and lymphocyte infiltration. Numerous granulomas consisting primarily of epithelioid cells, lymphocytes and occasional foreign body giant cells were present; some showed evidence of necrosis at the centers. Branching fungal hyphae were observed in many of the air capillaries as well as in the granulomas of lung sections stained by the periodic acid-Schiff technique. Hyphae also were evident, frequently without direct host reaction, in many of the air capillaries of the hematoxylin and eosin stained sections.

Blood agar plates were inoculated with lung and air sac lesions from the sick drake which died shortly after capture and with air sac lesions of another fresh carcass. Aspergillus, typical of *A. fumigatus*, was isolated from each lesion. Cultures of heart blood, liver and contents of

---

[1] Originally published in Bull. Wildl. Dis. Assoc. 5(4):404–405, 1969.

small intestine of the sick drake did not reveal the presence of pathogenic bacteria.

Although a possible source of the infection appeared to have been corn used in baiting the trap site, no grain was present at the time losses were noted. However, examination of the corn supply which was used revealed extensive mold growth on many of the ears. A diet consisting solely of this corn failed to produce infection in penned mallards. This may have been a reflection of a different route of infection or the absence of factors which may have reduced resistance to infection (Herman and Sladen, Trans. N. Amer. Wildl. Conf. 23:187–191, 1958). The relatively low number of banded ducks among those found dead and the incomplete information of the ducks' activities prior to the observed losses suggest that other possible sources of infection cannot be excluded.

Epornitics of aspergillosis in free-flying wild waterfowl have been reported in mallards (Herman, Calif. Fish and Game 29:204, 1943; Neff, J. Wildl. Mgmt. 19:415–416, 1955), wood ducks (Bellrose et al., J. Wildl. Mgmt. 9:325–326, 1945), and Canada geese (McDougle and Vaught, J. Wildl. Mgmt. 32:415–417, 1968). This outbreak appears to differ from the above in that a higher mortality (at least 13%) occurred in the course of only a few days.

ACKNOWLEDGMENTS

The author is indebted to Charles Schroeder and George Enyeart of the North Dakota Game and Fish Department and to William McClure, U.S. Game Management Agent, for assistance in gathering specimens and information, and to Dr. Louis N. Locke of the Patuxent Wildlife Research Center for reviewing histological interpretations.

FOWL CHOLERA IN WATERFOWL AT SQUAW CREEK NATIONAL WILDLIFE REFUGE, MISSOURI[1]

RICHARD W. VAUGHT, Missouri Department of Conservation, Columbia
HAROLD C. McDOUGLE, Department of Veterinary Microbiology, University of Missouri, Columbia
HAROLD H. BURGESS, U. S. Bureau of Sport Fisheries and Wildlife, Squaw Creek National Wildlife Refuge, Mound City, Mo.

Abstract: An epizootic of fowl cholera (*Pasteurella multocida*), in lesser snow geese (*Chen h. hyperborea*), blue geese (*Chen caerulescens*), mallards (*Anas platyrhynchos*), and other waterfowl occurred on Squaw Creek National Wildlife Refuge, Holt County, Missouri, during early January, 1964. More than 1,000 geese died in one night. Symptoms and previous case histories of fowl cholera, an infrequently reported disease among wild waterfowl, are reviewed. Pertinent field observations and methods of diagnosis are described. Observations indicated that mallard ducks were the probable early carriers of the disease. Snow, blue, and small Canada geese (*Branta c. hutchinsii*) were quite susceptible while large Canada geese (*Branta c. interior* and *maxima*) were not involved. Stresses caused by limited open water, overcrowding of birds, and inclement weather may have been conducive to the epizootic. Direct mortality from fowl cholera on wintering areas is not indicative of total mortality. Losses may continue along the migration routes. Secondary effects may result in loss of productivity.

This paper describes an epizootic of fowl cholera (*Pasteurella multocida*) in lesser snow and blue geese and other waterfowl on Squaw Creek National Wildlife Refuge, Holt County, Missouri, during late 1963 and early 1964.

Fowl cholera is a serious disease of domestic fowl, but it is infrequently reported as an epizootic disease of wild waterfowl. The earliest documented record of fowl cholera in wild ducks was reported by Quortrup et al. (1946) in Texas. Petrides and Bryant (1951) reported that periodic outbreaks of fowl cholera among ducks have occurred there since. The largest reported losses occurred in California where Sperry (1949 unpublished report filed at Patuxent Wildlife Research Center, Laurel, Maryland) estimated a die-off of 36,000 ducks. Rosen and Bischoff (1950) reported losses of coots, ducks, and gulls to *Pasteurella multocida* over a broad coastal area near San Francisco Bay. More recently, in Maine, a fowl cholera outbreak in eider ducks (*Somateria mollissima*) was reported by Gershman et al. (1964).

The absence of signs of disease before death from fowl cholera has been recorded in numerous cases. Curtice (1902) reported a case in domestic geese where some specimens in prime condition were found dead with scarcely any appearance of previous sickness. Quortrup et al. (1946:99) observed that 10 minutes before death, ducks were apparently in good health except that normal reflexes were not as sensitive as in healthy birds, and they did not become frightened so easily. They also noted, "Many birds died with their heads up in a natural sitting position and rigor mortis was immediate." Rosen and Bischoff (1949: 186) observed ducks in normal flight or in loafing attitudes, or else the carcasses were seen floating on the ponds or lying along the shoreline.

Barger et al. (1958) reported that, when the disease was very acute, the first indication of infection was the finding of dead chickens that had not shown any signs before death. They also found that ex-

[1] This project was supported by Federal Aid to Wildlife Restoration, Surveys and Investigation Projects, Missouri 13-R; by funds from the Department of Veterinary Microbiology, University of Missouri; and by funds from the Bureau of Sport Fisheries and Wildlife, Squaw Creek National Wildlife Refuge.

Originally published in J. Wildl. Manage. 31(2):248–253, 1967.

tremely fat fowl were particularly susceptible to the peracute form of the malady, and outbreaks in chickens were more prevalent during inclement weather. Comparing fowl cholera mortality rates with climatological data, Petrides and Bryant (1951: 209–215) found "little correlation . . . with any condition other than wind" and summarized: "Comparisons of population levels and mortality rates throughout the epizootic period revealed a general increase in severity of the disease throughout the period, though most waterfowl died early in the season because of their great abundance then." Curtice (1902) found considerable quantities of mucus in the throat and mouth, and a tenacious mucus in the nose in chickens. Similar symptoms of fowl cholera were reported by Barger et al. (1958:408) and Dorsey and Harshfield (1953).

Acknowledgment is due Dr. H. M. Wallace, Jr., D. V. M., Mound City, Missouri, Dr. J. R. Anderson, Iowa State University, Ames, and Dr. L. N. Locke, Patuxent Wildlife Research Center, Laurel, Maryland, for necropsies, diagnoses, and chemical studies, and to Dr. A. A. Case and Dr. G. B. Garner, University of Missouri, for chemical analyses. We thank J. A. Hague and Glen McCloud for assistance in collecting specimens, and Lena K. Thornton for laboratory assistance.

FIELD OBSERVATIONS

Waterfowl losses at the Squaw Creek Refuge began in early December, 1963, and continued through the migration period until mid-April, 1964. Dead waterfowl collected for disposal during this period included 1,169 snow and blue geese, 66 Canada geese, one white-fronted goose (*Anser albifrons*), 5,615 mallards, 23 black ducks (*Anas rubripes*), 23 American widgeon (*Mareca americana*), 38 green-winged teal (*Anas carolinensis*), 48 wood ducks (*Aix sponsa*), one pintail (*Anas acuta*), and one canvasback (*Aythya valisineria*). Recorded losses were considered minimal because dead birds in inaccessible areas were not tabulated. Recorded causes of mortality included crippling and lead poisoning.

Mallards were the principal species involved during early December, 1963. Standard diagnostic procedures (Torrey et al. 1934) were used to identify lead poisoning in most cases. A sample of sick and dead birds collected in mid-December indicated that something other than lead poisoning was prevalent. These birds appeared to be in good body condition. Abnormal behavior was observed with lack of fear response, associated with equilibrium difficulties; some ducks would swim in small circles.

Water being pumped from a deep well was suspected to contain lethal levels of inorganic salts or heavy metals that might cause such behavior. Water sample analyses showed less than 1 ppm of nitrate and only a trace of nitrite, both non-dangerous levels. Tests for lead, arsenic, mercury, phenol, phosphates, cyanide, and strychnine were negative.

On January 7, 1964, an apparently healthy flock of 20,000 lesser snow and blue geese returned to the refuge from an early evening feeding flight and separated into four groups. When the flock departed to feed the next morning 1,110 dead geese were distributed throughout the roosting sites. The distribution of dead geese indicated that the entire flock had been exposed to the same fatal agent. Also, the absence of sick geese before and after the die-off suggested that the deaths resulted from an extremely virulent pathogen or potent toxin.

Geese examined externally appeared to be in excellent body condition and the crops of some birds contained corn, an indica-

Table 1. Waterfowl examined for pasteurellosis, Squaw Creek Refuge, 1964.

SAMPLE No.	NUMBER AND SPECIES		DATE (1964)	WHERE COLLECTED	NECROPSY PERFORMED	PASTEURELLOSIS	
						Negative	Positive
1	2 snow geese	(dead)	1-10	Squaw Creek Refuge	Dr. Wallace (in practice)	2	0
2	8 blue and snow geese	(dead)	1-10	Squaw Creek Refuge	Univ. of Mo.	0	8
3	5 blue and snow geese	(dead)	1-10	Squaw Creek Refuge	Patuxent Res.	0	5
4	2 mallards	(dead)	1-10	Squaw Creek Refuge	Patuxent Res.	0	2
5	5 blue and snow geese	(dead)	1-10	Squaw Creek Refuge	Univ. of Iowa	0	5
6	6 blue and snow geese	(dead)	1-15	Squaw Creek Refuge	Univ. of Mo.	0	6
7	1 snow goose	(live)	1-15	Squaw Creek Refuge	Univ. of Mo.	0	1
8	5 blue and snow geese	(dead)	4- 3	45 miles NW of Refuge	Univ. of Mo.	0	5
9	1 coot	(dead)	4- 3	45 miles NW of Refuge	Univ. of Mo.	0	1
10	3 coots	(live)	4-10	45 miles NW of Refuge	Univ. of Mo.	0	3
11	1 Canada goose	(dead)	4-10	45 miles NW of Refuge	Univ. of Mo.	0	1
12	1 coot	(live)	5- 1	Squaw Creek Refuge	Univ. of Mo.	1	0
13	4 coots	(dead)	5- 1	Squaw Creek Refuge	Univ. of Mo.	4	0
14	2 mallards	(dead)	5- 1	Squaw Creek Refuge	Univ. of Mo.	2	0
15	2 coots	(live)	5- 4	Squaw Creek Refuge	Univ. of Mo.	2	0

tion of their ability to fly from feeding areas shortly before death.

The position of the dead geese was remarkably uniform. Each was in sitting posture with the head and neck extended over the back. Dirt particles blown across the ice had settled into melted depressions under the carcasses, indicating the geese had remained in the same position throughout the night. A minimum temperature of 12 F and a maximum wind velocity of 23 mph was recorded during the night of the die-off.

DIAGNOSIS AND RESULTS

Necropsies were performed on two snow geese that retained body heat. Gross hemorrhaging of the digestive tract associated with abnormal mucus deposits was found, but a causative agent was not isolated (Sample 1, Table 1).

Myocardial hemorrhages were present in all eight blue and snow geese (Sample 2) examined at the poultry diagnostic laboratory, University of Missouri. The heart blood was dark and poorly clotted. Numerous bipolar microorganisms characteristic of *Pasteurella* were observed upon microscopic examination of stained smears of heart blood. Giemsa's blood stain provided better resolution than methylene blue, gentian violet, or Gram's method of staining.

Bipolar microorganisms did not multiply on salmonella–shigella media, yet grew profusely on tryptose and blood agar plates. Small, fluorescent colonies appeared on inoculated tryptose and blood agar plates in 24 hours at 37 C. A small drop of suspension prepared from a few colonies in sterile saline, injected subcutaneously into the dorsal area of two mice, caused death within 23 hours. Stained blood smears from the hearts of the mice yielded results identical to those found in heart blood from the geese.

Carbohydrates were inoculated from colonies of bipolar organisms isolated from mice and geese. Acid, without gas, was present in dextrose sucrose, and d-mannitol. The bipolar organisms were nonmotile in SIM medium (Difco). Growth on triple sugar iron medium (TSI) slants showed production of acid. Hydrogen-sulfite was not produced in TSI agar. SIM and lead acetate strips were not blackened. Diagnosis: *Pasteurella multocida.*

Seven birds examined at Patuxent Wildlife Research Center and 5 at Iowa State University (Samples 3, 4, and 5) were found to contain bipolar, rod-shaped microorganisms which were isolated from typical fowl cholera lesions. Severe catarrhal enteritis and yellowish colored water in the posterior portions of the esophagus and in the proventriculus were noted. Bacterial cultures of tissue revealed *Pasteurella multocida* in all cases.

Birds collected from January 15 to April 10 also proved positive for fowl cholera, (Samples 6–11). Some of these specimens were collected from a small waterhole 45 miles northwest of the Squaw Creek refuge. Old greyish-yellow lesions measuring up to 2.5 × 7 mm were present in the heart tissue. These birds apparently developed the acute septicemic form of the disease following some unknown previous infection.

A wintering flock of 7,000 large Canada geese showed no evidence of this disease. Deaths were not reported, although they associated with infected snow and blue geese and mallards. One small Canada goose (*Branta canadensis hutchinsii*) collected northwest of the refuge contained fowl cholera microorganisms.

Coots (*Fulica americana*) were absent on the refuge during the winter. After they arrived late in March evidence of the disease was noted among them. A specimen collected on April 3, 1964, (Sample 9) had both new and healed hemorrhages of the liver. A 72-hour broth culture from this bird injected into a domestic turkey (0.5 ml intramuscular and intravenous) caused death in 7 hours 20 min. A mouse injected subcutaneously died in approximately 13 hours. Three apparently healthy coots collected April 10 (Sample 10) contained fowl cholera microorganisms in their livers and spleens, suggesting that this species may be a potential carrier.

Coots and shovelers (*Spatula clypeata*) collected 60 miles southeast of the refuge were negative for fowl cholera. Fowl cholera microorganisms were not isloated from any birds after April 10, 1964.

DISCUSSION

The similarity of pasteurellosis case histories suggests that accumulated stresses including overcrowding may induce spread of the disease. Fowl cholera is spread by contact between healthy and infected birds and by contact between healthy birds and a contaminated environment. Harshfield (1965:363) reported, "The body excretions of diseased birds which contaminate soil, food, or water can be an important factor in dissemination of the disease." Quortrup et al. (1946:98) found that bacterial suspensions were as lethal when administered orally as when administered intranasally. They also found mortality among ducks that had access to drinking water that had been used by infected birds.

High duck densities, strong winds, rapid drop in temperatures, and low water levels are major factors influencing fowl cholera epizootics. Theoretically, every waterfowl concentration in the United States is subject to a fowl cholera epizootic under certain conditions. The source of infection in most wildlife epizootics is difficult to determine. Many birds and animals have been classified as carriers of fowl cholera. Kaschula and Truter (1951) found sea gulls as potential carriers of the infection. Hutyra et al. (1949:107–108) stated that the disease is mostly introduced into premises by the introduction of infected fowls, or by wild birds, particularly sparrows and pigeons as permanent bacilli carriers. Still others found wild ruffed grouse, (*Bonasa umbel-*

lus) quail, raptors, gallinules, and terns to have been disseminators of the disease. The behavior of mallards at the refuge, discussed earlier, is evidence that this species may have been the carrier in the Squaw Creek outbreak. Although coots were not present during the winter, spring migrants were found to be carriers.

Chronic carriers of fowl cholera may be present in any waterfowl concentration. Harshfield (1965) found that birds recovering from the disease may act as carriers for a year. Pritchett et al. (1930) isolated fowl cholera microorganisms from the upper respiratory tract of supposedly normal birds. Similar findings were reported by Van Es and Olney (1940). Evidently the disease may remain in the subacute or chronic stage for a lengthy period, and become acute only when conditions are favorable.

In fowl cholera epizootics, mortality of waterfowl on a single wintering area may not be indicative of total mortality, as the birds represent only a small localized segment of the migratory waterfowl population. Fowl cholera carriers may also infect populations along migration routes and on the nesting grounds. Mortality along migration routes may be misidentified as lead poisoning.

Secondary effects of chronic fowl cholera on productivity could cause additional losses more staggering than direct mortality. In discussing secondary effects of chronic cases in chickens, Beach and Freeborn (1927:25) concluded that chronic pasteurellosis in chickens may cause a rupture of the yolk sac when infection localizes in the ovary. Shook and Bunyea (1939) found ruptured yolks, salpingitis, and hemorrhages of the ovary in fowl cholera epizootics among chickens. Barger et al. (1958) also noted that ovarian changes in chickens are not infrequent in chronic cases of fowl cholera. Further studies are needed to determine whether, and to what extent, fowl cholera mortality is being attributed to lead poisoning, and whether secondary effects of fowl cholera limit or inhibit productivity in waterfowl.

CONTROL AND SANITATION MEASURES

A contributing factor in the Squaw Creek epizootic was the maintenance of open water by pumping during winter. This management technique concentrated large waterfowl populations on relatively small areas with disastrous results. If artificial ecological conditions conducive to fowl cholera can be eliminated or reduced in importance, significant losses to this disease may be prevented. Winter pumping has been curtailed at Squaw Creek to reduce disease potentials and to better distribute wintering waterfowl. Fowl cholera has not recurred there.

Sanitation measures were imposed immediately when the outbreak occurred. Cleanup of carcasses was necessary to avoid spreading the potential diseases. The carcasses were burned. It is suggested that contaminated vegetation be burned and water areas be drained and cultivated as soon after the epizootic as possible. Contaminated agricultural land should also be cultivated.

LITERATURE CITED

BARGER, E. H., L. E. CARD, AND B. S. POMEROY. 1958. Diseases and parasites of poultry. 5th ed. Lea & Febiger, Philadelphia. 408pp.

BEACH, J. R., AND S. B. FREEBORN. 1927. Diseases and parasites of poultry in California. California Agr. Ext. Circ. 8. 60pp.

CURTICE, C. 1902. Goose septicemia. Rhode Island Agr. Expt. Sta. Bull. 86. 12pp.

DORSEY, T. A., AND G. S. HARSHFIELD. 1953. Facts about fowl cholera. South Dakota Agr. Exptl. Sta. Circ. 100. 11pp.

GERSHMAN, M., J. F. WITTER, H. E. SPENCER, JR., AND A. KALVAITIS. 1964. Case report: epizootic of fowl cholera in the common eider duck. J. Wildl. Mgmt. 28(3):587–589.

Harshfield, G. S. 1965. Fowl cholera. Pp. 359–373. *In* H. E. Biester and L. H. Schwarte (Editors), Diseases of poultry. 5th ed. Iowa State Univ. Press, Ames. 1382pp.

Hutyra, F., J. Marek, and R. Manninger. 1949. Special pathology and therapeutics of the diseases of domestic animals. 5th ed. Vol. I. Alexander Eger Inc., Chicago. 962pp.

Kaschula, V. R., and D. E. Truter. 1951. Fowl cholera in sea-gulls on Dassen Island. J. South Africa Vet. Med. Assoc. 22(4):191–192.

Petrides, G. A., and C. R. Bryant. 1951. An analysis of the 1949–50 fowl cholera epizootic in Texas panhandle waterfowl. Trans. N. Am. Wildl. Conf. 16:193–216.

Pritchett, Ida W., F. R. Beaudette, and T. P. Hughes. 1930. The epidemiology of fowl cholera. IV. Further field observation of the spontaneous disease. J. Exptl. Med. 51(2): 259–274.

Quortrup, E. R., F. B. Queen, and L. J. Merovka. 1946. An outbreak of pasteurellosis in wild ducks. J. Am. Vet. Med. Assoc. 108(827):94–100.

Rosen, M. N., and A. I. Bischoff. 1949. The 1948–49 outbreak of fowl cholera in birds in the San Francisco Bay area and surrounding counties. California Fish and Game 35(3): 185–192.

———, and ———. 1950. The epidemiology of fowl cholera as it occurs in the wild. Trans. N. Am. Wildl. Conf. 15:147–154.

Shook, W. B., and H. Bunyea. 1939. The detection of carriers of fowl cholera, and its control, by means of a stained-antigen, rapid whole-blood test. Poul. Sci. 18(2):146–149.

Torrey, J. P., F. Thorp, Jr., and R. Graham. 1934. A note on pathological changes encountered in wild ducks. Cornell Vet. 24(4): 289–298.

Van Es, L., and J. F. Olney. 1940. An inquiry into the influence of environment on the incidence of poultry diseases. Nebraska Agr. Expt. Sta. Bull. 118. 57pp.

Received for publication May 31, 1966.

LEUCOCYTOZOONOSIS IN CANADA GEESE AT THE SENEY NATIONAL WILDLIFE REFUGE[1]

CARLTON M. HERMAN, U.S. Fish and Wildlife Service, Patuxent Research Center, Laurel, MD 20811
JAMES H. BARROW, JR.,[2] Biology Department, Hiram College, Hiram, OH 44234
I. BARRY TARSHIS, U.S. Fish and Wildlife Service, Patuxent Research Center, Laurel, MD 20811

Abstract: A history is given of the Seney National Wildlife Refuge and the losses of goslings of Canada geese (*Branta canadensis*) recorded since inception of the refuge in 1935. Since 1960, when more reliable data became available, losses have been extensive every 4 years. Gosling deaths are attributed to the infection with *Leucocytozoon simondi.* The blackfly (*Simulium innocens*) is considered to be the prime vector in the transmission of this blood parasite to goslings.

The Canada goose, *Branta canadensis* (L.), is native to North America, breeding in the northern reaches of the United States and Canada and overwintering in the south. At least 10 subspecies are recognized in the latest checklist of the American Ornithologists' Union (1957). Efforts have been made to manage these birds by regulating their harvest and by establishing refuges for breeding and wintering populations.

The Seney National Wildlife Refuge was established in 1935 on the northern peninsula of Michigan, between Germfask and Seney. It encompasses 38,678 ha, including 24,682 ha of marsh and 2,932 ha of open water (Sherwood 1968). Most of the open water area is contained in 21 impoundments that were created by diking; these impoundments range from 11 to over 400 ha. Water levels are manipulated by controlling the supply delivered through diversion ditches from three streams; transfer ditches enable water to flow from one impoundment to another. The ditches provide excellent larval habitat for some species of blackflies (Simuliidae).

HISTORY OF GOSLING LOSSES

According to Crawford (unpubl. rep., Seney National Wildlife Refuge, 1936), the region around Seney was the breeding ground for Canada geese until the summer of 1910 when their numbers rapidly diminished. The last geese were seen in Walsh Ditch (now part of the refuge) in 1929. No resident Canada geese inhabited the area until 332 pinioned birds were released into the new refuge in January, 1936. The birds were a gift from Henry M. Wallace (C. S. Johnson, unpubl. rep., Seney National Wildlife Refuge, 1944), who had raised Canada geese since the early 1920's on a 2,400 ha farm near Highland, Michigan, about 64 km west of Detroit. Wallace's flock was started with four wild birds obtained from Owatonna, Minnesota (Crawford, unpubl. rep., 1936; J. L. Sypulski, unpubl. rep., Seney National Wildlife Refuge, 1954). During the first breeding season at least five pairs of the newly stocked birds were successful in hatching a total of 19 goslings (Johnson, unpubl. rep., 1944; Johnson 1947). This marked the beginning of the Seney goose flock. All offspring of the pinioned flock at Se-

[1] Originally published in J. Wildl. Dis. 11(3): 404–411, 1975.

[2] During part of this study Dr. Barrow served on the summer staff of the University of Michigan Biological Station, Pellston, MI.

ney were allowed to fly free, and they eventually established a migrating and homing pattern. Hanson (1965) identified these birds as giant Canada geese, *Branta canadensis maxima.*

The Seney experiment was the first attempt to establish a major flock of breeding Canada geese on a national wildlife refuge. Records show that the flock increased yearly from the original 332 in 1936 to 3,000 in 1956. There was a poor gosling crop in 1939, followed by temporary setbacks in 1943–44 and again in 1951.

Johnson (unpubl. rep., 1944) reported that the 1942 population consisted of 422 birds, of which 199 were migrants that had returned to Seney to breed. He attributed the 1943 loss of many goslings in the last week of May and the first week of June to cold rainy weather at a time when the goslings were very young. He apparently recognized a population plateau and a slowing growth of the flock: "The Canada goose flock has passed through nonreproductiveness followed by various stages of growth and decimation." During most of these early years, the flock was disturbed as little as possible until the goslings were well along in the stage 2 age group (when the birds are about 45 days old and almost fully feathered) for fear the nests and young might be deserted by the parents. It was not clear in Johnson's reports whether nesting failures or brood failures were the cause of reduced production.

In 1945, dead and sick goslings were observed but very few field notes appear to have been made at that time; a Seney Refuge Quarterly Narrative Report estimated the goose population at 500–600 birds (Sherwood 1968). In 1949 a general increase in waterfowl in the Upper Peninsula was not reflected at the Seney Refuge. Reports for 1950 indicated a population drop from 600 to 500 birds.

By 1954 the population of Canada geese had grown to an estimated 2,700 with 250 breeding pairs producing 950 young, of which 750 survived to migration. According to Henry (unpubl. rep., Seney National Wildlife Refuge, 1954) "Our losses were heavier this year . . . . We had a terrific hatch of blackflies about the time of the gosling hatch."

The gosling yield was estimated to be low in 1955, 750 compared to 950 in the previous year. In 1956, however, the yield was 1,000 and there were no reports of sick goslings. In 1957, both the number of nests and number of goslings per brood decreased. The decrease in nests was attributed to heavy hunting pressure during the previous fall. The greatest losses were in the broods that hatched late.

Production was poor again in 1960. The estimated hatch was 790, about 30% less than the previous year. Heavy rains with rapid spring thawing produced floods that were thought to have caused the lower hatch. William French (unpubl. memorandum, Seney National Wildlife Refuge, 1960), refuge biologist, attributed the lower production to the "worst water conditions in 50 years in the Upper Peninsula of Michigan." But subsequent field checks showed little or no nest damage attributable to high water. During late June, over 50 gosling carcasses were recovered from areas that were above high water levels. On 5 September it was estimated that only 100 goslings remained, thus indicating a loss of approximately 690 goslings.

Early techniques for estimating populations and production were not standardized and were not consistently reliable. Population estimates were as great as 3,000 in 1956. Critical review of these techniques and increased emphasis on more adequate methods of determining population size led Sherwood (unpubl. rep., Seney National Wildlife Refuge, 1963) to conclude that estimates of the population prior to 1960 were probably too high by 500 to 1,000 birds.

Gosling mortality in 1960 was alarmingly high. We have since learned that heavy losses may be expected once every 4 years. Since census methods were not reliable prior to 1960, cyclic losses could have been missed. The early records, nevertheless, indicated that noticeable setbacks in flock growth occurred several times prior to 1960 (Sherwood 1968).

Gosling losses since 1960 are shown in Table 1. Improved counting methods and marking of individual birds with plastic neck bands identifiable at a distance provided a better base for censusing than in earlier years. Even the figures presented for recent years, however, should be considered to be estimates.

OCCURRENCE OF *LEUCOCYTOZOON*

The genus was first found in North America by Wickware (1915) who reported it from a domestic duck in Ontario, Canada. He named the parasite *L. anatis.* O'Roke (1934) observed *Leucocytozoon* in blood films from several species of wild ducks in northern Michigan and claimed that extensive losses occurred among ducklings. *Leucocytozoon* has been reported from a wide variety of birds in North America (Herman 1944) and elsewhere (Coatney 1937) and from many species of Anatidae from North America (Herman 1968*a,b*).

The first North American report of *Leucocytozoon* from a goose was from a domestic bird in Quebec in 1933 (Wickware 1941) but several investigators have reported *L. anseris* as a pathogen of domestic geese in central Europe (Knuth and Magdeburg 1922, 1924; Stephan 1922; Ivanic 1937). *Leucocytozoon* in a Canada goose was first reported from Cape Cod, Massachusetts (Herman 1938*b*); it has subsequently been reported in subspecies of *B. canadensis* from Michigan (Herman 1944, Barrow et al. 1968), Illinois (Levine and Hanson 1953), southern California (Wood and Herman 1943), Wisconsin (Trainer et al. 1962), Quebec (Laird and Bennett 1970), Northwest Territories (Bennett and MacInnes 1972), and Labrador (Bennett 1972). The species of parasite in the Canada goose is considered to be *L. simondi* (Herman 1938*a*). Several authors have mentioned the occurrence of *Leucocytozoon* at the Seney Refuge (Ivanic 1937; Wehr and Herman 1954; Herman 1957, 1963, 1966, 1968*a,b*; Tarshis and Herman 1965; Barrow et al. 1968; Tarshis 1968, 1972, 1973). The following observation was recorded in a 1936 Seney Refuge Quarterly Narrative Report in the Seney Refuge files: "The young goslings were noted to have a heavy infestation of blackflies at the base of their necks . . . . Dr. E. C. O'Roke suggested that our geese might be susceptible to the prevalent malaria-like disease, *Leucocytozoon,* found amongst our native ducks." This suspicion was confirmed in 1945 when O'Roke diagnosed *Leucocytozoon* in a dead gosling from Seney. Beard (unpubl. rep., Seney National Wildlife Refuge, 1949) observed sick goslings in 1949 and sent blood smears from 38 goslings and two adult Canada geese from Seney to the senior author who reported very heavy parasitemias with *Leucocytozoon* in the goslings and suggested this parasite might have been the main contributory factor in the losses.

Since 1950 the Patuxent Wildlife Research Center has given increasing attention to the problem at the Seney Refuge in an effort to determine the cause of the losses of goslings. The high incidence of *L. simondi* incriminates this agent above all others. Although other parasites and possible disease-causing agents have been recorded, they have had a relatively low incidence compared with the *Leucocytozoon*. Other organisms observed include trypanosomes and coccidia, *Trichomonas* spp., *Haemoproteus* (*Parahaemoproteus*) *nettionis*, *Plasmodium* spp., *Tetrameres* sp., *Amidostomum anseris*, *Aspergillus* and viruses. None of these has been shown to be a cause of the epizootic losses. Autopsies of dead goslings revealed less than 5% with aspergillosis as a possible cause of death (one or two birds per year, some years none), and no pathological condition, other than that attributed to *Leucocytozoon*, was observed that was suggestive of an infectious agent.

Goslings have been examined in every year since 1950, except in 1956, and *L. simondi* has been consistently present. Some birds usually die during the first week in June; goslings 2 to 7 weeks of age appear to be the most vulnerable. At the time of death, blood smears show a high level of parasitemia with the round forms of *L. simondi*. Occasionally, particularly in the youngest age group, death occurs without parasitemia. In such birds we have demonstrated overwhelming infection in the tissues with schizogonic stages of the parasite, which suggests death from the parasitic infection at an early stage prior to appearance of parasites in the blood. Experimental infection, either by exposure of sentinel birds or by inoculation with infected vector flies or sporozoites obtained from such flies, indicates a prepatent period of 4 to 7 days, occasionally up to 2 weeks, before parasitemia can be demonstrated. Surviving birds lose their heavy parasitemia within a matter of weeks, the level of parasitemia subsiding to one parasite per 100,000 red blood cells or lower. With such low intensity of infection, parasites are observed only occasionally in routine microscopic examination. When infected birds are maintained in captivity, the parasitemia remains at this low level until the following spring; routine periodic blood films examined during this period rarely show an occasional elongate form. Parasitemia increases about the time of egg-laying and parasites can be readily demonstrated. Chernin (1952) was the first to show that regulation of the day length under laboratory conditions could stimulate the female goose to lay eggs about a month early; under such treatment, both the male and female birds exhibited parasitemia a month earlier than under natural conditions. One of us (C.M.H.) was able to demonstrate that an increase in parasitemia could also be produced by stress stimuli at any time following initial recovery.

In the early 1950's, our observations were limited to examination of a few sick or dead birds submitted to the laboratory

Table 1. Annual estimates of production and mortality of Canada goose goslings at the Seney National Wildlife Refuge.

Year	Goslings hatched	Gosling mortality	Percent mortality
1960	790	690	87
1962	819	269	33
1963	609	134	22
1964	627	527	84
1965	676	186	28
1966	818	143	17
1967	912	150	16
1968	1,022	730	71
1969	1,091	545	50
1970	1,181	381	32
1971	1,035	335	32
1972	425	325	76

for examination, and to observations made during brief visits to the Seney Refuge at the height of the losses. Dead and sick birds that were examined in 1954, which was a year of heavy losses, demonstrated a very high level of parasitemia (many parasites observable in each microscopic field—often over 50 parasites per 100 red blood cells). No losses were recorded in 1956; however, no birds were examined for evidence of *L. simondi* during that year.

Data from the studies during the 1950's led to the assumption that all goslings became infected with *Leucocytozoon,* and the more extensive data of recent years substantiated this assumption. Beginning with the summer of 1959, more frequent visits were made to the study site. As a result, we were able to determine that most goslings died between June 3 and June 10.

In 1963, and again in 1964, we observed the goose flock upon its arrival at Seney in the spring. Pairs chose their nesting territories and settled down to defend them against intrusion by the rest of the flock. Unattached birds, however, continued to show excitable and aggressive behavior. Following a suggestion by Barrow (1962) we attempted to correlate behavior with the intensity of infection. A number of birds were captured by means of a cannon net and banded with colored plastic neck bands which made field identification possible. Examination of blood smears indicated that the unattached birds had an intensity of parasitemia 2 or 3 times the level in the birds that had already chosen nest territories. Just prior to egg-laying time more than 80% of all the birds had a readily demonstrable parasitemia with *L. simondi.*

On the basis of the knowledge currently available, we conclude that *L. simondi* is the prime cause of the die-off in the Canada goose gosling population at the Seney National Wildlife Refuge.

We have been unable to explain the cyclic fluctuation in the losses; all evidence points to 100% infection in the goslings every year. We have unsuccessfully attempted to correlate weather conditions, hunting pressure, predation rate, and other parasites (which may provide an additive or synergistic effect) with the fluctuation in losses. Immune response may contribute to the cycles, for there is an indication that younger birds succumb more readily, but the data are not conclusive. Some investigators claim that the number of sporozoites in initial or repeated exposures may be a factor to consider (Fallis et al. 1951).

VECTORS OF *LEUCOCYTOZOON*

O'Roke (1934) reported that *Leucocytozoon* of Anatidae is transmitted by simuliids. Studies in Ontario (Fallis et al. 1951, 1954, 1956) demonstrated that the prime natural vectors of *L. simondi* in ducks are *Simulium rugglesi* and *S.* (*E.*) *anatinum.* Studies at the University of Michigan Biological Station confirmed *S. rugglesi* as a prime vector (Barrow 1968). In 1960–64 it was determined that *S. rugglesi* was the dominant blackfly in the Seney area from early June through mid-July and was capable of transmitting *L. simondi* to geese as well as to ducks.

Before 1964 there were few studies of the blackflies of the Seney area; only four species had been reported in the literature. Since that time, over 100 species, of which 35 are ornithophilic, have been identified in and around the Seney Refuge (Tarshis 1973). Specimens were collected by sweeping (netting), by using birds as bait, and by collecting eggs, larvae, and pupae from breeding habitats in water courses. Studies of the occurrence of these flies at Seney indicate that S.

rugglesi is not present in substantial numbers until after the first week of June, by which time extensive deaths of goslings with heavy infections of *Leucocytozoon* have already occurred. It appears, therefore, that *S. rugglesi* is probably not involved initially in the transmission of *L. simondi* in the local goose population.

Of the species of Simuliidae prevalent in the region earlier in the season, we first considered *Cnephia invenusta* to be a potential natural vector (Tarshis and Herman 1965), but subsequent studies indicated that this was incorrect. Field and laboratory experiments demonstrated that *C. invenusta* is incapable of transmission (Tarshis 1972).

Although 35 ornithophilic species of blackflies were taken at Seney during our observations, only four were taken from birds (*C. invenusta, C. taeniatifrons, S. innocens* and *S. rugglesi*) in sufficient abundance to be suspect vectors. Of the potential vectors present during May, the prime suspect is *S. innocens*.[3] Both laboratory and field studies indicate that it is a potential candidate (Tarshis 1972). In some years, particularly 1972, it was the only ornithophilic species present just prior to and during the time of the seasonal epizootic. Though immature stages (larvae and pupae) of *S. euryadminiculum* have been taken at Seney, no adult flies have been taken from exposed ducks and geese. Further study of this species will be required to determine whether it may serve as a vector. In Algonquin Park it is restricted to feeding on loons and appears to be an unlikely natural vector (Lowther and Wood 1964, Bennett et al. 1972). Both *S. innocens* and *S. rugglesi* are able vectors (Tarshis 1972).

S. innocens is believed to be the prime vector in transmission of *Leucocytozoon* to the goslings. However, a high incidence of this parasite is recognized in *S. rugglesi* throughout June to mid-July, as at Algonquin Park in Ontario (Fallis and Bennett 1966). We, as well as many of our colleagues, have collected *S. rugglesi* in the northern peninsula of Michigan as late as the last week in July, taken them to the laboratory and successfully produced infected ducks and geese by inoculation of triturated flies. We have collected ducks which hatch later in the season, at both Seney Refuge and other areas of northern Michigan that demonstrate a parasitemia up to mid-September; it is more likely, therefore, that the heavy prevalence of *L. simondi* in these flies was obtained from ducks than from geese.

[3] The authors recognize that the epizootiological relationships of *S. anatinum* at Algonquin Park and *S. innocens* at the Seney Refuge follow the same pattern. Controversy on the morphological identity of these species presents conflicts of diagnosis which must await further clarification.

ACKNOWLEDGMENTS

The authors are indebted to many colleagues for assistance in gathering the data which form the basis of this report. Particular thanks are extended to U.S. Fish and Wildlife Service personnel in the Minneapolis regional office for their support and encouragement. We also acknowledge the technical assistance of the refuge managers and other personnel at the Seney National Wildlife Refuge, staff of the Section of Disease and Parasite Studies of the Patuxent Wildlife Research Center, and students at the University of Michigan Biological Station and Hiram College.

LITERATURE CITED

AMERICAN ORNITHOLOGISTS' UNION. 1957. Check-list of North American Birds, 5th ed. 691pp.

BARROW, J. H., JR. 1962. Behavioral factors in relapse of parasitic infections. Proc. 1st. Int. Conf. on Wildl. Dis., Wildl. Dis. Ass., pp. 61–64.

———, N. KELKER, AND H. MILLER. 1968. Transmission of *Leucocytozoon simondi* to birds by *Simulium rugglesi* in northern Michigan. Am. Midl. Nat. 79:197–204.

BENNETT, G. F. 1972. Blood parasites of some birds from Labrador. Can. J. Zool. 50:353–356.

———, A. M. FALLIS, AND A. G. CAMPBELL. 1972. The response of *Simulium* (*Eusimulium*) *euryadminiculum* Davies (Diptera: Simuliidae) to some olfactory and visual stimuli. Can. J. Zool. 50:793–800.

———, AND C. D. MACINNES. 1972. Blood parasites of geese of the McConnell River, N.W.T. Can. J. Zool. 50:1–4.

CHERNIN, E. 1952. The relapse phenomenon in the *Leucocytozoon simondi* infection of the domestic duck. Am. J. Hyg. 52:101–118.

COATNEY, G. R. 1937. A catalog and host-index of the genus *Leucocytozoon*. J. Parasit. 23:202–212.

FALLIS, A. M., R. C. ANDERSON, AND G. F. BENNETT. 1956. Further observations on the transmission and development of *Leucocytozoon simondi*. Can. J. Zool. 34:389–404.

———, AND G. F. BENNETT. 1966. On the epizootiology of infections caused by *Leucocytozoon simondi* in Algonquin Park, Canada. Can. J. Zool. 44:101–112.

———, D. M. DAVIES, AND M. A. VICKERS. 1951. Life history of *Leucocytozoon simondi* Mathis and Leger in natural and experimental infections and blood changes produced in the avian host. Can. J. Zool. 29:305–328.

———, J. C. PEARSON, AND G. F. BENNETT. 1954. On the specificity of *Leucocytozoon*. Can. J. Zool. 32:120–124.

HANSON, H. C. 1965. The Giant Canada Goose. Southern Illinois Univ. Press. 226pp.

HERMAN, C. M. 1938*a*. *Leucocytozoon anatis* Wickware, a synonym for *L. simondi* Mathis and Leger. J. Parasit. 24:472–473.

———. 1938*b*. The relative incidence of blood protozoa in some birds from Cape Cod. Trans. Am. Micr. Soc. 57:132–141.

———. 1944. The blood protozoa of North American birds. Bird-Banding 15:89–112.

———. 1957. The occurrence of blood protozoa in North American birds. J. Protozool. 4 (suppl.):6.

———. 1963. The occurrence of blood parasites in Anatidae. Trans. VIth Congr. Int. Union Game Biol. pp. 341–349.

———. 1966. Some disease problems in Canada geese. 2nd Annual Canada Goose Ecology Sem., Seney, Michigan, June 14–15, 1966. pp. 14–17.

———. 1968*a*. Blood protozoa of free-living birds. Symp. Zool. Soc. London 24:177–195.

———. 1968*b*. Blood parasites of North American waterfowl. Trans. 33rd N. Am. Wildl. Conf. pp. 348–359.

———. 1969. The impact of disease on wildlife populations. Biosci. 19:321–325.

IVANIC, M. 1937. Zur Kenntnis der gewohnlichen Zweiteilung und der in den Leberzellen der Hausgans (*Anser domesticus* L.) vorkommenden multiplen Teilung (Schizogonie) bei *Leucocytozoon anseris* Knuth u. Magdeburg. Archiv. fur Protistenk. 89:16–44.

JOHNSON, C. S. 1947. Canada goose management. Seney National Wildlife Refuge. J. Wildl. Mgmt. 11:21–24.

KNUTH, P., AND F. MAGDEBURG. 1922. Ueber ein durch Leukozytozoon verursachtes Sterben junger Ganse. Berl. Tierarzt. Wochenschr. 33:359–361.

———, AND ———. 1924. Ueber Leukozytozoen bei der Hausgans. Zeitschr. Inf-Kr. Haust. 26:42–52.

LAIRD, M., AND G. F. BENNETT. 1970. The subarctic epizootiology of *Leucocytozoon simondi*. J. Parasit. 56:198.

LEVINE, N. D., AND H. C. HANSON. 1953. The blood parasites of the Canada goose *Branta canadensis interior*. J. Wildl. Mgmt. 17:185–196.

LOWTHER, J. K., AND D. M. WOOD. 1964. Specificity of a blackfly, *Simulium euryadminiculum* Davies, towards its host, the common loon. Can. Entomol. 96:911–913.

MATHIS, C., AND M. LEGER. 1910. *Leucocytozoon* d'une tourterelle (*Turtur humilis*) et d'une sarcelle (*Querquedula crecca*) du Tonkin. C. R. Soc. Biol. 68:118–120.

O'ROKE, E. C. 1934. Malaria-like disease of ducks, caused by *Leucocytozoon anatis* Wickware. Univ. Mich. Sch. of Forestry & Cons. Bull. 4, 44pp.

SHERWOOD, G. A. 1968. Factors limiting production and expansion of local populations of Canada geese. Canada Goose Management. Dembar Educational Research Service, Madison, Wisc. pp. 73–85.

STEPHAN, J. 1922. Uber eine durch Leukozytozoen verusachte Ganse- und Putenerkrankung. Deutsche Tierarztl. Wochenschr. 45:589–592.

TARSHIS, I. B. 1968. Collecting and rearing black flies. Ann. Entomol. Soc. Am. 61:1072–1083.

———. 1972. The feeding of some ornithophilic black flies (Diptera: Simuliidae) in the laboratory and their role in the transmission of *Leucocytozoon simondi*. Ann. Entomol. Soc. Am. 65:842–848.

———. 1973. Annual Report, Bureau of Sport Fisheries and Wildlife, Patuxent Wildlife Research Center, Laurel, Md.

———, AND C. M. HERMAN. 1965. Is *Cnephia invenusta* (Walker) a possible important vector of *Leucocytozoon* in Canada geese? Bull. Wildl. Dis. Ass. 1:10–11.

TRAINER, D. O., C. S. SCHILDT, R. A. HUNT, AND L. R. JAHN. 1962. Prevalence of *Leucocytozoon simondi* among some Wisconsin waterfowl. J. Wildl. Mgmt. 26:137–143.

WEHR, E. E., AND C. M. HERMAN. 1954. Age as a

factor in acquisition of parasites by Canada geese. J. Wildl. Mgmt. 18:239–247.

WICKWARE, A. B. 1915. Is *Leucocytozoon anatis* the cause of a new disease in ducks? Parasitology 8:17–21.

———. 1941. Notes on miscellaneous diseases of geese. Can. J. Comp. Med. 5:21–24.

WOOD, S. F., AND C. M. HERMAN. 1943. The occurrence of blood parasites in birds from southwestern United States. J. Parasit. 29:187–196.

LEECH PARASITISM OF WATERFOWL IN NORTH AMERICA[1]

DAVID L. TRAUGER,[2] Northern Prairie Wildlife Research Center, U.S. Fish and Wildlife Service, Jamestown, ND 58401
JAMES C. BARTONEK, Office of Biological Services, U.S. Fish and Wildlife Service, Anchorage, AK 99501

Leech parasitism of waterfowl is apparently widespread in North America, but the incidence and significance of these infestations is poorly documented. McDonald (1969) catalogued the helminth parasites of waterfowl and listed 16 species of Anatidae and 14 species of other waterbirds, mostly from the Northern Hemisphere, reported to have been infested by leeches. Meyer and Moore (1954) and Moore (1964, 1966) have made important contributions towards understanding of leech parasitism of waterfowl in North America. Earlier records were published by Sooter (1937) and Low (1945). Considerable information on the relationship of leeches and aquatic birds was obtained by three Canadian workers studying the helminth fauna of grebes (Podicipitidae) (Gallimore 1964), the American Coot *Fulica americana* (Colbo 1965), and ducks (Anatinae) (Graham 1966). Recently, Bartonek and Trauger (1975) reported on the nature and incidence of leech infestations among a waterfowl population of the northern forest zone. Europeans have long been aware of leech parasitism of waterfowl (Weltner 1887, Büchli 1924) and have contributed much towards our knowledge of leech biology and ecology (Mann 1962). This paper presents a review of the distribution and significance of leech parasitism of waterfowl in North America.

[1] Originally published in Wildfowl 28:143–152, 1977.

[2] Address correspondence to this author.

IDENTIFICATION OF LEECHES

Leeches of the genus *Theromyzon* (=*Protoclepsis*) are often called 'duck leeches' in the literature (Herter 1929, Christiansen 1939, Mann 1962). The principal species of leech infesting North American waterfowl is *Theromyzon rude* (Meyer and Moore 1954; Moore 1964, 1966; Bartonek and Trauger 1975), but Sooter (1937), Butler (1940) and Low (1945) referred to *T. occidentalis*. Moore and Meyer (1951) studied some specimens previously regarded as *T. occidentalis* and found them to be *T. rude*. They noted that leeches obtained from dying ducks were so engorged with blood that specific identification was often impossible, but they believed that there were three or four species of *Theromyzon* leeches in North America whose distributions were related to waterfowl flyways. Moore (1964) considered *T. meyeri* as synonymous with *T. occidentalis*, but he cautioned that 'inasmuch as there has been considerable confusion with respect to the species of the genus *Theromyzon*, which are represented in the North American fauna, it seems not unlikely that at least some of the records . . . for *T. meyeri* actually refer to leeches now designated as *T. rude*.'

McDonald (1969) listed *T. maculosum*, *T. occidentale*, *T. rude*, *T. sexoculatum*, and *T. tessulatum* as leech parasites of waterfowl. Recently Klemm (1972) critically examined major leech collections and most type specimens in an attempt to clarify the nomenclature and identification of North American leeches. He recognized only three species of *Theromyzon*: *T. maculosum* (=*T. meyeri*), *T. rude* (=*T. occidentalis*) and *T. tessulatum*. *T. tessulatum* and *T. maculosum* have been found parasitizing waterfowl in Europe, including USSR (Herter 1929, Christiansen 1939, Rollinson et al. 1950, Mann 1951, Roberts 1955, Kuznetsova 1955, Lang 1969, Keymer 1969, Fjeldså 1972, Gräfner and Baumann 1974).

Although more host records exist for *T. rude* among various species of North American waterfowl (Meyer and Moore 1954), Moore (1964, 1966) concluded that *Placobdella ornata* also feeds on blood extracted from various aquatic birds. Bartonek and Trauger (1975) found both *T. rude* and *P. ornata* infesting ducks and other waterbirds. Mathers (1948) suggested that *Macrobdella decora, Haemopsis marmorata*, and *H. lateralis* parasitized wading birds. McDonald (1969), Sawyer (1972) and Davies (1973) presented additional information on the identification, taxonomy, distribution and hosts of leeches in North America.

Fig. 1. Leeches attached to the conjunctiva beneath the nictitating membrane. These were fairly common parasites of Ring-necked Ducks and other boreal breeding waterfowl. (David Trauger.)

NATURE OF PARASITISM

Herter (1929) and Mann (1962) described responses of leeches to a variety of stimuli. Responses of *Theromyzon* spp. which favour encounters with ducks included: (1) a positive phototactic movement by hungry leeches and the opposite for satiated leeches; (2) an attraction towards and attachment to an object warmed to 33–35°C; (3) an attraction towards a disturbance or vibration in the water; (4) a tendency for hungry leeches to congregate near the surface of the water; and (5) a chemotactic movement towards objects that have been in contact with the preen gland of ducks. We categorized leech infestations of waterfowl according to the site of attachment: (1) eyes; (2) nasal chamber; (3) body; and (4) elsewhere (Bartonek and Trauger 1975).

Eyes

Although several European workers have reported leeches infesting the eyes of ducks and geese (Herter 1929, Christiansen 1939, Roberts 1955, Lang 1969, Keymer 1969, Gräfner and Baumann 1974), this type of infestation was first reported in North American waterfowl by Bartonek and Trauger (1975). Leeches were found attached to the conjunctiva canthus of the eye beneath the nictitating membrane (Fig. 1). This position protected the leeches from scratching by the bird. Apparently leeches seldom, if ever, attached themselves to the cornea. Although no more than one adult leech was usually found per eye, its large size would restrict the vision of the bird or even blind it. Engorged leeches were readily apparent from a distance through binoculars or telescopes. Young leeches, often several per eye, were found beneath the nictitating membrane and eyelid, often detectable only by post-mortem examination.

Fig. 2. A leech *Theromyzon rude* engorged with blood. It partially protrudes through the nare of this adult female Lesser Scaup. (David Trauger.)

Adult leeches apparently gained access to the eyes from the plumage of the head. Young leeches also used at least two other methods: (1) being transported by the parent leech entering the eye; and (2) entering the nasal chamber, either independently or on the parent leech, and then moving to the eye via the lacrimal duct.

Pressure from a fingertip against the medial edge of the nictitating membrane causes it to slip back exposing the leech, which can then be pulled loose from the conjunctiva with forceps. After the leech is removed, the conjunctiva remains inflamed and swollen for several hours, but blood exudes from the wound for only a few minutes. The eyelid frequently remains closed for a time due to irritation from the anticoagulant hirudin secreted by the leech. Gräfner and Baumann (1974) also found that leech infections resulted in defective vision. Kuznetsova (1955) and Roberts (1955) reported that the cornea of waterfowl became opaque after leeches fed at the conjunctiva. The former also observed that sometimes the eye increased in size, even obtruding from the orbit. We did not observe any such signs of eye injury to ducks handled in our study.

Nasal Chamber

The nasal chamber is the most prevalent site of infestation (Fig. 2) according to a number of North American workers (Kalmbach and Gunderson 1934; Sooter 1937; Butler 1940; Low 1945; Erickson 1948; Meyer and Moore 1954; Mendall 1958; Banko 1960; Moore 1964, 1966; Bartonek and Trauger 1975). In Europe, Büchli (1924), Herter (1929), Rollinson et al. (1950), Mann (1951), Kuznetsova (1955), Lang (1969), Keymer (1969), and Fjeldså (1972) documented occurrences in nasal chambers of ducks and geese.

Leeches were attached to the mucosa anywhere within the bird's nasal chamber, but generally posterior from the nares up to, and occasionally inside, the lacrimal ducts (Bartonek and Trauger 1975). Those deep within the nasal chamber were usually detected only after postmortem examination, but some adults were visible through the nares. Engorged leeches protruding from the nares were swollen on both ends and constricted in the middle where the body passed through the nare. Such leeches were readily observed from a distance with the aid of binoculars or telescopes (Fig. 3).

Entrance to the nasal chambers by adult and young leeches was probably gained through the nares following attachment to the bill, and less frequently through the buccal cavity and pharynx following ingestion. In addition, young leeches were likely transported on adults.

Ducks reacted to the apparent discomfort by scratching at protruding leeches, shaking their heads, and sneezing, forcibly expelling air through the nares while the bill was immersed in water (Bartonek and Trauger 1975, Kuznetsova 1955). Although ducks may scratch and injure some protruding engorged leeches, we never observed a duck free itself of a

Fig. 3. Leeches protruding from the nares of juvenile Lesser Scaup (second from left). They were visible at considerable distance, particularly with the aid of binoculars or telescopes. (James Bartonek.)

leech through purposeful effort. Low (1945), however, reported that Redheads *Aythya americana* expelled the smaller leeches from their nasal chambers by sneezing.

We used forceps to remove conspicuous leeches from the nasal chambers of ducks captured for banding. Kuznetsova (1955) suggested as a prophylaxis rinsing with aqueous solutions of gastric juice, sodium chloride (10%), vinegar or ammonia. Lang (1969) treated infested ducks with Ophthaine.

Body

Leeches were also attached to the bird's body, on legs, feet, breast or cloaca (Bartonek and Trauger 1975). Leeches that had not yet fed were frequently seen moving on the plumage of recently killed birds. These movements were generally towards the head, suggesting that feather direction may stimulate a taxis movement towards sites which are more protected from the preening activities of the bird. Erickson (1948), Meyer and Moore (1954), Banko (1960), and Moore (1964,

Fig. 4. Distribution of leech parasitism of waterfowl in North America. Relative size of circles indicates the number of waterfowl species parasitized by leeches.

1966) also reported leeches on the body surfaces of waterfowl in North America, but there are few references to this type of infestation in Europe (Rollinson et al. 1950).

Elsewhere

Leeches have been reported to occupy the trachea (Herter 1929, Mann 1951, Moore 1966), bronchi (Quortrup and Shillinger 1941), buccal cavity (Erickson 1948, Meyer and Moore 1954), larynx (Herter 1929), oesophagus (Weltner 1887), and brain (Büchli 1924, Herter 1929). Kuznetsova (1955) found leeches more often in the upper respiratory tracts, especially the nasal chambers, than attached within the oesophagus or to the conjunctiva.

We found leeches in the buccal cavity, pharynx, and larynx of autopsied birds but believed that they probably move there from the nasal chamber after the birds died. In addition, leeches were found in some oesophagi, proventriculi, and ventriculi of ducks examined for food habits (Bartonek and Murdy 1970, Bartonek 1972). Although leeches were apparently eaten as food, they also may have been ingested during preening.

SIGNIFICANCE OF PARASITISM

Leech infestations among ducks, geese, and swans have apparently occurred widely in North America, especially in northern and western areas (Fig. 4). A review of the literature in conjunction with our own observations and communications with other workers revealed leech parasitism of twenty species of waterfowl in the United States and Canada (Table 1). A variety of other waterbirds have also been infested by leeches.

Sooter (1937) found four of six Blue-

Table 1. Species of North American waterfowl reported to have been parasitized by leeches.

	Source reporting leech infestation				
Host species	This review*	Bartonek and Trauger (1975)	McDonald (1969)	Moore (1966)	Other references
Whistling Swan *Cygnus columbianus*	+			+	
Trumpeter Swan *Cygnus cygnus buccinator*	+			+	+ Banko (1960)
White-fronted Goose *Anser albifrons frontalis*	+				
Lesser Snow Goose *Anser c. caerulescens*	+				
Canada Goose *Branta canadensis* ssp.	+				
Northern Pintail *Anas acuta*		+	+	+	+ Meyer and Moore (1954)
American Green-winged Teal *Anas crecca carolinensis*		+			
Mallard *Anas platyrhynchos*	+	+	+	+	+ Quortup and Shillinger (1941)
Gadwall *Anas strepera*	+			+	
American Wigeon *Anas americana*		+		+	
Blue-winged Teal *Anas discors*			+	+	+ Sooter (1937)
Shoveler *Anas clypeata*	+	+		+	
Canvasback *Aythya valisineria*	+	+			+ Erickson (1948)
Redhead *Aythya americana*	+		+		+ Low (1945)
Ring-necked Duck *Aythya collaris*	+	+			+ Mendall (1958)
Lesser Scaup *Aythya affinis*	+	+	+	+	+ Meyer and Moore (1954); Graham (1966)
Surf Scoter *Melanitta perspicillata*		+			
American White-winged Scoter *Melanitta fusca deglandi*		+			
Bufflehead *Bucephala albeola*		+			
North American Ruddy Duck *Oxyura j. jamaicensis*	+		+		+ Meyer and Moore (1954); Graham (1966)

* Previously unpublished observations contributed by McDonald, Johnson, Pospichal, Bromley, Weller, and Pearson as noted in text.

winged Teal *Anas discors* ducklings infested with leeches in north-west Iowa, but Bennett (1938) was unable to assess the severity of the parasitism. Sooter (1937) believed that the death of a 1-week-old American Coot was caused by a leech obstructing the respiratory tract, but Blue-winged Teal and Pied-billed Grebes *Podilymbus podiceps* were not adversely affected. F. J. Vande Vusse (pers. com.) states that *T. rude* is still commonly observed in nasal passages and on the plumages of Blue-winged Teal and Coots in north-western Iowa. Low (1945) also found that 80% of 4- to 11-week-old Redhead ducklings were infested with leeches in Iowa, but older juveniles appeared to be free of them. Although two adults that died from lead poisoning were heavily infested with leeches, he could not attribute any mortality directly to such parasitism.

Mendal (1958) frequently encountered both adult and young Ring-necked Ducks *Aythya collaris* with leeches attached around the bill and nares in Maine. Although he found no indication that they harmed the ducks, he suspected that suffocation could result if leeches blocked the nares. Erickson (1948) found only a few small leeches on the feathers of healthy Canvasbacks *Aythya valisineria* in Oregon but noted many in the buccal and nasal cavities of dead and sick waterfowl. Cornwell and Cowan (1963) made no mention of leeches parasitizing Canvasbacks in Manitoba, but M. W. Weller (pers. com.) observed leeches feeding on the brood patches of incubating Redheads on the Delta Marsh, Manitoba.

Banko (1960) reported observations of leeches in the nasal chambers of two cygnet Trumpeter Swans *Cygnus cygnus buccinator* of the Red Rock National Wildlife Refuge in Montana. Banko thought that leeches were little more than a nuisance to the larger swans but could contribute to the mortality of small cygnets, and Moore (1966) reported the death of a cygnet attributed to a leech in the trachea.

Leech infestations of the Pintail *Anas acuta*, Lesser Scaup *Aythya affinis*, and Ruddy Duck *Oxyura jamaicensis* were first reported by Meyer and Moore (1954) from specimens collected at Whitewater Lake in south-western Manitoba. Moore (1965) noted leech parasitism of a Mallard *Anas platyrhynchos* and four species of grebe (Horned Grebe *Podiceps auritus*, Pied-billed Grebe, Red-necked Grebe *Podiceps grisegena*, Eared Grebe *Podiceps caspicus*) in Alberta. Subsequently, Moore (1966) listed the Gadwall *Anas strepera*, Pintail, Shoveler *Anas clypeata*, American Wigeon *Anas americana*, Blue-winged Teal, Lesser Scaup, Mallard, Trumpeter Swan, and Whistling Swan *Cygnus columbianus* as well as the American Coot and Western Grebe *Aechmophorus occidentalis* parasitized by leeches. Both *T. rude* and *P. ornata* were identified as the parasites in the above infestations.

Graham (1966) reported a higher incidence of leech infestation among 96 Ruddy Ducks in Alberta than among 216 Lesser Scaup. Adults were more heavily infested than young. Among 348 grebes examined by Gallimore (1964), a higher percentage (20–30%) of adult Red-necked and Western Grebes were parasitized by leeches than Horned and Eared Grebes (10–20%). Of six Pied-billed Grebes, two were infested. Again, more adults were parasitized than young. Colbo (1965), who studied 371 American Coots, determined that about 10% of the adults and 20% of the immatures were infested with leeches.

Bartonek and Trauger (1975) observed leech infestations in Mallard, Pintail, Green-winged Teal *Anas crecca carolinensis*, American Wigeon, Shoveler, Ring-necked Duck, Canvasbacks, Lesser Scaup, Bufflehead *Bucephala albeola*, White-winged Scoter *Melanitta fusca deglandi*, and Surf Scoter *Melanitta perspicillata* near Yellowknife, Northwest Territories. In addition to these 11 species of ducks, the Red-necked Grebe,

Horned Grebe, and Black-throated Diver *Gavia arctica* were also parasitized. *T. rude* was the principal leech involved in the waterfowl infestations, but *P. ornata* was also encountered. High incidences of leeches were found in Lesser Scaup and American Wigeon.

Leon L. Johnson (pers. com.) found leeches infesting Ring-necked Duck captured by nightlighting for banding at Rice Lake National Wildlife Refuge in Aitken County, Minnesota. During late September leeches were found in one or both eyes of 22% of 293 ducks in 1970; 36% of 499 were infested in 1971. The leeches were non-selective for age or sex. Although these data suggest a fairly high incidence of leech infestation of Ring-necked Ducks, Johnson stated that 1,250 diving ducks annually captured by nightlighting in Roseau, Mahnomen and Beltrami Counties of Minnesota were unafflicted by leech parasitism. In addition, Lewis M. Cowardin (pers. com.) has annually captured about 1,000 ducks by nightlighting on the Chippewa National Forest about 120 km (75 miles) northwest of Rice Lake, but none of these birds was parasitized. Carl E. Pospichal (pers. com.) had previously observed Canvasbacks blinded by leeches at Rice Lake National Wildlife Refuge.

In south-central Alaska, Robert G. Bromley (pers. com.) removed leeches from under the nicitating membranes of three Dusky Canada Geese *Branta canadensis occidentalis*. These birds were captured with about 500 other geese on Alaganik Slough of the Copper River Delta between 23 July and 2 August 1974. An additional 40 nest-trapped females, captured in early June, were not infested.

Waterfowl weakened by disease are apparently more susceptible to leech infestations than healthy birds. Kalmbach and Gunderson (1934) and Quortrup and Shillinger (1941) reported that leeches aggravated cases of botulism, but they doubted that they were ever the primary cause of death. Sciple (1953) implied that leeches were commonly encountered among ducks suffering from botulism poisoning. Bartonek also has observed ducks afflicted with botulism poisoning and infested with leeches on marshes adjacent to the Great Salt Lake in Utah. Gary L. Pearson (pers. com.) told us that leeches have been observed in the eyes, nares, and cloaca of Mallard, Pintail, Shoveler, Gadwall and Blue-winged Teal affected with botulism in North Dakota. Meyer and Moore (1954) speculated that leeches were responsible for the deaths of ducks on Whitewater Lake, Manitoba. We suspect that the birds were also poisoned, as this lake has a history of outbreaks of botulism.

Between 1957 and 1968, Malcolm E. McDonald (pers. com.) routinely noted the occurrence of leeches infesting waterfowl necropsied for parasites (Table 2). *T. rude* was considered an active parasite of living birds, whereas *P. ornata* found in the nasal cavities of some birds was assumed to be a post-mortem invader. The large number of leeches observed in some specimens suggested that they might be a mortality factor, especially regarding the high loss of juvenile Trumpeter Swans at the Red Rock Lakes National Wildlife Refuge in Montana. Three young swans (4–7 weeks) were infested by 35, 71, and 72 leeches, respectively. McDonald noted that the frequency of leech parasitism varied in relation to season, habitat, and location. Summer birds collected in Montana (Red Rock Lakes NWR) and Idaho (Camas NWR) were infested at higher rates, 77% and 62% respectively, compared to 1–3% in Utah (Bear River MBR). Red Rock Lakes and

Table 2. Leech parasitism of waterfowl examined post-mortem by Dr. Malcolm E. McDonald, 1957–68.*

Species	Number of individuals infested (number examined)	Location	Number of leeches found
Whistling Swan	3 (35)	Utah	3–25
Trumpeter Swan	10 (14)	Montana	1–72
Lesser Snow Goose	2 (14)	California	5–7
White-fronted Goose	1 (8)	California	3
Canada Goose	1 (20)	Utah	2
Mallard	5 (68)	Utah, Idaho, Montana	1–74
Gadwall	3 (55)	Idaho	9–15
Shoveler	1 (13)	Montana	15
Canvasback	3 (14)	Montana	1–18
Redhead	2 (15)	Utah, Montana	9–23
Lesser Scaup	2 (9)	Nebraska	19–24
Ruddy Duck	2 (10)	Utah, Montana	2–16

* Detailed records filed at Bear River Research Station, U.S. Fish and Wildlife Service, Bear River, Utah.

Camas National Wildlife Refuges have lush, spring-fed wetlands where leech populations were very high. Bear River Migratory Bird Refuge is an alkaline marsh with restricted variety of life.

Meyer and Moore (1954) considered *T. rude* as a major cause of death among waterfowl, especially young birds, on prairie wetlands of Canada. Moore (1966) believed that *T. rude* was responsible for considerable mortality in young waterbirds in Alberta. Smith et al. (1964) noted that some ducklings on the North American prairies would die from suffocation caused by leeches. Bartonek and Trauger (1975) attributed the deaths of several young waterfowl to leech parasitism. Quortrup and Shillinger (1941) mentioned that occasional cases of verminous pneumonia developed in ducks infested with leeches in the bronchi.

Mortality to domestic and captive waterfowl from leech *T. tessulatum* infestations has been reported frequently in Europe. Kuznetsova (1955) characterized severe leech infestations of the upper respiratory system as usually causing short, laboured breathing and terminating in death from asphyxiation. He estimated mortality rates of 15–20% and 80–90% for two groups of ducks and geese on state-operated farms in the USSR. Hilprecht (1956) reported that leeches also contributed to mortality of swans on a large scale in Europe. Rollinson et al. (1950) and Mann (1951) attributed the deaths of 24 ducklings on a large millpond in England to leeches infesting the nasal cavity. Mann (1951) found no previous records of *Theromyzon* being associated with the deaths of birds in Great Britain, but Rollinson et al. (1950) cited several references to infestations causing extensive mortality among waterfowl elsewhere in Europe (Weltner 1887, Büchli 1924). A Falkland Flightless Steamer Duck *Tachyeres brachypterus* at the Wildfowl Trust (1950) died from leech parasitism. Keymer (1969) reported mortality of waterfowl infested by leeches.

NEED FOR RESEARCH

Although Mann (1962) reviewed existing knowledge of leech biology and ecology, further work is needed on the leeches infesting waterfowl, particularly *T. rude*. Moore and Meyer (1951) summarized available information on the description, anatomy, and distribution of this species and later presented additional findings pertaining to its life history (Meyer and Moore 1954). Although they considered the information relatively incomplete, they concluded that the behaviour of *T. rude* was similar to that of *T. tessulatum*, the biology of which has been studied in considerable detail by Herter (1929) and Christiansen (1939). Hagadorn (1962) reported on some aspects of the biology of *T. rude*, especially the physiology of the reproductive cycle.

Until Herrmann's (1970) work, no broad ecological studies of leeches had been published in North America. He found that *T. rude* and *P. ornata* were widely distributed in relation to several chemical and physical factors. Scudder and Mann (1968), investigating the distribution of leeches in relation to salinity, found that *T. rude* exhibited tolerance to the widest range of environmental conditions compared to nine other species of freshwater leech. Gallimore (1964), Colbo (1965) and Graham (1966) also examined some ecological factors influencing leech parasitism of aquatic birds. Herrmann (1970) noted an interesting relationship between *T. rude* and *P. ornata*; they were frequently found in close physical association in shallow waters inhabited by a variety of waterfowl.

Leech-waterfowl relationships are still poorly understood. Sawyer (1972) stated, 'there is little doubt that *T. rude*, like its European congenitor, *T. tessulatum*, can be a cause of morbidity and mortality of young waterfowl, but the economic significance of this problem requires critical examination.' Future studies should be directed toward investigating the effects of leech parasitism upon individual birds, with emphasis on evaluating the debilitating impact of leeches on the growth and development of ducklings and on determining the combined effects of leeches, other parasites, and diseases on the health and survival of young waterfowl. Although Graham (1966) has made an important start in studying the helminth ecology of breeding waterfowl, the nature and incidence of leech infestations in relation to host species, age, habitat, and season need to be investigated in other areas for comparison with our observations. In addition, such questions as the dynamics and duration of infestations, feeding rates and frequency, blood volumes extracted, gross pathology, and host selectivity are of particular interest.

Meyer and Moore (1954) noted that *T. rude* commonly occurred in the northern United States and southern Canada, especially along the Rocky Mountain duck flyway. Subsequent records have indicated that leech infestations of North American waterfowl are probably widespread throughout northern and western breeding grounds (Fig. 4). Although the incidence of infestation is high in some northern forest waterfowl populations, the evidence suggests that the mortality directly attributable to leeches is probably low (Bartonek and Trauger 1975). Nevertheless, the contributing causes to mortality of juvenile waterfowl are often difficult to detect; it is even more difficult to ascribe relative values to them.

Leeches may indirectly contribute to mortality rates of waterfowl. Ducks may die from predation because leeches impair their vision or hinder their escape. Blinded ducks may not feed effectively. The debilitating effects may also retard growth and development of ducklings, and might prevent migration before freeze-up or adversely affect reproduction the following year. A partial obstruction of the respiratory tract must surely hinder breathing and the diving abilities. Blood parasites or toxic substances may also be transmitted in the anticoagulant of vector leeches. Sick and disturbed birds are prone to leech infestations; sick birds may succumb from the additional stress caused by parasitism.

SUMMARY

Leech parasitism of waterfowl is widespread in North America. Twenty species of ducks, geese and swans have been infested by leeches, particularly *Theromyzon rude* and *Placobdella ornata*. Sites of attachment include the eyes, nasal passages, and body. Information is lacking on the biology and ecology of duck leeches. Their significance as morbidity and mortality factors and their continental distribution should be determined in relation to waterfowl habitats and populations.

ACKNOWLEDGMENTS

We thank Dr. Frederick J. Vande Vusse, Dr. Malcolm E. McDonald, and Ms. Ell-Piret Multer for assistance in identifying and obtaining several references. To those contributing personal observations of leech infestations, we express sincere gratitude. Dr. Gary L. Pearson, George A. Swanson, and Dr. Gary L. Krapu provided editorial assistance on earlier drafts. Dr. McDonald offered helpful suggestions for final improvements.

LITERATURE CITED

BANKO, W. E. 1960. The Trumpeter Swan. North American Fauna No. 63.

BARTONEK, J. C. 1972. Summer foods of American Widgeon, Mallards, and a Green-winged Teal near Great Slave Lake, Northwest Territories. Canad. Fd.-Nat. 86:373–376.

———, AND H. W. MURDY. 1970. Summer foods of Lesser Scaup in Subarctic taiga. Arctic 23:35–44.

———, AND D. L. TRAUGER. 1975. Leech (Hirudinea) infestations among waterfowl near Yellowknife, Northwest Territories. Canad. Fd.-Nat. 89:234–243.

BENNETT, L. J. 1938. The Blue-winged Teal: its ecology and management. Collegiate Press, Ames, Iowa.

BÜCHLI, K. 1924. Bloedzuigers in de neusholte van eenden. Tijdschrift voor Diergeneeskunde 51:153–155.

BUTLER, W. J. 1940. Leeches in ducks. Montana Livestock Sanitary Board Report, 1939–1940:12.

CHRISTIANSEN, M. 1939. *Protoclepsis tesselata* (O. F. Müller), der Entengel, als Ursache von Krankheit, u.s. Konjunktivtis, bei Gänsen und Enten. Zeitschrift für Infektionskrankheiten, Parasitäre Krankheiten und Hygiene der Haustiere 55:75–89.

COLBO, M. H. 1965. Taxonomy and ecology of the helminths of the American Coot in Alberta. Unpub. M.S. thesis. University of Alberta, Edmonton, Alberta.

CORNWELL, G. W., AND A. B. COWAN. 1963. Helminth populations of the Canvasback (*Aythya valisineria*) and host-parasite—Environmental interrelationships. Trans. N. Amer. Wildl. and Nat. Res. Conf. 28:173–199.

DAVIES, R. W. 1973. The geographic distribution of freshwater Hirudinoidea in Canada. Canad. J. Zool. 51:531–545.

ERICKSON, R. C. 1948. Life history and ecology of the Canvasback, *Nyroca valisineria* (Wilson) in southwestern Oregon. Unpublished Ph.D. thesis, Iowa State College, Ames, Iowa.

FJELDSÅ, J. 1972. Records of *Theromyzon maculosum* (Rathke 1862): Hirudinea, in N. Norway. Norw. J. Sc. 20:19–26.

GALLIMORE, J. R. 1964. Taxonomy and ecology of helminths of grebes in Alberta. Unpublished M.S. thesis, University of Alberta, Edmonton, Alberta.

GRÄFNER, V. G., AND H. BAUMANN. 1974. Blutegelbefall bein Wassergeflügel. Angew Parasitol. 15:121–124.

GRAHAM, L. C. 1966. The ecology of helminths in breeding populations of Lesser Scaup (*Aythya affinis* Eyton) and Ruddy Ducks (*Oxyura jamaicensis* Gmelin). Unpublished M.S. thesis, University of Alberta, Edmonton, Alberta.

HAGADORN, I. R. 1962. Functional correlates of neurosecretion in the rhynchodellid leech, *Theromyzon rude*. Gen. and Comp. Endocrinology 2:516–540.

HERRMANN, S. J. 1970. Systematics, distribution and ecology of Colorado Hirudinea. Amer. Midl. Nat. 83:1–37.

HERTER, K. 1929. Reizphysiologisches Verhalten and Parasitismus des Entenegels *Protoclepsis tesselata* O. F. Müller. Zeitschrift für vergleichende Physiologie 10:272–308.

HILPRECHT, A. 1956. Hockerschwan, Singschwan, Zwerschwan. Wittenburg Lutherstadt: A. Ziemsen Verlag.

KALMBACH, E. R., AND M. F. GUNDERSON. 1934. Western duck sickness, a form of botulism. U.S. Dep. Agric. Technical Bull. No. 411.

KEYMER, I. F. 1969. Infestation of waterfowl with leeches. Vet. Rec. 85:632–633.

KLEMM, D. J. 1972. Freshwater leeches (Annelida: Hirudinea) of North America. Biota of Freshwater Ecosystems Identification Manual No. 8. U.S. Environmental Protection Agency. Washington, D.C.

KUZNETSOVA, O. N. 1955. Piyaviki-parazitei vodoplavayuschei ptitsei. Ptitsevodstvo 5:32–34.

LANG, D. C. 1969. Infestation of ducklings with leeches. Vet. Rec. 85:566.

LOW, J. B. 1945. Ecology and management of the Redhead, *Nyroca americana*, in Iowa. Ecol. Mono. 15:35–69.

MANN, K. H. 1951. On the bionomics and distribution of *Theromyzon tessulatum* (O. F. Müller), 1774 (= *Protoclepsis tesselata*). Annals and Magazine Nat. Hist. 4:956–961.

———. 1962. Leeches (Hirudinea). Their structure, physiology, ecology, and embryology. New York: Pergamon Press.

MATHERS, C. K. 1948. The leeches of the Okoboji region. Iowa Academy of Science Proc. 55:397–425.

McDONALD, M. E. 1969. Catalogue of helminths of waterfowl (Anatidae). U.S. Bur. Sport Fish. Wildl. Spec. Sc. Rep. Wildl. No. 126.

MENDALL, H. L. 1958. The Ring-necked Duck in the Northeast. Univ. Maine Bull. 69:1–317.

MEYER, M. C., AND J. P. MOORE. 1954. Notes on Canadian leeches (Hirudinea) with the description of a new species. Wasmann J. Biol. 12:63–96.

MOORE, J. E. 1964. Notes on the leeches (Hirudinea) of Alberta. Nat. Mus. Canada, Nat. Hist. Papers 27:1–15.

———. 1966. Further notes on Alberta leeches (Hirudinea). Nat. Mus. Canada, Nat. Hist. Papers 32:1–11.

MOORE, J. P., AND M. C. MEYER. 1951. Leeches (Hirudinea) from Alaskan and adjacent waters. Wasmann J. Biol. 9:11–77.

QUORTRUP, E. R., AND J. E. SHILLINGER. 1941. 3,000 wild bird autopsies on western lake areas. J. Amer. Vet. Medical Assoc. 99:382–387.

ROBERTS, H. E. 1955. Leech infestation of the eye in geese. Vet. Rec. 67:203–204.

ROLLINSON, D. H. L., K. N. SOLIMAN, AND K. H. MANN. 1950. Deaths in young ducklings associated with infestations of the nasal cavity with leeches. Vet. Rec. 62:225–227.

SAWYER, R. T. 1972. North American freshwater leeches exclusive of the Piscicolidae, with a key to all species. Illinois Biol. Mono. 46:1–154.

SCIPLE, G. W. 1953. Avian botulism: information on earlier research. U.S. Bur. Sport Fish. Wildl. Spec. Sc. Rep. Wildl. No. 23.

SCUDDER, G. G. E., AND K. H. MANN. 1968. The leeches of some lakes in the Southern Interior Plateau region of British Columbia. Syesis 1:203–209.

SMITH, A. G., J. H. STOUDT, AND J. B. GOLLOP. 1964. Prairie potholes and marshes, pp. 39–50, in Waterfowl Tomorrow. Ed. J. P. Linduska. Washington, D.C.: U.S. Bur. Sport Fish. Wildl.

SOOTER, C. A. 1937. Leeches infesting young waterfowl in northwest Iowa. J. Parasitol. 23:108–109.

WELTNER, W. 1887. *Clepsine tesselata* O. Fr. Müll. aus dem Tegelsee bei Berlin lebend vorzeigen. Sitzungsberichte der Gesellschaft Naturforschender Freunde zu Berlin. 17:85.

WILDFOWL TRUST. 1950. Pathology: parasites. Wildfowl Trust Ann. Rep. 3:52.

EFFECTS OF ALDRIN EXPOSURE ON SNOW GEESE IN TEXAS RICE FIELDS

EDWARD L. FLICKINGER, U.S. Fish and Wildlife Service, Patuxent Wildlife Research Center, Gulf Coast Field Station, Victoria, TX 77901

Abstract: In 1972 and 1974, 112 dead or moribund snow geese (*Chen c. caerulescens*), mostly immature white-phase males, were found in a study area on the Garwood Prairie, Texas. Dying geese were observed within 2 days after rice fields planted with aldrin-treated seed were flooded by heavy rains on 21 March 1972 and 25 March 1974. Brains from 8 snow geese that were moribund when found contained an average of 8.2 ppm (4.9–14.0 ppm) of dieldrin (a metabolite of aldrin); brains of 14 geese found dead contained an average of 14.1 ppm (2.1–31 ppm). Because no mortalities occurred in 1973 when aldrin-treated rice seed was flooded after all geese had migrated or in 1975 and 1976 after the treatment of rice seed with aldrin was suspended, it appears certain that aldrin caused the mortalities.

J. WILDL. MANAGE. 43(1):94–101

During the spring of 1971, many geese died on the winter range in southeast Texas in areas where aldrin-treated rice seed was planted in early March and flooded in late March. More than 300 dead geese were counted in ground and aerial surveys in a 5-county area of the Texas rice-growing region; at least 180 of these were at reservoirs and in rice fields on the Garwood Prairie.

Goose mortality had been reported in this area in earlier years, and detailed investigations were undertaken in 1972–76. Circumstances under which goose losses occurred in these years, symptoms of dieldrin poisoning in moribund geese, and quantities of dieldrin and mercury residues in brains of dead or moribund geese are described.

I thank L. Krenek and R. Korenek, rice growers on the Garwood Prairie; and H. Baer (veterinarian), L. Blus, and G. Heinz (biologists), U.S. Fish and Wildlife Service, for review of the manuscript.

STUDY AREA CONDITIONS

The 11.3 × 4.8-km study area is on the Garwood Prairie, Colorado County, Texas, 4.8 km southwest of the town of Garwood about 100 km inland from the Gulf of Mexico. The land use consisted largely of rice fields and pastures, interspersed with woodland, and included 2 large reservoirs (about 4 km apart) and many small ponds.

Rice was planted in March or April of each year at about 112 kg/ha (100 lb/acre). Nearly all seed planted in 1972, 1973, and 1974 was treated with aldrin at 2.5 g/kg of seed (4 oz/100 lb). In October 1974, the U.S. Environmental Protection Agency suspended aldrin as a rice seed treatment; consequently, no aldrin-treated seed was planted in 1975 and 1976. Purpose of the treatments was to control rice water weevil (*Lissorhoptrus oryzophilus*) larvae. However, larvae in Texas had shown increased resistance to aldrin since 1964 (Bowling 1968, 1972).

Other seed treatments were used to control rice seedling blight. In February 1970 the U.S. Department of Agriculture suspended certain mercury-based seed treatments. Ceresan L, a mercurial fungicide, at about 0.75 g/kg (1.2 oz/100 lb) of seed was used in addition to aldrin until supplies were exhausted in 1972. Terra-Coat L-205, a nonmercurial fungicide applied at the rate of 1.38 g/kg (2.2 oz/100 lb) replaced Ceresan L from 1973–75. Vitavax-R (another nonmercurial fungicide) at 2.19 g/kg (3.5 oz/100 lb) of seed

Originally published in J. Wildl. Manage. 43(1):94–101, 1979.

replaced Terra-Coat L-205 in 1976 because it was less expensive.

Seed treatment and rainfall differed each year. In 1972 aldrin-Ceresan L treated seed was planted in all rice fields (treated fields) on the west side while seed treated only with Ceresan L was planted in several large fields (untreated fields) on the east side of the study area. A heavy rain on 21 March flooded all rice fields sufficiently for seed germination. Planting was delayed in 1973 by frequent rains in early March and planting of aldrin-treated seed did not begin until 3 April, after nearly all geese had migrated northward. In 1974, rain on 25 March flooded all fields planted with aldrin-treated rice seed. No aldrin-treated rice seed was planted in 1975 and 1976. Geese were exposed to aldrin-treated rice seed only in 1972 and 1974.

Snow geese and some white-fronted (*Anser albifrons*) and Canada geese (*Branta canadensis*) spent winters on the study area concentrated near the reservoirs. Most arrived in late October and left for nesting grounds in mid-March. They spent most of the fall and early winter gleaning rice stubble fields. In late winter they rested on the reservoirs during midday and fed in pastures and rice stubble fields in the morning and afternoon. Some geese preferred pastures for feeding. Few visited dry planted rice fields; most were attracted to newly planted rice fields only after flooding (in late March) which occurred from 3 to 24 days after they were planted. After rains on 21 March 1972 and 25 March 1974, and until the remaining geese left for nesting grounds, most geese fed in flooded, treated fields.

METHODS

Counts of geese in the Garwood Prairie study area were begun in early or mid-March each year and continued until almost all had migrated (early May in 1972 and early April in 1973–76). In 1972 and 1974 observations were made of flights from reservoir resting areas to feeding areas. Counts of geese feeding in treated fields were made to estimate the proportion of the population that was exposed to contamination before northward migration. Casualty counts were conducted on the same dates as live counts. Dead and dying geese were collected and their tissues analyzed for pesticide residues. When feasible whole carcasses of dead geese were collected. Two carcasses were consumed by predators and scavengers to the extent that only the brain was usable for residue analysis. Snow geese were collected by shooting at reservoirs, in or near treated fields, and near control fields on 29 March and 1 April 1972, 8 and 11 days after rice fields were flooded.

In 1972 and 1974, 37 geese in suitable condition for study were aged and sexed. Twenty-four were weighed and examined for body fat. Twenty geese found dead or moribund were examined for gunshot wounds and their stomachs (proventriculus and gizzard) were examined for treated rice. Gizzard contents of 13 geese found dead or dying were examined for lead shot. Blood serum samples were taken from 5 snow geese found moribund or dead and 14 were necropsied for signs of disease, especially for duck virus enteritis in 1974.

Tissues were analyzed at the Denver Wildlife Research Center by the methods of Peterson et al. (1976) for organochlorines and the methods of Okuno et al. (1972) for mercury. Of the organochlorines only dieldrin residues are reported here because others present were in such minute amounts that quantification and (in some tissues) identification were dif-

Table 1. Numbers of geese[a] on the Garwood Prairie, Texas study area in relation to dates of planting and flooding of rice fields, March–May in 1972–76.

Month and day	Number of live or (dead) geese, and planting or flooding of rice				
	Aldrin and Ceresan L	Aldrin and Terra-Coat L-205		Terra-Coat L-205	Vitavax-R
	1972	1973	1974	1975	1976
March					
5			Planted		18,400
7		9,450		4,400	14,700
10	Planted	10,250	15,400	6,300	Planted
14	14,050	4,100	10,650	4,400	14,250
15				Planted	
17	14,500	1,850		1,930	
18				Flooded	3,150
20		930		1,600	
21	Flooded				3,600
22	5,500 (12)[b]	710	2,870	1,195	
25	4,200 (9)		Flooded	410	3,700
27			1,950 (47)		
28	1,850 (9)	590	200 (10)	410	530
31			1 (3)		
April					
1	1,300 (7)	310			13
3		Planted			
4		0[c]	0	26	Flooded
7	675 (4)[d]			0[c]	
14	690 (3)				
20	230 (4)				
25	230 (4)				
30	165				
May					
5	13				

[a] Counts were usually made between 1130 and 1430. Snow geese averaged 78% (67–88%) of total live geese in 3 counts in April 1972 and 6 counts in March and April 1973. White-phase snow geese averaged 83% (79–86%) of total live snow geese in 15 counts in March 1972, 1973, and 1975, April 1972 and 1973, and November 1972.
[b] There were 3,000 geese in the treated area.
[c] There were 40–75 Canada and white-fronted geese within 1.6 km of the study area.
[d] All geese were concentrated in the treated area.

ficult. Some tissues were analyzed for lead residues by the method described by White et al. (1977).

Rice production in treated vs. untreated fields was compared in 1972.

RESULTS

Goose Mortality

The highest number of geese observed in the study area in early to mid-March ranged from 6,300 in 1975 to 18,400 in 1976 (Table 1). From 62 to 87% of the geese migrated northward before treated fields were flooded in 1972 and 1974.

In 1972, 52 dead or dying snow geese were found between 22 March and 25 April after heavy rains on 21 March. The first moribund geese (12) observed in 1972 were in the treated area the day after fields planted with aldrin-treated seed were flooded by rain. Less than a week after flooding, dead or dying geese were observed at reservoirs, in treated fields, and in pastures. Casualties were also found near the untreated area after some

Table 2. Body weights and body fat index of immature male snow geese collected in aldrin-treated and untreated rice fields within 1 week after flooding, Garwood Prairie, Texas, late March and April, 1972 and 1974.

Geese shot in 1972				Geese found dead or dying			
Untreated area		Treated area		Treated area, 1972		Treated area, 1974	
Weight (g)	Body fat	Weight (g)	Body fat	Weight (g)	Body fat	Weight (g)	Body fat
2,175	**[a]	2,085	****	1,950[b]	***	1,950	*
2,085	****	1,975	**	1,925[b]	**	1,815	*
2,070	**	1,740	***	1,770	*	1,680	*
2,065	***			1,750	*	1,570	*
1,950	***			1,680[b]	*	1,510	*
1,940	***					1,380	*
1,925	**					1,350	*
1,835	****						
1,740	**						
1,976[c]		1,933		1,815		1,608	

[a] Relative amount of adipose tissue, low (*) to high (****).
[b] Found dying, others were dead.
[c] Average weight.

fields were planted with treated rice seed in early April 1972. Known mortality extended from 1 day to 5 weeks after fields were flooded. In 1974, 60 dead or dying snow geese were observed from 2 to 6 days after treated fields were flooded by a heavy rain on 25 March.

Mortality differed according to sex and age; 74% of the affected snow geese were males and 93% of the males were immature. This observation corroborated our findings that all of 10 dead geese sexed in 1971 were males (Flickinger and King 1972).

Snow geese comprised about 78% of the total goose population on the Garwood Prairie, and 96% of the total goose mortality. White-phase birds represented 83% of the snow goose population and the observed snow goose mortalities.

No mortality of geese was observed on the Garwood Prairie in 1973 as all had left the study area by 4 April, before rice planting. Timing of rice planting and flooding, and feeding patterns of geese were essentially the same in 1975 as in 1972 and 1974, when large kills occurred; yet not 1 dead goose was found during 7 searches of the study area during 20 days after flooding (Table 1). The only obvious difference in conditions in 1975 was the discontinuation of planting of aldrin-treated rice seed. Meaningful data could not be collected in 1976, when, as in 1973, geese had left the area before most rice fields were flooded.

No dead or moribund geese collected in 1972 and 1974 had gunshot wounds, lead shot in gizzards, or signs of disease. Rice seed dyed red (treated with aldrin) was found in the stomach contents of 2 dead geese in 1972 and 1974.

Symptoms of Dieldrin Intoxication

Symptoms of moribund geese in 1972 and 1974 were similar to those described for dying geese in Texas by Bauder et al. (1972) and for experimental birds undergoing dieldrin poisoning (Tucker and Crabtree 1970). Symptoms of intoxication involved withdrawal (cessation of interactions with the flock), head nodding, and bobbing side-to-side head movements accompanied by abnormal nibbling and chattering bill movements.

Table 3. Residues of dieldrin and mercury in snow geese collected on the Garwood Prairie, Texas, late March and April 1972 and 1974.

Condition, year, and locality of collection	Residues (ppm fresh wet weight)											
	Dieldrin[a]						Mercury[b]					
	Brain			Breast muscle			Brain			Breast muscle		
	N	$\bar{x}$	Range	N	$\bar{x}$	Range	N	$\bar{x}$	Range	N	$\bar{x}$	Range
Dead												
1972	5	20.9	(12.6–31.0)	3	18.6	(14.8–25.0)	5	0.02	(0.01–0.04)	3	0.03	(0.02–0.04)
1974	9	10.3	(2.1–15.0)									
Moribund												
1972	5	7.4	(4.9–12.0)	1	3.0		1	0.02		1	0.03	
1974	3	9.6	(5.3–14.0)									
Shot, 1972												
Treated fields	6	0.8	(<0.1–2.2)	1	3.8		1	0.01		1	0.02	
Untreated fields	6	0.1	(<0.1–0.12)	2	0.1	(<0.1–0.1)	2	0.08	(0.02–0.14)	2	0.03	(0.02–0.04)

[a] Breast muscle analyzed for dieldrin in only 1 to 3 geese from each group.
[b] Mercury in kidneys of the 3 moribund geese in 1974 averaged 0.04 ppm (range 0.03–0.04 ppm). Mercury in livers of the same geese averaged 0.08 ppm (range 0.03–0.11 ppm). Kidney and liver contained 0.1 ppm of lead.

Geese in advanced stages of intoxication had dull, sunken eyes and lacked muscular coordination. Their gait was unsteady and they walked in circles until their legs became immobile. Terminal symptoms displayed in the prostrate position were violent body tremors, violent wing beat, kicking and jumping convulsions, arching and twisting of the neck far over the back, and loud vocalizations. Some fell over backward in rigid paralysis; many eventually died in that position with heads thrust far under their bodies. Immature males found dead or dying in 1972 weighed about 8% less than those shot in the untreated area during the same period (Table 2).

All geese that displayed bobbing side-to-side head movements eventually died. The time to death varied: some geese died quickly (probably from heavy doses of aldrin) and others slowly (possibly because they received lower dosage). An immature male snow goose died 4 days after hand-capture and removal from the treated area. He showed symptoms of intoxication continuously during capture and confinement; terminal convulsions persisted for about 40 minutes. Bauder et al. (1972) captured 8 sick snow geese in 1971, placed them in confinement, and reported that all died within 12 hours of capture. Death occurred within a few minutes after the onset of terminal symptoms.

Pesticide Residues

Pesticide residues were found in tissues of all 34 snow geese from the Garwood Prairie in 1972 and 1974 (Table 3). Dieldrin residues in brains averaged 8.2 ppm (4.9–14 ppm) in 8 moribund and 14.1 ppm (2.1–31 ppm) in 14 dead geese collected in late March and April. Brains of 6 geese shot during the same period in 1972 in the treated area contained an average of 0.8 ppm (<0.1–2.2 ppm), whereas in 6 geese shot near untreated fields the average was only 0.1 ppm. A Canada goose found dead in the study area in 1974 contained 5.6 ppm dieldrin in brain.

Mercury residues in brains averaged 0.02 ppm (0.01 to 0.04 ppm) in 6 dead and dying geese and 0.06 ppm 0.01 to <0.14 ppm) in 3 geese that were shot in 1972. Mercury in breast muscle of 4 dead and dying geese and of 3 geese shot averaged 0.03 ppm (0.02–0.04 ppm) for each group.

Mercury and lead residues were measured in the kidneys and livers of 3 dying snow geese collected in 1974, 2 years after the last use of Ceresan L rice seed treatment. The kidneys contained 0.03–0.04 ppm of mercury. If these levels are representative, mercury residues in snow geese declined sharply from 1971 to 1974. In 1971 mercury residues averaged 0.38 ppm (0.09–1.1 ppm) in kidneys of 6 snow geese (Flickinger and King 1972). It is doubtful that the low levels of mercury in geese in 1974 contributed significantly to observed mortality. Lead residues in kidneys and livers of these 3 geese in 1974 were less than 0.1 ppm. These residues are less than 1/10 of the lowest residue reported by Locke et al. (1967) and Bagley et al. (1967), who found that residues in livers of Canada geese dying from lead poisoning in Delaware and Wisconsin ranged from 1.2 to 53 ppm.

DISCUSSION

About 2,000–3,000 geese (13–21% of the wintering population) remained in treated areas when they were flooded in 1972 and 1974. Most geese were attracted to treated rice fields by the presence of water, and some accumulated enough dieldrin to cause death. The lower limit of the diagnostic lethal level of dieldrin in brains of experimental and wild birds dying from dieldrin exposure was 4–5 ppm (Stickel et al. 1969), a concentration exceeded in the brains of 20 of 22 dead or moribund geese from the Garwood Prairie. The experimental evidence verifies our correlative evidence that dieldrin, after being metabolized from aldrin, was responsible for mortality of geese on the Garwood Prairie.

Immature snow geese, white and blue phases, were more susceptible to dieldrin poisoning than adults, white-fronted, and Canada geese. Also this may be because more immatures than adults were in segments of the population in March. Late migrants that remained until 21 March were at a greater risk than those that migrated earlier.

Immature male snow geese were markedly underweight when found dead or dying from dieldrin poisoning. Flickinger and King (1972) reported that 2 male fulvous whistling ducks (*Dendrocygna bicolor*) that survived initial exposure to aldrin in a rice field pen test virtually stopped feeding. They had lost 10 and 34% of their body weight by the time they died 3 and 6 days after first exposure to aldrin. Five survivors lost an average of 13% of their body weight by the 3rd day. In the present study an immature male snow goose (terminal weight 1,545 g) displayed symptoms of intoxication during 4 days before death and apparently did not feed during this period. Tucker and Crabtree (1970), Hayes (1971), and Flickinger and King (1972) reported aldrin exposure caused a complete loss of appetite with resultant weight loss. Birds fed DDT and then starved for 5 to 7 days lost 18–20% of their prestress body weight and used 50–75% of total carcass lipid (Findlay and de Freitas 1971).

There is evidence that geese are adversely affected during northward migration (Babcock and Flickinger 1977). Single moribund geese were frequently observed some distance from rice fields. On 27 March 1974 a dying immature female snow goose and a blue-winged teal (*Anas discors*) were observed 5.6 km from the nearest rice field. They displayed symptoms of dieldrin poisoning and later died. The brain of the goose contained 14 ppm dieldrin and the brain of the teal 19 ppm. The goose was probably migrating because only migrating geese were observed in the area where it was found; the nearest wintering flock of geese was about 57.9 km southeast.

Dieldrin residues may affect reproductivity once geese reach their nesting grounds. Band returns indicate that many snow geese that spend the winter on the Garwood Prairie and other parts of southeast Texas nest near the McConnell River (Eskimo Point) on the west shore of Hudson Bay, Northwest Territories, Canada. Mortality of snow geese at the McConnell River nesting area in 1967, 1971, and 1972 coincided with goose mortality on the Garwood Prairie, whereas during 1968 and 1970 there was little mortality in either area. Four of 5 unsuccessful nesting females found dead at McConnell River in 1972 and 4 of 5 females from failed nests contained traces of dieldrin in their brains, but only 1 of 10 that nested successfully contained such traces. Mercury residues in breast muscle of females that were found dead or nested unsuccessfully ranged from less than 0.01 to 0.14 ppm (Ankney 1974).

Adverse effects of dieldrin were probably not limited to snow geese or to the Garwood Prairie. Dead geese were also observed in Chambers County in 1972 and in Victoria, Wharton, and Harris counties in 1974. Flickinger and King (1972) reported numerous dead individuals of many species associated with aldrin-dieldrin poisoning in 3 Texas counties between 1967 and 1971. Two white-fronted geese, a blue-winged teal, 2 mourning doves (*Zenaida macroura*), and 2 eastern meadowlarks (*Sturnella magna*) were found during searches for dead and dying snow geese in 1972. A white-fronted goose and a Canada goose were found in 1974.

Presence of dieldrin and mercury residues in dead geese could have been a hazard to bald eagles (*Haliaeetus leucocephalus*) and raccoons (*Procyon lotor*) that fed on them on the Garwood Prairie. However, brains of 2 raccoons that were shot (1 moribund) at a goose mortality site in 1972 contained only 1.1 and 0.2 ppm dieldrin and 0.4 and 0.3 ppm mercury.

No noticeable difference in rice yield occurred between treated and untreated fields nor was yield reduced after the uses of aldrin and mercury were suspended as rice seed treatments.

CONCLUSIONS

Dieldrin-induced mortality of snow geese and perhaps of a number of other species of wildlife occurred in Texas in years when aldrin-treated rice seed was planted and flooded early. Many surviving geese were exposed to levels of aldrin and dieldrin residues that may have affected them during migration and nesting. No mortality of geese or other birds occurred in 1973 when aldrin-treated rice was flooded after geese had migrated, nor in 1975 and 1976 after use of aldrin was suspended. Clearly the suspension of the use of aldrin for treatment of rice seed should be sustained.

LITERATURE CITED

ANKNEY, C. D. 1974. The importance of nutrient reserves to breeding blue geese (*Anser caerulescens*). Ph.D. Thesis. Univ. of Western Ontario, London. 232pp.

BABCOCK, K. M., AND E. L. FLICKINGER. 1977. Dieldrin mortality of lesser snow geese in Missouri. J. Wildl. Manage. 41:100–103.

BAGLEY, C. E., L. N. LOCKE, AND G. T. NIGHTINGALE. 1967. Lead poisoning in Canada geese in Delaware. Avian Dis. 11:601–608.

BAUDER, R. B., L. L. WEISHUHN, D. B. FRELS, AND B. K. CARROLL. 1972. Geese and pesticides. Tex. Parks Wildl. 30:20–22.

BOWLING, C. C. 1968. Rice water weevil resistance to aldrin in Texas. J. Econ. Entomol. 61:1027–1030.

———. 1972. Status of rice water weevil resistance to aldrin in Texas. J. Econ. Entomol. 65:1490.

FINDLAY, G. M., AND A. S. W. DE FREITAS. 1971. DDT movement from adipocyte to muscle cell during lipid utilization. Nature (London) 229: 63–65.

FLICKINGER, E. L., AND K. A. KING. 1972. Some effects of aldrin-treated rice on Gulf Coast wildlife. J. Wildl. Manage. 36:706–727.

HAYES, W. J. 1971. Clinical handbook on economic poisons. U.S. Environ. Prot. Agency, Washington, D.C. 144pp.

LOCKE, L. N., G. E. BAGLEY, AND L. T. YOUNG. 1967. The ineffectiveness of acid-fast inclusions in diagnosis of lead poisoning in Canada geese. Bull. Wildl. Dis. Assoc. 3:176.

OKUNO, I., R. A. WILSON, AND R. E. WHITE. 1972. Determination of mercury in biological samples by flameless atomic absorption after combustion and mercury-silver amalgamation. J. Assoc. Off. Anal. Chem. 55:96–100.

PETERSON, J. E., K. M. STAHL, AND D. L. MEEKER. 1976. Simplified extraction and cleanup for determining organochlorine pesticides in small biological samples. Bull. Environ. Contam. Toxicol. 15:135–139.

STICKEL, W. H., L. F. STICKEL, AND J. W. SPANN. 1969. Tissue residues of dieldrin in relation to mortality in birds and mammals. Pages 174–200 *in* M. W. Miller and G. G. Berg, eds. Chemical fallout: current research on persistent pesticides. Charles C Thomas, Springfield, Ill. 531pp.

TUCKER, R. K., AND D. G. CRABTREE. 1970. Handbook of toxicity of pesticides to wildlife. U.S. Bur. Sport Fish. Wildl. Resour. Publ. 84. 131pp.

WHITE, D. H., J. R. BEAN, AND J. R. LONGCORE. 1977. Nationwide residues of mercury, lead, cadmium, arsenic, and selenium in starlings, 1973. Pestic. Monit. J. 11:35–39.

Received 1 March 1978.
Accepted 24 July 1978.

EGGSHELL BREAKAGE BY INCUBATING BLACK DUCKS FED DDE

J. R. LONGCORE, Patuxent Wildlife Research Center, Laurel, Maryland 20810

F. B. SAMSON, Patuxent Wildlife Research Center, Laurel, Maryland 20810[1]

Abstract: Black duck (*Anas rubripes*) hens fed 10 ppm dry weight (approximately 3 ppm wet weight) of p,p′-DDE in the diet laid eggs with shells 22 percent thinner at the equator, 30 percent thinner at the cap, and 33 percent thinner at the apex than those of controls. Natural incubation increased shell cracking more than fourfold as compared with mechanical incubation. Hens removed cracked eggs from nests, and one hen terminated incubation. Hens fed DDE produced one-fifth as many ducklings as controls. DDE in eggs of dosed hens averaged 64.9 ppm wet weight.

J. WILDL. MANAGE. 37(3):390–394

Field observers have reported that eggs of raptors, gulls, and pelicans have been cracked, crushed, and sometimes eaten by parent birds (Ratcliffe 1958, 1960; Ludwig and Tomoff 1966, Jehl 1969, Keith et al. 1970). A close association between egg destruction and organochlorine residues has usually been noted (Ratcliffe 1967, Hickey and Anderson 1968, Fyfe et al. 1969, Cade et al. 1971, Blus et al. 1972).

Eggs of kestrels (*Falco sparverius*) fed dieldrin and DDT in combination disappeared from nests in greater proportion than eggs of controls (Porter and Wiemeyer 1969). Egg loss was attributed to breakage of thin-shelled eggs and egg eating by the adults.

Black ducks fed either 10 or 30 ppm of DDE (dry weight) in the diet laid eggs which had thinner shells and cracked more readily than controls (Longcore et al. 1971). Since eggs were gathered daily and placed in mechanical incubators, the effects of natural incubation were not evaluated.

In the present study, black ducks were allowed to nest as pairs in individual pens to approximate a natural nesting cycle and to compare shell cracking and hatching success of eggs incubated by nesting hens and those incubated mechanically.

[1] Present address: Department of Zoology, Utah State University, Logan 84321.

We acknowledge R. J. Diebolt for his care of these ducks; R. G. Heath advised on statistical procedures; R. Andrews and L. F. Stickel reviewed the manuscript; and E. H. Dustman contributed to initial study design.

MATERIALS AND METHODS

The black ducks used in this study were 2-year olds that had bred successfully in 1970 (Longcore et al. 1971). Ten pairs had received dietary dosage of 10 ppm of p,p′-DDE (approximately 3 ppm wet weight) from mid-November 1969 to mid-June 1970 and untreated food from mid-June 1970 to mid-November 1970, when dosage was resumed. Ten pairs of controls received untreated commercial duck breeder mash throughout. Details of pen facilities and food preparation are discussed by Longcore et al. (1971).

At the onset of egg laying about 5 months after initiation of dosage, nests were visited daily and eggs were numbered and examined for cracks. After completion of laying, eggs were examined for cracks at weekly intervals. Hens were allowed to incubate until they had exceeded the normal incubation period. Eggs were then removed and examined to ascertain development. The third egg laid by each hen was removed from the clutch to obtain shell measurements and residue analysis. Shells

Originally published in J. Wildl. Manage. 37(3):390–394, 1973.

were washed while maintaining membranes intact and air-dried to constant weight. Shell thickness was measured at the shell equator, cap, and apex with a micrometer graduated in 0.01 mm units. Shell surface area was determined by the methods of Romanoff and Romanoff (1949:110), and shell weight per unit area was calculated. Egg contents were analyzed for organochlorine pesticides and PCB's by WARF Institute, Inc., using gas chromatography. Egg contents were dried and ground with sodium sulphate; extracted with a mixture of ethyl ether and petroleum ether (70:170) for 8 hours in Soxhlet apparatus; cleaned and separated by two elutions through a Florisil column with ethyl ether and petroleum ether (3:97; 15:85). Analysis was by gas chromatography, using a Barber-Coleman Pesticide Analyzer Model 5360. Columns were glass, 1.219 m × 4 mm. For the first elution, the column packing was 5 percent DC 200 Gas Chrom Q (60/80 mesh); temperatures were: injector 230 C, column 200 C, and detector 240 C. For the second elution, packing was 3 percent OV-17 on Gas Chrom Q (80/100 mesh); and temperatures were: injector 230 C, column 200 C, and detector 240 C. Nitrogen flow rates were such that p,p′-DDT had a retention of 6–8 minutes. For PCB separation an aliquot of the first elution was placed on silicic acid-Celite column (Armour and Burke 1970). Typical elutions were petroleum ether followed by 1:19:80 solution of acetonitrile:hexane:dichloromethane.

Data were tested by analysis of variance; angular transformations were applied to the percentages before analysis (Snedecor and Cochran 1956:316–317). A split-plot analysis was used to evaluate shell cracking in dosage groups between years. Techniques of Cochran (1943) were used to determine that weighting of data was unnecessary. Treatment means were separated by methods of Duncan (1955) and Kramer (1956). Differences between yearly shell parameter means were tested by a *t* test.

RESULTS

Shells of eggs from hens fed 10 ppm of p,p′-DDE were thinner ($P < 0.01$) at the equator, cap, and apex than shells of eggs from undosed hens. They measured 21.7 percent thinner at the equator, 30.0 percent thinner at the cap, and 32.9 percent thinner at the apex (Table 2). Shells weighed 0.0693 gram/cm^2 for eggs of controls and 0.0522 gram/cm^2 (25 percent lower, $P < 0.01$) for those of hens fed DDE.

Eggshell cracking was evaluated in terms of the number of eggshells cracked during: the first day, establishment of the clutch, incubation, and the total nesting period. There was no difference ($P > 0.05$) in the percentage of shells cracked on the day laid (Table 1). In all subsequent periods, however, cracking of eggs from dosed hens exceeded cracking of eggs from controls ($P < 0.01$). Forty-two percent of the eggs disappeared from nests of the ducks fed DDE (Table 1). All of these eggs had been cracked before disappearance. All but one of the eggs which disappeared were found; most were in the water troughs. Eggs recovered from the water usually had shells with only the apex crushed, although some shells were highly fragmented. None of the eggs from control hens disappeared from the nests. Egg contents from a cracked eggshell fouled the nest of one dosed hen to the extent that the hen abandoned the nest after incubating 2 weeks.

Dosed hens laid more eggs than controls ($P < 0.05$) (Table 1). However, hatching success was reduced ($P < 0.01$). Only 19 percent of the eggs hatched as compared with 86 percent for the controls. Among

Table 1. A comparison of eggshell cracking in eggs that were mechanically incubated (1970) or incubated in nests (1971) by seven pairs of black ducks that were controls and seven pairs fed DDE. Reproduction and survival are compared in controls and black ducks fed DDE that incubated their own nests in 1971.

	Control		10 ppm DDE	
	1970	1971	1970	1971
First day laid				
Number of eggs	90	50	146	71*
Eggs cracked	2	0	12	1
Percentage cracked	2.2	0.0	8.2	1.4
During clutch establishment				
Eggs cracked	--	0	--	17
Percentage cracked	--	0.0	--	23.9**
During incubation				
Number of eggs[a]	82	43	135	64
Eggs cracked	0	6	4	24
Percentage cracked	0.0	14.0	3.0	37.5**
Total				
Eggs cracked	2	6	16	41
Percentage cracked	2.2	12.0	11.0*	57.7**
Removed from nest	--	0	--	27
Percentage removed	--	0.0	--	42.2**
Hatched	--	37	--	12
Percentage hatched	--	86.0	--	18.7**
Number of 3-week-old ducklings per incubating hen	--	3.0	--	0.57*

* $P < 0.05$.
** $P < 0.01$.
[a] Based on eggs incubated in contrast to total eggs laid.

dosed birds, only 0.6 young per hen survived to 3 weeks of age as compared with 3.0 for controls ($P < 0.05$). DDE averaged 64.9 (36.4–89.0) ppm wet weight in the eggs from dosed hens. Eggs from undosed hens contained an average of 0.24 (0.20–0.35) ppm of DDE. DDD, DDT, or BHC in the eggs did not exceed 0.28 ppm in either group. Polychlorinated biphenyls averaged 0.44 ppm. Extractable lipids averaged 12.8 percent of the wet weight of the eggs.

DISCUSSION

Some of the biological ramifications of eggshell thinning are evident in this study. Previously we (Longcore et al. 1971) found that DDE at levels as low as 10 ppm in the diet of black ducks produced significant shell thinning (17.6 percent at shell equator) and shell breakage (10 percent of the eggs were cracked on the day they were laid). In that study, a few eggs from dosed hens cracked during mechanical incubation, suggesting that the nesting activities of laying and incubating hens might drastically increase shell breakage. This, in fact, occurred in the present study. Among dosed hens, shell cracking during the entire nesting period was 11.0 percent in 1970 and 57.7 percent in 1971. Shell cracking during incubation and during laying of the clutch also increased. Between the 2 years, cracking of eggshells of control hens also increased (Table 1). This increase was apparently caused by the activity of the incubating hens.

Table 2. Thickness of eggshells (mm) of the third eggs in the clutch of each of seven pairs of black ducks fed DDE and seven pairs of controls that laid in 1970 and 1971.

	Control		10 ppm DDE	
	1970	1971	1970	1971
Equator				
Mean and SD	0.343 ± 0.034	0.359 ± 0.018	0.284 ± 0.011	0.281 ± 0.011
Range	0.27 – 0.38	0.33 – 0.38	0.27 – 0.30	0.27 – 0.30
% difference (year)		+ 4.7		– 1.1
% difference (treatment)			– 17.2**	– 21.7**
Cap				
Mean and SD	0.273 ± 0.034	0.313 ± 0.021	0.211 ± 0.028	0.219 ± 0.038
Range	0.22 – 0.32	0.29 – 0.35	0.17 – 0.25	0.18 – 0.26
% difference (year)		+14.7*		+ 3.8
% difference (treatment)			– 22.7**	– 30.0**
Apex				
Mean and SD	0.254 ± 0.047	0.277 ± 0.024	0.151 ± 0.022	0.186 ± 0.038
Range	0.20 – 0.30	0.25 – 0.32	0.13 – 0.19	0.15 – 0.25
% difference (year)		+ 9.1		+23.2*
% difference (treatment)			– 40.5**	– 32.9**

* $P < 0.05$.
** $P < 0.01$.

Among eggs laid by dosed birds, the percentage of shell cracking on the day laid was greater in 1970 than 1971. In 1970, when 8.2 percent of the eggs cracked on the day laid, 33 percent of the cracks were of the type in which the apex or cap was collapsed (Longcore et al. 1971). In 1971, when only 1.4 percent of the eggs cracked on the day laid, this type of cracking did not occur. These differences probably were the result of increased apical thickness of shells of eggs laid by hens in their second season (Table 2).

Twenty-four percent of the eggs laid by mallards (*Anas platyrhynchos*) fed 10 ppm of DDE (dry weight) for two laying seasons showed shell fractures varying from hairline cracks to obvious breaks (Heath et al. 1969). Intact shells (measured at equators) averaged 10.8 percent thinner than those of controls in the first season. In a second study, mallards fed 10 ppm of DDE laid 20 percent cracked eggs in the first season and 28 percent in the second (Heath et al. 1970). Thickness of intact eggs was 10 percent lower than those of controls in both seasons. This amount of thinning is minimal since cracked eggshells, which would most likely be thinner, were not measured in either season.

Eggs that were removed from the nest were found in the water troughs. The shells recovered from the water were usually intact except for the apex of the shell, which was missing. The fact that the shell apexes were thinned and frequently cracked suggests that hens poked their mandibles into the cracked apexes and carried eggs to the water. Oring (1964) recorded removal of intact eggs from disturbed nest sites by incubating pintails (*Anas acuta*) and a mallard hen. Removal of eggshells by incubating hens has been observed in wild-nesting waterfowl by Hochbaum (1959:92) and Sowls (1955:104–105). Sowls (1955:106–109) put cracked eggshells in wild duck nests and observed shoveler (*Spatula clypeata*) and pintail hens removing these eggshells from the nests. The hens carried the eggshells in their bills and deposited the shells in nearby water areas.

The significant increase in shell breakage among eggs incubated by the hens as compared to those incubated mechanically shows that mechanical incubation does not reveal the importance of shell thinning to reproductive failure. Thin-shelled eggs are much more susceptible to breakage when eggs are incubated naturally. Although widespread shell thinning among anatids has not been reported, this study, using the black duck as a model, portrays the reality of reproductive failure via shell thinning and shell breakage among susceptible species sufficiently exposed to DDE.

LITERATURE CITED

ARMOUR, J. A., AND J. A. BURKE. 1970. Method for separating polychlorinated biphenyls from DDT and its analogs. J. Assoc. Of. Anal. Chem. 53(4):761–768.

BLUS, L. J., C. D. GISH, A. A. BELISLE, AND R. M. PROUTY. 1972. Logarithmic relationship of DDE residues to eggshell thinning. Nature 235(5338):376–377.

CADE, T. J., J. L. LINCER, C. M. WHITE, D. G. ROSENEAU, AND L. G. SWARTZ. 1971. DDE residues and eggshell changes in Alaskan falcons and hawks. Science 172(3986):955–957.

COCHRAN, W. G. 1943. Analysis of variance for percentages based on unequal numbers. Am. Stat. Assoc. J. 38(223):287–301.

DUNCAN, D. B. 1955. Multiple range and multiple F tests. Biometrics 11(1):1–42.

FYFE, R. W., J. CAMPBELL, B. HAYSON, AND K. HODSON. 1969. Regional population declines and organochlorine insecticides in Canadian prairie falcons. Can. Field Nat. 83(3):191–200.

HEATH, R. G., J. W. SPANN, AND J. F. KREITZER. 1969. Marked DDE impairment of mallard reproduction in controlled studies. Nature 224(5214):47–48.

———, ———, ———, AND C. VANCE. 1970. Effects of polychlorinated biphenyls on birds. Proc. Int. Ornithol. Congr. 15:475–485.

HICKEY, J. J., AND D. W. ANDERSON. 1968. Chlorinated hydrocarbons and eggshell changes in raptorial and fish-eating birds. Science 162(3850):271–273.

HOCHBAUM, H. A. 1959. The canvasback on a prairie marsh. 2nd ed. The Wildlife Management Institute, Washington, D.C. 207pp.

JEHL, J. R., JR. 1969. A wonderful bird was the pelican. Oceans 2(3,4):11–19.

KEITH, J. O., L. A. WOODS, JR., AND E. G. HUNT. 1970. Reproductive failure in brown pelicans on the Pacific coast. Trans. N. Am. Wildl. Nat. Resour. Conf. 35:56–64.

KRAMER C. Y. 1956. Extensions of multiple range tests to group means with unequal numbers of replications. Biometrics 12(3):307–310.

LONGCORE, J. R., F. B. SAMSON, AND T. W. WHITTENDALE, JR. 1971. DDE thins eggshells and lowers reproductive success of captive black ducks. Bull. Environ. Contam. and Toxicol. 6(6):485–490.

LUDWIG, J. P., AND C. S. TOMOFF. 1966. Reproductive success and insecticide residues in Lake Michigan herring gulls. The Jack-Pine Warbler 44(2):77–85.

ORING, L. W. 1964. Egg moving by incubating ducks. Auk 81(1):88–89.

PORTER, R. D., AND S. N. WIEMEYER. 1969. Dieldrin and DDT: effects on sparrow hawk eggshells and reproduction. Science 165(3889):199–200.

RATCLIFFE, D. A. 1958. Broken eggs in peregrine eyries. Br. Birds 51(1):23–26.

———. 1960. Broken eggs in the nest of sparrowhawk and golden eagle. Br. Birds 53(3):128–130.

———. 1967. Decrease in eggshell weight in certain birds of prey. Nature 215(5097):208–210.

———. 1970. Changes attributable to pesticides in egg breakage frequency and eggshell thickness in some British birds. J. Appl. Ecol. 7(1):67–107.

ROMANOFF, A. L., AND A. J. ROMANOFF. 1949. The avian egg. John Wiley and Sons., Inc., New York. 918pp.

SNEDECOR, G. W., AND W. G. COCHRAN. 1956. Statistical methods. 5th ed., Iowa State University Press, Ames. 534pp.

SOWLS, L. K. 1955. Prairie ducks. The Stackpole Co., Harrisburg, Pa. 193pp.

Accepted 4 June 1973.

A SURVEY OF CHLORINATED PESTICIDE RESIDUES IN BLACK DUCK EGGS[1]

W. L. REICHEL and C. E. ADDY, Bureau of Sport Fisheries and Wildlife, U.S. Department of Interior, Patuxent Wildlife Research Center, Laurel, MD

Winter surveys conducted by the Bureau of Sport Fisheries and Wildlife have shown that the black duck population in the Atlantic Flyway has declined since 1955 and is now at the lowest level recorded during the past 20 years. In addition, analysis of wings mailed in by hunters indicates a smaller proportion of young birds in the population. In 1960, the ratio of immature to adult birds was 2.11; in 1961—1.75; 1962—1.32; 1963—1.51; 1964—1.47; and 1965—1.38. These ratios are weighted to allow for regional differences in the kill, but they have not been adjusted for possible annual variations in vulnerability to shooting.

An exploratory survey of chlorinated pesticide residues in field collected eggs was initiated to help determine if these compounds were involved in the decline of the duck population.

METHODOLOGY

In the spring of 1964, two eggs from each of 85 nests were collected by cooperators from Canada to Maryland (Fig. 1). One egg from each clutch was randomly selected for analysis except that all eggs from New Jersey were analyzed. All analyses were made by thin layer chromatography; results were confirmed by gas chromatography on specimens picked at random from each State.

Preparation of Samples.—Only specimens that were not cracked were analyzed. Egg contents were ground with anhydrous sodium sulfate in a blender and extracted for 7 hours with petroleum ether in Soxhlet apparatus. Extracts were concentrated, taken up in 50 ml hexane and partitioned four times with 50 ml portions of acetonitrile. The acetonitrile was evaporated to dryness at room temperature, and the pesticides were eluted on a 2 × 15 cm column of partially inactivated florisil with 200 ml of 3:1 hexane-benzene mixture. Recoveries of 90 to 99 percent were obtained from chicken eggs fortified with 100 μg each of DDE, DDD, and DDT.

Analysis.—The purified extracts were concentrated and a semiquantitative determination was performed by TLC using aluminum oxide G and hexane as the developing solvent. The sensitivity achieved for quantitation was approximately 0.2 ppm in these samples.

The gas chromatograph was equipped with an electron capture detector, ¼″ × 44″ glass column packed with 5 percent SE-30 on 80/90 mesh Anakrom ABS and nitrogen carrier gas at 30 pounds pressure.

RESULTS AND DISCUSSION

The eggs contained DDT, DDE, DDD, and dieldrin, as shown in Table 1. In addition, trace amounts of heptachlor epoxide were detected in 31 specimens. DDT and DDE were found in all samples analyzed. Because of the presence of heterogeneous variance between the area means, even after a square root transformation, a statistical analysis of the data could not be performed. However, it would appear from these data that eggs

[1] Originally published in Bull. Environ. Contam. Toxicol. 3(3):174–179, 1968.

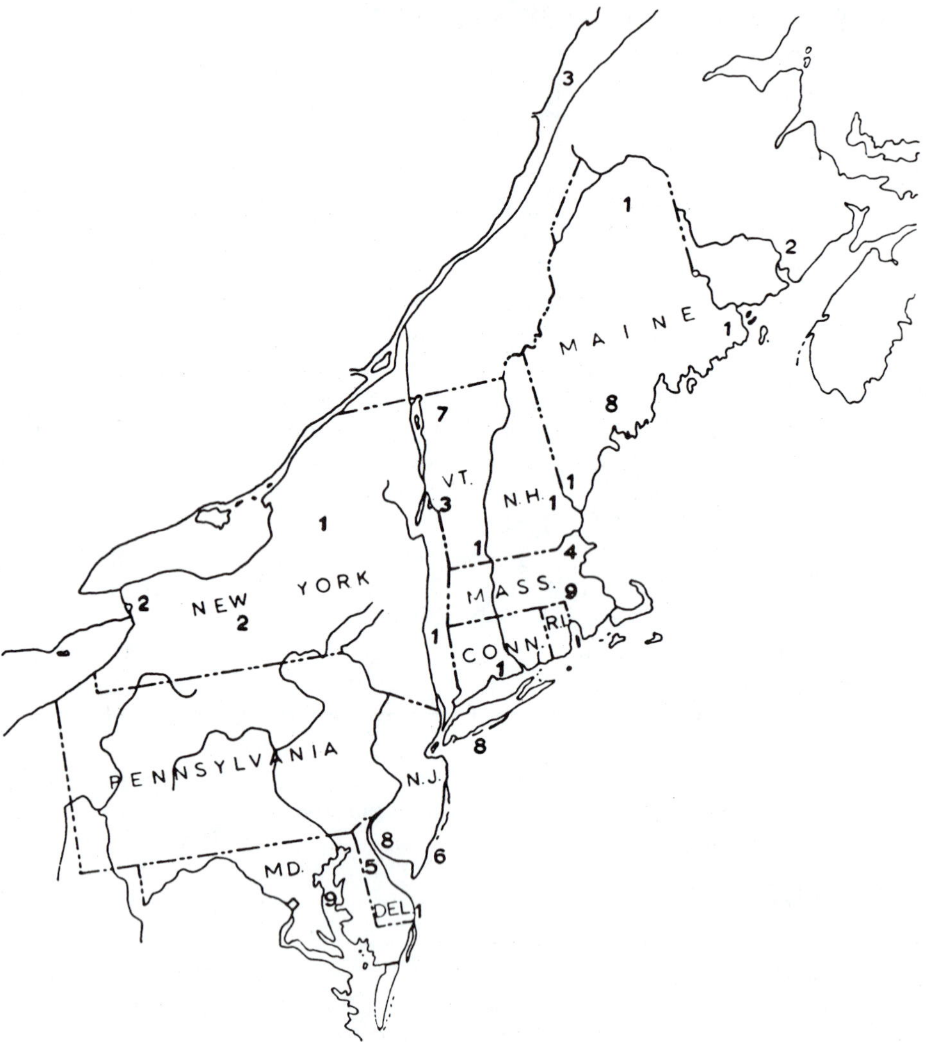

Fig. 1. Number and locations (within a 50 mile radius) of nests sampled.

from New Jersey, New York, and Massachusetts contained appreciably higher residues of DDT and metabolites than did those from other states.

The residue content of the pairs of eggs from the same nests are shown in Table 2. Results from the two eggs of a pair were randomly assigned to group A or B for presentation in the table. The eggs from the same nest compare favorably except for pair numbers 4, 5, and 6 where the differences are 5.3, 10.0, and 5.5 ppm, respectively.

This survey indicates that pesticide residues occur widely in the eggs of black ducks throughout the Atlantic Flyway. The quantity of these residues that will have an adverse effect on hatching and survival is not known, and will require experimental studies.

Table 1. Summary of mean residue values detected in black duck eggs.

Area	No. of eggs	ppm wet weight, ranges in parentheses[1]					
		DDE	SD	DDT	SD	DDD	Dieldrin
New Hampshire	1	1.4		0.5		T	0.2
Connecticut	1	2.1		2.1		T	0.2
Maryland	9	0.4 (0.1–1.2)	0.3	0.3 (T–0.8)	0.3	T (0–T)	T (0–0.2)
Vermont	11	1.2 (0.2–2.5)	0.8	0.5 (T–1.5)	0.4	0.1 (0–0.2)	T (0–T)
Maine	11	1.4 (0.2–2.4)	0.7	0.7 (T–1.6)	0.5	T (0–T)	T (0–0.5)
Canada	5	1.6 (0.9–2.5)	0.7	1.3 (0.5–3.1)	1.1	T (T–0.3)	T (0–0.2)
Delaware	6	1.7 (0.5–2.3)	0.7	1.7 (0.2–6.8)	2.6	0.2 (0–0.5)	T (0–T)
New York	14	4.4 (0.5–10.6)	3.3	3.1 (0.2–11.2)	3.4	1.3 (T–10.6)	0.3 (0–1.3)
New Jersey	23	4.6 (0.3–12.1)	3.5	2.3 (0.2–6.4)	2.0	0.3 (T–1.3)	0.2 (0–0.6)
Massachusetts	13	5.5 (1.4–10.5)	3.2	4.1 (0.5–10.5)	3.0	0.9 (T–2.5)	0.5 (0–2.0)

[1] SD = standard deviation, T = trace, less than 0.1 ppm.

Table 2. Residues in pairs of eggs collected in New Jersey.

Pair	ppm DDT + DDE + DDD		Difference
	Group A	Group B	
1	3.3	6.4	3.1
2	13.3	11.5	1.8
3	3.4	3.2	0.2
4	17.4	12.1	5.3
5	6.1	16.1	10.0
6	16.1	10.6	5.5
7	1.3	1.3	0.0
8	2.1	1.2	0.9
9	3.6	4.7	1.1

ACKNOWLEDGMENTS

We are indebted to the Biologist and Management personnel of the Fish and Wildlife Service, to Cooperators of the Atlantic Flyway, and Eastern Canada who submitted specimens and to Nancy C. Coon who prepared the area map.

SELECTED BIBLIOGRAPHY

Population Influences and Characteristics: Disease and Environmental Contaminants

ALBERS, P. H. 1980. Transfer of crude oil from contaminated water to bird eggs. Env. Res. 22:307–314.

ANDERSON, W. L. 1975. Lead poisoning in waterfowl at Rice Lake, Illinois. J. Wildl. Manage. 39(2):264–270.

ANDREWS, R., AND J. R. LONGCORE. 1969. The killing efficiency of soft iron shot. Trans. North Am. Wildl. Nat. Resour. Conf. 34:337–345.

AVERY, R. A. 1969. The ecology of tapeworm parasites in wildfowl. Wildfowl 20:59–68.

BELLROSE, F. C. 1959. Lead poisoning as a mortality factor in waterfowl populations. Ill. Nat. Hist. Survey Bull. 27(3):235–288.

BENNETT, G. F., AND C. D. MACINNES. 1972. Blood parasites of geese of the McConnell River, N.W.T. Can. J. Zool. 50(1):1–4.

———, A. D. SMITH, W. WHITMAN, AND M. CAMERON. 1975. Hematozoa of the Anatidae of the Atlantic flyway. II. The maritime provinces of Canada. J. Wildl. Dis. 11(2):280–289.

BLUS, L. J., C. J. HENNY, D. J. LENHART, AND E. CROMARTIE. 1979. Effects of heptachlor-treated cereal grains on Canada geese in the Columbia Basin. Pages 105–116 *in* R. L. Jarvis and J. C. Bartonek, eds. Management and biology of Pacific flyway geese. A symposium. Northwest Sect. of The Wildl. Soc. Oregon State Univ. Book Stores, Inc., Corvallis.

BRADSHAW, J. E., AND D. O. TRAINER. 1966. Some infectious diseases of waterfowl in the Mississippi flyway. J. Wildl. Manage. 30(3):570–576.

COCHRANE, R. L. 1976. Crippling effects of lead, steel and copper shot on experimental mallards. Wildl. Monogr. 51. 29pp.

CORNWELL, G. W., AND A. B. COWAN. 1963. Helminth populations of the canvasback (*Aythya valisineria*) and host-parasite-environmental interrelationships. Trans. North Am. Wildl. Nat. Resour. Conf. 28:173–199.

EASTIN, W. C., S. D. HASELTINE, AND H. C. MURRAY. 1980. Intestinal absorption of 5 chromium compounds in young black ducks. Toxicology Letters 6:193–197.

———, AND D. HOFFMAN. 1979. Biological effects of petroleum on aquatic birds. Pages 561–582 *in* C. Bates, Conference Chairman. Proc. Conf. on Assessment of Ecological Impacts of Oil Spills. Am. Inst. Biol. Sci., Arlington, VA.

ENRIGHT, C. A. 1971. A review of research on type "C" botulism among waterbirds. Colorado Coop. Wildl. Res. Unit, Colorado State Univ., Fort Collins. 22pp.

FALLIS, A. M. AND G. F. BENNETT. 1966. On the epizootiology of infections caused by *Leucocytozoon simondi* in Algonquin Park, Canada. Can. J. Zool. 44(1):101–112.

FLEMING, W. J. 1981. Environmental metal residues in tissues of canvasbacks. J. Wildl. Manage. 45:508–511.

FREDRICKSON, L. H., T. S. BASKETT, G.

K. BRAKHAGE, AND V. C. CRAVENS. 1977. Evaluating cultivation near duck blinds to reduce lead poisoning hazard. J. Wildl. Manage. 41(4):624–631.

FRIEND, M. 1981. Waterfowl management and waterfowl disease: independent or cause and effect relationship? Trans. N. Am. Wildl. Nat. Resour. Conf. 46. In Press.

HASELTINE, S. D., M. T. FINLEY, AND E. CROMARTIE. 1980. Reproduction and residue accumulation in black ducks fed Toxaphene. Arch. Environm. Contam. Toxicol. 9:461–471.

HEATH, R. G. 1969. Nationwide residues of organochlorine pesticides in wings of mallards and black ducks. Pestic. Monit. J. 3(2):115–123.

HERMAN, C. M. 1968. Blood parasites of North American waterfowl. Trans. North Am. Wildl. Nat. Resour. Conf. 33:348–359.

LOCKE, L. N., L. LEIBOVITZ, C. M. HERMAN, AND J. W. WALKER. 1968. Duck viral enteritis (duck plague) in North American waterfowl. Proc. Annu. Conf. S.E. Assoc. Game Fish Comm. 22:96–98.

———, V. STOTTS, AND G. WOLFHARD. 1970. An outbreak of fowl cholera in waterfowl on the Chesapeake Bay. J. Wildl. Dis. 6(4):404–407.

MCDOUGLE, H. C., AND R. W. VAUGHT. 1968. An epizootic of aspergillosis in Canada geese. J. Wildl. Manage. 32(2):415–417.

MIKULA, E. J., G. F. MARTZ, AND L. A. RYEL. 1977. A comparison of lead and steel shot for waterfowl hunting. Wildl. Soc. Bull. 5(1):3–8.

NEFF, J. A. 1955. Outbreak of aspergillosis in mallards. J. Wildl. Manage. 19(3):415–416.

NICKLAUS, R. H. 1976. Effects of lead and steel shot on shooting of flighted mallards. Wildl. Monogr. 51. 29pp.

SMITH, R. L., AND T. W. TOWNSEND. 1981. Attitudes of Ohio hunters toward steel shot. Wildl. Soc. Bull. 9(1):4–7.

STENDALL, R. C., E. CROMARTIE, S. N. WIEMEYER, AND J. R. LONGCORE. 1977. Organochlorine and mercury residues in canvasback duck eggs, 1972–73. J. Wildl. Manage. 41(3):453–457.

———, R. I. SMITH, K. P. BURNHAM, AND R. E. CHRISTENSEN. 1979. Exposure of waterfowl to lead: a nationwide survey of residues in wing bones of seven species, 1972–73. U.S. Dep. Inter. Fish and Wildl. Serv. Spec. Sci. Rep. 223. 12pp.

SZARO, R. C., N. C. COON, AND W. STOUT. 1980. Weathered petroleum: effects on mallard egg hatchability. J. Wildl. Manage. 44:709–713.

TRAINER, C. E. 1965. Lead poisoning of waterfowl on the Sauvie Island game management area. Proc. Annu. Conf. W. Assoc. State Game Fish Comm. 45:69–72.

WHITE, D. H., AND R. C. STENDELL. 1977. Waterfowl exposure to lead and steel shot on selected hunting areas. J. Wildl. Manage. 41(3):469–475.

Physiology and Energetics

THE BIOENERGETICS OF CAPTIVE BLUE-WINGED TEAL UNDER CONTROLLED AND OUTDOOR CONDITIONS[1]

RAY B. OWEN, JR.,[2] Department of Zoology, University of Illinois, Urbana, IL 61801

An understanding of avian bioenergetics is necessary before one can comprehend how birds utilize their natural resources. It is also important, from an evolutionary standpoint, for the understanding of how available energy regulates various activities during the yearly cycle and how it limits distribution. Until recently little work has been done to relate the energy requirements of birds in the field to those in the laboratory.

This investigation concerns the bioenergetics of caged Blue-winged Teal (*Anas discors*) held under controlled and outdoor conditions and was part of an attempt to find a method for estimating the energy requirements of free-living birds (Owen 1969). Special emphasis is placed on the comparison of outdoor and indoor birds and on the use of multiple regression analyses to partition the effects of numerous variables affecting metabolism.

Blue-winged Teal were selected for this study since there has been little bioenergetics work on waterfowl, or on 300–400 g birds. The teal were obtained from the breeding area around Delta, Manitoba, and Jamestown, North Dakota, and from fall migrants passing through Illinois. Blue-winged Teal breed predominantly in the northwest central part of the United States, through the prairie provinces of Canada, and up into British Columbia. They winter from the southern edge of the United States through Central America and the West Indies to the northern part of South America. They are one of the first waterfowl species to migrate south in the autumn and last to come north in the spring.

EXPERIMENTS UNDER CONTROLLED CONDITIONS

Methods

The relationships among photoperiod, temperature, and metabolism under laboratory conditions were determined by the method first developed by Kendeigh (1949). This method entails subtracting the caloric value of the excreta (excretory energy) from the caloric value of the food ingested (gross energy intake). The value obtained is equal to the amount of energy utilized (metabolized energy) and during periods of constant weight is called existence energy. Productive energy is that energy metabolized over and above that needed for existence. Efficiency of food utilization is equal to metabolized energy divided by gross energy intake.

The teal were held individually in metabolism cages 46 × 32½ × 45 cm. Some of the cages had a floating floor attached in each corner to a microswitch. Movement by the birds activated one of the switches and was recorded on an Esterline-Angus 20-point recorder. One unit of activity represented the activation of at least one microswitch during a 5-min period. Maximum activity was therefore 12 units per hr. A pan was placed under each cage to collect the feces, and a hole punched in one corner of the pan permitted drainage of excess water. Two male and three female teal (not always

[1] Originally published in Condor 72(2):153–163, 1970.

[2] Present address: 228 Forest Resources Bldg., University of Maine, Orono, ME 04473.

Table 1. Environmental characteristics within the temperature cabinets.

	Experimental temperatures		Relative humidity (%)	Light intensity (ft-c)
	Mean (°C)	Max. deviation (°C)		
High temperature walk-in	30, 35	1.5	35–50	20–70
Medium temperature walk-in	10, 20	2.0	85–95	75–85
Cold temperature walk-in	−18, −10, 0	2.5	80–90	75–80
Extreme cold reach-in unit	−28	4.0	90–98	10

the same birds) were used in all experiments and were acclimated to each experimental condition for about two weeks. Birds were fed Duck Growena, a prepared food in pellet form from Ralston Purina Company. The food had a nitrogen content of 3.02 ± 0.12 (mean ± SE) per cent and a caloric value of 4.38 ± 0.01 kcal/g.

Under each experimental condition three consecutive three-day periods of constant weight were obtained for each bird. Constant weight is defined as a change of less than 1.5 per cent in mean weight. Once acclimation had occurred, the birds were weighed to the nearest 0.1 g at 13:00 and given a known amount of food. Between 200 and 400 ml of water were given to each bird daily. At the end of each three-day period the teal were weighed and the number of feathers molted was recorded in grams, based upon previous determination of the weights of each type of feather. The unused food and excrement were also collected at this time and dried at 65°C to constant weight. Blem (1968) noted that there was no appreciable loss in the energy content of teal excrement dried at this temperature. The moisture content of the food supplied was determined for each period, and periodic determinations were made on a Parr oxygen-bomb calorimeter to determine its caloric value. The caloric value of the food not eaten subtracted from that of the initial amount of food gave the gross energy intake. The liquid effluent from the base pans was dried, weighed, and a caloric value obtained, which, when added to that of the excrement, gave excretory energy. Nitrogen content of the feces was obtained using the Kjeldahl method.

Photoperiods of 12 and 15 hr were chosen to determine the effects of photoperiod on metabolism. The former approximates the photoperiod encountered on the wintering grounds and during migration, while 15 hr is close to the photoperiod at the start of nesting. One group of birds was tested under each photoperiod at each of four temperatures (0, 10, 20, and 30°C). The 12-hr birds were tested at four additional temperatures (−28, −18, −10, and +35°C) to complete the relationship between temperature and energy utilization. In subsequent experiments temperature tolerances were studied by progressively acclimating two groups of teal to higher or lower temperatures.

The experiments were conducted in three walk-in temperature cabinets and a specially constructed refrigerator unit (Table 1). Humidity values at high temperatures were sufficiently low not to affect metabolism (Salt 1952, Wallgren 1954). At freezing temperatures small aquarium heaters kept the drinking water at about 1°C.

A probability level of 0.05 was required for significance in all statistical

Table 2. Data for controlled experiments.

Temperature (°C)	Weight: Male $\bar{x}$ g	SE	N	Weight: Female $\bar{x}$ g	SE	N	Feather loss/3 days $\bar{x}$ g	SE	N
12 hr photoperiod									
35	352.0	11.0	2	309.3	8.5	3	.0708	.0259	5
30	348.5	5.5	2	293.3	15.4	3	.1256	.0836	5
20	340.0	17.0	2	303.3	15.8	3	.0418	.0252	5
10	343.0	5.0	2	297.7	16.6	3	.1388	.0832	5
0	359.0		1	307.7	16.7	3	.4601	.2080	5
−10	360.0		1	316.3	2.6	3	.1437	.0904	5
−18	384.0	3.0	2	334.0	4.0	3	.0378	.0050	5
−28	360.0	11.0	2	321.5	2.5	3	.0428	.0101	4
15 hr photoperiod									
30	329.0		1	307.7	3.3	2	.4247	.1403	4
20	342.5	8.5	2	306.3	4.8	3	.2895	.1004	5
10	325.5	0.5	2	315.7	7.6	3	.1879	.0354	5
2	323.5	4.5	2	307.7	8.2	3	.1015	.0377	5
0	411.0		1	309.3	11.6	3	.2181	.0724	4

testing. The nonlinear multiple regression analyses were performed as suggested by Zar (1969).

Results and Discussion

Photoperiod.—Teal on a 12-hr photoperiod showed significant weight gains at lower temperatures (Table 2), and under both photoperiods mean weights of males and females were significantly different at all temperatures.

Between 0 and 30°C there was no significant difference between existence metabolism under 12- and 15-hr photoperiods. Williams (1965) obtained similar results with Canada Geese (*Branta canadensis*). The teal exhibited some nocturnal activity under all conditions, which may be characteristic of waterfowl (Williams 1965).

Temperature and Metabolism.—Regression lines calculated for gross energy intake and existence metabolism were significantly different between males and females when metabolism was placed on a per bird basis, although excretory energy values were the same for both sexes. The relationships between temperature and existence energy for each sex and between temperature and gross energy for males were linear (Fig. 1), while gross energy intake vs. temperature for females was best represented by a quartic equation. Excretory energy exhibited a quadratic regression on temperature, being low at high temperatures and leveling off at low temperatures.

The metabolic differences between males and females are apparently due to differences in mean weight (males, 362.84 ± 10.41 g; females, 329.6 ± 2.98 g). When existence energy is expressed on a per kilogram of body weight basis, females have a slightly higher value than males. When calculated per unit of surface area, or per weight$^{0.67}$, there was no

→

Fig. 1. Relationship of gross energy intake (GEI), existence energy, and excretory energy to ambient temperature in Blue-winged Teal under controlled conditions. All regression equations are shown ± standard error of estimate.

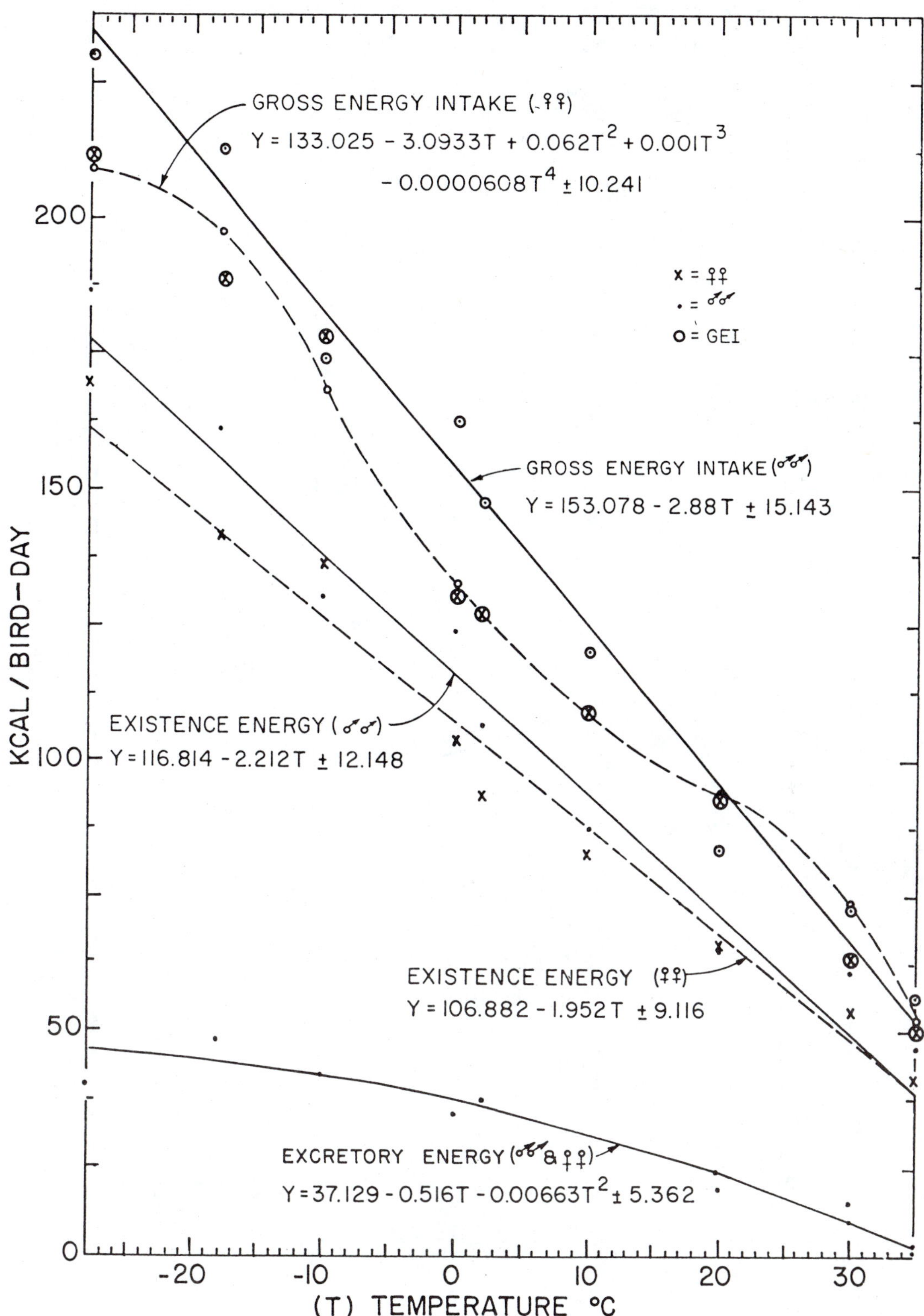
GROSS ENERGY INTAKE (♀♀)
Y = 133.025 - 3.0933T + 0.062T² + 0.001T³ - 0.0000608T⁴ ± 10.241
x = ♀♀
• = ♂♂
⊙ = GEI
GROSS ENERGY INTAKE (♂♂)
Y = 153.078 - 2.88T ± 15.143
EXISTENCE ENERGY (♂♂)
Y = 116.814 - 2.212T ± 12.148
EXISTENCE ENERGY (♀♀)
Y = 106.882 - 1.952T ± 9.116
EXCRETORY ENERGY (♂♂ & ♀♀)
Y = 37.129 - 0.516T - 0.00663T² ± 5.362
KCAL / BIRD-DAY
(T) TEMPERATURE °C
200
150
100
50
0
-20
-10
0
10
20
30

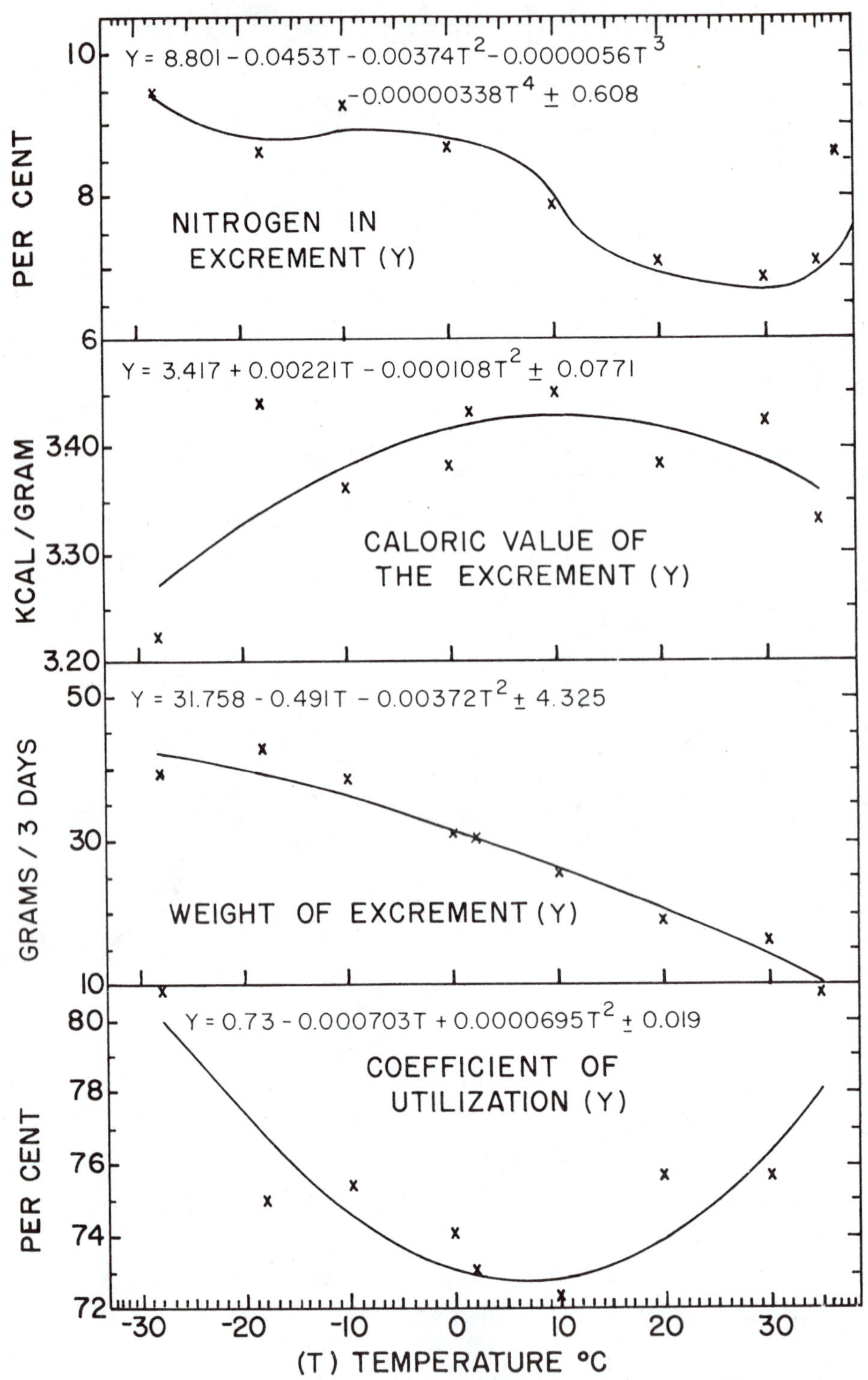
Y = 8.801 - 0.0453T - 0.00374T2 - 0.0000056T3
-0.00000338T4 ± 0.608
PER CENT
NITROGEN IN EXCREMENT (Y)
Y = 3.417 + 0.00221T - 0.000108T2 ± 0.0771
KCAL / GRAM
CALORIC VALUE OF THE EXCREMENT (Y)
Y = 31.758 - 0.491T - 0.00372T2 ± 4.325
GRAMS / 3 DAYS
WEIGHT OF EXCREMENT (Y)
Y = 0.73 - 0.000703T + 0.0000695T2 ± 0.019
PER CENT
COEFFICIENT OF UTILIZATION (Y)
(T) TEMPERATURE °C

difference between sexes for gross energy intake, excretory energy, or existence metabolism vs. temperature.

Excretory energy leveled off below −10°C, although a linear relationship has been shown in other species (Kendeigh 1949, Davis 1955, West 1960, Williams 1965). The curvilinear relationship in teal is due primarily to a drop in the actual amount of fecal material voided and partly to a decreased caloric value of the feces (Fig. 2). This decrease in the caloric value of the feces at lower temperatures brings an increase in the coefficient of utilization (Fig. 2). Except for an indication in geese (*Branta canadensis*; Williams 1965) and redpolls (*Acanthis* spp.; Brooks 1968), other species (all passerines) have failed to exhibit such an increase (Kendeigh 1949, Davis 1955, West 1960, Zimmerman 1965). The coefficient of utilization also increased at high temperatures. Both below and above 30°C the nitrogen content of the feces increased (Fig. 2).

At low temperatures the regression lines for gross energy intake and excretory energy diverge, indicating that there may be more protein assimilation at this extreme. Since the birds were at constant weight and presumably in nitrogen balance, the excess protein had to be broken down and the nitrogen excreted. This might account for the increased nitrogen in the excreta at this extreme and also the lowered caloric value, as uric acid contains less energy per gram than the food ingested.

Temperature Tolerance.—Blue-winged Teal can tolerate an unusually wide range of temperatures. The lower temperature limit was not obtained with the facilities available, but individual birds withstood mean temperatures ranging from −42 to −48°C with no apparent adverse effects. This is remarkable for a species that rarely encounters freezing temperatures in the field.

Perhaps even more remarkable is their ability to withstand high temperatures. Williams (1965) noted that the high lethal ambient temperature for Canada Geese was close to 41°C and Kendeigh (1969) stated that the ambient lethal temperature for some passerine species is 46–47°C. One Blue-winged Teal died at 46°C, but three others maintained weight at 48°C and tolerated 50°C for 24 hr, at which time the experiment was terminated. Teal are probably able to withstand high temperatures because of their ability to pant vigorously and also to consume large amounts of water. The birds which were least stressed by heat passed as much as one liter of water per day through the alimentary tract. The water in the dishes was 5–6°C below air temperature due to evaporative cooling.

The dense plumage of teal reduces the effects of both temperature extremes. At low ambient temperatures the outward movement of heat is retarded, while the reverse is true when ambient temperatures exceed body temperatures. There was no molt at either temperature extreme.

Weight Change and Metabolism.—The relationship of weight gain and weight loss to metabolized energy (ME) was calculated at four different temperatures: 30, 10, 0, and −10°C. The slopes of the linear regression lines for ME vs. weight

---

←

Fig. 2. Relationship of the nitrogen content, caloric value, and weight of the excrement, and coefficient of utilization to ambient temperature in Blue-winged Teal under controlled conditions.

gain or weight loss were not different at any temperature, nor were they different between temperatures. This permits the use of a single mean value, 5.0 kcal/g change in weight per day, to express the relationship between metabolism and weight change. This value is lower than some previous estimates (Odum 1960, 9.0 kcal; King 1961, 7.0 kcal) and may be attributed partially to changes in water balance.

A Modified Method for Determining Existence Energy.—The finding that the change in metabolism associated with weight gain and loss is the same and that this does not vary with temperature enables one to determine existence energy by a new, quick method. First a linear regression equation for metabolism vs. change in weight for each experimental condition is calculated. This not only gives information about the relationship of energy and weight change, as shown above, but, by plotting the Y-intercept for each temperature against temperature, a line for existence energy is obtained. A regression line calculated in this manner did not differ significantly from the line for existence metabolism calculated in the conventional way and given earlier in this paper.

EXPERIMENTS OUT-OF-DOORS

Methods

In early August 1966 two male and three female teal that had completed their postnuptial molt were placed in outdoor metabolism cages. The cages provided protection from rain, direct sunlight, and strong north winds. During the first week of December one female died and was replaced. Temperature, activity, molt, and metabolism were continuously recorded for 15 months; at the end of this period the birds had again completed the postnuptial molt.

The same methods were used to measure metabolism, activity, and molt as had been employed in the laboratory. The cages of one female and one male were wired for recording activity, but during midwinter the floating floors often froze and these periods were eliminated from all analyses. Activity was calculated as total daily activity and per cent of total possible nocturnal activity between civil sunset and civil sunrise. A thermocouple was placed next to one metabolism cage and temperatures were recorded automatically every 20 min. From these readings a mean temperature was obtained for each three-day period.

Outdoor existence energy was determined by plotting metabolized energy against temperature for all periods when the weight of the ducks held constant (±1.5 per cent). This was done on a seasonal and yearly basis. Annual changes in productive energy were obtained by comparing metabolized energy during a period with existence energy calculated for the temperature occurring during that period.

Results and Discussion

All birds exhibited the same general trends throughout the year (Fig. 3).

Metabolized Energy (ME).—The regression equation $Y = -0.962T + 5.81W^{0.512} + 5.316\Delta S - 0.224PT - 1.344P + 16.67M \pm 13.656$ (where Y = metabolized energy, T = temperature, W = body weight, ΔW = change in body weight, PT = preceding temperature, P = photoperiod, and M = molt) was calculated to determine the relationship between ME and the variables measured. Throughout the entire year major changes in ME were associated with changes in

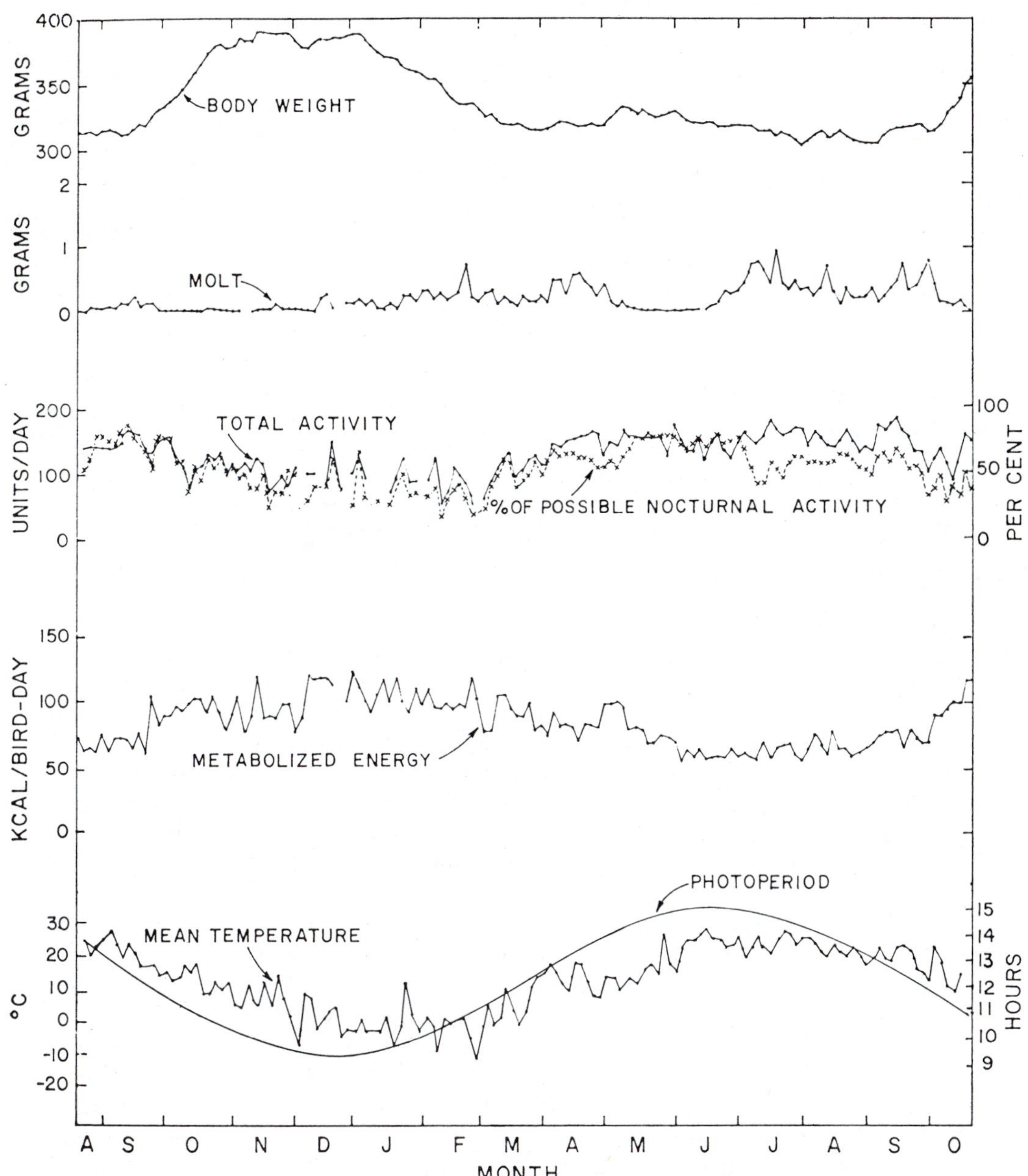

Fig. 3. Seasonal changes in body weight, molt, activity, and metabolized energy of five caged Blue-winged Teal held out-of-doors. Ambient temperature and photoperiod are given for comparison.

weight. The caloric value of 1 g change in weight varied between 2.9 and 7.0 during the year. Dolnik (1968), working with the Chaffinch (*Fringilla coelebs*), noted that the values varied between 2.0 and 9.0 kcal/g, depending on the season, obesity, energy balance, and degree of activity.

The relationship between ME and

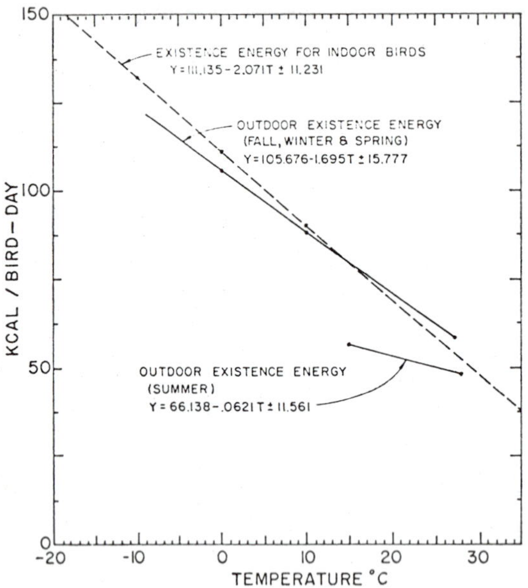

Fig. 4. Comparison of existence energy of five Blue-winged Teal held out-of-doors with birds tested under controlled conditions.

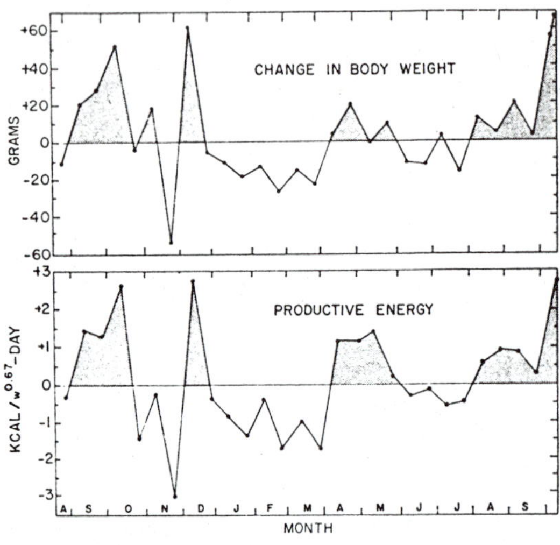

Fig. 5. Seasonal changes in body weight and productive energy for one Blue-winged Teal (R-12). Zero productive energy represents existence energy at the particular temperature occurring during the period of measurement.

temperature appears to be quite complex. Davis (1955) and Olson (1965) stated that caged song birds out-of-doors do not adjust their rate of food intake as fast as the temperature changes, especially when the temperature change is rapid. In the present study the mean temperature of the three-day period preceding the period for which data are given had a significant effect on ME, indicating that more than three days are required for complete metabolic adjustment. With a sudden drop in temperature, food intake often dropped initially or remained the same, as the birds relied on their fat reserves. After a few days the teal would then accelerate their rate of feeding, often continuing after the temperature again rose. This indicated that the birds in the field may attempt to "wait out" cold snaps, seeking additional food only when body reserves reach some low level.

Body weight and photoperiod both had a significant effect on ME. Although no dependence could be found for metabolism on weight of feathers dropped during each three-day period, the importance of molt was apparent when it was prorated over the period of new feather growth. Variation in total daily activity and nocturnal activity as measured had no significant effect on metabolism.

Existence and Productive Energy.—No significant differences were found between equations for outdoor existence energy vs. temperature, calculated separately for autumn, winter, and spring, but the regression line for summer had a significantly flatter slope (Fig. 4). During the summer the mean temperature range is small (12.5°C) and metabolic adjustments are slight in relation to changes in temperature. Perhaps physical regulation of body temperature is more important at this time. Both existence energy regression lines for outdoor birds have significantly flatter slopes than for indoor birds. Davis (1955) and West (1960) found sim-

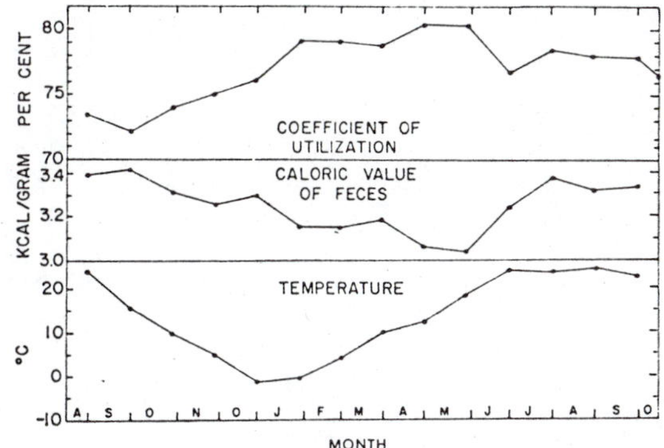

Fig. 6. Seasonal changes in the caloric value of the feces and coefficient of utilization of five Blue-winged Teal held out-of-doors. Ambient temperature is given for comparison.

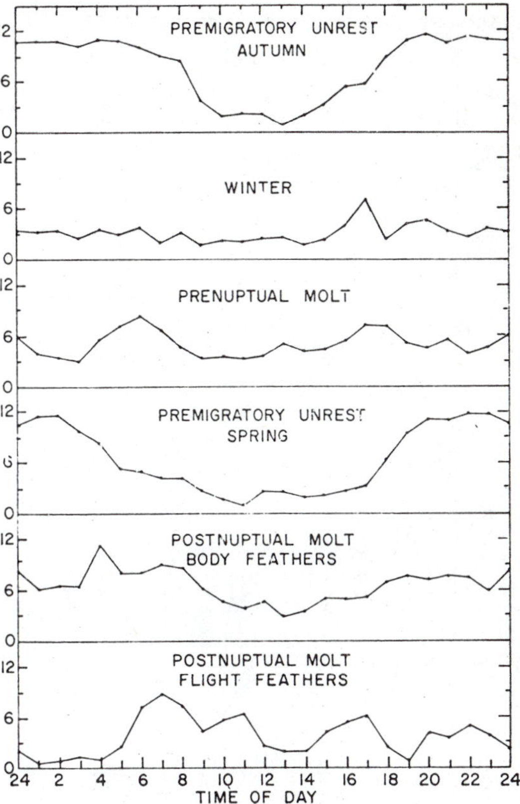

Fig. 7. Changes in the daily pattern of activity of Blue-winged Teal during premigratory periods, winter, and molt. Data are averaged for two caged birds held out-of-doors. Left hand scale is in counts per hour.

ilar results and attributed them to a lag effect, due to sluggish adjustment to variable ambient temperatures. Further evidence for this has been given in the preceding section.

Productive energy was calculated in two ways, first using the existence energy values from the indoor birds, and then using the seasonal existence energy values from the outdoor birds, but no difference could be detected between the two methods. There was a significant correlation between weight change and productive energy throughout the year (Fig. 5).

Coefficient of Utilization and Caloric Value of the Feces.—The coefficient of utilization and the caloric value of the feces show similar significant but opposite seasonal changes (Fig. 6). During winter, teal became more efficient in the digestion and utilization of food, and the caloric value per unit weight of the feces decreased as temperature decreased. Brooks (1965) noted a similar relation in redpolls (*Acanthis* spp.). This apparent temperature response is very much like the one exhibited by the teal maintained under constant conditions. The outdoor birds did not respond immediately to the increasing temperatures of spring but maintained their high efficiency until about 1 June.

Seasonal Changes in Body Weight, Molt, and Activity.—Body weight of the teal increased about 25 per cent during the fall (Fig. 3). The reaction to decreasing temperature is typical of many song birds wintering in the North Temperate Zone (Baldwin and Kendeigh 1938, Helms and Drury 1960, King and Farner 1966). Beginning in January, while ambient temperature continued low, however, the birds began gradually to lose weight. A small amount of vernal fat deposition began at the end of April and

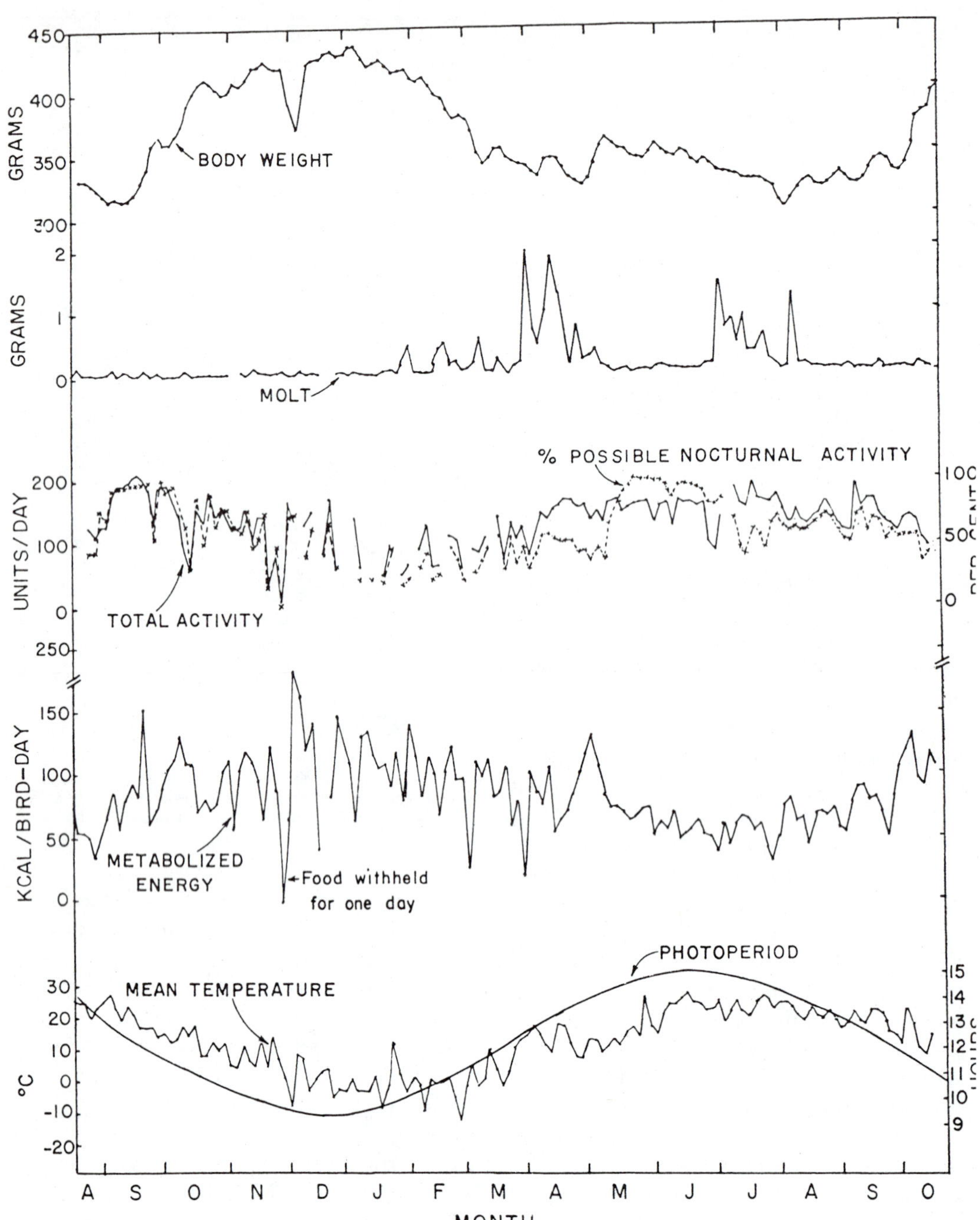

Fig. 8. Seasonal changes in body weight, molt, activity, and metabolized energy of one female Blue-winged Teal held out-of-doors.

lasted nearly two weeks. This premigratory response was delayed by the prenuptial molt and occurred almost one month after Blue-winged Teal normally begin migrating through the Champaign, Illinois, area (Smith 1930). Body weights were lowest during the summer.

The prenuptial molt, involving only body contour feathers, occurred mainly during April and ended abruptly nine days after the beginning of "premigratory" fat deposition. The postnuptial molt included body feathers and flight feathers. The body eclipse molt occurred in July. Only three ducks dropped their flight feathers, one in August and two in September. This delayed or non-occurrence of flight feather molt is typical of ducks confined in small cages and may have interfered with the development of an autumn "premigratory" fat deposition.

Throughout the year there were considerable changes in the amount of daily activity and its temporal pattern (Fig. 7). During migratory periods nocturnal activity increased. This type of response has been used to indicate a nocturnal migrant's physiological readiness to migrate. In the winter nocturnal activity was minimal. West (1962) noted that activity during cold weather reduces the insulative capacity of the feathers and increases heat loss. Molt has a depressing effect on nocturnal activity, especially during the flightless period. At this time teal in the wild are vulnerable to predation and become quite secretive.

Figure 8 shows the close relationship between the physiological, behavioral, and environmental changes during the spring migratory period. The prenuptial molt lasted three months but was heaviest during April. It was immediately followed by a period of hyperphagia and a 50-g increase in body weight. Nocturnal activity also increased at this time but only after the molt was completed and peak weight was reached. The sequence of events indicates that there may be some inhibitory effect of molt on prevernal fat deposition and nocturnal activity. Kendeigh et al. (1960) associated this with energy conservation.

CONCLUSION

The present study was an attempt to determine the effects of numerous variables on the energetics of a species. With the development of computer facilities and nonlinear multiple regression analyses (Zar 1969) it is now possible, as shown in this paper, to make detailed studies of caged birds held out-of-doors and to assign relative importance to each of the pertinent variables. These experiments better approximate field conditions and permit the study of variables rarely measured in the laboratory. The similarity in the effects of temperature, body weight, and weight change on metabolism under controlled and outdoor conditions in this study supports the use of outdoor experiments. Helms (1968) used a multiple regression analysis to study the metabolism of White-throated Sparrows (*Zonotrichia albicollis*) under outdoor conditions and came to a similar conclusion. When energy studies are made of free-living birds, this will be one way to partition the effects of the many variables occurring in the field.

With the aid of regression models, the yearly energy budget of an individual under natural conditions can be estimated. This is the ultimate aim of this general research program in bioenergetics. Obviously, when the energy budgets of individuals are known, this can be projected into energy budgets of whole populations to provide important information on the role of the species in the energy flow of the ecosystem.

SUMMARY

The bioenergetics of caged Blue-winged Teal were studied under controlled and outdoor conditions with special emphasis on the effects of different variables on metabolism. At temperatures above 0°C there was no difference in the existence metabolism of ducks held under 12- and 15-hr photoperiods. Existence metabolism was different for males and females and was associated with the differences in weight of the two sexes.

Excretory energy varied curvilinearly and inversely with temperature, leveling off at temperatures below −20°C. This relationship was due to a drop in the amount of fecal material voided and to a decrease in the caloric value of the feces at these temperatures. The coefficient of food utilization increased at both high and low temperatures, and opposite changes occurred in the caloric value of the feces. The nitrogen content of the feces increased both above and below 30°C.

Upper and lower lethal temperatures were not reached, but teal withstood ambient temperatures of −48 and +50°C.

The caloric equivalent of a gram change in weight was 5.0 kcal/bird-day for indoor birds. For outdoor birds the value varied between 2.9 and 7.0 with a yearly average of 5.3 kcal/bird-day.

A modified method for determining existence metabolism was developed which enables the use of birds that are not maintaining constant weight. Multiple linear and nonlinear regression analysis was used to determine the effects of different variables on the metabolism of caged teal kept out-of-doors. Body weight, change in body weight, and molt correlated positively with metabolism, while temperature and photoperiod exhibited a negative correlation with metabolism. Existence metabolism out-of-doors was the same during the autumn, winter, and spring but different during the summer. The slope for existence metabolism vs. temperature out-of-doors was flatter than indoors; the difference may be associated with the birds' inability to adjust completely to rapidly fluctuating temperatures.

Changes in body weight were positively correlated with changes in available productive energy. The coefficient of utilization and caloric value of the feces out-of-doors showed similar but opposite seasonal changes. The body weights of caged teal held out-of-doors increased about 25 per cent in the fall, decreased during the winter, and increased slightly at the end of April during the premigratory period.

Three molts occurred during the year: an extended prenuptial molt which peaked in April, a postnuptial molt of body feathers during July, and a delayed postnuptial molt of flight feathers during August and September. Total daily activity decreased during periods of molt and was lowest during the winter. Nocturnal activity increased sharply during premigratory periods.

ACKNOWLEDGMENTS

This report is based upon a thesis submitted in partial fulfillment of the requirement for the Ph.D. degree at the University of Illinois. I wish to express my appreciation to S. C. Kendeigh for suggesting the problem and for continued guidance throughout the course of the work. Thanks are also due to J. H. Zar for statistical aid and review of the manuscript. I am also grateful to C. Blem and R. Faber for laboratory assistance and to

H. A. Hochbaum, C. W. Dane, and F. C. Bellrose for supplying the birds. Finally, I wish to thank my wife, Sue, for her many weeks of data compilation and typing. The project was supported by NSF grants to S. C. Kendeigh. Use of the University of Illinois IBM 360/75 system was made possible by PHS funds granted to the Zoology Department by the University Research Board.

LITERATURE CITED

BALDWIN, S. P., AND S. C. KENDEIGH. 1938. Variation in the weights of birds. Auk 40:416–467.

BLEM, C. R. 1968. Determination of caloric and nitrogen content of excreta voided by birds. Poultry Sci. 47:1205–1208.

BROOKS, W. S. 1965. Bioenergetics of redpolls (*Acanthis*) in relation to their distribution. Ph.D. Thesis. Univ. Illinois, Urbana.

———. 1968. Comparative adaptations of the Alaskan redpolls to the Arctic environment. Wilson Bull. 80:253–280.

DAVIS, E. A. 1955. Seasonal changes in the energy balance of the English Sparrow. Auk 72: 385–411.

DOLNIK, V. R. 1968. Caloric value of the daily variation of body weight in birds. International studies on sparrows, I.B.P., P.T. Sect. 2:89–95.

HELMS, C. W. 1968. Food, fat, and feathers. Amer. Zool. 8:151–167.

———, AND W. H. DRURY, JR. 1960. Winter and migratory weight and fat studies of some North American buntings. Bird-Banding 31:1–40.

KENDEIGH, S. C. 1949. Effect of temperature and season on the energy resources of the English Sparrow. Auk 66:113–127.

———. 1969. Energy responses of birds to their thermal environments. Wilson Bull. 81:441–449.

———, G. C. WEST, AND G. W. COX. 1960. Annual stimulus for spring migration in birds. Anim. Behav. 8:180–185.

KING, J. R. 1961. The bioenergetics of vernal premigratory fat deposition in the White-crowned Sparrow. Condor 63:128–142.

———, AND D. S. FARNER. 1966. The adaptive role of winter fattening in the White-crowned Sparrow with comments on its regulation. Amer. Naturalist 100:403–418.

ODUM, E. P. 1960. Lipid deposition in nocturnal migrant birds. Proc. XII Int. Ornithol. Congr., Helsinki, pp. 563–576.

OLSON, J. B. 1965. Effect of temperature and season on the bioenergetics of the eastern Field Sparrow, *Spizella pusilla*. Ph.D. Thesis. Univ. Illinois, Urbana.

OWEN, R. B., JR. 1969. Heart rate, a measure of metabolism in Blue-winged Teal. Comp. Biochem. Physiol. 31:431–436.

SALT, G. W. 1952. The relation of metabolism to climate and distribution in three finches of the genus *Carpodacus*. Ecol. Monogr. 22:121–152.

SMITH, F. 1930. Records of spring migration of birds at Urbana, Illinois, 1903–1922. Illinois Nat. Hist. Sur. Bull. 19:105–117.

WEST, G. C. 1960. Seasonal variation in the energy balance of the Tree Sparrow in relation to migration. Auk 77:306–329.

———. 1962. Responses and adaptations of wild birds to environmental temperature. Pp. 291–333. *In* J. P. Hannon and E. Viereck [eds.] Comparative physiology of temperature regulation, Part 3. Arctic Aeromedical Laboratory, Fort Wainwright, Alaska.

WALLGREN, H. 1954. Energy metabolism of two species of the genus *Emberiza* as correlated with distribution and migration. Acta Zool. Fenn. 84:1–110.

WILLIAMS, J. E. 1965. Energy requirements of the Canada Goose in relation to distribution and migration. Ph.D. Thesis, Univ. Illinois, Urbana.

ZAR, J. H. 1969. The use of the allometric model for avian standard metabolism-body weight relationships. Comp. Biochem. Physiol. 29: 227–234.

ZIMMERMAN, J. L. 1965. Bioenergetics of the Dickcissel, *Spiza americana*. Physiol. Zool. 38: 370–389.

EVIDENCE OF STRESS RESPONSE IN BREEDING BLUE-WINGED TEAL[1]

H. J. HARRIS, JR., Iowa State University, Ames[2]

Abstract: Blue-winged teal hens (*Anas discors*) were studied under natural conditions during the reproductive season of 1966 and 1967 to investigate the hypothesis that reproduction predisposes female waterfowl to stress-associated mortality. Physiological parameters were monitored during prelaying, laying, and incubation periods.

A rapid loss in body weight was associated with the onset of incubation. The rate of loss was estimated to be 6.2 g/day from the time the 7th egg was laid until the 5th day of incubation; rate of weight loss declined after the 5th day of incubation.

A quadratic response of plasma-free fatty acids was associated with declining condition of incubating hens while glucose and non-protein nitrogen increased linearly with declining condition.

Acidophil levels were highest in incubating hens and lowest in prelaying hens. A gradual increase was observed over the reproductive period.

Plasma-free amino acids and acetoacetate could not be correlated with declining condition of incubating hens.

It is suggested that acidophilis and shifts in plasma constituents of incubating birds examined in this study are related to increased adrenal corticoid activity. It is further suggested that hypercortical adrenal (interrenal) activity is a response to energy demands accompanying reproduction.

A preponderance of drakes in spring populations of some North American waterfowl has been recognized for some time (Hochbaum 1959:15). Although this phenomenon is most marked in the inland diving ducks (tribe Aythyini) it also occurs among dabbling ducks (Anatini) such as the blue-winged teal (Sowls 1955:164, Bellrose et al. 1961). From analyses of band returns, Bellrose and Chase (1950) concluded that there was a higher rate of loss among mallard (*Anas platyrhynchos*) hens than among mallard drakes. Further analysis of year-class band data suggested that greater hen mortality occurred outside of the hunting season; this mortality was attributed to high vulnerability of hens during the reproductive season. Bellrose et al. (1961) later suggested that the differential mortality of hens may be due to stress as defined by Selye (1956:3). Bellrose et al. (1961:425) postulated that the physiological demands of reproduction "places the hens in much greater jeopardy to stress than the drakes, which experience marked depletion of energy only through the period of the post-nuptial molt." He further pointed out that little is known about the effects of stress as described by Selye in relation to waterfowl mortality. Hanson (1962) studied condition factors and seasonal stresses of Canada geese (*Branta canadensis*) and suggested that mobilization of body resources for egg production constituted a stress.

Blood level of non-protein nitrogen (NPN), free fatty acids (FFA), glucose and acidophils (both heterophils and eosinophils) in blue-winged teal were found to be responsive to corticosterone administration and fasting (Harris, unpublished manuscript). It was hypothesized that if female waterfowl undergo stress during the breeding season as a result of energy demands of laying or restricted feeding during incubation, then there should be an increased adrenal activity which would cause an alteration of the level of plasma constituents and formed elements of the

---

[1] Journal Paper No. J. 6596 of the Iowa Agriculture and Home Economics Experiment Station, Ames, Iowa. Project No. 1504.

[2] Current address: University of Wisconsin—Green Bay, Green Bay.

Originally published in J. Wildl. Manage. 34(4):747–755, 1970.

blood. More specifically, it was proposed that increased adrenal corticoid secretion would be reflected by increased levels of plasma (NPN), (FFA), glucose, aceto-acetate, free amino acids (FFA), and acidophilia. Body weight loss also should be expected to accompany utilization of energy stores.

The feasibility of the hypothesis was examined by studying wild blue-winged teal under natural conditions. Physiological parameters were followed in wild hens during all periods of the breeding season.

MATERIAL AND METHODS

Field studies were carried out in northwest Iowa during the spring and summer of 1966 and 1967. Blood samples and physical measurements were obtained from wild hens during prelaying, laying, and incubation periods. Birds were trapped on Dewey's Pasture, located in Clay and Palo Alto Counties of northwest Iowa. The study area has been described in detail elsewhere (Hayden 1943).

Traps and trapping

Birds were captured using single lead, baited funnel traps. During spring, when blood samples were secured from bait-trapped hens, trapping was confined to late morning hours.

Nests were found by observation from blinds and by searching. Nesting hens were captured with the Weller nest-trap (Weller 1957*b*) and the Salyer nest-trap (Salyer 1962). The traps were set between 4:30 and 6:30 AM. They were sprung manually about 11:00 AM or sometimes automatically by the return of an incubating hen to a Weller trap.

Night-lighting, as described by Cummings and Hewitt (1964), was employed to capture some blue-winged teal at the time of brood-rearing and molting.

Weights and measurements

Hens were weighed to the nearest gram and measured at the time of capture.

Culmen and keel measurements were taken with a vernier caliper to the nearest 0.1 mm. The chord of the culmen length was taken along the dorsal median line with the tip of the nail to the "V" of feathers on the forehead. The keel was measured from the anterior tip to the posterior margin along the ventral median surface of the sternum. Measurement was made to the nearest 0.1 cm.

Also noted at the time of capture was the number of eggs in the nest. In addition, the hen was palpated in the ventral abdominal region to ascertain whether there was an egg in the magnum or shell gland. Eggs were field-candled, using the technique described by Weller (1956), to establish the stage of embryonic development. Eggs of known stage of incubation were used as a standard.

Blood sampling and handling

Blood samples were drawn as soon after capture as possbible. When samples could not be taken immediately, the hens were held for less than 1 hour in a covered retaining box where they rested quietly. Each blood sample was drawn from the brachial vein into a 5 ml heparin treated syringe, transferred to a clean glass culture tube, sealed, and immediately chilled on ice. A sample was taken at this time for acidophil counts.

After birds had been sampled, the blood was taken to the field laboratory where the plasma was separated by centrifugation. The pipetted plasma samples were placed

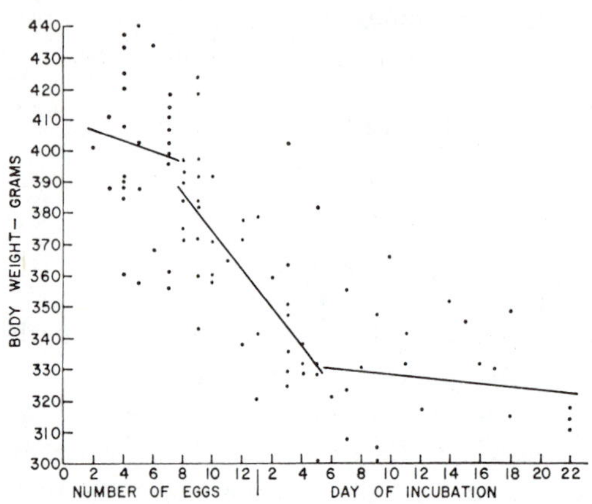

Fig. 1. Regression of body weight on number of eggs in nest or day of incubation.

in hard plastic vials and stored in deep freeze at –15 C until analyzed.

Acidophil counts

Acidophils were counted by the semi-indirect method of Wiseman (1931). The dilute solution (3 mg dye/100 ml) was used in conjunction with a 4–5 hour staining time. Mixing was accomplished with 10-minute minimum mixing time in a Bryan-Garrey pipette rotor. Counts were made in the standard manner (Wintrobe 1967).

Analysis of plasma constituents

Plasma analysis of acetoacetate (AcAc), free amino acids (FAA), non-protein nitrogen (NPN), free fatty acids (FFA), and glucose were conducted. Although desirable, the quantity of plasma available was insufficient to permit duplicate analyses of all plasma samples. As an alternate method of estimating precision and accuracy, control "plasma" purchased under the name of Lab-trol was analyzed in conjunction with the unknowns.

Plasma acetoacetate was estimated colorimetrically by the method of Schilke and Johnson (1965). Analysis of free amino acids was performed using the modified ninhydrin colorimetric method described by Fisher et al. (1963). The modified Folin and Wu method outlined by Henry (1965) was used for the determination of blood glucose. Non-protein nitrogen was estimated employing wet digestion with H_2SO_4 and the Berthelot color reaction (Henry 1965). Plasma-free fatty acids were determined using the modified method of Duncombe as described by Itaya and Ui (1965).

RESULTS

Weight changes during the reproductive cycle

Body-weight change provided a gross index of metabolic reserve. Body weight was plotted against the stage in the nesting cycle of each hen; that is, the number of eggs in the nest or estimated day of incubation. Regression lines then were fitted to the resulting points (Fig. 1). A separate regression line was fitted to the points from egg two to egg seven. This interval was chosen on the basis of Dane's observation (C. Dane, personal communication) that the reproductive tract of blue-winged teal hens starts regressing some time between the laying of the seventh egg and the start of incubation. The interval from egg eight to day 5 of incubation provided the points for the second regression and was separated on the basis of Phillips and van Tienhoven's (1962) observation that the reproductive tract of pintails (*A. acuta*) has completely regressed by day 5 of incubation. The third regression line was fitted to points from day 6 of incubation to day 22 of incubation. The regression equations of body weight on number of eggs or day of incubation for the three separate intervals are: egg two thru egg seven, $\hat{Y} = 410.7 + (-1.75X)$; egg eight

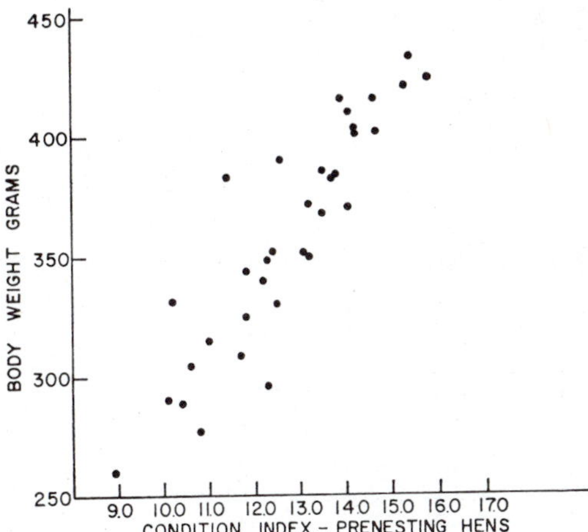

Fig. 2. Apparent association of body weight and condition index of prelaying hens.

thru day 5 incubation, $\hat{Y} = 436.7 + (-6.2X)$; day 6 incubation thru day 22 incubation, $\hat{Y} = 336.8 + (-0.64X)$. The most rapid weight loss, approximately 6 g per day, occurred during the interval from the eighth egg thru day 5 of incubation.

Condition index

It is evident from the scatter diagram (Fig. 1) that there was considerable variation of body weight between individuals at the same point in their reproductive cycle. It was theorized that some of this variation was due to structural differences of individual hens. Connell et al. (1960) studied the fat-free weight of some passerine birds and found that structural variation, as measured by wing length, was the most important factor influencing the fat-free weight. Therefore, it was thought that some compensation for structural variation could be made by creating a structural index and dividing it into the body weight. The structural index was taken as the product of the bill length times the keel length. The quotient resulting from the division of the body weight by the structural index was called the condition index. As can be seen in the scatter diagram (Fig. 2), structural variation is inherent in the population. Thus, it was believed that the condition index would provide a more meaningful measure of the metabolic reserves than would body weight.

Table 1. Known and estimated mean weight (in grams) of reproductive structures of lesser scaup and blue-winged teal.

	Body Weight 7th Egg	Ovary Weight 7th Egg	Oviduct Weight 7th Egg	Ovum Weight at Ovulation
Scaup	850	31	25	20
Blue-winged teal	400	Unknown	12	Unknown
Estimated				
Blue-winged teal		15[a]		10

[a] Ovary weight of BWT was estimated by constructing a simple proportion between known oviduct weights of scaup and BWT and ovary weight of scaup, then solving for the unknown: $25/12 = 31/X$. Utilization of known body weights and ovary weight of scaup yielded the same estimate. Ovum weight was estimated in a similar manner.

Weights of reproductive organs

Because birds could not be sacrificed in this study, the weights of female reproductive organs were estimated by indirect means. Ovary and ova weight at ovulation for blue-winged teal were estimated from known oviduct weight of blue-winged teal (C. Dane, personal communication) and body weight, ovary weight, and ova weight of lesser scaup (*Aythya affinis*) (D. Trau-

Table 2. Summary of mean condition indices and significant[a] differences between means at different stages of the reproductive cycle.

Laying		Molt	Prelay	Incubation	
Early	Late	(primaries)		Early	Late
13.5	12.7	12.5	12.0	11.7	10.9

[a] Any two means not underscored by the same line are significantly different, ($P < 0.01$).

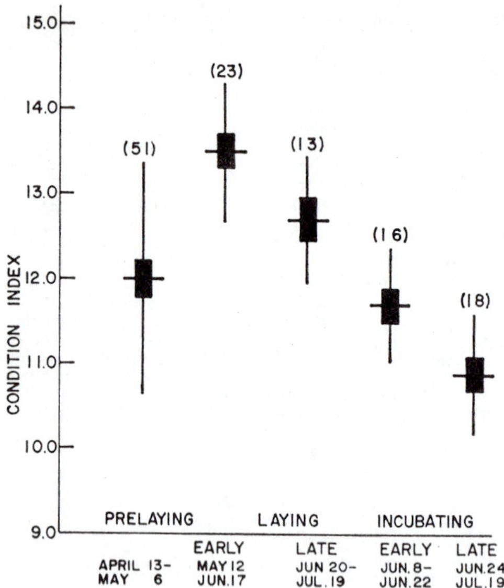

Fig. 3. Standard deviation and standard error of condition index for blue-winged teal hens at various reproductive stages (number of observations in parenthesis).

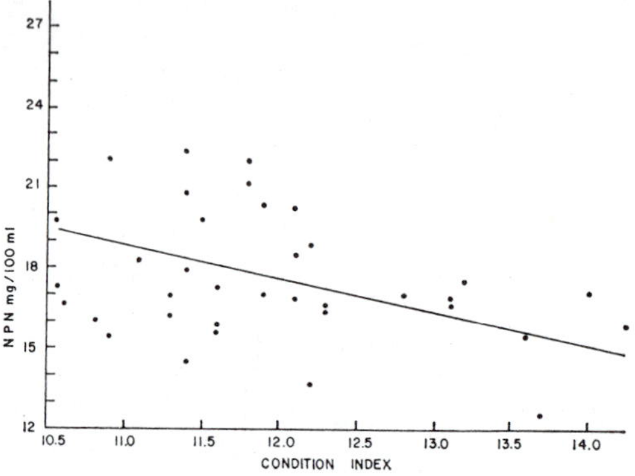

Fig. 4. Linear relationship of plasma NPN and condition index of incubating blue-winged teal hens.

ger, personal communication). These data are presented in Table 1.

Variation of condition index during the reproductive cycle

Condition index varied with respect to reproductive stage. The highest mean condition index was observed in hens during the early weeks of the laying stage while the lowest condition index was associated with the late weeks of the incubation stage (Fig. 3). A test of the results, when applied to the data using Duncan's New Multiple Range Test (Steel and Torrie 1960), is summarized in Table 2.

Variation of plasma constituents

Mean NPN levels were higher in incubating hens than in prelaying hens and mean FFA levels were higher in incubating hens than in laying hens (Table 3). However, there appeared to be little difference in plasma FAA levels of laying and incubating hens while plasma glucose levels were markedly higher in prelaying hens (Table 3). Only trace levels of acetoacetate were detected in the plasma of all birds collected during the study.

Mobilization of metabolic reserves prob-

Table 3. Level of plasma constituents during different stages of reproductive cycle.

	PRELAYING	LAYING	INCUBATING
FAA mg/100 ml	———	6.28 ± 0.18[a](27)	6.41 ± 0.26(25)[b]
NPN mg/100 ml	17.2 ± 0.54(23)	———	19.00 ± 0.63(32)
FFA meq/liter	———	557.8 ± 2.47(36)	669.1 ± 1.89(42)
Glucose mg/100 ml	384.9 ± 1.98(48)	259.2 ± 0.66(32)	275.7 ± 0.67(33)

[a] Standard error of sample.
[b] Number of observations.

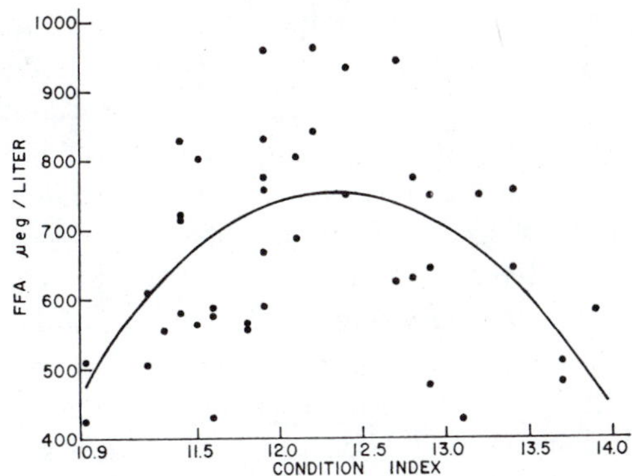

Fig. 5. Quadratic relationship of plasma FFA (meq/liter) and condition index of incubating blue-winged teal hens.

ably should have been reflected in changing levels of NPN, FFA and glucose during incubation because this period was associated with the lowest condition index (Fig. 3). Therefore, most effort was concentrated on analysis of plasma constituents of incubating hens. Plasma level of NPN in incubating hens was correlated with condition index as seen in Fig. 4. The regression of NPN on condition index is in the form of $Y = 28.0 + (-0.86X)$; the test of linearity showed $F = 5.38$ was significant ($P < 0.05$).

Plasma free fatty acid levels increased with decreasing condition index and then decreased as the condition index continued to decline (Fig. 5). A linear fit of the points was not significant; however, the fit of the data to the quadratic expression $\hat{Y} = -18{,}228 + 3{,}061.8X - 123.47X^2$ was significant ($P < 0.01$).

Plasma glucose was also related to decreasing condition index (Fig. 6). Although the linear fit was highly significant ($P < 0.01$), the second degree term ap-

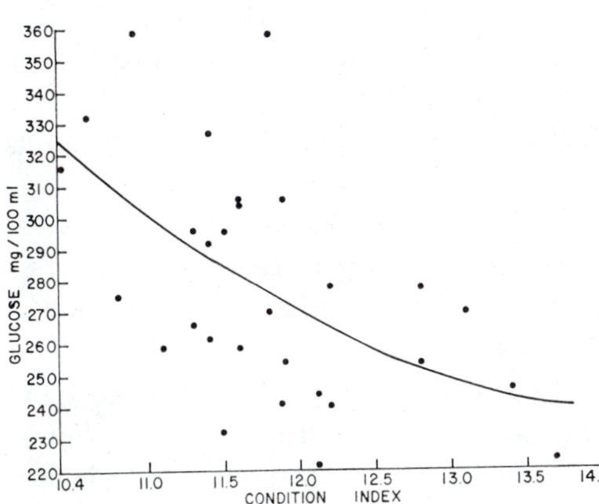

Fig. 6. Curvilinear relation of plasma glucose of incubating blue-winged teal hens to decreasing condition index.

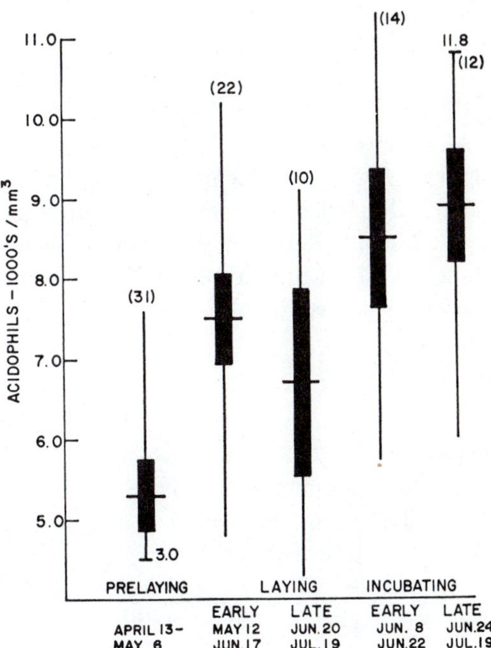

Fig. 7. Standard deviation and standard error of circulating acidophils of blue-winged teal hens at various reproductive stages (number of observations in parenthesis).

Table 4. Summary of mean acidophil levels (1000's/mm³) and significant[a] differences between means of various stages of reproductive cycle.

Incubation		Laying		Prelaying
Late	Early	Early	Late	
8.9	8.5	7.5	6.7	5.3

[a] Any two means not underscored by the same line are significantly different, ($P < 0.01$).

proached significance and the points were fitted to a slight curve.

Variation of acidophil levels

Mean level of circulating acidophils was higher (Fig. 7) in laying than prelaying hens, and reached peak levels in incubating hens. Mean differences were tested using Duncan's New Multiple Range Test; a summary is presented in Table 4.

DISCUSSION

Rapid loss of body weight during late laying and early incubation is evident from data presented in Figs. 1 and 3. What is not evident from these data is the physiological significance of this weight loss. An average of 70 g of body weight is lost from the laying of the seventh egg until day 5 of incubation (Fig. 1). Of these 70 g, approximately 37 g (53 percent) can be attributed to involution of ovary and oviduct (Table 1). The remaining weight lost during this period can be considered loss of metabolic reserves. The major portion probably is due to utilization of fat reserves. Mobilization of fat reserves was reflected in increasing levels of plasma FFA as hens underwent a decrease in condition index (Fig. 5).

As indicated by the level of FFA, lipid mobilization observed in blue-winged teal hens during early incubation may be due to decreasing levels of circulating estrogens coupled with reduced food intake during incubation. A decline in FFA as condition continues to decline (Fig. 5) suggests a depletion of fat reserves associated with incubation.

The increasing level of glucose during incubation (Fig. 6) is consistent with the hyperglycemic effect of corticosterone as demonstrated in chickens by Greenman and Zarrow (1961) and in ducks (Harris, unpublished manuscript). The concomitant increase in NPN (Fig. 4) is highly suggestive that gluconeogenesis is associated with the observed hyperglycemic response of incubating hens. The observed responses of NPN and glucose in incubating blue-winged teal hens also are consistent with similar responses observed in fasting pullets (Hazelwood and Lorenz 1959).

Acidophilia was associated with laying and incubating hens (Fig. 7). More specifically, the highest mean acidophil level was associated with the lowest mean condition index (Figs. 3 and 7) which occurred in incubating hens during the latter part of the nesting season. Undoubtedly, most hens incubating during this period (June 24–July 19) were renesting. Acidophil levels in domestic fowl are responsive to stressor and corticoid administration (Newcomer 1958, 1959).

Acidophilia in laying and incubating birds and the increase in blood level of NPN and glucose of incubating teal hens is evidence of increased adrenal (interrenal) activity resulting in mobilization of tissue reserves to meet the reproductive energy demands. Striking weight losses at cessation of laying can be interpreted as a loss of metabolic reserves. Similar weight changes have been recorded for the redhead (*Aythya americana*) (Weller 1957*a*) and mallard duck (Falk et al. 1966, Höhn 1947). A rapid decline in body weight of hen pheasants (*Phasianus colchicus*) during the later stage of laying has been documented by several investigators (Kirkpatrick 1944, Kabat et al. 1950, Breitenbach and Meyer 1959). Kabat et al. (1956) associated stress resistance of captive hen pheasants with available energy stores and found hens at their lowest level of physical condition after laying. Breitenbach and Meyer (1959) concluded that hen pheasants that have incubated a clutch and brooded young have depleted their energy reserves and are more vulnerable to stress factors.

It is clear that in waterfowl and gallinaceous birds studied to date, a loss of metabolic reserves is associated with the postlaying period. Although only a moderate weight loss was associated with egg production of wild blue-winged teal, the eggs produced represent expended energy. Clearly, the stress of reproduction is associated with energy demands of the reproductive processes.

In vertebrates producing polylecithal or mesolecithal eggs, protein and energy material must be mobilized and stored in the ova in a relatively short period of time. Other aspects associated with reproduction, such as migration, care of the young, and reduced feeding during all or part of the reproductive process, compound the energy demands of ova production. In forms subject to such rigors, adrenal corticoids are suggested to play a primary adaptive role in energy mobilization. The physiological information accumulated in this study suggests that the adrenal plays an adaptive role to meet the energy demands of reproduction in female teal. If adaptation to meet reproductive demands leads to degenerative changes, some postbreeding hen mortality would be expected.

The fact that corticosterone administration appeared to produce anemia in captive blue-winged teal (Harris, unpublished manuscript) suggests that hyperadrenal activity in wild blue-winged teal hens would have a similar result. Reduced oxygen-carrying capacity in wild hens would appear distinctly disadvantageous.

Lymphoid tissue (thymus) is suppressed by adrenal steroids (Garren and Statterfield 1957, Huble 1958, Höhn 1959, Newcomer and Connally 1960). Since lymphoid tissue is an integral part of the immunological system, any dysfunction of this system could result in lowered resistance to disease or parasitic infections. These possible deleterious side effects may accompany increased adrenal (interrenal) activity precipitated by the energy demands associated with reproduction. Although the adrenal functions primarily as an adaptive organ allowing the hen to meet the demands of the breeding season, unusual reproductive requirements may result in increased vulnerability of some hen blue-winged teal to natural mortality factors.

LITERATURE CITED

Bellrose, F. C., and Elizabeth B. Chase. 1950. Population losses in the mallard, black duck, and blue-winged teal. Illinois Nat. Hist. Survey Biol. Notes No. 22. 27pp.

———, T. G. Scott, A. S. Hawkins, and J. B. Low. 1961. Sex ratios and age ratios in North American ducks. Illinois Nat. Hist. Survey Bull. 27, Article 6. 391–474pp.

Breitenbach, R. P., and R. K. Meyer. 1959. Effect of incubation and brooding on fat, visceral weights and body weight of the hen pheasant. Poultry Sci. 38(5):1014–1026.

Connell, C. E., E. P. Odum, and H. Kale. 1960. Fat-free weights of birds. Auk 77(1):1–9.

Cummings, G. E., and O. H. Hewitt. 1964. Capturing waterfowl and marsh birds at night with light and sound. J. Wildl. Mgmt. 28(1): 120–126.

Falk, C., K. Hudec, and J. Toufar. 1966. The weight of the mallard, *Anas platyrhynchos*, and its changes in the course of the year. Zoologicke Listy 15(3):249–260.

Fisher, Lillian J., Sylvia L. Bunting, and L. E. Rosenberg. 1963. A modified ninhydrin colorimetric method for the determination of plasma alpha-amino nitrogen. Clin. Chem. 9(5):573–581.

Garren, H. W., and C. H. Satterfield. 1957. Attempt to stimulate lymphatic gland changes of fowl typhoid with adrenal cortex extract. Proc. Soc. Exptl. Biol. and Med. 95(4):716–719.

Greenman, D. L., and M. X. Zarrow. 1961. Steroids and carbohydrate metabolism in the domestic bird. Proc. Soc. Exptl. Biol. and Med. 106(3):459–462.

Hanson, H. C. 1962. The dynamics of condition factors in Canada geese and their relation to seasonal stresses. Arctic Inst. N. Am. Tech. Paper No. 12. 68pp.

HAYDEN, ADA. 1943. A botanical survey in the Iowa lake region of Clay and Palo Alto counties. Iowa State Coll. J. Sci. 17(3): 277–416.

HAZELWOOD, R. L., AND F. W. LORENZ. 1959. Effects of fasting and insulin on carbohydrate metabolism of the domestic fowl. Am. J. Physiol. 197(1):47–51.

HENRY, R. J. 1965. Clinical chemistry: principles and techniques. Harper and Row, New York. 1128pp.

HOCHBAUM, H. A. 1959. The canvasback on a prairie marsh. The American Wildlife Institute, Washington, D. C. 201pp.

HÖHN, E. O. 1947. Sexual behavior and seasonal changes in the gonads and adrenals of the mallard. Proc. Zool. Soc. of London. 117 (2 and 3):281–304.

———. 1959. Action of certain hormones on the thymus of the domestic hen. J. Endocrinol. 19(3):282–287.

HUBLE, J. 1958. Effect of hormones on endocrine and lymphepithelial glands in young fowl. Poultry Sci. 37(2):297–300.

ITAYA, K., AND M. UI. 1965. Colorimetric determination of free fatty acids in biological fluids. J. Lipid Research 6(1):16–20.

KABAT, C., R. K. MEYER, K. G. FLAKAS, AND R. L. HINE. 1956. Seasonal variation in stress resistance and survival in the hen pheasant. Wisconsin Conserv. Dept., Madison. Tech. Wildl. Bull. No. 13. 48pp.

———, D. R. THOMPSON, AND F. M. KOZLIK. 1950. Pheasant weights and wing molt in relation to reproduction with survival implications. Wisconsin Conserv. Dept., Madison. Tech. Wildl. Bull. No. 2. 26pp.

KIRKPATRICK, C. M. 1944. Body weights and organ measurements in relation to age and season in ring-necked pheasants. Anat. Rec. 89(2):175–194.

NEWCOMER, W. S. 1958. Physiologic factors which influence acidophilia induced by stressors in the chicken. Am. J. Physiol. 194(2): 251–254.

———. 1959. Adrenal and blood Δ^4–3^1-ketocorticosteroids following various treatments in the chick. Am. J. Physiol. 196(2):276–278.

———, AND J. D. CONNALLY. 1960. The bursa of Fabricius as an indicator of chronic stress in immature chickens. Endocrinology 67(2): 264–266.

PHILLIPS, R. E., AND A. VAN TIENHOVEN. 1962. Some physiological correlates of pintail reproductive behavior. Condor 64(4):291–299.

SALYER, J. W. 1962. A bow-net trap for ducks. J. Wildl. Mgmt. 26(2):219–221.

SCHILKE, RENOLD E., AND ROBERT E. JOHNSON. 1965. A colorimetric method for estimating actoacetate. Am. J. Clin. Pathol. 43(6):539–543.

SELYE, H. 1956. The stress of life. McGraw-Hill Book Company, Inc., New York. 324pp.

SOWLS, L. K. 1955. Prairie ducks. The Wildlife Management Institute, Washington, D. C. 193pp.

STEEL, R. G. D., AND J. H. TORRIE. 1960. Principles and procedures of statistics. McGraw-Hill Book Company, Inc., New York. 481pp.

WELLER, M. W. 1956. A simple field candler for waterfowl eggs. J. Wildl. Mgmt. 20(2): 111–113.

———. 1957*a*. Growth, weights, and plumages of the redhead, *Aythya americana*. Wilson Bull. 69(1):5–38.

———. 1957*b*. An automatic nest-trap for waterfowl. J. Wildl. Mgmt. 21(4):456–458.

WINTROBE, M. M. 1967. Clinical hematology. 6th ed. Lea and Febiger, Philadelphia. 1287pp.

WISEMAN, B. K. 1931. An improved method for obtaining white cell counts in avian blood. Proc. Exptl. Biol. and Med. Soc. 28(9):1030–1033.

Received for publication August 25, 1969.

ENERGY REQUIREMENTS AND GROWTH OF CAPTIVE LESSER SCAUP[1]

LAWSON G. SUGDEN,[2] Canadian Wildlife Service, Mobile #1, University of Saskatchewan Campus, Saskatoon, Saskatchewan, Canada
LORIN E. HARRIS, Department of Animal Science, Utah State University, Logan, UT 84321

Abstract: Energy requirements of captive Lesser Scaup ducks (*Aythya affinis*) were determined from hatching to 12 weeks using a feeding trial and comparative slaughter method. Food intake was measured directly; metabolizable energy intake by a chromic oxide indicator and calorimetry; net energy for gain by comparative slaughter; and total heat production by difference. Live weight growth was measured and dry matter growth estimated from a regression of percentage dry matter on age. Food intake (dry) increased from 6.7 g/duck/day during the 1st week to a peak of 52.5 g in the 5th week. Metabolizable energy intake averaged 5,575 kcal during the first 7 weeks, the assumed preflight period. Percentage carcass dry matter increased from 30 percent at 1 week to 45 percent at 12 weeks. A similar trend occurred in wild scaup though percentages were lower due to the lower fat content. Data are given for the proximate composition of carcasses for the first 12 weeks.

Little work has been done on the nutrition and bioenergetics of wild ducks. Holm and Scott (1954) and Scott and Holm (1964) showed that protein requirements of young Mallards (*Anas platyrhynchos*), Pintails (*A. acuta*) and Redheads (*Aythya americana*) were similar to those of domestic ducks and did not exceed 19 percent. The requirements of dabbling and diving ducks were apparently similar. Penney and Bailey (1970) reported on food consumption, growth and metabolizable energy intake of captive Black Ducks (*Anas rubripes*) during the first 8 weeks. The effects of temperature, photoperiod and activity on Blue-winged Teal (*A. discors*) metabolism were investigated by Owen (1969, 1970). The present study was undertaken to measure the energy requirements and growth of Lesser Scaup (*Aythya affinis*) from hatching to 12 weeks of age. It was done near Calgary, Alberta.

---

[1] Originally published in Poult. Sci. 51:625–633, 1972.

[2] Address correspondence to this author. Present address: Mig. Bird Res. Ctr., Univ. of SK CMPS, 115 Perimeter Road, Saskatoon, Saskatchewan S7N, 0X4, Canada.

MATERIALS AND METHODS

Scaup eggs were collected from wild nests and hatched in an electric incubator. Ducklings were transferred to 22 × 32 inch compartments in a poultry battery brooder 12 to 24 hours after hatching. There were 10 pens (5 for each sex), each containing four ducks. The brooder was kept in an unheated room where the temperature ranged from 18°C to 27°C. Each duck was weighed at the start of the trial and at weekly intervals thereafter.

Ducks were fed ad libitum a commercial duck starter with percentage composition of dry matter of 19.1 protein, 4.3 crude fat, 7.6 crude fiber, 6.1 ash, 1.55 calcium, and 0.97 phosphorus. For the first 2 weeks the diet was fed as crumbles. During the 3rd week, $^{5}/_{32}$-inch pellets were added, and after that, were fed exclusively. Chromic oxide was mixed into the diet at a level of 0.3 percent to measure the amount of excrement voided for a given amount of food (Dansky and Hill 1952). Chromic oxide concentrations were determined by the wet digestion procedure (Christian and Coup 1954), gross energy (G.E.) by oxygen bomb calorimeter, and total nitrogen by Kjeldahl apparatus.

Excreta were collected during the middle 3 days of each week. Weekly samples from each group were measured for gross energy, chromic oxide and nitrogen.

Metabolizable energy (M.E.) was calculated from the expression:

M.E. in kcal/g diet

$$= \text{G.E./g diet} - \left[\frac{Cr_2O_3/\text{g diet}}{Cr_2O_3/\text{g excreta}} \times \text{G.E./g excreta}\right]$$

Correction for nitrogen retained by the bird was made as follows (adapted from Vohra 1966):

N-corrected M.E. or $M.E._n$

$$= M.E. - 8.7N;$$

where N = nitrogen retention per gram of dry matter in the diet, and 8.7 = kilocalories of combustible energy in urinary nitrogen products;

$$N = \text{N/g diet} - \left[\text{N/g excreta} \times \frac{Cr_2O_3/\text{g diet}}{Cr_2O_3/\text{g excreta}}\right]$$

Net energy for gain ($N.E._g$ was estimated by multiplying the average daily growth increment of dry matter by the energy per unit of dry matter for each weekly period. These data were obtained from analysis of a series of ducks killed at weekly age intervals. Total heat production (H.P.) was calculated by subtracting $N.E._g$ from $M.E._n$. Net energy for maintenance ($N.E._m$) was estimated by Lofgreen's (1965) method. Using the recommended metabolic size of $W^{0.75}$ when W is weight in kilograms (Kleiber 1961), the logarithm of H.P. was plotted against $M.E._n$ intake, both expressed as kcal/kg of metabolic weight. To estimate $N.E._m$, the resulting line ($r = 0.95$) was extrapolated to zero energy intake. At that point the heat increment (H.I.) would be nil and theoretically, all heat production could be attributed to maintenance energy. The derived expression in kcal/duck/day is:

$$N.E._m = 111.5W^{0.75}$$

Heat increment was estimated by subtracting $N.E._g$ and $N.E._m$ from $M.E._n$.

Ducks for carcass analysis were reared under the same conditions as those used for the metabolism trial. Two of each sex were killed at zero-age and at weekly age intervals to 12 weeks. Before being killed they were fasted for 3 hours so that gullet and gizzard would contain little or no food. They were killed without blood loss and cooled in a refrigerator. Contents of the intestines and caeca were removed and the carcasses frozen. Four zero-aged ducks were pooled to make one sample and two 1-week-old birds for each of two samples. In addition to the captive ducks, 13 wild scaup were collected for analysis. To prepare it for analysis, a carcass was chopped into small pieces while still frozen and ground in a power meat grinder. This was done at below-freezing temperatures to reduce loss of fat which adheres to warm metal parts. It also minimizes moisture loss. Two samples were extracted for dry matter determinations. The remaining material was then vacuum freeze-dried prior to analyses which followed methods of the A.O.A.C. (1965).

Twenty-one Lesser Scaup were reared in a pen at the edge of a pond to obtain growth data which would approximate that of wild ducks. Measurements included weight, lengths of the ninth primary, sixth secondary, middle rectrix and longest scapular (Dzubin 1959).

RESULTS AND DISCUSSION

Growth of Scaup.—After 6 weeks of age, males weighed significantly

($P < 0.05$) more than females (Fig. 1). A weight decline occurred in all ducks between their 5th and 10th weeks. The weight knoll occurred in 16 at 6 weeks, 16 at 7 weeks, 5 at 8 weeks, and 3 at 9 weeks. These differences tend to mask the true weight losses when averages are used. Considering age, the average loss for males was 15 g and came at 8 weeks. However the average maximum loss regardless of age was 36 g. Corresponding losses in females were 11 g and 39 g. The average peak weight prior to each duck's loss was 556 g for males and 528 g for females. Because time of weighing would not always coincide with peak weights, these averages would be slightly low.

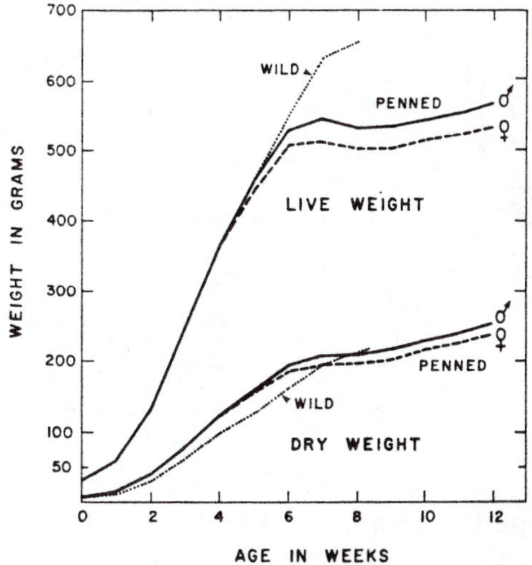

Fig. 1. Live weight and dry matter growth curves for penned and wild (estimated) Lesser Scaup.

Estimates for dry matter growth based on averages (Fig. 1) show that weight losses did not involve loss of dry matter. As previously explained, use of averages biased weight loss estimates and the actual average dry matter loss was probably close to 10 g.

Ducks reared indoors grew at a rate similar to those reared outside until after the 5th week, when weight gains of the former became smaller. A comparison of plumage and weight of wild scaup collected in the area with those of scaup reared outside indicated similar growth rates. The growth curve for the outside scaup (sexes averaged) is depicted (Fig. 1) and is believed to be close to the wild scaup curve.

After 3 weeks Alberta scaup grew considerably faster than those confined to a pond in Alaska—63°07′N, 142°36′W—(Schneider 1965). Just before flying age, wild Alberta scaup averaged almost 200 g heavier. Whether the Alaskan ducks represented free-living scaup is unknown.

Weight losses like those of the balance trial scaup were reported for several species of penned ducks (Veselovsky 1953), and for hatchery-reared Redheads (Weller 1957, Dane 1965) and Blue-winged Teal (Dane 1965). Veselovsky (1953) and Weller (1957) believed the weight loss was due to stress of remex formation. There is ample published evidence that molting in adult birds causes weight loss. Probably feather growth stress also influences weight declines of captive ducklings. However, there is reason to believe similar weight declines are not characteristic of wild young nor those reared outside. Only 2 of 21 scaup and 1 of 6 Gadwalls (*Anas strepera*) reared outside in this study lost weight before they were able to fly. Penned Black Ducks reared by Penney and Bailey (1970) showed no weight losses, but their data indicated that ducks kept outside grew faster during the critical period than those kept indoors. Lesser Scaup, Canvasbacks (*Aythya valisineria*) and Mallards confined to a small pond in Alaska with access only to natural foods lost no weight before their flight feathers devel-

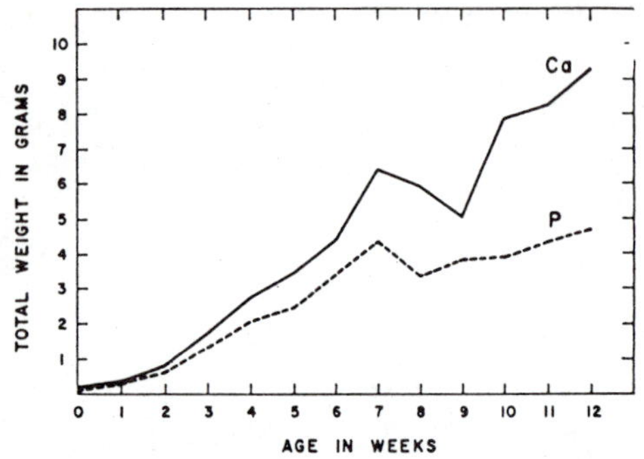

Fig. 2. Growth increments of calcium and phosphorus in penned Scaup.

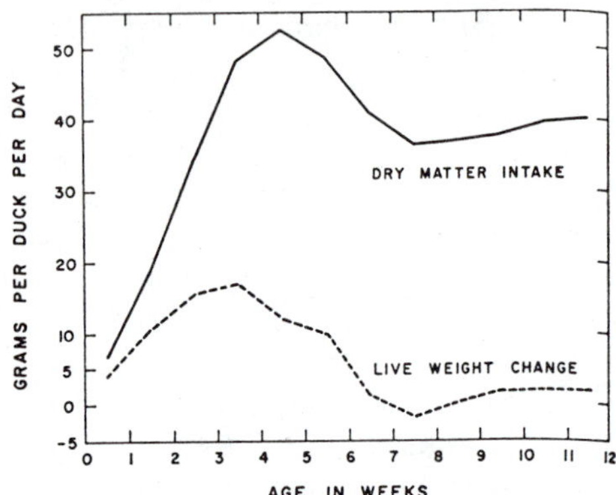

Fig. 3. Average daily intake of dry matter and live weight change in Scaup.

oped (Schneider 1965). A study of marked, free-living Canvasback ducklings disclosed no weight losses during the critical period (Dzubin 1959).

It is suggested there is a relation between the weight declines and a coincident negative balance of calcium and phosphorus in scaup raised indoors (Fig. 2). Excessive growth demands for phosphorus can result in inadequate retention of the two minerals which in turn can retard growth of other tissues (Maynard and Loosli 1962). Decreased food intake may also have been related to phosphorus deficiency. Calcium and phosphorus metabolism also involved vitamin D and manganese. In this case the deficient nutrient is unknown but it probably was vitamin D, since birds kept indoors require more of the vitamin than those with access to sunlight (Ewing 1951). Total energy requirements, rather than specific nutrient needs, tend to govern food intake, so if birds in indoor cages with lower energy requirements than those kept outside eat less food, a nutrient such as vitamin D

Table 1. Lesser Scaup energy balance data.

Week	Wt.[1] (g)	Diet intake (g/day)	M.E.$_n$ in diet (kcal/g)	Energy per duck per day (kcal)							E.E.[3] (%)
				G.E.	M.E.$_n$	H.P.	N.E.$_g$	N.E.$_m$[2]	N.E.$_{m+g}$	H.I.	
1	45	6.7	3.17	30.3	21.1	13.2	7.9	11.0	18.9	2.2	37.4
2	97	18.7	3.21	84.9	59.7	38.4	21.3	19.4	40.7	19.0	35.7
3	190	34.2	3.19	154.6	109.0	74.9	34.1	32.1	66.2	42.8	31.3
4	300	48.4	3.07	213.6	148.4	107.8	40.6	45.1	85.7	62.7	27.4
5	406	52.5	3.05	230.3	160.1	128.1	32.0	56.8	88.8	71.3	20.0
6	485	48.5	2.99	231.0	145.2	116.4	28.8	64.8	93.6	51.6	19.8
7	525	40.6	3.04	180.9	123.6	114.3	9.3	68.8	78.1	45.5	7.5
8	523	36.3	3.07	162.2	111.6	109.6	2.0	68.6	70.6	41.0	1.8
9	516	37.0	3.06	164.3	113.1	106.5	6.6	67.9	74.5	38.6	5.8
10	524	37.5	3.11	169.2	116.9	106.0	10.9	68.7	79.6	37.3	9.3
11	531	39.5	3.05	175.7	120.4	108.8	11.6	69.3	80.9	39.5	9.6
12	542	39.9	3.01	176.6	120.8	109.2	11.6	70.5	82.1	38.7	9.6

[1] Weight at midpoint of week.
[2] From expression, $111.5W^{0.75}$, when W = weight in kg.
[3] From expression, $N.E._g/M.E._n \times 100$ = energy efficiency.

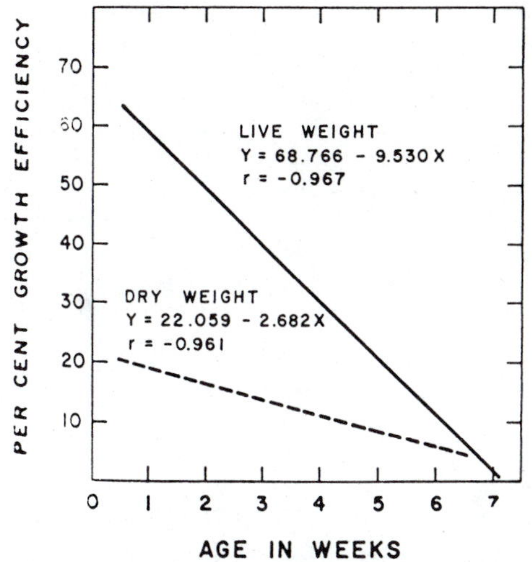

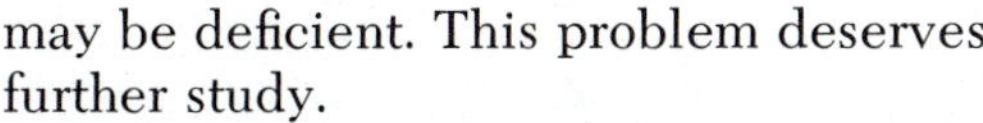
Fig. 4. Relationship of live and dry weight gain efficiencies to age of balance trial Scaup.

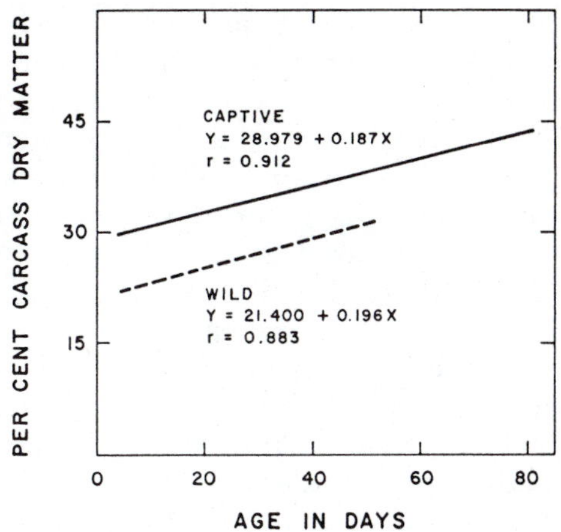

Fig. 5. Regression of carcass dry matter on age of 13 wild and 44 captive Scaup.

may be deficient. This problem deserves further study.

Food Consumption and Growth Efficiency.—During the 1st week, intake averaged 6.7 g dry matter per day. This increased to 52.5 g per day by the 5th week (Fig. 3, Table 1) and then declined for 3 weeks. After 5 weeks, the food intake curve closely paralled that for the live weight increment. The average intake for the first 7 weeks (the assumed preflight period) was 1,747 g of dry matter per duck.

The ratio of live weight gain to dry matter intake decreased lineally during the first 7 weeks (Fig. 4). The slope is similar (b = −9.53 vs. −9.49) to that derived for Black Ducks by Penney and Bailey (1970), but growth efficiency of the Black Ducks was about 6.6 percent

Table 2. Average[1] composition of penned Lesser Scaup ducklings.

Age in weeks	Dry matter in carcass			Energy retained (kcal)	Composition on a dry basis (%)				
	%	g	kcal/g		Protein	Fat	Ash	Ca	P
0	34.0	10.0	—	—	55.8	34.8	6.4	1.97	1.15
1	28.9	17.6	5.95	105	61.6	26.8	8.7	2.01	1.75
2	29.3	39.3	6.16	242	59.1	30.5	8.6	2.02	1.61
3	33.7	91.5	6.35	581	53.4	37.6	8.1	1.93	1.46
4	35.9	139.2	6.46	899	52.8	39.2	7.2	1.96	1.51
5	37.4	155.5	6.41	997	52.8	37.4	8.6	2.24	1.62
6	35.7	173.6	6.48	1,125	60.4	29.8	9.0	2.54	1.96
7	38.3	198.3	6.16	1,221	56.9	33.2	9.1	3.27	2.19
8	40.0	203.1	6.55	1,330	55.6	35.0	8.7	2.91	1.67
9	40.4	198.3	6.39	1,267	58.2	32.5	8.8	2.55	1.93
10	43.4	223.6	6.40	1,431	54.5	37.6	8.5	3.52	1.73
11	41.2	212.9	6.30	1,341	58.4	32.0	9.7	3.86	2.03
12	44.0	236.7	6.64	1,572	52.7	39.1	8.9	3.97	2.00

[1] Average of four ducks for each week except 11th, when there were two.

higher. This could be due to several factors including environmental temperatures, length of photoperiod (Seibert 1949, Cox 1961), nature of the diet (Scott et al. 1959), and species' differences. Growth efficiency in terms of dry matter gain also decreased lineally with age of ducks (Fig. 4). The initial energy efficiency of about 36 percent when duck weight was doubling (Table 1) is close to Rubner's theoretical value of 35 percent (Brody 1964) and agrees well with data for other species (Kleiber 1961).

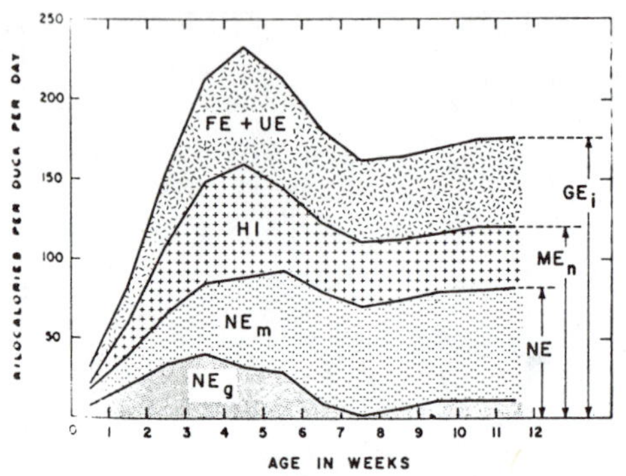

Fig. 6. Utilization of energy by an average penned Scaup.

Carcass Composition.—Dry Matter: Percentage dry matter in moth captive and wild Scaup increased with age (Fig. 5, Table 2). A similar trend for growing chickens was shown by Mitchell et al. (1931). Dry matter of captive Scaup increased from about 30 percent at 1 week, to 45 percent at 12 weeks. It averaged about 7 percent higher than that of wild ducks, the difference being attributed mainly to the higher fat content of the former.

Protein: Percentage of protein in live weight was similar in both captive and wild scaup and increased from 18 to 24 during the first 12 weeks. Protein in dry matter did not change significantly in either group, and averaged 56 percent in captive ducks and 69 percent in wild ducks, the difference reflecting the higher fat content of the former. Scott et al. (1959) analyzed Pekin ducklings and also found that protein content of carcasses remained relatively unchanged regardless of fat content.

Fat: Fat content was variable and largely accounted for variations in live weights; the heaviest birds of any age group contained relatively more fat. In four zero-aged ducks, 11.8 percent of live weight was fat, some of which the bird would use during its first few days. In captive Scaup 2 to 3 weeks old, fat averaged 8.6 percent (7.6–9.7) of live weight. Fat content of older ducks averaged 13.9 percent (9.2–22.8) and was significantly higher ($P < 0.05$). The average fat in dry matter of all ages was 34.4 percent.

Wild Scaup stored less fat which averaged 3.2 percent of live weight and 11.1 percent of dry weight. (These averages do not include figures for zero-aged ducks.) The difference in fat content between penned and wild Scaup can be attributed to two or three factors. Lower environmental temperatures and a lower M.E./protein ratio in the diet caused Pekin ducklings to deposit less fat (Scott et al. 1959). Wild Scaup experienced lower temperatures and probably ate a diet with a lower M.E./protein ratio than the penned ducks. A third factor may have been lower energy demands for activity by the penned ducks.

Ash, Calcium and Phosphorus: According to Maynard and Loosli (1962) calcium and phosphorus make up over 70 percent of body ash. Evidently this level is not reached in ducks until they are almost full grown. The two minerals made up about 45 percent of the ash during the first 5 weeks and increased thereafter until the last 3 weeks when the ratio exceeded 60 percent. It was 67 percent for the 12-week-old ducks. Although data on phosphorus are not included, similar ratios are apparent for chicks analyzed by Mitchell et al. (1931).

Percentages of calcium and phosphorus in dry matter of captive Scaup increased to 7 weeks, then calcium decreased for 2 weeks before again increasing. Phosphorus also decreased after 7 weeks, then fluctuated without reaching the peak of 7 weeks. Growth curves for calcium and phosphorus (Fig. 2) illustrate the negative balance after 7 weeks. The phosphorus decrease was significant at the 95 percent level, and calcium at the 80 percent level.

Calorific Content: Energy content of dry matter (Table 2) did not change significantly with age of penned ducks and averaged 6.436 ± 0.099 kcal/g. The average for wild Scaup, 5.574 ± 0.375 kcal/g, was significantly ($P < 0.01$) lower than the penned duck value, due to wild ducks' lower fat content. Gross energy per unit of live weight increased with age because of increasing percentage of carcass dry matter.

Utilization of Energy.—Data on energy use (Fig. 6, Table 1) are based on the average for all balance trial Scaup.

Metabolizable Energy: Corrections for N-retention decreased as the ducks grew (Fig. 7), conforming with results for chickens (Lockhart et al. 1963). The deviation from the trend during the 5th and 6th weeks was apparently caused by higher protein in the diet at that time. Lockhart et al. (1963) reported a similar relationship when varying amounts of protein were fed to chicks and turkey poults. That the deviation was not related to age of ducks was indicated by data from three younger groups that ate the higher protein diet at the same time as the seven groups in Fig. 7. The relatively high N-retention for the younger ducks corresponded to the change in dietary protein at an earlier age. The use of the N-retention correction factor for reducing variability of M.E. values requires further study. As Kleiber (1961) pointed out, the M.E. of protein is greater for protein growth than for heat production. Thus it may be invalid to use for growing birds an M.E. value which is essentially for nonproductive ducks.

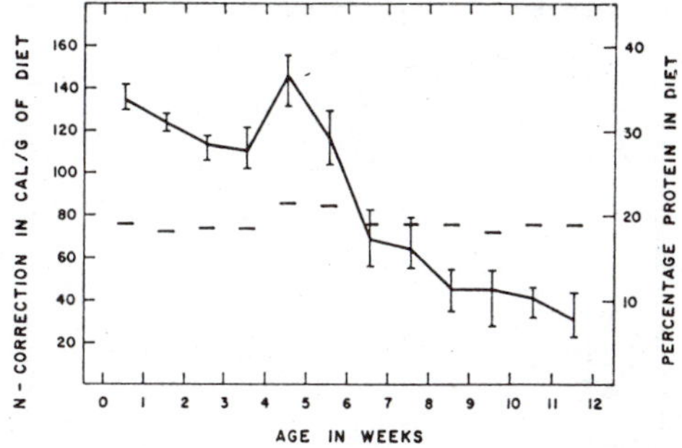

Fig. 7. Relationship of N-correction factor to age of Scaup and level of dietary protein. Vertical bars show range of correction values, and horizontal bars show level of protein.

The average $M.E._{n}$ value for the Scaup diet was 3.09 kcal/g dry matter and G.E. of the diet averaged 4.47 kcal/g dry matter. Thus, 69 percent of the dietary energy was metabolized. The corresponding figure for M.E. (uncorrected for N-retention) was 71 percent. Up to 7 weeks of age the cost per gram of live weight was 10.8 kcal $M.E._{n}$ or 11.2 kcal M.E. During its first 7 weeks, an average scaup used 5,370 kcal of $M.E._{n}$ or 5,575 kcal of M.E.

Heat Production: Total H.P. increased to the 5th week, decreased for 2 weeks, and then became relatively constant (Fig. 6, Table 1). The decrease in H.P. per unit of metabolic weight after the 4th week (Fig. 8) can be attributed to two factors. Relative H.I. of a food increased with an increased plane of nutrition (Brody 1964), so when food intake decreased, the rate of H.I. would also decrease. Also,

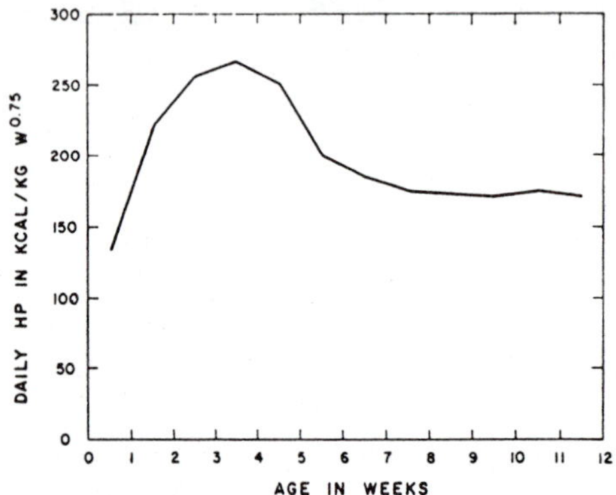

Fig. 8. Relationship of heat production per unit of metabolic weight to age of Scaup.

in chickens, the period of rapid growth was associated with relatively high basal heat production (Mitchell et al. 1927, Kibler and Brody 1944). A comparison of total H.P. (Table 1) with rate of H.P. (Fig. 8) illustrates the influence of the second factor. Heat production per kilogram of metabolic weight began to decrease after the 4th week, whereas energy intake, and presumably rate of H.I., increased for 1 more week. The declining rate of H.P. during the 4th week must have been caused by reduced maintenance energy, and since there is no reason to believe that the activity fraction decreased, a lower basal heat production must have been responsible. Mitchell et al. (1927) concluded that the metabolism per unit surface area of chickens was lower at hatching, increased to a peak at 30 to 40 days, and then decreased to the adult level. A similar trend is apparent for the ducks.

To be of practical use, energy requirement data should be expressed in terms of wild conditions. There is little information on requirements of free-living ducks and past estimates are complicated by temperature and activity differences. Owen (1969) concluded that the average metabolic difference of free-living Teal was 14.3 kcal/bird/day or about 13 percent higher than existence metabolism of caged ducks. Wild Scaup energy requirements should be higher than those of caged Scaup because of the formers' lower environmental temperature and greater activity. However, a captive Scaup stored more energy in the form of fat. Added to this is the H.I. produced while depositing the additional fat. Also, the H.I. fraction can be used to keep the body warm (Harris 1966), so wild Scaup may need little or no more energy than that metabolized by the captive ducks.

There are few data on the M.E. of wild duck foods. Amphipoda is an important food of Lesser Scaup and its M.E. has been measured as 2.45 kcal/g dry matter (Sugden, unpublished). Thus, it would require approximately 59 g of dry amphipods to meet the daily need of an 11–12-week-old scaup. Using 3.11 kcal/g dry weight as the M.E. in invertebrates eaten by Blue Grouse (*Dendragapus obscurus fuliginosus*) chicks (Stiven 1961), the equivalent requirement would be 39 g. With a daily intake of dry weight of 10 percent of the live weight of the duck (Sincock 1962), an 11–12-week-old Scaup would need about 54 g of dry plant food. Having an M.E. of 2.18 kcal/g dry weight (Stiven 1961) this would supply 118 kcal M.E. which is close to the captive scaup intake. More precise estimates must await additional information on the M.E. values of duck foods and the additional energy costs for free-living.

ACKNOWLEDGMENTS

We wish to acknowledge the helpful advice given by J. B. Gollop, Canadian Wildlife Service and J. B. Low, Utah Cooperative Wildlife Research Unit, Utah State University. C. M. Grieve, Department of Animal Science, University of Alberta, kindly supervised chromic oxide and calorific determinations. We thank H. J. Poston for technical assistance.

LITERATURE CITED

ASSOCIATION OF OFFICIAL AGRICULTURAL CHEMISTS. 1965. Official methods of analysis, 10th edition. A.O.A.C., Washington, D.C.

BRODY, S. 1964. Bioenergetics and growth, 2nd edition. Hafner Publishing Co., Inc., New York.

CHRISTIAN, K. R., AND M. R. COUP. 1954. Measurement of feed intake by grazing cattle and sheep. VI. The determination of chromic oxide in faeces. New Zealand J. Sci. Techol., Sec. A 36:328–330.

COX, G. W. 1961. The relation of energy requirements of tropical finches to distribution and migration. Ecology 42:253–266.

DANE, C. W. 1965. The influence of age on development and reproductive capability of the blue-winged teal (*Anas discors* Linnaeus). Ph.D. thesis, Purdue Univ.

DANSKY, L. M., AND F. W. HILL. 1952. Application of the chromic oxide indicator method to balance studies with growing chickens. J. Nutrition 47:449–459.

DZUBIN, A. 1959. Growth and plumage development of wild-trapped juvenile canvasback (*Aythya valisineria*). J. Wildl. Mgmt. 23:279–290.

EWING, W. R. 1951. Poultry nutrition, 4th edition. W. Ray Ewing (Publisher), South Pasadena, California.

HARRIS, L. E. 1966. Nutrient requirements of domestic animals. Glossary of energy terms and their biological interrelationships. National Acad. Sci. National Res. Council, Washington, D.C.

HOLM, E. R., AND M. L. SCOTT. 1954. Studies on the nutrition of wild waterfowl. New York Fish and Game J. 1:171–187.

KIBLER, H. H., AND S. BRODY. 1944. Metabolic changes in growing chickens. J. Nutrition 28:27–34.

KLEIBER, M. 1961. The fire of life. An introduction of animal energetics. John Wiley and Sons, Inc., New York.

LOCKHART, W. C., R. L. BRYANT, AND D. W. BOLIN. 1963. Factors affecting the use of classical metabolizable energy values in evaluation of poultry feeds. North Dakota State Univ., North Dakota Reserach, Research Rept. No. 10.

LOFGREEN, G. P. 1965. A comparative slaughter technique for determining net energy values with beef cattle, *in* Proc. Third Symposium on Energy Metabolism, K. L. Blaxter, Ed. Academic Press, London, pp. 309–317.

MAYNARD, L. A., AND J. K. LOOSLI. 1962. Animal nutrition, 5th edition. McGraw-Hill Book Co., Inc., New York.

MITCHELL, H. H., L. E. CARD, AND W. T. HAINES. 1927. The effect of age, sex, and castration on the basal heat production of chickens. J. Agr. Res. 34:945–960.

———, ———, AND T. S. HAMILTON. 1931. A technical study of the growth of White Leghorn chickens. Univ. of Illinois Agr. Exp. Sta. Bull. 367.

OWEN, R. B., JR. 1969. Heart rate, a measure of metabolism in blue-winged teal. Comp. Biochem. Physiol. 31:431–436.

———. 1970. The bioenergetics of captive blue-winged teal under controlled and outdoor conditions. Condor 72:153–163.

PENNEY, J. G., AND E. D. BAILEY. 1970. Comparison of the energy requirements of fledgling black ducks and American coots. J. Wildl. Mgmt. 34:105–114.

SCHNEIDER, K. B. 1965. Growth and plumage development of ducklings in interior Alaska. M.S. Thesis, Univ. Alaska.

SCOTT, M. L., F. W. HILL, E. H. PARSONS, JR., J. H. BRUCKNER, AND E. DOUGHERTY III. 1959. Studies on duck nutrition. 7. Effect of dietary energy: protein relationships upon growth, feed utilization and carcass composition in market ducklings. Poultry Sci. 38:497–507.

———, AND E. R. HOLM. 1964. Nutrition of wild waterfowl. Proc. Cornell Nutrition Conf. for Feed Manufacturers, pp. 149–155.

SEIBERT, H. C. 1949. Differences between migrant and non-migrant birds in food and water intake at various temperatures and photoperiods. Auk 66:128–153.

SINCOCK, J. L. 1962. Estimating consumption of food by wintering waterfowl populations. Proc. Ann. Conf. S.E. Assoc. Game and Fish Comm. 16:217–221.

STIVEN, A. E. 1961. Food energy available for and required by the blue grouse chick. Ecology 42:547–553.

VESELOVSKY, Z. 1953. Postembryonal development of our wild ducks. Translation from original Czech. paper in Sylvia 14:36–73. Ottawa, Indian Affairs and Northern Development Library.

VOHRA, P. 1966. Energy concepts for poultry nutrition. World's Poultry Sci. J. 22:6–24.

WELLER, M. W. 1957. Growth, weights and plumages of the redhead, *Aythya americana*. Wilson Bull. 69:5–38.

BREEDING STRESS OF FEMALE EIDERS IN MAINE[1]

CARL E. KORSCHGEN, Maine Cooperative Wildlife Research Unit, University of Maine, Orono 04473

Abstract: Physiological condition of breeding female American eiders (*Somateria mollissima dresseri*) was studied on islands in Penobscot Bay, Maine, from 1973 to 1975. Of particular interest was the hypothesis that stresses associated with reproduction predispose eiders to increased mortality and lowered productivity. Females established large nutrient reserves prior to egg laying and essentially terminated feeding before laying. They relied heavily on nutrient reserves for formation of eggs. Wet weights of the gizzard, liver, and intestine decreased significantly during follicular development before and during laying. There was no correlation between body weight and clutch size after egg laying, suggesting that clutch size was determined by size of nutrient reserves. Females fed little or not at all during incubation and lost 32 percent of their post-laying weight. Wet weights of the pectoral muscle decreased significantly. Based on fat and protein levels, most females probably could not continue to incubate when body weights approached 1.10 kg. Hematocrit percentages and levels of total plasma protein and free fatty acids were physiological parameters that indicated degenerative changes in incubating eiders. Levels of non-protein nitrogen in the blood plasma appeared to be considerably depressed but did not change during incubation. The renesting ability of American eiders appeared limited, at least in part, by the dysfunction of the digestive tract concomitant with egg laying. The digestive tract was so altered that even when a clutch was lost after only a few days of incubation, females required many days to reestablish reserves.

J. WILDL. MANAGE. 41(3):360–373

Female common eiders (*Somateria mollissima*) generally are believed to eat little or not at all during incubation (Milne 1963, 1976, Tinbergen 1958, Cooch 1965). By the time that the eggs hatch after an average of 26 days of incubation (Choate 1966, Guignion 1967) many females are emaciated. Some American eiders in Maine renest after the loss of an initial clutch (Sarbello 1973) and if the second clutch should be laid prior to reestablishment of optimum physiological condition, the stress to the females could be critical.

This study was initiated to evaluate the physiological condition of female eiders during the annual cycle, and to look at the relationship between behavioral and physiological strategies and productivity on the breeding ground. Lack (1954) suggested that delayed maturity is the result of breeding imposed strain on younger birds, which by natural selection results in the postponement of breeding. By marking European eiders (*S. m. mollissima*) as juveniles, Milne (1963:193) established that females in Scotland breed when 2 or 3 years old. American eiders are assumed also to be delayed breeders, although the age of usual first breeding is not known precisely. H. L. Mendall (Unpublished data) has determined that at least a few individuals in Maine nest when 2 years old. Bellrose et al. (1961) postulated that the physiological demand of reproduction in waterfowl, involving depletion of energy reserves, placed the female in greater jeopardy to stress than the male. Some aspects of the breeding stress of female eiders were reported by Milne (1963). Data collected on the natural mortality of European eiders at Sands of Forvie, Scotland, indicated that females were more vulnerable than males. Nearly one-half of the adult female mortality occurred during 2 months of the breeding season, when no corresponding increase in mortality oc-

[1] This paper describes parts of the results of studies undertaken during a Ph.D. program supported by the Maine Cooperative Wildlife Research Unit (U.S. Fish and Wildlife Service, Maine Department of Inland Fisheries and Wildlife, University of Maine, and Wildlife Management Institute, cooperating).

Originally published in J. Wildl. Manage. 41(3):360–373, 1977.

curred among other age and sex classes, suggesting that females were seriously weakened at that time of year. Milne found that the average weight of females decreased by as much as 30 percent over the egg-laying and incubation periods. In Quebec, incubating American eiders have lost as much as 45 percent of their body weight (Cantin et al. 1974).

I am indebted to H. Mendall for his assistance with the study and in preparation of the manuscript. Special thanks are due J. Zinkl and R. Hudson who analyzed the blood plasma, and personnel of the Maine Life Sciences and Agriculture Experiment Station for fat and protein analyses. I thank R. Owen, Jr., for his review of the manuscript.

STUDY AREA

Field studies were conducted in Penobscot Bay, in the midcoast region of Maine which is apparently the center of the breeding eider duck population in the state. Data were obtained from female eiders nesting on Mouse Island, Goose Island, East Goose Rock, and Robinson Rock. The general features and detailed descriptions of the flora of each of these islands were compiled by Choate (1966) and Clark (1968). Bourget (1970) described the island fauna. Generally the islands are small (less than 1 ha) and are covered by grasses and herbs. Great black-backed gulls (*Larus marinus*) and herring gulls (*L. argentatus*) are the most important breeding associates of the eiders. Sixteen wooden nesting shelters erected by Clark (1968) were on each of the study islands except East Goose Rock.

METHODS AND MATERIALS

Each island in the study area was visited 1 day per week, weather permitting. Female eiders nesting in vegetation were captured on the nests with traps or by netting them as they flushed from cover. Originally a modified Weller (1957) nest trap was used to catch birds; however, a more efficient, smaller, and simpler trap was designed which had a swinging drop-door that closed when the female returned to the nest. Early in the nesting season many birds nested under artificial shelters and trapping them was facilitated by the permanent attachment of welded-wire drop-doors to the front of each shelter.

Captured eiders were marked with metal leg bands of the U.S. Fish and Wildlife Service. Birds were weighed by suspending them by the metal hook of a 2.5 kg Pesola spring scale placed through the leg band. Weights were recorded to the nearest 10 gms. Each time a female was captured approximately 2 ml of blood were removed from the vein at the ulna-humeral joint with a heparinized disposable syringe. The blood sample was chilled over ice until it could be centrifuged. The stage of incubation was determined by calculation from the date of hatch and/or the day the clutch was completed. Complete clutch size was recorded for each female.

The seasons to which this paper refer are not those of the calendar year. The term *summer* covers the nesting and brooding season from 15 April to 1 September. *Fall* denotes the time of migration from the breeding grounds between 1 September and 15 November; *winter* was 15 November to 15 March. The short *spring* refers to the interval between 15 March and 15 April when eiders are returning to the nesting grounds.

All organ measurements were taken from fresh organs or those which had just been frozen. An incision was made so that the entire pectoral muscle could be removed and weighed. The viscera and reproductive organs were saved for measurement. Seventeen adult female eiders were prepared for

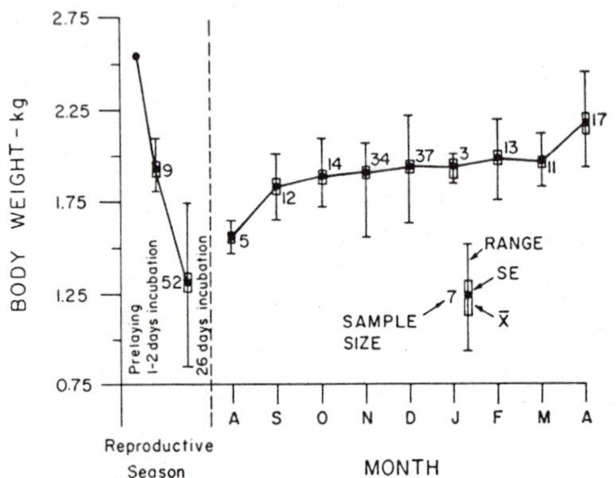

Fig. 1. Body weights of adult female American eiders.

total carcass fat and protein analysis by completely removing all feathers. The carcass was then frozen, thinly sliced with a meat saw, and homogenized with a blender. Subsamples of the homogenate were dried at 50 C to determine the percent moisture content. Eider eggs and gizzards were also analyzed. Duplicate samples of the carcass homogenate and the dried material were submitted to the Life Sciences and Agriculture Experiment Station of the University of Maine for analysis. Fat and protein content were measured by ether extraction and Kjeldahl nitrogen procedures. Eider diseases and parasites were studied in relation to the breeding cycle of females.

Statistical procedures were from Snedecor and Cochran (1967) and Nie et al. (1975). All hypotheses were tested at the 5 percent level of significance.

RESULTS

Changes in Body Weight

Changes in body weight provided an approximate index of the metabolic reserves (Harris 1970). By October, most birds had nearly completed the wing molt and had deposited subcutaneous fat. Mean weights of 124 adult female eiders increased but not significantly from October to March (Fig. 1). Mean weight from October to March was 1.91 ± 0.03 kg. In April, 17 birds had a mean weight of 2.14 ± 0.04 kg. Weights continued to increase until the maximum was attainted immediately prior to egg laying.

Since all female eiders were not synchronous in their time of nest initiation, consideration of weights during the reproductive cycle must be related to reproductive stage. The heaviest adult female, collected 9 May 1975, weighed 2.56 kg. Her ovary showed atretic follicles and developing follicles indicating that egg formation had been terminated, probably by unseasonable coldness around 1 May.

Lack of food in the digestive tract of laying and incubating eiders strongly indicated that they had ceased feeding. Therefore, the weight of prelaying females can be approximated by adding the weight of fresh eggs in the nest to the body weight. The average weight of 3 laying birds immediately prior to laying of the first egg was probably at least 2.53 kg, determined by adding 126 g for each egg in the nest to the body weight.

Mean weights of females during August, April, prelaying, and after 26 days of incubation were significantly different from each other and from mean weights in fall and winter.

During the 1974 and 1975 field seasons, data on 265 eider clutches was obtained. The mean clutch size was slightly more than 4 eggs.

Depending upon the initial prenesting condition of the female and the clutch size, a bird would be expected to weigh from 1.8 to 2.0 kg when the last egg was laid. However, no correlation ($r = 0.32$) existed between the weight of the female and clutch size after incubation had begun. Furthermore, the mean winter weight and weight after laying were quite similar, suggesting that eiders stored metabolic fuels to cover the expenditure of energy in the

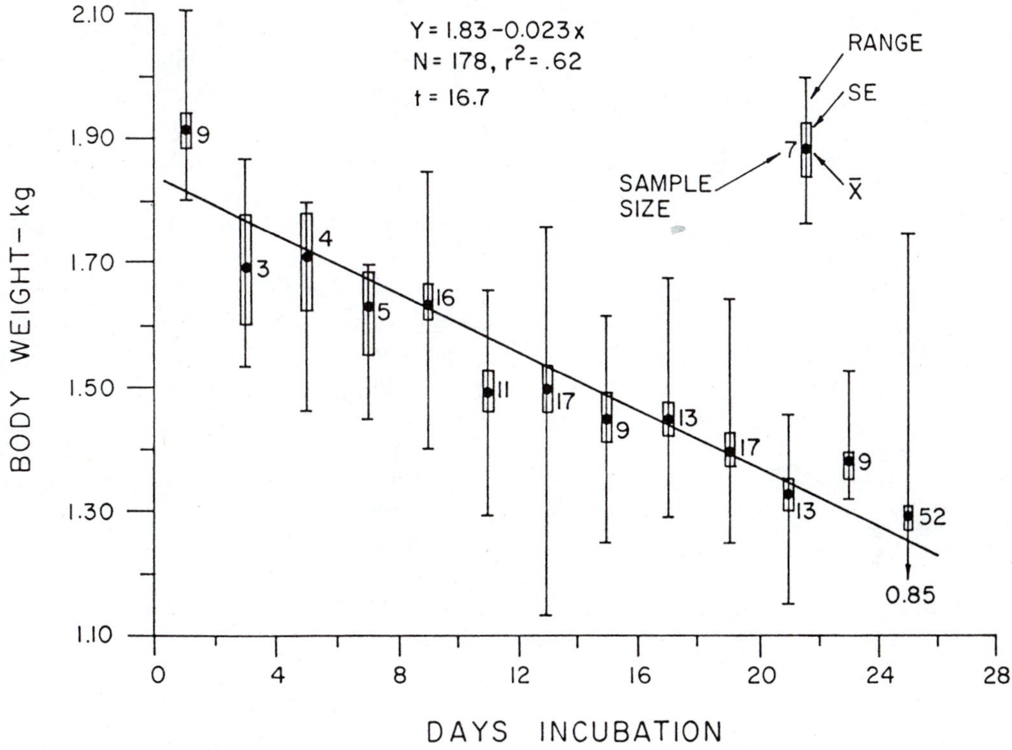

Fig. 2. Body weights of incubating American eiders.

eggs. Ankney (1974) found the same situation to be true for female blue geese (*Anser caerulescens*).

Based on regression analysis female eiders were estimated to weigh 1.83 kg at the start of incubation and 1.29 kg when the ducklings hatched (Fig. 2). This loss, plus the loss prior to egg laying, amounted to 50 percent of the maximum annual body weight or 32 percent of body weight after they started to incubate. Initial weight loss was due partly to the regression of the ovary and oviduct, which had a combined weight of less than 15 g after a few days of incubation.

Females at the end of incubation were in the worst physical condition experienced during the annual cycle. The greatest weight of a bird on the 26th day of incubation was 1.75 kg and the least was 0.85 kg. Obviously some females were better able to withstand the stress of egg production and incubation than were others. The date of hatching appeared to be an important factor in determining the condition of the eider. There was a significant decrease in the final weight of females as the season progressed. Probably the data included weights of renesting birds, although only 2 were confirmed as such.

In 3 field seasons 515 weights were obtained from 337 birds (assuming that each nesting season was independent, i.e., if 1 female was handled all 3 years of the study this was tabulated as 3 birds). Only twice were weights recorded less than 1.10 kg

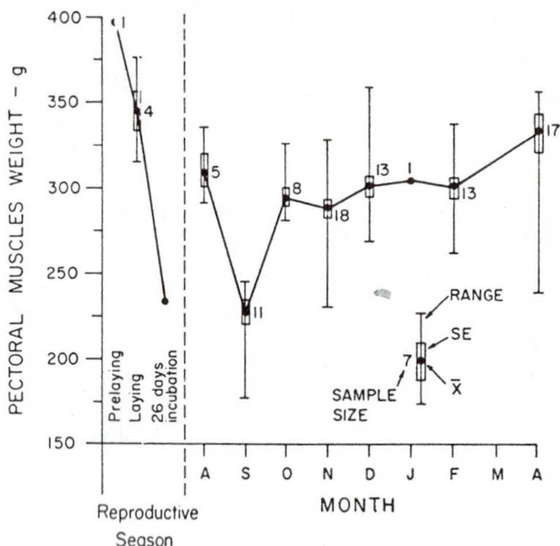

Fig. 3. Pectoral muscle wet weights of adult female American eiders. Information for the reproductive season is based on data from 12 incubating birds.

(1.06 and 0.85) and both records involved the same bird on the final day of incubation, in 2 different years.

Selected Organ Weights

Toward the end of incubation and during post-nuptial molt the most significant change in pectoral muscle wet weight occurred (Fig. 3). In early August the mean weight of the pectoral muscles was 310 g. The eiders collected at that time were molting the contour feathers of the belly and flank and no wing or tail molt was apparent. Females collected on 9 September had undergone a complete wing and tail molt and new flight feathers were beginning to emerge. The pectoral muscles then weighed 226 g, significantly less than in August, even though the total body weight was increasing. After completion of the wing molt, the weight of these muscles did not change significantly from October to April.

From a winter mean wet weight of 290 g, the pectorals increased to 397 g in the one prelaying female collected. Four birds collected during the egg-laying period had pectorals weighing an average of 345 g. Based on 12 incubating females, the pectorals weighed approximately 340 g at the start of incubation and decreased in weight during incubation by 34 percent to 227 g. The pectorals were the only organs measured, except the reproductive tract, which showed a significant loss of weight during incubation.

In spite of the decline in pectoral muscle weight, all incubating female eiders were capable of flying, although birds released after capture or that flushed from nests rarely flew more than 300 m before alighting on the water. Whether the females were reluctant to flee because of their innate broodiness or whether their physical endurance to make an extended escape flight was limited by the wasted condition of these muscles is not known. Egg-laying and incubating blue geese also were observed to fly very little (Ankney 1974).

After the reproductive season, the wet weight of the gizzard (Fig. 4) increased and it continued to increase through the winter and spring months. In April the birds with the largest gizzards were in a more advanced breeding condition as evidenced by ovarian development. Gizzard weights of birds immediately prior to egg laying were not obtained. The gizzard lost proportionally more weight during follicular development than during the incubation period. From 122 g on 20 April, mean gizzard weight dropped to only 42 g among laying females. No significant weight was lost during incubation, but by the 25th day of incubation, 2 gizzards averaged 26 g. Therefore, a total of 96 g was lost from the gizzard, 83 percent of which was lost before incubation began.

Gizzards were analyzed for water, fat, and protein content. Gizzards of various weights and collection times averaged 73 percent water. In terms of total fat and

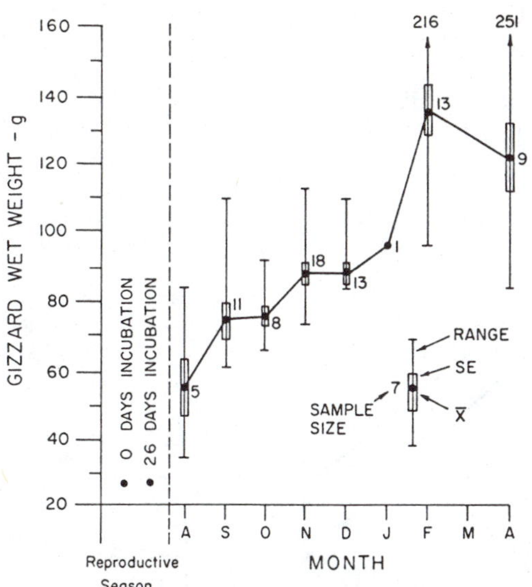

Fig. 4. Gizzard wet weights of adult female American eiders. Information for the reproductive season is based on data from 12 incubating birds.

protein reserves, the gizzard would be important primarily as a protein source. There was a strong linear relationship between the grams of protein available in gizzards and total wet weight (Fig. 5). Therefore, the rapid decrease in gizzard size during

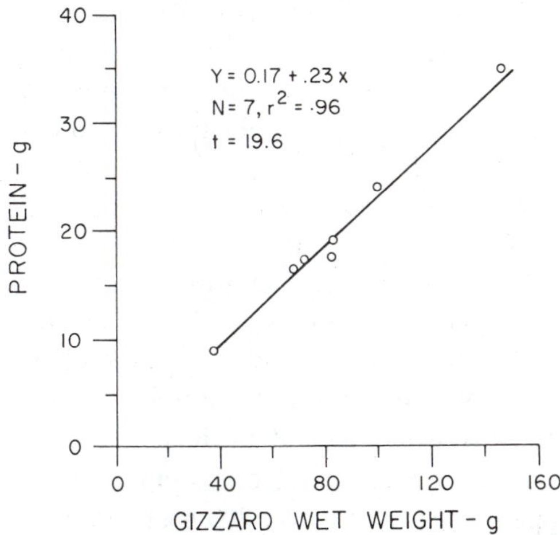

Fig. 5. Protein content of gizzards of adult female American eiders.

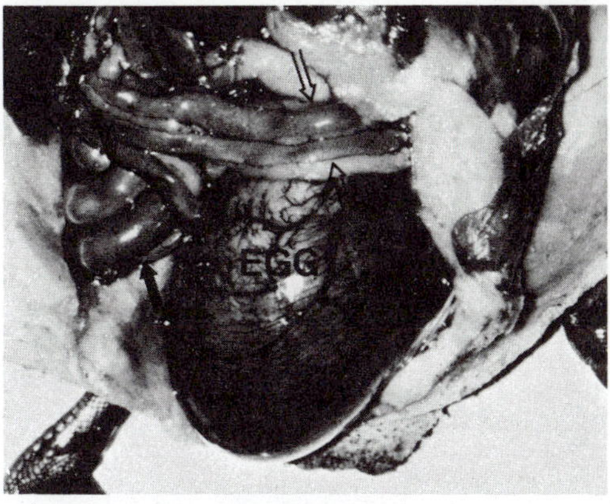

Fig. 6. Change in the intestines during egg laying. Note the reduced diameter of the lower segment of the small intestine (between outlined arrows) compared to the "functional" part of the anterior small intestine (between solid arrows).

laying may indicate utilization of tissue protein rather than atrophy from lack of use.

The wet weight of the liver in February appeared to be decreasing while the wet weight of the gizzard and intestine was increasing. From a post-reproductive wet weight in August of 52 g, mean weight of the intestine increased slowly through October, leveled off in November, and reached the maximum in February.

The average liver wet weight of 9 April eiders was 82 g, which represented an increase of about 20 g over the winter mean weight. Laying females had livers weighing 59 g. There was no significant weight loss from the liver or intestine during incubation. Shrinkage and decrease in the wet weight of the intestine occurred primarily during egg laying (Fig. 6). The posterior end of the small intestine and the entire large intestine were reduced initially.

Relation of Fat and Protein Reserves to Body Weight

Although fat and protein determinations were conducted on only 6 fall-spring female eiders, the results of these tests agreed closely with visual evaluation of fat depots

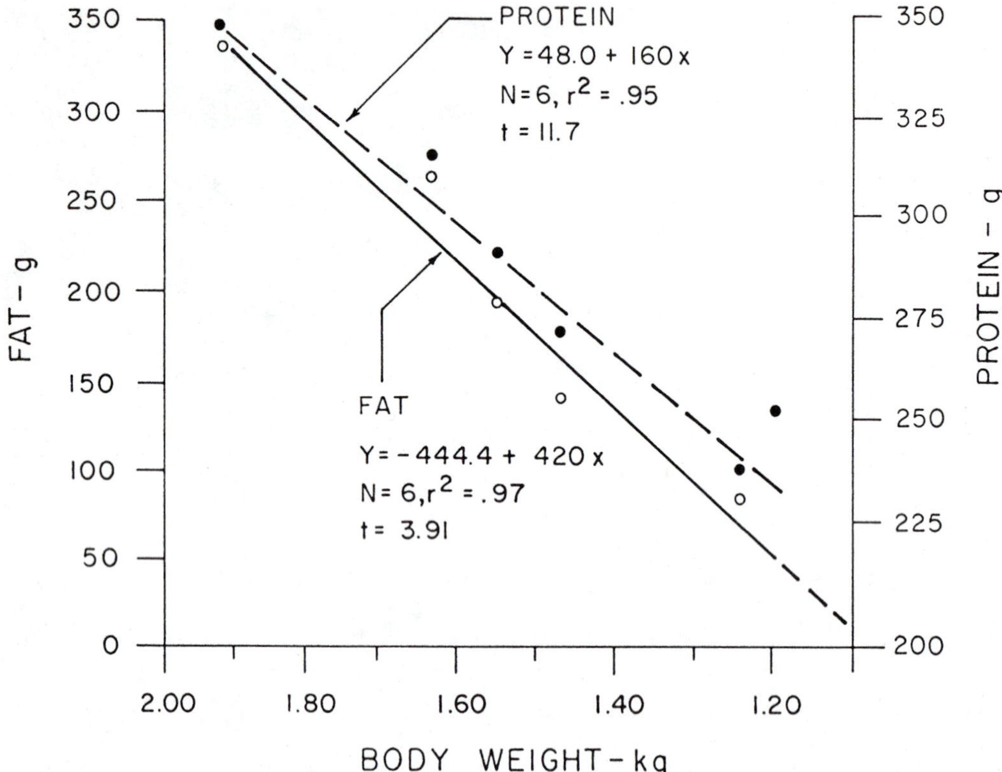

Fig. 7. Fat and protein content of incubating American eiders.

and the increase in weight of protein depots. An adult female was collected on 22 October; the carcass had very little subcutaneous and no visceral fat, and carcass analysis revealed that this bird had only 60 g of fat and 337 g of protein. Three females taken in winter all weighed within 30 g of each other. The grams of protein in each eider were essentially the same, and averaged 362. These birds contained an average of 175 g of fat. Two females collected 12 April had weights close to the April mean body weight. These females contained an average of 159 g of fat, and protein levels had increased to 418 g, 56 g more than found in winter birds. A visual rating of fat disclosed that female eiders in April were reducing the subcutaneous depots and increasing the visceral ones.

Eiders entered the egg-laying cycle with tremendous quantities of stored fat, both subcutaneous and visceral; 460 g in one prelaying bird was probably typical. Females divest a significant amount of fat and protein into eggs. Analyses of eggs showed that a female eider in Maine, laying an average clutch of 4 eggs, deposits 60 g of protein and 70 g of fat into the clutch. Laying birds, which had already deposited part of a clutch, had an average of 354 g of fat. During incubation, as body weight decreased, fat depots were significantly reduced (Fig. 7). During ova formation, laying, and the 26 days of incubation, the average female appeared to utilize over 300 g of stored fat and would have depleted all fat reserves when the body weight approached 1.10 kg.

Carcasses of laying birds had an average of 382 g of protein. However, the birds cannot physiologically mobilize their protein reserves to the same extent that fat depots are depleted. Females lost significant amounts of protein during incubation (Fig. 7).

Blood Plasma Constituents of Incubating Eiders

Successive hematocrits (2 or more) were obtained from 63 females. A paired *t*-test showed that there was a significant decrease in the hematocrit during incubation. A summary of the frequency of change in hematocrit was indicative of this trend. The hematocrit decreased in 48 (76%) of the birds, increased in 11 (18%), and remained the same in 4 (6%). Decreased hematocrit percentages were significantly correlated with lower total plasma protein levels.

No correlation was found between the concentration of plasma glucose and uric acid levels and the length of time the bird had been incubating or body weight. A paired *t*-test on the data collected from females captured and then recaptured indicated that there was not a significant change in plasma glucose or uric acid levels during incubation.

Total protein levels in the blood plasma of incubating eiders significantly declined as weight of the female declined. The combined data from 20 birds indicated that total protein was 12 percent less after the bird had been incubating. Plasma proteins are important for the maintenance of water balance and antibody production (Sturkie 1965:48) and are degraded only under extreme duress, the other tissues being sacrificed to maintain normal plasma protein levels (Keys et al. 1950). The plasma protein levels of the incubating eiders' blood reflected the degree to which they were stressed.

An increase in non-protein nitrogen (NPN) is associated with gluconeogenesis. NPN levels of incubating eiders could not be correlated with a decline in body weight. The mean NPN level of incubating eiders was 11.5 ± 0.65 mg/100 ml which was considerably lower than levels in breeding blue-winged teal (*Anas discors*) (Harris 1970) or wintering pintails (*A. acuta*) (Quortrup et al. 1957).

In breeding blue-winged teal, free fatty acid (FFA) levels increased and then decreased as body weight declined, suggesting a depletion of fat reserves (Harris 1970). In my study, FFA levels significantly increased as the body weight of eiders decreased, indicating that fat stores were not totally depleted in *incubating* birds.

In summary, the hematocrit, total plasma protein, and free fatty acid levels were physiological parameters that reflected degenerative changes in incubating eiders. Levels of NPN appeared to be considerably depressed but did not change during incubation. No changes were apparent in levels of plasma glucose or uric acid, although changes could have occurred before incubation began.

Effects of Reproductive Stress

Abandonment of Nests.—Desertion rates in all eider studies probably should be regarded as minimal figures. In the 3 field seasons of my study, a minimum of 42 of 372 (11%) of the nesting attempts were terminated by abandonment. These data are based only on nests of captured females. If the incubation period is divided roughly into thirds, 7 of 25 of the clutches were deserted in the first third (days 1–9), 14 in the second third (days 10–18), and 4 in the final third (days 19–26). Predictions of the birds' weight on the 26th day of incubation, based on an average loss of 23 g/

day from their weight when captured, gave the following results: 8 of 25 had predicted weights of less than 1.10 kg; 16 had predicted weights less than the mean final weight of 1.29 kg over the entire season, and only 1 had a weight greater than the mean weight on the 26th day of incubation.

Renesting Potential.—Milne (1963:101) and Paynter (1951) felt that once an eider lost a clutch she normally did not lay a second one. However, Cooch (1965) reported that some northern eiders (*S. m. borealis*) had the ability to renest. Sarbello (1973) found that only 16 of 112 (14 percent) marked female eiders in Penobscot Bay renested following the loss of initial clutches, although some others probably renested but were not captured.

I trapped 6 females during this study that were known to have renested. Three of these successfully completed their renesting attempts. Two of these females were recaptured on the day their renest clutches hatched and weighed 1.10 and 1.15 kg, significantly less than the mean weight of other birds that presumably hatched initial clutches the same week.

Except in 1 instance, renesting females lost at least 23 g of body weight for each day they incubated their second clutch, which is equal to or greater than loss during initial attempts. Two renesting females caught in the early stages of incubation had predicted final weights of less than 1.10 kg and both of these birds deserted their clutches.

Sarbello (1973) found the interval between the destruction of the first nest and the laying of the first egg in the renest to average 23 days for 14 renesting American eiders. Practically all of the renesting birds would have hatched their second clutch, if successful, after 1 July and some as late as August. Sarbello (1973:49) stated that the mean renest interval observed for American eiders was the longest of any waterfowl species yet studied. During my study the mean renesting intervals for 3 females was 21 days, similar to the 23 days that Sarbello observed. These renest clutches also would have hatched very late in the season—15 July or later.

Age-Related Productivity.—Some American eiders live at least 13 years (Wakeley and Mendall 1976); therefore, physiological maturity may be important in determining the reproductive efficiency of eiders. Banding of nesting adults provides the only means of separating eiders into 2 age-based classes—previously banded birds (returns) and a formerly unbanded group. The return group is composed of known older individuals that have nested at least once, while the latter group contained young females nesting for the first time plus an unknown percentage of older birds that evaded capture in previous years.

The eiders that first came ashore to nest on the Islesboro study area usually chose sites under artificial shelters. A total of 23 banded birds initiated nests under shelters in 1975. The mean minimum age for this entire group was 6 years and the mean clutch size was 5 eggs. Fifty unbanded females (i.e., mean minimum age of 2 years) that initiated nests in vegetation had significantly smaller clutches averaging 3.9 eggs. Whether the birds that nested in vegetation were losing a few eggs from their clutches due to gull predation during laying, or fewer eggs actually were laid is not known. In any event, the mean clutch size of the older group is larger than the mean clutch size for American eiders reported by Paynter (1951), Choate (1966), and Guignion (1967).

Vulnerability to Diseases and Parasites.—The physiological stresses related to egg laying and incubation undoubtedly render the female eiders more susceptible to disease. Evidence for such lies in the fact that during recent years there have been, among American eiders in Maine and Quebec, 4 major outbreaks of avian cholera (*Pasteurella multocida* infection) (Gershman et al. 1964, Reed and Cousineau 1967, H. L. Mendall, unpublished data), plus several minor ones. The most recent outbreak of avian cholera in Maine, in 1974, was apparently confined to a few islands in Penobscot Bay.

Avian cholera epidemics appear to occur when populations of physiologically stressed birds come in contact with the disease organism. Cholera outbreaks in Maine have peaked during mid- or late June when the greatest number of birds were in continually decreasing physical condition. Other observations made while autopsying females that had been incubating revealed that their spleen, one of the primary immunological organs, appeared to be markedly smaller in size. This organ possibly may lose part of its function or be less effective during and after incubation, thereby making the eiders more susceptible to any kind of stressing agent. Likewise, the levels of total protein, which would include some of the immunologically important globulins, decreased during incubation.

Recent studies of the parasite fauna of eiders have been conducted by Persson et al. (1974) in Sweden, Bishop and Threllfall (1974) in Newfoundland and Liat (1971) in Scotland. These studies pointed out the frequent and severe infestations of the acanthocephalid worm, *Polymorphus botulus.* Persson et al. (1974) stated that *Polymorphus* spp. seemed to be more pathogenic to eider ducks than any other parasite. One severe infestation of this parasite has occurred among Maine eider ducks (Clark et al. 1958). Fortunately for adult female eiders, any infections of intestinal parasites acquired during the period of hyperphagia prior to egg laying, will, in themselves, be of little consequence. I found that intestinal parasites were killed during the starvation associated with the incubation period.

DISCUSSION

Arctic nesting geese (Ankney 1974, MacInnes et al. 1974, Ryder 1970) and American eiders (my study) have similar reproductive strategies: (1) they rely heavily upon protein and fat reserves during laying and (2) they lay small clutches. However, the strategy may have evolved for different reasons. Arctic nesting geese are laying the largest clutch that the birds can possibly lay—given the constraints of accumulating fat and protein reserves and poor feeding at the time of laying (MacInnes et al. 1974). Milne (1976) implies that the pattern of reproduction in which eider females abstain from feeding throughout the 26 days, has almost certainly evolved in relation to severe egg predation which can occur when the females leave the nest. I agree with Milne, especially in view of the fact that eiders in Maine undergo the period of hyperphagia in the vicinity of nesting islands. The possibility of predation upon an incomplete clutch is reduced because laying of the complete clutch occurs in a shorter time. Species laying small clutches also can be more attentive to their nests during incubation, whereas those laying large clutches probably would deplete their nutrient reserves and leave their nests for long periods of time while feeding.

Female eiders appear to take advantage of all possible opportunities to prepare themselves for the reproductive cycle. My data show that, starting in April, the organs of female eiders hypertrophy. These tissues are probably increasing in size during a period of hyperphagia, which Gorman and Milne (1971) observed in European eiders. At this time hyperphagia also results in hyperlipogenesis that may produce extreme fatness in a few days (Odum 1960, King and Farner 1965).

Female eiders have, therefore, adapted to terminate feeding and to complete the clutch as fast as possible. Thus, the birds draw upon their stored energy resources to lay eggs. The weight lost from the gizzard alone during the period of egg formation would fulfill the protein requirements of nearly 1.5 eggs, or 38 percent of the protein requirement of the entire clutch. Similar, but smaller, decreases in the mass of the pectoral muscles and intestine probably contribute much of the entire requirement for the clutch. The lipid requirements of the clutch are fulfilled by mobilization of stored fat.

The eiders must have an energy reserve to maintain themselves during incubation, and basically have 2 sources, the skeletal muscles and stored fat. According to Hanson (1962) a bird cannot reduce its fat depots during a period of starvation without simultaneous reduction of its protein "pool." Data on incubating eiders in Maine showed that they utilized nearly 300 g of fat and 120 g of protein while incubating and that the average bird had only limited stored energy at the time the clutch hatched.

Literature regarding the importance of protein and fat reserves to metabolism was summarized by Hanson (1962:33). In times of starvation, liver and intestinal proteins are the most labile, with muscle proteins next (Fisher 1954). Benedict and Lee (1937:40) observed that increases in body weight of adult geese above the normal weight were chiefly additions of water and fat and were not accompanied by a corresponding increase in protein. However, other workers emphasize that there is a temporary pool of intracellular amino acids (Hoffman 1954) and that "deposit protein" is not a specialized storage product but the cytoplasm itself (Fisher 1954). Kendall et al. (1973) observed that the pectoralis major of red-billed queleas (*Quelea quelea*) is a labile protein-rich component that could be drawn upon during protein demanding processes such as egg production and molt, as well as during periods of fasting.

Benedict and Lee (1937:106) and Hanson (1962) observed that, even after prolonged fasting, geese usually had stores of visible fat. Gorman and Milne (1971) observed that European eiders at the end of incubation contained only about 10 g of fat, indicating that many nesting eiders had totally depleted fat depots.

If the weight loss percentage prior to death observed for other waterfowl (Hanson 1962, Jordan 1953, Trautman et al. 1939) are applied to eiders, they could not tolerate a loss of more than 56 percent of prelaying body weight (2.50 kg) or 44 percent of weight at the start of incubation (1.83 kg). On this basis, eiders during pre- and post-egg laying would have terminal death weights of 1.10 and 1.04 (average 1.07) kg, respectively. Actual data collected on the weights of birds on the 26th day of incubation and of birds abandoning clutches, and levels of carcass fat, confirmed my impression that most females physiologically could not afford to incubate after their body weight approached 1.10 kg. Birds that hatched clutches between 12 and 18 July weighed an average of 1.18 kg, only 80 g above the critical weight. Based on the relative amounts of protein and fat available for metabolism, the birds probably could not have extended incubation, had it been necessary, for more than 2 additional days.

Choate (1966) studied nesting success of eiders on the same islands as in my investigation. In the 2 years of his study, nest success increased to the last part of June, after which it declined until the season ended around 20 July. He assumed that greater loss of late nests indicated a lack of success in renests. However, Sarbello (1973) found that renests were more successful than initial nests. Milne (1963:203) observed that the percentage of nests destroyed by predators increased as the nesting season advanced, presumably because crows (*Corvus* sp.) learned to find eider nests or, alternatively, and less likely, he felt, as a result of an increasing inattentiveness among eider females with the advancing season.

Eiders may desert nests much more frequently than reported because many abandoned clutches are probably destroyed by predators. All field studies, but especially those conducted in the latter part of the eider nesting season, may disrupt birds with nearly depleted nutrient reserves. Tinbergen (1958) observed incubating European eiders that became so weak they abandoned their nests, even clutches of pipped eggs. Natural selection would be against those birds that sacrifice themselves in favor of their broods, for neither benefits. American eiders are long-lived birds (Wakeley and Mendall 1976) and total production over the life of an individual female would be little affected by abandonment of the clutch in 1 year. Milne (Personal communication) found that European eiders that had died (cause unknown) on the nest in Scotland weighed between 1.0 and 1.2 kg, indicating that they were in the latter stages of the incubation. Eleven dead eiders found in nesting cover in my study were not in fresh enough condition for me to determine their cause of death or procure meaningful weight data. However, it is possible that a few eiders may remain on the nest too long to insure survival. Ankney (1974) observed that approximately 200 female blue geese died of starvation on his study area in 1 year. Death in blue geese occurred right at or just before hatch.

Choate (1966) stated that human disturbance did not appear to cause nest desertion, which averaged 5 percent during the 2 years of his study. Milne's (1963:120) observations supported Choate's data. Milne found that about 12 percent of the eiders abandoned their nests each year, about one-half as many as were lost due to predation. He observed that females deserting nests had a lower mean clutch size than those that had their nests destroyed. He felt this reflected the tendency for eiders to desert more readily during the early stages of egg laying than at any other time, or possibly indicated that some females that lay small clutches are more likely to desert than are other females. Females in poor condition may lay smaller clutches and be more likely to desert them (Milne 1963:118, MacInnes et al. 1974).

The physiological changes that occur in the breeding female eider, even before incubation begins, probably result in the long renest interval. The observed reduction and nearly complete termination of function of the alimentary tract during egg laying would limit the ability to replenish nutrient reserves readily. Females would be limited initially to feeding on food items much smaller than normally taken, and a less than normal quantity of food could be processed by the abnormally small gizzard at any one time. A renesting bird probably must feed as much as possible during the renest interval and, unless fat and protein stores are reestablished, she will not be able to produce a clutch of eggs and have sufficient energy reserves to fast throughout the incubation period. Eiders that renest successfully are more likely older birds that have learned to exploit fully the food resource and nest early. Only females that can establish optimum conditions quickly will have an opportunity to obtain a mate, lay eggs, and incubate a second time.

Schamel (1974) stated that after loss of an incomplete clutch, it was quite possible that female Pacific eiders (*Somateria mollissima v-nigra*) continued their nesting efforts at either the same nest or another. Schamel did not consider this renesting but rather a continuation of a single clutch of eggs. He therefore felt that eider productivity was not as greatly affected by gulls as indicated by the low nesting success, but he did not present any data on the physical condition of females. From my study, I suspect that American eiders in Maine that continue to lay eggs, even twice the number of a normal clutch, might not have the energy reserve to incubate them.

CONCLUSION

Although the overall productivity is increased by the eider's reproductive strategy, productivity of individuals may be limited. Reproduction is stressful and under certain conditions becomes potentially dangerous to female American eiders. These birds attain peak physical condition before egg laying so that a small clutch of large eggs can be laid rapidly. The eggs are incubated almost constantly as the female utilizes metabolic reserves for energy; thus the eggs are protected. Females that initiate the cycle without sufficient reserves are forced to abandon their clutches, and occasionally females may even die due to starvation. Only females that nest early and can establish optimum condition quickly will have time to renest after loss of the initial clutch.

In addition to stresses found to be important in this investigation, other factors such as disease, parasites, and toxological contaminants could directly or indirectly cause mortality or limit productivity. These factors may become even more important in the future.

LITERATURE CITED

ANKNEY, C. D. 1974. The importance of nutrient reserves to breeding blue geese, *Anser caerulescens*. Ph.D. Thesis. Univ. Western Ontario, London. 212pp.

BELLROSE, F. C., T. G. SCOTT, A. S. HAWKINS, AND J. B. LOW. 1961. Sex ratios and age ratios in North American ducks. Illinois Nat. Hist. Surv. Bull. 27(6):391–474.

BENEDICT, F. G., AND R. C. LEE. 1937. Lipogenesis in the animal body, with special reference to the physiology of the goose. Carnegie Inst. Wash. Publ. 489. 232pp.

BISHOP, C. A., AND W. THRELLFALL. 1974. The helminth parasites of the common eider (*Somateria mollissima*) in Newfoundland and Labrador. Helminth. Soc. Wash. 41(1):25–35.

BOURGET, A. A. 1970. Interrelationships of eiders, herring gulls, and black-backed gulls nesting in mixed colonies in Penobscot Bay, Maine. M.S. Thesis. Univ. of Maine, Orono. 121pp.

CANTIN, M., J. BEDARD, AND H. MILNE. 1974. The food and feeding of common eiders in the St. Lawrence estuary in summer. Can. J. Zool. 52(3):319–334.

CHOATE, J. S. 1966. The breeding biology of the American eider in Penobscot Bay, Maine. M.S. Thesis. Univ. of Maine, Orono. 173pp.

CLARK, G. M., D. O'MEARA, AND J. W. VAN WEELDEN. 1958. An epizootic among eider ducks involving acanthocephalan worm. J. Wildl. Manage. 22(2):204–205.

CLARK, S. H. 1968. The breeding ecology and experimental management of the American eider in Penobscot Bay, Maine. M.S. Thesis. Univ. of Maine, Orono. 169pp.

COOCH, F. G. 1965. The breeding biology and management of the northern eider (*Somateria mollissima borealis*) in the Cape Dorset area, Northwest Territories. Can. Wildl. Serv. Bull. Ser. 2, No. 10. 68pp.

FISHER, R. B. 1954. Protein metabolism. Methuen and Co., London. 198pp.

GERSHMAN, M., J. F. WITTER, H. E. SPENCER, AND A. KALVAITUS. 1964. Case report: Epizootic of fowl cholera in the common eider duck. J. Wildl. Manage. 28(3):587–589.

GORMAN, M. L., AND H. MILNE. 1971. Seasonal changes in the adrenal steroid tissue of the common eider (*Somateria mollissima*) and its relation to organic metabolism in normal and oil-polluted birds. Ibis 113(2):218–228.

GUIGNION, D. L. 1967. A nesting study of the common eider (*Somateria mollissima*) in the St. Lawrence estuary. M.S. Thesis. Laval Univ., Quebec. 131pp.

HANSON, H. C. 1962. The dynamics of condition factors in Canada geese and their relation to seasonal stresses. Arct. Inst. N. Am. Tech. Pap. 12. 68pp.

HARRIS, H. J. 1970. Evidence of stress response in breeding blue-winged teal. J. Wildl. Manage. 34(4):747–755.

HOFFMAN, W. S. 1954. The biochemistry of clinical medicine. The Year Book Publishers, Chicago. 681pp.

JORDAN, J. S. 1953. Effects of starvation on wild mallards. J. Wildl. Manage. 17(3):304–311.

KENDALL, M. D., P. WARD, AND S. BACCHUS. 1973. A protein reserve in the pectoralis major flight muscle of *Quelea quelea.* Ibis 115 (4):600–601.

KEYS, A., J. BORZEK, A. HENSCHEL, O. MICKELSEN, AND H. L. TAYLOR. 1950. The biology of human starvation. Univ. Minnesota Press, Vols. 1 and 2. 1385pp.

KING, J. R., AND D. S. FARNER. 1965. Studies of fat deposition in migratory birds. Pages 422–440 *in* H. Wipple, ed. Adipose tissue metabolism and obesity. Ann. New York Acad. Sci. 131.

LACK, D. 1954. The natural regulation of animal numbers. Oxford Univ. Press, London. 343pp.

LIAT, L. B. 1971. Ecological studies of the acanthocephalan, *Profilicollis botulus* (van Cleave, 1916), in the eider duck, *Somateria mollissima* (L.), and shore crab, *Carcinus maenas* (L.), from the Ythan estuary, Aberdeenshire. M.S. Thesis. Aberdeen Univ., Scotland. 52pp.

MACINNES, C. D., R. A. DAVIS, R. N. JONES, B. C. LIEFF, AND A. J. PAKULAK. 1974. Reproductive efficiency of McConnell River small Canada geese. J. Wildl. Manage. 38(4):686–707.

MILNE, H. 1963. Seasonal distribution and breeding biology of the eider, *Somateria mollissima mollissima* L., in the north-east Scotland. Ph.D. Thesis. Aberdeen Univ., Scotland. 235pp.

———. 1976. Body weights and carcass composition of the common eider. Wildfowl 27: 115–122.

NIE, H. H., C. H. HALL, J. G. JENKINS, K. STEINBRENNER, AND D. H. BENT. 1975. SPSS: Statistical package for the social sciences. McGraw-Hill Book Co., New York. 675pp.

ODUM, E. P. 1960. Premigratory hyperphagia in birds. Am. J. Clin. Nutr. 8(5):621–629.

PAYNTER, R. A., JR. 1951. Clutch size and egg mortality of Kent Island eiders. Ecology 32(3):497–507.

PERSSON, L., K. BORG, AND H. FALT. 1974. On the occurrence of endoparasites in eider ducks in Sweden. Viltrevy Swedish Wildl. 9(1): 1–24.

QUORTRUP, E. R., M. E. GOETZ, AND J. W. DUNSING. 1957. Studies on the incidence of poultry diseases in wild ducks. California Fish Game 43(2):139–141.

REED, A., AND J. G. COUSINEAU. 1967. Epidemics involving the common eider (*Somateria mollissima*) at Ile Blanche, Quebec. Trans. Northeast Section Wildl. Soc. 24. 13pp.

RYDER, J. P. 1970. A possible factor in the evolution of clutch size in Ross' goose. Wilson Bull. 82(1):5–13.

SARBELLO, W. 1973. Renesting of the American eider in Penobscot Bay colonies. M.S. Thesis. Univ. of Maine, Orono. 67pp.

SCHAMEL, B. S. 1974. The breeding biology of the Pacific eider (*Somateria mollissima v-nigra* Bonaparte) on a barrier island in the Beaufort Sea, Alaska. M.S. Thesis. Univ. of Alaska, Fairbanks, 95pp.

SNEDECOR, G. W., AND W. G. COCHRAN. 1967. Statistical methods, 6th ed. The Iowa State Univ. Press, Ames. 593pp.

STURKIE, P. D. 1965. Avian physiology. Cornell Univ. Press, Ithaca, N.Y. 766pp.

TINBERGEN, N. 1958. Curious naturalists. Country Life Ltd., London. 280pp.

TRAUTMAN, M. B., W. E. BILLS, AND E. L. WICKLIFF. 1939. Winter losses from starvation and exposure of waterfowl and upland game birds in Ohio and other northern states. Wilson Bull. 51(2):86–104.

WAKELEY, J. S., AND H. L. MENDALL. 1976. Migrational homing and survival of adult female eiders in Maine. J. Wildl. Manage. 40(1): 15–21.

WELLER, M. W. 1957. An automatic nest trap for waterfowl. J. Wildl. Manage. 21(4):456–458.

Received 19 May 1976.
Accepted 1 February 1977.

THE USE OF NUTRIENT RESERVES BY BREEDING MALE LESSER SNOW GEESE *CHEN CAERULESCENS CAERULESCENS*

C. DAVISON ANKNEY, Department of Zoology, University of Western Ontario, London, Ontario N6A 5B7, Canada

Abstract: Breeding male lesser snow geese were collected at the McConnell River, Northwest Territories, and the size of their nutrient reserves (fat and protein) were indexed. The males use these reserves during nesting but protein use is less than that reported for females. It is argued that males use food available on the territory and thus remain in better condition than females. This allows them to protect the female and to become guardian of the family after hatch.

Male birds, unlike females, require little energy for gonadal growth (King 1973). Nevertheless, males of many species lose weight during the breeding season. Although little is known about the physiological stresses incurred by breeding males (Roseberry and Klimstra 1971), male weight loss is thought to reflect the demands of courtship and (or) territory defense (e.g. Anderson 1972, Brenner 1968, Hanson 1962, Murton et al. 1974, Oring 1969, Ryder 1975). In certain species incubation is an energetic cost for males (El-Wailly 1966). Weight loss by breeding males is usually assumed to reflect fat utilization, although in spruce grouse (*Dendragapus canadensis*) male weight changes primarily reflect changes in muscle mass (Pendergast and Boag 1973).

Tundra-nesting geese are heavy and have large fat reserves on arrival at the breeding grounds and show reduced feeding during egg laying and incubation (Barry 1962, 1967; Cooch 1958; Hanson 1962; Ryder 1970, 1975). Weight loss, by both sexes, occurs during breeding in several species (brant *Branta bernicla*) (Barry 1962); Canada goose (*B. canadensis*) (Hanson 1962); lesser snow geese (*Chen caerulescens caerulescens*) (Cooch 1958); Ross' goose (*C. rossi*) (Ryder 1970, 1975). Ankney and MacInnes (unpublished manuscript) showed that weight loss in nesting female lesser snow geese results from use of nutrient reserves (mainly fat and protein) for egg production and incubation. However, detailed information about changes in the weight of nutrient reserves of male geese has not been published. My purposes are to present such data for male lesser snow geese (which here includes the blue and white color phases) and to explain their significance to the reproductive strategy of this species. These data provide some support for Ryder's (1975) hypothesis about the evolution of territory size for colonial nesting geese.

METHODS

Data are from male lesser snow geese collected from mid-May through mid-July 1971 and 1972, at the nesting colony at the mouth of the McConnell River (60°50′N, 94°25′W), Northwest Territories, Canada. The area was described by MacInnes (1962). Breeding phenology and timing of collection periods were nearly identical in the 2 years (Table 1) and the data have been combined. I assigned birds to the following categories (collection methods are given by Ankney 1974): *arriving*, males arriving on the

---

[1] Originally published in Can. J. Zool. 55: 1984–1987, 1977. Reproduced by permission of the National Research Council of Canada.

Table 1. Breeding phenology and collection periods.

	1971	1972
Peak of arrival	27 May–28 May	26 May–27 May
Collected arriving ♂♂	23 May–29 May	23 May–31 May
Peak of laying	28 May– 3 June	27 May– 2 June
Collected laying ♂♂	30 May– 1 June	30 May– 7 June
Collected early incubation ♂♂	5 June–15 June	5 June–14 June
Collected failed nesters ♂♂	—	22 June–24 June
Collected late incubation ♂♂	26 June–27 June	19 June–26 June
Peak of hatch	27 June–29 June	26 June–28 June
Collected posthatch ♂♂	6 July–13 July	6 July –13 July

breeding ground; *laying*, males mated to females that had just completed laying; *early incubation*, males mated to females that had incubated 6–11 days (incubating geese were collected from nests with known histories); *late incubation*, males mated to females that had incubated at least 17 days of the 23-day incubation period; *posthatch*, males collected 7–14 days after the peak of the egg-hatching period; *failed nesters*, males mated to females that were collected feeding, away from the colony, at the end of incubation.

I used body weight, i.e., the fresh weight of a gander minus the weight of intestinal contents, as an overall index of its nutrient reserves. The protein reserve index (protein RI) is the total day weight of sternal muscles (pectoralis, supracoracoideus, and coracobrachialis), leg muscles (all muscles having either their origin or insertion on the femur or tibiotarsus), and gizzard (minus contents). The fat reserve index (fat RI) is the total wet weight of subcutaneous, mesenteric, and abdominal fat. Sternal and leg muscles were excised unilaterally and dry weights were doubled to compute the protein RI. Muscles were freeze-dried in 1971 and oven-dried (22 h at 105°C) in 1972; these techniques did not remove significantly different amounts of water from comparable samples (Ankney 1974). The components of the protein RI are presented separately and in total as they did not show simultaneous weight changes.

I did not measure intracellular fat in the muscles for two reasons. Firstly, most intracellular fat is not an energy reserve (Hoar 1966). Secondly, Hanson (1962) showed that variation in intracellular fat

Table 2. Changes in body and nutrient-reserve weights (grams) of breeding males. Mean ± SE.

	Arriving (N = 45)	P[a]	Laying (N = 18)	P[a]	Early incubation (N = 18)	P[a]	Late incubation (N = 22)	P[a]	Posthatch (N = 22)
Body weight	2,810 ± 40	NS	2,680 ± 60	***	2,400 ± 40	**	2,250 ± 40	NS	2,250 ± 40
Protein RI	246.2 ± 4.7	NS	247.2 ± 9.3	NS	228.7 ± 5.3	*	211.3 ± 5.3	NS	212.6 ± 5.6
Gizzard	34.1 ± 0.7	***	29.2 ± 1.1	NS	27.0 ± 1.0	NS	25.7 ± 0.8	***	29.6 ± 0.8
Breast muscle	135.5 ± 3.2	NS	136.9 ± 5.8	NS	124.2 ± 3.6	*	114.4 ± 2.8	***	99.1 ± 2.9
Leg muscle	76.6 ± 2.0	NS	81.1 ± 3.2	NS	77.2 ± 3.2	NS	70.8 ± 2.6	**	83.9 ± 3.4
Fat RI	398.5 ± 18.1	***	272.3 ± 24.3	***	116.1 ± 17.9	***	46.1 ± 6.1	—	—

[a] P = probability (from one-way ANOVA between each pair of adjacent means) that means in adjacent columns are different by chance.
* $P < 0.05$, ** $P < 0.01$, *** $P < 0.001$, NS indicates $P > 0.05$.
[b] None had a measurable amount of fat.

content of leg and breast muscles of Canada geese accounted for little of their weight changes.

Statistical tests follow Sokal and Rohlf (1969); significance was set at the 5% level.

RESULTS

Breeding male lesser snow geese used nutrient reserves after arrival on the breeding ground (Table 2). Mean body weight was highest at arrival (Table 2); in laying males, collected an average of 7 days later, mean body weight was lower, but not significantly ($0.1 > P > 0.05$). Mean body weight decreased significantly during the nesting period (weight loss averaged 20% from arriving through late incubation) but no change occurred during posthatch. The fat RI decreased significantly during successive periods and was depleted by the middle of posthatch (Table 2). The only significant change in the protein RI occurred between early and late incubation. However, changes in the components of the protein RI were sometimes in different directions and thus cancelled each other (e.g. between arriving and laying, and between late incubation and posthatch).

I compared failed nesters with late incubation males as both groups were collected during the same period (Table 1). They differed significantly ($P < 0.05$) only in mean gizzard weight; the heavier gizzards of failed nesters result from increased feeding by these birds (Ankney 1977).

DISCUSSION

Feeding by male lesser snow geese declines after they arrive on the breeding ground until midway through incubation but increases late in incubation (Ankney 1977). Males arrived with large nutrient reserves and used them, especially fat, during the breeding season (Table 2).

Nutrient reserve use by a male reflects the demands of territory maintenance plus his existence energy; courtship and copulation are completed before lesser snow geese arrive and males do not incubate (Cooch 1958). The energy cost of establishing and defending a territory must be relatively high for these geese because they nest in colonies (often more than 1,000 pairs/km^2 (C. von Barlowen, personal communication)); fights between neighboring males are common during egg laying and incubation.

The decline in protein reserves during incubation was considerably less in males (14% (Table 2)) than in females (35% (Ankney and MacInnes, unpublished manuscript)) even though males are more active than females during incubation. There are two, not mutually exclusive, explanations for that: (1) the nitrogen conserving effect of androgens inhibits protein catabolism in males; and (2) males probably feed more than females during incubation (Ankney 1977) and the oxalacetate required for fat metabolism is mostly derived from dietary carbohydrates rather than from protein catabolism (see Hanson 1962 for a review of avian intermediary metabolism). The former explanation may give a proximate factor in less use of protein reserves by males, but the latter one suggests an ultimate factor: that males establish territories large enough to provide some food during incubation because it is important that they remain physically strong.

Ryder (1975) hypothesized that, in colonial nesting geese, a male should acquire a territory small enough to defend against conspecifics but large enough to provide him with supplemental food. He argued that supplemental food was necessary so that the gander would not have to leave the territory and thus leave the incubating goose undefended from attacks by neighboring ganders. Attacks by ganders on undefended females are a major cause of nest desertion in Canada geese (Ewaschuck and Boag 1972). I agree with Ryder and suggest that food that the male gets on his territory enables him to maintain the large muscles which are important for defending the female.

I have no evidence that males ever deplete their reserves to the point where starvation is the alternative to leaving the territory to feed. Starved males have not been found and reserves of failed nester males were not lower than those of late incubation males. This is not so in females because they occasionally starve to death (Harvey 1971, Ankney 1975) and failed nester females have significantly smaller reserves than late incubation females (Ankney and MacInnes, unpublished manuscript). Even successful females are extremely emaciated at the end of incubation.

In lesser snow geese the strategy of nutrient reserve use during reproduction is as follows. Females rely almost solely on their nutrient reserves for egg production and energy during incubation. This allows them to devote maximal attention to the eggs but they complete incubation in poor physical condition. Males also use nutrient reserves during nesting but that use is mitigated by food eaten on the territory. The gander thus is able to defend the territory and is in relatively good condition at hatch. That is important because he then becomes the guardian of the female and brood and this allows the female to spend much time feeding (Harwood 1975). As a result, females gain weight after hatch (mean increase = 11% (Ankney and MacInnes, unpublished manuscript)) but males do not (Table 2). Thus, large nutrient reserves are very important to breeding lesser snow geese; the male–female 'cooperation' in using these reserves is noteworthy.

ACKNOWLEDGMENTS

I am grateful to Charles MacInnes for advice, encouragement, and assistance during this study. Larry Patterson provided excellent field assistance. This research was supported by the Canadian Wildlife Service, the National Research Council of Canada, and the University of Western Ontario.

LITERATURE CITED

ANDERSON, W. L. 1972. Dynamics of condition parameters and organ measurements in pheasants. Ill. Nat. Hist. Surv. Bull. 30:455–497.

ANKNEY, C. D. 1974. The importance of nutrient reserves to breeding blue geese (*Anser caerulescens caerulescens*). Ph.D. Thesis, University of Western Ontario, London.

———. 1975. Neckbands contribute to starvation in female lesser snow geese. J. Wildl. Manage. 39:825–826.

———. 1977. Feeding and digestive organ size in breeding lesser snow geese. Auk 94:275–282.

BARRY, T. W. 1962. Effects of late seasons on Atlantic brant reproduction. J. Wildl. Manage. 26:19–26.

———. 1967. The geese of the Anderson River delta, Northwest Territories. Ph.D. Thesis, University of Alberta, Edmonton.

BRENNER, F. J. 1968. Energy flow in two breeding populations of redwing blackbirds. Am. Midl. Nat. 79:289–310.

COOCH, F. G. 1958. The breeding biology and management of the blue goose *Chen caerulescens*. Ph.D. Thesis, Cornell University, Ithaca.

EL-WAILLY, A. J. 1966. Energy requirements for egg laying and incubation in the zebra finch *Taeniopygia castonotis*. Condor 68:582–594.

EWASCHUK, E., AND D. A. BOAG. 1972. Factors affecting hatching success of densely nesting Canada geese. J. Wildl. Manage. 36:1097–1106.

HANSON, H. C. 1962. The dynamics of condition factors in Canada geese and their relation to seasonal stresses. Arct. Inst. North Am. Tech. Pap. No. 12.

HARVEY, J. M. 1971. Factors affecting blue goose nesting success. Can. J. Zool. 49:223–234.

HARWOOD, J. 1975. The feeding strategies of blue

geese, *Anser caerulescens*. Ph.D. Thesis, University of Western Ontario, London.

HOAR, W. S. 1966. General and comparative physiology. Prentice-Hall, Englewood Cliffs. p. 226.

KING, J. R. 1973. Energetics of reproduction in birds. *In* Breeding biology of birds. Edited by D. S. Farner. Natl. Acad. Sci., Washington, D.C. pp. 78–107.

MACINNES, C. D. 1962. Nesting of small Canada geese near Eskimo Point, Northwest Territories. J. Wildl. Manage. 26:247–256.

MURTON, R. R., N. J. WESTWOOD, AND A. J. ISAACSON. 1974. Factors affecting egg weight, body weight and moult of the woodpigeon, *Columbia palumbus*. Ibis 116:52–73.

ORING, L. W. 1969. Summer biology of the gadwall at Delta, Manitoba. Wilson Bull. 88:44–54.

PENDERGAST, B. A., AND D. A. BOAG. 1973. Seasonal changes in the internal anatomy of spruce grouse in Alberta. Auk 90:307–317.

ROSEBERRY, J. L., AND W. D. KLIMSTRA. 1971. Annual weight cycles in male and female bobwhite quail. Auk 88:116–123.

RYDER, J. P. 1970. A possible factor in the evolution of clutch size in Ross' goose. Wilson Bull. 82:5–13.

———. 1975. The significance of territory size in colonial nesting geese—An hypothesis. Wildfowl 26:114–116.

SOKAL, R. R., AND F. J. ROHLF. 1969. Biometry. W. H. Freeman, San Francisco.

SELECTED BIBLIOGRAPHY

Population Influences and Characteristics: Physiology and Energetics

ANKNEY, C. D., AND C. D. MACINNES. 1978. Nutrient reserves and reproductive performance of female lesser snow geese. Auk 95:459–471.

BATT, B. D. J. 1977. Individual variation and the analysis of mallard populations. Pages 95–102 *in* T. A. Bookhout, ed. Waterfowl and wetlands—An integrated review. Proc. Symp. at 39th Midwest Fish and Wildl. Conf., Madison, WI. LaCrosse Printing Co., Inc. LaCrosse.

———, AND G. W. CORNWELL. 1972. The effects of cold on mallard embryos. J. Wildl. Manage. 36(3):745–751.

BRADLEY, E. L., AND W. N. HOLMES. 1972. The role of the nasal glands in the survival of ducks (*Anas platyrhynchos*) exposed to hypertonic saline drinking water. Can. J. Zool. 50:611–617.

COOCH, F. G. 1964. A preliminary study of the survival value of a functional salt gland in prairie Anatidae. Auk 81(3):380–393.

COOK, P. A., W. R. SIEGFRIED, AND P. G. H. FROST. 1977. Some physiological and biochemical adaptations to diving in three species of ducks. Comp. Biochem. Physiol. A Comp. Physiol. 57(2):227–228.

DROBNEY, R. D. 1980. Reproductive bioenergetics of wood ducks. Auk 97:480–490.

DWYER, T. J. 1975. Time budget of breeding gadwalls. Wilson Bull. 87(3):335–343.

KEAR, J. 1965. The internal food reserves of hatching mallard ducklings. J. Wildl. Manage. 29(3):523–528.

KOSKIMIES, J., AND L. LAHTI. 1964. Cold-hardiness of the newly hatched young in relation to ecology and distribution in ten species of European ducks. Auk 81(3):281–307.

KRAPU, G. L. 1977. Nutrition of female dabbling ducks during reproduction. Pages 59–70 *in* T. A. Bookhout, ed. Waterfowl and wetlands—An integrated review. Proc. Symp. at 39th Midwest Fish and Wildl. Conf., Madison, WI. LaCrosse Printing Co., Inc. LaCrosse.

———. 1981. The role of nutrient reserves in mallard reproduction. Auk 98:29–38.

———, AND G. A. SWANSON. 1975. Some nutritional aspects of reproduction in prairie nesting pintails. J. Wildl. Manage. 39(1):156–162.

MCLANDRESS, R. M., AND D. G. RAVELING. 1981. Changes in diet and body composition of Canada geese before spring migration. Auk 98:65–79.

ORING, L. W. 1968. Growth, molts, and plumages of the gadwall. Auk 85(3):355–380.

OWEN, M., AND W. A. COOK. 1977. Variation in body weight, wing length and condition of mallard, *Anas platyrhynchos platyrhynchos*, and their relationship to environmental changes. J. Zool. 183:377–395.

OWEN, R. B., JR., AND K. J. REINECKE. 1977. Bioenergetics of breeding dabbling ducks. Pages 71–93 *in* T. A. Bookhout, ed. Waterfowl and wetlands—An integrated review. Proc. Symp. at 39th Midwest Fish and Wildl. Conf., Madison, WI. LaCrosse Printing Co., Inc. LaCrosse.

PENNEY, J. G., AND E. D. BAILEY. 1970. Comparison of the energy requirements of fledgling black ducks and American coots. J. Wildl. Manage. 34(1):105–114.

PRINCE, H. H. 1977. Bioenergetics of postbreeding dabbling ducks. Pages 103–117 *in* T. A. Bookhout, ed. Waterfowl and wetlands—An integrated review. Proc. Symp. at 39th Midwest Fish and Wildl. Conf., Madison, WI. LaCrosse Printing Co., Inc. LaCrosse.

RAVELING, D. G. 1979. The annual energy cycle of the cackling goose. Pages 81–93 *in* R. L. Jarvis and J. C. Bartonek, eds. Management and biology of Pacific flyway geese. A symposium. Northwest Sect. of The Wildl. Soc. Oregon State Univ. Book Stores, Inc., Corvallis.

SMITH, K. G., AND H. H. PRINCE. 1973. The fasting metabolism of subadult mallards acclimatized to low ambient temperatures. Condor 75(3):330–335.

SUGDEN, L. G. 1979. Grain consumption by mallards. Wildl. Soc. Bull. 7:35–39.

THOMAS, V. G., AND J. P. PREVETT. 1980. The nutritional value of arrow-grasses to geese at James Bay. J. Wildl. Manage. 44:830–836.

WELLER, M. W. 1957. Growth, weights, and plumages of the redhead, *Aythya americana*. Wilson Bull. 69(1):5–38.

WYPKEMA, R. C., AND C. D. ANKNEY. 1979. Nutrient reserve dynamics of lesser snow geese staging at James Bay, Ontario. Can. J. Zool. 57:213–219.

FOOD HABITS AND FEEDING ECOLOGY

FOODS OF BREEDING PINTAILS IN NORTH DAKOTA

GARY L. KRAPU, Department of Zoology and Entomology, Iowa State University, Ames 50010[1]

Abstract: Food habits of breeding pintails (*Anas acuta*) were studied relative to sex, land use, and reproductive condition during the spring and summer of 1969, 1970, and 1971 in eastern North Dakota. Hens and drakes, respectively, consumed 79.2 percent and 30.0 percent animal matter on nontilled wetlands and consumed 16.6 percent and 1.1 percent animal matter on tilled wetlands. Aquatic dipterans (primarily larval forms), snails, fairy shrimp, and earthworms accounted for 71 percent of the diet of hens on nontilled wetlands, while barnyard grass (*Echinochloa crusgalli*) seeds formed 71 percent of the diet of hens on tilled wetlands. Cereal grain seeds formed 84 percent of the diet of 10 hens feeding on cropland. The diet of hens was influenced by reproductive status. Animal foods were predominant during the laying period (77.1 percent) but were less important in the postlaying diet (28.9 percent). Invertebrates formed 83.9 percent of the diet of renesting hens; 61.0 percent were dipteran larvae and snails. High consumption of animal foods during egg formation presumably is related to invertebrates being superior to plants in providing certain nutrients required for production of viable eggs. Research findings suggest that food requirements of prairie-nesting pintails can be met most effectively by providing pairs access to shallow, nontilled wetland habitat subject to periodic drawdowns.

J. WILDL. MANAGE. 38(3):408–417

Information on food habits of breeding pintails is scant. Studies of the food habits of the North American pintail have dealt almost exclusively with nonbreeding pintails and have shown this species to be primarily vegetarian (Anderson 1959, Chamberlain 1959, Glasgow and Bardwell 1962, Mabbott 1920, Martin et al. 1951, McGilvrey 1966, McMahan 1970, Munro 1944). Recent food habit investigations on other species of breeding waterfowl have indicated that invertebrates consistently account for a greater proportion of the diet of hens than drakes (Perret 1962, Bartonek and Hickey 1969, Swanson and Nelson 1970). Their findings provided an impetus for determining the magnitude of invertebrate consumption by pintails during the breeding period.

The present study was initiated to determine the diet of drake and hen pintails in three major foraging habitats used during spring and early summer. These foraging habitats were nontilled shallow wetland, tilled wetland, and cropland. Information on reproductive condition of foraging hens was gathered concurrently to provide an assessment of dietary needs associated with reproduction and the capability of selected foraging habitats to provide these needs. This study was supported by the U. S. Fish and Wildlife Service at the Northern Prairie Wildlife Research Center. I am indebted to M. W. Weller, G. A. Swanson, and H. K. Nelson for useful advice and constructive criticism throughout the study, and to P. F. Springer and J. C. Bartonek for critical review of the manuscript.

STUDY AREA

Birds were sampled in an eight-county area of eastern North Dakota; most were collected in Stutsman and Barnes Counties. Collecting occurred primarily on private lands within the Missouri Coteau and Drift Prairie areas. The Coteau is typically a rolling landscape with almost no natural drainage and consequently has tens of thousands of prairie potholes. The Drift Prairie is less rolling, so wetlands tend to be shallow and less permanent. The shallow

[1] Present address: U. S. Fish and Wildlife Service, Northern Prairie Wildlife Research Center, Jamestown, North Dakota 58401.

Originally published in J. Wildl. Manage. 38(3):408–417, 1974.

wetlands of the Drift Prairie are highly utilized by pintails during wet years.

METHODS

Collection of birds and initial handling of samples followed closely the procedures described by Swanson and Bartonek (1970). Only pintail hens whose reproductive condition was unknown were collected. Birds were observed feeding for a minimum of 10 minutes before collection. Immediately after each bird was shot its esophagus was removed and the esophageal contents were flushed into a glass bottle containing 80 percent ethanol to minimize postmortem digestion. Gizzard contents were excluded from these analyses since Swanson and Bartonek (1970) had demonstrated that the use of gizzard contents inflates the importance of seeds in the diet.

Drakes and hens were collected while feeding on nontilled and tilled wetlands and cropland. Nontilled wetland habitat includes the low prairie, wet meadow, and shallow marsh zones as described by Stewart and Kantrud (1971). Tilled wetland habitat refers to wetland basins cultivated prior to reflooding during the current year or after midsummer of the previous year.

Reproductive condition of hens was determined in the laboratory by examining the ovary and by checking for a brood patch. Ovaries were removed, weighed to the nearest 0.1 gram on a triple-beam balance, and examined for ruptured follicles.

On the basis of this information, hens were placed into one of three reproductive stages: prelaying, laying, and postlaying. A few hens did not fit into these categories and were excluded from comparisons involving reproductive condition. Hens placed in the prelaying stage had ovaries weighing a minimum of 3 grams and showing evidence of follicular enlargement, but had not initiated laying. Hens were considered to be in the laying stage when one or more ruptured follicles of an enlarged ovary indicated that laying had begun while at least one enlarged follicle remained to be ovulated or an egg remained in the oviduct. Postlaying hens had ovaries that showed no evidence of recent follicular growth but contained a series of regressing ruptured follicles and/or a well-developed brood patch. Examination of ovary and brood patch made it possible to distinguish many of the renesting hens. Hens with a brood patch that were in the prelaying stage or had one to four recently ruptured follicles were considered renesters. The brood patch forms late in the laying cycle and during incubation so its presence earlier in the cycle was considered indicative of one or more previous clutches.

The brood patch was utilized as an indicator of reproductive condition because changes in the ovary following laying soon make it unsuitable for distinguishing postlaying hens. Phillips and van Tienhoven (1962:296) note that the condition of the ovary changes rapidly so that, by the 6th to 8th day of incubation, the ovary is as small as in hens taken from migratory flocks. Ovulated follicles regress, and their lips fuse quickly making them indistinguishable from small atretic follicles.

Differences in the consumption of animal matter among groups were tested for statistical significance using Student's *t*-test (Snedecor 1956). The 95 percent confidence interval is given with certain volumetric data presented in the text. Plant foods were identified to genus and frequently to species with the aid of the manual by Martin and Barkley (1961). All invertebrates were identified to order and some to family using the keys in Pennak (1953).

Table 1. Esophageal contents of 53 breeding pintails collected while feeding on shallow, nontilled wetlands in North Dakota during 1969, 1970, and 1971.

Food item		Male (14[a])		Female (39)	
Scientific name	Common name[b]	Percent occurrence	Percent volume	Percent occurrence	Percent volume
Plant					
Riccia fluitans	Liverwort (vegetative)	7	0.2		
Potamogeton spp.	Pondweeds (achenes)	14	4.9	5	1.5
Zannichellia palustris	Horned pondweed (nutlets)			5	0.1
Alisma spp.	Water plaintains (seed)	21	1.9	8	0.1
Sagittaria sp.	Arrowhead (tubers, seed)	7	4.6	5	tr
Glyceria spp.	Mannagrasses (caryopses)	21	6.5	15	1.7
Scolochloa festucacea	Whitetop (caryopses)	14	tr[c]	13	1.7
Hordeum jubatum	Wild barley (caryopses)	7	0.9	5	1.8
Hordeum vulgare	Barley (caryopses)	7	4.2	5	0.3
Triticum aestivum	Wheat (caryopses)	7	7.0	10	1.9
Beckmannia syzigachne	Sloughgrass (caryopses)	7	6.6	13	2.5
Phalaris arundinacea	Reed canary grass (caryopses)	7	7.1	3	tr
Echinochloa crusgalli	Barnyard grass (caryopses)	43	4.3	26	1.8
Setaria spp.	Foxtails (caryopses)			7	0.2
Zea mays	Corn (caryopses)			3	2.4
Eleocharis spp.	Spikerushes (achenes)	21	0.7	8	0.7
Scirpus spp.	Bulrushes (achenes)			5	tr
Carex spp.	Sedges (achenes)			13	0.2
Rumex spp.	Docks (achenes)	14	0.2	18	0.5
Polygonum spp.	Smartweeds (achenes)	28	0.2	5	tr
Chenopodium album	Lambsquarters (utricles)	21	1.4	5	0.2
Suaeda depressa	Seablite (seed)	14	13.5		
Ambrosia spp.	Ragweeds (achenes)	7	3.0	10	0.7
Other			2.8		2.5
Total plant matter		86	70.0	62	20.8
Animal					
Oligochaeta	Earthworms	7	0.1	13	10.1
Hirudinea	Leeches			8	0.5
Anostraca	Fairy shrimp	21	3.8	21	10.9
Conchostraca	Clam shrimp	29	0.2	10	2.2
Cladocera	Waterfleas			5	1.2
Ostracoda	Seed shrimp	7	0.2	5	0.1
Odonata	Damselflies (naiads)			5	0.1
Hemiptera	Water boatman	14	tr	8	0.1
Trichoptera	Caddis flies (larvae)			8	0.6
Coleoptera	Water beetles (adults, larvae)	50	0.6	51	3.0
Diptera	Flies (larvae and pupae)	43	20.5	64	27.9
Gastropoda	Snails	50	4.6	62	22.5
Total animal matter		93	30.0	100	79.2

[a] Total number of specimens analyzed.
[b] Part or type in parentheses.
[c] Trace (tr) less than 0.1 percent.

Table 2. Esophageal contents of 21 breeding pintails collected while feeding on shallow tilled wetlands in North Dakota during 1969, 1970, and 1971.

Food item		Male (7[a])		Female (14)	
Scientific name	Common name[b]	Percent occurrence	Percent volume	Percent occurrence	Percent volume
Plant					
Glyceria spp.	Mannagrasses (caryopses)	14	4.5		
Scolochloa festucacea	Whitetop (caryopses)			7	1.0
Triticum aestivum	Wheat (caryopses)	14	14.1	21	1.3
Avena sativa	Oats (caryopses)			7	0.4
Beckmannia syzigachne	Sloughgrass (caryopses)			21	0.1
Setaria glauca	Foxtail (caryopses)	43	14.6	50	8.5
Setaria viridis	Green foxtail (caryopses)			14	0.1
Echinochloa crusgalli	Barnyard grass (caryopses)	57	55.1	93	71.1
Eleocharis acicularis	Spikerush (achenes)	43	2.2		
Scirpus spp.	Bulrushes (achenes)			14	tr[c]
Carex spp.	Sedges (achenes)			14	tr
Rumex spp.	Docks (achenes)			21	0.1
Polygonum spp.	Smartweeds (achenes)	57	0.5	71	0.3
Chenopodium album	Lambsquarters (utricles)	29	1.0		
Amaranthus sp.	Pigweed (seed)			28	0.2
Linum usitatissimum	Flax (caryopses)			14	0.1
Ambrosia spp.	Ragweeds (achenes)	29	0.3		
Other			6.7		0.3
Total plant matter		100	99.0	100	83.5
Animal					
Oligochaeta	Earthworms			7	1.2
Anostraca	Fairy shrimp			29	2.8
Conchostraca	Clam shrimp			7	0.2
Trichoptera	Caddisflies (larvae)			14	0.3
Coleoptera	Water beetles (adults, larvae)			57	2.3
Diptera	Flies (larvae and pupae)	14	0.1	43	8.4
Gastropoda	Snails	14	0.9	43	1.3
Other			0.1		0.1
Total animal matter		29	1.1	86	16.6

[a] Total number of specimens analyzed.
[b] Part or type in parentheses.
[c] Trace(tr) less than 0.1 percent.

RESULTS

Food Habits in Nontilled Wetland Habitat

Food habits of pintails feeding in nontilled wetland habitat are shown in Table 1. Invertebrates comprised 66.2 ± 11.0 percent of the diet of the 53 pintails collected while feeding in nontilled wetland habitat. Invertebrate consumption differed significantly between sexes ($P < 0.001$). Esophageal contents of 39 hens averaged 79.2 ± 9.9 percent animal matter, while 14 drakes averaged 30.0 ± 24.2 percent. Aquatic dipterans (primarily larval forms), snails, fairy shrimp, and earthworms accounted for 71 percent of the diet of females. Midge

Table 3. Esophageal contents of 10 field-feeding pintail hens collected during spring and early summer of 1969 and 1970 in eastern North Dakota.

Food item			
Scientific name	Common name[a]	Occurrence (%)	Volume (%)
Plant			
Hordeum vulgare	Barley (caryopses)	20	10.0
Triticum aestivum	Wheat (caryopses)	90	68.4
Avena sativa	Oats (caryopses)	10	5.2
Beckmannia syzigachne	Sloughgrass (caryopses)	10	tr[b]
Echinochloa crusgalli	Barynyard grass (caryopses)	10	0.1
Linum usitatissimum	Flax (caryopses)	10	tr
Other		10	0.1
Total plant matter		100	83.8
Animal			
Nematoda	Roundworms	10	0.1
Oligochaeta	Earthworms	10	0.7
Conchostraca	Clam shrimp	10	1.0
Odonata	Damselflies (naiads)	10	0.7
Trichoptera	Caddisflies (larvae)	20	3.9
Coleoptera	Water beetles	20	2.3
Diptera	Flies (larvae, pupae)	20	0.2
Gastropoda	Snails	20	7.3
Total animal matter		30	16.2

[a] Part or type in parentheses.
[b] Trace (tr) less than 0.1 percent.

larvae, the principal dipteran consumed, formed 16 percent of the total diet.

Twenty-two plant genera were identified in the diet of pintails collected while feeding in nontilled wetland habitat, but most plant foods were present in very limited quantity (Table 1). On a volumetric basis, seeds of sloughgrass (*Beckmannia syzigachne*), corn (*Zea mays*), wheat, barnyard grass, wild barley (*Hordeum jubatum*), mannagrass (*Glyceria* spp.), and whitetop (*Scolochloa festucacea*) were the dominant plant foods of hens.

Food Habits in Tilled Wetland Habitat

Food habits of pintails feeding in tilled wetland habitat are shown in Table 2. Plant foods formed 88.6 ± 10.4 percent of the diet of 21 pintails collected while feeding in tilled wetland habitat. Barnyard grass accounted for 55 percent of the diet of drakes and 71 percent of the diet of hens and occurred in 57 and 93 percent of the birds, respectively. Barnyard grass seed was the food item most frequently taken by both sexes during spring and summer. This plant is well adapted to wetland tillage since it germinates after water levels recede in late spring and summer and produces seed prior to fall tillage.

Invertebrate consumption by hens was significantly lower in tilled wetland habitat than in nontilled habitat ($P < 0.001$), but consumption by drakes did not differ significantly ($P > 0.05$). Invertebrates comprised 1.1 ± 2.2 percent of the diet of seven

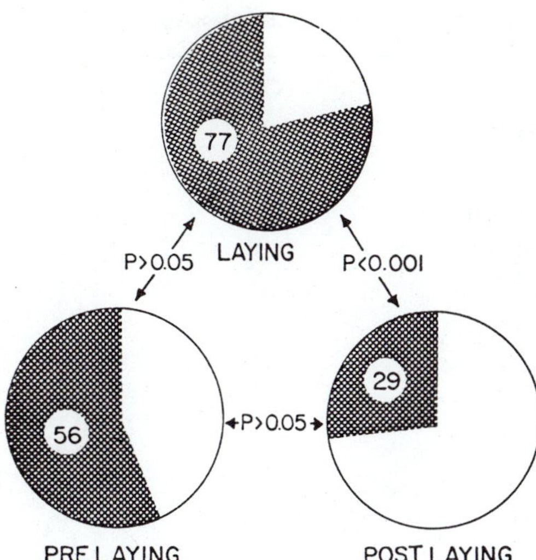

Fig. 1. Invertebrate consumption by pintail hens in North Dakota during certain stages of the reproductive cycle. Percentage of animal matter is shaded.

drakes taken while feeding in this habitat. In comparison to nontilled wetlands the mud bottoms of tilled wetlands generally contained low numbers of the invertebrates consumed by pintails. In late spring and early summer, midge larvae did become relatively abundant in some tilled ponds and were consumed by hens at that time.

Food Habits in Cropland

Pintails regularly field-feed in North Dakota during spring and early summer. This trait has existed for at least several decades because Mabbott (1920:33) indicated the occurrence of wheat, barley (*Hordeum vulgare*), and oats (*Avena sativa*) in the pintail diet by 1920. He referred to a pintail consuming oats in North Dakota in June. Bossenmaier and Marshall (1958:8) suggested that major changes in harvesting methods led to increased field-feeding by ducks in southern Manitoba. During this study pintails observed and collected while field-feeding in spring and early summer had consumed both seed remaining after planting and waste grain from the previous harvest. Field-feeding was observed most frequently during spring migration and after planting in May and June.

For the pintails collected while feeding on cropland, plant foods, principally wheat, accounted for 83.8 ± 18.8 percent of the diet of 10 hens (Table 3), and wheat was the entire diet of two drakes. The frequent occurrence of wheat in the diet of field-feeders probably is related to its high availability on the study area. Statistics of the North Dakota Crop and Livestock Reporting Service (1971) indicate that wheat is the principal cereal crop raised in eastern North Dakota. Preference may also be involved; Hammond (1961:72) reported that pintails consumed wheat more rapidly than barley and that both wheat and barley were preferred to oats.

Food choice on cropland appeared limited, cereal grain providing most of the available food. The 16 percent animal matter in the esophageal contents of the 10 hens consisted entirely of aquatic invertebrates that had been consumed prior to field-feeding.

Diet Relative to Reproductive Status

Animal foods comprised 56.0 ± 27.1 percent of the diet during prelaying (14 hens); 77.1 ± 11.6 percent during laying (31 hens); and 28.9 ± 21.1 percent during postlaying (16 hens). The percentage of plant and animal foods consumed by hens varied significantly from laying to postlaying (Fig. 1). Invertebrates formed 46.5 ± 57.7 percent and 4.6 ± 4.6 percent, respectively, of the diet of 4 laying and 10 nonlaying pintail hens collected while feeding on tilled wetlands. Invertebrates comprised 86.6 ± 10.9 percent of the diet of 20 laying hens collected in the wet-meadow and shallow marsh zones of nontilled wetlands.

Table 4. Esophageal contents of 11 renesting pintail hens collected in eastern North Dakota during 1969 and 1970.

Food item			
Scientific name	Common name[a]	Occurrence (%)	Volume (%)
Plant			
Alisma spp.	Water plaintains (seed)	9	0.2
Glyceria spp.	Mannagrasses (caryopses)	9	0.1
Scolochloa festucacea	Whitetop (caryopses)	9	1.2
Triticum aestivum	Wheat (caryopses)	9	1.3
Beckmannia syzigachne	Sloughgrass (caryopses)	9	tr[b]
Echinochloa crusgalli	Barnyard grass (caryopses)	27	11.0
Scirpus spp.	Bulrushes (achenes)	9	tr
Carex sp.	Sedge (achenes)	27	0.1
Rumex spp.	Docks (achenes)	9	0.2
Amaranthus sp.	Pigweed (seed)	9	0.2
Ambrosia sp.	Ragweed (achenes)	9	1.8
Total plant matter		64	16.1
Animal			
Hirudinea	Leeches	9	0.1
Conchostraca	Clam shrimp	9	0.4
Cladocera	Water fleas	9	4.2
Amphipoda	Scuds	9	0.1
Odonata	Damselflies	18	8.3
Hemiptera	Water boatman	9	0.2
Trichoptera	Caddisflies	9	2.2
Coleoptera	Water beetles	73	7.4
Diptera	Flies	82	40.7
Gastropoda	Snails	36	20.3
Total animal matter		100	83.9

[a] Part or type in parentheses.
[b] Trace(tr) less than 0.1 percent.

The esophageal contents of 11 renesting pintail hens collected from 18 May to 19 June are shown in Table 4. Diptera larvae and snails accounted for 61 percent of the diet of renesting hens. Midge larvae, the principal dipteran consumed, comprised 33 percent of the esophageal contents. Aquatic coleopterans occurred frequently in the diet but biomass ingested was low in comparison to dipteran and snail intake.

Consumption of midge larvae increased as pintails shifted from drying temporary ponds to seasonal wetlands and the shallow marsh zone of more permanent wetlands. During periods following extensive flooding within the low prairie zone, midge larvae were a major food of pintails feeding in this habitat.

Observed differences in animal matter consumption among reproductive stages suggest that segregation of food habits data by reproductive status can prevent major dietary trends from being obscured. Animal foods comprised 59.6 ± 42.2 percent of the diet when data on hens from all reproductive stages were combined.

DISCUSSION

Data indicating consumption of invertebrates is highest during egg formation and occurs principally on nontilled shallow wetland basins have important implications concerning pintail productivity in the prairie pothole region if current land use trends continue. In recent years, livestock-small grain farms have been converted extensively to single purpose grain operations. This change has stimulated widespread drainage and other alterations of prairie wetland basins. Wetland drainage is increasingly affecting the distribution and availability of the aquatic food supply of pintails and other waterfowl. The rate and magnitude of wetland losses are reflected in statistics presented by Aus (1969:317). He reported that 21 percent of all Type III, IV, and V wetlands in a 12-county area of northeastern North Dakota were drained from 1966 through 1968. Many of the remaining wetlands in the prairie pothole region are being used as depositories for water previously held in surrounding wetlands of varying depths. Food habits information indicates pintails feed primarily on organisms characteristic of those wetlands which undergo frequent drying. Loss of part of the wetland complex and increased depth and permanency of the remaining basins reduces availability of pintail foods. Hydrological changes lead to the disappearance of certain preferred foods and increased depth prevents the birds from obtaining other foods still existing on or near the bottom of ponds.

Tillage of wetland basins occurs widely and influences food availability and wetland use by breeding pairs. Stewart and Kantrud (1973:44) indicated that 29 percent of the area and 52 percent of the total number of all wetlands in North Dakota had cultivated bottom soils in 1967. They reported that 24 percent of the breeding pintails were sighted in wetlands with tilled basins from 1967 through 1969. Summer fallowing, fall plowing, and other tillage practices during periods when wetlands are dry destroy the wetland vegetation. Removal of the aquatic plants eliminates the niches of herbivorous and detritus feeding invertebrates that form the bulk of the diet of laying hens. Tillage also affects wetland water levels. Removal of the vegetation from a wetland and/or its watershed in late summer and fall reduces snow accumulation during the following winter leading to a reduction or elimination of spring runoff from snow melt. Runoff into wetlands from rain increases following removal of watershed vegetation but this change is accompanied by increased siltation of wetlands. The water that does accumulate in tilled basins is often turbid particularly during periods of high wind velocity and following heavy rains. In summary, annual tillage of a shallow wetland and the surrounding watershed creates and maintains a harsh environment for those aquatic invertebrates that are consumed regularly by breeding hens. Barnyard grass seeds are often plentiful in basins subjected to frequent tillage and are the principal food of pintails feeding there. Nutrient data reported by Krapu and Swanson (1975) suggest that barnyard grass and other plant foods consumed on wetlands and cropland are inadequate to meet the nutrient needs of breeding hens.

Pintails are attracted to recently flooded shallow wetland habitat and will breed at high densities when such habitat is abundant during the nesting period. Hochbaum and Bossenmaier (1972) noted that when high precipitation flooded 4200 acres (1700 ha) of St. Andrews Bog, an area in southern Manitoba with only 150 acres (61 ha) of permanent marsh in April of 1969, migrant pintails moved into the area in large numbers and an estimated 149 broods were raised per square mile (58 broods/km^2) on the 6.6-square-mile (17.1-km^2) area. Duplication of optimum natural water conditions through controlled water level manipulation, where feasible, can help insure high production of those food organisms consumed by breeding hens. Water level manipulation may be particularly useful for increasing the renesting effort because midge larvae, a major food of renesting pintail hens, respond favorably to controlled water level manipulation. McKnight and Low (1969:311) indicated that the bottom of a diked section of a spring-fed salt marsh in Utah that was dried during August and September of 1967 contained a midge larvae population in July of 1968 that was 18 times that of a nearby site flooded continuously for 3 years. The favorable invertebrate response achieved with artificial drying of wetlands reemphasizes the importance of maintaining natural wetland complexes. A natural wetland complex in a nontilled state provides a long term capability to maintain an adequate food base for breeding waterfowl present in that area. The broad range of water conditions that exist within a complex insures that, during most years, one or more wetlands will be highly productive of fairy shrimp, midge larvae, and/or certain other invertebrates sought by breeding hens.

CONCLUSIONS AND MANAGEMENT RECOMMENDATIONS

Breeding pintail hens obtain animal foods primarily from nontilled, temporary, and seasonal wetland habitats. The need of this species for animal foods during egg formation underscores the importance of maintaining nontilled shallow wetlands as an integral component of wetland complexes in the prairie pothole region.

LITERATURE CITED

ANDERSON, H. G. 1959. Food habits of migratory ducks in Illinois. Illinois Nat. Hist. Surv. Bull. 27(4):289–344.

AUS, P. B. 1969. What is happening to the wetlands? Trans. N. Am. Wildl. Nat. Resour. Conf. 34:315–323.

BARTONEK, J. C., AND J. J. HICKEY. 1969. Food habits of canvasbacks, redheads, and lesser scaup in Manitoba. Condor 71(3):280–290.

BOSSENMAIER, E. F., AND W. H. MARSHALL. 1958. Field-feeding by waterfowl in southeastern Manitoba. Wildl. Monogr. 1. 32pp.

CHAMBERLAIN, J. L. 1959. Gulf coast marsh vegetation as food of wintering waterfowl. J. Wildl. Manage. 23(1):97–102.

GLASGOW, L. L., AND J. L. BARDWELL. 1962. Pintail and teal foods in southern Louisiana. Proc. Southeastern Assoc. Game and Fish Commissioners 16:175–184.

HAMMOND, M. C. 1961. Waterfowl feeding stations for controlling crop losses. Trans. N. Am. Wildl. Nat. Resour. Conf. 26:67–79.

HOCHBAUM, G. S., AND E. F. BOSSENMAIER. 1972. Response of pintails to improved breeding habitat in southern Manitoba. Can. Field Nat. 86(1):79–81.

KRAPU, G. L., AND G. A. SWANSON. 1975. Some nutritional aspects of reproduction in prairie nesting pintails. J. Wildl. Manage. (In press.)

MABBOTT, D. C. 1920. Food habits of seven species of American shoal-water ducks. U. S. Dept. Agric. Bull. 862. 67pp.

MARTIN, A. C., AND W. D. BARKLEY. 1961. Seed identification manual. University of California Press, Berkeley. 221pp.

———, H. S. ZIM, AND A. L. NELSON. 1951. American wildlife and plants. McGraw-Hill, New York. 500pp.

MCGILVREY, F. B. 1966. Fall food habits of ducks near Santee Refuge, South Carolina. J. Wildl. Manage. 30(3):577–580.

MCKNIGHT, D. E., AND J. B. LOW. 1969. Factors affecting waterfowl production on a spring-fed salt marsh in Utah. Trans. N. Am. Wildl. Nat. Resour. Conf. 34:307–314.

MCMAHAN, C. A. 1970. Food habits of ducks wintering on Laguna Madre, Texas. J. Wildl. Manage. 34(4):946–949.

MUNRO, J. A. 1944. Studies of waterfowl in British Columbia. Pintail. Can. J. Res. 22(3): 60–86.

NORTH DAKOTA CROP AND LIVESTOCK REPORTING SERVICE. 1971. North Dakota crop and livestock statistics 1970. U. S. Dept. Agric. and North Dakota State Univ., Fargo, N. Dak. 81pp.

PENNAK, R. W. 1953. Fresh-water invertebrates of the United States. Ronald Press, New York. 769pp.

PERRET, N. G. 1962. The spring and summer foods of the common mallard (*Anas platyrhynchos platyrhynchos* L.) in south central Manitoba. M. S. Thesis. Univ. British Columbia. 82pp.

PHILLIPS, R. E., AND A. VAN TIENHOVEN. 1962. Some physiological correlates of pintail reproductive behavior. Condor 64(4):291–299.

SNEDECOR, G. W. 1956. Statistical methods. 5th ed. Iowa State University Press, Ames. 534pp.

STEWART, R. E., AND H. A. KANTRUD. 1971. Classification of natural ponds and lakes in the glaciated prairie region. U. S. Bur. Sport Fish. Wildl. Resour. Publ. 92. 57pp.

———, AND ———. 1973. Ecological distribution of breeding waterfowl populations in North Dakota. J. Wildl. Manage. 37(1):39–50.

SWANSON, G. A., AND J. C. BARTONEK. 1970. Bias associated with food analysis in gizzards of blue-winged teal. J. Wildl. Manage. 34(4): 739–746.

———, AND H. K. NELSON. 1970. Potential influence of fish rearing programs on waterfowl breeding habitat. Pages 65–71 *in* E. Schneberger, ed. A symposium on the management of midwestern winter-kill lakes. American Fisheries Society, North Central Division. 75pp.

Accepted 26 November 1973.

FEEDING ECOLOGY OF WOOD DUCKS IN SOUTH CAROLINA

J. LARRY LANDERS, School of Forest Resources, University of Georgia, Athens 30602
TIMOTHY T. FENDLEY, Savannah River Ecology Laboratory, Aiken, S. C. 29801
A. SYDNEY JOHNSON, Institute of Natural Resources and School of Forest Resources, University of Georgia, Athens 30602

Abstract: Wood ducks (*Aix sponsa*) were studied from August 1973 to August 1975 at the Savannah River Plant of the U. S. Energy Research and Development Administration in South Carolina. Two hundred feeding wood ducks were collected for study of food habits and nutrition in relation to foraging habitat use. Animal matter in the diet of females increased markedly during the breeding season and was greater ($P<0.05$) than for males. Dietary protein and ash peaked during egg-laying but decreased sharply in May when nitrogen-free extract was lowest of any month and crude fiber was highest; low weights of ducks also indicated a lean period. Percent dietary protein and fat, and weights of ducks were higher during fall of 1973 when there was a good mast crop than during 1974 when a mast failure occurred. Females fed on invertebrates in shallow, open water in spring. Both sexes used deeper water areas for feeding on succulent vegetation during early summer and concentrated in Carolina bays to feed on seeds of pad plants in late summer and early fall. As fall progressed, foraging shifted to seasonally flooded stream swamps.

J. WILDL. MANAGE. 41(1):118–127

Feeding habits of wood ducks in the southeastern United States are known mostly from studies of hunter-killed birds (e.g., Conrad 1965, McGilvrey 1966*a, b,* Kerwin and Webb 1971, Landers et al. 1976). This information has been of value for managing wintering waterfowl, but little is known of dietary and habitat requirements of resident wood ducks from spring through early fall. This study provides information on (1) year-round diet and nutrient intake, (2) differences in diet related to sex, (3) seasonal needs and preferences shown by use of various habitats, and (4) influence of thermal stress on food plants and habitats.

Support for this study was provided by the Institute of Natural Resources and School of Forest Resources of the University of Georgia, and the U. S. Energy Research and Development Administration (Contract AT [38-1]-810). We extend our appreciation to W. H. Duncan and V. T. Prevost, University of Georgia, and F. M. Uhler, U. S. Fish and Wildlife Service, for identifying unknown foods. We are grateful to Savannah River Ecology Laboratory personnel for assistance in collecting ducks, and to I. L. Brisbin, Jr., R. L. Carlton, M. C. Peed, and J. G. Wiener, University of Georgia, for critically reviewing the manuscript.

STUDY AREAS

The U. S. Energy Research and Development Administration's (ERDA) Savannah River Plant (SRP) includes 78,000 ha in the upper Coastal Plain northeast of the Savannah River in Aiken, Allendale, and Barnwell counties, South Carolina. The SRP was not open to waterfowl hunting, and because ducks were undisturbed, their preferences should be reflected by habitat use. The area was not managed for waterfowl except for maintenance of 99 nest boxes distributed through the aquatic habitats. In addition to resident wood ducks, migrating waterfowl used the area; the total waterfowl count reached 20,000 during some winters. The area used most by dabbling ducks (subfamily Anatinae) occupied less than 5 percent of the total SRP area and included river swamp, stream swamps with beaver (*Castor canadensis*) ponds, Carolina bays, and man-made ponds. Vegetational composition of these habitats at sites receiving

Originally published in J. Wildl. Manage. 41(1):118–127, 1977.

Table 1. Habitat composition of wood duck collection sites on the ERDA Savannah River Plant.

Habitat	Coverage (%)			
	Abundant		Common	
Permanently Flooded				
Carolina bay	*Panicum hemitomon*	35	Open water	5
	Brasenia schreberi	25	*Utricularia inflata*	5
	Nymphaea odorata	20	*Leersia oryzoides*	+[a]
			Nelumbo lutea	+
			Polygonum spp.	+
			Scirpus cyperinus	+
Man-made pond	Open water	50	*Potamogeton* spp.	6
	Brasenia schreberi	20	*Quercus* spp.	+
	Hydrochloa caroliniensis	10	*Leersia oryzoides*	+
			Spirodela polyrrhiza, *Lemna* spp.	+
			Sacciolepis striata	+
Fluctuating Waters[b]				
Post-thermal swamp	*Aneilema keisak*	30	*Quercus* spp.	5
	Polygonum punctatum	20	*Ceratophyllum demersum*	5
	Open water	10	*Boehmeria cylindrica*	5
	Leersia oryzoides	10	Mixed aquatic plants[c]	5
	Scirpus cyperinus	10	*Cephalanthus occidentalis*	+
Thermal swamp	*Echinochloa* spp.	30	Open water (channel)	7
	Aneilema keisak	25	*Polygonum lapathifolium*	5
	Ludwigia leptocarpa	10	*Sagittaria* spp.	5
			Cephalanthus occidentalis	+
			Salix nigra	+
			Ampelopsis arborea, *Vitis* spp.	+
			Panicum spp.	+
			Potamogeton spp.	+
Cool swamp	*Polygonum* spp.	25	Open water (channel)	8
	Aneilema keisak	25	*Sagittaria* spp.	6
	Cyperus odoratus	10	*Quercus* spp.	5
			Echinodorus cordifolius	5
			Scirpus cyperinus	+
			Panicum spp.	+
			Typha latifolia	+
			Ludwigia palustris	+
			Echinochloa spp.	+
			Scleria spp.	+
			Planera aquatica	+

[a] Plants were common in or marginal to collection sites but occupied less than 5 percent of the total area.
[b] These swamps have associated beaver ponds; water levels rise 1–2 m from December to April, increasing available feeding sites.
[c] Composed of *Spirodela polyrrhiza*, *Lemna* spp., *Myriophyllum brasiliense*, and *Azolla caroliniana*.

greatest use by wood ducks is presented in Table 1.

The Savannah River swamp supports a mature cypress-gum (*Taxodium-Nyssa*) swamp forest. Water levels in the swamp fluctuate about 2 m, with low water from April to December. Portions of the river swamp have been affected by reactor cooling water.

Other stream swamp habitats involved in this study were along three sluggish streams, interrupted by beaver dams, flowing into the Savannah River: (1) a stream delta-swamp modified by previous thermal effluent (post-thermal swamp); (2) a stream intensively altered by and still receiving thermal effluent (thermal swamp); and (3) a cool water, slightly altered stream (cool swamp).

The post-thermal swamp and associated beaver ponds received reactor effluent that killed most woody vegetation in this delta region prior to 1968 (Sharitz et al. 1974*a, b*). By 1975 higher areas were nearly covered by a reed-marsh of perennial herbs, mainly woolgrass (*Scirpus cyperinus*), and scattered clumps of shrubs, mainly buttonbush (*Cephalanthus occidentalis*). Rafts of tiny-leaved submerged and floating plants and leafy debris were common in open water, and edges were matted with emergent herbs such as Asiatic dayflower (*Aneilema keisak*), dotted smartweed (*Polygonum punctatum*), rice cutgrass (*Leersia oryzoides*), and duck-potato (*Sagittaria* spp.).

The thermal swamp received production reactor cooling water with temperatures at 45°C or more (Sharitz et al. 1974*b*), much cooler than that once received by the post-thermal swamp. Most perennials were dead except for widely scattered buttonbush and willows (*Salix* spp.) and a few small cypress trees away from the stream bed. Pondweeds (*Potamogeton* spp.) were common in slightly cooler, deeper water lateral to the stream bed. Wild millet (mostly *Echinochloa walteri*), Asiatic dayflower, primrose willow (*Ludwigia leptocarpa*), annual panic grasses (*Panicum* spp.), and nodding smartweed (*Polygonum lapathifolium*) were abundant along the channel edges.

The cool swamp floodplain was covered by 0.1–0.5 m of water during fall. During late spring and summer, water receded except where impounded by beaver dams, leaving a moist bed supporting southern smartweed (*Polygonum densiflorum*), Asiatic dayflower, flat sedge (*Cyperus odoratus*), panic grasses, duck-potato, and water plantain (*Echinodorus cordifolius*). Conditions for annuals were improved by rooting feral swine and by seasonal flooding.

Carolina bays are shallow, elliptic depressions of unknown origin (Murray 1961:512–519). They commonly support dense growth of hardwood species, many of them evergreen. The bay most used by ducks held slightly stained, very acid water generally less than 1.2 m deep. Woody vegetation in the interior occupied less than 1 percent of the cover. White waterlily (*Nymphaea odorata*) and watershield (*Brasenia schreberi*) covered most of the surface. Vegetation on the margins of the bay was mainly maidencane (*Panicum hemitomon*), with scattered rice cutgrass, floating paspalum (*Paspalum fluitans*) and smartweed.

The man-made pond from which we collected ducks had not been maintained since the SRP was established, and had undergone encroachment by shrubs and perennial herbs. It was surrounded by hardwood forest.

METHODS

Habitats most used each month were located by observations from helicopter or small boat or by reconnaissance on foot. Two hundred feeding wood ducks were collected by shooting during early afternoon hours from August 1973 to August 1975. An attempt was made to collect with minimum disturbance at least 10 mature or subadult birds per month. Contents from the esophagus and proventriculus were removed for food habits and proximate chemical analyses.

Foods were separated with sieves, hand-sorted, measured to the nearest 0.1 cc, and identified. Proximate chemical analyses of each major food were performed by the State Chemist, Georgia Department of Agriculture. Chemical composition of the diet by month was calculated from chemical composition of major foods, weighted by their monthly intake. Differences between sexes in intake of animal matter, and differences in weights of ducks, were tested for statistical significance using Student's *t*-test (Snedecor 1956:45).

Plant species composition and average water depths where important food plants grew at each duck collection site were estimated visually. Supplemental information was obtained on use of nest boxes in various habitats, breeding and nesting dates, and relative abundance. Telemetry data (Fendley, unpublished data) on movements of six wood ducks in and between various habitats were useful in interpreting feeding ecology.

RESULTS AND DISCUSSION

Feeding Habits

Seasonal Use of Foraging Habitats.—Relative use of different foraging habitats changed with seasonal availability of important foods, but was similar in corresponding months of the two years.

All three swamp areas (thermal, post-thermal and cool) were used intensively by migrating wood ducks from October through February. The cool swamp contributed acorns (*Quercus hemisphaerica* and *Q. nigra*), Asiatic dayflower, southern smartweed, panic grasses, and water elm (*Planera aquatica*) to the diet. The post-thermal area was used intensively in October and November when it provided Asiatic dayflower and dotted smartweed, two of the foods taken in greatest volume during those months. The thermal area provided Asiatic dayflower, annual panic grasses, and nodding smartweed during January and February.

With the departure of migrants, relative use of the thermal area declined, and use of the post-thermal and cool swamps increased during March to May, the peak of nesting and brood-rearing (Cunningham 1969, Odum 1970, Beshears 1974). Female wood ducks foraged for invertebrates in these habitats more than in any other. During early summer, post-thermal and thermal swamps provided pondweeds, blackberry (*Rubus cuneifolius*), and wild millet.

Beginning in July, resident wood ducks moved to the more open cool swamp and to the upland Carolina bays. Ducks fed in Carolina bays and man-made ponds mostly during early morning from late July until mid-October and in late afternoon from November to December. They fed intensively on white waterlily, watershield, rice cutgrass, and floating paspalum.

Wood ducks were never abundant in the mature cypress-tupelo river swamp below the post-thermal area nor along flooded hardwood bottomlands and streams having a closed canopy. Man-made ponds also attracted few wood ducks.

Plant Foods.—Monthly use of the major food items is presented in Table 2. Seventy-five other foods occurring in trace amounts (<0.1 percent of the diet each month) were identified but are not listed. Plant foods composed most of the diet each month. Acorns were the most important fall and early winter food in 1973. They made up 40.4 percent of the winter diet in 1973 but only 3.7 percent in 1974. The reduced intake during 1974 coincided with a general mast failure in the region. The portion of the diet formed by acorns in 1973 was replaced in 1974 primarily by seeds of primrose willow, sticktight (*Bidens frondosa*), St. John's wort (*Hypericum walteri*), bald cypress (*Taxodium distichum*), and false nettle (*Boehmeria cylindrica*). These were available for several months prior to their use, were taken in trace amounts during 1973, and ranked low in other studies.

The food taken most consistently during late fall and winter was Asiatic dayflower

Table 2. Major foods[a] by month of 200 wood ducks collected on the ERDA Savannah River Plant from August 1973 to August 1975.

Food Item	Aggregate Percentage[b]											
	(10)[c] J	(14) F	(10) M	(10) A	(13) M	(10) J	(10) J	(20) A	(24) S	(21) O	(41) N	(17) D
Aneilema keisak	17	41	16			28			1	13	21	14
Panicum spp.	32		11		27	9			7	2	1	4
Paspalum fluitans									7	1		
Liquidambar styraciflua	9											1
Animal matter	7	5	23	4	9	4	8	9	6	4	1	1
Sagittaria graminea	4	2	9									1
Planera aquatica			9	70								
Scleria reticularis					9	1						
Paspalum urvillei					6	2	4					
Rubus cuneifolius					1	13	2					
Potamogeton spp.					28	13	30				2	
Spirodela polyrrhiza	1						30	2	10	5	2	11
Echinochloa walteri		1				20	34	5	15	1	2	
Nymphaea odorata								64	41	18		
Polygonum spp.	11	40	3	3	4	4	8	8	6	27	11	1
Leersia oryzoides			3		5	1		3	2	3	2	5
Brasenia schreberi								10	8	1		
Vitis rotundifolia									5	2	1	
Quercus spp.	20									11	32	25
Ludwigia leptocarpa	1									11	2	1
Taxodium distichum						2					1	16
Hypericum walteri										1	2	
Boehmeria cylindrica	1											1
Bidens frondosa									1		2	

[a] These composed collectively at least 98.0 percent of the total diet each month.
[b] Aggregate percentage is the average of individual volumetric percentages as defined by Martin et al. (1946) and Larimore (1957). Percentages are rounded to the nearest whole number. Values less than 0.51 are omitted.
[c] Numbers in parentheses indicate sample sizes.

seed. Martin and Uhler (1939) reported it in only one individual in a sample of 1,213 ducks from the Atlantic Coast, but it has become a major waterfowl food in freshwater drawdown impoundments in South Carolina (Conrad 1965) and in beaver ponds and marshes elsewhere in the lower Atlantic Flyway (F. M. Uhler, personal communication). Where present, it appears to be preferred by wood ducks second only to acorns.

Smartweed seeds were taken inconsistently but were important during all months. Seeds of panic grasses and floating paspalum, not reported as major wood duck foods in the Southeast, were important from late fall to spring. These three genera were abundant and appeared to be staple items during some months.

Fruits of water elm were taken soon after falling (mostly in April), when major seed supplies of other species evidently were depleted. At times producing excellent waterfowl food in the lower Mississippi bayou region (Martin and Uhler 1939), this tree generally occurs infrequently in South Carolina (Radford et al. 1968). Slough grass (*Scleria reticularis*) was taken primarily in May when other seeds were scarce and before summer fruits ripened. It had been available for at least 8 months before use.

Blackberry, uncommon in aquatic habitats and not previously reported as a wood duck food, was an important food in June when it was most available. Our data and those of Hocutt and Dimmick (1971), who found wild cherry (*Prunus serotina*) important to juveniles, indicated that fleshy fruits may be important during summer. With the disappearance of blackberry from the diet, intake of succulent vegetation, especially pondweeds and big duckweed (*Spirodela polyrrhiza*), increased and was most important during July.

Wild millet and rice cutgrass were common and among the earliest available seed foods during late summer and fall. However, they were taken inconsistently and quickly replaced in the diet when other foods became available.

During August and September, seeds of white waterlily were eaten in large quantity. White waterlily usually is rated as a poor food for waterfowl other than ring-necked ducks (*Aythya collaris*). Watershield was as abundant as white waterlily, but its seeds were taken in relatively small amounts. The shift from white waterlily foraging ponds corresponded with availability and use of muscadines (*Vitis rotundifolia*) late in September. With the departure of wood ducks from Carolina bays, ring-necked ducks arrived and fed intensively on seeds of white waterlily and watershield (Landers, unpublished data), which probably had dropped to the bottom and become unavailable to wood ducks.

Three plant foods were significant but not major items: sweetgum (*Liquidambar styraciflua*) seeds in January, duck-potato (*Sagittaria graminea*) tubers in late winter, and vasey grass (*Paspalum urvillei*) seeds in May. These were not abundant enough to be evaluated properly, but sweetgum mast was taken soon after falling and can be an important late winter food (McGilvrey 1966*a*).

Animal Foods.—Animal foods made up 23 percent of the diet in March but accounted for less than 10 percent in other months (Table 2). Crayfish (Decapoda) formed 12 percent and snails (Gastropoda) formed 5 percent of the diet in March. Major insect foods were Trichoptera (6% in January), Hymenoptera (4% in February), Odonata (5% in March), Hemiptera (7% in May) and Coleoptera, which occurred in the diet in all months except March. Beetles were most important from July to September when they averaged 4 percent of the diet. Many of the insects eaten were not aquatic and probably were collected from emergent vegetation, stumps, logs, and water margins.

The importance of invertebrate intake to wood ducks during breeding, nesting, and brood-rearing is unclear. Increased feeding on invertebrates in early spring may be related simply to availability relative to plant foods. From mid-January to early April, the period just before and during nesting season, females in our samples consumed more animal foods than did males ($P<0.05$). During other times, intake of invertebrates never differed significantly between sexes (Fig. 1). Pronounced intake of invertebrates by females agrees with results of other studies on breeding waterfowl (Swanson et al. 1974, Krapu 1974).

Nutritional Relationships

Results of proximate chemical analyses of important foods are given in Table 3, and monthly intake of the various chemical fractions is shown in Figure 2.

The importance of proper nutritional balance has been demonstrated for several duck species. A diet of animal matter is high in calcium and essential amino acids (Table 3) and is important for conditioning female blue-winged teal (*Anas discors*) and pintails (*A. acuta*) for breeding (Swanson et al. 1974, Krapu and Swanson 1975).

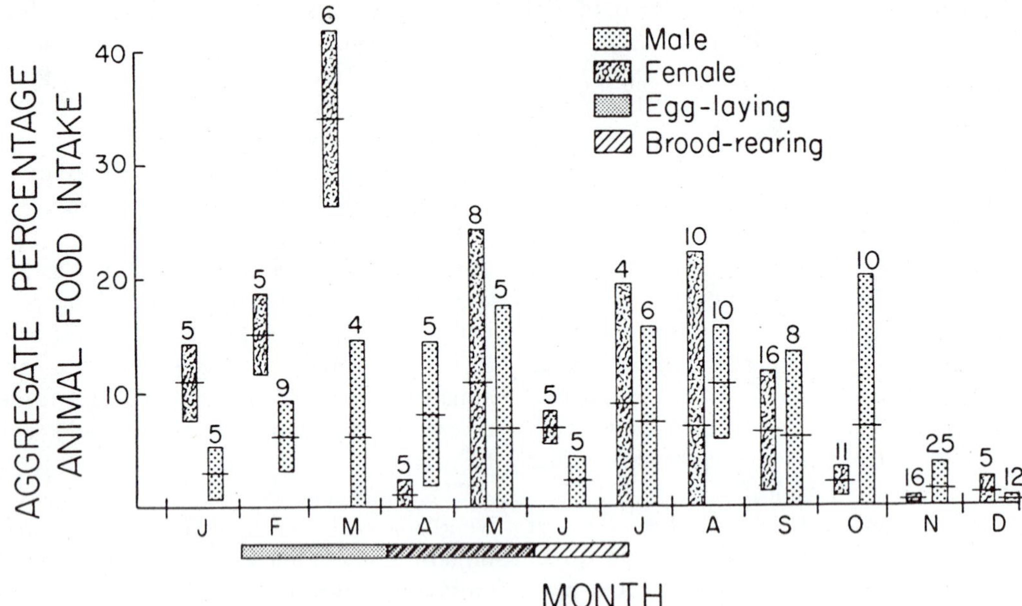

Fig. 1. Mean monthly aggregate percentage of animal food intake of male and female wood ducks collected on the ERDA Savannah River Plant from August 1973 to August 1975. Bars represent means ± 2 standard errors. Numbers are sample sizes.

Cook (1964) reported that wood ducks fail to reproduce without a high protein diet.

In our study, intake of protein (mostly from invertebrate foods) and ash peaked during the egg-laying season (Fig. 2); calcium and phosphorus intake also peaked at 2.5 and 1.6 percent, respectively, of dry weight of the diet during this time. Nitrogen-free extract (NFE) was also high at this time but, with protein and ash, intake decreased greatly in May as crude fiber peaked, suggesting a diet of low digestibility. Average body weights of both sexes were lowest during and shortly after this period (Fig. 3). Late spring appears to be a lean period following depletion of residual fall seeds and fruits and before production of nutritious succulent vegetation and fruits.

Seasonal differences in intake of animal matter may be a reflection of availability but are more likely related to dietary needs. More dietary protein and calcium, which were much higher in animal matter than in any plant food (Table 3), are necessary for laying breeders. A maintenance diet after the breeding period should contain enough protein for tissue replacement and more carbohydrates to maintain body weight (Holm and Scott 1974).

During late summer intake of NFE (Fig. 2) increased with consumption of succulent vegetation and fruits and was followed by an increase in average body weight of wood ducks (Fig. 3). From fall to early winter, intake of NFE slowly decreased, while fat and, to a lesser degree, protein intake increased (Fig. 2). The fall (1973) diet with more acorns included much more fat (14%) and NFE (48%) than the diet during 1974, the year of mast failure (8% and 41%, respectively). Goodrum (1959) discussed the value of acorns as high energy food for wild animals and their importance for conditioning animals for the winter. In our study, the good mast crop of 1973 was reflected in higher average fall body

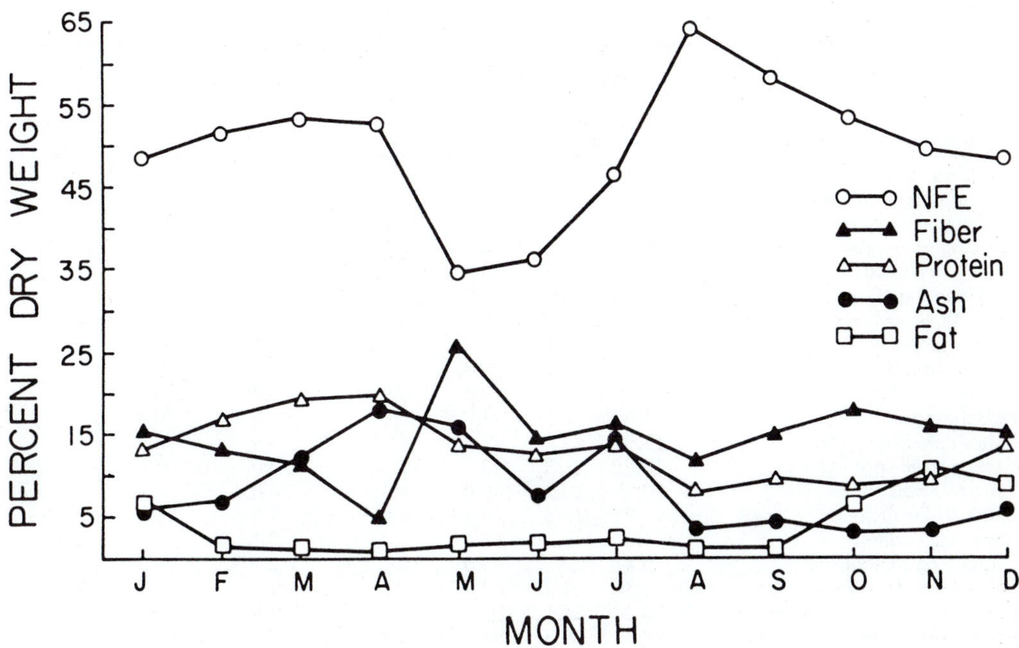

Fig. 2. Monthly nutrient content of the diet of 200 wood ducks collected on the ERDA Savannah River Plant from August 1973 to August 1975. NFE is nitrogen-free extract. Percentages are projected from average nutrient content percentages in major foods (Table 2), weighted by their monthly intake in grams.

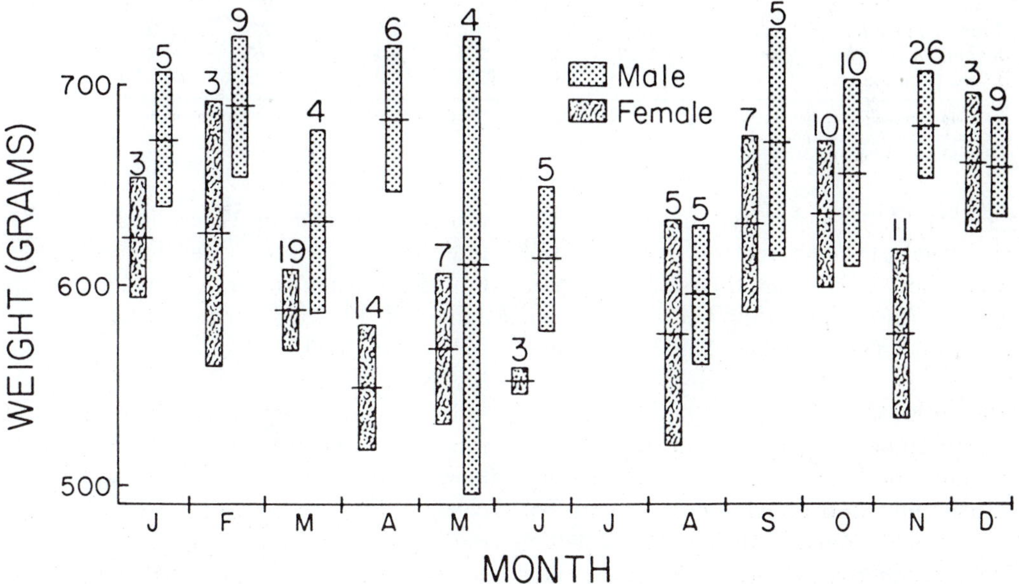

Fig. 3. Mean monthly weights of 173 mature wood ducks collected on the ERDA Savannah River Plant from August 1973 to August 1975. Bars represent means ± 2 standard errors. Numbers are sample sizes.

Table 3. Nutrient composition of major foods[a] of wood ducks collected on the ERDA Savannah River Plant from August 1973 to August 1975.

Food Item	% by dry weight						
	Crude Protein	Carbohydrates		Fat	Ash	Ca	P
		Crude Fiber	NFE				
Aneilema keisak	21.3	10.8	49.0	0.5	8.1	0.30	0.50
Panicum dichotomiflorum	14.4	21.1	48.4	1.7	5.6	0.27	0.37
Panicum verrucosum	18.1	12.6	51.7	1.1	7.1	0.25	0.31
Panicum gymnocarpon	13.1	21.6	43.5	0.5	13.1	0.25	0.23
Paspalum fluitans	13.1	25.4	44.9	1.0	6.4	0.33	0.37
Liquidambar styraciflua[b]	26.0	18.0	33.6	13.9	8.7	1.22	0.57
Animal matter (total)	39.4	5.3	28.8	3.1	22.1	5.20	0.63
Sagittaria graminea (tubers)	15.9	16.1	54.9	1.5	6.8	0.42	0.27
Planera aquatica (fruit)	19.7	4.5	58.0	0.8	7.4	0.26	0.25
Scleria reticularis	12.5	35.1	22.8	0.9	25.7	0.20	0.67
Paspalum urvillei	11.9	30.3	41.0	6.4	6.6	0.30	0.35
Rubus cuneifolius (fruit)	13.1	24.7	47.1	8.0	3.4	0.31	0.17
Potamogeton spp. (veg.)	15.9	25.3	43.1	2.8	10.0	2.40	0.40
Spirodela polyrrhiza (veg.)	10.6	13.2	48.0	1.8	16.0	1.31	0.23
Echinochloa walteri	17.2	13.2	49.9	4.2	7.2	0.25	0.49
Nymphaea odorata	7.8	10.4	68.4	1.0	2.1	0.24	0.14
Polygonum punctatum	9.4	16.1	59.0	2.7	2.9	0.32	0.27
Polygonum densiflorum	8.8	18.3	57.9	2.7	2.6	0.32	0.28
Polygonum hydropiperoides	8.4	20.1	57.9	1.9	2.0	0.30	0.18
Leersia oryzoides	13.8	9.3	57.8	1.9	7.6	0.35	0.25
Brasenia schreberi	6.0	36.7	45.9	1.1	0.9	0.25	0.08
Vitis rotundifolia (fruit)	6.0	19.9	50.7	1.8	3.1	0.53	0.13
Quercus hemisphaerica	4.4	16.0	52.8	17.3	1.2	0.38	0.06
Quercus nigra	3.8	17.2	48.7	14.6	1.6	0.40	0.06
Ludwigia leptocarpa	20.6	36.3	21.9	6.0	8.6	1.25	0.56
Taxodium distichum	8.7	45.6	25.8	8.4	2.2	0.66	0.30
Hypericum walteri	19.4	37.9	21.0	5.5	7.3	0.37	0.79
Boehmeria cylindrica	16.3	43.4	20.4	3.4	9.3	2.35	0.39
Bidens frondosa	26.6	18.5	27.5	11.9	8.8	0.74	0.34

[a] Food samples were whole seeds or nuts unless otherwise designated, and percentages represent averages of 3 to 7 samples taken from esophageal contents.
[b] Data from King and McClure, 1944.

weights (13% higher for males and 15% for females) compared to those of 1974 when mast failed, but this difference was not significant probably because migrant wood ducks were included in our samples.

Conclusions

Data from this study demonstrate the importance of habitat diversity for meeting year-round nutritional requirements of wood ducks. Females during the breeding and reproductive seasons require areas with good production and availability of invertebrate foods to satisfy high requirements for protein and calcium. Wood ducks will feed intensively on white waterlily seeds in sustained level ponds during late summer and early fall. Flooded hardwood bottoms provide acorns and other important mast during fall and winter. These late summer and fall foods are generally high in NFE and fats, providing energy for winter maintenance and for breeding. Lean periods may occur in late spring, and in fall and winter during years when acorn crops fail. The stress imposed by heated effluent destroys important mast trees but can favor production of important annual food plants.

LITERATURE CITED

BESHEARS, W. W., JR. 1974. Wood ducks in Alabama. Alabama Dept. Conserv. Nat. Resour. Special Rep. 4. 45pp.

CONRAD, W. B., JR. 1965. A food habits study of ducks wintering on the Lower Pee Dee and Waccamaw Rivers, Georgetown, South Carolina. Proc. Southeastern Assoc. Game and Fish Commissioners 19:93–98.

COOK, A. H. 1964. Better living for ducks—through chemistry. Pages 569–578 *in* J. P. Linduska, ed. Waterfowl Tomorrow. Bur. Sport Fish. Wildl., U. S. Government Printing Office, Washington, D. C. 770pp.

CUNNINGHAM, E. R. 1969. A three year study of the wood duck on the Yazoo National Wildlife Refuge. Proc. Southeastern Assoc. Game and Fish Commissioners 22:145–155.

GOODRUM, P. D. 1959. Acorns in the diet of wildlife. Proc. Southeastern Assoc. Game and Fish Commissioners 13:54–57.

HOCUTT, G. E., AND R. W. DIMMICK. 1971. Summer food habits of juvenile wood ducks in East Tennessee. J. Wildl. Manage. 35(2):286–292.

HOLM, E. R., AND M. L. SCOTT. 1974. Dietary needs. Pages 155–167 *in* D. O. Hyde, ed. Raising wild ducks in captivity. E. P. Dutton and Co., Inc. New York. 319pp.

KERWIN, J. A., AND L. G. WEBB. 1971. Foods of ducks wintering in coastal South Carolina, 1965–1967. Proc. Southeastern Assoc. Game and Fish Commissioners 25:223–245.

KING, T. R., AND H. E. MCCLURE. 1944. Chemical composition of some American wild feedstuffs. J. Agric. Res. 69(1):33–46.

KRAPU, G. L. 1974. Foods of breeding pintails in North Dakota. J. Wildl. Manage. 38(3): 408–417.

———, AND G. A. SWANSON. 1975. Some nutritional aspects of reproduction in prairie nesting pintails. J. Wildl. Manage. 39(1):156–162.

LANDERS, J. L., A. S. JOHNSON, P. H. MORGAN, AND W. P. BALDWIN. 1976. Duck foods in managed tidal impoundments in South Carolina. J. Wildl. Manage. 40(4) (in press).

LARIMORE, W. R. 1957. Ecological life history of the warmouth (Centrarchidae). Illinois Nat. Hist. Surv. Bull. 27(1):1-83.

MARTIN, A. C., R. H. GENSCH, AND C. P. BROWN. 1946. Alternative methods in upland gamebird food analysis. J. Wildl. Manage. 10(1): 8–12.

———, AND F. M. UHLER. 1939. Food of game ducks in the United States and Canada. U. S. Fish Wildl. Serv. Res. Rep. 30. 308pp.

MCGILVREY, F. B. 1966*a*. Fall food habits of wood ducks from Lake Marion, South Carolina. J. Wildl. Manage. 30(1):193–195.

———. 1966*b*. Fall food habits of ducks near Santee Refuge, South Carolina. J. Wildl. Manage. 30(3):577–580.

MURRAY, G. E. 1961. Geology of the Atlantic and Gulf Coastal Province of North America. Harper and Row. New York. 692pp.

ODUM, R. R. 1970. Nest box production and brood survival of wood ducks on the Piedmont National Wildlife Refuge 1969. Proc. Southeastern Assoc. Game and Fish Commissioners 24:108–116.

RADFORD, A. E., H. E. AHLES, AND C. R. BELL. 1968. Manual of the vascular flora of the Carolinas. Univ. North Carolina Press, Chapel Hill. 1183pp.

SHARITZ, R. R., J. W. GIBBONS, AND S. C. GAUSE. 1974*a*. Impact of production-reactor effluents on vegetation in a Southeastern swamp forest. Pages 356–362 *in* J. W. Gibbons and R. R. Sharitz, eds. Thermal ecology. U. S. At. Energy Comm. Symp. Ser. CONF-730505. 670pp.

———, J. E. IRWIN, AND E. J. CHRISTY. 1974*b*. Vegetation of swamps receiving reactor effluents. Oikos 25(1):7–13.

SNEDECOR, G. W. 1956. Statistical methods. 5th Ed. Iowa State University Press, Ames. 534pp.

SWANSON, G. A., M. I. MEYER, AND J. R. SERIE. 1974. Feeding ecology of breeding blue-winged teals. J. Wildl. Manage. 38(3):396–407.

Received 22 March 1976.
Accepted 17 September 1976.

IMPACT OF FLUCTUATING WATER LEVELS ON FEEDING ECOLOGY OF BREEDING BLUE-WINGED TEAL

GEORGE A. SWANSON, U.S. Fish and Wildlife Service, Northern Prairie Wildlife Research Center, Jamestown, North Dakota 58401

MAVIS I. MEYER, U.S. Fish and Wildlife Service, Northern Prairie Wildlife Research Center, Jamestown, North Dakota 58401

Abstract: Foods consumed by breeding blue-winged teal (*Anas discors*) before and after a hydrological change are compared on a study area located in the glaciated prairie pothole region of south-central North Dakota. Food selection shifted from a diet high in snails consumed on seasonal wetlands to one dominated by midge larvae consumed on semi-permanent lakes entering a drawdown phase. Total invertebrate contribution to the diet was similar for the two periods and varied from 89 percent (1967–71) to 97 percent (1973).

Animal foods dominated the diet of laying females accounting for 99 percent by volume, of which snails comprised 38 percent, crustacea 14 percent, and insects 44 percent.

J. WILDL. MANAGE. 41(3):426–433

The semi-arid climate of the glaciated prairie pothole region of North America is a dominant factor in the ecology of prairie wetlands. The annual moisture deficit in this area results in unstable water levels and in water high in dissolved solids (Langbein 1961, Leitch 1964, Kuznetsov 1970:22, Sloan 1972, Eisenlohr 1972, Stewart and Kantrud 1972, Swanson et al. 1974*b*). In response to this water regime aquatic biotic communities are continually adjusting to changing water levels. The hydrological and geological interactions on the glaciated prairie have produced a unique and highly attractive aquatic habitat for breeding waterfowl (Smith et al. 1964). The purpose of this paper is to describe the impact of changing wetland conditions on the feeding ecology of breeding blue-winged teal in the prairie pothole region of south-central North Dakota.

Appreciation is extended to F. B. Lee, D. S. Gilmer, H. F. Duebbert, J. T. Lokemoen and A. D. Kruse for critical review of the manuscript.

METHODS

Breeding birds were collected while feeding actively on wetlands in the ground and stagnation moraines of Stutsman and Kidder Counties in south-central North Dakota during the spring and early summer of 1973. Procedures for collecting and tabulating esophageal contents were similar to those described by Swanson et al. (1974*a*,*b*). An effort was made to collect birds in proportion to their feeding use of wetland classes. Only birds that were observed to feed consistently for a period of at least 5 min. were collected.

Ovaries were examined so that food consumption could be correlated with reproductive status. Data on laying females collected in this study were combined with those from a previous study (Swanson et al. 1974*b*) to increase sample size and provide data from both wet and dry years. Laying females were defined as birds that contained: (1) an egg in the oviduct, (2) large recently ruptured follicles, or (3) follicles of a size that would rupture within one day. The latter was determined by measuring the diameter of the largest follicle attached to the ovary of females which had an egg in the oviduct.

On selected wetlands within the two county study area a concurrent study was conducted of seasonal and annual changes in aquatic biotic communities and water quality. A study of the renesting potential

Originally published in J. Wildl. Manage. 41(3):426–433, 1977.

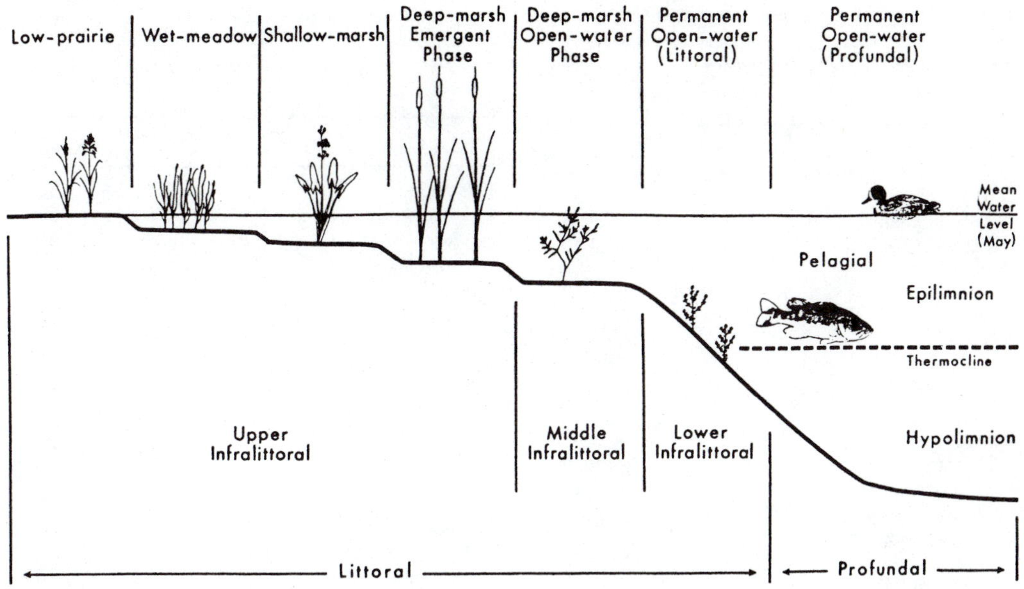

Fig. 1. Zonation of a Type V Prairie Wetland based on discussions by Hutchinson (1967:240), and Stewart and Kantrud (1971) (Swanson and Meyer 1973).

of known age blue-winged teal in relation to food availability was undertaken concurrently on experimental ponds at the Northern Prairie Wildlife Research Center.

Invertebrates, seeds, and vascular plants were identified with the aid of several guides by Baker (1928), Pennak (1953), Ward and Whipple (1959), Martin and Barkley (1961), and Stevens (1963). Wetland classes and zones illustrated in Fig. 1 are defined by Stewart and Kantrud (1971).

RESULTS

During the spring and early summer of 1973, wetlands within the study area had low water levels as carryover from the fall of 1972, and were supplied with only small volumes of water from precipitation. As a result, seasonal wetlands dried early in the spring of 1973 and blue-winged teal used semi-permanent lakes that were entering a drawdown phase. This change in the class structure of wetlands was reflected in the food consumption of breeding blue-winged teal. Midge larvae (Diptera: Chironomidae) that over-wintered on semi-permanent wetlands became available as water levels began to decline and accounted for 46 percent of the total volume of the diet (Table 1). Fingernail clams (Pelecypoda) were also available under these conditions and made up 7 percent of the diet. Snails (Gastropoda) accounted for 16 percent and adult midges 6 percent of the foods consumed. Midges made up 52 percent of the diet as compared with 9 percent during a wetter period (Swanson et al. 1974*b*). Although the amount of available surface water within the wetland complex was reduced and resulted in a change in the species of invertebrates consumed, the proportion of animal food in the diet remained similar to that found during wetter years. Animal foods accounted for 97 percent of the diet in 1973 and 89 percent of the diet during 1967–71 (Swanson et al. 1974*b*).

Table 1. Proportion by volume of animal and plant foods contained in the esophagus of 24 breeding blue-winged teal collected during the spring and summer 1973 in south-central North Dakota.

Food items	Aggregate[a] %	% Occurrence
Gastropoda	16	58
Lymnaeidae	13	21
Planorbidae	3	46
Physidae	*tr*	4
Pelecypoda	7	17
Sphaeriidae	7	17
Crustacea	9	54
Ostracoda	*tr*	25
Copepoda	*tr*	8
Cladocera	9	50
Insecta	65	92
Ephemeroptera	*tr*	4
Odonata	5	13
Hemiptera	*tr*	13
Trichoptera	7	13
Coleoptera	1	29
Haliplidae	*tr*	8
Dytiscidae	1	21
Hydrophilidae	*tr*	8
Curculionidae	*tr*	4
Diptera	52	92
Culicidae	*tr*	4
Chironomidae imm.	46	92
Chironomidae adult	6	13
Ceratopogonidae	*tr*	8
Tetanoceridae	*tr*	8
Terrestrial insects	*tr*	4
Seeds	3	46
Plant parts	*tr*	29
Total plant	3	50
Total animal	97	100

[a] As defined by Martin et al. 1946.

Table 2. Proportion by volume of animal and plant foods contained in the esophagus of 20 laying blue-winged teal collected during the spring and summer in south-central North Dakota.

Food items	Aggregate[a] %	% Occurrence
Gastropoda	38	70
Lymnaeidae	28	50
Planorbidae	7	50
Physidae	3	25
Pelecypoda	2	10
Sphaeriidae	2	10
Crustacea	14	55
Amphipoda	8	15
Ostracoda	1	20
Copepoda	*tr*	10
Cladocera	*tr*	30
Conchostraca	*tr*	20
Anostraca	5	10
Annelida	1	15
Insecta	44	90
Ephemeroptera	*tr*	5
Odonata	1	15
Hemiptera	1	15
Trichoptera	7	30
Coleoptera	3	60
Haliplidae	*tr*	35
Dytiscidae	3	55
Hydrophilidae	*tr*	5
Diptera	32	85
Tipulidae	1	5
Culicidae	5	15
Chironomidae imm.	19	75
Chironomidae adult	1	15
Ceratopogonidae	4	20
Stratiomyiidae	2	15
Tabanidae	*tr*	10
Tetanoceridae	*tr*	5
Seeds	1	60
Plant parts	*tr*	20
Total plants	1	65
Total animal	99	100

[a] As defined by Martin et al. 1946.

Animal foods accounted for 99 percent of the diet of female blue-winged teal during laying (Table 2). Snails (primarily *Stagnicola caperata* and *S. palustrus*) accounted for 38 percent, crustacea (primarily *Hyalella azteca*) 14 percent and insects (predominately midges) 44 percent of the diet. The plant foods consumed were seeds which accounted for 1 percent by volume of the total foods.

DISCUSSION

The unstable water conditions that are characteristic of the glaciated prairie require that breeding waterfowl utilizing this habitat respond each spring to an unpredictable water regime. Even during years that may be considered average in precipitation some breeding area on the prairies will usually contain extremes in either wet or dry conditions. Water conditions in turn reflect major changes in the abundance and availability of animal foods that are produced in temporary, seasonal and semipermanent wetlands.

Birds responding to this unpredictable water regime must be flexible, opportunistic, and possess a reproductive potential that can compensate for periods of drought through rapid expansion during ideal conditions (Pianka 1974:90). Evidence of prairie waterfowl response to changing water conditions were presented by Murdy (1966), Krapu et al. (1970), Smith (1970), Henny (1973) and Brewster et al. (1976). Stewart and Kantrud (1973) demonstrated that the distribution of breeding waterfowl on the prairie pothole region is closely related to yearly variations in the frequency of seasonal ponds with surface water.

Wetland Ecology

Seasonally flooded wetlands dry by midsummer during years of average precipitation and runoff. They have been referred to as ephemeral, temporary or seasonal wetlands (Pennak 1953, Stewart and Kantrud 1971). A second group contains water year around during years of normal precipitation and runoff and was called semi-permanent lakes (Stewart and Kantrud 1971). They may become dry once or twice within a 10-year period. Factors influencing the water regime include basin morphology, size and condition of the drainage basin, ground water, and precipitation:evaporation ratios.

Seasonal wetlands support plant and animal communities that are adapted to an aquatic environment that contains water for only a limited period of time each year. Invertebrates that thrive on a detritus and algal food chain are abundant during the waterfowl breeding season, and because of the shallow water depths are available to anatids. Seasonal wetlands due to their abundance also provide ideal sites for pairs to establish territories and as a result reduce interspecific strife.

Semi-permanent and permanent lakes undergoing various stages of drawdown often do not contain water within the low-prairie, wet-meadow, shallow-marsh, or deep-marsh zones (Fig. 1). Seasonal wetlands are composed of low-prairie, wet-meadow, and shallow-marsh zones (Stewart and Kantrud 1971), and it is likely that similar zones within a semi-permanent lake will also not contain surface water during most years when seasonal wetlands are prematurely dry. The loss of shallow feeding zones within a wetland complex may be a more important factor to waterfowl feeding ecology during a dry spring than just the loss of seasonal water areas per se. Although semi-permanent lakes in drawdown do not appear to compensate for the loss of seasonal wetlands, they are an important element in the wetland complex during wet years for late nesting species, renesting pairs, and broods. They also maintain a segment of the breeding population during dryer periods.

When water levels fall as they did on semi-permanent lakes in 1973, a short term increase in invertebrate availability to waterfowl may result due to the shallow water conditions and the concentration of organisms by a reduced water volume. In the long run, however, if complete drawdown occurs, aquatic invertebrates are eliminated or greatly reduced and food conditions for breeding ducks rapidly deteriorate. Falling water levels permit the cycle to be completed and provide the conditions that support high invertebrate populations following a subsequent rise in water levels. The effect of the duration and magnitude of a drawdown is not well understood and water level fluctuations can be detrimental to invertebrates that are utilized by waterfowl if they are of short duration (Kadlec 1962). Most invertebrates associated with permanent water cannot adjust to short term drawdowns that expose and inundate mud flats. Drawdowns on prairie lakes generally occur over a period of several years and the receding water is followed by the germination of plants. When water levels rise and drown the plants invertebrates become abundant.

When water levels rise to flood drawdown vegetation, shallow marsh and wet meadow zones and occasionally terrestrial vegetation, invertebrates are stimulated to increased rapidly by the abundant organic food base (Frey 1967:32, Petr 1975:44). Invertebrates (Gastropods) on experimental ponds responded to a rising water level by depositing a large number of egg masses within recently flooded vegetation. They responded similarly, within an aquarium environment, to an increase in food availability.

Wetlands on the glaciated prairie region achieve naturally, through a dynamic moisture regime, periodic drawdowns which have been observed to be advantageous to waterfowl where water levels are manipulated (McKnight and Low 1969, McKnight 1974, Whitman 1974, 1976). The natural prairie wetland, however, has an added advantage in that the salt levels, due to nonintegrated drainage, often exceed the tolerance levels of certain plants (*Typha* spp.) that can seriously limit wetland management on some fresh water impoundments (Whitman 1974). The ecology of seasonal and semi-permanent wetlands in the glaciated prairie region is unique because the morphological and climatic factors involved, which are in turn reflected in the biotic communities, are not readily duplicated by fresh integrated waters associated with most artificial impoundments. The moisture deficit associated with the semi-arid climate of the glaciated prairie is an integral part of the ecology of prairie wetlands and subsequently prairie waterfowl ecology.

Duck Response

Semi-permanent lakes may provide the dominant surface water available to breeding pairs during years when rain or snow melt is limited. Under these conditions different foods are consumed because different plant and animal communities are available (Table 1). Blue-winged teal shifted from a diet high in snails when seasonal wetlands were relatively abundant during the breeding season in 1967–71 (Swanson et al. 1974*b*) to one dominated by midge larvae in 1973 when semi-permanent lakes were dominant. In 1973, 10 pairs of blue-winged teal were observed competing for space on a 1.2 ha semi-permanent lake that contained an abundant population of midge larvae and fingernail clams. The pairs were evenly spaced around the wetland on a mud flat that had developed on the outer edge of the deep marsh zone (Fig. 1).

During the summer of 1973 the number of blue-winged teal broods observed was unusually low on the study area. Paired blue-winged teal and broods were also the lowest levels observed during a 10 year period (1965–1974) on the Woodworth Study Area in Stutsman County, North Dakota (L. M. Kirsch, personal communication). Duebbert and Lokemoen (1976) studied duck nest distribution and pair use on a study area in Edmunds County, South Dakota during 1971–73. Seasonal wetlands comprised an average of 70 percent of the basins and 44 percent of the area in surrounding wetland complexes. Blue-winged teal nests on the cover plots they studied decreased from 136 in 1972 to 28 in 1973. Blue-winged teal pairs dropped from 22.7 per km^2 to 7.0 per km^2 during the same period. This change in bird use was highly correlated with a reduction in available surface water during May and June.

Blue-winged teal arrive late on the breeding grounds and therefore may be more susceptible to deteriorating water conditions than an early nesting species like the mallard (*Anas platyrhynchos*) (Krapu et al. 1970). Leitch (1964) and Murdy (1966) suggested that when prairie ducks are displaced by drought to less productive northern lakes reproduction is impaired.

During periods of drought, reduction in food availability may be reflected in a reduction in renesting attempts as well as a displacement of breeding pairs. Pospahala et al. (1974:41) pointed out that late nesting or renesting efforts seemed strongest during years when midsummer water conditions were good. Blue-winged teal females provided with a high protein diet or an abundant invertebrate food supply, on experimental ponds, produced 4 and 5 clutches of eggs in response to imposed nest destruction. Reduced food availability, on the other hand, caused females to terminate renesting attempts (Swanson, unpublished data). Bengtson and Ulfstrand (1971:239) presented evidence that food availability influenced egg production in the harlequin duck (*Histrionicus histrionicus*): "The fact that a high proportion of the harlequin females did not lay eggs in 1970 may reasonably be connected with the relative food scarcity throughout that year. However, they remained on the breeding grounds throughout the summer, so the food resources were apparently adequate for their own survival." Bengtson (1971) reported that lower than average clutches were produced by 4 species of diving ducks in an apparent response to a reduction in invertebrate availability. Perret (1962), Krapu (1974), Swanson et al. (1974*b*), Serie and Swanson (1976) and Landers et al. (1977) have demonstrated an increase in invertebrate consumption by females during the breeding season. Milne (1976) reviewed factors affecting egg production in waterfowl populations. Marshall (1951) discussed food availability as a timing factor in the sexual cycle of birds.

Anderson and Glover (1967), McKnight and Low (1969), Whitman (1974), Schroeder (1975), and Schroeder et al. (1976) demonstrated an increase in waterfowl production on newly created aquatic habitat. McKnight (1974), and Whitman (1974) speculated that this increase was a response by breeding birds to an abundant invertebrate population.

Land-use practices on the prairies have favored drainage of shallow, non-permanent wetlands into drainage systems or into wetlands located at lower elevations. This practice is altering the natural wetland complex of the prairies by eliminating temporary, seasonal, and semi-permanent wetlands and creating larger, and more permanent water areas that are less attractive to breeding Anatinae.

Because of the high nest destruction that is known to occur on agricultural lands of the prairies (Kirsch 1969, Higgins 1977), breeding waterfowl can only be successful in a given year through a persistent renesting effort which requires a high quality wetland base that can supply an abundant and readily available high protein diet. It is therefore imperative that the integrity of those unique prairie aquatic ecosystems be preserved.

LITERATURE CITED

ANDERSON, D. R., AND F. A. GLOVER. 1967. Effects of water manipulation on waterfowl production and habitat. Trans. N. Am. Wildl. Nat. Resour. Conf. 32:292–300.

BAKER, F. C. 1928. The fresh water mollusca of Wisconsin. Part 1. Gastropoda. Wisconsin Acad. Sci., Arts and Letters. Madison. 507pp.

BENGTSON, S. A. 1971. Variations in clutch-size in ducks in relation to the food supply. Ibis 113(4):523–526.

———, AND S. ULFSTRAND. 1971. Food resources and breeding frequency of the harlequin duck *Histrionicus histrionicus* in Iceland. Oikos 22(2):235–239.

BREWSTER, W. G., J. M. GATES, AND L. D. FLAKE. 1976. Breeding waterfowl populations and their distribution in South Dakota. J. Wildl. Manage. 40(1):50–59.

DUEBBERT, H. F., AND J. T. LOKEMOEN. 1976. Duck nesting in fields of undisturbed grass-legume cover. J. Wildl. Manage. 40(1):39–49.

EISENLOHR, W. S. 1972. Hydrologic investigations of prairie potholes in North Dakota, 1959–68. U.S. Geol. Surv. Prof. Pap. 585-A. 102pp.

FREY, D. G. 1967. Reservoir research—objectives and practices with an example from the Soviet Union. Pages 26–36 *in* Reservoir Fishery Resources Symposium. Southern Div. Am. Fish. Soc. 569pp.

HENNY, C. J. 1973. Drought displaced movement of North American pintails into Siberia. J. Wildl. Manage. 37(1):23–29.

HIGGINS, K. F. 1977. Duck nesting in intensively farmed areas of North Dakota. J. Wildl. Manage. (in press).

HUTCHINSON, G. E. 1967. A treatise on limnology, Vol. II. John Wiley and Sons, Inc., New York. 1115pp.

KADLEC, J. A. 1962. Effects of a drawdown on a waterfowl impoundment. Ecology. 43(2):267–281.

KIRSCH, L. M. 1969. Waterfowl production in relation to grazing. J. Wildl. Manage. 33(4): 821–828.

KRAPU, G. L., D. R. PARSONS, AND M. W. WELLER. 1970. Waterfowl in relation to land use and water levels on the spring run area. Iowa J. Sci. 44(4):437–452.

———. 1974. Feeding ecology of pintail hens during reproduction. Auk 91(2):278–290.

KUZNETSOV, S. I. 1970. The microflora of lakes and its geochemical activity. (Transl. from Russian). Israel Program for Sci. Transl., Jerusalem. C. H. Oppenheimer, Ed, Univ. Texas Press, Austin. 503pp.

LANDERS, J. L., T. T. FENDLEY, AND A. S. JOHNSON. 1977. Feeding ecology of wood ducks in South Carolina. J. Wildl. Manage. 41(1):118–127.

LANGBEIN, W. B. 1961. Salinity and hydrology of closed lakes. U.S. Geol. Surv. Prof. Pap. 412. 20pp.

LEITCH, W. G. 1964. Water. Pages 273–281 *in* Waterfowl Tomorrow. U.S. Govt. Printing Office, Washington, D.C. 770pp.

MILNE, H. 1976. Some factors affecting egg production in waterfowl populations. Wildfowl 27:141–142.

MARTIN, A. C., AND W. D. BARKLEY. 1961. Seed identification manual. University California Press, Berkeley. 221pp.

———, R. H. GENSCH, AND C. P. BROWN. 1946. Alternative methods in upland gamebird food analysis. J. Wildl. Manage. 10(1):8–12.

MARSHALL, A. J. 1951. Food availability as a timing factor in the sexual cycle of birds. Emu. 50(4):267–282.

MCKNIGHT, D. E. 1974. Dry-land nesting by redheads and ruddy ducks. J. Wildl. Manage. 38(1):112–119.

———, AND J. B. LOW. 1969. Factors affecting waterfowl production on a spring-fed salt marsh in Utah. Trans. N. Am. Wildl. Nat. Resour. Conf. 34:307–314.

MURDY, H. W. 1966. When the prairies go dry. Naturalist 17(1):8–13.

PIANKA, E. R. 1974. Evolutionary ecology. Harper & Row, New York. 356pp.

PENNAK, R. W. 1953. Fresh-water invertebrates of the United States. Ronald Press Co., New York. 769pp.

PERRET, N. G. 1962. The spring and summer foods of the common mallard (*Anas platyrhynchos*) in south central Manitoba. M.S. Thesis, Univ. British Columbia. 82pp.

PETR, T. 1975. On some factors associated with the initial high fish catches in new African man-made lakes. Arch. Hydrobiol. 75(1): 32–49.

POSPAHALA, R. S., D. R. ANDERSON, AND C. J. HENNY. 1974. Population ecology of the mallard. II. Breeding habitat conditions, size of the breeding populations, and production indices. U.S. Fish Wildl. Serv. Resour. Publ. 115. 73pp.

SCHROEDER, L. D. 1975. Effects of invertebrate utilization on waterfowl production. Page 63 *in* O. B. Cope, ed. Colo. Game Research Review 1972–1974. Game Research Section Colo. Div. of Wildl. 76pp.

———, D. R. ANDERSON, R. S. POSPAHALA, G. G. W. ROBINSON, AND F. A. GLOVER. 1976. Effects of early water application on waterfowl production. J. Wildl. Manage. 40 (2):227–232.

SERIE, J. R., AND G. A. SWANSON. 1976. Feeding ecology of breeding gadwalls on saline wetlands. J. Wildl. Manage. 40(1): 69–81.

SLOAN, C. E. 1972. Ground-water hydrology of prairie potholes in North Dakota. U.S. Geol. Surv. Prof. Pap. 585-C. 28pp.

SMITH, A. G., J. H. STOUDT, AND J. B. GALLOP. 1964. Prairie potholes and marshes. Pages 39–50 *in* J. P. Linduska, ed. Waterfowl Tomorrow. U.S. Govt. Printing Office, Washington, D.C. 770pp.

SMITH, R. I. 1970. Response of pintail breeding populations to drought. J. Wildl. Manage. 34 (4):943–946.

STEVENS, O. A. 1963. Handbook of North Dakota plants. Cushing-Malloy, Ann Arbor, Mich. 324pp.

STEWART, R. E., AND H. A. KANTRUD. 1971. Classification of natural ponds and lakes in the glaciated prairie region. U.S. Fish Wildl. Serv. Resour. Publ. 92. 57pp.

———, AND ———. 1972. Vegetation of prairie potholes, North Dakota, in relation to quality of water and other environmental factors. U.S. Geol. Surv. Prof. Pap. 585-D. 36pp.

———, AND ———. 1973. Ecological distribution of breeding waterfowl populations in North Dakota. J. Wildl. Manage. 37(1):39–50.

SWANSON, G. A., G. L. KRAPU, J. C. BARTONEK, J. R. SERIE, AND D. H. JOHNSON. 1974*a*. Advantages in mathematically weighting waterfowl food habits data. J. Wildl. Manage. 38 (2):302–307.

———, AND M. I. MEYER. 1973. The role of invertebrates in the feeding ecology of Anatinae during the breeding season. Pages 143–185 *in* The Waterfowl Habitat Manage. Symp., Moncton, N.B. 306pp.

———, ———, AND J. R. SERIE. 1974*b*. Feeding ecology of breeding blue-winged teals. J. Wildl. Manage. 38(3):396–407.

WARD, H. B., AND G. C. WHIPPLE. 1959. Freshwater biology. W. Edmondson, ed. John Wiley and Sons, New York. 1248pp.

WHITMAN, W. R. 1974. The response of macroinvertebrates to experimental marsh management. Ph.D. thesis. Univ. Maine, Orono. 114pp.

———. 1976. Impoundments for waterfowl. Can. Wildl. Serv. Occasional Paper No. 22. 22pp.

Received 14 July 1976.
Accepted 5 April 1977.

FOOD HABITS OF CANVASBACKS, REDHEADS, AND LESSER SCAUP IN MANITOBA[1]

JAMES C. BARTONEK,[2] Northern Prairie Wildlife Research Center, Bureau of Sport Fisheries and Wildlife, Jamestown, ND 58401
JOSEPH J. HICKEY, Department of Wildlife Ecology, University of Wisconsin, Madison, WI 53706

The purpose of this paper is to present information on food habits of 175 Canvasbacks (*Aythya valisineria*), 99 Redheads (*A. americana*), and 71 Lesser Scaup (*A. affinis*) collected in southwestern Manitoba during the late spring, summer, and early fall, from 1959 to 1964. Primary emphasis is on juveniles and spring- and summer-collected adults.

Studies of food habits lead to a better understanding of a species' environmental and nutritional requirements, its diseases caused by parasitic infestation and food poisoning, its role in the biological transportation or concentration of envirionmental contaminants, and its economic relationship with man. Relatively little waterfowl food-habit information is based upon juveniles and adults collected during the summer; most information of this type is based upon birds collected during either the hunting season, winter, or early spring.

Information on the food habits of adult Canvasbacks, Redheads, and Lesser Scaup on their breeding grounds is very limited. Cottam (1939) summarized food habits of many Canvasbacks, Redheads, and Lesser Scaup taken throughout the year, but sexual, seasonal, and regional differences could not always be evaluated. Yocom (1951:172–176) and Keith (1961:34) examined a combined total of 2 Canvasbacks, 12 Redheads, and 9 Lesser Scaup collected during the summer; however, they lumped these data in with data from other species and, in doing so, obscured possible interspecific differences. Specific data on foods of adults during spring and summer are available for 6 Canvasbacks, 1 Redhead, and 51 Lesser Scaup (Pirnie 1935:308, 310; Munro 1941:134–137; Erickson 1948:282; Rogers and Korschgen 1966:259–261). Published data on juveniles are available for 9 Canvasbacks, 8 Redheads, and 32 Lesser Scaup (Cottam 1939, Munro 1941:135, Yocom 1951:174, Collias and Collias 1963:7).

Cottam (1939), in his presentation of the food habits of North American diving ducks, summarized the data accumulated by the Bureau of Biological Survey over many years. Much of the published information on food habits of Canvasbacks, Redheads, and Lesser Scaup has been based wholly or partly on these data (Phillips 1911, 1925; McAtee 1917, 1939; Preble and McAtee 1923; Kubichek 1933; Gabrielson and Jewett 1940; Martin et al. 1951).

COLLECTING AREAS IN SOUTHWESTERN MANITOBA

The ducks used in this study were collected primarily from the following areas in southwestern Manitoba.

Minnedosa-Erickson Pothole Area.—Located mainly within the aspen parkland but extending into the prairies, the Minnedosa-Erickson area with its numerous potholes (kettle hole ponds and lakes) and associated upland woods, pastures, and cereal crops provides some of

[1] Originally published in Condor 71(3):280–290, 1969.

[2] Address correspondence to this author. Present address: 17445 Crownview Dr., Gladstone, OR 97027.

the most productive, unmanaged, waterfowl nesting habitat remaining in North America. Canvasbacks, Redheads, and Lesser Scaup use this area primarily for breeding and nesting. None of the adults, both male and female, of these three species were known to have remained on the potholes during their postnuptial molt. Descriptions of this area and its use by waterfowl were given by Evans et al. (1952:2–16), Dzubin (1955:281), Kiel (1955:189–190), Rogers (1959:218), and Stoudt (1962–64). The general ecology of the aspen parkland was described by Bird (1961).

Delta-Lake Francis Marshes.—The two adjacent and somewhat similar marshes of Delta and Lake Francis are located between Lake Manitoba and the fertile agricultural lands of the Portage la Prairie plain. The Delta marsh is important to Canvasbacks, Redheads, and Lesser Scaup as a breeding area and a stopover during spring and fall migration but it is relatively unimportant as a molting area (Hochbaum 1959). Hochbaum (1959:3–12) and Olsen (1959:40–41) described the general ecology of the Delta marsh, Löve and Löve (1954) described its emergent vegetation, and Collias and Collias (1963:9–13) presented data on some invertebrates that were potential foods for waterfowl.

Lake Winnipegosis.—Lake Winnipegosis is a large (5,200 km^2), shallow (6-m mean depth), eutrophic lake lying within the southern edge of the boreal forest. This lake is important to Canvasbacks, Redheads, and Lesser Scaup as a stopover during the spring and as both a stopover and a staging area during the fall; in July and August, Redheads use it as a molting area (Bartonek 1965:18–19). All three species nest here to a limited extent. The Manitoba Department of Mines and Natural Resources, the Wildlife Management Institute, the U.S. Fish and Wildlife Service (1948), and McLeod and Bondar (1953:2–4) described the lake; Bajkov (1930) listed its plankton and bottom fauna.

METHODS

Of the 345 ducks used in our analyses, 330 were shot and 15 were drowned in gill nets of commercial fishermen. Prior to 1963 we placed most of the birds, immediately after collecting, in ice until they were autopsied or could be frozen. In 1963 and 1964 we minimized the effects of post-mortem digestion of foods by either injecting digestive tracts with Formalin, or removing the tracts and placing them in Formalin immediately after collection. The various foods were identified, segregated, and volumetrically measured while wet by water-displacement. Grit was analyzed separately from foods. Because of biases resulting from food digesting at different rates in certain parts of the upper digestive tract, we analyzed the contents of the esophagus separately from that of the accompanying proventriculus and gizzard. Dillon (1958:114) recognized that "gullet material reflects recent consumption and stomach material may distort the importance of some hard seeded plants." We noted that data on certain invertebrates are similarly distorted and that the composition of most foods found in the esophagus is significantly different from the composition in either the proventriculus or gizzard. Because many of the earlier waterfowl food-habit studies included the proventriculus and gizzard in their analyses, the esophagus-proventriculus-gizzard data and the preferred esophageal data are presented for comparative purposes. "Per cent of volume" (the "aggregate volume method" of Martin et al. 1946) and "per cent of occurrence" are used in presenting these data. "Percentage of bulk method" data (the "aggregate percentage method" of Martin et al. 1946) were used to compare our findings with those of others who had used this method of analysis.

FOOD HABITS OF CANVASBACKS

The spring-summer food habits of Canvasbacks were determined from 120 juveniles collected between mid-June and the first of September and from 42 adults collected between May and the end of August. Fall food habits were determined from 13 birds collected in the last part of September and in October during the hunting season.

During summer, food habits of juvenile and adult female Canvasbacks were similar in their high percentages of invertebrates and differed appreciably from those of adult males, which were high in plant material (Table 1). Indexes of Similarity (Curtis 1959:82–83) were used to compare diets among the various groups of birds. An I S value of 1.00 would indicate that diets were identical, while a value of 0.00 would indicate that diets had nothing in common. We compared "per cent of volume" of the items in the esophageal material and obtained I S values of 0.32 for juveniles and female adults, 0.03 for juveniles and male adults, and 0.09 for female and male adults. Corresponding values determined from esophagus-proventriculus-gizzard contents were 0.52, 0.13, and 0.25. I S values are highest in this latter group of comparisons because these food materials contained items common in most ducks, i.e., hard-coated seeds that tend to be retained by the gizzard.

Mostly immature aquatic insects and various gastropods (Lymnaeidae, Physidae, and Planorbidae) formed 87 per cent of the volume of foods found in the esophagi of juvenile Canvasbacks (Table 1). Trichoptera larvae and cases, Tendipedidae larvae, pupae and an occasional adult, and Ephemeroptera nymphs were the most abundant insects found in these young birds. Zygoptera and Anisoptera nymphs, Corixidae nymphs and adults, Haliplidae and Dytiscidae larvae and adults, Stratomyidae larvae, and an adult Mallophaga were the remaining insects, and totaled only one per cent. Other invertebrates (Hirudinea, cladoceran ephippia, ostracods, arachnids, etc.) formed less than one per cent volume. Consumption of *Zannichellia palustris* nutlets by two flying juveniles accounted for 62 percent of the plants found in esophageal material from the juvenile sample, and unduly influenced the values of both *Zannichellia* and the total plant material. Oögonia and vegetative branches of *Chara*, tubers and rootstalks of *Potamogeton pectinatus*, and seeds and vegetative parts from numerous emergent and subemergent species formed the remainder of the plant material in the esophagi.

As juvenile Canvasbacks grow older, they rely less and less upon animal food. By fall their diet and that of adults consists primarily of plant material (Table 2). The percentage (aggregate percentage method) of animal material found in the esophageal contents of birds aged 0 to 5 weeks was 99 ± 1 (95% C.L.); at 5 to 9 weeks of age, 86 ± 11; and at flying time, but before the fall hunting season, only 38 ± 22.

Cottam (1939:30) examined eight juveniles from Alberta and Saskatchewan. Three older birds, taken in September but still flightless, had fed almost entirely upon *Potamogeton* and *Scirpus*, while animal material comprised 56 per cent of the food found in the five younger duck-

Table 1. Foods from Canvasbacks collected during the spring and summer in southwestern Manitoba.

Source of material Food item	Common name (part or type)	% occurrence			% aggregate vol.		
		Juvenile	Adult female	Adult male	Juvenile	Adult female	Adult male
Esophageal contents (*N*)		(86)	(16)	(13)	(86)	(16)	(13)
Zannichellia sp.	Horned pondweed (nutlets)	2			8		
Chara spp.	Muskgrass (oögonia, vegetative)	5	6		2	tr.	
Potamogeton spp.	Pondweeds (tubers)	12	44	62	1	7	95
Other plants	Various seeds	45	25	46	2	tr.	tr.
	Misc. vegetative parts	34	6	15	tr.	tr.	2
Total plant material		73	75	100	13	8	98
Trichoptera	Caddis flies (larvae, cases)	53	44		59	10	
Gastropoda	Pond snails	22	38		18	66	
Tendipedidae	Midges (larvae, pupae)	37	31	31	8	2	2
Ephemeroptera	Mayflies (nymphs)	6	6		1	13	
Misc. Insecta	Misc. aquatic insects	26	12		1	tr.	
Other animals	Other aquatic invertebrates	12			tr.		
Total animal material		79	88	31	87	92	2
Esophagus-proventriculus-gizzard contents (*N*)		(120)	(23)	(19)	(120)	(23)	(19)
Potamogeton spp.	Pondweeds (tubers, winter buds)	12	35	68	3	13	81
	Pondweeds (nutlets)	52	87	79	2	6	4
Zannichellia sp.	Horned pondweed (nutlets)	2			4		
Chara spp.	Muskgrass (oögonia, vegetative)	8	9		4	2	
Scirpus spp.	Bulrushes (achenes)	83	87	79	3	4	3
Ceratophyllum sp.	Coontail (nutlets)	11	17	16	3	tr.	tr.
Carex spp.	Sedges (achenes, perigynia)	32	35	63	1	tr.	2
Myriophyllum sp.	Water milfoil (nutlets)	43	87	79	tr.	1	1
Chenepodium sp.	Lamb's-quarter (utricles)	5	9	21	tr.	tr.	5
Miscellaneous	Various seeds	31	52	58	1	1	tr.
	Vegetation	33	17	32	tr.	tr.	tr.
Total plant material		98	100	100	21	27	96
Trichoptera	Caddis flies (larvae, cases)	72	61	37	61	24	1
Gastropoda	Pond snails	22	30		10	33	
Tendipedidae	Midges (larvae, pupae)	34	44	37	4	5	3
Odonata	Damselflies, Dragonflies (nymphs)	16	17		1	tr.	
Ephemeroptera	Mayflies (nymphs)	8	4		1	8	
Other animals	Misc. aquatic invertebrates	39	9	11	1	1	tr.
	Unidentified animal material	12	17		1	2	
Total animal material		91	91	58	79	73	4

lings. Percentages of the more important food items found by Cottam were: *Potamogeton,* 37; *Scirpus,* 5; *Sparganium,* 7; *Myriophyllum* and *Hippuris,* 4; Trichoptera, 19; Corixidae, 8; Coleoptera, 4; and Tendipedidae larvae, 2. In comparing our data with Cottam's but excluding both miscellaneous and unidentified materials in the comparison, we obtained an I S value of 0.47. Yocom (1951:174) reported that a juvenile Canvasback collected at the end of July in Washington had fed entirely upon *Ruppia maritima* and *Potamogeton* spp.

Of food found in the esophagi of adult female Canvasbacks during spring–summer, 92 per cent was animal (Table 1). Lymnaeidae snails formed 99 per cent of the gastropods. Immature forms of Trichoptera, Tendipedidae, Ephemeroptera, and Zygoptera comprised the remainder of the animal food

Table 2. Foods from Canvasbacks collected in late September and early October during the hunting season in southwestern Manitoba.

Source of material Food item	Common name (part or type)	% occurrence	% aggregate vol.
Esophageal contents (*N*)		(7)	(7)
Potamogeton spp.	Pondweeds (tubers)	71	71
Chara spp.	Muskgrass (vegetative)	14	5
Myriophyllum sp.	Water milfoil (nutlets)	14	1
Other plants	Misc. vegetative parts and seeds	14	1
Total plant material		100	78
Ephemeroptera	Mayflies (nymphs)	14	18
Zygoptera	Damselflies (nymphs)	14	3
Other animals	Misc. aquatic invertebrates	29	1
Total animal material		29	22
Esophagus-proventriculus-gizzard contents (*N*)		(13)	(13)
Potamogeton spp.	Pondweeds (tubers, winter buds)	77	51
	Pondweeds (nutlets)	92	20
Scirpus spp.	Bulrushes (achenes)	62	4
Chara spp.	Muskgrass (vegetative)	15	4
Myriophyllum sp.	Water milfoil (nutlets, vegetative)	38	1
Other plants	Various seeds	23	1
	Unidentified vegetative parts	8	5
Total plant material		100	86
Ephemeroptera	Mayflies (nymphs)	8	12
Zygoptera	Damselflies (nymphs)	8	1
Other animals	Misc. aquatic invertebrates	15	1
Total animal material		15	14

and 26 per cent of the esophageal contents. Ephippia of cladocerans, corixids, Haliplidae adults and larvae, and arachnids were the "miscellaneous invertebrates" found in the esophagus-proventriculus-gizzard contents. *Potamogeton pectinatus* tubers were utilized by the females, but not as extensively as by the adult males. Miscellaneous plant items included *Lemna trisulca*, leaf segments of *Myriophyllum exalbescens*, and the seeds of *Sparganium, Hordeum, Eleocharis, Rumex,* and *Ranunculus*. Apparently, animal material forms the bulk of the adult females' diets during nesting, incubation, and brood-rearing, but plant material later increases in importance.

Adult male Canvasbacks consumed primarily (97 per cent) the vegetative parts and nutlets of *Potamogeton*, the tubers being mainly utilized (Table 1). Although animal matter was found in four males, it comprised only two per cent of the esophageal food items.

Sexual differences in food habits, as observed between adult male and female Canvasbacks during summer, have not previously been reported. Only once before has this aspect of waterfowl food habits been examined, i.e. for the Mallard, *Anas platyrhynchos* (Perret 1962:38–39). Atlhough the reason for this difference is unknown, a high protein diet simply may not be a necessity for the adult males.

The food found in Canvasbacks collected during the hunting season was similar to that in adult males collected during the spring and summer (I S = 0.71; Table 2). Vegetative parts of aquat-

Table 3. Quantities of *Potamogeton* spp., other Najadaceae, *Vallisneria americana,* and total plant material found in Canvasbacks (esophagus-proventriculus-gizzard content), as presented in reports involving 10 or more birds.

Location	N	Season	% vol. or (% occurrence) *Potamogeton*	Other Najadaceae	*Vallisneria*	Total plants	Reference
26 states, 5 provinces	427	Sept.–June	18	1	9	81	Cottam (1939:25)
Mostly southern states	381[a]	Winter–Spring	——18——		11	85	Phillips (1925:130–131)
Northeastern U.S.	71[a]	Fall–Spring	10–25	tr.–2	25–20		Martin et al. (1951:68)
Southeastern U.S.	64[a]	Winter	10–25	tr.–2			Martin et al. (1951:68)
Western U.S.	109[a]	All seasons	53	2–5			Martin et al. (1951:68)
Oregon	12[a]	Fall?	(62)	(8)		60	Gabrielson and Jewett (1940:157)
Minnesota	88	Fall?	(95)	tr.			Smith (1946:74)
Tennessee	38	Fall	38			74	Rawls ([1958]:65–66)
Illinois	28	Oct.–Dec.	46			65	Anderson (1959:320)
California	17	Oct.–April	16	3		19	Yocom and Keller (1961:48–49)
Missouri	10	Oct.–Dec.	45	1		95	Korschgen (1955:16)
Manitoba	175	April–Oct.	23	3		37	this study

[a] These data are also incorporated into Cottam's (1939:25) data based upon 427 birds.

ic plants, especially tubers of *Potamogeton pectinatus,* formed 77 per cent of the esophageal material. One juvenile male Canvasback, shot in late September on the Delta Marsh, contributed 21 of the total 22 per cent of animal material for esophageal contents and 13 of 14 per cent of esophagus-proventriculus-gizzard contents.

Cottam (1939:24–29) found that animal matter comprised 21 per cent of the food consumed by birds collected during April, May, June, and September (48 "stomachs"). Insects, nearly two-thirds of which were Trichoptera larvae and cases, were taken primarily during summer; mollusks were taken primarily during winter. Najadaceae (pondweeds) formed 33 per cent of the summer foods. Preble and McAtee (1923:47) reported that an adult male Canvasback, collected in the Pribilof Islands in May, had fed exclusively upon Trichoptera larvae and cases. Erickson (1948:282) examined six spring migrants that died from lead poisoning and found *Scirpus acutus* and *Potamogeton pectinatus* fruits in limited quantities.

If today's information on the food habits of Canvasbacks throughout their range had been available to Alexander Wilson, he might well have named them "*Anas potamogeton*" instead of "*A. valisineria.*" The published reports, which are either reviewed subsequently or listed in Table 3, indicate that potamogetons and other Najadaceae are more important to Canvasbacks than is the much acclaimed *Vallisneria americana.* Stewart (1962:51, 170–173) reported the food habits of 86 Canvasbacks taken from the Chesapeake region of Delaware and Maryland between October and March. Combining Stewart's findings from four different areas, the "percentages of occurrence" for Najadaceae species were: *Potamogeton* vegetative parts, 28, and fruit, 31; *Zostera marina* vegetative parts, 13; *Ruppia maritima* vegetative parts, 6, and fruit, 8; and *Najas* vegetative parts, 1. *Vallisneria americana* was found in 24 per cent of the birds. In four birds from Maryland, Warren (1890:43) found only vegetable substances that he "judged" to be "remains of Vallisneria." H. L. Skavlem found *Potamogeton* tubers to form 60 to 80 per cent of the Canvasbacks' food on Lake Koshkonong (McAtee 1917:14). He discredited the importance of *Vallisneria* as a food in Wisconsin by taking some of the alleged "wild-celery" buds from esophagi of Canvasbacks and growing them; in reality, they proved to be a *Potamogeton* (Kumlien and Hollister 1903:22). Zimmerman (1953:172) indicated that *Potamogeton* and *Vallisneria* were among the foods eaten by six birds examined in Wisconsin. Seven of eight birds collected by Pirnie (1935:307–308) in Michigan contained, in addition to other items, either the tubers, winter buds, or nutlets of potamogetons. Longcore and Cornwell (1964) successfully maintained Canvasbacks and Lesser Scaups in Michigan by feeding them "natural foods" which included 64 per cent (oven-dried weight) *Vallisneria.*

Additional references indicate that plants other than *Vallisneria* are extensively utilized by Canvasbacks. Nuttall (1834:431) claimed that in Massachusetts Bay the Canvasbacks' principal foods were *Zostera marina* and *Ruppia maritima* instead of *Vallisneria.* McAtee (1917:21) reported that the tubers of *Sagittaria platyphylla* were important in attracting large numbers of Canvasbacks into the Mississippi Delta in Louisiana. Grinnell et al. (1918:154), not mentioning any Najadaceae, reasoned that "in California the Canvasback partakes of more animal food, for wild celery does not grow in this state."

The succulent leaves, stems, rootstalks, tubers, and to a lesser extent the fruits, of *Potamogeton* spp., *Ruppia maritima, Zostera marina, Vallisneria americana,* and *Sagittaria* spp. appear to be the plant foods most utilized by Canvasbacks. While the extent to which "preference" in the wild determines their relative utilization has not been studied, plant distribution provdes a partial explanation for differences noted in utilization. *Potamogeton,* being more widely distributed in continental range than *Vallisneria* (Martin and Uhler 1939:25–35, 43), logically should form a greater proportion of Canvasbacks' diets, as it apparently does.

Most of the previously mentioned references on Canvasback food habits indicate that consumption of animal material is not uncommon. Additional references reporting Canvasbacks feeding extensively upon animal material are those of Dawson and Bowles (1909:793) in Washington, Trautman (1940:192) in Ohio, and Saunders (1964:257) in the coastal waters of México.

FOOD HABITS OF REDHEADS

The spring-summer food habits of Redheads were determined from 59 juveniles, collected between the end of June and the first week of September, and 24 adults collected between mid-May and late August. Information on fall food habits was provided by 2 juveniles and 14 adults shot during the hunting season.

Differences between the food habits of juveniles and adult females and those of adult males were not as great among Redheads as among Canvasbacks (Table 4). I S values for esophageal contents were 0.21 for juveniles and female adults, 0.24 for juveniles and male adults, and 0.74 for female and male adults. Corresponding values determined from esophagus-proventriculus-gizzard data were 0.52, 0.52, and 0.57, respectively.

Various foods were consumed by juvenile Redheads and no particular item was utilized extensively by the entire group (Table 4). The algae, Characeae and Chlorophyceae, comprised 26 per cent of the esophageal contents and were found in 12 of the 37 esophagi examined. Hard-coated seeds and Trichoptera lar-

Table 4. Foods from Redheads collected during the spring and summer in southwestern Manitoba.

Source of material Food item	Common name (part or type)	% occurrence			% aggregate vol.		
		Juvenile	Adult female	Adult male	Juvenile	Adult female	Adult male
Esophageal contents (*N*)		(37)	(6)	(6)	(37)	(6)	(6)
Chara spp.	Muskgrass (oögonia)	8			16		
	Muskgrass (vegetative)	11			2		
Scolochloa sp.	Whitetop grass (grains)	16	17	17	17	tr.	tr.
Chlorophyceae	Green algae	19		17	8		tr.
Ranunculus spp.	Buttercups (achenes)	5			5		
Scirpus spp.	Bulrushes (achenes)	51	50	33	3	4	tr.
Potamogeton spp.	Pondweeds (winter buds)	11	33	17	3	15	12
Lemna spp.	Duckweeds (vegetative)	11	17	17	2	tr.	tr.
Other plants	Misc. plants (seeds)	32	67	50	1	tr.	2
Total plant material		81	100	83	57	19	14
Trichoptera	Caddis flies (larvae, cases)	41	50	50	18	80	62
Gastropoda	Pond snails	11			11		
Cladocera	Water fleas (adults, ephippia)	16			7		
Tendipedidae	Midges (larvae, pupae)	24	17	17	1	tr.	22
Other animals	Invertebrate eggs	11			5		
	Misc. aquatic invertebrates	30	33	33	1	tr.	2
Total animal material		76	50	50	43	81	86
Esophagus-proventriculus-gizzard contents (*N*)		(59)	(10)	(14)	(59)	(10)	(14)
Chara spp.	Muskgrass (oögonia)	5			11		
	Muskgrass (vegetative)	10			1		
Potamogeton spp.	Pondweeds (winter buds)	8	30	43	7	19	50
	Pondweeds (nutlets)	44	60	33	3	1	tr.
Scolochloa sp.	Whitetop grass (grains)	10	10	7	7	2	9
Scirpus spp.	Bulrushes (achenes)	95	60	57	6	5	2
Ranunculus spp.	Buttercups (achenes)	19		7	5		tr.
Chlorophyceae	Green algae	17	10	7	5	tr.	tr.
Misc.	Various seeds and vegetative parts	51	80	57	2	tr.	2
Total plant material		97	100	100	46	27	64
Trichoptera	Caddis flies (larvae, cases)	64	50	50	36	72	33
Cladocera	Waterfleas (adults, ephippia)	14			5		
Gastropoda	Pond snails	7	10		4	tr.	
Tendipedidae	Midges (larvae, pupae)	24	20	7	1	1	3
Corixidae	Water boatmen (adults, nymphs)	20	10		1	tr.	
Other animals	Invertebrate eggs	7			5		
	Misc. aquatic invertebrates	44	30	29	tr.	tr.	tr.
Total animal material		85	70	57	54	73	36

vae with their cases comprised a greater percentage of the foods in the esophagus-proventriculus-gizzard contents than in the esophageal contents. Zygoptera nymphs, Haliplidae and Dytiscidae adults and larvae, Hydracarina, Chonchostraca, Ephemeroptera nymphs, and eggs of various invertebrates formed the "miscellaneous invertebrates" in the esophagus.

The only other references on juvenile Redheads reported plant material to form the bulk of the foods. Cottam's (1939:13–14) three downy Redheads contained primarily *Potamogeton* (33 per cent), *Scirpus* (31 per cent), and animal material (31 per cent); of the latter group, Corixidae, Coleoptera, Orthoptera, and Odonata were most important. Collias and Collias (1963:7) reported that five one-week-old Redheads collected on the

Table 5. Foods from Redheads collected in late September and early October during the hunting season in southwestern Manitoba.

Source of material Food item	Common name (part or type)	% occurrence	% aggregate vol.
Esophageal contents (*N*)		(5)	(5)
Chara spp.	Muskgrass (vegetative)	80	99
Hordeum sp.	Squirrel-tail grass (grain)	20	tr.
Total plant material		100	100
Esophagus-proventriculus-gizzard contents (*N*)		(16)	(16)
Chara spp.	Muskgrass (vegetative)	88	96
Potamogeton spp.	Pondweeds (vegetative, nutlets)	12	1
Misc.	Various seeds	12	2
	Unidentified vegetative parts	6	1
Total plant material		100	100

Delta marshes had eaten primarily the nutlets of *Potamogeton.*

Animal material found in our small samples of adult males and females comprised 86 and 81 per cent, respectively, of esophageal volumes (Table 4). Trichoptera larvae and cases and Tendipedidae larvae and pupae comprised the bulk of animal foods consumed by these adults. Zygoptera nymphs, Haliplidae and Dytiscidae adults and larvae, amphipods, and Sphaeridae were the "miscellaneous animal" foods eaten. Winter buds of *Potamogeton* were almost the exclusive item eaten by a group of 11 flightless adults drowned in gill nets during late August on Lake Winnipegosis. In addition to those plant items listed in Table 4, fruits from the following plants were found in small quantities: *Myriophyllum, Chenepodium, Eleocharis, Sparganium, Ruppia, Hordeum,* and *Echinochloa.*

Chara, with its musky odor and limy incrustation, is at times an important food of Redheads. Vegetative branches of *Chara* were found in all 14 birds shot on Lake Winnipegosis during the hunting season (Table 5). Both oögonia and, to a lesser extent, vegetative parts from these plants were eaten by six juveniles (Table 4). Kubichek (1933:108) reported that *Chara* comprised 91 per cent of the food found in the "stomachs" of 83 Redheads collected at Okanagan Landing, British Columbia, during the winter. We disagree with Kubichek's conclusion that Redheads resort to *Chara* because other foods are scarce. Eleven Canvasbacks, also collected with the Redheads during the hunting season on Lake Winnipegosis, had fed primarily upon *Potamogeton* tubers and nutlets, suggesting to us that although *Potamogeton* was available as a potential food for Redheads, *Chara* was preferred. Cottam (1939:10) also considered *Chara* to be an acceptable food in many areas where other excellent duck foods were available. At Swan Lake, British Columbia, Munro (1939:183), found *Chara*'s vegetative branches and oöspores to comprise 31 and 17 per cent, respectively, of the foods found in eight Redheads collected in the fall. Cornwell and Cowan (1963:186), examining the same 14 birds from Lake Winnipegosis used in this study, noted a paucity of intestinal parasites and suggested that *Chara* serves as a natural means to deworm the birds either mechanically or chemically.

Cottam (1939:7–13) considered Redheads to be predominantly vegetarians;

Table 6. Foods from Lesser Scaup collected during the spring and summer in southwestern Manitoba.

Source of material Food item	Common name (part or type)	% occurrence			% aggregate vol.		
		Juvenile	Adult female	Adult male	Juvenile	Adult female	Adult male
Esophageal contents (*N*)		(25)	(7)	(7)	(25)	(7)	(7)
Misc. plants	Various seeds	16	29	29	tr.	tr.	tr.
	Misc. vegetative	32	43	29	tr.	1	tr.
Total plant material		40	57	57	tr.	2	tr.
Amphipoda	Scuds	52	43	29	49	46	8
Gastropoda	Pond snails	4	14	43	39	4	4
Tendipedidae	Midges (larvae, pupae)	20	43	29	8	41	6
Corixidae	Water boatmen (adults, nymphs)	40	14	14	2	2	1
Coleoptera	Aquatic beetles (adults, larvae)	8		29	tr.		2
Hirudinea	Leeches	4		14	tr.		61
Trichoptera	Caddis flies (larvae, cases)	8	14	29	tr.	2	16
Other animals	Misc. aquatic invertebrates	16	29	14	1	1	1
Total animal material		80	86	100	99	98	99
Esophagus-proventriculus-gizzard contents (*N*)		(47)	(12)	(12)	(47)	(12)	(12)
Myriophyllum sp.	Water milfoil (nutlets)	47	92	92	12	7	5
Scirpus spp.	Bulrushes (achenes)	92	100	100	6	4	7
Other plants	Various seeds	51	17	75	1	2	2
	Misc. vegetative parts	15	25	25	tr.	tr.	tr.
Total plant material		96	100	100	19	13	14
Amphipoda	Scuds	32	25	17	39	19	7
Gastropoda	Pond snails	2	17	33	20	2	3
Tendipedidae	Midges (larvae, pupae)	17	25	25	9	34	12
Corixidae	Water boatmen (adults, nymphs)	38	17	25	4	1	tr.
Coleoptera	Aquatic beetles (adults, larvae)	6	8	25	1	tr.	2
Trichoptera	Caddis flies (larvae, cases)	6	25	25	tr.	5	24
Hirudinea	Leeches	2	8	8	tr.	2	31
Misc. Crustacea	Misc. crustaceans	13	25	8	tr.	2	tr.
Misc. Insecta	Misc. aquatic insects	4	25	8	tr.	2	1
Unident. animals	Unidentified animal material	32	17	17	7	20	6
Total animal material		68	58	64	81	87	86

plant material comprised 90 per cent of the "stomach" contents found in his 364 adults. Najadaceae (32 per cent) and Characeae (21 per cent) were the most important plant families represented in the foods consumed. Insects, including Orthoptera, Tendipedidae, and Trichoptera, and mollusks, including Gastropoda and Pelecypoda, comprised six and four per cent, respectively, of the total foods consumed. Animal material comprised 24 per cent of the food in June and 20 per cent in July; no adults were collected during May or August.

FOOD HABITS OF LESSER SCAUP

Data on spring and summer food habits of Lesser Scaup are based upon 47 juveniles collected during July, August, and the first week in September, and 24 adults collected in each month from May through August. We did not collect scaup during the hunting season.

Animal matter was more important than plants to duckling and adult Lesser Scaup; and, as was expected, animal food decreased in importance when material from proventriculi and gizzards were included with the contents of the esophagi (Table 6). I S values for esophageal data were 0.20 for juveniles and female adults, 0.20 for juveniles and male adults, and 0.22 for female and male adults; corresponding values determined from esophagus-proventriculus-gizzard contents were 0.50, 0.34, and 0.46, respectively.

Amphipods, gastropods, and Tendipedidae larvae formed 96 per cent of the esophageal material found in 25 juvenile Lesser Scaup. The esophagus-proventriculus-gizzard contents of 47 juveniles increased the importance of such plants as *Myriophyllum* and *Scirpus*. Chlorophyceae, *Potamogeton* vetetation and nutlets, and the fruits of *Ruppia, Sparganium, Scolochloa, Hordeum, Eleocharis, Carex, Rumex, Ceratophyllum, Ranunculus*, and *Sonchus* were among the group of "miscellaneous plants" that formed only one per cent of the total foods. Ephippia of cladocerans, ostracods, nymphs of Ephemeroptera and Zygoptera, and the larvae of Culicidae formed the "miscellaneous invertebrates."

Eighty-nine per cent of the "stomach" contents of 17 juvenile Lesser Scaup collected in the Prairie Provinces was animal material (Cottam 1939:45–46). Aquatic beetles, Tendipedidae larvae, Corixidae, and Odonata nymphs were the most important groups of animals eaten by this group. In spite of a preponderance of Dytiscidae beetles eaten by Cottam's birds and amphipods by ours, an I S value of 0.24 was obtained in a comparison of esophagus-proventriculus-gizzard data from the two groups.

We compared our findings based upon 20 adult Lesser Scaup collected in the pothole area with those of Rogers and Korschgen (1966:260) who collected 39 adults in the same area. An I S value of 0.39 was obtained. In spite of using esophagus-proventriculus-gizzard contents which usually greatly inflate the importance of plant material, the percentages of animal material in both studies were high—86 per cent for ours and 91 per cent for theirs. Three of Rogers and Korschgen's birds ate *Daphnia*, which amounted to eight per cent of the foods. None of our scaup contained these mature cladocerans, but 7 of the 71 birds (47 juveniles and 24 adults) did contain trace amounts of their ephippia. Leeches were eaten by birds in both studies.

The amphipods, *Gammarus* and *Hyalella*, are important foods for many adult and juvenile Lesser Scaup in potholes and marshes of southwestern Manitoba. Of 71 scaup we examined, 20 contained these crustaceans (Table 6). Rogers and Korschgen (1966:259–261) found 21 of 39 adults had eaten amphipods. Amphipods composed most of the food found by Munro (1941:134–137) in 10 juveniles and 9 adults taken during the summer in British Columbia. Cottam (1939:40–46), however, found them relatively unimportant in birds that he examined.

DISCUSSION

Cottam (1939:5, 53), whose information was based upon specimens collected largely from fall to spring, was probably justified in concluding that the food habits of *Aythya*, excepting those of the Greater Scaup (*A. marila*), are predominantly vegetarian. The present study during the spring and summer, however, shows that Canvasbacks (excepting adult males), Redheads, and Lesser Scaup in southwestern Manitoba consumed chiefly animal material. Other investigations tend to corroborate the importance of animal foods for diving ducks during summer. Martin et al. (1951:66, 68–69) reported percentages of animal material among summer-collected birds to be 37 for Canvasbacks, 21 for Redheads, and 52 for Lesser Scaup. Keith's (1961:34) data from Redheads, Lesser Scaup, Ruddy Ducks (*Oxyura jamaicensis*), and Canvasbacks taken during the spring and summer in Alberta showed that animal material comprised 59 per cent of the foods found in 24 "stomachs." Rogers and Korschgen (1966:262–263), who presented seasonal data and reviewed studies following Cottam's (1939), concluded that the food habits of Lesser Scaup were more akin to those of Greater Scaup in that both consisted mainly of animal material.

During the summer, Canvasback and Redhead juveniles ate progressively less animal material as they became older. Lesser Scaup juveniles, however, maintained diets high in animal material. Chura (1961:124–126) noted that juvenile Mallards also consumed progressively less animal material as they became older. Perret (1962:61–62), however, did not find a similar change in the diets of the juvenile Mallards he examined. Mendall (1958:187) believed the diets of half-grown juvenile Ring-necked Ducks (*Aythya collaris*) were more similar to those of adults (more plant material) than to those of downy young (more animal material).

Studies in which "stomachs" or "gullets and gizzards" were used in analyses of food habits have probably over-estimated the importance of plant material because of the bias resulting from the inclusion of the proventriculus and gizzard contents in with the more meaningful esophageal contents. Some plant foods found in the ducks were probably ingested incidentally. Filamentous algae (Chlorophyceae) were frequently ingested when ducks fed upon amphipods, corixids, Tendipedidae larvae, and Trichoptera larvae, since these plants adhered to the invertebrates that were being eaten by the birds. The seeds of *Eleocharis, Scirpus, Carex, Myriophyllum, Hippuris, Ranunculus, Chenepodium,* and *Rumex,* and the oögonia of *Chara,* and the vegetative parts of *Myriophyllum, Ceratophyllum,* and *Lemna* were frequently incorporated into the larval cases of Trichoptera, and were therefore incidentally ingested by those birds that fed upon the larvae. Of course seeds are eaten as a food or as a substitute for grit, but their importance as a summer food is often overrated.

Aquatic invertebrates formed the bulk of foods eaten by the Canvasbacks, Redheads, and Lesser Scaup during the spring and summer months in southwestern Manitoba. Trichoptera larvae with cases, Tendipedidae larvae, and gastropods were important items for all three species; amphipods were additionally important to scaup. Immature rather than adult insects were most frequently consumed. Although juvenile birds were occasionally seen chasing flying insects across the water, flying forms of insects were rarely encountered in the examination of food contents.

Potamogeton, with its tubers, winter buds, rootstalks, and nutlets, was the most important plant genus. *Chara* was often consumed in large quantities by particular groups of birds, but it was not found in a majority. *Scirpus* and *Myriophyllum* were found in most birds, but seldom in large quantities. With the possible exception of two birds feeding upon caryopses of *Scolochloa* that were still attached to this emergent, seeds were taken from the bottom of the pond.

There were greater similarities in food habits between ducks of all three species collected from potholes and marshes (I S = 0.34) than ducks from either potholes and lakes (0.13) or marshes and lakes (0.13). The fruits of upland and emergent vegetation such as *Scirpus*, *Carex*, *Eleocharis*, *Scolochloa*, *Hordeum*, *Ranunculus*, *Rumex*, *Chenepodium*, *Meliotus*, and *Senecio* were more frequently consumed by ducks from the potholes and marshes than by those from the lakes. Conversely, aquatic vegetation such as the vegetative branches and oögonia of *Chara* and the winter buds of *Potamogeton* was more frequently found in birds from the lakes than in those from either potholes or marshes. These differences may in part reflect the higher ratios of edge to open-water associated with potholes and marshes in comparison with lakes.

Use of foods, with respect to quantity and availability and interspecific relations of the food habits among diving ducks, will be discussed in a separate paper (Bartonek and Hickey, unpublished).

SUMMARY

Among 162 summer-collected Canvasbacks, animal material formed the bulk of esophageal contents in both juveniles (87 per cent) and adult females (92 per cent), but it was less important to both adult males (2 per cent) and 13 fall-collected birds (22 per cent). Trichoptera larvae with cases, Tendipedidae, Ephemeroptera nymphs, and gastropods were the animal items found in greatest quantities. Tubers of *Potamogeton* comprised 95 per cent of the esophageal contents of summer-collected adult males, and 71 per cent of the fall-collected birds. A review of literature on food habits indicated that *Potamogeton*, probably because of its continent-wide distribution, is a more important food of Canvasbacks than the often acclaimed *Vallisneria americana*.

The esophagi from 83 summer-collected juvenile and adult female and male Redheads contained, respectively, 43, 81, and 86 per cent animal material. Trichoptera larvae, Tendipedidae, Cladocera, and gastropods were the most abundant animal items. *Chara* oögonia and vegetative branches, Chlorophyceae, and the fruits of *Scolochloa*, *Ranunculus*, *Scirpus*, and *Potamogeton* were among the more important plant items consumed by these summer-collected birds. Vegetative branches of *Chara* were almost the only item found in 16 fall-collected Redheads.

Animal material formed 99, 98, and 99 per cent, respectively, of esophageal contents in 71 summer-collected juvenile and adult female and male Lesser Scaup. Amphipods were particularly important to these diving ducks, but gastropods, Tendipedidae and Trichoptera larvae, corixids, and leeches were also used.

With the possible exception of adult male Canvasbacks that fed mainly upon tubers of *Potamogeton*, the three species of *Aythya* used animal material extensively throughout the summer. By fall, however, plant material formed the bulk of the diets of Canvasbacks and Redheads. Lesser Scaup probably maintain a diet high in animal material throughout the year. Juvenile Canvasbacks and Redheads consumed progressively greater quantities of plant material as they became older.

Trichoptera larvae with cases, Tendipedidae larvae, pupae, and adults, gastropods, amphipods, Ephemeroptera and Odonata nymphs, and corixids were among the most important animal items consumed by the three species of birds. The vegetative parts and fruits of *Potamogeton* and *Chara* were the most frequently consumed plant items; fruits of *Scirpus*, *Myriophyllum*, *Scolochloa*, *Chenepodium*, and *Carex* were occasionally important to this group of birds.

ACKNOWLEDGMENTS

We wish to thank G. W. Cornwell, L. B. Keith, R. A. McCabe, D. P. Olson, J. H. Stoudt, and P. Ward for advice and assistance received during this study. We wish to acknowledge N. G. Perret's (unpublished M.S. thesis) work on the food habits of Mallards in the Minnedosa pothole area, which importantly influenced the nature of this study. H. A. Hochbaum is especially thanked for his guidance and assistance during this study. We received financial support from the Wildlife Management Institute, operating through the Delta Waterfowl Research Station, Delta, Manitoba, and from the University of Wisconsin. We gratefully acknowledge the time and assistance made available to us by the Bureau of Sport Fisheries and Wildlife during the preparation of this manuscript.

LITERATURE CITED

ANDERSON, H. G. 1959. Food habits of migratory ducks in Illinois. Illinois Nat. Hist. Surv. Bull. 27(4):289–344.

BAJKOV, A. 1930. Biological conditions of Manitoba lakes. Contrib. Can. Biol. and Fish., N.S. 5:381–422.

BARTONEK, J. C. 1965. Mortality of diving ducks on Lake Winnipegosis through commercial fishing. Can. Field-Naturalist 79:15–20.

BIRD, R. D. 1961. Ecology of the aspen parkland of western Canada in relation to land use. Can. Dept. Agr., Res. Branch, Res. Sta. Contrib. 27. 155 pp.

CHURA, N. J. 1961. Food availability and preferences of juvenile Mallards. Trans. N. Amer. Wildl. and Nat. Resources Conf. 26:121–134.

COLLIAS, N. E., AND E. C. COLLIAS. 1963. Selective feeding by wild ducklings of different species. Wilson Bull. 75:6–14.

CORNWELL, G. W., AND A. B. COWAN. 1963. Helminth populations of the Canvasback (*Aythya valisineria*) and host-parasite-environmental interrelationships. Trans. N. Amer. Wildl. and Nat. Resources Conf. 28:173–199.

COTTAM, C. 1939. Food habits of North American diving ducks. U.S. Dept. Agr. Tech. Bull. 643. 140 pp.

CURTIS, J. T. 1959. The vegetation of Wisconsin. Univ. Wisconsin Press, Madison. 657pp.

DAWSON, W. L., AND J. H. BOWLES. 1909. The birds of Washington. Vol. 2. Occidental Publ. Co., Seattle. Pp. 459–997.

DILLON, O. W., JR. 1958. Food habits of wild ducks in the rice-marsh transition area of Louisiana. Proc. Ann. Conf. Southeastern Assoc. Game Fish Comm. 11:114–119.

DZUBIN, A. 1955. Some evidences of home range in waterfowl. Trans. N. Amer. Wildl. Conf. 20:278–298.

ERICKSON, R. C. 1948. Life history and ecology of the Canvasback, *Nyroca valisineria* (Wilson), in southeastern Oregon. Ph.D. thesis, Iowa State College, Ames. 324pp.

EVANS, C. D., A. S. HAWKINS, AND W. H. MARSHALL. [1952] Movements of waterfowl broods in Manitoba. U.S. Fish and Wildl. Serv. Spec. Sci. Rep.: Wildl. 16. 47pp. (multilithed)

GABRIELSON, I. N., AND S. G. JEWETT. 1940. Birds of Oregon. Oregon State Coll., Corvallis. 650pp.

GRINNELL, J., H. C. BRYANT, AND T. I. STORER. 1918. The game birds of California. Univ. California Press, Berkeley. 642pp.

HOCHBAUM, H. A. 1959. The Canvasback on a prairie marsh. 2nd ed. Stackpole Co., Harrisburg, and Wildl. Mgmt. Inst., Washington, D.C. 207pp.

KEITH, L. B. 1961. A study of waterfowl ecology on small impoundments in southeastern Alberta. Wildl. Monogr. 6. 88pp.

KIEL, W. H., JR. 1955. Nesting studies of the Coot in southwestern Manitoba. J. Wildl. Mgmt. 19:189–198.

KORSCHGEN, L. J. 1955. The fall food habits of waterfowl in Missouri. Missouri Conserv. Comm., Fish and Game Div. P.-R. Ser. 14. 41pp. (multilithed)

KUBICHEK, W. F. 1933. Report on the foods of five of our most important game ducks. Iowa State Coll. J. Sci. 8:107–126.

KUMLIEN, L., AND N. HOLLISTER. 1903. The birds of Wisconsin. Bull. Wisconsin Nat. Hist. Soc. 3(1–3):1–143.

LONGCORE, J. R., AND G. W. CORNWELL. 1964. The consumption of natural foods by captive Canvasbacks and Lesser Scaups. J. Wildl. Mgmt. 28:527–531.

LÖVE, A., AND D. LÖVE. 1954. Vegetation of a prairie marsh. Bull. Torrey Bot. Club 81:16–34.

MANITOBA DEPT. MINES AND NAT. RESOURCES, GAME AND FISH BRANCH; WILDL. MGMT. INST.; AND U.S. FISH AND WILDL. SERV. 1948. A report on fish and wildlife resources in relation to the Manitoba Central Basin project. A portion of the Saskatchewan River plan. 144pp. (mimeographed)

MARTIN, A. C., R. H. GENSCH, AND C. P. BROWN. 1946. Alternative methods in upland gamebird food analysis. J. Wildl. Mgmt. 10:8–12.

———, AND F. M. UHLER. 1939. Food of game

ducks in the United States and Canada. U.S. Dept. Agr. Tech. Bull. 634. 157pp.

———, H. S. ZIM, AND A. L. NELSON. 1951. American wildlife and plants. McGraw-Hill, New York. 500pp.

MCATEE, W. L. 1917. Propagation of wild-duck foods. U.S. Dept. Agr. Bull. 465. 40pp.

———. 1939. Wildfowl food plants. Collegiate Press, Ames, Iowa. 141pp.

MCLEOD, J. A., AND G. F. BONDAR. 1953. A brief study of the Double-crested Cormorant on Lake Winnipegosis. Can. Field-Naturalist 67:1–11.

MENDALL, H. L. 1958. The Ring-necked Duck in the northeast. Univ. Maine Stud., Second Ser. 73, Univ. Maine Bull. 60(16):1–317.

MUNRO, J. A. 1939. Food of ducks and coots at Swan Lake, British Columbia. Can. J. Res. 17(D):178–186.

———. 1941. Studies of waterfowl in British Columbia. Greater Scaup duck, Lesser Scaup duck. Can. J. Res. 19(D):113–138.

NUTTALL, T. 1834. A manual of the ornithology of the United States and of Canada. Vol. 2. The water birds. Hilliard, Gray, and Co., Boston. 627pp.

OLSEN, P. F. 1959. Muskrat breeding biology at Delta, Manitoba. J. Wildl. Mgmt. 23:40–53.

PERRET, N. G. 1962. The spring and summer foods of the common Mallard (*Anas platyrhynchos platyrhynchos* L.) in south central Manitoba. M.S. thesis, Univ. British Columbia, Vancouver. 82pp.

PHILLIPS, J. C. 1911. Ten years of observation on the migration of Anatidae at Wenham Lake, Massachusetts. Auk 28:188–200.

———. 1925. A natural history of the ducks. Vol. 3. Houghton Mifflin Co., Boston. 383pp.

PIRNIE, M. D. 1935. Michigan waterfowl management. Michigan Dept. Conserv., Game Div., Lansing. 328pp.

PREBLE, E. A., AND W. L. MCATEE. 1923. A biological survey of the Pribilof Islands, Alaska. Part I. Birds and mammals, pp. 1–128. Dept. Agr., Bur. Biol. Surv. N. Amer. Fauna no. 46.

RAWLS, C. K., JR. [1958.] Reelfoot Lake waterfowl research. Tennessee Game and Fish Comm., Fed. Aid Wildl. Restoration Final Rep. Proj. W-22-R. 80pp.

ROGERS, J. P. 1959. Low water and Lesser Scaup reproduction near Erickson, Manitoba. Trans. N. Amer. Wildl. and Nat. Resources Conf. 24:216–224.

———, AND L. J. KORSCHGEN. 1966. Foods of Lesser Scaups on breeding, migration, and wintering areas. J. Wildl. Mgmt. 30:258–264.

SAUNDERS, G. B. 1964. South of the border, pp. 253–262. *In* J. P. Linduska, ed. Waterfowl tomorrow. U.S. Bur. Sport Fish. and Wildl., Washington, D.C. 770pp.

SMITH, J. D. 1946. The Canvas-back in Minnesota. Auk 63:73–81.

STEWART, R. E. 1962. Waterfowl populations in the upper Chesapeake region. U.S. Bur. Sport Fish. and Wildl. Spec. Sci. Rep.: Wildl. 65. 208pp. (multilithed)

STOUDT, J. H. 1962–64. Habitat requirements of Canvasback ducks during prenesting, nesting, brooding, rearing, and moulting periods. U.S. Bur. Sport Fish. Wildl., Branch Wildl. Res., Prog. Rep. Denver Wildl. Res. Center 1962:1–48, 1963:1–61, 1964:1–73. (multilithed)

TRAUTMAN, M. B. 1940. The birds of Buckeye Lake, Ohio. Misc. Publ. Mus. Zool. Univ. Michigan, 44. 466pp.

WARREN, B. H. 1890. Report on the birds of Pennsylvania. 2nd ed. E. K. Meyers, Harrisburg. 434pp.

YOCUM, C. F. 1951. Waterfowl and their food plants in Washington. Univ. Washington Press, Seattle, 272pp.

———, AND M. KELLER. 1961. Correlation of food habits and abundance of waterfowl, Humboldt Bay, California. California Fish and Game 47:41–53.

ZIMMERMAN, F. R. 1953. Waterfowl habitat surveys and food habit studies, 1940–1943. Wisconsin Conserv. Dept., Game Mgmt. Div., Final Rep. P.-R. Proj. 6-R. 176pp. (multilithed)

SEGREGATION IN FEEDING BEHAVIOUR OF FOUR DIVING DUCKS IN SOUTHERN MANITOBA[1]

W. R. SIEGFRIED, FitzPatrick Institute, University of Cape Town, Rondebosch, South Africa

Abstract: The canvasback, *Aythya valisineria*; redhead, *A. americana*; scaup, *A. affinis*; and ruddy duck, *Oxyura jamaicensis*, are sympatric on the small wetlands of the Canadian prairie region. The four species did not occur randomly and each species tended to occur by itself more often than with any other species. Each species tended to forage in a particular part of a pond. Selection for different foraging sites appears to be important in segregating those species whose diets overlap most.

Some of the various ways in which bird species differ from each other in their use of resources have been described by Lack (1971). For one of his examples of ecological segregation, Lack (1971) analysed, qualitatively, differences between congeneric species of waterfowl (family Anatidae) all of which were considered to be separated by feeding. However, variation in feeding behaviour, as a mechanism for reducing overlap in diet of congeneric species, has seldom been quantified for waterfowl (Stott and Olson 1973).

Cody (1974) examined, quantitatively, the way competition is avoided in bird species that live together. Within the same habitat, coexisting species may separate their ecological activities in several ways. There is often a tendency for different species to select different parts of a uniform habitat patch in which to feed.

The small wetlands that now characterize glaciated regions of the North American prairie accommodate dense concentrations of a diverse community of breeding waterfowl (Stewart and Kantrud 1974). Within southern Manitoba, in terms of species and absolute numbers of individuals, dabbling ducks (Anatini) predominate, but, in addition, at least four species of diving ducks (Aythyini and Oxyurini) occur together abundantly (Dzubin 1969*a*, Kiel et al. 1972). Somewhat surprisingly, relatively little is known about the ecological requirements of many species of North American ducks, and even less is known about how these requirements influence habitat use or population density (Dzubin 1969*b*).

This paper gives quantitative information on spatial segregation in relation to feeding behaviour among four species of North American diving ducks, and contributes towards an understanding of the way competition is avoided in these species. The species are canvasback, *Aythya valisineria*; redhead, *A. americana*; lesser scaup, *A. affinis*; and ruddy duck, *Oxyura jamaicensis*.

METHODS

I studied diving ducks in the pothole region near Minnedosa, Manitoba, during 20 May–8 July 1971. Descriptions of this area and its use by waterfowl appear in Evans et al. (1952), Bird (1961), Dzubin (1969*a*), and Bartonek and Hickey (1969).

I recorded diving ducks encountered while carrying out censuses of waterfowl on ponds within a 259-ha study area, 10 km south of Minnedosa, and while travelling by car along 250 km of road at bi-

[1] Originally published in Can. J. Zool. 54(5): 730–736, 1976. Reproduced by permission of the National Research Council of Canada.

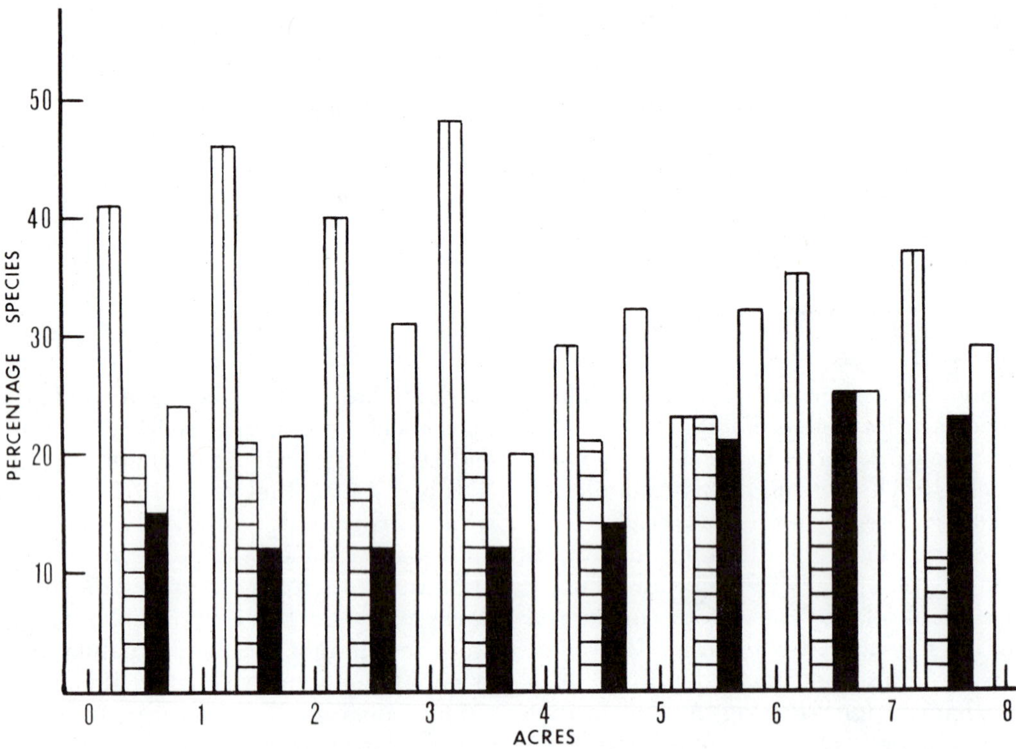

Fig. 1. Percentage occurrence of four species of diving ducks in relation to size of ponds (open water area in acres) utilized for feeding. Scaup (clear columns), canvasback (solid shading), redhead (horizontal hatching), and ruddy duck (vertical hatching). Data based on 196 ponds containing one or more of the four species.

weekly intervals. When I encountered diving ducks that were *feeding undisturbed for not less than 5 min,* I noted their locations with respect to position on pond surface. Cody (1971) used a similar method to study habitat separation in Chilean coots (*Fulica* spp.). The ducks' foraging behaviour was recorded on ciné film. Observations were made mainly in the morning and evening hours, when many female ducks were off their nests. No difference in spatial feeding behaviour between males and females was noted. I recorded singletons and pairs of

Table 1. Percentage of the ponds censused in which at least one of four species of diving ducks foraged either alone or together with one or more of the three other species.

Species	One species alone	Two species together	Three species together	Four species together	No. ponds in which species foraged
Ruddy duck	48	26	15	11	185
Canvasback	28	34	21	17	116
Scaup	42	26	20	12	171
Redhead	41	28	17	14	143

Table 2. Percentage of the ponds censused, partitioned according to size, in which at least one of four species of diving ducks foraged either alone or together with one or more of the three other species.

Pond size, acres open water	One species alone	Two species together	Three species together	Four species together	No. ponds in which species foraged
0.1–1.9	67	23	6	4	101
2.0–3.9	56	25	11	8	43
4.0–5.9	33	19	33	15	21
6.0–7.9	39	29	19	13	31

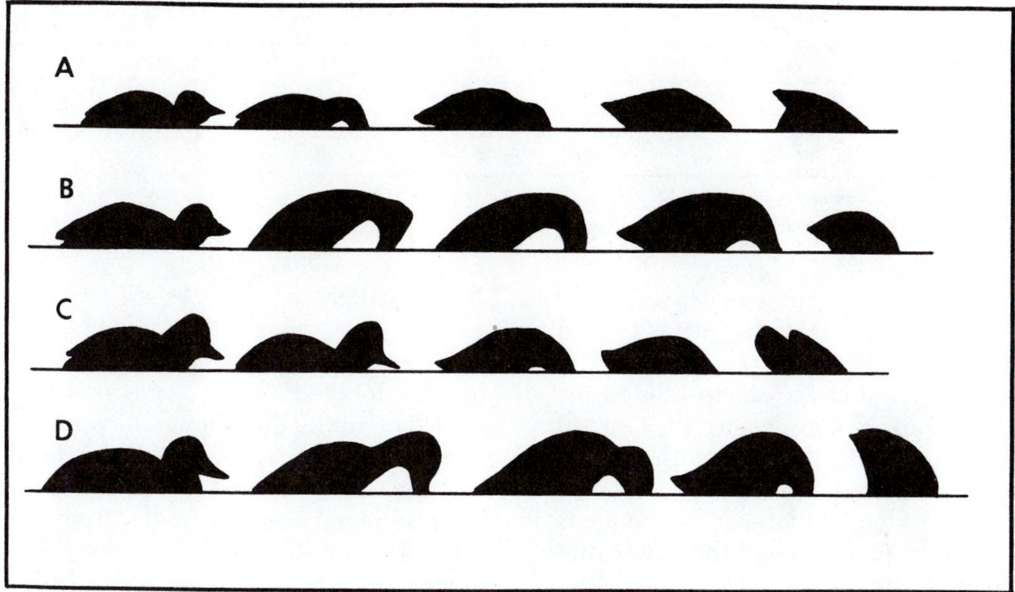

Fig. 2. Sequences of diving actions in the ruddy duck (A), redhead (B), scaup (C), and canvasback (D). Silhouettes were traced from ciné film.

birds feeding. Postbreeding aggregations of males and of females with broods were omitted from the records.

RESULTS

Table 1 gives data on the proportion of ponds, irrespective of size, utilized by a particular species recorded foraging alone or together with one or more of the three other species. Two or more species foraged together in 143 (36%) of the 395 ponds containing one or more species. I used the data in Table 1 in statistical analyses (details in Appendix A), showing that the four species did not occur randomly with respect to each other. Each species tended to occur by itself more often than with any other species. I could not detect a tendency for any two particular species not to occur together in the same pond (Appendix B). Table 2 shows that most small ponds (<4 acres (1 acre = 0.4047 ha)) contained only one species at a time and that all four species occurred together most frequently on large ponds (>4 acres). The ruddy duck tended to forage in small ponds (Fig. 1).

Table 3 shows frequency of foraging by each of the four species in relation to their distribution within ponds. The sig-

Table 3. Number of times each species of diving ducks was recorded foraging in different zones of 79 ponds.

Species	Central zone, open water	¼–¾ zone, open water	0 (bank)–¼ zone: Within and on edge of emergent plants	0 (bank)–¼ zone: Open water >2 m from emergents	Totals
Ruddy duck	5 (9.50)	2 (4.54)	3 (4.96)	17 (7.99)	27
Canvasback	13 (9.86)	7 (4.70)	7 (5.16)	1 (8.29)	28
Scaup	23 (13.37)	9 (6.38)	3 (7.00)	3 (11.25)	38
Redhead	3 (11.26)	3 (5.38)	10 (5.88)	16 (9.47)	32
Totals	44	41	23	37	125

Note: Figures in parentheses are computed expected values, on the assumption that there is no relation between species and pond zone.

Table 4. Mean duration (seconds) ± its standard deviation of foraging dives in four species of diving ducks.

Redhead		Canvasback		Scaup		Ruddy duck	
Males	Females	Males	Females	Males	Females	Males	Females
10.4 ± 2.7 (5)	11.6 ± 3.1 (5)	17.6 ± 2.7 (6)	15.6 ± 4.6 (6)	10.3 ± 2.7 (5)	13.2 ± 3.1 (6)	17.1 ± 3.2 (6)	20.4 ± 2.4 (5)

Note: Figures in parentheses represent number of separate bouts of diving recorded. Each bout consisted of 10 consecutive dives by an individual bird.

nificant conclusion ($\chi^2_9 = 54.54$, $P \leq 0.001$) is that each species tended to forage in a particular part of a pond. The canvasback and the scaup tended to restrict their foraging activities to open water near the centre of the body of water, whereas the ruddy duck and the redhead foraged mainly in open areas of shallower water near the edge of the pond.

Individual foraging dives tended to last longer in the canvasback and the ruddy duck than in the scaup and the redhead (Table 4). The canvasback and the redhead lift the foreparts of their bodies clear of the water and arch their necks at the beginning of every foraging dive (Fig. 2). Consequently, the birds tend to submerge vertically. Underwater swimming movements in the horizontal plane were restricted, the birds normally surfacing close to the original place of submergence (Table 5). The scaup and the ruddy duck both tend to dive obliquely (Fig. 2), and they swam relatively greater distances underwater (Table 5).

DISCUSSION

The ruddy duck and the redhead frequently foraged in the same part of a pond. The ruddy duck moves forward underwater using its specialized beak (Goodman and Fisher 1962) to strain out small sedentary invertebrates from the soft mud overlying the bottoms of ponds (Siegfried 1973). The redhead also takes animal food, but its diet includes submerged plant material (Bartonek and Hickey 1969). The canvasback and the scaup foraged in the same part of a pond, but each species takes different food and feeds differently. The scaup moves about at midwater levels and above the bottoms of ponds, capturing mainly free-swimming invertebrates such as amphipods (Bartonek and Hickey 1969, Bartonek and Murdy 1970); its beak is modified for this mode of feeding (Goodman and Fisher 1962). The canvasback uses its specialized beak (Goodman and Fisher 1962) to grasp and pull submerged vegetable material, chiefly tubers (Bartonek

Table 5. Mean distance (metres) ± its standard deviation separating places of submergence and surfacing of foraging dives in four species of diving ducks.

Redhead		Canvasback		Scaup		Ruddy duck	
Males	Females	Males	Females	Males	Females	Males	Females
0.6 ± 0.6 (46)	0.8 ± 0.7 (56)	0.5 ± 0.5 (54)	0.4 ± 0.5 (52)	2.1 ± 1.0 (28)	1.7 ± 0.8 (41)	1.6 ± 0.9 (81)	1.4 ± 1.1 (69)

Note: Figures in parentheses represent number of dives.

and Hickey 1969), from the substrate. The canvasback is a much bigger bird than the scaup, and the redhead is bigger than the scaup and the ruddy duck, which is smaller than the scaup (Kortright 1942). These differences might correlate with the species' diets, insofar as the size of food items should be proportional to size of bird (Hespenheide 1971). This needs to be investigated.

While the basic diets of the four species are different, there is overlap with respect to food items; also, the diets of conspecific males and females are not the same (Appendix C). The extent of overlap appears greatest between scaup and ruddy duck on the one hand, and redhead and canvasback on the other. Within the migratory populations of the four species of ducks considered here there is little opportunity for isolation, and genetic intermixing precludes the evolution of morphologically distinct subpopulations. The redhead and the canvasback presumably evolved separately in different geographic areas: the redhead in southwestern North America and the canvasback in the north (Weller 1964). Weller (1964) suggested that the redhead has only recently invaded the prairie pothole region. Similar histories can be argued for the ruddy duck and the scaup: the scaup presumably evolved as a northern species and the ruddy duck in the south, only recently having colonized the northern prairie (Siegfried 1976). If these generalizations are correct, they provide a basis for predicting interference competition between redhead and canvasback and between scaup and ruddy duck in those parts of their breeding ranges that overlap. In this case, if evolutionary constraints operate to inhibit change in morphology, particularly body size and trophic apparatus, then an alternative strategy for coexistence resorts in behavioural adaptations for spatial division of food and other resources. In each of the species pairs, overlap in food appears greater than in the division of preferred foraging space. This suggests that space is more easily partitioned than food. While this accords with theory developed by MacArthur and Wilson (1967), the conclusion is based on qualitative appraisal of the available data and confirmation must await more precise studies of the food and feeding habits of the four species.

Of interest is the similarity in basic plumage pattern between the two species comprising each pair, particularly the redhead and the canvasback. Because these species are congeners, it is difficult to distinguish possible character convergence (Cody 1969) from phylogenetic affiliation. One might, however, predict the occurrence of interspecific behavioural (agonistic) interactions, and that interactions would be particularly frequent between the two species that most resemble each other. Although my field work was not designed to test this, I did observe a number of aggressive supplants between canvasback and redheads. Scaup and ruddy duck were seldom involved in aggressive encounters either between each other or canvasback and redhead.

In conclusion, it is clear that the ruddy duck, canvasback, redhead, and scaup occur sympatrically on the small wetlands of the prairie pothole region, and that selection for different foraging sites appears to be important in segregating those species whose diets overlap most.

ACKNOWLEDGMENTS

I am grateful to Martin Cody, John Field, Les Underhill, and an anonymous referee for criticism and advice. I am indebted to the following bodies for financial support: the Frank M. Chapman Fund, the Wildlife Management Institute, the Delta Waterfowl Research Station, the South African Council for Scientific and Industrial Research, and the University of Cape Town.

LITERATURE CITED

BARTONEK, J. C., AND J. J. HICKEY. 1969. Food habits of canvasbacks, redheads and lesser scaup in Manitoba. Condor 71:280–290.

———, AND H. W. MURDY. 1970. Summer foods of lesser scaup in subarctic taiga. Arctic 23:35–44.

BIRD, R. D. 1961. Ecology of the aspen parkland of western Canada in relation to land use. Can. Dep. Agric. Res. Branch Res. Stn. Contrib. 27.

CODY, M. L. 1969. Convergent characteristics in sympatric populations: a possible relation to interspecific territoriality. Condor 71:222–239.

———. 1971. Chilean bird distribution. Ecology 51:459–464.

———. 1974. Competition and the structure of bird communities. Princeton University Press, Princeton.

DZUBIN, A. 1969*a*. Assessing breeding populations of ducks by ground counts. *In* Saskatoon wetlands seminar. Can. Wildl. Serv. Rep. Ser. No. 6. Pp. 178–230.

———. 1969*b*. Comments on carrying capacity of small ponds for ducks and possible effects of density on mallard production. *In* Saskatoon wetlands seminar. Can. Wildl. Serv. Rep. Ser. No. 6. Pp. 138–160.

EVANS, C. D., A. S. HAWKINS, AND W. J. MARSHALL. 1952. Movements of waterfowl broods in Manitoba. U.S. Fish Wildl. Serv. Spec. Rep. Wildl. No. 16.

GOODMAN, D. C., AND H. I. FISHER. 1962. Functional anatomy of the feeding apparatus in waterfowl (Aves: Anatidae). Southern Illinois University Press, Carbondale.

HESPENHEIDE, H. A. 1971. Food preference and the extent of overlap in some insectivorous birds, with special reference to the Tyrannidae. Ibis 113:59–72.

KIEL, W. H., A. S. HAWKINS, AND N. G. PERRET. 1972. Waterfowl habitat trends in the aspen parkland of Manitoba. Can. Wildl. Serv. Rep. Ser. No. 18.

KORTRIGHT, F. H. 1942. The ducks, geese and swans of North America. Stackpole, Harrisburg.

LACK, D. 1971. Ecological isolation in birds. Blackwell, Oxford.

MACARTHUR, R. H., AND E. O. WILSON. 1967. The theory of island biogeography. Princeton University Press, Princeton.

SIEGFRIED, W. R. 1973. Summer food and feeding of the ruddy duck in Manitoba. Can. J. Zool. 51:1293–1297.

———. 1976. Social organization in Ruddy and Maccoa Ducks. Auk. In press.

STEWART, R. E., AND H. A. KANTRUD. 1974. Breeding waterfowl populations in the prairie pothole region of North Dakota. Condor 76:70–79.

STOTT, R. S., AND D. P. OLSON. 1973. Food-habitat relationship of sea ducks on the New Hampshire coastline. Ecology 54:996–1007.

SWANSON, G. A., G. L. KRAPU, J. C. BARTONEK, J. R. SERIE, AND D. H. JOHNSON. 1974. Advantages in mathematically weighting waterfowl food habits data. J. Wildl. Manage. 38:302–307.

———, AND M. I. MEYER. 1973. The role of invertebrates in the feeding ecology of Anatinae during the breeding season. *In* Waterfowl habitat management symposium. Moncton, New Brunswick, July 30–Aug. 1, 1973. Pp. 143–185.

WELLER, M. W. 1964. Distribution and migration of the redhead. J. Wildl. Manage. 28:64–103.

APPENDIX A

Let A = ruddy duck, B = canvasback, C = scaup, and D = redhead. Using data in Table 1, the probability that A occurs in any particular pond is 185 (no. ponds in which A occurred)/395 (total no. ponds) = 0.47, and the probability that A does not occur is 0.53($1 - P_A = P_{\bar{A}}$). Corresponding figures for species B, C, and D are $P_B = 0.29$, $P_{\bar{B}} = 0.71$; $P_C = 0.43$, $P_{\bar{D}} = 0.57$; and $P_D = 0.36$, $P_{\bar{D}} = 0.64$.

Assuming that the species occur independently of each other in the ponds, then the probability that, for example, A and C occur in a pond is equal to $P_A \times P_C \times P_{\bar{B}} \times P_{\bar{D}} = 0.091$. The expected number of ponds for which species A and C occur is, therefore, equal to 395 × 0.091. Probabilities, expected and adjusted values are given below.

	Observed	Probability	Expected	Adjusted
A	89	0.12	47.3	54.7
B	33	0.06	22.3	25.8
C	72	0.10	41.0	47.4
D	58	0.08	30.4	35.2
AB	13	0.05	19.7	22.8
AC	19	0.09	36.1	41.8
AD	16	0.07	26.8	31.0
BC	14	0.04	17.0	19.7
BD	12	0.03	12.7	14.7
CD	12	0.06	23.2	26.8
ABC	12	0.04	15.0	17.4
ACD	13	0.05	20.5	23.7
ABD	3	0.03	11.1	12.8
BCD	9	0.02	9.6	8.5
ABCD	20	0.02	8.5	9.8

The expected number of ponds in which no species occur is 53.6. The equation $[1 - (53.6/395)]^{-1} = 1.16$ gives the adjusted expected values, whose sum is 395. Comparing observed values with the expected values yields a chi-squared value of 94, which is significant at a confidence level far greater than 99.9%.

APPENDIX B

The expected values were computed by scaling down the expected values given in Appendix A so that their sum is 86, the number of ponds with exactly two species. A chi-squared value of 4.14 was obtained, which is not significant. This shows that there was no tendency for any particular species not to occur together on a feeding pond.

	AB	AC	AD	BC	BD	CD	Totals
Observed	13	19	16	14	12	12	86
Expected	12.50	22.91	17.01	10.79	8.06	14.72	86

APPENDIX C

The following is a comparison of plant and animal foods reported consumed in spring and summer by adults of four diving duck species (from oesophageal contents only). These data are adapted after Swanson and Meyer 1973. Also see Swanson et al. (1974) for weighting of similar data and recommendations for reducing bias in use of percentage aggregate volume vs. percentage aggregate percent.

	% aggregate vol.					
	Animal material		Plant material		Main animal group (%)	
	Males	Females	Males	Females	Males	Females
Canvasback[a]	2	92	98	8	Tendipedidae (2)	Gasteropoda (66) Ephemeroptera (13) Trichoptera (10)
Redhead[a]	86	81	14	19	Trichoptera (62) Tendipedidae (22)	Trichoptera (80)
Lesser scaup[a]	99	98	trace	2	Hirudinea (61) Trichoptera (16)	Amphipoda (46) Tendipedidae (41)
Ruddy duck[b]	95	90	9	4	Tendipedidae (82)	Tendipedidae (63) Gasteropoda (22)

[a] Bartonek and Hickey (1969).
[b] Siegfried (1973).

FOOD-HABITAT RELATIONSHIP OF SEA DUCKS ON THE NEW HAMPSHIRE COASTLINE[1,2]

RICHARD S. STOTT, Department of Animal Sciences, University of New Hampshire, Durham, NH 03824
DAVID P. OLSON, Institute of Natural and Environmental Resources, University of New Hampshire, Durham, NH 03824

Abstract: Use of habitat, food preferences, and food availability were studied for seven species of waterfowl (white-winged scoter (*Melanitta deglandi*), surf scoter (*M. perspicillata*), common scoter (*Oidemia nigra*), oldsquaw (*Clangula hyemalis*), common goldeneye (*Bucephala clangula*), bufflehead (*B. albeola*), and red-breasted merganser (*Mergus serrator*)) on a 34-km section of the New England coastline during 1968–70. The three scoters selectively used areas of sandy substrate and had very similar food habits. The principal foods were the Atlantic razor clam (*Siliqua costata*) and Arctic wedge clam (*Mesodesma arctatum*), which were characteristic of, and abundant in, sandy substrate. In contrast to scoters, goldeneye preferred areas of rocky substrate associated with rocky headlands. They fed primarily on amphipods, isopods, crabs, and gastropods, which were commonly found in the Irish moss (*Chondrus crispus*) covering of the rocky sublittoral areas. Red-breasted mergansers, like goldeneye, also used the rocky areas. They fed primarily on several small fish species that were observed among the Irish moss and crevices of the rocky substrate. Bufflehead had the most restrictive distribution, being confined mostly to estuaries. Bufflehead fed primarily on sand shrimp, which were found only in harbors with soft ooze bottoms. Oldsquaw had the most generalized diet of all the sea ducks. The major food items consisted of bivalves, gastropods, sand shrimp, and isopods, which were found throughout the study area and accounted for the generalized distribution of oldsquaw along the coastline and in the harbors. Sea ducks were concentrated near the mouths of the estuaries, where more abundant food resources, particularly bivalves, were found. Although the species vary, the types of foods eaten by sea ducks were similar to those described in other studies. Thus, food availability, coupled with the physical structure of the substratum in the different coastal habitats, is apparently a major determinant in the way that coastal waterfowl selectively use habitat types. The described patterns of habitat usage appear to have implications for other wide geographical areas.

Several waterfowl species that are commonly called sea ducks winter along the coastline of the northeastern United States. They include white-winged scoter, surf scoter, common scoter, and oldsquaw. In addition, common goldeneye, bufflehead, and redbreasted merganser are found in the same coastal habitats and are included as "sea ducks" in this investigation.

Little is known about the wintering habitats used by these coastal species. The areas are being used at an increasing rate for transportation, power production sites, and recreation; associated pollution problems such as oil spillage and heated water discharges are common. In addition to threats to or actual changes in the environment from these causes, there is a continuing decline in the productive salt marsh habitats through filling and increased domestic and industrial pollution. These changes, and especially the losses in productivity, will undoubtedly affect sea duck populations and their invertebrate foods.

The few general food habit studies concerning sea duck species (Martin et al. 1961, McGilvrey 1967) merely report the food items eaten; they give no ecological relationship to the environment in which the animal was collected. A knowledge of food habits is essential in understanding a species' environmental and nutritional requirements, and also the degree of competition for a food resource among species that are part of the same ecosystem.

This study was a detailed analysis of

[1] Originally published in Ecology 54(5):996–1007, 1973.

[2] Published with the approval of the Director of the New Hampshire Agricultural Experiment Station as Scientific Contribution No. 609.

the way in which seven species of waterfowl utilize the various habitat types and food resources of a section of the New England coastline. The objectives were to describe patterns of habitat usage among the different species of coastal waterfowl on the New Hampshire coastline, to analyze their food habits, and to measure and describe food availability and abundance in the coastal sublittoral zone. This was the third and major part of a larger investigation concerning the winter ecology of sea ducks on the New Hampshire coastline (Stott 1972).

METHODS

The study area comprises 34 km of coastline from Portsmouth, New Hampshire, to Salisbury, Massachusetts (Fig. 1). A census of waterfowl on the study area was conducted each week from September to May from 41 observation points (Fig. 1) located so that complete coverage of the study area was assured, with no duplicated counts between observation points. We visited all observation points each week, using binoculars and a spotting scope as an aid in identifying species. We recorded flying sea ducks separately from birds that were resting or feeding on the water. The number of waterfowl, sex and age composition, and distance from shore were also recorded. For this census, distance intervals of 0–457 m from shore, 457–914 m from shore, and over 914 m (1,000 yards) from shore were used. A comparison of simultaneous aerial and ground censuses (Stott and Olson 1972*a*) revealed that 98% of all waterfowl counted from the air were located in the 0–457 m distance interval. Waterfowl species in this range can be counted easily from the ground.

Each observation point was classified into one of several habitat categories. Location of activity or concentration areas of sea ducks was ascertained from weekly censuses and noted under the appropriate observation point.

Sampling of Sublittoral Fauna and Flora

We used scuba to sample the sublittoral substrate of the various types of coastal habitat in order to determine the abundance and availability of food items. During March, April, May, and June 1970, 450 0.1-m^2 bottom samples were collected in the sublittoral: sandy substrate (150 samples), rocky substrate (150), and the three harbors (150). Bottom fauna and flora were collected either by shoveling the top 8 or 10 cm of soft substrate or by scraping off animals and seaweeds covering hard substrate and placing the material in large-mouthed diving bags with a fine mesh (approximately 1 mm) liner. This enabled silt and fine sand to pass through the bag but kept small organisms inside. These bottom samples were processed through several sieves (2, 1, 0.5 mm) and then the organisms were identified and separated into species.

For bottom sampling, five sandy areas and five rocky areas were selected on the basis of consistent sea duck usage as determined from weekly censuses during December and January, the period of least movement and most stable sea duck population levels. At each of these 10 areas (Fig. 1), 30 bottom samples were collected in a haphazard pattern in an area of approximately 1 acre. Each of the three harbors was also sampled by taking 0.1-m^2 samples along transects through areas of most consistent sea duck use. We collected 10 samples from Hampton Harbor, 60 from Rye Harbor, and 80 from Little Harbor.

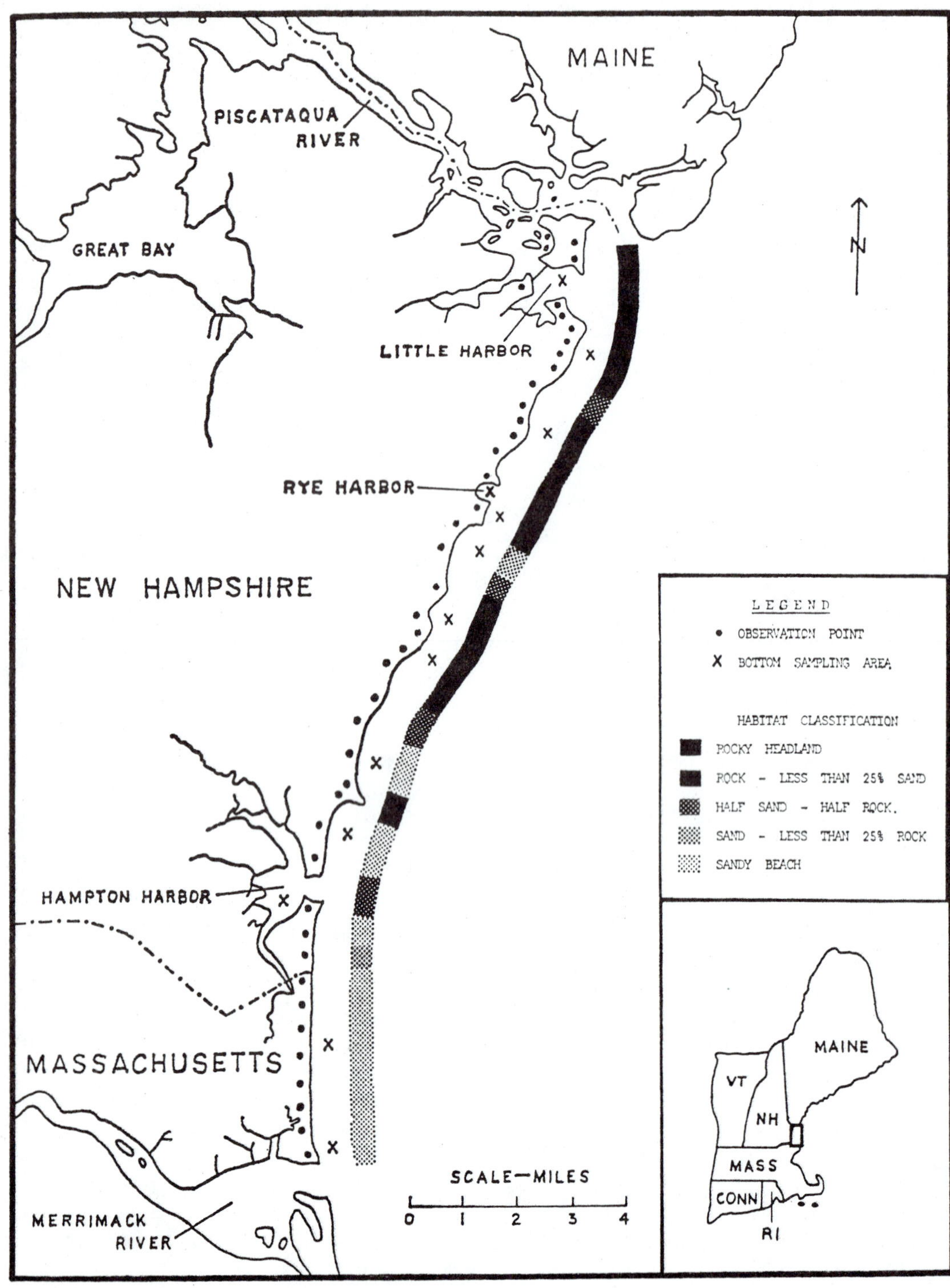
MAINE
PISCATAQUA RIVER
GREAT BAY
LITTLE HARBOR
RYE HARBOR
NEW HAMPSHIRE
HAMPTON HARBOR
MASSACHUSETTS
MERRIMACK RIVER
SCALE—MILES
0 1 2 3 4
N
LEGEND
OBSERVATION POINT
X BOTTOM SAMPLING AREA
HABITAT CLASSIFICATION
ROCKY HEADLAND
ROCK - LESS THAN 25% SAND
HALF SAND - HALF ROCK.
SAND - LESS THAN 25% ROCK
SANDY BEACH
MAINE
VT
NH
MASS
CONN
RI

Food Habits Analysis of Sea Ducks

During the 1968 and 1969 hunting seasons (September 25 to January 10), 585 sea duck carcasses were obtained from coastal waterfowl hunters and by selective shooting. Of these, 491 (84%) contained sufficient food material in the gullet (esophagus and proventriculus) or gizzard or both and were used in the food habits analysis. Food items were removed from each sea duck specimen and were then identified and separated into species. Frequency of occurrence of each food item and volume in cubic centimeters by water displacement were recorded. The birds analyzed included 166 white-winged scoter, 133 surf scoter, 42 common scoter, 40 oldsquaw, 48 goldeneye, and 62 bufflehead.

RESULTS

Habitat Usage of Sea Ducks

Coastline.—During the December and January censuses, the location of every sea duck was plotted and analyzed for five categories of coastal habitat. These habitat types consisted of 11.3 km of sandy beach, 2.2 km of sandy areas with less than 25% rocky outcrops, 5.5 km of approximately half sand and half rock, 1.6 km of rocky areas with less than 25% sandy patches, and 13.2 km of rocky headland (Fig. 1). Sandy or silty sublittoral substrate was found offshore of sandy beaches, and rocky bottoms were associated with rocky headlands. The areas with mixtures of rock and sand on the shoreline had mixtures of rock, sand, and silty sand offshore. This habitat classification for each observation point was formulated from personal observations at low tide, selective scuba diving, aerial observations, U.S. Geographical Survey topographical maps, and information from lobstermen in the area.

We conducted 15 ground censuses of the coastline during December and January (1968–70) and obtained approximately 15,000 locations of sea ducks in specific habitats. Only December and January census figures were used because of the more stable wintering populations of all species during this period. However, each sea duck species used the same habitat type from its arrival in the fall until its departure in the spring. This consistent habitat usage was also observed in the three harbors.

The average density of each sea duck per linear kilometer of coastline is listed in Table 1. These data revealed distinct differences in habitat usage for the five groups of sea ducks.

Scoters (white-winged, surf, and common) preferred sandy beaches (50.8 birds/km·census) to rocky headlands (0.62 birds/km) and there was a decreasing density of these species as the proportion of rocky substrate increased. Goldeneye, on the other hand, preferred the rocky areas (15.8 birds/km) to sandy beaches (0.15 birds/km), and the figures indicated an increasing density from sandy to rocky areas. Red-breasted mergansers were similar to goldeneye in using rocky areas (2.7 birds/km) more than sandy areas (0.19 birds/km).

←

Fig. 1. The study area consists of several distinct habitat types that are utilized differently by the seven species of sea ducks. The southern half of the area has predominantly wide sandy beaches whereas the northern half has predominantly rocky headlands and offshore ledges. There are also areas of rock and sand mixtures as well as three estuaries or harbors (Hampton Harbor, Rye Harbor, and Little Harbor). Thus, the study area has components of the different coastal habitats of New England and is transitional between the predominant rocky headlands and offshore ledges of northern New England and the prevailing sandy beaches of southern New England.

Table 1. Winter distribution of waterfowl for five categories of habitat on 34 km of the New Hampshire and Massachusetts coastline, 1968–70.

	Number of waterfowl per linear km of coastline					
Habitat	km	Scoter	Goldeneye	Red-breasted merganser	Oldsquaw	Bufflehead
Sandy beach	11.3	50.8 ± 7.5[a]	0.15 ± 0.14	0.19 ± 0.11	1.3 ± 0.6	—
Sand with less than 25% rock	2.2	11.0 ± 4.5	1.8 ± 1.1	1.1 ± 0.9	0.87 ± 0.75	0.09 ± 0.14
Half sand and half rock	5.5	4.7 ± 1.4	6.0 ± 1.2	1.0 ± 0.4	0.93 ± 0.37	0.10 ± 0.14
Rock with less than 25% sand	1.6	1.6 ± 0.9	19.4 ± 6.0	2.0 ± 1.5	1.2 ± 0.8	0.50 ± 0.45
Rocky headland	13.2	0.62 ± 0.31	15.8 ± 2.4	2.7 ± 0.7	1.9 ± 0.6	0.55 ± 0.22

[a] 95% confidence limits.

Although oldsquaw never appeared in large numbers, there were no clear habitat preferences; they were found well distributed over all the habitat types.

Only an occasional bufflehead was seen on the coastline proper and this species used the rocky areas (0.55 birds/km) or rocky area with less than 25 percent sandy patches (0.50/km) rather than sandy beaches (no birds observed). However, bufflehead used the harbors more readily than the coastline proper, and weekly censuses of the entire study area during December and January (1968–70) revealed that 74% of all bufflehead were found in the harbors or estuaries.

Harbors.—Sea duck usage of Hampton, Rye, and Little Harbors was recorded separately from the coastline proper, and the harbors were analyzed as three individual units. The portion of Hampton Harbor covered by the census was 126 ha; of Rye Harbor, 20 ha; and Little Harbor, 106 ha. These measurements were based on open water at mean high tide. The extensive salt marsh and tidal creek areas, which were frequented by black ducks (*Anas rubripes*), were not included in the areas studied. For convenience, the open water areas of these three estuaries are referred to as harbors in this investigation. They are used by many commercial and private boat owners for moorings and pleasure and business interests.

We conducted 28 censuses of the three harbors during December and January (1966–70). From these counts approximately 2,500 locations of sea ducks in specific habitats were obtained. Data for 1966–67 and 1967–68 were taken from field notes obtained by the first-named author and Nevers.

The average density of each sea duck per 100 ha for each of the three harbors is listed in Table 2. These data revealed that scoters seldom used harbors, goldeneye and red-breasted mergansers were usually found in all three harbors but in varying numbers, oldsquaws did not use

Table 2. Winter distribution of waterfowl in three harbors on the New Hampshire coastline, 1966–70.

	Number of waterfowl/100 ha of water					
	ha	Scoter	Goldeneye	Red-breasted merganser	Oldsquaw	Bufflehead
Hampton Harbor	125.6	0.35 ± 0.25[a]	29.7 ± 10.1	9.6 ± 4.9	—	0.02 ± 0.05
Rye Harbor	20.3	—	6.2 ± 5.7	0.17 ± 0.37	2.5 ± 2.0	36.8 ± 16.6
Little Harbor	105.3	0.17 ± 0.17	6.9 ± 3.7	0.79 ± 0.49	0.91 ± 0.62	19.5 ± 5.7

[a] 95% confidence limits.

Hampton Harbor but were observed in small numbers in Rye and Little Harbors, and bufflehead used all three harbors but chiefly Rye and Little Harbors. As already noted, buffleheads used the harbors more readily than they did the coastline proper.

Sublittoral Fauna and Flora

Marine invertebrates, which had a density of at least one animal per square meter in the various substrates, are listed in Table 3. A complete listing of all animal and plant species collected on the study area is given in Stott (1972). These data revealed marked differences in marine invertebrate species found in sandy areas and rocky areas, and also among the three harbors. The nomenclature for bivalves and gastropods was taken from Abbott (1968); all other invertebrates and classification are from Smith (1964).

Sandy Substrate.—Bottom samples from sandy and silty substrate off the sandy beaches were collected at depths of approximately 9–12 m since these were the depths in the areas where most sea ducks (especially scoters) were observed. The Atlantic razor clam (*Siliqua costata*), with an average volume of 1.6 cc and an average density of 6.6 individuals/m^2, and the Arctic wedge clam (*Mesodesma arctatum*), 0.6 cc and 10.3 individuals, were most frequently found in the areas sampled. The three next most important invertebrates were the Atlantic surf clam (*Spisula solidissima*), 1.7 cc and 2.5 individuals; northern moon snail (*Lunatia heros*), 4.2 cc and 2.4 individuals; and sand dollar (*Echinarachnius parma*), 9.5 cc and 2.9 individuals (Table 3). These five species made up 85% of the animal volume and are characteristic of sandy areas (Smith 1964).

Rocky Substrate.—In contrast to the sandy areas, bottom samples in this habitat were collected at water depths of 3–6 m since waterfowl using these areas were observed to be closer to shore than those using the sandy areas. The important marine invertebrates found commonly in the rocky areas were the northern lacuna periwinkle (*Lacuna vincta*), volume 2.5 cc and density 72.7 individuals/m^2; isopods (*Idotea baltica* and *I. phosphorea*), 16.7 cc and 234.9 individuals; amphipod (*Ampithoe rubricata*), 2.9 cc and 56.5 individuals; common periwinkle (*Littorina littorea*), 29.2 cc and 17.5 individuals; and the rock crab (*Cancer irroratus*), 4.3 cc and 1.9 individuals (Table 3). These six species made up 67% of the animal volume. Although no fish were collected, several species of small size were observed swimming about the rocky crevices and seaweeds.

Most of these animals were found in the cover supplied by Irish moss (*Chondrus crispus*), a red alga that covered most of the rocky bottom (1,720 cc/m^2). This algal species rapidly thinned out with deepening water because of lack of light penetration and the resultant decrease in photosynthetic activity. We saw no Irish moss at depths in excess of 9 m. This reduction in the invertebrate cover is probably the reason that goldeneye and red-breasted mergansers, which used rocky areas, were most often observed close to shore.

Hampton Harbor.—This harbor is a large basin of silty sand with a vast expanse of salt marsh (approximately 1,215 ha). Only the basin area of this harbor was observed for sea duck usage because of access limitations and the impossibility of visually covering the large section of salt marsh. Only a small part of the basin was bottom sampled. The only invertebrate species collected were the blue mussel (*Mytilus edulis*), volume 3,915.0 cc and density 1,180.0 individuals/m^2;

Table 3. Density and volume of marine invertebrates collected during sublittoral sampling at selected stations on a 34-km section of the New Hampshire and Massachusetts coastline during the spring of 1970. (Only invertebrates of a density of one or more animals/m² are listed.)

	Sandy substrate		Rocky substrate		Hampton harbor		Rye harbor		Little harbor	
Species	No.	cc	No.	cc	No.	cc	No.	cc	No.	cc
Siliqua costata (Biv.)[a]	6.6	1.6	–	–	–	–	–	–	–	–
Spisula solidissima (Biv.)	2.5	1.7	–	–	–	–	–	–	–	–
Lunatia heros (Gast.)	2.4	4.2	–	–	–	–	–	–	–	–
Chiridotea tuftsi (Crus.)	4.7	tr[b]	–	–	–	–	–	–	–	–
Tryphosella sp. (Crus.)	4.9	0.2	–	–	–	–	–	–	–	–
Haustoriidae (Crus.)	104.5	0.5	–	–	–	–	–	–	–	–
Echinarachnius parma (Ech.)	2.9	9.5	–	–	–	–	–	–	–	–
Nassarius trivittatus (Gast.)	1.1	0.2	–	–	–	–	–	–	+[c]	0.1
Undetermined Cumacea (Crus.)	12.7	tr	–	–	–	–	2.0	tr	–	–
Mesodesma arctatum (Biv.)	10.3	0.6	–	–	–	–	2.5	tr	–	–
Edotea triloba (Crus.)	4.6	tr	–	–	–	–	2.7	tr	+	tr
Undetermined Polychaeta (Poly.)	*[d]	2.1	*	tr	*	3.0	*	1.9	*	1.1
Lacuna vincta (Gast.)	–	–	72.7	2.5	–	–	–	–	–	–
Margarites helicinus (Gast.)	–	–	27.5	0.3	–	–	–	–	–	–
Idotea phosphorea (Crus.)	–	–	46.3	2.4	–	–	–	–	–	–
Ampithoe rubricata (Crus.)	–	–	56.5	2.9	–	–	–	–	–	–
Ischyrocerus anguipes (Crus.) / *Jassa falcata* (Crus.)	–	–	30.9	0.5	–	–	–	–	–	–
Pontogeneia inermis (Crus.)	–	–	10.8	0.2	–	–	–	–	–	–
Gammarellus homari (Crus.)	–	–	6.7	0.3	–	–	–	–	–	–
Cancer irroratus (Crus.)	–	–	1.9	4.3	–	–	–	–	–	–
Asterias vulgaris (Ast.)	–	–	7.5	1.1	–	–	–	–	–	–
Stronglyocentrotus drobachiensis (Ech.)	–	–	12.9	1.7	–	–	–	–	–	–
Idotea baltica (Crus.)	–	–	188.6	14.3	–	–	+	tr	–	–
Nucella lapillus (Gast.)	–	–	4.6	1.3	–	–	–	–	1.9	3.8
Gammarus oceanicus (Crus.)	–	–	10.1	1.7	18.0	2.5	+	tr	+	tr
Littorina littorea (Gast.)	–	–	17.5	29.2	75.0	45.0	18.0	15.3	79.5	26.9
Carcinus maenas Crus.)	–	–	–	–	7.0	5.0	+	tr	+	tr
Mytilus edulis (Biv.)	–	–	+	19.7	1180.0	3915.0	83.0	203.0	107.6	145.6
Anonyx sersi (Crus.)	–	–	–	–	–	–	1.3	tr	+	tr
Macoma balthica (Biv.)	–	–	–	–	–	–	28.3	2.9	40.0	8.0
Gammarus spp. (Crus.)	–	–	–	–	–	–	1.2	tr	1.9	tr
Odostomia bisuturalis (Gast.)	–	–	–	–	–	–	2.0	tr	53.8	0.3
Crangon septemspinosus (Crus.)	–	–	–	–	–	–	1.3	tr	6.1	0.5
Mya arenaria (Biv.)	–	–	–	–	+	tr	24.0	1.3	13.1	1.7
Acmaea testudinalis (Gast.)	–	–	+	tr	–	–	2.5	0.3	1.9	0.3
Ilyanassa obsoleta (Gast.)	–	–	–	–	–	–	–	–	7.8	1.4
Gemma gemma (Biv.)	–	–	–	–	–	–	–	–	7.6	tr
Microdeutopus gryllotalpa (Crus.)	–	–	–	–	–	–	–	–	1.4	tr

[a] Species classification: Biv. = Bivalvia, Gast. = Gastropoda, Crus. = Crustacea, Ech. = Echinoidea, Poly. = Polychaeta, and Ast. = Asteroidea.

[b] Less than 0.1 cc.

[c] Present but less than one organism/m².

[d] Present but no number available.

common periwinkle, 45.0 cc and 7.50 individuals; amphipod (*Gammarus oceanicus*), 2.55 cc and 18.0 individuals; green crab (*Carcinus maenas*), 5.0 cc and 7.0 individuals; soft-shell clam (*Mya arenaria*), and sand worms (polychaetes). The soft-shell clam and polychaetes occurred infrequently: fewer than one per square meter (Table 3). The soft-shell clam density in Table 3 is probably low, however,

Table 4. Major food items found in three species of scoters collected on the New Hampshire and Massachusetts coastline, 1968 and 1969.

Food items	White-winged scoter		Surf scoter		Common scoter	
	Volume	Occurrence	Volume	Occurrence	Volume	Occurrence
Siliqua costata	54%	61%	24%	55%	55%	62%
Mytilus edulis	5%	11%	8%	19%	19%	33%
Mesodesma arctatum	20%	8%	60%	16%	23%	12%
Lunatia heros	5%	35%	1%	15%	1%	12%
Balanus sp.	P[a]		P		1%	21%
Echinarachinus parma	3%	11%	P		P	
Idotea baltica	P		1%	5%	NP[b]	
Undetermined Bivalvia	8%	42%	2%	32%	P	
Total	95%		96%		99%	

[a] Present but not a major food item (less than 1% of total food volume).
[b] Not present in food items.

because the larger individuals of this species burrow deeply. The harbor contains large beds of clams that are harvested by the general public. That part of the harbor included in the study area consisted mostly of soft-shell clam beds and large beds of blue mussels on the surface of intertidal areas. There were also deep channels in the harbor, but their shifting coarse sands and strong currents made animal life sparse in these areas.

Rye Harbor and Little Harbor.—These two harbors were similar both in animals present and also in having a substrate of sandy mud, unlike Hampton Harbor. Both of these harbors had areas of salt marsh (each approximately 71 ha) and tidal creeks. Both harbor basins and some of the tidal creeks were sampled. The five most common invertebrate species found in Rye and Little Harbors were the blue mussel, common periwinkle, balthic macoma (*Macoma balthica*), soft-shell clam, and the Atlantic plate limpet (*Acmaea testudinalis*). These species made up 99% of the animal volume in Rye Harbor and 96% in Little Harbor.

The only species found in Little Harbor but not in Rye Harbor were the Atlantic dogwinkle (*Nucella lapillus*), volume 3.8 cc and density 1.9 individuals/m^2; eastern mud nassa (*Illyanassa obsoleta*), 1.4 cc and 7.8 individuals; amethyst gem clam (*Gemma gemma*), trace and 7.6 individuals; and the amphipod (*Microdeutopus gryllotalpa*), trace and 1.4 individuals (Table 3).

The sand shrimp (*Crangon septemspinosus*), although not shown in Table 3 to occur in large numbers, was one of the most abundant species of both these harbors. This species burrows near the surface of the soft substrate. While bottom samples were being taken, this species was observed to dart out of the substrate and swim away. This was especially true in eel grass beds (*Zostera marina*) in Little Harbor. Because of their mobility, these shrimp were difficult to collect and thus density figures for shrimp are biased downwards.

Food Habits of Sea Ducks

White-winged, Surf, and Common Scoter.—These three species had similar diets (Table 4). The most important food items was the Atlantic razor clam, followed by the Arctic wedge clam and the blue mussel. Although many other food items were found in scoters collected on the study area, bivalves made up 89%,

Table 5. Major food items found in oldsquaw, bufflehead, and goldeneye collected on the New Hampshire and Massachusetts coastline, 1968–69.

Food items	Oldsquaw		Bufflehead		Goldeneye	
	Volume	Occurrence	Volume	Occurrence	Volume	Occurrence
Animal food						
Siliqua costata	6%	30%	–	–	–	–
Mesodesma arctatum	2%	5%	–	–	–	–
Undetermined *Cumacea*	1%	18%	–	–	–	–
Edotea triloba	1%	30%	P[a]		–	–
Lacuna vincta	54%	40%	P		5%	44%
Crangon septemspinosus[b]	31%	8%	75%	65%	5%	6%
Littorina littorea	3%	13%	2%	55%	P	
Calliopius laeviusculus	1%	8%	P		P	
Idotea baltica	P		–	–	6%	35%
Ampithoe rubricata	P		–	–	4%	4%
Mytilus edulis	P		P		2%	19%
Idotea spp.	–	–	10%	24%	1%	17%
Gammarus oceanicus	–	–	2%	2%	1%	8%
Littorina obtusata	–	–	1%	16%	P	
Odostomia bisuturalis[b]	–	–	1%	15%	P	
Cancer irroratus	–	–	–	–	2%	15%
Idotea phosphorea	–	–	–	–	1%	25%
Undetermined animal food	P		6%	18%	54%	60%
Plant food						
Zostera marina (seed)[b]	P		P		17%	10%
Total	99%		97%		98%	

[a] Present but not a major food item (less than 1% of total food volume).
[b] Food item found only in birds collected in Little Harbor.
[c] Goldeneye fed primarily on soft-bodied animals (isopods and amphipods), which are ground up more readily than bivalves and gastropods, thus resulting in a large amount of undetermined animal material.

96%, and 97% of the total volume of food items found in white-winged, surf, and common scoters respectively (Stott 1972).

Several previous studies of scoters have indicated a predominately bivalve diet. Cronan and Halla (1968) in their analysis of 18 white-winged scoters from Rhode Island waters found that the northern quahaug (*Mercenaria mercenaria*) and other bivalve species made up the majority (90.7%) of the total volume of all food eaten. Mackay (1891) described the similar bivalve foods of the three scoter species in New England, which consisted of the black mussel (*Modiolus modiolus*), small sea clams (*Spisula solidissima*), scallops (*Pecten concentricus*), and short razor shells (*Siliqua costata*) about 2.5 to 3.8 cm long. In the present study, razor clams up to 5 cm in length have been found in the gullets of white-winged scoters, with smaller individuals being found in the surf and common scoters. Grosz (1966), in his analysis of 21 white-winged scoters, collected on the ocean outside of Humboldt Bay, California, found that the razor clam (*Solen sicarius*) accounted for 91% of the occurrence and 92% of the total food volume.

McGilvrey (personal communication) provided food habits data for 43 scoters collected on the present study area in 1964 which were part of a larger investigation (1967). His data revealed that these sea ducks had taken mainly three species of *Yoldia*, a bivalve. However, in the present study, no *Yoldia* were found in 427 scoters collected on the study area in 1968 and 1969. Nor were *Yoldia* found in the numerous bottom samples collected on the present study area although the area is included in the range of all three species of *Yoldia* (Abbott 1968).

The sizes of food items (razor and wedge clams, moon snails), ingested by scoters were within the range of sizes of these species obtained from bottom samples collected by scuba diving in areas of consistent scoter use.

Common Goldeneye.—There were marked differences among food items of goldeneye collected in Little Harbor (23 birds) and on the coastline proper (25 birds). The goldeneye taken in the harbors had eaten seeds of eel grass and sand shrimp; in contrast, the birds collected on the coastline proper had eaten isopods, *Idotea baltica*; amphipods, *Ampithoe rubricata,* and the rock crab. Some foods were found in birds collected from both the harbor and the coastline. These included the northern lacuna periwinkle, common periwinkle, and undetermined polychaetes. Food items of all goldeneye collected on the study area are listed in Table 5.

On the Pacific coast, Dawson (1909) found that the diet of the goldeneye included mussels, crabs, marine worms, and the remains of decayed salmon. Bent (1962) stated that goldeneye on the coast fed largely on small mussels and other molluscs, and also to some extent on the seeds of eel grass. Half of the 22 goldeneye examined by Cronan and Halla (1968) contained undetermined Decapoda (crab) remains. Olney and Mills (1963) collected 14 goldeneye on the coastline and estuaries of a part of Great Britain during the months of November to February. The green crab (*Carcinus maenas*) was found to be the most important food item and accounted for 66% of the total food volume and 64% of the occurrence. Madsen (1954) examined 90 specimens collected from October to February in Denmark and found that crustaceans were frequently eaten. These included shrimp (*Crangon vulgaris*), *Idotea* sp., *Gammarus* sp., and the green crab. *Littorina* sp. and the blue mussel were also found. Olney and Mills (1963) cited Witherby et al., who in 1940 stated that the diet of goldeneye of Great Britain consisted chiefly of animal material that included molluscs (*Littorina* sp., *Rissoa* sp., *Lacuna* sp.); crustaceans (*Crangon* sp., *Idotea* sp., *Gammarus* sp., *Talitrus* sp.); and some small fish.

Bufflehead.—This species was found to depend largely on the sand shrimp (*Crangon septemspinosus*) for its food supply. Shrimp accounted for 75% of the total food volume and 65% of the occurrence. Four other foods were important: isopods, *Idotea baltica* and *I. phosphorea*; common periwinkle; and eel grass seeds (Table 5).

Bent (1962) cited Audubon's 1840 statement that bufflehead in the seacoast estuaries fed on shrimps, small fry, and bivalve shells. Yocum and Keller (1961) found that bufflehead in Humboldt Bay, California, were feeding on a variety of animal species that included bivalves, crab, shrimp, and several gastropod species. Wiemeyer (1967) in his study of food habits of bufflehead in Humboldt Bay found that bivalves, crustaceans, fish, and gastropods made up the diet of this species. Although shrimp were found in these last two studies, they do not appear to be as important a food item as in the present investigation.

Oldsquaw.—The diet of this species contained a wide variety of food items and this is probably related to the generalized distribution of oldsquaw along the coastline. The northern lacuna periwinkle was the most important food. The Atlantic razor clam, sand shrimp, common periwinkle, and the isopod, *Edotea triloba,* were also of importance in the diet of this sea duck (Table 5).

Mackay (1892) in his description of oldsquaw in New England indicated that a small unidentified bivalve, sand fleas, short Atlantic razor clams, penny shells (*Astarte castanea*), shrimps, mussels, and small blue-claw crabs made up this species' marine diet. In the present study, razor clams up to 2 cm in length were found in the gullets of oldsquaw. It appears that oldsquaws were selectively feeding only on the smaller razor clams, whereas scoters can ingest razor clams up to 5 cm long. Lagler and Wienert (1948) also found a varied diet for oldsquaw of Lake Michigan consisting of small bivalves, deep water crustaceans, crayfish, gastropods, insect larvae, and a small amount of vegetable matter.

Red-breasted Merganser.—This species is known largely as a fish eater. Although only five red-breasted mergansers were collected on the study area and these in the harbors, they contained either killifish (*Fundulus* sp.) or silversides (*Menidia menidia*). Cronan and Halla (1968) found that the blueback herring (*Alosa aestevalis*) made up 99.6% of the total food volume of 15 mergansers collected in Rhode Island. Kortright (1953) and Bent (1962) also indicated that this species was primarily a fish eater.

Summary of Food-Habitat Relationship

In summary, the food habits data for sea ducks revealed contrasting differences among species in that scoters fed primarily on bivalves, bufflehead ate primarily sand shrimp, goldeneye fed on invertebrates characteristic of rocky substrate and harbors, and oldsquaw had the most generalized diet consisting of food items from all habitat types. These differences in food usage closely matched the relative abundance of the food items in various habitats and indicated that the type of foods present may be a primary cause for sea duck use of particular habitat types.

DISCUSSION

The distinct differences in food habits and the habitat preferences of waterfowl species observed in this study have broader implications than the present investigation. In previous New Hampshire studies, Richards (1952) stated that the majority of scoters were found off Hampton Beach (a coastal sandy area), that goldeneye were observed in large flocks off Great Boar's Head (a coastal rocky area), and that bufflehead used Rye and Little Harbors but not Hampton Harbor. Dearborn (1902) indicated that the three scoters were plentiful at Hampton.

In other New England areas, W. Blandin (personal communication) in his aerial surveys of coastal waterfowl for the Massachusetts Division of Fisheries and Game stated that his observations of the habitats used by sea ducks generally agreed with the present findings. W. Snow and R. Billard (personal communication) in their aerial surveys of coastal waterfowl also found scoters off sandy beach areas in Maine and Connecticut.

In New England and particularly on the study area, scoters are often hunted and observed from rocky headlands and points, and there is a common tendency to associate scoters with these rocky areas. This erroneous association is due to the fact that scoters have to pass these areas to get from one food resource to another.

W. Snow (personal communication) in his aerial surveys of the subarctic Labrador coast (54° latitude 57° long.) found several thousand scoters in a large shallow sandy bay on several occasions during late July of 1969 and 1972.

These similarities in the habitat usage of sea ducks in Maine, New Hampshire, Massachusetts, and Connecticut and possibly the subarctic coastal area indicate that the food and habitat preferences may apply to the entire Atlantic coastline.

The tendency of scoters to use sandy areas may be similar on the Pacific coast as well. Grosz (1966) in his study of white-winged scoter food habits found that the razor clam (*Solen sicarius*), which is found in sandy or silty substrate, made up the major portion of that species' diet.

Food habits of goldeneye described for the Pacific coast (Dawson 1909) and also the coasts of Denmark (Madsen 1954) and Great Britain (Olney and Mills 1963) were similar to the food habits of goldeneye in the present study and suggest that the habitat used by goldeneye in these geographical areas were probably similar to those observed in New England.

Food Competition and Changing Scoter Populations

The three scoters (white-winged, surf, and common) had primarily bivalve diets consisting mostly of Atlantic razor clams and Arctic wedge clams. These scoter species also used the same habitats and were frequently observed together in feeding flocks. Thus, the scoters occupied the same habitat for approximately 8 months and it is possible that food resources could be depleted if large populations of sea ducks were present. Glude (1967) found that an increase in the number of scoters in a coastal shell-fish area of Washington caused a reduction in numbers of a commercial soft-shell clam.

Further study is needed of the food requirement of scoters and other sea ducks and also a measure of the food resources that are being utilized by these waterfowl species. The bottom sampling of the present study area was probably not intensive enough for a reliable calculation of total food resources.

An evaluation of scoter populations and hunting (Stott and Olson 1972*b*) indicated that the common scoter was the most vulnerable to hunting on the New Hampshire coastline, followed by the surf scoter and then the white-winged scoter. The distribution of the common scoter appears to have shifted from its former range of the New England coast to its present southern Atlantic coast distribution because of past hunting pressures and its extreme vulnerability to the gun in New England. Presently, the mid-Atlantic coastal area appears to winter the majority of surf scoters, whereas the white-winged scoter appears to be the most abundant species along the New England coast. Thus these differential vulnerability patterns in scoters, besides causing probable shifts in the winter distribution of the species, may well be responsible for reduction in competition among scoters for a common food resource.

Although the bottom sampling of sandy substrate of the present study area was limited and was conducted in May and June when most scoters have left the area, results indicated that Atlantic razor clams and Arctic wedge clams were still common there, but in varying densities. Superficially, it appeared that the food resource had not been severely depleted by the scoter population. Thus, the extreme differences in vulnerability of scoters to hunting and resulting differences in populations and distribution may prevent or mask any real competition for food resources.

Food Resources of Harbors

Goldeneye, oldsquaw, and bufflehead were found together in Rye and Little Harbors, and their food habits reflected the food resources of these estuaries. There may be some competition for sand shrimp and perhaps other invertebrate species. Bufflehead depended on sand shrimp for a large part of their diet and they occupied the harbors almost the entire time they were on the study area. Although oldsquaw also fed on sand shrimp, they were found in these harbors only in very low numbers. Also oldsquaws had the most generalized food diet of all sea ducks, with foods characteristic of rocky areas, sandy areas, and harbors. Goldeneye utilized sand shrimp but occurred mostly on the coastline proper, where amphipods and isopods were abundant. Thus, bufflehead in these harbors were probably not greatly affected by the other two species, which had broader food preferences than the narrow food diet of the bufflehead.

There may be a relationship between the higher rate of activity and mobility of bufflehead and their primary food resource, sand shrimp. Whitlow (1965) stated that the metabolic rate per unit of body weight (for example, kcal/kg·24 h) decreased with increasing body weight in adult birds. Bufflehead, the smallest and most active of the sea ducks, appeared to eat the least proportion of shell material, hence probably obtaining maximum utilization of food items eaten as compared to the larger scoters, which ingested a larger proportion of shell.

Effect of Estuaries in Concentrating Sea Ducks

The largest concentration of scoters was consistently observed at Hampton Beach near the mouth of the Hampton River and at Salisbury Beach near the mouth of the Merrimack River. Bottom sampling in these areas revealed a greater density of Atlantic razor clams at Hampton Beach and a greater density of Arctic wedge clams at Salisbury Beach than in all other areas sampled. These bivalves were the two most important scoter foods. It is likely that these two estuaries and their associated cordgrass (*Spartina* spp.) marshes interlaced with tidal creeks are having an effect on these bivalve populations by increasing productivity. Massmann (1971) stated that crustaceans and molluscs are the principal direct beneficiaries of the particulate detritus provided by cordgrass, the protein content of which may actually quadruple during the decaying process (Odum and de la Cruz 1967).

A preponderance of Arctic wedge clams was found at Salisbury Beach near the estuary mouth (40 clams/m^2). This bivalve species was found in very low densities in all the other sandy areas that were bottom-sampled. Davis (1963) found wedge clams in the Merrimack estuary but no living clams on the beaches a short distance away from the estuary mouth. He also found wedge clams in Hampton Harbor, but only dead shells on the beach outside of the harbor. It appears that on the study area this wedge clam occurs only in or near estuaries. Atlantic razor clams at Hampton Beach occurred at a density of 10 animals/m^2, the highest density in all the areas sampled. These highly productive bivalve areas concentrated scoters from September to May.

Similarly, the productive influence of estuaries may concentrate goldeneye outside the mouth of Rye and Little Harbors. Goldeneye observed in or at the mouths of estuaries were mostly adult males and these bigger and stronger males may be able to cope with the estuary currents and take advantage of its increased productivity.

Further study is needed of the effect of estuaries on coastal waterfowl, as well as the effect of nutrients from marsh ecosystems and from pollutants on bivalve and crustacean (such as the sand shrimp) populations. Shrimp, which spend part of their life cycle in estuaries, have a low toxicity tolerance to pesticides (Butler and Springer 1963). Wallace (1971) and Salo and Stober (1971) indicated that pollution has detrimental effects on bivalve populations and other aspects of estuarine biology. Since the food resources in or near estuaries appear to attract and concentrate sea ducks, the future pollution of rivers and estuaries would affect the most productive areas for sea ducks.

Problems in Food Habits Analysis

Procedures for food habits analyses, such as those used in this study, have many limitations and biases. Many older food habits investigations used only gizzards of waterfowl in their analyses, whereas some more recent studies have used only gullets (esophagus and proventriculus). Until recently, post mortem digestion of food items in birds collected was not considered a source of bias in food items present. Apparently, few food habits investigations have looked into the possibility of food items actually being debris from an organism's environment. A serious limitation of many previous food habits studies is that the results are not related to the environment where the animal was collected. Several comparisons between the present study and other similar studies are in order.

Difference in Rates of Digestion.—Several food habits investigations have stressed the biases resulting from the different digestive rates of animal and plant food in the gullet (esophagus and proventriculus) and the gizzard (Dillon 1957, Perrett 1962, Dirshl 1969, Bartonek and Hickey 1969). These studies revealed that hard-seeded plants in the diet remained longer in the gizzard than did soft-bodied animals, thus inflating the importance of plant foods. Swanson and Bartonek (1970) indicated that soft foods, such as amphipods, broke down within minutes, whereas hard seeds were retained for days. This is the reason that some recent food habits analyses were restricted to the gullet only, whose content was assumed to provide a realistic measure of the diet.

However, all these investigations have dealt with birds in a freshwater environment. In the present study, no differences were observed in food items present between gullet and gizzard in the sea ducks examined. McGilvrey (1967) also found this to be true in his food habits analyses of sea ducks of the northeastern United States. In the present investigation, 28 sea ducks (6 surf scoter, 5 white-winged scoter, 5 goldeneye, 7 oldsquaw, and 5 bufflehead) had the same food items present in the gullet and gizzard of a given individual, and there were no apparent differences of food items in these specimens as compared to food items from gizzards only.

Post Mortem Digestion.—Post mortem digestion of soft-bodied animals (Dillery 1965) was not evident during this study. Since goldeneye fed primarily on soft-bodied animals and we collected all these specimens, a comparison was made. We opened approximately half of the 48 collected goldeneye immediately after death and froze the rest after a day or two to examine at a later date. Results for both treatments indicated that amphipods and isopods in these latter birds were perfectly intact and showed no sign of post mortem digestion in gullet and/or gizzard. A good example of the lack of post mortem digestion occurred when a goldeneye that had been left outdoors for 8 days contained perfectly intact soft-bodied amphipods and isopods in its gullet and gizzard.

Soft-bodied animals, such as amphipods and isopods, that live in the ocean may require a more complex or longer digestive process than do comparable organisms from freshwater. Marine invertebrates live in a saline environment and are ingested into a somewhat similar saline digestive environment. The body structure of these marine invertebrates may also be different from freshwater organisms in that the amphipods and isopods that goldeneye fed upon were usually found at a water depth (6 to 9 m) where the pressure is approximately 25–30 psi.

Ingestion of Debris.—Food habits, bottom sampling, and habitat usage information for the three scoters (white-winged, surf, and common) indicated that these species preferred a diet of bivalves, which were found in a sandy substrate. However, the food items taken from scoter gullets and gizzards indicated that they were also ingesting parts of a few animals found only in rocky areas, such as several species of gastropods, barnacles (*Balanus* sp.), and sea urchins (spines only). Bottom samples collected from the sandy areas revealed that food items characteristic of rocky areas were found as debris or dead organisms in the sandy areas and occurred in small amounts. It is likely that these dead items were ingested by scoters while searching for or ingesting live organisms. There is also the possibility that the birds did indeed ingest these as live organisms but in rocky areas. However, from personal observation, we think the first possibility more realistic. In examining scoter specimens we frequently found a gizzard with razor clams, a piece of gastropod, a sea urchin spine, or a piece of barnacle. Since it was not always possible to distinguish between dead and living material in the scoter specimens, we included all food items in the food habits tables.

Crab Movements and Utilization.—Although the green crab was found in the diet of goldeneye in several European food habits investigations it was not found in any specimens collected on the study area. Only the rock crab was found and this species accounted for only a small portion of the total diet. R. Croker (personal communication) stated that the green crab was the most common of all crabs on the study area, but it migrated offshore in the fall to breed and returned in the spring. He also stated that during the winter period only a few green crabs of small size could possibly be found and these in shallow water areas. Bottom sampling of the study area in March and April (Table 3) indicated that this species was found in the harbors and was of small size. It appears that although only a few rock crabs were present (1.9 animals/m^2), this was the species utilized by the sea ducks.

ACKNOWLEDGMENTS

We wish to acknowledge the assistance of E. E. Lang, class of 1970, Institute of Natural and Environmental Resources, for aiding in scuba diving; E. S. Moses and D. G. Grover, Parker River National Wildlife Refuge, Newburyport, Massachusetts and D. H. Swendsen, U.S. Game Management Agent (New Hampshire) for use of their boats and assistance during the scuba diving-sublittoral substrate sampling operation; M. F. Gable and R. A. Croker, Department of Zoology, for aid in identifying the amphipods obtained from sea ducks and sublittoral substrate sampling; H. P. Nevers, Department of Forest Resources, for use of his field notes of coastal waterfowl during 1967–68; F. B. McGilvrey, Patuxent Wildlife Research Center, Laurel, Maryland, for his food habits data of sea ducks collected on the study area in 1964; and the numerous sea duck hunters who donated their birds and also shared with us their knowledge of sea ducks on the New Hampshire coastline. The New Hampshire Agricultural Experiment Station gave partial financial support during this investigation.

LITERATURE CITED

ABBOTT, R. T. 1968. Seashells of North America. Western Publishing Co., Inc., Golden Press, New York. 280pp.

BARTONEK, J. C., AND J. J. HICKEY. 1969. Food habits of canvasbacks, redheads, and lesser scaup in Manitoba. Condor 71:280–290.

BENT, A. C. 1962. Life histories of North American wild fowl. Vol. I and II. Dover Publications, Inc., New York. 685pp.

BUTLER, P. A., AND P. F. SPRINGER. 1963. Pesticides—A new factor in coastal environment. Trans. N. Am. Wildl. Nat. Resour. Conf. 28:378–390.

CRONAN, J. M., AND B. F. HALLA. 1968. Fall and winter foods of Rhode Island waterfowl. Rhode Island Dept. of Natural Resources, wildlife pamphlet No. 7. 40pp.

DAVIS, J. D. 1963. A study of the arctic wedge clam, *Mesodesma deuratum* and *Mesodesma arctatum,* on the northwestern Atlantic. Ph.D. Thesis. Univ. New Hampshire, Durham. 144pp.

DAWSON, W. L. 1909. The birds of Washington. Occidental Publishing Co., Seattle. 997pp.

DEARBORN, N. 1902. The birds of Durham and vicinity. D.Sci. Thesis. New Hampshire College of Agric. and Mech. Arts, Durham. 121pp.

DILLERY, D. G. 1965. Post-morten digestion of stomach contents in the savannah sparrow. Auk 82:281.

DILLON, O. W., JR. 1957. Food habits of wild ducks in the rice-marsh transition area of Louisiana. Proc. Ann. Conf. Southeast Assoc. Game and Fish Comm., Mobile, Ala. 11:114–119.

DIRSCHL, H. J. 1969. Foods of lesser scaup and blue-winged teal in the Saskatchewan River delta. J. Wildl. Manage. 33:77–87.

GLUDE, J. B. 1967. The effect of scoter duck predation on a clam population in Dabob Bay, Washington. Proc. Natl. Shellfish Assoc. 55:73–86.

GROSZ, T. 1966. Food habits and parasites of the Pacific white-winged scoter (*Melanitta fusca dixori*) in the Humboldt Bay area. M.S. Thesis. Humboldt State College, Arcata, Calif. 44pp.

KORTRIGHT, F. H. 1953. The ducks, geese, and swans of North America. Wildlife Management Institute, Washington, D.C., and The Stackpole Co., Harrisburg, Pa. 476pp.

LAGLER, K. F., AND CATHERINE C. WIENERT. 1948. Food of the oldsquaw in Lake Michigan. Wilson Bull. 60:118.

MACKAY, G. H. 1891. The scoters (*Oidemia americana, O. deglandi,* and *O. perspicillata*) in New England. Auk 8:279–290.

———. 1892. Habits of the oldsquaw (*Clangula hyemalis*) in New England. Auk 9:330–337.

MADSEN, F. J. 1954. On the food habits of the diving ducks in Denmark. Danish Rev. Game Biol. 2:157–266.

MARTIN, A. C., H. S. ZIM, AND A. L. NELSON. 1961. American wildlife and plants—A guide to wildlife food habits. Dover Publications, Inc., New York. 500pp.

MASSMAN, W. H. 1971. The significance of an estuary on the biology of aquatic organisms of the middle Atlantic region. pp. 96–109. *In* P. A. Douglas and R. H. Stroud, eds. A symposium on the biological significance of estuaries. Sport Fishing Institute, Washington. 111pp.

MCGILVREY, F. B. 1967 (1965–66). Food habits of sea ducks from the northeastern United States. Wildfowl Trust 18:142–145.

ODUM, E. P., AND A. A. DE LA CRUZ. 1967. Particulate organic detritus in a Georgia salt marsh estuarine ecosystem. *In* G. H. Lauff, ed. Estuaries. Am. Acad. Adv. Sci. Publ. No. 83:383–388.

OLNEY, P. J. S., AND D. H. MILLS. 1963. The food and feeding habits of goldeneye (*Bucephala clangula*) in Great Britain. Ibis 105:293–300.

PERRET, N. G. 1962. The spring and summer foods of the common mallard (*Anas platyrhynchos platyrhynchos* L.) in south central Manitoba. M.S. Thesis. Univ. British Columbia, Vancouver. 82pp.

RICHARDS, T. 1952. The waterfowl of New Hampshire, their history and present status. M.S. Thesis. Univ. Michigan, Ann Arbor. 194pp.

SALO, E. O., AND Q. J. STOBER. 1971. The effects of pollution on estuaries of the northwest Pacific coast, pp. 86–95. *In* P. A. Douglas and R. H. Stroud, eds. A symposium on the biological significance of estuaries. Sport Fishing Institute, Washington. 111pp.

SMITH, R. I. 1964. Keys to marine invertebrates of the Woods Hole region. Spaulding Co., Boston. 209pp.

STOTT, R. S. 1972. Habitat usage and populations of sea ducks on the New Hampshire coastline. M.S. Thesis. Univ. New Hampshire, Durham. 120pp.

———, AND D. P. OLSON. 1972*a*. An evaluation of

waterfowl surveys on the New Hampshire coastline. J. Wildl. Manage. 36:468–477.

———, AND ———. 1972*b*. Differential vulnerability patterns among three species of sea ducks. J. Wildl. Manage. 36:775–783.

SWANSON, G. A., AND J. C. BARTONEK. 1970. Bias associated with food analysis in gizzards of blue-winged teal. J. Wildl. Manage. 34:739–746.

WALLACE, D. H. 1971. The biological effects of estuaries on shellfish of the middle Atlantic, pp. 76–85. *In* P. A. Douglas and R. H. Stroud, eds. A symposium on the biological significance of estuaries. Sport Fishing Institute, Washington. 111pp.

WHITLOW, G. C. 1965. Energy metabolism, pp. 244–260. *In* P. D. Sturkie, ed. Avian physiology 2nd ed. Cornell Univ. Press, Ithaca, New York. 766pp.

WIEMEYER, S. N. 1967. Bufflehead foot habits, parasites, and biology in northern California. M.S. Thesis. Humboldt State College, Arcata, Calif. 99pp.

YOCUM, C. F., AND M. KELLER. 1961. Correlation of food habits and abundance of waterfowl, Humboldt Bay, California. Calif. Fish Game 47:41–54.

SUMMER FEEDING ECOLOGY OF LESSER SNOW GEESE

JOHN HARWOOD, Zoology Department, University of Western Ontario, London, Canada N6A 3K7.

Abstract: Changes in the characteristics of the available vegetation at the mouth of the McConnell River, N.W.T. (60°50′N, 94°25′W), during the arctic summer were measured in 1971 and 1973. The concurrent variations in the feeding behavior of adult lesser snow geese (*Chen caerulescens*) were measured in 1973. Standing crop of vegetation in both grazed and ungrazed sites reached a maximum in the first week of August. The crude protein content of ungrazed vegetation showed a maximum value in late July, with a rapid decline in August. Grazed vegetation showed a similar rise, but with little decline in protein content in August. Snow geese and their goslings had access to a food supply increasing both in quantity and quality during the critical post-incubatory period. In this period adult female geese spent 17 hours per day feeding, probably as much time as was physically possible. Other parameters of feeding behavior varied predictably with the changes in vegetation characteristics.

J. WILDL. MANAGE. 41(1):48–55

Members of the Hudson Bay population of lesser snow geese breed in colonies on coastal, tundra marshes (Cooch 1961). Throughout the summer, breeding adults feed almost exclusively on the green shoots of *Gramineae, Cyperaceae*, and *Juncaceae*. Arctic grasslands traditionally have been considered to have a low annual primary productivity and a low vegetational nitrogen content (Russell 1940, Wilson 1954, Bliss 1971).

Paired adults arrive on the breeding grounds in late May or early June. Winter snow rarely melts by this time. Nesting starts as soon as suitable sites are available. There is little feeding by nesting adults during incubation, and females may lose more than 30 percent of their body weight during this period—including a large proportion of their breast muscle (Ankney 1974:102–107). This protein drain is exacerbated further by a major molt that occurs within 3 weeks of the end of incubation. Breeding geese must recover their lost body weight, replace their flight feathers, and prepare for southward migration in a two-month period. They must do this while feeding on what is considered to be a nutrient-poor food supply.

Compared to most grazing vertebrates, geese have a simple alimentary tract. Vegetation passes through the gut in 2 to 4 hours (Marriott and Forbes 1970, Ziswiler and Farner 1972:397), and large plant fragments are visible in the faeces. This rapid passage of food leaves little opportunity for any digestive process more complex than the simple absorption of cell solutes. Mattocks (1971) found no evidence of cellulose digestion in the digestive caecae of *Anser anser.*

In the post-incubatory period breeding snow geese need a high intake of protein, yet they lack major morphological adaptations for herbivory (possibly because such adaptations are incompatible with long migratory flights). Natural selective processes therefore favor individuals which show behavioral patterns that maximize protein intake per unit of energy expended in feeding. Maximization could be achieved by variation in the individual components of grazing behavior, such as the length of a feeding bout or the rate of pecking, in response to changes in vegetation characteristics. During the arctic summer, breeding snow geese feed on an easily defined and measured food resource that changes in character during the summer. If snow goose feeding behavior is adapted to ensure a maximum intake of protein during the post-incubatory period, the various parameters

Originally published in J. Wildl. Manage. 41(1):48–55, 1977.

of feeding behavior should vary in a predictable way with variations in the quantity of vegetation available, and its protein content. Measurement of these features of the vegetation provides an indication of the food resources available to arctic nesting geese. If this measurement is combined with some method of excluding feeding geese from particular areas, the impact of goose grazing on the tundra vegetation can be assessed.

I measured the changes in available vegetation and its crude protein content during the breeding season at the large McConnell River colony (60°50′N, 95°25′W) in 1971 and 1973. In 1973 the variations in the feeding behavior of adult snow geese were also recorded.

The research reported in this paper was funded by a contract from the Canadian Wildlife Service, and National Research Council grants to M.H.A. Keenleyside and C. D. MacInnes. The author was supported by a National Research Council studentship and a National Research Council scholarship.

METHODS

Complete details of all sampling methods and analytical techniques are given in Harwood (1975:9–18). The principal characteristics of the vegetation chosen for measurement were standing crop of green vegetation and crude protein content (6.25 × total nitrogen). This choice was made on the basis of the assumed importance of these characteristics to grazing geese, and their relative ease of measurement.

Six study areas were used, three in each year. All were wet meadow areas characterized by the presence of hairgrass-like reed-grass (*Calamagrostis deschampsiodes*) and were used regularly by grazing geese. Three 1-ha subareas were marked out in each area; subareas were chosen so as to have little standing water and relatively uniform vegetation composition. Within each subarea sample plots were randomly located. Each plot consisted of a pair of 5 m × 2 m subplots, one of which (the ungrazed subplot) was surrounded by a fence of 95 mm mesh wire netting to prevent the entry of grazing geese. Plots were sampled at approximately 10-day intervals, when 5 randomly located 500 mm × 200 mm quadrats were clipped to the moss level in each subplot. In 1971 samples were weighed, sorted into green monocotyledon, dicotyledon, and litter components, and then oven-dried to constant weight. In 1973 each sample was weighed and oven-dried to constant weight; a subsample of each dried sample was sorted into the three components. Some of the 1973 samples were completely sorted to determine the average percentage of green monocotyledons in the vegetation. The total nitrogen content of the dried, green monocotyledon component of each sample was then determined in triplicate using a modified Kjeldahl method (Johnson 1941).

Feeding behavior was studied only in 1973. Observations in the post-incubatory period were made on the study areas used for the vegetation sampling from raised, permanent observation towers (Lieff 1973: 7–8). Other observations were made from portable canvas blinds. The following parameters of feeding behavior were measured: (1) percentage of the daylight hours spent feeding; (2) length of a feeding bout; this was defined as the interval between the lowering of a goose's head into the vegetation to feed and the first raising of the head above the long axis of the body for more than one second; (3) rate of pecking while feeding; and (4) rate of walking while feeding.

Time spent feeding was measured by slightly different methods in the incubation and post-incubation periods. During May and June observations were made on individual feeding females. Birds were kept under observation for periods of 10 to 30 minutes, and their behavior was recorded at 1-minute intervals. The mean percentage of feeding records was used as an estimate of the percentage time spent feeding away from the nest. In July and August a scan-sampling technique (Altmann 1974) was used. Feeding flocks of adults with young were scanned at 5-minute intervals during 1-hour sampling periods evenly distributed throughout the daylight hours. The total number of adults visible, and the number feeding were recorded. The mean percentage of birds feeding was an estimate of the percentage of the observation time spent feeding by an individual. Bout length was measured to the nearest 1-second with a stopwatch; the total number of pecks directed at the vegetation was counted mentally; and the number of steps taken was recorded on a hand counter. When the bout terminated these values were transferred to a data sheet, with the sex and color phase of the bird under observation. These data were then used to calculate the number of pecks and steps per minute of feeding. All observations were made with a 30-power telescope or 8×40 binoculars at distances of 50 to 200 m.

RESULTS

Vegetation

All data are presented as mean values from several plots on different study areas. Such pooling, without any statistical test for homogeneity, precludes the drawing of precise statistical inferences about variation in time. It is, nonetheless, useful for descriptive purposes, providing an indication of the overall variation with time in the different parameters for the whole colony.

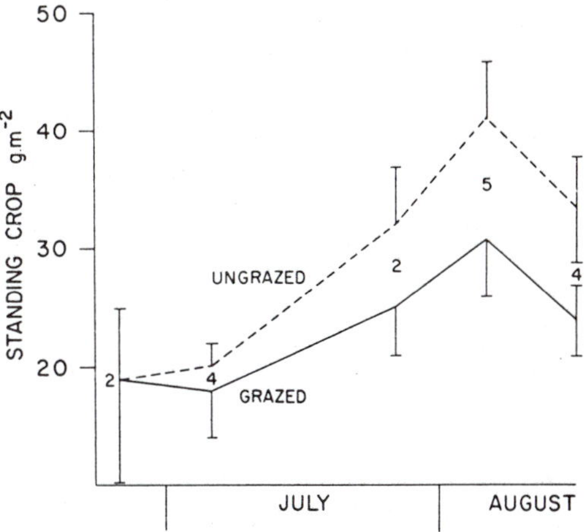

Fig. 1. Variation with time in dry weight standing crop of green monocotyledons at the McConnell River, N.W.T., in 1971. Figures between curves indicate the number of pairs of subplots sampled, vertical lines indicate ± one standard error.

However, statistical tests to determine the effects of grazing are valid if the pairs of values from grazed and ungrazed subplots are compared.

Attention was focused on the variation in the standing crop of green monocotyledons, because geese were observed only once feeding on dicotyledons. In 1971 only the variation in monocotyledon dry weight was recorded (Fig. 1). In 1973 the variation in fresh and dry weight of all vegetation was recorded (Fig. 2). In both years standing crop attained its maximum value in the first week of August and then declined (Figs. 1, 2). The amount of vegetation removed by grazing animals is indicated by the discrepancy between the lines for grazed and ungrazed vegetation. Snow geese were responsible for the vast majority of this removal. The two other large, grazing herbivores present at the McConnell River (Canada geese [*Branta canadensis*] and caribou [*Rangifer tarandus*]) were rare in relation to snow goose numbers. Lemmings (*Dicrostonyx groenlandicus*) could, and did, pass through the mesh of the exclosure wire. In

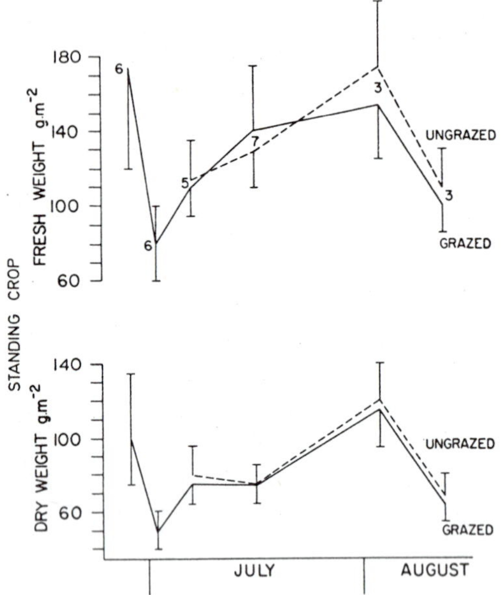

Fig. 2. Variation with time in fresh weight (upper figure) and dry weight (lower figure) standing crop of all vegetation at the McConnell River, N.W.T., in 1973. Notation as in Fig. 1.

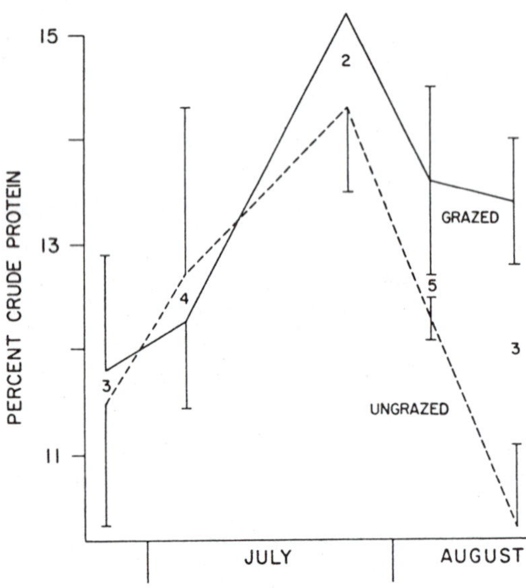

Fig. 3. Variation with time in the crude protein content of green monocotyledons at the McConnell River, N.W.T., in 1971. Notation as in Fig. 1.

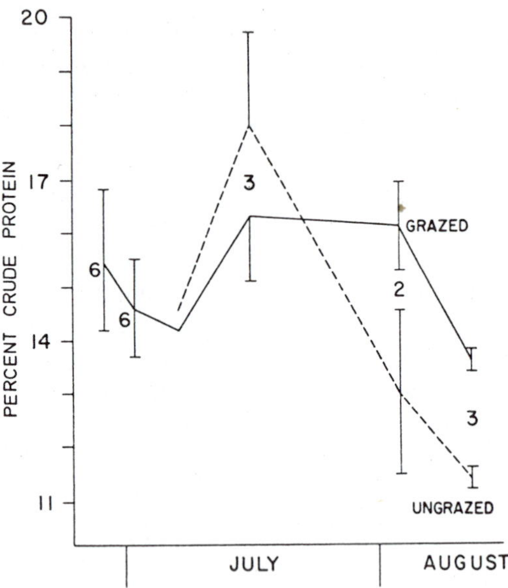

Fig. 4. Variation with time in the crude protein content of green monocotyledons at the McConnell River, N.W.T., in 1973. Notation as in Fig. 1.

1971 grazing removed 25 percent of the maximum standing crop (dry weight) of green monocotyledons. This component constituted 13 percent of the dry weight of the total standing crop in ungrazed subplots in 1973. In this year grazing removed 32 percent of the maximum standing crop of green monocotyledons, which was 16 $g.m^{-2}$ (dry weight). The constancy of the difference between the standing crop of grazed and ungrazed vegetation throughout July and August indicated the maintenance of a balance between removal by herbivores and new growth, because geese were present throughout the sampling period, and primary productivity ceased on the ungrazed subplots in the first week of August. Despite the impact of grazing, the available food supply for geese was increasing until the middle of August.

The crude protein content of the ungrazed monocotyledons reached a peak value in late July in both years, it then de-

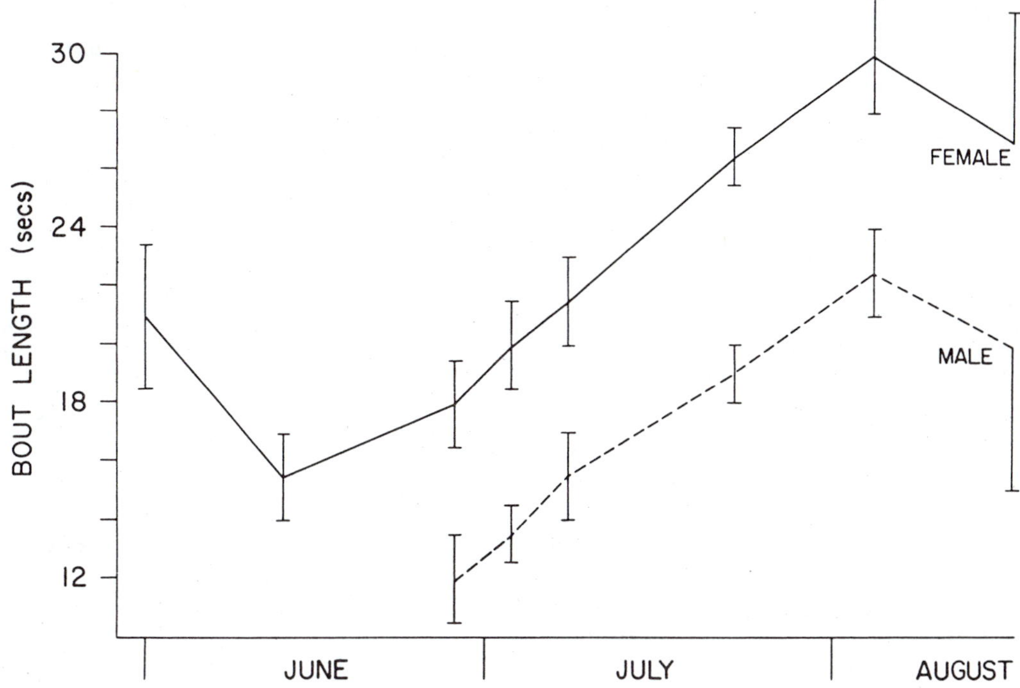

Fig. 5. Variation with time in the mean duration of a feeding bout for male and female, adult lesser snow geese at the McConnell River, N.W.T., in 1973. Vertical lines indicate ± one standard error.

clined in August (Figs. 3, 4). The peak probably corresponded to the period just before maximum growth. The grazed monocotyledons also had a maximum crude protein content in late July, but there was little decline in August (Figs. 3, 4). By the end of the sampling period, in both years, the vegetation in the grazed subplots had a significantly higher crude protein content than that in the ungrazed subplots ($P < 0.05$, paired t-test).

Behavior

In 1971 and 1973 the majority of breeding geese arrived at the colony in the last week of May. At this time more than 40 percent of the ground was snow-covered. Female geese were observed feeding on monocotyledon roots in suitable areas, although no quantitative observations were made. During the incubation period I observed only females feeding, while males remained alert nearby. Females spent 65 percent of the time away from the nest feeding, and were not observed to feed while incubating. After the eggs hatched, both sexes fed extensively, and spent 77 percent of the daylight hours feeding during July and August. This was equivalent to 15 hours of feeding per day.

The variation in the length of a feeding bout of both males and females (Fig. 5) showed a similar pattern to the variation in vegetation standing crop, with a maximum value in the first week of August. Throughout the summer female bouts were consistently 7 seconds longer than male bouts. This difference is explained by the organization of behavioral acts in feeding. Feeding consists of strictly alternating bouts of actual pecking and being alert. In a sample of 10 pairs of birds observed on

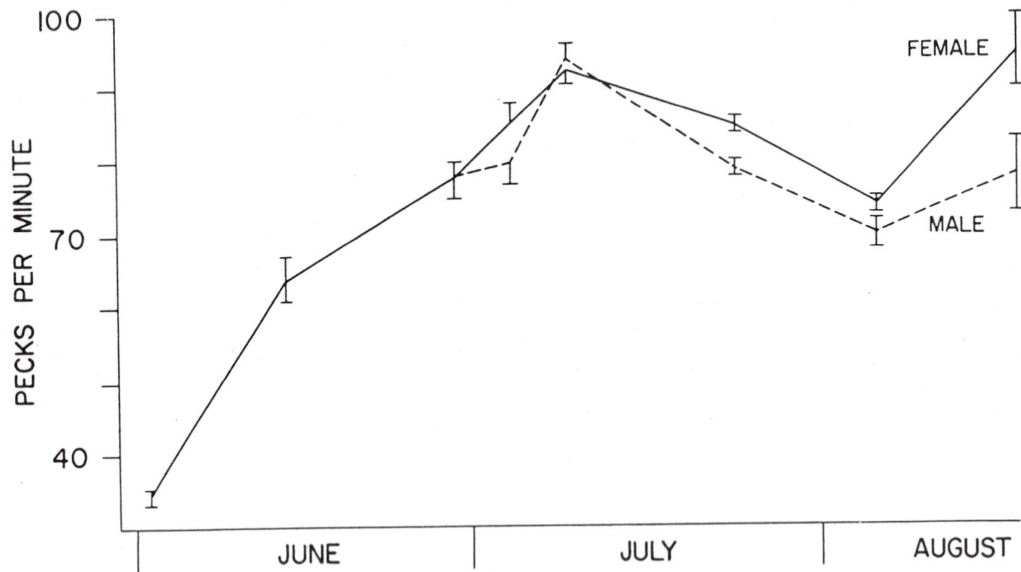

Fig. 6. Variation with time in the mean rate of pecking while feeding for adult, male and female lesser snow geese at the McConnell River, N.W.T., in 1973. Notation as in Fig. 5.

the same day, the average duration of a male bout of being alert was 4.8 ± 0.41 seconds, whereas female bouts averaged 2.5 ± 0.30 seconds. This difference was highly significant ($P < 0.001$, two-way analysis of variance) and indicated that males spent nearly twice as much time being alert as did females. If it is assumed that both sexes were equally alert when not feeding, it can be shown that females spent 85 percent of the daylight hours feeding and males spent 74 percent (Harwood 1975:51).

Variations in the rate of pecking (Fig. 6) showed a similar pattern to the variations in the crude protein content of the grazed monocotyledons, with a maximum value in mid-July and little decline in August. Walking rate showed no consistent pattern of variation, the average rate was 24 steps per minute of feeding.

DISCUSSION

The variations in vegetation characteristics recorded at the McConnell River during the summer are similar to those observed at comparable sites in the western Arctic. A quantitatively similar pattern to that shown by the ungrazed vegetation—but with higher overall values—was recorded by Tieszen (1972) for a wet sedge meadow at Barrow, Alaska, where there are no breeding snow geese. Haag (1974) found that the protein content of green vegetation in a sedge meadow at Tuktoyaktuk, N.W.T., showed a peak in mid-July similar to that at the McConnell River. However, he sampled the vegetation only three times during the summer, so the exact location of the peak could not be determined. Chapin et al. (1975), working at Barrow, found a peak in grass and sedge total nitrogen preceding a peak in standing crop. This pattern was similar to that shown by the ungrazed vegetation at the McConnell River, although the Barrow maxima occurred approximately 14 days earlier. Thus the variations in the ungrazed vegetation at the McConnell River seem to be representative of arctic tundra vegetation. Both Haag (1974) and Chapin et al. (1975) suggested that the decline in protein content that they observed in July and August represented the withdrawal of nitrogen and phosphorus to the root and shoot systems in anticipation of leaf senescence. The presence of a high crude protein concentration in the leaves of grazed monocotyledons at the McConnell River throughout August indicated that goose activity probably is maintaining the grazed vegetation in a pre-flowering state, thus prolonging the period of maximum productivity. A similar mechanism was suggested by Vesey-FitzGerald (1960) for the grazing regimes of the East African savannas, although he had no quantitative evidence. Nothing is known about the long-term effects of an annual removal of up to 30 percent of the maximum standing crop of dicotyledons by geese. Kuyken (1969) and Kear (1970) found that intensive grazing by geese in winter had no significant effect on primary productivity in the following spring, but these situations are not strictly comparable to that at the McConnell River. The maximum standing crop of green monocotyledons at the McConnell River was lower in 1973 than in 1971, but this was more likely to have been due to the extremely low rainfall in 1973 than to the long-term effects of goose grazing.

It is probable that in the post-incubatory period adults devote as much time as is physically possible to feeding. Owen (1972) recorded white-fronted geese (*Anser albifrons*) spending more than 90 percent of the daylight hours feeding. However, this was during short winter days when there were no goslings to brood and protect from predators. Even during the summer, when these activities are necessary, female snow geese spent 85 percent of the daylight hours feeding during a 20-hour day. This was made possible by the behavior of the males, who spent nearly twice as much time being alert as the females. The efficacy of this strategy is indicated by the fact that females increased their body weight by 30 percent during July and August, while the weight of males remained constant (Ankney 1974: 166, 174).

Both the length of a feeding bout, and the rate of pecking varied in a regular way with the variation in vegetation standing crop and its crude protein content, respectively. Such variations were predicted from the hypothesis that snow geese should attempt to maximize their protein intake by behavioral variations. It remains to be shown that the recorded variations could maximize protein intake. The pecking rate of snow geese feeding on an experimental pasture consisting of patches of vegetation of different protein contents was positively correlated with the crude protein content of the patch on which they were grazing (Harwood 1975:86). Such behavior serves to maximize the protein intake per unit feeding effort of birds which spend the majority of their time feeding, and which must cover a wide area to do so. The variations in pecking rate recorded at the McConnell River are of the same form as the experimental observations.

The observed variations in bout length are more difficult to interpret. Under experimental conditions, bout length was positively correlated with percentage time spent feeding (Harwood 1975:79, 124). However, because birds at the McConnell River probably were devoting as much time as possible to feeding, no such relationship could have been operating. In addition, intake per unit of feeding effort should have increased with increasing vegetation standing crop. Therefore, it might be anticipated that bout length could decrease as standing crop increased. The results indicate the problem of testing hypotheses with field data, where it is impossible to control extraneous variables. Breeding snow geese should have two priorities: to maximize their daily protein intake, and to ensure the survival of their goslings. Gosling deaths due to predation can be avoided partly by parental alertness. Goslings are most vulnerable to predation during their first three weeks of life. The best protection during this period is provided by those adults which look up frequently while feeding. This inevitably leads to feeding bouts being short. These ideas are supported by the fact that bouts of feeding were longer in early June than they were after hatch in late June (Fig. 5). As goslings become less vulnerable to predation the length of a feeding bout can be safely increased. Longer feeding bouts ensure a more thorough sampling of the available vegetation, and the detection of patches of vegetation of high protein content.

At the McConnell River, snow geese and their goslings have available a food resource that increases in both quantity and quality throughout July and August. The grazing activities of the birds seem to ensure that the protein content of the vegetation remains high during August. Sexual variation in feeding behavior results in a maximum amount of time being available for females to feed. Additional variations in feeding behavior appear to be a compromise between the need to maximize daily protein intake and to maximize the survival of goslings.

LITERATURE CITED

ALTMANN, J. 1974. Observational studies of behavior: sampling methods. Behaviour 49(3–4):227–267.

ANKNEY, C. D. 1974. The importance of nutrient reserves to breeding blue geese, *Anser caerulescens*. Ph.D. Thesis. Univ. of Western Ontario, London. 232pp.

BLISS, L. C. 1971. Arctic and alpine plant life cycles. Ann. Rev. Ecol. Syst. 2:405–438.

CHAPIN, F. S. III, K. VAN CLEEVE, AND L. L. TIESZEN. 1975. Seasonal nutrient dynamics of tundra vegetation at Barrow, Alaska. Arct. Alpine Res. 7(3):209–226.

COOCH, F. G. 1961. Ecological aspects of the blue-snow goose complex. Auk 78(1):72–89.

HAAG, R. W. 1974. Nutrient limitations to plant production in two tundra communities. Can. J. Bot. 52(1):103–116.

HARWOOD, J. 1975. The feeding strategies of blue geese, *Anser caerulescens*. Ph.D. Thesis. Univ. of Western Ontario, London. 186pp.

JOHNSON, M. J. 1941. Isolation and properties of pure yeast polypeptides. J. Biol. Chem. 137(2):575–586.

KEAR, J. 1970. The experimental assessment of goose damage to agricultural crops. Biol. Conserv. 2(3):206–212.

KUYKEN, E. 1969. Grazing of geese on grasslands at Damme, Belgium. Wildfowl 20:47–54.

LIEFF, B. C. 1973. Summer feeding ecology of blue and Canada geese at the McConnell River, N.W.T. Ph.D. Thesis. Univ. of Western Ontario, London. 230pp.

MARRIOTT, R. W. AND D. K. FORBES. 1970. The digestion of lucerne chaff by Cape Barren geese, *Cereopsis novaehollandiae* Latham. Aust. J. Zool. 18(2):257–263.

MATTOCKS, J. G. 1971. Goose feeding and cellulose digestion. Wildfowl 22:107–113.

OWEN, M. 1972. Some factors affecting food intake and selection in white-fronted geese. J. Anim. Ecol. 41(1):79–92.

RUSSELL, R. S. 1940. Physiological and ecological studies on an Arctic vegetation: II. The development of vegetation in relation to nitrogen supply and soil micro-organisms on Jan Mayen Island. J. Ecol. 28(2):269–288.

TIESZEN, L. L. 1972. The seasonal course of above-ground production and chlorophyll distribution in a wet arctic tundra at Barrow, Alaska. Arct. Alpine Res. 4(4):307–324.

VESEY-FITZGERALD, D. F. 1960. Grazing succession among East African game animals. J. Mammal. 41(2):161–172.

WILSON, J. W. 1954. The influence of "midnight sun" conditions on certain diurnal rhythms in *Oxyria digyna*. J. Ecol. 42(1):81–94.

ZISWILER, V., AND D. S. FARNER. 1972. Digestion and the digestive system. Pages 343–430 *in* D. S. Farner and J. R. King, eds. Avian biology. Vol. II. Academic Press, New York. 612pp.

Received 22 March 1976.
Accepted 28 August 1976.

HIERARCHY OF WATERFOWL FEEDING WITH WHISTLING SWANS[1]

ROBERT O. BAILEY[2] and BRUCE D. J. BATT, Delta Waterfowl Research Station, Delta, Manitoba R1N 3A1, Canada

The wasteful feeding habits of swans have recently been described by Owen and Kear (1972). Some earlier authors (Bent 1925:286, Bruette 1930) believed that swans wasted valuable food plants by rooting up more than they consumed. Sherwood (1960) suggested that by exploiting the feeding behavior of swans, other waterfowl are able to obtain food that would normally be unavailable to them. He reported Canada Geese (*Branta canadensis*), Snow Geese (*Chen caerulescens*), Mallards (*Anas platyrhynchos*), Pintails (*A. acuta*), Gadwalls (*A. strepera*), Canvasbacks (*Aythya valisineria*), Redheads (*A. americana*), and Buffleheads (*Bucephala albeola*), regularly feeding with Whistling Swans (*Olor columbianus*), in Utah. In the Chesapeake Bay wintering area, R. E. Munroe (pers. comm.) found Pintails, American Wigeons (*Anas americana*), Black Ducks (*A. rubripes*), Mallards, Gadwalls, Canada Geese, Canvasbacks, Common Goldeneyes (*Bucephala clangula*), Buffleheads, and American Coots (*Fulica americana*) taking advantage of Whistling Swan feeding activities. In Utah, Ryder (1959) noted coots defending a feeding area near the swans from Redheads.

From 30 April to 7 June 1972, we studied Whistling Swans and other waterfowl in feeding and loafing associations on the Delta Marsh in Manitoba. We were particularly interested in the degree of association by different species and the effect of interspecific aggression in determining a hierarchy of the species.

METHODS

Observations were made in a region of potholes, channels, and "borrow pits" on the Delta Marsh, 3 miles west of the village of Delta. This site was easily accessible by elevated dike roads that afforded a clear view without disturbing the birds. Observations were made from a vehicle or on foot, with the aid of a 20× spotting scope or 7 × 35 binoculars. Field notes were recorded on a portable tape recorder or by a helper. Neither swans nor ducks were collected for food examination, but presumably the swans were feeding on *Potamogeton* sp. common to the area. This food plant is highly rated as swan food by Owen and Kear (1972). The ducks were obviously feeding on material stirred up by the swans.

RESULTS

Ducks were seen associating with swans 33 times during the study period. Flock size varied from 1 to 53 swans attended by 2 to 136 ducks. Generally larger groups of swans attracted higher numbers of ducks.

Level of Association.—Three significantly different ($P < 0.01$) levels of association were noted for the species of ducks common to the area at this time of year (Table 1). Group 1 species most readily accompanied swans during feeding and loafing periods. Group 2 showed more variation. For example Blue-winged

---

[1] Originally published in Auk 91(3):488–493, 1974.

[2] Address correspondence to this author. Present address: Department of Wildlife, MacDonald College, St. Anne de Bell, Quebec H9X 1C0, Canada.

Table 1. Relative occurrence of ducks in feeding association with Whistling Swans.

Level 1		Level 2		Level 3	
Species	% occurrence[1]	Species	% occurrence	Species	% occurrence
Canvasback	63	Mallard	18	Northern Shoveler	0
Redhead	66	Pintail	36	American Green-winged Teal	0
Gadwall	81	Blue-winged Teal	36	Ruddy Duck	0
American Wigeon	72				
Lesser Scaup	75				

[1] Calculated from the number of times a species occurred in 33 associations.

Teals (*Anas discors*) loafed with swans but seldom participated in feeding activities. Group 3 did not associate although they were common in the immediate vicinity. Shorebirds and other water birds such as grebes did not join these feeding groups.

Windblown floating food material formed a feeding zone around the swans. This zone extended approximately 5 m downwind in the form of a "V." Floating food was most plentiful directly behind individual swans and competition for this position was intense among the ducks.

Rank in the Hierarchy.—We recorded the outcome of all aggressive encounters in the feeding zone. These consisted of threats and chases across the top of the water with one bird usually retreating from the other. The dominant species commanded a position nearest the feeding swan. Other species were spaced according to their rank in the hierarchy. Table 2 shows the rank of each species as determined by the relative numbers of successful chases in the feeding zone.

Canvasbacks and Mallards consistently occupied the best position. They had the most successful encounters and fewest submissions of all species studied. Canvasbacks were particularly intolerant of intruders, dividing their time equally between chasing and pecking for food. Mallards, when present, were the only species exempt of Canvasback aggression.

The Redhead ranked second in the hierarchy. Redheads chased all other species except Mallards and Blue-winged Teals. Occasionally Redheads chased Canvasbacks but Canvasbacks won significantly more ($P < 0.01$) interactions between these two species.

Pintails placed third in the hierarchy as they chased only Gadwalls, wigeons, and Lesser Scaups (*Aythya affinis*), but submitted to the three higher ranking species. During one study period a male Pintail responded aggressively to a threat issued by a male Mallard in the feeding zone. In the fight that followed the Mallard drove the Pintail from the feeding ground.

Gadwalls were fourth in the hierarchy. They chased wigeons and scaups but submitted to higher ranking species. We also watched a fight between a male Gadwall and a male Pintail in the feeding zone, in which case the Pintail successfully drove off the Gadwall.

We recorded 44 encounters between wigeons and Gadwalls in the feeding zone. Gadwalls were significantly ($P < 0.05$) more successful in these bouts. Wigeons rarely chased any other species but, because of their unique feeding behavior, they were frequently chased by higher ranking birds.

Table 2. Hierarchy of species feeding in association with Whistling Swans.[1]

Species submitting[2]	Species chasing							
	Canvasback	Mallard	Redhead	Pintail	Gadwall	American Wigeon	Lesser Scaup	Blue-winged Teal
Canvasback	21[3]	—	3	—	—	—	—	—
Mallard	—	—	—	—	—	—	—	—
Redhead	15	—	3	—	—	—	—	—
Pintail	5	1	1	3	—	1	—	—
Gadwall	4	4	2	7	6	15	—	—
American Wigeon	10	6	5	6	29	23	1	—
Lesser Scaup	10	—	15	4	2	2	—	—
Blue-winged Teal	—	3	—	—	—	1	—	—

[1] Determined from the number of successful aggressive encounters in the feeding zone.
[2] Listed in order of rank in the hierarchy.
[3] The number of aggressive encounters observed in 33 observation periods.

Lesser Scaups placed sixth in the hierarchy because they were chased by almost all higher ranking species. Only one successful chase was recorded for scaup. This encounter was between a male scaup and a male wigeon.

Blue-winged Teals avoided encounters with other ducks. They occupied a position in the feeding zone farthest away from the swans.

The most aggressive species were not necessarily highest ranking in the hierarchy. Ranking the species according to the number of aggressive gestures made, the order is as follows: Canvasback, Gadwall, Redhead, American Wigeon, Pintail, Mallard, Lesser Scaup, Blue-winged Teal. Females of all species were significantly less aggressive than were the males.

Canada and Snow Geese have been reported feeding in association with swans (Sherwood 1960). On seven occasions during our study, one to three Canada Geese joined a feeding group. The swans paid little attention to the geese, but the ducks avoided them. Geese immediately assumed the best position behind the swans and pecked for food. The geese could have fed independently of the swans but preferred not to in each case.

Swans were remarkably tolerant of ducks crowding around them. No aggressive encounters were recorded between swans and any other waterfowl, but sudden movement by a swan made ducks and geese retreat.

A Spearman rank correlation with adult male body weights (Kortright 1942:383) yielded a coefficient of 0.97 ($P < 0.01$) with the heaviest species assuming the highest position in the hierarchy. Evidently dominance in the hierarchy is determined to a great measure by body size.

Feeding Behavior.—Keen competition for food maintained a high level of excitement among the birds participating in the feeding association. Each species demonstrated a unique method of exploiting the feeding situation. The wigeon was the most opportunistic. This alert duck patroled the feeding zone, actively searching the surface for food and darting close to the swan where it was frequently chased away by larger birds. Wigeons did not steal food directly from Canvasbacks as noted by Bent (1923:195), nor did they attempt this behavior with the swans or other ducks.

Pintails and Gadwalls hunted the surface in a manner similar to the wigeons, but at a slower pace. Blue-winged Teals remained entirely at the feeding zone perimeter. These small ducks seemed to exhibit considerable caution when approaching the feeding zone.

Typically the swans fed in water too deep for dabbling ducks. None of the five dabbler species "tipped up" or otherwise probed for food while feeding with the swans. The ducks pecked at floating food objects dislodged from the bottom. Canvasbacks and Redheads also pecked for food although they were capable of diving to the bottom. When feeding with swans these two species dived half as frequently as when feeding alone. Lesser Scaups preferred to dive directly under feeding swans rather than peck for food at the surface.

Frequently, birds crowded so close to a "tipped up" swan that the big bird landed on them while righting itself. Lesser Scaups often dived as soon as the swan submerged its head. This resulted in an occasional underwater collision and the startled swan would rapidly lift its head.

Loafing Behavior.—Loafing situations differed from feeding associations in that interspecific aggression was negligible. The ducks appeared randomly spaced about the swans on loafing bars and intermingled regardless of their position in the hierarchy.

Ducks showed a definite preference to loaf with swans rather than on other suitable sites in the same water body. When the swans loafed in water too deep for ducks to stand, the ducks used the nearest shoreline or mudbar.

During some observation periods, opportunity was available to watch a group of ducks and swans feeding and a group loafing simultaneously. Ducks moved freely between each group. Each instance of exchange illustrated an interesting change in the birds' behavior. Ducks coming from the feeding group lost their aggressiveness and loafed peacefully among other birds. Ducks leaving the loafing site became intolerant of others once in the feeding zone.

DISCUSSION

Swans did not appear to benefit from associations with ducks. Swans attracted ducks from the vicinity but there was little evidence that they were drawn to water bodies occupied by other waterfowl. Advantages of this behavior are more apparent for the ducks. Primarily the swans provide a readily gathered source of food. This increases the efficiency of the ducks' feeding patterns and may be of particular importance during the early season when low temperatures occur and food is probably not plentiful.

The advantages for ducks loafing with swans are not clear. Swans may be more efficient sentinels. We believe the ducks are waiting for the swans to feed so they can take immediate advantage of the food.

The stage in the reproductive cycle of each species may have influenced the level of association. All highly associated species (group 1) were at the prenesting stage. High energy requirements at this time may have been satisfied more efficiently by feeding with swans.

With the exception of the Blue-winged Teal, group 2 species were actively involved with nesting duties during the observation period. Birds bounded to certain areas at this time are less apt to participate in associations. Nesting waterfowl are not generally gregarious during nest initiation and laying (McKinney 1965). This may account for the total lack of participation by the Northern Shoveler (*Anas clypeata*) as our observation period corresponded with the shoveler's nesting cycle. During most of the nesting season, the shoveler is a highly aggressive bird (McKinney 1970).

We believe interspecific dominance in the feeding zone is dependent upon mean body weight of each species. Our observations were limited to species common to the Delta Marsh in the spring. As other species of ducks are known to associate with swans, we suggest they would rank in the hierarchy primarily according to their body weights.

ACKNOWLEDGMENTS

We thank Robert E. Jones for making suggestions on this manuscript. The data reported here were collected while both of us were being supported by the North American Wildlife Foundation through the Delta Waterfowl Research Station, Manitoba, Canada. The senior author was also supported by a grant from the National Research Council of Canada.

LITERATURE CITED

BENT, A. C. 1923. Life histories of North American wild fowl. U.S. Natl. Mus. Bull. 126.

———. 1925. Life histories of North American wild fowl. U.S. Natl. Mus. Bull. 130.

BRUETTE, W. 1930. American duck, goose and brant shooting. New York, Charles Scribners and Sons.

KORTRIGHT, F. H. 1942. The ducks, geese and swans of North America. Washington, D.C., Amer. Wildl. Inst.

MCKINNEY, F. 1965. Spacing and chasing in breeding ducks. Wildfowl Trust Ann. Rept. 16:92–106.

———. 1970. Displays of four species of blue-winged ducks. Living Bird 19:29–64.

OWEN, M., AND J. KEAR. 1972. Food and feeding habits. Pp. 57–77 *in* The swans, P. Scott, ed. London, Fletcher & Son Ltd.

RYDER, R. A. 1959. Interspecific intolerance of the American Coot in Utah. Auk 76:424–442.

SHERWOOD, G. A. 1960. The Whistling Swan in the west with particular reference to Great Salt Lake Valley, Utah. Condor 62:370–377.

FEEDING ECOLOGY OF PINTAIL, GADWALL, AMERICAN WIDGEON AND LESSER SCAUP DUCKLINGS IN SOUTHERN ALBERTA[1]

LAWSON G. SUGDEN,[2] Canadian Wildlife Service, Saskatoon, Saskatchewan, Canada

Abstract: Objectives were to determine the diet of flightless young Pintails (*Anas acuta*), Gadwalls (*A. strepera*), American Widgeons (*Mareca americana*) and Lesser Scaups (*Aythya affinis*); investigate factors which influence food use; and determine nutritional composition of duck foods. Diet was determined from dry weight of esophagus-proventriculus contents from 144 Pintails, 167 Gadwalls, 129 Widgeons and 135 Scaups.

Up to 5 days, Pintails ate mostly insects captured on the water surface. Older ducklings ate aquatic invertebrates and plants. Pintails ate a variety of invertebrates; gastropods, chironomid larvae and cladocerans were most important. Diet during the prefledgling period contained 33 per cent plants, chiefly seeds of Gramineae and Cyperaceae.

Gadwalls first ate chiefly surface invertebrates. As they grew, they ate proportionately more aquatic invertebrates and plants, and by 3 weeks, were essentially herbivorous. Most important animal foods were chironomid larvae and adults, corixids, coleopterans and cladocerans. The prefledgling diet comprised 90 percent plants, the most important being leaves of *Potamogeton pusillus*, Cladophoraceae and *Lemna minor*.

Prefledgling Widgeons ate 89 per cent plant food. Despite similar diets, feeding methods, feeding habitat and seasons of use, Widgeons and Gadwalls had sufficient food and did not compete.

Young Scaups ate 96 per cent invertebrates of which amphipods, chironomid larvae and gastropods contributed 52, 16 and 16 per cent, respectively. As they grew, Scaups ate relatively more amphipods and fewer bottom larvae, because broods moved to larger ponds where amphipods were more prevalent.

Changes in methods and sites used by dabbling ducklings paralleled and confirmed diet changes. Diet data indicated that extensive surface feeding observed in newly-hatched Scaups was inefficient compared with diving for food. Feeding Pintails favoured the shallows near shore, Gadwalls and Widgeons fed mostly over submersed plants and Scaups preferred deeper water.

A comparison of food available with food eaten showed ducklings ate the most available invertebrates, considering the ducks' characteristic feeding adaptations. Gastropods were an exception and though often available, were seldom eaten. Use of plants was determined more by preference. Ducks sought a mixed diet and this may be related to selection of foods which provided a nutritionally balanced diet. Few of 21 duck foods analysed would provide the nutrient requirements of ducklings in adequate proportions. Chironomid larve, *Gammarus* and corixids contained the highest quality protein in terms of amino acid requirements of chicks.

The prairies and parklands of southern Canada are dotted with millions of water areas where more than half the continent's waterfowl are produced. To the casual observer the myriad of wetlands might seem unlimited but this is not so. Each year some wetlands are permanently lost through man's activities. As wetlands are eliminated from the landscape, ducks also disappear. If we wish to maintain duck populations at present-day levels, then we must learn to produce several ducks where one is now produced.

A detailed understanding of wetlands and how ducks use them is needed to do this. Ducks require food, water, cover and space to reproduce successfully. My objectives dealt with food of ducklings, an aspect that had been neglected until recent years. I studied the Pintail, Gadwall, American Widgeon and Lesser Scaup and have shown how the diet of each species changes as they grow and how these changes are related to shifts in

[1] Originally published in Can. Wildl. Serv. Rep. Ser. No. 24. Ottawa, 43pp., 1973. Reproduced by permission of the Minister of Supply and Services Canada.

[2] Present address: Mig. Bird Res. Ctr., U. of SK CMPS, 115 Perimeter Road, Saskatoon, Saskatchewan S7N 0X4, Canada.

feeding methods and habitat use. These features also differ among species. A diverse habitat will produce the greatest variety and probably the greatest number of ducks.

An understanding of the food requirements of any wildlife species is basic to its management and the need for such knowledge grows as management becomes more intensive. As hunting regulations suggest, the supply of North American waterfowl no longer exceeds demand. Increased demand helped to create this situation, but loss of habitat is potentially more serious. Various authors in *Waterfowl Tomorrow* (Linduska 1964) stressed the need not only to preserve existing waterfowl habitat but also to make it more productive. Despite programs to create and preserve wetlands, the number dwindles because of competing land uses. To maintain waterfowl populations similar to those of the 1960's, future management must involve habitat manipulation, and this must be based on a knowledge of each species' requirements. One major requirement is food for growing young. What does each species eat? How do diets change with age of ducks? How adaptable is each species to changes in available food? How much energy in the various foods is available to ducks? What kinds of ponds produce adequate food? Answers to such questions will provide guidelines for improved habitat acquisition and development.

Waterfowl biologists do not know enough about diets of ducks, particularly flightless young. There are numerous brief accounts of foods eaten by ducklings, but many are of doubtful value because they include results based on small samples and on gizzard material which causes serious bias (Dillon 1959, Perret 1962). Only four significant studies of duckling diets have been reported. Chura (1961) discussed foods found in esophagus-proventriculus-gizzard samples from 94 young Mallards (*Anas platyrhynchos*) collected at Bear River Refuge, Utah. The sample included ducklings less than 1 week old through to flying age. Immediately after hatching, the birds ate chiefly terrestrial insects but took more aquatic invertebrates and plant food as they grew. After 18 days, they ate few terrestrial insects. The proportion of plant foods continued to increase until, at flying age, the ducklings were eating almost 100 per cent plants. The change in diet was accompanied by a change in feeding methods.

Perret (1962) analysed esophagus-proventriculus contents of 62 young Mallards collected during 3 years near Minnedosa, Manitoba. There, invertebrates dominated the diets of all ages of flightless young and animal foods made up 91 per cent of the total diet. Flying young ate significantly more plant food, principally grain. Perret (1962) measured availability of foods and concluded that, to a large extent, Mallards ate those most available.

Esophageal contents of 86 young Canvasbacks (*Aythya valisineria*), 37 Redheads (*A. americana*) and 25 Lesser Scaups (*A. affinis*) from southwestern Manitoba were reported by Bartonek and Hickey (1969*a*). Canvasbacks ate larger proportions of plant food as they grew. Canvasbacks and Redheads tended to select bottom fauna, whereas amphipods were most important for Scaups. Bartonek and Hickey (1969*b*) studied selective feeding by the same sample of juvenile Canvasbacks and Redheads.

Bartonek and Murdy (1970) analysed esophageal contents of 38 flightless young Lesser Scaups collected near Yellowknife, Northwest Territories. The ducks had eaten almost 100 per cent invertebrates. In late July and early August they had eaten mostly Culicidae larvae and pupae, and Conchostraca. Amphipods, odonate naiads and corixids were the most important items eaten by Scaups collected in early September. The authors suggested that the difference in diets may reflect a tendency for older ducklings to feed at greater depths.

My study, carried out from 1963 through 1967, involves four species: Pintail (*Anas acuta*), Gadwall (*A. strepera*), American Widgeon (*Mareca americana*) and Lesser Scaup. Objectives were to determine the diet of the four species from hatching to flying; to investigate factors which influence food selection and to determine nutritional composition of natural foods.

The four species were chosen for several reasons. All are relatively common on the prairie breeding grounds and are important game ducks in terms of numbers shot. Little was known about their food habits. The four species often use different parts of the same ponds. Pintails prefer the shallow edges; Gadwalls and Widgeons are intermediate and are seen more often away from the shore; Scaups, being diving ducks, favour the deeper areas. Thus the four are a good combination for comparative study.

STUDY AREA

The study area is a north-south rectangle about 10 by 22 miles (16 by 35 km) surrounding Strathmore, Alberta (51°02′N, 113°23′W). The block coincides with the main part of the Western Irrigation District. Elevation at Strathmore is 3,192 feet (972.9 m) above sea level.

The area lies within the Dark Brown Soil Zone (Wyatt et al. 1942). Soils vary from sandy to light loam in texture. Topography is undulating to gently rolling. According to Moss (1944, 1955) vegetation of the region is characterized by a *Stipa-Bouteloua* climax association. However, Coupland (1961) stated that the grassland of the Dark Brown Soil Zone is of the Mixed Prairie Association dominated by a *Stipa-Agropyron* Faciation. Probably no part of the area has been undisturbed. Poston (1969) gave percentages of 1966 land use on a 2,726-acre (1,103-hectare) block within my study area as: pasture 66, grain 14, alfalfa 9, summer-fallow 2, roads and farmyards 2, brush and trees 2 and water 5 per cent. For the entire study area, I estimate there was 5 to 10 percent more acreage in grain and correspondingly less in pasture.

Annual precipitation averages about 15 inches (38 cm). Using 29°F (−1.7°C) as the limit of a killing frost, Wyatt et al. (1942) reported that the area averaged about 115 frost-free days.

Water areas ranged in size from less than 1 acre (0.4 ha) to 2,880 acres (1,165 ha). Approximately 20 exceeded 50 acres (20 ha). The number of water areas fluctuated from year to year and usually water levels and pond numbers declined throughout summer. Most water areas drying up each summer were under 1 acre (0.4 ha) in size. George Freeman, Ducks Unlimited (pers. comm.) collected water area data each year from a 25-mile (40.2-km), east-west transect bisecting my study area and sampling 6.25 sq miles (16.19 km^2). During the 5-year period, the density of mid May water areas averaged 9.8 ± 1.5 (SE) per sq mile (3.8/km^2). The mid July average was 8.4 ± 1.2 water areas per sq mile (3.2/km^2). Ducks Unlimited (Canada) had modified several of the permanent lakes and recharged them with irrigation water each summer. The ponds seldom exceeded 48 inches (1.2 m) in depth. Mean maximum depth in July and August of 50 water areas used for

Table 1. Percentage occurrence of plants on 52 water areas used for collecting ducks.

Item	Percent occurrence
Cladophoraceae	48
Characeae *Chara* sp.	2
Musci	6
Equisetaceae *Equisetum arvense* L.	2
Typhaceae *Typha latifolia* L.	13
Sparganiaceae *Sparganium eurycarpum* Engelm.	8
Zosteraceae	
Potamogeton vaginatus Turcz.	8
P. pectinatus L.	73
P. pusillus L.	63
P. gramineus L.	2
P. Richardsonii (Ar. Benn.) Rydb.	21
Zannichellia palustris L.	6
Juncaginaceae *Triglochin maritima* L.	25
Alismataceae *Sagittaria* sp.	10
Hydrocharitaceae *Elodea canadensis* Michx.	6
Gramineae	
Puccinellia Nuttalliana (Schultes) Hitchc.	40
Glyceria grandis S. Wats.	31
Scolochloa festucacea (Willd.) Link	2
Distichlis stricta (Torr.) Rydb.	38
Hordeum jubatum L.	79
Calamagrostis canadensis (Michx.) Nutt.	15
Alopecurus aequalis Sobol.	11
Spartina gracilis Trin.*	2
Beckmannia syzigachne (Steud.) Fern.	36
Cyperaceae	
Eleocharis acicularis (L.) R. & S.	8
E. macrostachya Britt.	79
Scirpus americanus Pers.	38
S. validus Vahl.	35
S. paludosus Nels.	13
Carex spp.	75
Lemnaceae	
Lemna trisulca L.	13
L. minor L.	36
Juncaceae	
Juncus tenuis Willd.	2
J. balticus Willd.	60
Polygonaceae	
Rumex spp.	29
Polygonum spp.	29
Ceratophyllaceae	
Ceratophyllum demersum L.	10
Ranunculaceae	
Ranunculus subrigidus W. B. Drew	15
R. Cymbalaria Pursh	23
R. Gmelini DC.	2
Haloragaceae *Myriophyllum exalbescens* Fern.	71
Hippuridaceae *Hippuris vulgaris* L.	13
Umbelliferae *Sium suave* Walt.	13
Labiatae *Mentha arvensis* L.	10

* Specific name from Hitchcock (1950).

duck collections was 23 inches (0.58 m) with a range of 8–54 inches (0.2–1.4 m). Average mean depth was 16 inches (0.4 m) with a range of 5–45 inches (0.13–1.14 m).

Type and abundance of vegetation varied widely among the water areas. Table 1 shows the per cent occurrence of plants on 52 water areas used for duck collections. None of the areas sampled was without some emergent and submersed plants. Trees were restricted to irrigation ditches and canals and farm windbreaks. Common trees along the watercourses were poplars (*Populus* spp.) and willows (*Salix* spp.). A variety of grasses and forbs grew on pastures. Commonest shrubs were wolfberry (*Symphoricarpos occidentalis*), silverberry (*Elaeagnus commutata*) and common rose (*Rosa Woodsii*). I placed specimens of plants collected on the study area in the CWS Herbarium, Saskatoon, and the Intermountain Herbarium, Utah State University, Logan.

METHODS AND MATERIALS

Nomenclature and Definitions

Nomenclature for vascular plants follows Fernald (1950). I have followed the common usage of the term "seed" as it usually includes the entire fruit of a plant. Borror and DeLong (1964) was used for Insecta and Pennak (1953) for other invertebrates. Names of birds are taken from American Ornithologists' Union (1957).

Some definitions of terms used here are needed because of the vast array of ecological terms referring to aquatic organisms and their habitats. I distinguish among three groups of invertebrates depending on where they are usually taken by feeding ducks. Bottom fauna are those associated with the bottom mud and the solid-liquid interface. Planktonic invertebrates are those occurring in the free water whether or not plants are present. Collectively, bottom fauna and planktonic invertebrates make up aquatic invertebrates. Surface invertebrates are those forms not normally occurring below the water surface and include terrestrial forms. When measuring proportions of aquatic and surface invertebrates eaten by ducks, I arbitrarily divided unidentified animal material proportionately between the two. The calculated proportion of invertebrates taken from the surface represents minimum figures because many aquatic forms such as Corixidae, Culicidae larvae and Dytiscidae are sometimes captured at the surface. Amphipods are often associated with bottom fauna. In this study I consider them plankton or, more properly, nektoplankton which are motile plankton (Hutchinson 1967). They regularly occurred throughout the entire planktonic zone. Hutchinson (1967:696) cited studies which showed that *Gammarus pulex* lived as nektoplankton in closed Tibetan lakes which lacked fish.

I have departed from an apparent tradition by not including Trichoptera larval cases in the analysis. Some cases may contribute a minor amount of food but most are valueless. By eliminating cases, the weight of Trichoptera included is more realistic. The exclusion of cases makes a greater difference when the food is measured by weight rather than by volume because of the high specific gravity of much case material. In a sample of 159 Leptoceridae, larvae made up 20 per cent of the combined dry weight of larvae and cases. All these cases appeared to be made of fine sand.

Food of Ducklings

Collection and Treatment of Material.—We collected ducks for food study on the study area from 1963 through 1967. Most were shot and the rest were captured on land by a retriever dog. A usable specimen was one that contained at least 1 mg dry weight of food in the combined esophagus and proventriculus. In the first year most ducks were taken in early morning or evening, but enough were collected during midday to demonstrate a diurnal feeding pattern as reported by Chura (1963). The proportion of specimens with food (37 per cent) was significantly ($P < 0.01$) lower in those taken between 7:00 A.M. and 7:00 P.M. After 1963, no midday collections were made. Near the end of the study, as samples increased in number, we noted that a higher proportion of usable specimens were collected in evening than in morning (88 vs. 76 per cent; $P < 0.01$). The best evening collections were made at dusk on clear warm days. Ducks fed more throughout cool and overcast days and their activity did not peak at dusk, except on calm evenings preceded by wind and rain. After such storms considerable feeding activity was evident.

To ensure the highest possible proportion of usable specimens, I tried to collect only feeding ducks. Although this method increases the number of usable ducks, it does not guarantee food above the gizzard. I tried to restrict each collection to two to four ducklings. Sometimes one duck, collected and examined immediately was not usable, so I took no further specimens. Generally, if one contained nothing, other members of the brood would be the same. Because the study involved a comparison of food used by four species, we collected more than one species at the same time and place when possible. Certain ponds proved more productive than others. Collections on these were restricted so that no pond contributed more than one-half of any species' plumage class, as defined by Gollop and Marshall (1954).

To eliminate post-mortem digestion that may take place in the digestive tract (Koersveld 1951, Dillery 1965), we injected about 50 drops of 10 per cent formaldehyde into the gullet with a rubber-tipped syringe within 10 minutes of the kill. Usually within 1 hour specimens were refrigerated or the digestive tracts were removed and frozen.

Specimens were weighed on a triple-beam balance and aged according to plumage classes (Gollop and Marshall 1954). Lengths of culmen and tarsus were measured to the nearest millimeter (Dzubin 1959). Although plumage classes were used as a guide to age of ducklings while collecting, they were not used in the final analysis because the time intervals[3] for each class vary among species, making quantitative comparisons difficult. Moreover, I found that I tended to overage specimens in the hand when using the technique which was developed for field observations. I used age categories based on weight as shown in Tables 2 to 5. The age-weight data are based on estimated growth curves. The Gadwall curve was derived from six ducks raised from hatching to flying in an outside pen. The results agreed well with weights of wild Gadwalls of comparable plumage classes and were similar to those of Oring (1968) who presented data for a small number of hatchery-raised Gadwalls. I obtained the age-weight figures for Pintails and Widgeons from growth curves based on weight at hatching (Smart 1965), mean weight of Class III ducks collected during the study and the assumption that the growth pattern is similar to that of Gadwalls. The Lesser Scaup growth curve was derived from average weights of 13 ducks reared in the outside pen. Comparisions with weights and plumages of wild Scaups indicated similar growth rates. I collected flying young only in Pintails and assigned these to the oldest age group regardless of weight. To calculate the composition of the prefledgling diet, I assumed 50 days represented the flightless period for the four species.

In the laboratory, contents of esophagi and proventriculi were sorted separately[4] into weighing pans, identified, oven-dried for 12 to 18 hours at 80°C and weighed to the nearest 0.1 mg on a Type H4 Mettler balance. Grit was not included. Because of bias caused by different rates of digestion of different foods in the gizzard (Dillon 1959, Perret 1962), gizzard material was not used. James Bartonek (pers. comm.) believed that similar bias could result from use of proventriculus material and for that reason I tabulated data for esophagus and proventriculus contents separately and compared them with results for combined samples.

Sample Size.—Davison (1940) and Hanson and Graybill (1956) have discussed methods for determining sample size in food habit studies. As in most waterfowl diet studies, practical considerations rather than statistical requirements dictated sample sizes in this study. After

[3] Gollop and Marshall (1954). See Tables 15, 17, 18, 19 of this report for age ranges of Pintails, Gadwalls, American Widgeons, Lesser Scaups in each plumage class.

[4] In 1963, contents of esophagi and proventriculi were not separated.

Table 2. Pintail data. By age group for weights; numbers of specimens, collections and collecting sites; animal and plant food dry weights; and the largest percentage contribution of one collection to each food type. (The number of specimens in each collection is shown in parentheses.)

	Age, days							Totals
	0–5	6–10	11–15	16–20	21–30	31–40	41+	
Weight, g	to 50	51–120	121–220	221–350	351–560	561–670	671+	
Usable specimens	10	25	18	14	38	14	25	144
Collections	5	14	10	12	23	12	18	77
Different sites	5	14	9	12	19	9	17	54
Total animal food, g	0.894	3.529	4.345	1.984	9.693	8.881	13.518	42.844
Total plant food, g	0.020	0.132	0.407	0.447	15.383	0.834	13.321	30.544
Avg wt of total food, g/duck	0.091	0.146	0.264	0.174	0.660	0.694	1.074	0.510
Range in food wt, g/duck	0.002–0.297	0.002–1.175	0.024–0.926	0.011–0.659	0.011–2.118	0.001–7.547	0.003–10.214	0.001–10.214
Largest % contribution of one collection:								
Animal food	33 (1)	55 (3)	39 (2)	31 (1)	21 (1)	79 (1)	72 (1)	39 (2)
Plant food	*	30 (1)	57 (3)	49 (2)	66 (3)	64 (1)	86 (2)	37 (2)
Total food	32 (1)	54 (3)	38 (2)	27 (1)	49 (3)	78 (1)	52 (2)	24 (2)

* Insufficient material.

Table 3. Gadwall data. By age group for weights; numbers of specimens, collections and collecting sites; animal and plant food dry weights; and the largest percentage contribution of one collection to each food type. (The number of specimens in each collection is shown in parentheses.)

	Age, days							Totals
	0–5*	6–10	11–15	16–20	21–30	31–40	41+	
Weight, g	to 45	46–100	101–165	166–280	281–510	511–650	651+	
Usable specimens	22	32	35	31	15	14	18	167
Collections	11	16	14	12	8	8	9	60
Different sites	8	14	10	10	8	8	9	32
Total animal food, g	0.445	0.878	2.010	0.967	0.050	0.303	0.066	4,719
Total plant food, g	0.027	0.631	0.839	3.652	2.279	6.131	7.372	20.931
Avg wt of total food, g/duck	0.021	0.047	0.081	0.149	0.155	0.460	0.413	0.154
Range in food wt, g/duck	0.001–0.086	0.001–0.253	0.001–0.589	0.001–0.496	0.007–0.591	0.009–1.345	0.002–1.547	0.001–1.547
Largest % contribution of one collection:								
Animal food	27 (3)	48 (4)	78 (4)	49 (3)	†	94 (3)	†	32 (4)
Plant food	†	61 (2)	35 (4)	45 (7)	57 (3)	44 (3)	21 (1)	13 (2)
Total food	26 (3)	28 (2)	65 (4)	36 (7)	56 (3)	56 (3)	21 (1)	12 (3)

* Weight of 0- to 3-day-old ducks estimated to 33 g; 4- to 5-day-old ducks, 34 to 45 g.
† Insufficient material.

Table 4. American Widgeon data. By age group for weights; numbers of specimens, collections and collecting sites; animal and plant food dry weights; and the largest percentage contribution of one collection to each food type. (The number of specimens in each collection is shown in parentheses.)

	Age, days							
	0–5	6–10	11–15	16–20	21–30	31–40	41+	Totals
Weight, g	to 44	45–90	91–150	151–255	256–460	461–590	591+	
Usable specimens	8	29	13	12	20	25	22	129
Collections	3	16	8	7	9	15	14	58
Different sites	3	11	8	6	8	14	14	38
Total animal food, g	0.780	2.392	0.965	0.083	0.043	0.065	0.156	4.484
Total plant food, g	0.005	0.065	0.114	1.541	2.301	4.787	3.210	12.023
Avg wt of total food, g/duck	0.098	0.085	0.083	0.135	0.117	0.194	0.153	0.128
Range in food wt, g/duck	0.047–0.216	0.001–0.373	0.005–0.239	0.010–0.371	0.004–0.497	0.003–0.779	0.001–0.908	0.001–0.908
Largest % contribution of one collection:								
Animal food	51 (3)	26 (2)	41 (2)	*	*	*	94 (3)	14 (2)
Plant food	*	*	47 (1)	54 (3)	29 (4)	32 (3)	57 (3)	21 (4)
Total food	51 (3)	26 (2)	37 (2)	54 (3)	29 (4)	32 (3)	54 (3)	15 (4)

* Insufficient material.

Table 5. Lesser Scaup data. By age group for weights; numbers of specimens, collections and collecting sites; animal and plant food dry weights; and the largest percentage contribution of one collection. (The number of specimens in each collection is shown in parentheses.)

	Age, days							
	0–5	6–10	11–15	16–20	21–30	31–40	41+	Totals
Weight, g	to 45	46–90	91–150	151–230	231–395	396–535	536+	
Usable specimens	19	22	15	16	24	23	16	135
Collections	7	10	9	9	12	15	11	45
Different sites	7	10	7	7	11	10	7	24
Total animal food, g	0.716	1.059	1.092	4.085	4.760	13.786	7.198	32.696
Total plant food, g	0.004	0.006	0.017	0.008	0.439	0.228	0.409	1.111
Avg wt of total food, g/duck	0.038	0.048	0.074	0.256	0.217	0.609	0.475	0.250
Range in food wt, g/duck	0.01–0.151	0.002–0.195	0.002–0.567	0.001–0.621	0.005–2.459	0.005–3.155	0.003–1.361	0.001–3.155
Largest % contribution of one collection:								
Animal food	57 (3)	45 (3)	52 (1)	49 (4)	52 (1)	48 (3)	35 (3)	20 (3)
Plant food	*	*	*	*	79 (3)	51 (1)	56 (2)	42 (4)
Total food	57 (3)	45 (3)	51 (1)	49 (4)	47 (1)	42 (1)	33 (3)	19 (3)

* Insufficient material.

the first season it was apparent that amounts and composition of food recovered from ducks were so variable that one would have to make serious inroads upon the duck population of the study area to satisfy acceptable statistical standards. Probably no species' population on the area could sustain the rate of collection needed to obtain an adequate sample in 5 years. Thus, for each species, I set an arbitrary objective of a minimum of 10 ducks, each with at least 10 mg dry weight of food, for each of the seven plumage classes (Gollop and Marshall 1954). These would be in addition to usable specimens containing less than 10 mg. At the other extreme, an arbitrary objective was set to collect enough birds so that no collection contributed more than 35 per cent of the total food weight in any plumage class. More often than not, this objective was not met.

Samples meeting the above quota would permit, among the various plumage classes, such comparisons as plant vs. animal foods, surface invertebrates vs. aquatic invertebrates, etc.

Expression of Results.—Hartley (1948) and Bartonek (1968) have reviewed methods for measuring diet composition. Because moisture in duck foods varies widely—from about 10 to 90 per cent—I chose to oven-dry and weigh them and express results as percentage of dry weight. This also facilitated conversion of data into terms of gross energy. I also calculated percentage of occurrence of each food item because, in combination with weight data, this method can reveal bias caused by inadequate samples. It may also show which items are eaten regularly but incidentally to more important foods. Although not considered a problem here, differential digestion rates of foods influence percentage of occurrence data less than volumetric or gravimetric data. For comparative purposes, diet composition is also expressed in terms of percentage of calorific (gross) energy contributed by each food. Calorific values were obtained for the more important foods in connection with nutritional analyses. Values for other items were taken from averages compiled by Cummins and Wuycheck (1971). Ideally, the relative importance of different foods would best be expressed in terms of metabolizable energy contributed. However, reliable

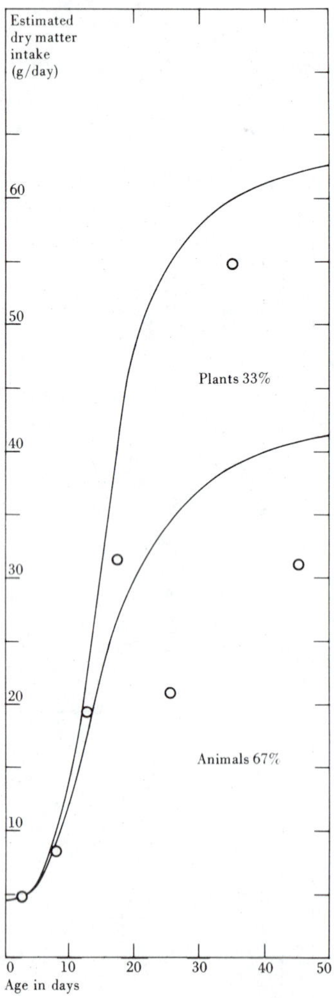

Fig. 1. Changes in plant and animal food intake by young Pintails.

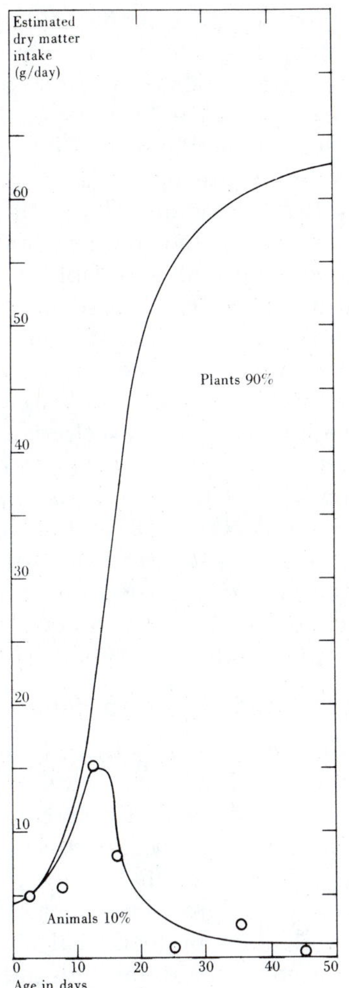

Fig. 2. Changes in plant and animal food intake by young Gadwalls.

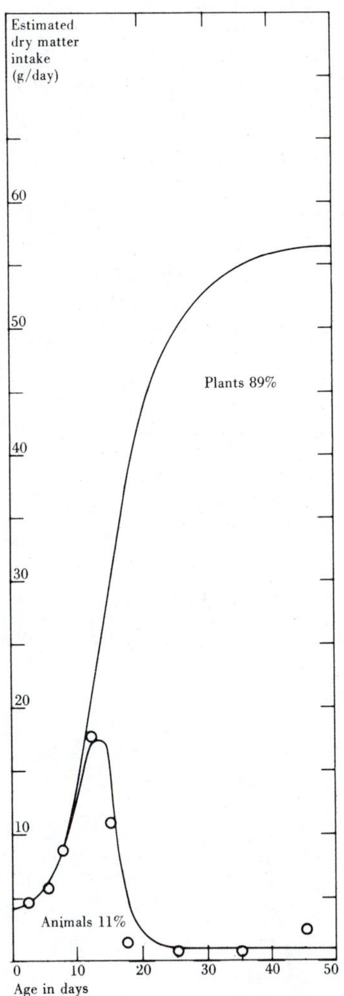

Fig. 3. Changes in plant and animal food intake by young American Widgeons.

values for wild waterfowl foods are not available.

I calculated the composition of the prefledgling diet by weighting the percentage of weight data according to the total estimated percentage of food actually eaten by each subsample or age group. This compensated for unequal numbers of specimens in different age groups and the fact that food intake did not increase with age at the same rate as average weight of food recovered from ducks. (For example, a 40-day-old duck ate about four times as much as a 10-day-old duck, but average[5] weight of food recovered was about eight times greater.) Thus, if diet composition changes with age—one aspect under study—the two factors could bias unweighted diet esti-

[5] Weights of food recovered from Widgeons and Pintails differed less.

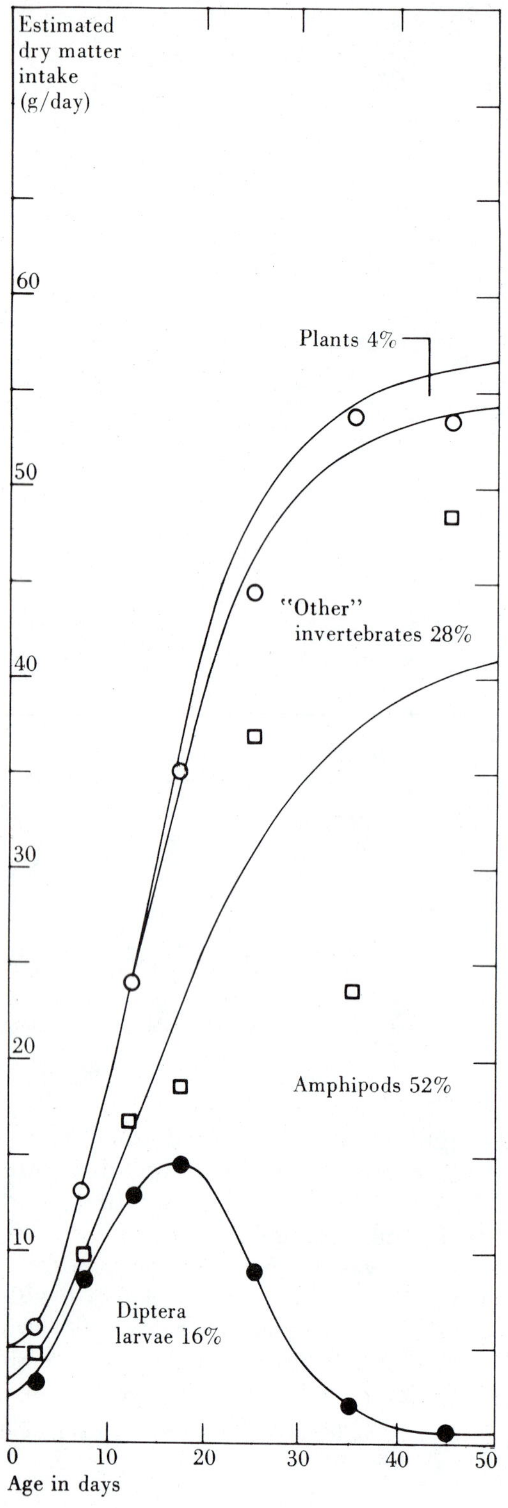

mates for the entire prefledgling period. Estimates of the food consumption are based on intake of a commercial diet eaten by captive Lesser Scaups (Sugden and Harris 1972), and the scant information in the literature (Sincock 1962, Penney and Bailey 1970). Scott and Holm (1964) concluded that basic food requirements were the same for diving and dabbling ducks, so the use of Scaup data seems justified for all species. A peak in food intake, which accompanies the latter stages of exponential growth at 5 to 7 weeks, has been found in Mallards (Jordan 1953), Black Ducks (*Anas rubripes*) (Penney and Bailey 1970), and Lesser Scaups (Sugden and Harris 1972), but does not appear in Figs. 1 to 4. The fact that a knoll is not shown in the food intake curves, should not significantly affect estimates for the prefledgling diet composition.

Factors Affecting Food Use

Feeding Behaviour.—In early morning and in evening when activity was highest, I observed feeding broods to determine methods and locations used by different ages of each species. These observations were not associated with birds collected for food analysis. I observed a brood for 10 minutes (min.) at a time, if possible, and for not more than 30 min. during 1 day. After each 1 min. of observation I recorded activity of the majority of the brood, their feeding method, water depth at the feeding site and the type of plants—emergent or submerged. Feeding methods were categorized as follows: diving, dabbling in mud (including tipping up), surface feeding, subsurface feeding in water, pecking at emergent plants, feeding on mud flats

←

Fig. 4. Trends in the diet of average Lesser Scaup ducklings.

and chasing flying insects. Water depth and plants were checked after the 10-minute observation period if not obvious at the time.

The categories of feeding methods are largely those associated with the different feeding zones—above water, water surface, subsurface water, bottom mud and mud flat—and do not always reflect the method of ingesting food. Goodman and Fisher (1962:35) divided anatids into two groups, based on feeding methods. One group uses a *grasping-action* to secure most of its food and includes grazers, such as Widgeons. The second group, which includes Scaups, uses the *straining-action* that involves a rapid opening and closing of the jaws. Both groups use a *gaping-action* at times—"... an opening and closing of the jaws that is simultaneous with the forward thrust of the head, to move large pieces of food back into the pharynx and possibly to enlarge the pharyngeal cavity." At a distance I could seldom determine which method a duck was using when it fed below the surface.

To increase the number of usable observations, I arbitrarily assigned 5 minutes to each observation when details could be noted but when it was not possible to watch a brood for any length of time, e.g., when broods became frightened and stopped feeding shortly after being sighted. This was justified because observations had shown that the features being measured changed little over a 30-minute period.

The feeding activity data were weighted to obtain averages for the prefledgling period in the same way as diet data. To do this, I asumed that different foraging methods were equally efficient. The assumption is not entirely valid; however, differences should not be great enough to obscure broad comparisons.

To supplement field data, I observed Lesser Scaup ducklings feeding in an aquarium. In addition to general observations on Scaup feeding behaviour, I made six tests using different pre-counted live aquatic invertebrates. The ducks were allowed to feed for a predetermined time, after which the uneaten items were counted. The relative selection rate was measured.

Food Sampling.—To compare foods in the diet with foods in the habitat, I sampled aquatic invertebrates at each site where ducks containing significant amounts of animal foods had been shot. It was possible to sample within 15 minutes of most collections. The two methods used to sample invertebrates available to ducks are similar to those described by Bartonek and Hickey (1969*b*). I sampled planktonic organisms with a mesh cone having an 8.3 inch (21 cm) opening. A piece of nylon mesh was fastened to the small end to collect each sample. A *sweep* consisted of passing the cone through 10 feet (3 m) of water which sampled about 3.7 cubic feet (0.1 m^3). I tried to sample those zones available to ducks, considering the species, age and characteristic method of feeding. When sampling for dabbling ducks which had been feeding on or close to the surface of deep water, I sampled close to the surface including some of the surface zone. Conversely, samples for Scaups were taken by making an arcing sweep from surface to bottom to surface.

I sampled bottom fauna with a 6-sq-inch (15.2-cm^2) Eckman dredge during the first 3 years, and later I took sweep samples which included mud bottom. Initially, and with little success, I tried to separate organisms from the bottom debris by immersing the sample in a sugar solution with a specific gravity of 1.12 (Anderson 1959). Most samples were preserved in their entirety and sorted by screening and hand-picking in the laboratory. Invertebrate samples were oven-dried and weighed in the same way as samples of food recovered from ducks. I pooled the weight data from samples for each collection site and expressed the composition of invertebrates in percentage of dry weight. Usually four samples were taken at a collection site although it varied from one to 16. A comparison of food in the diet with food available could be no better than the data gained from the duck specimens, so more intensive food sampling would add little precision.

I obtained data on available plant foods in two ways. Each of 52 water areas randomly selected from the 95 collecting sites was thoroughly searched and plant species present recorded. This provided an estimate of the percentage of occurrence for each species on the study area.

To measure plant cover where collected ducks had been feeding I used a 1-foot-square (30-cm-square) frame (divided into 100 equal squares with a wire grid) placed at about 1-yard (1-meter) intervals along a transect crossing the area occupied by the ducks, usually from shore part way out. The percentage of area covered by each plant species was used for comparison with plant foods found in the ducks. When ducks have been feeding on plants it is difficult to set limits for measuring the food available to them. Whether one samples the entire pond or only the vicinity of the feeding site can make a considerable difference in the ratios of *available* plant foods. I sampled the vicinity of the feeding site, and that seems to have been the best approach, though occasionally I missed an item eaten by the ducks.

Selection Categories.—To measure the degree to which ducks selected different items, I compared diet composition and relative abundance of foods sampled at collecting sites. Animal and plant foods were compared separately. To obtain food rankings, data from several collections are customarily pooled but this is justified only when the various features—the collecting period, collecting area and species' food niches—are relatively restricted. My study did not meet these conditions. I collected ducks over a 5-year period at many different sites, often containing different foods and in varying proportions. Each duck species used several feeding zones and classes of foods. I used different methods to sample bottom fauna, planktonic fauna and plants. The results from these different measurements are not comparable in terms of density or availability of foods. Also, significant correlations between food present in the habitat and food eaten for a single collection may be obscured when data are pooled. Consequently, I chose to calculate food ranks based on individual collections and, rather than pool original data, combined individual results. In each collection for which there were usable specimens as well as food measurements, I assigned each major item in the ducks and field samples to a selection category based on the ratio of the item in the diet to the item in the field samples as follows:

$$\frac{\text{Percent of item in diet}}{\text{Percent of item as available}}$$

Percentage of dry weight was used for eaten samples and samples of available aquatic invertebrates, and percentage of all cover measured along the transect was used for available plant samples. I arbitrarily chose nine categories with the following ranges: (1) 0.01–0.22, (2) 0.23–0.44, (3) 0.45–0.66, (4) 0.67–0.88, (5) 0.89–1.14,

(6) 1.15–1.52, (7) 1.53–2.27, (8) 2.28–4.55 and (9) 4.56–100.00. Since 1.00 was to occupy a central position there would be 4.5 categories below it and 4.5 above. Using percentages no lower than 1, there are 99 possible values below 1.00 (i.e., 0.01 to 0.99, inclusive), or a range of 0.22 per category; hence the ranges shown above. Ranges for categories above 1.00 are the reciprocals of corresponding values below it. Thus if a selection rating of 0.25 (20 per cent in diet/80 per cent in field sample) were reversed, the value becomes 4.00 (80 per cent in diet/20 per cent in field sample). The first value in this sample falls in category (2) the second in (8). To give the results greater significance, I ranked only those items occurring in either ducks or field samples in proportions greater than 3 per cent. A separate category (0) was used to designate those items present (over 3 per cent) but not eaten. Higher categories reflect positive selection on the part of the ducks. Average selection ratings were calculated by weighting the observation on the basis of category numbers, i.e., a rating falling in category (9) carried the weight of 9, one in category (8), the weight of 8, etc.

Feeding Overlap

To measure overlap between two species, one must compare their diets quantitatively as well as such factors as feeding sites, feeding methods and season of use (MacArthur 1958). Using the method of Horn (1966) and Orians and Horn (1969), I calculated for each combination of two species, overlap of diets, methods of feeding, range of water depths at feeding sites and the feeding sites (emergent plants, submerged plants, open water, mud flat).

Diet overlap between two species X and Y, in which the percentage of food *i* in each is represented by x_i and y_i, respectively, is calculated from the formula:

$$\text{Overlap} = \frac{2\sum_{i=1} xy}{\sum_{i=1} x^2 + \sum_{i=1} y^2}$$

Overlap calculated this way can vary from 0, with no overlap, to 1.00, with complete overlap. When feeding methods, water depths and feeding sites used by each species are reduced to percentages, overlap for these factors can be calculated in the same way. If proportions of food items obtained from the different sites or habitats are estimated, total overlap between two species can be calculated (Orians and Horn 1969). My data are insufficient for this purpose.

Nutrient Composition of Duck Foods

Foods for chemical analysis were collected from the field in a fresh state. Prior to drying, invertebrates were placed in a 1 per cent solution of boric acid for about 5 hours to reduce loss of nitrogen (Alex Dzubin, pers. comm.). Foods were oven-dried at 65°C for 24 hours, or, in the case of some plant material, air-dried in the sun. Proximate analyses for moisture, crude protein (nitrogen × 6.25), crude fat (ether extract), crude fibre, ash, calcium and phosphorous were contracted to the Provincial Analyst, University of Alberta. The nitrogen free extract (N.F.E.) part of the carbohydrate content was calculated by subtracting the sum of percentages for protein, fat, fibre, moisture and ash from 100. The Department of Animal Science, University of Alberta, measured gross energy by oxygen bomb calorimeter. The

Table 6. Frequency of collections from different sites for usable specimens.

Number of collections per site	Number of sites for Pintail	Gadwall	Widgeon	Scaup
1	39	19	26	11
2	6	8	8	8
3	4	2	3	3
4	2	1		1
5		3		1
6	1			
7			1	
Total sites	52	33	38	24

Chemistry Department, Utah State University, made amino acid determinations.

RESULTS

Food of Ducklings

Source of Material.—In 5 years I collected 175 Pintails, 213 Gadwalls, 153 American Widgeons, and 165 Lesser Scaups. Specimens containing usable amounts of food comprised 82 per cent of Pintails, 78 per cent of Gadwalls, 84 per cent of Widgeons and 82 per cent of Scaups. The lower average for Gadwalls resulted from those taken in 1963 (60 per cent of 91 were usable) before improved techniques were developed. After 1963, 92 per cent of the Gadwalls were usable. Larger birds contained more food on the average so more older than younger ducklings were usable, though the difference was slight. Males made up 49 per cent in Pintail, 47 in Gadwall, 52 in Widgeon and 53 in Scaup.

Ducks were collected from 95 sites (water areas). The numbers of usable specimens and collecting sites for each species are shown in Tables 2 to 5. All four species were collected (not necessarily simultaneously) on each of 4 sites, three species on 13 sites, two on 22 sites and one on 56 sites. Seven was the maximum number of collections for one species from one site during the study (Table 6). For a single year, the maximum number of collections from one site was four each for Pintail and Gadwall, three for Widgeon and five for Scaup. Collecting periods for each species' age groups (Table 7) do not necessarily represent the actual dates when each category of duckling was most abundant because collections were sometimes selective.

Sources of Error.—Excessive amounts of one food: In his study of surface feeding ducks, Coulter (1955) found a major source of error in the occurrence of a few specimens containing large amounts of one food. Such distortions occurred in all species in the present study. There was also a marked similarity of food composition in all specimens from any one collection; thus an entire collection could be considered a sampling unit. This illustrates the group behaviour characteristic of many vertebrates (Etkin 1964).

Table 7. Collecting periods for seven age groups of four duckling species.

Age group in days	Pintail	Gadwall	American Widgeon	Lesser Scaup
0–5	June 2–June 30	July 9–July 29	June 29–July 30	July 9–Aug 11
6–10	June 2–July 17	July 10–July 30	June 25–Aug 12	July 7–Aug 13
11–15	June 2–July 6	June 30–July 30	July 6–July 26	July 20–Aug 22
16–20	June 8–July 26	July 9–Aug 15	July 5–July 28	July 24–Aug 18
21–30	June 21–Aug 16	July 26–Sept 1	July 18–Aug 13	July 29–Sept 3
31–40	July 7–Aug 23	July 26–Sept 13	Aug 2–Sept 6	Aug 3–Sept 15
41+	June 29–Aug 12	Aug 8–Sept 14	Aug 4–Sept 11	Aug 21–Sept 15

Table 8. The influence of some individuals collections on percentages of certain food items in the diets of four duckling species shown by comparing values before and after the collections have been excluded (tr < 0.5%).

Species	No.* of Collections	No.* of Specimens	Food item	% of total dry food Before	% of total dry food After†
Pintail	1	2	Gastropoda	36	15
	1	2	*Hordeum vulgare*	9	0
	1	3	*Puccinellia* seeds	6	1
Gadwall	2	2	Cladocera	2	tr
	1	4	Coleoptera larvae	3	tr
	1	2	Cladophoraceae	19	12
	1	3	*Beckmannia* seeds	10	1
	1	3	*Potamogeton pusillus*	34	28
	1	3	*Ceratophyllum demersum*	3	0
Widgeon	1	3	*Carex lanuginosa*	9	0
	1	3	Cladophoraceae	18	11
	1	4	*Potamogeton pusillus*	47	39
Scaup	1	3	Gastropoda	16	4

* Total numbers of usable specimens and collections are given in Tables 2 to 5.
† Percentages would vary if more than one collection were eliminated.

The influence of excessive amounts of one food was measured in terms of the maximum percentage contribution of a single collection to the various food-type–age-group situations (Tables 2–5). More often than not, the largest contribution exceeded the arbitrary 35 per cent objective. Not all such collections caused distortions in final results because some involved items which were commonly found in the ducks in question. Some individual collections did, however, have a significant influence on the final breakdown of diet composition (Table 8). This indicates the large samples needed to obtain accurate estimates in waterfowl diet studies.

Proventriculus Material: Comparisons of several items found in esophagi, proventriculi and the two combined are made in Table 9. Items chosen for comparison are those that would be expected to reflect differences in digestion rates between the two organs should they occur. That is, soft material would disappear first and therefore occur in lower

Table 9. Comparison of some food proportions in esophagi and proventriculi, separately and combined in Pintail, Gadwall, Widgeon and Scaup ducklings.

Item, %	Pintail (141)* Esoph.	Proven.	Comb.	Gadwall (117) Esoph.	Proven.	Comb.	Widgeon (120) Esoph.	Proven.	Comb.	Scaup (127) Esoph.	Proven.	Comb.
Plant food	33.7	34.3	33.8	80.0	83.6	81.6	70.6	74.4	72.5	1.0	6.5	3.4
Scirpus nutlets	0.8	7.5	1.9									
Potamogeton nutlets	0.3	2.2	0.6									
All seeds	32.4	33.1	32.5	3.0	7.8	5.2	3.1	6.6	4.8	0.3	4.5	2.1
Gastropods	37.5	21.6	35.0	0.2	0.1	0.1				25.1	16.3	21.3
Coleoptera adults	0.8	1.3	0.9	0.8	0.7	0.8	0.8	1.3	1.0	0.4	0.4	0.4
Diptera larvae, pupae	14.2	25.6	16.0	2.5	3.7	3.1	5.1	4.7	4.9	13.5	17.0	15.0
Total dry weight of food, g	52.2	9.7	61.9	12.1	10.2	22.3	7.6	7.5	15.1	18.5	14.0	32.5

* Number of specimens.

Table 10. Percentages of surface invertebrates (SI), aquatic invertebrates (AI), and plant foods (PF) eaten by different age groups of four duckling species (tr < 0.5%).

	Pintail (144)*			Gadwall (167)			American Widgeon (129)			Lesser Scaup (135)		
Age group, days	SI	AI	PF	SI	AI	PF	SI	AI	PF	SI	AI	PF
0–3	73	25	2	74	26	0	79	20	1	3	96	1
4–5				41	48	11						
6–10	14	83	3	24	34	42	62	35	3	3	97	tr
11–15	19	72	9	56†	15	29	55	34	11	tr	98	2
16–20	2	80	18	2	19	79	3	2	95	1	99	tr
21–30	4	35	61	tr	2	98	1	1	98	1	91	8
31–40	1	91	8	3	2	95	1	1	98	tr	98	2
41+	tr	50	50	tr	1	99	4	tr	95	0	95	5
Prefledgling avg.	4	63	33	5	5	90	7	4	89	1	95	4

* Number of specimens.
† Curculionid larvae in four ducks made up 88 per cent of total surface invertebrates.

proportions in the proventriculi if more digestion took place there. The distribution of items in the esophagus and proventriculus was similar in all species. Proportionately more seeds occurred in the proventriculi. These were mostly nutlets of *Scirpus, Potamogeton, Myriophyllum, Carex* and *Eleocharis*. Diptera larvae were also highest in that organ. Conversely, gastropods tended to be proportionately lower in proventriculi. Percentages of adult Coleoptera differed little between the two organs.

Because one would not use proventriculus contents alone for food study, but rather esophagus material alone or the combined samples, proportions for the latter are included for comparison. Necessarily, differences are less than those between esophagus and proventriculus proportions. For the most part, minor items are involved. A higher proportion of an item in the proventriculus does not prove that other items disintegrated faster. It may simply mean that certain items—nutlets in particular—pass down the esophagus into the proventriculus faster. Seeds were higher by percentage of dry weight in the proventriculus, but gastropods and adult beetles were similar or lower in that organ. Such hard-bodied invertebrates are among the most resistant to gizzard digestion (Perret 1962), so

Table 11. Percentage of dry weight intake of animal and plant food by 10-day periods in four duckling species (tr < 0.05%).

	Percentage of 50-day intake											
	Pintail (144)*			Gadwall (167)			Widgeon (129)			Scaup (135)		
Age period, days	Animal	Plant	Total	Animal	Plant	Total	Animal	Plant	Total	Animal	Plant	Total
0–10	3.3	0.1	3.4	2.3	1.1	3.4	3.2	0.1	3.3	5.0	tr	5.0
11–20	10.3	3.9	14.2	5.6	8.5	14.1	5.5	8.8	14.3	14.9	0.1	15.0
21–30	15.9	9.5	25.4	0.6	24.8	25.4	0.5	24.8	25.3	22.2	2.0	24.2
31–40	18.1	9.8	27.9	1.3	26.7	28.0	0.4	27.7	28.1	27.0	0.4	27.4
41–50	19.0	10.1	29.1	0.3	28.8	29.1	1.3	27.7	29.0	26.9	1.5	28.4
Totals	66.6	33.4	100.0	10.1	89.9	100.0	10.9	89.1	100.0	96.0	4.0	100.0

* Number of specimens.

Table 12. Frequency of animal and plant foods occurring in seven age groups of four duckling species.

Age group, days	Percentage with animal food				Percentage with plant food			
	Pintail	Gadwall	Widgeon	Scaup	Pintail	Gadwall	Widgeon	Scaup
0–5	100	100	100	95	50	23	25	26
6–10	100	94	100	95	76	72	37	14
11–15	100	86	100	100	89	71	77	33
16–20	93	100	83	100	93	90	100	31
21–30	92	73	65	96	95	100	100	58
31–40	71	71	48	91	93	100	92	70
41+	60	67	45	94	96	95	96	75
Sample size	144	167	129	135	144	167	129	135

they should also occur in higher proportions in the proventriculus if differential digestion is a fact. Moreover, dipterous larvae—principally chironomids—were equal or even higher in the proventriculi and since these would be among the most susceptible to digestion, the observed ratios indicate an absence of differential digestion. If seeds do move down the esophagus faster than other items, then not including proventriculus material could introduce bias. But if the accumulation of seeds in the proventriculus is caused by their slower passage into the gizzard, then proventriculus material would add bias, though not because of differential digestion. Furthermore, it is possible that the injection of preservative into the gullet helped to flush small items into the proventriculus.

For these reasons and because differences between esophagus and combined proportions were small and involved minor items, there was no justification for excluding proventriculus material. Including it increased the food weight and number of usable specimens, respectively, by 19 and 22 per cent in Pintail, 84 and 27 per cent in Gadwall, 98 and 28 per cent in Widgeon, and 75 and 55 per cent in Scaup. The relatively small contribution of Pintail proventriculus material is probably because the Pintail's longer neck provides relatively more storage capacity in its esophagus.

Pintail Foods.—During the first 5 days Pintails ate chiefly surface invertebrates and, as they grew, consumed greater proportions of aquatic invertebrates and plants (Table 10). Surface invertebrates made up about 4 per cent of the prefledgling diet. Altogether, Pintails ate more than half animal food on the average (Table 10, Fig. 1), though the ratio was extremely variable. I estimated the average intake of animal food during the first 50 days at 67 per cent of the total diet (dry weight). Proportions of animal and plant foods eaten by Pintails during each of their first five 10-day periods (Table 11) were calculated from Fig. 1 with a dot grid. All Pintails ate some animal food during their first 15 days and two-thirds continued to do so during the last 20 days of the flightless period (Table 12). The use of plant food was almost the reverse.

Pintails ate many kinds of invertebrates, though a few accounted for most of the animal diet (Table 13). Gastropods made up 36 per cent by weight of the total diet, but as one collection contributed so much of the gastropod weight (Table 8), the estimate is too high. Moreover, the contribution of gastropods to a duck's nutrition tends to be overrated when presented on a gravimetric basis

Table 13. Diet composition of young Pintails (P), Gadwalls (G), Widgeons (W), and Scaups (S), expressed as percentages of dry weight, frequency of occurrence and gross energy (tr < 0.5%).

	Dry weight				Occurrence				Gross energy			
Item	P	G	W	S	P	G	W	S	P	G	W	S
Nematoda*	tr		tr		5		8		tr		tr	
Hirudinea*	tr	tr		1	2	1		7	tr	tr		1
Crustacea												
Cladocera*	4	2	tr	1	26	26	6	9	3	1	tr	1
Podocopa*	tr	tr	tr	tr	13	5	1	4	tr	tr	tr	tr
Eucopepoda*	tr	tr	tr		1	2	1		tr	tr	tr	
Amphipoda*	tr	tr	tr	52	3	2	1	34	tr	tr	tr	56
(Crustacea subtotal)	(4)	(2)	(tr)	(53)	39	30	9	41	(3)	(1)	(tr)	(57)
Insecta												
Collembola*	tr	tr	tr		6	9	3		tr	tr	tr	
Ephemeroptera adults†	tr	tr	1		3	2	4		tr	tr	tr	
Ephemeroptera naiads*	tr	tr	tr	tr	2	1	1	7	tr	tr	tr	tr
Anisoptera naiads*	1			tr	8			1	2			tr
Zygoptera adults†	tr	tr	1	tr	4	2	4	1	tr	tr	1	tr
Zygoptera naiads*	1	tr	tr	3	10	5	2	19	2	tr	tr	4
Thysanoptera†		tr		tr		1		1		tr		tr
Orthoptera†	1				2				2			
Mallophaga†	tr				1				tr			
Hemiptera*†	tr	1	1	3	23	34	26	44	tr	1	1	4
Homoptera†	tr	tr	tr	tr	10	2	5	3	tr	tr	tr	tr
Coleoptera adults*†	1	tr	tr	tr	37	28	23	18	2	1	tr	1
Coleoptera larvae*†	1	3	tr	1	37	22	6	20	2	4	tr	2
Trichoptera adults†	tr	tr	1	tr	10	5	12	2	tr	tr	1	tr
Trichoptera larvae*	2			2	14			20	3			4
Lepidoptera adults†			tr				4				tr	
Diptera adults†	2	2	4	tr	40	45	38	15	4	2	5	tr
Diptera larvae, pupae*	16	2	1	16	66	59	37	57	22	2	1	18
Hymenoptera†	tr	tr	tr	tr	5	7	5	5	tr	tr	tr	tr
Unidentified Insecta*†	tr	tr	tr	tr					tr	tr	tr	tr
(Insecta subtotal)	(26)	(8)	(9)	(26)	86	85	71	86	(39)	(11)	(11)	(33)
Arachnoidea												
Araneida†	tr	tr	tr		8	1	1		tr	tr	tr	
Hydracarina*	tr	tr	tr	tr	10	7	4	10	tr	tr	tr	tr
Gastropoda*	36	tr	2	16	35	4	2	16	10	tr	tr	4
Unidentified animal food*†	tr	tr	tr	tr					tr	tr	tr	tr
Total animal food	67	10	11	96	88	88	74	96	53	12	11	95
Cladophoraceae	tr	19	18	tr	7	23	16	2	tr	16	16	tr
Characeae *Chara* sp.												
foliage		3				2				3		
oögonia				1								1
Cyanophyceae	tr	tr		tr	3	1		1	tr	tr		tr
Musci	tr	tr	tr		1	1	1		tr	tr	tr	
Equisetaceae *Equisetum* sp. stem	tr				1				tr			
Typhaceae *Typha* sp. seeds	tr				1				tr			
Zosteraceae												
Potamogeton pectinatus												
foliage		1	1			3	2			1	1	
spikes		tr	1			4	3			1	1	
tubers	tr	tr	tr		1	1	2		tr	tr	tr	

Table 13. Continued.

Item	Dry weight				Occurrence				Gross energy			
	P	G	W	S	P	G	W	S	P	G	W	S
Potamogeton pusillus												
foliage	tr	34	47		3	31	32		tr	33	46	
spikes		3	tr			3	2			3	tr	
buds	tr	tr	tr		3	2	2		tr	tr	tr	
Potamogeton Richardsonii												
foliage		tr	tr			1	2			–	–	
spikes		tr	3			2	2			–	4	
Potamogeton sp.												
foliage	tr	tr	tr	tr	1	5	2	2	tr	tr	tr	tr
nutlets	1	tr	tr	tr	18	5	9	10	1	tr	tr	1
Zannichellia palustris foliage, seeds	2	2	1	tr	10	11	2	1	2	2	tr	tr
Juncaginaceae *Triglochin* sp. seeds	1				1				1			
Gramineae												
Puccinellia Nuttalliana seeds	6	tr	2	tr	6	1	5	1	8	tr	2	tr
Glyceria sp. seeds	tr				1				tr			
Distichlis stricta seeds	tr				6				tr			
Agropyron sp. seeds	tr				3				tr			
Hordeum jubatum seeds	2	tr	tr	tr	13	1	1	4	3	tr	tr	tr
Hordeum vulgare grain	9				1				12			
Agrostis sp. seeds	tr	tr			3	1			tr	tr		
Alopecurus aequalis seeds	tr	1			2	2			tr	1		
Beckmannia syzigachne seeds	1	10	tr		5	2	3		2	11	tr	
Unidentified Gramineae												
seeds	tr	tr			2	1			tr	tr		
foliage	tr	tr			1	1			tr	tr		
(Gramineae subtotal)	(19)	(11)	(2)	tr	21	4	9	4	(25)	(12)	(2)	(tr)
Cyperaceae												
Eleocharis sp. nutlets	4	tr	tr	tr	15	3	1	1	6	tr	tr	tr
Scirpus spp. nutlets	3	2	1	tr	57	10	8	8	5	tr	tr	tr
Carex lanuginosa perigynia, nutlets			9				2				11	
Carex spp. nutlets	1	tr	tr	tr	28	2	7	1	1	tr	tr	tr
(Cyperaceae subtotal)	(8)	(2)	(10)	(tr)	60	13	13	10	(12)	(tr)	(11)	(tr)
Lemnaceae												
Lemna trisulca		tr	1			5	4			tr	1	
Lemna minor	tr	7	4		4	13	7		tr	7	4	
Juncaceae *Juncus balticus* seeds	tr				3				tr			
Polygonaceae												
Eriogonum sp. seeds	tr				3				tr			
Rumex maritimus achenes	tr	tr		tr	5	1		1	tr	tr		tr
Polygonum spp. achenes	tr	tr		tr	8	1		1	tr	tr		tr
Ceratophyllaceae												
Ceratophyllum demersum foliage		3	tr			2	1			3	tr	
Chenopodiaceae *Chenopodium* sp. seeds	tr	tr		tr	16	2		6	tr	tr		tr
Leguminosae *Medicago* sp. seeds	tr				1				tr			

Table 13. Continued.

Item	Dry weight				Occurrence				Gross energy			
	P	G	W	S	P	G	W	S	P	G	W	S
Ranunculaceae												
Ranunculus subrigidus foliage		1		tr		2		1		1		tr
Ranunculus Cymbalaria foliage			tr				2				tr	
Haloragaceae												
Myriophyllum exalbescens												
foliage	tr	tr	tr	tr	3	7	5	6	tr	tr	tr	tr
spikes		tr				2				tr		
nutlets	1	tr	tr	2	18	1	1	23	2	tr	tr	3
Caprifoliaceae												
Symphoricarpos sp. nutlets	tr				3				tr			
Compositae												
Cirsium sp. achenes	tr				1				tr			
Sonchus sp. achenes		tr				1				tr		
Taraxacum sp. achenes	tr	tr	tr		4	1	1		tr	tr	tr	
Unidentified foliage	1	1	1	tr					1	2	1	tr
Unidentified seeds	tr	tr	tr	tr					tr	tr	tr	tr
Total plant food	33	90	89	4	88	78	78	44	47	88	89	5
Number of specimens	144	167	129	135	144	167	129	135	144	167	129	135

* Aquatic invertebrates.
† Surface invertebrates.

because of their relatively high ash content. This relationship is apparent when weight and calorific percentages are compared in Table 13.

Insects made up 26 per cent of the total diet. Most important were dipterans which contributed 18 per cent.[6] Of that, larvae and pupae made up 16 per cent. A breakdown of insect orders shows that Chironomidae (15 per cent) was the dominant Diptera family (Table 14). Insect orders of lesser importance were Odonata (2 per cent), Coleoptera adults and larvae (2 per cent) and Trichoptera larvae (2 per cent) (Table 13).

Cladocerans were the only crustaceans eaten in significant amounts (4 per cent) by young Pintails.

Three downy Pintails collected by Munro (1944) in British Columbia contained 99 per cent Zygoptera naiads by volume.

Most plant foods in Pintails less than 15 days old were seeds that the ducks probably had ingested accidentally while feeding on invertebrates, particularly bottom fauna. There appeared to be no deliberate selection of plant foods during the first 2 weeks. As they grew, Pintails selected more plant material as evidenced by relatively large amounts that could not have been swallowed accidentally. Plants made up 33 per cent of the diet and of that, seeds and nutlets comprised 30 per cent (Table 13). Grass (Gramineae) seeds contributed 19 per cent. The 9 per cent estimate for barley (*Hordeum vulgare*) is probably high as it was all found in two specimens (Table 8). *Puccinellia* seeds made up 6 per cent of the diet, *Hordeum jubatum* 2 per cent

[6] Unless otherwise specified, percentage of total prefledgling diet.

Table 14. Some invertebrate families and their percentage of dry weight contribution to the total diets of four duckling species (tr < 0.05%).

Item	Pintail		Gadwall		Widgeon		Scaup	
Hemiptera		(0.136 g)*		(0.255 g)		(0.234 g)		(0.986 g)
Corixidae		0.1		0.6		0.6		2.9
Notonectidae				tr				0.1
Gerridae		tr		tr				
Miridae						tr		
Lygaeidae		tr		tr		tr		
Saldidae		tr		tr		tr		tr
Mesoveliidae		tr						
	Adults	Larvae	Adults	Larvae	Adults	Larvae	Adults	Larvae
Coleoptera	(0.656 g)	(0.633 g)	(0.189 g)	(1.467 g)	(0.135 g)	(0.188 g)	(0.117 g)	(0.340 g)
Carabidae	tr		tr					
Haliplidae	tr	tr	tr	0.1	0.1	tr	0.1	0.7
Dytiscidae	0.3	0.6	0.1	0.1	tr	tr	0.2	0.3
Noteridae	tr							
Gyrinidae	tr							
Silphidae		0.1						
Hydrophilidae	0.1	0.1	tr	tr	tr		0.1	tr
Staphylinidae	tr		tr					
Elateridae	tr							
Malachiidae								
Heteroceridae	tr							
Coccinellidae	tr							
Anthicidae							tr	
Scarabaeidae	tr		tr					
Curculionidae	0.6		0.3	2.7	0.1	0.2	tr	
Trichoptera (larvae)		(1.053 g)						(0.904 g)
Phryganeidae								0.1
Limnephilidae		0.1						tr
Leptoceridae		1.5						2.4
	Adults	l + p†	Adults	l + p	Adults	l + p	Adults	l + p
Diptera	(1.670 g)	(11.133 g)	(0.563 g)	(0.896 g)	(1.121 g)	(0.812 g)	(0.035 g)	(4.947 g)
Tipulidae		0.8	tr					
Psychodidae		tr						
Culicidae	tr	0.2	tr	tr		tr		0.1
Ceratopogonidae	tr	0.2	tr	0.2	0.1	0.8		
Chironomidae	2.0	13.6	1.5	1.6	3.8	0.5	0.2	15.3
Mycetophilidae			tr					
Stratiomyidae	tr	0.5			tr			0.1
Tabanidae		0.3	0.1					
Dolichopodidae	tr		tr		tr			
Sepsidae					tr			
Syrphidae	tr	0.5						
Otitidae			tr					
Ephydridae	tr	0.5	tr	tr	tr	tr		
Chlorophidae	tr		tr		tr			
Anthomyiidae	0.1		0.1		0.1			
Gastropoda		(21.806 g)		(0.027 g)		(0.286 g)		(7.510 g)
Physidae		31.6		0.1				1.9
Lymnaeidae		3.9				1.1		13.7
Planorbidae		0.4		tr		0.4		tr

* Weight of identified material.
† l = larvae, p = pupae.

and *Beckmannia* 1 per cent. Grass seeds formed a major part of the diet of Pintails wintering in Louisiana (Glasgow and Bardwell 1962). At Gem, Alberta, Keith (1961) examined stomach contents of 19 adult Pintails, 9 flying young and 33 flightless young. Seeds of aquatic plants made up the bulk of the identifiable material in the three groups and very few grass seeds had been eaten. Munro (1944) reported on stomach contents of 45 fall and winter adult Pintails collected in British Columbia—25 from the interior and 20 from the coastal region. In a few specimens grass seeds constituted a minor part of the recovered food.

Fallen seeds from previous years made up about 10 per cent of the Pintails' diet in this study. Cyperaceae contributed 8 per cent of these seeds as follows: *Eleocharis* 4, *Scirpus* 3 and *Carex* 1 per cent. Because such hard-coated fruits are not easily digested (Bartonek 1968), their nutritional value may be much less than indicated by consumption rate.

A variety of items, foliage and attached seeds of *Zannichellia* and winter buds of *Potamogeton pusillus* predominating, made up the remaining 3 per cent of plant food.

Seven of the 41+ day group Pintails were flying young—six taken in late July and one in early August. They had eaten essentially the same as flightless ducks of the same age group. Perret (1962) found significantly more plant food in a sample of eight young Mallards which could fly (early August) than in their flightless counterparts. He attributed it to their greater access to fields. Flying adult and young Pintails in the Strathmore area characteristically fed on sites similar to those used by flightless ducks. Several times they were seen feeding together. I observed no field feeding by ducks in July or August during this study; however, there was relatively less land in grain in the Strathmore area. Significantly, the only two Pintails that had eaten cultivated barley were flightless. They were taken from a roadside ditch and had apparently eaten spilled barley.

In summary, Pintails ate about 67 per cent invertebrates during the prefledgling period. Although a wide variety was eaten, gastropods and dipterous larvae accounted for half the total diet. Surface invertebrates comprised 73 per cent of the diet during the first 5 days but gradually were replaced by aquatic invertebrates and plants. Seeds and nutlets dominated the plant portion of the diet and accounted for 30 per cent of the prefledgling diet. Most prevalent were seeds of Gramineae and Cyperaceae.

Gadwall Foods.—Gadwalls showed a trend from a predominantly invertebrate diet immediately after hatching to an almost exclusive plant diet after 3 weeks of age (Table 10, Fig. 2). None of six ducks considered less than 3 days old contained plant material. The frequency of plant food increased with age and after 3 weeks, over 90 per cent had eaten plants (Table 12). Chura (1961) reported a trend from an animal to plant food diet for young Mallards at Bear River Refuge, Utah, though the transition was not as rapid. The comparison is not entirely valid because Chura used gizzard material and Dillon (1959) and Perret (1962) have shown that the practice overrates plant proportions. The fact that the plant food in Chura's Mallards was mostly seeds of aquatic plants further indicates distortion. Although the proportion of animal food in the Gadwall diet decreased as the ducks grew, the actual intake of animal food would not start to decrease until about 2 weeks of age due to the rapidly increasing food intake (Fig. 2). Close to 80 per cent of the prefledgling animal food was eaten during the first 20 days, with about half taken in the 11- to 20-day period (Table 11). Intake of plant food increased until about 3 weeks of age when it levelled off. Altogether, Gadwalls ate 10 per cent animal and 90 per cent plant food.

Animal food eaten by Gadwalls during their first 3 days was mostly surface invertebrates (Table 10). After 3 days of age, the ducklings ate more aquatic invertebrates. Although invertebrates make only a small contribution to the prefledgling diet, ducklings depend on them almost entirely during their first few days. Close to 80 per cent of the animal food eaten by Gadwalls was insects (Table 13), primarily Diptera and Coleoptera. One dipterous family, Chironomidae, was dominant and made up about one-third of the animal food (Table 14). The families Curculionidae, Dytiscidae and Haliplidae accounted for most of the Coleoptera eaten by Gadwalls. Four ducks contained unusually large numbers of curculionid larvae (Table 8) that had infested immature spikes of *Myriophyllum* and *Potamogeton* which were also eaten. The contribution of Coleoptera larvae may thus be overrated. Corixidae comprised most of the Hemiptera eaten by Gadwalls.

Cladocera made up about 16 per cent of the animal food. Most of the Cladocera occurred in two specimens (Table 8), and the high frequency in Gadwalls (Table 13) resulted from trace amounts in many. The ingestion of such minor amounts—sometimes a single ephippium—probably occurred incidentally to swallowing other foods.

Gadwalls ate proportionately more plant food as they grew and plants made up 90 per cent of the diet (Table 13). *Potamogeton* foliage was the most important item and of that, *P. pusillus* contributed 34 per cent. Leaves of aquatic plants were also important in the autumn diet of the Gadwalls in Utah (Gates 1957). In that study, Gadwalls ate *P. pectinatus*, *Ruppia maritima* and *Zannichellia palustris*. Keith (1961) examined stomach contents of 12 adult, 3 flying young and 3 flightless young Gadwalls collected near Gem, Alberta. He believed that foliage of *Potamogeton pusillus* and *P. Friesii* were among the most important foods eaten by those specimens.

Green alga (Cladophoraceae), at 19 per cent, was the second most important plant food in the Strathmore Gadwall diet, followed by *Beckmannia* seeds (10 per cent) and *Lemna minor* (7 per cent). The percentage for *Beckmannia* may be too high because one duck contained most of the seeds recovered (Table 8). Single collections contained considerable quantities of some items: leaves of *Chara*, *Ceratophyllum* and *Ranunculus*; current seeds of *Alopecurus*; and immature spikes of *Potamogeton pectinatus* infested with curculionid larvae. Leaves and attached seeds of *Zannichellia* and *Scirpus* nutlets each contributed 2 per cent to the diet.

To recapitulate, Gadwalls ate chiefly surface invertebrates during their first few days. These were replaced by aquatic invertebrates and plants as they grew. By 3 weeks of age the ducks were essentially vegetarian. Insects dominated the animal diet, with chironomid larvae being the most important. *Potamogeton pusillus* foliage and Cladophoraceae were the most important plants and contributed 34 and 19 per cent, respectively. I estimated the average prefledgling Gadwall diet as containing 10 per cent animal and 90 per cent plant food.

American Widgeon Foods.—Animal foods dominated the Widgeon diet at first but were largely replaced with plants by

3 weeks of age (Table 10, Fig. 3). About 80 per cent of the animal food was taken during the first 20 days of the flightless period (Table 11). By 30 days, the food intake had almost levelled off and comprised mostly plants. As they grew, fewer Widgeons ate animal food and more ate plants (Table 12).

The ratio of surface invertebrates to aquatic invertebrates declined with age of ducks, though the former remained more important throughout the flightless period (Table 10). The diet contained 11 per cent animal food—7 per cent surface and 4 per cent aquatic invertebrates. The animal food eaten by Widgeons was 82 per cent insects (Table 13). Diptera—adults, pupae and larvae—made up 48 percent of the animal food; no other insect order contributed more than 10 per cent. Chironomids were the most common adult dipterans, ceratopogonids (chiefly pupae) and chironomids the most common immature dipterans (Table 14).

Gastropods comprised 14 per cent of the animal diet but only three of 129 ducks ate them; thus, the percentage may be too high. Widgeons ate trace amounts of crustaceans.

Munro (1949) reported that 10 stomachs of downy American Widgeons collected in British Columbia contained 88 per cent (by volume) animal matter, chiefly insects.

The Widgeon diet contained 89 per cent plant material and the composition of the plant diet did not change as the ducks grew. Older birds contained a greater variety because they ate more plants more frequently. *Potamogeton pusillus* foliage, the most important item, made up 47 per cent of the total diet, followed by Cladophoraceae at 18 per cent (Table 13). The 9 per cent for *Carex lanuginosa* is probably too high since three ducks from one collection accounted for all of it (Table 8). Other plants that contributed at least 1 per cent were: *Lemna minor* and *L. trisulca, Potamogeton Richardsonii* and *P. pectinatus* (principally spikes), *Puccinellia* seeds, *Zannichellia* foliage and seeds and *Scirpus* nutlets.

Keith's (1961) opinion concerning the importance of *Potamogeton* foliage to Gadwalls apparently also held for a similar number of Widgeon specimens pooled with the Gadwall sample. In interior British Columbia, Munro (1949) found that stomachs of 38 adult Widgeons collected during autumn contained 6 per cent (by volume) animal matter, 29 per cent alga and 65 per cent *vegetation.* Major foods included *Potamogeton, Utricularia, Ceratophyllum, Elodea* and *Chara*; the last four were insignificant or absent in this study.

In summary, invertebrates dominated the Widgeon diet up to 2 weeks. By 3 weeks, they were eating over 90 per cent plants, and an estimated 89 per cent of the prefledgling diet comprised plants. Surface invertebrates were more important than aquatic invertebrates throughout the flightless period, particularly during the first 10 days. Insects made up 82 per cent of animal food. The major plant items were *Potamogeton pusillus* and Cladophoraceae which contributed 47 and 18 per cent, respectively, to the total diet.

Lesser Scaup Foods.—Flightless Scaup ducklings in this study ate principally animal food (Tables 10, 11, Fig. 4) as did young Scaups in Manitoba (Bartonek and Hickey 1969*a*) and near Yellowknife, Northwest Territories (Bartonek and Murdy, 1970). Animal food—entirely invertebrates—comprised 96 per cent of the Strathmore Scaup diet. More than 90 per cent of Scaups in all age groups ate animal food (Table 12). Unlike the three

Table 15. Feeding activity by Pintail broods. Figures show percentage of observations (tr < 0.5%).

	Age class						
	Ia	Ib	Ic	IIa	IIb	IIc	III
Age in days*	1–5	6–12	13–18	19–23	24–33	34–43	44–51
Number of broods	12	11	9	11	5	10	10
Total observations†	165	148	97	207	52	124	135
Feeding method							
Surface	84	51	28	tr			
Subsurface:							
Bill-dip	14	7	21	24		10	
Head-duck		1	24	25	37	10	34
Tip-up						25	
Bottom:							
Head-duck						22	5
Tip-up		30	15	44	63	33	57
Diving	1	9		6			4
Peck at emergent plant	tr	tr				tr	
On mud flat	1	1	12				
Chase flying insect	tr	1					
Maximum depth at site							
0–6 in. (0–16 cm)	26	32	20	27	10	32	50
7–12 in. (17–31 cm)	47	42	33	47	90	30	16
13–18 in. (32–46 cm)	23	24	35	12		22	23
19–24 in. (47–62 cm)	4	2		9		16	11
25–30 in. (63–77 cm)				5			
31–36 in. (78–92 cm)			12				
Feeding site							
Open water	36	56	36	23	60	9	48
Emergent plants	48	27	21	48	13	36	19
Submerged plants	15	16	31	29	27	55	33
Mud flat	1	1	12				

* From Gollop and Marshall (1954).
† One observation per minute.

dabbling species, Scaup ducklings did not make heavy use of surface invertebrates in early life, though they did spend considerable time surface feeding. This disparity will be discussed under Feeding Behaviour. Figure 4 shows diet changes with ages of Scaups. As they grew, the ducks ate higher proportions of amphipods, mostly at the expense of dipterous larvae. Cause of the change is discussed under Food Selection.

The most important item in the diet of Scaups was Amphipoda which made up 52 per cent (Table 13). Insects contributed 26 per cent, with dipterous larvae being most important (16 per cent). Chironomids were the principal dipterans eaten (Table 14). Other insect orders eaten in significant amounts were Hemiptera (3 per cent and chiefly corixids), Zygoptera naiads (3 per cent) and Trichoptera larvae (2 per cent, mainly leptocerids). Coleoptera, principally haliplids and dytiscids, made up 1 per cent. Gastropods formed 16 per cent of the diet (12 per cent from one collection). Cladocerans were eaten in appreciable amounts by three Scaups from two collections and made up 1 per cent of the diet.

Scaup ducklings of all ages ate only 4

Table 16. Feeding activity by four duckling species. Figures show percentage of observations weighted on the basis of prefledgling food intake (tr < 0.5%).

	Pintail	Gadwall	Widgeon	Scaup
Feeding method				
Surface	5	12	22	1
Subsurface	39	86	74	0
Bottom	53	2	3	0*
Diving	2	0	0	99
Miscellaneous	1	tr	1	tr
Maximum depth at surface				
0–6 in. (0–16 cm)	29	8	12	0
7–12 in. (17–31 cm)	45	29	28	0
13–18 in. (32–46 cm)	17	44	19	11
19–24 in. (47–62 cm)	8	11	35	60
25–30 in. (63–77 cm)	tr	7	5	23
31–36 in. (78–92 cm)	1	1	1	2
37–42 in. (93–107 cm)	0	0	0	2
43–48 in. (108–122 cm)	0	0	0	2
Feeding site				
Open water	37	6	7	53
Emergent plants	26	6	10	tr
Submerged plants	36	87	82	46
Mud flat	1	tr	tr	0

* An unknown amount of bottom feeding would be recorded as *diving*.

per cent plant food (Tables 10, 13). Most of the plant material came from six ducks in two collections which contained *Chara* oögonia and *Myriophyllum* nutlets, respectively.

Strathmore Scaups ate food similar to that of 25 young collected in Manitoba by Bartonek and Hickey (1969*a*). There, amphipods, gastropods and Tendipedidae (chironomid) larvae formed 49, 39 and 8 per cent by volume, respectively, of all food eaten. Amphipods and chironomid larvae were the most important items in 14 adults in the same study. The diet of 39 adult Scaups from the Manitoba pothole area was also dominated by amphipods (Rogers and Korschgen 1966). Similarly, Munro (1941) found chiefly amphipods in stomachs of 15 young and 9 adult Lesser Scaups collected in British Columbia. Amphipods were also major items eaten by 108 adults from the Saskatchewan River Delta (Dirschl 1969). However, Dirschl noted seasonal differences and during the July to September period amphipods were secondary to other foods, principally Hirudinea and *Nuphar*. Bartonek and Murdy (1970) reported that 19 Class Ia–IIa Scaups collected during late July and early August in the Northwest Territories ate mostly culicid larvae and pupae (54 per cent by volume) and Conchostraca (30 per cent), and 19 Class IIa–III Scaups collected in early September had eaten mostly amphipods (57 per cent), odonate naiads (17 per cent) and corixids (11 per cent). In contrast to these results, amphipods were insignificant in stomachs of 17 juveniles collected by Cottam (1939) in the Prairie Provinces; the bulk of the food was insects. Cladocerans, which comprised 1 per cent of the Strathmore Scaup diet, were not found in Manitoba Scaups by Bartonek and Hickey (1969*a*) though trace amounts of cladoceran ephippia were found in a few. In the Northwest Territories, cladocerans contributed 8 per cent of the food in 23 adult Scaups, but only trace amounts in 38 juveniles (Bartonek and Murdy 1970). Three of 39 adults examined by Rogers and Korschgen (1966) had eaten significant amounts of adult Cladocera.

In summary, Scaups ate 96 per cent invertebrates. Dipterous larvae were important to early age classes but older ducklings ate more amphipods. Altogether, amphipods contributed 52 per cent; insects 26 per cent; and gastropods 16 per cent.

Factors Affecting Food Use

Feeding Behaviour.—Pintail Feeding: Young Pintails used a variety of methods to secure food (Tables 15, 16). They frequently fed among emergent plants where they were not readily observed so I may have underestimated the amount of activity there. Class Ia ducks fed mostly by pecking items from the water surface. This is the gaping-action of Goodman and Fisher (1962). Surface feeding was not observed in Class IIb and older Pintails. Diet data (Table 10) show, however, that older Pintails ate some surface invertebrates. Subsurface feeding either by dipping the bill, ducking the head or tipping up, and bottom feeding by head-ducking or tipping, gradually replaced surface feeding.

Of 68 Pintail broods on which I made feeding observations, seven included ducklings that were diving for food. I cannot recall seeing them diving during numerous unrecorded observations in the past. Johnsgard (1965) and Kear and Johnsgard (1968) reported that mature Pintails frequently dived for food, though Smith (1966) did not observe any diving during a 3-year study. The abundance of shallow water and submerged vegetation in the Strathmore areas used by Pintails may have reduced the incidence of diving.

As expected, water under 12 inches (31 cm) deep was favoured by feeding Pintails. Virtually all bottom feeding occurred there. Feeding activity was about evenly distributed among sites with no vegetation, sites with emergent plants and sites with submersed plants. Surface feeding appeared unrelated to the presence of vegetation, but caution must be used when relating feeding activity to such features as depth and vegetation because other factors such as the proximity of escape cover and the feeding behaviour of the hen also influence duckling distribution.

The manner in which Pintail ducklings obtained grass seeds illustrates their adaptability in securing food. Most *Hordeum jubatum* was apparently taken from the pond bottom while the ducks fed on other items. In at least one collection, *Beckmannia* seeds were also taken by bottom feeding. In other cases, I assumed that seeds floating on the water had been strained out by the ducks. *Beckmannia* on the study area usually grew tall and in most cases the spikes would be out of reach of a duckling. Pintails apparently strip the seeds from *Puccinellia* and, possibly, *Alopecurus*. I have not seen them do this, but duck tracks, dislodged seeds and stripped spikes evinced this method. Nowhere have I seen enough fallen seeds to account for large quantities sometimes eaten. Evidently Canada Geese (*Branta canadensis*) commonly strip grass seeds from plants, particularly *Poa* (Hanson 1965).

Gadwall Feeding: Class Ia–Ib Gadwalls fed most often from the water surface (Table 17). The rest of the time they fed just below the surface, principally by the bill-dip method. There is little differ-

Table 17. Feeding activity by Gadwall broods. Figures show percentage of observations (tr < 0.5%).

	Age class						
	Ia	Ib	Ic	IIa	IIb	IIc	III
Age in days*	1–6	7–14	15–18	19–27	28–38	39–44	45–50
Number of broods	9	7	10	8	8	8	10
Total observations†	122	120	115	110	80	132	144
Feeding method							
Surface	94	76	44		9		7
Subsurface:							
Bill-dip		24	22	60	71	48	30
Head-duck	6		8	26	20	22	5
Tip-up				14		30	58
Bottom:							
Head-duck			26				
Peck at emergent plant						tr	
Chase flying insect		tr					tr
On mud flat							tr
Maximum depth at site							
0–6 in. (0–16 cm)	3		26	18			15
7–12 in. (17–31 cm)	26	54	24	18	28	48	19
13–18 in. (32–46 cm)	50	17	33	36	72	36	24
19–24 in. (47–62 cm)	13	17		15		8	28
25–30 in. (63–77 cm)	8	12		13		8	14
31–36 in. (78–92 cm)			17				
Feeding site							
Open water	16	23	8	4	4		13
Emergent plants	7	4	1			19	14
Submerged plants	77	73	91	96	96	81	73
Mud flat							tr

* From Gollop and Marshall (1954).
† One observation per minute.

ence between surface feeding and bill-dipping below the surface and often a brood used both methods. The high incidence of surface feeding by Class I ducklings explains the dominance of surface invertebrates in their diet. The ducks largely replaced surface feeding with subsurface feeding as they grew. This change paralleled the diet change from invertebrates to plants.

About 73 per cent of Gadwall feeding occurred where water was 7 to 18 inches (17 to 46 cm) deep (Table 16). The data do not show any trends with changing age of ducks. Whether the depths over which Gadwalls fed reflect random use of existing depths is unknown. However, the 8 per cent use shown for the 0- to 6-inch (0- to 16-cm) zone is considerably less than the actual area occupied by that zone in the ponds so it appears they tended to avoid the shallow zone.

Feeding sites (emergent plants, submersed plants and open water) varied with age of ducks. Class Ia and Ib Gadwalls fed at random at least with regard to open water and submersed plants, the per cent use being similar to proportions estimated from vegetation transects. This kind of use would be expected for ducks which eat chiefly surface invertebrates. As the ducks grew and ate more aquatic invertebrates and plants, they fed less on open water and more over submersed

Table 18. Feeding activity by American Widgeon broods. Figures show percentage of observations (tr < 0.5%).

	Age class						
	Ia	Ib	Ic	IIa	IIb	IIc	III
Age in days*	1–7	8–12	13–18	19–26	27–35	36–41	42–50
Number of broods	12	10	8	6	6	6	7
Total observations†	152	155	112	100	102	102	142
Feeding method							
Surface	75	79	57	13	34	10	3
Subsurface:							
Bill-dip	14	21	36	62	42	33	48
Head-duck	1			12	8	43	38
Tip-up				13	13	2	11
Bottom:							
Tip-up					3	12	
Peck at emergent plant		tr	7				tr
Chase flying insect	10		tr				tr
On mud flat				tr			
Maximum depth at site							
0–6 in. (0–16 cm)	tr			50	3	12	
7–12 in. (17–31 cm)	3	11	32	23	3		75
13–18 in. (32–46 cm)	38	23	28	12	20	29	11
19–24 in. (27–62 cm)	30	56	31	15	74	39	11
25–30 in. (63–77 cm)	11	10				20	3
31–36 in. (78–92 cm)	18		9				
Feeding site							
Open water	35	25	30	13			3
Emergent plants	24	20	9	15	17	5	2
Submerged plants	41	55	61	72	83	95	95
Mud flat				tr			

* From Gollop and Marshall (1954).
† One observation per minute.

aquatics. Such plants attract and provide habitat for aquatic invertebrates (Moyle 1961, Sculthorpe 1967) and, perhaps more significantly, are selected as food, particularly by older Gadwalls.

I estimated that 16 per cent of the animal food eaten by Class I Gadwalls was chironomid larvae. Though usually considered bottom fauna, these slow-moving larvae were invariably collected in sweep samples in water; similarly they could be captured by ducklings. I conclude that most chironomid larvae eaten by small Gadwalls were taken from the water near the surface. The complete absence of Trichoptera larvae in Gadwalls in contrast to Pintails and Scaups also indicates little bottom feeding.

American Widgeon Feeding: Surface feeding, prevalent in the early Widgeon age classes, was replaced largely by subsurface feeding and bottom feeding was negligible (Table 18). My observations confirm data which showed that Class Ia Widgeons ate mostly surface insects while older age classes concentrated on aquatic plants. In a Michigan study of duck broods, Beard (1964) reported that American Widgeon ducklings at first fed mostly by surface feeding and dabbling (bill-dipping?). After 4 weeks of age they also began tipping for food, but Beard did not say whether it involved bottom feeding. Tipping in this study involved both subsurface and bottom feeding, though the former was more prevalent.

Feeding Widgeons tended to avoid the shore. Munro (1949) commented on this preference for areas free of emergent plants and suggested it was an adaptive behaviour related to the species' commensal association with diving ducks and coots. He stated that the commensal association began soon after the Widgeons hatched, though the amount of food obtained during summer in this way was much less than that obtained in autumn and winter. I suggest that the Widgeon's preference for water free of emergent plants is primarily an adaptation to its plant diet. Plants sought by Widgeons are not restricted to the shallow margins of ponds and, moreover, occur less frequently among emergent plants. Thus, it is to the species' advantage to seek food over the entire pond. The two characteristics—preference for plant food and preference for open water—have permitted the Widgeon to develop the commensal association with diving ducks. Such an association was not observed in this study, probably because the principal diving duck, Lesser Scaup, was carnivorous. Also, plants eaten by Widgeons were readily available.

As the ducks grew, they fed more over submersed plants. Again, the feeding sites changed as the diet changed from surface insects to aquatic plants. Younger ducklings tended to feed more at random, indicating that their food was more or less distributed throughout the entire pond habitat. Indeed, it was not uncommon to see members of a Class I brood scattered widely over a pond (e.g., up to 10 acres [4 ha]), simultaneously surface feeding on areas of open water, submersed plants, emergent plants and a variety of water depths.

Lesser Scaup Feeding: After 1 week of age, Scaups obtained virtually all their food by diving (Table 18). Although I did not observe it, diet samples showed that Class II Scaups occasionally took surface insects. Scaup ducklings could make dives of short duration within a day or so after hatching. Dives by Class Ia ducks usually lasted 3 to 4 seconds and most were apparently shallow. Bartonek and Hickey (1969*b*) observed a 3-day-old Scaup remain submerged in a tank for 9 seconds. Dives by Class II and III Scaups averaged about 6 seconds in this study. Duration of dives appeared related to water depth and perhaps the mode of feeding. Deeper water and bottom feeding are probably associated with longer dives. On one occasion, Class IIb ducks, known to be bottom feeding in about 4 feet (1.2 m) of water, averaged 14 seconds per dive. Those were the longest dives timed and occurred on one of the deepest ponds. Maximum depth measured on each of 17 Scaup collecting sites varied from 18 to 54 inches (0.46 to 1.37 m) and averaged 29 inches (0.74 m). Bartonek and Murdy (1970) found diet differences between Class I–IIa and IIa–III Scaups and suggested that the older ducks may have fed at greater depths. Sites used by feeding Scaups in that study averaged about 4 feet (1.2 m) in depth.

The diet of Class Ia Scaups and their observed methods of feeding showed little correlation. Over 40 per cent of their feeding took place on the surface, yet less than 5 per cent of their food contained items that occurred there. That this disparity resulted from different ingestion rates was evident on several occasions when ducklings which had been actively surface feeding were collected, only to

Table 19. Feeding activity by Lesser Scaup broods. Figures show percentage of observations (tr < 0.5%).

	Age class						
	Ia	Ib	Ic	IIa	IIb	IIc	III
Age in days*	1–6	7–13	14–20	21–28	29–33	34–42	43–50
Number of broods	17	6	7	7	12	6	6
Total observations†	193	70	105	120	185	110	95
Feeding method							
Surface	41	1	tr				
Chase flying insect	3						
Diving	56	99	100	100	100	100	100
Maximum depth at site							
13–18 in. (32–46 cm)	21			17	5	14	16
19–24 in. (47–62 cm)	45	57	76	67	46	68	53
25–30 in. (63–77 cm)	18	43	24	4	27	18	31
31–36 in. (78–92 cm)	8				11		
37–42 in. (93–107 cm)	8			12			
43–48 in. (108–122 cm)					11		
Feeding site							
Open water	66	70	71	33	68	53	37
Emergent plants	10					1	
Submerged plants	24	30	29	67	32	46	63

* From Gollop and Marshall (1954).
† One observation per minute.

find little or no food in them. Generally, ducklings which had been diving contained more food. The observed feeding activity was not a reliable index to food intake in this case and surface feeding was less efficient than diving for food.

Feeding Scaups preferred deeper areas of ponds probably because plants were sparse or absent in those areas. Data from vegetation surveys showed there was a high probability that open water occurred in the deeper zones of ponds. The feeding site data in Tables 16 and 19 suggest that the absence of submersed plants is not why deeper areas are chosen. However, during observations it was seldom possible to evaluate densities of submersed plants and, if any plants were in the vicinity of the ducks, they were simply recorded as present. Such a crude measurement would not reveal patches of open water present on many ponds. Whether or not the ducks were diving among submersed plants was a rather subjective consideration.

Bartonek and Hickey (1969*b*) reported that most of the lymnaeid and physid snails eaten by Canvasbacks and Redheads were crushed and the shell material washed away. Scaups in my study did not do this and gastropods were intact when removed from the esophagi and proventriculi. This was also true for the three dabbling duck species.

Food Selection.—To understand why ducks eat certain foods and not others, one must first compare the food they eat with that which is available. The comparison is made under the assumption that food sampling data reflect the relative availability of items present. The assumption is not always valid because standard sampling methods fail to duplicate activities of a feeding duck. So-called indexes of preference must be interpreted with this in mind. Probably the

Table 20. Average selection categories* of invertebrates available to the young of four duck species. (Number of collections shown in parentheses.)

Item	Pintail (43)	Gadwall (26)	Widgeon (16)	Scaup (34)
Hirudinea	9.0 (1)	2.5 (4)		6.0 (3)
Anostraca	0 (2)			
Cladocera	1.5 (25)	3.2 (16)	0 (6)	0.7 (14)
Podocopa	3.3 (3)	7.0 (1)		
Eucopepoda		0 (1)		0 (1)
Amphipoda	4.5 (2)	0.2 (5)	0.5 (2)	6.0 (15)
Collembola		9.0 (2)	9.0 (1)	
Ephemeroptera naiads	0 (1)	0 (2)	0 (2)	4.0 (5)
Anisoptera naiads	6.0 (6)		0 (2)	5.0 (1)
Zygoptera naiads	1.8 (9)	0.3 (4)	0.3 (4)	2.4 (14)
Hemiptera	1.6 (20)	3.2 (23)	4.3 (13)	3.5 (25)
Coleoptera adults, larvae	6.7 (20)	7.4 (14)	3.3 (7)	8.1 (9)
Trichoptera larvae	7.6 (5)			9.0 (4)
Diptera larvae, pupae	7.4 (30)	7.7 (21)	6.6 (12)	5.7 (24)
Hydracarina		0.3 (3)	1.0 (2)	2.0 (2)
Gastropoda	1.6 (34)	0.1 (20)	0 (12)	1.4 (26)

* Highest selection indicated by category 0; no selection indicated by 0.

greatest shortcoming occurs when foods must be sampled by more than one method because more than one feeding zone or category of food is involved. How much area of water surface is equivalent to a cubic meter below the surface in terms of available food? How much mud bottom must be sampled to equal a cubic meter of water? How does one compare availability of floating *Lemna* with a stand of seed-bearing *Puccinellia*? Thus, though precise measurements of available foods can be made, it is impossible to escape some subjective interpretation of results.

In determining food selection by ducks in this study, I did not combine animal and plant food data because of the difficuly of comparing availability. When because of age or species characteristics, the ducks were either essentially carnivorous or vegetarian, this posed no problem. However, there were times when invertebrates were obviously selected over plants and vice versa. No satisfactory method was devised to sample surface insects so that valid comparisons with aquatic invertebrates could be made. Nor did I attempt to compare availability of grasses with that of submersed and floating plants. By and large, comparisons are most valid for those items of like habit. Because the ratings are relative, the presence of other items will influence the rating for a given item. When the available food includes mostly unimportant items measured in the habitat, other items will be given a higher rating. Despite its shortcomings, I believe the method does provide a useful guide with which to interpret diet results.

Pintail Food Selection: Pintails appeared to select those items most available to them in terms of their characteristic feeding adaptations (Table 20). The diversity of the Pintail diet further suggests that they ate what was available. This was also evident in individual ducks, some of which had eaten as many as 25 different kinds of animal and plant items. All of the more common invertebrates were selected at least occasionally by Pintails. Considering only those items available in at least four collections (Table 20), highest selection was shown for Trichoptera larvae, Diptera larvae, Coleoptera, and Anisoptera naiads. Lower selection was evident for Zygoptera naiads, Hemiptera, Gastropoda and Cladocera. On the basis of diet analysis and field samples, surface invertebrates were evidently selected over aquatic forms when the former were relatively abundant and available. Low selection of gastropods is believed to reflect low preference rather than availability. Otherwise selection values appeared related to availability. Because Pintails did much of their feeding in shallow areas close to shore and in the mud bottom, organisms characteristic of those zones had highest selection ratings.

I did not attempt to rank plant foods eaten by Pintails because the plant diet varied widely and was obtained from different zones: nutlets from the mud bottom, rooted and unrooted foliage from water and grass seeds from bottom, surface and land. I believe most of the nutlets taken from the bottom were ingested accidentally while the ducks fed on bottom fauna. They were seldom taken in quantities which would indicate that they represented selected items. The frequency of plants on 52 sites (Table 1) provides a measure of abundance with which to compare diet data (Table 13). The following common plants occurred on at least one site from which Pintails over 20 days old were collected and Pintails showed little or no tendency to select them: Cladophoraceae, *Potamogeton, Triglochin, Distichlis, Lemna, Juncus, Rumex, Polygonum, Ranunculus* and *Myriophyllum*. Evidence from two collections indicated that Pintails had selected winter buds of *Potamogeton pusillus*. Some preference was also shown for *Zannichellia*, seeds of *Puccinellia, Beckmannia* and perhaps *Alopecurus*. Generally, if *Zannichellia* was present, it was almost always found in usable specimens. Such was not the case with the grass seeds which were taken sporadically. Data for *Hordeum jubatum* are not conclusive. It comprised a significant amount of the food eaten but seldom occurred in large quantities. It was also one of the most common plants at collecting sites, so it may have been taken largely through accident. Pintails apparently ate little grass seed in Keith's (1961) study. This is significant because, of the grasses for which Pintails in my study showed some preference (*Puccinellia, Beckmannia,* and *Alopecurus*), the last two were not recorded in Keith's plant surveys and *Puccinellia* occurred infrequently on his study area.

Pintails ate a wide variety of foods—animal and plant—and demonstrated an ability to exploit markedly different food resources. Perret (1962) found this was the case with young Mallards. Pintails did show high selection for invertebrates associated with the shallow areas close to shore which they most frequently used. Much of their food was taken from the mud bottom, and their long neck is considered an adaptation for bottom feeding (Olney 1964). It would also be an advantage when stripping seeds from grasses.

Gadwall Food Selection: Selection ratings for invertebrates eaten by Gadwalls (Table 20) do not include surface invertebrates. During periods of emergence when they were abundant, adults of Diptera, Trichoptera and Ephemeroptera were obviously selected over aquatic invertebrates and that depressed values for the latter. As previously discussed, surface invertebrates were most frequently eaten by ducks less than 15 days old.

Trends are apparent for some of the more common items. Gadwalls tended not to select Cladocera though there were two exceptions when cladocerans or their ephippia were apparently abundant enough to be selected. One duck had gorged itself on ephippia that had been concentrated along the shore by wind action. Keith (1961) collected an adult male Gadwall under similar circumstances. Another duckling that I examined had eaten immature cladocerans about 0.3 mm in diameter and contained an estimated 25,000 individuals. Collias and Collias (1963) tested Gadwall ducklings and concluded that they were inept at straining small items from the water.

Amphipods were seldom selected, apparently for a different reason. These mobile crustaceans occur throughout the entire pond, and ducks must pursue and capture them individually. Thus they are largely unavailable to non-diving ducks such as Gadwalls. The same is probably true of insect naiads which do not surface for air. Gadwalls tended to select Coleoptera adults and larvae and Diptera larvae and pupae. Most of the Coleoptera were probably captured when they surfaced for air. Most dipterous larvae were probably taken close to the surface. They move slowly and, hence, are easy prey. There was no trend shown in selection for Hemiptera, principally corixids. They were often present and selection ratings were distributed through all categories (0–9). Notonectids were virtually never taken and accounted for two category "0" ratings for Hemiptera. They are rapid swimmers and probably difficult to capture when they do surface. Gadwalls tended to ignore gastropods which were among the commoner invertebrates. This was clearly out of preference because most gastropods would be available given the feeding anatomy or behaviour of the ducks.

A change in the type of animal foods eaten by Gadwalls, from mainly surface invertebrates during the first few days, to mainly aquatic invertebrates in older birds, was described in the section on Gadwall foods. Chura (1961) reported a similar trend in young Mallards. Because only animal food is involved this comparison is probably valid. As with the Mallards, the change in Gadwall foods was associated with changing feeding methods. Perret (1962) found no such trend in the diet of young Mallards in Manitoba and believed that Chura's (1961) results, with regard to declining use of surface fauna and increasing use of plants, reflected a paucity of aquatic fauna in the habitat. That was not the case in this study and I conclude that the trend in Gadwall diet resulted from a normal change in food selection.

Gadwalls appeared to discriminate more among plant foods (Table 21). Ducklings can exercise more choice in selection of plants since these represent a more stable and uniform food resource. Thus, differences in selection ratings reflect preferences more than with invertebrates. Positive selection was evident for *Lemna minor*, *Zannichellia* and *Potamogeton pusillus*. *Lemna trisulca* and Cladophoraceae occupied an intermediate position and their degree of selection appeared to depend on what else was present. Gadwalls appeared to reject Musci, *Potamogeton pectinatus*, *P. Richardsonii* and *Myriophyllum*. Two cases where spikes of *Potamogeton pectinatus* and *Myriophyllum* were selected also involved beetle larvae.

The one time they were selected in large amounts, *Beckmannia* seeds were apparently taken from the water surface where they were readily available.

A selection hierarchy can be calculated based on food rankings from each collection, though a much larger sample is desirable. To illustrate, *Zannichellia* and

Cladophoraceae occurred simultaneously at collection sites on four occasions and each time *Zannichellia* was selected over Cladophoraceae. Selection for Cladophoraceae usually occurred when such favoured foods as *Potamogeton pusillus*, *Zannichellia* and *Lemna* were absent. On two occasions when *Potamogeton pusillus* and *Lemna minor* were both present, the latter was apparently the preferred food. A selection ranking, based on this method, for the nine most common plants (Gadwall column, Table 21) does not differ significantly from the ranking based on the average selection ratings as given.

American Widgeon Food Selection: Invertebrate selection values for Widgeons are fewer (Table 20) but the pattern is similar to that of Gadwalls. One difference was the Widgeons' non-selection of cladocerans the six times these crustaceans were present in appreciable amounts. Apparently Widgeons are even less inclined than Gadwalls to strain small items. Only three items—Diptera, Hemiptera and Coleoptera—showed significant selection by Widgeons. In one collection, not included in Table 20 for lack of food samples, Widgeons apparently selected gastropods over other invertebrates. This appeared to be an exceptional case.

Selection of plant foods was also similar in Widgeons and Gadwalls. One possible difference was the lower rating for Cladophoraceae in Widgeon collections. In one collection three Class IIc Widgeons had eaten large amounts of combined perigynia and nutlets from *Carex lanuginosa* growing in shallow water. This was the only time that ducks were known to feed on standing Cyperaceae. Why it was selected in this case is not clear but it may be because the pond contained very little of the usual foods eaten by Widgeons.

Table 21. Average selection categories* of plants available to young Gadwalls and Widgeons. (Number of collections shown in parentheses.)

Item	Gadwall (22)	Widgeon (17)
Cladophoraceae	3.7 (7)	1.1 (7)
Chara sp.	9.0 (1)	
Musci	0.3 (3)	3.0 (1)
Potamogeton pectinatus foliage	0.2 (12)	0.2 (12)
Potamogeton vaginatus foliage	0 (1)	0 (1)
Potamogeton Richardsonii foliage	0.2 (4)	0 (1)
Potamogeton pusillus foliage	5.4 (12)	7.2 (10)
Zannichellia palustris foliage, seeds	6.0 (4)	
Lemna trisulca	4.5 (4)	7.5 (2)
Lemna minor	7.8 (5)	7.0 (4)
Ceratophyllum demersum	9.0 (1)	
Ranunculus subrigidus foliage	5.0 (1)	
Myriophyllum exalbescens foliage	0.2 (13)	0.2 (12)

* Highest selection indicated by category 9; no selection indicated by 0.

Lesser Scaup Food Selection: The diet data indicated that food selection by Scaups changed as they grew (Fig. 4). The trend from predominantly bottom larvae to predominantly amphipods was related to movement of the broods to larger ponds. Generally, collections were random and lake size did not restrict collecting. I collected Class I Scaups from all types of water areas, including shallow, temporary ponds covered with emergent plants, and altogether on 16 ponds, of which eight were less than 2 acres (0.8 ha) in size. Older ducklings were seldom found on small ponds and, when they were, the pond was invariably deeper than average. Only three of 15 Class II–III (Scaup) ponds were less than 2 acres. Larger ponds were used by both Class I and older ducks. Low (1945), Smith (1953), Berg (1956), Evans and

Black (1956), Keith (1961), Lokemoen (1966) and Wright (1968) have described a tendency for duck broods to move from small to larger water areas. Low (1945) and Lokemoen (1966) studied Redheads, but in the other studies dabbling ducks contributed most of the data. It is reasonable to assume that Lesser Scaups would show a greater preference than dabbling ducks, for large, deep, open water areas, though they might show less tendency to move overland than some. In the Strathmore area, irrigation ditches and canals facilitated movement by flightless ducks between ponds.

Amphipods also occurred more often in larger and deeper ponds based on invertebrate samples from 54 collecting ponds for all species—the nearest I have to a random sample. They were found in 29 per cent of 38 ponds in the 0- to 3-acre (0- to 1.2-ha) range 56 per cent of 9 ponds in the 4- to 11-acre (1.6- to 4.5-ha) range and all of 7 ponds over 11 acres. Little is known about the over-winter requirements of amphipods. Pennak (1953) implied that they need water, which would mean permanent water areas that do not freeze to the bottom. If that is true, and since water depth and permanency tend to be related to surface area, the observed distribution of amphipods was to be expected. As predictable from the distribution of Scaups and amphipods, the latter occurred more often in ponds used by older ducklings. They occurred in 44 per cent of 16 Class I (Scaup) ponds, and 73 per cent of 15 Class II–III ponds, the difference not being significant ($P > 0.05$). The difference between amphipod occurrence in the 15 Class II–III ponds and that in the 54 collecting ponds that were sampled (73 vs. 43 per cent) is not quite significant at the 5 per cent level ($\chi^2 = 3.29$ with Yate's correction). However, the 54 ponds were not a random sample of water areas since they were chosen because ducks—including older Scaups—were using them. Poston's (1969) data indicate that ponds of less than 3 acres were much more prevalent than the 70 per cent shown above (38 of 54 ponds). Thus there would be fewer amphipods in a random sample of water areas.

I believe Scaups shifted to larger ponds not to seek food but rather, for security and freedom from harassment on larger and deeper ponds. (At least one collection pond dried up before the Scaups would have reached flying age.) The food in small ponds was adequate. Moreover, older Scaups regularly used larger ponds (4 to 15 acres; 1.6 to 6.1 ha) which were without amphipods. There, they ate chiefly bottom larvae.

Considering only items which were available at least four times, Scaups' selection ratings were highest for Trichoptera larvae and Coleoptera adults and larvae (Table 20). These were followed by Amphipoda and Diptera larvae. Scaups of all ages tended to select amphipods when available and, generally, these were chosen over all other invertebrates. Selection of dipterous larvae was variable and often appeared to be influenced by the presence of amphipods. Only once did Scaups select larvae over amphipods. In contrast, larvae were available to some extent virtually every time amphipods were taken. Rogers and Korschgen (1966) also believed that adult Scaups selected amphipods over the more abundant dipterous larvae. They suggested that the amphipods may have been more conspicuous and therefore easier prey. Perhaps amphipods were more palatable to Scaups.

Data for individual collections showed that selection of Hemiptera, Ephemeroptera naiads and Zygoptera naiads was variable and probably reflected their relative availability. On the other hand, gastropods and Cladocera were often present but seldom chosen by Scaups (Table 20), indicating low preference.

Scaups selected a plant food, *Chara* oögonia, only once, on the only site where the plant was found. While this does not prove that *Chara* is a preferred food, it does indicate some preference for diversity. The two ducks which contained *Chara* had evidently strained the oögonia from the water or mud, as no other parts were ingested.

Results of six feeding tests made with various combinations of aquatic invertebrates in the aquarium indicate that ability of prey to escape influenced selection rate by Scaups in the wild. In the confined tank there was nowhere to escape to and the invertebrates were almost equally available. Although too few tests were made for statistical analysis, the selection pattern was consistent for most items. Assigning the value of 100 to the item with the highest selection rate, the following values were obtained from the feeding tests:

Hemiptera (Notonectidae)	100
Anisoptera naiad	100
Zygoptera naiad	90
Hemiptera (Corixidae)	65
Coleoptera (Dytiscidae l.)	60
Coleoptera (Dytiscidae a.)	60
Amphipoda (Gammaridae)	40
Gastropoda (Physidae)	25

The results show that the selection values derived from field data do not necessarily reflect preferences. Amphipods, frequently selected in the ponds, were among the last to be taken in the presence of other items in the tank. In contrast, Zygoptera naiads and notonectids were among the first taken in the tank, but had relatively low selection values in the wild. Gastropods, relatively available in both situations, were least preferred both in the tank and in the ponds.

In the tank, young Scaups tended to prey on the largest items first. Whether or not these attracted their attention first was not determined, but the impression gained from watching them was that size and movement did influence their choice. Where availability is equal, selection of larger items has obvious survival value. Less effort is expended for a given amount of food. I have no data on whether or not wild Scaups select larger items.

Dirschl (1969) concluded that seasonal changes in food selection by adult Lesser Scaups reflected changes in the relative abundance of foods. Bartonek and Murdy (1970) also detected seasonal differences in the diet of young Scaups. However, they suggested that the changes may have resulted from changing feeding methods (i.e., older ducklings may have been diving deeper) because their data did not reveal marked changes in relative food abundance.

In summary, Lesser Scaup ducklings tended to select the most available invertebrates, considering their feeding methods and capabilities. Gastropods were an exception and, though generally available, were not preferred. Apparently amphipods were most often selected because they were frequently the most abundant prey.

Feeding Overlap

Overlap indexes for diet, method of feeding, depth and feeding site for each combination of two species (Table 22) provide but a rough measure of total overlap between species because not all factors that influence it were measured. Distribution of food within the habitat should be measured (Orians and Horn 1969) because food items are seldom ran-

Table 22. Calculated overlap of diet, feeding methods, depth at feeding sites, and feeding sites (emergent plants, submerged plants, open water and mud flat), between combinations of four duckling species (tr < 0.005).

Species	Diet	Method	Depth	Site
Pintail vs. Gadwall	.05	.59	.77	.64
Pintail vs. Widgeon	.05	.61	.77	.69
Pintail vs. Scaup	.34	.03	.18	.88
Gadwall vs. Widgeon	.90	.98	.78	.99
Gadwall vs. Scaup	.02	tr	.35	.69
Widgeon vs. Scaup	.02	tr	.72	.71

domly distributed. Time of use should also be considered (Pianka 1969). For example, populations of certain invertebrates available to Pintails may be different from those available to Scaups—Scaups being 4 to 6 weeks later (Hochbaum 1944; Keith 1961; this study, Table 7). Some invertebrates, such as adult Ephemeroptera, are extremely temporary (2 to 3 days) and use of such food by two species with dissimilar hatching peaks would tend to reduce total overlap. Also, each species tended to choose a certain type of pond. While some ponds were used by all species, others were used little or not at all by one or more; Pintails and Scaups differed most in their choices. The indexes of depth overlap are valid only when the feeding methods are also considered. For example, a Scaup diving in deep water and a Widgeon surface feeding at the same place would have the same depth designation as used here but would be feeding from different zones. Rather broad taxa—orders and classes—were used in the animal food lists. That would bias overlap indexes upward because similarity of invertebrate orders in the diets does not necessarily mean species or even families were the same. Some differences are apparent in proportions given in Table 14, e.g., gastropods in Pintails and Scaups.

Two species combinations—Pintail–Scaup and Gadwall–Widgeon—had significant diet overlaps (Table 22). In the case of Pintail and Scaup, the low overlap for depth as well as factors discussed above would probably make the total overlap insignificant. The actual feeding method overlap between the two species is probably higher than the given estimate because some Scaup activity recorded as *diving*, undoubtedly involved bottom feeding. However, any similarity in foraging methods would not have much bearing on the total overlap between Pintails and Scaups because of the dissimilarity of their habitat use.

Gadwalls and Widgeons showed a high overlap in all factors measured, and I believe the total overlap would also be high. The significance of this will be considered under Discussion. Most of the diet overlap resulted from the similarity of their plant diets. Gadwalls ate a greater variety of plants than Widgeons, but the larger sample of Gadwalls (167 vs. 129) may be the reason. Even during the last year after most Gadwalls had been collected, I found new items in some. Thus a larger sample of Widgeons would also probably contain greater variety.

Another way to compare food selection by different species is to collect more than one species at the same time and place (Talbot and Talbot 1963) so differences in food eaten reflect choice rather than availability. There were 11 mixed collections from which species comparisons could be made (Table 23). Some minor items have been omitted. Of the seven times Gadwalls and Widgeons were collected together, only twice had they eaten the same food in appreciable amounts. Overlap indexes calculated for the Gadwall–Widgeon collections in order of appearance in Table 23 are 0.04, 1.00, 0.03, 0.33, 0.07, 0.08 and 0. The average of these is 0.22 which is considerably lower than the value of 0.90 (Table

Table 23. Comparisons of major foods eaten by two or more species collected at the same time and place. Figures show percentage of dry weight (tr < 0.5%).

	3 IIc–III Gadwalls (1.008 g)*	3 IIc–III Widgeons (0.127 g)
Potamogeton pusillus foliage	0	90
Ceratophyllum demersum foliage	71	tr
Lemna minor	29	8

	1 IIa Gadwall (0.175 g)	3 IIb Widgeons (0.684 g)
Cladophoraceae	99	98

	3 III Gadwalls (1.036 g)	3 III Widgeons (0.071 g)
Cladophoraceae	93	0
Potamogeton pectinatus foliage	3	96
Potamogeton pusillus foliage	3	0
Invertebrates	tr	4

	2 III Gadwalls (1.249 g)	3 IIc Widgeons (0.195 g)
Lemna minor	98	25
Chrinomidae adults	2	75

	1 Ic Gadwall (0.346 g)	2 Ib Widgeons (0.022 g)
Cladophoraceae	73	0
Ranunculus Cymbalaria foliage	0	15
Trichoptera adults	0	38
Chironomidae adults	tr	18
Chironomidae larvae	26	12
Corixidae	0	16

	4 IIa Gadwalls (0.343 g)	3 IIa Widgeons (0.879 g)
Cladophoraceae	38	tr
Lemna minor	46	tr
Potamogeton pusillus foliage	5	90
Other plants	1	6
Invertebrates	9	4

	2 Ib Gadwalls (0.117 g)	2 IIb Widgeons (0.631 g)	6 IIa Scaups (0.810 g)
Cladophoraceae	0	97	0
Cladocera	88	0	46
Diptera larvae	9	1	51

	1 IIc Widgeon (0.051 g)	5 IIa Scaups (0.735 g)
Potamogeton pusillus foliage	98	0
Hirudinea	0	30
Amphipoda	0	58
Other invertebrates	0	12

Table 23. Continued.

	3 IIc–III Gadwalls (1.008 g)*	3 IIc–III Widgeons (0.127 g)
	2 Ic Widgeons (0.288 g)	4 Ib Scaups (0.168 g)
Amphipoda	0	68
Ephemeroptera naiads	0	6
Diptera larvae	0	16
Hemiptera	0	7
Gastropoda	98	0
	1 Ic Widgeon (0.076 g)	1 IIc Pintail (0.378 g)
Lemna trisulca	3	0
Scirpus nutlets	91	1
Carex nutlets	0	24
Alopecurus seeds	0	64
Diptera adults	6	0
Diptera larvae	0	9
	2 IIc Widgeons (0.465 g)	1 III Pintail (0.004 g)
Lemna minor	98	0
Diptera larvae	tr	87
Coleoptera larvae	tr	13

* Total dry weight of food.

22) calculated from diet lists. The difference in foods eaten by the two species collected at the same time and place is surprising considering the similarity of their diets. Age differences in one collection could have accounted for the dissimilar foods eaten. It is also true that the two species were not always taken from a mixed flock and that available food can vary considerably over a portion of a pond. That could account for some of the differences. However, in the first example (Table 23), both species were the same age and had been feeding at the same end of a small pond, yet had selected different foods. Perhaps a larger sample of mixed collections would show fewer differences in food selection by the two species.

There were fewer collections involving other species combinations. In one collection of Class I Gadwalls and Class II Scaups, both had eaten appreciable amounts of Cladocera. Widgeons and Scaups in three collections ate different foods, as did Widgeons and Pintails from two collections.

Nutrient Composition of Duck Foods

Chemical and energy data for 21 duck foods are given in Table 24. Some samples were too small for complete analysis. Except for Corixidae and Coleoptera, each sample was taken from a single site. The calorific content of living organisms is influenced by genetic constitution, nutritive condition and life history which in turn may vary with season, species and environmental conditions (Golley 1961). Thus, average values are good only for extensive surveys of biomass. By the

Table 24. The nutrient and energy content of some duck foods.

Item	Dry matter		Composition on a dry basis,%						
	%	kcal/g	Crude protein	Crude fat	N.F.E.*	Crude fibre	Ash	Ca	P
Cladophoraceae (cf. *Cladophora*)		3.57	16.0	0.2	41.3	22.4	20.1	2.9	0.6
Potamogeton pectinatus foliage	14	3.74	13.3	0.9	57.8	14.7	13.3	2.0	0.6
P. pusillus foliage	15†	3.99	13.7	1.6	56.7	11.4	16.6	1.2	0.8
P. pusillus foliage	15†		13.4	1.1	64.3	13.9	7.3	1.1	0.5
P. pusillus foliage	15†		15.0	1.2	53.3	17.1	13.4	2.7	0.6
P. pusillus winter buds	23	4.99	24.6						
Zannichellia palustris foliage, seeds	18†	4.06	20.3	9.2	47.6	1.3	21.6	1.5	0.7
Puccinellia Nuttalliana seeds	88	4.34	11.1	0.4	70.6	13.1	4.7	0.3	0.5
Glyceria grandis seeds	80†		6.0	1.4	76.1	7.9	8.5	0.3	0.5
Beckmannia syzigachne seeds	90†		7.0	6.5	59.6	20.0	6.9	0.5	0.4
Beckmannia syzigachne seeds	90†	4.73	8.9	4.9	53.3	27.4	5.5		
Scolochloa festucacea seeds	90	4.43	8.8	1.9	67.9	16.1	5.4	0.4	0.4
Alopecurus aequalis seeds	90†		15.5	9.1	51.6	15.5	8.3		
Carex lanuginosa perigynia, nutlets	90†		11.1	4.7	47.6	31.1	5.5		
Lemna trisulca	23	2.47	15.2	0.8	56.2	7.7	20.1	2.0	0.8
Lemna minor	9	4.09	37.1	4.2	37.1	8.8	12.8	1.2	1.2
Cladocera	13	2.71	31.8	1.5	10.9	7.3	48.4	11.8	1.2
Amphipoda *Gammarus* sp.	15	4.02	47.0	5.9	16.5	8.4	22.2		
Zygoptera naiads	19	5.72							
Hemiptera Notonectidae adults	21		62.9	9.4	12.8	9.0	5.9	0.4	1.3
Hemiptera Corixidae adults	20†	5.31	71.5	9.2	0.7	11.5	7.1	0.7	1.0
Coleoptera aquatic adults, larvae	24†	5.93							
Diptera Chironomidae larvae	16	4.30	56.0						
Gastropoda Lymnaeidae	17	0.92	16.9	0.7	5.8	12.4	64.2	26.1	0.3

* Nitrogen-free extract.
† Estimated.

same token, isolated samples may not be representative of average conditions. Variations in plant ash can be caused by calcareous deposits on the leaves in certain lakes (Sculthorpe 1967). This was evident in the samples of *Potamogeton pusillus* (Table 24) in which leaves of two samples were visibly coated. Variations in the nutrient and calorific contents of a series of freshwater plants are summarized from the literature by Straškraba (1968). Cummins and Wuycheck (1971) have compiled an extensive list of calorific values for various animals and plants. Straškraba (1968) demonstrated some correlation between the chemical composition of plants and their ecological category—emergent, submerged and those with floating leaves. Variability of invertebrate composition is well illustrated by the ash content of *Daphnia*. Comita and Schindler (1963) reported no ash after combustion of cladocerans. Ash in Wisconsin *Daphnia* ranged from 2.6 to 25.8 per cent of dry matter (Welch 1952, Wissing and Hasler 1968). In my sample of Cladocera (mostly, if not all, *Daphnia*) ash made up 48 per cent.

The moisture content of natural duck foods is a rather meaningless variant and does not seem to influence food selection. Since the energy available in a food usually governs the amount eaten, those foods with a high water content are probably eaten in greater quantities (wet weight) than are the low-moisture foods. An exception would be when the latter are lower in digestibility. Pulliainen, Paloheimo and Syrjälä (1968) demonstrated this with Willow Grouse (*Lagopus lago-*

Table 25. Partial amino acid composition of 13 duck foods.

	Amino acids on a dry basis, %								
	Dry matter	Alanine	Arginine	Asparagine*	½ Cystine	Glutamic acid	Glycine	Histidine	Isoleucine
Chick requirements†			1.2		0.35‡		1.0	0.3	0.6
Chironomidae larvae	16	6.0	3.2	4.9	0.3	5.2	4.3	2.4	2.2
Corixidae adults	20	10.1	4.4	5.1	0.3	9.0	6.4	3.2	2.8
Gammarus sp.	15	5.5	2.2	3.3	0.3	5.0	4.3	1.4	1.5
Cladocera	13	1.7	1.3	1.3	0.2	3.1	1.4	0.6	0.9
Zannichellia palustris foliage, seeds	18	2.0	1.5	2.2	0.1	2.7	2.1	0.5	0.8
Potamogeton pusillus foliage	15	1.5	1.9	3.1	0.2	2.9	1.5	0.7	0.9
Lemna minor	9	1.5	1.7	4.3	0.1	3.4	1.4	0.5	0.9
Potamogeton pectinatus foliage	14	1.2	1.1	2.5	0.1	2.3	1.2	0.3	0.8
Scolochloa festucacea seeds	90	0.4	0.6	0.7	1.0	1.6	0.4	0.2	0.3
Cladophoraceae cf. *Cladophora*		0.7	0.7	1.7	0.3	2.1	0.8	0.1	0.4
Lemna trisulca	23	0.6	0.6	1.2	0.1	1.2	0.6	0.2	0.4
Puccinellia Nuttalliana seeds	88	0.5	0.6	0.6	0.1	2.0	0.4	0.2	0.3
Lymnaeidae	17	1.2	0.4	1.4	0.0	1.5	0.6	0.2	0.4

	Amino acids on a dry basis, %								
	Leucine	Lysine	Methionine	Phenylalanine	Proline	Serine	Threonine	Tyrosine	Valine
Chick requirements†	1.4	1.0	0.8§	1.4‖			0.6		0.8
Chironomidae larvae	3.3	6.3	0.7	4.9	2.4	2.7	2.5	1.5	2.5
Corixidae adults	5.5	6.2	1.2	1.8	3.8	4.0	3.5	7.5	4.6
Gammarus sp.	2.7	4.3	0.8	1.5	2.6	2.1	2.0	2.9	2.2
Cladocera	1.8	1.7	0.4	2.1	1.2	1.0	0.8	2.0	1.1
Zannichellia palustris foliage, seeds	1.8	1.5	0.4	0.9	0.8	1.6	1.3	0.7	1.2
Potamogeton pusillus foliage	1.8	1.8	0.3	1.3	1.1	1.5	1.3	1.2	1.4
Lemna minor	2.0	1.5	0.4	1.2	1.2	1.2	0.5	0.9	1.2
Potamogeton pectinatus foliage	1.7	1.3	0.3	1.1	1.1	1.1	1.0	0.7	0.9
Scolochloa festucacea seeds	0.5	0.3	0.1	0.6	0.4	0.4	0.3	0.2	0.3
Cladophoracea cf. *Cladophora*	0.7	0.6	0.1	0.6	0.8	0.4	0.6	0.5	0.6
Lemna trisulca	0.8	0.7	0.2	0.6	0.5	0.6	0.5	0.4	0.5
Puccinellia Nuttalliana seeds	0.6	0.4	0.1	0.5	0.5	0.4	0.3	0.3	0.4
Lymnaeidae	0.8	0.6	0.0	0.5	0.6	0.6	0.6	0.4	0.5

* Amide corresponding to aspartic acid.
† Essential amino acid requirements of chicks, 0–8 weeks old; 20 per cent protein in diet (Bolton 1963:79). Tryptophan was not measured in duck foods so is omitted.
‡ Given as cystine.
§ Can be 0.45 per cent if cystine is 0.35 per cent.
‖ Can be 0.7 per cent if tyrosine is 0.7 per cent.

pus). Although *Vaccinium* berries had a higher digestibility than stems, the berries contained more moisture and the wet weight consumption of both was similar.

Evidentally nutrient requirements of wild ducklings are similar to those of domestic ducklings (Holm and Scott 1954, Scott and Holm 1964). A comparison of these requirements (Dean and Scott 1965) with the composition of foods in Table 24 shows that few foods by themselves would supply the basic nutrients in adequate proportions, though increased intake might compensate for certain deficient nutrients in some foods. The number of adequate foods would no doubt be smaller were other essential nutrients (amino acids, vitamins and additional minerals) considered. Apparently a mixture of foods is necessary to supply ducklings with a nutritionally balanced diet.

The little work which has been done on amino acid requirements of waterfowl (Demers and Bernard 1950) and the fact that the protein requirement of ducks is similar to that of chicks (Anonymous 1962) indicate that amino acid requirements of chicks and ducklings are similar. Consequently, I included the essential amino acid requirements of chicks (Bolton 1963) in Table 25 for comparison. Tryptophan is an essential amino acid for chicks but was not measured in the duck foods, so is excluded. In chicks, requirements for some amino acids vary with the level of protein in the diet (Bolton 1963), so any list must be interpreted with that in mind.

There is considerable variation in amino acid composition among the different foods. None of the plant foods meets all the requirements. Of all 13 foods, chironomid larvae, corixids and gammarids would appear to provide the most complete range of amino acids as based on chick requirements. The high quality protein provided by chironomid larvae is significant because these invertebrates seem important in the diets of most, if not all young ducks. Likewise, amphipods are the most important items in their diet. I believe corixids would be equally important were they similarly available. High glycine such as found in corixids can retard growth in chicks when nicotinic acid is inadequate (Bolton 1963), and the same might occur in ducks not eating mixed foods.

Cladocera, *Zannichellia* and *Potamogeton pusillus* are deficient only in cystine and methionine, the sulfur amino acids essential for feather growth. They as well as threonine, are also low in *Lemna minor*. *Potamogeton pectinatus* is low in arganine, cystine and methionine. Evidently a relatively high level of arganine is needed by the duck for rapid growth before feathering (Hegsted and Stare 1945). The remaining five foods are deficient in most essential amino acids.

DISCUSSION

This and other studies have shown that ducklings depend principally on invertebrate foods immediately after hatching. Moreover, during their first few days, dabbling ducks, at least, eat chiefly invertebrates which they capture on or close to the water surface. Veselovsky (1953) believed that during their first few days, ducklings took only items which they could see. Hochbaum (1944) stated that, although newly-hatched Canvasbacks could dive, they obtained most of their food from the surface during their first 2 weeks. During the first few days there was considerable overlap among the diets of the four species. The average diet of Scaups differed most, but the diet of some Scaups was indistinguishable from that of the three dabbling species.

The similarity of diets during the first few days is paralleled by a similarity in feeding behaviour and feeding apparatus. Veselovsky (1953) reported that at hatching the different duckling species have gills similar in structure. I examined a series of bills from each of the four species in this study and agree. The bill of a newly-hatched duckling is relatively unspecialized and appears adapted primarily for the gaping-action (Goodman and Fisher 1962), common to all anatids. As a duckling grows its bill becomes more specialized. In the three dabbling species there was a concomitant change of feeding behaviour and diet with bill specialization. No doubt other changes occur which parallel the dietary transition. Increased size would bring more underwater food within reach. There may be physiological changes enabling older ducks to remain submerged longer. Muscles required for adult feeding methods (Goodman and Fisher 1962) may be ineffective in small ducklings. The ability to digest plant foods may increase with age.

Unspecialized feeding apparatus and behaviour early in the life of ducklings could be considered an adaptation in itself. Because of their small size and buoyancy in the water, downy ducklings are largely confined to a narrow feeding zone close to the water surface and they must all share a limited supply of animal food. An overlap in diet by several species of young ducks using the same habitat at first appears to belie the concept of species' ecological niches. However the degree of overlap would be more apparent than real as it occurs when food intake is at a minimum. The need for adaptations that ecologically isolate species from one another becomes greater as the birds grow, eat more food and the potential for interspecific competition increases.

Although measurements are lacking, I believe surface invertebrates on the average study lake were not dense enough to sustain a duck beyond its first few days. Because surface feeding involves much moving about, the energy required to obtain food would increase with age (size). A comparison of the Scaup diet with feeding activity data indicated that surface feeding on invertebrates was inefficient for Scaups. Certainly terrestrial (flying) insects, which constitute most of the surface fauna available to ducks, were not a stable source of food when compared with aquatic invertebrates. During periods of emergence on calm days, adults of Chironomidae, Ephemeroptera and Trichoptera were abundant and taken in large numbers by ducks of all ages. But more often, and particularly on windy days, they were sparse on the water surface. When a duckling's energy requirements are minimum, it can obtain sufficient invertebrate food from the surface most of the time. But as its requirements increase, it soon reaches the point where it cannot secure enough food to meet its needs. Then it must either seek food in other zones or change to a diet of the more abundant plant foods. To varying degrees, both methods were used by the dabbling species studied.

Closely related bird species in the same area usually differ in habitat, food selection or other features which prevent competition for food (Lack 1954). In this study, only the Gadwall and Widgeon showed sufficient feeding overlap to suggest possible competition. Similarity of diet does not mean that two species are competing for food (Crombie 1947, Lack 1954, Milne 1961). Competition occurs when two or more animals use a resource which is insufficient to meet the needs of all. It also occurs when animals seeking a common resource harm one another in the process, despite an adequate supply (Birch 1957) and when behavioural interactions prevent an animal from using an otherwise plentiful resource (Gibb 1961). This latter aspect was not investigated, but casual observations suggest that it was unimportant. Gadwalls seemed tolerant towards Widgeons and vice versa. There was no evidence that Gadwalls and Widgeons were competing for food despite the similarity of their diets. The co-existence of sympatric species, of course, is dependent on the absence of competition (Lack 1944, 1945). Generally there appeared to be an abundance of foods, plant foods in particular, and, except for the removal of seeds from a few grasses, nowhere could I find evidence of significant use of plants by ducks. Also, the overlap in the animal portion of their diets took place when food intake was minimum. It may be significant that the highest overlap occurred between two essentially herbivorous species. Data summarized from the literature by Moyle (1961) indicate that the standing crop of aquatic plants in lakes is several times greater than the invertebrate standing crop. Thus there would be more opportunity for herbivores to eat the same foods without competing. This is in keeping with the concept that herbivore populations are seldom limited by food resources (Hairston et al. 1960).

In the Strathmore area, the way breeding pairs are spaced throughout the habitat (McKinney 1965) results in populations of young which are well within the food carrying capacity. While the function of pair spacing may not be related to food of young, the effect is the same. Lack (1966) believed that limited food outside the breeding season was the most important density-dependent factor regulating numbers of wild birds. Most species share certain components of their ecological niches in varying degrees with other species. When a shared component is in good supply and, by itself, does not limit either species' population, then considerable overlap occurs as with foods of young Gadwalls and Widgeons. Absence of food competition between duckling species on my study area does not preclude interspecific competition in other habitats. The Strathmore area is probably atypical of prairie breeding habitat in that irrigation water helps to maintain water levels throughout the brood season. Ditches and canals also facilitate movement of ducks between water areas. The ratio of ponds available to broods to those available to breeding pairs would be higher than on most areas without irrigation. Thus the brood population in the Strathmore area would have access to more habitat than a similar population on prairie habitat with no irrigation.

My results show that both preference and availability influence ducks in their selection of food. Choice of invertebrates appears to depend more on availability than does choice of plants. Plants represent a more stable and usually more abundant source of food, so ducks have greater opportunity to exercise a choice when eating them. There is some evidence that ducks seek diversity in their diet. Because of varying supplies of available foods—particularly invertebrates—a mixed diet may have been imposed in some cases, whether or not it was preferred. However, there were times when each species selected certain foods for no apparent reason other than a preference for a change. The fact that gastropods or certain plants were sometimes selected but often ignored suggests a preference for diversity. Occasionally Pintails ate large quantities of grass seeds and there was every reason to believe they could have eaten these foods exclusively had they so chosen. Similar examples could be cited for the other species. The variety of foods sometimes found in ducks also suggested a preference for a mixed diet. Individual contents sometimes reflected an abrupt change in food selection. In three Pintails collected from a small pond, the esophagi were packed with food and contained *Puccinellia* seeds in the lower half and chironomid larvae in the upper half. The ducks seemed to have switched foods simply out of preference.

Other vertebrates prefer a mixed diet.

Tinbergen (1960) reported that Great Tits (*Parus major*) did not restrict their diet to one prey, despite the fact it was abundant and readily available. He believed the birds preferred a mixed diet. Holling (1959) showed that *Peromyscus* preferred a mixed diet: although sawfly pupae were preferred and available, the mice continued to eat some of the alternate foods. Young (1940) concluded that white rats selected food on the basis of food eaten beforehand. He established that rats consistently preferred sugar to wheat when given a choice. However, when they were pre-fed sugar ad libitum and then presented with a choice, the original preferences were reversed.

Ducks that select a mixed diet have two obvious advantages. First, they can adapt readily to changing food resources and secondly, they are more apt to obtain a balanced diet. Chemical analyses showed that few foods by themselves would provide all the nutritional requirements of ducks. Behaviourally, seeking a mixed diet may be the same as selecting foods that provide a balanced diet (Dove 1935, Young 1941, Treichler et al. 1946, Newton 1964, Rodgers and Rozin 1966, Miller 1968). Scott and Verney (1947) tested rats with diets containing variable amounts of B vitamins, and concluded that the rats associated certain adequate diets with a certain flavour. That is, the appetite for the diet containing the needed vitamin was learned (associated with well-being), and not innate. Much the same conclusion was reached by Young (1948) in his rat studies.

It is tempting to compare food quality and food selection by ducks in this study because data suggest that preferred foods were also among the highest in quality as measured by crude protein in dry matter. However, additional analyses are needed of both selected and non-selected foods before valid conclusions can be made. Moreover, I doubt if valid comparisons can be made from field data because other variables such as availability and palatability also influence selection. Stoudt (1944) and Spinner and Bishop (1950) pointed out that preference ratings of foods eaten by game animals during the hunting season may be biased when animals are forced into marginal habitat where they must subsist on low-preference foods. While this was not a factor in my study it does illustrate the type of variable encountered in field studies. Perhaps we are seeking the impossible when we try to correlate food selection with food quality when the latter is expressed in terms of crude protein or calorific energy. These tell nothing of the food value in terms of metabolizable energy, available amino acids, vitamins or minerals.

I did not compare the composition of duck diets throughout the season nor throughout the 5 study years because sample sizes for each species' age group were too small. However, changes in diets during the flightless period appeared largely due to changes in food selection as the ducks grew and not to changes in available food. Annual and seasonal differences in diets as found in young Mallards by Perret (1962) and in adult Lesser Scaups and Blue-winged Teals (*Anas discors*) by Dirschl (1969), respectively, could be expected if the foods available change over time. In the Strathmore area, there was greater variability of foods available among ponds at any one time, than throughout the season or between years for any one pond.

This study has reaffirmed the importance of invertebrates as food for small ducklings and, in particular, the dependence of ducklings on chironomids for much of their early diet. It also supports previous studies showing that young Lesser Scaups are chiefly carnivorous and eat mostly amphipods. Probably because Gadwalls and Widgeons previously had not been studied in detail, my results show that foliage of aquatic plants—particularly *Potamogeton pusillus* and Cladophoraceae—must be added to the list of important duckling foods. Use of grass seeds, particularly *Puccinellia* and *Beckmannia*, was also more prevalent in this study than in previous ones.

The degree of feeding overlap varies widely among the different combinations of species. Whether or not any species combinations which were not studied have greater feeding overlap is not known. Considering the many factors that tend to ecologically isolate species, it is reasonable to assume that no two species would show complete overlap during the flightless period, except perhaps during the first few days of life. Consequently, most, if not all habitats will be used most efficiently and completely when occupied by a variety of species. This, of course, is an established principle and has been demonstrated for a wide variety of species. Other comparative studies which have shown that sympatric duck species tend to eat different foods and/or use different parts of the habitat, are those of Collias and Collias (1963), Olney (1964), Dirschl (1969) and Bartonek and Hickey (1969*a*). By the same token, the most diversified habitat will meet the needs of the greatest variety and, hence, the largest number of ducks. Moreover, diversity is needed to meet the changing requirements of at least some species.

SUMMARY

1. The objectives of the 5-year study were to determine the prefledgling diets of Gadwalls, Pintails, American Widgeons and Lesser Scaups in the Strathmore area of southern Alberta; investigate factors which influence food use; and determine the nutritional composition of duck foods.

2. Esophagus-proventriculus samples from 144 Pintails, 167 Gadwalls, 129 Widgeons and 135 Scaups were collected for study. Diet analyses are based on percentage of dry weight. Percentages of occurrence and gross energy are included for comparison.

3. A comparison of esophagus material with that for esophagus and proventriculus combined showed that proportions of some seeds were lower in the former though differences were small and involved minor items. There was no direct evidence that differences were caused by differential digestion.

4. The early diet of Pintails was dominated by surface invertebrates that were later replaced by aquatic invertebrates and, to a lesser extent, plants. The prefledgling diet contained 67 per cent animal food. Gastropods, insects and cladocerans made up 36, 26 and 4 per cent of the total diet, respectively. The dominant insect order was Diptera (18 per cent), chiefly chironomid larvae. Seeds of Gramineae and Cyperaceae accounted for 19 and 8 per cent, respectively.

5. Gadwalls ate chiefly surface invertebrates during their first few days. These were gradually replaced by aquatic invertebrates and plants until, by 3 weeks of age, Gadwalls were essentially herbivorous. The prefledgling diet contained 10 per cent animals—entirely invertebrates. The most important invertebrates eaten by Gadwalls were chironomid larvae and adults, aquatic beetles, cladocerans and corixids. *Potamogeton pusillus* foliage, Cladophoraceae, *Beckmannia* seeds and *Lemna minor* made up 34, 19, 10 and 7 per cent of the diet, respectively.

6. Widgeons had a diet similar to that of Gadwalls. It contained 11 per cent animal and 89 per cent plant food. At first Widgeons ate predominantly animal food, chiefly surface invertebrates. By 3 weeks they were eating less than 10 per cent animal food. Diptera adults, principally chironomids, were the most important invertebrates and made up 4 per cent of the total diet. *Potamogeton pusillus* foliage, Cladophoraceae, *Carex lanuginosa* and *Lemna minor* contributed 47, 18, 9 and 4 per cent, respectively.

7. Lesser Scaups were essentially carnivorous. Amphipods, dipterous larvae and gastropods made up 52, 16 and 16 per cent, respectively, of their diet. Chironomids were the most important Diptera. Older Scaups ate relatively more amphipods and less bottom larvae. This was attributed to brood movements to larger ponds where amphipods were more prevalent.

8. Changes in feeding methods and site use by dabbling species paralleled diet changes. As they grew, Pintails did more bottom feeding and necessarily, most of their feeding occurred in water less than 12 inches (31 cm) deep. In contrast, young Gadwalls and Widgeons replaced surface feeding principally by subsurface feeding. They tended to feed in areas deeper than those used by Pintails and much of their feeding occurred over submersed plants. Although newly-hatched Scaups did considerable surface feeding, it was not reflected in their diet, indicating that surface feeding was inefficient compared with diving for food. After the first week, virtually all feeding was done by diving. Scaups tended to use deeper parts of ponds than the dabbling ducks.

9. A comparison of food available with food eaten showed that the ducks selected the most available invertebrates considering their characteristic feeding adaptations. An exception was the low selection of gastropods which were apparently not preferred. Use of plants was influenced more by preference. There was some evidence that ducks sought a mixed diet and this may be related to selection of foods providing a nutritionally balanced diet.

10. Overlap indexes for combinations of the four species were calculated for diet, feeding method, depth at feeding site and feeding site (open water, emergent plants, submerged plants and mud flat). Only two combinations—Pintail–Scaup and Gadwall–Widgeon—had a significant diet overlap. These were 0.34 and 0.90, respectively. Total overlap between Pintails and Scaups would be insignificant because of differences in habitat and seasonal use. Total overlap between Gadwalls and Widgeons was high because of similarities in habitat and seasonal use. There appeared to be an abundance of the two species' major foods and they did not compete.

11. Newly-hatched ducklings of the three dabbling species were unspecialized in their feeding adaptations and behaviour and ate the same kinds of food. This overlap in diet occurred when food intake was minimum and when, for various reasons, the available food was restricted. Since surface invertebrates were generally insufficient to maintain them beyond their first few days, ducklings either sought more of their food in other zones, or switched to more abundant plant foods, or both.

12. Proximate analysis and calorific content of 21 duck foods and amino acid composition of 13 foods are given. Few foods by themselves would supply the nutritional requirements in adequate proportions, and a mixed diet may be needed to meet the needs of ducklings. Chironomid larvae, *Gammarus*, and co-

rixids contained the highest quality protein in terms of amino acid requirements of chicks. Of eight plant foods anlaysed, *Zannichellia* and *Potamogeton pusillus* had the highest quality protein, though they did appear deficient in cystine and methionine.

13. This and previous studies have shown that a diverse habitat will meet the needs of the greatest variety of species and, hence, the largest number of ducks. Each species requires diversity of food to meet its changing requirements throughout the prefledgling period.

ACKNOWLEDGMENTS

This study was carried out as a Canadian Wildlife Service research project. Of my many colleagues who provided stimulation, special thanks are due J. B. Gollop, CWS, who gave helpful advice throughout the project and reviewed the manuscript. I wish also to acknowledge the advice and encouragement of J. B. Low, Utah State University, and D. A. Munro, former director, CWS. Thanks are also proffered to H. J. Poston and K. Vermeer for their assistance in the field.

Others aided in diverse ways: A. H. Holmgren and H. M. Nielsen, Utah State University, checked plant identifications and supervised amino acid determinations, respectively; C. M. Grieve, University of Alberta, and J. M. Bell, University of Saskatchewan, each supervised certain laboratory analyses; Vera M. Reynolds, Canada Department of Agriculture, checked identification of seeds; W. J. Hanson, Utah State University, helped with invertebrate identifications; and G. Freeman, Ducks Unlimited Canada, contributed to the success of field work.

LITERATURE CITED

AMERICAN ORNITHOLOGISTS' UNION. 1957. Check-list of North American birds. 5th ed. A.O.U. Port City Press, Inc. Baltimore, Maryland. 691pp.

ANDERSON, R. O. 1959. A modified flotation technique for sorting bottom fauna samples. Limnol. Oceanogr. 4:223–225.

ANONYMOUS. 1962. Nutrient requirements of domestic animals. Number 1. Nutrient requirements of poultry. Nat. Acad. Sci. Nat. Res. Council. Washington, D.C. Pub. 827. 33pp.

BARTONEK, J. C. 1968. Summer foods and feeding habits of diving ducks in Manitoba. Unpublished Ph.D. dissertation. Univ. Wisconsin. Madison, Wisconsin. 113pp.

———, AND J. J. HICKEY. 1969*a*. Food habits of Canvasbacks, Redheads, and Lesser Scaup in Manitoba. Condor 71:280–290.

———, AND ———. 1969*b*. Selective feeding by juvenile diving ducks in summer. Auk 86:443–457.

———, AND H. W. MURDY. 1970. Summer foods of Lesser Scaup in subarctic taiga. Arctic 23:35–44.

BEARD, E. B. 1964. Duck brood behavior at the Seney National Wildlife Refuge. J. Wildl. Mgmt. 28:492–521.

BERG, P. F. 1956. A study of waterfowl broods in eastern Montana with special reference to movements and the relationship of reservoir fencing to production. J. Wildl. Mgmt. 20:253–262.

BIRCH, L. C. 1957. The meanings of competition. Amer. Natur. 91:5–18.

BOLTON, W. 1963. Poultry nutrition. U.K. Min. Agr., Fisheries and Food. Bull. No. 174. 99pp.

BORROR, D. J., AND D. M. DELONG. 1964. An introduction to the study of insects. 2nd ed. Holt, Rinehart and Winston, Inc. New York. 819pp.

CHURA, N. J. 1961. Food availability and preferences of juvenile mallards. N. Amer. Wildl. Conf. Trans. 26:121–133.

———. 1963. Diurnal feeding periodicity of juvenile mallards. Wilson Bull. 75:90.

COLLIAS, N. E., AND E. C. COLLIAS. 1963. Selective feeding by wild ducklings of different species. Wilson Bull. 75:6–14.

COMITA, G. W., AND D. W. SCHINDLER. 1963. Calorific values of Microcrustacea. Science 140:1394–1396.

COTTAM, C. 1939. Food habits of North American diving ducks. U.S. Dep. Agr., Tech. Bull. No. 643. 140pp.

COULTER, M. W. 1955. Spring food habits of surface-feeding ducks in Maine. J. Wildl. Mgmt. 19:263–267.

COUPLAND, R. T. 1961. A reconsideration of grassland classification in the northern Great Plains of North America. J. Ecol. 49:135–167.

CROMBIE, A. C. 1947. Interspecific competition. J. Anim. Ecol. 16:44–73.

CUMMINS, K. W., AND J. C. WUYCHECK. 1971. Caloric equivalents for investigations in ecological energetics. Mitt. Int. Verein. Limnol. No. 18. 158pp.

DAVISON, V. E. 1940. A field method of analyzing game bird foods. J. Wildl. Mgmt. 4:105–116.

DEAN, W. F., AND M. L. SCOTT. 1965. Nutrient requirements of ducks. Cornell Feed Serv. No. 60:1–5.

DEMERS, J. M., AND R. BERNARD. 1950. Further work on the nutrition of ducklings. A. Lipotropic factors. B. Sulphur amino acid requirements. Can. J. Res. E 28:202–211.

DILLERY, D. G. 1965. Post-mortem digestion of stomach contents in the savannah sparrow. Auk 82:281.

DILLON, O. W., JR. 1959. Food habits of wild mallard ducks in three Louisiana parishes. N. Amer. Wildl. Conf. Trans. 24:374–382.

DIRSCHL, H. J. 1969. Foods of lesser scaup and blue-winged teal in the Saskatchewan River Delta. J. Wildl. Mgmt. 33:77–87.

DOVE, W. F. 1935. A study of individuality in the nutritive instincts and of the causes and effects of variations in the selection of food. Amer. Natur. 69:469–544.

DZUBIN, A. 1959. Growth and plumage development of wild-trapped juvenile canvasback (*Aythya valisineria*). J. Wildl. Mgmt. 23:279–290.

ETKIN, W., editor. 1964. Social behavior and organization among vertebrates. Univ. Chicago Press. Chicago, Illinois. 307pp.

EVANS, C. D., AND K. E. BLACK. 1956. Duck production studies on the prairie potholes of South Dakota. U.S. Dep. Interior. Fish and Wildl. Serv. Spec. Sci. Rep. No. 32. 59pp.

FERNALD, M. L. 1950. Gray's manual of botany. 8th ed. American Book Co. New York. 1632pp.

GATES, J. M. 1957. Autumn food habits of the gadwall in northern Utah. Utah Acad. Proc. 34:69–71.

GIBB, J. A. 1961. Bird populations, pp. 413–446. *In* A. J. Marshall, ed. Biology and comparative physiology of birds, 1961. Vol. II. Academic Press. New York. 468pp.

GLASGOW, L. L., AND J. L. BARDWELL. 1962. Pintail and teal foods in south Louisiana. Annu. Conf. SE Ass. Game and Fish Comm. Proc. 16:175–184.

GOLLEY, F. B. 1961. Energy values of ecological materials. Ecology 42:581–584.

GOLLOP, J. B., AND W. H. MARSHALL. 1954. A guide for aging ducklings in the field. Mississippi Flyway Council Tech. Sec. Mimeo. 14pp.

GOODMAN, D. C., AND H. I. FISHER. 1962. Functional anatomy of the feeding apparatus in waterfowl. Aves: Anatidae. Southern Illinois Univ. Press. Carbondale, Illinois. 193pp.

HAIRSTON, N. G., F. E. SMITH, AND L. B. SLOBODKIN. 1960. Community structure, population control, and competition. Amer. Natur. 94:421–425.

HANSON, H. C. 1965. The giant Canada Goose. Southern Illinois Univ. Press. Carbondale, Illinois. 226pp.

HANSON, W. R., AND F. GRAYBILL. 1956. Sample size in food-habits analyses. J. Wildl. Mgmt. 20:64–68.

HARTLEY, P. H. T. 1948. The assessment of the food of birds. Ibis 90:361–381.

HEGSTED, D. M., AND F. J. STARE. 1945. Nutritional studies with the duck. I. Purified rations for the duck. J. Nutrition 30:37–44.

HITCHCOCK, A. S. 1950. Manual of the grasses of the United States. 2nd ed. U.S. Dep. Agr. Washington, D.C. 1051pp.

HOCHBAUM, H. A. 1944. The canvasback on a prairie marsh. Am. Wildl. Inst. Washington, D.C. 201pp.

HOLLING, C. S. 1959. The components of predation as revealed by a study of small mammal predation of the European pine sawfly. Can. Entomol. 91:293–320.

HOLM, E. R., AND M. L. SCOTT. 1954. Studies on the nutrition of wild waterfowl. New York Fish and Game J. 1:171–187.

HORN, H. S. 1966. Measurement of "overlap" in comparative ecological studies. Amer. Natur. 100:419–424.

HUTCHINSON, G. E. 1967. A treatise on limnology. Vol. II. John Wiley and Sons, Inc. New York. 1115pp.

JOHNSGARD, P. A. 1965. Handbook of waterfowl behavior. Cornell Univ. Press. Ithaca, New York. 378pp.

JORDAN, J. S. 1953. Consumption of cereal grains by migratory waterfowl. J. Wildl. Mgmt. 17:120–123.

KEAR, J., AND P. A. JOHNSGARD. 1968. Foraging dives by surface-feeding ducks. Wilson Bull. 80:231.

KEITH, L. B. 1961. A study of waterfowl ecology on small impoundments in southeastern Alberta. Wildl. Monogr. 6:1–88.

KOERSVELD, E. VAN. 1951. Difficulties in stomach analysis. Int. Ornith. Congr. Proc. 10:592–594.

LACK, D. 1944. Ecological aspects of species formation in passerine birds. Ibis 86:260–286.

———. 1945. The ecology of closely related species with special reference to cormorant (*Phalacrocorax carbo*) and shag (*P. aristotelis*). J. Anim. Ecol. 14:12–16.

———. 1954. The natural regulation of animal numbers. Oxford Univ. Press. London. 343pp.

———. 1966. Population studies of birds. Oxford Univ. Press. London. 341pp.

LINDUSKA, J. P., editor. 1964. Waterfowl tomorrow. U.S. Dep. Interior. Washington, D.C. 770pp.

LOKEMOEN, J. T. 1966. Breeding ecology of the redhead duck in western Montana. J. Wildl. Mgmt. 30:668–681.

LOW, J. B. 1945. Ecology and management of the redhead, *Nyroca americana*, in Iowa. Ecol. Monogr. 15:35–69.

MACARTHUR, R. H. 1958. Population ecology of

some warblers of north-eastern coniferous forests. Ecology 39:599–619.

MCKINNEY, F. 1965. Spacing and chasing in breeding ducks. pp. 92–106. *In* Wildfowl Trust annual report for 1964.

MILLER, G. R. 1968. Evidence for selective feeding on fertilized plots by red grouse, hares, and rabbits. J. Wildl. Mgmt. 32:849–853.

MILNE, A. 1961. Definition of competition among animals. Soc. Exp. Biol. Symp. 15:40–61.

MOSS, E. H. 1944. The prairie and associated vegetation of southwestern Alberta. Can. J. Res. C 22:11–31.

———. 1955. The vegetation of Alberta. Bot. Rev. 21:493–567.

MOYLE, J. B. 1961. Aquatic invertebrates as related to larger water plants and waterfowl. Minnesota Dep. Conserv. Invest. Rep. No. 233. 24pp.

MUNRO, J. A. 1941. Studies of waterfowl in British Columbia. Greater scaup duck, lesser scaup duck. Can. J. Res. D 19:113–138.

———. 1944. Studies of waterfowl in British Columbia. Pintail. Can. J. Res. D 22:60–86.

———. 1949. Studies of waterfowl in British Columbia. Baldpate. Can. J. Res. D 27:289–307.

NEWTON, I. 1964. Bud-eating by bullfinches in relation to the natural food-supply. J. Appl. Ecol. 1:265–279.

OLNEY, P. J. S 1964. The autumn and winter feeding biology of certain sympatric ducks. Intern. Union Game Biol. Trans. 6:309–322.

ORIANS, G. H., AND H. S. HORN. 1969. Overlap in foods and foraging of four species of blackbirds in the Potholes of central Washington. Ecology 50:930–938.

ORING, L. W. 1968. Growth, molts, and plumages of the gadwall. Auk 85:355–380.

PENNAK, R. W. 1953. Fresh-water invertebrates of the United States. Ronald Press Co. New York. 769pp.

PENNEY, J. G., AND E. D. BAILEY. 1970. Comparison of the energy requirements of fledgling black ducks and American coots. J. Wildl. Mgmt. 34:105–114.

PERRET, N. G. 1962. The spring and summer foods of the common mallard (*Anas p. platyrhynchos* L.) in south central Manitoba. Unpublished M. Sc. Thesis. Univ. B.C. Vancouver. 82pp.

PIANKA, E. R. 1969. Sympatry of desert lizards (*Ctenotus*) in western Australia. Ecology 50:1012–1030.

POSTON, H. J. 1969. Home range and breeding biology of the shoveler. Unpublished M.S. Thesis. Utah State Univ. Logan, Utah. 86pp.

PULLIAINEN, E., L. PALOHEIMO, L. SYRJÄLÄ. 1968. Digestibility of blueberry stems (*Vaccinium myrtillus*) and cowberries (*Vaccinium vitis idaea*) in the willow grouse (*Lagopus lagopus*). Annales Acad. Sci. Fennicae, Ser. A. IV Biol. No. 126. 15pp.

RODGERS, W., AND P. ROZEN. 1966. Novel food preferences in thiamine-deficient rats. J. Comp. Physiol. Psychol. 61:1–4.

ROGERS, J. P., AND L. J. KORSCHGEN. 1966. Foods of lesser scaups on breeding, migration, and wintering areas. J. Wildl. Mgmt. 30:258–264.

SCOTT, E. M., AND E. L. VERNEY. 1947. Self selection of diet. VI. The nature of appetites for B vitamins. J. Nutrition 34:471–480.

SCOTT, M. L., AND E. R. HOLM. 1964. Nutrition of wild waterfowl. Cornell Nutrition Conf. for Feed Manufacturers. Proc. 149–155.

SCULTHORPE, C. D. 1967. The biology of aquatic vascular plants. Edward Arnold (Publishers) Ltd. London. 610pp.

SINCOCK, J. L. 1962. Estimating consumption of food by wintering waterfowl populations. Annu. Conf. SE Ass. Game and Fish Comm. 16:217–221.

SMART, G. 1965. Body weights of newly hatched Anatidae. Auk 82:645–648.

SMITH, R. H. 1953. A study of waterfowl production on artificial reservoirs in eastern Montana. J. Wildl. Mgmt. 17:276–291.

SMITH, R. I. 1966. Review of Handbook of Waterfowl Behavior by P. A. Johnsgard. Wilson Bull. 78:483–484.

SPINNER, G. P., AND J. S. BISHOP. 1950. Chemical analysis of some wildlife foods in Connecticut. J. Wildl. Mgmt. 14:175–180.

STOUDT, J. H. 1944. Food preferences of mallards on the Chippewa National Forest, Minnesota. J. Wildl. Mgmt. 8:100–112.

STRAŠKRABA, M. 1968. Der Anteil der höheren Pflanzen an der Produktion der stehenden Gewässer. Mitt. Int. Verein. Limnol. 14:212–230.

SUGDEN, L. G., AND L. E. HARRIS. 1972. Energy requirements and growth of captive lesser scaup. Poul. Sci. 51:625–633.

TALBOT, L. M., AND M. H. TALBOT. 1963. The high biomass of wild ungulates on East African Savanna. N. Amer. Wildl. Conf. Trans. 28:465–476.

TINBERGEN, L. 1960. The dynamics of insect and bird populations in pine woods. Arch. Néerlandaises Zool. 13:265–336.

TREICHLER, R., R. W. STOW, AND A. L. NELSON. 1946. Nutrient content of some winter foods of ruffed grouse. J. Wildl. Mgmt. 10:12–17.

VESELOVSKY, Z. 1953. Postembryonal development of our wild ducks. [Translation from original Czech paper *in* Sylvia 14:36–73.] Northern and Indian Affairs Library, Ottawa. No. 42586 CZECH.

WELCH, P. S. 1952. Limnology. 2nd ed. McGraw-Hill Book Co. New York. 538pp.

WISSING, T. E., AND A. D. HASLER. 1968. Calorific values of some invertebrates in Lake Mendota, Wisconsin. J. Fisheries Res. Board of Can. 25:2515–2518.

WRIGHT, E. M. 1968. A comparative study of farm dugouts and natural ponds and their utilization by waterfowl. Unpublished M.Sc. Thesis. Univ. Alberta. Edmonton. 145pp.

WYATT, F. A., J. D. NEWTON, W. E. BOWSER, AND W. ODYNSKY. 1942. Soil survey of Blackfoot and Calgary sheets. Dep. Ext. Univ. of Alberta. Edmonton. Bull. 39. 44pp.

YOUNG, P. T. 1940. Reversal of food preferences of the white rat through controlled pre-feeding. J. Gen. Psychol. 22:33–66.

———. 1941. The experiment analysis of appetite. Psychol. Bull. 38:129–164.

———. 1948. Appetite, palatability and feeding habit: a critical review. Psychol. Bull. 45:289–320.

AQUATIC PLANT-MACROINVERTEBRATE ASSOCIATIONS AND WATERFOWL[1]

JOHN N. KRULL, Department of Forest Zoology, State University of New York, College of Forestry, Syracuse[2]

Abstract: An ecological study was conducted to determine the association of macroinvertebrates with 12 species of submerged aquatic plants common in central New York. The abundance and kind of animals associated with each plant species and with their substrates were determined. An Ekman dredge was used in obtaining the samples, which totaled 543 for the plants and 181 for the combined plant-substrate samples. These were taken in the shallows of five aquatic areas during the period of April–October, 1966. A total of 114 different taxonomic categories of animals was collected. Some plants harbored a larger biomass, greater numbers, and a greater taxonomic diversity than other hydrophytes. Three plant species harbored nearly 60 percent of the animal species found. Macroinvertebrates appeared to be many times more abundant in vegetated areas than in non-vegetated areas. On the average, 1 g of animal life was found associated with 100 g of plant material. Hydrophytes believed to be poor waterfowl food plants almost assuredly are indirectly important to waterfowl production, because they harbor large quantities of macroinvertebrates which furnish a source of animal protein.

The primary objective of this study was to relate the abundance, diversity, and seasonal occurrence of macroinvertebrates to several species of submerged aquatic plants. Abundance and diversity of benthos beneath the plants was also ascertained.

The capacity of waterfowl habitats to provide food for ducks has, in the past, been considered almost exclusively on the basis of plant resources. Small animal life associated with the plants, free swimming animal life, and animal life on or in the hydrosol, all serving as potentially important food for ducks, have been, until very recently, almost entirely disregarded.

In general, we know that immature and adult insects, snails, and crustaceans are eaten, but few definitive studies have been conducted on the food habits of egg-laying females, downy young, or molting adults. Beard (1953:424) stated that, "Ducklings of all species rely almost entirely upon animal foods during the first two or three weeks of their existence." Collias and Collias (1963:7) related that ten species of ducks, both in the field and in the laboratory, "all readily captured and ate many daphnids, amphipods, and various aquatic insects." Bartonek and Hickey (1969:455) demonstrated that of the food consumed by juvenile canvasbacks (*Aythya valisineria*) and redheads (*A. americana*), 96 and 43 percent respectively, consisted of animal material.

Little is known regarding the specific nutritional requirements of wild ducks. Hawkins (1964:193) related that, "Before and during the nesting period, protein demands of the hen are especially high. They continue to be high for ducklings and for moulting adults." Holm and Scott (1954:171) reported that young wild ducklings of several different species developed satisfactorily on 19 percent total protein or 8 percent animal protein. These authors also found that breeding and egg-laying mallards (*Anas platyrhynchos*) exhibited satisfactory egg production and hatchability of fertile eggs when a diet containing 19.6 percent protein was fed, but unsatisfactory results were obtained with a 17 percent protein diet.

[1] This work was partially financed by the State University of New York, College of Forestry, Syracuse, and the Bureau of Sport Fisheries and Wildlife, Division of Wildlife Refuges, Boston.

[2] Present address: Department of Zoology, Southern Illinois University, Carbondale.

Originally published in J. Wildl. Manage. 34(4):707–718, 1970.

Moyle (1961:3) reported that the protein content of the leaves and stems of water plants is between 1 and 2 percent of the wet weight, rhizomes and tubers average about 2 percent, and seeds and fruits may average 10 percent protein. Aquatic invertebrates on the other hand, usually are between 10 and 25 percent protein. It is becoming sufficiently evident that egg-laying hens, ducklings, and molting adults cannot obtain their necessary protein (and specific amino acid) requirements entirely from aquatic plants. It then becomes practical to know what plant species or plant communities harbor the greatest quantities of invertebrates so that management can favor these hydrophytes.

Many investigators have commented on the general relationships that exist between the abundance of aquatic invertebrates and the presence of hydrophytes. Shelford (1918), Surber (1930), Pirnie (1935), Berg (1949), McGaha (1952), Dineen (1953), and Leitch (1964) have qualitatively described these plant-animal associations. Few studies, however, focus attention on the quantitative aspects of plant-invertebrate associations of the aquatic environment. Needham (1929), Krecker (1939), Andrews and Hasler (1943), Rosine (1955), Gerking (1957), Collias and Collias (1963), and Gillespie and Brown (1966) are notable exceptions.

Moyle (1961:6) has summed up the voluminous literature on bottom fauna production by stating that, "production of bottom fauna differs greatly in waters of different quality, on different soil types and in different physical and chemical situations in the same body of water." There is practically no differentiation in the literature, however, between bottom fauna abundance in plant-free areas and in areas exhibiting a growth of submerged hydrophytes. Gerking (1957) employed a sampling apparatus which differentiated benthos from phytomacrofauna. Beatty and Hooper (1958) and Schneider (1965) were able to demonstrate that definite associations exist between aquatic vegetation and benthic invertebrates. Keiper (1965:24), in an analysis of macroscopic bottom fauna, stated that, "the distribution and abundance of the aquatic vegetation determined both the type and concentration of the bottom fauna."

Sincere thanks are due M. M. Alexander, State University of New York, College of Forestry, Syracuse, for guiding the study to a successful completion. W. M. Lewis, Southern Illinois University, Carbondale, made valuable manuscript improvements. G. Cummings and J. Morse, former Montezuma Refuge managers, aided in several ways during the execution of the field work.

THE STUDY AREAS

The 12 species of hydrophytes selected for study were chosen for two reasons: (1) their common occurrence in central New York and much of northeastern United States, and (2) their availability in nearly pure stands, in water less than 2 ft deep. Shallow areas like these are prime feeding locations for dabbling ducks. In order to study these plants, it was necessary to sample in five bodies of water located on four different study areas, as no single water unit could be found containing all 12 species in fairly large, pure stands.

The Montezuma National Wildlife Refuge is a 6,300-acre tract located at the north end of Cayuga Lake in Seneca County. It was established primarily for migratory waterfowl, but is secondarily important as a waterfowl production area.

The several shallow impoundments found on the area receive their water from rainfall, springs, diversion of water from two streams, and by pumping water from the nearby New York State Barge Canal. Dry and wet cattail (*Typha* sp.) marsh is prominent around the open water communities where sampling was accomplished. Eight plant species were sampled in two distinct portions of the several-hundred-acre main pool complex; these two sampling sites will be called the "Main Pool" (six plants sampled here) and the "Spring Hole" (two plants sampled here). General physical and biological characteristics of these areas are described by Alexander (1949) and Cowardin (1965).

The Howland Island Game Management Area is a 3,000-acre parcel of land located in north-central Cayuga County, about 12 miles northeast of the Montezuma Refuge. It is maintained by the New York State Conservation Department with primary emphasis placed on natural production of waterfowl. More than 300 acres of shallow, artificial ponds are present on the area in 17 distinct, but variously sized impoundments. Runoff is the main water source, but some pumping from the Barge Canal is done. Two plant species were sampled in Black Duck Pond, a 2.5-acre unit surrounded mostly by a second-growth hardwood forest. Uptegraft (1959) has summarized many of the physical and biological aspects of the area.

Reagan Pond is a small (3.5-acres), shallow, artificial impoundment located on the Heiberg Memorial Forest in Cortland County, approximately 35 miles southeast of the first two study areas. The Forest is administered by the State University of New York, College of Forestry, for teaching, research, and demonstration purposes. The 80-acre watershed of the Pond consists mostly of conifer plantations and second-growth hardwood forests. The Pond is almost entirely spring-fed. One plant species was sampled here. Petri (1965) and Cole (1966) have described many of the overall aspects of this area.

Labrador Pond (150 acres) is a shallow-water area in the extreme southern part of Onondaga County, about 5 miles northeast of Reagan Pond. The land surrounding the Pond is all privately owned. It receives its water from a small stream and the steep, forested slopes bordering the two sides. One plant species was also sampled here. Spiker (1931) offers some general information on the area.

METHODS

Physical and chemical information on each of the five sampling areas was collected: (1) to help characterize each area more fully, and (2) to help explain observed differences in the animal populations both seasonally on a particular study area and concurrently between the five areas. Water temperature and dissolved oxygen were determined with a Yellow Springs Instrument Company oxygen meter. Turbidity was measured with a Hellige turbidimeter. Hydrosol samples were taken with an Ekman dredge and the percentage of ignition and non-ignitable products in the substrates was determined by employing a drying oven, a muffle furnace, and a balance. Total alkalinity was measured by using an indicator (methyl orange) and titrating with N/50 sulfuric acid. A portable pH meter (manufactured by the Analytical Measurements Company) was employed in determining hydrogen-ion concentration. Free carbon dioxide was determined by using pH-alkalinity nomography. Except for the hydrosol samples that were taken only once in mid-July, physico-chemical data were recorded each time biological samples were taken.

Field work was accomplished from April–October, 1966. Sampling of the submerged plant beds commenced in late spring or early summer as soon as each species of plant had grown enough to occupy an area of several m². Since the different species of plants did not all begin their growth at the same time in the spring, grow and spread at the same rate during the summer, or degenerate at the same time in late summer or early fall, the animals associated with them were not all sampled the same number of weeks. The mean number of weeks that each plant species was sampled was 15(9–22). Three plant samples and one plant-plus-substrate sample were taken each week for each of the submerged aquatics. A total of 543 plant samples and 181 plant-plus-substrate samples was taken.

Sampling the organisms associated with the various aquatic plants was accomplished with an Ekman dredge. As the dredge was lowered into a stand of plants, the jaws were quickly released and a mass of plants (usually from 50–125 g) and associated animals were retained inside. Once a particular stand of submerged plants was chosen for study, the same stand was sampled throughout the investigation. All collections were made in water less than 12 inches deep. The dredge was rigged with a stronger-than-normal spring-releasing mechanism so that the jaws closed with a greater than normal force and there was no real problem because of incomplete closure. Those few samples taken when a poor closure was obtained were discarded. Each sample was placed in a 12-×18-inch plastic bag and taken to the laboratory for analysis.

Although hand picking the animals from the plants was found to be time-consuming, it was the only method that furnished useful data. Once removed from the samples, the organisms were placed in 70 percent ethyl alcohol and the plants were lightly wrapped in paper toweling to remove the excess water before weighing. Since the animals were stored in alcohol for up to several months before weighing, there was a loss in weight primarily due to dehydration. Weight loss averaged about 5 percent for all animals; therefore, the weights given in the analyses are a minimum. The following classifications were followed: aquatic invertebrates, Pennak (1953); terrestrial arachnids, Eddy and Hodson (1961); terrestrial insects, Ross (1956); terrestrial molluscans, Robertson and Blakeslee (1948); and aquatic vertebrates, Blair et al. (1957).

Although aquatic insects, molluscans, and crustaceans comprise the bulk of the animal food known to be consumed by waterfowl, all invertebrate and vertebrate animals were recorded, as they may be potentially important as waterfowl food. Of the invertebrates, only macroforms (those retained in a No. 18 U. S. Standard Sieve) were included. The abundance of animals associated with the 12 plant species was expressed as the wet weight and number of macroinvertebrates per 100 g of aquatic plant. Since each sample seldom consisted of exactly 100 g of plant, the raw data were adjusted upwards or downwards so that all weight and number figures were comparable. This adjustment was deemed reliable for two reasons: (1) experimental sampling evaluations indicated that, in general, macroinvertebrates increased proportionately with increasing amount of plant material, and (2) linear correlation analyses have indicated that animal abundance and plant abundance have a high degree of association (Gerking 1957:222). Wet weights (mg of animals and g of plants) best represent the natural status of animals and plants as they actually exist in the water and so all data are expressed in this manner; the values can be approximately converted to dry weights by dividing them by 10 (Moyle 1961:15).

RESULTS

Physico-Chemical Data

Considerable variability was present in the several physical-chemical factors recorded on the five sampling areas. Water temperatures were quite uniform, with seasonal (April–October) means ranging from 16–20 C. Seasonal mean turbidities were similar (5–16 Hellige turbidity units) on four of the five areas, the Main Pool having a considerably higher mean value of 51. Turbidity was caused by both non-living suspended matter and planktonic blue-green algae (*Anabaena* sp.), the latter being primarily responsible for the high turbidity values recorded in the Main Pool (Krull 1969:293–294). Seasonal mean dissolved oxygen concentrations (values always recorded in mid-morning) ranged from 6.2–9.8 ppm, all values being near or at saturation. Seasonal mean free carbon dioxide values ranged from 1.3–3.6 ppm. pH values were not recorded below 6.7 or above 10.0 on any of the sampling sites; most recordings were around 8.1. Seasonal mean total alkalinity values were similar (96–151 ppm) on four of the five areas, Reagan Pond having a much lower mean value of 29. The percent ignition products —percent non-ignitable products in the hydrosol samples, ranged from 3–97 in Black Duck Pond to 62–38 in the Spring Hole, indicating that the substrates of the five areas were quite different. Mean organic-inorganic percents were 27–73.

For some statistical comparisons, between sampling area variability was significant, and in other cases it was not. I have concluded that animal population differences between plants growing on different study areas is primarily attributable to inherent characteristics of the plants rather than to diverse physico-chemical factors. The five sampling sites are not limnologically identical, however, so comparisons between plants sampled on the same area may be the only desirable ones.

Animal Abundance and Diversity

The 12 species of submerged aquatic plants supported a wide range of invertebrate biomass and numbers (Table 1). The seasonal mean weight of organisms per 100 g of plant ranged from 2,059 mg in *Lemna trisulca* to 71 mg in *Myriophyllum spicatum*, with an overall mean of 931 mg. The average ratio of the weight of the plants to that of the animals, therefore, was approximately 100 to 1.

The seasonal mean number of organisms per 100 g of plant ranged from 161 in *Ceratophyllum demersum* to 36 in *M. spicatum* and *Najas flexilis*, with an overall mean of 82. On the average, therefore, every gram of plant supported something less than one animal.

From the time the plants appeared until they disappeared several weeks or months later, qualitative samples revealed that macroinvertebrates were at least several, and probably many, times more abundant in vegetated areas than in non-vegetated areas. Abundance of water-inhabiting macroinvertebrates and/or microinvertebrates before the plants appeared was not determined. Data were collected on the abundance of benthic animals during the period from ice-thaw to appearance of plants, but are not presented.

Considering all 12 plants for the entire sampling period, univalves (especially

Table 1. Weight, number, and taxonomic diversity of animals associated with the 12 species of submerged aquatic plants.

SAMPLING AREA	PLANT	SEASONAL (APRIL–OCTOBER) MEAN WEIGHT OF ANIMALS (mg)/100 G OF PLANT	SEASONAL (APRIL–OCTOBER) MEAN NUMBER OF ANIMALS/100 G OF PLANT	TOTAL (SEASONAL) NUMBER OF DIFFERENT TAXONOMIC GROUPS OF ANIMALS	MEAN (WEEKLY) NUMBER OF DIFFERENT TAXONOMIC GROUPS OF ANIMALS
Montezuma Main Pool	*R. hieroglyphicum*	306 ± 50[a]	60	32	9
	C. demersum	1,501 ± 577	161	18	5
	P. foliosus	533 ± 84	66	31	8
	P. pectinatus	786 ± 135	101	28	9
	L. trisulca	2,059 ± 462	152	46	15
	H. dubia	1,530 ± 388	103	30	11
Montezuma Spring Hole	*C. vulgaris*	587 ± 137	44	25	6
	N. marina	910 ± 168	85	31	9
Black Duck Pond	*U. vulgaris*	761 ± 141	80	37	10
	E. canadensis	1,117 ± 163	58	45	13
Reagan Pond	*N. flexilis*	1,003 ± 168	36	35	6
Labrador Pond	*M. spicatum*	71 ± 16	36	18	5
	Mean	931	82	31	9
	Range	1,988(71–2,059)	125(36–161)	28(18–46)	10(5–15)
	Variance	288,628	1,579	71	9
	Standard deviation	537	40	8	3
	Coefficient of variability	58	49	26	33

[a] One standard error of the mean.

Physa sp.), dragonflies, (Odonata), backswimmers, (Notonectidae), and water boatmen (Corixidae) were of outstanding importance, both in respect to biomass and numbers produced. Leeches (Hirudinea), amphipods, decapods, and giant water bugs (Belostomatidae) were of secondary importance. Many other animals, primarily insects, were abundant at various times of the year, but were of lesser overall importance and were associated with fewer plants.

An analysis of the plant distribution of invertebrates reveals that only five animals (Hirudinea, *Haliplus* sp., Tendipedidae, *Physa* sp., and *Gyraulus* sp.) were common to all 12 plant species. Six other organisms were associated with 11 plants, and three more with 10 plants. On the other hand, 33 organisms were associated with only one plant species, 12 more were associated with two plant species, and seven others with three plant species. Therefore, nearly 60 percent of the animals were found on three or fewer plant species.

Thirteen kinds of animals (nine insects, three snails, and one fish) were associated only with the substrate beneath one or more of the plant species. Twelve kinds of invertebrates (six snails, three insects, two annelids, and one crustacean), common to both the plant samples and the plant-plus-substrate samples, were the only ones that were at times more abundant on or in the substrate. During most samplings even these, however, were many times more abundant within the plants above the substrate, than they were with the substrate itself. Another 12 kinds of invertebrates (nine insects and three snails) were terrestrial forms that were encountered in the samples from time to time.

During this study 114 taxonomic groups of animals were recorded. Of these, 102 (89 percent) were aquatic representatives, and 12 (11 percent) were of terrestrial origin. There were 88 taxonomic groups of animals associated directly with the 12 species of submerged aquatic plants. The most common aquatic taxa were Hemiptera (9 families and 13 genera), Coleoptera (5 and 19+), Diptera (5 and 6+), Odonata (3 and 10), and Pulmonata (3 and 5). Dytiscidae had nine genera, Hydrophilidae had six genera, and Libellulidae had five genera. Coenagrionidae, Corixidae, Phryganeidae, Planorbidae, and Sphaeriidae each had three genera.

Organismic diversity can also be observed in Table 1. *L. trisulca* had the largest total (seasonal) and mean (weekly) number of taxonomic groups of organisms (46 and 15), *Elodea canadensis* had the second largest (45 and 13), and *C. demersum* and *M. spicatum* had the lowest (18 and 5). Mean values for all 12 plants were 31 and 9.

Relative to weight, number, and taxonomic diversity of animals, Table 1 indicates that variability between mean weight and mean number of organisms, and variability between total and mean number of different taxonomic groups of organisms is relatively small. However, variability between overall animal abundance (weight and number of organisms) and overall taxonomic diversity (total and mean) is quite large. This would indicate that in some instances a few species were present in large biomass or numbers, whereas in other instances a small total population contained many species.

Seasonal Availability of Animals

Table 2 lists the 12 plant species and the animals that were generally encountered throughout the entire period of sampling. One plant (*L. trisulca*) had nine kinds of animals associated with it throughout the 14-week sampling period, while another plant (*N. flexilis*), had only one animal associate during its 22 weeks of existence. The mean number of organisms associated with the 12 plant species for the duration of their samplings was four. These were the animals that were available as a potential source of food for ducks from the beginning to the end of the plants' existence.

In addition to the several animals available to ducks for the duration of each plants' existence, there generally were several additional kinds of animals associated with each plant for somewhat shorter periods of time. Animal associates of *E. canadensis* (sampled 22 weeks) and *M. spicatum* (sampled 17 weeks) will serve as extreme examples. For the former, *Caenis* sp. was present primarily during the first half of sampling, while *Siphlonurus* sp. occurred mainly during the middle few weeks of sampling. *Sympetrum* sp. was collected primarily during the first three-quarters of the sampling period, while *Leucorrhinia* sp. was encountered mainly during the last half of sampling, indicating a possible replacement of one genus by another closely related one. *Pachydiplax longipennis* was encountered only during the last half of sampling. *Ischnura* sp. was collected primarily during the last three-quarters of sampling, while the few individuals of *Enallagma* sp. were encountered mainly during the early sampling weeks. *Notonecta* sp. was encountered during the last half of sampling, while *Buenoa* sp. was collected mainly during the middle two-thirds of sampling. *Haliplus* sp. was encountered primarily during the last two-thirds of sampling, while *Laccophilus* sp. was collected mainly during the middle three-quarters of sampling. *Lymnaea* sp.

Table 2. Seasonal availability of animals associated with 12 species of submerged aquatic plants.

PLANT	ANIMAL AVAILABILITY PERIOD	ANIMALS
R. hieroglyphicum	Mid-June–Early Sept.	*H. azteca* *Enochrus* sp. Tendipedidae *Physa* sp.
C. demersum	End of June–Mid-Sept.	*Trichocorixa* sp. *Physa* sp. *Gyraulus* sp.
P. foliosus	Mid-June–Mid-Aug.	Hydracarina *Physa* sp. *Gyraulus* sp.
P. pectinatus	Mid-June–Early Sept.	*H. azteca* *Trichocorixa* sp. Tendipedidae *Physa* sp.
L. trisulca	Mid-June–Early Sept.	*H. azteca* *Ischnura* sp. *P. striola* *Belostoma* sp. *Trichocorixa* sp. *Haliplus* sp. Tendipedidae *Physa* sp. *Gyraulus* sp.
H. dubia	End of June–End of Aug.	*G. fasiatus* *Caenus* sp. *Ischnura* sp. Tendipedidae *Physa* sp.
C. vulgaris	Mid-June–End of Sept.	*Trichocorixa* sp. *Physa* sp. *Gyraulus* sp.
N. marina	Early July–Early Sept.	*Trichocorixa* sp. Tendipedidae *Physa* sp.
U. vulgaris	Mid-June–Early Oct.	*P. striola* Tendipedidae *Physa* sp. *Helisoma* sp. *Gyraulus* sp.
E. canadensis	Early June–End of Oct.	*P. striola* Tendipedidae *Physa* sp. *Gyraulus* sp.
N. flexilis	Early June–End of Oct.	Hirudinea
M. spicatum	Mid-June–Early Oct.	*H. azteca* *Gyraulus* sp.

and *Helisoma* sp. occurred intermittently throughout the sampling period. For the latter plant, Curculionidae and Tendipedidae were collected primarily during the first half of sampling, while *Amnicola* sp. was collected intermittently throughout the sampling period.

Finally, there was a somewhat larger complement of animals that were generally sporadic in occurrence and were either associated with a plant for a few weeks or had no regular pattern of existence. In total, although some similarities in animal associates between plants exist, a large amount of variability is readily apparent.

DISCUSSION

Data gathered in this study indicate that, on the average, 1 g of animal material is associated with 100 g of plant material. Soft-water lakes may average 500 k of bottom flora per hectare (standing crop, wet weight, ash-free basis) of lake surface, whereas hard-water lakes may average 10 times this amount (Juday 1942). Therefore, from 5 to 50 k of animal material per hectare of lake surface would be the corresponding standing crop of invertebrate life. These figures do not include benthos, zooplankton, or open-water microinvertebrates or macroinvertebrates, which may well exceed the standing crop of plant-associated animal material. In all probability, prairie potholes and marshes and many other shallow-water units produce animal material equal to or in excess of the above figures. This would seem to be an ample protein-rich food source for ducks. However, it remains to be determined why incubating hens seemingly choose from many available sites, one particular water area to which they take their broods upon hatching. I believe this is not a random choice on the part of the hen.

Although only 13 kinds of animals were confined to the bottom sediments, and none of these were particularly abundant, preliminary analysis of other available benthic data (not presented in this paper) collected before the submerged hydrophytes appeared, indicates a considerable abundance and diversity of potential animal food from approximately April 1–June 1. These organisms are probably valuable to incubating hens. Gerking (1957:222) revealed that of the animals common to plant samples and plant-plus-substrate samples, most were many times more abundant within the masses of plants above the substrate. My data support this conclusion. Although the terrestrial invertebrates did not comprise a large biomass, they may be a potentially important waterfowl food source under certain conditions and should not be overlooked.

McGaha (1952) found 58 species of insects living in association with 13 species of aquatic flowering plants. Berg (1949) encountered 32 species of insects directly associated with 17 species of the genus *Potamogeton*. These authors concluded that some aquatic insects are restricted to one or a few closely related species of plants with floating or emergent parts, while insects on submerged hydrophytes show almost no specificity. The 12 plants that I sampled harbored a greater diversity of animals and my data indicate a greater plant-animal specificity than other authors have reported.

Seasonal availability of animals between plants is quite variable. Each plant species, however, generally has several kinds of animals associated with it throughout its entire period of existence. Several additional kinds of animals are associated with each plant for shorter periods of time. Most important, though, is the fact that

Table 3. A comparison of waterfowl food plant rankings with weight and taxonomic diversity of animals encountered in this study.

PLANT	VOLUMETRIC PERCENT CONSUMED; 74.36 TOTAL (FROM MARTIN AND UHLER, 1939)	NUMERICAL RANK; 41 TOTAL (FROM MARTIN AND UHLER, 1939)	SEASONAL (APRIL–OCTOBER) MEAN WEIGHT OF ORGANISMS (mg) PER 100 G OF PLANT	NUMERICAL RANK	TOTAL (SEASONAL) NUMBER OF DIFFERENT TAXONOMIC GROUPS OF ORGANISMS	NUMERICAL RANK
Potamogeton (*P. foliosus* and *P. pectinatus*)	13.29	1	660	8.5	29.5	7.5
Lemna (*L. trisulca*)	2.97	6	2,059	1	46	1
Chara et al. (*C. vulgaris* and *N. flexilis*)	1.87	10	795	7	30	7
Algae (*R. hieroglyphicum*)	0.87	18	306	11	32	5
C. demersum	0.77	20	1,510	3	18	11.5
Myriophyllum (*M. spicatum*)	0.38	27	71	12	18	11.5
Heteranthera (*H. dubia*)	0.36	29	1,530	2	30	8
Elodea (*E. canadensis*)	0.07	37	1,117	4	45	2

organismic abundance reaches its peak soon after the plants appear and apparently provide an ecological substrate on and among which the animals can dwell. Both weight and numbers of animals tend to decline somewhat as the season progresses.

The relative position of those aquatic plants known to have a direct food value for numerous species of waterfowl is given in Table 3, along with their rankings for weight and taxonomic diversity of organisms as determined in the present study. Martin and Uhler (1939) did not list *N. marina* or *Utricularia vulgaris* in their analysis. They stated, however (p. 38), that *N. marina* is usually too scarce and too localized to have appreciable value as a duck food, but that under some circumstances it has a fair to slight value as food. As for *Utricularia* sp., they stated (p. 95) that there are no definite records of its use, but field observations indicate the possibility of a limited local value to ducks. The figures in Table 3, therefore, may have important waterfowl management implications. Probably the outstanding exemplification of this statement are the figures for *Elodea* sp. This hydrophyte seems to be a poor waterfowl food plant at best, and yet it harbors the second largest total number of taxonomic groups of organisms and the fourth largest mean weight of organisms of any of the plants sampled in the present investigation. If poor waterfowl food plants harbor large quantities of invertebrate organisms, and the results indicate that many of them do, then these plants may be *indirectly* very important to waterfowl production. This indirect value is based upon the assumption that the invertebrate organisms are important, and possibly even necessary, for waterfowl.

Potamogeton sp. is by far the best food plant, but is relatively poor in production of invertebrate fauna. Similar comparisons can also be made for the other plants listed in Table 3.

In conclusion, two questions can logically be asked. First, why is there so much weekly variability in both numbers and weight of organisms for all 12 species of submerged aquatic plants? I believe that increased sampling would not appreciably reduce this variability. The various animal populations seemed to be naturally fluctuating, probably due to such factors as normal die-off, hatching of eggs, pupation, emergence of mature insects, and an intricately complicated pattern of predation, local movement, and uneven distribution. Variability seemed to be the rule rather than the exception.

Second, why do some plants harbor more taxonomic groups, higher numbers, and greater weights of organisms than do other plants? There seems to be some correlation with the total amount of surface area characteristic of a plant species, those with more surface area harboring more organisms. It is among these plants that the animals find food and several kinds of shelter. It is nearly impossible, however, to determine even crudely, the surface area of those aquatic plants with finely divided leaves and complicated configurations. Some of the organisms that dwell on or among the masses of hydrophytes obviously feed upon the plants themselves, while others browse on the attached periphyton. Still others find their prey associated with the plants or avoid being preyed upon. Some plant species may also produce metabolites that have inhibitory effects on some or all aquatic animals, and this phenomenon may be seasonal. Ultimate animal abundance is undoubtedly dependent upon the abundance and kind of the various components of these intricate, ecological communities.

LITERATURE CITED

ALEXANDER, M. M. 1949. The development of the muskrat on the Montezuma National Wildlife Refuge. Ph.D. Thesis. State Univ. of New York, Syracuse. 161pp.

ANDREWS, J. D., AND A. D. HASLER. 1943. Fluctuations in the animal populations of the littoral zone in Lake Mendota. Trans. Wisconsin Acad. Sci., Arts and Letters 35:175–185.

BARTONEK, J. C., AND J. J. HICKEY. 1969. Selective feeding by juvenile diving ducks in summer. Auk 86(3):443–457.

BEARD, ELIZABETH B. 1953. The importance of beaver in waterfowl management at the Seney National Wildlife Refuge. J. Wildl. Mgmt. 17(4):398–436.

BEATTY, L. D., AND F. F. HOOPER. 1958. Benthic associations of Sugarloaf Lake. Papers Michigan Acad. Sci., Arts and Letters. 43: 89–106.

BERG, C. O. 1949. Limnological relations of insects to plants of the genus *Potamogeton*. Trans. Am. Microscop. Soc. 68(4):279–291.

BLAIR, W. F., A. P. BLAIR, P. BRODKORB, F. R. CAGLE, AND G. A. MOORE. 1957. Vertebrates of the United States. McGraw-Hill Book Co., Inc., New York. 819pp.

COLE, R. A. 1966. The distribution of small mammals in relation to artificial ponds. M.S. Thesis. State Univ. of New York, Syracuse. 119pp.

COLLIAS, N. E., AND ELSIE C. COLLIAS. 1963. Selective feeding by wild ducklings of different species. Wilson Bull. 75(1):6–14.

COWARDIN, L. M. 1965. Flooded timber as waterfowl habitat at the Montezuma National Wildlife Refuge. New York Cooperative Wildl. Res. Unit, Final Rept. 2. 124pp.

DINEEN, C. F. 1953. An ecological study of a Minnesota pond. Am. Midland Naturalist 50(2):349–376.

EDDY, S., AND A. C. HODSON. 1961. Taxonomic keys to the common animals of the north central states. 3rd ed. Burgess Publishing Co., Minneapolis. 162pp.

GERKING, S. D. 1957. A method of sampling the littoral macrofauna and its application. Ecology 38(2):219–226.

GILLESPIE, D. M., AND C. J. D. BROWN. 1966. A quantitative sampler for macroinvertebrates associated with aquatic macrophytes. Limnology and Oceanogr. 11(3):404–406.

HAWKINS, A. S. 1964. Mississippi flyway. Pp. 185–207. *In* J. P. Linduska (Editor), Waterfowl tomorrow. U. S. Government Printing Office, Washington, D. C. 770pp.

HOLM, E. R., AND M. L. SCOTT. 1954. Studies on the nutrition of wild waterfowl. New York Fish and Game J. 1(2):171–187.

JUDAY, C. 1942. The summer standing crop of plants and animals in four Wisconsin lakes. Trans. Wisconsin Acad. Sci., Arts and Letters 34:103–135.

KEIPER, R. R. 1965. Analysis of macroscopic bottom fauna in three different age beaver ponds. Massachusetts Cooperative Wildl. Res. Unit Quart. Rept. 18(4):22–24.

KRECKER, F. H. 1939. A comparative study of the animal population of certain submerged aquatic plants. Ecology 20(4):553–562.

KRULL, J. N. 1969. Factors affecting plant die-offs in shallow water areas. Am. Midland Naturalist 82(1):293–295.

LEITCH, W. G. 1964. Water. Pp. 273–281. *In* J. P. Linduska (Editor), Waterfowl tomorrow. U. S. Government Printing Office, Washington, D. C. 770pp.

MARTIN, A. C., AND F. M. UHLER. 1939. Food of game ducks in the United States and Canada. U. S. Dept. Agr. Tech. Bull. 634. 308pp.

MCGAHA, Y. J. 1952. The limnological relations of insects to certain aquatic flowering plants. Trans. Am. Microscop. Soc. 71(4):355–381.

MOYLE, J. B. 1961. Aquatic invertebrates as related to larger water plants and waterfowl. Minnesota Dept. Conserv. Invest. Rept. 233. 24pp.

NEEDHAM, P. R. 1929. Quantitative studies of the fish food supply in selected areas. New York State Conserv. Dept. Suppl. Eighteenth Annual Rept. 1928. 244pp.

PENNAK, R. W. 1953. Fresh-water invertebrates of the United States. The Ronald Press Co., New York. 769pp.

PETRI, M. G. 1965. The ecology of three artificial marsh ponds on the Tully Forest. M.S. Thesis. State Univ. of New York, Syracuse. 166pp.

PIRNIE, M. D. 1935. Michigan waterfowl management. Franklin DeKleine Co., Lansing. 328pp.

ROBERTSON, I. C. S., AND C. L. BLAKESLEE. 1948. The mollusca of the Niagara frontier region. Bull. Buffalo Soc. Nat. Sci. 19(3):191pp.

ROSINE, W. N. 1955. The distribution of invertebrates on submerged aquatic plant surfaces in Muskee Lake, Colorado. Ecology 36 (2):308–314.

ROSS, H. H. 1956. A textbook of entomology. 2nd ed. John Wiley and Sons, Inc., New York. 519pp.

SCHNEIDER, J. C. 1965. Further studies on the benthic ecology of Sugarloaf Lake, Washtenaw County, Michigan. Papers Michigan Acad. Sci., Arts and Letters 50:11–29.

SHELFORD, V. E. 1918. Conditions of existence. Pp. 21–60. *In* H. B. Ward and G. C. Whipple (Editors), fresh-water biology. John Wiley and Sons, Inc., New York. 1111pp.

SPIKER, C. J. 1931. A biological reconnaissance of the Peterboro Swamp and the Labrador Pond areas. Roosevelt Wildl. Bull. 6(1): 101–151.

SURBER, E. W. 1930. A method of quantitative bottom fauna and faculative plankton sampling employed in a year's study of slough biology. Trans. Am. Fisheries Soc. 60:187–198.

UPTEGRAFT, D. D. 1959. The ecology and deer-carrying capacity of the Howland Island Game Management Area. M.S. Thesis. State Univ. of New York, Syracuse. 92pp.

Received for publication October 16, 1969.

SELECTED BIBLIOGRAPHY

Food Habits and Feeding Ecology

ANDERSON, B. W., M. G. REEDER, AND R. L. TIMKEN. 1974. Notes on the feeding behavior of the common merganser (*Mergus merganser*). Condor 76(4):472–476.

ANDERSON, M. G., AND J. B. LOW. 1976. Use of sago pondweed by waterfowl on the Delta Marsh, Manitoba. J. Wildl. Manage. 40(2):233–242.

BARTONEK, J. C. 1972. Summer foods of American widgeon, mallards, and a green-winged teal near Great Slave Lake, N.W.T. Can. Field-Nat. 86(4): 373–376.

———, AND J. J. HICKEY. 1969. Selective feeding by juvenile diving ducks in summer. Auk 86(3):443–457.

———, AND H. W. MURDY. 1970. Summer foods of lesser scaup in subarctic Taiga. Arctic 23(1):35–44.

BELLROSE, F. C. 1941. Duck food plants of the Illinois River valley. Ill. Nat. Hist. Survey Bull. 21(8):235–280.

———, AND H. G. ANDERSON. 1943. Preferential ratings of duck food plants. Ill. Nat. Hist. Survey Bull. 22(5):417–433.

BOSSENMAIER, E. F., AND W. H. MARSHALL. 1958. Field-feeding by waterfowl in southwestern Manitoba. Wildl. Monogr. 1. 32pp.

CANTIN, M., J. BÉDARD, AND H. MILNE. 1974. The food and feeding of common eiders in the St. Lawrence Estuary in summer. Can. J. Zool. 52(3):319–334.

CHURA, N. J. 1961. Food availability and preferences of juvenile mallards. Trans. North Am. Wildl. Conf. 26:121–134.

———. 1963. Diurnal feeding periodicity of juvenile mallards. Wilson Bull. 75:90.

COLLIAS, N. E., AND E. C. COLLIAS. 1963. Selective feeding by wild ducklings of different species. Wilson Bull. 75:6–14.

CORNELIUS, S. E. 1977. Food and resource utilization by wintering redheads on lower Laguna Madre. J. Wildl. Manage. 41(3):374–385.

COTTAM, C. 1939. Food habits of North American diving ducks. U.S. Dep. Agric., Tech. Bull. 643. 139pp.

DILLON, O. W., JR. 1959. Food habits of wild mallard ducks in three Louisiana parishes. Trans. North Am. Wildl. Conf. 24:374–382.

DIRSCHL, H. J. 1969. Foods of lesser scaup and blue-winged teal in the Saskatchewan River Delta. J. Wildl. Manage. 33(1):77–87.

DROBNEY, R. D., AND L. H. FREDRICKSON. 1979. Food selection by wood ducks in relation to breeding status. J. Wildl. Manage. 43:109–120.

DURANT, A. J. 1956. Impaction and pressure necrosis in Canada geese due to eating dry hulled soybeans. J. Wildl. Manage. 20(4):399–404.

HOCUTT, G. E., AND R. W. DIMMICK. 1971. Summer food habits of juvenile wood ducks in East Tennessee. J. Wildl. Manage. 35:286–292.

KAMINSKI, R. M., AND H. H. PRINCE. 1981. Dabbling duck activity and foraging responses to aquatic invertebrates. Auk 98:115–126.

KERWIN, J. A., AND L. G. WEBB. 1972. Foods of ducks wintering in coastal

South Carolina, 1965–1967. Proc. Annu. Conf. S.E. Assoc. Game Fish Comm. 25:223–245.

KRAPU, G. L. 1974. Feeding ecology of pintail hens during reproduction. Auk 91(2):278–290.

———, AND G. A. SWANSON. 1977. Foods of juvenile, brood hen, and post-breeding pintails in North Dakota. Condor 79(4):504–507.

LANDERS, J. L., T. T. FENDLEY, AND A. S. JOHNSON. 1977. Feeding ecology of wood ducks in South Carolina. J. Wildl. Manage. 41(1):118–127.

———, A. S. JOHNSON, P. H. MORGAN, AND W. P. BALDWIN. 1976. Duck foods in managed tidal impoundments in South Carolina. J. Wildl. Manage. 40(4):721–728.

MARTIN, A. C., AND F. M. UHLER. 1939. Food of game ducks in the United States and Canada. U.S. Dept. Agric. Tech. Bull. 634. 156pp.

MCGILVREY, F. B. 1967. Food habits of sea ducks from the north-eastern United States. Wildfowl Trust 18th Annu. Rep. pp. 142–145.

MCMAHAN, C. A. 1970. Food habits of ducks wintering on Laguna Madre, Texas. J. Wildl. Manage. 34(4):946–949.

MENDALL, H. L. 1949. Food habits in relation to black duck management in Maine. J. Wildl. Manage. 13(1):64–101.

MILLER, M. R. 1975. Gut morphology of mallards in relation to diet quality. J. Wildl. Manage. 39(1):168–173.

PETERSON, S. R., AND R. S. ELLARSON. 1977. Food habits of oldsquaws wintering on Lake Michigan. Wilson Bull. 89(1):81–91.

REINECKE, K. J., AND R. B. OWEN. 1980. Food use and nutrition of black ducks nesting in Maine. J. Wildl. Manage. 44:549–559.

ROGERS, J. P., AND L. J. KORSCHGEN. 1966. Foods of lesser scaups on breeding, migration, and wintering areas. J. Wildl. Manage. 30(2):258–264.

SCHROEDER, L. D. 1973. A literature review on the role of invertebrates in waterfowl management. Colorado Div. Wildl. Spec. Rep. 29. 13pp.

SERIE, J. R., AND G. A. SWANSON. 1976. Feeding ecology of breeding gadwalls on saline wetlands. J. Wildl. Manage. 40(1):69–81.

SIEGFRIED, W. R. 1973. Summer food and feeding of the ruddy duck in Manitoba. Can. J. Zool. 51(12):1293–1297.

SINCOCK, J. L. 1962. Estimating consumption of food by wintering waterfowl populations. Proc. Annu. Conf. S.E. Assoc. Game Fish Comm. 16:217–221.

SWANSON, G. A., AND J. C. BARTONEK. 1970. Bias associated with food analysis in gizzards of blue-winged teal. J. Wildl. Manage. 34(4):739–746.

———, G. L. KRAPU, J. C. BARTONEK, J. R. SERIE, AND D. H. JOHNSON. 1974. Advantages in mathematically weighting waterfowl food habits data. J. Wildl. Manage. 38(2):302–307.

———, ———, AND J. R. SERIE. 1977. Foods of laying female dabbling ducks on the breeding grounds. Pages 47–57 *in* T. A. Bookhout, ed. Waterfowl and wetlands—An integrated review. Proc. Symp. at 39th Midwest Fish and Wildl. Conf., Madison, WI. LaCrosse Printing Co., Inc., LaCrosse.

———, AND M. I. MEYER. 1973. The role of invertebrates in the feeding ecology of Anatinae during the breeding season. Pages 143–185 *in* The Waterfowl Habitat Manage. Symp. at Moncton, New Brunswick, Canada.

———, ———, AND J. R. SERIE. 1974. Feeding ecology of breeding blue-winged teals. J. Wildl. Manage. 38(3):396–407.

———, AND A. B. SARGEANT. 1972. Observation of nighttime feeding behavior of ducks. J. Wildl. Manage. 36(3):959–961.

THOMPSON, D. 1973. Feeding ecology of diving ducks on Keokuk Pool, Mississippi River. J. Wildl. Manage. 37: 367–381.

TIMKEN, R. L., AND B. W. ANDERSON. 1969. Food habits of common mergansers in the Northcentral United States. J. Wildl. Manage. 33(1):87–91.

MANAGEMENT AND ECONOMICS
Marsh Management

© '80 D.R. BARRICK

EFFECTS OF A DRAWDOWN ON A WATERFOWL IMPOUNDMENT[1,2]

JOHN A. KADLEC,[3] Rose Lake Wildlife Experiment Station, Michigan Department of Conservation, East Lansing, MI

More than 40 major waterfowl impoundments, flooding 18,476 acres, were built by the Michigan Department of Conservation between 1948 and 1959 (Davenport 1959). For the first few years after construction, waterfowl-use of most of these impoundments was excellent. Seasonal duck-use began to decline in some flowages after 4 or 5 years. Workers in other states (Hartman 1949, MacNamara 1957) have also found that impoundments reach a peak in use by waterfowl soon after flooding and then slowly lose their attractiveness to ducks. Clearly these older unproductive impoundments need rejuvenating. Since the national wildlife refuges have successfully used the drawdown, or temporary drainage, to maintain a high level of marsh productivity, the technique seemed promising for Michigan impoundments.

This report covers an evaluation of a pilot drawdown on the Backus Lake flooding project in north-central lower Michigan and its effect on vegetation, waterfowl, soil, water, and bottom fauna. The investigation included two growing seasons before and one after the temporary drainage during the summer of 1958.

The research program was jointly sponsored by the Michigan Department of Conservation and the University of Michigan. I am most grateful to W. W. Chase, G. S. Hunt, D. C. Chandler, and S. A. Graham of the University of Michigan and to F. F. Hooper, R. A. MacMullan, and R. I. Blouch of the Michigan Department of Conservation for their advice and cooperation. Student aides G. G. Hofmaster, J. M. Meehan, D. D. Doell, P. F. Olsen, B. F. Tullar, D. Dimmers, and M. E. Rosasco helped with portions of the field work. I wish to thank C. T. Black of the Rose Lake Wildlife Experiment Station, Michigan Department of Conservation, for assistance in preparing the manuscript.

REVIEW OF LITERATURE

Many workers have observed the decline in waterfowl populations in impoundments some years after initial flooding. Hartman (1949) believed that the basic cause of the decline was the exhaustion or unavailability of soil nutrients. Cook and Powers (1958) studied marsh soils before and after flooding and found an accumulation rather than an exhaustion of soil nutrients. However, they found potentially toxic accumulations of iron and manganese. DiAngelo (1953) considered aquatic plant succession responsible for the pattern of use by waterfowl. He associated high early use of flooding projects in Michigan with an abundance of pioneer plants, such as duckweeds (Lemnaceae), which are highly preferred foods for waterfowl. Succession proceeds in the direction of more stable rooted aquatics, such as pondweeds (*Potamogeton* sp.), which do not produce as much food for waterfowl (Low and Bellrose 1944).

---

[1] Originally published in Ecology 43(2):267–281, 1962.

[2] A contribution from Federal Aid in Wildlife Restoration Project, Michigan 95-R.

[3] Present address: Dept. of Wildlife Science, Utah State University, UMC 52, Logan, UT 84322.

The amount and density of emergent cover is an important factor in duck production (Griffith 1948, Sowls 1955, Harris 1957). Cover is first provided in newly inundated habitat by the vegetation present before flooding (DiAngelo 1953). Subsequently, the amount and density of cover depends on the survival of preflooding vegetation and the development of new vegetation adapted to the increased water level.

These studies suggest that a successful technique to prolong the attractiveness of new waterfowl floodings should alter aquatic plant succession and have beneficial effects on the soil. Many studies of drawdowns in waterfowl marshes (Griffith 1948, Hartman 1949, Uhler 1956) emphasize the value of replacing the complex of true aquatic plants with moist soil species which provide food preferred by waterfowl. Kadlec (1956) and Harris (1957), studying the changes in marsh and aquatic vegetation produced by a drawdown, found that one of the more important results of a drawdown was the improvement of interspersion of cover and water.

Cover development by water-level management has been mentioned by Dozier (1953), Bell (1953), and Nelson (1955) but to my knowledge it has not been related to breeding populations of ducks. Allan and Anderson (1955) state that drawdowns are not likely to encourage nesting. After study of small impoundments in Alberta, Keith (1961) suggested that water-level fluctuations could be used to attract breeding waterfowl by making more food available in spring.

The effect of drainage on submerged soils is uncertain. Neess' (1946) review of fish-pond culture implies that commercial fish culturists in Europe periodically drain their ponds to increase the soil fertility. In contrast, Cook and Powers (1958) found drainage reduced the nutrient content of marsh soils.

STUDY AREAS

The primary area studied was the Backus Lake flooding, east of Houghton Lake in Roscommon County, Mich., in an almost level till plain interspersed with morainic ridges (Leverett and Taylor 1915). The upland cover is primarily oak (*Quercus* sp.), aspen (*Populus* sp.), and jack pine (*Pinus banksiana*) forest. Lowland areas commonly are bogs, lowland shrub swamps, or coniferous swamps.

In 1938 a dam built by the Civilian Conservation Corps raised the level of the 170-acre Backus Lake and flooded an additional 350 acres. The average depth of water in the old lake is now 3.8 feet and in the flooded area 1.8 feet. In the 350 acres of new aquatic habitat, there were approximately 144 acres of trees, 178 acres of sweet gale (*Myrica gale*), and 28 acres of grasses (Gramineae) and sedges (*Carex* sp.) prior to flooding.

Comparative studies were made in four other floodings, on Denton, Bear, Robinson, and Backus Creeks in Roscommon County.

METHODS

Vegetation

A series of permanent transects yielded detailed data on vegetation in July and August of each year. Each transect was subdivided into units 5 feet long to permit computation of frequency for each species. Each transect was 6 inches wide. In 1956, 1958, and 1959 data were gathered on 927 plots on 15 transects. In 1957 low water levels following a dike failure permitted access to only 593 plots.

The major vegetation types were mapped each year. The 1956 and 1957 maps were similar enough to combine into a single map of pre-drawdown conditions. Cover types were based primarily on the emergent species. Aerial photographs, both standard vertical and low altitude obliques, facilitated cover mapping. Plant names in this paper follow Fernald (1950).

Bottom Fauna

Two bottom fauna sample stations represented two types of habitat. Ten samples were taken at each station in mid-August before the drawdown and after reflooding. All samples were poured through a No. 30 sieve in the field and the residual material preserved. The Institute for Fisheries Research of the Michigan Department of Conservation separated the organisms from the detritus by flotation.

Soil and Water

Soil and water at permanent stations were sampled on Sept. 10, 1956, Sept. 5, 1958, and Sept. 8, 1959. The Soil Testing Service of Michigan State University analyzed the samples for nutrients. The Institute for Fisheries Research analyzed the water. Standard limnological tests were made for dissolved oxygen, carbon dioxide, total alkalinity, pH, water transparency, and temperature of the water twice a month each summer.

Samples of mud collected on April 11, 1958, and April 20, 1959, were filtered through successively finer filters, and the filtrate was analyzed for mineral nutrients in the same manner as other water samples.

Core Samples

On April 21, 1958, four pairs of cores of bottom sediments were procured at the soil sampling stations with a suction-type sampler equipped with plastic insert tubes. These tubes permitted examination of each core with a minimum of disturbance.

In the laboratory the pairs of cores were mounted in a 55-gallon drum filled with tap water, one member of each pair with the column of soil submerged (a control), and the other raised with part or all of the soil above water. After 4 months the raised cores were submerged. Four days later the water above the cores was siphoned into sample bottles. The Institute for Fisheries Research analyzed these samples for mineral nutrients.

FINDINGS AND ANALYSES

Water Levels

The water levels in the Backus Lake flooding averaged 7.9 feet (based on assumed datum) gauge height during the growing season prior to 1957. In 1957 heavy rains in early July caused a flood peaking at 9.0 feet on July 12. As the water receded, the cofferdam built to retain water levels during construction of a new water-control structure failed on July 24. The water at the dam dropped almost 3 feet by July 28, when the break was repaired; it then rose gradually to normal levels by late November.

The drawdown began in mid-April 1958. The level dropped to about 4 feet below full pool level by mid-May and remained there, with minor fluctuations, until about Sept. 1. At this time the stoplogs were replaced. The water level increased with autumn rains to 6.7 feet gauge height, 1.3 feet below normal, by winter. Thus, the drawdown lasted about 3½ months in the deepest part of the flooding.

In general, during the growing season water levels in 1959 were 8–10 inches lower than in 1956.

Minor water-level changes occurred in all years in relation to the pattern of rainfall.

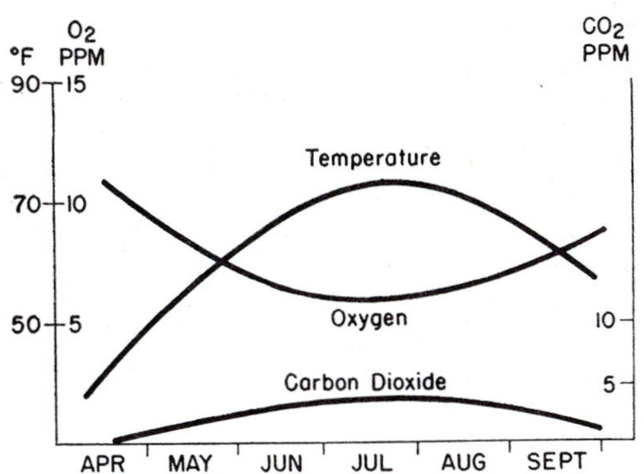

Fig. 1. Seasonal changes in water temperature, dissolved oxygen, and carbon dioxide in the Backus Lake flooding.

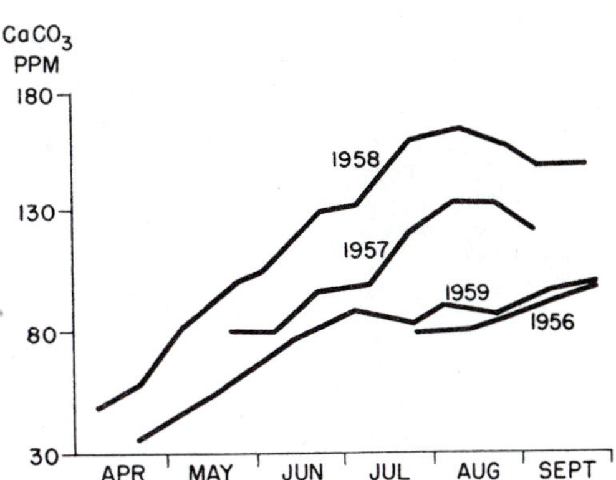

Fig. 2. Seasonal and annual changes in total alkalinity in the Backus Lake flooding.

Limnological Changes

Figures 1 and 2 show the seasonal variations in dissolved oxygen, carbon dioxide, total alkalinity, and temperature of the water in the Backus Lake impoundment. The pH and Secchi-disc readings are not graphed because of their low variability. The pH usually was 7.2–8.0, with a slight tendency to increase late in summer. The Secchi disc was almost invariably visible to the bottom.

Seasonal changes in oxygen, carbon dioxide, and temperature from 1956 through 1959 are summarized in curves eye-fitted to a plot of all individual measurements (Fig. 1). The curves indicate a low in dissolved oxygen and high in dissolved carbon dioxide related to the higher temperature of midsummer. Apparently decay processes in warm, shallow water overshadow photosynthetic production of oxygen and utilization of carbon dioxide.

Strong thermal gradients occurred only on calm days and did not cause pronounced chemical stratification.

Total alkalinity (Fig. 2) varied from year to year and showed a marked tendency to increase from spring through summer. The yearly variations are related to water-level changes. Thus, the alkalinity was highest in 1958 during the extremely low water levels of the drawdown and lowest during normal levels in 1956. Low water level following the dike failure in late July 1957 was reflected in a rise in alkalinity, as was the slightly lower water level in 1959.

An inverse relationship between water levels and total alkalinity was also observed in New York marshes by Cook and Powers (1958). Their graphs of these two variables against time are almost mirror images. They conclude that this strong inverse relationship between total alkalinity and water level was accidental. They believe, however, that the concentrating effect of evaporation and the increase in carbon-dioxide production with increasing temperatures, which would bring insoluble carbonates into solution as bicarbonates, adequately explain these apparent correlations.

In the Backus Lake flooding the ratio of surface or near-surface runoff to ground water in the water supply at a given time probably affects the total alkalinity. Water movement through the marsh, as indicated by outflow, was usually present during most of the year. Thus an in-

Table 1. Effects of temporary drainage on soil and water nutrients (mean values of number of samples indicated).

Item	Number of samples	Ca (ppm)	K (ppm)	Total P[1] (ppb)	Total N[1] (ppm)	Specific conductivity (μmhos)[2]
A. Soil (Fall)						
Before drainage	6	133	36.9	2,000	2.7	—
Drained	5	106	7.7	500	15.9	—
After reflooding	6	138	22.5	1,800	1.8	—
Soil solution (Spring)						
Before drainage	5	24.8	1.9	89.1	0.05	196
After reflooding	5	24.4	13.4	52.3	15.05	246
Water						
Spring						
Before drainage	6	17.6	0.8	23.1	0.05	93
After reflooding	5	11.7	1.6	43.8	0.16	86
Fall						
Before drainage	5	33.1	0.5	15.2	0.16	225
Drained	2	40.8	1.1	34.5	0.07	263
After reflooding	6	29.6	0.3	10.9	0.62	179
B. Core experiment (Soil solution)						
Control	4	31.9	3.5	148.5	—	244
Severely dried	2	28.5	3.4	104.5	—	263
Partially dried	2	93.1	2.9	64.5	—	478

[1] Except soil (fall) which is chiefly inorganic.
[2] Reciprocal megohms.

terchange of water occurred almost continuously. In the area studied surface runoff is practically absent, but heavy movement of water at or near the ground surface from swamp areas into the flooding is common during periods of abundant water. This water is almost certainly relatively soft and of low pH. In contrast, ground water in this region is very hard, as shown by well-water analyses (Mich. Dept. of Health 1948). My test of water from a flowing well at Backus Lake showed an alkalinity of 205 ppm $CaCO_3$. Thus, during periods of base flow, such as late in summer, the water supply of floodings built on permanent streams will be very high in total alkalinity. In spring, with the tremendous volume of water from snow melt, the amount of soft water entering a flooding must far overshadow the ground water contribution, resulting in relatively soft water.

Limnological observations, especially alkalinities, at other floodings in the Houghton Lake area were similar to those made at about the same time at Backus Lake. This indicates that the regional water supply was the predominating factor in determining the chemistry of the water rather than more variable features such as the type of vegetation or soils in the basin.

Soil and Water Fertility

The submerged soil of the Backus Lake impoundment was almost entirely organic. Sand bottom existed only as a narrow margin along a few portions of the shoreline. The organic sediments varied from finely divided to coarse fibrous material.

Prior to the drawdown the surface of the organic soil was loose and easily stirred into suspension. Drying during the drawdown consolidated the organic material to the point of bearing a man's weight in many areas. Reflooding had little immediate physical effect on these firmer bottoms.

Nutrient analyses of the soil and water in the Backus Lake impoundment are shown in Table 1. Movements of ions, or mineral nutrients, occur within the system depending on organic utilization and decay and various types of equilibria. Movements in and out of the system occur mainly through rain and water movements. In flooding projects such as Backus Lake, where outflow is normal through most of the year, water movement is of considerable importance.

Seasonal variations in quality of water supply resulted in low concentrations of bases, such as calcium and potassium, and in lower conductivity in spring as compared to fall.

Most of the other changes in nutrient availability (Table 1-A) can be attributed to the drawdown. During the drawdown a decline in bases in the soil was probably due to leaching. A strong increase in nitrogen throughout the system is clearly the result of active microbiological nitrification, under aerobic conditions, in an organic soil (Lyon and Buckman 1943). In the water, phosphorus and bases made notable gains during the drawdown, as shown during the fall. The decrease of potassium in the soil and the increase in the soil solution and free water indicate a release of this substance from the sediments to the dissolved form. The decrease in nitrogen in the water in the fall of 1958 during reflooding is puzzling unless organic utilization and deposition in the sediments were greatly increased in the warm shallow water.

By the fall of 1959 soil fertility had returned to essentially pre-drawdown levels. Nutrients in the water in the spring of 1959 had also returned to predrawdown conditions except for phosphorus and nitrogen. The latter increased, undoubtedly reflecting the buildup in phosphorus in the water and vigorous soil nitrification during the drawdown. Fall water analyses 1 year after reflooding show nutrient concentrations close to pre-drawdown levels, with the exception of nitrogen. This high nitrogen level in the water in the fall of 1959 is interesting in that other floodings also showed this change. Hence, this change in the Backus Lake flooding was probably not the result of the drawdown.

The experiments with core samples (Table 1-B) indicate that the extent of drying has a marked effect on the amount of nutrients released from bottom soils. In general, the largest increases in conductivity and calcium were associated with cores which maintained a high moisture content, by capillary action, throughout the period of drying. The decline of phosphorus as a result of drying was unexpected. Since there was a considerable increase in phosphorus in the water in the first spring following flooding (Table 1-A), it seems likely that phosphorus was released from the sediment, as shown by a decrease in the soil extracts, into the free water. The level of phosphorus in the water over the control cores seems to be excessive, however. Increased aeration of the sediment in these cores, due to turbulence created by bubbling air into the water to prevent stagnation, might have created this abnormal state.

Field and experimental data indicate that a drawdown increases the amount of soluble or, possibly, suspended mineral nutrients. The amount of increase or decrease is closely related to soil moisture and the amount of leaching during the drawdown.

The mechanism for release of nutrients is of considerable interest. The most obvious possibility is by decomposition of organic material. Since this is largely a bacterial process it is most vigorous in moist areas. Release of nutrients by decay assumes that these substances accumulate in the sediments. Lyon and Buckman (1943) indicate that in terrestrial soils the residual material after decay is largely fats, resins, and lignins, in combination with protein and allied nitrogenous compounds. The resultant complex is largely carbohydrate but contains considerable nitrogen, sulfur, and phosphorus. Most other organic matter, including some nitrogen, phosphorus, and sulfur, decomposes relatively easily into soluble form. Without oxygen, however, decay is often incomplete and may stop at stable intermediate stages (Ruttner 1953). Since anaerobic conditions exist in most of the submerged organic soil profile, decomposition is commonly incomplete in marsh sediments.

Several other explanations of the changes in nutrients are possible. Table 1-A indicates that the soils tested had a large reserve of mineral nutrients, chiefly in adsorbed form. The increase in dissolved nutrients following a drawdown might have been the result, in part, of the release of adsorbed ions. This in turn implies destruction of part of the colloidal fraction of the sediment. Less colloidal material in the soil would also permit increased losses of nutrients through leaching.

The colloidal fraction may be an important regulator of marsh productivity. Neess (1946) indicated that the colloidal material in the soil of European fish ponds is believed to govern the distribution of nutrients among pond organisms. Ideal fish-pond management requires developing a bottom soil neither so adsorptive as to impoverish the water of nutrients nor so inactive as to permit the loss of nutrients by seepage and outflow. The decline in productivity of old impoundments might be partly explained by an increasing colloid content of the soil with age.

The deleterious effect of high colloidal content of the bottom mud on higher aquatic plant growth is also illustrated by Misra (1938). He shows a high percentage saturation of bases for productive muds, but a low percentage saturation with bases in sterile subaqueous peat, and yet about the same amount of replaceable calcium (a base) in both soils. Hence, the productive mud must have had considerably higher colloidal content than the sterile soil. However, Gorham (1958) doubts the accuracy of Misra's data.

Increased colloidal content is logical in incompletely decomposed sediments. Agricultural peat soils show an increase in total exchange capacity of about 3 meq for each 1% increase in organic matter (Lyon and Buckman 1943). Peat soils usually have an exchange capacity 10–20 times greater than mineral soils. The accumulation of a partially decomposed organic layer on the bottom of an impoundment would therefore tremendously increase the capacity of the sediment to adsorb ions.

In a drained pond, decomposition of the organic colloids should be most active in the wetter areas. This process would be identical to that postulated earlier for nutrient release from organic compounds. It is quite possible that nutrient release in these wet areas is due to a combination of decomposition and reduced adsorption.

Exactly how the colloidal content of the soil controls nutrient availability for higher aquatic plants is not clear. The preceding discussion implies that adsorbed ions are not as available to aquatic plants as dissolved ions, but this is not necessarily true. Bonner and Galston (1952) show that terrestrial plants readily obtain adsorbed bases. In aquatic situations, however, dissolved nutrients are probably more abundant than in upland soils. Many aquatic plants utilize dissolved nutrients extensively, or even exclusively (Pond 1918). The improved growth of submerged plants after the drawdown in Backus Lake is good circumstantial evidence that an increase in soluble nutrients benefited these plants.

The infertility of organic soils may involve something more complicated than simple availability of major nutrients. Misra (1938) suggested the greater availability of iron may cause poor aquatic plant growth. Cook and Powers (1958) also considered increases in iron after flooding toxic to plant growth. They believed iron may be available under anaerobic conditions even in the presence of sulfides with which it usually forms an insoluble precipitate. This availability of iron can result from the formation of soluble complexes with the products of anaerobic decomposition of organic matter.

If iron affects aquatic soil productivity, it is most likely that iron-organic complexes are important, since most inorganic iron compounds are highly insoluble. Here again the accumulation of the products of incomplete decomposition of organic material is a dominant feature. The nature of the iron-organic compounds is not well known, but it certainly appears that aerobic destruction of the organic part of the complex should reduce the availability of iron.

The foregoing data and discussion have dealt with organic sediments. The principles discussed should apply to other soil types. In the case of a coarse sand bottom, leaching during a drawdown would be severe. Accelerated decay would deplete the already deficient organic content. Frequent and severe drying of a coarse sand bottom would be detrimental to marsh fertility. The effect of drawdown on other mineral soils will depend on porosity, particle size, and organic content.

Table 2. Numbers of bottom organisms per square foot, Backus Lake flooding, based on ten ¼-square-foot samples.

	Station I 4 feet deep, vegetation sparse		Station II 1 foot deep, vegetation dense	
Organism	1956	1959	1956	1959
Oligochaeta	6.4	0.0	11.2	25.6
Crustacea	3.2	0.4	5.2	3.2
Insecta				
Tricoptera	6.0	0.0	30.4	0.4
Ephemeroptera	4.0	0.0	45.6	0.0
Odonata	9.6	0.0	12.0	2.0
Diptera[1]	785.6	51.2	540.0	206.8
Mollusca				
Gastropoda	6.0	0.0	1.6	0.0
Pelecypoda				
Sphaeridae	95.2	0.0	37.2	0.0
Miscellaneous	4.0	0.0	5.2	0.0
Total	920.0	51.6	688.4	238.0

[1] Mostly Tendipedidae.

Invertebrates

The drawdown in 1958 was extremely detrimental to invertebrate life (Table 2). Mollusks were absent and other invertebrates were sparse in 1959. Since most of these forms could not have survived during the drawdown in 1958, the 1959 data must be interpreted either as slow repopulation or the effect of an altered environment. Mollusks in particular would probably repopulate slowly. The soil, solidifed by the drawdown, may have provided a less suitable habitat for insects.

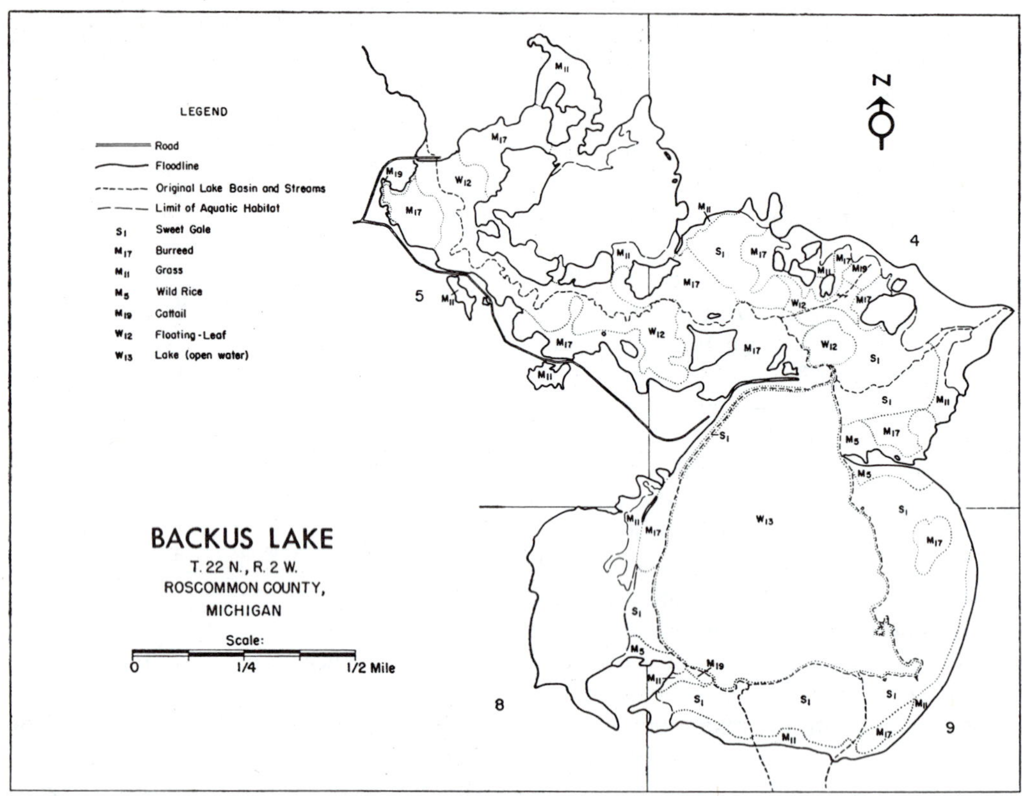

Fig. 3. Cover map of pre-drawdown vegetation—1956–57.

The effect of a deficiency of invertebrates on populations of waterfowl is difficult to assess. Literature on food habits of waterfowl (Martin and Uhler 1939, Martin et al. 1951, Zimmerman 1953, Coulter 1955, Korschgen 1955) indicates that about 10–30% of the food of puddle ducks and ring-necked ducks (*Athya collaris*) is animal material. In the floodings studied these species utilized about 30–50% animal food. A supply of invertebrate food is important to waterfowl. Further, immature ducks usually use more animal food than adults (Beard 1953, Mendall 1958, Chura 1961).

The reduced population of invertebrates after a drawdown could be detrimental to waterfowl production. Marshes treated with insecticides (Hanson 1952) have shown decreased use by waterfowl. In the Backus Lake area, however, factors other than food, such as cover, were probably more important in limiting waterfowl breeding. Beard (1953) also emphasized that factors other than animal food were involved in the brood productivity of beaver ponds. Shallow water areas in general probably produce more invertebrate food than can possibly be consumed by even the densest populations of breeding waterfowl. Sharp reductions in this food supply are important only if associated with extraordinarily high breeding populations.

Some modification of drawdown procedure may be required to leave ade-

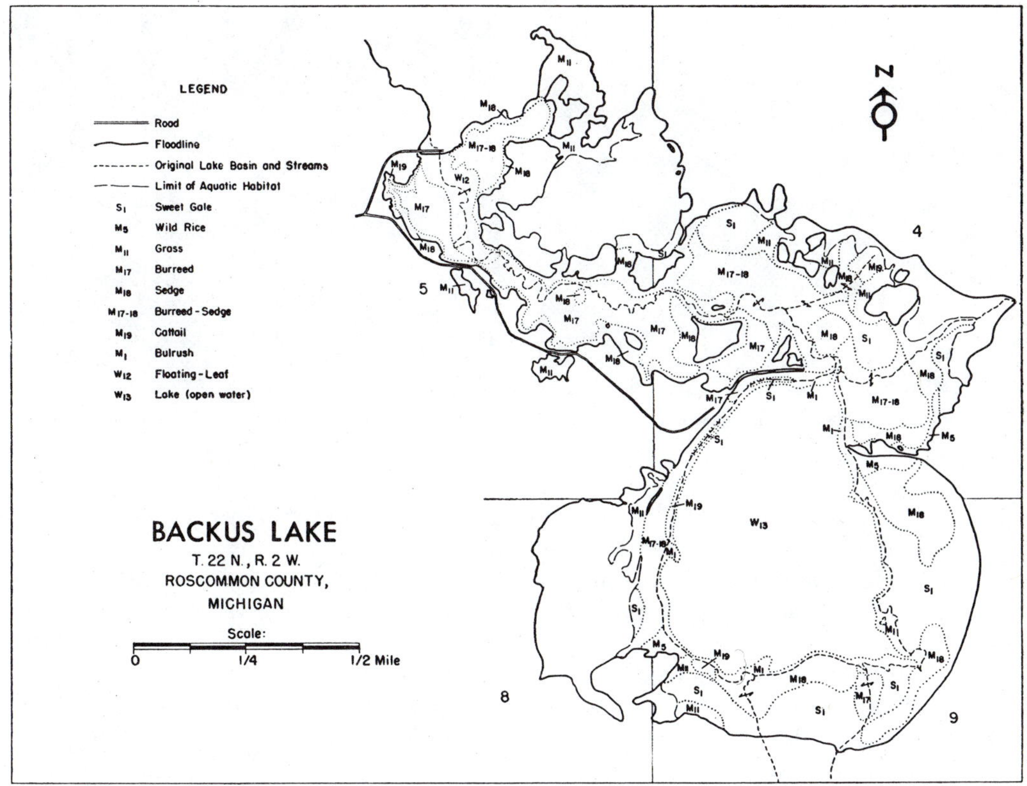

Fig. 4. Cover map of post-drawdown vegetation—1959.

quate residual vegetated water areas for invertebrate food production.

Vegetation

Cover Types.—The areas and average water depths of the cover types (Figs. 3, 4) distinguished in the Backus Lake flooding reflect a water level 8 inches lower in 1959 than in 1956 (Table 3).

Parts of the 1956 and 1957 grass type were included in the 1958 sweet gale type because of increased vigor of sweet gale during the drawdown. In a considerable portion of the sweet gale type, the sweet gale was dead in 1959 and was replaced by sedge (Figs. 5, 6). Sweet gale died in areas subjected to prolonged (19 years) deep flooding prior to the drawdown and severe drying during the drawdown (5 months). Apparently this combination was responsible for the death of the sweet gale, since it will survive either deep flooding or dry site conditions for a long time.

In 1958 sedges invaded many areas which were severely dried during the drawdown. In combination with the converted sweet gale area, this resulted in a sedge type of 91 acres in 1959, the largest post-drawdown type.

During the drawdown sedges invaded the entire burreed (*Sparganium chlorocarpum*) type, and I reclassified it as the burreed-sedge type (Figs. 7, 8). Reflooding drowned the sedges out of a portion of this area. Burreed invaded deeper

Fig. 5. Sweet gale type before drawdown, August 29, 1956.

Fig. 6. Sweet gale type after reflooding, August 5, 1959.

parts of the basin while the impoundment was drained. The net result of these changes, after reflooding, was a burreed type in deeper water than before the drawdown.

The floating-leaf type occurred in deep water near the old stream channel in the lower portion of the flooding and in a shallow area of dense, nearly pure watershield (*Brasenia Schreberi*). In the deep water, floatingleaf pondweed (*Potamogeton natans*) and yellow waterlily (*Nuphar variegatum*) were characteristic plants.

In all cover types, presence of plants other than the type species was determined primarily by water depth. In water less than 1 foot deep (grass, sedge, cattail, and part of sweet gale type), spikerush (*Eleocharis acicularis*), rice cutgrass (*Leersia oryzoides*), mannagrasses (*Glyceria* sp.), and leafy pondweed (*Potamogeton foliosus*) were most abundant. In water over 2 feet deep (burreed and bur-

Table 3. Areas and characteristic water depths of cover types, Backus Lake flooding.

	Year				
	1956 and 1957		1958	1959	
Cover type	Area (acres)	Characteristic water depth (inches)	Area[1] (acres)	Area[1] (acres)	Characteristic water depth (inches)
Grass	48	12	28 (−41.7)	30 (+7.1)	6
Burreed	98	24	—	51 (−47.9)	30
Floating-leaf	56	30	14 (−75.0)	11 (−21.4)	34
Sweet gale	129	18	151 (+17.1)	87 (−42.4)	8
Sedge	—	—	44	91 (+106.8)	8
Cattail	4	6	4 (0.0)	5 (+25.0)	2
Wild rice	13	24	10 (−23.1)	7 (−30.0)	14
Bulrush	—	—	20	14 (−30.0)	25
Burreed-sedge	—	—	97	67 (−30.9)	24
Lake (open water)	168	45	148 (−11.9)	153 (+3.4)	40
Total	516	—	516	516	—

[1] Percentage change from previous year in parentheses.

Table 4. Percentage occurrence of selected plants, Backus Lake flooding.

Plant	Year			
	1956	1957	1958	1959
Submerged species				
Potamogeton foliosus	20.2	14.7	0.2	4.1
Najas flexilis	18.3	12.1	—	23.5
Ceratophyllum demersum	7.9	14.1	—	4.2
Floating-leaf species				
Potamogeton natans	35.8	35.6	1.4	23.2
Brasenia Schreberi	26.6	4.8	—	2.4
Nuphar variegatum	14.5	24.7	7.2	20.3
Polygonum amphibium	1.9	3.4	21.9	32.1
Lemnaceae	1.9	0.3	0.1	11.0
Emergent species				
Sparganium chlorocarpum	33.2	24.9	20.7	34.4
Pontederia cordata	3.0	1.8	8.6	6.1
Zizania aquatica	3.8	3.7	1.7	1.5
Carex spp.[1]	11.2	13.1	76.8	50.6
Leersia oryzoides	10.9	10.2	44.8	52.0
Bidens spp.	4.3	—	46.8	10.6
Eleocharis acicularis	15.7	12.8	41.7	28.3
Scirpus cyperinus[1]	—	—	—	29.6
Sagittaria latifolia	8.6	11.5	13.1	22.4
Dulichium arundinaceum	3.5	5.5	8.3	21.1
Typha latifolia	1.4	2.2	4.5	3.1
Scirpus validus and *acutus*	0.3	—	2.2	1.4
Woody species				
Myrica gale	30.6	28.7	28.2	17.8

[1]*Scirpus cyperinus* included in *Carex* spp. in 1958.

reed-sedge types), floatingleaf pondweed and yellow waterlily were associated with the type species. Burreed occurred in all types but was densest in areas typed as burreed. Watershield, bushy pondweed (*Najas flexilis*), and water smartweed (*Polygonum amphibium*) were distributed among various types, apparently depending on soil fertility and competition.

Changes in Species Composition.— The percentages of occurrence of 21 of the most common plants determined by weighting transect data by cover type areas reveal the striking constancy of the species from year to year (Table 4). Only during the drawdown did a few plants disappear completely or new plants appear. Differences are restricted, with these few exceptions, to changes in abundance. This is not too surprising, since almost all of the species listed are perennials with structures which enable them to survive fluctuating water levels. Only bushy pondweed (Pond 1918), wild rice (*Zizania aquatica*), and sticktights (*Bidens* sp.) are annuals.

There were relatively few changes in vegetation between 1956 and 1957 in spite of the water-level fluctuations (Table 4). Some of the more sensitive aquatics, notably bushy pondweed, leafy pondweed, watershield, and burreed, were less common in 1957. The increase in yellow waterlily in 1957 is inexplicable. The increase in coontail (*Cerato-*

Fig. 7. Burreed type before drawdown, August 28, 1956.

Fig. 8. Burreed-sedge type after reflooding, August 28, 1959.

phyllum demersum) is unusual; its occurrence may be erratic because it reproduces by fragmentation. The best conclusion from a comparison of the 1956 and 1957 data is that the variations in plant abundance are probably normal for large annual differences in environmental conditions other than a planned drawdown.

The changes in vegetation between 1957 and 1958 were the result of the drawdown. Submergent plants persisted only in the residual water areas. All the floating-leaf species were reduced in some degree. Watershield was completely eliminated and floatingleaf pondweed almost so, but the waterlilies showed a remarkable ability to survive in very dry situations. Their extreme hardiness under adverse environmental changes was also found in a European species by Heslop-Harrison (1955). Individual plot records indicate that waterlily mortality occurred only in areas subjected to extreme drying, such as part of the sweet gale type.

Most emergent species increased in 1958, mainly due to seedling reproduction. Wild rice did not, as a result of insufficient water. Burreed was reduced in the drier areas but increased greatly in the wetter areas. The only common woody plant, sweet gale, remained virtually unchanged.

The most abundant plants during the drawdown (sedges, rice cutgrass, water smartweed, mannagrasses, spikerush, and sticktights) volunteered and increased in all cover types. Some zonation was evident, however, in relation to moisture conditions and date of soil exposure. The densest growth of sedge (including woolgrass, *Scirpus cyperinus*) was concentrated in a marginal band on the driest soil. Rice cutgrass and spikerush occurred predominantly in the grass type and in areas where seepage or the ground water level kept the soil moist. Sticktights were widely distributed but were densest on moist areas exposed early in the growing season.

An extensive volunteer stand of tree seedlings mostly birch (*Betula* sp.) and aspen, also invaded during the drawdown. Reflooding in 1959 eliminated them.

A good stand of softstem bulrush (*Scirpus validus*) appeared along the rim of the old lake basin. It was poorly sampled by the transects, and the cover type map provides a more accurate appraisal of its relative importance.

For production of a large amount of duck food from wetland plants such as millets (*Echinochloa* sp.) and smartweeds (*Polygonum* sp.), the drawdown of the Backus Lake flooding must be considered a failure. Only one highly regarded food plant, rice cutgrass, grew in large quantities, and it produced little seed. There are probably two reasons for the poor stand of more productive food plants on the exposed bottoms. First, the drawdown resulted in very dry soil conditions in over half of the flooded area, a situation further accentuated by a very dry summer. The presence of cattail (*Typha latifolia*) seedlings indicates proper moisture conditions for the growth of desirable wetland plants, since it requires a wet soil for establishment. Cattail seedlings occurred only between 2 and 10 inches above the water level prevailing at the time of seedling establishment. Much of the area was too dry for a good stand of wetland vegetation.

A second factor determining the type of vegetation which will volunteer on drained pond bottoms is the availability of seed (Uhler 1956). In general, bottom soils contain ample quantities of seed which germinate when conditions are favorable (Penfound 1953). In the Backus Lake impoundment, however, there was apparently a deficiency of seed of such plants as smartweeds, millet, and soft stem bulrush. Sticktights were abundant in spite of an apparently minimal seed source.

The vegetation of 1959 (Table 4) shows an interesting mixture of recovered perennial aquatics and persistence of plants which invaded during the drawdown. Burreed and waterlilies returned to a level of abundance closely approximating pre-drawdown conditions. Most other submergents and floating-leaf species, including floatingleaf pondweed, watershield, leafy pondweed, and coontail, showed increases over 1958 but were still far below pre-drawdown levels. These are perennials and will probably return to approximately their former abundance in time, unless the drawdown altered the environment permanently.

All but a few of the remaining plants in Table 4 are perennial emergents which spread during the drawdown and with some changes survived reflooding in 1959. The exceptions were the annuals bushy pondweed, wild rice, and sticktights; the amphibious water smartweed; the woody sweet gale; and the floating duckweeds. Wild rice, unfavorably affected by the drawdown, occupied about the same area in 1959 as in 1958, but it was much more dense, reflecting more favorable water levels. Denser emergent growth, providing more sheltered water, resulted in a better stand of duckweeds than before the drawdown. Improved fertility of the water in the spring of 1959 may also have favored this growth. Slightly lower water levels in 1959, together with an abundant seed supply from 1958, resulted in the growth of more sticktights in 1959 than before the drawdown.

Most of the effects of the drawdown on vegetation noted in the first year of reflooding were related to survival, regrowth, and seedling reproduction through the simple removal and replacement of water. Only bushy pondweed and water smartweed showed growth in 1959 which indicated an improved environment. The spread of water smartweed began with seedling reproduction during the drawdown. It flourished in 1959, however, producing a fine stand. During the major period of blossoming in July, large areas were pink with flowers, in

Table 5. Waterfowl populations, Backus Lake flooding.

Item	Year 1956	1957	1958	1959	1960
Spring migration peak population[1]	—	—	50	75	1,500
Breeding pairs[1]	—	3	5	5	10
Broods observed[1]	3	0	2	1	—
Average number observed daily:					
June and July[1]	6	4	12	5	—
August–September peak population[1]	200	35	150	560	—
Early September air census	—	30	50	10	—
Kill per 100 hunter hours on first day of season[2]	16.2	5.7	13.1	10.7	—

[1] Based on frequent shore and boat counts.
[2] Based on hunter bag checks.

areas supported an extremely dense stand of bushy pondweed mixed with some leafy pondweed. Changed soil conditions must have produced this growth, since other areas in the lake of almost densities more than one head per square foot over many acres. Large amounts of seed matured later in the summer. Prior to the drawdown the small amounts of water smartweed bloomed very late in summer and rarely produced seed. There can be little doubt that the excellent response of water smartweed was the result of improved growing conditions.

The response of bushy pondweed to the drawdown was striking. Since it is an annual, its growth in any one year can be considered an indication of suitable environmental conditions. Although abundance of bushy pondweed on the transects in 1959 was not greatly different than before the drawdown, its presence was clearly related to two factors—competition and changes in soil nutrients. Competition probably prevented it from becoming more abundant. The relation of bushy pondweed to soil fertility was clearest in the old lake basin. Drainage of this area was incomplete in 1958, with only a small proportion of the bottom exposed as mud flats saturated with water. In 1959 each of these former mud bar identical depth and water quality produced little aquatic growth. Moist soils, such as these mud flats, are conducive to the greatest changes in plant nutrients. This characteristic probably accounts for the maximum development of bushy pondweed.

Use by Waterfowl

Mallards (*Anas platyrhynchos*), black ducks (*Anas rubripes*), and blue-winged teal (*Anas discors*) comprise most of the population of the Backus Lake flooding at all seasons (Table 5). This area was used mainly as a gathering point for ducks in late August. Low breeding population and brood production were probably the result of the absence of suitable emergent cover in early spring. The food, open-water loafing spot, and nesting-cover requirements for territories of mated pairs postulated by Hochbaum (1944) appeared to be adequately provided. Upland grass areas, favored for nesting by mallards and blue-winged teal, were limited to thinly stocked portions of forest stands. This may have restricted nesting, but other floodings with favorable stands of emergent vegetation produced well in spite of the same limitation. Evans and Black (1956) believed that dispersal and the need for isolation are important factors in determining the distribution of breeding waterfowl in the prairie potholes. Emergent cover may provide this isolation factor in large waterfowl impoundments. It must be present in early spring for maximum use.

Emergent cover which does not break down during the winter also may have an important influence on breeding populations by affecting the time of the spring thaw. The emergent shoots trap drifting snow, increasing the depth of snow cover. The ice under the insulating blanket of snow is not as thick. Ice under emergent cover thawed and provided open water as much as 1 week before areas lacking emergent vegetation. Since the potential nesting pairs of blacks and mallards often arrive during this week, the earlier open water must influence the selection of breeding areas.

Cover is also of primary importance for broods (Bennett 1938, Hochbaum 1944, Griffith 1948). The importance of sedge marshes as brood habitat was studied by Mendall (1958) and Bear (1953). About 70% of the broods observed on floodings were associated with sedge cover. My food-habits studies and Beard's (1953) indicate that kind and amount of food available has little influence on the number of broods produced in such areas.

Since emergent cover is so important to brood production, the large increase in sedges in Backus Lake as a result of the drawdown must be considered a very valuable improvement in the habitat.

The absence of an increase in breeding waterfowl in 1959 seems to contradict the preceding conclusion, but the sedge cover was not available until June of that year. Reflooding in the fall of 1958 submerged the stand developed during the drawdown, and sedges did not appear above the water until after the main breeding period in 1959. Spring floods submerged this cover again in 1960, but as the water receded cover was available and the number of breeding pairs of each species increased. This increase might have been due to carry-over of large quantities of duck food from the first year of reflooding (1959), attractiveness to pairs of improved brood cover, improved isolation between pairs of the same species, or relatively earlier open water. Because of the low density of each species, the isolation factor was probably not very important.

Beginning in early August, ducks move about restlessly (Hochbaum 1955). Sharp daily changes in the number of waterfowl observed on the Backus Lake flooding during this period were probably due to movements into and away from the marsh. Gradually the aggregations became large and concentrated more heavily on the better food areas. In early September most ducks were apparently on a few favored feeding grounds. The ducks preferred floodings containing duckweed regardless of the kind of cover. Wild rice, bushy pondweed, and leafy pondweed areas were highly attractive. Wild rice in 1956 and bushy pondweed in 1959 apparently were responsible for the high waterfowl populations observed on Backus Lake.

Disturbance can affect the use of an area by waterfowl at all seasons (Pirnie 1935). Hunting forces ducks into inaccessible areas. Any flooding, such as Backus Lake, which is entirely accessible to hunters soon becomes devoid of waterfowl. During the gunning season areas of flooded timber too deep to wade and too dense to traverse by boat will hold ducks. Such areas frequently also support dense stands of duckweed.

DISCUSSION

A consideration of the list of common plants in Backus Lake (Table 4) indicates that the plants of a good waterfowl marsh were present prior to the drawdown. Food plants were adequately represented, particularly pondweeds. Cover in the form of sedge and cattail was limited but present. The shrubby sweet gale type provided a large area of cover but it apparently was not desirable since waterfowl use of this shelter was limited.

The primary deficiency of the Backus Lake marsh was probably improper distribution and quantity of plants. In general, two factors are responsible for the lack of desirable quantities of food and cover. Changes in availability of mineral nutrients following initial flooding altered the relative amounts of submerged and floating-leaf plants such as pondweeds and waterlilies. Excessive water depths and lack of suitable conditions for establishment limited the stands of emergent plants and precluded the development of good interspersion. These factors are probably of common importance in the ecology of waterfowl impoundments.

Cover is very important to waterfowl, especially during the breeding season; consequently, the development of cover is of major importance in flooding projects. In Backus Lake, and probably other floodings, the tendency is for cover to diminish as long as stable water levels are maintained. This decline is frequently related to water depths in excess of the tolerance of the cover plants common to flooding sites. Bulrush and narrow-leaved cattail (*Typha angustifolia*) tolerate deep water but are rare in the floodings studied. Burreed also grows in deep water, but its emergent shoots are present only for a brief period in summer, which seriously reduces its value as a cover plant.

Emergent plants may also be absent because they have not had an opportunity to become established. Many emergent plants, including cattail and bulrush, must have a bare mud flat as a seedbed. In impoundments with stable water levels, this condition is never met. Some emergent plants, notably burreed and pickerelweed (*Pontederia cordata*), will become established on bottoms under water. These species, however, do not provide much needed cover in early spring. Their emergent shoots break down completely over winter and new growth does not appear until late June or July.

Since stable water levels usually prohibit the establishment of desirable herbaceous emergent plants, adequate cover is provided only as long as flooded trees and shrubs persist. The effective life of woody species has been studied in some detail and is summarized by DiAngelo (1953). In general, within 10 years this cover has lost its value. Only cedar sometimes persists longer. A decline in productivity must be expected quite soon if woody cover is not replaced by herbaceous emergents.

The changes which occur in non-cover aquatic species with continued stable water levels are less distinct. In part, there seems to be a rapid plant succession. The initial abundance of duckweed is related to calm and sheltered water. A dense mat of these floating plants may provide conditions conducive to high productivity. Jacobs (1947) found anaerobic conditions prevalent under such a mat; my results confirm this. Anaerobiosis will result in the release of nutrients from the bottom muds (Mortimer 1941, 1942; Ruttner 1953; Hutchinson 1957). A high concentration of nutrients in the water, as would be expected under such circumstances, is undoubtedly essential to the continued development of duckweeds.

Jacobs (1947) observed that anaerobiosis under duckweeds usually killed associated submerged aquatics in midsummer. Shading probably helps keep submerged growth at a minimum under a dense layer of these floating plants. In either case the development of submergent vegetation is inhibited until the duckweeds become more sparse as the cover provided by woody plants is reduced by decay and fall. Mineral nutrients probably decline in the water at about the same time due to better aeration. A probably corresponding increase in nutrients in the soil would tend to favor rooted aquatic plants.

A shift from rooted submerged aquatic plants to rooted floating-leaf forms, notably waterlilies, occurs with time. In the classic view of succession (Weaver and Clements 1938) invasion by floating-leaf plants is associated with siltation and reduced water depths. Water depths in waterfowl impoundments are rarely beyond the limits of these species, however. Two explanations are possible for the delay in their appearance. First, the time involved, which is not well defined but appears to be at least 5 years, may merely be the time required for these plants to invade a new area. Second, further changes in the fertility of the soil may be necessary before these species can thrive. Possibly they invade as soil conditions become unfavorable for submerged species, thus reducing competition. Since waterlilies and floatingleaf pondweed will tolerate highly organic, often loose, soils (Martin and Uhler 1939, Moyle 1945), it may be that they are able to grow in soils too poor in available nutrients for other aquatics.

Misra (1938) discussed in detail the relation of soil changes to aquatic plant succession. He concluded (and this study helps confirm) that increases in the organic content of the soil reduce the availability of mineral nutrients, which in turn are major factors in determining plant succession. Factors such as light, water temperature, and competition may alter the rate of change or the plant species composition at any stage, but the process goes on inexorably, *as long as water levels remain stable.* Further, in shallow water, such as in waterfowl impoundments, the shift from a productive to nonproductive condition is rapid.

THE DRAWDOWN AS A MARSH MANAGEMENT TECHNIQUE

The drawdown is a natural and effective method of maintaining the productivity of a waterfowl marsh. Many of the most productive waterfowl areas are subject to natural "drawdown" as a result of droughts. Outstanding in this respect are the marshes of the northern prairies and in Michigan the marshes of the Great Lakes. Although these fluctuations are sometimes the subject of considerable concern, they are probably important in maintaining the productivity of the marshes. Early in the waterfowl impoundment program, floodings with poorly stabilized water levels were observed to be more productive than those with stable levels (Hartman 1949).

The effects of a drawdown fall into three categories. First, in some instances the drawdown produces a temporary abundance of food in the form of seeds of wetland plants. Second, it provides suitable conditions for the establishment of emergent cover. Last, it may result in soil improvement and in improved aquatic plant food production upon reflooding. Increased soil fertility depends on retaining adequate moisture during the period surface water is absent. Generally, this means reducing the water level only enough to expose the soil surface. In sandy soils, too frequent or too severe drainage may be harmful.

SUMMARY

This study was conducted to determine the effects of a drawdown on the soil, water, vegetation, invertebrates, and populations of waterfowl of an impoundment.

Soil and water analyses indicated a definite increase in plant nutrients. A marked increase in soil nitrates occurred during the drawdown as a result of aerobic nitrification. This effect persisted at least until the spring of the first year of reflooding. The response of other nutrients was less definite, but increases were noted and plant growth improved. The most favorable increase in fertility was obtained when the organic portion of the soil remained moist or even very wet during the drawdown.

Invertebrate populations, a potential food supply for waterfowl, were considerably reduced after the drawdown.

The plant species composition was not notably affected. Most of the common species prior to the drawdown were perennials and apparently able to survive drainage for one growing season. Many of the submerged and floating-leaf species were reduced in abundance. Waterlilies are extremely hardy and were little affected except in areas of very severe drying. Water smartweed and bushy pondweed growth was luxuriant after the drawdown, apparently in response to increases in nutrients.

Most emergent species spread and increased in abundance as a result of the drawdown. Many of these plants require an exposed soil seed bed for germination and early growth and respond rapidly to these conditions provided by a drawdown. Sedges and woolgrass were most abundant on portions of the study area which became very dry. Cattail, bulrush, and burreed were more abundant in areas where considerable soil moisture was retained throughout the drawdown. Rice cutgrass and mannagrasses were more generally distributed.

Wetland food production during the drawdown was disappointing. Poor millet and smartweed growth was probably due to the absence of an adequate seed supply and to excessive drying of the bottom soil. Rice cutgrass was abundant but did not produce seed.

Waterfowl utilization of the area increased in the late summer of 1959. Abundant food, principally bushy pondweed, was very attractive to ducks. Observations on other areas indicated that brood production is closely associated with emergent cover of suitable density which persists through the winter. The increased cover developed by the 1958 drawdown in Backus Lake was submerged by reflooding and was not available in early spring of 1959. Use by breeding waterfowl increased in 1960 when the newly developed emergent cover was available.

LITERATURE CITED

ALLAN, P. F., AND W. L. ANDERSON. 1955. More wildlife from our marshes and wetlands, pp. 589–596. *In* Water, Yearbook of Agr., U.S. Dept. Agr. 751pp.

BEARD, ELIZABETH B. 1953. The importance of beaver in waterfowl management at the Seney National Wildlife Refuge. J. Wildl. Mgmt. 17:398–436.

BELL, J. G. 1953. Horicon marsh—A decade of management. Wisconsin Conserv. Bull. 17:7–10.

BENNETT, L. J. 1938. The blue-winged teal, its ecology and management. Collegiate Press, Inc., Ames, Iowa. 144pp.

BONNER, J., AND A. W. GALSTON. 1952. Principles of plant physiology. W. H. Freeman and Co., San Francisco, Calif. 494pp.

CHURA, N. J. 1961. Food availability and preferences of juvenile mallards. Trans. N. Am. Wildl. Conf. 26:121–134.

COOK, A. H., AND C. F. POWERS. 1958. Early biochemical changes in the soils and water of artificially created marshes in New York. New York Fish and Game J. 5:9–65.

COULTER, M. W. 1955. Spring food habits of surface feeding ducks in Maine. J. Wildl. Mgmt. 19:263–267.

DAVENPORT, L. A. 1959. Dams, dikes, and ducks, Michigan Conserv. 28:6–11.

DIANGELO, S. 1953. Aquatic plant succession at certain waterfowl flooding projects in Michigan. M.S. Thesis. Univ. of Michigan, Ann Arbor, Mich. 112pp.

DOZIER, H. L. 1953. Muskrat production and management. U.S. Fish and Wildl. Serv., Circ. 18. 42pp.

EVANS, C. D., AND K. E. BLACK. 1956. Duck production studies on the prairie potholes of South Dakota. U.S. Dept. Interior, Fish and Wildl. Serv., Spec. Sci. Rept., Wildl. No. 32. 59pp.

FERNALD, M. L. 1950. Gray's manual of botany. American Book Co., N.Y. 1632pp.

GORHAM, E. 1958. Observations on the formation and breakdown of the oxidized microzone at the mud surface in lakes. Limnol. Oceanog. 3:291–298.

GRIFFITH, R. 1948. Improving waterfowl habitat. Trans. N. Am. Wildl. Conf. 13:609–617.

HANSON, W. R. 1952. Effects of some herbicides and insecticides on biota of North Dakota marshes. J. Wildl. Mgmt. 16:229–308.

HARRIS, S. W. 1957. Ecological effects of drawdown operations for the purpose of improving waterfowl habitat. Ph.D. Thesis. Univ. of Minnesota, St. Paul, Minn. 209pp.

HARTMAN, G. F. 1949. Management of central Wisconsin flowages. Wisconsin Conserv. Bull. 14:19–22.

HESLOP-HARRISON, YOLANDE. 1955. *Nuphar* Sm. J. Ecology 43:342–364.

HOCHBAUM, H. A. 1944. The canvasback on a prairie marsh. The American Wildl. Inst., Washington, D.C. 201pp.

———. 1955. Travels and traditions of waterfowl. Univ. of Minnesota Press, Minneapolis, Minn. 301pp.

HUTCHINSON, G. E. 1957. A treatise on limnology, Vol. I. John Wiley and Sons, New York. 1015pp.

JACOBS, D. L. 1947. An ecological life history of *Spirodela polyrhiza* with emphasis on the turion phase. Ecol. Monographs 17:437–469.

KADLEC, J. A. 1956. The effects of water level management on two central Wisconsin marshes. M.S. Thesis. Univ. of Michigan, Ann Arbor, Mich. 84pp.

KEITH, L. B. 1961. A study of waterfowl ecology on small impoundments in southeastern Alberta. Wildl. Monographs No. 6. 88pp.

KORSCHGEN, L. J. 1955. Fall foods of waterfowl in Missouri. Missouri Conserv. Comm. P-R Series No. 14. 41pp.

LEVERETT, F., AND F. B. TAYLOR. 1915. The Pleistocene of Indiana and Michigan and the history of the Great Lakes. U.S. Geol. Survey, Monograph 53. U.S. Gov't. Printing Office, Wash., D.C. 529pp.

LOW, J. B., AND F. C. BELLROSE, JR. 1944. The seed and vegetative yield of waterfowl food plants in the Illinois River valley. J. Wildl. Mgmt. 8:7–22.

LYON, T. L., AND H. O. BUCKMAN. 1943. The nature and properties of soils. The MacMillan Co., New York. 499pp.

MACNAMARA, L. G. 1957. Potentials of small waterfowl areas. Trans. N. Am. Wildl. Conf. 22:92–96.

MARTIN, A. C., AND F. M. UHLER. 1939. Food of game ducks in the United States and Canada. U.S. Dept. Agr. Tech. Bull. 634. Reprinted 1951 as Research Report 30, U.S. Gov't. Printing Office, Washington, D.C. 308pp.

———, H. S. ZIM, AND A. L. NELSON. 1951. American wildlife and plants. McGraw-Hill Book Co., Inc., New York. 500pp.

MENDALL, H. L. 1958. The ring-necked duck in the Northeast. Univ. of Maine Bull. 60(16). 317pp.

MICHIGAN DEPARTMENT OF HEALTH. 1948. Chemical analyses and their interpretations—Public water supplies in Michigan. Engineering Bull. No. 4. 23pp.

MISRA, R. D. 1938. Edaphic factors in the distribution of aquatic plants in English Lakes. J. Ecology 26:411–451.

MORTIMER, C. H. 1941. The exchange of dissolved substances between mud and water in lakes. J. Ecology 29:280–329.

———. 1942. The exchange of dissolved substances between mud and water in lakes. J. Ecology 30:147–201.

MOYLE, J. B. 1945. Some chemical factors influencing the distribution of aquatic plants in Minnesota. Am. Midland Naturalist 34:402–420.

NEESS, J. C. 1946. Development and status of pond fertilization in central Europe. Trans. Am. Fisheries Soc. 76:335–358.

NELSON, N. F. 1955. Factors in the development and restoration of waterfowl habitat at Ogden Bay Refuge, Weber County, Utah. Utah Dept. Fish and Game, Publ. No. 6 of Fed. Aid Div. 87pp.

PENFOUND, W. T. 1953. Plant communities of Oklahoma lakes. Ecology 34:561–583.

PIRNIE, M. D. 1935. Michigan waterfowl management. Michigan Dept. Conserv., Lansing, Mich. 328pp.

POND, R. H. 1918. The larger aquatic vegetaion, pp. 178–209. *In* H. B. Ward and G. C. Whipple, Freshwater biology, John Wiley and Sons, Inc., New York.

RUTTNER, F. 1953. Fundamentals of limnology. Univ. of Toronto Press, Toronto, Ont. 242pp.

SOWLS, L. K. 1955. Prairie ducks. Stackpole Co.,

Harrisburg, Pa. and Wildl. Mgmt. Inst., Washington, D.C. 193pp.

UHLER, F. M. 1956. New habitats for waterfowl. Trans. N. Am. Wildl. Conf. 21:453–469.

WEAVER, J. E., AND F. E. CLEMENTS. 1938. Plant ecology. McGraw-Hill Book Co., Inc., New York. 601pp.

ZIMMERMAN, R. F. 1953. Waterfowl habitat surveys and food habit studies 1940–43. Wisconsin Conserv. Dept. Final Report Pittman-Robertson Project 6-R. 176pp.

THE EFFECT OF DRAWDOWN DATE ON WETLAND PLANT SUCCESSION

ROBERT L. MEEKS, Winous Point Club, Port Clinton, Ohio

Abstract: A 7-year study was begun on the Winous Point Shooting Club in 1956 to determine the effect of drawdown date on plant succession. An 80-acre marsh was diked into four units, one of which was drained yearly in mid-March, one in mid-April, one in mid-May, and one in mid-June. All the units were reflooded during September. Plant succession followed the same general trend on all units, going from semi-aquatic species to predominantly annual weeds. Fewer years were required with early drawdowns for annual weeds to replace semi-aquatic species. The May drawdown unit had the best plant associations for wildlife after 7 seasons. Draining during mid-to-late May should allow muskrats (*Ondatra zibethica*) to raise two litters without interruption, and not interfere with duck nesting.

Wetland managers are able to exert much control over the environment. Remove all the water from a marsh and plant succession rapidly advances from a hydric state toward more zeric conditions. Flood an area and the reverse occurs. Neither situation will maintain wetland wildlife habitat at its optimum. Although water is an obvious requisite for ducks, food and cover are also necessary. Therefore periodic drawdowns may be used to increase the production of natural foods and cover and thereby enhance the value of an area to wildlife.

Harris (1957) found that for the establishment of emergent vegetation, 1-year drawdowns were usually better than most 2-year drawdowns, providing the water was removed by June 15th; and that during longer drawdowns of 3 to 5 years, the bottoms became thoroughly dried and the vegetation progressed from weeds to nearly solid willow stands. Uhler (1956) preferred a biennial drawdown to an annual de-watering because the latter may permit the excessive development of undesirable plants. Givens and Atkeson (1957) maintained that units drained during part or all of the growing season produced more food than permanent-level pools. Hopkins (1962) said that too-early drawdowns may have reduced effectiveness because unwanted plants became established before conditions were suitable for the germination of smartweeds and other desirable plants.

Shallow impoundments constructed on areas having no previous history of wetland wildlife use rapidly decreased in waterfowl productivity after several years due to aquatic plant succession (DiAngelo 1953). As succession proceeds, fewer waterfowl foods are available (Low and Bellrose 1944). Kadlec (1960) found that properly managed 1-year drawdowns could improve food, cover, and the basic fertility of a marsh. Green et al. (1964) recommended the use of drawdowns as a management tool.

I extend my most sincere thanks to J. M. Anderson, T. J. Peterle, R. Donahoe, R. Winner, C. Hanson, and C. Bampton for their help. This study was financed by the Winous Point Research Committee in cooperation with the North American Wildlife Foundation and the Ohio Cooperative Wildlife Research Unit.

STUDY AREA

The study was conducted on the Winous Point Shooting Club property located near Port Clinton, Ohio, at the southwestern end of Lake Erie where Muddy Creek and the

Originally published in J. Wildl. Manage. 33(4):817–821, 1969.

Sandusky River join to form Sandusky Bay. The club has maintained several thousand acres of prime marsh at this location for over a century. During the summer of 1956, an 80-acre study area was separated from the main marsh by diking and then subdivided into four units. A large pump was installed to drain and reflood the units through a system of canals, dikes, and flumes.

PROCEDURES

The entire area was first drained in July, 1956, and reflooded in September. In each of the next 6 years, one of the units was drained in mid-March, one in mid-April, one in mid-May, and one in mid-June; a given unit always being drained in the same month. No unit was redrained after the water was initially removed; therefore, due to rain, water was often present well into the growing season. The units were reflooded in September with from several inches to 2 ft of water depending upon the topography

The vegetation on the entire 80 acres was cover-mapped each August. As the dominant species, determined by area occupied or cover, on a study unit changed, a new community was delineated. Within each community all species were listed in their order of dominance. The first appearance of a plant and all subsequent changes in its distribution could be readily traced.

RESULTS AND MANAGEMENT IMPLICATIONS

The following nine cover types included all the dominant species: (1) nodding smartweed (*Polygonum lapathifolium*); (2) cattail (*Typha* sp.); (3) Walter's millet (*Echinochloa Walteri*); (4) semi-aquatic species: bur-reed (*Sparganium eurycarpum*), arrowhead (*Sagittaria latifolia*), soft-item bulrush (*Scirpus validus*), chufa (*Cyperus* sp.), needle-rush (*Eleocharis acicularis*);

Table 1. Percentage of each cover type occurring on the drawdown units from 1956–1962.

	1956	1957	1958	1959	1960	1961	1962
March drawdown							
Nodding smartweed		16	28	13	12	2	6
Cattail	2	3	2	2	2	3	3
Walter's millet		16	31	45	3	20	16
Semi-aquatic species		62	7	1	3	5	6
Rose mallow		1	2	3	13	14	14
Annual weeds		1	2	7	20	22	39
Rice-cutgrass		1	27	25	41	29	10
Blue-joint grass			1	4	6	5	6
Water lotus	36						
April drawdown							
Nodding smartweed		15	21	30	1	1	16
Cattail	9	11	12	9	12	14	15
Walter's millet		9	10	12	16	6	10
Semi-aquatic species		57	20	8	10	48	1
Rose mallow				6		1	2
Annual weeds			5	1	20	6	44
Rice-cutgrass		7	30	30	37	21	8
Blue-joint grass		1	2	5	4	3	4
Water lotus	27						
May drawdown							
Nodding smartweed		44	12	5		6	7
Cattail	3	14	10	3	2	3	4
Walter's millet		2	2	4		3	6
Semi-aquatic species		37	40	17	9	14	3
Rose mallow				1	1	4	6
Annual weeds			1	7	7	6	22
Rice-cutgrass		1	30	60	76	54	40
Blue-joint grass		1	2	3	4	9	11
Water lotus	10						
June drawdown							
Nodding smartweed		8		6			
Cattail	8	10	13	13	5	6	6
Walter's millet			15	28	17	1	6
Semi-aquatic species		82	69	26		23	5
Rose mallow			3	20	46	64	43
Annual weeds							1
Rice-cutgrass				6	31	5	38
Blue-joint grass							1
Water lotus	7						

(5) rose mallow (*Hibiscus palustris*); (6) annual weeds: sow-thistle (*Sonchus* sp.), touch-me-not (*Impatiens* sp.), swamp milkweed (*Asclepias incarnata*), monkey-flower (*Mimulus* sp.), stick-tight (*Bidens* sp.), boneset (*Eupatorium perfoliatum*), fireweed (*Erechtites hieracifolia*); (7) rice-cutgrass (*Leersia oryzoides*); (8) blue-joint grass (*Calamagrostis canadensis*); and (9) water lotus (*Nelumbo lutea*).

Plant succession followed the same general trend on all units, going from semiaquatic species with various amounts of nodding smartweed, Walter's millet, and rice-cutgrass to predominantly annual weeds (Table 1). An exception occurred on the June unit where rose mallow became dominant rather than annual weeds. The earlier the drawdown, the more rapidly annual weeds replaced the other species.

Well-established water lotus beds were no longer a dominant type on any unit after the first complete drawdown season. They were entirely replaced by other species following 2 years of March drawdowns. An additional year was required for them to completely die on the other units.

Blue-joint grass became established only on sites slightly covered by water during the non-drawdown period. Therefore, to initiate the growth of this excellent duck-nesting cover some relatively dry areas should be maintained most of the time.

Woody plants never became a nuisance as they sometimes have on similar drawdowns in other areas. Interspecific competition, soil chemistry, rapidity of soil drying following drawdown, depth of water after reflooding, and seed availability are probably all involved in determining which plants invade an area. Rarely are these factors identical at different geographical locations.

Cattail increased slightly on the March and April units during the study. It remained almost constant on the May unit and increased on the June unit for 3 years but then decreased, seemingly because of rose mallow competition.

Nodding smartweed grew in dense stands in all the units during the first 3 years. The invasion of annual weeds greatly reduced the value and extent of most smartweed stands after 3 years of annual draining.

Walter's millet and rice-cutgrass were important waterfowl food plants throughout the study. They usually grew together, with the millet more abundant on drier edges and cutgrass in wetter areas. As with nodding smartweed, annual weeds reduced their abundance in later years.

Rose mallow occurred in all units, but only on the June drawdown did it become dense enough to be considered a pest. Its predominance in that unit during later years was attributed to the late drawdown.

One- to 5-acre openings were sometimes mowed in the Walter's millet and rice-cutgrass stands in the late summer. These made excellent waterfowl feeding areas when flooded with 12–18 inches of water.

Waterfowl established territories on the study area and nested along the dikes, on muskrat houses, and in artificial structures above the water. Some broods hatched successfully in the structures and on the muskrat houses, but predators destroyed most of those nests on the dikes. March and April drawdowns during the egg-laying period seemed to disrupt territorial pairs. Further study with marked individuals is needed to determine the total effect of removing water from territorial ducks.

Muskrats were seen on the area during the entire year. When units were drained, they lived in dike dens and were encountered running along trails in dense vegetation. This was true even when there was no water in the canals adjacent to the dikes. After the units were reflooded, many additional muskrats from the surrounding marsh moved into the units and constructed houses in all vegetation types except annual weeds and blue-joint grass. The March drawdown reduced the number of young produced in houses almost to zero. Several litters were successfully produced in the June unit. Breeding pairs apparently moved to the canals and dikes around a unit following drainage. The study area froze completely to the bottom during a period of extreme cold in January, 1959. This caused the death from starvation or exposure of almost the entire muskrat population. A water depth of at least 2 ft would be necessary to prevent such uncommon winter losses. This is deeper than the ideal feeding depth for dabbling ducks.

Marsh and shore birds were common just after the drawdowns and remained as long as some open water was present. They probably sought small fish and invertebrate life that was exposed by the lowered water levels. Where vegetation rather than mud flats existed around the periphery of such areas, bird use was reduced.

During the project, the May unit had the best vegetation for wildlife. Semi-aquatic species, rice-cutgrass, and nodding smartweed were the most abundant plants. Annual weeds did not cover large areas until the last year. Walter's millet was always present in the rice-cutgrass stands.

The undesirable aspects of certain drawdown dates must be considered when planning management programs. The trend of plant succession toward annual-weed dominance on the March and April units, and rose-mallow dominance on the June unit, was objectionable. In addition, early drawdowns were considered harmful to breeding muskrats and ducks on territory prior to incubation.

Removing the water from an area in mid-to-late May does not have these disadvantages. Plant associations are good, muskrats could probably raise two litters uninterrupted, and most ducks would be incubating eggs so that pair territories are less important. Lowering the water level after nesting is well under way is not usually detrimental to ducks (Hopkins 1962) and would eliminate any chance of high water destroying the nests.

Partial drawdowns might be more valuable than total drawdowns on some areas because more wildlife used the study units during the summer when standing water was present. With partial drawdowns, annual weed succession could be restricted and openings would not have to be mechanically cut prior to reflooding.

Management practices on surrounding wetlands, amount of open water, values assessed different wildlife species, and dates of waterfowl concentration should be given consideration in any drawdown program.

LITERATURE CITED

DIANGELO, S. 1953. Aquatic plant succession at certain waterfowl flooding projects in Michigan. W.M. Thesis. Univ. Michigan, Ann Arbor. 112pp.

GIVENS, L. S., AND T. Z. ATKESON. 1957. The use of dewatered land in southeastern waterfowl management. J. Wildl. Mgmt. 21(4): 465–467.

GREEN, W. E., L. G. MACNAMARA, AND F. M. UHLER. 1964. Water off and on. Pp. 557–568. *In* J. P. Linduska (Editor), Waterfowl tomorrow. U. S. Government Printing Office Washington, D. C. 770pp.

HARRIS, S. W. 1957. Ecological effects of drawdown operations for the purpose of improving waterfowl habitat. Ph.D. Thesis. Univ. Minnesota, Minneapolis. 209pp.

HOPKINS, R. C. 1962. Drawdown for ducks. Wisconsin Conserv. Bull. 27(4):18–19.

KADLEC, J. A. 1960. The effect of a drawdown on the ecology of a waterfowl impoundment. Michigan Dept. Conserv., Lansing. 181pp.

LOW, J. B., AND F. C. BELLROSE, JR. 1944. The seed and vegetative yield of waterfowl food plants in the Illinois River Valley. J. Wildl. Mgmt. 8(1):7–22.

UHLER, F. M. 1956. New habitats for waterfowl. Trans. N. Am. Wildl. Conf. 21:453–469.

Received for publication August 16, 1968.

MANAGEMENT OF FRESHWATER MARSHES FOR WILDLIFE[1]

MILTON W. WELLER, Department of Entomology, Fisheries, and Wildlife, University of Minnesota, St. Paul, MN 55108

Abstract: Although commonly practiced on wildlife management areas, marsh management is poorly founded in theory and as a predictive science. Major objectives have been to preserve marshes in a natural state and to maintain their productivity. System or community-oriented management techniques are encouraged as most likely to meet diverse public needs, whereas species-specific management is more difficult, costly and limited in application.

The structure of a marsh is a product of basin shape, water regimes, cover–water interspersion, and plant species diversity. Resultant vegetative patterns strongly influence species composition and size of bird populations. Food resources influence mammals as well as birds. Species richness (i.e., number of species) may be the most simple index to habitat quality, although various diversity indices need further evaluation.

Marshes are in constant change, and wildlife species have evolved adaptations of wide tolerance or mobility. Throughout the Midwest, water levels and muskrats (*Ondatra zibethicus*) induce most vegetative change, and the pattern of vegetation, muskrat and avian responses are predictable in a general way. This short-term successional pattern in marshes forms a usable management strategy. Various ramifications are discussed that may enhance or perpetuate the most beneficial stages.

Artificial management practices are discouraged as costly and of short-term value whereas systems based on natural successional patterns produce the most ecologically and economically sound results. Public pressures for single-purpose management often increase as management potential increases, but such problems often can be avoided by advance planning and public relations.

Marsh management projects for wildlife have rarely been adequately evaluated because of cost, manpower, and inadequate experimental study areas. Some high priority, management-oriented research goals are suggested.

The major objective of this paper should be to summarize the "state of the art" concerning the theory and practice of marsh management for wildlife. I hope this objective will be met but it is difficult because the theory has never been well-formulated, and the practice has developed by trial and error. Therefore, I will attempt (1) to summarize what is known of the marsh as a habitat for wildlife (especially birds), (2) examine the dynamics of marsh habitat that influence management potentials, and (3) outline evaluation efforts and research needs.

In addition to extensive use of the literature, my summary is based mainly on studies of the birds, muskrats, vegetation and invertebrates of glacial marshes in the Midwest. These marshes are characterized by dramatic seasonal as well as year-to-year changes, and with strong herbivore influences. The studies have focused on behavioral and population responses by wildlife to changes in the vegetative substrate produced by both natural and experimental manipulations. These studies lend support to some current practices and discourage the use of others. Above all, they dramatize the need for large-scale, experimental studies to develop a better understanding of marsh fauna and flora.

MANAGEMENT OBJECTIVES AND PRIORITIES

Most of the large individual marshes or marsh complexes preserved today are due to interests of state and federal wildlife conservation agencies or private groups interested in waterfowl hunting. Although these groups still may represent the majority of active managers, many additional agencies and private groups or individuals now are interested

[1] Originally published in R. Good, D. Whigham, and R. Simpson, eds. Freshwater wetlands, pages 267–284. Academic Press, New York, 1978.

in maintaining marshes in a natural state, and in understanding their role in man-influenced as well as pristine systems. In establishing objectives, there is then a tendency to ask "Who is managing the marsh and for what purpose?" In most cases, this is a less significant question than "How can we maintain maximal productivity in this natural system?"

Because the best management may be merely protection via a fence, I include as the first objective of management the preservation of marshes in a natural and esthetically-pleasing state (with or without manipulation) as habitat for wildlife. A second objective is to maintain high productivity of characteristic flora and fauna in marsh units, whether for harvest, enjoyment, or natural biological processes.

In development of a management plan, a marsh should first be classified according to its mean condition or marsh type, and the program for it based on maintenance of the natural values for which it was protected. While this may sound obvious, it is often not the case. Commonly, marshes are viewed as basins that can be changed to a unit more productive of a single species or complex of species other than those found there at a given time. Subsequently, management of the marsh as a system or community should produce a wetland attractive to botanists, ornithologists, hunters, photographers and others. Such system or community management requires an understanding of how wildlife species use a marsh, how dynamics in the marsh system affect wildlife, and how natural processes can be used for the benefits of wildlife.

STRUCTURE OF MARSHES AND THEIR USE BY WILDLIFE

Marshes are known for their concentric zones of plants of various life forms surrounding a deeper, often open, water area. Several detailed studies of marsh vegetation have been conducted in the prairie pothole region (Millar 1969, Stewart and Kantrud 1972). The usual pattern is one of robust, deep-marsh emergents like cattail (*Typha* spp.) or bulrush (*Scirpus* spp.) surrounded by wet-meadow taxa like sedges (*Carex* spp.). In some marshes, taller *Phragmites* dominate the edge. Zonation is produced by varying water depths and results in a horizontal plant diversity attractive to different forms of wildlife. An example of wildlife use of a Midwestern marsh is shown in Fig. 1. How these species are ecologically separated is an exciting and complex subject but one outside the scope of this paper.

Beecher (1942) first demonstrated that the number of bird nests was positively correlated with the number of plant communities in marshes. His studies infer general benefits to wildlife by the presence of several plant zones rather than homogeneous stands. Steel et al. (1956) reported larger duck nesting populations in broken than in solid emergent vegetation, suggesting that edge was an important attractant to waterbirds. Patterson (1974) found wetland heterogeneity important in waterfowl productivity. Weller and Spatcher (1965) noted that many marsh bird species nested near water–cover interfaces or the meeting of 2 cover types. Moreover, most species favor marshes in a "hemimarsh" stage with a ratio of about 1:1 cover–water interspersion. Weller and Fredrickson (1974) noted a positive correlation between bird species and the percent open water or the number of open pools in the emergent cover. They also noted that good interspersion was important, but found that greatest species richness and greatest density of nests ranged from 1:1 to 1:2

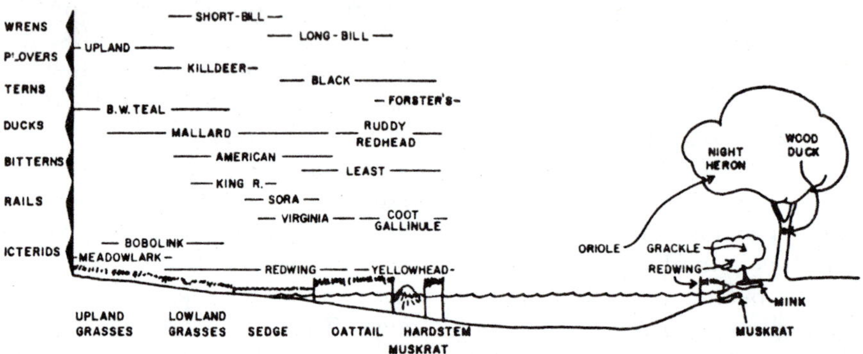

Fig. 1. A schematic drawing of habitat utilization by several families of marsh birds (from Weller and Spatcher 1965).

cover–water interspersion for different species. The studies of MacArthur (1958) on warblers of forest areas focused on the role of layers as an influence on available niches—and, therefore, on species diversity. A marsh with a complex plant zonation also has several heights or layers of vegetation as shown in Fig. 1. Open water acts as another layer, attracting the swimming birds which feed in the open, but use the cover–water edge for nesting. One of these species, the Pied-billed Grebe (*Podilymbus podiceps*), builds a completely floating nest of debris.

Most studies (Beecher 1942, Weller and Spatcher 1965) indicate that it is the structure rather than the taxonomic composition of emergent marsh plants that is of greatest importance to nesting birds. Bird species that choose a particular habitat niche (tall and robust emergents, for example) tend to use that life form regardless of the species. Hence, Yellow-headed Blackbirds (*Xanthocephalus xanthocephalus*) may use cattail, hardstem bulrush (*Scirpus acutus*), *Phragmites* or small willows (*Salix* spp.) for nests when such stands are in water and adjacent to open water. They rarely use low sedges. Red-winged Blackbirds (*Agelaius phoeniceus*), however, are much more adaptable and will use low trees, cattail or sedges but clearly favor cattail-sized plants (Fig. 1). When Red-winged and Yellow-headed blackbirds are together, competition enters the picture to a limited degree, as may also be true of Short-billed (*Cistothorus platensis*) and Long-billed marsh wrens (*Cistothorus palustris*).

However, plant species are important when serving as food for wildlife. Cattail seems to be a better food plant for muskrats than is hardstem bulrush. Wet-meadow plants are better food for birds than is cattail. Whereas emergent vegetation may be crucial for nest sites for birds or food for muskrats, submergent plants are substrates for the invertebrates that serve as food for ducks (Krull 1970). Biologists are just beginning to appreciate how vital certain food needs are to ducks during the reproductive phase (Krapu 1974). Hence, each plant fills a different role depending upon the wildlife need and season. Therefore, various types of wetlands may serve wildlife needs that differ with season and reproductive cycle.

CLASSIFICATION OF WETLANDS IN RELATION TO WILDLIFE USE

Various wetland classification systems have been developed, mostly by wildlife biologists, as an aid to quantitating wildlife uses of various wetland types to establish wildlife relationships (Shaw and Fredine 1956, Stewart and Kantrud 1971, Cowardin and Johnson 1973, Golet and Larson 1974, Jeglum et al. 1974, Bergman et al. 1977, Millar 1976). These systems are based mainly on water permanence and vegetation types. A new system is under development with the aid of specialists from many fields that should serve a still more diverse audience (Sather 1976). The system formulated by Shaw and Fredine (1956) has been much used to classify purchased or leased areas, and is integrated into laws concerning the protection of wetlands. However, in actual fact, very little use has been made of such systems to evaluate habitat for wildlife or even to correlate use by birds in a quantitative way.

In addition to vegetation type, size of a wetland is vital to maintenance of a marsh fauna, especially when the marsh is a relict. In much-drained regions of northern Iowa, several isolated units suggest that a typical wildlife fauna can be preserved in wetlands ≈100 ha in size. Rush Lake near Ayreshire, Iowa is 162 ha and it attracted a typical complement of marsh birds when a 162-ha wetland complex serving as a control was totally dry and unattractive to most marsh wildlife (Weller and Fredrickson 1974). Goose or Anderson Lake near Jewell, Iowa is 55 ha and is nearly as typical in bird fauna but a 110-ha lake and marsh nearby certainly serves as an attractant (Weller and Spatcher 1965). Minimal functional sizes need to be established to aid in acquisition of typical marsh areas for wildlife conservation. Many marsh areas now are "habitat islands" due to drainage of surrounding areas, and the outlook for the future is ominous.

However, to preserve a typical marsh avifauna, it is best to have several wetland types, as well as upland areas, present. Heterogeneity of wetland types in a complex creates habitat diversity inducing high species richness. In general, high species richness can be equated to periods of high productivity in a single marsh or in an area (Weller and Fredrickson 1974), and this index or other mathematical calculations of bird-species diversity may be simple, useful tools to measure habitat quality for some groups of marsh birds (Bezzel and Reichholf 1974). Because of the need for rapid and inexpensive assessments of marsh bird habitats in evaluating marsh management, considerable work needs to be done on this topic.

THE MARSH AS A DYNAMIC WILDLIFE HABITAT

Marshes usually are in constant change, and those in unstable climates change most readily, and probably are more productive as a consequence. Stability seems deadly to a marsh system, at least where terrestrial or semiaquatic faunas are preferred to open marsh or lake faunas. The pattern of change from dense marsh to open lake is so regular that it may be regarded as a successional trend. This short-term "cycle" tends to be the reverse of the classical textbook concept of marsh succession which is a directional change from an eutrophic lake to a sedge meadow or forest bog in a geologic time frame. Few studies estimate the longevity of long-term wetland succession but one 10-ha pond studied by McAndrews et al. (1967) had a history of ≈11,000 years and was still extant. However, management strategies must aim at exploiting short-term changes in marshes which are the products of water levels and herbivores. The chronology of such short-term successional changes usually involves the development of submer-

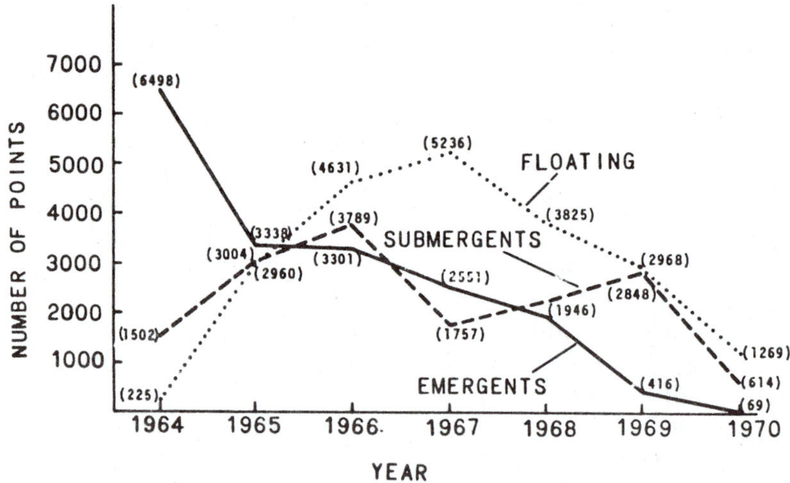

Fig. 2. Numerical changes in plant life-forms along point-count transects at Rush Lake, Iowa, 1964–70 (from Weller and Fredrickson 1974).

gents and the elimination of many of the emergents over a period of 3 to 7 years (see example in Fig. 2), but there are natural reversals due to reduced water levels, and similar management strategies may lengthen the process.

Dramatic changes in vegetation are caused by plant–water relationships as demonstrated in both observational and experimental studies: Bourn and Cottam 1939; Crail 1951; Dane 1959; Kadlec 1960, 1962; Harris and Marshall 1963; Weller and Spatcher 1965; Harter 1966; Meeks 1969. Many emergent plants (e.g., cattail) germinate only in shallow water or on mud flats, and revegetation of an open marsh occurs rapidly only when water levels are low. Even vegetative propagation of cattail is more rapid in low than in high water (Weller 1975). Deep basins or those with stable water levels may remain open because vegetative propagation does not equal losses at such levels, and are open marshes or lakes rather than typical marshes.

In a marsh that has been naturally devegetated and is open, a natural or artificial dewatering ("drawdown") produces a subsequent "germination" phase. At first, sedges and other shallow-marsh plants dominate the plant community. These are gradually replaced by the more water-tolerant species such as cattail (Weller and Fredrickson 1974), resulting in a shallow, "dense-marsh" stage dominated by robust aquatic emergents. A gradual reopening due to flotation or herbivores may result in excellent interspersion of emergent cover and water ("hemimarsh"). Continued devegetation results in a "deep-water" or "open marsh" phase, which resembles a lake system. Variations in the pattern result from timing of drawdown, germination, and reflooding sequence.

Herbivores are the second-most important influence on the structure of Midwestern marshes and, although there are countless invertebrates consuming marsh plants, it is the cutting of vegetation by muskrats (or nutria, *Myocaster coypus*, in the South), that induces dramatic changes especially impacting upon birds. Much of this cutting by muskrats is for construction of "lodges" rather than for direct consumption (Fig. 3), although stored

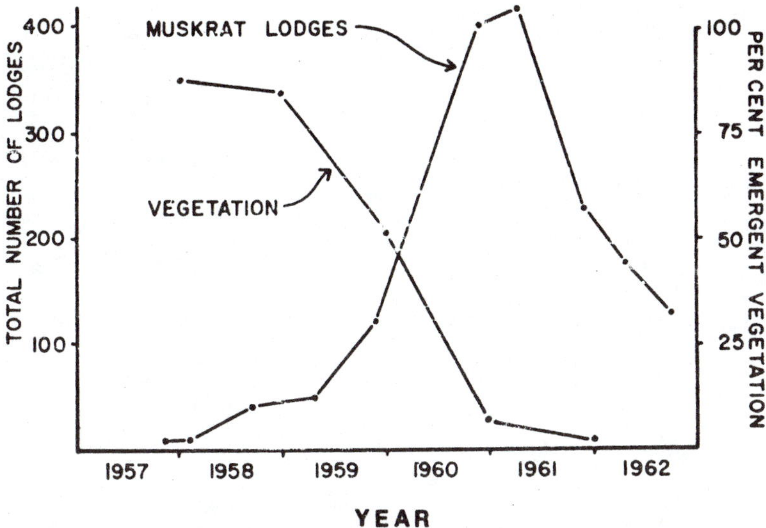

Fig. 3. The relationship between muskrat lodges and the percentage emergent cover at Goose Lake near Jewell, Iowa, 1957–62 (from Weller and Spatcher 1965).

plant tubers later may be eaten. Errington et al. (1963) traced the population history of an especially dramatic muskrat "eat-out," and Weller and Spatcher (1965) recorded its impact on the vegetation (Fig. 3) and on bird populations. Lynch et al. (1947) observed the habitat consequences of herbivory by both geese and muskrats.

Marsh invertebrates clearly respond to water and vegetation as do other consumer-level taxa and seem to be a direct influence of bird species using the area. The general pattern of population change in some major invertebrate groups is related to a schematic pattern of marsh habitat phases in Fig. 4 (from Voigts 1976). Although additional data are badly needed, especially from experimental manipulation, the patterns help to explain why the hemimarsh is so productive of many nesting bird species, and why many bird species concentrate to feed in semiopen marshes for both invertebrates and submergent plants.

Wildlife responses to dramatic changes in vegetation and water have been reported by several workers based on observational studies: Wolf (1955), Evans and Black (1956), Johnsgard (1956), Yeager and Swope (1956), Weller et al. (1958), Boyer and Devitt (1961), Bednarik (1963), Rogers (1964), Weller and Spatcher (1965), Anderson and Glover (1967), Krapu et al. (1970), Smith (1970), and Stewart and Kantrud (1974). Fewer experimental studies have successfully assessed wildlife responses to marsh changes (Schroeder et al. 1976, Weller and Fredrickson 1974). However, these observations demonstrate the responsiveness and adaptiveness of wildlife species associated with dynamic habitats.

Species like Red-winged Blackbirds are adaptable to a wide range of marsh nest sites and are regularly recorded each year despite dramatic differences in water level and vegetation (Beecher 1942). Niche-specific birds like certain ducks and Yellow-headed Blackbirds can be totally eliminated in some years. In abandoning unsuitable habitats, it is also

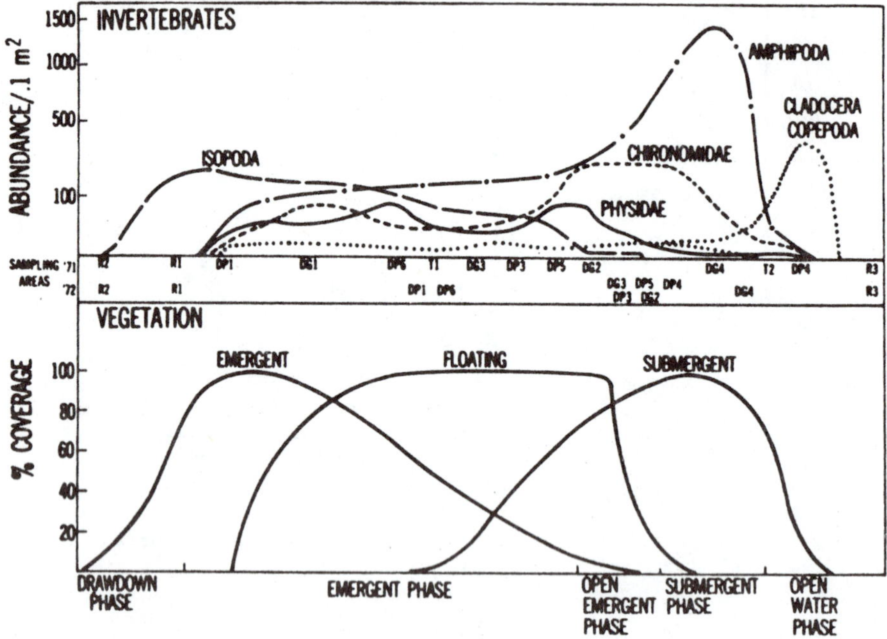

Fig. 4. Generalized vegetation macrofauna associations along a gradient of natural vegetation change in freshwater marshes (from Voigts 1976).

obvious that birds invade newly available or suboptimal areas readily. The invasion rate of pioneering species in new habitats is an important component of a management strategy. Species with wide ranges in tolerance pioneer easily, but those with specific requirements are forced to pioneer to fill those needs. Information on the rates and causes of pioneering are sparse. Pioneering is a product of a complex evolutionary history involving marsh instability, interspecific competition, geography, and geologic influences.

Population shifts must occur regularly between marshes in a wetland cluster, but they also are seen in areas as widespread as the prairie potholes versus the Alaskan and Siberian tundra. Pintails (*Anas acuta*) and other ducks seem to shift to suboptimal and marginal ranges when the optimal habitats go dry (Hansen and McKnight 1964, Henny 1973, Pospahala et al. 1974). However, one must be cautious not to infer that reproductive success in those areas is equal to that in optimal areas; it undoubtedly isn't, but it may be sufficient to warrant the energy required to shift as opposed to total failure or even lack of survival of breeding stock that would result by remaining in drought-stricken areas.

Another form of adaptability is in chronology of nesting. In my studies of waterbirds in northwest Iowa, I have seen 2 cases where Coots did not abandon a devegetated marsh, but remained in flocks until new vegetation appeared late in the season. Then, at least some of the population nested. Late migration and breeding by Short-billed Marsh Wrens also may be an adaptive response to suitable habitat conditions. There are cases, however, where ducks flock during a drought and seemingly never nest (Smith 1971).

Muskrats also respond quickly to changing conditions. New habitats are invaded promptly, probably as a product of population shifts after the breeding season and prior to winter establishment (Errington 1963). Reproductive rates vary markedly with habitat conditions with a density-dependent growth rate that influences population regulation. Very often, however, their numbers exceed estimates based on house counts made from shore, and destruction of emergent vegetation progresses so rapidly that population control comes after-the-fact. For this reason, regular surveys of lodge-building and feeding activities by muskrats requires travel by foot or canoe.

Although year-to-year water levels regulate major vegetation growth and wildlife responses, this does not mean that water levels must change constantly. Indeed, stable levels are important during breeding of birds that nest overwater (Low 1945) and muskrats rearing young in lodges (Errington 1937).

THE USE OF NATURAL PROCESSES IN MARSH MANAGEMENT

The short-term marsh habitat cycle based on water and herbivores as dominant causal factors, and the response of consumer-level organisms like invertebrates, muskrats and birds, is a natural dynamic pattern that is predictable and reproducible in a general way. It is, therefore, the theoretical basis on which we can establish management procedures. The resultant management practices may be very drastic to untrained eyes and they are commonly misinterpreted, but they are totally natural and, as such, are the most ecologically and economically sound methods. Some general principles of marsh management for wildlife are as follows:

1) System, rather than species management, results in widespread benefits to all plants and wildlife. Although there is some evidence of competition in birds, losses in production of game species due to high species richness of nongame species have not been demonstrated.
2) Manipulation to produce early plant successional stages results in longer lasting benefits, and creates diverse habitat niches. A marsh then proceeds through various phases with productivity of any one species being a dynamic component of the system. Methods producing long-term results are less expensive and more natural. Usually, this means use of natural tools for management.
3) To maintain heterogeneity in wetland complexes, all marsh units in an area should not be managed in the same way at the same time, even with extreme climatic conditions. This permits local population shifts of wildlife to more optimal niches.
4) Tools such as remote sensing offer exciting opportunities to enhance and document marsh management (Olson 1964, Cowardin and Myers 1974) but there is no substitute for the manager getting into the marsh.

Water-level regulation is the ideal way to influence marsh vegetation, but many wetlands lack a regular supply of water or suitable control structures. Where water control is possible, the following steps outline procedures for management of the plant community based mainly on observation by Weller and Fredrickson (1974):

1) When a marsh has become so open

that it no longer provides cover and food for wildlife, revegetation comes most readily via drawdown of water levels to produce the germination phase. Overwinter drawdowns seem to stimulate greater growth than single-growing season drawdowns. Timing of the drawdown influences plant species composition, as does soil moisture (Meeks 1969).

2) Following germination, water levels must be increased slowly in late summer or fall to avoid excessive loss of plants due to flotation or shading.
3) Similar water-level management during the following growing season will reduce bird use by some groups but will foster the greatest vegetative response. By the fall of the second growing season, water level management will be related more to wildlife use than to plant growth.
4) Vegetative propagation of emergents can be stimulated secondarily by lowering water levels. Whether the rate of growth can compensate losses to herbivores is dependent on their population status at the time. Further study is essential, especially in reference to soil and water chemistry, nutrient cycling and invertebrate populations, because few marshes seem to remain productive with continuous inundation.
5) Establishment of submergents vital to invertebrate production usually requires several years of stable levels of moderate depths. Flooding during the growth phase should be avoided because of clouding of the water with silt and other particulate matter that reduces light penetration.

To enhance the growth or regulation of populations of major marsh wildlife, the timing and degree of water-level manipulations are very important:

1) Dramatic drawdowns should take place in early spring prior to bird territory establishment or in fall prior to muskrats lodging for winter. If properly timed, lowered water levels enhance harvest of muskrats and prevent wasteful mortality.
2) Low water levels essential to survival of plants may induce use mainly by wet-meadow birds or, in larger units, restrict deep-marsh birds and muskrats to deeper, central areas of the marsh.
3) Drastic manipulation of water levels following vegetation establishment may aid in regulating muskrat populations that threaten the vegetation. Habitat conditions influence reproductive rates and trapability.
4) As central portions of the marsh are opened by muskrats and flotation, raising water levels makes peripheral areas more suitable for use by wildlife.
5) Some small fish live in marshes but the consequences of drawdowns do not seem to have been documented. Marshes associated with lakes often are major spawning beds and are, therefore, of importance in planning marsh drawdowns. Nongame fish like carp are detrimental to survival of emergents and development of submergents (Robel 1961) and may be controlled by drawdown procedures.

Several other natural processes have been adapted in marsh management. Grazing of a less intensive nature than performed by muskrats occurred naturally by deer (*Odocoileus virginianus*) and bison (*Bison bison*); now cattle may fill a similar role. Their indirect actions via the trails they make usually are more impacting than is their direct food consumption. There has been little experimental study of grazing impacts on freshwater marsh vegetation but careful studies of salt marsh have been made (Reimold et al. 1975). Some serious consequences of grazing on duck populations were reported during severe drought (Weller et al. 1958), and considerable effort has been devoted to measuring negative effects of grazing on ducks that nest in upland vegetation (Kirsch 1969).

Burning in permanent marshes, especially those where *Phragmites* is dominant, has produced some benefits in nutrient recycling and regrowth attractive to nesting ducks (Ward 1968), but careless burning of marsh vegetation during the nesting season produces direct losses (Cartwright 1942). Burns in northern peat-bottomed marshes may produce deep potholes that prevent growth of emergents (Linde 1969).

Modification of water salinity to achieve freshwater and freshwater vegetation is a common procedure along coastal areas (Palmisano 1972). Natural drainages often are blocked in barrier wetlands and the accumulating freshwater leaches out salt. A resulting shift of freshwater vegetation attracts different wildlife species. Similar techniques have been used in marshes around Great Salt Lake where impoundment and leaching are necessary to produce freshwater marsh vegetation (Nelson 1954, Christiansen and Low 1970). A potential conflict thus exists between groups interested in the preservation and management of these 2 marsh types.

ARTIFICIAL PROCEDURES USED FOR MODIFYING MARSHES

It is possible to simulate advanced successional stages in marshes that lack water control structures. Openings can be created in dense stands of cattail and emergents if they are cut during drought or on ice at low water levels and the cut ends are flooded during the next growing season (Nelson and Dietz 1966). Herbicides are perhaps still easier to use on large areas (Martin et al. 1957) and water levels are insignificant, but side effects are uncertain and, due to time for natural decay of standing plants, openings are not evident until the following year. Obviously, the interspersion thus created may last a shorter time. Theoretically, a more permanent cover–water interspersion could be produced by creating a marsh basin of uneven depth during construction, but this is rarely done because contour data are gross and equipment operation is expensive. It often occurs by accident where streams are the water source and where stream meanders remain in the upper portion of the basin, but this usually affects only a small area. A common practice is to create islands for nesting birds in artificially constructed marshes (Uhler 1956, Linde 1969). Level ditching combines some benefits of both of these concepts (see Mathiak and Linde 1956) but the product is esthetically questionable.

The use of dynamite to open dense marshes has been common (Provost 1948) with some evaluation of longevity and bird use (Strohmeyer and Fredrickson 1967). Blasting with ammonium nitrate or other less expensive explosives, and bulldozing have revitalized this effort (Mathiak 1965). In most cases, too little of the bottom is modified to create cover–water interspersion comparable to hemimarsh. Such newly created ponds are attractive to certain birds at certain stages, but a more significant issue is whether such areas should be permanently modified. Sedge marsh areas, the wetland type most commonly blasted, may serve different wildlife than those for which many agencies tend to manage (e.g., Short-billed Marsh Wrens instead of ducks). Moreover, such marshes also may change marsh types from shallow to deeper marsh during high water levels, and attract species that have shifted from marshes then less attractive due to water levels and muskrats.

In marshes that tend to remain too long in the open phase, there have been efforts to plant perennial cover such as bulrushes and cattail (Steenis 1939, Addy and MacNamara 1948). This is expensive in manpower and time, is rarely successful, and opposes natural successional trends.

In wet meadows, dewatering, cutting and fertilizing have been used to stimulate growth of goose foods (Givens and Atkeson 1957, Owen 1975). Experimental fertilization of freshwater marshes seems to have been tried only rarely, but its value may be more tied to understanding nutrient cycles than for any feasible management procedure.

The most intensive, species-oriented form of management is the use of artificial nest sites for ducks. These have been used where natural sites are not present regularly or for increased protection against predators. Such platforms, baskets or boxes attract ducks and they are resonably successful (Bishop and Barratt 1970), and such birds return to these sites in subsequent years (Doty and Lee 1974). This method appeals to sportsmen but is esthetically unsatisfying and is less sound either ecologically or economically when more natural management systems are possible. It is unlikely that a harvestable continental population of any duck can be retained on the basis of this type of management. The widespread practice of erecting nest boxes has successfully attracted Wood Ducks (*Aix sponsa*) and, although duck nesting success is higher than in natural cavities (Bellrose et al. 1964), the proportion of the total national production that occurs in such boxes must be modest.

SOCIOLOGICAL ASPECTS OF MARSH MANAGEMENT

In spite of the potential of managing marshes for a diverse public, it is impossible to please all interest groups. Many individuals and some organized private groups object to management in any form and one has difficulty in arguing against a pursuit of natural values. Realistically, there are large areas where protection alone is the only available management option. However, many of the most sought-after marshes are relicts with far-from-natural watersheds, flora or fauna. In such cases, management is essential and can be accomplished with natural tools in an esthetically pleasing manner. Conflicts over the issue of manipulation are most likely to occur where artificial and esthetically questionable systems are used.

A still more common conflict is between management-oriented groups with different goals, or those attempting decisions on the basis of insufficient knowledge of a complex subject. In semipermanent marshes, fishing may be an important local activity. Dramatic drawdowns designed to revegetate the marsh produce a direct conflict that is not easily resolved if the wetland is in public ownership. Such problems often are worsened when a water control structure is added, when the water supply is stabilized, or when a dredge is readily available because public pressure by fishermen, boaters, waterskiers and cabin owners may be to change a marsh to an open marsh or lake. Advance public relations programs are essential to prevent the development of such local pressures. As greater appreciation of marshes develops, this may be less of a problem, but it is an issue worthy of consideration as management strategies are developed for specific areas.

EVALUATING MARSH MANAGEMENT TECHNIQUES AND PROGRAMS

Because of the long period required for experimental work, and the lack of readily available controls for demonstrating cause and effect in a complex ecosystem, too little effort has been devoted to evaluation. An assessment of the size of a given wildlife population has been the major means of judging habitat quality or management results, but this is an expensive procedure for a large project of long duration. Qualitative judgements of before and after conditions, especially of marsh vegetation, often replace quantitative pre- and post-population data. While these procedures may have been adequate for gross management operations, they have not made marsh management a quantitative effort. More quantitative data are needed for modeling the system so that the consequences of manipulations can be predicted more precisely. Data on plant germination during drawdowns are fairly extensive but are not representative of a great variety of marsh types. The literature contains some data on muskrat densities but usually not with a quantitative and concurrent measurement of the food resource. Of the references reporting increased duck use after reflooding, few demonstrate increases in the foods that attracted them there. Quantitative data on songbird breeding populations in marshes are surprisingly uncommon. Such observational data gathered with clear-cut management objectives would be very valuable.

What is most needed to advance marsh management theory and practice are experimental data gathered concurrently by a team of specialists in marsh plants, limnology, hydrology, invertebrates, and vertebrates. If such a group also had an isolated, artificial, multi-unit marsh complex designed exclusively for experimentation on the ecology of marshes and wildlife, the potential for understanding marsh systems and devising proper marsh management procedures for marsh wildlife would be unsurpassed. Among the many topics that need to be addressed by careful experimental study are:

1) Habitat stimuli that attract wildlife to marshes
2) The development of indices to wildlife production in marshes
3) The size of isolated areas essential to the development and/or maintenance of marsh fauna (i.e., the marsh as a habitat "island")
4) The diversity or heterogeneity of wetland areas in a complex essential to attract and maintain marsh wildlife
5) Wetland : upland ratios conducive to preservation of typical prairie-wetland biotas
6) Germination conditions that make marsh drawdowns or other water manipulations more effective and predictable
7) A better understanding of water and soil chemistry of marsh systems to expand on the work of Cook and Powers (1958) and Harter (1966)
8) The role of siltation, fertilizers and other man-made products in modifying productivity of wetland areas
9) Objective experimentation on grazing, burning and other natural procedures to assess their role in marsh management for wildlife
10) The relationship of invertebrates to marsh dynamics
11) Detailed studies of the biology of dominant aquatic plants, such as the work of Linde et al. (1976).

Freshwater marshes often have been viewed as transient stages of either terrestrial or aquatic ecosystems. They are, however, unique, long-lived, and highly productive systems. They are a valuable resource and have not received the sophisticated and intensive study necessary to understand, manage and preserve them for posterity. Wildlife are among the most attractive components of the marsh, and their study in relation to their habitat will induce broadly applicable concepts and understanding of this complex system.

LITERATURE CITED

ADDY, C. E., AND L. G. MACNAMARA. 1948. Waterfowl management on small areas. Wildl. Manage. Inst., Washington, D.C. 80pp.

ANDERSON, D. R., AND F. A. GLOVER. 1967. Effects of water manipulation on waterfowl production and habitat. Trans. N. Am. Wildl. Nat. Resour. Conf. 32:292–300.

BEDNARIK, K. E. 1963. Marsh management techniques, 1960. Ohio Dep. Nat. Resour. Game Res. Ohio 2:132–144.

BEECHER, W. J. 1942. Nesting birds and the vegetation substrates. Chicago Ornithol. Soc. Chicago, Illinois. 69pp.

BELLROSE, F. C., K. L. JOHNSON, AND T. V. MEYERS. 1964. Relative value of natural cavities and nesting boxes for wood ducks. J. Wildl. Manage. 28:661–675.

BERGMAN, R. D., R. L. HOWARD, K. F. ABRAHAM, AND M. W. WELLER. 1977. Waterbirds and their wetland resources in relation to oil development at Storkersen Point, Alaska. U.S. Fish Wildl. Serv. Resour. Publ. 129. 38pp.

BEZZEL, E., AND J. REICHHOLF. 1974. Die Diversität als Kriterium zur Bewertung der Reichhaltigkeit von Wasservogel-Lebensräumen. J. Ornithol. 115:50–61.

BIHSOP, R. A., AND R. BARRATT. 1970. Use of artificial nest baskets by mallards. J. Wildl. Manage. 34:734–738.

BOURN, W. S., AND C. COTTAM. 1939. The effect of lowering water levels on marsh wildlife. Trans. N. Am. Wildl. Nat. Resour. Conf. 4:343–350.

BOYER, G. F., AND O. E. DEVITT. 1961. A significant increase in the birds of Luther Marsh, Ontario, following fresh-water impoundment. Can. Field-Nat. 75:225–237.

CARTWRIGHT, B. W. 1942. Regulated burning as a marsh management technique. Trans. N. Am. Wildl. Nat. Resour. Conf. 7:257–263.

CHRISTIANSEN, J. E., AND J. B. LOW. 1970. Water requirements of waterfowl marshlands in Northern Utah. Salt Lake City, Utah Div. Fish Game Publ. No. 69-12. 108pp.

COOK, A., AND C. F. POWERS. 1958. Early biochemical changes in the soils and waters of artificially created marshes in New York. New York Fish and Game J. 5:9–65.

COWARDIN, F., AND V. MYERS. 1974. Remote sensing for identification and classification of wetland vegetation. J. Wildl. Manage. 38:308–314.

COWARDIN, L. M., AND D. H. JOHNSON. 1973. A preliminary classification of wetland plant communities in north-central Minnesota. U.S. Fish Wildl. Serv. Spec. Sci. Rep.—Wildl. 168. 33pp.

CRAIL, L. 1951. Viability of smartweed and millet seed in relation to marsh management in Missouri. Missouri Conserv. Comm. 16pp.

DANE, C. W. 1959. Succession of aquatic plants in small artificial marshes in New York State. New York Fish and Game J. 6:57–76.

DOTY, H. A., AND F. B. LEE. 1974. Homing to nest baskets by wild female mallards. J. Wild. Manage. 38:714–719.

ERRINGTON, P. L. 1937. Drowning as a cause of mortality in muskrats. J. Mammal. 18:497–500.

———. 1963. Muskrat populations. Ames, Iowa. Iowa State Univ. Press.

———, R. SIGLIN, AND R. CLARK. 1963. The decline of a muskrat population. J. Wildl. Manage. 27:1–8.

EVANS, C. D., AND K. E. BLACK. 1956. Duck production studies on the prairie potholes of South Dakota. U.S. Fish Wildl. Serv. Spec. Sci. Pre.-Wildl. No. 32. 59pp.

GIVENS, L. S., AND T. Z. ATKESON. 1957. The use of dewatered land in southeastern waterfowl management. J. Wildl. Manage. 21:465–467.

GOLET, F. C., AND J. S. LARSON. 1974. Classification of freshwater wetlands in the glaciated northeast. U.S. Fish Wild. Serv. Resour. Publ. 116. 56pp.

HANSEN, H. A., AND D. E. MCKNIGHT. 1964. Emigration of drought-displaced ducks to the Arctic. Trans. N. Am. Wildl. Nat. Resour. Conf. 29:119–127.

HARRIS, S. W., AND W. H. MARSHALL. 1963. Ecology of water-level manipulations on a northern marsh. Ecology 44:331–343.

HARTER, R. D. 1966. The effect of water levels on soil chemistry and plant growth of the Magee Marsh Wildlife Area. Ohio Dep. Nat. Res. Game Monogr. No. 2. 36pp.

HENNY, C. J. 1973. Drought displaced movement of North American pintails to Siberia. J. Wildl. Manage. 37:23–29.

JEGLUM, J. K., A. N. BOISSONNEAU, AND V. F. HAAVISTO. 1974. Toward a wetland classification for Ontario. Can. For. Serv., Sault Saint Marie, Ont. Inf. Rep. O-X-215. 54pp.

JOHNSGARD, P. A. 1956. Effects of water fluctuations and vegetation change on bird populations, particularly waterfowl. Ecology 37: 689–701.

KADLEC, J. A. 1960. The effect of a drawdown on the ecology of a waterfowl impoundment. Mich. Dep. Cons. Game Div. Rep. 2276. 181pp.

———. 1962. Effects of a drawdown on a waterfowl impoundment. Ecology 43:267–281.

KIRSCH, L. M. 1969. Waterfowl production in relation to grazing. J. Wildl. Manage. 33:821–828.

KRAPU, G. L. 1974. Feeding ecology of pintail hens during reproduction. Auk 91:278–290.

———, D. R. PARSONS, AND M. W. WELLER. 1970. Waterfowl in relation to land use and water levels on the Spring Run area. Iowa State J. Sci. 44:437–452.

KRULL, J. N. 1970. Aquatic plant macroinvertebrate associations and waterfowl. J. Wildl. Manage. 34:707–718.

LINDE, A. F. 1969. Techniques for wetland management. Wisconsin Dep. Nat. Resour. Res. Rep. 45. 156pp.

———, T. JANISCH, AND D. SMITH. 1976. Cattail—The significance of its growth, phenology and carbohydrate storage to its control and management. Wisconsin Dep. of Nat. Resour. Tech. Bull. No. 94. 27pp.

LOW, J. B. 1945. Ecology and management of the redhead, *Nyroca americana,* in Iowa. Ecol. Monogr. 15:35–69.

LYNCH, J. J., T. O'NEIL, AND D. W. LAY. 1947. Management significance of damage by geese and muskrats to Gulf Coast marshes. J. Wildl. Manage. 11:50–76.

MARTIN, A. C., R. C. ERICKSON, AND J. H. STEENIS. 1957. Improving duck marshes by weed control. U.S. Fish Wildl. Serv. Circ. 19—Revised. 60pp.

MATHIAK, H. A. 1965. Pothole blasting for wildlife. Wisconsin Cons. Dep. Publ. 352. 31pp.

———, AND A. F. LINDE. 1956. Studies on level ditching for marsh management. Wisconsin Cons. Dep. Tech. Wildl. Bull. No. 12. 48pp.

MACARTHUR, R. H. 1958. Population ecology of some warblers of northeastern coniferous forests. Ecology 39:599–619.

MCANDREWS, J. H., R. E. STEWART, JR., AND R. C. BRIGHT. 1967. Paleoecology of a prairie pothole; a preliminary report. Pp. 101–113. *In* "Mid-western Friends of the Pleistocene Guidebook" 185th Ann. Field Conf. Clayton, Lee, and Freers, eds. North Dakota Geol. Surv. Misc. Ser. 30.

MEEKS, R. L. 1969. The effect of drawdown date on wetland plant succession. J. Wildl. Manage. 33:817–821.

MILLAR, J. B. 1969. Observations on the ecology of wetland vegetation. Pp. 49–56. *In* Saskatoon Wetlands Seminar. Can. Wildl. Serv. Rep. Ser. 6. 262pp.

———. 1976. Wetland classification in western Canada: a guide to marshes and shallow open water wetlands in the grasslands and parklands of the Prairie Provinces. Can. Wildl. Serv. Rep. Ser. No. 37. 38pp.

NELSON, N. F. 1954. Factors in the development and restoration of waterfowl habitat at Ogden Bay Refuge, Weber County, Utah. Utah Dep. Fish Game Publ. No. 6. 87pp.

———, AND R. H. DIETZ. 1966. Cattail control methods in Utah. Utah Dep. Fish Game Publ. No. 66-2. 31pp.

OLSON, D. P. 1964. The use of aerial photographs in studies of marsh vegetation. Maine Agric. Exp. Stn. Bull. 13, Tech. Ser. 62pp.

OWEN, M. 1975. Cutting and fertilizing grassland for winter goose management. J. Wildl. Manage. 39:163–167.

PALMISANO, A. W., JR. 1972. The effect of salinity on the germination and growth of plants important to wildlife in the Gulf Coast marshes. Proc. Ann. Conf. SE Assoc. Game and Fish Comm. 25:215–223.

PATTERSON, J. H. 1974. The role of wetland heterogeneity in the reproduction of duck populations in eastern Ontario. Can. Wildl. Serv. Rep. Ser. No. 29:31–32.

POSPAHALA, R. S., D. R. ANDERSON, AND C. J. HENNY. 1974. Population ecology of the Mallard II. Breeding habitat conditions, size of the breeding population, and production indices. U.S. Fish Wildl. Serv. Resour. Publ. No. 115. 73pp.

PROVOST, M. W. 1948. Marsh-blasting as a wildlife management technique. J. Wildl. Manage. 12:350–387.

REIMOLD, R. J., R. A. LINTHURST, AND P. L. WOLF. 1975. Effects of grazing on a salt marsh. Biol. Cons. 8:105–125.

ROBEL, R. J. 1961. The effects of carp populations on the production of waterfowl food plants of a western waterfowl marsh. Trans. N. Am. Wildl. Conf. 26:147–159.

ROGERS, J. P. 1964. Effect of drought on reproduction of the Lesser Scaup. J. Wildl. Manage. 28:213–220.

SATHER, J. H., editor. 1976. Proceedings of the national wetland classification and inventory workshop. U.S. Fish. Wildl. Serv. 110pp.

SCHROEDER, L. D., D. R. ANDERSON, R. S. POSPAHALA, G. W. ROBINSON, AND F. A. GLOVER. 1976. Effects of early water application on waterfowl production. J. Wildl. Manage. 20: 227–232.

SHAW, S. P., AND C. G. FREDINE. 1956. Wetlands of the United States. U.S. Fish Wildl. Serv. Circ. 39. 67pp.

SMITH, A. G. 1971. Ecological factors affecting waterfowl production in the Alberta Parklands. U.S. Fish Wildl. Serv. Resour. Publ. No. 98. 49pp.

SMITH, R. I. 1970. Response of pintail breeding

populations to drought. J. Wildl. Manage. 34:934–946.

STEEL, P. E., P. D. DALKE, AND E. G. BIZEAU. 1956. Duck production at Gray's Lake, Idaho, 1949–1951. J. Wildl. Manage. 20:279–285.

STEENIS, J. H. 1939. Marsh management on the Great Plains waterfowl refuges. Trans. N. Am. Wildl. Conf. 4:400–405.

STEWART, R. E., AND H. A. KANTRUD. 1971. Classification of natural ponds and lakes in the glaciated prairie region. U.S. Bur. Sport Fish Wildl. Resour. Publ. 92. 57pp.

———, AND ———. 1972. Vegetation of prairie potholes, North Dakota in relation to quality of water and other environmental factors. U.S. Dep. Int. Geol. Survey Professional Paper. 585-D.

———, AND ———. 1974. Breeding waterfowl populations in the prairie pothole region of North Dakota. Condor 76:70–79.

STROHMEYER, D. L., AND L. H. FREDRICKSON. 1967. An evaluation of dynamited potholes in northwest Iowa. J. Wildl. Manage. 31:525–532.

UHLER, F. M. 1956. New habitats for waterfowl. Trans. N. Am. Wildl. Conf. 20:453–469.

VOIGTS, D. K. 1976. Aquatic invertebrate abundance in relation to changing marsh vegetation. Am. Midl. Nat. 95:313–322.

WARD, P. 1968. Fire in relation to waterfowl habitat of the Delta marshes. Proc. Tall Timbers Fire Ecol. Conf. 8:254–267.

WELLER, M. W. 1975. Studies of cattail in relation to management for marsh wildlife. Iowa State J. Sci. 49:333–412.

———, AND L. H. FREDRICKSON. 1974. Avian ecology of a managed glacial marsh. Living Bird 12:269–291.

———, AND C. E. SPATCHER. 1965. Role of habitat in the distribution and abundance of marsh birds. Iowa Agric. Home Econ. Exp. Stn. Spec. Rep. No. 43. 31pp.

———, B. WINGFIELD, AND J. B. LOW. 1958. Effects of habitat deterioration on bird populations of a small Utah marsh. Condor 60:220–226.

WOLF, K. E. 1955. Some effects of fluctuating and falling water levels on waterfowl production. J. Wildl. Manage. 19:13–23.

YEAGER, L. E., AND H. M. SWOPE. 1956. Waterfowl production during wet and dry years in North-Central Colorado. J. Wildl. Manage. 20:442–446.

SELECTED BIBLIOGRAPHY

Management and Economics: Marsh Management

ATLANTIC FLYWAY COUNCIL. 1972. Techniques handbook of waterfowl habitat development and management. 2nd Ed. Atlantic Flyway Council. Bolton, MA. 218pp.

BURGESS, HAROLD H. 1969. Habitat management on a midcontinent waterfowl refuge. J. Wildl. Manage. 33(4):843–847.

CHABRECK, R. H. 1960. Coastal marsh impoundments for ducks in Louisiana. Proc. Annu. Conf. S.E. Assoc. Game Fish Comm. 14:24–29.

CHOATE, J. S. 1972. Effects of stream channeling on wetlands in a Minnesota watershed. J. Wildl. Manage. 36(3):940–944.

HARRIS, S. W., AND W. R. MARSHALL. 1963. Ecology of water-level manipulations on a northern marsh. Ecology 44:331–343.

KADLEC, J. A. 1977. Nitrogen and phosphorus dynamics in inland freshwater wetlands. Pages 17–41 *in* T. A. Bookhout, ed. Waterfowl and wetlands—An integrated review. Proc. Symposium at 39th Midwest Fish and Wildl. Conf., Madison, WI. LaCrosse Printing Co., Inc. Lacrosse.

KADLEC, J. A. AND W. A. WENTZ. 1974. Evaluation of marsh plant establishment techniques: Induced and natural. Tech. paper U.S. Army Coastal Engineering Research Center and Waterways Exp. Station. N.T.I.S. report A012837, Vol. I. 266 pp.

LINDE, A. F. 1969. Techniques for wetland management. Wisconsin Dep. Nat. Resour. Res. Rep. 45. 156pp.

MATHIAK, H. A., AND A. F. LINDE. 1956. Studies on level ditching for marsh management. Wisconsin Cons. Dep. Tech. Bull. 12. 48pp.

MENDALL, H. L. 1948. Water levels and waterfowl management. Proc. N.E. Game Conf. 1948:86–88.

NEWSOM, J. D., editor. 1968. Proc. marsh and estuary management symposium. Louisiana State Univ., Baton Rouge. 250pp.

ROBEL, R. J. 1961. The effects of carp populations on the production of waterfowl food plants on a western waterfowl marsh. Trans. North Am. Wildl. Conf. 26:147–159.

SANDERSON, G. C., AND F. C. BELLROSE. 1969. Wildlife habitat management of wetlands. An. Acad. Brasil Ciênc. 41(supplement):153–204.

SCHROEDER, L. D., D. R. ANDERSON, R. S. POSPAHALA, G. G. W. ROBINSON, AND F. A. GLOVER. 1976. Effects of early water application on waterfowl production. J. Wildl. Manage. 40(2): 227–232.

VOIGTS, D. K. 1976. Aquatic invertebrate abundance in relation to changing marsh vegetation. Am. Midl. Nat. 95:313–322.

WELLER, M. W., AND L. H. FREDRICKSON. 1974. Avian ecology of a managed glacial marsh. Living Bird 12:269–291.

———, AND C. S. SPATCHER. 1965. Role of habitat in the distribution and abundance of marsh birds. Spec. Rep. 43, Ag. and Home Econ. Exp. Sta. Iowa State Univ., Ames. 31pp.

———, B. H. WINGFIELD, AND J. B. LOW.

1958. Effects of habitat deterioration on bird popuations of a small Utah marsh. Condor 60:220–226.

WELLER, M. W. 1981. Freshwater marshes: ecology and wildlife management. Univ. Minnesota Press, Minneapolis. 146pp.

WENTZ, W. A., R. L. SMITH, AND J. A. KADLEC. 1974. Annotated bibliography on aquatic and marsh plants and their management. Tech. paper U.S. Coastal Engineering Research Center and Waterway Exp. Station. N.T.I.S. Report A012837, Vol. II. 206pp.

Establishing Local Populations

HIGH SURVIVAL AND HOMING RATE OF HAND-REARED WILD-STRAIN MALLARDS

FORREST B. LEE, U.S. Bureau of Sport Fisheries and Wildlife, Northern Prairie Wildlife Research Center, Jamestown, North Dakota 58401

ARNOLD D. KRUSE, U.S. Bureau of Sport Fisheries and Wildlife, Northern Prairie Wildlife Research Center, Jamestown, North Dakota 58401

Abstract: In the summer of 1970, 648 (329 males and 319 females) hand-reared wild-strain mallards (*Anas platyrhynchos*) were banded and released at the Arrowwood National Wildlife Refuge, Edmunds, North Dakota. The females were also marked with numbered nasal saddles. Liberation was by the *gentle release* method, and no special effort was made to isolate or condition the ducklings prior to release. Ducklings were placed in an enclosed pond area at 25 to 45 days of age. Altogether, 627 (97 percent) ducklings reached flight age and dispersed gradually into the wild. All had left the release area by 25 November. First-year band recovery reports indicated that 68 (11 percent) of the birds were shot in 15 states. Their migration pattern was similar to that for immature wild mallards banded in North Dakota in 1970.

Eighty-nine (33 percent) of a possible 270 marked females returned to Arrowwood Refuge during 1971. When consideration is given to assumed normal natural mortality and crippling loss, an estimated minimum of 43 percent of the surviving females returned to the release area. Returning birds not observed would raise this figure even higher. This potential homing rate is considerably higher than rates reported for other studies using various strains of mallards. Numerous observations of nests and broods indicated that breeding behavior and nesting success were similar to those of wild mallards in the area.

The success of this release is attributed to the inherent capability of hand-reared, wild-strain mallards to revert to their wild behavior, and to the high survival to flight age and first fall migration afforded by the gentle release in a sanctuary area. Indications are that releases of this type under the described conditions can be used to increase the breeding population of mallards in a local area.

J. WILDL. MANAGE. 37(2):154–159

Liberating hand-reared waterfowl to establish or supplement local breeding populations has been advocated by many, including Pirnie (1935), McCabe (1947), Foley (1954), Hunt and Smith (1966), and Borden and Hochbaum (1966), and has received qualified rejection by others, including Lincoln (1934), Brakhage (1953), Hunt et al. (1958), and Bednarik and Hanson (1965). Survival of mallards released into the wild is described by Benson (1939) and Kiel (1970).

Most of these studies dealt with domestic or semidomestic strains of mallards in which the observed survival and homing was low. Better success was achieved in gentle-release studies by Brakhage (1953) involving wild-strain mallards and by Doty and Kruse (1972) involving wild-strain wood ducks (*Aix sponsa*) at Arrowwood National Wildlife Refuge in 1968. In view of the scarcity of information but encouraging success achieved from releases of this type, it was decided to conduct further studies with wild-strain mallards, incorporating the best features of the previous studies and several additional features. Emphasis was placed upon assessing the migration, homing, and nesting of the released birds.

We acknowledge the assistance of personnel at the Arrowwood National Wildlife Refuge in caring for the ducklings, and of various personnel of the Northern Prairie Wildlife Research Center: R. A. Madson and Karl L. Hansen in banding, marking and other aspects of the study; Paul F. Springer for editorial assistance; and Harvey K. Nelson and George V. Burger for providing encouragement and help in planning the study.

Originally published in J. Wildl. Manage. 37(2):154–159, 1973.

STUDY AREA AND METHODS

The release of hand-reared wild-strain mallards was made at the headquarters area of the Arrowwood Refuge. This refuge was established in 1935 on 6439.5 hectares of prairie grassland intermingled with lakes, marshes, and farmland along a 25.7-km stretch of the James River in east-central North Dakota. Only short segments of natural river channel remain among four large impoundments on the floor of the river valley. Tree growth is limited to a narrow band along the perimeter of the lakes and river.

The birds were hatched in incubators at the Northern Prairie Wildlife Research Center over a 46-day period. The eggs came from clutches produced by a captive flock of wild-strain mallards at the Center and from clutches salvaged in the wild. Newly hatched ducklings were placed in brooders containing infrared heat lamps, starter mash, and water, and were kept there for 8 to 12 days before being moved to 2.1- by 11.0-m outside pens. The birds were transported to the Arrowwood Refuge at from 25 to 45 days of age and all were banded before being placed in the release pen. Females were also marked with white plastic nasal saddles, each individually identified with black numerals. After liberation into the release pen the ducklings were not handled again except for those that were retrapped the next summer.

The release pen consisted of an open-topped, 0.2-hectare, woven-wire enclosure located near the shore of Arrowwood Lake in the refuge headquarters area. It contained a 18.3- by 30.5-m pond which was 0.6 m deep and contained a small island. Grower pellets and grain were provided in poultry feeders in the release pen throughout the summer and fall. Dense vegetation within the release pen and on the island provided protective cover, and supplementary natural foods were available from the pond and the vegetation. Mammalian predators were controlled on the outside perimeter of the release pen site by live trapping and removal.

Thus, control over the ducklings lessened progressively from indoor brooders to outdoor pens and finally to the partly controlled environment of the release pen. Final liberation was achieved when the ducks were able to fly out of the release pen. No attempt was made to isolate the ducklings from human activity.

Observations of released birds were made at the refuge from the summer of 1970 through the fall of 1971. Observations in the spring and summer of 1971 were made with 20× spotting scopes from blinds located at the release pen. No special effort was directed toward locating nests or broods; however, observations of these were made by refuge personnel while conducting routine refuge work.

In order to catch and identify marked females which had lost their nasal saddles, bait trapping was conducted from 7 to 19 October 1971. Wheat and shelled corn were used in the release pen for several days before funnel traps were set over the baited area.

RESULTS

Flight and Migration

Of the 648 young ducks moved from the Center to the refuge, 21 died in the release pen from various causes. The remaining 627 ducks (306 females and 321 males) survived to flight age.

Flight was first noted on 20 July when the oldest group was 55 days old. By mid-August, groups of marked mallards were seen at different locations up to 2.4 km from the release site. The last group reached flight stage by early September.

In September and October, large groups of marked birds were noted feeding on mud flats and the shorelines of Arrowwood Lake in the vicinity of the release pen. During mornings and evenings throughout the fall, many marked birds continued to utilize the feed provided in the release pen. The majority of the marked birds had left the refuge by late October and early November. Seven marked birds seen on 23 November constituted the last observation in 1970.

Band Recoveries

The earliest direct band recovery reported by hunters was from the vicinity of the refuge on 4 October and the latest was from Arkansas on 30 January 1971. The percentages of direct recoveries by states are shown in Figure 1. This distribution pattern indicates that 68 released birds migrated along the same routes as 13 immature wild mallards banded in North Dakota in 1970. Brakhage (1953) reported no major differences in departure dates, migration patterns, and rate of progress down the flyway between hand-reared and wild mallards.

The direct recovery rate by hunters for released birds (0.107) was not significantly different ($P > 0.10$) from that for the immature wild mallards (0.071). No significant difference ($P > 0.10$) was noted in the recovery rates of hand-reared (0.102) and wild (0.106) males, but there was a significant difference ($P < 0.05$) in the recovery rates of hand-reared (0.113) and wild (0.034) females. We believe the difference in recovery rates in the females may be due in part to a higher band reporting rate for birds with markers.

Lincoln (1934) concluded from band recoveries that hand-reared, game farm mallards did not disperse from the point of release and had a poor survival rate. Errington and Albert (1936) cited a similar

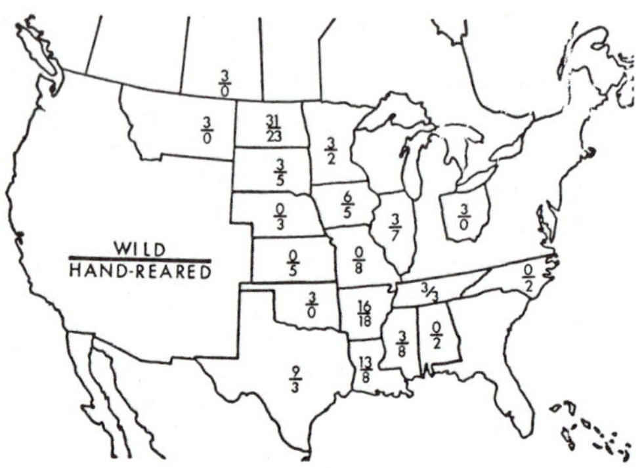

Fig. 1. Percentage of direct recoveries of immature wild and hand-reared mallards banded in North Dakota in 1970.

failure of game farm mallards to migrate. Brakhage (1953) found that local mortality of hand-reared, wild-stock mallards was 40 percent higher than that of wild mallards and that mortality was consistently higher for hand-reared than for wild-trapped ducks of other species also. Foley (1954) was optimistic about New York's program for establishment of waterfowl released as ducklings. He found that, of six species released, survival to flight age and subsequent return as breeders the following year was sufficient to repopulate some depleted nesting areas.

Survival and Homing

In the spring of 1971, returning females were first seen on 7 April. Observations became common by 10 April when six marked females were noted on Arrowwood Lake in the vicinity of the release pen. A minimum of 89 out of a possible 270 marked females returned to the refuge during 1971 (Table 1). This is a potential homing rate of 33 percent. If we assume a crippling loss of 25 percent and a nonhunting mortality of 20 percent (Geis et al. 1969), the estimated minimum survival (homing) rate is 43 percent. We feel 43 percent is minimal since 13 (46 percent) of the 28 marked females

Table 1. Fate and homing of female hand-reared mallards released at Arrowwood Refuge in 1970.

	Number	Number Remaining
Females banded	319	319
Total losses in release pen	13	306
Hunting mortality	36	270
Assumed crippling loss (25%)	12	258
Assumed nonhunting mortality (20%)	52	206
Birds assumed alive to return in spring	206	
Birds observed returning	89	
Percent returning	43	

trapped in the fall of 1971 were not previously observed during the spring and summer.

All marked females were paired when they returned in the spring. In only one instance was a banded drake observed with a marked female, indicating that most pairing was with wild drakes. The pairs were wary and easily flushed, making observation of marker numbers difficult. The birds were well distributed on the refuge and generally came to the release pen only in early morning or late evening to feed on grain placed there. Only a few pairs would enter the pen at one time, and if the markers had not been numbered, we probably would have concluded that only about 15 females returned. At other times of the day no marked females were present in the pen.

Sowls (1955) found that 5 percent of 20 hand-reared female mallards and 13 percent of 115 hand-reared female pintails returned the following spring to the marsh where they were released. Sellers (1973) found that approximately 25 percent of 821 wild-stock female mallard ducklings released at about 5 weeks of age in pothole habitat near Minnedosa, Manitoba in 1969 returned in 1970 to breed on or within 8.0 km of the 10.4-km^2 release area.

Table 2. Mallard breeding population data for Arrowwood Refuge 1967–72.

Year	Pairs	Young Produced
1967	133	290
1968	96	377
1969	158	754
1970	196	612
1971	351	1,184
1972	185	501

Nesting Behavior and Success

The first egg laying was noted on 26 April. Seventeen nests were found during the spring and summer of 1971. The nests were located as follows: seven on two islands in Arrowwood Lake, two in the release pen, three near the release pen, three in artificial nesting structures, and two on upland sites some distance from the release pen. The upland nests were in vegetative types normally used by wild mallards at the refuge. Thirty-five percent of the nests hatched. Hatching success was highest for nests on islands and lowest for nests on upland.

Thirteen observations of marked females with ducklings, representing a minimum of eight different broods, were made up to 3.2 km from the release site. The average number of ducklings in these broods was similar to that for 40 wild mallard broods observed on the refuge. In most instances marked females and their broods were seen in places also being used by wild mallards with broods. The behavior of marked females with broods was similar to that of the wild birds, and ducklings raised by marked females survived as well as those raised by wild hens.

Arrowwood Refuge has a history of supporting wild breeding mallards so the release in 1971 supplemented an established population. Both the number of mallard breeding pairs and young produced increased substantially in 1971 (Table 2) but decreased again in 1972. The increase in 1971 was probably only partially a response to the 1970 release since other management techniques have been applied on the refuge in recent years to make the area more attractive to breeding waterfowl. The decline in 1972 was due in part to poor habitat conditions which resulted in reduced breeding duck densities and production on and in the general area of the refuge.

DISCUSSION

The homing of these hand-reared mallards and the similarity of their behavior to that of wild birds suggest that this type of program can be used to increase the breeding population of mallards in a local area. It is interesting to speculate as to the factors which contributed to this apparently successful release. The genetic capability of the wild stock may be important in achieving normal migration and homing and a general reversion to wild behavior. The gentle release method provided food and protection from predators up to flight age. After achieving flight capability, the birds returned frequently to the release pen to feed and changed gradually to natural foods. Finally, release into the large sanctuary area provided security from hunting in the area of release during much of the fall, and also enabled the released birds to mingle with a large concentration of wild mallards.

The costs of producing and releasing wild-strain mallards by the methods used in this experiment are undoubtedly higher than for the more conventional type of releases of game birds at 3 or 4 weeks of age. Wild-strain mallards can be expected to produce less than half as many eggs as a flock of game farm birds. Considering only the direct expenses of an operational program (labor, feed, materials, etc.), we estimate the cost to produce a wild-strain mallard to flight age at from $1.50 to $3.00 depending on the size of the operation and other factors. While the gentle release of wild-strain mallards may be more expensive, the increased costs are probably offset by the better survival and general performance in the wild.

Additional research on propagation and release methods is contemplated. While no effort was made to shield the released mallards from human activity, isolation and various types of behavioral and other conditioning may have enabled even better survival in the wild. The role of genetic capability of stock, natural food supply, and predation in relation to the success of a release also needs further study.

LITERATURE CITED

BEDNARIK, K. E., AND C. L. HANSON. 1965. Ohio's waterfowl pioneering program. Game Res. in Ohio. 3:153–171.

BENSON, D. 1939. Survival studies of mallards liberated in New York State. Trans. N. Am. Wildl. Conf. 4:411–415.

BORDEN, R., AND H. A. HOCHBAUM. 1966. Gadwall seeding in New England. Trans. N. Am. Wildl. Nat. Resour. Conf. 31:79–88.

BRAKHAGE, G. K. 1953. Migration and mortality of ducks hand-reared and wild-trapped at Delta, Manitoba. J. Wildl. Manage. 17(4): 465–477.

DOTY, H. A., AND A. D. KRUSE. 1972. Techniques for establishing local breeding populations of wood ducks. J. Wildl. Manage. 36 (2):428–435.

ERRINGTON, P. L., AND W. E. ALBERT. 1936. Banding studies of semidomesticated mallard ducks. Bird-banding 7(2):69–73.

FOLEY, D. 1954. Survival and establishment of waterfowl released as ducklings. New York Fish Game J. 1(2):206–213.

GEIS, A. D., R. K. MARTINSON, AND D. R. ANDERSON. 1969. Establishing hunting regulations and allowable harvest of mallards in the United States. J. Wildl. Manage. 33(4): 848–859.

HUNT, R. A., L. R. JAHN, R. C. HOPKINS, AND G. H. AMELONG. 1958. An evaluation of artificial mallard propagation in Wisconsin. Wisconsin Conserv. Dept. Tech. Wildl. Bull. 16. 79pp.

———, AND C. F. SMITH. 1966. An evaluation of hand-reared wood ducks at Goose Island, Mississippi River, Wisconsin. Pages 132–140 *in* L. R. Jahn, ed. Wood duck management and research: A symposium. Wildl. Manage. Inst., Washington, D.C. 212pp.

KIEL, W. H., JR. 1970. A release of hand-reared mallards in south Texas. Texas Agric. Exp. Stn. Publ. MP-968. 12pp.

LINCOLN, F. C. 1934. Restocking of marshes with hand-reared mallards not proved practicable. Pages 310–313 *in* M. S. Eisenhower, ed. USDA Yearb. of Agric. 783pp.

MCCABE, R. A. 1947. The homing of transplanted young wood ducks. Wilson Bull. 59(2):104–109.

PIRNIE, M. D. 1935. Michigan waterfowl management. Michigan Dept. Conserv., Lansing. 328pp.

SELLERS, R. A. 1973. Mallard releases in understocked prairie pothole habitat. J. Wildl. Manage. 37(1):10–22.

SOWLS, L. K. 1955. Prairie Ducks. Wildl. Manage. Inst., Washington, D.C. 193pp.

Accepted 1 March 1973.

ESTABLISHING BREEDING POPULATIONS OF WOOD DUCKS BY RELOCATING WILD BROODS[1]

DAVID E. CAPEN, Maine Cooperative Wildlife Research Unit, University of Maine, Orono 04473[2]
WILLIAM J. CRENSHAW, Maine Cooperative Wildlife Research Unit, University of Maine, Orono 04473[3]
MALCOLM W. COULTER, Maine Cooperative Wildlife Research Unit, University of Maine, Orono 04473

Abstract: A procedure was developed for moving recently hatched broods of wild wood ducks (*Aix sponsa*) to stock suitable habitats. The most satisfactory technique utilized a release box, from which a wing-clipped hen and her ducklings were liberated together. Hens moved with newly hatched broods remained with their offspring and successfully reared them on the new areas. Eight of 87 female ducklings released were known to return to nest in later years.

J. WILDL. MANAGE. 38(2):253–256

Ducklings are often released to establish or restore breeding populations of waterfowl. Pen-reared birds have been stocked with the expectation that they would return to the release areas to nest in later years. McCabe (1947) reported one of the early successes in stocking wood ducks. Other wood duck release studies were discussed by Bellrose (1958), Lee and Nelson (1966), Lane et al. (1969), McGilvrey (1971), and by Doty and Kruse (1972).

It is sometimes difficult to use pen-reared birds for stocking. High losses during hatching and rearing have been reported (Hanson 1951, Hunt and Smith 1966). Also low survival rates after release are common (Brakhage 1953), particularly in northern, nonrefuge areas. Providing the proper facilities, food, and care, such as described by Lane et al. (1969) and Doty and Kruse (1972), is expensive and not always possible.

The purpose of the present study was to develop methods for moving wild hen wood ducks and their young to different locations where hens could raise their broods naturally in the wild. It was believed that the resulting broods would be more likely to establish nesting populations in future years than would pen-reared ducks. We also felt that a method for transplanting wild broods might be comparatively less expensive and easier than artificial propagation and release, in situations where wild stock is available.

The study was conducted in south-central Maine during four seasons, 1970–1973. The help of several people in the Maine Department of Inland Fisheries and Game was valuable. H. E. Spencer, Jr. and J. W. Peppard encouraged us to experiment with methods for transplanting wild birds and made helpful suggestions. G. G. Donovan, G. E. Hocutt, F. B. Hurley, and J. A. Dorso assisted with many phases of the project. W. B. Krohn, Bureau of Sport Fisheries and Wildlife, also provided assistance. The study was financed by Federal Aid to Wildlife Restoration Project W–62–R.

METHODS

Selecting Hens for Relocation

Hen wood ducks and their clutches or broods were taken from marshes where

[1] A contribution from the Maine Cooperative Wildlife Research Unit—University of Maine, Maine Department of Inland Fisheries and Game, Wildlife Management Institute, and U.S. Bureau of Sport Fisheries and Wildlife cooperating.

[2] Present address: Utah Cooperative Wildlife Research Unit, Utah State University, Logan 84322.

[3] Present address: Vermont Fish and Game Department, Sandbar Refuge, Milton 05468.

Originally published in J. Wildl. Manage. 38(2):253–256, 1974.

wooden nesting boxes were commonly used. Broods and clutches to be moved were selected from more than 200 occupied nest boxes.

Females tolerant of handling were selected for relocation. These were hens which generally remained quietly in the nest boxes when approached, struggled very little when caught, and remained in the boxes after being handled. This tolerant behavior was observed in both yearling and older hens suggesting that it may be an individual trait not necessarily related to age.

Nest boxes were checked at weekly intervals throughout the nesting season and a rough schedule of probable hatching dates was prepared based on a 30-day incubation period (Grice and Rogers 1965). The schedule was often modified by checking the eggs during the last 8–10 days of incubation with a simple field candler. The precise day of hatching was estimated by candling during the final 3–4 days of incubation and comparing the candled eggs to a series of photographs in Hanson (1954).

Experimental Techniques

Two methods for transporting wood ducks were tested. Basically, the first attempts consisted of moving a hen and her clutch in their nest box to a different marsh during the last days of incubation. During later tests, hens with newly hatched broods were transplanted.

Results from the first experiments indicated that it might be advantageous to make the hens flightless to prevent desertion from the release area. About 5 cm were clipped from the primary and secondary feathers of one wing of each bird. We also decided to release the ducklings from a box which allowed them to see the hen on the water and leave the box with little effort. Several kinds of boxes for releasing the hens and their ducklings together were tried. The most simple and effective technique utilized a box with a hinged bottom, suspended 15–20 cm above the water. The bottom was lowered slowly with a cord operated by a person well concealed 30–60 m away. Generally, the hen and the ducklings slid into the water gently, and then proceeded directly to the nearest cover.

Marking and Tagging

The adult hens which were moved were marked for individual identification by applying paint to the tails or wings as described by Sowls (1949) and by Coulter and Miller (1968). A satisfactory mark resulted from painting a rectangular patch on the secondaries and the secondary wing coverts.

A small, monel metal tag was placed in the web of each foot of the ducklings. The tags were modified and inserted as described by Grice and Rogers (1965). They were obtained in duplicate sets, each numbered consecutively, thus two identical tags were attached to each duckling.

Efforts were made to trap broods 4–5 weeks after release to obtain data about duckling survival and to band birds for future identification.

RESULTS

Two wood duck nests and 30 broods were moved during the study. In the first nest moved, the eggshells had not yet pipped, but frequent peeping could be heard from each egg; whereas in the second nest all eggs had pipped. In both cases, the females abandoned the release areas immediately after they had left the nest boxes. The first hen returned within 8 hours to the area from which she was taken, 48 km away, and renested successfully in a nest box about 200 m from the original site.

Five additional females and their newly hatched young were moved while still in the original nest boxes. In two instances, the transplants were successful. The females left the nests and began calling their young. The ducklings quickly climbed to the entrances of the nest boxes and jumped to the water. The other three trials were unsuccessful, although the same methods were used. The females abandoned their new areas and left the young in the nest boxes.

In the final 25 cases, the hens were wing-clipped and moved with their broods in a release box. Twenty-two of the 25 trials were successful. A release was considered successful if the hen and the brood were observed together later, or if there was evidence from bait trapping and band recoveries that any duckling from a brood survived to flying age.

The broods were taken from nest boxes, transported an average of 70 km, then released on a marsh where wood duck nests had not been found. The release areas had nest boxes available and were thought to be excellent sites for breeding wood ducks.

An estimated 87 female ducklings were transplanted to new areas. Eight tagged, yearling hens from the releases were found nesting in boxes the following years. Each hen was nesting on the area where she had been reared as a member of a relocated brood. The approximate 9 percent observed return was a favorable homing rate, since it had been expected that about 8 percent might return, a figure computed from data presented by Grice and Rogers (1965), Barden (1968), and McGilvrey (1969). In other states a larger proportion might be expected to return since annual mortality for immature wood ducks appears to be higher in Maine than in many states (Grice and Rogers 1965; unpublished administrative report, 1963, U.S. Bureau of Sport Fisheries and Wildlife).

The procedure developed appears to be feasible for establishing breeding populations of wood ducks. If the birds are available for transplant, moving wild birds promises to be more effective and economical than programs of artificial propagation and release. Furthermore, this technique can be used without the advance preparation necessary to hatch and rear ducklings artificially.

LITERATURE CITED

BARDEN, L. S. 1968. A population analysis of Maine-banded wood ducks. M.S. Thesis. Univ. of Maine, Orono. 109pp.

BELLROSE, F. C. 1958. The orientation of displaced waterfowl in migration. Wilson Bull. 70(1):20–40.

BRAKHAGE, G. K. 1953. Migration and mortality of ducks hand-reared and wild-trapped at Delta, Manitoba. J. Wildl. Manage. 17(4): 465–477.

COULTER, M. W., AND W. R. MILLER. 1968. Nesting biology of black ducks and mallards in northern New England. Vermont Fish Game Dept. Bull. 68-2. 74pp.

DOTY, H. A., AND A. D. KRUSE. 1972. Techniques for establishing local breeding populations of wood ducks. J. Wildl. Manage. 36 (2):428–435.

GRICE, D., AND J. P. ROGERS. 1965. The wood duck in Massachusetts. Massachusetts Div. Fish. Game. 96pp.

HANSON, H. C. 1951. Notes on the artificial propagation of wood duck. J. Wildl. Manage. 15(1):68–72.

———. 1954. Criteria of age of incubated mallard, wood duck and bobwhite quail eggs. Auk 71(3):267–272.

HUNT, R. A., AND C. F. SMITH. 1966. An evaluation of hand-reared wood ducks at Goose Island, Mississippi River, Wisconsin. Pages 132–140 *in* L. R. Jahn, ed. Wood duck management and research: a symposium. Wildlife Management Institute, Washington, D.C.

LANE, P. W., G. W. BOND, JR., AND W. H. JULIAN, JR. 1969. Wood duck production and transplants on national wildlife refuges in the south Atlantic states. Proc. Southeastern Assoc. Fish Game Commissioners Conf. 22:202–208.

LEE, F. B., AND H. K. NELSON. 1966. The role

of artificial propagation in wood duck management. Pages 140–150 *in* L. R. Jahn, ed. Wood duck management and research: a symposium. Wildlife Management Institute, Washington, D.C.

McCABE, R. A. 1947. The homing of transplanted young wood ducks. Wilson Bull. 59 (2):104–109.

McGILVREY, F. B. 1969. Survival in wood duck broods. J. Wildl. Manage. 33(1):73–76.

———. 1971. Increasing a wood duck nesting population by releases of pen-reared birds. Proc. Southeastern Assoc. Fish Game Commissioners Conf. 25:202–205.

SOWLS, L. K. 1949. A preliminary report on renesting in waterfowl. Trans. N. Am. Wildl. Conf. 14:260–275.

Accepted 5 February 1974.

EXPERIMENTAL RELEASE OF CANVASBACKS ON BREEDING HABITAT

LAWSON G. SUGDEN, Canadian Wildlife Service, Saskatoon, Saskatchewan S7N 0X4

Abstract: Of 43 female canvasbacks (*Aythya valisineria*) released as flightless young on a 15.5-km^2 study area near Saskatoon, Saskatchewan, in 1971, 3 returned to the general area of release in 1972. There was no evidence that they nested. A majority of 50 hand-reared females, spring-released as yearlings in 1972, formed brief pair bonds with wild males. None apparently produced broods though two attempted to nest. Three returned as 2-year-olds and at least 1 nested. No released birds were seen in second or subsequent years after release. There was no advantage in overwintering the ducklings before they were released as yearlings. Because the area may have been fully stocked with wild canvasbacks, similar releases should be evaluated on obviously understocked habitat.

J. WILDL. MANAGE. 40(4):716–720

Persistently low populations of canvasbacks dictate a need to investigate all facets of the species' ecology and to test management practices for improving its status. Artificial stocking as a way to increase canvasback breeding populations has received little attention and only one attempt has been reported. In that study, an insufficient number of ducklings was released to evaluate the technique (Foley 1954).

This paper describes an experiment to increase breeding densities of canvasbacks artificially by transplanting flightless young and by spring release of yearlings. I thank J. B. Gollop, J. H. Patterson, and *Journal of Wildlife Management* referees for their helpful comments.

STUDY AREA

The study area (52 N, 106 W), 48 km east of Saskatoon, Saskatchewan, was a block of 6 sections (15.5 km^2) in 1971 and 1972, and 12 sections from 1973 through 1975. The area is in the aspen parkland (Bird 1961), soils are dark brown, and topography is rolling to gently rolling. Annual precipitation averages about 36 cm. Most of the land is cultivated; barley and wheat are the main crops. Ponds averaged 20/km^2 and comprised 9 percent of the area. Size of ponds ranged from less than 0.04 to 7.5 ha. Most ponds were wholly or partly bordered by trees, mainly willows (*Salix* spp.) and aspen (*Populus tremuloides*).

METHODS

In late July and August 1971, 90 flightless young canvasbacks (47 M, 43 F) were banded, marked with nasal saddles (Sugden and Poston 1968), and released on the study area. They were at least Plumage Class IIB or about 5 weeks old (Dzubin 1959). Sixteen, including five females, had been hatched from wild-collected eggs and reared in captivity; the others were caught by night-lighting from ponds near the study area.

From 3 to 11 May 1972, 36 male and 50 female canvasbacks also were released on the study area. These had been reared from eggs collected in the wild in 1971 and held over winter at the Delta Waterfowl Research Station in Manitoba. The 1972 releases were made on 36 different Type IV and V ponds (Shaw and Fredine 1956) throughout the 6 sections. In addition to casual observations throughout the summer by 4 people in the field, the study area was covered systematically 10 times in May and at least once each June, July, and August. Also, two complete nest searches were made. Similar coverage was made from

Originally published in J. Wildl. Manage. 40(4):716–720, 1976.

1973 through 1975 but included an additional three sections on either side of the original six.

RESULTS AND DISCUSSION

Of the 90 young canvasbacks released in 1971, 8 males and 4 females were shot and reported during the 1971 hunting season. Four returns were from Saskatchewan, two from North Dakota, and one each from Ontario, Minnesota, Wisconsin, Virginia, Louisiana, and California. That year, the daily bag limit in Canada and the United States was one canvasback or one redhead (*Aythya americana*).

In May 1972, 2 of the females released in 1971 were each observed twice on the study block and another was seen 4 times, 11 km south of its release site. All were birds that had been wild-caught prior to release. I do not know if any of the three attempted to nest. Each was seen both paired and alone. None of the 1971 releases was seen after 1972.

Three of the yearling canvasbacks were flightless and in poor condition when released in May 1972. They were not seen after release, presumably because they died. The remainder exhibited a wide range of mobility. Two males apparently remained on their release pond for over 80 days. On the other hand, 1 male and 2 females were seen more than 8 km from their release site 78 days after release. Females tended to be more mobile than males. Relatively fewer females were seen during censuses on the study area, whereas more were seen off the area. Individual females were observed on more ponds, and the greatest distances between ponds that they used averaged higher than for males (Table 1). I postulate that females were generally more mobile than males because a majority of females formed brief pair bonds with wild males and, therefore, behaved more like wild canvasbacks (Dzubin 1955).

Table 1. Statistics illustrating differences in mobility between released male and female canvasbacks.

	% of birds seen off block	Mean % of times birds not seen during census	Mean no. of ponds occupied[a]	Mean max. distance (km) between occupied ponds[a]
Male	5.5	23.1	3.9	1.4
Female	18.0	39.1	4.9	2.2
χ^2	2.91			
t		2.41	1.84	2.86
df	1	81	60	60
P	<0.1	<0.05	<0.1	<0.01

[a] For birds seen 8 or more times.

Thirty-two of the females released in 1972 were seen paired with wild drakes that year. These pair bonds were apparently weak and brief, lasting but a few days in most cases. Thus, brief pairings by additional females may have occurred without detection. Of 40 females for which there were adequate records, only 2 were known to have attempted nesting. One started a nest on 7 June in company with a wild drake but the nest was never finished. The hen was seen in July and August with up to eight other marked canvasbacks on the block. Another was paired with a wild drake from 23 May through 2 June. She initiated a nest about 20 June, incubated a clutch, but deserted close to hatching and was not seen after 25 July. The failure of canvasback hens, released as yearlings, to bring off broods in their first year was in marked contrast to the minimum of 6 broods produced by 23 female gadwalls (*Anas strepera*) released as yearlings at Concord, Massachusetts, by Borden and Hochbaum (1966). There were few if any wild gadwalls using the Massachusetts area, whereas my area had a mean density of 1.7 wild canvasback pairs/km^2. Perhaps the different response of these two species was due to the presence or absence of wild pairs. Also, differences in innate behavior might have been responsible.

No marked drakes were seen paired. During 314 times they were seen on a pond occupied by either released or wild females, only twice did marked drakes display courtship behavior. Both times the drakes performed the "neck stretch" (Hochbaum 1944: 23) while in company with a marked female and a wild drake.

Unlike wild canvasbacks, released ducks frequently rested on shore, and this no doubt resulted from their experience in captivity. Generally, released birds were also tamer than wild canvasbacks, permitting closer approach before flight. However, females paired with wild drakes usually flushed with the drake. Both their propensity to rest on shore and their lack of wildness could lead to greater mortality of released birds, the first through increased predation and the second through increased hunting mortality.

In late May 1972, the released birds tended to form small flocks that sometimes included wild canvasbacks, predominantly drakes. One month after release, 84 percent of the marked ducks were present on the 6-section block; 60 percent were present after 2 months, and 55 percent after 3 months. No systematic counts were made after mid-August, but casual observations showed a few still present in early September. Based on birds seen and those known to have been alive because they were either shot or observed later, a minimum of 60 percent were alive in mid-August, 3 months after release.

Except for females with broods, virtually all adult wild canvasbacks had left the study area by August, presumably to molt elsewhere. Released birds that remained later on the area apparently did not molt there, for none was seen that was flightless or in eclipse plumage. The fact that these were nonbreeding birds may have contributed to their delayed molt (Hochbaum 1944:113).

In 1972 there was no hunting season on canvasbacks in the United States. In Canada, the daily bag limit remained at one. Eight ducks (5 M, 3 F) released in 1972 were shot and reported that autumn within 129 km of the study area. One female was reported shot in Mexico.

In May 1973, two females were seen on the study block four times; another was seen twice. One nested on the block and the others, also paired when seen, may have nested off the block. None was seen in 1974 or 1975.

The low rate of homing (3 of 43) of female canvasbacks released as flightless young in 1971 is not surprising in view of the continent-wide hunting season on canvasbacks that year and the high mortality experienced by young canvasbacks (Geis 1959). The similar low homing rate (3 of 50) for females released as yearlings in the spring of 1972 is perhaps more significant in view of the 1972 closed season in the United States. Trauger and Stoudt (1974: 44) reported that 25 percent of the females wild-caught and marked when young on their Manitoba study area in 1972 returned as yearlings in 1973. Reasons for the low rate of homing by hand-reared canvasbacks released as yearlings are not clear. Studies of other species, hand-reared and released directly into the wild as ducklings, have shown that they suffer greater hunting mortality than their wild counterparts, particularly near the release area (Brakhage 1953, Weller and Ward 1959, Schladweiler and Tester 1972), though survival can be increased by using a "gentle release" method (Doty and Kruse 1972, Lee and

Kruse 1973). Canvasbacks released directly into the wild are apparently no exception and, moreover, it appears that delaying their release until their first spring provides little or no advantage in terms of survival. In fact, one may postulate that the longer a duck is kept in captivity the more vulnerable it becomes to all forms of mortality when released into the wild. Many of the canvasbacks released as yearlings apparently had a delayed molt that also may have reduced survival.

It is well-known that female ducks tend to return to the area where they learned to fly. The mechanism of this learning is imperfectly understood, particularly the relationship between the strength of this "bond" and age of first flight. Sellers (1973) found a significantly higher homing rate for mallards (*Anas platyrhynchos*) released as ducklings before 23 July than those released after that date in the same year, and suggested that time available to become familiar with their release area influenced the precision of homing by the ducks. The ability of a duckling to learn the following-reaction is highly age-specific and declines rapidly in the duck's early life (Thorpe 1963:128). Perhaps the ability of a duck to "imprint" to its area of first flight also declines with age, and those released as yearlings would never have a homing rate equal to that of ducks released as flightless young.

Failure of released females to return and settle on the area also may have been related to existing densities of wild pairs. Mean densities on the 15.5-km^2 area were 1.7 and 3.1 pairs/km^2 in 1972 and 1973, respectively. The relationship between pairs and habitat can be expressed as pairs/100 Type IV and V ponds, because these were the ponds most often used. The average was 19.4 in 1972 and 38.9 in 1973. The increase in 1973 (the highest value recorded in 5 years) was caused partly by a reduction in pond numbers due to drought and mostly by an increase in pair numbers, the latter believed to represent birds displaced from deteriorated habitat elsewhere. Biologists generally agree that each pond habitat has a carrying capacity for each duck species, but such capacities have been difficult to measure and define (Dzubin 1969). The relationship likely involves more than pair densities and may be reflected in parameters such as nesting effort, nesting success, and brood survival. The relatively high density of wild canvasbacks in 1973 may well have prevented the establishment of more released birds, these perhaps less fit behaviorally to compete for space.

Regardless of the reasons for low homing rate, there was no advantage in holding the ducks over winter prior to release, under conditions of this experiment. Resulting production on the study area by released canvasbacks was negligible both in the year of release and subsequent years. Because the method failed in this instance, it does not follow that it is without value. Its true worth will not be known until experimental releases are evaluated on obviously understocked habitat (Sellers 1973). As our understanding of canvasback ecology and social behavior grows, so will our ability to choose management strategies with confidence.

LITERATURE CITED

BIRD, R. D. 1961. Ecology of the aspen parkland of western Canada. Can. Dept. Agric. Publ. 1066. 155pp.

BORDEN, R., AND H. A. HOCHBAUM. 1966. Gadwall seeding in New England. Trans. N. Am. Wildl. Nat. Resour. Conf. 31:79–88.

BRAKHAGE, G. K. 1953. Migration and mortality of ducks hand-reared and wild-trapped at Delta, Manitoba. J. Wildl. Manage. 17(4): 465–477.

DOTY, H. A., AND A. D. KRUSE. 1972. Techniques for establishing local breeding populations of wood ducks. J. Wildl. Manage. 36(2):428–435.

DZUBIN, A. 1955. Some evidences of home range in waterfowl. Trans. N. Am. Wildl. Conf.. 20: 278–298.

———. 1959. Growth and plumage development of wild-trapped juvenile canvasback (*Aythya valisineria*). J. Wildl. Manage. 23 (3):279–290.

———. 1969. Comments on carrying capacity of small ponds for ducks and possible effect of density on mallard production. Pages 138–160 *in* Saskatoon wetlands seminar. Can. Wildl. Serv. Rep. Ser. 6.

FOLEY, D. 1954. Survival and establishment of waterfowl released as ducklings. New York Fish Game J. 1(2):206–213.

GEIS, A. D. 1959. Annual and shooting mortality estimates for the canvasback. J. Wildl. Manage. 23(3):253–261.

HOCHBAUM, H. A. 1944. The canvasback on a prairie marsh. The American Wildlife Institute, Washington, D.C. 201pp.

LEE, F. B., AND A. D. KRUSE. 1973. High survival and homing rate of hand-reared wild-strain mallards. J. Wildl. Manage. 37(2):154–159.

SCHLADWEILER, J. L., AND J. R. TESTER. 1972. Survival and behavior of hand-reared mallards released in the wild. J. Wildl. Manage. 36(4):1118–1127.

SELLERS, R. A. 1973. Mallard releases in understocked prairie pothole habitat. J. Wildl. Manage. 37(1):10–22.

SHAW, S. P., AND C. G. FREDINE. 1956. Wetlands of the United States: their extent and their value to waterfowl and other wildlife. U.S. Fish Wildl. Serv. Circ. 39. 67pp.

SUGDEN, L. G., AND H. J. POSTON. 1968. A nasal marker for ducks. J. Wildl. Manage. 32(4): 984–986.

THORPE, W. H. 1963. Learning and instinct in animals. Rev. ed. Harvard University Press, Cambridge, Mass. 558pp.

TRAUGER, D. L., AND J. H. STOUDT. 1974. Looking out for the canvasback. Part II: Canvasbacks of the aspen parklands. Ducks Unlimited 38(4):30–31, 42, 44–45, 48, 60.

WELLER, M. W., AND P. WARD. 1959. Migration and mortality of hand-reared redheads (*Aythya americana*). J. Wildl. Manage. 23(4): 427–433.

Accepted 24 May 1976.

RE-ESTABLISHMENT OF THE GIANT CANADA GOOSE IN IOWA[1]

RICHARD A. BISHOP[2] and RONALD G. HOWING, Wildlife Section, Iowa State Conservation Commission

Abstract: Giant Canada geese (*Branta canadensis maxima*) were common nesters in Iowa before 1900 but were exterminated through overexploitation about that time. Recent efforts by the Iowa Conservation Commission to re-establish these birds have been successful. By providing protection and nesting areas this flock has been increased from a few pair in 1964 to 800–1,000 birds in 1970. The birds have adapted to the surrounding habitat and established a migration tradition. The goal is to increase the flock to 7,000 birds.

Giant Canada geese (*Branta canadensis maxima*) were common nesters in Iowa in early times (Hanson 1965), but overexploitation exterminated most wild nesting populations of Canada geese about 1900.

The ever increasing demand for Canada geese by both the hunter and the general public has generated a response in conservation agencies throughout the Mississippi Flyway. Many states have been working diligently to increase certain flocks of Canada geese that are providing shooting for their hunters. Also several states have embarked upon homegrown flocks of the giant Canada goose with striking success. Free-flying Canada geese have been successfully re-established in Missouri, Ohio, Wisconsin and other states (Dill and Lee 1970). These flocks are providing additional birds for the hunter while fulfilling a demand by the general public to see these magnificent birds. This paper reports an attempt in Iowa to re-establish the giant Canada.

PROCEDURE

Sixteen adult pairs of pinioned *maximas* were bought in 1964 from private goose raisers in Minnesota and South Dakota. These geese were probably progeny of Canada geese that originally nested in Iowa, Minnesota, and South Dakota. They were kept captive in an enclosure at Ingham Lake in Emmet County. Most of the young raised during the years 1964–66 were pinioned to build up the captive breeding flock.

Elevated artificial nesting structures and man-made dirt islands were constructed in the Ingham Lake breeding pen. Elevated structures were installed on marshes in the vicinity of Ingham Lake for use by free-flying geese. In many states with Canada goose projects, predation has been a serious limiting factor. By providing safe man-made nesting sites in the breeding pen, it was hoped that the young geese raised there would be imprinted and would select safe nesting sites in the wild.

Before 1967 many of the free-flying young and adults were harvested by sportmen hunting around the periphery of the small refuge. The flock was barely maintaining its numbers because of this high local harvest. In 1967 a Canada goose refuge, 120 square miles in size, was established around the Ingham Lake breeding pen by closing parts of Emmet and Palo Alto counties to Canada goose hunting. With adequate protection from hunting, all young Canada geese raised at Ingham Lake since 1967 have been released as free-fliers.

---

[1] Originally published in Proc. Iowa Acad. Sci. 79:14–16, 1972.

[2] Address correspondence to this author. Present address: 1004 South 14th Street, Clear Lake, IA 50428.

Table 1. Ingham Lake captive Canada goose flock breeding and production data, 1964–70.[1]

Year	Number nests	Average clutch	Percent successful	Number eggs	Percent hatched	Average brood size	Goslings raised	Number goslings banded
1964	—	—	—	—	—	3.4[2]	24[2]	—
1965	12	—	—	—	—	—	17[2]	—
1966	21	—	—	—	—	—	60[2]	—
1967	19	—	68	—	—	4.1[2]	54[2]	52
1968	26	5.1[3]	69	96[3]	82[3]	4.2[4]	79[4]	83
1969	22	—	—	—	—	—	52[2]	48
1970	52	5.3	71	274	52	3.9[4]	144[4]	101
Total	152	5.2	70	—	60	4.0	430	284

— Complete data not available.
[1] Data from flightless adults held in 24.3 acre pen.
[2] Based on brood counts.
[3] Eggs from 19 of the 26 nests—number of eggs from 7 nests unknown.
[4] Based on eggs counted that hatched from successful nests.

Young wing-clipped Canada geese bought from goose raisers in northwest Iowa during the period 1967–69 were used as a call flock at the Red Rock Refuge east of Des Moines, and then brought to Ingham Lake by December each year. Canada geese from Red Rock, numbering 153 in 1968, 66 in 1969, and 128 in 1970, were allowed free-flight when they moulted as yearlings to supplement geese raised at Ingham Lake.

RESULTS

Breeding and Production from the Ingham Lake Captive Flock

The results of 7 years of nesting activity from the captive flock at Ingham Lake are summarized in Table 1. Most of the geese nested on the islands, platforms or in barrels. Many of the ground nests were destroyed by raccoon or skunk until 1970. During 1970 the area around the goose pen was intensively trapped to reduce predation of ground nests. No ground nests were destroyed by predators during 1970. However, abandonment of ground nests was high during 1970 due to overcrowding and territorial conflicts between geese. Nest abandonment was lower on the elevated nesting sites where it appeared that the geese were able to defend a smaller territory and possibly felt more secure.

Dogs broke into the goose pen twice before nesting during 1969 and killed several breeding pairs of captive geese. Nesting activity was curtailed in 1969 because of this unfortunate incident.

Mortality of Young Released as Free-fliers

Hunting does not appear to be limiting the re-establishment of nesting flocks in northwest Iowa. Only 11 recoveries were reported from 183 Canada geese banded in the period 1967–69. Mortality rates for these birds until 1970 were very low, indicating that most young remained with the family group within the goose refuge until most hunting seasons were over. In past years they have left northwest Iowa in December and have experienced very light gunning pressure. A few birds taken as 2-year-old birds (all males) have been scattered through neighboring states with no clear cut pattern.

As more birds are produced, an earlier migration and higher mortality rates are expected. Preliminary analysis of 1970 band returns shows 54 recoveries; how-

Table 2. Reproductive data on the free-flying Ingham Lake flock, 1966–70.[1,2]

Year	Number nests	Site of nests	Average clutch	Percent successful	Number eggs	Percent hatched	Average brood size	Estimated number goslings
1966	1	M. Hut	6.0	100	6	100	6.0[3]	6[3]
1967	2	M. Hut	—	100	—	—	5.0[3]	12[3]
1968	3	M. Hut	—	100	—	—	5.0[3]	15[3]
1968	4	Unknown	—	—	—	—	5.0[3]	20[3]
1969	2	Basket	5.5	100	11	100	5.5[4]	11[4]
1969	4	Barrel	5.7	100	23	73	4.2[4]	17[4]
1969	3	M. Hut	5.0	60	15	60	4.5[4]	9[4]
1969	1	Ground	5.0	100	5	100	5.0[4]	5[4]
1969	2	Unknown	—	—	—	—	5.0[3]	10[3]
1970	10	Basket	5.0	60	50	56	4.8[4]	28[4]
1970	7	Barrel	5.6	100	39	100	5.6[4]	39[4]
1970	11	M. Hut	5.4	91	59	90	5.3[4]	53[4]
1969	1	Ground	2.0	100	2	100	2.0[4]	2[4]
1970	3	Ditch Bank	3.7	66	11	82	4.5[4]	9[4]
1970	1	Duck Blind	6.0	100	6	100	6.0[4]	6[4]
1970	4	Island	3.2	75	13	70	3.0[4]	9[4]
1970	4	Unknown	—	—	—	—	4.0[3]	16[3]
Total	63		5.0	76[1]	240[1]	81[1]	4.7	267

— Complete data not available.
[1] Data from observed nests only.
[2] All young were left in the wild as free-fliers.
[3] Based on brood counts.
[4] Based on eggs counted that hatched from successful nests.

ever, recoveries will continue to be turned in throughout the year. Of these, 54% were first year recoveries. A total of 264 young geese were banded in 1970 giving an 11.7% direct recovery rate the first year. Correcting these data for reporting rate (approximately 50%) gives a first year direct recovery rate of at least 23.4%. Additional returns will increase the recovery rate. This recovery rate is comparable to rates experienced by immatures of the Eastern Prairie Population of Canada geese (Vaught and Kirsch 1966). If mortality rates do not increase greatly over what was experienced in 1970, the population should continue to increase.

Establishment of Breeding Free-flying Geese in Northwest Iowa

A summary of observations of free-flying breeding Canada geese in northwest Iowa is presented in Table 2. Breeding Canada geese were occasionally observed in the wild before 1966. However, it is believed that most of these geese escaped from local goose raisers.

It appears that most geese are selecting relatively safe nesting sites (Table 2). Muskrat huts, when available, appear to be the best nesting sites. Barrels appear to be next best with islands, ditch banks, basket nests and others ranking in that order. Approximately 75% of the nesting is occurring within 5 miles of the Ingham Lake breeding pen. The geese have pioneered surrounding marshes and private small sloughs indicating their ability to utilize available habitat. This ability was one aspect known to be very important to the success of enlarging the flock.

Another obstacle envisioned was the lack of migrational behavior. If the flock failed to migrate, considerable problems could arise. However, the birds did develop a migration desire and established a fall migration, but the pattern has not been determined.

DISCUSSION

The Ingham Lake goose flock has only recently increased to the population level capable of providing some birds for shooting plus expanding nesting activities over adjacent marshes and private sloughs. This project has met with much interest and public support which gives considerable justification for the project on aesthetic values alone.

Because of the hunting aspect and increased demand by the general public to see these birds re-established as common nesting birds, plans have been made to expand this project to establish these birds as a prominent species. In order to increase the population, additional key refuges are needed to maintain a breeding nucleus. These birds are quite vulnerable to the gun on their natal areas and thus must be given adequate protection. It is believed that two additional refuge areas and breeding flocks (one in the Spirit Lake area at Kettleson Hogsback, and one near Ruthven on Smith's Slough) will provide protection for sufficient birds to maintain a population level high enough to utilize the surrounding habitat. These three refuges will triangulate the biggest portion of the marsh country in northwest Iowa. An addition flock may be established at Rice Lake near Lake Mills at a later date. It is planned that the overall adult flock will be built to about 7,000 birds of which about 3,000 would be adult breeders producing an annual crop in excess of 2,000 goslings. Results of nesting indicate that the giant geese can and will successfully pioneer new areas and rear young. At this point, production is not considered to be a problem.

The ultimate success of this management endeavor will depend on mortality rates. If the three refuge areas are large enough to protect a sizable portion of the flock and the birds do not undergo excessive harvest outside Iowa, the population should increase to the desired level.

ACKNOWLEDGMENTS

This project was conducted as part of a research program on waterfowl in the Wildlife Section of the Iowa State Conservation Commission. Funds were provided from hunting and fishing license fees.

LITERATURE CITED

DILL, HERBERT, H., AND F. B. LEE. 1970. Home grown honkers. Bur. Sport Fish, and Wildl. Washington, D.C. 154pp.

HANSON, HAROLD C. 1965. The giant Canada goose. So. Ill. Univ. Press, Carbondale. 226pp.

VAUGHT, RICHARD W., AND L. M. KIRSCH. 1966. Canada geese of the Eastern Prairie population with special reference to the Swan Lake Flock. Missouri Dept. Conserv., Tech. Bull. 3. 91pp.

TRUMPETER SWAN MANAGEMENT[1]

HENRY A. HANSEN, Area Office, U.S. Bureau of Sport Fisheries and Wildlife, 813 "D" Street, Anchorage, AK 99501

By 1920, following more than a century of exploitation and intolerable human encroachment, the magnificent Trumpeter Swan *Cygnus cygnus buccinator* was conceded by many to be on the brink of extinction, in all likelihood past the point of no return. Fifty years later this native of the North American continent, the largest waterfowl in the world, had recovered sufficiently for it to be officially declared no longer an endangered species, even though the population is still small by many standards.

This remarkable recovery is, in part, the result of protection from legalized hunting, intensive management of remnant populations, and the beginning of a successful transplanting programme. Entirely independent of man's heroic restoration effort in this area, an undiscovered Trumpeter Swan population in Alaska and along the North Pacific Coast was concurrently thriving. Subsequently, detailed studies of these two major population groups were conducted and reported in detail (Banko 1960, Hansen et al. 1971). Therefore, this will be a brief summary of the current population status of the Trumpeter Swan in North America and of the attempt to re-establish this species throughout its ancestral range.

In comparison with the Arctic-nesting Whistling Swan *Cygnus c. columbianus*, the Trumpeter, North America's only other native swan, probably never maintained numerically strong populations. Furthermore, its habits and range rendered it far more susceptible to human exploitation. By 1932 there were only sixty-nine Trumpeter Swans known to exist in the United States, south of Canada. These were in the remote high mountain valleys where the States of Montana, Idaho, and Wyoming join. The precarious condition of the Trumpeter led to the acquisition of the Red Rock Lakes National Wildlife Refuge in Montana in 1935 by the U.S. Government. With the protection afforded the Trumpeters there and in the adjacent Yellowstone National Park, the population quickly began to increase and continued to grow until about 1950 when the nesting habitat became too crowded. The population in that area has become stabilized since then at about 300 swans with a very low reproduction rate (Table 1, Fig. 1).

The Trumpeter Swan is notoriously slow to pioneer new areas, particularly where there are long distances between suitable areas of breeding habitat or geographical barriers such as mountain ranges. Thus, by the time the habitat at Red Rock Lakes became saturated, the limited number of suitable nesting areas within a 100-mile radius were also filled. From the outset it was obvious that the Trumpeter needed additional help to come back all the way. It was this knowledge and a desire to accelerate the return of the Trumpeter that led to the transplanting programme. Monnie (1964) and Marshall (1968) have reported the Government's effort to relocate breeding colonies of Trumpeter Swans. The following summary is taken from their accounts.

The first transplant of Trumpeters was made in 1938 when four cygnets from the Red Rock Lakes Refuge were moved to

[1] Originally published in Wildfowl 24:27–32, 1973.

[2] Present address: 1563 E. Polnell Road, Oak Harbor, WA 98277.

Table 1. Trumpeter Swan populations south of Canada, 1932–68.

	Red Rock Lakes Refuge			Yellowstone Park			All other areas			Total, all areas		
	Adults	Cygnets	Total	Adults	Cygnets	Total	Adults	Cygnets	Total	Adults	Cygnets	Total
1932	19	7	26	29	2	31	9	3	12	57	12	69
1933	15	9	24	27	8	35	7	0	7	49	17	66
1934	16	26	42	16	17	33	16	6	22	48	49	97
1935	30	16	46	16	11	27	No census		—	46	27	73
1936	31	26	57	38	13	51	7	2	9	76	41	117
1937	34	51	85	38	26	64	9	0	9	81	77	158
1938	28	42	70	40	4	44	25	9	34	93	55	148
1939	50	59	109	47	17	64	26	0	26	123	76	199
1940	58	48	106	39	14	53	26	6	32	123	68	191
1941	52	44	96	44	15	59	47	10	57	143	69	212
1942	45	43	88			*	53	10	63	98	53	151
1943	88	25	113			*	49	9	58	137	34	171
1944	106	58	164	41	8	49	60	6	66	207	72	279
1945	113	50	163			*	67	5	72	180	55	235
1946	124	46	170	43	8	51	122	18	140	289	72	361
1947	131	49	180	45	8	53	116	3	119	292	60	352
1948	121	73	194	49	13	62	142	20	162	312	106	418
1949	132	61	193	54	21	75	162	21	183	348	103	451
1950	106	40	146	57	16	73	140	17	157	303	73	376
1951	170	76	246	63	11	74	184	31	215	417	118	535
1952	184	55	239	58	10	68	236	28	264	478	93	571
1953	211	38	249	51	10	61	216	51	267	478	99	577
1954	352	28	380	64	23	87	144	31	175	560	82	642
1955	242	41	283	58	10	68	195	44	239	495	95	590
1956	293	39	332	48	9	57	166	33	199	507	81	588
1957	159	45	204	44	16	60	196	28	224	399	89	488
1958	270	40	310	64	18	82	231	80	311	565	138	703
1959	271	40	311	62	8	70	249	51	300	582	99	681
1960	163	34	197	56	7	63	353	53	406	572	94	666
1961	155	14	169	71	3	74	310	66	376	536	83	619
1962	179	53	232	44	7	51	296	56	352	519	116	635
1963	145	122	275	49	7	56	294	98	392	488	227	715
1964	180	22	202	61	8	69	458	35	493	699	65	764
1965	190	16	206	60	5	65	433	78	511	683	99	782
1966	240	54	294	57	12	69	418	99	517	713	165	878
1967	184	20	204	55	2	57	464	71	535	701	93	794
1968	155	90	245	57	4	61	489	112	601	701	206	907

* No census.

the National Elk Refuge at Jackson, Wyoming, approximately 160 km south. During the next 3 years, six more cygnets were released among these original four. In 1944, 6 years after the initial release, a pair nested successfully and raised one cygnet. From this modest beginning swans quickly filled the available breeding habitat in western Wyoming and adjacent Idaho. The population has been more or less stabilized in this area since about 1950.

Other transplants initiated at about the same time took much longer to bear fruit. Between 1939 and 1955 a total of 137 Trumpeters were translocated from Red Rock Lakes to the Malheur National Wildlife Refuge in southeastern Oregon, and eighty-four were moved to Ruby Lake National Wildlife Refuge in northeastern Nevada between 1949 and 1955. The first successful nesting in each of these areas occurred in 1958 from 3-year-old swans which had arrived as cygnets

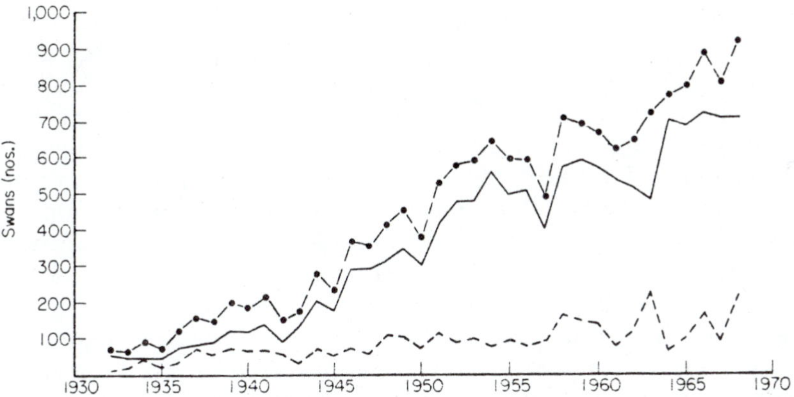

Fig. 1. Trumpeter Swan population, south of Canada, 1932–68. ——, Adults; – – –, cygnets; – · – · – ·, total swans.

in the 1955 transplant. As happened with the earlier transplant on the National Elk Refuge in Wyoming, these swans soon utilized the nesting habitat available to them, not only on the refuges but in surrounding marshes, and have maintained static populations for several years.

The most recent successful transplant in this general area of the continent was at the Turnbull National Wildlife Refuge in eastern Washington. Thirty-six swans from Red Rock Lakes were released at Turnbull from 1964 through 1966. The first brood was raised from one of these pairs in 1967. Since then, nesting has occurred off the refuge as well, up to 32 km from the original release site. As in the west, limited habitat will not allow for a greatly expanded population in eastern Washington.

Although Nevada and southern Oregon, where Trumpeter Swans are now breeding in limited numbers are both outside the historical breeding range of this species, and eastern Washington is at the western limit, much was learned from these initial attempts that has facilitated reintroductions elsewhere. Banko (1960) was of the opinion that the chief factor contribuing failure in the early transplanting efforts was the practice of pinioning and confining the flock to a single large pool. Intraspecific strife and spatial competition not only created a situation unfavourable for breeding, but it led to significant losses from accident and disease. On the other hand, liberating the transplanted individuals unrestricted into the large open marsh resulted in the liberated birds quickly dispersing and they disappeared.

Consistent success has since been achieved, with transplanted Trumpeters breeding as early as their third year of life. The technique consists of transplanting cygnets prior to flight in September. The birds are wing-clipped to render them flightless throughout the winter and until the following moult, and held semi-captive in spring-fed enclosures. Supplemental feeding is provided as required. This method allows the swan to become familiar with the new environment slowly and to develop a traditional attachment to the area. When they regain flight the following summer, they are then free to explore the surrounding marshes from a home base and complete their maturation under entirely natural conditions.

With little change for more than limited ultimate success on the western edge of the Trumpeters' breeding range, U.S.

Fish and Wildlife Service biologists turned their attention eastward to the plains States. The initial reintroduction of Trumpeters into this heartland of their ancestral breeding range was made on the Lacreek National Wildlife Refuge, in south-central South Dakota, which contains about 40 sq. km, over half of which is water and marsh. Despite severe winter weather, fresh water flows through the refuge during the entire year from constant springs in nearby hills. A large winter holding pen was built, with food-hoppers to supplement the natural feed available in the open marsh.

In the 3-year period 1960–62, a total of fifty-seven cygnets (twenty, seventeen, and twenty respectively) were transplanted from Red Rock Lakes to Lacreek during the month of September each year. Each of the three flocks was wing-clipped upon arrival and released into the holding pen. During the summer of 1963 two pairs from the 1960 release raised young on the refuge. These same two pairs plus another again produced young on the refuge in 1964 and three other pairs nested successfully off the refuge. One nest was located about 96 km north and another 29 km southeast. The third nesting pair was not located but they returned to the refuge in the fall with cygnets. This population has continued to prosper. In the summer of 1969 there were six nests on the Lacreek Refuge and four others located within a radius of 96 km. Eighty swans returned to the refuge that fall, but only seventy survived the winter.

The success at numerous Federal refuges under a wide variety of conditions indicated that the technique of managing transplanted populations into sustained reproduction was sound and warranted wider application. Thus was born the first Trumpeter Swan restoration project in the United States (outside zoological parks) by an agency other than the Federal Government. The Hennepin County Park Reserve District has established a producing flock of Trumpeters from Red Rock Lakes stock in Carver County, Minnesota, about 25 miles from the City of Minneapolis. The first pair was acquired by the Park Reserve in 1966, twenty more in 1967 and ten cygnets in 1968. From this beginning the first known nesting of Trumpeter Swans in Minnesota since the 1880s resulted in the hatching of one cygnet on 21 June 1969. Although this cygnet disappeared shortly before it was a month old this initial attempt gave reason for optimism. In 1970 a pair again nested on the Park Reserve (presumably the same pair) and hatched five cygnets. Another pair nested on a 12-ha marsh outside the Reserve. Unfortunately, there is an unnecessarily high loss of swans in this area, probably resulting from a large human population oriented toward outdoor recreation both summer and winter.

Inasmuch as several healthy, widely-scattered populations of Trumpeter Swans now exist and the species is no longer threatened, it is desirable, both for the welfare of the birds and for public enjoyment, to re-establish swans at other locations within their former breeding range. In order to ensure maximum success and provide adequately for the welfare of the birds, guidelines are being established for all new releases.

Several important factors are limiting the rate at which Trumpeter Swans can be restored throughout their traditional breeding range. Experience has shown that, to achieve reproduction at the earliest possible age, swans should be transplanted as cygnets prior to attaining flight, preferably in September of their natal year.

The Trumpeter Swan has large territorial requirements during the breeding season, free of competition from its own kind and relative isolation from human intrusion. Marsh habitat must be reasonably stable with no marked fluctuations in water level. These basic requirements have been observed in all populations of Trumpeters throughout their range, including Alaska. For example, it has been estimated that the 20 sq. km of marsh habitat on the Lacreek Refuge will successfully accommodate no more than ten Trumpeter nesting territories. Marshall (1968) states that . . . it appears as though the total number of nesting Trumpeters which can be supported on the 180,000-acre Malheur Refuge is only about 50. Malheur Refuge is one of the largest in the 48 contiguous States and contains the largest natural marsh remaining in the west outside Alaska. In his extensive study at Red Rock Lakes, Banko (1960) found the highest concentration of nests on a shallow lake where the irregular shoreline combined with numberous stable sedge islands to provide the greatest variety and interspersion of water and marsh habitat. This lake of about 200 ha supported seven nesting pairs of Trumpeters in 1957, about 30 ha of territory per pair. On a deeper, less attractive lake of 600 ha on the refuge only ten pairs nested, about 60 ha per pair. Banko noted that a certain amount of water space, presumably to meet flight take-off requirements, appears necessary within each territory and the large number of potholes over the refuge which often produce considerable food are not an important segment of the breeding habitat. We found territorial requirements in Alaska, where crowding has not yet become a serious factor, to be generally larger than at Red Rock Lakes and the other refuges.

Perhaps one of the most serious limiting factors to population growth and a more rapid extension of range is the non-migrant trait of Trumpeter Swans which live south of Canada. It is ironic that this inhibiting trait may well have been the most important single factor that saved the species from extinction. Those swans which were forced by weather to migrate annually from the northern breeding grounds in Canada south into the path of American settlers were soon extirpated, whereas the sedentary birds in the high mountain valleys of southwestern Montana were much less subject to man's relentless pursuit and, thus, survived.

A by-product of the non-migrant trait of Trumpeters, as they are gradually restored farther north across their ancestral range, is the necessity to provide them with adequate food and open water during the winter months. Up to a point, food can be supplied in any quantity that economics and logistics allow. But an adequate supply of open water, in the absence of natural springs, is next to impossible especially from the Canadian border northward east of the Rocky Mountains. A wintering population now numbering about 400 Trumpeters is maintained through an artificial feeding programme on Lonesome Lake in British Columbia (lat 52°30′N). The source of these birds is conjectural at present. It seems likely that they derive from the Alaska breeding grounds, however, inasmuch as there are no known breeding populations of that size in British Columbia. Be that as it may, a wintering flock of 400 swans maintained artificially in the north is cause for concern. Not only is it costly and difficult to supply adequate food at such a remote location, but such a large concentration of birds under artificial conditions with a limited water supply might be conducive to serious outbreaks of disease.

The Trumpeter Swans which nest in

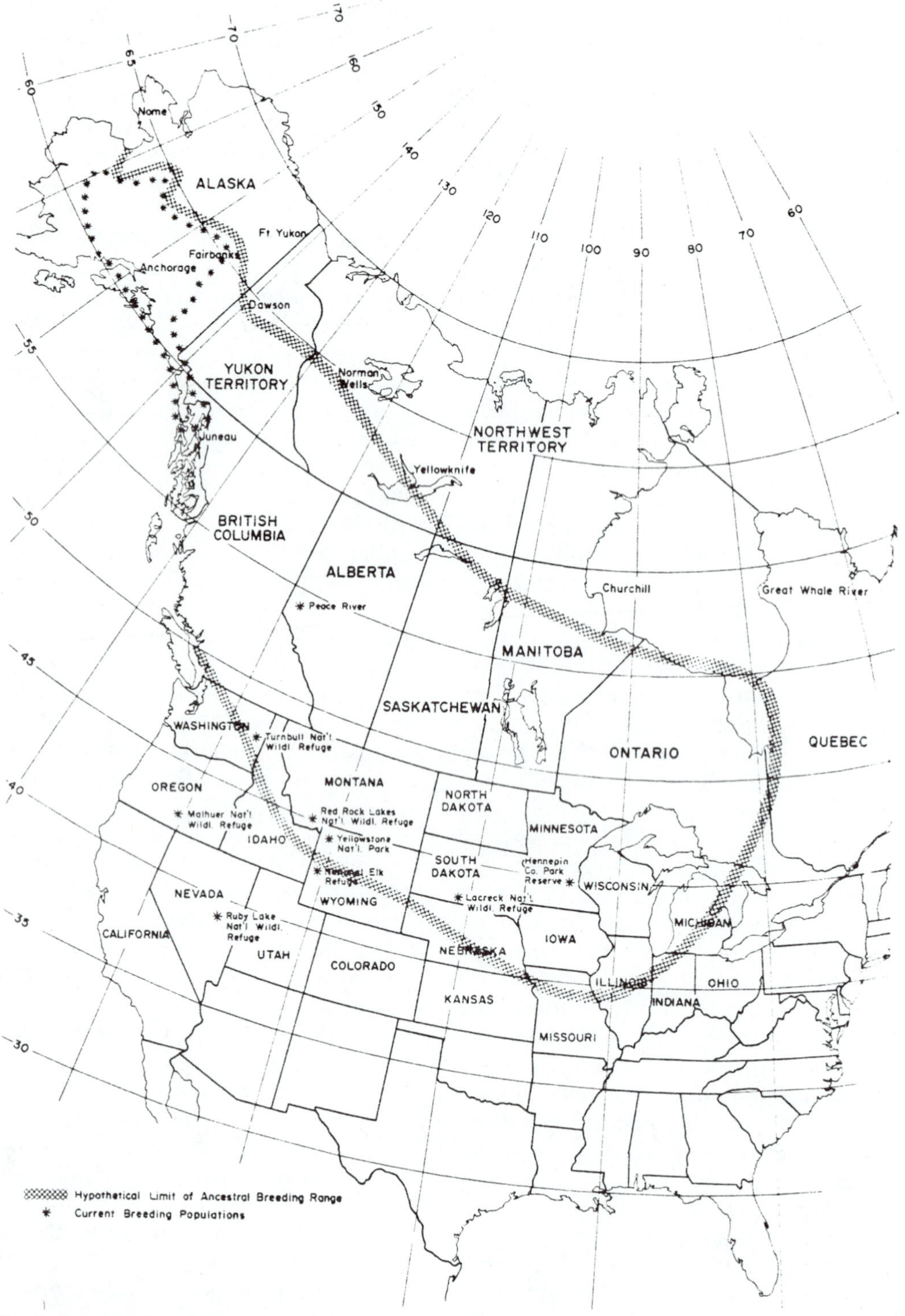

Fig. 2. Trumpeter Swan breeding boundaries.

Alaska must migrate as their breeding marshes are frozen from late September through April. However, they tend to move down the Pacific Coast only as far as necessary to find adequate wintering conditions. In recent years, as that population has grown to an estimated 3,500–4,000 birds, some Trumpeters move south as far as the mouth of the Columbia River which was part of their traditional wintering ground prior to settlement of the west coast (Hansen et al. 1971) (Fig. 2).

If a migrating tradition could be re-established in the Trumpeter Swan and adequate propagating techniques developed, the greatest potential for restoring this species in relatively large numbers lies in the prairie provinces of Canada north of the current agricultural belt. This area appeared to contain the greatest abundance of Trumpeters prior to white man's exploitation and the potential for favourable production remains. Large, stable marshes in a wilderness setting are available in reasonable numbers and human disturbance during the critical nesting season would be minimal.

Some discussion has centered around the possibility of using Alaskan stock with its migratory tradition, in lieu of the sedentary Red Rock Lakes' Trumpeters, to accelerate the northward spread of the species into Canada. Although this may seem to be meritorious at a hasty glance, there may be an overriding reason against it. From the detailed studies conducted both at Red Rock Lakes and in Alaska, it appears that these two widely-separated populations of Trumpeters may be distinct subspecies. There are significant physical differences, the Alaska Trumpeters being larger, starting from the egg. Based on a limited amount of banding and colour marking in both populations, we have no evidence of an interchange between the two. It appears likely that these two populations have evolved distinct from each other.

As long as the possibility of subspeciation between these diverse populations exists, or until disproved, there seems to be no justification for such a major tampering.

One possibility remains. A small, apparently static, breeding population of Trumpeters exists in the Peace River area northwest of Edmonton, Alberta, in Canada. This population numbers approximately 100 birds. It has been speculated that these swans may contribute to the wintering population at Lonesome Lake in British Columbia. From banding of a few swan families on the Peace River breeding grounds, subsequent recoveries at Red Rock Lakes and in the Dakotas indicate that these Trumpeters move south down the eastern side of the Rocky Mountains instead of west (Mackay 1957). In fact, attrition from illegal hunting may be the limiting factor to the natural expansion of these population, just as it inhibits population growth elsewhere.

Movement some 1,760 km south from their natal marshes during two consecutive autumns subsequent to banding shows a rather firm migrating tradition in this Peace River population. This, then, could provide the proper nucleus stock from which to re-establish Trumpeter Swans on their northern ancestral marshes.

The task would be neither simple nor quickly accomplished. The techniques for transplanting cygnets and successfully initiating reproduction in 3-year-old swans in the south of Canada may not be applicable in the north. Until the reasons why the Peace River population remains more or less static are identified and corrected, if possible, there may be too few cygnets to risk further loss through unsuccessful experimentation. Meanwhile it is imperative that adequate protection be afforded to all the nucleus flocks we have established so that the species can increase and spread naturally to its innate potential. A continuing campaign must be maintained to develop public awareness of and sympathy for the Trumpeter Swan restoration project. The physical characteristics of a swan in flight should be so well indoctrinated in hunters that mistaken identity can no longer be an excuse for shooting one. For example, in early October 1971, a mated pair of Trumpeter Swans from the newly established population in the Hennepin County Park Reserve District were mistakenly shot for snow geese when they wandered beyond the refuge boundary. To his credit, however, the errant hunter reported himself to the authorities when he realized his mistake.

To see Trumpeter Swans once again complete the array of North American wildfowl in their traditional manner will be worth all the ingenuity and whatever effort man can muster.

LITERATURE CITED

BANKO, W. E. 1960. The Trumpeter Swan. N. Amer. Fauna No. 63. Fish and Wildlife Service, Wash., D.C.

HANSEN, H. A., P. E. K. SHEPHERD, J. G. KING, AND W. A. TROYER. 1971. The Trumpeter Swan in Alaska. J. Wildl. Mgmt. Monograph Series No. 26.

MACKAY, R. H. 1957. Movement of Trumpeter Swans shown by band returns and observations. Condor 59:339.

MARSHALL, D. B. 1968. Return of the Trumpeter Swan. Naturalist J. Nat. Hist. Soc. Minn. 19.

MONNIE, J. B. 1964. A successful reintroduction of the Trumpeter Swan to its former prairie breeding range. Trans. 26th Mid. Wildl. Conf., Dec. 9, 1964.

PRODUCTIVITY AND MANAGEMENT OF FERAL MUTE SWANS IN CHESAPEAKE BAY

JAN G. REESE, Box 298, St. Michaels, Maryland 21663

Abstract: One or two mated pairs of pinioned mute swans (*Cygnus olor*) escaped from impoundments along tributaries of east central Chesapeake Bay in 1962. These feral swans and their offspring have bred successfully in the wild each year since and increased their numbers to about 151 during the last decade. In the past 7 years, the breeding pairs hatched 54 percent of their eggs, fledged 86 percent of their young, and achieved 80 percent nesting success. This has caused a rapid population increase which presents waterfowl biologists with new problems in management. Ecological implications for the Chesapeake Bay are discussed.

J. WILDL. MANAGE. 39(2):280–286

European mute swans have established themselves in Michigan and New England after being released or having escaped into the wild. These adaptable, highly productive, and aggressive birds have increased in numbers from a single pair to over 500 birds both in Rhode Island (Willey 1968) and in Traverse City, Michigan (Gelston, unpublished data), since 1948. With rapidly expanding swan populations, state waterfowl biologists are faced with several new problems in management.

In the Chesapeake Bay, a similar population increase is underway. During a destructive northeasterly storm on 7 March 1962, unusually high tides enabled one or two mated pairs of pinioned mute swans to escape from their waterfront impoundments at private estates along the Miles River in Talbot County, Maryland. These swans successfully bred in the wild that summer and increased their numbers severalfold during the following decade. A preliminary report on expansion of this population was given in Reese (1969).

This study was self-financed with assistance from G. Fenwick, P. Fowler, P. Gorman, M. LaMotte, and D. Meritt. W. J. L. Sladen, Johns Hopkins University, supplied plastic coded neck collars and advice. W. L. Gelston generously loaned his unpublished 1970–72 data for Michigan mute swans. R. K. Price and R. Vojvoda made timely observations and notes of swans nesting near their homes.

METHODS

Established territories and active nests were visited six or more times during each breeding season. Nest contents and behavior of the adults were recorded on each visit. Eggs were marked with a felt-tipped pen when first observed, and addled eggs and dead swans were collected for autopsy. Personal observations of nesting swans were solicited from local residents. Since 1971, 127 swans were marked with U. S. Fish and Wildlife Service aluminum tarsus bands and with plastic neck collars. Neck collars conformed to the continental swan neck collar scheme devised by W. J. L. Sladen. Collars were black, engraved several times around in contrasting color with a code of two letters followed by two numbers. This code could be read as far away as 350 m with a 25× spotting scope and enabled recognition of individual swans without recapture.

RESULTS

Nesting Periods

Since tributaries in the area seldom freeze over, mated pairs remain in their

Originally published in J. Wildl. Manage. 39(2):280–286, 1975.

home range year-round. Defense of defined territories begins in late February as mated pairs chase their young of the year and any other waterfowl from territories. The earliest nest building was observed on 15 March. Extreme egg dates during the study were 13 March and 23 June, with 61 percent of the nests having eggs between 9 and 16 April. The earliest date young were seen was 4 May. Young remained with their parents until the following nesting season. Between 11 and 25 May, 51 percent of the pairs studied had young; fewer nests with young were found thereafter.

Nests

After making necessary repairs, most swans use the previous year's nest if it is basically intact. The female does most of the nest building and is the principal incubator of the eggs. Nests were made of coarse grasses piled in a mound about 0.5 m above the high tide mark and were located in *Spartina alterniflora* and *S. patens* marshes just back from the shoreline along brackish tributaries of eastern Chesapeake Bay. High tides were known to have destroyed six nests during the study. Of the 45 nests studied, 96 percent contained eggs and 80 percent had young (Table 1). Willey (1968:50) found 76 percent of the nests he studied contained eggs. Gelston (Unpublished data) reported 61 percent of the nests in his study had young. In British studies, Eltringham (1966:204,206) observed young at 62 percent of the nests he studied and Minton (1968:55) found young in 58 percent.

Eggs

Average clutch size ranged from 4.2 to 8.0 annually and was 6.1 for the 7 years (Table 1). This average is comparable with those reported by Willey (1968), Campbell (1960), Eltringham (1963), Reynolds (1965), and Perrins and Reynolds (1967). Gelston (Unpublished data) reported an average clutch size of only 4.4. Incubation period ranged from 34 to 37 days for 10 eggs, 7 of which hatched at 35 days.

The percentage of eggs hatching from 1968 through 1974 varied from 27 to 75 percent annually and averaged 54 percent for the 7 years (Table 1). This success was better than the 48 percent Gelston (Unpublished data) found in Michigan but was far below the 87 percent given by Willey (1968:35) and 94 percent reported by Reynolds (1965:128). The percentage of eggs resulting in fledglings averaged 46 percent for the 7 years; this was slightly below the single year value of 49 percent observed by Willey (1968:39) and 48 percent found by Reynolds (1965:128), but well above the 28 percent reported by Gelston (Unpublished data).

Table 2 shows some of the reasons why 132 (46 percent) eggs failed to hatch. Most notable were eggs disappearing between nest visits and those inundated or washed away by high tides. All the eggs disappearing involved only part of a clutch, suggesting accidental breakage by the incubating bird or theft for souvenirs. Perrins and Reynolds (1967), Willey (1968), and Gelston (Unpublished data) believed flooding was a major cause of egg failure. Minton (1968) found harassment by humans was a primary cause of egg failure.

Young

Young fledged between 120 and 145 days with the 5 best estimates between 125 and 132 days. Of the 132 young observed, 81 percent were gray phase. The average brood size for the 7-year period was 4.3 (Table 1), which was well above the 3.1 to 3.5 observed by Perrins and Reynolds

Table 1. Nesting success of mute swans in Chesapeake Bay, 1968–74.

	1968	1969	1970	1971	1972	1973	1974	Mean	Totals
Pairs on territories	3	5	7	7	8	10	10		50
Active nests	3	5	3	7	7	10	10		45
Nests with eggs[a]	3(100)	4(80)	3(100)	7(100)	6(86)	10(100)	10(100)	6.1(96)	43
Nests with young[a]	3(100)	4(80)	3(100)	7(100)	5(71)	5(50)	9(90)	5.1(80)	36
Eggs known	17	19	30	40	48	71	61		286
Eggs hatched[b]	7(41)	12(63)	14(47)	30(75)	26(54)	19(27)	46(75)	22.0(54)	154
Eggs fledged[b]	7(41)	11(58)	11(37)	27(68)	19(40)	16(23)	41(67)	18.9(46)	132
Average clutch size	4.2[c]	4.7	6.0[d]	5.7	8.0	6.4[e]	6.1	6.1[f]	
Percent hatchlings fledged	100	92	79	90	73	84	89	86	
Average brood size	2.3	3.0	4.7	4.3	5.2	1.9	4.6	4.3	
Average number of fledglings per nest with eggs	2.3	2.7	3.7	3.9	3.2	1.6	4.1	3.1	

[a] Figure in parentheses indicates percent, based on active nests.
[b] Figure in parentheses indicates percent, based on eggs known.
[c] Based on 4 clutches—one pair laid 2 clutches.
[d] Based on 5 clutches—two pairs laid 2 clutches.
[e] Based on 11 clutches—one pair laid 2 clutches.
[f] Based on 47 clutches—four pairs laid 2 clutches.

(1967:81), Minton (1968:57), and Gelston (Unpublished data), but below the 4.8 given by Eltringham (1963:21) and 5.2 found by Willey (1968:35). Of the hatchlings observed, 86 percent fledged. This success was much higher than the 49 to 51 percent reported by Reynolds (1965:128), Willey (1968:39), and Gelston (Unpublished data). The average number of fledglings (young at least 110 days old) per active nest (a nest with eggs) was 3.1. This ratio measured the productivity of the population and was well above the 2.0 to 2.5 found in British studies (Rawcliffe 1958:52, Eltringham 1966:204, Perrins and Reynolds 1967:80, Minton 1968:57) and far above the 1.2 and 1.6 given for studies in this country (Willey 1968:37,39, Gelston, unpublished data).

Mortality

Mortality of young ranged from zero to 27 percent annually and averaged 14 percent for the 7 years. This is considerably

Table 2. Mute swan egg losses, Chesapeake Bay, 1968–74.

	1968	1969	1970	1971	1972	1973	1974	Total
Disappeared between nest visits		7	2	6	13	16	5	49
Flooded by high tides	4		13	3		13	2	35
Addled			1	1	2	6	3	13
Abandoned[a]					7	3		10
Found as fragments in nest						5	3	8
Destroyed by children	6							6
Stolen						5		5
Found outside nest						2	2	4
Accidentally broken[b]						2		2
Totals	10	7	16	10	22	52	15	132

[a] Incubating female died of aspergillosis.
[b] Male stepped on eggs while defending nest against investigator.

below averages between 41 and 51 percent reported by Reynolds (1965:128), Ogilvie (1967:68), Perrins and Reynolds (1967: 82), Willey (1968:39) and Gelston (Unpublished data). Nearly all mortality involved young less than three weeks old and occurred between my visits to territories and nests. As a result, the causes could not be determined. During the seven years, two people reported seeing single dead hatchlings on nests shortly after the brood left the nest for the first time. Three people observed turtles pulling young beneath the water. Willey (1968) and Gelston (Unpublished data) found snapping turtles (*Chelydra serpentina*) a serious factor in mortality of young. Snapping turtles were common in fresh headwaters of tributaries in the study area, and huge populations of diamondback terrapins (*Malaclemys terrapin*) were present throughout the tributaries. Harassment and theft by people, terrestrial predation, lead poisoning, and chilling during cold, wet weather are important causes of mortality in young (Reynolds 1965, Minton 1968, Willey 1968, Gelston, unpublished data) and are suspected of occurring in the Chesapeake swans.

Of seven dead adult swans examined, three had heavy fungus infections in the lungs and air sacs. These infestations were identified as typical *Aspergillus* nodules after microscopic examination at Johns Hopkins University. One swan was killed by a red fox (*Vulpes fulva*), one died from dog bites, one was shot, and one died from unknown causes. Collision with utility wires, severe weather, lead poisoning, oil spills, fighting with other swans, and starvation were important factors responsible for mortality of adult swans in other studies (Jennings et al. 1961, Eltringham 1963, Ogilvie 1967, Willey 1968, Gelston, unpublished data) and may be applicable to Chesapeake Bay swans.

Renesting

During the seven years, three pairs of swans were involved in four incidences of renesting after their original nest and eggs washed away during abnormally high tides. An additional pair incubated an addled egg for 30 days after people placed the egg in remains of the original nest that had been washed out by high tides. Average size of first and second clutches for all renestings was 6.0 and 5.5, respectively. Reynolds (1965) and Willey (1968) found only one or two incidences of relaying, but Minton (1968) found renesting in all years of his study. Data from renesting were included in Table 1, but the renestings were not counted as additional nests.

Desertion

In mid-May 1972, the female of one nesting pair was suspected of deserting her seven, three-day-old hatchlings and mate. The male stayed with the young about six weeks; then he also disappeared. This was the first time either member of the pair nested. Both had been banded the previous year as subadults. The nest was located directly in front of a waterfront home whose occupants watched the swans daily but never observed any abnormal behavior prior to desertion. I was unable to find either marked adult on any subsequent surveys of the area that year, but the male of the pair appeared with a new mate in a new territory 8 km away the following spring. The deserted young eluded two of my surveys after departure of the male but eventually reappeared trying to join another family 10 km away on 20 July. During this time three of the original seven young had disappeared. The remaining four young were captured and penned after being rescued from attacks by the foster parents. Minton (1968) observed a similar situation, but one of the deserted young was accepted by foster parents. Gelston (Unpublished data) reported several incidences of parent desertion, most of which he associated with aberrant young. I saw no abnormalities in the seven deserted young. In 1969 and 1971, I found a young swan with a permanently injured wing, but in neither instance was it deserted by its parents.

Dispersal

Since 1970, mute swans have been seen in all the Maryland tidewater counties north of latitude 38° 40′N. All of these sightings involved nonbreeding swans, and most took place in late February or early March when mated pairs begin courtship and aggressive defense of their territories. Neck-collared individuals have been seen 72 km north and 17 km south of their point of banding. Nonbreeding swans remain dispersed until July when they form molting groups in favorite marshy areas.

Mated pairs seldom were seen away from their home range. Temporary displacements of mated pairs were observed in mid-July, but all returned to their respective home ranges in late fall.

DISCUSSION

Mute swans may pair when two or three years old and breed for the first time when three or more years old (Perrins and Reynolds 1967, Minton 1968, Willey 1968). Progeny of the escaped swans should have begun to breed in 1965 or 1966 if they hatched in 1962. This was suggested by Reese (1969), who first observed additional pairs in 1966. Table 1 shows that territorial pairs increased annually after 1968. A rapidly increasing population is indicated by the fact that 80 percent of the nests were successful (nests where at least one young was fledged) and a productivity ratio of 3.1 was attained, both values far exceeding those reported in other studies.

From banding recoveries, Ogilvie (1967: 68) computed an annual mortality of 39 percent for British mute swans after one year of age. If the Chesapeake Bay swans had a similar mortality rate, they presently (late 1974) would number approximately 92 birds. I saw as many as 71 mute swans at one time in the fall of 1972, when a 39 percent mortality rate would have meant only 60 birds were in the population. Furthermore, 85 percent of the swans neck-collared in 1971 through 1973 were resighted a year later; however, 13 swans are known to have lost their neck collars shortly after banding. These facts suggest a very low annual mortality for the postfledging portion of the population.

A marked mute swan from Rhode Island was seen in the Chesapeake Bay in 1967, suggesting immigration to the Bay from the New England population (Willey 1968). The Rhode Island swan banding program was discontinued in 1968 and the Michigan mute swans have never been banded; thus, any immigration to the Chesapeake from those populations would go undetected.

The estimated population of mute swans in Chesapeake Bay in 1974 was 151 birds, based on reproductive and postfledging success and census counts made during that year. The population may exceed this estimate, however, with the possibility of immigration from the New England and Michigan populations.

IMPLICATIONS

The mute swan presents several problems to be considered by Chesapeake Bay waterfowl biologists as the population of this exotic species increases. The influence of a large sedentary mute swan population on our native waterfowl is unknown. Most important are whistling swans (*Olor columbianus*), for over half the continental population of 90,000 winters in the Chesapeake Bay. Both species of swans are primarily vegetarians as are most native puddle ducks and geese. Mute swans do not migrate and thus consume Chesapeake Bay vegetation year-round. Willey (1968:61) found that mute swans consume at least 3.8 kg (wet weight) of aquatic vegetation per day. Gillham (1956) reported mute swans are wasteful and destroy large amounts of aquatic vegetation when feeding. They also dislodge shallow-rooted species and remove vast amounts of vegetation for nest building. Since 1970, whistling swans have been seen feeding in fields, suggesting preferred aquatic vegetation is scarce in the Bay. Mute swans are very aggressive towards other waterfowl and defend their nesting territories from March to October. Eltringham (1963), Willey (1968), Stone and Marsters (1970), and Gelston (Unpublished data) reported mute swan attacks on other waterfowl, some of which were fatal.

Some mute swans exhibit interspecific aggression outside the breeding season (Willey 1968, Stone and Marsters 1970). May (1947) watched a mated pair confine a group of intruder swans to less than 4,000 m^2 of a pond for 11 weeks. During the seven years, three waterfront residents reported wintering whistling swan and Canada geese (*Branta canadensis*) were seldom tolerated in the home range of paired mute swans near their property. I have not observed any serious attacks by mute swans on other waterfowl; Eltringham (1963), Willey (1968), and Gelston (Unpublished data) believed attacks are rare in an otherwise peaceful coexistence with other waterfowl.

The relationship between mute swans and man is one of contrasts. Citizens claiming guardianship of the swans nesting near their homes violently opposed disturbing and banding the swans. The mute swans' tameness, acceptance of food handouts, and graceful appearance may be responsible for engendering such strong aesthetic attachment. In contrast, encounters between young children and male swans defending nests or young have resulted in injury to swans and destruction of eggs and nests. Swans nesting along park pathways or near waterfront homes may cause injury by attacking children or adults passing into the swan's territory. Swans which are fed regularly can become belligerent if the food supply is discontinued (Willey 1968). In Rhode Island, Willey (1968) found people who considered mute swans a nuisance and such a threat to native waterfowl that they initiated a campaign of egg destruction. Fishermen consider mute swans a nuisance because they eat chum bait, swallow lures, and become entangled in and break fishing lines (Eltringham 1963, Gelston, unpublished data). Overhead utility cables may be broken by a swan collision, causing local loss of electrical power.

Destruction of aquatic vegetation not only lessens the amount available to native waterfowl but also removes necessary cover for insects and fish. Losses of vegetation are not restricted to aquatic species. Gillham (1956), Berglund et al. (1963), Eltringham (1963), and Willey (1968) reported mute swans feeding in marsh meadows and fields. Gillham (1956) found swans selectively choose the most succulent marsh plants for consumption, pull up many grasses besides those eaten, and trample many others. The British Farmers' Union claimed mute swan damage to spring grasses was of serious economic concern in some portions of Great Britain (Eltringham 1963). Willey (1968) suspected water quality in public water supply reservoirs may deteriorate when feather and fecal matter accumulate from large flocks of mute swans.

State waterfowl biologists in Maryland have not established a program to study or regulate mute swans. In view of the potential disadvantages of a rapidly growing population of mute swans, it seems imperative that some authoritative agency be designated to study the ecological impact of this bird upon the Chesapeake Bay. In establishing a management program the most urgent needs are: (1) to undertake a study to determine what species and quantities of aquatic vegetation are being removed by mute swans in Chesapeake Bay, (2) to rigidly control productivity and dispersal of the present population, (3) to assign ownership of or responsibility for the mute swans to a proper authority, (4) to decide whether mute swans are to be protected for aesthetic reasons or hunted for game, and (5) to mount an educational campaign to inform the general public that mute swans are an exotic species presently not protected by any federal or Maryland laws and that there are potential dangers in permitting their continued existence in the Chesapeake Bay.

LITERATURE CITED

BERGLUND, B. E., K. CURRY-LINDAHL, H. LUTHER, V. OLSSON, W. RODHE, AND G. SELLERBERG. 1963. Ecological studies on the mute swan (*Cygnus olor*) in southeastern Sweden. Acta Vertebr. 2:167–288.

CAMPBELL, B. 1960. The mute swan census in England and Wales 1955–56. Bird Study 7 (4):208–223.

ELTRINGHAM, S. K. 1963. The British population of the mute swan in 1961. Bird Study 10(1):10–28.

———. 1966. The survival of mute swan cygnets. Bird Study 13(2):204–207.

GILLHAM, M. E. 1956. Feeding habits and seasonal movements of mute swans on two south Devon estuaries. Bird Study 3(3):205–212.

JENNINGS, A. R., E. J. L. SOULSBY, AND C. B. WAINWRIGHT. 1961. An outbreak of disease in mute swans at an Essex reservoir. Bird Study 8(1):19–24.

MAY, D. J. 1947. Notes on wintering territories of a pair of mute swans. Br. Birds 40:326–327.

MINTON, C. D. 1968. Pairing and breeding of mute swans. Wildfowl Trust Annu. Rep. 19: 41–60.

OGILVIE, M. A. 1967. Population changes and mortality of the mute swan in Britain. Wildfowl Trust Annu. Rep. 18:64–73.

PERRINS, C. M., AND C. M. REYNOLDS. 1967. A preliminary study of the mute swan (*Cygnus olor*). Wildfowl Trust Annu. Rep. 18:74–84.

RAWCLIFFE, C. P. 1958. The Scottish mute swan census 1955–56. Bird Study 5(2):45–55.

REESE, J. G. 1969. Mute swan breeding in Talbot County, Maryland. Maryland Birdlife 25 (1):14–16.

REYNOLDS, C. M. 1965. The survival of mute swan cygnets. Bird Study 12(2):128–129.

STONE, W. B., AND A. D. MARSTERS. 1970. Aggression among captive mute swans. New York Fish Game J. 17(1):50–52.

WILLEY, C. H. 1968. The ecology, distribution and abundance of the mute swan (*Cygnus olor*) in Rhode Island. M.S. Thesis. Univ. Rhode Island, Kingston. 93pp.

Accepted 11 October 1973.

SELECTED BIBLIOGRAPHY

Management and Economics: Establishing Local Populations

BENSON, D., AND S. D. BROWNE. 1972. Establishing breeding colonies of redheads in New York by releasing hand-reared birds. N.Y. Fish and Game J. 19(1):59–72.

BORDEN, R., AND H. A. HOCHBAUM. 1966. Gadwall seeding in New England. Trans. North Am. Wildl. Nat. Resour. Conf. 31:79–87.

CHABRECK, R. H., H. H. DUPUIE, AND D. J. BELSOM. 1975. Establishment of a resident breeding flock of Canada geese in Louisiana. Proc. Annu. Conf. S.E. Assoc. Game Fish Comm. 28:442–455.

DOTY, H. A., AND A. D. KRUSE. 1972. Techniques for establishing local breeding populations of wood ducks. J. Wildl. Manage. 36(2):428–435.

FOLEY, D. D., D. BENSON, L. W. DEGRAFF, AND E. R. HOLM. 1961. Waterfowl stocking in New York. N.Y. Fish Game J. 8(1):1.

GORE, J. F., AND C. J. BARSTOW. 1969. Status of a free flying, resident flock of Canada geese (*Branta canadensis*) in Tennessee. Proc. Annu. Conf. S.E. Assoc. Game Fish Comm. 23:101–104.

JONES, R. E., AND A. S. LEOPOLD. 1967. Nesting interference in a dense population of wood ducks. J. Wildl. Manage. 31(2):221–228.

LANE, P. W., G. W. BOND, JR., AND W. H. JULIAN, JR. 1968. Wood duck production and transplants on national wildlife refuges in the South Atlantic states. Proc. Annu. Conf. S.E. Assoc. Game Fish Comm. 22:202–208.

MCGILVREY, F. B. 1972. Increasing a wood duck nesting population by releases of pen-reared birds. Proc. Annu. Conf. S.E. Assoc. Game Fish Comm. 25:202–206.

MONNIE, J. B. 1966. Reintroduction of the trumpeter swan to its former prairie breeding range. J. Wildl. Manage. 30(4):691–696.

NELSON, H. K. 1963. Restoration of breeding Canada goose flocks in the north central states. Trans. North Am. Wildl. Conf. 28:133–150.

SELLERS, R. A. 1973. Mallard releases in understocked prairie pothole habitat. J. Wildl. Manage. 37(1):10–22.

SUGDEN, L. G. 1976. Experimental release of canvasbacks on breeding habitat. J. Wildl. Manage. 40(4):716–720.

Artificial Structures

USE OF NEST BOXES BY WOOD DUCKS IN MISSISSIPPI

THOMAS H. STRANGE, South Carolina Wildlife Resources Department, Columbia
EARL R. CUNNINGHAM, Bureau of Sport Fisheries and Wildlife, Memphis, Tennessee
JOHN W. GOERTZ, Department of Zoology, Louisiana Tech University, Ruston

Abstract: Nest data for wood ducks (*Aix sponsa*) were obtained from 55 to 253 boxes, checked from 1966 to 1969 at Yazoo National Wildlife Refuge, Glen Alan, Mississippi. Contingent factors such as amount of utilization, nest success, and predation were compared. As a supplementary project, 30 nest boxes were erected on Bayou D'Arbonne Lake, Louisiana, to determine the primary acceptance of nest boxes in an unmanaged area. A total of 15,273 eggs were laid in the nest boxes on Yazoo National Wildlife Refuge, and 6,036 ducklings left the boxes. Thirty-five natural cavities were located on 10 line transects, each 1 chain wide, and from 3,700 to 18,000 feet in length, but none of these cavities were used as nesting sites. Nineteen of the cavities were in willows (*Salix nigra*), the most abundant of the 22 species of trees found on the transects. The main predators of 1,292 wood duck eggs were the yellow-shafted flicker (*Colaptes auratus*), the raccoon (*Procyon lotor*), and the rat snake (*Elaphe obsoleta*).

This investigation involves a comparison of data obtained on the nesting of wood ducks in man-made nest boxes and includes a survey of the occurrence and availability of natural cavities in an area where boxes were available.

According to Weier (1966:91), "Little information is available on the species or sizes of trees most likely to contain suitable cavities." Others (Bent 1923, Grice and Rogers 1965:16) list the trees in which wood duck nests were found but did not indicate their relative abundance. Bellrose et al. (1964) found that the black oak (*Quercus velutina*) was the predominant species and the best cavity producer. Other studies (Baumgartner 1939, Gysel 1961) provided information on cavity formation, density, size, and usage, but these studies were not oriented toward management of wood ducks. In Missouri, Weier (1966:101, 104) studied cavity abundance in relation to tree species and size in different associations. Cavities were found to be most abundant in older upland hardwood associations such as elm–ash–maple (*Ulmus–Fraxinus–Acer*), even though these species were scarce on his study area. None of the cavities found in Weier's investigation were utilized by wood ducks during the nesting season.

A program of installing nest boxes for wood ducks has been under way on Yazoo National Wildlife Refuge since 1966. The program has been successful, with utilization exceeding 90 percent during 1 year and a known breeding population of wood ducks that increased over 100 percent in the first 3 years. This degree of utilization of nest boxes raises some questions with regard to the nesting of wood ducks in natural cavities. Are suitable natural cavities available? To what extent are these natural cavities supplementing production in nest boxes? If cavities are available and are being used, why did production not increase to a higher level previous to installation of the nest boxes? These questions must be considered before management by the use of nest boxes continues, for, although successful, this program is expensive.

With the above questions in mind, there were four objectives of our investigation: (1) to determine if and to what extent natural cavities were used by wood ducks on areas with nest boxes; (2) to consider the reproductive rates and losses of nests;

Originally published in J. Wildl. Manage. 35(4):786–793, 1971.

(3) to establish a basis for future forest management by determining the size, species, and priority of trees used; and (4) to determine the degree of acceptance of artificial nest structures by wood ducks in an area where nest boxes had not previously been available (Bayou D'Arbonne Lake).

We thank J. L. Savage and R. G. Strain, students at Louisiana Tech University, for their assistance in checking nest boxes and transects. Drs. B. J. Davis, Department of Zoology, and J. C. White, Department of Botany, Louisiana Tech University, reviewed the manuscript. This study was supported, in part, by the Bureau of Sport Fisheries and Wildlife, Louisiana Tech Wildlife Club, and Louisiana Tech University.

DESCRIPTION OF STUDY AREAS

Yazoo National Wildlife Refuge, containing 11,000 acres, is located in south-central Washington County, 25 miles south of Greenville, Mississippi. The area is characterized by flat to slightly undulating terrain with rich alluvial soils averaging 46 feet in depth. Yazoo is superimposed upon an old oxbow channel of the Mississippi River, with the main channel flowing 5 miles to the west. Containing some 4,500 acres, the old channel is about 15 miles long and 0.3 to 1.5 miles wide. The agricultural portion of the refuge, comprising 4,500 acres, contains numerous sloughs and waterfowl impoundments, which, along with the old oxbow channel, remain flooded most of the year. These sloughs are primarily cypress–willow (*Taxodium–Salix*) swamps. The lower elevations, perennially flooded, contain an abundance of aquatic plants in the open water areas (Cunningham 1969).

Bayou D'Arbonne Lake, located in Union Parish, Louisiana, 20 miles north of Ruston, contains some 15,000 acres of water. The construction of Bayou D'Arbonne Dam resulted in the flooding of hardwood and pine (*Pinus* spp.) forests and the eventual killing of the trees. The flooded areas away from the main channel of the lake are now tangled with stumps and snags of dead and dying trees. The surrounding lands are the typical rollings hills of north Louisiana with red, sandy soil and a predominance of pine trees. Stands of cypress and willow and other hardwoods such as water oak (*Quercus nigra*), willow oak (*Q. phellos*), sweet gum (*Liquidambar styraciflua*), elm (*Ulmus* spp.), and sycamore (*Platanus occidentalis*) are found in the upper and lower reaches of all streams that converge to form Bayou D'Arbonne.

MATERIALS AND METHODS

The first nest boxes were erected on Yazoo National Wildlife Refuge in the early months of 1966, with 20 of the total of 55 being erected in mid-March. Erection of additional boxes increased the total number of boxes to 135 in 1967, 202 in 1968, and 253 in 1969. Boxes used were the standard-size wooden boxes described by Bellrose (1955), constructed of 1-inch cypress lumber and erected on iron posts, usually with two boxes to each post. Most boxes were partially protected from terrestrial and aquatic predators by 30-inch conical sheet-metal shields or 24-gauge *sandwich*-type shields, 30 inches tall by approximately 16 inches wide as described by Cunningham (1969).

As a basis for comparing the economics of variously spaced nest boxes, three test sites were prepared during the winter of 1968–69. These sites consisted of 40, 24, and 23 boxes each, spaced in 50-foot grids, with two boxes erected back to back on each pole. The size of the nest grids ranged from one-third to three-quarters of an acre. Placed on dry land, yet in close proximity to brooding habitat, they were readily accessible from the tail gate of a pickup truck. Boxes over land and in close proximity to one another were more readily available to the investigator, thereby saving both time and funds. Some of the pole-box units were transferred from other areas to form the grids.

The boxes on Bayou D'Arbonne Lake were erected during January 1969. These and the Yazoo boxes were checked every 10–14 days throughout the nesting season. Boxes were erected in groups of five, in several different habitats, ranging from heavily wooded sloughs to open water of the lake proper. All were nailed onto trees over water at an average height of 12 feet—to discourage inquisitive fisherman. Predator shields were not used. All of these boxes were reached by boat.

A search for natural cavities at Yazoo was accomplished by laying out belt transects along compass lines over the entire refuge. Ten of these transects, covering all types of land area found on the refuge, were laid out equal distances apart. Six transects ran east and west across the lower part of the refuge, which is composed largely of agricultural fields; four transects ran north and south across the upper end of the old horseshoe lake, known as Swan Lake. All transects thus ran perpendicular to the bodies of water. Transects, 1-chain wide, varied from 3,700 feet to 18,000 feet in length.

Species composition and size of timber were sampled by tallying trees within the transects. All trees with a dbh of 9.5 inches were tallied. Cavity searching was done by two to four men walking along the transects. All cavities found were termed suitable or unsuitable for wood ducks, according to the combined size of the entrance and nesting platform. For wood ducks, the minimum acceptable dimensions for the entrance of cavities in use were 3 × 4 inches (Grice and Rogers 1965), and the minimum dimensions of a nest cavity in use were 5 × 7 inches (Bellrose et al. 1964). Usage of cavities by wood ducks was determined by the presence of nesting materials such as down. Many of the cavities located were unsuitable because they had open tops and could easily fill with water.

RESULTS AND DISCUSSION

Number of Boxes Available

One or two nest boxes were periodically checked for data at over 100 different stations on Yazoo National Wildlife Refuge and at 30 stations on Bayou D'Arbonne Lake. The results of these observations are shown in Table 1. The data from the 87 nest boxes erected in colonies are also recorded.

Boxes were erected on Yazoo as a management procedure to study their effect on the breeding population of wood ducks. Refuge files from 1960 to 1965 indicated an average breeding population of 30 to 35 pairs. As indicated by the number of boxes used, there may have been as many as 35 pairs using the area in 1966. The increase in the number of boxes used each year, through 1969, tends to indicate that the population increased yearly. This increase may have been the direct result of increasing the number of boxes available for use by ducks as well as the placement of boxes in new areas, including 2,000 acres added to the refuge in 1966.

Number of Boxes Used

McLaughlin and Grice (1952:245) indicated that unless 50 percent of the boxes

Table 1. Production of wood ducks in nest boxes at Yazoo National Wildlife Refuge and Bayou D'Arbonne Lake.

Location and Year	Number of Boxes Available	Number of Boxes Used	Number of Eggs Laid	Number of Eggs Hatched	Percentage of Eggs Hatched	Number of Ducklings Leaving Boxes	Number of Eggs Destroyed by Predators	Percentage of Eggs Destroyed by Predators
Yazoo (isolated boxes)								
1966	55	35	599	548	91	547	—	—
1967	135	120	2,652	1,659	63	1,648	—	—
1968	202	194	4,986	2,016	40	1,894	—	—
1969	166	160	5,971	1,866	31	1,786	691	10
Yazoo (colonial boxes)								
1969								
East Gin Slough	24	20	335	44	13	44	213	64
West Gin Slough	23	12	190	10	5	10	41	22
Alligator Pond	40	39	540	110	20	107	265	49
Bayou D'Arbonne Lake								
1969	30	16	243	115	47	114	82	34
Total (1969)	283	247	7,279	2,145	29	2,061	1,292	18

are used the first year they are erected, there are too many boxes for the area. They reasoned that if less than 50 percent are used, many would be in poor condition before the population reached a point where the extra boxes would be needed. Utilization of 66 percent at Yazoo the first year (547 ducklings produced) was well above the 50 percent level. As a result of this success, the number of available boxes was increased to a maximum of 253 by 1969. In addition, the percentage of boxes used increased yearly, even with the addition of extra boxes, to a high of 96 percent in 1968.

Twenty-eight nests were incubated in the 87 available boxes erected in colonies. There were also 67 dump nests, as defined by Morse and Wight (1969), in these boxes. Six of these dump nests were abandoned, and 61 were destroyed by predators. Fifteen of the 28 nests incubated were classed as dump nests because of the large number of eggs and an abnormal deposition rate. The remaining nests were classed as normal nests, having a normal deposition rate and a normal clutch size.

A total of 168 nests were incubated in the individual boxes. There were 55 dump nests in these boxes, of which 31 were destroyed by predators and 24 were abandoned. A total of 109 of the 168 nests were classed as dump nests—49 dump nests were not incubated. Clutches of as few as 2 to as many as 50 eggs were incubated.

Some of the boxes were used consistently; others were never used even though they seemed to be in ideal habitat. It is possible that the unused boxes were not visible to the ducks from their established flight lanes. Thus, the ducks may not have recognized the unused boxes as available nesting sites. Since newer boxes are more readily visible than the older, weathered ones, the newer boxes probably will be inspected first by prospecting ducks.

Number of Eggs Laid

A total of 5,971 eggs were laid during 1969 in the 166 isolated boxes at Yazoo. An additional 1,065 eggs were laid in colonial boxes. The mean clutch size incubated in the individual boxes was 22.3 with a range of 2–50. In colonial boxes, the mean was 16.7 with a range of 4–31. These data support McLaughlin and Grice (1952), who suggested that boxes erected over water received more use than nests over land.

A total of 2,030 eggs hatched during the 1969 nesting season at Yazoo, an average of 29.3 percent of the eggs laid. Of the 2,996 eggs that were incubated, 67.0 percent hatched.

Some eggs hatched after the female abandoned the entire clutch, or they hatched after the female left the nest with most of a hatched brood. Thus, 83 ducklings hatched and died without leaving the boxes (Table 1). Webster (1955) stated that he found such an occurrence on the Patuxent Research Refuge in Maryland. Partial incubation, in addition to solar insolation, may provide the heat necessary for hatching.

A total of 3,857 eggs did not hatch and were not destroyed by predators during 1969. Some of these eggs may have been infertile, but the number was probably insignificant, since McLaughlin and Grice (1952) found that a minimum of 92 percent of the eggs wood ducks laid in nest boxes were fertile. Thus, abandonment may account for most of these eggs.

A number of factors may be responsible for abandonment. Antagonism among ducks may be a cause, especially under densely populated conditions (McLaughlin and Grice 1952). Their study showed that abandonment increased with increased clutch size and usage, regardless of the fact that other boxes were available. In our study, casual observations of places where adult ducks were seen most frequently indicated that clutch size and dump nests were higher in areas frequently used or passed by ducks. In part, the greater number of ducks present in 1969 may be the reason that only 32 percent of the eggs hatched as compared with 92 percent in 1966, when the duck population on the area was lower. Also, as indicated by Stewart (1957), large clutch sizes, partly the result of overpopulation, retard incubation, since peripheral eggs are more subject to chilling. The unhatched peripheral eggs would be abandoned. The largest dump nest at Yazoo contained 50 eggs. Our study indicated that small clutches were often abandoned, presumably because abandonment occurred before the clutch was completed. In addition, many eggs, though not broken, were parts of clutches destroyed by predators. Thus, these eggs, although deserted, were abandoned because of predation.

Predation

Lack (1954:74–75) believed cavity nesters suffered fewer losses from predators than open nesters. Nice (1957) found 77 percent hatching success among cavity nests of altricial birds. The cavities used by many small altricial nesters may not be as easily accessible to predators as are the nests in the larger cavities used by wood ducks. Bellrose et al. (1964) found 40–49 percent success among wood ducks, and Bolen (1967) found 44 percent success among black-bellied tree ducks (*Dendrocygna autumnalis*) nesting in cavities.

The three main predators of wood duck eggs in boxes at Yazoo were the yellow-shafted flicker, the raccoon, and the rat snake.

Birds pecked 814 eggs during 1969. Most of this damage was done by the yellow-shafted flicker. The adverse influence upon the nest box program by the flicker cannot be overstated. In 1968, flickers were responsible for the destruction of 54 nests. Certainly the flicker problem must be considered in evaluating the causes and effects of crowding nest boxes.

Bellrose (1955) and Decker (1959) ranked the raccoon as the foremost predator of wood duck eggs, and McLaughlin and Grice (1952) ranked the raccoon as the foremost predator of eggs of black-bellied tree ducks. Llewellyn and Webster (1960: 182) stated that "Raccoons may not visit nest boxes the first year or two after they are erected. But it is the usual experience that one eventually will investigate and discover a nest of eggs. Thereafter it apparently seeks eggs in each box it finds." Miller (1952) noted that raccoons destroyed 32 percent of 50 clutches of eggs the second year, a low water year, after the boxes were erected.

At Yazoo, the colony on East Gin Slough sustained the most damage by raccoons of any single area, with 213 eggs destroyed. The boxes on this area were over land a short distance from water. The raccoons must have gained entrance by jumping over the conical-type shield on the poles supporting the boxes. Colonial boxes, over land, lend themselves to raccoon damage because of their close proximity to one another. However, properly mounted, conical-type shields at an adequate distance above the ground and sufficiently removed from objects that provide the predator a *jumping* base, are virtually 100 percent protected from terrestrial predators. In our study, it developed that some of the shields were inadequately mounted or maintained.

Similarly, over a period of years, we found the sandwich-type shield to be inadequate. Climbing mammals and snakes seemed to circumvent the sandwich shields at an increasing rate.

In Connecticut, Beckley (1956) found that predation was low where boxes were located in small, isolated groups of one to four. This was also true at Yazoo, where isolated boxes over water had less than 10 percent damage by raccoons, whereas the colonial boxes over land had 42 percent of the eggs destroyed by raccoons.

Excessive predation by snakes in boxes was noticed for the first time at Yazoo during 1969. Several snakes, many of which were engorged with eggs, were found in boxes over water. Snakes apparently gained entrance to the boxes over water by rising out of the water and attaching themselves to the rivets that hold the sandwich shields together.

Occurrence of Natural Cavities

During the 10-transect survey for natural cavities, 1.4 (100.7 acres) percent of the total timbered acreage was sampled at Yazoo. Suitable cavities for wood ducks occurred at the rate of about one per 4 acres of timber, but no wood ducks were found to occupy the 27 suitable (eight cavities were unsuitable) cavities located and inspected. Of the 22 species of trees examined, the largest percentage of suitable cavities occurred at the rate of 1.6 percent ($N = 18$) in 1,141 willows and 0.5 ($N = 4$) percent in 741 cypresses.

Nest Boxes on Bayou D'Arbonne Lake

The 30 nest boxes on Bayou D'Arbonne Lake were placed in three different types of habitat including densely wooded sloughs, wooded areas along Little D'Arbonne Creek, and on trees along the edge of open water (Table 1).

The main purpose in erecting these boxes was to determine acceptance in an area where, previously, boxes had not been available and where ducks nested in natural cavities. Abundance of cavities was evident on this area in that many acres of timber were flooded when this lake was formed, thereby killing most of the trees standing in the water. The larger dead trees are ideal nesting sites for pileated woodpeckers (*Dryocopus pileatus*) that inhabit the area. They frequently excavate one or more cavities in a single tree. One wood duck nest in a natural cavity was checked frequently during the 1969 nesting season. It contained a clutch of 12 eggs that were abandoned because of flooding during a rainstorm.

Sixteen (53 percent) of the boxes available were used the first year. Use was similar to the 51.9 percent utilization obtained for first-year boxes in Illinois by Bellrose et al. (1964). The high percentage of utilization at D'Arbonne during the first year is probably attributed to at least three factors. The nest boxes, constructed of planed lumber, were conspicuous, the locations were acceptable, and there may have been a dense breeding population of ducks prospecting for nesting sites.

Of 243 eggs laid, 115 (47 percent) hatched. This is a higher figure than the 36 percent listed by Bellrose et al. (1964) as the nesting success in unprotected boxes in Illinois. Eighty-two of 243 eggs (34 percent) were destroyed by predators, mainly raccoons. The remaining unhatched eggs were abandoned.

Breckenridge (1947) stated that field observations of conflicts between squirrels and wood ducks are rare. No conflict or competition was observed at Yazoo, but some competition for nest boxes did occur at D'Arbonne. One box contained a fox squirrel (*Sciurus niger*), and three boxes were found to contain as many as six flying squirrels (*Glaucomys volans*). Other competitors for nest boxes on both areas included several species of Hymenoptera, Carolina wrens (*Thyothorus ludovicianus*), tufted titmice (*Parus bicolor*), screech owls (*Otus asio*), bluebirds (*Sialis sialis*), and, at Yazoo, two hooded mergansers (*Lophodytes cucullatus*).

CONCLUSIONS

Although the number of nest boxes has been increased on the Yazoo National Wildlife Refuge and egg production has subsequently increased, natality rates and production are declining. This is largely because of increased, especially avian, predation. Further studies of avian predation are paramount to the continued growth or maintenance of the Yazoo nest box program.

Even though 1.08 suitable natural cavities per 4 acres are present at Yazoo, it appears that wood ducks prefer the man-made nest boxes. This is also true for the Bayou D'Arbonne Lake area; 53.3 percent of the boxes were utilized the first year on an area that presumably has many natural cavities.

If predation can be reduced and brood habitat maintained, nest boxes, if evenly spread over a wide area, should be more beneficial than the natural cavities, especially since boxes seem to be preferred as nesting sites by wood ducks.

LITERATURE CITED

BAUMGARTNER, L. L. 1939. Fox squirrel dens. J. Mammal. 20(4):456–465.

BECKLEY, O. E. 1956. Wood duck nesting box program: progress report 1953–1955. Connecticut State Board Fisheries and Game. 21pp. Mimeo.

BELLROSE, F. C. 1955. Housing for wood ducks. Illinois Nat. Hist. Survey Circ. 45. 48pp.

———, K. L. JOHNSON, AND T. U. MYERS. 1964. Relative value of natural cavities and nesting houses for wood ducks. J. Wildl. Mgmt. 28(4):661–676.

BENT, A. C. 1923. Life histories of North American wildfowl, order Anseres (Part 1). U. S. Natl. Museum Bull. 126. 250pp.

BOLEN, E. G. 1967. Nesting boxes for black-bellied tree ducks. J. Wildl. Mgmt. 31(4): 794–797.

Breckenridge, W. J. 1947. Wood ducks versus squirrels. Auk 64(4):621.

Cunningham, E. R. 1969 (1968). A three year study of the wood duck on the Yazoo National Wildlife Refuge. Proc. Southeastern Assoc. Game and Fish Commissioners Conf. 22:145–155.

Decker, E. 1959. A 4-year study of wood ducks on a Pennsylvania marsh. J. Wildl. Mgmt. 23(3):310–315.

Grice, D., and J. P. Rogers. 1965. The wood duck in Massachusetts. Massachusetts Div. Fisheries and Game, Boston. 96pp.

Gysel, L. W. 1961. An ecological study of tree cavities and ground burrows in forest stands. J. Wildl. Mgmt. 25(1):12–20.

Lack, D. 1954. The natural regulation of animal numbers. Clarendon Press, Oxford. 343pp.

Llewellyn, L. M., and C. G Webster. 1960. Raccoon predation on waterfowl. Trans. N. Am. Wildl. and Nat. Resources Conf. 25:180–185.

McLaughlin, C. L., and D. Grice. 1952. The effectiveness of large-scale erection of wood duck boxes as a management procedure. Trans. N. Am. Wildl. Conf. 17:242–259.

Miller, W. R. 1952. Aspects of wood duck nesting box management. Trans. Northeastern Fish and Wildl. Conf. 8. 6pp. Mimeo.

Morse, T. E., and H. M. Wight. 1969. Dump nesting and its effect on production in wood ducks. J. Wildl. Mgmt. 33(2):284–293.

Nice, Margaret M. 1957. Nesting success in altricial birds. Auk 74(3):305–321.

Stewart, P. A. 1957. The wood duck, *Aix sponsa* (Linnaeus), and its management. Ph. D. Thesis. Ohio State Univ. 372pp.

Webster, C. G. 1955. Hatching of wood duck eggs after abandonment. Wilson Bull. 67(4):306.

Weier, R. W. 1966 (1965). A survey of wood duck nest sites on Mingo National Wildlife Refuge in southeast Missouri. Pages 91–108. *In* Wood duck management and research: a symposium. Wildlife Management Institute, Washington, D. C. 212pp.

Received for publication June 8, 1970.

USE OF ELEVATED NEST BASKETS BY DUCKS

HAROLD A. DOTY, ***U.S. Fish and Wildlife Service, Northern Prairie Wildlife Research Center, Jamestown, North Dakota 58401***

FORREST B. LEE, ***U.S. Fish and Wildlife Service, Northern Prairie Wildlife Research Center, Jamestown, North Dakota 58401***

ARNOLD D. KRUSE, ***U.S. Fish and Wildlife Service, Northern Prairie Wildlife Research Center, Jamestown, North Dakota 58401***

Abstract: Open-top nest baskets were mounted on upright metal poles in various wetlands to assess the value of baskets as a potential technique for increasing duck nest success. Observations were made from 1966–1968 in North and South Dakota, Minnesota, and Wisconsin, and were continued through 1973 in North Dakota. Baskets were used most readily in the prairie pothole region; of the 1,038 basket nest sites provided during 1966–68, 392 contained clutches of eggs (38 percent), and 324 (83 percent) hatched. Mallards (*Anas platyrhynchos*) initiated 98 percent of these nests. Factors affecting nest success included human disturbance, nesting material, egg freezing, and avian predation.

In recent years, predators and farming activities have limited nest success by ground-nesting ducks in North Dakota to about 30 percent (Martz 1967, Kirsch 1969, Higgins and Kantrud 1973). In this study, we sought to determine if wild ducks would use elevated nest baskets and if baskets would provide safer nest sites. Elevated nest structures for waterfowl are not new; they were used in St. James Park in London as early as 1665 (Eley Game Advisory Station 1969:49). Mallards have used various man-made structures in New York (Cummings 1960), Maryland (Burger and Webster 1964), Ohio (Bandy 1965), Iowa (Bishop and Barratt 1970), Ontario (Young 1971), and other locations.

Mallards used baskets in North Dakota the first year (1966) baskets were installed (Lee et al. 1968). Study areas were added in 1967 and 1968 in North Dakota, South Dakota, Minnesota, and Wisconsin. Investigations continued in North Dakota through 1973, dealing with (1) effects of human disturbance on nest success and hatchability of eggs, (2) preference for different nesting materials, (3) egg destruction by freezing, and (4) egg destruction by predators.

Field work was done cooperatively with the Divisions of Wildlife Refuges and Wildlife Services of the U.S. Fish and Wildlife Service (FWS), U.S. Forest Service, North Dakota Game and Fish Department, and South Dakota Department of Game, Fish and Parks. R. Barratt and H. Johnson of the Iowa Conservation Commission provided information leading to initiation of the study. W. H. Thornsberry and H. H. Dill provided basket designs that were modified versions of those used by the Iowa Conservation Commission (Barratt 1966). We thank C. W. Dane and J. T. Lokemoen for manuscript review and D. H. Johnson for statistical analyses.

STUDY AREAS

Nest baskets were placed in 18 areas in North and South Dakota, Minnesota, and Wisconsin. Seven areas were composed of one or more FWS waterfowl production areas (WPA): wetland tracts in the prairie pothole region described by Stewart and Kantrud (1973). A representative WPA study area in Stutsman County, North Dakota included 41 WPA tracts averaging 200 ha in size; each tract contained 1–10 wetlands. On four FWS refuge

---

Originally published in Wildl. Soc. Bull. 3(2):68–73, 1975.

areas, baskets were placed in large impoundments with regulated water levels. Cooperating state agencies in North and South Dakota set out baskets in prairie marshes, a prairie lake, man-made impoundments, and ponds in a forested region. On two national forests, baskets were placed in natural marshes, man-made impoundments, beaver ponds, lakes, and rivers. Baskets on the Little Missouri River National Grassland were placed in man-made livestock watering ponds.

PROCEDURES

Nest baskets were made from galvanized hardware cloth (0.7 or 1.3-cm mesh wire) or molded fiberglass. Wire baskets were cone-shaped with a 66-cm top diameter and a depth of 30 cm, supported in a frame of 0.7-cm-diameter steel rods. Fiberglass baskets of similar dimensions were made by Kenco Plastics, Necedah, Wisconsin, and by the Tamarac Job Corps Center in Minnesota. Baskets were attached atop metal posts (2.1-m-long aluminum alloy pipes with 5-cm O.D.) which were set vertically about 0.4 m deep in firm clay-bottomed wetlands and about 1.0 m deep in soft muck-bottomed wetlands.

Baskets in three areas in 1966–68 were originally adjusted so that their bottoms were 0.5 or 1.0 m above water, where water depths ranged from 0.4 to 1.3 m. Each wetland had both "high" and "low" baskets, but water level fluctuations during the 1966 and 1967 nesting seasons resulted in basket conditions ranging from dry to nearly submerged. Ducks used baskets in all situations. In 1969, all baskets in areas where field studies were continued were set at heights from 0.8 m to 1.7 m above water surfaces to avoid inundation.

An average of four baskets was installed in one wetland (4–100 ha) per WPA tract, with baskets generally not closer than 60 m to one another. One WPA study area was unique in that it was a single WPA tract with a high density of baskets—77 baskets were maintained annually in 25 prairie wetlands covering 31 ha (1–13 baskets per wetland) in the 186-ha tract. Baskets were usually spaced evenly around the perimeter of each wetland, and distances from the nearest shoreline ranged from 10 to 100 m. In national forests and national wildlife refuges, baskets were set in clusters of four with 60–100 m spacing. Only two baskets were installed in each livestock watering pond on the National Grassland.

Nest baskets in most study areas were provided with flax straw (*Linum usitatissimum*) nesting material. A 5- to 10-cm-thick lining was wired to the inside of each basket, and loose nesting material was pressed into the center of the basket to a central depth of 25–30 cm, approximately level with the basket rim. On five prairie pothole areas, different nesting materials were evaluated. Comparisons included flax straw (66 and 40 baskets) versus smooth brome (*Bromus inermis*) hay (66 and 40 baskets) on two different areas for 1 year each, flax (79) versus barley straw (*Hordeum vulgare*) (77) on one area for 2 years, and flax (18 and 17) versus wild hay (20 and 17) on two different areas for 1 year each. In each wetland, flax straw was placed in two baskets and the other nesting material in the other two baskets. Chi-square tests were used to compare rates of duck usage among the various nesting materials.

Nesting results were recorded during three basket inspections in May–July each year. "Successful" nests were those with at least one egg hatched; hatchability in successful nests was determined from the proportion of presumed fertile eggs that hatched. Unsuccessful nesting was caused mainly by predation on eggs and by nest desertion attributed to human disturbance.

Our observations indicated that avian predators usually spilled egg fluids in the nests, while mammalian predators consumed the total contents of the eggs.

Nest failures were attributed to human disturbance when egg-laying and/or incubation was terminated immediately after nests were examined. This effect was most apparent in one area during 1968–71 when nesting mallards were captured and marked with nasal saddles (Doty and Lee 1974). The effect of human disturbance was measured by comparing the percentage of successful nests and hatchability in 1970 between an area of disturbance and one of no disturbance (where nest checks were delayed until after the breeding season). The student's t test was used to compare average nest success with average hatchability of presumed fertile eggs in successful nests.

To determine if eggs in nest baskets might be more vulnerable to freeze damage than eggs in ground nests, we obtained air (at basket height), soil (at nest bowl level), and simulated nest temperatures eight times during a 50-hour period in early April 1968 (2–3 weeks before wild ducks nested in the area). Temperature probes were placed alongside fresh, game-farm mallard eggs in four simulated nests representing all combinations of wire versus fiberglass baskets and barley versus flax straw nesting material.

RESULTS AND DISCUSSION

Durability and Cost of Baskets

Galvanized wire and fiberglass baskets were structurally sound after weathering 7 years; both appeared to be usable for 20 years or more, and the aluminum alloy support posts were considered at least equally durable. Retaining wires for nesting material usually needed replacement after 3 years. Observations showed that (1) 2.1 m support posts were too short for many muck-bottomed marshes or for water deeper than 1 m; (2) large, open bodies of water presented special hazards from wind, waves, and ice which bent or broke some support poles (rendering an average of 7 percent of the baskets unusable); and (3) flax straw was usable for 3–5 years, but other nesting materials had to be replaced or supplemented annually.

Cost (1974 prices) of the wire mesh, steel rods, and assembly pipe was about $8.00 per basket; cutting, welding and other labor costs are additional. A 2.4 m length of 5-cm O.D. supporting pipe will cost about $9.00.

Waterfowl Use of Baskets

Ducks nested in only 3 (0.4 percent) of 750 usable baskets located in forested wetlands in Minnesota, Wisconsin, and the Wakopa State Game Management Area in North Dakota (six areas with an average of 1.83 years per area). Only 2 (1.4 percent) of 146 baskets were utilized in 2 years in stockponds of the Little Missouri River National Grassland. In the prairie pothole region, however, duck nests were initiated in 392 (37.8 percent) of 1,038 usable baskets (11 areas with an average of 1.54 years per area), even though ducks used only 1 of 15 baskets along the shoreline of a prairie lake and none of 19 baskets in one drought-stricken area of prairie wetlands in 1968. A total of 329 (83 percent) of the 397 nests initiated in baskets were successful. Baskets also have high use in the prairie region of Iowa (Bishop and Barratt 1970).

Of the 397 nesting attempts in 1966–1968, 389 (98 percent) were by mallards. Other basket nesters included one blue-winged teal (*Anas discors*), one gadwall (*Anas strepera*), two pintails (*Anas acuta*), and four redheads (*Aythya americana*). Two canvasbacks (*Aythya valisineria*) used nest baskets after this period.

There was no apparent difference in usage by ducks with respect to wire or fiberglass construction, height over water, water depth, or distance from shore. Baskets located in small openings in emergent vegetation appeared to be used most often by ducks.

Nesting Material Preference

In areas previously without baskets, usage was significantly ($P < 0.01$) higher in baskets with barley straw (36 of 77) or smooth brome hay (20 of 40) than in those with flax straw (23 of 119). Where flax straw was provided for 4 years and then compared with smooth brome in the 5th year, brome hay was used more often (42 of 66) ($P < 0.10$) than straw (31 of 66). This might be considered significant since mallards nesting or hatching in baskets with flax straw in the previous 4 years may have been preconditioned to using flax straw. The comparative rates of nesting on wild hay (11 of 37) and flax straw (5 of 25) were not significantly different ($P > 0.10$).

Effect of Human Disturbance

We attributed a high proportion of unsuccessful nesting attempts to human disturbance in one area during 1968–71 when most hens were caught for marking. In that period, nest failures resulting from human activities averaged 18.5 percent of 251 nesting attempts, while in 1966, 1967, and 1972 when 144 nests were checked once or twice during laying and/or incubation, nest failures from human disturbance averaged only 1.7 percent. In 1970, nest success and hatchability of eggs in successful nests were significantly ($P < 0.05$) higher in an undisturbed area (where nests were not checked until after the breeding season) than in the area on which hens were trapped. On the latter area, 16 percent of 74 nests failed because of human disturbance, and an additional 11 percent were destroyed by predators; whereas on the control area, only 1 of 23 nests was unsuccessful, being deserted for an unknown reason. Hatchability of presumed fertile eggs was 95 percent in the control area and 84 percent in the area of disturbance.

Effect of Temperature

Our field check of simulated nests on April 3–5, 1968 showed that temperatures adjacent to eggs in nest baskets approximated air temperatures. At the same time, the temperature near eggs on the ground fluctuated very little and tended to parallel the more stable soil temperature. All the eggs were frozen and shells were cracked, but only those in baskets suffered ruptured egg membranes; some eggs may withstand freezing and remain viable if the egg membrane is not broken (Greenwood 1969). Egg laying normally began 3 weeks later than our test period. Eggs in only two wild mallard nests were destroyed by freezing during our study; however, extensive losses could occur if freezing temperatures were prolonged during egg laying. Bishop and Barratt (1970) found numerous eggs frozen in nest baskets in Iowa. The occurrence of rapid cooling of eggs in nest baskets and/or prolonged absence of females may have led to the death of some embryos where humans disturbed incubation during our study.

Effect of Predators

In the initial study area, nest losses to predators averaged 5 percent in 1966–69 and increased to 16 percent in 1970–72. Mammalian predation of eggs in basket nests was believed to be limited to raccoon (*Procyon lotor*) and accounted for 0 to 11 percent of the nest loss. The percentage of nests lost to mammalian predators did not increase with years and may have remained low because the round metal support posts proved difficult to climb. In five nests where raccoons were suspected predators, duckling embryos were consumed after the eggs were pipped. It seemed probable that the raccoons were attracted by the sounds of ducklings in the process of hatching. If this presumed attraction was common, it would further indicate that few of the animals were able to climb the support posts.

Egg destruction by avian predators increased annually after the first 3 years in the two areas where observations were continued. Nest loss due to avian predators increased from 2 percent in 1968 to 23 percent in 1972 in the initial study area. In the high-density basket installation area, avian predation increased from 0 and 8 percent in 1967 and 1968, respectively, to 36 percent of 28 nests in 1970; rate of loss averaged 49 percent (55, 47 and 86 percent) of 114 nests in that area in 1971–73. Ring-billed gulls (*Larus delawarensis*) were seen consuming eggs in baskets in these two study areas in five instances. Eggs usually were destroyed during the egg-laying period in late April and early May; nests initiated later in the season were usually successful.

SUMMARY AND CONCLUSIONS

Nest basket usage by ducks, principally mallards, was confined to the unforested prairie pothole region. Rejection of baskets for nest sites outside of this region may have resulted from differences in behavioral response to open-top structures, avoidance of flax straw for nesting material, or unknown factors. We agree with Bishop and Barratt (1970) that for best results, nest baskets should be elevated about 1 m above water and located in openings in stands of emergent vegetation in shallow marshes. While nest success of basket nesting ducks was high, total productivity was not measured.

Baskets and support posts proved durable beyond 7 years, but retaining wires for nesting material needed replacement after 3 years. An annual prebreeding season check of baskets was desirable to ensure usability of the structures. Although barley straw or smooth brome was preferred as nesting material, when only flax straw was provided it appeared to be adequate, and required less maintenance.

Our study objectives were met; ducks accepted baskets as nest sites, at least in the prairie pothole region, and nest success was substantially increased over that of duck nests on the ground in North Dakota. We identified avian predation of eggs in baskets as a potential but not insurmountable problem. Preventive measures might include removal of particular predators, use of nonlethal egg baits, and chemical or mechanical scare devices to condition predators to avoid baskets.

We believe that most nest baskets could be maintained in usable condition for a minimum of 20 years. At the predetermined cost of $17.00 per structure, plus our estimate of $60.00 for 20 years of maintenance, the average annual cost would be $3.85 per unit. Based on our results, each 10 nest baskets would—during their 20-year lifespan—hold 76 nests (38 percent usage), hatch 63 clutches of eggs (83 percent nest success), and yield 517 ducklings (88-nest sample averaged 8.2 ducklings per successful nest). Production per basket per year would be 2.6 ducklings for $3.85, or $1.48 per duckling hatched. If baskets could be maintained for 25 years with the same costs, the price would drop to $1.18 per duckling hatched. Further cost reduction would result with increased basket usage rates. In conclusion, we believe that nest baskets offer one method for increasing localized mallard production in the prairie pothole region.

LITERATURE CITED

BANDY, L. W. 1965. Colonization of artificial nesting structures by wild mallards and black ducks. M.S. Thesis. Ohio State Univ. 67pp.

BARRATT, R. 1966. Predator proof nests. Iowa Conserv. 25(3):23.

BISHOP, R. A. AND R. BARRATT. 1970. Use of artificial nest baskets by mallards. J. Wildl. Manage. 34(4):734–738.

BURGER, G. V. AND C. G. WEBSTER. 1964. Instant nesting habitat. Pages 655–666 *in* J. P. Linduska, ed. Waterfowl tomorrow. Gov. Printing Office, Washington, D.C. 770pp.

CUMMINGS, G. E. 1960. Housing for ducks. New York Conserv. 14(4):22.

DOTY, H. A. AND F. B. LEE. 1974. Homing to nest baskets by wild female mallards. J. Wildl. Manage. 38(4):714–719.

ELEY GAME ADVISORY STATION. (1969). Annu. Rev. 1967/68:49.

GREENWOOD, R. J. 1969. Mallard hatching from an egg cracked by freezing. Auk 86(4):752–754.

HIGGINS, K. F. AND H. A. KANTRUD. 1973. Increasing bird nesting success on cultivated lands. North Dakota Outdoors 35(9):18–21.

KIRSCH, L. M. 1969. Waterfowl production in relation to grazing. J. Wildl. Manage. 33(4):821–828.

LEE, F. B., A. D. KRUSE AND W. H. THORNSBERRY. 1968. New fashions for the duck marsh. Naturalist 19(1):27–32.

MARTZ, G. F. 1967. Effects of nesting cover removal on breeding puddle ducks. J. Wildl. Manage. 31(2):236–247.

STEWART, R. E. AND H. A. KANTRUD. 1973. Ecological distribution of breeding waterfowl populations in North Dakota. J. Wildl. Manage. 37(1):39–50.

YOUNG, C. M. 1971. A nesting raft for ducks. Can. Field Nat. 85(2):179–181.

USE OF ARTIFICIAL ISLANDS BY NESTING WATERFOWL IN SOUTHEASTERN ALBERTA

JEAN-FRANÇOIS GIROUX,[1] Department of Zoology, University of Alberta, Edmonton, Alberta T6G 2E9, Canada

Abstract: From 1976 to 1978, the use of artificial islands by nesting waterfowl was investigated in southeastern Alberta. A total of 1,205 nests of 12 species of ducks and 144 nests of Canada geese (*Branta canadensis*) was found on 203 islands. Mallards (*Anas platyrhynchos*), gadwalls (*A. strepera*), and lesser scaup (*Aythya affinis*) selected islands as nesting sites more than other species of ducks. The average density of ducks on the islands ranged from 1.8 to 29.1 nests/ha, with nesting success of 43–59%. Canada geese nested on 53% of the islands, with a mean of 1.35 nests/island; their nesting success averaged 70%. Smaller islands, farther from shore and with greater vegetative cover, were most productive. Means of improving construction, positioning, and vegetation of islands are suggested.

J. WILDL. MANAGE. 45(3):669–679

Construction of artificial islands as a management technique to overcome loss of nesting habitat (Merriam 1978) has been proposed by Hammond and Mann (1956), Keith (1961), Mihelsons et al. (1967), Sherwood (1968), and Bellrose and Low (1978). Greater production can be achieved on islands because waterfowl nest at higher densities and suffer less mammalian predation than on the mainland (Hammond and Mann 1956, Hildén 1965, Vermeer 1970*a*, Ewaschuk and Boag 1972). Few studies have provided specific information on the characteristics of islands that make them more attractive to nesting waterfowl. Kaminski and Prince (1977) used multivariate analyses to quantitatively distinguish factors that influenced selection of natural islands by nesting Canada geese.

This study used the Kaminski-Prince approach to identify factors important in limiting the number and nesting success of ducks and Canada geese using artificial islands in southeastern Alberta. I also measured the effect of nest density on nesting success of ducks and geese, and the effect of interactions among geese when selecting their nest sites.

I thank N. Foy, E. Haldorson, and D. Henbest for field assistance. Financial and logistic support were provided by Ducks Unlimited (Canada), The University of Alberta, and La Société Zoologique de Québec, through a graduate scholarship. I gratefully acknowledge the advice and editorial assistance of D. Boag, who supervised the study. E. Ewaschuk, K. Vermeer, and W. Wishart made critical comments on an early draft of this manuscript.

STUDY AREA

The islands studied were located in 7 impoundments created by Ducks Unlimited (Canada) near Brooks (50.6°N, 111.9°W) in southeastern Alberta (Table 1). This is in a region of mixed prairie 50 km southeast of the area described by Keith (1961).

Impoundments A and B were 2 adjacent irrigation reservoirs. Artificial islands, ranging in size from 0.13 to 6.6 ha, were created before flooding by isolating tips of peninsulas through excavation of 20-m wide and 40-cm deep ditches or by increasing the height of natural elevations. The cut peninsulas were covered with native mixed-prairie vegetation, and

[1] Present address: Ducks Unlimited (Canada), 1190 Waverley Street, Winnipeg, Manitoba R3T 2E2, Canada.

Originally published in J. Wildl. Manage. 45(3):669–679, 1981.

Table 1. Characteristics of 7 impoundments and artificial islands constructed by Ducks Unlimited (Canada) near Brooks, Alberta, 1977.

	Basin			Artificial islands			
						Total	
Impoundment	Area flooded (km^2)	Perimeter (km)	Maximum depth (m)	*N*	Date of construction	Area (ha)	Perimeter (km)
Tilley A (A)[a]	4.6	33.9	1.8	8	1971–72	19.1	5.4
Tilley B (B)	13.0	30.9	5.3	17	1973	11.7	6.1
Tilley H (C)	1.1	7.6	0.5	8	1973	2.1	2.0
Tilley O (D)	0.7	4.2	0.3	8	1975	1.3	1.3
Tilley P (E)	0.2	2.3	0.8	3	1975	0.6	0.5
Kininvie F (F)	2.3	17.5	0.9	14	1968	2.5	2.5
Kininvie S (G)	1.4	9.8	0.8	17	1974	4.7	3.7

[a] Impoundments are referred to in the text by letters in parentheses.

the scooped earth was placed on them in one or more heaps. The 5 other impoundments (C, D, E, F, and G) were located in shallow basins approximately 15 km southeast of reservoir B (Table 1). In each basin a series of islands was created with earth scrapers before flooding. Most were built by piling earth scooped out of a 10-m wide moat to a depth of about 75 cm. Other islands were made by piling earth from an adjacent borrow pit. The resulting islands were rectangular in shape, 1–2 m high, and 0.09–0.47 ha in size. Between the moat and the pile of earth, a 3–5-m berm was left intact. This was covered by common spikerush (*Eleocharis palustris*) and marsh knotweed (*Polygonum coccineum*), and was subject to flooding.

Pioneer vegetation that invaded the piles of exposed earth was common Russianthistle (*Salsola kali*), flixweed tansymustard (*Descurainia sophia*), slimleaf goosefoot (*Chenopodium leptophyllum*), common tumblemustard (*Sisymbrium altissimum*), fireweed summercypress (*Kochia scoparia*), lambsquarters goosefoot (*Chenopodium album*), bull thistle (*Cirsium vulgare*), curlycup gumweed (*Grindelia squarrosa*), and grasses such as foxtail barley (*Hordeum jubatum*), western wheatgrass (*Agropyron smithii*), and crested wheatgrass (*A. cristatum*). Crested wheatgrass was seeded on the islands at impoundments A and B in 1974, and islands in basins D and E were seeded with a mixture of crested wheatgrass (40%), wildrye (*Elymus* sp.) (40%), and sweetclover (*Melilotus* sp.) (20%) in spring 1977.

Water levels in both reservoirs were regulated—from early May to the end of July they were drawn down in response to irrigation requirements, and were refilled in fall and early spring with water from the Bow River. The shallow basins were also flooded in fall and early spring with water from reservoir B through a series of canals. Water levels decreased in these shallow ponds during the summer at a rate of approximately 15 cm/month through evapotranspiration. In some years, water disappeared over most of each basin, remaining only in the moats around the islands by July.

METHODS

Nesting habitat (37 ha) on 75 islands was annually searched during the first 2 years, and a sample of 53 of these islands (13 ha) was searched during the 3rd summer. Nests were located by systematic searches made at monthly intervals by 1 or 2 observers walking a series of parallel transects on each island. Transects were 2–3 m apart, depending on vegetation density. A short stake was used to separate dense vegetation.

A nest was recorded if it contained 1 or more eggs. If whole eggs were absent because of predation, presence of fresh down, nest material, and eggshell fragments was taken as evidence that a nest had been initiated that season. Nests were classified as active if hens were laying or incubating, and inactive if clutches had been hatched, deserted, or destroyed. The species of waterfowl occupying a nest was identified either by observing the female as it flushed or by characteristics of the nest, eggs, down, and contour feathers. Locations of nests were plotted on field maps; markers were not used because they could have attracted avian predators (Picozzi 1975). A nest was considered successful if at least 1 egg hatched.

In 1977, a series of independent variables was measured on each island to identify which physical characteristics explained the most variation of dependent variables (density and nesting success of ducks and geese). Area and length of island shoreline were calculated with a planimeter and a map measurer either from aerial photos or from maps drawn by the compass transverse method (Mosby 1971). Vegetation of the islands was classified into 7 types (Table 2) and mapped in July; the proportion of each island covered by the different types was calculated with a planimeter. By comparing availability of each type and its use by nesting ducks, I determined that forbs and grass-forbs were preferred by nesting waterfowl (Table 2). The proportion of each island covered by these 2 types was then included in the set of independent

Table 2. Observed and expected frequencies of duck nests in 7 types of vegetative cover on artificial islands near Brooks, Alberta, 1976–77.

Type[a]	% total island area	Obs (N)	Exp (N)	P[b]
Forbs	17.3	441	171	<0.005
Grass	2.5	34	25	>0.05
Grass-forbs	18.9	298	186	<0.005
Moist soil	11.9	83	117	<0.005
Sparse	7.9	57	78	<0.025
Emergent	4.8	11	47	<0.005
Grassland	36.7	62	362	<0.005
Totals	100.0	986	986	

[a] Forbs: stands (≥9 m²) of broad-leaved annuals or perennials; Grass: stands (≥9 m²) of grasses; Grass-forbs: heterogeneous stands (≥9 m²) of the 2 previous types; Moist soil: colonizing vegetation on muddy shores; Sparse: grasses or forbs colonizing the piled earth; Emergent: vegetation between moat and piled earth; Grassland: mixed-grass prairie vegetation.

[b] Based on chi-square goodness-of-fit test.

variables. Water depth and distance between each island and the mainland were measured in both early May and July. The age of each island was based on the number of summers since construction.

Variations in density and nesting success of ducks were analyzed by stepwise multiple regression (Draper and Smith 1966). The criterion for retaining or deleting a variable was based on the 5% probability level; aptness of the models was examined through study of the residuals (Draper and Smith 1966). A logarithmic transformation was used to linearize the regression function and to stabilize the variance of the error terms, and an angular transformation was applied to data represented by percentages (Sokal and Rohlf 1969).

Because the number of Canada geese nesting on each island was limited, discriminant analysis was used to compare islands used and unused by nesting geese, and islands with successful and unsuccessful goose nests. The independent variables were selected by a stepwise procedure on the basis of their discriminant power; the selection criterion

Table 3. Species composition of ducks nesting on artificial islands located in reservoirs and shallow basins near Brooks, Alberta, 1976–78.

	Reservoirs		Shallow basins	
Species	No. of nests	%	No. of nests	%
Mallard	118	17	94	21
Gadwall	139	20	69	15
Pintail (*Anas acuta*)	60	9	107	24
Teal[a]	69	10	62	14
Northern shoveler (*A. clypeata*)	35	5	25	5
American wigeon (*A. americana*)	39	5	15	3
All dabblers	460	66	372	82
Lesser scaup	210	30	57	13
Redhead (*Aythya americana*)	17	2	18	4
White-winged scoter (*Melanitta deglandi*)	12	2	1	tr[b]
Ruddy duck (*Oxyura jamaicensis*)	0	0	4	1
All divers	239	34	80	18
All ducks	699	100	452	100

[a] All 3 species of teal (*Anas discors, A. crecca,* and *A. cyanoptera*) were grouped together. However, blue-winged teal was the most common species.
[b] Less than 1%.

Table 4. Densities of nesting ducks on artificial islands near Brooks, Alberta, 1976–78.

	No. of nests/ha			
Impoundment	1976	1977	1978	Weighted average[b]
A	3.9	14.9	a	9.4
B	7.3	26.1	23.6	17.3
C	5.0	31.0	11.7	14.2
D	0.0	3.1	2.4	1.8
E	1.7	0.0	8.5	3.3
F	23.6	36.0	27.1	29.1
G	15.4	11.3	13.2	14.4
Weighted average[b]	7.1	19.4	16.4	13.8

[a] Islands in impoundment A were not searched in 1978.
[b] Area searched within years and impoundments was the weighting coefficient.

was the smallest Wilks' lambda (Nie et al. 1975).

RESULTS AND DISCUSSION

Species Composition

One thousand two hundred five nests of 12 species of ducks and 144 nests of Canada geese were found on 203 islands. Lesser scaup, mallards, and gadwalls were the most common ducks using the islands (Table 3). Other studies have also reported that mallards (Drewien and Fredrickson 1970, Vermeer 1970*b*), gadwalls (Henry 1948, Hammond and Mann 1956, Duebbert 1966, Vermeer 1968), and lesser scaup (Keith 1961, Vermeer 1968, Long 1970) nest at high densities on islands. Islands in the larger and deeper reservoirs (A and B) supported a greater proportion ($P < 0.005$) of diving ducks, which comprised 34% of the nesting birds (Table 3). In contrast, divers comprised only 18% of the nesting population in the shallow basins (C, D, E, F, and G).

Density of Duck Nests

Nesting density over the 3 years averaged 13.8 nests/ha, and varied from 1.8 nests/ha on the recently created islands (D) to 29.1 nests/ha on the older islands (F) (Table 4). Annual variation in density was recorded; the greatest number of nests was found during a drought in 1977. Water persisting in the artificial basins that year seemed to attract waterfowl to nest on the islands (Giroux 1979). Density of nesting ducks observed in this study was somewhat lower than other densities reported on islands (Table 5). However, it appears that when high densities of islands are present (Long 1970, Vermeer 1970*b*, this study), they are used differentially. These data support the conclusion that islands, even artificial ones, are attractive to ducks. The number of nests/ha on mainland habitat varies from 0.0 to 4.3 (Oetting and Dixon 1975).

Density of nesting ducks was inversely correlated with size of island in the res-

Table 5. Densities and success of ducks nesting on islands.

No. of islands[a]	Total area (ha)	Density (nests/ha)	Success (%)	Location	Reference
1	0.32	494.2		North Dakota	Henry 1948
			76	Alberta	Keith 1961
14	20.60	2.0	82	Saskatchewan	Townsend 1966
2	5.70	35.1	90	North Dakota	Duebbert 1966
1	42.50	16.1	61	Scotland	Boyd and Campbell 1967
5	20.00	16.3		USSR	Mihelsons et al. 1967
4	8.90	29.0	90	Alberta	Vermeer 1968
1	7.70	21.4		South Dakota	Drewien and Fredrickson 1970
22	32.70	12.6	70	Alberta	Long 1970
19	59.50	3.8	51	Alberta	Vermeer 1970*b*
8	15.20	19.4		Alberta	Dwernychuk and Boag 1973
2	4.37	65.7	82	Saskatchewan	Hines 1975
20[b]	0.81	64.2	65	Saskatchewan	Hines 1975
56[b]	0.14	135.7	63	North Dakota	Johnson et al. 1978
203[b]	87.60	13.8	49	Alberta	This study

[a] The same island can be observed for more than one year and can be counted more than once.
[b] Man-made islands.

ervoirs and shallow basins (Table 6). A similar relationship was reported by Mihelsons et al. (1967) and Vermeer (1970*b*). My smallest island (0.09 ha) supported 10 duck nests in 1977 (111 nests/ha), the highest density recorded. Smaller islands may have more nests/ha (e.g., Johnson et al. 1978). However, the minimum size that would permit establishment of more than 1 pair/island remains undetermined.

Density of nesting ducks on islands in reservoirs A and B was positively correlated with distance of island from shore in May (Table 6). Islands located far from the mainland had greater densities (46.8 nests/ha) than islands of similar size located close to shore (33.7 nests/ha).

The proportion of an island covered by preferred vegetation (Table 2) explained 70% of the variation in density of duck nests in the shallow basins (Table 6). Older islands had a greater proportion of their area covered by preferred vegetation ($r = 0.75$, df $= 33$, $P < 0.01$). Moreover, the proportion of the island covered by preferred vegetation was also correlated with depth of water around the is-

Table 6. Physical characteristics of islands that best explained the observed density and nesting success of ducks in reservoirs and shallow basins near Brooks, Alberta, 1977 (+ = positive influence; − = negative influence).

Dependent variables	Type of impoundment (no. of islands)	Independent variables (% variation explained)	*F* value
Density of nesting ducks on islands	Reservoir ($N = 25$)	− Size (54)*** + Distance in May (8)*	18.05***
	Shallow basin ($N = 35$)	+ Vegetative cover (70)*** − Size (7)**	54.94***
Nesting success of ducks on islands	Reservoir ($N = 25$)	+ Distance in July (30)**	9.80***
	Shallow basin ($N = 24$)	+ Distance in July (29)**	9.05***

* $P < 0.05$, ** $P < 0.01$, *** $P < 0.005$.

lands at F ($r = 0.58$, df $= 12$, $P < 0.05$) and at G ($r = 0.75$, df $= 15$, $P < 0.01$). This indicates that presence of water around islands may promote growth of vegetation, a suggestion supported by greater density of vegetation near the water (on the slopes) than on the tops of the islands.

Density of Canada Goose Nests

Canada geese used 107 (53%) of 203 islands as nesting sites, and initiated 1.35 nests/island. Geese preferred artificial islands; only 1 goose nest was found on the mainland adjacent to a basin. Between 1976 and 1978, the proportion of 53 islands used by Canada geese for nesting increased from 43 to 62 to 75%. This increased use was associated with a progressive colonization of the more recently created islands, which may reflect either immigration into the study area or an increase in the local breeding population. The average density of island-nesting geese over the 3-year period was 1.6 nests/ha, and ranged between 0.2 and 7.1 nests/ha in the different basins. Densities greater than 25 nests/ha have been reported for Canada geese nesting on islands (Naylor 1953, Munro 1960, Ewaschuk and Boag 1972). However, the number of islands/impoundment in these studies was much lower than at Brooks.

Depth of surrounding water and percentage of island covered with forbs and grass-forbs were most influential in separating islands used and unused as nesting sites by Canada geese (Wilks' lambda $= 0.783$, df $= 2$ and 46, $F = 6.37$, $P < 0.01$). Geese selected islands ($N = 36$) that were characterized by deeper surrounding water ($\bar{x} = 68.8$ cm, SE $= 5.4$) and greater coverage of forbs and grass-forbs ($\bar{x} = 52.3\%$, SE $= 0.4$). Islands surrounded by deeper water may represent safer nesting sites for geese. Greater density of vegetation may also be advantageous through lowering visual stimuli and, hence, decreasing interactions among nesting geese (Munro 1960, Ewaschuk and Boag 1972). However, this seems to contradict the findings of Kaminski and Prince (1977) in southeastern Michigan. They found that islands selected by nesting geese had a lower density of vegetation and, hence, good visibility. However, the vegetation found on the islands investigated in this study was short (30–70 cm), and allowed geese to observe the surrounding area when standing near their nests, whereas vegetation in Michigan ranged from 1.5–2.4 m in height. Moreover, visual barriers probably were less important in their study area because density of the breeding population was much lower than in mine (1.2 vs. 9.6 pairs/10 km^2).

Establishment of more than 1 nest/island was recorded when visual barriers were provided by vegetative cover or by physiognomy of the island. In March and April 1977, geese selecting nest sites were observed for 250 hours from an elevated blind located in the vicinity of the islands at F. In general, a pair of geese defended an entire island. However, 2 nests were initiated on each of the 3 islands with the greatest proportion (89, 98, and 99%) of their surface covered with forbs and grass-forbs. On those islands, dry vegetation of the previous year completely concealed the geese constructing their nests or laying. This reduced ($P < 0.005$) the number of agonistic interactions between pairs trying to establish nests on those islands. On 3 islands where 2 pairs were successful in establishing nests, I recorded 8.5 interactions/pair/island. In contrast, I recorded 16.6 interactions on 9 islands where only 1 pair became established. Thus, good forb cover over the entire island may permit establishment of more than one goose nest/island.

Nesting Success of Ducks

Fifty-nine percent of 220 active duck nests found in 1976 and 1977 on islands in shallow basins were successful. On islands in reservoirs A and B, 43% of 367 nests hatched at least 1 egg. This level of success is somewhat lower than expected on islands (Table 5). In all impoundments, decreasing water levels because of evapotranspiration and irrigation draw-down reduced the security of islands against mammalian predators. Of 301 nesting failures, 3% were deserted, 57% were lost to mammalian predators (striped skunks, *Mephitis mephitis*; badgers, *Taxidea taxus*; and coyotes, *Canis latrans*), 1% were lost to avian predators, and 40% had unknown causes.

Nesting success of ducks was positively correlated with distance of island from the mainland in early July (Table 6). Although it explained only 30% of the variation, this factor was the most important at both types of impoundments. Depth of water surrounding an island did not contribute to the variation in nesting success.

The effect of duck nesting density on nesting success was investigated because interactions between birds might decrease their success, or high concentrations of ducks might be more vulnerable to predation. Such a relationship was not found. Nesting success correlated positively with density ($r = 0.54$, df = 47, $P < 0.01$). More females selected islands that were safer for nesting. Duebbert (1966) noted that hatching success of gadwalls was not reduced at nesting densities as high as 43 nests/ha. However, Long (1970) reported that nesting behavior was abnormal at densities of 130 nests/ha, and that dropped eggs, nest desertion, and nest parasitism were frequent.

In 1977, 12% of 743 nests contained eggs that appeared to have been laid by 2 or more females (inter- or intraspecific parasitism). Nest parasitism was positively correlated with the density of nests in the different basins ($r = 0.95$, df = 4, $P < 0.01$). Joyner (1976) has shown that eggs in parasitized nests have lower hatching success than eggs in unparasitized nests. Nesting success based on the percentage of nests producing at least 1 young was not negatively related to density in this study. Perhaps data on egg success (percentage of eggs that hatched) would have given a different result.

Nesting Success of Canada Geese

One hundred one nests (70%) of Canada geese hatched successfully, 25 (17%) were preyed upon, and 18 (13%) were deserted during the 3 years. This level of nesting success is equivalent to the 67% calculated for 4,919 nests reported in several studies on islands (Naylor 1953, Sherwood 1968, Vermeer 1970*a*, Hanson and Eberhardt 1971, Ewaschuk and Boag 1972). All desertions occurred on islands in shallow basins where density of nesting geese was greater and where social interactions between pairs may have been the cause (Ewaschuk and Boag 1972). This hypothesis is supported by the greater success ($P < 0.005$) recorded for geese nesting singly on islands (80% of 60 nests) than for geese nesting on islands where there was more than 1 nest (53% of 43 nests). Nevertheless, the number of goslings produced/island was greater on islands with 2 than with 1 nest.

Distance between island and mainland in May and percentage of island covered with forbs and grass-forbs were the most important variables separating islands with at least 1 successful goose nest from those without a successful nest (Wilks' lambda = 0.795, df = 2 and 34, $F = 4.38$, $P < 0.05$). Islands with successful nests ($N = 24$) had denser vegetation ($\bar{x} = 58.2\%$, SE = 0.6) and were located farther from shore ($\bar{x} = 53.6$ m, SE = 9.7). Importance of distance of islands from mainland may reflect the same effect of discouraging mammalian predation as has been suggested for ducks in this study. Also, vegetative cover may reduce the number of interactions between pairs of geese, and consequently lower their rate of desertion (Ewaschuk and Boag 1972).

MANAGEMENT RECOMMENDATIONS

Comparison of island characteristics and productivity showed that smaller islands located farther from shore with greater vegetative cover were most productive. Keith (1961) observed that preferred islands were at least 15 m in diameter (0.02 ha), whereas Hammond and Mann (1956) suggested islands of 0.12–0.4 ha. From this study, I would recommend that islands encompass about 0.1 ha.

Rectangular islands are most appropriate because they have greater perimeter/area than circular, elliptical, or square islands. The greater the ratio of water–land edge to land mass the more attractive the insular habitat (Hammond and Mann 1956). Moreover, rectangular islands require limited surveying and are easier to build, especially with a scraper. Heavy equipment traveling and unloading material on the central pile of earth also results in a more compacted and erosion-resistant island. Therefore, I recommend artificial islands approximately 25 m wide and 40 m long.

Keith (1961) claimed that a moat 45–60 cm deep and about 10 m wide was adequate to deter skunks. Hammond and Mann (1956) suggested a depth of 30–45 cm with ". . . several hundred feet of open water . . . ," and Sherwood (1968) recommended locating islands more than 60 m from the mainland and at a minimal depth of 30 cm. However, coyotes (Hanson and Eberhardt 1971) and badgers (Duebbert 1967) have been observed to swim over 200 m without apparent stress. I observed a skunk swimming between islands over a distance of more than 200 m. Based on the relationships between nesting success of ducks and distance of islands from mainland, I would recommend a distance of at least 170 m between islands and the mainland. Because geese used islands surrounded by a mean of 69 cm of water, I consider that a depth of about 70 cm should be adequate to make an island attractive, providing it is sufficiently far from shore.

Islands created by increasing natural elevations in reservoirs had 52.7 nests/ha (SE = 8.6, $N = 9$) and 53% nesting success ($N = 91$). This was greater ($P < 0.01$) than the average of 25.1 nests/ha (SE = 5.3, $N = 16$) and the 34% nesting success ($N = 230$) on the large cut peninsulas. If peninsulas are used to create nesting islands, only a small portion should be isolated with wide ditches.

Islands created in the shallow basins by piling earth from an adjacent borrow pit were surrounded by flooded emergent vegetation except on the borrowed side, where there was open water. Density of duck nests on these islands averaged 8.2 nests/ha (SE = 2.5, $N = 12$), which was lower ($P < 0.05$) than the average of 19.4 nests/ha (SE = 4.0, $N = 22$)

on the islands with a complete moat. Thus, islands should be constructed with a complete moat so there is open water around the island.

Nesting waterfowl selected stands of broad-leaved annuals and perennials mixed with grasses. Establishment of vegetation on islands could be promoted by seeding a mixture of grasses and legumes (Duebbert and Lokemoen 1976). Type of soils and moisture conditions particular to each area will determine the species to seed. Most seeding done on islands in the Brooks area was unsuccessful or slow to become established, probably because of the dry conditions of the islands. Under such conditions, I suggest that watering the islands at time of seeding will accelerate establishment of nesting cover. Flooding of the basin will raise the water table under the islands, but can be detrimental to islands through erosive action of waves against unprotected shores.

Erosion is the most important factor influencing longevity and productivity of an island. The effect of erosion in my study was more marked in reservoirs than in shallow basins. However, actual reduction in size of eroded islands was usually limited, because the islands were all recently constructed. To minimize erosion, I suggest that islands be oriented parallel to the prevailing winds. Hammond and Mann (1956) suggested that emergent vegetation around the island can be used as natural breakwaters. However, Mihelsons et al. (1967) observed that islands surrounded by a dense belt of tall emergent vegetation offered no access to open water and were avoided by waterfowl. The importance of free access to open water was observed during nest-site selection at F, where I noted that geese approached or left islands more often ($P < 0.005$) by swimming than by flying (80% of 535 observations). I suggest that dense emergent vegetation be left only on the windward side of an island. In large impoundments where wave action is significant, islands should be located along the lee shore. Riprapping the windward shores of islands subjected to erosion is a costly possibility, and its effect on waterfowl is unknown.

Hammond and Mann (1956) suggested that close spacing of islands protects them from wind and wave action. However, clustering of islands can increase their vulnerability to predators (Sherwood 1968), a phenomenon also recorded in this study. At F, greater nesting success of ducks ($P < 0.005$) was recorded on islands that were separated by more than 100 m (89% of 28 nests) than on islands at less than 100 m (54% of 41 nests). Because these islands were the same distance from shore, their close spacing may have decreased their productivity. Sherwood (1968) suggested that small islands constructed for nesting Canada geese should be more than 45 m apart; results of this study indicate that islands of 0.1–0.2 ha should be no closer than 100 m.

Increase in the breeding population and progressive colonization of more recently created islands by Canada geese indicate that availability of nesting sites may be a limiting factor on the prairies of Alberta. It also shows the potential of constructing islands in different impoundments to increase local populations of geese.

Current costs involved in construction of islands range from \$1.00 to 2.00/m^3 of earth moved depending upon equipment, quality of material, and working conditions. An average of 2.2 goslings and 21.8 ducklings/island are produced annually, based on 4.5 goslings and 7.5

ducklings/successful nest (Vermeer 1970*a,b*). Considering an actual expenditure of \$2,300/island (\$1.50/m^3), the cost/bird hatched over a 20-year period would be \$4.80 (1980 Canadian funds). Because the life expectancy of these islands is more than 20 years, each additional year of production would reduce the cost/bird produced.

Compared to other techniques such as idle cropland (Duebbert and Lokemoen 1976) or artificial nesting structures (Rienecker 1971, Doty et al. 1975), islands are more expensive. However, they require less maintenance, more ducklings and goslings are hatched/unit area on them, and they are used by a greater diversity of species. Even if birds nesting on islands are only drawn from other parts of the marsh, they may enjoy greater nesting success than on the mainland. Moreover, any vacancies created by the movement of birds to islands may be filled by other breeding pairs.

Construction of islands may enhance productivity of wetlands for waterfowl in areas where nesting cover is a limiting factor. The technique is promising and should be used more extensively on the breeding grounds of North America.

LITERATURE CITED

BELLROSE, F. C., AND J. B. LOW. 1978. Advances in waterfowl management research. Wildl. Soc. Bull. 6:63–72.

BOYD, H., AND C. R. G. CAMPBELL. 1967. A survey of the ducks breeding at Loch Leven in 1966. Wildfowl 18:36–42.

DOTY, H. A., F. B. LEE, AND A. D. KRUSE. 1975. Use of elevated nest baskets by ducks. Wildl. Soc. Bull. 3:68–73.

DRAPER, N. R., AND H. SMITH. 1966. Applied regression analysis. John Wiley & Sons, Inc., New York, N.Y. 407pp.

DREWIEN, R. C., AND L. H. FREDRICKSON. 1970. High density mallard nesting on a South Dakota island. Wilson Bull. 82:95–96.

DUEBBERT, H. F. 1966. Island nesting of the gadwall in North Dakota. Wilson Bull. 78:12–25.

———. 1967. Swimming by a badger. J. Mammal. 48:323.

———, AND J. LOKEMOEN. 1976. Duck nesting in fields of undisturbed grass-legume cover. J. Wildl. Manage. 40:39–49.

DWERNYCHUK, L. W., AND D. A. BOAG. 1973. Effect of herbicide-induced changes in vegetation on nesting ducks. Can. Field-Nat. 87:155–165.

EWASCHUK, E., AND D. A. BOAG. 1972. Factors affecting hatching success of densely nesting Canada geese. J. Wildl. Manage. 36:1097–1106.

GIROUX, J.-F. 1979. A study of waterfowl nesting on artificial islands in southeastern Alberta. M.S. Thesis. Univ. Alberta, Edmonton. 98pp.

HAMMOND, M. C., AND G. E. MANN. 1956. Waterfowl nesting islands. J. Wildl. Manage. 20:345–352.

HANSON, W. C., AND L. L. EBERHARDT. 1971. A Columbia River Canada goose population, 1950–1970. Wildl. Monogr. 28. 61pp.

HENRY, C. J. 1948. Summer on the Souris Marsh. Audubon Mag. 50:242–249.

HILDÉN, O. 1965. Habitat selection in birds. A review. Ann. Zool. Fenn. 2:53–75.

HINES, J. E. 1975. Gadwall nesting and brood ecology at Waterhen Marsh, Saskatchewan. M.S. Thesis. Univ. Regina, Regina, Saskatchewan. 218pp.

JOHNSON, R. F., JR., R. O. WOODWARD, AND L. M. KIRSCH. 1978. Waterfowl nesting on small man-made islands in prairie wetlands. Wildl. Soc. Bull. 6:240–243.

JOYNER, D. E. 1976. Effects of interspecific nest parasitism by redheads and ruddy ducks. J. Wildl. Manage. 40:33–38.

KAMINSKI, R. M., AND H. H. PRINCE. 1977. Nesting habitat of Canada geese in southeastern Michigan. Wilson Bull. 89:523–531.

KEITH, L. B. 1961. A study of waterfowl ecology on small impoundments in southeastern Alberta. Wildl. Monogr. 6. 88pp.

LONG, R. J. 1970. A study of nest-site selection by island-nesting anatids in central Alberta. M.S. Thesis. Univ. Alberta, Edmonton. 123pp.

MERRIAM, G. 1978. Changes in aspen parkland habitats bordering Alberta sloughs. Can. Field-Nat. 92:109–122.

MIHELSONS, H., J. VIKSNE, AND G. LEJINS. 1967. Experience in waterfowl management under the conditions prevailing in the Latvian S.S. R. Wildfowl 18:146–149.

MOSBY, H. S. 1971. Reconnaissance mapping and map use. Pages 119–134 *in* R. H. Giles, Jr., ed. Wildlife management techniques. The Wildl. Soc., Washington, D.C.

MUNRO, D. A. 1960. Factors affecting reproduction of the Canada goose (*Branta canadensis*). Proc. Int. Ornithol. Congr. 12:542–546.

NAYLOR, A. E. 1953. Production of the Canada goose on Honey Lake Refuge, Lassen County, California. Calif. Fish and Game 39:83–94.

NIE, N. H., C. H. HULL, J. G. JENKINS, K. STEINBRENNER, AND D. H. BENT. 1975. SPSS. Statistical package for the social sciences. McGraw-Hill Book Co., New York, N.Y. 675pp.

OETTING, R. B., AND C. C. DIXON. 1975. Waterfowl nest densities and success at Oak Hammock Marsh, Manitoba. Wildl. Soc. Bull. 3:166–171.

PICOZZI, N. 1975. Crow predation on marked nests. J. Wildl. Manage. 39:151–155.

RIENECKER, W. C. 1971. Canada goose nest platforms. Calif. Fish and Game 57:113–123.

SHERWOOD, G. A. 1968. Factors limiting production and expansion of local populations of Canada geese. Pages 73–85 *in* R. L. Hine and C. Schoenfeld, eds. Canada goose management. Dembar Educ. Res. Serv., Madison, Wis. 195pp.

SOKAL, R. R., AND F. J. ROHLF. 1969. Biometry. W. H. Freeman Co., San Francisco, Calif. 776pp.

TOWNSEND, G. H. 1966. A study of waterfowl nesting on the Saskatchewan River Delta. Can. Field-Nat. 80:74–88.

VERMEER, K. 1968. Ecological aspects of ducks nesting in high densities among larids. Wilson Bull. 80:78–83.

———. 1970*a*. A study of Canada geese, *Branta canadensis,* nesting on islands in southeastern Alberta. Can. J. Zool. 48:235–240.

———. 1970*b*. Some aspects of the nesting of ducks on islands in Lake Newell, Alberta. J. Wildl. Manage. 34:126–129.

Received 29 June 1979.
Accepted 20 August 1980.

A NESTING RAFT FOR DUCKS[1]

COLIN M. YOUNG, Department of Biology, Laurentian University, Sudbury, Ontario, Canada

Abstract: A simple nesting raft for Mallards and Black Ducks is described. Structural details are discussed, plus the results of five years of field testing.

There are thousands of small lakes and beaver ponds in northern Ontario but these water areas produce surprisingly few ducks. This situation appears to be due, in part at least, to a scarcity of predator-free nesting sites. The few ducks which do nest successfully in this area usually choose offshore islands in the larger lakes, in order to escape from mammalian predators (Young 1968). For the wildlife manager, the obvious solution to this problem is to provide safe, artificial nesting sites. Elsewhere in North America, artificial nesting devices have been used extensively to increase wetland utilization by ducks. Most of the earlier types were modifications of European designs, such as the pitcher-shaped wicker baskets from the Netherlands and the woven reed wigwams from Denmark (Burger and Webster 1964). One of the more successful North American models is a type of open-ended cylinder which is either attached to trees in flooded swamplands or mounted on poles (Boyer 1958). There are no recorded instances of any of these devices having been used successfully in the forested regions of Ontario. The Sudbury Game and Fish Protective Association erected a large number of nesting cylinders around a small lake near Sudbury in 1963 and 1964 but none was used. The birds appeared to avoid all unnatural-looking structures. In order to overcome this aversion, a more rustic, brush-covered raft was tried. This design proved to be readily acceptable to both Mallards (*Anas platyrhynchos*) and Black Ducks (*Anas rubripes*).

Figures 1 and 2 illustrate the main structural details of the nesting raft. It is made of 6 foot long cedar logs held together with 'two by fours.' The nest box, which is placed near the centre of the raft, is 18 inches square and 6 inches deep. It is filled with leaf litter and screened with brush. The whole raft is then covered over with cedar boughs to protect the nest from crows and owls and is anchored several hundred feet from shore by means of a large rock and a length of ¼ inch polypropylene rope. Mink, which are the most serious predators of duck nests in this area, will not swim out to the rafts if they are placed well out in the lake. The spacing of the rafts is not critical. Since these birds do not generally nest within their defended territories, there is no problem with individual spacing; indeed, two or three nest boxes may be placed side by side on the same raft without risk of conflict between occupants. The usual inclination is to anchor the rafts in small sheltered bays or narrow creek mouths but this simply increases the chances of predation. It was found that the nesting birds are remarkably tolerant of wind and wave action, provided of course that the nest boxes do not actually become flooded. One should emphasize the importance of getting the rafts out on the lake as soon as

[1] Originally published in Can. Field-Nat. 85(2):179–181, 1971.

Fig. 1. Duck nesting raft showing the construction of the platform and the nest box.

Fig. 2. The completed raft, camouflaged with cedar boughs.

possible after spring break-up. At this latitude, the lakes are usually ice-free by the first week of May and the ducks take possession of the rafts as soon as they are made available. In the majority of cases the first egg is laid within three to four days of the rafts being set out; in several instances the first egg was laid on the same day. As for cost, the only real expense is labour. All of the building materials are available locally at little or no cost. One man working full time can put together 6 to 8 of these rafts per day once the materials have been gathered on the site.

In 1965, six rafts were tested. They were put in place on the third of May and within three days, three of the rafts were occupied. The attractiveness of at least one of the rafts was demonstrated by the fact that three different ducks used it during the same season. First a Black Duck laid a full clutch of 12 eggs in the nest box, then a Mallard added another 11 eggs and finally a second Mallard arrived and shared in the incubation of the huge clutch after having added a few eggs of its own. In 1966, twelve rafts were set out and six were used, three by Mallards and three by Black Ducks. In 1967, fourteen

Table 1. The use of duck nesting rafts, by species, at Laurentian Lake, Sudbury, Ontario, 1965–69.

Year	Number of rafts set out	Number of rafts used	Number of clutches laid				
			Mallard	Black	Unknown species	Hybrid	Total
1965	6	3	2	2			4
1966	12	6	3	3			6
1967	18	14	6	7	2		15
1968	20	18	12	8	3		23
1969	20	20	8	9	6	3	26

of the eighteen available rafts were occupied. Again in 1967, one of the rafts was used by two different birds, in this case one after the other and both brought off broods successfully. Table 1 summarizes the nesting data up to the present time. The records indicate that there were often more clutches laid than there were rafts available. This can be explained by the fact that some of the rafts had more than one nest box and that individual boxes were sometimes occupied by a succession of nesting birds.

The nesting rafts appear to be equally acceptable to Black Ducks and Mallards; their usage by the two species reflects the species composition of the local population. This overlap in nesting requirements may be partly responsible for the high incidence of hybridization between Mallards and Black Ducks in this area.

CONCLUSIONS AND RECOMMENDATIONS

The nesting raft described in this paper has been used successfully for five years on lakes and ponds in the Sudbury district in northern Ontario. It is suitable for both Black Ducks and Mallards. It is inexpensive and simple to construct and provided that it is properly constructed and anchored well out from shore, is effectively predator-proof. Exceptional situations may arise in which individual predators may "learn" to associate the rafts with the presence of duck eggs. In such cases a limited amount of selective predator control may be warranted. A management program involving rafts of this type is particularly well suited to intensively managed areas such as those that are frequently administered by local conservation groups and fish and game clubs.

LITERATURE CITED

BOYER, G. F. 1958. Duck nesting baskets. Ontario Department of Lands and Forests, Fish and Wildlife Management Report 41:27–28.

BURGER, G. V., AND C. G. WEBSTER. 1964. Instant nesting habitat. *In* J. P. Linduska, editor. Waterfowl tomorrow. U.S. Fish and Wildlife Service, Washington. 770pp.

YOUNG, C. M. 1968. Island nesting of ducks in northern Ontario. Canadian Field-Naturalist 82(3):209–212.

EVALUATING THE USE OF AERIAL NESTING PLATFORMS BY CANADA GEESE[1]

JOHN J. CRAIGHEAD and DWIGHT S. STOCKSTAD, U.S. Fish and Wildlife Service, Missoula; and Montana Fish and Game Department, Kalispell, Montana

In 1953, we began a long-range population study of Canada geese (*Branta canadensis*) in the Flathead Valley, Montana. We were working with a relatively small breeding population with clearly defined geographic limits described by Geis (1956). We believed that during the course of this intensive study we could test the value of artificial elevated platforms as nesting sites for geese by recording changes in the nesting habits of the population induced by the platforms.

Yocom (1952) showed that Canada geese will nest in artificial platforms and indicated that such platforms could be used to increase the number of Canada geese nesting in a given area. Yocom, however, did not present data to support his contention that artificial nests increased the total number of nesting Canada geese and improved the welfare of geese in the area. Such information is necessary before the use of platforms can be precisely evaluated as a management practice. The purpose of this paper is to present such an evaluation. To do this, a frame of reference had to be established prior to the erection of nesting platforms. Also the nesting histories of geese using the platforms had to be followed from year to year while changes in nesting habits of the population were recorded.

The authors are grateful to Bob Brown, Bob Gustafson, Ralph Stockstad, John Morrison, Glen Beckman, and Maurice Hornocker for helping us to erect, maintain, and check the platforms during the period of study. H. E. Reinhardt, Mathematics Department, Montana State University, performed the statistical treatment. The interpretation and conclusions are the responsibility of the authors.

To determine the value of aerial platforms for goose nesting, we sought answers to the following questions:

1. Is there a progressive increase in use of platforms from year to year?
2. Will geese shift from using natural elevated sites such as osprey or heron nests to using platforms?
3. Is there a percentage increase in the use of all aerial goose-nesting sites, including platforms, when platforms are made available?
4. Will platforms induce geese to change from ground to aerial nesting sites, from islands to lake and river shore lines, from island ground sites to island elevated sites?
5. Will nesting platforms increase the total nesting population by providing desirable nest sites where none previously existed or by attracting migratory geese to settle?
6. Will geese nesting in elevated platforms show a higher reproductive rate, better hatching success, and fewer nest failures than ground-nesting geese?
7. How are aerial platforms selected by geese and what is the pattern of use?
8. Is there considerable mortality of goslings when leaving elevated sites?

Two standards were used to compare data and to evaluate the effects of aerial platforms on the Canada goose population. One was population data obtained prior to

[1] Contribution from the Montana Cooperative Wildlife Research Unit, U.S. Fish and Wildlife Service, Montana State Fish and Game Department, Montana State University, and Wildlife Management Institute cooperating. The study was partially supported with Federal Aid in Wildlife Restoration funds under Pittman-Robertson Project W-71-R, Montana State Fish and Game Department.

Originally published in J. Wildl. Manage. 25(4):363–372, 1961.

the erection of platforms. This included number of nesting pairs, number of nests, nest-site locations, total eggs laid and hatched, and mortality during the nesting period (Geis, 1956). The second standard was a 6-yr. average of the same type of data, involving 1,267 nests. The number of nests annually under observation varied from a low of 160 to a high of 296. Each year very nearly all nests in the population were kept under observation; thus the totals shown in Table 1 are not samples but represent closely the total number of nests comprising the population for each of the 6 years.

In this way changes in the population unit caused by the introduction of artificial nesting platforms for any one of 5 years could be compared against the original 1953 situation, against a 6-yr. mean, and against progressive changes from year to year.

The study area included Flathead Lake, which is approximately 30 mi. long and averages 8 mi. in width, a 50-mi. stretch of the Flathead River and the Flathead Valley south of Flathead Lake.

Methods

In 1954, we erected artificial platforms along Flathead Lake, in Nine Pipe Reservoir, and along the Flathead River, Montana. Platform elevations varied from 4 to 45 ft. Platforms were placed on rock islands, in cattail marshes, and on heavily timbered shore lines, where nesting density was heavy as well as where few or no geese were nesting. Forty-five platforms were on small islands, 21 on large islands and 17 on shore lines. Over a 5-yr. period an average of 73 of the original 83 platforms were available each year to nesting geese. Fifty-three percent were at heights of 3 to 10 ft., 30 percent were at heights of 11 to 20 ft., and 17 percent were at heights of 21 to 45 ft. (Fig. 1).

The platforms were 30 in. long by 26 in. wide by 6 in. deep, constructed of wood and securely fastened to trees (Fig. 2). Soil and

Fig. 1. Canada goose nesting platform erected about 20 ft. above the ground on an island in Flathead Lake.

duff were placed in these so that the geese could make scrapes. Since some platforms were found to be destroyed or in disrepair each season, prior to the establishment of nesting territories the boxes were repaired and replenished with soil and duff. This proved to be an essential task if any number of platforms were to be kept attractive to geese. The first 2 years some platforms were camouflaged, others were not. There was no preference for camouflaged sites; consequently they were discontinued.

Changes Induced by Artificial Platforms

In 1953, prior to the erection of platforms, 96 percent of 225 nests were located on islands; 93 percent of these were ground nests (Table 1). With this information as a basic frame of reference, data gathered over a 6-yr. period involving 1,267 nests showed that the percentage of all nests on islands dropped from 96 percent in 1953 to 92 percent in 1958, with a 6-yr. average of 95 percent. Except for 1954, the decrease was progressive year by year. The percent-

FIG. 2. Platforms must be filled with soil or duff. The goose makes a scrape, lines it with down.

age of island ground nests dropped from 93 in 1953 to 83 in 1958 and showed a 6-yr. average of 90 percent. This decrease was also progressive year by year. The percentage of nests located on lake and river shore lines increased from 3 to 8 percent, averaging 5 percent for the period. This increase was progressive year by year.

These changes in location and distribution of goose nests by habitat over a 6-yr. period (Table 1) show that the nesting platforms caused definite and measurable changes in the nesting habits of the goose population.

Shore line ground nests showed no essential change, and no progressive pattern during the 6 years (Table 1).

The use by geese of natural elevated sites such as nests of ospreys, red-tailed hawks, eagles, and herons showed no essential change. The 6-yr. average showed a 1 percent decline over the 1953 standard, but there was considerable variation from year to year with no recognizable pattern (Table 1). Successful defense of nest structures by ospreys, eagles, herons, and red-tailed hawks during some years and inability to deter geese from using these at other times probably accounted for the varied use pattern.

The percentage of all nesting geese in the population that used nesting platforms increased progressively from 1 percent in 1954, when platforms were first erected, to 9 percent in 1958. The percentage of all nesting geese that used elevated nest sites, including platforms and natural structures, increased from 5 percent in 1953 to 18 percent in 1958. The actual increase in use was 11, 15, 13, 15, 23, and 30, respectively, or an increase of nearly 3 times the 1953 standard (Table 1). Since there was no essential change in the number of natural structures used, this increase in use of all elevated sites by the goose population could not have been a shifting from natural elevated structures to the artificial nesting platforms. The percentage of geese in the population that used aerial sites for nesting thus increased nearly threefold as a result of the platforms. This indicates that geese recognized the aerial platforms as desirable nest sites.

Table 1 shows that very few geese in the population unit made ground nests on the lake and river shore lines and that of this number, two-thirds used natural elevated sites. When artificial elevated platforms were made available along lake and river shore lines, geese were induced to use these areas to a greater extent. Supporting this conclusion is the 10-percent decrease of island ground nests from 1953 to 1958 with a corresponding increase of lake and river shore line nests from 3 to 8 percent during the same period.

STATISTICAL EVALUATION

We have attempted to answer two basic questions:

1. Is there a difference in nest-site choice when platforms are available?
2. Can the difference be attributed to nesting platforms?

Making decisions in the face of uncertain evidence is the province of statistical inference. We know that tradition is strong in Canada geese and that established ground-nesting habits are not easily broken. We assume, however, that there are random

TABLE 1.—DISTRIBUTION OF CANADA GOOSE NESTS BY HABITAT, FLATHEAD VALLEY, MONTANA

Nest Sites	AREA TOTALS						6-Year Total	6-Year Percent
	1953	1954	1955	1956	1957	1958		
Island nests								
All nests	216	246	282	152	151	155	1,202	
Percent	96	97	95	95	92	92		95
Ground nests only	210	236	275	142	137	139	1,139	
Percent	93	93	93	89	84	83		90
Lake and river shore line nests								
Number	7	7	12	8	13	13	60	
Percent	3	3	4	5	8	8		5
Ground nests only	2	2	6	3	4	1	18	
Percent	1	1	2	2	2	0.5		1.5
Tree nests								
Number	11	10	5	3	9	12	50	
Percent	5	4	2	2	6	7		4
Cliff nests								
Number	0	2	2	1	1	2	8	
Percent	0	1	1	1	1	1		1
Nesting platforms								
Number	Not	3	6	11	13	16	49	
Percent	erected	1	2	7	8	9		5
Total elevated nest sites								
Number	11	15	13	15	23	30	107	
Percent	5	6	4	9	14	18		8
Marsh nests								
Number	2	1	2	0	0	0	5	
Percent	1	5	1	0	0	0		0.5
Totals	225	254	296	160	164	168	1,267	

unexplained variations in nesting habits of geese, that these variations result in somewhat different nesting habits from year to year, and that these variations make Chi-square tests appropriate. Since we cannot predict with any certainty what the geese would have done if platforms had not been erected, we have applied statistical analysis to the first four questions posed.

1. There was a progressive increase in use of platforms from year to year. This was significant at the 99-percent level ($x^2 >$ 15.68 at 5 d.f.).

2. The progressive use of the platforms did not significantly affect the use of natural elevated sites ($x^2 = 9.25$; $x^2 = 11.07$ would be significant at the 95-percent level at 5 d.f.). The inference is that the use of platforms was not a shift from natural elevated sites to platforms. Thus the platforms were responsible for increasing the total number of pairs using aerial structures for nesting.

3. The increase in use of all elevated sites over ground nests was highly significant ($x^2 > 33.96$ at 5 d.f.) and indicates that some geese recognized the aerial sites as being more favorable than ground sites.

4. The change from island ground nests to island elevated nests was highly significant ($x^2 > 17.70$ at 5 d.f.). All evidence indicates this change was induced by platforms.

The decrease in island nesting and corresponding increase in use of shore lines was not statistically significant ($x^2 = 10.71$ at 5 d.f.), but a trend is evident.

Forty-one percent of all platforms erected along lake and river shore lines were used as nesting sites by geese; however, evidence of increase in use of lake and river shore lines for nesting, due to availability of aerial platforms, is not conclusive ($x^2 = 10.88$ with 5 d.f.). But again a trend is apparent.

The large Chi-square values indicate that something other than chance changed the nesting habits; we attribute these changes to the presence of nesting platforms.

USE RELATED TO HEIGHT AND HABITAT

Thirty-six percent of platforms erected at 3- to 10-ft. elevation were utilized by geese for nesting; 28 percent of those at 11 to 20 ft. were used, and 57 percent at 21 to 45 ft. There appeared to be a definite preference for the higher sites, especially when these were on lake and river shore lines. Platforms at lower heights were more readily utilized on islands, especially the small islands. Craighead and Craighead (1949), Geis (1956), and others have shown that Canada geese have a strong preference for nesting on islands. A wide variety of nesting cover was used by the 1,267 nesting pairs observed in this study, but plant cover did not appear to be an important factor in nest-site selection. For the purposes at hand we can, therefore, disregard cover in relation to nesting habitat and classify nest sites into three major habitat categories: small islands, large islands, and lake and river shore lines.

To compare the utilization of platforms by habitat we must consider the density of nesting geese in these three major habitat categories. On the small islands, 1 to 6 a. in extent, nesting density was greatest, averaging 5 nests per acre in 1953 and 1954 (Geis, 1956). Theoretically, at least, there was greater opportunity for a platform to be used, but only 31 percent of the platforms placed on small islands served as nests for geese. On the large islands, averaging 20 to 30 a. and larger, where nesting density was ½ nest per acre, 43 percent of the platforms were used. Along lake and river shore lines, where only 3 percent of the entire goose population nested in 1953, 41 percent of all platforms were used. There was no relationship between the use of platforms and the density of nesting geese where the platforms were erected. Quite different results might occur where nesting density is at a high level and competition for sites greater. We can conclude that in the Flathead Valley platforms were utilized by geese at all heights and in all major habitats, but platforms placed more than 20 ft. above ground and those on large islands and lake and river shore lines proved most attractive.

EFFECT ON POPULATION LEVEL

In 1953 there were 200 nesting pairs in the Flathead Valley study area, with an increase to 216 and 285 in 1954 and 1955 respectively. The population then dropped sharply in 1956 to 154 nesting pairs and remained at that level through 1958. This reduction was largely attributed to overshooting.

Any effect the nesting platforms might have had on population level was masked by the drastic changes caused by hunting pressure. There is no evidence, however, that nesting platforms did or will induce more geese to nest by attracting birds from other population units. We have evidence that nesting during most years is confined almost exclusively to locally reared geese and that tradition, breeding age, migration, survival of adults and subadults, and behavior patterns are probably more important than nest sites in determining population level. Nevertheless, it is conceivable that nesting platforms might increase the population level where a population is not heavily harvested and where suitable nesting sites are a limiting factor. This situation does not exist in the Flathead Valley.

In 1955, when the nesting population was 285 pairs, only 6 out of 71 (8.5 percent) of

TABLE 2.—USE OF NESTING PLATFORMS BY CANADA GEESE, FLATHEAD VALLEY, MONTANA

	AREA TOTALS					5-Year Total	5-Year Average
	1954	1955	1956	1957	1958		
No. of platforms	66	71	78	75	76	366	73
No. platforms showing goose use[1]	15	33	14	15	13	90	18
Percent platforms showing goose use	22.7	46.5	17.9	20.0	17.1	—	24.6
No. platforms used for nesting	3	6	11	13	16	49	—
Percent platforms used for nesting	4.5	8.5	14.1	17.3	21.1	—	13.4
Total no. eggs	14	33	60	77	79	263	—
Average no. eggs per nest	4.67	5.50	5.45	5.92	4.94	—	5.37
No. successful nests	0	6	6	12	11	35	—
Percent nests successful	0.0	100.0	54.6	92.3	68.8	—	71.4
No. eggs hatched	0	31	31	60	56	178	—
Percent eggs hatched	0.0	93.9	51.7	77.9	70.9	—	67.7
No. deserted nests	3	0	3	1	4	11	—
No. nests lost to predation	0	0	0	0	1	1	—
No. nests lost to other causes	0	0	2	0	0	2	—

[1] Includes platforms used for loafing spots and those where scrapes were made but does not include platforms where nesting occurred.

the platforms were used for nesting. In 1958, with a nesting population of 159 pairs, 16 out of 76 platforms (21 percent) were used.

Nesting habitat conditions remained remarkably constant over the years and no relation could be drawn between use of nesting platforms and spring runoff conditions, high water periods, or weather conditions. The degree of use was directly related to time. Progressively greater utilization of platforms occurred from year to year; this amounted to 3, 6, 11, 13, and 16 from 1954 to 1958. The increase in use rose from 4.5 percent in 1954 to 21 percent in 1958 with a 5-yr. average of 13.4 percent (Table 2).

EFFECT ON REPRODUCTIVE RATE AND NESTING SUCCESS

The fact that geese showed a preference for artificial nesting platforms and other elevated sites when these were available suggests that such sites may increase productivity. This can be tested by comparing reproductive rate, hatching success, and percentage of nests successful of those geese using nesting platforms with similar data obtained for the entire population unit.

Over the 6-yr. period, 1,105 pairs of nesting geese (where clutch size was known) produced 5,739 eggs for a reproductive rate of 5.19 eggs per breeding pair. The 49 pairs of geese using nesting platforms during a 5-yr. period produced 263 eggs for a reproductive rate of 5.37 eggs per breeding pair. The ninety-five percent confidence interval for differences in average number of eggs per nest is – 0.48 to + 0.84. There is thus no strong evidence that platforms directly affected the number of eggs per nest. The 1,113 pairs, for which we have complete hatching data, produced 3,408 goslings for a hatching success of 3.06 per pair of adults, whereas the 49 pairs nesting in platforms produced 172 goslings for a hatching success of 3.63. The ninety-five percent confidence interval for difference in average number of goslings per nest is 0.03 to 1.11—evidence that hatching success increased with use of platforms.

One nesting platform placed 25 ft. high in a ponderosa pine on Bull Island in Flathead Lake was occupied 6 consecutive years (1955 through 1960), with 100-percent hatching success. During this period 36 eggs were laid and 36 goslings hatched. There was no indication of mortality occurring during the descent. Whether the same pair of geese utilized the platform each year is not known.

TABLE 3.—NEST FAILURES

Cause of Nesting Failure	Population Unit		Platforms	
	Number	Percent	Number	Percent
Desertion	113	28	11	79
Predation	247	61	1	7
Other causes	44	11	2	14
Total	404		14	

Over a 6-yr. period 65 percent of 1,163 known-fate nests were successful, whereas 71 percent of nests in platforms were successful during a 5-yr. period ($x^2 = 0.603$ at the 95-percent level with 1 d.f. and is not significant).

Causes of Nesting Failure

The major causes of nesting failure were predation and desertion (Table 3). Desertion that occurred before predation took place could not always be detected; thus desertion as a primary cause of nesting failure may be greater than the figures suggest. On the other hand, there is evidence that some mammalian predation may cause desertion but leave the nest and eggs intact. A striking effect of the nesting platforms is revealed by data on cause of nesting failure (Table 3).

In the population unit, desertion accounted for 28 percent of nesting failures over the 6-yr. period. Desertion among geese using the platforms was considerably greater and represented 79 percent of all failures during a 5-yr. period.

Predation was the major cause of nest failure in the population unit, accounting for 247 failures out of 404 or 61 percent. However, only one platform nest was known to have been destroyed by predation; this represented 7 percent. Chi-square tests show that the decreased predation in platform versus non-platform nests is significant at the 99-percent level ($x^2 = 5.74$ with 1 d.f.). When desertion and all other causes of nest failure are compared for platform and non-platform nests, $x^2 = 18.47$ at the 99-percent level and 1 d.f. This is highly significant and indicates that platforms were probably largely responsible for the increase in desertion.

Other causes of nest failure in the population unit and among geese using the platforms showed no noticeable difference, 11 and 14 percent respectively being lumped in this category.

It appears that the exposed position of many of the nest boxes invited greater desertion but greatly reduced predation by the added security of an elevated site. Much of the desertion could be attributed to the disruptive influence of fishermen and sightseers who frequently passed close to the exposed nesting platforms in Flathead Lake or upon occasion inspected them at close range. There is little doubt that this human interference could be reduced by selecting more secluded sites.

We can thus state, in answer to questions 5 and 6, that there was no positive evidence that platforms increased the total nesting population by increasing nest sites or by attracting migratory geese; but the geese using platforms showed a slight increase in reproductive rate, significantly better hatching success, and a higher percentage of nests successful.

The nesting boxes increased desertion as a cause of nest failure, but reduced predation. Since, as we have shown, hatching success increased with use of platforms, increased desertion did not compensate for decreased predation. We can conclude there was a significant net gain in goslings hatched. Furthermore, we believe the loss from desertion can be reduced by more selective placement of the nesting platforms.

Selection of Aerial Platforms

We had hoped to determine under what conditions nesting platforms were selected as nest sites, and the age and sex of the geese involved. From 1955 through 1958, 548 goslings were color-marked with this purpose in mind. However, an average of only 15 percent of the marked geese were present and recognizable in the population at the end of the first year of life. We know a very small number lost neck markers, some may have moved to other population units, but heavy mortality from hunting accounted for most of the 1-yr.-old birds that did not return. Those marked which attained sexual maturity were considerably fewer than those surviving 1 year, and did not provide an adequate sample to work with. It may be significant that of the three color-marked known-age geese using elevated nest sites (two in platforms and one in an osprey nest), all three were 3-yr.-old birds for which our records indicate nesting for the first time. We have no record of a marked goose abandoning an established nest site of former years and then selecting a platform. We have much evidence both among marked and unmarked geese that change of nesting area is not a common practice and probably normally occurs only when the initial site has proved unfavorable. Flooding and predation seem to be major factors causing such changes. As pointed out earlier, geese used a higher percentage of nest platforms on lake and river shore lines and on large islands than those on small islands, and showed a preference for the higher sites; this we believe is largely a response to the threat of predation.

More information is needed on this point and can be obtained only from marked known-age birds. It would be particularly valuable from the standpoint of management to determine to what extent unsuccessful nesters select and use aerial platforms. Preliminary evidence from unmarked birds indicates this may happen. It seems probable that both learning (Thorpe, 1951) and social facilitation (Crawford, 1939) are involved. The authors propose to discuss this in greater detail in a paper on tradition and nest site selection.

A pair of geese tend to return to the same nest site year after year. This tradition has an important effect on the population level and on the distribution of nest sites; it appears to be so basic that, once established, it is not quickly altered by the attraction of elevated nesting platforms.

PATTERN OF PLATFORM USE

Of 75 platforms erected and available to geese for 1 year or longer, 30 were used as nests. Some platforms were used the first year they were constructed while others were not utilized until the fifth year. The pattern of first use was first year 3, second year 8, third year 8, fourth year 3, and fifth year 8. Each year additional platforms were used by geese and some previously used ones were vacated. Eighteen platforms were used only 1 year, 8 were used 2 years, 3 used 3 years, and 1 was used for 6 consecutive years.

After termination of the intensive phase of the study, the artificial nesting platforms were checked for occupancy during 1959 and 1960 to determine if use decreased as unrepaired platforms became untenable. In spite of a reduction in the number of platforms available and/or suitable for nesting, 12 platforms were occupied in 1959 and 13 in 1960. This represents a 25 and 19 percent reduction respectively over the peak year of 1958 (Table 2). The number of natural aerial structures used during these years was 9 and 11 respectively and thus showed no marked change from the situation that existed from 1954 through 1958. We believe the decrease in use of platforms was directly related to their disrepair. To obtain maximum use by geese, platforms should be repaired and filled with soil or duff each year.

MORTALITY OF GOSLINGS DESCENDING FROM AERIAL NESTS

One hundred and seven nests, or 8.4 percent of 1,267 nests, under observation were in elevated sites. (This does not include 45 aerial nests recorded in 1959 and 1960.)

Observation at many of the 107 aerial nests yielded only one incident where a gosling was killed in making the descent. A sharp stick protruding from the sand impaled the gosling when it struck the ground. Craighead and Stockstad (1958) reported an observation of goslings leaving an elevated nest. Since then the senior author and Ralph Stockstad made a second observation of this interesting behavior, and a third was reported to us by Maurice Hornocker. These bear accounting since they shed further light on the survival of goslings reared in aerial nests.

In one instance in late afternoon a Canada goose was observed on an osprey nest some 80 ft. above the ground. Closer inspection showed there were goslings in the nest. Rapping the tree flushed the gander and revealed the goose which hitherto had been concealed in the cup of the nest. It was anticipated that the goose would flush, fly to the water, and call the goslings, and that they would jump as observed on a previous occasion (Craighead and Stockstad, 1958). The goose proved very difficult to dislodge, refusing to leave until the observer had climbed a nearby tree to nest height. The goose left suddenly, and simultaneously with her departure, the three goslings launched themselves over the brink of the nest. All three goslings hit limbs as they fell, but the fall was not effectively broken for any of them. Less than 60 sec. after striking the ground the goslings were carefully examined. None appeared injured. All three could walk and, when taken to the lake shore, swam several hundred yards to join their parents; the family proceeded to swim several miles eastward until lost from sight. The fall sustained by these goslings was as formidable as any that would have been experienced by goslings from the 107 aerial nests under observation. On another occasion six goslings jumped from the top of a dead stub 40 ft. above the ground. One of the six landed on its back in a brush pile and appeared injured, but examination showed no broken bones or external injuries. In about 3 min. it seemed normal and when released swam off to join the goose.

The direct evidence of successful descents is further supported by indirect evidence. We were able to make gosling track counts in sand beneath some tree nests to compare with egg numbers and goslings hatched in these nests. Similarly, counts of 2- and 3-day-old goslings in the vicinity of aerial nests were compared with data on clutch size and hatch. Such data must be interpreted with caution, but the information indicated that most goslings get safely out of aerial nests—even the very high ones.

Management Suggestions

Artificial nesting platforms can be used effectively in the management of Canada geese, providing the platforms are erected at secluded sites and repaired and replenished with soil and duff each season prior to the establishment of nesting territories. In this study they did not cause an increase in general population level, but brought about a change in nesting habitat that was beneficial to the population.

They should prove most effective if placed on large islands or on lake and river shore lines or wherever suitable nesting sites are limited or where natural sites are subjected to flooding or heavy predation. It is recommended that platforms be constructed as described in the methods section, but any large platform securely fastened and filled with soil will suffice. The structures should be placed 20 to 50 ft. above the ground, preferably at isolated sites so as to minimize desertion.

Summary

During a 5-yr. period 73 aerial platforms, on an average, were available each year to Canada geese. One hundred and seven aerial nests of all types were observed; 49 of these were located in the aerial platforms and 58 in natural elevated sites. Since there was no decrease in the use of natural aerial structures during this time but a decrease in ground nests did occur, it was concluded that the platforms caused a greater number of geese to select aerial sites. The percentage of all nesting geese in the population that used nesting platforms increased progressively from 1 percent in 1954, when platforms were first erected, to 9 percent in 1958. The use of all elevated nest sites, including platforms and natural structures, increased from 5 percent in 1953 to 18 percent in 1958. There was no evidence that the nesting platforms increased the number of geese nesting in the study area. However, platforms caused significantly measurable effects in nest-site selection, mortality factors, and hatching success. Use of platforms caused a decrease in island ground nests and an increase in island aerial nests. A general decrease in island nesting and a corresponding increase in use of lake and river shore lines, though not statistically significant, showed a trend and is believed to be due to use of platforms. Supporting this belief is the fact that 41 percent of all platforms erected along shore lines were used as nesting sites. Geese using aerial platforms showed a slight increase in reproductive rate, significantly better hatching success, and a higher percentage of nests successful. The platforms significantly increased desertion as a cause of nest failure, but significantly reduced predation. This was not compensatory as there was a net gain is goslings hatched. Gosling mortality incurred while getting out of elevated nests was negligible. It is concluded that construction of aerial platforms benefited the geese, but to be most effective, platforms should be rehabilitated annually, erected 20 to 50 ft. above the ground, and located in situations remote from human activities.

LITERATURE CITED

CRAIGHEAD, F. C., JR. AND J. J. CRAIGHEAD. 1949. Nesting Canada geese on the Upper Snake River. J. Wildl. Mgmt., 13:51–64.

CRAIGHEAD, J. J. AND D. S. STOCKSTAD. 1958. Goslings descend from aerial nest. J. Wildl. Mgmt., 22:206–207.

CRAWFORD, M. P. 1939. The social psychology of vertebrates. Psych. Bull., 36:407–446.

GEIS, MARY B. 1956. Productivity of Canada geese in the Flathead Valley, Montana. J. Wildl. Mgmt., 20:409–419.

THORPE, W. H. 1951. The learning abilities of birds. Ibis, 93:252–296.

YOCOM, C. F. 1952. Techniques used to increase nesting of Canada geese. J. Wildl. Mgmt., 16:425–428.

Received for publication November 21, 1960.

SELECTED BIBLIOGRAPHY

Management and Economics: Artificial Structures

BELLROSE, F. C. 1953. Housing for wood ducks. Ill. Nat. Hist. Surv. Cir. 45. 47pp.

———, K. L. JOHNSON, AND T. U. MEYERS. 1964. Relative value of natural cavities and nesting houses for wood ducks. J. Wildl. Manage. 28(4):661–676.

———, AND F. B. MCGILVREY. 1966. Characteristics and values of artificial nesting cavities. Pages 125–131 *in* J. B. Trefethen, ed. Wood duck management and research, a symposium. The Wildl. Manage. Inst., Washington, D.C. 212pp.

BISHOP, R. A., AND R. BARRATT. 1970. Use of artificial nest baskets by mallards. J. Wildl. Manage. 34(4):734–738.

BOLEN, E. G. 1967. Nesting boxes for black-bellied tree ducks. J. Wildl. Manage. 31(4):794–797.

BRAKHAGE, G. K. 1966. Tub nests for Canada geese. J. Wildl. Manage 30(4):851–853.

BRENNER, F. J., AND J. J. MONDOK. 1979. Waterfowl nesting rafts designed for fluctuating water levels. J. Wildl. Manage. 43:979–981.

DOTY, H. A. 1979. Duck nest structure evaluations in prairie wetlands. J. Wildl. Manage. 43:976–978.

GORE, J. F. 1974. Forcing Canada geese into elevated nesting structures. Proc. Annu. Conf. S.E. Assoc. Game Fish Comm. 27:324–328.

GRABILL, B. A. 1977. Reducing starling use of wood duck boxes. Wildl. Soc. Bull. 5(2):69–70.

JOHNSON, L. L. 1967. The common goldeneye duck and the role of nesting boxes in its management in north-central Minnesota. J. Minn. Acad. Sci. 34(2):110–113.

LUMSDEN, H. G., R. E. PAGE, AND M. GAUTHIER. 1980. Choice of nest boxes by common goldeneyes in Ontario. Wilson Bull. 92:497–505.

RIENECKER, W. C. 1971. Canada goose nest platforms. Calif. Fish and Game J. 57:113–123.

SUGDEN, L. G. 1971. Rate of loafing raft use by ducks. Can. Field-Nat. 85(4):324–325.

WILL, G. C., AND G. I. CRAWFORD. 1970. Elevated and floating nest structures for Canada geese. J. Wildl. Manage. 34(3):583–586.

Economic Impacts

WATERFOWL IN THE ECONOMY OF THE ESKIMOS ON THE YUKON-KUSKOKWIM DELTA, ALASKA[1]

DAVID R. KLEIN,[2] Alaska Cooperative Wildlife Research Unit, College, AK 99735

Abstract: Use of waterfowl by Eskimos on the Yukon-Kuskokwim Delta amounts to approximately 83,000 geese and brant and 38,000 ducks annually with the greatest take occurring during the spring hunting period. About 5,500 swans and 1,000 cranes are also taken throughout the area and 40,000 eggs are gathered for use as food. Egg gathering and village drives of molting, flightless adult birds have decreased in importance in recent years, but spring hunting of waterfowl continues to be important as it coincides with the period of greatest need for food by the Eskimos.

Most of the inhabitants of the Yukon-Kuskokwim Delta (Fig. 1) are Eskimos who traditionally have killed ducks and geese for food without regard to the time of year or other restriction. Historically, the harvest was accomplished by egg gathering during the nesting period, by clubbing flightless birds during the molt, and by taking on the wing with bolas and bird spears. The introduction of firearms to this region began in the early nineteenth century and today the Eskimo hunter is well equipped with modern arms and ammunition limited only by his ability to pay. Available to him are methods and means of transportation giving him greater mobility than ever before.

This study was undertaken from April to June 1964 and during February 1965 to provide basic information for an objective appraisal of the problem of seasonal use of waterfowl by Eskimos in the Yukon-Kuskokwim Delta. Letters were written in advance to each village council within the study area, explaining the nature of the study and asking their cooperation when I visited the villages shortly after the spring hunting period.

Mr. Ray Christiansen, who operates an air charter service out of Bethel and is a representative in the Alaska State Legislature, flew me to most of the villages. He was of great help for, being an Eskimo, he acted as interpreter, and the fact that many of the people in the villages were his personal friends established a rapport that otherwise would not have been possible. Samuelson Flying Service of Bethel, which is owned, operated, and almost exclusively staffed by Eskimos, flew me to the other villages.

Upon arriving at a community, the village council president (chief) or other council member was contacted and arrangements were made to meet the men of the village, usually at the National Guard armory, but sometimes in trading posts, school and church buildings, community houses, or out-of-doors. Although the meetings were held at short notice, generally 20 to 30 men attended. Actual attendance varied from 8 at Akiak to 45 at Hooper Bay. At the meetings, which were held in 23 different villages (see footnote, Table 5), the reason for the study was explained; it was pointed out that everyone would benefit from an objective appraisal of the problem based on facts. Specific questions were then asked about the numbers by species of waterfowl obtained by the average hunter during the spring and fall shooting periods and these values were then related to the

[1] Originally published in Arctic 19(4):319–336, 1966.

[2] Present address: SR Box 20059, Fairbanks, AK 99701.

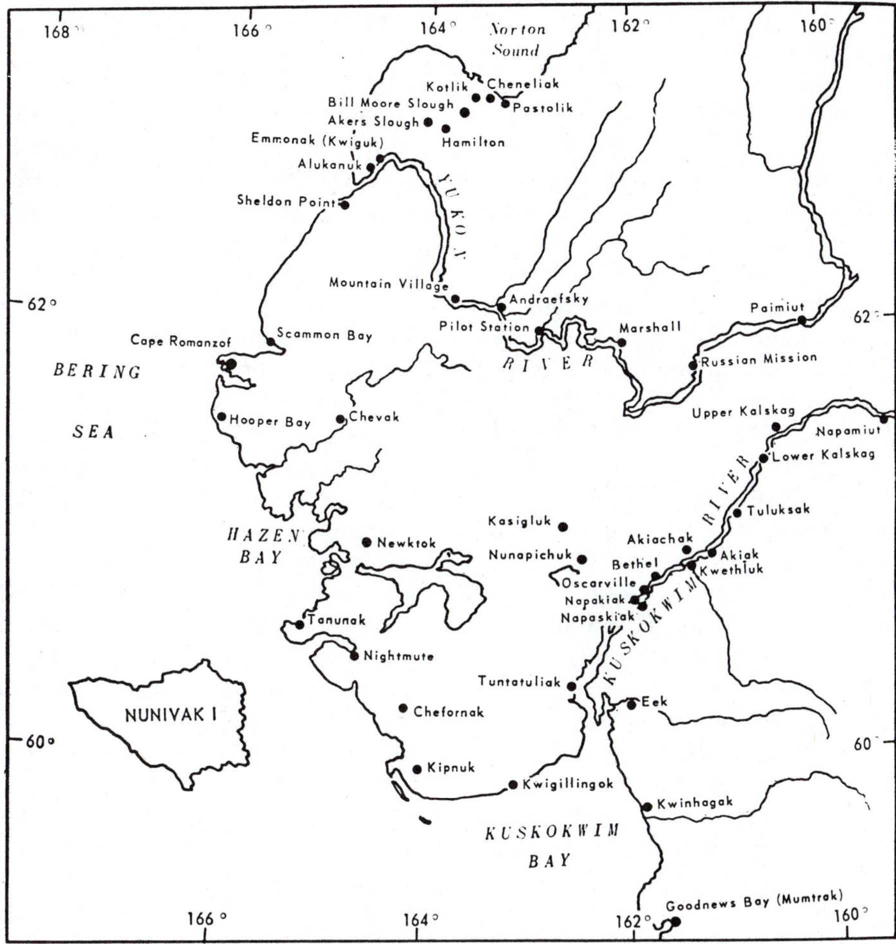

Fig. 1. The Yukon-Kuskokwim Delta area of Alaska.

average take per household. Information on the number of eggs gathered per household and the primary species involved was also sought as well as the number and species of birds caught in summer drives of flightless adults. The men were also questioned as to the use made of the birds; the numbers eaten fresh and the amount preserved and methods employed; trends in recent years in the take and use of waterfowl; the types and amounts of other wildlife resources available to the people, such as fish, marine mammals, moose, fur bearers, and small game.

The cooperation of the people in the villages was excellent. In one instance, in response to my preliminary letter, each hunter in the village reported his daily take of waterfowl during the spring hunt to the scribe of the local National Guard platoon. The scribe in turn tallied the total take for each man and presented the record to me when I visited the village. In another area, where the people had physically resisted enforcement attempts by U.S. Fish and Wildlife Service agents in the spring of 1961, the men were extremely cautious about divulging information about their use of waterfowl. Generally, however, the people freely provided the information I requested about their spring and fall harvest of geese and ducks. This is substantiated by comparison of these data for villages on the lower Yukon with similar data collected by Branch of River Basin Studies (BRBS) personnel during 1956 (U.S. Fish and Wildlife Service 1957). The fact that I used an interpreter who was an Eskimo, well known to the people, and further, that I was not identified with the U.S. Fish and Wildlife Service, undoubtedly contributed to the reliability of the data I collected. It is noteworthy that data from this study and the BRBS study for Emmonak and Mountain Village, where BRBS personnel spent considerable time, are similar, whereas the data for Pilot Station, where BRBS personnel had very limited contact, show wide differences. These comparisons of average waterfowl harvest per household are as follows:

	Total geese reported taken		Total ducks reported taken	
	This study	BRBS	This study	BRBS
Emmonak	30	23	15	5
Mountain Village	38	22	12	12
Pilot Station	170	23	75	11

The Eskimos of the Yukon-Kuskokwim Delta region feel strongly about their need and *right* to hunt geese and ducks in the spring, but they feel less justified in their spring hunting of swans and cranes, egg gathering, and summer drives of molting flightless waterfowl. This is presumably because they cannot usually justify these activities on the basis of need, and they harbour some concern about the possible harmful effects on the waterfowl populations. The data on the latter are therefore less reliable than the data on the goose and duck harvest.

Population and economic data for the study area have been obtained from the various published and mimeographed reports cited in the text; Kozely's work (1964) has been of particular value.

Ethnological and historical information about the Eskimo people of the area was obtained from the literature. Oswalt (1963*a,b*) gives detailed descriptions of the cultural changes taking place, the roots of origin and historical cultures of the people, and the ethnography of the Eskimo.

This report deals primarily with the seasonal use of waterfowl by Eskimos on the Yukon-Kuskokwim Delta, and the demographic, economic, sociologic, and ethnographic information presented is only that related to the problem.

THE PEOPLE

The Yukon-Kuskokwim Delta area has an average population density of about one person per 3 square miles; 97 per cent are Eskimos. The area supports the largest concentration of Eskimo people existing in the world today. With the exception of less than 25 people living in 3 isolated locations, the entire population of the area, estimated at 9,521 in 1963, lives in 35 villages and the town of Bethel. The population of Bethel in 1963 was 1,538 and the other villages ranged in size from 31 to 531. In 1963 only 6 villages had a population of less than 100, whereas 13 were in the 100–200 range, 11 in the 200–300 range, 7 in the 300–400 range, and only Hooper Bay had a population in excess of 500 people (Table 1). The average annual crude rate of natural increase in the area was 4.18 per cent in 1964. This compares with 1.4 per cent for

Table 1. Yukon-Kuskokwim Delta village populations (data from U.S. Bureau of the Census 1962, U.S. Bureau of Indian Affairs (BIA), and Kozely 1964).

Village	U.S. census 1960	BIA village census			No. households 1962
		1961	1962	1963	
Yukon River					
Russian Mission	102			123*	20**
Marshall	166			201*	32**
Pilot Station	219	248	247	251	44
Andraefsky	225			272*	44**
Mountain Village	300	316	325	351	66
Hamilton	35	31	31	31	4
Kotlik	57	119	123	165	18
Cheneliak	97	22	23	31	7
Pastolik		16		10	1***
Bill Moore Slough		32		4	2***
Akers Slough		12		5	1***
Emmonak (Kwiguk)	358	393	384	388	63**
Alukanuk	278	332	343	362	60
Kuskokwim River					
Upper Kalskag	147	155	151	121	26
Lower Kalskag	122	140	140	148*	31
Tuluksak	137	146	155	165*	30
Akiak	187	180	184	194	29
Akiachak	229	237	252	277*	45
Kwethluk	325	345	356	366	63
Bethel	1,258			1,538	203**
Oscarville	51			61	10**
Napaskiak	154	168	163	186*	35
Napakiak	190	244	246	254	43
Tuntatuliak	144	152	160	169	24
Eek	154	209	216	212	39
Kwigillingok	344	310	299	318	50
Kwinhagak	228	252	264	280	45**
Nunapichuk	327	368	387	392	62
Kasigluk	244	253	345	229	39
Bering Sea					
Sheldon Point	125			138*	22**
Scammon Bay	115	155	163	169	26
Hooper Bay	460	482	509	531	72
Chevak	315	348	358	372	63
Newktok	129	148	146	144	20
Tanunak	183	204	215	232	36
Nightmute	237	246	262	258	47
Chefornak	133	133	143	139	30
Kipnuk	221	256	265	274	45
Goodnews Bay (Mumtrak)	154	153	167	159	33****
Total				9,521	1,530

* Estimates based on average population change of other villages.
** Estimates based on average household size of 6.2; in the case of Bethel, it includes only the Eskimos population.
*** 1963.
**** 1961.

the entire United States and rates of 2 per cent for India and 3.5 per cent for Mexico during the current decade.

Since the introduction of aspects of Western culture and economy there has been a general abandonment of the smaller villages where subsistence hunting and fishing were the only means of livelihood. Kozely (1964) lists over 50 villages within the study area that have been abandoned during the past 3 decades; many of these villages were on the tundra of the Delta at some distance from the 2 main rivers. As a result vast areas are now unpopulated, and the Eskimo people are now concentrated in the larger villages along the Kuskokwim and Yukon Rivers, and on the coast of the Bering Sea where there are schools, churches, and stores.

In a U.S. Public Health Service study (from Kozely 1964) of a sample of 10 villages in the Yukon-Kuskokwim Delta area, including 420 housing units, it was found that 86 per cent of the houses had only 1 room, 10 per cent had 2 rooms, and 4 per cent had 3 rooms. The typical family consisted of 8 persons; the mother's age was 25 to 29, she had 5 living children; and 40 per cent of the mothers studied had tuberculosis.

ECONOMIC STATUS OF AREA

The basic economy of the entire Yukon-Kuskokwim Delta area is that of subsistence hunting, fishing, and gathering. The major portion of the food consumed by the people and their dogs comes from wildlife resources; virtually all the fuel for cooking and heating is locally obtained wood or seal oil, and much of the Eskimo clothing is made from hides of the marine and the land mammals of the area.

By far the most important single item in the subsistence economy is salmon. All of the villages, with the exception of those in the coastal areas, are dependent for their primary food source upon the annual migratory runs of salmon up the Yukon and Kuskokwim rivers. With the beginning of the fish runs, the people disperse from the villages to fishing camps along the rivers. These are traditionally-used fishing sites each occupied by one or several families, and with permanent fish drying racks and storage sheds. People at Kasigluk and Nunapichuk annually travel down the Johnson River to its confluence with the Kuskokwim where they fish for salmon. Other fish are also available seasonally throughout the area.

The people of the coastal villages of Scammon Bay, Hooper Bay, Tanunak, Nightmute, Newktok, Kipnuk, Chefornak, Kwigillingok, Kwinhagak, and Goodnews Bay (Fig. 1), derive much of their subsistence from the sea, although not to the same extent as the Eskimos on the islands of the Bering Sea or those on the Arctic coast of Alaska. Fish, primarily tomcod (*Microgadus proximus*), and seals (primarily *Phoca vitulina*) are the resources on which they draw most heavily. Other marine mammals, such as walrus (*Odobenus divergens*) and beluga whales (*Delphinapterus leucas*) are taken when available but they are not abundant in this region. Normally, a few men from the villages on the Yukon Delta, the villages of Chevak, Tuntatuliak and Eek, and as far up the Kuskokwim as Napaskiak (Fig. 1), travel by dog sled to the coastal areas to hunt seals. Seal hunting is an important winter activity and continues into the spring and early summer until the sea ice leaves the coastal areas.

Other food resources of the area include moose (*Alces alces*), ptarmigan (*Lagopus lagopus*), snowshoe and arctic hare (*Lepus americanus* and *L. othus*), carcasses of mammals taken for their

Table 2. Sources and amounts of earned income within villages on the Yukon-Kuskokwim Delta, 1962 (data from Kozely 1964).

Village	Wages	Fishing	Hunting and trapping	Arts and crafts	Other activities	Private business	Total
Yukon River							
Pilot Station	32,993	6,250	16,115	2,990	340	8,500	67,188
Mountain Village	37,000	150,000	15,700	770	1,600		205,070
Kotlik	19,500	5,000	10,500	1,400			36,400
Alukanuk	124,000	25,000	16,800	3,200	220	5,000	174,220
Kuskokwim River							
Kwethluk	21,000	40,000	21,660	21,500	3,200	1,000	108,360
Napaskiak	20,500	15,000	18,050	3,700	1,050		58,300
Napakiak	39,895	12,000	12,242	3,372	1,200		68,709
Tuntatuliak	21,035	13,090	13,641	3,611	3,268	1,900	56,545
Kwigillingok	46,225	30,000	19,810	3,090	8,970	3,000	111,095
Kasigluk	15,000	61,000	25,500	5,000	7,000	10,000	123,500
Bering Sea							
Scammon Bay	18,800	13,500	11,085	6,500	1,200	7,000	58,085
Hooper Bay	28,000	10,000	28,470	1,400	3,000	3,000	73,870
Newktok	19,700		5,512	1,670	575		27,457
Tanunak	70,000	6,020	15,200	5,175	1,020	7,000	104,415
Nightmute	19,900	1,600	8,150	11,100	1,500	8,500	50,750
Chefornak	26,500	12,500	22,650	2,790	700	1,000	66,140
Kipnuk	98,000	7,500	32,200	5,700	7,150	6,000	156,550
Goodnews Bay (Mumtrak)	100,000	4,400	3,860	1,620	75	400	110,355
Percentage of total	45.7	24.9	17.9	5.1	2.5	3.8	

pelts (such as muskrat, *Ondatra zibethica* and mink *Mustela vison*), berries and greens from wild plants, and the limited produce of leaf and root crops in home gardens.

The cash economy of the area is supplementary to the subsistence economy which meets many of the basic needs of the people. Nevertheless, cash is essential to purchase the many staple food items such as tea, coffee, salt, flour, milk and sugar introduced into the Eskimo diet by whites; it is also required for clothing, outboard motors and fuel, fish nets, rifles and ammunition, household items, etc. Less basic to the needs of the people, but important to their psychological well-being, are such things as food delicacies from the trading post, dress clothing to be worn at church and social events, radios, occasional air transportation, money for movies, and religious items and offerings.

Sources and amounts of cash income for 18 villages in the Yukon-Kuskokwim Delta area are presented in Table 2. Wages are derived mainly from fish-processing work, National Guard participation, work for the local village traders, maintenance work for U.S. Bureau of Indian Affairs and State school facilities, and longshoring. Commercial fishing is an important source of income on the Kuskokwim River downstream from Kwethluk, and on the Yukon River from Andraefsky to the sea. King, silver, and chum salmon are the three species of fish upon which the commerical fisheries are based. There is no commercial fishery in the coastal areas between the Yukon Delta and the Kuskokwim River.

Income is derived from the shooting of

muskrats and trapping of mink for their pelts, and from the sale of seal hides. Mink trapping has been by far the most important activity of this nature and averages annually 15,000 to 20,000 mink valued at between $375,000 and $500,000 (Burns 1964). Mink from the Yukon-Kuskokwim Delta are among the largest and of the best quality in North America, and the command premium prices at fur auctions. Oswalt (1963*b*) indicates that $250 to $375 was the average value of mink to each trapper in 1956 at Napaskiak. In the past two years the harvest has been considerably below these levels owing to poor weather conditions during the trapping season and a pronounced reduction in the value of mink on the market. Hair seal pelts have increased in value in the last few years and now bring prices of $20 to $30 per pelt. Muskrats have yielded a reduced income in recent years due to low value of pelts and the consequent decreased interest in spring rat hunting. Oswalt states that during 1956, which was a poor year with local prices of only $0.40 to $0.85 per pelt, the range in income by Napaskiak muskrat hunters was $20 to $200. Other fur bearers of lower abundance and frequently only locally available throughout the area, but which contribute to the overall income from trapping, are weasel, beaver, marten, river otter, snowshoe hare, lynx, wolf, and fox.

Income from arts and crafts is derived from the sale of women's handicraft such as baskets of grasses, sedges, and roots; parkas and mukluks; dolls and beadwork. In some of the coastal villages, men do limited ivory and wood carving. Utilitarian articles constructed for local sale by some men with special craft abilities include river boats, kayaks, and dog sleds.

Total personal income within the study area can only be estimated from the incomplete data available; however, it exceeds $4 million annually. Earned income constitutes approximately 85 per cent of the total income of the area, the remainder being welfare income from state and federal sources (Table 3). Welfare money is available mainly in the following categories: old age assitance, aid to dependent children, aid to the blind, unemployment compensation, social security, and direct Bureau of Indian Affairs and State of Alaska payments to individuals without other sources of income and unable to subsist from the land. Of the total welfare moneys coming into the area, approximately 80 per cent are from the State of Alaska, and most of the remainder is through the Bureau of Indian Affairs. It is interesting that the distribution of welfare money to the villages appears to be correlated with the proximity of the village to the town of Bethel, where the district welfare agency offices are located. For example, the village of Napaskiak, which is only 7 miles from Bethel, has a per capita income $17 above the average for the area and 30.2 per cent of its income is derived from welfare. While Pilot Station, approximately 90 miles from Bethel and on the Yukon River, has a per capita income $106 below the area average, yet only 9.1 per cent of its income is from welfare. In addition to direct welfare payments, those individuals with Eskimo blood are also given medical care through the auspices of the U.S. Public Health Service, which has a large staffed hospital in Bethel and sends nurse and doctor teams on frequent visits to the villages.

The per capita cash income for the area is obviously one of the lowest in the nation. The average per capita income of $432 for the villages, for which complete data is available, can be compared to the 1963 averages of $2,839 for all of Alaska,

Table 3. Total cash income within villages on the Yukon-Kuskokwim Delta (data from Kozely 1964).

Village	1963 welfare		1962 total earned income	Per capita income	Income per household
	BIA	State			
Yukon River					
Pilot Station	1,425	13,296	67,188	326	1,862
Mountain Village	256	20,312	205,070	643	3,419
Kotlik		6;765	36,400	262	2,398
Cheneliak	639	2,340			
Emmonak (Kwiguk)		13,840			
Alukanuk	798	28,552	174,220	562	3,393
Kuskokwim River					
Upper Kalskag	2,444	10,712			
Lower Kalskag	4,054				
Tuluksak	988				
Akiak	2,529	9,920			
Akiachak	84	17,608			
Kwethluk	1,983	14,344	108,360	341	1,979
Napaskiak	344	24,936	58,300	449	2,388
Napakiak	1,693	16,452	68,709	342	2,020
Tuntatuliak	480	13,752	56,545	419	2,958
Eek	666	10,572			
Kwigillingok	468		111,095		
Kwinhagak	1,517	3,296			
Nunapichuk		9,081			
Kasigluk	8,828	12,568	123,500	633	3,715
Bering Sea					
Scammon Bay	511	9,636	58,085	404	2,624
Hooper Bay	6,191	21,412	73,870	191	1,409
Chevak	1,280	17,468			
Newktok	580	6,144	27,457	237	1,709
Tanunak	3,543	10,228	104,415	509	3,283
Nightmute	134	10,492	50,750	238	1,306
Chefornak	68	12,696	66,140	568	2,630
Kipnuk	2,842	20,428	156,550	656	3,996
Goodnews Bay (Mumtrak)	857	11,720	110,355	773	3,725
Average				432	2,611

$2,500 for all 50 states and $1,390 for Mississippi, which has the lowest average in the nation. The contrast is obviously great and is reflected in the standard of living of the Eskimo people. However, a direct comparison of cash income of this nature does not take into consideration the value of the subsistence commodities that the Yukon-Kuskokwim Delta produces and the extent to which these commodities supplant the need for cash expenditures. The fish, wildlife, and plant resources of the area are all the more important to the Eskimo people because of the high cost of imported items which reduces the buying power of the dollar to less than one half of what it is in Seattle or other West Coast cities.

PATTERNS OF WATERFOWL USE

Although the bow with blunt-tipped arrow, bird spear, and bolas, once used by the Eskimos for taking waterfowl on the wing, were relatively inefficient in contrast to the shotgun a much greater effort was expended in the pursuit of waterfowl over a longer duration of time than at present. Egg gathering and drives

Table 4. Earliest dates of arrival of waterfowl species in the Yukon-Kuskokwim Delta region (data from Gabrielson and Lincoln 1959).

Species	Dates	Locations
Cackling goose	Apr. 24	Bethel
	Apr. 29	Mt. Village
Lesser Canada goose	Apr. 17	Bethel
Emperor goose	May 15	Hooper Bay
White-fronted goose	Apr. 17	Bethel
	Apr.17	Chevak
	Apr. 25	Mt. Village
Black brant	May 5	St. Michael*
	May 20	Hooper Bay
	May 25	Mt. Village
Snow goose	Apr. 29	Mt. Village
Mallard	Apr. 13	Bethel
	Apr. 16	Mt. Village
	Apr. 23	Pilot Station
Pintail	Apr. 14	Marshall
	Apr. 19	Eek
	Apr. 20	St. Michael*
	May 8	Hooper Bay
Whistling swan	Mid-April	St. Michael*
	Apr. 21	Mt. Village
	May 7	Bethel
Lesser sandhill crane	Apr. 29	Mt. Village
	May 2	St. Michael*
Pacific eider	May 4	Hooper Bay
King eider	May 4	Hooper Bay
Spectacled eider	May 2	Cape Romanzof
	May 5	Hooper Bay
	May 6	St. Michael*

* Not included in Fig. 1 as at 63°29′ N., 162°03′ W.

of flightless adult birds in the summer are still undertaken in essentially the same manner as they were in the past, although the use of outboard motors had added to the mobility of the Eskimo and motor powered boats are a definite asset in conducting drives on large lakes or lake systems. The patterns of waterfowl use by the Eskimos of the Delta region vary considerably from the coastal areas to the upriver regions where the tundra intergrades with the shrub type and spruce forests. Aboriginal techniques of hunting waterfowl show remarkably little variation throughout the arctic and subarctic tundra regions. In this respect, Chard's (1963) description of methods of hunting waterfowl employed by the Nganasan of the Taimyr Peninsula of Siberia is also applicable to the Eskimos of the Yukon-Kuskokwim Delta.

Spring Hunting

During early spring (late April and early May, see Table 4), large numbers of northward-migrating eider ducks become available to seal hunters. The birds come in almost continuous flocks of a few to several hundred each and fly low over the open leads adjacent to the shore ice. Seal hunters are reluctant to shoot eiders when seals are present in the area because they feel their shooting will frighten the seals; however, the eiders are readily taken during periods when seals may be temporarily unavailable. They are an important source of food for seal hunters in the field and are also taken back to the villages when the birds can be killed in sufficient quantity. Because the eiders are among the first waterfowl available after a long winter of living on fish and seal, their arrival is welcomed by the people as a pleasant diet variation, and in those years when winter stores are becoming depleted they are an important supplementary food.

Whereas firearms have enabled seal hunters to take larger numbers of eiders on any one hunt than was possible before, in recent years the cash economy has resulted in increased dependence on purchased foods with a corresponding reduction in the effort expended on seal hunting. Even with a substantial increase in the cash value of raw seal hides, only an average of about 20 per cent of the men of the coastal villages continue to hunt seals. Seal hunting is of greatest importance in the villages of Scammon Bay, Hooper Bay, and Tanunak.

As the spring progresses in the coastal

areas, other early-arriving species become available (Tables 4–7). The cackling (*Branta canadensis minima*) and white-fronted geese (*Anser albifrons frontalis*) arrive in abundance in early May, but a few birds may be seen in late April. The emperor goose (*Philacta canagica*) usually comes a little later except to the Goodnews Bay area where they congregate in large numbers in late April. The emperor goose is taken in greater numbers than any other goose in all of the coastal villages from Goodnews Bay to Newktok. In Chevak, Hooper Bay, and Scammon Bay, the cackling and white-fronted geese constitute the larger portion of the spring take.

Pintail ducks (*Anas acuta*) are also taken in large numbers throughout the coastal area (Table 6). They are not as eagerly sought as geese, because they represent less meat but they are the easier bird to obtain after the tundra ponds and lakes are free of ice. Mallards (*Anas platyrhynchos platyrhynchos*) are not taken in appreciable numbers by Eskimos in the coastal villages, but they are more plentiful in the areas further back from the coast.

During the early spring immediately after the birds first start arriving on the tundra, hunting is most intensive. At this time, the people are eager for a change of diet, other food is in shorter supply than at any other time of the year, and after a winter of unemployment, financial reserves are at a yearly low. The men generally travel 10 to 20 miles daily by dog team to bluffs and high cutbanks where shooting in flight is possible or to exposed mud bars where the geese rest before open water is available. Blinds of snow and ice or dead vegetation are used as well as decoys of mud and sticks or dead birds.

Further in from the coast and on the lower Yukon and Kuskokwim rivers, the pattern of spring hunting is similar to that on the coast. Species composition, however, shows more variation from area to area. On the Kuskokwim River, including the tundra villages of Nunapichuk and Kasigluk, the Canada goose varieties (cackling and lesser Canada geese, *Branta canadensis leucopareia*), and to a slightly lesser extent the white-fronted goose, are the only geese taken in numbers during the spring hunt (Table 5). Although among the ducks, pintails are taken in greatest number, mallards assume increasing importance in the upriver areas. Most of the early spring hunting is done along the Kuskokwim River itself, which is an important flightway for migrating geese and ducks.

The species of waterfowl taken during the spring hunting period on the Yukon River vary considerably more from area to area than on the Kuskokwim River. At Russian Mission, the Canada geese varieties are taken in greatest numbers while hunters from Marshall and Pilot Station take more brant (*Branta nigricans*) and fewer white-fronted and Canada geese. At Andraefsky, white-fronted geese predominate in the bag; and at Mountain Village, snow geese (*Chen hyperborea hyperborea*) and white-fronted geese are taken in almost equal numbers with brant and the Canada varieties being of lesser importance. Pintails and mallards are taken in equal numbers on the Yukon from Russian Mission to the mouth.

Without doubt, the importance to the Eskimo of spring hunting on the Yukon-Kuskokwim Delta, and the take of waterfowl associated with it, have increased substantially since the introduction of modern firearms. Because of the increased human population throughout the entire Delta and its concentration in relatively few villages, a greater pressure

Table 5. Take of geese and brant by Eskimos on the Yukon-Kuskokwim Delta.

	Spring							Fall						
			Relative importance							Relative importance				
Village	Total village	Total house-hold	Canada	Whitefront	Emperor	Snow	Black brant	Total village	Total house-hold	Canada	Whitefront	Emperor	Snow	Black brant
Yukon River														
Russian Mission	240	12	1					120	6	1				
Marshall	1,120	35		2			1	1,600	50	3	2			1
Pilot Station	2,640	60	3	2			1	4,840	110	3	2			1
*Andraefsky	1,892	43	3	1		4	2	2,728	62	2	1			3
Mountain Village	1,650	25	3	1		1	4	858	13	2	1			
*Hamilton	92	23	3	2		1		36	9	2	1			
*Kotlik	414	23	3	2		1		162	9	2	1			
*Cheneliak	161	23	3	2		1		72	9	2	1			
*Pastolik	23	23	3	2		1		9	9	2	1			
*Bill Moore Slough	46	23	3	2		1		18	9	2	1			
*Akers Slough	23	23	3	2		1		9	9	2	1			
Emmonak (Kwiguk)	1,260	20	3	2		1		630	10	2	1			
Alukanuk	1,500	25	3	2		1		480	8	1	2			3
Kuskokwim River														
*Upper Kalskag	520	20	1	1				130	5	1				
Lower Kalskag	620	20	1	1				155	5	1				
Tuluksak	750	25	2	1				390	13	2	1			
Akiak	870	30	1	2				232	8	1	2			
Akiachak	2,250	50	1	2				450	10	1	2			
*Kwethluk	2,520	40	1	2				567	9	1	2			
*Bethel	812	4	1	2				406	2	1	2			
*Oscarville	250	25	1					100	10	1				
*Napaskiak	875	25	1					350	10	1				
Napakiak	1,075	25	1					430	10	1				
*Tuntatuliak	480	20	1					120	5	1				
Eek	780	20	1	1				195	5	1				
Kwigillingok	1,250	25	2		1			500	10					
Kwinhagak	810	18	2		1	3		135	3				1	
Nunapichuk	4,960	80	1	2				3,720	60	1	2			
*Kasigluk	3,120	80	1	2				2,340	60	1	2			

Table 5. Continued.

Village	Spring							Fall						
			Relative importance							Relative importance				
	Total village	Total house-hold	Canada	Whitefront	Emperor	Snow	Black brant	Total village	Total house-hold	Canada	Whitefront	Emperor	Snow	Black brant
Bering Sea														
Sheldon Point	330	15	3	1		2		110	5	2	1			
Scammon Bay	2,600	100	1	3	2	4	5	2,600	100	1	3	2		
Hooper Bay	6,480	90	1	2	4		3	7,200	100	1	2	4		3
Chevak	1,134	18	1	2	3	4		819	13	1	2	3	4	
*Newktok	420	21	2		1			240	12	1				
Tanunak	900	25			1			540	15	1				
*Nightmute	987	21	2		1			564	12	1				
Chefornak	450	15	2	3	1			240	8	1	2			
*Kipnuk	1,125	25	2		1			675	15	1				
Goodnews Bay (Mumtrak)	429	13			1		2	165	5	1				
Total	47,858							34,935						
Approx. take by species			20,000	13,500	6,500	5,400	2,500			18,200	9,100	1,700	400	5,500
Average per hunter		31							23					

* Villages not visited; the basis for extrapolating data between ecologically similar villages to obtain estimates for those villages which were not visited was as follows:

Andraefsky = average of Pilot Station and Mountain Village
Hamilton, Kotlik, Cheneliak, Pastolik, Bill Moore Slough, Akers Slough = average of Emmonak and Alukanuk
Upper Kalskag = Lower Kalskag
Kwethluk = average of Akiak and Akiachak
Bethel (native) = estimate based on FWS, BIA, and other reports
Oscarville, Napaskiak = Napakiak
Tuntatuliak = Eek
Kasigluk = Nunapichuk
Nightmute, Newktok = average of Chefornak, Tanunak, and Kipnuk

Table 6. Take of ducks by Eskimos on the Yukon-Kuskokwim Delta.

Village	Spring					Fall			
	Total village	Total house-hold	Relative importance			Total village	Total house-hold	Relative importance	
			Mallard	Pintail	Eider			Mallard	Pintail
Yukon River									
Russian Mission	540	27	2	1		260	13	2	1
Marshall	320	10	1	2		160	5	1	2
Pilot Station	1,100	25	2	1		2,200	50	2	1
*Andreafsky	704	16	2	1		1,188	27	2	1
Mountain Village	462	7	1	2		330	5	1	2
*Hamilton	24	6	2	1		48	12	1	1
*Kotlik	108	6	2	1		216	12	2	1
*Cheneliak	42	6	2	1		84	12	2	1
*Pastolik	6	6	2	1		12	12	2	1
*Bill Moore Slough	12	6	2	1		24	12	2	1
*Akers Slough	6	6	2	1		12	12	2	1
Emmonak (Kwiguk)	315	5	1			630	10		
Alukanuk	420	7	2	1		900	15	2	1
Kuskokwim River									
*Upper Kalskag	260	10	1	2		130	5	1	2
Lower Kalskag	310	10	1	2		155	5	1	2
Tuluksak	300	10	2	1		210	7	2	1
Akiak	870	30	2	1		493	17	2	1
Akiachak	315	7	2	1		675	15	2	1
*Kwethluk	1,134	18	2	1		1,008	16	2	1
*Bethel	609	3	2	1		203	1	2	1
*Oscarville	150	15		1		30	3		1
*Napaskiak	525	15		1		105	3		1
Napakiak	645	15		1		129	3		1
*Tuntatuliak	288	12		1		72	3		1
Eek	468	12		1		117	3		1
Kwigillingok	750	15	3	2	1	250	5	2	1
Kwinhagak	450	10		1	2	225	5		1
Nunapichuk	1,860	30	2	1		930	15	2	1
*Kasigluk	1,170	30	2	1		585	15	2	1
Bering Sea									
Sheldon Point	110	5		1		286	13	2	1
Scammon Bay	650	25	3	2	1	520	20	2	1
Hooper Bay	1,080	15		1	2	864	12		1
Chevak	504	8		1	2	945	15		1
*Newktok	540	27		2	1	200	10		1
Tanunak	720	20		2	1	468	13		
*Nightmute	1,269	27		2	1	470	10		1
Chefornak	600	20	3	2	1	390	13	2	1
*Kipnuk	1,800	40			1	225	5		1
Goodnews Bay (Mumtrak)	264	8			1	66	2		1
Total	21,700					15,815			
			4,700	12,000	3,300			4,800	10,500
Average per hunter		14					10		

* Data calculated from ecologically similar villages. See footnote Table 5.

is exerted upon the land resources available to any one village. Consequently, although the resources of the land in the more remote areas are not exploited as they were in the past, land in the vicinity of the villages cannot provide the abundance of subsistence foods necessary to feed the population throughout the year. As food shortages are most likely to coincide with the spring arrival of waterfowl, it is understandable that use of the birds is greatest at that time.

The most intense spring hunting is immediately after the birds first arrive and until thaw conditions render travel by dog team on the rivers, sloughs, and tundra no longer possible. During the breakup of ice (early May on the Kuskokwim and late May on the Yukon) and until it ceases to flow in the rivers, travel is greatly restricted and hunting is naturally curtailed. Only a few years ago it was the custom of virtually all of the Eskimos of the river and tundra villages to leave before spring breakup and travel as family units to individual hunting camps dispersed throughout the tundra of the Delta. At these camps, muskrat hunting was the primary occupation, although waterfowl were shot for food. The families generally stayed there until salmon were beginning to run in the rivers, and travel back to the villages was possible by boat. Now, because of the decreased interest in muskrat hunting and the reluctance of parents to take their children out of school, there are at present only a few families in each village who continue to make the annual move to the spring hunting camps. This trend has accordingly reduced the late spring hunting of waterfowl, which has in the past been dispersed over a wider area than the early spring shooting, and results in the taking of birds that may have already begun nesting.

During the summer, an occasional bird may be shot for food in the Delta region, but generally the abundance of fresh fish prevents any shortage of food and the people are usually occupied with the many activities associated with the catching and preservation of fish. Also in recent years, increasing numbers of men in the lower Yukon and Kuskokwim River areas have become engaged in commercial fishing and many travel annually from the villages of the coast near the mouth of the Kuskokwim to the Bristol Bay area to be employed in salmon canneries. These cash-yielding occupations, which are important to the economy of the villages, obviously take precedence over subsistence hunting.

Egg Gathering

The gathering of eggs from the nests of waterfowl has traditionally been practised throughout the Delta region; however, it has been of greatest importance in the coastal tundra where nesting densities are highest (Table 7). It seems likely that in spite of the increased human population, fewer eggs are gathered now than in the past; for with most of the people concentrated in the villages, the total area searched is much less. There is no significant amount of waterfowl nesting in the shrub and forest zones adjacent to the upriver villages on the Yukon and Kuskokwim rivers, consequently, egg gathering is practised only by the few Eskimos who travel to spring hunting camps on the tundra.

Egg-gathering is undertaken primarily by the women and children of the coastal and tundra villages. Although the eggs are important as food, the traditional significance in the culture of the people and the recreational aspect of egg-gathering undoubtedly add incentive. While most of the eggs are gathered in the vicinity of

Table 7. Take of swans, cranes, and bird eggs by Eskimos on the Yukon-Kuskokwim Delta.

Village	Swans		Cranes		Eggs	
	Total village	Total household	Total village	Total household	Total village	Total household
Yukon River						
Russian Mission	60	3	5		n.s.	
Marshall	128	4	10		240	
Pilot Station	352	8	30		90	
*Andraefsky	308	7	30		225	
Mountain Village	330	5	30		n.s.	
*Hamilton	12	3	2		26	
*Kotlik	54	3	7		119	
*Cheneliak	21	3	3		46	
*Pastolik	3	3	n.s.		7	
*Bill Moore Slough	6	3	n.s.		13	
*Akers Slough	3	3	n.s.		7	
Emmonak (Kwiguk)	252	4	30		500	
Alukanuk	120	2	20		310	
Kuskokwim River						
*Upper Kalskag	52	2	5		n.s.	
Lower Kalskag	62	2	5		n.s.	
Tuluksak	30	1	10		144	24
Akiak	116	4	8		120	24
Akiachak	450	10	135	3	312	24
*Kwethluk	441	7	126	2	336	
*Bethel	40		10		n.s.	
*Oscarville	20	2	2		48	
*Napaskiak	70	2	6		192	
Napakiak	86	2	8		216	
*Tuntatuliak	96	4	25		864	36
Eek	156	4	30		1,404	36
*Kwigillingok	200	4	45		1,800	36
*Kwinhagak	180	4	42		1,620	36
Nunapichuk	620	10	186	3	2,976	48
*Kasigluk	390	10	117	3	1,872	48
Bering Sea						
Sheldon Point	110	5	22	1	100	
Scammon Bay	78	3	10		1,248	48
Hooper Bay	216	3	15		7,200	100
Chevak	189	3	13		3,780	60
Newktok	60	3	5		1,200	60
Tanunak	72	2	10		3,600	100
*Nightmute	94	2	13		2,820	60
Chefornak	10		5		3,000	100
*Kipnuk	90	2	13		2,700	60
Goodnews Bay (Mumtrak)	8		n.s.		660	20
Totals	5,585		1,033		39,795	

* Data calculated from ecologically similar villages. See footnote Table 5.
n.s.—amount taken not significant.

these villages, it is not uncommon in favourable weather for groups of women and children to be transported several miles by boat for a day of egg-gathering in a more productive habitat. In the spring hunting camps of upriver Eskimos, eggs are also gathered by the men during their muskrat hunting excursions.

The eggs of the various species of geese nesting throughout the region are preferred because of their size, but even the smallest eggs of passerine species are acceptable. In the coastal fringe of tundra from Scammon Bay to Kwinhagak, the eggs of emperor geese are readily available and constitute the major proportion of eggs taken. The eggs of cackling geese are also fairly abundant throughout this same region and at Chevak and possibly Newktok, they are most frequently taken. Those of sea gulls (*Larus* spp.) comprise a significant part of the total eggs taken; and at Scammon Bay, Tanunak, Tiksik Bay (new site of Nightmute), and Goodnews Bay, the eggs of murres (*Uria* spp.), puffins (*Fratercula corniculata* and *Lunda cirrhata*), and other sea birds may be available in limited numbers. In the tundra areas of the Delta further back from the coast, eggs collected represent a more random assortment of species.

Drives of Flightless Birds

An important method of taking waterfowl in the past has been that of staging drives of flightless birds in midsummer when adults are molting their flight feathers and before juveniles have attained flight. These drives, involving large numbers of people (usually all those in a village who are physically able), were usually conducted among the lake systems where the ducks and geese congregate during the molt. In recent years drives have lost much of their significance to the economy of the villages and each year sees a reduction in their number.

Drives require considerable organization and advance planning within the village. Boats must be committed to transport the people to the area chosen and to be used in the actual operations on the lakes. The birds are herded into one large flock by boats and kayaks and are then forced onto the land where additional people frighten the birds ahead of them into fish nets in which they become entangled, or through a line of waiting people who kill the birds with clubs. The social aspect of the drives, the thrill of the chase, and the general excitement all contribute to making them a pleasant diversion from the summer's fishing activities. The number of birds taken in a single drive, of course, varies with the habitat in which it is conducted as well as with the number of people and boats involved and the efficiency of the organization. Generally, to be worthwhile, a drive involving most of the people of a village would have to yield at least several hundred birds. From reports of the distribution of birds per family, the average take per drive very likely falls between one and two thousand birds. Small drives yielding from 20 to 100 birds may also occasionally be undertaken by several men with boats when they are afield in the summer and conditions are favourable.

Traditionally, at least one drive was conducted annually by the people in each of the villages of the coastal, tundra and downriver areas, but they were not generally undertaken by the people in the upriver regions because suitable areas were at too great a distance. The social and recreational aspects of drives have perhaps always been of a significance nearly equal to the actual need for food, at a time when other food is quite abundant. With the increase in wage employment in recent years, the demands of commercial and subsistence fishing, and the more frequent absence of men from the village during the summer months, there is less opportunity and incentive to organize village drives. Also, the Eskimos realize this activity is in violation of Federal laws, and because they cannot justify it in their own minds on the basis of need for food, there is increasing hesitation among them to undertake a drive which requires advance decision and planning. It is always more difficult to rationalize a questionable action before than after the fact. Furthermore, there is concern by the people that they may be apprehended by Federal agents, because an organized drive on the treeless tundra involving several boats and dozens of people is readily visible from a plane flying over the area.

Organized village drives during 1963 were apparently restricted to a few coastal villages including Scammon Bay and Chefornak, the two tundra villages of Kasigluk and Nunapichuk, and Napaskiak. The estimated total take in the Scammon Bay drive was 2,500 birds, whereas the estimated take from that at Napaskiak in 1961 was 1,400 birds. The Chefornak drive, on the other hand, appeared to involve less than 200 birds, mostly emperor geese. Other organized drives may have taken place during 1963, but we are not aware of them. In the coastal areas, emperor geese are the birds taken most frequently, while in the tundra villages and at Napaskiak, ducks (greater scaup [*Nyroca marila*] and old squaw [*Clangula hyemalis*]) apparently predominant with some lesser Canada geese also being taken.

Fall Hunting

Fall hunting of waterfowl is of considerably lesser importance throughout most of the Delta region than is spring hunting (Tables 5, 6). The exceptions are the Yukon River villages of Marshall, Pilot Station, and Andraefsky, where fall hunting results in a greater take of birds than does spring hunting, and the coastal villages of Scammon Bay and Hooper Bay where fall and spring hunting are about equal. There are several reasons for the general reduction in take of waterfowl in the fall, including the availability and abundance of other food at that time, the demands of other activities, such as subsistence fishing and fish preservation, moose hunting in upriver areas, the high cost of salt for preservation of birds for winter use, the greater wariness of the birds, and the absence of well defined flightways in the fall.

Geese are not as readily available for hunting in the fall as in the spring; consequently, there is a much greater reduction in the number of geese taken during the fall than of ducks; particularly in the villages of the Kuskokwim River above Bethel. The take of swans (*Olor columbianus*) and cranes (*Grus canadensis canadensis*) during the fall is relatively insignificant in contrast to the spring take.

There are a few individuals in some of the villages who preserve birds for use during the winter, but most of the birds taken are for immediate consumption. Because of the damp rainy autumn weather, birds usually cannot be preserved by drying as is sometimes done in the spring, and cold storage facilities are not available. Instead, salt is used as a preservative and the carcasses are stored in wooden barrels. As the required salt and barrels are quite expensive in these remote villages, only the occasional, more affluent Eskimo can afford to preserve for winter use birds that are shot in the autumn.

In the past, in addition to the meat of waterfowl, use was made of unplucked bird skins for making parkas; goose and eider down was used to a limited extent as insulation in garments; showy feathers were used to decorate mammal-skin parkas as well as fans and other ceremonial objects; and needles and other imple-

Table 8. Comparison of waterfowl population estimates for the Yukon-Kuskokwim Delta with the estimated take by Eskimos.

Species	Source	Waterfowl population	Take by Eskimos		
			Spring	Fall	Total
Cackling geese	Nelson and Hansen 1959	(spring) 80,000 (fall) 250,000	20,000	18,200	38,200
White-fronted geese	Dzubin et al. 1964	200,000	13,500	9,100	22,600
Black brant	Hansen and Nelson 1957	100–200,000	2,500	5,500	8,000
	Barry 1964	100–175,000			
Emperor geese	Barry 1964	200,000	6,500	1,700	8,200
Snow geese	Cooch 1964	300,000	5,400	400	5,800
Whistling swans	Banko and Mackay 1964	70–90,000			5,585

ments were made from bird bones. Bird-skin parkas were common throughout the Yukon-Kuskokwim Delta area as recently as 30 to 20 years ago. They were most frequently made from the vental surface skins of geese, brant, and eider ducks; and while extremely warm, they did not wear as well as most mammal-skin parkas. Bird-skin parkas are now very rare throughout the area. Feathers are still used to some extent for decoration on parkas and in the making of ceremonial fans and masks which are exported for sale to tourists. Metal implements have completely replaced those previously made of bird bone.

THE WATERFOWL POPULATIONS

Waterfowl population data for the Yukon-Kuskokwim Delta area are sketchy. For species such as the emperor and cackling geese that for the most part nest only in this area, population estimates are available based on counts of birds in their wintering areas or on aerial or ground counts of breeding pairs on the nesting grounds. For more cosmopolitan nesters, such as the lesser Canada and white-fronted geese, estimates of the Yukon-Kuskokwim component of their populations are either lacking or are empirical guesses by workers familiar with the particular species. Available population estimates for waterfowl species taken by Eskimo hunters in the Yukon-Kuskokwim Delta area are listed in Table 8 in comparison with the Eskimo harvest.

Cackling geese and white-fronted geese receive greater hunting pressure than any other waterfowl species on the Delta. The spring take by Eskimos may approach 15 per cent of the total spring population of each species. Lesser Canada geese, which are included with cackling geese in the utilization data, apparently are considerably less numerous throughout the Delta than cackling geese, and therefore represent the smaller component of the Canada goose varieties reported taken. Black brant, emperor, and snow geese are only locally available in the Delta area and harvests of these species are accordingly lower than for Canadas and white-fronts which are more widely distributed during the spring migration. Although species populations of brant, emperor, and snow geese inhabiting or passing through the Delta area are comparable to the white-fronted and cackling geese populations, the numbers harvested by Eskimos are considerably less than those of the white-fronts and cacklers. This is apparently directly related to their more restricted local availability. Probably not more than 2 to 3 per cent of the total spring population of black brant is taken by Eskimo hunters each year, while the fall harvest is perhaps 3 per cent. The maximum spring harvest of emperor geese by Eskimos would not be likely to exceed 6 per cent of the spring population of these birds, whereas the fall harvest accounts for about 1 per cent of the population at that time of the year. Snow geese do not nest on the Delta, but about 300,000 migrate in the spring along the coast and across the Yukon Delta to nesting areas on Wrangell Island and the northeast coast of the Chukchi Peninsula of Siberia (Cooch 1964). On the basis of this population estimate, the spring harvest by Eskimos on the Yukon-Kuskokwim Delta amounts to approximately 1 to 2 per cent of this segment of the total lesser snow goose population.

No population estimates are available for the species of ducks involved in the harvest. Eiders, which are taken in significant numbers only in early spring, represent a very small percentage of the total number of the eiders that migrate northward along the coast each spring. Pintails and Mallards, although taken in greater numbers than eiders, are not as eagerly sought as geese. Their harvest is both a product of availability and hunting effort. The take of over twice as many pintails as mallards is the direct result of the relative abundance of these two species throughout the Delta area. Because there is considerably less hunting of ducks than of geese, it is doubtful if the harvest of any species of duck approaches 5 per cent of the spring population.

Most of the harvesting of swans by Eskimos on the Yukon-Kuskokwim Delta is in the spring. As far as is known, only whistling swans are taken, as apparently there are no trumpeters (*Olor buccinator*) in the area. This harvest accounts for approximately 6 to 8 per cent of the total whistling swan population in North America.

ACKNOWLEDGMENTS

Financial support for this study was made available through the Alaska Cooperative Wildlife Research Unit by the U.S. Bureau of Sport Fisheries and Wildlife. I am indebted to the members of the village councils of the communities throughout the study area, without whose assistance the study would not have been possible. I am also grateful to Mr. Ray Christiansen who provided advice and background information about the area and acted as interpreter in many of the villages visited, and to Mr. Ray Woolford, Mr. Neil Argy, Mr. Ray Tremblay, Mr. Darwin Seim, and innumerable others, who provided useful advice and information. Mr. James King and Dr. Wendell Oswalt kindly read the manuscript and provided many useful comments.

LITERATURE CITED

BANKO, W. E., AND R. H. MACKAY. 1964. Our native swans. Waterfowl tomorrow. J. P. Linduska, ed. U.S. Fish & Wildlife Ser. pp. 155–164.

BARRY, T. W. 1964. Brant, Ross' goose, and emperor goose. Waterfowl tomorrow. J. P. Linduska, ed. U.S. Fish & Wildlife Ser. pp. 145–154.

BURNS, J. J. 1964. The ecology, economics and management of mink in the Yukon-Kuskokwim Delta, Alaska. Unpub. M.S. thesis, Univ. of Alaska. 114pp.

CHARD, C. S. 1963. The Nganasan: wild reindeer hunters of the Taimyr Peninsula. Arctic Anthro. 1(2):105–121.

COLLINS, H. B. 1954. Arctic area. Program of the

History of America. Instituto Pan Americano de Geografía e Historia. Comisión de Historia. Mexico. 152pp.

COOCH, F. G. 1964. Snows and blues. Waterfowl tomorrow. J. P. Linduska, ed. U.S. Fish & Wildlife Ser. pp. 125–133.

DZUBIN, A., H. W. MILLER, AND G. V. SCHILDMAN. 1964. White-fronts. Waterfowl tomorrow. J. P. Linduska, ed. U.S. Fish & Wildlife Ser. pp. 135–143.

GABRIELSON, I. N., AND F. C. LINCOLN. 1959. The birds of Alaska. Stackpole Co., Harrisburg. 922pp.

HANSEN, H. A., AND U. C. NELSON. 1957. Brant of the Bering Sea—Migration and mortality. North Am. Wildl. Conf. 22:237–256.

KOZELY, L. A. 1964. Overall economic development plan, the Yukon-Kuskokwim River Basins. U.S. Bureau of Indian Affairs, Bethel Dist. Off. 220pp.

NELSON, E. W. 1900. The Eskimo about Bering Strait. Govt. Print. Off., Wash., D.C. 518pp.

NELSON, U. C., AND H. A. HANSEN. 1959. The cackling goose—Its migration and management. North Am. Wildl. Conf. 24:174–187.

OSWALT, W. H. 1963*a*. Mission of change in Alaska. San Marino, Cal.: Huntington Library. 170pp.

———. 1963*b*. Napaskiak; an Alaskan Eskimo community. Tucson: Univ. of Arizona Press. 178pp.

U.S. BUREAU OF CENSUS. 1962. U.S. census of population: 1960. Detailed characteristics. Alaska. U.S. Govt. Print Off., Wash., D.C.

U.S. FISH AND WILDLIFE SERVICE. 1957. Fish and wildlife resources of the lower Yukon River. Progress Report No. IV. Juneau, Alaska. 33pp.

WATERFOWL DAMAGE TO CANADIAN GRAIN: CURRENT PROBLEMS AND RESEARCH NEEDS[1]

LAWSON G. SUGDEN[2]

Abstract: Waterfowl damage to crops in Alberta, Saskatchewan and Manitoba first became severe in the 1940's when the practice of swathing grain became prevalent. Mallards (*Anas platyrhynchos*) cause the most damage, which is sustained primarily by barley and wheat. Loss of grain is most severe in wet autumns that delay the harvest and tends to be chronic near large wetlands that harbour ducks in autumn. Losses have averaged about 1% of the crop value, and currently exceed $10 million annually. The threat of damage can also inhibit the programs for habitat preservation and development on private farmlands that are vital to North American duck production. Efforts to reduce losses to farmers have included both damage prevention and compensation programs, on which government agencies are currently spending over $1 million annually. Damage prevention has consisted of cultural methods, scaring devices, and provision of feeding stations and lure crops. Continuing losses by grain farmers plus the high costs of compensation and crop protection programs demand further research into economical ways of protecting crops. Combinations of control methods have the most potential for solving the overall damage problem. Therefore, a broad spectrum of related questions might profitably be investigated, including the field-feeding behaviour and the grain consumption of ducks, better ways of measuring the severity and distribution of damage, encouragement of farmers to make more use of available control methods, evaluation of new methods, the role that shelterbelts might have in damage prevention, and the relationship between the field-feeding habits of ducks and the features of the marshes they use. Small advances in crop protection will probably be the rule.

Cereal crop damage by waterfowl on the Canadian prairies was recognized as a problem in the 1940's (Hochbaum 1944; Soper 1944, 1948). Increasing damage and perhaps greater awareness soon brought warnings that the problem was acute and needed attention (Munro 1950*a*, Colls 1951, Leitch 1951, Mair 1953, Munro and Gollop 1955). During the past two decades, governments and others have undertaken research and developed programs to give farmers some relief from crop losses (Hochbaum et al. 1954; Paynter 1955; Beck 1959; Stephen 1961*a*, 1965*a*, 1967; Smith 1968; Renewable Resources Consulting Services [RRCS] 1969; MacLennan 1973). This paper reviews the current problem of waterfowl crop damage and identifies the need for further research.

Waterfowl have fed on upland grain fields since settlers first cropped the land (Sowls 1955, Denny 1956, Bossenmaier and Marshall 1958), but severe damage did not become prevalent until the mid-1940's. The change was believed caused by the new practice of allowing grain to ripen in swaths before threshing (Colls 1951, Bossenmaier and Marshall 1958), and possibly by the increased acreage of durum wheat and barley, which ducks prefer to common wheat (Bossenmaier and Marshall 1958, MacLennan 1973).

Crop damage on the Canadian prairies is caused mainly by mallards (*Anas platyrhynchos*) and pintails (*A. acuta*). Mallards do the most damage because they remain later in autumn (Hochbaum 1944), have a greater tendency to field-feed (Bossenmaier and Marshall 1958),

---

[1] Originally published as Can. Wildl. Serv., Occas. Paper 24, 1976. 25pp. Reproduced by permission of the Minister of Supply and Services Canada.

[2] Present address: Migratory Bird Research Center, University of Saskatchewan CMPS, 115 Perimeter Road, Saskatoon, Saskatchewan S7N 0X4, Canada.

and are more abundant. Geese that migrate through the Prairie Provinces (Alberta, Saskatchewan, and Manitoba) damage some grain crops in autumn, but such damage is localized (Bossenmaier and Marshall 1958, MacLennan 1973). Sandhill cranes (*Grus canadensis*) also damage crops in a few areas (principally in Saskatchewan) where they concentrate in the fall (Munro 1950*b*, Stephen 1967, MacLennan 1973).

NATURE OF DAMAGE

Wheat, barley, and oats comprise over 75% of the cropped acreage in prairie Canada (Statistics Canada 1972) and receive virtually all of the waterfowl damage. Bossenmaier and Marshall (1958) believed ducks preferred barley to common wheat because the unthreshed barley kernels were easier to extract. However, according to Hammond (1950), when the grain was threshed, common wheat was preferred to barley. RRCS (1969) suggested that barley received relatively more damage because it was swathed earlier than wheat. Oats are preferred less by ducks and much smaller acreages are planted, so that the monetary loss from oat damage is small compared with that for barley or wheat.

Most damage is done when grain is lying in the swath, where it is eaten, trampled, and fouled by ducks. As a rule, ducks waste more grain than they eat and mainly during their first few visits, when they dislodge grain while trampling the swaths. Extrapolations by Hammond (1950) and Benson (1952) indicated that waste grain exceeded eaten grain by four to six times, though the ratio was as low as 1.5 with damp grain (Hammond 1961). But if ducks feed on swathed grain long enough, they recover most of the fallen kernels (MacLennan 1973). Standing grain is seldom damaged except when flooded (Bossenmaier and Marshall 1958) or if it is short-stemmed (McWhorter 1961).

Crop damage by ducks varies both in time and space. Autumn precipitation appears to be the most important variable affecting the severity of damage (RRCS 1969, MacLennan 1973). Damage increases when wet weather delays harvesting, and especially when crops remain drying in the swath for long periods. Damage tends to be greater and more frequent in northern areas (e.g., Meadow Lake, Saskatchewan; The Pas, Manitoba; Peace River, Alberta) when late springs dictate a relatively late harvest (Stephen 1965*a*, RRCS 1969). Late harvests result, too, from delayed seeding caused by wet spring conditions. Northern areas may also receive relatively more damage simply because ducks delay their migration when food is abundant (RRCS 1969), though the evidence appears to be circumstantial.

Damage is also greater near large wetlands used by ducks in the fall (Bossenmaier and Marshall 1958, Stephen 1961*b*, RRCS 1969; MacLennan 1973), and its severity tends to be inversely proportional to the distance between the wetlands and susceptible fields. Although damage has occurred over most of the grain-growing region of prairie Canada, some areas consistently receive more damage than others (Stephen 1965*b*; RRCS 1969, 1970). These chronic damage areas are invariably associated with large wetlands.

Over the years, the severity of crop damage has not been related to the size of the duck population (Kalmbach 1935, RRCS 1969, MacLennan 1973). Indeed, duck populations were comparatively low when some of the worst damage occurred because weather conditions made crops vulnerable for long periods. Notwithstanding the lack of correlation between provincial mallard and pintail numbers, and damage intensity, on a local basis *many* ducks undoubtedly cause greater damage than *few* ducks.

COST OF DAMAGE

From mail surveys, damage for the three Prairie Provinces was estimated at $12.6 million in 1959 and from $5.7 million to $8.2 million in 1960 (Stephen 1961*b*). A 1955 survey in Saskatchewan showed a damage loss of $10.6 million (Paynter and Stephen 1964). Losses in Alberta for 1966, 1967, and 1968 were given as $5.8 million, $3.6 million, and $6.0 million respectively (RRCS 1969). The comparable bushel loss nowadays would be more costly because of the currently high market value of grains. The value of lost grain averages about 1% of the crop value. The authors caution that estimates based on their mail surveys may be biased upwards, though part of this bias may be offset by damage that goes unnoticed. Regardless of bias, the estimates are what the farmer believes he has lost and this dictates the seriousness of the problem (Stephen 1961*b*).

The impact of duck damage is aggravated when losses are not uniformly distributed among farms. In a 1964 prairie-wide survey, 16% of 5,327 respondents reported duck damage valued at $227,749 (Stephen 1965*b*), but only 5.6% reported losses in excess of $200 each. Similarly, 12% of Alberta farmers reporting damage in 1968 gave a figure over $500 each (RRCS 1969). That report suggested that $500 represented the approximate upper threshold of tolerable dollar loss from waterfowl damage. High loss by relatively few farmers is the cause of the greatest animosity (Munro 1958).

Crop losses due to waterfowl are low compared with losses from other causes. The average annual loss from hail in Saskatchewan was estimated at 4% of the provincial crop (University of Saskatchewan 1975) and one storm in 1957 caused about $17 million damage. Annual losses from hail in Alberta also average about 4% of the crop value (Summers and Wojtiw 1971), and from 1961 through 1968 averaged $23 million. The highest loss in that period was $58 million in 1966. The 1955 survey that estimated duck damage in Saskatchewan at $10.6 million also placed insect damage at $60 million.

In monetary terms, waterfowl damage may be overshadowed by damage from other causes, but the nature of the agent puts it in a different light. Hail is considered a natural farming hazard, and crops can be insured against it as well as other hazards. In Alberta hail damage is concentrated and substantial research on weather modification is being undertaken. Considerable research has also been done on methods of forecasting insect damage and techniques for control. Pest control is often subsidized by government programs.

The farmer views grain-eating waterfowl differently. Migratory game birds are protected by the Migratory Birds Convention Act and are managed primarily for their use by hunters and birdwatchers. The grain farmer identifies waterfowl with the users and believes that they should accept the responsibility. While it is doubtful that the damage situation would change were the mallard officially declared a pest and not protected (Murton 1968), the question is academic. Wildlife management agencies accept a major role in efforts to reduce losses from waterfowl depredations. Such involvement is imperative because their interests extend beyond the legal or moral aspects. Any program to alleviate duck damage is likely to affect recreational opportunities and, of more importance, the damage impedes efforts to preserve and develop waterfowl habitat on the Canadian prairies (Leitch 1951). Close to half the ducks in North America are produced on the privately-owned lands of prairie farmers, but no program to preserve or develop wetland or upland habitat can win the co-operation of farmers who continue to suffer severe crop losses from waterfowl. The cost of waterfowl damage in terms of debilitated habitat management programs is unknown and is probably unmeasurable, but periodic opposition to wetland development and requests to drain large wetlands in severe damage areas show that the problem exists.

Although the value of lost grain can only be estimated, the costs of reducing farmers' losses are measurable. Payments to farmers in Alberta and Saskatchewan through compensation and insurance claims have each exceeded $500,000 in recent years of severe damage. Details of these costs as well as damage control programs are discussed later. The programs cover but a fraction of the total crop loss because of ceilings on damage claims and incomplete participation by farmers.

Efforts to reduce the loss to farmers have been many and varied. One main approach is to reduce the damage to crops; another allows the farmer to recover part of his loss through compensation.

Methods and devices for reducing crop damage by ducks are discussed in many papers (Kalmbach 1935; Wagar 1946; Horn 1949; Biehn 1951; Hochbaum et al. 1954; Lostetter 1956, 1960; Bossenmaier and Marshall 1958; Hammond 1961, 1964; Stephen 1961*a*, 1965*a*, 1967; Paynter and Stephen 1964; Buckley and Cottam 1966; Dykstra 1966; Williams and Neff 1966; Anderson 1969; Cowan 1970; Kozicky and McCabe 1970; MacLennan 1973; Canadian Wildlife Service 1973).

Sources of scaring devices and repellents are listed in U.S. Fish and Wildlife Service (1964) and Anderson (1969). Additional bird control information appears in the literature on conflicts between birds and aircraft and other human activities (e.g., Aldrich et al. 1961, Kilgore and Doutt 1967, Murton and Wright 1968).

CULTURAL PRACTICES

These practices include growing non-susceptible crops such as flaxseed or rapeseed, growing grain varieties that can be harvested earlier or straight-combined (no swaths), using shatter-resistant varieties, leaving a high stubble to discourage ducks, and delaying cultivation of harvested fields until nearby susceptible crops have been harvested. The last practice provides a place for ducks to feed where they can do no harm, as they would be eating waste grain. On areas of marginal farmland that suffer chronic waterfowl damage it may be practical to put the land to other uses, including damage abatement and recreation.

The extent of farmers' attempts to reduce crop damage through cultural practices is not precisely known but appears slight. In Manitoba, Bossenmaier and Marshall (1958) found such practices almost non-existent. In the Alberta survey (RRCS 1969) cultural methods were not listed in the questionnaire, though some were included by a few respondents under *other methods* used to prevent damage, so the insignificant number of responses may not be representative. These mentioned speeding up the harvest, straight-combining, and growing non-susceptible crops. None reported leaving harvested fields uncultivated until harvesting was finished, though this is a widely recommended technique.

The reasons for infrequent use of cultural practices that reduce crop damage are not clear. Certain techniques (planting early-ripening varieties and an early and swift harvest) are useful regardless of the damage threat, so would not be considered a special measure for damage prevention. Likewise, spring cultivation (as opposed to fall cultivation) is beneficial where soil erosion by wind is a problem (University of Saskatchewan 1975) so cultivation would be delayed in any case. Conversely, postponing cultivation is often impractical in northern areas with short growing seasons (Stephen 1961*a*) or for fields with heavy straw cover. Finally, the efficient farmer who has completed his harvest may entertain no obligation to maintain alternative feeding sites for ducks that might damage his less efficient neighbour's crops.

Because ducks waste so much grain through trampling, biologists have suggested growing shatter-resistant varieties where such damage occurs. After reviewing studies by Truscott (1950) and Beck (1951), Gollop (1950) concluded that the grains most resistant to shattering were already in common use and were also among those most preferred by ducks. Kalmbach (1943) stated that waterfowl showed some aversion to unnaturally coloured grain, though in Stephen's (1959) experiment, ducks continued to eat swathed grain that was treated with green lawn paint.

One significant tract of marginal farmland in prairie Canada has been converted to an area primarily for wildlife use because of severe crop damage by sandhill cranes and ducks. This is the Last Mountain Lake Wildlife Area in Saskatchewan comprising over 8,000 ha (20,000 acres) (Hatfield 1971). The conversion eliminated over 3,000 ha (8,000 acres) of marginally commercial cropland that were susceptible to chronic damage and provided land for an extensive feeding crop program that helps to protect adjacent farmlands. Additional benefits accrue from livestock grazing and recreational uses of the area. Stephen (1965*a*) stated that cultivated land in the vicinity of Quill Lakes, Saskatchewan and Big Grass Marsh, Manitoba were similar by reason of poor soils and high waterfowl damage and could be considered possible candidates for a similar conversion. The long-term economics of land-use conversion on such areas need more study.

SCARING WATERFOWL

Techniques and devices used or tested for scaring ducks from fields include shooting (to scare or kill), *cracker shells* fired from shotguns, tracer cartridges, Very signals, acetylene exploders, firecrackers, ground bomb mortars, *sky rockets*, hand grenades, rifle grenades, sirens, wind-powered noisemakers, scarecrows and other strange objects such as barrels or farm implements, flashing lights, road flares, rotating beacons, spotlights, *spirillum whirlers*, fires, smoke bombs, fog-making machines, gas-filled balloons, and herding by foot, horseback, or aircraft. Frequently, two or more methods are used in combination.

No universal technique or device for keeping waterfowl out of susceptible crops has been discovered that is quick, cheap, easy to use, effective, and acceptable to the grain grower. Because crop damage on the Canadian prairies is widespread and often unpredictable, scaring is frequently attempted only after the foraging ducks have been discovered. By then considerable damage may have occurred, as much of the waste grain is lost during initial feedings. For this reason, biologists point out that scaring ducks from field to field actually increases total damage if alternative non-commercial feeding sites are not available in the vicinity. Nevertheless, the success of a feeding scheme often depends on a simultaneous scaring program.

Shooting permits have been issued to farmers at times to scare and kill troublesome ducks. In theory these permits enable busy farmers to enlist the help of hunters, who, as primary waterfowl users, would contribute to the management program. The practice has had mixed public relations values, but there is no evidence that it has substantially reduced crop damage (RRCS 1969). Permit-holders were concentrated near urban centres rather than in frequently damaged areas, tending to confirm the belief of many that their motive was unlimited pre-season shooting. Among farmers claiming compensation, the damage intensity was similar for those who had shooting permits and those who did not. Finally, much damage occurs after the waterfowl season opens and when special permits are no longer needed.

Automatic acetylene exploders have had considerable use in damage control programs, though mainly by wildlife agencies (Gollop 1960; Krentz 1960; Stephen 1961*a*, 1967; Burgess 1973). Experiments with acetylene exploders to control damage by ducks (Stephen 1961*a*) and sandhill cranes (Stephen 1967) showed that exploders effectively kept the birds from swathed grain. Generally, one exploder was needed for each one-quarter section (65 ha or 160 acres). In the crane study the cost to operate an exploder for an average season was about $44 (in 1965) including depreciation. As with other scaring methods, the effectiveness of exploders in reducing damage tended to be proportional to the availability of non-commercial feeding sites.

The modern acetylene exploder with automatic electric timing appears to come closest to the ideal scaring device. It is comparatively inexpensive, requires infrequent maintenance, and is reasonably effective for keeping waterfowl from crops. Nevertheless it has had little acceptance by farmers experiencing crop damage. In the RRCS (1969) survey, only about 2% of those with damage stated that they used exploders. Why so few use them is not clear, but cost is probably the answer. Often, insurance or compensation may be a *better buy* than an acetylene exploder, because the programs are financed largely by hunters and government revenue (Stephen 1965*a*). Perhaps not enough effort has been devoted to selling the technique to farmers, or further study may prove that it would pay wildlife agencies to subsidize part of the cost of exploders purchased by grain farmers (Stephen 1961*b*). The difficulty in obtaining acetylene gas in rural areas may also discourage farmers from buying exploders (S. Woynarski, pers. comm.).

None of the many other devices for keeping waterfowl out of crops has had much success for a variety of reasons. Some are not effective over a wide enough range of conditions; others are too costly or time-consuming. The homemade scarecrow in its many varieties seems as useful as any and has been the most used. Most farmers agree that it is more effective if parts of it move and flash in the wind. Like all devices, it does a better job if erected before waterfowl start feeding on the crop, as they are more easily frightened when they first arrive.

Hochbaum et al. (1954) experimented with combined patrols and scaring to reduce crop damage on a Manitoba area.

Shooting and scarecrows were used to frighten the ducks after they had been discovered. The authors estimated that one man could patrol about 80 sq. km (30 sq. miles) during an average season with a resulting reduction in crop damage. RRCS (1969) concluded that the method would be too costly to control the widespread damage in Alberta.

Herding field-feeding waterfowl, principally by aircraft, has been used extensively in the United States but only experimentally in Canada. It has served mostly to drive large numbers of ducks from fields and wetlands to nearby refuges that supply supplementary food (Horn 1949, Biehn 1951, Lostetter 1960, Hammond 1961). Lostetter (1960) reported that two aircraft could protect about 12,000 ha (30,000 acres) of rice crop in California.

Gollop (1951) described 22 flights near The Pas, Manitoba to drive ducks from crops. Flares were used during some flights. Because the cropland was interspersed with many wetlands, the method did not effectively move ducks from the vicinity of susceptible crops. Previously, Gollop (1950) had noted that ducks feeding at dark in the early morning or evening would be difficult to detect or herd by aircraft. Experiments to drive sandhill cranes from crops using up to three aircraft were also unsuccessful (Gollop 1960). During three years that feeding stations were used near Delta, Manitoba, Krentz (1960) successfully herded ducks onto the feeding station marshes with an aircraft. Regardless of effectiveness, herding waterfowl by aircraft or other means on the Canadian prairies would be extremely expensive because the damage areas are many and dispersed.

FEEDING PROGRAMS

Feeding methods for preventing damage provide grain and undisturbed feeding sites to keep ducks out of susceptible crops. One method provides threshed grain for ducks at *feeding stations*, usually on the shore of major resting places. Another supplies grain which is cut and left lying in the field. These fields are often called *lure crops* but the term implies more active attraction than in fact occurs. A crop may be planted in anticipation of ducks feeding on it or a commercial crop may be purchased after they have started damaging it. In the latter instance, the wildlife agency might not pay for any grain that the farmer can harvest after the field is no longer needed for damage control.

Many forms of recompense for farming services are used, such as standard crop sharing, cash payment for services, harvest of residual grain, cash payment for grain, and combinations of these. In no known instance are the farming operations carried out by government employees, in contrast to the practice on many National Wildlife Refuges in the United States. Hunting or other harassment is prohibited on feeding areas. Protecting ducks from disturbance while they feed in harvested fields could be considered as a third method in this category, though it would not be necessary to provide extra feed.

Feeding stations for keeping waterfowl out of commercial crops have had more use in the United States than in Canada. Hammond (1961) described the extensive feeding station program at Lower Souris Refuge, North Dakota and concluded that it was economically justified with 50,000 or more ducks. Ancillary benefits included the greater use of natural foods by ducks, less field-feeding, and favourable public reaction. Hammond (1961) gave useful information on feeding station operations, including site selection and preparation.

Feeding stations on a smaller scale

were used from 1957 through 1959 in a Manitoba area (Krentz 1959). The project involved four to six stations and some scaring, and cost $27,000 to $36,000 per year. Crop damage in the area was apparently reduced but it was not evaluated.

RRCS (1969) identified several chronic damage areas in Alberta and recommended the use of feeding stations in pilot programs. Evaluations of feeding stations on two Alberta areas—3 years at one and 2 years at the other—(Burgess 1973) showed that crop damage was significantly reduced and that the projects were economically justified. Benefit/cost ratios (farmer's loss prevented in relation to project cost plus compensation paid despite the program) averaged between two and four. Costs included scaring from nearby commercial crops. The average feeding station accommodated 439,500 duck-days of use (range, 162,380 to 845,000) and stations attracted ducks daily for an average of 57 days (range, 35 to 80). Average feeding station cost was 1.8¢ per duck per day (range, 0.6¢ to 4.4¢). Burgess (1973) estimated that one feeding station used for 35 days would cost $5,677. This estimate included feed for close to 6,000 ducks daily as well as costs of a complementary scaring program. Altogether there were 18 areas in Alberta believed suitable for the described treatment. These would require about 37 feeding sites.

Lure crops to control damage have been used to varying degrees in the Prairie Provinces. For example, in 1970 there were 4 in 2 Alberta damage areas, 29 in 5 Saskatchewan damage areas (18 of these were on the Last Mountain Lake Wildlife Area), and 10 in 5 Manitoba damage areas. A reduction in damage was evident in most cases and costs of operating lure-crop programs are fairly well documented, but few benefit/cost evaluations are available. Eleven lure crops used in Stephen's (1967) sandhill crane study near the north end of Last Mountain Lake, Saskatchewan included some grown on public lands, some purchased in entirety from farmers, and some partially purchased from farmers. Costs averaged $8.25 per acre (0.4 ha). Stephen concluded that, when combined with scaring (acetylene exploders), lure crops improved an already favourable benefit/cost ratio.

J. P. Hatfield (pers. comm.) estimated that 1 acre (0.4 ha) of lure-crop barley grown on publicly-owned land cost $7.00 in 1969 and that it would feed 20 sandhill cranes or 40 ducks for 2 weeks. If land had to be purchased, MacLennan (1973) calculated that 1 acre (0.4 ha) of lure crop would cost $10.30 annually. Capital costs were amortized over a 20-year period and it was assumed that two-thirds of the land would be cropped annually. From insured crop losses—thought to be one-third to one-half of the actual loss—MacLennan (1973) conservatively estimated that there were about 20 areas in Saskatchewan feasible for lure-crop programs, including 5 already treated. The 10 areas studied by MacLennan varied from about 31 to 130 sq. km (12 to 50 sq. miles) and were among the worst damage areas in the province.

Burgess (1973) used higher land and farming costs and assumed that all the land would be cropped annually when he calculated that an acre of lure crop would cost $23.50. If the crop were purchased it would cost $35.00 an acre (0.4 ha). Using the last figure for crop costs and combining it with costs for posting, patrolling, scaring, etc., Burgess estimated that a *crop damage control unit* involving a 65-ha (160-acre) lure crop would cost about $8,000 for 35 days of control. Cost per duck per day for the 10 lure crops evaluated averaged 3.2¢. High variability

(0.5¢ to 41.0¢) resulted from the erratic numbers of ducks using the different sites.

The most efficient size and number of lure crops depend on the number and distribution of ducks in the area, the length of time for which protection is needed (harvest progress), and the number of ducks each lure site may attract. Since this information cannot be predicted accurately, only experience will show what is needed to give a margin of safety. If one always manages for a *bad* damage year, lure crops will more often than not be inefficient in terms of grain uneaten, though at times some of the uneaten (and untrampled) grain can be harvested. An alternative is to prepare for an average year and, in the event of greater threats, convert commercial crops into lure crops (MacLennan 1973).

Burgess (1973) studied 10 lure crops ranging from 28 to 65 ha (70 to 160 acres). Three were completely used by ducks. Unharvestable grain on the remainder amounted to 13 to 39% of the original crop. Eighteen lure crops on the Last Mountain Lake Wildlife Area ranged from 12 to 24 ha (30 to 60 acres) of barley (J. P. Hatfield, pers. comm.). MacLennan (1973) assumed a lure crop size of about 40 ha (100 acres)—two-thirds of 65 ha (160 acres) in crop, one-third fallow—to estimate the needs for damage control on Saskatchewan areas. A Manitoba proposal recommended lure crops of 16 to 24 ha (40 to 60 acres) each. The reasons for differences in sizes recommended or used presumably relate to different crop rotation practices on the standard land unit, the *quarter-section* or 65 ha (160 acres). Growing a non-susceptible crop on part of the field can help offset the cost of owning a large acreage, as at the Last Mountain Lake Wildlife Area, where forage revenue more than offsets lure-crop costs.

Attempts to attract ducks to lure crops have included using decoys, flooding the field, and burning the crop. There is little information on the effectiveness of these methods, or indeed the need for them. The fact that there have been few trials, indicates little need. Bossenmaier and Marshall (1958) believed that burning straw on harvested fields made them more attractive to ducks, and a similar effect might be expected when swaths were burned. The flooded lure crop monitored by Burgess (1973) for three years was no better than crops on dry land judging by the number of ducks attracted and the quantity of grain eaten. Presumably, decoys on lure crops would be as effective as those used extensively by hunters and those used by Krentz (1960) and McWhorter (1961) to attract ducks to harvested grain fields. A well-placed lure crop may rarely need additional measures to attract ducks. Features of good sites have been described as: a large field (not necessarily all lure crop) devoid of trees, an open field with a high spot in it, at least 0.4 km (0.25 mile) from buildings and busy roads, a history of duck use, located on traditional flight lanes used by ducks flying from their resting places, and near principal resting places. Early ripening grains are best because the lure crop should be available before commercial crops are swathed. Short stubble may be more attractive to ducks once they land (Bossenmaier and Marshall 1958). Mowing, rather than swathing, lure grain may result in less wastage, but ducks may not recognize mowed grain as readily (Gallop 1950). Mowing would also make it impractical to salvage uneaten grain. More grain can be exposed by turning the swath with a side delivery rake (Krentz

1960) or disking the field after about a month's use (J. P. Hatfield, pers. comm.).

Both feeding stations and lure crops will probably be used more in future programs to reduce waterfowl damage on the Canadian prairies, and a careful analysis of their relative merits should precede any choice between the two. The Alberta experiment (Burgess 1973) showed that capital and operating costs for feeding stations were less than those for lure crops with equal protection. The difference increases with extended control because, during late harvests, an additional lure crop may have to be purchased. Feeding stations attracted ducks daily for longer periods than did lure crops, though there was not much difference in the number of ducks fed each day. Feeding stations can be started when needed and kept operating as long as necessary. They require little land and grain is seldom wasted. Provision of feed can be flexible and adapted to existing conditions. MacLennan (1973) believed that lure crops would provide cheaper protection than feeding stations in Saskatchewan. Since the damage areas are many and dispersed, the equipment and staff necessary to service them all with feeding stations would cost too much. Also, road conditions in wet seasons would make it difficult and costly to service feeding stations when they are most needed. Experience and careful record-keeping as done by Burgess (1973) will show where each feeding method is best used.

Burgess (1973) warned that the effect of feeding programs on duck populations and hunting opportunities must be measured and corrected if found detrimental. Feeding projects may alter migration patterns that, in turn, could affect crop damage or hunting opportunities elsewhere; though in one Alberta area feeding projects apparently made no measurable change in duck migration patterns in three years (Burgess 1973). But in the area located near a large urban centre, the feeding projects did make large numbers of ducks unavailable to hunters. Finally, ducks concentrated at feeding stations are more vulnerable to disease outbreaks.

Production of natural foods that would keep potential field-feeding ducks on marshes has had little investigation, probably because the method is thought to hold little promise. Hochbaum (1944), Horn (1949), and Bossenmaier and Marshall (1958) concluded that ducks fed on grain fields despite an abundance of natural foods in the marshes. Conversely, Leitch (1951) believed development of a smartweed bed (*Polygonum* sp.) in certain Alberta wetlands helped to keep pintails out of crops. Gollop (1950) made experimental plantings of sago pondweed (*Potamogeton pectinatus*), millet (*Echinochloa crusgalli*) and wild rice (*Zizania aquatica*) in southern Alberta. As the resulting plant production was insignificant, it could not be evaluated.

PAYMENTS TO FARMERS

Payments for losses from waterfowl damage have been made to farmers in Saskatchewan since 1953 in a form of insurance (Paynter 1955) and in Alberta since 1961 as compensation (Smith 1968, RRCS 1969). In both provinces revenues have been derived mainly from imposts on hunting licenses—$1 in Saskatchewan and $3 in Alberta ($2 before 1969). Farmers in Saskatchewan pay a 2% premium on the insured value of the crop, with a maximum of $25 an acre (0.4 ha). Policies have to be purchased prior to 10 August. Alberta farmers can claim damage compensation up to a maximum of three-quarters of the crop value or $25 an acre (0.4 ha), whichever is less ($15 an acre or one-half of the value before 1973) upon payment of a $25 adjustor's fee.

From 1956 through 1967, insurance claims for crop damage in Saskatchewan averaged $87,000 annually; the average for 1968 through 1971 was $428,000 (MacLennan 1973). The program could not be supported in recent years ($521,800 in 1971) by annual revenue of $140,000 to $180,000 from hunting license imposts, and had to be subsidized by other government funds. MacLennan (1973) could not definitely determine if the rise in claims reflected more severe damage in recent years or simply greater participation by farmers. The first reason was indicated by the increase in the percentage of policy-holders making claims between the two periods (41 vs. 54%) and the rise in average claim ($433 vs. $741). However these measurements could have been affected by changes in average acreage insured, an unknown figure. Although the reasons for the rise in insurance claims in recent years may be unclear, there has been a definite trend toward greater participation by farmers over the years.

Using 1971 insurance claim figures and assuming that the actual damage was two or three times the insured damage (RRCS 1969), MacLennan (1973) predicted that a compensation scheme for Saskatchewan would cost between $1.1 and $1.7 million annually. Apparently he assumed no change in farmers' participation. The crop damage insurance program in Saskatchewan has not been entirely acceptable to farmers, as is shown by perennial recommendations to abolish premiums, raise the insurable ceiling, and abolish the time limit for purchasing policies (Stephen 1965*a*).

Annual compensation for crop damage in Alberta was not over $6,000 during the first 3 years, 1961 to 1963 (RRCS 1969). It exceeded $300,000 in 1964, and from 1964 through 1968 averaged about $224,000. Figures in annual reports of the Alberta Department of Lands and Forests indicate that payments averaged about $500,000 from 1969 through 1973. As in Saskatchewan, annual revenue from hunting licence imposts, which has amounted to about $360,000 since 1969, could not alone support such high levels of compensation. The RRCS (1969) report concluded that the compensation program fell short of its objectives of reducing farmers' losses from crop damage and improving the attitude of farmers toward waterfowl and their users. First, a small proportion (12% in 1968) of farmers with damage were submitting claims. Some were not aware of the program and others were apparently willing to accept a certain level of crop loss. Second, the fixed ceiling of $15 an acre (0.4 ha) did not provide for fluctuating market values of grain nor for regional differences in crop yields. Farmers in low yield areas might recover close to one-half of their crop value, but those in high yield areas recovered much less. For those making claims, compensation payments averaged about one-third of the loss sustained.

The report recommended greater publicity for the compensation program and the use of a sliding scale for payments based on current grain values rather than the dollar ceiling. Maximum compensation could be based on one-half of the crop value, but the scheme could include an option allowing a farmer to insure the balance of his crop. These recommendations were made on the assumption that an extensive damage control program could accompany the more realistic levels of compensation.

Manitoba has had a compensation scheme since 1972. Before then the government was prepared to purchase damaged crops in special cases and use them for lure crops. Compensation payments in 1972 were $5,000 and in 1973, $33,000 (S. Woynarski, pers. comm.). The program is supported by a *wildlife control fund* to which hunters contribute by purchasing a $2.25 annual wildlife certificate. Revenue from this source amounted to $149,000 during the first year, 1970.

Despite efforts to solve it, much of the waterfowl damage problem remains. Part of the burden has been shifted from the farmer to the government agency and the waterfowl user, who supports abatement programs through imposts. This has helped to reduce the antipathy of grain farmers, but the shift of responsibility does not make the problem disappear. It seems probable that a majority of farmers will always tolerate a certain level of damage though, in doing so, they are not likely to regard waterfowl as anything but pests. Also, despite programs to protect crops, severe damage will occur periodically, particularly during delayed harvests, and nothing short of compensation or insurance will ease the problem then (Farmes 1969); but, as Cummings (1971) stated: "It cannot be regarded as an ultimate solution as it ignores the reason for the wildlife conflict." A solution can exist only when economical ways are found to reduce crop damage.

Not all factors that affect waterfowl damage or the success of control measures will be fully understood without more study of the behaviour of the birds. How long do individuals remain in one area? How much flock turnover is there? How far do birds fly to fields and how often do they feed? Are there differences in field-feeding habits between ages or sexes? More knowledge of the birds' behaviour and ecology would provide a stronger base on which to plan research and management projects aimed at damage control (Murton 1968, 1974).

Better ways must be found to measure the distribution and severity of damage so that its relationship to the variables that affect it can be accurately determined. Questionnaires, records of compensation or insurance claims, and scaring permits all have biases that render them useful only for broad surveys. Reliable data on damage are needed to plan crop protection programs.

FARMING PRACTICES

Forty years ago Leopold (1933) stated: "Only the landholder can practice game management cheaply." Leopold's *theorem* is no less valid today and, logistically, the grain farmer is in the best position to protect his crops. Some useful methods are available but little used. Reasons for this should be determined and ways devised to achieve more participation. In some cases it may simply mean better communication between wildlife agencies and the agricultural community. Some known crop protection techniques may need retesting; some never have been adequately tested. New devices and methods should be sought. The more techniques available, the better the chance that one will be used.

Growing non-susceptible crops on high-risk fields is one obvious way for the individual farmer to prevent losses from waterfowl. In some regions, however, it may not be culturally possible or economically advantageous to grow anything but wheat or barley. There are other limitations to changes in farming practices, such as the farmer's existing capital investment in equipment or the lack of capital to invest in alternatives. One may postulate, however, that tradition or inadequate information are the only reasons why wheat and barley are persistently grown in areas that experience chronic duck damage.

The use of chemicals to hasten ripening of standing grain and thereby eliminate the need for swathing was investigated briefly in North Dakota in the 1950's (Hammond 1955). Reports on the final results are not available, but preliminary results suggested that further research would be justified. Even without treatment, it may pay farmers to straight-combine grain in areas where waterfowl damage is an annual hazard. Usually the advantages of swathing grain outweigh the disadvantages (Dodds 1967), but the difference is small enough that its elimination could be seriously considered for chronic damage areas. Crop scientists have been successful in breeding grain varieties resistant to insects and diseases. Could they also produce a variety resistant to duck damage (Kozicky and McCabe 1970)?

REPELLING WATERFOWL

One gains the impression that the search for new and better ways to repel waterfowl died with the development of the improved acetylene exploder. Development of feeding schemes now seems to be the popular approach. The fact that scaring often increases total damage has dampened enthusiasm in the search for better methods, but scaring is often a necessary adjunct to feeding projects and so will always have a role in damage control. Moreover, feeding programs are economically feasible only in restricted areas with persistent severe damage. Elsewhere damage must be controlled by other means. Many farmers willingly devote reasonable effort to protecting their crops, and providing them with better techniques would help solve the crop damage problem.

The array of scaring devices that has been tried is impressive and seems to cover all possible stimuli that might deter waterfowl. But I believe that all possibilities have not been exhausted and that further research on scaring methods is justified. Some devices have been suggested but have not been adequately tested, e.g., the ways that hawk models might be used to scare ducks (Melzack et al. 1959). Seemingly innocuous objects might prove effective. In one study (Pfeifer and Keil 1963) a variety of birds were tested with reflecting glass balls, but only raptors were repelled. There appeared to be no explanation for this response peculiar to raptors. The use of chemical repellents to protect crops from ducks is suggested in the literature, but little research has been done. Generally, results from a traditional approach to repel ducks chemically have been disappointing (Kear 1965). But the success with chemicals that cause flock-disturbing behaviour in other species (Goodhue and Baumgartner 1965, De Grazio et al. 1972) indicates a need for parallel studies with ducks.

Scaring devices that produce loud sounds other than explosions have had little testing. Thiessen et al. (1957) obtained conflicting results when they used a siren to scare mallards and pintails from wetlands, and concluded that the method would not be economically practical for crop protection. Perhaps the ducks' response threshold would have been lower had they been field-feeding during the tests (Boudreau 1968). Development of amplified recorded sounds (Frings 1964) might make some acoustical methods more attractive as a means of scaring waterfowl. Any sound, including shotgun blasts, could be projected over large areas with suitable equipment. A tape recorder could be programmed to broadcast a variety of high-intensity sounds at varying intervals; the mixed noises should delay habituation, wherein lies the weakness of most scaring devices (Frings and Frings 1967).

Bio-acoustics, using recorded alarm and distress calls to scare birds, have shown promise in some situations, but most research has been confined to larids, sturnids, icterids, and corvids (Frings 1964, Boudreau 1968, Busnel and Giban 1968). Particularly fascinating is the possible use of synthetic *super-signals* that may suppress habituation to the stimulus. The use of broadcast predator calls (Frings and Frings 1967) may also deserve investigation. Bio-acoustics that frighten waterfowl seem to have been dismissed as a crop protection method, probably because damage is dispersed and traditional equipment is costly. But perhaps we have been too preoccupied with the costs of the tools at hand when contemplating options for crop protection research. Discovery of a technique that requires an inexpensive device to be practical need not await development of the device itself. Demonstrated utility will stimulate technology to look for it, as witnessed in the development of biotelemetry aids.

Field-feeding ducks prefer large open fields free of tree or shrub growth (MacLennan 1973) and lure crops may never attract waterfowl if placed close to trees, shelterbelts, etc. There is little doubt that, above a certain density, shelterbelts would give protection from waterfowl damage, though this has not been evaluated. The effective density should be determined, and also whether the altered habitat increases damage by other vertebrates such as blackbirds (Howard 1967). Although their value for reducing waterfowl damage remains uncertain, shelterbelts on cultivated farmland are useful for soil and moisture conservation (Staple and Lehane 1955), and increase the presence of passerine birds (Stewart and Kantrud 1972) and upland game birds (Hunt 1974). Provision of multiple benefits makes any technique more attractive. More study is needed on the relationship between the field-feeding habits of waterfowl and landscape features, including shelterbelts and natural tree growth.

Another practice in biological control alters habitat to attract natural enemies of troublesome species (Howard 1967). Would the addition of perching sites attract raptors to grain fields and, if so, would it help to reduce duck damage? This, too, may warrant some investigation.

ALTERNATIVE FEEDING SITES

Techniques for operating feeding-station and lure-crop projects are well known, though future experiences are likely to reveal new problems and innovations. To illustrate, Hammond (1955) recommended that low-cost bulky feeds, including oats, be tested as substitutes or additives to the usual grains distributed at feeding stations. Although the ratio of grain eaten to grain wasted is of little concern to the farmer who loses both ways, it is important to the lure-crop manager who tries to make the most efficient use of the grain. Verified measurements of consumption by field-feeding ducks are lacking, and estimates commonly used seem to be based on the grain found in a small number of mallard crops and the assumption that all ducks feed on the grain twice a day. Some mallards may feed on grain but once daily (Gollop 1950, Sterling 1952). Also, estimates based on feeding-station records may not be applicable to swathed grain because of differences in availability. The popular figures used for a mallard's daily consumption—198 to 227 g (7 to 8 oz.)—seem high in view of the measured intake of 73 g (2.6 oz.) daily by male mallards penned outdoors in Illinois in October (Jordan, 1953), as well as predicted values based on indirect measurements (Kendeigh 1970, Owen 1970, Sugden 1971). Studies are needed to determine if realistic estimates of grain consumption are being used, as these measurements are critical when evaluating feeding programs.

It would be useful to know if feeding projects do delay movements of ducks southward. A project in the north that reduces damage along the flyways to the south should reap greater benefits than one in the south.

Although culture of natural foods as a technique to keep ducks out of commercial grain appears to have limited utility, there is little quantitative evidence upon which to base the conclusion. Reliable information on the autumn diets of mallards and pintails that feed in prairie marshes is almost non-existent, most studies being based on gizzard material that may give biased results (Swanson and Bartonek 1970). Few attempts have been made to measure the abundance and availability of foods in marshes used by field-feeding ducks. We do not know how the features of a marsh are related to the tendencies of the ducks to forage in grain fields (Gollop 1951). At Delta, Manitoba, Hochbaum (1944) observed that some mallards obtained most of their food from fields, while others were strictly marsh-feeders. Elsewhere, some mallards apparently fed in fields twice daily, while others visited fields once each day (Sterling 1952).

Severely damaged areas are invariably associated with large wetlands harbouring flocks of ducks. But not all large wetlands have associated damage, despite the fact that some have comparable fall populations of mallards and pintails (D. J. Nieman, pers. comm.). Hammond (1955) believed years of good pondweed (*Potamogeton* spp.) seed production at Lower Souris Refuge, North Dakota were associated with low crop damage because mallards and pintails depended more on natural foods. These observations suggest that marshes differ in their ability to hold potential field-feeding ducks. Observations made in the past were largely of ducks that habitually fed in fields. Even less is known about ducks that do not field-feed or the wetlands they utilize. Further study might reveal important clues concerning the relationship between natural food stocks and field-feeding intensity. Demonstration of such a relationship would justify research on natural food management (Toth et al. 1972).

CONCLUSIONS

The urgency of the problem tends to generate short-term research projects seeking quick solutions, yet some questions will be answered only after years of careful data collection or experimentation. Examples of these would be the relationship between damage severity and the distribution, numbers, and movements of waterfowl; the relationship between field-feeding activity and the wetlands used by the ducks; the influence of landscape features on the behaviour of field-feeding ducks; and the application of bio-acoustics to scare ducks. The testing of some techniques may require several years to produce meaningful results.

Small gains in crop protection will probably be the rule and should not be dismissed. A reduction in crop damage as small as 5% could save a million dollars in grain in some years. No single approach is likely to solve the entire damage problem and programs will always be multiform, if for no other reason than that more than one group of people is involved. Benefits from multiple techniques tend to be additive.

ACKNOWLEDGMENTS

I thank the following persons for their help through discussions and/or manuscript review: W. J. D. Stephen, J. B. Gollop, D. J. Neave, and R. W. Prach.

LITERATURE CITED

ALDRICH, J. W., C. S. ROBBINS, AND W. W. DYKSTRA. 1961. Bird hazard to aircraft. U.S. Dept. Interior. Wildl. Leafl. 429. 10pp.

ANDERSON, T. E. 1969. Identifying, evaluating, and controlling wildlife damage. Pages 497–520 *in* R. H. Giles, Jr., ed. Wildlife management techniques. Wildl. Soc., Washington, D.C. 623pp.

BECK, R. A. 1959. Duck depredation studies in the Canadian prairie pothole country. Delaware Conserv. 4(1):13–15.

BECK, T. V. 1951. A study of shattering and weathering in wheat and barley. M.S. Thesis. Univ. Sask., Saskatoon. 42pp.

BENSON, W. A. 1952. Results of attempts to control duck damage in the Marengo area of western Saskatchewan, August–September, 1952. Sask. Dept. Natur. Resources. Typescript. 20pp.

BIEHN, E. R. 1951. Crop damage by wildlife in California with special emphasis on deer and waterfowl. Calif. Dept. Fish and Game. Game Bull. 5. 71pp.

BOSSENMAIER, E. F., AND W. H. MARSHALL. 1958. Field-feeding by waterfowl in southwestern Manitoba. Wildl. Monogr. 1. 32pp.

BOUDREAU, G. W. 1968. Alarm sounds and responses of birds and their application in controlling problem species. The Living Bird 7:27–46.

BUCKLEY, J. L., AND C. COTTAM. 1966. An ounce of prevention. Pages 454–459 *in* A. Stefferud, ed. Birds in our lives. U.S. Dept. Interior, Washington, D.C. 561pp.

BURGESS, T. E. 1973. A summary of Alberta crop damage control effort with considerations for a province-wide programme. Alberta Fish Wildl. Div. Typescript. 43pp.

BUSNEL, R. G., AND J. GIBAN. 1968. Prospective considerations concerning bio-acoustics in relation to bird-scaring techniques. Pages 17–28 *in* R. K. Murton and E. N. Wright, eds. The problems of birds as pests. Acad. Press, London and New York. 254pp.

CANADIAN WILDLIFE SERVICE. 1973. Uninvited guests. The prairie duck problem. Ottawa. 12pp.

COLLS, D. G. 1951. The conflict between waterfowl and agriculture. Trans. N. Amer. Wildl. Conf. 16:89–93.

COWAN, J. B. 1970. The role of the wildlife refuge in relief of vertebrate pest damage in agriculture. Proc. Vertebrate Pest Conf. 4:150–155.

CUMMINGS, M. W. 1971. Wildlife damage problems. Pages 85–89 *in* R. D. Teague, ed. A manual of wildlife conservation. Wildl. Soc., Washington, D.C. 206pp.

DEGRAZIO, J. W., J. F. BESSER, T. J. DECINO, J. L. GUARINO, AND E. W. SCHAFER, JR. 1972. Protecting ripening corn from blackbirds by broadcasting 4-aminopyridine baits. J. Wildl. Manage. 36(4):1316–1320.

DENNY, C. 1956. Animals of the early west. (Part II). Alberta Hist. Rev. 4(3):21–27.

DODDS, M. E. 1967. A review of research on the use of the windrower for harvesting cereal crops. Can. Agr. Eng. 9(2):95–97, 108.

DYKSTRA, W. W. 1966. To kill a bird. Pages 446–453 *in* A. Stefferud, ed. Birds in our lives. U.S. Dept. Interior, Washington, D.C. 561pp.

FARMES, R. E. 1969. Crop insurance for waterfowl depredation. Trans. N. Amer. Wildl. Natur. Resources Conf. 34:332–337.

FRINGS, H. 1964. Sound in vertebrate pest control. Proc. Vertebrate Pest Contr. Conf. 2:50–56.

———, AND M. FRINGS. 1967. Vertebrate pests. Behavioral manipulation (visual, mechanical, and acoustical). Pages 387–454 *in* W. W. Kilgore and R. L. Doutt, eds. Pest control. Biological, physical, and selected chemical methods. Acad. Press, New York and London. 477pp.

GOLLOP, J. B. 1950. Report on investigation of damage to cereal crops by ducks. Can. Wildl. Serv. Typescript. 63pp.

———. 1951. Report on investigation of damage to cereal crops by ducks—1951. Can. Wildl. Serv. Typescript. 22pp.

———. 1960. An experiment to alleviate crop losses due to sandhill cranes in Saskatchewan. Can. Wildl. Serv. Typescript. 17pp.

GOODHUE, L. D., AND F. M. BAUMGARTNER. 1965. Applications of new bird control chemicals. J. Wildl. Manage. 29(4):830–837.

HAMMOND, M. C. 1950. Waterfowl damage and control measures, Lower Souris Refuge and vicinity. U.S. Fish Wildl. Serv. Typescript. 30pp.

———. 1955. Waterfowl damage and control measures, Lower Souris Refuge 1954. U.S. Fish Wildl. Serv. Typescript. 32pp.

———. 1961. Waterfowl feeding stations for controlling crop losses. Trans. N. Amer. Wildl. Natur. Resources Conf. 26:67–78.

———. 1964. Ducks, grain, and American farmers. Pages 417–427 *in* J. P. Linduska, ed. Waterfowl tomorrow. U.S. Dept. Interior, Washington, D.C. 770pp.

HATFIELD, J. P. 1971. Waterfowl habitat in western Canada—Last Mountain Lake. Page 40 *in* Canadian Wildlife Service '71. Dept. Environ., Ottawa. 87pp.

HOCHBAUM, H. A. 1944. The canvasback on a prairie marsh. Amer. Wildl. Inst., Washington, D.C. 201pp.

———, S. T. DILLON, AND J. L. HOWARD. 1954. An experiment in the control of waterfowl depredations. Trans. N. Amer. Wildl. Conf. 19:176–181.

HORN, E. E. 1949. Waterfowl damage to agricultural crops and its control. Trans. N. Amer. Wildl. Conf. 14:577–585.

HOWARD, W. E. 1967. Vertebrate pests. Biocontrol and chemosterilants. Pages 343–386 *in* W. W. Kilgore and R. L. Doutt, eds. Pest control. Biological, physical, and selected chemical methods. Acad. Press, New York and London. 477pp.

HUNT, H. M. 1974. Habitat relations and reproductive ecology of Hungarian Partridge in a hedgerow complex in Saskatchewan. Sask. Dept. Tourism and Renewable Resources. Wildl. Rep. 3. 51pp.

JORDAN, J. S. 1953. Consumption of cereal grains by migratory waterfowl. J. Wildl. Manage. 17(2):120–123.

KALMBACH, E. R. 1935. Protecting grain crops from damage by wild fowl. U.S. Dept. Agr. Wildl. Res. Manage. Leafl. BS-13. 7pp.

———. 1943. Birds, rodents, and colored lethal baits. Trans. N. Amer. Wildl. Conf. 8:408–416.

KEAR, J. 1965. The reaction of captive mallard to grain treated with a commercial bird repellent. Wildfowl Trust Annu. Rep. 16:47–48.

KENDEIGH, S. C. 1970. Energy requirements for existence in relation to size of bird. Condor 72(1):60–65.

KILGORE, W. W., AND R. L. DOUTT, editors. 1967. Pest control. Biological, physical, and selected chemical methods. Acad. Press, New York and London. 477pp.

KOZICKY, E. L., AND R. A. MCCABE. 1970. Birds in pest situations. Pages 58–82 *in* Nat. Acad. Sci. publ. Principles of plant and animal pest control. Vol. 5. Vertebrate pests: problems and control. Washington, D.C. 153pp.

KRENTZ, H. 1959. Duck feeding program—1959. Man. Game Br. Typescript. 8pp.

———. 1960. Duck feeding program—1960. (Delta.) Man. Game Br. Typescript. 7pp.

LEITCH, W. G. 1951. Saving, maintaining, and developing waterfowl habitat in western Canada. Trans. N. Amer. Wildl. Conf. 16:94–99.

LEOPOLD, A. 1933. Game management. Charles Scribner's Sons. New York and London. 481pp.

LOSTETTER, C. H. 1956. Environmental control in waterfowl. Trans. N. Amer. Wildl. Conf. 21:199–209.

———. 1960. Management to avoid waterfowl depredations. Trans. N. Amer. Wildl. Nat. Resources Conf. 25:102–109.

MACLENNAN, R. 1973. A study of waterfowl crop depredation in Saskatchewan. Sask. Dept. Nat. Resources. Wildl. Rep. 2. 38pp.

MAIR, W. W. 1953. Ducks and grain. Trans. N. Amer. Wildl. Conf. 18:111–116.

MCWHORTER, R. E. 1961. Crop depredation control—Portage Plains and Big Grass Marsh. Man. Game Br. Typescript. 10pp.

MELZACK, R., E. PENICK, AND A. BECKETT. 1959. The problem of "innate fear" of the hawk shape: An experimental study with mallard ducks. J. Comp. Physiol. Psychol. 52(6):694–698.

MUNRO, D. A. 1950*a*. Review of waterfowl conditions in Canada. Trans. N. Amer. Wildl. Conf. 15:94–98.

———. 1950*b*. A study of the economic status of sandhill cranes in Saskatchewan. J. Wildl. Manage. 14(3):276–284.

———. 1958. Crop damage by birds. Can. Wildl. Serv. Typescript. 7pp.

———, AND J. B. GOLLOP. 1955. Canada's place in flyway management. Trans. N. Amer. Wildl. Conf. 20:118–125.

MURTON, R. K. 1968. Some predator-prey relationships in bird damage and population control. Pages 157–169 *in* R. K. Murton and E. N. Wright, eds. The problems of birds as pests. Acad. Press, London and New York. 254pp.

———. 1974. The use of biological methods in the control of vertebrate pests. Pages 211–232 *in* D. Price Jones and M. E. Solomon, eds. Biology in pest and disease control. Blackwell Scientific Publications, London, Edinburgh, and Melbourne. 398pp.

———, AND E. N. WRIGHT, editors. 1968. The problems of birds as pests. Acad. Press, London and New York. 254pp.

OWEN, R. B., JR. 1970. The bioenergetics of captive blue-winged teal under controlled and outdoor conditions. Condor 72(2):153–163.

PAYNTER, E. L. 1955. Crop insurance against waterfowl depredations. Trans. N. Amer. Wildl. Conf. 20:151–157.

———, AND W. J. D. STEPHEN. 1964. Waterfowl in the Canadian breadbasket. Pages 409–416 *in* J. P. Linduska, ed. Waterfowl tomorrow. U.S. Dept. Interior, Washington, D.C. 770pp.

PFEIFER, S., AND W. KEIL. 1963. Defense against bird damage through glass balls. (Transl. from Ger.) Can. Wildl. Serv. GER-10. 4pp.

RENEWABLE RESOURCES CONSULTING SERVICES LTD. (RRCS). 1969. A study of waterfowl damage to commercial grain crops in Alberta. Rep. for Alberta Fish Wildl. Div. Multilith. 166pp.

———. 1970. A preliminary study of waterfowl

damage to grain crops in Saskatchewan. Rep. for Can. Wildl. Serv. Typescript. 67pp.

SMITH, S. B. 1968. Wildlife damage legislation in Alberta. Trans. Fed.–Prov. Wildl. Conf. 32:43–46.

SOPER, J. D. 1944. Canadian waterfowl management problems. Trans. N. Amer. Wildl. Conf. 9:277–281.

———. 1948. Canada looks at waterfowl. Trans. N. Amer. Wildl. Conf. 13:52–56.

SOWLS, L. K. 1955. Prairie ducks. A study of their behavior, ecology, and management. Stackpole Co. and Wildl. Manage. Inst., Harrisburg, Pa. and Washington, D.C. 193pp.

STAPEL, W. J., AND J. J. LEHANE. 1955. The influence of field shelterbelts on wind velocity, evaporation, soil moisture, and crop yield. Can. J. Agr. Sci. 35(5):440–453.

STATISTICS CANADA. 1972. Canada year book. Statistical annual of the resources, demography, institutions, and social and economic conditions of Canada. Min. Ind. Trade Com., Ottawa. 1404pp.

STEPHEN, W. J. D. 1959. 1959 co-operative waterfowl depredation investigation. Can. Wildl. Serv. Typescript. 11pp.

———. 1961*a*. Experimental use of acetylene exploders to control duck damage. Trans. N. Amer. Wildl. Natur. Resources Conf. 26:98–110.

———. 1961*b*. Status of duck damage control research on the Canadian prairies. Proc. Conv. Int. Ass. Game, Fish Conserv. Comm. 51:64–67.

———. 1965*a*. Migratory waterfowl damage in the prairie provinces. Trans. Fed.–Prov. Wildl. Conf. 29:82–87.

———. 1965*b*. Survey of wildlife damage in the prairie provinces. Can. Wildl. Serv. Typescript. 10pp.

———. 1967. Bionomics of the sandhill crane. Can. Wildl. Serv., Rep. Ser. 2. 48pp.

STERLING, T. 1952. Prevention of crop depredation by ducks and cranes in the Last Mountain Lake area of south central Saskatchewan, August–September, 1952. Ducks Unlimited (Canada). Typescript. 16pp.

STEWART, R. E., AND H. A. KANTRUD. 1972. Population estimates of breeding birds in North Dakota. Auk 89(4):766–788.

SUGDEN, L. G. 1971. Metabolizable energy of small grains for mallards. J. Wildl. Manage. 35(4):781–785.

SUMMERS, P. W., AND L. WOJTIW. 1971. The economic impact of hail damage in Alberta, Canada and its dependence on various hailfall parameters. Amer. Meteorol. Soc. Severe Local Storms Conf. 7:158–163.

SWANSON, G. A., AND J. C. BARTONEK. 1970. Bias associated with food analysis in gizzards of blue-winged teal. J. Wildl. Manage. 34(4):739–746.

THIESSEN, G. J., E. A. G. SHAW, R. D. HARRIS, J. B. GOLLOP, AND H. R. WEBSTER. 1957. Acoustic irritation threshold of Peking ducks and other domestic and wild fowl. J. Acoust. Soc. Amer. 29:1301–1306.

TOTH, S. J., F. TOURINE, AND S. J. TOTH, JR. 1972. Fertilization of smartweed. J. Wildl. Manage. 36(4):1356–1363.

TRUSCOTT, J. D. 1950. A study of shattering resistance in cereal crops. M.S. Thesis. Univ. Sask., Saskatoon. 41pp.

UNIVERSITY OF SASKATCHEWAN, EXTENSION DIV. 1975. Guide to farm practice in Saskatchewan. Saskatoon. 177pp.

U.S. FISH AND WILDLIFE SERVICE. 1964. Bird control devices—Sources of supply. Wildl. Leafl., Washington, D.C. 409 rev. 4pp.

WAGAR, J. V. K. 1946. Colorado's duck-damage, grain-crop problem. Trans. N. Amer. Wildl. Conf. 11:156–160.

WILLIAMS, C. S., AND J. A. NEFF. 1966. Scaring makes a difference. Pages 438–445 *in* A. Stefferud, ed. Birds in our lives. U.S. Dept. Interior, Washington, D.C. 561pp.

PRIVATE WATERFOWL SHOOTING CLUBS IN THE MISSISSIPPI FLYWAY[1]

JOHN BARCLAY,[2] Cooperative Wildlife Research Unit, The Ohio State University, Columbus, OH
KARL E. BEDNARIK, Division of Wildlife, Ohio Department of Natural Resources, Columbus, OH

A cloud of uncertainty has obscured the role of private duck clubs in waterfowl management for many years. In the Mississippi Flyway, the paucity of information about such clubs has hampered guidance of private management efforts on a broad scale.

A major step toward resolving the unknowns was taken in 1963 when the Mississippi Flyway Council initiated an extensive study of the contribution of private clubs to the overall waterfowl management program. This paper reviews that effort, presents basic findings, and attempts to provide some comparison of the public and private waterfowl management roles.

The Mississippi Flyway embraces 14 states or one-fourth of the area of the 48 contiguous United States. One-fourth of North America's migratory waterfowl winter within the confines of the flyway, sharing the area with one-third of the nation's human population.

Despite substantial and continuing losses of wetlands, the Mississippi Flyway contains 42 percent (31 million acres as of 1956) of the nation's waterfowl habitat and 56 percent of its high-value habitat (Shaw and Fredine 1956). As of 1962, approximately 10 percent of the total habitat was under state or federal management (Ledin 1967). An estimated 5,000 private duck and goose hunting clubs control an additional 2.5 million acres (Barclay 1966).

[1] Originally published in Trans. North Am. Wildl. Nat. Resour. Conf. 33:130–142, 1968.

[2] Address correspondence to this author. Present address: 2402 W. 8th, Stillwater, OK 74074.

Forty percent of the duck hunters in this country pursue their sport in the Mississippi Flyway states, harvesting roughly one-fourth of the annual bag of geese and ducks (Hawkins 1964). One-third of the 664,000 flyway hunters are thought to hunt sometime during the season on private clubs as members, guests, or paid permit holders. These club hunters, in turn, may account for roughly one-third of the flyway's waterfowl harvest.

OTHER STUDIES

Although periodic surveys of existing and potential wetlands have been conducted, notably by the U.S. Fish and Wildlife Service, extensive flywaywide studies of the contribution of private clubs appear to have been non-existent. Anderson and Kozlik (1964) provide a useful overview of the role of private holdings on a national scale as well as by flyways, but found that many states were unable to offer substantial information. Bryant's (1965) report on private holdings in Southern Ontario is an excellent treatment of such lands on a regional basis. Braun (1965) obtained new and useful data on the financial and management aspects of private clubs in all four flyways, although his objectives varied considerably from the present study. Stimulated in part by efforts in the Mississippi Flyway, the other flyways have conducted similar surveys for the preparation of a nationwide report on private holdings by the Wildlife Management Institute.

OBJECTIVES

The Mississippi Flyway Council, in its 1960 report, recognized private waterfowl club lands as one of ten major aspects of the total waterfowl program which should receive special consideration in the subsequent decade. Thus in 1963, after a preliminary investigation by the Planning Committee, the Technical Section of the Council launched a flywaywide questionnaire-interview survey. The inventory was designed to aid in evaluating the role of private holdings through determination of:

1. The number of clubs plus the amount and type of habitat under private control in the flyway.
2. The contribution of such clubs to the overall waterfowl management program.
3. The extent of waterfowl utilization.
4. Recreational use and waterfowl harvest.
5. Financial investment in club operations and waterfowl management.

METHODS AND LIMITATIONS

A questionnaire-interview approach was adopted as being most feasible for meeting the above objectives. Conservation officers, game managers, biologists, and in some cases club representatives themselves, completed the questionnaires on the basis of personal contacts.

A private club in this study was defined as "any group, firm, corporation, association, organization, or individual renting, leasing, controlling, or operating any tract of land or body of water for taking wild ducks and/or geese (this excludes landowners who hunt casually on their lands, but includes all fee hunting areas)."

All responses were numerically coded and transferred to code sheets from which two cards per questionnaire were machine punched. Computer programming facilitated summarization of the data categorically for each state. A portion of the responses were further stratified by states according to type of operation, hunting emphasis, and the decade in which the clubs were organized. After machine processing, the data were tabulated and a report prepared.

Due to reasons discussed below, a thorough statistical analysis was not conducted. Consequently, totals, percentages, and means were utilized in the results section of the report.

Two states, Mississippi and Louisiana, were unable to participate in the questionnaire survey. Minnesota, having completed a private holdings study in 1962, did not use the questionnaire but submitted findings from a much briefer form than used in this survey. Some states were unable to obtain information for certain categories, such as age of club and annual waterfowl harvest.

In addition to providing questionnaires on 120 individual clubs throughout the state, Wisconsin personnel prepared a special report summarizing information for 257 goose clubs adjacent to the Horicon National Wildlife Refuge. Although the goose club data were included in the Wisconsin and flyway tabulations, they had to be excluded from the stratifications by club type.

Conditions under which the data were acquired made a sophisticated statistical treatment unjustified. Some statistically doubtful sample estimates, failure of states to conduct the survey simultaneously, variations in sampling effort and competence by field personnel, and difficulties with the questionnaire itself all served to restrict the analysis and reduce statistical reliability.

Incomplete responses and misinterpretation of questions caused considerable difficulty in the analysis. A minority of responses appear to have been influ-

Table 1. Number of private waterfowl hunting clubs in Mississippi Flyway states.

State	Clubs reported*	Estimated percent sample	Estimated total clubs
Minnesota	92 (87)	−10	920
Wisconsin	120 (120) + 257**	50–75	628 ± 125
Michigan	54 (53)	70	77
Iowa	36 (35)	95	38
Illinois	212 (212)	15	1,413
Indiana	21 (21)	90	23
Ohio	63 (63)	100	63
Sub-total	598 (591) + 257	27	3,162
Missouri	169 (167)	60–65	271 ± 11
Kentucky	10 (9)	75	13
Arkansas	129 (129)	37	350
Tennessee	29 (29)	80	36
Louisiana	— —	—	(1000)***
Mississippi	— —	—	(36)***
Alabama	25 (24)	23	109
Sub-total	362 (358)	46	779 + (1,036)
Total	960 (949) + 257 1,217	31 ± 4	3,941 + (1,036) 4,977

* Parentheses denote total usable questionnaires.
** Horicon area goose clubs not represented by questionnaires.
*** Estimate from Anderson and Kozlik (1964).

enced by either survey personnel or the clubs themselves. A few exceptionally large or active clubs probably exert undue influence on determined values. Also, the Wisconsin survey excluded clubs under 20 acres while other states did not.

Despite the drawbacks, the data as a whole are thought to provide a new and substantially more reliable dimension in our knowledge of private holdings. Critical examination of the nearly 1,000 questionnaires evoked a definite, but unprovable, belief that the bulk of the information accurately portrays the private clubs surveyed.

RESULTS AND DISCUSSION

Due to the nature of the study and the data obtained, many of the results are tentative and subject to future revision. The information acquired only partially fulfills the stated objectives. A brief resume of the findings is presented below, followed by an examination of certain data in terms of public and private aspects of the flyway management picture.

Sample Size

Estimates of numbers of clubs reported and total clubs in each state are presented in Table 1. The survey representative in each state, except for Arkansas, Louisiana, and Mississippi, provided the percentages of clubs reported. These estimates range from less than 10 percent in Minnesota to 100 percent in Ohio.

A total of 960 questionnaires, including 11 not usable for analysis, plus the 257 Horicon area goose clubs provide a total sample of 1,217 clubs. On the basis of sample estimates from each state, it is calculated that 31 percent of a minimum 3,941 clubs in 12 states were included in this survey. Anderson and Kozlik (1964) estimate that, in addition, approximately 1,000 clubs are to be found in Louisiana, while Mississippi may have 36. The com-

Table 2. Percentage composition of the major Mississippi Flyway waterfowl hunting clubs for type of operation, hunting emphasized, and year initiated.

Type of operation (1,187 clubs)	%*	Hunting emphasized (1,017 clubs)	%*	Year initiated (621 clubs)	%**
Owner-guest	28	Duck	52	1850–1939	20
Membership	50	Goose	11	1940–1966	80
Daily fee	19	Combination	38		
Other	2				
	99		101		100

* Values do not add to 100 due to rounding.
** Excluding Horicon.

bined estimates suggest that 4,977 clubs may exist in the flyway.

Clubs in the seven northern states (Table 1) comprise 64 percent of the nearly 5,000 clubs in the 14 states. Seventy percent of the surveyed clubs were also in the northern half. However, in terms of sample size, only 27 percent of the northern clubs were surveyed as compared to a 46 percent sample for the five southern states.

Club Characteristics

Clubs were examined from the standpoint of major characteristics such as club type (age, type operation, type hunting), acreage controlled, hunting effort and harvest, waterfowl use, waterfowl management, and economics. The data and highlights discussed generally represent the Mississippi Flyway picture exclusive of Louisiana, Mississippi, and Horicon goose clubs.

Club Type

Fifty percent of the clubs are membership clubs. Approximately 28 percent are owner-guest clubs (Table 2). Operation type does not appear to be related to club age. However, in terms of longevity, 25 percent of the membership clubs were organized before 1940. Only 15 percent of the owner-guest clubs and 10 percent of the fee clubs were organized before that year. These percentages are based on known aged clubs only and exclude Arkansas and Minnesota. From the standpoint of type of hunting emphasized, there is little difference in type of operations, except that a large percentage (35 percent) of daily fee clubs concentrate on geese.

Approximately 80 percent of the classifiable clubs were organized after 1939. Goose clubs, including those at Horicon, generally date back only to 1950. Nearly 20 percent of the duck clubs and 25 percent of the combination goose-duck clubs were organized before 1940.

Acreage

The inventoried clubs report owning or leasing 290,000 acres. Excluding the smaller Horicon goose clubs, the average club size is 304 acres, three-fourths of which is actually owned by the club.

Clubs organized before 1940 are larger (561 acres) than the newer clubs (203 acres) and control four times as much marsh habitat. Daily fee and "courtesy" type[3] clubs are nearly twice as large as the more numerous and typical membership (319 acres) or owner-guest (272 acres) clubs. Duck clubs average 354 acres compared to the combination clubs (285 acres) and goose clubs (124 acres).

[3] Industrial ownership, usually maintained for customers or employees.

Table 3. Hunting effort and success for major type of waterfowl clubs in the Mississippi Flyway. All figures are expressed as weighted means.

Club type	Average number per club*			
	Hunters	Ducks bagged	Geese bagged	Man days hunting
Old clubs	46	239	8	188
New clubs	44	134	27	143
Owner-guest	40	116	15	101
Membership	34	182	15	166
Daily fee	163	117	118	256
Other	134	189	13	219
Duck clubs	45	182	0.4	130
Goose clubs	48	2	59	176
Combination	58	147	31	170
Combined average	49	159	24	154

* No data on age, hunters, harvest or days effort for Arkansas,Minnesota, and Horicon goose clubs.

Hunting Effort and Harvest

More than 37,000 hunters spent 175,000 days hunting waterfowl, bagging more than 92,000 ducks and 14,000 geese annually on the surveyed clubs. Horicon goose club hunters add approximately 5,000 more geese to the total. On a weighted mean basis, the "average" club has 49 hunters (20% members, 53% guests, 27% daily fee) who account for the annual club harvest of 159 ducks and 24 geese in 154 man days of hunting. Illinois, Missouri, and Wisconsin account for 64 percent of the total waterfowl harvest reported by the ten states responding.

Only 62 percent of the annual man days use of the average club is reportedly spent in waterfowl hunting. Approximately 38 percent of the remaining recreational activity is devoted to other forms of hunting, fishing, bird-watching and picnicking. The owner-guest and "courtesy" type clubs hunt waterfowl 55 percent of the time, while 95 percent of the man days use of daily fee clubs are devoted to waterfowling. It is of interest that 55 percent of the man days use of duck clubs are devoted to activities *other* than waterfowl hunting compared to 35 percent for combination clubs and four percent for goose clubs.

Waterfowl Use

The migration, wintering, and nesting use data reported are highly variable and often unreliable. Briefly, an estimated 9,323 nesting pairs, 2.4 million migrant waterfowl (74% mallards, 10% geese) and 509,000 wintering waterfowl (16% geese) were reported aside from obviously aberrent figures which were discarded. Most wintering waterfowl (61%) were reported from Arkansas, while Missouri accounted for 38 percent of the migrants.

Waterfowl Management Practices

A total of 366 clubs reported 22,000 acres of their lands reserved as sanctuary. Over 700 clubs have an additional 14,000 acres planted to crops attractive to waterfowl. More than 98,000 acres were reported as having water level control involving 700 miles of dikes and 567 pumps.

At least 567 clubs employ 705 persons, mostly managers, with some of the larger clubs hiring guides and trappers. Sixty-seven clubs utilize special management techniques such as vegetative control. Excluding Minnesota and the Horicon goose clubs, 35 percent of 860 clubs adhere to self-imposed hunting restrictions, primarily observance of special rest days and/or shooting hours.

Club Economics

A total annual budget of $424,249 was reported by 347 clubs in ten states, exclusive of Arkansas and Minnesota, for an average budget of $1,223. Most of these clubs are the membership type. Approximately 45 percent of the membership

Table 4. Acreage distribution of public and private wetlands in Mississippi Flyway states.

State	Wetlands acreage in thousands			
	Total[1]	Total high and moderate value[1]	Total public state and federal waterfowl areas[2]	Estimated club control[3]
Minnesota	5,045	2,053	540	324
Wisconsin	2,791	438	457	102
Michigan	3,217	2,324	558	32
Iowa	138	109	108	9
Illinois	427	272	200	243
Indiana	283	200	51	9
Ohio	98	51	55	24
Sub-total	11,999	5,466	1,969	743
Missouri	377	199	90	63
Kentucky	273	112	24	5
Arkansas	3,785	1,626	178	181
Tennessee	828	576	138	13
Louisiana	9,647	2,413	887	1,500
Mississippi	2,589	998	81	25
Alabama	1,598	276	114	27
Sub-total	19,098	6,200	1,512	1,814
Total	31,098	11,666	3,481	2,558

[1] Shaw and Fredine (1956).
[2] Ledin (1967).
[3] Mississippi Flyway Survey data, 1966.

clubs reported on both membership and annual dues. These 232 clubs report 3,255 members for an average membership of 14. Average dues per member were $111, providing $1,754 per club annually. The average dues assessments per member ranged from five dollars in Kentucky to $454 in Ohio, with a ten state *median* value of $92.

Braun (1965) reported an annual charge per member of $275 and management costs of $3.72 per acre for the Mississippi Flyway, 1962–63. He also calculated an average club size of 862 acres with an average membership of 28, but indicated (p. 28) that smaller clubs may not have been included in his sample.

Clubs and the Flyway

Private clubs are frequently criticized as constituting a drain on the waterfowl resource, an impedance of sound management programs, and for withholding recreational lands from the hunting public. Whatever the case may be, information obtained in this survey fails to substantiate the first two contentions on a broad basis. The alternative for the third contention is that private clubs complement and supplement State and Federal Government programs aimed at preserving habitat for waterfowl. But neither the survey nor this report were designed to debate the philosophies involved in private clubs holding lands.

The following discussion of acreage distribution, hunting effort and harvest, and financial investments is presented as an aid to compare public-private roles in waterfowl management programs.

Acreage Distribution

Private clubs maintain a substantial acreage of waterfowl habitat in the Mississippi Flyway. As shown in Table 4, the estimated 4,000 clubs in 12 states control

Table 5. Average hunting activity and success ratios for Mississippi Flyway waterfowl hunters.

	Annual values per hunter		
	Day/hunter	Ducks/day	Ducks/hunter
Flyway			
North	5.54	0.74	4.11
South	5.41	0.81	4.37
Total	5.55	0.76	4.21
Private clubs*			
North	4.24	1.10	4.65
South	2.76	0.92	2.54
Total	3.45	1.03	3.55

* Excluding Arkansas, Louisiana, Minnesota, Mississippi and Horicon area goose clubs (private club portion only).

Table 6. Regional comparison of club investments per acre annually, based on total reported acreage and annual budgets.[1]

	Clubs reporting	Acres owned, leased or other	Annual budget	Cost per acre
North	170	45,665	$285,459	$6.25
South	92	24,806	113,159	4.56
Total	262	70,471	$398,618	$5.66

[1] No data for Arkansas, Louisiana, Minnesota, or Mississippi.

an estimated 1,032,900 acres of waterfowl habitat. Additional acreage in Louisiana raises the private total to a minimum estimate of slightly over 2.5 million acres. This is very close to Braun's 1965 estimate of over 2.3 million acres.

The private area is substantially more than the 1.7 million acres of waterfowl habitat (marsh + water + cropland) contained in 34 federal and 398 state management areas in the Mississippi Flyway, but less than the 3.5 million acres which comprise these same public areas (National Flyway Council 1967).

Shaw and Fredine (1956) reported a total of 11.7 million acres of high and moderate value habitat in the flyway, roughly divided between north and south. If it is assumed that private clubs occur primarily on high and moderate value habitats, then the private club acreage is roughly equivalent to 22 percent of the total. By regions, the seven northern states contain an estimated 743,362 acres of club lands, or 14 percent of the valued habitat. The southern states, in turn, account for 1,814,538 acres, or 29 percent, of valued habitat. If our original assumption is valid, private clubs play a major role in maintaining key waterfowl habitat.

Hunting Effort and Harvest Comparisons

Analysis of the survey data suggest that club hunters hunt less frequently in a season, bag more ducks per day, and bag fewer ducks per man annually than does the average flyway hunter (Table 5). These conclusions are based on comparison of calculated survey ratios with similar ratios found in the U.S. Fish and Wildlife Service Waterfowl Status Reports (Glover and Smith 1963, Hansen 1964, Hansen and Hudgins 1965).

The survey ratios were determined from weighted mean values per club. For example, ducks per man was determined by dividing the average number of hunters per club for a given state into the average ducks killed per club for the same state. Flyway ratios were selected from waterfowl status reports containing data for the year prior to that year in which the survey was conducted in any given state. This was done to offset differences in survey timing, since it was assumed that club responses would most accurately reflect the hunting effort and success of the previous season.

Regionally, club hunters in the North spend more days hunting, have a slightly better success ratio per day, and bag more birds per season than do their southern counterparts. Flyway hunters, on the other hand, fare slightly better in the South in terms of ducks per day and ducks per season. It must be remembered that the flyway values include club hunters and harvest, tending to offset differences between the average flyway hunter and the club hunter.

The data tend to indicate, therefore, that club hunters are not securing a disproportionate share of the annual waterfowl harvest. Hunting on clubs does seem to insure more productive results for the effort expended.

Public and Private Investments

The only investment criteria available to the authors for comparison of the public and private outlays is in terms of costs per acre. Club costs per acre were necessarily determined in a rather crude fashion by using acreages of clubs which provided budget estimates. They cannot be considered truly representative, but do provide a rough yardstick. Publicly owned lands, state and federal, and the associated acquisition and development costs were obtained from Ledin (1967). The results are shown in Table 7.

A total of 262 clubs provided data on both acreage and annual budget (Table 6). Those clubs controlled 70,471 acres and reported a total budget of $398,618 for an average budget of $1,521. Northern club budgets averaged $1,679 versus the southern club value of $1,230. These values differ from the average of $1,223 reported by 347 clubs which were discussed earlier, many of whom did not report acreage.

The average budget cost per acre, excluding the one respondent for Kentucky, ranged from a low of $1.51 per acre in Iowa to a high of $10.35 per acre in Ohio. Per acre investment for land which is owned is higher ($5.61) than that for clubs which lease ($4.86) land in both the northern and southern regions. When the average cost per acre was applied to the total estimated club acreage, in each state, and the results added, a total of 2.9 million dollars was calculated as a rough estimate of annual club investments in the ten states submitting data.

Table 7. Calculated value of private holdings based on estimated private acreage and governmental acquisition and development costs per acre.[1]

	Govt. cost per acre	Estimated private acres	Estimated private value
1962			
North	$22.17	743,362	$16,480,034
South	10.33	1,814,538	18,744,178
Total	$18.12	2,557,900	$35,224,212
1967			
North	$57.04	743,362	$42,401,368
South	10.36	1,814,538	18,798,614
Total	$30.09	2,557,900	$61,199,982

[1] Ledin (1967).

The Mississippi Flyway Council's Habitat Committee 1962 report (Ledin 1967) was used to determine state and federal acquisition and development costs per acre of waterfowl habitat for 1962 and 1967 (Table 7). These figures reveal an increase from $18 per acre in 1962 to $30 per acre in 1967. Multiplying the public cost per acre for each period times the total estimated private acreage provides some measure of the general value of club lands (Table 7). The estimated value of 35 million dollars in 1962 rose to 61 million dollars by 1967, as calculated from average governmental costs per acre.

CONCLUSIONS

1. A minimum of 3,941 private waterfowling clubs control an estimated 1,032,900 acres of wetland and upland in 12 of the 14 Mississippi Flyway states. Information on clubs from Louisiana and Mississippi is excluded from these figures.

2. An estimated 5,000 waterfowling

clubs control a minimum of 2.5 million acres of waterfowl habitat in the Mississippi Flyway. Two-thirds of the clubs controlling one-third of the acreage are found in the seven states of the northern region of the flyway.

3. The minimum estimate of slightly over 2.5 million acres controlled by private clubs is less than the approximate 3.5 million acres in the national wildlife refuges and state waterfowl management areas in the Mississippi Flyway. This is more than the approximate 1.7 million acres of waterfowl habitat (water + marsh + cropland) in 34 federal and 398 state waterfowl management areas.

4. As much as 22 percent of the moderate- to high-value habitat may be under private duck club control. If so, private clubs play a major role in perpetuating valued waterfowl habitat in the Mississippi Flyway.

5. The data suggests that club hunters are not securing a disproportionate share of the annual waterfowl harvest. Hunting effort on club lands does appear to insure more productive results for the efforts expended.

6. Canada goose hunting is important to clubs in Illinois, Wisconsin, and Missouri. Duck hunting is important in every state; however, clubs devote a substantial portion of their recreational use to activities other than waterfowl hunting. Thirty-eight percent of the man days are devoted to fishing, bird-watching, picnicking and other activities.

7. Rapidly accelerating acquisition and development costs emphasize the need for continued selective acquisition programs and intensified efforts to stimulate and guide private wetlands and waterfowl management.

In addition to providing hunting opportunities, private waterfowling clubs contribute materially to the waterfowl management effort in the Mississippi Flyway by (1) preserving, directly and indirectly, valuable habitat, (2) increasing the attractiveness of habitat through management, primarily water level manipulation and vegetation control, (3) encouraging production of waterfowl, (4) aiding in waterfowl distribution, primarily by maintaining refuges and restriction on daily and weekly shooting, (5) providing, on many areas, opportunities for a variety of recreational activities, and (6) investing substantial funds to maintain the quality of recreation. They complement and supplement state and federal programs aimed at preserving waterfowl habitat. Such investments would be difficult to match on a per acre basis under public ownership.

LITERATURE CITED

ANDERSON, JOHN M., AND FRANK M. KOZLIK. 1964. Private duck clubs. pp. 519–526. *In* J. P. Linduska, ed., Waterfowl tomorrow. U.S. Dept. Interior, Fish and Wildl. Serv., Washington, D.C. 770pp.

BARCLAY, JOHN S. 1966. A survey of the waterfowl management role of private shooting clubs in the Mississippi Flyway. The Technical Section, Mississippi Flyway Council. 104pp.

BRAUN, CLAIT E. 1965. A survey of the land values directly attributed to waterfowl within the contiguous United States. Montana State University, Missoula. M.S. Thesis. 132pp.

BRYANT, J. E. 1965. Private marshes in southwestern Ontario. Canadian Wildlife Service progress report on project 02-5-1. 65pp.

GLOVER, FRED A., AND J. DONALD SMITH. 1963. Waterfowl status report, 1963. U.S. Fish and Wildl. Serv. Special Sci. Rept.—Wildlife No. 75. 178pp.

HANSEN, HENRY A. 1964. Waterfowl status report, 1964. U.S. Fish and Wildl. Serv. Special Sci. Report—Wildlife No. 86. 142pp.

———, AND MILDRED R. HUDGINS. 1965. Waterfowl status report, 1965. U.S. Fish and Wildl. Serv. Special Sci. Report—Wildlife No. 90. 110pp.

HAWKINS, ARTHUR S. 1964. Mississippi Flyway. Pages 185–207. *In* J. P. Linduska, ed., Waterfowl tomorrow. U.S. Dept. Interior, Fish and Wildl. Serv., Washington, D.C. 770pp.

LEDIN, DONALD. Habitat Committee report, Mississippi Flyway Council. 6pp.

NATIONAL FLYWAY COUNCIL. 1967. Summary of private waterfowl hunting clubs in the United States. Washington, D.C. 8pp.

SHAW, SAMUEL P., AND C. GORDON FREDINE. 1956. Wetlands of the United States, their extent and their value to waterfowl and other wildlife. U.S. Dept. Interior, Fish and Wildlife Service, Circular 39. 67pp.

SELECTED BIBLIOGRAPHY

Management and Economics: Economic Impacts

CLARK, S., AND R. JARVIS. 1978. Effects of winter grazing by geese on yield of ryegrass seed. Wildl. Soc. Bull. 6(2):84–87.

COMMITTEE ON AGRICULTURAL LAND USE AND WILDLIFE RESOURCES. 1970. Special problems of waters and watersheds. Pages 149–180 *in* Land use and wildlife resources. Natl. Acad. of Sci., Washington, D.C.

GOLDSTEIN, J. H. 1971. Competition for wetlands in the Midwest: an economic analysis. The Johns Hopkins Press, Baltimore, MD, and London. 105pp.

HORN, E. E. 1949. Waterfowl damage to agricultural crops and its control. Trans. North Am. Wildl. Conf. 14:577–586.

KEAR, J. 1970. Experimental assessment of goose damage to agricultural crops. Biol. Conserv. 2(3):206–212.

MACLENNAN, R. 1973. A study of waterfowl crop depredation in Saskatchewan. Saskatchewan Dep. Nat. Resour. Wildl. Rep. 2. 33pp.

SHANNON, W. T. 1965. Private clubs and the waterfowl resource. Trans. North Am. Wildl. Nat. Resour. Conf. 30:255–259.

UHLIG, H. G. 1961. Survey of leased waterfowl hunting rights in Minnesota. J. Wildl. Manage. 25(2):204.

WOMACH, J. 1977. National evaluation of the water bank program. Trans. North Am. Wildl. Nat. Resour. Conf. 42:246–254.

MOVEMENT AND MIGRATION

NEST-SITE TENACITY AND HOMING IN THE BUFFLEHEAD[1,2]

ANTHONY J. ERSKINE,[3] Canadian Wildlife Service, Sackville, New Brunswick E0A 3E0, Canada

Banding data for the Bufflehead (*Bucephala albeola*) have not previously been summarized. In this paper, nest-site tenacity and homing tendencies are discussed on the basis of evidence from banding, and some of the shortcomings of Bufflehead banding are pointed out. Many generalizations for that species may have some application to other ducks.

The Bufflehead is more suitable than most other ducks for a study of nest-site tenacity. Its nests in cavities made by Flickers (*Colaptes*) are easily found, at least in favored breeding areas in British Columbia and Alberta. Previously, such studies (e.g., Sowls 1955) have used ground-nesting species, but tree nests have a major advantage in that they are fixed in location and may be revisited in subsequent years without need for further search. Other ducks that nest in trees require larger cavities, which, except when nest boxes are used, are much less easy to locate. The Bufflehead is relatively long-lived, so that individual birds may be recaptured in several successive years.

SOURCES OF DATA

Banding of Buffleheads may be classified as systematic or fortuitous. Most important in the former category is the work of the Department of Zoology, University of British Columbia, and of the British Columbia Game Commission. Flightless young and molting adult Bufflehead were banded in the central plateau region of British Columbia, where the Bufflehead is an abundant breeder, using a drive-trapping technique developed for diving ducks (Cowan and Hatter 1952). Much of the material presented in this paper is derived from retraps and recoveries of the approximately 2,000 Bufflehead banded in that area in 1948–55 and 1957–59. The writer studied the Bufflehead during the summers of 1958 and 1959, while preparing a thesis at the University of British Columbia (Erskine 1960). Nests located during those summers were rechecked in 1960 by Lawson G. Sugden (formerly with the B.C. Game Commission), Canadian Wildlife Service, Edmonton, Alberta.

Other banding of Buffleheads has been classed as fortuitous in that those birds were caught during drive- or bait-trapping operations aimed at other species. Most work in that category was done by Ducks Unlimited co-operators in the Prairie Provinces (1939–50), and by the state game departments of New York (1955–59), Maryland (1956–59), and Oregon (1947–59). Banding by Ducks Unlimited was mostly in August and September, although a few birds were banded in late May and early June. Banding in the other regions was almost exclusively carried out from January through March.

USAGE OF NEST SITES

In central British Columbia a turnover of about 50 per cent was found in usage

---

[1] Originally published in Auk 78(3):389–396, 1961.

[2] This study is a contribution from the Department of Zoology, University of British Columbia, and from Canadian Wildlife Service. This paper was delivered in essence at the Seventy-eighth Stated Meeting of the American Ornithologists' Union, on 26 August 1960, in Ann Arbor, Michigan.

[3] Present address: P.O. Box 1327, Sackville, New Brunswick E0A 3E0, Canada.

Table 1(a). Nest usage by Buffleheads.

Year[1]	Nests used	Nests reused next year	Nests unusable next year
1952	6	1	2
1953	2	2	—
1954	3	—	2
1955	2	—	—
1957	16	9	—
1958	39	25	2
1959	71	33	2
Total[2]	139	70	8

[1] Data for 1952–54 were provided by Miss Mary F. Jackson, and those for 1955 and 1957 (in part) by M. Timothy Myres.

[2] Forty-eight nests occupied in 1960 were omitted from the table, since no data on subsequent use were available.

Table 1(b). Reuse of individual nests.

	Number of consecutive years in which nest used			Used more than once in broken sequence
	4	3	2	
No. of nests	6	10	34	6

of Bufflehead nests. Tables 1(a) and 1(b) present the available data on reuse.

Table 1(a) shows that part of the annual turnover is due to nests becoming unusable, usually because the tree fell down or the cavity became unsuitable. Nests in Aspen (*Populus tremuloides*) are much less durable than nests in Douglas Fir (*Pseudotsuga menziesii*) stubs. One site in Douglas Fir was used by Bufflehead in 1941 (Munro 1942), and again in 1954 (Jackson, in litt.), and the site was still suitable for occupation by Buffleheads in 1960.

SITE TENACITY OF INDIVIDUAL BIRDS

Some investigators (e.g., Munro 1958; H. W. Burns, in litt.) have stated that Bufflehead nests may be used for many years in succession. However, that is not always true, and occupation of a given site in consecutive years need not always involve the same bird. Table 2 gives the known histories of female Buffleheads captured on nests in more than one year.

Only two birds (505–50476 and 515–42803) were caught in three consecutive years on the same nest, while 19 others have been caught twice in the same nest, all but one (38–520622) in two consecutive years. One bird (505–50254 = 505–50497) was caught twice each in two nests, while two others (515–42801 and 515–42804) were also caught in four consecutive years, and one (515–13721) in three of four years in broken sequence. Those data are similar to the histories of individual birds obtained by Sowls (1955) for ground-nesting ducks.

In all, Table 2 includes 35 cases of birds caught in two consecutive years. Table 3 shows the relative numbers of previously banded Buffleheads, handled on nests in earlier years, which were found on the same nest as before or on a different nest in 1958–60. With one exception nest trapping began in 1957.

Actually, the proportion of birds moving is probably lower under natural conditions. In 1957 and 1958 techniques for the nest study were being developed, and much more disturbance of nests resulted in those years than in 1959. However, desertion during the 1957 and 1958 nesting seasons was no more frequent than in 1959.

SURVIVAL OF BUFFLEHEADS

It is worth noting that birds first trapped on the nest in 1957 were frequently recaptured in later years (see Table 2). Mortality rates calculated from shot recoveries (cf. Hickey 1952) are impossibly high, exceeding even the most optimistic estimates of production, but the samples are too small to be satisfactory. Of eight females first trapped on the nest in 1957, seven were alive in 1958,

Table 2. Histories of female Buffleheads.

Band number	Known history of bird
38–520461	Banded as young 1949; rebanded 515–42805 on nest at same lake 1957; on same nest 1958.
38–520622	Banded as young 1950; on nest at lake 1 km away 1952; on same nest 1954; but not 1953.
505–50120	Banded as molting adult 1952; on nest at lake 155 km away 1957; moved 265 m W to new (re-)nest 1958.
505–50254	Banded as subadult (?) 1955; on nest at same lake 1957; on same nest 1958; also trapped with brood on same lake 1957 and 1958; rebanded 505–50497 on new nest 67 m E in 1959 (renest); on same nest 1960.
505–50471	Banded on nest 1958; on same nest 1959.
505–50472	Banded on nest 1958; on same nest 1959.
505–50473	Banded on nest 1958; on same nest 1959.
505–50474	Banded on nest 1958; on same nest 1959.
505–50476	Banded on nest 1958; on same nest 1959 and 1960.
505–50477	Banded on nest 1958; moved 82 m SE to new nest 1959.
505–50478	Banded on nest 1958; moved 450 m SSE to next lake to new (re-)nest 1959; on same nest 1960.
505–50483	Banded on nest 1958; moved 1,100 m ESE to new nest 1959.
505–50486	Banded on nest 1959; on same nest 1960.
505–50491	Banded on nest 1959; moved 5 km ESE to next lake to new nest 1960.
505–50493	Banded on nest 1959; on same nest 1960.
505–50494	Banded on nest 1959; on same nest 1960.
505–50495	Banded on nest 1959; on same nest 1960.
505–50498	Banded on nest 1959; on same nest 1960.
515–13721	Banded as young 1955; on nest at same lake 1957 (1958?, bird on same nest not caught); moved 70 m SE to new nest 1959; moved 1,200 m W to new nest 1960.
515–13790	Banded on nest 1959; on same nest 1960.
515–13794	Banded on nest 1959; on same nest 1960.
515–42801	Banded on nest 1957; moved 900 m E to new nest 1958; moved 180 m S to new nest 1959; on same nest 1960.
515–42803	Banded on nest 1957; on same nest 1958 and 1959.
515–42804	Banded on nest 1957; moved 134 m NW to new (re-)nest 1958; moved (from 1958) 255 m ESE to new (re-)nest 1959; on same nest 1960.
525–19630	Banded as young 1957; on nest at same lake 1959; moved 75 m W to new nest 1960.
525–19725	Banded on nest 1958; on same nest 1959.
545–40538	Banded as adult with brood 1958; on nest at same lake 1959; on same nest 1960.

five in 1959, and four in 1960, a mortality rate of about 17 per cent. Smaller portions of birds first handled in 1958 and 1959 have been recaptured in subsequent years, however, and much more data are needed before such mortality rates can be accepted as representative of that population.

MOVEMENTS OF BUFFLEHEADS

The most important study of the movements of female ducks dealt with the renesting of dabbling ducks (Sowls 1955). For the Pintail (*Anas acuta*) Sowls measured movements between original nests and renests of the same bird in 15 cases; distances varied from 78 to 1,370 meters, and averaged 258 meters. For the Buffle-

Table 3. Relative site tenacity of the Bufflehead, 1958–60.

Year	Birds caught: In same nest as before	Birds caught: In another nest
1958	3	3
1959	7	6
1960	13	3
	23	12

head only movements between the nests in successive years are known, but the results appear comparable to those found by Sowls. Table 2 includes data on 12 such movements. Three were of less than 100 meters, four of 100–300 meters, and three of 900–1,200 meters; two others involved movements between lakes, one of 450 meters, and one of five km. The average distance was 797 meters; since the chances of recapturing birds at distances of over two km are so slight as to be negligible, the one such value is best omitted from the calculation, leaving an average of 428 meters. The data given here suggest that a renesting study on Bufflehead could provide much valuable data in a short time.

HOMING

As shown in Table 3, homing by the adult female Bufflehead is often very precise; 23 cases out of 35 cited involving returns to the precise nesting site used previously. Breeding females usually return to their natal lake. Of nine birds banded as flightless young and recaptured on nests two to nine years later, six were at the lakes where they were banded and two others at lakes within one km of the banding lake; one bird was found nesting five km away in the next valley. Three other birds banded by drive trapping were also recaptured on nests later, while three more were captured with broods in two consecutive years, all captures of each individual being at the same lake. As shown above, 18 females banded on nests were later captured on nests at the same lakes, while two others had moved to other lakes. The one record of a female (505–50120) having molted 155 km from a later nesting area indicates that in Bufflehead, as in other species (cf. Hochbaum 1955), molting may take place far from the breeding areas.

Table 4. Homing to wintering areas.

Area	Sex	Recaptures (live)	Recoveries (shot) (distance from point of banding) Under 15 km	15–50 km	50–80 km
Ore.	M	3	3		
	F	3	1	1	
N.Y.	M	24	11	3	3
	F	8	8	5	5
Md.	M	22	18		1
	F	4	4		1

HOMING TO MOLTING AREAS

The molting areas of the male Bufflehead in British Columbia are unknown, but some data are available for females. Fourteen females banded while molting and five banded as young were later taken as molting adults. Ten were recaptured on the same lake, and five others within five km of the points of banding. The other four, including two banded as young, were recaptured between 25 and 65 km away. A tendency to return to the same molting area is suggested.

HOMING TO WINTERING AREAS

Considerable numbers of Buffleheads have been banded on wintering areas and later shot or recaptured in the same general area. Data from Oregon, New York, and Maryland are summarized in Table 4, all birds included having been recaptured or shot in subsequent winter seasons.

For comparison, it may be worth mentioning that from New York bandings only six Buffleheads were recovered at localities more than 80 km from the banding areas, during the months of December through March, and only one similarly from Maryland bandings.

Those data indicate that males as well as females are capable of homing to a precise locality, and males may well also

Table 5. Sex ratios of Buffleheads during migration.

Date(s)	No. adult males	No. females	Sex ratio (males/100 females)	Source of data
(a) Early in migration (just after lakes became open)				
5–6 Apr. 1958	132	9	1,466/100	The writer
10 Apr. 1959	149	22	677/100	Sugden, in litt.
(b) Later in migration (in 1959 about one week before the first eggs were laid)				
16–24 Apr. 1941	318	123	258/100	Munro (1942)
19 Apr. 1959	235	104	226/100	Sugden, in litt.

home to breeding and molting areas (cf. Cartwright and Law 1952).

EVIDENCE AGAINST WINTER PAIRING OF BUFFLEHEADS

The most generally accepted hypothesis is that most pairing of waterfowl takes place on the wintering grounds (cf. Hochbaum 1955), and that homing depends mainly upon the female. Banding data alone neither support nor refute that hypothesis.

One basis for the hypothesis is the repeated observation of courtship among most species in such areas. However, it is known that courtship is also very common during migration and after birds arrive on the breeding areas. In the Bufflehead, courtship, including precopulatory displays, has been noted in wintering areas, but copulation has only been seen on the breeding grounds (Myres 1959; Drury, verbal). This suggests that pairs are not consummated until the breeding grounds are reached, and further evidence suggests that frequently pair formation is also delayed.

Sex ratios of Buffleheads during spring migration in British Columbia provide evidence for migration of unpaired males. Such data are given in Table 5.

On 5–6 April 1958 flocks of 10–20 males were seen on several occasions unaccompanied by females, so even the possibility that several males may accompany one female (cf. Munro 1942) does not cover the observations. The evidence presented suggests that many, if not most, male Buffleheads must commence migration before pairing.

In order to prove or disprove the homing tendency in male ducks, whether Buffleheads or other species, it will be necessary to develop methods for capturing the males on their territories. To date that problem has been generally ignored.

SUMMARY

Female Buffleheads exhibit a tendency to home to their natal lake, often returning to the precise nest site used in previous years. Reuse of a given nest site may be prevented by its having become unusable, or disturbance during the previous nesting season may induce a move to another site. The homing tendency and the distance of moves between nests are similar to those established earlier for other species of ducks.

Female Buffleheads also tend to return to molting areas, while both sexes return to wintering ground used in previous years. Evidence is presented to suggest that male Buffleheads may home to the breeding grounds, often independently of the female.

Banding male ducks on their territories seems the logical way to prove homing in drakes, but this is lacking for the Bufflehead and for other ducks.

AUTHOR'S NOTE

Additional work was done in 1961–66 and ultimately a monograph on the species resulted (1972). Points made in my 1961 paper which required modification in the light of added data were as follows:

—the durability of nest sites was documented much more fully in the Monograph, and was extended considerably following a later visit in 1975;

—site tenacity and homing were documented in much greater detail in the Monograph, and the suspicion that the 1960 data (in Table 3) were more representative than those for 1958–59 was confirmed; and

—the evidence for pairing during migration and on breeding areas (rather than in winter) was much more complete, and confirmed that such is the general rule.

ACKNOWLEDGMENTS

The writer wishes to thank the following individuals or organizations who contributed to this study. Work in 1958 and 1959 was supported by postgraduate Wildlife Fellowships awarded by Canadian Industries Limited; equipment was provided by the Department of Zoology, University of British Columbia, Vancouver, B.C., and the study was supervised by Dr. I. McT. Cowan, Head, Zoology Department, University of British Columbia. The 1960 studies were supported by the Canadian Wildlife Service, Department of Northern Affairs and National Resources, Ottawa, Ontario. Data on the bandings in areas other than British Columbia were provided by the organizations involved. The help of Miss Mary F. Jackson, M. Timothy Myres, A. James Wiggs, William D. McLaren, and Lawson G. Sugden is gratefully acknowledged.

LITERATURE CITED

CARTWRIGHT, B. W., AND J. T. LAW. 1952. Waterfowl banding 1939–1950 by Ducks Unlimited. Publ. by Ducks Unlimited, Winnipeg, Man. 53pp.

COWAN, I. MCT., AND J. HATTER. 1952. A trap and technique for the capture of diving waterfowl. Jour. Wildl. Mgt. 16:438–441.

ERSKINE, A. J. 1960. A discussion of the distributional ecology of the Bufflehead (*Bucephala albeola*; Anatidae; Aves) based upon breeding biology studies in British Columbia. M.A. thesis, University of British Columbia.

HICKEY, J. J. 1952. Survival studies of banded birds. United States Department of the Interior, Fish and Wildlife Service. Spec. Sci. Rpt. 15. 177pp.

HOCHBAUM, H. A. 1955. Travels and traditions of waterfowl. Univ. Minn. Press, Minneapolis. xx + 301pp.

MUNRO, J. A. 1942. Studies of waterfowl in British Columbia. Bufflehead. Can. Jour. Res. 20D:133–160.

———. 1958. The status of nesting waterfowl in the Cariboo Parklands, British Columbia, in 1958. B.C. Game Comm., mimeo rpt.

MYRES, M. T. 1959. Display behaviour of Bufflehead, Scoters, and Goldeneyes at copulation. Wilson Bull. 71:159–168.

SOWLS, L. K. 1955. Prairie ducks. The Stackpole Co., Harrisburg, Pa., and Wildl. Mgt. Inst., Washington, D.C. xii + 193pp.

THE MOBILITY OF BREEDING PINTAILS[1]

SCOTT R. DERRICKSON, Department of Ecology and Behavioral Biology, University of Minnesota, Minneapolis, MN 55455

Abstract: During 1971, 1972, and 1973 the mobility of breeding Pintails (*Anas acuta*) was studied in the pothole region of central North Dakota. A total of 5 unpaired males, 8 paired males, and 15 females were marked and followed for periods long enough to enable home range estimation. The mean home range sizes for unpaired males, paired males, and paired females were 579 ha, 896 ha, and 480 ha, respectively. Males were generally more mobile than females at all stages of the reproductive cycle.

Mobility was found to vary with reproductive chronology, usually decreasing from the prenesting to the nesting period. Seven pair ranges that included both the prenesting and nesting period averaged 509 ha, while four pair ranges that included only the nesting period averaged 167 ha. Female mobility was found to be greatest during the period preceding laying, and home range estimates for the prenesting period were significantly larger than home ranges calculated for the laying period. Females that renested were found to have reduced mobility throughout the renest interval.

Home range estimates for breeding Pintails are generally larger than those previously recorded for other *Anas* species. Interspecific variation in breeding home range size is apparent, and reflects differences in social behavior and feeding ecology.

The spacing behavior of breeding ducks has received much attention in the literature. Hochbaum (1944) suggested that breeding ducks are territorial, each pair occupying and defending a particular area. Although the behavioral responses among breeding pairs and the seasonal timing of pursuit behavior support this view (McKinney 1965), the application of this concept to some species has been repeatedly questioned (Bezzel 1959, Lebret 1961, Hori 1963). Data obtained on pair mobility have shown specific differences in spacing patterns. While some species approach the classical territoriality described by Hochbaum, other more mobile species clearly do not (Sowls 1955; Dzubin 1955; McKinney 1965; Seymour 1974*a,b*). Such specific differences in mobility and home range size are correlated with differences in feeding and social behavior and appear to reflect rather subtle differences in evolved breeding strategies (McKinney 1965, 1973, 1975).

Information on mobility and breeding home range size has been collected for many *Anas* species. Despite qualitative statements in the literature regarding Pintail (*Anas acuta*) mobility, only two references have provided limited quantitative data (Dzubin 1955, Drewien 1967). The present paper discusses the mobility and home range size of breeding Pintails. The data used in this analysis were gathered during an investigation of this species' social system.

STUDY AREA AND METHODS

The 93-km^2 study area is in west-central Stutsman County, North Dakota, approximately 10 km south of Medina. This area falls within the Coteau du Missouri, a physiographic region of dead-ice moraine resulting from extensive stagnation following late Wisconsin glaciation. Resultant topography consists of closely spaced low hills interspersed with numerous shallow basin wetlands. The climate, geology, hydrology and aquatic plant communities of this region are described in detail by Winters (1963, 1967), Clayton (1967), Eisenlohr (1969), Eisen-

[1] Originally published in Auk 95(1):104–114, 1978.

[2] Present address: Endangered Species Program, Patuxent Wildl. Res. Center, Laurel, MD 20811.

lohr et al. (1968, 1972), Sloan (1972), and Stewart and Kantrud (1971, 1972).

The central 41 km² of the study area contains approximately 331 wetland basins. According to the classification of Stewart and Kantrud (1971), which is based on surface water permanence, approximately 10% of the wetlands are ephemeral, 33% temporary, 35% seasonal, and 15% semipermanent (Dwyer 1974). Tilled wetlands of unknown class, permanent wetlands, and several fens comprise the remaining wetland percentages. Although few basins have been drained for agricultural purposes, about 19% of the basins are tilled annually. Many of the temporary and seasonal wetlands are hayed during mid or late summer.

All the land within the study area is privately owned and is subjected to rather intensive agricultural use. Excluding wetland acreages, current land-use is approximately 60% cropland and 40% pasture and hayland.

Pintails were captured at baited shoreline sites using projection nets (Dill and Thornsberry 1950) and floating treadle traps (Thornsberry and Cowardin 1971). Upon capture, birds were marked with adjustable, back-mounted radio packages (Dwyer 1972) and/or nasal saddles (Sugden and Poston 1968). Transmitter circuitry design was similar to that described by Cochran and Lord (1963).

The positions of marked birds were determined by triangulation and/or visual sighting. Approximately one third of the recorded locations involved visual contact. All plotting was done on aerial photograph maps, and point locations were recorded using a superimposed ordinate grid system. Most locations were obtained between dawn and dusk.

In analyzing home range I relied upon the methodology of previous workers to facilitate cross-species comparison. Period and cumulative home ranges have been calculated according to the minimum area method of Mohr (1947). A more conservative estimate of the home range, or "primary range," was calculated according to the method of Gilmer (1971), which involves the elimination of all peripheral fix locations prior to home range calculation. A location was designated as peripheral if it was 0.16 km or more from any other location recorded on a different day. Other quantitative measures used to characterize home range and mobility were maximum length (cf. Dzubin 1955) and mean activity radius (Hayne 1949). To be included in the analysis of home range an individual had to have at least one fix for each of 15 consecutive days and a minimum of 20 fix locations.

RESULTS

A total of 20 adult male and 20 adult female pintails were captured: 8 in 1971, 23 in 1972, and 9 in 1973. Eleven of these birds failed to meet the minimum criteria for analysis, and one late-caught female was excluded because she joined a postbreeding flock soon after capture. The remaining 28 birds included 5 unpaired males, 8 paired males, and 15 females. The mean number of fix locations was 63 for unpaired males, 90 for paired males, and 93 for females; tracking times averaged 32 days, 52 days, and 45 days, respectively.

Breeding home range in waterfowl has generally been defined as the area occupied between the breakup of postmigratory spring flocks and the completion of breeding (Sowls 1955:48, Dzubin 1955). In the present study not all birds were captured immediately after arrival or at the same reproductive stage, and measurements of home range were often more restricted. For males "home range"

Table 1. Comparison of home range and primary range characteristics in unpaired male, paired male, and female Pintails.

Home range measurement	Unpaired males (N = 5)	Paired males (N = 8)	Females (N = 15)
Home range size (ha)			
Max.	1,067	1,477	1,387
Min.	234	498	177
$\bar{x} \pm$ SE	579 ± 145	896 ± 137	480 ± 88
Primary range size (ha)			
Max.	771	1,017	649
Min.	234	400	46
$\bar{x} \pm$ SE	412 ± 98	596 ± 72	299 ± 50
Home range length (km)			
Max.	5.2	8.2	8.2
Min.	2.7	4.0	1.5
$\bar{x} \pm$ SE	4.0 ± 0.5	5.5 ± 0.5	3.7 ± 0.5
Primary range length (km)			
Max.	4.5	5.8	4.0
Min.	2.7	2.9	1.3
$\bar{x} \pm$ SE	3.7 ± 0.3	4.2 ± 0.3	2.9 ± 0.3

includes the area occupied from capture until departure from the study area, and for females the area used from capture until hatching, departure, or postreproductive flocking.

Several pairs captured early in the breeding season typically spent most of the day on the study area, but moved 11 km or more to rejoin large flocks for night-time roosting. Such locations were not considered as part of the normal breeding home range and were subsequently omitted from home range analyses after breeding status was determined. Inclusion of these locations would have more than tripled the home range size of several pairs. Similarly, telemetric locations of questionable quality and locations that were noted to be the result of aerial pursuit activity were deleted prior to home range calculation.

Home Range and Mobility of Unpaired Males, Paired Males, and Females.—Home range and primary range estimates varied considerably between individuals. I originally thought that much of this variation was due to individual differences either in the duration of tracking or in the number of recorded fix locations, but neither home range nor primary range estimates correlated significantly with either of these factors.

Home ranges and primary ranges tended to be largest among paired males, intermediate among unpaired males, and smallest among females (Table 1). Differences between the means for paired and unpaired males and for unpaired males and females were not significant, but the differences between the means for paired males and females were significant for both home range and primary range (t = 2.90, df = 21, $P < 0.05$; t = 3.73, df = 21, $P < 0.05$, respectively). Primary range typically included between 84 and 100% of the locations recorded for an individual bird. In terms of area, the primary range accounted for approximately 70% of the cumulative home range in paired males, 76% in unpaired males, and 67% in females.

Maximum length of the home range was positively correlated with home range size (r = 0.89, $P < 0.05$), and maximum length of the primary range was correlated with primary range size (r = 0.66, $P < 0.05$). As with home range and primary range size estimates, the mean maximum lengths for both home range and primary range were larger for paired males than for either unpaired males or females (Table 1).

As an additional measure of mobility, frequency distributions based on the length of activity radii from the geometric center of activity were calculated for each individual (Hayne 1949, Tester and Siniff 1965). Such a procedure allows additional comparison of mobility without the biases associated with area determinations. Means and standard errors for un-

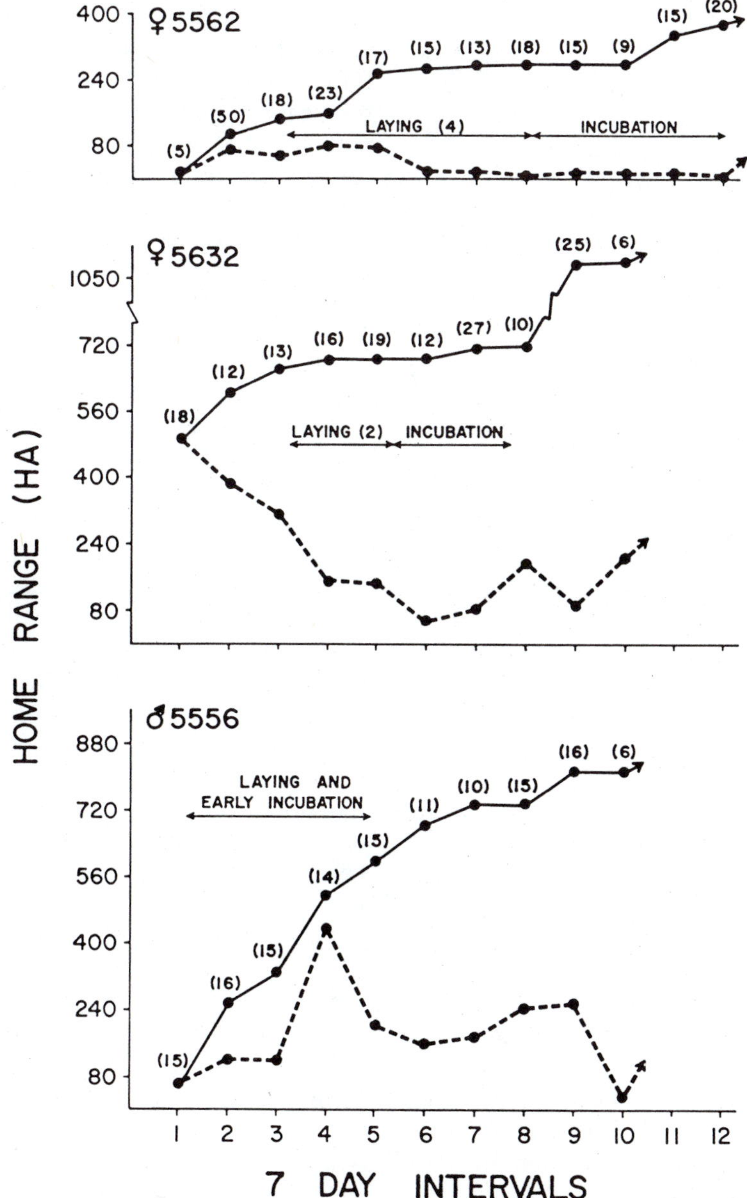

Fig. 1. Relationship between breeding chronology, cumulative home range, and period home range for three individual pintails. Solid line represents cumulative home range and the dotted line period range. Numbers in parentheses above the solid line represent the number of locations in each interval. Numbers in parentheses on the breeding chronology line represent number of documented nests.

paired males, paired males, and females were 1.03 ± 0.21 km, 1.13 ± 0.19 km, and 0.81 ± 0.11 km, respectively. Although the differences between these mean activity radii are not significant (*t*-test, $P < 0.05$), the observed pattern is consistent with that recorded for both home range and primary range. When the activ-

Table 2. Comparison of home range stability in unpaired male, paired male, and female Pintails.

	N	No. of individuals showing		
		Stability	Temp. stability	No stability
Unpaired males	5	0	1	4
Paired males	8	2	4	2
Females	15	7	6	2

ity radii for all individuals are combined the resultant distribution has a mean activity radius of 0.90 km, with approximately 58% of all recorded locations falling within a 0.81-km radius of the geometric center of activity.

Home Range Stability.—Following the method of Gilmer (1971) I checked for the possibility that individuals may tend to limit their movements during the breeding period. By calculating both the minimum area home range and the cumulative increase in home range size for every 7-day interval, a graph similar to the "observation area" curve of Odum and Keunzler (1955) could be constructed for each individual (Fig. 1).

Graphs for individuals fell into one of three categories: (1) continuous increase in cumulative home range—no stability, (2) step-like increases in cumulative home range—temporary stability, and (3) unchanging cumulative home range size over prolonged periods—stability. On this basis 29% of the Pintails demonstrated no stability, 39% demonstrated temporary stability, and 32% demonstrated stability.

Stabilization of the cumulative home range occurred more frequently among females than among either paired males or unpaired males (Table 2). As will be discussed below, reduced mobility during laying and incubation accounts for this trend in females. Among paired males, temporary stability, if achieved, usually occurred during the laying period and/or the postbreeding flocking period following pair-bond dissolution. It is interesting to note that both the paired males that demonstrated prolonged stability were paired to females that made several nesting attempts. The only unpaired male that demonstrated any stability remained on the study area much longer than the other unpaired males. Most of his activity was restricted to a complex of seasonal wetlands frequented by other Pintails.

The recorded "period" minimum area ranges were highly variable and indicated that during any 7-day interval individuals utilized only a portion of their cumulative home range. This pattern was consistent for all individuals regardless of sex and breeding status.

Mobility of Nesting Hens.—Documentation of changes in female mobility in relation to nesting chronology was complicated by several factors: (1) not all females were captured at the same stage of the breeding cycle; and (2) many nests were lost as a result of predation. To test for differences in prenesting and nesting mobility, minimum area ranges were calculated for each period on the basis of nest chronology. Prenesting ranges included all fix locations from the time of capture until the initiation of laying, and nesting ranges included all locations from the initiation of laying until hatching or nest destruction. Laying periods for individual females included more than one nest in three cases, and observed incubation times ranged from 6 to 23 days. Nine females with known nesting chronologies were tracked for periods long enough to enable calculation of either one or both period ranges.

Female mobility tended definitely to decrease once nesting began. Means and standard errors for the prenesting and nesting ranges were 605 ± 197 ha and 124 ± 25 ha, respectively. The difference between the means is significant (t = 3.06, df = 11, $P < 0.05$). Maximum lengths of the prenesting ($\bar{x}$ = 4.2 km) and nesting ($\bar{x}$ = 1.8 km) ranges also differed significantly (t = 3.47, df = 11, $P < 0.05$). Only one female (#5515) demonstrated a slight increase in home range size during the nesting period. I believe that this was because her first documented nest was actually a renest. This seems likely because (1) her mobility during the recorded "prenesting" interval was comparable to that of other renesting females, and (2) she was observed giving Repulsion calls and postures (Lorenz 1953, Smith 1968), indicating previous laying and/or incubation soon after capture.

Female mobility appeared to be even further reduced during incubation. Differences between laying and incubation ranges were not tested because of the considerable variation in the duration of observed incubation times as a result of predation. However reduced mobility during the incubation period would be expected, as females leave the nest only a few times a day to feed, drink, and bathe.

Five females that initiated several nests showed reduced mobility throughout the nesting and renesting periods, although two of these females made shifts in the primary wetlands being utilized. Available data concerning the distances between successive nests for several *Anas* species (Sowls 1955, Gates 1962, Stotts and Davis 1960, Coulter and Miller 1968) likewise suggest that reduced mobility during the renesting interval is common. Several females that left the study area immediately after nest destruction may have moved to new areas before renesting. Such movements have previously been suggested by Coulter and Miller (1968) and Stoudt (1969) for other *Anas* species.

Mobility of Paired Males During Laying and Incubation.—Paired males are more mobile than their mates during the laying and incubation period. Home ranges of five males during this period averaged 316 ha (range 132 ha to 591 ha). Male #0631 had the smallest recorded nesting home range, but as this male was marked only with a nasal-saddle his mobility was certainly underestimated. Frequent checks of the usual feeding and loafing spots used by the pair indicated that he was often absent when his mate was known to be on the nest. My observations indicate that the mobility of paired males is at its minimum during the first few days of laying, but as the female spends more and more time on the nest as laying nears completion, site attachment by the male rapidly wanes, and male mobility and sociability increase.

Home Range and Mobility of Pairs.—During this study, home ranges were obtained for 11 Pintail pairs. In instances where both members of the pair were radio-marked, home range was calculated on the basis of locations recorded when the pair was together. In cases where only one member of the pair was radio-marked and the other member of the pair was either nasal-saddled or unmarked, home range was calculated solely on the basis of visual sightings.

Recorded pair ranges varied considerably with much of this variation directly attributable to female reproductive chronology. Pair ranges that included both prenesting and nesting periods averaged 509 ± 73 ha (N = 7), while pair ranges that included only the nesting period averaged 167 ± 36 ha (N = 4). Pair ranges in the latter category closely approximate the nesting ranges calculated for nesting hens as would be expected.

Female #5527, originally marked in 1971 as a laying female, returned to occupy essentially the same areas in both 1972 and 1973. During the spring of 1973, the prenesting movements of this female and her unmarked mate encompassed an area of about 607 ha. Following nesting, the pair was observed on only four different wetlands and associated upland sites in an area of about 122 ha. Reduced mobility was also apparent in the unmarked incubating hen paired to male #5566. No pair range was calculated in this case as the birds were observed together on only two wetlands, though the male used others when not accompanied by the female.

The home ranges of both individual males and females exceeded the calculated pair ranges in nearly all cases. Much of this is attributable to the greater mobility of males throughout the nesting period and to the movements of females outside the pair range following pair-bond dissolution.

Number of Utilized Wetlands.—Pintail populations fluctuate dramatically with spring water conditions. Low water levels and drought conditions appear to cause emigration (Smith 1970) or nonbreeding (Leitch 1964), whereas high water levels and concomitant flooding result in pioneering and high population levels (Hochbaum and Bossenmaier 1972). Because Pintails forage primarily in the bottom sediments of shallow wetlands that are subject to seasonal flooding and drying, such population fluctuations are probably related directly to increases or decreases in shallow wetland habitat (Krapu 1974*a*). In wet years this foraging habitat is greatly increased not only by the flooding of temporary and seasonal basins, but also by the reflooding of the shallow marsh zones of semipermanent and permanent wetlands. This would appear to explain observed correlations between spring Pintail populations and seasonal wetlands, semipermanent wetlands, and total wetlands as found by Stewart and Kantrud (1974).

All of the individuals used in this analysis utilized water areas of several different classes. The number of wetlands used by individual birds varied considerably, averaging 13 and ranging from 3 to 27. Paired males, unpaired males, and females utilized averages of 17, 12, and 11 ponds, respectively. The number of wetlands used by females reflected primarily reproductive chronology, with more wetlands being used during the prelaying period than during the nesting period. Females of known breeding chronology used an average of 10 different wetlands during the prenesting period and 5 wetlands during the nesting period. The difference between the means is significant ($t = 3.29$, $\mathrm{df} = 11$, $P < 0.05$). While laying females often used water areas not utilized previously, this was observed only twice for incubating females. No incubating female was known to frequent more than four different wetlands, and the choice of particular wetlands during this period often appeared to be influenced by male sexual harassment.

DISCUSSION

Throughout the preceding sections I have emphasized the variability in individual home range estimates. Although factors such as wetland distribution and quality, population density, and social interactions undoubtedly affect individual and pair mobility, much of the observed variation can be related to sex, breeding status, and stage of the breeding cycle.

Unpaired male Pintails demonstrated great variation in mobility. Only two of five marked individuals remained on the study area for more than 21 days, and only one male showed long-term localization of activities. All of these males were observed associating with other males and pairs, and engaging in courtship activities. Similar behavior has been reported for unpaired male Northern Shovelers (*Anas clypeata*) (Poston 1974; Seymour 1974*a,b*), Blue-winged Teal (*Anas discors*) (Drewien 1968), and Gadwalls (*Anas strepera*) (Dwyer 1974).

For both paired males and females, the early season prenesting period was characterized by high mobility and short-term use of many wetlands. As for any specific individual many of these movements were certainly missed, I generally consider individual and pair home range estimates to be rather conservative. Despite this bias, home range estimates calculated for this stage of breeding were consistently larger than those calculated for the nesting period.

In general the mobility of paired males and females decreases through the prenesting period as movements become more localized. While female mobility becomes even further reduced during laying and incubation, male mobility tends to increase during the latter part of the laying period. This difference between males and females is reflected in the tendency for female home range size to stabilize once nesting begins, whereas male home ranges normally exhibited only temporary stabilization.

This pattern of decreasing mobility has been documented in many *Anas* species (Dzubin 1955, Sowls 1955, Drewien 1968, Titman 1971, Poston 1974, Seymour 1974*b*, Dwyer 1974, Gilmer et al. 1975), but major interspecific differences exist in the degree of activity localization and in the degree and duration of male site attachment (McKinney 1965, 1973). When compared to other species studied thus far, it is apparent that Pintail pairs are much more mobile during the laying and incubation periods, and that site attachment in male Pintails is normally reduced and brief. The lack of strong site attachment, the frequent erratic movements and the pronounced sociability that characterize male Pintails have previously been noted by Dzubin (1955, 1969), McKinney (1965, 1973), and Smith (1968). Male mobility was undoubtedly greater than female mobility at all stages of the breeding cycle, as males frequently left their mates to associate with other males and pairs and to court and/or chase "strange" females.

Working in the pothole region of South Dakota, Drewien (1967, 1968) found the home ranges of a Pintail pair and a Pintail female to be approximately 486 ha and 283 ha, respectively. Although the reproductive chronologies of these birds were unknown, the home range estimate for the pair probably included the prenesting and nesting periods as the pair was followed for about 6 weeks. These estimates are quite similar to the home range estimates obtained in this study.

Although home range information has been gathered for relatively few *Anas* species to date, species-specific mobility patterns are already becoming apparent. Recorded pair home range estimates for Cinnamon Teal (*A. cyanoptera*), Blue-winged Teal, Shovelers, and Gadwalls have generally been less than 130 ha (Gates 1962; Drewien 1967, 1968; Evans and Black 1956; Dzubin 1955; Sowls 1955; Poston 1974; Seymour 1974*b*). Pair home range estimates for the Mallard (*A. platyrhynchos*) range from 200 to 283 ha (Dzubin 1955, Drewien 1968, Gilmer et al. 1975), and a single pair of Green-winged Teal (*A. crecca*) was found to have a home range of approximately 243 ha (Drewien 1967). In comparison with these species, the breeding home range of a pair of Pintails is quite large.

Such comparative differences between species are also consistent for other measures of mobility such as maximum home range length and mean activity radius. Previously reported home range lengths vary from 1.0 km for Blue-winged Teal (Dzubin 1955) to 2.6 km for Mallards (Gilmer et al. 1975); while reported mean activity radii range from 0.29 km for Blue-winged Teal (Evans and Black 1956) to 0.58 km for Mallards (Gilmer 1971). As with home range size, estimates of these parameters are comparatively greater for Pintails than the other species studied thus far.

Mobility, as reflected by breeding home range size, is an important component of a species social system, and is related to many other aspects of social behavior. As McKinney (1973, 1975) pointed out, species with low mobility tend to be more territorial and demonstrate pronounced male-male hostility, distant threat displays, long-lasting pair-bonds, well developed three-bird chases and a low frequency of promiscuous copulations. Conversely more mobile species like the Pintail are less territorial and correspondingly male-male hostility is reduced, pair bonds are weaker, aerial pursuit behavior is more variable, and promiscuous copulations are more frequent.

While many factors have certainly been involved in the evolution of specific *Anas* social systems (cf. McKinney 1973), several lines of evidence suggest that much of the observed diversity may be related to the spatial and temporal aspects of available food resources and whether or not these resources are "economically defensible" (Brown 1964, Brown and Orians 1970). It is now apparent that egg-laying is energetically demanding for ducks (King 1973) and large amounts of protein in the form of aquatic invertebrates are required (Holm and Scott 1954; Krapu 1972, 1974*a,b*; Swanson and Meyer 1974; Swanson et al. 1974). These energetic and dietary demands are reflected in dietary shifts during the prelaying, laying, and postlaying periods (Krapu 1972) as well as in increased feeding rates during the laying period (Bengston 1972, Dwyer 1974, Swanson et al. 1974). As a result, both McKinney (1973, 1975) and Dwyer (1974) have postulated that in territorial species such as the Shoveler and the Gadwall chasing serves to secure a food supply and to provide undisturbed feeding time for the female.

Although Young (1970) has demonstrated a relationship between resource levels and exclusive feeding areas for the Common Sheld-Duck (*Tadorna tadorna*), no equivalent studies have been carried out thus far for any *Anas* species, but research to date indicates that: (1) different *Anas* species are utilizing different food resources even when occupying the same wetland habitat (Krapu 1972, Swanson et al. 1974); (2) individuals often respond quickly to shifts in food availability in space and time; and (3) specific invertebrate populations fluctuate seasonally within and between wetlands (Swanson et al. 1974). Additional research on resource patchiness is clearly warranted, and may provide a better understanding of the specific differences in mobility and social behavior within the genus *Anas*.

ACKNOWLEDGMENTS

During this study I was supported by a N.I.H. Training Grant (No. 5 TO1 GMO1779) from the National Institute of General Medical Sciences. Field work was conducted in cooperation with the

Northern Prairie Wildlife Research Center, Jamestown, North Dakota. I especially thank T. J. Dwyer and D. S. Gilmer for their assistance in the field, and D. W. Mock, J. R. Tester, H. B. Tordoff, and F. McKinney for critically reviewing the manuscript.

LITERATURE CITED

BENGSTON, S. A. 1972. Breeding ecology of the Harlequin Duck *Histrionicus histrionicus* (L.) in Iceland. Ornis. Scandinavica 3:1–19.

BEZZEL, E. 1959. Beitrage zur Biologie der Geschlechter bei Entenvogeln. Anz. Orn. Ges. Bayern. 5:269–355.

BROWN, J. L. 1964. The evolution of diversity in avian territorial systems. Wilson Bull. 76: 160–169.

———, AND G. H. ORIANS. 1970. Spacing patterns in mobile animals. Ann. Rev. Ecol. System. 1:239–262.

CLAYTON, L. 1967. Stagnant-glacier features of the Missouri Coteau in North Dakota. Pp. 25–46 *in* Glacial geology of the Missouri Coteau and adjacent areas. L. Clayton and T. F. Freers, eds. North Dakota Geol. Surv. Misc. Ser. 30.

COCHRAN, W. W., AND R. D. LORD. 1963. A radiotracking system for wild animals. J. Wildl. Mgmt. 27:9–24.

COULTER, M., AND W. MILLER. 1968. Nesting biology of Black Ducks and Mallards in northern New England. Vermont Fish and Game Dept. Bull. No. 68-2.

DILL, H. H., AND W. H. THORNSBERRY. 1950. A cannon-projected net trap for capturing waterfowl. J. Wildl. Mgmt. 14:132–137.

DREWIEN, R. C. 1967. Ecological relationships of breeding waterfowl to prairie potholes. Pierre, South Dakota P-R Rept., 1965–66, W-75R-8.

———. 1968. Ecological relationships of breeding Blue-winged Teal to prairie potholes. Unpubl. M.S. Thesis, Brookings, South Dakota State Univ.

DWYER, T. J. 1972. An adjustable radio-package for ducks. Bird-Banding 43:282–284.

———. 1974. Social behavior of breeding Gadwalls in North Dakota. Auk 91:375–386.

DZUBIN, A. 1955. Some evidence of home range in waterfowl. Trans. North Amer. Wildl. Conf. 20:278–298.

———. 1969. Assessing breeding populations of ducks by ground counts. Pp. 178–230 *in* Saskatoon Wetlands Seminar, Canad. Wildl. Serv. Rept., Ser. No. 6.

EISENLOHR, W. S. 1969. Hydrology of small water areas in the prairie pothole region. Pp. 35–39 *in* Saskatoon Wetlands Seminar, Canad. Wildl. Serv. Rept., Ser. No. 6.

———, AND C. E. SLOAN. 1968. Generalized hydrology of prairie potholes on the Coteau du Missouri, North Dakota. U.S. Geol. Surv. Circ. 558.

———, ———, AND J. B. SHJEFLO. 1972. Hydrologic investigations of prairie potholes in North Dakota, 1959–1968. U.S. Geol. Surv. Prof. Pap. 585-A.

EVANS, C. D., AND K. E. BLACK. 1956. Duck production studies on the prairie potholes of South Dakota. U.S. Dept. Interior, Fish Wildl. Serv., Spec. Sci. Rept.—Wildl. No. 32.

GATES, J. M. 1962. Breeding biology of the Gadwall in northern Utah. Wilson Bull. 74:43–67.

GILMER, D. S. 1971. Home ranges and habitat-use of breeding Mallards (*Anas platyrhynchos*) and Wood Ducks (*Aix sponsa*) in north-central Minnesota as determined by radio-tracking. Unpublished Ph.D. Dissertation, Univ. Minneapolis, Minnesota.

———, I. J. BALL, L. M. COWARDIN, J. H. REICHMANN, AND J. R. TESTER. 1975. Habitat use and home range of mallards breeding in Minnesota. J. Wildl. Mgmt. 39:781–789.

HAYNE, D. W. 1949. Calculation of size of home range. J. Mammal. 30:1–18.

HOCHBAUM, G. S., AND E. F. BOSSENMAIER. 1972. Response of pintails to improved breeding habitat in southern Manitoba. Canadian Field Naturalist 86:79–81.

HOCHBAUM, H. A. 1944. The canvasback on a prairie marsh. Washington, D.C., Wildl. Mgmt. Inst.

HOLM, E. R., AND M. L. SCOTT. 1954. Studies on the nutrition of wild waterfowl. New York Fish and Game J. 1:171–187.

HORI, J. 1963. Three-bird flights in the Mallard. Wildfowl 14:124–132.

KING, J. R. 1973. Energetics of reproduction in birds. Pp. 78–107 *in* Breeding biology of birds. D. S. Farner, ed. Washington, D.C., Natl. Acad. Sci.

KRAPU, G. L. 1972. Feeding ecology of the Pintail (*Anas acuta*) in North Dakota. Unpubl. Ph.D. Dissertation, Ames, Iowa State Univ.

———. 1974*a*. Feeding ecology of pintail hens during reproduction. Auk 91:278–290.

———. 1974*b*. Foods of breeding pintails in North Dakota. J. Wildl. Mgmt. 38:408–416.

LEBRET, T. 1961. The pair formation in the annual cycle of the Mallard, *Anas platyrhynchos*, L. Ardea 49:97–158.

LEITCH, W. G. 1964. Water. Pp. 273–281 *in* Waterfowl tomorrow. J. P. Linduska and A. L. Nelson, eds. Washington, D.C., U.S. G.P.O.

LORENZ, K. 1953. Comparative studies on the behavior of the Anatinae. Reprinted from Avicult. Mag. 57:157–182; 58:8–17, 61–72, 86–94, 172–184; 59:24–34, 80–91.

MCKINNEY, F. 1965. Spacing and chasing in breeding ducks. Wildfowl 16:92–106.

———. 1973. Ecoethological aspects of reproduction. Pp. 6–21 *in* Breeding biology of birds. D. S. Farner, ed. Washington, D.C., Natl. Acad. Sci.

———. 1975. The evolution of duck displays. Pp. 331–357 *in* Function and evolution of behavior. G. Baerends, C. Beer, and A. Manning, eds. Oxford, Clarendon Press.

MOHR, C. O. 1947. Table of equivalent populations of North American small mammals. Amer. Midl. Naturalist 37:223–249.

ODUM, E. P., AND E. J. KEUNZLER. 1955. Measurement of territory and home range size in birds. Auk 72:128–137.

POSTON, J. H. 1974. Home range and breeding biology of the Shoveler. Can. Fish Wildl. Serv. Rept., Ser. No. 25.

SEYMOUR, N. R. 1974*a*. Site attachment in the Northern Shoveler. Auk 91:423–427.

———. 1974*b*. Territorial behavior of wild Shovelers at Delta, Manitoba. Wildfowl 25:49–55.

SLOAN, C. E. 1972. Ground-water hydrology of prairie potholes in North Dakota. U.S. Geol. Surv., Prof. Pap. 585-C.

SMITH, R. I. 1968. The social aspects of reproductive behavior in the pintail. Auk 85:381–396.

———. 1970. Response of Pintail breeding populations to drought. J. Wildl. Mgmt. 34:943–946.

SOWLS, L. K. 1955. Prairie ducks. Washington, D.C., Wildl. Mgmt. Inst.

STEWART, R. E., AND H. A. KANTRUD. 1971. Classification of natural ponds and lakes in the glaciated prairie region. U.S. Dept. Interior, Fish and Wildl. Sev., Res. Publ. No. 92.

———, AND ———. 1972. Vegetation of prairie potholes, North Dakota, in relation to quality of water and other environmental factors. U.S. Geol. Surv., Prof. Pap. 585-D.

———, AND ———. 1974. Breeding waterfowl populations in the prairie pothole region of North Dakota. Condor 76:70–79.

STOTTS, V. D., AND D. E. DAVIS. 1960. The Black Duck in the Chesapeake Bay of Maryland: breeding behavior and biology. Chesapeake Sci. 1:127–154.

STOUDT, J. H. 1969. Relationships between waterfowl and water areas on the Redvers waterfowl study area. Pp. 123–131 *in* Saskatoon Wetlands Seminar, Can. Wildl. Serv. Rept., Ser. No. 6.

SUGDEN, L. G., AND H. J. POSTON. 1968. A nasal marker for ducks. J. Wild. Mgmt. 32:984–986.

SWANSON, G. A., AND M. I. MEYER. 1974. The role of invertebrates in the feeding ecology of Anatinae during the breeding season. Pp. 143–185 *in* Waterfowl habitat mgmt. symp., July 30–August 1, 1973, Moncton, New Brunswick.

———, ———, AND J. R. SERIE. 1974. Feeding ecology of breeding Blue-winged Teals. J. Wildl. Mgmt. 38:396–407.

TESTER, J. R., AND D. B. SINIFF. 1965. Aspects of animal movement and home range data obtained by telemetry. Trans. North Amer. Wildl. Nat. Res. Conf. 30:379–392.

THORNSBERRY, W. H., AND L. M. COWARDIN. 1971. A floating bait trap for capturing individual ducks in spring. J. Wildl. Mgmt. 35:837–839.

TITMAN, R. D. 1971. The role of the pursuit flight in the breeding biology of the Mallard. Unpubl. Ph.D. Dissertation, New Brunswick, Univ. New Brunswick.

WINTERS, H. A. 1963. Geology and ground water resources of Stutsman County, North Dakota, part 1, geology: North Dakota. North Dakota Geol. Surv. Bull. 41.

———. 1967. The extent of the Coteau du Missouri in south-central North Dakota. Pp. 63–72 *in* Glacial geology of the Missouri Coteau, Field Conf., 1967. North Dakota Geol. Surv. Misc. Ser. 30.

YOUNG, C. M. 1970. Territoriality in the Common Shelduck *Tadorna tadorna*. Ibis 112:330–335.

DIVING DUCK MOVEMENTS ON KEOKUK POOL, MISSISSIPPI RIVER

DENNIS D. THORNBURG, Department of Zoology and Entomology, Iowa State University, Ames 50010[1]

Abstract: A study was initiated in 1969 to determine the patterns and causes of local movements of diving ducks on the Keokuk Pool and to relate diurnal activity to hunter harvest and food availability. Within a week of arrival, diving ducks on the Keokuk Pool established a diurnal rhythm of movement. The general pattern was a morning flight at dawn from the highly disturbed middle and upper sections to the less disturbed lower section where birds loafed throughout the day. A return flight upstream to choice feeding areas in the middle and upper sections occurred at dusk. Over 60 percent of the population using the pool participated in this daily movement. Human disturbance was the major factor inducing mass movements. Hunting activity was most intense in the middle and upper sections and the initiation of mass movements to the lower segment and a concurrent decrease in use of areas in the middle and upper sections was correlated with the opening of the hunting season. Minimal feeding occurred on the pool during the day. Birds fed extensively at night in the middle and upper sections of the Keokuk Pool. Areas in the middle and upper sections were more productive in bottom invertebrates than areas in the lower section. In general, the distribution of diving ducks was correlated with the greatest abundance of benthic organisms used for food.

J. WILDL. MANAGE. 37(3):382–389

Intensive use of Pool 19 or the Keokuk Pool, Mississippi River, by migrating diving ducks has stimulated several ecological studies. Thompson (1969) reported that diving duck use of the Keokuk Pool was as high as 20 million duck-days per year. Such intense utilization of the Keokuk Pool by migrating waterfowl has been attributed by Gale (1969) and Thompson (1969) to the abundance of benthic organisms, especially fingernail clams (*Sphaerium transversum*). Mills et al. (1966) reported the simultaneous decline in diving duck use and the disappearance of the fingernail clam resource in the Illinois River.

The objectives of this study were to determine the pattern and causes of local diving duck movements that might be related to hunter harvest, and to locate feeding areas and relate use to food availability. The study was financed by the Iowa State Conservation Commission through Pittman–Robertson Project W-108-R in 1968 and 1969.

I am indebted to M. W. Weller of Iowa State University for supervision and guidance, F. C. Bellrose of the Illinois Natural History Survey for aerial census data, G. Yates of the Iowa Conservation Commission for support to the Project, and S. Wilds for field assistance.

STUDY AREA

The study area was the same as that used and described by Thompson (1969). Division of the lower 26 miles of the Keokuk Pool into three sections corresponding with those of Thompson's enabled convenient comparison of data.

METHODS

Flock Movements and Activity

Throughout the 1969 fall migration, diving duck distribution, diurnal activity, and daily movements were monitored by observations made at preselected sites along the Illinois side of the river. Observations of 30 minutes duration were made during all daily time periods at each of seven sites overlooking the river. Observation points

[1] Present address: Illinois Department of Conservation, Union County Refuge, R.R. 2, Jonesboro, Illinois 62952.

Originally published in J. Wildl. Manage. 37(3):382–389, 1973.

were numbered progressively from 1 to 7 proceeding upriver from Hamilton, Illinois, at the lower boundary of the study area to Dallas City at the upper boundary. Observation sites 1, 2, and 3 were spaced along the lower section of the study area below Nauvoo, Illinois. Sites 4 and 5 were located above Nauvoo along the middle section and sites 6 and 7 were located above Niota and below Dallas City, Illinois, along the upper section of the study area. The map of the study area (Thompson 1969) assists in visualizing the placement of observation sites in relation to section divisions. During the observation period, the number of flocks and the size of each flock passing the observer were recorded on a field data form. Flight direction and species identification were also noted.

On-water concentrations of diving ducks were mapped daily. Flock movements were related to behavior on the water by recording the activity of diving ducks on an area of concentration during an observation period. Relative abundance by species and percentages of birds engaged in feeding, loafing, swimming, or maintenance activities were recorded. Weekly aerial surveys were made to aid in mapping diving duck distribution and to assist in censusing the diving duck population. Aerial counts made by F. C. Bellrose were used to refine my estimates.

The relationship between hunter activity and diving duck movements was determined by plotting locations of duck blinds on maps of the study area.

Food Availability

The procedure used to determine the standing crop of benthos was similar to that used by Thompson (1969). Using a 9- × 9-inch Ponar dredge, 112 random bottom samples were taken within the major diving duck concentration areas. Samples were screened through a wash bucket of 10 grids to the inch and preserved in 10 percent formalin solution. In the lab each sample was sorted and the number of clams (Pelecypoda), snails (Gastropoda), and Mayfly larvae (Ephemeroptera) were counted and weighed. Anderson (1959), Rogers and Korschgen (1966), and Thompson (1969) found these three groups of benthos to be of primary importance in the diet of diving ducks on the Mississippi River.

Because of the extremely large size of the sample taken by the Ponar dredge (81 square inches), numbers of molluscs were determined by sampling rather than by counting the total. The bottom of a 10- × 15-inch porcelain pan was gridded into 80 equal 1.25- × 1.50-inch squares. Using strainers of the proper grid size, molluscs were separated into three size classes on the basis of length: 1–2 mm, 2–5 mm, and 5 mm. Each size class of every sample was placed in the pan, and the number of pelecypods and gastropods were counted in eight randomly-selected squares. An average number per square was calculated and multiplied by 80 to obtain an estimate of the total number of pelecypods and gastropods in each sample.

Average weights were obtained for each size class of clams, snails and mayfly larvae. To convert the number of organisms in a sample to weight, the number of organisms was multiplied by the conversion factor for the group. Mean standing crop in pounds per acre was calculated for each area by totaling the weights of the three groups of benthos.

RESULTS

Populations and Movements

The first major migration of diving ducks into the Keokuk Pool area was observed at

Table 1. Size and distribution of the population of diving ducks using the Keokuk Pool throughout the fall migration season, 1969.

Date (1969)	Total number of diving ducks[a]			
	Upper section	Middle section	Lower section	Total
1 Oct.	0	0	0	0
7 Oct.	0	0	0	0
14 Oct.	0	200	8,070	8,270
21 Oct.	500	31,600	9,000	41,100
28 Oct.	12,700	151,875	269,690	434,265
5 Nov.	0	136,970	691,200	828,170
11 Nov.	2,950	215,300	90,625	308,875
12 Nov.	0	76,150	151,350	227,500
25 Nov.	2,900	21,200	90,575	114,675
29 Nov.	14,250	24,000	9,100	47,350
2 Dec.	12,000	59,400	10,450	81,850
Total	45,300	716,695	1,330,060	2,092,055

[a] Weekly aerial counts by F. C. Bellrose during fall of 1969.

daybreak 19 October 1969. Prior to this date, fewer than 10,000 diving ducks were on the pool. During 21–28 October, the population increased from under 45,000 to over 425,000 and continued upward until a peak of over 825,000 was reached the first week in November (Table 1). Peak numbers of the six most important species of diving ducks are shown in Table 2.

Throughout the period 18 October–12 December, 259 flock movements were observed. The first large scale movements between sections were observed on the morning of 26 October 1969. In the following weeks, flocks of diving ducks on the Keokuk Pool displayed a well-defined pattern of diurnal movements. Once established, little deviation in the daily pattern of movements occurred throughout the entire season. Intensity of movement was greatest during the early morning and late evening (Fig. 1). Minimal movement between sections of the pool occurred during midday except when hunters, fishermen, or pleasure boaters disturbed diving ducks on concentration areas. The magnitude of the daily flights was in direct proportion to the size of the population of diving ducks on the Keokuk Pool (Fig. 2).

Table 2. Peak numbers of six species of diving ducks using the Keokuk Pool, Mississippi River during fall migration, 1969.

Species	Peak numbers[a]
Lesser scaup (*Aythya affinis*)	670,000
Canvasback (*A. valisineria*)	148,500
Ring-necked duck (*A. collaris*)	45,000
Common goldeneye (*Bucephala clangula*)	4,850
Redhead (*A. americana*)	250
Bufflehead (*B. albeola*)	150

[a] Figures taken from aerial counts made by F. C. Bellrose 5 September–2 December 1969.

The early morning flight consisted primarily of diving ducks leaving the middle section and flying downstream to the middle region of the lower section. At other time periods an insignificant amount of movement in this direction was recorded. The evening flight was composed of diving ducks leaving the lower section and flying upstream to a destination primarily in the middle section (Table 3).

The morning flight consistently occurred at the break of day or shortly before, and the typical evening flight did not begin

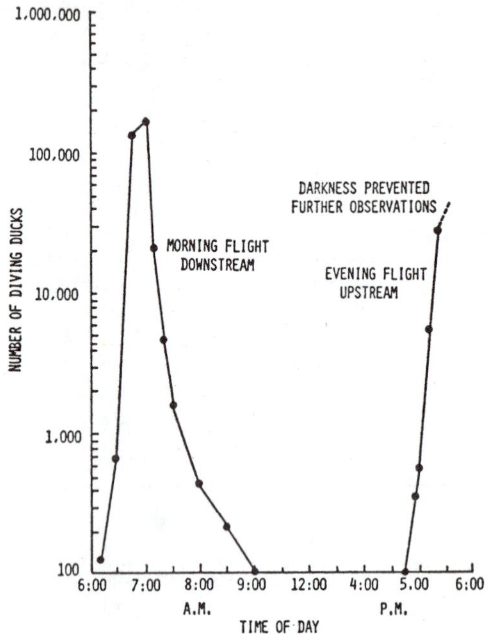

Fig. 1. Diurnal pattern of waterfowl movements on the Keokuk Pool.

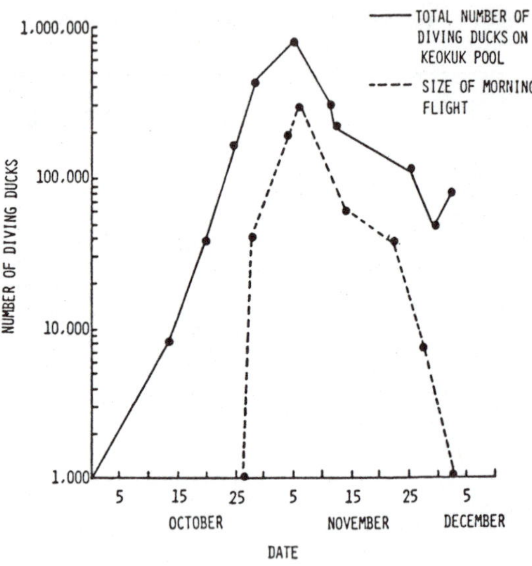

Fig. 2. Relationship of total numbers of diving ducks to those involved in the morning flight downstream, Keokuk Pool.

until shortly after sunset. As light intensity decreased, the population became more alert and preflight behavior often was observed. The destination of upstream flights was sometimes difficult to determine because of darkness.

Distribution and Activity

Throughout the fall of 1969, diving ducks congregated in 13 distinct areas of the Keokuk Pool. Of these, seven were used for the entire season, three were used for only a short period in early fall, and three were used only during the last few weeks of the season (Figs. 3, 4, 5). These areas corresponded closely with those mapped by Thompson in 1966 and 1967 except for three that were not used during the fall of 1969 (Thompson 1969).

Predominate species and magnitude of use varied between concentration areas. Area L-1 (area no. 1 of lower section) was intensely utilized by ring-necked ducks, possibly because of the presence of one of the few beds of sago pond weed (*Potamogeton pectinatus*) in this region. Area L-2 was used almost exclusively by canvasbacks. Area L-3 was one of the three most important concentration areas on the Keokuk Pool. Over 90 percent of the early morning flight landed in area L-3 and numbers exceeding 100,000 were recorded on this area by F. C. Bellrose during the first week of November when peak numbers of diving ducks were on the Keokuk Pool. Large numbers of all species utilized this area.

Areas M-3 and M-6 in the middle section also were used intensively by all species of diving ducks. Area M-2 was utilized throughout October but was abandoned until late November and areas M-4 and M-5 were not used until late November and early December. Area M-4 was utilized extensively by common goldeneyes, whereas

Table 3. Indices to the magnitude of diving duck diurnal flock movements upstream and downstream between the three sections of the Keokuk Pool, fall 1969.

Flight direction	Mean number of flocks and mean number of diving ducks observed per 30 minute observation period							
	0600–0900		0900–1200		1200–1500		1500–1800	
	Flocks	Ducks	Flocks	Ducks	Flocks	Ducks	Flocks	Ducks
Downstream	280	130,011	66	5,585	0	0	33	1,502
Upstream	27	431	14	139	1	6	108	19,075

M-5 was used almost exclusively by canvasbacks late in the season.

The upper section received the least use by diving ducks. Lesser scaup and canvasbacks used area U-1 only early in the season. Area U-2 received slight use by canvasbacks in late November and early December whereas area U-3 was utilized intensively the first few weeks of the season but received no later use.

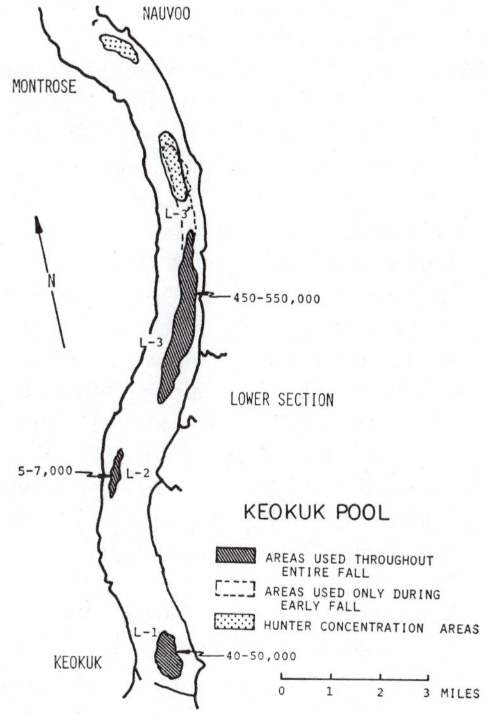

Fig. 3. Waterfowl concentration areas in the lower section, Keokuk Pool.

It was readily apparent from flock activity on the three major concentration areas that the diving duck population on the Keokuk Pool used the lower section as a loafing rather than feeding site during the day (Table 4). Two days of continuous observation from sunrise to sunset, and numerous observations at all daily time periods throughout the fall resulted in only three sightings of flocks engaged in moderate feeding (30–80 percent of the flock diving). The daily behavior pattern of diving ducks

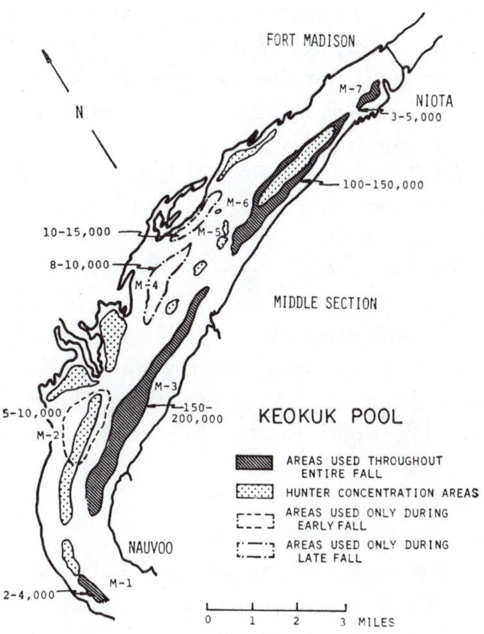

Fig. 4. Waterfowl concentration areas in the middle section, Keokuk Pool.

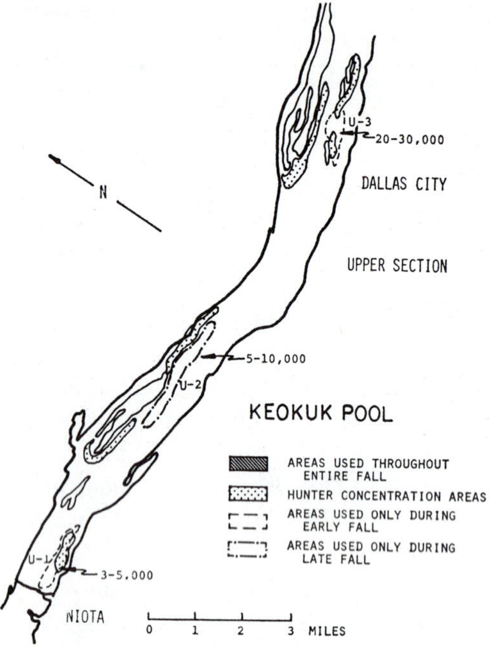

Fig. 5. Waterfowl concentration areas in the upper section, Keokuk Pool.

on the lower section of the pool was uniform: immediately upon arrival in the lower section at dawn, thousands of diving ducks began sleeping with their heads under their wings. This loafing activity was exhibited daily regardless of high waves and adverse weather and was continued until late evening.

Feeding activity during the day in the middle section was only slightly more common. One can only conclude that intensive feeding by an extensive percentage of the population occurred at night after the mass evening flight to the middle and upper section.

Food Availability

Bottom samples taken randomly in 9 of the 13 diving duck concentration areas revealed a significant difference between standing crops in weight of the three groups

Table 4. Intensity of diurnal feeding by diving ducks on three major concentration areas (M-3, M-6, and L-3) on the Keokuk Pool, fall 1969.

Time periods	Number of observations	Number feeding	Mean percent diving	Mean percent loafing
0600–0900	156	5	7.3	92.7
0900–1200	120	6	5.3	94.7
1200–1500	110	2	3.7	96.3
1500–1800	132	13	17.0	83.0

of benthic organisms (Table 5). The middle and upper sections clearly were the most productive of bottom invertebrates. Concentration areas M-3, M-6, and U-3 possessed the largest biomass of bottom fauna.

On the basis of 120 random Ponar dredge samples taken in late September 1967, Gale (1969) recorded a mean standing crop in numbers for the entire study area of 18,000 sphaerids/m^2. Mean standing crop in numbers for all areas sampled in 1969 was 17,332 sphaerids/m^2. Although these means for the entire pool are comparable for 1967 and 1969, mean standing crop in numbers for each section differed markedly (Fig. 6). Sampling differences may explain this variation because the entire pool was sampled in September of 1967, whereas sampling was restricted to concentration areas within sections in late November 1969.

The mean standing crop in weight was converted to kilograms per hectare for each of the three sections to allow comparison with data recorded by Gale in 1967 (Fig. 6). The discrepancy between standing crops recorded in terms of weight in September 1967 and November 1969 probably was due to differences in the size classes of the fingernail clam population.

Factors Influencing Flock Movements

Movements and distribution of diving ducks on Pool 19 apparently were determined by two important factors: human disturbance, especially hunting activity,

Table 5. Mean standing crop in weight of three groups of benthic organisms in nine diving duck concentration areas on the Keokuk Pool, late November 1969.

	Standing crop (lb/acre)			
Area	Pelecypods	Gastropods	Mayfly larvae	Total
L-1	767.3	0	0	767.3
L-3	2,456.5	110.4	45.1	2,612.0
M-1	2,414.2	773.1	74.9	3,262.2
M-3	6,325.6	773.1	255.4	7,354.1
M-4	1,148.6	110.4	60.5	1,319.5
M-6	7,236.9	993.9	90.3	8,321.1
M-7	3,858.6	662.6	29.8	4,551.0
U-1	3,218.0	110.4	270.8	3,599.2
U-3	8,238.6	547.4	29.9	8,815.9

and food availability. Initiation of early morning movements from the middle and upper sections and a corresponding increase in the use of the less disturbed lower section was associated with the opening of the Iowa waterfowl season on 25 October. Hunting activity was most intense on the upper and middle sections because shallow water was suitable for building blinds in open water. Following the opening of the Illinois waterfowl season on 1 November, an even greater percentage of diving ducks concentrated on the lower section throughout the day (Table 1). Diving duck use of several areas on the Keokuk Pool was terminated by hunting activity or initiated following the close of the waterfowl seasons (Figs. 3, 4, 5). Early morning and late evening flights consistently occurred before and after shooting hours. Girard (1941) and Bellrose (1944) reported that disturbances due primarily to hunting caused rapid alteration of waterfowl flight and feeding routines. Cronan (1957) also found that selection of feeding sites by scaup in Connecticut was influenced by disturbances such as hunters, fishermen, and pleasure boaters. On numerous occasions, mass flights of diving ducks on the Keokuk Pool were initiated by continued harassment by boaters.

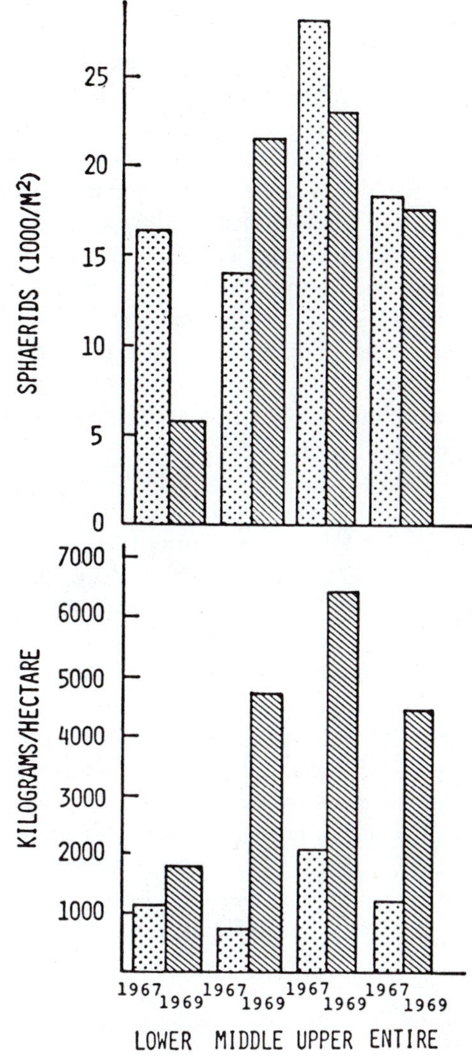

Fig. 6. Weights and densities of fingernail clams for the three sections and the entire Keokuk Pool.

In the absence of disturbance, diving ducks showed a definite preference for the middle and upper sections in the fall of 1969 and the spring of 1970. Apparently this was due to a more abundant food supply in certain areas of the middle and upper sections. Late evening flights to these sections during fall allowed undisturbed feeding throughout the night.

DISCUSSION

Probably no other inland area in North America is more important to migrating diving ducks than is the Keokuk Pool. During spring and fall, hundreds of thousands of diving ducks utilize the open water for resting and the abundant molluscan bottom fauna for restoring energy reserves expended during migration. This study has shown the ability of a population of diving ducks to adapt to hunting disturbance by deviating from typical patterns of diurnal activity. Intensive hunting activity near preferred feeding areas resulted in early morning flights to less disturbed locations. Fortunately, diving ducks could escape intensive disturbance by rafting in the lower section of Keokuk Pool where deep water prevented building blinds and staking decoys.

Increased hunting activity and other disturbances could pose a serious threat to the continued use of the Keokuk Pool by great numbers of migrating waterfowl. Monitoring disturbance as well as food resources is essential to the preservation of this unique area. Eventually, restrictions on boating activity may be necessary in some areas, and the value and effectiveness of establishing a refuge on the Keokuk Pool should be thoroughly studied and seriously considered.

LITERATURE CITED

ANDERSON, H. G. 1959. Food habits of migratory ducks in Illinois. Illinois Nat. Hist. Surv. Bull. 27(4):287–344.

BELLROSE, F. C. 1944. Duck populations and kill. Illinois Nat. Hist. Surv. Bull. 23(2): 327–372.

CRONAN, J. M., JR. 1957. Food and feeding habits of scaups in Connecticut waters. Auk 74(4):459–468.

GALE, W. F. 1969. Bottom fauna of Pool 19, Mississippi River with emphasis on the life history of the fingernail clam (*Sphaerium transversum*). Ph.D. Thesis. Iowa State Univ. Science and Technology, Ames, Iowa. 238pp.

GIRARD, G. L. 1941. The mallard its management in western Montana. J. Wildl. Manage. 5(3):233–259.

MILLS, H. B., W. C. STARRETT, AND F. C. BELLROSE. 1966. Man's effect on the fish and wildlife of the Illinois River. Illinois Nat. Hist. Surv. Biol. Notes 57. 24pp.

ROGERS, J. P., AND L. J. KORSCHGEN. 1966. Foods of lesser scaups on breeding, migration, and wintering areas. J. Wildl. Manage. 30(2): 258–264.

THOMPSON, J. 1969. Feeding behavior of diving ducks on Keokuk Pool, Mississippi River. M.S. Thesis. Iowa State Univ. Science and Technology. 79pp.

Accepted 20 June 1973.

THE MOULT MIGRATION[1]

FINN SALOMONSEN, Universitetets Zoologiske Museum, Universitetsparken 15, Copenhagen, Denmark

The flight- and tail-feathers are shed simultaneously in wildfowl, auks, divers, rails and a number of other groups, thus rendering the birds flightless and rather helpless for a period each year. The birds withdraw at this critical time to special areas where they are safe, usually to secluded places in dense marshes, lakes, coastal waters or the open sea. The main requirements of such areas are sufficient food, safety from predation, and (in water birds) an adequate depth of water. If these conditions are not met on the breeding ground or its immediate vicinity, the birds make a pre-moult shift to areas further away. This has in some cases resulted in a mass transfer of individuals in a fixed direction towards localised moulting places. This so-called 'Moult Migration' is particularly highly developed in wildfowl.

A comparative analysis of our recent, and incomplete, knowledge of moult migration has hitherto not been attempted.

HISTORY

The existence of moult migration was unknown until 30–40 years ago, but in recent years many investigations have been carried out. The first to draw attention to this form of migratory movement was the Swedish zoologist Sven Ekman, who in 1922 described it in the Eider (scientific names will be found in the section dealing with individual species), the Mute Swan and the Lesser White-fronted Goose (Ekman 1922). He called it *ruggnings-flyttning* in Swedish, and this term is now used in all languages (English: *moult migration,* French: *migration de mue,* German: *Mauserzug,* Danish: *fældningstræk*). The importance of this phenomenon was not realised until 10–20 years later. In 1937–39 the Russians Vuczeticz and Tugarinov published the results of wildfowl ringing in the Soviet Union and demonstrated that enormous numbers of dabbling ducks originating from northern Europe and Asia, gathered in the Volga delta in order to moult their flight-feathers there. Subsequently, Stresemann (1940) described a similar phenomenon from a lake on the border between Tibet and Sikkim where, at an altitude of about 4,500 m, a number of dabbling ducks and Tufted Duck shed their flight-feathers after a migration of about 2,000 km from their breeding places in northern Siberia.

Not until 1942, however, was the moult migration of a species in Europe described, i.e. that of the Shelduck (Hoogerheide and Kraak 1942). In North America no real movements to moulting areas were described until well after 1950.

GENERAL REMARKS

In the best developed form, moult migration is from the breeding place to a special moulting area, common to a large number, in some cases hundreds of thousands, of birds. When the flightless stage is over the ordinary autumn migration to the winter quarters starts. This form of moult migration cannot be regarded as the first part of the autumn movement for three reasons. Firstly, the flight direction is often different, sometimes the opposite of the autumn migration. Secondly, certain sections of the breeding population, usually the adult females, do not partici-

[1] Originally published in Wildfowl 19:5–24, 1968.

pate in the moult migration. Thirdly, the sharply circumscribed geographical situation and enormous population density in the moulting area are something quite unique. In the winter quarters the birds scatter over larger areas. In populations with typical moult migration the individuals adhere to a rigid schedule, which is followed regularly year after year. In other populations the system is less clear or only slightly developed.

The timing of the moult migration is dependent on that of breeding. When in late springs or unfavourable summers breeding is postponed, the moult migration falls correspondingly late, as demonstrated in various dabbling ducks and diving ducks in America (Hochbaum 1955) and in Europe (Bezzel 1964). The moult migration may in certain years be so delayed that the birds are forced to stop and shed their flight-feathers en route. This has been described in the Shelduck, which occasionally moults in Kent on its way to Germany (Eltringham and Boyd 1960), and in Steller's Eider, which sometimes moults in eastern Siberia on its way to Alaska (Jones 1965).

Some species (or populations) of ducks have no moult migration. The males remain in the breeding place and withdraw to a quiet, remote spot in a marsh or lake, sometimes within their own breeding territory. Here they carry out the wing-moult solitarily or in small groups, but never in large flocks. An example is the Pintail in Denmark, and, probably, in the whole of Scandinavia. At any rate I have observed solitary wing-moult in Swedish Lappland. This also illustrates the geographical variation in moulting behaviour, for this species performs extensive moult migrations in Russia and northern Asia and also in America.

Some species undergo wing-moult in the winter quarters and mass congregations may develop. In others, for example Brent Geese, immature birds may halt on the spring migration for this purpose.

It is possible therefore to distinguish between the following situations during the post-nuptial moult when an individual may shed the flight- and tail-feathers:

A. In the breeding territory or in the immediate surroundings.

B. During the ordinary autumn migration, or immature birds during spring migration.

C. In the winter quarters.

D. In a special area which is reached through a pre-moult migration starting in adult birds from the breeding range and in immature birds often directly from the winter quarters or from intermediate stations during spring migration.

It is clear that only in case D is it possible to speak about a genuine moult migration.

The size of the moulting flocks is another important character of the moult migration. Individuals may during the post-nuptial moult shed their flight- and tail-feathers:

I. On their own or in very small groups.

II. Assembled in comparatively small flocks, usually no more than a few hundred, occasionally up to a thousand birds.

III. Gathered in huge aggregates, in extreme cases numbering more than a hundred thousand birds.

All combinations of the classes A–D and I–III occur, except that the combination A III is found only in immature birds. If falling within class D, individuals belonging to all three groups I–III may be said to carry out a moult migration, but type D III represents moult migration as generally understood.

An obvious question is what purpose

is served by concentrating in huge flocks in a special moulting area, sometimes situated more than 3,000 km from the breeding area, when in other areas the same species can perform the moult on the breeding ground, solitarily or in small groups? It is evident that both forms of behaviour have certain advantages. In northern countries with short summers and early onset of cold the birds may run a considerable risk if they moult their flight-feathers on the breeding ground. Under such conditions selection for development of moult migration must be strong because it is, obviously, advantageous to transfer the time of wing-moult to areas with a milder climate situated nearer to the winter quarters, or even to postpone it until after the arrival in the winter quarters. There is also a high selective advantage when a part of the population (adult males and/or non-breeders) perform a moult migration, leaving the breeding areas and their food resources for the female and the ducklings. It is probable that in many (or most) species the ultimate cause of the development of moult migration has been a potential shortage of food on the breeding grounds.

It is possible that the enormous concentrations of individuals within a small moulting area may serve some social function (Wynne-Edwards 1962). Traditions, which play an important role in the ecology of wildfowl, may also be of significance in mass moult gatherings. Such traditions need not even be genetically fixed, although they evidently must be so in populations with a pronounced moult migration. In such populations the direction of the moult migration and the position of the moulting area are rigidly determined and the same area is used by the birds one year after another. The biological reason for choosing this particular area may date back to a distant past, the original migration pattern being maintained where it is still advantageous. In other species or populations the situation is more unstable. The populations then segregate in a number of moulting areas, each of which is frequented by a comparatively small number of birds, at most a few thousand individuals. Such minor concentrations may move, suddenly or gradually, to another place for no apparent reason.

A well-documented case of locality change has been demonstrated at the Ismaninger Reservoir in Bavaria. A small number of dabbling and diving ducks traditionally underwent wing-moult in this lake area, but when in 1955 the water surface was raised 2 m artificially the number of moulting diving ducks increased considerably in the subsequent years. The Red-crested Pochard from 10–90 to over 300, the Tufted Duck from 100–200 to about 2,000, and the Pochard from 500–1,000 to no less than 9,000–11,000 individuals (Bezzel 1964).

In the majority of dabbling and diving ducks the post-nuptial (eclipse) moult in the males is initiated on the breeding ground. In the Mallard in Denmark the first body-feathers are shed as early as the middle of April. In species with moult migration the males leave the breeding place at a certain time, usually solitarily, but as a rule soon gather in small flocks. These gatherings increase gradually to some hundreds and occasionally to more than a thousand. At the same time the flocks move to intermediate resting places. During this movement the males perform the greater part of the eclipse moult, excepting the wing-moult which in the dabbling ducks constitutes the final stage. When this stage is imminent the birds leave for the moulting area together. The biggest moulting flight ever described was observed at Mud Lake,

Idaho, where during one night (5th August) no less than 52,000 dabbling ducks, belonging to six species, arrived (Oring 1964). The postponement of the final flight until shortly before the wing-moult makes it possible to reduce the time spent in the moulting area to about three to four weeks. The moulting area is then abandoned, but new flocks are continuously pouring in and moulting males of a particular species are present for much longer, from two months in high arctic species (such as the King Eider) to four months in the Shelduck.

The final phase of the moult migration in ducks takes place rapidly and must be controlled by a very strong migratory urge. This is contrary to the usual more leisurely movements of ducks, interrupted by long pauses in resting places. The distance between the gathering place of the males (near the breeding place) and the moulting area is usually covered by a non-stop flight without deviations. The entire moult migration of the vast majority of the population is sometimes concentrated into a few days.

Many marine species, which during their usual migrations keep to coastal waters and avoid the interior, may cross large land-masses during the moult migration. The best known examples are the crossing of England by the Shelduck, the migration over the mountains of Baffin Island by the King Eider, and the crossing of Jutland by the Shelduck, Common Scoter and Eider (although the latter three species may occasionally cross the mainland during spring and autumn migration).

A review of the known moult migrations in the different groups of wildfowl is now given.

Swans and Geese (Anserini)

The moult migrations of the swans and those of the geese have much in common. Moult migration is restricted to non-breeders, mostly to young, immature birds. Breeding birds remain with their young and indeed, in most swans and in many geese, the immature birds themselves undergo wing-moult in the vicinity of the breeding ground, usually gathered in small flocks (type A II), which means that such populations have no moult migration.

Swans Cygnus.—The adult birds perform the wing-moult in the breeding period, first the female and then the male. In this way there is always one of the parents to defend the nest or the young. The wing-moult certainly takes place in this way in the Mute Swan *Cygnus olor* (Szijj 1965), the Whooper Swan *Cygnus cygnus* (Scott and Fisher 1953) and the Trumpeter Swan *Cygnus buccinator* (Banko 1960).

In the post-breeding period the swans roam about with the young, which still need parental care. The wing-moult cannot, therefore, be postponed until after the young are fledged because the flightless adult birds could not then follow their offspring.

From the point of view of moult migration the adult swans represent a primitive stage.

The non-breeding one year old and (usually) two year old swans gather in summer in flocks, numbering up to some hundreds of birds, occasionally many more. In most species the flocks remain in the vicinity of the breeding area (moulting type A II) and, evidently, do not carry out a real moult migration which is known only in the Mute Swan. The immature Mute Swans usually frequent shallow water along low and protected sea-coasts, performing the moult rather slowly, from the end of May to the end of August, the flight-feathers being shed in the latter half of July and the first days of August. In Denmark and southern

Sweden smaller congregations of moulting birds are found in various places along sea-coasts with a water depth less than one metre. The southern Sound and adjacent areas off the island of Amager and in Køge Bay form a very important moulting area (type A III). This moulting area has been known for centuries because the shooting of the flightless birds was formerly a prerogative of the Danish kings and, the hunt being a spectacular performance, was often described, the first time being in 1557. The royal hunting stopped about 1750 but subsequently shooting of the flightless swans was for many years practised on the Swedish side of the Sound where it was a privilege of the prefect of Scania (Schiøler 1925, Weismann 1931). In the beginning of the 20th century the swans were virtually exterminated, particularly by excessive winter shooting. In 1926, however, full protection was given to the swans by the Danish and Swedish governments, and this resulted in an immense increase, which has continued to the present day. Probably climatic influences have also been involved in this population explosion.

In the 17th century moulting swans were numerous in late July from Gedser along the east coast of the islands of Falster, Møen and Zealand right to Amager and Saltholm in the southern part of the Sound, but in recent years the centre of the moulting area has shifted to the Swedish side of the Sound. According to Mathiasson (1964) more than 10,000 moulting birds were gathered in 1963 along the east coast of the southern Sound, and a further 200 in Skälderviken and 1,200 in Kungsbacka Fjord in Halland, further north (Fig. 2). In another paper Mathiasson (1963) concludes that this enormous number of moulting swans comprises not only the entire population of non-breeding swans from Zealand and Scania, but also large numbers of birds from more remote breeding places. In this he is undoubtedly correct and the majority of the immature swans of southern Sweden, eastern Denmark and the northern coastland of East Germany probably gather there. Future ringing must decide whether this view is correct. Presumably, non-breeding Mute Swans come from all directions to the moulting area in the Sound, the moult migration thus resembling that of the Shelduck, although on a smaller scale.

The flightless period in the swans lasts for about seven weeks. During the wing-moult the birds must have access to firm land or at least to very shallow water as they cannot preen while swimming.

Geese Anser, Branta.—The adult breeding geese have no moult migration. Both sexes share the parental care, as in the swans, and both remain with the goslings on the breeding places, in late summer undergoing the wing-moult which, contrary to the ducks, begins the post-nuptial moult. Generally the moult of the female precedes that of its mate by about a week. The immature birds, joined (or led) by a small number of adult non-breeders, gather in flocks usually of some hundreds but occasionally amounting to several thousand individuals. They often remain within the breeding area of the population (type A II, A III) but in many species a real moult migration has developed of the type D II or even D III. It is noteworthy that this movement, at least in all known cases, invariably goes in a northerly direction, leading to areas situated beyond the boundary of the population's normal breeding range.

All known cases of moult migration in non-breeding geese are briefly outlined below and shown in Fig. 1, represented by the numeral included in the description.

Pink-footed Goose *Anser fabalis*

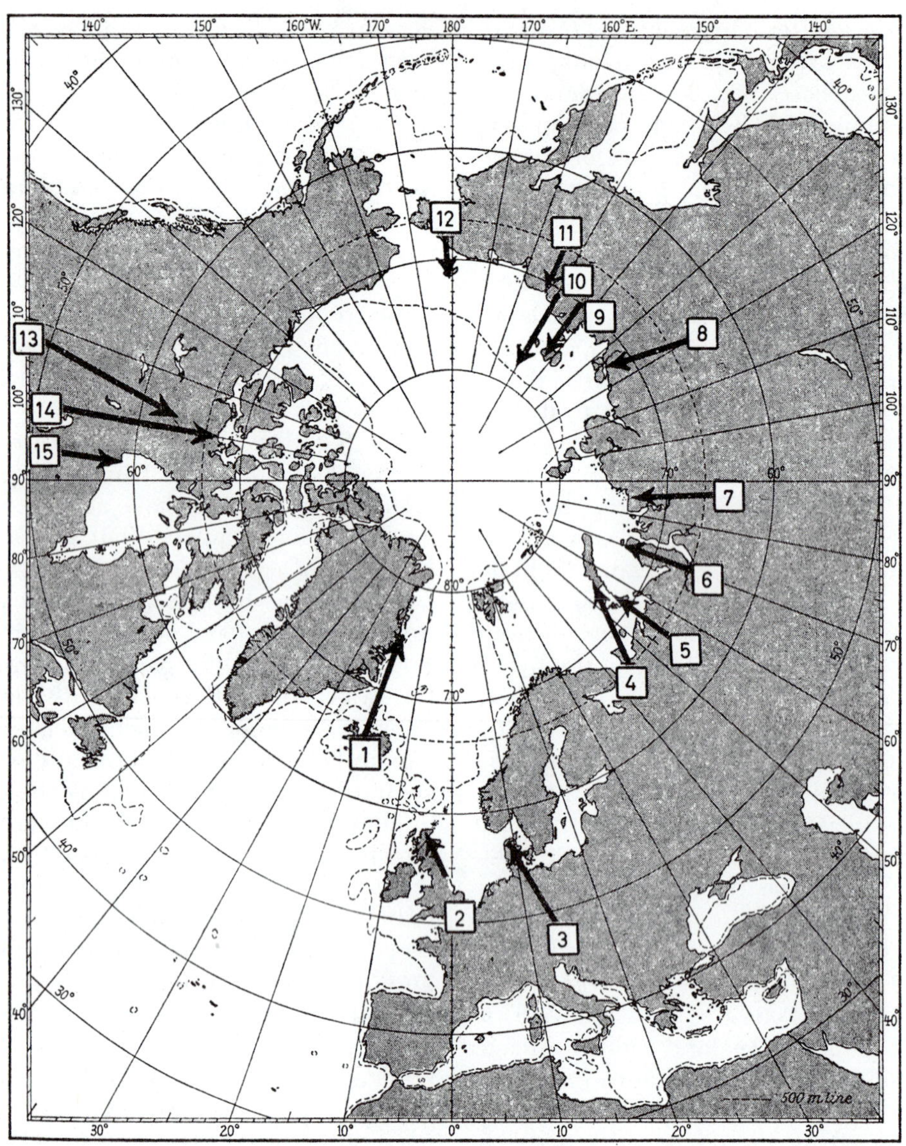

Fig. 1. All known cases of moult migration in non-breeding geese. The arrows show direction and distance from origin to destination of the migration. The numerals refer to literature statements enumerated in the text pp. 1114–1118.

brachyrhynchus: Moves from Iceland to northeast Greenland, the migration involving more than 10,000 birds (1) (Taylor 1953, Christensen 1967).

Bean Goose *Anser fabalis*, various subspecies: Moves from northern Russia to southern Novaya Zemlya in great numbers (5) (Johansen 1945, Portenko 1959, Uspenski 1965*a*). Very important moulting places are found in northern Siberia on the tundra in central Yamal (6), western Taymyr (7) and the delta of Indigirka (11) (Uspenski 1965*a*). Portenko (1959) adds the Lena delta (8). All these places are situated in the northern part of the breeding range. Pleske (1928) states that moulting birds are found in small numbers on the New Siberian Islands (9), north of the regular breeding range of the Bean Goose.

White-footed Goose *Anser albifrons*: This makes similar movements in the Eurasian tundra to the Bean Goose, often mixing with that species in the moulting areas. Great moulting concentrations are found in Novaya Zemlya (5), central Yamal (6), western Taymyr (7), and the delta of Indigirka (11) (Uspenski 1965*a*) and moulting birds are also found in considerable numbers on the New Siberian Islands (9) (Pleske 1928), where the species breeds only rarely. Immature birds of the Greenland population *flavirostris* are strictly stationary, moulting in the breeding areas, assembling in small companies of at most a dozen individuals, probably the offspring of a few pairs. A similar situation is, apparently, present in North America.

Lesser White-fronted Goose *Anser erythropus*: According to Ekman (1922) the moulting birds of the alpine zone of Scandinavia withdraw to the uppermost parts of the mountains, where they gather in large flocks. No moult migration has been recorded from Siberia.

Greylag Goose *Anser anser*: The only known case of moult migration is found in the Danish population, of which the non-breeding birds moved to Vejlerne, an extensive marshland in northern Jutland. From ringing results it seems probable that many of these moulting birds originated from northern Germany, Poland and Austria (3) (Paludan 1965). The species did not breed in Vejlerne until about 1925 and individuals from other places did not use the area for moulting until the 1930's. In 1934–37 at most 200 non-breeding birds were moulting there, in 1934 500 (Salomonsen 1943) and in 1955 about 3,000 (Paludan 1965). The numbers began to decrease in 1959 and now only few are left. In 1959 summering Greylag Geese suddenly began to turn up in Holland, and in 1964 the number of moulting non-breeders at the lagoon Saltbækvig in Zealand (Denmark) increased considerably. It is probable, therefore, that these and other areas have now replaced Vejlerne as moulting areas (Paludan 1965).

Brent Goose *Branta bernicla*: During the spring migration of the nominate form from Europe towards the breeding range in northern Siberia, many immature birds remain to moult in eastern Kola Peninsula and northern Kanin Peninsula (type B II), while others divert from the eastward flight direction of the breeding birds and turn northwards to Novaya Zemlya, where they occur on both the southern and northern island (4). Many thousands moult in the New Siberian Islands (9), originating from the coast of NE. Siberia between Yana and Kolyma Rivers (Uspenski 1960). According to Uspenski there are many observations of birds flying north over the Polar Sea north of the New Siberian Islands and at Henrietta and Bennett Islands (10). It is very unlikely that they continue across the central parts of the Polar Sea to North Greenland or to some sterile ice-island. Uspenski's view that they turn eastwards to moulting areas in Alaska is borne out by recoveries in the New Siberian Islands, on Wrangel Island, and at the Kolyma Delta of birds ringed in previous years at moulting stations in western Alaska (Uspenski 1960, 1965*b*). Finally Wrangel Island (12) forms the moulting area of at least 10,000 non-breeding Brents, coming from the south, while only 1,000–2,000 pairs breed there (Uspenski 1965*b*).

No case of moult migration has been described in the North American populations. Apparently the immature birds moult in small flocks in the breeding areas of the adult birds (Scott 1951). Uspenski (1960, 1965*a*), however, reports that Brent Geese ringed during the moult in Alaska are recovered in subsequent moulting periods in eastern Siberia.

Canada Goose *Branta canadensis*: Moult migrations are known to go northwards to the Thelon River district (13), to Perry River (14) and to the western coastland of Hudson Bay (15) (Scott 1951, Hanson 1965, Sterling and Dzubin 1967). The last named authors have delineated the movements of the different races, and banding results (the earliest being those of Kuyt 1962) have now indicated the movements of localised populations. The number of moulting birds is considerable, at Thelon River up to 16,000 individuals have been observed. In Great Britain numbers of moulting birds gather in Inverness-shire, Scotland, and ringing has demonstrated that at least some of them originate as far south as Yorkshire (2) (Dennis 1964).

The Canada Goose was introduced to Great Britain and the moult migration to Inverness, therefore, must be a comparatively recent phenomenon, certainly less than 300 years old, and probably of much more recent origin. It is reasonable to assume that it is a result of an ancient adaptation based on hereditary factors.

Very likely moult migration will be discovered in other species than those mentioned above, but it does not appear to be the case in those species which have been thoroughly studied. Uspenski (1965*a*), however, is of the opinion that the non-breeding Snow Geese *Anser caerulescens* of Wrangel Island perform a moult migration.

The flightless period in geese covers about 35–40 days, but less than a month in the Snow Goose (Uspenski 1965*a*). The non-breeders begin the moult a fortnight earlier than the breeding birds, in most arctic species in the middle of July, compared with early August in the breeding birds, but according to Uspenski (1965*a*) the two groups moult simultaneously in the high-arctic Brent and Snow Goose. Cooch (1957), however, states that in the Snow Goose in Southampton Island the non-breeders moult much earlier than the breeding birds.

It is my belief that the ultimate cause of the moult migration of non-breeding geese is an endeavor to avoid heavy competition for food on the breeding places, but it is difficult to understand why the migration invariably moves in a northern direction while all other moult migrations in wildfowl lead to regions with a milder climate. There are three alternative explanations:

(1) It may have something to do with so-called 'prolongation of migration.' The immature birds are still in a migratory state when the time comes for them to leave the breeding grounds only a few weeks after arrival. Under such circumstances it is most likely that the choice of a flight direction will be the same as used during the spring migration, i.e. northerly. If the northern direction is genetically fixed it will be kept provided that selective forces do not favour any other direction.

(2) I was at first inclined to believe that the northerly direction of the moult migration in geese expressed a phenomenon similar to the so-called nonsense orientation in British and American Mallard, which demonstrates an instinctive selection of a northerly flight direction under certain circumstances. However, recent investigations by Matthews, Eygenraam and Hoffmann (1963) and

Bellrose (1963) have shown that other species of wildfowl choose other directions during nonsense orientation, and that different populations of the same species may do likewise (Matthews 1963). I am now satisfied, therefore, that nonsense orientation is not involved in the northward moult migration in geese.

(3) The north direction may be the result of climatic influences. In arctic regions the length of time of snow-cover is of decisive significance for many ground-feeding birds and mammals. According to Uspenski (1965*a*) a snow-free period of three months is necessary for a successful accomplishment of the breeding cycle in most species of geese. Only the Snow Goose and the Brent Goose are able to manage the full breeding cycle in slightly over two months, owing to a particularly rapid development of the goslings and an accelerated wing-moult in the adults. Although the snow-free period in high-arctic areas is too short to permit breeding in most species of geese, the food resources can be utilized by non-breeding birds when the snow-melt in the latter part of June has made the food plants available to them. A high selective premium is paid to such populations in which the immature birds move north to the high-arctic region in June, leaving the food resources on the breeding places to the goslings and their parents, in this way enabling the breeding population to raise its productivity.

Shelduck (Tadornini)

The moult migration of the Shelduck *Tadorna tadorna* in northern Europe is of impressive dimensions. In this species both the immature non-breeding individuals as well as the adult breeding birds participate in the moult migration. Male and female share the parental care, but many leave the ducklings before they are fledged. Shelducks from the British Isles, the North Sea countries, Scandinavia and the Baltic countries move in the summer from all points of the compass to the German Waddensea coast in order to perform the wing-moult there (type D III). The biggest concentration of birds is found on the tidal flats Knechtsand, east of Cuxhaven, where at the peak about 100,000 gather. Smaller centres are found off the North Sea coast of Schleswig-Holstein, northward to the Ejdersted Peninsula. Before the migration the Shelduck collect in flocks and then leave at sunset, probably covering the whole distance in a single night. The migration usually follows a straight line, these normally coastal birds crossing the mainland of England and Jutland. The moult migration begins in Denmark in June (immature birds) and continues until September–October, but in England virtually the entire migration takes place in July. When the post-nuptial moult has finished, the autumn migration takes place more leisurely. It covers the period October–November and, paradoxically enough, transfers the British population back to its breeding range, while the Scandinavian and East European populations scatter, to winter in the coastal areas of the southern North Sea, France and the British Isles (as shown by ringing of Danish birds; cf. Salomonsen 1967). Some flocks move northwards in the North Slesvig Waddensea or to the lagoons in western Jutland, but many thousands of birds winter within the moulting area proper.

The moult migration of the Shelduck, which in recent years has attracted much attention, has been studied particularly by Hoogerheide and Kraak (1942), Coombes (1950), Goethe (1957, 1961*a,b*) and Lind (1957).

It is noteworthy that a moulting congregation of Shelduck, totalling more than 3,000 birds, was recently discovered in Bridgwater Bay, Somerset, in England, possibly being of Irish origin (Eltringham and Boyd 1960). Apart from this, apparently all European Shelduck west of the Soviet border perform the wing-moult in the German Waddensea. In Lake Rezaiyeh in Iranian Azerbaijan about 300 flightless Shelduck were observed in August by Savage (1964). This locality serves probably as a local moulting centre for Shelduck which assemble here from wide areas within Iran.

Dabbling Ducks (Anatini)

The dabbling ducks breed when they are one year old (Wigeon often not until they are two years old) and it is, therefore, not necessary to distinguish between the moult migration of immature and adult birds. The males do not participate in brooding and parental care, but soon leave the female in order to perform the eclipse moult. Only the males perform a moult migration, whereas the females stay with the ducklings. A few females may join the males but only those which have given up breeding for the year.

The time for the males' desertion of the females varies somewhat. In the Mallard *Anas platyrhynchos* and Pintail *Anas acuta* the female is abandoned as soon as the clutch is complete, before incubation. In the Mallard in Europe this is in the second half of April. In most other species the males remain near the female until various stages of incubation. According to Hochbaum (1955) and Oring (1964) the Shoveler *Anas clypeata*, Blue-winged Teal *Anas discors* and Cinnamon Teal *Anas cyanoptera* sometimes remain even until hatching, in spite of well developed body-moult. The males of most holarctic species moult the wing-feathers in the period from the middle of June to the end of August. The Mallard is on average slightly but not significantly earlier than other species. The flightless period covers three to four weeks, and is shortest in the small species.

The females remain with the ducklings until they are more or less independent. They then withdraw to suitable areas in the same marsh or in its vicinity and perform the wing-moult, much later, of course, than the males. They may sometimes assemble in small parties, but never in big flocks, and usually they are solitary. The wing-moult in most species takes place from the middle of July to September or even October.

The females may in exceptional cases remain with the ducklings during the flightless stage, or they may occasionally commence the autumn migration before the moult, performing the wing-moult alone or in small groups during the migration (type B I) or in the winter quarters (C I). In the winter quarters of the Gadwall *Anas strepera* in Louisiana, Chabreck (1966) found two or three dozen females in the flightless stage in October. Lebret (1952) records a single flightless female of Gadwall in September and a number of flightless females of Wigeon *Anas penelope* in October, during their migration in Holland. However, no breeding females of any species of dabbling duck perform a real moult migration.

The extension and proportions of the moult migrations in the males is subject to considerable variation, both specifically, individually and geographically. In Denmark the greater number of males of all species moult on the breeding place proper, either solitarily or in very small groups (A I). Only the Mallard, and in some places also the Shoveler, has something approaching a moult migration. The males within an area collect in small flocks, usually less than two dozen birds, but occasionally up to about 200 (type A II). The same behaviour is displayed in most other European countries where the Mallard is non-migratory. It is even the case in Greenland, where the largest concentration of flightless males I ever saw amounted to only eleven birds. In western Europe also all other species of dabbling ducks evidently adhere to the moulting types A I or A II. In the flightless stage they prefer large marshes, also densely overgrown lakes, the Mallard even lagoons or quiet bays in fjords.

Populations breeding in regions with a continental or arctic climate carry out regular and often long migrations to winter quarters. In these populations the males have highly developed moult migrations, leading to large moulting centres where individuals coming from very extensive areas collect in a restricted locality, usually 50,000–100,000 birds together, occasionally even more. These moulting areas, frequented year after year, are as a rule situated on the migration route (B III) or in the winter quarters (C III). True moult migrations of the type D III are hardly known within the dabbling ducks. A number of species assemble on these moulting places and form part of the huge congregations, but there are definite local and specific differences. Usually the Mallard and the Pintail predominate, but this is not always so.

In the Old World particularly large concentrations of moulting males are found in the West Siberian lakes, the Transuralian forested steppes, northern Kazakstan, Kuban flats, Rybinski Reservoir (north of Moscow), Volga delta, Russian-Finnish lakes, and Matsalu National Park in Estonia (Ottow 1956, Teplov and Kartashev 1958, Kumari 1962, Wolff 1966). In Matsalu Park there were formerly (until the 1930's) 'many hundreds of thousands' of birds, mostly Mallard and Teal, but also some Wigeon, Shoveler and Garganey *Anas querquedula*, but now, owing to human interference, only about 10,000 birds (Kumari 1962).

In North America great moulting centres are the Delta Marsh at Lake Manitoba (Hochbaum 1955) and the Camas Reserve in Idaho (Oring 1964), and probably many more. The main species moulting in Delta Marsh are Mallard, Pintail, American Wigeon *Anas americana*, and American Green-winged Teal *Anas crecca carolinensis*. In the Camas Reserve all these species moult, also Cinnamon Teal and Blue-winged Teal. Some of these may be local birds (probably only a small fraction) but certainly Pintail and Wigeon are not found breeding until many hundred kilometres further north. The greatest moulting concentrations are probably found in the American Green-winged Teal and American Wigeon, of which species Sowls (cited by Bezzel 1964) records congregations of 125,000 individuals in a particular locality.

Moulting congregations of this order of magnitude are not found in western Europe, as said already, but some localities approach them. In the Lake Tåkern in southern Sweden males of Mallard and Wigeon gathered in summer at least in hundreds (Lönnberg 1935) and the same is evidently the case with other lakes in south Sweden, such as Hornborgasjön. While Mallard, at least partially, may belong to local populations, Wigeon are uncommon breeders so far south in Sweden, and the greater part of them must obviously have originated from further north, now performing the wing-moult at a resting place situated on the ordinary autumn flyway (type B II).

The other known moulting areas in western Europe are principally of the same kind as Tåkern, holding some hundreds of moulting males, the majority of which having performed a B II migration, but a small fraction being local birds with an A II moult. A typical B II locality is Ijsselmeer in Holland, in which Mallard, Gadwall, Teal, Garganey, Pintail, Wigeon and Shoveler spend the flightless stage (Lebret 1950). In Lake Constance some hundred individuals of Mallard, Teal, Gadwall, Garganey and Shoveler moult the flight-feathers, but apparently no Pintail or Wigeon (Szijj 1965). The Ismaninger Reservoir in Bavaria is characterised by the large number of moulting Gadwall (about 400), but only a few of other species of dabbling ducks (Bezzel 1964). The Himalayan lake, described by Stresemann (1940), in which many dabbling ducks spent the flightless period is of a similar B II type as the above-mentioned European lakes. Even the locality in Scotland (Beauly River in Inverness-shire) described by Dennis (1964) as being full of moulting male Mallard may belong to this type, but it is more probable that the birds observed are of local origin (A II type). There are, of course, other localities of this kind in Europe than those mentioned, but the wildfowl ecology in these places has not yet been thoroughly studied.

I have selected three species for some special comments.

Pintail *Anas acuta*: Individual variation in moult migration comprises the types A I, A II, B II, B III. In Scandinavia and Denmark the males usually moult the wing-feathers in the breeding range, solitarily or in small parties. In other places they gather in large flocks in the breeding area, such as described by Scott (1951) from Perry River in arctic Canada. As a rule, however, arctic and sub-arctic Pintail make very extensive pre-moult migrations in a southerly direction, spending the flightless stage on intermediate resting stations, from which they continue the migration southwards when their wings can again carry them. These moult migrations are generally longer than in most other dabbling ducks. Sometimes the Pintail collect in hundreds in the moulting areas (type B II), as in Ijsselmeer in Holland, but in Soviet and U.S.A. the moulting congregations usually reach enormous dimensions (type B III). In Bear River, Utah, 7,500 individuals have been recorded, in Camas Reserve, Idaho, 20,000 (Oring 1964), in lakes in Kazakstan, 30,000 (Cuisin 1966). The autumn passage migrants of this species in Denmark, originating from Scandinavia, north Russia and some even from western Siberia (as demonstrated by recoveries of ringed birds; cf. Salomonsen 1967) belong to populations which perform the wing-moult in the breeding areas or in resting stations north of Denmark. The males pass through Denmark, all with new wing-feathers, from the end of August to the middle of September, well ahead of the adult females and juvenile birds; the rear party, passing after the middle of October, consists exclusively of juveniles (Schiøler 1925). The segregation on the migration of the two sexes reflects the different timing of the wing-moult, and is the rule also in Teal and Wigeon.

Teal *Anas crecca*: Like the males of the Pintail, those of the Teal moult either in the breeding area or on suitable resting places on the southward migration in autumn. The flight-feathers are shed within the period from the middle of June to the middle of August, usually in early August (Wolff 1966). There is a notable difference in the movements between Pintail and Teal, at any rate in the passage migrants passing Denmark. A substantial part of the males of northern Teal leave the breeding places soon after incubation has started and appear in Denmark, in small flocks, as early as the middle of June on their way to moulting areas further south or south-west (Palm 1950). Such an early passage has not been noticed in Denmark in any other dabbling duck. The Teal apparently do not spend the flightless period in Denmark, but are known to do so in some numbers in Holland and a flightless male ringed in Holland was recovered next autumn in Poland (Wolff 1966). Flightless males have often been obtained in Denmark in August but they may be local birds. During the ordinary autumn migration, starting in August, males (with new wings) arrive in advance of females, just as in the Pintail (Schiøler 1925). In Russia and U.S.A. huge concentrations of moulting males (type B III) have been recorded, as mentioned before.

Wigeon *Anas penelope*: This species differs from most other dabbling ducks by the postponement of breeding in most individuals until the second year. Many of the one year old non-breeding birds may spend the summer and moult the flight-feathers in areas south of the breeding range. The adult males moult the flight-feathers in June–July, the females in August–October. The majority of the males evidently leave the breeding ranges very soon after incubation, shedding the flight-feathers in areas further south, gathering in flocks (type B II). Lebret (1950) during a visit in August to the breeding places in Jämtland, in northern Sweden, observed hundreds of females with young, but virutally no males. The latter had already left and were moulting the wing-feathers in lakes situated further south or south-west on the flyways of the subsequent autumn migration. Flocks of moulting males are known in north-west Europe from the end of June onwards in Estonia (Matsalu), southern Sweden (Tåkern and Hornborgasjön), Denmark (Vejlerne, N. Jutland) and Holland (Ijsselmeer). The males leave the moulting areas and begin the genuine autumn migration as soon as the flightless period is over, usually in August. In Denmark as well as in Holland males (with new wings) predominate during the early stages of the autumn migration, while females and juveniles follow later.

The moulting areas of the dabbling ducks are wetlands with dense vegetation and very shallow water, usually open reed beds or other plant formations along the shore, furnishing cover and sufficient food. The really big moulting centres are extensive and secluded. The moulting birds must have access to firm land because they do not preen while swimming.

Diving Ducks (Aythyini)

The diving ducks resemble the dabbling ducks in being able to breed at one year old and have, therefore, no distinct moult migration of immature birds. The general character of the moult migration is also very similar. The most striking difference is the participation of a certain number of adult females, but these are always much fewer than the males and they migrate considerably later. The moult migration of both sexes belongs to type B II, but moulting congregations of more than 10,000 individuals (type B III) are occasionally found. Probably a large number of individuals of both sexes remain in the breeding territory, spending the flightless period there (type A I or A II), but only scanty information is available. The performance of moult migration in females may have something to do with the fact that the females sometimes leave the brood before the young can fly. This has been observed in the Redhead

Aythya americana, and the Canvasback *A. valisneria,* whereas in the Lesser Scaup *A. affinis* the females remain with the young until they are fledged (Oring 1964).

These three American species, as well as a fourth, the Ring-necked Duck *A. collaris,* perform striking moult migrations, sometimes gathering in concentrations of more than 10,000 birds. Among the Palaearctic species the Tufted Duck *A. fuligula* and the Pochard *A. ferina* have moult migration, at least in some populations. Both species appear in large numbers on the Ijsselmeer in Holland in July–August but breed only sparsely in Holland (Lebret 1950). In Ismaninger Reservoir in Bavaria about 9,000–11,000 Pochard and more than 2,000 Tufted Duck spend the flightless period. The males arrive in June–July, the females (less than 10% of the numbers) not until August. Just as in Holland the two species are only scattered breeders in Bavaria, and the large flocks must have originated from rather remote breeding places (Bezzel 1964). The occurrence of these two species in central European moulting areas is probably the result of a pre-moult migration due east-west because northern birds apparently spend the flightless period in the breeding range, or at any rate on localities situated much further north. Extensive ringing in Denmark of Tufted Duck during autumn migration has demonstrated that these birds breed in Scandinavia, north Russia and NW. Siberia, and winter in Germany, France and England, occasionally in Italy (Salomonsen 1967). They do not arrive in Denmark until October, with new wings, and consequently must have spent the flightless period further north. Something similar can be said about the Pochard which appears as a passage migrant in Denmark in September–October. No moulting areas for these species are known in Scandinavia, but a great number of Tufted Duck and a smaller number of Pochard are known to moult their flight-feathers in Matsalu National Park in Estonia (Kumari 1962).

Possibly the well-known strict sexual segregation in the winter quarters (allohiemy) in the Pochard and the Tufted Duck is a consequence of the difference in the moult migration in males and females. The males, having finished the wing-moult much in advance of the females, arrive earlier in the winter quarters where they apparently occupy all available space within the specific niches and pre-empt the food resources. The females, consequently, are forced to continue their migration to areas beyond, the two sexes performing a so-called leapfrog migration (Salomonsen 1955). Such a situation is unknown in dabbling ducks.

The Red-crested Pochard *Netta rufina* has a moult migration similar in many respects to that of the *Aythya* species. A comparatively large number spend the flightless period in various lakes in central Europe, about 300 individuals in the Ismaninger Reservoir, and about twice this number in Lake Constance. The males begin to arrive in the last part of June, the majority in July and early in August, the females not until August. The males moult the flight-feathers in July–August, the females in August and the first half of September (Bezzel 1964, Szijj 1965). In Ismaninger all birds leave in September for the autumn migration, while in Lake Constance, on the contrary, a new influx of birds which have finished the moult occurs in September–October, when about 4,000 birds can be present. In November they all leave again (Zink 1964). Ringing has definitely shown that the birds moulting in Lake Constance originate from the

Carmargue in southern France (Mayaud 1966). In certain years they do not move so far eastwards, but use lakes in Lorraine as a moulting area. The autumn migration, which takes place in September–November, goes the opposite way, towards the south-west, the main wintering places extending from the Camargue to Albufera de Valencia in eastern Spain. The ducklings from the Camargue move directly to Spain, naturally without performing any moult migration (Mayaud 1966). The eastward moult migration and subsequent westward return migration in the autumn strikingly resembles the situation in the British population of the Shelduck. The individuals which arrive in Lake Constance in September–October must originate from eastern breeding places (Balkans, S. Russia, SW. Siberia). Just as in the *Aythya* species mentioned above, these individuals perform a moult migration to Central Europe in a due western direction. Even so they winter probably somewhere in Spain. Ringing of Red-crested Pochard at breeding places in Denmark has demonstrated that the greater part of this population spend the winter in SE. France and NE. Spain (Preuss 1965) but apparently they perform the wing-moult in the breeding area.

The Scaup *Aythya marila*, although belonging to the same genus as the Pochard and its allies, is a marine species, which mainly frequents coastal waters. Nothing is known about its moulting behaviour.

The moulting areas of the diving ducks are fresh-water lakes of varying size, though not very small ones. The moulting birds frequent the areas of open water off the riparian zone of vegetation (reed beds, etc.), usually in shallow water with a depth of less than 5 m, not too far outside the belt of vegetation. They do not need access to firm land, being able to preen while swimming. The Red-crested Pochard differs by preferring open reed beds, much like the dabbling ducks.

Eiders, Scoters and Sawbills (Somaterini and Mergini)

The moult migrations of the marine ducks are more diverse and better developed than in any other group of wildfowl. Those of the eiders and scoters are, however, similar. In the marine ducks, contrary to the situation in the dabbling ducks and the diving ducks, the one year old birds and in some species even the two year old birds do not breed but join the males in their comprehensive moult migration. The participation of the adult females in the moult migration varies considerably from one species to the other. They may spend the flightless period on the breeding places (type A I) or in the winter quarters (type C I), or they may participate in the moult migration together with the males, or more usually join them later in the autumn. Part of the female population at any rate must remain in the breeding places because the young are too small to be left alone. The departure of some of the females is compensated for by individuals which remain and are possessed of a strongly developed tendency to collect and keep large flocks of ducklings, as in the eiders. It is also developed in the Shelduck in which both sexes show 'crèching' behaviour.

The Common Scoter *Melanitta nigra* breeds in the arctic and northern high-boreal areas of the Old World. It has been known for a long time that summering and moulting individuals occurred in small flocks in the inner Danish waters and in the Limfjord, but only fairly recently was it pointed out that the actual moulting area was in the North Sea just off the west coast of Jutland (Salomonsen 1950*a*). Moulting birds occur in flocks of varying size right from the Danish-German boundary northward to the Skaw (Fig. 2). The moult migration to this area, which is very spectacular and has been known for a long time, passes through the southern Baltic Sea, south of Denmark, and crosses Jutland along the fjord Slien (Jørgensen 1941), going westwards to the Waddensea of North Slesvig where the flocks gradually spread northward along the west coast of Jutland. The greatest concentrations of moulting birds are found, therefore, along the southern part of the west coast of Jutland; the flocks off Rømø Island amount to about 150,000 individuals, according to an aerial census made by Joensen (1964). A smaller proportion of the migrating birds pass somewhat further northward and have been recorded over southern Zealand (Sjaelland), in the Little Belt and at the town of Ribe, following the south-eastern fjords in Jutland westward (Flensburg Fjord, Åbenrå Fjord, Vejle Fjord) the most northerly observations being from Horsens Fjord (Schiøler 1926, Behrends 1955). Small flocks of some hundred birds, have been observed in early August to pass northwards through the Great Belt (Bruun and Schelde 1957), possibly heading towards moulting areas in the western Kattegat. By far the majority, however, spend the flightless period off the west coast of Jutland, and the densely packed flocks congregating there comprise undoubtedly the greater part of the Scandinavian and north Russian breeding population. It should be noted that the Common Scoter is the only species of wildfowl occurring off the sandy coast of West Jutland. The shedding of the flight-feathers takes place in August and early in September. The birds frequent the zone of shallow water over sand, with a water depth of less than 10 m, usually less than 5 m, often just off the heavy surf.

The moult migration across Jutland takes place at sunset or during the night and passes at a considerable height. It is initiated as early as the middle of May by the one year old birds which have curtailed their spring migration to the northeast before reaching the breeding range. Some individuals probably move directly from the winter quarters to the moulting area. The immature birds are joined by the adult males from the beginning of July until the middle of August. In the last part of this period some adult females probably participate in the migration, but this has not been observed with certainty. The greater part of the moulting birds disappear in September or October, spreading in the surrounding waters or continuing the autumn migration to the English Channel or the Bay of Biscay.

It is not known whether some individuals make a return flight across Jutland to winter quarters in the Kattegat, but it is unlikely. During spring migration part of the population may perhaps cross Jutland on their way to Scandinavian-Russian breeding places but there are no certain records. On the other hand, in the early part of April many thousands daily pass the Skaw on migration northeast (Hansen and Christensen 1954), and it is probable, therefore, that the main spring migration passes north of Jutland, not across the country.

No other moulting areas of the Common Scoter are known except in Great Britain. According to Atkinson-Willes (1963) large congregations of moulting males have been recorded off east Scotland in late summer 'and others may be found elsewhere.' These birds are either of Icelandic origin, or constitute flocks which have continued the pre-moult migration from Jutland across the North Sea.

Velvet Scoter *Melanitta fusca* also spend the flightless period in Danish waters. Flocks of immature birds occur commonly in the coastal waters. They are most numerous in the southern Kattegat, in the Little Belt and in the western Limfjord, where they are particularly common in Løgstør Bredning (Fig. 2). A number of adult males join the immature birds in July and August, but quantitatively the moult migration of this species in Danish waters is much less pronounced and much more scattered than that of the Common Scoter. The adult females do not arrive until much later. I have examined flightless females obtained in the Little Belt and in the southern Kattegat in October. Part of the population remains in Danish waters in winter but many continue the migration to western Europe in November–December. The Velvet Scoter occurs only exceptionally along the western caost of Jutland.

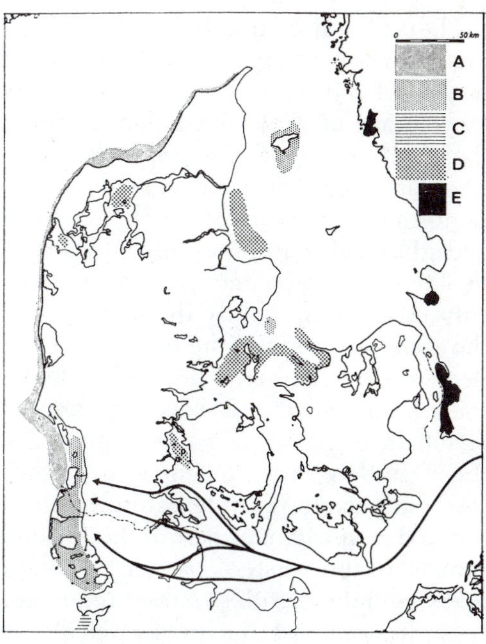

Fig. 2. Moulting areas of northern wildfowl in Danish waters. A, Common Scoter *Melanitta nigra.* B, Eider *Somateria mollissima.* C, Shelduck *Tadorna tadorna.* D, Velvet Scoter *Melanitta fusca.* E, Mute Swan *Cygnus olor.* The solid lines (with arrow-heads) indicate the most important migration routes for the species A, B, and C.

In the Eider *Somateria mollissima* the immature birds and males perform large-scale moult migrations to the Danish waters, where they collect in great numbers in a restricted area. The population of Bohuslän in western Sweden and, possibly, of southern Norway, gather in the Læsø area, particularly off the northeastern coast of this island. Large flocks are seen also off Hjelm Island further south in the Kattegat. The large population of the Baltic segregates in various moulting areas, situated off Gotland and along the coast of Estonia and Latvia. The majority, however, perform a moult migration south-west through Kalmar Sound (Svärdson 1959), across the southern parts of the Danish islands or just south of them, and across southern Jutland to the North Sea coast. Tens of thousands of birds spend the flightless period in the North Slesvig Waddensea, from Fanø and Rømø Islands south along the German coast (Fig. 2). The moult migration across Jutland takes place from the end of June until early August, usually following Flensburg Fjord westwards, i.e. somewhat further north than the main migration of the Common Scoter. However, flocks of Eider on moult migration have been met with frequently right from Eckernförde as far north as Åbenrå, incidentally the same area in which the Shelduck of the Baltic region move towards the moulting area in the Bay of Helgoland. Many ornithologists have observed the impressive east-to-west Eider migration across North Slesvig; I have personally once observed a single flock moving westward across southern Zealand.

The Eider migration across North Slesvig has been carefully followed and mapped by Behrends (1955, 1966). The movements take place predominantly in the evening hours, just as in the Shelduck and the Common Scoter, and are performed, primarily by immature birds and adult males, in June–July with a peak (3,300 observed in one evening) in early July. At the end of July the migration of the males ceases, and the immature birds decrease in number. The adult females then begin to arrive, reaching a peak (1,400 in one day) in early August, and the migration then soon comes to an end. Behrends made the interesting observation that a substantial part of the females remain in the western part of the Baltic and spend the flightless period there, i.e., they do not cross the peninsula of Jutland.

The more northern populations, which have undergone the wing-moult in the Baltic region proper, arrive in the southwestern Baltic Sea and the eastern fjords of North Slesvig in September–October during their ordinary autumn migration but do not continue across Jutland to the North Sea. The three migration peaks (early July, early August, and September-October) correspond exactly with those which have been demonstrated for the migration along the coast of Kalmar Sound in southern Sweden (Svärdson 1959).

The moult migration of the Eider in Scotland, recently studied by Milne (1965), is much smaller than that in the Danish waters, but agrees with it on certain points. The migration passes southwards along the east coast, but only over short distances, at most 100 km, and quite slowly. The females follow one month after the males and go through the wing-moult more rapidly than the latter. The males move further generally than the females. Immature birds do not have such a well-defined moulting area as the adult birds, but spread more evenly along the coast. The moult migration in Scotland is of the type B II, but the winter quarters are situated only about 50 km further to the south. The condition in Great Britain is thus interesting in demonstrating the moult migration in an initial stage.

The Eider performs a moult migration, to a greater or lesser degree, in other areas, i.e. in Canada, the White Sea and the Baltic Sea (Milne 1965) and probably elsewhere. In Greenland and Norway the extensive areas of rocky skerries along the coast furnish, evidently, sufficient food and satisfactory protection to the moulting birds and, as far as is known, the flightless period is everywhere spent within the breeding range of the population (type A II).

The autumn migration of the population which spends the flightless period in the Waddensea off Slesvig, has not been investigated. A fair proportion of the birds remain in the area in winter but the greater part, undoubtedly, move gradually further south into the German and Dutch Waddensea. These two groups must, then, have performed a moult migration of type C III and B III, respectively. The birds do not winter off the open North Sea coast of Jutland north of Skallingen Peninsula and the moulting population of the Waddensea has never been observed to return across Jutland in an eastward direction in order to spend the winter in the Kattegat area, nor is this likely. The great number of Eider wintering in these waters do not arrive until October–November, having performed the wing-moult somewhere else. Ringing has demonstrated that these birds mainly belong to the breeding populations of Bornholm and south-eastern Sweden (Salomonsen 1967).

The spring migration of the Waddensea birds appears to pass across Jutland, judging from the fact that they do not then pass the Skaw. There are some observations on flocks of Eider passing eastwards across the eastern Danish islands.

It appears from Fig. 2 that three species of ducks, differing considerably from each other in life habits and feeding biology, have divided the Danish North Sea coast between each other, using separate regions as moulting areas, the Shelduck in the Bay of Helgoland, the Eider in the Waddensea of Slesvig, and the Common Scoter off the west coast of Jutland. To these species should be added the other species which spend the flightless period in the eastern Danish waters, i.e., the Velvet Scoter and the Goldeneye (discussed below) in the Limfjord region and the southern Kattegat, the Mute Swan in the southern Sound and elsewhere, and the scattered flocks of Mallard in shallow water off the coasts of eastern Jutland, Zealand and other eastern islands as well as in freshwater lakes and marshes.

The King Eider *Somateria spectabilis*, which breeds in the high-arctic zone, performs a moult migration of an even more grandiose character (Fig. 3). The entire population (i.e. the immature birds and the adult males) of the greater part of arctic Canada, the Canadian Archipelago and North Greenland congregate in a comparatively restricted area of western Greenland, extending from the southern Upernavik District southwards to Egedesminde District, with a maximum density in the Disko Bay. The males leave the brooding females early and by the first week of July the first have arrived in the moulting area. This is only about three weeks after the last breeding pairs passed on the northward spring migration. During the moult migration the males may move north or south of Baffin Island, but the majority cross through the mountain passes in the middle of the island, south of the ice-cap. In the latter half of July flock after flock numbering hundreds of birds, all adult males, flew in a north-eastern direction from Clyde Inlet, often at a height of 1,000–1,200 m (Wynne-Edwards 1952). The number of King Eider in the moulting area reaches a peak in early August when some hundred thousand individuals are gathered there. This figure includes the immature birds, of which part move directly to the moulting area from the winter quarters. Others approach the breeding range, but interrupt the migration and return to the moulting area early in summer (June).

After the flightless period, in September–October, the King Eider begin the autumn migration which leads due south along the west coast of Greenland to the ice-free coasts of SW. Greenland, to Labrador and Newfoundland. This implies that the Canadian population changes the flight direction from east (during moult migration) to south (during autumn migration), demonstrating that the moult migration, at least that of the adult males, belongs to the type D III.

When previously describing the tremendous concentrations of King Eider in the moulting area in West Greenland (Salomonsen 1950*b*) I advanced the opinion, for several reasons, that the majority of these birds must originate in Canada. The correctness of my assumption has now been proved by the extensive ringing of flightless King Eider in West Greenland, carried out in recent years under my direction. The recoveries in the breeding places are shown in Fig. 3. The birds breeding farthest to the west must migrate about 2,500 km before reaching the moulting area in Greenland.

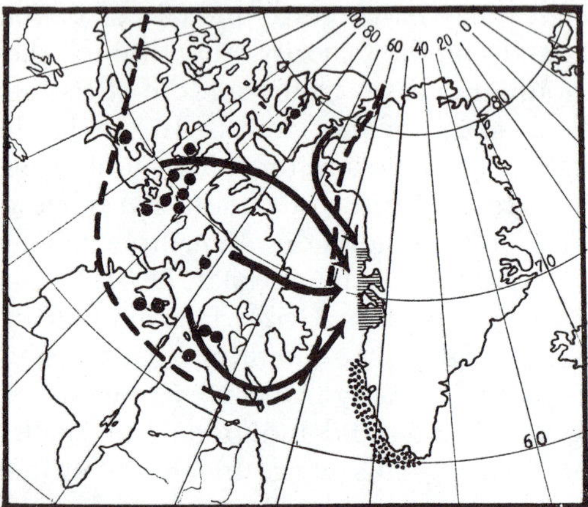

Fig. 3. Moult migration of King Eider *Somateria spectabilis* in Canada and Greenland. From the breeding area within the dashed line males and non-breeders move along the routes indicated by solid lines (with arrow-heads) to moulting area (horizontally hatched). Solid circles give localities for recoveries in the breeding places (not in the winter quarters) of individuals ringed when flightless in the moulting area in West Greenland. The dotted area represents the winter quarters.

The adult females do not participate in the moult migration to West Greenland, where they occur in the area only exceptionally. Some of the females, however, perform a separate moult migration which takes place later than in the males and does not go so far. In the middle of August 1934 Dalgety (1936) observed thousands of females in Clyde Inlet where they probably intended to spend the flightless period. This resembles the situation in the Common Eider in Slesvig, where at least some of the females halted their moult migration on the east coast of Jutland.

The males of the King Eider must possess a strong urge to leave the high-arctic region before they lose the power of flight. Being marine birds they cannot fly southwards into the interior of America, but must choose to fly either eastwards or westwards from the Canadian breeding places to reach low-arctic regions where they do not risk being overtaken by the new ice in the flightless stage. The nearest low-arctic area is central West Greenland and the Bering Sea, respectively. The ringing recoveries have demonstrated that the migratory divide between the two diametrically opposite movements (to W. Greenland and the Bering Sea) is situated near Victoria Island, exactly the geographical centre between W. Greenland and the Bering Sea. This shows that selection for the most appropriate (i.e. the shortest) route of moult migration has operated very precisely. The moult migration of the western population, which moves to the Bering region, has long been known as a spectacular phenomenon at Point Barrow in Alaska, but the position of the moulting area is unknown. It is probable that it is situated on the Soviet side of the Bering Strait.

Evidently there is a similar migratory divide in Siberia, the immature birds in particular collecting in enormous numbers in easternmost Siberia and near Kolguyev in north Russia, respectively (Portenko 1959), but the phenomenon has not been closely studied.

Steller's Eider *Polysticta stelleri*, breeding in high-arctic east Siberia and west Alaska, winters in a comparatively restricted area at the easternmost Aleutian Islands and the outer (western) part of Alaska Peninsula. It arrives there usually as early as August and immediately begins the wing-moult, i.e. it spends the flightless period in the winter quarters (type C III). It resembles the King Eider in congregating in enormous flocks, amounting to some hundred thousand individuals, within a restricted area. Ringing of flightless birds has been carried out also in this species (Jones 1965) and recoveries have demonstrated that the majority of the birds originate from the east Siberian polar coast, westwards to the Lena delta which is situated 3,200 km away. In unfavourable summers, when the breeding cycle is delayed, the moult migration is also postponed. The birds are then unable to reach the usual moulting area and are forced to perform the wing-moult at some (unknown) place en route (type B II or B III). In such years they do not arrive in the winter quarters until November (Jones 1965). A variation of this kind is not found in the King Eider in Greenland, and is altogether unknown in other species of ducks with large and compact aggregates of moulting birds. According to Jones both males and females participate in the moult migration and arrive simultaneously at the moulting area, although in separate flocks. The males, therefore, are probably not dependent on the females in their moult migration. It is incomprehensible to me, however, how the adult females can arrive in the moulting area as early as August. Jones does not mention the presence of immature birds and may probably have confused females with immature birds.

Evidently the Goldeneye *Bucephala clangula* has developed a moult migration but our knowledge about it is very fragmentary. Large flocks of males are known to gather and moult in the Matsalu National Park in Estonia (Kumari 1962) and a smaller number is known to spend the flightless period in Lake Tåkern in Sweden (Lönnberg 1935). In Denmark, which is situated much to the south of the Goldeneye's breeding range, one year old birds are commonly present from May to August in the Limfjord region in northern Jutland, frequenting the shallow brackish water of the coasts of the fjord as well as nearby fresh-water lakes. The Goldeneye is a numerous winter visitor in this area, and the young birds are probably remaining in the winter quarters through the subsequent summer, performing the wing-moult there without making any migrations. Certainly flightless specimens have been obtained in July and August. Adult females arrive in the Limfjord in September and a number of flightless individuals have been obtained there (Schiøler 1926). The scanty information available indicates that the moult migration of the males belongs to type B II, that of the females and immature birds to C I and C II. Apparently this species does not usually gather in large aggregates in the moulting areas.

The Long-tailed Duck *Clangula hyemalis* is a circumpolar species, breeding in the entire arctic zone. Everywhere in its breeding range this species is known to moult the flight-feathers in the breeding area proper, either solitarily (A I) or in small flocks (A II). Strangely enough the east Siberian population differs from this general pattern. Non-breeding birds, i.e. the males joined by the immature non-breeders, from Anadyr Land and the Tchuktch Peninsula perform an extensive northward moult migration across the Arctic Ocean to Wrangel Island where they gather in thousands although the species does not breed there (Portenko 1959). It has been mentioned already that this big island also forms an important moulting area for the Brent Goose.

CONCLUDING REMARKS

The description above has shown that the moult migration differs widely in the wildfowl. Within each tribe, however, the migration pattern is basically similar, at any rate as far as the participation of the sex and age groups is concerned. The migration pattern, therefore, can be used as an additional taxonomic character (Table 1).

It is a common character in most species of ducks (not geese) with a separate moult migration that the individuals

Table 1. Participation in moult migration according to sex and age. xx: all individuals of group in question participate. x: only a small fraction of group in question participates.

	Adult males	Adult females	Immature birds
Anserini			xx
Tadornini	xx	xx	xx
Anatini[1]	xx		
Aythyini	xx	x	
Somateriini[2]	xx	x	xx
Mergini[2]	xx	x	xx

[1] Only the Wigeon has a tendency to moult migration in immature birds.
[2] These two tribes have been united in many recent studies, for example by Johnsgard (1960).

gather in moulting areas which have a milder climate than the breeding areas. In some cases they even perform the wing-moult in the winter quarters. It has been mentioned already that the high-arctic King Eider has a low-arctic moulting area, and the same holds good for the high-arctic Steller's Eider. The low-arctic and north-boreal species, such as Common Scoter, Velvet Scoter and Eider, move to south-boreal (temperate) moulting areas, and the same holds good for various dabbling ducks. Only the Mute Swan, the Shelduck and the Red-crested Pochard, which as breeding birds belong mainly to the south-boreal zone, have their moulting areas in Europe situated in the same climatic zone. Apparently in these southern latitudes, with a milder climate, the necessity for moult migration is not so pronounced. Most species of wildfowl moult here in the breeding place proper or in its near vicinity. It also appears to be a general rule that stationary populations do not have any moult migration either. This may explain the fact that, so far as is known, no tropical species have developed a moult migration.

The moulting area is not always the first climatically suitable to be passed by the population during its post-nuptial migration. Traditions, historic factors or other circumstances may have caused it to be placed in areas which are further removed from the breeding area than appears to be necessary. The choice of moulting area is to a considerable degree dependent on the suitability of the locality and on biotic factors, primarily on peace from predators (foxes, man). The water depth is highly significant, for dabbling ducks as well as for diving ducks; the latter evidently has the capability of diving considerably reduced in the flightless stage. Extensive areas of shallow water, rich in food, and difficult of access or with good cover constitute the optimal conditions.

Some tendencies towards a development of moult migration are found also in other groups of birds made vulnerable by a simultaneous loss of flight-feathers. In all other groups than wildfowl it appears, however, to be developed only to a slight degree and in most species it awaits further study. The phenomenon is best known in the Coot, both the European species *Fulica atra* and the North American one *F. americana*. It has been noticed in many places (also in Denmark) that in certain suitable lakes the number of Coot increases in the summer time, and large flocks are known to congregate and spend the flightless period in places like Delta, Manitoba (Hochbaum 1955), and Ismaninger in Germany (Bezzel 1964). At the latter locality also the Water Rail *Rallus aquaticus* and probably even the Little Crake *Porzana parva* collect in order to perform the wing-moult. Apparently grebes *Podicipedes* sometimes have a moult migration, but only to a slight degree and not yet demonstrated with certainty. Savage (1964) observed that small flocks of Flamingo *Phoenicopterus ruber* spent the flightless period, in early September, in the salt Lake Rezaiyeh in north Iran, where they evidently did not breed. Elsewhere flamingos appear to moult the flight-feathers near the breeding place just before or after the breeding period. A most interesting case of moult migration in the Crane *Grus grus* has recently come to light. During a visit in May 1962 to the salt Lake Selety-Tengis, in Kazakstan, Gavrin observed a flock of about 3,500 flightless individuals, probably constituting birds which did not breed that year (Cuisin 1966, Stresemann 1967). Cranes apparently do not breed each year and perform a moult of the flight-feathers only in those years in which they do not breed. Gavrin's observation is the only known record of wing-moult in the Crane in the field (outside zoos) and this species must be extremely secretive during the flightless period.

Moult migration is definitely not developed in divers Gaviae and in auks Alcae. The latter may sometimes perform the autumn migration in the flightless stage, swimming very large distances, which in the case of Brünnich's Guillemot *Uria lomvia* off West Greenland may be more than 1,000 km (Salomonsen 1967).

Birds with a gradual replacement of the flight-feathers do not perform moult migrations in the way that has been defined above. Nevertheless, some shore birds with extensive migrations divide the autumn migration into two parts separated by a resting period during which the wing-moult takes place in a definite moulting area. This parallels the situation in many species of wildfowl. Such a moult migration has been described only in one species, the Wood Sandpiper *Tringa glareola,* but it is undoubtedly developed similarly in some other related species, at least in the genus *Tringa.* The northern European breeding Wood Sandpipers leave the breeding area during high summer, usually in the latter part of July, and move in a non-stop flight southwards to southern Europe, for example the Camargue, where they temporarily interrupt the migration and, during a long resting period, perform the wing-moult before they start on the actual autumn migration to tropical Africa (Hoffmann 1957).

The moult migration is still imperfectly known and there is in most species much to be done before it is properly understood. The present review may, I hope, encourage further study of this interesting biological phenomenon.

LITERATURE CITED

ATKINSON-WILLES, G. L., editor. 1963. Wildfowl in Great Britain. London: H.M.S.O.

BANKO, W. E. 1960. The Trumpeter Swan. Its history, habits and population in the United States. Washington, D.C.

BEHRENDS, O. 1955. Maritimt sommertræk over det østlige Sønderjylland. Flora og Fauna 61:1–16.

———. 1966. Om ederfuglenes (*Somateria mollissima* (L.)) sommertræk over Sønderjylland. Flora og Fauna 72:101–104.

BELLROSE, F. C. 1963. Orientation behavior of four species of wildfowl. Auk 80:257–289.

BEZZEL, E. 1964. Zur Okologie der Brutmauser bei Enten. Anz. Ornith. Ges. Bayern 7:43–79.

BRUUN, B., AND O. SCHELDE. 1957. The autumn migration at Stigsnæs, S.W. Zealand. Dansk Ornith. Foren. Tidsskr. 51:149–167. (Danish, with English summary)

CHABRECK, R. H. 1966. Molting Gadwall (*Anas strepera*) in Louisiana. Auk 83:664.

CHRISTENSEN, N. H. 1967. Moult migration of Pink-footed Goose (*Anser fabalis brachyrhynchus* Baillon) from Iceland to Greenland. Dansk Ornith. Foren. Tidsskr. 61:56–66.

COOCH, G. 1957. Mass ringing of flightless Blue and Lesser Snow Geese in Canada's Eastern Arctic. Wildfowl Trust Ann. Rep. 8:58–67.

COOMBES, R. A. H. 1950. The moult-migration of the Sheld-duck. Ibis 92:405–418.

CUISIN, M. 1966. Les oiseaux-gibier du Kazakhstan (faunistique, écologie, valeur économique). (Review.) L'Oiseau 36:292.

DALGETY, C. T. 1936. Notes on birds observed in Greenland and Baffin Land. Ibis 13(3):580–591.

DENNIS, R. H. 1964. Capture of moulting Canada Geese in the Beauly Firth. Wildfowl Trust Ann. Rep. 15:71–74.

EKMAN, S. 1922. Djurvärldens utbredningshistoria på skandinaviska halvön. Stockholm.

ELTRINGHAM, S. K., AND H. BOYD. 1960. The Shelduck population in the Bridgwater Bay moulting area. Wildfowl Trust Ann. Rep. 11:107–117.

GOETHE, F. 1957. Uber den Mauserzug der Brandenten (*Tadorna tadorna* L.) zum Grossen Knechtsand. *In* Meise, W., ed., Fünfzig Jahre Seevogelschutz (pp. 96–106). Hamburg.

———. 1961*a*. A survey of moulting Shelduck on Knechtsand. Brit. Birds 54:106–115.

———. 1961*b*. The moult gatherings and moult migrations of Shelduck in north-west Germany. Brit. Birds 54:145–161.

HANSEN, E., AND N. H. CHRISTENSEN. 1954. The spring-migration at the Skaw. Dansk Ornith. Foren. Tidsskr. 48:156–172. (Danish, with English summary)

HANSON, H. C. 1965. The Giant Canada Goose. Carbondale, Illinois.

HOCHBAUM, H. A. 1955. Travels and traditions of waterfowl. Minneapolis.

HOFFMANN, L. 1957. Le passage d'automne du Chevalier sylvain (*Tringa glareola*) en France méditerranéenne. Alauda 25:30–42.

HOOGERHEIDE, J., AND W. K. KRAAK. 1942. Voorkomen en trek von de Bergeend, *Tadorna tadorna* (L.), naar aanleiding van veldobservaties aan de Gooije kust. Ardea 31:1–19.

JOENSEN, A. H. 1964. An investigation of the moulting areas of the Common Scoter (*Melanitta nigra*) at the south-west coast of Jutland, Denmark, 1963. Dansk Ornith. Foren. Tidsskr. 58:127–136. (Danish, with English summary)

JOHANSEN, H. 1945. Races of Bean-Geese. Dansk Ornith. Foren. Tidsskr. 39:106–127. (Danish, with English summary)

JOHNSGARD, P. A. 1960. Classification and evolutionary relationships of the sea ducks. Condor 62:426–433.

JONES, R. D., JR. 1965. Returns from Steller's Eiders banded in Izembek Bay. Wildfowl Trust Ann. Rep. 16:83–85.

JØRGENSEN, J. 1941. Sortandens (*Melanitta nigra*) Juli-Augusttræk. Dansk Ornith. Foren. Tidsskr. 35:137–143.

KUMARI, E. 1962. The wildfowl in the Matsalu National Park. Wildfowl Trust Ann. Rep. 13:109–116.

KUYT, E. 1962. Northward dispersion of banded Canada Geese. Canad. Field Nat. 76:180–181.

LEBRET, T. 1950. The sex-ratios and the proportion of adult drakes of Teal, Pintail, Shoveler and Wigeon in the Netherlands, based on field counts made during autumn, winter and spring. Ardea 38:1–18.

———. 1952. Pre-moult migration of a female Gadwall, *Anas strepera* L., and two female Wigeon, *Anas penelope* L. Ardea 40:75–76.

LIND, H. 1957. A study of the movements of the Sheld-Duck (*Tadorna tadorna* (L.)). Dansk Ornith. Foren. Tidsskr. 51:85–114. (Danish, with English summary)

LØNNBERG, E. 1935. Svenska jåglars flyttning. Stockholm.

MATHIASSON, S. 1963. Untersuchungen über jährliche Fluktuationen nichtbrütender Höckerschwäne, *Cygnus olor* (Gm.) in Schonen, Südschweden. Lunds Univ. Årsskr. N. F. Avd. 2. 58. Nr. 13.

———. 1964. Ett bidrag till kännedomen om knölsvanens, *Cygnus olor*, ruggningsansamlingar i Sverige. Göteborgs Naturhist. Mus. Årstryck 1964:15–19.

MATTHEWS, G. V. T. 1963. 'Nonsense' orientation as a population variant. Ibis 105:185–197.

———, J. A. EYGENRAAM, AND L. HOFFMANN. 1963. Initial direction tendencies in the European Green-winged Teal. Wildfowl Trust Ann. Rep. 14:120–123.

MAYAUD, N. 1966. Contribution a l'histoire de *Netta rufina* (Pallas), La Nette a Huppe rousse en Europe occidentale. Alauda 34:191–199.

MILNE, H. 1965. Seasonal movements and distribution of Eiders in northeast Scotland. Bird Study 12:170–180.

ORING, L. W. 1964. Behavior and ecology of certain ducks during the post-breeding period. J. Wildl. Mgmt. 28:223–233.

OTTOW, B. 1956. Ergebnisse der Vogelberingung in Sowjetrussland. (Review.) Vogelwarte 18:226–230.

PALM, B. 1950. The migration of Teal (*Anas crecca* L.) in Denmark. Dansk Ornith. Foren. Tidsskr. 44:147–150. (Danish, with English summary)

PALUDAN, K. 1965. Migration and moult-migration of *Anser anser*. Danske Vildtundersøgelser 12:1–54. (Danish, with English summary)

PLESKE, T. 1928. Birds of the Eurasian Tundra. Mem. Boston Soc. Nat. Hist. 6:111–485.

PORTENKO, L. A. 1959. Peculiarities of bird-migration in the Arctic. Aquila 66:119–134. (Hungarian, with English summary)

PREUSS, N. O. 1965. The migration of Danish Red-crested Pochards (*Netta rufina* (Pallas)). Dansk Ornith. Foren. Tidsskr. 59:38–40. (Danish, with English summary)

SALOMONSEN, F. 1943. Grågæssene (*Anser anser* (L.)) på Vejlerne. Dansk Ornith. Foren. Tidsskr. 37:188–189.

———. 1950*a*. Common Scoters (*Melanitta nigra* (L.)) summering off the west-coast of Jutland. Dansk Ornith. Foren. Tidsskr. 44:171–172. (Danish, with English summary)

———. 1950*b*. The birds of Greenland. Copenhagen: Ejnar Munksgaard.

———. 1955. The evolutionary significance of bird-migration. Dan. Biol. Medd. 22, No. 6:1–62.

———. 1967. Fugletrækket og dets gåder. 2nd ed. Copenhagen.

SAVAGE, C. 1964. Lake Rezaiyeh: a specialised

summer habitat for Shelduck and Flamingos. Wildfowl Trust Ann. Rep. 15:108–113.

SCHIØLER, E. L. 1925. Danmarks Fugle. Vol. 1. Indledning og Andefugle (*Anseriformes*). Copenhagen.

———. 1926. Danmarks Fugle. Vol. 2. Oversigt over Grønlands Fugle og Andefugle (*Anseriformes*) II, Dykænder (*Fuligulinae*). Copenhagen.

SCOTT, P. 1951. The Perry River Expedition, 1949. Wildfowl Trust Ann. Rep. 3:56–64.

———, AND J. FISHER. 1953. A thousand geese. London.

STIRLING, T., AND A. DZUBIN. 1967. Canada Goose molt migrations to the North-west Territories. Trans. N. Amer. Wildlife & Nat. Res. Conf. 31:355–373.

STRESEMANN, E. 1940. Zeitpunkt und Verlauf der Mauser bei einigen Entenarten. Journ. Ornith. 88:288–333.

———. 1967. Ein sammelplatz mausernder Kraniche (*Grus grus*). Journ. Ornith. 108:81–82.

SVARDSON, G. 1959. Sjöfågelsträcket i Kalmarsund 1958. Svensk Jakt. 97:128–130.

SZIJJ, J. 1965. Okologische Untersuchungen an Entenvögeln (Anatidae) des Ermatinger Beckens (Bodensee). Vogelwarte 23:24–71.

TAYLOR, J. 1953. A possible moult-migration of Pink-footed Geese. Ibis 95:638–642.

TEPLOV, V. F., AND N. N. KARTASHEV. 1958. Wildfowl research in Russia. Biological Foundations for the regulation of wildfowling in the central districts of the European part of the U.S.S.R. Wildfowl Trust Ann. Rep. 9:157–169.

USPENSKI, S. M. 1960. The Brent Goose (*Branta bernicla* L.) in the Soviet Union. Wildfowl Trust Ann. Rep. 11:80–93.

———. 1965*a*. Die Wildgänse Nordeurasiens. Wittenberg Lutherstadt.

———. 1965*b*. The geese of Wrangel Island. Wildfowl Trust Ann. Rep. 16:126–129.

VUCZETICS, V., AND A. TUGARINOV. 1937–39. Seasonal distribution and migration of ducks (subfam. Anatinae) on the base of bird ringing in the U.S.S.R. Moscow. (Quoted after Stresemann, E. 1940)

WEISMANN, C. 1931. Vildtets og Jagtens Historie i Danmark. Copenhagen.

WOLFF, W. J. 1966. Migration of Teal ringed in the Netherlands. Ardea 54:230–270.

WYNNE-EDWARDS, V. C. 1952. Zoology of the Baird Expedition (1950). I. The birds observed in Central and South-East Baffin Island. Auk 69:353–391.

———. 1962. Animal dispersion in relation to social behaviour. Edinburgh and London.

ZINK, G. 1964. Ein ungelöstes Rätsel: der Herbstzug der Kolbenente. Kosmos 1964:134–136.

WATERFOWL MIGRATION CORRIDORS EAST OF THE ROCKY MOUNTAINS IN THE UNITED STATES[1,2]

FRANK C. BELLROSE, Section of Wildlife Research, Illinois Natural History Survey, Havana, IL 62644

It has been over three decades since Frederick Lincoln (1935) defined and mapped the four waterfowl flyways of North America. Since then maps of the flyways with their attendant routes have been published innumerable times, in most instances almost without modification from the original presentation. Lincoln based his flyway maps entirely upon data resulting from bandings of waterfowl before 1935.

Although a tremendous amount of banding data has been obtained since Lincoln initially mapped the waterfowl flyways of North America, no attempt has been made to update the maps of routes within the flyways. Numerous papers showing waterfowl bands recovered from bandings of particular species in given states have provided evidence that flyway routes as outlined by Lincoln are in need of revision.

Recently I was requested to prepare a report, *Establishing Certain Parameters of Hazards to Aircraft by Migrating Birds in the Mississippi Flyway,* for the Bureau of Sport Fisheries and Wildlife (Bellrose 1967). Part of the report was devoted to establishing the migration paths of waterfowl within the Mississippi Flyway and across this flyway to the Atlantic Coast. Waterfowl biologists who saw various drafts of the maps suggested improvements and extensions of the regions covered. Consequently, this project grew to include all areas of the United States east of the Rocky Mountains.

The greatest quantity of available data pertained to the Mississippi Flyway, and next largest quantity to the Atlantic Flyway, and the smallest quantity to the Central Flyway. Therefore, I believe the material is likewise most sound for the Mississippi Flyway, next for the Atlantic, and least sound for the Central Flyway.

The maps represent an attempt to show myriads of migration paths with clarity. A presentation of all the details available on the flight routes of waterfowl would result in maps either approaching incomprehensibility or drawn on such a large scale as to limit reproduction.

I prefer to refer to the mapped patterns of waterfowl movement as "flight corridors" rather than routes. I believe a route represents a path only a mile or two wide which waterfowl follow consistently from year to year. Each corridor, on the other hand, consists of a web of routes, some of which may cross or crisscross within a single flight corridor. The corridors do not have sharp boundaries; rather there may be gradual changes from the center of a flight corridor to its margins in the numbers of waterfowl using it. If the adjacent corridor has a greater abundance of waterfowl, then the number of birds increases from the center toward the margin. On the other hand, if the adjacent corridor has fewer birds, the number decreases from the center to the periphery.

Because numerous sources of data which had no common denominator were used, the presentations of flight corridors

---

[1] Originally published as Illinois Natural History Survey Biological Notes, No. 61. 24pp., 1968.

[2] This paper is published by authority of the State of Illinois, IRS Ch. 127, Par. 58.12, and is a contribution from the Section of Wildlife Research of the Illinois Natural History Survey. Frank C. Bellrose is a Survey Wildlife Specialist.

are my interpretation of the available data. Unquestionably the maps can be improved as more information becomes available. Therefore, this paper is presented as an interim report. A detailed analysis of the findings on bird migration from radar surveillance is in preparation.

METHODS

This paper is based upon seven kinds of information sources from which waterfowl migration patterns and magnitudes of passage were deduced:

1) recoveries of bands from waterfowl;
2) visual sightings of waterfowl in migration by ground observers;
3) visual sightings of waterfowl in migration from light aircraft;
4) radar surveillance of waterfowl in migration;
5) periodic waterfowl censuses conducted in Illinois, 1938–66; in all states of the Mississippi Flyway, 1954–56; and in several states of the flyway, 1954–66;
6) reports on the annual winter inventory of waterfowl by states in the Atlantic, Mississippi, and Central flyways, 1960–66;
7) review of the material prepared for this report and consequent suggestions for improvement by the Technical Committee of the Mississippi Flyway Council and by waterfowl biologists in the Atlantic and Central flyways.

Band Recoveries

Band recovery data are the most important information source from which to deduce waterfowl migration patterns, because these data are more extensive than other kinds and deal with identifiable population elements. The principal disadvantage in using band data for this purpose is that they are discontinuous; that is, recoveries occur in relation to the distribution of hunting areas and numbers of hunters. Frequently waterfowl stop in tremendous numbers on large water areas, such as Lake Michigan, where there is little or no hunting. Other waterfowl cross nonstop over hundreds of miles of terrain devoid of suitable habitat, such as the Appalachian Mountains. Moreover, bands attached to ducks at a northern station and recovered far down the flyway do not necessarily show the deviations from a straight line which the birds may have taken to reach the point of recovery. Nevertheless, in this paper the judicious interpretation of band data forms the principal base for determining the migration paths of waterfowl.

Often a point of confusion in using waterfowl banding data per se to map migration paths arises from a wide dispersal of recoveries. This occurs for some species more frequently than for others. In this respect redheads, lesser scaups, and canvasbacks are most notorious among ducks; however, even such a strong homing species as the Canada goose has been banded in one flyway and later killed in another. This creates the impression that some species of waterfowl do not move along well defined routes of migration but scatter over broad regions of the continent.

However, I believe that these "misplaced" waterfowl have indeed migrated along well defined routes of travel for the species. It seems apparent that the transfer of individuals from one flight route to another within a flyway or to routes in other flyways occurs because they are carried along by larger assemblages of migrating waterfowl. Especially on the breeding grounds, where waterfowl gather on staging areas before departing in migration, it is likely that birds which ordinarily use a given flyway route may be captivated by a flock or assemblage of birds using a different route.

Anyone who has watched departing flocks of migrating waterfowl and flocks in actual migration is aware of the diversity of orientations among members of some flocks. Small groups may break away from large groups and head in entirely different directions, or they may separate from large flocks only to recombine and continue in one direction. This separating and sometimes recombining among migrating flocks of waterfowl suggests to me that one population element may at times influence the migration behavior of other elements. When flocks combine into migratory assemblages on staging areas, a small segment of a population may change flight routes and even flyways, thus accounting for a wider dispersal of bands than would seem warranted by the distribution of flight routes.

Both published and unpublished material on recoveries of bands attached to waterfowl were carefully reviewed. In addition, I analyzed band recoveries from over 100,000 mallards at five locations in Illinois and those made at the Squaw Creek National Wildlife Refuge in northwest Missouri. Band recovery data on Canada geese recently compiled by the Migratory Bird Population Center, Bureau of Sport Fisheries and Wildlife, were also examined.

Visual Sightings by Ground Observers

For the past 10 years the Technical Committee of the Mississippi Flyway Council has assisted me in recording the visual sightings of waterfowl throughout the flyway. During a 20-year period with the assistance of numerous cooperators I have recorded the passage of waterfowl through Illinois.

Visual sightings reveal details of diurnal flight routes not evident from banding analysis. They are especially useful in determining routes used by Canada and blue and lesser snow geese, species which migrate diurnally more often than do most other species of waterfowl.

Visual Sightings from Aircraft

From a light aircraft I have observed flocks of ducks and geese in migration on numerous occasions during the 20 years I have been making weekly censuses of waterfowl in Illinois. On several occasions I have followed migrating flocks of ducks and geese for over 50 miles.

Many pilots, particularly of light aircraft, report migrating flocks of waterfowl to the nearest FAA station. These reports, called Pireps, are sent by teletype to other stations on the regional circuit. For 5 years I have collected Pireps on waterfowl sightings in the north-central United States as received by the FAA station at Burlington, Iowa. These reports are most valuable for plotting the lines of flight of Canada and blue and snow geese and, to a lesser extent, ducks.

Actually following migrating flocks of waterfowl with a light airplane provides details of flight routes used more precisely than other methods described here. I have used this procedure on numerous occasions in Illinois.

Radar Surveillance

Radar surveillance of waterfowl migration proved to be valuable in determining the direction and magnitude of movement. Because radar can "see" at night and through clouds not laden with water droplets, it provided information obtainable by no other technique. The princi-

Fig. 1. Locations of U.S. Weather Bureau and Illinois Natural History Survey radar stations used in obtaining data on waterfowl migration corridors.

pal disadvantages of radar are that it rarely allows the observer to identify waterfowl species, and the records are geographically discontinuous.

Dr. Richard Graber and I employed an APS-42A radar at Havana and Champaign, Ill., and a mobile unit in Illinois, Indiana, Iowa, and Missouri during the waterfowl migration periods, 1960–64. In addition I had the cooperation (1963–65) of U.S. Weather Bureau WSR-57 radar surveillance of waterfowl migrations at 27 stations (Fig. 1).

The Illinois Natural History Survey's small radar provided a window on the passage of waterfowl which extended only 4 miles, but WSR-57 radar furnished a window on waterfowl passage that usually extended 40 miles and occasionally up to 100 miles.

Periodic Waterfowl Censuses

Estimates of waterfowl populations were made periodically throughout the Mississippi Flyway during the autumn, 1954–56, under the coordination of the Technical Committee of the Mississippi Flyway Council. In Illinois I have made waterfowl censuses from a light aircraft over much of the state, 1946–66. Several states, notably Missouri, Tennessee, and Louisiana, have made periodic waterfowl censuses from 1954 through 1966.

Data on the distribution of waterfowl populations within these states provided information from which to deduce much about the magnitudes of waterfowl migrations.

Winter Inventory

The distributions of waterfowl populations at the time of the winter inventories in early January provided information on the ultimate destinations of waterfowl moving through the Mississippi, Atlantic, and Central flyways during the fall migration. The sizes of the various waterfowl population elements on wintering areas compared with the sizes of the same population elements on important migration areas provided the principal means of determining the magnitudes of movement along the migration corridors.

Review of Material

The Technical Committee of the Mississippi Flyway Council has twice reviewed late "editions" of the flyway maps. Some representatives of the Atlantic and Central flyway committees have also reviewed them, as has the Migratory Bird Population Center of the Bureau of Sport Fisheries and Wildlife.

Besides these groups, a host of persons—refuge managers, game agents, game biologists—have reviewed various drafts of the maps and have made numerous suggestions toward improving their validity.

Species Groupings

The most meaningful presentations of waterfowl migrations were obtained by using four categories: dabbling ducks, diving ducks, Canada geese, and blue and lesser snow geese.

Migration corridors used by diving ducks are quite distinct from the corridors used by dabbling ducks. Therefore, I have separated these two groups. Flight corridors of Canada geese are in some regions nearly the same as but in other regions quite distinct from those of the blue and snow geese, and so they are shown separately.

I considered showing separate flight corridors for each of the more numerous species of ducks, but there are many similarities in their migration corridors among those species of dabbling ducks and among those species of diving ducks whose breeding grounds are on the northern Great Plains. The eastern-breeding black duck is an exception, but its migration corridors are so distinct as to be evident on the map for dabbling ducks. It appeared more practical to group species of dabbling ducks and to group diving ducks than to present each species separately. Important differences in the movements of species within the two groups are discussed in the text.

Population Estimates

Three types of population figures were used to estimate the magnitudes of waterfowl passage.

1) Figures presented for populations heading south down the flyways into the United States are based upon win-

ter inventory data, 1959–66, to which 25 percent has been added to compensate for hunting and other mortality.

2) Peak population figures at rest areas along each corridor are the averages of maximum numbers of waterfowl observed during the fall over a period of years. Because of migration turnover, peak populations of waterfowl usually represent only from one-fourth to one-half of the numbers of waterfowl actually passing through an area.
3) Based upon the distribution of waterfowl habitats and known waterfowl concentrations, the winter inventory data for each state, 1960–66, were broken down by regions of the state so that the population densities of migration corridors could be indicated as precisely as possible.

All population data should be considered relative rather than definitive. Population data are only approximations of species abundance in the various migration corridors. Maps of migration corridors are based upon population densities and species composition.

FALL MIGRATION PATTERNS

In the past decade duck populations have been depressed by drought and unseasonable temperatures on the breeding grounds. Mallards and pintails have suffered more than other species. Yet, each fall, 1960–66, about 17,500,000 ducks, excluding the blue-winged teal and the sea ducks, have migrated down flight corridors in the United States east of the Rocky Mountains. The largest portion, about 12,275,000, entered the geographical confines of the Mississippi Flyway from the northern Great Plains, and 2,475,000 of them continued across the Mississippi Flyway to the Atlantic Flyway. Almost 4,500,000 ducks moved south along corridors terminating on wintering grounds of the Central Flyway.

Although most of these ducks originated their southward passage from the northern Great Plains, many started in the Yukon and the Northwest Territories of Canada and some even in Alaska. In addition to the nearly 17,000,000 ducks migrating from or through the northern Great Plains, about 650,000 black ducks moved south from Ontario, Quebec, New Brunswick, and northern states from Wisconsin eastward.

In spite of their depressed populations mallards and pintails made up half of the typical fall flight, with mallards composing about 40 percent. Scaups, the most abundant of the diving ducks, composed about 15 percent of the usual fall flight in the three flyways.

Because flight corridors used by ducks often transcend flyways, I have found it expedient to discuss the passage of each group of ducks from breeding grounds to wintering grounds according to the migration corridors they use. The discussion begins with the westernmost corridors, because of their proximity to the breeding ground, and proceeds eastward. The flight corridors of geese, however, are discussed from east to west.

Dabbling Ducks

Western Plains Corridor.—The westernmost migration corridor for dabbling ducks that breed on the Great Plains commences in eastern Alberta and western Saskatchewan (Fig. 2). It slopes south-southeast along the eastern edge of the Rocky Mountains to the lower Texas coast and the northern portion of the gulf coast of Mexico. It might be termed the Western Plains Corridor.

An approximation of the dabbling

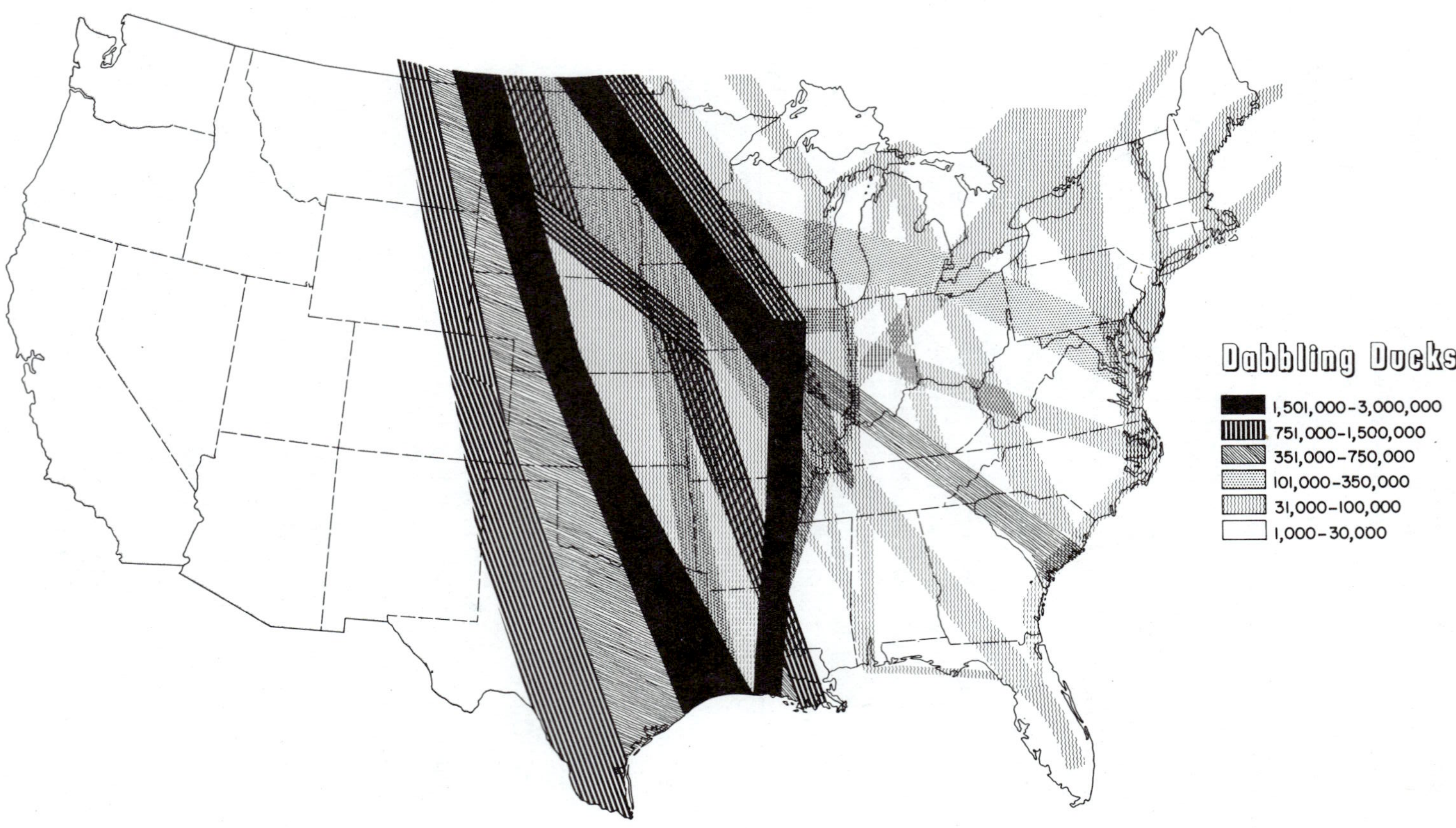

Fig. 2. The migration corridors used by dabbling ducks during their fall migrations.

ducks using this corridor is 1,500,000, made up as follows: mallards, 550,000; pintails, 450,000; baldpates, 200,000; green-winged teals, 125,000; gadwalls, 90,000; and shovelers, 30,000.

Some mallards winter almost at the northern end of this corridor near Malta, Mont., where usually about 2,000 stay during the cold months. Up to 15,000 mallards also winter along the Yellowstone River of Montana where it runs through this corridor and on east into the next one. One hundred thousand mallards winter just east of the Front Range in northern Colorado, with an additional 30,000 along the Arkansas River in the southeastern part of that state. Other thousands winter farther east in the area embraced by the adjacent corridor. By far the largest concentration of wintering mallards in the Western Plains Corridor occurs in the Texas panhandle where about 300,000 usually concentrate.

The Texas panhandle is also an important wintering ground for several other species: pintails, 160,000; green-winged teals, 90,000; baldpates, 60,000; gadwalls, 15,000; and shovelers, 8,000.

About 600,000 dabbling ducks continue southward in this corridor to winter along the lower Texas gulf coast and the upper Mexican gulf coast. Most of these are pintails, numbering almost 75,000 on the Texas coast and 187,000 on the Mexican coast (Saunders 1964:259). Other important dabbling ducks wintering in this area are: baldpates, 108,000, of which about 105,000 occur on the Mexican coast; gadwalls, 62,000, of which 56,000 are on the Mexican coast; 19,000 green-winged teals; and 17,000 shovelers.

Mid-Plains Corridor.—Immediately east of the Western Plains Corridor lies the Mid-Plains Corridor. It extends from western Saskatchewan to the Texas coast between Galveston Bay and Corpus Christi.

About 700,000 dabbling ducks migrate along this corridor. Mallards predominate, numbering, at the start of the hunting season, about 500,000. Pintails are next in abundance with 110,000, followed by 40,000 green-winged teals, 18,000 baldpates, 15,000 gadwalls, and 7,000 shovelers.

Mallards, about 10,000 of them, winter in this corridor as far north as Fort Peck, Mont. Along the North Platte River, in western Nebraska and eastern Wyoming, nearly 75,000 mallards winter, while almost 125,000 congregate along the South Platte and Republican rivers in northeastern Colorado. Lake McKinney and the Cimarron River in southwestern Kansas are the wintering areas of about 125,000 mallards. A rough estimate is 50,000 mallards wintering in this corridor in Texas, largely in the northern part of the state; only about 7,000 mallards reach the Gulf Coast where this corridor terminates. Almost all of the other species of dabbling ducks using this corridor winter along the Texas coast.

Eastern Plains Corridor.—The easternmost Great Plains corridor extends from central Saskatchewan across eastern Montana and western South Dakota to the gulf coast of eastern Texas and western Louisiana. It is termed the Eastern Plains Corridor.

Almost 3,000,000 dabbling ducks head down this corridor in the fall. About 1,000,000 are mallards, 600,000 are pintails, 460,000 are gadwalls, 400,000 are green-winged teals, 300,000 are baldpates, and 225,000 are shovelers.

Mallards in this corridor winter as far north as the hot springs adjacent to the Black Hills of South Dakota, where 20,000 stay. Farther south about 40,000 winter along the Platte River in central Nebraska and 14,000 in Harlan the County Reservoir area in the southern part of that state. In this corridor in Kansas about 45,000 mallards winter, 20,000 at the Quivira National Wildlife Refuge and Cheyenne Bottoms, and 25,000 at the Jamestown Management Area. Almost 160,000 mallards winter on artificial reservoirs in Oklahoma. A rough estimate of 45,000 is made for mallards wintering in eastern Texas, north of its gulf coast, and only 4,000 for the Gulf Coast. The largest concentration of mallards using this flight corridor winters in Louisiana; nearly 400,000 are concentrated along the coastal marshes adjacent to rice fields in the western part of the state.

Practically all of the other dabbling duck species, about 1,500,000 birds, winter in the coastal marshes between Galveston Bay, Texas, and Vermilion Bay, La. About 10 percent of these ducks winter in east Texas and 90 percent in western Louisiana.

Missouri River Corridor.—The Missouri River has a pronounced effect on migrating waterfowl. It attracts ducks because it offers rest areas and food and a guideline in migration. Almost 1,500,000 dabbling ducks appear to use this extremely narrow corridor, creating a great density of passage.

The Missouri River Corridor extends from northwest North Dakota along the river course to Kansas City, Mo. Most of the ducks leave the river there, apparently because it turns abruptly eastward. The main branch of the corridor continues southeastward to eastern Louisiana, while a subbranch extends southward to western Louisiana.

Mallards migrating along the Missouri River Corridor number about 1,100,000 along with 150,000 pintails, 100,000 green-winged teals, 50,000 baldpates, and 50,000 gadwalls.

Mallards in the Missouri River Corridor winter in numbers as far north as the Fort Randall Reservoir and Lake Andes, S. Dak. About 250,000 stay there. At the Squaw Creek National Wildlife Refuge in northwest Missouri the wintering mallard population usually averages about 200,000. About 11,000 winter on the Platte River in Nebraska near its confluence with the Missouri River. In eastern Kansas about 20,000 winter on the Marais-des-Cygnes Management Area and nearly 100,000 winter on the Neosho Management Area.

Probably not more than 300,000 of the 1,100,000 mallards wintering in Arkansas arrive by this corridor. However, most of the 150,000 mallards wintering on the Holla Bend National Wildlife Refuge near Russellville, Ark., use this corridor. Others also arrive there by flying directly south from the Swan Lake National Wildlife Refuge in north-central Missouri.

Available evidence suggests that most of the 55,000 pintails, 23,000 gadwalls, 18,000 baldpates, 18,000 green-winged teals, and 13,000 shovelers which winter in southeast Arkansas arrive by this corridor. Others of these species migrating down this corridor probably use the western branch to reach coastal marshes in western Louisiana.

Mississippi River Corridor.—The next corridor, the Mississippi River Corridor, starts on the Manitoba border in central North Dakota and stretches southeastward to the Mississippi River in southeast Iowa and northeast Missouri. From there it extends eastward to the Illinois River valley. At this point the corridor changes direction to the south to terminate on the gulf coast of Louisiana.

Because of its narrowness, this corridor

has the greatest density of dabbling duck passage of any migration corridor east of the Rocky Mountains. The upper section, from Manitoba to the Mississippi River, is followed by almost 2,500,000 dabbling ducks of which 2,000,000 are mallards, 200,000 are pintails, 125,000 are baldpates, 70,000 are green-winged teals, 50,000 are gadwalls, and 20,000 are shovelers.

The lower section of the Mississippi Migration Corridor, from western Illinois southward, is used by smaller numbers of waterfowl because of the corridors which stem from it. These corridors extend southeastward to terminate in North Carolina, South Carolina, and Florida.

The northernmost concentrations of mallards wintering in this flight corridor are on the Mississippi River near New Boston, Ill., and on the upper Illinois River. About 25,000 winter near New Boston and 60,000 on the Illinois River above Peoria. Other concentrations of wintering mallards are: lower Illinois River near Havana, 140,000; Mississippi River, Hannibal, Mo., to Alton, Ill., 200,000; southern Illinios, 150,000; southeast Missouri, 40,000; Reelfoot Lake, Tenn., 50,000; northeast Arkansas, 400,000; Stuttgart, Ark., area, 300,000; eastern Mississippi, 60,000; Louisiana (by this corridor), about 200,000 some at Catahoula Lake but most in the southeastern part of the state.

Most of the other species of dabbling ducks migrating along the Mississippi Corridor through the Iowa-Illinois-Missouri area winter on the southeast Atlantic Coast. Details of the corridors used to reach specific wintering areas will be described later.

Mid-Prairie Corridor.—A corridor used by far fewer ducks is shown paralleling the Mississippi Corridor to the west and south. This is the Mid-Prairie Corridor. It is estimated that 250,000 dabbling ducks use this route in similar proportions by species to the species using the Mississippi Corridor. Two of the most important stopping places on this corridor are the Fountain Grove Wildlife Area and the Swan Lake National Wildlife Refuge in north-central Missouri; there mallards usually reach a peak of 75,000 during the fall.

Mid-Minnesota Corridor.—To the north and east of the Mississippi Corridor a corridor extends from eastern Manitoba to the upper Mississippi River south of Minneapolis. This is termed the Mid-Minnesota Corridor; it is followed by about 760,000 dabbling ducks. Most of the mallards, about 600,000, follow the general course of the upper Mississippi southward; however, at the peak of migration nearly 100,000 land to feed on the Upper Mississippi River National Wildlife and Fish Refuge between Red Wing, Minn., and Rock Island, Ill. From the upper Mississippi River the bulk of the mallards move both south to the upper Illinois River valley and southeast to northwestern Indiana.

Chesapeake Bay Corridor.—However, an estimated 65,000 mallards, 35,000 baldpates, and 25,000 pintails move eastward from the upper Mississippi River to eastern Wisconsin, especially the Horicon National Wildlife Refuge. This corridor then continues eastward to encompass the marshes of Lake Erie from Monroe, Mich., to Sandusky Bay, Ohio. From the Lake Erie marshes it is a nonstop flight of about 400 miles to Delaware and Chesapeake bays, where most of these ducks winter.

North Carolina Corridor.—From north-central Illinois a corridor followed by 65,000 dabbling ducks extends southeastward to wintering grounds in northern coastal North Carolina. It is used by approximately 35,000 pintails, 18,000 mallards, 8,000 baldpates, and 2,000 gadwalls.

South Carolina Corridor.—The largest flight corridor for dabbling ducks to the Atlantic Coast is used by about 400,000 birds. It extends from west-central Illinois on the Mississippi River to the coast of South Carolina. The approximate species composition is 140,000 mallards, 125,000 pintails, 70,000 baldpates, 40,000 gadwalls, and 25,000 shovelers.

Mid-Florida Corridor.—The most southern corridor extends southeast from southern Illinois on the Mississippi River to central Florida. Most of the ducks using this corridor proceed no farther than the Cross Creeks and Tennessee national wildlife refuges, Tenn., and the Wheeler National Wildlife Refuge, Ala., where 300,000 mallards have wintered in recent years. About 35,000 pintails, 25,000 baldpates, and 5,000 mallards continue southeastward to Florida.

Mobile Bay Corridor.—Flight corridors extend from the north and northwest to wintering grounds in the Mobile Bay delta area of Alabama. About 35,000 dabbling ducks winter in the Mobile delta area, including almost equal numbers of baldpates (8,500), pintails (8,000), and gadwalls (7,000), with lesser numbers of green-winged teals, mallards, and black ducks. Formerly mallards wintered in greater numbers in the Mobile delta area, but in recent years increasing numbers have stopped for the winter at the Noxubee National Wildlife Refuge in eastern Mississippi. About 60,000 mallards winter at the Noxubee Refuge along with 3,000 baldpates, 2,600 green-winged teals, 1,500 black ducks, and 1,300 gadwalls.

Black Duck Corridors.—A corridor extends across western Lake Superior and south-southeast through eastern Wisconsin to northeastern Illinois and northwestern Indiana. About 25,000 black ducks and 10,000 mallards use this corridor as far as southeastern Wisconsin, where, at the Horicon National Wildlife Refuge, additional mallards join the passage south.

Other corridors extend southward through western and eastern Michigan. A total of approximately 150,000 black ducks and 50,000 mallards follows these corridors. The western corridor divides in southwestern Michigan, one branch swinging southwest to the Kankakee and Willow Slough management areas of Indiana, and the other branch turning south-southeast to the TVA lakes in eastern Tennessee. The easternmost corridor in Michigan continues south-southeast to the coastal marshes of South Carolina.

A corridor followed almost entirely by black ducks extends southwestward from eastern Ontario, across the west end of Lake Erie to the confluence of the Wabash and Ohio rivers, and on south to the Arkansas River in eastern Arkansas. Perhaps 35,000 black ducks use this path.

Of the approximately 50,000 black ducks which winter in South Carolina, Georgia, and Florida, most reach these states by a corridor extending south from eastern Ontario to coastal South Carolina and thence down the coast to Florida.

A most important corridor for migrating black ducks extends from eastern Ontario across central New York to Chesapeake Bay. From the distribution of band recoveries, I estimate that three-fourths of the 100,000 black ducks wintering from Chesapeake Bay, Md., south through Pamlico Sound, N.C., arrive by this corridor.

About one-third of the 60,000 black ducks wintering in New Jersey appear to arrive by the corridor which extends from western Quebec down the Lake Champlain and Hudson River valleys. Probably half of New Jersey's wintering population of black ducks arrives by the corridor running down the Atlantic coast. This corridor channels about 150,000 black ducks southward, including the black ducks wintering up the coast from New Jersey. In addition, the bulk of the 80,000 green-winged teals wintering along the Atlantic Flyway use this coastal corridor from the Maritime Provinces of Canada to reach their principal wintering grounds in southeastern South Carolina, where about 60,000 congregate.

Diving Ducks

About 4,200,000 diving ducks migrate south into the United States east of the Rocky Mountains. Slightly over 60 percent of these divers are scaup ducks, mostly lesser scaups. Redheads are second in abundance, composing almost 20 percent; canvasbacks and ring-necked ducks each form about 7 percent of this population.

Western Plains Corridor.—Not only are the densities of diving duck passage along migration corridors different from those of dabbling species, but the migration corridors are arranged somewhat differently (Fig. 3). The Western Plains Corridor of the diving ducks extends along the east flank of the Rocky Mountains from eastern Alberta to the upper gulf coast of Mexico.

Rough approximations of the diving ducks following the Western Plains Corridor are: lesser scaups, 50,000; redheads, 15,000; and canvasbacks, 5,000. Most of the redheads using the lower half of this corridor originate from breeding grounds in the Great Salt Lake basin of Utah.

Mid-Plains Corridor.—The Mid-Plains Corridor for diving ducks extends from western Saskatchewan to the lower Texas coast between Aransas Pass and Brownsville. About 150,000 lesser scaups and 5,000 canvasbacks follow this corridor. Radar at Brownsville, Texas, indicates that most of these ducks proceed south along the Gulf Coast to winter in Mexico. Only 8,000 scaups and 2,000 canvasbacks winter along the Aransas Pass-Brownsville stretch of coast.

Eastern Plains Corridor.—The Eastern Plains Corridor for diving ducks differs in directional axis from that of the dabblers. This corridor extends almost north-south from western Manitoba and eastern Saskatchewan to the Texas coast below Matagorda Bay. Of the 450,000 divers using this corridor fully 95 percent are redheads. Indeed, almost three-fourths of the redheads in North America fly along this corridor to reach their wintering grounds on the Laguna Madre along the Texas and Mexican coast. About 15,000 lesser scaups and 6,000 canvasbacks join the 425,000 redheads using this corridor.

East Texas Corridor.—Between the Eastern Plains Corridor and the Missouri River Corridor is a small, wedge-shaped corridor used by about 55,000 divers in migration from lakes in the eastern Dakotas to the Texas coast between Sabine Lake and Matagorda Bay. Practically no redheads migrate along this corridor, but about 50,000 lesser scaups, 4,000 ring-necked ducks, and 2,000 canvasbacks use it.

Missouri River Corridor.—The Missouri River Corridor for diving ducks enters North Dakota farther east than its counterpart for dabbling ducks. It extends through the Waubay Hills of north-

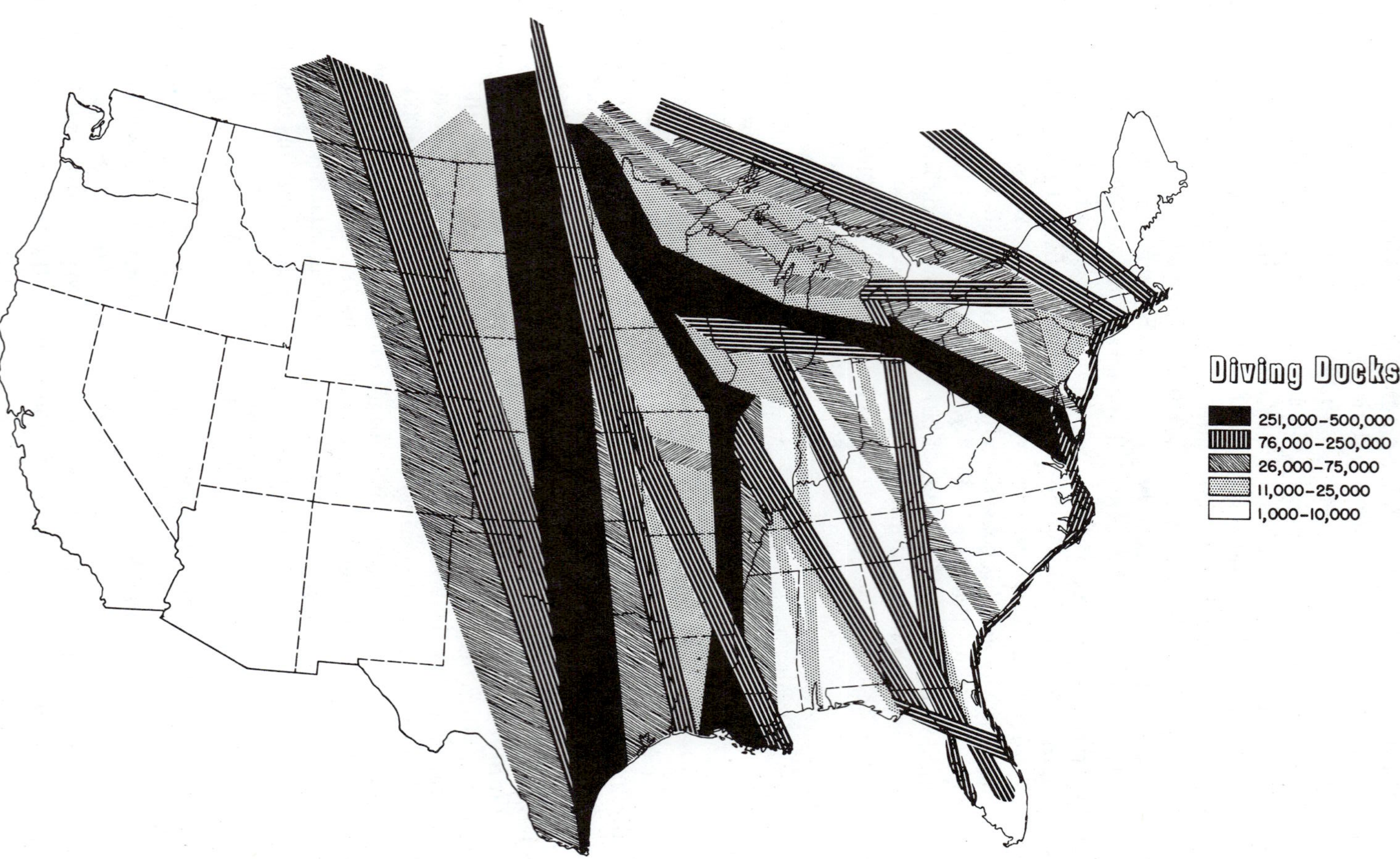

Fig. 3. The migration corridors used by diving ducks during their fall migrations.

eastern South Dakota to the vicinity of Kansas City, Mo., where the corridor divides three ways: one branch continues almost straight south to the gulf coast of western Louisiana, the second branch swings southeasterly to lakes Pontchartrain and Borgne in eastern Louisiana, and a third branch follows the Missouri River eastward across Missouri.

Above Kansas City, Mo., this corridor is used by about 175,000 lesser scaups, 50,000 ring-necked ducks, 2,000 redheads, and lesser numbers of canvasbacks. Perhaps 30,000 of the lesser scaups turn eastward at Kansas City along with about 5,000 ring-necked ducks. It seems probable that the remaining population of lesser scaups, some 145,000, divides about equally between the south and southeast branches of the corridor. The remaining 45,000 ring-necked ducks follow the south branch to the Lacassine National Wildlife Refuge in southwestern Louisiana. Most of the canvasbacks and redheads follow the southeast branch to southeastern Louisiana.

Prairie Corridor.—Between the Missouri River and Mississippi River corridors is a smaller flight corridor used by perhaps 20,000 lesser scaups and 5,000 ring-necked ducks to pass from southwestern Minnesota across central Iowa, Missouri, and Arkansas to the Louisiana coast.

Mississippi River Corridor.—The diving duck corridor most comparable to the Mississippi River Corridor for dabbling ducks enters the United States farther east in northwestern Minnesota from lakes Manitoba and Winnipeg in Manitoba. This corridor divides in central Minnesota, one branch taking an east-southeast direction, the other branch continuing south-southeast to where the Mississippi River borders southern Iowa.

The key concentration point of the more westerly branch of this corridor is the Mississippi River's Keokuk Navigation Pool, which includes the 30 miles between Dallas City, Ill., and Keokuk, Iowa. Peak populations of diving ducks in this area (1960–66) averaged 320,000 lesser scaups, 31,000 ring-necked ducks, and 22,000 canvasbacks. Probably twice these numbers pass through this area in the fall.

Also included in this corridor are lakes of the Illinois River valley, which lie about 100 miles east of the Mississippi River. At one time diving duck populations were higher in the Illinois valley than in the Mississippi valley. Pollution of the water diminished the food supply (Mills et al. 1966), resulting in a tremendous decline in the number of diving ducks in the Illinois valley. During the fall migration peak numbers now include only 13,000 lesser scaups, 12,000 ring-necked ducks, and 2,000 canvasbacks.

From this west-central area of Illinois, the Mississippi Corridor divides into two branches; the larger branch extends directly south to the Louisiana coast, and a smaller branch extends southeastward to Florida.

As judged from the direction taken by departing flocks, the branch which stretches toward Louisiana is followed by about 500,000 lesser scaups, 30,000 ring-necked ducks, and 30,000 canvasbacks. No more than 50,000 of the 500,000 lesser scaups winter north of the Gulf Coast, primarily along the lower Mississippi River; the rest winter off the coast of Louisiana, largely east of Grand Chenier and west of Marsh Island. About 10,000 ring-necked ducks go no farther than southeastern Arkansas, and 5,000 stop in central Louisiana, especially at Catahoula Lake. The remaining 15,000 ring-necked ducks winter in southeastern Louisiana, particularly in the Mississippi River delta.

About 7,500 canvasbacks winter on the Mississippi River just south of the Keokuk Navigation Pool and north of Alton, Ill. Farther south, in southeastern Arkansas, western Mississippi, and northeastern Louisiana, old oxbow lakes of the Mississippi River provide wintering areas for about 10,000 canvasbacks. Another 10,000 canvasbacks go on to winter on Wax Lake southwest of Morgan City, La.

West Florida Corridor.—The flight corridor from west-central Illinois southeastward, terminating in Florida, is followed by about 100,000 lesser scaups, 25,000 ring-necked ducks, and 10,000 canvasbacks. The first wintering area of significance for these ducks is Reelfoot Lake, Tiptonville, Tenn., and the Tennessee National Wildlife Refuge near Paris. About 3,500 scaups, 10,000 ring-necked ducks, and 2,000 canvasbacks winter on these areas. Except for those using a subbranch to Mobile Bay, most of the remaining ducks fly on to Florida.

Mobile Bay Corridors.—The subbranch extending south-southeast from Reelfoot to Mobile Bay, Ala., is used by about 7,000 ring-necked ducks, 4,500 scaups, and 3,500 canvasbacks. Most of these ducks winter in the Mobile Bay area, but about 5,000 of the 7,000 ring-necked ducks stop to winter at the Noxubee National Wildlife Refuge in eastern Mississippi.

A small flight corridor extending south from northeastern Illinois is followed by about 12,000 ring-necked ducks. Some winter at the Tennessee National Wildlife Refuge, and others continue south to the Mobile delta area.

Now we must return to Minnesota to pick up the pattern of diving duck passage to the east. The principal corridor extends east from central Minnesota across central Wisconsin to lakes Poygan, Butte des Morts, Winneconne, Winnebago, Mendota, and Michigan.

South Carolina Corridor.—From southeastern Wisconsin a corridor extends to coastal South Carolina. About 35,000 ring-necked ducks and, perhaps, several thousand lesser scaups follow this corridor.

Mid-Florida Corridor.—Radar observations at Chicago point to a large south-southeasterly departure of lesser scaups from along the Illinois and Wisconsin shore of Lake Michigan. As many as 250,000 have been known to concentrate there during the fall migration, but unknown is the proportion migrating east as opposed to south-southeast. Perhaps one-third of this population migrates southeast to Florida. Probably the bulk of the 70,000 ring-necked ducks which winter in Florida also use this corridor. An additional 15,000 ring-necked ducks reach Florida largely by way of a corridor extending from the eastern part of Michigan's upper peninsula south along the Indiana-Ohio border, across eastern Kentucky and Tennessee, and through central Georgia.

Southern Michigan Corridors.—From eastern Wisconsin the main flow of diving duck passage, other than that of the ring-necked duck, is east to east-southeast across Michigan to the Saginaw Bay and Lake St. Clair–Detroit River–Lake Erie areas.

Diving ducks congregate on Saginaw Bay to the extent that peak numbers include 22,000 lesser scaups, 22,000 redheads, and 7,000 canvasbacks. One hundred miles to the south peak populations of 380,000 lesser scaups, 260,000 canvasbacks, and 42,000 redheads have been recorded on Lake St. Clair, the Detroit River, and western Lake Erie by the Michigan Department of Conservation (1954–58). More recent aerial surveys over Lake Erie have revealed several hundred thousand diving ducks spread as far east as Long Point, Ontario. About 8,000 scaups, 6,500 canvasbacks, and 2,000 redheads winter in the Detroit River area, but at least 700,000 diving ducks fly on from Lake Erie to wintering grounds in the Atlantic Flyway.

Central Ohio Corridor.—A flight corridor extends southward from Lake Erie to Florida. Radar observations of diving ducks moving south past Columbus, Ohio, and band recoveries from lesser scaups and redheads point to a passage of over 100,000 divers along this corridor. Most of the 75,000 redheads which usually winter in Florida stay on the upper west coast. It appears that practically all of these ducks arrive by this corridor.

During the fall of 1966 unusually large numbers of redheads appeared on Lake Erie. Subsequently, in the midwinter waterfowl population survey, 200,000 redheads were found on Apalachee Bay, Fla. The absence of an unusually large concentration of redheads during the fall along the Atlantic Coast implies that these birds flew directly south from Lake Erie to Apalachee Bay, Fla. About half of the 11,000 canvasbacks wintering in Florida also appear to use this corridor when flying south from Lake Erie.

About 358,000 scaups, almost all lesser scaups, wintered in Florida, 1960–66. Major concentrations were: 200,000 on the Indian River, Oak Hill to Vero Beach; 60,000 on interior lakes, largely between Palatka and Orlando; 40,000 on Tampa and Sarasota bays and Charlotte Harbor. The lesser scaups wintering on the Indian River reached that area along four flight corridors: the Atlantic Coast from Chesapeake Bay, the Central Ohio from Lake Erie, the Mid-Florida from Lake Michigan, and the Mississippi River from west-central Illinois. For lesser scaups wintering elsewhere in Florida the corridors other than the Atlantic Coast are the principal passageways.

Ring-necked ducks winter largely in peninsular Florida lakes from Lake City south through Lake Okeechobee.

Chesapeake Bay Corridors.—The principal passage of diving ducks to the Atlantic Coast occurs along a corridor from Lake St. Clair, the Detroit River, and Lake Erie to Chesapeake Bay. At least 250,000 lesser scaups, 130,000 canvasbacks, and 50,000 redheads use this corridor.

Other corridors channel smaller numbers of diving ducks to Chesapeake Bay. One corridor extends southeast from Saginaw Bay, Mich.; another extends east from Saginaw Bay to the Central Lakes region of New York and then south-southeast to Chesapeake Bay.

At peak population in the fall about 13,000 diving ducks are found in the Central Lakes region of New York (including the major and minor Finger Lakes, Oneida Lake, and Montezuma Marsh) (Benson et al. 1957:200). The population turnover in the fall is probably several times this number, for an average of 5,000 redheads and 4,000 canvasbacks winter there, and censuses show that many thousands pass through on the way to wintering grounds on the Atlantic Coast.

Atlantic Coast Corridor.—From Chesapeake Bay tens of thousands of diving ducks migrate south along the Atlantic Coast, some as far as Florida. About 100,000 canvasbacks remain to winter in Chesapeake Bay along with 60,000 lesser scaups and 40,000 redheads. Almost 14,000 canvasbacks, 8,000 lesser scaups, and 6,000 redheads winter on Albemarle and Pamlico sounds, N.C. Along the coast of South Carolina and Georgia about 40,000 lesser scaups and 4,000 canvasbacks winter, but only 400 redheads stay there.

In addition to the corridor extending south-southeast from the Central Lakes region of New York, a corridor continues eastward to the Atlantic Coast. This is followed by an estimated 25,000 lesser scaups, and 7,000–10,000 canvasbacks.

Long Island Sound Corridor.—I have somewhat tentatively placed corridors for the passage of scaups, almost entirely greater scaups, from Lake Winnipegosis, Manitoba, across the northern reaches of Lake Superior and Georgian Bay, to the eastern end of Lake Ontario. From the Lake Ontario–St. Lawrence River area the corridor continues southeast to Long Island Sound. Another corridor apparently brings greater scaups from Alaska and the Northwest Territories of Canada via the west coast of James Bay to Lake St. Francis (near Montreal), Lake Champlain, and Long Island Sound. The mapping of these corridors is based upon bandings of greater scaups on Long Island Sound by the New York State Conservation Department and upon field observations of duck flights over New York state.

Winter inventory estimates, 1960–66, show that 225,000 scaups stayed between Boston and Delaware Bay. Most of these are greater scaups, according to Dirck Benson, New York State Conservation Department. He reported (personal communication) that the proportion of greater to lesser scaups varies from 6:1 in the New York City area to 10:1 off the coasts of Massachusetts, Connecticut, and Rhode Island.

It seems evident that sizeable numbers of greater scaups move from Long Island Sound southward along the Atlantic Coast as far as Florida. Small numbers of greater scaups also appear to migrate along other corridors in the company of lesser scaups to reach the southeast Atlantic Coast and the Gulf of Mexico.

Canada Geese

More than any other species of waterfowl, Canada geese have radically altered their migration routes during the past decade. This great change in migration habits has resulted from this species' rapid adaptation to newly created waterfowl refuges and feeding grounds. Since they are still in the process of evolving new migration corridors, probably this analysis of migration paths will be outmoded in a few years.

Airplane pilot and ground observer reports were especially useful in plotting migration corridors used by Canada geese. Radar observations from Buffalo; Washington, D.C.; Detroit; Cincinnati; and Evansville, Ind., also aided materially in mapping Canada goose flight routes. There were several wintering populations about which the evidence was conflicting as to the paths followed from staging areas at Hudson and James bays. Banding data suggested rather involved, circuitous routes, while observation reports suggested more direct paths. Perhaps, it was speculated, Canada geese traveled both the direct corridors (Fig. 4) and the circuitous corridors. However, the observed flight corridors were across terrain devoid of suitable habitat, and therefore, band recoveries would be few or wanting.

Because band recoveries often reflect a shift in the wintering grounds of a particular banded sample, they must be interpreted with caution. There is an intermixing of Canada goose wintering populations on staging areas at James and Hudson bays. It appears that geese that

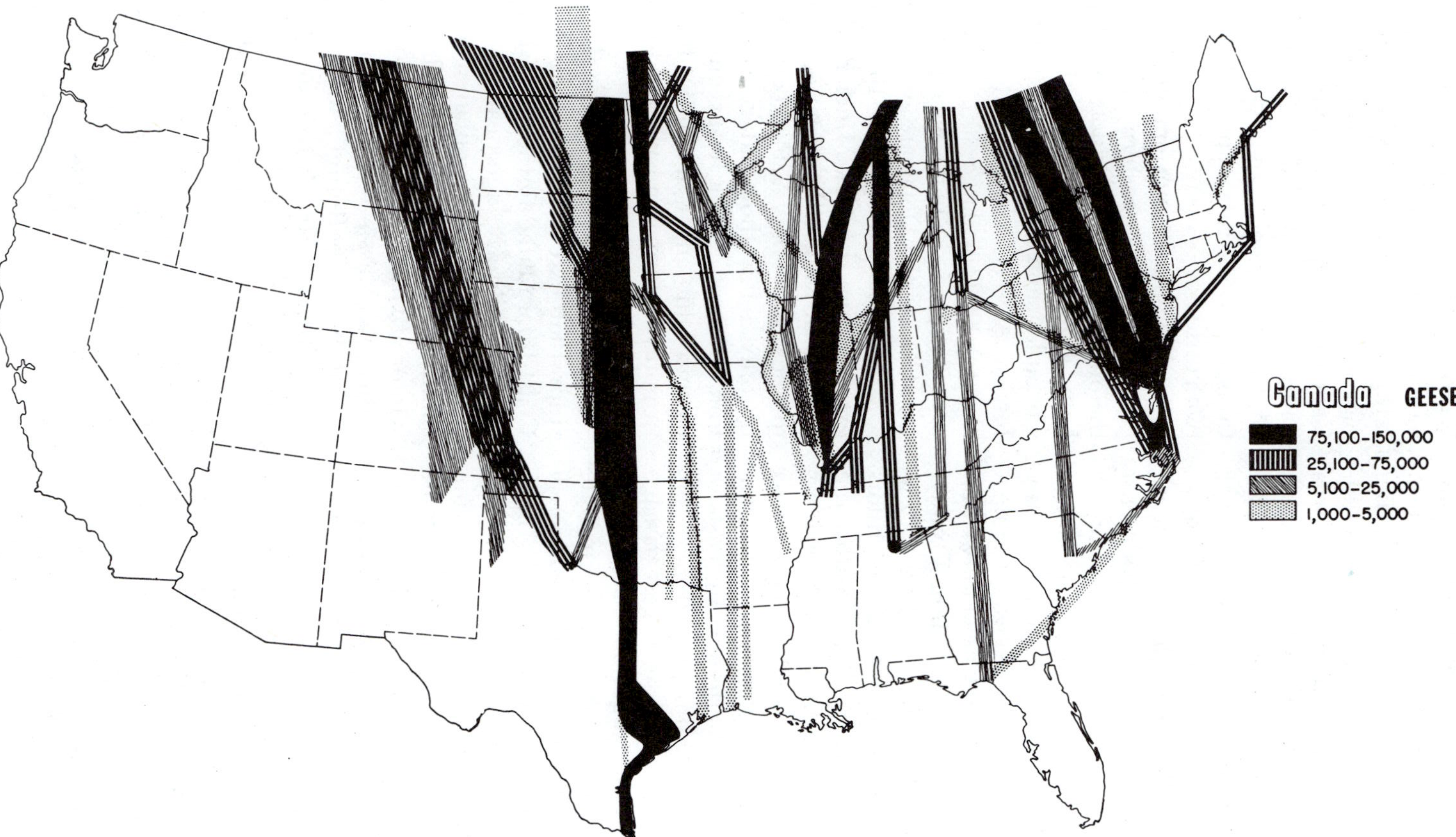

Fig. 4. The migration corridors followed by Canada geese during their fall migrations.

usually visit one wintering ground are frequently carried along by population elements bound for a different wintering area. Thus, band recoveries may not always reflect the flight course used by a given Canada goose population passing from a particular breeding area to a particular wintering area.

Each fall about 1,300,000 Canada geese (winter inventory plus 25 percent hunter kill, 1960–66) leave Canada east of the Rocky Mountains for wintering grounds in the United States. The largest number, 600,000, head for wintering grounds in the Atlantic Flyway; the next largest number, 475,000, head for wintering grounds in the Mississippi Flyway; and 250,000 use routes within the Central Flyway. Because the flight corridors of Canada geese generally fall within the established flyways, these flight corridors are discussed flyway by flyway. Canada goose corridors are also dealt with from east to west, because those in the east are closest to the breeding grounds.

Atlantic Flyway.—The largest passage of Canada geese, about 500,000, crosses central and western New York en route to wintering grounds along the shores of Delaware Bay, Chesapeake Bay, Back Bay, Currituck Sound, Albemarle Sound, and Mattamuskeet Lake. The most important single flight corridor is one across the central part of Lake Ontario and the Finger Lake region of central New York. The second most important corridor skirts the east end of Lake Ontario, passes over Oneida Lake, and proceeds south to Delaware and Chesapeake bays. The third most important corridor crosses the west end of Lake Ontario with most geese migrating south-southeast to Chesapeake Bay. Radar and visual observations indicate that a branch of this corridor extends straight south from Buffalo to Gadde's Pond, N.C., and the Carolina Sandhills and Santee national wildlife refuges, S.C. Band recoveries show a passage of geese from Chesapeake Bay to Gadde's Pond, Carolina Sandhills, and Santee. This population totals about 25,000 Canada geese, and it is impossible to ascertain relative numbers using the two corridors.

Samll migratory movements of Canada geese occur across eastern New York, but the only significant corridor, used by perhaps 4,000 birds, is one along Lake Champlain and the Hudson River to New Jersey. A very small corridor used by about 2,000 Canada geese extends south over Tupper Lake in the west-central Adirondacks to the Delaware River valley.

A corridor used by about 10,000 geese extends from the Jack Miner Bird Sanctuary, near Kingsville, Ontario, southeast to Chesapeake Bay. A small corridor used by only a few thousand geese extends from Mosquito Creek Reservoir in northeastern Ohio and Pymatuning Reservoir in northwestern Pennsylvania to Chesapeake Bay.

About 30,000 Canada geese use a corridor that extends along the Atlantic Coast from Maine to the Pea Island National Wildlife Refuge near Nags Head, N.C. As this goose population proceeds southward, various elements drop off to winter at Great Bay, N.H., 2,000; Plymouth Bay, Mass., 1,000; Monomoy National Wildlife Refuge, Mass., 6,000; Long Island, 2,800; Brigantine National Wildlife Refuge and adjacent coastal areas of New Jersey, 4,500; and Pea Island, N.C., 10,000.

Mississippi Flyway.—The main migration corridor for Canada geese in the Mississippi Flyway extends down the west shore of Lake Michigan to the Horicon National Wildlife Refuge about 50 miles northwest of Milwaukee. About 150,000 Canada geese use this corridor. Upon departing from Horicon most of the geese fly slightly west of south, between the Fox and Rock rivers, and on south for 400–450 miles to three waterfowl refuges in southern Illinois located near Carbondale, Ware, and Cairo.

Another important corridor extends down the east shore of Lake Michigan. According to a study by Wilson and Weiss (1961:4), it is used by about 90,000 Canada geese. Wilson and Weiss's computations show that about 28,600 geese stopped at the Swan Creek Marsh near Fennville in southwestern Michigan, indicating that the bulk of the migrants passed without stopping.

In southwestern Michigan the Lake Michigan Corridor divides three ways. One branch swings southwestward to join the corridor in eastern Illinois extending to the Crab Orchard National Wildlife Refuge near Carbondale. A second branch extends south-southwest to the Wabash River in Indiana and follows it south to its mouth, where some flocks of geese head due south for Kentucky Lake, Tenn., and other flocks continue along the Ohio River to the Horseshoe Lake State Wildlife Refuge near Cairo, Ill. Almost 20,000 of these geese continue southward along the Mississippi River to Reelfoot Lake, Tenn. The third branch extends almost straight south from southwestern Michigan, passing over Indianapolis, Ind., and slightly east of Nashville, Tenn., to the Wheeler National Wildlife Refuge in Alabama, where about 40,000 geese winter.

A small flight corridor enters central Michigan via the Straits of Mackinac. It extends south near Petoskey and Battle Creek, Mich., and Fort Wayne, Ind.; continues east of Louisville, Ky.; and terminates at Guntersville Lake near Scottsboro, Ala. A Canada goose population of 3,000–5,000 follows this flight corridor.

A third corridor extends through eastern Michigan south to the Shiawassee National Wildlife Refuge and Saginaw Bay, where it divides. One branch, used by 10,000–15,000 Canada geese, extends to the southwest, skirts Lake Michigan, and terminates at the Crab Orchard National Wildlife Refuge near Carbondale, Ill. At the peak of migration as many as 4,000 of this group stop at the Willow Slough Wildlife Area in northwestern Indiana. The other branch continues due south, through western Ohio and near Cincinnati, to the Hiwassee Wildlife Area north of Chattanooga, Tenn., where about 5,000 geese winter. Some geese continue along the Tennessee River to Scottsboro, Ala., and the Wheeler National Wildlife Refuge at Decatur, Ala.

A fourth flight corridor extends southward from James Bay across the west end of Manitoulin Island and down Lake Huron to a refuge near Pontiac, Mich., and the Jack Miner Bird Sanctuary near Kingsville, Ontario.

This corridor divides there, one branch extending south-southwest to the Lake Erie marshes of Ohio and Grand Lake near Celina, Ohio. About 4,000 winter at Grand Lake and 1,500 on the Lake Erie marshes. Pilot reports and sightings from the ground indicate that another branch extends due south from the Jack Miner Sanctuary along the Scioto River valley through central Ohio and across the Great Smoky Mountains to areas near Tallahassee, Fla., including the St. Marks National Wildlife Refuge. Band recoveries tell another story. They show the flight corridor extending from Jack Miner's to Chesapeake Bay, going south along the Atlantic Coast to Georgia, and then swinging southwestward to the Tallahassee area. About 7,500 Canada geese winter in that area, but it is difficult to determine the relative magnitudes of passage along the two corridors.

West of the large Lake Michigan corridor, a small corridor extends southwest through Wisconsin to the Necedah National Wildlife Refuge in the west-central part of that state. It continues south to the Mississippi River and across country to the Louisa unit of the Mark Twain National Wildlife Refuge near Muscatine, Iowa. From the Louisa refuge some flocks of geese continue south along the Mississippi River to a point northwest of St. Louis where they leave the river to proceed south-southeast to the Mingo National Wildlife Refuge in southeast Missouri. From 5,000 to 7,000 Canada geese stop at the peak of migration at the Necedah Refuge, and peak numbers at the Louisa refuge are from 1,000 to 2,000. About 5,000 winter at the Mingo Refuge.

Another small corridor reaches the upper Mississippi River via the north shore of Lake Superior and the St. Croix River. It follows the Mississippi to the Spring Lake National Wildlife Refuge, Savanna, Ill. From there it extends south to the lower Illinois River. About 2,000 geese follow this corridor.

A small corridor used by about 6,000 giant Canada geese runs southeast from their Manitoba breeding ground in the region between Lake Manitoba and Lake Winnipeg to their wintering ground at Silver Lake in Rochester, Minn. Another population of about 4,000 giant Canada geese migrates southeastward from the Whiteshell Provincial Park region of southeastern Manitoba to its wintering grounds on the Rock Prairie area near Beloit, Wis.

In addition to those using the Great Lakes corridors, the largest passage of Canada geese in the Mississippi Flyway moves south through western Minnesota and Iowa and eastern South Dakota to the Swan Lake National Wildlife Refuge in north-central Missouri (Vaught and Kirsch 1966:21). The Red River provides a corridor to the Big Sioux River. About at its confluence with the Missouri River the geese turn from south to southeast and proceed across country to the Swan Lake Refuge.

Another branch of this corridor follows the Minnesota River from Big Stone Lake to near Mankato, Minn., where it turns almost due south to the Swan Lake Refuge. The importance of the Minnesota River to migrating Canada geese is shown by the fact that on the Lac qui Parle Refuge on that river from 7,000 to 12,000 geese have stopped in the past 2 years.

From 1960 to 1966 an average of 65,000 Canada geese have wintered at the Swan Lake National Wildlife Refuge, Mo., while about 8,000 have migrated farther south to winter at the White River and Holla Bend national wildlife refuges in Arkansas and in western coastal Louisiana.

Central Flyway.—Migration patterns of small Canada geese in the Great Plains have been reported by Ryder (1955), Marquardt (1962), Rutherford (1965), and MacInnes (1966). In addition, I have studied the geographic distribution of these geese as indicated by winter inventories and reports of fall populations based on coordinated censuses made along their flight paths. Indirect recovery data from bandings of Canada geese at the Sand Lake National Wildlife Refuge, S. Dak., 1952–64, were also used in this analysis.

In addition to the small Canada geese,

which nest in the Arctic, larger forms, nesting farther south, use the same flight corridors. Other flight corridors are not presented because of lack of information.

Of the two principal Canada goose corridors in the Central Flyway the easternmost was termed the tall-grass prairie route by Marquardt (1962:48–49) and the westernmost the short-grass prairie route. About 150,000 Canada geese (1964–67) moved south from Manitoba in the region between Lake Manitoba and Lake Winnipeg down the eastern Great Plains Corridor. The first large gathering, from 12,000 to 20,000, occurs in the vicinity of Devils Lake, N. Dak. Farther south about 18,000 Canada geese concentrate at the peak of migration on the Sand Lake National Wildlife Refuge in South Dakota. From 500 to 1,500 stop in Nebraska, mostly along the Missouri River. About 5,000 gather in Kansas, largely at the Kirwin and Quivira national wildlife refuges and the Cheyenne Bottoms Wildlife Area. Just south of the Kansas border, at the Salt Plains National Wildlife Refuge in Oklahoma, about 18,000 Canada geese are found at the height of migration.

Across Oklahoma to the south the Tishomingo and Hagerman national wildlife refuges on Lake Texoma are the focal points for aggregations of about 28,000 Canada geese. Most of these small Canada geese continue southward to the Texas coast, the bulk of the migrants reaching it between Galveston and Matagorda bays. From there a sizeable number of geese move along the Gulf Coast as far south as Tampico, Vera Cruz, Mexico.

About 40,000 small Canada geese winter along the Texas coast and 5,000 along the Mexican coast. On Lake Texoma in northern Texas about 12,000 geese belonging to this population winter, largely on the Hagerman National Wildlife Refuge. Others, about 16,000, winter as far north as the Salt Plains National Wildlife Refuge in northern Oklahoma.

The westernmost of the Great Plains flight corridors for Canada geese extends from southeastern Alberta and southwestern Saskatchewan to the panhandle of Texas. A population totaling about 100,000 of these geese enters the United States to fly almost nonstop down this broad corridor complex to western Nebraska and southeastern Colorado. In the fall of 1966 about 10,000 were observed on the North Platte River in Nebraska and 48,000 in southeastern Colorado, largely on Eads, Blue, Lake Meredith, Henry, John Martin, Horse Creek, and Two Buttes reservoirs. On the average 35,000 remain to winter on these reservoirs, while about 33,000 winter farther south—5,000 in northeastern New Mexico, 8,000 at Buffalo Lake and Muleshoe national wildlife refuges in the Texas panhandle, and 20,000 at the Waggoner Ranch and Winchester Lake near Vernon, Texas. In recent years 5,000 have wintered as far north as the North Platte River in western Nebraska.

A population of perhaps 50,000 Canada geese, referred to as the Western Prairie group, migrates from the Saskatchewan River delta and other areas in Saskatchewan and Manitoba to the Fort Randall Reservoir on the Missouri River in southern South Dakota. About 28,000 occur there and on nearby Lake Andes at the peak of the fall migration; almost 18,000 winter there.

From the Fort Randall Reservoir two principal corridors are used by Canada geese migrating farther south. One corridor follows the Missouri River to the Squaw Creek National Widlife Refuge in northwest Missouri, where, at the height of the fall flight, about 8,000 geese are found. The wintering population numbers about 4,500 Canada geese. Another 7,000 migrate farther southward to winter on the Gambill Refuge near Paris, Texas, and in southeast coastal Texas.

The other corridor, followed by about 15,000 geese, extends almost straight south from the Fort Randall Reservoir to the Cheyenne Bottoms Wildlife Area and the Kirwin and Quivira national wildlife refuges in Kansas. About 7,500 winter in these areas, and smaller numbers continue to the Salt Plains and Tishomingo national wildlife refuges in northern and southern Oklahoma, respectively. About 3,500 geese of this population winter at these two refuges, while several hundred continue south to the Texas coast to winter near Tivoli.

Almost 6,000 Canada geese nest in the Great Plains of the United States and Canada. These birds breed in numerous scattered colonies from southeastern Saskatchewan to central Nebraska. Most migrate only short distances along dispersed lanes of travel.

Blue and Lesser Snow Geese

Each October from 400,000 to 450,000 blue and lesser snow geese migrate through the Mississippi Flyway to reach their wintering grounds on the coastal marshes of Louisiana (Fig. 5). An additional 300,000 migrate across the Great Plains to winter along the Texas coast. Of the two principal contingents of these geese the eastern departs from southern James Bay and the western contingent from Hudson Bay between York Factory and Cape Henrietta Maria (Cooch 1955:171).

There is some variation in the migration pattern of these geese from year to year. During the last 15 years there have been 2 years, 1955 and 1959, when unusual numbers of blue and lesser snow geese appeared east of their customary flight lanes. As many as 500 blue and lesser snow geese appeared in early November, 1955, in the Lake Erie marshes of Ohio and 2,200 in the interior of that state. At the same time 4,000 were found on TVA reservoirs in Tennessee, 1,400 on TVA reservoirs in Alabama, and 1,200 in Mississippi.

The easternmost flight corridor, customarily used by small numbers of blue and lesser snow geese, runs from the south end of James Bay slightly west of south to the Lake Erie marshes of Ohio; there it turns southwestward across Indiana along the White River to the Wabash River, where it turns due south to Mobile Bay, Ala. From there the corridor turns south-southwestward to the Mississippi River delta. About 10,000–15,000 blue and snow geese follow this corridor, according to the Alabama Department of Conservation. An offshoot of this corridor is used by about 1,800 blue and snow geese which winter at the Wheeler National Wildlife Refuge, Decatur, Ala. In recent years small numbers of blue and snow geese have been observed migrating down the Chattahoochee River on the border of Alabama and Georgia.

A somewhat larger number of blue and lesser snow geese use a corridor that extends through Saginaw Bay, Mich., southwestward to the Wabash River. This corridor then follows the Wabash to its confluence with the Ohio River, follows the Ohio to the Mississippi River, and the Mississippi to its delta southeast of New Orleans.

The number of blue and lesser snow geese stopping at Saginaw Bay has varied from 700 in 1955 to 2,100 in 1956. Few stop elsewhere along this route, but many flocks are seen and heard passing down the Wabash River.

A flight corridor of approximately the

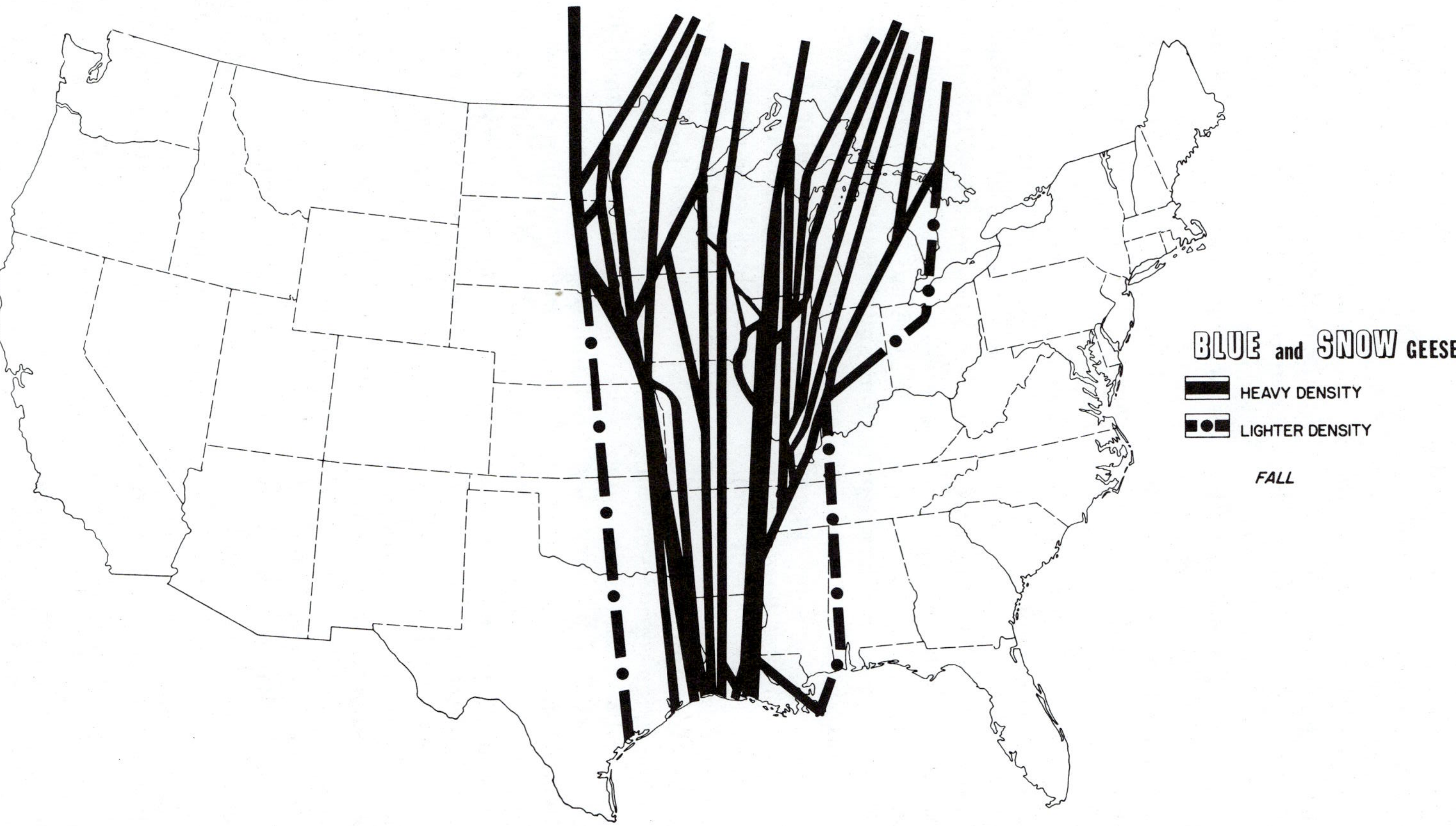

Fig. 5. The migration corridors followed by blue and lesser snow geese during their fall migrations from staging areas on Hudson and James bays to the Gulf Coast.

same size enters Michigan east of Sault Ste. Marie. It proceeds south-southwest across Michigan, across the northeast corner of Indiana (where it passes over the Willow Slough Wildlife Area), and along the Kaskaskia River in Illinois to the Mississippi River. There it usually cuts due south across country to pick up the Mississippi again near Reelfoot Lake, Tenn.

The only consistent stopping place for blue and lesser snow geese on this corridor is the Willow Slough Wildlife Area near Morocco, Ind. Numbers resting and feeding there have averaged at their peaks about 3,600, 1954–60.

Another corridor enters Michigan west of Sault Ste. Marie, running southwestward across Grand Traverse Bay and southern Lake Michigan. (Numerous pilots have reported these geese at 5,000–10,000 feet over the southern end of the lake.) Upon reaching the west side of Lake Michigan, it turns south-southwestward to the Kaskaskia River which it follows to the Mississippi River.

As with the migration corridors of Canada geese, the blue and lesser snow goose corridors immediately to the west of Lake Michigan are followed by more geese than are those to the east. Of the Wisconsin corridors, the one probably used by the largest number of blue and snow geese follows the Lake Michigan shore about to the Illinois border, where the corridor turns southwest to the upper Illinois River.

A large corridor also extends along the west side of Green Bay to Lake Winnebago, where its direction changes from south-southwest to almost due south, passing over the Horicon Marsh National Wildlife Refuge (where from a few hundred to several thousand geese stop) to the upper Illinois River valley.

Of all the corridors coming from James Bay, the farthest one to the west appears to extend south-southwest across the center of Lake Superior to the Keweenaw Peninsula of Michigan. There it apparently divides, one branch continuing south-southwest to central Wisconsin where it turns southward to reach the Mississippi and Illinois rivers. This branch brings at least 12,000 blue and lesser snow geese to the Mississippi River along the borders of Iowa and Missouri, and 10,000 to the Illinois River valley between Banner and Meredosia (based on peak numbers from censuses of 1954–66). The other branch arrives at the Illinois River valley near Bureau and is used by at least 6,000 blue and snow geese.

Seldom are more than a few hundred blue and lesser snow geese observed above Dubuque, Iowa, either on the Mississippi River or migrating down it. Thus, it is apparent that most of these birds observed south of Dubuque and above St. Louis in the Mississippi River valley use this Central Wisconsin Corridor. About 10,000 geese using this corridor winter near the mouth of the Illinois River at Grafton, Ill.

This corridor continues in two branches slightly west of south through west-central Illinois and along the adjacent reach of the Mississippi River to recombine near Ste. Genevieve, Mo. It continues in the same direction across the southeast corner of Missouri and northeast corner of Arkansas to return to the Mississippi River near Rosedale, Miss. There this flight corridor is joined by one which results from the merger of several smaller corridors between the mouth of the Ohio River and Memphis, Tenn.

At this juncture this corridor probably accommodates the passage of about 150,000 blue and lesser snow geese. The corridor approximates the course of the Mississippi River, but splits about where the Louisiana border extends east of the river. One branch continues along the river to the Mississippi delta; the other branch heads directly south to Marsh Island on the coast.

The group of flight corridors used by blue and lesser snow geese west of Lake Superior appears to stem from Hudson Bay. A corridor, used by relatively small numbers of blue and snow geese, crosses the western tip of Lake Superior, proceeds over the Mississippi River near Winona, Minn., and continues south over Little Rock, Ark., and Alexandria, La., to the Gulf coastal marshes. Few of these geese stop en route, and so it is difficult to approximate the magnitude of this flight.

A second corridor, farther west, enters the United States near Ely, Minn., and divides near Duluth. One branch extends south over the Crex Meadows Wildlife Area, Wis., to the Swan Lake National Wildlife Refuge in north-central Missouri. The other branch extends south-southwest along the Minnesota River to Mankato, Minn., where it turns slightly east of south to pass over Des Moines, Iowa, on its way to the Swan Lake Refuge. There it recombines with its easterly branch. An average peak fall population of 8,000 blue and lesser snow geese occurred at the Swan Lake Refuge, 1954–60, but probably two to three times this number passed through the area during the entire migration period.

A third corridor from Hudson Bay extends southwest over Sioux Lookout, Ontario, enters the United States near International Falls, Minn., and continues to the vicinity of Leech Lake, Minn., where it turns southward to pass over Spirit Lake, Iowa, and reach the Squaw Creek National Wildlife Refuge in northwest Missouri.

A fourth corridor extends south-southwest over Quibell, Ontario, crosses the United States-Canadian border near Rainy River, Ontario, and continues in the same direction to Lake Traverse and Big Stone Lake on the South Dakota-Minnesota border. There the corridor turns south to follow the Big Sioux and Missouri rivers to the Squaw Creek Refuge. A branch of this corridor extends to the Tewaukon National Wildlife Refuge in the southeast corner of North Dakota. It turns south there extending over the Waubay Hills of South Dakota to reach the Missouri River near Yankton, S. Dak. From 1956 to 1964 peak numbers of blue and lesser snow geese at the Tewaukon Refuge during the fall averaged about 9,000.

A fifth corridor extends south-southwest from Hudson Bay over Kenora, Ontario, and along the west shore of Lake of the Woods to the Sand Lake National Wildlife Refuge in northeastern South Dakota. The sixth corridor reaches the Sand Lake Refuge from the region between Lake Manitoba and Lake Winnipeg in Manitoba via the Devils Lake region of North Dakota and the James River.

Peak numbers of blue and lesser snow geese at the Sand Lake Refuge have averaged about 60,000 during the fall, 1954–64. Not only is the population turnover probably two to three times this number, but numerous flocks bypass the refuge.

From the vicinity of Sand Lake National Wildlife Refuge flight corridors stretch southward across Nebraska, central Kansas, and Oklahoma to the Texas coastal plain. About 300,000 blue and lesser snow geese winter on the coastal plain of Texas (1963–67), most (170,000) between Galveston and Corpus Christi. Only 5,500 winter between Corpus Christi and Brownsville. On the upper coastal plain, between Galveston and the Louisiana border, about 125,000 winter. Most of these geese probably arrive by flight corridors from the Squaw Creek National Wildlife Refuge in northwest Missouri.

The bulk of the blue and snow geese which funnel into the Squaw Creek Refuge come from the Sand Lake Refuge. However, other flight corridors reach Squaw Creek through the Waubay Hills of northeastern South Dakota and by way of Lake Traverse and Big Stone Lake on the western border of Minnesota. Peak populations at Squaw Creek average 55,000 geese (1954–61), with probably two to three times this number passing through the region. The number passing through is indicated by the census of the fall of 1960 when at one time 130,000 blue and lesser snow geese were on the Squaw Creek Refuge. During late November, 1967, 120,000 blue and lesser snow geese were on the Squaw Creek Refuge. During late November 1967, 120,000 blue and snow geese were estimated at the De Soto Bend National Wildlife Refuge on the Missouri River near Omaha, Nebr.

An average of 18,000 blue and lesser snow geese winter at Squaw Creek; indeed, in Janaury of 1966, 48,000 were recorded. However, the bulk of the blue and snow geese move south from Squaw Creek to winter on the coastal plains of eastern Texas and western Louisiana.

SPRING MIGRATION PATTERNS OF BLUE AND LESSER SNOW GEESE

Much less is known about the flight corridors used by waterfowl migrating northward in the spring than is known about the corridors used in fall migrations. Band recoveries are few, not many observers are in the field, and there is much less interest in observing the northward migration of waterfowl because hunting is not involved.

However, circumstantial evidence indicates that some of the pintails migrating through California in the fall migrate northward through the western basin of the Mississippi River in the spring (Aldrich et al. 1949:13–16). Radar surveillance of early spring migration of ducks indicates a pronounced northeastward movement throughout the interior of the southern and central United States. Since this is not the reverse of a comparable fall passage, it suggests that some species of ducks use one migration corridor in the fall and another in the spring. Findings from radar surveillance of spring waterfowl movements will be presented in detail in a later report.

Here I wish to describe only the spring migration of blue and lesser snow geese because it is well known and is so utterly different from the fall migration. What makes it unusual is the shift of the eastern contingent of geese westward to the Missouri River (Fig. 6).

Numerous flight corridors extend slightly west of north from points of concentration between Galveston, Texas, and the delta of the Mississippi River. As the corridors from eastern Louisiana proceed north, they turn more westward, especially in southern Missouri.

Most of the spring flight corridors focus on the Missouri River in the vicinity of the northwest Missouri and southeast Iowa borders, particularly at the Squaw Creek National Wildlife Refuge. By early March the concentration of blue and snow geese at Squaw Creek alone amounts to 200,000–250,000. Additional thousands of geese are scattered over other areas in that general region.

As the snow and ice melt in the Missouri River valley, these geese gradually move northward to the vicinity of Onawa,

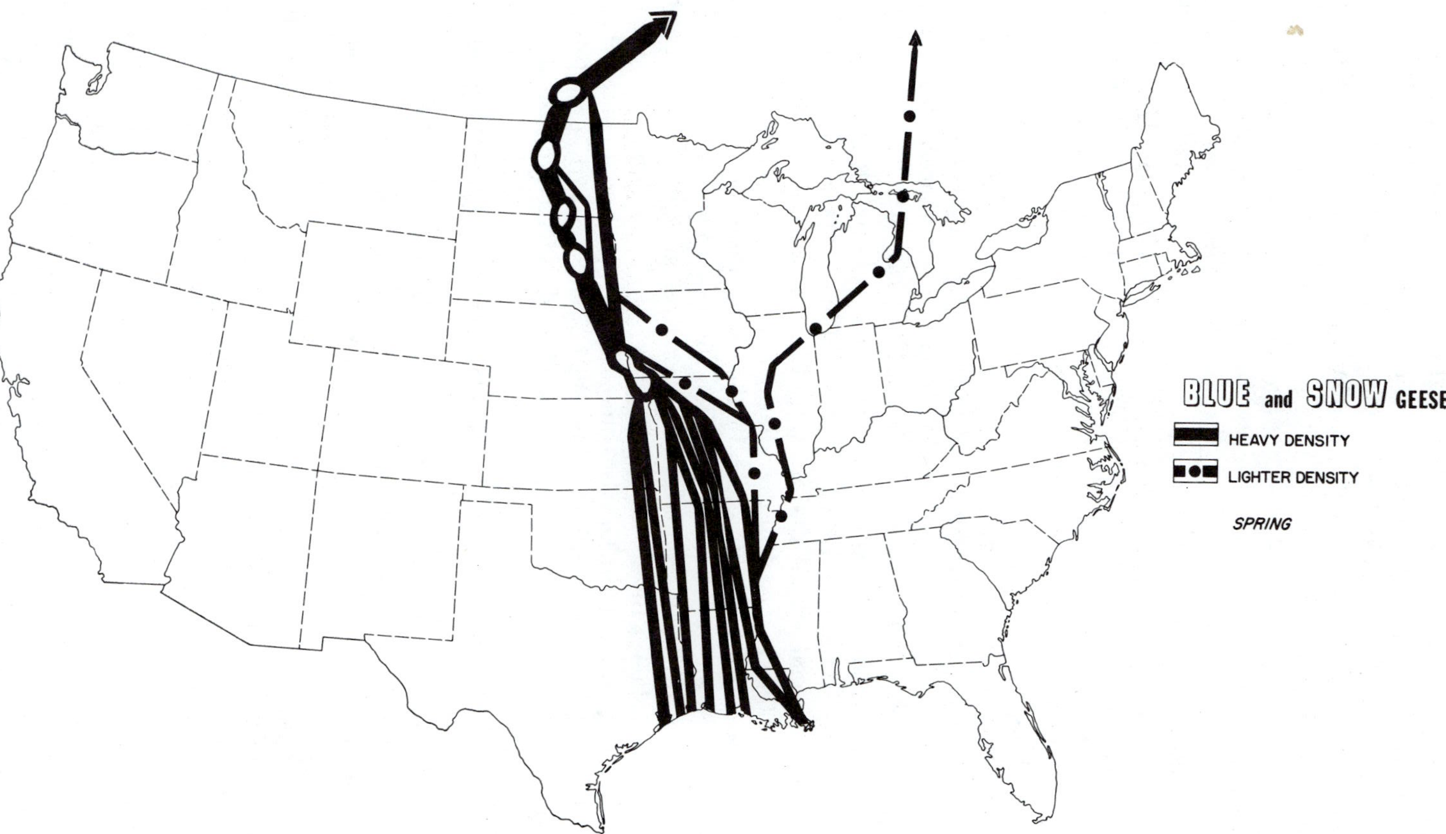

Fig. 6. The migration corridors followed by blue and lesser snow geese during their spring migrations from the Gulf Coast to southern Canada. The areas enclosed by heavy lines between northwestern Missouri and southern Manitoba are important concentration and feeding areas.

Iowa. From there a small branch corridor continues northward to Big Stone Lake and Lake Traverse on the Minnesota–South Dakota border. A secondary branch extends north over the Waubay Hills of South Dakota to the Tewaukon National Wildlife Refuge in southeastern North Dakota.

The bulk of the population, however, continues north-northwest from Onawa, Iowa, to the Sand Lake National Wildlife Refuge northeast of Aberdeen, S. Dak. In those springs when the ice is late leaving the Sand Lake Refuge, the geese stop about midway between Onawa and the Sand Lake Refuge in the area of De Smet, S. Dak.

Between 200,000 and 500,000 blue and snow geese stop to feed in the vicinity of the Sand Lake Refuge in the spring. Peak numbers are usually reached April 10–15. From 15,000 to 20,000 form a peak at the Tewaukon Refuge, usually about mid-April.

From Sand Lake most of this population continues up the James River valley to rest and feed in the area about Devils Lake, N. Dak. As the weather permits, they proceed northeastward to agricultural fields and water area northwest of Winnipeg, Manitoba.

In addition to the flight corridors already described (used by 90 percent or more of the blue and lesser snow geese migrating in the spring) a small corridor follows the Mississippi River. Usually the geese using this corridor number about 5,000–15,000. They leave the river between Hannibal, Mo., and Burlington, Iowa, flying northwestward and apparently bound for the principal concentration of the species along the Missouri River.

Occasionally a small passage of blue and lesser snow geese occurs on the Illinois River. Apparently these birds leave the Illinois River near Bureau and head northeastward to Saginaw Bay, Mich. Prior to the spring of 1967 this group numbered only a few hundred. However, on March 15, 1967, an estimated 7,000 appeared in the lower Illinois River valley. On March 17 these geese moved up the valley to Clear Lake near Pekin, Ill. They departed Clear Lake the night of March 18–19. Michigan Department of Conservation biologists reported that an estimated 5,000 blue and snow geese were at Fish Point, Saginaw Bay, Mich., on March 24, and on March 28 they counted 6,400. Unknown are the exact days of arrival and departure.

The conclusion that the flock of geese at Saginaw Bay was the one that left Clear Lake is based upon the unusually large number of geese east of the Mississippi River in the spring of 1967, the similarity in estimates of the number of birds in the flock, the compatibility of dates when the geese were last noted on the Illinois River and first detected at Saginaw Bay, and the absence of any flock of blue and snow geese of comparable size in Wisconsin even though biologists were alerted to watch for this flock.

SUMMARY AND DISCUSSION

Waterfowl in migration cover the breadth of the United States east of the Rocky Mountains. However, there are great differences in the densities of their passages over the country. Evidently the differences in densities of waterfowl in passage stem from the productivity and locations of the breeding grounds from which the migrations originate, the distribution of favorable habitats en route to the wintering areas, the locations and carrying capacities of the wintering grounds, and the evolutionary processes by which species reduce competition with each other. Species of waterfowl with similar food preferences appear to reduce competition by concentrating on different wintering areas (Weller 1964:99).

The migration corridors outlined in this paper represent passageways, each connecting a series of waterfowl habitats extending from the breeding grounds to the wintering grounds. The directions taken by corridors between waterfowl habitats have been deduced from band recoveries, radar surveillance, and visual sightings from the ground and from aircraft. Population estimates on migration rest areas and winter areas of concentration provide a means of determining comparative densities of passage by species.

Migration corridors differ from flyways in being smaller and more precisely defined as to species and population elements using them. I consider the flyways as proposed by Lincoln (1935) to be primarily geographical and secondarily biological. Migration corridors, on the other hand, are primarily biological and secondarily geographical.

It is evident from this presentation that many flight corridors which cross a large section of the Central Flyway terminate on wintering grounds in the Mississippi Flyway. Likewise it is evident that most migration corridors leading to wintering grounds in the Atlantic Flyway first cross the Mississippi Flyway.

The migration corridors of prairie-nesting dabbling ducks tend to slope in a general northwest-southeast direction. Population elements from the eastern part of the prairie breeding grounds tend to winter on the eastern and northern fringes of the principal wintering grounds. As the prairie breeding grounds occur farther and farther west, the ducks using them tend to winter either farther and farther down the Atlantic Coast to Florida or farther and farther west and south along the Gulf of Mexico.

Unlike dabbling ducks, a large proportion of the diving ducks nesting on the Great Plains of Canada migrate east from Alberta and western Saskatchewan to eastern Saskatchewan and Manitoba before entering the United States. Therefore, their flight corridors in the United States do not slope toward the east as greatly as do those of dabbling ducks. An important exception, of course, is the large eastward passage of divers through the Great Lakes region to the northeast Atlantic Coast.

Migration corridors of ducks become increasingly complex from west to east. Those on the Great Plains are relatively simple and are shown on the basis of densities of passage and changes in species composition. The pattern of migration corridors in the Midwest becomes more complex because corridors end in wintering areas in both the Mississippi and Atlantic flyways. Important wintering grounds east of the Great Plains receive migrating ducks from two, occasionally three, and rarely, four corridors. The more corridors leading to wintering grounds, such as those in Florida, the greater the difficulty in appraising relative densities of passage in those corridors.

The flight corridors of Canada geese are more directly along a north-south axis than are those of most ducks. Consequently, the corridors of Canada geese fall within specific flyway boundaries more readily than do those of most duck species. The black duck is an exception, for its migration corridors also fall quite well into either the Mississippi or Atlantic flyways as a result of its easterly breeding grounds.

Within the last decade we have witnessed the development of hunting regulations governing the take of waterfowl for each of the four flyways. Regional adjustments have been made in the hunting regulations to bring waterfowl production and kill into greater balance between broad regions of the United States. As waterfowl management becomes more and more refined, it will become feasible to manage the kill on smaller regional bases than the present flyways. The migration corridors outlined in this paper provide bases for considering regional units smaller than flyways.

ACKNOWLEDGMENTS

A report covering a region as extensive as this one does could only have been developed because many persons and agencies contributed information. Without the splendid collaboration of those cited here, this report would be much more limited in scope, a mere skeleton of its present form.

I wish to thank Dr. John Seubert, Bureau of Sport Fisheries and Wildlife, for suggesting to the Federal Aviation Agency the study which led to this report; Mr. Walter Crissey, Dr. Aelred Geis, Mr. R. Kahler Martinson, and Mr. Earl Baysinger, Bureau of Sport Fisheries and Wildlife, for unpublished band recovery data; the National Science Foundation for financial support of radar studies of bird migration and the U.S. Weather Bureau, particularly Mr. Stuart Bigler and many radar meteorologists, for cooperation in radar surveillance of bird migration at 27 Weather Bureau stations.

My thanks go also to these Illinois Natural History Survey personnel: Dr. Glen Sanderson, Head, Section of Wildlife Research, for counsel throughout the study; Mr. Robert M. Zewadski, Associate Technical Editor, for editing the manuscript; and Mr. Richard M. Sheets, Technical Illustrator, for drawing the maps and designing the cover.

Waterfowl migration data pertaining to specific regions were contributed by the following persons whose generous sharing of information made this study possible:

Atlantic Flyway.—Bureau of Sport Fisheries and Wildlife, Donald Hankla and C. E. Addy

Dirck Benson, New York State Conservation Department

Mississippi Flyway.—Bureau of Sport Fisheries and Wildlife, Arthur Hawkins, Rossalius Hanson, Harold Burgess, Richard Toltzmann, Burton Webster, Carrell Ryan, and James Gillett

Alabama, Walter Beshears, Alabama Department of Conservation

Arkansas, David Donaldson, Arkansas Conservation Commission

Illinois, George Arthur, Illinois Department of Conservation

Indiana, William Barnes, Indiana Department of Natural Resources

Louisiana, Clark Hoffpauer, Louisiana Wildlife and Fisheries Commission

Michigan, Edward Mikula and Herbert Miller, Michigan Department of Conservation

Minnesota, Robert Jessen, Minnesota Division of Game and Fish

Missouri, Richard Vaught and George Brakhage, Missouri Department of Conservation

Ohio, Karl Bednarik, Ohio Department of Natural Resources

Tennessee, Calvin Barstow, Tennessee Conservation Commission

Wisconsin, Richard Hunt, Wisconsin Conservation Department; Laurence Jahn, Wildlife Management Institute

Central Flyway.—Bureau of Sport Fisheries and Wildlife, Ray Buller, Harvey Nelson, and Lyle Schoonover.

LITERATURE CITED

ALDRICH, JOHN W., ET AL. 1949. Migration of some North American waterfowl. A progress report on an analysis of banding records. U.S. Department of the Interior, Fish and Wildlife Service Special Scientific Report (Wildlife) 1. 48pp. + 31 maps.

BELLROSE, FRANK C. 1967. Establishing certain parameters of hazards to aircraft by migrating birds in the Mississippi Flyway. U.S. Department of the Interior, Bureau of Sport Fisheries and Wildlife, Division of Wildlife Research. 74pp.

BENSON, DIRCK, DONALD D. FOLEY, AND DONALD L. SCHIERBAUM. 1957. The problem of setting duck hunting seasons in New York. New York Fish and Game Journal 4(2):194–202.

COOCH, GRAHAM. 1955. Observations on the autumn migration of blue geese. Wilson Bulletin 67(3):171–174.

LINCOLN, FREDERICK C. 1935. The waterfowl flyways of North America. U.S. Department of Agriculture Circular 342. 12pp.

MACINNES, C. D. 1966. Population behavior of eastern arctic Canada geese. Journal of Wildlife Management 30(3):536–553.

MARQUARDT, RICHARD EARL. 1962. Ecology of the migrating and wintering flocks of the small white-cheeked geese within the south central United States. Ph.D. Thesis. Oklahoma State University, Stillwater. 179pp.

MILLS, HARLOW B., WILLIAM C. STARRETT, AND FRANK C. BELLROSE. 1966. Man's effect on the fish and wildlife of the Illinois River. Illinois Natural History Survey Biological Notes 57. 24pp.

RUTHERFORD, WILLIAM H., editor. 1965. Description of Canada goose populations common to the Central Flyway. Central Flyway Waterfowl Council Technical Committee. n.p.

RYDER, RONALD A. 1955. A preliminary analysis of waterfowl recoveries in Colorado with notes on trapping and banding. Colorado Department of Game and Fish, Game Management Division Federal Aid Project W-37-R Completion Report. 72pp.

SAUNDERS, GEORGE B. 1964. South of the border, pp. 253–262. *In* Joseph P. Linduska, editor, Waterfowl tomorrow. U.S. Department of the Interior, Bureau of Sport Fisheries and Wildlife, Fish and Wildlife Service.

VAUGHT, RICHARD W., AND LEO M. KIRSCH. 1966. Canada geese of the eastern prairie population, with special reference to the Swan Lake flock. Missouri Department of Conservation Technical Bulletin 3. 91pp.

WELLER, MILTON W. 1964. Distribution and migration of the redhead. Journal of Wildlife Management 28(1):64–103.

WILSON, H. LEE, AND ROBERT F. WEISS. 1961. Fall migration, populations, and flight trails of Canada geese in southwestern Michigan in 1959. Michigan Department of Conservation, Game Division Report 2349. 6pp.

LITERATURE CONSULTED

In addition to the literature cited in the text, the literature listed here was consulted in preparing the maps showing the corridors used by migrating waterfowl. Because it was impossible to cite these references in appropriate places in the text, they are listed as a bibliography.

ADDY, C. E. [1953.] Fall migration of the black duck. U.S. Department of the Interior, Fish and Wildlife Service Special Scientific Report (Wildlife) 19. 63pp. + 31 fig.

———. 1960–66. Winter surveys, Atlantic Flyway. [U.S. Department of the Interior, Bureau of Sport Fisheries and Wildlife.] Mimeographed reports.

BELLROSE, FRANK C. 1957. A spectacular waterfowl migration through central North America. Illinois Natural History Survey Biological Notes 36. 24pp.

———, AND JAMES G. SIEH. 1960. Massed waterfowl flights in the Mississippi Flyway, 1956 and 1957. Wilson Bulletin 72(1):29–59.

[BULLER, RAYMOND J.] 1960, 1964–66. Summary of Central Flyway midwinter waterfowl population survey. [U.S. Department of the Interior, Bureau of Sport Fisheries and Wildlife.] Mimeographed reports.

CARTWRIGHT, BERTRAM W., AND JEAN T. LAW. 1952. Waterfowl banding 1939–1950 by Ducks Unlimited. Ducks Unlimited, Winnipeg. 53pp.

GREEN, WILLIAM E. 1963. Waterfowl utilization and hunting kill 1946 through 1960 Upper Mississippi River Wildlife and Fish Refuge and Mark Twain National Wildlife Refuge. U.S. Department of the Interior, Fish and Wildlife Service Special Scientific Report—Wildlife 71. 62pp.

HANDLEY, DELMAR E. 1958. Waterfowl band recoveries for Ohio 1939–1956. Ohio Department of Natural Resources, Division of Wildlife Technical Bulletin 3. 94pp.

HANSON, HAROLD C., AND ROBERT H. SMITH. 1950. Canada geese of the Mississippi Flyway. Illinois Natural History Survey Bulletin 25(3):67–210.

HANSON, ROSSALIUS C. 1963. Tabulation of periodic Canada goose surveys in the Atlantic and Mississippi flyways, 1960–1963. [U.S. Department of the Interior] Bureau of Sport Fisheries and Wildlife [Minneapolis]. Mimeographed report. n.p.

———. 1965. Tabulation of periodic Canada goose

surveys in the Atlantic and Mississippi flyways 1960–1965. [U.S. Department of the Interior, Bureau of Sport Fisheries and Wildlife, Minneapolis.] Mimeographed report. n.p.

———. 1966. Tabulation of Canada goose surveys in the Mississippi Flyway by populations and flocks fall and winter 1964–1966. [U.S. Department of the Interior, Bureau of Sport Fisheries and Wildlife, Minneapolis.] Mimeographed report. n.p.

———. 1967. Tabulation of Canada goose surveys in the Mississippi flyway by populations and flocks fall and winter 1965–1967. [U.S. Department of the Interior, Bureau of Sport Fisheries and Wildlife, Minneapolis.] Mimeographed report. n.p.

HAWKINS, ARTHUR S. 1964. The January 1964 waterfowl population survey in Mississippi Flyway states. [U.S. Department of the Interior, Bureau of Sport Fisheries and Wildlife, Minneapolis.] Mimeographed report. n.p.

———. 1965. The 1965 mid-winter waterfowl survey in the Mississippi Flyway states. [U.S. Department of the Interior, Bureau of Sport Fisheries and Wildlife, Minneapolis.] Mimeographed report. n.p.

———, AND ROSSALIUS C. HANSON. 1960. Results of the January 1960 waterfowl survey in the Mississippi Flyway states. U.S. Department of the Interior, Bureau of Sport Fisheries and Wildlife, Minneapolis. Mimeographed report. n.p.

———, AND ———. 1961. Results of the January 1961 waterfowl survey in the Mississippi Flyway states. U.S. Department of the Interior, Bureau of Sport Fisheries and Wildlife, Minneapolis. Mimeographed report. n.p.

———, AND ———. 1962. Results of the January 1962 waterfowl survey in the Mississippi Flyway states. U.S. Department of the Interior, Bureau of Sport Fisheries and Wildlife, Minneapolis. Mimeographed report. n.p.

———, AND ———. 1966. The 1966 mid-winter waterfowl survey in the Mississippi Flyway states. [U.S. Department of the Interior, Bureau of Sport Fisheries and Wildlife, Minneapolis.] Mimeographed report. n.p.

———, AND DONALD E. WIELAND. 1963. Results of the January 1963 waterfowl survey in the Mississippi Flyway states. U.S. Department of the Interior, Bureau of Sport Fisheries and Wildlife, Minneapolis. Mimeographed report. n.p.

HICKEY, JOSEPH J. 1951. Mortality records as indices of migration in the mallard. Condor 53(6):284–297.

———. 1956. Autumnal migration of ducks banded in eastern Wisconsin. Wisconsin Academy of Sciences, Arts and Letters Transactions 45: 59–76.

HYDE, ROBERT K. 1958. Florida waterfowl band recoveries 1920–1957. Florida Game and Fresh Water Fish Commission. 23pp. + 34 maps.

JAHN, LAURENCE R., AND RICHARD A. HUNT. 1964. Duck and coot ecology and management in Wisconsin. Wisconsin Conservation Department Technical Bulletin 33. 212pp.

KEELER, JAMES E. 1956. Alabama waterfowl band recoveries 1929–1956. Alabama Department of Conservation, Division of Game and Fish Federal Aid in Wildlife Restoration Special Report 1. n.p.

LEE, FORREST B., GERALD T. BUE, NORMAN J. ORDAL, AND ROBERT E. FARMES. 1954. Minnesota bands ducks. Conservation Volunteer 18(102):5–18.

LENSINK, CALVIN J. 1964. Distribution of recoveries from bandings of ducklings. U.S. Department of the Interior, Bureau of Sport Fisheries and Wildlife Special Scientific Report—Wildlife 89. 146pp.

LOW, SETH H. 1957. Waterfowl banding in the Canadian prairie provinces. U.S. Department of the Interior, Bureau of Sport Fisheries and Wildlife Special Scientific Report—Wildlife 36. 30pp.

MISSISSIPPI FLYWAY COUNCIL TECHNICAL SECTION. 1954–56. Unpublished periodic waterfowl census reports by individual states.

MOISAN, GASTON, ROBERT I. SMITH, AND R. KAHLER MARTINSON. 1967. The green-winged teal: its distribution, migration, and population dynamics. U.S. Department of the Interior, Bureau of Sport Fisheries and Wildlife Special Scientific Report—Wildlife 100. 248pp.

MUMFORD, RUSSELL E. 1954. Waterfowl management in Indiana. Indiana Department of Conservation Pittman-Robertson Bulletin 2. 99pp.

MURDY, RAY. 1955. Analysis of first-year recoveries of mallards and Canada geese banded at Lake Andes and in the Black Hills during the winter of 1950–51. South Dakota Department of Game, Fish and Parks Project W-17-R-9 Job Completion Report. 20pp.

NELSON, HARVEY K. 1958. Factors in whistling swan management. U.S. Department of the Interior, Bureau of Sport Fisheries and Wildlife, Minneapolis. Mimeographed report. 11pp.

SCHIERBAUM, DONALD, DIRCK BENSON, LEE W. DEGRAFF, AND DONALD D. FOLEY. 1959. Waterfowl banding in New York. New York Fish and Game Journal 6(1):86–102.

SINGLETON, J. R. 1953. Texas coastal waterfowl survey. Texas Game and Fish Commission Federal Aid in Wildlife Restoration Project 29-R Final Report. 128pp.

[SMITH, MORTON M.] 1961. Louisiana waterfowl population study. Louisiana Wild Life and Fisheries Commission Pittman-Robertson Projects W-17R and W-29R Final Report. 49pp. + 63 figs.

STEWART, ROBERT E. 1962. Waterfowl populations

in the upper Chesapeake region. U.S. Department of the Interior, Bureau of Sport Fisheries and Wildlife Special Scientific Report—Wildlife 65. 208pp.

———, AELRED D. GEIS, AND CHARLES D. EVANS. 1958. Distribution of populations and hunting kill of the canvasback. Journal of Wildlife Management 22(4):333–370.

YANCEY, RICHARD K., MORTON M. SMITH, LAURENCE R. JAHN, AND HERBERT J. MILLER. 1958. Waterfowl distribution and migration in the Mississippi Flyway. Mississippi Flyway Council Technical Section Report. 20pp. + 39 fig.

APPENDIX

The common and scientific names of waterfowl referred to in the text are:

Geese

Common name	Scientific name
Canada Goose	*Branta canadensis*
Lesser Snow Goose (Blue Goose)	*Anser caerulescens*

Dabbling Ducks

Common name	Scientific name
Mallard	*Anas platyrhynchos*
Black Duck	*Anas rubripes*
Gadwall	*Anas strepera*
Pintail	*Anas acuta*
Green-winged Teal	*Anas carolinensis*
Baldpate	*Mareca americana*
Shoveler	*Spatula clypeata*

Diving Ducks

Common name	Scientific name
Redhead	*Aythya americana*
Ring-necked Duck	*Aythya collaris*
Canvasback	*Aythya valisineria*
Greater Scaup	*Aythya marila*
Lesser Scaup	*Aythya affinis*

RADIAL DISPERSAL AND SOUTHWARD MIGRATION OF WOOD DUCKS BANDED IN VERMONT[1]

PAUL A. STEWART, 203 Mooreland Drive, Oxford, NC 27565

This paper involves an analysis of the dispersal and migratory movements of Wood Ducks (*Aix sponsa*) with use of recoveries of birds banded in Vermont. Data from Vermont were chosen because this state is located in the more northern part of the Wood Duck's range and because a relatively large number of recoveries were available of birds banded there. All of the recoveries available on 10 March 1976 of Wood Ducks banded in Vermont were obtained from the Bird Banding Laboratory, Migratory Bird Populations Station, Laurel, Maryland, for use in this study.

METHODS AND MATERIALS

The data were selected to include only birds recovered before a second migratory period passed after banding. Thus, the recoveries show what can be assumed to be direct flights from Vermont, the hatching or breeding grounds, to recovery sites. Selection was made also to include only birds shot by hunters. The time and rate of the major southward migration was determined by averaging recovery dates.

RESULTS AND DISCUSSION

A total of 3,096 recoveries was obtained, and 1,403 of these were selected for use in this study. The distribution of the 1,403 recoveries is shown in Fig. 1. The largest proportion of the recoveries was made in Vermont or elsewhere nearby, but some birds were scattered over a wide area in southeastern Canada and the eastern United States, a substantial part of the eastern portion of the range of the Wood Duck. Some few birds made relatively long flights, with one going more than 2,250 km to Texas and one more than 1,290 km to Newfoundland.

The band recoveries show the largest number of birds moving southward; however, they also show movements in other directions than southward. Single birds went in a northerly direction each to Newfoundland and Nova Scotia, and 13 birds went in a westerly direction to Ontario. These were direct flights showing northward and westward movements after the breeding season. Earlier I noted northward movement of Wood Ducks after the breeding season (Stewart 1972) and pointed out that Wood Ducks in Ohio make a radial movement in late September and early October, flying various distances in all compass directions (Stewart 1958). The dispersal flight is made ahead and independently of recognized southward migration.

In their southward migration the banded Wood Ducks started their movement in early or mid-November and continued it at least until mid-December, the average date on which the birds were shot being progressively later to the southward (Fig. 2). The progressively later dates to the southward suggest that the birds moved southward with the advancing season. The largest percentages of recoveries were taken in the Atlantic coastal states, partly because the birds were funnelled into a lane by the Atlantic Ocean. However, more importantly it seems probable that these birds followed

---

[1] Originally published in Bird-Banding 48(4):333–336, 1977. Reproduced by permission of the Northeastern Bird-Banding Association.

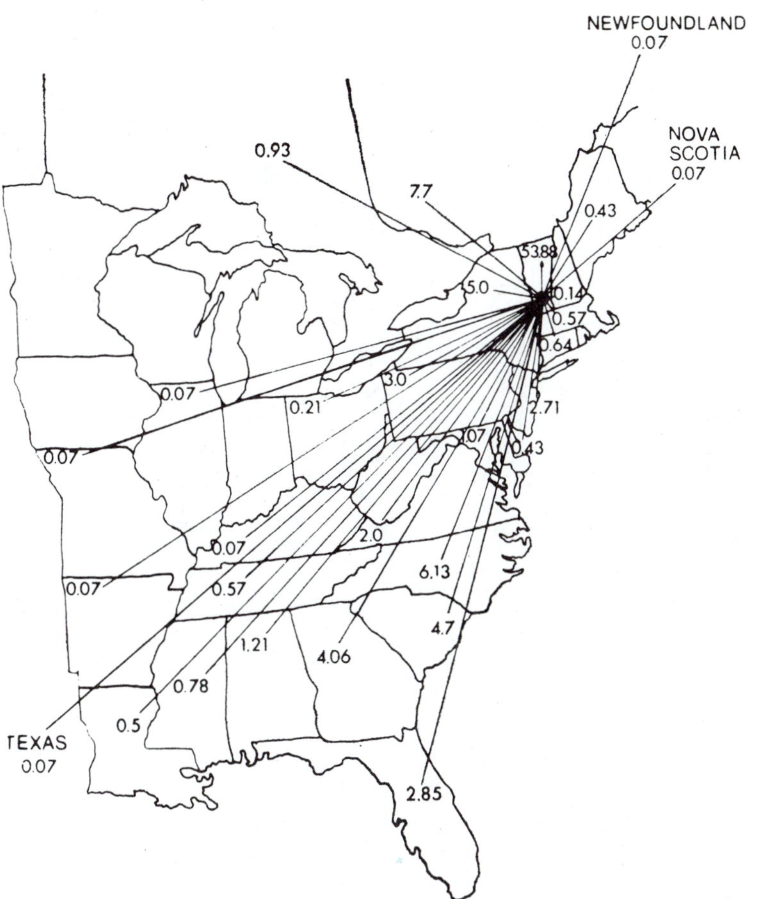

Fig. 1. Percentages of 1,403 Wood Ducks recovered in different states and provinces after one dispersal and one migratory period.

their preferred habitat southward. Wooded swamps provide favored habitat for Wood Ducks, and these birds moved southward largely on a strip of land containing swampy habitat, the Princess Anne, Pamlico, Talbot, Penholoway, Wicomico, and Sunderland terraces. According to Fenneman (1938) the greatest swamps are on the Princess Anne and Pamlico terraces, but the other terraces also contain an abundance of swampy habitat.

Dispersal movements of Wood Ducks are characterized by marked differences in the length of the flights made by different birds. Likewise, some birds may remain throughout the winter where they went in their dispersal flight, even far north of their breeding grounds. Thus, the Wood Duck recovered in Newfoundland on 2 December 1968 was banded in Vermont on 6 September 1968. The literature also contains numerous reports of Wood Ducks remaining in the more northern regions beyond the usual time for southward migration, with such occurrences being reported during mid-January in Ontario (Bailie 1951), during

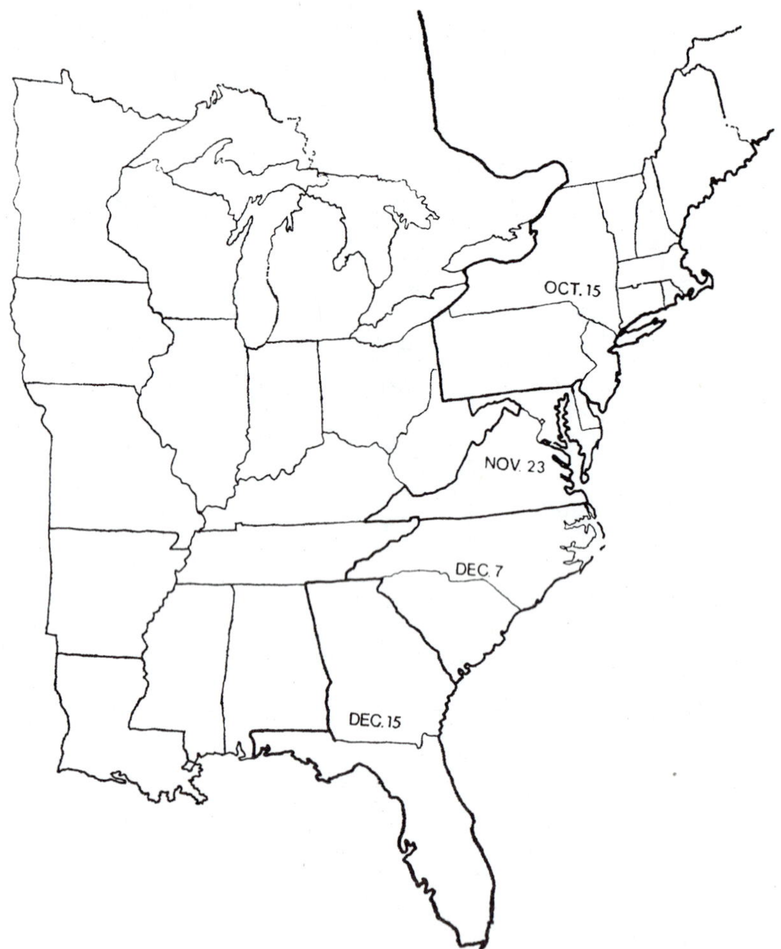

Fig. 2. Average dates on which banded Wood Ducks were shot in different regions, the regions being outlined with heavier lines than state boundaries.

January in Massachusetts (Morgan and Emery 1956), and during late January in Idaho (Low 1952).

SUMMARY

With use of 1,403 recoveries of Wood Ducks banded in Vermont, an analysis was made of movements of the species. The birds made radial movements after the nesting season and before the regular southward migration, with a small part of the population making relatively long flights but most making short flights. Birds on their southward migration appeared to move gradually southward, following swampy habitat. Some Wood Ducks remained beyond the migration season far north of their hatching or breeding grounds.

ACKNOWLEDGMENTS

I gratefully acknowledge the help of the Bird Banding Laboratory in making these banding and recovery records available for my use in this study. Also, the help of the Vermont Department of

Fish and Game in granting me permission to use the data resulting from their banding efforts is gratefully acknowledged. David E. Stewart aided by making the two maps.

LITERATURE CITED

BAILIE, J. L. 1951. Ontario-western New York region. Aud. Field Notes 5:201–203.

FENNEMAN, N. M. 1938. Physiography of the Eastern United States. New York, McGraw-Hill.

LOW, J. B. 1952. Great Basin-central Rocky Mountain region. Aud. Field Notes 6:207–208.

MORGAN, A., AND R. P. EMORY. 1956. Northeastern maritime region. Aud. Field Notes 10:234–236.

STEWART, P. A. 1958. Local movements of Wood Ducks (*Aix sponsa*). Auk 75:157–168.

———. 1972. Northward movement of Wood Ducks after the nesting season. Raven 43:28–29.

MIGRATION REVERSAL: A REGULAR PHENOMENON OF CANADA GEESE[1]

DENNIS G. RAVELING,[2] Canadian Wildlife Service, Winnipeg, Manitoba R3T 2N6, Canada

Abstract: Migration from a nesting to a wintering ground and back again in autumn was detected each year during a 3-year study of individually identifiable Canada geese (*Branta canadensis*). Reverse migrants were primarily yearling, nonbreeding individuals and others of nonfamily status.

Bird migration is normally considered as an orderly departure and return to the same area with the changing seasons. Flocks migrating opposite to the usual direction are uncommon, and causes are usually attributed to untoward weather conditions (Hochbaum 1955, Dorst 1962). My study of Canada geese (*Branta canadensis*) demonstrated regular occurrence of migration to wintering grounds and return to the nesting area in autumn among a small portion of the population. Reverse migrants were primarily 1-year-old, nonbreeding individuals and others not associated with families, which dominate goose society.

During July, August, and early September of 1968, 1969, and 1970, 1,523 geese were captured and marked with individually identifiable plastic neck collars (Sherwood 1966) and released at a marsh on the southeastern shore of Lake Manitoba (50°30′N, 98°W) 96 km northwest of Winnipeg, Manitoba, Canada. Age and sex of geese were determined by plumage and cloacal characters (Hanson 1962). Marked geese were observed at the marsh for an average of 2 days per week between 20 September and 20 November, during which all normal and reverse autumn migrations of this flock occurred. The main wintering site for this population was at Rochester, Minnesota (44°N, 92°20′W), 855 km southeast of the banding site (Hanson 1965, Gulden and Johnson 1968). Marked geese observed in Rochester during autumn were recorded sporadically by me and by cooperators.

Canada geese mature sexually at 2 years of age (Hanson 1962). Three age classes were identified: immatures—banded and observed during the summer and autumn in which they hatched; yearlings—1½ years of age; adults—more than 2½ years of age. Most yearlings were away from the marsh at banding time at a distant molting site (Sterling and Dzubin 1967), but they returned to their natal marsh in autumn. Most observations (94.1 percent) of yearlings were made in 1969 and 1970 and represent surviving geese banded when immature the previous year.

Twenty-eight of 1594 marked geese (1.8 percent) identified in Manitoba during autumn 1968, 1969, and 1970 migrated to, and were seen at, Rochester, Minnesota, and then seen again in Manitoba in the same autumn. The length of stay of these geese at Rochester was imprecisely known because of irregular observation, but different individuals remained at least 2, 8, 10, 17, 42 and 61 days before returning to Manitoba. Irregular observation at Rochester also indi-

---

[1] Originally published in Science 193(4248): 153–154, 1976. Copyright 1976 by the American Association for the Advancement of Science.

[2] Present address: Wildlife and Fisheries Biology, University of California–Davis, Davis, CA 95616.

cates that there could have been other reverse migrants that were undetected. Reverse migrants were predominantly yearlings ($\chi^2 = 26.56$; 2 df; $P < 0.001$) (Table 1). There were no differences within any age class in the proportions of the sexes that participated in reverse migration.

Table 1. Number of marked Canada geese in relation to migration pattern.

Age	Migration	
	Normal	Reverse
Adult	477	10 (2.1 percent)
Yearling	223	13 (5.5 percent)
Immature	866	5 (0.6 percent)

Canada geese have a complex social organization. Goslings normally stay with parents for the first year of life and yearlings may rejoin parents, form pairs or sibling groups, or be unattached (Raveling 1968, 1969*a,b,c,* 1970). Some families include goslings other than those hatched by the adult pair, and these associations are termed gang brood families (Williams and Marshall 1938, Miller and Collins 1953, Brakhage 1965). Marked geese observed in autumn in Manitoba were categorized as to their social relations based on stereotyped displays and unity in aggression, flying, and feeding, which indicate familial bonds (Raveling 1968, 1969*a,b,c,* 1970)—as well as on repeated observation of associations of the identifiable birds of known age, sex, and history (Table 2).

Reverse migrant adults were primarily of unidentifiable social status and not birds with families ($\chi^2 = 21.64$; 5 df; $P < 0.001$). Single adults and even pairs were unaggressive (Raveling 1968, 1969*a,b,c,* 1970) and therefore difficult to identify as to social relations, especially if mates were unmarked, because of the low frequency of behaviors used to identify social positions. One adult male participated in reverse migration in both 1969 and 1970 and was a single in one year and of unidentified status in the other.

There was not a significant difference among social classes of yearlings that participated in reverse migration ($\chi^2 = 3.16$; 5 df; $P > 0.5$). As with adults, single yearlings were difficult to identify. Even sibling groups were difficult to ascertain when all members were not marked and identified from observations as immatures. Yearlings that formed a pair bond were usually together and none participated in reverse migration. Yearlings in sibling groups usually stayed together, and one of these groups participated in reverse migration. Yearlings rejoining their parents and new young were variable in behavior and not always in association with their families; these were probably singles when they participated in reverse migration because their parents were not observed with them.

Immatures in identified families did not reverse migrate in proportion to those unclassified as to status or those which were singles ($\chi^2 = 8.34$; 3 df; $P < 0.02$). Immatures in families were frequently separated temporarily from their parents during feeding because of the large numbers of geese crowded into a small area where food was artificially provided. It was during these feeding periods that most observations of marked birds were made and, as a result, I was indecisive on the status of many young.

Single geese, particularly yearlings are much more variable in daily roost and feeding locations and flight patterns than are families (Raveling 1968, 1969*a,b,c,* 1970). They tend to join in flight with geese taking off near them, whereas adults with young maintain consistent patterns. Return to previously used areas

Table 2. Social status of marked Canada geese in relation to migration pattern.

	Migration					
	Adult		Yearling		Immature	
Status	Normal	Reverse	Normal	Reverse	Normal	Reverse
Family*	252	0	1	0	432	1
Gang brood family	11	2			135	0
Paired—no young	60	1	19	0		
Sibling group	5	0	27	3†		
Rejoin parents			34	2‡		
Single	17	1	19	2	23	1
Unknown	132	6	123	6	276	3
Total	477	10	223	13	866	5

* Includes pairs with 1-year-old (or older) young with or without immatures.
† Three siblings always together migrated back as a group.
‡ Variable behavior—sometimes with parents, sometimes as a single or with a sibling.

is a major mechanism of reunificiation of family members. Yearlings are also less traditional in migration patterns than adults (Vaught and Kirsch 1966). The strong gregarious nature of geese, coupled with the following behavior of yearling and nonfamily geese, results in some interchange with other flocks and populations and probably accounts for the unusual but regular occurrence of these reverse migrations. Strong attachments to, and seeking of, family members (Fischer 1965; Raveling 1968, 1969*a,b,c,* 1970) probably motivated their return to the natal marsh or autumn concentration locality.

Of the 28 reverse migrants, 21 returned again in the same autumn to Rochester, Minnesota. Of the other seven, the fate of two was unknown, one was shot in Manitoba and another in Iowa, one was observed in Missouri, and two were observed in Kansas. Irregular migration behavior by yearlings and singles could provide a major mechanism of gene flow, even though one of small proportions, between populations as localized and traditional as Canada geese, which exhibit marked isolationism and show geographic variation in morphology (Delacour 1954, Hanson 1965, Gulden and Johnson 1968).

ACKNOWLEDGMENTS

I thank the P. D. Curry and A. J. Vincent families for permission to study on their property; many personnel of the Manitoba Department of Mines, Energy, and Natural Resources and the Minnesota Department of Natural Resources for assistance in the field; M. R. Petersen for assistance in preparation and analysis of data.

LITERATURE CITED

BRAKHAGE, G. K. 1965. J. Wildl. Manage. 29:751.
DELACOUR, J. 1954. The waterfowl of the world. Volume 1. Country Life, London. Pages 150–178.
DORST, J. 1962. The migrations of birds. Houghton Mifflin, Boston. Pages 239, 240.
FISCHER, H. 1965. Z. Tierpsychol. 22:247.
GULDEN, N. A., AND L. L. JOHNSON. 1968. Page 59 *in* R. L. Hine and C. Schoenfeld, eds. Canada goose management. Dembar Educational Research Service, Madison, Wis.
HANSON, H. C. 1962. Ill. Nat. Hist. Surv. Biol. Notes 49:1.
———. 1965. The giant Canada goose. Southern Illinois Univ. Press, Carbondale. Pages 97–99.
HOCHBAUM, H. A. 1955. Travels and traditions of waterfowl. Univ. Minnesota Press, Mineapolis. Pages 112, 113, 132, 133.
MILLER, A. W., AND B. D. COLLINS. 1953. Calif. Fish and Game 39:385.

RAVELING, D. G. 1968. Page 87 *in* R. L. Hine and C. Schoenfeld, eds. Canada goose management. Dembar Educational Research Service, Madison, Wis.

———. 1969*a*. Auk 86:671.

———. 1969*b*. J. Wildl. Manage. 33:304.

———. 1969*c*. J. Wildl. Manage. 33:330.

———. 1970. Behaviour 37:291.

SHERWOOD, G. A. 1966. J. Wildl. Manage. 30:853.

STERLING, T., AND A. DZUBIN. 1967. Trans. North Am. Wildl. Nat. Resour. Conf. 32:355.

VAUGHT, R. W., AND L. M. KIRSCH. 1966. Canada geese of the eastern prairie population. Mo. Dep. Conserv. Tech. Bull. 3.

WILLIAMS, C. S., AND W. H. MARSHALL. 1938. J. Wildl. Manage. 2:17.

SELECTED BIBLIOGRAPHY

Movement and Migration

ABRAHAM, K. F. 1980. Moult migration of lesser snow geese. Wildfowl 31:89–93.

BELLROSE, F. C. 1957. A spectacular waterfowl migration through central North America. Ill. Nat. Hist. Surv. Biol. Notes 36. 24pp.

———. 1958. Celestial orientation by wild mallards. Bird-Banding 29(2):75–90.

———. 1958. The orientation of displaced waterfowl in migration. Wilson Bull. 70(1):20–40.

———. 1963. Orientation behavior of four species of waterfowl. Auk 80:257–289.

———. 1964. Radar studies of waterfowl migration. Trans. North Am. Wildl. Nat. Resour. Conf. 29:128–143.

———. 1972. Mallard migration corridors as revealed by population distribution, banding, and radar. Pages 3–26 *in* Population ecology of migratory birds; a symposium. U.S. Dep. Inter. Bur. Sport Fish and Wildl. Res. Rep. 2. 278pp.

———. 1974. The effects of short-term weather on the migration of waterfowl. Fed. Aviation Adm. Final Rep. Wash., D.C. 42pp.

———, AND R. D. CROMPTON. 1970. Migrational behavior of mallards and black ducks as determined from banding. Ill. Nat. Hist. Surv. Bull. 30(3):167–234.

———, AND ———. 1981. Migration speeds of three waterfowl species. Wilson Bull. 93:121–124.

BERGMAN, R. D. 1973. Use of southern boreal lakes by postbreeding canvasbacks and redheads. J. Wildl. Manage. 37(2):160–170.

BISHOP, R. A., D. D. HUMBURG, AND R. D. ANDREWS. 1978. Survival and homing of female mallards. J. Wildl. Manage. 42(1):192–196.

BRAKHAGE, G. K. 1953. Migration and mortality of ducks hand-reared and wild-trapped at Delta, Manitoba. J. Wildl. Manage. 17(4):465–477.

COOKE, W. W. 1906. Distribution and migration of North American ducks, geese, and swans. U.S. Dep. Agric. Biol. Surv. Bull. 26. 90pp.

CRISSEY, W. F. 1955. The use of banding data in determining waterfowl migration and distribution. J. Wildl. Manage. 19(1):75–84.

DAU, C. P., AND P. G. MICKELSON. 1979. Relation of weather to spring migration and nesting of cackling geese on the Yukon-Kuskokwim Delta, Alaska. Pages 94–104 *in* R. L. Jarvis and J. C. Bartonek, eds. Management and biology of Pacific flyway geese. A symposium. Northwest Sect. of The Wildl. Soc. Oregon State Univ. Book Stores, Inc., Corvallis.

DOTY, H. A., AND F. B. LEE. 1974. Homing to nest baskets by wild female mallards. J. Wildl. Manage. 38(4):714–719.

DZUBIN, A. 1955. Some evidences of home range in waterfowl. Trans. North Am. Wildl. Conf. 20:278–298.

———. 1965. A study of migrating Ross geese in western Saskatchewan. Condor 67(6):511–534.

ERSKINE, A. J. 1972. Buffleheads. Can. Wildl. Serv. Monogr. Ser. 4. 240pp.

FLICKINGER, E. L. 1981. Weather conditions associated with beginning of northward migration departures of snow geese. J. Wildl. Manage. 45:516–520.

HANKLA, D. J., AND R. R. RUDOLPH.

1967. Changes in the migration and wintering habits of Canada geese in the lower portion of the Atlantic and Mississippi flyways—With special reference to national wildlife refuges. Proc. Annu. Conf. S.E. Assoc. Game Fish Comm. 21:133–144.

HEIN, D., AND A. O. HAUGEN. 1966. Illumination and wood duck roosting flights. Wilson Bull. 78(3):301–308.

JOHNSGARD, P. A. 1961. Wintering distribution changes in mallards and black ducks. Am. Midl. Nat. 66(2):477–484.

KOERNER, J. W., T. A. BOOKHOUT, AND K. E. BEDNARIK. 1974. Movements of Canada geese color-marked near southwestern Lake Erie. J. Wildl. Manage. 38(2):275–289.

KROHN, W. B., AND E. G. BIZEAU. 1979. Molt migration of the Rocky Mountain population of the western Canada goose. Pages 130–140 *in* R. L. Jarvis and J. C. Bartonek, eds. Management and biology of Pacific flyway geese. A symposium. Northwest Sect. of The Wildl. Soc. Oregon State Univ. Book Stores, Inc., Corvallis.

MACINNES, C. D. 1966. Population behavior of eastern Arctic Canada geese. J. Wildl. Manage. 30(3):536–553.

MANN, G. E. 1950. Reverse Fall migration. J. Wildl. Manage. 14(3):360–362.

MCCABE, R. A. 1947. The homing of transplanted young wood ducks. Wilson Bull. 59(2):104–109.

MELINCHUK, R., AND J. P. RYDER. 1980. The distribution, fall migration routes and survival of Ross's geese. Wildfowl 31:161–171.

RATTI, J. T., AND D. E. TIMM. 1979. Migratory behavior of Vancouver Canada geese: recovery rate bias. Pages 208–212 *in* R. L. Jarvis and J. C. Bartonek, eds. Management and biology of Pacific flyway geese. A symposium. Northwest Sect. of The Wildl. Soc. Oregon State Univ. Book Stores, Inc., Corvallis.

SCHLADWEILER, J. L., AND J. R. TESTER. 1972. Survival and behavior of hand-reared mallards released in the wild. J. Wildl. Manage. 36:1118–1127.

STERLING, T., AND A. DZUBIN. 1967. Canada goose molt migrations to the Northwest Territories. Trans. North Am. Wildl. Nat. Resour. Conf. 32:355–373.

WELLER, M. W. 1964. Distribution and migration of the redhead. J. Wildl. Manage. 28(1):64–103.

———, AND P. WARD. 1959. Migration and mortality of hand-reared redheads (*Aythya americana*). J. Wildl. Manage. 23(4):427–433.

WINNER, R. W. 1959. Field-feeding periodicity of black and mallard ducks. J. Wildl. Manage 23(2):197–202.

WOOLINGTON, D. W., P. F. SPRINGER, AND D. R. YPARRAGUIRRE. 1979. Migration and wintering distribution of Aleutian Canada geese. 1979. Pages 299–309 *in* R. L. Jarvis and J. C. Bartonek, eds. Management and biology of Pacific flyway geese. A symposium. Northwest Sect. of The Wildl. Soc. Oregon State Univ. Book Stores, Inc., Corvallis.

ZICUS, M. C. 1981. Molt migration of Canada geese from Crex Meadows, Wisconsin. J. Wildl. Manage. 45:54–63.

WINTERING WATERFOWL

© D. R. BARRICK

DISTRIBUTION AND ABUNDANCE OF WATERFOWL WINTERING IN SOUTHERN QUEBEC[1]

AUSTIN REED and ANDRÉ BOURGET, Canadian Wildlife Service, Environment Canada, P.O. Box 10 100, Ste.-Foy, Quebec G1V 4H5, Canada

Abstract: In January and February of 1974, 1975, and 1976, surveys of wintering waterfowl were conducted through most open-water areas of southern Quebec. These surveys indicated the presence of at least 171,000 ducks, mostly diving and sea ducks in the estuary and Gulf of St. Lawrence. Inland freshwater areas, mainly in the Montreal region, supported many Common Goldeneye (*Bucephala clangula*), Common Merganser (*Mergus merganser*), and Black Duck (*Anas rubripes*). The most abundant ducks on the estuarine portion were Oldsquaw (*Clangula hyemalis*), Common and Barrow's (*Bucephala islandica*) Goldeneyes, and Black Duck. In the gulf, Common Eider (*Somateria mollissima*), Oldsquaw, Common and Barrow's Goldeneyes were abundant. The area of the estuary and gulf is of international importance as a sea- and diving-duck wintering ground. Further study and close surveillance are required owing to the birds' apparently great vulnerability to oil pollution and habitat change in a very rigorous climate.

Several species of water birds overwinter in southern Quebec, principally along the St. Lawrence river, estuary, and gulf. Heavy ship traffic during the winter and expanding urban and industrial development along the shores are posing an ever increasing threat to those birds and to their habitats. The paucity of published information prompted us to assemble recent unpublished reports and to conduct surveys to document the distribution and abundance of waterfowl inhabiting that area during the winter.

STUDY AREA AND METHODS

In early February 1974, 1975, and 1976, we attempted to cover all open-water areas in southern Quebec by ground and/or aerial counts.

Regional differences in accessibility, habitat type, and species composition prevented the use of a standard survey procedure for the entire study area. We subdivided the area into 10 zones based on these regional differences (Fig. 1).

The 1974 survey was carried out from 31 January to 20 February, in 1975 from 3 to 6 February, and in 1976 from 1 to 12 February. Ground crews (P. Blais, A. Bourget, H. Briard, G. Chapdelaine, P. Dupuis, G. Fortin, P. Lamothe, M. Laverdière, D. Lehoux, P. Rancourt, A. Reed, L.-G. de Repentigny, J. Rosa, J.-P. Savard, and G. Tremblay) methodically scanned all open-water areas with telescopes and binoculars in all zones except part of zone F. Dupuis and Tremblay conducted aerial surveys that covered mainly zones E and F. In most flights a Cessna 337 was flown at an altitude of approximately 60 m parallel to, and about 70 m seaward from, the edge of the shoreline of permanent ice. At some coastal sites flights were conducted up to 15 km from shore to check for offshore flocks of sea ducks.

Supplementary observations were available from previous years for the Montreal area and the north shore of the estuary, mainly since 1964. Files of the Canadian Wildlife Service and the Quebec Wildlife Service yielded unpublished results of various winter surveys conducted from 1952 to 1963, mainly in the Montreal area. The winter season was

---

[1] Originally published in Can. Field-Nat. 91(1):1–7, 1977.

[2] Address correspondence to this author. Present address: 16 Place Valcourt, Neufchatel, Quebec, Canada.

considered to extend from 1 January to 28 February.

RESULTS

The combined results of the 1974, 1975, and 1976 surveys are presented in Table 1 and Fig. 1. We believe that we consistently underestimated the bird populations because (1) exhaustive surveys were not possible over such a vast and partly inaccessible area, (2) many of the species inhabited offshore areas and were difficult to detect from aircraft (see Stotts and Olson 1972), and (3) cold air temperatures and ice conditions reduced the efficiency of the observers. For these reasons, the largest number of birds recorded in each zone over the three winters can be considered as the best estimate of that population; we have presented those maximum counts in Table 1. The data, in summarized form, are plotted in Fig. 1 to show major concentration areas. Those results, and previous data, form the basis for the description which follows for each area.

(A) Ottawa River

Most of this area was frozen over in winter; only a few natural pools and areas below a hydroelectric dam remained open. In 1974 (no counts in 1975–76) three species of ducks occurred but only in small groups: Black Ducks (*Anas rubripes*), Common Goldeneyes (*Bucephala clangula*), and Common Mergansers (*Mergus merganser*).

(B) Montreal

This region has large areas of open water, principally at the inlets and outlets of its two largest bodies of water, Lake St. Francis and Lake St. Louis. The Lachine rapids were particularly important. The Montreal region possessed the most important winter-bird concentrations in freshwater areas in Quebec. The Common Merganser was the most abundant species in the Montreal region; more than 3,500 birds spent the winters of 1974 and 1975 in open water below the Cornwall hydroelectric dam, feeding on fish which had passed through the turbines. The Common Goldeneye was second in importance and the Black Duck third.

(C) Eastern Townships

All areas south of Lake St. Peter and east of Montreal were included in this zone. Open-water areas were found along fast-flowing streams and rivers in this rolling countryside. In contrast to the ice-free areas of the St. Lawrence, which were relatively consistent in size and location from year to year, open water was highly variable in extent and location within and between winters. No large concentrations of ducks were encountered. Common Mergansers, Common Goldeneyes, and Black Ducks occurred regularly.

(D) Lake St. Peter

This zone had no appreciable areas of permanent open water and no waterfowl were observed.

(E) Estuary

This portion of the St. Lawrence had large expanses of open water throughout the winter. Of particular importance were large sections of tidal flats near the mouth of the Saguenay River where tides and river currents prevented the formation of permanent ice. Along most of the south shore, water areas suitable for aquatic bird use were frozen over.

This vast area included some of the most important wintering sites for waterfowl in the province, especially along the north shore of the St. Lawrence. The most important concentration of winter-

Table 1. Estimated numbers of aquatic birds that overwinter in the St. Lawrence River system, Quebec. Each number represents the maximum count obtained. Surveys were conducted in most regions in February 1974, 1975, and 1976.

Species	Regions									
	Ottawa River	Montreal	Eastern townships	Estuary	North shore	Gaspésie	Baie des Chaleurs	Matapédia River	Lake St. John	Total
Black Duck (*Anas rubripes*)	56	506	71	1,906				4		2,543
Common Goldeneye (*Bucephala clangula*)	160	2,908	164	8,328[1]	979[1]	332	111	12	8	13,002
Barrow's Goldeneye (*Bucephala islandica*)	1		4	1,394	869	260	19			2,547
Bufflehead (*Bucephala albeola*)		1	2	69		1				73
Oldsquaw (*Clangula hyemalis*)				6,451	2,411	46,782	48			55,692
Surf Scoter (*Melanitta perspicillata*)					185					185
Common Eider (*Somateria mollissima*)				9	91,035	505				91,549
Common Merganser (*Mergus merganser*)	16	5,300	196	19		5	5	7	2	5,550
Red-breasted Merganser (*Mergus serrator*)			2	91	74	98	23	1		289
Miscellaneous duck species[2]	1	72	12	3	1					89
Sub total—ducks	234	8,787	451	18,270	95,554	47,983	206	24	10	171,519
Great Cormorant (*Phalacrocorax carbo*)						21	91			112
Black Guillemot (*Cepphus grylle*)				78		57	42			177
Total	234	8,787	451	18,348	95,554	48,061	339	24	10	171,808

[1] May include some *B. islandica*.

[2] Miscellaneous duck species by order of importance are as follows: Ottawa River, Mallard (*Anas platyrhynchus*); Montreal, Mallard, Pintail (*Anas acuta*), Canvasback (*Aythya valisineria*), Redhead (*Aythya americana*), Lesser Scaup (*Aythya affinis*), Ring-necked Duck (*Aythya collaris*), American Wigeon (*Anas americana*); Eastern Townships, Mallard, Hooded Merganser (*Lophodytes cucullatus*); Estuary, Harlequin Duck (*Histrionicus histrionicus*), Mallard; North Shore, Black Scoter (*Melanitta nigra*).

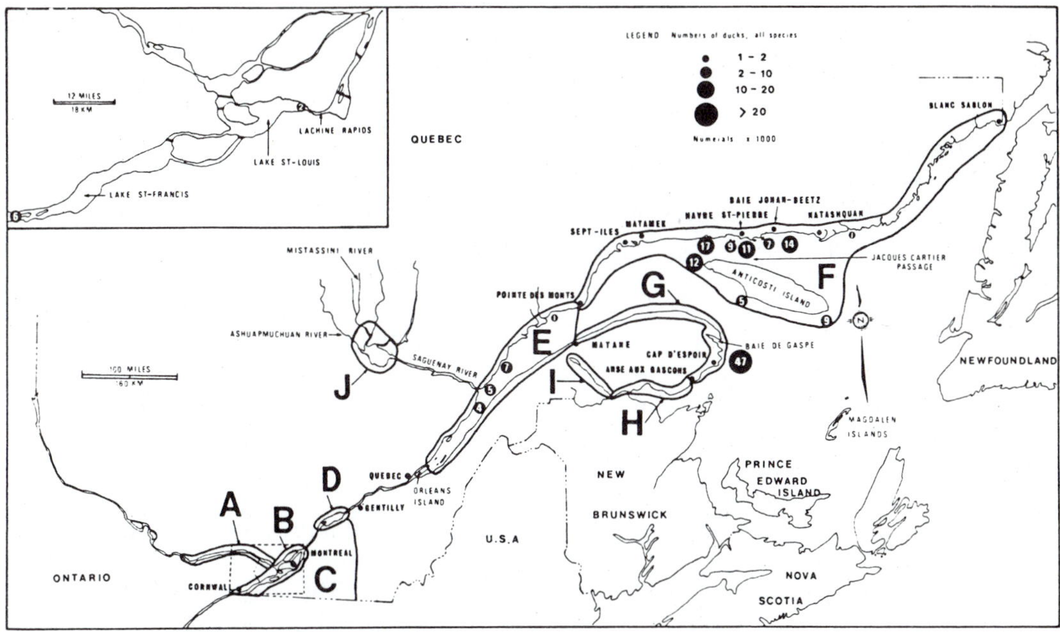

Fig. 1. Southern Quebec, showing major duck wintering sites (dark circles) and survey zones (outlined and identified by large letters). The Montreal area is shown in a larger scale on the inset at the upper left of the figure. The survey zones are (A) Ottawa River, (B) Montreal, (C) Eastern Townships, (D) Lake St. Peter, (E) St. Lawrence estuary, (F) North shore, Gulf of St. Lawrence, (G) Gaspésie, (H) Baie des Chaleurs, (I) Matapedia (J) Lake St. John.

ing Black Ducks in Quebec was found on the tidal flats near the mouth of the Saguenay River, where more than 75% of the Black Ducks counted in 1974 were found. The Common Goldeneye was the most widely distributed duck on the north shore of the estuary and was the most abundant species. The Oldsquaw (*Clangula hyemalis*) was also important but it was difficult to appraise its distribution and abundance because it often frequented areas too far from shore to be seen by ground crews and because it took flight early and dispersed rapidly at the approach of an aircraft; it was undoubtedly more abundant than our figures indicated. The Barrow's Goldeneye (*Bucephala islandica*) was also encountered frequently. Buffleheads (*Bucephala albeola*) occurred regularly (although in small numbers) only near the mouth of the Saguenay River. Two other species of aquatic birds also occurred regularly: the Red-breasted Merganser (*Mergus serrator*) and the Black Guillemot (*Cepphus grylle*).

(F) North Shore of the Gulf

This region extends from Pointe des Monts to Blanc Sablon on the Quebec-Labrador border (about 800 km) and includes Anticosti Island. Because of the vastness of the area and inaccessibility of certain portions, its coverage cannot be considered exhaustive. The inner part from Pointe des Monts to Matamek was surveyed both from the ground and from the air; east of Matamek was surveyed only from an aircraft. Ice conditions are generally heavy in this region although the area of Natashquan and the eastern tip of Anticosti Island is characterized by less severe conditions (Simpson 1973).

Sea ducks represented the most important component of the wintering population of aquatic birds. The Common Eider (*Somateria mollissima*) was recorded along the outer north shore of the gulf; most birds of this species were seen in the Jacques-Cartier passage in areas of slushy ice. The Oldsquaw and Goldeneyes (Common and Barrow's combined) were also abundant.

(G) Gaspésie

Ice conditions in this zone were highly variable. Water areas were completely covered by large sheets of floating ice when inshore winds prevailed. The eastern tip of the peninsula, however, was more consistently ice-free; most large flocks were observed there.

The Oldsquaw was by far the most abundant bird species observed in 1974 and 1976; most birds of this species were in Baie de Gaspé, which was clear of ice. In 1975, that site was choked with ice and only a small number of Oldsquaws was observed in the entire zone. Similarly, our counts of goldeneye (Common and Barrow's) varied from year to year, apparently reflecting different conditions of ice cover.

(H) Baie des Chaleurs

This large bay was characterized by heavy ice conditions (Simpson 1973), but occasionally strong west winds opened up large expanses of the bay. Despite different ice conditions (1974 heavy, 1975 and 1976 light) few birds were observed. Common and Barrow's Goldeneyes, Oldsquaw, Red-breasted (*Mergus serrator*) and Common Mergansers, and Great Cormorants (*Phalacrocorax carbo*) were encountered regularly in all years.

(I) Matapédia

Many sections of the river remained open through the winter, but were not heavily used by wintering waterfowl. The Common Goldeneye was the main species encountered.

(J) Lake St. John

The only open-water areas in this zone were found on fast-flowing sections of rivers, principally the Ashuapmuchuan and the Mistassini which flow into the lake. Very few birds were present in this area in 1974 (no census in 1975 and 1976). Common Goldeneyes and Common Mergansers were the only species observed.

DISCUSSION

The abundance and diversity of the wintering population is remarkable for an area with such a harsh and rigorous climate. In winter waterfowl require open water that can offer an abundant food supply and suitable resting areas (Nilsson 1972). Several species can be accommodated in southern Quebec because there is a wide variety of habitats, ranging from inland-freshwater to coastal-saltwater, which are kept open by tides, winds, and currents. Food is available in the form of aquatic organisms, which are notably abundant in intertidal and sublittoral zones in the St. Lawrence estuary and gulf.

Of the nine species of waterfowl which wintered regularly in this region the Common Eider, the Oldsquaw, and the Common Goldeneye were, in that order, the most numerous. Large flocks of eiders were present in saltwater along the north shore of the gulf, particularly off Natashquan, Baie Johan-Beetz, Havre St.-Pierre, and around Anticosti Island. Flocks of several thousand Oldsquaw were found in salt and brackish waters in Baie de Gaspé, the estuary, and along the north shore of the gulf. Common Goldeneyes occurred in fresh, brackish, and saltwater

Table 2. Summary of counts of selected species of wintering ducks on the Atlantic coast of North America.

Species	St. Lawrence[1]	Nova Scotia and New Brunswick[2]	United States[3]
Black Duck (*Anas rubripes*)	2,500	11,800	304,500
Common Goldeneye (*Bucephala clangula*)	13,000	4,400	68,200
Oldsquaw (*Clangula hyemalis*)	55,700	850	12,200
Common Eider (*Somateria mollissima*)	91,500	2,100	72,600

[1] This study, based on maximum of mid-winter counts 1974–76 (from Table 1, rounded to nearest 100).
[2] Bateman (1974)—Jan. and Feb. 1974 (Atlantic and Fundy coasts).
[3] Unpublished results of mid-winter waterfowl surveys in the Atlantic Flyway, coordinated by the United States Fish and Wildlife Service. Average 1964–73.

habitats, the largest concentrations being located in the vicinity of the mouth of the Saguenay River (north shore of the estuary) and in the Lachine Rapids near Montreal.

The great abundance of Common Goldeneye and Oldsquaw in the estuary and gulf was heretofore unrecognized (Bellrose 1976, Johnsgard 1975). Similarly, Barrow's Goldeneye was believed to be relatively rare on the east coast of North America (Bellrose 1976, Johnsgard 1975, Palmer 1976, Hasbrouck 1944); our data indicate that the St. Lawrence estuary and gulf represent a stronghold of an unexpectedly large population.

Our counts in January and February (1974–76) indicated an annual wintering population of about 171,000 ducks, despite incomplete coverage. Clearly our eider estimates must be very low owing to the inaccessibility of many of the known or suspected haunts of this bird; the same applies to the Oldsquaw, with the added complication of its known ability to escape detection by aerial observers (Stotts and Olson 1972). The estimates of goldeneye from coastal areas are undoubtedly low as well. Although precise adjustments cannot be made at this time, it seems likely that the area covered must harbor at least a quarter of a million ducks and it is conceivable that half a million could be involved.

Clearly the most important part of the study area was the estuary and gulf of St. Lawrence (Zones E, F, G, and H), which accounted for 94% of the ducks recorded. Some areas of the gulf which were not covered by this study also support important populations of wintering ducks. Average winter populations (1972–74) on Prince Edward Island were 3,070 Black Ducks, 1,540 goldeneye (apparently almost all *B. clangula*), 1,450 mergansers (species not indicated), and small numbers of Oldsquaw (Bateman, M., Mid-winter aerial waterfowl surveys of the Maritime Provinces, unpubl. rep., Canadian Wildlife Service, Sackville, N.B., mimeogr., 13pp., 1974). The Magdalen Islands support a few hundred Oldsquaw (A. Smith, personal communication), while Newfoundland is an important gathering area for Common Eiders (Gillespie and Learning 1974). Unfortunately there are too many gaps in the data to allow estimation of the winter duck population of the entire gulf.

Other areas along the Atlantic coast of North America are also important wintering areas. Various data from aerial surveys in Nova Scotia, New Brunswick (Bateman, loc. cit.) and the Atlantic Flyway (winter surveys coordinated by the United States Fish and Wildlife Service) for selected species are presented in Table 2 along with comparative data from the present study. Although those more southerly areas harbor large numbers of surface-feeding ducks it is evident that the St. Lawrence is of great importance to sea and diving ducks.

Comparison with European counts is more difficult because a more complete coverage is obtained there by using a network of ground observers (Atkinson-Willes 1969). In terms of total ducks present, however, few areas of equivalent size harbor as many ducks as the St. Lawrence. For example, a comparison of our figures with those from the Baltic Sea, indicated by Atkinson-Willes (1969:Fig. 2, p. 105), suggest wintering duck populations of similar magnitude. Also, much of the North Sea has fewer ducks than does the St. Lawrence (Atkinson-Willes 1969, Milne and Campbell 1973). That area of the North Sea encompassing Denmark, the Netherlands and northern Germany, however, has a much larger overwintering duck population. The latter area is probably the only European site of greater importance than the St. Lawrence to diving and sea ducks (Atkinson-Willes 1969, Joensen 1974). Clearly the St. Lawrence must be considered one of the major duck wintering areas of the North Atlantic.

Industrial and urban development along the St. Lawrence pose a constant threat to the birds and to their habitats. Port facilities for supertankers have been proposed for the estuary and gulf, which would increase the likelihood and gravity of oil spills which could have disastrous effects. In the past two years, 102 cases of oil pollution have been reported in these regions; it is only through good luck that none has had serious effects. In the Lachine Rapids near Montreal, a hydroelectric dam has been proposed which, through major changes in the hydrography and biology of the area, could lead to drastic reduction in the Common Goldeneye population. Some habitat changes may lead to an increase in the numbers of some species. The proposed Lachine Rapids dam might increase the numbers of Common Mergansers, as has occurred further upriver near Cornwall. The Lake St. Peter area, which presently has no open water, may eventually serve as a new wintering ground if warm water effluents from nearby nuclear power plants at Gentilly prevent the freezing over of expanses of the St. Lawrence in that area.

This investigation has permitted the identification of the more important areas of the system and provided an approximate estimate of numbers of the various species of wintering birds, but further work is required. In particular, the surveys along the remote outer north shore cannot be considered as exhaustive. Further work is proposed to obtain more accurate counts of sea ducks in the estuary and gulf, to document further the present status of the Barrow's Goldeneye in winter, and to clarify the racial status of Common Eiders (two races, *Somateria mollissima dresseri* and *S. m. borealis*, are known to overwinter in the gulf (Ouellet 1969, 1975; Gillespie and Learning 1974)). Also it is hoped that a survey can soon be undertaken to cover the entire gulf. The continued and increasing threats from industrial and urban development provide ample justification for close surveillance and further study.

ACKNOWLEDGMENTS

We are extremely grateful to H. Ouellet, National Museum of Natural Sciences, Ottawa, to M. Lepage, Quebec Wildlife Service, Montreal, and to Y. Lafleur, Parks Canada, for providing data from unpublished reports. Thanks are due to the many wildlife technicians, pilots, and volunteers who participated in the censuses, often under very difficult conditions. The Ministry of Transport kindly permitted us to place an observer on board its helicopter during a lighthouse inspection in the gulf in 1974. H. Ouellet, H. Boyd, and J. Bryant made valuable comments on the manuscript.

LITERATURE CITED

ATKINSON-WILLES, G. L. 1969. The mid-winter distribution of wildfowl in Europe, northern Africa and south-west Asia, 1967 and 1968. Wildfowl 20:98–111.

BELLROSE, F. C. 1976. Ducks, geese and swans of North America. Stackpole Books, Harrisburg. Pennsylvania. 544pp.

GILLESPIE, D. I., AND W. J. LEARNING. 1974. Eider numbers and distribution off Newfoundland. *In* Candian Wildlife Service waterfowl studies in eastern Canada 1969–73. Edited by H. Boyd. Canadian Wildlife Service Report Series Number 29. pp. 73–78.

HASBROUCK, E. M. 1944. The status of Barrow's Goldeneye in the eastern United States. Auk 61:544–554.

JOENSEN, A. H. 1974. Waterfowl populations in Denmark, 1965–1973. Danish Review of Game Biology 9(1). 206pp.

JOHNSGARD, P. A. 1975. Waterfowl of North America. Indiana University Press, Bloomington, Indiana. 575pp.

MILNE, H., AND L. H. CAMPBELL. 1973. Wintering sea-ducks off the east coast of Scotland. Bird Study 20:153–172.

NILSSON, L. 1972. Habitat selection, food choice, and feeding habits of diving ducks in coastal waters of South Sweden during the non-breeding season. Ornis Scandinavica 3:55–78.

OUELLET, H. 1969. Les oiseaux de l'Ile d'Anticosti, province de Québec, Canada. Musée national des sciences naturelles, publications en zoologie Numéro 1. 79pp.

———. 1975. Contribution à l'étude des oiseaux d'hiver au Parc National de Forillon, Québec. Revue Géographique de Montréal 29(4): 289–304.

PALMER, R. S., editor. 1976. Handbook of North American birds. Volume 3, Waterfowl (Part 2). Yale University Press, New Haven, Connecticut. 560pp.

SIMPSON, W. 1973. Gulf of St. Lawrence water uses and related activities. Lands Directorate, Environment Canada, Geographical Paper Number 53. 20pp.

STOTTS, R. S., AND D. P. OLSON. 1972. An evaluation of waterfowl surveys on the New Hampshire coastline. Journal of Wildlife Management 36(2):468–477.

INVESTIGATIONS OF MALLARDS OVERWINTERING AT CALGARY, ALBERTA[1]

LAWSON G. SUGDEN,[2] Canadian Wildlife Service, Saskatoon, Saskatchewan S7N 0X4, Canada
WILLIAM J. THURLOW, Environmental Control Consultants Ltd., Ottawa, Ontario K1P 5W7, Canada
ROBERT D. HARRIS, Canadian Wildlife Service, 5421 Robertson Road, Delta, British Columbia, Canada
KEES VERMEER, Canadian Wildlife Service, 10025 Jasper Avenue, Edmonton, Alberta T5J 1S6, Canada

Abstract: Mallards (*Anas platyrhynchos*) were investigated intermittently from 1957 through 1967 to determine why they failed to migrate and to test methods for controlling their numbers which increased from 2,000 in the early 1950's to a peak of 14,000 in 1964–65. Band returns showed that most Mallards originated from breeding grounds north of Calgary and most returned there the following spring. More than one half of the direct band recoveries from Mallards transferred from Calgary to coastal British Columbia were made in Alberta and a significant fraction of survivors returned to Calgary the next winter. Data are given on sex and age ratios, weight trends, and the incidence of shot wounds. Available food, open water, and protection from hunting were considered the main factors causing Mallards to forego migration. Of the control methods tried (no supplementary feeding, removal by transfer, scaring with acetylene exploders, and winter shooting within the city), cessation of feeding was the most acceptable and efficient way to reduce numbers.

Each year flocks of Mallards (*Anas platyrhynchos*) attempt to overwinter at various places in southern Alberta. These places feature open water and a nearby source of food, harvested grain fields usually. Depending on weather conditions, many of these ducks apparently survive. Although the overwintering flocks form a minor part of the provincial or flyway Mallard populations, they do create special public-relations and management problems, particularly those wintering close to population centers, airfields, etc.

The largest and most persistent flock has wintered on the Bow River at Calgary (51°N, 114°W). The Bow River, which flows through the city, never completely freezes because of industrial and domestic sewage entering it there. Protection from hunting within the city and a feeding program by the Alberta Fish and Game Association also induced Mallards to winter at Calgary. Stockyards in the city and grain fields nearby also provided food.

This paper describes results of various investigations of the Calgary flock from 1957 through 1967. Objectives were to determine factors responsible for the flock build-up and to recommend control methods. Later, data were collected during control efforts. RDH banded 698 Mallards during two winters, 1957–59. LGS banded 2,441 in two winters, 1963–65, and weighed and fluoroscoped samples. That project was halted prematurely because of the urgency to reduce the flock. During the 1965–66 winter, WJT took part in a cooperative scare program, and eventually trapped and transferred 1,262 Mallards to British Columbia. The following winter, KV collected data on 506 ducks shot during a control experiment.

THE STUDY AREA

The two main areas used by Mallards were the Inglewood Bird Sanctuary and an area near the Consolidated Mining and Smelting Company's (Cominco) fer-

---

[1] Originally published in Can. Field-Nat. 88(2):303–311, 1974.

[2] Address correspondence to this author. Present address: Migratory Bird Research Center, University of Saskatchewan CMPS, 115 Perimeter Road, Saskatoon, Saskatchewan S7N 0X4, Canada.

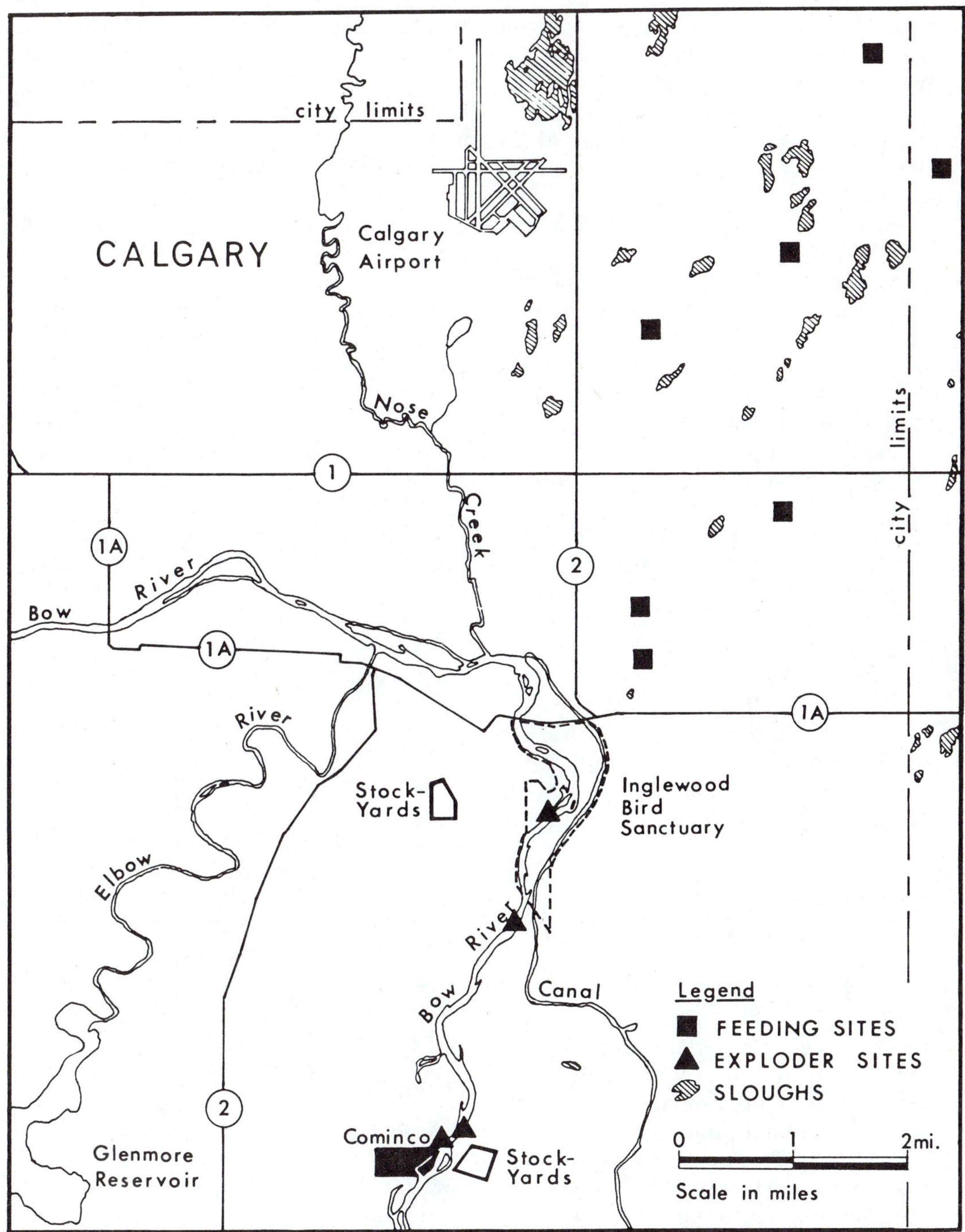

Fig. 1. Map of study area.

tilizer plant (Fig. 1). At Inglewood, the ducks used a 2-acre pond most of the time, as it contained the main feeding station. When the pond froze during prolonged sub-zero weather, they used the Bow River and a small sewer discharge stream that entered the river on the sanctuary. Warm water flowed through a large ditch from the Cominco plant to the river, providing open water at all temperatures. Feed was also distributed here. Depending on snow conditions, Mallards fed in harvested grain fields northeast of the sanctuary (Fig. 1).

Climate at Calgary is classed as "cold temperate" but is modified most winters by chinook winds from the Rocky Mountains (Anonymous 1959). This feature results in variable temperatures. The normal winter mean temperature at Calgary Municipal Airport (3,540 feet elevation) is 17°F while extreme means of 4°F and 32°F have been recorded. Extreme high and low temperatures prevailed during the winters of 1963–64 and 1964–65, respectively. The mean minimum temperature for the months of December, January, and February was 12.2°F in 1963–64 and −1.3°F in 1964–65. The long-term average was 6.7°F. Snow depth at Calgary seldom exceeds 12 inches. In 1963–64 maximum depth at the airport was 6 inches; in 1964–65 it was 9 inches.

METHODS

Estimates of flock size were obtained by ground counts, aerial counts, and use of the Lincoln Index (Adams 1951). Mallards were captured in bait traps on land and with cannon projectile net traps on ice and land. Traps were baited with barley or wheat. The optimum temperature range for trapping appeared to be −10°F to 10°F. Below that, ducks were reluctant to leave the water. Pulliainen (1963) described similar behavior. At higher temperatures, Mallards at Calgary tended to disperse along the river, and few were attracted to the bait. When bait-trapping in 1964–65 became unproductive, we set a cannon net, 25 × 75 feet, on the pond ice. The ice was chopped out to receive the recoil blocks and launching rods. At Cominco the net was set on an unused road that served as a feeding station. Because the ground was frozen, cannons were mounted on concrete recoil blocks that also served as anchors for the trailing edge of the net.

All Mallards were banded; samples were weighed to the nearest 10 grams; some were also fluoroscoped with an apparatus similar to the unit described by Elder (1955). Samples of drakes were aged (Hochbaum 1942) during the first visits of the 1963–64 and 1964–65 winters.

RESULTS AND DISCUSSION

Flock Size

Mallards overwintering at Calgary numbered about 2,000 in the early 1950's and reached a peak of 14,000 in 1964–65. In October 1965 there were about 12,000 present, but by January 1966, only 3,500 remained. Similarly, 12,000 were estimated the next fall, but the number remaining in January was about 4,000. Since then the number has fluctuated but never exceeded 4,000. The effect of the control program started in 1965–66 is discussed later.

Migration

Mild fall weather delays Mallard migrations from the southern Canadian prairies (Low 1957), and reports of wintering flocks in Alberta are more prevalent in such years. Although most migrants have left the province by early December, later flights sometimes occur.

To illustrate, in late December 1969, over 200,000 Mallards were concentrated on two lakes and the Bow River about 30 miles east of Calgary (G. Freeman, personal communication). Most left on 3 January and an estimated 36,000 were present on 8 January. Most of these left soon after. An exceptionally late grain harvest, coupled with light snow cover, contributed to the delayed migration.

Most Alberta breeding areas probably contribute Mallards that winter at Calgary, though those north of Calgary apparently contribute a majority. This conclusion is based on the banding locations of birds recovered within 12 miles of Calgary during November and December of the banding year, and the distribution of direct recoveries in autumn of Mallards banded at Calgary in winter. Some originate in western Saskatchewan, as evinced from one banded 27 July at 51°40′N, 110°00′W and retrapped the following winter at Calgary. Another banded at 51°20′N, 109°20′W on 16 August was shot at Calgary on 6 December. A few may undergo a reverse fall migration (Mann 1950) and attempt to winter in Alberta. One banded 9 September in Montana was retrapped that winter in Calgary 335 miles NW of its banding site. Another banded in Washington (46°10′N, 118°50′W) in August was shot near Calgary the following October.

That a substantial portion of surviving Mallards returned to winter at Calgary is suggested by the relatively large number of late-season direct and indirect recoveries made in the vicinity. More conclusive evidence is the number of banded birds retrapped the next winter. Of 1,844 trapped in 1964–65, 3.6% were from the 695 banded there the previous winter. Using our most conservative estimates of flock size and survival rate, we estimate that a majority of 1963–64 survivors (perhaps as high as 80%) returned the next winter. The estimate is supported by the low proportion of direct recoveries (31%) made in the United States. This is in contrast to 77% direct recoveries occurring in the United States for adult males banded elsewhere in southwestern Alberta (Anderson and Henny 1972).

During late winter, Mallards tended to disperse along the Bow River, then ice-free, southeast of Calgary. Distribution of direct fall recoveries simply shows that many Mallards were shot north of Calgary—some as much as 200 miles—suggesting a northward spring migration, though northward shifts in late summer and early fall cannot be discounted. Eleven spring and early summer direct recoveries, however, clearly indicate a northward dispersal. All of them were made north of Calgary and distances ranged from 190 to 620 miles. The fact that there were no similar recoveries for the more densely settled southern areas supports our contention that most Mallards migrate north from Calgary in spring.

Dispersal of Displaced Mallards

In January and February 1966, 881 male and 381 female Mallards were trapped at Calgary, air-freighted to Vancouver, British Columbia, banded, and released near the mouth of the Fraser River. During the 1966 hunting season, 66 banded birds were recovered in Canada; 37 of these came from Alberta and 29 from British Columbia. Because of differences in hunting effort it is impossible to make a quantitative comparison of recovery rates for the two provinces. It is clear, however, that a substantial portion of the ducks returned to Alberta, and most of these appear to have returned to the Calgary area.

In addition to the direct recoveries mentioned above, 13 were made by the

Table 1. Percentage of drakes in Mallards examined at Calgary.

Winter	Number examined	Percent drakes
1957–58	620[a]	75.3
1958–59	89[a]	78.7
1963–64	697[a]	75.8
1964–65	1,247[a]	74.7
1964–65	611[b]	69.9
1965–66	1,268[b]	69.8
1966–67	506[c]	71.8

[a] Bait trap.
[b] Common net trap.
[c] Shot by control team.

control team at Calgary during the 1966–67 winter. These comprised 2.6% of the shot sample of 506 ducks. This can be projected to provide a crude estimate of the proportion of survivors that returned to winter at Calgary. Assuming a flock size of 4,000 during the collecting period and 50% survival for the 1,262 displaced Mallards, then about 104, or 16%, of the survivors returned. More may have stayed had there been no scare program that winter.

The return to Alberta is not surprising in view of Munro's (1943) recoveries from 16,789 fall- and winter-banded Mallards on the coastal plain of British Columbia from 1938 through 1940. A small but consistent number was recovered in Alberta, mainly in the Peace River and central areas. Our displaced Mallards that crossed the Continental Divide would probably migrate south along traditional routes east of the mountains rather than return to coastal British Columbia. Evidence that this would happen is provided by Bellrose (1958) who reported on movements of drake Mallards transferred in November from Illinois in the Mississippi Flyway to Utah in the Pacific Flyway. Recoveries made the next fall showed that about two-thirds of the adults returned to the Mississippi Flyway. Bellrose (1958) believed the ducks migrated north in spring, probably with Pacific Flyway ducks, to Alberta and Saskatchewan breeding grounds. Here, if not already on familiar terrain, they were close to it and many were able to return to their original flyway.

Since our recoveries tended to be concentrated near the British Columbia release site or near Calgary, there is no definite pattern indicating the route taken by returning ducks. Munro's (1943) data indicated that Mallards wintering on the coastal plain reached Alberta by crossing the mountains in the Peace River area. Eight of our recoveries support this route; none discount it.

Proportionately more females than males were shot in British Columbia, suggesting that females showed less tendency to disperse to former migration routes. These percentages (52% vs. 33%) are not significantly different ($P > 0.1$) for the smaller sample of first-year recoveries but are for total recoveries (55% vs. 30%; $P < 0.01$). This difference also could be due to differences between sexes in vulnerability to hunting.

Sex Ratios

A striking feature of Mallard flocks that overwinter in Alberta is the preponderance of males, which may exceed 70%. Because of bias associated with bait traps (Bellrose et al. 1961), our percentage of drakes in bait-trap samples (Table 1) may be too high. They were significantly higher ($P < 0.05$) than percentages of drakes taken in net traps in the same winter. We believe the latter gave the more reliable estimate. The sample of shot ducks in 1966–67 is believed free of bias because shooters did not select either sex.

Pulliainen (1963) observed that winter

Table 2. Mean weight of Mallards, in grams, with two standard deviations. Figure in brackets after weights represents number of ducks weighted.

Date	Weight	
	Females	Males
7–9 Jan. 1964	1,077 ± 243 (28)	1,226 ± 206 (95)
27–30 Jan. 1964	1,066 ± 187 (114)	1,229 ± 210 (291)
24, 25 Feb. 1964	1,035 ± 180 (27)	1,167 ± 169 (136)
30 Nov.–3 Dec. 1964	1,023 ± 185 (138)	1,198 ± 183 (160)
5–8 Jan. 1965	1,022 ± 236 (84)	1,228 ± 219 (167)
11 Feb. 1965	952 ± 154 (56)	
17, 18 Mar. 1965	973 ± 157 (68)	1,128 ± 162 (155)
1, 2 Feb. 1966	1,081 ± 185 (45)	1,206 ± 190 (112)
10 Nov. 1966	1,218 ± 92 (12)	1,339 ± 92 (48)
6, 7 Dec. 1966	1,061 ± 68 (65)	1,224 ± 75 (137)
4 Jan. 1967	1,104 ± 66 (23)	1,250 ± 86 (60)
30, 31 Jan. 1967	1,026 ± 39 (21)	1,170 ± 74 (38)
6, 7 Mar. 1967	1,029 ± 55 (22)	1,209 ± 71 (80)

Mallard flocks in Finland were male-predominant. The 10-year average for one flock was 58%. He suggested the unbalanced sex ratio resulted from higher hen mortality and greater tendency for hens to migrate. Composition of wintering flocks apparently reflects that of late migrants and since the latter are male-predominant (Gollop 1965), the observed sex ratios are to be expected. Gollop (1965) had significantly more direct male than female recoveries north of his Kindersley, Saskatchewan (51°N, 109°W) banding block. Such dispersal would contribute to the unbalanced sex ratio in late fall.

Age Ratios

Our ratios indicate considerable year-to-year variation in the proportion of immatures (birds hatched the preceding summer) in the flock. A sample of 95 drakes aged in early January 1964 showed 63% immatures. That ratio is probably low because some immature drakes may assume adult characters as early as mid-November (Hochbaum 1942). The next winter, 151 drakes were aged 5 to 6 weeks earlier, but the indicated immature portion was only 12%. Assuming 67% immatures in 1963–64, the immature/adult ratio dropped 93% between winters. Based on wing samples, Smart (1966) reported declines in immature/adult ratios from 1963 to 1964 in the Central and Pacific Flyways of 37% and 27%, respectively. Although this would account for some of the observed decline at Calgary, it is unlikely that it was the sole reason. The mild fall weather in 1963 in contrast to 1964 may have caused a greater proportion of immatures to remain.

Mallard Weights

Mean weights of Mallards declined during winter (Table 2), and though some declines were significant none was serious. Decreases in mean weights did not exceed 16%, indicating that most of the birds wintered well. This was true whether or not they were fed.

The coefficient of variation was significantly lower ($P < 0.01$) in samples of shot ducks than in trapped ducks, indicating a more uniform sample in the for-

Table 3. Percentage of combined reported bands and retrapped Mallards from different banding periods.

Banding period	Number with bands[a]	Percent of bands reported and Mallards retrapped[b]
7–9 Jan. 1964	123	26.8
27–30 Jan. 1964	417	23.5
24–25 Feb. 1964	155	25.8
30 Nov.–3 Dec. 1964	530[c]	20.7
17–19 Dec. 1964	304	17.1
5–7 Jan. 1965	343	18.4
8–11 Feb. 1965	460	18.3
17–18 Mar. 1965	181	16.0

[a] 1964–65 samples include 1963–64 ducks retrapped at Calgary.
[b] If a retrapped duck was later shot and reported, it was counted only once.
[c] 513 newly banded; 6 shot and reported same season; we arbitrarily assume 7 were shot and not reported; hence 500 plus 30 1963–64 retraps gives sample of 530.

mer. Absent from the shot samples were ducks of extremely low weight that occurred in trap samples. Such birds would be relatively sedentary and less likely to be shot.

During late winter virtually all female Mallards were paired and on mild days, considerable courtship activity was evident. There was nothing to suggest that the birds were anything but normal.

Winter Mortality

Banded samples suitable for calculating mortality rates are limited as a result of effects of the control program after banding. Hickey (1952) showed there was some correlation between direct recovery and mortality rates, and Martinson (1966) developed a regression equation for this relationship based on post-season male Mallard bandings at United States wintering areas. For a sample of 525 drakes banded at Calgary in 1958 and 1959, the calculated mortality rate was 47% (Lauckhart 1956) and the direct recovery rate, 5.3%. Based on this recovery rate, Martinson's (1966) regression predicts a mortality rate of 36%. The difference indicates that non-hunting mortality may have been comparatively high in our Mallards. When the climatic differences between Calgary and United States wintering areas are considered, this is a reasonable expectation.

If samples of ducks are banded during different periods of a given winter, differences in survival among samples should be reflected in subsequent band recovery rates, or retrap rates in later winters. This assumes the only variable is survival rate between banding periods, and all ducks surviving the banding winter have equal chances of being either shot and reported or retrapped. Banding spanned only a 7-week period in 1963–64, so little or no difference in survival could be expected, as was the case (Table 3). The next winter, there was no significant difference in survival indexes among samples banded from early December through to mid-March. We could detect no mortality over the 3½-month period by this means. Some mortality did occur, however, as evinced by dead ducks we found each visit. It appeared there was a consistent but small loss of ducks that became too weak to obtain food.

Incidence of Shot Wounds

One popular reason for the failure of Mallards to migrate was that the ducks were wounded. To check this, we fluoroscoped 488 live Mallards and 34 found dead in 1964–65. Close to 90% of the drakes had survived at least two hunting seasons. Most Mallards were not wounded (Table 4), and the incidence of shot wounds was probably close to that of birds that migrate from the area. Similar percentages have been found for migratory Mallards elsewhere (Elder 1950, 1955, Bellerose 1953). The lower incidence in females reflects their smaller size (Elder 1955).

In a sample of Mallards fluoroscoped and weighed 30 November–3 December, wounded males averaged 38 grams lighter than shot-free males ($P < 0.02$); wounded females averaged 50 grams less than shot-free females ($P < 0.01$). It appeared that only a few of the wounded birds were seriously affected and their low weight depressed the mean. If trapping favored stronger birds, the difference between mean weights in the population may have been greater than indicated. Bellerose (1953) however, found no difference in mean weights between much larger samples of wounded and shot-free Mallards trapped in Illinois. He noted there was an unknown loss that occurred between the time ducks were hit, but continued in flight and migration, and the time they were live-trapped. We believe our sample included at least part of this "loss" and it was represented by ducks in such poor condition that they would fail to migrate and would not be available for live-trapping farther south. If the weight below which Mallards would not migrate is arbitrarily set at 900 grams for females and 1,070 grams for males, 16% of the females and 15% of the drakes were in that category of wounded birds. Corresponding ratios for shot-free ducks were 5% and 9% for females and males, respectively. The relationship holds regardless of level set for critical weight. This difference indicates that failure to migrate because of shot wounds could account for little more than 2% of the total flock.

Based on band recoveries, there was little or no difference in survival between Mallards with and without shot wounds. Accumulative band recovery rate for 120 that carried shot was 12.5% compared with 14.0% for 357 shot-free ducks. Including retraps the resulting indexes were 18.2% for wounded birds and 21.8%

Table 4. Incidence of shot wounds in Mallards.

Sex	Numbers with 0 to 6 pellets[a]							Percent with shot
	0	1	2	3	4	5	6	
Male	176	39	16	4	5	2	1	27.6
Female	189	39	10	5	2	0	0	22.9
Totals	365	78	26	9	7	2	1	25.2

[a] None with more than six pellets.

for shot-free birds, the difference not being significant. Samples are too small to conclude that small differences in survival exist as suggested by weight data. Thirty-four ducks died on the sanctuary; they had a shot-wound incidence of 32.4%. Live Mallards had a shot-wound incidence of 25.2%. While not statistically significant, the difference again suggests that shot wounds were responsible for the early death of a few Mallards. Bellerose's (1953) band recovery data revealed no difference in survival between wounded and shot-free Mallards, but some loss of wounded birds could have occurred before he sampled the population.

Control Experiments

In 1963–64, 18 tons of grain was distributed to Mallards at Calgary by the Alberta Fish and Game Association. The next winter, 70 tons was distributed at a cost of $3,723. The volume increased in the second winter partly because more ducks were being fed, but mostly because the second winter was much more severe. The ducks depended on supplied grain for a longer period and their daily food requirement would be higher in 1964–65 as a result of lower temperatures (Kendeigh 1945).

In view of the large flock size in 1964–65, agencies and individuals concerned agreed that some control was necessary to avoid similar concentrations in future winters. The ducks represented a potential hazard to aircraft at the Calgary airfield and the feeding program could not be justified as sound management.

Feeding itself undoubtedly aided the build-up by encouraging Mallards to remain in the protected areas and by increasing the number of survivors that might return in successive years. Wintering flocks elsewhere in Alberta[3] were not fed and none increased from 1963–64 to 1964–65 as did the Calgary flock. Most appeared to decrease.

The two main recommendations for 1965–66 were to discontinue feeding and to conduct a scare program. It was also recommended that late-fall hunting should be encouraged in problem areas and that, where possible, effluents responsible for open water be eliminated, or at least rendered unavailable to ducks. Nothing could be done about the effluents, and hunting regulations remained unchanged that autumn.

The scare program started on 2 October and involved 10 acetylene exploders (Stephen 1961) located along the Bow River (Fig. 1). At first, weekend use of exploders was sufficient to scare most of the ducks from the city, but by late October an increase in ducks necessitated daily continuous use of exploders. In early December, about 5,000 Mallards were present and the exploders were having no apparent effect on flock size, so scaring was discontinued. Likewise, a resumption of scaring from 3 to 21 January did not reduce the number of Mallards (3,500) then present.

To determine the feasibility of reducing the flock by transplanting, 1,262 Mallards were net-trapped from 22 January to 3 February, and released in British Columbia. Costs for trapping and airlifting averaged about $1.70 per duck. Dispersal of these ducks has already been discussed.

In 1966–67 there was no artificial feeding; the hunting season was extended from 4 to 31 December and the regulation prohibiting hunting within 100 yards of the Bow River was removed. Permission was obtained to shoot within city limits and teams of shooters comprised of wildlife agency personnel and city police shot Mallards under permit on dates given in Table 2. Altogether, 506 were shot.

Except for the outright removal of ducks, results of the various management practices are difficult to evaluate because factors such as weather and natural food supply can affect migration. Also, more than one technique was used simultaneously. In both winters there was a substantial reduction in flock size, suggesting that harassment did cause many ducks to migrate. This is in contrast to the two previous winters when, with no scaring, the numbers remained relatively high throughout fall and winter. On the other hand, the ducks were fed the first two winters but not the last two, so lack of supplementary feeding may have been largely responsible for the declines accompanying scaring and shooting. This is supported by events in later years when, with no feeding, scaring or shooting, flock numbers have remained relatively low.

A comparison of the distribution of direct hunting recoveries made after 1 October 1965 (after scaring started) with that for 1964 reveals no increased movement of Mallards to the United States that might be related to the scaring. Relatively more direct recoveries were made within 20 miles of Calgary in 1965 (66%) than in 1964 (21%). The direct recovery rate for this area increased from 1.1% in 1964 to 4.3% in 1965, suggesting that control measures increased local hunting

[3] Counts of other flocks were made by Alberta Fish and Wildlife Division Officers.

mortality. Even allowing for non-reported bands (Geis and Atwood 1961), however, any increased kill attributable to control measures would probably not exceed 10% of the flock.

Removal of ducks by trapping and transplanting would be economically impractical even if enough could be caught to reduce materially a large flock. It also has dubious public-relations value. Finally, it did not prevent a significant portion of the transplanted ducks from returning the next winter. Shooting ducks within city limits is not practical for administrative reasons and is undesirable for public relations. It appeared to accomplish little more than the scare program, which also created public relations problems.

Open water, available food, and protection from hunting are the main factors that cause Mallards to forego migration in Alberta. Little can be done to eliminate open water in winter. But all deliberate feeding and probably some accidental feeding (e.g., in stockyards) can be prevented. If ducks are forced to seek food outside the protected area, harassment by hunters will be an added stimulus for migration.

ACKNOWLEDGMENTS

Many individuals and organizations contributed to these investigations. Special thanks go to R. Webb, formerly with Alberta Fish and Wildlife Division; B. Stewart, formerly with Alberta Fish and Game Association; and G. Freeman, Ducks Unlimited (Canada). We appreciate the cooperation of other personnel from those organizations, as well as of the Canadian Wildlife Service, Consolidated Mining and Smelting Company, Royal Canadian Mounted Police, and Calgary City Police. We would be remiss if we did not acknowledge the goodwill of Calgary residents who tolerated the barrage of scaring devices.

LITERATURE CITED

ADAMS, L. 1951. Confidence limits for the Petersen or Lincoln index used in animal population studies. Journal of Wildlife Management 15(1):13–19.

ANDERSON, D. R., AND C. J. HENRY. 1972. Population ecology of the Mallard. I. A review of previous studies and the distribution and migration from breeding areas. United States Department of the Interior, Bureau of Sport Fisheries and Wildlife. Resource Publication 105. 166pp.

ANONYMOUS. 1959. Annual meteorological summary 1958. Long term meteorological records 1885–1958. Calgary, Alberta. Meteorological Branch, Department of Transport, Canada. 38pp.

BELLEROSE [sic], F. C. 1953. A preliminary evaluation of cripple losses in waterfowl. Transactions of North American Wildlife Conference 18:337–360.

BELLROSE, F. C. 1958. The orientation of displaced waterfowl in migration. Wilson Bulletin 70(1):20–40.

———, T. G. SCOTT, A. S. HAWKINS, AND J. B. LOW. 1961. Sex ratios and age ratios in North American ducks. Illinois Natural History Survey Bulletin 27(6):387–474.

ELDER, W. H. 1950. Measurement of hunting pressure in waterfowl by means of X-ray. Transactions of North American Wildlife Conference 15:490–503.

———. 1955. Fluoroscopic measures of hunting pressure in Europe and North America. Transactions of North American Wildlife Conference 20:298–321.

GEIS, A. D., AND E. L. ATWOOD. 1961. Proportion of recovered waterfowl bands reported. Journal of Wildlife Management 25(2):154–159.

GOLLOP, J. B. 1965. Dispersal and annual survival of the Mallard (*Anas platyrhynchos*). Ph.D. thesis, University of Saskatchewan, Saskatoon, Saskatchewan. 174pp.

HICKEY, J. J. 1952. Survival studies of banded birds. United States Fish and Wildlife Service, Special Scientific Report Wildlife 15. 177pp.

HOCHBAUM, H. A. 1942. Sex and age determination of waterfowl by cloacal examination. Transactions of North American Wildlife Conference 7:299–307.

KENDEIGH, S. C. 1945. Resistance to hunger in birds. Journal of Wildlife Management 9(3): 217–226.

LAUCKHART, J. B. 1956. Calculating mortality rates for waterfowl. Murrelet 37(3):31–34.

LOW, S. H. 1957. Waterfowl banding in the Canadian prairie provinces. United States Fish and Wildlife Service, Special Scientific Report Wildlife 36. 30pp.

MANN, G. E. 1950. Reverse fall migration. Journal of Wildlife Management 14(3):360–362.

MARTINSON, R. K. 1966. Some characteristics of wintering Mallard populations and their management. United States Bureau of Sport Fisheries and Wildlife, Administrative Report 116. 11pp.

MUNRO, J. A. 1943. Studies of waterfowl in British Columbia. Mallard. Canadian Journal of Research D 21:223–260.

PULLIAINEN, E. 1963. On the history, ecology and ethology of the Mallards (*Anas platyrhynchos* L.) overwintering in Finland. Ornis Fennica 40(2):45–66.

SMART, G. 1966. Age ratios of some important duck species killed during the 1965–66 hunting season compared with those of prior years. United States Bureau of Sport Fisheries and Wildlife, Administrative Report 111. 14pp.

STEPHEN, W. J. D. 1961. Experimental use of acetylene exploders to control duck damage. Transactions of North American Wildlife and Natural Resources Conference 26:98–110.

STRESS RESPONSE IN WINTERING GREEN-WINGED TEAL[1]

JAMES W. BENNETT, Department of Range and Wildlife Management, Texas Tech University, Lubbock 79409[2]
ERIC G. BOLEN, Department of Range and Wildlife Management, Texas Tech University, Lubbock 79409[3]

Abstract: Stress levels of green-winged teal (*Anas crecca carolinensis*) wintering on the High Plains region of Texas were determined by measuring a Condition Index and determining blood glucose, urea nitrogen and uric acid concentrations. The onset of severe weather, particularly when accompanied by high wind velocities, precipitated increased stress levels as shown by our parameters. Condition Index proved the most useful and reliable parameter for measuring stress. A differential sex ratio, 76:24, was observed apparently because females moved out of the census area in response to adverse weather and the associated stress. Management implications include maintenance of wind breaks as a means of reducing weather-induced stress on the wintering grounds.

J. WILDL. MANAGE. 42(1):81–86

For several months each year thousands of ducks assemble on their wintering grounds, yet biological considerations within these seasonally concentrated populations remain largely unexplored. Indeed, the extent and causes of nonhunting mortality in wintering waterfowl populations are among the least known statistics in waterfowl management (Stout 1967). Friend (1976) estimated that nonhunting winter losses may be twice those inflicted by sport hunting. Stress-induced losses are an unstudied factor in nonhunting mortality for wintering waterfowl populations. We, therefore, measured the effects of weather-induced stress on green-winged teal by determining a "Condition Index" and by measuring selected blood parameters.

In this study, stress is considered the syndrome induced by nonspecifically-induced changes within the organism as it tries to maintain homeostasis against the pressures of environmental stressors (Selye 1956:53–64).

Our gratitude is extended to the Rob and Bessie Welder Wildlife Foundation and, especially, to the late Clarence Cottam for financial support of this study. Additional financial assistance was provided by the Institute of University Research, Texas Tech University, through a grant administered by J. Knox Jones, Jr. Bert Blair provided access at Muleshoe National Wildlife Refuge, and J. A. Crawford and J. R. Alford assisted with the field work. John Jones conducted the blood analyses in the laboratory at Methodist Hospital, Lubbock. An early draft of this paper was thoughtfully reviewed by R. B. Owen, Jr.

STUDY AREAS

The study areas were located on the southern High Plains region of the Texas Panhandle. This region is the most important wintering ground for green-winged teal in the Central Flyway (Bellrose 1976:222). The High Plains are characterized by a native short-grass prairie, much of which is now under cultivation, and by thousands of playa lake basins. These small shallow lakes are unique features of the region; they provide the nuclei of the winter habitat for waterfowl, although agricultural activities and periodic drought may impair their suitability (Rollo and Bolen 1969). In addition, Muleshoe National Wildlife Refuge and Buffalo Lake National Wildlife Refuge are important concentration points for win-

[1] Contribution Number 200, Rob and Bessie Welder Wildlife Foundation, and Paper T-9-172, College of Agricultural Sciences, Texas Tech University.

[2] Present address: College of Forestry, Wildlife and Range Sciences, University of Idaho, Moscow 83843.

[3] Present address: Rob and Bessie Welder Wildlife Foundation, Sinton, Texas 78387.

Originally published in J. Wildl. Manage. 42(1):81–86, 1978.

tering waterfowl on the High Plains. Much of our field work was conducted on 2 playa lakes located in Lubbock County, Texas. Our study covered the periods September 1972 through March 1973 and September 1973 through February 1974.

METHODS

Population surveys and sex ratios for green-winged teal were determined weekly from flocks of loafing birds on the 2 playa lakes. The visual field of a spotting scope comprised a random sample; repeated sweeps were made until a cumulative sample size of not less than 100 birds had been classified (Alford and Bolen 1977).

Periodic surveys were made of the shoreline at both playa lakes and at Muleshoe National Wildlife Refuge for the carcasses of dead birds; plumage, trachael structure, and other physical features were used whenever possible to identify the sex and species of the carcasses. The remains were then sprayed with red paint to avoid duplication in later carcass censuses.

Green-winged teal were live-trapped using baited funnel traps. The birds were banded, weighed to the nearest gram on a 500 gram Pesola scale and keel-length measurements were determined to the nearest 0.01 cm with a vernier caliper. These data were used to derive the Condition Index formulated by Harris (1970), as follows:

$$\text{Condition Index} = \frac{\text{Body Weight (g)}}{\text{Bill Length} \times \text{Keel Length (cm)}}$$

Blood samples were drawn from the brachial vein into 10 ml heparin-treated syringes. This technique was used satisfactorily on blue-winged teal (*Anas discors*) by Harris (1970) and Canada geese (*Branta canadensis*) by Raveling (1970). Blood was centrifuged in the field within 30 minutes of extraction to separate the plasma from the red blood cells; this prevented the breakdown of the glucose fraction by bacterial action. The plasma samples were stored at −15 C until analyzed for glucose concentration and 2 non-protein nitrogens, uric acid and urea. The urea (blood urea nitrogen or BUN) concentration was determined according to procedures outlined by Crocker (1967). The uric acid concentration was measured on a Technicon AutoAnalyzer; the automated procedure was adapted from the manual method described by Hawk et al. (1923:282–283). The glucose concentration was determined colorimetrically using a procedure developed at the Methodist Hospital Laboratory in Lubbock, Texas. These blood factors were then correlated with weather data from the records of the U.S. National Weather Service at Lubbock to determine the presumed physiological response to weather-induced stress.

Harris (1970) used blood glucose and the total non-protein nitrogen fraction as stress indicators, and determined that gluconeogenesis plays a major role in the hyperglycemia of stressed birds. Uric acid, a component of the total blood non-protein nitrogen, is the end product of protein metabolism in birds and represents the bulk of waste nitrogen eliminated by the bird (Sturkie 1965:44–45). Also, as urea is a precursor to uric acid synthesis in birds, it, too, comprises an important fraction of the total plasma non-protein nitrogen.

RESULTS

Weather-Related Response

The 2 winter study periods differed considerably in their relative severity. The 1972–73 winter was both colder and wetter than that of 1973–74. This difference is also reflected by the green-winged teal stress indicator parameters shown in Table 1. Dur-

Table 1. Yearly averages and standard deviations for Condition Index (including structural index and weight), glucose, uric acid, and urea for green-winged teal wintering near Lubbock, Texas, 1972–74. Average winter climatological data for September–February are also shown for each year.

Parameter	N	1972–73	N	1973–74	(P)
Structural index[a]	183	23.74 ± 1.69	60	23.54 ± 2.05	
Weight (gms)	183	322 ± 39	60	335 ± 50	
Condition index	183	13.61 ± 1.80	60	14.21 ± 1.62	<0.05
Glucose (mg/100 ml)	78	275 ± 100	18	253 ± 59	<0.20
Uric acid (mg/100 ml)	72	11.4 ± 4.0	18	9.4 ± 2.3	<0.13
Urea (mg/100 ml)	51	5.7 ± 5.7	18	2.6 ± 1.8	<0.08
Maximum temperature (°F)		56 ± 10		67 ± 10	
Minimum temperature (°F)		33 ± 9		38 ± 14	
Wind at maximum temperature (knots)		13 ± 3		14 ± 2	
Wind at minimum temperature (knots)		8 ± 1		8 ± 1	
Maximum chill index (°F)		45 ± 11		59 ± 14	
Minimum chill index (°F)		22 ± 11		26 ± 18	
Snow (inches)		0.8 ± 1.0		0.1 ± 0.1	
Rainfall (inches)		1.86 ± 1.13		0.36 ± 0.40	
Relative humidity (%)		86 ± 4		68 ± 12	

[a] Structural index = bill length (cm) × keel length (cm).

ing the more severe winter (1972–73), green-winged teal showed a higher stress level, as indicated by elevated blood parameters and a significantly ($P < 0.05$) lower Condition Index, than was manifested during the more moderate winter (1973–74).

The relationship between Condition Index and average monthly weather values was determnied with multiple regression analyses. A significant ($P < 0.05$, $r^2 = 0.91$) relationship existed. Average monthly stress levels were affected to the largest degree by increased wind velocities and higher relative humidities. Blood parameters, although generally to a lesser degree, were also related to weather changes. Of these, uric acid levels were significantly ($P < 0.05$) related to weather changes ($r^2 = 0.80$) as were levels of BUN ($P < 0.01$, $r^2 = 0.97$). As with the Condition Index, wind velocity and relative humidity again played the dominant environmental role in affecting these measurements of stress in wintering green-winged teal. Additionally, snowfall greatly affected increased blood urea levels. Individual correlations and multiple regression equations are given in Table 2 for these relationships. Blood glucose levels were not statistically related to weather changes in our analysis.

Harris (1970) found that stress in blue-winged teal was manifested by a lowering of the Condition Index and elevation of blood glucose and non-protein nitrogen levels. Our study of green-winged teal indicated that both wind velocity and relative humidity had a negative correlation with Condition Index and a positive correlation with uric acid and urea levels, suggesting that the combination of these weather parameters has the greatest overall effect on inducing stress on wintering green-winged teal (Table 2). However, other weather variables, such as temperature and precipitation, may irregularly have great impact on the stress levels of green-winged teal, as shown below for temperature.

The percentage of green-winged teal in the overall duck population on the High Plains study areas was not related to

Table 2. Correlation coefficients (r) for weather variables (X_1–X_9) and Condition Index, glucose, uric acid and urea (Y_1–Y_4) and for selected population parameters (Y_5–Y_7) of green-winged teal wintering near Lubbock, Texas, 1972–74.

Parameters	X_1[a]	X_2	X_3	X_4	X_5	X_6	X_7	X_8	X_9
Condition index (Y_1)**[b]			0.22	−0.38	0.13	−0.18		0.35	−0.62
Plasma glucose (Y_2)			0.32	0.17	−0.49			0.05	0.36
Uric acid (Y_3)**			0.45	0.58				0.13	0.43
Urea (Y_4)**		−0.18		0.35	−0.52		0.78		0.57
Percent green-winged teal in overall duck population (Y_5)	0.19	0.18	−0.09	−0.21	0.23	0.18	−0.26	−0.05	−0.08
Percent dead green-winged teal in overall carcass population (Y_6)*	−0.38		−0.35	−0.17	−0.34		0.09		
Percent male green-winged teal in overall green-winged teal population (Y_7)**			0.52			−0.54	0.20	−0.32	−0.17

[a] The weather variables are: maximum daily temperature (X_1), minimum daily temperature (X_2), wind velocity at daily maximum temperature (X_3), wind velocity at daily minimum temperature (X_4), maximum daily chill index (X_5), minimum daily chill index (X_6), accumulated snow (X_7), rainfall (X_8), and relative humidity at daily minimum temperature (X_9).

[b] Significant ($P < 0.10 =$ *, $P < 0.05 =$ **) equations, as follows:

$$Y_1 = 3.71 + 0.37X_3 - 0.64X_4 + 0.23X_5 - 0.22X_6 + 0.79X_8 + 0.04X_9$$
$$Y_3 = -15.76 + 0.93X_3 - 0.16X_4 - 0.57X_8 + 0.20X_9$$
$$Y_4 = -23.79 - 0.33X_2 + 2.01X_4 + 0.30X_5 + 4.27X_7 + 0.07X_9$$
$$Y_6 = 144.07 + 10.32X_1 - 19.37X_3 + 10.65X_4 - 10.82X_5 - 29.90X_7$$
$$Y_7 = 13.80 + 2.11X_3 + 0.31X_6 + 18.52X_7 - 14.32X_8 + 0.41X_9.$$

weather changes. However, the percentage of green-winged teal in the population of carcasses examined was significantly ($P < 0.10$, $r^2 = 0.79$) related to weather changes. Of the 9 weather variables measured, temperature and Chill Index, a function of both temperature and wind velocity, showed the strongest correlations ($r = -0.38$) and ($r = -0.34$), respectively. As temperature and Chill Index decreased, the proportion of dead green-winged teal increased in the carcass census (Table 2). This relationship suggests that a sudden cold snap accompanied by high winds may have a disproportionate effect on green-winged teal survival in winter in comparison with other species.

Differential Sex Response to Weather Changes

The average green-winged teal sex ratio on our study areas during the 2 winter periods was 74:26 (Table 3) whereas a 57:43 sex ratio has been reported as the overall sex ratio for teal shot in the United States (Bellrose 1976:219). Multiple regression analysis indicated that the percentage of males in the population we studied was significantly ($P < 0.01$, $r^2 = 0.98$) related to weather changes (Table 2). Again, it was high wind velocities that played a major role in increasing the percentage of males in the population. Our data showed no significant ($P > 0.15$) sex-related stress differences as indicated by Condition Index or blood parameters for the green-winged teal remaining on the High Plains. Bellrose et al. (1961:432) concluded that green-winged teal males found dead in winter, presum-

Table 3. Sex ratios for green-winged teal wintering near Lubbock, Texas, 1972–74.

Year	No. weekly observations	No. green-winged teal		% male
		Total	Male	
1972–73	17	5,760	4,224	73 (54–85)[a]
1973–74	16	2,367	1,756	74 (60–80)
Totals	33	8,127	5,980	74 (54–85)

[a] Range shown in parentheses.

Table 4. Percentage of male green-winged teal in the wintering teal population in comparison with the percentage of dead males in the carcass censuses. Data for the Lubbock area and for Muleshoe National Wildlife Refuge, 1971–74.

Year	% males in green-winged teal population	Green-winged teal carcasses		
		Total	No. males	% males
1971–72[a]	58	29	19	66
1972–73	73	88	63	72
1973–74	74	10	7	70

[a] Data courtesy of John R. Alford for January–March 1972.

ably from fowl cholera, in the Texas Panhandle suffered mortality rates proportionately no greater than those of females. Thus, from the imbalance of winter sex ratios we observed in our study, it appears that females may move away from adverse weather as opposed to "sitting-out" rigorous winter conditions. Furthermore, there is no difference ($P > 0.25$) between the percentage of male green-winged teal in the living population and that in the teal carcass census (Table 4), indicating that the overall winter mortality for green-winged teal is not selective by sex.

DISCUSSION

Condition Index, glucose, uric acid and urea all reflected, to varying degrees, weather-induced stresses on green-winged teal. However, Condition Index was the best parameter of these as it is the least expensive and easiest to employ. Since stages of the General Adaptation Syndrome (Selye 1956:31–33) need not be considered in calculating the Condition Index, it also becomes the most reliable measurement of stress in green-winged teal and, likely, other waterfowl.

Condition Index may enable quantification of stress effects for waterfowl stopping on refuges north of traditional winter ranges. Presumably, green-winged teal and other waterfowl in better condition relative to stress would be found in the more southern regions of their winter range whereas birds held in more northern, extralimital areas might exhibit poor body conditions and a predisposal to stress-induced losses.

The behavioral response of female green-winged teal to adverse weather (i.e., their apparent movement out of our census area) seems a sexually differentiated migration of biological significance; such movements protect females that might otherwise suffer greater losses than males in static wintering conditions.

If, as Jones (1971) proposed, the condition of waterfowl when they leave the wintering grounds each spring provides a baseline for their productivity during the breeding season, it then seems imperative that proper wintering ground management be considered (e.g., reduction in shortstopping; habitat management in traditional wintering areas; etc.). A study correlating reproductive success with the preceding winter conditions would provide insight into this hypothesis.

At wintering areas where high wind velocities occur, as on the High Plains, windbreaks provide loafing ducks with protection that presumably enhances their welfare in winter. On the High Plains, windbreaks should prove particularly effective where large numbers of birds are concentrated in relatively small areas; our observations of teal and other wintering waterfowl clustered in the lee of the windward shoreline suggest the value of such protection on playa lakes. Salt cedar (*Tamarix gallica*), a common shoreline species on the alkali lakes of the High Plains, may serve a heretofore unappreciated purpose in reducing wind-induced stress on wintering waterfowl. The removal of salt cedar has been a traditional management practice because of its excessive water utilization; however, we believe that consideration is needed for a replacement plant with low water requirements that would continue as a wind break before the wholesale removal of salt cedar is undertaken.

LITERATURE CITED

ALFORD, J. R., AND E. G. BOLEN. 1977. Influence of winter temperatures on pintail sex ratios. Southwestern Natl. 21(4):554–556.

BELLROSE, F. C. 1976. Ducks, geese and swans of North America. Stackpole Books, Harrisburg, Pa. 543pp.

———, T. G. SCOTT, A. S. HAWKINS, AND J. B. LOW. 1961. Sex ratios and age ratios in North American ducks. Illinois Nat. Hist. Survey Bull. 27(6):391–474.

CROCKER, C. L. 1967. Rapid determination of urea nitrogen in serum of plasma without deproteinization. Am. J. of Med. Tech. 33(5): 361–365.

FRIEND, M. 1976. Diseases: a threat to our waterfowl. Ducks Unlimited 40(2):36–37.

HARRIS, H. J., JR. 1970. Evidence of stress response in breeding blue-winged teal. J. Wildl. Manage. 34(4):747–755.

HAWK, P. B., B. L. OSER, AND W. H. SUMMERSON. 1923. Practical physiological chemistry. P. Blakiston's and Son and Co., Philadelphia. 693pp.

JONES, R. E. 1971. Fall newsletter, Delta Waterfowl Research Station. 30 November 1971. 8pp.

RAVELING, D. G. 1970. Survival of Canada geese unaffected by withdrawing blood samples. J. Wildl. Manage. 34(4):941–943.

ROLLO, J. D., AND E. G. BOLEN. 1969. Ecological relationships of blue- and green-winged teal on the High Plains of Texas in early fall. Southwestern Natl. 14(2):171–188.

SEYLE, H. 1956. The stress of life. McGraw-Hill Book Co., Inc., New York. 324pp.

STOUT, I. J. 1967. The nature and pattern of non-hunting mortality in fledged North American waterfowl. M.S. Thesis. Virginia Polytech. Inst. 329pp.

STURKIE, P. D. 1965. Avian physiology. Cornell Univ. Press, Ithaca, N.Y. 766pp.

Received 3 November 1976.
Accepted 25 August 1977.

BODY WEIGHT AND WEIGHT CHANGES OF WINTERING DIVING DUCKS[1]

RICHARD A. RYAN, Biology Department, Hobart and William Smith Colleges, Geneva, New York

Abstract: Weights of 1,281 diving ducks of five species livetrapped on Seneca Lake, Ontario County, New York, during January, February, and March of 1960, 1961, 1962, 1965, and 1971 are reported. Body weights drop significantly from early January through late February and March. The weight loss by redheads (*Aythya americana*) is emphasized with significant differences shown in the 11-year time span between 1960 and 1971. To make conjectures as to this difference, it is suggested that periods of zero to subzero temperatures occurring in 1971 and not in 1960 influenced weight loss. Also, dramatically different, and possibly less suitable, food resources dominating the aquatic environment of the lake in 1971 contributed to weight loss.

After a flurry of attention given to publishing records of the body weights of birds in the 1920's and 1930's, little new information appeared. With some notable exceptions, waterfowl, largely neglected during the early period, have continued to be neglected. Leopold (1919) recorded weights of a number of species shot during the gunning seasons of 1917 and 1918 in the Rio Grande Valley near Albuquerque, New Mexico, and offered some generalizations regarding weight changes during fall and winter.

Kortright (1942) serves with Bent (1923) as a good starting point for many aspects of the life histories of waterfowl. However, Bent offers little or nothing on body weight, and Kortright's data, although based on sizable numbers of individuals and divided on the basis of sex, do not indicate the time of year when the records were made nor any distinctions relative to age. Both of these are factors of significance.

Dzubin (1959) recorded the weights of both adult and young canvasbacks (*Aythya valisneria*) in Manitoba. Weller's (1957) work with redheads, most of it done at Delta Waterfowl Research Station in southern Manitoba, offers good records of the body weights of this species. His data included weights of both sexes, adults and immatures, and spring, summer, and fall records. He also included weights of redheads from Utah and Michigan. Bellrose and Hawkins (1947) tabulated the average weights of ducks shot in the Illinois River Valley from 1938 through 1940 and included the weights of small numbers of redheads and canvasbacks and good samples of lesser scaup (*Aythya affinis*). Weights were categorized by age and sex. Longcore and Cornwell (1964) gave the weights of captive, immature canvasbacks and lesser scaups in conjunction with their study of the consumption of natural foods by these two species. In August 1962, near Fort Yukon, Alaska, approximately 10,000 flightless ducks were driven into a large trap on Ohtig Lake. One objective was to weigh large numbers of diving ducks. Yocom (1970) reported this remarkable effort and gave the weights of 355 adult diving ducks of seven species.

The object of the present paper is to place on record the body weights of over 1,200 individual diving ducks of five species recorded during the winter period of January, February, and early March, and, in a number of cases, in late March. In 1960, weights were recorded as late as mid-April.

[1] This is a contribution of the Federal Aid to Wildlife Restoration Program, New York Pittman–Robertson Project W–39–R.

Originally published in J. Wildl. Manage. 36(3):759–765, 1972.

The time span covered by these records is 11 years, from 1960 through 1971. Attention is given to weight changes that occur during the winter period, and some attempt is made to explain some of the more dramatic and significant changes in body weight.

I thank L. DeGraff, S. Browne, and E. Fried of the New York Department of Environmental Conservation for their support and cooperation. The assistance of C. Beach, S. Ryan, and M. MacNamara in the operation of the diving duck banding station at Seneca Lake was appreciated.

THE STUDY AREA

Seneca Lake is the largest in total area, being approximately 67 square miles, and the deepest (over 600 feet) of the Finger Lakes of central New York State. Approximately 35 miles long and over 3 miles across at its widest point, the lake points north, like a long finger, at Lake Ontario 25 miles to the north. The long, north–south exposure nearly assures open water even during the coldest winters, since strong south winds frequently occur. Cold temperatures and absolute calm for an extended period are required for any extensive ice cover to form. Seneca Lake has been frozen over completely, or nearly so, only four times in the past 100 years. Ice shelves reaching about 100 feet from shore are not uncommon, but they do not persist for more than a few days. The usual winter condition is one of open water and exposed feeding grounds for diving ducks.

Seneca Lake generally serves as the winter quarters for 2,000 to 10,000 diving ducks (unpublished January aerial surveys, New York State Dept. of Environmental Conservation). All the species in this study apparently winter as far north as open water and food are available. The mean maximum and minimum air temperatures for January and February of the winters involved in this study were strikingly similar, usually varying only a few degrees Fahrenheit. Water temperatures during January and February seldom exceeded 5 C (41 F).

METHODS

All the waterfowl weighed in this study were livetrapped at Kashong Bay, 7 miles south of the north end of Seneca Lake on the west shore. The weighing was done in conjunction with an ongoing waterfowl banding program begun in 1953 under the direction of the New York State Department of Environmental Conservation and the U.S. Bureau of Sport Fisheries and Wildlife. This program has emphasized the banding of diving ducks.

The traps used were comparable to those described by Schierbaum and Talmage (1954) except that the wire mesh was 1 × 1 inch instead of 1 × 2 inches. The smaller mesh prevented damage to bills and wings and reduced loss by drowning. One (sometimes two) trap was placed in 2.5 to 3 feet of water on a rubble bottom and baited with wheat or corn, or both. Trapped birds were retrieved twice each day, in late morning and before dark. Age and sex were determined by cloacal examination (Hochbaum 1942). Most birds were weighed in late morning because of more available time and better light. Ducks were never in the traps more than a few hours and were released no more than 0.5 hour after removal from the trap. The duck was placed in a cone of hardware cloth suspended from a Chatillon autopsy scale and weighed to the nearest 10 grams. Immature birds of all species weighed were easily distinguished from the adults through January, February, and early March on the basis of the immature penis and the presence of the bursa of Fabricius.

Table 1. Weights of wintering diving ducks livetrapped on Seneca Lake, Ontario County, New York.

SPECIES, AGE, AND SEX	YEAR	WEIGHING PERIOD[a]	NUMBER	WEIGHT (grams)	
				Range	Mean[b]
REDHEAD					
Adult					
Male	1960	Jan. 6–15	40	1,000–1,420	1,220 ± 16[c]
	1960	Feb. 15–Mar. 1	40	1,070–1,310	1,200 ± 10[c]
Female	1960	Jan. 6–17	15	1,020–1,250	1,126 ± 16[c]
	1960	Feb. 8–28	15	1,010–1,130	1,133 ± 23[c]
Adult					
Male	1961–62, 1965	Jan. 13–Mar. 6	101	860–1,380	1,143 ± 9
Female	1961–62, 1965	Jan. 7–Mar. 12	58	900–1,250	1,048 ± 8
Immature					
Male	1960–62, 1965	Jan. 8–Mar. 1	24	980–1,270	1,098 ± 10
Female	1961, 1965	Jan. 11–Mar. 3	14	910–1,250	988 ± 30
Adult					
Male	1971	Jan. 11–13	50	1,100–1,380	1,230 ± 10***
	1971	Feb. 22–Mar. 2	50	970–1,280	1,110 ± 9***
Female	1971	Jan. 11–16	9	970–1,290	1,100 ± 30**
	1971	Feb. 22–28	9	820–1,120	970 ± 37**
Immature					
Male	1971	Jan. 11–12	16	1,110–1,340	1,210 ± 17***
	1971	Feb. 22–Mar. 2	16	960–1,210	1,060 ± 18***
REDHEAD					
Immature					
Female	1971	Jan. 11–12	12	1,040–1,170	1,070 ± 13***
	1971	Feb. 22–28	12	880–1,090	950 ± 17***
CANVASBACK					
Adult					
Male	1960–62, 1965, 1971	Jan. 9–Mar. 31	191	850–1,600	1,252 ± 9
Female	1960–62, 1965, 1971	Jan. 9–Mar. 31	54	900–1,530	1,154 ± 14
Immature					
Male	1960–62, 1965, 1971	Jan. 9–Mar. 29	57	1,020–1,510	1,250 ± 11
Female	1960–62, 1965, 1971	Jan. 13–Mar. 24	26	950–1,390	1,149 ± 29
LESSER SCAUP					
Adult					
Male	1960–62, 1965	Jan. 6–Mar. 31	147	600–1,040	838 ± 6
Female	1960–62, 1965	Jan. 7–Mar. 28	21	570–970	801 ± 29
Immature					
Male	1960–62, 1965	Jan. 7–Mar. 30	92	670–970	813 ± 5
Female	1960–62	Jan. 7–Mar. 28	35	600–940	761 ± 10
GREATER SCAUP					
Adult					
Male	1960–62, 1965, 1971	Jan. 7–Mar. 30	44	850–1,350	1,054 ± 13

Table 1. *Continued.*

Table 1. *Continued.*

Species, Age, and Sex	Year	Weighing Period[a]	Number	Weight (grams) Range	Mean[b]
Female	1960–62, 1965, 1971	Jan. 7–Mar. 29	23	740–1,260	976 ± 36
Immature					
Male	1960–62, 1965, 1971	Jan. 7–Mar. 29	40	830–1,150	990 ± 8
Female	1960–62, 1965, 1971	Jan. 7–Mar. 31	29	830–1,170	987 ± 27
BUFFLEHEAD					
Adult					
Male	1960–62, 1965	Jan. 8–Apr. 16	21	400–550	468 ± 11
Female	1960–62, 1965	Jan. 6–Mar. 26	20	310–570	397 ± 19

[a] Earliest and latest dates are given for the years in which data have been pooled.
[b] ± one standard error.
[c] No significant differences ($P > 0.50$), within each sex and each age-group, between the two periods.
** Weight changes, for adult females, were significant ($P < 0.025$) between the two periods.
*** Weight changes, within each sex and each age-group, were highly significant ($P < 0.001$) between the two periods.

RESULTS

The weights recorded (Table 1) were those of unbanded birds or, if of banded birds, were of individuals handled for the first time that banding season. Thus, I avoided a bias from successive exposure to traps. For any species, sex, or age-group, the mean weights sometimes showed large differences from year to year. These differences, in part, reflected the difference in the time when most of the birds were weighed. January birds weighed more than February birds, and these weighed more than the March birds. If the time span over which weights were taken was an extensive one, and if many of the birds were late-season birds, the mean weight was less than if the time span was short and early in the season. These observations supported those of others (Leopold 1919, Raveling 1968) and indicated that waterfowl tended to lose weight over the winter, a phenomenon observed by Roseberry and Klimstra (1971) in bobwhite quail (*Colinus virginianus*). This tendency is graphically shown for adult male redheads in Fig. 1. The upward trend in body weight in late March of 1965 may be the consequence of ameliorating weather conditions and an influx of heavier male redheads migrating from more southerly winter areas. The data in Table 1 show quite clearly that for all species recorded, where samples were adequate, males were heaviest and immature females were lightest. Among canvasbacks and redheads, immature males tended to be slightly heavier than adult females, whereas in les-

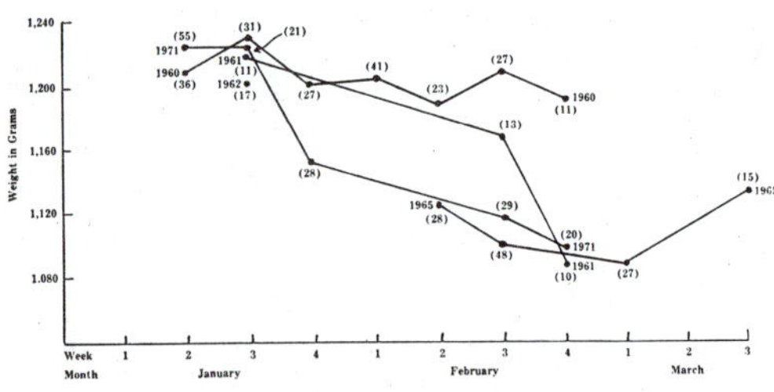

Fig. 1. Mean weights of livetrapped, adult male redheads in four winter periods spanning 11 years on Seneca Lake, Ontario County, New York. Sample sizes are in parentheses.

ser scaup and greater scaup (*A. marila*) the two were more nearly the same. Weller (1957) found much the same tendency in the redhead in mid-September at Lake Winnipegosis, Manitoba.

The body weights of diving ducks in January, as recorded here, were as heavy, or heavier; than those reported by Leopold (1919), Kortright (1942), Bellrose and Hawkins (1947), Dzubin (1959), Longcore and Cornwell (1964), and Yocom (1970) for various species of diving ducks in different localities and times of the year.

Because more redheads were trapped on Seneca Lake than any of the other diving ducks, they have been treated in more detail. The changes in weight (Table 1) that occurred in this species in 1971 in each sex and age category were highly significant ($P < 0.001$ except for the adult females where $P < 0.025$ and > 0.010). When the results for 1971 were compared with similar data taken 11 years earlier, during the corresponding winter periods for adult males and adult females (inadequate samples of immature birds were secured in 1960), the differences were striking. The adult females (Table 1) in 1960 showed no significant weight change for early and late winter periods ($P > 0.50$). The adult females in both January 1960 and 1971 were of comparable weight. There was no significant difference in the weights of these two populations ($P > 0.40$). As with the adult females, no significant difference was found between the weights of adult males trapped in early and in late winter in 1960 (Table 1) nor between these and the adult male redheads trapped in early winter in 1971. However, the weight change that occurred in the adult males by late winter in 1971 was highly significant. The data for the adult males trapped in early and in late winter in 1960 and 1971 were treated to an anlysis of variance ($F = 20$, df $= 1, 176$, $P < 0.01$), which indicated the highly significant difference of the mean weight of the adult males in late February 1971 relative to the other mean weights.

Whether the other species behaved similarly to the redheads in the winter periods of 1960 and 1971 has not been ascertained because of limited numbers of individuals weighed during the same time periods. The weight data were, therefore, pooled for the various years for each of the age and sex categories (Table 1). Likewise, redhead weights, including those of immature males from 1960 and all other age and sex categories for the years 1960–62 and 1965, were pooled.

DISCUSSION AND CONCLUSION

Diving ducks wintering at the northern extremes of their winter ranges are subjected to rigorous environmental conditions. These conditions place considerable demands on the metabolic machinery of the ducks in terms of the maintenance of their normally high internal temperatures that have been measured (author's unpublished data): as high as 44 C (111 F) in the lesser scaup, greater scaup, and bufflehead (*Glaucionetta albeola*) and 43 C (110 F) in the redhead and canvasback. The average cloacal temperatures of 72 redheads of both sexes, including the temperatures of immature and adult birds taken between February 12 and March 1, 1965, was 41.4 C (106 F).

Crissey (1955) has mentioned the relative sedentary nature of some species of waterfowl during midwinter, and Weller (1964) refers to the limited shifting of redheads from one winter area to another. From banding data obtained at Seneca Lake and from neighboring Canandaigua Lake, Benson and DeGraff (1968) showed that redheads of both sexes remained stable, with some movement between these two lakes.

Of a total of 328 diving ducks wearing bands at the times of their capture in 1960 on Seneca Lake, 174 (53 percent) had been banded at the Seneca Lake trap site during previous years. In 1971, of a total of 590 already banded birds, 183 (31 percent) had been banded at the Seneca Lake trap site in past years. In both instances, the great majority of the remaining banded birds had been originally banded on Canandaigua Lake 15 miles to the west of Seneca Lake. Diving ducks of the species represented here apparently remained as individuals on the lake throughout the winter period, feeding on the aquatic animal and plant life available to them.

The general downward trend in body weight in wintering diving ducks in the northern part of their winter range may be accounted for in part by a negative energy balance during the cold winter months. This condition was demonstrated by Raveling (1968) in adult Canada geese (*Branta canadensis interior*) during the winter even under ad libitum food and water conditions.

Nilsson (1969) and Sincock (1965) have offered a means of estimating the total food consumption of wintering waterfowl. Both of their estimates are based on a daily food consumption equal to a percentage of the average body weight of the species under consideration. Neither author had reliable average weights available to him; nevertheless, the estimates appear to be reasonable and show strikingly the tremendous quantities of food consumed by populations of wintering waterfowl.

The rooted aquatic vegetation of Seneca Lake has changed dramatically in the past 10 years. Scattered beds of *Chara* and different species of pondweeds (*Potamogeton*), eel grass (*Vallisneria americana*), coontail (*Ceratophyllum demersum*), and water milfoil (*Myriophyllum spicatum*) once occurred (Muenscher 1928). Milfoil has now, as a consequence of explosive growth, occupied nearly all of the littoral zone of Seneca Lake. The major waterfowl food habit studies of Martin and Uhler (1939: 89–91) and Cottam (1939) revealed milfoil to be relatively unimportant as a food source for ducks, and Krull (1970) found milfoil to be a poor habitat for macroinvertebrates, important in the diet of many diving ducks. I can only surmise that this dramatic shift in food resources, plus 10 zero to subzero temperature readings (recorded at the New York State Agricultural Experiment Station at Geneva, 8 miles north of the Seneca Lake trap site) during January and February 1971, where no such low readings were recorded in 1960, contributed to the weight differences in redheads in 1960 and 1971. There are no available data to support these conjectures nor other environmental variables known that might have contributed to the weight differences.

LITERATURE CITED

BELLROSE, F. C., AND A. S. HAWKINS. 1947. Duck weights in Illinois. Auk 64(3):422–430.

BENSON, D., AND L. W. DEGRAFF. 1968. Distribution and mortality of redheads banded in New York. New York Fish and Game J. 15(1):52–70.

BENT, A. C. 1923. Life histories of North American wild fowl. Vol. 1. U. S. Natl. Museum Bull. 126. Dover Publications, New York. 243pp.

COTTAM, C. 1939. Food habits of North American diving ducks. U. S. Dept. Agr. Tech. Bull. 643. 140pp.

CRISSEY, W. F. 1955. The use of banding data in determining waterfowl migration and distribution. J. Wildl. Mgmt. 19(1):75–84.

DZUBIN, A. 1959. Growth and plumage development of wild-trapped juvenile canvasback (*Aythya valisneria*). J. Wildl. Mgmt. 23(3): 279–290.

HOCHBAUM, H. A. 1942. Sex and age determination of waterfowl by cloacal examination. Trans. N. Am. Wildl. Conf. 7:299–307.

KORTRIGHT, F. H. 1942. The ducks, geese and

swans of North America. The American Wildlife Institute, Washington, D. C. 476pp.

KRULL, J. N. 1970. Aquatic plant-macroinvertebrate associations and waterfowl. J. Wildl. Mgmt. 34(4):707–718.

LEOPOLD, A. 1919. Notes on the weights and plumages of ducks in New Mexico. Condor 21(3):128–129.

LONGCORE, J. R., AND G. W. CORNWELL. 1964. The consumption of natural foods by captive canvasbacks and lesser scaups. J. Wildl. Mgmt. 28(3):527–531.

MARTIN, A. C., AND F. M. UHLER. 1939. Food of game ducks in the United States and Canada. U. S. Dept. Agr. Tech. Bull. 634. 156pp.

MUENSCHER, W. C. 1928. Vegetation of Cayuga and Seneca Lakes. Biological Survey of the Oswego River System. Appendix XII. New York State Conserv. Dept. Suppl. to Rept. 17(1927):243–248.

NILSSON, L. 1969. Food consumption of diving ducks wintering at the coast of south Sweden in relation to food resources. Oikos 20(1): 128–135. (Russian abstract.)

RAVELING, D. G. 1968. Weights of *Branta canadensis interior* during winter. J. Wildl. Mgmt. 32(2):412–414.

ROSEBERRY, J. L., AND W. D. KLIMSTRA. 1971. Annual weight cycles in male and female bobwhite quail. Auk 88(1):116–123.

SCHIERBAUM, D., AND E. TALMAGE. 1954. A successful diving duck trap. New York Fish and Game J. 1(1):116–117.

SINCOCK, J. L. 1965 (1962). Estimating consumption of food by wintering waterfowl populations. Proc. Southeastern Assoc. Game and Fish Commissioners Conf. 16:217–221.

WELLER, M. W. 1957. Growth, weights, and plumages of the readhead, *Aythya americana.* Wilson Bull. 69(1):5–38.

———. 1964. Distribution and migration of the redhead. J. Wildl. Mgmt. 28(1):64–103.

YOCOM, C. F. 1970. Weights of ten species of ducks captured at Ohtig Lake, Alaska—August 1962. Murrelet 51(2):20–21.

Received for publication October 7, 1971.

DYNAMICS OF DISTRIBUTION OF CANADA GEESE IN WINTER[1]

DENNIS G. RAVELING, Division of Wildlife and Fisheries Biology, University of California, Davis, CA 95616

The present distribution of Canada geese (*Branta canadensis*) in the United States in autumn and winter is easy to describe. They are concentrated in large numbers on refuges and they have declined or become extinct in some areas previously occupied, especially in southern portions of the range (Crider 1967, Hankla and Rudolph 1967, Hine and Schoenfeld 1968). These changes have resulted in many programs aimed at altering distribution of geese (e.g. Hankla 1968, Reeves et al. 1968). Frequently, the justification for these programs rested on the administrative desire to spread the benefits of geese more equitably among people in different political units and was based on the assumption that "short-stopping" resulted in the changed distribution. Short-stopping is usually taken to mean that individual geese have shortened or delayed their migration behavior in their lifetime. An alternative explanation is that changes in distribution reflect the results of differential survival of populations or their subunits (Crissey 1968).

This paper examines distribution and survival of neck-banded giant Canada geese (*B. c. maxima*, Hanson 1965). Segments of the banded population having different migration paths and wintering locations were identified. These data were compared to recoveries of banded birds shot and reported by hunters. The comparison makes possible an analysis of differential survival of population subunits in relation to distribution patterns.

[1] Originally published in Trans. North Am. Wildl. Nat. Res. Conf., 43:206–225, 1978.

METHODS

Individually identifiable plastic neck collars (cf. Sherwood 1966) were placed on 1,406 giant Canada geese at the Marshy Point Goose Sanctuary on the southeast shore of Lake Manitoba about 65 miles (105 km) northwest of Winnipeg, Manitoba, Canada (50°30′N, 98°W). This location is at the edge of the breeding range of the giant Canada goose in Manitoba (Raveling 1976*b*). Neck-bands were also placed on 118 geese captured at Dog Lake, Moosehorn Lake, and Sleeve Lake which are about 50 miles (80 km) north of Marshy Point. An additional 145 geese received leg bands only. Collars were not sealed after placement on the geese; thus, they came off if pulled against a solid object. All banding was done before the opening of Manitoba hunting seasons in 1968, 1969, and 1970. Geese were captured in July when they were flightless by herding them into a corral trap, and in August and early September with a drop-gate, walk-in trap or with cannon-nets.

Marked geese were observed in Manitoba on an average of 2 days per week between their arrival in late March and early April until their final departure in mid-November between 1968 and 1970. From 1971 through 1974, I made one-week trips to Manitoba in early April and in mid-September when geese were concentrated at accessible locations at Marshy Point. I made 22 visits of about 1 week each to Rochester, Minnesota between 1968 and December 1975. Of most importance were visits each year (8) in late November, after all geese had migrated from Manitoba and most of the population was concentrated in the refuge at Rochester. Other visits to Rochester were made in October (3), December (2), January (1), February (1), and March (7). The staff at the Kirwin National Wildlife Refuge near Kirwin, Kansas searched for and reported neck-bands on a weekly basis. I also visited Kirwin National Wildlife Refuge and other Kansas reservoirs in January and December 1970, and Swan Lake National Wildlife Refuge, Missouri in December 1970. Cooperators and student assistants provided records through the winter at Rochester, Swan Lake, and other locations throughout the study. Assistants recorded neck-banded geese for about three months in summer and autumn in Manitoba in 1973 and 1974.

Geese allowed humans to approach them closely enough at Marshy Point and Rochester to record leg-band numbers. Thus, individuals which had lost their collars were often identified.

The proportion of marked geese that were alive, but not seen, during a winter was determined by subsequently observing these geese. In every case where subsequent data became available, a marked goose that had not been seen for 2 years was found to have died or lost its collar. Data came from: retrapping, reading leg-band numbers, contacting hunters who reported shooting geese for information on the presence or absence of a collar, finding a carcass or collar, and learning of geese that had been killed by hunters who did not report the bands to the banding office. Therefore, geese which had not been seen for 2 years were eliminated from the marked sample available to be seen or killed in a particular year in the following analysis. An occasional individual dispersed widely (e.g. one to Colorado and one to New York), but the effect of omitting them from the results is negligible in relation to the records of 897 geese which were seen in their traditional locations on migration and in winter.

RESULTS

Distribution of Band Recoveries

Banded geese were shot in 15 states and were known to occur in two other states from which no recoveries by hunters were reported (Fig. 1). No single location accounted for more than 11 percent of recoveries and no state accounted for more than 19 percent of recoveries (Table 1) (away from the breeding ground banding site). The direct recovery rate was 8.3 percent which would indicate that mortality caused by hunting was moderate and that population expansion could be expected.

Distribution of Neck-banded Geese Observed

Locations of banded geese observed during the hunting season (primarily late November) (Table 2) were much different than the distribution of geese shot by hunters. Thus, over the years 1968–76, nearly 73 percent of neck-banded geese known to be alive and retaining their collar were at Rochester and about 12 percent were at Kirwin, Kansas. Only about 10 percent were unaccounted for in any one winter and some of these were, no doubt, at Rochester and Kirwin but were not seen.

Time of Migration in Relation to Band Recoveries

Migration away from Manitoba began about September 20 and was completed between November 10 to 20. Peak populations at Rochester were present during the last week of November. About 15

Fig. 1. Locations of 327 recoveries from giant Canada geese banded in the Interlake of Manitoba between 1968 and 1970 and recovered through the winter of 1975–76.

Table 1. Distribution of 327 recoveries from giant Canada geese banded in Manitoba between 1968 and 1970 and recovered through the winter of 1975–76.

Location	Number of recoveries (percent)
Canada	151 (46.2)
Manitoba	146 (44.6)
Saskatchewan	4 (1.2)
Alberta	1 (0.3)
Mississippi Flyway	113 (34.6)
Minnesota	61 (18.7)
Wisconsin	2 (0.6)
Iowa	14 (4.3)
Missouri	13 (4.0)
Arkansas	1 (0.3)
Illinois	16 (4.9)
Kentucky	5 (1.5)
Tennessee	1 (0.3)
Central Flyway	63 (19.3)
North Dakota	5 (1.5)
South Dakota	15 (4.6)
Nebraska	14 (4.3)
Kansas	25 (7.6)
Colorado	1 (0.3)
Oklahoma	1 (0.3)
Texas	2 (0.6)

to 30 percent of the peak population at Rochester departed between mid-December and mid-January (Gulden and Johnson 1968). More recent records of departure were: 1968–69—17 percent between December 19 and January 6; 1969—30 percent in early to mid-December; 1973–74—29 percent between December 29 and January 2. Locations of 110 geese observed after they left Rochester revealed that they went to Swan Lake. Missouri (52 percent), Kirwin, Kansas (39 percent), and the southern Illinois–Ballard County, Kentucky area (7 percent).

Over 89 percent of recoveries in states other than Minnesota occurred before the usual detectable major departures from Rochester had occurred (Fig. 2). Therefore, harvest by hunters in states other than Minnesota was heavily concentrated on those geese that did not stop at, or

Table 2. Fate and migration pattern of 1,524 neck-banded giant Canada geese in winter.

	Year (winter)								
	1968–69	1969–70	1970–71	1971–72	1972–73	1973–74	1974–75	1975–76	Totals
Maximum number available	448	958	1,233	774	382	204	117	59	4,175
Died previous winter		16	47	60	23	9	6	2	163
Died in Manitoba in summer-autumn	25	57	52	29	11	5	1	1	181
Lost collar[a]	9	50	91	55	39	10	12	2	268
Dead or lost collar[b]	19	120	269	248	105	63	39	15	878
Available for observation	395	715	774	382	204	117	59	39	2,685
Seen in:									
Rochester	274 (69.4)[c]	510 (71.3)	502 (64.9)	297 (77.8)	170 (83.3)	109 (93.2)	56 (94.9)	38 (97.4)	1,956 (72.8)
Other Mississippi flyway states	16 (4.1)	41 (5.7)	37 (4.8)	5 (1.3)	1 (0.5)	1 (0.9)	0	1 (2.6)	102 (3.8)
Kansas	66 (16.7)	104 (14.5)	117 (15.1)	23 (6.0)	3 (1.5)	0	0	0	313 (11.7)
Other central flyway states	3 (0.8)	7 (1.0)	24 (3.1)	7 (1.8)	1 (0.5)	0	1 (1.7)	0	43 (1.6)
Alive-location unknown	36 (9.1)	53 (7.4)	94 (12.1)	50 (13.1)	29 (14.2)	7 (6.0)	2 (3.4)	0	271 (10.0)

[a] Retrapped or leg-band number read—see text.
[b] Never seen again—see text.
[c] Figures in parentheses are percentages.

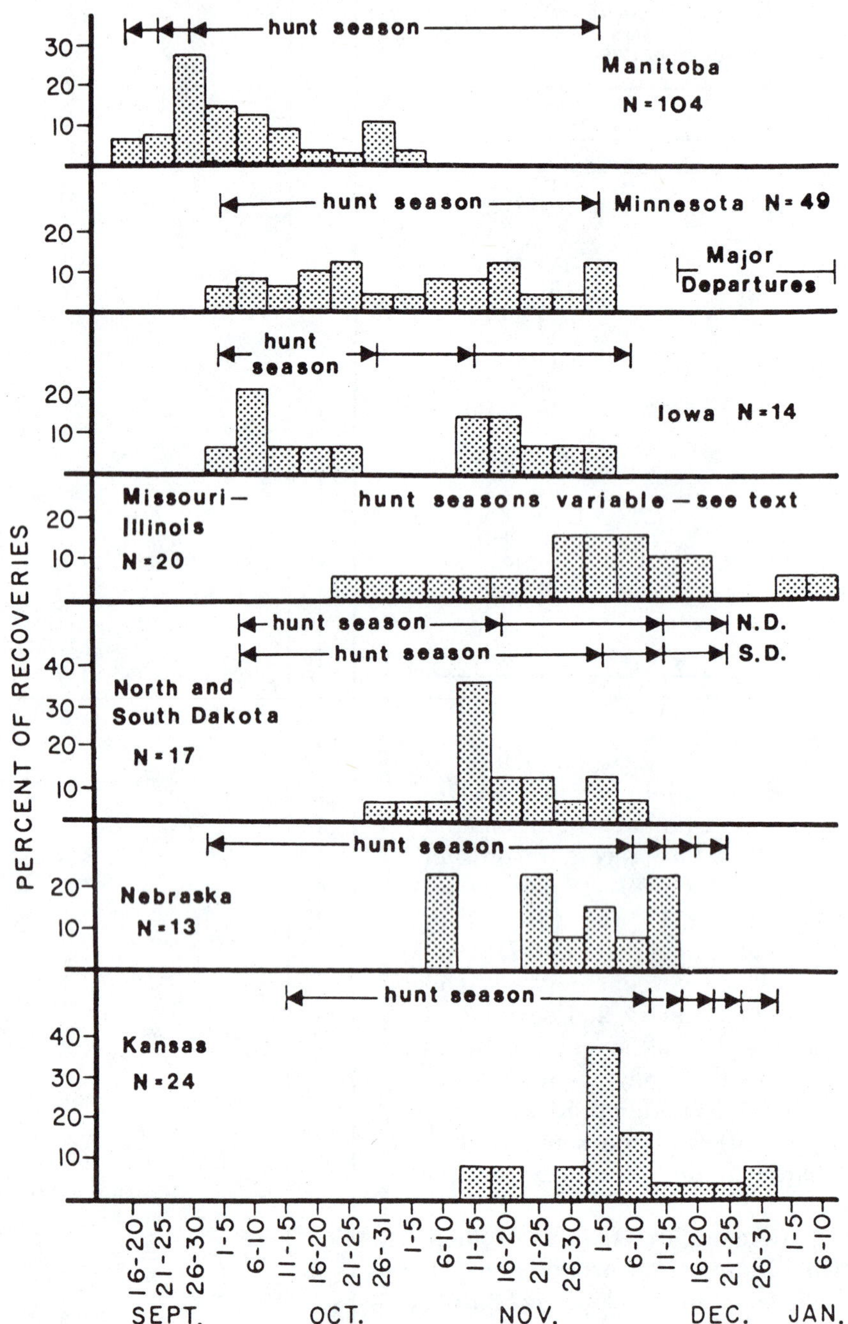

Fig. 2. Chronology of recoveries from giant Canada geese banded in the Manitoba Interlake.

stayed only for a few days or less at, Rochester.

The segment of the marked population which migrated in the central flyway through the Dakotas and Nebraska to Kansas was consistently the bulk of the last migration departure from Manitoba in mid-November. In the Mississippi flyway, in contrast, recoveries (Fig. 2) show that migrants were going past Minnesota into Iowa, Missouri, and Illinois at the same time the population was building up rapidly at Rochester.

Vulnerability by Geographic Area

Geese which migrated through the central flyway and those that bypassed Rochester in the Mississippi flyway were respectively, 4.7 and 5.5 times more likely to be shot than geese in Minnesota (Table 3). These values are slight overestimates because some geese left Rochester. The bias is small, however, because over 89 percent of recoveries in states other than Minnesota were from birds shot before detectable departures from Rochester occurred (Fig. 2).

Mortality Rates of Population Subunits

The much greater vulnerability of geese to being shot at locations other than Rochester might not be indicative of overharvest because of the low overall harvest (8.3 percent direct recovery rate) and known very low kill of geese around Rochester (estimated to be less than 5 percent of the flock by local Department of Natural Resource officials). Thus, I used the direct recovery rate (birds shot and reported in the first hunting season after banding) and reporting rate (proportion of banded birds shot that are reported voluntarily to the banding office) in relation to the proportion of the marked population available to be shot to estimate mortality rates of population segments with different migration patterns.

Reporting Rate.—Although there are several estimates of band reporting rates (e.g. Martinson and McCann 1966, Henny and Burnham 1976), they tend to vary geographically and are thought to be higher for color-banded or neck-banded birds than for just leg-banded birds. Therefore, I used data from the disappearance rates of neck-banded geese to estimate reporting rate (Table 4).

The numbers of marked geese shot and not reported by hunters would be contained in the category of geese never seen again (dead or lost collar row of Table 2 and row *g* in Table 4). The proportion of geese in this category that lost their collar can be estimated from recaptures of marked geese. Eight of 29 geese (28 percent) recaptured one year after banding had lost their collars and 9 of 20 geese recaptured two years after banding had lost their collars (23 percent per year). These results are close to the 16 to 24 percent loss per year by giant Canada geese with the same type collars in Michigan, calculated from data presented by Fjetland (1973). I conclude that a 25 percent rate of collar loss is a reasonable estimate for the marked population of this study. Most of the collar loss was apparently because of weathering which caused the plastic to become brittle and crack.

Deducting the number of geese known to have lost their collars from the total expected to have lost their collars results in an estimate of the proportion of the never-seen-again population that was caused by collar loss (Table 4). The remainder of those geese never seen again are considered dead. The portion of these dead geese which can be attributed to

Table 3. Distribution of recoveries from banded giant Canada geese in relation to availability by geographic area.

Location	*a* Proportion of recoveries ($N = 327$)[a]	*b* Proportion of banded population available (autumn)	*c* Expected proportion of recoveries if shot at same rate as in Minnesota	*d* Vulnerability to being shot compared to geese in Minnesota ($a \div c$)
Manitoba	44.6%	100% → 0% by close of hunting	25.7	+1.7
Minnesota	18.7%	72.8%[b]		
Other Mississippi flyway states	15.9%	11.4%[c]	2.9	+5.5
Kansas	7.6%	11.7%[c]	3.0	+2.5
Other central flyway states	11.6%	15.8%[c]	4.1	+2.8
Central flyway as a whole	19.3%	15.8%	4.1	+4.7

[a] Through 1975–76 hunting seasons—from Table 1.
[b] From Table 2.
[c] The 10 percent of the geese that were in unknown winter locations were apportioned to the Mississippi and central flyways in accordance with the distribution of marked geese at known locations (77:14 = 85 percent Mississippi flyway, 15 percent central flyway). For the central flyway, the 12 percent in Kansas was also added to availability in other central flyway locations because 89 percent of the harvest in the flyway away from Kansas was to the north (Table 1).

nonreported harvest by hunters can be estimated by multiplying by 0.85, which allows for a 10 to 15 percent crippling loss (Hunt 1968) and 5 percent to negligible non-hunting loss (see also Crissey 1968). The excellent visibility and accessibility to investigators of the main concentration areas, coupled with the relatively rare occurrence of finding dead geese that did not show evidence of being shot, supports the use of the above calculation. Thus, in total, there were 120 banded geese reported shot in the years where sufficient data were available to calculate a reporting rate and an estimated 254 banded geese shot and not reported for a reporting rate of 32 percent (Table 4). This value is close to the calculation of 36 percent by Martinson and McCann (1966) or the 24 to 35 percent

Table 4. Estimation of reporting rate of hunter-killed giant Canada geese.

	Year 1970–71	1971–72	1972–73	Totals
a Maximum number of marked geese available[a]	668	714	359	1,741
b Known dead[b]	45	49	20	114
c Number of marked geese remaining to be observed, lose collar, or die ($a - b$)	623	665	339	1,627
d Number expected to have lost collar[c] ($c \times 0.25$)	156	166	85	407
e Known to have lost collar[a]	79	55	39	173
f Remainder expected to have lost collar ($d - e$)	77	111	46	234
g Number of geese never seen again (dead or lost collar)[a]	180	248	105	533
h Number dead ($g - f$)	103	137	59	299
i Number shot and not reported[c] ($h \times 0.85$)	88	116	50	254
j Bands reported	42	51	27	120
k Band reporting rate ($j/i + j \times 100$)	32.3%	30.5%	35.1%	32.1%

[a] From Table 2. For 1970–71, includes only 1968 and 1969 banded geese to allow for 1 year of collar loss; 1971–72 and 1972–73 data include geese banded in 1968, 1969, and 1970.
[b] Birds dying in Manitoba that autumn plus those known to die during that winter (Table 2).
[c] See text.

Table 5. Direct recovery rates and estimated mortality of giant Canada geese in relation to geographic area in 1968, 1969, and 1970.

a Location	*b* Proportion of direct recoveries ($N = 139$)	*c* Direct recovery rate (1,669 banded)	*d* Proportion of the original total population kill taken from	*e* Direct recovery rate in relation to availability ($c \div d$)	*f* Estimated mortality by hunting (at 32.1% reporting rate)
Manitoba	48.9%	4.1%	100%	4.1%	12.8%
Minnesota	14.4%	1.2%	59%[a]	2.0%	6.2%
Other Mississippi flyway states	17.3%	1.4%	11%[a]	12.7%	39.6%
Kansas	9.4%	0.8%	13%[a]	6.2%	19.3%
Other central flyway states	10.1%	0.8%	16%[a,b]	5.0%	15.6%
Totals	100%	8.3%	100%	8.3%	25.9%

[a] Percent of original flock—13 percent die in Manitoba, 87 percent remaining were distributed in autumn as in Table 2 (average of 1968, 1969, and 1970 years of direct recoveries; thus, e.g., 0.683 × 0.87 = 0.59 for proportion in Rochester). Geese in unknown locations (9.7 percent) were apportioned as in Table 3.

[b] Includes Kansas total as these birds migrated through the other states and were potentially available before reaching Kansas.

depressed rates around banding sites discussed by Henny and Burnham (1976). This suggests that reporting rate of marked geese was not materially different than for just leg-banded birds as also suggested by Koerner et al. (1974).

Mortality Rates.—The distribution of direct recoveries and direct recovery rates are presented in Table 5. The proportion of the population from which the kill was extracted is based on the observed distribution in autumn and corrected for mortality which occurred in Manitoba. If the kill in Manitoba did not differentially affect the different migratory population subunits, the results show that the subunit which went to Rochester sustained a mortality rate from hunting of about 19 percent (13 percent in Manitoba and 6 percent in Minnesota). Such a low rate of harvest should have allowed large population expansion. Indeed, the peak population at Rochester increased 29, 41, and 28 percent in 1968, 1969, and 1970, respectively (those years for which direct recoveries are available which are proportioned in Table 5) (from 9,500 to 12,300 to 17,400, to 22,260 between 1967 to 1968 to 1969 to 1970, respectively).

In contrast to the low mortality rate of geese going to Rochester, hunters in the Mississippi flyway states other than Minnesota killed an estimated 40 percent of the marked birds available and hunters in the central flyway states killed about 35 percent of their available segments. Addition of 13 percent mortality in Manitoba shows that about one-half the population subunits associated with these migration paths were shot.

These mortality rates are obviously beyond the reproductive capability of geese and these subunits should have been declining rapidly. Two other lines of evidence support this conclusion:

1. The proportion of the surviving neck-banded geese that went to Rochester became progressively greater and the proportion in other locations (including unknown) became less (Table 2). This was not because of a shift of survivors to Rochester, but because Rochester geese were the only ones surviving that long. Survival of geese traditionally associated with Rochester was 61 percent for 1-year old birds and 62 to 89 percent for adults (Table 6). In contrast, survival of 1-year old geese which went to Kirwin was 33 percent and survival of adults was 57

Table 6. Disappearance of neck-banded geese that were seen every year of their life at Rochester, Minnesota or Kirwin, Kansas.

	Winters after banding[a]					
Banded as adults and seen at:	1	2	3	4	5	6
Rochester						
Maximum number available[b]		143	95	56	37	18
Number seen	190	126	74	49	24	16
Survival[c]		88%	78%	88%	65%	89%
Kirwin						
Maximum number available[b]		35	15	5	2	0
Number seen	46	20	7	2	0	0
Survival[c]		57%	47%	40%		
Banded as immatures and seen at:						
Rochester						
Maximum number available[b]		376	171	95	62	29
Number seen	501	228	126	82	38	24
Survival[c]		61%	74%	86%	62%	83%
Kirwin						
Maximum number available[b]		73	18	7	1	0
Number seen	97	24	9	1	1	0
Survival[c]		33%	50%	14%		

[a] Seventh and eighth year records not presented because data from 1969 and 1970 banded birds not complete yet.
[b] Previous year's total × 0.25 to account for loss of collars.
[c] Number seen ÷ maximum number available.

percent or less (Table 6). These figures are in close agreement with the mortality estimated by comparing numbers of band recoveries to numbers of geese available (Table 5) because the latter records refer to mortality without respect to age. Immatures are more vulnerable to hunting than adults and they are included in the data in Table 5, but not, of necessity, in Table 6. A few geese did shift their wintering locations from year to year (Table 7). However, the number of geese leaving Kirwin for Rochester was nearly equalled by geese leaving Rochester to spend a subsequent winter at Kirwin. An additional 15 geese spent from 3 to 6 years moving between Rochester, Kirwin, and yet other locations. The details of migration dispersal by age and social status are to be the subject of a future report (see also Raveling 1976*a*).

The point here is to demonstrate that shifts to Kirwin were nearly as prevalent as shifts away from Kirwin. Records of geese which moved to Rochester would be expected to predominate in the categories where 4 or more years of data were available because geese associated with other locations experienced a much greater mortality than those associated with Rochester (Tables 5, 6).

2. The expansion of the Rochester proportion of the marked population and the heavy mortality of marked geese associated with other winter areas represent powerful selection pressures by man. This should have been reflected in occupation of the breeding grounds by an increasing population of geese going to Rochester and a decreasing proportion having other migration traditions. For reasons to be explained below, only geese banded

Table 7. Numbers of geese shifting their wintering location in different years between Rochester, Minnesota and Kirwin, Kansas.

Years seen	Type of shift	Number of geese shifting
2	Kirwin to Rochester	19
2	Rochester to Kirwin	15
3	Kirwin 1 year and Rochester 2 years	5
3	Rochester 1 year and Kirwin 2 years	3
4	Kirwin 1 year and Rochester 3 years[a]	4
4	Rochester 1 year and Kirwin 3 years	1
5	Kirwin 1 year and Rochester 4 years	1
5	Kirwin 3 years and Rochester 2 years[b]	1
7	Kirwin 3 years and Rochester 4 years	1
7	Kirwin 1 year and Rochester 6 years	1
8	Kirwin 1 year and Rochester 7 years[c]	1

[a] Three moved to Rochester after spending one winter at Kirwin; one moved to Kirwin after spending three winters at Rochester.
[b] 1969 and 1970—Kirwin; 1971—Rochester; 1972—Kirwin; 1973—Rochester.
[c] 1968 and 1969—Rochester; 1970—Kirwin; 1971–75—Rochester.

at Marshy Point while flightless in July can be used to test this hypothesis (Table 8). In ensuing years more of the newly banded population went to Rochester, a smaller proportion was known to depart Rochester, and a smaller portion was seen in Kansas, but these proportions only approach statistical significance in a 3×3 χ^2 contingency test ($P = 0.12$). Sample sizes for 1970 were small. If the categories of geese leaving Rochester and those in Kansas are combined, the proportions of geese exhibiting a different pattern among years become significantly different ($\chi^2 = 6.29$, 2 df, $P < 0.05$).

Origin of Distribution Pattern

As far as I know, giant Canada geese nesting in southeast Manitoba (east and south of Lake Winnipeg) have always been associated with a migration path to southeast Wisconsin with some going on to southern Illinois (Raveling 1976*b*). Geese breeding at Delta, Manitoba on the south shore of Lake Manitoba and west of Lake Manitoba have always been associated with a central flyway migration path to the Missouri River in South Dakota, to Kansas, and some as far south as Texas (see recovery patterns in Hanson 1965:84; Vaught and Kirsch 1966; and unpublished recoveries from the Delta Waterfowl Research Station and Kirwin, Kansas National Wildlife Refuge). Small numbers of Canada geese have apparently always wintered in the river bottoms around Rochester, Minnesota and the first bandings there in the early 1960's showed that they were from the region of Manitoba between Lakes Manitoba and Winnipeg (Interlake) (Gulden and Johnson 1968).

Marshy Point, where the bulk of the geese were marked during this study, did not contain breeding geese until part of the breeding flock from Delta was held captive there in the mid-1950's (as were their resulting young). Flightless goslings were also transported to Marshy Point at that time from Dog Lake where geese have been known to be present

Table 8. Migration pattern of giant Canada geese neck-banded at Marshy Point Goose Sanctuary, Manitoba in successive years.

Time of banding	Number observed in winter	Migration pattern: To Rochester	Migration pattern: To Rochester, then elsewhere in same winter	Migration pattern: To Kansas
July 1968	84	56 (66.7%)	15 (26.8%)[a]	28 (33.3%)
July 1969	285	204 (71.6%)	46 (22.5%)[a]	81 (28.4%)
July 1970	47	38 (80.9%)	2 (5.3%)[a]	9 (19.1%)

[a] As a percent of geese at Rochester.

Table 9. Migration pattern of neck-banded giant Canada geese in relation to time and location of banding.

Month and location of banding	Migration pattern		
	To Rochester	To Rochester, then elsewhere in same winter	To Kansas
July—Marshy Point	298	63 (21.1)[a]	118 (39.6)[a]
August—Marshy Point	347	30 (8.6)[a]	71 (20.5)[a]
September—Marshy Point	161	16 (9.9)[a]	23 (14.2)[a]
July—Dog, Moosehorn, and Sleeve Lakes[b]	91	1 (1.1)[a]	1 (1.1)[a]

[a] As a percent of geese observed at Rochester.
[b] See text.

from the time of settlement in the early 1900's (R. Otto, personal communication). The Dog Lake area was a major recovery location of geese banded at Rochester (Gulden and Johnson 1968).

Expansion of the population at Rochester began slowly in the mid-1950's and has been rapid since 1959 (Gulden and Johnson 1968, Raveling, unpublished data). This expansion was coincident with the enlargement of the refuge at Rochester in 1961 and the success of the introduction of breeding geese to East Meadows Ranch where they were virtually invulnerable to hunting because of the creation of a 55 square mile (142 km^2) Marshy Point Goose Sanctuary. The breeding flock was allowed to become free-flying in 1959, although escapes had occurred since 1953.

By 1967, when this study began, giant Canada geese were breeding in a continuum through the Interlake with Marshy Point representing the south-west edge of the range of this population. As soon as geese were at Marshy Point, migrants began using the area in August and in autumn. Subsequent data (censuses and records of geese neck-banded at Dog Lake, Moosehorn Lake, and Sleeve Lake) demonstrated that up to 75 percent of the peak autumn concentration were giant Canada geese from further north in the Interlake (Raveling, unpublished data).

It seems obvious that at least part of the original breeding population at Marshy Point resumed their association with Delta and the central flyway and that dispersal from the expanding Interlake-Rochester population occupied Marshy Point where nesting was enhanced by provision of artificial nest structures. Thus, this study captured and marked breeding geese and their young in July at Marshy Point which had two different migration paths, one to Kansas and one to Minnesota. Geese captured in August and September would represent increasing proportions of birds from the Rochester population subunit as they increasingly congregated at Marshy Point from other Interlake locations. This is clearly demonstrated by the distribution of geese observed in winter in relation to their month and location of banding (Table 9; $\chi^2 = 69.7$, 7 df, $P < 0.001$).

DISCUSSION

Band Recoveries and Distribution

This study demonstrated that recoveries of banded birds can be misleading because of the effects of varying vulnerability of birds to hunters in different geographic areas. Caution is needed in interpretation of banding data. Without observation of the neck-collared geese, erroneous, but defensible, conclusions would have been drawn. What appeared to be wide distribution with moderate and equitable harvest obscured the dynamics of decline or expansion of numbers and geographic range of segments of the total population.

Mississippi Flyway

Although the large increase in numbers of geese at Rochester was obvious, the reverse, i.e., the very high mortality and, thus, predictable decline of the population segments occupying areas away from Rochester was not obvious. Geese in the Mississippi flyway which bypassed or stopped for a few days only at Rochester were associated primarily with refuge complexes occupied by 100,000 to 300,000 geese of other races (Swan Lake, Missouri and southern Illinois; see Hanson and Smith 1950, Vaught and Kirsch 1966, Reeves et al. 1968, Kennedy and Arthur 1974). Even dramatic decline or extinction of these subunits would be undetectable because of the small numbers of giant Canadas involved in relation to the overall numbers of the wintering geese from other breeding populations in these areas.

The powerful force of hunting causing changes in distribution becomes obvious only when related to the numbers of geese available from a population and the cumulative effects of harvest on that population in many areas. While the total population was undergoing gratifying expansion, that segment with a tradition for migrating further south during the hunting season was in the process of being exterminated by hunting.

Central Flyway

Essentially, it was only the Marshy Point breeding flock which contributed Interlake giant Canada geese to the central flyway and the wintering flock at Kirwin, Kansas (only about 500 to 1,000 geese at most in the fall—based on distribution of neck-banded geese from Marshy Point in relation to the size of the breeding population at Marshy Point). Giant Canadas in Kansas originate primarily from Manitoba west of Lake Manitoba and from Saskatchewan and Alberta (based on recoveries of geese banded at Kirwin and on observation of geese neck-banded in Saskatchewan and Alberta by Ducks Unlimited). Thus, again, the number of geese undergoing the high mortality found in this study was small compared to the total numbers in the flyway and at Kirwin (10,000 to 15,000 large Canadas—Kirwin National Wildlife Refuge censuses). Therefore, unless these marked birds represented what was happening over a much larger range representing different breeding populations, the decline of this population subunit would be undetectable in Kansas.

In this case what appeared to be an equitable distribution of geese from North Dakota to Kansas with some contribution even as far as Texas, with only modest harvest in any one area, was actually excessive mortality in summation. The results of this pattern may lead to extinction of this subunit or will inevitably result in favoring those individuals which winter as far north as they are physiologically capable of doing so. The giant Canada has the best capability of all the Canadas of withstanding severe winter conditions if water and food are available (see LeFebvre and Raveling 1967).

Implications for Manitoba Breeding Range

Declines or extinction of geese going beyond Rochester or into the central flyway would be undetected by assessment of the breeding population in Manitoba, provided that Rochester geese reproduced as well or better than birds with different migration traditions. The favorable survival pattern of the geese staying at Rochester resulted in a reservoir of geese which could occupy habitat made available by high mortality of some birds within their range (subunit) and of those adjacent to their range. I have records of marked geese raising young 50 miles (80 km) from where they were, themselves, reared as goslings. Their dispersal capability may be even greater but this is certainly sufficient to result in rapid expansion of a population subunit by occupation of territories or adjacent ranges made available by high mortality of other subunits in the population. Thus, from the viewpoint of numbers of geese on the breeding grounds, the total population expanded; but destination of those birds was changing because of occupation of the range by birds of a specific migration behavior tradition allowing high survival.

I previously suggested that the expanding Interlake population may have come to occupy range east of Lake Winnipeg which probably was occupied historically by geese going to southeast Wisconsin or beyond (Raveling 1976*b*). I also predict that geese in the tradition of migrating to Rochester will, or probably have already begun to, expand west of Lake Manitoba which had previously been occupied only by geese migrating through the central flyway.

Implications for Other Populations

While this study was conducted on only a small population, and the subunits were particularly small and, therefore, "unimportant" relative to numbers of geese in most political units, I believe the results reiterate what has occurred in many areas with many populations. Geese do not survive long hunting seasons, especially when their migrations involve stopping at one or more locations along their way to a winter terminus.

Refuges have played a major role in the distribution of geese. The term "short-stopping" must be defined more precisely. It is obvious that geese respond to restoration or creation of habitat along their migration path. I submit that one of the major changes caused by refuges, however, is in timing and length of migration stop-overs with attendant mortality caused by hunters, not the extinction of traditional destinations of individuals that survive. The extinction of destinations is then caused by excessive mortality on population subunits which are harvested at each successive migration stopping place.

In a more general, but prescient, review of needs in Canada goose research, Crissey (1968) proposed that harvest by hunters beyond the reproductive capacity of the birds could account for distributional changes, especially the decline of geese going to Florida and south of Missouri. The results of this study demonstrate this phenomenon and strongly support Crissey's recommendations and Kennedy and Arthur's (1974) that the foundation of Canada goose management lies in controlling the timing and magnitude of hunter-caused mortality on population subunits.

The threat of over-shooting Canada geese is commonly referred to, but almost always with respect to the large concentrations that have developed at refuges (cf. Hine and Schoenfeld 1968:8). While this is true (e.g. see Reeves et al. 1968), it is clear that management has controlled kill around these refuges because population size and magnitude of the kill can be measured in local areas (e.g. Brakhage et al. 1971, Kennedy and Arthur 1974).

In contrast to the concern about over-harvest around concentration areas, most managers have considered the relatively small harvest of geese away from concentration areas as opportunistic and of high and desirable quality. The problem clearly seems to be that a change in emphasis in thinking about overharvest is needed. The traditional 70-day, or even longer, hunting seasons that have existed in most areas away from goose refuges overharvest the small population subunits not going directly to refuges. To the extent that expansion of populations on refuges supplies a surplus to disperse, this may continue to provide a widespread kill (as indicated by the recoveries in this study, e.g.). However, I suggest that a wider distribution of increased numbers of geese in areas away from refuges, or on "underpopulated" refuges in the south, will only result from flyway wide agreements to severely restrict hunting of geese away from refuges.

Hazing and transplants of geese at concentration areas, as attempts to force geese into administratively determined distribution patterns, have been obvious failures (e.g. Hankla 1968), as well as having had an inhumane aspect and having helped to create an adverse public opinion towards management. The best chance to obtain the desired distribution of geese, especially in the south, is to protect the remnant population subunits from harvest before they reach their winter terminals. This will require the capture and identification of these populations and subunits and an extraordinary degree of cooperation among political units in restricting harvest of this international resource as recommended with force and insight by Crissey (1968) and Jahn (1968).

Specific Management Approaches

The following deals only with recommendations which could be implemented to assist the general goals of wide distribution and population growth as an example based on the results of mortality on population subunits. It is recognized the particular management actions undertaken may vary widely depending on judgments yet to be made on the philosophy of deriving share and responsibility and the relative importance of populations or subunits to overall programs in any political unit. Successful precedent exists for discussing "fair share" of resource allocation between states in the form of harvest quotas on certain populations of Canada geese (see Reeves et al. 1968).

Mississippi Flyway.—Mortality on the subunit bypassing or moving quickly through Rochester in autumn would have to be cut by one-half, or more, to allow stabilization or growth. Superficially, the obvious solution would be to close hunting in early November in Iowa and late November or early December in Missouri and Illinois (see Fig. 2 for timing of recoveries). The problem lies with the fact that the main Canada goose populations of importance to these states are *B. c. interior* and seasons and management decisions of necessity will be dictated by needs for these populations (see Vaught and Kirsch 1966, Reeves et al. 1968, Kennedy and Arthur 1974).

The kill in Iowa, however, is widespread (Fig. 1) and establishment of restrictive regulations in certain small geographic areas may be feasible, if they did not unduly restrict access of hunters to Eastern Prairie Population (EPP) *B. c. interior*. Local study of harvest areas could provide assistance.

Two programs in Missouri and Illinois would seem feasible to consider within the constraints imposed by management for *B. c. interior*. Giant Canadas occupy areas other than the main refuges in both states, particularly along the Mississippi River (Fig. 1). As for Iowa, restrictive regulations in these small geographic units could assist these population subunits.

Or, as suggested above, a restrictive rather than a permissive view of statewide harvest away from refuges would benefit subunits of many populations. Secondly, my own observations of giant Canadas at both the Missouri and Illinois refuges lead me to believe that they occupy localized and specific areas within a refuge in a fashion reported earlier for *B. c. interior* (Raveling 1969). Identification of these roost areas could potentially allow a limited feeding or crop manipulation scheme to protect these geese (and other subunits of interest). Such a program would represent the logical culmination of the direction of management that has proceeded from species to flyway to subspecies to refuge and now to refuge subflock.

Central Flyway.—Again, harvest would need to be cut by one-half, or more, to produce favorable status for this population subunit. Small Canadas (*B. c. parvipes-hutchinsii* complex of MacInnes 1966) are the most numerous and important Canadas to hunters in these states and they have, for the most part, migrated through the states involved by the time the bulk of the giant Canadas appear. Closure of hunting in mid-November in the Dakotas, in late November in Nebraska and in early December in Kansas would favor these giant Canadas (see Fig. 2).

Banding.—This study supports almost totally the recommendations emphasized by Crissey (1968), Jahn (1968), and Kennedy and Arthur (1974). In addition to the need for banding and identifying all local winter populations, especially those "remnant" groups, I would add breeding ground banding to obtain the benefit of direct recoveries. Serious consideration should be given to exchanging routine agency banding programs for color-marking programs and the assignment of a biologist to "live" with each population or subunit of interest to obtain consistency in records of marked individuals. I believe the information gathered would be of more use, and would not necessarily cost that much more, if such a marking program were a substitute for traditional banding, especially where small samples make interpretation of mortality estimates tenuous, if not worthless (cf. Johnson 1974), or completely misleading as to distribution as revealed in this study.

SUMMARY

Individually identifiable neck-bands were placed on 1,524 giant Canada geese (*Branta canadensis maxima*) in southern Manitoba in 1968, 1969, and 1970. Recoveries of banded birds shot by hunters showed a wide distribution of these geese into 15 states in the Mississippi and central flyways with a modest overall rate of kill (8.3 percent direct recovery rate). No one specific location away from the breeding grounds accounted for more than 11 percent of recoveries. About 90 percent of the neck-banded geese alive in any one winter were observed and their distribution was markedly different than that indicated by band recoveries. About 73 percent of the marked population were in Rochester, Minnesota and 12 percent were in Kirwin, Kansas and only minor fractions occupied other locations. Those geese going south of Minnesota in the Mississippi flyway or through the central flyway were, respectively, 5.5 and 4.7 times more likely to be shot than geese in Minnesota. Annual mortality of the Rochester population subunit was estimated at 19 percent in contrast to about 50 percent for subunits going elsewhere. The total breeding population expanded because of the favorable survival of the large Rochester population subunit, while other subunits were being exterminated.

Changes in distribution were the result of overharvest on some population segments and low harvest on others. Geese wintering the farthest north were favored. What appeared to be modest harvest in any one location resulted in overharvest in summation as the birds traveled farther south. Similar results could account for much of the changed distribution of geese in association with refuges. Suggestions for alternatives to present management programs are offered.

ACKNOWLEDGMENTS

This study was a Canadian Wildlife Service project for 1967 through 1970. The project continued from 1971 through 1976 in my present position, supported by the University of California, Davis Agricultural Experiment Station, the Canadian Wildlife Service, and the Minnesota Department of Natural Resources. This research benefited from exceptional cooperation of many agencies and individuals to whom I am most grateful. Special acknowledgment is due to the P. Curry and A. Vincent families, owners of the East Meadows Ranch, Clarkleigh, Manitoba and L. King, ranch manager; to C. Dixon, L. Bidlake, and several of their assistants of the Manitoba Department of Mines, Resources, and Environmental Protection; to A. Dzubin, R. Halladay, G. Adams, R. Hutchison, and student assistants D. Hatch and R. McLandress, Canadian Wildlife Service; to R. Osika, Royal Canadian Mounted Police; to R. Jessen, R. Holmes, N. Gulden, J. Gilbertson, D. Ondler, A. Stegen, and J. Heather, Minnesota Department of Natural Resources; to K. Hansen and S. Cornelius, U.S. Fish and Wildlife Service, Kirwin National Wildlife Refuge, Kansas and M. Schwilling, Kansas Forestry, Fish and Game Commission; to R. Vaught and K. Babcock, Missouri Department of Conservation; and to many student assistants at the University of California, Davis, especially M. Wege, R. McLandress, and M. Petersen. C. D. MacInnes, Ontario Ministry of Natural Resources, provided much helpful criticism of the manuscript.

LITERATURE CITED

BRAKHAGE, G.K., H. M. REEVES, AND R. A. HUNT. 1971. The Canada goose tagging program in Wisconsin. Trans. N. Amer. Wildl. and Nat. Resour. Conf. 36:275–295.

CRIDER, E. D. 1967. Canada goose interceptions in the southeastern United States, with special reference to the Florida Flock. Proc. S.E. Assoc. Game and Fish Comms. Annu. Conf. 21:145–155.

CRISSEY, W. F. 1968. Informational needs for Canada goose management programs. Pages 141–147 *in* R. L. Hine and C. Schoenfeld, eds. Canada goose management. Dembar Educational Research Services, Inc., Madison, Wisc.

FJETLAND, C. A. 1973. Long-term retention of plastic collars on Canada geese. J. Wildl. Manage. 37(2):176–178.

GULDEN, N. A., AND L. L. JOHNSON. 1968. History, behavior, and management of a flock of giant Canada geese in southeastern Minnesota. Pages 59–71 *in* R. L. Hine and C. Schoenfeld, eds. Canada goose management. Dembar Educational Research Services, Inc., Madison, Wisc.

HANKLA, D. J. 1968. Summary of Canada goose transplant program on nine national wildlife refuges in the southeast, 1953–1965. Pages 105–111 *in* R. L. Hine and C. Schoenfeld, eds. Canada goose management. Dembar Educational Research Services, Inc., Madison, Wisc.

———, AND R. R. RUDOLPH. 1967. Changes in the migration and wintering habits of Canada geese in the lower portion of the Atlantic and Mississippi flyways—With special reference to national wildlife refuges. Proc. S.E. Assoc. Game and Fish Comms. Annu. Conf. 21:133–144.

HANSON, H. C. 1965. The giant Canada goose. Southern Illinois Univ. Press, Carbondale. 226pp.

———, AND R. H. SMITH. 1950. Canada geese of the Mississippi flyway: with special reference to an Illinois flock. Ill. Nat. Hist. Surv. Bull. 25:67–210.

HENNY, C. J., AND K. P. BURNHAM. 1976. A reward band study of mallards to estimate band reporting rates. J. Wildl. Manage. 40(1):1–14.

HINE, R. L., AND C. SCHOENFELD, eds. 1968. Canada goose management. Dembar Educational Research Services, Inc., Madison, Wisc. 195pp.

HUNT, R. A. 1968. Shell limits and other regulations used in managed goose hunting. Pages 123–139 *in* R. L. Hine and C. Schoenfeld, eds. Canada goose management. Dembar Educational Research Services, Inc., Madison, Wisc.

JAHN, L. R. 1968. Summary: requirements and opportunities for managing Canada geese. Pages 168–173 *in* R. L. Hine and C. Schoenfeld, eds. Canada goose management. Dembar Educational Research Services, Inc., Madison, Wisc.

JOHNSON, D. H. 1974. Estimating survival rates from banding of adult and juvenile birds. J. Wildl. Manage. 38(2):290–297.

KENNEDY, D. D., AND G. A. ARTHUR. 1974. Subflocks in Canada geese of the Mississippi Valley population. Wildl. Soc. Bull. 2(1):8–12.

KOERNER, J. W., T. A. BOOKHOUT, AND K. E. BEDNARIK. 1974. Movements of Canada geese color-marked near southwestern Lake Erie. J. Wildl. Manage. 38(2):275–289.

LEFEBVRE, E. A., AND D. G. RAVELING. 1967. Distribution of Canada geese in winter as related to heat loss at varying environmental temperatures. J. Wildl. Manage. 31(3):538–545.

MACINNES, C. D. 1966. Population behavior of eastern arctic Canada geese. J. Wildl. Manage. 30(3):536–553.

MARTINSON, R. K., AND J. A. MCCANN. 1966. Proportion of recovered goose and brant bands that are reported. J. Wildl. Manage. 30(4):856–858.

RAVELING, D. G. 1969. Roost sites and flight patterns of Canada geese in winter. J. Wildl. Manage. 33(2):319–330.

———. 1976*a*. Migration reversal: a regular phenomenon of Canada geese. Science 193(4248):153–154.

———. 1976*b*. Status of giant Canada geese nesting in southeast Manitoba. J. Wildl. Manage. 40(2):214–226.

REEVES, H. M., H. H. DILL, AND A. S. HAWKINS. 1968. A case study in Canada goose management: the Mississippi Valley Population. Pages 150–165 *in* R. L. Hine and C. Schoenfeld, eds. Canada goose management. Dembar Educational Research Services, Inc., Madison, Wisc.

SHERWOOD, G. A. 1966. Flexible plastic collars compared to nasal discs for marking geese. J. Wildl. Manage. 30(4):853–855.

VAUGHT, R. W., AND L. M. KIRSCH. 1966. Canada geese of the eastern prairie population, with special reference to the Swan Lake flock. Missouri Dep. Conserv., Tech. Bull. No. 3, Jefferson City. 91pp.

WEIGHTS OF LESSER SNOW GEESE TAKEN ON THEIR WINTER RANGE

EDWARD L. FLICKINGER, U.S. Fish and Wildlife Service, Patuxent Wildlife Research Center, Gulf Coast Field Station, Victoria, TX 77901
ERIC G. BOLEN,[1] Rob and Bessie Welder Wildlife Foundation, Sinton, TX 78387

Geese are assumed to accumulate fat on the winter range (Bent 1962, Williams 1967) to sustain them through the long northward migration and early part of the nesting season. However, there are no weights given in the literature of lesser snow geese (*Anser c. caerulescens*) on their winter ranges to compare with weights on the breeding grounds. For many years biologists relied on Kortright (1942) for weights of lesser snow geese, and more recently on Bellrose (1976). In the present study, snow geese from the Garwood Prairie, a rice growing area in Colorado County, Texas, were weighed to determine if weights increased before northward migration. The Garwood Prairie is a segment of the snow goose winter range near the Gulf Coast of Texas.

METHODS

Snow geese shot by hunters were weighed between late October and mid-January 1974–76. We also shot geese in February through early April 1972–76 for weight data. Geese were weighed in the field with a graduated (25-g) tubular spring scale or at a commercial goose cleaner shortly after they were shot. Body weight, sex, and age (on the basis of plumage) were recorded for each goose. Weights of geese collected in all months were separated into 3 biologically meaningful time periods: postfall migration (Oct–Nov), wintering (Dec–Feb), and prespring migration (Mar–Apr). Because some sample sizes were small and means and ranges were usually similar for identical age and sex classes and collection periods among the years, samples for all years were combined. Other physical characteristics, e.g., amount of abdominal or knee strip fat (both legs), were weighed. Condition of sternal muscles or gonad size of males was determined by visual examination in at least 2 of the 5 years of study. Weights were not different ($P > 0.05$) between blue and white color phases or between some sex and age-groups (such as immature males) among periods and therefore are not discussed.

RESULTS AND DISCUSSION

Weights of 196 geese are shown in Table 1 (164 white phase and 32 blue phase). Immature females were lighter ($P < 0.05$) than adult females in the postfall migration period but the sample of adults was small. However, immature females were also lighter ($P < 0.01$) than adult females in the winter. Immature females weighed less than immature males ($P < 0.02$) during winter and during the prespring migration period ($P < 0.001$). Adult females weighed less than adult males ($P < 0.02$) in March and April. In the prespring migration period, adult males ($P < 0.05$), adult females ($P < 0.001$), and immature females ($P < 0.05$) all weighed less than in the postfall migration period. The greatest decrease was in adult females but the sample sizes were small.

Adult males and females contained low amounts of abdominal fat in February

[1] Present address: Dean's Office, The Graduate School, Texas Tech University, Lubbock, TX 79409.

Originally published in J. Wildl. Manage. 43(2):531–533, 1979.

Table 1 Weight comparisons of lesser snow geese on a segment of the winter range, Garwood Prairie, Texas, 1972–76.

	Weight (g)			
	$\bar{x}$	SE	(*N*)	Range
Oct–Nov Postfall migration period				
Imm. males	1,994	53	(36)	1,430–2,660
Imm. females	1,918	56	(30)	1,225–2,510
Adult males	2,224	83	(8)	1,970–2,630
Adult females	2,260	45	(5)	2,100–2,360
Dec–Feb Wintering period				
Imm. males	1,937	48	(16)	1,625–2,325
Imm. females	1,758	45	(24)	1,505–2,200
Adult males	2,086	66	(12)	1,625–2,370
Adult females	1,972	53	(12)	1,500–2,185
Mar–Apr Prespring migration period				
Imm. males	1,955	34	(27)	1,580–2,215
Imm. females	1,691	32	(9)	1,623–1,840
Adult males	2,009	59	(10)	1,750–2,350
Adult females	1,786	52	(7)	1,582–1,995

through April of 1975 and 1976 (mean for males 11.7 g, range 0–17.7 g; mean for females 9.5 g, range 0–16.7 g), but 9 immature males were moderately fat in March 1972. Male knee strip deposits in March averaged 5.7 g (range 0–8.9 g) and females averaged 3.8 g (range trace–6.4 g). Sternal muscles were atrophied on all 26 immature and adult males examined in March of 1973 through 1976 as compared to some geese examined in the postfall migration period. Testes of males were small in late March indicating that they were not in breeding condition.

Lesser snow geese arrived on the Texas winter range weighing less than those weighed by Bellrose (1976) in Ontario, Canada, and South Dakota. There, males averaged 2,749 g and females 2,500 g in early October. In late October and November, adult females were the heaviest geese weighed in Texas, averaging 2,260 g. Adult males averaged 2,224 g.

In March and April, at the onset of northward migration to the breeding grounds, adult males and immature and adult females weighed less than they did in October and November. The heaviest geese in Texas in March were much lighter than those weighed in May by Ankney (1974) when they arrived on the breeding ground at the McConnell River, Northwest Territories, Canada. In March and April adult males averaged 2,009 g and adult females averaged 1,786 g. In May of 1971 and 1972 in the Northwest Territories, males averaged 2,881 g and 2,769 g respectively; females averaged 2,930 g and 2,960 g (Ankney 1974). Geese generally contained low amounts of fat in March. The weights of adult male and female geese and the amount of fat on geese on the Garwood Prairie in March were similar to late incubation period measurements of geese at the McConnell River in late June. Both sexes rely on fat and other reserves through the incubation period (Ankney 1974). Twelve immature males dead or dying from pesticide poisoning on the Garwood Prairie in late March and April of 1972 and 1974 averaged 1,694 g (range 1,350–1,950).

Geese were lighter on the Garwood Prairie segment of the winter range in March and April than in October and November. When geese arrived in Missouri in March during the spring migration period there was very little food for them to eat (K. Babcock, Missouri Department of Conservation, personal communication). But geese were heavy when they arrived on the breeding ground in late May and had been feeding heavily before their arrival (Ankney 1974). Weight loss occurs on the nesting ground by early June (Ankney 1974), but geese were heavy again when they reached South Dakota in early October. Therefore, lesser snow geese must make weight gains while in migration. Perhaps this gain occurs shortly before they reach the breeding ground in the spring and shortly after they leave it in the late summer. Hanson (1962) found that Canada geese (*Branta canadensis*) spending the winter in southern Illinois gained no appreciable weight by early March, shortly before they began their northward flight. He concluded that Canada geese normally initiate migration before acquiring appreciable fat reserves. Once migration began, fat reserves were put on quite rapidly. Body weights of Canada geese reached the annual maximum at the termination of their spring migration (Hanson 1962).

The lighter weight of lesser snow geese on the Garwood Prairie in the prespring migration period does not appear to be the result of extreme physiological or behavioral stress associated with the prebreeding period as discussed by Anderson (1972). Some immature lesser snow goose males were light in April, and the testes of adult males were undeveloped in late March.

Acknowledgments.—We thank H. D. Lobpries of Lobpries Goose Cleaner, Garwood, Texas, who allowed us to weigh and examine geese brought to the cleaner by guides and hunters. We also thank D. H. White, U.S. Fish and Wildlife Service for statistical analysis of the data; G. H. Heinz, R. C. Szaro, and C. M. Glenn of U.S. Fish and Wildlife Service, and C. D. Stutzenbaker of the Texas Parks and Wildlife Department for helping improve the manuscript.

LITERATURE CITED

ANDERSON, W. L. 1972. Dynamics of condition parameters and organ measurements in pheasants. Ill. Nat. Hist. Surv. Bull. 30:451–498.

ANKNEY, C. D. 1974. The importance of nutrient reserves to breeding blue geese (*Anser caerulescens*). Ph.D. Thesis. Univ. of Western Ontario, London. 232pp.

BELLROSE, F. C. 1976. Ducks, geese & swans of North America. Stackpole Books, Harrisburg, Pa. 544pp.

BENT, A. C. 1962. Life histories of North American wild fowl. Part Two. Dover Publications, Inc., New York. 314pp.

HANSON, H. C. 1962. The dynamics of condition factors in Canada geese and their relation to seasonal stresses. Arct. Inst. North Am. Tech. Pap. 12. 68pp.

KORTRIGHT, F. H. 1942. The ducks, geese and swans of North America. The Stackpole Co., Harrisburg, Pa. 476pp.

WILLIAMS, C. S. 1967. Honker. D. Van Nostrand, Inc. Princeton. 179pp.

Received 6 June 1977.
Accepted 17 October 1978.

SELECTED BIBLIOGRAPHY

Wintering Waterfowl

CHABRECK, R. H. 1977. Winter habitat of dabbling ducks—Physical, chemical, and biological aspects. Pages 133–142 *in* T. A. Bookhout, ed. Waterfowl and wetlands—An integrated review. Proc. Symp. at 39th Midwest Fish and Wildl. Conf., Madison, WI. LaCrosse Printing Co., Inc., La-Crosse.

FREDRICKSON, L. H. 1978. Wildlife values in hardwood habitats. *In* P. E. Greeson, V. R. Clark, and J. E. Clark, eds. Wetland functions and values: the state of our understanding. Proc. Natl. Symp. on Wetlands. Am. Water Resour. Assoc., Minneapolis, MN.

HARTMAN, F. E. 1963. Estuarine wintering habitat for black ducks. J. Wildl. Manage. 27(3):339–347.

LEFEBVRE, E. A., AND D. G. RAVELING. 1967. Distribution of Canada geese in winter as related to heat loss at varying environmental temperatures. J. Wildl. Manage. 31(3):538–546.

NICHOLS, J. D., AND G. M. HARAMIS. 1981. Sex-specific differences in winter distribution patterns of canvasbacks. Condor 82:406–416.

OWEN, M. 1975. Cutting and fertilizing grassland for winter goose management. J. Wildl. Manage. 39(1):163–167.

RAVELING, D. G. 1968. Weights of *Branta canadensis interior* during winter. J. Wildl. Manage. 32(2):412–414.

———. 1969. Roost sites and flight patterns of Canada geese in winter. J. Wildl. Manage. 33(2):319–330.

———, W. E. CREWS, AND W. D. KLIMSTRA. 1972. Activity patterns of Canada geese during winter. Wilson Bull. 84(3):278–295.

RYAN, R. A. 1972. Body weight and weight changes of wintering diving ducks. J. Wildl. Manage. 36(3):759–765.

SMITH, I. D., AND D. A. BLOOD. 1972. Native swans wintering on Vancouver Island over the period 1969–71. Can. Field-Nat. 86(3):213–216.

STEWART, R. E., AND J. H. MANNING. 1958. Distribution and ecology of whistling swans in the Chesapeake Bay region. Auk 75(2):203–211.

WHITE, D. H., AND D. JAMES. 1978. Differential use of fresh water environments by wintering waterfowl of coastal Texas. Wilson Bull. 90(1):99–111.

EVOLUTION, HYBRIDIZATION, AND SPECIATION

COMPARATIVE BEHAVIOUR OF THE ANATIDAE AND ITS EVOLUTIONARY IMPLICATIONS[1]

PAUL A. JOHNSGARD[2]

Abstract: An attempt has been made to summarize, in broad outline, the variations encountered in the behaviour of the Anatidae, and to relate these variations to their probable evolutionary significance. In particular, variations in manner of pair formation and pair bond length, in geographic distribution and ecology, and the related conditions of allopatry or sympatry with other species are discussed and their probable effects on behaviour are suggested. Instances are mentioned where a knowledge of behaviour would be helpful in judging evolutionary relationships that have thus far eluded taxonomists (e.g., *Stictonetta, Heteronetta, Thalassornis*), and likewise examples are pointed out where behavioural evidence suggests different relationships from those which are currently accepted (e.g., "*Lophonetta*," "*Anas*" *leucophrys*, and the eiders).

The critical use of instinctive, or "species-typical," behaviour in systematic studies is a relatively recent, but increasingly important, taxonomic tool. Mayr (1958) has summarized the most important literature in this field, and has shown that behavioural information can often help to solve difficult evolutionary problems. Some of the classical contributions of behaviour to avian systematics, such as those of Heinroth (1911), Lorenz (1941, 1951–53), and Delacour and Mayr (1945), have concerned waterfowl, and this group is particularly well suited to such a comparative approach.

An understanding of the significance of pair formation, pair bond strength, and the effects of sexual selection is vital to a proper taxonomic evaluation of instinctive, and especially sexual, behaviour, particularly because it varies greatly within the Anatidae. Thus in the subfamilies Anseranatinae and Anserinae (Delacour 1954) the pair bond is normally lifelong, whereas in most of the Anatinae (except the Tadornini) the pair bond frequently lasts only for a single breeding season. As a result the former groups possess a much smaller capacity for genetic mixing in a large population. This is strengthened in geese and swans (Anserini) by the tendency for a pair's progeny to return to their place of hatching and to mate with closely related individuals, resulting in local inbreeding and thus favouring subspeciation (Mayr 1942). In migratory ducks of the genus *Anas*, however, males normally mate on the wintering grounds and follow their mates to the females' natal homes, which may be a great distance from the males' birthplaces. This, of course, increases the tendency towards panmixia in duck populations and thus reduces subspeciation. Geese and swans do not become sexually mature until several years after hatching, resulting in a longer life cycle and a correspondingly reduced potential rate of genetic change. Most ducks, however, mature in their first year, and thus evolutionary adaptation is potentially much more rapid. This is also enhanced by the larger average clutch size of ducks, which may provide a greater opportunity for selection to act on favourable genotypes. Finally, since in the Anseranatinae, Anserinae and possibly, the Tadornini pair bonds are permanent, mate selection nor-

---

[1] Originally published in Eleventh Annual Rep. of Wildfowl Trust, pages 31–45, 1958–59.

[2] Present address: Department of Life Sciences, University of Nebraska, Lincoln, NE 68588.

mally takes place only once, and seems to be a very gradual process which allows for the "correction" of incipient mating errors between species. Correlated with this is the fact that in most species of these groups there is but a single moult per year (there is less need for a nuptial plumage after a pair bond is once formed), sexual dimorphism is generally almost lacking (apparently because of reduced sexual selection) and sexual displays are normally simple and are mutually performed by both sexes, since their primary function is probably sexual synchronization. In the rest of the Anatinae sexual selection is enhanced by the fact that mate selection generally occurs yearly, there is much sympatry of closely related species, and females "select" their mates (which are usually in surplus numbers and hence must compete for mates). These factors result in selection for species-recognition signals and male heterosexual stimuli, which generally include elaborate plumage and/or soft part colouration and conspicuous prenuptial displays. These morphological specializations and displays must differ enough among closely related, sympatric species to provide for species recognition and thus prevent hybridization. The evolution of male nuptial plumages, the compression of the winter plumage into the short "eclipse" plumage, the staggered period of pair formation among different species, and the other mechanisms which have been evolved as a result of these selective pressures have been described by Sibley (1957), and will not be further elaborated on here. Sibley has also reviewed the interesting examples of isolated populations (such as *Anas acuta eatoni* and *Anas platyrhynchos wyvilliana*) that have lost their sexual dimorphism as a probable result of the diminished selective pressures for species recognition in areas where no other closely related forms occur.

Summarizing these points, we should expect to find in inbreeding species with a long life cycle and permanent pair bond a relatively slow rate of adaptation, but a fairly strong tendency towards speciation and simple, mutual displays combined with sexual monomorphism and nonelaborate plumages. Conversely, in outbreeding species with a short pair bond and short life cycle we should expect a comparatively rapid rate of evolutionary adaptation but a relatively weak tendency towards continental speciation, and heterosexual, elaborate displays combined with plumage dimorphism. Males of sympatric, closely related species should differ in plumages and/or displays, although one would expect that the most closely related forms would share the greatest number of homologous, if somewhat modified, behaviourial patterns. We may now examine the anatid groups, by tribes, to correlate these generalizations with individual cases. Except where recent evidence has suggested modifications, the groupings and scientific nomenclature used is that of Delacour and Mayr (1945) or Delacour (1954–59).

SUBFAMILY ANSERANATINAE

The monotypic Magpie Goose, *Anseranas semipalmata*, differs from all other members of the Anatidae in numerous anatomical respects and in its general behaviour as well. Males and females are coloured alike, and differ only slightly in voice and head shape; one would thus expect that any displays would be of a mutual nature. Delacour and Mayr (1945) state that there is no sign of any real display in the species, and the lack of any close relatives probably reduces selective pressures for species-specific behaviour. McKinney (1953) recorded wing-shaking derived from comfort movements as an epigamic display, but no detailed information on sexual behaviour is yet available. It would be of great interest to compare copulatory behaviour in this species with that of the South American screamers (Anhimidae) and the true geese.

SUBFAMILY ANSERINAE

Tribe Anserini

Sexual display in the geese and swans is mutual, and the sexes are generally almost identical in appearance. Sexual recognition and pair formation behaviour seems to have evolved from derivations of the threat displays towards other birds into mutual "triumph ceremonies," described well by Heinroth (1911). Precopulatory behaviour is essentially the same throughout the whole group, involving a rapid head-dipping in and out of the water by both sexes, reminiscent of and probably derived from bathing movements or, possibly, nest-building movements. Post-copulatory behaviour is also mutual and varies considerably among different species. Thus it may serve as an isolating mechanism, since "incorrect" post-copulatory responses can inhibit the formation of a permanent pair bond between two species (Heinroth 1911).

The swans of the genus *Cygnus* can be divided behaviourally into two major groups. In one group (*olor*, *atratus*, and *melanocoryphus*) vocalizations are reduced, the wings are closed (*melanocoryphus*) or raised while folded (*atratus*, *olor*) during threat display, and the wings remain closed during post-copulatory display. In addition the species wing-flap with the bill pointed upwards (Poulsen 1949), and in some species at least this wing flapping appears to be modified, or "ritualized" into a threat. The Black-necked Swan (*C. melanocoryphus*) deviates considerably from the other two, but all three species carry their young on the parents' backs, which the other species apparently never do. In the second group (*buccinator*, *cygnus*, *bewickii*, *columbianus* and *jankowskii*) vocalizations are elaborate (and visual plumage signals are correspondingly reduced), the wings are spread during threat display, and are flapped or waved during post-copulatory display and during triumph ceremonies. Species in this group wing-flap with a curved neck (as in geese).

Geese differ mainly from swans in their greater vocal versatility; their behaviour has been described at length by Heinroth (1911). Heinroth felt that the triumph ceremony serves an important role in pair formation, family bond development, sexual synchronization, and other important functions. Blurton Jones and Gillmor (1954) have investigated the components of the triumph displays of *Branta* and *Anser*, and have found that species differ in the number and elaboration of these various components, indicating their probable importance in species recognition. Pre-copulatory display consists of the typical head-dipping found in the swans, and post-copulatory display is also mutual. The genus *Branta* appears to have fewer vocal signals than does *Anser*, and shows a corresponding increase in plumage pattern differentiation. This is especially true of head patterns, where the cheek and throat patches of *Branta* seem to be associated with flight intention head-tossing. Many species of *Branta* and *Anser* have striations on the neck feathering, which seems associated with the vibrating of the neck feathers in threat situations. All species of *Branta* and *Anser* but one (*A. canagicus*) have white under tail coverts, which is undoubtedly related to the male's courtship behaviour of swimming ahead of the female with the rear part of the body high in the water. Balham's (1954) exhaustive study of the Canada Goose (*Branta canadensis*) provides a basis for specific behavioural comparisons with other species.

The Cape Barren Goose (*Cereopsis novae-hollandiae*) has been placed, because of its general aggressiveness and downy young pattern, in the Tadornini, but numerous skeletal features indicate a closer relationship with the true geese (Verheyen 1953). A conspicuous triumph ceremony is present in this species, and the similarity of the sexes in voice and display also suggests anserine affinities.

The Coscoroba (*Coscoroba coscoroba*) somewhat resembles the Mute Swan (*Cygnus olor*) in its threat and sexual behaviour, but it apparently forms a true link between the Anserini and the whistling ducks (Dendrocygnini). Pre-copulatory display is of the typical anserine type, although copulation occurs in shallow water (as in the Tadornini). Following copulation there is a mutual display in which both sexes stand together with their necks outstretched and their heads held high, as in the true geese.

Tribe Dendrocygnini

The whistling, or tree, ducks comprise eight species in the single genus *Dendrocygna*. As is true of geese, they are gregarious, highly vocal, and they pair for life. Thus there is little or no sexual dimorphism in plumage or voice, and their visual displays are simple and mutual. All species are very similar in their threat behaviour, which resembles that of true geese, but, as in the geese, these threat displays differ somewhat among different species and may provide clues to intrageneric relationships. No detailed behavioural studies have been done on the group, but evidently pre-copulatory display is the same as in geese and swans. Following copulation, the birds rise up side by side, call, and open one (the far) wing (Finn 1919, Meanley and Meanley 1958). Wing colouration in this group is very uniform, usually being black, which may be related to this display, although other body parts vary greatly in plumage and colour pattern. Their specialized downy pattern and tracheal structure indicate that they are more advanced than the Anserini, and are distinctly isolated from them and from the shelduck group.

Stictonetta

There is considerable anatomical evidence that the Freckled Duck (*Stictonetta naevosa*) is more closely related to the geese and swans than to the Anatinae (Verheyen 1953), as indicated by its large lacrymal, reticulated tarsus, palatine shape, lack of tracheal bulla and the number of cervical vertebrae. If this is true, it possibly should be accorded a monotypic tribal rank ("Stictonettini"). Its sexual behaviour is still unknown, and a knowledge of it would doubtless aid much in determining the relationships of this extremely aberrant species.

SUBFAMILY ANATINAE

Tribe Tadornini

The sheldgeese and shelducks form a smooth transition between the Anserinae and the Anatinae, indicating the largely artificial distinction between the groups. Like geese and swans, most species pair for life, and in some the sexes are coloured alike. However, in the shelducks at least, there are two molts per year (as in true ducks), and pair bonds are not always permanent (Heinroth 1911). In most species the pre-copulatory display is of the typical anserine type. However, the sexes differ in their vocalizations, threat, and sexual displays, and in some forms the sexes are coloured very differently. Threat displays usually involve a lifting of the folded wings, the upper and under coverts of which are generally white and very conspicuous. Metallic coloured wing specula (and associated mock preening) are also first encountered in this group, as is the "Inciting" behaviour of females; these characteristics are typical of most of the Anatinae.

The group seems most closely linked with the true geese (and *Cereopsis*) through the Abyssinian Blue-winged Goose (*Cyanochen cyanopterus*), which lacks white wing coverts and, a sharply distinct speculum, both sexes having very similar voices and displays. In the closely related genus *Chloëphaga* there is a remarkable, and as yet unexplained, variation between plumage monomorphism and dimorphism in the two sexes. In all, however, the sexes' voices and displays are very different, the female exhibiting typical inciting behaviour and the male possessing various threat postures. These threat postures reach their highest degree of elaboration in the Andean Goose (*C. melanoptera*). Modifications of the anserine dipping movements are used in pre-copulatory display, which occurs on land or calm water. The closely related genera *Neochen* and *Alopochen* link the typical sheldgeese with the shelducks (*Tadorna*) both in behaviour and morphology. In *Tadorna* the pre-copulatory behaviour may involve mutual bathing, head-dipping, or head-bobbing motions, or the female may assume the receptive posture without previous mutual display (Poulsen 1957). Pre-copulatory preening occurs in *T. tadorna*; ritualized preening is typical of most of the other Anatinae. Post-copulatory display in *Tadorna* usually consists of the male raising one wing while the female remains crouched, as is also true in *Alopochen* and *Chloëphaga*.

The steamer ducks of South America (*Tachyeres*) are of dubious relationships; Moynihan (1958) found that their threat and pre-copulatory displays are of the typical Tadornini pattern, but that other displays are distinct enough to warrant their placement in a special, separate tribe ("Tachyerini"). Post-copulatory displays involve both sexes swimming apart in an alert posture, with "Head-flagging" and "Grunting."

Tribe Cairinini

The perching ducks were placed by Delacour and Mayr (1945) between the Aythyini and the Mergini, apparently largely because their nesting habits are similar to the latter, but hybridization evidence indicates, rather, that they belong between the Tadornini and the Anatini (Johnsgard 1960*a*). The group consists of about a dozen species which possess a strange mixture of very generalized, or "primitive," and highly specialized features. Part of the tribe (*Plectropterus*, *Cairina*, and *Sarkidiornis*) seems, in fact, to represent a group of "relict" species which probably most closely approximate the generalized anatine condition, from which the more specialized groups have radiated. In this more generalized group plumages are generally metallic in both sexes and lack specialized patterns, vocalizations are poorly developed, displays are rudimentary, and pair bonds are weak or absent. No eclipse plumage is present, and even during the breeding season the sexes rarely associate. Copulation in at least two genera (*Cairina* and *Sarkidiornis*) is characterized by the male brutally attacking and raping the female, and the great size dimorphism of the sexes in these species seems to be related to this fact. The African Hartlaub's Duck (*"Cairina" hartlaubi*) shows little behavioural similarity to the other species of *Cairina*; likewise both the adult and downy plumages deviate from that genus and suggest affinities with the Anatini. It seems likely that it should be maintained in a separate genus (*Pteronetta*) until its relationships are better understood.

The rest of the Cairinini consists of several genera which show striking similarities to representatives of other tribes (e.g., *Chenonetta* with Tadornini, *Aix* with *Anas*, *Amazonetta* with *Aythya*), thus emphasizing the central position of the Cairinini in the subfamily Anatinae. Unlike the previous group, plumages are usually different in the two sexes, and metallic colouration usually occurs in restricted areas (usually wing and head regions) and in highly specialized patterns. Vocalizations are relatively complex, displays are often elaborate, and pair bonds are stronger. An eclipse plumage occurs in two genera (*Aix* and *Nettapus*), and the sexes associate throughout the year.

There is little known about the behaviour and displays of the pigmy geese (*Nettapus*), but apparently the striking wing patterns are displayed in some species (Delacour and Mayr 1945). Delacour's (1945) description of the Maned Goose's (*Chenonetta jubata*) displays indicate affinities with *Aix*, and the post-copulatory behaviour consists of an exaggerated and prolonged raising of the male's hindquarters as it swims away from the female, an action only slightly indicated in *Aix* (D. F. McKinney, pers. comm).

The behaviour of the Wood Duck (*Aix sponsa*) has been thoroughly discussed by Heinroth (1910) and Lorenz (1951–53); these authors have also provided the most complete account of the Mandarin Duck's (*Aix galericulata*) behaviour. The males of these species possess the most elaborate plumage patterns to be found in the Anatidae, and a knowledge of their behaviour contributes to the understanding of this remarkable plumage specialization. Additional comments on the relations between the plumage and behaviour of these species are presented by Dilger and Johnsgard (1959).

The behaviour of the Brazilian Teal (*Amazonetta brasiliensis*) provides a fascinating mixture of components found in species of several different tribes. The male's wheezy whistle is reminiscent of *Aix*, but the female's inciting is rather like some species of *Anas* or *Aythya*. Female pre-copulatory behaviour is an *Anas*-like head-pumping rather than the soliciting posture of female *Aix*, and following copulation the male swims away in a rigid posture astonishingly like the post-copulatory display of *Netta* and *Aythya* (D. F. McKinney, pers. comm.) and *Anas angustirostris*.

The Ringed Teal (*"Anas" leucophrys* of Delacour and Mayr 1945) seems to belong to the perching duck tribe rather than the Anatini (von Boetticher 1952), as indicated by its hole-nesting habits, hybridization with *Amazonetta brasiliensis*, and other evidence. Furthermore, the behaviour and voice of the female Ringed Teal is extremely like that of *Aix*, and the copulatory behaviour of the species is also very similar to that of *Aix*, but is totally unlike *Anas*. I therefore believe that the Ringed Teal should be placed in a separate genus *Callonetta* (as originally proposed by Delacour, 1936) and be included in the perching duck tribe adjacent to *Aix*.

Tribe Anatini

This large tribe of typical surface-feeding ducks is comprised of one large genus

Anas (about 35 species) and several aberrant monotypic genera of dubious relationships. Although males of most species of *Anas* differ greatly in appearance the females tend to be more similar. Display patterns are also similar, and the remarkable degree of interspecific hybrid fertility indicates a closely knit evolutionary group that justifies a broad generic concept. This tribe also typifies the mating situation outlined for ducks earlier, namely a short pair bond, strong sexual selection resulting from male competition for mates, and a high capacity for rapid evolutionary changes by means of a short life cycle and high fecundity.

The displays of two of the monotypic genera, *Hymenolaimus* and *Malacorhynchus,* are so poorly known that they can be omitted here. According to Delacour and Mayr (1945) the major display of the now-extinct Pink-headed Duck (*Rhodonessa caryophyllacea*) was a wheezy neck-stretching, probably corresponding to the "Burp" of male *Anas,* or possibly to the courtship call of male *Aythya,* to which it may be more closely related, as is indicated by its tracheal structure. The highly specialized Torrent Duck (*Merganetta armata*) is also poorly known, but the descriptions of Phillips (1953) and Scott (1954) indicate that the species' behaviour is unique, and shows no distinct similarity to typical *Anas* behaviour.

The behaviour of 14 species in the genus *Anas* (sensu Delacour and Mayr) has been carefully investigated by Lorenz (1941, 1951–53). He has pointed out numerous behavioural homologies among related species, and has thus determined the probable major evolutionary relationships within the group. This important work cannot be adequately summarized here, and should be read in its complete form for details. Most species studied by Lorenz are characterized by numerous display patterns, the number and form of which are usually shared by other species in direct proportion to their degree of evolutionary relationships as suggested by other characters. However, some species (such as *Anas georgica spinicauda*) lack individual displays that are found in closely related species, and it appears probable that this is the result of a secondary loss of such displays, possibly under the impact of selection for isolating mechanisms under conditions of sympatry. Recent research (Lorenz 1958) has indicated that the genetic factors governing such displays may be present in a latent condition in these species, and the displays may only appear in hybrid matings. It would be expected that such a secondary loss of an individual display pattern might occur in a region of sympatry with another closely related form in which this pattern forms an important part of its species-recognition system.

Certain behavioural patterns have been found in all the species of *Anas* thus far studied. For example, female inciting has been found in every species observed, and it appears to play a basic role in the pair-formation process of at least some species of *Anas* (Johnsgard 1959, 1960*b*). Likewise in the case of males the orientation of the back of the head towards a "courted" female appears to be of primary significance in many species, and special head feather patterns are often exhibited during this display. Precopulatory display in all species studied involves a mutual head-bobbing. No special female post-copulatory displays have been recorded, but in males these vary from elaborate displays (as in the mallard group) to those species where such displays are rudimentary or lacking. Major male social displays in *Anas* include (in Lorenz's 1951–53 terminology) "Burping," the "Grunt-whistle," "Head-up-tail-up," "Down-up," "Bridling," "Chin-lifting," and others. Generalized patterns typical of nearly all species include ritualized preening, drinking, and shaking movements. Correlated with these behavioural patterns, males of many species possess erectile crests or otherwise specialized head plumage, many have elaborate scapular feathering or tail feathers, and nearly all have metallic-coloured specula. Bright bill colouration is also typical of many species.

Behavioural evidence (such as the presence of a "Grunt-whistle") indicates that the Andean Crested Duck (*"Lophonetta" specularioides*) should be regarded as a member of the genus Anas, probably most closely related to *specularis*, rather than an aberrant shelduck such as Delacour and Mayr (1945) considered it to be.

Tribe Aythyini

The diving duck tribe is much like the preceding one in that the pair bond is short, there are numerous sympatric and closely related species, and there is a one or two year period to maturity. All species exhibit sexual dimorphism, particularly in the head and iris colouration. Metallic-coloured specula are lacking in all species, but white specula are characteristic of most, and mock preening occurs in most if not all species.

Sexual displays in the group show remarkable uniformity, and justify the broad generic concept of Delacour and Mayr (1945). In fact, *Netta rufina* shows such great similarities to some of the Anatini and *Netta erythropthalma* shows so many characteristics of *Aythya* that any distinct generic separation is difficult. The sexual behaviour is outwardly rather different from that of *Anas*, but the fact that fertile *Anas* × *Aythya* hybrids have been reared on several occasions (Gray 1958) indicates that the two groups must actually be fairly closely related. In at least one species (*Netta rufina*), pre-copulatory behaviour approaches *Anas*-like head-bobbing, but in most species of *Aythya* thus far studied the female assumes a receptive posture without previous mutual head-bobbing display. Post-copulatory display in all species of *Netta* and *Aythya* thus far observed is essentially identical, but different from that of *Anas*. The male calls, then swims in a rigid posture with the head pointed downwards and the bill pressed against the breast. Females of most, and probably all, species have inciting displays which contain a strong chin-lifting component (as in the blue-winged ducks and shovelers), alternating with pointing movements.

Almost no comparative behavioural studies on the Aythyini have been published. Lind's (1958) study of the Red-crested Pochard (*Netta rufina*) provides almost the only information on that genus, and Hochbaum's (1944) account of Canvasback (*Aythya vallisneria*) displays is the most complete description of typical *Aythya* behaviour. A courtship call, emitted with a curved neck or head-throw is the major *Aythya* display, and is probably homologous with the "Sneeze" of *Netta rufina* and, possibly, the "Burp" of *Anas*. Neck-stretching occurs in both sexes of many species, and is apparently equivalent to the "Chin-lifting" of *Anas*. The posture Hochbaum termed the "Sneak" is also typical of many species.

Male head-throws have been recorded for all species of *Aythya* except *innotata* (the displays of which are undescribed), as well as for *Netta erythropthalma* and *N. peposaca*. Group chases over the water surface by several males after a female are typical of this group, and seem to represent a ritualized version of the rape chases that are found in many species of *Anas*.

The Eiders

The four species of eiders were placed by Delacour and Mayr (1945) in the Tribe Mergini, but Delacour later (1956) stated that they belong in a separate tribe, the Somateriini, adjacent to the Anatini. This decision was apparently based on Humphrey's (1958) studies on tracheal anatomy, in which aspect the eiders do resemble the *Anas* group. However apart from this detail of anatomy, and a superficial similarity in female plumages to *Anas* (which is probably the result of selection for concealing colouration in similar nesting habitats), there seems to be little reason to suspect any close relationships between these groups. Myres' recent (1959) comparative behavioural study of the group resulted in his conclusion that the eiders show no behavioural similarity with *Anas*, and also are fairly distinct from the other sea ducks. Females show the inciting behaviour found in the Anatini, Aythyini, and the goldeneyes (*Bucephala*) and mergansers (*Mergus*), and likewise solicit copulation in a prone posture as do the Aythyini and the Mergini. Male displays deviate from those of all other ducks, and thus shed no light on relationships. Male pre- and post-copulatory behaviour greatly resembles that of the goldeneyes (*Bucephala*), with many ritualized comfort movements included in the displays (Hoogerheide 1950).

Tribe Mergini

This tribe of sea ducks differs from the Aythyini mainly in that the species do not achieve sexual maturity until their second or, possibly, third year (in scoters), and they also tend to subsist to a greater degree on a diet of animal matter. Most forms are Northern Hemisphere in distribution, and there is much sympatry of ranges. Some of the most elaborate displays and male plumage patterns in the entire family Anatidae are found in this tribe. Only two species (the isolated Southern Hemisphere mergansers *Mergus australis* and *M. octosetaceus*) lack sexual dimorphism. Specialized colour patterns tend to occur on the heads, bills, and wings. Erectile crests occur on some species, and sexual dimorphism is frequent in bill, foot, and eye colouration.

Displays in the group are often extremely complex, and it is difficult to generalize on them or to point out homologies. Detailed information is not available for many species, but Myres (1959*a*) has well summarized the published information and added many additional observations. It may be said that the scoters (*Melanitta*) are the most generalized of the group, and their displays tend to be derived from simple comfort movements. In this group, as in the eiders, bill shape and colouration probably plays an important role in species recognition. McKinney (1959) and Myres (1959*b*) have described copulatory behaviour of scoters, which is comprised primarily of ritualized comfort movements, such as drinking, preening, stretching and shaking.

The behaviour of the Old-squaw, or Long-tailed Duck (*Clangula hyemalis*) and Harlequin (*Histrionicus histrionicus*) is still inadequately known, but both species appear to have head-throw displays and other displays associated with loud and elaborate calls.

The goldeneyes and Bufflehead of the genus *Bucephala* show striking variations in their behavioural patterns, and Myres feels that the Bufflehead (*B. albeola*) probably deserves generic separation from the goldeneyes on this basis. The displays of the goldeneyes are exceedingly complex, and have been studied by several workers, including Myres (1957), B. Dane et al. (1959) and others. Myres (1959*b*) has also described the copulatory behaviour of the Bufflehead, which is essentially like that of the goldeneyes and scoters.

Behaviourally, the goldeneyes seem to be linked to the mergansers through the Smew (*Mergus albellus*) (Lebret 1958), which exhibits characteristics of both groups and has frequently hybridized in the wild with goldeneyes. The Hooded Merganser (*Mergus cucullatus*) appears to be similar to the Smew in its displays, but the Red-breasted Merganser (*M. serrator*) and Goosander (*M. merganser*) show surprising differences in their male display patterns. However, the mating behaviour of the females of these species is relatively uniform. Nothing is known concerning the displays of the Chinese Mergansers (*M. squamatus*), and very little is known concerning the Southern Hemisphere species. Copulatory behaviour of the mergansers is only very poorly understood. In all species where it has been described the female assumes a receptive posture after mutual drinking display (as in goldeneyes), and the males of at least some species perform ritualized preening and drinking movements, which in the Hooded Mergansers are linked into a sequence almost identical with that found in the goldeneyes.

Subspeciation is very evident in some species of sea-ducks such as the Common and Velvet Scoters (*Melanitta nigra* and *M. fusca*) and the Common Eider (*Somateria mollissima*). This is probably the result of the wide ranges of these forms and the numerous disjunct breeding and wintering areas. It is interesting that in these cases the American races, which are subjected to the greatest amount of sympatry with other species, have the most elaborate male signal characters of bill form and colouration, whereas the Atlantic races tend to have these characters reduced. It appears likely that in these species the recognition characters have been reinforced in the areas where possibilities for incorrect mate selection are greatest.

Tribe Oxyurini

The stiff-tail group represents a unique section of the Anatidae that has deviated greatly from the remainder of the family in morphology, ecology, and behaviour. The tribe consists of a diverse group of genera which are of uncertain relationships to one another and to the rest of the family. In contrast to nearly all of the other Anatinae, males of all species lack a tracheal bulla, and correlated with this there has been the development of a sound-producing tracheal air sac system. Sexual behaviour has become modified for sound production by this means, and it is a significant fact that in this group, which inhabits weedy, overgrown ponds, auditory rather than visual displays appear to be of prime importance. Although males differ in appearance from females in most species, visual display characters mainly involve bill colour and, in some forms, head colouration. The relatively minor importance of plumage in species-recognition is shown by the fact that in South America two species (*Oxyura vittata* and *O. jamaicensis ferruginea*) occur sympatrically which have almost identical male plumage patterns. However, according to Dr. Martin Moynihan (in litt.) these species' displays (and associated vocalizations) are much more different than the degree of difference found in most species of *Anas*. In this group taxonomists must therefore rely on behavioural characteristics and the anatomical basis of display (the œsophagus and tracheal air sac) rather than upon external features. In this respect, the North American Ruddy Duck (*Oxyura j. jamaicensis*) and the Peruvian Ruddy Duck (*O. j. ferruginea*) have essentially identical displays (Moynihan, in litt.), but differ greatly from the Argentine Ruddy Duck (*O. vittata*). Correlated with this, the Argentine Ruddy Duck has an inflatable œsophagus and a weakly developed tracheal air sac (Wetmore 1926), indicating a different means of sound production. By inflating the œsophagus and using jerky head and neck movements to produce sounds, the Argentine Ruddy Duck appears to be similar in its displays to the African Maccoa Duck (*O. maccoa*) and possibly the Australian Blue-billed Duck (*O. australis*). In the North American Ruddy Duck (*O. j. jamaicensis*) the sound produced during display is for the most part a mechanical one, caused by the bill striking the inflated air sac.

No comparative behavioural studies have been done on the tribe as a whole, and to date not even a single species' behaviour has been adequately described. The nearly completed studies of Miss Helen Hays on the North American Ruddy Duck will, however, provide an important contribution to our understanding of the group. Some behavioural information is available for *Oxyura australis* (Brown 1949, Wheeler 1953, Scott 1958) and *Biziura lobata* (Serventy 1946). In those species where display has been observed, the tail is cocked upwards and some kind of head jerking or bobbing is utilized to produce sound. A backward foot-kicking has also been observed in several species. Wheeler (1953) has provided the only published account of copulatory behaviour for any species in the group, which in *Oxyura australis* involves an underwater chase, with the female being completely submerged during copulation. According to Miss Helen Hays (pers. comm.), this is entirely different from copulatory behaviour in *O. j. jamaicensis*, in which "Bill-flicking" is the primary male pre-copulatory display, and the usual head-bobbing, or "Bubble," display follows copulation.

Practically no behavioural information is available regarding the Black-headed Duck (*Heteronetta atricapilla*) and the White-backed Duck (*Thalassornis leuconotus*), both of which are only dubiously included in the stiff-tail group. A knowledge of the Black-headed Duck's behaviour would be of great interest, not only because of its uncertain affinities, but also because of its parasitic nesting behaviour, which must certainly have modified sexual behaviour and pair formation.

PROSPECTS FOR FUTURE BEHAVIOURAL RESEARCH

As is all too evident from the above discussion, great gaps still remain in our knowledge of the general behavioural patterns of many species, to which any interested person could contribute much. In no case, even in the commonest species, is any waterfowl species so thoroughly understood that it would not be worthy of additional detailed study. Indeed, careful quantitative study of a single form or a few closely related forms is more likely to greatly increase our knowledge of the function and evolution of behavioural differences than simply pursuing broad-scale qualitative studies. Examples of situations which could be studied especially profitably are (1) geographic variations in the behaviour of well-marked subspecies and (2) variations in the behaviour of closely related, sympatric forms. In the former case, D. F. McKinney's uncompleted studies on the races of the Common Eider (*Somateria mollissima*) will be of great interest, and other promising examples include the races of Common Teal (*Anas crecca*), Velvet Scoter (*Melanitta fusca*) and Canada Goose (*Branta canadensis*), to mention only a few. Examples of studies where the effects of secondary contact in closely related, but rarely hybridizing, forms might be profitably investigated include Grey and Chestnut-breasted Teal (*Anas gibberifrons* and *A. castanea*), Greater and Lesser Scaup (*Aythya marila* and *A. affinis*), and the Goldeneyes (*Bucephala clangula* and *B. islandica*). Cases where secondary contact of incipient species is accompanied by frequent hybridization are especially instructive, as, for example, where the Mallard (*Anas platyrhynchos*) is in contact with the Black Duck (*A. rubripes*) and the Grey Duck (*A. superciliosa*). Finally, the comparison of mainland forms with island races that have lost most of their secondary sexual characteristics of plumage could provide an insight into a similar secondary loss of behavioural characteristics which might have occurred.

ACKNOWLEDGMENTS

This paper was written while the author was being supported by a National Science Foundation Postdoctoral Fellowship. I would also like to state my appreciation to the following persons with whom I have exchanged ideas and observations on various species: J. Delacour, H. Hays, P. Humphrey, H. Lind, K. Lorenz, D. F. McKinney, M. Moynihan, D. Ripley, P. Scott, C. G. Sibley and W. Von de Wall. W. C. Dilger kindly read and commented on an early version of the manuscript.

LITERATURE CITED

BALHAM, R. W. 1954. The behaviour of the Canada Goose (*Branta canadensis*) in Manitoba. Ph.D. Dissertation, Univ. of Missouri. 244pp.

BLURTON JONES, N. G., AND R. A. F. GILLMOR. 1954. Triumph display in geese. Wildfowl Trust Sixth Annual Report: 82.

BROWN, G. 1949. Display of Blue-billed Ducks. Emu 48:315.

DANE, B., C. WALCOTT, AND W. H. DRURY. 1959. The form and duration of the display actions of the Goldeneye (*Bucephala clangula*). Behaviour 14:265–281.

DELACOUR, J. 1936. Note sur la classification des Anatidés. Oiseau 6:366–379.

———. 1945. The display of the Maned Goose. Wilson Bull. 57:129.

———. 1954, 1956, 1959. The waterfowl of the world. 3 vol. Country Life, London.

———, AND E. MAYR. 1945. The family Anatidae. Wilson Bull. 57:3–55.

DILGER, W. C., AND P. A. JOHNSGARD. 1959. Comments on "species recognition" with special reference to the Wood Duck and the Mandarin Duck. Wilson Bull. 71:46–53.

FINN, F. 1919. Bird behaviour. London, 363pp.

GRAY, A. P. 1958. Bird hybrids. Commonwealth Agricultural Bureau of England. 390pp.

HEINROTH, O. 1910. Beobachtungen bei einem Einbürgerungsversuch mit der Brautente (*Lampronessa sponsa* (L.)). Journ. für Ornith. 58:101–156.

———. 1911. Beiträge zur Biologie, namentlich Ethologie und Psychologie der Anatiden. Verh. V Int. Orn. Kongr., Berlin. 1910. pp. 598–702.

HOCHBAUM, H. A. 1944. The canvasback on a prairie marsh. Amer. Wildl. Inst., Washington. 201pp.

HOOGERHEIDE, C. 1950. De Eidereenden. *Somateria mollissima* L., of Vlieland. Ardea 37:139–160.

HUMPHREY, P. S. 1958. Classification and systematic position of the eiders. Condor 60:129–135.

JOHNSGARD, P. A. 1959. Evolutionary relationships of the North American mallards. Ph.D. Dissertation, Cornell University. 153pp.

———. 1960*a*. Hybridization in the Anatidae and its taxonomic implications. Condor 62:25–33.

———. 1960*b*. A quantitative behavioural study of the Mallard and the Black Duck. Wilson Bull. (In Press).

LEBRET, T. 1958. Baltsbewegingen van het Nonnetje, *Mergus albellus* L. Ardea 46:75–79.

LIND, H. 1958. Eine untersuchung über das Balzverhalten der Kolbenente (*Netta rufina* Pallas). Zeitschrift für Tierpsychologie 15:99–111.

LORENZ, K. Z. 1941. Vergliechende Bewegung studien an Anatinen. Journ. für Ornith. 89(suppl.):194–294.

———. 1951–53. Comparative studies on the behaviour of the Anatinae. Avic. Mag. 57:157–182; 58:8–17, 61–72, 86–94, 172–184; 59:24–34, 80–91.

———. 1958. The evolution of behaviour. Sci. Amer. 199(6):67–78.

McKINNEY, D. F. 1953. Studies on the behaviour of the Anatidae. Ph.D. Dissertation, University of Bristol. 227pp.

———. 1959. Waterfowl at Cold Bay, Alaska, with notes on the display of the Black Scoter. Wildfowl Trust Tenth Annual Report: 133–140.

MAYR, E. 1942. Systematics and the origin of species. Columbia Univ. Press, New York. 334pp.

———. 1958. Behaviour and systematics. *In* Behaviour and evolution. Yale University Press, New Haven. 557pp.

MEANLEY, B., AND A. G. MEANLEY. 1958. Post-copulatory display in Fulvous and Black-bellied Tree Ducks. Auk 75:96.

MOYNIHAN, M. 1958. Notes on the behaviour of the Flying Steamer Duck. Auk 75:183–202.

MYRES, M. T. 1957. An introduction to the behaviour of the goldeneyes (*Bucephala islandica* and *B. clangula* (Class Aves, Family Anatidae)). M.A. Thesis, University of British Columbia. 254pp.

———. 1959*a*. The behaviour of the sea-ducks and its value in the systematics of the tribes Mergini and Somateriini, of the family Anatidae. Ph.D. Dissertation, University of British Columbia. 504pp.

———. 1959*b*. Display behaviour of Bufflehead, scoters and goldeneyes at copulation. Wilson Bull. 71:159–168.

PHILLIPS, S. 1953. An incident concerning the Peruvian Torrent Duck. Avic. Mag. 59:134.

POULSEN, H. 1949. Bidrag til Svanerne Ethologi. Dansk. Ornith. Foren. Tidsskr. 42:173–201.

———. 1957. Notes on the mating behaviour of the Sheld-duck. (*Tadorna tadorna* (L.)). Dansk. Ornith. Foren. Tidsskr. 51:115–118.

SCOTT, P. 1954. Behaviour of the Bolivian Torrent Duck. *In* Wildfowl Trust Sixth Annual Report: 69–72.

———. 1958. Notes on Anatidae seen on world tour. Wildfowl Trust Ninth Annual Report: 86–112.

SERVENTY, V. N. 1946. Display in the Musk Duck. Emu 45:318–321.

SIBLEY, C. G. 1957. The evolutionary and taxonomic significance of sexual dimorphism and hybridization in birds. Condor 59:166–191.

VERHEYEN, R. 1953. Contribution à l'Ostéologie at à la Systématique des Ansériformes. Gerfaut 43(suppl.):373–497.

VON BOETTICHER, H. 1952. Gänse und Entenvögel aus aller Welt. Die Neue Brehm-Bücherei, Heft 73. 95pp.

WETMORE, A. 1926. Observations on the birds of Argentina, Paraguay, Uruguay and Chile. Bull. U.S. Nat. Mus., Washington. 448pp.

WHEELER, J. R. 1953. Notes on the Blue-billed Ducks at Lake Wendouree, Ballarat. Emu 53:280–282.

MALLARD-BLACK DUCK RELATIONSHIPS IN THE NORTHEAST

H. W. HEUSMANN, ***Massachusetts Division of Fisheries and Game, Westboro 01581***

Abstract: During the past 100 years, the status of the mallard (*Anas platyrhynchos*) in the Northeast has changed from that of rare migrant to major game bird, a change associated both with release of game farm stock and an eastward expansion of the mallard's breeding range. The close relationship between mallards and black ducks (*Anas rubripes*) is leading to increasing hybridization as the species come in contact, particularly in inland park situations. The black duck possesses few traits to prevent hybridization, and its continued existence as a distinct species is threatened.

In 1969, for the first time, more mallards than black ducks were shot in the Atlantic Flyway. That year, mallards made up 18.5 percent of the total. The percent of mallards in the kill steadily increased until 1972 (latest available figures), when mallards made up 22.6 percent of the flyway kill and black ducks made up only 14.5 percent. This shift is due in part to the black duck's decline in recent years, but more important is the great increase in mallards in the northern half of the flyway.

HISTORICAL BACKGROUND

Prior to 1900, the mallard was listed for New England only as a wanderer in western sections (Samuel 1870). Howe and Allen (1901), Knight (1908), and Allen (1909) reported that mallards were uncommon even as migrants at the turn of the century, with no confirmed breeding records. Forbush (1929:129) reported that the mallard was becoming increasingly common during the 1920's ". . . due largely to recent propagation of the bird by park commissioners, sportsmen and game keepers," adding that escaped or released birds mated with wild mallards or other escaped birds. Griscom (1949) indicated that mallards continued to increase during the 1930's and early 1940's and that feral mallards were breeding in eastern Massachusetts.

The release of mallards has been accelerated in recent years by state programs. In the Northeast, both New York (Browne 1971) and Pennsylvania (Pratt 1971) have had programs involving the release of large numbers of game-farm mallards. Such releases are not the only reason for the mallard's range expansion, however. The mallard began moving eastward on its own initiative in the late 1800's. Johnsgard (1959), reviewing Audubon Christmas-count data, discovered that the mallard had extended its range eastward some 300 miles between 1900 and 1950. Mallards currently move from east to west and presumably vice versa on an annual basis as well. Mallards banded in Massachusetts parks during winter months have been recovered the following hunting season in Minnesota, Iowa, and Illinois (Heusmann and Burrell 1974).

Eastward range expansion among waterfowl is not unique to the mallard. The ring-necked duck (*Aythya collaris*) was long considered a breeding bird of the West and Midwest with Michigan constituting the eastern limit of its nesting range. However, between 1930 and 1935, the bird became increasingly common in the Northeast as a migrant and was first found breeding in New England in 1936. At present the ringneck is an established breeder in Maine and other areas of the Northeast (Mendall 1958). The baldpate or American wigeon (*Anas americana*) is

Originally published in Wildl. Soc. Bull. 2(4):171–177, 1974.

another western duck that is moving east, presently breeding in limited numbers in New Jersey and elsewhere (Wayne F. MacCallum, personal communication). The gadwall (*Anas strepera*) was not recorded as a breeder on the Atlantic coast prior to 1939, but now nests in at least 30 locations from Prince Edward Island to South Carolina (Charles J. Henny, personal communication).

EVOLUTIONARY THEORY

The colonization of the Northeast by the mallard poses a provocative question: what will be the effect on New England's black duck? The mallard inhabits almost the whole of the northern hemisphere and is found across the North American continent except (until recently) in the Northeast where its place was taken by the black duck (Kortright 1953). In order to discover why this was so, we must go back to the Pleistocene.

The exact ancestry of the black duck is in question. Ernst Mayr (personal communication) believes that the mallard and the black duck descended from a common ancestor in the recent past. Johnsgard (personal communication) is convinced that the black duck is a direct descendant of the mallard.

Kendeigh (1961) theorizes that during the Pleistocene, North American biota were segregated into eastern and western populations by the Great Plains in the south and by repeated glaciation in the north. The western section continued to have contact with the Eurasian biociation, but the eastern section was too remote. It would then be possible that a group of mallards or mallard-like ducks became isolated in the Northeast, perhaps by a glacier that lingered in the Appalachians long after it had receded from lower elevations.

Unlike the rich postglacial pothole country of mid-America, the lands of the Northeast were rocky and thin-soiled. Year-round precipitation allowed the rapid reinvasion of glacier-despoiled lands by forests, resulting in generally acidic soil and water conditions. Despite the rigorous climate and poor fertility, ducks adapted to the region through generations of natural selection, gradually moving their breeding range from coastal freshwater marshes to wooded ponds, retreating each winter to the open waters of coastal bays.

Because of relatively poor habitat, the region's waterfowl species were few. Aside from blue-winged teal (*Anas discors*) nesting along open inland marshes, the only other waterfowl with which mallard-like ducks came in contact were wood ducks (*Aix sponsa*), hooded mergansers (*Lophodytes cucullatus*), buffleheads (*Bucephala albeola*), and goldeneyes (*Bucephala clangula*). The biology of these cavity nesters was such that it rendered inbreeding with the mallard types almost impossible. Hence, there was no selection toward brightly colored males such as existed on western prairies, where species recognition was important. As selective pressures shifted toward protective coloration for both males and females, sexual dimorphism was lost, a situation frequently occurring in isolated island-nesting species (Johnsgard 1968). Darker birds were less conspicuous to predators in the shadowy ponds and bogs of the forest, and gradually the dark plumage of the black duck we know today evolved.

MALLARD-BLACK DUCK HYBRIDIZATION

Some Possibilities

One of the stipulations usually included in the definition of the term "species" is "reproductively isolated" (Kendeigh 1961; Mayr 1942; Pettingill 1970). According to Lack (1971), the three major ways in which bird species are segregated from one another are by range, habitat, and feeding. Extensive land clearing in New England during the mid-1800's drastically altered habitat. Land clearing elsewhere in the East, together with the construction of numerous farm ponds, may have created a corridor which allowed the mallard to expand eastward into the black duck's range.

The mallard readily hybridizes with other ducks and has done so with approximately 40 other species (Johnsgard 1968). In most cases, hybrid offspring are sterile. However, Phillips (1915) crossed mallards with black ducks and found that the offspring were completely fertile; crossing the offspring to one another as well as back-crossing to pure mallards and blacks gave no evidence of decreasing fertility.

Offspring of the original mallard-black duck cross were "dark, intermediate types, plainly showing all mallard characteristics, but obscured by the plain dark brownish color of the black parent duck" (Phillips 1915:76). When hybrids were allowed to cross with one another, female offspring looked the same as before: simply a dark mallard female. Males, however, ranged from individuals with green heads, mottled cheeks, no neck ring, and a rich chestnut chest to individuals even darker than their hybrid father, with no anterior white wing bar. Furthermore, sex feathers on the rump varied greatly. They were absent on some males and small, medium, or large on others (Phillips 1915:77–78). When the hybrids were back-crossed to mallards, the second generation ran from dark males with green skull caps to mallard types with spotted faces, reduced or absent neck rings, and reduced wing bars. When hybrids were back-crossed to black ducks, it was difficult to distinguish the young from pure blacks (Phillips 1915:79).

Will such hybridization occur in the wild? Johnsgard (1959:120) records that C. E. Goodwin, observing a resident population of mallards and black ducks in the Toronto area, noted that since the introduction of a small stock of mallards and black ducks in 1931, the two forms hybridized freely, with the mallards increasing rapidly in proportion to black ducks. Goodwin postulated that a selection against black ducks might be operating through a tendency toward non-selective mating, or toward cross-mating in the case of the female blacks. Johnsgard (1959:119) reports further that Konrad Lorenz found that females of the sexually nondimorphic Meller's duck (*Anas melleri*), very similar in appearance to New England's black duck, mated as readily with male mallards as with their own species.

Most waterfowl species have elaborate courtship displays wherein an action on the part of the male elicits a specific response from the female which, in turn, causes a response from the male and so on. If any one step is omitted, the final mating will not take place. In this way, hybridization between most species is largely prevented. Johnsgard (1959) found no difference between display patterns of black ducks and mallards, eliminating one roadblock to interbreeding. Therefore, it is possible that given the choice between a drab male black duck and a brightly colored male mallard, the female black duck may choose the mallard often enough to affect the black duck's reproductive status.

Johnsgard (1959:34) points out that by the late 1950's there were 6 times as many mallards wintering in the combined Atlantic and Mississippi Flyways as there were black ducks. With continued expansion of the mallard's range eastward, he believes it may be possible that the black duck gene pool will eventually be swamped by the mallard. This occurrence will be prevented only if the present breeding and wintering habitat of the black duck differs significantly enough from that of the mallard to avoid contact during pair-bond formation. Since most of the black duck's pair formation takes place on the wintering ground (Wright 1954), the ratio of mallards to blacks on wintering areas will be important in determining chances of hybridization.

Hybridization in Massachusetts

During January 1973, the Massachusetts Division of Fisheries and Game conducted coastal waterfowl inventory flights (Heusmann 1973a) and an inland park mallard census. For the census purposes, a *park mallard* was defined as a duck that had access to artificial feed and spent at least part of the day during part of the year in the close company of humans (Heusmann 1973b). From the two censuses, it was determined that approximately 21,000 black ducks and 10,000 mallards were wintering in Massachusetts. Of the black ducks, 19,000 were observed along the coast; about 2,000 wintered inland. Less than 500 mallards were observed on the coast.

It would thus appear that the maritime proclivities of the black duck limit its contact with mallards during the time of year most important in pair-bond formation, in turn limiting chances of hybridization and subsequent gene-pool dilution. However, the number of mallards that winter along the coast has been increasing for several years. While many mallards are missed during winter inventory flights (because of the difficulty the observer has in separating individual mallards from flocks of black ducks), Massachusetts waterfowl crew members have noticed an increasing number of mallards and hybrids among captured black ducks during coastal winter banding work. Between 1972 and 1974, the proportion of mallards in bandings has increased from 7.4 to 12.4 percent. This is not to imply that mallards make up 12 percent of coastal mallard-black duck populations; mallards seem to be easier to trap. It may be pertinent that one mallard subspecies, the Greenland mallard (*A. p. conboschas*), winters in the rigorous climate of Greenland and is adapted to a maritime situation, implying that the common mallard may also possess this potential.

More important are the effects of mallard-black duck intermingling on inland sites. Black ducks are common in park situations, frequently making up 5 to 35 percent of a mallard-black duck flock. Mixed pairs are not unusual, and I have observed several cases where an apparently pure mallard drake was paired with a hybrid hen, obviously of mallard × black duck origin, indicating an intermixing of genes beyond the first generation.

The importance of inland sites to mallard-black duck hybridization is evident from Massachusetts trapping data. Hybrids comprised 8.1 percent of the blacks and mallards banded on the coast during the winters of 1971–1974. During this same period, 12.9 percent of the mallard and black ducks banded inland were hybrids, a rate 59 percent higher than that for the coast. Furthermore, the coastal hybrid figure is unusually high because of the large proportion of hybrids captured in the Boston Harbor area. The hybrid rate for southeastern Massachusetts is only 6.5 percent.

Factors Complicating Hybrid Statistics

Unfortunately, the ability to determine accurately the degree of mallard-black duck hybridization in nature is complicated by

2 factors: the complete interfertility of the two species and their close evolutionary relationship. The plumage of mallard × black hybrids of other than a 50-50 combination may differ only minutely from either of the species' standards. Further, black ducks apparently retain latent mallard characteristics as first described by Phillips (1912), who found that 20–30 percent of male black ducks taken in late fall in Massachusetts possessed some mallard-like variation of plumage. He argued that if such characters signified a slight infusion of mallard blood, one would expect a corresponding variation in the mallard; such was not the case. Phillips therefore postulated that black ducks were carrying slight mallard tendencies in a latent condition.

One of the criteria currently used by the U.S. Fish and Wildlife Service's Migratory Bird Population Station to determine mallard × black duck hybrids, based on wing samples, is the presence of an indistinct line anterior to the speculum of black-duck type wings (S. M. Carney, personal communication). W. F. MacCallum and I visited the Harvard Museum of Comparative Zoology and examined 103 black duck study skins collected from New England and the Canadian Maritime provinces prior to 1916. Forty of the 103 specimens had some form of partial buff or white line along the anterior edge of the speculum. Since mallards were rare in the Northeast prior to the 1920's (as indicated by an almost complete lack of mallard specimens collected from New England prior to 1930), we assume that the aberrant specimens represent latent mallard characteristics or at least a natural plumage variation in the black duck.

In 1971, Massachusetts received several dozen black duck eggs from the Delaware Division of Fish and Wildlife. The eggs were from game-farm held black ducks that, in turn, had been hatched the previous year from eggs collected on the Brigantine National Wildlife Refuge in New Jersey. Of 43 black ducks hatched from the Delaware eggs, only 42 percent possessed "perfect" type black duck wings; the rest had some type of buff or white line along the anterior edge of the speculum. When 7 of the "perfect"-winged females were crossed with 5 perfect males, 36 (70.6 percent) of the progeny were of the perfect-wing type. These, in turn, produced young in the ratio of 36:12 perfects to aberrants based on wing plumage. The F_3 generation consisted of 15:5 perfects to aberrants. Only 2 of the 32 F_1, F_2 and F_3 aberrant winged birds, however, actually had a white line along the anterior edge of the speculum; all the others possessed buff markings.

The fact that in all three filial generations at least a quarter of the birds possessed some types of partial or complete buff line along the anterior edge of the speculum indicates that such a line is a normal plumage characteristic in black duck populations. For practical purposes, most biologists would call such birds black ducks. The designation "perfect" is just that: a wing with no trace of an anterior wing-bar. However, in F_3 generation birds that were not bred from "perfect" stock, signs of anterior wing bars were both more prevalent (about 40 percent of the birds) and more distinct—either speckled with white, broader, or both—indicating that genetic factors may intensify the wing markings. Pedigree data suggest that a thin buff line along the anterior edge of a black-duck speculum may indicate an infusion of mallard blood, but it is not a sign that the bird is a hybrid.

Johnsgard (1959:87) presents further evidence on the close evolutionary relationship between blacks and mallards, based on the extremely similar electrophoretic profiles of their egg-white proteins. The profile of the domestic Pekin mallard actually exhibits a greater difference from the wild mallard than does the black duck.

THE FUTURE

Whether or not the black duck will continue to exist as a distinct species is uncertain. One factor necessary to a species' continued existence is reproductive isolation by range, habitat, feeding mechanisms, or structural features. The population from which the black duck evolved was originally separated from other populations by distance (range). The duration of the separation, however, apparently was not great enough to allow the black duck to evolve into a completely different species from the mallard. Feeding mechanisms, courtship display patterns, and size and structure remained similar between the two; only habitat occupied differed. Now man has modified the habitat sufficiently to enable the mallard to colonize the Northeast.

Parks in urban areas have become refuges for large numbers of mallards, acting as wintering areas where birds are provided with corn and bread, even in the most inclement weather, and serving as refuges for local birds during the hunting season. Low mortality rates compensate for low reproduction in parks (Heusmann and Burrell 1974). Insect populations in urban areas are frequently lower than in the surrounding countryside, meaning fewer vectors to carry diseases. In a sample of 259 blood smears from mallards banded in park situations in Massachusetts, 25 percent were infected with one or more blood parasites; during the same period, 48 percent of a sample of 327 mallards banded on outlying "wild" areas were infected (Gordon F. Bennett, personal communication). While the black duck is losing habitat to urban development, the mallard is fitting into the new environment.

The black duck evolved to fill an unutilized niche. If that niche is altered or disappears, the purpose for the black duck's existence will disappear with it. The cosmopolitan mallard is adapting to man's modifications of the environment; whether or not the mallard will continue to adapt as fast as these modifications occur remains to be seen.

LITERATURE CITED

ALLEN, G. M. 1909. Fauna of New England; List of *Aves*. Occas. Pap., Boston Soc. Nat. Hist. 230pp.

BROWNE, S. 1971. The New York hand-reared duck program. Pages 9–19 *in* Symposium on the role of hand-reared ducks in waterfowl management. Max McGraw Wildl. Fndn., Dundee, Ill. 174pp.

FORBUSH, E. H. 1929. Birds of Massachusetts and other New England states. Part I: Waterbirds, marshbirds and shorebirds. Norwood Press, Norwood, Mass. 481pp.

GRISCOM, L. 1949. The birds of Concord. Harvard Univ. Press, Cambridge, Mass. 340pp.

HEUSMANN, H. W. 1973a. Waterfowl inventory flights. Mass. Div. Fish. Game. P-R Prog. Rep. W-42-R-6 VI-1. 7pp. Mimeogr.

———. 1973b. The 1973 Massachusetts park mallard census. Mass. Div. Fish. Game. 5pp. Mimeogr.

———, AND R. G. BURRELL. 1974. Park mallards. Pages 77–86 *in* Symposium on wildlife in an urbanizing environment. Coop. Ext. Serv., Univ. of Mass., Amherst. 182pp.

HOWE, R. H., JR. AND G. M. ALLEN. 1901. The birds of Massachusetts (by subscription). Cambridge, Mass. 154pp.

JOHNSGARD, P. A. 1959. Evolutionary relationships among the North American mallards. Ph.D. thesis. Cornell Univ. 159pp.

———. 1968. Waterfowl: their biology

and natural history. Univ. Nebr. Press, Lincoln. 138pp.

KENDEIGH, S. C. 1961. Animal biology. Prentice Hall, Inc., Englewood Cliffs, N.J. 468pp.

KNIGHT, O. W. 1908. The birds of Maine. Charles H. Gloss and Co., Bangor, Me. 693pp.

KORTRIGHT, F. H. 1953. The ducks, geese, and swans of North America. Stackpole Co., Harrisburg, Pa., and Wildl. Manage. Inst., Washington. 476pp.

LACK, D. 1971. Ecological isolation in birds. Harvard Univ. Press, Cambridge, Mass. 404pp.

MAYR, E. 1942. Systematics and the origin of species. Columbia Univ. Press, New York, N.Y. 334pp.

MENDALL, H. L. 1958. The ring-necked duck in the Northeast. Univ. Press, Orono, Me. 313pp.

PETTINGILL, O. S., JR. 1970. Ornithology in laboratory and field. Burgess Publishing Co., Minneapolis, Minn. 524pp.

PHILLIPS, J. C. 1912. A reconsideration of the American black ducks with special reference to certain variations. Auk 29 (2):295–306.

———. 1915. Experimental studies of hybridization among ducks and pheasants. J. Exp. Zool. 18(1):69–144.

PRATT, H. R. 1971. The mallard stocking program in Pennsylvania. Pages 21–42 *in* Symposium on the role of hand-reared ducks in waterfowl management. Max McGraw Wildl. Fndn., Dundee, Ill. 174pp.

WRIGHT, B. S. 1959. High tide and an east wind. Stackpole Co., Harrisburg, Pa. and Wildl. Manage. Inst., Washington. 162pp.

OCCURRENCES OF DUCK HYBRIDS AT JAMES BAY[1]

R. M. ALISON,[2] Wildlife Branch, Ministry of Natural Resources, Whitney Block, Queen's Park Crescent, Toronto, Ontario M7A 1W3, Canada
J. P. PREVETT, Ministry of Natural Resources, Moosonee District Office, Moosonee, Ontario, Canada

Wing collections in 1973 and 1974 sampling approximately 95% of those ducks shot by hunters in the vicinity of the Moose River estuary (51°20′N, 80°30′W) provided information on the frequency of hybridization (Table 1). Although those ducks shot in the fall in James Bay may not be positively assigned to a specific breeding area, it is likely that a substantial number of Black Ducks (*Anas rubripes*), Mallards (*A. platyrhynchos*), and Pintails (*A. acuta*) nest in the Hudson-James Bay lowlands. Thus the rates of hybridization may apply generally to breeding populations in that region.

The frequency of occurrence of Mallard × Black Duck hybrids is of particular interest. Unfortunately, it is not entirely possible to distinguish all Mallard × Black Duck hybrids and thus determine accurately, based upon wing plumage criteria, the degree of hybridization in nature. The observed frequency of 2.6% exceeds significantly the hybridization frequencies reported by Johnsgard (Amer. Midl. Naturalist 77:53, 1967) in those states south and east of the Great Lakes during the period 1960–64. Nonetheless hybrids comprised 8.1% of the Blacks and Mallards banded on the Massachusetts coast during the winters of 1971–74 and 12.9% of the birds banded inland (Heusmann, Wildl. Soc. Bull. 2:174, 1974).

Banding data suggest that Mallard and Black Ducks staging on the James Bay coast of Ontario winter in both the Mississippi and Atlantic Flyways where, in the late 1950's, Mallards outnumbered Blacks six to one (Johnsgard, unpublished Ph.D. dissertation, Ithaca, New York, Cornell Univ., 1959). Increased frequencies of occurrence of hybridization might reflect increasing Mallard and decreasing Black Duck populations in those regions from which the individuals that stage on James Bay are derived. In the absence of specific breeding data, the relatively high frequency of hybrid occurrence at James Bay suggests that Mallards, in addition to being adapted to survive in agricultural and heavily populated habitats, are also able to survive and breed in significant numbers in the Hudson and James Bay lowlands. Data collected by staff of the Ontario Ministry of Natural Resources in 1960 indicate that the frequency of occurrence of Mallard × Black hybrids in southwestern Ontario was about 2.1% (2,185 wings examined) of the combined total. Thus the observed ratio at James Bay is consistent with ratios from southern Ontario and may only reflect declining Black Duck population rather than significant differences in the operation of selective mechanisms related to pair formation for those birds breeding in northern Ontario.

On 1 October 1974 an apparent Pintail × Black Duck hybrid (probably immature female) was shot by an unknown hunter approximately 8 miles north of Moosonee, Ontario (51°20′N, 80°30′W). The specimen was not kept but one wing was removed and preserved during routine data collection at the West River Waterfowl Check Station. The wing

[1] Originally published in Auk 93(3):643–644, 1976.
[2] Address correspondence to this author.

Table 1. Frequency of occurrence of wings of major species, Moose River, James Bay.

	1973	1974	Total
Normal wings			
Black Duck	113	196	309
Mallard	378	797	1,175
Pintail	378	826	1,204
American Wigeon (*Anas americana*)	41	109	150
Hybrid wings			
Black Duck × Pintail	—	1	1
Mallard × Black Duck	7	22	29
Mallard × Pintail	—	1	1
American Wigeon × Pintail	2	1	3

shows plumage characteristics intermediate between the two species. Whereas the under surface was almost indistinguishable from that of a normal Pintail, the upper surface vaguely resembled that of a Black Duck. The speculum was purple and poorly defined. The secondary coverts closely resembled those of an immature Black Duck. The remainder of the upper surface was uniform dark gray-brown. The measurements conformed to those of immature Pintail wings at the Royal Ontario Museum. Check Station staff reported that the bird appeared similar to a normal wild Pintail.

This is the first record of a wild-taken hybrid between these two species. A captive hybrid has been reported (Sibley, Condor 59:166, 1957). Although isolating mechanisms (e.g. distinct courtship displays), normally prevent the frequent formation of mixed pairs, hybridization among the Anatinae has been frequently reported for nearctic waterfowl (Sibley 1957).

PROXIMATE AND ULTIMATE DETERMINANTS OF CLUTCH SIZE IN ANATIDAE[1]

PAUL A. JOHNSGARD, Department of Zoology, Oldfather Hall, The University of Nebraska–Lincoln, Lincoln, NE 68588

In a stimulating analysis, Lack (1967, 1968*a*) reviewed waterfowl clutch size and egg size data, and concluded that interspecific variations in average clutch size are generally inversely related to those of relative egg size. Thus, he suggested that the average clutch size of each waterfowl species has evolved in relation to the average availability of food to the female around the time of nesting. He hypothesized that in waterfowl, relatively large eggs have probably evolved to provide the newly-hatched young with a large food supply (an idea he subsequently (1968*b*) questioned) or with an adequate insulating layer of fat. He also suggested that, since annual, seasonal, and local variations in clutch size exist, proximate factors, such as the food supply of individual females, may be more likely to influence a bird's date of laying than either its egg size or clutch size. Since the publication of Lack's study, several additional reviews of avian clutch sizes have appeared, notably those of Klomp (1970), von Haartman (1971) and Cody (1971). Klomp considered the problems posed by the Anatidae in some detail, and generally agreed that the food supplies available to the female are probably the ultimate factor influencing clutch size in this group.

Because of the large amount of information available for waterfowl, and since Lack did not concern himself with proximate influences on clutch sizes of individuals, I have given these matters some attention and have reached somewhat different conclusions. No simple explanation for inter- and intraspecific variations in clutch sizes seems possible at present, but a summary of the evidence relating to these phenomena nevertheless appears worthwhile.

PROXIMATE FACTORS INFLUENCING CLUTCH SIZES OF INDIVIDUAL BIRDS

It is well established that intrapopulation variations in clutch size of waterfowl do exist, which probably reflect proximate environmental influences that vary with time. Klomp (1970) listed thirteen species of Anatidae that have been reported to exhibit declines in average clutch size during a single breeding season, and Bengtson (1972) reported this trend in all of ten species of ducks in his study. Except for Koskimies' (1957) suggestion that such individual clutch size variations might be the result of genetic polymorphism having adaptive value, it has been generally believed that these seasonal differences are mainly the result of proximate influences. The lowered hormonal levels after the reproductive peak (Hilden 1964), or the reduced stimulating by temperature or photoperiod effects (Dane 1966), might reduce the clutch size of late-nesting birds. Their smaller clutch sizes might also simply reflect renesting, since repeat clutches are generally smaller than the original ones (Sowls 1959). This, in turn, may result from exhaustion of the female's reserves (Wagner 1960). Again, the smaller, later clutches may be produced by younger females nesting for the first time and thus

[1] Originally published in Wildfowl 24(1):144–149, 1973.

not in peak reproductive condition (Lemieux 1959). Kossack (1950) provided some data for the Canada Goose *Branta canadensis* favouring this view.

Variations in average clutch of a single population in different years also occur in the Anatidae, and clearly must be controlled by proximate factors. The possibility that these might be related to annual variations in food availability has recently been supported by Bengtson (1971) who observed that during a year of relative food scarcity, four species of diving ducks and the European Wigeon *Anas penelope* produced significantly smaller clutches than normal. This finding clearly runs counter to Lack's suggestion that annual variations in food supply influence laying date rather than clutch size, but does support his view that the average clutch size may be basically attuned to normal food availability.

Annual variations in clutch size and nonbreeding, related to weather conditions during the egg-laying period, have also been established for the Anatidae, particularly among arctic breeders. Evidence on this point has been provided for the Atlantic Brent Goose *Branta bernicla hrota*, the White-fronted Goose *Anser albifrons*, Black Brant *Branta bernicla orientalis* and Lesser Snow Goose *Anser caerulescens caerulescens* by Barry (1962), for the Lesser Snow and "Blue" Geese by Cooch (1961), and for the Ross' Goose *Anser rossii* by Ryder (1970b).

If females breeding for the first time tend to have smaller clutches than experienced breeders, then variations in the percentage of young females in a population might result in between year variations in average clutch size. Mendall (1958) suggested this possibility for the Ring-necked Duck *Aythya collaris*, when he found a limited correlation between poor hatching success in one year and large average clutches of Ring-necked Duck. Hilden (1964) provided supporting evidence among Tufted Ducks *Aythya fuligula* and Greater Scaups *Aythya marila*.

Population density is, theoretically, another factor controlling clutch size. Hilden (1964) found no evidence for this among the two *Aythya* species just mentioned. The only example I have encountered is that of Marshall (1967), who reported that increased clutch size (but reduced nesting success) was associated with increased nesting densities in the European Eider *Somateria m. mollissima*. Ryder (1970b) found that Ross' Geese nested earlier in high-density concentrations, but that clutch size was not influenced by the breeding density.

Interpopulation variations in clutch size might, of course, be a reflection of either proximate or ultimate factors. If the populations are geographically well isolated, the probability of genetic control for these differences would seem to be higher, and indeed Lack (1967) provided some examples among various races of certain ducks. However, continuous clines in clutch size might well be geared to such proximate factors as photoperiod or temperature gradients. Weller (1964) was unable to find any evidence for such geographic variation in the clutch size of the Canada Goose. The suggestion of Paynter (1951) that the American Eider *S. m. dresseri* has intraspecific clinal variation was based on data from various investigators and, as Weller indicated, is therefore of questionable value as well as being only over a range of less than ten degrees of latitude. A more general comparison of average clutch size of this species (Table 1) is not indicative of increased clutch size with increasing latitude; if anything, the

Table 1. Breeding latitude and reported clutch sizes of the Common Eider *S. mollisima*.

Latitude (°N)	Average clutch-size	Total nests	Locality	Authority
79	2.95	2,993	Kongsfjord, Spitzbergen	Ahlen and Andersson 1970
65	2.74	42	Iceland	Gudmundsson 1932
64	3.44	1,598	Cape Dorset, NWT	Cooch 1965
63	4.6[a]	193	Valassaaret, Finland	Hildén 1964
62	4.89	89	Yukon-Kuskokwim Delta	Lensink (personal communication)
61	4.32	734	Green Is., Que	Lemieux (cited in Cooch 1965)
60	3.13	73	Payne, Bay, Que.	Edwards (cited in Cooch 1965)
56	4.47	120	Belcher Is., NWT.	Freeman 1970
51	3.6	60	Amchitka Is., Alaska	Kenyon 1961
48	4.04	1,131	Saquénay Co., Que.	Lewis 1939
45	3.53	134	Kent Is., Me.	Gross 1938
44	3.25	44	Penobscot Bay, Me.	Paynter 1951

[a] Excludes clutches of less than three eggs.

average clutch size is largest at intermediate latitudes.

To summarize, it would appear that proximate factors are as likely to influence anatid clutch size as to account for variations in laying dates, at least in temperate or arctic species.

ULTIMATE FACTORS INFLUENCING AVERAGE CLUTCH SIZES OF ANATID SPECIES

Lack (1967) advanced the view that the average clutch size of each anatid species has evolved in relation to average available food supplies for the female, as influenced by the size of the species' eggs. He and, earlier, Heinroth (1922) have also pointed out that larger-bodied birds channel relatively less food material into the production of individual eggs, resulting in a negative correlation between average adult female weight and the weight of the species' eggs. An even clearer negative correlation may be seen between the average adult female weight and the proportional weight of the average total clutch. This ratio provides a useful index to the relative energy drain on the female during laying. Lack's (1968*a*) tabular data indicate that in eight taxa (species or subspecies) of swans, the equivalent of from 16 to 34% (average 24%) of their adult weight is deposited in an average clutch of eggs. For sixteen taxa of true geese the calculated range is from 20 to 40% (average 28%), for forty-seven surface-feeding ducks from 35 to 106% (average 60%), and for sixteen sea ducks from 20 to 109% (average 63%). The larger species, geese and swans, which have the greatest available energy reserves of body fat, thus actually experience the smallest relative energy drain from egg-laying. Their generally small clutch size is therefore unlikely to be attributable to limited food supplies during laying.

Several hypotheses have been proposed to explain this problem. Ryder (1970*a*) has suggested that, at least in the Ross' Goose, the total pre-breeding food reserves needed by the female for both egg-laying and during incubation might limit the average clutch size of this unusually small goose, which usually lays only four eggs. Thus, for this and perhaps other arctic nesting geese, the female's energy supplies must allow the female to provide maximum protection to the clutch during incubation and ensure the survival of the young until they can forage. This theory is essentially an extension of Lack's basic views on clutch size controls.

A second hypothesis is that egg predation during the egg-laying period may limit effective clutch size. Thus the dangers of leaving the nest exposed prior to incubation may outweigh the advantages of adding additional eggs. The probability of this occurring increases with increasing clutch size, especially in species vulnerable to preincubation predation of the entire clutch. Lack has rejected predation as an ultimate control of avian clutch size, on the grounds that natural predation levels are normally too low to be effective and in general this would seem to be true. Bengtson (1972) provided data for ten Icelandic duck species, showing that pre-incubation nest predation caused 55% of the nest failures in 2,889 nests, or a total of about 19% of the nests under study. This would suggest a daily predation rate of little more than 2% per day during a 10-day egg-laying period, too low effectively to limit clutch size. However, Choate's (1967) study of American Eiders indicated that 66% of the entire nest predation in 1 year (totalling 58% of 448 nests) occurred on incompleted nests, implying a 12–15% daily nest loss during the 3- or 4-day period required to complete a clutch. If they are at all typical, such predation rates might easily account for the low average clutch size of this species.

Thirdly, it is possible that average clutch size may be limited by decreasing parental effectiveness. Mendall (1958) reported decreased hatching success among large clutches of Ring-necked Duck. Hilden (1964) had similar results for Tufted Ducks and Greater Scaups, and Bengtson (1972) for Greater Scaups. Ryder (1970*a*) has cited some additional examples. Likewise, larger than normal broods may suffer relatively higher mortality rates than normal sized ones, as indicated by Eygenaraam (1957) for Mallard *Anas platyrhynchos.* Cooch (1961) noted that Lesser Snow Goose goslings hatched from eggs laid late in large clutches survived less well. Similarly, Parsons (1970) reported that Herring Gulls *Larus argentatus* hatched from smaller eggs, usually the third-laid ones, exhibited the poorest survival. If this trend is general, it might well be a source of increasing selective disadvantage for enlarging the clutch size.

Fourthly, a restricted optimum breeding period, or the need to synchronize hatching with an optimum hatching date, may limit average clutch size. Koskimies (1957) found laying date and clutch size to be individually constant among female Velvet Scoters *Melanitta fusca,* and believed this ensured uniform hatching times of different-sized clutches. Cooch (1961) similarly pointed out that, in the Lesser Snow Goose, smaller clutches are "necessary" in retarded breeding seasons or towards the end of normal ones if reproduction is to be efficient. Hilden (1964) mentioned that, since the period of both egg-laying and hatching are undesirably prolonged in large clutches, and since late-hatched broods generally survive poorly, selection may limit clutch size below the female's physiological limits or her incubation abilities. Dane (1966) similarly pointed out that each egg added to a duck's clutch delays hatching another day, both increasing the problems of egg and chick survival and shortening the available time for maturation prior to migration. There is considerable evidence from a variety of waterfowl species that broods hatching relatively late usually survive more poorly than

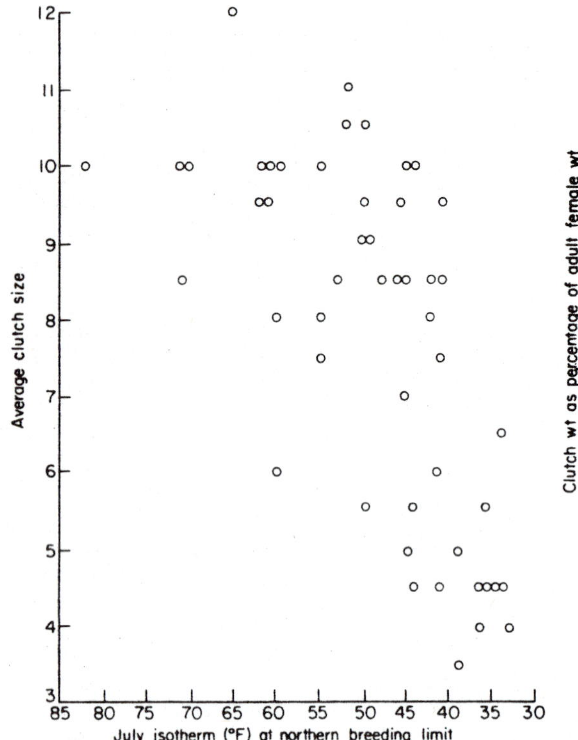

Fig. 1. The relationship between average clutch size and northern breeding limits in fifty northern hemisphere Anatidae.

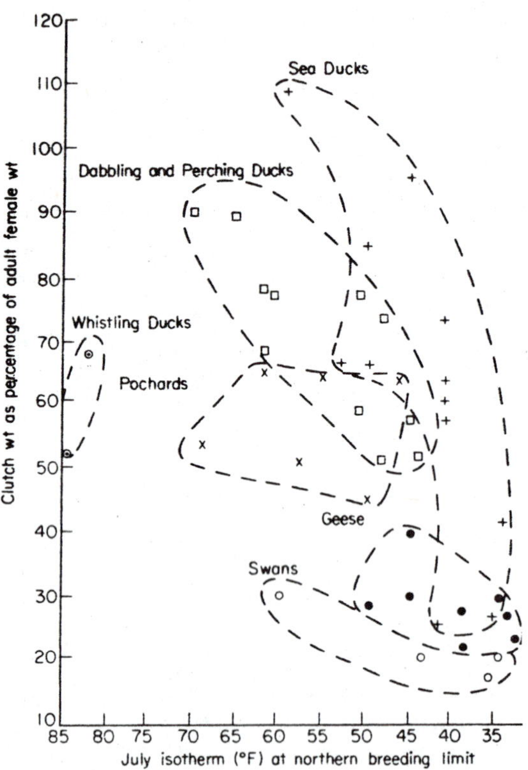

Fig. 2. The relationship between the total average clutch weight relative to adult female weight in the northern breeding limits in forty-three northern hemisphere Anatidae.

those hatched fairly early in the season (Grice and Rogers 1965, Bengtson 1972).

This influence of a restricted optimum breeding period is most likely to be exerted in arctic or subarctic areas. If one compares the average clutch size of a number of northern hemisphere waterfowl as given by Lack with average July isotherms (°F) representing the northern limit of these species' breeding ranges primarily as reported by Voous (1960), an interesting relationship may be seen (Fig. 1). Species having small average clutches nearly all are arctic or subarctic breeding, while those with large average clutches tend to be more temperate or subtropical. If one calculates clutch weight as a percentage of adult female weight for such species and again plots the results against July isotherms at the northern limits of distribution, a greater taxonomic spread may be seen (Fig. 2). Although collectively there is a strong tendency to reduce the relative amount of energy put into the clutch the further north they breed, the trend is clearer in some groups than in others. This may be due to restricted breeding periods, possibly to increased egg-predation dangers, to other demands on energy reserves associated with breeding in arctic environments, or to other factors.

In general, those anatid species having

the smallest average clutch size (swans, geese, eiders) are not likely to encounter food shortages at the time of laying. Nor are their clutch sizes likely to be limited by ecological needs for relatively large eggs. Increased average food availability seem to play little part in the evolution of increased average clutch size in waterfowl. Instead, I would suggest that, where food supplies are not a limiting factor, clutch size is likely to be limited by decreasing parental effectiveness, decreased available optimum breeding time, and increased probability of nest predation. These four selective factors are in turn further obscured by proximate factors which produce the individual, seasonal and local variations in clutch size encountered by field biologists.

SUMMARY

A review of Anatidae clutch-size data and an analysis of David Lack's hypothesis that food availability to the female around the time of her nesting can account for the evolution of average waterfowl clutch-sizes suggest several additions to or modifications of his theory. First, in contrast to Lack's suggestion, proximate factors do influence anatid clutch-sizes and result in measureable seasonal, yearly and perhaps also interpopulational variations in these. Secondly, indirect evidence suggests that several factors in addition to average food supplies may have influenced clutch-size evolution. These include needs for efficient partitioning of energy reserves between the incubating female and her eggs, dangers of pre-incubation clutch losses in those species that are unusually susceptible to nest predation, and decreasing parental effectiveness as well as possible decreased available optimum breeding periods associated with increases in clutch-sizes. Several or all of these may have placed upper limits on anatid clutch-sizes independently of or in conjunction with food supply effects.

LITERATURE CITED

AHLEN, I., AND A. ANDERSSON. 1970. Breeding ecology of an Eider population on Spitzbergen. Ornis Scand. 1:83–106.

BARRY, T. 1962. Effects of late seasons on Atlantic Brant reproduction. J. Wildl. Mgmt. 26:19–26.

———. 1967. The geese of the Anderson River Delta, N.W.T. Unpublished Ph.D. thesis, Univ. Alberta, Edmonton.

BENGTSON, S.-A. 1971. Variations in clutch-size in ducks in relation to food supply. Ibis 113: 523–526.

———. 1972. Reproduction and fluctuations in the size of duck populations at Lake Myvatn, Iceland. Oikos 23:35–58.

CHOATE, J. S. 1967. Factors influencing nesting success of eiders in Penobscot Bay, Maine. J. Wildl. Mgmt. 31:769–777.

CODY, M. L. 1971. Ecological aspects of reproduction. *In* Avian biology. Pp. 461–512. New York: Academic Press.

COOCH, F. G. 1961. Ecological aspects of the Blue-snow Goose complex. Auk 78:72–79.

———. 1965. The breeding biology and management of the Northern Eider (*Somateria mollissima borealis*) in the Cape Dorset area, Northwest Territories. Can. Wildl. Serv., Wildl. Mgmt. Bull., Ser. 2, No. 10.

DANE, C. W. 1966. Some aspects of the breeding biology of the Blue-winged Teal. Auk 83:389–402.

EYGENRAAM, J. A. 1957. The sex-ratio and the production of the Mallard, *Anas platyrhynchos* L. Ardea 45:177–243.

FREEMAN, M. M. R. 1970. Observations on the seasonal behavior of the Hudson Bay Eider. Can. Fld. Nat. 84:145–153.

GRICE, D., AND J. P. ROGERS. 1965. The Wood Duck in Massachusetts. Mass. Div. Fisheries and Game, Final Rept. Proj. No. W-19-R. 96pp.

GROSS, A. O. 1938. Eider ducks of Kent's Island. Auk 55:387–400.

GUDMUNDSSON, F. 1932. Beobachtungen an islandischen Eiderenten (*Somateria m. mollissima*). Beitr. Fortpfe. Biol. Vögel 9:85–93, 142–147.

HAARTMEN, L. VON. 1971. Population dynamics. *In* Avian biology. Vol. 1, pp. 391–459. New York: Academic Press.

HEINROTH, O. 1922. Die Beziehungen zwischen Vogelgewicht, Eigewicht, Gelegewicht und Brutauer. J. Orn., Lpz. 70:172–285.

HILDEN, O. 1964. Ecology of duck populations in

the island group of Valassaaret, Gulf of Bothnia. Ann. Zoologici 1:153–279.

KLOMP, O. 1970. The determination of clutch-size in birds. A review. Ardea 58:1–124.

KOSKIMIES, J. 1957. Polymorphic variability in clutch size and laying date of the Velvet Scoter, *Melanitta fusca* (L.). Ornis Fennica 34:118–128.

KOSSACK, C. W. 1950. Breeding habits of Canada Geese under refuge conditions. Am. Midl. Nat. 43:627–649.

LACK, D. 1967. The significance of clutch-size in waterfowl. Wildfowl Trust Ann. Rep. 18: 125–128.

———. 1968*a*. Ecological adaptations for breeding in birds. London: Methuen.

———. 1968*b*. The proportion of yolk in the eggs of waterfowl. Wildfowl 19:67–69.

LEMIEUX, L. 1959. The breeding biology of the Greater Snow Goose on Bylot Island, Northwest Territories. Can. Fld. Nat. 73:117–128.

LEWIS, H. F. 1939. Size of sets of eggs of the American Eider. J. Wildl. Mgmt. 3:70–73.

MARSHALL, I. K. 1967. The effects of high nesting density on the clutch-size of the Common Eider *Somateria mollissima* L. (abstract). J. Ecol. 55(3):59pp.

MENDALL, H. L. 1958. The Ring-necked Duck in the Northeast. U. Maine Studies, 2nd Ser., No. 73. U. Maine Bull. 60(16):1–317.

PARSONS, J. 1970. Relationship between egg size and post-hatching chick mortality in the Herring Gull (*Larus argentatus*). Nature, Lond. 228:1221–1222.

PAYNTER, R. A. 1951. Clutch-size and egg mortality of Kent Island eiders. Ecology 32:497–507.

RYDER, J. F. 1970*a*. A possible factor in the evolution of clutch size in Ross's Goose. Wilson Bull. 82:5–13.

———. 1970*b*. Timing and spacing of nests and breeding biology of Ross' Goose. Unpublished Ph.D. dissertation, Univ. of Saskatchewan, Saskatoon.

SOWLS, L. K. 1959. Prairie ducks. Washington, D.C.: Wildlife Mgmt. Inst.

VOOUS, K. H. 1960. Atlas of European birds. New York: Nelson.

WAGNER, H. O. 1960. Beziehungen zwischen Umweltfactoren under der Brutziet, Zahl der Gelege sowie ihres Grösse. Zool. Anz. 16:161–172.

WELLER, M. W. 1964. The reproductive cycle. *In* The waterfowl of the world. Vol. 4, pp. 35–79. London: Country Life.

OLDSQUAWS NESTING IN ASSOCIATION WITH ARCTIC TERNS AT CHURCHILL, MANITOBA[1]

ROGER M. EVANS, Department of Zoology, University of Manitoba, Winnipeg, Manitoba R3T 2N2, Canada

The tendency for the Oldsquaw (*Clangula hyemalis*) to nest in close association with the Arctic Tern (*Sterna paradisaea*) has been noted in several geographic regions, including Alaska (Bailey 1925, 1943), Southampton Island (Sutton 1932), Greenland (Salomonsen *in* Larson 1960), and Spitsbergen (Lovenskiold 1954, Burton and Thurston 1959). Taverner and Sutton (1934) reported both species as common breeders along the west coast of Hudson Bay, near Churchill, Manitoba, but did not refer explicitly to association of nests of the two species. That such associations do occur in this region, however, is indicated by the observations of Twomey (*in* Taverner and Sutton 1934) that populations of both species nested on a single small offshore island. Hawksley (1957:66) states that "the Old-squaw is commonly found nesting with Arctic Terns in North America," and implies that such associations occur at Churchill, but does not indicate the locations or extent of the association in this region. Evidence that close associations between nests of Oldsquaw and Arctic Tern are common on the mainland at Churchill, and particularly on small islands in fresh-water ponds, is presented below.

Larson (1960) has suggested that nest associations such as those mentioned above are commensal, the Oldsquaw deriving a degree of protection from potential nest predators as a result of the well-developed nest defense behavior of the Arctic Tern. The interpretation that protection from nest predators is derived by the Oldsquaw or other species, notably the eider (*Somateria*) and brant (*Branta bernicla*; *B. nigricans*) when they nest in association with Arctic Terns, has also been advanced by several other investigators, including Lovenskiold (1954), Gudmundsson (1956), Burton and Thurston (1959), Hilden (1965), and Cooch (1967). Koskimies (1957) and Vermeer (1968) have advanced the further hypothesis that imprinting of ducklings to gulls or terns nesting in the same vicinity may constitute the proximate cause of these and other similar associations.

The hypothesis that nest associations between Arctic Terns and Oldsquaws are commensal relationships that develop locally as a result of imprinting does not appear to have been subject to rigorous experimental tests. In the absence of such data, extensive documentation of the occurrence or nonoccurrence of such nest associations in various local areas, including those where avian nest predators are common as well as those where such predators are rare or absent, would appear to be useful. The following observations of the nest sites selected by Oldsquaws, the extent of their association with Arctic Terns, and the relationships of these associations to the more common avian predators in the Churchill region are presented here as a contribution towards such documentation.

DESCRIPTION OF NEST SITES

According to Phillips (1925), "there is nothing characteristic about the (Oldsquaw) nest or its site. It is usually near

[1] Originally published in Wilson Bull. 82(4): 383–390, 1970.

Table 1. Distance between Oldsquaw nests and nearest open water.

Nest location	Number of nests	Distance to water (meters)		
		Mean	Median	Range
Mainland beach	3	9.0	9	8–10
Mainland tundra	9	28.6	1	0.2–200
Islands in fresh water	16	2.1	2	0.1–6.7

the water, though sometimes far away from it . . . and is placed under thick bushes . . . when such cover is found." Oldsquaws may nest as isolated pairs, or "practically in colonies" (1925:362). This description applies with validity to the Oldsquaw nests observed at Churchill, where nests were found in virtually all major terrestrial areas, including (1) mainland beach, (2) mainland tundra, (3) islands in fresh-water ponds, and (4) offshore islands. The present observations, conducted during June and July of 1967 and 1968, were concerned primarily with the first three of these nest habitats; confirmation of the observations cited in Taverner and Sutton (1934) of Oldsquaws nesting on offshore islands was provided by Mr. Carroll Littlefield (pers. comm.), who counted seven Oldsquaw nests on a small island off the coast of Cape Churchill on 27 June 1968.

Although the Oldsquaw is said typically to nest along the edges of small fresh-water ponds or on islands in such ponds (Phillips 1925, Bent 1925), records of nests placed some distance away from the nearest open water are not uncommon. Bent (1925), for example, cited observations by Hersey of a nest placed 20 feet from the edge of a pond, and a report by Palmer of a nest 40 feet from a fresh-water pond. He further cited Ekblaw that nests are "sometimes in the grass near the pools, but more frequently . . . at considerable distances from any water" (Bent, 1925:38). At Churchill, the distances to the nearest open water were also variable, ranging from as little as 0.1 m to at least 200 m for the 28 nests measured (Table 1).

The distance between Oldsquaw nests and the nearest open water at Churchill was found to vary according to the area in which the nests were located (Table 1). Average distances were least on the small islands in fresh-water ponds (average for 16 nests, 2.1 m), somewhat greater along the beach (average for three nests, 9.0 m), and greatest in the mainland tundra (average for nine nests, 28.6 m). The average distance to water for the mainland tundra is skewed due to a number of extreme values well above the median distance of 1 m. Except for these extreme values on the mainland tundra, nest sites tended to be close to the shore for both fresh-water islands (median 2 m) and mainland tundra (median 1 m), and somewhat farther from water for nests located along the beach (median 9 m). These results suggest that Oldsquaws at Churchill exhibit a definite tendency to nest near the edge of water, but not exclusively so. This tendency is necessarily reinforced when small islands no more than a few meters in diameter are selected for nest sites, but may be relaxed when mainland tundra locations are selected. For nests located along the beach the minimum distance to water appeared to be set by the maximum extent of wave action at high tide.

In each of the three areas described above, Oldsquaws were found nesting in association with Arctic Terns. A similar

Table 2. Distance between Oldsquaw nests and nearest Arctic Tern nest.

Nest location	Number of nests	Distance to nearest tern nest (meters)		
		Mean	Median	Range
Mainland beach	3	13	12	10–17
Mainland tundra	5[a]	72	70	18–178
Islands in fresh water	16	2.3	2	0.8–6

[a] Does not include three nests located in the vicinity of Arctic Terns but for which distances to tern nests were not determined, and one nest that was not in association with terns.

association was also present on the small offshore island visited by Littlefield (pers. comm.). On islands in fresh-water ponds, Oldsquaw nests were found exclusively on islands that also contained Arctic Terns. In consequence, minimum distances between nests of the two species on these islands were necessarily small (average for 16 nests, 2.3 m), with none exceeding 6 m (Table 2). In the other areas, and particularly on mainland tundra, distances between Oldsquaw and Arctic Tern nests were greater, ranging up to at least 178 m (Table 2). In addition, one Oldsquaw nest was found on mainland tundra in an area that apparently lacked a local population of breeding terns. This latter finding, coupled with the greater distances between nests of the Oldsquaw and Arctic Tern on the mainland tundra (Table 2), suggests a relaxation in the tendency for association between the two species on mainland tundra compared to islands in fresh-water ponds.

It should be noted that nest hunting for Oldsquaws was concentrated in areas that contained Arctic Terns, and random sampling of large areas of habitat was not done. The high frequency of association between Arctic Terns and Oldsquaws found at Churchill may therefore be biased upwards, due to an undetermined number of Oldsquaw nests being located well away from areas containing terns. Several considerations suggest, however, that the possibility of such a bias does not negate the conclusion that an association between the species does in fact occur, especially for those nests located on islands in fresh-water ponds. As indicated above, all 16 Oldsquaw nests found on such islands were in close association with Arctic Terns. While searching for nests in these areas, many islands in addition to those found to contain tern nests were inspected, yet in no instance was an Oldsquaw nest found on an island that lacked terns. Nests located on islands in one small fresh-water pond are illustrative: In 1967, two islands in the pond each had one Oldsquaw nest and one tern nest. In 1968, one of these islands had an Arctic Tern nest and two Oldsquaw nests; the other island contained nests of neither species. From considerations such as these, coupled with the measurements listed in Table 2, it seems reasonable to conclude that a definite positive association between Oldsquaw and Arctic Tern nests was present at Churchill in 1967 and 1968. An exact determination of the frequency of this association on mainland tundra remains lacking, however, pending a more complete and random sampling of the potential nesting habitat.

AVIAN PREDATORS

At least three potential avian predators of Oldsquaw eggs were present at Churchill: Herring Gull (*Larus argenta-*

tus), Parasitic Jaeger (*Stercorarius parasiticus*), and Common Raven (*Corvus corax*). Of these species, the Herring Gull was most common; 15 and 22 breeding pairs were found, widely scattered, throughout the study area in 1967 and 1968 respectively. In addition, mixed flocks composed largely of non-breeders of this and other large *Larus* gulls totalling several hundred in number could be observed daily at the local garbage dump located near the middle of the study area.

Egg predation of ground-nesting species by Herring Gulls is considered by some authorities to be infrequent (Bent 1921:112). They are, however, known to take eggs of various ground-nesting species (Tinbergen 1953), including those of the Oldsquaw (Sutton 1932:263–264). This latter fact, coupled with the high numbers of Herring Gulls known to be present at Churchill, suggests that it would be unrealistic to exclude the Herring Gull as a potential egg predator of Oldsquaws in this region.

Although less abundant than the Herring Gull, Parasitic Jaegers and Ravens were observed throughout the area in both 1967 and 1968. According to Kortwright (1953:283), jaegers, along with various other predators, may "take a heavy toll" of Oldsquaw eggs. Sutton (1932) also cited the Parasitic Jaeger as a predator of Oldsquaw eggs, and cited observations of jaegers taking Oldsquaw young. The Raven, according to Larson (1960), may also constitute an important egg predator of the Oldsquaw.

Despite the presence of the above predators, loss of Oldsquaw clutches at Churchill was limited. On islands in fresh-water ponds, no predator-destroyed clutches were found in 1967, even when nests were visited repeatedly, every one to two days, by one or more observers. In 1968, two clutches, found prior to the onset of nesting by the terns, were missing on subsequent visits to the islands, and may therefore have been destroyed by predators. On the beach, one nest was destroyed within an abandoned tern colony. This loss, however, was apparently due to wave action rather than to predation. On the mainland tundra, at least two, and possibly three, nests were destroyed, presumably by predators. Taken together, these figures indicate that at most, no more than five of the 28 nests (18 per cent) were destroyed by predators. This percentage loss of clutches compares favorably with egg loss (average 22.9 per cent) of several anatid species nesting in larid colonies located on islands in the Gulf of Bothnia (Hilden 1964), but is somewhat greater than that for Gadwall (*Anas strepera*) and Lesser Scaup (*Aythya affinis*) nesting in association with *Larus* spp. in Alberta, where 89–90 per cent of the nests hatched (Vermeer 1968).

DISCUSSION

In the absence of comparative data from areas where egg predators are absent or where terns and Oldsquaws do not nest together, definite conclusions concerning the extent of nest protection derived by the Oldsquaws that nest in association with Arctic Terns are not warranted. Indirect evidence, however, is provided by instances in which avian predators have been attacked and driven away by Arctic Terns, as described for the Herring Gull by Sutton (1932), Bullough (1942), and Sutton and Parmelee (1956). Active defense by Arctic Terns of their nest sites against Parasitic Jaegers (Anderson 1913, Sutton 1932, Lovenskiold 1954) and Ravens (Sutton 1932, Larson 1960) have also been documented. Instances in which Arctic Terns attacked and chased these species were also observed during the present study at Churchill. There thus seems little reason to doubt the interpretation of Anderson (1913), Larson (1960) and others that such attacks by Arctic Terns provide a measure of protection for birds that nest in or near their colonies, and that such nest associations are therefore commensal relationships. The data obtained at Churchill suggest, however, that the commensal relationship between Oldsquaws and Arctic Terns is of significance primarily for nests located on islands (cf. also Larson 1960, Delacour 1959:174–175), and possibly for those located on the beach, but is probably of less importance for nests located on the mainland tundra.

The most parsimonious explanation of the proximate mechanisms underlying the association between Oldsquaws and Arctic Terns is that of similar habitat preferences by two compatible species. At Churchill, this simple interpretation would seem sufficient for nests located on the mainland tundra, where distances between nests of the two species were comparatively great, but it does not appear sufficient to account for the close association in other habitats, particularly on islands in fresh-water ponds. In these latter areas, some form of active selection of one species by the other seems likely.

According to the general hypothesis advanced by Koskimies (1957), the development of positive associations between Oldsquaws and Arctic Terns could be attributed to the active selection of tern colonies by Oldsquaws that have been imprinted, as ducklings, to terns that were present in the vicinity of their nest. At Churchill, it was evident that opportunities for auditory or visual imprinting of Oldsquaw ducklings to Arctic Terns typically occurred at hatching. The extent to which such imprinting might influence subsequent choice of nest site by the ducks remains problematical, however, in part due to the early arrival of the Oldsquaw, which may precede the arrival of the terns on the breeding grounds (Taverner and Sutton 1934). In addition, in at least six instances in 1968, Oldsquaws at Churchill had laid clutches prior to the onset of laying by terns on the same islands.

A possible supplement to the imprinting hypothesis was suggested by observations at Churchill of Oldsquaw nest cups, remaining from previous years, on the islands in fresh-water ponds. These old nests, which numbered as high as 10 on a single island measuring no more than 10 by 5 m in size, indicate that, like the Arctic Tern (Cullen 1956), Oldsquaws may use traditional nesting areas from year to year. Where this tendency is prevalent, then once a nesting Oldsquaw became established in or near a tern colony, association in the same area would be perpetuated in subsequent years regardless of which species commenced nesting first in any particular year. The initial association, according to this interpretation, could presumably arise either as a chance result of similar habitat preferences of the two species or as a result of imprinting.

According to evidence reviewed by Hilden (1965:68) fidelity to a traditional nest site is more likely to occur in the absence of nest disturbance or predation. If true for Oldsquaws, then nests located away from tern colonies, if destroyed by predators, would tend to be shifted to a different location in the following year, whereas those located in tern colonies, where predation is less likely, would tend to be placed in the same location in subsequent years. Such differential predation and nest site fidelity cannot therefore be excluded as a possible additional mechanism favoring the accretion of Oldsquaw nests in or near tern colonies.

If imprinting alone constituted the proximate cause of associations between Oldsquaws and Arctic Terns, a more or less random distribution of local areas in which associations do or do not occur would be expected. In particular, it would not be expected that the occurrence of associations would necessarily be concentrated in those areas where avian nest predators are locally abundant. According to the alternative view, that associations may be initiated either by similar habitat preferences or imprinting, but are then favored by the tendency of Oldsquaws to use traditional nest sites that are protected from nest predators by Arctic Terns, maximum association in areas where nest predators are abundant would be expected. Further investigations of association between these species, with particular reference to the presence or absence of local populations of avian nest predators, should therefore provide information as to the relative importance of these various mechanisms, all of which must be considered tenable on the basis of existing data.

SUMMARY

A high incidence of nest association between Arctic Terns and Oldsquaws was found at Churchill, Manitoba, in 1967 and 1968. Distances between nests of these species averaged only 2.3 m on islands in fresh-water ponds, increased to an average of 13 m on mainland beach sites, and reached 72 m on mainland tundra.

Potential avian predators of Oldsquaw eggs included the Herring Gull, Parasitic Jaeger, and Common Raven. Clutches lost to predators did not exceed a maximum of five of 28 nests observed. Observations of Arctic Terns attacking potential predators suggested that Oldsquaws derived protection from nearby terns. It is suggested that such protection, coupled with a tendency to return to successful nest sites in successive years, affords a possible supplement to habitat preferences and imprinting of ducks to terns as the proximate mechanism responsible for the maintenance of nest associations between these species.

ACKNOWLEDGMENTS

This study was financed by grants from the Northern Studies Committee, University of Manitoba, and the National Research Council (Ottawa). M. McNicholl and D. Krindle provided valuable assistance in the field. Thanks are extended to the staff of the Churchill Research Range for providing facilities and ready access to the study area. Comments on an earlier draft of the manuscript by D. A. Boag are gratefully acknowledged.

LITERATURE CITED

ANDERSON, R. M. 1913. Report on the natural history collections of the expedition. pp. 436–527, *In* V. Stefansson. My life with the Eskimo. Revised ed., 1951. The Macmillan Co., New York.

BAILEY, A. M. 1925. A report on the birds of northwestern Alaska and regions adjacent to Bering Strait. Part IV. Condor 27:164–171.

———. 1943. The birds of Cape Prince of Wales, Alaska. Proc. Colorado Mus. Nat. Hist. 18:1–113.

BENT, A. C. 1921. Life histories of North American gulls and terns. U.S. Natl. Mus. Bull. 113. Reprinted 1963, Dover Publ. Inc., New York.

———. 1925. Life Histories of North American Wild Fowl, Part II. U.S. Natl. Mus. Bull., 130. Reprinted 1962, Dover Publ., Inc., New York.

BULLOUGH, W. S. 1942. Observations on the colonies of the Arctic Tern (*Sterna macrura* Naumann) on the Farne Islands. Proc. Zool. Soc. London (A) 112:1–12.

BURTON, P. J. K., AND M. H. THURSTON. 1959. Observations on Arctic Terns in Spitsbergen. Brit. Birds 52:149–161.

COOCH, F. G. 1967. Review of: Delacour, The waterfowl of the world. Vol. 4, 1964. Auk 84:135–138.

CULLEN, J. M. 1956. A study of the behaviour of the Arctic Tern (*Sterna macrura*). Unpubl. D. Phil. Thesis, Oxford.

DELACOUR, J. 1959. The waterfowl of the world. Vol. 3. Country Life Ltd., London.

GUDMUNDSSON, F. 1956. Islenzikir fuglar XIV Kria (*Sterna paradisaea*). Natturufraedingurinn 26:206–217.

HAWKSLEY, O. 1957. Ecology of a breeding population of Arctic Terns. Bird-Banding 28:57–92.

HILDEN, O. 1964. Ecology of duck populations in the island group of Valassaaret, Gulf of Bothnia. Ann. Zool. Fenn. 1:153–279.

———. 1965. Habitat selection in birds. Ann. Zool. Fenn. 2:53–75.

KORTRIGHT, F. H. 1953. The ducks, geese and swans of North America. Stackpole Co., Harrisburg.

KOSKIMIES, J. 1957. Terns and gulls as features of habitat recognition for birds nesting in their colonies. Ornis Fenn. 34:1–6.

LARSON, S. 1960. On the influence of the Arctic Fox *Alopex lagopus* on the distribution of Arctic birds. Oikos 11:276–305.

LOVENSKIOLD, H. L. 1954. Studies on the avifauna of Spitsbergen. Norsk. Polarinst. Skrifter 103:1–131.

PHILLIPS, J. C. 1925. A natural history of the ducks. Vol. III. Houghton Mifflin Co., New York.

SUTTON, G. M. 1932. The birds of Southampton Island. Mem. Carnegie Mus., Vol. 12, Part II, Sect. 2.

———, AND D. F. PARMELEE. 1956. On certain Charadriiform birds of Baffin Island. Wilson Bull. 68:210–223.

TAVERNER, P. A., AND G. M. SUTTON. 1934. The birds of Churchill, Manitoba. Ann. Carnegie Mus. 23:1–83.

TINBERGEN, N. 1953. The Herring Gull's world. Collins, London.

VERMEER, K. 1968. Ecological aspects of ducks nesting in high densities among larids. Wilson Bull. 80:78–83.

LOCOMOTOR MECHANISMS IN NORTH AMERICAN DUCKS[1]

ROBERT J. RAIKOW, Department of Biology, University of Pittsburgh, Pittsburgh, PA 15213

The Anatinae of North America may be divided into two general adaptive types, the dabbling ducks and the diving ducks. The dabbling ducks (Tribe Anatini) are primarily surface feeders, and feed from the bottom only as deep as they can reach by tipping up, without entirely submerging. Thus they feed mainly in shallow, inshore waters. In contrast, the diving ducks (Tribes Aythyini, Mergini, and Oxyurini) feed mainly by diving in deeper offshore waters. The dabbling ducks can walk on land with relative ease, and different species feed there to a greater or lesser extent. The diving ducks, however, walk on land poorly at best, and seldom feed there. The dabblers frequently utilize areas bordered by trees or containing emergent vegetation, where the extent of open water is limited. Their flying abilities are suited to the use of these spatially restricted areas, particularly in taking off and landing. They take off by "rocketing" upward, aided by an initial jump and climbing vertically clear of obstructions. This requires the immediate production of powerful lift forces. Most diving ducks cannot take off in this manner, but must instead use the method called "skittering." They travel across the water surface paddling with their feet and flapping their wings, gaining speed and lift until they are able to rise from the surface. This is adequate for their needs because they usually remain in open water where the necessary space is available. Rocketing and skittering may be compared to the takeoff of helicopters and fixed-wing aircraft respectively. In landing the dabbling ducks are again more proficient. They can fly more slowly than divers and thus drop with greater agility into restricted spaces. Diving ducks typically use a faster, flatter approach and generally land only on water. Weller (1964) describes these movements in some detail.

Several workers have studied the locomotor system of birds by means of quantitative comparisons. The most extensive study is that of Hartman (1961) who measured heart, muscle, and body weights as well as wing and tail areas in many groups. Poole (1938) recorded weights and wing areas for 143 species. Greenwalt (1962) reprinted similar data from several earlier workers. All of these studies contain some data on the Anatidae but are primarily concerned with formulating general principles of dimensional relationships with respect to flight. None concentrates on a single group of birds. Storer (1955) studied weight, wing area, and skeletal proportions in three species of hawks. No comparable study has been done on waterfowl.

This paper will describe certain morphological variations in ducks which are correlated with differences in locomotor abilities. The muscular and skeletal systems are very important in locomotion, and have been discussed elsewhere (Raikow 1970, 1971). In the present paper I will consider size, shape, and slotting of the wings, and the size of the paddles relative to the behavioral distinction noted above between dabbling and diving ducks.

MATERIALS AND METHODS

Measurements were made on forty-five specimens collected in the vicinity of San

[1] Originally published in Wilson Bull. 85(3):295–307, 1973.

Table 1. Measurements of fifteen species of North American ducks.

Species	No. of specimens	Body weight (g)		Wing area (cm^2)		Paddle area (cm^2)	
		Mean	Range	Mean	Range	Mean	Range
Anatini							
Anas cyanoptera	1	320.0		481.7		28.1	
Anas clypeata	2	514.6	457.1–572.0	578.8	566.9–590.6	37.4	36.2–38.6
Anas acuta	2	712.5	625.0–800.0	800.7	701.3–900.1	46.4	45.9–46.8
Anas americana	2	800.4	743.6–857.1	638.5	629.5–647.6	39.7	39.0–40.4
Anas platyrhynchos	5	961.3	828.5–1,057.1	869.8	752.0–1,018.4	56.9	48.2–64.4
Aythyini							
Aythya affinis	1	665.0		454.4		63.4	
Aythya valisineria	1	910.0		700.8		93.6	
Mergini							
Somateria fischeri	1	1,457.1		718.6		67.6	
Somateria spectabilis	2	1,700.0	1,571.4–1,828.5	824.4	748.0–900.7	76.5	74.4–78.5
Somateria mollisima	1	2,342.7		1,014.9		108.6	
Melanitta perspicillata	5	826.9	614.3–977.0	649.2	517.0–699.7	81.3	72.6–88.9
Melanitta fusca	2	1,167.8	1,164.0–1,171.5	735.4	710.8–760.0	104.1	100.6–107.6
Bucephala albeola	5	396.2	343.2–486.2	326.9	259.2–368.6	47.8	44.6–51.6
Bucephala clangula	3	764.0	618.0–914.2	566.0	499.4–621.0	75.7	59.8–80.6
Oxyurini							
Oxyura jamaicensis	12	520.8	414.3–714.3	325.7	301.2–374.8	65.4	54.5–73.2

Table 2. Buoyancy Index and Paddle Index in fifteen species of North American ducks.

Species	No. of specimens	Buoyancy Index		Paddle Index	
		Mean	Range	Mean	Range
Anatini					
Anas cyanoptera	1	3.20		0.77	
Anas clypeata	2	3.02	2.87–3.16	0.77	0.73–0.81
Anas acuta	2	3.17	2.85–3.50	0.77	0.73–0.80
Anas americana	2	2.73	2.64–2.81	0.48	0.47–0.50
Anas platyrhynchos	5	2.99	2.70–3.24	0.77	0.68–0.86
Aythyini					
Aythya affinis	1	2.44		0.91	
Aythya valisineria	1	2.73		1.00	
Mergini					
Somateria fischeri	1	2.36		0.73	
Somateria spectabilis	2	2.40	2.35–2.45	0.73	0.72–0.73
Somateria mollisima	1	2.40		0.79	
Melanitta perspicillata	5	2.72	2.48–3.05	0.97	0.92–1.00
Melanitta fusca	2	2.58	2.53–2.62	0.97	0.95–0.98
Bucephala albeola	5	2.46	2.24–2.67	0.94	0.88–0.96
Bucephala clangula	3	2.65	2.57–2.74	0.95	0.91–0.98
Oxyurini					
Oxyura jamaicensis	12	2.26	1.96–2.41	1.01	0.92–1.10

The Buoyancy Index equals the square root of wing area divided by the cube root of body weight. The Paddle Index equals the square root of the paddle area divided by the cube root of the body weight.

Francisco Bay, California, and (*Somateria*) Barrow, Alaska. These represent six genera and fifteen species. The wing was spread and pinned down on a sheet of paper, and its outline traced. The outline was then measured with a planimeter to obtain the wing area. In several specimens both wings were measured but gave nearly identical results, so in most cases only one wing was measured and this value was doubled to give the wing area of the specimen (Table 1). The wing was spread so that the leading edge was as nearly as possible perpendicular to the body axis, and the wing extended to the maximum degree possible short of damaging the tissues. This standardized method gave repeatable results, insuring that a comparable measurement was made in each case. This is important since wing area varies continuously with the degree of wing spreading, and comparisons are valid only if a uniform method is used. For this reason I have not attempted to pool my data with those of other authors (noted above) who have also measured wing areas in waterfowl.

Relative wing area is expressed as Buoyancy Index following Hartman (1961). This equals the square root of the wing area divided by the cube root of the body weight.

Paddle area (Table 1) was determined by spreading one foot and pinning it to a piece of paper. The outline was then traced around all four digits and their webbing. The area was measured with a planimeter and doubled to give the paddle area of the specimen. Relative paddle size is expressed as the Paddle Index, which equals the square root of the paddle area divided by the cube root of the body weight. The length of the alula and the areas of wingtip slots were measured on the wing tracings. The primary emarginations were measured on study skins.

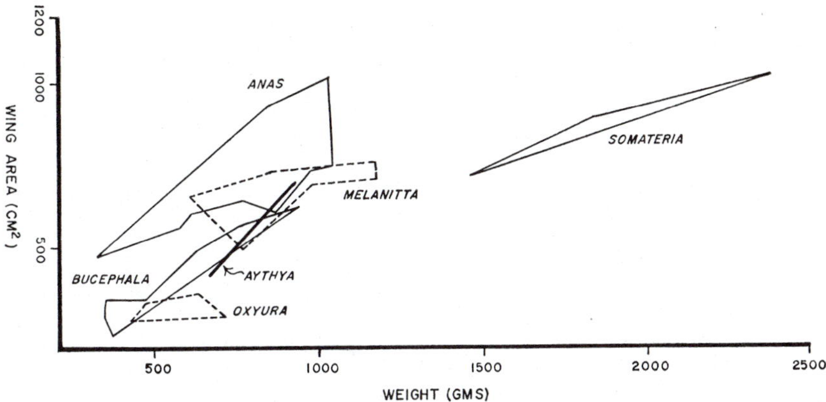

Fig. 1. The weights and wing areas for 45 specimens of 15 species of ducks were plotted, and the outermost points for each genus connected. *Aythya* is represented by a line since only two specimens were measured. The species and number of specimens included here are listed in Table 1. The illustration demonstrates that wing area is not a simple function of weight, but is different in genera with similar weights. The functional significance of the relationship between weight and wing area in the different genera is discussed in the text.

RESULTS

Wing Size.—The wing area relative to body weight (Buoyancy Index) is larger in *Anas* than in the diving ducks (Table 2). The highest value for diving ducks equals the lowest value for *Anas*. Other things being equal, the amount of lift produced by a bird is proportional to its wing area. The larger area in *Anas* is one factor providing for the greater lift needed in its special flying abilities as discussed above.

Since the species studied varied considerably in weight (Table 1) it is possible that differences in Buoyancy Index are related merely to body size and not to behavioral differences. It is well known that larger birds tend on the whole to have relatively smaller wings than do smaller birds (Poole 1938). (See Storer [1955] for an example among hawks.) This follows from the surface-volume relationship, i.e. that area varies as the square of a linear dimension while weight varies as the cube.

I plotted the weight against the wing area for the forty-five specimens of fifteen species considered in this study, and then connected the outside points for all individuals of each genus to give a polygon for each genus (Fig. 1). It is apparent that at any given body weight, the different genera have different wing areas. In a given weight range *Anas* has the largest wings and *Oxyura* the smallest, the other diving ducks being intermediate. *Somateria* falls outside the weight range of the other genera, yet its wing areas fall almost entirely within the range of *Anas*. Figure 1 shows that the relative wing area *between* genera is independent of body weight, so the correlation between wing area and habits is not an artifact of the surface-volume relationship, but is presumably biologically significant. *Within* a genus, however, wing area does increase with weight in a ratio roughly consistent with that expected from the surface-volume relationship, namely that weight increases more rapidly than area.

Wing Shape.—The shape of a bird's wing is aerodynamically suited to its method of flight. Savile (1957) recognized four basic wing shapes which have

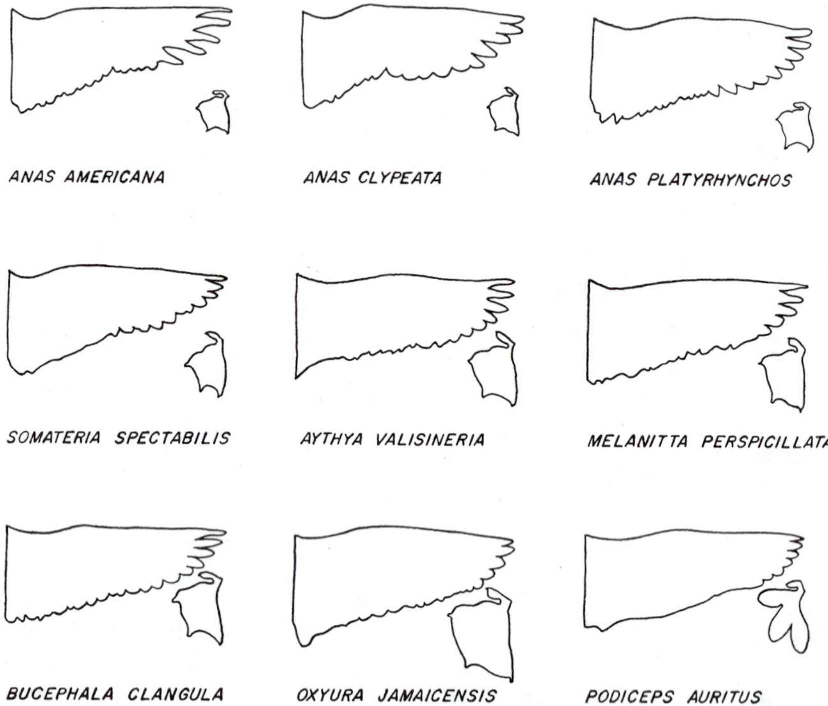

Fig. 2. Outline tracings of the wings and paddles of eight representative species of ducks and a grebe. The drawings are adjusted to equal wing lengths, so that the relative size of wing and paddle may be directly compared between species. The evolution of diving habits is accompanied by an increased paddle size, and by a more pointed, less slotted wing. *Anas americana* and *Oxyura jamaicensis* illustrate extremes of these features in dabbling and diving ducks respectively. The wing of *Oxyura* more closely resembles that of a grebe (*Podiceps*) than that of a dabbling duck (*Anas*).

evolved many times in different avian groups. The *slotted soaring wing* and the *high aspect-ratio wing* are characteristic of terrestrial and oceanic soaring birds respectively. The *elliptical wing* is "adapted to operation in confined spaces" (Savile 1957:224) since it provides high lift and good control under various conditions. It is found in birds which fly through restricted areas in the vegetation of forest or scrub, such as many Passeriformes, Galliformes, Piciformes, and Columbiformes. The wing type commonly has well-developed slotting, which increases lift at low speeds. The *high-speed wing* has a moderately high aspect ratio, a slender elliptical tip, a swept-back leading edge, a lack of tip slots, and other features. It is efficient for relatively direct, rapid flight, but not for slow flight or great maneuverability.

Savile (1957) reported that ducks have a moderately developed high-speed wing. While this is adequate to characterize the subfamily of ducks as a whole, detailed comparison shows that within this group the different genera have subtle differences in wing shape which are of functional importance (Fig. 2). In general, the diving ducks have a more typical high-speed wing, with reduced slotting (discussed below), and a more pointed tip resulting from a relatively straight trailing edge. *Anas* has a more rounded trailing edge, with greater wingtip slotting. Thus its shape more closely approaches

Table 3. Relative length of the alula in fifteen species of North American ducks.

Species	Alula/Total Wing Length			Alula/Standard Wing Length		
	Mean	Range	No. of specimens	Mean	Range	No. of specimens
Anatini						
Anas cyanoptera	0.24		1	0.35		1
Anas clypeata	0.23		1	0.32		1
Anas acuta	0.21	0.19–0.23	2	0.31	0.29–0.33	2
Anas americana	0.22		1	0.29		1
Anas platyrhynchos	0.24	0.21–0.27	5	0.33	0.32–0.35	4
Aythyini						
Aythya affinis	0.23		1	0.34		1
Aythya valisineria	0.24		1	0.36		1
Mergini						
Somateria fischeri	0.24		1	0.32		1
Somateria spectabilis	0.22		1	0.33		1
Somateria mollisima	0.27		1	0.36		1
Melanitta perspicillata	0.22	0.20–0.25	5	0.32	0.31–0.33	5
Melanitta fusca	0.23	0.23–0.23	2	0.33		1
Bucephala albeola	0.24	0.22–0.29	4	0.36	0.34–0.38	4
Bucephala clangula	0.23	0.22–0.24	2	0.33	0.32–0.35	3
Oxyurini						
Oxyura jamaicensis	0.24	0.19–0.28	9	0.38	0.32–0.43	12

Total Wing Length is measured from shoulder to wing tip; Standard Wing Length is measured from wrist to wing tip.

the elliptical type than does that of divers, especially when the wing is extended, as during take-off. In level flight the wing is less fully extended, so that the ends of the primaries converge to close the slots, and the wing presents a more pointed appearance.

Wing Slotting.—Wing slots are devices which increase lift and lower the minimum flight speed by delaying stalling. Their aerodynamic characteristics are described by Savile (1957) and Jack (1953). Avian wing slots occur along the leading edge and at the wing tip. The leading-edge slot is formed when the alula is lifted away from the wing. In order to compare the size of the leading-edge slot between species I measured the length of the alula and divided this by the total wing length, from shoulder to tip, and by the standard measurement of wing length, from wrist to tip (Table 3). Measured either way the length of the leading-edge slot varies but little between species. Thus is does not seem to be functionally significant in the different flying abilities of dabbling and diving ducks. The scoters (*Melanitta*) have the peculiar habit of holding the alula extended while diving (Brooks 1945), possibly as a diving plane. This habit is not associated with any change in length of the alula (Table 3).

Wingtip slots are formed by the spaces between the separated tips of the primaries. They are usually accentuated by emargination of the feathers. The size and shape of the slots depends on the length of the emarginated segment, the depth of the emargination, and the shape of the proximal end of the slot. I measured the length of the emargination of the outer primary and divided this value by the wing length (Table 4). There is a slight increase in *Melanitta perspicillata,* but the difference is small. In gen-

Table 4. Measurements of wingtip slots in fifteen species of North American ducks.

Species	Emarginated segment/wing length			Wingtip slot area/wing area		
	Mean	Range	No. of specimens	Mean	Range	No. of specimens
Anatini						
Anas cyanoptera	0.14	0.13–0.15	5	0.023		1
Anas clypeata	0.16	0.15–0.17	5	0.027		1
Anas acuta	0.14	0.12–0.15	5	0.021	0.021–0.021	2
Anas americana	0.16	0.15–0.16	5	0.053	0.030–0.075	2
Anas platyrhynchos	0.16	0.14–0.17	5	0.031	0.022–0.040	5
Aythyini						
Aythya affinis	0.12	0.11–0.13	5	0.022		1
Aythya valisineria	0.15	0.12–0.18	5	0.026		1
Mergini						
Somateria fischeri	0.16	0.15–0.18	3	0.014		1
Somateria spectabilis	0.15	0.13–0.17	5	0.009	0.006–0.011	2
Somateria mollisima	0.17	0.15–0.18	5	0.024		1
Melanitta perspicillata	0.24	0.22–0.27	5	0.021	0.006–0.033	5
Melanitta fusca	0.16		1	0.014	0.009–0.018	2
Bucephala albeola	0.16	0.14–0.18	5	0.008	0.004–0.010	4
Bucephala clangula	0.18	0.15–0.20	5	0.030	0.018–0.037	3
Oxyurini						
Oxyura jamaicensis	0.15	0.12–0.17	5	0.010	0.003–0.017	12

eral there is no pattern of increased emargination in any genus or tribe. In contrast to this there are great differences in the depth of the emarginated region (Fig. 3). It is very deep in *Anas*, thus forming well defined slots. In divers the emarginated portion is more shallow, though varying between genera (Fig. 3). Furthermore among divers the emargination may be nearly or entirely obliterated in worn plumage, a condition which I did not note in *Anas*.

In an attempt to quantify the somewhat subjective impression of differences in depth of emargination, I measured the area of the slots as shown on the wing tracings. This was divided by the wing area to give a measurement of relative wingtip slot area (Table 4). A complete division between dabblers and divers was not found, but the largest slot areas are in some species of *Anas*, while some divers have considerably smaller slot areas. This is most marked in the smaller species, *Bucephala albeola* and *Oxyura jamaicensis*. *Anas cyanoptera* and *A. clypeata* are in the same weight range as these diving species, but have more than twice the wingtip slot area. The largest slots were in *Anas americana*, which also has the smallest wings in its genus (Table 2) among the species studied. Possibly the increased slot area compensates for this to some extent.

In *Anas* the transition from emarginated to unemarginated regions is abrupt, so that the proximal end of the slot is U-shaped. In contrast the transition in divers is more gradual, giving a more V-shaped slot. The latter condition denotes a less efficient slotting mechanism (Savile 1957).

Paddle Area.—Ducks are propelled through the water by the use of their feet, though dabblers and eiders may use the wings as an aid in diving. The main propulsive structure is thus the paddle, by which I mean the second through fourth digits and their webbing, plus the hallux, whose surface area is slightly increased

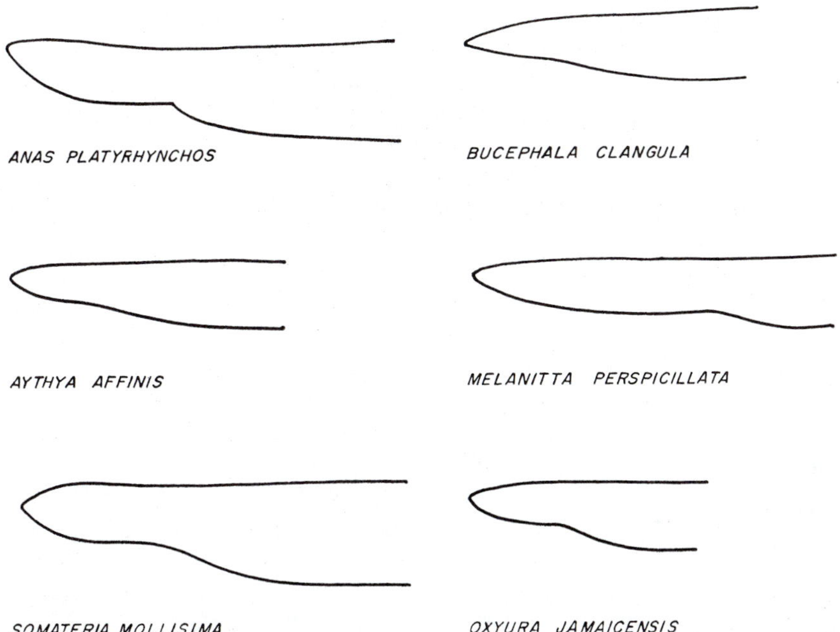

Fig. 3. Outline tracings of the distal end of the outer primary in six species of ducks. One species of each genus studied is included. All are from fresh plumaged birds. The efficiency of wingtip slots depends upon the depth of the emargination, and on the shape of the proximal end of the emarginated region of the feather. This region is deepest in *Anas*, and shallower in diving ducks. The transition from emarginated to unemarginated regions is abrupt in *Anas*, but more gradual in diving ducks. The emarginated region is unusually long in *Melanitta perspicillata*.

in diving ducks by having an enlarged lobe. The Paddle Index indicates the surface area of the paddles relative to body weight. Table 2 shows that in most divers the surface area of the paddles is relatively larger than in *Anas*, which is of obvious functional significance in increasing the efficiency of swimming and diving. It results primarily from a lengthening of the second through fourth digits and a corresponding increase in web area. The progressive evolution of this feature in the tribe Oxyurini has been discussed previously (Raikow 1970).

DISCUSSION

Ecological isolation in *Anas* is accomplished largely by differences in feeding habits and correlated structural specializations of the head and bodily proportions. Differences in feeding behavior which reduce interspecific competition have not been studied in detail, but some broad differences are obvious. For example, the long-necked Pintail (*Anas acuta*) can feed from the bottom in deeper water than other species, the Shoveler (*A. clypeata*) is specialized for straining food through its well-developed lamellae, etc. (Kortwright 1942, Lack 1971). Most such differences are not reflected in the locomotor features considered here. A large deviation from the generally similar measurements in the five species of *Anas* studied is the relatively small paddle in the Am. Widgeon (*A. americana*) (Table 2). This is correlated with the fact that the Am. Widgeon is the most terrestrial species studied, a good deal of its feeding being done by grazing. Kortwright (1942) says that "they are active on land, where they trot about and graze like little geese." The smaller paddle is clearly an adaptation to agility on land. Reduced foot size is characteristic of cursorial forms, e.g. the Secretarybird (*Sagittarius serpentarius*) has toes only one-fifth as long as those of most hawks (Welty 1964).

The diving ducks as a group have smaller wings and larger paddles than do the dabbling ducks. The larger wings of dabblers, together with their more elliptical shape and increased slotting, are adapted to the use of small bodies of water, and inshore areas of larger bodies which may be spatially broken up by surrounding or emergent vegetation. This type of wing is aerodynamically suited to permit their habit of rocketing upward from these areas where a long clear distance for a running start may be absent. This relationship between wing type and habitat was pointed out by Savile (1957:218) who, however, did not document his statement. The paddle size in ducks is for each species a compromise between the optimally small paddle best suited for walking on land, and at the other extreme, the optimally large paddle best suited for aquatic locomotion.

Among the diving ducks studied two genera deserve special mention. The eiders (*Somateria*) alone among the divers, lack an enlarged paddle (Table 2). Its relative size is comparable to that of *Anas*, although a lobed hallux is present. This implies that eiders are less efficient divers than other members of the Mergini. Little is known about their underwater actions, but Humphrey (1958) reports that they use their wings underwater like Anatini, a sign that foot propulsion alone is not adequate. The eiders are ground nesters and walk efficiently on land, so the *Anas*-like paddle size is clearly adaptive. The wing size of eiders is reduced as in other divers (Table 2), which is correlated with the open waters which they frequent.

The Ruddy Duck (*Oxyura jamaicensis*) has the relatively smallest wings of the fifteen species studied. In shape they most nearly conform to Savile's (1957) characterization of the high-speed type, being small, pointed, and minimally slotted. Bent (1925:158) comments on the "grebelike" nature of the flight, swimming, and diving habits of Ruddy Ducks. Figure 2 shows that the wing shape in Ruddy Ducks is more like that of a grebe than that of a dabbling duck. Ruddy Ducks have the relatively largest paddles of all species studied except *Aythya valisineria* (Table 2). While they swim excellently, both on the surface and beneath it, they are clumsy and incompetent on land, being unable to walk more than a few steps (Kortwright 1942:369). This is in part due to the posterior placement of the feet and their specialized musculoskeletal system (Raikow 1970), but the very large paddles undoubtedly add to their clumsiness on land. The Ruddy Duck represents an extreme in a spectrum of specialized conditions illustrated by the species investigated in this study.

It is believed that the diving ducks evolved from dabbling ducks, i.e. that the common ancestor of present-day dabblers and divers closely resembled the former. Thus the differences between the two represent primitive conditions in the dabblers and derived conditions in the divers. The divers are not a monophyletic group, however (Delacour and Mayr 1945), rather it is probable that the three tribes of divers studied here arose separately from the Anatini and evolved into divers independently of one another. The similarity of their modifications is a result of parallel evolution. Nevertheless, while the general pattern is similar in each case, the details vary. Each character has diverged from the primitive condition to different degrees in different groups. Relative paddle size, for example, has not increased at all in *Somateria*, but has increased from a lesser to a greater degree in the other diving genera studied. The same is true of the reduction of wing area and slotting, and conversion to a more pointed wing shape. In each species a particular combination of characters is thus in a sense a visible reflection of its ecological niche.

SUMMARY

The relationship between locomotor morphology and feeding ecology was studied in fifteen species of North American ducks. Two general adaptive types are recognized. Dabbling ducks (Anatini) feed on the surface, seldom dive, walk and feed on land, feed in shallow, inshore waters, and take off from restricted areas by rocketing upward. Diving ducks (Aythyini, Mergini, Oxyurini) feed underwater by diving, walk on land poorly if at all, feed in open, offshore waters, and take off by running along the surface. These ecological differences are correlated with morphological differences.

Dabbling ducks have the largest wing areas relative to body weight, the most rounded wings, and the best developed wingtip slotting. This improves their ability to land and take off from spatially restricted areas. They have the relatively smallest paddles, which is correlated with their lesser aquatic adaptations but giving them greater agility in walking on land. The smallest paddles are in *Anas americana*, the most terrestrial of the species studied.

Diving ducks have smaller, more pointed, less slotted wings. These are adequate for rapid, direct flight, but inadequate for a rocketing take-off, thus limiting these birds to more open waters. They have the relatively largest paddles, however, in relation to their efficient diving abilities. The Ruddy Duck (*Oxyura jamaicensis*) is a superb diver but helpless on land. Its structural characteristics reflect this condition. Eiders, the most cursorial diving ducks studied, have paddle areas comparable to those of dabbling ducks. Similarities in the different tribes of separately derived diving ducks are due to parallel evolution in relation to similar adaptive specializations.

ACKNOWLEDGMENTS

I am grateful to Kenneth C. Parkes and Mary H. Clench of the Carnegie Museum for allowing me to examine study skins in their care, to James Lynch, Paul Covel, William Arvey, and John Cowan for assistance in collecting specimens, and to Harvey I. Fisher for suggesting improvements in the analysis of the data.

LITERATURE CITED

Bent, A. C. 1925. Life histories of North American wild fowl, Part II. Reprint Ed. 1962. Dover Publications, Inc., New York.

Brooks, A. 1945. The underwater actions of diving ducks. Auk 62:517–523.

Delacour, J., and E. Mayr. 1945. The family Anatidae. Wilson Bull. 57:3–55.

Greenwalt, C. H. 1962. Dimensional relationships for flying animals. Smithsonian Misc. Coll. 144:1–46.

Hartman, F. A. 1961. Locomotor mechanisms of birds. Smithsonian Misc. Coll. 143:1–91.

Humphrey, P. S. 1958. Classification and systematic position of the eiders. Condor 60:129–135.

Jack, A. 1953. Feathered wings. Methuen & Co., Ltd., London.

Kortwright, F. H. 1942. The ducks, geese, and swans of North America. Amer. Wildlife Inst., Washington, D.C.

Lack, D. 1971. Ecological isolation in birds. Harvard Univ. Press, Cambridge, Mass.

Poole, E. L. 1938. Weights and wing areas in North American birds. Auk 55:511–517.

Raikow, R. J. 1970. Evolution of diving adaptations in the stifftail ducks. Univ. California Publ. Zool. 94:1–52.

———. 1971. The osteology and taxonomic position

of the White-backed Duck, *Thalassornis leuconotus*. Wilson Bull. 83:270–277.

SAVILE, D. B. O. 1957. Adaptive evolution in the avian wing. Evolution 11:212–224.

STORER, R. W. 1955. Weight, wing area, and skeletal proportions in three accipiters. Acta XI Congr. Internatl. Ornithol. 287–290.

WELLER, M. W. 1964. General habits, *in* J. Delacour, The waterfowl of the world, vol. 4, Country Life Ltd., London, pp. 15–34.

WELTY, J. C. 1964. The life of birds. W. B. Saunders Co., Philadelphia and London.

TIMING AND SUCCESS OF BREEDING IN TUNDRA-NESTING GEESE[1]

I. NEWTON, The Nature Conservancy, 12 Hope Terrace, Edinburgh EH9 2AS, Scotland

This chapter is concerned with the factors that influence breeding output by tundra-nesting geese, and is a review of published information. In recent years, many detailed studies on individual species have been made but, to my knowledge, no synthesis of ideas. The main ideas favoured here are (1) that breeding in such geese depends largely on reserves of body fat and protein accumulated at wintering and migration areas, and (2) that its timing and success is influenced by the date in spring when snow melts and nest sites become available. The first idea is an extension of David Lack's (1967, 1968) last contribution on the evolution of clutch size in birds, while the second interested him many years earlier (Bertram et al. 1934). Regarding geese, major contributors to the field discussed here have included Cooch (1958), Barry (1962), Hanson (1962), MacInnes (1962, 1966), Ryder (1970) and F. Cooke (papers in preparation).

BACKGROUND

Some 12 species of goose in the genera *Anser* (including *Chen*) and *Branta* are involved; for Latin names of species mentioned see Table 1. These are large, robust waterfowl, which inhabit relatively open landscapes and feed entirely, or almost entirely, on plant material. They nest at high latitudes, in tundra and forest tundra, and migrate south for the winter. Only the Canada goose in North America and the Greylag in Eurasia also breed south of the Boreal Zone.

North of the treeline, geese are restricted to damp fertile areas where sedges (*Carex* spp.) predominate, such as river deltas or near sea coasts. They nest either solitarily, or in loose colonies, which in some species usually contain only a few pairs and in others hundreds or thousands of pairs. The same species may breed solitarily in one area and colonially in another (Nyholm 1965, Uspenski 1965*a*, King 1970). The largest concentration of Snow geese (on Wrangel Island, Siberia) has numbered more than 400,000 birds (Uspenski 1965), and several other colonies in northern Canada contained more than 300,000 (R. H. Kerbes, in litt.). Within such colonies, the ganders defend territories of a few metres radius around a nest, and remain there while the females incubate (Cooch 1958, Lemieux 1959, Ryder 1972).

The actual nest sites of geese are often on islets surrounded by water (MacInnes 1962, Ryder 1967, King 1970), on cliffs or bluffs (Kessel and Cade 1958, Blurton Jones and Gillmor 1959, Kumari 1971), near nests of birds of prey (Uspenski 1965, Cade 1964), or in other places which supposedly offer protection against mammalian predators. Birds nesting solitarily or in small groups are usually in less accessible sites than those in large colonies, where the sheer numbers and synchrony of breeding confer protection (Kerbes et al. 1971). Nesting usually occurs in habitats which differ from, but are adjacent to, good feeding areas. The commonest clutch sizes are 3–5 eggs.

After hatching, the family may move

[1] Originally published in B. Stonehouse and C. Perrins, eds. Evolutionary ecology, pages 113–126. University Park Press, Baltimore, MD, 1977.

many kilometres to good feeding areas, where they may live on their own or in groups of families. While the young grow, the adults moult their flight feathers, starting about 2 weeks after the eggs have hatched, so for a time the whole family is flightless. Some Greylag broods walked and swam more than 25 km in the early brood-rearing period (Paakspuu 1972), and some broods of Snow geese more than 100 km (MacInnes and Lieff 1968), but these were exceptionally far. Such movement was necessary because local food supplies were insufficient for all the birds that nested.

ADAPTATIONS TO ARCTIC NESTING

For geese nesting in the tundra, the main constraint is the shortness of the season. To produce young that are strong on the wing in the period between spring melt and autumn freeze up, such geese show three main adaptations:

(1) They conform to the widespread trend among birds that the further north they breed, the shorter their individual breeding cycles, and the more they are synchronised with one another (Newton 1972). This is shown by comparing tundra nesting populations with temperate zone ones, and among tundra ones by comparing the northern Brent, Barnacle and Snow geese with the rest (Table 1). The main shortening of breeding seasons is due to a reduction in the spread of the starting dates of individuals, rather than in the shortening of individual cycles. In most tundra species, individuals need three months to complete a breeding cycle, but the three most northerly ones only require 2.5 months.

(2) Courtship and copulation occur either on winter quarters or at stopping places on northward migration (Barry 1962, MacInnes 1962, Ryder 1967, Kistchinski 1971). The birds arrive in pairs, the females already fertilised; if conditions are right they can lay within a week (Barry 1962, Ryder 1967, 1971). The males' testes have already begun to regress (Barry 1962, Ryder 1967). If the clutch is destroyed after completion, a second is not laid, but if some eggs are destroyed before the clutch is completed, the remaining eggs may be laid in a new nest, with no longer break than usual between eggs (Barry 1962, MacInnes 1962). The completion of the pre-nesting phase of breeding before arrival may be usual in other northern waterfowl, but is apparently not the norm in other birds.

(3) All breeding activities before the eggs hatch are accomplished almost entirely on reserves accumulated at wintering and migration areas (see below). Successful females evidently lay down enough reserves for migration (or at least for the last stage of it), for producing the eggs and for their own maintenance during incubation (Ryder 1967, 1970; Harvey 1971). The males expend less energy than the females (see below), but are more active, establishing and defending the nest area until hatch. These demanding activities together take a minimum of 4–6 weeks in each successful bird. The dependence of migration on body reserves is well known among other bird families at all latitudes (Moreau 1972), and at least a partial dependence of breeding on reserves is known in some other waterfowl (Milne 1974) and other birds (Fogden 1974) further south. But northern geese (and swans) seem extreme in the number and duration of activities which they accomplish on reserves, with little opportunity for replenishment.

EVIDENCE FOR DEPENDENCE ON RESERVES

The evidence for such heavy and prolonged dependence on reserves is of two

Table 1. The duration of the breeding cycle (days) in different species of geese. As far as possible, species (or races) are listed according to their breeding distributions north to south.

Species	Locality	Spread in start of laying	Usual clutch size	Incubation period	Fledging period	Total egg[a] period of population	Breeding period of individual	Total breeding period of population	Source
Brent *B. bernicla*	Southampton Island	6	4	24	45–50	34	73–78	83	Barry 1962
Greater snow goose *A. hyperboreus*	Bylot Island	7	4	23–25	44	36	71–73	79	Lemieux 1959
Snow goose *A. caerulescens*	Eastern Arctic Canada	7–14	4	22–23	42	34–43	68–69	75–84	Cooch 1964 Ryder 1971
Ross's goose *A. rossii*	Central Arctic Canada	6–11	4	22	—	32–37	—	—	Ryder 1967, 1972
Barnacle *B. leucopsis*	Spitzbergen	—	4	24	49	—	78	—	Norderhaug et al. 1964
Canada goose *B. c. hutchinsii*	Eastern Arctic Canada	8–10	4	24–25	—	37–39	—	—	MacInnes 1962
Pinkfooted goose *A. brachyrhynchus*	Iceland	—	4–5	26	58	—	88–90	—	Witherby et al. 1938 Scott et al. 1955 Norderhaug et al. 1965
Emperor goose *A. canagicus*	Northeast Siberia	13	5–6	25	—	45	—	—	Barry 1964 Kistchinski 1971
White-fronted goose *A. albifrons*	Alaska	21	5	27	42–49	54	75–82	102	Lack 1968 Dzbuin et al. 1964
Bean goose *A. fabalis*	Northern Europe	—	5	28	—	—	—	—	Lack 1968
Canada goose *B. c. maxima*	Missouri	38	5–6	28	65–70[b]	73	99–104	141	Brakhage 1965 Yocum and Harris 1965
Greylag *A. anser*	Temperate Europe	49	6–7	27–28	56	86	90–93	141	Hudec and Rooth 1970 Newton and Kerbes 1974

[a] From first egg laid to last hatched by population, assuming each bird lays one egg every 1.5 days (Barry 1962; Brakhage 1965; Kossoch 1950; Klopman 1958; Lemieux 1959; MacInnes 1962; Yocum and Harris 1965; Ryder 1967; 1971).
[b] Calculated for *B. c. moffiti.*

types. First, successful birds feed little or not at all until after the eggs hatch (Harvey 1971, MacInnes et al. 1975). When the geese arrive, the ground may be snow covered and they do not start nesting until bare patches have appeared (Lemieux 1959, Barry 1962, Uspenski 1965); solitary nesters wait until ice around nesting islets has melted, thus making them safer from mammalian predators (MacInnes 1962). The amount of feeding by geese depends partly on the interval between arrival and nesting; this is shortest at the highest latitudes, and in any one area is shortest in the warmest springs. It depends also on whether food is available, that is, on snow cover and habitat, and on the condition of the female, which is partly dependent on local weather (Harvey 1971). Feeding can occur only on places clear of snow, and at first the food is of poor quality because new growth does not begin for another 2–3 weeks, well after incubation has started. Also, the birds often nest in areas of low scrub or heath, which are deficient in food plants. During incubation the female spends nearly all her time on the nest (Salomonsen 1950, Harvey 1971), but she may leave occasionally for short periods to obtain what little food is available nearby, and very rarely she may fly to feed elsewhere, accompanied by her mate. At this stage the male is more free to feed than the female, but is still restricted to a small area near his mate.

Spring migration of geese is normally accomplished in a series of long flights, each of several hundred kilometres, between traditional stopover points (Cooch 1964, Dzubin 1965, MacInnes 1966, Prevett and MacInnes 1972). The extent to which birds can feed on migration varies between populations and whether they migrate over favourable terrain, but in general the nearer to their destination, the less their chance of getting fresh protein-rich vegetation. The Pinkfooted geese, which fly the 1,100 km over water between Scotland and central Iceland in spring, have no access to good feeding for several weeks after setting off. Other populations that move over land feed at stopping places (MacInnes 1966, Drobovtsev 1972, Kumari 1971), but the bulk of the reserve needed for breeding is almost certainly laid down earlier.

Secondly, the weights of breeding birds show a massive loss between the dates of arrival and hatching, irrespective of weather and snow cover. Female Ross's geese lost about 25 per cent of their initial weight over the few days of egg laying, and another 25 per cent during the 22 days of incubation, then gained rapidly when they began to feed again after hatching (Ryder 1967). The males lost about 25 per cent of their weight between arrival and hatching and then, like the females, gained weight again. Female Snow geese lost about 25 per cent of their weight between arrival and hatching, males about 17 per cent (Cooch 1964). Also, while nesting female Brent geese lost 25 per cent of their weight, non-nesting females lost only about half as much as this. The enormous fat reserves present in geese on arrival on their breeding areas have been noted in Brent geese (Barry 1962), Snow geese (Cooch 1958), White-fronted and Canada geese (Hanson et al. 1964). Carcass analyses of nesting Canada and Snow geese showed that weight loss resulted from metabolism of both fat and protein stores, the latter mainly in the pectoral muscles (Hanson 1962, Harvey 1971). Female Snow geese became extremely emaciated. Their breast muscles were resorbed until "only vestiges of stringy gelatinous tissues remained," and the keel protruded sharply. Their necks also became thin and their bill linings blackened and dried (Harvey 1971).

TIMING AND SUCCESS OF BREEDING

The arrival of geese on their breeding areas does not always coincide with the dates of snow melt, which can vary by up to three weeks from year to year. Generally, arrival dates are much more constant from year to year than melt dates (Goodhart and Wright 1958, Barry 1962, Kerbes 1969). In years when the ground has begun to clear at the time of arrival, geese begin nesting within a week, but in other years they remain on the breeding areas and wait (Barry 1962, Uspenski 1965), all the time depleting their reserves. The more of the reserves used in prior maintenance, the less that can be allocated to eggs (Ryder 1970). In these circumstances, breeding output might be influenced both by the initial size of the reserves (hence, on conditions further south) and also on how long the geese have to wait between accumulating their reserves and laying their eggs. Peak laying dates of several populations have been up to two weeks later in late than in early years (Hardy 1967, Uspenski 1965); after even more delay, the birds did not attempt to nest (Barry 1962, Cooch 1964).

To my knowledge, the only attempt to relate breeding output in tundra nesting geese with previous conditions on winter quarters is that of Cabot and West (1973), with the Greenland Barnacle that winter on the Inishkea Islands, off western Ireland. Using data for 13 years, they found a significant positive correlation ($P < 0.05$) between mean brood sizes in any one winter and mean temperatures over the preceding winter. Temperature had a major influence on the production of winter food (grass) and thus, it was presumed, on the condition of the geese. MacInnes et al. (1974) also provided indirect evidence that conditions south of breeding areas were partly responsible for annual variations in production by two populations of Canada geese. Further work of this type is much needed.

The relationship between the date of snow melt and the timing and success of breeding in geese has been well documented in White-fronted, Canada and Brent geese (Barry 1962), Snow geese (Cooch 1964, Kerbes 1969, Uspenski 1965*b*), Ross's geese (Ryder 1970), Pink-footed and Barnacle geese (Goodhart and Wright 1958), and by casual observations on other species. In general, the later that nest-sites become available, the smaller the proportion of birds that lay, the smaller the clutches and (at least in Snow geese) the poorer the hatching success (see later). Availability of nest sites in spring is influenced not only by temperatures, but also by snow depth, flooding and other factors.

Resorption of ova is evidently the mechanism by which clutch sizes are reduced, or, in very late years, breeding is prevented (see photographs in Barry 1962). The importance of this is not so much the nutrients the female reclaims at the time, but rather those she saves through not committing herself to a larger clutch and a later incubation. In some female Brents killed off nests in a late year, 60 per cent of ova had been resorbed, compared with 95 per cent in birds killed from nonbreeding flocks (Barry 1962). The few eggs laid by the latter were probably "dumped," that is, laid in another bird's nest or on the ground.

In all species in which it was studied,

mean clutch size was smaller in late than in early years (Barry 1964, Cooch 1964), and it declined as each season progressed, sometimes by more than 50 per cent in a few days. Thus in 1967 on Baffin Island, the mean clutch size of Snow geese was 5.0 for birds starting on June 17, 3.9 for birds starting on June 18, 3.5 on June 19, 2.6 on June 20 and 2.1 on June 21 (Kerbes 1969). Seasonal declines of similar magnitude were noted in other populations of Snow geese (Ryder 1971), and in Ross's geese (Ryder 1967); less marked ones were noted in *A. c. atlantica* (Lemieux 1959), and Brent geese (Barry 1962). In Snow geese they also occurred within particular age groups, and could not be wholly attributed to younger birds (which laid smaller clutches) nesting later than older birds (Finney and Cooke, in press). The depletion of reserves may not be the only factor involved, moreover, for a late bird laying a small clutch will also hatch its eggs earlier than if it laid a large clutch, and in a short season the few days saved could be crucial (see later).

Once they have bred, individual marked female geese have usually returned to breed in the same area year after year (Barry 1962, Cooch 1958, MacInnes and Lieff 1966, Cooke et al. 1975). In late years, competition for what snow-free ground was available led to much fighting, as seen in Brent geese, Snow geese (Barry 1962) and White-fronted geese (Dzubin et al. 1964). The youngest potential breeders (22 and 34 months old) among Snow geese nested chiefly in early springs, when nest sites were superabundant from the start of the season (Cooch 1964). Young birds nested a few days later, on average, than did older, experienced breeders, even when not constrained by shortage of sites; they also laid smaller clutches than older birds nesting at the same date (Finney and Cooke, in press).

HATCHING SUCCESS

Whether a bird's reserves will last through incubation depends not only on their extent, but also on their rate of loss, which in turn depends on the weather and its effect on heat loss (Harvey 1971). In one cold year at the McConnell River, some female Snow geese were found dead on their eggs, which were near to hatching. On average, they weighed 43 per cent less than did breeders on arrival. Other geese interrupted incubation to feed, thus exposing their nest to predation. Among individuals that were closely watched from a hide, predation was highest among birds which interrupted incubation to feed. Most losses occurred late in incubation, when there were fewer predators present, but when females left their nests most often. Usually the whole clutch was taken, even though covered with down. Hence, a bird's condition influenced not only the number of eggs it laid, but also its chance of hatching them.

In some studies, the mean hatching success was found to be better in early than in late springs when availability of nest sites was delayed. Cooch (1964) estimated the usual success of Snow goose nests to be around 81 per cent in early seasons, 64 per cent in average seasons, and 51 per cent in late seasons, attributing the losses to predation; L. Maltby (in litt.) found equivalent figures of 97, 79 and 16 per cent; while Kerbes (1969) found 76 per cent in an average year and 26 per cent in a late year. On the other hand, Ryder (1971) found no reduction in nesting success of Ross's geese in a late season. MacInnes (1962) gave figures of 75 and 90 per cent for *B. c. hutchinsii* in two early years.

Problems arise in assessing predation rates, however, because the main predators on the eggs of arctic-nesting geese are skuas (mainly Arctic skuas) and gulls (mainly Herring gulls). These are mainly opportunists, unable to drive a goose off a nest, but able to get in quickly and take unguarded eggs. They are thus greatly assisted in their efforts by the presence of a biologist working in the area. Hence, predation rates recorded in the literature are probably higher than they would be in natural conditions, and they do not usually distinguish clutches that were deserted before being eaten. MacInnes and Misra (1972) thought that the partial depletion of clutches in *B. c. hutchinsii*, which accounted for 55 per cent of all eggs lost, occurred only under human disturbance, and that an average of 0.65 eggs was lost from each nest at every visit by the observer. Otherwise predation rates would have been around 10 per cent, would not have varied much in the five years studied, and would have been restricted to whole clutches.

Arctic foxes *Alopex lagopus* have locally accounted for a large number of clutches. In one study, a single fox was seen to destroy all the 200 Snow goose clutches in 3 km² in 5 days. The fox systematically removed the eggs from one nest after another and buried them (MacInnes and Misra 1972). The heavy destruction of Snow goose and Brent goose eggs in another area was associated with the presence of an active fox den in the colony (Barry 1964). These effects were local and, unless foxes were numerous and short of normal food over a wide area, they would be unlikely to have any major impact on goose populations or breeding success, especially where geese nest in a more dispersed manner. Grizzly Bears *Ursus horribilis* have been known to have a heavy local impact: two ate the contents of 295 goose nests in 6 days (Barry 1964).

FLEDGING SUCCESS

This has usually been assessed by comparing the mean brood sizes in a population at different dates between hatching and fledging, ignoring pairs without young. The survival of young *B. c. hutchinsii* in two early seasons near McConnell River was thus estimated at 85 and 90 per cent (MacInnes 1962), that of young Ross's geese in two early seasons near Perry River at about 67 per cent and that of young Pinkfooted geese between hatching in Iceland and arrival in Britain in October at 67 per cent or more (Scott et al. 1955). All these figures imply good survival, but are almost certainly overestimates because they take no account of broods which failed entirely. In general, losses were greatest in the week after hatching, when the young were still small. The main predators were large gulls (especially Herring gulls), which in *B. c. hutchinsii* took any young that strayed more than about 3 m from their parents (MacInnes 1962). On Baffin Island, survival among Snow geese was poorer in a late year than in an average year (Kerbes 1969), a finding that needs more investigation.

BREEDING SUCCESS AND POPULATION TRENDS

The result of varying seasons is that production of young has varied enormously from year to year. This was especially so in high Arctic nesters, like Brent and Snow geese, in which the proportion of young in the autumn populations varied from <1 to >50 per cent

Table 2. Annual variations in production of young, judged from brood counts in winter quarters. As far as possible, species are listed according to their breeding distributions, north to south.

	Breeding/wintering area	No. of years of observation	Range of values from different years in: Percentage young in population	Range of values from different years in: Mean brood size	Source
Brent goose *B. bernicla*	Northern Siberia/ Britain, France	15	<1–53	—	Ogilvie and Matthews, 1969
Snow goose *A. caerulescens*	Northeast Canada/ Southern United States	11	2–55	1.6–2.7	Lynch and Singleton, 1964
Barnacle goose *B. leucopsis*	Northeast Greenland/ Western Scotland	9	8–31	1.4–2.8	Boyd, 1968
	Northeast Greenland/ Western Ireland	12	1–14	1.5–2.4	Cabot and West, 1973
Pinkfooted goose *A. brachyrhynchus*	Iceland/Britain	19	11–49	1.3–3.3	Boyd and Ogilvie, 1969
Greylag *A. anser*	Iceland/Britain	12	6–44	1.3–3.8	Boyd and Ogilvie, 1972
White-fronted goose *A. albifrons*	Northern Russia/ England	17	11–47	2.5–3.9	Boyd, 1965

(Table 2), and in which poor years were most frequent. In general, there was a good correlation between mean brood size and percentage of young in the population, but the latter was also influenced by the number of immature birds, and hence on breeding success in previous years. Good production was often associated with big increases in population and vice versa; several good years in succession led to a massive increase in numbers, and several poor years to a decline. Differences also occurred within a breeding population wintering in different areas. The population of Brent geese that winter on the Inishkea Islands remained stable for 12 years, with a mean adult loss of 8.3 per cent and a mean production of 7.8 per cent young, while the Islay ones increased continuously for at least 18 years, with a 10.1 per cent adult loss and 16.5 per cent production of young (Cabot and West 1973; H. Boyd, in litt.) Both populations breed in eastern Greenland. Such increases are presumably possible only until populations become limited by shortage of breeding or wintering habitat.

Icelandic populations of Pinkfooted and Greylag geese more than doubled in size in 20 years and, while production of young varied greatly from year to year, on average the proportion of mature birds producing young declined (Boyd and Ogilvie 1969, 1971). This implied some steadily increasing restriction in production of young as numbers rose. One way in which this might have occurred is through competition for limited areas of breeding habitat, an idea supported by the recent finding that nesting and feeding habitat of Pinkfooted geese was occupied at very high density (Kerbes et al. 1971).

NON-BREEDERS

Probably most geese nest for the first time at 3 years (34 months), but some at 4 years (46) or 2 years (22). This is the case with *Anser* and *Branta* species in captivity (Scott et al. 1955), and has been confirmed in the wild in Canada geese (Craighead and Stockstad 1964, Martin 1964), Brent geese (Barry 1962) and Snow geese (Finney and Cooke, in press); it has not been confirmed in European White-fronted geese, most of which bred at 4 yr and only a few at 3 years (Boyd 1965). These generalisations may of course be upset by seasonal phenology, by the intensity of competition for breeding places and other factors (Cooch 1958; Finney and Cooke, in press); even during its breeding life, a bird may not nest every year (MacInnes et al. 1974).

Geese that do not breed moult their feathers 2–3 weeks earlier than those that do. They may remain in the breeding area, in flocks separated from breeders (Hardy 1967, Newton and Kerbes 1974), or migrate up to several hundred kilometres northwards to traditional areas where they gather in flocks containing up to several thousand birds. They are ready for autumn migration, and in some species leave well before the breeders. Moult migrations are regular in all species of geese (see Salomonsen [1968] for Greylag, White-fronted, Lesser white-fronted, Bean, Pinkfooted, Canada, Brent and Snow geese, and Kistchinski [1971] and Blurton Jones [1972] for Emperor geese).

DISCUSSION

Breeding Season

The short and more synchronised breeding cycles of arctic geese, compared with those of the temperate zone have parallels in other bird families that breed in both regions (Newton 1972), though geese in general have longer breeding cycles than most other land birds at similar latitudes, largely because their young take longer to reach the flying stage. This may in turn be linked with their almost wholly vegetarian diet in which (with swans) geese seem unique. The completion of the pre-nesting phase of breeding before arrival may be usual in other northern waterfowl, but it is apparently not usual in other tundra nesting birds. Also geese seem extreme in the number and duration of activities that they accomplish almost entirely on reserves (though again swans *Cygnus* spp. may provide parallels). Both features could be interpreted as adaptations to save time.

The period needed to complete a breeding cycle is probably a major feature preventing any one goose species from extending its range northwards, for the further north a species breeds, the smaller the proportion of summers in which it can raise young (Lensink 1973). It is not clear to me what prevents a species from breeding further south, unless perhaps some competition is experienced from related species. Reduced competition was probably also involved in the evolution of moult migrations. By leaving the nesting areas, non-breeding geese avoid competing for food with families of their own species and, by flying north, they also gain the advantage of longer days. Some populations also get two spring flushes of plant-growth, the first on the breeding area and the second on the moulting area. The flightless period of non-breeding geese lasts less than half as long as a successful breeding cycle, so individuals can moult well to the north of where they can breed.

Clutch Size and Non-breeding

Lack (1967) proposed that clutch size in waterfowl had evolved in relation to the average amount of food available to the female at the time (and place) of laying, modified by the relative size of the eggs. Starting with this idea, Ryder (1970) proposed that clutch size in Ross' geese had evolved to correspond with the maximum that the female could normally produce on her reserves, that resorption of ova allowed adjustment of clutch size to depleted reserves, and that the female usually retained a certain reserve to enable her to incubate effectively. The female was thus largely independent of food supplies at the time and place of laying. Not only should this view now be extended to other species of geese, but annual variations in spring body reserves may also be considered partly responsible for annual variations in production.

When reserves are falling, resorption allows the transfer of food materials from the ova back to the female. Further, it prevents the female from committing herself to extra breeding effort, and from nesting so late that she would have little chance of raising young. Selection operates against late and repeat nesting; Barry (1962) found 21 Brent geese that had hatched in a late spring, frozen in the ice the following spring. They were well preserved, and had nothing wrong with them except that their feather development was 4–5 days short of allowing them to fly. When birds fail to nest, they do not suffer a big energy drain, are able to feed all summer and moult earlier, and thus presumably enhance their own chances of surviving to attempt to breed again. Since individual geese nest in several seasons, they might produce most young by skipping a year in return for greater success the following year.

Breeding Success

Greater egg loss in late years results from less sustained incubation (facilitating greater predation from skuas and gulls), and perhaps also from shortage of sites at laying time forcing more birds than usual to nest in unsuitable places (Cooch 1964). The greater numbers of avian predators often seen around large goose colonies in late years (Barry 1964, Kerbes 1969) has usually been attributed to shortage of the predator's normal food. The alternative view, that they are attracted there by more vulnerable (exposed and dumped) eggs, has seldom been considered. The survival of young after hatching may also be poorer in late years, irrespective of any being frozen in, but needs more study.

The relationship between the timing and success of breeding also holds in waterfowl nesting in temperate regions. Thus the Greylag geese resident in the snowfree environment of the Outer Hebrides Islands, off northwest Scotland, nested earlier and more successfully in warm than in cold springs and, within each season, the first birds to nest were also the most successful (Newton and Kerbes 1974). Here nest sites were unrestricted and the differences between years were due mainly to differential predation, which occurred only when the nest was left unattended. The same association within a season also held in at least four species of duck nesting at Loch Leven, in east-central Scotland (Newton and Campbell 1975). Disastrously poor seasons for production of young have also occurred in temperate zone waterfowl. They were frequent in Scottish Eiders *Somateria molissima* (Milne 1974) and Shelducks *Tadorna tadorna* (Jenkins et al. 1975), but in these species the failures were due to heavy mortality of small young, rather than to widespread failure to lay, as in arctic geese.

Further Research

The model presented here, based on links between the level of body reserves accumulated on winter quarters, on the availability of nest sites in spring, and the timing and success of breeding, is probably oversimplified and likely to be modified by further work. Whether events before or after arrival on breeding areas have most effect on production of young may also vary between populations and between years in the same population. A major research need is for more study of the relationship between winter food supplies and the spring condition and breeding success of the birds. Future studies on breeding areas could also include some good measure of progressive nest site availability each year. Different years from the same and different studies could then be more precisely compared with one another, and the relationship between timing and success of breeding examined more rigorously. In studies of gosling survival, some account must also be taken of broods depleted to nil, and some assessment made of the quality of summer grazings.

ACKNOWLEDGMENTS

I thank H. Boyd, F. Cooke and C. D. MacInnes for giving me the opportunity to study breeding geese in arctic Canada, H. Boyd, F. Cooke, J. P. Dempster, G. Finney, M. Harris, D. Jenkins, R. H. Kerbes and L. Maltby for many constructive comments on the manuscript, and F. Cooke, G. Finney, C. D. MacInnes and L. Maltby for allowing me to quote from their unpublished work.

LITERATURE CITED

BARRY, T. W. 1962. Effect of late seasons on Atlantic Brant reproduction. J. Wildl. Mgmt. 26:19–26.

———. 1964. Brant, Ross' Goose and Emperor Goose, *in* Waterfowl tomorrow, ed. J. P. Linduska, US Government Printing Office, Washington, pp. 145–154.

BERTRAM, G. C. L., D. LACK, AND B. B. ROBERTS. 1934. Notes on East Greenland birds, with a discussion of the periodic non-breeding among arctic birds. Ibis 4(13):816–831.

BLURTON JONES, N. G. 1972. Moult migration of Emperor geese. Wildfowl 23:92–93.

———, AND R. GILLMOR. 1959. Some observations on wild geese in Spitsbergen. Wildfowl Trust Ann. Rep. 10:118–132.

BOYD, H. 1965. Breeding success of White-fronted geese from the Nenets National Area. Wildfowl Trust Ann. Rep. 16:34–40.

———. 1968. Barnacle geese in the West of Scotland, 1957–67. Wildfowl 19:96–107.

———, AND M. A. OGILVIE. 1969. Changes in the British-wintering population of the Pinkfooted goose from 1950 to 1975. Wildfowl 20:33–46.

———, AND ———. 1972. Icelandic Greylag geese wintering in Britain in 1960–1971. Wildfowl 23:64–82.

BRAKHAGE, G. K. 1965. Biology and behaviour of tub-nesting Canada geese. J. Wildl. Mgmt. 29:751–771.

CABOT, D., AND B. WEST. 1973. Population dynamics of Barnacle geese, *Branta leucopsis*, in Ireland. Proc. R.I.A. 73B:415–443.

CADE, T. 1960. Ecology of the Peregrine and Gyrfalcon populations in Alaska. Univ. Calif. Publ. Zool. 63:151–290.

COOCH, F. G. 1958. The breeding biology and management of the Blue goose (*Chen caerulescens*). PhD thesis, Cornell University, Ithaca, New York.

COOCH, G. 1964. Snows and Blues, *in* Waterfowl tomorrow, ed. J. P. Linduska, US Government Printing Office, Washington, pp. 125–133.

COOKE, F., C. D. MACINNES, AND J. P. PREVETT. 1975. Gene flow between breeding populations of Lesser snow geese. Auk 92:493–510.

CRAIGHEAD, J. J., AND D. S. STOCKSTAD. 1964. Breeding age of Canada geese. J. Wildl. Mgmt. 28:57–64.

DROBOVTSEV, V. 1972. Character of the spring and autumn passage of geese in the North-Kazakhstan Region, *in* Geese in the USSR, ed. E. Kumari, Tartu. pp. 132–138. Russian, with English summary.

DZUBIN, A. 1965. A study of migrating Ross geese in western Saskatchewan. Condor 67:511–534.

———, H. W. MILLER, AND G. V. SCHILDMAN. 1964. Whitefronts, *in* Waterfowl tomorrow, ed. J. P. Linduska. US Government Printing Office, Washington, pp. 135–143.

FINNEY, G., AND F. COOKE. In Press. Reproductive strategies in the Snow goose: the influence of female age. Ibis.

FOGDEN, M. P. L. 1974. The seasonality and population dynamics of Equatorial forest birds in Sarawak. Ibis 114:307–342.

GOODHART, J., AND T. WRIGHT. 1958. North-east Greenland expedition 1956. Wildfowl Trust Ann. Rep. 9:180–192.

HANSON, H. C. 1962. The dynamics of condition

factors in Canada geese and their relation to seasonal stresses. Arct. Inst. Tech. Pap. 12. 68pp.

HARDY, D. E. 1967. Observations on the Pink-footed Goose in Central Iceland, 1966. Wildfowl Trust Ann. Rep. 18:134–141.

HARVEY, J. M. 1971. Factors affecting Blue goose nesting success. Can. J. Zool. 49:223–234.

HUDEC, K., AND J. ROOTH. 1970. Die Graugans (*Anser anser* L.). Die Neue Brehm-Bucherei, Wittenberg Lutherstadt. 148pp.

JENKINS, D., M. G. MURRAY, AND P. HALL. 1975. Structure and regulation of a Shelduck population. J. Anim. Ecol. 44:201–231.

KERBES, R. H. 1969. Biology and distribution of nesting Blue geese on Koukdjuak Plain, N.W.T. MSc thesis, University of Western Ontario, London, Ontario, Canada.

———, M. A. OGILVIE, AND H. BOYD. 1971. Pink-footed geese of Iceland and Greenland: a population review based on an aerial nesting survey of Thjorsarvar in June 1970. Wildfowl 22:5–17.

KESSEL, B., AND T. J. CADE. 1958. Birds of the Colville River, Northern Alaska. Biol. Papers Univ. Alaska, No. 2.

KING, J. G. 1970. The swans and geese of Alaska's arctic slope. Wildfowl 21:11–17.

KISTCHINSKI, A. A. 1971. Biological notes on the Emperor goose in north-east Siberia. Wildfowl 22:29–34.

KLOPMAN, R. B. 1958. The nesting of Canada geese at Dog Lake, Manitoba. Wilson Bull. 70:168–183.

KOSSACK, C. W. 1960. Breeding habits of Canada geese under refuge conditions. Am. Midl. Nat. 43:627–649.

KUMARI, E. 1971. Passage of the Barnacle goose through the Baltic area. Wildfowl 22:35–43.

LACK, D. 1967. The significance of clutch-size in waterfowl. Wildfowl Trust Ann. Rep. 18: 125–128.

———. 1968. Ecological adaptations for breeding in birds. Methuen, London. 409pp.

LEMIEUX, L. 1959. The breeding biology of the Greater Snow Goose on Bylot Island, Northwest Territories. Can. Field Nat. 73:117–128.

LENSINK, C. J. 1973. Population structure and productivity of Whistling swans on the Yukon Delta, Alaska. Wildfowl 24:21–25.

LYNCH, J. J., AND J. R. SINGLETON. 1964. Winter appraisals of annual productivity in geese and other water birds. Wildfowl Trust Ann. Rep. 15:115–126.

MACINNES, C. D. 1962. Nesting of small Canada geese near Eskimo Point, Northwest Territories. J. Wildl. Mgmt. 26:247–256.

———. 1966. Population behaviour of eastern Arctic Canada geese. J. Wildl. Mgmt. 30:536–553.

———, R. A. DAVIS, R. N. JONES, B. C. LIEFF, AND A. PAKULAK. 1974. Reproductive efficiency of McConnell River Small Canada geese. J. Wildl. Mgmt. 38:686–707.

———, AND B. C. LEIFF. 1968. Individual behaviour and composition of a local population of Canada geese, *in* Canada goose management, ed. R. L. Hine and C. Schoenfeld, Dembar, Madison, pp. 93–101.

———, AND R. K. MISRA. 1972. Predation on Canada goose nests at McConnell River, Northwest Territories. J. Wildl. Mgmt. 36:414–422.

MARTIN, F. W. 1964. Behaviour and survival of Canada geese in Utah. Utah State Dept. Fish Game, Dept. Inform. Bull. 89pp.

MILNE, H. 1974. Breeding numbers and reproductive rate of Eiders at the Sands of Forvie National Nature Reserve, Scotland. Ibis 116: 135–154.

MOREAU, R. E. 1972. The Palaearctic-African bird migration systems. Academic Press, London and New York. 384pp.

NEWTON, I. 1972. Finches. Collins, London. 288pp.

———, AND C. R. G. CAMPBELL. 1975. Breeding of ducks at Loch Leven, Kinross. Wildfowl 26: 28–102.

NEWTON, I., AND R. H. KERBES. 1974. Breeding of Greylag Geese (*Anser anser*) on the Outer Hebrides, Scotland. J. Anim. Ecol. 43:771–783.

NORDERHAUG, M., M. A. OGILVIE, AND R. J. F. TAYLOR. 1964. Breeding success of geese in West Spitzbergen. Wildfowl Trust Ann. Rep. 16:106–110.

NYHOLM, E. S. 1968. Ecological observations on the geese of Spitzbergen. Ann. Zool. Fenn. 2:197–207.

OGILVIE, M. A., AND G. V. T. MATTHEWS. 1969. Brent geese, mudflats and man. Wildfowl 20:119–125.

PAAKSPUU, V. 1972. Present-day status of the Greylag goose populations in the Matsalu Bay, *in* Geese in the USSR, ed. E. Kumari, Tartu. pp. 13–19 Russian, with English summary.

PREVETT, J. P., AND C. D. MACINNES. 1972. The number of Ross' geese in central North America. Condor 74:431–438.

RYDER, J. P. 1967. The breeding biology of Ross's goose in the Perry River region, Northwest Territories. Can. Wildl. Service Rep. Ser. 3. 56pp.

———. 1970. A possible factor in the evolution of clutch size in Ross's goose. Wilson Bull. 82:5–13.

———. 1971. Distribution and breeding biology of the Lesser snow goose in Central Arctic Canada. Wildfowl 22:18–28.

———. 1972. Biology of nesting Ross's geese. Ardea 60:185–215.

SALOMONSEN, F. 1950. The birds of Greenland. Munksgaavd, Copenhagen.

———. 1968. The moult migration. Wildfowl 19:5–25.

SCOTT, P., H. BOYD, AND W. J. L. SLADEN. 1955.

The Wildfowl Trust's second expedition to Central Iceland, 1953. Wildfowl Trust Ann. Rep. 7:63–98.

Uspenski, S. M. 1965*a*. The geese of Wrangel Island. Wildfowl Trust Ann. Rep. 16:126–129.

———. 1965*b*. Die Wildganse Nordeurasians. Wittenburg Lutherstadt, Ziemren.

Witherby, H. F., F. C. R. Jourdain, N. F. Ticehurst, and B. W. Tucker. 1938. The handbook of British birds. Vol. 3. Witherby, London.

Yocum, C. F., and S. W. Harris. 1965. Plumage descriptions and age data for Canada goose goslings. J. Wildl. Mgmt. 29:874–877.

ECOLOGICAL ASPECTS OF THE BLUE-SNOW GOOSE COMPLEX[1]

GRAHAM COOCH,[2] Canadian Wildlife Service, 900-269 Main Street, Winnipeg 1, Manitoba, Canada

The taxonomic relationship of the Blue Goose (*Chen caerulescens caerulescens*) and the Lesser Snow Goose (*Chen hyperborea hyperborea*) has long created controversy among avian systematists, e.g., Blaauw (1908), Soper (1930), Sutton (1932), Manning (1942), and Manning et al. (1956). I believe that the two forms are conspecific and that the species consists of two subspecies; a large form, *Chen caerulescens atlantica,* which has no color phases, and a smaller form, *Chen caerulescens caerulescens,* which is polymorphic and has two clearly defined color phases. The remainder of the discussion is concerned only with the latter race.

Because of slight pleiotropic differences between the phases, reflected especially in nesting and incubation behavior, some may prefer to follow the lead of Manning et al. (1956) and confer subspecific status on *hyperborea.* However, my opinion is that such differences should be considered as dichromatic polymorphs of a single subspecies *Chen c. caerulescens.*

The genetic basis of these color phases is at yet incompletely known and will not be stressed here (cf. Cooch and Beardmore 1959). Color phases are common among arctic vertebrates and in this case appear to be a form of adaptive polymorphism, which under present climatological conditions gives some selective advantages to blue-phase birds. I shall attempt to define some of the ecological factors influencing the genetic shift toward blue-phase birds.

DISTRIBUTION

The distribution of the 14 main breeding concentrations is shown in Fig. 1. All are located on flat, palaeozoic basins, drained by braided deltas and within five miles of salt water, with the exception of Egg River, Banks Island, which is 16 miles inland (McEwen 1958).

The percentage of blue-phase birds within any given population is presently greatest at Bowman Bay, Baffin Island, but is increasing rapidly elsewhere, especially within the Hudson Bay drainage. For example, in 1940 the percentages of blue-phase at each colony were as follows: Bowman Bay, 95; Cape Dominion, 50; Koukdjuak, 20; Boas River, 10; Eskimo Point, trace; Perry River, trace. In 1959 the percentages were: Bowman Bay, 97; Cape Dominion, 85; Koukdjuak, 50; East Bay, 35; Boas River, 30; Eskimo Point, 15; Perry River, 9; Banks Island, trace. Evidence of the westward extension of blue genes is the increased number of blue-phase geese reported in migration in recent years from Alberta and California. Details of the recent distributional changes will be presented elsewhere (Cooch 1960 MS), concomitantly with a discussion of introgression between the phases.

PLUMAGE

Plumage color within populations of *Chen c. caerulescens* ranges from white-phase, having six dark primaries and white alulae, to extremely melanistic blue-phase geese. The extent of this variation is most easily detected at colonies

[1] Originally published in Auk 78(1):72–89, 1961.

[2] Present address: 685 Echo Drive, Ottawa, Ontario K1S 1P2, Canada.

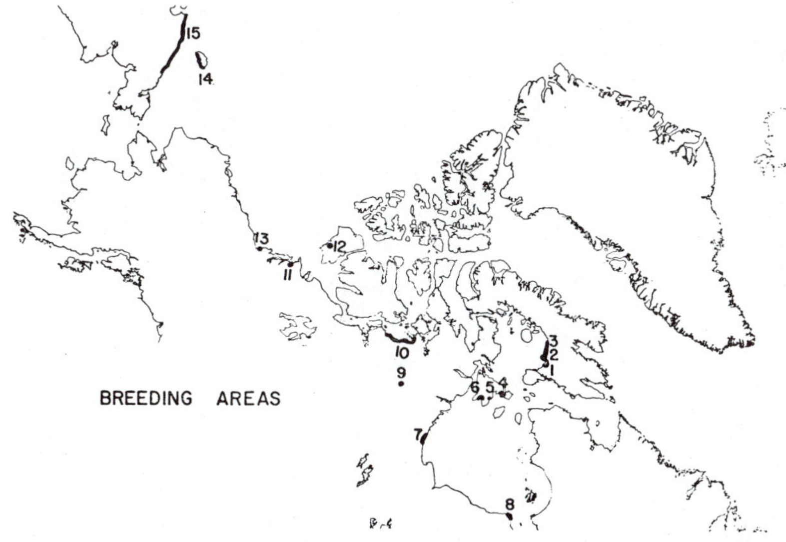

Fig. 1. Location of known major breeding concentrations of *Chen caerulescens caerulescens*. Localities are identified in Table 1.

such as Boas River, where both phases are relatively common. In white-phase birds, a cline of decreasing frequency of dark alulae can be detected northward and westward from Bowman Bay, similar in nature to the blue to white cline mentioned above. Dark alulae seem to be the first indication of the presence of blue genes in what otherwise would appear to be a pure population of white-phase *caerulescens*.

PAIRING

Pairing between phases is common but not random (Cooch and Beardmore 1959). Progeny from all types of mating are equally viable, and no difference in egg fertility has been detected. In areas where predominately blue-phase birds have apparently only recently penetrated, adult male heterozygous blues (white-bellied) mated to dark-alulaed white-phase females have pioneered. In most breeding areas where the populations are mixed and blues are in the minority, blue-phase individuals are increasing within those populations at a rate of from 1 to 2 per cent per annum.

NESTING

No differences have been detected between the phases with regard to the selection of nesting sites, manner of construction, or defense (Cooch 1958). Clutch sizes before predation and other loss are identical, averaging 4.42 eggs per complete attempt for both phases under comparable phenological conditions. This is referred to as the theoretical clutch size, since it would occur only in situations where no egg loss occurred.

Since blue- and white-phase birds are differentially affected by varying phenology, the nature of the nest-initiation curves is of utmost importance in analyzing the observed increase of blue-phase birds. *Chen c. caerulescens* constructs nests over a 10-day period, regardless of the phenology of the season, and 12 days after the first nest has been completed

Table 1. Size and population of the major breeding ground of *Chen caerulescens caerulescens*.

Locality[a]	Latitude	Longitude	Sq. miles	Population	% blue phase
1 Bowman Bay	65°20′N	73°35′W	250	165,000	97
2 Cape Dominion	65°50′N	74°W	240	100,000	85
3 Koukdjuak	66°20′N	73°55′W	200	75,000	50
4 East Bay	64° 0′N	82°10′W	20	20,000	35
5 Bear Cove	63°40′N	84°45′W	1	1,000	30
6 Boas River	63°42′N	85°45′W	30	25,000	30
7 Eskimo Point	60°30′N	94°50′W	25	15,000	14
8 Cape Henrietta Maria	55°10′N	82°50′W	?	25,000	?
9 Beverly Lake	64°50′N	100°10′W	?	?	?
10 Perry River	67°50′N	102°W	?	?	9
11 Anderson River	69°50′N	129°W	?	5,000	0
12 Egg River	71°50′N	124°50′W	16	20,000	TR
13 Kendall Island	69°10′N	136°W	2	5,000	0
14 Wrangel Island	72°N	180°W	?	?	0
15 Siberia	70°N	180°W	?	?	0

[a] Numbers before localities refer to the position of these localities on Fig. 1.

and laid in, all laying is terminated. Both phases begin and end their egg-laying activities within the same 12-day interval.

However, the nature of the nesting curve in terms of new nests begun and eggs laid is different for the two phases under differing phenological conditions. Three types of nesting curves are presented in Fig. 2, representing early (4–7 June, e.g., 1952), "normal" (8–11 June, e.g., 1953), and late or retarded (12–16 June, e.g., 1957, 1959) seasons. The three curves in Fig. 2 are based on all nesting attempts, regardless of phase. The difference between the phases in mean date of nest initiation in retarded seasons is similar to that depicted in Fig. 2, if 1957 represents white-phase and 1952 blue-phase nesting attempts. Data in Table 2 indicate that the increase in activity in the first part of a retarded season is clear cut, and the results of such activity will be apparent later in the paper. Throughout the investigation it has been evident that white-phase birds tend to nest earlier than do blue-phase birds except in a very early season (1952).

In itself, this variation is interesting. But its importance lies in the fact that predation and other forms of nesting loss are greatest early in the season and then quickly subside (Cooch 1956). At Eskimo Point in 1959, 100 per cent of all eggs laid on the first two days of the nest-initiation period were destroyed by Parasitic Jaegers (*Stercorarius parasiticus*) or by flooding. Since white-phase birds tend to nest earlier than do blue-phase birds, this would suggest that more nests and eggs of the former were destroyed. This does not take into account the number of nests completely destroyed, which increases in the same proportion. However, if a season is extremely retarded (after 14 June at Boas River), a higher proportion of white-phase birds is successful because of an inherent difference in the shape of the nesting curve exhibited by the phases—during an early season 50 per cent of white-phase and 75 per cent of blue-phase birds nest within two days of the mean date of nest initiation. Complete disruption of a mjor portion of the nesting pairs would thus affect relatively more blue-phase birds.

Figure 3 shows the effect of retarded seasons on clutch sizes of successful nest-

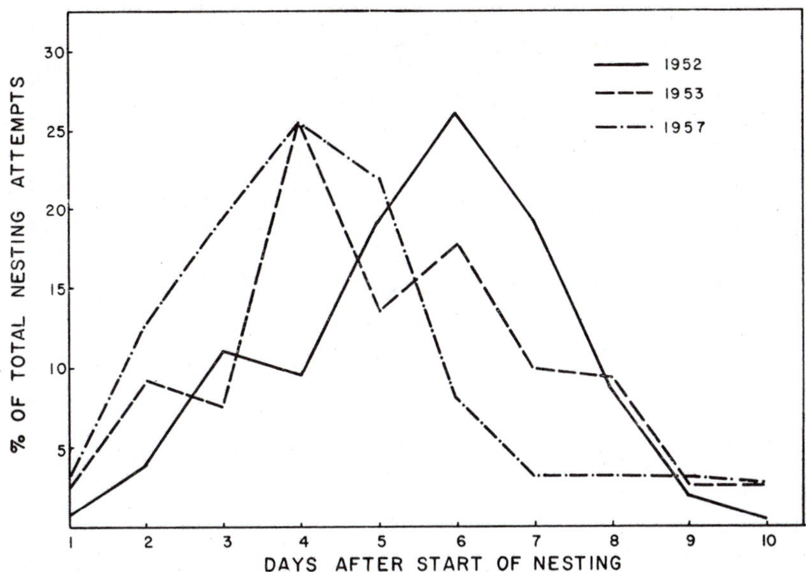

Fig. 2. Number of nesting attempts started on each day of nest initiation period expressed as a per cent of total attempts—data for both phases are combined.

ing attempts of blue- and white-phase birds. In early seasons the nest-initiation curves are nearly identical, and egg losses are also in the same order of magnitude; but as seasons become more retarded, a higher proportion of eggs from white-phase birds are destroyed.

Figure 4 represents the components of nesting loss in different seasons, based on a sample extrapolated to 1,000 eggs. The net effect of a retarded season appears to be that birds physiologically ready to nest early in the season are prevented from doing so because of weather or snow conditions. However, when extrinsic barriers are removed, competition for available nesting space is intensified, and all those birds still capable of nesting attempt to do so simultaneously. This frequently results in a breakdown of territoriality and leads to desertion and dumping of eggs in other nests, with concomitant decrease in intensity of nest defense. In short, in an early season (4 June) 190/1,000 eggs are destroyed before hatching, in a "normal" season (9 June) 365/1,000, and in a retarded season (13 June) 490/1,000. Complete destruction of a clutch causes the birds to enter their postnuptial molt earlier than do successful breeding pairs. No renesting is attempted, nor can it be induced (Cooch 1958).

CLUTCH SIZES

As stated previously, no difference exists between numbers of eggs laid by the

Table 2. Variation in mean date of nest initiation measured in number of days after first nesting attempt.

Year	Pair	First nest	No.	Mean	SD
1952	SXS	4 June	172	5.5	1.77
1953	SXS	9 June	105	4.0	2.28
1959	SXS	8 June[a]	238	3.7	1.92
1952	BXB	4 June	65	5.4	1.67
1953	BXB	9 June	11	4.7	1.96
1959	BXB	8 June[a]	42	4.6	1.83

[a] Data for 1952 and 1953 are from Boas River, for 1959, from Eskimo Point. At Eskimo Point 8 June is the phenological equivalent of 12 June at Boas River. Thus, the comparison of years 1952, 1953, and 1959 is effectively a comparison of early, normal, retarded seasons.

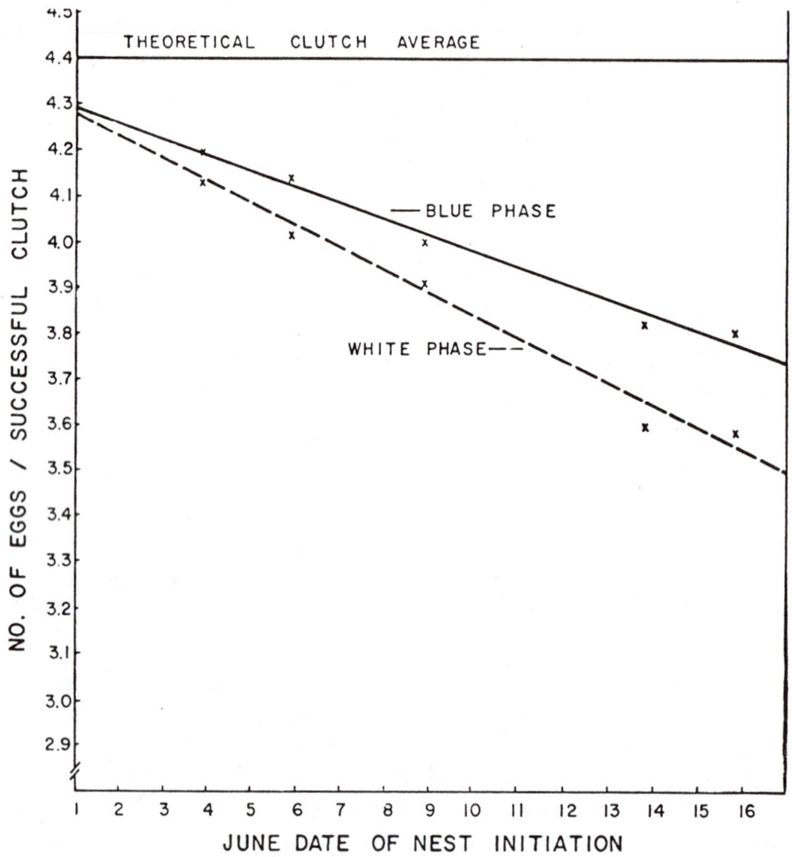

Fig. 3. Average number of eggs per successful clutch showing relationship between relative success of blue-phase and white-phase *caerulescens*, and successively later June date of nest initiation.

various pairing arrangements (BXB, BXW, WXB, or WXW). Significant differences (6 vs. 3) were found, however, between clutches initiated early in the season and those initiated later. In retarded seasons there is less difference (4.8 vs. 3.0) between early and late clutches. Predation and other forms of nesting loss tend to reduce the difference but never obliterate it. In teleological terms, smaller clutches are "necessary" in retarded seasons or at the end of a normal season in order that reproduction be speeded up. Under optimum conditions, *caerulescens* has 105 days in which to complete its reproductive activities. In a retarded season, the last birds to start laying have only 83 days.

Lack (1947) has postulated several theories on the evolutionary significance of clutch size, based mainly on the premise that, in altricial species, availability of food during brood rearing is a limiting factor. In the case of *caerulescens* and its precocial young, that thesis does not seem to hold. Factors limiting brood size are related to mortality caused by the physical nature of the environment and predation.

Birds laying large clutches do not lay

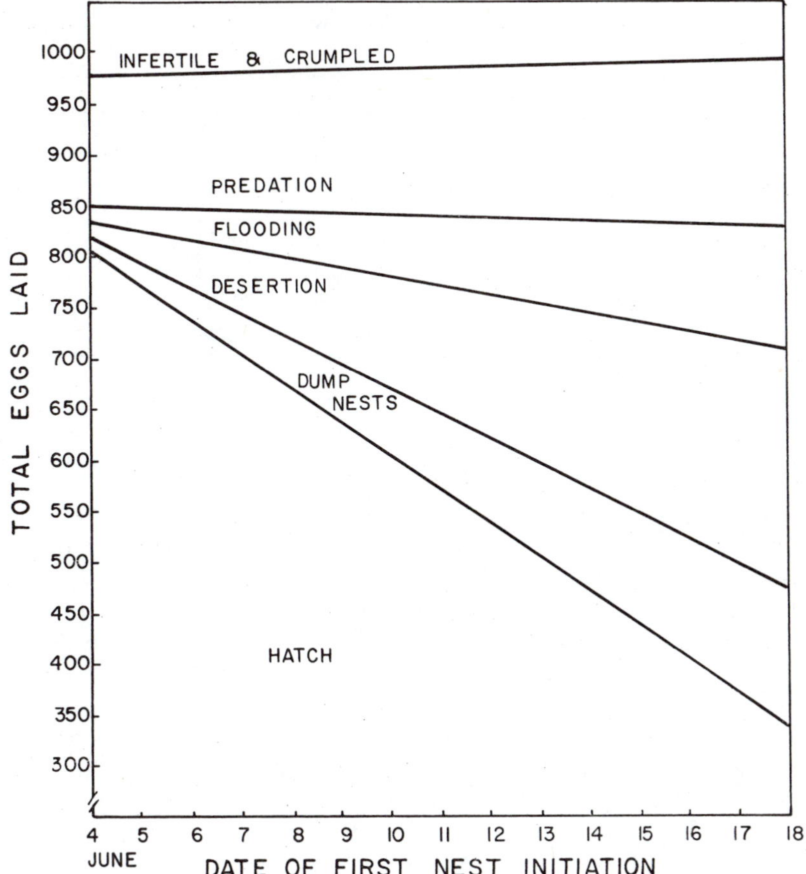

Fig. 4. Schematic presentation of components of nesting loss showing variation associated with variation in date of first nest initiation.

on consecutive days, but after the deposition of the fourth egg, tend to cease laying for two days. As a result nine days are required to lay seven eggs. The most important factor limiting brood size is the phenomenon of interrupted egg laying. Large clutches normally require two days to hatch, but in the event of inclement weather, three or more days may be required. The four eggs that were laid first hatch almost simultaneously. Frequently there is as much as a 96-hour difference in the ages of a seven-gosling brood. As a result, the first hatched are better able to keep up with the adults and do not straggle. The last hatched are weak, tend to straggle, and are unable to compete for brooding space with older members of the brood. The prognosis of survival for such goslings is poor.

There are some data based on serially marked eggs that strongly suggest that, in mixed pairing, white-phase progeny tend to hatch later in any given brood, and are therefore weaker and more susceptible to predation. These data are presented in Table 3. The observed decrease in frequency of white-phase young in mixed broods as the season progresses is presented in Table 4. The decrease noted in

Table 3. Relative proportion of white-phase goslings hatching in 64 serially marked, mixed-clutches, Boas River, 1952, 1953.

Clutch size	N	Egg sequence 1 B	1 W	2 B	2 W	3 B	3 W	4 B	4 W	5 B	5 W	%W
2	9	9	0	7	2							11.1
3	16	16	0	13	3	10	6					18.7
4	21	20	1	17	4	13	8	10	11			28.3
5	18	17	1	15	3	12	6	10	8	8	10	31.1
Total	64	62	2	52	12	35	20	20	19	8	10	26.2
% White		3.1		18.7		36.3		48.7		55.5		

B = blue-phase gosling; W = white-phase gosling.

the 10th week after hatching is partly attributable to selective hunting pressure south of the breeding grounds. Few mixed broods larger than four contain any white-phase young after the 10th week.

The reduction in white-phase goslings in mixed broods is apparently one mechanism by which the percentage of blue-phase birds is increasing. The reverse occurs when both birds of a pair are white-phase geese having dark alulae and laying more than five eggs. In 54 cases observed at Boas River in 1952 and 1953, the last egg laid produced an atypical blue-phase gosling, which eventually became an extreme white-bellied blue-phase adult. The ability of such a gosling to survive the critical posthatch period is slight, and few if any blue goslings are produced by such pairs. Such cases are uncommon except where both phases are relatively abundant.

AUTUMN MIGRATION

The direct differential effect of varying phenological conditions on nest initiation and reproductive success is one basic cause of the observed increase in the proportion of blue-phase birds. The date of nest initiation also affects autumn migration and produces predictable changes from the "norm" (Cooch 1955), which may bear more heavily on one phase than the other.

Figure 5 shows the relationship between date of nest initiation and all other phenological events. Band recoveries indicate that in early breeding seasons individuals of *Chen caerulescens* breeding at Boas River make a nonstop flight from Hudson Bay to Gulf of Mexico. However, when seasons are retarded, a higher percentage of the population interrupts its migration in the midwestern United

Table 4. Changes in phase composition of mixed broods from time of hatching until 12 weeks after hatching, 1952.

Time	Brood size 1	2	3	4	5	6	7	8	Average	% White
Hatch	0	1	3	16	12	1	0	0	4.22	25.5
First week	4	4	6	11	7	2	0	0	3.55	17.9
Tenth week	4	12	8	8	6	1	1	1	3.23	12.5
Twelfth week	3	8	8	6	5	2	0	0	3.33	11.3

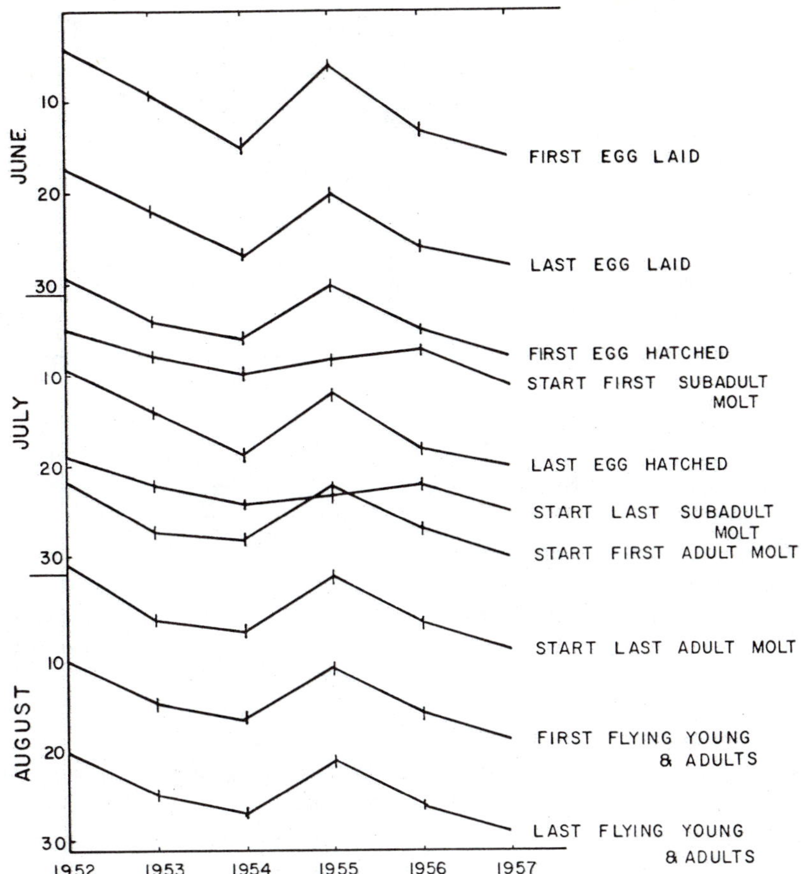

Fig. 5. Chronology of phenological events 1952–57 showing the relationship between date of first egg laying and all other events happening on the breeding grounds.

States. These data are given in Table 5, where recoveries of adult banded birds from northern states are expressed as a percentage of the total adult recoveries from the United States. In moderately retarded seasons, the rate of recovery for white-phase birds is greater than for blue-phase birds. In extremely retarded seasons, relatively more blue-phase birds are taken. This is apparently a result of the pattern of nest initiation: a high percentage of white-phase birds are geese that have failed to produce young that molt early, and that behave as subadults, i.e., make a nonstop flight to the Gulf Coast. Because blue-phase birds nest a little later, some at least are always successful, but since they are retarded by phenological events, their migration is severely interrupted. Following a phenologically early season, approximately 25 per cent of the total population is removed by hunting pressure: but in retarded seasons, the kill increases to nearly 35 per cent, with most of the increment made up of birds shot in the midwestern United States. Because blue-phase birds are in the minority, but are increasing,

Table 5. Variations in the number of bands from adult blue-phase and white-phase geese returned from the United States, 1952–58.

		Northern United States						Southern United States					
		Blue		White		Combined		Blue		White		Combined	
Year	Date[a] June	No.	%	No.	%	No.	%	No.	%	No.	%	No.	%
1952	4	0	0.00	2	11.0	2	5.0	22	100	16	90	38	95
1953	9	10	26.3	41	43.6	51	38.6	28	73.7	53	56.4	81	61.4
1954	14	30	66.6	85	59.0	115	60.8	15	33.3	59	41.0	74	39.2
1955	6	4	12.0	13	19.4	17	17.0	29	88.0	54	80.5	33	83.0
1956	12	19	65.5	46	55.3	65	58.0	10	34.5	37	44.7	47	42.0
1957	16	8	47.0	36	57	44	55.0	9	53.0	27	43.0	36	45.0
1958	12	12	50.0	74	69	86	65.5	12	50.0	33	31.0	45	34.4

[a] Date of first nest initiation.

adult cohorts contain fewer blue-phase birds than do younger cohorts. The increased attrition on breeding adults would speed up the process of eliminating white-phase birds even if hunting pressure were exerted randomly. Since 1952, 33 bands per hundred from white-phase adults have been returned for each 21 per hundred blue-phase bands. It has previously been shown that in the case of juveniles (which contain the highest proportion of blue-phase birds) white-phase goslings are selected against, both by natural and by hunting predation. This is an example of how man can influence the selection of a color phase by hunting pressure alone without changing the ecological aspect of the breeding habitat.

Another factor that influences the spread of blue genes is the distribution pattern of *caerulescens* during breeding, migration, and wintering. Perhaps the most important point is the behavior of the two phases during migration. Five primary aspects of migration apparently affect the recently observed shifts in the frequency of the blue genes. These are:

1. The relatively distinct routes used by the various populations (Fig. 6).
2. The observed tendency of blue-phase birds during migration to filter eastward and white-phase birds to filter westward within the bounds of the population flyway.
3. The tendency of blue-phase birds to make a nonstop flight from James Bay and Hudson Bay to the Gulf of Mexico more frequently than white-phase birds.
4. A greater hunter preference for white-phase birds.
5. Differences in migratory pattern associated with age, breeding success, and phenology.

The first two factors are isolating mechanisms that impede the rapid exchange of genes from one population to another, while the last three factors tend to contribute to selection pressure.

The cline of increasing blue and decreasing white to the north and to the west of Bowman Bay is difficult to explain unless migration by breeding population is considered. Apparently, predominately blue-phase geese have appeared only recently (possibly within the past 50 years) outside of the Baffin Island breeding areas. Salomonsen (1954) has summarized the various types of gene flow, showing lucidly how barriers to the spread of a particular gene need not necessarily be physical, spatial, or behavioral. In the case of *Chen c. caerulescens*,

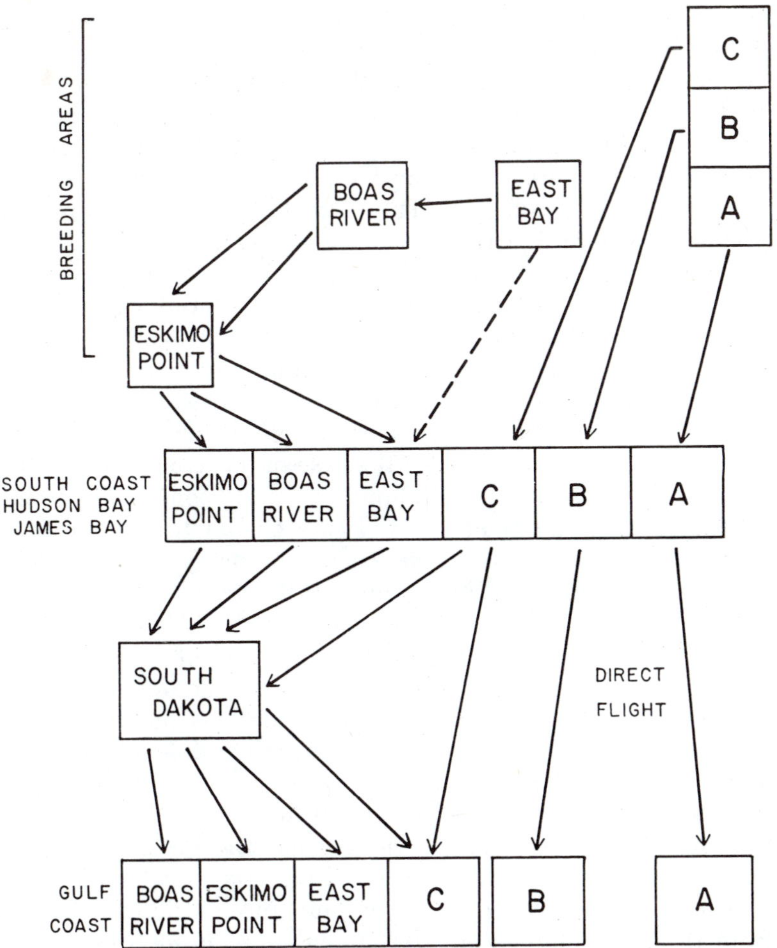

Fig. 6. A schematic presentation of migratory and wintering distribution of six populations of *Chen c. caerulescens* from the Hudson Bay drainage. A = Bowman Bay; B = Cape Dominion; C = Koukdjuak.

the spread of blue genes was impeded by the intrusion of other populations from Baffin Island, between Bowman Bay, and the breeding and wintering populations from Southampton Island and mainland colonies to the west (Fig. 6). Before blue genes from Baffin Island were able to reach Southampton Island, they had to work their way north along the Foxe Basin coast of Baffin Island. This process required not a single generation, but gene movement through a number of generations of geese. This was possible only with an amelioration in climate such as witnessed in the past 50 years. In arctic Canada, this amelioration is mostly found east of a line that runs roughly parallel to the west coast of Hudson Bay (cf. Hare 1955, Ahlmann 1955, Willett 1950, Lysgaard 1950). Although both phases begin and end their nesting activity in the same 12-day period, the relative success of white-phase birds in extremely retarded seasons would imply that northward extension of blue genes was inhibited until climatic amelioration occurred.

In addition, white-phase birds have a shorter incubation period (23.1 days vs. 23.6 days) than do blue-phase birds, and in regions where the length of the breeding season is reduced, this difference would confer an additional advantage to white-phase birds. The more northerly distribution of white-phase birds presently in existence might be taken as an indication that they are still better adapted for a rigorous environment.

Because geese have strong familial ties and during the first year at least these familial ties remain intact, there is reduced opportunity for new genes to be introduced into any population by the progeny from any given breeding season. Adults that have previously nested in a given area return to that area to breed in successive years (Cooch 1958). If the parents survive, their progeny also return, at least in their second year. Since *caerulescens* require two and possibly three years to reach sexual maturity, only those three-year-old individuals that have just reached breeding age or those two-year-old birds that have lost their parents are likely to wander to new areas. Such action by three-year-olds is, however, unlikely, since, during their first summer on the breeding grounds, subadults remain with their parents until the first stages of incubation, then molt on the periphery of the breeding colony. There they associate with second-year and failed-breeding adults. That cohort of the population migrates in mid-August and reaches the wintering areas in early October. Band recoveries from subadults have the same distributional pattern as those from adults and young banded at the same colony. In nearly all extracolonial shifting recorded to date (149/184), birds banded as locals have been involved. This is especially true in shifting between Eskimo Point and Perry River (7/7). Whether the shift occurred when the birds were subadults or of breeding age is not known. Band recoveries from the breeding grounds indicate that fewer than one band in 1,000 will be recovered from an area other than that where it was originally attached. This would indicate that each breeding population is relatively discrete. A larger gene flow can be expected from a continuous colony such as exists along the Foxe Basin coast. However, populations or segments of populations tend to resist movement from one locus into other loci.

Because of this conservatism, the Cape Dominion and Koukdjuak populations acted as a barrier to the spread of blue genes to Southampton Island until frequency of the genes in those populations had reached a level whereby a relatively high proportion of heterozygotes was available for emigration. It will be noted that the Koukdjuak population in winter is only partially allohemic with regard to the East Bay and Southampton Island populations. Once blue-phase birds reached the northern limit of the Baffin Island breeding area in numbers, they were then able to drift over into the East Bay population through association during migration and on the wintering grounds. Once that was accomplished, a major barrier to the spread of blue genes had been overcome.

A second factor that tends to act as an isolating mechanism for blue genes may be described as an observed tendency for like to attract like, especially during migration. This is also of importance on the breeding grounds and would have delayed the northward spread of blue genes on Baffin Island into regions of white abundance. It has been observed at Eskimo Point, Perry River, and Banks Island, that the first blue-phase individuals to colonize a new area are white-bellied blue-phase males mated to white-phase females (mostly with dark alulae). The latter are probably the true pioneers, but being predominately white-phase would not generally be detectable. All known westward shifting from Eskimo Point to Perry River has involved white-phase birds whose alulae color is unknown. As pointed out previously, a pair of dark alulaed white-phase birds having a large clutch (more than 4) are capable of producing an extreme white-bellied blue-phase gosling. It is thus within the realm of possibility that the heterozygotes involved in pioneering have actually been products of this pairing arrangement. This fact in no way changes previous arguments that the frequency of blue genes had to be relatively great before successful emigration could occur.

The fact that like tend to attract like has been clearly demonstrated in band recoveries from the Boas River population. In 1952 and 1953, a total of 13,400 geese were banded there in the ratio of 1 blue-phase to 2.4 white-phase. These birds migrate first to the south coast of Hudson Bay and are hunted from York Factory, Manitoba, eastward to Cape Henrietta Maria, Ontario; few are taken within James Bay proper. As one proceeds east from York Factory, the ratio steadily decreases from 1:2.4 to 1:2.1 at Severn, to 1:1.8 at Winisk, and 1:1 in James Bay. During migration through the United States, recoveries east of the Mississippi are in the ratio of 1:0.8 blue to white, and west of the Mississippi, the ratio is 1:4.0 blue to white. Along the wintering grounds, ratios change from 1:0.5 blue to white at the mouth of the Mississippi River, to 1:2.4 in east Texas, to 1:9.0 in Cameron County, Texas. The greatest rate of band return comes from east Texas, where birds are taken in the same ratio as they occur in the banded population. Segregation on the wintering grounds is important because coastal marshes of Louisiana are relatively less accessible than those of Texas. Blue-phase geese that tend to filter east therefore receive less hunting pressure than do white-phase birds that filter west along the Texas coast. As a result, white-phase birds again tend to be removed from the population at a faster rate than do the blue-phase birds.

SUMMARY

Blue Geese (*Chen c. caerulescens*) breed in 14 major concentrations from Baffin Island to Siberia. Blue Geese and Lesser Snow Geese (*Chen h. hyperborea*) are considered to be conspecific and color phases of *Chen c. caerulescens.* The center of blue-phase abundance is at Bowman Bay, Baffin Island, but the frequency of blue genes is increasing rapidly, especially in the Hudson Bay drainage. This increase is considered to be an example of adaptive polymorphism, which under present conditions favors blue-phase birds. Mixed pairing occurs but is not random. Progeny from mixed pairs are predominately blue-phase and follow Mendelian segregation. Selection pressure in mixed broods is greatest against white-phase goslings, but equal in pure broods of either phase.

No behavioral differences are noted between the phases, but there are slight differences in the nature of the nesting curve, which in some seasons selects against white-phase birds. Basic clutch size is 4.42, but the number of eggs surviving to hatching time is dependent upon the phenology of the season. A factor limiting brood size is interrupted egg laying and resulting differences in age of goslings within the brood. Since, in mixed clutches, the white-phase tend to be laid last, they are the last hatched and thus less likely to survive. Both phases are more successful in early breeding seasons than in retarded ones, but blue-phase birds and mixed pairs are more successful than white-phase birds, except in extremely retarded seasons. Populations breed, migrate, and winter as discrete entities with little gene exchange. White-phase birds are more likely to exhibit an interrupted migration and are therefore more frequently available to hunters in the United States.

ACKNOWLEDGMENTS

Grateful acknowledgment is made to the Arctic Institute of North America and the U.S. Office of Naval Research for financial assistance in 1952 and 1953. Investigations since that time have been sponsored by the Canadian Wildlife Service. The assistance of T. W. Barry, G. M. Stirrett, and G. F. Boyer, Canadian Wildlife Service, T. H. Manning and W. E. Godfrey, National Museum of Canada, J. J. Lynch, U.S. Fish and Wildlife Service, and Dr. O. H. Hewitt, Cornell University, in collecting and analyzing data was of immeasurable help. Dr. D. A. Munro, A. H. McPherson, Canadian Wildlife Service, and Dr. Kenneth C. Parkes, Carnegie Museum, Pittsburgh, read the final manuscript and offered detailed criticism and advice. They are in no way accountable for conclusions drawn by the author.

LITERATURE CITED

AHLMANN, H. W. 1953. Glacier variations and climatic fluctuations. Am. Geogr. Soc. Bowman Mem. Lect., Ser. 3. 51pp.

BLAAUW, F. E. 1908. On the breeding of some of the waterfowl at Gooilust in the year 1903. Ibis 4:67–75, Series 8.

COOCH, F. G. 1955. Observations on the autumn migration of the Blue Goose. Wilson Bull. 67:171–174.

———. 1956. The breeding biology and management of the Northern Eider, *Somateria mollissima borealis*. Typed report, Canadian Wildlife Service. 145pp.

———. 1958. The breeding biology and management of the Blue Goose, *Chen caerulescens*. Unpub. Ph.D. thesis, Cornell University. 235pp.

———. 1960. Recent changes in the distribution of color-phases of *Chen c. caerulescens*. Unpub. MS.

———, AND J. BEARDMORE. 1959. Assortative mating and reciprocal difference in the Blue-Snow Goose complex. Nature 183:1833–1834.

HARE, F. K. 1955. Weather and climate. *In* Geography of the northlands, ed. by D. Good and F. Kimble. Am. Geogr. Soc. Spec. Publ. No. 32. 58–83.

LACK, D. 1947. The significance of clutch size. Ibis 89:303–352 and 90:25–45.

LYSGAARD, L. 1950. On the present climatic variation. Cent. Proc. Meteor. Soc. 206–211.

MANNING, T. H. 1942. Blue and Lesser Snow Geese on Southampton and Baffin Islands. Auk 59:158–175.

———, O. HOHN, AND A. H. MACPHERSON. 1956. The birds of Banks Island. Nat. Mus. of Canada, Bull. 143:1–144.

MCEWEN, E. H. 1958. Observations on the Lesser Snow Goose nesting grounds Egg River, Banks Island. Can. Field-Nat. 72:122–127.

SALOMONSEN, F. 1954. The evolutionary significance of bird migration. Biol. Med. 22:1–62.

SOPER, J. D. 1930. The Blue Goose; an account of its breeding ground, migration, eggs, nests and general habits. Canada Dept. Int., Ottawa. 64pp.

SUTTON, G. M. 1932. The exploration of Southampton Island, Hudson Bay, Part II. Zoology, Section 2: The birds of Southampton Island. Carneg. Mus. Mem., 12:3–268.

WILLETT, H. C. 1950. Temperature trends of the past century. Cent. Proc. Roy. Met. Soc. 195–206.

WHITE GEESE INTERMEDIATE BETWEEN ROSS' GEESE AND LESSER SNOW GEESE[1]

DAVID L. TRAUGER,[2] Department of Zoology and Entomology, Iowa State University, Ames, IA 50010
ALEX DZUBIN, Prairie Migratory Bird Research Centre, Canadian Wildlife Service, Saskatoon, Saskatchewan, Canada
JOHN P. RYDER, Manitoba Wildlife Branch, Winnipeg, Manitoba, Canada

This paper describes white geese with morphological characteristics intermediate between the Ross' Goose (*Chen rossii*) and the Lesser Snow Goose (*Chen hyperborea hyperborea*). Although the parentage of these intermediate white geese is unknown, they apparently represent the hybridization of Ross' Geese and Lesser Snow Geese in the wild.

Johnsgard (1960) analyzed the occurrence of intratribal hybridization among Anserini based primarily on hybrids reported by Gray (1958). Ross' Goose is known to hybridize in captivity with both the Blue Goose (*Chen caerulescens*) and Lesser Snow Goose (Sibley 1938, Gray 1958:53). Intergeneric hybrids have been reported from avicultural collections between the Ross' Goose and the domesticated Greylag Goose (*Anser anser*), Emperor Goose (*Philacte canagicus*), and Cackling Goose (*Branta canadensis minima*) by Sibley (1938), and the Red-breasted Goose (*Branta ruficollis*) by Scott (1951:38). Sibley (1938) also documents the intertribal hybridization of a captive Ross' Goose and Blue-winged Goose (*Cyanochen cyanopterus*). Wild hybrids of Ross' Geese and these species have not been reported.

Scientific nomenclature follows the A.O.U. Check-list (A.O.U. 1957), although taxonomic revisions of the Anatidae suggested by Delacour and Mayr (1945), Delacour (1954), and Johnsgard (1968) have been accepted by an increasing number of waterfowl biologists. Terminology and concepts of hybridization conform with the definitions and descriptions of Mayr (1963) and Short (1969). The term "intermediate" is used to denote the apparent hybrids of Ross' Geese and Lesser Snow Geese.

SOURCE OF INTERMEDIATE WHITE GEESE

Twenty-four intermediate white geese were studied between 1962 and 1968 (Table 1). In addition, information is presented on 18 other intermediates to document further the occurrence and distribution of these geese.

While banding waterfowl at Teo Lake (51°35'N, 109°24'W) near Kindersley, Saskatchewan, on 4 October 1961, Dzubin captured a goose with characteristics intermediate between the Ross' and Lesser Snow Geese. This adult female goose was carefully examined but escaped before measurements were taken. Dzubin trapped and measured a second intermediate goose, an immature female, at Teo Lake on 24 October 1962.

Independently, Trauger captured an adult female intermediate goose on 29 December 1962 while cannon-netting geese at Squaw Creek National Wildlife Refuge (40°05'N, 95°15'W) near Mound City, Missouri. This goose was presented to the U.S. National Museum (No. 479427) where R. H. Manville identified it as a Ross' Goose × Lesser Snow Goose hybrid.

In subsequent years, Dzubin obtained

---

[1] Originally published in Auk 88(4):856–875, 1971.

[2] Address correspondence to this author. Present address: Northern Prairie Wildl. Res. Ctr., P.O. Box 1747, Jamestown, ND 58401.

Table 1. Source of intermediate white geese examined between 1962 and 1968.

Specimen no.	Location[1]	Date	Age[2]	Sex	Present status
1	A	24 October 1962	I	F	Escaped
2	C	29 December 1962	A	F	Specimen No. 479427 U.S. Natl. Mus.
3	C	16 October 1963	I	F	Escaped
4	B	1 October 1964	I	F	Killed in captivity
5	B	1 October 1964	I	F	Specimen No. 1401 Iowa State Univ.
6	B	1 October 1964	I	M	Captivity Iowa
7	A	12 October 1965	A	M	Captivity Saskatchewan
8	C	29 March 1966	A	F	Escaped
9	E	1 July 1966	A	F	Specimen JPR, No. 65–66[3]
10	B	13 October 1966	I	M	Specimen CWS-PMBRC[4]
11	B	13 October 1966	I	M	Specimen CWS-PMBRC
12	F	6 August 1967	A	M	Specimen JPR, No. 50–67
13	F	6 August 1967	A	M	Specimen JPR, No. 51–67
14	B	27 September 1967	A	M	Specimen CWS-PMBRC
15	D	30 September 1967	I	F	Killed by hunter
16	B	30 September 1967	A	M	Specimen CWS-PMBRC
17	B	30 September 1967	I	M	Specimen CWS-PMBRC
18	A	1 October 1967	A	M	Banded and released
19	A	19 October 1967	SA	F	Specimen CWS-Edmonton
20	A	22 October 1967	I	F	Banded and released
21	A	22 October 1967	I	M	Banded and released
22	G	1 August 1968	A	M	Specimen JPR, No. 44–68
23	A	5 October 1968	SA	F	Specimen CWS-PMBRC
24	A	21 October 1968	I	F	Specimen CWS-PMBRC

[1] A, Teo Lake, Kindersley, Saskatchewan (51°35′N, 109°24′W). B, Buffalo Coulee Lake, Coleville, Saskatchewan (51°46′N, 109°18′W). C, Squaw Creek National Wildlife Refuge, Mound City, Missouri (40°05′N, 95°10′W). D, Forney's Lake Game Management Area, Thurman, Iowa (40°45′N, 95°45′W). E, Karrak Lake, District of Keewatin, Northwest Territories (67°15′N, 100°15′W). F, Simpson River, District of Keewatin, Northwest Territories (67°40′N, 100°27′W). G, Perry River, District of Mackenzie, Northwest Territories (67°40′N, 102°15′W).
[2] I, immature; SA, subadult; A, adult.
[3] JPR, J. P. Ryder, Collection.
[4] CWS-PMBRC, Canadian Wildlife Service, Prairie Migratory Bird Research Centre, Saskatoon, Saskatchewan.

data on 15 additional intermediate geese in western Saskatchewan (Table 1). These geese were cannon-netted along with Ross', Lesser Snow, and White-fronted Geese (*Anser albifrons*) at Teo Lake and Buffalo Coulee Lake (51°46′N, 109°18′W) near Coleville, Saskatchewan. Nine of these intermediates were preserved as specimens, three were held in captivity, and three were banded and released.

H. H. Burgess provided two additional intermediate geese for study from northwestern Missouri (Table 1). One was trapped at Squaw Creek National Wildlife Refuge in October 1963; the other was found among 131 Lesser Snow and Blue Geese that struck a power line near Craig, Missouri (40°12′N, 95°24′W) in March 1966. Although several intermediate geese were seen on Squaw Creek National Wildlife Refuge during migration periods between 1963 and 1968, no additional specimens were obtained. However, L. Bates measured and photographed an immature female intermediate goose a hunter shot on 30 September 1967 at Forney Lake Game Management Area (40°45′N, 95°45′W) near Thurman in southwestern Iowa.

During February 1968 refuge personnel trapped two intermediate geese at Sabine National Wildlife Refuge (29°55′N, 93°25′W) near Cameron in southwestern Louisiana (J. M. Valentine, Jr., pers. comm.; James 1968). These geese were banded, photographed, and released. As many as four additional intermediate geese were seen near the banding site at Sabine National Wildlife Refuge by J. J. Lynch and K. McCartney between 23 January and 28 February 1968.

While inspecting flocks of Lesser Snow and Blue Geese for neck-collared individuals, J. P. Prevett (pers. comm.) made two definite sightings of intermediate geese. On 24 October 1968, he saw a family group consisting of an adult intermediate goose, and adult Ross' Goose, and four young at Sand Lake National Wildlife Refuge (45°45′N, 98°25′W) near Columbia, South Dakota. He also identified an adult intermediate goose on 20 November 1968 at Plattsmouth Waterfowl Management Area (41°05′N, 95°55′W) near Plattsmouth, Nebraska.

Ryder has observed intermediate white geese on the breeding grounds at three locations in the central Arctic (Table 1). He collected an adult female in a nesting colony of Ross' Geese at Karrak Lake, Northwest Territories (67°15′N, 100° 15′W) in July 1966 and trapped eight adult males while banding geese on the Simpson River, Northwest Territories (67°40′N, 100°27′W) in August 1967. Six of these geese were banded and released, two were collected. In 1968 Ryder studied a nesting pair of intermediate geese at Karrak Lake during June and July. This pair was successful in bringing off a brood of three goslings. He also collected another intermediate while banding Ross' Geese on the Perry River, Northwest Territories (67°40′N, 102°15′W) in August 1968. Intermediate geese are not restricted to the central arctic during the breeding season. In August 1967 J. P. Prevett and C. D. MacInnes (pers. comm.) reported trapping and banding an adult female intermediate goose accompanied by a brood on the McConnell River delta (60°50′N, 94°25′W) near Eskimo Point, Northwest Territories.

DESCRIPTION OF INTERMEDIATE WHITE GEESE

Measurements were made of 12 adult (including subadult) and 12 immature intermediate white geese following methods described by Palmer (1962:5) and the Canadian Wildlife Service (1963). These measurements were compared with similar data from 79 adult and 80 immature Ross' Geese, and 68 adult and 71 immature Lesser Snows obtained during the 1965 fall migration in western Saskatchewan. Although considerable overlap was found among mensural characteristics, intermediate geese were generally larger than Ross' Geese and smaller than Lesser Snow Geese for all age and sex categories (Table 2).

Heads and Bills.—Heads and bills most strikingly showed the intermediate nature of these geese in comparision with Ross' and Lesser Snow Geese (Fig. 1). Heads of intermediate geese are not so massive or angular in shape as those of Lesser Snow Geese nor as diminutive and rounded as in Ross' Geese. Feathers of the lores meet the base of the upper mandible in a slightly rounded arc in intermediate geese, whereas this juncture of feathers and mandible forms a straight line in Ross' Geese and a sharply curved arc in Lesser Snow Geese (Fig. 1).

Bills or intermediate geese are markedly shorter than bills of Lesser Snow Geese and are slightly longer than bills of Ross' Geese (Table 2). Culmen measurements of intermediate geese and Ross' Geese overlap, but measurements of the culmen for Lesser Snows and intermediate geese do not. Bills of inter-

Table 2. Comparison of measurements (mm) and weights (g) of intermediate white geese with Lesser Snow and Ross' Geese.

Age and sex	Culmen (exposed)			Tarsus (total)			Middle toe			Flat wing			Total length			Weight		
	Ross'	Inter.[1]	Snow	Ross'	Inter.	Snow	Ross'	Inter.	Snow	Ross'	Inter.	Snow	Ross'	Inter.	Snow	Ross'	Inter.	Snow
Adult male																		
No.	47	7	32	47	7	32	47	7	32	47	4	32	47	4	32	47	7	32
Min.	39	40	53	80	87	91	47	54	59	371	414	428	604	657	700	1,580	1,680	2,030
Max.	47	48	61	91	92	108	57	59	70	411	419	474	658	678	776	2,010	2,160	2,860
Mean	41.9	45.1	56.2	84.8	89.6	98.4	51.5	57.1	63.2	394.8	415.8	449.0	625.4	668.8	739.7	1,780.2	1,955.7	2,403.1
SE	0.3	1.2	0.4	0.4	0.8	0.7	0.3	0.8	0.4	1.3	1.2	2.0	1.8	4.4	3.7	14.6	81.5	34.8
SD	1.7	3.1	2.2	2.6	2.1	3.7	2.2	2.1	2.5	8.6	2.4	11.4	12.4	8.8	20.7	99.9	216.0	196.6
CV	4.0	6.8	3.9	3.1	2.3	3.7	4.1	3.7	3.9	2.1	0.6	2.5	1.9	1.3	2.8	5.6	11.0	8.1
Adult female																		
No.	32	5	36	32	4	36	32	5	36	32	4	36	32	4	36	32	4	36
Min.	37	45	50	74	84	90	44	54	58	362	382	413	571	570	678	1,390	1,334	1,890
Max.	44	50	59	85	90	101	53	61	67	391	404	461	616	662	742	1,840	2,240	2,590
Mean	39.0	46.6	53.5	79.9	86.5	94.7	49.4	56.2	61.7	376.0	393.5	430.2	591.2	626.3	708.4	1,583.1	1,778.5	2,274.4
SE	0.3	0.9	0.4	0.5	1.5	0.5	0.4	1.3	0.4	1.5	4.5	1.7	2.1	19.7	2.9	20.5	194.9	32.5
SD	1.5	2.1	2.2	3.0	3.0	2.7	2.3	2.9	2.1	8.3	9.0	9.9	11.9	39.4	17.4	116.0	389.7	194.9
CV	3.7	4.5	4.1	3.7	3.5	2.8	4.5	5.3	3.3	2.1	2.3	2.3	2.0	6.3	2.4	7.3	21.9	8.5
Immature male																		
No.	44	5	36	44	5	36	44	5	36	44	5	36	44	5	36	44	5	36
Min.	36	39	51	71	81	92	46	49	60	350	370	402	561	590	683	1,100	1,480	1,840
Max.	42	48	60	93	96	104	54	59	69	392	414	455	625	658	733	1,850	2,170	2,530
Mean	39.3	44.0	55.9	83.4	88.6	98.1	50.3	55.0	63.1	373.0	392.2	424.6	597.8	631.2	712.6	1,556.1	1,834.0	2,210.3
SE	0.2	1.5	0.4	0.5	2.7	0.5	0.3	1.7	0.4	1.4	6.9	1.6	2.3	11.4	2.3	22.7	131.3	30.3
SD	1.5	3.4	2.4	3.5	6.0	3.0	2.1	3.8	2.1	9.1	15.6	9.9	14.9	25.4	13.8	150.7	293.6	181.9
CV	3.7	7.7	4.2	4.2	6.7	3.0	4.2	6.9	3.2	2.4	4.0	2.3	2.4	4.0	1.9	9.6	16.0	8.2
Immature female																		
No.	36	7	35	36	5	35	36	6	35	36	7	35	36	6	35	36	7	35
Min.	34	39	49	72	83	88	45	53	56	347	377	384	546	578	643	1,250	1,077	1,790
Max.	41	46	56	86	87	99	55	57	66	380	402	434	592	635	710	1,640	1,880	2,350
Mean	37.9	42.9	52.6	78.9	85.2	93.5	48.4	55.2	61.3	360.9	386.9	409.0	568.3	623.2	679.7	1,465.0	1,556.3	2,030.0
SE	0.3	0.9	0.3	0.5	0.7	0.5	0.3	0.6	0.4	1.3	3.3	1.9	2.2	9.1	2.4	15.6	109.6	20.9
SD	1.6	2.5	1.9	2.8	1.5	2.8	2.0	1.5	2.3	7.9	8.6	11.4	13.4	22.2	14.3	93.8	289.9	123.4
CV	4.2	5.8	3.6	3.5	1.8	2.9	4.1	2.7	3.7	2.2	2.2	2.7	2.3	3.6	2.1	6.4	18.6	6.0

[1] In spite of small sample sizes, calculations of SD, SE, and CV were made to facilitate comparison.

Fig. 1. Comparison of heads and bills of adult Ross' (left), Intermediate, and Lesser Snow Geese. Note narrow tomia, slim mandible, and laterally, slightly rounded fusion of feathers with the upper mandible in the intermediate.

mediates are more slender and less massive in shape when compared with Lesser Snows but more elongate than bills of Ross' Geese.

Bill coloration of immature intermediate geese trapped in the fall closely resemble the bill coloration of young Ross' Geese. The sides of the upper mandible are gray with bright pink anterior to the nostril and on the dorsal surface. The lower mandible is generally pinkish-gray. Lesser Snow Geese normally have gray or black mandibles in autumn. The mandibles of adult intermediates are dark pink with a greenish-gray or bluish-gray area near the base of the upper mandible. This area of pigmentation generally is not as dark nor as extensive as in Ross' Geese and shows no evidence of swelling.

Warty protuberances between the nostrils and base of the upper mandible, characteristic of Ross' Geese, are reduced or absent on the bills of intermediate geese. Lesser Snows lack coloration, swellings, or protuberances on the upper mandible. Mandibles of both immature and adult intermediate geese have conspicuous black tomia, a character absent in Ross' Geese but distinctive of Lesser Snows. The black tomia of intermediates forms a thin (6–8 mm) "smile patch" about half as wide as the broad "grinning patch" of Lesser Snow Geese (Fig. 1).

Legs and Feet.—Legs and feet of intermediate geese are markedly smaller than those of Lesser Snows and are more delicate as in Ross' Geese. Although tarsal measurements overlap between intermediate geese and Ross' Geese, measurements of the tarsus are consistently larger in intermediates and overlap only slightly with comparable measurements in Lesser Snows (Table 2). Midtoe measurements are relatively larger in relation to tarsal measurements in intermediate geese, overlapping less with Ross' Geese and more with Lesser Snows. Thus, intermediate geese tend to have comparatively shorter legs than Lesser Snows and larger feet than Ross' Geese.

Coloration of legs and feet of adult intermediate geese is deep pink as in adult Ross' Geese rather than red as in adult Lesser Snow Geese. In immature intermediates, leg and foot coloration also closely resembles Ross' Goose immatures. In October legs are dark gray with

Table 3. Trends in wintering populations of Lesser Snow and Ross' Geese in North America.[1]

Winter	Lesser Snow Geese	Ross' Geese
1956–57	641,000	7,930
1957–58	617,000	12,800
1958–59	600,600	15,600
1959–60	657,200	18,000
1960–61	726,400	23,050
1961–62	732,200	27,920
1962–63	857,300	25,250
1963–64	830,200	32,450
1964–65	826,300	31,880
1965–66	752,400	30,400
1966–67	966,400	31,400

[a] After Dzubin (1965) and Lynch (1967, 1968).

light tan on webs and along toes in intermediates immatures whereas this coloration of legs and feet in Lesser Snow immatures develops during January.

Bodies and wings.—Intermediate geese are smaller and slimmer than Lesser Snows but larger than Ross' Geese. These differences in body size and shape are reflected in total length measurements and weights (Table 2). Maximum measurements of total length in Ross' Geese overlap with minimum measurements for intermediate geese, but total length measurements in Lesser Snow Geese and intermediate geese do not overlap. Total length measurements are particularly influenced by the relative length of the neck in intermediates. Intermediate geese have longer necks than Ross' Geese but shorter necks than Lesser Snow Geese in relation to overall body size.

Measurements of flattened wing show wingspread of intermediate geese greater than in Ross' Geese but considerably less than in Lesser Snows (Table 2). Although flat wing measurements overlap in immature intermediates and Lesser Snows, they do not in adults. Flat wing measurements in both adult and immature intermediate and Ross' Geese overlap.

Weights.—Although body weight provides the poorest criterion for distinguishing intermediate geese from Lesser Snow and Ross' Geese, weights reflect this bird's intermediate size (Table 2). Weights of intermediate geese average less than Lesser Snow Geese and more than Ross' Geese in spite of extreme variation in weight related to differences in seasonal status, i.e. breeding, molting, migrating, and wintering.

Plumages.—Immature intermediate white geese exhibit considerable variation in plumage coloration. Specimens examined had plumages ranging from the typical plumage of immature Lesser Snows to the typical plumage of immature Ross' Geese. In general, immature intermediates have more white feathering than Lesser Snows and more gray feathering than Ross' Geese of the same age. Plumages of adult intermediates are identical to plumages of adult Lesser Snow and Ross' Geese. Ferrous staining often observed in Lesser Snow Geese is absent from plumages of intermediate geese as in Ross' Geese.

ORIGIN OF INTERMEDIATE WHITE GEESE

The occurrence of white geese with morphological characteristics intermediate between the Ross' Goose and Lesser Snow Goose suggests either the hybridization of these species in the wild or the existence of a heretofore undescribed subspecies of white goose. Two recent observations of interbreeding involving Ross' and Lesser Snow Geese support the hypothesis that the intermediate geese are hybrids. Ryder observed a female Ross' Goose mated with a male Lesser Snow Goose at Karrak Lake, Northwest Territories, in 1967. During June this pair established a nest with two eggs on the largest nesting island. One egg hatched and a deep yellow-colored gosling was seen with the pair in early July. In late June 1968, J. P. Prevett (pers. comm.) found a nest with two eggs attended by a female Lesser Snow Goose and a male Ross' Goose on the McConnell River delta near Eskimo Point, Northwest Territories; both eggs hatched in early July. Hence fertile matings of Ross' Geese and Lesser Snow Geese have occurred in the wild. White geese with intermediate characteristics most likely represent hybrid offspring of these species.

BREAKDOWN OF ISOLATING MECHANISMS

An apparent breakdown of isolating mechanisms between the Lesser Snow and the Ross' Goose has resulted in the hybridization of these species in the wild. Undoubtedly, several factors have contributed to the loss of natural barriers preventing interbreeding, but recent changes in the distribution and abundance of Ross' Geese and Lesser Snow Geese seem particularly important.

Dzubin (1965:525) and Ryder (1967) have recently reviewed the population status of the Ross' Goose. During the past 20 years this species has apparently increased from an estimated 2,000 in 1949 (Hanson et al. 1956:55) to more than 30,000 in 1967 (Lynch 1967:19). Although MacInnes (1964) suggested that at least part of this increment was due to an increase in effort expended to study these birds and an expansion of the wintering areas censused by waterfowl biologists, the increase in the Ross' Goose population has paralleled ($r = +0.815$) an increase in the number of Lesser Snow Geese (Table 3). These population increases have occurred during a period of climatic amelioration in arctic Canada (Hare 1955; Cooch 1961, 1963) and may reflect a series of extremely favorable breeding seasons. Severe weather, particularly late seasons, is a major factor governing the productivity of arctic nesting geese (Barry 1962, 1964), including Ross' Geese (Hanson et al. 1956:53; Ryder 1964, 1967:45), and Lesser Snow and Blue Geese (Cooch 1961, 1964; Uspenski 1965).

Concomitant with the increase in continental populations of Ross' Goose, apparent changes have occurred in this species distribution. Although the Ross' Goose and the Lesser Snow Goose were apparently isolated geographically during the Pleistocene (Ploeger 1968:97), these species are now broadly sympatric throughout the Canadian Arctic (Barry 1964). Ross' Goose has been considered a relict species (Amadon 1953, Johansen 1956:98) restricted in its distribution to a narrow migratory route between nesting colonies in the Perry River region of the central Canadian Arctic and wintering grounds in the interior valleys of California (see Delacour 1954:134, Van Tyne and Berger 1959:191). Recently Ross' Geese have been seen nesting in colonies of Lesser Snow and Blue Geese in the eastern Arctic on Southampton Island and at the McConnell River, Northwest Territories (Cooch 1954, Barry and Eisenhart 1958, MacInnes and Cooch 1963), and in the western Arctic on Banks Island, Northwest Territories (Manning et al. 1956, Barry 1960). Whether these reports of Ross' Geese from areas other than the Perry River region represent extensions of the distributional range of this species or reflect increased activity by waterfowl biologists is unknown, but Sutton (1932), Manning (1942), and Bray (1943) did not report Ross' Geese in the eastern Arctic, and the Eskimos of Southampton Island have no name for this species (Cooch 1954). Furthermore,

Cooch (pers. comm.) states that moderate-sized breeding colonies of 50–100 Ross' Geese now exist at several locations in the eastern Arctic. He believes that these colonies are either new or, if Ross' Geese were present in the past, their numbers were so small as to be insignificant.

In addition, changes have apparently occurred in the distribution of Ross' Geese during migration and on wintering areas. Dzubin (1965) documented the transposition of the major migratory pathway of this species from central Alberta to western Saskatchewan. This eastward shift in the Ross' Goose migration route after 1960 was preceded by an eastward movement of Lesser Snow Geese about 1955. Recently Trauger (MS) summarized published (Buller 1955, Smart 1960, MacInnes and Cooch 1963, Moyle 1964, Sweet and Robertson 1966, and others) and unpublished records of Ross' Geese outside this species' traditional range east of the Rocky Mountains. Since 1960, Ross' Geese have been reported with increasing frequency in the Mississippi and Central Flyways. The upshot of these events has been increased interspecific contact between the Ross' Goose and the Lesser Snow Goose.

Because courtship, pair formation, and copulation in the Ross' Goose apparently take place on the wintering grounds and during the spring migration (Ryder 1967:21), recent changes in the distribution and abundance of this species have provided increased opportunities for interbreeding with the Lesser Snow. Trauger (MS) estimates that 200 to 400 Ross' Geese annually winter throughout the Mississippi and Central Flyways, particularly with large flocks of Lesser Snow and Blue Geese in Louisiana, Texas, and New Mexico. These Ross' Geese are isolated from the main wintering concentrations of this species in central California. Thus the relative scarcity of conspecific mates increases the probability of Ross' Geese mating with Lesser Snow Geese.

Certain factors are known to facilitate the breakdown of isolating mechanisms between closely related species. One important factor is the rarity of conspecific mates when individuals of a species occur beyond the principal range of the species or in areas without an adequate number of suitable mates of the same species (Mayr 1963:127–128). In the absence of conspecific individuals, the instinctive mating drive overcomes the inhibitory effect of incorrect species recognition, and individuals of different species form mixed pairs (Sibley 1961). This appears to be one of the mechanisms involved in the hybridization of Ross' Geese and Lesser Snow Geese. As courtship displays are similar among all the true geese (Delacour and Mayr 1945:9, Delacour 1954:94, Johnsgard 1965:25), there would be few behavioral barriers preventing pair formation in these closely related species. Although the incidence of these interspecies matings is not known, it does occur. In addition to the two observations of Ross' Geese mated with Lesser Snow Geese on the breeding grounds, Refuge Manager R. W. Rigby (pers. comm.) photographed a Ross' apparently mated with a Lesser Snow at Bosque del Apache National Wildlife Refuge near San Antonio, New Mexico.

The unusually late spring of 1967 provided insight to another possible mechanism facilitating the hybridization of Lesser Snow and Ross' Geese. Inclement weather delayed the arrival and nest initiation of both species at Karrak Lake, Northwest Territories. When the snow melted exposing the nesting habitat, Ryder noted considerable interaction between these species as nests were established. Later he found 16 nests containing eggs of both Ross' Geese and Lesser Snow Geese while studying 265 Ross' and Lesser Snow Goose nests during June on the largest nesting island. In early July, Trauger and J. B. Gollop found four additional mixed clutches on another island while determining clutch sizes in 155 Ross' and Lesser Snow Goose nests. With the exception of one nest, the incubating female of these mixed clutches was a Lesser Snow. Apparently Ross' Geese were displaced by Lesser Snows from nests established in preferred habitat. Ryder (1969) estimated more than twice as many Ross' than Lesser Snow Geese at Karrak Lake. Dump nesting by both species also may have occurred.

At present Ross' Geese nest in association with Lesser Snow Geese in at least 18 colonies in the central Arctic (Ryder 1969) and in 4 colonies in the eastern and western Arctic (Barry 1964; Cooch, pers. comm.). The incidence of mixed clutches of Ross' and Lesser Snow Goose eggs is unknown in other nesting colonies. It is also not certain if mixed clutches occur only in years when late seasons delay nesting in both species and provoke acute interspecific competition for preferred nesting sites. Perhaps a few mixed clutches are formed each year.

In context with the behavioral characteristics of the Anserini (Delacour and Mayr 1945:8–9, Delacour 1954:51, Johnsgard 1965:24–25), the occurrence of mixed clutches of Lesser Snow and Ross' Goose eggs has important implications as a possible mechanism contributing to the hybridization of these species. It is possible that goslings of Lesser Snow Geese or Ross' Geese hatched in nests of the opposite species become imprinted to the wrong species-specific characteristics. These morphological features and behavior patterns would be reinforced by the strong family bonds typical of this group, as families migrate and winter as a unit. In geese the young apparently remain with the parents until the beginning of a new breeding season.

Although detailed comparative studies of the ecological and behavioral differences between the Ross' and Lesser Snow Geese have not been undertaken, evidence suggests that few barriers to interbreeding exist other than imprinting to morphological and behavioral characteristics of the parents. Because plumage patterns are similar in both species, the shape of the heads and bills appear to provide the most significant species-specific characteristics in the Ross' Goose and the Lesser Snow Goose. The shape and coloration of the bill may be particularly important characteristics for species recognition in these geese. Johnsgard (1965) notes that hybridization is most likely to occur if the reproductive behavior is nearly identical in two species. Courtship displays in geese are simple and subtle and vary little among the species (Johnsgard 1963). Thus a Ross' Goose hatched in a Lesser Snow Goose nest could reach sexual maturity with little association with species-specific characteristics of its own species. The selection of a Lesser Snow as a mate and the production of hybrid offspring would be the ultimate natural consequence of mixed clutches whether competition for nesting habitat or dump nesting was the cause.

Interspecific brood adoptions (Wintle 1968) and promiscuous copulations (Smith 1968) observed in other waterfowl species are recognized as other possible mechanisms that could lead to the production of hybrid offspring of Ross' and Lesser Snow Geese, but these phenom-

Table 4. Relative abundance of intermediate white geese.

Location	Year	Number			
		Intermediate geese	Lesser Snow Geese	Blue Geese	Ross' Geese
Saskatchewan	1961	1	412		256
Saskatchewan	1962	1	227	1	762
Missouri	1962	1	342	348	
Missouri	1963[1]	1	772	370	
Saskatchewan	1964	3	932		793
Saskatchewan	1965	1	197		218
Missouri	1966	1	47	84	
Saskatchewan	1966	2	35		92
Northwest Territories	1967	8	10	4	927
Saskatchewan	1967	7	1,436	1	1,202
Iowa	1967	1	243	196	
Louisiana	1968	2	202	655	
Northwest Territories	1968	1	186	7	551
Saskatchewan	1968	2	1,448		670
Total		32	6,489	1,666	5,471

[1] No intermediates trapped in Saskatchewan in 1963, although 263 Lesser Snow and 333 Ross' Geese handled.

ena are normally intraspecific rather than interspecific when they occur in the wild. The shortage of suitable mates on the wintering grounds and the occurrence of mixed clutches on the breeding grounds appear to be the most important factors contributing to the breakdown of isolating mechanisms and the subsequent hybridization of Ross' and Lesser Snow Geese.

SIGNIFICANCE OF INTERMEDIATE WHITE GEESE

To appraise the significance of the intermediate white geese, a quantitative index of their relative abundance was needed. As intermediates were trapped along with Ross' Geese, Lesser Snow Geese, and Blue Geese for banding, the total capture of these geese provides data for estimating the total number of intermediate geese in the Lesser Snow and Ross' Goose populations (Table 4). Geese were captured with a cannon-net trap in Saskatchewan, Missouri, and Louisiana and in a corral drive trap in the Northwest Territories. The 1966 Missouri data are based on geese found killed or injured in the power line incident, and the 1967 Iowa data are based on geese checked a controlled public hunting area.

A total of 32 intermediate geese was found in a sample of 6,489 Lesser Snows and 5,471 Ross' Geese between 1961 and 1968 (Table 4). These data suggest a ratio of one intermediate goose to 203 Lesser Snows or one intermediate goose to 171 Ross' Geese. To estimate the total number of intermediates in the continental populations of Lesser Snow and Ross' Geese, the mean population of each species was determined for the 1961–68 period. Mean populations for these species were calculated from data presented in Table 3 and by Lynch (1968), but populations for Ross' Geese in 1967 and 1968 and Lesser Snow Geese in 1968 were unavailable. Continental wintering populations averaged 807,600 for the Lesser Snow Goose and 29,880 for the Ross' Goose during this period. Based on the apparent incidence of intermediate geese, estimates ranged from 175 intermediates using the Ross' Goose population to 3,978 intermediates using the Lesser Snow population.

The validity of these estimates depends on the following two assumptions: (1) The number of Lesser Snow and Ross' Geese in the sample is representative of the total populations of these species, and (2) the total number of intermediate geese in the sample is representative of the actual number of intermediates occurring in Lesser Snow and Ross' Goose populations. Because the proportion of Ross' Geese in relation to Lesser Snow Geese in the sample is greater than the relative proportion of these species in their continental wintering populations, the first assumption is not satisfied. Therefore it is believed that the estimated number of intermediate geese is low using the Ross' Goose data and high using the Lesser Snow Goose data.

When Ryder spent the 1965–66 winter studying Ross' Geese on the California wintering grounds he saw no intermediate geese, but he alerted waterfowl biologists to the existence of intermediates and solicited their assistance in obtaining specimens. Since then no intermediate geese have been identified in California where thousands of geese are checked in hunter's bags on state public hunting areas (F. M. Kozlik, pers. comm.). Theoretically hybrids should be rarest where the parent species are abundant and commonest where one species is rare (Johnsgard 1967). Therefore intermediate geese apparently are associated with geese of the Mississippi and Central Flyways, although this does not preclude the possibility of intermediate geese being observed in the Pacific Flyway in the future.

Hence the Lesser Snow Goose population of the Mississippi and Central Flyways between 1961 and 1967 was thought to provide a better basis for estimating the number of intermediate geese. During this period, the Gulf population of Lesser Snow Geese has ranged from 191,200 to 373,300 and has comprised 26 percent to 45 percent of the continental population of this species (Lynch 1968). The mean population of 288,400 Lesser Snow Geese was used to estimate the number of intermediate geese in these flyways. At the apparent rate of one intermediate goose to 200 Lesser Snows, an average of 1,442 intermediates has occurred in the Mississippi and Central Flyways each year between 1961 and 1968. This represents 0.5 percent of the Lesser Snow Goose population in these flyways and less than 0.2 percent of the continental population. Yet if 1,442 is a valid estimate, the intermediate goose population is 4.8 percent of the Ross' Goose population, suggesting a fairly high rate of hybridization.

Although the rate of hybridization appears to be increasing (Table 4), whether the increase in the number of intermediates is real or apparent is not known. This trend may merely reflect a larger number of observers familiar with intermediate geese and a greater effort made to identify them. Considerable evidence suggests that the hybridization of the Lesser Snow and Ross' Geese is a relatively recent event in view of the recent changes in the populations and distributions of these species. Nevertheless this does not rule out the possibility that these species crossed in the past but the hybrids were not recognized. Recent emphasis on banding waterfowl and the development of trapping techniques, particularly the cannon-net trap, have allowed waterfowl biologists to capture and handle large numbers of geese. Doubtless these factors contributed to the discovery of the Lesser Snow × Ross' Goose hybrids.

Although someone familiar with the characteristics of intermediate geese could make an accurate identification of these birds in the field, recent variability among intermediate geese will make this more difficult. Apparently, this variability is due to the presence of F_2 and F_3 generation hybrids and backcrosses in flocks of Lesser Snow and Ross' Geese. According to Mayr (1963), first-generation (F_1) hybrids are generally intermediate between the parental species and tend to be uniform in most characteristics, while F_2 hybrids generally exhibit increased variability. Phillips (1915, 1921) found that many recombinant individuals closely approached parental characteristics in F_2 and backcross generations. This wide variability suggest that introgressive hybridization is occurring on a broad scale between the Ross' and the Lesser Snow Geese, although Mayr (1963) contends that only a small fraction of hybrids backcross with either of the parent species. As early as 1966 Dzubin suspected that one of the intermediate geese captured in western Saskatchewan was an F_2 hybrid or an intermediate goose × Ross' Goose backcross. In 1967 white geese exhibiting a whole spectrum of intermediate characteristics appeared to be emerging. During October Dzubin examined at least three specimens with characters departing markedly from typical intermediate geese and approaching either Ross' Geese or Lesser Snows. In November Trauger captured an aberrant white goose in northwest Missouri that closely approached the Lesser Snow Goose in mensural and morphological characteristics but had several features typical of intermediate geese. This goose, the apparent offspring of a Lesser Snow × intermediate backcross, was also examined by H. H. Burgess and J. P. Prevett. In 1968 Dzubin caught eight geese that were the apparent progeny of F_2 or F_3 generation hybrids or backcrosses with the parent species.

Direct evidence of intermediate geese backcrossing with the parent species was obtained on the breeding grounds. In 1966 Ryder found a female intermediate goose mated with a male Ross' Goose at Karrak Lake. She laid three eggs. When D. F. Parmelee and G. M. Sutton visited the colony on 16 June, they confirmed Ryder's identification and photographed the unusual pair. On 1 July the eggs hatched and both the intermediate goose and the Ross' Goose mate were collected (JPR No. 65–66). The goslings weighed about 90 g at hatching whereas typical Ross' goslings weigh about 65 g (Ryder 1967). In addition, J. P. Prevett (pers. comm.) saw a definite family group consisting of an intermediate goose-Ross' Goose pair and four goslings on 24 October 1968 at Sand Lake National Wildlife Refuge near Columbia, South Dakota. The young were smaller and more advanced in molt than Lesser Snow Geese.

Thus hybridization and introgression between Ross' Geese and Lesser Snow Geese appear to be occurring on a broad scale at several locations in the Canadian Arctic. The hybrids and backcrosses appear to be fully fertile between each other and the parent species. Johnsgard (1960) concludes that evidence of hybrid sterility is infrequent among waterfowl. Delacour and Mayr (1945:9) state that hybrids from crosses between species of *Anser* (including *Chen*) usually are fertile, whereas intergeneric hybrids from crosses between *Anser* and *Branta* are sterile. According to Sibley (1961), hybridization proves genetic compatibility of the interbreeding gene pools and a close phylogenetic relationship. The hybridization of Lesser Snow and Ross'

Geese brings into question Ploeger's (1968:97) statement that "though resembling each other closely, they do not interbreed, not even in mixed colonies and, therefore, they have apparently passed the species limit." The evolutionary significance and taxonomic implications of avian hybridization have been thoroughly discussed by Sibley (1959, 1961), Mayr (1963), and Short (1969).

If the present trend of hybridization and introgression continues, several valid reasons suggest that Ross' Goose, one of the rarest North American geese, may be in serious jeopardy as a species. Hybridization may pose a potential threat to the Ross' Goose because of genetic swamping by the Lesser Snow Goose analogous to the situation postulated by Johnsgard (1967) for the Black Duck (*Anas rubripes*) and Mallard (*Anas platyrhynchos*). Because of its much smaller gene pool, Black Ducks are theoretically vulnerable to eventual swamping through hybridization and introgression with Mallards. Likewise Ross' Goose has an extremely small gene pool in comparison with the Lesser Snow Goose. The ratio of the continental populations of Black Ducks to Mallards is 1:6 (Johnsgard 1967), whereas the ratio of Ross' Geese to Lesser Snow Geese is 1:27 (Table 4). Hence the Black Duck is nearly five times more abundant in relation to the Mallard than Ross' Goose is to the Lesser Snow. Although the rate of hybridization in Black Ducks and Mallards has been analyzed in greater detail (Johnsgard 1961:35, 1967), the apparent rate of hybridization in Ross' Geese and Lesser Snow Geese may be more than twice this rate.

A comparative study of the behavioral and ecological isolating mechanisms of the Lesser Snow Goose and the Ross' Goose seems highly desirable, because genetic barriers to interbreeding apparently are lacking. There is a need to define more precisely the habitat requirements and preferences of these species where they are sympatric in order to determine if the degree of competition for food, nesting sites, and other requisites is having a deleterious effect on either species and is contributing to hybridization. There is also a need to determine further the distribution and abundance of intermediate white geese to follow changes in the rate of hybridization of Lesser Snow and Ross' Geese. This appears to be the only practical way of determining if the hybrids have behavioral or ecological advantages over the parent species that would be of selective importance. Field workers, especially those banding or handling samples of Lesser Snow, Blue, and Ross' Geese, are encouraged to record the number of intermediate geese in relation to the other species as shown in Table 4. These data will provide a quantitative measure of the relative abundance of intermediate white geese to appraise the significance of Lesser Snow and Ross' Goose hybridization in the future. The degree of biological success of hybrids depends upon the extent to which natural selection acts against them (Sibley 1961). There is no evidence that the hybrids of Lesser Snow Geese and Ross' Geese are selected against in obtaining mates or are inferior in producing young or adapting to the environment. Regardless of the overall genetic significance of hybridization to the Ross' Goose or the Lesser Snow Goose, more contact of these species on breeding and wintering areas and along migratory routes will probably result in the production of more intermediate white geese.

The intermediate white geese described in this paper have been recognized as the hybrids of Lesser Snow Geese and Ross' Geese by the Canadian Wildlife Service and United States Fish and Wildlife Service. Recently, the A.O.U. Number 170.3 was assigned to Ross' × Lesser Snow Goose hybrids by the Migratory Bird Populations Station for bird banding purposes.

SUMMARY

White geese with characteristics intermediate between Lesser Snow Geese and Ross' Geese were studied between 1961 and 1968. Although the parentage of these intermediate geese was unknown, they apparently represented the first wild hybrids reported for these species.

The 42 intermediate white geese examined by various individuals were obtained in all seasons: 17 were trapped in Saskatchewan during autumn, 12 migrating and wintering birds were captured or observed in Louisiana, Missouri, Iowa, Nebraska, and South Dakota from autumn through spring, and 13 were collected or studied on the breeding grounds of the central and eastern Canadian Arctic in summer.

We measured 24 intermediates for comparison with Lesser Snow and Ross' Geese. In spite of considerable variation, mensural characteristics of these geese are intermediate for all ages and sexes. Heads and bills provide the most obvious evidence suggesting that the intermediate geese are hybrids of Lesser Snow and Ross' Geese. Plumages of intermediates are identical to Lesser Snow and Ross' Geese in adults but are variable in immatures.

Recent changes in the distribution and abundance of Lesser Snow Geese and Ross' Geese have increased interspecific contacts throughout the annual cycle. The occurrence of Ross' Geese outside the traditional wintering range has possibly contributed to the breakdown of isolating mechanisms caused by a shortage of conspecific mates in large concentrations of Lesser Snow and Blue Geese in the Mississippi and Central Flyways. Interspecies pairs have been observed on breeding and wintering grounds. In addition, competition for nesting sites in large colonies where Lesser Snow and Ross' Geese are sympatric has resulted in mixed clutches, particularly in late springs. Young hatched in these nests may become imprinted to the wrong species-specific characteristics facilitating hybridization.

Based on the apparent incidence of intermediate white geese in samples of Lesser Snow and Ross' Geese, an estimated 1,400 hybrids may have been produced annually in recent years, and a hybrid complex appears to be forming between the two species. Intermediate white geese are known to be fully fertile with each other and the parent species. Because of its relatively small gene pool, the rare Ross' Goose may be vulnerable to eventual genetic swamping by the Lesser Snow Goose.

ACKNOWLEDGMENTS

Many individuals in several state, provincial, and federal organizations aided in various aspects of this study. We are especially grateful for the valuable contributions made by the following: Harold H. Burgess, Harvey W. Miller, John J. Lynch, Jacob M. Valentine, Jr., Richard W. Rigby, Glen A. Sherwood, Harvey K. Nelson, United States Fish and Wildlife Service; George Schildman and John Sweet, Nebraska Game and Parks Commission; J. Paul Prevett and Charles D. MacInnes, Western Ontario University; F. Graham Cooch, J. Bernard Gollop, Dennis G. Raveling, Canadian Wildlife

Service; Loren C. Bates and Paul A. Vohs, Jr., Iowa State University; Frank M. Kozlik, California Department of Fish and Game; Richard H. Manville, George E. Watson, and Richard C. Banks, United States National Museum. We are indebted to Milton W. Weller, Iowa State University, for helpful comments on the manuscript. Field work by Dzubin and Ryder was done under the auspices of the Canadian Wildlife Service; Trauger was employed by the United States Fish and Wildlife Service.

LITERATURE CITED

AMADON, D. 1953. Migratory birds of relict distribution: some inferences. Auk 70:461–469.

AMERICAN ORNITHOLOGIST'S UNION. 1957. Check-list of North American birds, fifth ed. Baltimore, Amer. Ornithol. Union.

BARRY, T. W. 1960. Waterfowl reconnaissance in the western Arctic. Arctic Circ. 13:51–58.

———. 1962. Effect of late seasons in Atlantic Brant reproduction. J. Wildl. Mgmt. 26:19–26.

———. 1964. Brant, Ross' Goose and Emperior Goose. Pp. 145–154 *in* Waterfowl tomorrow. Joseph P. Linduska, ed. Washington, D.C., U.S. Dept. Interior.

———, AND J. EISENHART. 1958. Ross' Geese nesting at Southampton Island., N.W.T., Canada. Auk 75:89–90.

BRAY, R. 1943. Notes on the birds of Southampton Island, Baffin Island, and Melville Peninsula. Auk 60:504–536.

BULLER, R. J. 1955. Ross's Goose in Texas. Auk 72:298–299.

CANADIAN WILDLIFE SERVICE. 1963. Goose measurements. (Mimeo.) Saskatoon, Saskatchewan, Canadian Wildl. Serv.

COOCH, F. G. 1954. Ross' Goose in the eastern Arctic. Condor 56:307.

———. 1961. Ecological aspects of the Blue-Snow Goose complex. Auk 78:72–89.

———. 1963. Recent changes in distribution of color phases of *Chen c. caerulescens.* Proc. 13th Intern. Ornithol. Congr. (1962) 2:1182–1194.

———. 1964. Snows and blues. Pp. 125–133 *in* Waterfowl tomorrow. Joseph P. Linduska, ed. Washington, D.C., U.S. Dept. Interior.

DELACOUR, J. 1954. The waterfowl of the world, vol. 1. London, Country Life Ltd.

———, AND E. MAYR. 1945. The family Anatidae. Wilson Bull. 57:1–55.

DZUBIN, A. 1965. A study of migrating Ross' Geese in western Saskatchewan. Condor 67:511–534.

GRAY, A. P. 1958. Bird hybrids. Franham Royal, Bucks, England, Commonwealth Agr. Bureaux.

HANSON, H. C., P. QUENEAU, AND P. SCOTT. 1956. The geography, birds and mammals of the Perry River region. Arctic Inst. North Amer., Spec. Publ. No. 3.

HARE, F. K. 1955. Weather and climate. Pp. 58–83 *in* Geography of the northlands. George H. T. Kimble and Dorothy Good, eds. Amer. Geogr. Soc., Spec. Publ. No. 32.

JAMES, F. C. 1968. Central Southern Region. Audubon Field Notes 22:445–448.

JOHANSEN, H. 1956. Revision and entstehung der arktischen Vogelfauna, part 1. Acta Arctica 8.

JOHNSGARD, P. A. 1960. Hybridization in the Anatidae and its taxonomic implications. Condor 62:25–33.

———. 1961. Evolutionary relationships among the North American Mallards. Auk 78:3–43.

———. 1963. Behavioral isolating mechanisms in the family Anatidae. Proc. 13th Intern. Ornithol. Congr. (1962) 1:531–543.

———. 1965. Handbook of waterfowl behavior. Ithaca, New York, Cornell Univ. Press.

———. 1967. Sympatry changes and hybridization incidence in Mallards and Black Ducks. Amer. Midl. Naturalist 77:51–63.

———. 1968. Waterfowl: their biology and natural history. Lincoln, Univ. Nebraska Press.

LYNCH, J. J. 1967. 1966 productivity and mortality among geese, swans, and brant. (Mimeo.) Lafayette, Louisiana, Res. Progr. Rept., Patuxent Wildlife Research Center.

———. 1968. 1967 productivity and mortality among geese, swans, and brant. (Mimeo.) Lafayette, Louisiana, Res. Progr. Rept., Patuxent Wildlife Research Center.

MACINNES, C. D. 1964. The status of Ross's Goose in 1962–63. Wildfowl Trust, Ann. Rept. 15:137–139.

———, AND F. G. COOCH. 1963. Additional eastern records of Ross' Goose (*Chen rossii*). Auk 80:77–79.

MANNING, T. H. 1942. Blue and Lesser Snow Geese on Southampton and Baffin Islands. Auk 59:158–175.

———, E. O. HÖHN, AND A. H. MACPHERSON. 1956. The birds of Banks Island. Natl. Mus. Canada, Bull. 143, Biol. Ser. No. 48.

MAYR, E. 1963. Animal species and evolution. Cambridge, Massachusetts, Belknap Press of Havard Univ. Press.

MOYLE, J. B., editor. 1964. Waterfowl in Minnesota. Minnesota Dept. Conserv., Tech. Bull. No. 7.

PALMER, R. S. 1962. Handbook of North American birds, vol. 1. New Haven, Connecticut, Yale Univ. Press.

PHILLIPS, J. C. 1915. Experimental studies of hybridization among ducks and pheasants. J. Exp. Zool. 18:69–144.

———. 1921. A further report on species crosses in birds. Genetics 6:366–383.

PLOEGER, P. L. 1968. Geographical differentiation in arctic Anatidae as a result of isolation during the last glacial. Ardea 56:1–159.

RYDER, J. P. 1964. A preliminary study of the breeding biology of Ross' Goose. Wildfowl Trust, Ann. Rept. 15:127–137.

———. 1967. The breeding biology of the Ross' Goose in the Perry River region Northwest Territories. Canadian Wildl. Serv. Rept., Ser. No. 3.

———. 1969. Nesting colonies of Ross' Goose. Auk 86:282–292.

SCOTT, P. 1951. Waterfowl collection. Wildl. Trust, Ann. Rept. 3.

SHORT, L. L. 1969. Taxonomic aspects of avian hybridization. Auk, 86:84–105.

SIBLEY, C. G. 1959. Hybridization in birds: taxonomic and evolutionary implications. Bull. Brit. Ornithol. Club 79:154–158.

———. 1961. Hybridization and isolating mechanisms. Pp. 69–87 *in* Vertebrate speciation, W. F. Blair, ed. Austin, Univ. Texas Press.

SIBLEY, C. L. 1938. Hybrids of and with North American Anatidae. Proc. 9th Intern. Ornithol. Congr., Rouen (1938):327–335.

SMART, G. 1960. Ross' Goose taken at Horeshoe Lake, Illinois. Wilson Bull. 72:288–289.

SMITH, R. I. 1968. The social aspects of reproductive behavior in the pintail. Auk 85:381–396.

SUTTON, G. M. 1932. The birds of Southampton Island. Mem. Carnegie Mus., No. 12, part 2, sect. 2.

SWEET, J. T., AND K. ROBERTSON. 1966. Ross' Geese in Nebraska. Nebraska Bird Review 34:70–71.

USPENSKI, S. M. 1965. The geese of Wrangel Island. Wildfowl Trust, Ann. Rept. 16:126–129.

VAN TYNE, J., AND A. J. BERGER. 1959. Fundamentals of ornithology. New York, John Wiley and Sons.

WINTLE, D. S. 1968. Adoption of young by Versicolor Teal and other wildlfowl. Wildfowl 19:81–82.

SELECTED BIBLIOGRAPHY

Evolution, Hybridization, and Speciation

BARASH, D. P. 1977. Sociobiology of rape in mallards (*Anas platyrhynchos*): response of the mated male. Science 197(4305):788–789.

COOCH, F. G. 1963. Recent changes in distribution of color phases of *Chen c. caerulescens*. Proc. XIII Int. Ornithol. Congr. pp. 1182–1194.

———, AND J. P. RYDER. 1971. The genetics of polymorphism in the Ross' goose (*Anser rossi*). Evolution 25:461–470.

COOKE, F., AND F. G. COOCH. 1968. The genetics of polymorphism in the goose *Anser caerulescens*. Evolution 22:289–300.

———, C. D. MACINNES, AND J. P. PREVETT. 1975. Gene flow between breeding populations of lesser snow geese. Auk 92(3):493–510.

———, AND P. J. MIRSKY. 1972. A genetic analysis of lesser snow goose families. Auk 89(4):863–871.

———, AND J. P. RYDER. 1971. The genetic polymorphism in the Ross' goose (*Anser rossii*). Evolution 25:483–496.

DELACOUR, J., AND E. MAYR. 1945. The family Anatidae. Wilson Bull. 57(1): 4–55.

JOHNSGARD, P. A. 1960. Classification and evolutionary relationships of the sea ducks. Condor 62:426–433.

———. 1960. Hybridization in the Anatidae and its taxonomic implications. Condor 62:25–33.

———. 1961. Evolutionary relationships among the North American mallards. Auk 78(1):3–43.

———. 1961. Taxonomy of the Anatidae—A behavioural analysis. Ibis 103a(1):71–85.

———. 1962. Evolutionary trends in the behavior and morphology of the Anatidae. 13th Annu. Rep. Wildfowl Trust 1960–61. pp. 130–148.

———. 1967. Sympatry changes and hybridization incidence in mallards and black ducks. Am. Midl. Nat. 77(1):51–63.

JOHNSON, D. H., D. E. TIMM, AND P. F. SPRINGER. 1979. Morphological characteristics of Canada geese in the Pacific Flyway. Pages 56–80 *in* R. L. Jarvis and J. C. Bartonek, eds. Management and biology of Pacific Flyway geese. A symposium. Northwest Sec. of The Wildl. Soc. Oregon State Univ. Book Stores, Inc., Corvallis.

LACK, D. 1967. The significance of clutch-size in waterfowl. 18th Annu. Rep. Wildfowl Trust 1965–66. pp. 125–128.

MENDALL, H. L. 1980. Intergradation of eastern American common eiders. Can. Field-Nat. 94:286–292.

PREVETT, J. P., AND C. D. MACINNES. 1973. Observations of wild hybrids between Canada and blue geese. Condor 75(1):124–125.

RAIKOW, R. J. 1970. Evolution of diving adaptations in the stifftail ducks. Univ. Calif. Publ. Zool. 94:1–52.

RAVELING, D. G. 1978. The timing of egg laying by northern geese. Auk 95:294–303.

ROCKWELL, R. F., AND F. COOKE. 1977. Gene flow and local adaptation in a colonially nesting dimorphic bird: the lesser snow goose (*Anser caerulescens caerulescens*). Am. Nat. 111(977):91–97.

RYDER, J. P. 1970. A possible factor in

the evolution of clutch size in Ross' goose. Wilson Bull. 82(1):5–13.

RYLANDER, M. K., AND E. G. BOLEN. 1970. Ecological and anatomical adaptations of North American tree ducks. Auk 87(1):72–90.

SIEGFRIED, W. R. 1976. Segregation in feeding behaviour of four diving ducks in southern Manitoba. Can. J. Zool. 54(5):730–736.

WHITE, D. H., AND D. JAMES. 1978. Differential use of fresh water environments by wintering waterfowl of coastal Texas. Wilson Bull. 90:99–111.

SELECTED LIST OF BOOKS RELATED TO WATERFOWL ECOLOGY AND MANAGEMENT

BANKO, W. E. 1960. The trumpeter swan: its history, habits, and population in the United States. North American Fauna 63, U.S. Fish and Wildlife Service, Washington, D.C. 214pp.

BELLROSE, F. C. 1976. Ducks, geese and swans of North America. Stackpole Co., Harrisburg, PA. 544pp.

BENNETT, L. J. 1938. The blue-winged teal: its ecology and management. Iowa State Univ. Press, Ames. 144pp.

BENT, A. C. 1962. Life histories of North American wildfowl. Part I. Dover Publications, New York. 244pp.

———. 1962. Life histories of North American wildfowl. Part II. Dover Publications, New York. 314pp.

DAY, A. M. 1949. North American waterfowl. Stackpole and Heck, Inc., New York. 329pp.

DELACOUR, J. 1954–64. The waterfowl of the world. 4 vol. Country Life, London. 1150 pp.

DILL, H. H., AND F. B. LEE, editors. 1970. Home grown honkers. U.S. Fish and Wildlife Service, Washington, D.C. 154pp.

EINARSEN, A. S. 1965. Black brant: sea goose of the Pacific Coast. Univ. of Washington Press, Seattle. 142pp.

EISENHAUER, D. I., AND D. A. FRAZER. 1972. Nesting ecology of the emperor goose in the Kokechik Bay region, Alaska. Department of Forestry and Conservation, Purdue Univ. Press, West Lafayette, IN. 66pp.

FRITH, H. J. 1967. Waterfowl in Australia. Halsted Press, Sydney. 328pp.

GOLDSTEIN, J. H. 1971. Competition for wetlands in the Midwest: an economic analysis. Resources for the Future, Inc., Washington, D.C. 105pp.

HAMMACK, J., AND G. M. BROWN, JR. 1974. Waterfowl and wetlands: toward bioeconomic analysis. Resources for the Future, Inc., Washington, D.C. 95pp.

HANSON, H. C. 1965. The giant Canada goose. Southern Illinois Univ. Press, Carbondale. 226pp.

HINE, R. L., AND C. SCHOENFELD. 1968. Canada goose management: current continental problems and programs. Dembar Education Research Services, Madison, WI. 195pp.

HOCHBAUM, H. A. 1944. The canvasback on a prairie marsh. The Wildlife Management Institute and Stackpole Co., Harrisburg, PA. 201pp.

———. 1956. Travels and traditions of waterfowl. Univ. of Minnesota Press, Minneapolis. 301pp.

———. 1973. To ride the wind. Richard Bonnycastle Book, Toronto, Canada. 120pp.

JOHNSGARD, P. A. 1965. Handbook of waterfowl behavior. Cornell Univ. Press, Ithaca, NY. 378pp.

———. 1968. Waterfowl: their biology and natural history. Univ. of Nebraska Press, Lincoln. 138pp.

———. 1975. Waterfowl of North America. Indiana Univ. Press, Bloomington. 575pp.

JOHNSGARD, P. A. 1978. Ducks, geese, and swans of the world. Univ. of Nebraska Press, Lincoln. 404pp.

KORTRIGHT, F. H. 1942. The ducks, geese and swans of North America. Wildlife Management Institute and Stackpole Co., Harrisburg, PA. 476pp.

LINDUSKA, J. P., editor. 1964. Waterfowl tomorrow. U.S. Fish and Wildlife Service, Washington, D.C. 770pp.

MENDALL, H. L. 1958. The ring-necked duck in the northeast. Univ. of Maine Bull. 60(16). Maine Univ. Press, Orono. 317pp.

MILLAIS, J. G. 1902. The natural history of the British surface-feeding ducks. Longmans Green, London.

———. 1913. British diving ducks. 2 vol. Longmans Green, London.

PHILLIPS, J. C. 1923–26. The natural history of the ducks. 4 vol. Houghton Mifflin Co., Boston, MA.

———, AND F. C. LINCOLN. 1930. American waterfowl: their present situation and the outlook for their future. Houghton Mifflin Co., Boston, MA. 312pp.

PIRNIE, M. D. 1935. Michigan waterfowl management. Michigan Department of Conservation, Lansing. 328pp.

SANDERSON, G. C., AND F. C. BELLROSE. 1969. Wildlife habitat management of wetlands. Supplemento Dos An. Acad. Brasil. Ciênc. 41:153–204.

SCOTT, P. 1968. A coloured key to the wildfowl of the world. Wildfowl Trust. W. R. Royle & Son Ltd., London. 95pp.

———, AND THE WILDFOWL TRUST. 1972. The swans. Houghton Mifflin Co., Boston, MA. 242pp.

SOWLS, L. K. 1955. Prairie ducks: a study of their behavior, ecology and management. Wildlife Management Institute and Stackpole Co., Harrisburg, PA. 193pp.

TODD, F. S. 1978. Waterfowl: ducks, geese and swans of the world. Sea World Press, San Diego, CA. 400pp.

TREFETHEN, J. B., editor. 1966. Wood duck management and research: a symposium. Wildlife Management Institute, Washington, D.C. 212pp.

U.S. FISH AND WILDLIFE SERVICE. 1975. Final environmental statement for the issuance of annual regulations permitting the sport hunting of migratory birds. U.S. Department of the Interior, Washington, D.C. 710pp.

WARD, P., AND B. BATT. 1973. Propagation of captive waterfowl: the Delta Waterfowl Research Station System. North American Wildlife Foundation and Wildlife Management Institute, Washington, D.C. 64pp.

WELLER, M. W. 1981. The island waterfowl. Iowa State Univ. Press, Ames. 144pp.

WILLIAMS, C. S. 1967. Honker: a discussion of the habits and needs of the largest of our Canada geese. Van Nostrand Co., Princeton, NJ. 179pp.

WRIGHT, B. S. 1954. High tide and an east wind: the story of the black duck. Wildlife Management Institute and Stackpole Co., Harrisburg, PA. 162pp.

YOCUM, C. F. 1951. Waterfowl and their food plants in Washington. Univ. of Washington Press, Seattle.